DrAP 1975	A Directory of American Poets (1975 edition)
EarAB	Early American Book Illustrators and Wood Engravers
EncM&D	Encyclopedia of Mystery and Detection
EncWL	Encyclopedia of World Literature in the 20th Century
EuAu	European Authors, 1000-1900
EvEuW	Everyman's Dictionary of European Writers
EvLB	Everyman's Dictionary of Literary Biography, English and American
FamAI	Famous Author-Illustrators for Young People
FamAYP	Famous Authors for Young People
FamSYP	Famous Storytellers for Young People
FemPA	The Female Poets of America
HsB&A	The House of Beadle and Adams and its Dime and Nickel Novels
IlBYP	Illustrators of Books for Young People (Second edition)
IlCB	Illustrators of Children's Books
IndAu	Indiana Authors and Their Works
JBA	The Junior Book of Authors
LivBAA	Living Black American Authors
LivFWS	Living Female Writers of the South
LongC	Longman Companion to Twentieth Century Literature
McGWD	McGraw-Hill Encyclopedia of World Drama
MnBBF	The Men Behind Boy's Fiction
MnnWr	Minnesota Writers
ModAL	Modern American Literature
ModBL	Modern British Literature
ModGL	Modern German Literature
ModRL	Modern Romance Literatures
ModSL	Modern Slavic Literatures
ModWD	Modern World Drama
MorBMP	More Books by More People
MorJA	More Junior Authors
MouLC	Moulton's Library of Literary Criticism of English and American Authors
NewC	The New Century Handbook of English Literature
Newb 1922	Newbery Medal Books, 1922-1955
NewbC 1956	Newbery and Caldecott Medal Books, 1956-1965
NewbC 1966	Newbery and Caldecott Medal Books, 1966-1975
OhA&B	Ohio Authors and Their Books
OxAm	The Oxford Companion to American Literature
OxCan	The Oxford Companion to Canadian History and Literature
OxCan Sup	Supplement to the Oxford Companion to Canadian History and Literature
OxEng	The Oxford Companion to English Literature
OxFr	The Oxford Companion to French Literature
OxGer	The Oxford Companion to German Literature
Pen Am	The Penguin Companion to American Literature
Pen Cl	The Penguin Companion to Classical, Oriental and African Literature
Pen Eng	The Penguin Companion to English Literature
Pen Eur	The Penguin Companion to European Literature
PiP	The Pied Pipers
PoCh	The Poets of the Church
PoIre	The Poets of Ireland
PoLE	The Poets Laureate of England
PueRA	Puerto Rican Authors
RAdv 1	The Reader's Adviser, volume 1
RCom	The Reader's Companion to World Literature
REn	The Reader's Encyclopedia
REnAL	The Reader's Encyclopedia of American Literature
REnWD	The Reader's Encyclopedia of World Drama
RGAfL	A Reader's Guide to African Literature
SenS	A Sense of Story
SixAP	Sixty American Poets, 1896-1944
SmATA	Something About the Author
St&VC	Story and Verse for Children
TexWr	Texas Writers of Today
ThBJA	Third Book of Junior Authors
TwCA	Twentieth Century Authors
TwCW	Twentieth Century Writing
WebEAL	Webster's New World Companion to English and American Literature
WhCL	The Who's Who of Children's Literature
WhGrA	Who's Who in Graphic Art
WhLA	Who's Who Among Living Authors of Older Nations
WhPNW	Who's Who Among Pacific Northwest Authors
WhTwL	Who's Who in Twentieth Century Literature
WhWNAA	Who Was Who Among North American Authors
WiscW	Wisconsin Writers
WorAu	World Authors, 1950-1970
WrD 1976	The Writers Directory, 1976-1978
YABC	Yesterday's Authors of Books for Children

Author Biographies Master Index

AUTHOR BIOGRAPHIES MASTER INDEX

A consolidated guide to biographical information concerning authors living and dead as it appears in a selection of the principal biographical dictionaries devoted to authors, poets, journalists, and other literary figures.

Edited by Dennis La Beau

First Edition

Volume 1: A - K

Gale Biographical Index Series No. 3

Gale Research Company • Book Tower • Detroit, Michigan

Editor: Dennis La Beau

Editorial Associates: Barbara Brandenburg,
Miranda Herbert, Kathleen D. Mailloux,
Barbara McNeil, Rita Runchock, Helen
Savage

Editorial Assistants: Katherine A. Foster,
Nancy Helen Moore

Production Supervisor: Laura Bryant

Production Manager: Michaeline Nowinski

Cover Design: Art Chartow

Library of Congress Cataloging in Publication Data

Main entry under title:

Author biographies master index.

   (Gale biographical index series ; no. 3)
   Bibliography: p. vii pp. vii-xxi
   Includes index.
   1. Authors--Biography--Indexes. I. La Beau,
Dennis. II. Series.
Z5304.A8A88   [PN452]   809   76-27212
ISBN 0-8103-1085-6

Computerized photocomposition by Computer Composition Corporation
Madison Heights, Michigan

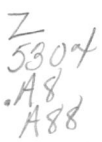

Introduction

The purpose of *Author Biographies Master Index* is a simple but valuable one: it enables the user to locate, without tedious searching, biographical information on a single person from among more than 413,000 entries in more than 140 biographical dictionaries and directories of writers. In function, but not content, it is a literary counterpart to Gale's *Biographical Dictionaries Master Index* published in 1975-76.

ABMI tells the user which edition of which publication to consult or, almost equally as helpful, it reveals that there is no listing for a given individual in any of the publications indexed. In cases where *ABMI* has multiple listings for the same person, the searcher is able to choose the source which is most convenient to him, or to locate multiple sketches to compare with one another.

All names in an indexed work are listed in *ABMI*, whether living or deceased. There is no need to consult the work itself if the desired name is not shown by *ABMI* to be in the work, since it has been the editorial policy to index every name found in a particular book.

How to Read a Citation

Each citation gives the author's name, followed by the years of birth and/or death. If there is no year of birth, the death date is preceded by a lower case *d*. After the dates researchers will find the codes for the books indexed that apply to that individual:

Johnson, David M 1858-1907 *BrAu, OxEng, TwCA*

A list of the works indexed in *ABMI,* and the codes used to refer to them, is printed on the endsheets, and complete bibliographic citations follow this introduction.

ABMI Is a Unique Reference Work

ABMI is the largest project of its kind ever undertaken. Although some similar efforts have appeared in the past, notably Wallace's *Dictionary of North American Authors,* the present work goes far beyond its predecessors in scope. (Wallace's *Dictionary* has itself been included in this index since it provides references to 70 sources not used in *ABMI.)*

The books indexed in *ABMI,* while they are of several distinct types (biographical dictionaries, collected criticism, etc.), all have one common characteristic: Each includes at least a moderate amount of biographical, critical, or career-related information on individual authors, and most include a substantial amount of information.

All of the books cited in *ABMI* are readily available and widely held in most reference collections. These books include, for example, Gale's *Contemporary Authors* series, the St. Martin's *Contemporary Writers in the English Language* series, Scribner's *American Writers,* the *Oxford Companions* to various literatures and genres, the H.W. Wilson biographical series on authors, and many more.

Two directories have been included even though they do not provide biographical data. They do, however, give addresses for lesser-known authors frequently overlooked by biographical dictionaries concerned with the more established writers. These publications are *The Directory of American Fiction Writers,* and *The Directory of American Poets.*

The entire *Library of Literary Criticism,* published by the Frederick Ungar Company, and Gale's *Contemporary Literary Criticism* are also included. Both of these series offer users a quick critical survey of a writer's works, which are usually helpful to an understanding of an author's life.

Editorial Practices

ABMI follows standard alphabetizing rules used by the Library of Congress, with the exception of *Mac* and *Mc,* which are filed strictly letter by letter. Not all source books use this method of alphabetizing. Some names, therefore, may have an alphabetic position in a source book different from this index.

Since *Author Biographies Master Index* includes so many diverse reference works, problems of alternate spellings of names and variant birth and death dates of authors listed became complex.

To simplify the listings, and to help the user, some standardization of names has been instituted when it appeared certain that the same person was referred to by the various forms. However, if a given author's name has spellings or dates that differ substantially from publication to publication, or if there is any other reason to believe that more than one person is referred to by the variant forms, the name has been retained in its variant forms.

Users should be careful, therefore, in searching for some citations. An individual author could have more than one listing if the various source books differ greatly in how that author's name appears.

Also, users may need to look in *ABMI* under all possibilities for listing a name, especially in the case of names with prefixes or suffixes, Spanish names which may be listed in sources under either part of the surname, Chinese names which may be entered in sources in direct or inverted order, transliterated names from non-Roman alphabets, etc.

In a very few cases, extremely long names have been shortened slightly because of typesetting system limitations, e.g., *Northcliffe, Alfred Charles William Harmsworth, Viscount* has been shortened to *Northcliffe, Alfred Harmsworth, Viscount.* The editors believe that such editing will not affect the usefulness of the individual entries.

Cross references appearing in the publications indexed have been retained in *ABMI.*

Years of birth and death are repeated as found in the source works. If a source has indicated that the dates may not be accurate, the questionable date(s) are followed by a question mark. As with variations in names, *ABMI* editors have not attempted to reconcile discrepancies between dates reported in the various source works.

Suggestions Are Welcome

Future editions of *ABMI* are planned. Additional sources will be added to new editions as their availability and usefulness become known. The editors will welcome suggestions from users for additional works which could be indexed, or any other comments and suggestions.

Bibliographic Key to Publication Codes
for Use in Locating Sources

Unless otherwise noted, the books indexed by *Author Biographies Master Index* provide biographical and bibliographical information.

Code	Book Indexed
AfA 1	✓ *African Authors; A Companion to Black African Writing, Volume 1: 1300-1973.* By Donald E. Herdeck. Washington, D. C., Black Orpheus Press, 1973.
Alli	Allibone, S. Austin: *A Critical Dictionary of English Literature and British and American Authors Living and Deceased from the Earliest Accounts to the Latter Half of the Nineteenth Century.* Containing over forty-six thousand articles (authors) with forty indexes of subjects. In three volumes. Philadelphia, J. B. Lippincott & Co., 1858-1871. Reprinted in 1965 by The Gale Research Company, Detroit. Also available from Gale on microfiche.

Most entries are biographical. There are some blind cross-references.

Alli Sup	*A Supplement to Allibone's Critical Dictionary of English Literature and British and American Authors.* Containing over thirty-seven thousand articles (authors), and enumerating over ninety-three thousand titles. By John Foster Kirk. In two volumes. Philadelphia, J. B. Lippincott & Co., 1891. Reprinted in 1965 by The Gale Research Company, Detroit. Also available from Gale on microfiche.
AmA

Ref. PS 21,K8 | *American Authors, 1600-1900; A Biographical Dictionary of American Literature.* Edited by Stanley J. Kunitz and Howard Haycraft. New York, The H. W. Wilson Company, 1938. |
| *AmA&B*

Ref. Z 1224.B87 1962 | *American Authors and Books, 1640 to the Present Day.* Third revised edition. By W. J. Burke and Will D. Howe. Revised by Irving Weiss and Anne Weiss. New York, Crown Publishers, Inc. (c1972). |

Provides dates of birth and death, occupation and brief bibliographies.

AmLY	*The American Literary Yearbook.* A biographical and bibliographical dictionary of living North American authors; a record of contemporary literary activity; an authors' manual and students' text book. Volume 1, 1919. Edited by Hamilton Traub. Henning, Minnesota, Paul Traub, Publisher (1919). Republished in 1968 by Gale Research Company, Detroit. Also available from Gale on microfiche.

Biographical dictionary begins on page 57. A list of pen names and pseudonyms begins on page 49, and is cited in this index by the code "XR".

AmNov	*American Novelists of Today.* By Harry R. Warfel. Westport, Connecticut, Greenwood Press, Publishers (1976). Reprinted from the 1951 edition published by the American Book Company, New York.

The Index of Married Names and Pseudonyms *begins on page 477, and is cited in this index by the code "XR".*

AmSCAP 66   *The ASCAP Biographical Dictionary of Composers, Authors and Publishers*. 1966 edition. Compiled and edited by the Lynn Farnol Group, Inc. New York, The American Society of Composers, Authors and Publishers (c1966).

Ref. ML 106.U3 A5 1966

> *This dictionary contains information on many writers and poets who have contributed to the music and theater worlds.*

AmWr   **American Writers: A Collection of Literary Biographies.** Edited by Leonard Unger. In four volumes. New York, Charles Scribner's Sons (c1974).

Ref. PS 129.A55

> *Originally published as* The University of Minnesota Pamphlets on American Writers.

AnCL   *Anthology of Children's Literature*. Compiled and edited by Edna Johnson, Evelyn R. Sickels and Frances Clarke Sayers. Fourth edition. Boston, Houghton Mifflin Company (c1970).

j808.8 Johns

> *Biographies begin on page 1217.*

AnMV 1926   *Anthology of Magazine Verse for 1926 and Yearbook of American Poetry*. Edited by William Stanley Braithwaite. Freeport, New York, Books for Libraries Press (Granger Index Reprint Series) (1972). Reprint of the 1926 edition.

> *A Biographical Dictionary of Poets in the United States is found in Part IV, at the back of this edition.*

ArizL   *Arizona in Literature; A Collection of the Best Writings of Arizona Authors from Early Spanish Days to the Present Time*. By Mary G. Boyer. Ann Arbor, Gryphon Books, 1971. Reprint of the 1935 edition published by The Arthur H. Clark Company, Glendale, California. Also available from Gale Research Company on microfiche.

> *Use the Index that begins on page 569 to find any given author.*

AtlBL   *Atlantic Brief Lives; A Biographical Companion to the Arts*. Edited by Louis Kronenberger. Boston, Little, Brown and Company (c1971) (An Atlantic Monthly Press Book)

Au&Wr   *The Author's and Writer's Who's Who*. Sixth edition. Darien, Connecticut, Hafner Publishing Company, Inc. (Published and copyrighted by Burke's Peerage Limited, London, 1971)

AuBYP   *Authors of Books for Young People*. Second edition. By Martha E. Ward and Dorothy A. Marquardt. Metuchen, N.J., The Scarecrow Press, Inc., 1971.

AuICB   *Authors and Illustrators of Children's Books: Writings on Their Lives and Works.* By Miriam Hoffman and Eva Samuels. New York, R. R. Bowker Company, 1972.

AuNews 1   *Authors in the News;* A compilation of news stories and feature articles from American newspapers and magazines covering writers and other members of the communications media. Volume 1. Edited by Barbara Nykoruk. (Biography News Library). Detroit, Gale Research Company (c1976).

Ref CT 215 .A9 v.1

> *Many of the articles give some biographical information.*

AuNews 2   *Authors in the News . . .* Volume 2. Detroit, Gale Research Company, (c1977).

Ref. CT 215 .A9 v.2

> *Many of the articles give some biographical information.*

BbD   *The Bibliophile Dictionary;* A biographical record of the great authors, with bibliographical notices of their principal works from the beginning of history. Originally published as volumes 29 and 30 of *The Bibliophile Library of Literature, Art and Rare Manuscripts*. Compiled and arranged by Nathan Haskell Dole, Forrest Morgan, and Caroline Ticknor. New York, London, The International Bibliophile Society (c1904). Republished in 1966 by the Gale Research Company, Detroit. Also available from Gale on microfiche.

BbtC   *Bibliotheca Canadensis; or A Manual of Canadian Literature.* By Henry J. Morgan. Ottawa, G. E. Desbarats, 1867. Reprinted in 1968 by the Gale Research Company, Detroit. Also available from Gale on microfiche.

BiB N   *Biographia Britannica Literaria; or Biography of Literary Characters of Great Britain and Ireland,* arranged in chronological order. *Anglo-Norman Period.* By Thomas Wright. London, John W. Parker, West Strand, 1846. Reprinted in 1968 by Gale Research Company, Detroit. Also available from Gale on microfiche.

Use index at back of book to locate biographies.

BiB S   *Biographia Britannica Literaria . . . Anglo-Saxon Period.* By Thomas Wright. London, John W. Parker, West Strand, 1842. Reprinted by Gale Research Company, Detroit, 1968. Also available from Gale on microfiche.

BiD&SB   *Biographical Dictionary and Synopsis of Books Ancient and Modern.* Edited by Charles Dudley Warner. Akron, Ohio, The Werner Company (c1902). Reprinted in 1965 by Gale Research Company, Detroit. Also available from Gale on microfiche.

BiDLA   *A Biographical Dictionary of the Living Authors of Great Britain and Ireland.* Comprising literary memoirs and anecdotes of their lives; and a chronological register of their publications, with the number of editions printed; including notices of some foreign writers whose works have been occasionally published in England. London, Printed for Henry Colburn; Public Library, Conduit Street, Hanover Square, 1816. Republished by the Gale Research Company, Detroit, 1966. Also available from Gale on microfiche.

A supplemental listing of authors begins on page 407, and is indicated in this index by the code Sup.

BiDPar   *Biographical Dictionary of Parapsychology, with Directory and Glossary, 1964-1966.* Edited by Helene Pleasants. New York, Garrett Publications, Helix Press, 1964.

BiDSA   *Biographical Dictionary of Southern Authors.* By Lucian Lamar Knight. Originally published as *Library of Southern Literature, volume XV, Biographical Dictionary of Authors.* Atlanta, Georgia, The Martin & Hoyt Company, 1929. Reprinted by Gale Research Company, Detroit, 1978. Also available from Gale on microfiche.

BkC   *The Book of Catholic Authors;* Informal self-portraits of famous modern Catholic writers. Edited by Walter Romig. Walter Romig & Company, Detroit (c1942-?).

BkC 1   First series (c1942)
BkC 2   Second series (c1943)
BkC 3   Third series (c1945)
BkC 4   Fourth series (n.d.)
BkC 5   Fifth series (n.d.)
BkC 6   Sixth series (n.d.)

BkCL   *A Book of Children's Literature.* Third edition. By Lillian Hollowell. New York, Chicago, Holt, Rinehart and Winston, Inc. (c1966).

Biographies of authors begin on page 553.

BkIE   *Book Illustrators in Eighteenth-Century England.* By Hanns Hammelmann. Edited and completed by T. S. R. Boase. Published for the Paul Mellon Centre for Studies in British Art (London) Ltd. New Haven and London, Yale University Press, 1975.

BkP   *Books are by People; Interviews with 104 Authors and Illustrators of Books for Young Children.* Edited by Lee Bennett Hopkins. New York, Citation Press, 1969.

Ref. Z 1229 .N39 R87

BlkAW   *Black American Writers Past and Present; A Biographical and Bibliographical Dictionary.* In two volumes. By Theressa Gunnels Rush, Carol Fairbainks Myers, Esther Spring Arata. Metuchen, N. J., The Scarecrow Press, Inc., 1975.

Br&AmS   *British and American Sporting Authors; Their Writings and Biographies.* By A. Henry Higginson. London, Hutchinson & Co. (Publishers) LTD, 1951.

Use index in back of book to locate authors.

Ref. PR 105 .K9

BrAu   *British Authors Before 1800; A Biographical Dictionary.* Edited by Stanley J. Kunitz and Howard Haycraft. New York, The H. W. Wilson Company, 1952.

Ref. PR 451 .K8 1936

BrAu 19   *British Authors of the Nineteenth Century.* Edited by Stanley J. Kunitz. New York, The H. W. Wilson Company, 1936.

Cald 1938   ✓ *Caldecott Medal Books: 1938-1957;* With the artist's acceptance papers & related material chiefly from the Horn Book Magazine. Edited by Bertha Mahony Miller and Elinor Whitney Field. Horn Book Papers, Volume II. Boston, The Horn Book, Incorporated, 1957.

CanNov   *Canadian Novelists, 1920-1945.* By Clara Thomas. Toronto, Longmans, Green & Company (c1946). Reprinted in 1970 by Folcroft Library Editions.

CanWr   *Canadian Writers; A Biographical Dictionary.* Edited by Guy Sylvestre, Brandon Conron, Carl F. Klinck. New edition, revised and enlarged. Toronto, The Ryerson Press (c1966).

Biographies of Quebec authors are in French.

CarSB   *The Carolyn Sherwin Bailey Historical Collection of Children's Books.* A Catalogue. Edited and compiled by Dorothy R. Davis. Southern Connecticut State College, 1966.

Some listings are not in strict alphabetical sequence. There is no index.

Ref. PN 41 .C3 1954

CasWL   *Cassell's Encyclopaedia of World Literature.* Edited by S. H. Steinberg in two volumes. Revised and enlarged in three volumes by J. Buchanan-Brown. New York, William Morrow & Company, Inc. (c1973).

Biographies are found in volumes two and three.

CatA 1947   *Catholic Authors; Contemporary Biographical Sketches, 1930-1947.* Edited by Matthew Hoehn. Newark, St. Mary's Abbey, 1957. (c1948).

CatA 1952   *Catholic Authors; Contemporary Biographical Sketches.* Edited by Matthew Hoehn. St. Mary's Abbey, 1952.

Ref. Z 1037 .A1 C48

ChLR 1   *Children's Literature Review;* Excerpts from reviews, criticism, and commentary on books for children and young people. Volume 1. Edited by Ann Block and Carolyn Riley. Detroit, Gale Research Company (c1976). Also available from Gale on microfiche.

A book of collected criticism.

ChLR 2   *Children's Literature Review . . .* Volume 2. Edited by Carolyn Riley. Detroit, Gale Research Company (c1976). Also available from Gale on microfiche.

A book of collected criticism.

ChPo   *Childhood in Poetry;* A catalogue, with biographical and critical annotations, of the books of English and American poets comprising the Shaw Childhood in Poetry Collection in the Library of the Florida State University, with lists of the poems that relate to childhood. By John Mackay Shaw. In four volumes. Detroit, Gale Research Company (c1967). Also available from Gale on microfiche.

There are some blind cross-references.

ChPo S1 — *Childhood in Poetry . . .* Supplement (One). By John Mackay Shaw. In three volumes. Detroit, Gale Research Company (c1972). Also available from Gale on microfiche.

ChPo S2 — *Childhood in Poetry . . .* Second Supplement. By John Mackay Shaw. Detroit, Gale Research Company (c1976). Also available from Gale on microfiche.

Chmbr 1-3 — *Chambers's Cyclopaedia of English Literature.* Edited by David Patrick. Revised by J. Liddell Geddie. In three volumes: Volume 1, 7th-17th century; Volume 2, 18th century; Volume 3, 19th-20th century. Philadelphia and New York, J. B. Lippincott Company (1938). To be reprinted by Gale Research Company. Available from Gale on microfiche.

Use the indexes found at the back of each of the three volumes to locate authors.

ClDMEuL — *Columbia Dictionary of Modern European Literature.* Edited by Horatio Smith. New York and London, Columbia University Press (c1947). Also published as *A Dictionary of Modern Europen Literature.* London, Oxford University Press, 1947.

CnDAL — *Concise Dictionary of American Literature.* Edited by Robert Fulton Richards. Philosophical Library, Inc. (c1955). Reprinted in 1969 by Greenwood Press, Publishers, New York.

CnE&AP — *The Concise Encyclopedia of English and American Poets and Poetry.* Edited by Stephen Spender and Donald Hall. New York, Hawthorn Books Inc (c1963).

Ref. PR 19 .S6

CnMD — *The Concise Encyclopedia of Modern Drama.* By Siegfried Melchinger. Translated from the German by George Wellwarth. Edited by Henry Popkin. New York, Horizon Press (c1964).

Ref. PN 1861 .M4

Biographies begin on page 159. A supplemental list of 21 playwrights with short biographical notices begins on page 287, and is cited in this index by the code Sup.

CnMWL — *The Concise Encyclopedia of Modern World Literature.* Edited by Geoffrey Grigson. Hutchinson of London (c1963).

Ref. PN 41 .C64

Biographical entries begin on page 29.

CnThe — *A Concise Encyclopedia of the Theatre.* By Robin May. (Reading, Berkshire, England) Osprey (c1974).

Use the index at the back of the book to locate biographies.

ConAmA — *Contemporary American Authors; A Critical Survey and 219 Bio-Bibliographies.* By Fred B. Millett. New York, Harcourt, Brace & World, Inc. (c1940). Reprinted 1970 by AMS Press, Inc., New York.

Author biographies begin on page 207.

ConAmL — *Contemporary American Literature; Bibliographies and Study Outlines.* By John Matthews Manly and Edith Rickert. Revised by Fred B. Millett. New York, Harcourt, Brace (1929). Reprinted 1974 by Haskell House Publishers Ltd., New York.

Biographical section begins on page 101.

ConAu — *Contemporary Authors.* A bio-bibliographical guide to current authors and their works. Detroit, Gale Research Company (c1962-1976). Available from Gale on microfiche.

Ref. Z 1224 .C6

ConAu 1R — Volume 1-4, 1st revision, 1967
ConAu 5R — Volume 5-8, 1st revision, 1969
ConAu 9R — Volume 9-12, 1st revision, 1974

ConAu 13	Volume 13-14, 1965
ConAu 13R	Volume 13-16, 1st revision, 1975 *1st ed*
ConAu 15	Volume 15-16, 1966
ConAu 17	Volume 17-18, 1967
ConAu 17R	Volume 17-20, 1st revision, 1976 *1st ed.*
ConAu 19	Volume 19-20, 1968
ConAu 21	Volume 21-22, 1969
ConAu 23	Volume 23-24, 1970
ConAu 25	Volume 25-28, 1971
ConAu 29	Volume 29-32, 1972
ConAu 33	Volume 33-36, 1973
ConAu 37	Volume 37-40, 1973 *Rev. ed 1979*
ConAu 41	Volume 41-44, 1974
ConAu 45	Volume 45-48, 1974
ConAu 49	Volume 49-52, 1975
ConAu 53	Volume 53-56, 1975
ConAu 57	Volume 57-60, 1976
ConAu 61	Volume 61-64, 1976
ConAu XR	Index to volumes 1-64, *found in back of volume 61-64. This code refers to pseudonym entries which appear only as cross references in the cummulative index to* Contemporary Authors.

ConAu P-1   *Contemporary Authors, Permanent Series;* A bio-bibliographical guide to current authors and their works. Edited by Clare D. Kinsman. Volume 1. Detroit, Gale Research Company (c1975). Also available from Gale on microfiche.

ConDr   *Contemporary Dramatists.* Edited by James Vinson. London, St. James Press; New York, St. Martin's Press (c1973).

Ref. PN 452 .V5 D7

> *Biographies are given in the following sections:* Contemporary Dramatists, *page 7;* Screen Writers, *page 847;* Radio Writers, *page 857;* Television Writers, *page 867;* Musical Librettists, *page 875;* The Theatre of Mixed Means, *page 889.*

ConICB   *Contemporary Illustrators of Children's Books.* Compiled and edited by Elinor Whitney and Bertha F. Mahony. Boston, The Bookshop for Boys and Girls, Women's Educational and Industrial Union, 1930. To be reprinted by Gale Research Company. Available from Gale on microfiche.

ConLC   *Contemporary Literary Criticism;* Excerpts from criticism of the works of today's novelists, poets, playwrights, and other creative writers. Detroit, Gale Research Company (c1973-1976). Also available from Gale on microfiche.

Ref. PN 771 .C59

ConLC 1	Volume 1, 1973
ConLC 2	Volume 2, 1974
ConLC 3	Volume 3, 1975
ConLC 4	Volume 4, 1975
ConLC 5	Volume 5, 1976
ConLC 6	Volume 6, 1976

A series of collected criticism.

ConNov 1972   *Contemporary Novelists.* Edited by James Vinson. London, St. James Press; New York, St. Martin's Press (c1972).

PN 452 .V5 N6

ConNov 1976   *Contemporary Novelists.* Second edition. Edited by James Vinson and D. L. Kirkpatrick. London, St. James Press; New York, St. Martin's Press (c1976).

Ref. PN 452 .V5 N6 197

> *Deceased authors are listed in the appendix, which begins on page 1565.*

ConP 1970   *Contemporary Poets.* Edited by Rosalie Murphie. London, St. James Press; New York, St. Martin's Press (c1970).

PN 452 .C6

ConP 1975
Ref. PN 452.C6 1975

Contemporary Poets. Second edition. Edited by James Vinson and D. L. Kirkpatrick. London, St. James Press; New York, St. Martin's Press (c1975).

Deceased poets are listed in the appendix, which begins on page 1745.

CrCAP
Ref. PS 323.5 .M3

Crowell's Handbook of Contemporary American Poetry. By Karl Malkoff. New York, Thomas Y. Crowell Company (c1973).

Biographical entries begin on page 43.

CrCD
PN 1861 .C7

Crowell's Handbook of Contemporary Drama. By Michael Anderson, Jacques Guicharnaud, Kristin Morrison, Jack D. Zipes, and others. New York, Thomas Y. Crowell Company (c1971).

CrE&SL

Crowell's Handbook of Elizabethan & Stuart Literature. By James E. Ruoff. New York, Thomas Y. Crowell Company (c1975).

CriT
Ref. PR 83 .C764

The Critical Temper; A survey of modern criticism on English and American Literature from the beginnings to the twentieth century. In three volumes. Edited by Martin Tucker. New York, Frederick Ungar Publishing Co. (c1969).

CriT 1 Volume 1: From Old English to Shakespeare
CriT 2 Volume 2: From Milton to Romantic Literature
CriT 3 Volume 3: Victorian Literature, and American Literature.

Authors are listed alphabetically within each period/division of literature.

CyAL 1-2

Cyclopaedia of American Literature; Embracing personal and critical notices of authors, and selections from their writings, from the earliest period to the present day. By Evert A. Duyckinck and George L. Duyckinck. In two volumes. Philadelphia, Wm. Rutter & Co. (1975). Republished 1965 by Gale Research Company, Detroit. Also available from Gale on microfiche.

Use index in back of volume 2 to locate authors.

CyWA
Ref. PN 41 .M26 1958a

Cyclopedia of World Authors. Edited by Frank N. Magill and Dayton Kohler. New York, Harper & Row, Publishers (c1958). Originally published under title of *Masterplots Cyclopedia of World Authors.*

DcAmA

A Dictionary of American Authors. By Oscar Fay Adams. Fifth edition, revised and enlarged. Boston and New York, Houghton Mifflin Company, 1904. Reprinted 1969 by Gale Research Company. Also available from Gale on microfiche.

DcBiA

A Dictionary of Biographies of Authors Represented in the Authors Digest Series; With a supplemental list of later titles and a supplementary biographical section. Edited by Rossiter Johnson. New York, The Authors Press (1927). Reprinted 1974 by Gale Research Company, Detroit. Also available from Gale on microfiche.

DcCLA

A Dictionary of Contemporary Latin American Authors. Compiled by David William Foster. Tempe, Center for Latin American Studies, Arizona State University, 1975.

DcEnA

A Dictionary of English Authors, Biographical and Bibliographical. By R. Farquharson Sharp. New edition, revised with an appendix bringing the whole up to date and including a large amount of new matter. London, Kegan Paul, Trench, Trubner & Co., Ltd., 1904. Reprinted 1978 by Gale Research Company, Detroit. Also available from Gale on microfiche.

Biographies found in the Appendix are indicated by the code Ap.

DcEnL

Dictionary of English Literature; Being a comprehensive guide to English authors and their works. By W. Davenport Adams. Second edition. London, Cassell Petter & Galpin (n.d.). Reprinted 1966 by Gale Research Company, Detroit. Also available from Gale on microfiche.

DcEuL	*A Dictionary of European Literature;* Designed as a companion to English studies. By Laurie Magnus. Second, revised edition. London, George Routledge & Sons, Ltd.; New York, E. P. Dutton & Co., 1927. Republished 1974 by Gale Research Company, Detroit. Also available from Gale on microfiche.
DcLEnL	*A Dictionary of Literature in the English Language, From Chaucer to 1940.* In two volumes. Compiled and edited by Robin Myers. Oxford, London, Pergamon Press (c1970).
	Biographical entries are found in volume 1. An author-title index is provided in volume 2.
DcNAA	✓ *A Dictionary of North American Authors Deceased Before 1950.* Compiled by W. Stewart Wallace. Toronto, The Ryerson Press (c1951). Reprinted 1968 by Gale Research Company, Detroit. Also available from Gale on microfiche.
	This is an index to biographical material found in standard reference sources, many of which are not included in this index.
DcOrL	*Dictionary of Oriental Literatures.* In three volumes. Jaroslav Prusek, General Editor. New York, Basic Books, Inc., Publishers (c1974).
DcOrL 1	Volume 1, East Asia. Edited by Zbigniew Slupski.
DcOrL 2	Volume 2, South and South-East Asia. Edited by Dusan Zbavitel.
DcOrL 3	Volume 3, West Asia and North Africa. Edited by Jiri Becka.
DcRusL	✓ *Dictionary of Russian Literature.* By William E. Harkins. New York, Philosophical Library, Inc. (c1956). Reprinted 1971 by Greenwood Press, Publishers, Westport, Connecticut.
	This book gives biographies of authors and appraises each author's contribution to Russian letters.
DcSpL	*Dictionary of Spanish Literature.* By Maxim Newmark. New York, Philosophical Library, Inc. (c1956). Republished in 1970 by Littlefield, Adams & Co., Totowa, New Jersey.
DrAF 1976	✓ *A Dictionary of American Fiction Writers, 1976 Edition;* Names and addresses of more than 800 contemporary fiction writers whose work has been published in the United States. New York, Poets & Writers, Inc., 1976.
	Provides addresses with mention of writer's latest published works. Use index which begins on page 123, to find author listings.
DrAP 1975	*A Directory of American Poets, 1975 Edition;* Names and addresses of more than 1,500 contemporary poets whose work has been published in the United States. New York, Poets & Writers, Inc., 1975.
	Provides addresses with mention of poet's latest work. Use index, which begins on page vii, to find listings.
EarAB	*Early American Book Illustrators and Wood Engravers 1670-1870;* Volume 1, Main Catalogue. A Catalogue of a collection of American books illustrated for the most part with woodcuts and wood engravings in the Princeton University Library. By Sinclair Hamilton. Princeton, New Jersey, Princeton University Press, 1968 (c1958).
	Use the index in the back of the book to locate entries.
EarAB Sup	*Early American Book Illustrators and Wood Engravers 1670-1870;* Volume 2, Supplement. By Sinclair Hamilton. Princeton, New Jersey, Princeton University Press, 1968.
	Use the index in the back of this volume to locate entries.

Ref. PJ 31 .D5

Ref. PQ 6006 .N4 1963

Ref. PN 3448 .D4 E5

EncM&D   *Encyclopedia of Mystery and Detection.* Edited by Chris Steinbrunner, Otto Penzler, Marvin Lachman and Charles Shibuk. New York, McGraw-Hill (c1976).

Ref. PN 774 .LH33

EncWL   *Encyclopedia of World Literature in the 20th Century.* In three volumes. Edited by Bernard Fleischmann. An enlarged and updated edition of the Herder *Lexikon der Weltliteratur im 20.Jahrhundert.* New York, Frederick Ungar Publishing Co. (c1967).

Ref. PN 774 .L433 v. 4

EncWL Sup   *Encyclopedia of World Literature in the 20th Centruy.* Volume 4, Supplement. Edited by Frederick Ungar and Lina Mainiero. New York, Frederick Ungar Publishing Co. (c1975).

Ref. PN 451 .K8

EuAu   *European Authors, 1000-1900; A Biographical Dictionary of European Literature.* Edited by Stanley J. Kunitz and Vineta Colby, New York, The H. W. Wilson Company, 1967.

Ref. PN 451 .H3

EvEuW   *Everyman's Dictionary of European Writers.* By W. N. Hargreaves-Mawdsley. London, J. M. Dent & Sons Ltd; New York, E. P. Dutton & Co. Inc. (c1968).

EvLB   *Everyman's Dictionary of Literary Biography, English & American.* Compiled after John W. Cousin by D. C. Browning. London, J. M. Dent & Sons Ltd; New York, E. P. Dutton & Co. Inc. (1960 revised edition).

FamAI   *Famous Author-Illustrators for Young People.* By Norah Smaridge. New York, Dodd, Mead & Company (c1973).

FamAYP   *Famous Authors for Young People.* By Ramon P. Coffman and Nathan G. Goodman. New York, Dodd, Mead & Company (c1943).

FamSYP   *Famous Storytellers for Young People.* By Laura Benet. New York, Dodd, Mead & Company (c1968).

FemPA   *The Female Poets of America;* With portraits, biographical notices, and specimens of their writings. By Thomas Buchanan Read. Seventh edition, revised. Philadelphia. E. H. Butler & Co., 1857. To be reprinted by Gale Research Company. Available from Gale on microfiche.

HsB&A   *The House of Beadle and Adams and its Dime and Nickel Novels; The Story of a Vanished Literature.* By Albert Johannsen. Norman, University of Oklahoma Press (c1950).

          Biographical entries are found in volume 2, beginning on page 6.

HsB&A Sup   *The House of Beadle and Adams and its Dime and Nickel Novels . . .* Volume 3, Supplement, Addenda, Corrigenda. By Albert Johannsen. Norman, University of Oklahoma Press (c1962)

          Corrections and additions to the biographies in volume 2 begin on page 15.

Ref. j920 Ward 1970

IlBYP   *Illustrators of Books for Young People.* Second edition. By Martha E. Ward and Dorothy A. Marquardt. Metuchen, N. J., The Scarecrow Press, Inc., 1975.

IlCB 1945   *Illustrators of Children's Books, 1744-1945.* Compiled and edited by Bertha E. Mahony, Louise P. Latimer and Beulah Folmsbee. Boston, The Horn Book Inc. (c1945, reprinted 1970).

Ref. j920 I1 1946-56

IlCB 1956   *Illustrators of Children's Books, 1946-1956.* Compiled and edited by Ruth Hill Viguers, Marcia Dalphin and Bertha Mahoney Miller. Boston, The Horn Book, 1958.

Ref. j920 I1 1957-66

IlCB 1966   *Illustrators of Children's Books, 1957-1966.* Compiled and edited by Lee Kingman, Joanna Foster and Ruth Giles Lontoft. Boston, The Horn Book, Inc., 1968.

IndAu 1816   *Indiana Authors and Their Books, 1816-1916;* Biographical sketches of authors who published during the first century of Indiana statehood with lists of their books. Compiled by R. E. Banta. Crawfordsville, Indiana, Wabash College, 1949.

IndAu 1917   *Indiana Authors and Their Books, 1917-1966;* A continuation of Indiana Authors and Their Books, 1816-1916, and containing additional names from the earlier period. Compiled by Donald E. Thompson. Crawfordsville, Indiana, Wabash College 1974.

JBA 1934   *The Junior Book of Authors;* An introduction to the lives of writers and illustrators for younger readers from Lewis Carroll and Louisa Alcott to the present day. Illustrated with 260 photographs and drawings. Edited by Stanley J. Kunitz and Howard Haycraft. New York, The H. W. Wilson Company, 1934 (first edition).

The 1934 edition contains many biographies that were not carried over into the second edition (see below).

JBA 1951   *The Junior Book of Authors.* Second edition, revised. Edited by Stanley J. Kunitz and Howard Haycraft. New York, The H. W. Wilson Company, 1951.

Ref. j920 Juni v.1

LivBAA   *Living Black American Authors; A Biographical Dictionary.* By Ann Allen Shockley and Sue P. Chandler. New York and London, R. R. Bowker Company, 1973.

Ref. PS 153 .N5 S5

LivFWS   *The Living Female Writers of the South.* Edited by the author of *Southland Writers.* Philadelphia, Claxton, Remsen & Haffelfinger, 1872. To be reprinted by Gale Research Company. Available from Gale on microfiche.

LongC   *Longman Companion to Twentieth Century Literature.* By A. C. Ward. (London) Longman (c1970).

McGWD   *McGraw-Hill Encyclopedia of World Drama.* An international reference work in four volumes. New York, McGraw-Hill Book Company (c1972).

Ref. PN 1625 .M3

MnBBF   *The Men Behind Boy's Fiction.* By W. O. G. Lofts and D. J. Adley. London, Howard Baker (c1970).

Most entries are biographical.

MnnWr   *Minnesota Writers.* A collection of autobiographical stories by Minnesota prose writers. Edited and annotated by Carmen Nelson Richards. Minneapolis, T. S. Denison & Company, Inc. (c1961).

Use the table of contents to locate authors.

ModAL   *Modern American Literature.* A Library of Literary Criticism. Fourth enlarged edition. In three volumes. Compiled and edited by Dorothy Nyren Curley, Maurice Kramer and Elaine Fialka Kramer. New York, Frederick Ungar Publishing Co. (c1969).

Ref. PS 221 .C8 1969

A book of collected criticism.

ModAL Sup   *Modern American Literature.* A Library of Literary Criticism. Volume IV, Supplement to the fourth edition. Compiled and edited by Dorothy Nyren, Maurice Kramer, and Elaine Fialka Kramer. New York, Frederick Ungar Publishing Co. (c1976).

Ref. PS 221 .C8 1969 v. 4

A book of collected criticism.

ModBL   *Modern British Literature.* A Library of Literary Criticism. In three volumes. Compiled and edited by Ruth Z. Temple and Martin Tucker. New York, Frederick Ungar Publishing Co. (c1966).

Ref. PR 473 .T4

A book of collected criticism.

ModBL Sup   *Modern British Literature.* A Library of Literary Criticism. Volume IV, Supplement. Compiled and edited by Martin Tucker and Rita Stein. New York, Frederick Ungar Publishing Co. (c1975).

Ref. PR 473 .T4 v. 4

A book of collected criticism.

ModGL   *Modern German Literature*. A Library of Literary Criticism. In two volumes. Compiled and edited by Agnes Korner Domandi. New York, Frederick Ungar Publishing Co. (c1972).

Ref. PT 401 .D6

A book of collected criticism.

ModRL   *Modern Romance Literatures*. A Library of Literary Criticism. Compiled and edited by Dorothy Nyren Curley and Arthur Curley. New York, Frederick Ungar Publishing Co. (c1967).

Ref. PN 813 .C8

A book of collected criticism.

ModSL 1   ✓ *Modern Slavic Literatures. Volume 1: Russian Literature*. A Library of Literary Criticism. Compiled and edited by Vasa D. Mihailovich. New York, Frederick Ungar Publishing Co. (c1972).

A book of collected criticism.

ModSL 2   ✓ *Modern Slavic Literatures. Volume 2: Bulgarian, Czechoslovak, Polish, Ukrainian and Yugoslav Literatures*. A Library of Literary Criticism. Compiled and edited by Vasa D. Mihailovich, Igor Hajek, Zbigniew Folejewski, Bogdan Czaykowski, Leo D. Rudnytzky and Thomas Butler. New York, Frederick Ungar Publishing Co. (c1976)

A book of collected criticism. Authors listed alphabetically by country/language. Use the alphabetical listing on page vii to locate authors.

ModWD   *Modern World Drama; An Encyclopedia*. By Myron Matlaw. New York, E. P. Dutton & Co., Inc., 1972.

Ref. PN 1851 .M36

MorBMP   *More Books by More People*. Interviews with sixty-five authors of books for children. By Lee Bennett Hopkins. New York, Citation Press, 1974.

MorJA   *More Junior Authors*. Edited by Muriel Fuller. New York, The H. W. Wilson Company, 1963.

Ref. j920 Juni v.2

MouLC   *Moulton's Library of Literary Criticism of English and American Authors;* Through the beginning of the twentieth century. In four volumes. Abridged, revised and with additions by Martin Tucker. New York, Frederick Ungar Publishing Co. (c1966).

Ref. PR 83 .M73 1959
8 v.

MouLC 1   Volume 1, The Beginnings to the Seventeenth Century.

Alphabetical listing of authors begins on page xv.

MouLC 2   Volume 2, Neo-Classicism to the Romantic Period.

Alphabetical listing of authors begins on page vii.

MouLC 3   Volume 3, The Romantic Period to the Victorian Age.

Alphabetical listing of authors begins on page vii.

MouLC 4   Volume 4, The Mid-Nineteenth Century to Edwardianism.

Alphabetical listing of authors begins on page vii.

NewC   *The New Century Handbook of English Literature*. Revised edition. Edited by Clarence L. Barnhart with the assistance of William D. Halsey. New York, Appleton, Century, Crofts (c1967).

Ref. PR 19 .NH 1956

Newb 1922   ✓ *Newbery Medal Books, 1922-1955*. With their author's acceptance papers & related material chiefly from the Horn Book Magazine. Edited by Bertha Mahony Miller and Elinor Whitney Field. Horn Book Papers, Volume 1. Boston, The Horn Book, Incorporated (c1955).

NewbC 1956   ✓*Newbery and Caldecott Medal Books, 1956-1965*. With acceptance papers, biographies & related material chiefly from the Horn Book Magazine. Edited by Lee Kingman. Boston, The Horn Book, Incorporated, 1965.

NewbC 1966   ✓*Newbery and Caldecott Medal Books, 1966-1975*. Edited by Lee Kingman. Boston, The Horn Book Incorporated, 1975.

OhA&B   *Ohio Authors and Their Books;* Biographical data and selective bibliographies for Ohio authors, native and resident, 1796-1950. Edited by William Coyle. Cleveland and New York, The World Publishing Company (c1962).

Ref. Z 1323 .C6

OxAm   *The Oxford Companion to American Literature*. Fourth edition. By James D. Hart. New York, Oxford University Press, 1965.

Ref. PS 21 .H3 1965

OxCan   *The Oxford Companion to Canadian History and Literature*. By Norah Story. Toronto, Oxford University Press, 1967.

Ref. PR 9106 .S7 1967

OxCan Sup   *Supplement to the Oxford Companion to Canadian History and Literature*. Edited by William Toye. Toronto, Oxford University Press, 1973.

Most entries are biographical.

OxEng   *The Oxford Companion to English Literature*. Compiled and edited by Sir Paul Harvey. Fourth edition revised by Dorothy Eagle. Oxford, New York, The Oxford University Press (c1967).

Ref. PR 19 .H3 1967

OxFr   *The Oxford Companion to French Literature*. Compiled and edited by Sir Paul Harvey and J. E. Heseltine. Oxford, Clarendon Press (c1959; 1966 corrected edition).

Ref. PQ 41 .H3 A59

OxGer   *The Oxford Companion to German Literature*. By Henry and Mary Garland. Oxford, Clarendon Press, 1976.

Ref. PT 41 .G3

Pen Am   *The Penguin Companion to American Literature*. Edited by Malcolm Bradbury, Eric Mottram and Jean Franco. New York, McGraw-Hill Book Company (c1971). On spine: *The Penguin Companion to World Literature*.

Ref. PN 843 .P4

In two alphabetical sections. One is for the USA, the other for Latin America.

Pen Cl   *The Penguin Companion to Classical, Oriental & African Literature*. Edited by D. M. Lang and D. R. Dudley. New York, McGraw-Hill Book Company (c1969). On spine: *The Penguin Companion to World Literature*.

Ref. PA 31 .P4 1971

In four alphabetical sections by period and/or region.

Pen Eng   *The Penguin Companion to English Literature*. Edited by David Daiches. New York, McGraw-Hill Book Company (c1971). On spine: *The Penguin Companion to World Literature*.

Ref. PN 849 .C5 P4

Pen Eur   *The Penguin Companion to European Literature*. Edited by Anthony Thorlby. New York, McGraw-Hill Book Company (c1969). On spine: *The Penguin Companion to World Literature*.

Ref. PN 41 .P43 1971

PiP   *The Pied Pipers; Interviews with the Influential Creators of Children's Literature*. Edited by Justin Wintle and Emma Fisher. New York, Paddington Press Ltd. —The Two Continents Publishing Group (n.d.).

PoCh   *The Poets of the Church; A Series of Biographical Sketches of Hymn-Writers with Notes on Their Hymns*. By Edwin F. Hatfield. New York, Anson D. F. Randolph & Company (c1884). To be reprinted by Gale Research Company. Available from Gale on microfiche.

PoIre   *The Poets of Ireland; A Biographical and Bibliographical Dictionary of Irish Writers of English Verse*. By D. J. O'Donoghue. Dublin, Hodges Figgis & Co., LTD.; London, Henry Frowde, Oxford University Press, 1912. Reprinted 1968 by Gale

Research Company, Detroit. Available from Gale on microfiche.

*Has two biographical sections. The main section begins on page 5. The appendix
starts on page 495.*

PoLE   *The Poets Laureate of England.* Being a history of the office of poet laureate, biographical notices of its holders, and a collection of the satires, epigrams, and lampoons
directed against them. By Walter Hamilton. London, Elliot Stock, 1879. Republished 1968 by Gale Research Company, Detroit. Available from Gale on
microfiche.

Use the index to locate entries.

PueRA   *Puerto Rican Authors; A Biobibliographic Handbook.* By Marnesba D. Hill and Harold
B. Schleifer. Translations of entries into Spanish by Daniel Maratos. Metuchen,
N. J., The Scarecrow Press, Inc., 1974.

A bilingual edition.

RAdv 1   *The Reader's Adviser; A Layman's Guide to Literature.* 12th edition. Volume 1, *The
Best in American and British Fiction, Poetry, Essays, Literary Biography, Bib-
liography, and Reference.* Edited by Sarah L. Prakken. New York and London,
R. R. Bowker Company, 1974.

Ref. Z 1035 B7 v 1

See the index for locations of author biographies and bibliographies.

RCom   *The Reader's Companion to World Literature.* Edited by Lillian Herlands Hornstein.
Second edition, revised and updated by Lillian Herlands Hornstein, Leon Edel
and Horst Frenz. New York, New American Library (c1973).

REn   *The Reader's Encyclopedia.* By William Rose Benet. Second edition. New York,
Thomas Y. Crowell Company (c1965).

Ref. PN 41 .B4 1965

REnAL   *The Reader's Encyclopedia of American Literature.* By Max J. Herzberg. New York,
Thomas Y. Crowell Company (c1962).

Ref. PS 21 .R4

REnWD   *The Reader's Encyclopedia of World Drama.* Edited by John Gassner and Edward
Quinn. New York, Thomas Y. Crowell Company (c1969).

Ref. PN 1625 .G3 1969

RGAfL   *A Reader's Guide to African Literature.* Compiled and edited by Hans M. Zell and
Helene Silver. New York, Africana Publishing Corporation (c1971).

Biographies begin on page 113.

SenS   *A Sense of Story; Essays on Contemporary Writers for Children.* By John Rowe
Townsend. (London) Longman (c1971).

SixAP   *Sixty American Poets 1896-1944.* Selected, with preface and critical notes by Allen
Tate. Washington, The Library of Congress, 1954. Reprinted 1969 by Gale
Research Company, Detroit. Available from Gale on microfiche.

A bibliographical study of major American poets.

SmATA   *Something About the Author.* Facts and pictures about contemporary authors and
illustrators of books for young people. Edited by Anne Commire. Detroit, Gale
Research Company (c1971-1976). Also available from Gale on microfiche.

Ref. j920 Som

SmATA 1	Volume 1, 1971
SmATA 2	Volume 2, 1971
SmATA 3	Volume 3, 1972
SmATA 4	Volume 4, 1973
SmATA 5	Volume 5, 1973
SmATA 6	Volume 6, 1974

SmATA 7	Volume 7, 1975
SmATA 8	Volume 8, 1976
SmATA 9	Volume 9, 1976
SmATA 10	Volume 10, 1976
SmATA XR	Index to volume 1-10, *found in back of volume 10. This code refers to pseudonym entries which appear only as cross references in the cumulative index to* Something About the Author.
St&VC	*Story and Verse for Children.* By Miriam Blanton Huber. Third edition. (New York) The Macmillan Company (c1965).

Biographies are located on pages 793-856.

TexWr	*Texas Writers of Today.* By Florence Elberta Barns. Ann Arbor, Gryphon Books, 1971 (Reprint of 1935 edition). Also available from Gale on microfiche.
ThBJA	*Third Book of Junior Authors.* Edited by Doris De Montreville and Donna Hill. New York, The H. W. Wilson Company, 1972.

Ref. j920 Juni v.3

TwCA	*Twentieth Century Authors; A Biographical Dictionary of Modern Literature.* Edited by Stanley J. Kunitz and Howard Haycraft. New York, The H. W. Wilson Company, 1942.

Ref. PN 771 . K86

TwCA Sup	*Twentieth Century Authors* ... First Supplement. Edited by Stanley J. Kunitz and Vineta Colby. New York, The H. W. Wilson Company, 1955.

Ref. PN 771 . K86s

TwCW	*Twentieth Century Writing; A Reader's Guide to Contemporary Literature.* Edited by Kenneth Richardson. (Levittown, N. Y.) Transatlantic Arts, Inc. (c1969).

Ref. PN 771 .R5 1971

WebEAL	*Webster's New World Companion to English and American Literature.* Edited by Arthur Pollard. New York, World Publishing (c1973).

Ref. PR 19 .W4 1973

WhCL	*The Who's Who of Children's Literature.* By Brian Doyle. New York, Schocken Books (c1968).
WhGrA	*Who's Who in Graphic Art.* An illustrated book of reference to the world's leading graphic designers, illustrators, typographers and cartoonists. Zurich, Amstutz & Herdeg Graphis Press (c1962).

Use the index, which begins on page 576, to locate citations.

WhLA	*Who's Who Among Living Authors of Older Nations.* Covering the literary activities of living authors and writers of all countries of the world except the United States of America, Canada, Mexico, Alaska, Hawaii, Newfoundland, the Phillipine Islands, the West Indies, and Central America. Volume 1, 1931-1932. Edited by A. Lawrence. Golden Syndicate Publishing Company (c1931). Republished 1966 by Gale Research Company, Detroit. Also available from Gale on microfiche.
WhPNW	*Who's Who Among Pacific Northwest Authors.* Second edition. Edited by Frances Valentine Wright. Pacific Northwest Library Association, Reference Division, 1969.

Biographies are alphabetical by state. Use the index, which begins on page 103, to locate citations.

WhTwL	*Who's Who in Twentieth Century Literature.* By Martin Seymour-Smith. New York, Holt, Rinehart and Winston (c1976).

Ref. PN 451 .S4

WhWNAA	*Who Was Who Among North American Authors, 1921-1939.* In two volumes. Gale Composite Biographical Dictionary Series Number 1. Detroit, Gale Research Company (c1976). Originally published as *Who's Who Among North American Authors,* volumes 1-7, by the Golden Syndicate Publishing Company (1921-1939). Also available from Gale on microfiche.

WiscW   *Wisconsin Writers; Sketches and Studies.* By William A. Titus. Detroit, Gale Research
                Company, 1974. (Reprint of 1930 edition published in Chicago). Also available
                from Gale on microfiche.

                Use the table of contents to locate authors.

WorAu   *World Authors, 1950-1970.* A companion volume to *Twentieth Century Authors.*
Ref. PN 451 .W3   Edited by John Wakeman. New York, The H. W. Wilson Company, 1975.

WrD 1976   *The Writers Directory, 1976-78.* London, St. James Press; New York, St. Martin's
Ref. PS 1 .W73   Press (c1976).

YABC 1   *Yesterday's Authors of Books for Children.* Facts and pictures about authors and
                illustrators of books for young people, from early times to 1960. Edited by Anne
                Commire. Volume 1. Detroit, Gale Research Company (c1977). Also available
                from Gale on microfiche.

A

A, F P *ConAmA*
A, H *PoIre*
A, M A *PoIre*
A A *LongC*
A D B *WhLA*
A G A P *WhWNAA*
A K H B *DcEnL*
A Kadosh *PueRA*
A L O E *ChPo, Chmbr 3, DcEnL, NewC, WhCL*
A M *ConAu 49*
A N *WhWNAA*
A R P M *NewC*
A Riposte *TwCA, TwCA Sup*
A Ying *DcOrL 1*
Aachen, C V *WhWNAA*
Aafjes, Lambertus Jacobus Johannes 1914- *EvEuW*
Aaker, David A 1938- *ConAu 49*
Aakjaer, Jeppe 1866-1930 *CasWL, ChPo, ClDMEuL, EncWL, EvEuW, Pen Eur, REn*
Aal, Johannes 1500?-1551? *OxGer*
Aanrud, Hans 1863- *ClDMEuL*
Aar, Alexis 1853- *BiD&SB*
Aardema, Verna 1911- *ConAu 5R, SmATA 4, WrD 1976*
Aarestrup, Carl Ludvig Emil 1800-1856 *CasWL, DcEuL, EvEuW*
Aarestrup, Emil 1800-1856 *BbD, BiD&SB, Pen Eur*
Aaron, Benjamin 1915- *ConAu 23*
Aaron, Charles Dettie 1866- *AmLY, WhWNAA*
Aaron, Charles Howard *Alli Sup*
Aaron, Chester 1923- *ConAu 21, SmATA 9*
Aaron, Daniel 1912- *AmA&B, Au&Wr, ConAu 13R*
Aaron, James Ethridge 1927- *ConAu 23, WrD 1976*
Aaron, Jonathan *DrAP 1975*
Aaron, Madeleine Germaine 1896- *WhWNAA*
Aaron, Richard I 1901- *Au&Wr*
Aaron, Samuel 1800-1865 *DcAmA, DcNAA*
Aaronovitch, Sam 1919- *Au&Wr, ConAu 13R, WrD 1976*
Aarons, Edward S 1916-1975 *ConAu 57, EncM&D*
Aarons, Slim 1916- *WrD 1976*
Aaronsohn, Michael 1896- *OhA&B*
Aaronson, Bernard S 1924- *ConAu 29*
Aaronson, Irving 1895-1963 *AmSCAP 66*
Aarsleff, Hans 1925- *ConAu 21*
Aasen, Ivar 1813-1896 *ClDMEuL, DcEuL, Pen Eur*
Aasen, Ivar Andreas 1813-1896 *BbD, BiD&SB, CasWL, EvEuW, REn*
Aaseng, Rolf E 1923- *ConAu 49*
Ab'-O'-Th'-Yate *NewC*
Abad, Pero *DcSpL*
Abaelard, Peter *NewC*

Abag *McGWD*
Abailard *OxFr*
Abailard, Peter *NewC*
Abailard, Pierre *EuA*
Abailard, Pierre 1079-1142 *OxFr*
Abano, Pietro D' 1250?-1316? *REn*
Abarbanel, Isaac Ben Jehudah 1437-1508 *CasWL, EvEuW*
Abarbanel, Judah 1460?-1535? *CasWL, EuA*
Abarbanel, Leone Ebreo 1460?-1535? *EvEuW*
Abarbanell, Jacob Ralph 1852-1922 *Alli Sup, AmA&B, DcNAA, HsB&A*
Abasheli, Aleksandre 1884-1954 *DcOrL 3*
Abashidze, Grigol 1913- *DcOrL 3*
Abasiyanik, Sait Faik 1906-1954 *DcOrL 3*
Abay *DcOrL 3*
Abba, Giuseppe Cesare 1838-1910 *BiD&SB, CasWL, EvEuW*
Abbad Y Lasierra, Inigo 1745-1813 *PueRA*
Abbagnano, Nicola 1901- *ConAu 33*
Abbas Effendi *CasWL*
Abbas, Ahmad 1914- *ConNov 1972, ConNov 1976, WrD 1976*
Abbas, Khwaja Ahmad 1914- *ConAu 57, DcLEnL, DcOrL 2*
Abbat, Per *DcSpL*
Abbati, Francesco *Alli Sup*
Abbatt, Richard *Alli Sup*
Abbatt, William 1851-1935? *AmA&B, AmLY, DcAmA, DcNAA, WhWNAA*
Abbay, Richard *Alli Sup*
Abbazia, Patrick 1937- *ConAu 57*
Abbe, Cleveland 1838-1916 *BbD, BiD&SB, DcAmA, DcNAA, OhA&B*
Abbe, Elfriede 1919- *ConAu 13R*
Abbe, Frederick Randolph 1827-1889 *Alli Sup, DcAmA, DcNAA*
Abbe, George 1911- *AmA&B, ConAu 25*
Abbe, Truman 1873- *WhWNAA*
Abbett, Robert W 1902- *WrD 1976*
Abbey, Charles John 1833- *Alli Sup, ChPo S1*
Abbey, Charlotte S *Alli Sup*
Abbey, Edward 1927- *ConAu 45, DrAF 1976*
Abbey, Edward Austin 1852-1911 *ChPo*
Abbey, Edwin Austin 1852-1911 *OxAm*
Abbey, Everett Lucius 1855-1945 *DcNAA, OhA&B*
Abbey, Henry 1842-1911 *Alli Sup, AmA, AmA&B, ChPo, ChPo S1, ChPo S2, CnDAL, DcAmA, DcNAA, REnAL*
Abbey, Merrill R 1905- *ConAu 1R, WrD 1976*
Abbey, Richard 1805-1901? *Alli Sup, BiDSA, DcAmA, DcNAA*
Abbey, Staton 1912- *Au&Wr*
Abbie, Andrew Arthur 1905- *Au&Wr*
Abbing, Justine *CasWL*
Abbo Of Fleury 945?-1004 *NewC, OxEng*
Abbon Of Fleury 945?-1004 *NewC*
Abbot SEE ALSO Abbott
Abbot *Alli*

Abbot, Abiel 1765-1859 *DcAmA, DcNAA*
Abbot, Abiel 1770-1828 *Alli, DcAmA, DcNAA*
Abbot, Anthony 1893-1952 *EncM&D*
Abbot, Charles *Alli*
Abbot, Charles 1757-1829 *Alli, DcEnL*
Abbot, Charles 1762-1832 *Alli, DcEnL*
Abbot, Charles, Baron Colchester 1798-1867 *Alli Sup*
Abbot, Charles Greeley 1872-1973 *ConAu 45, WhWNAA*
Abbot, Everett Vergnies 1862-1925 *DcNAA*
Abbot, Ezra 1819-1884 *Alli Sup, BbD, BiD&SB, CyAL 1, DcAmA, DcNAA*
Abbot, Francis Ellingwood 1836-1903 *Alli Sup, BiD&SB, ChPo S1, DcAmA, DcNAA*
Abbot, George 1562-1633 *Alli, DcEnL, NewC*
Abbot, George 1603?-1649 *Alli, NewC*
Abbot, George Jacob *Alli Sup*
Abbot, George Maurice *Alli Sup*
Abbot, Gorham Dummer 1807-1874 *DcAmA, DcNAA*
Abbot, Henry *Alli*
Abbot, Henry Larcom 1831-1927 *Alli Sup, DcAmA, DcNAA*
Abbot, Hull d1774 *Alli*
Abbot, Jacob 1803-1879 *EvLB*
Abbot, Joel 1766-1826 *DcNAA*
Abbot, John *Alli*
Abbot, L A *Alli Sup*
Abbot, Reginald Edward, Baron Colchester 1842- *Alli Sup*
Abbot, Robert *Alli*
Abbot, Robert 1560-1617 *Alli, DcEnL, NewC*
Abbot, Robert 1585-1653 *Alli*
Abbot, T Eastoc *Alli*
Abbot, William Ebenezer 1810-1888 *DcNAA*
Abbot, Willis John 1863-1934 *Alli Sup, AmA&B, BiD&SB, DcAmA, DcNAA, REnAL*
Abbott SEE ALSO Abbot
Abbott, A A *AmA&B*
Abbott, A F *Alli Sup*
Abbott, A O *Alli Sup*
Abbott, Abbott A *Alli Sup*
Abbott, Alexander C 1860-1935 *DcAmA, DcNAA*
Abbott, Alice *ConAu XR, SmATA 8*
Abbott, Alice I *Alli Sup*
Abbott, Allan 1876- *WhWNAA*
Abbott, Anne 1931- *Au&Wr*
Abbott, Anne W *Alli Sup*
Abbott, Anthony S 1935- *ConAu 17R*
Abbott, Arletta Maria 1856-1933 *DcNAA*
Abbott, Arthur Vaughan 1854-1906 *DcAmA, DcNAA*
Abbott, Augustus Levi 1858-1934 *DcNAA*
Abbott, Austin 1831-1896 *Alli Sup, Alli, AmA&B, DcAmA, DcNAA*
Abbott, Avery *WhWNAA*
Abbott, Barbara *ChPo*

Abeling, Theodor 1862- *WhLA*
Abell, Arunah Shepherdson 1806-1888 *AmA&B*
Abell, George O 1927- *ConAu 9R*, *WrD 1976*
Abell, John *Alli*
Abell, Joshua d1846 *PoIre*
Abell, Kathleen 1938- *ConAu 49*, *SmATA 9*
Abell, Kjeld 1901-1961 *CasWL*, *CIDMEuL*,
  CnMD, *CnThe*, *EncWL*, *EvEuW*,
  McGWD, *ModWD*, *Pen Eur*, *REn*,
  REnWD
Abell, Mrs. L G *Alli*
Abell, Lucia Elizabeth *Alli Sup*
Abell, Thomas d1540 *NewC*
Abell, Walter 1897-1956 *AmA&B*, *WhWNAA*
Abella, Irving Martin 1940- *ConAu 49*
Abelow, Samuel Philip d1948 *DcNAA*
Abels, Jules 1913- *ConAu 61*
Abelson, Raziel A 1921- *ConAu 9R*
Abelson, Robert P 1928- *ConAu 41*
Aben-Ezra *EvEuW*
Abencerrages *REn*
Abencerraje Y LaHermosa Xarifa, H Del'
  DcEuL
Abend, Hallett 1884-1955 *AmA&B*
Abend, Norman A 1931- *ConAu 33*
Aber 1884- *WhLA*
Aber, William M 1929- *ConAu 57*
Aberbach, Joel D 1940- *ConAu 45*
Aberconway, Lady Christabel 1890- *Au&Wr*
Abercrombie, Elizabeth 1848- *ChPo S1*
Abercrombie, James 1758-1841 *DcNAA*
Abercrombie, John *Alli Sup*, *Chmbr 3*
Abercrombie, John 1726-1806 *Alli*
Abercrombie, John 1780?-1844 *Alli*, *BbD*,
  BrAu 19, *DcEnL*, *EvLB*
Abercrombie, John William 1866-1940 *BiDSA*,
  DcNAA
Abercrombie, Lascelles 1881-1938 *ChPo*,
  ChPo S1, *Chmbr 3*, *DcLEnL*, *EncWL*,
  EvLB, *LongC*, *ModBL*, *NewC*, *OxEng*,
  Pen Eng, *REn*, *TwCA*, *TwCA Sup*,
  TwCW, *WebEAL*, *WhLA*
Abercrombie, Michael 1912- *Au&Wr*
Abercrombie, Nigel James 1908- *WrD 1976*
Abercrombie, Patrick 1656-1720 *Alli*, *DcEnL*,
  EvLB
Abercrombie, Patrick 1879-1957 *LongC*
Abercrombie, Robert *Alli Sup*
Abercromby, David *Alli*, *Alli*
Abercromby, James, Baron Dunfermline
  1776-1858 *Alli Sup*
Abercromby, Patrick 1656-1716 *CasWL*,
  Chmbr 2
Abercromby, Ralph 1842- *Alli Sup*
Aberdare, Lord *Alli Sup*
Aberdeen, Lady 1857-1939 *OxCan*
Aberdeen, Lord 1847-1934 *OxCan*
Aberdeen, George, Earl Of *Alli*
Aberdour, Alexander *Alli*
Aberg, Sherrill E 1924- *ConAu 21*
Aberhart, William *OxCan*
Aberigh-Mackay *Alli Sup*
Aberigh-Mackay, George Robert 1848-1881
  BrAu 19
Aberle, David F 1918- *ConAu 21*
Aberle, John Wayne 1919- *ConAu 1R*
Aberle, Kathleen Gough 1925- *ConAu 13R*
Aberle, Will *ChPo S2*
Abernathy, David M 1933- *ConAu 53*
Abernathy, Elton 1913- *ConAu 17R*
Abernathy, M Glenn 1921- *ConAu 13R*
Abernethie, Thomas *Alli*
Abernethy, Alonzo 1836-1915 *DcNAA*,
  OhA&B
Abernethy, Arthur Talmadge 1872- *BiDSA*
Abernethy, Cecil Emory 1908- *Au&Wr*
Abernethy, Francis Edward 1925- *ConAu 21*
Abernethy, George Lawrence 1910- *ConAu 1R*
Abernethy, J W *BiDSA*
Abernethy, John *Alli*, *BiDLA*, *BiDLA Sup*
Abernethy, John 1680-1740 *Alli*
Abernethy, John 1763-1831 *Alli*, *DcEnL*
Abernethy, Robert G 1927- *ConAu 21*,
  SmATA 5
Abernethy, Thomas Perkins 1890- *AmA&B*,
  ConAu P-1
Abernethy, Wealtha Vieth 1870-1956 *OhA&B*
Abershaw, Louis Jeremiah 1773?-1795 *NewC*

Abert, Josef Friedrich 1879- *WhLA*
Abert, Silvanus Thayer 1828-1903 *Alli Sup*,
  DcAmA
Abert, Sylvanus Thayer 1828-1903 *DcNAA*
Abeson, Marion 1914- *AmSCAP 66*
Abet, Adam 1867- *WhWNAA*
Abetti, Giorgio 1882- *Au&Wr*
Abhedananda, Swami 1866- *AmLY*
Abhinavagupta *DcOrL 2*
Abildgaard, Ove 1916- *CasWL*
Abingdon, Earl Of *Alli*, *NewC*
Abingdon, Thomas *Alli*
Abington, Frances 1737-1815 *NewC*
Abington, S J *Alli Sup*
Abington, Thomas *Alli*
Abington, William *Alli*
Abisch, Roslyn Kroop 1927- *ConAu 21*,
  SmATA 9
Abisch, Roz *ChPo S1*, *ConAu XR*,
  SmATA XR
Abish, Walter *DrAF 1976*, *DrAP 1975*
Ablancourt, Nicolas Perrot D' 1606-1664 *OxFr*
Ablass, Bruno 1866- *WhLA*
Able, Thomas d1540 *Alli*, *DcEnL*
Ableman, Paul 1927- *ConAu 61*, *ConDr*,
  ConNov 1972, *ConNov 1976*, *WrD 1976*
Abler, Ronald 1939- *ConAu 53*
Ables, Richard Louis 1911- *AmSCAP 66*
Ablesimov, Alexander Onisimovich 1742?-1783
  CasWL, *DcRusL*, *EvEuW*
Ablett, William H *Alli Sup*
Abney, A H *Alli Sup*
Abney, Louise *WhWNAA*
Abney, William DeWivesleslie 1843- *Alli Sup*
Aboab, Isaac 1300?- *CasWL*, *Pen Eur*
Abodaher, David J 1919- *ConAu 17R*
Abonyi, Lajos 1833- *BiD&SB*
About, Edmond Francois Valentin 1828-1885
  BbD, *BiD&SB*, *CasWL*, *CIDMEuL*,
  CyWA, *DcBiA*, *DcEuL*, *EvEuW*, *OxFr*,
  Pen Eur
Abovian, Khatchatur 1809-1848 *DcOrL 3*
Abrabanel, Judah Leon 1465?-1535 *REn*
Abrabanel, Solomon *Alli*
Abrahall, Bennet Hoskyns- *Alli Sup*
Abrahall, Chandos Hoskyns- *Alli Sup*
Abrahall, Clare Hoskyns *ChPo S1*,
  ConAu XR
Abrahall, John Hoskyns 1829-1891 *Alli Sup*,
  ChPo
Abraham *REn*
Abraham A Sancta Clara 1644-1709 *BiD&SB*,
  CasWL, *Pen Eur*
Abraham A Santa Clara 1644-1709 *OxGer*
Abraham Bedersi 1240?-1300? *CasWL*
Abraham Ben Meir Ibn Ezra 1092-1167 *BiD&SB*,
  EuA, *REn*
Abraham Ibn Ezra *CasWL*, *Pen Cl*
Abraham Ibn Hasdai d1240 *CasWL*
Abraham, Mrs. Ashley P *ChPo S2*
Abraham, Ashley Perry 1876- *ChPo S1*,
  WhLA
Abraham, Charles John 1815- *Alli Sup*
Abraham, Claude Kurt 1931- *ConAu 23*,
  WrD 1976
Abraham, Edward Penley 1913- *Au&Wr*,
  WrD 1976
Abraham, George Dixon 1872- *WhLA*
Abraham, Henry Augustus *Alli Sup*
Abraham, Henry Julian 1921- *ConAu 5R*,
  WrD 1976
Abraham, J H *Alli*
Abraham, James Johnston 1876- *WhLA*
Abraham, Philip *Alli Sup*
Abraham, Robert d1854 *BbtC*, *DcNAA*
Abraham, Samuel 1885- *WhWNAA*
Abraham, Willard 1916- *ConAu 13R*,
  WrD 1976
Abraham, William Emmanuel 1934-
  ConAu 13R, *WrD 1976*
Abraham, William I 1919- *ConAu 25*
Abrahams, Doris Caroline 1901- *ChPo S2*
Abrahams, Gerald 1907- *Au&Wr*
Abrahams, Harold Maurice 1899- *Au&Wr*
Abrahams, Hilary Ruth 1938- *IlBYP*,
  IlCB 1966
Abrahams, Howard Phineas 1904- *ConAu 57*
Abrahams, J *Alli Sup*

Abrahams, L B *Alli Sup*
Abrahams, Maurice 1883-1931 *AmSCAP 66*
Abrahams, Peter 1919- *AfA 1*, *Au&Wr*,
  CasWL, *ConAu 57*, *ConLC 4*,
  ConNov 1976, *Pen Eng*, *RGAfl*, *TwCW*,
  WebEAL, *WorAu*, *WrD 1976*
Abrahams, R G 1934- *ConAu 25*
Abrahams, Robert David 1905- *AmA&B*,
  AuBYP, *ConAu 33*, *SmATA 4*
Abrahams, Roger D 1933- *ConAu 9R*,
  WrD 1976
Abrahams, William Miller 1919- *ConAu 61*
Abrahamsen, David 1903- *AmA&B*
Abrahamson, Una *OxCan Sup*
Abram, E *Alli Sup*
Abram, H S 1931- *ConAu 29*
Abram, Theresa Williams 1903- *BlkAW*
Abram, William Alexander *Alli Sup*
Abram, William John *Alli Sup*
Abramov, Fyodor 1920- *TwCW*
Abramovitch, Sholem Jacob *CasWL*
Abramovitz, Moses 1912- *AmA&B*, *Au&Wr*
Abramowitz, Jack 1918- *ConAu 5R*
Abramowitz, Shalom Jacob 1836-1917 *EuA*
Abrams, Albert 1863?-1924 *DcNAA*,
  WhWNAA
Abrams, Alexander St. Clair *BiDSA*
Abrams, Charles 1901-1970 *AmA&B*,
  ConAu 23
Abrams, George J 1918- *ConAu 61*
Abrams, Harry N *AmA&B*
Abrams, Israel Aaron 1882- *WhWNAA*
Abrams, Leroy 1874- *AmLY*, *WhWNAA*
Abrams, Lester *IlBYP*
Abrams, Lisle Joseph 1903- *OhA&B*
Abrams, Mark 1906- *Au&Wr*
Abrams, Meyer Howard 1912- *AmA&B*,
  ConAu 57
Abrams, Peter D 1936- *ConAu 33*
Abrams, Richard M 1932- *ConAu 13R*,
  WrD 1976
Abrams, Robert J 1924- *BlkAW*
Abrams, Sam 1935- *ConAu 21*
Abrams, Stephen Irwin 1938- *BiDPar*
Abramson, Dolores *BlkAW*
Abramson, Doris E 1925- *ConAu 25*
Abramson, Harold J 1934- *ConAu 45*
Abramson, Joan 1932- *ConAu 25*
Abramson, Martin 1921- *ConAu 49*
Abramson, Paul R 1937- *ConAu 61*
Abrantes, Jean-Andoche Junot, Duc D'
  1771-1813 *OxFr*
Abrantes, Laure Permon, Duchesse D' 1785-1838
  OxFr
Abranyi, Emil 1851- *BiD&SB*
Abranyi, Kornel 1849- *BbD*, *BiD&SB*
Abrash, Merritt 1930- *ConAu 23*
Abravanel, Isaac 1437-1508 *CasWL*, *DcEuL*,
  Pen Eur
Abravanel, Judah 1460?-1535? *DcEuL*, *EuA*,
  Pen Eur
Abravanel, Judas *DcSpL*
Abreau, Maria Isabel 1919- *ConAu 45*
Abreu, Casimiro Jose Marques De 1839-1860
  Pen Am
Abricht, Johann *ChPo*
Abril, Mariano 1861-1935 *PueRA*
Abril, Xavier 1905- *DcCLA*
Abro, Jamaluddin 1924- *DcOrL 2*
Abromowitz, Sholem Yakob *CIDMEuL*
Abruquah, Joseph Wilfred 1940?- *AfA 1*
Abs, P Josef 1880- *WhLA*
Absalom, Roger Neil Lewis 1929- *Au&Wr*,
  WrD 1976
Abschatz, Hans Assmann, Freiherr Von
  1646-1699 *OxGer*
Abse, Dannie 1923- *Au&Wr*, *ChPo S1*,
  ConAu 53, *ConDr*, *ConNov 1976*,
  ConP 1970, *ConP 1975*, *DrAP 1975*,
  ModBL Sup, *WorAu*, *WrD 1976*
Abse, David Wilfred 1915- *Au&Wr*,
  ConAu 49
Abse, Davis Wilfred 1915- *WrD 1976*
Abshire, David M 1926- *ConAu 23*
Absinthe, Pere *DcNAA*
Absolom, Charles Severn *Alli Sup*
Absolon *OxGer*
Absolon, John 1815-1895 *ChPo*

Abt, Isaac Arthur 1867- *WhWNAA*
Abt, Lawrence Edwin 1915- *ConAu 33*
Abu 'Ali Ebne Sina *DcOrL 3*
Abu 'Ali Ibn Sina *CasWL*
Abu Bakr *DcOrL 3*
Abu Dulama Ibn Al-Djuan 720?-777? *AfA 1*
Abu Jaber, Kamel S 1932- *ConAu 21*
Abu 'l-Atahiya 748-825? *DcOrL 3*
Abu 'l-Fida, Isma'il 1273-1331 *DcOrL 3*
Abu-Lughod, Ibrahim Ali 1929- *ConAu 5R*
Abu Madi, Iliya 1889?-1957 *CasWL, DcOrL 3*
Abu-Nuwas 762?-815 *BiD&SB, CasWL,*
  DcOrL 3, Pen Cl
Abu Rayhan *CasWL*
Abu Risha, 'Umar 1910- *CasWL*
Abu Sa'id 967?-1049 *CasWL, DcOrL 3*
Abu Shabaka, Ilyas 1903-1947 *CasWL*
Abu Shadi, Ahmad Zaki 1892-1955 *DcOrL 3*
Abu Talib, Kalim Hamadani *DcOrL 2*
Abu Tammam *CasWL, DcOrL 3*
Abubacer *CasWL, DcOrL 3*
Abubakar, Alhaji Imam *CasWL*
Abubakar, Alhaji Sir Tafawa Balewa 1912-1966
  AfA 1, CasWL
Abubakar, Iman 1920?- *AfA 1*
Abu'l-Ala *ChPo S2*
Abu'l-'Ala Al-Ma'arri 973-1058? *CasWL,*
  Pen Cl
Abu'l-'Atahiyah *CasWL*
Abu'l-Faraj, 'Ali Ibn Husain, Al-I 879-967
  Pen Cl
Abu'l-Hasan, Mian d1711 *DcOrL 2*
Abu'l M'ali Nasr Allah *CasWL*
Abulafia, Todros 1247-1300? *CasWL, Pen Eur*
Abul'ala Ganjevi *DcOrL 3*
Abulfaragius 1226-1286 *BiD&SB*
Abulfaraj 1226-1286 *BbD, BiD&SB*
Abulfeda, Ismail Ibn Ali 1273-1331 *BiD&SB*
Abushady, Ahmad Zaki 1892-1955 *CasWL*
Abutsu 1233?-1283? *CasWL 1, DcOrL 1*
Academic Investor *ConAu XR*
Acadian, An *OxCan*
Acart DeHesdin, Jean *CasWL*
Acarya, Bhanubhakta 1814-1869 *DcOrL 2*
Acaster, John *Alli Sup*
Acca d740? *Alli, BiB S*
Accius, Lucius 170BC-085?BC *BiD&SB,*
  CasWL, Pen Cl
Accola, Louis W 1937- *ConAu 29*
Accolti, Bernardo 1458?-1535 *BbD, BiD&SB,*
  CasWL, REn
Accolti, Francesco 1416-1484? *CasWL*
Acconci, Vito 1940- *ConP 1970*
Accoramboni, Vittoria 1557?-1585 *NewC, REn*
Accum, Frederic *BiDLA, BiDLA Sup*
Accum, Frederick 1769-1838 *Alli*
Ace Williams *WhWNAA*
Ace, Daniel *Alli Sup*
Ace, Goodman 1899- *ConAu 61*
Acevedo Diaz, Eduardo 1851-1921? *CasWL,*
  DcSpL, EncWL, Pen Am, REn
Acevedo Diaz, Eduardo 1882- *EncWL*
Achard *Alli*
Achard, Eugene 1884- *WhWNAA*
Achard, F C *Alli*
Achard, George *ConAu XR*
Achard, Louis Amedee 1814-1875 *BbD,*
  BiD&SB, DcBiA
Achard, Marcel 1899-1974 *CasWL, CIDMEuL,*
  CnMD, ConAu XR, EncWL, EvEuW,
  McGWD, ModWD, OxFr, Pen Eur, REn
Acharya, Prasanna Kumar 1890- *WhLA*
Achchygyya, Amma 1906- *DcOrL 3*
Achdiat Karta, Mihardja *DcOrL 2*
Achebe, Chinua 1930- *AfA 1, Au&Wr,*
  CasWL, ConAu 1R, ConAu XR,
  ConLC 1, ConLC 3, ConLC 5,
  ConNov 1972, ConNov 1976, ConP 1975,
  EncWL Sup, LongC, Pen Cl, Pen Eng,
  RGAfl, TwCW, WebEAL, WhTwL,
  WorAu, WrD 1976
Acheley, Thomas *DcEnL*
Achelis, Elizabeth 1880- *AmA&B*
Achelis, Werner 1927- *WhLA*
Acher, Matthias *WhLA*
Acher, Virginia Pate *IndAu 1917*
Acherley, Roger *Alli, CyAL 1*
Achery, Luc D' 1609-1685 *DcEuL, OxFr*

Acheson, Alexander Wilson 1842-1934 *DcNAA*
Acheson, Arthur 1864-1930 *DcNAA*
Acheson, Dean 1893-1971 *AmA&B, ConAu 25,*
  ConAu 33, REnAL
Acheson, Edward 1902- *AmA&B*
Acheson, Edward Goodrich 1856-1931 *DcNAA*
Acheson, Harriet *PoIre*
Acheson, Lila Bell *AmA&B*
Acheson, Patricia Castles 1924- *AuBYP,*
  ConAu 1R
Acheson, Sam Hanna 1900- *TexWr*
Achesone, James *Alli*
Acheta Domestica *DcEnL*
Achilles Tatius *BiD&SB, CasWL*
Achilles, Edith Mulhall *WhWNAA*
Achilles, Tatius *BbD*
Achillini, Claudio 1574-1640 *Pen Eur*
Achintre, Auguste 1834-1886 *DcNAA*
Achleitner, Friedrich 1930- *OxGer*
Achler, Elsbeth *OxGer*
Achorn, Edgar Oakes 1859-1935 *DcNAA*
Achorn, John Warren 1857-1926 *DcNAA*
Achron, Isidor 1892-1948 *AmSCAP 66*
Achron, Joseph 1886-1943 *AmSCAP 66*
Achsharumov, Nikolei Dmitriyevich 1819-
  BiD&SB
Achtemeier, Elizabeth 1926- *ConAu 17R*
Achtemeier, Paul J 1927- *ConAu 17R*
Achterberg, Gerrit 1905-1962 *CasWL, EncWL,*
  Pen Eur, WhTwL
Achyut *ConAu XR*
Acilius, Gaius *Pen Cl*
Acindynus *CasWL*
Ackah, Christian Abraham 1908- *Au&Wr,*
  WrD 1976
Acker, Duane Calvin 1931- *ConAu 33*
Acker, Helen *AuBYP*
Acker, William R B 1910?-1974 *ConAu 49*
Ackerley, John Randolph 1896-1967 *ChPo S1,*
  ChPo S2, LongC, WorAu
Ackerman, Bruce A 1943- *ConAu 53*
Ackerman, Carl William 1890-1970? *AmA&B,*
  ConAu 29, IndAu 1917
Ackerman, Diane 1948- *ConAu 57,*
  DrAP 1975
Ackerman, Edward Augustus 1911-1973
  AmA&B, ConAu 41
Ackerman, Eugene 1888-1974 *SmATA 10*
Ackerman, Francis Eugene 1888- *IndAu 1917*
Ackerman, G E *Alli Sup*
Ackerman, Gerald M 1928- *ConAu 45*
Ackerman, J Mark 1939- *ConAu 53*
Ackerman, James S 1919- *ConAu 9R*
Ackerman, Nathan W 1908- *ConAu 29*
Ackerman, Robert E 1928- *ConAu 45*
Ackerman, William K 1832-1905 *DcNAA*
Ackerman, Zoe *ChPo*
Ackermann, Hans *OxGer*
Ackermann, Louise Victorine 1813-1890 *BbD,*
  BiD&SB, OxFr
Ackermann, Rudolph 1764-1834 *ChPo, NewC*
Ackernecht, Erwin 1880- *WhLA*
Ackers, Andrew Acquarulo 1919- *AmSCAP 66*
Ackerson, Duane 1942- *ConAu 33,*
  DrAP 1975, WrD 1976
Ackin, Joseph *Alli*
Ackland, J *Alli*
Ackland, Joseph *Alli Sup*
Ackland, Rodney 1908- *Au&Wr, ConAu 57,*
  ConDr, DcLEnL, LongC, NewC,
  WrD 1976
Ackland, Thomas Gilbank *Alli, BiDLA*
Ackland, Thomas Suter *Alli Sup*
Ackland, William *Alli*
Ackley, Alfred Henry 1887-1960 *AmSCAP 66*
Ackley, Bentley D 1872-1958 *AmSCAP 66*
Ackley, Charles Walton 1913- *ConAu 41*
Ackley, Gardner 1915- *ConAu 61,*
  IndAu 1917
Ackley, Mary Ellen 1842-1929? *DcNAA*
Ackley, Randall William 1931- *ConAu 53,*
  DrAP 1975, WrD 1976
Acklom, George *Alli*
Acklom, Mary *Alli Sup*
Ackman, Herman 1904- *AmSCAP 66*
Ackoff, Russell L 1919- *ConAu 41*
Ackroyd, Joyce Irene *WrD 1976*
Ackroyd, Laura G *ChPo S2*

Ackroyd, Peter Runham 1917- *Au&Wr,*
  ConAu 25
Ackroyd, W *Alli Sup*
Ackworth, George *Alli*
Ackworth, Robert Charles 1923- *ConAu 5R*
Acland, Alice 1912- *WrD 1976*
Acland, Arthur Herbert Dyke 1847- *Alli Sup*
Acland, Sir Henry Wentworth 1815- *Alli Sup*
Acland, Hugh Dyke *Alli*
Acland, James *Alli Sup*
Acland, James H 1917- *ConAu 41*
Acland, Peter Leopold Dyke *Alli Sup*
Acland, Sir Thomas Dyke 1809- *Alli Sup*
Acland-Troyte *Alli Sup*
Aclocque, Charles Paul Jacques 1832- *BiD&SB*
Acominatus *CasWL*
Acominatus, Michael *Pen Cl*
Acominatus, Nicetas *Pen Cl*
Aconzio, Jacopo 1500-1567? *EvEuW*
Acorn, Milton 1923- *ConP 1970, ConP 1975,*
  OxCan, OxCan Sup, WrD 1976
Acorn, Milton 1925- *CanWr*
Acosta, Jose De 1539-1600 *BiD&SB, CasWL,*
  DcEuL, Pen Am
Acosta, Jose Julian 1825-1891 *PueRA*
Acosta, Mercedes De 1900- *AmA&B,*
  WhWNAA
A'Court, Charles *Alli Sup*
Acquah, Gaddiel Robert 1884-1954 *AfA 1*
Acquaviva, Nicholas 1927- *AmSCAP 66*
Acquaye, Alfred Allotey 1939- *ConAu 25*
Acquroff, Helen 1833-1887 *ChPo S1*
Acre, Stephen *ConAu XR, EncM&D*
Acred, Arthur Henry 1926- *Au&Wr,*
  ConAu 25
Acree, Sharlie Fain *TexWr*
Acres, Joseph *Alli*
Acropolites, George 1217-1282 *CasWL, Pen Cl*
Acryse, L *Alli*
Actman, Irving 1907- *AmSCAP 66*
Acton *Alli*
Acton, Lord 1834-1902 *BrAu 19, Chmbr 3,*
  LongC, NewC
Acton, Lord ALSO Acton, Baron John E
Acton, C Penrhyn *Alli Sup*
Acton, C R 1893- *Br&AmS*
Acton, E De *Alli*
Acton, Edward Birt *Alli Sup*
Acton, Eliza 1799-1859 *Alli Sup, NewC*
Acton, Mrs F Stackhouse *Alli Sup*
Acton, George *Alli*
Acton, Harold Mario 1904- *Au&Wr,*
  ConAu 1R, DcLEnL, WorAu
Acton, Harry Burrows 1908- *Au&Wr*
Acton, Henry *Alli*
Acton, J *Alli*
Acton, Jay 1949- *ConAu 45*
Acton, Jeanie *Alli Sup*
Acton, Baron John Emerich Edward Dalberg
  1834-1902 *Alli Sup, AtlBL, DcEnA,*
  DcEnA Ap, DcEuL, DcLEnL, EvLB,
  OxEng, Pen Eng
Acton, Baron John E ALSO Acton, Lord
Acton, Llewellyn *Alli Sup*
Acton, Mary Harriet *ChPo S1*
Acton, Philip *Alli Sup, ChPo*
Acton, Richard *Alli Sup*
Acton, Roger *Alli Sup*
Acton, Rose *ChPo S1*
Acton, S *Alli*
Acton, Thomas 1948- *ConAu 57*
Acton, Thomas H *Alli, BiDLA*
Acton, W *Alli*
Acton, William *Alli, Alli Sup*
Acton-Bond, Acton And Eve *ChPo S2*
Aculeus *Alli*
Acuna, Hernando De 1518?-1580? *CasWL,*
  DcEuL, Pen Eur
Acuna, Manuel 1849-1873 *BiD&SB, CasWL,*
  DcSpL, Pen Am
Acuna DeFigueroa, Francisco 1791-1862 *BbD,*
  BiD&SB
Acworth, William *Alli Sup*
Aczel, Tamas 1921- *ConAu 49*
Ad-Din, Kamal Of Isfahan d1237 *ChPo S2*
Adachi, Barbara 1924- *ConAu 49*
Adair *Alli*

Adair, Bethenia Angelina 1840-1926 *DcNAA*
Adair, Cecil *WhCL*
Adair, D L *Alli Sup*
Adair, Hazel *Au& Wr*
Adair, Ian Hugh 1940- *Au& Wr*
Adair, Ian Hugh 1942- *WrD 1976*
Adair, James *BiDSA, PoIre*
Adair, James d1798 *Alli*
Adair, James 1709?-1783? *Alli, AmA,*
    AmA&B, CnDAL, OxAm, REnAL
Adair, James M 1728-1802 *Alli, BiDLA*
Adair, James R 1923- *ConAu 17R, WrD 1976*
Adair, John *Alli, ChPo S1*
Adair, John 1934- *Au& Wr, WrD 1976*
Adair, John 1933- *ConAu 49*
Adair, Margaret Weeks d1971 *ConAu P-1,*
    SmATA 10
Adair, Patrick *Alli Sup*
Adair, Sir Robert 1763-1855 *Alli, BiDLA,*
    Chmbr 2, DcEnL, PoIre
Adair, Robert 1802-1890 *DcNAA*
Adair, Sir Robert A S, Baron Waveney
    1811-1886 *Alli Sup*
Adair, Robert Kemp 1924- *IndAu 1917*
Adair, T *ChPo S2*
Adair, Thomas M 1913- *AmSCAP 66*
Adair, W James *Alli*
Adair, William *Alli*
Adalard *Alli, BiB S, DcEnL*
Adalbert, Monk Of Spalding 1140?- *BiB N*
Adali-Mortty, Geormbeeyi 1920?- *AfA 1*
Adam *DcEnL, EuA*
Adam, Madame 1836- *BbD*
Adam, Madame ALSO Adam, Juliette
Adam Billaut *OxFr*
Adam D'Arras 1250?-1306? *AtlBL*
Adam De La Bassee d1286 *CasWL*
Adam De La Hale 1240?-1288? *BiD&SB,*
    McGWD, REn
Adam De La Halle 1240?-1288? *AtlBL,*
    CasWL, DcEuL, EvEuW, OxFr, Pen Eur
Adam De Marisco *Alli*
Adam De St. Victoire *EvEuW*
Adam Du Petit Pont d1180 *BiB N*
Adam Le Bossu 1250?-1306? *AtlBL, CasWL*
Adam Of Bremen 1045?-1081? *CasWL*
Adam Of Dore *BiB N*
Adam Of Einesham *BiB N*
Adam Of Evesham d1161 *BiB N*
Adam Of Murimouth *Alli*
Adam Of Murimuth 1274?-1347 *NewC*
Adam Of St. Victor 1110?-1180? *CasWL,*
    Pen Eur
Adam Scotus d1180 *Alli, DcEnL*
Adam The Scot d1180 *BiB N*
Adam, Alexander 1741-1809 *Alli*
Adam, Archibald *Alli*
Adam, Ben *ConAu XR*
Adam, Charles *Alli Sup*
Adam, Sir Charles Elphinstone 1859- *Alli Sup*
Adam, Cornel *ConAu XR*
Adam, Dean *Alli*
Adam, E *Alli Sup*
Adam, G M *Chmbr 3*
Adam, George 1846- *DcNAA*
Adam, Graeme Mercer 1839-1912 *Alli Sup,*
    ChPo, DcLEnL, DcNAA, OxCan
Adam, Helen 1909- *ChPo S2, ConAu 17R,*
    ConP 1970, DrAP 1975
Adam, Helen Douglas 1912- *ChPo, ChPo S1*
Adam, Helen Pearl 1882- *WhLA*
Adam, J A Stanley *ChPo*
Adam, James *Alli, Alli Sup*
Adam, Jean 1710-1765 *ChPo, Chmbr 2, EvLB,*
    NewC
Adam, Jeu *OxFr*
Adam, John *Alli, Alli Sup*
Adam, John Douglas 1866- *AmLY*
Adam, Juliette 1836-1936 *BiD&SB, OxFr,*
    REn
Adam, Juliette ALSO Adam, Madame
Adam, Karl 1876- *CatA 1947*
Adam, Marcel *OxCan Sup*
Adam, Michael *ChPo*
Adam, Michael 1919- *ConAu 53*
Adam, Paul 1862-1920 *CasWL, ClDMEuL,*
    EuA, EvEuW, OxFr, REn
Adam, Robert 1728-1792 *Alli, AtlBL, NewC*

Adam, Robert 1770-1826 *Alli, BiDLA, DcEnL*
Adam, Robert Borthwick 1863-1940 *DcNAA*
Adam, Ruth Augusta 1907- *Au& Wr 23,*
    ConAu 23, WrD 1976
Adam, Thomas *Alli Sup*
Adam, Thomas 1701-1784 *Alli*
Adam, Thomas R 1900- *ConAu P-1*
Adam, W *Alli Sup*
Adam, William *Alli, Alli Sup, BiDLA,*
    BiDLA Sup
Adam, William Augustus 1866- *WhLA*
Adam Smith, Janet Buchanan 1905- *Au& Wr,*
    LongC
Adam-Smith, Patsy 1926- *Au& Wr, WrD 1976*
Adama VanScheltema, Carel Steven 1877-1924
    ClDMEuL
Adamczewski, Zygmunt 1921- *ConAu 13R*
Adamec, Ludwig W 1924- *WrD 1976*
Adamec, W Ludwig 1924- *ConAu 23*
Adami, Friedrich 1816-1893 *BiD&SB*
Adami, Jonn George 1862- *WhLA*
Adamic, Louis 1899-1951 *AmA&B, CnDAL,*
    ConAmA, DcLEnL, OxAm, REn,
    REnAL, TwCA, TwCA Sup
Adamnan, Saint 625?-704? *Alli, BiB 5,*
    CasWL, Chmbr 1, DcEnL, EvLB, NewC,
    OxEng, Pen Eng
Adamov, Arthur 1908-1970 *CasWL, CnMD,*
    CnThe, ConAu 17, ConAu 25, ConLC 4,
    CrCD, EncWL, McGWD, ModRL,
    ModWD, Pen Eur, REnWD, WorAu
Adamovich, Georgyi 1894- *EncWL*
Adams *BiDLA*
Adams, Miss *Alli Sup*
Adams, Mrs. A *Alli Sup*
Adams, A Don *ConAu XR*
Adams, A John 1931- *ConAu 33*
Adams, A M *WhWNAA*
Adams, Abigail 1744-1818 *Alli, AmA,*
    AmA&B, BbD, BiD&SB, CyAL 1,
    DcAmA, DcNAA, OxAm, REn, REnAL
Adams, Adeline Valentine Pond 1859- *ChPo*
Adams, Adrienne 1906- *BkP, ChPo, ChPo S1,*
    ChPo S2, ConAu 49, IlBYP, IlCB 1956,
    IlCB 1966, SmATA 8, ThBJA
Adams, Alger LeRoy *BlkAW*
Adams, Alice 1926- *ConLC 6*
Adams, Alice Dana 1864-1934 *DcNAA*
Adams, Alice M *ChPo*
Adams, Almeda C 1865-1949 *OhA&B*
Adams, Alva d1922 *DcNAA*
Adams, Alvin *BlkAW*
Adams, Amos 1728?-1775 *Alli, DcAmA,*
    DcNAA
Adams, Amy Belle 1904- *ChPo*
Adams, Andrew Leith d1892 *Alli Sup, OxCan*
Adams, Andrew Napoleon *Alli Sup*
Adams, Andy 1859-1935 *AmA&B, AmLY,*
    BiDSA, CnDAL, DcAmA, DcLEnL,
    DcNAA, IndAu 1816, JBA 1934,
    JBA 1951, OxAm, REnAL, TexWr,
    WhWNAA, YABC 1
Adams, Ann Olivia *Alli Sup*
Adams, Anne H 1935- *ConAu 41*
Adams, Annette *ConAu XR*
Adams, Ansel 1902- *AuNews 1, ConAu 21*
Adams, Arthur 1881- *Alli Sup, AmLY,*
    WhWNAA
Adams, Arthur Barto 1887- *WhWNAA*
Adams, Arthur E 1917- *ConAu 5R*
Adams, Arthur Henry 1872-1936 *ChPo,*
    ChPo S1, Chmbr 3, DcLEnL, EvLB,
    TwCW
Adams, Arthur Merrihew 1908- *ConAu 53*
Adams, Arthur T *OxCan*
Adams, Arthur White 1912- *Au& Wr*
Adams, Audri 1925- *AmSCAP 66*
Adams, Beresford *ChPo S1*
Adams, Bertha Leith *BiD&SB*
Adams, Bertram Martin 1879- *ChPo*
Adams, Betsy *ConAu XR*
Adams, Blanche E 1887-1933 *ArizL*
Adams, Braman Blanchard 1851-1944 *DcNAA*
Adams, Brooks 1848-1927 *Alli Sup, AmA,*
    AmA&B, BiD&SB, DcAmA, DcNAA,
    OxAm, Pen Am, REnAL
Adams, C *Alli*
Adams, C H *ChPo*

Adams, C Raymond 1898- *WhWNAA*
Adams, C Warren *Alli Sup*
Adams, Cedric M 1902-1961 *AmA&B, MnnWr*
Adams, Charles *Alli Sup*
Adams, Charles 1808-1890 *Alli Sup, BiD&SB,*
    DcAmA, DcNAA
Adams, Charles Abel 1854- *DcNAA*
Adams, Charles Baker 1814-1853 *Alli, DcAmA,*
    DcNAA
Adams, Charles Christopher 1873- *WhWNAA*
Adams, Charles Clarence 1883-1948 *DcNAA*
Adams, Charles Coffin 1810-1888 *Alli Sup,*
    DcAmA, DcNAA
Adams, Charles Collard 1836-1925 *DcNAA*
Adams, Charles Darwin 1856-1938 *DcNAA*
Adams, Charles Follen 1842-1918 *Alli Sup,*
    AmA, AmA&B, AmLY, BiD&SB, ChPo,
    ChPo S1, DcAmA, DcNAA, EvLB,
    OxAm, REnAL
Adams, Charles Francis 1807-1886 *Alli,*
    Alli Sup, AmA&B, BbD, BiD&SB,
    ChPo S1, CyAL 2, DcAmA, DcNAA,
    OxAm
Adams, Charles Francis 1854-1914 *DcNAA*
Adams, Charles Francis, Jr. 1835-1915 *Alli Sup,*
    AmA, AmA&B, BbD, BiD&SB, DcAmA,
    DcLEnL, DcNAA, OxAm, REn, REnAL
Adams, Charles H *Alli Sup*
Adams, Charles J 1924- *ConAu 17R*
Adams, Charles Josiah 1850-1924 *ChPo,*
    DcAmA, DcNAA, OhA&B
Adams, Charles Kendall 1835-1902 *Alli Sup,*
    AmA, AmA&B, BbD, BiD&SB, DcAmA,
    DcNAA
Adams, Charles Laban 1856-1914 *DcNAA*
Adams, Charles True 1900-1942 *DcNAA*
Adams, Charlotte *Alli Sup, ChPo*
Adams, Christopher *ConAu XR*
Adams, Cindy *ConAu 23*
Adams, Clarence Orvan 1893- *IndAu 1917*
Adams, Clayton *BlkAW*
Adams, Clement 1519?-1587 *NewC*
Adams, Cleve F 1895-1949 *EncM&D*
Adams, Clifton 1919- *ConAu 13R*
Adams, Clinton 1918- *ConAu 33*
Adams, Coker *Alli Sup*
Adams, Comfort Avery 1868- *WhWNAA*
Adams, Cyrus Cornelius 1849-1928 *AmLY,*
    DcAmA, DcNAA
Adams, Daniel 1773-1864 *DcNAA*
Adams, Don 1925- *ConAu 33, WrD 1976*
Adams, Doris B *BlkAW*
Adams, Dorothy *CatA 1952*
Adams, E F *ChPo S2*
Adams, E M 1919- *ChPo, ConAu 1R*
Adams, E R *Alli Sup*
Adams, Edward 1876- *AmA&B*
Adams, Edward C *MnBBF*
Adams, Edward Dean 1846-1931 *DcNAA*
Adams, Edward Francis 1839-1929 *AmLY,*
    DcNAA, WhWNAA
Adams, Edwin *Alli Sup*
Adams, Edwin Plimpton 1878- *WhWNAA*
Adams, Eleanor N *AmA&B*
Adams, Eliashib 1773-1855 *DcNAA*
Adams, Eliphalet 1676-1753 *Alli*
Adams, Elizabeth Kemper *ChPo S1*
Adams, Elizabeth Starbuck 1873- *WhWNAA*
Adams, Emily *Alli Sup*
Adams, Emma E *Alli Sup*
Adams, Emma Hildreth 1827-1900? *Alli Sup,*
    DcNAA, OhA&B
Adams, Ephraim 1818-1907 *DcNAA*
Adams, Ephraim Douglass 1865-1930 *AmA&B,*
    DcNAA, WhWNAA
Adams, Ernest Charles 1926- *WrD 1976*
Adams, Ernest Harry 1886-1959 *AmSCAP 66*
Adams, Ernest Kempton 1873-1904 *DcNAA*
Adams, Estella *IndAu 1816*
Adams, Estelle Davenport *Alli Sup*
Adams, Ethel Mathilda Green 1913-
    IndAu 1917
Adams, Eudora *ChPo*
Adams, Eunice *ChPo*
Adams, Eustace L 1891- *AmA&B, WhWNAA*
Adams, Evangeline Smith d1932 *DcNAA*
Adams, F A *Alli Sup*
Adams, F W L *Alli Sup, Chmbr 3*

Adams, Ferry 1906- *AnMV 1926*

Adams, Florence 1932- *ConAu 49*

Adams, Frances Davis 1908- *ArizL*

Adams, Francis *Alli, Alli Sup, BiDLA*

Adams, Francis 1796-1861 *Alli Sup*

Adams, Francis Alexandre 1874-1975 *ConAu 61, DcAmA*

Adams, Sir Francis Boyd 1888- *Au&Wr*

Adams, Francis Colburn 1850-1891? *Alli Sup, BbD, BiD&SB, BiDSA, DcAmA, DcNAA*

Adams, Sir Francis Ottiwell 1825-1889 *Alli Sup*

Adams, Francis William Lauderdale 1862-1893 *Alli Sup, BrAu 19, DcLEnL, EvLB*

Adams, Frank *ChPo, ChPo S1*

Adams, Frank 1875- *WhWNAA*

Adams, Frank Dawson 1859-1942 *DcNAA, WhWNAA*

Adams, Frank Mantell *Alli Sup*

Adams, Frank R 1883-1963 *AmA&B, AmSCAP 66, ConAu 5R, REnAL, WhWNAA*

Adams, Franklin Pierce 1881-1960 *AmA&B, ChPo, ChPo S1, ChPo S2, CnDAL, ConAmA, OxAm, REn, REnAL, TwCA, TwCA Sup, WhWNAA*

Adams, Fred Winslow 1866- *WhWNAA*

Adams, Frederick Hentz *ChPo, ChPo S1*

Adams, Frederick K *MnBBF*

Adams, Frederick Upham 1859-1921 *AmA&B, DcAmA, DcNAA*

Adams, Frederick W 1786-1858 *DcAmA, DcNAA*

Adams, Mrs. G M *Alli Sup*

Adams, G P 1882-1961 *AmA&B*

Adams, George *Alli, Alli Sup, BiDLA*

Adams, George 1904- *AmSCAP 66*

Adams, George Burton 1851-1925 *Alli Sup, AmA&B, BiD&SB, DcAmA, DcNAA*

Adams, George Matthew 1878-1962 *AmA&B, REnAL*

Adams, George Moulton 1824-1906 *DcNAA*

Adams, George Worthington 1905- *ConAu 41*

Adams, Georgia Sachs 1913- *ConAu 37*

Adams, Gerald Drayson *MnBBF*

Adams, Gertrude Leonard *ChPo S1*

Adams, Grace Marie 1926- *WrD 1976*

Adams, Graham, Jr. 1928- *ConAu 17R*

Adams, H C *Alli, ChPo, MnBBF*

Adams, H G *Alli*

Adams, H H *ChPo*

Adams, H M *ChPo*

Adams, H S *ChPo*

Adams, H W *Alli Sup*

Adams, Hampton 1897- *AmA&B*

Adams, Hannah 1755?-1832? *Alli, AmA, AmA&B, BbD, BiD&SB, CyAL 1, DcAmA, DcEnL, DcNAA, OxAm, REn, REnAL*

Adams, Harlen Martin 1904- *ConAu P-1, WrD 1976*

Adams, Harriet L 1838-1913 *OhA&B*

Adams, Harriet S *AmA&B, AuNews 2, ConAu 17R, EncM&D, SmATA 1*

Adams, Harrison *AmA&B, ConAu XR, DcNAA, WhWNAA*

Adams, Harry *MnBBF*

Adams, Hartly *Alli Sup*

Adams, Hazard 1926- *ConAu 9R, SmATA 6, WrD 1976*

Adams, Helen Simmons 1897- *AmA&B*

Adams, Henry *Alli Sup*

Adams, Henry And Adams, Arthur *Alli Sup*

Adams, Henry Austin 1861-1931 *AmA&B, DcNAA*

Adams, Henry Brooks 1838-1918 *Alli Sup, AmA, AmA&B, AmWr, AtlBL, BbD, BiD&SB, CnDAL, CyWA, DcAmA, DcBiA, DcLEnL, DcNAA, EvLB, LongC, ModAL, ModAL Sup, OxAm, OxEng, Pen Am, RAdv 1, RCom, REn, REnAL, WebEAL, WhTwL, TwCW*

Adams, Henry Cadwallader 1817- *Alli Sup*

Adams, Henry Carter 1852?-1921 *Alli Sup, BiD&SB, DcAmA, DcNAA*

Adams, Henry Charles 1873- *WhLA*

Adams, Henry F 1882- *WhWNAA*

Adams, Henry Gardiner *Alli Sup, ChPo*

Adams, Henry Gardner *ChPo S1, ChPo S2*

Adams, Henry H 1917- *ConAu 21*

Adams, Henry Joseph *WhLA*

Adams, Henry Kingman 1828-1903 *DcNAA*

Adams, Henry Mason 1907- *ConAu P-1*

Adams, Henry S 1864- *WhWNAA*

Adams, Henry T *ConAu XR*

Adams, Henry Wright 1818-1881 *DcNAA*

Adams, Herbert *ChPo*

Adams, Herbert 1874-1952 *EncM&D*

Adams, Herbert Baxter 1850-1901 *Alli Sup, AmA, BiD&SB, BiDSA, DcAmA, DcNAA, OxAm*

Adams, Herbert Mayow 1893- *ConAu 25*

Adams, Hervey Cadwallader 1903- *Au&Wr*

Adams, Howard *OxCan Sup*

Adams, Ian *OxCan Sup*

Adams, Isaac E *Alli Sup*

Adams, J *BbtC*

Adams, J Donald 1891-1968 *AmA&B, ConAu 1R, REnAL*

Adams, J Donald 1891- *WhWNAA*

Adams, J S *Alli Sup*

Adams, Mrs. J S *ChPo S1*

Adams, J Verney *MnBBF*

Adams, J W S *Alli Sup*

Adams, Jacob 1842-1930 *OhA&B*

Adams, James *Alli, BiDLA Sup, ChPo S2*

Adams, James Alonzo 1842-1925 *DcNAA, OhA&B*

Adams, James Barton 1843-1918 *ChPo S1, DcAmA, DcNAA, OhA&B*

Adams, James F 1927- *ConAu 17R, WrD 1976*

Adams, James Fenimore Cooper *HsB&A*

Adams, James Fowler 1888- *WhWNAA*

Adams, James Luther 1901- *AmA&B, ConAu 41*

Adams, James McKee 1886-1945 *DcNAA*

Adams, James Merrill Ryland *WhWNAA*

Adams, James Osgood 1818-1887 *Alli Sup*

Adams, James R 1934- *ConAu 41*

Adams, James Truslow 1878-1949 *AmA&B, ConAmA, DcLEnL, DcNAA, EvLB, OxAm, REn, REnAL, TwCA, TwCA Sup, WhWNAA*

Adams, Jasper 1793-1841 *BiDSA, DcAmA, DcNAA*

Adams, Jeanette *BlkAW*

Adams, Jedidiah Howe 1866-1919 *DcNAA*

Adams, Jesse Earl 1888-1945 *DcNAA, IndAu 1917, WhWNAA*

Adams, Jessie Janes *TexWr*

Adams, Joey 1911- *ConAu 49*

Adams, John *Alli, BiDLA, ChPo S2, DcEnL, MnBBF*

Adams, John d1719 *Alli*

Adams, John 1704-1740 *Alli, AmA, CnDAL, CyAL 1, DcAmA, DcNAA, OxAm, REnAL*

Adams, John 1735-1826 *Alli, AmA&B, BbD, BiD&SB, BiDLA Sup, ChPo S1, CyAL 1, CyWA, DcAmA, DcNAA, EvLB, OxAm, REn, REnAL*

Adams, John 1750?-1814 *CarSB*

Adams, John 1772-1863 *DcNAA*

Adams, John 1822-1877 *Alli Sup*

Adams, John 1872- *WhWNAA*

Adams, John B And Durham, Warren *Alli Sup*

Adams, John Clarke 1910- *ConAu 1R*

Adams, John Coleman 1849-1922 *Alli Sup, AmA&B, AmLY, DcAmA, DcNAA*

Adams, John Couch 1817- *Alli*

Adams, John Cranford 1903-1952 *AmA&B, TwCA Sup*

Adams, John D d1879 *WhWNAA*

Adams, John F 1930- *ChPo, ConAu 33*

Adams, John Greenleaf 1810-1887 *Alli, Alli Sup, ChPo S1, ChPo S2, DcAmA, DcNAA*

Adams, John Haslup 1871- *BiDSA*

Adams, John Jay *ChPo*

Adams, John Milton *Alli Sup*

Adams, John Paul *ConAu XR*

Adams, John Q, III 1938- *BiDPar*

Adams, John Quincy *Alli Sup*

Adams, John Quincy 1767-1848 *Alli, AmA&B, BbD, BiD&SB, BiDLA, ChPo, ChPo S1, CyAL 1, DcAmA, DcEnL, DcLEnL, DcNAA, OxAm, REn, REnAL*

Adams, John Quincy 1825-1881 *DcNAA*

Adams, John Quincy 1849-1940 *DcNAA*

Adams, Mrs. John Quincy *ChPo*

Adams, John R 1900- *ConAu 25*

Adams, John S *Alli Sup, ChPo, ChPo S1, ChPo S2*

Adams, Mrs. John S *Alli Sup*

Adams, John Stowell d1893 *DcNAA*

Adams, John T *ChPo*

Adams, John Turvill 1805-1882 *Alli Sup, AmA&B, DcAmA, DcNAA, OxAm*

Adams, John Wesley 1832- *ChPo S2*

Adams, John William 1862-1926 *DcNAA*

Adams, John Wolcott *ChPo S1*

Adams, Jonas *Alli*

Adams, Joseph *OxCan*

Adams, Joseph 1719-1783 *Alli*

Adams, Joseph 1756-1818 *Alli, BiDLA, BiDLA Sup*

Adams, Joseph Alexander 1803-1880 *EarAB, EarAB Sup*

Adams, Joseph Henry 1867-1941 *DcNAA*

Adams, Joseph Quincy 1881-1946 *AmA&B, AmLY, EvLB, NewC, REnAL, WhWNAA*

Adams, Josiah Quincy 1881-1946 *DcNAA*

Adams, Julia Davis 1900- *AmA&B, JBA 1934, JBA 1951*

Adams, Julian 1919- *ConAu 25*

Adams, Julian 1920- *WrD 1976*

Adams, Julius Walker 1812-1899 *Alli Sup, DcAmA, DcNAA*

Adams, Katharine *AmA&B, JBA 1934, JBA 1951*

Adams, Kenneth Menzies 1922- *Au&Wr, WrD 1976*

Adams, Kramer A 1920- *ConAu 9R*

Adams, L Jerold 1939- *ConAu 49*

Adams, Laura 1943- *ConAu 53*

Adams, Laurie 1941- *ConAu 53, WrD 1976*

Adams, Lawrence *MnBBF*

Adams, Lee 1924- *AmSCAP 66*

Adams, Mrs. Leith *Alli Sup*

Adams, Leon D 1905- *ConAu 45*

Adams, Leonie 1899- *AmA&B, Au&Wr, ChPo, ChPo S1, CnE&AP, CnMWL, ConAmA, ConAu P-1, ConP 1970, ConP 1975, DcLEnL, DrAP 1975, ModAL, OxAm, REn, REnAL Sup, SixAP, TwCA Sup, TwCW, WrD 1976*

Adams, Leta Zoe 1902- *WhWNAA*

Adams, Levi d1832 *BbtC, OxCan*

Adams, Lionel Ernest *Alli Sup*

Adams, Lowell *ConAu XR*

Adams, Loyce 1912- *TexWr*

Adams, Lucy Lockwood *AmA&B*

Adams, M A *Alli Sup*

Adams, M P *MnBBF*

Adams, Marguerite Janvrin 1889- *WhWNAA*

Adams, Marion 1932- *ConAu 41*

Adams, Marion Sheffield 1904- *IndAu 1917*

Adams, Mark *ChPo S1*

Adams, Mary *Alli Sup, DcNAA*

Adams, Mary Frances *ChPo*

Adams, Mary Jane Mathews 1840-1902 *AmA&B, ChPo S1, ChPo S2, DcAmA, DcNAA, PoIre*

Adams, Matthew d1753 *Alli*

Adams, Maude 1872-1953 *OxAm, REnAL*

Adams, Michael Evelyn 1920- *Au&Wr, ConAu 33, WrD 1976*

Adams, Moses *Alli Sup, AmA&B, DcNAA*

Adams, Myra Winchester *ChPo, ChPo S1*

Adams, Myron 1841-1895 *BiD&SB, DcAmA, DcNAA*

Adams, Myron Howell 1846-1929 *DcNAA*

Adams, Myron Winslow 1860-1939 *DcNAA*

Adams, Nathan Miller 1934- *Au&Wr, ConAu 45*

Adams, Nathaniel 1856-1929 *DcNAA*

Adams, Nehemiah 1806-1878 *Alli, Alli Sup, AmA, BiD&SB, DcAmA, DcNAA*

Adams, Nicholson Barney 1895- *AmA&B, DcSpL, WhWNAA*

Adams, Orville *WhWNAA*
Adams, Oscar Fay 1855-1919 *Alli Sup, AmA&B, BbD, BiD&SB, ChPo, ChPo S1, ChPo S2, DcNAA, OxAm, REnAL*
Adams, Oscar Sherman 1874- *WhWNAA*
Adams, Paul 1894- *TexWr*
Adams, Paul E 1922- *AmSCAP 66*
Adams, Paul L 1924- *ConAu 61*
Adams, Pauline Batcheler *IlBYP*
Adams, Percy G 1914- *ConAu 1R*
Adams, Perseus 1933- *ConP 1970*
Adams, Q *Alli, BiDLA*
Adams, R N *Alli*
Adams, Ramon Frederick 1889- *AmA&B, REnAL*
Adams, Randolph Greenfield 1892-1951 *AmA&B, ChPo, ChPo S2, WhWNAA*
Adams, Raymond 1898- *WhWNAA*
Adams, Rice *Alli*
Adams, Richard *Alli, Alli Sup*
Adams, Richard d1684 *Alli*
Adams, Richard 1920- *AuNews 1, AuNews 2, ChPo S2, ConAu 49, ConLC 4, ConLC 5, PiP, SmATA 7, WrD 1976*
Adams, Richard Laban 1883- *WhWNAA*
Adams, Richard N 1924- *ConAu 29*
Adams, Richard P 1917- *ConAu 33*
Adams, Robert *Alli*
Adams, Robert 1791-1875 *Alli Sup*
Adams, Robert Chamblet 1839-1892 *Alli Sup, ChPo, ChPo S1, DcAmA, DcNAA*
Adams, Robert H *ChPo S1*
Adams, Robert Martin 1915- *AmA&B, ConAu 5R*
Adams, Robert McCormick 1926- *AmA&B, ConAu 61*
Adams, Robert Morrill 1882-1931 *ChPo, DcNAA*
Adams, Robert P 1910- *ConAu 13R*
Adams, Roger 1889- *WhWNAA*
Adams, Romanzo 1868-1942 *DcNAA, WhWNAA*
Adams, Rufus W *OhA&B*
Adams, Russell L 1930- *ConAu 53, LivBA*
Adams, Ruth Joyce *AuBYP*
Adams, S *Alli*
Adams, St. Clair 1906- *ChPo, ChPo S1*
Adams, Sally Pepper *ConAu 41*
Adams, Sam 1934- *ConAu 57*
Adams, Samuel *Alli*
Adams, Samuel 1722-1803 *Alli, AmA, AmA&B, DcAmA, DcNAA, OxAm, REn, REnAL*
Adams, Samuel Hopkins 1871-1958 *AmA&B, AmLY, AmNov, AuBYP, CnDAL, EncM&D, OxAm, REn, REnAL, TwCA, TwCA Sup, WhWNAA*
Adams, Samuel Shugert 1853- *WhWNAA*
Adams, Sarah B *Alli Sup*
Adams, Sarah Flower Fuller 1805-1848 *Alli, BbD, BiD&SB, BrAu 19, DcEnL, DcLEnL, NewC, OxEng, PoCh*
Adams, Sarah Holland *Alli Sup*
Adams, Sebastian C *Alli Sup*
Adams, Sexton 1936- *ConAu 25*
Adams, Seymour Webster 1815-1864 *DcNAA, OhA&B*
Adams, Sherman 1899- *AmA&B*
Adams, Sherman Wolcott 1836-1898 *DcNAA*
Adams, Silas *Alli Sup*
Adams, Silas 1841-1926 *DcNAA*
Adams, Stanley 1907- *AmSCAP 66*
Adams, T *Alli, Alli Sup, BiDLA*
Adams, T A S *Alli Sup*
Adams, T W 1933- *ConAu 25, WrD 1976*
Adams, Terrence Dean 1935- *ConAu 33*
Adams, Theodore Floyd 1898- *Au&Wr, ConAu P-1*
Adams, Thomas *Alli*
Adams, Thomas d1670 *Alli*
Adams, Thomas Albert Smith 1839-1888 *BiDSA, DcNAA*
Adams, Thomas F 1927- *ConAu 13R*
Adams, Thomas Sewell 1873-1933 *DcNAA*
Adams, Valentine *ChPo, ChPo S1*
Adams, W L *Alli Sup*
Adams, W M *Alli Sup*

Adams, Walter 1922- *ConAu 1R, WrD 1976*
Adams, Walter Marsham *Alli Sup*
Adams, Walter R 1897- *TexWr, WhWNAA*
Adams, Walter Sydney 1876- *WhWNAA*
Adams, Warren Austin 1861- *WhWNAA*
Adams, Washington Irving Lincoln 1865- *Alli Sup, DcAmA*
Adams, Wellington Alexander *BlkAW*
Adams, William *Alli, Alli Sup, BiDLA, BiDLA Sup, PoIre*
Adams, Sir William *Alli*
Adams, William 1707-1749 *Alli*
Adams, William 1807-1880 *Alli Sup, BiD&SB, DcAmA, DcNAA*
Adams, William 1813-1897 *Alli Sup, DcAmA, DcNAA*
Adams, William 1814-1848 *Alli, BbD, DcEnL*
Adams, William 1820- *Alli Sup*
Adams, William Augustus 1865- *PoIre*
Adams, William Bridges 1797-1872 *Alli Sup*
Adams, William Davenport 1851-1904 *Alli Sup, BbD, BiD&SB, ChPo, ChPo S1, ChPo S2*
Adams, William E *Alli Sup*
Adams, William Edward 1866-1946 *OhA&B, WhWNAA*
Adams, William F 1838-1896 *HsB&A*
Adams, William Forbes 1898-1935 *DcNAA*
Adams, William Frederick 1848- *DcNAA*
Adams, William H *Alli Sup*
Adams, William Henry Davenport 1829-1891 *Alli Sup, BbD, NewC*
Adams, William Lysander 1821-1906 *DcNAA, OhA&B*
Adams, William Richard 1923- *IndAu 1917*
Adams, William Taylor 1822-1897 *Alli Sup, AmA, AmA&B, BbD, BiD&SB, CarSB, ChPo, ChPo S2, CnDAL, CyAL 2, DcAmA, DcEnL, DcNAA, HsB&A, HsB&A Sup, OxAm, REn, REnAL*
Adams, Winona Bernice *TexWr*
Adams, Zabdiel 1736?-1801 *Alli, DcNAA*
Adams-Walker *Alli Sup*
Adamson *Alli*
Adamson, Alexander 1858- *ChPo S1*
Adamson, Archibald R *ChPo S2*
Adamson, C M *Alli Sup*
Adamson, Cecil *MnBBF*
Adamson, David Grant 1927- *ConAu 13R*
Adamson, Donald 1939- *Au&Wr, ConAu 53, WrD 1976*
Adamson, Dorothy *ChPo S1*
Adamson, Ed 1915?-1972 *ConAu 37*
Adamson, Edward Hussey *Alli Sup*
Adamson, Gareth 1925- *ConAu 13R, WrD 1976*
Adamson, George Worsley 1913- *ChPo S1, ChPo S2, IlBYP, IlCB 1956, IlCB 1966*
Adamson, Graham *ConAu XR, SmATA XR*
Adamson, Hans Christian 1890-1968 *AmA&B, ConAu 5R*
Adamson, Harold 1906- *AmSCAP 66*
Adamson, Henry d1639 *Alli, DcEnL*
Adamson, Henry Thomas *Alli Sup*
Adamson, Joe *ConAu XR*
Adamson, John *Alli*
Adamson, John 1787-1855 *Alli, BiDLA, ChPo*
Adamson, Joseph, III 1945- *ConAu 45*
Adamson, Joy 1910- *Au&Wr*
Adamson, M *Alli*
Adamson, Margot Robert 1898- *ChPo S1, ConP 1970*
Adamson, Patrick 1536?-1592 *Alli, DcEnL*
Adamson, Robert *Chmbr 3*
Adamson, Robert 1832- *ChPo S1*
Adamson, Robert 1852-1902 *Alli Sup, BrAu 19, NewC, OxEng*
Adamson, W *Alli*
Adamson, Wendy Wriston 1942- *ConAu 53*
Adamson, William *Alli Sup*
Adamson, William Agar 1800-1868 *Alli Sup, BbtC, DcNAA, OxCan*
Adamson, William Augustus 1883- *WhWNAA*
Adamson, William Robert 1927- *ConAu 23*
Adamthwaite, John *Alli*
Adamus, Franz 1867-1948 *OxGer, WhLA*
Adan, Martin 1908- *DcCLA*
Adare, Allen *MnBBF*

Adas, Michael 1943- *ConAu 53*
Adawiyah, Rabiah Al- 714-801 *CasWL*
Aday *Alli*
Adburgham, Alison Haig 1912- *ConAu P-1*
Adburgham, M V Alison *Au&Wr*
Adcock, Almey St. John *Au&Wr, ChPo, ChPo S1, ChPo S2*
Adcock, Arthur St. John 1864-1930 *BbD, ChPo, ChPo S1, ChPo S2, LongC, WhLA*
Adcock, Betty *ConAu 57, DrAP 1975*
Adcock, C John 1904- *BiDPar, ConAu -P01*
Adcock, Elizabeth S 1938- *ConAu 57*
Adcock, Elver Forest 1898- *WhWNAA*
Adcock, Fleur 1934- *ConAu 25, ConP 1970, ConP 1975, WrD 1976*
Adcock, John *Alli Sup*
Adcock, Marion St. John *ChPo*
Adcock, St. John 1864-1930 *ChPo S1*
Addams, Charles 1912- *AmA&B, ConAu 61, WrD 1976*
Addams, Francis Holland *Alli Sup*
Addams, George Stanton 1869-1933 *DcNAA*
Addams, J *Alli*
Addams, Jane 1860-1935 *AmA&B, AmLY, DcAmA, DcLEnL, DcNAA, OxAm, REn, REnAL, WhWNAA*
Addarian, Garnik 1925- *DcOrL 3*
Adde, Leo 1927?-1975 *ConAu 57*
Addenbrooke, J *Alli*
Adderley, Sir Charles Bowyer 1814- *Alli Sup, BbtC*
Adderley, James Granville 1861- *Alli Sup, BbD, WhLA*
Adderley, Thomas *Alli*
Addey, Markinfield *Alli Sup*
Addicks, Lawrence 1878- *WhWNAA*
Addington, A *Alli*
Addington, Arthur Charles 1939- *Au&Wr, WrD 1976*
Addington, Henry *Alli*
Addington, Hugh M 1876- *WhWNAA*
Addington, John *Alli, BiDLA, BiDLA Sup*
Addington, Larry Holbrook 1932- *ConAu 33, WrD 1976*
Addington, Luther Foster 1899- *AmA&B*
Addington, R D *Alli Sup*
Addington, Robert Milford 1867- *WhWNAA*
Addington, Sarah 1891-1940 *AmA&B, DcNAA, OhA&B, WhWNAA*
Addington, Stephen 1729-1796 *Alli*
Addington, Thomas 1829- *IndAu 1816*
Addington, Sir William *Alli*
Addis, Harold Ahmed Noureddin 1884-1958 *OhA&B, WhWNAA*
Addis, Hugh 1909- *OhA&B*
Addis, John *Alli Sup*
Addis, Thomas *OhA&B*
Addis, Thomas 1881- *WhWNAA*
Addis, William E *Alli Sup*
Addiscombe, John *MnBBF*
Addison *BiDLA*
Addison, Captain *MnBBF*
Addison, The American 1768-1812 *DcEnL*
Addison Of The North *DcEnL, NewC, OxEng*
Addison, Albert *Alli Sup*
Addison, Alexander 1757-1807 *Alli*
Addison, Anthony *Alli*
Addison, C G *Alli*
Addison, D C *Alli Sup*
Addison, Daniel Dulany 1863-1936 *AmA&B, ChPo, ChPo S2, DcAmA, DcNAA*
Addison, Doris Maureen 1926- *WrD 1976*
Addison, Elinor d1948 *DcNAA*
Addison, Francis *Alli Sup*
Addison, Frederic *Alli Sup*
Addison, G Douglas *MnBBF*
Addison, G H 1793-1815 *Alli*
Addison, Gwen 1928- *ConAu XR*
Addison, Henry Robert 1805?-1876 *Alli Sup, PoIre*
Addison, Herbert 1889- *Au&Wr*
Addison, Mrs. J *Alli Sup*
Addison, James Thayer 1887-1953 *AmA&B, WhWNAA*
Addison, Joseph 1672-1719 *Alli, AtlBL, BbD, BiD&SB, BrAu, CasWL, ChPo, ChPo S1, ChPo S2, Chmbr 2, CriT 2, CyWA, DcEnA, DcEnL, DcEuL,*

*DcLEnL, EvLB, McGWD, MouLC 2,
NewC, OxEng, Pen Eng, PoCh, RAdv 1,
RCom, REn, WebEAL*
Addison, Julia *Alli Sup*
Addison, Julia DeWolf 1866- *AmA&B, AmLY,
WhWNAA*
Addison, Lancelot 1632-1703 *Alli*
Addison, Lloyd 1931- *BlkAW, DrAP 1975,
LivBAA*
Addison, Lloyd 1937- *ConAu 45*
Addison, Mister *ChPo S2*
Addison, Ottelyn *OxCan Sup*
Addison, P L *Alli Sup*
Addison, Phoebe Wilhelm 1897- *WhWNAA*
Addison, Robert B *ChPo S1*
Addison, Thomas 1793-1860 *Alli Sup*
Addison, W G *ChPo S1*
Addison, William *Alli, Alli Sup, ChPo S2*
Addison, William H F 1880- *WhWNAA*
Addison, William Wilkinson 1905- *ConAu 13R*
Addleshaw, George William Outram 1906-
Au&Wr
Addon, Esther *Alli Sup*
Addona, Angelo F 1925- *ConAu 25,
WrD 1976*
Addums, Mozis *DcAmA, REnAL*
Addy, Catherine Greaves 1892- *WhLA*
Addy, D C *Alli Sup*
Addy, G H *Alli Sup*
Addy, George M 1927- *ConAu 21*
Addy, Sidney Oldall 1848- *Alli Sup, WhLA*
Addy, Ted *ConAu XR, SmATA XR*
Addy, William *Alli*
Ade, George 1866-1944 *AmA&B, AmLY,
BbD, BiD&SB, CasWL, ChPo, ChPo S1,
Chmbr 3, CnDAL, ConAmL, DcAmA,
DcNAA, EvLB, IndAu 1816, McGWD,
ModWD, OxAm, Pen Am, REn, REnAL,
TwCA, TwCA Sup, TwCW, WhWNAA*
Ade, John 1828-1914 *DcNAA*
Ade, Walter Frank Charles 1910- *ConAu 53*
Adee, David Graham *Alli Sup*
Adee, Herbert *Alli*
Adee, Lucy A K *ChPo*
Adee, Nicholas *Alli*
Adee, S *Alli*
Adela 1062?-1137 *NewC*
Adelaide 1792-1849 *NewC*
Adelard Of Bath *NewC*
Adelberg, Doris *ChPo S1, ConAu XR,
SmATA 7*
Adelberg, Roy P 1928- *ConAu 17R*
Adelborg, Ottilia 1855- *ChPo*
Adelbrecht, Priester *OxGer*
Adeler, Max 1847-1915 *Alli Sup, AmA,
AmA&B, ChPo, Chmbr 3, DcAmA,
DcNAA, EvLB, OxAm, REnAL*
Adeline *ChPo S1*
Adeliza d1151 *NewC*
Adell, Ilunga 1948- *BlkAW*
Adelman, Clifford 1942- *ConAu 41,
WrD 1976*
Adelman, Gary 1935- *ConAu 33*
Adelman, Howard 1938- *ConAu 25*
Adelman, Irma Glicman *ConAu 5R*
Adelman, Irving 1926- *ConAu 21*
Adelman, Janet 1941- *ConAu 61*
Adelmann, Frederick J 1915- *ConAu 49*
Adelsberger, Lucie 1895-1971 *ConAu 33*
Adelson, Joseph 1925- *ConAu 17R*
Adelson, Leone 1908- *AuBYP, ConAu 61*
Adelstein, Michael E 1922- *ConAu 33*
Adelt, Leonhard 1881- *WhLA*
Adelung, Johann Christoph 1732-1806 *BiD&SB,
OxGer*
Ademola, Frances 1930?- *AfA 1*
Adenauer, Konrad 1876-1967 *OxGer, REn*
Adenet Le Roi 1240?-1300? *BbD, BiD&SB,
CasWL, EvEuW, OxFr*
Adeney, David Howard 1911- *ConAu 53*
Adeney, Walter Frederick *Alli Sup*
Ader, Paul 1919- *AmA&B, AmNov*
Aderman, Ralph M 1919- *ConAu 5R*
Adey *Alli*
Adey, William Thomas *ChPo S1*
Adger, John B 1810-1899 *BiDSA, DcNAA*
Adhelm *Alli*
Adickes, Frances Wood 1889- *AmSCAP 66*

Adidnac *DcNAA*
Adiga, Sopalakrishna 1918- *DcOrL 2*
Adis, Henry *Alli*
Adivar, Halide Edib 1884-1964 *DcOrL 3,
EncWL Sup, Pen Cl*
Adizes, Ichak 1937- *ConAu 33*
Adjutor, Rivard 1868- *WhWNAA*
Adkin, Knight 1879- *WhLA*
Adkin, Lancaster d1806 *Alli, BiDLA,
BiDLA Sup*
Adkins, Arthur William Hope 1929- *Au&Wr,
WrD 1976*
Adkins, Bernard 1903- *Au&Wr*
Adkins, Dorothy C 1912- *ConAu 13R*
Adkins, E *Alli Sup*
Adkins, Homer Burton 1892- *WhWNAA*
Adkins, Jan 1944- *ConAu 33, SmATA 8*
Adkins, W *Alli*
Adkins, Walter Scott 1890- *TexWr*
Adkins, William *Alli Sup*
Adkinson, Francis *Alli Sup*
Adkinson, Harvey E 1934- *AmSCAP 66*
Adlam, Basil G *AmSCAP 66*
Adlam, Samuel 1798-1880 *Alli Sup*
Adlard, George *Alli Sup*
Adlard, John 1929- *ConAu 57*
Adleman, Robert H 1919- *ConAu 25,
WrD 1976*
Adler, Alfred 1870-1937 *LongC, OxGer, REn,
TwCA, TwCA Sup, WhLA*
Adler, Anne *ChPo*
Adler, Bernard S *ChPo S2*
Adler, Betty 1918-1973 *ConAu P-1*
Adler, Bill *ConAu XR*
Adler, Carol 1938- *ConAu 61*
Adler, Cyrus 1863-1940 *AmA&B, DcAmA,
DcNAA*
Adler, David A 1947- *ConAu 57*
Adler, Diantha Warfel *IndAu 1917*
Adler, Elmer 1884-1962 *AmA&B, ChPo*
Adler, Emanuel 1873- *WhLA*
Adler, Felix 1851-1933 *Alli Sup, AmA&B,
BbD, BiD&SB, DcAmA, DcNAA, REn,
REnAL, TwCA, TwCA Sup, WhWNAA*
Adler, Frederick Henry Herbert 1885-1959
AnMV 1926, ChPo S1, OhA&B
Adler, Friedrich 1857- *WhLA*
Adler, Friedrich Wolfgang 1879- *WhLA*
Adler, George J 1821-1868 *Alli, Alli Sup,
CyAL 2, DcAmA, DcNAA*
Adler, Guido 1855- *WhLA*
Adler, H G 1910- *ConAu 25*
Adler, Hans A 1921- *ConAu 49*
Adler, Helmut E 1920- *ConAu 33, WrD 1976*
Adler, Hermann 1839- *Alli Sup, BiD&SB*
Adler, Irene *ConAu XR, SmATA XR*
Adler, Irving 1913- *AmA&B, Au&Wr,
AuBYP, ConAu 5R, SmATA 1, ThBJA*
Adler, Jacob 1873?-1974 *ConAu 53,
WhWNAA*
Adler, Jacob 1913- *ConAu 17R*
Adler, Jacob Henry 1919- *ConAu 13R,
IndAu 1917, WrD 1976*
Adler, Julius Ochs 1892-1955 *AmA&B*
Adler, Lucile *DrAP 1975*
Adler, Manfred 1936- *ConAu 49*
Adler, Max Kurt 1905- *Au&Wr, ConAu 9R*
Adler, Mortimer Jerome 1902- *AmA&B,
OxAm, REnAL, TwCA Sup, WhWNAA*
Adler, Nathan Marcus 1803-1890 *Alli Sup*
Adler, Peggy *AuBYP*
Adler, Polly 1900-1962 *AmA&B, Au&Wr*
Adler, Renata 1938- *AmA&B, ConAu 49,
DrAF 1976*
Adler, Richard 1921- *AmSCAP 66*
Adler, Robert *SmATA 1*
Adler, Ruth 1915-1968 *AuBYP, ConAu 5R,
ConAu 25, SmATA 1, ThBJA*
Adler, Samuel 1801-1891 *DcAmA*
Adler, Samuel 1928- *AmSCAP 66*
Adler, Selig 1909- *Au&Wr, ConAu 5R*
Adler, Sol 1925- *ConAu 17R*
Adler, Viktor 1852-1918 *OxGer*
Adler, William 1929- *ConAu 9R*
Adler-Karlson, Gunnar *OxCan Sup*
Adlerbeth, Gudmund Joran 1751-1818 *CasWL*
Adlerblum, Nina H 1882-1974 *ConAu 49,
WhWNAA*

Adlersfeld, Eufemia Von *BiD&SB*
Adlersfeld-Ballestrem, E Von 1854- *WhLA*
Adley, Charles C *Alli Sup*
Adlum, John 1759-1836 *DcNAA*
Admirable Crichton *DcEnL*
Admirable Doctor, The 1214?-1292? *DcEnL,
NewC*
Adney, Edwin Tappan 1868-1950 *AmLY,
ChPo S1, OhA&B, OxCan*
Adoff, Arnold 1935- *AuBYP, AuNews 1,
ChPo S1, ChPo S2, ConAu 41, MorBMP,
SmATA 5*
Adoki, G E 1910?- *AfA 1*
Adolf Von Nassau 1255?-1298? *OxGer*
Adolph *WhWNAA*
Adolph, Karl 1869-1931 *OxGer*
Adolphus, John 1768?-1845 *Alli, BiD&SB,
BiDLA, DcEnL, EvLB*
Adolphus, John Leycester 1795-1862 *Alli,
Alli Sup, ChPo S1*
Adolphus, Otto *Alli Sup*
Adolphus, Thomas *Alli Sup*
Adomnan, Saint *NewC*
Adonai *REn*
Adonias Filho 1915- *Pen Am*
Adonim Ha-Levi *CasWL*
Adonis 1930- *DcOrL 3*
Adony, Raoul *ConAu XR*
Adorjan, Carol 1934- *ConAu 41, SmATA 10*
Adorno, J N *Alli*
Adorno, Theodor Wiesengrund 1903-1969
CasWL, ConAu 25, EncWL Sup, OxGer
Adra *ChPo S1*
Adret, Solomon 1235?-1310? *CasWL*
Adrian IV 1100?-1159 *Alli, NewC, REn*
Adrian De Castello 1460?-1521? *NewC*
Adrian De Corneto 1460?-1521? *NewC*
Adrian, Arthur Allen 1906- *ConAu 19,
WrD 1976*
Adrian, Charles R 1922- *ConAu 1R*
Adrian, Diane *AmSCAP 66*
Adrian, Baron Edgar Douglas 1889- *DcLEnL*
Adrian, Mary *AuBYP, ConAu XR*
Adrian, Rhys *ConDr*
Adrian, Robert 1775-1843 *Alli*
Adriance, John S *Alli Sup*
Adshead, Gladys L 1896- *AmA&B, ConAu 29,
MorJA, SmATA 3*
Adshead, Mary 1904- *IlCB 1956*
Adshead, S D 1868- *WhLA*
Adshead, W P *Alli Sup*
Adso Von Toul *OxGer*
Adsuar, Jorge 1883-1926 *PueRA*
Aduamah, Enos Yao 1940?- *AfA 1*
Advtum *ConAu XR*
Adwaita 1863-1919 *CasWL*
Adwani, Sir Bheeromal Mehrchand 1876-1953
DcOrL 2
Ady, Endre 1877-1919 *CasWL, ClDMEuL,
EncWL Sup, EvEuW, Pen Eur, TwCW,
WhTwL*
Ady, Mrs. Henry *Chmbr 3*
Ady, John *Alli, BiDLA*
Ady, T *Alli*
Adye, Frederick *Alli Sup*
Adye, Sir John Miller 1819- *Alli Sup*
Adye, R W *Alli*
Adye, S P *Alli*
Adye, Willett L *Alli Sup*
AE 1867-1935 *AtlBL, CasWL, Chmbr 3,
DcLEnL, EvLB, ModBL, NewC, OxEng,
Pen Eng, REn, TwCA, TwCA Sup,
TwCW, WebEAL*
Aeby, Jacquelyn *ConAu 29*
Aedhan, Saint *NewC*
Aegidius Of Assisi d1262 *NewC*
Aegydius, Saint *NewC*
Aelfheah, Saint 954-1012 *NewC*
Aelfled *NewC*
Aelfred *BrAu, Chmbr 1*
Aelfric 955?-1020? *BrAu, CasWL, Chmbr 1,
DcEnL, EvLB, NewC, OxEng, Pen Eng,
REn, WebEAL*
Aelfthryth *NewC*
Aelian *CasWL*
Aelianus, Claudius *BiD&SB*
Aelius Donatus *NewC*
Aelius Herodianus *Pen Cl*

Aharoni, Johanan *ConAu XR*
Aharoni, Yohanan 1919- *ConAu 25*
Ahbez, Eden 1908- *AmSCAP 66*
Ahearn, Lillian M 1886- *AmSCAP 66*
Ahearn, Robert G *REnAL*
Aheart, Andrew Norwood *BlkAW*
A'Heath, Patrick *ChPo S2*
Ahern, Barnabas M 1915- *ConAu 5R*
Ahern, Emily M 1944- *ConAu 49*
Ahern, George Patrick 1859-1942 *DcNAA*
Ahern, James *McGWD*
Ahern, James F 1932- *ConAu 41*
Ahern, John F 1936- *ConAu 61*
Ahern, Margaret McCrohan 1921- *ConAu 13R,*
SmATA 10
Ahern, Michael Joseph 1844-1914 *DcNAA*
Ahern, Thomas Francis 1947- *ConAu 45*
Ahern, Tom *ConAu XR, DrAP 1975*
Aherne, Owen *ConAu XR*
Ahl, Florence Myrick 1874-1946 *IndAu 1917*
Ahlberg, Harry 1912- *AmSCAP 66*
Ahlers, C *Alli*
Ahlert, Fred E 1892-1953 *AmSCAP 66*
Ahlgren, Ernst 1850-1888 *BiD&SB, CasWL,*
EuA,   Pen Eur
Ahlin, Lars Gustaf 1915- *CasWL, EncWL,*
Pen Eur
Ahll, Arthur Crawshay Alliston 1847-1930
DcNAA
Ahlquist, August Engelbert 1826-1889 *BiD&SB*
Ahlsen, Leopold 1927- *CnMD, CrCD,*
McGWD,   ModWD
Ahlstroem, G W 1918- *ConAu 45*
Ahlstrom, G W *ConAu XR*
Ahlstrom, Sydney E 1919- *ConAu 21,*
WrD 1976
Ahlwardt, Theodor Wilhelm 1828- *BiD&SB*
Ahmad, 'Aziz 1914- *DcOrL 2*
Ahmad, Dorothy *BlkAW*
Ahmad, Ishtiaq 1937- *ConAu 53*
Ahmad, Mawlavi *DcOrL 2*
Ahmad, Nafis 1913- *ConAu 17R*
Ahmad, Nazir 1836-1912 *DcOrL 2*
Ahmad Faris Al-Shidyaq 1801-1887 *CasWL*
Ahmad Khan, Sir Saiyid 1817-1898 *DcLEnL*
Ahmad Khan, Sir Sayyid 1817-1898 *CasWL,*
DcOrL 2
Ahmadjan Khan Bahadur, Munshi 1882-1951
DcOrL 2
Ahmann, Mathew H 1931- *ConAu 9R*
Ahmasi *BlkAW*
Ahmed, Khan Bahadur Kazi Sir Azizuddin 1861-
WhLA
Ahmed Bey Shauki *CasWL*
Ahmed Hamdi Tanpinar 1901-1962 *CasWL*
Ahmed Hasim 1884-1933 *CasWL*
Ahmed Shauki *CasWL*
Ahmedi, Taceddin Ibrahim 1335?-1413
DcOrL 3
Ahnebrink, Lars 1915- *ConAu 5R*
Ahnstrom, Doris N 1915- *AuBYP, ConAu 5R*
Aho, Juhani 1861-1921 *CasWL, EncWL,*
EvEuW,   Pen Eur,   REn
Ahrem, Jacques *ChPo*
Ahrendts, Marinda Baines 1877-1935 *OhA&B*
Ahrenhold, Novie Moffat *IlBYP*
Ahsen, Akhter 1931- *ConAu 61*
Ahwas Al-Ansari, Al- 655?-723? *DcOrL 3*
Ai 1947- *ConLC 4, DrAP 1975*
Ai, Ching 1910- *CasWL, DcOrL 1*
Ai, Wu 1904- *CasWL, DcOrL 1*
Aias *RCom*
Aicard, Jean 1848-1921 *BiD&SB, OxFr*
Aicher, Otl 1922- *WhGrA*
Aichinger, Helga 1937- *ConAu 25, IlBYP,*
SmATA 4
Aichinger, Ilse 1921- *CasWL, EncWL,*
ModGL,   OxGer,   Pen Eur
Aichinger, Peter 1933- *ConAu 61*
Aickin, J *Alli*
Aickin, Joseph *PoIre*
Aickman, Robert Fordyce 1914- *Au&Wr,*
ConAu 5R,   WrD 1976
Aidan d606 *NewC*
Aidan, Saint d615 *NewC*
Aide, Hamilton 1829-1906 *Alli Sup, BbD,*
BiD&SB,   ChPo S1,   ChPo S2,   Chmbr 3,
DcBiA,   DcEnL,   LongC,   NewC

Aidenoff, Abraham 1913-1976 *ConAu 37,*
ConAu 61,   WrD 1976
Aidman, Charles 1925- *AmSCAP 66*
Aidoo, Christina Ama Ata 1942- *AfA 1,*
ConDr,   RGAfl,   TwCW,   WrD 1976
Aig-Imoukhuede, Frank Abiodun 1935- *AfA 1,*
ConP 1970
Aigle DeMeaux, L' *OxFr*
Aigler, Ralph W 1885- *WhWNAA*
Aiguillette *ConAu XR*
Aikawa, Jerry K 1921- *WrD 1976*
Aiken *Alli*
Aiken, Aaron Eugene 1868- *BlkAW*
Aiken, Albert W 1846?-1894 *AmA&B,*
HsB&A,   HsB&A Sup,   REnAL
Aiken, Charles Augustus 1827- *Alli Sup,*
CyAL 1
Aiken, Charles Francis 1863-1925 *DcNAA*
Aiken, Clarissa Lorenz 1899- *ConAu 21*
Aiken, Clementine Edith *Alli Sup*
Aiken, Cleveland 1859- *WhWNAA*
Aiken, Conrad Potter 1889-1973 *AmA&B,*
AmLY,   AmLY XR,   AmWr,   AnCL,
AuBYP,   CasWL,   ChPo,   ChPo S1,
ChPo S2,   Chmbr 3,   CnDAL,   CnE&AP,
CnMD,   CnMWL,   ConAmA,   ConAmL,
ConAu 5R,   ConAu 45,   ConLC 1,
ConLC 3,   ConLC 5,   ConNov 1972,
ConP 1970,   DcLEnL,   EncWL,   EvLB,
LongC,   ModAL,   ModAL Sup,   ModWD,
OxAm,   OxEng,   Pen Am,   RAdv 1,   REn,
REnAL,   SixAP,   SmATA 3,   TwCA,
TwCA Sup,   TwCW,   WebEAL,   WhTwL,
WhWNAA
Aiken, Ednah 1872- *AmA&B*
Aiken, George David 1892- *AmA&B*
Aiken, George L 1830-1876 *Alli Sup, AmA,*
AmA&B,   CnDAL,   DcNAA,   HsB&A,
McGWD,   OxAm,   REnAL,   REnWD
Aiken, Henry *AmLY XR*
Aiken, Henry David 1912- *ConAu 1R*
Aiken, Mrs. J G *BiDSA*
Aiken, James R *Alli Sup*
Aiken, Joan 1924- *Au&Wr, AuBYP, ChLR 1,*
ConAu 9R,   PiP,   SenS,   SmATA 2,
ThBJA,   WrD 1976
Aiken, John R 1927- *ConAu 33*
Aiken, Kenneth 1885- *AmSCAP 66*
Aiken, Lewis R, Jr. 1931- *ConAu 25,*
WrD 1976
Aiken, May *ChPo*
Aiken, Michael Thomas 1932- *ConAu 21*
Aiken, Peter Freeland *Alli Sup*
Aiken, Samuel Clark 1790-1879 *OhA&B*
Aiken, Solomon 1758-1833 *DcNAA*
Aikin, Anna Letitia *Alli, BrAu 19*
Aikin, Arthur *Alli, BiDLA, BiDLA Sup,*
ChPo,   ChPo S2
Aikin, Berkeley *Alli Sup*
Aikin, Charles 1901- *ConAu 5R*
Aikin, Charles Roguson 1774?- *Alli, BiDLA*
Aikin, Edmund *Alli, BiDLA*
Aikin, J *Alli*
Aikin, John 1747-1822 *Alli, BiDLA, BrAu 19,*
CasWL,   ChPo,   ChPo S1,   ChPo S2,
DcEnL,   EvLB,   NewC
Aikin, John F *Alli Sup*
Aikin, Lucy 1781-1864 *Alli, Alli Sup, BbD,*
BiD&SB,   BiDLA,   BiDLA Sup,   BrAu 19,
CasWL,   ChPo,   ChPo S1,   Chmbr 3,
DcEnL,   EvLB,   NewC
Aikins, Carroll *OxCan*
Aikins, Herbert Austin 1867-1946 *AmLY,*
DcNAA,   WhWNAA
Aikman, Ann *ConAu XR*
Aikman, Conrad Allison 1874- *WhWNAA*
Aikman, Duncan 1889-1955 *AmA&B,*
IndAu 1917,   TexWr
Aikman, Henry G *AmA&B*
Aikman, J Logan *Alli Sup*
Aikman, James *Alli, Alli Sup*
Aikman, William 1824-1909 *Alli Sup,*
BiD&SB,   DcAmA,   DcNAA
Aikman, William Robertson *Alli Sup*
Ailleboust DeC Et D'Argentenay, L D' 1612-1660
OxCan
Ailly, Pierre D' 1350-1420 *CasWL*
Ailmer Of Canterbury d1137 *BiB N*

Ailmer, John *Alli*
Ailred 1100-1167 *CasWL*
Ailred, Abbot Of Rievaulx 1109-1166 *DcEnL*
Ailred Of Rievaux 1109?-1166? *Alli, BiB N,*
NewC
Ailred, Saint *NewC*
Ailward, Simeon *DcEnL*
Ailwin *BiB N*
Aim, James B *Alli Sup*
Aimard, Gustave 1818-1883 *BiD&SB, EvEuW,*
HsB&A,   MnBBF,   OxAm
Aimeric De Belenoi *CasWL*
Aimeric De Peguilhan 1195?-1230 *CasWL,*
EuA,   EvEuW
Aimon *NewC*
Aimwell, Walter *Alli Sup, BiD&SB, DcAmA,*
DcNAA
Aina *WhWNAA*
Ainger, Alfred 1837-1904 *Alli Sup, BrAu 19,*
ChPo,   ChPo S1,   ChPo S2,   Chmbr 3,
EvLB,   LongC,   NewC,   OxEng
Ainger, Arthur Campbell 1841-1919 *Alli Sup,*
ChPo,   ChPo S1
Ainger, Thomas 1799-1863 *Alli Sup*
Ainsa Amigues, Fernando 1937- *DcCLA*
Ainsley, Ellis *Alli Sup*
Ainsley, Thomas Liddell *Alli Sup*
Ainslie, A Douglas *Alli Sup*
Ainslie, Alex *Alli*
Ainslie, Alexander Colvin *Alli Sup*
Ainslie, Charles N 1856- *WhWNAA*
Ainslie, Douglas 1865-1952 *ChPo, ChPo S1,*
NewC,   WhLA
Ainslie, Hew 1792-1878 *Alli, AmA, AmA&B,*
BiD&SB,   BiDSA,   ChPo,   CyAL 1,
DcAmA,   DcNAA,   OxAm
Ainslie, John *Alli, BiDLA*
Ainslie, Peter 1867-1934 *AmLY, DcNAA*
Ainslie, Philip Barrington *Alli Sup*
Ainslie, Ralph St. John *ChPo S1*
Ainslie, Robert *Alli, Alli Sup*
Ainslie, Sir Robert *Alli*
Ainslie, Rosalynde 1932- *ConAu 25*
Ainslie, Tom *ConAu XR*
Ainslie, W *Alli*
Ainsworth, Charles H 1935- *ConAu 49*
Ainsworth, Edward Maddin 1902-1968 *AmA&B,*
ConAu 5R
Ainsworth, Harriet *ConAu 57*
Ainsworth, Harrison 1805-1882 *HsB&A*
Ainsworth, Henry d1662 *Alli, CyAL 1,*
DcEnL
Ainsworth, J *Alli*
Ainsworth, Joseph *BiDLA*
Ainsworth, Katherine 1908- *ConAu 29*
Ainsworth, Lillian M 1876- *ChPo, WhWNAA*
Ainsworth, Mary D Salter 1913- *ConAu 21,*
WrD 1976
Ainsworth, Norma *ConAu 13R, SmATA 9*
Ainsworth, Patricia *WrD 1976*
Ainsworth, Percy Clough *ChPo S2*
Ainsworth, Robert 1660-1743 *Alli, DcEnL*
Ainsworth, Ruth Gallard 1908- *Au&Wr, ChPo,*
ChPo S1,   ConAu XR,   SmATA 7,   WhCL,
WrD 1976
Ainsworth, T *Alli*
Ainsworth, Thomas *Alli*
Ainsworth, William *Alli*
Ainsworth, William Francis 1807-1896 *Alli,*
Alli Sup,   BiD&SB,   DcEnL
Ainsworth, William Harrison 1805-1882 *Alli,*
Alli Sup,   BbD,   BiD&SB,   BrAu 19,
CasWL 19,   ChPo,   ChPo S1,   Chmbr 3,
CyWA,   DcBiA,   DcEnA,   DcEnA Ap,
DcEnL,   DcEuL,   DcLEnL,   EvLB,
MnBBF,   NewC,   OxEng,   Pen Eng,   REn,
WebEAL,   WhCL
Ainsworth-Davis, James Richard 1861- *WhLA*
Aio d974 *BiB S*
Airas DeSantiago, Joan *CasWL*
Airay, Christopher 1601-1670 *Alli*
Airay, Henry 1559-1616 *Alli*
Aird, Catherine 1930- *ConAu XR, EncM&D,*
WrD 1976
Aird, David Mitchell *Alli Sup*
Aird, Eileen M 1945- *ConAu 49*
Aird, James *Alli*

EuA
Alanus, H *Alli Sup*
Alaol 1597?-1673? *DcOrL 2*
Alarcon, Juan Ruiz De 1581?-1639 *CasWL,*
   CnThe, DcEuL, DcSpL
Alarcon, Pedro Antonio De 1833-1891 *BiD&SB,*
   CasWL, ClDMEuL, CyWA, EuA,
   EvEuW, Pen Eur, REn
Alarcon Y Ariza, Pedro Antonio De 1833-1891
   BbD, DcBiA, DcSpL
Alarcon Y Mendoza, Juan Ruiz De 1580?-1639
   BbD, BiD&SB, EvEuW, REn
Alaric I 370?-410 *OxGer, REn*
Alas, Leopoldo 1852-1901 *ClDMEuL, DcSpL,*
   Pen Eur
Alas Y Urena, Leopoldo 1852-1901 *CasWL,*
   EuA, EvEuW, REn
Alavi, Aqa Buzurg 1908- *CasWL*
Alavi, Bozorg 1904- *DcOrL 3*
Alaya, Flavia 1935- *ConAu 33, WrD 1976*
Alazraki, Jaime 1934- *ConAu 33, WrD 1976*
Alba, Nanina 1917-1968 *BlkAW*
Alba, Victor 1916- *ConAu 23, WrD 1976*
Albach, James R 1797-1865 *Alli Sup, OhA&B*
Alban, Saint d304? *DcEnL, NewC*
Albanel, Charles 1616-1696 *OxCan*
Albanesi, Madame 1859-1936 *LongC*
Albany, Ada *ChPo S1*
Albany, George *HsB&A, HsB&A Sup*
Albasini, Joao 1890?-1925 *AfA 1*
Albaugh, Benjamin Franklin 1836-1917?
   DcNAA, OhA&B
Albaugh, Dorothy Priscilla 1903- *OhA&B*
Albaugh, Noah H 1834-1907 *OhA&B*
Albaugh, Ralph M 1909- *ConAu P-1*
Albaum, Gerald 1933- *ConAu 37*
Albaum, Melvin 1936- *ConAu 53*
Albee, Edward 1927- *CnMD*
Albee, Edward 1928- *AmA&B, AmWr,*
   AuNews 1, CasWL, CnThe, ConAu 5R,
   ConDr, ConLC 1, ConLC 2, ConLC 3,
   ConLC 5, CrCD, EncWL Sup, LongC,
   McGWD, ModAL, ModAL Sup,
   ModWD, OxAm, Pen Am, RCom, REn,
   REnAL, REnWD, TwCW, WebEAL,
   WhTwL, WorAu, WrD 1976
Albee, Ernest 1865-1927 *AmA&B, DcNAA*
Albee, Fred Houdelet 1876- *WhWNAA*
Albee, George Sumner 1905-1964 *ConAu 1R*
Albee, Helen Rickey 1864-1939 *AmLY,*
   DcAmA, OhA&B, WhWNAA
Albee, John 1833-1915 *Alli Sup, AmA&B,*
   BiD&SB, ChPo, DcAmA, DcNAA
Albemarle, Earl Of 1799-1891 *Alli Sup,*
   BrAu 19, NewC 19
Albeniz, Isaac Manuel Francisco 1860-1909
   AtlBL
Alber *OxGer*
Alber, Mike 1938- *ConAu 25*
Alberdingk Thijm, Josephus Albertus 1820-1889
   BiD&SB, CasWL, EvEuW
Alberdingk Thijm, Karel Joan Lodewijk *CasWL*
Alberg, Albert *Alli Sup*
Albergati Capacelli, Francesco 1728-1804
   BiD&SB
Alberger, Cora Gaskill *ChPo*
Alberger, John *Alli Sup*
Alberic De Besancon *OxGer*
Alberic Von Bisinzo *CasWL*
Albericus De Vere *Alli, BiB N*
Albericus Gentilis *OxEng*
Alberry, Faxon Franklin Duane 1848-1930
   OhA&B
Albers, Anni *ConAu 1R*
Albers, Henry H 1919- *ConAu 1R*
Albers, Homer 1863- *WhWNAA*
Albers, John Kenneth 1924- *AmSCAP 66*
Albers, Josef 1888- *AmA&B, ConAu 1R,*
   REn
Albert *Alli, PoIre*
Albert Francis C A E, Prince Consort 1819-1861
   Alli Sup
Albert Of Aix *Pen Eur*
Albert Of Stade 1200?-1261 *CasWL*
Albert, Prince 1819-1861 *ChPo S1, NewC,*
   REn
Albert The Great *REn*

Albert Victor & George, Princes Of Wales
   Alli Sup
Albert Von Stade 1200?-1261 *EvEuW*
Albert, A Adrian 1905-1972 *ConAu 37*
Albert, Adrien 1907- *WrD 1976*
Albert, Bessie *Alli Sup*
Albert, Burton, Jr. 1936- *ConAu 61*
Albert, Calvin Dodge 1876- *WhWNAA*
Albert, Ethel M 1918- *ConAu 23*
Albert, George 1869- *WhLA*
Albert, Harold A *Au&Wr, ConAu 29,*
   WrD 1976
Albert, Heinrich 1604-1651 *CasWL, DcEuL,*
   OxGer
Albert, Karl 1878- *WhLA*
Albert, Leslie *BlkAW*
Albert, Marvin H *AuBYP*
Albert, Mary *Alli Sup*
Albert, Mimi Abriel *DrAF 1976*
Albert, Paul 1827-1880 *BiD&SB*
Albert, Thomas 1879-1924 *DcNAA*
Albert, Walter E 1930- *ConAu 23*
Albert, Wilhelm 1890- *WhLA*
Albert-Birot, Pierre 1876-1967 *CasWL*
Albert I Paradis, Catalina 1873-1966 *ClDMEuL*
Albert I Paradis, Catarina 1873-1966 *CasWL*
Albertanus Of Brescia *REn*
Albertazzi, Adolfo 1865-1924 *CasWL*
Alberti, Konrad 1862-1918 *BiD&SB, OxGer*
Alberti, Leon Battista 1404-1472 *AtlBL,*
   BiD&SB, CasWL, DcEuL, EuA, EvEuW,
   OxEng, Pen Eur, REn
Alberti, Luigi 1822- *BiD&SB*
Alberti, Rafael 1902- *CasWL, ClDMEuL,*
   CnMD, CnMWL, DcSpL, EvEuW,
   McGWD, ModRL, ModWD, Pen Eur,
   REn, TwCA Sup, TwCW
Alberti, Rafael 1903- *EncWL*
Alberti, Robert E 1938- *ConAu 61*
Alberti, Solon 1889- *AmSCAP 66*
Alberti, Sophie *BiD&SB*
Albertini, Eugene 1880- *WhLA*
Albertinus, Agidius 1560?-1620 *CasWL,*
   DcEuL, OxGer, Pen Eur
Alberto Yunque *PueRA*
Alberton, Edwin *BiDSA, DcNAA*
Alberts, Al 1922- *AmSCAP 66*
Alberts, David Stephen 1942- *ConAu 29*
Alberts, Frances Jacobs 1907- *ConAu 5R*
Alberts, Robert Carman 1907- *ConAu 33,*
   WrD 1976
Alberts, William W 1925- *ConAu 21*
Albertsen, Frank *Alli Sup*
Albertson, Charles Carroll 1865- *ChPo S2,*
   IndAu 1816, WhWNAA
Albertson, Chris 1931- *ConAu 57*
Albertson, Dean 1920- *ConAu 1R, WrD 1976*
Albertus Magnus 1193?-1280 *BbD, BiD&SB,*
   CasWL, DcEnL, DcEuL, EuA, EvEuW,
   NewC, OxGer, Pen Eur, REn
Alberus, Erasmus 1500-1553 *BiD&SB, CasWL,*
   DcEuL, OxGer
Albery, James 1832?-1889 *BiD&SB, BrAu 19,*
   Chmbr 3, DcEnL
Albery, Michael James *Au&Wr*
Albery, Peter 1912- *Au&Wr*
Albin, Eleazar *Alli*
Albin, J *Alli, BiDLA*
Albine, John *Alli*
Albini, Joseph L 1930- *ConAu 61*
Albino, Francis Edward *ChPo S2*
Albinovanus Pedo *Pen Cl*
Albinski, Henry Stephen 1931- *ConAu 23,*
   WrD 1976
Albinson, Jack *ConAu 57*
Albinson, James P 1932- *ConAu 57*
Albinus *BrAu, EvLB, NewC*
Albinus d732? *BiB S*
Albinus, Johann Georg 1624-1679 *OxGer*
Albion, Lee Smith *IlBYP, IICB 1966*
Albion, Robert Greenhalgh 1896- *AmA&B,*
   ConAu 1R, WrD 1976
Albis, Thomas De *Alli*
Albjerg, Esther Marguerite Hall 1895-1971
   IndAu 1917
Albjerg, Victor Lincoln 1892-1973 *IndAu 1917*
Albo, Joseph 1380?-1444 *CasWL, EuA,*
   Pen Eur

Albornoz, Aurora De *PueRA*
Albov, Mikhail Nilovich 1851-1911 *CasWL,*
   DcRusL, EvEuW
Albrand, Alberta *AmA&B*
Albrand, Martha 1911- *AmNov*
Albrand, Martha 1912- *AmA&B, Au&Wr,*
   EncM&D
Albrand, Martha 1913- *TwCA Sup*
Albrand, Martha 1914- *ConAu 13R*
Albrecht *OxGer*
Albrecht II 1397-1439 *OxGer*
Albrecht III, Der Fromme 1401-1460 *OxGer*
Albrecht I, Deutscher Konig 1255-1308 *OxGer*
Albrecht IV, Herzog Von Bayern 1447-1508
   OxGer
Albrecht, Marschall Von Rapperswil *OxGer*
Albrecht Von Eyb 1420-1475 *CasWL, OxGer*
Albrecht Von Halberstadt *CasWL, OxGer,*
   Pen Eur
Albrecht Von Johannsdorf *CasWL, EuA,*
   OxGer
Albrecht Von Kemnaten *OxGer*
Albrecht Von Koln *OxGer*
Albrecht Von Scharfenberg *CasWL, DcEuL,*
   OxGer, Pen Eur
Albrecht, Arthur Emil 1894- *WhWNAA*
Albrecht, C Milton 1904- *ConAu 33*
Albrecht, Elmer 1901-1959 *AmSCAP 66*
Albrecht, Friedrich Wilhelm 1774-1840 *CasWL*
Albrecht, Hans 1873- *WhLA*
Albrecht, Johann Friedrich Ernst 1752-1814
   OxGer
Albrecht, Lillie 1894- *ConAu 5R*
Albrecht, Robert C 1933- *ConAu 23*
Albrecht, Ruth E 1910- *ConAu 17R*
Albrecht, Sebastian 1876- *WhWNAA*
Albrecht, Sophie 1757-1840 *OxGer*
Albrecht, W A 1888- *WhWNAA*
Albrecht, William Price 1907- *ConAu 17,*
   WrD 1976
Albrecht-Carrie, Rene 1904- *AmA&B,*
   ConAu 1R
Albree, John 1859-1938 *DcNAA*
Albricius *Alli*
Albright, Bliss 1903- *ConAu 33*
Albright, Evelyn May 1880-1942 *OhA&B*
Albright, Guy Harry 1876- *WhWNAA*
Albright, Ivan LeLorraine 1897- *REn*
Albright, Jacob Dissinger 1870-1926 *DcNAA*
Albright, Rachel *ChPo S1*
Albright, Raymond W 1901-1965 *ConAu P-1*
Albright, Victor E 1878- *WhWNAA*
Albright, William Foxwell 1891-1971 *AmA&B,*
   ConAu 33
Albro, Addis 1855-1911 *DcNAA*
Albro, John Adams 1799-1866 *Alli Sup,*
   DcNAA
Albrow, Martin 1937- *ConAu 33*
Albu, Austen Harry 1903- *Au&Wr*
Albu, Leon 1880- *WhWNAA*
Album, Leon 1880- *WhWNAA*
Albumazar 805-885 *NewC*
Albuquerque, Afonso De 1461-1515 *CasWL*
Albyn *OxCan*
Albyn, B *Alli*
Albyne *Alli*
Alcaeus *AtlBL, BbD, BiD&SB, CasWL,*
   NewC, OxEng, Pen Cl, RCom
Alcaforado, Marianna *OxFr*
Alcala Galiano, Antonio 1789-1865 *CasWL*
Alcala Y Herrera, Alfonso De *DcEuL*
Alcala Yanez DeRibera, Jeronimo De 1563-1632
   CasWL
Alcalde, E L *ConAu XR*
Alcantara, Osvaldo 1904- *AfA 1, Pen Cl*
Alcantara-Chaves, Pedro Carlos De 1829-
   BiD&SB
Alcantara Machado, Antonio Castilho De
   1901-1935 *Pen Am*
Alcayaga, Lucila Godoy *DcSpL*
Alcazar, Baltasar Del 1530-1606 *BbD,*
   BiD&SB, CasWL, DcEuL, DcSpL,
   Pen Eur
Alcendor, Ralph R 1926- *AmSCAP 66*
Alceu Amoroso Lima 1893- *Pen Am*
Alcharisi *CasWL*
Alchfrith *NewC*
Alchin, Carolyn Alden 1857-1926 *DcNAA*
Alchorne, W B *Alli*

Alchuine 735-804 *OxGer*
Alciati, Andrea 1492-1550 *DcEuL*
Alciato, Andrea 1492-1550 *CasWL*
Alcibiades 450?BC-404BC *DcEnL*, *REn*
Alcidamas Of Elaea *CasWL*
Alcinous *REn*
Alcione *REn*
Alciphron *BbD*, *BiD&SB*, *CasWL*, *OxEng*, *REn*
Alcmaeon *NewC*
Alcmaer, Heinric Van *CasWL*
Alcman *BbD*, *BiD&SB*, *CasWL*, *NewC*, *OxEng*, *Pen Cl*, *REn*
Alcmar, H *ChPo*
Alcock, Colonel *Alli Sup*
Alcock, Miss *ChPo S1*
Alcock, Charles W *Alli Sup*
Alcock, Deborah 1835-1913 *Alli Sup*, *ChPo S1*
Alcock, Frederick James 1888- *WhWNAA*
Alcock, J B *Alli Sup*
Alcock, J Curtis 1881- *WhWNAA*
Alcock, John *Alli Sup*
Alcock, John d1500 *Alli*
Alcock, Mary 1741-1798 *Alli*, *ChPo*, *PoIre*
Alcock, Nathan *Alli*
Alcock, R H *Alli Sup*
Alcock, Sir Rutherford 1809- *Alli Sup*
Alcock, T *Alli*
Alcock, Thomas *BbtC*
Alcoforado, Mariana 1640-1723 *CasWL*, *EvEuW*
Alcofribas Nasier *NewC*, *OxEng*, *REn*
Alcorn, Henry *PoIre*
Alcorn, John 1935- *ChPo*, *ChPo S1*, *IlBYP*, *IlCB 1966*, *ThBJA*
Alcorn, Katherine S *ChPo*
Alcorn, Marvin D 1902- *ConAu 13R*
Alcorn, Robert Hayden 1909- *ConAu 5R*
Alcott, Abigail May *DcNAA*
Alcott, Amos Bronson 1799-1888 *Alli*, *Alli Sup*, *AmA*, *AmA&B*, *BbD*, *BiD&SB*, *CasWL*, *ChPo*, *ChPo S2*, *Chmbr 3*, *CnDAL*, *CyAL 2*, *DcAmA*, *DcLEnL*, *DcNAA*, *EvLB*, *OxAm Am*, *Pen Am*, *REn*, *REnAL*
Alcott, J *Alli*
Alcott, Louisa May 1832-1888 *Alli Sup*, *AmA*, *AmA&B*, *AtlBL*, *AuBYP*, *BbD*, *BiD&SB*, *CarSB*, *CasWL*, *ChLR 1*, *ChPo*, *Chmbr 3*, *CnDAL*, *CriT 3*, *CyAL 2*, *CyWA*, *DcAmA*, *DcBiA*, *DcEnL*, *DcLEnL*, *DcNAA*, *EvLB*, *FamAYP*, *JBA 1934*, *MouLC 4*, *OxAm*, *OxEng*, *Pen Am*, *REn*, *REnAL*, *St&VC*, *WhCL*, *YABC 1*
Alcott, May 1840-1879 *EarAB*
Alcott, Ten *DcNAA*
Alcott, William Andrus 1798-1859 *Alli*, *AmA*, *AmA&B*, *DcAmA*, *DcEnL*, *DcNAA*
Alcover, Joan 1854-1926 *CasWL*, *Pen Eur*
Alcover I Maspons, Joan 1854-1926 *ClDMEuL*, *EncWL*
Alcuin 735-804 *Alli*, *BbD*, *BiB S*, *BiD&SB*, *BrAu*, *CasWL S*, *Chmbr 1*, *DcEnL*, *EvLB*, *NewC*, *OxEng*, *OxFr*, *OxGer*, *Pen Eng*, *Pen Eur*, *REn*
Alcuin Of Tours *DcEnL*
Alcyone *ConAu XR*, *REn*
Aldam, W H *Alli Sup*
Aldan, Daisy 1923- *AmA&B*, *ConAu 13R*, *DrAP 1975*
Aldana, Francisco De 1537-1578 *CasWL*, *EvEuW*, *Pen Eur*
Aldana, Ramon 1832-1882 *BiD&SB*
Aldanov, Mark Aleksandrovich 1886?-1957 *AmA&B*, *CasWL*, *ClDMEuL*, *DcRusL*, *EncWL*, *Pen Eng*, *REn*, *TwCA*, *TwCA Sup*, *TwCW*
Alday, J *Alli*
Aldcroft, Arthur *MnBBF*
Aldcroft, Derek H 1936- *ConAu 25*
Aldebaran *BlkAW*
Alden, Agnes M *ChPo S1*
Alden, Amelia Daly *ChPo*
Alden, Augustus Ephraim 1837-1914 *DcNAA*
Alden, Betty *REnAL*, *WhWNAA*
Alden, Carlos Coolidge 1866- *DcAmA*,

WhWNAA
Alden, Carroll Storrs 1876- *OhA&B*, *WhWNAA*
Alden, Charles Henry 1836-1906 *DcNAA*
Alden, Cynthia May 1861-1931 *DcNAA*
Alden, Cynthia Westover *AmLY*, *WhWNAA*
Alden, Cyrus 1785-1855 *DcNAA*
Alden, E T *ChPo*
Alden, Ebenezer 1788-1881 *Alli Sup*, *DcNAA*
Alden, Ellen Tracy *Alli Sup*, *ChPo S2*
Alden, Emily Gillmore *ChPo S2*
Alden, George Henry 1866- *WhWNAA*
Alden, George Ira 1843-1926 *DcNAA*
Alden, Mrs. George R *DcNAA*
Alden, Harold Lee 1890- *WhWNAA*
Alden, Henry Mills 1836-1919 *Alli Sup*, *AmA*, *AmA&B*, *BbD*, *BiD&SB*, *CnDAL*, *DcAmA*, *DcNAA*, *OxAm*, *REnAL*
Alden, Isabella Macdonald 1841-1930 *Alli Sup*, *AmA&B*, *AmLY*, *BbD*, *BiD&SB*, *CarSB*, *DcAmA*, *DcNAA*, *LongC*, *OhA&B*, *OxAm*
Alden, Jack *ConAu XR*
Alden, John 1599-1687 *OxAm*, *REn*, *REnAL*
Alden, John 1810-1894 *DcNAA*
Alden, John 1869-1934 *AmA&B*
Alden, John Berry 1847-1924 *AmA&B*, *DcNAA*
Alden, John D 1921- *ConAu 17R*
Alden, John Richard 1908- *AmA&B*, *Au&Wr*, *ConAu 1R*, *WrD 1976*
Alden, John W 1895- *AmSCAP 66*
Alden, Joseph 1807-1885 *Alli*, *Alli Sup*, *AmA*, *AmA&B*, *BbD*, *BiD&SB*, *DcAmA*, *DcNAA*
Alden, Joseph G 1876- *WhWNAA*
Alden, Joseph Reed 1886-1951 *AmSCAP 66*
Alden, Joseph Warren *Alli Sup*
Alden, Lucia B *ChPo*
Alden, M A *ChPo*
Alden, Margaret Hamilton 1863- *ChPo*
Alden, Mary *ChPo*
Alden, Miriam *Alli Sup*
Alden, Raymond Macdonald 1873-1924 *Alli Sup*, *AmA&B*, *AmLY*, *ChPo*, *DcAmA*, *DcNAA*
Alden, Roberta *LongC*
Alden, T J F *Alli*
Alden, Timothy 1771-1839 *Alli*, *AmA&B*, *DcNAA*
Alden, W *Alli Sup*, *ChPo S2*
Alden, William Livingston 1837-1908 *Alli Sup*, *AmA*, *AmA&B*, *BbD*, *BiD&SB*, *CarSB*, *ChPo*, *ChPo S2*, *DcAmA*, *DcNAA*
Alder, Francis A 1937- *ConAu 61*
Alder, Henry 1922- *ConAu 49*
Alder, Robert *Alli*, *BbtC*
Alder, Thomas *Alli*, *BiDLA*
Alderdice, Eliza Winslow *Alli Sup*
Alderfer, Clayton P 1940- *ConAu 37*
Alderfer, Harold F 1903- *ConAu 9R*
Alderham, Joseph 1925- *AmSCAP 66*
Alderman, Clifford Lindsey 1902- *AuBYP*, *ConAu 1R*, *SmATA 3*
Alderman, Edwin Anderson 1861-1931 *AmA&B*, *BiDSA*, *DcAmA*, *DcNAA*
Alderman, Joy 1931- *ConAu 61*
Alderman, William Horace 1885- *WhWNAA*
Alders, Lucas 1915- *Au&Wr*
Aldersey, S *Alli*
Alderson, Althea Todd *ChPo S1*
Alderson, Brian W A *ChPo S1*, *ChPo S2*
Alderson, Sir Edward Hall 1787-1857 *Alli Sup*
Alderson, Sir Edwin Alfred Hervey 1859-1927 *Br&AmS*, *OxCan*
Alderson, Sir James 1794-1882 *Alli Sup*
Alderson, John *Alli*, *BiDLA*, *BiDLA Sup*
Alderson, Lady M A *Alli Sup*
Alderson, Stanley 1927- *ConAu 5R*
Alderson, Valerie *ChPo S2*
Alderson, Victor Clifton 1862- *WhWNAA*
Alderson, William Atkinson 1856-1938 *DcNAA*
Alderson, William T, Jr. 1926- *ConAu 9R*
Aldfrith d705 *NewC*
Aldhelm 640?-709 *Alli*, *BiB S*, *BrAu*, *CasWL*, *DcEnL*, *NewC*, *OxEng*
Aldin, Cecil Charles Windsor 1870-1935 *Br&AmS*, *ChPo S1*, *ChPo S2*, *ConICB*

Alding, Peter *EncM&D*
Aldinger, Wallace S 1905- *ConAu 1R*
Aldington, Major *Alli*
Aldington, Hilda Doolittle 1886- *AmA&B*, *ConAmA*, *SixAP*
Aldington, J *Alli*
Aldington, John *BiDLA*
Aldington, Richard 1892-1962 *CasWL*, *ChPo*, *ChPo S1*, *ChPo S2*, *Chmbr 3*, *CyWA*, *DcLEnL*, *EncWL*, *EvLB*, *LongC*, *ModBL*, *NewC*, *OxEng*, *Pen Eng*, *REn*, *TwCA*, *TwCA Sup*, *TwCW*, *WebEAL*
Aldington, Mrs. Richard 1886-1961 *ChPo S2*, *Chmbr 3*
Aldini, John *Alli*, *BiDLA*
Aldis, Charles James Berridge 1808-1872 *Alli Sup*
Aldis, Dorothy 1897?-1966 *AmA&B*, *AnCL*, *AuBYP*, *BkCL*, *ChPo*, *ChPo S1*, *ConAu 1R*, *JBA 1934*, *JBA 1951*, *SmATA 2*, *St&VC*, *WhWNAA*
Aldis, Elijah *Alli Sup*
Aldis, J A *Alli Sup*
Aldis, Mary Reynolds 1872-1949 *AmA&B*
Aldis, Mary Steadman *Alli Sup*
Aldis, William Steadman *Alli Sup*
Aldiss, Brian W 1925- *Au&Wr*, *ConAu 5R*, *ConLC 5*, *ConNov 1972*, *ConNov 1976*, *TwCW 1976*, *WrD 1976*
Aldolfo Nones *PueRA*
Aldon, Adair *AuBYP*, *ConAu XR*, *SmATA 6*
Aldouby, Zwy H 1931- *ConAu 33*
Aldous, Allan Charles 1911- *Au&Wr*
Aldred d1069? *Alli*
Aldred, Cyril 1914- *ConAu 57*
Aldred, Eric 1934- *Au&Wr*
Aldred, Jer *Alli*
Aldred, Margaret Gertrude 1914- *Au&Wr*
Aldred, Philip Foster *Alli Sup*
Aldred, W M *Alli Sup*
Aldred, W W *Alli Sup*
Aldrete, Bernardo 1560?-1640? *DcEuL*
Aldrich, Alan *ChPo S2*
Aldrich, Anne Reeve 1866-1892 *AmA&B*, *BiD&SB*, *ChPo*, *DcAmA*, *DcNAA*
Aldrich, Auretta 1829-1920 *DcNAA*
Aldrich, Bess Streeter 1881-1954 *AmA&B*, *AmNov*, *OxAm*, *REn*, *REnAL*, *TwCA*, *TwCA Sup*, *WhWNAA*
Aldrich, C *Alli*
Aldrich, C Knight 1914- *ConAu 25*
Aldrich, Charles 1828-1908 *DcNAA*
Aldrich, Charles Roberts 1877-1933 *DcNAA*, *IndAu 1917*
Aldrich, Clara Chapline Thomas d1967 *AmA&B*, *IndAu 1917*, *WhWNAA*
Aldrich, Darragh *AmA&B*, *MnnWr*, *WhWNAA*
Aldrich, Flora L 1859-1921 *DcNAA*
Aldrich, Fred Hampton 1861-1944 *OhA&B*
Aldrich, Frederic DeLong 1899- *ConAu P-1*
Aldrich, George 1816-1888 *DcNAA*
Aldrich, Henry 1647-1710 *Alli*, *Chmbr 2*, *DcEnA*, *DcEnL*
Aldrich, J K *Alli Sup*
Aldrich, James 1810-1856? *Alli*, *BiD&SB*, *ChPo*, *ChPo S1*, *CyAL 2*, *DcAmA*, *DcNAA*
Aldrich, Jeremiah Knight 1826-1905 *DcNAA*
Aldrich, John Merton 1866- *AmLY*, *WhWNAA*
Aldrich, Julia Carter 1834-1924 *OhA&B*
Aldrich, Lillian d1927 *DcNAA*
Aldrich, Loyal Blaine 1884- *WhWNAA*
Aldrich, M Almy *Alli Sup*
Aldrich, Marie Antoinette *AnMV 1926*
Aldrich, Mildred 1853-1928 *AmA&B*, *DcNAA*, *WhWNAA*
Aldrich, Myrtle Anna 1872- *ChPo*, *ChPo S1*
Aldrich, O W *Alli Sup*
Aldrich, Peleg Emory 1813-1895 *Alli Sup*, *DcNAA*
Aldrich, Perley Dunn 1863-1933 *DcNAA*
Aldrich, Richard 1863-1937 *AmA&B*, *DcNAA*, *WhWNAA*
Aldrich, Robert d1555 *Alli*
Aldrich, Talbot *ChPo S1*

Aldrich, Thomas Bailey 1836-1907 *Alli,*
Alli Sup, AmA, AmA&B Sup, BbD,
BiD&SB, CarSB, CasWL, ChPo,
ChPo S1, ChPo S2, Chmbr 3, CnDAL,
CyAL 2, CyWA, DcAmA, DcBiA,
DcEnA Ap, DcEnL, DcLEnL, DcNAA,
EncM&D, EvLB, JBA 1934, OxAm,
OxEng, Pen Am, REn, REnAL
Aldrich, Mrs. Thomas Bailey *DcNAA*
Aldrich, Virgil C 1903- *TexWr*
Aldrich, Wilbur d1922 *DcNAA*
Aldridge *Alli, BbtC*
Aldridge, A Owen 1915- *ConAu 17R,*
WrD 1976
Aldridge, Adele 1934- *ConAu 49, DrAP 1975*
Aldridge, Gordon James 1916- *AmA&B,*
WrD 1976
Aldridge, James 1918- *Au&Wr, ConAu 61,*
ConNov 1972, ConNov 1976, TwCA Sup,
WrD 1976
Aldridge, Jeffrey 1938- *ConAu 25*
Aldridge, John W 1922- *AmA&B, ConAu 1R,*
WorAu
Aldridge, Josephine Haskell *AuBYP*
Aldridge, R W *Alli Sup*
Aldridge, Reginald *Alli Sup*
Aldridge, Richard Boughton 1930- *ConAu 9R*
Aldridge, Robert d1555 *Alli*
Aldridge, W *Alli*
Aldus Manutius *NewC*
Ale Ahmad, Jalal 1920?-1971 *DcOrL 3*
Aleandro, Girolamo 1480-1542 *CasWL*
Aleandro, Girolamo 1574-1629 *BiD&SB*
Aleardi, Aleardo 1812-1878 *BbD, BiD&SB,*
CasWL, EuA, EvEuW, Pen Eur
Alecis, Guillaume 1425?-1486? *CasWL, OxFr*
Aleck, Adolph William 1899- *IndAu 1917*
Alecsandrescu, Grigoic 1812-1886 *BiD&SB*
Alecsandrescu, Grigore 1812-1886 *CasWL*
Alecsandri, Vasile 1821-1890 *BiD&SB, CasWL,*
EvEuW, McGWD, Pen Eur
Alee, Lycurgus J *BlkAW*
Alegre, Caetano DaCosta 1864-1890 *AfA 1*
Alegria, Alonso 1940- *DcCLA*
Alegria, Ciro 1909-1967 *CasWL, CyWA,*
DcSpL, Pen Am, TwCA Sup, TwCW
Alegria, Fernando 1918- *ConAu 9R, DcCLA*
Alegria, Jose S 1887-1965 *PueRA*
Alegria, Ricardo E 1921- *ConAu 25, PueRA,*
SmATA 6
Alegria Bazan, Ciro 1909-1967 *EncWL*
Aleichem, Shalom 1859-1916 *LongC, REn,*
TwCA, TwCA Sup
Aleichem, Sholem 1859-1916 *CasWL, EncWL,*
REn
Aleichem, Sholom 1859-1916 *AmA&B, AtlBL*
Aleix, L T Eulalie *BiDSA*
Aleixandre, Vicente 1898- *CasWL, EncWL,*
Pen Eur, REn, WorAu
Aleixandre, Vicente 1900- *ClDMEuL, DcSpL,*
EvEuW, TwCW
Alekhine, Alexandre 1892- *WhLA*
Aleksandrov *CasWL*
Aleman, Mateo 1547-1614? *CasWL, CyWA,*
DcEuL, DcSpL, EuA, EvEuW, Pen Eur,
REn
Aleman, Matteo 1550?-1609? *BbD, BiD&SB,*
DcBiA
Alemany, Joseph Sadoc 1814-1888 *Alli Sup,*
DcAmA, DcNAA
Alembert, Jean Baptiste LeRond D' 1717-1783
BbD, BiD&SB, CasWL, EuA, EvEuW,
OxFr, Pen Eur, REn
Alen, Edmond d1559? *Alli*
Alencar, Jose Martiniano De 1829-1877
BiD&SB, CasWL, Pen Am, REn
Alent, Rose Marie Bachem *ConAu 49*
Alepoudelis, Odysseus *WorAu*
Aleramo, Sibilla 1876?-1960 *CasWL,*
ClDMEuL
Alerding, Herman Joseph 1845-1924 *DcNAA,*
IndAu 1816
Aleri, Bishop Of *DcEuL*
Ales *Alli*
Ales, Alexander 1500-1565 *Alli*
Alesius, Alexander 1500-1565 *Alli, EvLB*
Alethitheras *DcNAA*
Alewijn, Abraham Martijnsz 1664-1721 *CasWL*

Alexander I 1777-1825 *REn*
Alexander II 1818-1881 *REn*
Alexander III d1181 *NewC*
Alexander III 1845-1894 *REn*
Alexander VI, Pope *REn*
Alexander De Hales d1245 *Alli*
Alexander De Villa Dei 1160?-1203? *Pen Eur*
Alexander Essebiensis *Alli*
Alexander Le Pargiter d1220 *BiB N*
Alexander Le Partiger d1220 *Alli*
Alexander Neckam 1157-1217 *Alli, BiB N,*
CasWL
Alexander Of Aphrodisias *CasWL*
Alexander Of Hales 1175?-1245 *BiD&SB,*
DcEnL, NewC, OxEng, REn
Alexander The Corrector 1701-1770 *DcEnL,*
REn
Alexander The Great 356BC-323BC *DcEuL,*
NewC, Pen Cl, REn
Alexander, A *Alli Sup*
Alexander, A J *Alli Sup*
Alexander, Addison *ChPo*
Alexander, Adelaide *Alli Sup*
Alexander, Albert 1914- *ConAu 25*
Alexander, Alexander Crichton 1845- *ChPo,*
ChPo S1
Alexander, Alexander Septimus 1860-1935
DcNAA
Alexander, Ann *Alli Sup*
Alexander, Anna B Cooke 1913- *ConAu 5R,*
ConAu 57, SmATA 1
Alexander, Anne 1913- *AuBYP, ConAu 57*
Alexander, Annie French 1825-1902 *DcBiA*
Alexander, Annie ALSO Alexander, Mrs.
Alexander, Anthony Francis 1920- *ConAu 1R*
Alexander, Archibald 1772-1851 *Alli, AmA,*
AmA&B, BbD, BiD&SB, BiDSA,
CyAL 1, DcAmA, DcEnL, DcNAA
Alexander, Archibald 1855-1917 *Alli Sup,*
DcAmA, DcNAA
Alexander, Arthur 1927- *ChPo S1, ConAu 5R*
Alexander, Augustus Washington *Alli Sup*
Alexander, B *Alli Sup*
Alexander, B d1768 *Alli*
Alexander, Boyd 1913- *Au&Wr, ConAu 53,*
WrD 1976
Alexander, Caleb 1775-1828 *Alli, CyAL 1,*
DcAmA, DcNAA
Alexander, Calvert Page 1900- *CatA 1947*
Alexander, Carter 1881- *WhWNAA*
Alexander, Mrs. Cecil Frances 1818-1895
Alli Sup, BiD&SB, BkCL, BrAu 19,
ChPo, ChPo S1, ChPo S2, Chmbr 3,
DcEnL, EvLB, PoCh, PoIre
Alexander, Charles *ConAu XR*
Alexander, Charles 1897- *WhWNAA*
Alexander, Charles Beatty 1849-1927 *Alli Sup,*
DcNAA
Alexander, Charles C 1935- *ConAu 13R*
Alexander, Charles Stevenson 1916- *ConAu 5R*
Alexander, Charles T *AnMV 1926*
Alexander, Charles Wesley 1837-1927 *DcNAA*
Alexander, Christine 1893-1975 *ConAu 61*
Alexander, Colin Cuthbert 1879- *WhWNAA*
Alexander, Colin James 1920- *ConAu 13R*
Alexander, Conel Hugh O'Donel 1909- *Au&Wr*
Alexander, D *Alli*
Alexander, D T *Alli*
Alexander, David 1907-1973 *Au&Wr,*
ConAu 1R, ConAu 41, EncM&D
Alexander, DeAlva Stanwood 1845-1925
DcAmA, DcNAA, OhA&B
Alexander, Dee *DrAP 1975*
Alexander, Denis 1945- *ConAu 45*
Alexander, Disney *BiDLA*
Alexander, E *Alli*
Alexander, E Porter *Alli Sup*
Alexander, Edward 1936- *ConAu 13R*
Alexander, Edward Porter 1835-1910 *AmA&B,*
BiDSA, DcNAA
Alexander, Edward Porter 1907- *Au&Wr,*
ConAu 33
Alexander, Edwin P 1905- *ConAu 29*
Alexander, Eleanor Jane *WhLA*
Alexander, Esther Frances 1840?- *DcAmA*
Alexander, Eugenie 1919- *WrD 1976*
Alexander, Evan *Alli Sup*
Alexander, F Russell 1902- *WhWNAA*

Alexander, Floyce 1938- *ConAu 33,*
DrAF 1976, DrAP 1975, WrD 1976
Alexander, Frances 1837-1917 *Alli Sup*
Alexander, Frances 1888- *AnCL, ConAu 25,*
SmATA 4, TexWr, WrD 1976
Alexander, Francesca 1837-1917 *Alli Sup,*
AmA&B, ChPo, ChPo S2, DcNAA
Alexander, Franklin Osborne 1897- *ConAu 25*
Alexander, Franz 1891-1964 *AmA&B,*
ConAu 5R
Alexander, Gabriel *Alli Sup*
Alexander, George 1858-1918 *LongC*
Alexander, George 1918- *AmSCAP 66*
Alexander, George Gardener *Alli Sup*
Alexander, George M 1914- *ConAu 5R*
Alexander, Georgina Stanley 1929- *WrD 1976*
Alexander, Gil *ConAu XR*
Alexander, Grace Caroline 1872- *IndAu 1816*
Alexander, Gross 1852-1915 *BiDSA, DcAmA,*
DcNAA
Alexander, Hartley Burr 1873-1939 *AmA&B,*
AmLY, DcNAA, WhWNAA
Alexander, Henry *PoIre*
Alexander, Henry Aaron 1874- *BiDSA*
Alexander, Henry Carrington 1835-1894
Alli Sup, DcNAA
Alexander, Herbert E 1927- *ConAu 41*
Alexander, Holmes Moss 1906- *AmA&B,*
ConAu 61
Alexander, Hubert G 1909- *ConAu 23*
Alexander, Hugh *PoIre*
Alexander, I J 1905?-1974 *ConAu 53*
Alexander, Ian Welsh 1911- *Au&Wr,*
ConAu 13R
Alexander, Irene *ChPo*
Alexander, J *Alli, Alli Sup*
Alexander, J Bell *BiDSA*
Alexander, J H *Alli Sup*
Alexander, J J G 1935- *ConAu 21*
Alexander, James *Alli Sup, BbtC, ChPo,*
PoIre
Alexander, Sir James Edward 1803-1885 *Alli,*
Alli Sup, BbD, BbtC, BiD&SB, OxCan
Alexander, James Lynne 1800-1879 *DcNAA,*
OxCan
Alexander, James McKinney 1835-1911 *DcNAA*
Alexander, James Waddel 1804-1859 *Alli,*
Alli Sup, BiDSA, CyAL 1, DcAmA,
DcNAA, PoCh
Alexander, James Waddel 1839-1915 *DcAmA,*
DcNAA
Alexander, Janet 1907- *Au&Wr, WrD 1976*
Alexander, Jean 1926- *ConAu 49*
Alexander, Jeff 1910- *AmSCAP 66*
Alexander, Jerome 1876- *AmLY, ChPo,*
DcEuL, WhWNAA
Alexander, Joan 1920- *Au&Wr, ConAu XR,*
WrD 1976
Alexander, Jocelyn Anne Arundel 1930- *AuBYP,*
ConAu 1R
Alexander, John *Alli Sup*
Alexander, John 1736-1765 *Alli*
Alexander, John A 1912- *ConAu 9R*
Alexander, John Brevard 1834-1911 *BiDSA,*
DcNAA
Alexander, John D 1839-1931 *IndAu 1816*
Alexander, John E 1815-1901 *DcNAA,*
OhA&B
Alexander, John H *BiDSA*
Alexander, John Henry 1812-1867 *Alli,*
Alli Sup, AmA, BiDSA, DcAmA,
DcNAA
Alexander, John Henry 1846- *DcNAA*
Alexander, John L 1875-1932 *DcNAA*
Alexander, John Romich 1849-1940 *OhA&B,*
WhWNAA
Alexander, John T *ChPo*
Alexander, John Thorndike 1940- *ConAu 33,*
WrD 1976
Alexander, John W 1918- *ConAu 5R*
Alexander, Jon 1940- *WrD 1976*
Alexander, Josef *AmSCAP 66*
Alexander, Joseph Addison 1809-1860 *Alli,*
Alli Sup, ChPo, ChPo S2, CyAL 1,
DcAmA, DcNAA
Alexander, Julius J *Alli Sup*
Alexander, Kenneth John Wilson 1922- *Au&Wr,*
ConAu 61, ConAu XR

Alexander, Kyle *ConAu XR*
Alexander, L *Alli, Alli Sup, BiDLA*
Alexander, L C *Alli Sup*
Alexander, Larry 1939- *AmSCAP 66*
Alexander, Lewis Grandison 1900-1945 *BlkAW*
Alexander, Lewis M 1921- *ConAu 21*
Alexander, Lillie d1943 *DcNAA*
Alexander, Linda Lewann 1935- *ConAu 23, SmATA 2, WrD 1976*
Alexander, Lloyd Chudley 1924- *AnCL, Au&Wr, AuBYP, ChLR 1, ConAu 1R, MorBMP, NewbC 1966, PiP, SmATA 3, ThBJA*
Alexander, Louis George 1932- *Au&Wr, WrD 1976*
Alexander, M E W *ChPo*
Alexander, Magnus Washington 1870-1932 *DcNAA*
Alexander, Maitland 1867-1940 *DcNAA*
Alexander, Marc 1929- *ConAu 5R*
Alexander, Marge *ConAu XR*
Alexander, Marianne *Alli Sup*
Alexander, Marion *BlkAW*
Alexander, Martha Kathleen 1910- *Au&Wr, IlBYP*
Alexander, Marthann 1907- *ConAu 53*
Alexander, Martin 1930- *ConAu 49*
Alexander, Mary Jean McCutcheon *ConAu 9R*
Alexander, Matilda Greathouse 1842-1892 *IndAu 1816*
Alexander, Michael J 1941- *ConAu 45*
Alexander, Milton 1917- *ConAu 17R*
Alexander, Mrs. 1825-1902 *Alli Sup, BbD, BiD&SB, LongC, NewC*
Alexander, Mrs. ALSO Alexander, Annie
Alexander, Patrick Proctor 1823-1886 *Alli Sup, ChPo S1*
Alexander, Perry 1895- *AmSCAP 66*
Alexander, Peter 1922- *Au&Wr*
Alexander, Ric *ConAu XR*
Alexander, Richard Thomas 1887- *WhWNAA*
Alexander, Richard W *DcNAA*
Alexander, Robert *Alli Sup*
Alexander, Robert 1837-1901 *OhA&B*
Alexander, Robert 1863-1941 *DcNAA*
Alexander, Robert J 1918- *ConAu 1R, WrD 1976*
Alexander, Robert Jocelyn *Alli Sup, PoIre*
Alexander, Russell George *ChPo S2*
Alexander, Ruth *ChPo S2*
Alexander, Samuel *Chmbr 3, PoIre*
Alexander, Samuel 1857?-1938 *LongC, WhLA*
Alexander, Samuel Davies 1819-1894 *Alli Sup, DcAmA, DcNAA*
Alexander, Shana 1925- *ConAu 61, WrD 1976*
Alexander, Sidney 1912- *ConAu 9R*
Alexander, Sidney Arthur 1866- *Alli Sup, WhLA*
Alexander, Sigmund B *Alli Sup*
Alexander, Stephen 1806-1883 *Alli, Alli Sup, DcAmA, DcNAA*
Alexander, Stuart *Alli Sup*
Alexander, Sue 1933- *ConAu 53*
Alexander, T H 1891-1941 *AmA&B, WhWNAA*
Alexander, Theron 1913- *ConAu 5R*
Alexander, Thomas *Alli Sup*
Alexander, Thomas 1887- *WhWNAA*
Alexander, Thomas S *Alli*
Alexander, Thomas Tyler *Alli Sup*
Alexander, Thomas W, Jr. 1930- *ConAu 9R*
Alexander, Van 1915- *AmSCAP 66*
Alexander, W *Alli, Chmbr 1*
Alexander, W F *ChPo S1*
Alexander, W L *Alli*
Alexander, William *Alli, Alli Sup, ChPo S1, Chmbr 3*
Alexander, William d1788 *BiDLA, BiDLA Sup*
Alexander, William 1602?-1638 *OxCan*
Alexander, William 1767?-1815 *BiDLA Sup, BkIE*
Alexander, William 1824-1911 *Alli Sup, ChPo, ChPo S1, ChPo S2, DcEnL, PoIre*
Alexander, William 1826-1894 *Alli Sup, Pen Eng*
Alexander, William 1848-1937 *DcNAA*

Alexander, Sir William, Earl Of Stirling 1567?-1640 *Alli, BbtC, BrAu, CasWL, ChPo, CrE&SL, DcEnA, DcEnL, DcLEnL, NewC, OxCan, OxEng, Pen Eng, REn*
Alexander, William D S *Alli Sup*
Alexander, William DeWitt 1833-1913 *Alli Sup, DcAmA, DcNAA*
Alexander, William John 1855-1944 *DcNAA*
Alexander, William Lindsay 1808-1884 *Alli Sup, DcEnL, DcNAA, PoCh*
Alexander, William M 1912- *ConAu 33*
Alexander, Sir William Picken 1905- *Au&Wr*
Alexander, Yonah 1931- *ConAu 61*
Alexandersson, Gunnar V 1922- *ConAu 17R*
Alexandra *NewC*
Alexandre De Bernai *CasWL*
Alexandre De Bernay *OxFr*
Alexandre De Paris *CasWL*
Alexandre Du Pont *CasWL*
Alexandre, Philippe 1932- *ConAu 41*
Alexandrescu, Grigore M 1812?-1885 *CasWL*
Alexandri, Vasile 1821-1890 *EuA*
Alexandrow, A *Alli Sup*
Alexandrow, F *Alli Sup*
Alexandrowicz, Charles Henry 1902- *Au&Wr, ConAu 1R, WrD 1976*
Alexeieff, Alexandre 1901- *WhGrA*
Alexeyev, Konstantin Sergeyevich *DcRusL, REn*
Alexeyev, Sergey Alexandrovich *CasWL*
Alexis 390?BC-280?BC *CasWL, OhA&B*
Alexis De Barbezieux, Father *OxCan*
Alexis, Guillaume 1425?-1486 *CasWL, OxFr*
Alexis, Jacques-Stephen 1922-1961? *CasWL*
Alexis, Joseph E A 1885- *WhWNAA*
Alexis, Paul 1847-1901 *ClDMEuL, OxFr*
Alexis, Willibald 1798-1871 *BbD, BiD&SB, CasWL, DcEuL, EuA, EvEuW, OxGer, REn*
Alexius Comnenus 1048-1118 *REn*
Alexopoulos, Constantine John 1907- *WrD 1976*
Aley, Howard C 1911- *OhA&B*
Aley, Maxwell 1889- *IndAu 1816, WhWNAA*
Aley, Robert Judson 1863-1935 *DcNAA, IndAu 1816*
Aleyn, Charles d1640 *Alli, DcEnL, NewC*
Aleyn, J *Alli*
Aleyrac, Jean-Baptiste *OxCan*
Alfandary-Alexander, Mark 1923- *ConAu 5R*
Alfani, Gianna 1260?-1320? *CasWL*
Alfarabius *CasWL*
Alfasi, Isaac Ben Jacob 1013-1103 *CasWL, Pen Eur*
Alfidi, Joseph 1961- *AmSCAP 66*
Alfieri, Count Vittorio 1749-1803 *AtlBL, BbD, BiD&SB, CasWL, CnThe, DcEnL, DcEuL, EuA, EvEuW, McGWD, OxEng, Pen Eur, RCom, REn, REnWD*
Alfonse DeSaintonge, Jean Fonteneau 1485?-1544 *OxCan*
Alfonsi, Petrus *DcSpL*
Alfonso V And I 1416-1458 *DcEuL*
Alfonso VII *DcSpL*
Alfonso X 1221?-1284 *BbD, BbD, CasWL, DcEuL, DcSpL, EuA Eur, Pen Eur, REn*
Alfonso XI *DcSpL*
Alfonso, Don 1899- *AmSCAP 66*
Alfonso, Mrs. Hector *AmNov XR*
Alfonso, Pedro *DcSpL*
Alford, Charles Richard 1816- *Alli Sup*
Alford, Daniel Pring 1838- *Alli Sup*
Alford, Elizabeth M *Alli Sup*
Alford, Fanny *Alli Sup*
Alford, Henry 1810-1871 *Alli, Alli Sup, BbD, BiD&SB, BrAu 19, CasWL 19, ChPo, ChPo S1, ChPo S2, Chmbr 3, DcEnA, DcEnL, EvLB, NewC*
Alford, Henry 1874- *WhLA*
Alford, J *Alli*
Alford, Joseph *Alli*
Alford, Leon Pratt 1877-1942 *DcNAA, WhWNAA*
Alford, Loyal Adolphus 1814-1883 *Alli Sup, DcNAA, IndAu 1816*
Alford, Marian *ChPo S1*

Alford, Lady Marian Margaret 1817-1888 *Alli Sup*
Alford, Michael 1587-1652 *Alli*
Alford, Norman William 1929- *ConAu 37, WrD 1976*
Alford, Robert R 1928- *ConAu 41*
Alford, Walter *Alli Sup*
Alfred *Alli, BiB N, Chmbr 1*
Alfred Ernest Albert, Prince 1844- *Alli Sup*
Alfred, King 849-901? *BiB S, BrAu, CasWL, DcEnL, EvLB, NewC, OxEng, Pen Eng, WebEAL Eng*
Alfred Of Beverley *BiB N*
Alfred Of Beverly 1100?- *Alli*
Alfred Of Malmsbury *Alli*
Alfred The Englishman *DcEuL*
Alfred The Glossator *BiB S*
Alfred The Great 849-901 *Alli, BbD, BiD&SB, CriT 1, REn*
Alfred, H J *Alli Sup*
Alfred, Richard 1931- *ConAu XR*
Alfred, Roy 1916- *AmSCAP 66*
Alfred, William 1922- *ConAu 13R, ConDr, CrCD, McGWD, WorAu, WrD 1976*
Alfred, William 1923- *ModAL*
Alfreda, Sister Mary *CatA 1952*
Alfric Bata d1051? *Alli, BiB S*
Alfric Of Canterbury d1006 *Alli, BiB S*
Alfric Of Malmsbury *Alli, BiB S*
Alfrid *Alli*
Alfriend, Edward Morrison 1843- *BiDSA*
Alfriend, Frank H *Alli Sup, BiDSA, DcNAA*
Alfriston, Louis *MnBBF*
Alfven, Hannes O G 1908- *ConAu 29*
Algar, Frederic *Alli Sup*
Algarotti, Francesco 1712-1764 *BiD&SB, CasWL, EvEuW, Pen Eur*
Algazel *CasWL*
Algeo, John 1930- *ConAu 17R, WrD 1976*
Alger, Abby Langdon *Alli Sup*
Alger, Catharine Jackson *ChPo S2*
Alger, F *BbtC*
Alger, Horatio 1834?-1899 *Alli Sup, AmA, AmA&B, BbD, BiD&SB, CarSB, CasWL, ChPo, ChPo S1, ChPo S2, CnDAL, CyAL 2, DcAmA, DcNAA, EvLB, OxAm, Pen Am, REn, REnAL, WebEAL, WhCL*
Alger, J G *Alli Sup*
Alger, Joseph *ChPo*
Alger, Leclaire Gowans 1898-1971 *AuBYP, ThBJA*
Alger, Philip Langdon 1894- *WrD 1976*
Alger, Philip Rounseville 1859-1912 *DcNAA*
Alger, Russell Alexander 1836-1907 *DcAmA, DcNAA, OhA&B*
Alger, William Rounseville 1822-1905 *Alli, Alli Sup, AmA&B, BbD, BiD&SB, CyAL 2, DcAmA, DcNAA*
Algernon *Alli*
Algery, Andre 1919- *ConAu XR*
Algie, James 1857-1928 *DcNAA, OxCan*
Algol *ChPo*
Algood, M *Alli*
Algren, Nelson 1909- *AmA&B, AmNov, CasWL, CnDAL, CnMWL, ConAu 13R, ConLC 4, ConNov 1972, ConNov 1976, DcLEnL, DrAF 1976, EncWL, ModAL, ModAL Sup, OxAm, Pen Am, RAdv 1, REn, REnAL, TwCA Sup, TwCW, WebEAL, WhTwL, WrD 1976*
Algrind *NewC*
Alguno, Senor *DcNAA*
Alhaique, Claudio 1913- *ConAu 29*
Alhaji, Abubakar Imam Kagara *AfA 1*
Alhamisi, Ahmed Akenwale 1940- *BlkAW*
Ali, Abdullah Gureh 1940?- *AfA 1*
Ali, Ahmad 1906- *Pen Cl*
Ali, Ahmed 1910- *Au&Wr, ConAu 25, ConNov 1972, ConNov 1976, WrD 1976*
Ali, Ahmed 1912- *CasWL, DcOrL 2*
Ali, Sabahattin 1906-1948 *DcOrL 3*
Ali, Tariq 1943- *Au&Wr, ConAu 25*
Ali Duuh *Pen Cl*
Ali Haji, Raja 1808-1868 *Pen Cl*
Ali Sikandar *DcOrL 2*
Ali Sir Nevai 1441-1501 *CasWL*
Aliaga, Luis De 1565-1626 *DcEuL*

Aliav, Ruth 1914- *WrD 1976*
Aliber, Robert Z 1930- *ConAu 23, WrD 1976*
Alibert, Francois Paul 1873-1953 *CasWL,*
ClDMEuL, REn
Alice, Aunt *DcAmA*
Alice, Cousin *DcAmA*
Alice Maud Mary, Princess Of Gt Britain
1843-1870 *Alli Sup*
Alien *DcNAA*
Aliesan, Jody 1943- *ConAu 57, DrAP 1975*
Aliger, Margarita Iosifovna 1915- *CasWL,*
DcRusL, EvEuW, Pen Eur, TwCW
Alighieri, Dante *BiD&SB, Pen Eur*
Alighieri, Jacopo d1348? *CasWL*
Alighieri, Pietro d1364 *CasWL*
Alihan, Milla *ConAu 29*
Aliki 1929- *AuBYP, ConAu XR, IlCB 1966,*
SmATA 2, ThBJA, WrD 1976
Alilunas, Leo John 1912- *ConAu 17R*
Alimayo, Chikuyo *ConAu 57*
Alimjan, Hamid *DcOrL 3*
Alin, Morris 1905- *AmSCAP 66*
Alinder, Martha Wheelock 1941- *ConAu 25*
Alingham *Alli*
Alington, Adrian 1895-1958 *LongC*
Alington, Argentine Francis 1898- *Au&Wr*
Alington, Cyril Argentine 1872-1955 *ChPo,*
ChPo S1, ChPo S2, LongC
Alington, Gillian *ChPo*
Alinsky, Saul 1909-1972 *AmA&B, ConAu 37*
Alioto, Robert F 1933- *ConAu 45*
Alis, Hippolyte Percher 1857- *BiD&SB*
Aliscans *CasWL*
Alishan, Ghevond 1820-1901 *DcOrL 3*
Alishan, Leon M 1820- *BbD, BiD&SB*
Alisjahbana, Sutan Takdir 1908- *DcOrL 2*
Alisky, Marvin Michael Howard 1923-
ConAu 13R, WrD 1976
Alison, Alexander 1812?- *Alli, Alli Sup*
Alison, Archibald 1757-1839 *Alli, BiD&SB,*
BiDLA, BiDLA Sup, Chmbr 2, DcEnL,
EvLB
Alison, Sir Archibald 1792-1867 *Alli, Alli Sup,*
BiD&SB, BrAu 19, CasWL, Chmbr 3,
DcEnA, DcEnL, EvLB, OxEng
Alison, Sir A ALSO Allison, Sir A
Alison, Sir Archibald 1826- *Alli Sup*
Alison, Francis 1705-1779 *CyAL 1*
Alison, George *ChPo S2*
Alison, R *Alli*
Alison, Somerville Scott *Alli Sup*
Alison, William Pulteney *Alli*
Alisov, Boris P 1892-1972 *ConAu 37*
Alister, R *Alli Sup*
Aliyu Dan Sidi *CasWL*
Aljama *DcEuL*
Alkazi, Roshen 1923- *ConP 1970*
Alkema, Chester Jay 1932- *ConAu 53*
Alken, H *Alli Sup*
Alker, Dorothy *ChPo S2*
Alker, Hayward R, Jr. 1937- *ConAu 17R*
Allaben, Frank 1867-1927 *DcNAA*
Allaby, Michael 1933- *ConAu 45*
Allain, Helen *BiDSA*
Allain, Marcel *OxFr*
Allainval, Leonor-J-C Soulas D' 1700-1753 *OxFr*
Allaire, Joseph L 1929- *ConAu 41*
Allais, Alphonse 1885-1905 *OxFr*
Allam, Andrew 1655-1685 *Alli*
Allama Prabhu *DcOrL 2*
Allamand *Alli*
Allan *Alli*
Allan, A D H *ChPo*
Allan, Adam *BbtC, OxCan*
Allan, Alfred K 1930- *ConAu 17R*
Allan, Billie Lamb *OxCan*
Allan, Catherine *ChPo, ChPo S2*
Allan, Charles *Alli*
Allan, D G C 1925- *ConAu 25*
Allan, David 1744-1796 *Alli, BkIE*
Allan, David Shea 1840- *ChPo S1*
Allan, Dot *WhLA*
Allan, Elizabeth Preston 1848-1933 *Alli Sup,*
AmA&B, BiDSA, CarSB, DcNAA
Allan, Elkan 1922- *Au&Wr, WrD 1976*
Allan, Eric *OxCan*
Allan, F Carney *MnBBF*
Allan, G W *BbtC*

Allan, George d1800 *Alli*
Allan, George 1768-1828 *Alli*
Allan, Harry T 1928- *ConAu 25*
Allan, Henry *Alli Sup*
Allan, Sir Henry Marshman Havelock- 1830-
Alli Sup
Allan, Herbert *Alli Sup*
Allan, Hugh *Alli Sup*
Allan, Sir Hugh *Alli Sup*
Allan, Iris *OxCan Sup*
Allan, J A *Alli Sup, BbtC*
Allan, J H *Alli*
Allan, James MacGregor *Alli Sup*
Allan, James Watson *Alli Sup*
Allan, John *Alli Sup, MnBBF*
Allan, John 1850- *ChPo*
Allan, John Andrew 1884- *WhWNAA*
Allan, John David 1945- *ConAu 41*
Allan, John David 1950- *WrD 1976*
Allan, Lewis *AmSCAP 66*
Allan, Mabel Esther 1915- *Au&Wr, AuBYP,*
ConAu 5R, SmATA 5, WrD 1976
Allan, Marguerite Buller *ChPo, ChPo S1*
Allan, Maud 1883-1956 *LongC*
Allan, Mea 1909- *Au&Wr, ConAu 5R,*
WrD 1976
Allan, Oswald *Alli Sup*
Allan, Peter John *Alli Sup, OxCan*
Allan, R *Alli*
Allan, Robert *Alli, BiDLA*
Allan, Robert 1774-1841 *ChPo*
Allan, Robert 1848- *Alli Sup, ChPo,*
ChPo S1
Allan, Ted 1916- *ConDr, OxCan, WrD 1976*
Allan, Thomas *Alli, BiDLA Sup*
Allan, William *Alli*
Allan, William d1939 *DcNAA*
Allan, William 1782-1850 *ChPo, ChPo S1*
Allan, William 1837-1889 *BiD&SB, BiDSA,*
ChPo S2, DcAmA, DcNAA
Allan, William 1844- *ChPo*
Allan-Fraser *Alli Sup*
Allana, G *ConP 1970*
Alland, Alexander, Jr. 1931- *ConAu 21*
Allanson *Alli*
Allanson, J A *Alli*
Allard, Dean C 1933- *ConAu 45*
Allard, Hafiz *Alli Sup*
Allard, Harry Ardell 1880- *WhWNAA*
Allard, Sven 1896- *ConAu 29*
Allardice, James Burns 1919- *OhA&B*
Allardyce, A *Alli*
Allardyce, Alexander 1846- *Alli Sup*
Allardyce, Elizabeth Winslow *Alli Sup*
Allardyce, Gilbert Daniel 1932- *ConAu 33*
Allardyce, Paul *Alli Sup*
Allardyce, Paula *WrD 1976*
Allart, Hortense 1801-1879 *OxFr*
Allarton, George *Alli Sup*
Allason, J *Alli*
Allason, T *Alli*
Allaun, Frank Julian 1913- *Au&Wr,*
WrD 1976
Allbeck, Willard Dow 1898- *ConAu 21,*
OhA&B
Allbeury, Ted 1917- *ConAu XR, WrD 1976*
Allbeury, Theodore Edward LeBouthillier 1917-
ConAu 53
Allbut *Alli*
Allbut, Robert *Alli Sup*
Allbutt, Thomas Clifford *Alli Sup*
Allchin, A M 1930- *Au&Wr, ConAu 25*
Allchin, Harry *ChPo*
Allchin, Richard *Alli, BiDLA*
Allcott, W A *Alli Sup*
Alldis, John 1849- *WhLA*
Alldredge, Ida R 1891- *ArizL*
Alldridge, James Charles 1910- *Au&Wr,*
ConAu 29
Alldridge, John Stratten 1914- *Au&Wr*
Alldridge, Lizzie *Alli Sup*
Alldridge, W J *BiDLA*
Alldridge, W T *Alli*
Alldritt, Keith 1935- *ConAu 25*
Alle, T *Alli*
Allee, Marjorie Hill 1890-1945 *AmA&B,*
DcNAA, IndAu 1917, JBA 1934,
JBA 1951, WhWNAA

Allee, Warder Clyde 1885-1955 *IndAu 1917,*
WhWNAA
Alleger, Daniel E 1903- *ConAu 33*
Allegra 1817- *NewC*
Allegro, John Marco 1923- *Au&Wr,*
ConAu 9R, WrD 1976
Allein, Joseph 1633-1688 *Alli*
Allein, Richard 1611-1681 *Alli*
Allein, Thomas *Alli*
Alleine, Joseph 1633-1688 *Alli, DcEnL*
Alleine, Richard 1611-1681 *Alli*
Allen *Alli, BiDLA*
Allen, Mrs. *PoIre*
Allen, A B *Alli Sup*
Allen, A Dale, Jr. 1935- *ConAu 21*
Allen, A J 1930- *Au&Wr, WrD 1976*
Allen, Miss A J *Alli Sup*
Allen, A P *Alli Sup*
Allen, Abel Leighton 1850-1927 *AmLY,*
DcNAA, OhA&B, WhWNAA
Allen, Adam *AuBYP, ConAu XR, MorJA,*
OhA&B, SmATA 1
Allen, Agnes d1959 *WhCL*
Allen, Albert J 1856- *IndAu 1816*
Allen, Alexander Viets Griswold 1841-1908
Alli Sup, AmA, AmA&B, BiD&SB,
DcAmA, DcNAA
Allen, Alfred 1866-1947 *Alli Sup, AmA&B,*
DcAmA
Allen, Alfred H *Alli Sup*
Allen, Alice C *ChPo*
Allen, Alice E *ChPo, ChPo S1, ChPo S2*
Allen, Allyn *AuBYP, ConAu XR, SmATA 2*
Allen, Andrew Hussey 1855-1921 *DcNAA*
Allen, Ann H *Alli Sup*
Allen, Anthony d1754 *Alli*
Allen, Arthur Augustus 1885-1964 *AmA&B,*
ConAu 1R
Allen, Arthur Bruce 1903- *Au&Wr, ConAu 23*
Allen, Arthur Francis 1867- *WhWNAA*
Allen, Arthur Watts 1879- *WhWNAA*
Allen, B *Alli*
Allen, Barbara *ConAu XR*
Allen, Barclay 1918- *AmSCAP 66*
Allen, Barney 1902- *CanNov*
Allen, Bean *ChPo S1*
Allen, Benjamin 1789-1829 *AmA&B, DcNAA*
Allen, Bennet Mills 1877-1963 *IndAu 1917*
Allen, Betsy *AuBYP, ConAu XR, SmATA 1*
Allen, Beverly Sprague 1881-1935 *DcNAA*
Allen, C *Alli Sup*
Allen, C Bruce *Alli Sup*
Allen, C Frank 1851- *WhWNAA*
Allen, C K 1887-1966 *LongC*
Allen, C W *Alli Sup*
Allen, Calvin Francis 1851- *AmLY*
Allen, Cecil J 1886- *ConAu 25*
Allen, Charles *Alli, Alli Sup, BiDLA*
Allen, Charles 1827-1913 *DcAmA, DcNAA*
Allen, Charles Dexter 1865-1926 *AmA&B,*
DcAmA, DcNAA
Allen, Charles Elmer 1872- *WhWNAA*
Allen, Charles Grant Blairfindie 1848-1899
Alli Sup, BbD, Chmbr 3, DcEnA,
DcEnA Ap, EvLB
Allen, Charles H *Alli Sup*
Allen, Charles Linnaeus 1828-1909 *DcNAA*
Allen, Charles R 1862- *WhWNAA*
Allen, Charles Richard 1885- *DcLEnL*
Allen, Charles Warrenne 1854-1906 *DcAmA,*
DcNAA
Allen, Charlotte *ChPo S1*
Allen, Chilion B And Mary A *Alli Sup*
Allen, Chris 1929- *ConAu 29, MnBBF*
Allen, Clabon Walter 1904- *WrD 1976*
Allen, Clay *ConAu XR*
Allen, Clifford *ChPo S1*
Allen, Clifford 1889- *WhLA*
Allen, Clifford Edward 1902- *Au&Wr,*
ConAu P-1, WrD 1976
Allen, Creighton 1900- *AmSCAP 66*
Allen, Cynthia M 1839-1901 *DcNAA*
Allen, D C *BiDSA*
Allen, David 1925- *ConAu 33*
Allen, David Elliston 1932- *Au&Wr,*
ConAu 25
Allen, David J 1936?- *IndAu 1917*
Allen, David Oliver 1799?-1863? *Alli, DcAmA,*

DcNAA
Allen, Devere 1891-1955 *AmA&B, WhWNAA*
Allen, Diarca Howe 1808-1870 *Alli Sup, DcNAA*
Allen, Dick 1939- *ConAu 33, DrAP 1975, WrD 1976*
Allen, Diogenes 1932- *ConAu 25, WrD 1976*
Allen, Don *DcNAA, OhA&B*
Allen, Don B 1889-1966 *AmA&B*
Allen, Don Cameron 1903-1966 *AmA&B, Au&Wr, ConAu 5R*
Allen, Donald Emerson 1917- *ConAu 45*
Allen, Donald M 1912- *AmA&B, ConAu 17R*
Allen, Donald R 1930- *ConAu 45*
Allen, Dotaline Elizabeth 1909-1969 *IndAu 1917*
Allen, Durward Leon 1910- *ConAu 41*
Allen, Durwood Leon 1910- *IndAu 1917*
Allen, Dwight W 1931- *ConAu 13R*
Allen, E *Alli*
Allen, E A *ChPo*
Allen, E C *ConAu XR*
Allen, Edgar 1892-1943 *DcNAA*
Allen, Edgar Johnson 1866- *WhLA*
Allen, Edith Beavers 1920- *ConAu 9R, WrD 1976*
Allen, Edith Louise *WhWNAA*
Allen, Edith Marion *ConAu P-1*
Allen, Edmond *Alli*
Allen, Edward *BiDLA, ChPo S2*
Allen, Edward Archibald 1843-1922 *BiDSA, DcNAA*
Allen, Edward D 1923- *ConAu 49*
Allen, Edward Frank 1885- *AmA&B, ChPo S2, WhWNAA*
Allen, Edward Heron- 1861- *Alli Sup*
Allen, Edward J 1907- *ConAu P-1*
Allen, Edward Lisle 1868- *WhWNAA*
Allen, Edward Monington 1899- *AmA&B*
Allen, Edward Weber 1885- *AmA&B, WhWNAA*
Allen, Edwin H *ChPo S2*
Allen, Edwin West 1864- *WhWNAA*
Allen, Egbert Chesley *OxCan*
Allen, Elisabeth Offutt 1895- *ConAu 57*
Allen, Elizabeth 1794?-1849 *ChPo, ChPo S1, DcNAA*
Allen, Elizabeth Ann Akers 1832-1911 *Alli Sup, AmA, AmA&B, BiD&SB, ChPo, ChPo S1, ChPo S2, CyAL 2, DcAmA, DcNAA*
Allen, Ella *ChPo S1*
Allen, Emma Sarah Gage 1859- *DcNAA, IndAu 1917*
Allen, Emory Adams 1853-1933? *DcNAA, OhA&B*
Allen, Ephraim *PoIre*
Allen, Eric William 1879-1944 *AmA&B, DcNAA, WhWNAA*
Allen, Ernest F *ChPo S2*
Allen, Esther Charlotte Anne *Alli Sup*
Allen, Ethan 1737-1789 *Alli, AmA&B, BbD, BbtC, BiD&SB, CyAL 1, DcAmA, DcNAA, OxAm, REn, REnAL, DcNAA*
Allen, Ethan 1831-1911 *DcNAA*
Allen, Ethan 1904- *OhA&B*
Allen, Eugene Thomas 1864- *WhWNAA*
Allen, Ezra 1870- *WhWNAA*
Allen, F *Alli*
Allen, F M *Alli Sup, WhLA*
Allen, Mrs. Fairchild *DcNAA*
Allen, Florence Ellinwood 1884- *OhA&B*
Allen, Fordyce A *Alli Sup*
Allen, Frances *ChPo*
Allen, Francis A 1919- *ConAu 13R, WrD 1976*
Allen, Francis Henry 1866-1953 *AmA&B, WhWNAA*
Allen, Frank 1874- *WhWNAA*
Allen, Frank G *Alli Sup*
Allen, Frank J *ChPo S1*
Allen, Frank Waller 1878- *AmA&B, WhWNAA*
Allen, Frank Wisdom 1887- *WhWNAA*
Allen, Fred 1894-1956 *ChPo, REnAL*
Allen, Fred Hovey 1845-1926 *AmLY, BiD&SB, DcAmA, DcNAA*
Allen, Frederic James 1864-1927 *DcNAA*

Allen, Frederic Sturges 1861-1920 *AmA&B, DcNAA*
Allen, Frederick DeForest 1844-1897 *Alli Sup, DcAmA, DcNAA, OhA&B*
Allen, Frederick G 1936- *ConAu 57*
Allen, Frederick H *Alli Sup*
Allen, Frederick James 1864-1894 *ChPo S2*
Allen, Frederick Lewis 1890-1954 *AmA&B, CnDAL, OxAm, REn, REnAL, TwCA, TwCA Sup*
Allen, Frederick Madison 1879- *WhWNAA*
Allen, Frederick Martin Brice 1898- *Au&Wr*
Allen, Freeman Harlow 1862- *WhWNAA*
Allen, G *Alli*
Allen, G Everett 1899- *AmSCAP 66*
Allen, G G *Alli Sup*
Allen, G W *Alli Sup*
Allen, Gardner Weld 1856- *AmA&B, WhWNAA*
Allen, Garland E 1936- *ConAu 53*
Allen, Gary *ConAu 57*
Allen, Gay Wilson 1903- *AmA&B, Au&Wr, ConAu 5R, REnAL, WrD 1976*
Allen, Geoffrey Francis 1902- *Au&Wr, ConAu P-1, WrD 1976*
Allen, George *Alli Sup*
Allen, George 1792-1883 *DcNAA*
Allen, George 1808-1876 *Alli Sup, DcAmA, DcNAA*
Allen, George 1832-1907 *LongC*
Allen, George Cyril 1900- *Au&Wr, ConAu 1R, WrD 1976*
Allen, George Francis 1907- *Au&Wr, ConAu P-1*
Allen, George J *MnBBF*
Allen, George Leonard 1905-1935 *BlkAW*
Allen, George Rollason 1923- *Au&Wr*
Allen, George Wood 1864-1950 *IndAu 1917*
Allen, Gertrude E 1888- *ConAu 61, SmATA 9*
Allen, Gina 1918- *AmA&B, ConAu 1R*
Allen, Glenn *WhWNAA*
Allen, Glover Morrill 1872- *WhWNAA*
Allen, Grace Barton *ChPo*
Allen, Graham *AmA&B*
Allen, Grant 1848-1899 *BiD&SB, BrAu 19, CanWr, ChPo S1, DcLEnL, EncM&D, NewC, OxCan*
Allen, Gwenfread Elaine 1904- *ConAu 61*
Allen, H *Alli, Alli Sup*
Allen, H C *Alli Sup*
Allen, H Fredericka *ConAu XR*
Allen, H G *ConAu 29*
Allen, Hamilton Ford 1867- *IndAu 1917*
Allen, Hans VanNes 1914- *OhA&B*
Allen, Harlan C 1891- *WhWNAA*
Allen, Harold B 1902- *ConAu 17R*
Allen, Harold J 1925- *ConAu 45*
Allen, Harrison 1841-1897 *Alli Sup, DcAmA, DcNAA*
Allen, Harry Cranbrook 1917- *Au&Wr, ConAu 5R, WrD 1976*
Allen, Hazel *ConAu XR*
Allen, Henry *ConAu XR*
Allen, Henry 1748-1784 *Alli*
Allen, Henry 1912- *AmA&B*
Allen, Henry, Jr. 1900- *AmSCAP 66*
Allen, Henry Clay 1836-1909 *DcNAA*
Allen, Henry Ellis *Alli Sup*
Allen, Henry Justin 1868- *WhWNAA*
Allen, Henry Tureman 1859-1930 *DcNAA, WhWNAA*
Allen, Henry Watkins 1820-1866 *BiDSA, DcNAA*
Allen, Herbert 1927- *AmSCAP 66*
Allen, Herbert Stanley *WhLA*
Allen, Herbert Warner *EncM&D*
Allen, Hervey 1899-1949 *AmA&B, AmNov, AnMV 1926, ChPo, ChPo S1, ChPo S2, Chmbr 3, CnDAL, ConAmA, ConAmL, CyWA, DcLEnL, DcNAA, EncWL, LongC, OxAm, Pen Am, REn, REnAL, TwCA, TwCA Sup, TwCW, WhWNAA*
Allen, Heywood 1935- *ConAu 33*
Allen, Hezekiah *Alli*
Allen, Horace Newton 1858-1932 *DcAmA, DcNAA, OhA&B, WhWNAA*
Allen, Horace R *Alli Sup*
Allen, Horatio 1802-1890 *DcNAA*

Allen, Howard W 1931- *ConAu 33*
Allen, Hubert Raymond 1919- *WrD 1976*
Allen, Hugh 1882- *DcNAA, OhA&B*
Allen, I N *Alli*
Allen, Ida Bailey 1885-1973 *AmA&B, REnAL, WhWNAA*
Allen, Ira 1751-1814 *Alli, CyAL 1, DcAmA, DcNAA*
Allen, Ira Wilder 1827-1896 *DcNAA, OhA&B*
Allen, Irene 1903- *ConAu P-1*
Allen, J *Alli*
Allen, Mrs. J *Alli Sup*
Allen, J Antisell *Alli Sup*
Allen, J A ALSO Allen, Joseph A
Allen, J R *Alli Sup*
Allen, J Romilly *Alli Sup*
Allen, Jack 1914- *ConAu 9R*
Allen, James *Alli, AmA&B, AmNov XR, BiDLA, ChPo*
Allen, James d1831 *BkIE*
Allen, James 1632-1710 *Alli*
Allen, James 1691-1747 *Alli*
Allen, James 1734-1804 *PoCh*
Allen, James 1739-1808 *Alli, CyAL 1*
Allen, James Adams *Alli Sup*
Allen, James E 1876- *WhWNAA*
Allen, James Egert 1896- *LivBA*
Allen, James L, Jr. 1929- *ConAu 33*
Allen, James Lane 1848- *BiDSA, DcAmA*
Allen, James Lane 1849?-1925 *AmA, AmA&B, AmLY, BbD, BiD&SB, BiDSA, CarSB, CasWL, ChPo S1, ChPo S3, CnDAL, ConAmL, DcAmA, DcBiA, DcLEnL, DcNAA, LongC, OxAm, REn, REnAL*
Allen, James Turney 1873-1949 *OhA&B, WhWNAA*
Allen, Jay 1922- *McGWD*
Allen, Jerome 1830-1894 *DcAmA, DcNAA*
Allen, Jerry 1911- *Au&Wr, ConAu 9R*
Allen, Jim *ConAu XR, ConDr*
Allen, Joel Asaph 1838-1921 *Alli Sup, BiD&SB, DcAmA, DcNAA*
Allen, Joel ALSO Allen, Joseph Asaph
Allen, Johannes 1916- *ConAu 29*
Allen, John *Alli, Alli Sup, BiDLA, ChPo S1, DcNAA, PoIre*
Allen, John 1476-1534 *Alli*
Allen, John 1596-1671 *Alli*
Allen, John 1770?-1843 *Alli, BrAu 19*
Allen, John 1790-1859 *Alli Sup*
Allen, John Alexander 1922- *ConAu 25*
Allen, John Alpheus 1863-1916 *DcNAA*
Allen, John B *Alli Sup*
Allen, John Bryan Lorton 1921- *Au&Wr*
Allen, Sir John Campbell 1817-1898 *DcNAA*
Allen, John D 1898- *ConAu 33*
Allen, John E 1921- *Au&Wr, WrD 1976*
Allen, John Edward 1889-1947 *DcNAA, WhWNAA*
Allen, John Fisk *Alli, Alli Sup*
Allen, John Gamaliel *Alli Sup*
Allen, John H *Alli Sup*
Allen, John Harden 1847- *DcNAA*
Allen, John Henry 1836-1890 *DcNAA*
Allen, John Jay 1932- *ConAu 33, WrD 1976*
Allen, John Mills 1846- *BiDSA*
Allen, John Piers 1912- *Au&Wr*
Allen, John Robert 1851-1937 *BiDSA, DcNAA*
Allen, John Robins 1869-1920 *DcNAA*
Allen, John S 1841-1923 *DcNAA*
Allen, John Taylor 1848-1919? *DcNAA*
Allen, John W, Jr. 1819-1903 *Alli Sup, AmA*
Allen, Jon L 1931- *ConAu 57*
Allen, Jonathan Adams 1787-1848 *DcNAA*
Allen, Jonathan Adams 1825?-1890 *DcAmA, DcNAA*
Allen, Joseph *Alli, Alli Sup*
Allen, Joseph 1790-1873 *Alli Sup, DcNAA*
Allen, Joseph 1870- *WhWNAA*
Allen, Joseph A *Alli Sup*
Allen, Joseph Antisell 1814-1900 *DcNAA, OxCan, PoIre*
Allen, J A ALSO Allen, J Antisell
Allen, Joseph Asaph 1838-1921 *BbD*
Allen, Joseph A ALSO Allen, Joel A
Allen, Joseph Henry 1820-1898? *Alli, Alli Sup, AmA*

Alleyne, Ellen *DcLEnL*
Alleyne, J *Alli*
Alleyne, John 1861-1933 *ChPo S2*
Alleyne, Mabel *ChPo*
Alleyne, Sarah Frances d1885 *Alli Sup*
Allfrey, Emily *Alli Sup*
Allfrey, Katherine *AuBYP*
Allgire, Mildred J 1910- *ConAu 25, IndAu 1917*
Allhands, Edmund Spencer 1862- *AnMV 1926*
Allibaco, W A *Alli Sup*
Allibond, John d1658 *Alli*
Allibond, Peter 1560-1629 *Alli*
Allibone, Samuel Austin 1816-1889 *Alli Sup, AmA, AmA&B, BbD, BiD&SB, CnDAL, CyAL 2, DcAmA, DcEnL, DcLEnL, DcNAA, OxAm*
Allid *CanWr, OxCan*
Allies, Jabez 1787-1856 *Alli Sup, BiD&SB*
Allies, Mary H *Alli Sup*
Allies, Thomas William 1813- *Alli, Alli Sup*
Alliluyeva, Svetlana 1926- *ConAu 57*
Allin, A *ChPo S2*
Allin, Abby *Alli, Alli Sup*
Allin, Arthur 1869-1903 *DcAmA*
Allin, C D *OxCan*
Allin, Cephas Daniel 1874-1927 *DcNAA*
Allin, John 1596-1671 *DcNAA*
Allin, Thomas 1784-1866 *Alli Sup*
Alline, Henry 1748-1784 *BbtC, DcLEnL, DcNAA, OxCan, PoCh*
Alling, Arthur Nathaniel 1862-1949 *DcNAA*
Alling, Ethan 1800-1868 *OhA&B*
Alling, Harold Lattimore 1888- *WhWNAA*
Allingham *Alli*
Allingham, Claud *MnBBF*
Allingham, Claude *MnBBF*
Allingham, Edward *PoIre*
Allingham, Helen *ChPo S2*
Allingham, Herbert John 1867-1935 *MnBBF*
Allingham, John Till *Alli, PoIre*
Allingham, John W *MnBBF*
Allingham, Margery 1904-1966 *ConAu 5R, ConAu 25, DcLEnL, EncM&D, EvLB, LongC, MnBBF, NewC Sup, TwCA, TwCA Sup, TwCW*
Allingham, W *Alli*
Allingham, William *Alli Sup*
Allingham, William 1824?-1889 *Alli Sup, AnCL, BbD, BiD&SB, BrAu 19, CasWL, ChPo, ChPo S1, ChPo S2, Chmbr 3, DcEnL, DcLEnL, EvLB, NewC, Pen Eng, PoIre, REn, St&VC, WebEAL*
Allington, John *Alli*
Allinson, Anne Crosby Emery 1871-1932 *AmA&B, DcNAA, WhWNAA*
Allinson, Beverley 1936- *ConAu 49*
Allinson, David 1774-1858 *DcNAA*
Allinson, Edward P And Penrose, Boies *Alli Sup*
Allinson, Edward Pease 1852-1901 *DcNAA*
Allinson, Francis Greenleaf 1856-1931 *AmA&B, DcNAA, WhWNAA*
Allinson, Thomas Richard *Alli Sup*
Allinson, William J *Alli Sup*
Alliot, Hector 1862-1919 *DcNAA*
Alliott, Richard 1804-1863 *Alli Sup*
Allis, Edward Phelps, Jr. 1851- *WhWNAA*
Allis, Marguerite 1886-1958 *AmA&B, AmNov*
Allis, Oswald Thompson 1880-1973 *AmA&B, ConAu 37*
Allison, A F *ChPo S2*
Allison, Alexander Ward 1919- *ConAu 5R*
Allison, Anne Osterstrom *AmA&B*
Allison, Anthony C 1928- *ConAu 29*
Allison, Sir Archibald 1792-1867 *BbD*
Allison, Sir A ALSO Alison, Sir A
Allison, B *Alli*
Allison, Bob *AuBYP*
Allison, Burgiss 1753-1827 *DcNAA*
Allison, Charles Elmer 1847-1908 *DcNAA*
Allison, Christopher Fitzsimons 1927- *ConAu 1R*
Allison, Clay 1914- *Au&Wr, ConAu XR*
Allison, David 1836-1924 *DcNAA, OxCan*
Allison, David P 1886- *OhA&B*
Allison, Drummond 1921-1943 *CnMWL*
Allison, Edwin Henry 1847-1919 *OhA&B*
Allison, Elizabeth 1824- *ChPo S1*

Allison, F 1705-1777 *Alli*
Allison, Franklin Elmer *WhWNAA*
Allison, George William 1887- *IndAu 1816*
Allison, Graham T, Jr. 1940- *ConAu 49*
Allison, Guy Selwin *ChPo*
Allison, Harrison C 1917- *ConAu 49*
Allison, Hughes *BlkAW*
Allison, Ivan Edward 1902- *Au&Wr, WhWNAA*
Allison, James Henry 1879- *TexWr, WhWNAA*
Allison, James Murray 1877- *ChPo*
Allison, John *BiDSA*
Allison, John 1845-1920 *DcNAA*
Allison, John A 1914- *AmSCAP 66*
Allison, John Maudgridge Snowden 1888-1944 *DcNAA*
Allison, John Murray 1889- *ConAu 21*
Allison, Joy *Alli Sup, ChPo*
Allison, Lydia W 1880-1959 *BiDPar*
Allison, M Sinclair *Alli Sup*
Allison, Margaret M *BlkAW*
Allison, Marian *ConAu XR*
Allison, Michael Frederick Lister 1936- *ConAu 57*
Allison, Mike *ConAu 57*
Allison, Nathaniel 1876-1931 *DcNAA*
Allison, Noah Dwight 1889- *TexWr*
Allison, Noah Dwight 1899- *WhWNAA*
Allison, P d1802 *Alli*
Allison, R *Alli*
Allison, R Bruce 1949- *ConAu 49*
Allison, Rand *ConAu XR*
Allison, Sam *ConAu XR*
Allison, Susan Whalley *ChPo*
Allison, T *Alli*
Allison, Thomas Jefferson 1850- *DcNAA*
Allison, William H 1910- *AmLY*
Allison, William Henry 1870-1941 *DcNAA, WhWNAA*
Allison, William Talbot 1874-1941 *ChPo S1, DcNAA, OxCan*
Allison, Young Ewing 1853-1932 *AmA&B, ChPo, DcNAA*
Allister, William *OxCan*
Allix, Peter 1641-1717 *Alli*
Allman, Drue 1893- *WhWNAA*
Allman, George James 1812- *Alli Sup*
Allman, George Johnston 1824- *Alli Sup*
Allman, Michael L 1911- *AmSCAP 66*
Allman, Norwood Francis 1893- *WhWNAA*
Allman, William *Alli*
Allmendinger, David F, Jr. 1938- *ConAu 61*
Allmers, Hermann 1821-1902 *BiD&SB, OxGer*
Allmond, Marcus Blakey 1851-1909 *Alli Sup, BiDSA, ChPo S1, DcAmA, DcNAA*
Allnatt, A Charles *BiDLA*
Allnatt, Charles F B *Alli Sup*
Allnatt, Elizabeth *Alli Sup*
Allnatt, Francis J Benwell *Alli Sup*
Allnatt, Maud Elizabeth Surtees- *Alli Sup*
Allnatt, Richard Hopkins *Alli Sup*
Allner, Walter H 1909- *WhGrA*
Allnut, A C *Alli*
Allnut, Mrs. Alfred *Alli Sup*
Allnut, G S *Alli*
Allnut, Henry *Alli Sup*
Allnut, Sidney *ChPo*
Allnut, Z *Alli*
Allnutt, W H *Alli Sup*
Allnutt, Zachariah *BiDLA*
Allon, Henry 1818- *Alli Sup*
Allot, Robert *Alli, DcEnL*
Allott, Kenneth 1912- *ChPo, ConP 1970*
Allott, Richard *Alli, BiDLA Sup*
Allott, Robert *CasWL, NewC*
Allouez, Claude-Jean 1622-1689 *OxCan*
Alloway, David Nelson 1927- *ConAu 23, WrD 1976*
Alloway, Lawrence 1926- *AmA&B, ConAu 41*
Alloway, Mary 1848-1919 *DcNAA, OxCan*
Alloway, Robert Morellet 1807- *PoIre*
Allport, Floyd Henry 1890- *REnAL, WhWNAA*
Allport, Frank 1856-1935 *DcNAA*
Allport, Gordon Willard 1897-1967 *AmA&B, ConAu 1R, ConAu 25, IndAu 1917, REnAL*
Allport, Herbert Roland *ChPo*

Allred, G Hugh 1932- *ConAu 61*
Allred, Gordon T 1930- *ConAu 17R, SmATA 10*
Allsen, Philip E 1932- *ConAu 53*
Allshorn, Adolph Hahnemann *Alli Sup*
Allshorn, G S *Alli Sup*
Allson, W *Alli Sup*
Allsop, Henry *ChPo*
Allsop, Kenneth 1920-1973 *Au&Wr, ConAu 1R, WorAu*
Allsop, Thomas 1795-1880 *Alli Sup*
Allsopp, Bruce 1912- *Au&Wr, ConAu 5R, WrD 1976*
Allsopp, Frederick William 1868-1946 *AmA&B, WhWNAA*
Allston, Joseph Blyth 1833-1904 *Alli Sup, BiDSA, OxAm, REnAL*
Allston, Margaret *DcAmA*
Allston, Robert Francis Withers 1801?-1864 *DcAmA, DcNAA*
Allston, Robert ALSO Alston, Robert
Allston, Washington 1779-1843 *Alli, AmA, AmA&B, BbD, BiD&SB, BiDLA, BiDSA, CasWL, ChPo, ChPo S1, Chmbr 3, CnDAL, CyAL 2, DcAmA, DcEnL, DcNAA, EvLB, OxAm, Pen Am, REnAL*
Allstorm, Oliver *ChPo S1*
Allswang, John M 1937- *ConAu 41*
Allton, Minette 1916- *AmSCAP 66*
Allum, Nancy 1920- *Au&Wr, ConAu P-1*
Allvine, Fred C 1936- *ConAu 61*
Allward, Maurice Frank 1923- *Au&Wr, ConAu 5R, WrD 1976*
Allwood, Inga Wilhelmsen *ChPo S1*
Allwood, Martin Samuel *ChPo S1*
Allwood, Philip *Alli, BiDLA, BiDLA Sup*
Allworthy, Thomas Bateson 1879- *WhLA*
Allyn, Avery *Alli Sup*
Allyn, Charles *Alli Sup*
Allyn, Eunice Eloisae Gibbs *OhA&B*
Allyn, Kate *ChPo*
Allyn, Lewis Benajah 1874-1940 *DcNAA*
Allyn, Paul *ConAu XR*
Allyne, Roy *MnBBF*
Allyson, Kym *ConAu XR*
Alma-Tadema, Laurence *Alli Sup, ChPo, WhLA*
Almack, Edward 1852-1917 *ChPo S1*
Almack, John Conrad 1883- *WhWNAA*
Almafuerte 1854-1917 *Pen Am*
Alman, David 1919- *AmA&B, AmNov, ConAu 9R*
Almaraz, Felix D, Jr. 1933- *ConAu 33*
Almedingen, E M 1898-1971 *Au&Wr, ConAu 1, LongC, SmATA 3, ThBJA, WorAu*
Almedingen, Martha Edith Von 1898-1971 *SmATA 3*
Almeida, Guilherme De 1890- *Pen Am*
Almeida, Jose Americo De 1887- *CasWL, Pen Am*
Almeida, Jose Maria *AfA 1*
Almeida, Jose Valentim Fialho De 1857-1911 *CasWL, EvEuW*
Almeida, Laurindo 1917- *AmSCAP 66*
Almeida, Manuel Antonio De 1831-1861 *CasWL, Pen Am*
Almeida, Nicolao Tolentino De 1741-1811 *BiD&SB*
Almeida, Nicolau Tolentino De 1740-1811 *CasWL*
Almeida Garrett, Joao Baptista DaSilva 1799-1854 *BbD, BiD&SB, CasWL, EuA, EvEuW*
Almella, Diego Rodriguez De 1426?-1492 *DcEuL*
Almon *Alli*
Almon, Mr. *Alli*
Almon, Bert *DrAP 1975*
Almon, Clopper, Jr. 1934- *ConAu 21*
Almon, John 1738-1805 *Alli*
Almond *Alli*
Almond, Hely Hutchinson *Alli Sup*
Almond, Linda Stevens *AmA&B*
Almond, Nina 1882-1964 *IndAu 1917*
Almond, R *Alli*
Almond, Richard 1938- *ConAu 53*

Almonte, Rosa *ConAu XR*
Almore, Caspar *Alli Sup*, *DcNAA*
Almquist, Carl Jonas Love 1793-1866 *CasWL*,
    EuA, *Pen Eur*
Almquist, Carl ALSO Almqvist, Carl
Almquist, Don *ChPo*, *IlBYP*
Almquist, Karl Jonas Ludvig 1793-1866
    BiD&SB
Almquist, L Arden 1921- *ConAu 29*
Almqvist, Carl Jonas L 1793-1866 *DcEuL*,
    EvEuW
Almqvist, Karl Jonas L 1793-1866 *BbD*
Almqvist, Karl ALSO Almquist, Carl
Almy, Amy Bruner 1875- *WhWNAA*
Almy, Annie Whittier *ChPo*
Almy, Charles, Jr. And Fuller, Horace W
    Alli Sup
Almy, John Edwin 1875- *WhWNAA*
Aloian, David 1928- *ConAu 25*
Aloise, Frank *IlBYP*
Aloma, Harold David 1908- *AmSCAP 66*
Alomar, Gabriel 1873-1941 *CasWL*, *ClDMEuL*,
    EncWL
Alone *Pen Am*
Aloni, Nissim 1926- *CnThe*, *REnWD*
Alonso, Amado 1896?-1952 *ClDMEuL*, *DcSpL*
Alonso, Damaso 1898- *CasWL*, *ClDMEuL*,
    DcSpL, *EncWL*, *EvEuW*, *Pen Eur*, *REn*
Alonso, Manuel A 1822-1889 *PueRA*
Alonso, William 1933- *ConAu 9R*
Alonso Cortes, Narciso 1875- *DcSpL*
Alonso Millan, Juan Jose 1936- *CrCD*
Alonzo, Cecil *BlkAW*
Alorna, Leonor DeAlmeida, Marquesa De
    1750-1839 *CasWL*
Aloysius, Sister Mary *ConAu 49*
Alper, Benedict S 1905- *ConAu 49*
Alper, Clifford Daniel *ChPo S2*
Alperin, David 1889- *WhWNAA*
Alpern, Gerald D 1932- *ConAu 53*
Alpern, Hymen 1895- *WhWNAA*
Alperovitz, Gar 1936- *ConAu 49*
Alpers, Antony 1919- *Au&Wr*, *ConAu 1R*,
    WrD 1976
Alpers, William Charles 1851-1917 *DcNAA*
Alperson, Edward Lee, Jr. 1925- *AmSCAP 66*
Alpert, Carl 1913- *WhWNAA*
Alpert, Hollis 1916- *AmA&B*, *ConAu 1R*
Alpert, Mark I 1942- *ConAu 61*
Alpert, Milton I 1904-1965 *AmSCAP 66*
Alpert, Paul 1907- *ConAu 41*
Alpert, Pauline *AmSCAP 66*
Alpha *OhA&B*
Alpha Of The Plough *NewC*, *WhLA*
Alphanus Of Salerno d1085 *CasWL*
Alphege, Saint *NewC*
Alphen, Hieronymus Van 1746-1803 *CasWL*
Alphonse, Mother *DcNAA*
Alphonso-Karkala, John B 1923- *ConAu 37*,
    WrD 1976
Alport, Lord 1912- *Au&Wr*
Alport, Cuthbert James McCall 1912-
    WrD 1976
Alpuche, Wenceslao 1804-1841 *BiD&SB*
Alram Von Gresten *OxGer*
Alroy, David *REn*
Alroy, Gil Carl 1924- *ConAu 41*
Alsager, C Martin 1871- *WhWNAA*
Alsberg, Carl Lucas 1877- *WhWNAA*
Alschuler, Rose H 1887- *ConAu 25*
Alsever, John Bellows 1908- *Au&Wr*
Alsington, Blanche *ChPo S1*
Alsop, Alfred *Alli Sup*
Alsop, Ann *Alli*
Alsop, Anthony d1726 *Alli*
Alsop, Benjamin *Alli*
Alsop, George 1638- *Alli*, *AmA&B*, *BiDSA*,
    DcAmA, *OxAm*, *REnAL*
Alsop, James R *Alli Sup*
Alsop, John 1776-1841 *Alli*, *CyAL 1*
Alsop, Joseph W 1910- *AmA&B*, *REn*,
    REnAL, *WorAu*
Alsop, Mary O'Hara 1885- *ConAu 9R*,
    SmATA 2
Alsop, N *Alli*
Alsop, Reese Fell *AuBYP*
Alsop, Richard 1761-1815 *Alli*, *AmA*,
    AmA&B, *BiD&SB*, *CyAL 1*, *DcAmA*,

DcLEnL, *DcNAA*, *OxAm*, *Pen Am*,
    REn, *REnAL*
Alsop, Samuel *Alli Sup*, *DcNAA*
Alsop, Stewart 1914-1974 *AmA&B*, *ConAu 49*,
    REn
Alsop, Vincent d1703 *Alli*
Alspach, Russell K 1901- *Au&Wr*
Alsted, Johann Heinrich 1586-1628 *DcEuL*
Alstern, Fred 1899- *ConAu XR*
Alstetter, Mabel Flick 1894- *WhWNAA*
Alston, Alfred Henry *Alli Sup*
Alston, Charles 1682-1760 *Alli*
Alston, J W *Alli*, *BiDLA*
Alston, Mary Niven 1918- *ConAu 33*
Alston, Patrick L 1926- *ConAu 25*
Alston, Rex 1901- *Au&Wr*, *WrD 1976*
Alston, Robert Francis Withers 1801-1864
    BiDSA
Alston, Robert ALSO Allston, Robert
Alston, Wallace McPherson 1906- *AmA&B*
Alston, William Payne 1921- *AmA&B*,
    ConAu 5R
Alt, David 1933- *ConAu 49*
Alt, Florence May *ChPo*
Alt, Georg *OxGer*
Alt, Simon *OxGer*
Alt, Tilo 1931- *ConAu 41*
Alta 1942- *ConAu 57*, *DrAF 1976*,
    DrAP 1975
Altabe, Joan B 1935- *ConAu 53*
Altamira, Rafael 1866-1951 *DcSpL*
Altamira Y Crevea, Rafael 1866-1951 *CasWL*,
    ClDMEuL, *EvEuW*
Altamirano, Ignacio Manuel 1834-1893 *BiD&SB*,
    CasWL, *CyWA*, *DcSpL*, *Pen Am*, *REn*
Altaroche, Marie Michel 1811-1884 *BiD&SB*
Altbach, Edith Hoshino 1941- *ConAu 57*
Altbach, Philip G 1941- *ConAu 25*
Altdorfer, Albrecht 1480-1538 *AtlBL*, *OxGer*
Alte Dessauer, Der *OxGer*
Alte Fritz, Der *OxGer*
Altemus, Jameson Torr *Alli Sup*
Altenberg, Peter 1859-1919 *ClDMEuL*, *EncWL*,
    ModGL, *OxGer*
Altenbernd, Lynn 1918- *ConAu 45*
Altendorf, Wolfgang 1921- *CnMD*, *CrCD*
Alter, Amos Joseph 1916- *IndAu 1917*
Alter, Dinsmore 1888- *WhWNAA*
Alter, J Cecil 1879-1964 *AmA&B*, *ConAu 5R*,
    IndAu 1917
Alter, James Leander *IndAu 1816*
Alter, Jean V 1925- *ConAu 45*
Alter, John E 1853-1934 *IndAu 1816*
Alter, Karl Joseph 1885- *OhA&B*
Alter, Louis 1902- *AmSCAP 66*
Alter, Nicholas M 1885- *WhWNAA*
Alter, Robert B 1935- *ConAu 49*
Alter, Robert Edmond 1925-1965 *AuBYP*,
    ConAu 1R, *SmATA 9*
Alterman, Nathan 1910-1970 *CasWL*,
    ConAu 25, *REnWD*, *WorAu*
Altgeld, Emma Ford 1849-1915 *OhA&B*
Altgeld, John Peter 1847-1902 *Alli Sup*,
    AmA&B, *DcAmA*, *OhA&B*, *OxAm*,
    REnAL
Altgelt, John Peter 1847-1902 *DcNAA*
Alth, Max O 1927- *ConAu 41*
Altham, Arthur *Alli*
Altham, Sir Edward 1856- *WhLA*
Althan, Roger *Alli*
Althaus, Aug Wilhelm Hermann Paul 1888-
    WhLA
Althaus, Julius *Alli Sup*
Althauser, Robert P 1939- *ConAu 57*
Althea *NewC*
Althoff, Phillip 1941- *Au&Wr*, *ConAu 33*
Altholz, Josef L 1933- *ChPo S1*, *ConAu 9R*
Althouse, LaVonne 1932- *ConAu 17R*
Althusius 1557-1638 *DcEuL*
Altick, Richard Daniel 1915- *ChPo*,
    ConAu 1R, *OhA&B*, *WrD 1976*
Altingdean, Edward *Alli Sup*
Altisonant, Lorenzo *Alli Sup*
Altizer, Thomas Jonathan Jackson 1927-
    ConAu 1R
Altman, Arthur *AmSCAP 66*
Altman, Dennis 1943- *ConAu 33*, *WrD 1976*
Altman, Edward I 1941- *ConAu 57*

Altman, Frances Evelyn 1937- *WrD 1976*
Altman, Jack 1938- *ConAu 21*
Altman, Nathaniel 1948- *ConAu 57*
Altman, Richard Charles 1932- *ConAu 41*
Altman, Robert A 1943- *ConAu 29*
Altmann, Wilfred 1927- *Au&Wr*, *ConAu P-1*
Altmann, Alexander 1906- *ConAu 61*
Altolaguirre, Manuel 1904?-1959 *CasWL*,
    ClDMEuL, *EncWL*, *EvEuW*, *Pen*
Altoma, Salih J 1929- *ConAu 49*
Alton *Alli*, *ChPo S2*
Alton, Edmund *Alli Sup*
Alton, John D' *Alli*
Alton, Maxine 1890- *WhWNAA*
Altrick, Richard Daniel 1915- *ChPo S1*
Altrocchi, Julia Cooley 1893-1972 *AmA&B*,
    ChPo S1, *ConAu P-1*, *WhWNAA*
Altrocchi, Rudolph 1882- *WhWNAA*
Altschul, Charles 1857-1927 *DcNAA*
Altsheler, Joseph Alexander 1862-1919 *AmA&B*,
    AuBYP, *BiDSA*, *DcAmA*, *DcNAA*, *JBA*,
    REnAL, *TwCA*, *TwCA Sup*, *YABC 1*
Altshuler, Edward A 1919- *ConAu 17R*
Altswert, Meister *OxGer*
Aluko, Timothy Mofolorunso 1920- *Pen Cl*
Aluko, Timothy Mofolorunso 1918- *AfA 1*,
    Au&Wr, *CasWL*, *ConNov 1972*,
    ConNov 1976, *RGAfl*, *TwCW*, *WebEAL*,
    WrD 1976
Alum, Hardly *DcNAA*
Alun 1797-1840 *CasWL*
Aluredis, Alredis *Alli*
Alurista 1947- *ConAu 45*, *DrAP 1975*
Alva, Martin *WhWNAA*
Alvarenga, Manuel Inacio DaSilva 1749-1814
    Pen Am
Alvarenga Peixoto, Inacio Jose De 1744-1793
    Pen Am
Alvares DeAzevedo, Manuel Antonio 1831-1852
    Pen Am
Alvares DoOriente, Fernao 1540?-1595? *CasWL*
Alvares ALSO Alvarez DoOriente, F
Alvarez, Alejandro Rodriguez *McGWD*
Alvarez, Alfred 1929- *Au&Wr*, *ConAu 1R*,
    ConLC 5, *ConP 1970*, *ConP 1975*,
    ModBL Sup, *REn*, *WorAu*, *WrD 1976*
Alvarez, Eugene 1932- *ConAu 57*
Alvarez, Francisco 1847-1881 *PueRA*
Alvarez, Jorge *DrAP 1975*
Alvarez, Jose Sixto 1858-1903 *Pen Am*
Alvarez, Joseph A 1930- *ConAu 33*
Alvarez, Julia 1950- *BlkAW*
Alvarez, Walter C *DrAP 1975*
Alvarez, Walter Clement 1884-1974 *AmA&B*,
    ConAu 61, *MnnWr*, *WhWNAA*
Alvarez-Altman, Grace 1926- *ConAu 33*
Alvarez DeCienfuegos, Nicasio 1764-1809
    CasWL, *EvEuW*
Alvarez DelVayo, Julio 1891-1975 *ConAu 61*
Alvarez DeToledo, Gabriel 1662-1714 *Pen Eur*
Alvarez DeToledo Pellicer Y Tovar, G 1662-1714
    CasWL
Alvarez DeVillasandino, Alfonso d1425? *CasWL*.
    DcSpL
Alvarez DoOriente, Fernan 1540-1599 *BbD*,
    BiD&SB
Alvarez ALSO Alvares DoOriente, F
Alvarez Espriella, Manuel *DcEnL*
Alvarez Gato, Juan 1440?-1510? *CasWL*
Alvarez Martin, Casimir 1873- *WhWNAA*
Alvarez Nazario, Manuel *PueRA*
Alvarez Quintero, Joaquin 1873-1944 *CasWL*,
    ClDMEuL, *DcSpL*, *EncWL*, *LongC*,
    McGWD, *ModRL*, *ModWD*, *Pen Eur*,
    REn, *TwCA*, *TwCA Sup*, *TwCW*
Alvarez Quintero, Serafin 1871-1938 *CasWL*,
    ClDMEuL, *DcSpL*, *EncWL*, *EvEuW*,
    LongC, *McGWD*, *ModRL*, *ModWD*,
    Pen Eur, *REn*, *TwCA*, *TwCA Sup*,
    TwCW
Alvaro *WhWNAA*
Alvaro, Corrado 1895-1956 *CasWL*, *ClDMEuL*,
    EncWL, *ModRL*, *Pen Eur*, *REn*, *WorAu*
Alvary, W C *Alli Sup*
Alver, Betti 1906- *EncWL*
Alverdes, Paul 1897- *ClDMEuL*, *OxGer*,
    TwCA, *TwCA Sup*
Alverson, Charles 1935- *ConAu 25*

Alves, Colin 1930- *ConAu 5R*
Alves, James *BiDLA*
Alves, Juliet *DcNAA*
Alves, Marcio Moreira 1936- *ConAu 45*
Alves, Robert d1794 *Alli*
Alvey, Edward, Jr. 1902- *ConAu 53*
Alvey, Thomas *Alli*
Alvin, Juliette Louise *Au&Wr*
Alvin, Louis Joseph 1806-1887 *BbD, BiD&SB*
Alvord, Benjamin 1813-1884 *Alli Sup, DcAmA, DcNAA*
Alvord, Clarence Walworth 1868-1928 *AmA&B, AmLY, DcNAA*
Alvord, Idress Head *WhWNAA*
Alvord, John Watson 1861- *WhWNAA*
Alvord, Samuel Morgan 1869-1943 *DcNAA*
Alwan, Ameen *DrAP 1975*
Alwin *BiB N*
Alwood, Lister *ChPo S2*
Alwood, William Bradford 1859-1946 *OhA&B*
Alworth, E P 1918- *ConAu 25*
Alxinger, Johann Baptist Von 1755-1797 *BiD&SB, DcEuL, OxGer*
Aly, Bower 1903- *Au&Wr, ConAu 5R, WrD 1976*
Aly, Lucile Folse 1913- *ConAu 23*
Aly, Wolfgang 1881- *WhLA*
Alyeshmerni, Mansoor 1943- *ConAu 29*
Alynton, Robert *Alli*
Alyoshin, Samuil 1913- *CnMD, ModWD*
Amabile, George 1936- *ConAu 33, ConP 1970, DrAP 1975, WrD 1976*
Amacher, Richard Earl 1917- *ConAu 1R*
Amadi, Elechi 1934- *AfA 1, CasWL, ConAu 29, RGAfl, WrD 1976*
Amadis De Gaula *CasWL*
Amadis Of Gaul *DcEuL*
Amado, Jorge 1912- *CasWL, CyWA, EncWL, Pen Am, REn, TwCW, WorAu*
Amadon, Dean 1912- *ConAu 61*
Amador DeLosRios, Jose 1818-1878 *DcSpL*
Amadou, Robert 1924- *BiDPar*
Amalia *DcSpL*
Amalie, Marie Friederike Auguste 1794-1870 *BiD&SB*
Amamoo, Joseph Godson 1931- *Au&Wr, ConAu 13R*
Aman, Mohammed M 1940- *ConAu 49, LivBAA*
Amanat, Sayyid Agha Hasan 1816-1859 *DcOrL 2*
Amand, George St. *Alli*
Amanda *ConAu XR*
Amann, Peter H 1927- *ConAu 61*
Amann, Victor F 1927- *ConAu 41*
Amanuddin, Syed 1934- *ConAu 49*
Amaral, Anthony 1930- *ConAu 21*
Amaral, Nestor 1913-1962 *AmSCAP 66*
Amarcius *CasWL*
Amaru *DcOrL 2*
Amary, Issam B 1942- *ConAu 61*
Amass, Arthur William 1880- *WhWNAA*
Amateur, An *DcEnL*
Amato, Joseph Anthony 1938- *ConAu 57*
Amatora, Sister Mary *ConAu 9R*
Amaya, Mario 1933- *ConAu 61*
Ambauen, Andrew Joseph 1847- *DcAmA, DcNAA*
Amber *AmA&B, ChPo S1*
Amberg, Emil 1868- *WhWNAA*
Amberg, Samuel 1874- *WhWNAA*
Amberley, Viscount *Alli Sup, NewC*
Amberley, Richard *WrD 1976*
Amberley, Simon *WrD 1976*
Ambesser, Axel Von 1910- *CnMD*
Ambient, Mark 1860- *ChPo S1*
Ambikatanayadatta *DcOrL 2*
Ambirajan, Srinivasa 1936- *ConAu 17R, WrD 1976*
Ambler, Benjamin George *Alli Sup*
Ambler, Charles *Alli*
Ambler, Charles Henry 1876-1957 *AmA&B, OhA&B, WhWNAA*
Ambler, Christopher Gifford 1886- *IlBYP, IlCB 1956*
Ambler, Eric 1909- *AmA&B, Au&Wr, CnMWL, ConAu 9R, ConLC 4, ConLC 6, ConNov 1972, ConNov 1976,*

DcLEnL, EncM&D, LongC, NewC, REn, TwCA Sup, TwCW, WrD 1976
Ambler, Henry Lovejoy 1843-1924 *OhA&B*
Ambler, John S 1932- *ConAu 49*
Ambler, R P *Alli Sup*
Ambras *DcEuL*
Ambree, Mary *NewC*
Ambrogini, Angelo *McGWD*
Ambroise *CasWL*
Ambroise D'Evreux *OxFr*
Ambros, August Wilhelm 1816-1876 *BbD, BiD&SB*
Ambrose, Saint 340?-397 *BiD&SB, CasWL, NewC, OxEng, Pen Cl, PoCh, REn*
Ambrose, Alice 1906- *ConAu 49, WrD 1976*
Ambrose, Bertie *BiDLA Sup*
Ambrose, Brother *DcNAA*
Ambrose, Cora Janet *ChPo*
Ambrose, Daniel Leib 1843-1922 *DcNAA*
Ambrose, Eric 1908- *Au&Wr, ConAu P-1*
Ambrose, Isaac d1664 *Alli*
Ambrose, John *BbtC*
Ambrose, John W, Jr. 1931- *ConAu 57*
Ambrose, Paul *DcNAA*
Ambrose, Stephen Edward 1936- *ConAu 1R*
Ambrose, W Haydn 1922- *ConAu 25*
Ambrosini, Maria Luisa *ConAu 33*
Ambrosio *REn*
Ambrosius Aurelianus 420?- *NewC*
Ambrosius, Johanna 1854- *BiD&SB, ChPo*
Ambross, Miss *Alli*
Ambroz, Oton 1905- *ConAu 41*
Ambrus, Victor G 1935- *ChPo S1, ChPo S2, ConAu 25, IlBYP, IlCB 1966, SmATA 1, ThBJA, WhCL*
Ambrus, Zoltan 1861-1932 *ClDMEuL, EncWL, Pen Eur*
Ameer Ali, Syed 1848- *Alli Sup*
Ameipsias *CasWL*
Amelesagoras *Pen Cl*
Amelia *AmA&B, DcNAA*
Amelio, Ralph J 1939- *ConAu 37*
Amend, Victor E 1916- *ConAu 33*
Amenemhet I 991?BC-962BC *DcOrL 3*
Amenemope *DcOrL 3*
Amenhotep *DcOrL 3*
Ament, Wilhelm 1876- *WhLA*
Amergin *DcEnL*
American Shipmaster 1814-1900 *AmA*
Americo Amador *PueRA*
Amerie, Robert *Alli*
Amerine, Maynard A 1911- *ConAu 41*
Ameringer, Charles D 1926- *ConAu 57*
Ameringer, Oscar 1870-1942 *DcNAA*
Amerman, Lockhart 1911-1969 *AuBYP, ConAu 29, SmATA 3*
Amery, C F *Alli Sup*
Amery, Harold Julian 1919- *Au&Wr*
Amery, Julian 1919- *ConAu 61*
Amery, Leopold Stennett 1873-1955 *LongC, NewC, WhLA*
Ames *Alli*
Ames, Azel 1845-1908 *Alli Sup, DcAmA, DcNAA*
Ames, Charles Edgar 1895- *ConAu 25*
Ames, Charles Gordon 1828-1912 *Alli Sup, AmA, BiD&SB, ChPo, DcAmA, DcNAA*
Ames, Chester Winthrop *ChPo S2*
Ames, Delano 1906- *Au&Wr, MnBBF, OhA&B*
Ames, Edith T *ChPo*
Ames, Edward *Alli*
Ames, Edward Scribner 1870-1958 *AmA&B, WhWNAA*
Ames, Eleanor Maria 1830?-1908 *Alli Sup, AmA&B, BiD&SB, DcAmA, DcNAA*
Ames, Elinor *WhWNAA*
Ames, Evelyn 1908- *ConAu 57*
Ames, Miss F S D *Alli Sup*
Ames, Felicia *ConAu XR, WrD 1976*
Ames, Fisher 1758-1808 *Alli, Alli Sup, AmA, AmA&B, BbD, BiD&SB, CyAL 1, DcAmA, DcNAA, OxAm, REnAL*
Ames, Fisher 1838-1918 *DcNAA*
Ames, Francis Herbert 1900- *ConAu 17R, WhPNW*
Ames, Gerald 1906- *BkP, ThBJA*
Ames, Herman Vandenburg 1865-1935 *DcNAA*

Ames, J *Alli Sup*
Ames, James Barr 1846-1910 *Alli Sup, DcNAA*
Ames, Jennifer *LongC*
Ames, Jocelyn Green *ConAu 5R*
Ames, John H *Alli Sup*
Ames, Joseph 1689-1758? *Alli, DcEnL*
Ames, Joseph Bushnell 1878-1928 *DcNAA*
Ames, Joseph Sweetman 1864-1943 *DcAmA, DcNAA*
Ames, Lee Judah 1921- *AuBYP, ConAu 1R, IlCB 1956, IlCB 1966, SmATA 3*
Ames, Leslie *WrD 1976*
Ames, Lilia *Alli Sup*
Ames, Louise Bates 1908- *AmA&B, ConAu 1R*
Ames, Lucia True 1856- *Alli Sup, DcAmA*
Ames, Lucille Perry 1892- *WhWNAA*
Ames, Mary 1853-1929 *DcNAA*
Ames, Mary Clemmer 1839-1884 *Alli Sup, AmA&B, BiD&SB, ChPo, ChPo S1, CyAL 2, DcAmA, DcNAA*
Ames, Nathan 1825-1865 *DcNAA*
Ames, Nathaniel d1835 *AmA&B, DcNAA*
Ames, Nathaniel 1708-1764 *AmA, AmA&B, BiD&SB, ChPo S2, CyAL 1, DcAmA, DcNAA, OxAm, REnAL*
Ames, Noel *ConAu XR*
Ames, Norma 1920- *ConAu 29*
Ames, Ruth M 1918- *ConAu 29*
Ames, Samuel 1806-1865 *Alli, Alli Sup*
Ames, Seth *CyAL 1*
Ames, Van Meter 1898- *AmA&B, ConAu P-1, OhA&B*
Ames, William 1576-1633 *Alli*
Ames, William Homer 1876- *WhWNAA*
Ames, Winslow 1907- *ConAu 25*
Ames, Woodforde *WhWNAA*
Amesbury, Joseph *Alli*
Amesbury, Marion G *ChPo S1*
Amescua, Antonio Mira De 1578?-1644 *DcEuL*
Amesse, John W 1874- *WhWNAA*
Amey, Lloyd Ronald 1922- *ConAu 45*
Amfiteatrov, Alexander Valentinovich 1862-1923? *CasWL, DcEuL, EvEuW*
Amfitheatrof, Daniele 1901- *AmSCAP 66*
Amgis 1786-1867 *AmA*
Amherst, Francis Kerril 1819-1883 *Alli Sup*
Amherst, J H 1776-1851 *AmA&B*
Amherst, Jeffrey 1717-1797 *NewC, OxCan*
Amherst, William *OxCan*
Amherst, William Joseph 1820- *Alli Sup*
Amhurst, Nicholas 1706-1742 *Alli*
Ami, Henry Marc 1858-1931 *DcNAA*
Ami DesHommes, L' *OxFr*
Amicis, Edmondo De 1846-1905 *BbD, BiD&SB, CasWL, CyWA, EuA*
Amick, Robert Gene 1933- *ConAu 33, WrD 1976*
Amicus *DcEnL*
Amid, John *WhWNAA*
Amidon, Bill 1935- *ConAu 45, DrAF 1976*
Amidon, Royal W *Alli Sup*
Amiel, Denys 1884- *ClDMEuL, McGWD, OxFr, Pen Eur, REn*
Amiel, Henri Frederic 1821-1881 *BbD, BiD&SB, CasWL, ClDMEuL, DcEuL, EuA, EvEuW, OxEng, OxFr, Pen Eur*
Amihai, Jehuda 1924- *CasWL*
Amilcar Barca *PueRA*
Amini, Johari M 1935- *BlkAW, ConAu 4173, DrAP 1975, LivBA*
Amir, Aharon 1923- *CasWL*
Amir, Menachem 1930- *ConAu 45*
Amir Hamzah 1911-1946 *Pen Cl*
Amir Khosrou 1253-1325 *DcOrL 3*
Amir Khusrau *CasWL*
Amir Mina'i, Munshi Ahmad 1928-1900 *DcOrL 2*
Amira, Karl 1848- *WhLA*
Amiri, Mirza Sadeq Khan 1860?-1917 *DcOrL 3*
Amis, Breton *ConAu XR*
Amis, Kingsley 1922- *Au&Wr, AuNews 2, CasWL, CnMWL, ConAu 9R, ConLC 1, ConLC 2, ConLC 3, ConLC 5, ConNov 1972, ConNov 1976, ConP 1970, ConP 1975, EncM&D, EncWL, LongC, ModBL, ModBL Sup, NewC, Pen Eng,*

*RAdv 1, REn, TwCW, WebEAL,
WhTwL, WorAu, WrD 1976*
Amis, Lola Elizabeth Jones 1930- *BlkAW,
LivBAA*
Amis, Martin 1949- *WrD 1976*
Amis, Martin 1950?- *ConLC 4*
Amis, Pfaffe *DcEuL*
Amishai-Maisels, Ziva *ConAu 49*
Amlund, Curtis Arthur 1927- *ConAu 21*
Amman Dihlavi, Mir 1745?-1806 *DcOrL 2*
Ammar, Abbas 1907?-1974 *ConAu 53*
Amme, Carl H, Jr. 1913- *ConAu 25*
Ammen, Daniel 1820-1898 *Alli Sup, BbD,
BiD&SB, DcAmA, DcNAA, OhA&B*
Ammer, Dean S 1926- *ConAu 17R*
Ammerman, David L 1936- *ConAu 57*
Ammerman, Leila Tremaine 1912- *ConAu 33,
WrD 1976*
Ammerman, Robert R 1927- *ConAu 13R*
Ammers-Kuller, Jo Van 1884- *CyWA, EncWL,
REn, TwCA, TwCA Sup*
Ammianus Marcellinus 330?-400? *CasWL,
Pen Cl*
Ammidown, Holmes *Alli Sup*
Ammirato, Scipione 1531-1601 *CasWL*
Ammon, Hermann 1888- *WhLA*
Ammonius Saccas 175?-242? *Pen Cl, REn*
Ammons, A R 1926- *AmA&B, AuNews 1,
ConAu 9R, ConLC 2, ConLC 3,
ConLC 5, ConP 1970, ConP 1975,
CrCAP, DrAP 1975, ModAL Sup,
RAdv 1, WorAu, WrD 1976*
Amner, John *Alli*
Amner, Richard 1736-1803 *Alli*
Amo, Antonius Guilielmus 1703-1750? *AfA 1*
Amoaku, J K 1936- *ConAu 45*
Amoers, Jan *CasWL*
Amon, Aline 1928- *ConAu 61, SmATA 9*
Amor, Amos *ConAu XR*
Amorie VanDerHoeven, Abraham Des, Jr.
1821-1848 *CasWL*
Amorie VanDerHoeven, Abraham Des, Sr.
1798-1855 *CasWL*
Amorim, Enrique 1900-1960 *CasWL, EncWL,
Pen Am*
Amoros, Juan Bautista 1856-1912 *CasWL,
ClDMEuL*
Amorosi, Ray *DrAP 1975*
Amory, Anne Reinberg 1931- *ConAu 17R*
Amory, Cleveland 1917- *AmA&B, AuNews 1,
REnAL, TwCA Sup, WrD 1976*
Amory, Frances *ChPo*
Amory, Mark *ChPo S2*
Amory, Martha Babcock 1812-1880 *Alli Sup,
DcNAA*
Amory, Robert 1842-1910 *Alli Sup, DcNAA*
Amory, Thomas 1691?-1788 *Alli, BiD&SB,
BrAu, Chmbr 2, DcEnA, DcEnL,
DcLEnL, EvLB, NewC, OxEng*
Amory, Thomas 1701-1774 *Alli, DcEnL*
Amory, Thomas Coffin 1812-1889 *Alli Sup,
AmA&B, BiD&SB, ChPo S2, DcAmA,
DcNAA*
Amos *Alli, DcOrL 3*
Amos, A *BbtC*
Amos, Andrew *Alli*
Amos, J *Alli*
Amos, James *Alli Sup, BiDLA*
Amos, Sheldon 1835-1887 *Alli Sup*
Amos, Stanley William 1915- *Au&Wr*
Amos, William *Alli, BiDLA*
Amos, William E 1926- *ConAu 17R*
Amos, Winsom 1921- *ConAu 49*
Amoss, Berthe 1925- *ConAu 21, SmATA 5*
Amoss, Harold Edwin *WhWNAA*
Amoss, Harold Lindsay 1886- *WhWNAA*
Amoss, Harry 1880- *WhWNAA*
Amoyt, Jacques 1513-1594 *DcEuL*
Ampere, Andre Marie 1775-1836 *OxFr, REn*
Ampere, Jean Jacques Antoine 1800-1864 *BbD,
BiD&SB, OxCan, OxFr*
Amphibian *WhLA*
Amphlett, John *Alli Sup*
Amphlett, W *ChPo S1*
Amphlett, William *Alli, BiDLA*
Amprimoz, Alexandre 1948- *ConAu 37*
Ampzing, Samuel 1590-1632 *CasWL*
Amram, David 1930- *ConAu 29*

Amram, David Werner 1866-1939 *DcNAA*
Amrine, Michael 1919?-1974 *ConAu 49*
Amru'u'l-Qais *Pen Cl*
Amsbary, Mary Anne 1921- *OhA&B*
Amsbary, Wallace Bruce 1867- *ChPo,
ChPo S1*
Amsden, Charles Avery 1899-1941 *DcNAA*
Amsden, Gloria *ChPo*
Amsden, Mrs. H L *ChPo*
Amsden, Samuel 1820-1867 *BbtC*
Amsinck, P *Alli*
Amstead, B H 1921- *ConAu 23*
Amster, Linda 1938- *ConAu 45*
Amsterdam, Chet 1926- *AmSCAP 66*
Amsterdam, Morey 1912- *AmSCAP 66*
Amstutz, Arnold E 1936- *ConAu 21*
Amstutz, Peter B 1846-1938 *OhA&B*
Amulree, Lord 1860- *WhLA*
Amulree, Lord 1900- *Au&Wr*
Amundsen, Kirsten 1932- *ConAu 37*
Amundsen, Richard E *IlBYP*
Amundsen, Roald Engelbregt Gravning
1872-1928 *OxCan, REn*
Amuzegar, Jahangir 1920- *ConAu 41*
Amway, John C 1904- *AmSCAP 66*
Amy, Francisco J 1837-1912 *PueRA*
Amy, S *Alli*
Amy, William Lacey *CanNov, OxCan*
Amyand, C *Alli*
Amyntor, Gerhard Von 1831- *BiD&SB*
Amyot, Jacques 1513-1593 *BiD&SB, CasWL,
EuA, EvEuW, NewC, OxEng, OxFr,
Pen Eur*
Amyot, Thomas 1775-1850 *Alli, BiDLA*
An-Ski, Sh 1863-1920 *CasWL, EuA, Pen Eur*
Anacreon 570?BC-485?BC *AtlBL, BbD,
BiD&SB, CasWL, DcEuL, NewC,
OxEng, Pen Cl, RCom*
Anacreon Moore 1779-1852 *DcEnL*
Anacreon Of The Twelfth Century 1150-1196
DcEnL
Anacreon, The Scottish *DcEnL*
Anagnos, Julia R 1844-1886 *Alli Sup, BbD,
BiD&SB, ChPo S1, DcAmA, DcNAA*
Anagnos, Michael 1837-1906 *DcNAA*
Anahory, Terencio 1934- *AfA 1*
Anak Sungei *WhLA*
Anakreontiker *DcEuL*
Analyticus *WhWNAA*
Anand, Mulk Raj 1905- *Au&Wr, CasWL,
ConNov 1972, ConNov 1976, DcOrL 2,
Pen Eng, REn, WebEAL, WorAu,
WrD 1976*
Anandavardhana *DcOrL 2*
Anang, Dei *AfA 1*
Anania, Michael 1939- *ConAu 25, ConP 1975,
DrAP 1975, WrD 1976*
Ananou, David 1930?- *AfA 1*
Ananta Thuriya 1112?-1173 *DcOrL 2*
Anastaplo, George 1925- *ConAu 37*
Anastas, Peter 1937- *ConAu 45*
Anastasi, Anne 1908- *AmA&B, Au&Wr,
ConAu 5R*
Anastasio El Pollo *DcSpL*
Anastasiou, Clifford 1929- *ConAu 49*
Anastasius Of Sinai *CasWL*
Anati, Emmanuel 1930- *Au&Wr, WrD 1976*
Anau, Benjamin *CasWL*
Anaxagoras 500?BC-428?BC *BbD, BiD&SB,
CasWL, Pen Cl, REn*
Anaxandrides *CasWL*
Anaximander 611?BC-547?BC *BbD, BiD&SB,
CasWL, Pen Cl, REn*
Anaximenes *BiD&SB, CasWL, Pen Cl, REn*
Anaximenes Of Lampsacus 380?BC-320?BC
REn
Anaya, A *Alli*
Anaya, Rudolfo A 1937- *ConAu 45,
DrAF 1976*
Anburey, Thomas *BiDLA*
Anbury, Thomas *Alli*
Ancell, Henry *Alli Sup*
Ancell, Samuel d1802 *Alli, PoIre*
Ancelot, Jacques Arsene 1794-1854 *BiD&SB,
OxFr*
Ancey, Georges 1860-1917 *ModWD, OxFr*
Anchell, Melvin 1919- *ConAu 25*
Anchieta, Padre Jose De 1534-1597 *Pen Am*

Anchoran, J *Alli*
Anchors, Don *ChPo S2*
Anchusa *WhWNAA*
Ancien, Monsieur L' *OxCan*
Anckarsvard, Karin 1915-1969 *AuBYP,
ConAu 9R, SmATA 6, ThBJA*
Anckettill, W R *Alli Sup*
Ancona, Alessandro D' *CasWL*
Ancona, Ciriaco D' *CasWL*
Ancona, George 1929- *ConAu 53*
Ancram, Earl Of *Alli*
Ancre, Marechal D' *OxFr*
Ancrum, Earl Of *Chmbr 1*
Ancrum, Robert Kerr, Earl Of 1578-1654 *DcEnL*
Anczyc, Vladislav Ludvig 1823-1883 *BbD,
BiD&SB*
Andalina, Michael J 1925- *AmSCAP 66*
Anday, Melih Cevdet 1915- *DcOrL 3,
EncWL Sup, REnWD*
Andelman, Eddie 1936- *ConAu 57*
Andelson, Robert V 1931- *ConAu 33,
WrD 1976*
Anderdon, John Lavicount 1792-1874 *Alli Sup*
Anderdon, William Henry 1816- *Alli Sup*
Anderegg, Frederick 1852-1922 *DcNAA*
Anderegg, Frederick Osband 1887- *WhWNAA*
Andereich, Justus *ConAu XR*
Anders, Edith Mary England 1899- *ConAu P-1,
WrD 1976*
Anders, Evelyn 1916- *ConAu 29*
Anders, Howard S 1866- *WhWNAA*
Anders, James Meschter 1854-1936 *Alli Sup,
DcAmA, DcNAA*
Anders, Leslie 1922- *ConAu 13R, WrD 1976*
Anders-Richards, Donald 1928- *ConAu 25,
WrD 1976*
Andersan, James Arthur 1857- *WhWNAA*
Andersch, Alfred 1914- *CasWL, ConAu 33,
EncWL, ModGL, OxGer, Pen Eur*
Andersch, Elizabeth Genevieve 1913-
ConAu 5R
Andersen, Andreas 1782?- *BiDLA*
Andersen, Arlow W 1906- *ConAu P-1*
Andersen, Arthur Olaf 1880-1958 *AmSCAP 66*
Andersen, Doris 1909- *ConAu 23*
Andersen, Hans Christian 1805-1875 *AnCL,
AtlBL, AuBYP, BbD, BiD&SB, CarSB,
CasWL, ChPo, ChPo S1, ChPo S2,
CyWA, DcBiA, DcEnL, DcEuL, EuA,
EvEuW, FamAYP, FamSYP, JBA 1934,
JBA 1951, NewC, OxEng, Pen Eur,
RCom, REn, St&VC, WhCL, YABC 1*
Andersen, Ib 1907- *WhGrA*
Andersen, Johannes C *ChPo S1*
Andersen, Karl 1828-1883 *BbD, BiD&SB*
Andersen, Kenneth E 1933- *ConAu 37*
Andersen, Lale *OxGer*
Andersen, Marion Lineaweaver 1912?-1971
ConAu 29
Andersen, Michael 1938- *AmSCAP 66*
Andersen, R Clifton 1933- *ConAu 33*
Andersen, Richard 1931- *ConAu 57*
Andersen, Ted *ConAu XR*
Andersen, Tryggve 1866-1920 *EvEuW*
Andersen, Trygve 1866-1920 *ClDMEuL*
Andersen, Uell Stanley 1917- *ConAu 1R*
Andersen, Wayne V 1928- *ConAu 9R*
Andersen, Wilhelm 1911- *ConAu 29*
Andersen, Yvonne 1932- *ConAu 29*
Andersen Nexo, Martin 1869-1954 *CasWL,
EncWL, EvEuW, Pen Eur, TwCA,
TwCA Sup*
Anderson, Abraham Archibald 1847-1940
DcNAA
Anderson, Ada Woodruff 1860- *AmA&B*
Anderson, Adam d1867 *Alli Sup*
Anderson, Adam 1692-1765 *Alli*
Anderson, Adrienne Adams *ThBJA*
Anderson, Aeneas *Alli, BiDLA*
Anderson, Alan Ross 1925-1973 *ConAu 17,
ConAu 45*
Anderson, Alex *Alli*
Anderson, Alexander *Chmbr 3*
Anderson, Alexander d1813 *Alli*
Anderson, Alexander 1775-1870 *AmA&B,
ChPo, ChPo S1, CyAL 1, DcAmA,
DcNAA, EarAB, EarAB Sup*
Anderson, Alexander 1845-1909 *Alli Sup,*

BrAu 19, ChPo, ChPo S1, ChPo S2, EvLB, LongC

Anderson, Alexander Caulfield 1814-1884 *DcNAA*

Anderson, Alexander Dwight 1843-1901 *Alli Sup, DcNAA*

Anderson, Alice D *BlkAW*

Anderson, Alpha E 1914- *ConAu 23*

Anderson, Alston 1924- *BlkAW*

Anderson, Andrew *Alli Sup*

Anderson, Andrew A *Alli Sup*

Anderson, Andrew Ferguson *Alli Sup*

Anderson, Anne *ChPo S1*

Anderson, Anthony Keith 1929- *Au&Wr*

Anderson, Archer *BiDSA*

Anderson, Arthur G 1886- *WhWNAA*

Anderson, Barbara 1894- *AmA&B, AmNov*

Anderson, Barry 1935- *ConAu 17R*

Anderson, Basil S 1861- *ChPo*

Anderson, Benjamin *Alli Sup*

Anderson, Benjamin M, Jr. 1886- *WhWNAA*

Anderson, Bern 1900-1963 *ConAu 1R*

Anderson, Bernard Eric 1936- *ConAu 53*

Anderson, Bernhard Word 1916- *AmA&B, Au&Wr, ConAu 57*

Anderson, Bernice 1894- *WhWNAA*

Anderson, Bernice Gibbs 1900- *ChPo S1*

Anderson, Bertha Moore 1892- *ConAu 5R*

Anderson, Bessie Wayne 1867-1955 *OhA&B*

Anderson, Bill *ChPo S2*

Anderson, Brad Jay 1924- *AmA&B*

Anderson, C *Alli*

Anderson, C Cuyler *Alli Sup*

Anderson, C H *Alli Sup*

Anderson, C L 1901- *ConAu 25*

Anderson, C W 1891-1971 *BkP, JBA 1951, St&VC, ThBJA*

Anderson, C W ALSO Anderson, Clarence

Anderson, Camilla M 1904- *ConAu 33*

Anderson, Carl 1875-1943 *IndAu 1816*

Anderson, Carl Dicmann 1912- *ConAu 33*

Anderson, Carl E 1892- *AmSCAP 66*

Anderson, Carl L 1919- *ConAu 41*

Anderson, Carl Thomas 1865-1948 *AmA&B*

Anderson, Caroline Dorothea *Alli Sup*

Anderson, Catherine Corley 1909- *ConAu 1R*

Anderson, Charles *Alli Sup, BiDLA*

Anderson, Charles C 1931- *ConAu 29*

Anderson, Charles Henry *Alli Sup*

Anderson, Sir Charles Henry John 1804- *Alli Sup*

Anderson, Charles L 1938- *BlkAW*

Anderson, Charles Palmerston 1864-1930 *DcNAA, WhWNAA*

Anderson, Charles Roberts 1902- *AmA&B, ConAu 1R*

Anderson, Charles W 1934- *ConAu 9R*

Anderson, Chester G 1923- *ConAu 25*

Anderson, Christine *ChPo*

Anderson, Christopher 1782-1852? *Alli, BiDLA Sup, DcEnL*

Anderson, Chuck 1933- *ConAu 49*

Anderson, Clarence William 1891-1971 *AuBYP, ConAu 29, IlCB 1945, IlCB 1956, IlCB 1966*

Anderson, Clarence ALSO Anderson, C W

Anderson, Clifford *ConAu XR*

Anderson, Colena M 1891- *ConAu 21*

Anderson, Courtney 1906- *ConAu P-1, WrD 1976*

Anderson, D *Alli*

Anderson, D F *ChPo S1*

Anderson, Dave *AuNews 2*

Anderson, David *Alli Sup, BbtC, BiDLA*

Anderson, David 1814-1885 *Alli Sup, BbtC, OxCan*

Anderson, David 1875-1947 *DcNAA*

Anderson, David Allen 1874- *WhWNAA*

Anderson, David Daniel 1924- *ConAu 13R, WrD 1976*

Anderson, David John *Alli Sup*

Anderson, David L 1919- *ConAu 5R*

Anderson, David Wilson *IndAu 1816*

Anderson, David Wulf 1878-1938 *IndAu 1917*

Anderson, Dewey 1897- *AmA&B, ConAu 57*

Anderson, Dice Robins 1880-1942 *DcNAA, WhWNAA*

Anderson, Dillon 1906-1973 *ConAu 1R,*

ConAu 45

Anderson, Donald F 1938- *ConAu 53*

Anderson, Donald K, Jr. 1922- *ConAu 37, WrD 1976*

Anderson, Doris *OxCan Sup*

Anderson, Douglas *DrAP 1975*

Anderson, Douglas 1942- *Au&Wr*

Anderson, Duncan 1828-1903 *Alli Sup, ChPo, ChPo S1, DcNAA*

Anderson, Dwight 1882-1953 *OhA&B*

Anderson, Mrs. E M *BiDSA*

Anderson, Edgar 1920- *ConAu 33*

Anderson, Sir Edmund d1605 *Alli*

Anderson, Edmund 1912- *AmSCAP 66*

Anderson, Edna *BlkAW*

Anderson, Edna A *MnnWr*

Anderson, Edward D *ChPo*

Anderson, Edward H *BlkAW*

Anderson, Edward Lowell 1842-1916 *Alli Sup, DcAmA, DcNAA, OhA&B*

Anderson, Edward Pretot 1855-1887 *DcAmA, DcNAA*

Anderson, Einar 1909- *ConAu 13R*

Anderson, Elam Jonathan 1890-1944 *DcNAA*

Anderson, Elizabeth 1837- *Alli Sup*

Anderson, Ella *WrD 1976*

Anderson, Elm J 1890- *WhWNAA*

Anderson, Eloise Adell 1927- *ConAu 53, SmATA 9*

Anderson, Emil V 1875-1958 *IndAu 1917*

Anderson, Emma Frances 1842-1868 *Alli Sup*

Anderson, Eric John 1919- *Au&Wr*

Anderson, Erica 1914- *ConAu 57*

Anderson, Ethel 1883-1958 *ChPo S1*

Anderson, Ethel Todd *AuBYP, OhA&B*

Anderson, Eugene N 1900- *AmA&B, ConAu 29*

Anderson, Eustace *Alli Sup*

Anderson, Eva Greenslit 1889- *WhPNW*

Anderson, Everett L 1900- *AmSCAP 66*

Anderson, Ferguson 1911- *WrD 1976*

Anderson, Lady Flavia 1910- *Au&Wr, WrD 1976*

Anderson, Florence *BiDSA, LivFWS*

Anderson, Florence Mary Bennett 1883- *AmA&B, AmA&B*

Anderson, Floyd Edward 1906- *BkC 6*

Anderson, Forrest Clayton 1903- *WhPNW*

Anderson, Fortescue L M *Alli Sup*

Anderson, Frank *MnBBF*

Anderson, Frank H, Jr. 1895-1952 *AmSCAP 66*

Anderson, Frank J 1919- *ConAu 9R*

Anderson, Frank Maloy 1871- *AmA&B, WhWNAA*

Anderson, Frank Marion 1863- *WhWNAA*

Anderson, Frederick Irving 1877-1947 *AmA&B, DcNAA, EncM&D, TwCA, TwCA Sup, WhWNAA*

Anderson, Frederick Lincoln 1862- *AmLY, WhWNAA*

Anderson, Freeman B 1922- *ConAu 41*

Anderson, G J B *MnBBF*

Anderson, G M *Alli, BiDLA*

Anderson, G W *Alli Sup*

Anderson, G W 1856- *ChPo S1*

Anderson, Galusha 1832-1918 *DcNAA*

Anderson, Mrs. Galusha *Alli Sup, DcNAA*

Anderson, Garland 1886-1939 *BlkAW, DcNAA*

Anderson, George *Alli, Alli Sup, ChPo S2, ConAu XR, SmATA XR*

Anderson, George And Anderson, Peter *Alli Sup*

Anderson, George And Finley, John *Alli Sup*

Anderson, Sir George Campbell *Alli Sup*

Anderson, George Christian 1907- *ConAu 29*

Anderson, George K 1901- *ConAu 23*

Anderson, George Laverne 1905- *Au&Wr, ConAu 5R, ConAu 13R*

Anderson, George Lucius 1849- *WhWNAA*

Anderson, George S *BiDSA*

Anderson, George Washington 1816-1903 *DcNAA*

Anderson, George Wishart 1913- *Au&Wr*

Anderson, George Wood 1873- *OhA&B*

Anderson, Gerald H 1930- *ConAu 17R*

Anderson, Gunnar *IlBYP*

Anderson, H Dewey 1897-1975 *ConAu 61*

Anderson, Harold H 1897- *ConAu 21*

Anderson, Harry Edwin 1900- *IndAu 1917*

Anderson, Helen Acker *MnnWr*

Anderson, Henry *Alli*

Anderson, Henry J *Alli, CyAL 1*

Anderson, Henry L N 1934- *BlkAW*

Anderson, Henry P 1927- *ConAu 33*

Anderson, Henry Tompkins 1812-1872 *DcNAA*

Anderson, Howard Peter 1932- *ConAu 61*

Anderson, Hugh 1920- *Au&Wr, ConAu 9R*

Anderson, Idella Alderman 1880- *WhWNAA*

Anderson, Isabel Harriet *Alli Sup*

Anderson, Isabel Weld 1876-1948 *AmA&B, ChPo S1, ChPo S2, WhWNAA*

Anderson, J *Alli Sup*

Anderson, J 1939- *Au&Wr*

Anderson, J Grant 1873- *WhWNAA*

Anderson, J K 1924- *ConAu 17R*

Anderson, J Redwood *ChPo S2*

Anderson, J S *Alli*

Anderson, J W *Alli, Alli Sup, BiDLA, OxCan Sup*

Anderson, Jack 1922- *AuNews 1, ConAu 57, WrD 1976*

Anderson, Jack 1935- *AmA&B, ConAu 33, DrAP 1975*

Anderson, Jacob Peter 1874- *WhWNAA*

Anderson, James *Alli, Alli Sup, BbtC, OxCan*

Anderson, James 1662-1728 *Alli, DcEnL*

Anderson, James 1739-1808 *Alli*

Anderson, Sir James 1824- *Alli Sup*

Anderson, James Arthur 1857- *AmLY, WhWNAA*

Anderson, James Blythe 1868- *WhWNAA*

Anderson, James D *OxCan Sup*

Anderson, James D 1933- *ConAu 49*

Anderson, James E 1933- *ConAu 9R*

Anderson, James F 1910- *ConAu 41*

Anderson, James G 1936- *ConAu 25, WrD 1976*

Anderson, James L 1941- *Au&Wr*

Anderson, James M 1933- *ConAu 33*

Anderson, James Maitland *Alli Sup*

Anderson, James Nesbitt 1864- *AmLY, WhWNAA*

Anderson, James Norman Dalrymple 1908- *Au&Wr, ConAu 9R*

Anderson, James Richard 1919- *IndAu 1917*

Anderson, James Thomas Milton 1878-1946 *DcNAA*

Anderson, James Turnbull *Alli Sup*

Anderson, James Wallace *Alli Sup*

Anderson, Jean 1930- *ConAu 41*

Anderson, Jennifer 1942- *ConAu 57*

Anderson, Jerome A 1847-1903 *DcNAA, IndAu 1917*

Anderson, Jerry M 1933- *ConAu 41*

Anderson, Jessica Queale *ConAu 9R*

Anderson, Jessie Annie 1861- *ChPo, ChPo S2*

Anderson, Jessie Macmillan *ChPo*

Anderson, Johannes Carl 1873-1959 *DcLEnL*

Anderson, John *Alli, Alli Sup, ChPo S1*

Anderson, Sir John *Alli Sup*

Anderson, John 1726-1796 *Alli*

Anderson, John 1822- *ChPo, ChPo S1*

Anderson, John 1840- *Alli Sup*

Anderson, John 1896-1943 *AmA&B, DcNAA*

Anderson, John 1909- *WrD 1976*

Anderson, John Bayard 1922- *ConAu 33*

Anderson, John Benjamin 1869- *AmLY, WhWNAA*

Anderson, John Bennett *Alli Sup*

Anderson, John Corbet *Alli Sup*

Anderson, John Edward 1893- *WhWNAA*

Anderson, John Edward 1903- *Au&Wr, ConAu 37*

Anderson, John Eustace *Alli Sup*

Anderson, John F 1945- *ConAu 53*

Anderson, John George 1866- *WhWNAA*

Anderson, John Henry *Alli Sup*

Anderson, John Jacob 1821-1906 *Alli Sup, DcAmA, DcNAA*

Anderson, John M 1914- *ConAu 17R*

Anderson, John Murray 1886-1954 *AmSCAP 66*

Anderson, John Parker *Alli Sup*

Anderson, John Parker 1841- *ChPo*

Anderson, John Q 1916- *ConAu 1R*

Anderson, John Redwood 1883- *ChPo*
Anderson, John Richard Lane 1911- *Au&Wr,*
ConAu 25, WrD 1976
Anderson, Jon 1940- *ConAu 25, ConP 1970,*
DrAP 1975
Anderson, Joseph *Alli Sup*
Anderson, Joseph 1836-1916 *DcNAA*
Anderson, Joy 1928- *ConAu 25, SmATA 1*
Anderson, Kate *Alli Sup*
Anderson, Katherine Finnigan *ChPo S2*
Anderson, Ken 1917- *ConAu 25*
Anderson, Kenneth *ChPo S1*
Anderson, Kenneth Douglas Stuart 1910-
Au&Wr
Anderson, L B *BiDSA*
Anderson, Larz 1866-1937 *OhA&B*
Anderson, Mrs. Larz 1876- *WhWNAA*
Anderson, Lawrence *Alli Sup*
Anderson, Lee 1896-1972 *ConAu 1R,*
ConAu 37
Anderson, Leroy 1866- *WhWNAA*
Anderson, Leroy 1908- *AmSCAP 66*
Anderson, Lester William 1918- *ConAu 5R*
Anderson, Lewis Flint 1866-1932 *DcNAA,*
OhA&B, WhWNAA
Anderson, Linsay *MnBBF*
Anderson, Lizzie R *ChPo S1*
Anderson, Lonzo 1905- *BkP, ConAu 25,*
SmATA 2, ThBJA
Anderson, Lou Eastwood *IndAu 1917,*
WhWNAA
Anderson, Louie *TexWr*
Anderson, Lucia 1922- *ConAu 41, SmATA 10*
Anderson, M *Alli*
Anderson, Madeleine Paltenghi 1899-
ConAu P-1
Anderson, Malcolm 1934- *ConAu 33,*
WrD 1976
Anderson, Margaret 1917- *ConAu 21*
Anderson, Margaret 1920- *BiDPar*
Anderson, Margaret Bartlett 1922- *ConAu 9R*
Anderson, Margaret C 1892?-1973 *AmA&B,*
ConAu 45, IndAu 1917, REnAL
Anderson, Margaret Johnson 1909- *ConAu 1R*
Anderson, Margaret Steele 1875-1921 *ChPo,*
ChPo S1, DcNAA
Anderson, Marian 1902- *REn*
Anderson, Marjorie 1892-1954 *ChPo S2,*
OhA&B
Anderson, Mark French *Alli Sup*
Anderson, Martin 1936- *ConAu 13R*
Anderson, Martin Brewer 1815-1890 *DcAmA,*
DcNAA
Anderson, Marvin Walter 1933- *ConAu 41*
Anderson, Mary 1939- *ConAu 49, SmATA 7*
Anderson, Mary A 1859- *BbD, BiD&SB,*
DcAmA
Anderson, Mary Audientia Smith 1872-
WhWNAA
Anderson, Mary Desiree 1902- *Au&Wr,*
ConAu 9R
Anderson, Mary Eleanor 1840-1916 *Alli Sup,*
ChPo, ChPo S2, DcNAA
Anderson, Matthew *ChPo*
Anderson, Matthew Smith 1922- *Au&Wr,*
ConAu 13R, WrD 1976
Anderson, Maxwell 1888-1959 *AmA&B,*
AmSCAP 66, CasWL, CnDAL, CnMD,
CnThe, ConAmA, ConAmL, CrCD,
CyWA, DcLEnL, EncWL, EvLB, LongC,
McGWD, ModAL, ModWD, OxAm,
Pen Am, REn, REnAL, REnWD, TwCA,
TwCA Sup, TwCW, WebEAL
Anderson, May M *ChPo, ChPo S1*
Anderson, Melville B *Alli Sup*
Anderson, Melville Best 1851-1933 *AmA&B,*
DcNAA
Anderson, Meta L *WhWNAA*
Anderson, Mildred Napier *ChPo*
Anderson, Mildred Travers *ChPo*
Anderson, Mona 1910- *ConAu 57, WrD 1976*
Anderson, Neal Larkin 1865-1931 *DcNAA*
Anderson, Neil *AuBYP*
Anderson, Norman 1907- *WrD 1976*
Anderson, Norman Dean 1928- *ConAu 33*
Anderson, Norman G *MnnWr*
Anderson, O Roger 1937- *ConAu 33*
Anderson, Odie 1943- *BlkAW, LivBA*

Anderson, Odin W 1914- *ConAu 25*
Anderson, Olive Ruth 1926- *Au&Wr,*
WrD 1976
Anderson, Olive San Louie 1842-1886 *Alli Sup,*
DcNAA, OhA&B
Anderson, Oscar Edward 1918- *IndAu 1917*
Anderson, Owen *OxCan Sup*
Anderson, P Howard 1947- *ConAu 61*
Anderson, Paris *PoIre*
Anderson, Patrick *Alli*
Anderson, Patrick 1915- *Au&Wr, ConP 1970,*
ConP 1975, OxCan, REnAL, WrD 1976
Anderson, Patrick 1936- *AmA&B, ConAu 33*
Anderson, Paul E 1925- *ConAu 33*
Anderson, Paul Johnson 1884- *WhWNAA*
Anderson, Paul Lewis 1880- *WhWNAA*
Anderson, Paul Russell 1907- *AmA&B*
Anderson, Paul Seward 1913- *ConAu 1R*
Anderson, Paul Y *WhWNAA*
Anderson, Peggy 1938- *WrD 1976*
Anderson, Philip *Alli Sup*
Anderson, Poul 1926- *ConAu 1R, WorAu,*
WrD 1976
Anderson, Poul 1936- *AmA&B*
Anderson, Quentin 1912- *ConAu 1R, REnAL*
Anderson, R *Alli, Alli Sup*
Anderson, R Alex 1894- *AmSCAP 66*
Anderson, R C *Alli Sup*
Anderson, Rachel *ConAu 21, WrD 1976*
Anderson, Ralph *Alli, BiDLA*
Anderson, Randall C 1934- *ConAu 41*
Anderson, Rasmus Bjorn 1846-1936 *Alli Sup,*
AmA&B, AmLY, BbD, BiD&SB,
DcAmA, DcNAA, WhWNAA, WiscW
Anderson, Richard *Alli Sup*
Anderson, Richard Clough 1872-1916 *DcNAA,*
OhA&B
Anderson, Richard Lloyd 1926- *ConAu 37,*
WrD 1976
Anderson, Richard Loree 1915- *IndAu 1917*
Anderson, Robert *Alli, Alli Sup, PoIre*
Anderson, Robert 1751?-1830? *Alli, ChPo S2,*
DcEnL
Anderson, Robert 1770-1833 *BiD&SB,*
BrAu 19, ChPo, ChPo S2, DcEnL, EvLB
Anderson, Robert 1805-1871 *Alli Sup, DcNAA*
Anderson, Robert 1841- *Alli Sup*
Anderson, Robert 1917- *AmA&B, AuNews 1,*
CnMD, ConAu 21, ConDr, CrCD,
McGWD, ModAL, ModWD, OxAm,
Pen Am, REn, REnAL, WorAu,
WrD 1976
Anderson, Robert E *Alli Sup*
Anderson, Robert Gordon 1881-1950 *AmA&B,*
CatA 1952, WhWNAA
Anderson, Robert H 1918- *ConAu 49*
Anderson, Robert L *ChPo S1*
Anderson, Robert Newton 1929- *ConAu 49*
Anderson, Robert Patrick *Alli Sup*
Anderson, Robert Phillips 1866- *WhWNAA*
Anderson, Robert Stuart Guthrie *ChPo S1*
Anderson, Robert T 1926- *ConAu 9R*
Anderson, Robert VanVleck 1884- *WhWNAA*
Anderson, Robert W 1926- *ConAu 17R*
Anderson, Rosa *WhLA*
Anderson, Ross Peter 1887- *WhWNAA*
Anderson, Roy 1905- *WhWNAA*
Anderson, Roy 1936- *ConAu 13R, WrD 1976*
Anderson, Roy Allan 1895- *ConAu 13R*
Anderson, Roy Claude 1931- *Au&Wr*
Anderson, Rudolph John 1879- *WhWNAA*
Anderson, Rudolph Martin 1876-1961 *OxCan,*
WhWNAA
Anderson, Rufus *Alli*
Anderson, Rufus 1796-1880 *Alli Sup, DcAmA,*
DcNAA
Anderson, Ruth Irene 1919- *AuBYP,*
ConAu 1R, WrD 1976
Anderson, S E 1943- *BlkAW*
Anderson, Samuel G 1854-1900 *OhA&B*
Anderson, Samuel H 1888- *WhWNAA*
Anderson, Sarah Marie L Marshall *ChPo S1*
Anderson, Scarvia 1926- *ConAu 41*
Anderson, Sherwood 1876-1941 *AmA&B,*
AmWr, AtlBL, CasWL, Chmbr 3,
CnDAL, CnMWL, ConAmA, ConAmL,
CyWA, DcLEnL, DcNAA, EncWL,
EvLB, LongC, ModAL, ModAL Sup,

OhA&B, OxAm, OxEng, Pen Am,
RAdv 1, REn, REnAL, TwCA,
TwCA Sup, TwCW, WebEAL, WhTwL,
WhWNAA
Anderson, Stanford 1934- *ConAu 25*
Anderson, Stanley Edwin 1900- *ConAu 1R*
Anderson, Stanley V 1928- *ConAu 21*
Anderson, T Diane *BlkAW*
Anderson, T S *Alli Sup*
Anderson, T W 1918- *ConAu 49*
Anderson, Tempest *Alli Sup*
Anderson, Theodore R 1927- *ConAu 41*
Anderson, Theophilus D *Alli Sup*
Anderson, Thomas *Alli, Alli Sup*
Anderson, Thomas 1819-1874 *Alli Sup*
Anderson, Thomas 1832-1870 *Alli Sup*
Anderson, Thomas 1929- *ConAu 1R*
Anderson, Thomas Carnegy *Alli Sup*
Anderson, Thomas Gordon Terry 1805-1856
ChPo
Anderson, Thomas M 1836-1917 *Alli Sup,*
DcNAA, OhA&B
Anderson, Thomas McCall *Alli Sup*
Anderson, Thomas Scott 1853- *Br&AmS*
Anderson, Tommy 1918- *ConAu 45*
Anderson, Totton J 1909- *ConAu 1R*
Anderson, Troyer Steele 1900-1948 *DcNAA*
Anderson, Verily 1915- *Au&Wr, ConAu 5R,*
WrD 1976
Anderson, Vernon Ellsworth 1908- *ConAu 1R,*
WrD 1976
Anderson, Violet Louise 1906- *ConP 1970*
Anderson, Virgila Antris 1899- *ConAu 1R*
Anderson, Virginia 1920- *ConAu 21,*
WrD 1976
Anderson, Vivienne 1916- *ConAu 17R,*
WrD 1976
Anderson, W *Alli, Au&Wr*
Anderson, W E 1875- *WhWNAA*
Anderson, W J *Alli, BbtC*
Anderson, Mrs. W J 1843-1868 *ChPo*
Anderson, W Monro *ChPo*
Anderson, W Theodore *PoIre*
Anderson, Waldron W *ChPo*
Anderson, Wallace Ludwig 1917- *ConAu 17R*
Anderson, Walter d1800 *Alli*
Anderson, Walter V 1903- *WhWNAA*
Anderson, Warren DeWitt 1920- *ConAu 17R*
Anderson, Warwick *MnBBF*
Anderson, Wayne Jeremy 1908- *ConAu 49*
Anderson, Wilbert Lee 1859-1915 *DcNAA*
Anderson, William *Alli, Alli Sup,*
BiDLA Sup, BlkAW, ChPo S1, PoIre
Anderson, William 1799?-1873 *Alli, Alli Sup*
Anderson, William 1805?-1866? *Alli Sup,*
ChPo S1, ChPo S2
Anderson, William 1842- *Alli Sup*
Anderson, William 1888- *AmA&B, MnnWr*
Anderson, William 1916- *AmSCAP 66*
Anderson, William A 1927- *LivBA*
Anderson, William Ashley *OxCan*
Anderson, William Brennan 1868-1940 *DcNAA*
Anderson, William Caldwell 1852-1910 *DcNAA*
Anderson, William Charles 1920- *ConAu 5R*
Anderson, William Davis 1938- *ConAu 33*
Anderson, William Francis Desnaux 1935-
Au&Wr
Anderson, William Franklin 1860- *WhWNAA*
Anderson, William G *Alli Sup*
Anderson, William Gibson 1874- *WhWNAA*
Anderson, William Gilbert 1860-1947 *DcNAA*
Anderson, William H 1905-1972 *ConAu 49*
Anderson, William Hugh 1874-1932 *ArizL*
Anderson, William James *Alli Sup*
Anderson, William James 1813-1873 *DcNAA*
Anderson, William Robert 1921- *ConAu 5R*
Anderson, William Scovil 1927- *ConAu 61*
Anderson, William T *Alli Sup*
Anderson, Wilton T 1916- *ConAu 17R*
Anderson, Winslow 1861?-1917 *DcNAA*
Anderson, Yarborough 1850- *Alli Sup*
Anderson-Imbert, Enrique 1910- *ConAu 17R*
Anderson Imbert, Julio 1910- *DcCLA*
Anderson-Scott, Natalie 1906- *Au&Wr*
Andersons, Edgars *ConAu XR*
Andersson, Charles John 1827-1867 *Alli Sup*
Andersson, Dan 1888-1920 *CasWL, ClDMEuL,*
Pen Eur

Andrews, John N *Alli Sup*
Andrews, John Richard *Alli Sup*
Andrews, John W *Alli Sup*
Andrews, John Williams 1898-1975 *AmA&B, ChPo, ChPo S1, ConAu 57*
Andrews, Joseph *Alli*
Andrews, Julie 1935- *ConAu 37, SmATA 7, WrD 1976*
Andrews, Justin 1902- *WhWNAA*
Andrews, Keith 1930- *ConAu 33*
Andrews, Kenneth R 1916- *ConAu 1R*
Andrews, Lancelot 1555-1626 *Alli*
Andrews, Launcelot Winchester 1856-1938 *DcAmA, DcNAA, WhWNAA*
Andrews, Laurie Wilfred 1919- *Au&Wr*
Andrews, Lilian Herbert *Alli Sup*
Andrews, Lincoln Clark 1867- *WhWNAA*
Andrews, Sir Linton 1886- *Au&Wr*
Andrews, Lorenzo Frank 1828-1915 *DcNAA*
Andrews, Loring d1805 *Alli*
Andrews, Lorrin 1795-1868 *Alli Sup, DcNAA*
Andrews, Lyman 1938- *ConAu 49, WrD 1976*
Andrews, M W *Alli, BiDLA*
Andrews, Mabel H *ChPo*
Andrews, Margaret E *ConAu 33*
Andrews, Margaret Lovell *ChPo S1*
Andrews, Marietta Minnegerode 1869-1931 *ChPo S1, ChPo, DcNAA*
Andrews, Mark 1875-1939 *AmSCAP 66*
Andrews, Mark Edwin 1903- *ConAu P-1*
Andrews, Marshall 1899?-1973 *ConAu 45*
Andrews, Martin Register 1842-1913 *DcNAA, OhA&B*
Andrews, Mary Evans *ConAu 5R*
Andrews, Mary H *Alli Sup*
Andrews, Mary Raymond Shipman 1865?-1936 *AmA&B, ChPo, ConAmL, DcNAA 1, JBA 1934, REnAL, TwCA, WhWNAA*
Andrews, Matthew Page 1879-1947 *AmA&B, AmLY, BiDSA, ChPo, DcNAA, WhWNAA*
Andrews, Matthew Thomas 1869-1939 *DcNAA*
Andrews, Mervyn *MnBBF*
Andrews, Michael F 1916- *ConAu 49*
Andrews, Miles Peter d1814 *BiDLA, BiDLA Sup*
Andrews, Peter 1931- *ConAu 17R*
Andrews, Peter Miles d1814 *Alli, DcEnL*
Andrews, Philip Walter Sawford 1914- *Au&Wr*
Andrews, R *Alli*
Andrews, Ralph Warren 1897- *ConAu 9R, WhPNW*
Andrews, Regina *BlkAW*
Andrews, Richard *Alli Sup, BiDLA*
Andrews, Robert D *AmA&B, ConAu XR*
Andrews, Robert Douglas 1908- *ConAu P-1*
Andrews, Robert Hardy 1903- *AmA&B, AmNov*
Andrews, Robert William 1846- *Alli Sup*
Andrews, Roy Chapman 1884-1960 *AmA&B, AuBYP, EvLB, REnAL, TwCA, TwCA Sup, WhWNAA*
Andrews, S *Alli, Alli Sup*
Andrews, S C *Alli Sup*
Andrews, Samuel *Alli Sup*
Andrews, Samuel d1901 *PoIre*
Andrews, Samuel James 1817-1906 *Alli Sup, DcAmA, DcNAA*
Andrews, Sidney 1837?-1880 *Alli Sup, DcAmA, DcNAA*
Andrews, Sirl *ChPo S2*
Andrews, Stanley 1894- *ConAu 45*
Andrews, Stephen Pearl 1812-1886 *Alli, Alli Sup, AmA, BbD, BiD&SB, BiDSA, ChPo S1, DcAmA, DcNAA, OxAm, REnAL*
Andrews, T *Alli*
Andrews, T Maud *ChPo S2*
Andrews, Thomas *Alli, Alli Sup, WhWNAA*
Andrews, Thomas Sheldon 1829-1891 *DcNAA*
Andrews, Tom 1863- *Br&AmS*
Andrews, W E *Alli*
Andrews, W S *Alli Sup*
Andrews, W T *ChPo S2*
Andrews, W W *Alli Sup*
Andrews, Wayne 1913- *AmA&B, ConAu 9R*
Andrews, William *Alli*
Andrews, William 1848-1908 *Alli Sup,*

ChPo S1, ChPo S2
Andrews, William A *Alli Sup*
Andrews, William D 1853-1903 *DcNAA*
Andrews, William G 1930- *ConAu 5R*
Andrews, William Given 1835-1912 *DcNAA*
Andrews, William Halstead 1913- *IndAu 1917*
Andrews, William Linton 1886- *ConAu 9R*
Andrews, William Loring 1837-1920 *AmA, AmA&B, DcNAA*
Andrews, William Page 1848-1916 *ChPo, ChPo S1, DcAmA, DcNAA*
Andrews, William R 1937- *ConAu 53*
Andrews, William Symes 1847-1929 *DcNAA*
Andreyev, Leonid Nikolayevich 1871-1919 *CasWL, ClDMEuL, CnMD, CnThe, CyWA, DcRusL, EncWL, EvEuW, LongC, McGWD, ModSL 1, Pen Eur, REn, REnWD, TwCA, TwCA Sup, TwCW*
Andreyev, Leonid ALSO Andreev, Leonid
Andreyevich *CasWL*
Andreyevsky, Sergey Arkadyevich 1847-1920? *CasWL, DcRusL*
Andrezel, Pierre *ConAu XR, LongC, Pen Eur, TwCA Sup*
Andrian-Werburg, Leopold, Freiherr Von 1875-1951 *ClDMEuL, OxGer*
Andric, Ivo 1892-1975 *Au&Wr, CasWL, ClDMEuL, ConAu 57, EncWL, EvEuW, ModSL 2, Pen Eur, REn, TwCW, WhTwL, WorAu*
Andriekus, Leonardas 1914- *ConAu 25*
Andrieu Contredit d1248 *CasWL*
Andrieux, Francois Jean Stanislas 1759-1833 *BbD, BiD&SB, EvEuW, OxFr*
Andrist, Ralph K 1914- *ConAu 9R*
Androcles *NewC, REn*
Androclus *NewC, REn*
Andronicus, Livius 284?BC-204?BC *BbD, BiD&SB*
Andros, Sir Edmund 1637-1714 *Alli, OxAm*
Andros, Richard Salter Storrs 1817-1868 *DcNAA*
Andros, Stephen Osgood 1876- *WhWNAA*
Andros, Thomas 1759-1845 *DcNAA*
Androse, R *Alli*
Androtion *Pen Cl*
Androzzo, Alma B 1912- *AmSCAP 66*
Andrus, Hyrum Leslie 1924- *ConAu 37, WrD 1976*
Andrus, Vera 1895- *ConAu 21*
Andruss, Harvey Adolphus 1902- *Au&Wr*
Andry, Laure *BiDSA*
Andrzejewski, Jerzy 1909- *CasWL, ConAu 25, EncWL, ModSL 2, Pen Eur, TwCW, WhTwL*
Andrzeyevski, George 1909- *ConAu XR, WorAu*
Anduze-Dufy, Raphael 1919- *ConAu XR*
Aneau, Barthelemy 1500?-1561? *CasWL, OxFr*
Aneirin *BrAu, CasWL, NewC, OxEng, Pen Eng*
Anelay, H *ChPo, ChPo S2*
Aneley, Samuel 1620?-1696 *Alli*
Aner, Karl August 1879- *WhLA*
Anesaki, Masaharu 1873- *WhLA*
Anet, Claude *TwCA, TwCA Sup*
Anethan, Baroness E Mary *WhLA*
Aneurin *BbD, BiD&SB, BrAu, DcEnL, NewC, OxEng*
Angas, George French *Alli, Alli Sup*
Angas, John *MnBBF*
Angel, Clara Louise *ChPo S1*
Angel, Daniel D 1939- *ConAu 33*
Angel, John *Alli*
Angel, John d1655 *Alli*
Angel, Marie 1923- *ChPo S1, ChPo S2, ConAu 29, IlBYP*
Angel, Moses *Alli Sup*
Angel, Myron 1827-1911 *DcNAA*
Angel, Rosa Evangeline d1895 *ChPo, DcNAA*
Angeles, Carlos A Filipino 1921- *ConP 1970, ConP 1975, WrD 1976*
Angeles, Jose 1930- *ConAu 33*
Angeles, Juan DeLos 1536?-1609 *CasWL, DcEuL, DcSpL*
Angeles, Peter A 1931- *ConAu 33*
Angeles, Philip 1909- *ConAu 5R*

Angeli, Marguerite De *JBA 1951*
Angeli, Pietro Angelo 1517-1596 *CasWL*
Angelic Doctor *DcEnL*
Angelico, Fra 1387?-1455 *AtlBL, REn*
Angelicus, Doctor *NewC*
Angelilli, Frank Joseph *ConAu XR*
Angelique DeSaint-Jean, LaMere *OxFr*
Angelique DeSainte-Madeleine, LaMere *OxFr*
Angell, Branford Bryan *ChPo*
Angell, Ernest 1889-1973 *ConAu 37, OhA&B*
Angell, Frank 1857- *WhWNAA*
Angell, Frank Joseph 1919- *ConAu 17R*
Angell, George Nelson 1887- *WhWNAA*
Angell, George Thorndike 1823-1909 *DcNAA*
Angell, H J *ChPo*
Angell, Henry *Alli Sup*
Angell, Henry Clay 1829-1911 *Alli Sup, DcAmA, DcNAA*
Angell, Hildegarde d1933 *DcNAA, OhA&B*
Angell, James 1915- *Au&Wr*
Angell, James Burrill 1829-1916 *Alli Sup, AmA&B, BbD, BiD&SB, CyAL 1, CyAL 2, DcAmA, DcNAA*
Angell, James Rowland 1869-1949 *AmA&B, DcNAA, WhWNAA*
Angell, James Waterhouse 1898- *AmA&B*
Angell, John *Alli, Alli Sup*
Angell, John d1655 *Alli*
Angell, Joseph K 1794-1857 *Alli, CyAL 1, DcAmA, DcNAA*
Angell, Lewis *Alli Sup*
Angell, Sir Norman 1874?-1967 *ConAu P-1, DcLEnL, EvLB, LongC, NewC, OxEng, TwCA, TwCA Sup, WhLA*
Angell, Oliver 1787-1858 *DcNAA*
Angell, Richard B 1918- *ConAu 13R*
Angell, Robert Cooley 1899- *AmA&B*
Angell, Roger 1920- *ConAu 5776, DrAF 1976*
Angell, Tony 1940- *ConAu 53*
Angell, Warren M 1907- *AmSCAP 66*
Angellier, Auguste 1848-1911 *OxFr*
Angellotti, Marion Polk *AmA&B, AmLY, WhWNAA*
Angelo, C A *Alli Sup*
Angelo, Frank 1914- *ConAu 53*
Angelo, Henry 1760-1839? *Alli, OxEng*
Angelo, Michel *BiD&SB*
Angelo, Nancy Carolyn Harrison 1928- *IndAu 1917*
Angelo, Valenti 1897- *AmA&B, AuBYP, BkC 6, CatA 1952, ChPo, IlCB 1945, IlCB 1956, IlCB 1966, JBA 1951*
Angelocci, Angelo 1926- *ConAu 23*
Angeloni, Battista *DcEnL*
Angelopolous, Angelo 1919?-1962 *IndAu 1917*
Angelou, Maya 1928- *BlkAW, DrAP 1975, LivBAA, WrD 1976*
Angelus Silesius 1624-1677 *BiD&SB, CasWL, DcEuL, EuA, EvEuW, OxGer, Pen Eur, PoCh, REn*
Angely, Louis 1787-1835 *BiD&SB, OxGer*
Angennes, Julie D' *OxFr*
Anger, Joseph Humfrey 1862-1913 *DcNAA*
Angermann, William G *ChPo*
Angermayer, Fred Antoine 1889- *WhLA*
Angers, Charles 1854-1929 *DcNAA*
Angers, F A *OxCan Sup*
Angers, Felicite 1845-1924 *CanWr, DcNAA, OxCan*
Angers, Francois Real 1813-1860 *BbtC, DcNAA*
Angers, Pierre *OxCan*
Angersbach, Adam Lorenz 1861- *WhLA*
Anghel, Dimitrie 1872-1914 *CasWL, ClDMEuL, EncWL, EvEuW*
Anghiera, Pietro Martire D' *CasWL, EvEuW, OxAm*
Angier, Lord *Alli*
Angier, Annie Lanman *Alli Sup*
Angier, Belle Sumner 1870- *WhWNAA*
Angier, Bradford *ConAu 5R*
Angier, John *Alli*
Angier, Samuel *Alli*
Angier, Vena And Bradford *OxCan*
Angilbert *Pen Eur*
Angioletti, Giovanni Battista 1896-1961 *CasWL*
Angiolieri, Cecco 1260?-1312? *CasWL, EvEuW*

Angle, Edward Hartley 1855-1930 *DcNAA*
Angle, Edward John 1864- *WhWNAA*
Angle, Paul McClelland 1900-1975 *AmA&B*,
ConAu 21, *ConAu 57*, *NewC*, *REnAL*,
TwCA Sup
Anglerius *CasWL*
Anglesey *Alli*
Anglesey, Arthur, Earl Of *Alli*
Anglesey, George C Paget, Marquess Of 1922-
Au&Wr, *ConAu XR*, *WrD 1976*
Angley, John Godfrey *PoIre*
Anglicus, Bartholomaeus *NewC*
Anglicus, Gilbertus *Alli*
Anglicus, Richard *Alli*
Anglin, Arthur Henry 1850- *WhLA*
Anglin, Douglas G 1923- *ConAu 37*,
WrD 1976
Anglin, Robert Alton 1910- *IndAu 1917*
Anglund, Joan Walsh 1926- *AmA&B*, *Au&Wr*,
AuBYP, *ChLR 1*, *ChPo S1*, *ChPo S2*,
ConAu 5R, *FamAI*, *IlCB 1966*,
SmATA 2, *ThBJA*
Angly, J Edward 1898- *TexWr*
Angoff, Allan 1910- *BiDPar*, *ConAu 45*
Angoff, Charles 1902- *AmA&B*, *Au&Wr*,
ConAu 5R, *DrAF 1976*, *DrAP 1975*,
REnAL, *WhWNAA*, *WrD 1976*
Angouleme, Duchesse De *OxFr*
Angove, Emily 1837- *Alli Sup*
Angove, Grace *Alli Sup*
Angress, Ruth K 1931- *ConAu 37*, *WrD 1976*
Angress, Werner T 1920- *ConAu 13R*
Angrist, Shirley S 1933- *ConAu 25*
Angrist, Stanley W 1933- *ConAu 25*,
SmATA 4
Angstadt, L Jean 1931- *BiDPar*
Anguish, Thomas *Alli*
Anguita, Eduardo 1914- *DcCLA*
Angus *DcNAA*
Angus, A D *OxCan*
Angus, Alfred Henry 1873- *WhLA*
Angus, Carl *WhWNAA*
Angus, Don *ChPo S1*
Angus, Douglas Ross 1909- *ConAu 1R*
Angus, Henry Forbes *OxCan*
Angus, Ian 1936- *ConAu XR*, *WrD 1976*
Angus, James *ChPo*
Angus, John Colin 1907- *WrD 1976*
Angus, Joseph 1816- *Alli*, *Alli Sup*
Angus, Margaret 1908- *ConAu 21*, *WrD 1976*
Angus, Marion 1866-1946 *CasWL*, *ChPo*,
ChPo S1, *ChPo S2*, *EvLB*, *Pen Eng*,
WhLA
Angus, Marion Isabel *WhWNAA*
Angus, Samuel 1881- *WhLA*
Angus, Sylvia 1921- *ConAu 61*
Angus, Tom *ConAu XR*
Angus, W *Alli*
Angus, William *Alli*, *BiDLA*
Angus, William Cargill 1870- *ChPo S1*
Angus-Butterworth, Lionel Milner 1900-
Au&Wr, *ConAu 53*, *WrD 1976*
Anhava, Tuomas 1927- *Pen Eur*
Anheisser, Roland 1877- *WhLA*
Anicet-Bourgeois, Auguste 1806-1871 *BiD&SB*
Anicetus *DcNAA*
Anichkov, Evgeny Vasilyevich 1866-1937
CasWL
Anis, Mir Babar 'Ali 1802-1874 *DcOrL 2*
Anjos, Augusto Dos 1884-1914 *Pen Am*
Ankenbrand, Frank, Jr. 1905- *ConAu 19*
Ankenbrand, Ludwig 1888- *WhLA*
Anker Larsen, Johannes 1874-1957 *CasWL*,
EvEuW, *Pen Eur*, *TwCA*, *TwCA Sup*,
REn
Anketell, John 1750?- *PoIre*
Anketell, John 1835- *PoIre*
Ankrom, Thelma Eileen 1931- *AmSCAP 66*
Anley, Miss *Alli*
Anmar, Frank *ConAu XR*
Ann Knish *WhWNAA*
Ann, Mother *REn*
Anna Amalia, Herzogin 1739-1807 *OxGer*
Anna Comnena 1083-1148? *CasWL*, *EuA*,
NewC, *OxEng*, *Pen Cl*, *REn*
Anna Matilda *NewC*
Annan, Lord 1916- *LongC*
Annan, Anne M F *ChPo S1*, *FemPA*

Annan, Annie R *ChPo*
Annan, Noel Gilroy 1916- *ConAu 61*, *WorAu*,
WrD 1976
Annan, William *Alli Sup*
Annand, A McKenzie 1905- *Au&Wr*
Annand, Alex *Alli*
Annand, Douglas 1903- *WhGrA*
Annand, James King 1908- *ChPo S2*,
WrD 1976
Annand, William 1633-1689 *Alli*
Annand, William 1808-1887 *BbtC*, *DcNAA*
Annandale, Charles *Alli Sup*
Annandale, Thomas 1838- *Alli Sup*
Annarino, John 1929- *AmSCAP 66*
Annaturai, C N 1909-1969 *DcOrL 2*
Anne 1665-1714 *NewC*
Anne Boleyn 1507?-1536 *NewC*, *REn*
Anne Bullen 1507?-1536 *NewC*
Anne D'Autriche 1602-1666 *OxFr*
Anne-Mariel *ConAu XR*
Anne Of Austria 1602-1666 *REn*
Anne Of Bohemia 1366-1394 *NewC*
Anne Of Cleves 1515-1557 *NewC*, *REn*
Anne Of Denmark 1574-1619 *NewC*
Annenkov, Pavel Vasilyevich 1812-1887 *CasWL*,
DcRusL
Annensky, Innokenty Fyodorovich 1856-1909
CasWL, *ClDMEuL*, *DcRusL*, *EncWL*,
EuA, *EvEuW*, *ModSL 1*, *Pen Eur*, *REn*
Annerson, James *Alli*
Annesley *Alli*
Annesley, Alexander *Alli*, *BiDLA*
Annesley, Arthur, Earl Of Anglesey 1614-1686
Alli
Annesley, Charles *Alli Sup*
Annesley, Sir Francis *Alli*
Annesley, George 1769-1844 *PoIre*
Annesley, Sir James *Alli*
Annesley, James 1715-1760 *NewC*
Annesley, Miss M *Alli Sup*
Annesley, Samuel 1620?-1696 *Alli*
Anneson, James *Alli*
Anness, Milford Edwin 1918- *ConAu 17R*,
IndAu 1917
Annet *Alli*
Annet, Peter *Alli*
Annett, Albert 1861- *ChPo*
Annett, Cora *AuBYP*, *ConAu XR*
Annett, John 1930- *ConAu 29*
Annette, Sister Mary *ConAu XR*
Anniceris *Pen Cl*
Annie Laurie *WhWNAA*
Annigoni, Pietro *Au&Wr*
Annixter, Jane *AuBYP*, *ConAu XR*,
SmATA 1
Annixter, Paul *ConAu XR*, *SmATA 1*
Anno, Saint 1010?-1075 *OxGer*
Anno, Mitsumasa 1920?- *ConAu 49*, *IlBYP*,
SmATA 5
Anno, Mitsumasa 1926- *ChLR 2*
Annunzio, Gabriele D' 1864?-1938 *BbD*,
BiD&SB, *CasWL*, *DcBiA*, *EuA*, *EvEuW*,
LongC, *ModRL*, *RCom*, *TwCA Sup*,
TwCW
Anobile, Richard J 1947- *ConAu 53*
Anoff, I S 1892- *ConAu 45*
Anon *Br&AmS*, *Pen Eur*
Anonyme De Bethune *OxFr*
Anonymous *WhWNAA*
Anouilh, Jean 1910- *Au&Wr*, *CasWL*, *CnMD*,
CnMWL, *CnThe*, *ConAu 17R*, *ConLC 1*,
ConLC 3, *CrCD*, *CyWA*, *EncWL*,
EvEuW, *LongC*, *McGWD*, *ModRL*,
ModWD, *OxEng*, *OxFr*, *Pen Eur*, *RCom*,
REn, *REnWD*, *TwCA Sup*, *TwCW*,
WhTwL
Anozie, Sunday Ogbonna 1942- *AfA 1*
Anquetil-Duperron, Abraham-Hyacinthe
1731-1805 *OxFr*
Anrooy, Frans Van *SmATA 2*
Ansari, Abd Allah *CasWL*
Ansari, Bayazid *DcOrL 3*
Ansari, Sheykh Ol-Eslam Abu Esma'il 'A
1006-1074 *DcOrL 3*
Ansbacher, Heinz L 1904- *ConAu P-1*
Ansberry, William F 1926- *ConAu 33*
Anschel, Eugene 1907- *ConAu 53*
Anschel, Kurt R 1936- *ConAu 41*

Anschutz, Everett LeRoy 1913- *TexWr*
Anschutz, Heinrich 1785-1865 *OxGer*
Ansel, Walter 1897- *ConAu 45*
Ansell, Charles d1795? *BkIE*
Ansell, George Frederick 1826-1880 *Alli Sup*
Ansell, Helen 1940- *ConAu 25*
Ansell, Jack 1925- *ConAu 17R*
Ansell, Michael 1905- *WrD 1976*
Anselm Of Aosta 1033-1109 *Pen Eng*
Anselm Of Canterbury *DcSpL*
Anselm, Saint 1033-1109 *Alli*, *BiB N*, *CasWL*,
DcEnL, *NewC*, *OxEng*
Anselm, Felix *ConAu XR*
Ansen, Alan 1922- *ConAu 1R*, *ConP 1970*
Anshen, Melvin Leon 1912- *AmA&B*
Anshutz, Edward Pollock 1846-1918 *DcNAA*,
OhA&B
Ansky, S 1863-1920 *CnMD*, *CnThe*, *McGWD*,
ModWD, *REnWD*
Ansley, Clarke Fisher 1869-1939 *AmA&B*,
DcNAA
Ansley, Gladys Piatt 1906- *ConAu 5R*
Anslijn, Nicolaas Nzn 1777-1838 *CasWL*
Anslinger, Harry Jacob 1892-1975 *ConAu 61*,
ConAu P-1
Anslo, Reimer 1622?-1669 *BiD&SB*
Anslo, Reyer 1626-1669 *CasWL*
Anslo, Roger 1626-1669 *DcEuL*
Anson, Augustus Henry Archibald 1835-1877
Alli Sup
Anson, Bill 1907- *AmSCAP 66*
Anson, Cyril J 1923- *ConAu 49*
Anson, George *AmSCAP 66*
Anson, Lord George 1697-1762 *Alli*, *DcEnL*
Anson, Jack Lee 1924- *IndAu 1917*
Anson, Peter Frederick 1889- *Au&Wr*, *BkC 2*,
CatA 1947, *ConAu 9R*, *WrD 1976*
Anson, Piers *MnBBF*
Anson, W S W *Alli Sup*, *ChPo S1*
Anson, Sir William Reynell 1843-1914 *Alli Sup*,
BrAu 19, *NewC*, *OxEng*
Ansorge, Sir Eric Cecil 1887- *Au&Wr*
Anspach, Elizabeth, Margravine Of 1750-1828
Alli, *BiD&SB*, *BiDLA*, *BiDLA Sup*
Anspach, Frederick Rinehart 1815?-1867 *Alli*,
BiD&SB, *BiDSA*, *DcAmA*, *DcNAA*
Anspach, J M *Alli Sup*
Anspach, Lewis A *Alli*, *BbtC*, *BiDLA*,
OxCan
Anspacher, Helen M *ChPo*
Anspacher, Louis Kaufman 1878-1947 *AmA&B*,
AmLY, *ChPo*, *DcNAA*, *OhA&B*,
REnAL, *WhWNAA*
Anspacher, Mrs. Louis Kaufman *ChPo S1*
Ansted, David Thomas 1814?-1880 *Alli*,
Alli Sup
Anster, John 1793-1867 *Alli*, *Alli Sup*,
CasWL, *ChPo*, *NewC*, *PoIre*
Anstey, Christopher 1724-1805 *Alli*, *BbD*,
BiD&SB, *BrAu*, *CasWL*, *ChPo*,
Chmbr 2, *DcEnL*, *DcLEnL*, *EvLB*,
NewC, *OxEng*, *Pen Eng*, *REn*, *WebEAL*
Anstey, Edgar 1917- *Au&Wr*, *ConAu 5R*,
WrD 1976
Anstey, F 1856-1934 *Alli Sup*, *BiD&SB*,
ChPo, *ChPo S2*, *ChPo S3*, *DcBiA*,
DcEnA Ap, *DcLEnL*, *EvLB*, *LongC*,
MnBBF, *ModBL*, *NewC*, *OxEng*, *REn*,
TwCA, *TwCA Sup*, *WhCL*
Anstey, Henry 1827- *Alli Sup*
Anstey, John *Alli*, *BiDLA*, *DcEnL*
Anstey, Roger T 1927- *ConAu 13R*
Anstey, Thomas Chisholm *Alli*, *Alli Sup*
Anstey, Vera 1889- *ConAu P-1*
Anstice, Henry 1841-1922 *DcNAA*
Anstice, Joseph 1808-1836 *PoCh*
Anstice, Robert *Alli*, *BiDLA*
Anstie, Francis Edmund 1833-1874 *Alli Sup*
Anstie, John *Alli*, *Alli Sup*, *BiDLA*
Anstis, John 1699-1745 *Alli*, *DcEnL*
Anstruther, Alexander *Alli*, *BiDLA*
Anstruther, B *Alli Sup*
Anstruther, George Elliot 1870-1940 *CatA 1947*,
WhLA
Anstruther, Godfrey 1903- *Au&Wr*
Anstruther, Sir John *Alli*
Anstruther, Joyce *LongC*
Anstruther, Mace *Alli Sup*

Anstruther, Sir W *Alli*
Antal *DcOrL 2*, *Pen Cl*
Antar 550?-615? *AfA 1*, *BbD*, *BiD&SB*,
CasWL
Antara *BbD*, *CasWL*
Antara B Shaddad *DcOrL 3*
Antarah, Ben Shedad El Absi d615? *BiD&SB*
Antarah, Obi 1943- *BlkAW*
Antcliffe, Herbert, Jr. 1875- *CatA 1947*
Antell, Gerson 1926- *ConAu 53*
Antepara, J M *BiDLA*
Antequera, Fernando De *DcSpL*
Antequera, Narvaez De *DcSpL*
Antes, J *Alli*
Antevs, Ernst Valdemar 1888- *WhWNAA*
Antheil, George 1900-1959 *AmSCAP 66*,
REnAL
Anthem, Chris *ChPo*
Anthes, Otto Wilhelm Johannes Eugen 1867-
WhLA
Antheunis, Gentil Theodoor 1840- *BiD&SB*
Anthon, Charles 1797-1867 *Alli*, *AmA*,
AmA&B, *BbD*, *BiD&SB*, *CyAL 1*,
DcAmA, *DcNAA*
Anthon, Charles Edward 1823-1883 *Alli*,
DcNAA
Anthon, Henry *Alli*
Anthon, John 1784-1863 *Alli*, *CyAL 2*,
DcAmA, *DcNAA*
Anthondyke, Harry *MnBBF*
Anthony Of Padua, Saint 1195-1231 *REn*
Anthony, Saint *REn*
Anthony, Mrs. A S *Alli Sup*
Anthony, Alfred Williams 1860-1939 *AmLY*,
DcAmA, *DcNAA*, *WhWNAA*
Anthony, Andrew Varick Stout 1835-1906
AmA&B, *ChPo*, *ChPo S2*, *EarAB*
Anthony, Barbara 1932- *Au&Wr*
Anthony, C L *Chmbr 3*, *ConAu XR*,
DcLEnL, *LongC*, *NewC*, *SmATA 4*,
WrD 1976
Anthony, Catherine *ConAu 49*
Anthony, Charles H *Alli Sup*
Anthony, Charles Hartshorn *Alli Sup*
Anthony, David *BlkAW*, *ConAu 49*
Anthony, E 1907- *Au&Wr*
Anthony, Earl *BlkAW*, *LivBA*
Anthony, Edward 1895-1971 *AmA&B*, *AuBYP*,
BkCL, *ChPo*, *ConAu 33*, *REnAL*
Anthony, Edwyn 1844- *Alli Sup*
Anthony, Elliot *Alli*
Anthony, Elliott 1827-1898 *DcNAA*
Anthony, Evelyn 1928- *Au&Wr*, *ConAu XR*,
WrD 1976
Anthony, Francis 1550-1623 *Alli*
Anthony, Frank S 1891-1925 *DcLEnL*, *TwCW*
Anthony, Gardner Chace 1856-1937 *DcNAA*
Anthony, Geraldine d1912 *DcNAA*
Anthony, Harold Elmer 1890- *WhWNAA*
Anthony, Henry Bowen 1815-1884 *Alli Sup*,
AmA&B, *DcNAA*
Anthony, Irvin 1890- *Au&Wr*, *WhWNAA*
Anthony, J Garner 1899- *ConAu 61*
Anthony, James R 1922- *ConAu 49*,
WrD 1976
Anthony, John *ConAu XR*
Anthony, John 1587-1655 *Alli*
Anthony, Joseph 1897- *AmA&B*, *ChPo*,
ChPo S1, *ChPo S2*
Anthony, Katharine Susan 1877-1965 *AmA&B*,
AmLY, *ChPo S2*, *ConAu 25*, *TwCA*,
TwCA Sup, *WhWNAA*
Anthony, Luther B 1876- *AmLY*, *WhWNAA*
Anthony, Mother Mary *ConAu XR*
Anthony, Mary Borden 1864-1947 *DcNAA*
Anthony, Matilda *Alli Sup*
Anthony, Michael 1932- *Au&Wr*, *CasWL*,
ConAu 17R, *ConNov 1972*, *ConNov 1976*,
LongC, *WebEAL*, *WrD 1976*
Anthony, Paul *BlkAW*
Anthony, Peter 1929- *Au&Wr*, *WrD 1976*
Anthony, Piers 1934- *AmA&B*, *Au&Wr*,
ConAu XR, *WrD 1976*
Anthony, Robert N 1916- *ConAu 13R*
Anthony, Roy David 1884- *WhWNAA*
Anthony, Susan Brownell 1820-1906 *BbD*,
DcNAA, *OxAm*, *REn*
Anthony, Susanna 1726-1791 *Alli*, *DcNAA*

Anthony, W B *Alli Sup*
Anthony, William Arnold 1835-1908 *DcNAA*
Anthony, William G 1934- *ConAu 17R*
Anthrops *DcNAA*
Anticaglia, Elizabeth 1939- *ConAu 45*
Antico, John 1924- *ConAu 29*
Antier, Benjamin *OxFr*
Antikainen, Kosti Aukusti 1930- *WhGrA*
Antill, Ed *Alli*
Antill, James Macquarie 1912- *ConAu 33*,
WrD 1976
Antillano, El *PueRA*
Antilon 1722-1797 *AmA*
Antimachus *BbD*, *BiD&SB*, *CasWL*, *Pen Cl*
Antin, David 1932- *ConP 1970*, *DrAF 1976*,
DrAP 1975
Antin, Esther *ChPo S1*
Antin, Louis-Antoine, Duc D' 1665-1736 *OxFr*
Antin, Mary 1881-1949 *AmA&B*, *DcAmA*,
DcNAA, *OxAm*, *REn*, *TwCA*,
TwCA Sup, *WhWNAA*
Antinous *NewC*
Antipater *Pen Cl*
Antipater Of Sidon *BiD&SB*, *CasWL*
Antiphanes 408?BC-334?BC *CasWL*
Antiphon 480?BC-411BC *CasWL*, *Pen Cl*,
REn
Antiphon Of Athens *CasWL*
Antiquary, The 1809-1865 *AmA*
Antisell, Thomas 1817-1893 *Alli*, *Alli Sup*,
DcNAA
Antisthenes Of Athens 443?BC-366?BC *CasWL*,
NewC, *Pen Cl*
Antliff, William *ChPo S2*
Antoine De La Salle 1398?-1461? *DcEuL*
Antoine, Andre 1858-1943 *CIDMEuL*, *LongC*,
OxFr, *REn*
Antoine-Dariaux, Genevieve 1914- *ConAu 57*
Antoinette, Marie *REn*
Antokol'sky, Pavel Grigoryevich 1896- *CasWL*,
EvEuW, *Pen Eur*
Anton Ulrich, Duke Of Brunswick 1633-1714
BiD&SB, *CasWL*, *EuA*
Anton Ulrich, Herzog Von Braunschweig
1633-1714 *OxGer*
Anton, Frank Robert 1920- *ConAu 41*
Anton, John P 1920- *ConAu 21*
Anton, Michael J 1940- *ConAu 57*
Anton, Peter *Alli Sup*
Anton, Rita 1920- *ConAu 9R*
Anton, Robert *Alli*
Antona-Traversi, Camillo 1857-1934 *BiD&SB*,
McGWD
Antona-Traversi Grismondi, Giannino 1860-1939
McGWD
Antonacci, Robert J 1916- *ConAu 5R*
Antoncich, Betty 1913- *AuBYP*, *ConAu 13R*
Antonelli, Luigi 1882-1942 *EncWL*, *McGWD*
Antonello Da Messina 1430?-1479 *AtlBL*, *REn*
Antoni *ConAu 49*
Antonia *WhWNAA*
Antonick, Robert J 1939- *ConAu 37*
Antonides, Joannes *CasWL*, *DcEuL*
Antonides VanDerGoes, Joannes 1647-1684 *BbD*,
BiD&SB
Antoninus, Brother 1912- *ConAu XR*,
ConLC 1, *ConP 1970*, *ConP 1975*,
OxAm, *Pen Am*, *WorAu*, *WrD 1976*
Antoninus Pius 086-161 *NewC*
Antoninus, Marcus Aurelius *BiD&SB*, *DcEnL*
Antonio Da Ferrara *CasWL*
Antonio, Mario 1934- *AfA 1*
Antonio, Nicolas 1617-1684 *CasWL*, *DcEuL*
Antonius, Marcus 143BC-087BC *Pen Cl*
Antoniutti, Ildebrando 1898-1974 *ConAu 53*
Antonovsky, Aaron 1923- *ConAu 29*
Antony, Jonquil 1916- *Au&Wr*, *ConAu 13R*
Antony, Marc 082?BC-030BC *REn*
Antony, Peter 1926- *ConAu XR*, *EncM&D*
Antonych, Bohdan Ihor 1909-1937 *ModSL 2*
Antrim, Doron Kemp 1889- *OhA&B*
Antrim, Ernest Irving 1869-1953 *OhA&B*,
WhWNAA
Antrim, George Doyle 1867-1958 *OhA&B*
Antrim, Harry T 1936- *ConAu 33*
Antrim, Joshua 1820?- *OhA&B*
Antrim, Minna Thomas 1861- *AmA&B*
Antrobus, Augustus M 1839- *DcNAA*

Antrobus, Benjamin *Alli*
Antrobus, E C *Alli Sup*
Antrobus, Frederick Ignatius *Alli Sup*
Antrobus, John *Alli*, *Alli Sup*
Antrobus, John 1831- *ChPo*
Antrobus, John 1933- *ConAu 57*, *ConDr*,
WrD 1976
Antrobus, R *Alli*
Antrobus, Suzanne *BiDSA*, *DcAmA*
Antrobus, Thomas *Alli*
Antschel, Paul *OxGer*, *WorAu*
Anttila, Raimo 1935- *ConAu 33*
Antupit, Louis 1896- *WhWNAA*
Anvari, Auhad-Al-Din 'Ali d1191? *CasWL*
Anvari, Ouhadoddin 'Ali B Vahidoddin M
1126?-1189? *DcOrL 3*
Anvers, Alicia D' *Alli*
Anvers, Caleb D' *Alli*
Anvers, Henry D' *Alli*
Anvers, K D' *Alli*
Anville, J-B-L-F-De-R DeLaR, Duc D'
1709-1746 *OxCan*
Anwar *DcOrL 2*
Anwar, Chairil 1922-1949 *DcOrL 2*
Anwick *Alli*
Anwyl, John Bodvan 1875- *WhLA*
Anwyl-Davies, Thomas *Au&Wr*
Anyan, T *Alli*
Anyon, G Jay 1909- *ConAu 5R*
Anza, Juan Bautista De 1735-1788 *OxAm*,
REnAL
Anzengruber, Ludwig 1839-1889 *BbD*,
BiD&SB, *CasWL*, *CIDMEuL*, *EuA*,
EvEuW, *McGWD*, *OxGer*, *Pen Eur*,
REn, *REnWD*
Anzer, Richard C *OxCan*
Aoki, Haruo 1930- *ConAu 49*
Apaque, L H *Alli Sup*
Apel, Johann August 1771-1816 *BiD&SB*,
OxGer
Apel, Paul 1872-1946 *OxGer*, *WhLA*
Apel, Willi 1893- *AmA&B*, *Au&Wr*,
ConAu 1R, *REnAL*
Apelfeld, Aharon 1932- *CasWL*
Apelian, Albert S 1893- *WhWNAA*
Apelles *NewC*
Apelt, Otto 1845- *WhLA*
Apes, William 1798- *AmA*, *AmA&B*, *BiDSA*,
DcNAA, *OxAm*, *REnAL*
Apgar, Austin Craig 1838-1908 *DcAmA*,
DcNAA
Apgar, Catherine H *ChPo S1*
Apgar, Ellis A d1905 *DcNAA*
Apgar, Virginia 1909-1974 *ConAu 53*
Apgeorge, George *Alli Sup*
Aphthonius *CasWL*
Apicius, Marcus Flavius *REn*
Apicius, Marcus Gavius *CasWL*
Apilado, Tony *IlBYP*
Apilentz *WhWNAA*
Apin, Rivai 1927- *DcOrL 2*
Apion d048 *AnCL*
Apitz, Bruno 1900- *CasWL*
Apjohn, A *Alli Sup*
Apjohn, Lewis *Alli Sup*
Apletre, J *Alli*
Apley, George *REnAL*
Apley, John 1908- *Au&Wr*, *WrD 1976*
Apolinar, Danny 1934- *ConAu 61*
Apollinaire, Guillaume 1880-1918 *AtlBL*,
CasWL, *CIDMEuL*, *CnMD*, *CnMWL*,
EncWL, *EvEuW*, *LongC*, *McGWD*,
ModRL, *ModWD*, *OxEng*, *OxFr*,
Pen Eur, *RCom*, *REn*, *REnWD*, *TwCA*,
TwCA Sup, *TwCW*, *WhTwL*
Apollodorus *REn*
Apollodorus Of Carystus *CasWL*, *Pen Cl*
Apollodorus Of Gela *CasWL*, *Pen Cl*
Apollon, Gerald *BlkAW*
Apolloni, Livio 1904- *WhGrA*
Apollonios Tyanaios *REn*
Apollonius Of Rhodes 295?BC-230?BC *REn*,
BiD&SB, *RCom*
Apollonius Of Tyana *Pen Cl*, *REn*
Apollonius Rhodius 295?BC-230?BC *CasWL*,
DcEnL, *NewC*, *OxEng*, *Pen Cl*
Apostata *OxGer*
Apostle, Chris N 1935- *ConAu 21*

Apostle Of The Indies *DcSpL*

Apostolius, Michael 1422-1480 *REn*

App, Austin Joseph 1902- *AmA&B*, *BkC 5*, *CatA 1952*, *WrD 1976*

App, Frank 1886- *WhWNAA*

Appach, Francis Hobson 1827- *Alli Sup*

Appar *DcOrL 2*, *Pen Cl*

Apparaw, Gurajtada Wenkata 1862-1915 *DcOrL 2*

Appareti, Luigi 1924- *AmSCAP 66*

Appel, Benjamin 1907- *AmA&B*, *AmNov*, *ConAu 13R*, *DcLEnL*, *OxAm*, *TwCA*, *TwCA Sup*

Appel, Carl 1857- *WhLA*

Appel, David *AuBYP*

Appel, John J 1921- *ConAu 33*

Appel, Joseph Herbert 1873-1949 *AmA&B*, *WhWNAA*

Appel, Kenneth E 1896- *WhWNAA*

Appel, Theodore 1823-1907 *Alli Sup*, *DcAmA*, *DcNAA*

Appel, Theodore Burton 1871-1937 *DcNAA*

Appelbee, A S *MnBBF*

Appelfeld, Aharon *CasWL*

Appelius, J *Alli*

Appelius, David 1922- *AmSCAP 66*

Appell, Don *ConDr*

Appell, Johann Wilhelm *Alli Sup*

Appelman, Hyman 1902- *ConAu 5R*

Appelmans, Gheraert *CasWL*

Apperley *Alli*

Apperley, Mister *BiDLA*

Apperley, Charles James 1777?-1843 *Alli*, *Br&AmS*, *BrAu 19*, *DcEnL*, *NewC 19*, *OxEng*

Apperley, Newton Wynne 1846-1925 *Br&AmS*

Apperley, T *Alli*

Apperson, George Latimer 1857- *WhLA*

Appiah, Peggy 1921- *Au&Wr*, *ConAu 41*, *WrD 1976*

Appian *CasWL*, *DcEnL*, *OxEng*, *Pen Cl*

Appignanesi, Lisa 1946- *ConAu 49*

Appius *DcEnL*

Appius Claudius *REn*

Applbaum, Ronald L 1943- *ConAu 57*

Apple, Joseph Henry 1865- *WhWNAA*

Apple, Max *DrAF 1976*

Applebaum, Stanley 1922- *AmSCAP 66*, *ChPo S2*

Applebaum, Stella Balaban 1897- *WhWNAA*

Applebaum, William 1906- *ConAu 9R*, *WrD 1976*

Appleby, C J *Alli Sup*

Appleby, John *Alli*

Appleby, John T 1909?-1974 *ConAu 53*

Appleby, Jon 1948- *ConAu 33*

Appleby, Thomas *Alli Sup*

Applegarth, H *Alli*

Applegarth, Margaret Tyson 1886- *AmA&B*, *WhWNAA*

Applegarth, Robert *Alli*, *BiDLA*

Applegate, Albert Angelo 1889- *WhWNAA*

Applegate, Frank Guy 1882-1932? *AmA&B*, *DcNAA*, *WhWNAA*

Applegate, George *HsB&A*, *HsB&A Sup*

Applegate, James 1923- *ConAu 33*, *WrD 1976*

Applegate, Jesse 1811-1888 *AmA&B*, *DcNAA*

Applegate, John Stilwell 1837-1916 *DcNAA*

Appleman, Charles Orville 1878- *WhWNAA*

Appleman, John Alan 1912- *AmA&B*, *ConAu 5R*

Appleman, Mark J 1917- *ConAu 29*

Appleman, Philip 1926- *ConAu 13R*, *DrAF 1976*, *DrAP 1975*, *IndAu 1917*, *WrD 1976*

Appleman, Roy Edgar 1904- *ConAu P-1*

Appler, A *Alli Sup*

Appler, Augustus C *Alli Sup*

Appleseed, Johnny 1774-1845 *AmA&B*, *OxAm*, *REn*, *REnAL*

Appleton, Anna E *Alli Sup*

Appleton, Arthur 1913- *Au&Wr*, *WrD 1976*

Appleton, Cecil *MnBBF*

Appleton, Charles Edward Cutts Birchall 1841-1879 *Alli Sup*

Appleton, Daniel 1785-1849 *AmA&B*

Appleton, Edward Victor 1892- *WhLA*

Appleton, Elizabeth Haven 1815-1890 *Alli*,

Alli Sup, *BiDLA Sup*, *DcNAA*, *OhA&B*

Appleton, Emily *AmA&B*

Appleton, Everard Jack 1872-1931 *ChPo*, *ChPo S1*, *DcNAA*, *OhA&B*

Appleton, Floyd 1871- *WhWNAA*

Appleton, G Webb *Alli Sup*

Appleton, George Washington 1805-1831 *EarAB Sup*

Appleton, Honor C *ChPo*, *ChPo S1*

Appleton, J W *Alli Sup*

Appleton, James Henry 1919- *ConAu 5R*

Appleton, Jesse 1772-1819 *Alli*, *CyAL 1*, *DcAmA*, *DcNAA*

Appleton, John *Alli*, *Alli Sup*, *WhWNAA*

Appleton, John 1804-1891 *DcAmA*, *DcNAA*

Appleton, John Hoblyn And Sayce, A H *Alli Sup*

Appleton, John Howard 1844-1930 *Alli Sup*, *DcAmA*, *DcNAA*

Appleton, John Reed And Jones, Morris C *Alli Sup*

Appleton, Lewis *Alli Sup*

Appleton, Lilla Estelle 1858-1937 *DcNAA*, *WhWNAA*

Appleton, Lydia Ann *BbtC*

Appleton, Nathan 1779-1861 *Alli Sup*, *DcNAA*

Appleton, Nathan 1843-1906 *DcNAA*

Appleton, Nathaniel 1693-1784 *Alli*, *DcNAA*

Appleton, Richard *Alli Sup*

Appleton, Sally *ChPo S1*

Appleton, Sarah *ConAu XR*, *DrAP 1975*

Appleton, Sheldon Lee 1933- *ConAu 1R*, *WrD 1976*

Appleton, Thomas E *OxCan Sup*

Appleton, Thomas Gold 1812-1884 *Alli Sup*, *AmA*, *AmA&B*, *BiD&SB*, *DcAmA*, *DcNAA*, *OxAm*, *REnAL*

Appleton, Victor *AmA&B*, *ConAu 19*, *SmATA 1*

Appleton, Victor, II *AmA&B*, *ConAu 17R*, *SmATA 1*

Appleton, William Henry 1814-1899 *AmA&B*

Appleton, William Hyde 1842-1926 *DcNAA*

Appleton, William Sumner 1840-1903 *Alli Sup*, *DcNAA*

Appleton, William Worthen 1845-1924 *AmA&B*

Applewhite, James W *DrAP 1975*

Appley, M H 1921- *ConAu 13R*

Appleyard, Charles *Alli Sup*

Appleyard, Dev *IlBYP*

Appleyard, Donald 1928- *ConAu 5R*

Appleyard, Ernest Silvanus *Alli Sup*

Appleyard, Jose-Luis 1927- *DcCLA*

Appleyard, Reginald Thomas 1927- *ConAu 17R*

Applezweig, M H *ConAu XR*

Applin, Arthur G T 1883-1948? *MnBBF*

Appolonius Dyscolus *CasWL*

Appreece *Alli*

Apps, Edwin 1931- *Au&Wr*

Apps, Jerold W 1934- *ConAu 49*

Apps, Jerry *ConAu 49*

Appuleius, Lucius *NewC*

Aprhys, R *Alli Sup*

Aprilov, Vassil 1789-1847 *CasWL*

Aprily, Lajos 1887-1967 *Pen Eur*

Apronti, Jawa 1940- *AfA 1*

Apsey, Ruby Lloyd 1881- *WhWNAA*

Apsler, Alfred 1907- *ConAu 5R*, *SmATA 10*, *WhPNW*, *WrD 1976*

Apsley, Lady 1897- *Br&AmS*

Apsley, Sir Allen *Alli*

Apt, Leon 1929- *ConAu 53*

Apte, Hari Narayan 1864-1919 *CasWL*, *DcOrL 2*

Apted, M R 1919- *ConAu 25*

Apter, David Ernest 1924- *ConAu 1R*, *WrD 1976*

Apter, Michael John 1939- *Au&Wr*, *ConAu 29*, *WrD 1976*

Aptheker, Bettina 1944- *ConAu 29*, *WrD 1976*

Aptheker, Herbert 1915- *AmA&B*, *ConAu 5R*

Apthomas, Ifan 1917- *Au&Wr*, *WrD 1976*

Apthorp, East 1832?-1816 *Alli*, *BiDLA*

Apthorp, George Frederick *Alli Sup*

Apthorp, William Foster 1848-1913 *Alli Sup*, *AmA*, *AmA&B*, *BiD&SB*, *DcAmA*,

---

DcNAA

Apthorpe, East 1733-1816 *CyAL 1*

Aptorp, East 1732-1816 *Alli*

Apukhtin, Alexey Nikolayevich 1841-1893 *ClDMEuL*, *CasWL*, *DcRusL*

Apuleius, Lucius 125?-175? *AtlBL*, *BbD*, *BiD&SB*, *CasWL*, *CyWA*, *DcEnL*, *NewC*, *OxEng*, *RCom*, *Pen Cl*, *REn*

Aql, Sa'id 1912- *DcOrL 3*

Aqqad, 'Abbas Mahmud Al- 1889-1964 *CasWL*, *DcRusL 3*

Aquilano, Serafino 1466-1500 *CasWL*

Aquin, Hubert 1929- *CanWr*, *CasWL*, *OxCan*, *OxCan Sup*

Aquina, Sister Mary *ConAu XR*

Aquinas, Sister Mary *WrD 1976*

Aquinas, Thomas, Saint 1225?-1274 *BbD*, *BiD&SB*, *CasWL*, *CyWA*, *DcEuL*, *EuA*, *EvEuW*, *NewC*, *OxEng*, *OxFr*, *Pen Eur*, *RCom*, *REn*

Aquino, Rinaldo D' *Pen Eur*

A'Rabbit, Shamus *ChPo S1*

Arago, Dominique Francois 1786-1853 *BbD*, *BiD&SB*

Arago, Etienne Vincent 1802-1892 *BiD&SB*

Arago, Francois 1786-1853 *OxFr*

Arago, Jacques Etienne 1790-1855 *BbD*, *BiD&SB*

Aragon, Agustin 1870- *AmLY*

Aragon, Louis 1897- *CasWL*, *ClDMEuL*, *ConLC 3*, *EncWL*, *EvEuW*, *LongC*, *ModRL*, *ModWD*, *OxEng*, *OxFr*, *Pen Eur*, *REn*, *TwCA*, *TwCA Sup*, *TwCW*, *WhTwL*

Aragona, Tullia D' 1508-1556 *CasWL*

Aragvispireli, Shio 1867-1926 *DcOrL 3*

Araki, James Tomomasa 1925- *ConAu 13R*, *WrD 1976*

Arakida, Moritake 1473-1549 *CasWL*, *DcOrL 1*

Aram, Eugene d1759 *NewC*

Aramis *PueRA*

Arana, Felipe N 1902-1963 *PueRA*

Arana Soto, Salvador 1908- *PueRA*

Araneta, Gregorio *WhWNAA*

Araneta, Salvador 1902- *WhWNAA*

Arango, Abel Villegas 1893- *WhWNAA*

Arango, Jorge Sanin 1916- *ConAu 61*

Aranha, Jose Pereira DaGraca 1868-1931 *Pen Am*, *REn*

Aranha, Ray 1939- *BlkAW*

Aranow, Edward Ross 1909- *ConAu 41*

Arany, Janos 1817-1882 *BbD*, *BiD&SB*, *CasWL*, *ClDMEuL*, *EuA*, *EvEuW*, *Pen Eur*

Arany, Laszlo 1844- *BiD&SB*

Aranzadi Y Unamuno, Telesforo De 1860- *WhLA*

Arapoff, Nancy 1930- *ConAu 29*

Arason, Bishop Jon 1484?-1550 *CasWL*, *EuA*, *EvEuW*

Arason, Steingrimur *AuBYP*

Arator *CasWL*, *Pen Eur*

Aratus 315?BC-240BC *BiD&SB*, *CasWL*, *Pen Cl*

Araujo Porto-Alegre, Manoel De 1806-1879 *BbD*, *BiD&SB*

Arbasino, Alberto 1930- *WorAu*

Arbaud, Joseph D' 1874- *ClDMEuL*, *REn*

Arbaugh, George Bartholomew 1905- *AmA&B*, *IndAu 1917*

Arbeely, Abraham Joseph 1852- *DcAmA*

Arbeiter, Petronius *WhWNAA*

Arber, Agnes 1879- *WhLA*

Arber, Edward 1836-1912 *Alli Sup*, *BrAu 19*, *ChPo*, *Chmbr 3*, *DcEuL*, *LongC*, *NewC*, *OxEng*, *REn*

Arberg, Peter, Graf Von *OxGer*

Arberry, Arthur J 1905- *ConAu 1R*, *ConP 1970*

Arbes, Jan Jakub 1840-1914 *CasWL*, *EvEuW*

Arbib, Robert 1915- *ConAu 33*

Arbib-Costa, Alfonso 1869- *WhWNAA*

Arbingast, Stanley A 1910- *ConAu 17R*

Arblastier, William *NewC*

Arblay, Madame D' *BiD&SB*, *BrAu 19*, *DcEnL*, *NewC*

Arbois DeJubainville, Henri D' 1827- *BiD&SB*

Arboleda, Julio 1817-1862? *BbD, BiD&SB, CasWL*

Arbouin, James *Alli Sup*

Arbrams, Mark 1906- *WrD 1976*

Arbuckle, Dorothy Fry 1910- *AmSCAP 66, IndAu 1917*

Arbuckle, Dugald S 1912- *ConAu 13R*

Arbuckle, Howard Bell 1870- *WhWNAA*

Arbuckle, James 1700-1746? *Alli, DcEnL, PoIre*

Arbuckle, Mary *TexWr*

Arbuckle, May Adams Dayton 1885-1964 *IndAu 1917*

Arbuckle, Robert D 1940- *ConAu 61*

Arbuckle, Wanda Rector 1910- *ConAu 41*

Arbuckle, Wendell Sherwood 1911- *IndAu 1917*

Arbusov, Alexey Nikolayevitch 1908- *CnMD*

Arbuthnot, Alexander 1538-1583? *Alli, DcEnL, NewC*

Arbuthnot, Sir Alexander John 1822- *Alli Sup*

Arbuthnot, Arch *Alli*

Arbuthnot, F F *Alli Sup*

Arbuthnot, George *Alli Sup*

Arbuthnot, James *Alli Sup*

Arbuthnot, John 1667-1735 *Alli, BbD, BiD&SB, BrAu, CasWL, Chmbr 2, DcEnA, DcEnL, DcLEnL, EvLB, NewC, OxEng, Pen Eng, REn Eng, WebEAL*

Arbuthnot, May Hill 1884-1969 *AuBYP, ChPo, ChPo S2, ConAu 9R, OhA&B, SmATA 2*

Arbuthnott, Mrs. Elrington *Alli Sup*

Arbuzov, Alexey Nikolayevich 1908- *CasWL, CnThe, McGWD, ModWD, Pen Eur*

Arc, Joan Of *NewC*

Arcadelt, Jakob 1505?-1571? *AtlBL*

Arcand, Adrien *OxCan*

Arce, Juan De *DcSpL*

Arce DeVazquez, Margot 1904- *DcCLA, PueRA*

Arcellana, Francisco 1916- *DcOrL 2*

Arceneaux, Thelma Hoffmann Tyler *AuNews 1*

Arcesilaus *Pen Cl*

Arch, E L *ConAu 49*

Archambault, Anna Margaretta *WhWNAA*

Archambault, Germain *OxCan Sup*

Archambault, Gilles *OxCan Sup*

Archambault, J P *OxCan Sup*

Archambault, Joseph Louis 1849-1925 *DcNAA*

Archambault, Louis Misael 1812-1894 *DcNAA*

Archard *Alli, BiDLA*

Archard, George *WrD 1976*

Archbold, Ann 1820?- *OhA&B*

Archbold, J F *Alli, BiDLA*

Archbold, John *Alli, BbtC*

Archbold, Thomas E *PoIre*

Archdale, John *Alli, BiDSA, CyAL 1*

Archdall, Mervyn 1723-1791 *Alli*

Archdeacon, Matthew 1800?-1853? *PoIre*

Archdeacon, Matthew 1843- *PoIre*

Archdeacon, Spencer *ChPo*

Archdekin, Richard 1619-1690? *Alli*

Archenholz, Johann Wilhelm Von 1743-1812 *BiD&SB, OxGer*

Archer, Major *Alli*

Archer, A *Alli*

Archer, A A *ConAu XR*

Archer, Benjamin Edgar 1898- *WhWNAA*

Archer, Branch T 1790-1856 *BiDSA*

Archer, C *Alli*

Archer, C P *Alli*

Archer, Clement *BiDLA*

Archer, E *Alli*

Archer, E M *Alli Sup*

Archer, E Margaret DuP *ChPo*

Archer, E Tracey *ChPo, ChPo S1*

Archer, Edmond *Alli*

Archer, Edward 1816- *Alli Sup*

Archer, Edward W *HsB&A*

Archer, Faye Bishop *TexWr*

Archer, Frank *ConAu XR*

Archer, Fred 1915- *ConAu 57, WrD 1976*

Archer, Fred C 1916?-1974 *ConAu 53*

Archer, Frederic 1838-1901 *DcAmA*

Archer, G W *BiDSA*

Archer, George W *Alli Sup*

Archer, George Washington d1907 *DcNAA*

Archer, Gladys Merritt *ChPo*

Archer, Gleason Leonard 1916- *WrD 1976*

Archer, H Richard 1911- *ConAu 13R*

Archer, Hannah *Alli Sup*

Archer, Harry 1888-1960 *AmSCAP 66*

Archer, Henry Playsted *PoIre*

Archer, Isabel *REnAL*

Archer, J W *ChPo*

Archer, James *Alli, BiDLA*

Archer, James Henry Laurence d1889 *Alli Sup*

Archer, Jean C *ChPo S1*

Archer, John *Alli, OxCan Sup*

Archer, John Clark 1881- *WhWNAA*

Archer, Joseph *Alli, BiDLA*

Archer, Jules 1915- *AuBYP, ConAu 9R, SmATA 4*

Archer, Kate Rennie *ChPo S2*

Archer, L A *Alli Sup*

Archer, Lane *AmA&B, DcNAA, WhWNAA*

Archer, Lou Ella 1891- *ArizL*

Archer, Mrs. M A *ChPo*

Archer, Marion Fuller 1917- *ConAu 5R*

Archer, Mark *Alli Sup*

Archer, Peter Kingsley 1926- *ConAu 5R, WrD 1976*

Archer, Peter Kingsley 1928- *Au&Wr*

Archer, Richard *Alli Sup*

Archer, Richard Lawrence 1874- *WhLA*

Archer, Ron *ConAu XR*

Archer, Ruby Cole *ChPo S2, TexWr*

Archer, S E *ConAu XR*

Archer, Sara F *ChPo*

Archer, Sellers G 1908- *ConAu 17R*

Archer, Sir Simon 1581- *Alli*

Archer, Stephen H 1928- *ConAu 17R*

Archer, Thomas *Alli Sup, BiD&SB, DcEnL*

Archer, Thomas 1830-1893 *Alli Sup, ChPo*

Archer, Thomas Croxen *Alli, Alli Sup*

Archer, W G 1907- *ConAu 57*

Archer, W N *Alli*

Archer, William *ChPo S1, Chmbr 3*

Archer, William d1874 *PoIre*

Archer, William 1843- *ChPo*

Archer, William 1856-1924 *Alli Sup, BiD&SB, CasWL, ChPo, CnMD, DcEnA, DcEnA Ap, DcLEnL, EvLB, LongC, ModBL, ModWD, NewC, OxEng, Pen Eng, TwCA, WebEAL*

Archer, William Clifford 1876-1950 *OhA&B*

Archer, William Henry *Alli Sup*

Archer Houblon, Doreen 1899- *Au&Wr*

Archibald, A K *BbtC*

Archibald, Sir Adams George 1814-1892 *OxCan*

Archibald, Andrew Webster 1851-1926 *DcAmA, DcNAA, WhWNAA*

Archibald, C D *BbtC*

Archibald, C M *MnBBF*

Archibald, Douglas 1919- *ConDr, WrD 1976*

Archibald, Eben Henry 1873- *WhWNAA*

Archibald, Edith Jessie 1854-1934 *CanNov, DcNAA, OxCan, WhWNAA*

Archibald, Sir Edward Mortimer 1810-1884 *OxCan*

Archibald, Francis A *Alli Sup*

Archibald, Mrs. George 1854-1928 *AmA&B, ChPo, ChPo Sup, DcAmA, WhWNAA*

Archibald, George Hamilton *ChPo S1*

Archibald, James Francis Jewell 1871-1934 *DcNAA*

Archibald, Joe 1898- *AuBYP, ConAu XR*

Archibald, John Felton 1856-1919 *DcLEnL*

Archibald, John J 1925- *ConAu 5R*

Archibald, Joseph S 1898- *ConAu 9R, SmATA 3*

Archibald, Kathleen *OxCan Sup*

Archibald, Raymond Clare 1875- *AmLY, WhWNAA*

Archibald, Samuel George William 1777-1846 *OxCan*

Archibald, William *Alli Sup*

Archibald, William 1924-1970 *ConAu 29, McGWD*

Archibald, William Charles 1824-1924 *DcNAA*

Archibald, William Frederick Alphonse 1846- *Alli Sup*

Archil 1647-1713 *DcOrL 3*

Archilochus *BbD, BiD&SB, CasWL, NewC,*

OxEng, Pen Cl

Archimedes 287?BC-212BC *CasWL, DcEnL, NewC, Pen Cl, REn*

Archipenko, Alexander Porfirievich 1887-1964 *REn*

Archipoeta *OxGer*

Archpoet, The 1130?-1165? *CasWL, Pen Eur*

Arciniegas, German 1900- *ConAu 61, DcCLA, DcSpL, Pen Am*

Arcipreste De Hita *DcSpL, Pen Eur*

Arcipreste De Talavera 1398?-1470? *DcSpL, Pen Eur*

Arcone, Sonya 1925- *ConAu 21*

Arcos, Rene 1881- *OxFr, REn*

Arctander, John William 1849-1920 *DcNAA*

Arcticum Polo *WhWNAA*

Arctinus *Pen Cl*

Arcy, D'Azile *Alli*

Ard, Ben Neal, Jr. 1922- *ConAu 33, WrD 1976*

Ard, William 1922-1962? *ConAu 5R*

Ardagh, Edward Gowan Russell *WhWNAA*

Ardagh, John 1928- *ConAu 25*

Ardagh, W D *BbtC*

Ardebeili, Achmed *ChPo S2*

Arden, Albert Henry *Alli Sup*

Arden, Barbie *ConAu XR, SmATA 3, ThBJA*

Arden, C L *ChPo S1*

Arden, Edwin Hunter Pendleton 1864-1918 *AmA*

Arden, Francis *ChPo*

Arden, George *Alli Sup*

Arden, Gothard Everett 1905- *ConAu P-1*

Arden, Hazelfoot *Alli Sup*

Arden, J E M *ConAu XR*

Arden, J R *Alli Sup*

Arden, Jane *ConAu 61, ConDr, WrD 1976*

Arden, John 1930- *Au&Wr, CasWL, CnMD, CnThe, ConAu 13R, ConDr, ConLC 6, CrCD, LongC, McGWD, ModBL Sup, ModWD, NewC, Pen Eng, REnWD, TwCW, WebEAL, WhTwL, WorAu, WrD 1976*

Arden, Maurice *Alli Sup*

Arden, William *EncM&D*

Ardener, Edwin *ConAu 5R*

Ardern, John *Alli*

Arderne, James d1691 *Alli*

Arderon, William *Alli*

Ardesoif, J P *Alli*

Ardies, Tom 1931- *ConAu 33*

Ardizonne, Edward 1900- *ChPo, ChPo S1, ChPo S2, WrD 1976*

Ardizzone, Edward 1900- *Au&Wr, AuBYP, AuICB, ConAu 5R, IlCB 1945, IlCB 1956, IlCB 1966, LongC, MorJA, PiP, SmATA 1, WhCL*

Ardley, George *Alli, BiDLA*

Ardmore, Jane Kesner 1915- *ConAu 5R*

Ardoin, John 1935- *ConAu 57*

Ardouin-Dumazet, Victor Eugene 1852- *WhLA*

Ardrey, Robert 1908- *AmA&B, BlkAW, CnMD, ConAu 33, ConDr, ModWD, TwCA Sup, WrD 1976*

Areeda, Phillip E 1930- *ConAu 23, WrD 1976*

Afef, Mirza Abolqasem Qazvini 1882-1934 *DcOrL 3*

Arehart-Treichel, Joan 1942- *ConAu 57*

Arellanes, Audrey Spencer 1920- *ConAu 33*

Arellano, George I 1923- *AmSCAP 66*

Arena, John I 1929- *ConAu 45*

Arenas, Braulio 1913- *DcCLA*

Arenas, Reinaldo 1943- *DcCLA*

Arendt, Erich 1903- *OxGer*

Arendt, Hannah 1906-1975 *AmA&B, ConAu 17R, ConAu 61, Pen Am, REn, WorAu, WrD 1976*

Arendzen, John Peter 1873- *CatA 1947*

Arene, Paul Auguste 1843-1893? *BbD, BiD&SB, CasWL, EvEuW, OxFr*

Arens, Richard 1921- *WrD 1976*

Arensberg, Conrad Maynadier 1910- *AmA&B, ConAu 61*

Arensberg, Walter Conrad 1878-1954 *AmA&B, WhWNAA*

Arenson, Saul Bryan 1895- *WhWNAA*

Arent, Arthur 1904-1972 *Au&Wr, CnMD,*

ConAu 23, ConAu 33, McGWD,
ModWD
Ares, Richard OxCan, OxCan Sup
Areskoug, Kaj 1933- ConAu 29
Aresty, Esther Bradford ConAu 9R,
WrD 1976
Areta, Mavis ConAu XR, WrD ·1976
Arethas, Archbishop Of Caesarea 850?-932?
CasWL, Pen Cl
Aretino CasWL
Aretino, Francesco CasWL
Aretino, Leonardo Pen Eur
Aretino, Pietro 1492-1556 AtlBL, BiD&SB,
CasWL, CnThe, CyWA, DcEuL, EuA,
EvEuW, McGWD, NewC, OxEng,
Pen Eur, REn, REnWD
Aretino, Unico CasWL
Aretz, Gertrude 1886- WhLA
Arevalo Martinez, Rafael 1884- CasWL,
DcCLA, DcSpL, EncWL, Pen Am, REn
Arey, Harriet Ellen 1819-1901 Alli Sup,
AmA&B, ChPo, ChPo S1, ChPo S2,
DcAmA, DcNAA, HsB&A, OhA&B
Arey, Henry W Alli Sup
Arey, James A 1936- ConAu 41
Arey, Leslie Brainerd 1891?- AmA&B,
WhWNAA
Arfwedson, C D BbtC
Argall, John d1606 Alli
Argall, Richard Alli
Argall, Sir Samuel d1626 Alli, OxCan
Arganston, J Alli
Argens, Jean-Baptiste, Marquis D' 1704-1771
OxFr
Argensola, Bartolome Leonardo De 1561?-1631
BiD&SB, CasWL, DcEuL, EvEuW,
Pen Eur
Argensola, Lupercio Leonardo De 1559?-1613
BbD, BiD&SB, CasWL, DcEuL, EvEuW,
Pen Eur
Argenson, Marc-Pierre, Comte D' 1694-1764
OxFr
Argenson, Pierre DeVoyer, Vicomte D' 1625-1709
OxCan
Argenson, Rene-Louis Voyer, Marquis D'
1694-1757 DcEuL, OxFr
Argent, Henry David James 1907- Au&Wr
Argent, Sophie Alli Sup
Argenti, Philip 1891?-1974 ConAu 49
Argentina, Sareno S 1917- AmSCAP 66
Argento, Dominick 1927- AmSCAP 66
Argenton, Monsieur D' OxFr
Argenzio, Victor 1902- ConAu 53
Arghezi, Tudor 1880-1967 CasWL, EncWL,
Pen Eur, WhTwL
Argiro, Larry 1909- ConAu 5R
Argles, Mrs. Alli Sup
Argles, Napoleon Alli Sup
Argonautos DcSpL
Argote DeMolina, Gonzalo 1548?-1598? CasWL,
DcEuL
Argow, Waldemar 1916- ConAu 23
Argow, Wendelin Waldemar Wieland 1891-
OhA&B, WhWNAA
Arguedas, Alcides 1879-1946 CasWL, DcSpL,
EncWL, Pen Am, REn
Arguedas, Jose Maria 1911-1969 CasWL,
EncWL Sup, Pen Am, WorAu
Arguelles, Jose A 1939- ConAu 45
Arguelles, Miriam Tarcov 1943- ConAu 45
Arguijo, Juan De 1565?-1623 CasWL, DcEuL,
Pen Eur
Argus ConAu XR
Argus, Arabella Alli, CarSB
Argyle, Anna Alli Sup
Argyle, Aubrey William 1910- ConAu P-1
Argyle, George Douglas Campbell 1823-1900
Alli, BiD&SB
Argyle, Michael 1925- ConAu 21, WrD 1976
Argyle, Ruth ChPo, ChPo S1
Argyll, Duchess Of NewC
Argyll, George Douglas Campbell, Duke Of
1823-1900 Alli Sup, BbD, BiD&SB,
BrAu 19, ChPo S2, Chmbr 3, DcEnL,
EvLB
Argyll, John Douglas S Campbell, Duke Of 1845-
BiD&SB
Argyrakis, Minos 1920- WhGrA

Argyris, Chris 1923- ConAu 1R
Argyris, John 1913- Au&Wr, WrD 1976
Argyropoulos, Joannes 1416-1484 DcEuL
Argyropoulos, Johannes 1410-1490 REn
Argyropulos, John Pen Cl
Ari EuA
Ari Thorgilsson 1067-1148 BiD&SB, DcEuL,
EuA
Ariake DcOrL 1
Arian, Alan 1938- ConAu 49
Arian, Edward 1921- ConAu 33
Arias, Ron DrAF 1976
Arias Montano, Benito 1527-1598 CasWL
Arias Robalino, Augusto 1903- DcCLA
Aribau, Bonaventura Carles 1798-1862 CasWL,
EvEuW
Aricha, Yoseph 1906- CasWL
Arici, Cesare 1782-1836 BiD&SB
Arida, Nasib 1887-1946 CasWL
Aridjis, Homero 1940- DcCLA
Ariel ConAu XR
Arienti, Giovanni Sabadino d1540 CasWL
Aries, Philippe 1914- Au&Wr
Arieti, Silvano 1914- ConAu 21
Arif, Abu'l-Qasim 1882-1933 CasWL
Arif, Ahmed DcOrL 3
Arigo OxGer
Arihara No Narihira 825-880 CyWA
Aring, Charles D 1904- ConAu 49
Arinos, Affonso 1868-1916 Pen Am
Arion CasWL, NewC, OxEng, Pen Cl
Ariosto, Lodovico 1474-1533 CnThe, DcEnL,
EvEuW, NewC, REn, REnWD
Ariosto, Ludovico 1474-1533 AtlBL, BbD,
BiD&SB, CasWL, CyWA, DcEuL, EuA,
McGWD, NewC, OxEng, Pen Eur,
RCom
Ariosto Of The North DcEnL
Arishima, Takeo 1878?-1923 CasWL,
DcOrL 1
Aristaenetus CasWL
Aristarchus 217?BC-144?BC CasWL, NewC,
Pen Cl, REn
Aristarchus Of Samos 280?BC-230BC CasWL,
NewC
Aristeides BiD&SB
Aristides 530?BC-468?BC BiD&SB, DcEnL,
DcNAA, NewC, REn
Aristides Of Miletus REn
Aristides, The British 1620-1678 DcEnL
Aristides, Aelius 120?-189 CasWL, Pen Cl
Aristippus 435?BC-356?BC NewC, REn
Aristobulus 350?BC- Pen Cl
Aristocles BiD&SB
Aristogiton NewC
Ariston Pen Cl
Aristophanes 448?BC-385?BC AtlBL, BbD,
BiD&SB, CasWL, CnThe, CyWA,
DcEnL, McGWD, NewC, OxEng,
Pen Cl, RCom, REn, REnWD
Aristophanes Of Byzantium 257?BC-180?BC
CasWL, Pen Cl, REn
Aristophanes, The English 1722-1777 DcEnL
Aristotle 384BC-322BC AtlBL, BbD,
BiD&SB, CasWL, CnThe, CyWA,
DcEnL, DcEuL, NewC, OxEng, Pen Cl,
RCom, REn, REnWD
Aristoxenus 370?BC- CasWL
Arius 256?-336 REn
Ariwara, Narihira 825-880 CasWL, DcOrL 1,
Pen Cl
Arizona Cy HsB&A
Arjan Mal 1581-1606 CasWL, DcOrL 2
Arjona, Juan De DcEuL
Arjona, Manuel Maria DcSpL
Arjona Y DeCubas, Manuel Maria De 1771-1820
CasWL, Pen Eur
Arjun 1581-1606 CasWL
Ark, Henry REnAL
Arkell, Anthony John 1898- Au&Wr
Arkell, Reginald 1882-1959 ChPo, ChPo S1,
ChPo S2, LongC, NewC, WorAu
Arkell, Roderick 1892- WhWNAA
Arkell, William J 1856-1930 DcNAA
Arkhurst, Frederick S 1920- AfA 1, ConAu 29
Arkhurst, Joyce Cooper 1921- BlkAW,
ConAu 17R, LivBA, WrD 1976
Arkin, Alan 1934- AmSCAP 66

Arkin, David 1906- AmSCAP 66, ConAu 21,
WrD 1976
Arkin, Frieda DrAF 1976
Arkin, Herbert 1906- ConAu 5R
Arkin, Joseph 1922- ConAu 5R
Arkin, Marcus 1926- ConAu 53, WrD 1976
Arkin, Robert B 1923- AmSCAP 66
Arkley, Arthur James 1919- WrD 1976
Arkley, Patrick Alli Sup
Arkwright, John Stanhope 1872- ChPo S1
Arkwright, Peleg DcAmA
Arkwright, T Alli
Arland, Marcel 1889- CasWL
Arland, Marcel 1899- EncWL, Pen Eur
Arlandson, Leone 1917- ConAu 29
Arlen, Harold 1905- AmSCAP 66
Arlen, Jeanne Burns 1917- AmSCAP 66
Arlen, Michael 1895-1956 DcLEnL, EncM&D,
EvLB, LongC, ModBL, Pen Eng, REn,
TwCA, TwCA Sup, TwCW
Arlen, Michael J 1930- AmA&B, ConAu 61
Arleo, Joseph 1933- ConAu 29
Arles, Henri D' 1870-1930 CanWr, OxCan
Arlett, Vera Isabel 1896- Au&Wr
Arley, Catherine 1935- ConAu 45
Arlincourt, Victor Prevost, Vicomte D' 1789-1856
BiD&SB, OxFr
Arling, Emanie Nahm AmA&B
Arlington, Earl Of Alli
Arlisienne WhWNAA
Arliss, George 1868-1946 ChPo, NewC
Arlitt, Ada Hart 1890- WhWNAA
Arlott, John 1914- Au&Wr, ConAu 9R,
WrD 1976
Arlotto, Anthony 1939- ConAu 33
Arlow, Jacob A 1912- ConAu 53
Arlt, Gustav Otto 1895- AmA&B
Arlt, Roberto 1900-1942 CasWL, Pen Am,
WhTwL
Armagnac, Arthur S 1877- WhWNAA
Armah, Ayi Kwei 1936- ConLC 5
Armah, Ayi Kwei 1938- AfA 1
Armah, Ayi Kwei 1939- CasWL, ConAu 61,
ConNov 1972, ConNov 1976, EncWL Sup,
RGAfl, WrD 1976
Arman, Abraham Alli Sup
Armand CasWL, OxAm, OxGer
Armand, Louis 1905-1971 ConAu 29,
ConAu 33
Armando Duval PueRA
Armatage, George Alli Sup
Armatas, James P 1931- ConAu 41
Armattoe, Raphael Ernest Grail Glikpo
1913-1953 AfA 1, Pen Cl
Armbruster, C Alli Sup
Armbruster, Carl J 1929- ConAu 33
Armbruster, Charles Hubert 1874- WhLA
Armbruster, F O 1929- ConAu 49
Armbruster, Francis E 1923- ConAu 29
Armbruster, Frank ConAu XR
Armbruster, Ludwig 1886- WhLA
Armbruster, Maxim Ethan 1902- ConAu 1R
Armbruster, Robert AmSCAP 66
Arme Mann Im Toggenburg, Der OxGer
Armen, Kay AmSCAP 66
Armenheim, Gregory WhWNAA
Armens, Sven 1921- ConAu 21
Armentrout, James Sylvester 1887- WhWNAA
Armentrout, Lee 1909- AmSCAP 66
Armentrout, William W 1918- ConAu 33
Armentrout, Winfield Dockery 1889-
WhWNAA
Armer, Alberta Roller 1904- ConAu 5R,
IndAu 1917, SmATA 9
Armer, Laura Adams 1874-1963 AmA&B,
AuBYP, ConAmA, IlCB 1945, JBA 1934,
JBA 1951, Newb 1922
Armer, Sidney 1871- IlCB 1945
Armerding, Hudson Taylor 1918- ConAu 23
Armes, Ellen Elizabeth 1847-1904 DcNAA
Armes, Ethel Marie AmA&B
Armes, George Augustus 1844-1919 DcNAA
Armes, Roy 1937- WrD 1976
Armfield, Henry Thomas Alli Sup
Armfield, Lucile BiDSA
Armfield, Maxwell 1881?- Au&Wr, ChPo S1,
IlCB 1945
Armi, Anna Maria ChPo

Armiger, Charles 1800?- *Br&AmS*
Armigix, T *Alli*
Armijn Pane *DcOrL 2*
Armin, Robert 1568?-1615 *Alli, CasWL, DcEnL, NewC*
Armington, John Calvin 1923- *ConAu 53*
Arminius 018?BC-019?AD *DcEuL, OxGer, REn*
Arminius, Jacobus 1560-1609 *NewC*
Armistead, Samuel 1927- *ConAu 53*
Armistead, Wilson *Alli Sup*
Armit, Robert H *Alli Sup*
Armitage, Alfred *MnBBF*
Armitage, Angus 1902- *Au&Wr, ConAu P-1, WrD 1976*
Armitage, D *Alli Sup*
Armitage, Doris May *ChPo*
Armitage, E Liddall 1887- *ConAu P-1*
Armitage, E M *Alli Sup*
Armitage, Edward 1817-1896 *Alli Sup, ChPo*
Armitage, Ella S *Alli Sup*
Armitage, Evelyn Noble *ChPo S2*
Armitage, John 1910- *Au&Wr, CanNov, OxCan*
Armitage, Laura F *ChPo*
Armitage, Merle 1893-1975 *AmA&B, ConAu 61*
Armitage, Mrs. R A *Alli Sup*
Armitage, Thomas 1819-1896 *Alli Sup, BiD&SB, DcAmA, DcNAA*
Armitage, Thomas Rhodes *Alli Sup*
Armitage, Vincent *MnBBF*
Armitage, William *Alli Sup*
Armitage, William James 1860-1929 *DcNAA*
Armitt, Annie *Alli Sup*
Armocida, William Francis 1922- *AmSCAP 66*
Armor, William C *Alli Sup*
Armor, William Crawford *DcNAA*
Armory, Thomas 1692-1789 *BbD*
Armour, Edward Douglas 1851-1922 *DcNAA*
Armour, George Denholm 1864-1949 *Br&AmS*
Armour, James *Alli Sup*
Armour, John *ConAu XR*
Armour, John M *Alli Sup*
Armour, Jonathan Ogden 1863-1927 *DcNAA*
Armour, Lloyd R 1922- *ConAu 29*
Armour, Margaret d1943 *CarSB, ChPo S2*
Armour, R Coutts *MnBBF*
Armour, Richard Willard 1906- *AmA&B, AnCL, Au&Wr, AuBYP, ChPo, ChPo S1, ChPo S2, ConAu 1R, REnAL, WrD 1976*
Armour, Robert, Jr. 1809-1845 *BbtC*
Armour, Rollin Stely 1929- *ConAu 33, WrD 1976*
Armour, Samuel Crawford *Alli Sup*
Armour, W T *OxCan Sup*
Armour, William *Alli Sup*
Arms, George Warren 1912- *AmA&B, ConAu 5R, REnAL*
Arms, Goodsil Filley 1854-1932 *DcNAA*
Arms, Jane *ChPo S2*
Arms, Mary L 1836- *DcNAA*
Arms, Suzanne 1944- *ConAu 57*
Armsby, Henry Prentiss 1853-1921 *Alli Sup, DcNAA*
Armstrong *Alli*
Armstrong, A Joseph 1873-1954 *AmA&B, TexWr, WhWNAA*
Armstrong, A W *PoIre*
Armstrong, Alexander *OxCan*
Armstrong, Sir Alexander *Alli Sup*
Armstrong, Andrew 1934- *Au&Wr*
Armstrong, Andrew Campbell 1860-1935 *DcNAA, WhWNAA*
Armstrong, Andrew James 1848- *ChPo S1*
Armstrong, Ann Seidel 1917- *ConAu 9R*
Armstrong, Anne 1924- *ConAu 13R*
Armstrong, Anne W 1872- *WhWNAA*
Armstrong, Annie *Alli Sup, ChPo*
Armstrong, Annie E *Alli Sup*
Armstrong, Anthony 1897- *Au&Wr, DcLEnL, EncM&D, EvLB, LongC, MnBBF*
Armstrong, Archibald d1672 *Alli, NewC*
Armstrong, Arthur Hilary 1909- *Au&Wr*
Armstrong, Brice W *TexWr*
Armstrong, Charles *Alli, BiDLA*
Armstrong, Charles 1886- *WhWNAA*

Armstrong, Charles Edward *Alli Sup*
Armstrong, Charlotte 1905-1969 *AmA&B, ConAu 1R, ConAu 25, EncM&D, WorAu*
Armstrong, Clara J *IndAu 1917*
Armstrong, Claude Blakeley 1889- *Au&Wr*
Armstrong, David M 1944- *ConAu 57*
Armstrong, David Maitland 1836-1918 *DcNAA*
Armstrong, David Malet 1926- *Au&Wr, ConAu 25, WrD 1976*
Armstrong, Donald Budd 1886- *WhWNAA*
Armstrong, Douglas Albert 1920- *Au&Wr, ConAu 9R*
Armstrong, Dwight LeRoy 1854-1927 *IndAu 1816*
Armstrong, Edmund John 1841-1865 *Alli Sup, BiD&SB, ChPo S1, PoIre*
Armstrong, Edward Allworthy 1900- *Au&Wr, ConAu 5R, WrD 1976*
Armstrong, Edward Cooke 1871-1948 *DcNAA, WhWNAA*
Armstrong, Elizabeth 1917- *ConAu 25, OxCan*
Armstrong, F Claudius *Alli, Alli Sup*
Armstrong, F L *Alli Sup*
Armstrong, Fannie *Alli Sup*
Armstrong, Florence A *WhWNAA*
Armstrong, Florence C 1843- *Alli Sup, PoIre*
Armstrong, Frances Charlotte *Alli Sup*
Armstrong, Francis *Alli*
Armstrong, Frank P *HsB&A*
Armstrong, Frederick H 1926- *ConAu 33*
Armstrong, G *Alli Sup*
Armstrong, George *Alli*
Armstrong, George D 1927- *SmATA 10*
Armstrong, George Dodd 1813-1899 *Alli Sup, BiDSA, DcAmA, DcNAA*
Armstrong, George Francis 1845-1906 *Alli Sup, BbD, BiD&SB, ChPo S1, PoIre*
Armstrong, George Henry 1858-1938 *DcNAA*
Armstrong, Gerry 1929- *ConAu 13R, SmATA 10*
Armstrong, Gregory T 1933- *ConAu 9R*
Armstrong, Hamilton Fish 1893-1973 *AmA&B, ChPo, ConAu 41, TwCA, TwCA Sup, WhWNAA*
Armstrong, Mrs. Hamilton Fish *AmNov XR*
Armstrong, Harold Hunter 1884- *AmA&B*
Armstrong, Harry 1879-1951 *AmSCAP 66*
Armstrong, Helen B *ChPo S2*
Armstrong, Henry *BlkAW*
Armstrong, Henry Edward *Alli Sup*
Armstrong, Henry H *ConAu 57*
Armstrong, Henry T *Alli Sup*
Armstrong, Miss I T *Alli Sup*
Armstrong, J L *Alli Sup*
Armstrong, J Scott 1937- *ConAu 45*
Armstrong, J W 1812-1878 *Alli Sup*
Armstrong, Jack *MnBBF*
Armstrong, Jack 1914- *Au&Wr*
Armstrong, Jack Roy 1902- *Au&Wr*
Armstrong, James *Alli, Alli Sup, BbtC*
Armstrong, James 1821-1888 *DcNAA*
Armstrong, James 1924- *ConAu 29*
Armstrong, James Clayton 1847- *DcNAA*
Armstrong, James Edward 1830-1908? *DcNAA*
Armstrong, James Elder 1855-1936 *DcNAA*
Armstrong, Jessie F *Alli Sup*
Armstrong, John *Alli, BbtC, Chmbr 2*
Armstrong, John d1528? *NewC*
Armstrong, John 1709-1779 *Alli, BrAu, CasWL, ChPo, ChPo S1, ChPo S2, DcEnL, DcLEnL, EvLB, NewC, OxEng, Pen Eng, REn*
Armstrong, John 1758-1843 *BiD&SB, CyAL 1, DcAmA, DcNAA*
Armstrong, John 1771-1797 *Alli*
Armstrong, John 1784-1829 *Alli*
Armstrong, John 1813-1856 *DcEnL*
Armstrong, John 1839- *Alli Sup*
Armstrong, John Alexander 1922- *Au&Wr, ConAu 1R, WrD 1976*
Armstrong, John Borden 1926- *ConAu 33*
Armstrong, John Byron 1917- *ConAu 5R*
Armstrong, John Echlin *Alli Sup*
Armstrong, Joseph 1848-1907 *DcNAA*
Armstrong, Joseph L 1857- *BiDSA*
Armstrong, Keith F W 1950- *ConAu 29*
Armstrong, L C *Alli Sup*

Armstrong, Lebbeus 1775-1860 *Alli Sup, DcNAA*
Armstrong, Leroy 1854-1927 *DcAmA, DcNAA*
Armstrong, Leslie *Alli, BiDLA*
Armstrong, Lillian Hardin 1902- *AmSCAP 66*
Armstrong, Louis 1900-1971 *AmSCAP 66, ConAu 29*
Armstrong, Louis E *Alli Sup*
Armstrong, Mrs. M F And Ludlow, Helen W *Alli Sup*
Armstrong, M J *Alli*
Armstrong, Macartney *Alli*
Armstrong, Margaret 1867-1944 *AmA&B, ChPo, DcNAA, TwCA, TwCA Sup, WhWNAA*
Armstrong, Martin Donisthorpe 1882-1974 *ChPo, ChPo S1, ConAu 49, DcLEnL, LongC, ModBL, NewC, TwCA, TwCA Sup*
Armstrong, Mary Frances d1903 *DcNAA*
Armstrong, Mary K *TexWr*
Armstrong, Maurice *OxCan*
Armstrong, Mildred Bowers *ChPo*
Armstrong, Moses Kimball 1832-1906 *DcNAA, OhA&B*
Armstrong, Nancy 1924- *WrD 1976*
Armstrong, Nevill Alexander Drummond 1878?- *OxCan*
Armstrong, Nicholas *Alli Sup*
Armstrong, Ogle *Alli*
Armstrong, Orland Kay 1893- *WhWNAA*
Armstrong, Paul 1869-1915 *AmA&B, DcNAA, REnAL, TwCA, TwCA Sup*
Armstrong, Paul 1912- *ConAu 37*
Armstrong, Perry A 1823- *DcNAA*
Armstrong, Philander Banister 1847- *IndAu 1917*
Armstrong, R A *Alli*
Armstrong, Richard 1903- *Au&Wr, AuBYP, ThBJA, WhCL*
Armstrong, Richard Acland *Alli Sup*
Armstrong, Mrs. Richard F *Alli Sup*
Armstrong, Robert *Alli, Alli Sup, BiDLA*
Armstrong, Robert 1901- *Au&Wr, WrD 1976*
Armstrong, Robert Allen 1860-1936 *AmA&B, DcNAA*
Armstrong, Robert Bruce *Alli Sup*
Armstrong, Robert Grenville 1888-1956 *OhA&B*
Armstrong, Robert Laurence 1926- *ConAu 29, WrD 1976*
Armstrong, Robert Plant 1919- *ConAu 41*
Armstrong, Robert S *ChPo S1*
Armstrong, Roger D 1939- *ConAu 17R*
Armstrong, Ruth Gallup 1891- *ConAu P-1*
Armstrong, Samuel Chapman 1839-1893 *DcNAA*
Armstrong, Selene Ayer 1883- *BiDSA*
Armstrong, Simon *Alli*
Armstrong, Sinclair 1912- *AmSCAP 66*
Armstrong, Skeffington *Alli Sup*
Armstrong, T *Alli Sup*
Armstrong, Terence Iam Fytton 1912-1970 *ChPo, ChPo S1, ChPo S2, ConAu 17, ConAu 29, ConP 1970, EvLB, LongC*
Armstrong, Thomas 1899- *Au&Wr, ConAu 5R, LongC, WrD 1976*
Armstrong, Tom *IlBYP*
Armstrong, W *Alli Sup*
Armstrong, W P *Alli Sup*
Armstrong, Walter *Alli Sup*
Armstrong, Walter 1850- *Alli Sup*
Armstrong, William *Alli, BbtC, BiDLA, NewC, PoIre*
Armstrong, William 1856-1942 *Alli Sup, AmA&B, DcNAA*
Armstrong, William A 1912- *ConAu 13R*
Armstrong, William A 1915- *ConAu 17R*
Armstrong, William H 1914- *AuBYP, AuNews 1, ChLR 1, ConAu 17R, MorBMP, NewbC 1966, SmATA 4, ThBJA, WrD 1976*
Armstrong, William Jackson 1841-1913 *DcNAA, OhA&B*
Armstrong, William M 1919- *ConAu 9R, ConAu 49*
Armstrong, William Nevins 1835-1905 *DcNAA*
Armstrong, Z Starr 1887- *TexWr*
Armytage *MnBBF*
Armytage, Charles *ChPo*

Armytage, Dudley *Alli Sup*
Armytage, Fenella *Alli Sup*
Armytage, George John *Alli Sup*
Armytage, Sydney *Alli Sup*
Armytage, Walter Harry Green 1915- *Au&Wr,*
ConAu 9R
Arnaboldi, Alessandro 1827- *BiD&SB*
Arnaboldi, Joseph P 1920- *AmSCAP 66*
Arnade, Charles W 1927- *ConAu 33,*
WrD 1976
Arnall, Richard 1696?-1756 *Alli*
Arnall, William *Alli*
Arnarson, Orn 1884-1942 *EncWL*
Arnason, H H 1909- *ConAu 61*
Arnason, Jon 1819-1888 *BiD&SB, CasWL,*
EuA
Arnatt, Ronald 1930- *AmSCAP 66*
Arnau, Frank 1894- *Au&Wr*
Arnaud, Francois 1721-1784 *OxFr*
Arnaud, Francois-Thomas DeBaculard D'
1718-1805 *OxFr*
Arnaud, Georges 1917- *McGWD*
Arnaud, Jasper *Alli*
Arnaudov, Mihail 1878- *CasWL*
Arnauld, Antoine 1612-1694 *CasWL, DcEuL,*
OxFr, REn
Arnauld, Jacqueline-Marie-Angelique 1591-1661
OxFr
Arnauld, Jeanne-Catherine-Agnes 1594-1671
OxFr
Arnauld D'Andilly, Angelique 1624-1684 *OxFr,*
REn
Arnauld D'Andilly, Robert 1589-1674 *OxFr*
Arnault, Antoine Vincent 1766-1834 *BiD&SB,*
DcEuL, EvEuW, OxFr
Arnaut Daniel *CasWL, EuA, Pen Eur*
Arnaut De Mareuil 1170-1200 *CasWL, EuA*
Arndell, W *BiDLA*
Arndt *ChPo*
Arndt, Ernest Moritz 1769-1860 *BbD, EuA*
Arndt, Ernst Heinrich Daniel 1899- *Au&Wr,*
ConAu 23, WrD 1976
Arndt, Ernst Moritz 1769-1860 *BiD&SB,*
CasWL, ChPo S1, DcEuL, EvEuW,
OxGer, REn
Arndt, Felix 1889-1918 *AmSCAP 66*
Arndt, Heinz Wolfgang 1915- *ConAu 21,*
WrD 1976
Arndt, Johann 1555-1621 *EvEuW, OxGer*
Arndt, Karl John Richard 1903- *ConAu 17R,*
WrD 1976
Arndt, Margaret *ChPo S1*
Arndt, Nola *AmSCAP 66*
Arndt, Paul 1870- *WhLA*
Arndt, Ruth E 1890- *WrD 1976*
Arndt, Ursula *ChPo S1, IlBYP*
Arndt, Walter Tallmadge 1872-1932 *DcNAA*
Arndt, Walter W 1916- *ConAu 13R*
Arndt, William Frederick 1880- *WhWNAA*
Arne, Michael 1741-1786 *NewC*
Arne, Sigrid 1900- *OhA&B*
Arne, Thomas Augustine 1710-1778 *Alli, AtlBL,*
NewC, REn
Arner, Ernst Nils Sivar Erik 1909- *CasWL*
Arner, Sivar 1909- *Pen Eur*
Arneson, Ben Albert 1883-1958 *OhA&B,*
WhWNAA
Arneth, Alfred Von 1819-1897 *BiD&SB*
Arnett, Alexander Mathews 1888-1945 *AmA&B,*
DcNAA
Arnett, Braithwaite *Alli Sup*
Arnett, Caroline *SmATA X*
Arnett, Carroll 1927- *ConAu 21, DrAP 1975*
Arnett, Harold E 1931- *ConAu 21*
Arnett, J A *Alli*
Arnett, Laura Vivian Belvadere *WhWNAA*
Arnett, Ross H, Jr. 1919- *ConAu 49*
Arnez, Nancy Levi 1928- *BlkAW, ConAu 29,*
LivBAA
Arngrim, Jonasson 1568-1648 *DcEuL*
Arnheim, Daniel D 1930- *ConAu 9R*
Arnheim, Gus 1897-1955 *AmSCAP 66*
Arnheim, Rudolf 1904- *AmA&B, Au&Wr,*
ConAu 1R, WrD 1976
Arnholter, Ethelwynne 1902- *IndAu 1917*
Arni Magnusson 1663-1730 *DcEuL*
Arniches, Carlos 1866-1943 *CasWL, CnMD,*
DcSpL, EvEuW

Arniches Y Barrera, Carlos 1866-1943
ClDMEuL, EncWL, McGWD
Arnim, Countess Von *EvLB, LongC, NewC*
Arnim, Grafin Von *REn*
Arnim, Achim Von 1781-1831 *BbD, BiD&SB,*
OxGer
Arnim, Anna Leffler *Alli Sup*
Arnim, Bettina Von 1785-1859 *BiD&SB,*
CasWL, DcEuL, EuA, EvEuW, OxGer,
Pen Eur
Arnim, Elisabeth Von 1785-1859 *REn*
Arnim, Harry, Graf Von 1824-1881 *OxGer*
Arnim, Ludwig Achim Von 1781-1831 *DcEuL,*
EuA, Pen Eur
Arnim, Ludwig Joachim Von 1781-1831 *CasWL,*
EvEuW, OxGer, REn
Arnim, Robert *DcEnL*
Arnimal *DcOrL 2*
Arnison, Jim 1925- *WrD 1976*
Arno, Enrico 1913- *ChPo S1, ChPo S2,*
IlBYP, IlCB 1956, IlCB 1966
Arno, Peter 1904?-1968 *AmA&B, ConAu 25,*
LongC
Arnobius *CasWL, Pen Cl*
Arnold, Ewart *OxGer*
Arnold, Priester *OxGer*
Arnold Von Immessen *CasWL*
Arnold, A *Alli Sup*
Arnold, A B *Alli Sup*
Arnold, A C L *Alli*
Arnold, A K *Alli Sup*
Arnold, A S *Alli Sup*
Arnold, Abraham B 1820-1904 *DcNAA*
Arnold, Abraham Kerns 1837-1901 *DcNAA*
Arnold, Adlai F 1914- *ConAu 33*
Arnold, Alan 1922- *ConAu 5R*
Arnold, Albert Nicholas 1814-1883 *Alli Sup,*
DcAmA, DcNAA
Arnold, Alexander S *Alli Sup*
Arnold, Alexander Streeter 1829- *DcNAA*
Arnold, Amelia *Alli Sup*
Arnold, Anthony Brown 1791-1885 *DcNAA*
Arnold, Armin H 1931- *ConAu 9R*
Arnold, Arnold 1921- *ChPo S2, ConAu 17R*
Arnold, Sir Arthur 1833-1902 *Alli Sup,*
BiD&SB, BrAu 19, DcEnL, NewC
Arnold, August Gottfried 1666-1714 *DcEuL*
Arnold, Augusta Foote 1844-1903 *DcAmA,*
DcNAA
Arnold, Augustus C L *Alli Sup*
Arnold, Benedict 1741-1801 *OxAm, OxCan,*
REn, REnAL
Arnold, Bernard 1915- *AmSCAP 66*
Arnold, Birch *AmA&B, DcAmA, DcNAA,*
OhA&B
Arnold, Blake *MnBBF*
Arnold, Bruce 1936- *Au&Wr*
Arnold, C *Alli*
Arnold, C H *Alli*
Arnold, Carl *ConAu XR*
Arnold, Cecil *Alli Sup*
Arnold, Charlotte *Alli Sup*
Arnold, Charlotte E Cramer *ConAu 57*
Arnold, Clara *ChPo, ChPo S1*
Arnold, Clement *MnBBF*
Arnold, Constantine Peter 1860- *WhWNAA*
Arnold, Corliss Richard 1926- *ConAu 49*
Arnold, Denis Midgley 1926- *Au&Wr,*
ConAu 5R
Arnold, Earl Caspar 1884- *WhWNAA*
Arnold, Eben *MnBBF*
Arnold, Edgar *MnBBF*
Arnold, Edmund *Alli*
Arnold, Edmund Clarence 1913- *ConAu 1R,*
WrD 1976
Arnold, Edmund Samuel Foster -1907
Alli Sup, DcNAA
Arnold, Edward A *Alli Sup*
Arnold, Edward Carleton 1868- *WhLA*
Arnold, Sir Edwin 1832-1904 *Alli, Alli Sup,*
BbD, BiD&SB, BrAu 19, ChPo,
ChPo S1, ChPo S2, Chmbr 3, DcEnA,
DcEnA Ap, DcEnL, DcEuL, DcLEnL,
EvLB, LongC, NewC, OxEng, REn
Arnold, Edwin Lester 1856- *Alli Sup, BiD&SB,*
MnBBF, WhLA
Arnold, Elliott 1912- *AmA&B, AmNov,*

Au&Wr, AuBYP, ConAu 17R,
SmATA 5, TwCA Sup, WrD 1976
Arnold, Emmy 1884- *ConAu 23*
Arnold, Eric *Alli Sup*
Arnold, Ernst Hermann 1865- *WhWNAA*
Arnold, Ethel Nishua *BlkAW*
Arnold, F R *ChPo*
Arnold, Faith Stewart *WhWNAA*
Arnold, Felix 1879-1927? *DcNAA*
Arnold, Francena H 1888- *ConAu P-1*
Arnold, Frances R *ChPo S1*
Arnold, Frank *MnBBF*
Arnold, Frank Russell 1871- *WhWNAA*
Arnold, Frank S *Alli Sup*
Arnold, Fred *Alli*
Arnold, Frederick *Alli Sup*
Arnold, Frederick 1833- *Alli Sup*
Arnold, Frederick Henry *Alli Sup*
Arnold, G *ChPo*
Arnold, G L *ConAu XR*
Arnold, George 1834-1865 *Alli Sup, AmA,*
AmA&B, BiD&SB, ChPo, ChPo S1,
ChPo S2, CyAL 2, DcAmA, DcLEnL,
DcNAA, OxAm, REnAL
Arnold, George Carpenter 1868- *WhWNAA*
Arnold, George M Brock *Alli Sup*
Arnold, Gottfried 1666-1714 *CasWL, OxGer*
Arnold, Guy 1932- *ConAu 25, WrD 1976*
Arnold, Hans 1850- *BiD&SB*
Arnold, Harry John Philip 1932- *Au&Wr,*
ConAu 5R, WrD 1976
Arnold, Harry L, Jr. 1912- *WrD 1976*
Arnold, Henrietta And Charlotte *Alli Sup,*
PoIre
Arnold, Mrs. Henry *Alli Sup*
Arnold, Henry Harley 1886-1950 *AmA&B*
Arnold, Henry Lucian d1915 *DcNAA*
Arnold, Henry Vernon 1848- *DcNAA*
Arnold, Herbert 1935- *ConAu 37*
Arnold, Howard Payson 1831-1910 *Alli Sup,*
DcAmA, DcNAA
Arnold, Ida *LongC*
Arnold, Isaac Newton 1815-1884 *Alli Sup,*
AmA, BiD&SB, DcAmA, DcNAA
Arnold, J E *MnBBF*
Arnold, J L *Alli Sup*
Arnold, James Loring 1868-1935 *DcNAA*
Arnold, James Newell 1844-1927 *DcNAA*
Arnold, James Oliver 1838-1905 *OhA&B*
Arnold, Jane E *Alli Sup*
Arnold, Janet 1932- *WrD 1976*
Arnold, Johann Georg Daniel 1780-1829
BiD&SB, OxGer
Arnold, John *Alli*
Arnold, John Muehleisen *Alli Sup*
Arnold, John Paul 1854-1931 *DcNAA*
Arnold, Joseph H *ConAu XR, WrD 1976*
Arnold, Josiah Lynden 1768-1796 *Alli*
Arnold, Josias Lyndon 1768-1796 *AmA&B,*
ChPo S1, CyAL 1, DcNAA
Arnold, Julian T Biddulph 1864- *Alli Sup,*
WhWNAA
Arnold, June 1926- *ConAu 21*
Arnold, L J *ConAu XR*
Arnold, Lauren Briggs 1814-1888 *Alli Sup,*
DcAmA, DcNAA
Arnold, LeRoy 1881- *WhWNAA*
Arnold, Levi McKeen 1813-1864 *DcNAA*
Arnold, Lloyd R 1906-1970 *ConAu 25*
Arnold, M E *Alli Sup*
Arnold, Miss M J *Alli Sup*
Arnold, Magda B 1903- *ConAu 5R,*
WrD 1976
Arnold, Malcolm *MnBBF*
Arnold, Mary Augusta 1851-1920 *DcEuL*
Arnold, Mary ALSO Ward, Mrs. Humphrey
Arnold, Mary ALSO Ward, Mary Augusta
Arnold, Matthew 1822-1888 *Alli, Alli Sup,*
AtlBL, BbD, BiD&SB, BrAu 19, CasWL,
ChPo, ChPo S1, ChPo S2, CasWL 3,
CnE&AP, CriT 3, CyWA, DcEnA,
DcEnA Ap, DcEnL, DcEuL, DcLEnL,
EvLB, MouLC 4, NewC, OxAm, OxEng,
Pen Eng, RAdv 1, RCom, REn, REnAL,
WebEAL
Arnold, Milo Lawrence 1903- *ConAu 57*
Arnold, Muller Johann *OxGer*
Arnold, Nason Henry 1874- *WhWNAA*

CasWL, *ChPo*, *ChPo S1*, *ChPo S2*, *CyAL 2*, *DcAmA*, *DcBiA*, *DcEnL*, *DcNAA*, *OxAm*, *Pen Am*, *REn*, *REnAL*
Arthur, William *ConAu XR*
Arthur, William 1797-1875 *Alli Sup*, *DcNAA*, *MnBBF*
Arthur, William 1819- *Alli Sup*
Arthur, William Reed 1876- *WhWNAA*
Arthur, Zua Bearss 1900?- *IndAu 1917*
Arthurs, Harry *MnBBF*
Arthy, Elliot *BiDLA*
Arthy, Elliott *Alli*
Artieda, Andres Rey De 1549-1613 *DcEuL*
Artifex *WhLA*
Artigue, Jean D' *OxCan*
Artioli, Alfonso 1913- *WhGrA*
Artis, Edmund Tyrrell *Alli*
Artis, Vicki Kimmel 1945- *ConAu 53*
Artiss, Percy Harold 1903- *Au&Wr*
Artman, Adelia Cobb 1869-1936 *IndAu 1816*
Artman, Joseph Manson 1879-1952 *IndAu 1917*, *WhWNAA*
Artman, Samuel R 1866-1930 *IndAu 1816*
Artmann, Hans Carl 1921- *CasWL*, *ModGL*, *OxGer*
Artom, Benjamin *Alli Sup*
Artom, Guido 1906- *ConAu 29*
Artsybashev, Mikhail Petrovich 1878-1927 *CasWL*, *ClDMEuL*, *CnMD*, *CyWA*, *DcRusL*, *EncWL*, *EvEuW*, *ModWD*, *REn*, *TwCA*, *TwCA Sup*
Artz, D A C 1894- *ChPo*
Artz, Frederick Binkerd 1894- *AmA&B*, *ConAu 1R*, *OhA&B*
Artzybasheff, Boris Mikhailovich 1899-1965 *AmA&B*, *AnCL*, *AuBYP*, *ChPo S2*, *ConICB*, *IICB 1945*, *JBA 1934*, *JBA 1951*, *St&VC*, *WhGrA*
Aruego, Ariane *ConAu 49*, *SmATA 7*
Aruego, Jose 1932- *ChPo S2*, *ConAu 37*, *IlBYP*, *SmATA 6*
Arumukam, Nallur Kantappillai 1822-1879 *DcOrL 2*
Arunacalakavi *DcOrL 2*
Arunakirinatar *DcOrL 2*
Arundale, F *Alli*
Arundale, Pamela Constance 1919- *Au&Wr*
Arundel, Anne, Countess Of d1630 *Alli*, *AuBYP*
Arundel, Honor Morfydd 1919-1973 *Au&Wr*, *ConAu 21*, *ConAu 41*, *SmATA 4*
Arundel, Jocelyn 1930- *AuBYP*, *ConAu XR*
Arundel, John Francis, Baron Of Wardour 1831- *Alli Sup*
Arundel, Louis *CarSB*
Arundel, Mary, Countess Of *Alli*
Arundel, Thomas 1353-1414 *NewC*
Arundel & Surrey, A Talbot, Countess Of *Alli*
Arundel Of Wardour, Lord Henry *Alli*
Arundell, F V J *Alli*
Arundell, James Whitton *Alli Sup*
Arundell, John *Alli*, *BiDLA*
Arundell, Thomas 1562-1639 *NewC*
Arundell, Thomas 1817-1880 *Alli Sup*
Arundell, William Arundell Harris 1794-1865 *Alli Sup*
Arvay, Harry 1925- *ConAu 57*
Arvers, Alexis Felix 1806-1850 *CasWL*, *EvEuW*, *OxFr*
Arvey, Verna 1910- *AmSCAP 66*
Arvin, Newton 1900-1963 *AmA&B*, *IndAu 1917*, *TwCA*, *TwCA Sup*, *WhWNAA*
Arvine, Kazlitt 1819-1851 *Alli*, *DcNAA*
Arwaker, Edmund *PoIre*
Arwaker, Edmund d1684 *PoIre*
Arwarker, E *Alli*
Arwidson, Adolf Ivar 1791-1858 *BiD&SB*
Arx, Caesar Von 1895-1949 *OxGer*
Ary, Donald E 1930- *ConAu 41*
Ary, Sheila M 1929- *ConAu 13R*
Arya Sura *CasWL*, *DcOrL 2*
Arymaer, Henry G *Alli Sup*
Arzak, Nikolay *TwCW*
Arzola, Marina 1939- *PueRA*
Arzt, Max 1897-1975 *ConAu 61*
Asabore *WhWNAA*
Asachi, Gheorghe 1788-1869 *CasWL*

Asadi, Abu Mansur 'Ali B Ahmad 1010?-1080? *DcOrL 3*
Asadi, 'Ali Ibn Ahmad Tusi *CasWL*
Asakawa, Kwan-Ichi 1873-1948 *DcNAA*
Asalache, Khadambi 1934- *AfA 1*, *ConP 1970*
Asam, Cosmas Damian 1686-1739 *OxGer*
Asamani, Joseph Owusu 1934- *ConAu 49*
Asan *DcOrL 2*
Asana, Jehangir Jamasji 1890-1954 *BiDPar*
Asanger, Florian 1878- *WhLA*
Asare, Bediako 1930?- *AfA 1*
Asare, Konadu *AfA 1*
Asare, Meshack 1945- *ConAu 61*
Asbaje, Juana Ines *DcSpL*
Asbell, Bernard 1923- *ConAu 45*
Asbjornsen, Peter C, And Moe, Jorgen E *St&VC*
Asbjornsen, Peter Christen 1812-1885 *AnCL*, *CarSB*, *CasWL*, *DcEuL*, *EuA*, *EvEuW*, *WhCL*
Asbjornsen, Peter Kristen 1812-1885 *BbD*, *BiD&SB*
Asbury, Francis 1745-1816 *AmA&B*, *BiDSA*, *DcNAA*, *OxAm*, *REnAL*
Asbury, Henry 1810-1896 *DcNAA*
Asbury, Herbert 1891-1963 *AmA&B*, *REnAL*, *TwCA*, *TwCA Sup*, *WhWNAA*
Asbury, Samuel E *TexWr*
Asbury, Samuel Ralph *Alli Sup*
Ascasubi, Hilario 1807-1875 *CasWL*, *DcSpL*, *Pen Am*
Asch, Frank 1946- *ConAu 41*, *SmATA 5*, *WrD 1976*
Asch, Nathan 1902-1964 *AmA&B*, *OxAm*, *REnAL*, *TwCA*, *TwCA Sup*
Asch, Schalom 1880-1957 *EncWL*
Asch, Shalom 1880-1957 *AmA&B*, *Pen Am*
Asch, Sholem 1880-1957 *AmNov*, *CasWL*, *ClDMEuL*, *CnDAL*, *CnMD*, *CnThe*, *CyWA*, *LongC*, *McGWD*, *ModWD*, *OxAm*, *REn*, *REnAL*, *REnWD*, *TwCA*, *TwCA Sup*, *TwCW*, *WhLA*
Aschaffenburg, Gustav 1866- *WhLA*
Ascham, Anthony *Alli*
Ascham, Anthony d1650 *Alli*
Ascham, John Bayne 1873-1957? *AmA&B*, *OhA&B*
Ascham, Roger 1515-1568 *Alli*, *AtlBL*, *BbD*, *BiD&SB*, *BrAu*, *CasWL*, *Chmbr 1*, *CrE&SL*, *CriT 1*, *DcEnA*, *DcEnL*, *DcEuL*, *DcLEnL*, *EvLB*, *NewC*, *OxEng*, *Pen Eng*, *REn*, *WebEAL*
Asche, Albert 1881-1959 *IndAu 1917*
Ascheim, Skip 1943- *ConAu 53*
Aschenborn, Hans Anton 1888- *WhLA*
Ascher, Emil 1859-1922 *AmSCAP 66*
Ascher, Isidore G 1835-1914 *BbtC*, *ChPo*, *DcLEnL*, *OxCan*
Ascher, Rhoda G *BlkAW*
Ascher, Sheila *DrAF 1976*
Ascherson, Neal 1932- *ConAu 13R*
Ascheton, William *Alli*
Aschmann, Helen Tann *ConAu 13R*
Aschoff, Ludwig 1866- *WhLA*
Asclepiades *OxEng*, *Pen Cl*
Asclepiades Of Samos *CasWL*, *NewC*
Ascoli, Anna Maria M P Gracinta 1899- *ChPo*
Ascoli, Max 1898- *AmA&B*
Asconius Pedianus 009BC-076AD *CasWL*
Ascott, John *MnBBF*
Ascu, E *Alli*
Asellio, Sempronius 120?BC- *Pen Cl*
Asena, Orhan 1922- *REnWD*
Asenjo, Conrado 1881- *PueRA*
Asenjo, Federico 1831-1893 *PueRA*
Asenjo Barbieri, Francisco *CasWL*
Aseyev, Nikolay Nikolayevich 1889-1963 *CasWL*, *ClDMEuL*, *DcRusL*, *EncWL*, *Pen Eur*, *TwCW*
Asgill, John *Alli*, *Chmbr 2*
Asgill, John 1659-1738 *Alli*, *DcEnL*, *EvLB*
Asgrimsson, Eysteinn d1361 *CasWL*, *EuA*
Ash, Anthony Lee 1931- *ConAu 49*
Ash, Bernard 1910- *Au&Wr*, *ConAu P-1*
Ash, Charles *Alli*
Ash, Christopher 1914- *ConAu 1R*
Ash, David Fuller 1898- *IndAu 1917*
Ash, David W 1923- *ConAu 9R*
Ash, Derek *MnBBF*

Ash, Douglas 1914- *Au&Wr*, *ConAu 5R*, *WrD 1976*
Ash, Edward d1829 *Alli*, *BiDLA*
Ash, Edward 1797-1873 *Alli Sup*
Ash, Fenton *MnBBF*
Ash, John *Alli*
Ash, John 1723-1798 *Alli*
Ash, John 1724?-1779 *Alli*, *NewC*
Ash, Mark *MnBBF*
Ash, Paul 1891-1958 *AmSCAP 66*
Ash, Pauline *WrD 1976*
Ash, Peter *AmA&B*, *DcNAA*, *WhWNAA*
Ash, Rene Lee 1939- *ConAu 57*
Ash, Russell John 1946- *WrD 1976*
Ash, Sarah Leeds 1904- *ConAu P-1*
Ash, Sholem 1880-1957 *Pen Eur*
Ash, St. George 1658-1717 *Alli*
Ash, T *Alli*
Ash, William Franklin 1917- *ConAu 5R*
A'sha, Al- *CasWL*
A'sha Maymun, Al- *DcOrL 3*
Ashabranner, Brent 1921- *ConAu 5R*, *SmATA 1*
Ashabranner, James H 1861-1936 *IndAu 1917*
Ashanti, Baron J *BlkAW*
Ash'ari, Abu'l-Hasan Al- 873?-935? *DcOrL 3*
Ashbaugh, Ernest James 1883- *IndAu 1917*, *WhWNAA*
Ashbee, Charles Robert 1863-1942 *ChPo*, *ChPo S1*, *WhLA*
Ashbee, Paul 1918- *Au&Wr*
Ashberry, Anne 1914- *Au&Wr*
Ashbery, John 1927- *AmA&B*, *ConAu 5R*, *ConLC 2*, *ConLC 3*, *ConLC 4*, *ConLC 6*, *ConP 1970*, *ConP 1975*, *CrCAP*, *DrAP 1975*, *ModAL Sup*, *Pen Am*, *RAdv 1*, *WebEAL*, *WorAu*, *WrD 1976*
Ashbolt, Allan Campbell 1921- *WrD 1976*
Ashbrook, Harriette 1898-1946 *DcNAA*
Ashbrook, James Barbour 1925- *ConAu 37*, *WrD 1976*
Ashbrook, John *WrD 1976*
Ashbrook, William 1922- *ConAu 29*
Ashbrook, William Albert 1867-1940 *OhA&B*, *WhWNAA*
Ashburn, Gene Holmes *BlkAW*
Ashburn, Joseph Nelson 1838-1919 *OhA&B*
Ashburn, Percy Moreau 1872-1940 *DcNAA*, *OhA&B*, *WhWNAA*
Ashburn, Thomas D' *DcEnL*
Ashburn, Thomas Quinn 1874-1941 *OhA&B*
Ashburne, Jim G 1912- *ConAu 1R*
Ashburner, A M *Alli*
Ashburner, John *Alli Sup*
Ashburner, R W *Alli Sup*
Ashburnham, John 1603-1671 *Alli*
Ashburnham, William *Alli*, *BiDLA*
Ashburnham, Sir William *Alli*
Ashburton, Lord d1848 *BbtC*
Ashburton, A *ChPo S2*
Ashby, Aubrey Leonard 1886- *WhWNAA*
Ashby, C *Alli Sup*
Ashby, Cliff 1919- *Au&Wr*, *ConAu 25*
Ashby, Mrs. E *Alli Sup*
Ashby, Eric 1904- *ConAu 61*
Ashby, George *Alli*, *DcEnL*
Ashby, George 1724-1808 *Alli*
Ashby, Gwynneth Margaret 1922- *Au&Wr*, *ConAu 25*, *WrD 1976*
Ashby, Henry *Alli Sup*
Ashby, J T *Alli Sup*
Ashby, Sir John *Alli*
Ashby, Joseph *Alli Sup*
Ashby, LaVerne 1922- *ConAu 21*, *IndAu 1917*
Ashby, LeRoy 1938- *ConAu 33*
Ashby, Livia Miller 1888- *IndAu 1917*
Ashby, Maude *ChPo S2*
Ashby, Paul W 1893- *IndAu 1917*
Ashby, Philip Harrison 1916- *ConAu 17R*, *WrD 1976*
Ashby, R C 1899- *EncM&D*
Ashby, Richard *Alli*
Ashby, Samuel *Alli*
Ashby, Thomas 1874- *WhLA*
Ashby, Thomas Almond 1848-1916 *DcNAA*
Ashby, William Mobile 1889- *BlkAW*
Ashby, William Ross 1903- *Au&Wr*

Ashby, Winifred M 1879- *WhWNAA*
Ashby-Sterry, Joseph 1838-1917 *Alli Sup,*
  ChPo, ChPo S1, DcEnA Ap, NewC
Ashcraft, Allan Coleman 1928- *ConAu 9R*
Ashcraft, Morris 1922- *ConAu 45*
Ashcroft, Peggy 1907- *NewC*
Ashdown, Clifford 1860-1936 *EncM&D*
Ashdowne, J *Alli*
Ashdowne, William *Alli, BiDLA*
Ashe *Alli*
Ashe, E *Alli Sup*
Ashe, E D *BbtC*
Ashe, F M *ChPo*
Ashe, Geoffrey Thomas 1923- *Au&Wr,*
  ConAu 5R, WrD 1976
Ashe, Gordon *ConAu XR, EncM&D, LongC,*
  WorAu
Ashe, Isaac *Alli, Alli Sup, PoIre*
Ashe, Isaac d1891 *PoIre*
Ashe, J *Alli*
Ashe, John Harold 1907- *WrD 1976*
Ashe, Jonathan *Alli, BiDLA*
Ashe, Nicholas *Alli, BiDLA, PoIre*
Ashe, Penelope 1936- *AmA&B, ConAu XR*
Ashe, Robert Hoadly *Alli, BiDLA*
Ashe, Robert Pickering 1875- *DcNAA*
Ashe, Samuel A'Court 1840-1938 *AmA&B,*
  BiDSA, DcNAA, WhWNAA
Ashe, Simeon d1662 *Alli*
Ashe, Thomas *Alli, BiDSA, CyAL 1*
Ashe, Thomas 1770- *BiDLA, REnAL*
Ashe, Thomas 1836-1889 *Alli Sup, BrAu 19,*
  ChPo, ChPo S1, PoIre
Ashe, Waller *Alli Sup*
Asheburne, Thomas *Alli*
Asheim, Lester Eugene 1914- *AmA&B,*
  ConAu 17R
Ashenafi, Kebede 1937- *AfA 1*
Ashenden *REn*
Ashenfelter, Orley C 1942- *ConAu 61*
Ashenhurst, Thomas R *Alli Sup*
Asher Ben Yechtel 1250?-1327 *CasWL*
Asher, Alvin Julian 1903- *WhWNAA*
Asher, David *Alli Sup*
Asher, George Michael d1905 *Alli Sup,*
  DcNAA
Asher, Harry 1909- *ConAu 5R, WrD 1976*
Asher, John Alexander 1921- *ConAu 23,*
  WrD 1976
Asher, John William 1927- *IndAu 1917*
Asher, Philip 1876-1920 *DcNAA*
Asher, Robert Eller 1910- *ConAu 61*
Asheri, Rosh 1250?-1327 *CasWL*
Asherman, Edward M 1913- *AmSCAP 66*
Asherman, Nat 1909- *AmSCAP 66*
Asheton, William *Alli*
Ashey, Bella 1927- *ConAu XR*
Ashford, Bailey Kelly 1873-1934 *DcNAA,*
  WhWNAA
Ashford, Daisy 1881?-1972 *CarSB, ConAu 33,*
  DcLEnL, EvLB, LongC, Pen Eng, REn,
  SmATA XR, WhCL
Ashford, F C 1909- *Au&Wr*
Ashford, Gerald 1907- *ConAu 41*
Ashford, Jeffrey 1926- *Au&Wr, AuBYP,*
  ConAu 1R, EncM&D, WrD 1976
Ashford, John *Alli Sup*
Ashford, Margaret Mary 1881-1972 *NewC,*
  SmATA 10
Ashhurst, Astley Paston Cooper 1876-
  WhWNAA
Ashhurst, Sir H *Alli*
Ashhurst, John 1839-1900 *Alli Sup, DcAmA,*
  DcNAA
Ashhurst, Richard Lewis 1838-1911 *DcNAA*
Ashhurst, Sir W H *Alli*
Ashi 352-427 *CasWL*
Ashibi *DcOrL 1*
Ashlee, Ted *OxCan Sup*
Ashleigh, Rose *Alli Sup*
Ashley *Alli, BiDLA, WhGrA*
Ashley, Baron *NewC*
Ashley, Lord *NewC*
Ashley, Anthony *Alli*
Ashley, Barnas Freeman 1833-1915 *DcAmA,*
  DcNAA, OhA&B
Ashley, Carlos *ChPo S2*
Ashley, Charles Sumner 1864-1925 *OhA&B*

Ashley, Clarence Degrand 1851-1916 *DcNAA*
Ashley, Clifford Warren 1881-1947 *AmA&B,*
  DcNAA, WhWNAA
Ashley, Elizabeth *WrD 1976*
Ashley, Ernest 1906- *ConAu P-1*
Ashley, Evelyn 1836- *Alli Sup*
Ashley, Florence Emily *Alli Sup*
Ashley, Franklin 1942- *ConAu 45,*
  DrAF 1976
Ashley, Fred *MnBBF*
Ashley, Frederick William 1863-1943? *AmA&B,*
  OhA&B
Ashley, George Hall 1886- *WhWNAA*
Ashley, Gladys *WrD 1976*
Ashley, Graham *ConAu XR*
Ashley, Henry *Alli*
Ashley, Jack 1922- *WrD 1976*
Ashley, James M 1824-1896 *OhA&B*
Ashley, John *Alli, Alli Sup*
Ashley, John Marks *Alli Sup*
Ashley, Jonathan 1713-1780 *Alli*
Ashley, Kate *ChPo*
Ashley, Leonard R N 1928- *WrD 1976*
Ashley, Leonard R N 1929- *ConAu 13R*
Ashley, Lillah A *AnMV 1926*
Ashley, Margaret Lee *ChPo*
Ashley, Martin *BlkAW*
Ashley, Mary 1832-1901 *AmA*
Ashley, Maurice Percy 1907- *Au&Wr,*
  ConAu 41, WrD 1976
Ashley, Ossian Doolittle 1821-1904 *DcNAA*
Ashley, Paul P 1895- *ConAu 21*
Ashley, R K *Alli Sup*
Ashley, Robert 1565-1641 *Alli*
Ashley, Robert Paul, Jr. 1915- *AuBYP,*
  ConAu 17R
Ashley, Roscoe Lewis 1872- *DcAmA,*
  WhWNAA
Ashley, Schuyler 1897-1927 *DcNAA*
Ashley, William *BlkAW*
Ashley, William Henry 1778?-1838 *OxAm*
Ashley, William James 1860- *Alli Sup,*
  DcAmA
Ashley-Montagu, Montague Francis *ConAu XR,*
  TwCA Sup
Ashlin, John *ConAu XR*
Ashlock, Patrick 1937- *ConAu 61*
Ashlock, Robert B 1930- *ConAu 29*
Ashmall, William E *ChPo*
Ashman, Joseph *Alli Sup*
Ashman, Margaret *ChPo S2*
Ashmand, J M *Alli*
Ashmead, Albert Sydney d1911 *DcNAA*
Ashmead, Gordon *AuBYP*
Ashmead, Henry Graham 1838-1920 *DcNAA*
Ashmead, John, Jr. 1917- *ConAu 1R*
Ashmead, John W *Alli*
Ashmead, William Harris 1858-1908 *DcNAA*
Ashmead-Bartlett *Alli Sup*
Ashmole, Elias 1617-1692 *Alli, Chmbr 1,*
  DcEnA, DcEnL, EvLB, NewC, OxEng
Ashmont *DcNAA*
Ashmore *Alli*
Ashmore, Annie *Alli Sup*
Ashmore, Basil Norton 1915- *Au&Wr*
Ashmore, Dorothy Emily Augusta *ChPo,*
  ChPo S2
Ashmore, Harry S 1916- *AmA&B,*
  ConAu 13R
Ashmore, Jerome 1901- *ConAu 33*
Ashmore, John *Alli, DcEnL*
Ashmore, Otis 1853- *BiDSA, DcNAA*
Ashmore, Owen 1920- *Au&Wr, WrD 1976*
Ashmore, Ruth *DcAmA, DcNAA*
Ashmore, Sidney Gillespie 1852-1911 *DcNAA*
Ashmore, Thomas *Alli, BiDLA*
Ashmore, William 1824-1909 *DcNAA*
Ashmun, Jehudi 1794-1828 *Alli, DcNAA*
Ashmun, Margaret Eliza d1940 *AmA&B,*
  DcNAA, JBA 1934, JBA 1951,
  WhWNAA, WiscW
Ashner, Sonie Shapiro 1938- *ConAu 57*
Ashpitel, Arthur 1807-1869 *Alli Sup*
Ashpitel, Francis *Alli Sup*
Ashplant, Henry Brinsmead 1863- *AmLY,*
  WhWNAA
Ashraf Khan Khatak, Hijri 1635-1693 *DcOrL 3*
Ashton, Adrian Olsson 1906- *WrD 1976*

Ashton, Agnes Amelia 1906- *Au&Wr*
Ashton, Algernon Bennet Langton 1859- *WhLA*
Ashton, Charles 1665-1752 *Alli, DcEnL*
Ashton, Charles Hamilton 1866-1936 *DcNAA,*
  WhWNAA
Ashton, Dore 1928- *AmA&B, ConAu 5R,*
  WrD 1976
Ashton, Elyzabeth Hickey 1889- *WhWNAA*
Ashton, Frederick T *Alli Sup*
Ashton, G *Alli*
Ashton, Sir George Grey 1861- *WhLA*
Ashton, H A *Alli Sup*
Ashton, Helen Rosaline 1891-1958 *ChPo S2,*
  DcLEnL, LongC, NewC, REn, TwCA,
  TwCA Sup
Ashton, J *Alli*
Ashton, Jane *Alli Sup*
Ashton, John *Alli Sup*
Ashton, John 1834?-1911 *Alli Sup, ChPo,*
  ChPo S1
Ashton, Joseph Nickerson 1868-1946 *DcNAA*
Ashton, Laurence 1847- *DcAmA*
Ashton, P *Alli*
Ashton, R *Alli*
Ashton, Robert *PoIre*
Ashton, Robert 1924- *ConAu 1R*
Ashton, Robert Stone *Alli Sup*
Ashton, Samuel Elkanah *Alli Sup*
Ashton, Sophia Goodrich 1819- *Alli, Alli Sup,*
  DcNAA
Ashton, Thomas 1631- *Alli*
Ashton, Thomas 1716-1775 *Alli*
Ashton, Thomas John *Alli Sup*
Ashton, Walter *Alli*
Ashton, Warren T *Alli Sup, DcNAA*
Ashton, William *Alli*
Ashton, William Easterly 1859-1933 *DcNAA*
Ashton, William Lawrence 1931- *Au&Wr*
Ashton, William Thomas 1832- *Alli Sup*
Ashton, Winifred *DcLEnL, EvLB, LongC,*
  McGWD, NewC, TwCA, TwCA Sup
Ashton-Warner, Sylvia 1905?- *Pen Eng*
Ashton-Warner, Sylvia 1908- *ConNov 1972,*
  ConNov 1976, LongC, RAdv 1, TwCW,
  WorAu, WrD 1976
Ashtown, Lord *ChPo S1*
Ashwell, Arthur Rawson 1824-1879 *Alli Sup*
Ashwell, George 1612-1693 *Alli*
Ashwell, John *Alli, DcEnL*
Ashwell, Lena 1869- *WhWNAA*
Ashwell, Samuel *Alli*
Ashwell, Thomas *Alli*
Ashwood, Bart *Alli*
Ashwood, John *Alli*
Ashworth, Caleb 1721-1775 *Alli*
Ashworth, Chadwick *MnBBF*
Ashworth, Edward Montague *OxCan*
Ashworth, Henry 1794-1880 *Alli Sup, BbtC*
Ashworth, James George *Alli Sup*
Ashworth, John 1813-1875 *Alli Sup, BrAu 19*
Ashworth, John Hervey *Alli Sup*
Ashworth, Kenneth H 1932- *ConAu 41*
Ashworth, Mae Hurley *IndAu 1917*
Ashworth, Mary Wells Knight 1903- *ConAu 5R*
Ashworth, Philip Arthur 1854- *Alli Sup*
Ashworth, Thomas *Alli Sup*
Ashworth, Wilfred 1912- *ConAu 13R*
Ashworth, William 1920- *ConAu 5R*
Asimov, Isaac 1920- *AmA&B, Au&Wr,*
  AuBYP, CasWL, ConAu 1R, ConLC 1,
  ConLC 3, ConNov 1972, ConNov 1976,
  DrAF 1976, EncM&D, LongC, Pen Am,
  REn, REnAL, SmATA 1, ThBJA,
  TwCW, WebEAL, WorAu, WrD 1976
Asin Palacios, Miguel 1871-1944 *CasWL,*
  ClDMEuL, REn
Asinius Pollio *CasWL*
Asinof, Eliot 1919- *ConAu 9R, SmATA 6,*
  WrD 1976
Ask, Upendranath 1910- *DcOrL 2*
Askari, Hussaini Muhammad *ConAu XR*
Aske, James *Alli, DcEnL*
Aske, Robert d1537 *NewC*
Aske, Sir Robert 1872- *WhLA*
Askelof, Johan Christoffer 1787-1848 *CasWL*
Askerc, Anton 1856-1912 *CasWL*
Askew, Anthony 1722-1772 *Alli, DcEnL*
Askew, William C 1910- *ConAu 49*

Atkeson, Thomas Clark 1852-1935 *AmLY,*
DcNAA
Atkeson, William Oscar 1854- *DcNAA*
Atkey, A *Alli*
Atkey, Bertram 1880-1952 *EncM&D*
Atkey, Philip *EncM&D, MnBBF*
Atkin, George Duckworth *ChPo S2*
Atkin, J Myron 1927- *ConAu 45*
Atkin, Randolph Henry *ChPo S2*
Atkin, Ronald Harry 1926- *Au&Wr*
Atkin, William 1882- *WhWNAA*
Atkins *Alli, BiDLA*
Atkins, Anna *Alli Sup*
Atkins, Chester G 1948- *ConAu 45*
Atkins, Dudley 1898-1945 *DcNAA*
Atkins, Edward *Alli Sup*
Atkins, Edwin Farnsworth 1850-1926 *DcNAA*
Atkins, Elizabeth Mary 1891- *WhWNAA*
Atkins, F J *MnBBF*
Atkins, Frank A *MnBBF*
Atkins, Frederick Anthony 1864- *WhLA*
Atkins, G Pope 1934- *ConAu 33*
Atkins, Gaius Glenn 1868- *IndAu 1816,*
WhWNAA
Atkins, H *Alli*
Atkins, Harry 1933- *ConAu 25*
Atkins, Sir Hedley John Barnard 1905- *Au&Wr*
Atkins, J *Alli Sup*
Atkins, Jack *ConAu XR*
Atkins, James *Alli, BiDLA*
Atkins, James B *Alli Sup*
Atkins, James G 1932- *ConAu 17R*
Atkins, Jim *ConAu XR*
Atkins, John *Alli, PoIre*
Atkins, John Alfred 1916- *Au&Wr,*
ConAu 9R, WrD 1976
Atkins, John Black 1871- *WhLA*
Atkins, John Ringwood *Alli Sup*
Atkins, Mary A *Alli Sup*
Atkins, Mary Sayles 1879-1966 *IndAu 1917*
Atkins, Paul Moody 1892- *WhWNAA*
Atkins, Richard *Alli Sup*
Atkins, Robert *Alli, BiDLA*
Atkins, Russell 1926- *BlkAW, ConAu 45,*
DrAP 1975, LivBA, WrD 1976
Atkins, Samuel *Alli*
Atkins, Stuart 1914- *AmA&B, ConAu 25,*
WrD 1976
Atkins, Suemma Vajen 1883-1924 *IndAu 1917*
Atkins, Thomas *Alli Sup, BlkAW*
Atkins, Thomas 1939- *ConAu 61*
Atkins, Thomas Astley 1839-1916 *DcNAA*
Atkins, W G *Alli Sup*
Atkins, Walter B *Alli Sup*
Atkins, Willard Earl 1889- *WhWNAA*
Atkins, William *Alli*
Atkins, William Ringrose Gelston 1884- *WhLA*
Atkinson *Alli*
Atkinson, Miss *Alli Sup*
Atkinson, Albert Algernon 1867- *WhWNAA*
Atkinson, Alice Minerva *AmLY, AmLY XR*
Atkinson, Anna Lindley *TexWr*
Atkinson, B A *Alli*
Atkinson, Basil Ferris Campbell 1895- *Au&Wr,*
ConAu 5R
Atkinson, Brian Hebblewhite 1914- *Au&Wr*
Atkinson, Brooks 1894- *ConAu 61, OxAm,*
REnAL, TwCA, TwCA Sup, WhWNAA,
WrD 1976
Atkinson, Bruce W 1941- *Au&Wr*
Atkinson, Caroline Penniman *ChPo, ChPo S1*
Atkinson, Carroll 1896- *ConAu P-1*
Atkinson, Charles Edwin 1884- *WhWNAA*
Atkinson, Charles Prescott 1867- *BiDSA*
Atkinson, Chris *Alli*
Atkinson, D H *Alli Sup*
Atkinson, E C *Alli Sup*
Atkinson, E M *ChPo S1*
Atkinson, Edmund *Alli Sup*
Atkinson, Edward 1827-1905 *Alli Sup, AmA,*
BbD, BiD&SB, DcAmA, DcNAA
Atkinson, Eleanor 1863-1942 *AmA&B,*
DcNAA, IndAu 1816, JBA 1934, TwCA,
TwCA Sup, WhWNAA
Atkinson, Emma Willsher *Alli Sup*
Atkinson, Francis Blake d1930 *DcNAA*
Atkinson, Fred Washington 1865-1945 *DcNAA*
Atkinson, Frederick *Alli Sup*

Atkinson, G F *Alli Sup*
Atkinson, Geoffroy 1892- *WhWNAA*
Atkinson, George *Alli, Alli Sup*
Atkinson, George Francis 1854-1918 *AmA,*
DcAmA, DcNAA
Atkinson, George Franklin *Alli Sup*
Atkinson, George Henry 1819-1889 *DcNAA*
Atkinson, George Wesley 1845-1925 *Alli Sup,*
AmA&B, BiDSA, DcAmA, DcNAA
Atkinson, Henry *Alli*
Atkinson, Henry 1786?-1831 *Alli*
Atkinson, Henry Avery 1877- *AmLY,*
WhWNAA
Atkinson, Hugh Craig 1933- *ConAu 49*
Atkinson, I Priestman *Alli Sup*
Atkinson, Israel *Alli Sup*
Atkinson, J J *Alli Sup*
Atkinson, J P *ChPo*
Atkinson, James *Alli, BiDLA*
Atkinson, James 1914- *Au&Wr, ConAu 25,*
WrD 1976
Atkinson, James Augustus *Alli Sup*
Atkinson, Jane *Alli Sup*
Atkinson, Janet *ChPo*
Atkinson, Jasper *Alli, BiDLA*
Atkinson, John *Alli*
Atkinson, John 1835-1897 *Alli Sup, DcAmA,*
DcNAA
Atkinson, John Augustus *BiDLA*
Atkinson, John Augustus & Walker, James *Alli*
Atkinson, John Christopher 1814-1900 *Alli Sup,*
NewC
Atkinson, John W 1923- *ConAu 23*
Atkinson, Joseph 1743-1818 *BiDLA, DcEnL,*
PoIre
Atkinson, Joseph 1846-1924 *Alli Sup, DcNAA*
Atkinson, Joseph Beavington 1822-1886
Alli Sup
Atkinson, Justin Brooks 1894- *AmA&B,*
TwCA, TwCA Sup
Atkinson, Louisa *Alli Sup*
Atkinson, M *Alli*
Atkinson, Margaret Fleming *AuBYP*
Atkinson, Marian A *ChPo*
Atkinson, Mary *ConAu 49*
Atkinson, Mary Ellen *Alli Sup, ChPo,*
ChPo S1
Atkinson, Mary Evelyn 1899- *Au&Wr,*
ConAu XR, SmATA 4, WhCL
Atkinson, Mary Jourdan 1898- *TexWr*
Atkinson, Matthew 1827-1913 *OhA&B*
Atkinson, Nancy 1910- *WrD 1976*
Atkinson, Oriana *AmA&B, ChPo*
Atkinson, Owen 1898- *WhWNAA*
Atkinson, Peter Righton d1888 *Alli Sup*
Atkinson, Philip *Alli Sup*
Atkinson, Phillip S 1921- *ConAu 25*
Atkinson, R C 1929- *ConAu 17R*
Atkinson, Ralph Waldo 1887- *WhWNAA*
Atkinson, Reginald *MnBBF*
Atkinson, Richard Stuart 1927- *WrD 1976*
Atkinson, Robert *Alli Sup*
Atkinson, Robert J 1820-1871 *OhA&B*
Atkinson, Ron 1932- *ConAu 57, DrAP 1975*
Atkinson, Ronald Field 1928- *ConAu 17R,*
WrD 1976
Atkinson, S *Alli*
Atkinson, T *BbtC*
Atkinson, Thomas *ChPo S1*
Atkinson, Thomas d1639 *Alli, DcEnL*
Atkinson, Thomas 1770- *Alli, BiDLA, PoIre*
Atkinson, Thomas Witlam 1799-1861 *Alli,*
Alli Sup
Atkinson, Mrs. Thomas Witlam *Alli Sup*
Atkinson, W A *MnBBF*
Atkinson, W Christopher *BbtC, OxCan*
Atkinson, W D *BiDSA*
Atkinson, Willard S 1874- *WhWNAA*
Atkinson, William *Alli, Alli Sup, BiDLA*
Atkinson, William Biddle 1832-1909 *Alli Sup,*
DcAmA, DcNAA
Atkinson, William Blake *Alli Sup, ChPo S1,*
ChPo S2
Atkinson, William C 1902- *DcSpL*
Atkinson, William Davis 1850- *DcNAA*
Atkinson, William Parsons 1820-1890 *Alli Sup,*
DcAmA, DcNAA
Atkinson, William Walker 1862-1932 *DcNAA*

Atkinson, Wilmer 1840-1920 *AmA&B,*
DcNAA
Atkinson And Clarke *Alli*
Atkisson, Arthur A 1930- *ConAu 61*
Atkyns, Glenn C 1921- *ConAu 49*
Atkyns, John *Alli*
Atkyns, John Tracy *Alli*
Atkyns, Richard 1615?-1677 *Alli, DcEnL,*
NewC
Atkyns, Sir Robert 1621-1709 *Alli*
Atkyns, Sir Robert 1647-1711 *Alli, DcEnL*
Atlas *ConAmA*
Atlas, James *DrAP 1975*
Atlas, Martin 1914- *ConAu 5R*
Atlay, Joseph *Alli, BiDLA*
Atlee, Benge 1890- *WhWNAA*
Atlee, Edwin Augustus 1776-1852 *DcNAA*
Atlee, Washington Lemuel 1808-1878 *Alli,*
Alli Sup, DcAmA
Atley, H *Alli Sup*
Atmore, Anthony 1932- *ConAu 25*
Atmore, Charles *Alli, BiDLA*
Atom, Ann *AmA*
Atre, Prahlad Kesav 1898-1970 *DcOrL 2*
Atreya, Bhikhan Lal 1897- *BiDPar*
Atson, William *Alli Sup*
Attaleiates *CasWL*
Attaliates, Michael *Pen Cl*
Attar, Farid Al-Din Abu Hamid 1119?-1230
CasWL, Pen Cl
Attar, Faridoddin d1220? *DcOrL 3*
Attar, Ferid Ed Din 1119-1229? *BbD, BiD&SB*
Attaway, Robert J 1942- *ConAu 49*
Attaway, William A 1912- *AmA&B, BlkAW,*
LivBAA, LivBA
Attea, Mary 1929- *ConAu 57*
Atteberry, William L 1939- *ConAu 53*
Attenberry, Bernard George *Au&Wr,*
ConAu 49
Attenborough, David Frederick 1926- *Au&Wr,*
Co Au 1R, WrD 1976
Attenborough, Florence G *ChPo S2*
Atter, Gordon Francis 1905- *WrD 1976*
Atterbom, Per Daniel Amadeus 1790-1855 *BbD,*
BiD&SB, CasWL, EuA, EvEuW,
Pen Eur
Atterbom, Peter Daniel Amadeus 1790-1855
DcEuL
Atterbury *Alli*
Atterbury, Anson Phelps 1854-1931 *DcAmA,*
DcNAA
Atterbury, Francis 1662-1732 *Alli, BrAu,*
Chmbr 2, DcEnL, EvLB, NewC, OxEng
Atterbury, Lewis 1631-1693 *Alli*
Atterbury, Lewis 1656-1731 *Alli*
Atterbury, Marguerite *ChPo*
Atterbury, Stella 1899- *Au&Wr*
Atteridge, Andrew Hilliard *Alli Sup, NewC*
Atteridge, Harold Richard 1886-1938 *AmA&B,*
AmSCAP 66
Atteridge, Helen *Alli Sup, ChPo S1, PoIre*
Atteridge, Mary Ellen *Alli Sup*
Atterley, Joseph *DcNAA*
Attersol, William *Alli*
Attfield, John 1835- *Alli Sup*
Attfield, William *Alli Sup*
Atthill, Barbara Joyce 1907- *Au&Wr*
Atthill, Lombe *Alli Sup*
Atthill, Robert Anthony 1912- *WrD 1976*
Atthill, Robin 1912- *Au&Wr, WrD 1976*
Atticus *ConAu XR, DcEnL, SmATA XR*
Atticus, Titus Pomponius 109BC-032BC *CasWL,*
Pen Cl, REn
Attila d453 *NewC, OxGer, REn*
Attius *Pen Cl*
Attix, James Conner 1870- *WhWNAA*
Attlee, Clement Richard 1883-1967 *LongC*
Attneave, Carolyn L 1920- *ConAu 45*
Atton *Alli*
Attree, H R *BiDLA*
Attucks, Crispus *REn*
Attwater, Donald 1892- *Au&Wr, BkC 2,*
CatA 1947
Attwater, J P *ChPo S1*
Attwell, Arthur A 1917- *ConAu 49*
Attwell, Henry 1834- *Alli Sup, ChPo*
Attwell, Mabel Lucie 1879-1964 *ChPo,*
ChPo S1, WhCL

Attwell, Mable Lucie 1879-1964 *LongC*
Attwill, R I And Schofield, W J *Alli Sup*
Attwood, A A *ChPo*
Attwood, Charles 1898- *Au&Wr*
Attwood, F G *ChPo*
Attwood, George *Alli Sup*
Attwood, Thomas 1784-1856 *DcEnL*
Attwood, William 1919- *AmA&B, ConAu 21*
Atty, P T S *BbtC*
Atwater, C Elizabeth 1923- *ConAu 13R*
Atwater, Caleb 1778-1867 *DcNAA, OhA&B*
Atwater, Caroline *WhWNAA*
Atwater, Edward Elias 1816-1887 *Alli Sup, DcNAA*
Atwater, Florence Hasseltine Carroll *MorJA*
Atwater, Francis 1858-1935 *DcNAA*
Atwater, George Parkin 1874-1935? *AmLY, DcNAA, OhA&B*
Atwater, Helen Woodard *WhWNAA*
Atwater, Horace Cowles 1819-1879 *Alli Sup, DcAmA, DcNAA*
Atwater, Isaac 1818-1906 *DcNAA*
Atwater, Jeremiah *CyAL 1*
Atwater, John Birdseye 1855-1921 *DcNAA*
Atwater, Lyman Hotchkiss 1813-1883 *Alli Sup, DcAmA, DcNAA*
Atwater, Mary Meigs 1878- *WhWNAA*
Atwater, Montgomery Meigs 1904- *AuBYP, MorJA, WhPNW*
Atwater, Richard Tupper 1892-1948 *AmA&B, BkCL, ChPo S1, MorJA*
Atwater, Wilbur Olin 1844-1907 *Alli Sup, DcAmA, DcNAA*
Atwell, B W *Alli Sup*
Atwell, Clarence Allen 1891- *WhWNAA*
Atwell, George *Alli*
Atwell, Joseph d1768 *Alli*
Atwell, Roy 1878-1962 *AmSCAP 66, ChPo*
Atwell, William Erskine *Alli Sup*
Atwill, Lionel 1885-1946 *REn*
Atwood, Ann Margaret 1913- *ConAu 41, SmATA 7*
Atwood, Anthony 1801-1888 *Alli Sup, DcAmA, DcNAA*
Atwood, Clara E *ChPo*
Atwood, Daniel T *Alli Sup*
Atwood, David 1815-1889 *DcNAA*
Atwood, Drucy *ConAu XR*
Atwood, E W *Alli Sup*
Atwood, Edward S *Alli Sup*
Atwood, Frederick Julius 1857- *ChPo S1*
Atwood, G *Alli*
Atwood, George 1745-1807 *Alli*
Atwood, Harry Fuller 1870-1930 *DcNAA, WhWNAA*
Atwood, Henry Dean 1839-1921 *DcNAA*
Atwood, Horace 1869- *WhWNAA*
Atwood, Isaac Morgan 1838-1917 *Alli Sup, BiD&SB, DcAmA, DcNAA*
Atwood, Mae *OxCan Sup*
Atwood, Margaret 1939- *Au&Wr, ConAu 49, ConLC 2, ConLC 3, ConLC 4, ConNov 1976, ConP 1970, ConP 1975, DrAF 1976, DrAP 1975, OxCan, OxCan Sup, WrD 1976*
Atwood, Millard VanMarter 1886-1941 *AmA&B, DcNAA, WhWNAA*
Atwood, Nora 1866-1948 *DcNAA*
Atwood, Robert B *AuNews 2*
Atwood, Thomas *Alli*
Atwood, Thomas 1765-1838 *Alli*
Atwood, Wallace Walter 1872-1949 *AmA&B, DcNAA, WhWNAA*
Atwood, William *Alli*
Atwood, Winfred McKenzie 1883- *WhWNAA*
Atze, Gerhard *OxGer*
Atzler, Edgar 1887- *WhLA*
Auale, Lemeke *Alli*
Aub, Max 1903- *REn, TwCW*
Aubanel, Theodore 1829-1886 *BiD&SB, CasWL, ClDMEuL, EuA, EvEuW, OxFr, Pen Eur*
Auber, Daniel François Esprit 1782-1871 *AtlBL, OxFr, REn*
Auber, Harriet 1773-1862 *NewC, PoCh*
Auber, Peter *Alli*
Aubert, Alex V 1729-1805 *Alli*
Aubert, Alvin 1930- *BlkAW, ConP 1975,*

DrAP 1975, WrD 1976
Aubert, Brenda *ChPo*
Aubert, Joachim Marie Jean Jacques A J 1804-1890 *BiD&SB*
Aubert, R P *BbtC*
Aubert, Thomas *OxCan*
Aubert DeGaspe, Philippe 1786-1871 *CanWr, DcNAA, OxCan, REnAL*
Aubert DeGaspe, Philippe 1814-1841 *DcNAA, OxCan*
Aubert DeLaChesnaye, Charles 1630-1702 *OxCan*
Aubert DeLaChesnaye DesBois, F-A *OxFr*
Aubertin, J J *Alli Sup*
Aubery, Pierre 1920- *ConAu 37*
Aubey, Robert T 1930- *ConAu 21*
Aubignac, Francois Hedelin, Abbe D' 1604-1676 *BiD&SB, CasWL, DcEuL, OxFr, Pen Eur, REn*
Aubigne, Theodore Agrippa D' 1552?-1630 *BiD&SB, CasWL, DcEuL, EuA, EvEuW, OxFr, REn*
Aubin, Hermann Carl William 1885- *WhLA*
Aubin, Napoleon 1812-1890 *BbtC, DcNAA, OxCan*
Aubin, P *Alli*
Aubourg, Michel 1921- *BiDPar*
Aubrey, Charles E 1822-1852 *ChPo*
Aubrey, D *Alli Sup*
Aubrey, Edwin Ewart 1896- *WhWNAA*
Aubrey, Frank *MnBBF*
Aubrey, Frederick *Alli Sup*
Aubrey, John 1626-1697 *Alli, AtlBL, BrAu, CasWL, Chmbr 1, CrE&SL, DcEnA, DcEnL, DcLEnL, EvLB, MouLC 1, NewC, OxEng, Pen Eng, REn, WebEAL*
Aubrey, William 1529-1595 *Alli*
Aubrey, William Hickman Smith *Alli Sup*
Aubrey-Fletcher, Henry Lancelot *EncM&D*
Aubry, Auguste Eugene 1819- *BbtC*
Aubry, Claude *OxCan Sup*
Aubry, M *Alli, BbtC*
Aubry, Octave 1881-1946 *EvEuW, TwCA, TwCA Sup, WhLA*
Aubusson, Pierre D' 1423-1503 *OxFr*
Auchincloss, J *Alli, BiDLA*
Auchincloss, Louis 1917- *AmA&B, Au&Wr, ConAu 1R, ConLC 4, ConLC 6, ConNov 1972, ConNov 1976, DrAF 1976, ModAL, ModAL Sup, OxAm, Pen Am, RAdv 1, REn, REnAL, TwCW, WebEAL, WorAu, WrD 1976*
Auchincloss, William Stuart 1842-1928 *Alli Sup, AmLY, DcNAA*
Auchinleck, Lord *NewC*
Auchinleck, Gilbert *BbtC, OxCan*
Auchinleck, Hugh B *Alli*
Auchmuty, Arthur Compton *Alli Sup*
Auchmuty, James Johnston 1909- *WrD 1976*
Auchmuty, Robert d1750 *Alli*
Auchter, Eugene Curtis 1889- *WhWNAA*
Auchterlonie, Dorothy 1915- *ConP 1970*
Auckinleck, Sydney E *PoIre*
Auckland, Lord William Eden d1814 *Alli, BiDLA, BiDLA Sup*
Auclair, Joseph 1813-1887 *DcNAA*
Auclair, Marie Gabrielle Marcelle *Au&Wr*
Aucoin, Peter *OxCan Sup*
Audain, R *Alli Sup*
Audax *WhWNAA*
Aude, Joseph, Chevalier 1755-1841 *OxFr*
Audefroi Le Bastart *CasWL, EvEuW*
Audelay, John *CasWL, ChPo, DcEnL*
Audemars, Pierre 1909- *ConAu 17R*
Auden, J E 1860-1946 *Br&AmS*
Auden, W H 1907-1973 *AmA&B, AmSCAP 66, Au&Wr, CasWL, ChPo, ChPo S1, ChPo S2, Chmbr 3, CnE&AP, CnMD, CnMWL, ConAu 9R, ConAu 45, ConLC 1, ConLC 2, ConLC 3, ConLC 4, ConLC 6, ConP 1970, ConP 1975, CyWA, DcLEnL, EncWL, EvLB, LongC, McGWD, ModAL, ModAL Sup, ModBL, ModBL Sup, ModWD, NewC, OxAm, OxEng, Pen Eng, RAdv 1, RCom, REn, REnAL, TwCA, TwCA Sup, TwCW, WebEAL, WhTwL*

Auden, William Henry 1867-1940 *DcNAA*
Audet, Francois Joseph 1867-1943 *DcNAA, WhWNAA*
Audet, Philippe *OxCan Sup*
Audiberti, Jacques 1899-1965 *CasWL, ClDMEuL, CnMD, CnThe, ConAu 25, CrCD, EncWL, EvEuW, McGWD, ModWD, OxFr, Pen Eur, REn, WorAu*
Audisio, Gabriel 1900- *CasWL*
Audley, Captain *MnBBF*
Audley, E H 1895- *Au&Wr*
Audley, Lady Eleanor *Alli*
Audley, J *Alli*
Audley, Lord James, Earl Of Castlehaven *Alli*
Audley, John *Alli, BiDLA*
Audley, Matt *Alli*
Audouard, Olympe 1830-1890 *BiD&SB*
Audourad, Olympe 1830-1890 *BbD*
Audoux, Marguerite 1863-1937 *LongC, OxFr*
Audsley, George Ashdown 1838-1925 *Alli Su, BiD&SB, DcAmA, DcNAA*
Audsley, James Edward Lawrence 1911- *Au&Wr*
Audsley, William James *Alli Sup*
Audubon, John James 1785?-1851 *Alli, AmA, AmA&B, AtlBL, BbD, BiD&SB, BiDSA, CnDAL, CyAL 1, DcAmA, DcLEnL, DcNAA, MouLC 3, OhA&B, OxAm, OxCan, OxEng, Pen Am, REn, REnAL*
Audubon, Lucy Bakewell d1874 *BiDSA*
Audubon, Maria R d1925 *BiDSA, DcNAA*
Audus, Leslie John 1911- *Au&Wr, WrD 1976*
Aue, Hartmann Von *BiD&SB, REn*
Auer, Adelheid Von 1818- *BiD&SB*
Auer, Harry A *OxCan*
Auer, Heinrich Joachim 1884- *WhLA*
Auer, J Jeffery 1913- *ConAu 9R*
Auer, Leopold 1845-1930 *AmSCAP 66*
Auerbach, Arnold 1898- *Au&Wr*
Auerbach, Arnold M 1912- *ConAu 17R*
Auerbach, Berthold 1812-1882 *BbD, BiD&SB, CasWL, DcBiA, DcEnL, DcEuL, EuA, EvEuW, OxGer, REn*
Auerbach, Erich 1892-1957 *EncWL, ModGL, WorAu*
Auerbach, Erna d1975 *ConAu 61*
Auerbach, George 1905?-1973 *ConAu 45*
Auerbach, Jerold S 1936- *ConAu 21*
Auerbach, Joseph Smith 1855-1944 *DcNAA*
Auerbach, Marjorie 1932- *ConAu 9R, IlCB 1966*
Auerbach, Stevanne 1938- *ConAu 57*
Auerbach, Sylvia 1921- *ConAu 53*
Auerell, William *Alli*
Auernheimer, Raoul 1876-1948 *OxGer, WhLA*
Auersperg, Anton Alexander Graf Von 1806-1876? *BbD, BiD&SB, CasWL, DcEuL, EvEuW, OxGer*
Auezov, Mukhtar 1897-1961 *DcOrL 3*
Auf Der Maur, Nick *OxCan Sup*
Auffenberg, Josef, Freiherr Von 1798-1857 *OxGer*
Auffenberg, Baron Joseph Von 1798-1857 *BiD&SB*
Aufi, Muhammad *CasWL, DcOrL 3*
Aufidius Bassus *Pen Cl*
Aufrecht, Simon Theodor 1822- *Alli Sup*
Aufrere, Anthony *BiDLA*
Aufricht, Hans 1902- *ConAu 45*
Aufsesser, Hans *ChPo*
Auge, Claude *OxFr*
Augelli, John P 1921- *ConAu 17R*
Auger, H A 1917- *Au&Wr*
Auger, Joseph Cyrille 1836-1891 *DcNAA*
Auger, Louis-Simon 1772-1829 *OxFr*
Auger, Pierre Victor 1899- *Au&Wr*
Augereau, Pierre-Francois-Charles *OxFr*
Aughey, John Hill 1828-1911 *Alli Sup, DcNAA, OhA&B*
Aughey, Samuel 1831-1912 *DcNAA*
Aughiltree, Ruth *AnMV 1926*
Aughinbaugh, William Edmund 1871-1940 *DcNAA, WhWNAA*
Aughtry, Charles Edward 1925- *ConAu 5R*
Augier, Emile 1820-1889 *BbD, BiD&SB, CasWL, CnThe, DcEuL, EuA, EvEuW, McGWD, OxFr, Pen Eur, REn, REnWD*
Augsberger, David W 1938- *ConAu 33*

39

Augsburg, Paul Deresco 1897- *WhWNAA*
Augsburger, A Don 1925- *ConAu 21*
Augsburger, Myron S 1929- *ConAu 13R*
Augspurger, Marie M 1898- *OhA&B*
Augur, Herbert Bassett 1874-1938 *DcNAA*
Augur, Ruth Monro *ChPo S1*
August III 1696-1763 *OxGer*
August II, Der Starke 1670-1733 *OxGer*
August, Eugene R 1935- *ConAu 49*
August, Garry J 1894- *IndAu 1917*
August, John *AmNov XR, LongC*
Augusta, Clara 1856- *ChPo*
Augustenburg, Friedrich, Herzog Von 1829-1880 *OxGer*
Augustijnken Van Dordt *CasWL*
Augustin Von Hamersteten *OxGer*
Augustin, Ann Sutherland 1934- *ConAu 57*
Augustin, Ernst 1927- *OxGer*
Augustin, George *BiDSA*
Augustin, James M *BiDSA*
Augustin, John Alcee 1838-1888 *BiDSA, DcNAA*
Augustin, Marie *BiDSA*
Augustin, Pius 1934- *ConAu 17R*
Augustine, Saint 354-430 *AtlBL, BbD, BiD&SB, CasWL, CyWA, NewC, OxEng, Pen Cl, RCom, REn*
Augustine Of Canterbury, Saint d604? *REn, NewC*
Augustine, Erich 1950- *ConAu XR*
Augustine, Jane *DrAP 1975*
Augustson, Ernest *WhWNAA*
Augustus *AmLY XR*
Augustus 063BC-014AD *NewC, Pen Cl, REn*
Augustus, John 1785-1859 *DcNAA*
Augustus, Timothy Bell *BlkAW*
Auhadi 1337?- *CasWL*
Auhadi, Taqi 1565-1630 *DcOrL 2*
Aukerman, Robert C 1910- *ConAu 33, WrD 1976*
Aukrust, Olav 1883-1929 *CasWL, ClDMEuL, EncWL, Pen Eur*
Aulaire, Edgar Parin D' *AnCL, JBA 1951*
Aulaire, Ingri D' *AnCL, JBA 1951*
Aulaire, Ingri D' And Edgar Parin D' *JBA 1934*
Aulard, Alphonse 1849-1928 *OxFr*
Auld, Agnes *ChPo S2*
Auld, Alexander *Alli Sup*
Auld, Alexander 1816-1889? *AmA&B, DcNAA*
Auld, Georgie 1919- *AmSCAP 66*
Auld, Philip 1915- *Au&Wr, WrD 1976*
Auld, Robert Campbell MacCombie 1857-1937 *ChPo S1, DcNAA*
Auleta, Michael S 1909- *ConAu 25*
Auletta, Richard P 1942- *ConAu 53*
Aulick, June L 1906- *ConAu 25*
Aulls, Joseph A *IndAu 1816*
Aulnay-Charnisay, Charles DeM, Sieur D' 1604?-1650 *OxCan*
Aulneau, Jean-Pierre *OxCan*
Aulnoy, Marie-Catherine, Comtesse D' 1650?-1705 *BiD&SB, CarSB, CasWL, DcEuL, OxFr*
Ault, Norman 1880-1950 *ChPo, ChPo S1, ConICB, IlCB 1945*
Ault, Susan Mary 1934- *Au&Wr*
Ault, Warren Ortman 1887- *WhWNAA*
Aultman, Donald S 1930- *ConAu 17R*
Aultman, Dwight Edward 1872-1929 *DcNAA*
Aulus Gellius *OxEng*
Aumale, Henri Eugene P, L D'o, Duc D' 1822-1897 *BiD&SB*
Aumann, Francis Robert 1901- *ConAu 41, OhA&B*
Aumbry, Alan *ConAu XR*
Aumonier, Stacy 1887-1928 *EncM&D, EvLB, LongC, NewC, TwCA, TwCA Sup*
Aumont, Jean-Pierre 1913- *ConAu 29*
Aung, Htin 1909- *ConAu 5R*
Aungell, John *Alli*
Aungerville, Richard 1281?-1345 *Alli, BrAu, DcEuL, NewC*
Aungervyle, Richard *DcEnL*
Aunt Carrie *DcNAA*
Aunt Carry *ChPo*
Aunt Clara *ChPo*
Aunt Effie *ChPo*

Aunt Elmina *DcNAA*
Aunt Este *WhWNAA*
Aunt Fanny *AmA, AmA&B, ChPo, OhA&B*
Aunt Hattie *AmA&B*
Aunt Irene *NewbC 1966*
Aunt Judy *ChPo, ChPo S1*
Aunt Kitty *CyAL 2*
Aurand, Harold Wilson 1940- *ConAu 41*
Aurand, L W 1920- *ConAu 53*
Aurandt, Paul Harvey 1918- *AmA&B*
Aurbacher, Ludwig 1784-1847 *BiD&SB*
Aurednicek, Anna 1873- *WhLA*
Aureli, Mariano 1820- *BiD&SB*
Aurelia *DcNAA*
Aurelius, Abraham *Alli*
Aurelius, Marcus 121-180 *BbD, BiD&SB, CasWL, DcEnL, Pen Cl, RCom*
Aurelius Victor, Sextus *CasWL, Pen Cl*
Aurell, Tage 1895- *CasWL*
Auriac, Jules Berlioz D' 1820- *BiD&SB*
Auric, Georges 1899- *REn*
Auringer, Obadiah Cyrus 1849-1937 *Alli Sup, AmA&B, BiD&SB, DcAmA, DcNAA, WhWNAA*
Aurispa, Giovanni 1375?-1459 *CasWL, DcEuL, REn*
Aurner, Clarence Ray 1861- *WhWNAA*
Aurner, Nellie Slayton 1873- *WhWNAA*
Aurner, Robert Ray 1898- *ConAu 5R, WhWNAA, WrD 1976*
Aurobindo, Sri *CasWL, DcLEnL, WebEAL*
Aurora Esmeralda *AmA&B*
Aurthur, Robert Alan 1922- *AmA&B*
Aus, Carol 1868- *ChPo*
Auslaender, Rose 1907- *CasWL*
Auslander, Joseph 1897-1965 *AmA&B, ChPo, ChPo S1, CnDAL, OxAm, REn, REnAL, TwCA, TwCA Sup, WhWNAA*
Ausonius, Decimus Magnus 310?-395? *BiD&SB, CasWL, OxEng, Pen Cl*
Ausserer, Carl 1883- *WhLA*
Austen *Alli*
Austen, Adelaide *Alli Sup*
Austen, Evelyn *Alli Sup*
Austen, Frances Vescelius *ChPo*
Austen, Henry Haversham Godwin 1834- *Alli Sup*
Austen, Jane 1775-1817 *Alli, AtlBL, BbD, BiD&SB, BrAu 19, CasWL 19, Chmbr 2, CriT 2, CyWA, DcBiA, DcEnA, DcEnL, DcEuL, DcLEnL, EvLB, MouLC 2, NewC, OxEng, Pen Eng, RAdv 1, RCom, REn, WebEAL*
Austen, John 1886- *ChPo, ChPo S1, ChPo S2, IlCB 1945*
Austen, Peter Townsend 1852-1907 *Alli Sup, DcAmA, DcNAA*
Austen, R *EarAB*
Austen, Ralph d1676 *Alli*
Austen, Ralph A 1937- *ConAu 25*
Austen, Samuel Cooper *Alli Sup*
Austen-Leigh *Alli Sup*
Auster, George *Alli Sup*
Austerlitz, Emanuel H 1838-1927 *OhA&B*
Austgen, Robert Joseph 1932- *ConAu 23, IndAu 1917, WrD 1976*
Austin Of Canterbury, Saint *NewC*
Austin, Adam *Chmbr 2*
Austin, Alfred 1835-1913 *Alli Sup, BbD, BiD&SB, BrAu 19, ChPo, ChPo S1, ChPo S2, Chmbr 3, DcEnA, DcEnA Ap, DcEnL, DcEuL, DcLEnL, EvLB, LongC, NewC, OxEng, Pen Eng, TwCW*
Austin, Allen C 1922- *ConAu 33, WrD 1976*
Austin, Anne *TexWr*
Austin, Anthony 1919- *ConAu 33*
Austin, Arthur Everett 1861- *WhWNAA*
Austin, Arthur Williams 1807-1884 *Alli Sup, ChPo, ChPo S2, DcAmA, DcNAA*
Austin, Aurelia *ConAu 53*
Austin, B C *Alli Sup*
Austin, Barbara Leslie *ConAu XR*
Austin, Benjamin *Alli*
Austin, Benjamin 1752-1820 *Alli, DcAmA, DcNAA*
Austin, Benjamin Fish 1850-1932 *AmLY, DcNAA*
Austin, Billy 1896-1964 *AmSCAP 66*

Austin, Blanche Friend 1886- *WhWNAA*
Austin, Brett *ConAu XR, WrD 1976*
Austin, Caroline *Alli Sup*
Austin, Cedric Ronald Jonah 1912- *Au&Wr, WrD 1976*
Austin, Charles E *Alli Sup*
Austin, Coe Finch 1831-1880 *Alli Sup, DcAmA, DcNAA*
Austin, David 1759-1831 *DcNAA*
Austin, David E 1926- *ConAu 29*
Austin, E *Alli Sup*
Austin, E P *Alli Sup*
Austin, Edmund *BlkAW*
Austin, Elizabeth S 1907- *ConAu 25, SmATA 5*
Austin, F W G *BbtC*
Austin, Mrs. Francis M 1885- *WhWNAA*
Austin, Francis Marion 1862-1922 *DcNAA*
Austin, Frank Eugene 1873- *WhWNAA*
Austin, Frederick Britten 1885-1941 *MnBBF, NewC, WhLA*
Austin, Gene 1900- *AmSCAP 66*
Austin, George Lowell 1849-1893 *Alli Sup, BiD&SB, ChPo S1, DcAmA, DcNAA*
Austin, Mrs George Lowell *Alli Sup, ChPo*
Austin, George McKendree 1856-1930 *OhA&B*
Austin, Gilbert *Alli, BiDLA*
Austin, Grace Jewett 1872-1948 *DcNAA, WhWNAA*
Austin, Grace M *ChPo*
Austin, Harry *ConAu XR*
Austin, Henry 1858-1918 *Alli Sup, BiD&SB, DcAmA, DcNAA*
Austin, Henry Wilfred 1906- *WrD 1976*
Austin, Henry Willard 1858-1912 *Alli Sup, BbD, BiD&SB, DcAmA, DcNAA*
Austin, Herbert Douglas 1876- *WhWNAA*
Austin, Herbert Henry 1868- *WhLA*
Austin, Hilda *ChPo S1, ChPo S2*
Austin, Sir Horatio Thomas d1865 *OxCan*
Austin, J A *Alli Sup*
Austin, J B *Alli Sup*
Austin, J Harold 1883- *WhWNAA*
Austin, James C 1923- *ConAu 13R*
Austin, James G *Alli Sup*
Austin, James T 1784-1870 *Alli, BiD&SB, CyAL 1, DcAmA, DcNAA*
Austin, Jane Goodwin 1831-1894 *Alli Sup, AmA, AmA&B, BbD, BiD&SB, CarSB, DcAmA, DcBiA, DcNAA, JBA 1934, OxAm, REnAL*
Austin, John *Alli, ChPo, Chmbr 3*
Austin, John 1613-1669 *Alli, ChPo, DcEnL, PoCh*
Austin, John 1790-1859 *Alli Sup, BrAu 19, CasWL, DcEnL, DcEuL, EvLB, NewC, OxEng*
Austin, John 1922- *ConAu 61*
Austin, Mrs. John *Chmbr 3*
Austin, John Langshaw 1911-1960 *LongC, OxEng*
Austin, John Mather 1805-1880 *Alli, DcAmA, DcNAA*
Austin, John Osborne 1849-1918 *Alli Sup, AmA&B, DcAmA, DcNAA*
Austin, Jonathan Loring 1748-1826 *Alli*
Austin, Joseph 1808-1836 *ChPo, ChPo S1*
Austin, Kenneth Ashurst 1911- *WrD 1976*
Austin, Leonard Strong 1846-1929 *DcNAA, WhWNAA*
Austin, Lettie J 1925- *LivBA*
Austin, Lewis *Alli Sup*
Austin, Linda 1943- *ConAu 29*
Austin, Lloyd James 1915- *Au&Wr, ConAu P-1*
Austin, Louis Winslow 1867-1932 *DcNAA*
Austin, Lucie *Chmbr 3*
Austin, Margot *AuBYP, ConAu P-1, MorJA*
Austin, Maria Theresa *BiDSA*
Austin, Martha W *BiDSA*
Austin, Mary C 1915- *ConAu 5R*
Austin, Mary F *ChPo S1*
Austin, Mary Hunter 1868-1934 *AmA&B, AmLY, AnCL, BkCL, ChPo, ChPo S1, ChPo S2, CnDAL, ConAmA, ConAmL, DcAmA, DcLEnL, DcNAA, OxAm, REnAL, St&VC, TwCA, TwCA Sup, WhWNAA*

Austin, Mortimer *MnBBF*
Austin, Muriel Howard *Au&Wr*
Austin, Neal F 1926- *ConAu 25*
Austin, Oliver Luther, Jr. 1903- *ConAu 49, SmATA 7*
Austin, Oscar Phelps 1848?-1933 *AmLY, DcAmA, DcNAA, WhWNAA*
Austin, P T *Alli Sup*
Austin, Phil *IlBYP*
Austin, Richard Joseph Byron 1926- *Au&Wr, WrD 1976*
Austin, Richard Wilson 1857-1919 *DcNAA*
Austin, Robert Cecil 1828- *Alli Sup*
Austin, Robert S 1895- *ChPo, ChPo S1*
Austin, Samuel 1760-1830 *Alli, CyAL 1, DcAmA, DcEnL, DcNAA*
Austin, Samuel, The Elder 1606- *Alli*
Austin, Samuel, The Younger 1636-1665? *Alli*
Austin, Sarah 1793-1867 *Alli, Alli Sup, DcEnL, DcEuL, NewC, OxEng*
Austin, Stanley E d1950? *MnBBF*
Austin, Stella *Alli Sup*
Austin, Stephen Fuller 1793-1836 *AmA&B, REnAL*
Austin, Sumner Francis *Au&Wr*
Austin, Thomas *Alli Sup, PoIre*
Austin, Thomas J *Alli Sup*
Austin, Tom *ConAu XR*
Austin, W F *Alli Sup*
Austin, Mrs. W L *TexWr*
Austin, Walter 1864-1929 *DcNAA*
Austin, William *Alli*
Austin, William d1793 *Alli*
Austin, William 1587-1634 *NewC*
Austin, William 1778-1841 *Alli, AmA, AmA&B, BiD&SB, CyAL 1, DcAmA, DcLEnL, DcNAA, OxAm, REn, REnAL*
Austin, William W 1920- *ConAu 23, WrD 1976*
Austin, Wiltshire S, Jr. And Ralph, J *Alli Sup*
Austral *ChPo, ChPo S1*
Austrian, Charles Robert 1885- *WhWNAA*
Austwick, John *ConAu XR*
Ausubel, Herman 1920- *Au&Wr, ConAu 1R*
Auten, James H 1938- *ConAu 41*
Auteroche, Chappe D' *BbtC*
Auther, John *Alli*
Auton, C *Alli Sup, DcNAA*
Auton, Jean D' 1465?-1528 *CasWL, OxFr*
Autran, Joseph 1813-1877 *BbD, BiD&SB, EvEuW, OxFr*
Autran Dourado, Waldomiro *ConAu XR*
Autrey, C E 1904- *ConAu 1R*
Autrey, Herman 1904- *AmSCAP 66*
Autry, Ewart 1900- *ConAu 13R*
Autry, Gene 1907- *AmSCAP 66*
Autton, Norman William James 1920- *Au&Wr, WrD 1976*
Auty, Phyllis 1910- *Au&Wr, ConAu 5R*
Auvergne, E D' *Alli*
Auvergne, Martial D' 1430?-1508 *CasWL, EvEuW*
Auvert-Eason, Elizabeth 1917- *ConAu 37*
Auvil, Kenneth W 1925- *ConAu 17R*
Auzias-Turenne, Raymond *OxCan*
Ava, Frau d1127 *CasWL, OxGer*
Avakumoric, Ivan 1926- *ConAu 41*
Avakumovic, Ivan *OxCan Sup*
Avalle-Arce, Juan Bautista 1927- *ConAu 33*
Avallone, Michael Angelo, Jr. 1924- *Au&Wr, ConAu 5R, EncM&D, WrD 1976*
Avancini, Nicolaus Von 1612-1686 *CasWL*
Avancini, Nikolaus 1611-1686 *OxGer*
Avary, Myrta Lockett *AmA&B, BiDSA, WhWNAA*
Avaugour, Baron Pierre DuBois D' d1664 *OxCan*
Avdyeyev, Michael Vassilyevich 1821-1876 *BiD&SB*
Avebury, Baron John Lubbock 1834-1913 *BrAu 19, ChPo S2, DcEnA Ap, EvLB, NewC*
Aveline, Claude 1901- *Au&Wr, CasWL, ConAu 5R*
Aveline, E L *ChPo, ChPo S1*
Aveling, Edward Bibbins 1851-1898 *Alli Sup, PoIre*
Aveling, Eleanor *Alli Sup*
Aveling, Frederic Wilkins *Alli Sup*

Aveling, Henry *Alli Sup*
Aveling, James Hobson *Alli Sup*
Aveling, S T *Alli Sup*
Aveling, Thomas *Alli Sup*
Aveling, Thomas William Baxter 1815-1884 *PoCh, Alli Sup*
Avellaneda *DcSpL*
Avellaneda, Alonso Fernandez De *CasWL, DcEuL, OxEng*
Avellaneda, Gertrudis Gomez De *CasWL*
Avellaneda, Luis *WhWNAA*
Avellaneda Y Arteaga, Gertrudis Gomez De 1814-1873 *BbD, BiD&SB*
Avellino, Alfred 1913- *AmSCAP 66*
Avenant, D' *Alli*
Avenarius, Ferdinand 1856-1923 *OxGer*
Avencebrol 1028?-1058? *BiD&SB*
Avendano, Francisco De *DcEuL*
Avenel, Paul 1823-1902 *BbD, BiD&SB*
Aventinus, Johannes 1477-1534 *CasWL, EvEuW, OxGer*
Averanches, Henry D' *DcEnL*
Averbach, Albert 1902- *ConAu 21*
Averbakh, Leopold Leonidovich 1903- *CasWL, DcRusL*
Averbury, Lord *Chmbr 3*
Averchenko, Arkady Timofeyevich 1881-1925 *CasWL, ClDMEuL, DcRusL, EvEuW*
Averill, Anna Boynton 1843- *ChPo, ChPo S1*
Averill, Charles E *AmA&B, DcNAA*
Averill, E W 1906- *ConAu 53*
Averill, Elise *ArizL*
Averill, Esther Cunningham 1895- *BkCL, WhWNAA*
Averill, Esther Holden 1902- *AmA&B, AuBYP, ConAu 29, IlCB 1956, IlCB 1966, JBA 1934, SmATA 1, WrD 1976*
Averill, Lawrence Augustus 1891- *AmA&B, WhWNAA*
Averill, Lloyd J 1923- *ConAu 23*
Averitt, Robert T 1931- *ConAu 23*
Averitt, Will F 1889- *IndAu 1917*
Averitte, Ruth *ChPo, TexWr*
Averkiyev, Dmitry Vassilyevich 1836- *BbD, BiD&SB*
Averrhoes 1126-1198 *BbD, BiD&SB, REn*
Averroes 1126-1198 *BbD, BiD&SB, CasWL, DcEuL, DcOrL 3, EuA, EvEuW, OxEng, REn*
Avery, A S *Alli Sup*
Avery, Al *AmA&B, AuBYP, ConAu XR, SmATA 3, WrD 1976*
Avery, Benjamin Parke 1828?-1875 *Alli, Alli Sup, AmA, AmA&B, BiD&SB, ChPo, DcAmA, DcNAA*
Avery, Carlos 1868- *WhWNAA*
Avery, Catherine B 1909- *ConAu 57*
Avery, Claribel Weeks *ChPo S1*
Avery, David *WrD 1976*
Avery, Elizabeth *Au&Wr*
Avery, Elroy McKendree 1844-1935 *Alli Sup, AmLY, DcAmA, DcNAA, OhA&B, WhWNAA*
Avery, Emma Gage *ChPo*
Avery, Emmett Langdon 1903- *IndAu 1917*
Avery, Frank *ChPo S1*
Avery, George C 1926- *ConAu 25*
Avery, Gillian Elise 1926- *AuBYP, ConAu 9R, SmATA 7, WhCL*
Avery, H N *Alli Sup*
Avery, Harold 1867-1943 *MnBBF, WhCL*
Avery, Harold 1903- *Au&Wr*
Avery, Henry M 1840- *HsB&A*
Avery, Isaac Erwin 1871-1904 *BiDSA, DcNAA*
Avery, Isaac Wheeler 1837-1897 *BiDSA, DcAmA, DcNAA*
Avery, Jane G *Alli Sup*
Avery, John 1819-1902 *DcNAA*
Avery, John W *ChPo*
Avery, Kay 1908- *ConAu 1R, SmATA 5*
Avery, Laurence G 1934- *ConAu 33*
Avery, Lynn *AuBYP, ConAu XR, SmATA XR*
Avery, M A *Alli Sup*
Avery, Mary 1907- *WhPNW*
Avery, Peter William 1923- *Au&Wr, ConAu 13R*
Avery, Robert Sterling 1917- *ConAu 13R*

Avery, Samuel 1731-1806 *DcNAA*
Avery, Samuel P *Alli Sup, ChPo*
Avery, Samuel Putnam 1822-1904 *DcNAA*
Avery, Samuel Putnam 1847-1890 *DcNAA*
Avery, Susan Look 1817- *BiDSA*
Avery, W B *Alli Sup*
Avesbury, Robert De d1356 *Alli, DcEnL*
Avesta *CasWL*
Avey, Albert Edwin 1886-1963 *ConAu P-1, OhA&B*
Avi-Yonah, M 1904- *ConAu 5R*
Avianus, Flavius *BiD&SB, CasWL, NewC, OxEng*
Avice, Claude 1925- *ConAu 61*
Avicebron 1028?-1058? *BiD&SB, CasWL, DcEuL, EuA, EvEuW*
Avicenna 980-1037? *BiD&SB, CasWL, DcOrL 3, OxEng, Pen Cl, REn*
Avidan, David 1934- *CasWL*
Avienius, Rufius Festus *CasWL*
Avienus, Rufius Festus *CasWL, Pen Cl*
Avil, John D *BbD*
Avila, Juan De 1500-1569 *CasWL, DcEuL*
Avila, Lilian Estelle *ConAu 45*
Avila Y Zuniga, Luis De 1490?-1560? *DcEuL*
Avineri, Shlomo 1933- *ConAu 25*
Avinoff, Andrey 1884- *IlCB 1945*
Avirett, James Battle 1837?-1912 *BiDSA, DcNAA*
Avison, Charles 1710-1770 *Alli*
Avison, George 1885- *ConICB, IlBYP, IlCB 1945, IlCB 1956*
Avison, Margaret 1918- *CanWr, ConAu 17R, ConLC 2, ConLC 4, ConP 1970, ConP 1975, OxCan, OxCan Sup, WhTwL, WrD 1976*
Avison, N Howard 1934- *ConAu 29*
Avni, Abraham Albert 1921- *ConAu 33, WrD 1976*
Avocat, Un *OxCan*
Avola, Alexander Albert 1914- *AmSCAP 66*
Avon, W *Alli Sup*
Avotcja *BlkAW*
Avram, Mois H 1880- *WhWNAA*
Avramovic, Dragoslav 1919- *ConAu 41*
Avrelin, M *ConAu XR*
Avrett, Robert William 1901- *ChPo S1, ConAu 1R, DcSpL, TexWr*
Avrich, Paul 1931- *ConAu 49*
Avril, Pierre 1930- *ConAu 29*
Avseyenko, Vasily Grigoryevich 1842-1913 *CasWL*
Avvakum, Archpriest 1621?-1682 *DcRusL, EuA, Pen Eur, REn*
Avvakum, Protopop 1621?-1682 *CasWL*
Awa, Eme Onuoha 1921- *ConAu 13R*
Awad, Elias M 1934- *ConAu 17R*
Awazu, Kiyoshi 1929- *WhGrA*
Awbhatha, U 1758?-1798? *DcOrL 2*
Awbrey, Tim *Alli*
Awde, James *Alli Sup*
Awde, Robert *Alli Sup*
Awdelay, John *ChPo, NewC*
Awdeley, John *Alli, CasWL, NewC*
Awdry, Frances *Alli Sup*
Awdry, H *Alli Sup*
Awdry, Richard Charles 1929- *WrD 1976*
Awdry, Wilbert Vere 1911- *Au&Wr, WhCL, WrD 1976*
Awe, Chulho 1927- *Au&Wr, ConAu 33*
Aweusi, Alli *BlkAW*
Awolowo, Obafemi Awo 1909- *AfA 1*
A'Wood, Anthony *EvLB*
Awoonor, Kofi 1935- *AfA 1, BlkAW '2, CasWL, ConAu 29, ConP 1970, ConP 1975, DrAF 1976, EncWL Sup, RGAfl, WrD 1976*
Awoonor-Williams, George 1935- *AfA 1, CasWL, Pen Cl, TwCW*
Awsby, Edith *Alli Sup*
Awsiter, John *Alli*
Axe, J Wortley *Alli Sup*
Axelrad, Jacob 1899- *ConAu 61*
Axelrod, David B 1943- *ConAu 45, DrAP 1975*
Axelrod, George 1922- *AmA&B, CnMD, ConDr, McGWD, ModAL, WorAu, WrD 1976*

Axelrod, Herbert Richard 1927- *Au&Wr*
Axelrod, Joseph 1918- *ConAu 33*
Axelrod, Robert 1943- *ConAu 33*
Axelrod, Susan *DrAP 1975*
Axelson, Eric 1913- *ConAu 21*, *WrD 1976*
Axelson, Mary McDougal *AnMV 1926*,
    WhWNAA
Axeman, Lois *IlBYP*
Axford, John *Alli*
Axford, H William 1925- *ConAu 37*
Axford, Joseph Mack 1879- *ConAu 25*
Axford, Lavonne B 1928- *ConAu 33*
Axford, Roger W 1920- *ConAu 33*
Axelrod, David 1937- *AmSCAP 66*
Axline, W Andrew 1940- *ConAu 25*
Axling, William 1873- *WhWNAA*
Axon, William Edward Armytage 1846-1913
    Alli Sup, *ChPo S1*
Axson, Stockton 1867- *TexWr*
Axt, William 1888-1959 *AmSCAP 66*
Axtell, Harold L 1876- *WhWNAA*
Axton, W F 1926- *ConAu 21*
Ayal, Igal 1942- *ConAu 37*
Ayala, Adelardo Lopez De 1829-1879 *BbD*,
    BiD&SB
Ayala, Francisco 1906- *CasWL*, *TwCW*
Ayala, Pedro Lopez De 1332-1407 *BbD*,
    BiD&SB, *CasWL*, *DcEuL*, *DcSpL*,
    EvEuW
Ayala, Ramon Perez De *CnMWL*, *ModRL*,
    TwCA, *TwCA Sup*
Ayandele, E A 1936- *ConAu 21*
Ayanque, Simon *DcSpL*
Ayars, Albert Leo 1917- *ConAu 29*,
    WrD 1976
Ayars, James Sterling 1898- *AuBYP*,
    ConAu 5R, *SmATA 4*, *WrD 1976*
Ayars, Thomas H *ChPo*
Ayatey, Siegfried B Y 1934- *ConAu 25*
Ayaz, Shaikh Mubarak 1922- *DcOrL 2*
Aybar, Trudy *BlkAW*
Aybek *DcOrL 3*
Ayckbourn, Alan 1939- *ConAu 21*, *ConDr*,
    ConLC 5, *WrD 1976*
Ayckbourn, Hubert *Alli*, *Alli Sup*
Aydelott, Benjamin P 1795?-1880 *Alli Sup*,
    DcNAA, *WhWNAA*
Aydelotta, Frank 1880- *WhWNAA*
Aydelotte, Dora 1878- *WhWNAA*
Aydelotte, Frank 1880-1956 *AmA&B*,
    IndAu 1816
Aydelotte, Marian *ChPo S1*
Aydelotte, William Osgood 1910- *ConAu 57*,
    IndAu 1917
Ayearst, Morley 1899- *ConAu 29*
Ayer, Alfred Jules 1910- *Au&Wr*, *ConAu 5R*,
    DcLEnL, *LongC*, *OxEng*, *REn*, *WorAu*,
    WrD 1976
Ayer, Anne Chandler *ChPo*
Ayer, Brian *ConAu XR*
Ayer, Fred Carleton 1880- *TexWr*, *WhWNAA*
Ayer, Frederick 1822-1918 *DcNAA*
Ayer, Frederick 1917?-1974 *ConAu 45*
Ayer, Frederick Fanning d1942 *ChPo S1*,
    DcNAA
Ayer, Harriet 1854-1903 *DcAmA*, *DcNAA*
Ayer, Isaac Winslow *DcNAA*
Ayer, Jacqueline Brandford 1930- *IlBYP*,
    IlCB 1966, *ThBJA*
Ayer, James Cook 1818-1878 *Alli Sup*,
    DcNAA
Ayer, Jean Young *ChPo*
Ayer, John *AmA&B*
Ayer, Joseph Cullen 1866-1944 *DcAmA*,
    DcNAA
Ayer, Louisa M *Alli Sup*
Ayer, Margaret *IlBYP*, *IlCB 1956*, *MorJA*
Ayer, Mary Allette 1859- *WhWNAA*
Ayer, Mary True *ChPo*
Ayer, V A K 1911- *Au&Wr*
Ayerigg, Benjamin *Alli*
Ayerra Y Santa Maria, Francisco De 1630-1708
    PueRA
Ayers, A *Alli Sup*
Ayers, Donald Murray 1923- *ConAu 17R*
Ayers, E T *Alli Sup*
Ayers, Eben A 1890- *WhWNAA*
Ayers, Edward Augustus 1855-1917 *DcNAA*

Ayers, Harry Morgan 1881-1948 *DcNAA*,
    WhWNAA
Ayers, Howard 1859- *DcAmA*
Ayers, John H 1868?-1943 *DcNAA*
Ayers, M R 1935- *ConAu 25*
Ayers, Minnie Maud 1880-1942 *ChPo S1*,
    DcNAA
Ayers, Ph *Alli*
Ayers, Robert H 1918- *ConAu 45*
Ayers, Ronald 1948- *ConAu 61*
Ayers, Thomas *Alli Sup*
Ayers, Vivian *BlkAW*
Ayerst, David George Ogilvy 1904- *Au&Wr*,
    WrD 1976
Ayerst, William *Alli*, *Alli Sup*
Ayesha 611?-678? *NewC*
Ayguals, DeIzco, Wenceslao *DcSpL*
Aykroyd, Wallace Ruddell 1899- *WrD 1976*
Aylen, Elise 1904- *WhWNAA*
Aylen, Leo *WrD 1976*
Aylesbury, Thomas *Alli*
Aylesbury, William *Alli*
Aylesworth, Allen Bristol 1854-1952 *OxCan*
Aylesworth, Barton Orville 1860- *DcAmA*
Aylesworth, Thomas Gibbons 1927- *ConAu 25*,
    IndAu 1917, *SmATA 4*
Aylett, George *Alli*
Aylett, Robert *Alli*, *DcEnL*
Ayleway, William *Alli*
Ayleworth, William *Alli*
Ayliffe, Agnes *ChPo S1*
Ayliffe, John *Alli*
Ayling, Stanley 1909- *ConAu 45*
Aylmer, Lady *OxCan*
Aylmer, Lord 1775-1850 *BbtC*, *OxCan*
Aylmer, Sir Felix 1889- *Au&Wr*, *ConAu XR*
Aylmer, Mrs. Fenton *Alli Sup*
Aylmer, G E 1926- *ConAu 13R*, *WrD 1976*
Aylmer, Mrs. G E *Alli Sup*
Aylmer, George James *Alli*, *BiDLA*
Aylmer, John *Alli*
Aylmer, John 1521-1594 *Alli*, *DcEnL*, *NewC*
Aylmer, Justin *Alli*
Aylmer, William *Alli*
Aylmer-Gowing, Emilia 1846- *BiD&SB*
Ayloffe, Sir Joseph 1709-1781 *Alli*
Aylsworth, William Prince 1844- *WhWNAA*
Aylward, Alfred *Alli Sup*
Aylward, James Ambrose Dominic 1813-1872
    Alli Sup, *PoIre*
Aylward, William James 1875- *IlCB 1945*
Aymar, Brandt 1911- *ConAu 1R*, *WhWNAA*
Aymar, Gordon Christian 1893- *Au&Wr*,
    ConAu 5R, *WrD 1976*
Ayme, Isaac *Alli*
Ayme, Marcel 1902-1967 *CasWL*, *CIDMEuL*,
    CnMD, *CnThe*, *EncWL*, *EvEuW*, *LongC*,
    McGWD, *ModRL*, *ModWD*, *OxFr*,
    Pen Eur, *REn*, *TwCA Sup*, *TwCW*
Aymer De Valence 1265?-1324 *NewC*
Aymes, John *Alli*
Aymes, Sister Maria DeLaCruz *ConAu 23*
Aymon *NewC*
Aymot, Jacques 1513-1593 *REn*
Aynes, Edith A 1909- *ConAu 45*
Aynes, Pat Edith *ConAu XR*
Aynesworth, Cecil *MnBBF*
Ayni, Sadriddin 1878-1954 *DcOrL 3*
Aynsley, Mrs. H G Murray- *Alli Sup*
Ayr, Esther *Alli Sup*
Ayraud, Pierre *WorAu*
Ayrault, Evelyn West 1922- *ConAu 9R*
Ayray, James *Alli*
Ayre, John *Alli*, *Alli Sup*
Ayre, Joseph *Alli*
Ayre, Legh Richmond *Alli Sup*
Ayre, Robert Hugh 1900- *AuBYP*, *ConAu 1R*,
    OxCan, *OxCan Sup*
Ayre, William *Alli*
Ayrenhoff, Cornelius Hermann Von 1733-1819
    DcEuL, *OxGer*
Ayrenhoff, Kornelius Hermann Von 1733-1819
    CasWL
Ayrer, Jacob 1543-1605 *CasWL*, *EuA*,
    REnWD
Ayrer, Jakob 1543-1605 *CasWL*, *DcEuL*,
    OxGer, *Pen Eur*
Ayres, Alfred *Alli Sup*, *DcAmA*, *DcNAA*,

OhA&B
Ayres, Amelia Price *ChPo*
Ayres, Anne 1816-1896 *Alli Sup*, *BiD&SB*,
    DcAmA, *DcNAA*
Ayres, Atlee Bernard 1874- *OhA&B*
Ayres, Brown 1856- *BiDSA*
Ayres, Clarence Edwin 1891- *AmA&B*, *TexWr*,
    WhWNAA
Ayres, Daisy Fitzhugh *BiDSA*
Ayres, Elizabeth *DrAP 1975*
Ayres, Esther W *ChPo*
Ayres, Eugene Edmond 1859-1920 *DcNAA*
Ayres, George B *Alli Sup*
Ayres, Gilbert Haven 1904- *IndAu 1917*
Ayres, Mrs. H M E Sharp- *Alli Sup*
Ayres, Harry Morgan 1881- *ChPo*, *WhWNAA*
Ayres, Henry *Alli Sup*
Ayres, J A *Alli*
Ayres, James *PoIre*
Ayres, Jared Augustus 1814-1886 *DcNAA*
Ayres, John *Alli*, *DcEnL*
Ayres, Juanita *TexWr*
Ayres, Leonard Porter 1879-1946 *DcNAA*,
    OhA&B
Ayres, Milan Church 1850-1920 *DcNAA*
Ayres, Mitchell 1910- *AmSCAP 66*
Ayres, Paul *EncM&D*
Ayres, Philip 1638-1712 *Alli*, *DcEnL*, *CasWL*,
    ChPo, *DcLEnL*
Ayres, Ruby Mildred 1883-1955 *LongC*, *NewC*,
    TwCW
Ayres, Samuel Gardiner 1865-1942 *AmA&B*,
    DcAmA, *WhWNAA*
Ayres, Steven Beckwith 1861-1929 *DcNAA*
Ayres, W T *Alli*
Ayres, Warren Joyce 1908- *AmSCAP 66*
Ayrinhac, Henry Amans 1867-1930 *DcNAA*
Ayrshire Bard, The *DcEnL*
Ayrton, Edmund d1808 *Alli*
Ayrton, Elisabeth Walshe 1918- *Au&Wr*,
    ConAu 5R, *WrD 1976*
Ayrton, J Calder *Alli Sup*
Ayrton, John *Alli*
Ayrton, Matilda 1846-1883 *Alli Sup*
Ayrton, Michael 1921-1975 *Au&Wr*, *ChPo S1*,
    ConAu 5R, *ConAu 61*, *WrD 1976*
Ayrton, S *Alli*
Ayrton, William *Alli Sup*
Ayrton, William Edward *Alli Sup*
Ayscough, Florence 1878-1942 *AmA&B*,
    LongC, *TwCAS*, *TwCA Sup*
Ayscough, Francis *Alli*
Ayscough, George Edward *Alli*, *DcEnL*
Ayscough, John 1858-1928 *LongC*, *NewC*,
    TwCA, *TwCA Sup*
Ayscough, Philip *Alli*
Ayscough, Samuel 1745-1804 *Alli S2*,
    ChPo S2, *DcEnL*
Ayscu, Edward *Alli*
Ayshford, Henry *Alli*, *BiDLA*
Aytmanov, Chingiz 1928- *DcOrL 3*
Ayton, Richard *Alli*, *BiDLA Sup*
Ayton, Sir Robert 1570-1638 *Alli*, *BiD&SB*,
    BrAu, *ChPo*, *ChPo S2*, *Chmbr 1*, *DcEnL*,
    EvLB, *NewC*, *Pen Eng*, *REn*
Aytoun, Sir Robert 1570-1638 *Alli*, *BiD&SB*,
    BrAu, *CasWL*, *DcLEnL*, *EvLB*, *NewC*,
    Pen Eng, *REn*
Aytoun, William Edmondstoune 1813-1865 *Alli*,
    Alli Sup, *BbD*, *BiD&SB*, *BrAu 19*,
    CasWL, *ChPo*, *ChPo S1*, *ChPo S2*,
    Chmbr 3, *DcEnA*, *DcEnL*, *DcEuL*,
    DcLEnL, *EvLB*, *NewC*, *OxEng*, *Pen Eng*,
    REn, *WebEAL*
Ayub Khan, Mohammad 1907- *ConAu 23*
Ayyub, Dhu'n-Nun 1908- *DcOrL 3*
Aza, Vital 1851-1912 *CasWL*
Azad, Muhammad Husain 1830-1910 *DcOrL 2*
Azana, Manuel 1880-1940 *CasWL*, *CIDMEuL*
Azana Y Diaz, Manuel 1880-1940 *EvEuW*
Azar, Edward E 1938- *ConAu 49*
Azarias, Brother 1847-1893 *Alli Sup*, *AmA&B*,
    BiD&SB, *DcAmA*, *DcNAA*
Azarowicz, Marjory Frances Brown 1922-
    WrD 1976
Azat Jamaldini, 'Abdu'l-Vahid 1918- *DcOrL 2*
Azcarate, Gumersindo De 1840-1917 *CasWL*

Azeglio, Massimo Taparelli, Marchese D'
  1798?-1866 *BiD&SB, CasWL, DcBiA,
  DcEuL, EvEuW, Pen Eur, REn*
Azevedo, Alonso De *DcEuL*
Azevedo, Aluisio De 1857-1913 *Pen Am*
Azevedo, Aluizio 1857-1913 *CasWL, REn*
Azevedo, Artur 1855-1908 *REnWD*
Azevedo, Guilherme De 1839-1882 *Pen Eur*
Azevedo, Manoel Antonio Alvares De 1831-1852
  BiD&SB
Azevedo, Pedro Corsino De 1905-1942 *AfA 1*
Azhayev, Vasili Nikolayevich 1915- *DcRusL*
Azikiwe, Benjamin Nnamdi 1904- *AfA 1*
Aziz Nesin 1915- *CasWL*
Azneer, J Leonard 1921- *ConAu 33,
  WrD 1976*
Azorin 1873?-1967 *CasWL, ClDMEuL,
  ConAu XR, DcSpL, EncWL, EvEuW,
  ModRL, Pen Eur, TwCA, TwCA Sup,
  TwCW*
Azoy, A C M 1891- *ConAu P-1*
Azrin, Nathan H 1930- *ConAu 45*
Azuela, Mariano 1873-1952 *CasWL, CyWA,
  DcSpL, EncWL, Pen Am, REn, TwCW,
  WhWNAA, WorAu*
Azulai, Hayim David *BiD&SB*
Azumi, Koya 1930- *ConAu 29*
Azurara *CasWL*

B

B *Poire*
B 1770-1827 *DcEnL*
B, A W *ChPo S1*
B, C D *ChPo S1*
B, H M *Poire*
B, J *Poire*
B, J B *Poire*
B, J G *Poire*
B, J T *Poire*
B, M G *ChPo S1*
B, R *Poire*
B, W W *ChPo S1*
B B 1905- *Br&AmS, LongC, SmATA 6, ThBJA, WhCL*
B L T *AmA&B*
B V *BrAu 19, CasWL, LongC, NewC*
B W *WhLA*
Ba, Mallam Amadou Hampate 1920?- *AfA 1*
Ba, Oumar 1900?- *AfA 1*
Baa Lamb, The *WhWNAA*
Baade, Herman Joseph 1887- *WhWNAA*
Baader, Franz Xaver 1765-1841 *OxGer*
Ba'al Ha-Turim *CasWL*
Ba'al Shem Tov, Israel 1700?-1760? *CasWL*
Baal-Teshuva, Jacob 1929- *ConAu 5R*
Ba'albakki, Layla 1937- *DcOrL 3*
Baar, Jindrich Simon 1869-1925 *CasWL*
Baarnhielm, Miss E W *Alli Sup*
Baars, Conrad W 1919- *ConAu 57*
Baart, P A *Alli Sup*
Baasch, Ernst 1861- *WhLA*
Baastad, Babbis Friis *ConAu XR, SmATA 7*
Baath, Albert Ulrik 1853-1912 *CasWL, ClDMEuL*
Bab, The, Siyyid Ali Muhammad 1819-1850 *CasWL, NewC*
Baba, Ahmad Al-Tinbukhti 1556-1627 *AfA 1*
Baba Taher 'Oryan 1000?-1055? *DcOrL 3*
Baba Tahir Hamadani *CasWL*
Babalola, Solomon Adeboye Q 1930?- *AfA 1*
Babar *NewC*
Babar, Zehir-Eddin Mohammed 1483-1530 *BiD&SB*
Babasinian, V S 1876- *WhWNAA*
Babayevski, Semyon Petrovich 1909- *CasWL, DcRusL*
Babazon, E J *Alli Sup*
Babb, C E *Alli Sup*
Babb, Clement Edwin 1821-1906 *DcNAA*
Babb, Cyrus Cates 1867- *WhWNAA*
Babb, Hattie *Alli Sup*
Babb, Howard S 1924- *ConAu 13R*
Babb, Hugh Webster 1887-1970? *ConAu P-1*
Babb, Kroger 1906- *WhWNAA*
Babb, Lawrence 1902- *ConAu 33*
Babb, Sanora 1907- *Au&Wr, ConAu 13R, WrD 1976*
Babb, Stanley E 1899- *TexWr*
Babbage, Charles 1790- *Alli*
Babbage, Charles 1792-1871 *Alli Sup, BiD&SB, BrAu 19, DcEnL*

Babbage, Stuart Barton 1916- *Au&Wr, ConAu 5R, WrD 1976*
Babbidge, Homer Daniels, Jr. 1925- *ConAu 61*
Babbie, Earl 1938- *ConAu 61*
Babbington, Charles *Alli Sup*
Babbis, Eleanor *ConAu XR, SmATA 7, ThBJA*
Babbitt, Adeline *ChPo*
Babbitt, Charles Jacob 1856-1913 *DcNAA*
Babbitt, Edwin Dwight 1828-1905 *Alli Sup, DcAmA, DcNAA, OhA&B*
Babbitt, Eugene Howard 1859-1927 *DcNAA*
Babbitt, Frank Cole 1867-1935 *DcNAA*
Babbitt, Harold Eaton 1888- *WhWNAA*
Babbitt, Irving 1865-1933 *AmA&B, AmLY, CasWL, CnDAL, ConAmA, ConAmL, DcLEnL, DcNAA, LongC, ModAL, OhA&B, OxAm, OxEng, Pen Am, REn, REnAL, TwCA, TwCA Sup, WebEAL, WhTwL*
Babbitt, James Bradford 1827- *DcNAA*
Babbitt, Natalie 1932- *ChLR 2, ChPo S2, ConAu 49, MorBMP, SmATA 6, WrD 1976*
Babbitt, Robert *WrD 1976*
Babbitt, Samuel Fisher 1929- *Au&Wr*
Babbler *ConAu XR*
Babcock, Augustus Dwight 1852- *IndAu 1816*
Babcock, Bernie 1868- *AmLY, BiDSA, DcAmA, OhA&B, WhWNAA*
Babcock, C Merton 1908- *ChPo S2, ConAu 1R, ConAu 5R*
Babcock, Charles Alamanzo 1847-1922 *DcNAA*
Babcock, Charlotte Farrington *ChPo*
Babcock, Dennis Arthur 1948- *ConAu 61*
Babcock, Edwina Stanton *AmA&B, WhWNAA*
Babcock, Emma S *Alli Sup*
Babcock, Emma Whitcomb *Alli Sup*
Babcock, Ernest Brown 1877- *WhWNAA*
Babcock, Frederic 1896- *AmA&B, Au&Wr, ConAu 5R, WhWNAA*
Babcock, George DeAlbert 1875-1942 *DcNAA*
Babcock, Harmon Seeley 1849-1937 *Alli Sup, DcNAA*
Babcock, Harold Lester 1886- *WhWNAA*
Babcock, J S *Alli*
Babcock, James Staunton 1815-1847 *AmA&B, ChPo S2, DcNAA*
Babcock, John M L *Alli Sup*
Babcock, John Martin Luther 1822-1894 *DcNAA*
Babcock, Kendric Charles 1864-1932 *AmLY, DcNAA, WhWNAA*
Babcock, Maltbie Davenport 1858-1901 *ChPo, ChPo S2, DcAmA, DcNAA*
Babcock, N P *ChPo*
Babcock, Robert Hall 1851-1930 *DcNAA, WhWNAA*
Babcock, Robert J 1928- *ConAu 13R*

Babcock, Robert Weston 1893-1963 *IndAu 1917*
Babcock, Rufus 1798-1875 *Alli Sup, DcAmA, DcNAA*
Babcock, Sarah A *Alli Sup*
Babcock, Stephen 1832-1916 *DcNAA*
Babcock, Theron C 1925- *AmSCAP 66*
Babcock, William Henry 1849-1922 *Alli Sup, BiDSA, DcAmA, DcNAA*
Babcock, William Wayne 1872- *WhWNAA*
Babcock, Winnifred 1879- *AmA&B*
Babel, Isaak Emanuilovich 1894-1941? *AtlBL, CasWL, ClDMEuL, CnMD, CnMWL, DcRusL, EncWL, EvEuW, LongC, McGWD, ModSL 1, ModWD, Pen Eur, REn, TwCA, TwCA Sup, TwCW, WhTwL*
Babenroth, Adolph Charles 1882?-1928 *ChPo, ChPo S1, DcNAA, WhWNAA*
Baber 1483-1530 *NewC*
Baber, Asa 1936- *ConAu 29, DrAF 1976*
Baber, Carroll Preston 1885- *WhWNAA*
Baber, Douglas Gordon 1918- *Au&Wr*
Baber, Edward Colborne *Alli Sup*
Baber, Edward Cresswell *Alli Sup*
Baber, H H *Alli*
Baber, Henry Hervey *BiDLA*
Baber, Jack 1821- *IndAu 1816*
Baber, Zehir-Eddin Mohammed 1483-1530 *BiD&SB*
Babeuf, Francois-Emile 1760-1797 *OxFr*
Babeuf, Francois Noel 1760-1797 *BiD&SB, REn*
Babin, David E 1925- *ConAu 23*
Babin, Maria Teresa 1910- *DcCLA, PueRA*
Babin, Victor 1908- *AmSCAP 66*
Babington, Anthony 1561-1586 *NewC*
Babington, Anthony Patrick 1920- *Au&Wr, ConAu 61, WrD 1976*
Babington, Arthur *Alli Sup*
Babington, Benjamin Guy 1794-1866 *Alli, Alli Sup, Poire*
Babington, Charles Cardale 1808- *Alli Sup, DcEnL*
Babington, Churchill 1821- *Alli Sup, DcEnL*
Babington, Mrs. E *Alli Sup*
Babington, E R *Alli Sup*
Babington, Gervase d1610 *Alli*
Babington, Humphrey *Alli*
Babington, John 1820?- *Alli, Br&AmS*
Babington, R *Alli*
Babington, William 1756-1833 *Alli, BiDLA*
Babington, Zachary *Alli*
Babington Smith, Constance *Au&Wr*
Babits, Linda 1940- *AmSCAP 66*
Babits, Mihaly 1883-1941 *CasWL, ClDMEuL, EncWL, EvEuW, Pen Eur, WhTwL*
Babitz, Sol 1911- *ConAu 41*
Babladelis, Georgia 1931- *ConAu 23*
Babli, Hillel 1893-1961 *CasWL*
Babo, Joseph Marius Von 1756-1822 *BbD,*

BiD&SB, OxGer
Baboeuf, Francois Noel 1760-1797 *BiD&SB*
Babris, Peter J 1917- *ConAu 21, WrD 1976*
Babrius *BbD, BiD&SB, CasWL, Pen Cl*
Babson, David Leveau 1911- *Au&Wr*
Babson, Emma Mortimer *ChPo*
Babson, John J *Alli Sup*
Babson, John James 1809-1886 *DcAmA, DcNAA*
Babson, Naomi Lane 1895- *AmA&B, AmNov, WhPNW*
Babson, Roger Ward 1875- *AmLY, WhWNAA*
Babson, Thomas Everett 1895- *Au&Wr*
Babst, Diederich Georg 1741-1800 *CasWL*
Babur *NewC*
Babur 1483-1530 *Pen Cl*
Babur, Muhammad Zahiruddin 1483-1530 *DcOrL 3*
Babur, Zahiruddin Muhammed 1483-1530 *CasWL*
Baby, William Lewis 1812-1897 *DcNAA*
Bacal, Harvey 1915- *AmSCAP 66*
Bacal, Melanie Ella 1948- *AmSCAP 66*
Bacarisse, Mauricio 1895-1931 *CasWL, EvEuW*
Baccalar Y Sana, Marquis Of St. Philip d1726 *BiD&SB*
Baccan 1907- *DcOrL 2*
Bacchelli, Riccardo 1891- *CasWL, ClDMEuL, CnMD, ConAu 29, CyWA, EncWL, EvEuW, ModRL, Pen Eur, REn, TwCW, WorAu*
Bacchus, E W *LivFWS*
Bacchus, Lizzie W *Alli Sup*
Bacchylides 516?BC-450?BC *CasWL, NewC, OxEng, Pen Cl*
Bacciocco, Edward J, Jr. 1935- *ConAu 45*
Bacevicius, Vytautas 1905- *AmSCAP 66*
Bach, Alberto B *Alli Sup*
Bach, Bert C 1936- *ConAu 23*
Bach, Carl Philipp Emanuel 1714-1788 *AtlBL*
Bach, George Leland 1915- *AmA&B, ConAu 1R*
Bach, Johann Christian 1735-1782 *AtlBL*
Bach, Johann Sebastian 1685-1750 *AtlBL, NewC, OxGer, REn*
Bach, Marcus Louis 1906- *AmA&B*
Bach, Richard David 1936- *AuNews 1, ConAu 9R, WrD 1976*
Bach, Wilfrid 1936- *ConAu 61*
Bacharach, Alfred L 1891-1966 *ConAu P-1*
Bacharach, Burt F 1928- *AmSCAP 66*
Bacharach, Herman Ilfeld 1899- *ConICB*
Bachaumont, Francois De 1624-1702 *OxFr, REn*
Bachaumont, Louis Petit De 1690-1771 *EvEuW, OxFr*
Bache, Alexander Dallas 1806-1867 *Alli, Alli Sup, BbD, BiD&SB, CyAL 1, DcAmA, DcNAA*
Bache, Ann *ChPo, ChPo S2*
Bache, Anna *Alli, Alli Sup*
Bache, Benjamin Franklin 1769-1798 *AmA&B, OxAm*
Bache, Franklin 1792-1864 *Alli, BiD&SB, CyAL 1, DcAmA, DcNAA*
Bache, R *Alli*
Bache, Richard 1794-1836 *Alli*
Bache, Richard Meade *Alli Sup*
Bache, Samuel 1804-1876 *Alli Sup*
Bache, William *Alli*
Bache, William B 1922- *ConAu 25*
Bachelard, Gaston 1884?-1962 *CasWL, Pen Eur, WhTwL, WorAu*
Bachelder, John B *Alli Sup*
Bacheler, Irving *BbD*
Bacheler, John Badger 1825-1894 *DcNAA*
Bacheler, O R *Alli Sup*
Bacheller, Irving 1859-1950 *AmA&B, BiD&SB, ChPo, ChPo S1, ChPo S2, Chmbr 3, ConAmL, DcAmA, DcBiA, DcLEnL, JBA 1934, OxAm, REn, REnAL, TwCA Sup, WhWNAA*
Bachelor, Joseph Morris 1889- *ChPo, WhWNAA*
Bachelot DeLaPylaie, M *BbtC*
Bachem, Albert 1888- *WhWNAA*

Bachem, Bele *WhGrA*
Bachem, Renate Gabriele 1916- *WhGrA*
Bachem Alent, Rose M *ConAu 49*
Bacher, Edward Leonard 1889- *WhWNAA*
Bacher, Julius 1810- *BiD&SB*
Bacher, Otto Henry 1856-1909 *DcNAA, OhA&B*
Bacheracht, Therese Von 1804-1852 *BbD, BiD&SB, OxGer*
Bacherl, Franz 1808-1869 *OxGer*
Bachi, Amurath-Effendi Hekim *CasWL*
Bachi, Pietro 1787-1853 *DcNAA*
Bachler, Wolfgang 1925- *OxGer*
Bachman, Catharine Louise *BiDSA*
Bachman, Frank Peterbaugh 1871-1934 *AmLY*
Bachman, Frank Puterbaugh 1871-1934 *DcNAA*
Bachman, Fred 1949- *ConAu 53*
Bachman, Ingeborg 1926-1973 *ConAu 45*
Bachman, Jerald G 1936- *ConAu 41*
Bachman, John 1790-1874 *Alli, AmA, BiD&SB, BiDSA, DcAmA, DcNAA*
Bachman, John Walter 1916- *ConAu 5R, WrD 1976*
Bachman, Mariana 1907- *TexWr*
Bachmann, Freda M 1878- *WhWNAA*
Bachmann, Georg Philipp 1864- *WhLA*
Bachmann, Ingeborg 1926-1973 *CasWL, EncWL, ModGL, OxGer, Pen Eur, TwCW, WorAu*
Bachmann, Jean George 1877- *WhWNAA*
Bachmann, Zacharius *OxGer*
Bachmura, Frank T 1922- *ConAu 45*
Bachner, Louis 1882-1946 *DcNAA*
Bachofen, Johann Jacob 1815-1887 *CasWL, EuA, REn*
Bachtold, A *Pen Eur*
Bachur, Elijah 1468-1549 *CasWL, Pen Eur*
Bachya Ben Joseph d1080? *CasWL*
Bachya Ibn Pakuda d1080? *CasWL*
Back, Ernest Adna 1880- *WhWNAA*
Back, Sir George 1796-1878? *Alli, BiD&SB, OxCan*
Back, Joe W 1899- *ConAu 17*
Back, Kurt W 1919- *ConAu 13R*
Back, Philip 1858- *Br&AmS*
Back, William d1920? *MnBBF*
Backer, George De *OxFr*
Backer, John H 1902- *ConAu 33*
Backer, Morton 1918- *ConAu 17R*
Backham, Oscar *Alli Sup*
Backhouse, Edward 1808-1879 *Alli Sup*
Backhouse, James *Alli*
Backhouse, Julius Brockman *Alli Sup*
Backhouse, Katharine *Alli Sup*
Backhouse, Sally 1927- *ConAu 23*
Backhouse, Sarah *Alli Sup*
Backhouse, Thomas *Alli, BbtC, BiDLA*
Backhouse, W *Alli, Alli Sup*
Backhouse, William *Alli*
Backhouse, William 1593-1662 *Alli*
Backler, L L McL *Alli Sup*
Backman, Carl W 1923- *ConAu 17R*
Backman, Jules 1910- *AmA&B, Au&Wr, ConAu 1R, WrD 1976*
Backman, Melvin 1919- *ConAu 21*
Backman, Milton V, Jr. 1927- *ConAu 33*
Backstrom, Charles H 1926- *ConAu 13R*
Backstrom, Per Johan Edvard 1841-1886 *BiD&SB, CasWL*
Backus, Azel 1765-1816 *Alli, CyAL 2*
Backus, Azel 1765-1817 *DcNAA*
Backus, Charles 1749-1803 *Alli, DcNAA*
Backus, Charles K *Alli Sup*
Backus, Edwin Burdette 1888-1955 *OhA&B*
Backus, Emma Henriette Schiermeyer 1877?- *OhA&B, WhWNAA*
Backus, Mrs. Henry *WhWNAA*
Backus, Isaac 1724-1806 *Alli, DcAmA, DcNAA, OxAm*
Backus, J *Alli*
Backus, Jean L 1914- *Au&Wr, ConAu 33*
Backus, Joseph 1764-1838 *DcNAA*
Backus, L W *ChPo*
Backus, Oswald P, III 1921-1972 *ConAu 33, ConAu 37*
Backus, Richard C 1890- *WhWNAA*
Backus, Truman Jay 1842-1908 *AmA&B, DcAmA, DcNAA*

Backus, William Woodbridge 1803-1892 *DcNAA*
Backwell, Edward d1683 *NewC*
Backwoodsman, A *OxCan*
Bacmeister, Ernst 1874- *EncWL*
Bacmeister, Rhoda W 1893- *ChPo, ConAu P-1*
Bacon *Alli*
Bacon, Mister *Alli*
Bacon, A M *Alli Sup*
Bacon, A O *Alli Sup*
Bacon, Albert Montreville 1827-1898 *DcNAA*
Bacon, Albion Fellows 1865-1933 *AmA&B, DcNAA, IndAu 1816, WhWNAA*
Bacon, Alexander Samuel 1853-1920 *AmLY, DcNAA*
Bacon, Alice Mabel 1858-1918 *AmA&B, DcAmA, DcNAA*
Bacon, Anne 1528-1600 *Alli, DcEnL*
Bacon, Anthony 1558- *Alli*
Bacon, Augustus Octavius 1839-1914 *BiDSA, DcNAA*
Bacon, Avery D *BbtC*
Bacon, Benjamin C *Alli Sup*
Bacon, Benjamin Wisner 1860?-1932 *DcAmA, DcNAA*
Bacon, Bob *DrAP 1975*
Bacon, Charles David 1840-1905 *DcNAA*
Bacon, Charles Sumner 1856?-1947 *DcNAA, WhWNAA*
Bacon, Charles Vincent 1885- *WhWNAA*
Bacon, Charles William 1856-1938 *DcNAA*
Bacon, Daisy Sarah *AmA&B*
Bacon, David Francis 1813-1865 *DcNAA*
Bacon, Delia Salter 1811-1859 *Alli, AmA, AmA&B, BiD&SB, CnDAL, DcAmA, DcEnL, DcLEnL, DcNAA, NewC, OhA&B, OxAm, REnAL*
Bacon, Dolores Marbourg *ChPo, DcNAA*
Bacon, Mrs. E A *Alli Sup*
Bacon, Edgar Mayhew 1855-1935 *AmA&B, ChPo, ChPo S2, DcAmA, DcNAA*
Bacon, Edmund *Alli Sup*
Bacon, Edmund Norwood 1910- *ConAu 41, WrD 1976*
Bacon, Edward *Alli Sup*
Bacon, Edward 1830-1901 *DcNAA*
Bacon, Edward 1906- *ConAu 29*
Bacon, Edwin Faxon 1832-1910 *DcNAA*
Bacon, Edwin Munroe 1844-1916 *Alli Sup, AmA, AmA&B, DcAmA, DcNAA*
Bacon, Eleanor Warfield 1875-1927 *ChPo S1*
Bacon, Elizabeth 1914- *ConAu 29, SmATA 3*
Bacon, Elizabeth E 1904- *ConAu P-1*
Bacon, Ernst 1898- *AmSCAP 66*
Bacon, Eugenia Jones 1840- *BiDSA, DcNAA*
Bacon, Ezekiel 1776-1870 *DcNAA*
Bacon, Frances Atchinson 1903- *ConAu 1R*
Bacon, Sir Francis 1561-1626 *Alli, AtlBL, BbD, BiD&SB, BrAu, CasWL, ChPo, ChPo S2, Chmbr 1, CrE&SL, CriT 1, CyWA, DcEnA, DcEnL, DcEuL, DcLEnL, EvLB, MouLC 1, NewC, OxEng, Pen Eng, RAdv 1, RCom, REn, WebEAL*
Bacon, Frank 1864-1922 *AmA&B, DcNAA, ModWD, REn, REnAL*
Bacon, Frederick Hampden 1849-1928 *Alli Sup, DcNAA*
Bacon, Gaspar Griswold 1886-1947 *DcNAA*
Bacon, George Blagden 1836-1876 *Alli Sup, DcNAA*
Bacon, George Edward 1917- *WrD 1976*
Bacon, George Mackenzie *Alli Sup*
Bacon, George Vaux *ChPo*
Bacon, George Washington *Alli Sup*
Bacon, Gorham 1855-1940 *DcNAA*
Bacon, Harry E 1900- *Au&Wr*
Bacon, Henry *ChPo S1*
Bacon, Henry 1813- *Alli*
Bacon, Henry 1839-1912 *DcAmA, DcNAA*
Bacon, Henry 1840-1924 *Alli Sup, ChPo, ChPo S1*
Bacon, Henry Bowman *Alli Sup*
Bacon, J *Alli Sup*
Bacon, J H *Alli Sup*
Bacon, James *Alli, BiDLA*
Bacon, John *Alli, BiDLA, DcEnL*
Bacon, John 1740-1799 *Alli*

Bacon, John 1940- *ConAu 53*
Bacon, John Harwood 1875- *BiDSA*
Bacon, John Henry Frederick 1865-1914
  ChPo S1
Bacon, John Mackenzie *Alli Sup*
Bacon, John R *ChPo*
Bacon, Josephine Dodge Daskam 1876-1961
  AmA&B, ChPo, ChPo S2, DcAmA,
  REnAL, St&VC, TwCA, TwCA Sup,
  WhWNAA
Bacon, Julia *Alli Sup, BiDSA, LivFWS*
Bacon, Lenice Ingram 1895- *ConAu 45*
Bacon, Leonard 1802-1881 *Alli, Alli Sup,*
  AmA&B, BiD&SB, DcAmA, DcEnL,
  DcNAA, OhA&B, PoCh
Bacon, Leonard 1887-1954 *AmA&B, ChPo,*
  ChPo S1, ChPo S2, DcLEnL, OxAm,
  REn, REnAL, TwCA, TwCA Sup,
  WhWNAA
Bacon, Leonard Woolsey 1830-1907 *Alli Sup,*
  BiD&SB, DcAmA, DcNAA
Bacon, Louise Lee 1861- *DcAmA*
Bacon, Margaret Hope 1921- *ConAu 25,*
  SmATA 6, WrD 1976
Bacon, Marion 1901?-1975 *ConAu 57*
Bacon, Martha Sherman *ChPo S1*
Bacon, Mary *Alli Sup, TexWr*
Bacon, Mary A *Alli*
Bacon, Mary Applewhite 1863- *BiDSA*
Bacon, Mary Schell 1870-1934 *AmA&B, ChPo,*
  DcNAA
Bacon, Matthew *Alli, BiDLA*
Bacon, Nathaniel *Alli, OxAm, REn*
Bacon, Sir Nathaniel *Alli*
Bacon, Nathaniel 1647-1676 *REnAL*
Bacon, Nathaniel Terry 1858- *WhWNAA*
Bacon, Sir Nicholas 1510-1579 *Alli*
Bacon, Oliver N *Alli Sup*
Bacon, Paul 1913- *AuBYP*
Bacon, Peggy 1895- *AmA&B, ChPo,*
  ChPo S2, ConAu 23, ConICB, IlBYP,
  IlCB 1945, IlCB 1956, IlCB 1966,
  OxAm, REnAL, SmATA 2, St&VC
Bacon, Phanuel 1700-1783 *Alli, DcEnL,*
  NewC
Bacon, Phillip 1922- *ConAu 41*
Bacon, R *Alli*
Bacon, R N *Alli*
Bacon, Ralph *ChPo*
Bacon, Raymond Foss 1880- *IndAu 1816,*
  WhWNAA
Bacon, Robert *Alli*
Bacon, Robert 1168?-1248 *Alli*
Bacon, Robert 1860-1919 *DcNAA*
Bacon, Roger 1214-1294? *Alli, BbD, BiD&SB,*
  BrAu, CasWL, Chmbr 1, DcEnL,
  DcEuL, EvLB, NewC, OxEng, Pen Eng,
  REn
Bacon, Selden 1861-1946 *DcNAA*
Bacon, Theodore *Alli Sup*
Bacon, Theodore 1834-1900 *DcNAA*
Bacon, Theodore Davenport 1863-1930 *DcNAA*
Bacon, Thomas *Alli*
Bacon, Thomas 1700?-1768 *DcNAA*
Bacon, Thomas Scott 1825-1904 *Alli Sup,*
  BiD&SB, DcAmA, DcNAA
Bacon, Vincent *Alli*
Bacon, Virginia Cleaver *WhWNAA*
Bacon, Wallace A 1914- *ConAu 17R*
Bacon, William *Alli, Alli Sup*
Bacon, William 1789-1863 *DcNAA*
Bacon, William Johnson *Alli Sup*
Bacon, William Plumb 1837-1918 *DcNAA*
Bacon, William Thompson 1812-1881 *ChPo,*
  DcNAA
Bacondorp, John d1346 *Alli*
Baconthorp, John d1346 *Alli*
Bacot, J T W *MnBBF*
Bacot, John Thomas Watson *Alli Sup*
Bacot, Mary E *Alli Sup*
Bacote, Clarence A 1906- *ConAu 33*
Bacovia, George 1881-1957 *CasWL, Pen Eur,*
  WhTwL
Bacovia, Gheorghe 1881-1957 *EncWL*
Bacque, James 1929- *OxCan Sup*
Bacsanyi, Janos 1763-1845 *BiD&SB*
Baculard D'Arnaud, Francois-Thomas De
  1718-1805 *BiD&SB, CasWL, EvEuW*

Baczko, Ludwig Franz Josef Von 1756-1823
  OxGer
Baczynski, Krzysztof Kamil 1921-1944 *CasWL*
Badash, Lawrence 1934- *ConAu 37*
Badawi, M M 1925- *ConAu 49*
Badawi, Muhammad Mustafa *ConAu 49*
Badcock, John *Alli Sup, DcEnL*
Badcock, R *Alli*
Badcock, Samuel 1747-1788 *Alli*
Badcock, Winnifred 1879- *DcAmA*
Baddam, Benjamin *Alli*
Baddeley, F H *BbtC*
Baddeley, John James *Alli Sup*
Baddeley, Montford John Byrde 1843- *Alli Sup*
Baddeley, P F H *Alli Sup*
Baddeley, Richard Wheildon *Alli Sup*
Baddeley, Robert 1733?-1794 *NewC*
Baddeley, Welbore St. Clair 1856- *Alli Sup*
Baddeley, George *Alli*
Baddely, R *Alli*
Baddiley, James 1918- *Au&Wr*
Bade, Josse 1461?-1535 *CasWL*
Bade, William Frederic 1871-1936 *AmLY,*
  DcNAA, WhWNAA
Badeau, Adam 1831-1895 *Alli Sup, AmA&B,*
  BbD, BiD&SB, DcAmA, DcNAA
Badelly, John *Alli*
Baden, Katia 1898- *WhWNAA*
Baden-Powell *Alli Sup*
Baden-Powell, Sir George Smyth 1847-1898
  BiD&SB
Baden-Powell, Sir Robert 1857-1941 *LongC,*
  MnBBF, WhCL, WhLA
Badeni, June 1925- *WrD 1976*
Badenoch, James Greig *Alli Sup*
Badenock, James *Alli*
Bader, Barbara *ChPo S2*
Bader, Charles *Alli Sup*
Bader, Georgia C 1876- *AnMV 1926, TexWr,*
  WhWNAA
Badeslade, Thomas *Alli*
Badford, E *Alli Sup*
Badger, A G *Alli Sup*
Badger, Alfred Bowen 1901- *Au&Wr*
Badger, C *Alli*
Badger, Mrs. C M *Alli Sup*
Badger, Charlotte *BiDLA*
Badger, Mrs. E M *BiDSA*
Badger, George Henry *AmLY*
Badger, George Percy 1815-1888 *Alli Sup*
Badger, Henry Clay *Alli Sup*
Badger, J *Alli*
Badger, John D'Arcy 1917- *ConAu 45*
Badger, Joseph 1757-1846 *OhA&B*
Badger, Joseph E, Jr. 1848-1909 *HsB&A*
Badger, Ralph E 1890- *ConAu 21*
Badger, Ralph F 1890- *WhWNAA*
Badger, S T *ChPo*
Badger, Stephen *Alli*
Badgley, John Herbert 1930- *ConAu 37,*
  WrD 1976
Badgley, Jonathan 1837?- *Alli Sup, DcNAA*
Badgley, Robin F *OxCan Sup*
Badham, C D *Alli*
Badham, Charles *Alli, Alli Sup, BiDLA*
Badham, Charles 1780-1845 *NewC*
Badham, Charles 1813-1884 *Alli Sup*
Badham, Leslie 1908- *WrD 1976*
Badian, Ernst 1925- *ConAu 37, WrD 1976*
Badian, Seydou Kouyate 1928- *AfA 1*
Badin, Stephen Theodore 1768-1853 *DcNAA*
Badinguet d1883 *NewC*
Badlam, Anna B 1887?- *ChPo S2, DcNAA*
Badlam, Anna E *ChPo, ChPo S1*
Badland, Thomas *Alli*
Badley, Brenton Hamline *Alli Sup*
Badley, Brenton Thoburn 1876-1949 *DcNAA,*
  WhWNAA
Badley, John Haden 1865- *WhLA*
Badmin, Stanley Roy 1906- *IlCB 1956*
Badnall, Hopkins *Alli Sup*
Badnall, James *Alli Sup, ChPo S1*
Badonicus *BrAu*
Badruddin Chachi d1346 *DcOrL 2*
Badt, Kurt Ludwig 1890- *Au&Wr*
Baducing, Biscop *NewC*
Badura-Skoda, Eva 1929- *ConAu 37*
Baeda *BrAu, Chmbr 1, EvLB, NewC*

Baedeker, Karl 1801-1859 *NewC, REn*
Baedeker, Karl 1910- *Au&Wr*
Baege, M H 1875- *WhLA*
Baehr, George 1887- *WhWNAA*
Baekelmans, Lode 1879-1965 *CasWL*
Baen, Chadwyn *WhWNAA*
Baena, Antonio 1795?-1850 *BiD&SB*
Baena, Cancionero De *REn*
Baena, Juan Alfonso De *CasWL, DcEuL,*
  DcSpL, EvEuW, Pen Eur
Baensch, Willy E 1893-1972 *ConAu 37*
Baenziger, Hans 1917- *ConAu 49*
Baer, Mrs. *HsB&A*
Baer, Abel 1893- *AmSCAP 66*
Baer, Arthur 1886-1969 *REnAL*
Baer, Mrs. Benjamin F *Alli Sup*
Baer, Charles E 1870-1962 *AmSCAP 66*
Baer, Curtis O 1898- *ConAu 49*
Baer, Daniel J 1929- *ConAu 33*
Baer, Earl E 1928- *ConAu 57*
Baer, Edith Ruth 1920- *Au&Wr*
Baer, Eleanora A 1907- *ConAu 9R*
Baer, Gabriel 1919- *ConAu 5R*
Baer, George Webster 1935- *ConAu 21*
Baer, Jean L *ConAu 13R*
Baer, John 1886-1970 *ConAu 29*
Baer, Karl Ernst Von 1792-1876 *BiD&SB*
Baer, Leo 1880- *WhLA*
Baer, Libbie C Riley 1849-1929 *OhA&B*
Baer, Lucy A d1925? *HsB&A Sup*
Baer, Max Frank 1912- *ConAu 9R*
Baer, Rosemary 1913- *ConAu 41*
Baer, W *Alli Sup*
Baer, Werner 1931- *ConAu 9R*
Baerg, Harry John 1909- *ConAu 9R,*
  WrD 1976
Baerle, Caspar Van 1584-1648 *CasWL*
Baerle, Kasper Van 1584-1648 *EvEuW*
Baerlein, Henry 1875-1960 *NewC, WhLA*
Baermann, Jurgen Niklas 1785-1850 *CasWL*
Baerwald, Hans H 1927- *ConAu 33,*
  WrD 1976
Baerwald, Sara 1948- *ConAu 61*
Baesecke, Georg 1876- *WhLA*
Baeta, H X *Alli*
Baetjer, Frederick Henry 1874- *WhWNAA*
Baetzhold, Howard G 1923- *ConAu 29*
Baeuml, Franz H 1926- *ConAu 49*
Baez, Joan 1941- *ConAu 21*
Baffico, Giuseppe 1852-1927 *McGWD*
Baffin, William 1584-1622 *Alli, BiD&SB,*
  DcEnL, NewC, OxCan
Bagby, Albert Morris 1859-1941 *AmA&B,*
  DcAmA, DcNAA
Bagby, Alfred *BiDSA*
Bagby, Alfred 1828- *DcNAA*
Bagby, Alfred, Jr. 1866- *WhWNAA*
Bagby, Arthur T 1879-1949 *OhA&B*
Bagby, David Young 1849- *DcNAA*
Bagby, David Young 1859- *BiDSA*
Bagby, George *ConAu XR, EncM&D*
Bagby, George William 1828-1883 *Alli Sup,*
  AmA   AmA&B, BiD&SB, BiDSA,
  CnDAL, DcAmA, DcLEnL, DcNAA,
  OxAm
Bagby, Wesley M 1922- *ConAu 1R*
Bagdasarian, Ross 1919- *AmSCAP 66*
Bagden, J O *Alli Sup*
Bagdikian, Ben Haig 1920- *AmA&B,*
  ConAu 9R, WrD 1976
Bagdon, J C *Alli Sup*
Bage, Robert 1728-1801 *Alli, BiD&SB, BrAu,*
  CasWL, Chmbr 2, DcEnL, DcLEnL,
  EvLB, NewC, OxEng
Bagehot, Walter 1826-1877 *Alli Sup, AtlBL,*
  BbD, BiD&SB, BrAu 19, CasWL,
  Chmbr 3, CriT 3, DcEnA, DcEnL,
  DcEuL, DcLEnL, EvLB, NewC, OxEng,
  Pen Eng, REn, WebEAL
Bagenal, Philip Henry Dudley 1850- *Alli Sup*
Bagford, John 1650-1716 *Alli, NewC*
Bagg, Graham 1917- *ConAu 57*
Bagg, Helen F *AmA&B, WhWNAA*
Bagg, J N *Alli Sup*
Bagg, Lyman Hotchkiss 1846-1911 *Alli Sup,*
  DcAmA, DcNAA
Bagg, Moses Mears 1816-1900 *DcNAA*
Bagg, Robert *DrAP 1975*

Bagg, Robert Ely 1835- *AmA&B*
Bagg, Rufus Mather 1869- *WhWNAA*
Bagg, Stanley Clark 1820- *BbtC*
Baggaley, Andrew R 1923- *ConAu 13R*
Baggaly, William 1808-1879 *Alli Sup*
Baggarly, Franklin Clyde *WhWNAA*
Bagge, Henry Theodore James *Alli Sup*
Bagger, Carl Christian 1807-1846 *CasWL*
Bagger, Eugene 1892- *BkC 4, CatA 1947*
Baggesen, Jens Immanuel 1764-1826 *BbD,
    BiD&SB, CasWL, EuA, EvEuW, ChPo,
    ChPo S1, DcEuL, OxGer, Pen Eur*
Baggs, Jeffrey *Alli*
Baggs, Jeffry *BiDLA*
Baggs, John *Alli, BiDLA*
Baggs, Mae d1922 *DcNAA*
Baggs, Mae Lacy 1875-1922 *OhA&B*
Baghdadi, Shawqi 1928- *DcOrL 3*
Baghdigian, Bagdasar Krikor 1888- *WhWNAA*
Bagioli, Antonio 1795-1871 *DcNAA*
Bagley, Clarence Booth 1843-1932 *DcNAA*
Bagley, David T *Alli Sup*
Bagley, Desmond 1923- *Au&Wr, ConAu 17R,
    WrD 1976*
Bagley, Edward R 1926- *ConAu 53*
Bagley, George *Alli, Alli Sup*
Bagley, John Joseph 1908- *Au&Wr,
    ConAu 5R, WrD 1976*
Bagley, William *Alli*
Bagley, William Alfred 1910- *Au&Wr*
Bagley, William Chandler 1874-1946 *AmA&B,
    AmLY, DcNAA, REnAL, WhWNAA*
Bagnal, Gibbon *BiDLA*
Bagnal, Thomas *Alli*
Bagnall *Alli*
Bagnall, George *Alli Sup*
Bagnall, James E *Alli Sup*
Bagnall, John Nock *Alli Sup*
Bagnall, William Rhodes 1819-1892 *DcNAA*
Bagnel, Joan 1933- *ConAu 49*
Bagnol *Alli*
Bagnol, Robert *Alli*
Bagnold, Miss E S H *Alli Sup, ChPo S1*
Bagnold, Enid 1889- *AuBYP, ChPo S2,
    CnMD, ConAu 5R, ConDr,
    ConNov 1976, DcLEnL, EvLB, LongC,
    ModWD, NewC, OxEng, REn,
    SmATA 1, TwCA, TwCA Sup, TwCW,
    WhCL, WrD 1976*
Bagnold, Joseph *Alli*
Bagot, A G 1830?- *Alli Sup, Br&AmS*
Bagot, Alan *Alli Sup*
Bagot, Sir Charles 1781-1843 *OxCan*
Bagot, Mrs. Charles Walter *Alli Sup*
Bagot, Daniel 1805-1891 *Alli, Alli Sup,
    BiDLA, PoIre*
Bagot, John *Alli Sup*
Bagot, Lewis 1740-1802 *Alli*
Bagot, Richard 1860- *Alli, BiD&SB*
Bagritsky, Eduard 1895?-1934 *CasWL,
    ClDMEuL, DcRusL, EncWL, EvEuW,
    Pen Eur*
Bagryana, Elisaveta 1893- *CasWL, ModSL 2,
    Pen Eur*
Bagrynowski, S *EvEuW*
Bagshaw, Edward 1604-1662 *Alli*
Bagshaw, Edward 1629-1671 *Alli*
Bagshaw, Henry *Alli*
Bagshaw, John *Alli*
Bagshaw, Samuel *Alli Sup*
Bagshaw, William 1628-1702 *Alli*
Bagshawe, Edward Gilpin 1829- *Alli Sup*
Bagshawe, Francis Lloyd *Alli Sup*
Bagshawe, J L *ChPo S1*
Bagshawe, John B *Alli Sup*
Bagshawe, Thomas Wyatt 1901- *Au&Wr*
Bagshotte, Annerley *MnBBF*
Bagstad, Anna Emilia 1876- *WhWNAA*
Bagster, C Birch *OxCan*
Bagster, G Birch *Alli Sup*
Bagster, Hubert *ConAu XR*
Bagwell, Philip S 1914- *ConAu 33*
Bagwell, Richard *Alli Sup*
Bagwell, William *Alli*
Bagwell, William Francis, Jr. 1923- *ConAu 33,
    WrD 1976*
Bahadur, K P 1924- *ConAu 57*
Bahar, Mohammad Taqi 1886-1950 *DcOrL 3*

Bahar, Muhammad Taqi 1886-1951 *CasWL*
Baha'u'llah, Mirza Husain-'Ali 1817-1892
    CasWL
Bahdanovich, Maxim 1891-1917 *DcRusL*
Bahe, Liz Sohappy *DrAP 1975*
Bahelele, Jacques N 1911- *AfA 1*
Bahithat Al-Badiyah *CasWL*
Bahl, Roy W 1939- *ConAu 23*
Bahlke, George W 1934- *ConAu 29*
Bahlke, Valerie Worth 1933- *ConAu 41*
Bahm, Archie J 1907- *ConAu 9R, WrD 1976*
Bahmer, William J 1872-1953 *ChPo, OhA&B*
Bahn, Eugene 1906- *ConAu 23*
Bahn, Margaret Linton 1907-1969 *ConAu 25*
Bahnc, Salcia *ChPo*
Bahr, Ehrhard 1932- *WrD 1976*
Bahr, Erhard 1932- *ConAu 33*
Bahr, Hermann 1863-1934 *BiD&SB, CasWL,
    ClDMEuL, CnMD, EncWL, EvEuW,
    McGWD, ModGL, ModWD, OxGer,
    Pen Eur, REn*
Bahr, Howard M 1938- *ConAu 29*
Bahr, Jerome 1909- *ConAu 33, WrD 1976*
Bahr, Johann Christian 1798-1872 *BiD&SB*
Bahram Gur *DcOrL 3*
Bahrdt, Karl Friedrich 1741-1792 *BiD&SB*
Bahryanyy, Ivan 1906-1963 *ModSL 2*
Bahti, Tom *IlBYP*
Bahya, Ben Joseph Ben Pakoda *BbD, BiD&SB*
Bahya, Ben Joseph Ibn Pakuda *EuA*
Bahya, Ibn Paquda *EvEuW*
Baierl, Helmut 1926- *CrCD, EncWL Sup*
Baif, Jean Antoine De 1532-1589 *BiD&SB,
    CasWL, DcEuL, EuA, EvEuW, OxFr,
    Pen Eur, REn*
Baif, Lazare De 1485-1547 *CasWL, DcEuL,
    OxFr*
Baigent, Francis Joseph *Alli Sup*
Baihaqi, Muhammad Abu'l-Fazl 995-1077
    CasWL
Baikie, Edwin Simpson- *Alli Sup*
Baikie, William Balfour 1825-1864 *Alli Sup*
Bail, Hamilton Vaughan *ChPo*
Bailden, Henry Bellyse 1849- *ChPo S1*
Baildon, Henry Bellyse *Alli Sup*
Baildon, John *Alli*
Baildon, Joseph *Alli*
Baildon, Samuel *Alli Sup*
Bailes, Dale Alan *DrAP 1975*
Bailey *Alli*
Bailey, A G *OxCan Sup*
Bailey, Abigail 1746-1815 *DcNAA*
Bailey, Abraham *Alli*
Bailey, Albert Hopson 1821-1891 *DcNAA*
Bailey, Alexander Mabyn *Alli*
Bailey, Alfred 1829- *Alli Sup*
Bailey, Alfred Goldsworthy 1905- *CanWr,
    ConAu 25, ConP 1970, DcLEnL, OxCan*
Bailey, Alfred M 1894- *ConAu 41*
Bailey, Alice 1857- *DcNAA*
Bailey, Alice Cooper 1890- *ConAu P-1*
Bailey, Ambrose Moody 1875- *WhWNAA*
Bailey, Anthony 1933- *ConAu 1R*
Bailey, Arthur Low 1867-1940 *DcNAA*
Bailey, Arthur Scott 1877-1949 *DcNAA,
    WhWNAA*
Bailey, B *Alli*
Bailey, Benjamin *Alli Sup*
Bailey, Benjamin Franklin 1875- *WhWNAA*
Bailey, Benson *Alli Sup*
Bailey, Bernadine Freeman 1901- *AuBYP,
    ConAu 5R*
Bailey, Bert Heald 1875-1917 *DcNAA*
Bailey, Betty *WrD 1976*
Bailey, Caroline Hubbard 1890- *WhWNAA*
Bailey, Carolyn A 1876-1961 *ChPo*
Bailey, Carolyn Sherwin 1875-1961 *AmA&B,
    AnCL, AuBYP, BkCL, CarSB, ChPo,
    ChPo S1, ChPo S2, JBA 1951,
    Newb 1922, St&VC*
Bailey, Cecil Henry 1899- *Au&Wr*
Bailey, Charles *Alli Sup, AmA&B*
Bailey, Charles Waldo, II 1929- *ConAu 1R,
    WrD 1976*
Bailey, Clyde H 1887- *WhWNAA*
Bailey, Cyril 1871- *WhLA*
Bailey, David *Alli Sup, ChPo S2*
Bailey, David C 1930- *ConAu 45*

Bailey, David Roy Shackleton 1917- *Au&Wr,
    ConAu 5R, WrD 1976*
Bailey, Dennis *WhGrA*
Bailey, Derrick Sherwin 1910- *Au&Wr,
    ConAu 5R*
Bailey, Douglas *OxCan Sup*
Bailey, Dudley 1918- *ConAu 17R*
Bailey, Ebenezer 1795-1839 *Alli Sup, AmA,
    ChPo S1, DcNAA*
Bailey, Edgar Henry Summerfield 1848-1933
    DcAmA, DcNAA
Bailey, Edmund *Alli Sup*
Bailey, Edward *Alli, Alli Sup*
Bailey, Edward Lucas 1823-1869 *DcNAA*
Bailey, Eli Stillman 1851-1926 *DcNAA*
Bailey, Eliza Randall *WhWNAA*
Bailey, Elizabeth Rainier *Alli Sup*
Bailey, Elmer James *ChPo S1*
Bailey, Emily Pearson *ChPo S1*
Bailey, Emma F *ChPo*
Bailey, Eric 1933- *Au&Wr, ConAu 33*
Bailey, F *Alli Sup*
Bailey, F M *Alli Sup*
Bailey, F W N *Alli Sup, ChPo*
Bailey, Flora *AuBYP*
Bailey, Florence Augusta Merriam 1863-
    AmA&B, AmLY, DcAmA
Bailey, Francis 1735-1815 *AmA&B, REnAL*
Bailey, Frank Albert 1909- *Au&Wr*
Bailey, Frederic William d1918 *DcNAA*
Bailey, Frederick George 1924- *ConAu 13R*
Bailey, Frederick Marshman 1882-1967
    ConAu P-1
Bailey, Frederick Randolph 1871-1923 *DcNAA*
Bailey, G H *Alli Sup*
Bailey, Gamaliel 1807-1859 *AmA&B,
    BiD&SB*
Bailey, George *Alli Sup*
Bailey, George 1919- *ConAu 25*
Bailey, George Taylor 1887- *WhWNAA*
Bailey, George W *Alli Sup*
Bailey, Gerald Earl 1929- *ConAu 25*
Bailey, Gilbert Ellis 1852-1924 *DcNAA*
Bailey, Gilbert Stephen 1822-1891 *Alli Sup,
    DcNAA*
Bailey, Gordon Keith 1936- *Au&Wr,
    WrD 1976*
Bailey, H *Alli*
Bailey, H C 1878-1961 *EncM&D*
Bailey, Harold *WhWNAA*
Bailey, Harry A, Jr. 1932- *ConAu 23*
Bailey, Harry L 1879-1934 *ChPo*
Bailey, Harry P 1912- *AmSCAP 66*
Bailey, Helen Miller 1909- *ConAu 13R*
Bailey, Henry *Alli, Alli Sup*
Bailey, Henry Christopher 1878-1961 *EvLB,
    LongC, NewC, TwCA, TwCA Sup,
    WhLA*
Bailey, Henry Ives *Alli, Alli Sup*
Bailey, Henry Mercer *Alli Sup*
Bailey, Henry Turner 1865-1931 *DcNAA,
    OhA&B*
Bailey, Hillary G 1894- *ConAu 57*
Bailey, Hollis Russell 1852-1934 *DcNAA*
Bailey, Hugh C 1929- *ConAu 9R*
Bailey, I Temple d1953 *AmA&B*
Bailey, Isaac d1824 *DcNAA*
Bailey, J *Alli Sup, BbtC*
Bailey, J H *Alli Sup*
Bailey, J Martin 1929- *ConAu 49*
Bailey, J O 1903- *ConAu 17R*
Bailey, Jackson Holbrook 1925- *ConAu 45*
Bailey, Jacob *BbtC*
Bailey, Jacob 1731-1808 *Alli, CyAL 1,
    OxCan*
Bailey, Jacob 1797-1853 *CyAL 2*
Bailey, Jacob Whitman 1811?-1857 *Alli,
    Alli Sup, DcNAA*
Bailey, James *Alli, Alli Sup*
Bailey, James Montgomery 1841-1894 *Alli Sup,
    AmA, AmA&B, BiD&SB, CnDAL,
    DcAmA, DcEnL, DcNAA, OxAm,
    REnAL*
Bailey, James R A 1919- *ConAu 53*
Bailey, James Robinson 1868- *TexWr,
    WhWNAA*
Bailey, James W *Alli Sup*
Bailey, Jane H 1916- *ConAu 53*

Bailey, Jessie Emerson *AmA&B*
Bailey, Joan H 1922- *ConAu 21*
Bailey, Joe A 1929- *ConAu 37*
Bailey, John *Alli, AuBYP, BiDLA, ChPo S2*
Bailey, John A 1929- *ConAu 37*
Bailey, John Burn *Alli Sup*
Bailey, John C W *Alli Sup*
Bailey, John Cann 1864-1931 *LongC, WhLA*
Bailey, John Eglington 1840-1888 *Alli Sup*
Bailey, John J *Alli Sup*
Bailey, John J d1873 *DcNAA*
Bailey, John Jay 1833-1913 *DcNAA*
Bailey, John M *Alli Sup*
Bailey, John Read 1833-1910 *DcNAA*
Bailey, John William 1873- *IndAu 1816*
Bailey, Joseph *BlkAW*
Bailey, Joseph Weldon 1863- *BiDSA*
Bailey, Joseph Whitman 1865-1932 *DcNAA*
Bailey, Josiah William 1873- *BiDSA, WhWNAA*
Bailey, Kenneth Claude 1896- *WhLA*
Bailey, Kenneth K 1923- *ConAu 23*
Bailey, Kenneth P 1912- *ConAu 53*
Bailey, L H, Jr. *Alli Sup*
Bailey, Lawrence 1925- *WrD 1976*
Bailey, Ledyard M *WhWNAA*
Bailey, Liberty Hyde 1858-1954 *AmA&B, AmLY, ChPo, DcAmA, WhWNAA*
Bailey, Loring Woart 1839-1925 *Alli Sup, BbtC, DcAmA, DcNAA*
Bailey, Lucy D *ChPo*
Bailey, M *Alli Sup*
Bailey, M E *Alli Sup*
Bailey, M Thomas *ConAu 57*
Bailey, Mabel *ChPo S1*
Bailey, Maralyn Collins 1941- *ConAu 53*
Bailey, Margaret Emerson 1880-1949 *AmA&B, ChPo S2, DcNAA, WhWNAA*
Bailey, Margaret Jewett 1837?- *DcNAA*
Bailey, Margaret L 1812- *Alli, ChPo*
Bailey, Margery 1891- *AmA&B, WhWNAA*
Bailey, Mark 1827-1911 *DcNAA*
Bailey, Matilda *ConAu XR, SmATA 6*
Bailey, Matilda A *LivFWS*
Bailey, Maurice 1925- *Au&Wr*
Bailey, Maurice Charles 1932- *ConAu 53*
Bailey, Middlesex Alfred 1856-1923 *DcNAA*
Bailey, Nathaniel d1742 *Alli, BiD&SB, BrAu, DcEnL, NewC, OxEng, REn*
Bailey, Norman Alishan 1931- *ConAu 21, WrD 1976*
Bailey, Norman Thomas John 1923- *Au&Wr, WrD 1976*
Bailey, Patrick 1925- *ConAu 57*
Bailey, Paul 1885- *WhWNAA*
Bailey, Paul 1937- *Au&Wr, ConAu 21, ConNov 1972, ConNov 1976, WhTwL, WrD 1976*
Bailey, Paul Dayton 1906- *ConAu 5R*
Bailey, Pearce 1865-1922 *DcAmA, DcNAA*
Bailey, Pearl 1918- *AmSCAP 66, ConAu 61, LivBAA*
Bailey, Peter d1823 *Alli*
Bailey, Philip James 1816-1902 *Alli, Alli Sup, BbD, BiD&SB, BrAu 19, CasWL, ChPo, ChPo S1, ChPo S2, Chmbr 3, DcEnA, DcEnA Ap, DcEnL, DcEuL, DcLEnL, EvLB, NewC, OxEng, Pen Eng, REn, WebEAL*
Bailey, Prentiss 1873-1939 *DcNAA, WhWNAA*
Bailey, Rae 1879-1958 *OhA&B*
Bailey, Ralph Edgar 1893- *ConAu P-1*
Bailey, Raymond H 1938- *ConAu 61*
Bailey, Richard *BlkAW*
Bailey, Richard 1911- *Au&Wr*
Bailey, Richard Eugene 1907- *Au&Wr*
Bailey, Richard W 1939- *ConAu 25*
Bailey, Robert, Jr. 1945- *ConAu 49*
Bailey, Robert Ernest *MnBBF*
Bailey, Roberta *BlkAW*
Bailey, Robeson *ChPo S1*
Bailey, Ronald W *LivBA*
Bailey, Roy F 1883- *WhWNAA*
Bailey, Rufus William 1793-1863 *Alli, DcNAA*
Bailey, Samuel 1787- *Alli*
Bailey, Samuel 1791-1870 *Alli Sup, BbD, BiD&SB*

Bailey, Sarah Loring 1836-1896 *Alli Sup, DcNAA*
Bailey, Solon Irving 1854-1931 *DcNAA*
Bailey, Stephen Kemp 1916- *ConAu 1R*
Bailey, T *Alli, BiDLA*
Bailey, T Arthur *ChPo S1, ChPo S2*
Bailey, Temple 1880-1953 *REnAL, TwCA, TwCA Sup, WhWNAA*
Bailey, Thomas 1785-1856 *Alli*
Bailey, Thomas Andrew 1902- *ConAu 17R*
Bailey, Thomas D 1897- *ChPo S2*
Bailey, Thomas John *Alli Sup*
Bailey, Thomas Pearce 1867-1949 *AmLY, BiDSA, DcNAA, WhWNAA*
Bailey, Urania Locke 1820-1882 *Alli Sup, ChPo, DcAmA, DcNAA*
Bailey, Vernon 1864-1942 *DcAmA, DcNAA*
Bailey, Vernon 1864- *WhWNAA*
Bailey, Vernon Howe 1874-1953 *AmA&B*
Bailey, W B *Alli Sup*
Bailey, W E *Alli Sup*
Bailey, W T *Alli Sup*
Bailey, Walter *Alli*
Bailey, Warren Worth 1855-1928 *DcNAA, WhWNAA*
Bailey, Wellesley C *Alli Sup*
Bailey, Whitman *WhWNAA*
Bailey, William *Alli, Alli Sup*
Bailey, William Bacon 1873- *AmLY, WhWNAA*
Bailey, William Edgar *BlkAW*
Bailey, William Francis 1842-1915 *DcNAA*
Bailey, William H *Alli Sup*
Bailey, William Henry 1831-1908 *BiDSA, DcAmA, DcNAA*
Bailey, William Louis 1885- *WhWNAA*
Bailey, William Theodore 1828-1896 *DcNAA*
Bailey, William Whitman 1843-1914 *Alli Sup, DcAmA, DcNAA*
Bailey-Jones, Beryl 1912- *IlBYP, IlCB 1956*
Bailie, J K *Alli*
Bailie, Victoria Worley 1894- *ConAu P-1*
Bailie, William 1899- *AmLY*
Bailin, Harriett 1923- *AmSCAP 66*
Bailkey, Nels M 1911- *ConAu 33*
Baillairge, C P F *BbtC*
Baillarge, Charles 1825-1906 *DcNAA*
Baillarge, F-A *OxCan*
Baillarge, Frederic Alexandre 1854-1928 *DcNAA*
Baillargeon, Charles Francois 1798-1870 *BbtC, DcNAA*
Baillargeon, G E *OxCan Sup*
Baillargeon, Pierre 1916-1967 *CanWr, OxCan*
Baillargeon, Samuel *OxCan*
Baillen, Claude 1934- *ConAu XR*
Baillet, Adrien 1649-1706 *EvEuW, OxFr*
Baillie, Captain *Alli*
Baillie, A D R Cochrane-Wishart- *Alli Sup*
Baillie, Alex *Alli*
Baillie, Alexander F *Alli Sup*
Baillie, Mrs. E C C *Alli Sup*
Baillie, E J *Alli Sup*
Baillie, Frank 1927- *WrD 1976*
Baillie, George *Alli, BiDLA*
Baillie, Lady Grisell 1665-1746 *ChPo, EvLB, Pen Eng*
Baillie, Lady Grizel 1665-1746 *BrAu, CasWL, Chmbr 2, EvLB, NewC, Pen Eng*
Baillie, Helen *Alli Sup*
Baillie, Hugh *Alli, BbtC*
Baillie, J *BiDLA*
Baillie, James Black *WhLA*
Baillie, Joanna 1762-1851 *Alli, BbD, BiD&SB, BiDLA, BrAu 19, CasWL, ChPo, ChPo S1, Chmbr 2, DcEnA, DcEnL, DcLEnL, EvLB, NewC, OxEng, Pen Eng*
Baillie, John *Alli*
Baillie, John d1890 *Alli Sup*
Baillie, John 1886- *WhWNAA*
Baillie, Marianne *Alli*
Baillie, Matthew 1761-1823 *Alli, BiDLA, BiDLA Sup*
Baillie, Neil Benjamin Edmonstone *Alli Sup*
Baillie, Peter 1889-1914 *ChPo*
Baillie, Robert 1599?-1662 *Alli, BrAu, Chmbr 1, DcEnL, DcLEnL, EvLB, NewC, OxEng*

Baillie, Thomas 1797?-1863 *BbtC, OxCan*
Baillie, William *Alli, Alli Sup*
Baillie-Grohman, William A 1851-1921 *Alli Sup, Br&AmS, OxCan*
Baillieu, Vera Latham *ChPo S1*
Bailly, J S *Alli*
Bailly, James *Alli*
Bailly, Jean Sylvain 1736-1793 *BiD&SB, OxFr*
Bailor, Edwin Maurice 1890- *WhWNAA*
Baily, Alfred *Alli Sup*
Baily, Caleb *Alli*
Baily, D E And Hammond, John D *Alli Sup*
Baily, E H *ChPo S1*
Baily, Florence *Alli Sup*
Baily, Francis *Alli Sup, BiDLA*
Baily, Francis 1774-1844 *Alli, BiD&SB*
Baily, Francis Gibson 1868- *WhLA*
Baily, Hannah Lavinia 1837- *ChPo*
Baily, J *Alli Sup*
Baily, John *Alli Sup*
Baily, John 1643-1697 *Alli*
Baily, Laurence R *Alli Sup*
Baily, Leslie 1906- *Au&Wr, ConAu 25, WrD 1976*
Baily, Nathan A 1920- *ConAu 9R*
Baily, Samuel L 1936- *ConAu 29*
Baily, Thomas L *Alli Sup*
Baily, Thomas Lloyd 1884-1914 *AmA&B*
Baily, Thomas Loyd 1824-1914 *DcNAA*
Baily, William Hellier *Alli Sup*
Baily, William L *Alli Sup*
Baily, William Lloyd 1861- *WhWNAA*
Bailyn, Bernard 1922- *AmA&B, ConAu 61, WrD 1976*
Bailzie, William *Alli*
Bain *Alli*
Bain, Alexander *Chmbr 3*
Bain, Alexander 1811-1877 *Alli Sup*
Bain, Alexander 1818-1903 *Alli Sup, BbD, BiD&SB, BrAu 19, CasWL, DcEnA Ap, DcEnL, EvLB, NewC, OxEng*
Bain, C *ChPo S1*
Bain, Charles M *Alli Sup, ChPo S1*
Bain, Charles Wesley 1864-1915 *BiDSA, DcNAA*
Bain, Chester A 1912- *ConAu 29*
Bain, Cyril William Curtis 1895- *Au&Wr*
Bain, E *Alli Sup*
Bain, Edgar C 1891- *WhWNAA*
Bain, Edward Ustick *AuBYP*
Bain, Foster 1871- *WhWNAA*
Bain, Francis 1842-1894 *DcNAA*
Bain, Francis William 1863-1940 *ChPo, LongC, WhLA*
Bain, George *Alli Sup*
Bain, George Grantham 1865- *WhWNAA*
Bain, George William 1901- *WrD 1976*
Bain, Harry Foster 1872-1948 *IndAu 1917*
Bain, Iain *ChPo S2*
Bain, J *BiDLA*
Bain, J A Kerr *Alli Sup*
Bain, J W *Alli Sup*
Bain, James 1842-1908 *DcNAA*
Bain, James Watson 1875- *WhWNAA*
Bain, Joe S 1912- *ConAu 33*
Bain, John, Jr. *ChPo S1*
Bain, John Wallace 1833-1910 *DcNAA*
Bain, Joseph And Rogers, C *Alli Sup*
Bain, Kenneth Ross 1923 *Au&Wr*
Bain, R Nisbet 1854-1909 *St&VC*
Bain, Richard 1811-1875 *Alli Sup*
Bain, Robert *ChPo, ChPo S2*
Bain, Sylvia *ChPo S2*
Bain, Willard S, Jr. 1938- *ConAu 25*
Bain, William *Alli*
Bainbridge, Beryl 1933?- *ConAu 21, ConLC 4, ConLC 5, ConNov 1976, WrD 1976*
Bainbridge, Bryant *HsB&A*
Bainbridge, C G *Alli*
Bainbridge, Geoffrey 1923- *Au&Wr, ConAu 5R*
Bainbridge, John 1582-1643 *Alli*
Bainbridge, John 1913- *AmA&B, ConAu 13R, WrD 1976*
Bainbridge, Katharine 1863- *AmSCAP 66*
Bainbridge, Lucy Seaman 1842-1928 *Alli Sup, DcNAA, OhA&B*
Bainbridge, Stella Marguerite 1896- *WhWNAA*

Bainbridge, William *Alli, Alli Sup*
Bainbridge-Hoff, William *DcNAA*
Bainbrigge, William Henry *Alli Sup*
Baine, A C *Alli Sup*
Baine, Bernard *Alli*
Baine, Colin T *MnBBF*
Baine, Duncan *Alli*
Baine, James *Alli*
Baine, Paul *Alli*
Baine, W B *Polre*
Baines, Anthony C 1912- *Au&Wr, ConAu 5R*
Baines, Edward *Alli*
Baines, Edward 1774-1848 *Alli, Alli Sup, DcEnL*
Baines, Sir Edward 1800-1890 *Alli, Alli Sup, DcEnL*
Baines, John *Alli, Alli Sup*
Baines, John 1786?-1835 *Alli*
Baines, John M 1935- *ConAu 41*
Baines, M A *Alli Sup*
Baines, Minnie Willis 1845- *ChPo S2, DcNAA*
Baines, R Read *MnBBF*
Baines, T B *Alli Sup*
Baines, Thomas *Alli Sup*
Baines, Thomas 1802- *Alli*
Baines, Thomas 1806-1881 *Alli Sup*
Baines, Thomas 1822-1875 *Alli Sup*
Baines, Wilhelmina *Alli Sup*
Baines-Miller, Minnie Willis 1845- *AmA&B, DcAmA*
Bainsmead, Hesba Fay Hungerford 1922- *Au&Wr*
Bainton, Roland Herbert 1894- *Au&Wr, ConAu 1R, WhWNAA, WrD 1976*
Bainville, Jacques 1879-1936 *CasWL, ClDMEuL, OxFr*
Bair, Joseph H *ChPo S1*
Baird, Albert Craig 1883- *ConAu P-1, IndAu 1917, WhWNAA*
Baird, Alexander *ChPo S2*
Baird, Alexander John 1925- *Au&Wr, ConAu 9R, ConP 1970, WrD 1976*
Baird, Andrew Cumming *WhLA*
Baird, Andrew J d1884 *DcNAA*
Baird, Andrew Wilson *Alli Sup*
Baird, Bil *ChPo S2*
Baird, Catherine *ChPo S2*
Baird, Charles Washington 1828-1887 *Alli Sup, AmA&B, BiD&SB, ChPo, CyAL 1, DcAmA, DcNAA*
Baird, E J C *Alli Sup*
Baird, Edwin 1886- *WhWNAA*
Baird, Forrest J 1905- *ConAu 19, ConAu P-1*
Baird, Frank *OxCan*
Baird, G *ChPo, ChPo S1, MnBBF*
Baird, George Washington 1843-1930 *DcNAA*
Baird, Henry Carey 1825- *Alli Sup, AmA&B, BiD&SB, DcAmA*
Baird, Henry Martyn 1832-1906 *Alli Sup, AmA, AmA&B, BiD&SB, CyAL 1, CyAL 2, DcAmA, DcNAA*
Baird, Hugh *Alli Sup*
Baird, Irene *CanNov, OxCan*
Baird, J Arthur 1922- *ConAu 5R*
Baird, James *Alli Sup, BbtC*
Baird, James Skerrett Shore *Alli Sup*
Baird, Jane *ChPo*
Baird, Jay William 1936- *ConAu 41*
Baird, Jean Katherine 1872-1918 *DcNAA*
Baird, Jesse Hays 1889- *ConAu 13R*
Baird, John *Alli Sup*
Baird, John Edward 1922- *ConAu 17R*
Baird, John Logie 1888-1946 *LongC*
Baird, Joseph Armstrong 1922- *ConAu 33*
Baird, Keith A *BlkAW*
Baird, Marie-Terese 1918- *ConAu 57*
Baird, Martha 1921- *ConAu 61*
Baird, Sister Mary Julian *BkC 6*
Baird, Robert 1798-1863 *Alli, Alli Sup, BiD&SB, CyAL 1, DcAmA, DcNAA*
Baird, Robert D 1933- *ConAu 53*
Baird, Robert H *Alli Sup*
Baird, Ronald J 1929- *ConAu 53*
Baird, Russell Norman 1922- *ConAu 17R, WrD 1976*
Baird, Samuel John 1817-1893 *Alli Sup, BiDSA, DcAmA, DcNAA, OhA&B*
Baird, Spencer Fullerton 1823-1887 *Alli,*

Alli Sup, BiD&SB, CyAL 2, DcAmA, DcEnL
Baird, Spencer Fullerton 1823-1888 *DcNAA*
Baird, Thomas 1923- *Alli, AmA&B, ConAu 53, WrD 1976*
Baird, Thomas Dickson 1773-1839 *DcNAA*
Baird, W David 1939- *ConAu 41*
Baird, William *Alli Sup*
Baird, William 1803-1872 *Alli Sup*
Baird, William 1924- *ConAu 13R*
Baird, William Britton 1904- *AmA&B*
Baird, William Raimond 1858-1917 *Alli Sup, DcNAA*
Baird, William Thomas 1819?-1897 *DcNAA, OxCan*
Bairdy, John *Alli*
Bairn *Alli*
Bairn, John *Alli*
Bairnsfather, Bruce 1888?-1959 *ChPo S1, LongC*
Bairstow, J O *Alli Sup*
Bairstow, Jeffrey N 1939- *ConAu 61*
Baitman, George *Alli*
Baitsell, George Alfred 1885- *WhWNAA*
Baity, Elizabeth Chesley 1907- *AmA&B, AnCL, ConAu 29, MorJA, SmATA 1*
Bajema, Carl Jay 1937- *ConAu 33*
Bajza, Joseph 1804-1858 *BiD&SB*
Bajza, Jozef Ignac 1755-1836 *CasWL, EvEuW*
Bak, Wojciech 1907-1961 *Pen Eur*
Bakacs, George *IlBYP*
Bakal, Carl 1918- *ConAu 23*
Bakan, David 1921- *ConAu 25*
Bakan, Paul 1928- *ConAu 23*
Bakeless, John Edwin 1894- *AmA&B, Au&Wr, AuBYP, ConAu 5R, REnAL, SmATA 9, TwCA, TwCA Sup, WhWNAA, WrD 1976*
Bakeless, Katherine Little 1895- *Au&Wr, ConAu 5R, SmATA 9, WrD 1976*
Baker *Alli*
Baker, Lady *Alli Sup*
Baker, A *ChPo, MnBBF*
Baker, A George 1840?- *DcAmA*
Baker, A H *Alli Sup*
Baker, A R *ChPo S2*
Baker, Aaron *Alli*
Baker, Abigail d1923 *DcNAA*
Baker, Abijah Richardson 1805-1876 *Alli Sup, DcAmA, DcNAA*
Baker, Adelaide Nichols 1894- *ConAu 45, WhWNAA*
Baker, Adolph 1917- *ConAu 53*
Baker, Al *AuNews 1*
Baker, Albert Rufus 1858-1911 *OhA&B*
Baker, Alfred 1848-1942 *DcNAA*
Baker, Alice 1849-1913 *DcNAA*
Baker, Alonzo Lafayette 1894- *WhWNAA*
Baker, Alton Wesley 1912- *ConAu 33*
Baker, Amy *Alli Sup*
Baker, Andrew Jackson 1832- *DcNAA*
Baker, Anne *Alli*
Baker, Anselm 1834-1885 *Alli Sup*
Baker, Arthur *Alli, Alli Sup*
Baker, Arthur John *Alli Sup*
Baker, Arthur Latham 1853-1934 *DcNAA*
Baker, Arthur Lempriere Lancey 1904?- *Au&Wr, WrD 1976*
Baker, Arthur M *Alli Sup*
Baker, Arthur Mulford 1880-1941 *DcNAA, OhA&B, WhWNAA*
Baker, Asa *EncM&D*
Baker, Augusta 1911- *BlkAW, ConAu 1R, LivBAA, SmATA 3*
Baker, Augustus *MnBBF*
Baker, Barbara *ChPo, ChPo S1*
Baker, Benjamin *Alli Sup*
Baker, Benjamin 1915- *ConAu 1R*
Baker, Benjamin A 1818-1890 *AmA, AmA&B, CnDAL, OxAm*
Baker, Benjamin Franklin 1811-1889 *Alli, Alli Sup, DcNAA*
Baker, Benson *Alli Sup*
Baker, Betty 1928- *AmA&B, AuBYP, ConAu XR, SmATA 5, ThBJA*
Baker, Betty D 1916- *ConAu 9R*
Baker, Bill *ConAu 57*

Baker, Bill Russell 1933- *ConAu 57*
Baker, C *Alli Sup*
Baker, C 1905- *WrD 1976*
Baker, C William 1919- *ConAu 57*
Baker, Carlos Heard 1909- *AmA&B, ChPo, ConAu 5R, REnAL, WhWNAA, WorAu, WrD 1976*
Baker, Caroline Horwood *ChPo*
Baker, Charles *Alli, Alli Sup*
Baker, Charles 1803-1874 *Alli Sup*
Baker, Charles Conyers Massey 1847- *Alli Sup*
Baker, Charles Edmund *Alli Sup*
Baker, Charles H, Jr. 1895-1968 *AmA&B*
Baker, Charles R *Alli Sup*
Baker, Charles Richard 1842-1898 *DcAmA, DcNAA*
Baker, Charles Whiting 1865-1941 *AmLY, DcAmA, DcNAA, WhWNAA*
Baker, Charlotte 1910- *AuBYP, ConAu 17R, IlCB 1956, SmATA 2*
Baker, Charlotte Alice 1833-1909 *Alli Sup, DcNAA, OxCan*
Baker, Chauncey Brooke 1860-1936 *DcNAA*
Baker, Christina Hopkinson 1873- *ChPo, WhWNAA*
Baker, Colgate d1940 *AmA&B*
Baker, Cornelia 1855-1930 *DcNAA, OhA&B*
Baker, Cyril Clarence Thomas 1907- *Au&Wr, WrD 1976*
Baker, D *Alli, Alli Sup*
Baker, D B *Alli*
Baker, D W C *BiDSA*
Baker, Daniel 1791-1857 *Alli, Alli Sup, BiDSA, CyAL 2, DcNAA*
Baker, David 1575-1641 *Alli*
Baker, David Erskine d1767 *Alli*
Baker, Denys Val 1917- *ConAu 9R*
Baker, DeWitt Clinton 1832-1881 *Alli Sup, DcNAA*
Baker, Don 1903- *AmSCAP 66*
Baker, Donald G 1932- *ConAu 33*
Baker, Donald N 1936- *ConAu 23*
Baker, Donald W *DrAF 1976, DrAP 1975*
Baker, Dorothea *Alli Sup*
Baker, Dorothy 1907-1968 *AmA&B, AmNov, ChPo, ChPo S1, ChPo S2, ConAu 1R, ConAu 25, DcLEnL, OxAm, Pen Am, TwCA, TwCA Sup, WhTwL*
Baker, E *Alli Sup*
Baker, Edna Dean *WhWNAA*
Baker, Edward B *Alli Sup*
Baker, Eleanor Z 1932- *ConAu 57*
Baker, Elinor *Alli Sup*
Baker, Elizabeth *DcLEnL*
Baker, Elizabeth 1923- *ConAu 1R, WrD 1976*
Baker, Elizabeth Faulkner 1886?-1973 *ConAu 41, ConAu P-1, WhWNAA*
Baker, Elizabeth W *WhWNAA*
Baker, Ella Anthony *ChPo*
Baker, Ella M d1888 *Alli Sup*
Baker, Ellen Maria 1848-1884 *ChPo, ChPo S1*
Baker, Elliott 1922- *AmA&B, ConAu 45, ConNov 1972, ConNov 1976, DrAF 1976, WrD 1976*
Baker, Elsie Gorham *ChPo*
Baker, Elsworth Frederick 1903- *ConAu 25, WrD 1976*
Baker, Emilie Kip *AmA&B, St&VC*
Baker, Eric Wilfred 1899-1973 *Au&Wr, ConAu 45*
Baker, Ernest Everhart *ChPo*
Baker, Ernst A 1869- *WhLA*
Baker, Etta Anthony *AmA&B, AmLY, WhWNAA*
Baker, Ezekiel *Alli*
Baker, F *Alli Sup*
Baker, F M *ChPo*
Baker, F P And Furnas, R W *Alli Sup*
Baker, Francis A *Alli Sup*
Baker, Frank *ChPo S1*
Baker, Frank 1840-1916 *DcNAA*
Baker, Frank 1908- *LongC, TwCA Sup*
Baker, Frank 1910- *Au&Wr, ConAu 9R, WrD 1976*
Baker, Frank 1936- *ConAu 49*
Baker, Frank, D O N *Alli Sup*
Baker, Frank S 1910- *ConAu 17R*
Baker, Frank Sheaffer 1910- *IndAu 1917*

Baker, Frank Tarkington 1878-1924 *IndAu 1816*
Baker, Franklin 1800-1867 *Alli Sup*
Baker, Franklin Thomas 1864-1949 *AmA&B, DcNAA*
Baker, Fred Abbott 1846- *DcNAA*
Baker, Mrs. G *Alli Sup*
Baker, G M *Alli Sup*
Baker, Gary G 1939- *ConAu 23*
Baker, Geoffrey *Alli*
Baker, George *Alli, BiDLA*
Baker, Sir George 1722-1809 *Alli*
Baker, George 1781-1851 *DcEnL*
Baker, George 1915-1975 *AmA&B, ConAu 57*
Baker, George Augustus 1849-1906 *Alli Sup, BiD&SB, ChPo, DcAmA, DcNAA*
Baker, George Barr 1870-1948 *AmA&B, ChPo*
Baker, George Cornelius 1881- *WhWNAA*
Baker, George E 1816- *CyAL 2*
Baker, Sir George E Dunstan Sherston 1846- *Alli Sup*
Baker, George G *Alli Sup*
Baker, George Hall 1850-1911 *DcNAA*
Baker, George Holbrook 1827-1906 *EarAB Sup*
Baker, George Melville 1832-1890 *Alli Sup, AmA&B, ChPo, DcAmA, DcNAA*
Baker, George Pierce 1866-1935 *AmA&B, ChPo, CnDAL, DcAmA, DcNAA, LongC, McGWD, OxAm, Pen Am, REnAL, TwCA, TwCA Sup, WhTwL*
Baker, George Shereton *Alli Sup*
Baker, George W 1915- *ConAu 21*
Baker, Georgina M A *Alli Sup*
Baker, Gladys *CatA 1952*
Baker, Gladys L 1910- *ConAu 41*
Baker, Gordon Harrington 1878- *WhWNAA*
Baker, Gordon Pratt 1910- *ConAu 1R*
Baker, Grace Hackel 1888- *TexWr*
Baker, H S *MnBBF*
Baker, Harold 1914- *AmSCAP 66*
Baker, Harriette Newell 1815?-1893 *Alli Sup, AmA&B, BbD, BiD&SB, CarSB, DcAmA, DcNAA*
Baker, Harry James 1894- *IndAu 1917*
Baker, Harry Torsey 1877- *WhWNAA*
Baker, Hendrik Maurice Ruitenga 1910- *Au&Wr*
Baker, Henry *Alli, Alli Sup, BbtC, HsB&A*
Baker, Henry 1703-1774 *Alli, DcEnL*
Baker, Henry Barton *Alli Sup*
Baker, Henry F *Alli Sup*
Baker, Henry Felt 1797-1857 *DcNAA*
Baker, Henry Moore 1841-1912 *DcNAA*
Baker, Sir Henry Williams 1821-1877 *Alli Sup, ChPo, PoCh*
Baker, Herbert G 1920- *AmSCAP 66, ConAu 41*
Baker, Herschel Clay 1914- *ConAu 61*
Baker, Houston Alfred, Jr. 1943- *BlkAW, ConAu 41, LivBA, WrD 1976*
Baker, Howard 1905- *ConAu 19, ConP 1970, ConP 1975, Pen Am, SixAP, WrD 1976*
Baker, Hugh D R 1937- *ConAu 25*
Baker, Humphrey *Alli*
Baker, I O *Alli Sup*
Baker, Ira Osborn 1853-1925 *DcNAA, IndAu 1917, WhWNAA*
Baker, J *Alli, Alli Sup*
Baker, J A 1926- *ConAu 25*
Baker, J B *Alli*
Baker, J M *Alli Sup*
Baker, J Percy 1859- *WhLA*
Baker, J S *Alli Sup*
Baker, J W *BiDLA*
Baker, James *Alli, Alli Sup, BiDLA*
Baker, James 1847- *Alli Sup*
Baker, James Franklin Bethune *Alli Sup*
Baker, James Heaton 1829-1913 *OhA&B*
Baker, James Hutchins 1848-1925 *AmLY, DcAmA, DcNAA*
Baker, James L *Alli Sup*
Baker, James Lawrence 1941- *ConAu 53*
Baker, James Loring d1886 *DcNAA*
Baker, James Rupert 1925- *ConAu 29, WrD 1976*
Baker, James Volant 1903- *ConAu 57*
Baker, Janice E 1941- *ConAu 57*
Baker, Jean Hogarth H 1933- *ConAu 41*

Baker, Jeffrey J W 1931- *ConAu 49, SmATA 5*
Baker, Jehu *Alli Sup*
Baker, Jerry *AuNews 2*
Baker, Jessie M *ChPo*
Baker, John *Alli*
Baker, John Alec 1926- *WrD 1976*
Baker, John Clapp 1828-1912 *DcNAA*
Baker, John Clark 1884- *WhWNAA*
Baker, John Clifford Yorke 1905- *Au&Wr*
Baker, John F *Alli Sup*
Baker, John Fleetwood 1901- *WrD 1976*
Baker, John Gilbert 1834- *Alli Sup*
Baker, John H 1936- *ConAu 33*
Baker, John Milton 1895- *WhWNAA*
Baker, John Randal 1900- *Au&Wr, ConAu 49, WrD 1976*
Baker, John Victor T 1913- *WrD 1976*
Baker, John W *Alli*
Baker, John W 1920- *ConAu 61*
Baker, Johnny *MnBBF*
Baker, Joseph Brogden *Alli Sup*
Baker, Joseph E 1905- *ConAu 33*
Baker, Joseph Eugene 1827-1914 *DcNAA*
Baker, Josephine Katherine Turck *AmLY*
Baker, Josephine L *ChPo*
Baker, Josephine R *Alli Sup*
Baker, Josephine Turck d1942 *AmA&B, ChPo, WhWNAA*
Baker, Julia Keim 1858- *DcAmA*
Baker, Julia Wetherill 1858- *BiDSA*
Baker, Karle Wilson 1878- *AmA&B, BiDSA, ChPo, ChPo S1, ChPo S2, TexWr, WhWNAA*
Baker, Keith Michael 1938- *ConAu 57*
Baker, Kenneth F 1908- *ConAu 49*
Baker, Lafayette Curry 1826-1868 *Alli Sup, DcNAA*
Baker, Laura Nelson 1911- *Au&Wr, AuBYP, ConAu 5R, MnnWr, SmATA 3, WrD 1976*
Baker, Lawrence M 1907- *ConAu P-1*
Baker, Leonard *Alli Sup*
Baker, Leonard 1931- *ConAu 23, WrD 1976*
Baker, Letha Elizabeth 1913- *ConAu 33*
Baker, Levi Wood *Alli Sup*
Baker, Lewis Carter 1831-1915 *DcNAA*
Baker, Liva 1930- *ConAu 29*
Baker, Lon *WhWNAA*
Baker, Loren Lynn 1884-1934 *DcNAA*
Baker, Mrs. Louie Alien 1858- *DcNAA*
Baker, Louise *REnAL*
Baker, Louise 1909- *AmA&B, AmNov*
Baker, Louise Regina 1868- *AmA&B, ChPo*
Baker, Louise Southard 1846-1896 *DcNAA*
Baker, M E Penny *ConAu 45*
Baker, Magdalena D H 1897- *OhA&B*
Baker, Marc *AuNews 1*
Baker, Marceil Genee 1911- *AuNews 1*
Baker, Marcus 1849-1903 *DcNAA*
Baker, Margaret 1890- *Au&Wr, ChPo S2, ConAu 13R, JBA 1951, SmATA 4, WrD 1976*
Baker, Margaret And Mary *JBA 1934*
Baker, Margaret Joyce 1918- *Au&Wr, AuBYP, ConAu 13R, MorJA, WrD 1976*
Baker, Marvin G 1925- *IndAu 1917*
Baker, Mary *JBA 1951*
Baker, Mary 1897- *ConICB, IlCB 1945, IlCB 1956*
Baker, Mary Elizabeth Gillette 1923- *SmATA 7*
Baker, Mary Gladys Steel 1892-1970? *ConAu P-1*
Baker, Mary Louise *ChPo*
Baker, Mattie W *ChPo*
Baker, May Allread 1897- *ChPo, OhA&B*
Baker, Melyn D 1800-1852 *OhA&B*
Baker, Michael 1938- *ConAu 25, SmATA 4, WrD 1976*
Baker, Michael H C 1937- *ConAu 57*
Baker, Moses Nelson 1864- *DcAmA, WhWNAA*
Baker, Myla Jo Closser 1880-1962 *IndAu 1917*
Baker, Myron Eugene d1901 *DcNAA*
Baker, Naaman Rimmon 1868- *AmLY, OhA&B*
Baker, Nelson Blaisdell 1905- *ConAu 17R,*

Baker, *WrD 1976*
Baker, Newman Freese 1898-1941 *IndAu 1917*
Baker, Newton Diehl 1871-1937 *AmA&B, DcNAA, OhA&B*
Baker, Nina Brown 1888-1957 *AmA&B, AuBYP, JBA 1951*
Baker, O *Alli Sup*
Baker, Olaf *JBA 1934, JBA 1951, MnBBF*
Baker, Oliver 1856- *WhLA*
Baker, Oliver Edwin 1883- *WhWNAA*
Baker, Orlando Harrison 1830-1913 *IndAu 1816*
Baker, Osman Cleander 1812-1871 *Alli, Alli Sup, DcAmA*
Baker, Osmon Cleander 1812-1871 *DcNAA*
Baker, P *Alli Sup*
Baker, Paul R 1927- *ConAu 9R*
Baker, Paul T 1927- *ConAu 33*
Baker, Pearl Biddlecome 1907- *ConAu 17R*
Baker, Peter *Alli*
Baker, Peter 1928- *ConAu 23*
Baker, Peter Gorton 1926- *Au&Wr, WrD 1976*
Baker, Phil 1896-1963 *AmSCAP 66*
Baker, Sir R *Chmbr 1*
Baker, R J 1924- *ConAu 33*
Baker, Rachel *Alli*
Baker, Rachel 1903- *BkCL, MorJA*
Baker, Rachel 1904- *AuBYP, ConAu 5R, SmATA 2*
Baker, Ray 1890- *WhWNAA*
Baker, Ray Palmer 1883- *AmA&B, OxCan, WhWNAA*
Baker, Ray Stannard 1870-1946 *AmA&B, AmLY, CarSB, ChPo S2, ConAmL, DcAmA, DcLEnL, DcNAA, EvLB, LongC, OxAm, REn, REnAL, TwCA, TwCA Sup, TwCW, WhWNAA, WiscW*
Baker, Reginald O 1909- *Au&Wr*
Baker, Richard *Alli, BiDLA*
Baker, Sir Richard 1568-1645 *Alli, CasWL, EvLB, NewC*
Baker, Richard E 1916- *AmSCAP 66*
Baker, Richard M, Jr. 1924- *ConAu 13R*
Baker, Richard St. Barbe 1889- *Au&Wr, ConAu P-1*
Baker, Richard Terrill 1913- *ConAu 1R*
Baker, Richard Thomas 1854- *WhLA*
Baker, Robert *Alli, Alli Sup*
Baker, Robert d1580? *Alli*
Baker, Robert And York, Shelton *Alli Sup*
Baker, Robert B 1937- *ConAu 53*
Baker, Robert H 1883- *WhWNAA*
Baker, Robert Melville 1868- *ChPo*
Baker, Robert Milum *BlkAW*
Baker, Robin Campbell 1941- *ConAu 17R*
Baker, Roger 1934- *Au&Wr, ConAu 25*
Baker, Ross Allen 1886- *WhWNAA*
Baker, Ross K 1938- *ConAu 29*
Baker, Russell Wayne 1925- *AmA&B, ConAu 57*
Baker, S *Alli, BiDLA*
Baker, Miss S H *ChPo*
Baker, S Josephine *WhWNAA*
Baker, S W *Alli*
Baker, Samm S 1909- *ConAu 5R*
Baker, Samuel *Alli*
Baker, Sir Samuel White 1821-1893 *Alli Sup, BbD, BiD&SB, BrAu 19, Chmbr 3, DcEnL, EvLB, MnBBF, NewC, OxEng*
Baker, Sarah Schoonmaker 1824-1906 *Alli Sup, CarSB, ChPo, DcAmA, DcNAA*
Baker, Sheridan 1824-1890 *DcNAA*
Baker, Sheridan 1918- *ConAu 5R*
Baker, Smith 1836-1917 *DcNAA*
Baker, Stacy E *ChPo*
Baker, Stephen 1921- *ConAu 1R*
Baker, T *Alli*
Baker, T Barwick Lloyd *Alli Sup*
Baker, T F 1935- *Au&Wr, ConAu 25*
Baker, T H *Alli Sup*
Baker, T R *Alli Sup*
Baker, Mrs. Tabbet *Alli Sup*
Baker, Tarkington 1878-1924 *DcNAA*
Baker, Theodore 1851-1934 *ChPo, DcNAA*
Baker, Thomas *Alli, Alli Sup*
Baker, Thomas 1625-1690 *Alli*
Baker, Thomas 1656-1740 *Alli, DcEnL*

Baker, Thomas 1680- *NewC*
Baker, Sir Thomas 1810-1886 *Alli Sup*
Baker, Thomas 1819- *Alli Sup*
Baker, Thomas Bagnall *Alli Sup*
Baker, Thomas Francis Timothy 1935-
  WrD 1976
Baker, Thomas Harrison 1933- *ConAu 33,*
  WrD 1976
Baker, Thomas Rakestraw 1837-1930 *DcNAA*
Baker, Thomas Stockham 1871-1939 *DcNAA,*
  WhWNAA
Baker, Thomas Turner *Alli Sup*
Baker, Tom *MnBBF*
Baker, Valentine 1825- *Alli Sup*
Baker, Virginia 1859- *AmLY, ChPo S1*
Baker, W *Alli Sup*
Baker, W B *Alli Sup*
Baker, W B And Ainsworth, W F *Alli Sup*
Baker, W H *Alli Sup*
Baker, Walter 1849-1897 *DcNAA*
Baker, Wesley C *ConAu 23*
Baker, William *Alli, Alli Sup*
Baker, William 1742-1785 *Alli*
Baker, William 1841- *Alli Sup*
Baker, William Adolphus *Alli Sup*
Baker, William Arthur Howard 1925- *MnBBF*
Baker, William Avery 1911- *ConAu 5R,*
  WrD 1976
Baker, William C 1891- *AuBYP*
Baker, William Deal 1812-1876 *DcNAA*
Baker, William E 1935- *ConAu 23*
Baker, William E S *Alli Sup*
Baker, William Franklin 1878- *WhWNAA*
Baker, William Hosier d1911 *Alli Sup, PoIre*
Baker, William Howard *ConAu XR*
Baker, William James Furneaux Vashon 1851-
  WhLA
Baker, William King *ChPo S1*
Baker, William M *ChPo*
Baker, William Mumford 1825-1883 *Alli Sup,*
  AmA, AmA&B, BiD&SB, BiDSA,
  CyAL 2, DcAmA, DcLEnL, DcNAA,
  OxAm
Baker, William Richard 1798-1861 *Alli Sup*
Baker, William S 1925- *AmSCAP 66*
Baker, William Spohn 1824-1897 *Alli Sup,*
  DcAmA, DcNAA
Baker, William Thurlow *Alli Sup*
Baker, William W *Alli Sup*
Baker, Wilson 1900- *Au&Wr*
Baker, Woods *Alli Sup*
Baker White, John 1902- *Au&Wr, WrD 1976*
Baketel, Oliver Sherman 1849-1937 *DcNAA*
Bakewell *Alli, BiDLA*
Bakewell, Charles Montague 1867- *WhWNAA*
Bakewell, Esther *Alli Sup*
Bakewell, F C *Alli*
Bakewell, Frederick C *Alli Sup*
Bakewell, John 1721-1819 *Alli Sup, PoCh*
Bakewell, Kenneth Graham Bartlett 1931-
  Au&Wr, WrD 1976
Bakewell, Paul, Jr. 1889-1972 *ConAu P-1*
Bakewell, Robert *Alli, BiDLA*
Bakewell, Thomas *Alli*
Bakewell, William J 1823?- *DcNAA*
Bakhuizen VanDenBrink, Reinier C 1810-1865
  CasWL
Baki, Mahmud Abdulbaki 1526-1600 *BiD&SB,*
  CasWL, DcOrL 3
Bakin 1767-1848 *CasWL, DcOrL 1,*
  Pen Cl
Bakish, David 1937- *ConAu 45*
Bakjian, Andy 1915- *ConAu 53*
Bakke, Arthur Lawrence 1886- *WhWNAA*
Bakke, Mary S 1904- *ConAu 37*
Bakke, Mildred *ChPo*
Bakker, Cornelius B 1929- *ConAu 57*
Baklanoff, Eric N 1925- *ConAu 33*
Bakr, Khaula R *BlkAW*
Bakri, Abu'l-Hasan Al- *DcOrL 3*
Baksi, Candrakant *DcOrL 2*
Bakula, William J, Jr. 1936- *ConAu 49*
Bakunin, Mikhail Alexandrovich 1814-1876
  CasWL, DcRusL, EuA, REn
Bakunts, Aksel 1899-1937 *DcOrL 3*
Bakwell, Robert Hall *Alli Sup*
Bakwin, Harry 1894-1973 *ConAu 19,*
  ConAu 45

Bakwin, Ruth Morris 1898- *ConAu 17R*
Balaam *ConAu XR, SmATA XR,*
  WrD 1976
Balabkins, Nicholas 1926- *ConAu 9R*
Balagon, Kuwasi *BlkAW*
Balagtas, Francisco 1788-1862 *Pen Cl*
Balaguer, Victor 1824-1901 *BiD&SB, EvEuW*
Balam, R *Alli*
Bal'ami, Abu 'Ali Mohammad B Mohammad
  DcOrL 3
Bal'ami, Muhammad Abu 'Ali d974? *CasWL*
Balandier, Georges 1920- *ConAu 61*
Balantyn *Alli*
Balantyne, Robert Michael 1825-1894 *MnBBF*
Balart, Federico 1831-1905 *ClDMEuL*
Balas, David L 1929- *ConAu 33, WrD 1976*
Balassa, Balint 1554-1594 *EvEuW, Pen Eur*
Balassa, Bela 1928- *ConAu 1R*
Balassi, Baron Balint 1554-1594 *CasWL*
Balawyder, Aloysius 1924- *ConAu 41,*
  OxCan Sup
Balbernie, A *Alli*
Balbernie, Arthur, Jr. *BiDLA*
Balbi, Gasparo *BiD&SB*
Balbi, Gerolamo d1530? *CasWL*
Balbin, Bohuslav 1621-1688 *CasWL*
Balbirnie, John *Alli, Alli Sup*
Balbo, Count Cesare 1789-1853 *BiD&SB,*
  CasWL, Pen Eur
Balboa, Miguel Cabello De 1525?-1586?
  BiD&SB
Balboa, Vasco Nunez De 1475-1519? *NewC,*
  REn
Balbontin, Jose Antonio 1893?- *Au&Wr,*
  ConAu P-1
Balbuena, Bernardo De 1568?-1627 *BiD&SB,*
  CasWL, DcEuL, DcSpL, EvEuW,
  Pen Am, PueRA, REn
Balbus *ConAu 57, ConAu XR*
Balcanqual, W *Alli*
Balcanquhall, Dean *Alli*
Balcarras, Earl Of *Alli*
Balcarres, Earl Of *NewC*
Balcescu, Nicolae 1819-1852 *CasWL*
Balch, Edwin Swift 1856-1927 *DcNAA,*
  WhWNAA
Balch, Mrs. Edwin Swift *AmA&B*
Balch, Elizabeth 1843?-1890 *Alli Sup, DcAmA,*
  DcNAA
Balch, Ernest Berkeley 1860- *WhWNAA*
Balch, Francis V *Alli Sup*
Balch, Frederick Homer 1861-1891 *DcNAA*
Balch, George Thacher 1828-1894 *DcNAA*
Balch, Glenn 1902- *AmA&B, AuBYP,*
  ConAu 1R, MorJA, SmATA 3, WhPNW
Balch, Lewis 1847-1909 *DcNAA*
Balch, Thomas *Alli Sup*
Balch, Thomas 1821-1877 *DcNAA*
Balch, Thomas Bloomer 1793-1878 *DcNAA*
Balch, Thomas Willing 1866-1927 *DcNAA*
Balch, William 1704-1792 *Alli*
Balch, William Monroe 1871- *WhWNAA*
Balch, William Ralston 1852-1923 *Alli Sup,*
  DcNAA
Balch, William S *Alli Sup*
Balch, William Stevens 1806-1887 *DcAmA,*
  DcNAA
Balchen, Bernt 1899-1973 *ConAu 45*
Balchin, Nigel Marlin 1908-1970 *ConAu 29,*
  DcLEnL, EvLB, LongC, ModBL,
  Pen Eng, REn, TwCA Sup, TwCW
Balchin, William George Victor 1916- *Au&Wr,*
  WrD 1976
Balcomb, Amelia *Alli Sup*
Balcomb, Raymond E 1923- *ConAu 23*
Bald, F Clever 1897-1970 *ConAu P-1*
Bald, R C 1901-1965 *ConAu 5R*
Bald, Robert *Alli, BiDLA*
Baldanza, Frank 1924- *ConAu 1R*
Balde, Jacobus 1604-1668 *Pen Eur*
Balde, Jakob 1604-1668 *CasWL, DcEuL,*
  EvEuW, OxGer
Baldelli, Giovanni 1914- *ConAu 45*
Baldemar Von Peterweil *OxGer*
Baldensperger, Fernand 1871- *ClDMEuL*
Balderson, Margaret *ConAu 25*
Balderston, George *Alli*
Balderston, John L 1889-1954 *CnMD, LongC,*

  AmA&B, McGWD, ModWD, WhWNAA
Balderston, Lloyd 1863- *WhWNAA*
Balderston, R R *Alli*
Balderston, R R And Ingleton, Margaret
  Alli Sup
Balderston, Ray *WhWNAA*
Balderston, Robert W 1882- *WhWNAA*
Balderstone, R R *BiDLA*
Baldgrave, O *Alli*
Baldi, Bernardino 1553-1617 *DcEuL, EvEuW*
Baldick, Robert Andre Edouard 1927- *Au&Wr*
Baldie, W D *Alli Sup*
Balding, Mortimer *Alli Sup*
Baldinger, Albert Henry 1876- *WhWNAA*
Baldinger, Stanley 1932- *ConAu 29*
Baldini, Antonio 1889-1962 *CasWL,*
  ClDMEuL, EncWL, Pen Eur
Baldner, Leonhard 1612-1694 *OxGer*
Baldock, Ralph De d1314 *Alli*
Baldovini, Francesco 1635-1716 *BiD&SB*
Baldree, J Martin, Jr. 1927- *ConAu 53*
Baldridge, Mrs. C LeRoy *AmA&B*
Baldridge, Cyrus LeRoy 1889- *IlBYP,*
  IlCB 1945, IlCB 1956, WhWNAA
Baldridge, Samuel Coulter 1829-1898 *DcNAA*
Baldrige, Letitia *ConAu 25*
Baldry, Bernard 1886- *ChPo S2*
Baldry, Enid *WrD 1976*
Baldry, Harold Caparne 1907- *ConAu 17R,*
  WrD 1976
Baldry, James *ChPo*
Balducci, Carolyn Feleppa 1946- *ConAu 33,*
  SmATA 5
Balducci, Ernesto 1922- *ConAu 29*
Balduf, Walter Valentine 1889- *WhWNAA*
Balduin Von Trier 1285-1354 *OxGer*
Baldus, Aloys Gregor 1871- *WhLA*
Baldus, Simon Alexander 1872-1957 *BkC 2,*
  OhA&B, WhWNAA
Baldwin, Archbishop Of Canterbury d1190
  BiB N
Baldwin I 1058?-1118 *NewC*
Baldwin II d1131 *NewC*
Baldwin, A C *Alli Sup*
Baldwin, A H *Alli Sup*
Baldwin, A W *ChPo S2*
Baldwin, A W I *ChPo*
Baldwin, Aaron Dwight 1850-1912 *DcNAA*
Baldwin, Alpha Wright 1866-1929 *OhA&B*
Baldwin, Anne Norris 1938- *ConAu 29,*
  SmATA 5, WrD 1976
Baldwin, Arthur H *AuBYP*
Baldwin, Astley H *ChPo S1, ChPo S2*
Baldwin, Basil *MnBBF*
Baldwin, Bates *ConAu XR*
Baldwin, Bird Thomas 1875-1928 *DcNAA,*
  WhWNAA
Baldwin, Byron A *Alli Sup*
Baldwin, C C *Alli Sup*
Baldwin, Caleb C 1820-1911 *DcNAA*
Baldwin, Charles Candee 1834-1895 *DcNAA,*
  OhA&B
Baldwin, Charles Jacob 1841-1921 *DcNAA,*
  OhA&B
Baldwin, Charles Sears 1867-1935 *AmA&B,*
  CatA 1947, DcNAA
Baldwin, Clara *ConAu 61*
Baldwin, Cyrus d1909 *DcNAA*
Baldwin, Daniel Pratt 1837-1908 *DcNAA,*
  IndAu 1816
Baldwin, David A *Alli Sup, OxCan Sup*
Baldwin, David Allen 1936- *ConAu 17R,*
  IndAu 1917
Baldwin, David Dwight 1831-1912 *DcNAA*
Baldwin, Dorothy Anne Clare 1934- *Au&Wr*
Baldwin, Douglas *WhWNAA*
Baldwin, Ebenezer 1745-1776 *DcNAA*
Baldwin, Ebenezer 1790-1837 *DcNAA*
Baldwin, Edward *Alli*
Baldwin, Edward 1756-1836 *DcEnL*
Baldwin, Edward Chauncey 1870?-1940 *DcNAA,*
  WhWNAA
Baldwin, Edward R 1935- *ConAu 45*
Baldwin, Edward Robinson 1864- *WhWNAA*
Baldwin, Edward Thomas 1846- *Alli Sup*
Baldwin, Elbert Francis 1857-1927 *AmLY,*
  DcNAA, OhA&B, WhWNAA
Baldwin, Eleanor *ChPo S2*

Baldwin, Elihu Whittlesey 1789-1840 *DcNAA*
Baldwin, Ellen Frances *ChPo*
Baldwin, Emily And Driver, Paulina *Alli Sup*
Baldwin, Emily Foote *Alli Sup*
Baldwin, Ernest Hickok 1869-1922 *DcNAA*
Baldwin, Eugene Francis 1840-1937 *DcNAA*
Baldwin, Evelyn Briggs 1862-1933 *DcNAA*
Baldwin, Ewart Merlin 1915- *WhPNW*
Baldwin, F *Alli Sup*
Baldwin, Faith 1893- *AmA&B, AmNov,
    AuNews 1, ChPo, ConAu 5R, LongC,
    OxAm, REn, REnAL, TwCA,
    TwCA Sup, WhWNAA, WrD 1976*
Baldwin, Foy Spencer 1870- *DcAmA*
Baldwin, Frances Elizabeth 1899-1931 *DcNAA,
    WhWNAA*
Baldwin, Fred Clare 1861-1939 *ChPo, DcNAA*
Baldwin, George *Alli, BiDLA*
Baldwin, George Colfax 1817-1899 *Alli Sup,
    DcAmA, DcNAA*
Baldwin, Gertrude *ChPo*
Baldwin, Gordon C 1908- *ConAu 1R*
Baldwin, Gordo *ConAu XR*
Baldwin, H *Alli Sup*
Baldwin, Hanson Weightman 1903- *AmA&B,
    Au&Wr, ConAu 61, REnAL, TwCA Sup*
Baldwin, Harmon Allen 1869-1936 *DcNAA,
    OhA&B, WhWNAA*
Baldwin, Harold 1888- *CanNov, OxCan*
Baldwin, Henry *ChPo*
Baldwin, Henry 1780?-1844 *Alli, DcNAA*
Baldwin, Henry 1832-1905 *DcNAA*
Baldwin, Henry 1846-1911 *DcNAA*
Baldwin, Honor *ChPo*
Baldwin, J *Alli Sup, OxCan Sup*
Baldwin, J E *Alli Sup*
Baldwin, J W *Alli Sup*
Baldwin, James *Alli, Alli Sup, DrAF 1976*
Baldwin, James 1841-1925 *AmA&B, AmLY,
    AnCL, AuBYP, CarSB, ChPo, DcNAA,
    IndAu 1816, JBA 1934, JBA 1951,
    REnAL*
Baldwin, James 1924- *AmA&B, BlkAW,
    CasWL, ConAu 1R, ConDr, ConLC 1,
    ConLC 2, ConLC 3, ConLC 4, ConLC 5,
    ConNov 1972, ConNov 1976, CrCD,
    EncWL, LivBA, LongC, McGWD,
    ModAL, ModAL Sup, ModWD, OxAm,
    Pen Am, RAdv 1, REn, REnAL,
    SmATA 9, TwCW, WebEAL, WhTwL,
    WorAu, WrD 1976*
Baldwin, James Fairchild 1850-1936 *DcNAA*
Baldwin, James Fosdick 1871- *AmLY*
Baldwin, James Mark 1861-1934 *Alli Sup,
    AmA&B, AmLY, BiDSA, DcAmA,
    DcNAA*
Baldwin, John *Alli Sup*
Baldwin, John Cook 1887-1939 *DcNAA*
Baldwin, John Denison 1809-1883 *Alli Sup,
    AmA&B, BiD&SB, DcAmA, DcEnL,
    DcNAA*
Baldwin, John Henry 1841- *Alli Sup*
Baldwin, John Loraine *Alli Sup*
Baldwin, Joseph *Alli Sup*
Baldwin, Joseph 1827-1899 *DcAmA, DcNAA*
Baldwin, Joseph Glover 1815-1864 *Alli Sup,
    AmA, AmA&B, BiDSA, CasWL,
    DcAmA, DcLEnL, DcNAA, OxAm,
    REnAL*
Baldwin, Joyce G 1921- *ConAu 61*
Baldwin, Joyce Margaret 1905- *Au&Wr*
Baldwin, L *Alli Sup*
Baldwin, Leland Dewitt 1897- *AmA&B,
    ConAu 41*
Baldwin, Loammi 1780-1838 *DcNAA*
Baldwin, Lydia Wood 1836- *Alli Sup, DcAmA,
    DcNAA*
Baldwin, Marshall W 1903-1975 *ConAu 57,
    ConAu 61*
Baldwin, Mary *ChPo, ChPo S1*
Baldwin, Mary Briscoe *Alli Sup*
Baldwin, Mary H 1841- *IndAu 1816*
Baldwin, Mary R *Alli Sup*
Baldwin, Maurice Scollard 1836-1904 *Alli Sup,
    DcNAA*
Baldwin, Michael 1930- *Au&Wr, ChPo S2,
    ConAu 9R, NewC*
Baldwin, Ned *ConAu XR*

Baldwin, Neil *DrAP 1975*
Baldwin, R *Alli*
Baldwin, R A *TexWr*
Baldwin, R M *OxCan Sup*
Baldwin, Ralph Lyman 1872- *WhWNAA*
Baldwin, Robert 1804-1858 *OxCan*
Baldwin, Robert E 1924- *ConAu 41*
Baldwin, Robert Macqueen 1904- *Au&Wr*
Baldwin, Roger E 1929- *ConAu 49*
Baldwin, Ruth M *ChPo S2*
Baldwin, Samuel *Alli*
Baldwin, Samuel D *Alli Sup*
Baldwin, Samuel Prentiss 1868- *WhWNAA*
Baldwin, Sidney 1885- *ChPo S2, WhWNAA*
Baldwin, Simeon Eben 1840-1927 *DcAmA,
    DcNAA*
Baldwin, Simon E *Alli Sup*
Baldwin, Stan 1929- *ConAu 49*
Baldwin, Stanley, Earl 1867-1947 *NewC, REn*
Baldwin, Stephen Livingstone 1835-1902
    DcNAA
Baldwin, Thomas *Alli, Alli Sup, BiDLA*
Baldwin, Thomas d1190 *Alli*
Baldwin, Thomas 1753-1825 *Alli, DcAmA,
    DcNAA*
Baldwin, Thomas 1819- *DcAmA*
Baldwin, Thomas H *WhWNAA*
Baldwin, Thomas Whitfield 1890- *AmA&B,
    WhWNAA*
Baldwin, Thomas Williams 1849-1926 *DcNAA*
Baldwin, Sir Timothy *Alli*
Baldwin, W J *Alli Sup*
Baldwin, Walter *Alli*
Baldwin, Walter J *BiDLA*
Baldwin, William *Alli, CasWL, OxEng*
Baldwin, William d1564 *NewC*
Baldwin, William 1518?- *DcEnL*
Baldwin, William 1527?- *CrE&SL*
Baldwin, William Charles *Alli Sup*
Baldwin, William Henry 1851-1923 *DcNAA,
    OhA&B*
Baldwin, William James St. John 1844-1924
    DcNAA
Baldwin, William Lee 1928- *ConAu 1R*
Baldwin, William Russell 1926- *IndAu 1917*
Baldwin, William Warren 1775-1844 *OxCan*
Baldwin, Willis 1860-1926 *DcNAA*
Baldwin-Brown *Alli Sup*
Baldwin-Ford, Pamela *IlBYP*
Baldwyn, Augusta 1821?-1884 *BbtC, DcNAA,
    OxCan*
Baldwyn, Edward *Alli, BiDLA*
Baldwyn, William *Alli*
Bale, Don 1937- *WrD 1976*
Bale, George Gilley Pritchett *Alli Sup*
Bale, John, Bishop Of Ossory 1495-1563 *Alli,
    BiD&SB, BrAu, CasWL, Chmbr 1,
    CrE&SL, CyWA, DcEnA, DcEnL,
    DcLEnL, EvLB, McGWD, NewC,
    OxEng, Pen Eng, REn*
Bale, Joy *DrAP 1975*
Bale, M Powis *Alli Sup*
Bale, Robert Osborne 1912- *ConAu 1R*
Bales, Carol Ann 1940- *ConAu 45*
Bales, James D 1915- *ConAu 5R*
Bales, Peter *Alli*
Bales, Peter 1547-1610? *Alli, DcEnL*
Bales, Richard 1915- *AmSCAP 66*
Bales, Thomas *Alli Sup*
Bales, William Alan 1917- *ConAu 5R*
Balestier, Charles Wolcott 1861-1891 *Alli Sup,
    AmA, AmA&B, BiD&SB, DcAmA,
    DcBiA, DcLEnL, DcNAA*
Balestier, Joseph Neree *Alli Sup, DcNAA*
Balestier, Josephine *ChPo*
Balestier, Wolcott 1861-1891 *AmA, CnDAL,
    LongC, OxAm, REnAL*
Balet, Jan B 1913- *AuBYP, IlCB 1956,
    ThBJA*
Baley, James A 1918- *ConAu 13R*
Baley, Walter 1529-1592 *Alli*
Balfern, W Poole *Alli Sup, ChPo S1,
    ChPo S2*
Balforeus, Robert *Alli*
Balfour *Alli*
Balfour, Earl Of *Chmbr 3*
Balfour, A J 1848-1930 *LongC*
Balfour, Alexander *Alli Sup*

Balfour, Alexander 1767-1829 *Alli, BbD,
    BiD&SB, ChPo, ChPo S2, DcEnL,
    NewC*
Balfour, Andrew *ChPo*
Balfour, Sir Andrew 1630-1694 *Alli*
Balfour, Sir Andrew 1873- *WhLA*
Balfour, Arthur James Balfour, Earl Of
    1848-1930 *Alli Sup, BbD, BiD&SB,
    BiDPar, DcLEnL, EvLB, NewC, OxEng,
    TwCA, TwCA Sup*
Balfour, Lady Betty *ChPo S2*
Balfour, Clara Lucas 1808-1878 *Alli Sup,
    NewC*
Balfour, Conrad George 1928- *ConAu 53*
Balfour, David S *MnBBF*
Balfour, Donald Church 1882- *WhWNAA*
Balfour, Edward G 1813- *Alli Sup*
Balfour, Fairfax *Alli Sup*
Balfour, Francis Maitland 1851-1882 *Alli,
    Alli Sup, BiDLA, BrAu 19*
Balfour, Frederic Henry *Alli Sup*
Balfour, Sir George 1809- *Alli Sup*
Balfour, George William *Alli Sup*
Balfour, Gerald William 1853-1945 *BiDPar*
Balfour, Graham 1859-1928 *ChPo S1*
Balfour, Grant *DcNAA, WhWNAA*
Balfour, Isaac Bayley 1853- *Alli Sup*
Balfour, James *Alli Sup*
Balfour, Sir James 1600-1657 *Alli, NewC*
Balfour, James 1703-1795 *Alli, DcEnL*
Balfour, James 1925- *ConAu 25*
Balfour, John *ChPo S1*
Balfour, Baron John d1688 *REn*
Balfour, John Hutton 1808-1884 *Alli, Alli Sup,
    DcEnL*
Balfour, Mary 1775?-1820? *ChPo, PoIre*
Balfour, Michael Leonard Graham 1908-
    Au&Wr, ConAu 9R
Balfour, Patrick *ConAu XR*
Balfour, Robert *Alli*
Balfour, Thomas Alexander Goldie *Alli Sup*
Balfour, Walter 1776-1852 *Alli, DcNAA*
Balfour, William *Alli, Alli Sup, BiDLA Sup*
Balfour, William Raymond John Evelyn 1923-
    Au&Wr
Balfour, Willoughby T *Alli Sup*
Balfour-Browne, V R *ChPo*
Balfour-Kinnear, George Purvis Russell 1888-
    ConAu 5R
Balg, G H *Alli Sup*
Balgarnie, Robert *Alli Sup*
Balgrave, J *Alli*
Balguy, Charles *Alli*
Balguy, John 1686-1748 *Alli, DcEnL*
Balguy, Thomas 1716-1795 *Alli*
Balhorn, Johann 1528-1603 *OxGer*
Balian, Lorna 1929- *ChPo, ConAu 53,
    SmATA 9, WrD 1976*
Baligh, Helmy H 1931- *ConAu 21*
Balikci, Asen 1929- *ConAu 29*
Balinky, Alexander 1919- *ConAu 21*
Balinski, Stanislaw 1898- *ClDMEuL*
Balint, Gyorgy 1906-1943 *Pen Eur*
Balint, Michael 1896-1970 *Au&Wr, BiDPar,
    ConAu P-1*
Baliol, Edward De d1363 *NewC*
Baliol, John De d1269? *NewC*
Balk, Alfred 1930- *ConAu 25*
Balkavi 1890-1918 *DcOrL 2*
Balke, Clarence William 1880- *WhWNAA*
Balkrsna Sama *DcOrL 2*
Balkwill, Francis H *Alli Sup*
Ball *Alli*
Ball, Alexander M W *ChPo*
Ball, Alice Eliza 1867-1948 *ChPo S1, DcNAA,
    OhA&B*
Ball, Armine *WhWNAA*
Ball, B L *Alli Sup*
Ball, B N *ConAu XR*
Ball, Benjamin West 1823-1896 *Alli Sup,
    ChPo S1, DcNAA*
Ball, Birdie Jayroe 1899- *TexWr*
Ball, Brian N 1932- *ConAu 33*
Ball, Mrs. C A *ChPo*
Ball, Carleton Roy 1873- *WhWNAA*
Ball, Caroline Augusta 1823- *BiDSA, DcNAA,
    LivFWS*
Ball, Charles *Alli Sup*

Ball, Charles B *Alli Sup*
Ball, Charles Backus 1854-1928 *DcNAA*
Ball, Charles James *Alli Sup*
Ball, Charles Richard *Alli Sup*
Ball, Clive 1941- *WrD 1976*
Ball, Doris Bell 1897- *Au&Wr, ConAu 1R, EncM&D*
Ball, E A R *Alli Sup*
Ball, Edmund Ferdinand 1905- *IndAu 1917*
Ball, Edward *Alli*
Ball, Eliza Craufurd *Alli Sup*
Ball, Enid *Au&Wr*
Ball, Ernest R 1878-1927 *AmSCAP 66*
Ball, Eustace Hale 1881?-1931 *DcNAA, OhA&B*
Ball, F C *ConDr*
Ball, F Carlton 1911- *ConAu 17R*
Ball, Farlin Quigley 1838-1917 *DcNAA*
Ball, Francis Kingsley 1863-1940 *AmA&B, AmLY, DcNAA, WhWNAA*
Ball, Frank Clayton 1857-1943 *DcNAA, OhA&B*
Ball, Frederick Cyril 1905- *Au&Wr*
Ball, George Harvey 1819-1907 *DcNAA*
Ball, George W 1909- *ConAu 23*
Ball, George W I *Alli Sup*
Ball, Henry William *Alli Sup*
Ball, Howard 1937- *ConAu 33*
Ball, Hugo 1886-1927 *CasWL, EncWL, ModGL, OxGer, Pen Eur, REn, WhTwL*
Ball, J *Alli, BiDLA*
Ball, James *Alli Sup*
Ball, James Moores 1863-1929 *DcNAA*
Ball, Jane Eklund 1921- *ConAu 33*
Ball, John *Alli*
Ball, John d1381 *NewC*
Ball, John d1812 *PoIre*
Ball, John 1585-1640 *Alli, DcEnL*
Ball, John 1794-1884 *DcNAA*
Ball, John 1818-1889 *Alli Sup*
Ball, John 1911- *Au&Wr, AuBYP, ConAu 5R, EncM&D, WrD 1976*
Ball, John C 1924- *ConAu 5R*
Ball, John Cecil Hawley 1923- *Au&Wr*
Ball, John Dudley, Jr. 1911- *AmA&B*
Ball, John M 1923- *ConAu 33*
Ball, John Thomas 1815- *Alli Sup*
Ball, Joseph H 1905- *ConAu 23*
Ball, Julia E *ChPo*
Ball, M J *ChPo S2*
Ball, M Margaret 1909- *ConAu 25*
Ball, Margaret 1878- *WhWNAA*
Ball, Maria Elsie *ChPo*
Ball, Nathaniel *Alli*
Ball, Nelson 1942- *ConP 1970*
Ball, Nicholas 1828-1896 *DcNAA*
Ball, Peter William *Au&Wr*
Ball, Rachel Stutsman 1894- *IndAu 1917*
Ball, Richard *Alli*
Ball, Richard Francis 1860?- *Br&AmS*
Ball, Robert *Alli Sup, ChPo S2, IlBYP, IlCB 1956*
Ball, Sir Robert 1840-1913 *EvLB*
Ball, Robert Hamilton 1902- *ConAu 9R, WrD 1976*
Ball, Sir Robert Stawell 1840-1913 *Alli Sup, BbD, BiD&SB, BrAu 19, Chmbr 3, LongC*
Ball, S E *ChPo S1*
Ball, Samuel *Alli Sup*
Ball, Sydney Hobart 1877- *WhWNAA*
Ball, Sylvia Patricia 1936- *ConAu 57*
Ball, T Frederick *Alli Sup*
Ball, Thomas *Alli, BiDLA, ChPo*
Ball, Thomas 1590-1659 *Alli*
Ball, Thomas 1819-1911 *DcNAA*
Ball, Thomas Frederick *PoIre*
Ball, Thomas Hanly *Alli Sup*
Ball, Thomas Horatio *Alli Sup*
Ball, Thomas Isaac *Alli Sup*
Ball, Timothy Horton 1826-1913 *DcNAA, IndAu 1816*
Ball, V *Alli Sup*
Ball, Walter Savage 1875- *WhWNAA*
Ball, Walter William Rouse 1851- *Alli Sup*
Ball, Wayland Dalrymple 1858-1893 *DcNAA*
Ball, Wilfred 1853-1917 *ChPo S1*
Ball, William *Alli, Alli Sup*

Ball, William d1824 *PoIre*
Ball, William Antony 1904- *Au&Wr*
Ball, William David 1885- *WhWNAA*
Ball, William Edmund *Alli Sup*
Ball, William I *Alli Sup*
Ball, Zachary *AuBYP, ConAu XR, SmATA 3*
Ball-Hennings, Emmy 1885-1948 *OxGer*
Ballagas, Emilio *Pen Am*
Ballagh, James Curtis 1866?-1944 *AmA&B, AmLY, BiDSA, DcNAA, WhWNAA*
Ballance, Charles 1800- *DcNAA*
Ballanche, Pierre Simon 1776-1847 *DcEuL, OxFr*
Ballantine, Edward D 1907- *AmSCAP 66*
Ballantine, Elisha 1810-1886 *DcNAA, IndAu 1816*
Ballantine, G J *ChPo S1*
Ballantine, Henry *Alli Sup*
Ballantine, Henry 1846-1914 *DcNAA*
Ballantine, Henry Winthrop 1880- *WhWNAA*
Ballantine, Jack *MnBBF*
Ballantine, James *Chmbr 3*
Ballantine, James 1808-1877 *Alli Sup, BiD&SB, BrAu 19, ChPo, ChPo S1, ChPo S2, DcEnL, EvLB, NewC*
Ballantine, James 1835- *ChPo S1*
Ballantine, John 1920- *ConAu 53*
Ballantine, Joseph W 1890?-1973 *ConAu 41*
Ballantine, Leslie Frost *ChPo S2*
Ballantine, R H *ChPo S1*
Ballantine, Richard 1940- *ConAu 45*
Ballantine, Stuart 1898-1944 *DcNAA*
Ballantine, William *Alli, BiDLA*
Ballantine, William 1812-1887 *Alli Sup*
Ballantine, William Gay 1848-1937 *AmA&B, ChPo, ChPo S1, DcAmA, DcNAA, OhA&B, WhWNAA*
Ballantyne, Archibald *Alli Sup*
Ballantyne, David Watt 1924- *Au&Wr, ConNov 1972, ConNov 1976, LongC, TwCW, WrD 1976*
Ballantyne, Dorothy Joan 1922- *ConAu 5R*
Ballantyne, James *Alli Sup*
Ballantyne, James 1772-1833 *Alli, NewC*
Ballantyne, James Methven 1877- *WhWNAA*
Ballantyne, James Robert 1813-1864 *Alli Sup*
Ballantyne, John *NewC*
Ballantyne, John 1774-1821 *Alli, NewC*
Ballantyne, John 1778-1830 *DcEnL*
Ballantyne, John Chalmers 1917- *Au&Wr, WrD 1976*
Ballantyne, Lereine 1891- *WhWNAA*
Ballantyne, Randall H *Alli Sup*
Ballantyne, Robert Michael 1825-1894 *Alli Sup, BbD, BbtC, BiD&SB, BrAu 19, CarSB, CasWL, ChPo, ChPo S1, Chmbr 3, DcEnL, DcLEnL, EvLB, NewC, OxCan, OxEng, Pen Eng, WhCL*
Ballantyne, Thomas 1806-1871 *Alli Sup, NewC*
Ballard *Alli*
Ballard, A *Alli Sup*
Ballard, Addison 1822- *DcAmA*
Ballard, Addison 1822-1914 *DcNAA*
Ballard, Allen B 1930- *ConAu 61*
Ballard, Charles Rollin 1828?-1906 *ChPo, ChPo S1, DcNAA*
Ballard, Charles W 1887- *WhWNAA*
Ballard, Colin 1868- *WhLA*
Ballard, Cyrus *WhWNAA*
Ballard, Dean *ConAu XR*
Ballard, Dorothy Scott *ChPo*
Ballard, E *BiDLA*
Ballard, Edward *Alli, Alli Sup*
Ballard, Edward 1840-1870 *DcNAA*
Ballard, Edward Goodwin 1910- *ConAu 33*
Ballard, Ellis Ames 1861-1938 *Alli Sup, ChPo, DcNAA*
Ballard, Eric Alan *MnBBF*
Ballard, Eva F Clodfelter *IndAu 1816*
Ballard, Mrs. F L *ChPo*
Ballard, Francis Drake 1899-1960 *AmSCAP 66*
Ballard, Fred 1884- *AmA&B*
Ballard, George d1755 *Alli*
Ballard, George Edward 1791-1860 *ChPo S1*
Ballard, Granville Mellen 1833-1926 *IndAu 1816*

Ballard, H C *ChPo*
Ballard, Harlan Hoge 1853-1934 *Alli Sup, AmA&B, ChPo, DcAmA, DcNAA, OhA&B*
Ballard, Isaac Fowler *Alli Sup*
Ballard, J *Alli Sup*
Ballard, J G 1930- *Au&Wr, ConAu 5R, ConLC 3, ConLC 6, ConNov 1972, ConNov 1976, DrAF 1976, WorAu, WrD 1976*
Ballard, J Z *Alli Sup*
Ballard, James Graham 1930- *TwCW*
Ballard, Joan Kadey 1928- *ConAu 5R*
Ballard, John *PoIre*
Ballard, John Woods 1831- *PoIre*
Ballard, Julia Perkins 1828-1894 *Alli Sup, ChPo, ChPo S1, ChPo S2, DcAmA, DcNAA*
Ballard, K G *ConAu XR, EncM&D*
Ballard, Lowell Clyne 1904- *ConAu P-1*
Ballard, Marshall 1879- *WhWNAA*
Ballard, Martin 1929- *Au&Wr, ConAu 25, SmATA 1*
Ballard, P D *ConAu XR, WrD 1976*
Ballard, Reave *Alli*
Ballard, Robert *Alli Sup*
Ballard, Robert H 1913- *AmSCAP 66*
Ballard, S J *Alli Sup*
Ballard, Thomas *Alli Sup*
Ballard, Todhunter 1903- *ConAu 13R, WrD 1976*
Ballard, W T *ConAu XR, WrD 1976*
Ballard, William 1780-1827 *DcNAA*
Ballard, William Roberts *Alli Sup*
Ballard, Willis Todhunter 1903- *ConAu XR, OhA&B, WrD 1976*
Ballaseyus, Virginia 1893- *AmSCAP 66*
Balle, John 1585-1640 *Alli*
Ballenden, Sir John d1550 *Alli, DcEnL, NewC*
Ballenger, Howard Charles 1886- *IndAu 1917*
Ballenger, L *Alli Sup*
Ballenger, William Lincoln 1861-1915 *DcNAA, IndAu 1917*
Baller, Richard *Alli*
Ballester, Manuel Mendez 1909- *DcCLA*
Ballestrem, Countess Eufemia Von 1859- *BbD, BiD&SB*
Balley, Elisha *Alli Sup*
Ballhorn, Johann 1528-1603 *OxGer*
Ballidon, J *Alli*
Balliett, Whitney 1926- *AmA&B, ConAu 17R, WrD 1976*
Ballin, Miss *Alli, BiDLA*
Ballin, Ada S *Alli Sup*
Ballin, Caroline *ConAu 17R*
Ballin, F L *Alli Sup*
Ballingal, James *Alli Sup*
Ballingall, Sir George d1855 *Alli*
Ballingall, William *Alli Sup*
Ballinger, Bill S 1912- *ConAu XR, EncM&D, WrD 1976*
Ballinger, Harry 1892- *ConAu 23*
Ballinger, James Lawrence 1919- *ConAu 17R*
Ballinger, Louise Bowen 1909- *ConAu 13R*
Ballinger, Margaret 1894- *ConAu 61*
Ballinger, Raymond A 1907- *ConAu 5R*
Ballinger, Richard Achilles 1858-1922 *DcNAA*
Ballinger, William A *ConAu XR, MnBBF*
Ballinger, William Sanborn 1912- *Au&Wr, ConAu 1R*
Balliol *NewC*
Ballmer, Edwin 1883- *AmLY*
Ballmer, Walter 1923- *WhGrA*
Ballon, Robert J 1919- *ConAu 45*
Ballonoff, Paul A 1943- *ConAu 57*
Ballou, Addie Lucia 1837-1916 *DcNAA*
Ballou, Adin 1803-1890 *Alli Sup, AmA, ChPo S1, DcAmA, DcNAA, OxAm, REnAL*
Ballou, Arthur W 1915- *ConAu 25*
Ballou, C H *ChPo S2*
Ballou, Charles H 1890- *WhWNAA*
Ballou, Ellen B 1905- *ConAu 29*
Ballou, Elsie Aultman 1894- *OhA&B*
Ballou, Frank Washington 1879- *WhWNAA*
Ballou, Helen B *ChPo S1*
Ballou, Henry Arthur 1872- *WhWNAA*
Ballou, Hosea 1771-1852 *Alli, AmA&B,*

CyAL 1, DcAmA, DcNAA, OxAm
Ballou, Hosea 1796-1861 Alli, BbD, BiD&SB, CyAL 1, DcAmA, DcNAA
Ballou, Luman Adolphus 1844-1919? ChPo, DcNAA
Ballou, Maturin Murray 1820-1895 Alli, Alli Sup, AmA, AmA&B, BbD, BiD&SB, DcAmA, DcNAA, OxAm
Ballou, Moses 1811-1879 Alli, DcAmA, DcNAA
Ballou, Robert Oleson 1892- AmA&B
Ballou, William Hosea 1857-1937 AmA&B, DcNAA, WhWNAA
Ballou, William Rice 1864-1893 DcNAA
Ballowe, James 1933- ConAu 29
Bally, George Alli
Balma, Michael J 1930- ConAu 17R
Balmain, W Alli
Balman, Thomas Alli Sup
Balmanno, Mary Alli, ChPo
Balmanno, Robert 1780- Alli
Balme, David Mowbray 1912- WrD 1976
Balme, Edward Balme Wheatley 1819- Alli Sup
Balme, Joshua Rhodes Alli Sup
Balme, Maurice 1925- ConAu 61
Balmer, Edwin 1883-1959 AmA&B, EncM&D, REnAL, WhWNAA
Balmer, Robert 1787-1844 Alli
Balmer, Thomas C Alli Sup
Balmes, Jaime Luciano 1810-1848 DcSpL, EuA
Balmes Urpia, Jaime Luciano 1810-1848 CasWL, EvEuW
Balmford, James Alli
Balmforth, Henry 1890- Au&Wr
Balmont, Konstantin Dmitriyevich 1867-1943 CasWL, ClDMEuL, DcRusL, EncWL, EvEuW, ModSL 1, Pen Eur, REn
Balmori, Jesus 1886-1948 DcOrL 2
Balnaves, Henry d1579 Alli
Balogh, Erno 1897- AmSCAP 66
Balogh, Joseph 1893- WhLA
Balogh, Penelope 1916- Au&Wr, ConAu 25, SmATA 1, WrD 1976
Balogh, Lord Thomas 1905- Au&Wr, ConAu 57, WrD 1976
Balogun, Ola 1945- AfA 1
Baloian, James C DrAP 1975
Baloucci, Francesco d1642 BiD&SB
Balow, Tom 1931- ConAu 45
Balsamo, Giuseppe REn
Balsamo, Joseph OxFr
Balsamon CasWL
Balsdon, Dacre ConAu XR, WrD 1976
Balsdon, John Percy Vyvian Dacre 1901- Au&Wr, ConAu 5R, WrD 1976
Balseiro, Jose Agustin 1900- AuNews 1, DcSpL, PueRA
Balsiger, David W 1945- ConAu 61
Balsley, Howard L 1913- ConAu 1R
Balsley, Irol Whitmore 1912- ConAu 13R
Baltazar, Eulalio R 1925- ConAu 17R, WrD 1976
Baltazar, Francisco 1788-1862 DcOrL 2
Balterman, Marcia Ridlon 1942- ConAu 25
Baltes, Peter Joseph 1827-1886 DcNAA
Baltharpe, John Alli
Balthazar, Earl E 1918- ConAu 53
Balticus, Martin 1532-1600 OxGer
Baltimore, Lord Alli, OxAm
Baltimore, Lord 1580?-1632 REnAL
Baltimore, Lord Fred Calvert d1772 Alli
Baltor, Harold 1915- AmSCAP 66
Baltrusaitis, Jurgis 1873-1944 CasWL, DcRusL, EncWL
Baltz, Howard B 1930- ConAu 29
Baltzell, E Digby 1915- ConAu 33
Baltzell, Winton James 1864-1928 AmLY, DcNAA
Baltzer, Hans 1900- IlBYP, IlCB 1966
Balucki, Michael 1837-1901 BbD, BiD&SB, ClDMEuL, ModWD
Balue, Jean DeLa 1422-1491 REn
Baluze, Etienne 1630-1718 OxFr
Balward, John Alli
Baly, Denis 1913- ConAu 17R
Baly, Joseph Sugar Alli Sup
Baly, Monica Eileen 1914- WrD 1976
Baly, Price Richard Alli Sup

Baly, William Alli Sup
Balza, Jose 1939- DcCLA
Balzac, Honore De 1799-1850 AtlBL, BbD, BiD&SB, CasWL, ChPo S2, CyWA, DcBiA, DcEuL, EncM&D, EuA, EvEuW, McGWD, NewC, OxEng, OxFr, Pen Eur, RCom, REn
Balzac, Jean Louis Guez De 1597-1654 BiD&SB, CasWL, DcEuL, EvEuW, OxFr, Pen Eur
Balzani, Ugo Alli Sup
Balzano, Jeanne 1912- ConAu 5R
Balzer, Richard J 1944- ConAu 45
Bambara, Toni Cade 1939- BlkAW, ConAu 29, LivBAA
Bamber, E F Alli Sup
Bamber, Wallace Rugene 1895- WhWNAA
Bamberger, A J And L J Alli Sup
Bamberger, Bernard Jacob 1904- AmA&B, ConAu 13R
Bamberger, Carl 1902- ConAu 21
Bamberger, Florence Eilau WhWNAA
Bamberger, Fritz 1902- WhLA
Bamberger, Laura Owen Miller 1914- IndAu 1917
Bamboccio, Il NewC
Bamboche 1613-1674? OxFr
Bamboschek, Giuseppe 1890- AmSCAP 66
Bambote, Pierre Makambo 1932- AfA 1
Bambrough, Renford 1926- ConAu 61
Bamdad, Ahmad 1925- CasWL
Bamer, F Alli Sup
Bamfield, Joseph Alli
Bamfield, S A Alli
Bamfield, Thomas Alli
Bamfield, Veronica 1908- Au&Wr
Bamford, Alfred J Alli Sup
Bamford, Brian Reginald 1932- WrD 1976
Bamford, Mrs. C E Alli Sup
Bamford, H A Alli Sup
Bamford, J Alli Sup
Bamford, James Alli
Bamford, John M Alli Sup
Bamford, Joseph Alli
Bamford, Margaret Alli Sup
Bamford, Mary E Alli Sup
Bamford, Mary Ellen 1857- DcNAA
Bamford, Paul W 1921- ConAu 41
Bamford, Samuel 1788-1872 Alli Sup, NewC
Bamfylde, Francis d1684 DcEnL
Bamfylde, John Alli, DcEnL
Bamm, Peter 1897-1975 CasWL, ConAu XR, EncWL, ModGL, OxGer, Pen Eur
Bamman, Henry A 1918- ConAu 5R
Bampfield, Francis d1684 Alli
Bampfield, George Frederick Lewis Alli Sup
Bampfield, John Alli
Bampfield, R W Alli
Bampfylde, Francis d1684 Alli
Bampton, Charles Alli Sup
Bampton, John Alli
Bampton, John 1689-1751 Alli, NewC
Bampton, Joseph M 1854- WhLA
Ban, Joseph D 1926- ConAu 23
Ban, Mathias 1818-1903 BiD&SB
Ban, Thomas Arthur 1929- ConAu 21, WrD 1976
Bana CasWL, DcOrL 2, Pen Cl
Banani, Amin 1926- ConAu 33
Banaphul 1899- DcOrL 2
Banaster, Gilbert Alli
Banastre, Gilbert Alli
Banbury, G A Lethbridge- Alli Sup
Banbury, Philip 1914- WrD 1976
Bances Candamo, Francisco Antonio De 1662-1704 CasWL, DcSpL, EvEuW, Pen Eur
Bances Y Lopez-Candamo, Francisco A 1662-1704 McGWD
Banchs, Enrique 1888-1968 CasWL, DcSpL, EncWL, Pen Am
Bancks, G W MnBBF
Bancks, J Alli
Bancks, Robert Alli
Bancroft, A Alli
Bancroft, Aaron 1755-1839 Alli, BiDLA, CyAL 1, DcAmA, DcNAA
Bancroft, Anne 1923- ConAu 57, WrD 1976

Bancroft, Caroline 1900- ConAu 21
Bancroft, Charitie Lees 1841- PoCh, PoIre
Bancroft, Charles BbtC, ChPo
Bancroft, E N Alli
Bancroft, Edgar Addison 1857-1925 DcNAA
Bancroft, Edward 1744-1821 Alli, CyAL 1, DcAmA, DcNAA
Bancroft, Edward Nathaniel BiDLA
Bancroft, Frederic 1860-1945 AmA&B, AmLY, DcAmA, DcNAA
Bancroft, George Alli, BbtC, Chmbr 3
Bancroft, George 1800-1891 Alli, Alli Sup, AmA, AmA&B, BbD, BiD&SB, ChPo, CyAL 2, DcAmA, DcEnA Ap, DcEnL, DcLEnL, DcNAA, EvLB, OxAm, OxEng, Pen Am, REn, REnAL, WebEAL
Bancroft, George Pleydell 1868-1956 LongC, WhLA
Bancroft, George Russell 1878- WhWNAA
Bancroft, Griffing 1907- AuBYP, AuNews 1, ConAu 29, SmATA 6
Bancroft, Hester ChPo
Bancroft, Hubert Howe 1832-1918 Alli Sup, AmA&B, BbD, BiD&SB, Chmbr 3, DcAmA, DcLEnL, DcNAA, OhA&B, OxAm, OxCan, REnAL
Bancroft, Hugh 1879-1933 DcNAA, WhWNAA
Bancroft, Jessie Hubbell 1867- ChPo S2, WhWNAA
Bancroft, John Alli
Bancroft, Laura ThBJA
Bancroft, Margaret 1854-1912 DcNAA
Bancroft, Marie Effie Alli Sup
Bancroft, Peter 1916- ConAu 41
Bancroft, R M And Francis, J Alli Sup
Bancroft, Richard 1544-1610 Alli, DcEnL
Bancroft, Robert ConAu XR
Bancroft, Sir Squire 1841-1926 Alli Sup, NewC
Bancroft, Thomas Alli, BiDLA
Bancroft, Thomas 1600?- Alli, DcEnL
Bancroft, Timothy Whiting 1837-1890 DcNAA
Bancroft, Wilder Dwight 1867- DcAmA
Bancroft, William Henry 1858-1921 DcNAA
Bancroft, William Wallace 1893-1947 DcNAA
Band, Moriz 1864- WhLA
Bandas, Rudolph G 1896- CatA 1947
Bandeira, Manuel 1886?-1968 Pen Am, TwCW, WorAu
Bandeira Filho, Manuel Carneiro DeSousa 1886-1968 CasWL, EncWL
Bandelier, Adolph Francis Alphonse 1840?-1914 Alli Sup, AmA, AmA&B, BiD&SB, DcAmA, DcNAA, OxAm, REnAL
Bandello DcEnL
Bandello, Matteo 1480?-1561? BbD, BiD&SB, CasWL, CrE&SL, DcEuL, EuA, EvEuW, NewC, OxEng, OxFr, Pen Eur, REn
Bander, Edward J 1923- ConAu 13R
Bander, James Wynne MnBBF
Bander, Peter 1930- WrD 1976
Bandera, V N 1932- ConAu 33
Bandi, Hans-Georg OxCan Sup
Bandinel, Bulkeley Alli
Bandinel, J Alli
Bandinel, James Alli Sup
Bandinell, Bulkeley BiDLA, BiDLA Sup
Bandinell, James Alli
Bandinelli, Ranuccio Bianchi 1901?-1975 ConAu 53
Bandini, Albert Jacovino 1916- AmSCAP 66
Bandini, Albert R 1882- CatA 1947
Bandler, Samuel Wyllis 1869-1932 DcNAA
Bandlow, Heinrich Johann Theodor 1855- WhLA
Bandman, Bertram 1930- ConAu 21
Bandmann, Daniel Edward 1837?-1905 Alli Sup, DcNAA
Bandrowski, Juljusz 1885-1945 ClDMEuL
Bandura, Albert 1925- ConAu 13R, WrD 1976
Bandy, Eugene Franklin 1914- ConAu 33
Bandy, W T 1903- ConAu 37
Bandyopadhyay, Bibhutibhusan 1894-1950 DcOrL 2
Bandyopadhyay, Manik 1908-1956 DcOrL 2

Bandyopadhyay, Tarasankar 1898-1971
 DcOrL 2
Bane, Lita 1887- *WhWNAA*
Bane, Martin J 1900- *AmSCAP 66*
Banel, Joseph 1943- *ConAu 45*
Baner, Johan Gustav Runeskiold 1861-
 WhWNAA
Baner, Skulda Vanadis 1897-1964 *ConAu P-1,*
 SmATA 10
Banerje, Bibhuti Bhusan 1894-1950 *CasWL*
Banerje, Tarasankar 1898- *CasWL*
Banerjea, H K M *Alli Sup*
Banerjee, H N 1929- *BiDPar*
Banerjee, Tarashankar 1898- *REn*
Banerji, Bibhuti-Bhusan 1894-1950 *EncWL Sup*
Banerji, Ranan B 1928- *ConAu 29*
Banes, Charles Henry 1830-1897 *Alli Sup*
Banes, Charles Henry 1831-1897 *DcNAA*
Baness, J Frederick *Alli Sup*
Banet, Charles Henry 1922- *IndAu 1917*
Banet, Doris Beatrice Robinson 1925-
 ConAu 5R, MnnWr
Banfield, A W Frank 1918- *ConAu 61,*
 WrD 1976
Banfield, Edith Colby 1870-1903 *AmA&B,*
 ChPo S1, ChPo S2, DcNAA
Banfield, Edward Christie 1916- *AuNews 1,*
 ConAu 57
Banfield, Edward James 1852-1923 *DcLEnL*
Banfield, F *MnBBF*
Banfield, Frank *Alli Sup*
Banfill, Bertha J *OxCan*
Banfill, S *Alli*
Banfill, Samuel *BiDLA*
Bang, Herman Joachim 1857-1912 *CasWL,*
 ClDMEuL, EncWL, EuA, EvEuW,
 Pen Eur, REn, TwCA, TwCA Sup
Bangay, Evelyn Dorrington 1889- *Au&Wr*
Bangert, Carl F 1897- *AnMV 1926*
Bangert, Ethel E 1912- *ConAu 45*
Bangert, William V 1911- *ConAu 45*
Bangham, Mary Dickerson 1896- *ChPo,*
 ConAu 23
Bangs, Mrs. Bleecker *DcNAA*
Bangs, Carl 1922- *ConAu 17R*
Bangs, Charlotte Rebecca 1867-1920 *DcNAA*
Bangs, Edward 1756-1818 *ChPo*
Bangs, Egbert L *ChPo S2*
Bangs, Ella Matthews *ChPo*
Bangs, Heman 1790-1869 *Alli Sup, DcNAA*
Bangs, J K And Sherman, F D *Alli Sup*
Bangs, Janet Norris 1885- *AnMV 1926*
Bangs, John 1781-1849 *DcNAA*
Bangs, John Kendrick 1862-1922 *AmA&B,*
 BbD, BiD&SB, CarSB, ChPo, ChPo S1,
 ChPo S2, DcAmA, DcLEnL, DcNAA,
 EncM&D, OxAm, REnAL, St&VC,
 TwCA, TwCA Sup
Bangs, Lemuel Bolton 1842-1914 *DcAmA,*
 DcNAA
Bangs, Nathan 1778-1862 *Alli, AmA&B,*
 DcAmA, DcNAA
Bangs, Outram 1863-1932 *DcNAA*
Bangs, Robert Babbitt 1914- *ConAu 37,*
 WrD 1976
Banham, Katharine M 1897- *BiDPar*
Banham, Reyner 1922- *Au&Wr, ConAu 29*
Banigan, Leon F 1887- *WhWNAA*
Banim, John 1798-1842 *Alli, BbD, BiD&SB,*
 BrAu 19, CasWL, ChPo S1, ChPo S2,
 Chmbr 3, DcBiA, DcEnA, DcEnL,
 DcLEnL, EvLB, NewC, OxEng, PoIre
Banim, Michael 1796-1874 *Alli Sup, BbD,*
 BiD&SB, BrAu 19, Chmbr 3, DcEnA,
 DcLEnL, EvLB, NewC
Banister, A *Alli, Alli Sup*
Banister, Gary L 1948- *ConAu 57*
Banister, Gilbert *DcEnL*
Banister, Henry *Alli Sup*
Banister, Henry C *Alli Sup*
Banister, James *Alli*
Banister, John d1692 *Alli, BiDSA, DcAmA*
Banister, Manly 1914- *ConAu 41*
Banister, Richard *Alli*
Banister, Thomas *Alli Sup*
Banister, William *Alli Sup*
Bank, Arnold 1908- *WhGrA*
Bank, Ted 1923- *ConAu 41, WrD 1976*

Bank, Theodore P, II 1923- *ConAu 41*
Bank, W Dane *WhLA*
Bank-Jensen, Thea *ConAu XR*
Banker, Howard James 1866- *WhWNAA*
Banker, Luella G *ChPo S2*
Bankes, G N *Alli Sup*
Bankes, George 1788-1856 *Alli Sup*
Bankes, Henry 1757?-1835 *Alli*
Bankes, Sir John *Alli*
Bankes, Sir Joseph 1743- *BiDLA Sup*
Bankes, Lawrence *Alli*
Bankes, Thomas *Alli*
Bankes, W H *Alli, BiDLA, BiDLA Sup*
Bankole, Timothy 1920?- *AfA 1*
Bankowsky, Richard James 1928- *AmA&B,*
 ConAu 1R
Banks *Alli*
Banks, A Polan 1906- *AmA&B*
Banks, Alice *Alli Sup*
Banks, Arthur Geoffrey 1922- *Au&Wr*
Banks, Arthur S 1926- *ConAu 33*
Banks, Augustus *Alli Sup*
Banks, Brenda C 1947- *BlkAW*
Banks, Charles Edward 1854-1931 *AmA&B,*
 DcNAA
Banks, Charles Eugene 1852-1932 *AmA&B,*
 ChPo, ChPo S2, DcAmA, DcNAA,
 WhWNAA
Banks, Charles O 1899-1944 *AmSCAP 66*
Banks, E Gripper *Alli Sup*
Banks, Edgar James 1866-1945 *AmA&B,*
 AmLY, DcNAA, WhWNAA
Banks, Edward *Alli Sup*
Banks, Elizabeth 1870-1938 *AmA&B, DcNAA*
Banks, Elliot V *Alli Sup*
Banks, Florence Aiken *WhWNAA*
Banks, Francis Richard 1912- *Au&Wr*
Banks, George Linnaeus 1821-1881 *Alli Sup,*
 ChPo, ChPo S1, ChPo S2, NewC
Banks, Mrs. George Linnaeus *ChPo S1,*
 ChPo S2
Banks, George Nugent *Alli Sup*
Banks, Helen Ward *AmA&B*
Banks, Isabella 1821-1897 *Alli Sup, ChPo S1,*
 NewC
Banks, J Houston 1911- *ConAu 33*
Banks, Sir Jacob *Alli*
Banks, James *Alli Sup*
Banks, James Albert 1941- *ConAu 33,*
 WrD 1976
Banks, John *Alli, BiDLA, DcEnL*
Banks, John 1650?-1706 *NewC, REn*
Banks, John 1709-1751 *Alli*
Banks, John A *ChPo S1*
Banks, John Shaw *Alli Sup*
Banks, John Tatham *Alli Sup*
Banks, Jona *Alli*
Banks, Joseph *Alli Sup*
Banks, Sir Joseph 1743-1820 *Alli, BiDLA,*
 DcEnL, DcLEnL, NewC
Banks, Louis Albert 1855-1933 *BiD&SB,*
 DcAmA, DcNAA, OhA&B, WhWNAA
Banks, Lynne Reid *ConNov 1972,*
 ConNov 1976, TwCW
Banks, Marsh *MnBBF*
Banks, Martha Burr *ChPo, ChPo S1,*
 ChPo S2
Banks, Mary Ross 1846- *Alli Sup, BiDSA,*
 DcNAA
Banks, Mattie B *Alli Sup*
Banks, Nancy 1850?- *DcNAA*
Banks, Nancy H *BiDSA*
Banks, Olive 1923- *Au&Wr*
Banks, P W *Alli*
Banks, Percival Weldon *DcEnL*
Banks, Richard L 1920- *ConAu 9R*
Banks, Robert *Alli*
Banks, Robert W *BiDSA*
Banks, Ronald F 1934- *ConAu 29*
Banks, Russell *DrAF 1976, DrAP 1975*
Banks, T C *BbtC*
Banks, Talcott Miner *ChPo*
Banks, Theodore Howard 1895- *AmA&B,*
 WhWNAA
Banks, Thomas Christopher 1760?-1854 *Alli,*
 BiDLA, DcEnL
Banks, William d1920 *DcNAA*
Banks, William Augustus 1894- *BlkAW,*

 ChPo S1, WhWNAA
Banks, William John 1906- *WhWNAA*
Banks, William Stott 1820-1872 *Alli Sup*
Banks-Henries, A Doris *AfA 1*
Bankson, Douglas 1920- *ConAu 45*
Bankson, Russell Arden 1889- *AmA&B,*
 OxCan
Bankton, Lord Andrew McDouall *Alli*
Bankwitz, Philip Charles Farwell 1924-
 ConAu 33
Banmo Tin Aun *DcOrL 2*
Banna'i *DcOrL 3*
Bannantine, James *Alli, BiDLA*
Bannard, Charles H *Alli Sup*
Bannard, Edward Yorke 1919- *Au&Wr*
Bannatyne, Alexander M *Alli Sup*
Bannatyne, Dugald *Alli*
Bannatyne, Dugald J *Alli Sup*
Bannatyne, George 1545-1608? *Alli, DcEnL,*
 EvLB, NewC, Pen Eng
Bannatyne, Jack *WrD 1976*
Bannatyne, John *NewC*
Bannatyne, John Millar *Alli Sup*
Bannatyne, Richard *Alli, Chmbr 1*
Bannatyne, Richard d1605 *EvLB*
Bannatyne, Sir William 1743-1834 *Alli*
Bannehr, J *Alli Sup*
Banneker, Benjamin 1731-1806 *DcAmA*
Banner, Angela 1923- *ConAu XR,*
 SmATA XR, WrD 1976
Banner, Edgar Harold Walter 1897- *Au&Wr*
Banner, Edward Gregson *Alli Sup*
Banner, Hubert Stewart 1891-1964 *ConAu P-1*
Banner, James M, Jr. 1935- *ConAu 49*
Banner, Lois W 1939- *ConAu 49*
Banner, Melvin Edward 1914- *ConAu 53*
Banner, Patricia 1900- *IndAu 1917*
Banner, Richard *Alli*
Banner, William Augustus 1915- *ConAu 45*
Bannerman, Anne *Alli, BiDLA, ChPo*
Bannerman, D Douglas *Alli Sup*
Bannerman, David Armitage 1886- *Au&Wr,*
 WrD 1976
Bannerman, Helen Brodie Cowan 1862?-1946
 CarSB, IICB 1945, JBA 1951, WhCL
Bannerman, Henry *Alli Sup*
Bannerman, James 1807-1868 *Alli Sup*
Bannerman, Jean Elisabeth 1904- *WrD 1976*
Bannerman, Patrick *Alli Sup*
Bannick, Nancy 1926- *ConAu 41*
Banning, Edmund Prior 1810- *DcNAA*
Banning, Edward P *Alli Sup*
Banning, Evelyn Irene 1903- *ConAu 19,*
 WrD 1976
Banning, Henry Thomas 1844- *Alli Sup*
Banning, Hubert A And Arden, Henry *Alli Sup*
Banning, Kendall 1879-1944 *AmA&B,*
 AnMV 1926, ChPo, ChPo S2, DcNAA,
 WhWNAA
Banning, Margaret Culkin 1891- *AmA&B,*
 AmNov, BkC 6, ConAu 5R, MnnWr,
 OxAm, REnAL, TwCA, TwCA Sup,
 WhWNAA
Banning, N A *Alli Sup*
Banning, Pierson Worrall 1879-1927 *DcNAA*
Banning, William Peck 1885-1962 *ChPo*
Bannister, Arthur Thomas 1962- *WhLA*
Bannister, Christopher *ChPo S1*
Bannister, Donald 1928- *ConAu 61*
Bannister, J T *Alli Sup*
Bannister, James *Alli, BiDLA*
Bannister, John *BiDLA*
Bannister, John 1816-1873 *Alli Sup*
Bannister, John William *BbtC, OxCan*
Bannister, M E *ChPo*
Bannister, Nathaniel Harrington 1813-1847
 AmA, AmA&B, DcLEnL, DcNAA,
 OxAm, REnAL
Bannister, Robert C, Jr. 1935- *ConAu 23*
Bannister, Roger Gilbert 1929- *Au&Wr,*
 WrD 1976
Bannister, S *Alli*
Bannister, Saxe 1790-1877 *Alli Sup*
Bannister, Sybil Louise 1910- *Au&Wr*
Bannock, Graham 1932- *ConAu 33,*
 WrD 1976
Bannon, Henry Towne 1867-1950 *OhA&B*
Bannon, John Francis 1905- *CatA 1952,*

ConAu 1R, WrD 1976
Bannon, Laura May d1963 AuBYP,
ConAu 1R, IlCB 1945, IlCB 1956,
IlCB 1966, MorJA, SmATA 6
Bannon, Peter ConAu XR
Bannow, Waldemar Alli Sup
Banse, Ewald 1883- WhLA
Bansley, Charles Alli, DcEnL
Banson, John Alli
Banta, Arthur Mangun 1877-1946 IndAu 1917,
WhWNAA
Banta, David Demaree 1833-1896 DcAmA,
DcNAA, IndAu 1816
Banta, Frank Graham 1918- IndAu 1917
Banta, George 1857-1935 IndAu 1816
Banta, Melissa Elizabeth Riddle 1834-1907
DcNAA, IndAu 1816, OhA&B
Banta, Nathaniel Moore 1867-1932 DcNAA,
IndAu 1816, WhWNAA
Banta, Richard Elwell 1904- ConAu 33,
IndAu 1917
Banti, Anna 1895- WorAu
Banting, Sir Frederick Grant 1891-1941 LongC
Banting, William 1797-1878 Alli Sup
Bantista, Rudy Michael DrAP 1975
Bantleman, Lawrence 1942- ConP 1970,
WebEAL
Bantock, G H 1914- ConAu 25
Bantock, Gavin Marcus August 1939- Au&Wr,
ConAu 33, ConP 1970, ConP 1975,
WrD 1976
Bantock, Geoffrey Herman 1914- Au&Wr
Bantock, George Granville AHi Sup
Bantock, Miles DcNAA
Banton, Coy ConAu XR, WrD 1976
Banton, Michael Parker 1926- Au&Wr,
ConAu 5R
Banuelos, Juan 1932- DcCLA
Banvard, A ChPo
Banvard, James Alli Sup
Banvard, John 1820?-1891 Alli Sup, AmA&B,
BiD&SB, DcAmA, DcNAA
Banvard, Joseph 1810-1887 Alli, Alli Sup,
AmA&B, BiD&SB, DcAmA, DcNAA
Banville, Theodore Faullain De 1823-1891 BbD,
BiD&SB, CasWL, ClDMEuL, DcEuL,
EuA, EvEuW, McGWD, OxFr, Pen Eur,
REn
Bany, Mary A 1913- ConAu 9R
Banyer, Edward Alli
Banyer, Henry Alli
Banyer, Josiah Alli
Banz, George 1928- ConAu 29
Banziger, Hans ConAu 49
Baour-Lormian, Louis Pierre Marie F
1772?-1854 BbD, BiD&SB, EvEuW, OxFr
Baptie, D Alli Sup
Bapu ConAu XR
Bar Hebraeus 1226-1286 Pen Cl
Bar-Natan, Moshe ConAu XR
Bar-Yosef, Yehoshua 1912- CasWL
Bar-Zohar, Michael 1938- ConAu 23
Barab, Seymour 1921- AmSCAP 66
Barabas, Steven 1904- Au&Wr, ConAu 5R
Barabe, Paul-Henri 1904- BkC 2
Barach, Frederica Pisek 1904- AmA&B
Barach, Joseph H 1882- WhWNAA
Barack, Nathan A 1913- ConAu 13R,
WrD 1976
Barackman, Paul F 1894- ConAu 1R
Barada, Bill ConAu XR
Barada, William Richard 1913- ConAu 45
Baraga, Friedric 1797-1868 DcAmA
Baraga, Irenaeus Friedrich 1797-1868 DcNAA
Barahini, Reza CasWL
Barahona DeSoto, Luis 1548?-1595 CasWL,
EvEuW
Baraka, Amiri Imamu WebEAL
Baraka, Imamu Amiri 1934- BlkAW,
ConAu XR, ConDr, ConLC 1, ConLC 2,
ConLC 3, ConLC 5, ConNov 1972,
ConNov 1976, ConP 1975, CrCAP,
DrAP 1975, EncWL Sup, LivBA,
McGWD, WorAu, WrD 1976
Barakovic, Juraj 1549-1628 EvEuW
Baral, Robert 1910- ConAu P-1, IndAu 1917
Baralt, Rafael Maria 1814-1860 BiD&SB
Baranauskas, Antanas 1835-1902 CasWL

Baranet, Nancy Neiman 1933- ConAu 41
Baranga, Aurel 1913- CasWL
Baranovich, Lazar 1620-1693 CasWL
Barante, Baron Aimable Guillaume P B De
1782-1866 BiD&SB
Barante, Baron Guillaume-P Brugiere De
1782-1866 OxFr
Barantsevich, Kazimir Stanislavovich 1851-1927
CasWL, DcRusL
Barany, George 1922- ConAu 25
Barany, Robert 1876- WhLA
Barasch, Frances K 1928- ConAu 37,
WrD 1976
Barash, Asher 1889-1952 CasWL, Pen Cl,
Pen Eur
Barash, Meyer 1916- ConAu 1R
Baratashvili, Nikoloz 1817-1845 DcOrL 3
Baratynsky, Evgeny Abramovich 1800-1844
CasWL, EuA, EvEuW
Baratynsky, Jevgen Abramovich 1800-1844
BiD&SB
Baratynsky, Yevgeni Abramovich 1800-1844
DcRusL, Pen Eur
Baraville, Mary Signe ChPo S1
Barba, Harry 1922- ConAu 1R, DrAF 1976,
WrD 1976
Barba Jacob, Porfirio 1883-1942 CasWL,
Pen Am
Barbach, Lonnie Garfield 1946- ConAu 61
Barbanell, Maurice 1902- BiDPar
Barbara AmA&B, DcNAA
Barbara, Dominick A 1914- ConAu 37
Barbaro, Hermolao 1454-1493 DcEuL
Barbarossa, Frederick 1123?-1190 DcNAA,
NewC, OxGer, REn
Barbary, James ConAu XR, SmATA XR
Barbash, Jack 1910- ConAu 1R
Barbauld, Anna Letitia 1743-1825 Alli, BbD,
BiD&SB, BiDLA, BrAu 19, CasWL,
ChPo, ChPo S1, ChPo S2, Chmbr 2,
DcEnA, DcEnL, DcLEnL, EvLB, NewC,
OxEng, Pen Eng, PoCh
Barbe, Louis A Alli Sup
Barbe, Waitman 1864-1925 AmA&B, BiDSA,
DcAmA, DcNAA
Barbe, Walter Burke 1926- ConAu 13R
Barbe, Wren 1913- ConAu 15
Barbeau, Arthur E 1936- ConAu 49
Barbeau, Charles Marius 1883- CasWL,
DcLEnL
Barbeau, Jean 1945- OxCan Sup
Barbeau, Marius 1883-1969 CanWr, ConAu 25,
OxCan, WhWNAA
Barbeau, Raymond OxCan
Barbeau, Victor 1896- CanWr, OxCan
Barbee, David E 1936- ConAu 57
Barbee, David Rankin 1874- WhWNAA
Barbee, William J 1816-1892 Alli Sup, BiDSA,
DcAmA, DcNAA, OhA&B
Barbelle, Albert ChPo
Barbellion, W N P 1889-1919 Chmbr 3,
DcLEnL, EvLB, LongC, TwCA,
TwCA Sup
Barber Alli
Barber, Captain Alli
Barber, Anna Penney WhWNAA
Barber, Benjamin R 1939- ConAu 29,
WrD 1976
Barber, Bernard 1918- AmA&B
Barber, Catharine Webb BiDSA
Barber, Charles 1915- ConAu 17R
Barber, Charles Alfred 1860- WhLA
Barber, Charles Laurence 1915- WrD 1976
Barber, D F 1940- ConAu 61
Barber, Daniel 1756-1834 DcNAA
Barber, Ed Alli
Barber, Edward C Alli Sup
Barber, Edward Gordon 1920- Au&Wr
Barber, Edwin 1878-1914 DcNAA
Barber, Edwin Atlee 1851-1916 DcAmA,
DcNAA
Barber, Elizabeth Gertrude Alli, ChPo S1
Barber, Elmer DeVergne 1858-1900? DcNAA
Barber, Elsie Oakes 1914- AmA&B, AmNov
Barber, Emily S ChPo
Barber, Frances ChPo S1
Barber, Francis 1751- CyAL 1

Barber, G M Alli Sup
Barber, George Alli Sup
Barber, George Duckett Alli Sup
Barber, Gershom Morse 1823-1903 DcAmA,
DcNAA
Barber, Harriet Boomer Alli Sup
Barber, Harry Clark 1881- WhWNAA
Barber, Henry Alli Sup
Barber, J T Alli
Barber, James Alli, Alli Sup
Barber, James David 1930- ConAu 13R,
WrD 1976
Barber, John Alli, BlkAW
Barber, John Warner 1798-1885 Alli, Alli Sup,
AmA&B, ChPo, DcAmA, DcNAA,
EarAB, EarAB Sup
Barber, Jonathan 1784-1864 DcNAA
Barber, Joseph Alli
Barber, Joseph 1864?- DcNAA
Barber, L E Alli Sup
Barber, Lucius Israel 1806-1889 DcNAA
Barber, Lucy L 1882?-1974 ConAu 9
Barber, Margaret Browning ChPo S1
Barber, Margaret Fairless 1869-1901 DcLEnL,
EvLB, LongC, TwCA, TwCA Sup
Barber, Mary 1690?-1757? Alli, ChPo, PoIre
Barber, Mary A S Alli Sup
Barber, Mary Finette ChPo
Barber, Melanie Gordon ChPo S2
Barber, Richard 1941- ConAu 33
Barber, Richard J 1932- ConAu 29
Barber, S Alli Sup
Barber, Samuel 1848-1918 DcNAA
Barber, Samuel 1910- AmSCAP 66, OxAm
Barber, Theodore Xenophon 1927- BiDPar,
ConAu 41
Barber, Thomas Alli Sup
Barber, W C Alli Sup
Barber, W Howard 1886- WhWNAA
Barber, W R ChPo
Barber, Willard F 1909- ConAu 21
Barber, William Alli, Alli Sup, BiDLA
Barber, William Henry 1918- ConAu 5R
Barber, William Joseph 1925- ConAu 61
Barbere, John d1396 Alli
Barberino, Andrea Da 1370?-1432? CasWL,
EvEuW, REn
Barberis ConAu XR
Barberis, Franco 1905- ConAu 25
Barbero, Yves Regis Francois 1943- ConAu 57
Barbet, Pierre ConAu XR
Barbette, Jay WorAu
Barbey D'Aurevilly, Jules Amedee 1808-1889
AtlBL, BiD&SB, CasWL, ClDMEuL,
EuA, EvEuW, OxFr, Pen Eur, REn
Barbi, Michele 1867-1941 CasWL
Barbier, Antoine-Alexandre OxFr
Barbier, Auguste 1805-1882 DcEuL, EuA,
OxFr, Pen Eur
Barbier, Edmond-Jean-Francois 1689-1771 OxFr
Barbier, Henri Auguste 1805-1882 BbD,
BiD&SB, CasWL, EvEuW
Barbier, J Alli
Barbier, John Alli
Barbier, Jules 1822-1901 BiD&SB
Barbiera, Raphael 1851- BiD&SB
Barbieri, Francisco 1823-1894 CasWL
Barbieri, Giovanni Maria 1519-1574 CasWL,
EvEuW
Barbieri, Giuseppe 1783-1852 BiD&SB
Barbilian, Dan CasWL
Barblan, Gudench 1860-1916 CasWL
Barbon, Nicholas Alli
Barbosa, Domingos Caldas 1738?-1800 AfA 1
Barbosa, Jorge 1902- AfA 1
Barbosa DeOliveira, Antonio Rui 1849-1923
Pen Am
Barbot, John Alli
Barbotin, Edmond 1920- ConAu 57
Barbour, Mrs. A DcAmA
Barbour, A Maynard DcNAA
Barbour, Alexander Hugh Freeland Alli Sup
Barbour, Anna Maynard d1914 AmA&B,
DcNAA
Barbour, Arthur Joseph 1926- ConAu 57
Barbour, Brian M 1943- ConAu 49
Barbour, Clarence Augustus 1867-1937 DcNAA
Barbour, D Alli Sup

Barbour, David 1912-1965 *AmSCAP 66*
Barbour, David Nevill 1895- *Au&Wr*
Barbour, Douglas 1940- *ConP 1975,*
OxCan Sup, WrD 1976
Barbour, Floyd *BlkAW, LivBA*
Barbour, Frances Martha 1895- *ConAu 17R*
Barbour, Mrs. G F *Alli Sup*
Barbour, George Brown 1890- *WhLA,*
WhWNAA
Barbour, George Freeland 1882- *WhLA*
Barbour, George M *Alli Sup*
Barbour, George T *Alli Sup*
Barbour, Heman Humphrey 1820-1875 *DcNAA*
Barbour, Henry Gray 1886-1943 *DcNAA,*
WhWNAA
Barbour, Hugh 1921- *ConAu 23, WrD 1976*
Barbour, Ian G 1923- *ConAu 21*
Barbour, J *Alli Sup*
Barbour, J Murray 1897-1970 *ConAu P-1*
Barbour, James 1775-1842 *BiDSA*
Barbour, John 1316?-1396 *Alli, BbD,*
BiD&SB, BrAu, CasWL, ChPo,
Chmbr 1, CriT 1, DcEnL, DcLEnL,
EvLB, MouLC 1, NewC, OxEng,
Pen Eng, REn, WebEAL
Barbour, John Gordon *Alli Sup*
Barbour, John Humphrey 1854-1900 *DcAmA*
Barbour, Kenneth Michael 1921- *ConAu 5R*
Barbour, Lewis Green 1829-1907 *DcNAA*
Barbour, Lola 1864- *WhWNAA*
Barbour, Mrs. M F *Alli Sup*
Barbour, Michael G 1942- *ConAu 49*
Barbour, Nevill 1895- *ConAu 5R*
Barbour, Oliver Lorenzo 1811-1889 *Alli,*
Alli Sup, DcAmA, DcNAA
Barbour, Philip L 1898- *ConAu 9R*
Barbour, Philip Pendleton 1783-1841 *BiDSA*
Barbour, Ralph Henry 1870-1944 *AmA&B,*
AuBYP, CarSB, ChPo, DcAmA, DcNAA,
JBA 1934, JBA 1951, REnAL
Barbour, Robert *Alli*
Barbour, Robert W *Alli Sup*
Barbour, Roger W 1919- *ConAu 61*
Barbour, Ross 1928- *AmSCAP 66*
Barbour, Russell B 1906- *ConAu 23*
Barbour, Thomas 1884-1946 *DcNAA, REnAL,*
WhWNAA
Barbrook, Alec *ConAu XR*
Barbrook, Alexander Thomas 1927- *ConAu 45*
Barbu, Eugen 1924- *CasWL*
Barbu, Ion 1895-1961 *CasWL, EncWL,*
Pen Eur
Barbud *DcOrL 3*
Barbusse, Henri 1873?-1935 *CasWL,*
CIDMEuL, CyWA, EncWL, EvEuW,
LongC, NewC, OxFr, Pen Eur, REn,
TwCA, TwCA Sup, TwCW, TwCW Sup,
WhLA
Barce, Elmore 1872- *IndAu 1917*
Barchek, James Robert 1935- *ConAu 41*
Barchilon, Jacques 1923- *ConAu 13R*
Barchnam, John 1572-1642 *Alli*
Barcia, Andres Gonzales De *BiDSA*
Barck, Lothar 1880- *WhLA*
Barck, Oscar Theodore, Jr. 1902- *ConAu 21*
Barckley, Sir Richard *Alli, DcEnL*
Barclay *BbtC*
Barclay, Alexander 1475?-1552 *Alli, AtlBL,*
BiD&SB, BrAu, CasWL, Chmbr 1,
CrE&SL, DcEnL, DcEuL, DcLEnL,
EvLB, NewC, OxEng, Pen Eng, REn
Barclay, Alexander 1896- *Au&Wr*
Barclay, Andrew Whyte 1817-1884 *Alli Sup*
Barclay, Anthony *Alli Sup, BiDSA*
Barclay, Barbara 1938- *ConAu 29*
Barclay, Charles *BbtC, OxCan*
Barclay, Cyril Nelson 1896- *Au&Wr,*
ConAu 5R, WrD 1976
Barclay, D R *Alli Sup*
Barclay, David *Alli*
Barclay, Edgar *Alli Sup*
Barclay, Edward *Alli Sup*
Barclay, Florence Louisa 1862-1921 *DcLEnL,*
EvLB, LongC, NewC, REn, TwCA,
TwCA Sup, TwCW
Barclay, George *Alli, Au&Wr*
Barclay, George Lippard 1868-1884 *DcNAA*
Barclay, H *Alli*

Barclay, H Maria *Alli Sup*
Barclay, Harold B 1924- *ConAu 9R*
Barclay, Henry d1765 *Alli*
Barclay, Hugh 1799-1884 *Alli Sup*
Barclay, Hugh Donald *Alli Sup*
Barclay, Isabel Marian *Au&Wr*
Barclay, Isobel *ConAu XR*
Barclay, James *Alli*
Barclay, James Turner 1807-1874 *Alli,*
Alli Sup, BiDSA, DcAmA, DcNAA
Barclay, Jean 1582-1621 *DcEuL*
Barclay, John *Alli, BbtC, BiDLA, Chmbr 1*
Barclay, John 1582-1621 *Alli, BiD&SB, BrAu,*
CasWL, CrE&SL, CyWA, DcEnA,
DcEnL, EvLB, NewC, OxEng, OxFr,
OxGer, Pen Eng
Barclay, John 1734-1798 *Alli, ChPo*
Barclay, John 1760-1826 *Alli*
Barclay, Joseph 1831-1881 *Alli Sup*
Barclay, Joseph Gurney *Alli Sup*
Barclay, Maurice Edward 1886- *Br&AmS*
Barclay, Oliver R 1919- *ConAu 57*
Barclay, P *Alli Sup*
Barclay, Patrick *Alli*
Barclay, Peter *Alli Sup*
Barclay, Rachel *ChPo*
Barclay, Robert *Alli Sup, Chmbr 2*
Barclay, Robert 1648-1690 *Alli, DcEnL,*
EvLB
Barclay, Robert 1779-1854 *Alli*
Barclay, Robert 1833-1876 *Alli Sup*
Barclay, Mrs. S *Alli Sup*
Barclay, Mrs. S M *Alli Sup*
Barclay, Sarah *BiDSA*
Barclay, Shepard 1889- *WhWNAA*
Barclay, Sidney *Alli Sup*
Barclay, Thomas *Alli*
Barclay, Thomas 1753-1830 *DcNAA*
Barclay, Thomas 1849- *WhLA*
Barclay, Sir Thomas 1853- *Alli Sup, ChPo S2,*
WhLA
Barclay, Vera Charlesworth 1893- *Au&Wr,*
CatA 1952
Barclay, William *Alli Sup*
Barclay, William 1546-1605? *Alli*
Barclay, William 1907- *Au&Wr*
Barclay, William Singer 1871- *WhLA*
Barclift, Nelson 1917- *AmSCAP 66*
Barcus, James E 1938- *ConAu 23*
Barcynska, Countess *NewC*
Bard, Bernard 1927- *ConAu 25*
Bard, Harry 1906- *ConAu 33*
Bard, Harry Erwin 1867-1955 *IndAu 1917*
Bard, John 1716-1799 *Alli*
Bard, Patti 1935- *ConAu 21*
Bard, Samuel 1742-1821? *Alli, CyAL 1,*
DcNAA
Bard, Samuel A 1821-1888 *DcEnL, DcNAA*
Bard, William Earl 1892- *IndAu 1917, TexWr,*
WhWNAA
Bardach, Hans, Edler Von Chlumberg *OxGer*
Bardach, John E 1915- *ConAu 41*
Bardaisan *DcOrL 3*
Bardarson, Hjalmar R 1918- *ConAu 57*
Barde, Alexandre *BiDSA*
Barde, Frederick Samuel 1869-1916 *DcNAA*
Bardeen, Charles Russell 1871- *WhWNAA*
Bardeen, Charles William 1847-1924 *Alli Sup,*
AmA&B, AmLY, DcAmA, DcNAA
Barden, Leonard William 1929- *Au&Wr,*
ConAu 1R
Bardens, Amey E 1894?-1974 *ConAu 53*
Bardens, Dennis Conrad 1911- *Au&Wr,*
ConAu 5R
Bardis, Panos D 1924- *ConAu 25, WrD 1976*
Bardley, Van Allen *ChPo S2*
Bardolph, Richard 1915- *ConAu 61*
Bardoly, Louis Stephen 1893- *OhA&B*
Bardon, Minna Feibleman 1900- *OhA&B*
Bardos, Marie 1935- *ConAu 13R*
Bardot, Louis 1896-1975 *ConAu 61*
Bardouin, F G *Alli*
Bardoux, Jacques 1874- *WhLA*
Bardsley, Charles Wareing *Alli Sup*
Bardsley, Cuthbert K N 1907- *ConAu 25*
Bardsley, James *Alli Sup*
Bardsley, James Wareing *Alli Sup*
Bardsley, John *MnBBF*

Bardsley, John Edwin Prince 1911- *Au&Wr*
Bardsley, Joseph *Alli Sup*
Bardsley, Samuel Argent *Alli, BiDLA*
Bardwell, Denver *MnBBF*
Bardwell, Francis 1867- *WhWNAA*
Bardwell, George E 1924- *ConAu 1R*
Bardwell, Thomas *Alli*
Bardwell, William *Alli Sup*
Bardy, Gustave 1881- *CatA 1952*
Bare, Arnold Edwin 1920- *IlBYP, IlCB 1945,*
IlCB 1956
Barea, Arturo 1897-1957 *CasWL, EvEuW,*
LongC, REn, TwCA Sup, TwCW
Barea, Tylon *BlkAW*
Barecroft, Charles *Alli*
Barecroft, J *Alli*
Bareham, John Derek 1928- *Au&Wr*
Bareiro Saguier, Ruben 1930- *DcCLA*
Bareis, George F 1852-1932 *OhA&B*
Barer, Marshall L 1923- *AmSCAP 66*
Barese, Sir Richard *Alli*
Baret, John *Alli*
Baret, Michael *Alli*
Baretti, Giuseppe Marc'Antonio 1719-1789
BiD&SB, CasWL, DcEuL, EuA, EvEuW,
NewC, OxEng, Pen
Bareynska, Helene *WhLA*
Barfett, John *Alli*
Barff, Frederick Settle 1823-1886 *Alli Sup*
Barfield, Arthur Owen 1898- *Au&Wr,*
ConAu 5R, DcLEnL, WrD 1976
Barfoot, Audrey Ilma 1918-1964 *ConAu 5R*
Barfoot, Henry *Alli Sup*
Barfoot, John *Alli Sup*
Barfoot, P *Alli*
Barford, Alfred Henry And Tilley, H A *Alli Sup*
Barford, Richard *Alli*
Barford, William d1792 *Alli*
Bargagli, Girolamo 1537-1586 *McGWD*
Bargar, B D 1924- *ConAu 17R*
Bargarag, Shibli *ConAu XR*
Bargebuhr, Frederick P 1904- *ConAu 33*
Bargellini, Piero 1897- *CatA 1952*
Bargeo, Pier Angelo *CasWL*
Barger, George 1878- *WhLA*
Barger, Harold 1907- *ConAu 19*
Barger, James 1947- *ConAu 57*
Barger, Marilee 1897- *WhWNAA*
Bargeron, Carlisle 1895-1965 *AmA&B*
Barghoorn, Frederick Charles 1911- *AmA&B*
Bargone, Charles *EvEuW*
Bargone, Edouard *OxFr*
Bargrave, Isaac 1586-1643 *Alli*
Barham, Alfred G Foster- *Alli Sup*
Barham, Francis Foster 1808-1871 *Alli,*
Alli Sup
Barham, George *Alli Sup*
Barham, Henry *Alli*
Barham, Joseph Foster *Alli, BiDLA*
Barham, Richard Harris *Chmbr 3*
Barham, Richard Harris 1788-1845 *Alli, BbD,*
BiD&SB, BrAu 19, CarSB, CasWL,
ChPo, ChPo S1, ChPo S2, DcEnA,
DcEnL, DcEuL, DcLEnL, EvLB, NewC,
OxEng
Barham, Richard Harris Dalton 1815-1887?
Alli Sup, ChPo S1
Barham, Thomas Foster- 1794-1869 *Alli,*
Alli Sup
Barhebraeus, Grigor Abu'l-Faraj Bar E
1225?-1286 *DcOrL 3*
Bari, Gwen 1927- *AmSCAP 66*
Barillet, Pierre 1923- *McGWD*
Barine, Francis, Jr. *ChPo*
Baring, Alexander, Lord Ashburton 1774-1848
Alli, BiDLA
Baring, Arnulf Matin 1932- *ConAu 41*
Baring, Charles *Alli, BiDLA, BiDLA Sup*
Baring, Sir Evelyn 1840- *Alli Sup*
Baring, Sir Francis 1740-1810 *Alli*
Baring, Maurice 1874-1945 *BkC 4, CasWL,*
CatA 1947, ChPo, ChPo S1, ChPo S2,
DcLEnL, EncWL, EvLB, LongC, ModBL,
NewC, OxEng, REn, TwCA, TwCA Sup,
TwCW, WebEAL
Baring, Thomas Charles 1831- *Alli Sup*
Baring, Thomas G, Earl Of Northbrook 1826-
Alli Sup

Baring-Gould *Alli Sup*
Baring-Gould, Cecil *ChPo*
Baring-Gould, Sabine 1834-1924? *BbD, BiD&SB, BrAu 19, CarSB, ChPo, ChPo S1, CatA S2, Chmbr 3, DcBiA, DcEnA, DcEnA Ap, DcEnL, DcLEnL, EvLB, LongC, NewC, OxEng, Pen Eng, WebEAL*
Baring-Gould, William S *ChPo, ChPo S2*
Baring-Gould, William Stuart 1913-1967 *ConAu 25*
Baringer, William Eldon 1909- *ConAu 1R, IndAu 1917, WhWNAA*
Barish, Jonas A 1922- *ConAu 23, WrD 1976*
Barish, Matthew 1907- *ConAu 57*
Baritz, Loren 1928- *ConAu 13R*
Barja, Cesar 1892-1952 *DcSpL*
Bark, William 1908- *ConAu P-1*
Barka, Vasyl' 1908- *ModSL 2*
Barkalow, Frederick Schenck, Jr. 1914- *ConAu 61*
Barkam, William *Alli*
Barkan, Elliott Robert 1940- *ConAu 23*
Barkan, Stanley H *DrAP 1975*
Barkan, Stanley Howard 1936- *AmSCAP 66*
Barkas, Janet 1948- *ConAu 57*
Barke, Lizzie *Alli Sup*
Barkee, Asouff *ConAu 41*
Barker *Alli*
Barker, Lady *DcEnL*
Barker, A *Alli Sup*
Barker, A J 1918- *ConAu 13R*
Barker, A L 1918- *ConAu 9R, ConNov 1972, ConNov 1976, WrD 1976*
Barker, Albert Smith 1843-1916 *DcNAA*
Barker, Albert W 1900- *SmATA 8*
Barker, Aldred Farrer 1868- *WhLA*
Barker, Alfred *Alli Sup*
Barker, Andrew *Alli*
Barker, Arthur E J *Alli Sup*
Barker, Arthur William 1866- *WhWNAA*
Barker, Audrey Lillian 1918- *TwCA Sup*
Barker, Benjamin *AmA&B, DcNAA*
Barker, Benjamin Fordyce 1818-1891 *DcNAA*
Barker, Bernard *Alli Sup*
Barker, Bertram *OxCan*
Barker, C Edward 1908- *WrD 1976*
Barker, C Hedley *MnBBF*
Barker, Carol M 1942- *ConAu 45*
Barker, Carol Minturn 1938- *ChPo S1, IlBYP, IlCB 1966*
Barker, Charles *Alli*
Barker, Charles Edward 1908- *Au&Wr*
Barker, Charles M, Jr. 1926- *ConAu 13R*
Barker, Charles T *BiDLA*
Barker, Christopher 1815- *Alli Sup*
Barker, Cicely Mary *ChPo, ChPo S2*
Barker, Cicely May *ChPo S1*
Barker, Colin *HsB&A*
Barker, D R 1930- *ConAu 5R*
Barker, Dale 1920- *AmSCAP 66*
Barker, David 1816-1874 *ChPo, ChPo S1, DcNAA*
Barker, Dennis 1929- *ConAu 25, WrD 1976*
Barker, Dudley 1910- *Au&Wr, ConAu 1R, WrD 1976*
Barker, E *ChPo S2*
Barker, E M *ConAu XR*
Barker, Edmund *Alli*
Barker, Edmund Henry 1788-1839 *Alli, BiDLA, ChPo*
Barker, Edward *Alli Sup*
Barker, Edward B B *Alli Sup*
Barker, Edward D *ChPo*
Barker, Edward Harrison *Alli Sup*
Barker, Edward Waller *Alli Sup*
Barker, Ellen 1850?- *Alli Sup, DcAmA, DcNAA*
Barker, Elmer Eugene 1886- *WhWNAA*
Barker, Elsa 1869-1954 *AmA&B, AmLY, ChPo, WhWNAA*
Barker, Elsa M 1906?- *Au&Wr, ConAu 17, WrD 1976*
Barker, Elver A 1920- *ConAu 25*
Barker, Eric *AmA&B*
Barker, Eric 1905-1973 *ConAu 1R, ConAu 41, ConP 1970*
Barker, Eric 1912- *Au&Wr*

Barker, Sir Ernest 1874-1960 *EvLB, LongC, NewC, Pen Eng, TwCA Sup, WhLA*
Barker, Ernest Franklin 1886- *WhWNAA*
Barker, Esther T 1910- *ConAu 49*
Barker, Eugene Campbell 1874- *AmA&B, TexWr, WhWNAA*
Barker, F C And Danforth, J S *Alli Sup*
Barker, Mrs. F Raymond *Alli Sup*
Barker, Fannie *ChPo S1*
Barker, Fordyce 1818-1891 *Alli Sup, AmA&B, DcAmA, DcNAA*
Barker, Francis *Alli Sup*
Barker, Frank Granville 1923- *Au&Wr, ConAu P-1*
Barker, Fred George 1890- *WhWNAA*
Barker, George *Alli*
Barker, George Fisher Rupert 1848- *Alli Sup*
Barker, George Frederic 1835-1910 *Alli Sup, DcAmA, DcNAA*
Barker, George Granville 1913- *Au&Wr, CasWL, ChPo S2, CnE&AP, CnMWL, ConAu 9R, ConP 1970, ConP 1975, DcLEnL, DrAF 1976, DrAP 1975, EncWL, LongC, ModBL, ModBL Sup, NewC, OxEng, Pen Eng, REn, TwCA Sup, TwCW, WebEAL, WhTwL, WrD 1976*
Barker, George M *Alli Sup*
Barker, George William Michael Jones d1855 *DcEnL*
Barker, Granville *Chmbr 3, TwCA, TwCA Sup*
Barker, H J *Alli Sup*
Barker, Harley Granville *CnThe, DcLEnL, LongC, Pen Eng, REn*
Barker, Harley Granville Granville *NewC, OxEng*
Barker, Henry Ames 1868-1929 *DcNAA*
Barker, Henry D 1893- *WhWNAA*
Barker, Henry H *Alli Sup*
Barker, Henry James 1852- *WhLA*
Barker, Howard *ConDr*
Barker, J *Alli*
Barker, J H *Alli Sup*
Barker, Mrs. J L *Alli Sup*
Barker, J T *Alli Sup*
Barker, J W *ChPo, ChPo S1*
Barker, Jack 1922- *AmSCAP 66*
Barker, Jacob 1779-1871 *Alli Sup, BiDSA, DcAmA, DcNAA*
Barker, James *Alli*
Barker, James 1918- *WrD 1976*
Barker, James Louis 1880- *WhWNAA*
Barker, James Nelson 1784-1858 *Alli, AmA, AmA&B, CasWL, ChPo, ChPo S1, CnDAL, DcAmA, DcLEnL, DcNAA, McGWD, OxAm, Pen Am, REn, REnAL, REnWD*
Barker, Jessie M *Alli Sup*
Barker, John d1748 *Alli*
Barker, John *Alli, BiDLA*
Barker, John G *Alli Sup*
Barker, John Marshall 1849-1930 *DcNAA*
Barker, John Marshall 1849-1928 *OhA&B*
Barker, John Theodore *Alli Sup*
Barker, John Thomas 1844- *ChPo S1*
Barker, John W 1933- *ConAu 17R*
Barker, Johnson *Alli Sup*
Barker, Joseph 1806-1875 *Alli Sup*
Barker, Joseph Henry *Alli Sup*
Barker, Kathleen F 1901- *Br&AmS*
Barker, Laura Emily Cooke 1866-1927 *OhA&B*
Barker, Lewellys Franklin 1867-1943 *DcAmA, DcNAA, WhWNAA*
Barker, Lillian *CatA 1947*
Barker, Lucy D Sale 1841- *Alli Sup*
Barker, Lady Mary Anne 1831-1911 *Alli Sup, CasWL, DcLEnL*
Barker, Mary Lucretia 1912- *OhA&B*
Barker, Matthew *Alli*
Barker, Matthew Henry 1790-1846 *BiD&SB, NewC*
Barker, Maurice Eugene 1894- *WhWNAA*
Barker, Melvern J 1907- *ConAu P-1, IlCB 1956*
Barker, Michael John Eustace 1915- *Au&Wr*
Barker, Myrtie Lillian 1910- *ConAu 5R, IndAu 1917*

Barker, Peter *Alli*
Barker, Philip C *Alli Sup*
Barker, Phoebe Alice Caywood 1868-1943 *IndAu 1917*
Barker, Ralph *Alli*
Barker, Ralph Hammond 1917- *Au&Wr, ConAu 1R*
Barker, Reginald Charles 1881-1937 *AmA&B, DcNAA, WhWNAA*
Barker, Richard *Alli*
Barker, Robert *Alli, BiDLA, PoIre*
Barker, Robert L 1937- *ConAu 25*
Barker, Rodney 1942- *ConAu 45*
Barker, Roger Garlock 1903- *ConAu P-1*
Barker, Ronald 1920- *Au&Wr*
Barker, Ronald Ernest 1920- *Au&Wr*
Barker, S *Alli*
Barker, S Omar 1894- *ConAu 17, SmATA 10, WhWNAA, WrD 1976*
Barker, Mrs. Sale 1841- *ChPo, ChPo S2*
Barker, Samuel *Alli, Alli Sup*
Barker, Shirley Frances 1911-1965 *AmA&B, ChPo, ChPo S1, ConAu 5R, TwCA Sup*
Barker, Stanley 1870- *WhWNAA*
Barker, T S 1941- *ConAu 45*
Barker, Theodore Cardwell 1923- *Au&Wr, ConAu 13R, WrD 1976*
Barker, Thomas *Alli, Alli Sup*
Barker, Thomas 1721-1809 *Alli*
Barker, Thomas B *Alli Sup*
Barker, Thomas Childe *Alli Sup*
Barker, Thomas Francis *Alli Sup*
Barker, Thomas Herbert *Alli Sup*
Barker, Thomas M 1929- *ConAu 23*
Barker, W Alan 1923- *ConAu 1R*
Barker, W H *Alli, BiDLA*
Barker, Walter Goodyer *Alli Sup*
Barker, Wharton 1846-1921 *DcNAA*
Barker, Will 1913- *Au&Wr, AuBYP, ConAu 9R, SmATA 8*
Barker, William *Alli, Alli Sup*
Barker, William Alan 1923- *Au&Wr*
Barker, William Burckhardt *Alli Sup*
Barker, William Gideon Michael Jones 1817-1855 *Alli Sup, ChPo S1*
Barker, William P 1927- *ConAu 9R*
Barkham *Alli*
Barkin, David Peter 1942- *ConAu 37*
Barkin, Kenneth D 1939- *ConAu 41*
Barkin, Solomon 1907- *ConAu 9R*
Barkins, Evelyn 1919- *ConAu 29*
Barkley, Alice *ChPo S1*
Barkley, Archibald Henry 1872-1937 *DcNAA, WhWNAA*
Barkley, Frederick R 1892- *WhWNAA*
Barkley, Henry C *Alli Sup*
Barkley, James Edward 1941- *IlBYP, SmATA 6*
Barkley, John Trevor *Alli Sup*
Barkley, Vada Lee 1919- *ConAu 57*
Barkly, A M *Alli Sup*
Barkman, Paul Friesen 1921- *ConAu 17R*
Barkow, Al 1932- *ConAu 53, WrD 1976*
Barks, Coleman Bryan 1937- *ConAu 25, DrAP 1975, WrD 1976*
Barksdale, Clement 1609-1687 *Alli, DcEnL*
Barksdale, E C 1944- *ConAu 57*
Barksdale, Emily Woodson *BiDSA*
Barksdale, George *BiDSA*
Barksdale, George 1882-1939 *DcNAA*
Barksdale, Hiram C 1921- *ConAu 9R*
Barksdale, Lena *AmA&B, AuBYP*
Barksdale, Richard K 1915- *BlkAW, ConAu 49, LivBA*
Barksdale, W H 1827- *Alli Sup*
Barkshire, Earl Of *Alli*
Barkstead, William *Alli*
Barksted, William *CasWL, NewC*
Barksteed, William 1591?- *NewC*
Barkton, R Rush *ConAu XR*
Barkwith, W *Alli*
Barlaam Y Josapha *CasWL*
Barlace, G *Alli*
Barlach, Ernst Heinrich 1870-1938 *CasWL, ClDMEuL, CnMD, EncWL, EvEuW, McGWD, ModGL, ModWD, OxGer, Pen Eur, REn*
Barlaeus, Caspar 1584-1648 *DcEuL*

Barlaeus, Kaspar Van 1584-1648 *BiD&SB*
Barland, Katherine *Alli Sup*
Barlay, Bennett *ConAu XR*
Barlay, Stephen 1930- *ConAu 25, WrD 1976*
Barlee *Alli*
Barlee, E *ChPo S1*
Barlee, Edward *Alli*
Barlee, Ellen *Alli Sup*
Barley, Leslie John 1890- *Au&Wr*
Barley, William *Alli*
Barling, Charles *ConAu XR*
Barling, F H *Alli Sup*
Barling, John 1804-1883 *Alli Sup*
Barling, Muriel Vere Mant 1904- *ConAu 5R*
Barlough, J Ernest 1953- *ConAu 49*
Barlow *EarAB*
Barlow, Alfred *Alli Sup*
Barlow, Mrs. C Y *Alli Sup*
Barlow, Charles *Alli Sup*
Barlow, Claude W 1907- *ConAu 33*
Barlow, Columbus 1847-1907 *DcNAA*
Barlow, Derrick 1921- *Au&Wr*
Barlow, Edward *Alli*
Barlow, Frank 1911- *Au&Wr, ConAu 9R, WrD 1976*
Barlow, Frederic *Alli*
Barlow, Genevieve 1910- *ConAu 21*
Barlow, George *Alli Sup*
Barlow, George 1847-1914 *Alli Sup, ChPo, ChPo S1, NewC*
Barlow, George 1948- *BlkAW, DrAP 1975*
Barlow, George Hilaro *Alli Sup*
Barlow, Harold 1915- *AmSCAP 66*
Barlow, Henry Clark 1806-1876 *Alli Sup*
Barlow, Howard 1892- *AmSCAP 66*
Barlow, J *Alli*
Barlow, J E M *ChPo S1*
Barlow, J Stanley 1924- *ConAu 41*
Barlow, James Henry Stanley 1921-1973 *Au&Wr, ConAu 41, ConAu P-1*
Barlow, James William *Alli Sup*
Barlow, Jane 1857?-1917 *BbD, BiD&SB, ChPo, ChPo S1, ChPo S2, Chmbr 3, DcEnA Ap, DcLEnL, NewC, PoIre, TwCA*
Barlow, Joel 1754-1812 *Alli, AmA, AmA&B, BiD&SB, CasWL, ChPo, Chmbr 3, CnDAL, CyAL 1, DcAmA, DcEnL, DcLEnL, DcNAA, EvLB, OxAm, OxEng, Pen Am, PoCh, REn, REnAL, WebEAL*
Barlow, John *Alli*
Barlow, John A 1924- *ConAu 21, WrD 1976*
Barlow, John Evelyn 1860- *Alli Sup*
Barlow, John Richard 1846- *DcNAA*
Barlow, John W 1838- *Alli Sup*
Barlow, Joseph Lorenzo 1818-1896 *Alli Sup, DcNAA*
Barlow, Nathan Pratt 1834-1920 *DcNAA*
Barlow, Nora 1885- *ConAu 25, WrD 1976*
Barlow, P W *Alli Sup*
Barlow, Peter 1776- *Alli, Alli Sup, BiDLA*
Barlow, Peter William *Alli Sup*
Barlow, R *Alli*
Barlow, Reuel R 1894- *WhWNAA*
Barlow, Sir Robert *Alli, BiDLA*
Barlow, Robert O *ConAu 49*
Barlow, Roger *ConAu XR*
Barlow, Samuel *Alli Sup*
Barlow, Samuel Latham Mitchell 1826-1889 *Alli Sup, DcNAA*
Barlow, Stephen *Alli, BiDLA*
Barlow, T *Alli Sup*
Barlow, T Disney *Alli Sup*
Barlow, T Edward 1931- *ConAu 45*
Barlow, Theodore *Alli*
Barlow, Thomas 1607-1691 *Alli, DcEnL*
Barlow, Thomas Worthington *Alli Sup*
Barlow, W H *Alli Sup*
Barlow, Warren Sumner *Alli Sup, ChPo S1, DcNAA*
Barlow, Wayne 1912- *AmSCAP 66*
Barlow, Wilfred 1915- *Au&Wr, WrD 1976*
Barlow, William *Alli, Alli Sup*
Barlow, William d1568 *Alli*
Barlow, William d1613 *Alli Sup, DcEnL*
Barlow, William d1625 *Alli*
Barlow, William Frederick *Alli Sup*
Barlow, William H *Alli Sup*

Barlow, William Henry *Alli Sup*
Barlow, William Ruxton *Alli Sup*
Barlowe, R *BiDLA*
Barlowe, Raleigh 1914- *ConAu 17R, WrD 1976*
Barlowe, William d1568 *Alli, DcEnL*
Barlowe, William d1625 *Alli*
Barmann, Lawrence Francis 1932- *ConAu 9R, WrD 1976*
Barmash, Isadore 1921- *ConAu 45*
Barmby, James *Alli Sup*
Barmby, John Goodwyn 1820-1881 *Alli Sup*
Barna, Yon 1927- *ConAu 53*
Barnaby, A *Alli*
Barnaby, Charles Frank 1927- *WrD 1976*
Barnaby, Frank 1927- *ConAu 33*
Barnaby, Sir Nathaniel 1829-1915 *Alli Sup, ChPo S1*
Barnaby, Ralph S 1893- *ConAu 61, SmATA 9*
Barnaby, Sydney W *Alli Sup*
Barnacle, Robert *AmA&B*
Barnard, Mrs. *Alli Sup, DcEnL*
Barnard, Alan 1928- *ConAu 9R*
Barnard, Alfred J 1878- *MnBBF*
Barnard, Andrew 1860- *ChPo S1*
Barnard, Lady Anne 1750-1825 *Alli, BbD, BiD&SB, BrAu, CasWL, ChPo, Chmbr 2, DcEnL, DcLEnL, EvLB, NewC, OxEng, Pen Eng*
Barnard, C D *MnBBF*
Barnard, Caroline *Alli, BiDLA*
Barnard, Charles 1835- *Alli Sup*
Barnard, Charles 1838-1920 *AmA&B, BiD&SB, DcAmA, DcNAA*
Barnard, Mrs. Charles 1830-1869 *PoIre*
Barnard, Charles Inman 1850-1942 *DcNAA*
Barnard, Charles N 1924- *ConAu 49*
Barnard, Charlotte Alington 1830-1869 *Alli Sup, BrAu 19, NewC*
Barnard, Christiaan 1922- *ConAu 61*
Barnard, Daniel Dewey 1796?-1861 *CyAL 2, DcNAA*
Barnard, Edna A *Alli Sup*
Barnard, Edouard Andre 1834-1898 *DcNAA*
Barnard, Edward 1721-1774 *Alli*
Barnard, Edward Emerson 1857-1923 *BiDSA, DcNAA*
Barnard, Edward W *ChPo S1*
Barnard, Ellsworth 1907- *ConAu 21*
Barnard, F E A *Alli Sup*
Barnard, F M 1921- *ConAu 25*
Barnard, Francis *Alli*
Barnard, Francis 1834- *ChPo*
Barnard, Francis Pierrepont 1854- *Alli Sup, WhLA*
Barnard, Frederick 1849-1896 *ChPo S1*
Barnard, Frederick Augustus Porter 1809-1889 *Alli, Alli Sup, AmA&B, BiDSA, CyAL 1, DcAmA, DcNAA, OxAm*
Barnard, George *Alli Sup*
Barnard, George Grey 1863-1938 *OxAm, REnAL*
Barnard, Harry 1906- *ConAu 5R*
Barnard, Henry 1811-1900 *Alli, Alli Sup, AmA, BbD, BiD&SB, CyAL 1, CyAL 2, DcAmA, DcNAA*
Barnard, Mrs. Henry *Alli Sup*
Barnard, J Darrell 1906- *ConAu 5R*
Barnard, James *Alli*
Barnard, James Lynn 1867-1941 *DcNAA, WhWNAA*
Barnard, James Underwood 1849- *DcNAA*
Barnard, Job 1844-1923 *DcNAA, IndAu 1917*
Barnard, John *Alli*
Barnard, John d1683 *Alli*
Barnard, John 1681-1770 *Alli, BiD&SB, CyAL 1, DcAmA, DcNAA*
Barnard, Sir John 1685-1764 *Alli*
Barnard, John 1690-1758 *Alli*
Barnard, John 1932- *ConAu 33*
Barnard, John Gross 1815-1882 *Alli Sup, DcAmA, DcNAA*
Barnard, Jonathan *Alli*
Barnard, Joseph *Alli Sup, ChPo S2*
Barnard, Leslie Gordon 1890-1961 *CanNov, CanWr, OxCan, WhWNAA*
Barnard, Leslie William 1924- *Au&Wr*

Barnard, Margaret E 1895- *WhWNAA*
Barnard, Marjorie Faith 1897- *DcLEnL, WrD 1976*
Barnard, Mary 1909- *ConAu 21, ConP 1970, DrAF 1976, DrAP 1975*
Barnard, Mordaunt Roger *Alli Sup*
Barnard, Oliver W 1828- *DcNAA, IndAu 1917*
Barnard, Richard Boyle *Alli, BiDLA Sup*
Barnard, Richard Innes *MnBBF*
Barnard, Robert J *MnBBF*
Barnard, S *Alli*
Barnard, Samuel, Jr. *BiDLA*
Barnard, Seymour *ChPo*
Barnard, T *ChPo*
Barnard, Thomas *Alli*
Barnard, Thomas 1714-1776 *Alli*
Barnard, Thomas 1728?-1806 *PoIre*
Barnard, Thomas 1748-1814 *Alli*
Barnard, Wilfred *MnBBF*
Barnard, William *Alli*
Barnard, William Francis *ChPo*
Barnard, William Francis 1865?-1947 *OhA&B*
Barnard, William Nichols 1875-1947 *DcNAA, WhWNAA*
Barnard-Smith, Catharine *ChPo*
Barnardiston, J *Alli*
Barnardiston, Thomas *Alli*
Barnardo, Thomas John 1845-1905 *ChPo S1, LongC, NewC*
Barnaval, Louis *Alli Sup*
Barnave, Antoine-Pierre-Joseph-Marie 1761-1793 *DcEuL, OxFr*
Barnby, Mrs. *Alli, BiDLA*
Barnd, Bertram 1883- *WhWNAA*
Barne, Kitty 1883-1957 *JBA 1951, WhCL*
Barne, Miles *Alli*
Barne, Thomas *Alli*
Barneby, W A *OxCan*
Barneby, W Henry *Alli Sup*
Barnefield, Richard 1574-1627 *ChPo*
Barnes, Major *Alli*
Barnes, Albert 1798-1870 *Alli, Alli Sup, AmA&B, BiD&SB, CyAL 2, DcAmA, DcEnL, DcNAA*
Barnes, Almont d1918 *DcNAA*
Barnes, Andrew Wallace 1878- *WhWNAA*
Barnes, Annie Marie 1857- *AmA&B, BiDSA, DcNAA*
Barnes, Arthur K 1909- *WhWNAA*
Barnes, Arthur Stapylton 1861-1936 *CatA 1947*
Barnes, Arthur Ward 1856- *ChPo*
Barnes, Aubrey *BlkAW*
Barnes, Barnabe 1569?-1609 *Alli, BiD&SB, BrAu, CasWL, ChPo, Chmbr 1, CnThe, CrE&SL, DcEnL, EvLB, NewC, OxEng, Pen Eng, REn, REnWD*
Barnes, C H *ChPo*
Barnes, C L *Alli Sup*
Barnes, C V *WrD 1976*
Barnes, Carman Dee 1912- *AmA&B, AmNov*
Barnes, Catherine J 1918- *ChPo, IlBYP, IICB 1956*
Barnes, Charles Cicero 1882-1946 *DcNAA*
Barnes, Charles R *Alli Sup*
Barnes, Charles Reid 1858-1910 *DcAmA, DcNAA, IndAu 1917*
Barnes, Charlotte Mary Sanford 1818-1863 *AmA, AmA&B, DcNAA, FemPA, OxAm*
Barnes, Chesley Virginia *ConAu XR*
Barnes, Clara Ernst 1895- *ConAu 5R*
Barnes, Clifford P 1897- *AmSCAP 66*
Barnes, Clive 1927- *AmA&B, AuNews 2*
Barnes, Culmer *ChPo*
Barnes, Cyril Charles 1913- *Au&Wr, WrD 1976*
Barnes, Daniel H d1818 *Alli*
Barnes, Dave *WhWNAA*
Barnes, David 1731-1811 *Alli*
Barnes, David M *Alli Sup*
Barnes, Demas 1827-1888 *Alli Sup, DcNAA*
Barnes, Derek Gilpin *ChPo S2*
Barnes, Diantha d1939 *DcNAA*
Barnes, Djuna 1892- *AmA&B, Au&Wr, CasWL, CnMD, ConAu 9R, ConDr, ConLC 3, ConLC 4, ConNov 1972, ConNov 1976, DcLEnL, EncWL, LongC, ModAL, ModAL Sup, OxAm, Pen Am,*

RAdv 1, REn, REnAL, TwCA,
TwCA Sup, TwCW, WhTwL, WrD 1976
Barnes, E *ChPo*
Barnes, E P *ChPo*
Barnes, E W *Alli*
Barnes, Miss E W *Alli Sup, ChPo S1*
Barnes, Earl 1861-1935 *DcNAA*
Barnes, Edgar G *Alli Sup*
Barnes, Edward John *Alli Sup*
Barnes, Edward Shippen 1887-1958
AmSCAP 66
Barnes, Edwin C *Alli Sup*
Barnes, Elliot *Alli Sup*
Barnes, Emily Ripley 1800- *Alli Sup, DcNAA*
Barnes, Emma J *Alli Sup*
Barnes, Eric Wollencott 1907-1962 *AmA&B,*
AuBYP
Barnes, Ernest William 1874- *WhLA*
Barnes, Everett d1930 *DcNAA*
Barnes, Faye King *OhA&B*
Barnes, Forrest 1905- *WhWNAA*
Barnes, Francis *Alli Sup*
Barnes, Francis Merriman, Jr. 1881-
WhWNAA
Barnes, Frank Coe 1867-1934 *DcNAA*
Barnes, Fred Asa 1876- *WhWNAA*
Barnes, G A *Alli Sup*
Barnes, G G *MnBBF*
Barnes, G H *ChPo*
Barnes, George *Alli*
Barnes, George Edward 1871- *WhWNAA*
Barnes, George Foster *ChPo*
Barnes, George Nicoll 1859- *WhLA*
Barnes, George Owen 1827-1908 *DcNAA*
Barnes, Gilbert Hobbs 1889-1945 *DcNAA,*
OhA&B
Barnes, Gregory Allen 1934- *ConAu 25*
Barnes, Harold *Au&Wr*
Barnes, Harry Aldrich 1872- *WhWNAA*
Barnes, Harry Elmer 1889-1968 *AmA&B,*
ConAu 25, OxAm, REnAL, TwCA,
TwCA Sup, WhWNAA
Barnes, Harry Lee 1877- *WhWNAA*
Barnes, Hazel E 1915- *ConAu 5R*
Barnes, Hellen 1908- *AmSCAP 66*
Barnes, Henry *Alli*
Barnes, Henry A 1906-1968 *ConAu P-1*
Barnes, Herbert *MnBBF*
Barnes, Homer Francis 1895- *ChPo*
Barnes, Howard McKent 1884-1945 *DcNAA*
Barnes, Howard Turner 1873- *WhWNAA*
Barnes, J *Alli, BiDLA, BiDLA Sup*
Barnes, J And Robinson, W *Alli Sup*
Barnes, Jack 1940- *ConAu 61*
Barnes, James *ChPo*
Barnes, James 1865-1936 *AmA&B, BiDSA,*
DcAmA
Barnes, James 1866-1936 *DcNAA*
Barnes, James A *IndAu 1816*
Barnes, James A 1898- *ConAu 9R*
Barnes, James J 1931- *ConAu 9R, WrD 1976*
Barnes, Jasper Converse 1861-1931 *DcNAA,*
WhWNAA
Barnes, Jeremiah Root 1808-1900 *OhA&B*
Barnes, Jim *DrAP 1975*
Barnes, Joanna 1934- *ConAu 57*
Barnes, John *Alli, BiDLA, MnBBF*
Barnes, John 1908- *ConAu 45*
Barnes, John A G 1909- *Au&Wr*
Barnes, John Arundel 1918- *WrD 1976*
Barnes, John B 1924- *ConAu 33*
Barnes, John Hindmarsh *Alli Sup*
Barnes, John S *Alli Sup*
Barnes, John Sanford 1836-1911 *DcNAA*
Barnes, Joseph *Alli*
Barnes, Josephine 1912- *Au&Wr, WrD 1976*
Barnes, Joshua 1654-1712 *Alli, DcEnL*
Barnes, Josiah *Alli Sup*
Barnes, Juliana *Alli, DcEnL, EvLB, NewC*
Barnes, Kenneth Charles 1903- *Au&Wr,*
WrD 1976
Barnes, Lemuel Call 1854-1938 *AmLY,*
DcNAA, OhA&B, WhWNAA
Barnes, Leola Christie 1889- *TexWr*
Barnes, Leonard 1895- *ConAu 29*
Barnes, M L *Alli Sup*
Barnes, Margaret Ayer 1886-1967 *AmA&B,*
ConAmA, ConAu 25, DcLEnL, OxAm,

REnAL, TwCA, TwCA Sup, WhWNAA
Barnes, Mary Downing 1850-1898 *DcAmA,*
DcNAA
Barnes, Melvyn 1942- *Au&Wr*
Barnes, Nathaniel Waring 1884- *WhWNAA*
Barnes, Nellie *AnMV 1926*
Barnes, Orlando Mack 1825-1899 *DcNAA*
Barnes, Peter 1931- *ConDr, ConLC 5,*
WrD 1976
Barnes, Philip Edward 1815- *Alli*
Barnes, Phoebe 1908- *ConAu 23*
Barnes, R G 1932- *ConAu 33*
Barnes, R S Fancourt *Alli Sup*
Barnes, Ralph *Alli*
Barnes, Ralph M 1900- *ConAu 17*
Barnes, Reginald Henry *Alli Sup*
Barnes, Richard John 1931- *Au&Wr*
Barnes, Richard William *Alli Sup*
Barnes, Robert *Alli Sup, ChPo, ChPo S1,*
ChPo S2
Barnes, Robert d1540 *Alli, DcEnL*
Barnes, Robert 1816- *Alli*
Barnes, Robert J 1925- *ConAu 21*
Barnes, Robert M 1940- *ConAu 45*
Barnes, Ronald Gorell 1884- *ChPo, NewC*
Barnes, S *Alli*
Barnes, Sam G 1913- *ConAu 13R*
Barnes, Samuel Henry 1931- *ConAu 23,*
WrD 1976
Barnes, Stephen Goodyear 1853-1931 *AmLY,*
DcNAA, WhWNAA
Barnes, Susan Rebecca *Alli, ChPo*
Barnes, Thomas *Alli*
Barnes, Thomas 1747-1810 *Alli*
Barnes, Thomas 1784-1841 *DcEnL, NewC*
Barnes, Thomas Garden 1930- *ConAu 1R*
Barnes, Thurlow Weed 1853- *Alli Sup, AmLY*
Barnes, Viola Florence 1885- *ConAu 1R*
Barnes, Wade 1917- *AmSCAP 66*
Barnes, Walter 1880-1969 *AmA&B, ChPo,*
OhA&B, REnAL, WhWNAA
Barnes, Warner *ChPo S1*
Barnes, William *Alli, Alli Sup, BiDLA,*
Chmbr 3
Barnes, William 1801?-1886 *Alli Sup,*
BiD&SB, BrAu 19, CasWL, ChPo,
ChPo S2, CnE&AP, DcEnA, DcEnL,
DcEuL, DcLEnL, EvLB, NewC, OxEng,
Pen Eng, REn, WebEAL
Barnes, William 1824-1913 *DcNAA*
Barnes, William 1927- *AmSCAP 66*
Barnes, Mrs. William C *OhA&B*
Barnes, William Croft 1858-1936 *ArizL,*
DcNAA, WhWNAA
Barnes, William Emery 1859- *WhLA*
Barnes, William George *Alli*
Barnes, William Horatio 1866?- *Alli Sup,*
DcNAA
Barnes, William Hutt 1877- *WhWNAA*
Barnes, William Robbins 1866-1945 *AmA&B,*
DcNAA
Barnesby, George J *Alli Sup*
Barnet *Alli*
Barnet, A *Alli*
Barnet, James *Alli Sup*
Barnet, Miguel 1940- *DcCLA*
Barnet, Richard J *ConAu 13R*
Barnet, Sylvan 1926- *ConAu 1R*
Barnetson, William Denholm 1917- *Au&Wr*
Barnett, Adam *ConAu XR*
Barnett, Alice 1886- *AmSCAP 66*
Barnett, Ann *Alli Sup*
Barnett, Arthur Doak 1921- *ConAu 5R,*
WrD 1976
Barnett, Correlli Douglas 1927- *Au&Wr,*
ConAu 13R, WrD 1976
Barnett, Edith A *Alli Sup*
Barnett, Edward *Alli Sup*
Barnett, Evelyn Scott Snead d1921 *DcNAA*
Barnett, Evelyn Scott Snead 1866- *BiDSA*
Barnett, Evelyn Scott Snead 1891- *AmLY*
Barnett, F S A *Alli Sup*
Barnett, George Ernest 1873-1938 *DcNAA*
Barnett, George Leonard 1915- *ConAu 29,*
IndAu 1917, WrD 1976
Barnett, Grace Treleven 1899- *WhPNW*
Barnett, Guy 1928- *ConAu 17R*
Barnett, H G 1906- *ConAu 45*

Barnett, Henrietta Octavia Weston 1851-
Alli Sup, WhLA
Barnett, Henry Green 1890- *WhWNAA*
Barnett, Homer Garner 1906- *WhPNW*
Barnett, Horace Leslie 1909- *IndAu 1917*
Barnett, Jack 1920- *AmSCAP 66*
Barnett, John *Alli Sup, MnBBF*
Barnett, John Francis 1837- *ChPo S1*
Barnett, John Pyer *Alli Sup*
Barnett, L David *ConAu XR*
Barnett, Leo 1925- *ConAu 29*
Barnett, Leonard Palin 1919- *Au&Wr,*
ConAu P-1, WrD 1976
Barnett, Lincoln Kinnear 1909- *AmA&B,*
WorAu
Barnett, Malcolm Joel 1941- *ConAu 45*
Barnett, Marva T 1913- *ConAu 57*
Barnett, Matilda J *Alli Sup*
Barnett, Mavis Clare 1898- *ChPo*
Barnett, Michael 1930- *ConAu 57*
Barnett, Moneta *IlBYP*
Barnett, Mrs. Percy Arthur *ChPo S1*
Barnett, Reginald *Alli Sup, ChPo S2*
Barnett, Richard *Alli, BiDLA*
Barnett, Richard C 1932- *ConAu 33*
Barnett, Richard David 1909- *Au&Wr*
Barnett, Robert W *Alli Sup*
Barnett, Samuel Anthony 1915- *Au&Wr,*
ConAu 13R, WrD 1976
Barnett, Samuel Augustus *Alli Sup*
Barnett, Violet Malcolm *ChPo S1*
Barnett, W *ChPo S1*
Barnette, Henlee H 1911- *ConAu 49*
Barnette, W Leslie, Jr. 1910- *ConAu P-1*
Barnevelt, Esdras *DcEnL*
Barnewall, R V *Alli*
Barney, Miss A M *Alli Sup*
Barney, Anna Louise *AnMV 1926*
Barney, C *Alli Sup*
Barney, Danford N *ChPo S2*
Barney, Eliam E 1807-1880 *OhA&B*
Barney, J Dellinger 1878- *WhWNAA*
Barney, John *BiDSA*
Barney, John Stewart 1868-1925 *DcNAA*
Barney, Laura D 1880?-1974 *ConAu 53*
Barney, LeRoy 1930- *ConAu 33, WrD 1976*
Barney, Maginel Wright 1881- *IlCB 1945*
Barney, Mary *BiDSA*
Barney, Natalie 1878?-1972 *ConAu 33*
Barney, Raymond Livingston 1891- *WhWNAA*
Barney, William L 1943- *ConAu 41*
Barnfield, Gabriel 1924- *Au&Wr*
Barnfield, Richard *ChPo, Chmbr 1*
Barnfield, Richard 1574-1627 *Alli, BrAu,*
CasWL, CnE&AP, CrE&SL, DcEnL,
DcLEnL, EvLB, NewC, OxEng, Pen Eng,
REn, WebEAL
Barnham, Sir Francis *Alli*
Barnham, Richard Harris 1788-1845 *DcEnA Ap*
Barnhart, Clarence L 1900- *AmA&B,*
ConAu 13R
Barnhart, Dean Leffel 1889- *WhWNAA*
Barnhart, Earl Wingert 1882- *WhWNAA*
Barnhart, Joe Edward 1931- *ConAu 41*
Barnhart, Nancy 1889- *ChPo, IlBYP,*
IlCB 1945, IlCB 1956
Barnhill, Celeste Jane Terrell 1864- *IndAu 1917*
Barnhill, James *Alli Sup*
Barnhill, John Finch 1865-1943 *DcNAA,*
IndAu 1917, WhWNAA
Barnhill, Myrtle Fait 1896- *ConAu P-1*
Barnhisel, Ethel Keeler Betts 1880- *WhWNAA*
Barni, Jules Romain 1818-1878 *BiD&SB*
Barnie, John 1941- *ConAu 57, WrD 1976*
Barnitt, Nedda Lemmon *ConAu 9R*
Barnitz, Albert Trovillo Siders 1833- *OhA&B*
Barnitz, Harry W 1920- *ConAu 25*
Barnivelt, Esdras *NewC*
Barnoon, Shlomo 1940- *ConAu 41*
Barnouw, Adriaan Jacob 1877- *AuBYP,*
ChPo S1, WhWNAA
Barnouw, Erik 1908- *AmA&B, ConAu 13R*
Barns, Cass Grove 1848-1932 *IndAu 1917*
Barns, Chancy R *Alli Sup*
Barns, Clara Elberta *TexWr*
Barns, Florence Elberta *AmA&B, TexWr,*
WhWNAA

Barns, John W B 1912-1974 *ConAu 49*
Barns, W E *Alli Sup*
Barns, William Eddy 1853-1915 *DcNAA, IndAu 1816*
Barnsley, Alan Gabriel 1916- *ConAu 13R, WorAu, WrD 1976*
Barnston, George *BbtC*
Barnston, James 1831-1858 *BbtC*
Barnstone, Aliki 1956- *ChPo S1*
Barnstone, Willis 1927- *ConAu 17R, DrAP 1975*
Barnum, Frances Courtenay Baylor 1848- *AmA&B, BiD&SB, DcAmA, DcNAA*
Barnum, Frances Aloysius 1849-1921 *DcNAA*
Barnum, H L *Alli Sup*
Barnum, Jay Hyde *AuBYP, IlCB 1956*
Barnum, Phineas Taylor 1810-1891 *Alli, Alli Sup, AmA&B, BbD, BiD&SB, DcAmA, DcNAA, MnBBF, OxAm, REn, REnAL*
Barnum, Richard *ConAu 19, SmATA 1*
Barnum, Samuel Weed 1820-1891 *Alli Sup, DcAmA, DcNAA*
Barnum, W Paul 1933- *ConAu 29*
Barnwall *BbtC*
Barnwell *DcNAA*
Barnwell, Annie M *LivFWS*
Barnwell, Charles H *Alli Sup*
Barnwell, D Robinson 1915- *ConAu 17R*
Barnwell, Desiree A *BlkAW*
Barnwell, Dot Robinson 1915- *WrD 1976*
Barnwell, Edward Lowry *Alli Sup*
Barnwell, Lily Ripley *BiDSA*
Barnwell, R G *Alli Sup*
Barnwell, Robert Woodward 1801-1882 *BiDSA*
Barnwell, Robert Woodward 1849-1900? *BiDSA, DcNAA*
Barnwell, Robinson *WrD 1976*
Baro 1600?-1696 *Alli*
Baro, Balthazar *DcEuL, OxFr*
Baro, Gene 1924- *ConP 1970, ConP 1975, WrD 1976*
Baro, Peter d1600? *Alli*
Baroja, Pio 1872-1956 *CnMWL, DcSpL, ModRL, TwCW, WhTwL*
Baroja Y Nessi, Pio 1872-1956 *CasWL, ClDMEuL, CyWA, EncWL, EvEuW, Pen Eur, REn, TwCA, TwCA Sup*
Barolini, Antonio 1910- *ConAu 1R*
Barolini, Helen *DrAF 1976*
Baron 1600?-1696 *Alli*
Baron, Alexander 1917- *ConAu 5R, LongC, TwCA Sup*
Baron, Anthony *MnBBF*
Baron, Cyril Faudel Joseph 1903- *Au&Wr, WrD 1976*
Baron, David *Alli Sup, ConAu XR*
Baron, Denis Neville 1924- *Au&Wr, WrD 1976*
Baron, Devorah 1887-1956 *CasWL*
Baron, George 1911- *Au&Wr*
Baron, Hans 1900- *ConAu 17R*
Baron, Herman 1941- *ConAu 61*
Baron, John *Alli, MnBBF*
Baron, John d1885 *Alli Sup*
Baron, John Thomas 1856- *ChPo S1*
Baron, Jonny 1925- *AmSCAP 66*
Baron, Joseph Alexander 1917- *Au&Wr, NewC*
Baron, Linda *BlkAW*
Baron, Mary 1944- *ConAu 49, DrAP 1975*
Baron, Maurice 1889-1964 *AmSCAP 66*
Baron, Michel Boyron 1653?-1729 *DcEuL, OxFr*
Baron, Peter *Alli*
Baron, Richard d1768 *Alli*
Baron, Robert *Alli*
Baron, Robert 1631?- *Alli, DcEnL*
Baron, Robert Alex 1920- *ConAu 41*
Baron, Salo W 1895- *AmA&B*
Baron, Samuel *Alli*
Baron, Samuel H 1921- *ConAu 9R*
Baron, Stephen *Alli*
Baron, Vic 1910- *AmSCAP 66*
Baron, Virginia Olsen 1931- *ConAu 25*
Baron, Wendy 1937- *ConAu 41*
Baron, William *Alli, ChPo*
Baron Mikan *ConAu XR*

Baronas, Aloyzas *CasWL*
Baronas, Antanas *CasWL*
Barondess, Sue K 1926- *ConAu 1R*
Barone, Allen G 1867-1947 *OhA&B*
Baronian, Hagop 1842-1891 *CasWL*
Baronio, Cesare 1538-1607 *CasWL, EvEuW, Pen Eur*
Baronius, Cardinal Cesare 1538-1607 *OxFr*
Barovick, Fred *AmSCAP 66*
Barquero, Efrain 1930- *DcCLA*
Barr *Alli, BbtC*
Barr, Albert E 1931- *AmSCAP 66*
Barr, Albert William Cleeve 1910- *Au&Wr*
Barr, Alfred Hamilton, Jr. 1902- *AmA&B, ConAu 49*
Barr, Alice Montgomery *WhWNAA*
Barr, Alwyn 1938- *ConAu 33, WrD 1976*
Barr, Amelia Edith Huddleston 1831-1919 *Alli Sup, AmA, AmA&B, BbD, BiD&SB, BiDSA, ChPo, ChPo S1, ChPo S2, DcAmA, DcBiA, DcLEnL, DcNAA, OxAm, REn, REnAL*
Barr, Anne F *ChPo*
Barr, Anthony 1921- *AmSCAP 66*
Barr, Arvil Sylvester 1892-1962 *IndAu 1917, WhWNAA*
Barr, Beverly *ConAu 61*
Barr, Carolyn *WhWNAA*
Barr, Densil *Au&Wr, WrD 1976*
Barr, Donald *DcLEnL*
Barr, Donald 1921- *ConAu 9R*
Barr, Doris W 1923- *ConAu 33*
Barr, George 1907- *AmA&B, AuBYP, ConAu 1R, SmATA 2*
Barr, Gladys Hutchison 1904- *ConAu 1R*
Barr, Granville Walter 1860?-1939 *AmLY, DcAmA, OhA&B*
Barr, Isaac *OxCan*
Barr, Isabel Harriss *BkC 6, TexWr*
Barr, J T *Alli Sup*
Barr, James *Alli Sup*
Barr, James 1862-1923 *ChPo S1, DcNAA, WhLA*
Barr, James 1913- *BiDPar*
Barr, James 1924- *ConAu 1R, WrD 1976*
Barr, Jene 1900- *AmA&B, AuBYP, ConAu 5R*
Barr, John *Alli, Alli Sup, ChPo S1, OxCan Sup*
Barr, John 1809-1889 *DcLEnL*
Barr, John 1858- *ChPo S1*
Barr, John Henry 1861-1937 *DcAmA, DcNAA, IndAu 1917, WhWNAA*
Barr, John J 1942- *ConAu 61*
Barr, John T *Alli Sup*
Barr, Lillie E *Alli Sup, ChPo, ChPo S1*
Barr, Martin W 1860-1938 *DcNAA*
Barr, Mary *ChPo*
Barr, Mary A *ChPo S1*
Barr, Matthias 1831- *Alli Sup, ChPo, ChPo S1, ChPo S2*
Barr, Michael 1927- *AmSCAP 66*
Barr, Nat *MnBBF*
Barr, O Sydney 1919- *ConAu 13R*
Barr, Patricia Miriam 1934- *Au&Wr, ConAu 23*
Barr, Robert 1850?-1912 *BbD, BiD&SB, Chmbr 3, EncM&D, EvLB, NewC, OxCan, REn, TwCA*
Barr, Robert M *Alli*
Barr, Stephen 1904- *ConAu P-1*
Barr, Stringfellow 1897- *AmA&B, ConAu 1R, OxAm, REnAL, TwCA Sup*
Barr, Thomas *Alli Sup*
Barr, Thomas E *Alli Sup*
Barr, William M *Alli Sup*
Barr, William Miller 1879?- *DcNAA*
Barr, William Monfort 1905- *IndAu 1917*
Barracand, Leon Henri 1844- *BbD, BiD&SB*
Barrack, William *Alli Sup*
Barraclough, Geoffrey 1908- *WorAu*
Barraclough, Henry *ChPo S1*
Barraclough, Solon L 1922- *ConAu 41*
Barradale-Smith, William *MnBBF*
Barraga, Natalie Carter 1915- *ConAu 41*
Barral, Mary-Rose 1925- *ConAu 33, WrD 1976*
Barralet, John James d1812? *BkIE*

Barrand *Alli*
Barrand, Philip *Alli*
Barranger, M S 1937- *ConAu 29, WrD 1976*
Barrantes, Vicente 1829- *BiD&SB*
Barras, Charles M 1826-1873 *REnAL*
Barras, Julius *Alli Sup*
Barras, Paul-J-F-Nicholas, Vicomte De 1755-1829 *OxFr*
Barrass, Edward 1821-1898 *BbtC, DcNAA*
Barratt, Alfred 1844-1881 *Alli Sup*
Barratt, Mrs. F Layland *Alli Sup*
Barratt, George *Alli Sup*
Barratt, Joseph *Alli Sup*
Barratt, Norris Stanley 1862-1924 *DcNAA*
Barratt, Robert C *Alli Sup*
Barratt Brown, Michael 1918- *Au&Wr, WrD 1976*
Barraud, Allan F *ChPo*
Barrault, Jean-Louis 1910- *OxFr, REn*
Barrax, Gerald William 1933- *BlkAW, DrAP 1975, LivBA*
Barre, George *OxCan Sup*
Barre, Henry Walter 1881- *WhWNAA*
Barre, Raoul 1874-1932 *DcNAA*
Barre, Uttere *Alli Sup*
Barre, W L 1830- *Alli Sup, DcNAA*
Barre, William *BiDLA*
Barrell, Miss *Alli*
Barrell, Andrew *Alli*
Barrell, Edmund *Alli*
Barrell, Geoffrey Richard 1917- *Au&Wr, WrD 1976*
Barrell, George 1809- *DcNAA*
Barrell, Joseph 1869-1919 *DcNAA*
Barrell, Sarah Sayward 1759-1855 *AmA&B, DcNAA, REnAL*
Barren, Charles 1913- *Au&Wr, ConAu 9R*
Barreno, Maria Isabel 1939- *AuNews 1*
Barrere, Albert *Alli Sup*
Barres, Maurice 1862-1923 *BiD&SB, CasWL, ClDMEuL, EvEuW, LongC, NewC, OxEng, OxFr, Pen Eur, REn, TwCA, TwCA Sup*
Barres, Oliver 1921- *ConAu 13R*
Barret *Alli*
Barret, B *Alli*
Barret, Mrs. J B *ChPo*
Barret, John *Alli, BiDLA*
Barret, LeRoy Carr 1877- *WhWNAA*
Barret, Onsow *Alli*
Barret, Phineas *Alli*
Barret, Pringle *ChPo*
Barret, Robert *Alli*
Barret, Stephen 1718-1801 *Alli*
Barreto, Affonso Henriques DeLima 1881-1922 *Pen Am*
Barreto, Rui Moniz *AfA 1*
Barreto DeMeneses, Tobias 1839-1889 *Pen Am*
Barrett, Alan *IlBYP*
Barrett, Albert Moore 1871- *WhWNAA*
Barrett, Albert Reed 1841-1936 *DcNAA*
Barrett, Alfred 1808-1876 *Alli Sup*
Barrett, Alfred 1906- *CatA 1947, ChPo S2*
Barrett, Alfred Walter 1869- *MnBBF*
Barrett, Anne Mainwaring 1911- *Au&Wr, ConAu 29, WrD 1976*
Barrett, Arrie *TexWr*
Barrett, Arthur Charles *Alli Sup*
Barrett, Ashley William *Alli Sup*
Barrett, B *Alli, BiDLA*
Barrett, Benjamin Fisk 1808-1892 *Alli Sup, BiD&SB, DcAmA*
Barrett, Benjamin Fiske 1808-1892 *DcNAA, OhA&B*
Barrett, Bryan *Alli, BiDLA*
Barrett, Carl Allen 1894- *IndAu 1917*
Barrett, Charles Kingsley 1917- *Au&Wr, ConAu 21, WrD 1976*
Barrett, Charles Leslie 1879- *DcLEnL*
Barrett, Charles Simon 1866-1935 *DcNAA*
Barrett, Clifford L 1894-1971 *ConAu 33, WhWNAA*
Barrett, Clifton Waller 1901- *ChPo S1, ConAu 41*
Barrett, Daniel William *Alli Sup*
Barrett, Don Carlos 1868-1943 *DcNAA, OhA&B*
Barrett, Donald N 1920- *ConAu 13R*

Barrett, E Boyd 1883- *AmA&B*, *WhWNAA*
Barrett, Eaton Stannard 1786-1820 *Alli*, *BiDLA*, *ChPo*, *EvLB*, *PoIre*
Barrett, Edna Dueringer 1896-1947 *OhA&B*
Barrett, Edward 1828-1881 *Alli Sup*, *DcNAA*
Barrett, Edward L, Jr. 1917- *ConAu 25*
Barrett, Edward W 1910- *WrD 1976*
Barrett, Elizabeth *DcLEnL*
Barrett, Elizabeth B *Alli*
Barrett, Elizabeth Gertrude Barber *Alli Sup*
Barrett, Ethel Cook 1892?- *IndAu 1917*, *WhWNAA*
Barrett, Eton Stannard d1820 *DcEnL*
Barrett, Eugene F 1921- *ConAu 57*
Barrett, Florence Magruder Wynne *TexWr*
Barrett, Frances H *ChPo*
Barrett, Francis *Alli*, *BiDLA*, *BiDLA Sup*
Barrett, Frank 1848- *Alli Sup*, *BbD*
Barrett, Fred W 1858-1951 *OhA&B*
Barrett, G S *Alli Sup*
Barrett, George 1796-1875 *OhA&B*
Barrett, George W 1908- *ConAu 17R*
Barrett, Gerald Van 1936- *ConAu 37*
Barrett, Guy Crossland 1925- *Au&Wr*
Barrett, Harrison Delivan 1863-1911? *DcNAA*
Barrett, Henry *Alli*, *BiDLA*
Barrett, Henry Charles 1923- *ConAu 53*
Barrett, Henry John *Alli Sup*
Barrett, Howard *Alli Sup*
Barrett, Hugh Gilchrist 1917- *Au&Wr*
Barrett, Ivan J 1910- *ConAu 49*
Barrett, J *Alli Sup*
Barrett, J Edward 1932- *ConAu 37*
Barrett, J Lee 1881- *IndAu 1917*
Barrett, J O *Alli Sup*
Barrett, James Francis 1888-1934 *CatA 1947*, *DcNAA*
Barrett, James H 1906- *ConAu 33*
Barrett, James Joseph 1867?- *PoIre*
Barrett, Jay Amos 1865-1936 *DcNAA*
Barrett, Jean *ChPo S2*
Barrett, John 1746?-1821 *Alli*
Barrett, John 1866-1938 *AmLY*, *DcAmA*, *DcNAA*
Barrett, John E *PoIre*
Barrett, John Erigena 1849- *DcNAA*
Barrett, John Gilchrist 1921- *ConAu 5R*, *WrD 1976*
Barrett, John Henry 1913- *WrD 1976*
Barrett, John Presley 1852-1924 *DcNAA*, *OhA&B*
Barrett, Jonathan *Alli Sup*
Barrett, Joseph *Alli*, *BiDLA*, *MnBBF*
Barrett, Joseph Hartwell 1824-1907? *DcNAA*, *OhA&B*
Barrett, Joseph Osgood d1898 *Alli Sup*, *DcNAA*
Barrett, Judi 1941- *WrD 1976*
Barrett, Kate 1858-1925 *DcNAA*
Barrett, Katharine Ellis 1879- *ChPo S2*
Barrett, Katherine Ruth Ellis 1870- *ChPo S1*
Barrett, Laurence I 1935- *ConAu 17R*
Barrett, Lawrence 1838-1891 *Alli Sup*, *DcNAA*
Barrett, Leonard Andrew 1874-1945 *DcNAA*, *OhA&B*, *WhWNAA*
Barrett, Lillian Foster 1884-1963 *AmA&B*, *WhWNAA*
Barrett, Lindsay *BlkAW*
Barrett, Linton Lomas 1904- *ConAu 5R*
Barrett, M *BbtC*
Barrett, Mary *Alli Sup*, *DcNAA*
Barrett, Mary Ellin 1927- *ConAu 17R*
Barrett, Monte *DcNAA*, *WhWNAA*
Barrett, Montgomery 1897-1949 *DcNAA*, *IndAu 1917*, *TexWr*, *WhWNAA*
Barrett, Nancy Smith 1942- *ConAu 37*, *WrD 1976*
Barrett, Nathan N 1933- *BlkAW*, *ConAu 17R*
Barrett, Otis Warren 1872- *WhWNAA*
Barrett, P *Alli Sup*
Barrett, Patricia 1914- *ConAu 5R*, *IndAu 1917*
Barrett, Phairis Worrell 1860-1936 *IndAu 1917*
Barrett, R S *Alli Sup*
Barrett, Raina *ConAu XR*
Barrett, Richard A F *Alli*
Barrett, Richmond Brooks 1895- *AmA&B*,

WhWNAA
Barrett, Robert John *OxCan*
Barrett, Robert N 1868- *BiDSA*
Barrett, Robert S *BiDSA*
Barrett, Robert South 1851-1896 *DcNAA*
Barrett, Robert South 1877- *WhWNAA*
Barrett, Ron *IlBYP*
Barrett, Rona 1936?- *AuNews 1*
Barrett, Russell H 1919- *ConAu 17R*
Barrett, S A 1879- *ChPo*, *WhWNAA*
Barrett, Selah Hibbard 1822-1883 *Alli Sup*, *DcNAA*, *OhA&B*
Barrett, Serenus *Alli*
Barrett, Solomon 1827?- *DcNAA*
Barrett, Stephen 1718-1801 *Alli*, *PoIre*
Barrett, Stephen Melvil 1865- *AmA&B*, *WhWNAA*
Barrett, Storrs B 1864- *WhWNAA*
Barrett, Susan Mary 1938- *Au&Wr*
Barrett, Sylvia 1914- *ConAu 25*
Barrett, Theodore H *WhWNAA*
Barrett, Thomas Squire *Alli Sup*
Barrett, W *Alli Sup*
Barrett, Walter *AmA&B*, *DcAmA*, *DcNAA*
Barrett, Walter, Clerk d1864 *DcEnL*
Barrett, Ward J 1927- *ConAu 29*
Barrett, William d1789 *Alli*
Barrett, William 1836-1888 *Alli Sup*, *DcNAA*
Barrett, William 1913- *AmA&B*, *ConAu 13R*
Barrett, William 1915- *REnAL*
Barrett, William Alexander 1836- *Alli Sup*
Barrett, William Edmund 1900- *AmA&B*, *Au&Wr*, *BkC 5*, *CatA 1952*, *ConAu 5R*, *REnAL*
Barrett, Sir William Fletcher 1844-1925 *BiDPar*
Barrett, William Garland *Alli Sup*
Barrett, William John *Alli Sup*
Barrett, Wilson 1846-1904 *BrAu 19*, *DcNAA*, *LongC*, *NewC*
Barrett, Wilton Agnew 1886-1940 *DcNAA*
Barrett-Lennard, Charles E *OxCan*
Barrette, George W 1896- *WhWNAA*
Barrette, Marilee Barger 1897- *WhWNAA*
Barretto, Larry 1890- *AmA&B*, *AmNov*, *ConAu XR*, *TwCA*, *TwCA Sup*, *WhWNAA*
Barretto, Laurence Brevoort 1890-1971 *ConAu 33*
Barretto, Lefty *DrAF 1976*
Barrey, Lod *Alli*
Barri, Giraldus De *BrAu*, *NewC*
Barrick, James Russell 1829-1867 *BiDSA*
Barrick, Mac E 1933- *ConAu 33*
Barrie, Alex *Alli*
Barrie, Alexander 1923- *Au&Wr*, *ConAu 1R*, *WrD 1976*
Barrie, Derek Stiven Maxwelton 1907- *Au&Wr*
Barrie, Donald C 1905- *Au&Wr*
Barrie, Sir James Matthew 1860-1937 *Alli Sup*, *AtlBL*, *BbD*, *BiD&SB*, *CarSB*, *CasWL*, *ChPo*, *ChPo S1*, *ChPo S2*, *Chmbr 3*, *CnMD*, *CnThe*, *CyWA*, *DcBiA*, *DcEnA*, *DcEnA Ap*, *DcLEnL*, *EncWL*, *EvLB*, *FamAYP*, *JBA 1934*, *LongC*, *McGWD*, *ModBL*, *ModWD*, *NewC*, *OxEng*, *Pen Eng*, *RAdv 1*, *REn*, *REnWD*, *TwCA*, *TwCA Sup*, *TwCW*, *WebEAL*, *WhCL*, *WhTwL*, *YABC 1*
Barrie, Jane *ConAu XR*, *WrD 1976*
Barrie, P 1833- *ChPo S1*
Barrie, S *MnBBF*
Barrier, Norman G 1940- *ConAu 53*
Barriere, Jean Francois 1786-1868 *BiD&SB*
Barriere, Theodore 1823-1877 *BiD&SB*, *EvEuW*, *OxFr*, *Pen Eur*
Barrifee, William *Alli*
Barrili, Antonio Giulio 1836-1908 *BiD&SB*, *CasWL*, *ClDMEuL*, *DcBiA*, *EvEuW*
Barringer, Daniel Moreau 1860-1929 *DcNAA*, *WhWNAA*
Barringer, Edwin C 1892- *OhA&B*
Barringer, Maria Massey *Alli Sup*
Barringer, Paul Brandon 1857-1941 *DcNAA*
Barringer, Rufus 1821-1895 *BiDSA*
Barrington, Daines 1727-1800 *Alli*, *NewC*
Barrington, E *DcNAA*, *LongC*, *NewC*, *OxCan*, *REn*, *TwCA*, *TwCA Sup*

Barrington, Ernest James William 1909- *Au&Wr*, *WrD 1976*
Barrington, F Clinton *Alli Sup*, *HsB&A*, *HsB&A Sup*
Barrington, George 1755-1840? *Alli*, *NewC*
Barrington, George W 1876- *TexWr*
Barrington, George Walter 1908- *Au&Wr*
Barrington, H W *ConAu XR*
Barrington, John *ConAu XR*
Barrington, John Shute 1678-1734 *Alli*, *NewC*
Barrington, Sir Jonah 1767?-1834 *Alli*, *BiDLA*, *DcEnL*, *NewC*
Barrington, Joseph Thomas *Alli Sup*
Barrington, Lowther John 1805- *Alli Sup*
Barrington, Maurice *EvLB*, *LongC*
Barrington, P V *ConAu XR*
Barrington, Pamela *ConAu XR*
Barrington, Pamela Vere *Au&Wr*
Barrington, Patrick *ChPo*
Barrington, Pauline B 1876- *WhWNAA*
Barrington, Shute 1732?-1826 *Alli*, *BiDLA*
Barrington-Ward, Robert McGowan 1891-1948 *LongC*
Barrio, Raymond 1921- *ConAu 25*, *DrAF 1976*, *WrD 1976*
Barrios, Daniel Levi De 1625?-1701 *EvEuW*
Barrios, David *IlBYP*
Barrios, Eduardo 1884-1963 *CasWL*, *DcSpL*, *EncWL*, *Pen Am*, *REn*, *TwCW*
Barrios, Miguel De 1625?-1701? *CasWL*, *DcEuL*
Barris, Alex 1922- *ConAu 61*
Barris, Amanda *ChPo*
Barris, Chuck *WrD 1976*
Barris, Harry 1905-1962 *AmSCAP 66*
Barrister, A *DcEnL*
Barritt, Denis P 1914- *ConAu 21*
Barritt, Frances Fuller 1826-1902 *AmA&B*, *DcNAA*, *HsB&A*
Barritt, Leon *Alli Sup*
Barroll, C *Alli Sup*
Barroll, Benjamin Crockett 1819-1908 *DcNAA*
Barron, A Elton *MnBBF*
Barron, A F *Alli Sup*
Barron, Alfred *Alli Sup*
Barron, Alfred Austin *Alli*
Barron, Arthur *Alli*, *ConDr*
Barron, Billy Malloy 1925- *AmSCAP 66*
Barron, Clarence Walker 1855-1928 *DcNAA*
Barron, D H *ChPo*
Barron, Douglas Gordon *ChPo S2*
Barron, E L *ChPo S1*
Barron, Eliza Mary *Alli Sup*
Barron, Elwyn Alfred 1855-1929 *Alli Sup*, *AmA&B*, *DcAmA*, *DcNAA*
Barron, Frank 1922- *ConAu 5R*
Barron, Hannah Eayrs 1809- *DcNAA*
Barron, Harry 1908- *Au&Wr*
Barron, Jerome A 1933- *ConAu 45*
Barron, John Augustus 1850-1936 *DcNAA*, *WhWNAA*
Barron, Joseph Thomas 1889-1939 *DcNAA*
Barron, Leonard 1868-1938 *AmLY*, *DcNAA*, *WhWNAA*
Barron, Milton Leon 1918- *AmA&B*, *ConAu 1R*, *WrD 1976*
Barron, Oswald 1868-1939 *LongC*
Barron, S B *BiDSA*
Barron, Samuel Benton 1834-1912 *DcNAA*
Barron, Ted 1879-1943 *AmSCAP 66*
Barron, Thomas 1924- *Au&Wr*
Barron, William *Alli*
Barros, Joao De 1496-1570 *BiD&SB*, *CasWL*, *EvEuW*, *Pen Eur*
Barrosse, Thomas 1926- *ConAu 9R*
Barrough, Philip *Alli*
Barroughby, W *Alli*
Barrow, Lady *ChPo S2*
Barrow, Edwin Pinder *Alli Sup*, *ChPo S2*
Barrow, Elfrida DeRenne 1884- *AnMV 1926*
Barrow, Frances Elizabeth 1822-1894 *Alli Sup*, *AmA&B*, *BiD&SB*, *BiDSA*, *CarSB*, *DcAmA*, *DcNAA*
Barrow, Geoffrey W S 1924- *ConAu 17R*
Barrow, Sir George 1806-1876 *Alli Sup*
Barrow, George Staunton *Alli Sup*
Barrow, Henry *Alli*
Barrow, Humphrey *Alli*

Barrow, Isaac 1630-1677 *Alli, BrAu, CasWL, Chmbr 1, DcEnL, DcLEnL, EvLB, NewC, OxEng*
Barrow, J *BiDLA, BiDLA Sup*
Barrow, James *Alli, BiDLA*
Barrow, John *Alli, Alli Sup, BbtC, BiDLA, BiDLA Sup*
Barrow, Sir John 1764-1848 *Alli, BbD, BiD&SB, BrAu 19, Chmbr 2, DcEnA, DcLEnL, NewC, OxCan*
Barrow, John, Jr. *Alli, Alli Sup*
Barrow, Sir John Croker 1833-1900 *Alli Sup, ChPo S2*
Barrow, John H d1858 *Alli*
Barrow, Kate 1860-1939 *DcNAA*
Barrow, Lyn Norman 1918- *Au&Wr*
Barrow, Raymond 1920- *ConP 1970*
Barrow, Rhoda Catharine 1910- *Au&Wr, ConAu 9R*
Barrow, Roscoe Lindley 1913- *Au&Wr*
Barrow, S *Alli, BbtC*
Barrow, Mrs. S L *ChPo, ChPo S1*
Barrow, Terence 1923- *ConAu 41*
Barrow, Thomas C 1929- *ConAu 23*
Barrow, William 1754?-1836 *Alli, BiDLA*
Barrow, William 1927- *ConAu XR*
Barrow, William Edward 1878- *WhWNAA*
Barrow-North, H *MnBBF*
Barrowcliffe, A J *Alli Sup*
Barrowes, Henry d1592 *Alli*
Barrows, Albert L 1883- *WhWNAA*
Barrows, Anita 1947- *ConAu 49, DrAP 1975*
Barrows, Charles Henry 1853-1918 *AmLY, DcNAA*
Barrows, Charles M *Alli Sup*
Barrows, Clarke *ChPo*
Barrows, Cliff *ChPo S1*
Barrows, David Prescott 1873- *AmLY, WhWNAA*
Barrows, Mrs. E A *Alli Sup*
Barrows, Edward Morley 1887-1940 *DcNAA*
Barrows, Elijah Porter 1805-1888 *Alli Sup, DcAmA, DcNAA, OhA&B*
Barrows, Harold Kilbrith 1873- *WhWNAA*
Barrows, Henry Robbins 1880-1935 *DcNAA*
Barrows, Isabel Chapin 1845- *Alli Sup, Alli Sup*
Barrows, J O *Alli Sup*
Barrows, John Henry 1847-1902 *AmA&B, BiD&SB, DcAmA, DcNAA, OhA&B*
Barrows, John Otis 1833-1918 *DcNAA*
Barrows, Katherine Isabel Hayes 1845?-1912 *DcAmA, DcNAA*
Barrows, L D *Alli Sup*
Barrows, Marjorie *AmA&B, AuBYP, ChPo, ChPo S1, ConAu 21, WhWNAA*
Barrows, Nathaniel A 1900-1949 *DcNAA*
Barrows, Ruth *ConAu XR*
Barrows, Samuel June 1845-1909 *Alli Sup, DcAmA, DcNAA*
Barrows, Walter Bradford 1855-1923 *DcNAA*
Barrows, Wayne Grove 1880- *AmA&B*
Barrows, William *Alli Sup*
Barrows, William 1815-1891 *Alli Sup, DcAmA, DcNAA*
Barrows, William Edward 1878- *WhWNAA*
Barrows, William Morton 1883- *WhWNAA*
Barrs, George *Alli, BiDLA*
Barruel-Bauvert, Antoine-Joseph 1756-1817 *OxFr*
Barrus, Clara 1864-1931 *DcNAA, WhWNAA*
Barrus, George Hale 1854-1929 *DcNAA*
Barrus, Hiram 1822-1883 *DcNAA*
Barrus, Mortimer Franklin 1879- *WhWNAA*
Barry, Comtesse Du *NewC*
Barry Cornwall *OxEng*
Barry, Miss *Alli Sup*
Barry, Al 1903- *AmSCAP 66*
Barry, Alfred 1826- *Alli Sup, DcEnL*
Barry, Alice Frances 1861-1951 *ChPo, ChPo S1, PoIre*
Barry, Ann 1734-1801 *NewC*
Barry, Arthur *MnBBF*
Barry, C A *Alli Sup*
Barry, C M *Alli Sup*
Barry, Charles *CatA 1947*
Barry, Charles A 1830-1892 *ChPo, ChPo S1, EarAB, EarAB Sup*

Barry, Charles Robert 1825- *Alli Sup*
Barry, Clive 1922- *Au&Wr, ConNov 1972, ConNov 1976, WrD 1976*
Barry, Colman J 1921- *ConAu 13R*
Barry, Dave 1918- *AmSCAP 66*
Barry, Sir David 1780-1835 *Alli*
Barry, David Sheldon 1859-1936 *DcNAA*
Barry, Donald Rex 1910- *Au&Wr, WrD 1976*
Barry, E *Alli Sup*
Barry, Earl Farnham *Alli*
Barry, Edward *BiDLA, BiDLA Sup*
Barry, Edward 1759?-1822 *Alli*
Barry, Sir Edward d1776 *Alli*
Barry, Edward Middleton 1830-1880 *Alli Sup*
Barry, Elizabeth 1658-1713 *NewC*
Barry, Ethelred Breeze 1870- *AmA&B, DcAmA, ChPo S2*
Barry, F W *Alli Sup*
Barry, Florence Valentine *ChPo, ChPo S1*
Barry, Garret *Alli*
Barry, George 1747-1804 *Alli*
Barry, Sir Gerald 1898-1968 *LongC*
Barry, Gerald R 1887- *MnBBF*
Barry, Gerry 1913- *AmSCAP 66*
Barry, Girald 1146?-1223? *Alli, DcEnL*
Barry, Giraldus De *NewC*
Barry, Henry *Alli Sup*
Barry, Henry Aloysius d1907 *DcNAA*
Barry, Herbert *Alli Sup*
Barry, Herbert, III 1930- *ConAu 37*
Barry, Hugh Collis 1912- *WrD 1976*
Barry, J B *PoIre*
Barry, J M *Alli*
Barry, Jack *DrAP 1975*
Barry, Jackson G 1926- *ConAu 29*
Barry, James *Alli Sup*
Barry, James 1741-1806 *Alli*
Barry, James, Lord Of Santry 1598-1673 *Alli*
Barry, James Donald 1926- *ConAu 33*
Barry, James E *IlBYP*
Barry, James P 1918- *ConAu 37, WrD 1976*
Barry, Jane 1925- *ConAu 5R, WrD 1976*
Barry, Jerome B 1894-1975 *ConAu 1R, ConAu 61*
Barry, Jocelyn 1925- *ConAu XR*
Barry, John Daniel 1866-1942 *AmA&B, AmLY, BiD&SB, DcAmA, WhWNAA*
Barry, John Melven *BiDLA*
Barry, John Stetson 1819-1872 *Alli Sup, DcAmA, DcNAA*
Barry, John Vincent William 1903- *ConAu 1R*
Barry, John Wolfe *Alli Sup*
Barry, Joseph *Alli Sup*
Barry, Joseph 1828?-1905 *DcNAA*
Barry, Joseph 1917- *ConAu 57*
Barry, Joseph Gayle Hurd 1858-1931 *DcNAA*
Barry, Katharina Watjen 1936- *AuBYP, ChPo, ConAu 9R, IlCB 1966, SmATA 4*
Barry, Kevin M 1932- *AmSCAP 66*
Barry, Lodowick *PoIre*
Barry, Lucy 1934- *ConAu 17R*
Barry, Ludowick *DcEnL*
Barry, M *Alli Sup*
Barry, M A *PoIre*
Barry, M J *Alli*
Barry, M L *Alli Sup*
Barry, Maltman *Alli Sup*
Barry, Margaret 1910- *Au&Wr*
Barry, Mary J 1928- *ConAu 49*
Barry, Michael 1820-1873 *PoIre*
Barry, Michael Joseph 1817-1889 *Alli Sup, ChPo S1, PoIre*
Barry, Noeline 1915- *ConP 1970*
Barry, Patrick *Alli Sup*
Barry, Patrick 1816-1890 *Alli Sup, DcAmA, DcNAA*
Barry, Philip 1896-1949 *AmA&B, CasWL, CatA 1947, CnDAL, CnMD, CnThe, ConAmA, DcLEnL, DcNAA, EvLB, LongC, McGWD, ModAL, ModWD, OxAm, Pen Am, REn, REnAL, REnWD, TwCA, TwCA Sup, TwCW, WebEAL*
Barry, Philip Francis Gould *Alli Sup*
Barry, R Milner- *Alli Sup*
Barry, Raymond Walker 1894- *ConAu P-1*
Barry, Richard Hayes 1881- *AmA&B*
Barry, Richard Hugh 1908- *Au&Wr*

Barry, Robert Everett 1931- *AuBYP, ConAu 5R, IlCB 1966, SmATA 6, WrD 1976*
Barry, Robertine 1866-1910 *DcNAA*
Barry, Spranger 1719-1777 *NewC*
Barry, Spranger 1916- *ConAu XR*
Barry, T A And Patten, B A *Alli Sup*
Barry, Theodore Augustus 1825-1881 *DcNAA*
Barry, Thomas *Alli, BiDLA*
Barry, Thomas De *Alli*
Barry, W *Alli Sup*
Barry, W Keogh *Alli*
Barry, William *Alli Sup*
Barry, William 1805-1885 *DcAmA, DcNAA*
Barry, William 1849- *BbD, PoIre*
Barry, William 1911- *AmSCAP 66*
Barry, William Edward 1846-1932 *DcNAA*
Barry, William F 1849-1930 *CatA 1947*
Barry, William Farquhar 1818-1879 *DcNAA*
Barry, William Francis *Chmbr 3*
Barry, William J *Alli Sup*
Barry, William Jackson 1819?- *Alli Sup*
Barry, William Taylor 1785-1835 *BiDSA*
Barry, William Whittaker *Alli Sup*
Barry, Wolfe *MnBBF*
Barry, Lord Yelverton *Alli*
Barrymore, John 1882-1942 *LongC*
Barrymore, Lionel 1878-1954 *AmSCAP 66, LongC*
Barrymore, Maurice 1847-1905 *LongC*
Barrymore Family *OxAm*
Barsac, Louis *ChPo, LongC*
Barsacq, Andre 1909-1973 *ConAu 41*
Barschak, Erna 1898-1958 *OhA&B*
Barsis, Max 1894?-1973 *ConAu 41*
Barsky, Philip 1914- *AmSCAP 66*
Barsness, Larry 1919- *WhPNW*
Barsotti, Charles 1850-1927 *AmA&B*
Barss, William 1916- *ChPo S1, IlBYP, IlCB 1966*
Barstable, C Francis *Alli Sup*
Barston, John *Alli*
Barstow, Amos C *Alli Sup*
Barstow, C H *Alli Sup*
Barstow, Charles Murray 1810?- *Br&AmS*
Barstow, Mrs. E *Alli Sup*
Barstow, George 1812-1883 *DcNAA*
Barstow, George Eames 1849- *AmLY*
Barstow, Ralph 1884- *WhWNAA*
Barstow, Stan 1928- *Au&Wr, ConAu 1R, ConNov 1972, ConNov 1976, ModBL Sup, NewC, TwCW, WrD 1976*
Barstow, William *Alli Sup*
Bart, Benjamin F 1917- *ConAu 25*
Bart, Jan 1919- *AmSCAP 66*
Bart, Lionel *ConDr*
Bart, Pauline B 1930- *ConAu 53*
Bart, Teddy 1936- *AmSCAP 66*
Bart-Williams, Gaston Nicholas Omoyele 1938- *AfA 1, Au&Wr, ConP 1970*
Bartas, Guillaume DeSalluste Du 1544-1590 *EuA, EvEuW, NewC, REn*
Bartek, Edward J 1921- *ConAu 37, WrD 1976*
Bartel, Roland 1919- *ConAu 17R*
Bartell, Edmund, Jr. *Alli, BiDLA*
Bartell, Ernest 1932- *ConAu 33*
Bartell, Floyd E 1883- *WhWNAA*
Bartelle, John Peter 1858-1946 *OhA&B*
Bartels, Adolf 1862-1945 *OxGer*
Bartels, Robert 1913- *ConAu 13R, WrD 1976*
Bartels, Robert A 1923- *ConAu 1R*
Bartels, Susan Ludvigson 1942- *ConAu 57*
Bartels, Wolfgang Von 1883- *WhLA*
Barten, Harvey H 1933- *ConAu 33*
Barter, A K 1918- *ConAu 57*
Barter, A R 1900- *Au&Wr*
Barter, Arthur Reginald 1900- *WrD 1976*
Barter, Catherine *Alli Sup*
Barter, Charles *Alli, Alli Sup*
Barter, Clement Smith *Alli Sup*
Barter, J *Alli Sup*
Barter, William Brudenell *Alli Sup*
Barter, William George Thomas 1808-1871? *Alli Sup, PoIre*
Barth, Agnar Johannes 1871- *WhLA*
Barth, Alan 1906- *AmA&B, Au&Wr, ConAu 1R*

Barth, Charles P 1895- *ConAu 25*
Barth, Christoph F 1917- *ConAu 29*
Barth, Edna 1914- *ConAu 41, SmATA 7*
Barth, Emil 1900-1958 *EncWL, ModGL, OxGer*
Barth, Hans 1897-1956 *AmSCAP 66*
Barth, Harold Bradshaw 1884- *OhA&B*
Barth, Heinrich 1821-1865 *Alli Sup*
Barth, John 1930- *AmA&B, AmWr, Au&Wr, AuNews 1, AuNews 2, CasWL, ConAu 1R, ConLC 1, ConLC 2, ConLC 3, ConLC 5, ConNov 1972, ConNov 1976, DrAF 1976, EncWL Sup, ModAL, ModAL Sup, OxAm, Pen Am, RAdv 1, TwCW, WebEAL, WhTwL, WorAu, WrD 1976*
Barth, John Robert 1931- *ConAu 29, WrD 1976*
Barth, Karl 1886-1968 *ConAu 25, LongC, OxGer, TwCA Sup*
Barth, Kaspar Von 1587-1658 *OxGer*
Barth, Lois *ConAu XR*
Barth, Lucena Jaeger 1918- *IndAu 1917*
Barth, M And Roger, H *Alli Sup*
Barth, Markus Karl 1915- *ConAu 5R, WrD 1976*
Barth, Roland S 1937- *ConAu 45*
Barthe, Georges Isidore 1834-1900 *BbtC, DcNAA, OxCan*
Barthe, Joseph Guillaume 1818?-1893 *BbtC, DcNAA, OxCan*
Barthe, Ulric 1853-1921 *DcNAA*
Barthel, Ernst *WhLA*
Barthel, Ludwig Friedrich 1898-1962 *CasWL, OxGer*
Barthel, Max 1893- *OxGer*
Barthelemy, Auguste Marseille 1796-1867 *BbD, BiD&SB, EvEuW*
Barthelemy, Jean Jacques 1716-1795 *BiD&SB, DcEuL, EvEuW, OxFr, REn*
Barthelemy, Nicolas 1478-1540? *CasWL*
Barthelemy-Saint-Hilaire, Jules 1805-1895 *BbD, BiD&SB*
Barthelet, A *Alli Sup*
Barthelme, Donald 1931- *DrAF 1976, AmA&B, ConAu 21, ConLC 1, ConLC 2, ConLC 3, ConLC 5, ConLC 6, ConNov 1972, ConNov 1976, ModAL Sup, Pen Am, RAdv 1, SmATA 7, WorAu, WrD 1976*
Barthes, Roland 1915- *CasWL, Pen Eur, WhTwL, WorAu*
Barthet, Armand 1820-1874 *BiD&SB*
Barthlet, J *Alli*
Bartholdi, Frederic Auguste *REn*
Bartholomaeus d1187 *Alli*
Bartholomaeus Angelicus *Alli*
Bartholomaeus Anglicus 1210?- *CasWL, DcEnL, NewC, OxEng*
Bartholomay, Julia A 1923- *ConAu 45*
Bartholomew Anglicus *REn*
Bartholomew, Bishop Of Exeter d1186? *BiB N*
Bartholomew De Glanville *CasWL*
Bartholomew, Saint *NewC, REn*
Bartholomew The Englishman *NewC*
Bartholomew, Mrs. *ChPo S1*
Bartholomew, Anne Charlotte d1862 *DcEnL*
Bartholomew, Annie E *Alli*
Bartholomew, C *Alli Sup*
Bartholomew, Cecilia 1907- *ConAu P-1*
Bartholomew, Charles *Alli Sup*
Bartholomew, Charles L 1869- *ChPo S1*
Bartholomew, Christopher Churchill *Alli Sup*
Bartholomew, Ed 1914- *ConAu 25*
Bartholomew, Edward Fry 1846-1946 *AmLY, DcNAA, WhWNAA*
Bartholomew, Elbert Thomas 1878- *WhWNAA*
Bartholomew, George Kellam 1835-1917 *DcNAA*
Bartholomew, Henry Sager Knapp 1862-1952 *IndAu 1917*
Bartholomew, John *Alli, Alli Sup, BiDLA*
Bartholomew, John Charge *Alli Sup*
Bartholomew, Lucille Keene 1888- *WhWNAA*
Bartholomew, Marshall Moore 1885- *AmSCAP 66*
Bartholomew, Paul Charles 1907- *ConAu 17R, IndAu 1917, OhA&B, WrD 1976*

Bartholomew, Mrs. Valentine *ChPo S2*
Bartholomew, Wallace Edgar 1877-1920 *DcNAA*
Bartholomew, William *Alli*
Bartholow, Roberts 1831-1904 *Alli Sup, DcAmA, DcNAA*
Bartier, Pierre 1945- *ConAu 23*
Bartimeus 1886- *DcLEnL, LongC, NewC, WhLA*
Bartle, George W *Alli Sup*
Bartleet, Samuel Edwin *Alli Sup*
Bartles, Alfred H 1930- *AmSCAP 66*
Bartlet, Richard *Alli*
Bartlet, Vernon 1863- *WhLA*
Bartlet, W S *OxCan*
Bartlet, William *Alli*
Bartlet, William Stoodley 1809-1883 *Alli, CyAL 2, DcNAA*
Bartlett *ChPo*
Bartlett, Mrs. A B *Alli Sup*
Bartlett, A E *Alli Sup*
Bartlett, A Jennie *Alli Sup*
Bartlett, Albert Leroy 1852-1934 *DcNAA*
Bartlett, Alden Eugene 1873- *WhWNAA*
Bartlett, Alfred Darling *Alli Sup*
Bartlett, Alice Elinor 1848-1920 *AmA&B, DcAmA, DcNAA, OhA&B*
Bartlett, Alice Hunt 1870-1949 *AmA&B, ChPo S2, DcNAA, WhWNAA*
Bartlett, Arthur Charles 1901-1964 *AmA&B, WhWNAA*
Bartlett, Barbara R *Alli Sup*
Bartlett, Sir Basil Hardington 1905- *Au&Wr*
Bartlett, Benjamin 1714-1787 *Alli*
Bartlett, Billie *ConAu XR*
Bartlett, Bob 1875-1946 *OxCan*
Bartlett, C *Alli Sup*
Bartlett, C J 1931- *ConAu 17R*
Bartlett, Cecil Richmond *OhA&B*
Bartlett, Charles 1921- *ConAu 29*
Bartlett, Charles C *MnBBF*
Bartlett, Charles Henry 1853-1937 *DcNAA, IndAu 1816*
Bartlett, Charles J 1864- *WhWNAA*
Bartlett, Christopher John 1931- *WrD 1976*
Bartlett, Clarence 1858-1935 *DcNAA*
Bartlett, Dana Prescott 1863-1936 *DcNAA, WhWNAA*
Bartlett, David *ConAu XR*
Bartlett, David Vandewater Golden 1828-1912 *DcNAA*
Bartlett, David W 1828- *Alli, Alli Sup, DcNAA*
Bartlett, E J *Alli Sup*
Bartlett, Edgar E 1856- *WhWNAA*
Bartlett, Edward Everett 1863-1942 *DcNAA*
Bartlett, Edward Payson 1884- *WhWNAA*
Bartlett, Edwards And Peters, John P *Alli Sup*
Bartlett, Edwin Julius 1851-1932 *DcNAA, OhA&B, WhWNAA*
Bartlett, Elisha 1804?-1855 *Alli, ChPo, DcAmA, DcNAA*
Bartlett, Elizabeth 1911- *ConAu 17R, DrAP 1975*
Bartlett, Ellis Ashmead- 1849- *Alli Sup*
Bartlett, Elsa Jaffe 1935- *ConAu 33*
Bartlett, Eric George 1920- *ConAu 5R, WrD 1976*
Bartlett, Ezra A *Alli Sup*
Bartlett, F L *Alli Sup*
Bartlett, Floyd A 1893- *AmSCAP 66*
Bartlett, Frank W 1856-1932 *DcNAA*
Bartlett, Frederic Huntington 1872-1948 *DcNAA*
Bartlett, Frederick Orin 1876- *AmA&B, DcAmA, WhWNAA*
Bartlett, George B *Alli Sup*
Bartlett, George Bradford 1832-1896 *ChPo, ChPo S1, DcNAA*
Bartlett, George Miller 1873-1936 *DcNAA, WhWNAA*
Bartlett, Gerald 1935- *ConAu 21*
Bartlett, Gertrude *DcNAA*
Bartlett, H Critchett *Alli Sup*
Bartlett, Helen 1884-1925 *DcNAA*
Bartlett, I J *ChPo S2*
Bartlett, Irving H 1923- *ConAu 23*
Bartlett, J *Alli*

Bartlett, J Allen *MnBBF*
Bartlett, J G *ChPo S2*
Bartlett, James A *ChPo*
Bartlett, James Arthur Stanhope 1915- *Au&Wr*
Bartlett, John 1820-1905 *Alli, Alli Sup, AmA, AmA&B, BiD&SB, ChPo, CnDAL, DcAmA, DcNAA, EvLB, LongC, OxAm, REn, REnAL*
Bartlett, John 1828- *Alli Sup*
Bartlett, John Pemberton *Alli Sup*
Bartlett, John Russell 1805-1886 *Alli, Alli Sup, AmA, AmA&B, ArizL, BiD&SB, CyAL 2, DcAmA, DcEnL, DcNAA*
Bartlett, John Spencer *Alli Sup*
Bartlett, John Thomas 1892-1947 *DcNAA*
Bartlett, Joseph 1762?-1827 *Alli, AmA&B, CyAL 1, DcAmA, DcNAA*
Bartlett, Joseph 1872-1927 *DcNAA*
Bartlett, Josiah 1759-1820 *Alli, Alli Sup*
Bartlett, Kathleen *ConAu XR*
Bartlett, L I *ChPo*
Bartlett, L L *ChPo*
Bartlett, Lanier 1879- *WhWNAA*
Bartlett, Lester William 1883- *WhWNAA*
Bartlett, Levi *Alli Sup*
Bartlett, Margaret Abbot 1892- *ChPo S1*
Bartlett, Margaret Farrington 1896- *ConAu 5R*
Bartlett, Margaret O *ChPo S2*
Bartlett, Marie 1918- *ConAu 21*
Bartlett, Maro Loomis 1847-1919 *DcNAA*
Bartlett, Mary Belle *Alli Sup*
Bartlett, Mary C *ChPo*
Bartlett, Nancy *AmA&B, WhWNAA*
Bartlett, Nancy W 1913-1972 *ConAu 23, ConAu 41*
Bartlett, Napier 1836-1877 *BiDSA, DcNAA*
Bartlett, Norman 1908- *Au&Wr*
Bartlett, Paul 1909- *ConAu 17*
Bartlett, Paul Alexander *DrAF 1976*
Bartlett, Philip A *ConAu 19, SmATA 1*
Bartlett, Phyliss *ChPo*
Bartlett, Phyllis 1908?-1973 *ConAu 41*
Bartlett, Richard A 1920- *ConAu 5R*
Bartlett, Robert Abram 1875-1946 *AmA&B, DcNAA*
Bartlett, Robert Edward *Alli Sup*
Bartlett, Robert Merrill 1899- *AmA&B, ConAu 5R, IndAu 1917*
Bartlett, Ruhl J 1897- *ConAu P-1*
Bartlett, Ruth *ConAu 17R*
Bartlett, Ruth Fitch *AnMV 1926*
Bartlett, Miss S F *ChPo*
Bartlett, S P *ChPo*
Bartlett, S T *ChPo*
Bartlett, Samuel Colcord 1817-1898 *Alli Sup, BiD&SB, DcAmA, DcNAA*
Bartlett, Stanley Foss 1902-1937 *DcNAA*
Bartlett, Thomas 1789- *DcEnL*
Bartlett, Mrs. Tom B *TexWr*
Bartlett, Truman Howe 1835-1923 *Alli Sup, DcNAA*
Bartlett, Vernon 1894- *Au&Wr, ConAu 61, LongC, NewC, TwCA, TwCA Sup, WhLA, WrD 1976*
Bartlett, W C *Alli Sup*
Bartlett, W H *BbtC*
Bartlett, W P 1855- *WhWNAA*
Bartlett, Wilfred H *ChPo S2*
Bartlett, Willard W 1884- *OhA&B*
Bartlett, William Abraham *Alli Sup*
Bartlett, William And Chapman, Henry *Alli Sup*
Bartlett, William Chambers 1839-1908 *DcNAA*
Bartlett, William Chauncey 1818-1907 *DcNAA*
Bartlett, William H C 1804- *Alli*
Bartlett, William Henry *OxCan*
Bartlett, William Henry d1904 *DcNAA*
Bartlett, William Henry 1809-1854 *Alli, DcEnL*
Bartlett, William Holms Chambers 1804?-1893 *DcAmA, DcNAA*
Bartlett, William Warren 1861-1893 *DcNAA*
Bartley, Mrs. *PoIre*
Bartley, Azie S 1877- *WhWNAA*
Bartley, Elias Hudson 1849-1937 *Alli Sup, DcAmA, DcNAA, WhWNAA*
Bartley, George C T *Alli Sup*
Bartley, J D *ChPo S1*
Bartley, James Avis 1830- *Alli Sup, BiDSA,*

ChPo S1, DcNAA
Bartley, Nalbro 1888- *AmA&B*
Bartley, Nehemiah *Alli, BiDLA*
Bartley, O W *Alli, BiDLA, BiDLA Sup*
Bartley, Robert T Hawley *Alli Sup*
Bartley, Theodore B *Alli Sup*
Bartley, Thomas Welles 1812-1885 *OhA&B*
Bartley, William Warren, III 1934- *ConAu 37, WrD 1976*
Bartlow, John Davis 1887-1954 *IndAu 1917*
Bartmann, Bernhard 1860- *WhLA*
Barto, Agnita L'vovna *ChPo, ChPo S1*
Bartocci, Gianni 1925- *ConAu 23*
Bartok, Bela 1881-1945 *AmSCAP 66, AtlBL, REn*
Bartok, Ludwig Von 1851- *BiD&SB*
Bartol, Cyrus Augustus 1813-1900 *Alli, Alli Sup, BbD, BiD&SB, ChPo S1, CyAL 2, DcAmA, DcNAA*
Bartol, William Cyrus 1847-1940 *DcNAA*
Bartole 1314-1357 *OxFr*
Bartoli, Adolfo 1833-1894 *BiD&SB*
Bartoli, Daniello 1608-1685 *CasWL*
Bartoli Natinguerra, Amerigo 1890- *WhGrA*
Bartolini, Louisa Grace *PoIre*
Bartolini, Luigi 1892- *EncWL*
Bartolome De Las Casas *EuA*
Bartolommeo, Fra 1472?-1517 *AtlBL, ChPo, REn*
Bartolozzi, Francesco 1725-1815 *BkIE*
Bartolus 1313?-1357 *DcEuL, OxFr*
Barton *Alli, MnBBF*
Barton, A S *ChPo*
Barton, Adelia M *ChPo S2*
Barton, Agnes *Alli Sup*
Barton, Alan 1913- *Au&Wr*
Barton, Albert Olaus 1871-1947 *DcNAA*
Barton, Allen H 1924- *ConAu 25*
Barton, Andrew *AmA&B, NewC*
Barton, Annie M *Alli Sup, ChPo S1*
Barton, Ardelia Maria 1843- *Alli Sup*
Barton, Arthur Willis 1873- *WhWNAA*
Barlow, Benjamin Smith 1766-1815 *Alli, AmA, BiDLA, CyAL 1, DcAmA, DcNAA, REnAL*
Barton, Benjamin Thomas 1840- *Alli Sup*
Barton, Bernard 1784-1849 *Alli, BiD&SB, BrAu 19, CasWL, ChPo, ChPo S1, ChPo S2, Chmbr 3, DcEnL, DcLEnL, EvLB, NewC, REn*
Barton, Betty *ChPo*
Barton, Bruce 1886-1967 *AmA&B, OhA&B, WhWNAA*
Barton, Byron 1930- *ConAu 57, SmATA 9*
Barton, Carl *OxCan Sup*
Barton, Charles *Alli, BiDLA*
Barton, Clara Harlowe 1821-1912 *AmA&B, DcNAA, REn, REnAL*
Barton, Cutts *Alli*
Barton, David *Alli*
Barton, Derek 1912- *Au&Wr*
Barton, Donald Clinton 1899- *TexWr*
Barton, Sir Dunbar Plunket 1853- *WhLA*
Barton, Eda 1908- *Au&Wr*
Barton, Edward *Alli*
Barton, Elizabeth 1506?-1534 *NewC*
Barton, Fanny M *Alli Sup, ChPo*
Barton, Frank Townend 1864- *Br&AmS*
Barton, Fred Bushnell 1891- *OhA&B*
Barton, George 1866-1940 *AmA&B, CatA 1947, DcNAA*
Barton, George Aaron 1859-1942 *AmA&B, DcNAA, WhWNAA*
Barton, George Burnett 1836-1901 *Alli Sup, DcLEnL*
Barton, George Elliott *Alli Sup*
Barton, George Hunt 1852- *WhWNAA*
Barton, Henry *Alli*
Barton, Humphrey 1900- *ConAu 19*
Barton, J A G *Alli Sup*
Barton, J King *BbtC*
Barton, James *Alli, BiDLA*
Barton, James Levi 1855-1936 *AmLY, DcNAA, WhWNAA*
Barton, Jerome *Alli Sup*
Barton, Joan 1908- *ChPo S2*
Barton, John *Alli, Alli Sup*
Barton, John Kellock *Alli Sup*

Barton, John Kennedy 1853-1921 *DcNAA*
Barton, John Mackintosh Tilney 1898- *CatA 1947, ConAu P-1*
Barton, John P *ChPo*
Barton, K *Alli Sup*
Barton, K C *Alli Sup*
Barton, Lucy *Alli, ChPo S1*
Barton, Margaret D 1902- *ConAu P-1*
Barton, Marie *TexWr, WhWNAA*
Barton, Mary Neill 1899- *ConAu 19*
Barton, May Hollis *ConAu 19, SmATA 1*
Barton, Nicholas J 1935- *Au&Wr*
Barton, Olive Roberts 1880-1957 *AmA&B, WhWNAA*
Barton, Otis 1899- *Au&Wr*
Barton, Philip *Alli*
Barton, R C *ChPo*
Barton, Ralph 1891-1931 *AmA&B, DcNAA*
Barton, Richard *Alli, PoIre*
Barton, Richard F 1924- *ConAu 61*
Barton, Robert T *Alli Sup*
Barton, Robert Thomas 1842-1917 *DcNAA*
Barton, S W *ConAu 41*
Barton, Samuel *Alli, Alli Sup*
Barton, Samuel Goodwin 1882- *WhWNAA*
Barton, Samuel Marx 1859-1926 *BiDSA, DcNAA*
Barton, Thomas *Alli*
Barton, Thomas 1730-1780 *Alli*
Barton, Thomas Frank 1905- *ConAu 45*
Barton, Thomas H 1828-1911 *OhA&B*
Barton, V Wayne *ConAu 1R*
Barton, Walter Elbert 1886- *IndAu 1917*
Barton, Weldon V 1938- *ConAu 21*
Barton, Wilfred Mason 1871-1930 *DcNAA, WhWNAA*
Barton, William *Alli, CyAL 1*
Barton, William d1817 *DcNAA*
Barton, William 1603?-1678 *PoIre*
Barton, William 1950- *ConAu 45*
Barton, William Eleazar 1861-1930 *AmA&B, AmLY, BiD&SB, ChPo S1, DcAmA, DcNAA, OhA&B, REnAL, WhWNAA*
Barton, William Gardner *ChPo S1*
Barton, William Henry, Jr. 1893-1944 *DcNAA, WhWNAA*
Barton, William Pawl Crillon 1786-1856 *Alli*
Barton, William Paul Crillon 1786-1856 *DcAmA, DcNAA*
Bartos-Hoeppner, Barbara 1923- *Au&Wr, ConAu 25, SmATA 5*
Bartow, Edward 1870- *WhWNAA*
Bartow, Evelyn Pierrepont 1846?-1902 *Alli Sup, DcNAA*
Bartram *Alli*
Bartram, Mister *BiDLA*
Bartram, G B *MnBBF*
Bartram, George *ChPo S1*
Bartram, Isaac *Alli*
Bartram, John 1699-1777 *Alli, AmA, AmA&B, BiD&SB, CyAL 1, DcAmA, DcNAA, OxAm, OxCan, REnAL*
Bartram, Moses *Alli*
Bartram, Richard *Alli Sup*
Bartram, William 1739-1823 *Alli, AmA, AmA&B, BiDLA, BiDSA, CasWL, CyAL 1, DcAmA, DcLEnL, DcNAA, OxAm, OxEng, Pen Am, REn, REnAL*
Bartran, Margaret 1910- *ConAu 29*
Bartrina, Joaquin Maria 1850-1880 *CasWL, CIDMEuL, EvEuW*
Bartrum, Douglas Albert 1907- *Au&Wr, ConAu 9R*
Bartrum, Edward *Alli Sup*
Bartrum, John Arthur 1885- *WhLA*
Bartrum, Katherine Mary *Alli Sup*
Bartsch, Jochen 1906- *IIBYP, IlCB 1966*
Bartsch, Paul 1871- *WhWNAA*
Bartsch, Rudolf Hans 1873-1952 *EvEuW, OxGer*
Bartscht, Waltraud 1924- *ConAu 41*
Bartu, Robert, Earl Of Lindsay *Alli*
Barty, James S *Alli Sup*
Bartz, Albert E 1933- *ConAu 23, WrD 1976*
Baruch *NewC*
Baruch, Bernard M 1870-1965 *AmA&B, REn, REnAL*

Baruch, Dorothy Walter 1899- *ChPo, St&VC, AmA&B*
Baruch, Lob *OxGer*
Baruch, Moyses *OxGer*
Baruch, Ruth-Marion 1922- *ConAu 29*
Baruch, Simon 1840-1921 *DcNAA*
Barudi, Mahmud Sami Al- 1839-1904 *CasWL, DcOrL 3*
Baruh, Raphael *Alli*
Barus, Carl 1856-1935 *DcNAA, WhWNAA*
Barville, John *Alli*
Barwell, Mrs. *Alli*
Barwell, Arthur Henry Sauxay *Alli Sup*
Barwell, Harold Shuttleworth 1875- *WhLA*
Barwell, Peggy *ChPo S1*
Barwell, Richard *Alli, Alli Sup*
Barwick, Alfred *Alli Sup*
Barwick, Edward *Alli, BiDLA Sup*
Barwick, George Frederick 1853- *WhLA*
Barwick, Henry *Alli, BiDLA*
Barwick, Humphrey *Alli*
Barwick, John 1612-1664 *Alli*
Barwick, Peter 1619-1705? *Alli*
Barwick, Steven 1921- *ConAu 13R*
Barwick, Walter d1906 *DcNAA*
Barwis, Jackson *Alli*
Barwis, John *Alli, BiDLA*
Barzanti, Sergio 1925- *ConAu 17R*
Barzelay, Walter Moshe 1924- *WrD 1976*
Barzini, Luigi 1908- *ConAu 13R, WorAu*
Barzman, Ben 1912- *Au&Wr*
Barzun, Henri-Martin 1881- *OxFr*
Barzun, Jacques 1907- *AmA&B, Au&Wr, ConAu 61, EncM&D, OxAm, RAdv 1, REn, REnAL, TwCA, TwCA Sup, WrD 1976*
Bas, Joe 1932- *ConAu 53*
Bas, William 1583?-1653? *EvLB, NewC*
Basanavicius, Jonas 1851-1927 *CasWL*
Basanier, M *BiDSA*
Basart, Ann Phillips 1931- *ConAu 1R*
Basavanna *DcOrL 2*
Basave, Agustin 1886- *WhWNAA*
Basche, James 1926- *ConAu 29*
Baschin, Otto 1865- *WhLA*
Bascom, Florence 1862-1945 *DcNAA, WhWNAA*
Bascom, Henry Bidleman 1796-1850 *Alli, BiDSA, DcAmA, DcNAA, OhA&B*
Bascom, John 1827-1911 *Alli Sup, AmA, AmA&B, BiD&SB, CyAL 1, DcAmA, DcEnL, DcNAA*
Bascom, Robert O 1855-1909 *DcNAA*
Bascom, Willard N 1916- *ConAu 1R*
Bascom, William Russel 1912- *ConAu 17R, WrD 1976*
Bascome, E *Alli*
Bascome, Edward *Alli Sup*
Basdekis, Demetrios 1930- *ConAu 25*
Base, A H *MnBBF*
Base, Daniel 1869-1926 *DcNAA*
Basedow, Johann Bernhardt 1723-1790 *BiD&SB, DcEuL, OxGer*
Baseley, Mrs. *Alli Sup*
Baseley, J *Alli*
Baseley, Thomas *Alli, BiDLA*
Basford, James Lendall *Alli Sup*
Basford-De-Wilson *Alli Sup*
Bash, Bertha Runkle *WhWNAA*
Bash, Ewald 1924- *IndAu 1917*
Bash, Mrs. Isadore S *Alli Sup*
Basham, William Richard 1804-1877 *Alli Sup*
Bashby, Henry Jeffreys *Alli Sup*
Basheer *DcOrL 2*
Basheikh Husein, Ahmad 1909-1961 *CasWL*
Bashevis, Isaac *ConAu XR, SmATA 3*
Bashford, Coles *Alli Sup*
Bashford, Sir Henry Howarth 1880-1961 *ChPo, ChPo S1, LongC, NewC, WhLA*
Bashford, Herbert 1871-1928 *AmLY, ChPo, ChPo S2, DcAmA, DcNAA*
Bashford, James Whitford 1842?-1919 *DcAmA, DcNAA*
Bashford, John L *Alli Sup*
Bashforth, Francis *Alli Sup*
Bashforth, G Reginald 1903- *Au&Wr*
Bashira, Damali 1951- *ConAu 57*
Bashirov, Gomar 1901- *DcOrL 3*

Batcheller, John M 1918- *ConAu 45*
Batcheller, Tryphosa Bates 1878-1952 *AmA&B*
Batchellor, Albert Stillman 1850-1913 *DcNAA*
Batchelor, Alfred Francis 1901- *Au&Wr*
Batchelor, George 1836-1923 *Alli Sup, AmLY, DcAmA, DcNAA*
Batchelor, George Keith 1920- *WrD 1976*
Batchelor, Henry *Alli Sup*
Batchelor, Jean M *ChPo S1*
Batchelor, John *BiDLA*
Batchelor, John 1942- *WrD 1976*
Batchelor, John M *Alli Sup*
Batchelor, Joseph Alexander 1909- *IndAu 1917*
Batchelor, Leon Dexter 1884- *WhWNAA*
Batchelor, Mary Kathleen 1927- *Au&Wr*
Batchelor, Paula Vivien *Au&Wr*
Batchelor, Rea *ConAu XR*
Batchelor, Richard A C *MnBBF*
Batchelor, T *BiDLA*
Batchelor, Thomas *Alli, BiDLA*
Batchelour, William *Alli Sup*
Batchilor, John *Alli*
Batdorf, John William 1852- *DcNAA*
Bate, Charles Spence 1819- *Alli Sup*
Bate, Edward *Alli*
Bate, Francis *Alli Sup*
Bate, George *Alli, Alli Sup*
Bate, George 1608-1668 *Alli*
Bate, Henry *Alli, BiDLA*
Bate, Henry 1846- *Alli Sup*
Bate, James *Alli*
Bate, James 1703-1755 *Alli*
Bate, John *Alli, Alli Sup*
Bate, John d1429 *Alli*
Bate, John Drew *Alli Sup*
Bate, Julius 1711?-1771? *Alli*
Bate, Ludwig 1892- *WhLA*
Bate, Norman Arthur 1916- *AuBYP, ConAu 1R, IlCB 1956, SmATA 5, WrD 1976*
Bate, R B *Alli*
Bate, Randall *Alli*
Bate, Richard Alexander 1871- *WhWNAA*
Bate, Sam 1907?- *Au&Wr, WrD 1976*
Bate, Thomas *Alli*
Bate, Walter Jackson 1918- *AmA&B, ConAu 5R, OxAm, WorAu*
Bate, William Brimage 1826-1905 *BiDSA*
Bate, William Stivers *ChPo*
Batecumbe, William *Alli*
Bateham, J C *ChPo*
Bateman, Lord *Alli Sup*
Bateman, A W *Alli*
Bateman, Alan M *WhWNAA*
Bateman, Barbara Dee 1933- *ConAu 41*
Bateman, Edmund *Alli*
Bateman, Frederick *Alli Sup, MnBBF*
Bateman, Frederick 1909- *Au&Wr, BiDPar*
Bateman, H *MnBBF*
Bateman, H M *ChPo*
Bateman, Harry 1882-1946 *DcNAA, WhWNAA*
Bateman, Henry *Alli Sup, ChPo, ChPo S1, PoCh*
Bateman, Henry Mayo 1887- *IlCB 1945*
Bateman, Mrs. J C *Alli Sup*
Bateman, James *Alli, Alli Sup*
Bateman, John *Alli Sup, ChPo*
Bateman, John Frederic Latrobe- 1810- *Alli Sup*
Bateman, John H 1892- *WhWNAA*
Bateman, Joseph *Alli*
Bateman, Josiah *Alli, Alli Sup*
Bateman, Newton 1822-1897 *Alli Sup, DcNAA*
Bateman, R T *Alli*
Bateman, Robert 1922- *Au&Wr, ConAu 5R*
Bateman, Sidney Frances 1823-1881 *AmA, AmA&B, DcNAA, OxAm, REnAL*
Bateman, Stephen *Alli*
Bateman, Stringer *ChPo S1*
Bateman, Thomas *Alli, BiDLA, BiDLA Sup*
Bateman, Thomas 1778-1821 *Alli*
Bateman, Thomas 1821-1861 *Alli Sup*
Bateman, Walter L 1916- *ConAu 29*
Bateman, William Fairbairn Latrobe *Alli Sup*
Bateman, William O *Alli Sup, DcNAA*
Baten, Anderson Monroe 1888-1943 *AmA&B,*

DcNAA, TexWr, WhWNAA
Baten, Charles Edwin 1890- *WhWNAA*
Baten, William Dowell 1892- *WhWNAA*
Bates *Alli*
Bates, Ada Board *TexWr*
Bates, Alan 1929- *Au&Wr, WrD 1976*
Bates, Alan Lawrence 1923- *ConAu 17R*
Bates, Albert Carlos 1865- *WhWNAA*
Bates, Antony *ChPo S1*
Bates, Arlo 1850-1918 *Alli Sup, AmA, AmA&B, BbD, BiD&SB, CarSB, ChPo, DcAmA, DcBiA, DcNAA, OxAm, REnAL*
Bates, Arthenia J 1920- *BlkAW, ConAu 57*
Bates, Barbara S 1919- *ConAu 17R*
Bates, Cadwallader John *Alli Sup*
Bates, Carlos Glazier 1885- *WhWNAA*
Bates, Charles Austin 1866- *IndAu 1917*
Bates, Charlotte Fiske 1838-1916 *Alli Sup, AmA&B, BiD&SB, ChPo, DcAmA, DcNAA*
Bates, Clara Doty 1838-1895 *Alli Sup, AmA&B, BiD&SB, ChPo, ChPo S1, ChPo S2, DcAmA, DcNAA*
Bates, Clement 1845-1931 *Alli Sup, DcNAA, WhWNAA*
Bates, Mrs. D B *Alli Sup*
Bates, Daisey *LivBA*
Bates, Daniel M 1849?-1899 *Alli Sup, DcAmA*
Bates, Darrell 1913- *Au&Wr, ConAu P-1, WrD 1976*
Bates, David 1810?-1870 *Alli, Alli Sup, AmA&B, ChPo, DcAmA, DcNAA*
Bates, David Homer 1837?-1926 *DcNAA, OhA&B*
Bates, David Robert 1916- *Au&Wr*
Bates, Dewey 1851-1899 *ChPo S1*
Bates, E Katharine *Alli Sup*
Bates, E P *Alli Sup*
Bates, Eleanor W F *ChPo*
Bates, Elisha 1779?-1861 *Alli, OhA&B*
Bates, Ely *Alli, BiDLA Sup*
Bates, Ernest Sutherland 1879-1939 *AmA&B, DcNAA, OhA&B, OxAm, REnAL, TwCA*
Bates, Fanny B *Alli Sup*
Bates, Fanny D *Alli Sup*
Bates, Fletcher *ChPo*
Bates, Frank Amasa 1858-1915 *DcNAA*
Bates, Frank Green *DcAmA*
Bates, Frank Greene 1868- *IndAu 1816*
Bates, Frederick John 1877- *WhWNAA*
Bates, G W *Alli Sup*
Bates, George Ferne *Alli*
Bates, George H *Alli Sup*
Bates, Gilbert H *Alli Sup*
Bates, Gordon *CarSB*
Bates, H E 1905-1974 *ConAu 45, ConNov 1972, EncWL, LongC, ModBL, NewC, Pen Eng, REn, TwCW, WhTwL*
Bates, H E ALSO Bates, Herbert Ernest
Bates, Harriet Leonora 1856-1886 *Alli Sup, AmA&B, BiD&SB, CarSB, DcAmA, DcNAA*
Bates, Henry Walter 1825-1892 *Alli Sup, BrAu 19, NewC, OxEng*
Bates, Herbert 1868-1929 *AmA&B, DcAmA, DcNAA*
Bates, Herbert Ernest 1905- *Au&Wr, CasWL, ChPo, ChPo S1, DcLEnL, EvLB, TwCA, TwCA Sup*
Bates, Herbert Ernest ALSO Bates, H E
Bates, J *Alli*
Bates, J C *Alli Sup*
Bates, J Leonard 1919- *ConAu 13R*
Bates, James Arthur 1926- *Au&Wr, WrD 1976*
Bates, James Hale 1826-1901 *DcNAA*
Bates, James L *Alli Sup*
Bates, James Lawrence 1815-1890 *OhA&B*
Bates, Jerome E 1917- *ConAu 17R*
Bates, Jerome Paine 1837-1915 *DcNAA*
Bates, Joah 1740-1799 *Alli*
Bates, John *Alli, PoIre*
Bates, John M 1846- *WhWNAA*
Bates, Joseph 1792-1872 *DcNAA*
Bates, Joseph Clement 1836-1913 *DcNAA*
Bates, Josephine W *Alli Sup, DcAmA*

Bates, Katharine Lee 1859-1929 *Alli Sup, AmA&B, AmLY, AnMV 1926, BiD&SB, CarSB, ChPo, ChPo S1, ChPo S2, CnDAL, DcAmA, DcNAA, EvLB, JBA 1934, OxAm, REnAL, TwCA, TwCA Sup, TwCW, WhWNAA*
Bates, Kenneth Francis 1904- *ConAu P-1*
Bates, Leo *ChPo*
Bates, Lieutenant *MnBBF*
Bates, Lindell Theodore 1890-1937 *DcNAA*
Bates, Mrs. Lindon *DcAmA*
Bates, Lindon Wallace 1858-1924 *DcNAA*
Bates, Lindon Wallace 1883-1915 *DcNAA*
Bates, Lizzie *Alli Sup*
Bates, Lloyd Vernon 1909- *Au&Wr*
Bates, Lois *ChPo*
Bates, Mrs. M E C *ChPo, ChPo S1*
Bates, Margaret Holmes Ernsperger 1844-1927 *AmLY, IndAu 1816, OhA&B*
Bates, Margaret J 1918- *ConAu 17R*
Bates, Margret Holmes 1844-1927 *AmA&B, DcAmA, DcNAA*
Bates, Marston 1906-1974 *AmA&B, ConAu 5R, ConAu 49*
Bates, Miner Searle 1897- *OhA&B*
Bates, Morgan 1848-1902 *DcAmA, DcNAA*
Bates, Myrtle *BlkAW*
Bates, Newton W *BiDSA*
Bates, Ola Aniese *TexWr*
Bates, Oric 1883-1918 *AmLY, DcNAA*
Bates, Paul A 1920- *ConAu 37*
Bates, Peter Watson 1920- *Au&Wr, WrD 1976*
Bates, Phaon Hilborn 1879- *WhWNAA*
Bates, Miss R *Alli Sup*
Bates, Ralph 1899- *DcLEnL, LongC, ModBL, Pen Eng, REn, TwCA, TwCA Sup, TwCW*
Bates, Ralph Orr 1847-1909 *OhA&B*
Bates, Ralph Samuel 1906- *ConAu 1R, WrD 1976*
Bates, Robert Chapman 1901-1942 *DcNAA*
Bates, Ronald Gordon 1924- *CanWr, ConAu 25, ConP 1970, OxCan, OxCan Sup*
Bates, Samuel Austin 1822-1897 *DcNAA*
Bates, Samuel Penniman 1827-1902 *Alli Sup, DcAmA, DcNAA*
Bates, Sarah B *Alli Sup*
Bates, Scott 1923- *ConAu 49, DrAP 1975*
Bates, Stockton *Alli Sup*
Bates, Sylvia Chatfield *AmA&B, AmNov*
Bates, Thomas *Alli, Alli Sup, BiDLA*
Bates, Timothy M 1946- *ConAu 53*
Bates, Walter 1760-1842 *AmA&B, DcNAA, OxCan*
Bates, William *Alli, Alli Sup, DcEnL*
Bates, William d1884 *ChPo S2*
Bates, William 1625-1699 *Alli*
Bates, William Henry 1840-1924 *DcNAA*
Bates, William Horatio 1860-1931 *DcNAA*
Bates, William Nickerson 1867-1949 *AmA&B, DcNAA, WhWNAA*
Bates, William Oscar 1852-1924 *AmLY, DcNAA, IndAu 1816*
Bates, William Wallace 1827-1912 *DcAmA, DcNAA*
Bateson, Charles Henry 1903- *Au&Wr*
Bateson, Frederick Wilse 1901- *Au&Wr, ConAu 5R, DcLEnL, ModBL, WorAu, WrD 1976*
Bateson, Gregory 1904- *AmA&B, ConAu 41, WrD 1976*
Bateson, Peter *Alli*
Bateson, Thomas *Alli*
Bateson-Wright *Alli Sup*
Batey, Richard 1933- *ConAu 33*
Bath, Earl Of *Alli*
Bath, Marquis Of *Alli Sup*
Bath, Cyril John 1890- *OhA&B*
Bath, Philip Ernest 1898- *Au&Wr, ConAu P-1*
Bath, Robert *Alli, BiDLA*
Bath, W Harcourt *Alli Sup*
Bath And Wells, Bishop Of *BiDLA*
Batham, Lucy *Alli Sup*
Bathe, Anthony *Alli Sup*
Bathe, William 1564-1614 *Alli*
Bather, Charles *Alli Sup*

Bather, Edward 1779-1847 *Alli*
Bather, Francis Arthur 1863- *WhLA*
Bather, Leslie 1930- *Au&Wr*
Bather, Lucy Elizabeth 1836-1864 *Alli Sup*
Bathgate, Alexander *Alli Sup*
Bathgate, Alexander W *ChPo*
Bathgate, John *Alli Sup*
Bathgate, William *Alli Sup*
Bathhurst, Henry *BiDLA*
Bathie, Arch *Alli*
Bathke, Edwin A 1936- *ConAu 57*
Bathke, Nancy E 1938- *ConAu 57*
Batho, Edith Clara 1895- *Au&Wr, ConAu P-1, WrD 1976*
Bathos, Robert L *Alli Sup*
Bathurst, Earl 1864-1943 *Br&AmS, WhLA*
Bathurst, Charles *Alli Sup*
Bathurst, Henry *Alli Sup, BiDLA Sup*
Bathurst, Henry 1744-1837 *Alli*
Bathurst, Henry, Earl 1714-1794 *Alli*
Bathurst, Maurice Edward 1913- *Au&Wr*
Bathurst, Ralph 1620-1704 *Alli*
Bathurst, Richard *DcEnL*
Bathurst, Selina *Alli Sup*
Bathurst, Theodore *Alli*
Bathurst, William Hiley 1796-1877 *Alli Sup, ChPo S1*
Batiffol, Pierre Henri 1861- *WhLA*
Batikuling *DcOrL 2*
Batilliat, Marcel 1871- *WhLA*
Batilo *DcSpL*
Batipps, Percy Oliver *BlkAW*
Batiray 1832-1910 *DcOrL 3*
Batki, John 1942- *ConAu 45, DrAF 1976, DrAP 1975*
Batkins, Jefferson Scattering *Alli Sup*
Batley, Samuel *Alli*
Batman, Stephen 1537-1587 *Alli, DcEnL*
Batmanson, John d1531 *Alli*
Batson, Alfred 1900- *CanNov, OxCan*
Batson, Edward 1906- *WrD 1976*
Batson, George 1918- *Au&Wr, ConAu 33*
Batson, Larry 1930- *ConAu 57*
Batson, Peter *Alli*
Batson, William Howard 1881- *WhWNAA*
Batt, C W *Alli*
Batt, Ethel D *ChPo S1*
Batt, Michael *Alli*
Batt, William *Alli*
Batt, William 1744-1812 *Alli*
Battaglia, Aurelius *IlBYP*
Battaglia, Elio Lee 1928- *ConAu 1R*
Battalia, O William 1928- *ConAu 45*
Battan, Louis J 1923- *ConAu 13R*
Battcock, Gregory 1937- *ConAu 23, WrD 1976*
Batte, Lelia McAnally *ChPo S2*
Battel, Andrew *Alli*
Battell, Joseph 1839-1915 *DcNAA*
Battell, Ralph *Alli*
Battelle, Adah Fairbanks *WhWNAA*
Battely, John 1647-1708 *Alli*
Battely, Nicholas *Alli*
Batten, Edmund Chisholm- 1817- *Alli Sup*
Batten, Harry Mortimer 1888- *MnBBF, WhCL, WhLA*
Batten, Jack 1932- *ConAu 49, OxCan Sup*
Batten, James William 1919- *ConAu 33, WrD 1976*
Batten, Jean Gardner 1909- *WrD 1976*
Batten, John, Jr. 1841- *Alli Sup*
Batten, John M *Alli Sup*
Batten, John Mullin 1837-1916 *DcNAA*
Batten, Joyce Mortimer *ConAu XR*
Batten, L H, Jr. *Alli Sup*
Batten, Lindsey Willett 1889- *Au&Wr*
Batten, Loring Woart 1859-1946 *AmA&B, DcNAA, WhWNAA*
Batten, Mary 1937- *ConAu 41, SmATA 5*
Batten, Peter W 1893- *MnBBF*
Batten, Roger Lyman 1923- *IndAu 1917*
Batten, Samuel Zane 1859-1925 *DcNAA*
Batten, Thomas Reginald 1904- *Au&Wr, ConAu 13R, WrD 1976*
Battenhall, Jesse Park 1851-1891 *DcAmA*
Battenhouse, Henry Martin 1885-1960 *AmA&B*
Battenhouse, Roy W 1912- *ConAu 13R, WrD 1976*

Batterfield, R *Alli*
Battersby, Mrs. *Alli Sup, ChPo S1, ChPo S2*
Battersby, C Maud *PoIre*
Battersby, Caryl James *ChPo S2*
Battersby, Charles *Alli Sup*
Battersby, Hannah S *Alli Sup, PoIre*
Battersby, Henry Francis Prevost 1862- *PoIre*
Battersby, I C *Alli Sup*
Battersby, James L 1936- *ConAu 41*
Battersby, John *Alli, Alli Sup, PoIre*
Battersby, Sydney Harold 1914- *Au&Wr*
Battersby, T Preston 1856- *Alli Sup, WhLA*
Battersby, T S Frank *Alli Sup*
Battersby, Thomas Dundas Harford *Alli Sup*
Battersby, William J d1873 *PoIre*
Battersby, William John 1904- *Au&Wr, BkC 6, ConAu 5R*
Battershall, Fletcher Williams 1866-1929 *DcAmA, DcNAA*
Battershall, Jesse Park 1851-1891 *Alli Sup, DcNAA*
Battershall, Walton Wesley 1840-1920 *DcAmA, DcNAA*
Battersie, John *Alli*
Batterson, Hermon Griswold 1827-1903 *Alli Sup, DcAmA, DcNAA*
Batterson, James Goodwin 1823-1901 *DcNAA*
Batteson, Philip *Alli*
Battestin, Martin Carey 1930- *ConAu 13R, WrD 1976*
Battey, Robert 1828- *BiDSA*
Battey, Sallie J *Alli Sup*
Battey, Sallie J H *LivFWS*
Battey, Thomas C *Alli Sup*
Battey, Thomas C 1851?- *DcNAA*
Battie, William *Alli*
Battier, Henrietta d1794 *PoIre*
Battin, R Ray 1925- *ConAu 9R*
Battin, William 1832- *DcNAA*
Batting, John *Alli*
Battis, Emery John 1915- *ConAu 1R*
Battiscombe, Esther Georgina 1905- *Au&Wr, ConAu P-1, WrD 1976*
Battishill, Jonathan 1738-1801 *Alli*
Battista Mantovano *CasWL*
Battista, O A 1917- *BkC 6, ConAu 13R*
Battisti, Eugenio 1924- *ConAu 37*
Battle, Allen Overton 1927- *ConAu 41*
Battle, Archibald John 1826-1907 *Alli Sup, BiDSA, DcNAA*
Battle, Edgar William 1907- *AmSCAP 66*
Battle, Effie T *BlkAW*
Battle, Gerald N 1914- *ConAu 57*
Battle, Jean Allen 1914- *ConAu 25*
Battle, John Rome 1889- *WhWNAA*
Battle, Kemp Plummer 1831-1919 *BiDSA, DcAmA, DcNAA*
Battle, Richard Henry 1835- *BiDSA*
Battle, Sol 1934- *BlkAW, ConAu 25, WrD 1976*
Battle, William H *Alli Sup*
Battle, William Horn 1803-1879 *DcNAA*
Battle, William James 1870- *TexWr*
Battles, Edith 1921- *ConAu 41*
Battles, Ford Lewis 1915- *ConAu 13R*
Battles, Jesse Moore 1935- *BlkAW, IndAu 1917*
Battles, Roxy Edith 1921- *SmATA 7*
Batto, Bernard Frank 1941- *ConAu 57*
Batts, Michael S 1929- *ConAu 41*
Batts, Robert Lynn 1864-1935 *DcNAA*
Battu, Zoe A 1898- *WhWNAA*
Batty, Mrs. *Alli Sup*
Batty, Adam *Alli*
Batty, Barth *Alli*
Batty, Beatrice *Alli Sup*
Batty, Charles David 1932- *Au&Wr, ConAu 17R*
Batty, David T *Alli Sup*
Batty, Dora M *ChPo*
Batty, E *Alli*
Batty, John *Alli Sup*
Batty, Joseph *Alli*
Batty, Joseph 1929- *Au&Wr*
Batty, Joseph H d1906 *Alli Sup, DcNAA*
Batty, Joyce D 1919- *ConAu 17R*
Batty, Linda Schmidt 1940- *ConAu 61*
Batty, R *Alli*

Batty, Richard d1758 *Alli*
Batty, Robert *Alli*
Batty, William *Alli*
Battye, Gladys 1915- *Au&Wr*
Battye, Louis Neville 1923- *Au&Wr, ConAu 5R*
Battye, Richard Fawcett *Alli Sup*
Battye, Thomas *Alli, BiDLA*
Batu, Selahattin 1905- *REnWD*
Baty, Gaston 1885?-1952 *ClDMEuL, OxFr, REn*
Baty, Gordon B 1938- *ConAu 57*
Baty, Richard d1758 *Alli*
Baty, Wayne 1925- *ConAu 13R*
Batyushkov, Konstantin Nikolayevich 1787-1855 *CasWL, DcEuL, DcRusL, EuA, EvEuW*
Bauby, Cathrina 1927- *ConAu 49*
Bauch, Bruno 1877- *WhLA*
Baucom, Mary Barrow *TexWr*
Baudart, Willem 1565-1640 *CasWL*
Baude, Henri 1430-1496? *CasWL, DcEuL, OxFr*
Baudelaire, Charles Pierre 1821-1867 *AtlBL, BbD, BiD&SB, CasWL, ClDMEuL, CyWA, DcEuL, EuA, EvEuW, NewC, OxEng, OxFr, Pen Eur, REn*
Baudelaire, Pierre Charles 1821-1867 *RCom*
Bauder, Levi F 1840-1913 *OhA&B*
Baudisch, Hans 1881- *WhLA*
Baudissin, Eva Von Grafin 1869- *WhLA*
Baudissin, Wolf Heinrich Von 1789-1878 *BiD&SB, DcEuL, EvEuW, NewC*
Baudouin *NewC*
Baudouin, Jean 1590-1650 *OxFr*
Baudouin, Joseph Albert 1875- *WhWNAA*
Baudouy, Michel-Aime 1909- *ConAu 33, SmATA 7, ThBJA*
Baudri Of Bourgueil 1046-1130 *CasWL, Pen Eur*
Baudrillart, Cardinal Henri Marie A 1859-1942 *CatA 1947*
Baudry De Bourgueil 1046-1130 *EvEuW*
Bauduc, Ray 1909- *AmSCAP 66*
Bauduy, Jerome K *Alli Sup*
Baudy, Nicolas 1904?-1971 *ConAu 33*
Bauer, Bruno 1809-1882 *BiD&SB*
Bauer, Clyde Max 1886- *IndAu 1917*
Bauer, Constantin 1883- *WhLA*
Bauer, E Charles 1916- *ConAu 9R*
Bauer, Erwin A 1919- *ConAu 9R*
Bauer, F *Alli*
Bauer, Ferdinand *BiDLA*
Bauer, Florence Marvyne *AmA&B, AmNov, ConAu 17*
Bauer, Fred 1934- *ConAu 29*
Bauer, Fred John 1878- *WhWNAA*
Bauer, Friedhold 1934- *CrCD*
Bauer, Georg Lorenz 1880- *WhLA*
Bauer, George Howard 1933- *ConAu 29*
Bauer, George N 1872- *WhWNAA*
Bauer, Hanna R 1918- *ConAu 57*
Bauer, Hans 1878- *WhLA*
Bauer, Harold 1873-1951 *AmSCAP 66*
Bauer, Harry C 1902- *ConAu P-1*
Bauer, Helen 1900- *ConAu 5R, SmATA 2*
Bauer, Josef Martin 1901- *ConAu 5R, EncWL, ModGL*
Bauer, Juliette *Alli Sup*
Bauer, Karl 1868- *WhLA*
Bauer, Karl Jack 1926- *ConAu 25, WrD 1976*
Bauer, Klara *BiD&SB*
Bauer, Louis *Alli Sup*
Bauer, Louis A 1865- *WhWNAA*
Bauer, Ludwig Amandus 1803-1846 *OxGer*
Bauer, Marion 1887- *WhWNAA*
Bauer, Mary T 1885-1949 *OhA&B*
Bauer, Oswald 1876- *WhLA*
Bauer, Peter Thomas 1915- *Au&Wr*
Bauer, Ralph Stanley 1883- *WhWNAA*
Bauer, Raymond Augustine 1916- *AmA&B, ConAu 61*
Bauer, Royal D M 1889- *ConAu 33*
Bauer, Stephen 1865- *WhLA*
Bauer, Walter 1904- *EncWL, ModGL, OxCan Sup, OxGer*
Bauer, Wilhelm 1877- *WhLA*
Bauer, William *OxCan Sup*
Bauer, William 1915- *AmSCAP 66*

Bauer, William Waldo 1892- *ConAu 5R*
Bauer, Wolfgang 1941- *CrCD*
Bauer, Wolfgang L 1930- *ConAu 13R*
Bauer, Wright *DcNAA*
Bauer, Yehuda 1926- *ConAu 29, WrD 1976*
Bauerle, Adolf 1786?-1859 *BiD&SB, OxGer*
Bauerle, Charles B *EarAB Sup*
Bauerman, Hilary *Alli Sup*
Bauernfeind, Harry B 1904- *ConAu 19*
Bauernfeld, Eduard Von 1802-1890 *BiD&SB, CasWL, OxGer*
Bauernschmidt, Marjorie 1926- *IlBYP, IlCB 1956*
Baugh, Albert Croll 1891- *AmA&B*
Baugh, Edward Ernest *Alli Sup*
Baughan, Blanche Edith 1870-1958 *ChPo S1, DcLEnL*
Baughan, Edward Algernon 1865- *WhLA*
Baughan, Peter Edward 1934- *Au&Wr, WrD 1976*
Baughan, Rosa *Alli Sup*
Baughe, Thomas *Alli*
Baughman, Abraham J 1838-1913 *DcNAA, OhA&B*
Baughman, Ernest W 1916- *ConAu 33*
Baughman, James P 1936- *ConAu 25*
Baughman, Millard Dale 1919- *ConAu 41, IndAu 1917*
Baughman, Ray Edward 1925- *ConAu 9R*
Baughman, Roland Orvil 1902- *ChPo S1*
Baughman, Theodore 1845- *DcNAA*
Baughn, William Hubert 1918- *ConAu 1R*
Baugy, Henri De d1720 *OxCan*
Bauke, Algernon Cooke *Alli Sup*
Baukhage, Hilmar Robert *AuNews 2*
Bauland, Peter 1932- *ConAu 25*
Baulch, Lawrence 1926- *ConAu 25*
Baum, Allyn Z 1924- *ConAu 17R*
Baum, Bernard H 1926- *ConAu 37, WrD 1976*
Baum, Bernie 1928- *AmSCAP 66*
Baum, Betty *AuBYP*
Baum, Claude 1928- *AmSCAP 66*
Baum, Daniel 1934- *ConAu 13R*
Baum, David William 1940- *ConAu 53*
Baum, Frank George 1870-1932 *DcNAA, WhWNAA*
Baum, Gregory *ConAu 25*
Baum, Henry Mason 1848- *Alli Sup, DcAmA*
Baum, Julius *WhLA*
Baum, Kurt 1876-1962 *CasWL*
Baum, Loren 1917- *WhWNAA*
Baum, Lyman Frank 1856-1919 *AmA&B, AuBYP, CarSB, ChPo, ChPo S2, CnDAL, DcAmA, DcNAA, FamSYP, LongC, OxAm, Pen Am, REn, REnAL, ThBJA, TwCA, WhCL*
Baum, Paull Franklin 1886-1964 *AmA&B, ConAu 5R, WhWNAA*
Baum, Richard 1940- *ConAu 57*
Baum, Richard Fitzgerald 1913- *ConAu 5R*
Baum, Vicki 1888?-1960 *AmA&B, AmNov, CasWL, CyWA, EvEuW, LongC, OxGer, TwCA, TwCA Sup, TwCW, WhLA*
Baum, Willi 1931- *ConAu 29, SmATA 4*
Bauman, Clarence 1928- *ConAu 45*
Bauman, Elizabeth Hershberger 1924- *IndAu 1917*
Bauman, H Carl 1913- *ConAu 9R*
Bauman, Louis 1880- *WhWNAA*
Bauman, M J *MnBBF*
Baumann, Amy 1922- *SmATA 10*
Baumann, Anthony *Alli Sup*
Baumann, Carol Edler 1932- *ConAu 33, WrD 1976*
Baumann, Emil J 1891- *WhWNAA*
Baumann, Emile 1868-1942 *CatA 1947*
Baumann, Gustave 1881- *ChPo S1*
Baumann, Hans 1914- *Au&Wr, ConAu 5R, SmATA 2, ThBJA*
Baumann, Walter 1935- *ConAu 29*
Baumbach, Jonathan 1933- *AmA&B, ConAu 13R, ConLC 6, DrAF 1976*
Baumbach, Rudolf 1840-1905 *BiD&SB, OxGer*
Baumback, Clifford M 1915- *ConAu 57*
Baumberger, James Percy 1892- *WhWNAA*
Baumberger, Otto 1889- *WhGrA*
Baume, Michael 1930- *ConAu 25*

Baumeler, Joseph Michael *OhA&B*
Baumer, Gertrud 1873-1954 *EncWL, OxGer*
Baumer, Lewis 1870- *ChPo, IlCB 1945*
Baumer, William H, Jr. 1909- *CatA 1947, ConAu 1R*
Baumgard, Herbert Mark 1920- *ConAu 13R*
Baumgardt, David 1890- *ConAu 1R*
Baumgardtner, Claude Chalmers 1883-1942 *IndAu 1917*
Baumgart, Johannes 1514-1578 *OxGer*
Baumgart, Reinhard 1929- *CasWL, ModGL*
Baumgarten, Alexander Gottlieb 1714-1762 *DcEuL, EvEuW*
Baumgarten, Moritz Julius Maximilian P M 1860- *WhLA*
Baumgartner, Edwin A 1889- *WhWNAA*
Baumgartner, John Stanley 1924- *ConAu 9R*
Baumgartner, Paul 1861-1917 *IndAu 1917*
Baumgartner, Samuel Henry 1860-1936 *IndAu 1816*
Baumgartner, Walter 1887- *WhLA*
Baumgartner, William J *WhWNAA*
Baumhauer, Hans 1913- *IlBYP, IlCB 1956*
Bauml, Franz H *ConAu 49*
Baumler, Christian Gottfried Heinrich 1836- *WhLA*
Baumol, William J 1922- *ConAu 13R, WrD 1976*
Baumrin, Bernard H 1934- *ConAu 9R*
Baumrin, Stefan *ConAu XR*
Baur, Emil Adolf 1873- *WhLA*
Baur, Ferdinand Christian 1792-1860 *BiD&SB*
Baur, Franz 1887- *WhLA*
Baur, John Edward 1922- *ConAu 9R, WrD 1976*
Baus, Herbert Michael 1914- *ConAu 25, IndAu 1917, WrD 1976*
Bausani, Alessandro 1921- *ConAu 45*
Bausch, Edward 1854-1944 *DcNAA*
Bausch, William J 1929- *ConAu 29*
Bausher, Mrs. J Lee *AmNov XR*
Bauslin, David Henry 1854-1922 *DcNAA, OhA&B*
Bausman, Benjamin 1824-1909 *Alli Sup, DcAmA, DcNAA*
Bausman, Frederick 1861-1931 *DcNAA*
Bauthumley, Jacob *Alli*
Bauza, Guillermo 1916- *PueRA*
Bauza, Obdulio 1907- *PueRA*
Bavaunde, W *Alli*
Baverstock, J *Alli, BiDLA*
Bavicchi, John 1922- *AmSCAP 66*
Bavink, Bernhard *WhLA*
Bawden, Edward 1903- *IlCB 1956, WhGrA*
Bawden, Harry Reginald 1921- *Au&Wr*
Bawden, Nina 1925- *Au&Wr, ChLR 2, ConAu XR, ConNov 1972, ConNov 1976, SmATA 4, WrD 1976*
Bawden, William *BiDLA*
Bawden, William d1816 *Alli*
Bawden, William T 1875- *WhWNAA*
Bawmer, Lewisiam 1870- *ChPo S1*
Bawn, Mary 1870- *ConAu XR*
Bawn, Mary Pamela 1917- *Au&Wr*
Bax *ConAu XR*
Bax, Sir Arnold 1883-1953 *LongC*
Bax, Arthur H *MnBBF*
Bax, Bonham W *Alli Sup*
Bax, Clifford 1886-1962 *ChPo, ChPo S1, ChPo S2, DcLEnL, LongC, McGWD, ModBL, NewC, REn, WhLA*
Bax, Emily 1882-1943 *DcNAA*
Bax, Ernest Belfort 1854-1926 *Alli Sup, LongC*
Bax, Percy William Frederick 1903- *Au&Wr*
Bax, Roger *ConAu XR, EncM&D, WorAu*
Baxendale, Walter *Alli Sup, ChPo, PoIre*
Baxley, Henry Willis 1803-1876 *Alli Sup, DcNAA*
Baxley, Isaac Rieman 1850-1930 *Alli Sup, DcAmA*
Baxley, Isaac Rieman 1850-1920 *DcNAA*
Baxt, George 1923- *ConAu 21*
Baxter, Albert 1823-1905 *DcNAA*
Baxter, Alexander *Alli*
Baxter, Alexander Duncan 1908- *Au&Wr*
Baxter, Andrew 1686-1750 *Alli, DcEnL*
Baxter, Andrew J *Alli Sup*

Baxter, Annette Kar 1926- *ConAu 1R*
Baxter, Arthur Beverley *Chmbr 3*
Baxter, Arthur George *Alli Sup*
Baxter, Batsell Barrett 1916- *ConAu 33*
Baxter, Benjamin *Alli*
Baxter, Sir Beverley 1891-1964 *LongC*
Baxter, Brian *Au&Wr, WrD 1976*
Baxter, Bruce *ChPo*
Baxter, C E *Alli Sup*
Baxter, Charles *DrAP 1975*
Baxter, Charles 1947- *ConAu 57*
Baxter, Charles R *Alli Sup*
Baxter, Craig 1929- *ConAu 25, WrD 1976*
Baxter, Edmund Dillahunty 1838-1910 *DcNAA*
Baxter, Edna May 1890- *ConAu P-1, WrD 1976*
Baxter, Edward John *Alli Sup*
Baxter, Eric George 1918- *ConAu 17R*
Baxter, Eric Peter 1913- *Au&Wr, ConAu 9R*
Baxter, Evan Buchanan 1844-1885 *Alli Sup*
Baxter, F *Alli Sup*
Baxter, Francis Willoughby *Alli Sup*
Baxter, George 1868-1917 *ChPo S1*
Baxter, George Owen *MnBBF*
Baxter, Gillian Jose Charlotte 1938- *Au&Wr*
Baxter, Glenn E 1926- *AmSCAP 66*
Baxter, Gordon F, Jr. 1923- *ConAu 45*
Baxter, Gregory Paul 1876- *WhWNAA*
Baxter, Hazel *ConAu XR*
Baxter, Henry Forster *Alli Sup*
Baxter, Horlyor *MnBBF*
Baxter, Hugo F *ChPo S1*
Baxter, Ian F G *ConAu 23*
Baxter, J *Alli, Alli Sup*
Baxter, J H *Alli Sup*
Baxter, J K *WebEAL*
Baxter, James *Alli Sup*
Baxter, James 1913-1964 *AmSCAP 66*
Baxter, James Keir 1926-1972 *CasWL, ChPo S1, ChPo S2, ConDr, ConP 1970, ConP 1975, LongC, Pen Eng, TwCW, WorAu*
Baxter, James Phinney 1831-1921 *Alli Sup, AmLY, DcAmA, DcNAA, OxAm*
Baxter, James Phinney, III 1893-1921 *AmA&B, ConAu 57, OxAm, TwCA Sup*
Baxter, Jedidiah Hyde 1837-1890 *DcNAA*
Baxter, Jere 1852-1904 *DcNAA*
Baxter, John *Alli, ConAu XR, EncM&D*
Baxter, John 1939- *ConAu 29*
Baxter, John A *Alli*
Baxter, John Babington Macaulay 1868-1946 *DcNAA, WhWNAA*
Baxter, John E *ChPo S2*
Baxter, Joseph 1676-1745 *Alli*
Baxter, Joseph Harvey Lowell *BlkAW*
Baxter, Katharine Schuyler 1845- *DcNAA*
Baxter, Katherine d1924 *DcNAA*
Baxter, Larry 1924- *AmSCAP 66*
Baxter, Les 1922- *AmSCAP 66*
Baxter, Lucy E *Alli Sup*
Baxter, Lydia 1809-1874 *Alli Sup, AmA&B, ChPo, DcAmA, DcNAA*
Baxter, Matthew *Alli Sup*
Baxter, Maurice *Alli Sup*
Baxter, Maurice Glen 1920- *ConAu 13R*
Baxter, Michael Paget *Alli Sup*
Baxter, N A *Alli*
Baxter, Phil 1896- *AmSCAP 66*
Baxter, R A *Alli*
Baxter, Richard 1615-1691 *Alli, BbD, BiD&SB, BrAu, CasWL, ChPo, Chmbr 1, CrE&SL, DcEnA, DcEnL, EvLB, NewC, OxEng, Pen Eng, PoCh, REn, WebEAL*
Baxter, Robert *Alli Sup*
Baxter, Robert Dudley 1827-1875 *Alli Sup*
Baxter, Samuel Alexander 1839-1908 *OhA&B*
Baxter, Shane V *ConAu XR, WrD 1976*
Baxter, Stephen B 1929- *ConAu 17R*
Baxter, Sylvester 1850-1927 *AmA&B, BiD&SB, DcAmA, DcNAA*
Baxter, Thomas *Alli, Alli Sup, BiDLA*
Baxter, W C *Alli Sup*
Baxter, W E *Alli*
Baxter, W R *Alli Sup*
Baxter, Walter 1915- *Au&Wr*
Baxter, William *Alli, Alli Sup, ChPo S2*

Baxter, William 1650-1723 *Alli*
Baxter, William 1820-1880 *AmA&B, BiD&SB, DcAmA, DcNAA, OhA&B*
Baxter, William 1823- *Alli Sup, BiDSA*
Baxter, William 1854- *DcNAA*
Baxter, William Edward 1825-1890 *Alli Sup, DcEnL*
Baxter, William Edwards 1863- *WhWNAA*
Baxter, William Joseph *Au&Wr*
Baxter, William L *Alli Sup*
Baxter, Wynne Edwin *Alli Sup*
Bay, Christian 1921- *ConAu 33*
Bay, E H *Alli*
Bay, James *DcNAA, WhWNAA*
Bay, W *Alli*
Bay, W V N *Alli Sup, BiDSA*
Bay Laurel, Alicia 1949- *ConAu 41*
Bayalinov, Kasymaly 1902- *DcOrL 3*
Bayard, Chevalier De 1475?-1524 *NewC*
Bayard, Alvred *ChPo*
Bayard, Elise Justine d1850? *Alli, CyAL 2*
Bayard, Emile Antoine 1837-1891 *ChPo*
Bayard, James *Alli*
Bayard, James A 1767-1815 *Alli*
Bayard, Jean Francois Alfred 1796-1853 *BiD&SB*
Bayard, Pierre DuTerrail, Chevalier De 1473?-1524 *OxFr, REn*
Bayard, R *BbtC*
Bayard, Samuel *Alli, Alli Sup*
Bayard, Samuel 1767-1840 *DcNAA*
Bayard, Samuel John d1879 *DcNAA*
Bayati, 'Abdalwahhab Al- 1926- *DcOrL 3*
Bayazid *NewC*
Bayazid Ansari, Pir Roshan 1524-1580? *DcOrL 3*
Baybars, Taner 1936- *ConAu 53, ConP 1970, ConP 1975, WrD 1976*
Bayer, Eleanor R 1914- *OhA&B*
Bayer, Herbert 1900- *WhGrA*
Bayer, Karl Robert Emerich Von *BiD&SB*
Bayer, Konrad 1932-1964 *CrCD*
Bayer, Leo G 1908- *OhA&B*
Bayer, Oliver Weld *OhA&B*
Bayer, William 1939- *ConAu 33, WrD 1976*
Bayerle, Gustav 1931- *ConAu 53*
Bayes, Alfred Walter 1832-1909 *ChPo*
Bayes, Joshua 1671-1761 *Alli*
Bayes, Ron *DrAP 1975*
Bayes, Ronald H 1932- *ConAu 25*
Bayes, Thomas *Alli*
Bayes, William *Alli Sup*
Bayfield, Mrs. *Alli, BiDLA*
Bayfield, A Carolyn *WhWNAA*
Bayfield, Henry Wolsey *Alli Sup, BbtC*
Bayfield, R *Alli*
Bayfield, Robert *Alli*
Bayfield, Samuel Joseph *Alli Sup*
Bayfield, William John 1871-1958 *MnBBF*
Bayford, A F *Alli*
Bayford, David *Alli*
Bayford, Thomas *Alli*
Bayh, Birch E, Jr. 1928- *ConAu 41*
Bayha, Charles A 1891-1957 *AmSCAP 66*
Bayha, Edwin F *ChPo*
Baykin, R C *BlkAW*
Baykurt, Fakir *CasWL*
Baylay, Charles Frederick Rogers *Alli Sup*
Bayldon, Arthur Albert Dawson 1865- *Alli Sup, DcLEnL*
Bayldon, George *Alli Sup*
Bayldon, J S *Alli*
Bayldon, Richard *Alli Sup*
Bayle, Pierre 1647-1706 *BbD, BiD&SB, CasWL, DcEnL, DcEuL, EuA, EvEuW, NewC, OxEng, OxFr, Pen Eur, REn*
Baylebridge, William 1883-1942 *ChPo, DcLEnL, Pen Eng*
Baylee, Joseph 1808-1883 *Alli, Alli Sup*
Baylen, Joseph O 1920- *ConAu 25, WrD 1976*
Bayles, Ernest E 1897- *ConAu 19, WrD 1976*
Bayles, George James 1869-1914 *DcAmA, DcNAA*
Bayles, James Copper 1845-1913 *Alli Sup, DcNAA*
Bayles, Michael D 1941- *ConAu 49*
Bayles, R B *BiDLA*

Bayles, Richard Mather *Alli Sup, DcNAA*
Bayles, W E *Alli Sup*
Bayles, William Harrison 1841- *DcNAA*
Bayley, Barrington John 1937- *ConAu 37, WrD 1976*
Bayley, C *Alli*
Bayley, Catherine *Alli, BiDLA*
Bayley, Charles Calvert 1907- *ConAu 33, WrD 1976*
Bayley, Cornelius *Alli*
Bayley, Cornwall *OxCan*
Bayley, David H 1933- *ConAu 13R*
Bayley, Denis *OxCan Sup*
Bayley, Dorothy *ChPo*
Bayley, Edward *Alli*
Bayley, Sir Edward Clive 1821-1884 *Alli Sup*
Bayley, F *Alli Sup*
Bayley, Fr *Alli*
Bayley, Francis *Alli*
Bayley, Frank William 1863-1932 *DcNAA*
Bayley, Frederick W N B 1807-1852 *Alli, PoIre*
Bayley, Frederick William Naylor 1808-1853 *ChPo*
Bayley, G James Roosevelt 1814-1877 *Alli Sup*
Bayley, G W R *Alli Sup*
Bayley, George *Alli*
Bayley, Mrs. H *BbtC*
Bayley, H V *Alli*
Bayley, J H R *Alli Sup*
Bayley, James Roosevelt 1814-1877 *DcAmA, DcNAA*
Bayley, James Roosevelt 1846-1917 *DcNAA*
Bayley, Joel *Alli*
Bayley, John *Alli, BiDLA*
Bayley, Sir John 1763?-1841 *Alli, BiDLA*
Bayley, John 1814-1880 *Alli, DcNAA*
Bayley, John B *Alli*
Bayley, Sir John Robert Laurie Emilius *Alli Sup*
Bayley, Jonathan *Alli Sup*
Bayley, L M Laning *Alli Sup*
Bayley, Peter 1778?-1823 *ChPo*
Bayley, Peter, Jr. *Alli, BiDLA*
Bayley, R B *Alli*
Bayley, Rafael Arroyo *Alli Sup*
Bayley, Richard 1745-1801 *Alli, DcNAA*
Bayley, Thomas *Alli Sup*
Bayley, Viola Clare Wingfield 1911- *Au&Wr*
Bayley, Viola Powles 1911- *ConAu 5R*
Bayley, William *Alli*
Bayley, William Henry *Alli Sup*
Bayley, William Henry And Huddleston, W *Alli Sup*
Bayley, William Shirley 1861-1943 *DcNAA, WhWNAA*
Baylie, John *Alli Sup*
Baylie, Richard *Alli*
Baylie, Robert *Alli*
Baylie, Thomas *Alli*
Baylies, Edwin 1840-1925 *Alli Sup, DcNAA*
Baylies, Francis 1783-1852 *DcAmA, DcNAA*
Baylies, Nicholas d1893 *DcNAA*
Baylies, Nicholas 1772?-1847 *DcNAA*
Baylies, William 1724-1787 *Alli*
Baylis, F G *Alli Sup*
Baylis, John *Alli, BiDLA*
Baylis, Joseph *ChPo S1*
Baylis, Lilian 1874-1937 *LongC*
Baylis, Samuel Mathewson 1854-1941 *DcNAA*
Baylis, Thomas Henry 1817- *Alli Sup*
Baylis, William 1724-1787 *Alli*
Bayliss, A E M *ChPo S2*
Bayliss, Alfred 1847-1911 *DcNAA*
Bayliss, Clara Kern 1848- *AmLY, DcAmA, DcNAA, WhWNAA*
Bayliss, Edwin *Alli Sup*
Bayliss, Eliza A *Alli Sup*
Bayliss, Fred W *ChPo S1*
Bayliss, John Clifford 1919- *ConAu 13R, ConP 1970*
Bayliss, Marguerite Farleigh 1895- *AmA&B, AmNov, REnAL*
Bayliss, Timothy 1936- *ConAu XR, ConP 1970, WrD 1976*
Bayliss, Wyke 1835- *Alli Sup*
Baylor, Adelaide Steele 1865?-1935? *DcNAA, IndAu 1816, WhWNAA*
Baylor, Frances Courtenay 1848-1920 *Alli Sup,*

AmA, AmA&B, BbD, BiD&SB, BiDSA, ChPo, DcAmA, DcBiA, DcNAA, OxAm
Baylor, Robert 1925- *ConAu 13R*
Bayly, Ada Ellen 1857-1903 *Alli Sup, BiD&SB, Chmbr 3, DcEnA Ap, EvLB, LongC, NewC*
Bayly, Anselm *Alli*
Bayly, Arthur *Alli*
Bayly, Benjamin d1720? *Alli*
Bayly, Charles *Alli Sup*
Bayly, Edward *Alli*
Bayly, Elizabeth Boyd *Alli Sup, ChPo S1*
Bayly, Ellen *DcLEnL*
Bayly, George *Alli Sup, MnBBF*
Bayly, Henry *PoIre*
Bayly, Hugh Wansey 1873- *WhLA*
Bayly, J A Sparvel *Alli Sup*
Bayly, James Dudgeon *Alli Sup*
Bayly, John 1595-1633 *Alli*
Bayly, Joseph 1920- *WrD 1976*
Bayly, Joseph T 1920- *ConAu 17R*
Bayly, Lewis d1632 *Alli*
Bayly, Mary *Alli Sup*
Bayly, Richard *Alli*
Bayly, Robert *Alli*
Bayly, Thomas *Alli*
Bayly, Thomas d1670 *Alli*
Bayly, Thomas *PoIre*
Bayly, Thomas Haynes 1797-1839 *Alli, BiD&SB, BrAu 19, ChPo, ChPo S1, ChPo S2, Chmbr 3, DcEnA Ap, DcEnL, DcLEnL, EvLB, NewC, OxEng*
Bayly, William d1810 *Alli*
Baylye, Thomas *Alli*
Baym, Max I 1895- *ConAu 41*
Bayma, Joseph *Alli Sup*
Bayman, Mary Ann *Alli Sup*
Baynam, William 1749-1814 *Alli*
Baynard, Edward *Alli*
Baynard, James B *Alli Sup*
Bayne, A D *Alli Sup*
Bayne, Alexander d1737 *Alli*
Bayne, Alicia *Alli Sup*
Bayne, Charles Joseph 1870- *BiDSA*
Bayne, Charles S 1876- *MnBBF*
Bayne, D *Alli*
Bayne, David C 1918- *ConAu 41*
Bayne, Emily *Alli Sup*
Bayne, H Paterson 1868- *ChPo S1*
Bayne, Henry Wyndell *WhWNAA*
Bayne, Hugh A *BiDSA*
Bayne, James 1710-1790 *Alli*
Bayne, John *BbtC*
Bayne, Julia Taft 1845- *ChPo, WhWNAA*
Bayne, K *Alli*
Bayne, Paul d1617 *Alli*
Bayne, Peter 1830-1896 *Alli, Alli Sup, ChPo S1, DcEnL, MnBBF, NcwC*
Bayne, Reed Taft 1885- *WhWNAA*
Bayne, Robert *Alli Sup*
Bayne, Samuel Gamble 1844-1924 *DcNAA*
Bayne, Stephen Fielding, Jr. 1908-1974 *Au&Wr, ConAu 45*
Bayne, W 1860?- *ChPo S1*
Bayne, W B *PoIre*
Bayne-Jardine, C C 1932- *ConAu 25*
Bayne-Powell, Rosamond 1879- *ChPo*
Baynes, Arthur Hamilton 1854- *WhLA*
Baynes, C R *Alli*
Baynes, D *Alli Sup*
Baynes, E D *Alli*
Baynes, Ernest Harold 1868-1925 *AmLY, DcNAA, JBA 1934, JBA 1951, St&VC*
Baynes, H S *Alli*
Baynes, Henry Samuel *Alli Sup*
Baynes, John *Alli Sup*
Baynes, John Christopher Malcolm 1928- *Au&Wr, ConAu 21, WrD 1976*
Baynes, Norman 1877-1961 *LongC*
Baynes, Paul d1617 *Alli*
Baynes, Pauline Diana 1922- *ChPo, ChPo S2, IlBYP, IlCB 1956, IlCB 1966, ThBJA, WhCL*
Baynes, Ralph d1559 *Alli*
Baynes, Robert *Alli, BiDLA*
Baynes, Robert Edward *Alli Sup*
Baynes, Robert Hall 1831-1895 *Alli Sup, ChPo, ChPo S1*

Baynes, Roger *Alli*

Baynes, Thomas Spencer 1823-1887 *Alli Sup, BrAu 19, DcEnL, EvLB, NewC*

Baynham, George Walter *Alli Sup*

Baynham, Henry Wellesley Forster 1933- *ConAu 29, WrD 1976*

Baynham, William *Alli*

Baynton, Barbara *Chmbr 3*

Baynton, Thomas *Alli, BiDLA, BiDLA Sup*

Bayr, Rudolf 1919- *CnMD, CrCD*

Bays, Carl Andrew 1914- *IndAu 1917*

Bays, Gwendolyn McKee *ConAu 13R*

Bays, W W *BiDSA*

Bayton, James A 1912- *LivBA*

Bazalgette, Charles Norman 1847- *Alli Sup*

Bazalgette, F E *Alli Sup*

Bazan, Emilia Pardo 1852- *BiD&SB, EvEuW, ModRL*

Bazancourt, Baron Cesar Lecat De 1810-1865 *BiD&SB*

Bazard, Armand 1791-1832 *OxFr*

Bazelon, David Thomas 1923- *AmA&B, ConAu 17R*

Bazelon, Irwin A 1922- *AmSCAP 66*

Bazhan, Mykola 1904- *ModSL 2, Pen Eur*

Bazhov, Pavel Petrovich 1879-1950 *CasWL*

Bazin, Germain 1907- *ConAu 5R*

Bazin, Herve 1911- *CasWL, EncWL, REn, TwCW, WorAu*

Bazin, Nancy Topping 1934- *ConAu 41*

Bazin, Nicholas 1636-1710 *ChPo*

Bazin, Rene 1853-1932 *CatA 1947, ClDMEuL, DcBiA, EvEuW, LongC, OxFr, Pen Eur, REn, TwCA, TwCA Sup*

Bazire, Pierre Victor And Cormack, J R *Alli Sup*

Bazley, Thomas Sebastian *Alli Sup*

BB 1905- *Br&AmS, ConAu XR, SmATA 6*

Beable, William Henry 1860- *ChPo*

Beach, Abel 1829-1899 *DcNAA*

Beach, Abraham d1828 *Alli*

Beach, Alfred Eli 1826-1896 *Alli Sup, DcNAA*

Beach, Allen C *Alli Sup*

Beach, Arthur Grandville 1870-1934 *OhA&B*

Beach, Arthur Granville 1870-1934 *DcNAA*

Beach, Belle 1875?- *Br&AmS*

Beach, Bert Beverly 1928- *ConAu 57*

Beach, Bruce C 1903- *AmSCAP 66*

Beach, Chandler Belden 1839-1928 *DcNAA*

Beach, Charles *Alli Sup*

Beach, Charles Amory *CarSB, ConAu 19, SmATA 1*

Beach, Charles F *Alli Sup*

Beach, Charles Fisk 1827-1908 *DcAmA, DcNAA*

Beach, Charles Fisk, Jr. 1854-1934 *Alli Sup, BiDSA, DcAmA, DcNAA*

Beach, D *Alli Sup*

Beach, D N *Alli Sup*

Beach, Dale S 1923- *ConAu 13R*

Beach, David 1819- *BbtC*

Beach, David Nelson 1848-1926 *DcAmA, DcNAA*

Beach, Earl F 1912- *ConAu 13R*

Beach, Edward Latimer 1867-1943 *AmLY, DcNAA, OhA&B, WhWNAA*

Beach, Edward Latimer 1918- *Au&Wr, ConAu 5R, WrD 1976*

Beach, Elizabeth T Porter *Alli Sup*

Beach, Floyd Orion 1898- *AmSCAP 66*

Beach, Mrs. H H A 1867-1944 *AmSCAP 66*

Beach, Harlan Page 1854-1933 *DcNAA*

Beach, Harlan Page 1864- *DcAmA*

Beach, Harriet Maria *Alli Sup*

Beach, John d1782 *Alli*

Beach, John Noble 1829-1897 *OhA&B*

Beach, John Sheldon 1819-1887 *DcNAA*

Beach, Joseph Warren 1880-1957 *AmA&B, AmLY, CnDAL, OxAm, TwCA Sup*

Beach, Lewis 1835-1886 *Alli Sup, DcNAA*

Beach, Liza Bet *WhWNAA*

Beach, Marion *BlkAW*

Beach, Moses Yale 1800-1868 *AmA&B, DcNAA*

Beach, Philip *Alli*

Beach, Rebecca Gibbons 1823-1893 *Alli Sup, DcNAA*

Beach, Rex Ellingwood 1877-1949 *AmA&B,*

CyWA, DcLEnL, DcNAA, EvLB, LongC, OxAm, REnAL, TwCA, TwCA Sup, TwCW, WhWNAA

Beach, Samuel Bellamy 1780?-1866 *DcNAA*

Beach, Seth Curtis 1837-1925 *DcNAA*

Beach, Stewart 1899- *AmA&B, AuBYP*

Beach, Sylvia 1887-1962 *CasWL, LongC, Pen Am, REnAL*

Beach, Thomas *Alli*

Beach, Vincent W 1917- *ConAu 33*

Beach, W B H And Hickey, Y *Alli Sup*

Beach, W W *Alli, Alli Sup*

Beach, Waldo 1916- *ConAu 61*

Beach, Walter Greenwood 1868- *WhWNAA*

Beach, William Dorrance 1856-1932 *DcNAA*

Beach, William H *ChPo S1*

Beach, William R *Alli Sup*

Beach, William Waldo 1916- *AmA&B*

Beach, Wooster 1794-1868 *DcNAA*

Beachcomber *WorAu*

Beachcroft, Robert Porter *Alli, BiDLA*

Beachcroft, Thomas Owen 1902- *Au&Wr, ConAu P-1, WrD 1976*

Beacher, L *Alli*

Beacon, George *Alli Sup*

Beacon, R *Alli*

Beacon, Thomas *Alli*

Beaconsfield, Benjamin Disraeli, Earl Of 1804-1881 *Alli Sup, AtlBL, BbD, BiD&SB, BrAu 19, CasWL, Chmbr 3, DcEnA, DcEnL, EvLB, NewC*

Beaconsfield, Earl ALSO Disraeli, B

Beade, Herman Joseph 1887- *WhWNAA*

Beadel, Harriett *ChPo S1*

Beadell, Len 1923- *WrD 1976*

Beadle, Delos White 1823-1905 *BbtC, DcNAA*

Beadle, Erastus Flavel 1821-1894 *AmA&B, DcNAA, OxAm, REnAL*

Beadle, Gwyneth Gordon 1908- *Au&Wr*

Beadle, John *Alli*

Beadle, John Hanson 1840-1897 *Alli Sup, DcNAA, IndAu 1816, OhA&B*

Beadle, Muriel McClure Barnett 1915- *AmA&B, Au&Wr, ConAu 21*

Beadle, Samuel Alfred *BlkAW*

Beadle, William Henry Harrison 1838-1915 *DcNAA, IndAu 1816*

Beadles, William T 1902- *ConAu 17R*

Beadnell, Charles Marsh 1872- *WhLA*

Beadnell, Henry *Alli Sup*

Beadon, Richard *Alli, BiDLA, BiDLA Sup*

Beagle, Peter Soyer 1939- *ConAu 9R, DrAF 1976, WrD 1976*

Beaglehole, John Cante 1901-1971 *CasWL, ChPo, ConAu 21, ConAu 33, DcLEnL, LongC, OxCan Sup*

Beak, Francis *Alli*

Beakes, Samuel Willard 1861-1927 *DcNAA*

Beakley, George Carroll, Jr. 1922- *ConAu 45*

Beal, Alvin Casey 1872- *WhWNAA*

Beal, Anthony Ridley 1925- *Au&Wr, ConAu 9R*

Beal, Arthur Floyd 1888- *WhWNAA*

Beal, Carl Hugh 1889- *WhWNAA*

Beal, Charles A 1891- *WhWNAA*

Beal, Charles E *Alli Sup*

Beal, Edward William *Alli Sup*

Beal, Edwin C *ChPo*

Beal, George *MnBBF*

Beal, George Charles 1918- *Au&Wr*

Beal, George M 1917- *ConAu 23*

Beal, H Martin *ChPo*

Beal, James 1829- *Alli Sup*

Beal, James Hartley 1861- *DcAmA*

Beal, John 1603-1683 *Alli*

Beal, John David 1921- *WrD 1976*

Beal, Joseph Carleton 1900- *AmSCAP 66*

Beal, M F *DrAF 1976*

Beal, Merrill D 1898- *ConAu 1R, WhPNW*

Beal, Nathan Stone Reed *Alli Sup*

Beal, Samuel 1825- *Alli Sup*

Beal, Samuel Benoni *Alli Sup*

Beal, William 1815-1870 *Alli Sup*

Beal, William James 1833-1924 *Alli Sup, DcAmA, DcNAA*

Bealby, Joseph *BiDLA*

Bealby, S T *Alli Sup*

Beale, Anne *Alli, Alli Sup, ChPo S1,*

ChPo S2

Beale, Bart *Alli*

Beale, Calvin L 1923- *ConAu 1R*

Beale, Charles Willing 1845-1932 *BiDSA, DcAmA, DcNAA*

Beale, Dorothea 1831-1906 *Alli Sup, LongC*

Beale, E H *Alli Sup*

Beale, Edgar 1916- *Au&Wr*

Beale, Elizabeth Ashcroft 1926-1963 *BiDPar*

Beale, George William 1842- *DcNAA*

Beale, Helen G *BiDSA, LivFWS*

Beale, Howard Kennedy 1899-1959 *AmA&B*

Beale, James *Alli Sup, PoIre*

Beale, John *Alli, BiDLA*

Beale, Joseph *Alli Sup*

Beale, Joseph Henry 1861-1943 *DcAmA, DcNAA*

Beale, Lionel John *Alli Sup*

Beale, Lionel S *Alli*

Beale, Lionel Smith 1828- *Alli Sup, DcEnL*

Beale, Maria Taylor 1849- *BiDSA, DcEnL, DcNAA*

Beale, Mary 1632-1697 *Alli*

Beale, Richard Lee Turberville 1819-1893 *DcNAA*

Beale, Robert d1601 *Alli*

Beale, S Sophia *Alli Sup*

Beale, Stephen *Alli Sup*

Beale, Thomas Willert 1831- *Alli Sup, DcEnL*

Beale, Thomas William *Alli Sup*

Beale, Truxtun 1856-1936 *DcNAA*

Bealer, Alex W 1921- *ConAu 45, SmATA 8*

Bealer, Alexander W *BiDSA*

Bealer, Gertrude Eloise *ChPo S1*

Beales, Arthur Charles Frederick 1905- *CatA 1947*

Beales, Edmond 1803-1881 *Alli Sup*

Bealey, Frank William 1922- *Au&Wr, WrD 1976*

Bealey, Joseph *Alli*

Bealey, Richard Rome 1828-1887 *Alli Sup, ChPo S1, ChPo S2*

Bealey, William 1922- *ConAu 5R*

Beall, Asa 1824-1863 *HsB&A*

Beall, Edgar C *Alli Sup*

Beall, Emma Jacobs Rebecca 1865- *OhA&B*

Beall, J Y *Alli Sup*

Beall, John Bramblett 1833-1917 *BiDSA, DcNAA*

Beall, Lester 1903- *WhGrA*

Beals, Alan R 1928- *ConAu 37*

Beals, Carleton 1893- *AmA&B, Au&Wr, AuBYP, ConAu 1R, DcLEnL, OxAm, REnAL, TwCA, TwCA Sup, WhWNAA, WrD 1976*

Beals, Frank Lee 1881- *AmA&B, Au&Wr, ConAu 5R, WhWNAA*

Beals, Helen Raymond Abbott 1888- *AmA&B, WhWNAA*

Beals, Jessie Tarbox *ChPo S1, WhWNAA*

Beals, Ralph Leon 1901- *AmA&B, ConAu 23*

Beam, C Richard *ConAu 45*

Beam, E M *Alli Sup*

Beam, Harriet M *ChPo S1*

Beam, Mary H *ChPo*

Beaman, Alexander Gaylord Emmons 1885-1943 *DcNAA, WhWNAA*

Beaman, Charles Cotesworth 1840-1900 *Alli Sup, DcNAA*

Beaman, Edmond Addison 1811- *Alli Sup, DcNAA*

Beaman, George *Alli Sup*

Beaman, Joyce Proctor 1931- *ConAu 29, WrD 1976*

Beaman, S G Hulme *WhCL*

Beame, Rona 1934- *ConAu 45*

Beames, John *Alli, Alli Sup, BiDLA, OxCan*

Beames, John 1889- *WhWNAA*

Beames, Thomas *Alli, Alli Sup*

Beamish, Annie O'Meara DeVic 1883- *ConAu 13R*

Beamish, Florence F *PoIre*

Beamish, Fred Earl 1901- *WrD 1976*

Beamish, Henry Hamilton d1872 *Alli Sup, PoIre*

Beamish, Huldine V 1904- *ConAu P-1*

Beamish, J S *Alli Sup, PoIre*

Beamish, N L *Alli*

Beamish, Noel DeVic *ConAu XR*
Beamish, Richard *Alli Sup*
Beamish, Richard Joseph 1869-1945 *DcNAA, WhWNAA*
Beamish, Sir Tufton Victor Hamilton 1917- *Au&Wr*
Beamish, William *Alli Sup*
Beamont, William *Alli Sup*
Beamont, William John 1828-1868 *Alli Sup*
Bean, Arthur John 1884- *WhWNAA*
Bean, Charles *Alli*
Bean, Charles Edwin 1879- *DcLEnL*
Bean, Charles Homer 1870- *WhWNAA*
Bean, Constance A *ConAu 41*
Bean, David 1932- *Au&Wr, WrD 1976*
Bean, E A *MnBBF*
Bean, Edward D *Alli Sup*
Bean, Elijah Harry 1875- *OhA&B*
Bean, Ernest F 1882- *WhWNAA*
Bean, Fannie d1894? *Alli Sup, DcNAA*
Bean, George Ewart 1903- *Au&Wr, ConAu 25*
Bean, Harriet C 1823-1897 *BiDSA*
Bean, Helen Mar *Alli Sup*
Bean, James *Alli, BiDLA*
Bean, Joseph *Alli*
Bean, Keith Fenwick 1911- *ConAu P-1*
Bean, Keith Fenwick 1910- *Au&Wr*
Bean, Lowell John 1931- *ConAu 41*
Bean, Tarleton Hoffman 1846-1916 *DcAmA, DcNAA*
Bean, Theodore Weber 1833-1891 *Alli Sup, DcNAA*
Bean, W W *Alli Sup*
Bean, Walton 1914- *ConAu 25*
Bean, William Jackson 1863- *WhLA*
Beanblossom, Moody Lewis 1885-1923 *IndAu 1917*
Beane, Florella H *ChPo*
Beane, S M *ChPo*
Beaney, James George *Alli Sup*
Beaney, Jan *SmATA XR*
Beanland, A *Alli Sup*
Beanland, Arthur DeMillichamp 1909- *Au&Wr*
Beans, E W *Alli Sup*
Beanus d1047 *Alli*
Bear, Donald Jeffries 1905-1952 *IndAu 1917*
Bear, Firman Edward 1884- *WhWNAA*
Bear, James A, Jr 1919- *ConAu 21*
Bear, Joan 1918- *ConAu 57*
Bear, John *Alli*
Bear, John W 1800-1880 *OhA&B*
Bear, Roberta Meyer 1942- *ConAu 21*
Bear, William E *Alli Sup*
Bearblock, James *Alli, BiDLA*
Bearce, George D 1922- *ConAu 9R*
Bearcroft, Philip 1697-1761 *Alli*
Bearcroft, William *Alli*
Beard, Adelia Belle 1857-1920 *ChPo S1, DcNAA, OhA&B*
Beard, Annie E S d1930 *DcNAA*
Beard, Arthur *Alli Sup*
Beard, Augustus Field 1833-1934 *DcNAA, WhWNAA*
Beard, Belle Boone 1898- *Au&Wr*
Beard, Charles 1827-1888 *Alli Sup*
Beard, Charles Austin 1874-1948 *AmA&B, ConAmA, DcLEnL, DcNAA, EvLB, IndAu 1816, LongC, OxAm, REn, REnAL, Pen Am, TwCA, TwCA Sup, WebEAL*
Beard, Charles Heady 1855-1916 *DcNAA*
Beard, Cyril *ChPo S1*
Beard, Daniel Carter 1850-1941 *Alli Sup, AmA&B, AmLY, BiD&SB, CarSB, ChPo, DcAmA, DcNAA, JBA 1934, OhA&B, OxAm, REnAL, TwCA, TwCA Sup, WhWNAA*
Beard, Emma Patten *AmLY, WhWNAA*
Beard, Frank *Alli Sup, ChPo, DcNAA, OhA&B*
Beard, George Miller 1839-1883 *Alli Sup, BbD, BiD&SB, DcAmA, DcNAA*
Beard, Harry *ChPo S1*
Beard, Henry *Alli, BiDLA*
Beard, J G 1888- *WhWNAA*
Beard, J R *Alli*
Beard, James Andrews 1903- *AmA&B,*

Beard, James Carter 1837-1913 *Alli Sup, AmA&B, ChPo, DcNAA, EarAB, EarAB Sup, OhA&B*
Beard, James F 1919- *ConAu 1R*
Beard, James Melville *Alli Sup*
Beard, James Thom, I 1855-1941 *DcNAA, WhWNAA*
Beard, James Thom, II 1889- *WhWNAA*
Beard, John 1760- *Br&AmS*
Beard, John Reilly 1800-1876 *Alli Sup*
Beard, Joseph Howard 1883- *WhWNAA*
Beard, Lina d1933 *DcNAA, WhWNAA*
Beard, Lina Adelia B *Alli Sup*
Beard, Mary 1876-1946 *DcNAA*
Beard, Mary Caroline 1853-1933 *OhA&B*
Beard, Mary Miller *TexWr*
Beard, Mary Ritter 1876-1958 *AmA&B, DcLEnL, IndAu 1816, OxAm, REnAL, TwCA, TwCA Sup, WhWNAA*
Beard, O T *Alli Sup*
Beard, Oliver Thomas 1832- *DcAmA, DcNAA*
Beard, Patten *AmA&B, AmLY XR, ChPo, ChPo S2, WhWNAA*
Beard, Peter H 1938- *ConAu 13R*
Beard, Reed 1862-1939 *IndAu 1816*
Beard, Richard 1799-1880 *Alli, BiDSA, DcAmA, DcNAA*
Beard, Sidney Hartnoll 1862- *WhLA*
Beard, Thomas *Alli*
Beard, Thomas Francis 1842-1905 *DcNAA, EarAB, OhA&B*
Beard, William 1907- *AmA&B*
Beard, William Holbrook 1825-1900 *Alli Sup, DcAmA, DcNAA, EarAB Sup, OhA&B*
Bearden, James Hudson 1933- *ConAu 23*
Bearden, Romare H 1914- *AmSCAP 66*
Beardmore, George Cedric 1908- *Au&Wr*
Beardmore, Nathaniel 1816-1872 *Alli Sup*
Beardmore, Septimus *Alli Sup*
Beardshear, William Miller 1850-1902 *DcNAA*
Beardslee, Clark Smith 1850-1914 *DcNAA*
Beardslee, John Walter 1837-1921 *DcNAA, OhA&B*
Beardslee, John Walter, Jr. 1879- *WhWNAA*
Beardslee, John Walter, III 1914- *ConAu 37*
Beardslee, L A *Alli Sup*
Beardsley, Aubrey Vincent 1872-1898 *AtlBL, BrAu 19, ChPo, ChPo S2, DcLEnL, NewC, REn, WebEAL*
Beardsley, Charles E *OxCan*
Beardsley, Charles Noel 1914- *ConAu 1R*
Beardsley, Daniel B 1832-1894 *OhA&B*
Beardsley, Eben Edwards 1808-1891 *Alli Sup, BiD&SB, DcAmA, DcNAA*
Beardsley, Elizabeth Lane *ConAu 29*
Beardsley, Frank Grenville 1870- *WhWNAA*
Beardsley, Isaac Haight 1831-1902 *DcNAA*
Beardsley, John *Alli Sup*
Beardsley, Katharine *ChPo S2*
Beardsley, Levi 1785-1857 *DcNAA*
Beardsley, Monroe Curtis 1915- *AmA&B, ConAu 17R*
Beardsley, Richard K 1918- *ConAu 17R*
Beardsley, Simeon 1872- *WhWNAA*
Beardsley, Theodore S, Jr. 1930- *ConAu 33, WrD 1976*
Beardsley, Wilfred Attwood 1889- *WhWNAA*
Beardsley, William Agur 1865-1946 *DcNAA*
Beardsworth, Millicent Monica 1915- *WrD 1976*
Beardsworth, Monica 1915- *Au&Wr*
Beardwood, Valerie Fairfield *ConAu 5R*
Beare, Francis Wright 1902- *Au&Wr, ConAu 1R*
Beare, John Isaac *Alli Sup*
Beare, M A Nikki 1928- *ConAu 37*
Beare, Matt *Alli*
Beare, Nicholas *Alli*
Bearne, David *ChPo S2*
Bearne, Edward *Alli*
Bearne, Lucy *Alli Sup*
Bearse, Richard Stuart 1939- *AmSCAP 66*
Bearss, Edwin C 1923- *ConAu 25*
Beart, John *BiDLA*
Beart, John A *Alli*
Beaslai, Piaras 1883- *CatA 1947*
Beasley, Benjamin *Alli Sup*

Beasley, Edward, Jr. 1932- *LivBA*
Beasley, Frederick 1777-1845 *Alli, BiDSA, DcAmA, CyAL 1, DcNAA*
Beasley, Frederick Williamson 1808-1878 *Alli Sup, DcNAA*
Beasley, Henry *Alli*
Beasley, Jerry C 1940- *ConAu 37*
Beasley, Kenneth Ephriam 1925- *IndAu 1917*
Beasley, M Robert 1918- *ConAu 9R*
Beasley, Mercer *Alli Sup*
Beasley, Rex 1925- *ConAu 9R*
Beasley, Richard Dunkley *Alli Sup*
Beasley, Thomas Dykes 1850- *DcNAA*
Beasley, W *BiDLA*
Beasley, W Conger, Jr. 1940- *ConAu 53*
Beasley, W G 1919- *ConAu 53*
Beasley, Walter Joseph 1889- *Au&Wr*
Beasley, William Gerald 1919- *WrD 1976*
Beasley-Murray, George Raymond 1916- *Au&Wr, WrD 1976*
Beasly, Thomas J *Alli*
Beasly, W *Alli*
Beath, Paul Robert 1905- *ConAu 5R, REnAL*
Beath, Robert Bruns 1839-1914 *DcNAA*
Beatley, Clara Bancroft 1858-1923 *ChPo, ChPo S1, ChPo S2, DcNAA*
Beatniffe, John *Alli*
Beaton, Alfred Charles *Alli Sup*
Beaton, Anne *ConAu XR*
Beaton, Cecil 1904- *Au&Wr, LongC, NewC, WrD 1976*
Beaton, David 1494-1546 *Alli*
Beaton, David 1848-1920 *DcAmA, DcNAA*
Beaton, George *ConAu XR*
Beaton, James 1517-1603 *Alli*
Beaton, Leonard 1929-1970 *ConAu 5R*
Beaton, Leonard 1929-1971 *ConAu 29*
Beaton, Maude Hill *CanNov*
Beaton, Maude Pettit *OxCan*
Beaton, Patrick *Alli Sup*
Beaton, Philip Cuyler 1897- *WhWNAA*
Beaton-Jones, Cynon 1921- *ConAu 5R*
Beatrice, Countess Of Die *CasWL, EvEuW*
Beatrice Portinari 1266-1290 *NewC*
Beatson, Alexander *Alli, BiDLA*
Beatson, D *Alli Sup*
Beatson, Elwyn Vivian 1913- *Au&Wr*
Beatson, John *Alli*
Beatson, R S *BbtC*
Beatson, Robert 1742-1818 *Alli, BiDLA*
Beatson, W F *Alli Sup*
Beattie *Alli*
Beattie, Carol 1918- *ConAu 29*
Beattie, David Johnstone *ChPo*
Beattie, Estelle Jeanne 1922- *Au&Wr*
Beattie, Francis Robert 1848-1906 *Alli Sup, BiDSA, DcAmA, DcNAA*
Beattie, George 1782?-1823 *ChPo, ChPo S1*
Beattie, James 1735-1803 *Alli, BbD, BiD&SB, BrAu, CasWL, ChPo, ChPo S1, ChPo S2, Chmbr 2, DcEnA, DcEnL, DcEuL, DcLEnL, EvLB, MouLC 2, NewC, OxEng, Pen Eng, REn, WebEAL*
Beattie, James Alexander 1895- *WhWNAA*
Beattie, James Hay 1768-1790 *Alli*
Beattie, Jessie Louise 1896- *Au&Wr, CanNov, ConAu 5R, OxCan, WhWNAA, WrD 1976*
Beattie, John Hugh Marshall 1915- *ConAu 37, WrD 1976*
Beattie, Lisa Redfield 1924- *ConAu 25*
Beattie, Pakenham *ChPo S1*
Beattie, Rolla Kent 1875- *WhWNAA*
Beattie, William *Alli*
Beattie, William 1793-1875 *DcEnL*
Beattie-Kingston, W *ChPo S1*
Beatty, Adam 1777-1858 *DcNAA*
Beatty, Albert R 1906- *WhWNAA*
Beatty, Arthur 1869-1943 *AmA&B, DcNAA, WhWNAA*
Beatty, Bessie 1886-1947 *AmA&B, DcNAA, WhWNAA*
Beatty, Bill *ConAu XR*
Beatty, Charles *Alli*
Beatty, Charles Clinton 1715?-1772 *AmA*
Beatty, Elizabeth *ConAu XR*
Beatty, Francis *Alli, BiDLA*
Beatty, Hetty Burlingame 1907?-1971 *AuBYP,*

ConAu 1R, IlCB 1956, IlCB 1966,
MorJA, SmATA 5
Beatty, Jerome 1886-1967 AmA&B,
WhWNAA
Beatty, Jerome, Jr. 1918- AuBYP, ConAu 9R,
SmATA 5
Beatty, John 1828-1914 Alli Sup, AmA&B,
DcNAA, OhA&B
Beatty, John 1922-1975 ConAu 5R, ConAu 57,
SmATA 6, ThBJA
Beatty, John Owen 1890-1961 AmA&B
Beatty, John Wesley 1851-1924 DcNAA
Beatty, Marion ChPo
Beatty, Morgan 1902-1975 ConAu 61
Beatty, Norman 1924- AmSCAP 66
Beatty, Pakenham Thomas 1855- PoIre
Beatty, Patricia Robbins 1922- AuBYP,
ConAu 1R, SmATA 1, ThBJA
Beatty, Paxenham Alli Sup
Beatty, Rita Gray 1930- ConAu 45
Beatty, Thomas Edward d1872 Alli Sup, PoIre
Beatty, W BiDLA
Beatty, W 1770-1843 Alli
Beatty, William Alfred 1907- Au&Wr
Beatty, William Alfred 1912- ConAu P-1
Beatty, William K 1926- ConAu 41
Beatty-Kingston Alli Sup
Beattys, Harry Harvey 1860-1939 DcNAA
Beatus Rhenanus 1485-1547 CasWL, OxGer
Beaty, David 1919- Au&Wr, ConAu 1R,
ConNov 1972, ConNov 1976, WrD 1976
Beaty, Janice J 1930- ConAu 13R
Beaty, John Owen 1890- ChPo, TexWr,
WhWNAA
Beaty, John Yocum 1884- AuBYP
Beau Brummell NewC
Beau Nash NewC
Beau, Henry J 1911- AmSCAP 66
Beaubien, Charles Philippe 1843-1914 DcNAA
Beaubien, Henri DesRivieres 1800?-1834 BbtC,
DcNAA
Beauchamp, Edward R 1933- ConAu 61
Beauchamp, Germain OxCan Sup
Beauchamp, J Alli Sup
Beauchamp, Jean Joseph 1852-1923 DcNAA
Beauchamp, Kathleen Mansfield 1888-1923
EvLB, LongC, TwCA, TwCA Sup
Beauchamp, Kenneth L 1939- ConAu 2R,
WrD 1976
Beauchamp, Lou Jenks 1851-1920 ChPo S1,
DcNAA, OhA&B
Beauchamp, M E Alli Sup
Beauchamp, Mary Annette LongC, REn,
TwCA, TwCA Sup
Beauchamp, Pat ConAu XR
Beauchamp, Shelsley Alli Sup
Beauchamp, W B 1870- WhWNAA
Beauchamp, William Alli Sup
Beauchamp, William 1772-1824 DcNAA
Beauchamp, William Martin 1830-1925
AmA&B, AmLY, DcAmA, DcNAA
Beauchamps, Lord Alli
Beauchemin, Neree 1850-1931 CanWr,
DcNAA, OxCan
Beauchene, Robert-Chevalier OxCan
Beauchesne, Arthur 1876- WhWNAA
Beauchesne, John Baldon Alli
Beauchesne, John De Alli
Beauclair, Gotthard De 1907- WhGrA
Beauclair, Henri 1860-1919 OxFr
Beauclerc, James d1787 Alli
Beauclerk, Lady Diana DeVere 1734-1808
Alli Sup, BkIE
Beauclerk, Helen DeVere 1892-1969 LongC,
TwCA, TwCA Sup
Beauclerk, William Nelthorpe 1849- Alli Sup
Beaude, Henri 1870-1930 DcNAA, OxCan
Beaudet, Henri CanWr
Beaudoin, Kenneth Lawrence 1913- ConAu 29,
DrAP 1975, WrD 1976
Beaudouin, Joseph Damase 1856-1917 DcNAA
Beaudry, David Hercule 1822-1876 DcNAA
Beaudry, Evien G 1894- OhA&B
Beaudry, Goldie OhA&B
Beaudry, Hercules BbtC
Beaudry, J U BbtC
Beaudry, Louis Napoleon 1833-1892 Alli Sup,
DcNAA

Beaudry, Rene OxCan Sup
Beaufey, Robert De DcEnL
Beauford, Fred BlkAW
Beauford, William BiDLA
Beaufort, Duke Of 1824-1899 Alli Sup,
Br&AmS
Beaufort, Augustus Alli Sup, PoIre
Beaufort, D A Alli
Beaufort, Daniel Augustus Alli, BiDLA
Beaufort, Sir Francis d1857 Alli
Beaufort, Francis Lestock 1815-1879 Alli Sup
Beaufort, John Alli, BiDLA
Beaufort, Margaret 1441-1509 Alli
Beaufort, Raphael Ledos De Alli Sup
Beaufort, W L Alli Sup
Beaufort, William Morris 1823- Alli Sup
Beaufoy BbtC
Beaufoy, Henry Alli, BiDLA
Beaufoy, Mark Alli
Beaufre, Andre 1902-1975 ConAu 57
Beaugrand, Honore 1849-1906 DcNAA, OxCan
Beauharnais, Josephine T DeLaPagerie
1763-1814 OxFr, REn
Beauharnais, Marie-Anne-Francoise 1738-1813
OxFr
Beauharnois, C DeLaB, Marquis De 1670-1749
OxCan
Beaujeu, Monongahela De 1870-1928 DcNAA
Beaujeu, Renaud De OxFr
Beaulac, Willard L 1899- ConAu 9R
Beaulieu, Andre OxCan Sup
Beaulieu, Emile F EarAB, EarAB Sup
Beaulieu, Luke De Alli
Beaulieu, Mario OxCan Sup
Beaulieu, Michel OxCan Sup
Beaulieu, Victor-Levy 1945- OxCan Sup
Beauman, Eric Bentley Au&Wr, ConAu 9R
Beauman, Katharine Burgoyne Bentley Au&Wr,
WrD 1976
Beauman, William Alli
Beaumanoir, Philippe DeRemi, Sire De
1250?-1296 OxFr
Beaumarchais, Eugenia De ChPo
Beaumarchais, Pierre Augustin Coron De
1732-1799 AtlBL, BbD, BiD&SB, CasWL,
CnThe, CyWA, DcEuL, EuA, EvEuW,
McGWD, NewC, OxEng, OxFr, Pen Eur,
RCom, REn, REnWD
Beaumont Alli, AtlBL
Beaumont, Madame De OxFr
Beaumont, Albanis BiDLA
Beaumont, Albert 1901- Au&Wr
Beaumont, Alex Alli
Beaumont, Alexander BiDLA
Beaumont, Anthony 1918- Au&Wr
Beaumont, Arthur Bishop 1887- WhWNAA
Beaumont, Averil Alli Sup
Beaumont, Mrs. B Alli Sup
Beaumont, Barber Alli
Beaumont, Betty 1828- DcNAA
Beaumont, Beverly 1931- ConAu XR
Beaumont, Brenchley MnBBF
Beaumont, Charles Alli
Beaumont, Charles 1820-1889 DcNAA
Beaumont, Charles 1929- ConAu 5R
Beaumont, Charles Allen 1926- ConAu 1R
Beaumont, Christophe De 1703-1781 OxFr
Beaumont, Cyril William 1891- Au&Wr, ChPo,
ConAu 13R, WrD 1976
Beaumont, Frances Alli Sup
Beaumont, Francis 1584-1616 Alli, BiD&SB,
BrAu, CasWL, ChPo, ChPo S1,
ChPo S2, Chmbr 1, CnE&AP, CnThe,
CrE&SL, CriT 1, DcEnA, DcEnL,
DcEuL, DcLEnL, EvLB, McGWD,
MouLC 1, NewC, OxEng, Pen Eng,
REnWD, WebEAL
Beaumont, Francis & Fletcher, John CyWA
Beaumont, Francis William C E 1814- Alli
Beaumont, G Alli
Beaumont, G D B Alli
Beaumont, George Alli Sup
Beaumont, George Ernest 1888-1974 Au&Wr,
ConAu 49
Beaumont, Grace Alli Sup
Beaumont, Sir Harry 1698-1768 Alli, DcEnL
Beaumont, Henry 1902-1947 DcNAA

Beaumont, Henry Francis 1878- BiDSA
Beaumont, J A Alli, Alli Sup
Beaumont, J F A Alli
Beaumont, J T Barber Alli, BiDLA
Beaumont, James L 1940- AmSCAP 66
Beaumont, John Alli, Alli Sup
Beaumont, Sir John 1582-1627 Alli, CasWL,
ChPo, ChPo S1, Chmbr 1, DcEnL,
DcLEnL, EvLB, NewC
Beaumont, John, Jr. Alli
Beaumont, Joseph Alli, Alli Sup
Beaumont, Joseph 1616-1699 Alli, CasWL,
ChPo, ChPo S2, DcEnL, DcLEnL, EvLB
Beaumont, R Alli Sup
Beaumont, Robert Alli
Beaumont, Simon Van 1574-1654 CasWL
Beaumont, Thomas Wentworth PoIre
Beaumont, W Alli Sup
Beaumont, William Alli, BiDLA
Beaumont, William 1785-1853 DcNAA
Beaumont, William 1796-1853 Alli
Beaumont And Fletcher DcEnA, DcEnL,
MouLC 1, REn
Beaumont DeLaBonniniere, Gustave-A De
1802-1866 OxFr
Beaunoir, Alexandre Louis Bertrand 1746-1823
BiD&SB
Beauregard, Alphonse 1885-1924 DcNAA
Beauregard, Pierre Gustave Toutant 1818-1893
Alli Sup, BiDSA, DcAmA, DcNAA
Beaurigout, J DcEuL
Beaurline, L A 1927- ConAu 21
Beausang, Michael F, Jr. 1936- ConAu 57
Beausay, Florence E 1911- ConAu 21,
WrD 1976
Beauvais, W ChPo S2
Beauvoir, Edouard Roger De 1806-1866 EvEuW
Beauvoir, Roger De 1806-1866 OxFr
Beauvoir, Simone De 1908- CasWL, CnMWL,
ConAu 9R, ConLC 1, ConLC 2,
ConLC 4, EncWL, EvEuW, LongC,
ModRL, OxEng, OxFr, Pen Eur, REn,
TwCA Sup, TwCW, WhTwL
Beauvois, Eugene OxCan
Beaux, Cecilia ChPo
Beavan, Charles Alli
Beavan, Mrs. E Alli Sup
Beavan, Edward Alli
Beavan, Mrs. F OxCan
Beavan, Harriet A ChPo S1
Beavan, James Alli
Beavan, R Alli Sup
Beaven, Mrs. BbtC
Beaven, Albert William 1882- WhWNAA
Beaven, James 1801-1875 BbtC, DcNAA,
OxCan
Beaver, Barrington Alli Sup, MnBBF
Beaver, Bruce 1928- ConP 1970, ConP 1975,
WrD 1976
Beaver, George Alli
Beaver, Harold 1929- ConAu 21
Beaver, Jack Patrick 1923- ConAu 33,
WrD 1976
Beaver, John Alli
Beaver, Paul Chester 1905- IndAu 1917
Beaver, Philip Alli
Beaver, Robert Pierce 1906- Au&Wr,
ConAu 5R, OhA&B
Beaver, William Carl 1896- Au&Wr
Beaverbrook, Lord 1879-1964 LongC
Beavers, Mary Fletcher ChPo
Beawes, Wyndham Alli
Beazell, William Preston 1877-1946 OhA&B,
WhWNAA
Beazley, Sir Charles Raymond Chmbr 3
Beazley, Sir John Davidson 1885-1970 LongC,
WhLA
Beazley, Lillian Elizabeth Stoll 1895-
WhWNAA
Beazley, Rosalind R d1924 DcNAA
Beazley, S, Jr. BiDLA
Beazley, Samuel 1786-1851 Alli, NewC
Bebb, Fisher MnBBF
Bebb, Russ, Jr. 1930- ConAu 49
Bebel, Ferdinand August 1840-1913 BbD,
BiD&SB, OxGer, REn
Bebel, Heinrich 1472-1518 BbD, BiD&SB,
CasWL, DcEuL, EvEuW, OxGer

WrD 1976

Beckham, Charles W *Alli Sup*
Beckham, Stephen Dow 1941- *ConAu 61*
Beckhard, Arthur J *AuBYP*
Beckhelm, Paul 1906- *AmSCAP 66* .
Beckinella, Janette *BlkAW*
Beckingham, Charles 1699-1730 *Alli, DcEnL*
Beckingham, Charles Fraser 1914- *ConAu 61, WrD 1976*
Beckington, Thomas d1464? *Alli*
Beckinsale, Robert Percy 1908- *Au&Wr, ConAu 5R, WrD 1976*
Beckler, Marion Floyd 1889- *ConAu P-1*
Beckles, S H *Alli Sup*
Beckles Willson, Robina Elizabeth 1930- *Au&Wr, WrD 1976*
Beckley, Henry *Alli Sup*
Beckley, Hosea 1779-1843 *DcNAA*
Beckman, Anders 1907- *WhGrA*
Beckman, Elizabeth Hurlock *WhWNAA*
Beckman, Gail McKnight 1938- *ConAu 53, WrD 1976*
Beckman, Gunnel 1910- *ConAu 33, SmATA 6*
Beckman, Kaj 1913- *IlCB 1956*
Beckman, Nellie d1936 *DcNAA*
Beckman, Per 1913- *IlCB 1956*
Beckman, Theodore N 1895- *OhA&B, WhWNAA*
Beckman, Wilhelm 1852- *WhLA*
Beckman, Mrs. William *DcNAA*
Beckmann, David M 1948- *ConAu 61*
Beckmann, George Michael 1926- *ConAu 5R*
Beckmann, Martin J 1924- *ConAu 37*
Beckmann, Max 1884-1950 *AtlBL, OxGer*
Beckmeyer, Clement d1921 *DcNAA*
Becknell, William 1790?-1832 *OxAm, REnAL*
Beckner, Welden 1933- *ConAu 33*
Beckovic, Matija 1939- *CasWL, ConAu 33*
Beckson, Karl 1926- *ConAu 5R*
Beckstrand, Elias Hyrum 1870- *WhWNAA*
Beckwith, Albert Clayton 1836-1915 *DcNAA*
Beckwith, Arthur *Alli Sup*
Beckwith, Burnham Putnam 1904- *ConAu 33, WrD 1976*
Beckwith, Charles E 1917- *ConAu 37*
Beckwith, Charles Minnigrode 1851-1928 *BiDSA, DcNAA*
Beckwith, Clarence Augustine 1849-1931 *DcNAA*
Beckwith, Edward Lonsdale *Alli Sup*
Beckwith, F L *Alli Sup*
Beckwith, George Cone 1800-1870 *DcNAA*
Beckwith, Hiram Williams 1832-1903 *DcNAA*
Beckwith, Isbon Thaddeus 1843-1936 *DcNAA*
Beckwith, John *Alli*
Beckwith, John Gordon 1918- *Au&Wr, ConAu 9R, WrD 1976*
Beckwith, John Watrus 1831-1891 *BiDSA*
Beckwith, Josiah 1734- *Alli, BiDLA*
Beckwith, Julia Catherine 1796-1867 *DcLEnL*
Beckwith, Lillian 1916- *ConAu XR, WrD 1976*
Beckwith, Paul *BiDSA*
Beckwith, Paul Edmond 1848-1907 *DcNAA*
Beckwith, Theodore Day 1879- *WhWNAA*
Beckwith, Thomas 1731-1799 *Alli*
Beckwith, William *Alli, BiDLA*
Beckwourth, James P 1798-1867? *Alli Sup, OxAm, REnAL*
Becon, Thomas 1510?-1570 *Alli, DcEnL*
Beconsall, Thomas *Alli*
Becque, Henri Francois 1837-1899 *BiD&SB, CnThe, EuA, EvEuW, OxFr*
Becque, Henry Francois 1837-1899 *CasWL, ClDMEuL, CnMD, McGWD, ModWD, Pen Eur, REn, REnWD*
Becquer, Gustavo Adolfo 1836-1870 *AtlBL, BiD&SB, CasWL, ClDMEuL, DcSpL, EuA, EvEuW, Pen Eur, REn*
Beda 672?-735 *Alli, · AtlBL, BrAu*
Beda, Noel d1536 *OxFr*
Bedard, Elzear 1799-1849 *OxCan*
Bedard, Isidore 1806?-1833 *BbtC, OxCan*
Bedard, Joseph Edouard 1845-1927 *DcNAA*
Bedard, P H *BbtC*

Bedard, Pierre 1763-1827 *BbtC*
Bedard, Pierre Joseph 1869-1905 *DcNAA*
Bedard, Pierre-Stanislas 1762-1829 *OxCan*
Bedard, Roger J *OxCan Sup*
Bedard, Theophile-Pierre 1837-1900 *DcNAA, OxCan*
Bedau, Hugo Adam 1926- *ConAu 9R*
Bedborough, George *ChPo S1*
Beddall, Barbara G 1919- *ConAu 33, WrD 1976*
Beddall-Smith, Charles John 1916- *ConAu 13R*
Bedding, S A *Alli Sup*
Beddington, Mrs. Claude *Au&Wr*
Beddington, Julian Roy 1910- *Au&Wr*
Beddington, Roy 1910- *WrD 1976*
Beddoe, Alan B *ChPo*
Beddoe, Ellaruth *ConAu XR*
Beddoe, John 1826- *Alli Sup*
Beddoes, Richard H 1926- *ConAu 37*
Beddoes, Thomas 1760-1808 *Alli*
Beddoes, Thomas Lovell 1803-1849 *Alli, BiD&SB, BrAu 19, CasWL, ChPo, ChPo S1, Chmbr 3, CnE&AP, CriT 2, DcEnA, DcEnL, DcEuL, DcLEnL, EvLB, MouLC 3, NewC, OxEng, Pen Eng, REn, WebEAL*
Beddome, Benjamin 1717-1795 *Alli, PoCh*
Beddome, Richard Henry *Alli Sup*
Beddow, Mrs. Charles Peter *BiDSA*
Beddy, Joseph Fawcett *Alli Sup*
Bede 672?-735 *AtlBL, BbD, BiB S, BiD&SB, BrAu, CasWL, CriT 1, DcEnL, DcEuL, EvLB, NewC, OxEng, OxFr, Pen Eng, REn*
Bede, Brother 1874-1939 *DcNAA*
Bede, The Venerable 672?-735 *Chmbr 1*
Bede, Andrew *ConAu XR*
Bede, Augustin *Alli Sup*
Bede, C *Alli Sup*
Bede, Cuthbert 1827-1889 *Alli Sup, BbD, BiD&SB, BrAu 19, CasWL, ChPo, ChPo S2, Chmbr 3, DcBiA, DcEnL, DcLEnL, EvLB, NewC, OxEng, REn*
Bedel, Henry *Alli*
Bedel, Maurice 1884-1954 *EncWL, TwCA, TwCA Sup*
Bedell, Cornelia Frances *ChPo*
Bedell, Edwin Augustus 1853-1908 *DcNAA*
Bedell, Frederick 1868- *WhWNAA*
Bedell, George C 1928- *ConAu 41*
Bedell, Gregory Thurston 1817-1892 *Alli Sup, DcAmA, DcNAA, OhA&B*
Bedell, Gregory Townsend 1793-1834 *Alli, DcAmA, DcNAA*
Bedell, L Frank 1888- *ConAu P-1*
Bedell, Mary Crehore 1870- *OhA&B, WhWNAA*
Bedell, Robert Leech 1909- *AmSCAP 66*
Bedell, William 1570-1641 *Alli*
Bedersi, Abraham *CasWL*
Bedersi, Jedaiah *CasWL*
Bedford, A N *ConAu XR, SmATA 3*
Bedford, Annie North *ConAu XR, SmATA 3*
Bedford, Arthur *Alli*
Bedford, Arthur 1668-1745 *Alli, DcEnL*
Bedford, Barbara *Alli Sup*
Bedford, C R *Alli Sup*
Bedford, Charles Harold 1929- *ConAu 57*
Bedford, Edward Henslowe *Alli Sup*
Bedford, Emmett G 1922- *ConAu 45*
Bedford, Francis Donkin 1864-1950 *ChPo, ChPo S1, ChPo S2, ConICB, IlCB 1945, WhCL*
Bedford, Frederick G D *Alli Sup*
Bedford, Gunning S *Alli*
Bedford, Gunning S 1806-1870 *BiDSA, DcAmA, DcNAA*
Bedford, Henry *Alli Sup*
Bedford, Henry Frederick 1931- *ConAu 9R, WrD 1976*
Bedford, Herbert 1867- *WhLA*
Bedford, Hilkiah 1663-1724 *Alli*
Bedford, J T *Alli Sup*
Bedford, Jessie *ChPo*
Bedford, John *Au&Wr, ConAu XR*
Bedford, Joseph Goodworth *Alli Sup*
Bedford, Kenneth *ConAu XR*
Bedford, Ledbury *Alli Sup*

Bedford, Lee *MnBBF*
Bedford, Lou Singletary *BiDSA*
Bedford, Mary *ChPo*
Bedford, Norton M 1916- *ConAu 5R*
Bedford, Paul 1798?-1871 *Alli Sup*
Bedford, Randolph 1862-1941 *DcLEnL*
Bedford, Ruth Marjory *ChPo S1*
Bedford, Scott Elias William 1876- *WhWNAA*
Bedford, Sybille 1911- *Au&Wr, ConAu 9R, ConNov 1972, ConNov 1976, ModBL, NewC, RAdv 1, WorAu, WrD 1976*
Bedford, T *Alli Sup*
Bedford, Thomas *Alli*
Bedford, Thomas d1773 *Alli*
Bedford, W K Riland *Alli*
Bedford, William *Alli*
Bedford, William Devaynes *Alli Sup*
Bedford, William Kirkpatrick Riland *Alli Sup*
Bedford-Jones, Henry James O'Brien 1887-1949 *AmA&B, AmLY, DcLEnL, DcNAA, TwCA, TwCA Sup, WhWNAA*
Bedi, Rajindar Singh 1915- *DcOrL 2*
Bediako, K A *ConAu XR*
Bediako, Kwabena Asare *AfA 1*
Bedier, Joseph 1864-1938 *ClDMEuL, DcSpL, OxFr, TwCA Sup*
Bedier, Julie *BkC 1*
Bedil, 'Abdulqadir 1644-1721 *DcOrL 2, DcOrL 3*
Bedil, Qadir Bakhsh Of Rohri 1814-1872 *DcOrL 2*
Bedinger, E W *Alli Sup*
Bedinger, Henry 1810- *BiDSA*
Bedinger, Margery 1891- *ConAu 57*
Bedinger, Singleton B 1907- *ConAu 49*
Bedingfield, James *Alli*
Bedingfield, Robert *ChPo S1*
Bedingfield, Thomas *Alli*
Bedini, Silvio A 1917- *ConAu 33*
Bedle, Joseph *Alli*
Bedle, Thomas *Alli*
Bedloe, William *Alli*
Bedlow, Henry 1821-1914 *DcAmA, DcNAA*
Bednall, Jeannie *ChPo S2*
Bednar, Alfonz 1914- *CasWL, ModSL 2*
Bedny, Demyan 1883-1945 *CasWL, ClDMEuL, DcRusL, REn*
Bedortha, N *Alli Sup*
Bedott, Widow 1814-1852 *AmA, OxAm, REnAL*
Bedregal DeConitzer, Yolanda 1916- *DcCLA*
Bedsole, Adolph 1914- *ConAu 13R*
Bedson, P Phillips And Williams, W C *Alli Sup*
Bedson, Peter Phillips 1853- *WhLA*
Bedwell, Cyril Edward Alfred 1877- *WhLA*
Bedwell, Thomas *Alli*
Bedwell, William 1562-1632 *Alli*
Bee, B H *Alli Sup*
Bee, Clair Francis 1900- *AuBYP, ConAu 1R*
Bee, David 1931- *ConAu 17R*
Bee, Jay *ConAu 57*
Bee, John David Ashford 1931- *Au&Wr*
Bee, Jon *DcEnL*
Bee, Jonathan *Alli*
Bee, Thomas 1720- *Alli, BiDSA*
Beearde, Richard *Alli*
Beebe, Ann 1919- *ConAu 41*
Beebe, B F 1920- *ConAu 1R, SmATA 1, WrD 1976*
Beebe, Catherine 1899- *BkC 2, CatA 1947*
Beebe, Dwight Eastman 1878- *WhWNAA*
Beebe, Ethel Fairmont 1881- *WhWNAA*
Beebe, Frank N And Lincoln, A W *Alli Sup*
Beebe, Frederick S 1914-1973 *ConAu 41*
Beebe, H Keith 1921- *ConAu 29*
Beebe, James Albert 1878-1934 *DcNAA*
Beebe, John W 1853-1938 *IndAu 1917*
Beebe, Katherine 1860- *DcNAA*
Beebe, Lizzie G *ChPo*
Beebe, Lucius Morris 1902-1966 *AmA&B, ChPo, ConAu 25, REn, REnAL*
Beebe, Maurice 1926- *ConAu 1R, WrD 1976*
Beebe, P O *Alli*
Beebe, Ralph K 1932- *ConAu 33, WrD 1976*
Beebe, Robb 1891- *BkC 2, CatA 1947*
Beebe, Velma Vanderburgh *ChPo*
Beebe, William 1877-1962 *AmA&B, AmLY, ConAmA, ConAmL, DcLEnL, EvLB,*

OxAm, REnAL, St&VC, TwCA,
TwCA Sup, WhWNAA
Beebe, Mrs. William *AmNov XR*
Beebee, Charles Washington *Alli Sup*
Beeby, Charles Evans *Alli Sup*
Beeby, Clarence Edward 1902- *WrD 1976*
Beeby, Daniel J 1872- *WhWNAA*
Beeby, Dorothea *WhWNAA*
Beeby, Otto 1906- *Au&Wr*
Beech, Alice A *Alli Sup*
Beech, George T 1931- *ConAu 9R*
Beech, Harold Reginald 1925- *ConAu 25,*
WrD 1976
Beech, John H *Alli Sup*
Beech, Keyes 1913- *ConAu 33*
Beech, Robert 1940- *ConAu 33*
Beech, Webb *ConAu XR, SmATA 5*
Beecham, Sir Thomas 1879-1961 *LongC, REn*
Beechcroft, T O 1902- *LongC*
Beeche, Don Gregorio *DcSpL*
Beecher, Catharine Esther 1800-1878 *Alli,*
Alli Sup, AmA, AmA&B, BiD&SB,
ChPo, CyAL 1, DcAmA, DcNAA,
FemPA, OhA&B, OxAm, REnAL
Beecher, Charles 1815-1900 *Alli, Alli Sup,*
AmA&B, BiD&SB, CyAL 1, CyAL 2,
DcAmA, DcNAA, OhA&B
Beecher, Charles Emerson 1865-1904 *DcAmA*
Beecher, Edward 1803?-1895 *Alli, Alli Sup,*
AmA&B, BbD, BiD&SB, CyAL 2,
DcAmA, DcNAA, REnAL
Beecher, Edward N 1846-1933 *OhA&B*
Beecher, Elizabeth *WhWNAA*
Beecher, Esther Catherine 1800- *CyAL 2*
Beecher, Eunice White 1812-1897 *Alli Sup,*
DcAmA, DcNAA
Beecher, George 1809-1843 *OhA&B*
Beecher, Harriet *Alli*
Beecher, Henry Ward 1813-1887 *Alli, Alli Sup,*
AmA, AmA&B, BbD, BiD&SB, CasWL,
Chmbr 3, CyAL 1, CyAL 2, DcAmA,
DcBiA, DcEnL, DcNAA, EvLB, OhA&B,
OxAm, OxEng, Pen Am, REn, REnAL
Beecher, Mrs. Henry Ward *CyAL 1, DcNAA*
Beecher, Johannes R 1891-1958 *CrCD*
Beecher, John 1904- *AuNews 1, BlkAW,*
ConAu 5R, ConLC 6, ConP 1970,
ConP 1975, WrD 1976
Beecher, Julia M *Alli Sup*
Beecher, Leonard James 1906- *Au&Wr*
Beecher, Lyman 1775-1863 *Alli, AmA,*
AmA&B, BbD, BiD&SB, CyAL 1,
DcAmA, DcEnL, DcLEnL, DcNAA,
OhA&B, OxAm, REn, REnAL
Beecher, Marion E 1887- *WhWNAA*
Beecher, Mary Howell 1854-1923 *DcNAA*
Beecher, May Howell *ChPo, DcNAA*
Beecher, Moritz *ChPo*
Beecher, Thomas Kinnicut 1824-1900 *Alli Sup,*
CyAL 2, DcAmA, DcNAA
Beecher, Thomas Kinnicutt 1824-1900 *BiD&SB,*
OhA&B
Beecher, William C And Scoville, S *Alli Sup*
Beecher, William Constantine 1849-1928
DcNAA
Beecher, William Gordon, Jr. 1904-
AmSCAP 66
Beecher, Willis Judson 1838-1912 *Alli Sup,*
DcAmA, DcNAA, OhA&B
Beecher-Stowe, Mrs. *DcEnL*
Beechey, Frederick S *Alli Sup*
Beechey, Sir Frederick William 1796-1856 *Alli,*
OxCan
Beechey, St. Vincent *Alli Sup*
Beechey, Sir William 1753-1839 *ChPo*
Beechhold, Henry F 1928- *ConAu 33*
Beeching, Amy 1922- *ConAu 21*
Beeching, Henry Charles 1859-1919 *Chmbr 3,*
ChPo, ChPo S1, ChPo S2, DcEnA Ap,
LongC
Beeching, Jack *ConAu 21*
Beechwood, Warwick *Alli Sup*
Beeck, Alfred 1855- *WhLA*
Beeckman, Daniel *Alli*
Beecroft, J J *Alli Sup*
Beecroft, John William Richard 1902-1966
AmA&B, AuBYP, ConAu 5R
Beede, Charles Gould d1906 *DcNAA*

Beede, Ivan 1897-1946 *DcNAA*
Beeding, Frances *MnBBF*
Beeding, Francis 1885-1944 *DcLEnL,*
EncM&D, EvLB, LongC, NcwC, TwCA,
TwCA Sup, TwCW
Beedle, Susannah *Alli Sup*
Beedle, Thomas *Alli Sup*
Beedome, Thomas d1641 *Alli, ChPo*
Beegle, Dewey Maurice 1919- *ConAu 5R*
Beehan, Jack Rogers *WhWNAA*
Beehler, William Henry 1848-1915 *Alli Sup,*
DcNAA
Beek, J *Alli*
Beek, Martin A 1909- *ConAu 13R*
Beeke, Henry 1751-1837 *Alli, BiDLA,*
BiDLA Sup
Beekman, Allan 1913- *ConAu 33, WrD 1976*
Beekman, E M 1939- *ConAu 33*
Beekman, James Spencer Cannon d1906
DcNAA
Beekman, John 1918- *ConAu 61*
Beekman, Ross *DcNAA*
Beelby, Malcolm 1907- *AmSCAP 66*
Beeler, Florence Ashley *AnMV 1926*
Beeler, Maxwell Newton 1888- *IndAu 1917,*
WhWNAA
Beeler, Nelson Frederick 1910- *AuBYP,*
MorJA
Beeley, Arthur Lawton 1890- *WhWNAA*
Beeley, Sir Harold 1909- *Au&Wr*
Beelo, Adrianus 1798-1878 *CasWL*
Beeman, Bess Odell *TexWr*
Beeman, T *Alli Sup*
Beeman, Thomas O *Alli Sup*
Beene, Greg *DrAP 1975*
Beenken, Hermann 1896- *WhLA*
Beer, Barrett L 1936- *ConAu 49*
Beer, Edwin 1876-1938 *DcNAA, WhWNAA*
Beer, Eloise C S 1903- *ConAu 13R*
Beer, Ethel S 1897-1975 *ConAu 25, ConAu 57,*
WrD 1976
Beer, Francis Anthony 1939- *ConAu 25*
Beer, G J *BiDLA*
Beer, George Louis 1872-1920 *AmLY, DcNAA*
Beer, Gretel *Au&Wr*
Beer, J W *Alli Sup*
Beer, Johann 1655-1700 *CasWL, EvEuW,*
OxGer, Pen Eur
Beer, John B 1926- *ConAu 5R*
Beer, Kathleen Costello 1926- *ConAu 25,*
WrD 1976
Beer, Lawrence W 1932- *ConAu 37*
Beer, Lisl *ConAu XR*
Beer, Michael 1800-1833 *OxGer*
Beer, Morris Abel 1887?-1936 *AnMV 1926,*
ChPo, ChPo S1
Beer, Patricia 1924- *Au&Wr, ConAu 61,*
ConP 1970, ConP 1975, WrD 1976
Beer, Richard *IlBYP, IlCB 1966*
Beer, Robert Carl *Alli Sup*
Beer, Samuel Hutchison 1911- *AmA&B,*
Au&Wr, ConAu 61, OhA&B
Beer, Stafford 1926- *Au&Wr, WrD 1976*
Beer, Thomas 1889-1940 *AmA&B, ConAmL,*
DcLEnL, DcNAA, EvLB, OxAm, REn,
REnAL, TwCA, TwCA Sup
Beer, William 1849- *BiDSA*
Beer-Hofmann, Richard 1866-1945 *CasWL,*
ClDMEuL, CnMD, EncWL, McGWD,
ModGL, ModWD, OxGer, Pen Eur, REn
Beerbohm, Henry Maximilian 1872-1956
EncWL
Beerbohm, Julius *Alli Sup*
Beerbohm, Sir Max 1872-1956 *AtlBL, CasWL,*
ChPo S1, Chmbr 3, CnMD, CnMWL,
CyWA, DcLEnL, EvLB, LongC, ModBL,
ModBL Sup, ModWD, NewC, OxEng,
Pen Eng, RAdv 1, REn, TwCA,
TwCA Sup, TwCW, WebEAL
Beerbower, James Richard 1927- *IndAu 1917*
Beere, Richard *Alli, BiDLA*
Beerman, *Alli*
Beers, Burton Floyd 1927- *ConAu 1R,*
WrD 1976
Beers, Clifford Whittingham 1876-1943 *DcNAA,*
REnAL
Beers, Dorothy Sands 1917- *ConAu 49,*
SmATA 9

Beers, Eli 1856-1946 *DcNAA*
Beers, Ethel Lynn 1827-1879 *AmA, AmA&B,*
BiD&SB, ChPo S2, EvLB, OxAm,
REnAL
Beers, Ethelinda 1827-1879 *Alli Sup, ChPo,*
DcAmA, DcNAA
Beers, Fannie A 1840?- *BiDSA, DcNAA*
Beers, George Emerson 1865- *WhWNAA*
Beers, Henry Augustin 1847-1926 *Alli Sup,*
AmA, AmA&B, BiD&SB, ChPo,
DcAmA, DcNAA, OxAm, REnAL
Beers, Henry Putney 1907- *ConAu 13R*
Beers, Jan Van 1821-1888 *BiD&SB, CasWL*
Beers, Lorna 1897- *ConAu 49*
Beers, R W *Alli Sup*
Beers, Timothy *CyAL 1*
Beers, V Gilbert 1928- *ConAu 49, SmATA 9*
Beers, William George 1843-1900 *Alli Sup,*
BbtC, DcNAA
Beery, Jesse 1861-1945 *OhA&B*
Beery, Mary 1907- *ConAu 5R, WrD 1976*
Beery, Pauline Gracia 1881- *WhWNAA*
Beesley, Augustus Henry *ChPo*
Beesley, Henry *Alli*
Beesley, Thomas Quinn 1891- *WhWNAA*
Beesly, Mrs. *Alli Sup*
Beesly, Augustus Henry *Alli Sup*
Beesly, Edward Spencer 1831- *Alli Sup,*
Chmbr 3
Beeson, Charles Henry 1870-1949 *IndAu 1917*
Beeson, Jack 1921- *AmSCAP 66*
Beeson, Jasper Luther 1867- *WhWNAA*
Beeson, John 1803- *DcNAA*
Beeson, Malcolm Alfred 1879- *WhWNAA*
Beeson, Trevor 1926- *Au&Wr, WrD 1976*
Beeston, C *Alli Sup*
Beeston, Edmund *Alli*
Beeston, L J *MnBBF*
Beeston, Sir William *Alli*
Beet, Joseph Agar 1840- *Alli Sup*
Beet, Josephine M *ChPo S1*
Beetham, Hutton *Alli Sup*
Beethoven, Ludwig Van 1770-1827 *AtlBL, BbD,*
BiD&SB, NewC, OxGer, REn
Beetle, David Harold 1908- *Au&Wr*
Beetles, Peggy *ChPo S1*
Beeton, Isabella Mary 1836-1865 *Alli Sup,*
EvLB, OxEng
Beeton, Samuel Orchart 1831-1877 *Alli Sup,*
ChPo S1, HsB&A, HsB&A Sup, MnBBF
Beets, Henry 1869-1947 *AmA&B, WhWNAA*
Beets, Nicolaas 1814-1903 *BiD&SB, CasWL,*
EuA, Pen Eur
Beever, Susannah *Alli Sup*
Beever, William Holt *Alli Sup*
Beevers, John 1911-1975 *ConAu 61*
Beevor, C E And Horsley *Alli Sup*
Beezley, P C 1895- *ConAu 5R*
Beezley, William H 1942- *ConAu 49*
Beffroy DeReigney, Louis Abel 1757-1811
EvEuW
Befu, Harumi 1930- *ConAu 53*
Beg, Toran *ConAu XR*
Begay, Harrison *IlBYP*
Begbie, Agnes H *ChPo, ChPo S2*
Begbie, Edward Harold 1871-1929 *ChPo,*
ChPo S1
Begbie, Elphinstone Waters *Alli Sup*
Begbie, Harold 1871?-1929 *ChPo S2, LongC,*
NewC
Begbie, J P *Alli Sup*
Begbie, James 1798-1869 *Alli Sup*
Begbie, James Warburton 1826-1876 *Alli Sup*
Begbie, Janet *ChPo*
Begbie, Sir Matthew Baillie 1819-1894 *OxCan*
Begeman, Louis 1865-1958 *IndAu 1917,*
WhWNAA
Begg, Alexander 1825-1905? *DcNAA, OxCan*
Begg, Alexander 1839?-1897? *OxCan, DcNAA*
Begg, Alexander Charles 1912- *WrD 1976*
Begg, Howard Bolton 1896- *ConAu 5R*
Begg, James 1808-1883 *Alli Sup*
Begg, James A *Alli*
Begg, John Henderson *Alli Sup*
Begg, Neil Colquhoun 1915- *WrD 1976*
Begg, W Proudfoot *Alli Sup*
Begg, John *Alli*
Beggerow, Hans A H 1874- *WhLA*

Beggs, David 1909- *WrD 1976*
Beggs, David, III 1931-1966 *ConAu P-1*
Beggs, Donald L 1941- *ConAu 33*
Beggs, George Erle 1883-1939 *DcNAA*
Beggs, Stephen R 1801-1895 *DcNAA*
Beggs, Thomas *Alli Sup*
Beggs, Thomas 1789-1847 *PoIre*
Beghtol, Charles Alexander 1869- *WhWNAA*
Begin, Louis Nazaire 1840-1925 *DcNAA*
Begley, Cornelius *Alli*
Begley, James 1929- *ConAu 25*
Beglinger, Nina Joy 1885- *WhWNAA*
Begner, Edith P *Au&Wr, ConAu 1R*
Begovic, Milan 1876-1948 *CasWL, EncWL, ModSL 2*
Beh-Azin, Muhammad 1915- *CasWL*
Beha, Ernest Andrew 1908- *Au&Wr, ConAu P-1*
Beha, Sister Helen Marie 1926- *ConAu 21*
Beha, Joseph L *WhWNAA*
Behagel, Otto 1854- *WhLA*
Behaim, Michael 1416-1472? *OxGer, Pen Eur*
Behaine, Rene 1880-1966 *CasWL*
Behan, Brendan 1923-1964 *CasWL, CnMD, CnThe, ConLC 1, CrCD, EncWL, LongC, McGWD, ModBL, ModBL Sup, ModWD, NewC, Pen Eng, REn, REnWD, TwCW, WebEAL, WhTwL, WorAu*
Behan, John Clifford Valentine 1881- *WhLA*
Behan, Leslie *ConAu XR*
Behara, Devendra Nath 1940- *ConAu 41*
Beharrell, Thomas G 1824- *Alli Sup, IndAu 1816*
Behazin, Mohammad E'temadzade 1915- *DcOrL 3*
Beheim, Michael 1416-1472? *CasWL, EvEuW, OxGer*
Beheim-Schwarzbach, Martin 1900- *OxGer*
Behemb, Martin 1557-1622 *OxGer*
Behle, William Harroun 1909- *ConAu 5R, WrD 1976*
Behler, Ernst 1928- *ConAu 41*
Behlmer, Reuben D 1903- *IndAu 1917*
Behlmer, Rudy 1926- *ConAu 57*
Behm, Heinrich 1853- *WhLA*
Behm, Martin *OxGer*
Behm, William H, Jr. 1922- *ConAu 13R*
Behme, Robert Lee 1924- *ConAu 57*
Behmen, Jakob *EvEuW*
Behn, Afra 1640-1689 *Alli, DcLEnL, NewC, OxEng, Pen Eng*
Behn, Aphara 1640-1689 *Alli, NewC, OxEng*
Behn, Aphra 1640-1689 *Alli, AtlBL, BbD, BiD&SB, BrAu, CasWL, ChPo, Chmbr 2, CyWA, DcBiA, DcEnA, DcEnL, DcEuL, EvLB, McGWD, MouLC 1, NewC, OxEng, Pen Eng, REn, WebEAL*
Behn, Ayfara 1640-1689 *OxEng*
Behn, Harry 1898-1973 *AnCL, ArizL, AuBYP, BkCL, ChPo, ChPo S1, ChPo S2, ConAu 5R, ConAu 53, IlCB 1956, IlCB 1966, MorBMP, MorJA, SmATA 2, St&VC*
Behn, Siegfried 1884- *WhLA*
Behne, Adolf 1885- *WhLA*
Behnke, Charles A 1891- *ConAu 19*
Behnke, Emil *Alli Sup*
Behnke, Frances L *ConAu 33, SmATA 8*
Behnken, Heinrich 1880-1960 *CasWL*
Behr, Edward 1926- *ConAu 1R*
Behr, H H *Alli Sup*
Behr, Hans-Georg 1937- *CrCD*
Behr, Hans Herman 1818-1904 *DcNAA*
Behr-Pinnow, Carl Von 1864- *WhLA*
Behramoglu, Ataol 1942- *DcOrL 3*
Behrend, Arthur C 1895- *Au&Wr, ChPo S1*
Behrend, Bernard Arthur 1875-1932 *DcNAA*
Behrend, Elisabeth 1887- *WhLA*
Behrend, Ernst 1882- *WhLA*
Behrend, Felix 1880- *WhLA*
Behrend, George 1922- *WrD 1976*
Behrend, George Henry Sandham 1922- *Au&Wr*
Behrend, Jeanne 1911- *ConAu 17R*
Behrends, Adolphus Julius Frederick 1839-1900 *Alli Sup, DcAmA, DcNAA, OhA&B*

Behrends, Cora E 1865- *TexWr*
Behrendt, Walter Curt 1884-1945 *DcNAA, WhLA*
Behrens, Bertha *BiD&SB, OxGer*
Behrens, Charles A 1885- *WhWNAA*
Behrens, Dietrich 1859- *WhLA*
Behrens, Ernst 1878-1970 *CasWL*
Behrens, Helen Kindler 1922- *ConAu 61*
Behrens, Herman D 1901- *ConAu 33*
Behrens, Jack 1935- *AmSCAP 66*
Behrens, John C 1933- *ConAu 37, WrD 1976*
Behrens, June York 1925- *AuBYP, ConAu 17R*
Behrisch, Ernst Wolfgang 1738-1809 *OxGer*
Behrman, Carol H 1925- *ConAu 61*
Behrman, Ethel Knapp 1800-1943 *OhA&B*
Behrman, Jack N 1922- *ConAu 29*
Behrman, Lucy C 1940- *ConAu 29*
Behrman, Robert G *TexWr*
Behrman, S N 1893-1973 *AmA&B, Au&Wr, CasWL, CnDAL, CnMD, CnThe, ConAmA, ConAu 45, ConAu P-1, ConDr, CrCD, DcLEnL, LongC, McGWD, ModAL, ModWD, OxAm, Pen Am, REn, REnAL, REnWD, TwCA, TwCA Sup, WebEAL*
Behrmann, Walter 1882- *WhLA*
Beichman, Arnold 1913- *ConAu 49*
Beichner, Paul Edward 1912- *ConAu 33, IndAu 1917*
Beier, Ernst G 1916- *ConAu 21*
Beier, Ulli 1922- *ConAu 9R, TwCW, WrD 1976*
Beigel, Hermann *Alli Sup*
Beigel, Hugo George 1897- *ConAu 37, WrD 1976*
Beighle, Nellie 1851-1916 *DcNAA*
Beighton, Mrs. *Alli Sup*
Beighton, Henry *Alli*
Beighton, John F *Alli Sup*
Beighton, Mary *ChPo, ChPo S2*
Beik, Paul H 1915- *ConAu 13R*
Beilby *Alli*
Beilby, Mister *BiDLA*
Beilby, J Wood *Alli Sup*
Beilby, John *Alli*
Beilby, Samuel d1813 *Alli, BiDLA, BiDLA Sup*
Beilby, William *Alli Sup*
Beilenson, Edna 1909- *AmA&B*
Beilenson, Laurence W 1899- *ConAu 29*
Beiler, Edna 1923- *ConAu 1R, IndAu 1917*
Beiler, Irwin Ross 1883- *OhA&B*
Beilharz, Edwin Alanson 1907- *ConAu 33*
Beim, Jerrold 1910-1957 *AuBYP, JBA 1951*
Beim, Lorraine 1909-1951 *JBA 1951*
Bein, Albert 1902- *CnMD, ModWD, OxAm*
Beinart, Ben Zion *WrD 1976*
Beinhacker, Ada Perry 1882-1952 *IndAu 1917*
Beinhart, Ernest George 1887- *WhWNAA*
Beining, Guy R *DrAP 1975*
Beirne, Bryan Patrick 1918- *Au&Wr*
Beirne, Joseph Anthony 1911-1974 *ConAu 45, ConAu 53*
Beirne, Brother Kilian 1896- *ConAu 21*
Beiser, Arthur *AuBYP*
Beiser, Germaine *AuBYP*
Beisly, Sidney *Alli Sup*
Beisner, Robert L 1936- *ConAu 25, WrD 1976*
Beissel, Henry Eric 1929- *ConP 1970, ConP 1975, OxCan Sup, WrD 1976*
Beissel, Johann Conrad 1690-1768 *AmA&B, CasWL*
Beisser, Arnold R 1925- *ConAu 25*
Beistle, Aldarilla Shipley 1896-1949 *OhA&B*
Beitel, Calvin G *Alli Sup*
Beith, Alexander 1799- *Alli Sup*
Beith, Sir John Hay 1876-1952 *Chmbr 3, DcLEnL, EvLB, LongC, MnBBF, NewC, REn, TwCA, TwCA Sup*
Beitler, Ethel Jane 1906- *ConAu 5R*
Beitler, Stanley 1924- *AuBYP, ConAu 5R*
Beitz, Charles R 1949- *ConAu 49*
Beitzinger, A J 1918- *ConAu 45*
Beja, Morris 1935- *ConAu 29, WrD 1976*
Bejart, Madeleine And Armande *OxFr*
Bejerot, Nils 1921- *ConAu 29*

Bejla, J *EvEuW*
Bek, Alexander Alfredovich 1903- *CasWL*
Beke, Charles Tilstone 1800-1874 *Alli, Alli Sup, DcEnL*
Beke, Emily *Alli Sup*
Bekenn, M L *Alli Sup*
Bekessy, Jean *TwCA Sup*
Bekhterev, Vladimir Mikhailovich 1857-1927 *BiDPar*
Bekinsau, John 1496-1559 *Alli*
Bekker, Balthasar 1634-1698 *CasWL*
Bekker, Elisabeth 1738-1804 *BiD&SB*
Bekker, Hugo 1925- *ConAu 41*
Bekker-Nielsen, Hans 1933- *ConAu 25*
Bekkh, Johann Joseph *OxGer*
Beklemishev, Yuri Solomonovich 1908-1941 *DcRusL*
Beklennishev, Yuriy *CasWL*
Bel, Sarah F *ChPo*
Bel, Thomas *Alli*
Bel, William *Alli*
Bel Geddes, Joan *ConAu 57*
Belafonte, Harold George, Jr. 1927- *AmSCAP 66*
Belaieff, Michael Vassilievitch *WhLA*
Belair, Richard L 1934- *ConAu 13R*
Belan, Cliff 1921- *AmSCAP 66*
Beland, Andre *OxCan*
Beland, Henri Severin 1869-1935 *DcNAA*
Belane, George *WhWNAA*
Belaney, Archibald *Alli Sup, PoIre*
Belaney, Archibald Stansfeld 1888-1938 *CanWr, LongC*
Belaney, George Stansfeld 1888-1938 *DcLEnL, OxCan*
Belaney, Robert *Alli Sup*
Belanger, Henri *OxCan Sup*
Belanger, Jean Amable 1832-1913 *DcNAA*
Belanger, Jeannine 1915- *OxCan*
Belanger, L *BbtC*
Belanger, Marcel *OxCan Sup*
Belanger, Rene *OxCan Sup*
Belanger-Gill, Georgiana *WhWNAA*
Belasco, David 1859?-1931 *AmA&B, CasWL, Chmbr 3, CnDAL, CnThe, DcAmA, DcLEnL, DcNAA, EvLB, LongC, McGWD, ModAL, ModWD, OxAm, REn, REnAL, REnWD, TwCA, TwCA Sup, TwCW, WhWNAA*
Belaval, Emilio S 1903- *DcCLA, PueRA*
Belben, May *ChPo S1*
Belbin, Harry *MnBBF*
Belbin, Peter *Alli*
Belcamp, J V *Alli*
Belcari, Feo 1410-1484 *CasWL, DcEuL, McGWD, REn*
Belcastro, Joseph 1910- *ConAu 19*
Belch, Caroline Jean 1916- *ConAu 45*
Belcher *Alli*
Belcher, Alexander Emerson 1844-1926 *DcNAA*
Belcher, Dabridgcourt d1621 *Alli, DcEnL*
Belcher, Lady Diana *Alli Sup*
Belcher, Sir Edward 1799-1877 *Alli, Alli Sup, BbtC, OxCan*
Belcher, Henry *Alli Sup*
Belcher, Hilda 1881- *ChPo*
Belcher, Mrs. J *Alli*
Belcher, John *Alli Sup*
Belcher, Jonathan 1681-1757 *CyAL 1*
Belcher, Jonathan 1710-1776 *BbtC, OxCan*
Belcher, Joseph 1794-1859 *Alli, Alli Sup, BbtC, ChPo, DcAmA, DcNAA*
Belcher, Robert Henry *Alli Sup*
Belcher, Ronald 1909- *Au&Wr*
Belcher, Samuel *Alli*
Belcher, Thomas Waugh *Alli Sup*
Belcher, William *Alli*
Belches, R *Alli*
Belchier, Dabridgcourt *Alli*
Belchier, John *Alli*
Belcikovski, Adam 1839- *BiD&SB*
Belcour, G *Alli Sup*
Belcourt, Georges Antoine 1803-1874 *BbtC, DcNAA, OxCan*
Belcourt, Napoleon Antoine 1860- *WhWNAA*
Beldam, Joseph *Alli Sup*
Belden, A Russell 1831?- *DcNAA*
Belden, Ezekiel Porter 1823-1911 *DcNAA*

Belden, George P 1845?- *Alli Sup, EarAB Sup, OhA&B*
Belden, Henry S 1840-1920 *OhA&B*
Belden, Jessie Perry 1857-1910 *DcAmA, DcNAA*
Belden, L W *Alli Sup*
Belden, Lemuel W 1801-1839 *DcNAA*
Belden, N H *Alli Sup*
Belden, Shirley *AuBYP*
Belding, Albert G 1870- *WhWNAA*
Belding, Robert E 1911- *ConAu 33*
Belev, Gyoncho 1889-1962 *CasWL*
Belew, M Wendell 1922- *ConAu 33*
Belfast, Earl Of *Alli Sup, PoIre*
Belfield, Eversley Michael Gallimore 1918- *Au&Wr, ConAu 25, WrD 1976*
Belfield, Harry Wedgwood *MnBBF*
Belfield, Henry Holmes 1837-1912 *DcNAA*
Belfield, W T *Alli Sup*
Belfield, William Thomas 1856-1929 *DcNAA*
Belfiglio, Valentine J 1934- *ConAu 49*
Belford, Ken *OxCan Sup*
Belford, Lee A 1913- *ConAu 17R*
Belfour, Hugo James 1802-1827 *Alli*
Belfour, John *Alli, BiDLA*
Belfour, O *BiDLA*
Belfour, Okey *Alli*
Belfrage, Cedric 1904- *AmA&B, AmNov, Au&Wr, ConAu 9R, TwCA, TwCA Sup, WrD 1976*
Belfrage, Henry 1774-1835 *Alli, DcEnL*
Belfrage, Sally 1936- *Au&Wr*
Belgiojoso, Princess Cristina Trivulzio 1808-1871 *OxFr*
Belgion, Montgomery 1892-1973 *Au&Wr, ConAu P-1*
Belgrave, Dalrymple J *Alli Sup*
Belgrave, Richard *Alli*
Belgrove, William *Alli*
Belgum, David 1922- *ConAu 13R*
Belhaven, Lord *Alli*
Beliashvili, A *DcOrL 3*
Belin, Prosper *Alli Sup*
Beling, Ernst Von 1866- *WhLA*
Beling, Richard 1613-1677 *Alli*
Beling, Willard A 1919- *ConAu 53*
Belinkov, Arkady Viktorovich 1922?-1970 *ConAu 29*
Belinski, Maxim *DcRusL*
Belinsky, Vissarion Grigoryevich 1811-1848 *BiD&SB, CasWL, DcRusL, EuA, EvEuW, Pen Eur, REn*
Belisario, A M *Alli, BiDLA*
Belisarius 505?-565 *NewC, REn*
Belisle, D W *Alli Sup, ChPo S1*
Belisle, David W *DcNAA*
Belitsky, A Harvey 1929- *ConAu 33*
Belitt, Ben 1911- *AmA&B, ConAu 13R, ConP 1970, ConP 1975, DrAP 1975, Pen Am, TwCA Sup, WrD 1976*
Belke, Thomas *Alli*
Belkin, Samuel 1911- *AmA&B, ConAu 1R*
Belkind, Allen 1927- *ConAu 29*
Belknap, B H *YABC 1*
Belknap, Boynton K *HsB&A*
Belknap, Charles Eugene 1846-1929 *DcNAA*
Belknap, D P *Alli Sup*
Belknap, Eugene McCamly 1898-1949 *OhA&B*
Belknap, George Eugene 1832- *ChPo S2*
Belknap, George Washington 1832-1903 *DcAmA*
Belknap, Ivan 1916- *ConAu 5R*
Belknap, Jeremy 1744-1798 *Alli, AmA, AmA&B, ChPo, ChPo S1, CyAL 1, DcAmA, DcLEnL, OxAm, REnAL*
Belknap, Jeremy 1774-1798 *DcNAA*
Belknap, Robert H 1917- *ConAu 45*
Belknap, Robert L 1929- *ConAu 33, WrD 1976*
Belknap, S Yancey 1895- *ConAu P-1*
Belknap, William Worth 1829-1890 *DcNAA*
Bell *Alli*
Bell, Mrs. *Alli Sup*
Bell, A *Alli Sup*
Bell, A Donald 1920- *ConAu 25*
Bell, A N *Alli Sup*
Bell, Acton *BiD&SB, DcEnA, DcLEnL, NewC*

Bell, Acton, Ellis, And Currer *REn*
Bell, Adam *NewC*
Bell, Mrs. Adolphus *Alli Sup*
Bell, Adrian Hanbury 1901- *DcLEnL, EvLB, LongC, TwCA, TwCA Sup*
Bell, Agnes Paton 1891- *Au&Wr*
Bell, Agrippa Nelson 1820-1911 *BiDSA, DcAmA, DcNAA*
Bell, Alan P 1932- *ConAu 33*
Bell, Alexander Graham 1847-1922 *AmLY, DcNAA, LongC, REnAL*
Bell, Alexander Melville 1819-1905 *Alli Sup, DcAmA, DcNAA*
Bell, Alexander Montgomerie 1808-1868 *Alli Sup*
Bell, Alvin Eugene 1882- *OhA&B*
Bell, Andrew *Alli Sup, BbtC, OxCan*
Bell, Andrew 1753-1832 *Alli, BiDLA, BiDLA Sup*
Bell, Andrew James 1856-1932 *DcNAA*
Bell, Annie Douglas *ChPo S1, ChPo S2*
Bell, Anthea *ChPo S1*
Bell, Archibald *Alli, BiDLA*
Bell, Archie 1877-1943 *AmA&B, AmLY, OhA&B, OxCan, WhWNAA*
Bell, Arnold Craig 1911- *Au&Wr*
Bell, Arthur Francis *ChPo S1, ChPo S2*
Bell, Arthur John *Alli Sup*
Bell, Arthur W *ChPo*
Bell, Arthur Wellington 1875-1945 *DcNAA*
Bell, Aubrey FitzGerald 1881-1950 *NewC*
Bell, Aubrey P G 1881-1950 *DcSpL*
Bell, Beaupre d1745 *Alli*
Bell, Benjamin *Alli, BiDLA*
Bell, Benjamin d1883 *Alli Sup*
Bell, Benjamin 1752-1836 *DcNAA*
Bell, Bernard Iddings 1886-1958 *AmA&B, OhA&B, TwCA Sup, WhWNAA*
Bell, C *ChPo S1*
Bell, C F Moberly 1847-1911 *Alli Sup, LongC*
Bell, Mrs. C M *Alli Sup*
Bell, Caroline *Alli Sup*
Bell, Carolyn *WrD 1976*
Bell, Carolyn Shaw 1920- *ConAu 29*
Bell, Catherine Douglas d1861 *Alli Sup, CarSB, DcEnL*
Bell, Sir Charles 1778-1842 *Alli, Alli Sup, BiDLA, DcEnL*
Bell, Charles Alfred 1870- *WhLA*
Bell, Charles Dent 1819?-1898 *Alli Sup, ChPo S2, PoIre*
Bell, Charles Frederic Moberly 1847-1911 *NewC*
Bell, Charles G 1929- *ConAu 37*
Bell, Charles Greenleaf 1916- *ConAu 1R, ConP 1970, ConP 1975, DrAF 1976, DrAP 1975, WrD 1976*
Bell, Charles Henry 1823-1893 *Alli Sup, AmA&B, DcAmA, DcNAA*
Bell, Charles N *Alli Sup*
Bell, Charles Napier 1854-1936 *DcNAA*
Bell, Charles U *Alli Sup*
Bell, Charles Wentworth 1858-1929 *Br&AmS*
Bell, Charles William 1876-1938 *DcNAA*
Bell, Chichester A *Alli Sup*
Bell, Clara *Alli Sup*
Bell, Clark 1832-1918 *DcNAA*
Bell, Clive 1881-1964 *DcLEnL, LongC, ModBL, NewC, OxEng, Pen Eng, REn, TwCA, TwCA Sup*
Bell, Colin Alexander 1919- *Au&Wr*
Bell, Colin John 1938- *ConAu 29, Au&Wr*
Bell, Corydon Whitten 1894- *AuBYP, ChPo, ConAu 5R, IlBYP, IlCB 1956, IlCB 1966, OhA&B, SmATA 3, ThBJA*
Bell, Currer 1816-1855 *BiD&SB, DcEnA, DcEnL, DcLEnL, NewC*
Bell, Currer, Ellis And Acton *ChPo, OxEng*
Bell, Cyril William Bowdler *Alli Sup*
Bell, Daniel 1919- *AmA&B, Au&Wr, ConAu 1R*
Bell, David Arthur 1911- *Au&Wr*
Bell, David Charles 1817-1902 *ChPo S1, DcAmA*
Bell, David S 1945- *ConAu 61*
Bell, David Victor John 1944- *ConAu 45*
Bell, Denys *ChPo S2*
Bell, Dita 1915- *AmSCAP 66*

Bell, Don *OxCan Sup*
Bell, Doyne Courtenay d1888 *Alli Sup*
Bell, Dugald *Alli Sup*
Bell, E C D *ChPo S1*
Bell, Earl H 1903-1963 *ConAu 1R*
Bell, Edward *Alli Sup*
Bell, Edward Price 1869-1943 *AmA&B, DcNAA, IndAu 1917*
Bell, Edwin 1860-1921 *DcNAA, WhWNAA*
Bell, Edwin C 1848-1923 *DcNAA*
Bell, Eileen *ConAu 33*
Bell, Elexious Thompson 1880- *WhWNAA*
Bell, Ellis *BiD&SB, DcEnA, DcLEnL, NewC*
Bell, Emily Ernst *Alli Sup*
Bell, Emily Mary *ConAu XR, SmATA XR*
Bell, Emma M *ChPo*
Bell, Eric Temple 1883-1960 *AmA&B, WhWNAA, REnAL, TwCA Sup*
Bell, Ernest *DcNAA*
Bell, Evans d1887 *Alli Sup*
Bell, Florence Eveleen 1851-1930 *ChPo, ChPo S1*
Bell, Frances Augusta 1809-1825 *ChPo*
Bell, Francis Jeffrey *Alli Sup*
Bell, Frank *OhA&B*
Bell, Frederick McKelvey 1878-1931 *DcNAA*
Bell, Gail Winther 1936- *ChPo S2, ConAu 41*
Bell, Geoffrey F 1896- *Au&Wr*
Bell, George *Alli, BiDLA, BiDLA Sup, MnBBF*
Bell, Sir George 1794-1877 *Alli Sup*
Bell, George 1814-1890 *NewC*
Bell, George 1828- *Alli Sup*
Bell, George Howard 1905- *Au&Wr*
Bell, George Joseph 1770-1847 *Alli, BiDLA*
Bell, George W 1832-1907 *Alli Sup, DcNAA*
Bell, George William 1873-1920 *DcNAA*
Bell, Gerald D 1937- *ConAu 49*
Bell, Gerard 1920- *Au&Wr*
Bell, Gertrude 1911- *ConAu 13R*
Bell, Gertrude Margaret Lowthian 1868-1926 *DcLEnL, EvLB, LongC, Pen Eng, REn*
Bell, Gina *ConAu XR, SmATA 7*
Bell, Goodloe Harper 1832-1899 *DcNAA*
Bell, Graham Keith Gallwey 1921- *Au&Wr*
Bell, H C P *Alli Sup*
Bell, Harold Idris 1879-1967 *ChPo, ConAu P-1*
Bell, Harry McAra 1899- *Au&Wr, ConAu P-1, WrD 1976*
Bell, Hattie F *ChPo*
Bell, Henry *Alli*
Bell, Henry Glassford 1803-1874 *Alli, Alli Sup, BrAu 19, ChPo, ChPo S1, ChPo S2, Chmbr 3, DcEnL, EvLB, NewC*
Bell, Mrs. Henry Glassford *Alli Sup*
Bell, Henry Nugent *Alli*
Bell, Henry Thomas Mackenzie 1856- *Alli Sup, ChPo S2, Chmbr 3*
Bell, Herbert Clifford Francis 1881- *CatA 1947*
Bell, Hill McClelland 1860-1927 *DcNAA*
Bell, Hiram Parks 1827-1908? *BiDSA, DcNAA*
Bell, Isaac 1878- *Br&AmS*
Bell, Sir Isaac Lowthian 1816- *Alli Sup*
Bell, Isabel *Alli Sup*
Bell, J *Alli, Alli Sup*
Bell, J Bowyer 1931- *ConAu 17R*
Bell, J C *Alli Sup*
Bell, J Cawdor *DcNAA, OxCan*
Bell, J Freeman *Alli Sup*
Bell, J H *Alli Sup*
Bell, J J 1871- *WhLA*
Bell, J M *BiDSA*
Bell, J S *Alli*
Bell, Jack L 1904-1975 *ConAu 1R, ConAu 61*
Bell, Jacob And Redwood, T *Alli Sup*
Bell, James *Alli, Alli Sup, BiDLA*
Bell, James 1769-1833 *Alli*
Bell, James 1846- *ChPo S1, ChPo S2*
Bell, James B *Alli Sup*
Bell, James Edward 1941- *ConAu 33, WrD 1976*
Bell, James Ford *ChPo*
Bell, James Kenton 1937- *ConAu 25, WrD 1976*
Bell, James Mackintosh 1877-1934 *DcNAA*
Bell, James Madison 1826-1902 *AmA, AmA&B, BlkAW, CnDAL, DcNAA,*

OhA&B
Bell, James Munsie 1880- *WhWNAA*
Bell, Janet *ConAu XR, SmATA XR*
Bell, Jeannie *Alli Sup*
Bell, John *Alli, BiDLA*
Bell, John d1801 *Alli*
Bell, John 1691-1780 *Alli*
Bell, John 1763-1820 *Alli*
Bell, John 1796-1872 *Alli, DcAmA, DcNAA*
Bell, John 1797-1869 *BiDSA*
Bell, John 1799?-1868 *OxCan*
Bell, John 1800- *Alli*
Bell, John 1811-1895 *ChPo*
Bell, John, Jr. 1783-1864 *ChPo, ChPo S2*
Bell, John Calhoun 1851-1933 *DcNAA*
Bell, John Gray *Alli*
Bell, John Herbert *ChPo S2*
Bell, John Joy 1871-1934 *ChPo, ChPo S1, EvLB, LongC, NewC, Pen Eng*
Bell, John Keble 1875-1928 *ChPo, MnBBF*
Bell, John Montgomerie *Alli Sup*
Bell, John Thomas 1842- *DcNAA*
Bell, Jonathan Anderson 1809-1865 *Alli Sup, ChPo S1*
Bell, Joseph 1837-1911 *Alli Sup, LongC*
Bell, Josephine 1897- *ConAu XR, EncM&D*
Bell, Joyce 1920- *ConAu 57, WrD 1976*
Bell, Joyce Denebrink 1936- *ConAu 17R*
Bell, Julian 1908-1937 *ChPo S1, DcLEnL, NewC, Pen Eng*
Bell, Kensil 1907- *AuBYP*
Bell, L Nelson 1894-1973 *ConAu 45, ConAu P-1*
Bell, Leland V 1934- *ConAu 49*
Bell, Lettice *CarSB*
Bell, Lilian Lida 1867-1929 *AmA&B, BiD&SB, ChPo S2, DcAmA, DcNAA*
Bell, Louis 1864-1923 *DcNAA*
Bell, Louise Price *ConAu P-1*
Bell, Lucia C *Alli Sup*
Bell, Lucia Osborne *AnMV 1926*
Bell, Lucile Anderson *AmSCAP 66*
Bell, Lura *DcNAA*
Bell, Luther Vose 1806-1862 *DcNAA*
Bell, M M *Alli Sup*
Bell, M W Meriwether *LivFWS*
Bell, Mackenzie 1856- *ChPo S1*
Bell, Mackenzie 1856-1930 *NewC, TwCA*
Bell, Mackintosh 1877-1934 *OxCan*
Bell, Margaret Elizabeth 1898- *AmA&B, AuBYP, ConAu 1R, MorJA, SmATA 2*
Bell, Margaret Thompson *ChPo S1*
Bell, Margaret VanHorn Dwight 1790-1834 *OhA&B*
Bell, Marguerite *PoIre*
Bell, Lady Marion *Alli Sup*
Bell, Martin 1918- *ConP 1970, ConP 1975, WrD 1976*
Bell, Marvin Hartley 1937- *AmA&B, ConAu 23, ConP 1970, ConP 1975, CrCAP, DrAP 1975, WrD 1976*
Bell, Mary *Alli Sup*
Bell, Mary C *ChPo*
Bell, Mary Hayley *Au&Wr, ConAu XR*
Bell, Mattie *ChPo*
Bell, Mymie *Alli Sup*
Bell, Nancy R E *Alli Sup*
Bell, Neil 1887-1964 *ChPo, DcLEnL, LongC, NewC, TwCA, TwCA Sup*
Bell, Norman 1899- *ConAu 61*
Bell, Norman W 1928- *ConAu 1R*
Bell, Oliver 1913- *ConAu 53*
Bell, Orelia Key 1864- *BiDSA*
Bell, Paul *Alli Sup, BrAu 19, NewC*
Bell, Pearl Doles *AmA&B, WhWNAA*
Bell, Peter Robert 1920- *Au&Wr*
Bell, Philip W 1924- *ConAu 29*
Bell, Quentin 1910- *ConAu 57, WrD 1976*
Bell, R A *ChPo S1*
Bell, R C 1917- *ConAu 17R*
Bell, Ralcy Husted 1869-1931 *DcNAA*
Bell, Raymond Martin 1907- *ConAu 29, WrD 1976*
Bell, Reginald William 1906- *Au&Wr*
Bell, Robert *Alli, Alli Sup, BiDLA*
Bell, Robert 1732?-1784 *AmA&B, CyAL 1*

Bell, Robert 1800-1867 *Alli, Alli Sup, BbD, BiD&SB, ChPo S1, ChPo S2, DcEnL, NewC, PoIre*
Bell, Robert 1841- *BbtC*
Bell, Robert, Jr. *Alli*
Bell, Robert Charles 1917- *WrD 1976*
Bell, Robert Eugene 1914- *ConAu 37, WrD 1976*
Bell, Robert Lowry *ChPo*
Bell, Robert Roy *ConAu 1R*
Bell, Robert Stanley Warren 1871-1921 *ChPo, MnBBF, WhCL*
Bell, Ronald McMillan 1914- *Au&Wr*
Bell, Roscoe Rutherford 1858- *DcNAA*
Bell, Rose 1939- *ConAu 29*
Bell, Rudolph M 1942- *ConAu 45*
Bell, S D *Alli*
Bell, S S *Alli, BbtC*
Bell, Sallie Lee Riley *ConAu 1R*
Bell, Sarah Fore 1920- *ConAu 53*
Bell, Seacombe *Alli Sup*
Bell, Sidney 1929- *ConAu 41*
Bell, Solomon *AmA&B*
Bell, Spurgeon 1880- *WhWNAA*
Bell, Susanna *Alli*
Bell, Sydney Smith *Alli, Alli Sup*
Bell, T George *Alli Sup*
Bell, T P *Alli Sup*
Bell, Thelma Harrington 1896- *AuBYP, ChPo, ConAu 1R, OhA&B, SmATA 3, ThBJA*
Bell, Thomas *Alli, Alli Sup*
Bell, Thomas 1792-1880 *Alli, Alli Sup*
Bell, Thomas 1903-1961 *AmA&B, REnAL*
Bell, Thomas J *Alli Sup*
Bell, Thornborough *Alli Sup*
Bell, Tony *ChPo*
Bell, Vanessa 1879-1961 *LongC, NewC*
Bell, Velma *ChPo S1*
Bell, Vereen McNeill 1911-1944 *DcNAA*
Bell, Vicars W 1904- *ConAu P-1, LongC*
Bell, W *Alli*
Bell, W H *Alli Sup*
Bell, Walker 1904- *Au&Wr*
Bell, Walter George 1867- *WhLA*
Bell, Walter Nehemiah d1921 *DcNAA*
Bell, Wendell 1924- *ConAu 1R*
Bell, Wilbur Cosby 1881-1933 *DcNAA, WhWNAA*
Bell, William *Alli, Alli Sup, BbtC, BiDLA*
Bell, William 1625-1683 *Alli*
Bell, William 1731-1816 *Alli*
Bell, William 1780-1857 *OxCan*
Bell, William 1860- *WhLA*
Bell, William Abraham *Alli Sup*
Bell, William Blair 1871- *WhLA*
Bell, William Bonar 1877- *WhWNAA*
Bell, William Dixon 1865- *WhWNAA*
Bell, William E *Alli Sup*
Bell, William Hemphill 1834-1906 *DcNAA*
Bell, William J *AuNews 1*
Bell, William Melvin 1860-1933 *DcNAA, IndAu 1816, WhWNAA*
Bell, William Morrison *Alli Sup*
Bell, William Stewart 1921- *ConAu 1R*
Bell, Winifred 1914- *ConAu 17R*
Bell, Winthrop *OxCan*
Bell, Zura *DcAmA*
Bell-The-Cat 1449?-1514 *NewC*
Bell-Zano, Gina *ConAu XR, SmATA 7*
Bellah, James Warner 1899- *AmA&B, AmNov, Au&Wr, ConAu 5R, REnAL, TwCA, TwCA Sup, WhWNAA*
Bellah, Robert N 1927- *ConAu 21*
Bellairs, Angus D'Albini 1918- *Au&Wr, WrD 1976*
Bellairs, Lady Blanche St. John *Alli Sup*
Bellairs, Carlyon 1871- *WhLA*
Bellairs, George 1902- *Au&Wr, EncM&D, WrD 1976*
Bellairs, Henry *Alli Sup*
Bellairs, Henry Spencer Kenrick *Alli Sup*
Bellairs, Henry Walford *Alli Sup*
Bellairs, John 1938- *ConAu 23, SmATA 2, WrD 1976*
Bellairs, Kenneth Ffarington *Alli Sup*
Bellairs, Nona *Alli Sup*
Bellaisis, Margaret *OxCan*
Bellaman, Katharine d1956 *ChPo*

Bellamann, Henry 1882-1945 *AmA&B, AnMV 1926, ChPo S2, CyWA, DcNAA, REnAL, TwCA, TwCA Sup, WhWNAA*
Bellamie, John *Alli*
Bellamont, Lord *Alli*
Bellamy, Blanche Wilder 1852-1919 *ChPo S2, DcNAA*
Bellamy, Charles J *Alli Sup*
Bellamy, Charles Joseph 1852-1910 *AmA&B, DcAmA, DcNAA*
Bellamy, D *Alli*
Bellamy, Daniel 1687- *ChPo S1*
Bellamy, Mrs. E W *LivFWS*
Bellamy, Edward *Chmbr 3*
Bellamy, Edward d1889 *Alli Sup*
Bellamy, Edward 1850-1898 *Alli Sup, AmA, AmA&B, BbD, BiD&SB, CasWL, CnDAL, CyWA, DcAmA, DcBiA, DcEnA Ap, DcLEnL, DcNAA, EvLB, MouLC 4, OxAm, OxEng, Pen Am, RAdv 1, REn, REnAL, WebEAL*
Bellamy, Elizabeth *Alli, BiDLA*
Bellamy, Elizabeth Whitfield 1837?-1900 *Alli Sup, AmA, AmA&B, BiD&SB, BiDSA, ChPo, DcAmA, DcNAA*
Bellamy, Emily Whitfield 1837?-1900 *Alli Sup*
Bellamy, Francis Rufus 1886-1972 *AmA&B, AmNov, ConAu 33*
Bellamy, G Somers *Alli Sup*
Bellamy, George Anne 1727?-1788? *Alli, NewC*
Bellamy, J *BiDLA, ChPo*
Bellamy, Jacobus 1757-1786 *BiD&SB, CasWL, DcEuL, EvEuW*
Bellamy, James A 1925- *ConAu 49*
Bellamy, James W *Alli*
Bellamy, Jeanne 1911- *AmA&B*
Bellamy, Joe David 1941- *ConAu 41, DrAF 1976, DrAP 1975*
Bellamy, John *Alli, BiDLA, ChPo S2*
Bellamy, Joseph 1719-1790 *Alli, BiD&SB, CyAL 1, DcAmA, DcNAA, EarAB Sup, OxAm*
Bellamy, Orlando Rollins 1856- *IndAu 1816*
Bellamy, Paul 1884-1956 *AmA&B*
Bellamy, R L *MnBBF*
Bellamy, Raymond Flavius 1885- *IndAu 1917*
Bellamy, Robert Lowe *ChPo*
Bellamy, Thomas *Alli*
Bellamy, Thomas 1745-1800 *Alli*
Bellamy, W H 1800-1866 *PoIre*
Bellamy, William 1846- *Alli, ChPo S1, DcAmA*
Bellan, Ruben Carl 1918- *ConAu 13R, WrD 1976*
Bellancourt, Max Edmond 1920- *Au&Wr*
Bellarmine, Robert Francis Romulus 1542-1621 *EvEuW, NewC*
Bellarmine, Roberto Francesco Romolo 1542-1621 *OxEng*
Bellarmino, Roberto Francesco Romolo 1542-1621 *NewC*
Bellars, Henry John *Alli Sup*
Bellars, William *Alli Sup*
Bellas, George *Alli*
Bellasis, Brian *MnBBF*
Bellasis, Edward 1800-1873 *Alli Sup*
Bellasis, Edward 1852- *Alli Sup*
Bellasis, Margaret Rosa *Au&Wr, CatA 1952*
Bellavance, Michel *OxCan Sup*
Bellaw, Americus Wellington 1842- *ChPo, HsB&A, OhA&B*
Bellay, Joachim Du 1522?-1560 *AtlBL, BiD&SB, EuA, EvEuW, REn*
Belle, Barbara 1922- *AmSCAP 66*
Belle, J A A *BbtC*
Belleau, Sir Narcisse-Fortunat 1808-1894 *OxCan*
Belleau, Remy 1528-1577 *BbD, BiD&SB, CasWL, DcEuL, EuA, EvEuW, OxFr, Pen Eur*
Bellefeuille, Joseph Edouard Lefebvre De 1840-1926 *DcNAA*
Belleforest, Francois De 1530-1583 *CrE&SL, DcEnL, OxFr*
Bellemans, Daniel 1642-1674 *CasWL*

Bemister, Margaret *OxCan*
Bemmann, Rudolf 1887- *WhLA*
Bemmelen, Willem Van 1868- *WhLA*
Bemont, Charles 1848- *WhLA*
Bemrose, William *Alli Sup*
Ben, Ilke *ConAu XR*
Ben-Ami 1858-1932 *Pen Eur*
Ben-Avigdor 1866-1921 *CasWL, Pen Eur*
Ben-Avraham, Chofetz Chaim *ConAu 57*
Ben-Dov, Meir *ConAu XR*
Ben-Ezer, Ehud 1936- *ConAu 61*
Ben Ezra *EvEuW*
Ben Ezra, Abraham *CasWL*
Ben-Gurion, David 1886-1973 *Au&Wr, ConAu 45*
Ben-Horav, Naphthali *ConAu 49*
Ben-Horin, Meir 1918- *ConAu 29, WrD 1976*
Ben-Israel-Kidron, Hedva *ConAu 33*
Ben Judah *EuA*
Ben Shimon Halevi, Zev *WrD 1976*
Ben Yehudah, Eliezer 1858-1922 *CasWL, EuA, Pen Cl, Pen Eur*
Ben-Yitzhak, Abraham 1883-1950 *CasWL*
Ben-Yosef, Avraham Chaim 1917- *ConAu 37, WrD 1976*
Ben-Zion, Sh 1870-1932 *CasWL*
Ben-Zion, Simcha 1870-1932 *Pen Eur*
Benade, W H *Alli Sup*
Benadum, Clarence Edward 1889- *IndAu 1917*
Benagh, Jim 1937- *ConAu 57*
Bena'i 1453-1512 *DcOrL 3*
Benamou, Michel J 1929- *ConAu 5R*
Benante, Joseph P 1936- *ConAu 33*
Benar, Andrew *Alli Sup*
Benard, Edmond Darvil 1914- *CatA 1947*
Benarde, Melvin Albert 1923- *ConAu 25*
Benarde, Melvin Albert 1922- *WrD 1976*
Benardete, Jane Johnson 1930- *ConAu 45*
Benario, Herbert W 1929- *ConAu 25*
Benarria, Allan *ConAu XR*
Benary, Margot *SmATA 2*
Benary-Isbert, Margot 1889- *AnCL, AuBYP, ConAu 5R, MorJA, SmATA 2*
Benasutti, Marion 1908- *ConAu 21, SmATA 6, WrD 1976*
Benatzky, Ralph 1894-1957 *AmSCAP 66*
Benauly *AmA&B, DcEnL*
Benavente, Jacinto 1866-1954 *CasWL, CatA 1947, ClDMEuL, CnMD, DcSpL, McGWD, ModRL, ModWD, Pen Eur, REn, REnWD, TwCW*
Benavente, Toribio De d1565 *Pen Am*
Benavente Y Martinez, Jacinto 1866-1954 *CyWA, EncWL, EvEuW, LongC, NewC, OxEng, TwCA, TwCA Sup*
Benawa, 'Abdurrauf 1913- *DcOrL 3*
Benazech, Charles 1767-1794 *BkIE*
Benbow, John 1653-1702 *NewC*
Benbow, John Glen 1884-1944 *DcNAA*
Benbrigge, John *Alli*
Bence, George Wright *Alli Sup*
Bence-Jones *Alli Sup*
Bence-Jones, Mark 1930- *Au&Wr, ConAu 13R, WrD 1976*
Benchley, Nathaniel Goddard 1915- *AmA&B, Au&Wr, ConAu 1R, SmATA 3, WorAu, WrD 1976*
Benchley, Peter B 1940- *AuNews 2, ConAu 17R, ConLC 4, SmATA 3*
Benchley, Robert Charles 1889-1945 *AmA&B, ChPo, ConAmA, DcLEnL, DcNAA, EvLB, LongC, ModAL, OxAm, Pen Am, RAdv 1, REn, REnAL, TwCA, TwCA Sup, TwCW*
Bencke, Albert Henry 1846- *Alli Sup*
Benda, Harry J 1919- *ConAu 9R*
Benda, Julien 1867-1956 *CasWL, ClDMEuL, EvEuW, LongC, OxFr, Pen Eur, REn, TwCA, TwCA Sup, WhLA*
Benda, Wladyslaw Theodore 1873- *ChPo, IlCB 1945*
Bendall, Cecil *Alli Sup*
Bendall, Gerard *Alli Sup, ChPo S1*
Bendall, Herbert *Alli Sup*
Bendall, J E *ChPo*
Bendavid, Avrom 1942- *ConAu 41*
Bendbow, Hesper *Alli Sup, DcNAA*
Bender, Arnold 1904- *Au&Wr*

Bender, C *Alli Sup*
Bender, Charles B *Alli Sup*
Bender, Charles E *Alli Sup*
Bender, Coleman C 1921- *ConAu 33, WrD 1976*
Bender, Eric J 1902-1966 *AmA&B, ChPo, OhA&B*
Bender, George H 1896-1961 *OhA&B*
Bender, H A 1895- *WhWNAA*
Bender, Hans 1907- *BiDPar*
Bender, Hans 1919- *ModGL, OxGer*
Bender, Harold H 1882-1951 *AmA&B, REnAL, WhWNAA*
Bender, Harold Stauffer 1897-1962 *IndAu 1917*
Bender, Henry E, Jr. 1937- *ConAu 33*
Bender, Henry Richard 1847- *DcNAA*
Bender, Horace *DcNAA*
Bender, Ida Catherine 1858-1916 *DcNAA*
Bender, J Terry *ChPo S2*
Bender, James F 1905- *AmA&B, ConAu 17R*
Bender, Jay *ConAu XR*
Bender, Joan *AmSCAP 66*
Bender, John S 1827-1912 *Alli Sup, IndAu 1816, OhA&B*
Bender, Louis W 1927- *ConAu 33*
Bender, Lucy Ellen 1942- *ConAu 25*
Bender, Marylin 1925- *ConAu 21*
Bender, Prosper 1844-1917 *Alli Sup, BiD&SB, DcAmA, DcNAA, OxCan*
Bender, Richard 1930- *ConAu 45*
Bender, Robert M 1936- *ConAu 33*
Bender, Ross Thomas 1929- *ConAu 61*
Bender, Stephen 1942- *ConAu 61*
Bender, Todd K 1936- *ConAu 21, WrD 1976*
Bender, Wilbur H 1860-1927 *DcNAA*
Bendezu, Francisco 1928- *DcCLA*
Bendick, Jeanne 1919- *AuBYP, BkP, ConAu 5R, IlCB 1956, IlCB 1966, MorJA, SmATA 2*
Bendick, Robert L 1917- *AuBYP, ConAu 61, MorJA*
Bendiener, Oscar 1870- *WhLA*
Bendiner, Elmer 1916- *ConAu 57*
Bendiner, Robert 1909- *AmA&B, Au&Wr, ConAu 9R*
Bendire, Charles Emil 1836-1897 *DcAmA, DcNAA*
Bendish, Sir Thomas *Alli*
Bendit, Gladys Williams 1889?- *Au&Wr, ConAu P-1*
Bendit, Laurence John 1898- *BiDPar, ConAu 25*
Bendit, Phoebe Daphne Payne 1939- *BiDPar*
Bendix, Reinhard 1916- *ConAu 1R, WrD 1976*
Bendixson, Terence 1934- *WrD 1976*
Bendloe, William *Alli*
Bendlowes, Edward 1602-1676 *Alli, DcEnL*
Bendow, Josef *WhWNAA*
Bendre, Dattatreya Ramacandra 1896- *DcOrL 2*
Bendyshe, Thomas *Alli Sup*
Benedeiz *CasWL, EvEuW*
Benedek, Ludwig August, Ritter Von 1804-1881 *OxGer*
Benedek, Therese 1892- *ConAu 41*
Benedetta, Mary 1909- *Au&Wr*
Benedetti, Mario 1920- *CasWL, DcCLA, Pen Am*
Benedetti, Robert L 1939- *ConAu 29*
Benedetta Da Mantova *CasWL*
Benedetto, Antonio Di 1922- *DcCLA*
Benedetto, Arnold J 1916-1966 *ConAu 5R*
Benedicks, Carl Axel Fredrik 1875- *WhLA*
Benedict *Alli*
Benedict d1193 *NewC*
Benedict 480-543 *DcEuL*
Benedict Biscop 629?-690 *Alli, BiB S, NewC*
Benedict Of Norwich d1340 *Alli*
Benedict Of Peterborough d1193 *Alli, BiB N, DcEnL*
Benedict Of Saint Peter's *BiB N*
Benedict, A L 1865- *WhWNAA*
Benedict, Agnes Elizabeth 1889-1950 *OhA&B*
Benedict, Anne Elizabeth Kendrick 1851-1922 *DcNAA, OhA&B*
Benedict, Bertram 1892- *WhWNAA*
Benedict, David 1779-1874 *Alli, Alli Sup,*

BiD&SB, DcAmA, DcNAA
Benedict, Dorothy Potter 1889- *ConAu P-1*
Benedict, Elsie Lincoln *AmA&B*
Benedict, Emma Lee *ChPo*
Benedict, Erastus Cornelius 1800-1880 *Alli, Alli Sup, ChPo, ChPo S2, DcAmA, DcNAA, PoCh*
Benedict, Ernest *Alli Sup*
Benedict, Fannie *ChPo*
Benedict, Francis Gano 1870- *WhWNAA*
Benedict, Frank Lee 1834-1910 *Alli Sup, AmA&B, BiD&SB, BiDSA, DcAmA, DcNAA*
Benedict, G H *Alli Sup*
Benedict, George Grenville 1826-1907 *Alli Sup, DcAmA, DcNAA*
Benedict, George L *ChPo*
Benedict, Harriet E *ChPo*
Benedict, Harry Yandell 1869-1937 *DcNAA, TexWr, WhWNAA*
Benedict, Henry Marvin 1827-1875 *Alli Sup, DcNAA*
Benedict, Mrs. Hester *Alli Sup*
Benedict, Hester A 1838- *ChPo, ChPo S1, OhA&B*
Benedict, J D *ChPo*
Benedict, Joel *Alli*
Benedict, Joel Tyler 1821-1892 *DcNAA*
Benedict, Joseph *Alli Sup, ConAu XR*
Benedict, Sir Julius 1804-1885 *Alli Sup*
Benedict, Leopold *REnAL*
Benedict, Lois Trimble 1902-1967 *ConAu 19*
Benedict, Lovina B 1826-1899 *DcNAA*
Benedict, Lady Mary C *Alli Sup*
Benedict, Michael Les 1945- *ConAu 45*
Benedict, Murray Reed 1892- *AmA&B*
Benedict, Noah *Alli*
Benedict, Ralph Curtiss 1883- *WhWNAA*
Benedict, Rex Arthur 1920- *ConAu 17R, SmATA 8, WrD 1976*
Benedict, Robert Dewey *Alli Sup*
Benedict, Robert P 1924- *ConAu 41*
Benedict, Roswell Alphonzo 1855- *DcNAA*
Benedict, Ruth Fulton 1887-1948 *AmA&B, DcNAA, REnAL, TwCA Sup*
Benedict, Stanley Rossiter 1884- *WhWNAA*
Benedict, Stewart H 1924- *ConAu 13R*
Benedict, Suzan Rose 1873-1942 *DcNAA*
Benedict, Verne Taylor *ChPo S2*
Benedict, Wayland Richardson 1848-1915 *DcNAA, OhA&B*
Benedict, William A And Tracy, Hiram A *Alli Sup*
Benedict, William H 1845-1929 *DcNAA*
Benedictoff, Vladimir Grigorjevich 1810-1873 *BbD, BiD&SB*
Benedictoff SEE ALSO Benediktov
Benedictsson, Victoria Maria 1850-1888 *BiD&SB, CasWL, ClDMEuL, EuA, EvEuW*
Benedictus, David Henry 1938- *Au&Wr, ConNov 1972, ConNov 1976, NewC, WrD 1976*
Benedikt, Michael 1935?- *AmA&B, ConAu 13R, ConLC 4, CrCAP, DrAF 1976, DrAP 1975*
Benedikt, Michael 1937- *ConP 1970, ConP 1975, RAdv 1, WrD 1976*
Benediktov, Vladimir Grigoryevich 1807-1873 *CasWL, DcRusL, EvEuW*
Benediktov SEE ALSO Benedictoff
Benediktsson, Einar 1864-1940 *CasWL, ClDMEuL, EncWL, REn*
Benedix, Roderich Julius 1811-1873 *BbD, BiD&SB, OxGer*
Benefiel, William Henry Harrison 1846-1923 *IndAu 1917*
Benefield, Barry 1877- *AmA&B, AmNov, ConAmL, DcLEnL, OxAm, REnAL, TexWr, TwCA, TwCA Sup*
Benefield, June 1921- *ConAu 45*
Benefield, Sebastian 1559-1630 *Alli*
Beneke, Rudolf 1861- *WhLA*
Beneke, Walter 1923- *DcCLA*
Benell, Florence B 1912- *ConAu 33*
Benelli, Sem 1877-1949 *CasWL, ClDMEuL, CnMD, McGWD, ModWD, REn, REnWD*

Benello, C George 1926- *ConAu 33*
Benemy, Frank William Georgeson 1909-
   Au&Wr
Benenson, Lawrence A *AuBYP*
Benes, Eduard 1884-1948 *REn*
Benes, Jan 1936- *ConAu 29*
Benesch, Kurt 1926- *CrCD*
Benese, Sir Richard De *Alli*
Benesova, Bozena 1873-1936 *CasWL, EncWL,*
   ModSL 2
Benet, Edouard *ConAu XR*
Benet, Gilbert *Alli*
Benet, James 1914- *ConAu 61*
Benet, Laura 1884- *AmA&B, AuBYP, ChPo,*
   ConAu 9R, JBA 1951, REn, REnAL,
   SmATA 3
Benet, Mary Kathleen 1943- *ConAu 57*
Benet, Rosemary 1900-1962 *ChPo*
Benet, Stephen Vincent 1827-1895 *Alli Sup,*
   BiDSA, DcNAA
Benet, Stephen Vincent 1898-1943 *AmA&B,*
   AnCL, BkCL, CasWL, ChPo, ChPo S1,
   ChPo S2, Chmbr 3, CnDAL, CnE&AP,
   CnMWL, ConAmA, ConAmL, CyWA,
   DcLEnL, ModAL, OxAm, OxEng,
   Pen Am, RAdv 1, REn, REnAL, SixAP,
   St&VC, TwCA, TwCA Sup, TwCW,
   WebEAL, WhTwL, WhWNAA, YABC 1
Benet, Sula 1903- *AuBYP*
Benet, William Rose 1886-1950 *AmA&B,*
   ChPo, ChPo S1, ChPo S2, CnDAL,
   ConAmA, ConAmL, DcLEnL, LongC,
   OxAm, OxEng, Pen Am, REn, REnAL,
   TwCA, TwCA Sup, WhWNAA
Benetar, Judith 1941- *ConAu 53, WrD 1976*
Benevente, Jacinto 1866-1954 *CnThe, WhLA*
Benevieno, Girolamo *DcEuL*
Benevolus *NewC*
Benezet, Anthony 1713-1784 *Alli, DcAmA,*
   DcNAA, OxAm
Benezra, Barbara 1921- *ConAu 13R,*
   SmATA 10
Benfante, Ignazio 1914- *AmSCAP 66*
Benfey, Theodore 1809-1881 *Alli Sup*
Benfield, Derek 1926- *Au&Wr, ConAu 23*
Benford, Lawrence 1946- *BlkAW*
Bengani, Redvus Robert 1899?- *AfA 1*
Benge, Eugene J 1896- *ConAu 57*
Bengelsdorf, Irving S 1922- *ConAu 57*
Bengengruen, Werner 1892-1964 *ModGL*
Benger, Elizabeth Ogilvy 1778-1827 *Alli,*
   BiDLA, ChPo S2, DcEnL, NewC
Bengough, Elisa 1877?- *DcNAA*
Bengough, Harcourt Mortimer *Alli Sup*
Bengough, I E *Alli Sup*
Bengough, John Wilson 1851-1923 *ChPo,*
   DcLEnL, DcNAA, OxCan
Bengtson, Vern L 1941- *ConAu 49*
Bengtsson, Arvid 1916- *ConAu 33*
Bengtsson, Frans Gunnar 1894-1954 *CasWL,*
   ClDMEuL, EncWL, EvEuW, Pen Eur,
   REn
Benhab, Edwin *Alli Sup*
Benham, Allen Rogers 1879- *WhWNAA*
Benham, Betty Chapman *ChPo S2*
Benham, Charles Edwin 1860-1929 *ChPo S1*
Benham, Daniel *Alli Sup*
Benham, David *Alli*
Benham, Dewitt Miles *ChPo S1*
Benham, Emma Caroline King 1857-1942
   IndAu 1816
Benham, George Chittenden *Alli Sup*
Benham, Ida Whipple *ChPo*
Benham, James Erle *Alli Sup*
Benham, Leslie 1922- *ConAu 9R*
Benham, Lois 1924- *ConAu 9R*
Benham, Thomas *Alli*
Benham, W Gurney *Alli Sup*
Benham, William 1831-1910 *Alli Sup, ChPo*
Benham, Sir William Gurney 1859-1944
   ChPo S1, EvLB, NewC
Beniak, Valentin 1894- *CasWL*
Benichou, Paul 1908- *ConAu 57*
Beniczky-Bajza, Illona 1840- *BiD&SB*
Benington, John 1921- *ConAu 5R*
Benisch, Abraham 1811-1878 *Alli Sup*
Benischke, Gustav 1867- *WhLA*

Benison, H W S Worsley- *Alli Sup*
Benison, Paul *Alli Sup*
Benitez, Conrado 1889- *WhWNAA*
Benitez, Francisco 1887- *WhWNAA*
Benitez, Jaime 1908- *PueRA*
Benitez, Lillie Kate Walker *BlkAW*
Benitez, Maria Bibiana 1783-1873 *PueRA*
Benitsky, Alexander Petrovich 1780-1809
   CasWL
Beniuc, Mihai 1907- *CasWL*
Benivieni, Girolamo 1453-1542 *REn*
Benjamin Ben Jonah, Of Tudela d1173 *EvEuW*
Benjamin Duval *PueRA*
Benjamin Of Tudela 1130?-1173 *CasWL,*
   NewC, OxEng, Pen Eur
Benjamin, Rabbi *DcEnL*
Benjamin, A Cornelius 1897- *WhWNAA*
Benjamin, Alice *ConAu 57*
Benjamin, Anna N *ChPo*
Benjamin, Anna Shaw 1925- *ConAu 41*
Benjamin, Annette Francis 1928- *ConAu 17R*
Benjamin, Asher 1773-1845 *DcNAA*
Benjamin, Bennie 1907- *AmSCAP 66*
Benjamin, Bry 1924- *ConAu 17R*
Benjamin, Charles *ChPo S1*
Benjamin, Charles Henry 1856-1937 *DcAmA,*
   DcNAA, WhWNAA
Benjamin, Charles Love *ChPo*
Benjamin, Claude 1911- *ConAu 9R*
Benjamin, Curtis G 1901- *AmA&B*
Benjamin, DeWitt Clinton 1820-1871 *DcNAA*
Benjamin, Earl W 1889- *WhWNAA*
Benjamin, Edward Bernard 1897- *Au&Wr,*
   WrD 1976
Benjamin, Elizabeth Dundas d1890 *Alli Sup,*
   DcAmA, DcNAA
Benjamin, Fannie Nichols *Alli Sup*
Benjamin, George 1799-1864 *BbtC*
Benjamin, Gerald 1945- *ConAu 49*
Benjamin, Gilbert Giddings 1874- *WhWNAA*
Benjamin, Harry 1885- *ConAu P-1*
Benjamin, Herbert S 1922- *ConAu 5R*
Benjamin, Hiram Bernard 1901- *Au&Wr*
Benjamin, Israel Joseph *Alli Sup*
Benjamin, Joseph 1921- *ConAu 57*
Benjamin, Joseph Louis *BlkAW*
Benjamin, Judah Philip 1811-1884 *Alli Sup,*
   BiD&SB, BiDSA, DcAmA, DcNAA
Benjamin, Kathy *BlkAW*
Benjamin, L N *Alli Sup, BbtC*
Benjamin, Lewis Saul 1874-1932 *LongC, NewC,*
   WhLA
Benjamin, Louis *Alli Sup*
Benjamin, Louis Nathan 1842?-1887 *DcNAA*
Benjamin, Marcus 1857-1932 *Alli Sup,*
   DcNAA, WhWNAA
Benjamin, Mary Gladding 1814-1871 *Alli Sup,*
   DcNAA
Benjamin, N D *Alli Sup*
Benjamin, Nora *ConAu XR*
Benjamin, Park 1809-1864 *Alli, AmA,*
   AmA&B, BiD&SB, ChPo, ChPo S1,
   ChPo S2, CyAL 2, DcAmA, DcEnL,
   DcNAA, OxAm
Benjamin, Park, Jr. 1849-1922 *Alli Sup,*
   AmA&B, BiD&SB, DcAmA, DcNAA
Benjamin, Paul *BlkAW*
Benjamin, Philip 1922-1966 *ConAu 5R,*
   ConAu 25
Benjamin, Ralph *WrD 1976*
Benjamin, Rene 1885- *ClDMEuL*
Benjamin, Reuben Moore 1833-1917 *DcAmA,*
   DcNAA
Benjamin, Robert C O 1855- *BlkAW*
Benjamin, Roger W 1942- *ConAu 37*
Benjamin, Samuel Green Wheeler 1837-1914
   Alli Sup, BiD&SB, DcAmA
Benjamin, Samuel Greene Wheeler 1837-1914
   AmA, AmA&B, DcNAA
Benjamin, Virginia Sarah *ChPo*
Benjamin, Walter 1892-1940 *CasWL, EncWL,*
   ModGL, OxGer, Pen Eur
Benjamin, William Evarts 1942- *ChPo,*
   ConAu 25
Benji, Thomas *ConAu 49*
Benjoin, George *Alli, BiDLA*
Benko, Nancy *WrD 1976*
Benko, Stephen 1924- *ConAu 9R*

Benkovitz, Miriam J 1911- *ConAu 9R,*
   WrD 1976
Benloe, William *Alli*
Benlowe *Alli*
Benlowes *Alli*
Benlowes, Edward 1602?-1676 *Alli, BrAu,*
   CasWL, DcLEnL, NewC, OxEng,
   WebEAL
Benn, Alfred William *Alli Sup*
Benn, Caroline DeCamp Wedgwood 1926-
   Au&Wr, ConAu 1R
Benn, Sir Ernest John Pickstone 1875- *WhLA*
Benn, George 1801-1882 *Alli Sup*
Benn, Gottfried 1886-1956 *CasWL, ClDMEuL,*
   CnMWL, EncWL, EvEuW, ModGL,
   OxGer, Pen Eur, REn, WhTwL, WorAu
Benn, Mary *Alli Sup, PoIre*
Benn, Matthew *WrD 1976*
Benn, William 1600-1680 *Alli*
Benn, William Wedgwood 1877- *WhLA*
Bennairde, Blanche *FemPA*
Bennani, B M 1946- *ConAu 61*
Bennard, George 1873-1958 *AmSCAP 66,*
   ChPo
Benndorf, Friedrich Kurt *WhLA*
Benndorf, Hans 1870- *WhLA*
Benne, Katherine Freeman 1908?- *IndAu 1917*
Benne, Kenneth D 1908- *ConAu 33*
Bennell, Florence M *ChPo*
Benner, Ralph Eugene 1932- *ConAu 33*
Benner, Samuel *Alli Sup*
Bennet, A *Alli*
Bennet, Mrs. A M d1808 *Alli*
Bennet, Agnes Maria d1805 *DcEnL*
Bennet, Benjamin 1674-1726 *Alli*
Bennet, Christopher 1617-1655 *Alli*
Bennet, Elizabeth *REn*
Bennet, Emerson 1822- *DcEnL*
Bennet, George *Alli, DcEnL*
Bennet, Georgiana *Alli Sup*
Bennet, Georgianna *ChPo*
Bennet, H *Alli*
Bennet, Henry *Alli*
Bennet, Henry 1618-1685 *Alli*
Bennet, Henry Grey *Alli*
Bennet, James *Alli, Alli Sup*
Bennet, James Henry 1816-1880? *Alli Sup*
Bennet, John *Alli, ChPo S1*
Bennet, John W *OxCan Sup*
Bennet, Jules *Alli*
Bennet, N C *ChPo*
Bennet, Philip *Alli*
Bennet, R *Alli*
Bennet, Robert d1687 *Alli*
Bennet, Robert Ames 1870-1954 *AmA&B,*
   ArizL, WhWNAA
Bennet, Sanford Fillmore 1836-1898 *DcNAA*
Bennet, Sol *Alli*
Bennet, T *Alli*
Bennet, Thomas *Alli*
Bennet, Thomas 1673-1728 *Alli, DcEnL*
Bennet, Mrs. W Ford *ChPo S1*
Bennet, W H *Alli*
Bennet, W W *BiDSA*
Bennet, William *Alli, Alli Sup*
Bennet, William Heath *Alli Sup*
Bennet, Zelotes R *Alli Sup*
Bennett *ChPo S2*
Bennett, A *BiDLA*
Bennett, A E 1898- *WrD 1976*
Bennett, A Hughes *Alli Sup*
Bennett, A J *Alli Sup*
Bennett, Addison C 1918- *ConAu 5R*
Bennett, Adrian A 1941- *ConAu 53*
Bennett, Alan 1934- *Au&Wr, CnThe, ConDr,*
   WrD 1976
Bennett, Albert A 1888- *WhWNAA*
Bennett, Alfred Allen 1850-1922 *DcAmA,*
   DcNAA
Bennett, Alfred Gordon 1901- *WhLA*
Bennett, Alfred William *Alli Sup*
Bennett, Alice *ConAu XR*
Bennett, Anna Elizabeth 1914- *ChPo,*
   ConAu 17R
Bennett, Archibald F 1896- *ConAu P-1*
Bennett, Arnold 1867-1931 *AtlBL, Chmbr 3,*
   CnMD, CnMWL, CyWA, DcBiA,
   DcLEnL, EncM&D, EncWL, LongC,

McGWD, ModBL, ModBL Sup, ModWD,
NewC, OxEng, Pen Eng, RAdv 1, REn,
TwCA, TwCA Sup, TwCW, WebEAL,
WhTwL
Bennett, Arthur 1862- WhLA
Bennett, Bernard 1915- AmSCAP 66
Bennett, Blossom TexWr
Bennett, Bob BlkAW
Bennett, Bruce L 1917- ConAu 25
Bennett, C C Alli Sup
Bennett, C N MnBBF
Bennett, Carlyle Wilson 1895- WhWNAA
Bennett, Carolyn Hill TexWr
Bennett, Charles 1854- Alli Sup
Bennett, Charles 1901- ConAu P-1
Bennett, Charles 1932- ConAu 25
Bennett, Charles Alpheus 1864-1942 DcNAA,
  WhWNAA
Bennett, Charles Andrew Armstrong 1885-1930
  DcNAA
Bennett, Charles E 1910- ConAu 9R
Bennett, Charles Edwin 1858-1921 AmA&B,
  ChPo, DcAmA, DcNAA
Bennett, Charles Fox OxCan
Bennett, Charles Henry 1829-1867 Alli Sup,
  ChPo, ChPo S1, ChPo S2
Bennett, Charles Moon 1899- Au&Wr,
  EarAB Sup, MnBBF, WrD 1976
Bennett, Charles Wesley 1828-1891 Alli Sup,
  BiD&SB, DcAmA, DcNAA
Bennett, Charles William 1886- WhWNAA
Bennett, Christine ConAu XR
Bennett, Claud Nathaniel 1866- BiDSA
Bennett, Cyril Alli Sup
Bennett, D M 1818-1882 AmA
Bennett, Daniel K 1830-1897 BiDSA, DcNAA
Bennett, Daphne Nicholson ConAu 41
Bennett, David 1897- AmSCAP 66
Bennett, David H 1935- ConAu 25
Bennett, Deborah Elizabeth 1932- Au&Wr
Bennett, Dennis J 1917- ConAu 49
Bennett, DeRobigne Mortimer 1818-1882
  DcNAA
Bennett, DeRobique Mortimer 1818-1882
  Alli Sup, DcAmA
Bennett, Donald Clifford Tyndall 1910- Au&Wr
Bennett, Dorothea ConAu XR
Bennett, Dorothy 1919- Au&Wr
Bennett, Dorothy Agnes 1909- ChPo S1
Bennett, Dwight AmA&B, ConAu XR
Bennett, E Alli Sup
Bennett, Edmund Hatch 1824-1898 DcAmA,
  DcNAA
Bennett, Edmund Henry Alli Sup
Bennett, Edward Alli Sup
Bennett, Edward 1876- WhWNAA
Bennett, Edward 1924- ConAu 5R
Bennett, Edward M 1927- ConAu 33,
  WrD 1976
Bennett, Ellen A Alli Sup
Bennett, Elsie M 1919- AmSCAP 66
Bennett, Emerson 1822-1905 Alli, Alli Sup,
  AmA, AmA&B, CyAL 2, DcAmA,
  DcNAA, OhA&B, OxAm, REnAL
Bennett, Emily T B Alli Sup
Bennett, Emily Thacher DcNAA
Bennett, Enoch Arnold 1867-1931 CasWL,
  EvLB
Bennett, Sir Ernest Nathaniel 1868-1947 BiDPar,
  WhLA
Bennett, Ernest Walter 1921- Au&Wr,
  WrD 1976
Bennett, Estelline d1948 DcNAA
Bennett, Ethel Hume 1881- OxCan,
  WhWNAA
Bennett, Ethel Mary Granger 1891- Au&Wr,
  ConAu P-1
Bennett, Eve AuBYP
Bennett, F I ChPo
Bennett, Florence Mary 1885- ChPo,
  WhWNAA
Bennett, Frances Grant 1899- ConAu 25
Bennett, Francis Graham Alli Sup
Bennett, Francis Oswald 1898- WrD 1976
Bennett, Francis W Alli Sup
Bennett, Frank Marion 1857-1924 DcAmA,
  DcNAA
Bennett, Frank Selwyn Macaulay 1866- WhLA

Bennett, Frederick E Alli Sup
Bennett, Fredna W 1906- ConAu P-1
Bennett, Fremont O Alli Sup
Bennett, G E ChPo, ChPo S2
Bennett, G J Alli
Bennett, G M Alli Sup
Bennett, Geoffrey Martin 1909- Au&Wr,
  ConAu 13R, WrD 1976
Bennett, George Alli Sup, BiDLA, ChPo,
  ChPo S1, ChPo S2
Bennett, George 1824- PoIre
Bennett, George 1920- ConAu 5R
Bennett, George Bright Alli Sup
Bennett, George Edward 1889- WhWNAA
Bennett, George J 1897- AmSCAP 66
Bennett, George W Alli Sup
Bennett, Gertrude Ryder AnMV 1926,
  ChPo S1, ConAu 53, WhWNAA,
  WrD 1976
Bennett, Gordon A 1940- ConAu 29
Bennett, Gordon C 1935- ConAu 33
Bennett, Grace Irene ChPo S1
Bennett, Granville G Alli Sup
Bennett, Gwendolyn B 1902- BlkAW, ChPo S1,
  LivBAA
Bennett, H BiDLA
Bennett, H O WrD 1976
Bennett, H S 1889- LongC
Bennett, Hal 1930- BlkAW, DrAF 1976,
  LivBAA
Bennett, Hal 1936- ConAu 41, ConLC 5
Bennett, Hall ConAu XR
Bennett, Harriett M ChPo, ChPo S1,
  ChPo S2
Bennett, Harriett M And Mack, Robert E
  Alli Sup
Bennett, Helen Christine 1881- WhWNAA
Bennett, Henry 1766?-1828 PoIre
Bennett, Henry 1813-1868 PoCh
Bennett, Henry Eastman 1873- WhWNAA
Bennett, Henry Holcomb 1863-1924 ChPo,
  DcNAA, OhA&B
Bennett, Henry Morden Alli Sup
Bennett, Hilda R MnBBF
Bennett, Hiram Rockwell 1886- Au&Wr
Bennett, Horace Wilson 1862-1941 AmA&B,
  DcNAA
Bennett, Howard Franklin 1911- ConAu 1R
Bennett, Hugh Hammond 1881- WhWNAA
Bennett, Ida Dandridge 1860-1925 DcNAA
Bennett, J W W ChPo
Bennett, Jack Arthur Walter 1911- Au&Wr,
  ConAu 9R, NewC
Bennett, James Alli, BiDLA
Bennett, James 1817- BbtC
Bennett, James D 1926- ConAu 61
Bennett, James Gordon 1795-1872 AmA&B,
  OxAm, REn, REnAL
Bennett, James Gordon 1841-1918 AmA&B
Bennett, James O'Donnell 1870-1940 AmA&B,
  DcNAA
Bennett, James R Alli Sup
Bennett, James Richard 1932- ConAu 33,
  WrD 1976
Bennett, Sir James Risdon 1809- Alli Sup
Bennett, James William 1891- AmA&B,
  IndAu 1917, WhWNAA
Bennett, Mrs. James William AmNov XR,
  WhWNAA
Bennett, Jean Frances ConAu XR
Bennett, Jeremy ConAu XR
Bennett, Jesse Lee 1885-1931 DcNAA,
  WhWNAA
Bennett, Joan 1896- LongC
Bennett, John Alli Sup, BiDLA, BiDSA,
  MnBBF
Bennett, John 1865-1956 AmA&B, BlkAW,
  CarSB, ChPo, ChPo S1, ConICB,
  DcAmA, IlCB 1945, JBA 1934,
  JBA 1951, OhA&B, OxAm, REnAL,
  YABC 1
Bennett, John 1920- ConAu 29, DrAP 1975,
  WrD 1976
Bennett, John Coleman 1902- AmA&B
Bennett, John E And Wakely, Charles Alli Sup
Bennett, John Godolphin 1897- Au&Wr,
  BiDPar
Bennett, John Hughes 1812-1875 Alli, Alli Sup

Bennett, John I Alli Sup
Bennett, John Jerome Nelson 1939- ConAu 21
Bennett, John Michael 1942- ConAu 49,
  DrAP 1975
Bennett, John William 1915- ConAu 1R
Bennett, Jonathan 1930- ChPo S2, ConAu 45
Bennett, Joseph Alli Sup, ChPo S1
Bennett, Joseph D 1922-1972 ConAu 1R,
  ConAu 33
Bennett, Josephine Waters 1899- Au&Wr,
  ConAu 1R
Bennett, Joyce W 1923- AmSCAP 66
Bennett, Kay Curley 1922- ConAu 17R
Bennett, Lerone, Jr. 1928- BlkAW, ConAu 45,
  LivBAA
Bennett, Louise 1919- CasWL, ConP 1970,
  ConP 1975, WrD 1976
Bennett, Lucy Ann Alli Sup, ChPo, ChPo S1
Bennett, M ChPo
Bennett, M E ChPo
Bennett, Margaret E 1893- ConAu 5R
Bennett, Margaret L Alli Sup
Bennett, Margot Au&Wr
Bennett, Marion T 1914- ConAu 9R
Bennett, Martha Haines Butt Alli Sup, BiDSA
Bennett, Martha T ChPo
Bennett, Mary Alli Sup, ChPo S1
Bennett, Mary E Alli Sup, DcNAA
Bennett, Mary E 1841- DcAmA, DcNAA
Bennett, Mavis Clare ChPo S1
Bennett, Melba Berry 1901- ConAu 19
Bennett, Meridan 1927- ConAu 25
Bennett, Mildred R 1909- ConAu 25
Bennett, Milo Lyman 1789-1868 DcNAA
Bennett, Miriam ChPo S2
Bennett, N C ChPo
Bennett, Noel 1939- ConAu 45
Bennett, Nora ChPo
Bennett, Norman Robert 1932- ConAu 9R
Bennett, Patrick PoIre
Bennett, Paul Lewis 1921- ConAu 1R
Bennett, Peggy ChPo
Bennett, Penelope Agnes 1938- Au&Wr,
  ConAu 13R
Bennett, Phil 1913- AmSCAP 66
Bennett, R B 1870-1947 OxCan
Bennett, R King OhA&B
Bennett, Rachel ConAu XR
Bennett, Rainey 1907- IlBYP, IlCB 1966,
  IndAu 1917
Bennett, Rebecca Maria 1895-1947 IndAu 1917
Bennett, Richard 1899- BlkAW, IlBYP,
  IlCB 1945, IlCB 1956, JBA 1951
Bennett, Richard M ChPo
Bennett, Robert 1855- ChPo S1
Bennett, Robert A 1927- ConAu 13R
Bennett, Robert Ames 1870- AmLY
Bennett, Robert L 1931- ConAu 41
Bennett, Robert Russell 1894- AmSCAP 66
Bennett, Rodney ChPo, ChPo S2
Bennett, Rolfe 1882- MnBBF
Bennett, Rowena 1896- ChPo, ChPo S1,
  ChPo S2
Bennett, Roy C 1918- AmSCAP 66
Bennett, Roy Coleman 1889- WhWNAA
Bennett, Mrs. S R I Alli Sup
Bennett, Samuel Alli Sup
Bennett, Samuel 1815-1878 Alli Sup
Bennett, Samuel A Alli Sup
Bennett, Sanford Fillmore 1836-1898 Alli Sup,
  AmA&B, ChPo S1, CatA S2, DcNAA,
  WiscW
Bennett, Scott 1939- ConAu 33
Bennett, Simon Harry ChPo S1
Bennett, Solomon BiDLA
Bennett, Susan IlBYP
Bennett, T J Wesley Alli Sup
Bennett, Thomas Alli, BiDLA
Bennett, Thomas Randle 1821- Alli Sup
Bennett, Victor 1919- ConAu 5R
Bennett, Mrs. W Ford Alli Sup
Bennett, W H Alli Sup
Bennett, Walter Alli Sup
Bennett, Walter Lee BlkAW
Bennett, Wendell Clark 1905-1953 IndAu 1917
Bennett, William Alli Sup, BiDLA
Bennett, William And Elizabeth Alli Sup
Bennett, William Cox 1820-1895 Alli Sup,

BiD&SB, BrAu 19, ChPo, ChPo S1, ChPo S2, Chmbr 3, DcEnL
Bennett, William Harper 1860-1931 *DcNAA*
Bennett, William Heath *Alli Sup*
Bennett, William Henry 1855-1920 *ChPo S1*
Bennett, William James Early 1805-1886 *Alli, Alli Sup*
Bennett, William L 1924- *ConAu 17R*
Bennett, William Robert 1921- *Au&Wr, ConAu 13R*
Bennett, William W *Alli Sup*
Bennett, William Wallace 1821-1887 *DcNAA*
Bennett, William Zebina 1856- *Alli Sup, DcAmA*
Bennett, Wilma 1904- *IndAu 1917*
Bennett-Edwards *Alli Sup*
Bennett-England, Rodney Charles 1936- *ConAu 61, WrD 1976*
Bennetts, Pamela 1922- *Au&Wr, ConAu 37, WrD 1976*
Bennie, James Noble *Alli Sup*
Bennigsen, Rudolf Von 1824-1902 *OxGer*
Benning, H T *Alli Sup*
Benning, Howe *Alli Sup*
Benning, Lee Edwards 1934- *ConAu 53*
Bennion, Adam S 1886- *WhWNAA*
Bennion, Edmund Baron 1901- *Au&Wr*
Bennion, John *Alli*
Bennion, Milton 1870- *WhWNAA*
Bennis, Warren G 1925- *ConAu 53, WrD 1976*
Bennison, Mrs. D M *ChPo*
Bennoch, Francis 1812-1890 *Alli Sup, ChPo, ChPo S2*
Benns, Frank Lee 1889-1967 *AmA&B, IndAu 1917*
Benny, Philip Berger *Alli Sup*
Benoff, Mac 1915?-1972 *ConAu 37*
Benois, Alexander Nikolayevich 1870-1960 *CasWL*
Benoist-Mechin, Jacques 1901- *Au&Wr*
Benoit *CasWL*
Benoit De Sainte-Maure *Alli, BiB N, BbD, BiD&SB, CasWL, EuA, EvEuW, OxEng, OxFr, Pen Eur, REn*
Benoit De Sainte-More *OxFr*
Benoit Of Sainte-More *DcEuL*
Benoit, Alice P *WhWNAA*
Benoit, Emile 1910- *ConAu 5R*
Benoit, Jacques *OxCan Sup*
Benoit, Joseph Paul Augustine 1850-1915 *DcNAA*
Benoit, Leroy James 1913- *ConAu 33*
Benoit, Pierre 1886-1962 *CasWL, ClDMEuL, EncWL, EvEuW, OxFr, TwCA, TwCA Sup*
Benoit, Pierre Maurice 1906- *ConAu 41*
Benoit, Real 1916- *CanWr*
Benoit, Richard Leroy 1898- *WhWNAA*
Benoliel, Jeanne Quint 1919- *ConAu 49*
Benrath, Henry 1882-1949 *OxGer*
Benrimo, Joseph Henry 1871-1942 *DcNAA*
Bense, Peter *Alli*
Bense, Walter F 1932- *ConAu 45*
Bensel, Anna B *ChPo S1*
Bensel, James Berry 1856-1886 *Alli Sup, BiD&SB, ChPo, DcAmA*
Bensell, E B *ChPo, EarAB, EarAB Sup*
Bensell, James Berry 1856-1886 *DcNAA*
Bensen, Donald R 1927- *ConAu 9R*
Benserade, Isaac De 1613?-1691 *CasWL, DcEuL, EvEuW, OxFr, REn*
Benskin, Samuel 1922- *AmSCAP 66*
Bensley, Benjamin Arthur 1875-1934 *DcNAA*
Bensley, Robert 1738?-1817 *NewC*
Bensly, Robert Lubbock 1831- *Alli Sup*
Bensman, Joseph 1922- *ConAu 23*
Bensol, Oscar *ConAu XR*
Benson, Miss *Alli, BiDLA*
Benson, Mrs. *Alli Sup*
Benson, Adolph Burnett 1881- *WhWNAA*
Benson, Allan Louis 1871-1940 *AmA&B, DcNAA*
Benson, Arthur Christopher 1862-1925 *Alli Sup, ChPo, ChPo S1, ChPo S2, Chmbr 3, DcEnA Ap, DcEuL, DcLEnL, EvLB, LongC, NewC, Pen Eng, REn, TwCA*
Benson, Arthur H 1919- *AmSCAP 66*

Benson, B A *ConAu XR*
Benson, Ben 1920?-1959? *EncM&D*
Benson, Bernard J 1891- *ChPo S2*
Benson, Blackwood Ketchum 1845- *BiDSA, DcNAA*
Benson, C Randolph 1923- *ConAu 29, WrD 1976*
Benson, C W 1909- *Au&Wr*
Benson, C W *Alli Sup*
Benson, Carl *Alli Sup, AmA&B, BiD&SB, DcAmA, DcNAA*
Benson, Carmen 1921- *ConAu 57*
Benson, Charles d1880 *PoIre*
Benson, Charles 1901- *Au&Wr*
Benson, Charles Emile 1881- *WhWNAA*
Benson, Charles S 1922- *ConAu 17R*
Benson, Christopher *Alli*
Benson, Clara Cynthia 1875- *WhWNAA*
Benson, Dennis C 1936- *ConAu 37*
Benson, Edward Frederic 1867-1940 *BbD, BiD&SB, Chmbr 3, DcEnA Ap, DcLEnL, EvLB, LongC, MnBBF, ModBL, NewC, OxEng, Pen Eng, TwCA, TwCW*
Benson, Edward White 1829- *Alli Sup*
Benson, Egbert 1746-1833 *Alli Sup, DcAmA, DcNAA*
Benson, Elizabeth *TexWr*
Benson, Eugene 1839?-1908 *Alli Sup, AmA&B, BiD&SB, DcAmA, DcNAA, EarAB*
Benson, Evelyn *Alli Sup*
Benson, Mrs. F R *ChPo S1*
Benson, Frank *ChPo S1*
Benson, Frank Atkinson 1921- *Au&Wr, WrD 1976*
Benson, Sir Frank Robert 1858-1939 *NewC*
Benson, Frederick R 1934- *ConAu 33, WrD 1976*
Benson, G *Alli*
Benson, George 1699-1763 *Alli, DcEnL*
Benson, George Charles Sumner 1908- *Au&Wr*
Benson, George Willard 1859-1944 *DcNAA*
Benson, Ginny *ConAu 57*
Benson, Godfrey Rathbone 1864-1945 *EncM&D, TwCA, TwCA Sup*
Benson, Hawtrey 1843- *WhLA*
Benson, Henry Clark 1815- *Alli Sup, DcNAA, OhA&B*
Benson, Henry Kreitzer 1877- *WhWNAA*
Benson, Jackson J 1930- *ConAu 25, WrD 1976*
Benson, James 1925- *Au&Wr*
Benson, James W *Alli Sup*
Benson, John *Alli Sup*
Benson, John Alfred 1899- *DcNAA*
Benson, John J 1915- *AmSCAP 66*
Benson, Joseph 1748-1821 *Alli, BiDLA, DcEnL*
Benson, Larry D 1929- *ConAu 37*
Benson, Lawrence Sluter *Alli Sup, DcNAA*
Benson, Louis Fitzgerald 1855-1930 *ChPo, DcNAA*
Benson, Luther 1847-1898 *Alli Sup, IndAu 1816*
Benson, Lyman 1909- *ConAu 49, WrD 1976*
Benson, M E *Alli Sup*
Benson, Margaret H Benson 1899- *ConAu 5R*
Benson, Martin *Alli, BiDLA*
Benson, Martin d1752 *Alli*
Benson, Mary 1919- *ConAu 49*
Benson, Mary Josephine 1887- *ChPo*
Benson, Mildred Wirt 1905- *AuBYP, OhA&B*
Benson, Nathaniel Anketell 1903-1966 *OxCan, WhWNAA*
Benson, Oliver Earl 1911- *AmA&B*
Benson, Oscar Herman 1875- *AmLY, WhWNAA*
Benson, P *ChPo S1*
Benson, P, Sr. *AmLY XR*
Benson, P G R *ChPo S2*
Benson, R B *Alli Sup*
Benson, Richard *Alli, ConAu XR, MnBBF, PoIre*
Benson, Richard Meux *Alli Sup, PoCh*
Benson, Robert *Alli, Alli Sup*
Benson, Robert G *ConAu 29*
Benson, Robert Hugh 1871-1914 *ChPo, ChPo S1, ChPo S2, EvLB, LongC, TwCA, TwCA Sup*

Benson, Robert S 1942- *ConAu 33*
Benson, Ruth Crego 1937- *ConAu 41*
Benson, Sally 1900-1972 *AmA&B, CnDAL, ConAu 37, ConAu P-1, OxAm, REn, REnAL, SmATA 1, TwCA Sup*
Benson, Stella 1892-1933 *ChPo, ChPo S2, Chmbr 3, DcLEnL, EvLB, LongC, ModBL, NewC, Pen Eng. REn, TwCA, TwCA Sup, TwCW, WhTwL*
Benson, Stephana Vere 1909- *Au&Wr, ConAu 13R*
Benson, Theodora 1906-1968 *LongC*
Benson, Therese *AmA&B, WhWNAA*
Benson, Thomas *Alli*
Benson, Thomas Godfrey 1899- *ConAu P-1*
Benson, Thomas W 1937- *ConAu 29*
Benson, Virginia 1923- *ConAu 57*
Benson, W H *Alli Sup*
Benson, Warren Frank 1924- *AmSCAP 66*
Benson, William *Alli, Alli Sup, BiDLA*
Benson, William 1682-1754 *Alli, DcEnL*
Benson, William Howard 1902- *ConAu 1R*
Benson, William Shepherd 1855-1932 *DcNAA*
Bensserade, Isaac De 1613-1691 *BiD&SB*
Benstead, Emma *ChPo S1*
Bensted, John *Alli*
Bensted-Smith, Richard Brian 1929- *Au&Wr, ConAu 13R*
Benstock, Bernard 1930- *ConAu 17R, WrD 1976*
Bensusan, Samuel Levy 1872- *ChPo S1, ChPo S2, WhLA*
Bent, Alan Edward 1939- *ConAu 49*
Bent, Allen Herbert 1867-1926 *DcNAA*
Bent, Arthur Cleveland 1866- *WhWNAA*
Bent, Charles N 1935- *ConAu 23*
Bent, J *Alli*
Bent, James H *Alli Sup*
Bent, James Theodore 1852-1897 *Alli Sup, BrAu 19*
Bent, John *BbtC*
Bent, Lancaster *ChPo*
Bent, O M *ChPo*
Bent, Rosetta Case 1918- *AmSCAP 66*
Bent, Rudyard K 1901- *ConAu 1R*
Bent, Samuel Arthur 1841-1912 *Alli Sup, DcNAA*
Bent, Silas *Alli Sup*
Bent, Silas 1820-1887 *DcNAA*
Bent, Silas 1882-1945 *AmA&B, DcNAA, REnAL, TwCA, TwCA Sup, WhWNAA*
Bent, Thomas *Alli*
Bent, William *Alli, BiDLA*
Bente, Frederick d1930 *WhWNAA*
Bentel, Pearl Bucklen 1901- *AuBYP, ConAu 21*
Benter, Charles 1887-1964 *AmSCAP 66*
Benthall, John *Alli Sup*
Benthall, Jonathan 1941- *ConAu 41*
Bentham, Edward 1707-1776 *Alli*
Bentham, George 1800-1884 *Alli Sup, BrAu 19*
Bentham, James 1709?-1794 *Alli*
Bentham, Jay *ConAu XR*
Bentham, Jeremy 1748-1832 *Alli, AtlBL, BbD, BiD&SB, BiDLA, BrAu 19, CasWL, Chmbr 2, DcEnA, DcEnL, DcEuL, DcLEnL, EvLB, NewC, OxEng, Pen Eng, REn, WebEAL*
Bentham, Jeremy ALSO Smith, Gamaliel
Bentham, Joseph *Alli*
Bentham, Lady Mary Sophia d1858 *Alli Sup*
Bentham, Thomas 1513?-1578 *Alli*
Benthian, Fritz *WhLA*
Benthic, Arch E *ConAu XR*
Benthul, Herman F 1911- *ConAu 33*
Bentinck, Lord Charles Cavendish 1868- *Br&AmS*
Bentinck, George Augustus F Cavendish 1821- *Alli Sup*
Bentinck, Lord Henry 1804-1870 *Br&AmS*
Bentinck, Henry Cavendish, Lord William 1774- *Alli*
Bentinck, Lady Norah *WhLA*
Bentinck, Lord William Henry Cavendish 1774- *BiDLA*
Bentine, Michael *WrD 1976*
Bentivoglio, Ercole 1507-1573 *CasWL, EvEuW*

Bentivoglio, Cardinal Guido 1579-1644 *BiD&SB,*
 CasWL, EvEuW
Bentleman, Lawrence 1942- *REn*
Bentley, A J *Alli Sup*
Bentley, Arthur Fisher 1870- *IndAu 1816,*
 WhWNAA
Bentley, Beth 1928- *DrAP 1975, WrD 1976*
Bentley, Charles 1806-1854 *ChPo S1*
Bentley, Edith A *ChPo*
Bentley, Edmund Clerihew 1875-1956 *ChPo,*
 ChPo S2, DcLEnL, EncM&D, EvLB,
 LongC, NewC, OxEng, REn, TwCA,
 TwCA Sup, TwCW
Bentley, Edward *Alli Sup*
Bentley, Edward R 1888- *WhWNAA*
Bentley, Edwin R 1888- *WhWNAA*
Bentley, Elizabeth 1767- *Alli, BiDLA, ChPo*
Bentley, Ella D *BiDSA*
Bentley, Eric 1916- *AmA&B, AmSCAP 66,*
 Au&Wr, ConAu 5R, NewC, REnAL,
 TwCA Sup, WrD 1976
Bentley, G E, Jr. 1930- *ConAu 1R*
Bentley, George *Alli Sup*
Bentley, Gerald Eades 1901- *ConAu 41,*
 IndAu 1917, WrD 1976
Bentley, Gordon Mansir 1876- *WhWNAA*
Bentley, H *Alli Sup*
Bentley, H Cumberland *ChPo S1, ChPo S2*
Bentley, Harry C 1877- *WhWNAA*
Bentley, Howard Beebe 1925- *ConAu 9R*
Bentley, Hugh *Alli*
Bentley, Mrs. James C *ConAu XR*
Bentley, James William Benedict 1914- *Au&Wr*
Bentley, Janice Babb 1933- *ConAu 13R*
Bentley, John *Alli, BiDLA*
Bentley, John, Jr. 1880- *WhWNAA*
Bentley, John Charles *Alli Sup*
Bentley, John Morgan *ChPo S1*
Bentley, Joseph *Alli Sup*
Bentley, Madison *WhWNAA*
Bentley, Margaret 1926- *WrD 1976*
Bentley, Max 1888- *TexWr*
Bentley, Nelson, Jr. 1918- *WhPNW*
Bentley, Nicolas Clerihew 1907- *Au&Wr,*
 ChPo, ChPo S1, ChPo S2, IlCB 1945,
 LongC, NewC
Bentley, Phyllis Eleanor 1894- *Au&Wr,*
 ConAu 1R, DcLEnL, EncM&D, EvLB,
 LongC, ModBL, NewC, Pen Eng,
 RAdv 1, REn, SmATA 6, TwCA,
 TwCA Sup, TwCW
Bentley, Richard *Alli, BiDLA, Chmbr 2*
Bentley, Richard d1782 *Alli, BkIE*
Bentley, Richard 1662-1742 *Alli, BiD&SB,*
 BrAu, CasWL, DcEnA, DcEnL, DcEuL,
 EvLB, NewC, OxEng, Pen Eng, REn
Bentley, Richard 1794-1871 *ChPo, NewC*
Bentley, Robert 1825- *Alli Sup*
Bentley, Samuel *Alli Sup*
Bentley, Thomas *Alli, Alli Sup, BiDLA*
Bentley, Virginia W 1908- *ConAu 57*
Bentley, W Holman *Alli Sup*
Bentley, W Perry 1880- *BiDPar*
Bentley, William 1759-1819 *Alli, AmA,*
 AmA&B, DcNAA
Bentley, William Preston 1862-1941 *OhA&B*
Bentley, Wilson Alwyn 1865-1931 *ChPo S1,*
 DcNAA, WhWNAA
Bently, Bessie *ChPo*
Bently, Samuel *Alli*
Bently, Thomas *Alli*
Bently, William *Alli*
Bento, Texeira 1556?-1600 *Pen Am*
Benton, Angelo Ames 1837-1912 *Alli Sup,*
 DcAmA, DcNAA
Benton, Ariel 1792-1883 *OhA&B*
Benton, Mrs. C C *Alli Sup*
Benton, Caroline French *WhWNAA*
Benton, Charles William 1852-1913 *DcNAA*
Benton, Clark *Alli*
Benton, Clive *MnBBF*
Benton, Dorothy Gilchrist 1919- *ConAu 57*
Benton, E C *Alli Sup*
Benton, Elbert Jay 1871-1946 *DcNAA,*
 OhA&B, WhWNAA
Benton, Frank 1852-1919 *DcAmA, DcNAA*
Benton, Guy Potter 1865-1927 *DcNAA,*
 OhA&B

Benton, J Rosalie *Alli Sup*
Benton, James Gilchrist 1820-1881 *Alli Sup,*
 DcAmA, DcNAA
Benton, Joel 1832-1911 *Alli Sup, AmA,*
 AmA&B, BbD, BiD&SB, ChPo,
 ChPo S1, DcAmA, DcNAA
Benton, John W 1933- *ConAu 29*
Benton, Joseph Augustine 1818-1892 *Alli Sup,*
 DcNAA
Benton, Josephine Moffett 1905- *ConAu 5R*
Benton, Josiah Henry 1843-1917 *DcNAA*
Benton, Josiah Henry, Jr. *Alli Sup*
Benton, Kenneth Carter 1909- *Au&Wr,*
 ConAu 49, WrD 1976
Benton, Lewis R 1920- *ConAu 17R*
Benton, Myron Beecher 1834-1902 *ChPo*
Benton, Patricia 1907- *ConAu 5R, WrD 1976*
Benton, Peggie 1906- *Au&Wr, ConAu 49,*
 WrD 1976
Benton, Philip *Alli Sup*
Benton, Reuben Clark 1830-1895 *DcNAA*
Benton, Rita 1881- *WhWNAA*
Benton, Robert 1932- *AmA&B, ConAu 1R,*
 ConDr
Benton, Samuel *Alli Sup*
Benton, Thomas Hart 1782-1858 *Alli, AmA&B,*
 BbD, BiD&SB, BiDSA, CyAL 1,
 DcAmA, DcNAA, OxAm, REn, REnAL
Benton, Thomas Hart 1889-1975 *AmA&B,*
 ConAu 53, IlCB 1945, IlCB 1956, OxAm,
 REn, REnAL
Benton, Walter J 1907- *AmA&B, OhA&B*
Benton, Wilbourn Eugene 1917- *ConAu 1R*
Benton, Will *ConAu XR*
Benton, William 1900-1973 *AmA&B,*
 ConAu 41, ConAu P-1
Bentwich, Herbert 1856- *WhLA*
Bentwich, Norman 1883- *Au&Wr*
Bentwright, Jeremiah *Alli Sup*
Bentz, Charles A 1897- *WhWNAA*
Bentz, William F 1940- *ConAu 53*
Bentzel-Sternau, Count Karl C E Von 1767-1843
 BiD&SB
Bentzon, Therese 1840-1908 *BbD, BiD&SB,*
 DcBiA
Benveniste, Asa 1925- *ConP 1975, WrD 1976*
Benveniste, Guy 1927- *ConAu 61*
Benvenisti, James Lincoln 1890- *BkC 2,*
 CatA 1947
Benvenuti, Fortune Francis *Alli Sup*
Benvras, David *Alli*
Benward, Bruce Charles 1921- *ConAu 9R,*
 IndAu 1917
Benwell, John *Alli, Alli Sup*
Beny, Roloff 1924- *Au&Wr, ConAu XR*
Beny, Wilfred Roy 1924- *ConAu 23*
Benz, Ernst 1907- *ConAu 13R*
Benz, Francis E 1899- *BkC 1, CatA 1947*
Benz, Frank L 1930- *ConAu 41*
Benz, Richard 1884-1966 *OxGer*
Benzelius, Erik 1675-1743 *DcEuL*
Benzie, William 1930- *ConAu 37, WrD 1976*
Benziger, James 1914- *ConAu 13R*
Benzinger, Immanuel Gustav Adolf 1865-
 WhLA
Benzon, Carl Otto Valdemar 1856-1927 *CasWL*
Beolco, Angelo 1502-1542 *CasWL, CnThe,*
 EvEuW, REn, REnWD
Beorse, Bryn 1896- *ConAu 45*
Beothy, Zeolton 1848- *BbD*
Beothy, Zoltan 1848- *BiD&SB*
Beowulf *CasWL, CriT 1, MouLC 1, NewC*
Beranek, Leo L 1914- *ConAu 5R*
Beranek, William 1922- *ConAu 5R*
Beranger, Jean-Pierre De 1780-1857 *CasWL,*
 RCom
Beranger, Pierre-Jean De 1780-1857 *BbD,*
 BiD&SB, ChPo, ChPo S1, ChPo S2,
 DcEuL, EuA, EvEuW, OxEng, OxFr,
 Pen Eur, REn
Berard, Augusta Blanche 1824-1901 *Alli Sup,*
 DcAmA, DcNAA
Berard, Claudius 1786-1848 *DcNAA*
Berard, J Aram 1933- *ConAu 17R*
Berard, J B *Alli*
Berard, Peter *Alli, BiDLA*
Berardo, Felix M 1934- *ConAu 57*
Berault, Peter *Alli*

Berberova, Nina 1901- *ConAu 33*
Berbrich, Joan D 1925- *ConAu 29, WrD 1976*
Berbusse, Edward J 1912- *ConAu 21*
Berceo, Gonzalo De 1195?-1252? *CasWL,*
 DcEuL, DcSpL, EuA, EvEuW, Pen Eur,
 REn
Berch, Jack 1907- *AmSCAP 66*
Berch, William O *ConAu XR*
Berchet, Giovanni 1783-1851 *BiD&SB, CasWL,*
 EuA, EvEuW, Pen Eur
Berchet, Peter 1659-1720 *BkIE*
Berchoux, Joseph 1765-1839 *OxFr*
Berchtold, Leopold, Graf 1863-1942 *OxGer*
Bercken, Arnold *WhLA*
Bercken, Erich VonDer 1885- *WhLA*
Berckman, Evelyn Domenica 1900- *Au&Wr,*
 ConAu 1R, EncM&D, WrD 1976
Bercovici, Konrad 1882-1961 *AmA&B,*
 AmNov, CnDAL, ConAmL, DcLEnL,
 OxAm, REnAL, TwCA, TwCA Sup,
 WhWNAA
Bercovitch, Sacvan 1933- *ConAu 41*
Berctwald d731 *BiB S*
Bercuire, Pierre d1362 *OxFr*
Berczeller, Richard 1902- *ConAu 9R*
Berdahl, Clarence Arthur 1890- *AmA&B,*
 WhWNAA
Berdan, John Milton 1873-1949 *ChPo, DcNAA,*
 OhA&B
Berdes, George R 1931- *ConAu 29*
Berdichevsky, Mikhah Yosef 1865-1921 *EuA*
Berdichewski, Micah Joseph 1865-1921 *Pen Eur*
Berdiczevsky, Micha Yoseph 1865-1921 *CasWL*
Berdie, Douglas R 1946- *ConAu 53*
Berdie, Ralph F 1916- *ConAu 17R*
Berding, Andrew H 1902- *ConAu 5R*
Berdmore, Samuel *Alli*
Berdmore, Septimus *Alli Sup*
Berdmore, Thomas *Alli*
Berdoe, Marmaduke *Alli*
Berdow, Lillian *ChPo*
Berdyayev, Nikolay Aleksandrovich 1874-1948
 CasWL, ClDMEuL, DcRusL, EncWL,
 EvEuW, LongC, REn, TwCA,
 TwCA Sup
Bere, Charles Sandford *Alli Sup*
Bere, Rennie Montague 1907- *Au&Wr,*
 WrD 1976
Bere, Thomas d1814 *Alli, BiDLA,*
 BiDLA Sup
Bereau, A M *Alli Sup*
Bereday, George Z F 1920- *ConAu 1R*
Berelson, Bernard R 1912- *AmA&B,*
 ConAu 5R, WrD 1976
Berelson, David 1943- *ConAu 25*
Berelson, Howard 1940- *IlBYP, SmATA 5*
Berenberg, David Paul 1890- *ChPo S1*
Berend, Alice 1878- *WhLA*
Berendsohn, Walter A 1884- *ConAu 33,*
 WhLA
Berendt, C H *Alli Sup*
Berendt, H C 1911- *BiDPar*
Berenger, Richard d1782 *Alli*
Berenice 028?-079? *NewC*
Berenice II *NewC*
Berens, Mrs. E M *Alli Sup*
Berens, Edward *Alli*
Berens, Louise *Alli Sup*
Berenson, Bernard 1865-1959 *AmA&B,*
 CasWL, LongC, OxAm, OxEng, Pen Am,
 REn, REnAL, TwCA Sup
Berenson, Bernhard 1865-1959 *DcAmA,*
 DcLEnL, TwCA
Berenson, Conrad 1930- *ConAu 9R*
Berenson, Mary 1864- *WhWNAA*
Berenstain, Janice 1923- *AmA&B, AuBYP,*
 ConAu 25
Berenstain, Stanley 1923- *AmA&B, AuBYP,*
 ChPo S1, ConAu 25
Berent, Waclaw 1873-1940 *CasWL, ClDMEuL,*
 EncWL, EvEuW, ModSL 2, Pen Eur
Bereny *Alli*
Beresford *Alli*
Beresford, A Von *Alli Sup*
Beresford, Anne 1929?- *ConP 1970,*
 ConP 1975, WrD 1976
Beresford, Benjamin *Alli, BiDLA*
Beresford, Blanche Elizabeth Adelaide *Alli Sup*

Beringause, Arthur F 1919- *ConAu 33*
Beringer, Joseph August 1862- *WhLA*
Beringer, Mrs. Oscar *Alli Sup*
Berington, Joseph *Alli*
Berington, Joseph 1743-1827 *Alli, DcEnL*
Berington, Simon *Alli*
Berjeau, Jean Philibert *Alli Sup*
Berjeau, Philibert Charles *Alli Sup*
Berjeu, John *Alli*
Berk, Ilhan 1916- *DcOrL 3*
Berk, Lew 1888- *AmSCAP 66*
Berk, Lotte 1913- *Au&Wr*
Berk, Morty 1900-1955 *AmSCAP 66*
Berkart, J B *Alli Sup*
Berke, Joseph H 1939- *ConAu 57*
Berkebile, Don H 1926- *ConAu 61*
Berkebile, Fred D 1900- *ConAu 5R*
Berkeley, Aikin *Alli Sup*
Berkeley, Anthony 1893-1970 *EncM&D,
   LongC, MnBBF, TwCA, TwCA Sup*
Berkeley, Comyns 1865- *WhLA*
Berkeley, David S 1917- *ConAu 41*
Berkeley, Edward *Alli*
Berkeley, Edward Stratton Fitzhardinge
   1827-1878 *Alli Sup*
Berkeley, Elizabeth 1750-1828 *NewC*
Berkeley, George *Chmbr 2*
Berkeley, George 1685-1753 *Alli, BbD,
   BiD&SB, BrAu, CasWL, ChPo,
   ChPo S1, CyAL 1, DcEnA, DcEnL,
   DcEuL, DcLEnL, EvLB, NewC, OxAm,
   OxEng, Pen Eng, PoIre, REn, WebEAL*
Berkeley, George 1733-1795 *Alli*
Berkeley, George, Earl Of d1698 *Alli*
Berkeley, George C Grantley Fitzhardinge
   1800-1881 *Alli, Alli Sup, DcEnL, NewC*
Berkeley, George Monck 1763-1793 *Alli, PoIre*
Berkeley, Grantley 1800-1881 *Br&AmS*
Berkeley, Hastings *Alli Sup*
Berkeley, John *Alli*
Berkeley, Joshua *Alli*
Berkeley, M F F, Baron Fitzhardinge 1788-1867
   Alli Sup
Berkeley, Mary, Countess Dowager Of *Alli,
   BiDLA*
Berkeley, May *ChPo S1*
Berkeley, Miles Joseph 1803- *Alli Sup*
Berkeley, Thomas *Alli*
Berkeley, Sir William 1606-1677 *Alli, BiDSA,
   CyAL 1, OxAm, REn, REnAL*
Berkeley, William Nathaniel 1868-1928 *DcNAA*
Berkeley, William Noland 1867-1945 *DcNAA,
   WhWNAA*
Berkemeyer, William C 1908- *ConAu 25*
Berkenhead, Sir John *Alli, NewC*
Berkenhout, Helena *BiDLA*
Berkenhout, Helina *Alli*
Berkenhout, John 1730?-1791 *Alli*
Berket, Henry *Alli*
Berkey, Charles Peter 1867-1955 *IndAu 1917,
   WhWNAA*
Berkey, Helen 1898- *ConAu 23*
Berkey, William Augustus 1823-1902 *Alli Sup,
   DcNAA*
Berkhey, Johannes LeFrancq Van 1729-1812
   CasWL
Berkhofer, Robert Frederick, Jr. 1931-
   ConAu 13R
Berkie, J James *Alli*
Berkley, Constance Elaine 1931- *BlkAW,
   DrAP 1975, LivBA*
Berkley, Cora *Alli Sup*
Berkley, E *Alli Sup*
Berkley, F M *ChPo*
Berkley, Helen 1819-1870 *AmA*
Berkley, Henry Johns 1860-1940 *DcNAA*
Berkman, Alexander 1870-1936 *DcNAA*
Berkman, Edward O 1914- *ConAu 61*
Berkman, Harold W 1926- *ConAu 53*
Berkman, Jack N 1905- *OhA&B*
Berkman, Richard Lyle 1946- *ConAu 45*
Berkman, Sue 1936- *ConAu 45*
Berkman, Sylvia Leah 1907- *Au&Wr,
   WrD 1976*
Berkman, Ted *ConAu XR*
Berkovits, Eliezer 1908- *AmA&B, ConAu 1R*
Berkovitz, Irving H 1924- *ConAu 57*
Berkovitz, Yitzchak Dov 1885-1967 *CasWL*

Berkowitz, Bernard 1909- *AuNews 1*
Berkowitz, David Sandler 1913- *AmA&B,
   ConAu 33, WrD 1976*
Berkowitz, Freda Pastor 1910- *AuBYP,
   ConAu P-1*
Berkowitz, Henry 1857-1924 *AmLY, DcNAA*
Berkowitz, Hyman Chonon 1895-1945 *DcNAA*
Berkowitz, Luci 1938- *ConAu 33*
Berkowitz, Marvin 1938- *ConAu 29*
Berkowitz, Morris Ira 1931- *ConAu 53*
Berkowitz, Pearl H 1921- *ConAu 23*
Berkowitz, Sol 1922- *AmSCAP 66, ConAu 45*
Berkowitz, Yitzhak Dov 1885-1967 *Pen Eur*
Berkson, Bill 1939- *AmA&B, ConAu XR,
   ConP 1970, ConP 1975, DrAP 1975,
   WrD 1976*
Berkson, Seymour 1905-1959 *AmA&B*
Berkson, William C 1939- *ConAu 21*
Berkson, William Koller 1944- *WrD 1976*
Berl, Ernst 1877- *WhLA*
Berl-Lee, Maria *ConAu XR*
Berlak, Harold 1932- *ConAu 33*
Berland, Theodore 1929- *ConAu 5R*
Berle, Adolf Augustus, Jr. 1895-1971 *AmA&B,
   ConAu 23, ConAu 29*
Berle, Milton 1908- *AmA&B, AmSCAP 66,
   AuNews 1*
Berle, Reidar Johan 1917- *WhGrA*
Berleant, Arnold 1932- *ConAu 29*
Berlichingen, Gottfried 1480?-1562 *OxGer*
Berlichingen, Gotz Von 1480?-1562 *BiD&SB,
   CasWL, EvEuW, OxGer, REn*
Berlin, Ellin 1895- *AmA&B*
Berlin, Ellin 1903- *AmNov*
Berlin, H S *Alli Sup*
Berlin, Irving 1888- *AmSCAP 66, ChPo S2,
   McGWD, OxAm, REn, REnAL*
Berlin, Irving N 1917- *ConAu 23*
Berlin, Sir Isaiah 1909- *Au&Wr, LongC,
   WorAu*
Berlin, Normand 1931- *ConAu 57*
Berlind, Bruce 1926- *ConAu 33, DrAP 1975*
Berliner, Emile 1851-1929 *DcNAA,
   WhWNAA*
Berliner, Franz 1930- *ConAu 29*
Berlinski, Herman 1910- *AmSCAP 66*
Berlioz, Louis-Hector 1803-1869 *AtlBL, BbD,
   BiD&SB, OxFr, REn*
Berlitz, Charles L Frambach 1913- *AmA&B,
   ConAu 5R*
Berlowitz, Max 1880- *WhLA*
Berly, J A *Alli Sup*
Berlye, Milton K 1915- *ConAu 49*
Berlyn, Phillippa Mary 1923- *ConP 1970*
Berlyne, Daniel Ellis 1924- *ConAu 13R,
   WrD 1976*
Berman, Art Harry 1902-1959 *AmSCAP 66*
Berman, Arthur Irwin 1925- *WrD 1976*
Berman, Benjamin Frank 1903- *WhWNAA*
Berman, Berel Vladimir 1896- *WhWNAA*
Berman, Bruce D 1944- *ConAu 41*
Berman, Cassia *DrAP 1975*
Berman, Claire 1936- *ConAu 25, WrD 1976*
Berman, Daniel M 1928- *ConAu 1R*
Berman, Edward 1897-1938 *DcNAA,
   WhWNAA*
Berman, Edward 1911- *AmSCAP 66*
Berman, Louise M 1928- *ConAu 21*
Berman, Marshall 1940- *ConAu 29*
Berman, Milton 1924- *ConAu 1R*
Berman, Morton 1924- *ConAu 5R*
Berman, Ronald 1930- *ChPo S2, ConAu 13R*
Berman, Sanford 1933- *ConAu 37, WrD 1976*
Berman, Simeon M 1935- *ConAu 49*
Berman, William C 1932- *ConAu 41*
Bermange, Barry 1933- *Au&Wr, ConAu 57,
   ConDr, WrD 1976*
Bermann, Patty Pemberton *ChPo S1*
Bermant, Chaim 1929- *Au&Wr, ConAu 57,
   ConNov 1976, WrD 1976*
Bermingham, Edward John 1853-1922 *Alli Sup,
   DcNAA*
Bermingham, Joseph Aldrich *Alli Sup*
Bermont, Georges 1901- *AmSCAP 66*
Bermont, Hubert Ingram 1924- *ConAu 9R*
Bermosk, Loretta Sue 1918- *ConAu 9R*
Bermudez, Geronimo 1530?-1590? *DcEuL*
Bermudez, Jeronimo 1530?-1590? *CasWL*

Bermudez DeCastro, Salvador 1817-1883
   CasWL, DcSpL, EvEuW
Berna, Paul 1910?- *Au&Wr, AuBYP, ThBJA*
Bernabe, Manuel *DcOrL 2*
Bernabo'-Brea, Luigi 1910- *Au&Wr*
Bernadette *ConAu XR, SmATA 4*
Bernadette Of Lourdes, Saint 1844-1879 *REn*
Bernadette Soubirous, Saint 1844-1879 *OxFr*
Bernadotte, Charles-Jean *OxFr*
Bernadou, John Baptiste 1858-1908 *DcAmA,
   DcNAA*
Bernagie, Pieter 1656?-1699 *CasWL, DcEuL,
   EvEuW*
Bernal, John Desmond 1901-1971 *Au&Wr,
   ConAu 33, LongC, WorAu*
Bernal, Judith F 1939- *ConAu 57*
Bernal, Ralph 1808?-1882 *ChPo, ChPo S1*
Bernal Y Garcia Y Pimentel, Ignacio 1910-
   ConAu 9R
Bernaldez, Andres 1480?- *DcEuL*
Bernanos, Georges 1888-1948 *CasWL,
   CatA 1947, CIDMEuL, CnMD, CyWA,
   EncWL, EvEuW, LongC, ModRL,
   ModWD, OxFr, Pen Eur, REn, TwCA,
   TwCA Sup, TwCW, WhTwL*
Bernaola, Pedro 1916-1972 *PueRA*
Bernard De Naisil *OxFr*
Bernard De Ventadour *BiD&SB, OxFr, REn*
Bernard Of Clairvaux, Saint 1091?-1153 *BbD,
   BiD&SB, CasWL, EuA, EvEuW, NewC,
   Pen Eur, PoCh, REn*
Bernard Of Cluny 1100?-1156? *BiD&SB,
   CasWL, NewC, Pen Eur, REn*
Bernard Of Morlaix 1100?-1156? *EvEuW,
   NewC, OxEng, OxFr, PoCh, REn*
Bernard Of Morlas *CasWL*
Bernard Of Tours *CasWL*
Bernard, Saint 1091?-1153 *BbD, BiD&SB,
   NewC, OxEng, OxFr*
Bernard Silvester *CasWL, EvEuW*
Bernard, Mrs. *Alli Sup*
Bernard, A G Farquhar- *Alli Sup*
Bernard, Al 1888-1949 *AmSCAP 66*
Bernard, Alexis Xyste 1847-1923 *DcNAA*
Bernard, Alice *Alli Sup*
Bernard, Andre *OxCan Sup*
Bernard, Andrew M d1523? *Alli, DcEnL,
   PoLE*
Bernard, Anne *OxCan Sup*
Bernard, Antoine 1890- *OxCan*
Bernard, Bayle *Alli Sup*
Bernard, Mrs. Bayle *Alli Sup*
Bernard, Charles *Alli*
Bernard, Charles De 1804?-1850 *BbD,
   BiD&SB, DcEuL, OxFr*
Bernard, Chris *Alli*
Bernard, Claude 1813-1878 *DcEuL, OxFr*
Bernard, David *Alli Sup*
Bernard, David 1798-1876 *DcNAA*
Bernard, Edward 1638-1697? *Alli, DcEnL*
Bernard, Felix 1897-1944 *AmSCAP 66*
Bernard, Florence Scott 1889-1948 *OhA&B,
   WhWNAA*
Bernard, Frances Fenton 1880- *WhWNAA*
Bernard, Sir Francis d1779 *Alli, CyAL 1*
Bernard, Francis 1900- *WhGrA*
Bernard, Franz *Alli Sup*
Bernard, G S *Alli Sup*
Bernard, George S 1837-1912 *BiDSA, DcNAA*
Bernard, H H *Alli*
Bernard, H Russell 1940- *ConAu 41*
Bernard, Harold W 1908- *ConAu 1R*
Bernard, Harry 1898?- *CanWr, OxCan,
   WhWNAA*
Bernard, Henry *ChPo S1*
Bernard, Henry F *Alli Sup*
Bernard, Henry Norris *Alli Sup*
Bernard, Herman Hedwig 1785-1857 *Alli Sup*
Bernard, Hugh Y, Jr. 1919- *ConAu 23*
Bernard, Jack F 1930- *ConAu 21*
Bernard, Jacqueline 1921- *ConAu 23,
   SmATA 8*
Bernard, Jean-Jacques 1888-1972 *CasWL,
   CIDMEuL, CnMD, CnThe, ConAu 37,
   EncWL, LongC, McGWD, ModWD,
   OxFr, Pen Eur, REn*
Bernard, Jean-Marc 1881-1915 *OxFr*
Bernard, Jean Paul *OxCan Sup*

IlCB 1966
Berrill, John *Alli Sup*
Berrill, N J 1903- *ConAu 17R*
Berriman, John 1689-1768 *Alli*
Berriman, Matthew *Alli Sup*
Berriman, William 1688-1750 *Alli, DcEnL*
Berring, Sir P *Alli Sup*
Berrington *Alli*
Berrington, B S *Alli Sup*
Berrington, Hugh Bayard 1928- *ConAu 49, WrD 1976*
Berrington, John *ConAu XR, SmATA 6, WrD 1976*
Berrington, Joseph *BiDLA, BiDLA Sup*
Berrisford, Judith Mary 1912- *Au&Wr, AuBYP, WrD 1976*
Berrow, Capel *Alli*
Berry, The Misses *DcEnL*
Berry, A Moore *Alli Sup*
Berry, Abel B *Alli Sup*
Berry, Adrian M 1937- *ConAu 57, WrD 1976*
Berry, Agnes 1764-1852 *NewC*
Berry, Alice *Alli Sup*
Berry, Barbara J 1937- *ConAu 33, SmATA 7, WrD 1976*
Berry, Brewton 1901- *Au&Wr, ConAu 1R, WrD 1976*
Berry, Brian J L 1934- *ConAu 13R*
Berry, C B *Alli Sup*
Berry, Catherine *Alli Sup*
Berry, Charles *Alli, BiDLA*
Berry, Charles, Duc De 1778-1820 *OxFr*
Berry, Charles Scott 1875- *WhWNAA*
Berry, Charles W 1872- *WhWNAA*
Berry, Chuck *ChPo S2*
Berry, Cicely 1926- *WrD 1976*
Berry, D C 1942- *ConAu 45, DrAP 1975*
Berry, David *Alli Sup*
Berry, David 1942- *Au&Wr, ConAu 29*
Berry, Edmund G 1915- *ConAu 1R*
Berry, Edward I 1940- *ConAu 57*
Berry, Edward Wilber 1875-1945 *DcNAA, WhWNAA*
Berry, Elizabeth 1920- *ConAu 21*
Berry, Elmer 1879- *WhWNAA*
Berry, Elwood Sylvester 1879-1954 *OhA&B*
Berry, Erick 1892- *AuBYP, ChPo, ConAu XR, ConICB, DcNAA, IlCB 1956, JBA 1934, JBA 1951, SmATA 2*
Berry, Faith 1939- *BlkAW*
Berry, Frances Miriam *REnAL*
Berry, Francis *Alli*
Berry, Francis 1915- *Au&Wr, ChPo S1, ChPo S2, ConAu 5R, ConP 1970, ConP 1975, WrD 1976*
Berry, George Ricker 1865-1935 *DcNAA, WhWNAA*
Berry, Gerald L *OxCan*
Berry, Grove *Alli Sup*
Berry, H W *ChPo*
Berry, Helen *ConAu XR*
Berry, Henry *Alli*
Berry, Jack 1918- *ConAu 37*
Berry, Sir James 1860- *WhWNAA*
Berry, James 1932- *ConAu 23*
Berry, James B 1880- *WhWNAA*
Berry, Jason 1949- *ConAu 45*
Berry, Jean 1883- *ChPo, WhWNAA*
Berry, Jim *ConAu XR*
Berry, John *Alli Sup*
Berry, John 1907- *Au&Wr*
Berry, John 1915- *REnAL*
Berry, Josie Graig *BlkAW*
Berry, Katherine F 1877- *ConAu 17*
Berry, Kelley-Marie *BlkAW*
Berry, Len *MnBBF*
Berry, Lillian Gay 1872- *IndAu 1917*
Berry, Lizzie 1847- *ChPo*
Berry, Lloyd Andrew *BlkAW*
Berry, Lloyd E 1935- *ConAu 13R*
Berry, Louise M *ChPo*
Berry, Lynn 1948- *ConAu 61*
Berry, Martha E *Alli Sup*
Berry, Mary 1763-1852 *Alli, BrAu 19, NewC*
Berry, Mary 1935- *Au&Wr*
Berry, Mary Frances 1938- *ConAu 33*
Berry, Michael F 1906- *Br&AmS*

Berry, Paul 1919- *Au&Wr, WrD 1976*
Berry, R J A 1867- *WhLA*
Berry, Richard *Alli*
Berry, Robert *Alli, BiDLA*
Berry, Robert Lee 1874- *WhWNAA*
Berry, Ron 1920- *ConAu 25, WrD 1976*
Berry, S Stillman 1887- *WhWNAA*
Berry, Stephen 1833- *DcNAA*
Berry, Thomas 1914- *ConAu 23, WrD 1976*
Berry, Thomas Elliott 1917- *ConAu 33*
Berry, W S *Alli Sup*
Berry, Wallace Taft 1928- *ConAu 17R, WrD 1976*
Berry, Wendell 1934- *AuNews 1, ConLC 4, ConLC 6, ConP 1970, ConP 1975, DrAF 1976, DrAP 1975, Pen Am, RAdv 1, WrD 1976*
Berry, William *Alli, BiDLA*
Berry, William 1902- *AnMV 1926*
Berry, William D *AuBYP*
Berry, William David 1926- *IlCB 1966*
Berry, William Turner 1888- *ConAu 23*
Berryer, Pierre Antoine 1790?-1868 *DcEuL*
Berryhill, S Newton 1830-1888 *AmA&B, BiDSA, ChPo, DcNAA*
Berryman, Cecil W 1888- *WhWNAA*
Berryman, E R P *ChPo S1, ChPo S2*
Berryman, John 1914-1972 *AmA&B, AmWr, Au&Wr, CasWL, CnE&AP, ConAu 33, ConAu P-1, ConLC 1, ConLC 2, ConLC 3, ConLC 4, ConLC 6, ConP 1970, ConP 1975, CrCAP, EncWL Sup, ModAL, ModAL Sup, OxAm, Pen Am, RAdv 1, REn, REnAL, TwCA Sup, WebEAL, WhTwL*
Berryman, John R *Alli Sup*
Berryman, John R 1849-1914 *DcNAA*
Berryman-Paap, Opal Leigh 1897- *WhWNAA*
Bersani, Leo 1931- *ConAu 53*
Berschadsky, Isaiah 1871-1910 *CasWL*
Berscheid, Ellen 1936- *ConAu 25*
Bersezio, Vittorio 1828-1900 *BiD&SB, CasWL, EvEuW*
Bershadsky, Isaiah 1872-1910 *Pen Eur*
Berson, Harold 1926- *ChPo, ConAu 33, IlBYP, IlCB 1966, SmATA 4*
Berssenbrugge, Mei-Mei *DrAP 1975*
Berst, Charles A 1932- *ConAu 41*
Berstl, Julius 1883- *WhLA*
Bersuire, Pierre 1290?-1362 *CasWL, OxFr*
Bert, Ed *Alli*
Bert, Josephina *Alli Sup*
Bertail, Inez *ChPo S1*
Bertaut, Jean 1552-1611 *BiD&SB, CasWL, DcEuL, EvEuW, OxFr*
Bertelli, Luigi 1858-1920 *CarSB*
Bertelson, David 1934- *ConAu 21*
Bertenshaw, Thomas Handel 1859- *ChPo S1*
Bertezen, S *Alli*
Bertha, Gus *BlkAW*
Berthelot, Amable 1777-1847? *BbtC, DcNAA*
Berthelot, Brunet *OxCan Sup*
Berthelot, Hector 1842-1895 *OxCan*
Berthelot, Joseph A 1927- *ConAu 21*
Berthelot, Marcelin 1827-1907 *OxFr*
Berthet, Elie 1815-1891 *BiD&SB*
Berthier, Louis-Alexandre *OxFr*
Berthoff, Rowland 1921- *ConAu 33*
Berthoff, Warner 1925- *AmA&B, ConAu 5R*
Berthold Von Holle *CasWL, OxGer*
Berthold Von Regensburg 1215?-1272 *CasWL, OxGer*
Berthold, Franz 1802-1839 *BiD&SB*
Berthold, Mary Paddock 1909- *ConAu 53*
Berthold, Victor Maximilian 1856-1932 *DcNAA*
Bertholf, Lloyd Millard 1899- *WhWNAA*
Berthollet, Claude-Louis, Comte 1748-1822 *OxFr*
Berthoud, Jacques 1935- *ConAu 17R*
Bertie *MnBBF*
Bertie, Willoughby 1740-1799 *Alli, NewC*
Bertillon, Alphonse 1853-1914 *LongC, OxFr*
Bertin *OxFr*
Bertin, Antoine 1753?-1790 *BiD&SB, OxFr*
Bertin, Celia 1920- *Au&Wr*
Bertin, Charles 1919- *CnMD, ModWD*
Bertin, George *Alli Sup*
Bertin, Leonard M 1918- *Au&Wr,*

ConAu 13R
Bertinoro, Obadiah Di 1450?-1500? *CasWL*
Bertken, Suster 1427?-1514 *CasWL*
Bertman, Stephen 1937- *ConAu 45*
Berto, Giuseppe 1914- *CasWL, EvEuW, ModRL, TwCA Sup*
Bertocci, Peter A 1910- *ConAu 17R*
Bertola De'Giorgi, Aurelio 1753-1798 *CasWL*
Bertolazzi, Carlo 1870-1916 *McGWD, REnWD*
Bertolino, James 1942- *ConAu 45, ConP 1970, ConP 1975, DrAP 1975, WrD 1976*
Bertolome Zorzi 1230?-1290 *CasWL, EvEuW*
Berton, G F S *BbtC*
Berton, Laura *OxCan*
Berton, P M *Alli Sup*
Berton, Pierre 1920- *Au&Wr, CanWr, ConAu 1R, OxCan, OxCan Sup, WrD 1976*
Berton, Ralph 1910- *ConAu 49*
Berton, William *Alli*
Bertram, Charles 1723-1765 *Alli, NewC, OxEng*
Bertram, Ernst 1884-1957 *EncWL, EvEuW, OxGer*
Bertram, George Colin Lawder 1911- *Au&Wr, ConAu 13R*
Bertram, H *Alli Sup*
Bertram, H C *Alli Sup*
Bertram, James G *Alli Sup*
Bertram, James Munro 1910- *Au&Wr, WrD 1976*
Bertram, Jean DeSales *ConAu 45*
Bertram, Robert Aitkin 1836- *Alli Sup*
Bertram, Robert F 1916- *AmSCAP 66*
Bertram-Cox, Jean DeSales *ConAu XR*
Bertran De Bar-Sur-Aube *EvEuW*
Bertran De Born 1140?-1215? *CasWL, EuA, EvEuW, Pen Eur, REn*
Bertrana, Prudenci 1867-1941 *ClDMEuL*
Bertrand De Bar-Sur-Aube *CasWL, OxFr*
Bertrand De Born 1140?-1215? *OxFr*
Bertrand, Aloysius 1807-1841 *CasWL, EvEuW*
Bertrand, Alvin L 1918- *ConAu 45*
Bertrand, Camille *OxCan*
Bertrand, Charles *ConAu XR*
Bertrand, Denis *OxCan Sup*
Bertrand, Henri-Gratien, Comte De 1773-1844 *OxFr*
Bertrand, Lewis 1897?-1974 *ConAu 53*
Bertrand, Louis 1866-1941 *CatA 1947, OxFr, WhLA*
Bertrand, Louis Jacques Napoleon 1807-1841 *DcEuL, EuA, OxFr, Pen Eur*
Bertron, Mrs. Ottilie *Alli Sup, BiDSA*
Bertsch, Fred S *ChPo*
Bertsch, Hugo 1851-1935 *CasWL*
Bertsche, Karl 1879- *WhLA*
Bertuch, Friedrich Justin 1747-1822 *OxGer*
Bertz, Edward *Alli Sup*
Berulle, Cardinal Pierre De *OxFr*
Berwald, William 1864-1948 *AmSCAP 66*
Berwanger, Eugene H 1929- *ConAu 21*
Berwick, Edward *Alli, BiDLA, BiDLA Sup*
Berwick, George *Alli Sup*
Berwick, James Fitzjames, Duke Of 1670-1734 *OxFr*
Berwick, Jean Shepherd 1929- *ConAu 9R*
Berwick, John *Alli*
Berwick, Keith 1928- *ConAu 33*
Berwick, Marshal, Duke Of 1670-1734 *Alli*
Berwick, Mary *NewC*
Berwick, Thurso *ChPo S1*
Berwick, William Edward Hodgson 1888- *WhLA*
Berwinski, Ryszard Wincenty 1819-1879 *CasWL, EvEuW*
Bery, John *Alli*
Berzelius, Baron Jons Jakob 1779-1848 *REn*
Berzsenyi, Daniel 1776-1836 *CasWL, Pen Eur*
Berzunza, Julius 1896- *WhWNAA*
Besanceney, Paul H 1924- *ConAu 45*
Besancon, Alberic De *OxFr*
Besant, Annie 1847-1933 *Alli Sup, Chmbr 3, DcLEnL, EvLB, LongC, NewC, REn, TwCA, TwCA Sup, WhLA*
Besant, Sir Walter 1836-1901 *Alli Sup, BbD, BiD&SB, BrAu 19, CasWL, Chmbr 3,*

DcBiA, DcEnA, DcEnA Ap, DcEuL,
DcLEnL, EvLB, HsB&A, MouLC 4,
NewC, OxEng, Pen Eng, REn, WebEAL
Besant, William Henry 1828- *Alli Sup*
Besch, Lutz 1918- *CnMD*
Bescherelle, Louis-Nicolas *OxFr*
Beschi, Constanzo Giuseppe 1680-1746
DcOrL 2
Besci, Kurt 1920- *CrCD, McGWD*
Besemeres, Jane *Alli Sup*
Besemeres, John Daly *Alli Sup*
Besemers, Jane *ChPo S1*
Besenval, Baron Pierre-Victor De 1722-1791
OxFr
Beshers, James M 1931- *ConAu 1R*
Beshoar, Michael 1833-1907 *DcNAA*
Besht *CasWL*
Besier, George *MnBBF*
Besier, Rudolf 1878-1942 *DcLEnL, EvLB,
LongC, ModWD, REn, TwCA, WhLA*
Besier, Rudolph 1878-1942 *McGWD*
Besiki 1750-1791 *DcOrL 3*
Beskow, Bernard Von 1796-1868 *CasWL,
DcEuL, EvEuW*
Beskow, Bo 1906- *ConAu 61*
Beskow, Elsa 1874- *AnCL, BkCL, ChPo S2,
ConICB, IlCB 1945, JBA 1934,
JBA 1951*
Besnard, Lucien 1872- *McGWD*
Besodun, John *Alli*
Besombe, Robert *Alli*
Besoyan, Rick 1924?-1970 *ConAu 25*
Bess, Elmer Allen 1869- *IndAu 1917*
Bess, Olean 1936- *BlkAW*
Bessa-Victor, Geraldo 1917- *AfA 1*
Bessarion 1403-1472 *DcEuL, Pen Cl, REn*
Bessarion 1858- *WhWNAA*
Bessarion, John 1395-1472 *CasWL*
Bessau, Oscar *EarAB*
Bessborough, Earl Of 1913- *Au&Wr,
ConAu XR*
Besse, Henry 1823-1901 *OhA&B*
Besse, Joseph *Alli*
Besse, Robert 1920- *AmSCAP 66*
Bessell, Adolf Wilhelm Lucian 1857- *WhLA*
Bessels, Emil 1847-1888 *Alli Sup*
Bessemans, Joseph Francois A Albert 1888-
BiDPar
Bessems, Josephine *WhWNAA*
Bessenyei, Gyorgy 1747-1811 *CasWL*
Besser, Gretchen R 1928- *ConAu 41*
Besser, Johann Von 1654-1729 *CasWL, DcEuL,
EvEuW, OxGer*
Besset, Jane M *Alli Sup*
Bessett, Sydney *Alli Sup*
Bessette, Gerard 1920- *CanWr, CasWL,
ConAu 37, OxCan, OxCan Sup*
Bessey, Charles Edwin 1845-1915 *Alli Sup,
DcAmA, DcNAA*
Bessey, Ernst Athearn 1877- *WhWNAA*
Bessey, Mabel A 1884- *WhWNAA*
Bessie, Alvah 1904- *AmA&B, AmNov,
ConAmA, ConAu 5R, TwCA,
TwCA Sup, WhWNAA, WrD 1976*
Bessieres, Jean-Baptiste *OxFr*
Bessinger, Jess B, Jr. 1921- *ConAu 13R*
Bessom, Malcolm E 1940- *ConAu 57*
Best, Adam *ConAu XR*
Best, Allena Champlin 1892- *AuBYP,
ConAu 25, IlCB 1945, IlCB 1956,
JBA 1934, JBA 1951, SmATA 2*
Best, Carol Ann *Au&Wr*
Best, Charles *ChPo*
Best, Charles Herbert 1899- *Au&Wr,
ConAu 45, WrD 1976*
Best, Elsdon 1856-1931 *DcLEnL*
Best, Eva *ChPo, ChPo S1*
Best, Flora L *ChPo*
Best, Gary A 1939- *ConAu 33*
Best, Geoffrey F A 1928- *Au&Wr*
Best, George *Alli, OxCan*
Best, George Payne *Alli Sup*
Best, Henry *Alli, BiDLA*
Best, Herbert 1894- *AmA&B, AmNov,
AuBYP, ConAu 25, JBA 1934,
JBA 1951, SmATA 2*
Best, James J 1938- *ConAu 37*
Best, John Wesley 1909- *ConAu 17R*

Best, L *Alli Sup*
Best, Mrs. M C *Alli Sup*
Best, Mary Agnes 1767-1942 *DcNAA*
Best, Matilda *Alli*
Best, Michael R 1939- *ConAu 37*
Best, Nolan Rice 1871-1930 *AmLY, DcNAA,
OhA&B*
Best, Rayleigh Breton Amis 1905- *Au&Wr,
ConAu P-1*
Best, Robert *Alli Sup*
Best, Rupert Jethro 1903- *Au&Wr*
Best, Samuel *Alli, Alli Sup*
Best, Susie Montgomery 1869-1944 *ChPo,
ChPo S2, OhA&B*
Best, Mrs. T *Alli*
Best, Tharratt Gilbert 1892- *WhWNAA*
Best, Thomas *Alli, Alli Sup, BiDLA*
Best, Thomas W 1939- *ConAu 29*
Best, W M *Alli*
Best, William *Alli*
Best, William Newton 1860-1922 *DcNAA*
Beste, John Richard Digby *Alli, Alli Sup*
Beste, Karl August Axel *WhLA*
Beste, Kenelm Digby- 1836- *Alli Sup*
Beste, Konrad 1890-1958 *CasWL, OxGer*
Beste, R Vernon 1908- *Au&Wr, ConAu 1R*
Bester, Alfred 1913- *AmA&B, ConAu 13R,
WrD 1976*
Besterman, Theodore 1904- *BiDPar, LongC*
Bestic, Alan Kent 1922- *ConAu 13R*
Beston, Henry 1888-1968 *AmA&B, ConAu 25,
JBA 1934, JBA 1951, OxCan, REnAL,
TwCA, TwCA Sup*
Beston, Mrs. Henry *AmA&B, AmNov XR*
Beston, John *Alli*
Bestor, Arthur, Jr. 1908- *AmA&B, Au&Wr,
ConAu 1R, WrD 1976*
Bestor, Don 1889- *AmSCAP 66*
Bestul, Thomas H 1942- *ConAu 53*
Bestuzhev, Alexander Alexandrovich 1797-1837
BbD, BiD&SB, DcRusL
Bestuzhev-Marlinsky, Alexander A 1797-1837
CasWL
Besuire, Pierre d1362 *DcEuL*
Besus, Roger 1915- *EncWL, Pen Eur*
Beswick, Samuel *Alli Sup*
Betab, Sufi 'Abdulhaqq Khan 1888-1969
DcOrL 3
Betagh, William *Alli*
Betances, Ramon Emeterio 1827-1898 *PueRA*
Betances, Samuel *DrAP 1975*
Betancourt, Jeanne 1941- *ConAu 49*
Betenson, Lula Parker 1884- *ConAu 61*
Beth, Karl 1872- *WhLA*
Beth, Loren Peter 1920- *ConAu 1R*
Beth, Marianne 1890- *WhLA*
Beth, Mary *ConAu XR, SmATA XR*
Betham, Mrs. *Alli Sup*
Betham, Charles Jepson *Alli Sup*
Betham, Ernest Burton *Alli Sup, ChPo*
Betham, John d1701 *Alli*
Betham, Mary Matilda 1776-1852 *ChPo*
Betham, Matilda *Alli, BiDLA*
Betham, Philip *Alli*
Betham, Robert *Alli*
Betham, Robert Mitchell 1864- *WhLA*
Betham, William *Alli, BiDLA*
Betham, Sir William 1779-1853 *Alli, DcEnL,
NewC*
Betham-Edwards, Matilda Barbara 1836-1919
*Alli Sup, BrAu 19, ChPo, ChPo S1,
ChPo S2, Chmbr 3, LongC, NewC*
Bethancourt, T Ernesto *ConAu XR*
Bethea, Jack 1892-1928 *DcNAA, WhWNAA*
Bethel, Dell 1929- *ConAu 29*
Bethel, Ellsworth 1863- *WhWNAA*
Bethel, Gar *DrAP 1975*
Bethel, J *ChPo S2*
Bethel, Paul D 1919- *ConAu 25*
Bethel, Slingsby *Alli*
Bethell, A J *Alli Sup*
Bethell, A P *Alli Sup*
Bethell, Augusta *Alli Sup*
Bethell, Christopher *Alli, Alli Sup*
Bethell, Jean 1922- *ConAu 9R, SmATA 8*
Bethell, Mary Ursula 1874-1945 *CnMWL,
DcLEnL, LongC, Pen Eng, TwCW,
WebEAL, WhTwL*

Bethell, Nicholas William 1938- *ConAu 45*
Bethell, Philip *ChPo S2*
Bethell, Samuel *Alli, BiDLA Sup*
Bethers, Ray 1902- *Au&Wr, AuBYP,
ConAu P-1, SmATA 6*
Bethge, Hans 1876-1946 *EncWL, OxGer*
Bethmann, Erich Waldemar 1904- *ConAu 23,
WrD 1976*
Bethmann-Hollweg, Theobald Von 1856-1921
OxGer, REn
Bethum, John *Alli*
Bethune, A M *Alli Sup*
Bethune, Alexander *ChPo S1*
Bethune, Alexander 1804-1843? *Alli, BrAu 19,
DcEnL*
Bethune, Alexander Neil 1800?-1879 *BbtC,
DcNAA*
Bethune, Charles J S *BbtC*
Bethune, George Ambrose *Alli Sup*
Bethune, George Washington 1805-1862 *Alli,
Alli Sup, AmA&B, BiD&SB, ChPo,
ChPo S1, ChPo S2, CyAL 2, DcAmA,
DcNAA, PoCh*
Bethune, J *ChPo S2*
Bethune, J G *HsB&A, YABC 1*
Bethune, John *Alli, BbtC*
Bethune, Lebert 1937- *BlkAW, DrAF 1976,
DrAP 1975*
Bethune, Mary *Au&Wr*
Bethune-Baker, James Franklin 1861- *Alli Sup,
WhLA*
Bethurum, F Dorothy 1897- *ConAu 17*
Beti, Mongo 1932- *AfA 1, CasWL,
EncWL Sup, Pen Cl, RGAfl, TwCW*
Betjeman, Sir John 1906- *Au&Wr, CasWL,
ChPo, ChPo S1, ChPo S2, CnE&AP,
CnMWL, ConAu 9R, ConLC 2,
ConLC 6, ConP 1970, ConP 1975,
DcLEnL, EvLB, LongC, ModBL,
ModBL Sup, NewC, OxEng, Pen Eng,
RAdv 1, REn, TwCA Sup, TwCW,
WebEAL, WhTwL, WrD 1976*
Betocchi, Carlo 1899- *CasWL, ConAu 9R,
WorAu*
Betsch, Roland 1888- *WhLA*
Bett, Henry *ChPo S1*
Bett, Walter Reginald 1903- *Au&Wr,
ConAu P-1*
Bettan, Israel 1889-1957 *OhA&B*
Bettany, G T *ChPo S1*
Bettany, George Kernahan Gwynne 1891-
WhLA
Bettany, George Thomas 1850- *Alli Sup*
Bettany, Mary Jean Hickling 1857- *Alli Sup*
Bettelheim, Bruno 1903- *AmA&B*
Bettelheim, Frederick A 1923- *ConAu 49*
Betteloni, Vittorio 1840-1910 *BiD&SB, CasWL,
ClDMEuL, EvEuW*
Betten, Francis Sales 1863-1942 *DcNAA,
OhA&B*
Betten, Francis Salesius 1863-1942 *CatA 1947,
WhWNAA*
Bettenson, Henry 1908- *ConAu 13R*
Betteridge, Anne *ConAu XR, WrD 1976*
Betteridge, Don *LongC*
Betteridge, H T 1910- *ConAu 5R*
Bettersworth, John K 1909- *ConAu 5R*
Betterton, Mrs. d1711 *NewC*
Betterton, Kathleen Diana 1912- *Au&Wr*
Betterton, Thomas 1635?-1710 *Alli, BrAu,
CasWL, DcEnL, DcLEnL, NewC,
OxEng, REn*
Bettesworth, Charles *Alli*
Bettesworth, John *Alli, BiDLA*
Betti, Ugo 1892-1953 *CasWL, ClDMEuL,
CnMD, CnMWL, CnThe, EncWL,
EvEuW, LongC, McGWD, ModRL,
ModWD, OxEng, Pen Eur, REnWD,
TwCW, WorAu*
Bettie, W *Alli*
Bettina 1903- *AuBYP, ConAu XR,
IlCB 1956, IlCB 1966, MorJA, REn,
SmATA 1*
Bettinelli, Saverio 1718-1808 *CasWL, EvEuW*
Bettis, Fannie E *TexWr*
Bettis, Joseph Dabney 1936- *ConAu 33*
Bettison, William James *Alli Sup*
Bettmann, Otto Ludwig 1903- *ConAu 17R*

Bettner, George Shonnard 1801-1860 *DcNAA*
Betton, T R *Alli*
Bettridge, William Craddock 1791-1879 *BbtC,* *DcNAA*
Betts, Anson Gardner 1876- *WhWNAA*
Betts, Charles Henry 1863- *AmLY,* . *WhWNAA*
Betts, Charles L 1908- *WrD 1976*
Betts, Charles Marsden *Alli Sup*
Betts, Charles Wyllys 1845-1887 *DcNAA*
Betts, Craven Langstroth 1853-1941 *Alli Sup,* *AmA&B, AmLY, BiD&SB, DcAmA,* *DcNAA, OxCan, WhWNAA*
Betts, Donni 1948- *ConAu 53*
Betts, Doris June Waugh 1932- *AmA&B,* *ConAu 13R, ConLC 6, DrAF 1976*
Betts, Edward William 1881- *Au&Wr*
Betts, Emmett Albert 1903- *ConAu 33,* *IndAu 1917, WrD 1976*
Betts, Ethel Franklin *ChPo, ChPo S1*
Betts, Frederick William 1858-1932 *DcNAA*
Betts, George 1944- *ConAu 45*
Betts, George Herbert 1868-1934 *AmLY,* *DcNAA, WhWNAA*
Betts, Henry John *Alli Sup*
Betts, John *Alli*
Betts, John Thomas *Alli Sup*
Betts, Joseph *Alli*
Betts, Nancy K 1880- *WhWNAA*
Betts, Raymond Frederick 1925- *ConAu 1R,* *WrD 1976*
Betts, Robert *Alli*
Betts, Ruth Morris *TexWr*
Betts, Samuel Rossiter 1787-1868 *Alli, DcAmA,* *DcNAA*
Betts, Thomas Jeffries 1894- *WhWNAA*
Betts, Victoria Bedford 1913- *WrD 1976*
Betts, William Wilson, Jr. 1926- *ConAu 33,* *WrD 1976*
Betty Bee *WhWNAA*
Betty, Joseph *Alli*
Betty, Mrs. William H *OhA&B*
Betty, William Henry West 1791-1874 *NewC*
Bettz, Anna Whelan *ChPo*
Betulejus, Xystus *OxGer*
Betz, Annette 1886- *WhWNAA*
Betz, Betty 1920- *AuBYP, ConAu 1R,* *MorJA*
Betz, Eva Kelly 1897-1968 *BkC 5, ConAu P-1,* *SmATA 10*
Betz, Hans Dieter 1931- *ConAu 53*
Betz, Johann Albert 1885- *WhLA*
Betzner, John F 1908- *AmSCAP 66*
Beulanius *Alli*
Beulanius, Samuel *Alli*
Beum, Robert Lawrence 1929- *ConAu 9R,* *OhA&B*
Beumelburg, Werner 1899-1963 *OxGer*
Beurdeley, Michel 1911- *ConAu 49*
Beutenmuller, William 1864- *DcAmA,* *WhWNAA*
Beuthien, Angelius Erich Wilhelm 1834-1926 *CasWL*
Bevan, Alistair *ConAu XR*
Bevan, Bryan Henry 1913- *Au&Wr,* *ConAu 13R*
Bevan, Charles Dacres 1805-1872 *Alli Sup*
Bevan, E Dean 1938- *ConAu 33*
Bevan, E F *Alli Sup*
Bevan, Edwyn Robert 1870-1943 *LongC,* *WhLA*
Bevan, Frances *Alli Sup*
Bevan, George Phillips d1889 *Alli Sup*
Bevan, Henry *Alli*
Bevan, Henry Bailey *Alli Sup*
Bevan, J A *Alli Sup*
Bevan, Jack 1920- *ConAu 13R*
Bevan, James Stuart 1930- *Au&Wr*
Bevan, John Aylwin *Alli Sup*
Bevan, Joseph Gurney d1814 *Alli,* *BiDLA,* *BiDLA Sup*
Bevan, Llewelyn David 1842- *Alli Sup*
Bevan, Philip *Alli Sup*
Bevan, R *Alli Sup*
Bevan, Ralph Hervey 1881- *WhWNAA*
Bevan, Richard *Alli*
Bevan, Robert Casper Lee *Alli Sup*
Bevan, Mrs. Robert Casper Lee *Alli Sup*

Bevan, Samuel *Alli Sup*
Bevan, Sylvanus *Alli*
Bevan, Thomas *Alli*
Bevan, Tom 1868-1938? *MnBBF, WhCL*
Bevan, William Latham *Alli Sup*
Bevan, Wilson Lloyd 1866-1935 *DcNAA*
Bevans, Gladys Huntington *WhWNAA*
Bevans, John *Alli, BiDLA*
Bevans, Margaret *AuBYP*
Bevans, Michael H *AuBYP*
Bevans, Neile *DcNAA*
Bevard, Camille *IndAu 1917*
Bever, Thomas 1725-1781 *Alli*
Bever, Thomas 1855- *Alli Sup*
Beveridge, Lord 1879-1963 *LongC*
Beveridge, Albert Jeremiah 1862-1927 *AmA&B,* *DcAmA, DcNAA, IndAu 1816, OhA&B,* *OxAm, REn, REnAL, TwCA,* *TwCA*
Beveridge, Albert Jeremiah, Jr. 1908- *WhWNAA*
Beveridge, Andrew *ChPo*
Beveridge, David *Alli Sup*
Beveridge, Henry *Alli Sup*
Beveridge, James *Alli Sup*
Beveridge, John *Alli Sup*
Beveridge, John d1767 *Alli, CyAL 1, DcNAA*
Beveridge, John Harrie 1869-1932 *DcNAA*
Beveridge, Mitchell Kilgour *Alli Sup*
Beveridge, Oscar Maltman 1913- *ConAu 9R*
Beveridge, Robert *Alli Sup*
Beveridge, Thomas *Alli*
Beveridge, Thomas G 1938- *AmSCAP 66*
Beveridge, William 1636?-1708 *Alli, DcEnL*
Beveridge, William Ian Beardmore 1908- *Au&Wr, WrD 1976*
Beverley, Charlotte *Alli, BiDLA*
Beverley, Constance *Alli Sup*
Beverley, John *Alli, BiDLA*
Beverley, John Of *Alli*
Beverley, May *Alli Sup*
Beverley, Peter *Alli*
Beverley, R M *Alli*
Beverley, Robert 1673-1722 *AmA, AmA&B,* *DcAmA, DcLEnL, DcNAA, OxAm,* *Pen Am, REnAL*
Beverley, Robert Mackenzie *Alli Sup*
Beverley, Thomas *Alli*
Beverley-Giddings, Arthur Raymond 1899- *AmA&B, AmNov*
Beverly, John *Alli*
Beverly, Katherine *BlkAW*
Beverly, R *Alli Sup*
Beverly, Robert *BiDSA*
Beverly, Robert 1673?-1722? *Alli, REn*
Beverly, Vivian *WhWNAA*
Beverton, Simon *Alli*
Bevier, Abraham Garret 1812-1861 *DcNAA*
Bevier, Isabel 1860-1942 *AmLY, DcNAA,* *WhWNAA*
Bevier, Louis 1857-1925 *DcNAA*
Bevier, R S *Alli Sup*
Bevilacqua, Alberto 1934- *ConAu 29*
Bevill, Robert *Alli, BiDLA*
Bevin, Elway *Alli*
Bevin, Philip 1811-1890 *IndAu 1816*
Bevington, David M 1931- *ConAu 1R*
Bevington, Helen Smith 1906- *AmA&B, ChPo,* *CnDAL, ConAu 13R, WorAu*
Bevington, Louisa S *Alli Sup*
Bevir, Edward Lawrence d1922 *ChPo S2*
Bevir, J L *Alli Sup*
Bevis, Alma Darst Murray 1888- *OhA&B*
Bevis, Em Olivia 1932- *ConAu 49*
Bevis, H U 1902- *ConAu 29*
Bevis, Henry J *Alli Sup*
Bevis, James *ConAu XR*
Bevis, John 1695-1771 *Alli*
Bevis, Sophia Cortoulde Hazlett 1846- *OhA&B*
Bevk, France 1890-1970 *CasWL, EncWL*
Bevlin, Marjorie Elliott 1917- *ConAu 9R*
Bewer, Julius August 1877-1953 *AmA&B,* *WhWNAA*
Bewes, Richad 1934- *WrD 1976*
Bewick, Benjamin *Alli*
Bewick, Jane 1787-1881 *Alli Sup*
Bewick, John 1760?-1795 *Alli, CarSB,* *ChPo S1*

Bewick, Joseph *Alli Sup*
Bewick, Thomas 1753-1828 *Alli, BkIE, CarSB,* *ChPo, ChPo S1, ChPo S2, DcLEnL,* *NewC, St&VC, WhCL*
Bewicke, Miss A E N *Alli Sup*
Bewicke, E H *Alli Sup*
Bewicke, Robert *Alli, BiDLA*
Bewkes, Eugene Garrett 1895- *ConAu 5R*
Bewley, Charles Henry 1888- *ConAu 5R*
Bewley, Christopher *MnBBF*
Bewley, Edward White *Alli Sup*
Bewley, Henry *Alli Sup*
Bewley, Loyal Vivian 1898- *Au&Wr*
Bewley, Marius 1918-1973 *Au&Wr,* *ConAu 5R, ConAu 41*
Bewley, Richard *Alli, BiDLA*
Bews, John W 1889- *WhLA*
Bewsher, Amelia *Alli Sup*
Bewsher, Frederick William 1886- *WhLA*
Bewsher, Mrs. M E *Alli Sup*
Bexell, John Andrew 1867- *WhWNAA*
Bey, Ali *DcNAA*
Bey, Isabelle *WrD 1976*
Bey, R R Hubbard *MnBBF*
Beyatli, Yahya Kemal 1884-1958 *DcOrL 3*
Beyea, Basil 1910- *ConAu 61*
Beyer, Audrey White 1916- *ConAu 13R,* *SmATA 9*
Beyer, David S 1880- *WhWNAA*
Beyer, Edward 1820-1865 *EarAB Sup*
Beyer, Ernestine Cobern 1893- *ChPo, ChPo S1,* *WhWNAA*
Beyer, Evelyn *ChPo*
Beyer, Evelyn M 1907- *ConAu 25*
Beyer, George Eugene 1861- *BiDSA*
Beyer, Glenn H 1913- *ConAu 1R*
Beyer, Howard 1929- *AmSCAP 66*
Beyer, Maximilian 1890- *TexWr*
Beyer, Oskar Fred Theodor 1882- *WhLA*
Beyer, Werner William 1911- *Au&Wr,* *ConAu 9R, IndAu 1917, WrD 1976*
Beyerle, Nellie Taneyhill *Alli Sup*
Beyerlein, Franz Adam 1871-1949 *OxGer*
Beyfus, Drusilla 1927- *Au&Wr, WrD 1976*
Beygrau, Frederick Reginald 1873- *WhWNAA*
Beyhaqi, Abu'l-Fazl Mohammad 996-1077 *DcOrL 3*
Beyle, Henri 1783-1842 *AtlBL, DcEuL,* *OxEng, OxFr*
Beyle, Herman Carey 1892-1956 *IndAu 1917*
Beyle, Marie Henri 1783-1842 *BiD&SB, EuA,* *EvEuW, NewC, REn*
Beyle, Thad L 1934- *ConAu 37*
Beynon, Huw 1942- *WrD 1976*
Beynon, John *MnBBF, WorAu*
Bezanson, A Maynard 1878-1958 *OxCan*
Bezbarua, Laksminath 1868-1938 *DcOrL 2*
Beze, Theodore De 1519-1605 *CasWL, DcEuL,* *EvEuW, OxFr, Pen Eur*
Bezeman, L 1865- *WhWNAA*
Bezruc, Petr 1867-1958 *CasWL, ClDMEuL,* *EncWL, ModSL 2, Pen Eur*
Bezucha, Vlastimil 1928- *BiDPar*
Bezwoda, Eva Susanne 1942- *ConP 1970*
Bezymenski, Alexander Ilyich 1898- *CasWL,* *ClDMEuL, DcRusL*
Bezzi, Giovanni Aubrey *Alli Sup*
Bezzola, Andrea 1840-1897 *CasWL, EvEuW*
Bezzola, Eduard 1875-1948 *CasWL*
Bha Shein, U *DcOrL 2*
Bhagat, Goberdhan 1928- *ConAu 29,* *WrD 1976*
Bhagat, Niranjan *DcOrL 2*
Bhagavatula, Murty S 1921- *ConAu 29*
Bhagwati, Jagdish N 1934- *ConAu 17R*
Bhalo, Ahmad Nassir Bin Juma *AfA 1*
Bhamaha *DcOrL 2*
Bhana, Surendra 1939- *ConAu 57*
Bhandarkar, D R 1875- *WhLA*
Bhanj, Upendra *DcOrL 2*
Bhanubhakta *DcOrL 2*
Bharata *CasWL, DcOrL 2, Pen Cl,* *REnWD*
Bharathidasan *DcOrL 2*
Bharathithasan *DcOrL 2*
Bharati *CasWL, Pen Cl*
Bharati, Agehananda 1923- *ConAu 1R,* *WrD 1976*

Bharati, S *DcOrL 2*
Bharavi 550?- *CasWL*, *DcOrL 2*
Bhardwaj, Surinder Mohan 1934- *ConAu 45*
Bhartendu *DcOrL 2*
Bhartrhari *CasWL*, *DcOrL 2*, *Pen Cl*
Bhasa *CasWL*, *DcOrL 2*, *REn*, *REnWD*
Bhaskaran, M P 1921- *ConP 1970*
Bhatia, Hans Raj 1904- *ConAu 53*
Bhatia, Jamunadevi 1919- *WrD 1976*
Bhatia, June 1919- *Au&Wr*, *OxCan Sup*, *WrD 1976*
Bhatia, Krishan 1926?-1974 *ConAu 53*
Bhatnagar, Joti 1935- *ConAu 41*
Bhatt, Udayasankar 1898- *DcOrL 2*
Bhatta, G *DcOrL 2*
Bhatta, Manisankar *DcOrL 2*
Bhatta, Motiram 1865-1896 *DcOrL 2*
Bhatta, Samal *DcOrL 2*
Bhatta Narayana *CasWL*, *DcOrL 2*
Bhattacharji, Sukumari 1921- *ConAu 33*
Bhattacharya, Bhabani 1906- *CasWL*, *ConAu 5R*, *ConNov 1972*, *ConNov 1976*, *DcLEnL*, *REn*, *WebEAL*, *WrD 1976*
Bhatti *BbD*, *BiD&SB*, *CasWL*, *DcOrL 2*
Bhavabhuti 750?- *BbD*, *BiD&SB*, *CasWL*, *CnThe*, *DcOrL 2*, *Pen Cl*, *REn*, *REnWD*
Bhely-Quenum, Olympe 1928- *AfA 1*, *Pen Cl*
Bhimnidhi *DcOrL 2*
Bhoja 1008-1060 *CasWL*, *DcOrL 2*
Bhosale, Yeshwantrao P 1904- *WhLA*
Bhutto, Zulfikar Ali 1928- *ConAu 53*
Bial, Morrison David 1917- *ConAu 61*
Bialik, Chaim Nachman 1873-1934 *CasWL*, *Pen Cl*, *WorAu*
Bialik, Hayyim Nahman 1873-1934 *ChPo*, *EncWL*, *Pen Eur*
Bialk, Elisa 1912- *ConAu XR*, *MorJA*, *SmATA 1*
Bialoszewski, Miron 1922- *CasWL*, *ModSL 2*
Bialy, Harvey 1945- *ConP 1970*, *DrAP 1975*
Bianchi, Eugene Carl 1930- *ConAu 25*, *WrD 1976*
Bianchi, George Henry *Alli Sup*
Bianchi, M A *BiDLA*
Bianchi, Martha Gilbert Dickinson 1866-1943 *AmA&B*, *ChPo*, *ChPo S1*, *DcNAA*, *WhWNAA*
Bianciardi, Elizabeth Dickinson Rice 1833?-1885 *Alli Sup*, *ChPo S1*, *DcAmA*
Bianco Da Siena 1350?-1412? *CasWL*, *EvEuW*
Bianco, Margery Williams 1881-1944 *AmA&B*, *AnCL*, *AuBYP*, *BkCL*, *DcNAA*, *JBA 1934*, *JBA 1951*, *NewC*, *St&VC*, *WhCL*
Bianco, Pamela 1906- *AuBYP*, *ChPo*, *ConICB*, *IlCB 1945*, *IlCB 1956*, *JBA 1934*, *JBA 1951*
Bianco, Robert 1934- *AmSCAP 66*
Biancolli, Louis 1907- *AmA&B*
Bianconi, Fulvio 1915- *WhGrA*
Bianki, Vitali *AuBYP*
Biard, Pierre 1567-1622 *OxCan*
Biart, Lucien 1829-1897 *BiD&SB*
Biasin, Gian-Paolo 1933- *ConAu 25*, *WrD 1976*
Bibaculus, Marcus Furius 103BC- *Pen Cl*
Bibaud Jeune *OxCan*
Bibaud, Francois Marie Uncas Maximilien 1824-1887 *Alli*, *BbtC*, *DcNAA*, *OxCan*
Bibaud, Michel 1782-1857 *Alli*, *BbtC*, *CanWr*, *DcNAA*, *OxCan*, *OxCan Sup*
Bibb, A Denee 1885-1934 *BlkAW*
Bibb, Eloise A *BlkAW*
Bibb, George M 1772-1859 *Alli*, *BiDSA*
Bibb, Kathleen C *ChPo S1*
Bibb, William Wyatt 1781-1820 *DcNAA*
Bibbiena, Il *CasWL*
Bibbiena, Bernard Dovizio Da 1470-1520 *BiD&SB*, *McGWD*, *REnWD*
Bibbs, Hart Leroi 1930- *BlkAW*
Bibbs, Paul *HsB&A*, *HsB&A Sup*
Bibby, Cyril 1914- *Au&Wr*, *ConAu 13R*, *WrD 1976*
Bibby, E *Alli Sup*
Bibby, John F 1934- *ConAu 45*
Bibby, Thomas 1799-1863 *PoIre*
Bibby, Thomas Geoffrey 1917- *Au&Wr*, *ConAu 1R*

Biber, George Edward 1801-1874 *Alli*, *Alli Sup*
Biberius, Caldius Mero *REn*
Biberman, Edward 1904- *ConAu 49*
Biberman, Herbert 1900-1971 *ConAu 33*, *ConAu P-1*
Bibesco,Princess Elizabeth Charlotte 1897-1945 *LongC*
Bibesco,Princess Martha Lucia 1887?-1973? *CatA 1952*, *ConAu 49*, *EncWL*, *LongC*, *TwCA*, *TwCA Sup*
Bibiena, Alessandro Galli Da 1687-1769 *AtlBL*
Bibiena, Antonio Galli Da 1700-1744 *AtlBL*
Bibiena, Ferdinando Galli Da 1657-1743 *AtlBL*
Bibiena, Giovanni Maria Galli Da 1625-1665 *AtlBL*
Bibiena, Giuseppe Galli Da 1696-1756 *AtlBL*
Bible, Charles 1937- *IlBYP*
Bible, G W *Alli Sup*
Bibo, Irving 1889-1962 *AmSCAP 66*
Bibolet, Edith Caddelle 1902- *WhWNAA*
Bibolet, Edith Cadelle 1902- *TexWr*
Bibolet, R H *WrD 1972*
Bicci, Ersilio 1845- *BiD&SB*
Bice, Clare 1909- *AuBYP*, *IlCB 1956*
Bicha, Karel D *OxCan Sup*
Bicheno, J E *Alli*
Bicheno, James *Alli*, *BiDLA*
Bichsel, Peter 1935- *ModGL*
Bickel, Alexander M 1924-1974 *ConAu 1R*, *ConAu 53*
Bickel, Konrad *OxGer*
Bickerdike, Joseph Fletcher *Alli Sup*
Bickerdyke, John 1858- *Alli Sup*, *NewC*, *WhLA*
Bickerman, Elias J 1897- *ConAu 25*, *WrD 1976*
Bickers, Daniel Garnett 1873?- *ChPo*, *ChPo S1*, *WhWNAA*
Bickers, Richard Leslie Townshend 1917- *ConAu 45*
Bickerstaff, Edwin Robert 1920- *Au&Wr*, *WrD 1976*
Bickerstaff, Isaac *CasWL*, *DcEnL*, *NewC*, *REnAL*
Bickerstaff, Isaac 1735?-1812? *Alli*, *BiDLA*, *DcEnL*
Bickerstaffe, Isaac 1735?-1812? *BrAu*, *CasWL*, *ChPo*, *Chmbr 2*, *DcEuL*, *DcLEnL*, *EvLB*, *McGWD*, *NewC*, *OxEng*, *PoIre*
Bickerstaffe, Mona B *Alli Sup*
Bickerstaffe-Drew, Count Francis B 1858-1928 *LongC*, *NewC*, *REn*, *TwCA*
Bickersteth, Charlotte *Alli Sup*
Bickersteth, Edward 1786-1850 *Alli*, *PoCh*
Bickersteth, Edward 1814- *Alli Sup*, *DcEnL*
Bickersteth, Edward Henry 1825-1906 *Alli Sup*, *BbD*, *BiD&SB*, *ChPo*, *ChPo S1*, *ChPo S2*, *DcEnL*, *NewC*, *PoCh*
Bickersteth, Emily *Alli Sup*
Bickersteth, Geoffrey Langdale 1884-1974 *ConAu 49*
Bickersteth, John *Alli Sup*
Bickersteth, Mona *Alli Sup*
Bickersteth, Montagu Cyril 1858- *Alli Sup*, *WhLA*
Bickersteth, Robert 1816-1884 *Alli Sup*, *DcEnL*
Bickerton, Derek 1926- *ConAu 61*
Bickerton, G *Alli*
Bicket, Zenas J 1932- *ConAu 37*
Bickford, Elwood Dale 1927- *ConAu 61*
Bickford, Ernest Leopold Trevenen Harris *Alli Sup*
Bickford, James *Alli Sup*
Bickford, Lelia B 1852-1873 *ChPo S1*
Bickham, George *Alli*
Bickham, George d1758 *ChPo*
Bickham, George d1769 *BkIE*
Bickham, George, Jr. d1749 *BkIE*
Bickham, Jack M 1930- *AmA&B*, *ConAu 5R*, *WrD 1976*
Bickham, Warren S 1861- *WhWNAA*
Bickham, William Denison 1827-1894 *Alli Sup*, *OhA&B*
Bickle, Judith Brundrett *Au&Wr*, *ChPo S2*, *ConAu P-1*
Bickley, Augustus Charles *Alli Sup*
Bickley, George W L 1823-1867 *OhA&B*

Bickley, Lloyd Wharton 1801-1855 *DcNAA*
Bickley, W B *Alli Sup*
Bickmore, Albert Smith 1839-1914 *Alli Sup*, *AmA&B*, *BbD*, *BiD&SB*, *DcAmA*, *DcNAA*
Bicknell, Alex *Alli*
Bicknell, Algernon Sidney *Alli Sup*
Bicknell, Amos J *Alli Sup*
Bicknell, Anna Louise 1835?- *DcAmA*, *DcNAA*
Bicknell, Charles F And Hawley, T P *Alli Sup*
Bicknell, Edward 1855-1922 *DcNAA*
Bicknell, Edward John 1882- *WhLA*
Bicknell, Emeline Larkin 1825-1916 *OhA&B*
Bicknell, Ernest Percy 1862-1935 *DcNAA*, *IndAu 1917*
Bicknell, Frank Martin 1854-1916 *DcAmA*, *DcNAA*
Bicknell, George Augustus 1815-1891 *Alli Sup*, *DcNAA*, *IndAu 1917*
Bicknell, Herman 1830-1875 *Alli Sup*
Bicknell, J L *Alli*
Bicknell, James 1862-1914 *DcNAA*
Bicknell, Minnie *OxCan*
Bicknell, Philip B *Alli Sup*
Bicknell, Thomas Williams 1834-1925 *Alli Sup*, *AmA&B*, *AmLY*, *DcAmA*, *DcNAA*
Bicknell, W N *ChPo*
Bicknell, Walter L *Alli Sup*
Bicknoll, Edmond *Alli*
Bida, Constantine 1916- *ConAu 61*
Biddell, Hurman *Alli Sup*
Bidder, George *ChPo S1*
Bidder, M *Alli Sup*
Bidders, George *ChPo*
Biddiss, Michael Denis 1942- *Au&Wr*, *ConAu 53*, *WrD 1976*
Biddle, Anthony Joseph Drexel 1874-1948 *AmA&B*, *BiD&SB*, *DcAmA*, *DcNAA*
Biddle, Arthur 1852-1897 *Alli Sup*, *DcAmA*, *DcNAA*
Biddle, Arthur W 1936- *ConAu 45*
Biddle, Bruce Jesse 1928- *ConAu 17R*, *WrD 1976*
Biddle, Charles John 1819-1873 *Alli*, *DcAmA*
Biddle, Clement *Alli Sup*
Biddle, Clement d1879 *DcNAA*
Biddle, Clement Cornell 1784-1854 *Alli*
Biddle, Clinton Poston 1897-1939 *DcNAA*
Biddle, Daniel *Alli Sup*
Biddle, Francis 1886- *AmA&B*, *ConAu 5R*
Biddle, George 1885-1968? *AmA&B*, *ConAu 45*, *WhWNAA*
Biddle, George And Paul, John Rodman *Alli Sup*
Biddle, George Washington 1843-1886 *Alli Sup*, *DcNAA*
Biddle, Horace Peters 1811-1900 *Alli Sup*, *AmA&B*, *DcAmA*, *DcNAA*, *IndAu 1816*, *OhA&B*
Biddle, Jacob Albert 1845-1914 *DcNAA*, *OhA&B*
Biddle, John *Alli Sup*
Biddle, John 1615-1662 *Alli*, *DcEnL*
Biddle, John B *Alli Sup*
Biddle, John Barclay 1815-1879 *DcNAA*
Biddle, Nicholas 1786-1844 *Alli*, *AmA*, *AmA&B*, *BiD&SB*, *CyAL 1*, *DcAmA*, *DcNAA*, *OxAm*, *REn*
Biddle, Owen *Alli*
Biddle, Perry H, Jr. 1932- *ConAu 57*
Biddle, Phillips R 1933- *ConAu 37*
Biddle, Richard 1796-1847 *Alli*, *DcAmA*, *DcNAA*
Biddle, Tyrrel E *Alli Sup*
Biddle, William W 1900- *ConAu 17*
Biddle-Cope *Alli Sup*
Biddlecombe, Sir George 1807-1878 *Alli Sup*
Biddulph, C E *Alli Sup*
Biddulph, J *Alli Sup*
Biddulph, Sir Michael Anthony Shrapnel 1823- *Alli Sup*
Biddulph, P *Alli Sup*
Biddulph, Thomas Tregenna 1763-1838 *Alli*, *BiDLA*, *BiDLA Sup*
Biddulph, Will And Pet *Alli*
Bideford, The Rural Postman Of 1819- *DcEnL*
Bidel *DcOrL 3*

Biden, James *Alli Sup*
Biden, William Downing *Alli Sup*
Biderman, Albert D 1923- *ConAu 5R*
Biderman, Sol 1936- *ConAu 25, WrD 1976*
Bidermann, Jakob 1578-1639 *CasWL, EvEuW, OxGer, Pen Eur*
Bideu, Lou 1919- *AmSCAP 66*
Bidez, Joseph 1867- *WhLA*
Bidie, George *Alli Sup*
Bidil *DcOrL 3*
Bidingfield, James *Alli*
Bidlake, John 1755-1814 *Alli, BiDLA, BiDLA Sup*
Bidlake, John 1775-1814 *ChPo S1*
Bidloo, Govert 1649-1713 *CasWL, EvEuW*
Bidney, David 1908- *ConAu 9R*
Bidston, Lester 1884- *MnBBF*
Bidulph, Miss Sidney *Alli*
Bidwell, Barnabas 1763-1833 *AmA&B, DcNAA, OxCan*
Bidwell, Charles Toll *Alli Sup*
Bidwell, Daniel Doane 1866?-1937 *AmA&B, DcNAA, WhWNAA*
Bidwell, Edwin M *Alli Sup*
Bidwell, Frederic David 1873-1947 *DcNAA*
Bidwell, George H *Alli Sup*
Bidwell, John 1819-1900 *OhA&B, OxAm*
Bidwell, Marshall Spring 1799-1872 *OxCan*
Bidwell, Percy Wells 1888- *Au&Wr, ConAu P-1*
Bidwell, R *Alli*
Bidwell, Shelford 1848- *Alli Sup*
Bidwell, Walter Hilliard 1798-1881 *Alli Sup, AmA&B*
Bidyalankarana, Prince 1876-1945 *Pen Cl*
Bidyasagar, Isvarcandra 1820-1891 *DcOrL 2*
Bie, Cornelis De 1627-1715 *CasWL*
Bieber, Margarete 1879- *ConAu 17R*
Biebl, Konstantin 1898-1951 *CasWL*
Biebuyck, Daniel P 1925- *ConAu 25, WrD 1976*
Biedermaier, Gottlieb *OxGer*
Biedermann, Karl 1812-1901 *BiD&SB*
Biedermann, Woldemar, Freiherr Von 1817-1903 *OxGer*
Biederwolf, William Edward 1867-1939 *DcNAA, IndAu 1816, WhWNAA*
Biedma, Luis Hernandez *BiDSA*
Biegel, John E 1925- *ConAu 49*
Biegel, Paul 1925- *Au&Wr, WrD 1976*
Biehl, Carlotta Dorothea d1788 *DcEuL*
Biehler, Robert F 1927- *ConAu 37*
Bielefeld, C F *Alli*
Bielenberg, Christabel 1909- *Au&Wr, ConAu 29*
Bieler, Ludwig J G 1906- *ConAu 5R, WrD 1976*
Bieler, Manfred 1934- *CasWL, ModGL*
Bielfeld, H *Alli Sup*
Bielinsky, Vissario Grigorievich 1811-1848 *DcEuL*
Bielovski, August 1806-1876 *BiD&SB*
Bielski, Alison Joy Prosser 1925- *ConP 1970, WrD 1976*
Bielski, Feliks *ConAu XR*
Bielski, Marcin 1495?-1575 *CasWL, EvEuW*
Biely, Andrei 1880-1934 *TwCW*
Bielyi, Sergei *ConAu XR*
Biemiller, Ruth Cobbett 1914- *ConAu 37*
Bien, David Duckworth 1930- *ConAu 5R*
Bien, H M *BiDSA*
Bien, Herman M 1831-1895 *Alli Sup, DcNAA*
Bien, Joseph Julius 1936- *ConAu 53*
Bien, Peter A 1930- *ConAu 9R, WrD 1976*
Biencourt DeSaint-Just, Charles De 1591?-1623? *OxCan*
Bienek, Horst 1930- *OxGer*
Bienkowski, Zbigniew 1913- *CasWL*
Bienstock, Mike *ConAu XR*
Bienstock, Myron Joseph 1922- *ConAu 9R*
Bienvenu, Bernard J 1925- *ConAu 25, ConAu 53*
Bienvenu, Richard 1936- *ConAu 61*
Bienville, Francois LeM, Sieur De 1666-1691 *OxCan*
Bienville, Jean B LeMoyne, Sieur De 1680-1768? *BiDSA, OxCan, REn*
Bier, Jesse 1925- *ConAu 5R, WhPNW*

Bier, William C 1911- *ConAu 33*
Bierbaum, F J *Alli Sup*
Bierbaum, Margaret 1916- *ConAu 33*
Bierbaum, Otto Julius 1865-1910 *BiD&SB, CasWL, ClDMEuL, EvEuW, OxGer, Pen Eur*
Bierbower, Austin 1844-1913 *Alli Sup, DcNAA*
Bierbower, Elsie Janis *OhA&B*
Bierce, Ambrose 1842-1914? *AmA, AmA&B, AmWr, AtlBL, CasWL, ChPo, ChPo S1, Chmbr 3, CnDAL, CriT 3, CyWA, DcAmA, DcLEnL, DcNAA, EncM&D, EvLB, LongC, ModAL, ModAL Sup, OhA&B, OxAm, OxEng, Pen Am, RAdv 1, REn, REnAL, WebEAL*
Bierce, Chloe B Conant 1802-1846 *OhA&B*
Bierce, Lucius Verus 1801-1876 *DcNAA, OhA&B*
Bierce, M A *DcEnL*
Bierce, M H *Alli Sup*
Bierhorst, John 1936- *ConAu 33, SmATA 6, WrD 1976*
Bieri, Arthur Peter 1931- *ConAu 61*
Bierly, Willis Reed *DcNAA*
Bierman, Bernard 1908- *AmSCAP 66*
Bierman, Harold, Jr. 1924- *ConAu 17R*
Bierman, Mildred Thornton 1912- *ConAu 5R*
Biermann, Lillian *ConAu XR*
Biermann, Wolf 1936- *CasWL, ModGL, OxGer*
Biernatzki, Johann Christoph 1795-1840 *BbD, BiD&SB, OxGer*
Biernatzki, William E 1931- *ConAu 57*
Bierstadt, Albert 1830-1902 *EarAB, OxAm*
Bierstadt, Edward Hale 1891- *AmA&B*
Bierstadt, O A *Alli Sup*
Bierstedt, Robert 1913- *AmA&B, ConAu 1R*
Biert, Cla 1920- *CasWL*
Bierwirth, Heinrich Conrad 1853-1940 *DcNAA*
Biery, James Solomon 1839-1904 *DcNAA*
Biery, William 1933- *ConAu 57*
Biesanz, John Berry 1913- *Au&Wr*
Biesanz, Mavis Hiltunen 1919- *Au&Wr, ConAu 33*
Biesele, John Julius 1918- *Au&Wr*
Biesele, Rudolph Leopold *TexWr*
Biester, Joao Ernesto 1829-1880 *BiD&SB*
Biesterveld, Betty Parsons 1923- *ConAu 1R*
Bieston, Roger *Alli*
Biezanek, Anne C 1927- *ConAu 17R*
Bifield *Alli*
Bifrun, Jacham U Tuetschet 1506-1572 *CasWL*
Big Bear d1888 *OxCan*
Big Eagle, Duane N *DrAP 1975*
Bigandet, Pierre *Alli Sup*
Bigard, Leon Albany 1906- *AmSCAP 66*
Bigart, Robert James 1947- *ConAu 33*
Bigby, Mary Catherine Dougherty 1839- *BiDSA*
Bigelow, Abijah 1775-1860 *DcNAA*
Bigelow, Allen Gilman 1854-1891 *ChPo*
Bigelow, Andrew 1795-1877 *Alli, DcAmA, DcNAA*
Bigelow, Artemas 1818- *Alli*
Bigelow, David 1806-1875 *ChPo*
Bigelow, Donald R 1918- *ConAu 41*
Bigelow, Edith Evelyn 1861-1932 *DcAmA, DcNAA*
Bigelow, Edward Fuller 1860-1938 *DcNAA*
Bigelow, Edwin Victor 1866-1929 *DcNAA*
Bigelow, Erastus Brigham 1814-1879 *Alli Sup, DcAmA, DcNAA*
Bigelow, Florence *WhWNAA*
Bigelow, Francis Hill 1859-1933 *DcNAA*
Bigelow, Frank Hagar 1851-1924 *DcAmA, DcNAA*
Bigelow, Frederick Southgate 1871- *WhWNAA*
Bigelow, George Bemis *Alli*
Bigelow, George Tyler *Alli*
Bigelow, Glenna Lindsley 1876- *WhWNAA*
Bigelow, Grace *Alli Sup*
Bigelow, Harold Eugene *WhWNAA*
Bigelow, Henry Bryant 1879- *WhWNAA*
Bigelow, Henry Jacob 1818-1890 *Alli Sup, DcNAA*
Bigelow, Herbert Seely 1870-1951 *IndAu 1917*
Bigelow, Horatio Ripley *Alli Sup*
Bigelow, Jacob 1787-1879 *Alli, Alli Sup,*

ChPo, CyAL 2, DcAmA, DcNAA
Bigelow, John 1817-1911 *Alli, Alli Sup, AmA, AmA&B, BbD, BiD&SB, CyAL 2, DcAmA, DcNAA, OxAm, REn, REnAL*
Bigelow, John, Jr. 1854-1939 *AmLY, DcAmA, DcNAA*
Bigelow, L J 1835-1870 *Alli Sup*
Bigelow, Lafayette Jotham 1835-1870 *DcAmA, DcNAA*
Bigelow, Lewis 1785-1838 *Alli, DcNAA*
Bigelow, Lottie S *ChPo*
Bigelow, Marguerite Ogden *ChPo*
Bigelow, Marion Albina *ChPo, ChPo S1*
Bigelow, Marshall Train 1822-1902 *Alli Sup, DcAmA, DcNAA*
Bigelow, Mary Ann Hubbard 1792-1870 *ChPo, DcNAA*
Bigelow, Marybelle S 1923- *ConAu 25*
Bigelow, Maurice Alpheus 1872-1955 *OhA&B*
Bigelow, Melville Madison 1846-1921 *Alli Sup, DcAmA, DcNAA*
Bigelow, Poultney 1855-1954 *AmA&B, BbD, BiD&SB, Chmbr 3, DcAmA, DcEnA Ap*
Bigelow, Mrs. Poultney *DcNAA*
Bigelow, Robert Payne 1863- *WhWNAA*
Bigelow, Robert S 1918- *Au&Wr, WrD 1976*
Bigelow, Robert Wilcox 1890-1965 *AmSCAP 66*
Bigelow, Mrs. S A *Alli Sup*
Bigelow, Samuel Fowler 1837-1915 *DcNAA*
Bigelow, Samuel Lawrence 1870-1947 *DcNAA*
Bigelow, Timothy 1767-1821 *Alli, OxCan*
Bigelow, W D 1866- *WhWNAA*
Bigelow, Walter Storrs *ChPo*
Bigelow, William Pingry 1867- *WhWNAA*
Bigelow, William Sturgis 1850-1926 *DcNAA*
Bigg, Charles *Alli Sup*
Bigg, Henry Heather *Alli Sup*
Bigg, James *Alli Sup, BiDLA*
Bigg, John Stanyan 1828-1865 *Alli, Alli Sup, BrAu 19, DcEnL, NewC, WebEAL*
Bigg, Louisa *Alli Sup*
Bigg, Patricia Nina 1932- *Au&Wr, WrD 1976*
Bigg, Robert Heather *Alli Sup*
Bigg, William *Alli Sup*
Bigg-Wither *Alli Sup*
Biggar, Charles Robert Webster 1847-1909 *DcNAA, OxCan*
Biggar, Emerson Bristol 1853-1921 *DcNAA*
Biggar, Henry Percival 1872-1938 *DcNAA, OxCan*
Biggar, Oliver Mowat 1876-1948 *DcNAA*
Biggar, Walter *Alli Sup*
Bigge, Morris L 1908- *ConAu 9R, WrD 1976*
Bigge, Thomas *Alli, BiDLA*
Bigger, David Dwight 1849-1932 *OhA&B*
Bigger, Finley 1807- *IndAu 1816*
Bigger, H Dunn *Alli*
Bigger, J *Alli*
Bigger, Samuel Lennox L d1891 *Alli Sup, PoIre*
Biggers, Earl Derr 1884-1933 *AmA&B, ChPo S1, DcNAA, EncM&D, EvLB, MnBBF, OhA&B, OxAm, Pen Am, REn, REnAL, TwCA, TwCW, WhWNAA*
Biggers, John Thomas 1924- *ConAu 1R*
Biggin, George *Alli*
Biggle, Lloyd, Jr. 1923- *ConAu 13R*
Biggs, Anselm G 1914- *ConAu 33*
Biggs, Arthur *Alli*
Biggs, Asa 1811-1878 *DcNAA*
Biggs, D *ChPo S1*
Biggs, Hermann M *Alli Sup*
Biggs, James *Alli*
Biggs, John, Jr. 1895- *AmA&B, WhWNAA*
Biggs, John Burville 1934- *ConAu 57, WrD 1976*
Biggs, Joseph 1776-1844 *BiDSA, DcNAA*
Biggs, Lottie Lovell 1913- *AmSCAP 66*
Biggs, Louis Coutier *Alli Sup*
Biggs, Louise Ogan 1882-1958 *OhA&B*
Biggs, Maude Ashurst *Alli Sup*
Biggs, Michael *Alli Sup*
Biggs, Noah *Alli*
Biggs, Richard *Alli*
Biggs, Richard Keys 1886-1962 *AmSCAP 66*
Biggs, T *Alli Sup*
Biggs, William *Alli*

Biggs, William Derrick 1923- *Au&Wr*
Biggs-Davison, John Alec 1918- *WrD 1976*
Biggs-Davison, John Alec 1918- *Au&Wr, ConAu 13R*
Bigham, John Charles *Alli Sup*
Bigham, Madge Alford 1874- *AmA&B, BiDSA, WhWNAA*
Bigham, Robert W *Alli Sup*
Bigham, Robert Williams 1824-1900 *BiDSA, DcNAA*
Bigiaretti, Libero 1906- *ConAu 29*
Bigland, John d1832 *Alli, BiDLA, BiDLA Sup*
Bigland, Ralph 1711-1784 *Alli*
Bigland, Richard *Alli, BiDLA*
Bigland, William *Alli, BiDLA*
Bigler, David 1806?-1875 *ChPo S1, DcNAA*
Bigler, Vernon 1922- *ConAu 21*
Bigler, William H 1840-1904 *DcNAA*
Biglow, William 1773-1844 *Alli, AmA&B, CyAL 1, DcAmA, DcNAA*
Bigly, Cantell A 1817-1859 *AmA, DcNAA*
Bigmore, Edward C And Wyman, C W H *Alli Sup*
Bigne, Gace DeLa *CasWL*
Bignell, Alan 1928- *WrD 1976*
Bignell, Effie 1855- *DcNAA*
Bignell, Henry 1611-1660? *Alli*
Bigney, Andrew J 1864- *WhWNAA*
Bigney, Mark Frederick 1817-1886 *Alli Sup, AmA&B, BbtC, BiDSA, ChPo, DcNAA*
Bignold, G S *ChPo*
Bigot, Sieur De *McGWD*
Bigot, Sir Francis *Alli*
Bigot, Francois 1703-1777? *BbtC, OxCan*
Bigot, Mary *Alli Sup*
Bigsby, B E S Drake *Alli Sup*
Bigsby, Bernard *ChPo*
Bigsby, Christopher William Edgar 1941- *ConAu 25, WrD 1976*
Bigsby, John Jeremiah 1792-1881 *Alli Sup, BbtC, OxCan*
Bigsby, Robert 1806- *Alli, Alli Sup, DcEnL*
Bigwood, John *Alli Sup*
Bihari Lal 1603-1663 *CasWL*
Biharilal 1595-1664 *DcOrL 2*
Bijns, Anna 1493?-1575 *BiD&SB, CasWL, DcEuL, Pen Eur*
Bijou, Sidney W 1908- *ConAu 37*
Bikel, Theodore 1924- *ConAu 1R*
Bikelas, Dimitrios 1835-1908 *BiD&SB*
Bikkers, A J W *Alli Sup*
Bikkers, Alexander V W *Alli Sup*
Bikkie, James A 1929- *ConAu 53*
Bikouta-Menga, Gaston-Guy *AfA 1*
Bilac, Olavo Bras Martins DosGuimaraes 1865-1918 *EncWL, Pen Am*
Bilainkin, George 1903- *Au&Wr*
Bilas, Richard A 1935- *ConAu 53*
Bilbasar, Kemal 1910- *DcOrL 3*
Bilbo, Queenie d1972 *ConAu 37*
Bilbow, Antony 1932- *ConAu 25*
Bilbrough, E Ernest *Alli Sup*
Bilby, Thomas *ChPo*
Bilder, Robert M 1913-1961 *AmSCAP 66*
Bilderdijk, Willem 1756-1831 *BiD&SB, CasWL, DcEuL, EvEuW, Pen Eur*
Bildersee, Adele 1883- *WhWNAA*
Bileck, Marvin 1920- *IlBYP, IlCB 1956, IlCB 1966*
Biles, Roy Edwin 1888-1941 *OhA&B*
Biley, Edward *Alli Sup*
Bilger, George McClellan 1861- *ChPo S1*
Bilgram, Hugo 1847-1933 *Alli Sup, DcNAA*
Bilhana *CasWL, DcOrL 2*
Bilik, Jerry H 1933- *AmSCAP 66*
Bilinsky, Yaroslav 1932- *ConAu 13R*
Bilkey, Warren J 1920- *ConAu 29*
Bill, Alfred Hoyt 1879- *AmA&B, JBA 1934, JBA 1951, MnnWr*
Bill, Anna *Alli*
Bill, Clarence Powers 1875- *WhWNAA*
Bill, Edward Lyman 1862-1916 *DcNAA*
Bill, Ingraham E 1805-1891 *DcNAA*
Bill, Ledyard 1836-1907 *Alli Sup, DcAmA, DcNAA*
Bill, Max 1908- *WhGrA*
Bill, Valentine T 1909- *Au&Wr, ConAu 13R*

Bill-Belotserkovsky, Vladimir Naumovich 1884?- *CasWL, ModWD, Pen Eur*
Bill-Bjelozerkowski, Vladimir 1884?- *CnMD*
Billaut, Adam 1602-1662 *BiD&SB, OxFr*
Billet, James *Alli Sup*
Billetdoux, Francois 1927- *CasWL, CnMD, CnThe, ConAu 21, CrCD, EncWL Sup, McGWD, ModWD, Pen Eur, REnWD, WorAu*
Billett, Roy O 1891- *ConAu 13R*
Billias, George Athan 1919- *ConAu 9R, WrD 1976*
Billig, Kurt 1907- *Au&Wr*
Billing, Archibald 1791-1881 *Alli Sup*
Billing, John Davis 1842- *DcNAA*
Billing, Noel Pemberton 1880-1948 *LongC*
Billing, Robert *Alli*
Billing, Sidney *Alli, Alli Sup*
Billinger, Richard 1893-1965 *ClDMEuL, CnMD, CrCD, EncWL, McGWD, ModWD, OxGer*
Billinghurst, George *Alli*
Billinghurst, Percy J *ChPo S1*
Billings, Addie M *Alli Sup*
Billings, Anna Hunt 1861-1944 *DcNAA*
Billings, B, Jr. *BbtC*
Billings, Buck *MnBBF*
Billings, Edward Everett 1855- *DcNAA*
Billings, Edwin T 1824-1893 *ChPo*
Billings, Elkanah 1820- *BbtC*
Billings, Frank 1854-1932 *DcAmA, DcNAA*
Billings, Frank Seaver 1845-1912 *Alli Sup, DcNAA*
Billings, Frederick Horatio 1869- *WhWNAA*
Billings, Georgina E *ChPo*
Billings, Hammatt 1818-1874 *ChPo, ChPo S1, EarAB, EarAB Sup*
Billings, Harold 1931- *ConAu 25*
Billings, Henry 1901- *AmA&B, IlCB 1956, MorJA*
Billings, John D *Alli Sup*
Billings, John Shaw 1838-1913 *Alli Sup, AmA&B, BbD, BiD&SB, DcAmA, DcNAA, IndAu 1816, OhA&B*
Billings, Joseph *Alli*
Billings, Josh 1818-1885 *Alli Sup, AmA, AmA&B, BbD, BiD&SB, CasWL, ChPo S1, Chmbr 3, CnDAL, DcAmA, DcEnL, DcLEnL, DcNAA, EvLB, OhA&B, OxAm, OxEng, Pen Am, REn, REnAL*
Billings, Peggy 1928- *ConAu 25*
Billings, Peter *Alli*
Billings, R W *Alli*
Billings, Warren M 1940- *ConAu 61*
Billings, William 1746-1800 *AmA&B, DcNAA, OxAm*
Billings, William Edward 1869-1952 *IndAu 1917*
Billingsley *Alli*
Billingsley, Amos Stevens 1818-1897 *Alli Sup, DcNAA, OhA&B*
Billingsley, Andrew 1926- *ConAu 57, LivBA*
Billingsley, Edward Baxter 1910- *ConAu 25*
Billingsley, Sir Henry d1606 *Alli*
Billingsley, John *Alli*
Billingsley, Martin *Alli*
Billingsley, Nicholas *Alli*
Billingsley, Paul 1887- *WhWNAA*
Billington, Dora May 1890-1968 *ConAu P-1*
Billington, John *ConAu XR*
Billington, Linus W 1802- *Alli*
Billington, Mary Frances *Alli Sup*
Billington, Michael 1939- *WrD 1976*
Billington, Monroe Lee 1928- *ConAu 21*
Billington, Rachel 1942- *Au&Wr, AuNews 2, ConAu 33, WrD 1976*
Billington, Ray 1930- *WrD 1976*
Billington, Ray Allen 1903- *AmA&B, Au&Wr, ConAu 1R*
Billington, Thomas *Alli Sup*
Billington, William 1827-1884 *Alli Sup*
Billman, Ira *ChPo, ChPo S2*
Billmeyer, Fred W, Jr. 1919- *WrD 1976*
Billon, Frederic Louis 1801-1895 *DcNAA*
Billon, Frederick Louis 1801-1895 *Alli Sup, BiDSA*
Billon, Pierre *OxCan Sup*

Billout, Guy Rene 1941- *SmATA 10*
Bills, Geneva Mills 1889- *TexWr*
Billson, Charles James *Alli Sup*
Billson, William Weldon 1847-1923 *DcNAA*
Billy, Andre 1882-1971 *CasWL, ConAu 29, Pen Eur*
Billy, Captain *AmA&B*
Billyns *Alli*
Bilodeau, Georges M 1895- *WhWNAA*
Bilodeau, Rosario *OxCan Sup*
Bilotti, Anton 1906-1963 *AmSCAP 66*
Bilotti, John J 1916- *AmSCAP 66*
Bilsby, Julian W *OxCan*
Bilsing, Sherman Weaver 1885- *TexWr, WhWNAA*
Bilsland, Guy Willis 1885- *WhWNAA*
Bilson, Thomas 1536-1616 *Alli, DcEnL*
Bilstone, John *Alli*
Bilton, Ernest *Alli Sup*
Bilton, Samuel Francis *Alli Sup*
Bilz, Jakob 1872- *WhLA*
Bimboni, Alberto 1882-1960 *AmSCAP 66*
Bimeler, Joseph Michael 1778?-1853 *OhA&B*
Bimler, Richard William 1940- *ConAu 41*
Bin Gorion, Micha Yoseph *CasWL, EuA, Pen Eur*
Bin Tah *PueRA*
Binawa *DcOrL 3*
Binchy, Daniel 1899- *CatA 1947*
Binck, James *Alli*
Binckes, William *Alli*
Binckley, Nellie *ChPo*
Binder, Aaron 1927- *ConAu 57*
Binder, Abraham Wolfe 1895- *AmSCAP 66*
Binder, Eando *AuBYP, ConAu XR*
Binder, Frederick M 1931- *ConAu 29*
Binder, Frederick Moore 1920- *ConAu 41*
Binder, Georg *OxGer*
Binder, Leonard 1927- *ConAu 61*
Binder, Otto Oscar 1911-1974 *AuBYP, ConAu 1R, ConAu 53*
Binder, Pearl 1904- *Au&Wr, IlCB 1945, IlCB 1956*
Binder, Rudolph M 1865- *WhWNAA*
Binding, Rudolf Georg 1867-1938 *ClDMEuL, EncWL, EvEuW, ModGL, OxGer*
Bindley, Charles 1795-1859 *Alli Sup, Br&AmS*
Bindley, James *Alli, BiDLA*
Bindley, T Herbert *Alli Sup*
Bindloss, Harold 1866-1945 *LongC, MnBBF, OxCan, TwCA, TwCA Sup, WhLA*
Bindman, Arthur J 1925- *ConAu 45*
Bindman, J S 1951- *WrD 1976*
Binfield, A D *Alli Sup*
Binfield, William *Alli*
Binford, John H 1844-1912 *IndAu 1816*
Binford, Laurence C 1935- *WrD 1976*
Bing, Rudolf 1902- *REn*
Bingaman, Ron 1936- *ConAu 61*
Binger, Carl Alfred Lanning 1889- *Au&Wr*
Binger, Norman H 1914- *ConAu 33*
Bingham, Alfred Mitchell 1905- *AmA&B, TwCA, TwCA Sup*
Bingham, Anne E 1840- *WhWNAA*
Bingham, Anson *Alli Sup*
Bingham, Arthur *MnBBF*
Bingham, Caleb 1757-1817 *Alli, AmA&B, ChPo S1, CyAL 1, DcAmA, DcNAA, OxAm, REnAL*
Bingham, Caroline 1938- *ConAu 57, WrD 1976*
Bingham, Carson *ConAu XR*
Bingham, Charles B *Alli Sup*
Bingham, Charles H *Alli Sup*
Bingham, Charlotte Mary Therese 1942- *Au&Wr, WrD 1976*
Bingham, Colin William Hugh 1898- *Au&Wr*
Bingham, David A 1926- *ConAu 53*
Bingham, Denis Arthur 1829- *Alli Sup*
Bingham, Edwin R 1920- *ConAu 5R*
Bingham, Ellice *Alli Sup*
Bingham, Eugene Cook 1878- *WhWNAA*
Bingham, George 1715-1800 *Alli*
Bingham, George Caleb 1811-1879 *AtlBL, OxAm, REn*
Bingham, George Charles, Earl Of Lucan 1800-1888 *Alli Sup*
Bingham, Graham Clifton 1859-1913 *ChPo,*

ChPo S1, ChPo S2
Bingham, Mrs. H A *Alli Sup*
Bingham, Helen M *Alli Sup*
Bingham, Hiram 1789-1869 *Alli Sup, AmA, AmA&B, DcNAA, EarAB, EarAB Sup, REnAL*
Bingham, Hiram 1831-1908 *AmA, DcNAA, REnAL*
Bingham, Hiram, Jr. 1875-1956 *Alli Sup, AmA&B, AmLY, REnAL, WhWNAA*
Bingham, J Elliot *Alli*
Bingham, J Foote 1827-1914 *Alli Sup, DcAmA*
Bingham, Jane M *Alli Sup*
Bingham, Jennie M *Alli Sup*
Bingham, Jennie Maria 1859- *DcNAA*
Bingham, Joel Foote 1827-1914 *DcNAA*
Bingham, John Michael Ward 1908-1960 *Au&Wr, ConAu 21, LongC*
Bingham, Jonathan Brewster 1914- *ConAu 33*
Bingham, Joseph *Alli*
Bingham, Joseph 1668-1723 *Alli, DcEnL, NewC*
Bingham, Joseph 1668-1923 *OxEng*
Bingham, Joseph Walter 1878- *IndAu 1917, WhWNAA*
Bingham, June Rossbach 1919- *AmA&B, ConAu 1R, WrD 1976*
Bingham, Kate Boyles 1876- *IncfAu 1816*
Bingham, L E *ChPo*
Bingham, Luther Goodyear 1798-1877 *Alli Sup, DcNAA*
Bingham, M P 1918- *ConAu 49*
Bingham, Madeleine 1912- *ConAu 13R*
Bingham, Millicent Todd 1880-1968 *AmA&B, ChPo*
Bingham, Peregrine *Alli, BiDLA*
Bingham, Richard 1798-1872 *Alli, Alli Sup, BiDLA*
Bingham, Robert C 1927- *ConAu 21*
Bingham, Robert E 1925- *ConAu 29*
Bingham, Robert F 1891- *WhWNAA*
Bingham, Robert Worth 1871- *BiDSA*
Bingham, Rowland V d1942 *DcNAA*
Bingham, S D *Alli Sup*
Bingham, S J *ChPo*
Bingham, Sallie *ConAu XR*
Bingham, Seth 1882- *AmSCAP 66*
Bingham, Stephen D 1828- *DcNAA*
Bingham, Theodore Alfred 1858-1934 *DcNAA*
Bingham, Thomas *Alli, BiDLA*
Bingham, Walter VanDyke 1880- *WhWNAA*
Bingham, William 1751-1804 *Alli, DcAmA, DcNAA*
Bingham, William 1835-1873 *BiDSA, DcAmA, DcNAA*
Bingham, William Philip Strong *Alli Sup*
Bingley, Clive Hamilton 1936- *Au&Wr, ConAu 17R, WrD 1976*
Bingley, David Ernest 1920- *ConAu 45*
Bingley, Thomas *Alli Sup, CarSB*
Bingley, William *Alli*
Bingley, William d1823 *Alli, BiDLA, BiDLA Sup*
Binh-Nguyen-Loc 1914- *DcOrL 2*
Binham, Philip Frank 1924- *Au&Wr, WrD 1976*
Binion, Rudolph 1927- *ConAu 1R, WrD 1976*
Binion, Samuel Augustus 1853-1914 *ChPo S2, DcNAA*
Binkerd, A D *Alli Sup*
Binkley, Luther John 1925- *ConAu 5R, WrD 1976*
Binkley, Olin T 1908- *ConAu 45*
Binkley, Robert Cedric 1897-1940 *DcNAA, OhA&B*
Binkley, Wilfred Ellsworth 1883- *OhA&B*
Binkley, William Campbell 1889- *AmA&B*
Binks, Rebecca *ChPo S1*
Binks, Robert *ChPo S2*
Binks, Sarah *CanWr*
Binmore, Henry *Alli Sup, DcNAA*
Binn, Mark *IlBYP*
Binnell, Robert *Alli*
Binnewies, Wilfred George 1879- *WhWNAA*
Binney, Alfred Jonathan *Alli Sup*
Binney, Amos *Alli*
Binney, Amos 1800-1847 *DcNAA*
Binney, Amos 1802-1878 *DcNAA*

Binney, Amos 1803-1847 *Alli, DcAmA, DcNAA*
Binney, Cecil 1897- *WhLA*
Binney, Charles Chauncey 1855-1913 *DcNAA*
Binney, Charles James Fox 1806-1888 *Alli Sup, DcNAA*
Binney, Earle *ChPo S1*
Binney, Ermyntrude 1896- *WhLA*
Binney, Ethel Mary 1913- *Au&Wr, WrD 1976*
Binney, Frederick Altona *Alli Sup*
Binney, George *OxCan*
Binney, Hibbert 1819- *BbtC*
Binney, Horace 1780-1875 *Alli, DcAmA, DcNAA*
Binney, Jonathan *OxCan*
Binney, Juliette Patterson *Alli Sup*
Binney, Thomas 1798-1874 *Alli, Alli Sup, DcEnL*
Binney, William Greene 1833- *Alli, Alli Sup, BbtC, DcAmA*
Binnie, John Fairbairn 1863-1936 *DcNAA*
Binnie, William 1823-1886 *Alli Sup*
Binnie-Clark, Georgina *OxCan*
Binning, Hugh 1627-1654 *Alli*
Binning, Robert B M *Alli Sup*
Binns, Abraham *Alli, BiDLA*
Binns, Archie 1899- *AmA&B, AmNov, OxAm, REnAL, TwCA, TwCA Sup, WhPNW*
Binns, Benjamin Pemberton *PoIre*
Binns, Charles Fergus 1857-1934 *DcNAA*
Binns, Elsie *ChPo S2*
Binns, Henry Bryan *ChPo S2*
Binns, J W 1940- *ConAu 53*
Binns, John 1772-1860 *Alli, AmA&B, DcNAA*
Binns, John Alexander 1761?-1813 *DcNAA*
Binns, Jonathan *Alli*
Binns, Richard William *Alli Sup*
Binns, Mrs. Wildon H *Alli Sup*
Binns, William *Alli Sup*
Binns, William S *Alli Sup*
Binoi *DcOrL 3*
Binski, Sigurd R 1921- *BiDPar*
Binsted, Raymond Horatio 1912- *Au&Wr*
Binyon, Laurence 1869-1943 *CasWL, ChPo, ChPo S1, ChPo S2, Chmbr 3, CnE&AP, LongC, ModBL, NewC, OxEng, REn, TwCA, TwCA Sup, TwCW, WebEAL, WhLA*
Binyon, Mary Elizabeth *ChPo*
Binyon, Robert Laurence 1869-1943 *DcEnA Ap, DcLEnL, EvLB, Pen Eng*
Binzer, August, Freiherr Von 1793-1868 *OxGer*
Bioletti, Frederic Theodore 1865- *WhWNAA*
Bion *BbD, BiD&SB, CasWL, DcEnL, NewC, OxEng, Pen Cl, RCom*
Bion 325?BC-255?BC *Pen Cl*
Biondello *DcEnL*
Biondo, Flavio 1392?-1463 *CasWL, DcEuL, REn*
Biot, Francois 1923- *ConAu 13R*
Bioy Casares, Adolfo 1914- *ConAu 29, ConLC 4, DcCLA, Pen Am*
Birabeau, Andre 1890- *CnMD, McGWD, ModWD*
Birbeck, Chris *Alli*
Birbeck, Geoffrey 1875- *WhLA*
Birbeck, Morris 1764-1825 *DcNAA*
Birch, Anthony Harold 1924- *Au&Wr, ConAu 13R, WrD 1976*
Birch, Busby *Alli*
Birch, C E 1875- *WhWNAA*
Birch, Charles *Alli*
Birch, Charles Allan 1903- *Au&Wr, WrD 1976*
Birch, Charlotte Maria *Alli Sup*
Birch, David L 1937- *ConAu 25*
Birch, Dorothy *Au&Wr*
Birch, Henry *Alli Sup*
Birch, Herbert G 1918-1973 *ConAu 41*
Birch, J *MnBBF*
Birch, J F *Alli, BiDLA*
Birch, J Weedon *MnBBF*
Birch, John d1815 *Alli, Alli Sup, BiDLA, BiDLA Sup*
Birch, John B *Alli*
Birch, Jonathan 1783-1847 *ChPo*

Birch, Leo Bedrich 1902- *ConAu 33, WrD 1976*
Birch, McLane *BlkAW*
Birch, Michele *DrAP 1975*
Birch, Peter 1652- *Alli*
Birch, Philip *Alli Sup*
Birch, R W Peregrine *Alli Sup*
Birch, Raymond Russell 1881- *WhWNAA*
Birch, Reginald Bathurst 1856-1943 *ChPo, ChPo S1, ChPo S2, ConICB, JBA 1951*
Birch, Robert Fairfax *AmSCAP 66*
Birch, Sampson *Alli*
Birch, Samuel 1757- *Alli, BiDLA*
Birch, Samuel 1813-1885 *Alli Sup, DcEnL*
Birch, Scholes Butler *Alli Sup*
Birch, Thomas *Alli*
Birch, Thomas 1705-1766? *Alli, DcEnL, NewC*
Birch, Thomas 1779-1851 *EarAB*
Birch, Thomas Bruce 1866- *WhWNAA*
Birch, Thomas Erskine 1760-1820 *DcNAA*
Birch, W A *ChPo*
Birch, Walter *Alli, BiDLA*
Birch, Walter DeGray *Alli Sup*
Birch, William *Alli, Alli Sup*
Birch, William G 1909- *ConAu 53*
Birch, William John *Alli Sup*
Birch, William Thomas *Alli Sup*
Birch-Pfeiffer, Charlotte 1800-1868 *BbD, BiD&SB, EvEuW, OxGer*
Birch-Reynardson *Alli Sup*
Birchal, John *Alli*
Birchall, James *Alli Sup*
Birchall, Samuel *Alli, BiDLA*
Birchall, Sara Hamilton *ChPo*
Bircham, Deric Neale 1934- *WrD 1976*
Birchedus *Alli*
Birchensha, John *Alli*
Birchfield, James D *ChPo S2*
Birchfield, Martha *ChPo S2*
Birchfield, Raymond *BlkAW*
Birchington, Stephen d1407? *Alli*
Birchley, William *Alli*
Birchmore, John W *Alli Sup*
Birchmore, John Woodbridge 1822-1900 *DcNAA*
Birchwood, Reginald *MnBBF*
Birck, Sixt 1501-1554 *CasWL, DcEuL, OxGer*
Birckbeck, Mrs. M H *Alli Sup*
Birckbeck, Simon 1584-1656 *Alli*
Birckhead, Nancy *ChPo S1*
Birckhead, William Lunper *Alli Sup*
Bird, Alice *IlBYP*
Bird, Anna M Pennock 1855-1946 *OhA&B*
Bird, Annie Laurie 1893- *WhPNW*
Bird, Anthony Cole 1917- *Au&Wr, ConAu 13R*
Bird, Mrs. Atherstone *ChPo S2*
Bird, Bessie Calhoun *BlkAW*
Bird, Brandon *ConAu XR*
Bird, Caroline 1915- *ConAu 17R, WrD 1976*
Bird, Charles *Alli Sup*
Bird, Charles Smith 1795-1862 *Alli, Alli Sup*
Bird, Claude Smith *Alli Sup*
Bird, Cyril Kenneth 1887-1965 *ConAu P-1, LongC, WhLA*
Bird, Dennis Leslie 1930- *Au&Wr, WrD 1976*
Bird, Dorothy Maywood 1899- *ConAu P-1, WrD 1976*
Bird, Edward *Alli*
Bird, F J *Alli Sup*
Bird, Frederic Mayer 1838-1908 *Alli Sup, AmA&B, DcAmA, DcNAA*
Bird, Frederick Spencer *Alli Sup*
Bird, Frederick Vincent Godfrey *Alli Sup*
Bird, G *Alli*
Bird, George Lloyd 1900- *Au&Wr, ConAu 5R, IndAu 1917*
Bird, George T 1900- *AmSCAP 66*
Bird, Golding 1815-1854 *Alli*
Bird, Grace Electa *WhWNAA*
Bird, Harrison *OxCan Sup*
Bird, Helen Louisa Bostwick 1826-1907 *OhA&B*
Bird, Henry 1869- *WhWNAA*
Bird, Henry Edward *Alli Sup*
Bird, Henry George *Alli Sup*
Bird, Henry Merttins *Alli, BiDLA*
Bird, Isabella L *Alli Sup, BrAu 19*

Bird, J *Alli, BiDLA*
Bird, James *Alli Sup*
Bird, James 1788-1839 *ChPo, ChPo S1, ChPo S2, NewC*
Bird, James Barry *Alli, BiDLA*
Bird, James Harold 1923- *WrD 1976*
Bird, John *Alli, Alli Sup, BiDLA, ChPo S1*
Bird, Joseph *Alli Sup, DcNAA*
Bird, Kenneth 1916- *Au&Wr*
Bird, Laura Lee *TexWr*
Bird, Lewis *MnBBF*
Bird, Lilian *ChPo S1*
Bird, Louisa *Alli Sup*
Bird, M *Alli Sup*
Bird, Mrs. M A *Alli Sup*
Bird, M B *Alli Sup*
Bird, Maria *WhCL*
Bird, Mary Pages 1866- *BiDSA*
Bird, May Golding *ChPo S2*
Bird, Michael J *OxCan*
Bird, Patricia Amy 1941- *ConAu 61*
Bird, Peter Graeme 1934- *Au&Wr*
Bird, Peter Hinckes *Alli Sup*
Bird, R *Alli*
Bird, R Wilberforce *Alli Sup*
Bird, Richard *ChPo, MnBBF*
Bird, Richard 1938- *ConAu 9R*
Bird, Robert *Alli Sup*
Bird, Robert 1854- *ChPo, ChPo S1, ChPo S2*
Bird, Robert Montgomery 1806-1854 *Alli, AmA, AmA&B, BiD&SB, CasWL, ChPo, ChPo S1, Chmbr 3, CnDAL, CnThe, CyAL 2, CyWA, DcAmA, DcBiA, DcEnL, DcLEnL, DcNAA, EvLB, McGWD, OxAm, Pen Am, REn, REnAL, REnWD*
Bird, Robert Montgomery 1867-1938 *DcNAA*
Bird, Samuel *Alli*
Bird, Samuel Doughan *Alli Sup*
Bird, Sarah *Alli Sup*
Bird, Thomas *Alli*
Bird, Ulmer S *TexWr*
Bird, Vivian 1910- *WrD 1976*
Bird, W Ernest 1890- *ConAu P-1*
Bird, Wilkinson Dent 1869- *WhLA*
Bird, Will R 1891- *ConAu 13R, DcLEnL, OxCan, OxCan Sup, WhWNAA*
Bird, William *Alli*
Bird, William 1889- *WhWNAA*
Bird, William Henry 1882- *Au&Wr*
Bird, William Richard 1891- *Au&Wr, CanNov*
Bird, Zenobia *AmA&B*
Birds, James Adey *Alli Sup*
Birdsall, Ralph 1871-1918 *DcNAA*
Birdsall, Steve 1944- *ConAu 53*
Birdsall, William Wilfred 1854-1909 *DcNAA*
Birdsell, Ella S *Alli Sup*
Birdsey, Emer *ChPo*
Birdseye, Charles F *Alli Sup*
Birdseye, Clarence Frank 1854-1927 *DcNAA*
Birdseye, George W 1844- *ChPo S1, ChPo S2*
Birdt, Robert 1935- *AmSCAP 66*
Birdwhistell, Ray L 1918- *ConAu 45*
Birdwood, Sir George C Molesworth 1839- *Alli Sup*
Birdwood, George F B 1929- *WrD 1976*
Bire, Edmond *DcEuL*
Birenbaum, Halina 1929- *ConAu 45*
Birenbaum, William M 1923- *ConAu 29*
Birge, Edward Bailey 1868- *IndAu 1816, WhWNAA*
Birge, Julius Charles 1839-1923 *DcNAA*
Birge, Raymond T 1887- *BiDPar, WhWNAA*
Birge, William Spoford 1857-1925 *DcNAA*
Birimisa, George 1924- *ConDr, WrD 1976*
Birinyi, Louis Kossuth 1887-1941 *OhA&B*
Birk, Julia 1907- *AnMV 1926*
Birk, Sixt 1500?-1554 *CasWL, EvEuW*
Birkbeck, Miss A M *Alli Sup*
Birkbeck, George 1776-1841 *Alli*
Birkbeck, John *Alli Sup*
Birkbeck, John A *ChPo S2*
Birkbeck, Morris 1764-1825 *Alli, BiDLA Sup, OxAm, REnAL*
Birkbeck, William Lloyd 1806-1887 *Alli Sup*
Birkby, Carel 1910- *Au&Wr*
Birkby, Thomas Simpson *Alli Sup*
Birkeland, Torger *WhPNW*

Birken, Siegmund 1626-1681 *OxGer*
Birken, Sigmund Von 1626-1681 *CasWL*
Birkenhead, Earl Of 1872-1930 *ChPo, LongC*
Birkenhead, Lord *ConAu 57*
Birkenhead, Elijah 1903- *Au&Wr*
Birkenhead, Sir John 1615?-1679 *Alli, NewC*
Birkenmayer, Sigmund Stanley 1923- *ConAu 23*
Birket-Smith, Kaj 1893- *ConAu P-1, OxCan*
Birkett, Lord 1883-1962 *ChPo S2, LongC*
Birkett, Mary *PoIre*
Birkett, Thomas *Alli Sup*
Birkhead, Henry *Alli*
Birkhead, Henry 1617- *Alli*
Birkhimer, William Edward 1848-1914 *Alli Sup, DcNAA, OhA&B*
Birkhoff, George David 1884-1944 *DcNAA, WhWNAA*
Birkin, Sir Charles 1907- *Au&Wr*
Birkin, William *Alli*
Birkinshaw, Maria Louisa *Alli Sup*
Birkitt, Edward *Alli*
Birkley, Marilyn 1916- *ConAu 41*
Birkmire, William Harvey 1860-1924 *DcAmA, DcNAA*
Birkos, Alexander S 1936- *ConAu 25*
Birks, A *Alli*
Birks, Herbert Alfred *Alli Sup*
Birks, J *Alli*
Birks, Thomas Rawson 1810-1883 *Alli, Alli Sup, DcEnL*
Birla, Lakshminiwas N 1909- *ConAu P-1*
Birland, Maud *ChPo*
Birley, Anthony Richard 1937- *Au&Wr*
Birley, Caroline *Alli Sup*
Birley, Julia 1928- *ConAu 13R*
Birley, R K *Alli Sup*
Birley, Sir Robert 1903- *Au&Wr*
Birley, William Hornby 1834- *Alli Sup*
Birmingham, A W *Alli Sup*
Birmingham, Andrew B *PoIre*
Birmingham, David 1938- *ConAu 17R*
Birmingham, Frances A 1920- *ConAu 17R*
Birmingham, Frederic Alexander 1911- *AmA&B, ConAu 17R*
Birmingham, George A 1865-1950 *DcLEnL, EvLB, LongC, NewC, REn, TwCA, TwCA Sup, TwCW, WhLA*
Birmingham, John 1816-1884 *Alli Sup, PoIre*
Birmingham, John 1951- *ConAu 45*
Birmingham, Maisie *WrD 1976*
Birmingham, Stephen 1932?- *AmA&B, Au&Wr, AuNews 1, ConAu 49, WrD 1976*
Birmingham, Walter 1913- *ConAu 17R, WrD 1976*
Birn, John Donald 1918- *Au&Wr*
Birn, Raymond Francis 1935- *WrD 1976*
Birnage, Derek A W *MnBBF*
Birnage, Dick *MnBBF*
Birnbach, Martin 1929- *ConAu 1R, WrD 1976*
Birnbaum, Ben *DrAF 1976*
Birnbaum, Bruno 1891- *WhLA*
Birnbaum, Eleazar 1929- *ConAu 37*
Birnbaum, Martin 1878-1970 *AmA&B, REnAL*
Birnbaum, Milton 1919- *ConAu 33*
Birnbaum, Nathan 1864- *WhLA*
Birnbaum, Norman 1926- *ConAu 53*
Birnbaum, Philip 1904- *ConAu 49*
Birnbaum, Salomo 1891- *WhLA*
Birne, Henry 1921- *ConAu 17R*
Birney, Alfred Earle 1904- *Au&Wr, CasWL*
Birney, Alice Lotvin 1938- *ConAu 33, WrD 1976*
Birney, Catherine H *Alli Sup*
Birney, Earle 1904- *CanWr, ChPo S1, ConAu 1R, ConLC 1, ConLC 4, ConLC 6, ConNov 1972, ConNov 1976, ConP 1970, ConP 1975, DcLEnL, DrAP 1975, LongC, OxCan, OxCan Sup, Pen Eng, REnAL, TwCW, WebEAL, WrD 1976*
Birney, Hoffman 1891-1958 *AmA&B*
Birney, James Gillespie 1792-1857 *BbD, BiD&SB, BiDSA, DcAmA, DcNAA,*

OxAm
Birney, William 1819-1890? *BiDSA, DcAmA, DcNAA*
Birnie, John Black Leslie *Alli Sup*
Birnie, Rogers 1851-1939 *DcNAA*
Birnie, William *Alli*
Birnin Gwari, Muhammadu Na *CasWL*
Biro, Balint S 1921- *ConAu 25, IlCB 1956*
Biro, Charlotte Slovak 1904- *ConAu 57*
Biro, Val 1921- *Au&Wr, IlBYP, IlCB 1966, ConAu 23, SmATA 1*
Biron, Armand-Louis, Duc De *OxFr*
Biron, Charles, Duc De 1562-1602 *OxFr*
Birotteau, Cesar *OxFr*
Birrell, Andrew *Alli, BiDLA*
Birrell, Augustine 1850-1933 *Alli Sup, BiD&SB, ChPo, ChPo S1, Chmbr 3, DcEnA Ap, DcLEnL, EvLB, LongC, NewC, OxEng, Pen Eng, REn, TwCA, TwCA Sup, TwCW*
Birrell, Charles Morton *Alli Sup*
Birrell, James Peter 1929- *WrD 1976*
Birrell, Olive M *Alli Sup*
Birrell, Thomas Anthony 1922- *Au&Wr*
Birrell, William Dunbar 1868- *ChPo, ChPo S1*
Birren, Faber 1900- *ConAu 13R*
Birren, James E 1918- *ConAu 17R*
Birse, A H 1889- *ConAu 23*
Birstein, Ann 1927- *AmA&B, ConAu 17R, DrAF 1976, WrD 1976*
Birt, Catherine 1917- *Au&Wr*
Birt, Isaiah *Alli, BiDLA*
Birt, John *Alli, BiDLA*
Birt, William Radcliff *Alli, Alli Sup*
Birtha, Jessie M *ChPo S1*
Birtles, William *Alli Sup*
Birtwistle, George 1877- *WhLA*
Biruni, Abu Al-Rayhan Muhammad Ibn Ahmad 973-1050? *CasWL*
Biruni, Abu'l-Rayhan Muhammad Al- 973-1050? *Pen Cl*
Biruni, Abu'r-Rayhan Muhammad B M Al- 973-1050? *DcOrL 3*
Biryukov, Pavel Ivanovich 1860-1931 *CasWL*
Bisbee, Frederick Adelbert 1855-1923 *DcNAA*
Bisbee, L H And Simons, J C *Alli Sup*
Bisbee, Lewis H 1839-1898 *DcNAA*
Bisbee, M D *Alli Sup*
Bisbee, Mariana M *Alli Sup, ChPo*
Bisbee, Marvin Davis 1845-1913 *DcNAA*
Bisbee, Susan A *Alli Sup*
Bisbee, William Henry 1840-1942 *DcNAA*
Bisbie, Nathaniel d1695 *Alli*
Bisby, Guy Richard 1889- *WhWNAA*
Bisby, Minnie K *ArizL*
Bisch, Edith *WrD 1976*
Bisch, Louis Edward 1885- *WhWNAA*
Bischof, Ledford Julius 1914- *ConAu 9R*
Bischoff, David *Alli*
Bischoff, E *Alli Sup*
Bischoff, Fred *Alli*
Bischoff, Friedrich 1894- *OxGer*
Bischoff, Helmut 1926- *WhGrA*
Bischoff, Ilse Marthe 1903?- *AuBYP, ChPo, ChPo S1, ChPo S2, ConICB, IlCB 1945, IlCB 1956, MorJA*
Bischoff, J E K *BiD&SB*
Bischoff, James *Alli*
Bischoff, Julia Bristol 1909- *AuBYP, ConAu 21*
Bischoffwerder, Johann Rudolf Von 1741-1803 *OxGer*
Bisco, John *Alli*
Biscoe, Miss A C *Alli Sup*
Biscoe, C *Alli*
Biscoe, Ellen L *Alli Sup*
Biscoe, Richard d1748 *Alli*
Biscop, Benedict 654?-690 *DcEnL, NewC*
Biscop Baducing, Benedict *NewC*
Bisgood, Mary *ChPo S1*
Biser, Benjamin Franklin 1868-1928 *DcNAA*
Bish, Robert L 1942- *ConAu 53*
Bishai, Wilson B 1923- *ConAu 33*
Bishenden, Charles James *Alli Sup*
Bisher, James F 1918- *ConAu 5R*
Bishin, William R 1939- *ConAu 61*

Bishir, John 1933- *ConAu 41*
Bishop, A *Alli Sup*
Bishop, A W *Alli Sup*
Bishop, Abraham 1763-1844 *DcNAA*
Bishop, Albert Webb *DcNAA*
Bishop, Alfred *Alli*
Bishop, Annette *ChPo, EarAB*
Bishop, Avard Longley 1875-1932 *DcNAA, WhWNAA*
Bishop, Bertha Thorne *Alli Sup, HsB&A*
Bishop, Blanche *ChPo*
Bishop, Carlton Thomas 1882- *WhWNAA*
Bishop, Charles *Alli*
Bishop, Charles Kenwick Kenelm *Alli Sup*
Bishop, Charles McTyeire 1862- *TexWr, WhWNAA*
Bishop, Claire Huchet *AuBYP, BkP, CatA 1952, JBA 1951*
Bishop, Cortlandt Field 1870-1935 *AmA&B, ChPo, DcNAA*
Bishop, Crawford M 1885- *ConAu 17*
Bishop, Curtis Kent 1912-1967 *AuBYP, ConAu P-1, SmATA 6*
Bishop, David Horace 1870- *BiDSA*
Bishop, Donald G 1907- *ConAu 1R, WrD 1976*
Bishop, E Morchard *ConAu XR*
Bishop, Elizabeth 1911- *AmA&B, Au&Wr, ChPo, ChPo S1, CnE&AP, ConAu 5R, ConLC 1, ConLC 4, ConP 1970, ConP 1975, CrCAP, DrAP 1975, EncWL, ModAL, ModAL Sup, OxAm, Pen Am, RAdv 1, REn, REnAL, TwCA Sup, TwCW, WebEAL, WrD 1976*
Bishop, Emily Montague 1858-1916 *DcNAA*
Bishop, Eric Francis Fox 1891- *Au&Wr, WrD 1976*
Bishop, Ernest Simons 1876-1927 *DcNAA*
Bishop, Evelyn Morchard *ConAu XR*
Bishop, Farnham 1886-1930 *DcNAA*
Bishop, Ferman 1922- *ConAu 23, WrD 1976*
Bishop, George *Alli, CyAL 1*
Bishop, George 1924- *ConAu 49*
Bishop, George Riker 1841-1937 *Alli Sup*
Bishop, George Riker 1841-1931 *DcNAA*
Bishop, George Sayles 1836-1914 *DcNAA*
Bishop, George W, Jr. 1910- *ConAu 13R*
Bishop, George Walter 1886- *WhLA*
Bishop, Giles d1925 *DcNAA*
Bishop, Gordon *DrAP 1975*
Bishop, Grace *AuBYP*
Bishop, H R *ChPo S2*
Bishop, Harriet E 1817-1883 *Alli Sup, DcNAA*
Bishop, Harry Gore 1874-1934 *DcNAA*
Bishop, Hawley *Alli*
Bishop, Henry Fitch 1820-1910 *DcNAA*
Bishop, Henry Halsall *Alli Sup*
Bishop, Sir Henry Rowley 1783-1855 *Alli*
Bishop, Hugh William Fletcher 1907- *Au&Wr*
Bishop, Ian Benjamin 1927- *Au&Wr, WrD 1976*
Bishop, Isabella Lucy Bird 1831-1904 *Alli Sup, BrAu 19, Chmbr 3, NewC*
Bishop, Jack *ConAu XR*
Bishop, James *Alli Sup*
Bishop, James Alonzo 1907- *AuNews 1, ConAu 17R*
Bishop, James Leander *Alli Sup*
Bishop, Jesse Phelps 1815-1881 *DcNAA, OhA&B*
Bishop, Jim 1907- *AmA&B, AuNews 1, AuNews 2, ConAu XR, DrAP 1975, REnAL*
Bishop, Joe 1907- *AmSCAP 66*
Bishop, Joel Prentiss 1814-1901 *Alli, Alli Sup, DcAmA, DcNAA*
Bishop, John *Alli, Alli Sup, DcEnL*
Bishop, John 1797-1873 *Alli Sup*
Bishop, John B *Alli Sup*
Bishop, John George *Alli Sup*
Bishop, John L 1913- *ConAu 33*
Bishop, John Leander 1820-1868 *DcNAA*
Bishop, John Peale 1892-1944 *AmA&B, CasWL, CnDAL, CnE&AP, ConAmA, DcLEnL, DcNAA, EncWL, ModAL, OxAm, Pen Am, REn, REnAL, SixAP, TwCA Sup*
Bishop, John S 1834- *Alli Sup*

Bishop, Joseph Bucklin 1847-1928 *AmLY, DcAmA, DcNAA, WhWNAA*
Bishop, Joseph W, Jr. 1915- *ConAu 33, WrD 1976*
Bishop, Josiah Goodman 1833-1922 *OhA&B*
Bishop, Judson Wade 1831-1917 *DcNAA*
Bishop, Julian Truitt *MnBBF*
Bishop, Leonard 1922- *AmA&B, ConAu 13R*
Bishop, Leslie G 1908- *CanNov*
Bishop, Levi 1815-1881 *Alli Sup, ChPo, DcNAA*
Bishop, Louis Bennett 1865- *WhWNAA*
Bishop, Louis Faugeres 1864-1941 *DcAmA, DcNAA, WhWNAA*
Bishop, M C *Alli Sup*
Bishop, Martha Carver 1867?-1950 *IndAu 1917*
Bishop, Mary *Alli, BiDLA*
Bishop, Mary Davidson d1957 *ChPo S2*
Bishop, Matthew *Alli, DcEnL*
Bishop, Maxine H 1919- *ConAu 25*
Bishop, Michael 1945- *AuNews 2, ConAu 61*
Bishop, Morchard 1903- *ConAu XR, WrD 1976*
Bishop, Morris Gilbert 1893?-1973 *AmA&B, ChPo, ChPo S1, ChPo S2, ConAu 1R, ConAu 45, OxAm, REnAL, TwCA Sup*
Bishop, Nathaniel Holmes 1837-1902 *Alli Sup, AmA&B, BiD&SB, DcAmA, DcNAA*
Bishop, Nicholas *Alli Sup*
Bishop, P P *Alli Sup*
Bishop, Percy Cook *MnBBF*
Bishop, Putnam Peter 1823-1896 *BiDSA, DcNAA*
Bishop, R *Alli*
Bishop, Richard E D 1925- *Au&Wr*
Bishop, Robert 1938- *WrD 1976*
Bishop, Robert Hamilton 1777-1855 *DcAmA, DcNAA, OhA&B*
Bishop, Robert Lee 1931- *ConAu 13R*
Bishop, Robert Roberts 1834-1909 *DcNAA*
Bishop, Ruth M *ChPo S1*
Bishop, Samuel 1731-1795 *Alli, Chmbr 2, DcLEnL, EvLB*
Bishop, Seth Scott 1852-1923 *DcAmA, DcNAA*
Bishop, Stanley Walter Edgar 1906- *Au&Wr*
Bishop, Tania Kroitor 1906- *ConAu 29*
Bishop, Thomas *Alli, Alli Sup*
Bishop, Thomas B *Alli Sup, ChPo S1*
Bishop, Thomas Brigham 1835-1905 *OxAm, REnAL*
Bishop, Thomas W 1929- *ConAu 1R*
Bishop, W A *OxCan*
Bishop, W Arthur 1923- *ConAu 21*
Bishop, Walter 1905- *AmSCAP 66*
Bishop, Washington Irving *Alli Sup*
Bishop, William *Alli*
Bishop, Sir William *Alli*
Bishop, William 1533-1624 *Alli*
Bishop, William Henry 1847-1928 *Alli Sup, AmA&B, AmLY, BbD, BiD&SB, DcAmA, DcNAA, WhWNAA, WiscW*
Bishop, William Samuel 1865-1944 *DcNAA, WhWNAA*
Bishop, William W, Jr. 1906- *ConAu 17R*
Bishop, William Warner 1871-1955 *AmA&B, ChPo S1*
Bishop-Collett, Beryl *WhWNAA*
Bishop Hatto *NewC*
Bishopp, F C 1884- *WhWNAA*
Bishopric, Robert *Alli*
Bishton, I *Alli*
Biskar, John L 1918- *AmSCAP 66*
Biskin, Miriam 1920- *ConAu 25*
Bisland, Elizabeth 1862?- *AmA&B, BbD, BiD&SB, DcAmA, DcNAA*
Bismarck, Prince Otto Edward Leopold Von 1815-1898 *BbD, BiD&SB, NewC, OxGer, REn*
Bismarck-Schonhausen, Prince O E L Von 1815-1898 *NewC*
Bisonius *WrD 1976*
Bispham, Caroline Russell *ChPo S1*
Bispham, David Scull 1857-1921 *DcNAA*
Bispham, George Tucker 1838-1906 *Alli Sup, DcAmA, DcNAA*
Bispham, Henry Collins 1841-1882 *EarAB Sup*
Bispham, Thomas *Alli*

Bisque, Anatole *ConAu XR*
Biss, Frederick *ChPo S2*
Bissart, Patrick 1500-1568 *Alli*
Bissat, Patrick 1500-1568 *Alli*
Bisse, James *Alli*
Bisse, Philip *Alli*
Bisse, Thomas d1731 *Alli*
Bisseker, Harry 1878- *WhLA*
Bissell, A H *Alli Sup*
Bissell, Allen Page 1835-1914 *Alli Sup, DcNAA*
Bissell, Arthur Dart 1858-1925 *DcNAA*
Bissell, Champion 1830-1899 *Alli Sup, ChPo, DcNAA*
Bissell, Claude T 1916- *CanWr*
Bissell, Edwin Cone 1832-1894 *Alli Sup, BbD, BiD&SB, DcAmA, DcNAA*
Bissell, Emily P d1948 *ChPo S1*
Bissell, James Dougal 1864- *WhWNAA*
Bissell, John N *Alli Sup*
Bissell, Josiah H *Alli Sup*
Bissell, Mary L *Alli Sup*
Bissell, Mary Taylor 1854-1936 *DcNAA*
Bissell, Richard 1913- *AmA&B, Au&Wr, ConAu 1R, REnAL, WorAu, WrD 1976*
Bissell, Richard Mervin 1862-1941 *DcNAA*
Bissell, Walter Lewis 1879-1957 *OhA&B*
Bissenden, Charles Norton 1906- *Au&Wr*
Bisset, Alexander Macdonald 1869- *ChPo, ChPo S2*
Bisset, Andrew 1800- *Alli, Alli Sup*
Bisset, Charles 1717-1791 *Alli*
Bisset, Donald 1910- *Au&Wr, ConAu 33, SmATA 7*
Bisset, J *Alli, BiDLA*
Bisset, Sir John Jarvis 1819- *Alli Sup*
Bisset, Patrick 1500-1568 *Alli*
Bisset, Robert d1805 *Alli*
Bisset, Thomas *Alli*
Bisset, William *Alli*
Bissett, Bill 1939- *ConP 1970, ConP 1975, OxCan Sup, WrD 1976*
Bissett, Clark Prescott 1875-1932 *DcNAA*
Bissing, Friedrich Wilhelm Freiherr 1873- *WhLA*
Bisson, Alexandre 1848- *BiD&SB*
Bisson, F Perronet *ChPo*
Bisson, Frederick S D DeCarteret *Alli Sup*
Bissoondoyal, Basdeo 1906- *ConAu 25, WrD 1976*
Bissot, Francois, Sieur De La Riviere 1612?-1673 *OxCan*
Bisticci, Vespasiano Da 1421-1498 *CasWL, DcEuL, Pen Eur*
Bistram, Ottilie Von 1859- *WhLA*
Bistrizki, Nathan *CasWL*
Bite, Ben *ConAu XR*
Biterolf *OxGer*
Biterswigg, Pendavid *Alli*
Bitgood, Roberta 1908- *AmSCAP 66*
Bithell, Richard *Alli Sup*
Bithnell, Jethro 1878- *ChPo, WhLA*
Bithray, Ebenezer *Alli Sup*
Bitner, Julia Grace 1902- *TexWr*
Bittel, Lester Robert 1918- *ConAu 13R*
Bittenbender, Ada Matilda 1848- *DcNAA*
Bitter, Arthur 1821-1872 *BiD&SB*
Bitterman, Henry J 1940- *WrD 1976*
Bitterman, Herbert 1914-1944 *ChPo, ChPo S1*
Bittermann, Henry J 1904- *ConAu 33*
Bitting, William Coleman 1857-1931 *DcNAA*
Bittinger, Benjamin F *Alli Sup*
Bittinger, Desmond W 1905- *ConAu 37*
Bittinger, Emmert F 1925- *ConAu 37*
Bittinger, John Quincy 1831-1895 *DcNAA*
Bittinger, Lucy Forney 1859-1907 *DcAmA, DcNAA, OhA&B*
Bittle, Celestine 1884- *CatA 1952*
Bittle, Leonard F *ChPo S2*
Bittle, William E 1926- *ConAu 53*
Bittleston, Adam Henry 1849- *Alli Sup*
Bittlinger, Arnold 1928- *ConAu 49*
Bittner, Herbert G d1960 *AmA&B*
Bittner, William 1921- *ConAu 5R*
Bitton, Davis 1930- *ConAu 33*
Bitzius, Albert *BiD&SB, CasWL, EuA, EvEuW, OxGer, REn*
Biven, W Carl 1925- *ConAu 21*

Bivens, Burke 1903- *AmSCAP 66*
Bivin, Virginia Pritchett 1922- *WrD 1976*
Bivona, Gus 1917- *AmSCAP 66*
Bivona, S Richard 1911-1964 *AmSCAP 66*
Bix *AmLY XR, WhWNAA*
Bixby, Ammi Leander 1856-1934 *AmLY, ChPo, DcNAA, WhWNAA*
Bixby, Amsori Leander 1856-1934 *WhWNAA*
Bixby, George Stephenson 1861-1937 *DcNAA*
Bixby, James Thompson 1843-1921 *Alli Sup, AmA&B, DcAmA, DcNAA*
Bixby, Jerome Lewis 1923- *ConAu 17R*
Bixby, John Munson 1800-1876 *DcAmA, DcNAA*
Bixby, Olive Jennie *Alli Sup*
Bixby, Ray Z *ConAu XR, WrD 1976*
Bixby, William Courtney 1920- *AmA&B, AuBYP, ConAu 1R, SmATA 6*
Bixby, William K *ChPo S2*
Bixby-Smith, Sarah *ChPo S1*
Bixler, Julius Seelye 1894- *AmA&B*
Bixler, Norma 1905- *ConAu 49*
Bixler, R Russell, Jr. 1927- *ConAu 61*
Bixler, William Allen 1876- *WhWNAA*
Biyidi, Alexandre 1932- *AfA 1, Pen Cl*
Bizardel, Yvon 1891- *ConAu 61*
Bizcarrondo, Indalego *Pen Eur*
Bizet, Alexandre Cesar Leopold 1838-1875 *OxFr, REn*
Bizet, Georges 1838-1875 *AtlBL*
Bizzarro, Salvatore 1939- *ConAu 53*
Bizzell, William Bennett 1876-1944 *AmA&B, DcNAA, TexWr, WhWNAA*
Bjelfvenstam, Nils Erik 1896- *BiDPar*
Bjerke, Jarl Andre 1918- *EncWL*
Bjerke, Robert Alan 1939- *ConAu 41*
Bjerknes, V 1862- *WhLA*
Bjerre, Jens 1921- *Au&Wr, ConAu 9R*
Bjerregaard, Carl Hendrick Andreas 1845-1922 *DcNAA*
Bjerregaard, Carl Henry Andrew 1845-1922 *AmA&B, AmLY*
Bjerregaard, Henrik Anker 1792-1842 *BiD&SB, CasWL, DcEuL*
Bjerrgaard, Carl Henry Andrew 1845-1922 *DcAmA*
Bjerring, Nicholas *Alli Sup*
Bjork, Kenneth O *MnnWr*
Bjorkhem, John 1910-1963 *BiDPar*
Bjorklund, Lorence F *IlBYP, IlCB 1956, IlCB 1966*
Bjorkman, Edwin August 1866-1951 *AmA&B, ConAmL, TwCA, TwCA Sup, WhWNAA*
Bjorkman, J Walther 1896- *WhLA*
Bjorling, Gunnar 1887-1960 *EncWL, Pen Eur*
Bjorling, Philip R *Alli Sup*
Bjorn Johnsson 1575-1656 *DcEuL*
Bjorn, Thyra Ferre 1905-1975 *AmA&B, ConAu 5R, ConAu 57*
Bjornard, Reidar B 1917- *ConAu 33*
Bjorneboe, Jens Ingvald 1920- *CasWL, CrCD*
Bjornson, Bjornstjerne Martinius 1832-1910 *AtlBL, BbD, BiD&SB, CasWL, ChPo S1, ClDMEuL, CnMD, CnThe, CyWA, DcBiA, DcEuL, EuA, EvEuW, LongC, McGWD, ModWD, Pen Eur, REn, REnWD*
Bjornstad, James 1940- *ConAu 29*
Bjornvig, Thorkild Strange 1918- *CasWL, Pen Eur*
Bjorset, Bryniolf *ConAu XR*
Blaauw, William Henry *Alli*
Blacam, Hugh De 1890?- *CatA 1947*
Blachford *BbtC*
Blachford, George 1913- *Au&Wr, ConAu 9R*
Blachford, M *BbtC*
Blachly, Clarence Dan 1881- *WhWNAA*
Blachly, Frederick Frank 1880?-1975 *ConAu 57, WhWNAA*
Blachly, Lou 1899- *ConAu P-1*
Black *Alli*
Black, Miss *CarSB*
Black, Mrs. *Alli Sup*
Black, Reverend *BiDLA*
Black, A E *Alli Sup*
Black, A W *ChPo S1*
Black, Adam *Alli Sup*

Black, Adam 1784-1874 *Alli Sup*
Black, Albert George 1928- *ConAu 45*
Black, Alexander 1859-1940 *Alli Sup, AmLY, DcAmA, DcNAA, REnAL*
Black, Algernon David 1900- *ConAu 1R*
Black, Amy E *Alli Sup*
Black, Angus 1943- *ConAu 29*
Black, Anna Robinson *IndAu 1816*
Black, Archibald Pollok *Alli Sup*
Black, Austin 1929- *BlkAW*
Black, B Coursin *WhWNAA*
Black, Ben 1889-1950 *AmSCAP 66*
Black, Buddy 1918- *AmSCAP 66*
Black, Caroline Adair 1887- *WhWNAA*
Black, Charles 1903- *AmSCAP 66*
Black, Charles Augustus Harold 1847- *Alli Sup*
Black, Charles Bertram *Alli Sup*
Black, Charles C *Alli Sup*
Black, Charles Christopher d1879 *Alli Sup*
Black, Charles Clarke 1858- *WhWNAA*
Black, Charles Ingham 1821?-1896 *Alli Sup, ChPo S1, PoIre*
Black, Charles Lund, Jr. 1915- *ConAu 1R, WrD 1976*
Black, Chauncey Forward d1904 *Alli Sup, DcNAA*
Black, Clementina *Alli Sup*
Black, Clinton Vane DeBrosse 1918- *Au&Wr, WrD 1976*
Black, Cornelius *Alli Sup*
Black, Cyril Edwin 1915- *AmA&B, ConAu 1R*
Black, Cyrus 1809-1898 *DcNAA*
Black, David *ConAu 57*
Black, David 1762-1806 *Alli*
Black, David Dakers *Alli Sup*
Black, David Macleod 1941- *ConAu 25, ConP 1970, ConP 1975, WrD 1976*
Black, Donald Campbell *Alli Sup*
Black, Dorothy 1914- *Au&Wr*
Black, Dorothy Delius *Au&Wr*
Black, Duncan 1908- *ConAu 19*
Black, Ebenezer Charlton 1861-1927 *Alli Sup, DcAmA, DcNAA*
Black, Edward Loring 1915- *Au&Wr, ConAu 9R*
Black, Effie Squier 1866-1906 *OhA&B*
Black, Emily Julia *Alli Sup*
Black, Eugene 1927- *ConAu 9R*
Black, Eugene R 1898- *ConAu 25*
Black, F Charlton 1861- *BiD&SB*
Black, Forrest Revere 1894-1943 *OhA&B*
Black, Frank J 1896- *AmSCAP 66*
Black, Franklyn *ChPo S2*
Black, G V *Alli Sup*
Black, Gavin *ConAu XR*
Black, George *Alli Sup*
Black, George Fraser 1866?-1948 *AmA&B, DcNAA*
Black, Glenn Albert 1900-1964 *IndAu 1917*
Black, Glenn G 1888- *OhA&B*
Black, Greene Vardiman 1836-1915 *DcNAA*
Black, Harold Stephen 1898- *WrD 1976*
Black, Harry George 1933- *ConAu 61*
Black, Helen *Alli Sup*
Black, Henry Campbell 1860-1927 *Alli Sup, DcAmA, DcNAA*
Black, Hermina Mary *Au&Wr*
Black, Hobart *ConAu XR*
Black, Hugh 1868-1953 *AmA&B*
Black, Hugh C 1920- *ConAu 37*
Black, Hugo Lafayette 1886-1971 *ConAu 33*
Black, Ian Stuart 1915- *Au&Wr, ConAu 9R, MnBBF*
Black, Irma Simonton 1906-1972 *AuBYP, ConAu 1R, ConAu 37, SmATA 2*
Black, Isaac J *BlkAW*
Black, Ivory 1849-1913 *AmA*
Black, James *Alli, Alli Sup, BbtC, BiDLA*
Black, James 1823-1894 *Alli Sup, DcAmA*
Black, James B *Alli Sup*
Black, James Menzies 1913- *ConAu 5R*
Black, James Rush 1827-1895 *Alli Sup, DcAmA, OhA&B*
Black, James William 1866-1934 *DcNAA*
Black, Jean Ferguson *ChPo*
Black, Jennie Prince 1868-1945 *AmSCAP 66*
Black, Jeremiah Sullivan 1810-1883 *Alli Sup,*

Black, John *Alli, Alli Sup, BiDLA, BiDLA Sup, ChPo S1*
Black, John 1777?-1825 *ChPo*
Black, John 1783-1855 *Alli, DcEnL, NewC*
Black, John 1847- *ChPo S1*
Black, John Bennett 1883- *WhLA*
Black, John Donald 1883-1960 *AmA&B, WhWNAA*
Black, John Janvier 1837-1909 *DcAmA, DcNAA*
Black, John N 1922- *ConAu 33*
Black, John R d1880 *Alli Sup*
Black, John Sutherland *Alli Sup*
Black, John Wilson 1906- *ConAu P-1, IndAu 1917*
Black, Joseph 1728-1799 *Alli*
Black, Joseph Burton 1924- *IndAu 1917*
Black, Joseph E 1921- *ConAu 9R*
Black, Josephine *Alli Sup*
Black, Kenneth, Jr. 1925- *ConAu 13R*
Black, Ladbroke Lionel Day 1877-1940 *ChPo S1, MnBBF*
Black, Lionel *ConAu XR, WrD 1976*
Black, Mansell *ConAu XR, WrD 1976*
Black, Margaret Horton 1881- *DcAmA, DcNAA*
Black, Margaret Katherine 1921- *Au&Wr, ConAu 29*
Black, Margaret Moyes *ChPo S2*
Black, Margaret Shafer 1859-1913 *OhA&B*
Black, Martha E 1901- *ConAu 33, WrD 1976*
Black, Martha Louise 1866-1957 *OxCan*
Black, Mary Childs 1922- *ConAu 21*
Black, Matthew W 1895- *ConAu 25*
Black, Max 1909- *AmA&B, ConAu 61*
Black, McKnight d1931 *DcNAA*
Black, Millard H 1912- *ConAu 25*
Black, Misha 1910- *Au&Wr, ConAu P-1*
Black, Norman Fergus 1876- *OxCan, WhWNAA*
Black, Patrick 1813-1879 *Alli Sup*
Black, Percy 1922- *Au&Wr, ConAu 33, WrD 1976*
Black, Robert *Alli Sup*
Black, Robert C, III 1914- *ConAu 41*
Black, Robert Lounsbury 1881-1954 *OhA&B*
Black, Robert Moffitt 1879- *WhWNAA*
Black, Robert Perry 1927- *WrD 1976*
Black, Ruby Aurora 1896- *WhWNAA*
Black, Ryland Melville 1867- *WhWNAA*
Black, Sally *BiDSA*
Black, Sam 1915- *Au&Wr*
Black, Samuel *Alli*
Black, Samuel 1785?-1841 *OxCan*
Black, Samuel Charles 1869-1921 *DcNAA, OhA&B*
Black, Sarah S *Alli Sup*
Black, Stanley Warren, III 1939- *ConAu 45*
Black, Stephen 1912- *Au&Wr*
Black, Stephen William 1881?-1932 *CasWL*
Black, Veronica *ConAu XR, WrD 1976*
Black, Vince *ConAu XR*
Black, W M P *ChPo*
Black, Warren Columbus 1848?-1915 *BiDSA, DcAmA, DcNAA*
Black, William *Alli, BiDLA, Chmbr 3, OxCan*
Black, William 1825?-1887 *ChPo S1*
Black, William 1841-1898 *Alli Sup, BbD, BiD&SB, BrAu 19, CasWL, ChPo, ChPo S1, DcBiA, DcEnA, DcEnA Ap, DcEnL, DcLEnL, EvLB, HsB&A, NewC, OxEng*
Black, William George *Alli Sup*
Black, William H 1868- *BiDSA*
Black, William Henry 1854-1930 *BiDSA, DcAmA, IndAu 1816*
Black, William Leslie 1843-1931 *DcNAA*
Black, William Murray 1855-1933 *DcAmA, DcNAA*
Black, William Nelson *Alli Sup*
Black, Winifred 1865- *WhWNAA*
Black Agnes *NewC*
Black Douglas, The *NewC*
Black Hawk 1767-1838 *DcNAA, OxAm*
Black-Michaud, Jacob 1938- *ConAu 61*
Blackadder, E *ChPo S1*

Blackadder, Edward 1869-1922 *DcNAA*
Blackadder, H H *Alli*
Blackadder, J *Alli*
Blackader, Alexander Dougall 1847-
  WhWNAA
Blackader, R B *Alli Sup*
Blackall, Anthony *Alli*
Blackall, C R *Alli Sup*
Blackall, C W *ChPo S1*
Blackall, Christopher Rubey 1830-1924 *AmLY,
  ChPo S1, DcNAA*
Blackall, Dorothy Brewer *ChPo*
Blackall, Elizabeth *PoIre*
Blackall, Emily Lucas 1832?-1892? *DcNAA,
  IndAu 1816*
Blackall, John *Alli, BiDLA*
Blackall, Offspring 1654-1716 *Alli*
Blackall, Theophilus *Alli*
Blackall, Thomas *Alli*
Blackamore, A *Alli*
Blackbeard *OxAm*
Blackbird, Andrew J 1820?- *Alli Sup, DcNAA*
Blackborrow, Peter *Alli*
Blackbourne, John 1683-1741 *Alli*
Blackburn, Barbara *ConAu XR*
Blackburn, Charles F *Alli Sup*
Blackburn, Charles Frederick Osborn 1870-
  ChPo S1
Blackburn, Charles S 1850-1929 *DcNAA*
Blackburn, Claire *ConAu XR*
Blackburn, D *Alli Sup*
Blackburn, Douglas 1857-1926? *CasWL,
  DcLEnL*
Blackburn, Edith H *AuBYP*
Blackburn, George Andrew 1861-1918 *BiDSA,
  DcNAA*
Blackburn, Grace *ChPo S2, OxCan*
Blackburn, Helen *Alli Sup*
Blackburn, Henry 1830-1897 *Alli Sup,
  ChPo S1, DcEnL*
Blackburn, Hugh *Alli Sup*
Blackburn, J *Alli*
Blackburn, John d1856 *Alli, Alli Sup*
Blackburn, John Fenwick 1923- *Au&Wr,
  ConAu 1R, WrD 1976*
Blackburn, John Fenwick 1924- *AmA&B*
Blackburn, John H *OxCan Sup*
Blackburn, John M 1914- *AmSCAP 66*
Blackburn, Joyce Knight 1920- *ConAu 17R,
  IndAu 1917*
Blackburn, Laura *AmLY XR, ChPo,
  ChPo S1, DcNAA*
Blackburn, Laurence Henry 1897- *ConAu 57*
Blackburn, Lloyd *ConAu XR*
Blackburn, Margaret Elizabeth 1847-1902
  DcNAA
Blackburn, Mary Johnson *ChPo*
Blackburn, Paul 1926-1971 *AmA&B, Au&Wr,
  ConAu 33, ConP 1970, CrCAP, Pen Am,
  RAdv 1*
Blackburn, Philip Conklin *ChPo S1*
Blackburn, Simon 1944- *ConAu 49*
Blackburn, Thomas 1916- *Alli Sup, Au&Wr,
  ChPo S1, ConP 1970, ConP 1975, REn,
  TwCW, WorAu, WrD 1976*
Blackburn, Vernon d1907 *ChPo*
Blackburn, Victoria Grace d1928 *CanNov*
Blackburn, William Maxwell 1828-1898?
  *Alli Sup, AmA&B, BiD&SB, DcAmA,
  DcNAA, IndAu 1816*
Blackburne, E L *Alli*
Blackburne, E Owens *Alli Sup*
Blackburne, Edward *Alli Sup*
Blackburne, Francis 1705-1787 *Alli, BiDLA*
Blackburne, Gertrude M Ireland *Alli Sup*
Blackburne, H G *ChPo S2*
Blackburne, J *Alli Sup*
Blackburne, Lancelot d1743 *Alli*
Blackburne, Mary Frances 1874- *AmA&B*
Blackburne, Neville Alfred Edmund 1913-
  ConAu 53, WrD 1976
Blackburne, Thomas d1782 *Alli*
Blackburne, William *Alli, BiDLA*
Blackenbury, E *Alli*
Blacker, Beaver Henry d1890 *Alli Sup*
Blacker, C P 1895-1975 *ConAu 57*
Blacker, Carmen Elizabeth 1924- *ConAu 9R*
Blacker, George Dacre 1791-1871 *Alli Sup,

  PoIre*
Blacker, Hereth *WrD 1976*
Blacker, Irwin R 1919- *ConAu 1R*
Blacker, James *Alli Sup*
Blacker, Maxwell Julius 1822-1888 *PoIre*
Blacker, Robert Shapland Carew *Alli Sup*
Blacker, Valentine d1823 *Alli, PoIre*
Blacker, Sir William *Alli*
Blacker, William 1777-1855 *PoIre*
Blackerby, Samuel *Alli*
Blacket, Joseph 1786-1810 *Alli, ChPo*
Blacket, W S *Alli Sup*
Blackett, B *Alli Sup*
Blackett, B E *Alli*
Blackett, Herbert Field *Alli Sup*
Blackett, Howard *Alli Sup*
Blackett, Mary D *Alli*
Blackett, Monica 1888- *WrD 1976*
Blackett, Patrick 1897-1974 *ConAu 49*
Blackett, Veronica Heath 1927- *Au&Wr,
  ConAu 53, WrD 1976*
Blackey, Robert 1941- *ConAu 53*
Blackford, C *Alli*
Blackford, Charles Minor 1833-1903 *DcNAA*
Blackford, Isaac *Alli*
Blackford, Katherine M H 1875- *WhWNAA*
Blackhall, David Scott 1910- *ConAu 5R,
  WrD 1976*
Blackhall, Offspring *Alli*
Blackham, H H *ChPo*
Blackham, G *Alli Sup*
Blackham, Garth J 1926- *ConAu 33,
  WrD 1976*
Blackham, Harold John 1903- *Au&Wr,
  ConAu 23, WrD 1976*
Blackham, R J *WhLA*
Blackie, A B *Alli Sup*
Blackie, Agnes A C *ChPo S1*
Blackie, Alexander *BbtC*
Blackie, Bruce L 1936- *ConAu 57*
Blackie, C *Alli Sup*
Blackie, Ernest Morell 1867- *WhLA*
Blackie, George S *Alli Sup*
Blackie, John Stuart 1809-1895 *Alli Sup, BbD,
  BiD&SB, BrAu 19, CasWL, ChPo,
  ChPo S1, ChPo S2, Chmbr 3, DcEnA,
  DcEnL, EvLB, NewC*
Blackie, Thomas Morell *Alli Sup*
Blackie, Walter Graham *Alli Sup*
Blacking, John 1928- *ConAu 9R*
Blackiston, J *Alli*
Blackith, C H F *Alli Sup*
Blacklaws, Peter Campbell 1929- *Au&Wr*
Blackleack, John *Alli*
Blackledge, Celize Foote 1857-1937 *OhA&B*
Blackledge, Ethel H 1920- *ConAu 23*
Blackledge, Katherine *DcNAA*
Blackledge, William James 1886- *MnBBF*
Blackley, Charles Harrison *Alli Sup*
Blackley, Thomas *Alli*
Blackley, William *Alli, Alli Sup*
Blackley, William Lewery 1830-1902 *Alli Sup,
  ChPo S1, PoIre*
Blacklock, Ambrose *Alli*
Blacklock, M Strickland *Alli Sup*
Blacklock, Thomas 1721-1791 *Alli, ChPo,
  ChPo S2, Chmbr 2, DcEnL, EvLB,
  NewC, Pen Eng, PoCh*
Blackloe, Thomas *Alli*
Blackman, Edwin Cyril 1908- *Au&Wr*
Blackman, Elmer Ellsworth 1863- *WhWNAA*
Blackman, Emily C *Alli Sup*
Blackman, John *Alli, Alli Sup, OxEng*
Blackman, Louis *BlkAW*
Blackman, Maulsby Willett 1876- *WhWNAA*
Blackman, Raymond Victor Bernard 1910-
  Au&Wr
Blackman, Sheldon 1935- *ConAu 33*
Blackman, Victor 1922- *WrD 1976*
Blackman, William Fremont 1855-1932 *BiDSA,
  DcAmA, DcNAA*
Blackmar, Armand E *ChPo S1*
Blackmar, Beatrice *AmA&B*
Blackmar, Frank Wilson 1854-1931 *DcAmA,
  DcNAA, WhWNAA*
Blackmer, Donald L M 1929- *ConAu 33,
  WrD 1976*
Blackmer, P W *ChPo S1*

Blackmon, C Robert 1925- *ConAu 33*
Blackmore, Anauta Ford 1890?-1965
  IndAu 1917
Blackmore, Carl 1904-1965 *AmSCAP 66*
Blackmore, Dorothy S *ConAu 41*
Blackmore, Fred *MnBBF*
Blackmore, John *Alli, Alli Sup*
Blackmore, John T 1931- *ConAu 41*
Blackmore, Peter 1909- *Au&Wr, ConAu 9R*
Blackmore, R W *Alli*
Blackmore, Sir Richard 1650?-1729 *Alli,
  BiD&SB, BrAu, CasWL, ChPo S1,
  Chmbr 1, DcEnL, DcLEnL, EvLB,
  NewC, OxEng, Pen Eng*
Blackmore, Richard Doddridge 1825-1900
  *Alli Sup, BbD, BiD&SB, BrAu 19, ChPo,
  ChPo S1, ChPo S2, Chmbr 3, CyWA,
  DcBiA, DcEnA, DcEnA Ap, DcEnL,
  DcEuL, DcLEnL, EvLB, JBA 1934,
  MouLC 4, NewC, OxEng, Pen Eng,
  REn, WebEAL*
Blackmore, Robert Long 1919- *Au&Wr*
Blackmore, Simon Augustine 1849?-1926
  AmLY, DcNAA, OhA&B
Blackmore, Thomas *BiDLA*
Blackmore, William *Alli Sup*
Blackmur, Richard Palmer 1904-1965 *AmA&B,
  CasWL, CnDAL, ConAu 25, ConAu P-1,
  ConLC 2, DcLEnL, EncWL, EvLB,
  LongC, ModAL, ModAL Sup, OxAm,
  Pen Am, RAdv 1, REn, REnAL, SixAP,
  TwCA, TwCA Sup, TwCW, WebEAL*
Blackoff, Edward M 1934- *ConAu 9R*
Blackrie, Alexander *Alli*
Blackshear, E J *BlkAW*
Blackshear, Helen F 1911- *ConAu 25*
Blackson, Lorenzo Dow 1817- *BlkAW*
Blackstock, Charity 1888- *Au&Wr, TwCW,
  WrD 1976*
Blackstock, Edward *Alli Sup*
Blackstock, Paul W 1913- *ConAu 13R*
Blackstock, Walter 1917- *ChPo, ConAu 5R*
Blackstone, Frederick Charles *Alli Sup*
Blackstone, Geoffrey Vaughan 1910- *Au&Wr,
  ConAu P-1*
Blackstone, Henry *Alli*
Blackstone, Jo *Alli*
Blackstone, Milton 1894- *WhWNAA*
Blackstone, Tessa 1942- *Au&Wr, WrD 1976*
Blackstone, Sir William 1723-1780 *Alli, AtlBL,
  BiD&SB, BrAu, CasWL, ChPo,
  Chmbr 2, DcEnA, DcEnL, EvLB, NewC,
  OxEng, REn*
Blackstone, William T 1931- *ConAu 17R*
Blackton, Jay S 1909- *AmSCAP 66*
Blackwall, Anthony 1674-1730 *Alli*
Blackwall, John 1790-1881 *Alli Sup*
Blackwall, Jonathan *Alli, BiDLA*
Blackwelder, Bernice Fowler 1902- *ConAu 1R*
Blackwelder, Boyce W 1913- *ConAu 17R*
Blackwelder, Eliot 1880- *WhWNAA*
Blackwell, Alex d1747 *Alli*
Blackwell, Alice Stone 1857-1950 *AmA&B,
  ChPo S1, TwCA, TwCA Sup,
  WhWNAA*
Blackwell, Anna *Alli Sup, ChPo S2*
Blackwell, Antoinette Louisa 1825-1921
  *Alli Sup, BbD, BiD&SB, DcAmA,
  DcNAA*
Blackwell, Betsy Talbot *AmA&B*
Blackwell, Bonnie *TexWr*
Blackwell, David 1919- *LivBA*
Blackwell, Dorothy F *BlkAW*
Blackwell, Elidad *Alli*
Blackwell, Elizabeth *Alli*
Blackwell, Elizabeth 1813-1897 *OhA&B*
Blackwell, Elizabeth 1821-1911? *Alli, Alli Sup,
  BiD&SB, DcAmA, DcNAA, OhA&B*
Blackwell, Ernest *Alli Sup*
Blackwell, George 1545-1612 *Alli*
Blackwell, George Lincoln 1861- *AmLY*
Blackwell, Henry *Alli*
Blackwell, Henry Brown 1825-1909 *OhA&B*
Blackwell, James *BlkAW*
Blackwell, James DeRuyter *Alli Sup, BiDSA*
Blackwell, John *Alli, WrD 1976*
Blackwell, Leslie 1885- *Au&Wr, ConAu 9R*
Blackwell, Louise 1919- *ConAu 37*

Blackwell, R *Alli Sup*
Blackwell, Sir Ralph *Alli*
Blackwell, Richard Joseph 1929- *ConAu 33, WrD 1976*
Blackwell, Robert *Alli, ChPo S1*
Blackwell, Robert Edward *Alli Sup*
Blackwell, Robert Emory 1854- *BiDSA*
Blackwell, Robert S 1823-1863 *Alli Sup, DcNAA*
Blackwell, Samuel *Alli*
Blackwell, Sarah Ellen 1828- *DcNAA*
Blackwell, Thomas d1728 *Alli*
Blackwell, Thomas 1701-1757 *Alli, DcEnL, NewC*
Blackwell, W H *Alli Sup*
Blackwell, William L 1929- *ConAu 23*
Blackwood, Mrs. *ChPo S1*
Blackwood, Adam 1539-1613 *Alli, DcEnL, NewC*
Blackwood, Alexander Leslie 1862-1924 *DcNAA*
Blackwood, Algernon 1869-1951 *ChPo, ChPo S1, Chmbr 3, DcLEnL, EncM&D, EvLB, LongC, NewC, Pen Eng, REn, TwCA, TwCA Sup, TwCW*
Blackwood, Lady Alicia 1818- *Alli Sup*
Blackwood, Andrew W 1882- *ConAu 5R*
Blackwood, Andrew W, Jr. 1915- *ConAu 1R, WrD 1976*
Blackwood, Basil T *ChPo*
Blackwood, Caroline 1931- *ConLC 6*
Blackwood, Christopher *Alli*
Blackwood, Easley 1903- *IndAu 1917*
Blackwood, Sir F T Hamilton-Temple- 1826- *Alli Sup*
Blackwood, Frederick H *BrAu 19*
Blackwood, George D 1919- *ConAu 13R*
Blackwood, Granby 1921- *BlkAW*
Blackwood, Helen Selina *BrAu 19*
Blackwood, Henry d1634 *Alli*
Blackwood, Henry 1526?-1614? *Alli*
Blackwood, James R 1918- *ConAu 23*
Blackwood, James Stevenson 1805-1882 *Alli Sup, PoIre*
Blackwood, John 1818-1879 *NewC*
Blackwood, Stevenson Arthur *Alli Sup*
Blackwood, Thomas *BbtC*
Blackwood, W S *Alli Sup*
Blackwood, William *MnBBF*
Blackwood, William 1776-1834 *ChPo, ChPo S2, NewC*
Blackwood, William 1804- *Alli Sup*
Blacow, Richard *Alli, BiDLA, BiDLA Sup*
Blade, James P 1907- *AmSCAP 66*
Bladen, Elizabeth S *Alli Sup*
Bladen, Martin d1746 *Alli*
Bladen, Thomas *Alli*
Bladen, V W 1900- *ConAu 61*
Blades, Ann *OxCan Sup*
Blades, James 1901- *Au&Wr, WrD 1976*
Blades, R H *Alli Sup*
Blades, William 1824-1890 *Alli Sup, ChPo, ChPo S1, DcEnL*
Bladow, Suzanne Wilson 1937- *ConAu 61*
Blaffer, Sarah C 1946- *ConAu 41*
Blaga, Lucian 1895-1961 *CasWL, CnMD, EncWL, Pen Eur*
Blagden, Sir Charles 1748-1820 *Alli*
Blagden, Cyprian 1906-1962 *ConAu 1R*
Blagden, David 1944- *ConAu 53*
Blagden, Francis William *BiDLA*
Blagden, Mrs. George *Alli Sup*
Blagden, Henry Charles *Alli Sup*
Blagden, Isabella 1816-1873 *Alli Sup, REn*
Blagden, Silliman 1846-1907 *DcNAA*
Blagdon, Francis William *Alli*
Blage, Thomas *Alli*
Blagg, Charles John 1832-1915 *Br&AmS*
Blagg, J W *Alli Sup*
Blagg, Michael Ward *Alli Sup*
Blagrave, J *Alli, BiDLA*
Blagrave, Sir John *Alli*
Blagrave, John d1611 *Alli*
Blagrave, Jonathan *Alli*
Blagrave, Joseph 1610-1679 *Alli*
Blagrave, Samuel *Alli*
Blagrove, G H *Alli Sup*
Blaher, Damian J 1913- *ConAu 21*

Blahoslav, Jan 1523-1571 *CasWL*
Blaich, H E *OxGer*
Blaich, Lydia Rebecca 1870-1933 *IndAu 1816*
Blaich, Theodore Paul 1902- *ConAu P-1*
Blaikie, Alexander *Alli Sup*
Blaikie, Francis *Alli*
Blaikie, James Andrew *Alli Sup*
Blaikie, John *Alli Sup*
Blaikie, John A And Gosse, Edmund W *Alli Sup*
Blaikie, John Arthur *ChPo*
Blaikie, Margaret *ChPo, ChPo S1*
Blaikie, Robert Henry *Alli Sup*
Blaikie, Robert Jackson 1923- *Au&Wr, ConAu 33*
Blaikie, William 1843-1904 *Alli Sup, BiD&SB, DcAmA, DcNAA*
Blaikie, William Garden 1820- *Alli Sup*
Blaikley, Ernest *MnBBF*
Blaiklock, Edward Musgrave 1903- *Au&Wr, ConAu 17R, MnBBF*
Blaiklock, George 1856- *WhLA*
Blain, W *MnBBF*
Blain DeSaint Aubin, Emm 1833- *BbtC*
Blaine, Delabere P 1800?- *Alli, BiDLA, Br&AmS*
Blaine, Delabere Roberton *Alli Sup*
Blaine, Eleanor *HsB&A*
Blaine, Harry G 1858-1930 *OhA&B*
Blaine, James Gillespie 1830-1893 *Alli Sup, AmA&B, BbD, BiD&SB, DcAmA, DcNAA, DcSpL, OxAm, REn, REnAL, WrD 1976*
Blaine, John *ConAu XR, SmATA 6*
Blaine, John, Jr. 1910- *TexAW*
Blaine, Margery Kay 1937- *ConAu 61*
Blaine, Robert Gordon *Alli Sup*
Blainey, Ann 1935- *ConAu 25*
Blainey, Geoffery Norman 1930- *Au&Wr, ConAu 25, WrD 1976*
Blair 1930- *ConAu XR*
Blair, Major *Alli*
Blair, Mrs. *Alli Sup*
Blair, Allan *MnBBF*
Blair, Andrew Alexander 1846-1932 *Alli Sup, BiDSA, DcAmA*
Blair, Andrew Alexander 1848-1932 *DcNAA*
Blair, Anthony *MnBBF*
Blair, Arthur *Au&Wr*
Blair, Brice *Alli*
Blair, Calvin Patton 1924- *ConAu 13R*
Blair, Carvel Hall 1924- *ConAu 49*
Blair, Charles *Alli Sup*
Blair, Charles E 1920- *ConAu 25*
Blair, Claude 1922- *Au&Wr, ConAu 5R, WrD 1976*
Blair, Clay, Jr. 1925- *AmA&B, AuNews 2*
Blair, D B *BbtC*
Blair, D Oswald Hunter *Alli Sup*
Blair, Daniel *Alli*
Blair, David *Alli, Alli Sup*
Blair, David 1768-1840 *DcEnL*
Blair, Dike 1919- *ConAu 9R*
Blair, Donald 1906- *Au&Wr*
Blair, Dorothy Sara 1913- *Au&Wr, WhWNAA, WrD 1976*
Blair, Duncan B 1815-1891 *DcNAA*
Blair, Edward *MnBBF*
Blair, Edward H 1938- *ConAu 17R*
Blair, Edward Payson 1910- *ConAu P-1*
Blair, Edward Tyler 1857-1939 *DcNAA*
Blair, Eliza 1859-1907 *DcAmA, DcNAA*
Blair, Emily Newell 1877- *WhWNAA*
Blair, Emma Helen d1911 *DcNAA*
Blair, Eric Arthur 1903-1950 *DcLEnL, EvLB, LongC, NewC, OxEng, Pen Eng, REn, WebEAL*
Blair, Erskine *MnBBF*
Blair, Ethel *ChPo*
Blair, Everetta Love 1907- *ConAu 25*
Blair, Francis Preston 1792-1876 *BiDSA*
Blair, Francis Preston 1821-1875 *BiDSA*
Blair, George S 1924- *ConAu 17R, WrD 1976*
Blair, Glenn Myers 1908- *ConAu 5R, WrD 1976*
Blair, Hal 1915- *AmSCAP 66*
Blair, Helen 1910- *IlBYP, IlCB 1956*
Blair, Henry William 1834-1920 *Alli Sup,*

DcAmA, DcNAA
Blair, Hugh 1718-1800 *Alli, BiD&SB, BrAu, CasWL, Chmbr 2, DcEnL, EvLB, NewC, Pen Eng, WebEAL*
Blair, James 1655?-1743 *Alli, AmA, AmA&B, BiDSA, CyAL 1, DcAmA, OxAm, REnAL*
Blair, James Law 1826-1881 *ChPo S1*
Blair, James R 1897- *WhWNAA*
Blair, James Stanley 1906- *Au&Wr*
Blair, Jane N 1911- *ConAu 57*
Blair, John *Alli, CyAL 1*
Blair, John d1771 *Alli*
Blair, John d1782 *Alli, DcEnL*
Blair, John 1818-1889 *ChPo S1*
Blair, John G 1934- *ConAu 13R*
Blair, John Paul *BlkAW*
Blair, Kay Kimery Reynolds 1942- *ConAu 33, WrD 1976*
Blair, L H *Alli Sup*
Blair, Leon Borden 1917- *ConAu 29*
Blair, Lucile *ConAu XR*
Blair, Mary Robinson 1911- *IlCB 1956*
Blair, Patrick d1728? *Alli*
Blair, Paxton 1892-1974 *ConAu 53*
Blair, Philip M 1928- *ConAu 41*
Blair, David 1768-1840 *DcEnL*
Blair, Robert *Alli, Chmbr 2, DcEnL*
Blair, Robert 1593-1666 *Alli*
Blair, Robert 1699-1746 *Alli, BiD&SB, BrAu, CasWL, ChPo, ChPo S2, DcEnL, DcEuL, DcLEnL, EvLB, NewC, OxEng, Pen Eng, WebEAL*
Blair, Sir Robert 1859- *WhLA*
Blair, Robert Dike 1919- *ConAu 17*
Blair, Robert Hugh *Alli Sup*
Blair, Ruth VanNess 1912- *ConAu 21, WrD 1976*
Blair, Sam 1932- *ConAu 53*
Blair, Samuel 1712-1751 *Alli, CyAL 1, DcNAA*
Blair, Samuel 1741-1818 *Alli*
Blair, Stephen *ChPo*
Blair, Sylvia *WhWNAA*
Blair, Thomas Stewart 1867-1939 *DcNAA*
Blair, Vilray Papin 1871- *WhWNAA*
Blair, Walter 1835-1909 *Alli Sup, DcNAA*
Blair, Walter 1900- *AmA&B, AuBYP, ChPo, ConAu 5R, REnAL, WrD 1976*
Blair, Walter Acheson 1856-1931? *DcNAA*
Blair, Wilfrid *ConAu XR*
Blair, William *Alli, Alli Sup, BiDLA, ChPo S1*
Blair, William 1765-1822 *Alli*
Blair, William 1782-1852? *DcNAA*
Blair, William Allen 1859- *BiDSA, WhWNAA*
Blair, William R 1874- *WhWNAA*
Blair-Fish, Wallace Wilfrid 1889-1968 *ChPo, ChPo S1, ConAu 29*
Blairman, Jacqueline *WrD 1976*
Blais, Andre *OxCan Sup*
Blais, Marie-Claire 1939- *CanWr, CasWL, ConAu 21, ConLC 2, ConLC 4, ConLC 6, OxCan, OxCan Sup, WorAu*
Blais, Martin *OxCan Sup*
Blaisdell, Mrs. A H *Alli Sup*
Blaisdell, Albert Franklin 1847-1927 *Alli Sup, DcAmA, DcNAA*
Blaisdell, Anne *ConAu XR, EncM&D*
Blaisdell, Donald Christy 1899- *AmA&B, ConAu 37*
Blaisdell, E Warde *ChPo, ChPo S1*
Blaisdell, Elijah Whittier 1825-1900 *DcNAA*
Blaisdell, Elinore 1904- *IlBYP, IlCB 1945, IlCB 1956*
Blaisdell, F A *ChPo*
Blaisdell, Frank Ellsworth, Sr. 1862- *WhWNAA*
Blaisdell, Paul H 1908- *ConAu 61*
Blaisdell, Thomas Charles 1867- *AmLY, WhWNAA*
Blaise, Lord *Alli*
Blaise, Clark 1940- *AuNews 2, ConAu 53, OxCan Sup*
Blake *Alli*
Blake, Lady *Alli Sup*
Blake, Mister *BiDLA*
Blake, A Harold 1896- *WhWNAA*
Blake, Alfred *ConAu XR*

Blake, Andrew *Alli, ConAu XR*
Blake, Barnett *Alli Sup*
Blake, Bebe 1925- *AmSCAP 66*
Blake, Bernard *MnBBF*
Blake, Brian 1918- *WrD 1976*
Blake, C J *ChPo, ChPo S2, MnBBF*
Blake, Caroline L *Alli Sup*
Blake, Cecilia *Alli Sup*
Blake, Charles *Alli, Alli Sup, PoIre*
Blake, Charles A *ChPo S2*
Blake, Charles Carter *Alli Sup*
Blake, Charles W *Alli Sup*
Blake, Clarence E *Alli Sup*
Blake, Clarence John 1843-1919 *DcNAA*
Blake, Clarice 1894- *WhWNAA*
Blake, David H 1940- *ConAu 41*
Blake, Dinny *PoIre*
Blake, Dominick T d1839 *DcNAA*
Blake, Douglas *ChPo*
Blake, E C 1912- *Au&Wr*
Blake, Mrs. E Vale *Alli Sup*
Blake, E Vinton *ChPo*
Blake, Edith *Alli Sup*
Blake, Edward *Alli*
Blake, Edward 1833-1912 *OxCan*
Blake, Edward Thomas *Alli Sup*
Blake, Eleanor 1899- *WhWNAA*
Blake, Eli Whitney 1795-1886 *Alli Sup, DcNAA*
Blake, Elizabeth 1770?- *PoIre*
Blake, Emilia Aylmer *Alli Sup, PoIre*
Blake, Emily Calvin *AmA&B, WhWNAA*
Blake, Emma M *ChPo*
Blake, Eubie 1883- *AmSCAP 66*
Blake, Euphemia 1817?-1904 *DcAmA, DcNAA*
Blake, Fay M 1920- *ConAu 53*
Blake, Francis *Alli*
Blake, Sir Francis *Alli, BiDLA*
Blake, Francis Everett 1839-1916 *DcNAA*
Blake, Frank Ringgold 1875- *WhWNAA*
Blake, Frederick Hyde *Au&Wr*
Blake, G T *Alli Sup*
Blake, George *Alli, BiDLA*
Blake, George 1893-1961 *CasWL, EvLB, LongC, NewC, Pen Eng, TwCA, TwCA Sup, TwCW*
Blake, George 1917-1955 *AmSCAP 66*
Blake, George M 1912- *AmSCAP 66*
Blake, Gladys *AmA&B, WhWNAA*
Blake, H J C *Alli*
Blake, Harlan Morse 1923- *ConAu 25*
Blake, Harrison Gray Otis 1816-1898 *AmA, OxAm, REnAL*
Blake, Henry Arthur *Alli Sup*
Blake, Henry Nichols 1838-1933 *Alli Sup, DcNAA*
Blake, Henry Taylor 1828-1922 *DcNAA*
Blake, Henry William 1865-1929 *DcNAA*
Blake, Israel George 1902- *ConAu 21, IndAu 1917*
Blake, J *Alli, BiDLA*
Blake, James *Alli, BlkAW*
Blake, James d1771 *Alli*
Blake, James Henry 1845- *WhWNAA*
Blake, James L *Alli Sup*
Blake, James S *PoIre*
Blake, James Vila 1842-1925 *Alli Sup, AmA&B, AmLY, BiD&SB, ChPo, ChPo S1, DcAmA, DcNAA*
Blake, James W 1862-1935 *AmSCAP 66, ChPo S1*
Blake, James Washington *DrAP 1975*
Blake, John *Alli*
Blake, John Frederick *Alli Sup*
Blake, John Lauris 1788-1857 *Alli, AmA, AmA&B, ChPo, DcAmA, DcNAA*
Blake, John Y Fillmore 1856-1907 *DcNAA*
Blake, Jonas 1910- *ConAu XR*
Blake, Jonathan 1780-1864 *Alli Sup, DcNAA*
Blake, Joseph Augustus 1864-1937 *DcNAA*
Blake, Judith 1926- *ConAu 1R*
Blake, Justin *WrD 1976*
Blake, Katherine *ConAu XR*
Blake, Katherine 1859- *DcNAA*
Blake, Kathleen 1944- *ConAu 57*
Blake, Kay *ConAu XR*
Blake, L H *Alli Sup*

Blake, Leslie James 1913- *Au&Wr, ConAu 25*
Blake, Lillie Devereux Umstead 1835-1913 *Alli Sup, AmA, AmA&B, BbD, BiD&SB, BiDSA, DcAmA, DcNAA, HsB&A, HsB&A Sup*
Blake, Louise Demaresque *ChPo S1*
Blake, Lucien Ira 1852-1916 *DcNAA*
Blake, Lucius O'Brien *Alli Sup*
Blake, Malachi d1760 *Alli*
Blake, Margaret *DcNAA*
Blake, Marian *ChPo S2*
Blake, Mark *Alli, BiDLA*
Blake, Martin *Alli*
Blake, Mary Elizabeth McGrath 1840-1907 *Alli Sup, AmA, AmA&B, BbD, BiD&SB, ChPo, ChPo S2, DcAmA, DcNAA, PoIre*
Blake, Mary Katharine Evans 1859-1923 *IndAu 1816*
Blake, Maurice Adin 1882- *WhWNAA*
Blake, Monica *ConAu XR*
Blake, Mortimer 1813-1884 *Alli Sup, DcNAA*
Blake, Myrtle Ann 1906- *AmSCAP 66*
Blake, Nelson Manfred 1908- *Au&Wr, ConAu 1R*
Blake, Nicholas 1904-1972 *ConAu XR, ConLC 1, ConNov 1972, DcLEnL, EncM&D, EvLB, LongC, NewC, PoIre, REn, TwCA, TwCA Sup, TwCW, WhTwL*
Blake, Norman Francis 1934- *Au&Wr, WrD 1976*
Blake, Patricia 1933- *ConAu 49*
Blake, Paul *Alli Sup, ChPo, ChPo S1, ChPo S2, MnBBF*
Blake, Paul C 1916- *ConAu 25*
Blake, Peter Jost 1920- *AmA&B*
Blake, Quentin 1932- *ChPo S1, ConAu 25, IlBYP, IlCB 1966, SmATA 9*
Blake, Redmond *HsB&A*
Blake, Reed H 1933- *ConAu 57*
Blake, Robert *Alli, Alli Sup, BiDLA, ConAu XR, MnBBF, PoIre*
Blake, Robert Howarth *Alli Sup*
Blake, Robert Norman William 1916- *Au&Wr, ConAu 9R, WorAu, WrD 1976*
Blake, Robert R 1918- *ConAu 23*
Blake, Robert W 1930- *ConAu 33*
Blake, Rodney *ChPo, DcNAA*
Blake, Royston *MnBBF*
Blake, S Leroy *Alli Sup*
Blake, Sally Mirliss 1925- *ConAu 17R, WrD 1976*
Blake, Samuel *Alli Sup*
Blake, Sexton *MnBBF*
Blake, Silas Leroy 1834-1902 *DcNAA*
Blake, Sophia Jex- *Alli Sup*
Blake, Stacey 1878-1964 *MnBBF*
Blake, Stephen *Alli*
Blake, T C *Alli Sup, BiDSA*
Blake, Thaddeus C *DcNAA*
Blake, Thomas 1597-1657 *Alli*
Blake, Thomas William Jex- 1832- *Alli Sup*
Blake, Vernon 1875- *WhLA*
Blake, Verschoyle B *OxCan Sup*
Blake, W *BiDLA*
Blake, W A *Alli Sup*
Blake, W W *Alli Sup*
Blake, Walker E *ConAu XR*
Blake, Walter E *SmATA 5*
Blake, William *Alli*
Blake, William 1757-1827 *Alli, AnCL, AtlBL, BbD, BiD&SB, BiDLA, BkIE, BrAu 19, CarSB, CasWL, ChPo, ChPo S1, ChPo S2, Chmbr 2, CnE&AP, CriT 2, CyWA, DcEnA, DcEnA Ap, DcEnL, DcEuL, DcLEnL, EvLB, MouLC 3, NewC, OxEng, Pen Eng, RAdv 1, RCom, REn, St&VC, WebEAL*
Blake, William Hume 1861-1924 *BbtC, CanWr, DcLEnL, DcNAA, OxCan*
Blake, William J *DcNAA*
Blake, William J 1894-1968 *ConAu 5R, ConAu 25*
Blake, William O *Alli Sup, DcNAA*
Blake, William P *Alli Sup*
Blake, William Phipps 1826-1910 *Alli Sup, DcAmA, DcNAA*

Blake, Wilson Wilberforce 1850-1918 *DcNAA*
Blake, Wilton *MnBBF, WhCL*
Blake, Winifred Ballard *ChPo*
Blake-Forster *Alli Sup*
Blakeborough, John Fairfax- 1883- *Br&AmS*
Blakelee, G E *Alli Sup*
Blakeley, All Etheered *BlkAW*
Blakeley, Henry *BlkAW*
Blakeley, Nora *BlkAW*
Blakeley, Peggy *ChPo S2*
Blakeley, Phyllis 1922- *ConAu 61, OxCan*
Blakeley, Thomas J 1931- *ConAu 9R*
Blakelock, Denys Martin 1901- *Au&Wr*
Blakelock, Ralph Albert 1847-1919 *OxAm*
Blakely *PoIre*
Blakely, Abram *Alli Sup*
Blakely, Edward T *Alli Sup*
Blakely, F Ray 1891?- *IndAu 1917*
Blakely, John *Alli Sup*
Blakely, Paul Lendrum 1880-1943 *CatA 1947, DcNAA*
Blakely, R J 1915- *ConAu 37*
Blakely, Sue *Alli Sup*
Blakely, Theophilus Alexander *Alli Sup*
Blakely, Ulysses Simpson Grant 1868- *WhWNAA*
Blakely, William Addison *Alli Sup*
Blakeman, Bessie C *Alli Sup*
Blakeman, E D *Alli Sup*
Blakeman, Phineas 1813-1870 *Alli Sup, DcNAA*
Blakeman, Rufus d1848 *DcNAA*
Blakeman, Rufus 1813-1870 *DcNAA*
Blakemore, Trevor Ramsay Villiers *ChPo S1, ChPo S2*
Blakeney, Edward Henry 1869- *ChPo, ChPo S1, ChPo S2, WhLA*
Blakeney, Mrs. Henry L *ChPo*
Blakeney, L *Alli, BiDLA Sup*
Blakeney, Richard Paul 1820-1884 *Alli, Alli Sup*
Blakeney, William *Alli Sup*
Blaker, Richard 1893-1940 *NewC, TwCA*
Blaker, Thomas Frederick Isaacson *Alli Sup*
Blakeslee, Erastus 1838-1908 *DcNAA*
Blakeslee, Fred Gilbert 1868- *WhWNAA*
Blakeslee, George Hubbard 1871-1954 *AmA&B*
Blakeslee, S V *Alli Sup*
Blakeslee, Victor Franklin 1898-1947 *DcNAA*
Blakesley, Joseph Williams 1808-1885 *Alli Sup, DcEnL*
Blakesley, Stephen *MnBBF*
Blakeway, John Brickdale 1765-1826 *Alli, BiDLA*
Blakeway, Robert *Alli*
Blakey *Alli, BiDLA*
Blakey, Nicholas *BkIE*
Blakey, Robert 1795-1878 *Alli, Alli Sup, DcEnL*
Blakey, Roy Gillispie 1880- *WhWNAA*
Blakey, William *Alli*
Blakiston, E F *Alli Sup*
Blakiston, Herbert Edward Douglas 1862- *WhLA*
Blakiston, John Richard *Alli Sup*
Blakiston, Noel 1905- *Au&Wr*
Blakiston, Perry *Alli*
Blakiston, Peyton *Alli Sup*
Blakiston, Thomas Wright *Alli Sup*
Blakston, W, Swaysland, W & Wiener, A F *Alli Sup*
Blakwell, Alexander *Alli*
Blalock, Grover Cleveland 1884- *WhWNAA*
Blalock, Hubert Morse, Jr. 1926- *ConAu 13R*
Blaman, Anna 1905-1960 *CasWL, EncWL*
Blamford, Samuel *Alli*
Blamire, Susanna 1747-1794 *Alli, CasWL, ChPo, ChPo S1, Chmbr 2, DcEnL, DcLEnL, EvLB, NewC*
Blamires, Harry 1916- *Au&Wr, ConAu 9R, WrD 1976*
Blanc, Charles 1813-1882 *BbD, BiD&SB*
Blanc, Henry *Alli Sup*
Blanc, L *Alli Sup*
Blanc, Louis 1811-1882 *OxFr, REn*
Blanc, Mel J 1908- *AmSCAP 66*
Blanc, Suzanne *WhPNW*
Blance, Ellen 1931- *ConAu 57*

Blanch, Gustavus W *Alli Sup*
Blanch, Josephine Mildred *WhWNAA*
Blanch, Lesley 1907- *Au&Wr, WrD 1976*
Blanch, Robert J 1938- *ConAu 21*
Blanch, William Harnett *Alli Sup*
Blanchan, Neltze *AmA&B*
Blanchard, Amos 1800-1869 *DcNAA*
Blanchard, Amy Ella 1856-1926 *BiD&SB,
    BiDSA, CarSB, ChPo, ChPo S1,
    ChPo S2, DcAmA, DcNAA*
Blanchard, Arthur Alphonzo 1876- *WhWNAA*
Blanchard, B Everard 1909- *ConAu 41*
Blanchard, Calvin *Alli Sup, DcNAA*
Blanchard, Caroline *ChPo*
Blanchard, Carroll Henry, Jr. 1928-
    ConAu 13R
Blanchard, Charles Albert 1814-1925 *DcNAA*
Blanchard, Charles Elton 1868-1945 *OhA&B*
Blanchard, Edith Richmond *ChPo*
Blanchard, Edward Litt Laman 1820-1889
    *Alli Sup, BiD&SB, BrAu 19, ChPo,
    Chmbr 3, DcEnL, NewC*
Blanchard, Ferdinand Quincy 1876- *OhA&B,
    WhWNAA*
Blanchard, Fessenden Seaver 1888-1963
    ConAu 5R
Blanchard, Frank LeRoy 1858-1936 *DcNAA,
    WhWNAA*
Blanchard, Frank Nelson 1888-1937 *DcNAA,
    WhWNAA*
Blanchard, Frederic Thomas 1878-1947
    AmA&B, DcNAA, WhWNAA
Blanchard, G *ChPo*
Blanchard, George A And Weeks, Edward P
    Alli Sup
Blanchard, Grace d1944 *DcNAA, WhWNAA*
Blanchard, Henry Percy 1862-1939 *DcNAA*
Blanchard, Howard L 1909- *ConAu 5R,
    WrD 1976*
Blanchard, J H *BiDLA*
Blanchard, Jonathan 1811-1892 *DcNAA,
    OhA&B*
Blanchard, Joseph-Henri *OxCan*
Blanchard, Joshua Pollard *Alli Sup*
Blanchard, Jotham 1800-1840 *BbtC, OxCan*
Blanchard, Julian 1885- *WhWNAA*
Blanchard, Laman 1804?-1845 *Alli, BrAu 19,
    Chmbr 3, DcEnL*
Blanchard, Lucy Mansfield 1869-1927 *DcNAA,
    OhA&B, WhWNAA*
Blanchard, M E *Alli Sup*
Blanchard, Orlando 1801- *DcNAA*
Blanchard, Peter *BiDLA*
Blanchard, Phyllis 1895- *WhWNAA*
Blanchard, Ralph Harrub 1890-1973 *ConAu P-1,
    WhWNAA*
Blanchard, Rufus 1821-1904 *Alli Sup, DcAmA,
    DcNAA*
Blanchard, Samuel Laman 1804-1845 *ChPo,
    NewC*
Blanchard, Sidney Laman 1825?- *Alli Sup*
Blanchard, W J *Alli*
Blanchard, William G 1905- *AmSCAP 66*
Blanchard, William Henry 1922- *ConAu 23,
    WrD 1976*
Blanchard, William Martin 1874-1942 *DcNAA*
Blanchard, William Martin 1874- *WhWNAA*
Blanchard, William Oscar 1886- *WhWNAA*
Blanchard, William Stinson 1813-1896 *DcNAA*
Blanchard And Ramsay *BiDLA*
Blanche, August Theodor 1811-1868 *BiD&SB,
    CasWL, EvEuW*
Blanche, Jacques-Emile 1861-1942 *OxFr*
Blanche, John F *Alli Sup*
Blanche, Pierre 1927- *ConAu 25*
Blanchefleur *REn*
Blancheflor *REn*
Blanchet, Clement Theophilus 1845- *WhWNAA*
Blanchet, Eileen 1924- *ConAu 57*
Blanchet, Francois Norbert 1795-1883 *DcNAA*
Blanchet, Francois Xavier 1776-1830 *BbtC,
    DcNAA*
Blanchet, Francois Xavier 1835-1906 *DcNAA*
Blanchet, Guy *OxCan*
Blanchet, John Baptiste 1856- *WhWNAA*
Blanchet, M Wylie *OxCan*
Blanchette, Oliva 1929- *ConAu 53*
Blanchot, Maurice 1907- *CasWL, EncWL,*

Pen Eur, WorAu
Blanck, Jacob Nathaniel 1906-1974 *AmA&B,
    ConAu 53, ConAu P-1, OxAm*
Blanck, Rubin 1914- *ConAu 25*
Blanckenburg, Christian Friedrich Von
    1744-1796 *OxGer*
Blanckenhorn, Max 1894- *WhLA*
Blanckensee, Irma *ChPo S1*
Blanckley, T R *Alli*
Blanco, Antonio Nicolas 1887-1945 *PueRA*
Blanco, Jeronimo *DrAP 1975*
Blanco, Richard L 1926- *ConAu 57*
Blanco, Tomas 1900- *PueRA*
Blanco Fombona, Rufino 1874-1944 *CasWL,
    DcSpL, Pen Am, REn*
Blanco White, Jose Maria 1775-1841 *CasWL,
    DcSpL, EvEuW*
Blanco White, Joseph 1775-1841 *EuA, Pen Eur*
Blancpain, Marc 1909- *CasWL*
Bland, Alden *BlkAW*
Bland, David Farrant d1970 *ChPo S2*
Bland, Doreen *ChPo*
Bland, Edith Nesbit 1858-1924 *AuBYP, ChPo,
    ChPo S1, ChPo S2, EvLB, JBA 1934,
    NewC, TwCA, TwCA Sup, YABC 1*
Bland, Edwarde *Alli*
Bland, Elizabeth 1660?- *Alli*
Bland, F *Alli Sup*
Bland, Fabian *LongC, YABC 1*
Bland, Harcourt *Alli Sup*
Bland, Henry Meade 1863-1931 *ChPo S1,
    DcNAA*
Bland, Hester Beth 1906- *ConAu 57*
Bland, Hubert 1856-1914 *LongC, NewC*
Bland, Mrs. Hubert *LongC*
Bland, Humphrey *Alli*
Bland, J *Alli, Alli Sup, BiDLA*
Bland, James A 1854-1911 *ChPo, ChPo S2,
    OxAm, REnAL*
Bland, Jennifer 1925- *ConAu XR, WrD 1976*
Bland, John *Alli, Alli Sup*
Bland, John Otway Percy 1863- *WhLA*
Bland, Lizzie *NewC*
Bland, M *Alli*
Bland, Miles Carlisle 1875-1926 *DcNAA*
Bland, Pascal Brooke 1875-1940 *DcNAA*
Bland, Peter *Alli*
Bland, Peter 1934- *ChPo S2, ConP 1970*
Bland, Philip *Alli*
Bland, R *BiDLA*
Bland, Randall Walton 1942- *ConAu 53*
Bland, Richard 1710-1776? *Alli, BiDSA,
    CyAL 1, OxAm*
Bland, Richard Parks 1835-1899 *BiDSA*
Bland, Robert *Alli, BiDLA, BiDLA Sup*
Bland, Robert 1779-1825 *Alli*
Bland, Salem Goldworth 1859- *WhWNAA*
Bland, T A *Alli Sup*
Bland, Theodoric *Alli*
Bland, Theodoric 1742-1790 *Alli, BiDSA,
    CyAL 1*
Bland, Thomas *Alli*
Bland, Thomas Augustus 1830- *DcNAA,
    IndAu 1816*
Bland, Tobie *Alli*
Bland, William *Alli Sup*
Bland, William, Jr. *Alli*
Bland-Sutton, Sir John 1855- *WhLA*
Blanden, Charles Granger 1857-1933 *Alli Sup,
    AmLY, AnMV 1926, ChPo, ChPo S2,
    DcNAA*
Blandford, George Fielding *Alli Sup*
Blandford, Gladys Winifred 1908- *Au&Wr*
Blandford, Percy William 1912- *Au&Wr,
    ConAu 9R, WrD 1976*
Blandie, William *Alli*
Blandin, Mrs. I M E *BiDSA*
Blanding, Donald Benson 1894-1957 *AmA&B,
    ChPo, WhWNAA*
Blandino, Giovanni 1923- *ConAu 23*
Blandy, Adam *Alli*
Blandy, William *Alli*
Blane, Sir Gilbert 1749-1834 *Alli, BiDLA*
Blane, Howard T 1926- *ConAu 25*
Blane, Ralph 1914- *AmSCAP 66*
Blane, William *Alli, BiDLA, Br&AmS*
Blane, William 1852- *ChPo S2*
Blane, William 1858- *ChPo S1*

Blaneford, Henry Of *DcEnL*
Blaney *BbtC*
Blaney, Charles E 1875?-1944 *OhA&B*
Blaney, Henry Robertson 1855-1913? *DcNAA*
Blanford, Henry Francis *Alli Sup*
Blanford, James T 1917- *ConAu 33*
Blanford, William Thomas *Alli Sup*
Blank, Blanche D *ConAu 41*
Blank, Charlie *IndAu 1917*
Blank, Leonard 1927- *ConAu 33*
Blank, Richard 1901- *WhGrA*
Blank, Sheldon Haas 1896- *Au&Wr,
    ConAu 1R*
Blankenburg, Lucretia M 1845-1937 *DcNAA*
Blankenship, A B 1914- *ConAu 13R,
    WrD 1976*
Blankenship, Edward Gary 1943- *ConAu 45*
Blankenship, Lela 1886- *ConAu 5R*
Blankenship, William D 1934- *ConAu 33*
Blankfort, Michael 1907- *AmA&B, AmNov,
    ConAu 1R*
Blankman, Howard Milford 1925- *AmSCAP 66*
Blankner, Frederika *AmA&B, Au&Wr,
    ChPo S2, WhWNAA*
Blanksten, George I 1917- *ConAu 1R*
Blanqui, Louis Auguste 1805-1881 *OxFr, REn*
Blanshard, Brand 1892- *AmA&B, Au&Wr,
    ConAu 1R, REnAL*
Blanshard, Henry *Alli*
Blanshard, Paul 1892- *AmA&B, TwCA Sup*
Blanshard, Richard *OxCan*
Blanshard, Thomas W *Alli Sup*
Blanshard, William *Alli*
Blanton, Annie Webb d1945 *DcNAA, TexWr,
    WhWNAA*
Blanton, Catherine 1907- *AuBYP, ConAu 1R*
Blanton, Lorenzo D *BlkAW*
Blanton, Margaret Gray 1887- *WhWNAA*
Blanton, Smiley 1882-1966 *AmA&B,
    WhWNAA*
Blanton, Wyndham B 1890- *WhWNAA*
Blanzaco, Andre C 1934- *ConAu 29*
Blaquiere, Edward *Alli, BiDLA*
Blaquiere, William *Alli, BiDLA*
Blas, Ruy *WhWNAA*
Blaschke, Wilhelm 1885- *WhLA*
Blasco Ibanez, Vicente 1867-1928 *CasWL,
    ClDMEuL, CyWA, DcSpL, EncWL,
    EvEuW, ModRL, Pen Eur, REn, TwCA,
    TwCA Sup, TwCW*
Blasdale, Walter Charles 1871- *WhWNAA*
Blase, Karl Oskar 1925- *WhGrA*
Blase, Melvin G 1933- *ConAu 33, WrD 1976*
Blaser, Robin Francis 1925- *ConAu 57,
    ConP 1970, ConP 1975, WrD 1976*
Blashfield, Albert Dodd *ChPo*
Blashfield, Edwin Howland 1848-1936 *AmA&B,
    ChPo, DcAmA, DcNAA*
Blashfield, Evangeline Wilbour d1918 *AmA&B,
    DcNAA*
Blashfield, John Marriott *Alli Sup*
Blashford-Snell, John Nicholas 1936-
    WrD 1976
Blasier, Cole 1925- *ConAu 23*
Blasius, William *Alli Sup*
Blass, Birgit A 1940- *ConAu 29*
Blass, Ernst 1890-1939 *OxGer*
Blassingame, John W 1940- *ConAu 49,
    LivBAA*
Blassingame, Wyatt Rainey 1909- *AuBYP,
    ConAu 1R, SmATA 1, WrD 1976*
Blasson, M C *ChPo S2*
Blatch, Harriot Stanton 1856-1940 *DcNAA,
    OxAm, WhWNAA*
Blatch, William *Alli Sup*
Blatchford, Ambrose Nichols 1842- *ChPo*
Blatchford, Eliphalet Wickes 1826-1914 *DcNAA*
Blatchford, Robert 1851-1943 *ChPo, ChPo S1,
    LongC, NewC*
Blatchford, Samuel 1820-1893 *Alli Sup,
    DcNAA*
Blatchford, Thomas Windeatt 1794-1866
    DcNAA
Blatchford, Willis Stanley 1859-1940 *DcAmA*
Blatchley, Willis Stanley 1859-1940 *AmLY,
    DcNAA, IndAu 1816, WhWNAA*
Blatchly, A *Alli Sup*
Blatherwick, Charles *Alli Sup*

Blathwayt, Jean 1918- *Au&Wr, WrD 1976*
Blathwayt, Maggie 1841- *Alli Sup*
Blathwayt, William 1882- *ChPo S2*
Blatt, Burton 1927- *ConAu 41*
Blatt, John Markus 1921- *WrD 1976*
Blatt, Sidney J 1928- *ConAu 37*
Blatt, William Mosher 1876- *WhWNAA*
Blatter, Dorothy 1901- *ConAu P-1*
Blatter, Ethelbert 1877- *WhLA*
Blatty, William Peter 1928- *ConAu 5R, ConLC 2, WrD 1976*
Blau, Joseph L 1909- *ConAu 9R*
Blau, Joshua *ConAu 13R*
Blau, Ludwig 1861- *WhLA*
Blau, Peter Michael 1918- *AmA&B, ConAu 1R, WrD 1976*
Blau, Robert *Alli*
Blau, Sheldon Paul 1935- *ConAu 57*
Blau, Yehoshua *ConAu XR*
Blau, Zena Smith 1922- *ConAu 45*
Blaufuss, Walter 1883-1945 *AmSCAP 66*
Blaug, Mark 1927- *ConAu 1R*
Blaumanis, Rudolfs 1863-1908 *CasWL*
Blauner, Robert 1929- *ConAu 17R*
Blaushild, Babette 1927- *ConAu 29*
Blaustein, Albert Paul 1921- *ConAu 1R, WrD 1976*
Blaustein, Arthur I 1933- *ConAu 25*
Blaustein, Elliott H 1915- *ConAu 41*
Blaustein, Esther 1935- *ConAu 45*
Blauth-Muszkowski, Peter Christopher 1919- *Au&Wr*
Blauvelt, Augustus 1832-1900 *Alli Sup, DcAmA, DcNAA*
Blauvelt, Mrs. J Remsen *Alli Sup*
Blauvelt, Mary Taylor 1869- *AmA&B*
Blauw, Johannes 1912- *ConAu 9R*
Blavatsky, Helena Petrovna 1831-1891 *Alli Sup, AmA&B, BbD, BiD&SB, DcAmA, NewC, OxAm, REn*
Blaxland, George *Alli*
Blaxland, Gregory 1918- *Au&Wr, ConAu 9R, WrD 1976*
Blaxland, John 1917- *ConAu 5R*
Blaxton, John *Alli*
Blay, J Benibengor 1900?- *AfA 1, Pen Cl*
Blaydes, Cecil S 1901- *IndAu 1917*
Blaydes, Frederick Henry Marvell *Alli Sup*
Blaydes, Glenn William 1900- *IndAu 1917*
Blayds, Charles Stuart *EvLB*
Blaymires, J *Alli*
Blayne, Roger *MnBBF*
Blayney, Lord *Alli*
Blayney, Allan *Alli*
Blayney, Benjamin d1801 *Alli*
Blayney, Frederick *Alli*
Blayney, Lindsey *TexWr*
Blayney, Margaret S 1926- *ConAu 53*
Blaze, Don *MnBBF*
Blaze, Wayne 1951- *ConAu 61*
Blaze DeBury, Ange Henri 1813-1888 *BiD&SB*
Blaze DeBury, Baroness Marie P Rose *Alli Sup*
Blazek, Douglas 1941- *ConAu 25, DrAP 1975*
Blazicek, Oldrich Jakub 1914- *Au&Wr*
Bleackley, Horace William 1868- *WhLA*
Bleakley, David Wylie 1925- *WrD 1976*
Bleamire, William *Alli*
Bleasdale, John Ignatius *Alli Sup*
Bleasdell, William *BbtC*
Bleby, A E *Alli Sup*
Bleby, Henry *Alli Sup*
Bleby, Henry William 1831- *Alli Sup*
Blecher, George *DrAF 1976*
Blecher, Wilfred *ChPo S1*
Blechfeldt, Emil Harry 1874- *AmLY*
Blechman, Burt 1927- *Au&Wr, ConNov 1972, ConNov 1976, Pen Am, WrD 1976*
Blechman, Burt 1932- *AmA&B, ConAu 21*
Blechynden, Richard *Alli*
Bleckley, John Mollan *Alli Sup*
Bleckley, Logan E 1827-1907 *BiDSA, ChPo S1*
Bleckly, Henry *Alli Sup*
Bledlow, John *ConAu XR*
Bledsoe, Albert Taylor 1809-1877 *Alli Sup, AmA, AmA&B, BiD&SB, BiDSA, DcAmA, DcEnL, DcNAA, OhA&B*
Bledsoe, Edna T *TexWr*
Bledsoe, George 1921- *AmSCAP 66*

Bledsoe, Joseph C 1918- *ConAu 33*
Bledsoe, Samuel Thomas 1868-1939 *DcNAA*
Bledsoe, Thomas 1914- *ConAu 13R*
Bledsoe, W C *BiDSA*
Bleeck, Arthur Henry 1827?-1877 *Alli Sup*
Bleeck, Oliver *ConAu XR, EncM&D, WrD 1976*
Bleecker, Ann Eliza 1752-1783 *Alli, AmA, AmA&B, CyAL 1, DcAmA, DcNAA, OxAm, REnAL*
Bleecker, Anthony 1770-1827 *Alli, AmA&B, DcNAA*
Bleek, Wilhelm Heinrich Immanuel 1827-1875 *Alli Sup*
Bleeker, Claas Jonco 1898- *Au&Wr*
Bleeker, Sonia 1909- *BkP, ConAu XR, MorJA, SmATA 2*
Blees, Robert A 1922- *ConAu 17R*
Blegborough, Ralph 1769-1827 *Alli, BiDLA*
Blegen, Carl 1887-1971 *ConAu 33*
Blegen, Theodore Christian 1891-1969 *AmA&B, ChPo, ConAu 5R, MnnWr*
Blegvad, Erik 1923- *ChPo, IlBYP, IlCB 1956, IlCB 1966, ThBJA*
Blegvad, Lenore 1926- *ThBJA*
Bleheris *CasWL*
Blehl, Vincent Ferrer 1921- *ConAu 9R*
Blei, Franz 1871-1942 *ModGL, OxGer*
Bleiberg, German 1915- *CasWL*
Bleibtreu, Carl 1859-1928 *OxGer*
Bleibtreu, Karl 1859-1928 *BiD&SB, ClDMEuL, REn*
Bleich, Alan R 1913- *ConAu 13R*
Bleicher, Michael N 1935- *ConAu 37*
Bleiler, E F *ChPo S2*
Bleksley, Arthur Edward Herbert 1908- *BiDPar*
Bleloch, Archibald *Alli Sup*
Blemmydes, Nicephorus 1197?-1272? *CasWL, Pen Cl*
Blemont, Emile 1839-1927 *OxFr*
Blench, John Wheatley 1926- *Au&Wr, ConAu 13R*
Blencowe, Mrs. *ChPo S1*
Blencowe, Edward *Alli*
Blencowe, George *Alli Sup*
Blencowe, R W *Alli*
Blend, Charles Daniels 1918- *ConAu 23, IndAu 1917*
Blender, Frances Jones 1894- *WhWNAA*
Blenerhasset, Thomas 1550?-1625? *Alli, CasWL, NewC*
Blenkarn, John *Alli Sup*
Blenkin, Hugh Linton 1916- *Au&Wr*
Blenkinsop, William Henry *Alli Sup*
Blenkinsopp, Edwin Clennell Leaton *Alli Sup*
Blenkinsopp, Joseph 1927- *ConAu 37, WrD 1976*
Blenkinsopp, Richard B George Leaton *Alli Sup*
Blenman, Richard *Alli*
Blennerhasset, Margaret 1778?-1842 *DcNAA, OxCan*
Blennerhassett, Harman 1765-1831 *AmA&B, REnAL*
Blennerhaysett, Thomas *Alli*
Blesen, Peter d1200? *Alli*
Blesenis, Peter d1200? *Alli*
Blesh, Rudi 1899- *AmA&B, ConAu XR, WrD 1976*
Blesh, Rudolph Pickett 1899- *ConAu 17R*
Blessing, George Frederick 1875-1921 *DcNAA*
Blessing, Richard Allen 1939- *ConAu 53*
Blessinger, Karl 1888- *WhLA*
Blessington, J P *Alli Sup*
Blessington, Marguerite, Countess Of 1789-1849 *Alli, BbD, BiD&SB, BrAu 19, CasWL, ChPo S1, ChPo S2, Chmbr 3, DcEnL, DcLEnL, EvLB, NewC, OxEng, PoIre, REn*
Blessitt, Bernadine *BlkAW*
Blest Gana, Alberto 1830-1920 *CasWL, DcSpL, Pen Am, REn*
Blethen, Alden Joseph, Jr. 1870- *ChPo S1*
Blethen, Joseph 1870-1937 *AmA&B, DcNAA*
Bleton, C *BiDSA*
Bletter, Robert 1933?-1976 *ConAu 61*
Bletter, Rosemarie Haag 1939- *ConAu 57*
Blevins, Leon W 1937- *ConAu 57*
Blevins, William L 1937- *ConAu 33*

Blevins, Winfred 1938- *ConAu 45*
Blew, R W *Alli Sup*
Blew, William Charles Arlington 1848- *Alli Sup, Br&AmS*
Blew, William John *Alli Sup*
Blewert, William *Alli*
Blewett, Duncan Bassett 1920- *BiDPar*
Blewett, George John 1873-1912 *DcNAA*
Blewett, Jean 1862-1934 *ChPo, ChPo S1, DcLEnL, DcNAA, OxCan*
Blewitt, Ann Roper *Alli Sup*
Blewitt, J *Alli*
Blewitt, Octavius *Alli*
Blewitt, R J *Alli*
Bleyer, Willard Grosvenor 1873-1935 *AmLY, DcNAA, WhWNAA*
Bleything, Dennis H 1946- *ConAu 61*
Blezard, T *ChPo S1*
Bleznick, Donald W 1924- *ConAu 21*
Blicher, Steen Steensen 1782-1848 *BbD, BiD&SB, CasWL, ChPo, DcEuL, EuA, EvEuW, Pen Eur*
Blichfeldt, Hans Frederik 1873- *WhWNAA*
Blick, Francis *Alli, BiDLA*
Blicke, Sir Charles *Alli, BiDLA*
Blicker, Seymour *BlkAW, OxCan Sup*
Blicq, Anthony 1926- *ConAu 33, OxCan Sup*
Bligger Von Steinach *CasWL, OxGer*
Bligh, Arthur *Alli, BiDLA*
Bligh, Edward Vesey 1829- *Alli Sup*
Bligh, Harris Harding 1842-1918 *DcNAA*
Bligh, Michael *Alli*
Bligh, Norman *ConAu XR*
Bligh, Richard *Alli*
Bligh, S T *ChPo S1*
Bligh, William 1754-1817 *Alli, BiDLA, NewC, REn*
Blight, Francis James 1858- *WhLA*
Blight, John 1913- *ChPo S2, ConP 1970, ConP 1975, WrD 1976*
Blight, John Thomas 1835- *Alli Sup*
Blight, Leslie 1931- *Au&Wr*
Blight, Reynold E 1879- *WhWNAA*
Blind, Mathilde 1841?-1896 *Alli Sup, BbD, BiD&SB, BrAu 19, ChPo, Chmbr 3, DcEnA, EvLB, NewC*
Blind Harry d1492? *Alli, BrAu, CasWL, Chmbr 1, DcEnL, EvLB, NewC*
Blind Preacher, The *DcEnL*
Blind Traveller, The *DcEnL*
Blinderman, Abraham 1916- *ConAu 53, ConAu 61*
Blinders, Belinda *MnBBF*
Blinman, Richard *Alli*
Blinn, Edward 1938- *AmSCAP 66*
Blinn, Henry Clay 1824-1905 *DcNAA*
Blinn, Mrs. Henry G *Alli Sup*
Blinn, Leroy J *Alli Sup*
Blinn, Lucy M *ChPo*
Blinn, Walter Craig 1930- *ConAu 61*
Blinshall, James *Alli*
Blish, James 1921-1975 *AmA&B, Au&Wr, ConAu 1R, ConAu 57, ConNov 1976, WorAu, WrD 1976*
Blish, Morris Joslin 1889- *WhWNAA*
Blishen, Bernard Russell 1919- *ConAu 1R*
Blishen, Edward 1920- *Au&Wr, ChPo, ConAu 17R, SmATA 8, WrD 1976*
Bliss, A Richard, Jr. 1889- *WhWNAA*
Bliss, Alan Joseph 1921- *Au&Wr*
Bliss, Annie Marie *ChPo S2*
Bliss, Anthony *Alli*
Bliss, C V F *Alli Sup*
Bliss, Carey E *ChPo*
Bliss, Carey S 1914- *ConAu 41*
Bliss, Charles Bemis 1868- *WhWNAA*
Bliss, Charles R *Alli Sup*
Bliss, Daniel 1823-1916 *DcAmA, DcNAA, OhA&B*
Bliss, E V *Alli Sup*
Bliss, Edgar J *ChPo S1*
Bliss, Edward, Jr 1912- *ConAu 41*
Bliss, Edwin Munsell 1848-1919 *DcAmA, DcNAA*
Bliss, Eugene Frederick 1836-1918 *Alli Sup, DcNAA*
Bliss, Florence *Alli Sup*
Bliss, Frank Chapman *Alli Sup, DcNAA*

Bliss, Frederick Jones 1859-1937 *DcAmA,*
DcNAA
Bliss, George *Alli*
Bliss, George 1793-1873 *DcNAA*
Bliss, George 1830-1897 *Alli Sup, DcAmA,*
DcNAA
Bliss, George Ripley 1816- *Alli Sup*
Bliss, Gilbert Ames 1876- *WhWNAA*
Bliss, Henry 1797-1873 *Alli Sup, BbtC,*
DcNAA
Bliss, Mrs. J Worthington *Alli Sup*
Bliss, John *Alli, BiDLA*
Bliss, Judah Lee *Alli Sup*
Bliss, Lena Edith *WhWNAA*
Bliss, Leonard 1811-1842? *DcNAA*
Bliss, Loretta Ann Deering *WhWNAA*
Bliss, Michael *OxCan Sup*
Bliss, Nathaniel d1764 *Alli, BiDLA,*
BiDLA Sup
Bliss, Orville Justus 1848-1875 *Alli Sup,*
DcNAA
Bliss, Paul Southworth 1889-1940 *AmA&B,*
ChPo, ChPo S1, WhWNAA
Bliss, Philemon 1813-1889 *Alli Sup, DcNAA,*
OhA&B
Bliss, Philip 1788-1857 *Alli, BiDLA, DcEnL*
Bliss, Philip Paul 1838-1876 *AmA&B, ChPo,*
ChPo S1
Bliss, Porter Cornelius 1838-1885 *Alli Sup,*
DcAmA
Bliss, Ronald G 1942- *ConAu 53*
Bliss, Seth *Alli Sup*
Bliss, Sylvester d1863 *DcNAA*
Bliss, Sylvia Hortense 1870- *AnMV 1926,*
OhA&B, WhWNAA
Bliss, Thomas *Alli*
Bliss, W H *ChPo S2*
Bliss, W W *Alli Sup*
Bliss, Ward R *Alli Sup*
Bliss, William Dwight Porter 1856-1926
BiD&SB, DcAmA, DcNAA
Bliss, William Julian Albert 1867- *DcAmA,*
WhWNAA
Bliss, William Root 1825-1906 *Alli Sup,*
DcAmA, DcNAA
Blissard, W *Alli Sup*
Blissett, Marlan 1938- *ConAu 41*
Blistein, Elmer M 1920- *ConAu 9R*
Blitch, Fleming Lee 1933- *ConAu 9R*
Blith, Walter *Alli*
Blithe, Nathaniel *Alli*
Blitz, Mrs. A *Alli Sup*
Blitz, Antonio 1810-1877 *Alli Sup, DcAmA,*
DcNAA
Blitzstein, Marc 1905-1964 *AmA&B,*
AmSCAP 66, CnMD, McGWD, ModWD,
OxAm, REn, REnAL
Bliven, Bruce 1889- *AmA&B, Au&Wr,*
AuBYP, ConAu 37, TwCA, TwCA Sup,
WrD 1976
Bliven, Bruce, Jr. 1916- *ConAu 17R,*
SmATA 2
Bliven, Naomi 1925- *ConAu 33*
Blix, Elias 1836-1902 *ClDMEuL*
Blixen, Baroness Karen 1885-1962 *CasWL,*
ConAu 25, EncWL, LongC, Pen Eng,
Pen Eur, REn, TwCA, TwCA Sup,
WhTwL
Blixen-Finecke, Karen 1885-1962 *EvEuW,*
TwCW
Blizard, Thomas 1722-1838 *Alli*
Blizard, Sir William 1743-1835 *Alli, BiDLA,*
BiDLA Sup
Blizzard, Alpheus Wesley 1884- *WhWNAA*
Bloch, Alexander 1881- *WhWNAA*
Bloch, Ariel A 1933- *ConAu 41*
Bloch, Chajim 1881- *WhLA*
Bloch, Chana *DrAP 1975*
Bloch, E Maurice *ConAu 25*
Bloch, Ernest 1880-1959 *AmSCAP 66, AtlBL,*
OxAm, REn
Bloch, Ernst 1885- *CasWL, ConAu 29,*
OxGer
Bloch, Henry Simon 1915- *AmA&B*
Bloch, Herbert Aaron 1904-1965 *AmA&B,*
ConAu 1R
Bloch, Herman D 1914- *ConAu 29*
Bloch, Ignaz 1878- *WhLA*

Bloch, Jean-Richard 1884-1947 *CasWL,*
EvEuW, OxFr, TwCA, TwCA Sup
Bloch, Joshua 1890- *WhWNAA*
Bloch, Leopold 1876- *WhLA*
Bloch, Lucienne 1909- *IlBYP, IlCB 1945,*
IlCB 1956, SmATA 10
Bloch, Marc 1886-1944 *OxFr*
Bloch, Marie Halun 1910- *Au&Wr, AuBYP,*
ConAu 1R, SmATA 6, WrD 1976
Bloch, Oscar *OxFr*
Bloch, Raymond 1914- *Au&Wr*
Bloch, Raymond A 1902- *AmSCAP 66*
Bloch, Robert 1917- *AmA&B, ConAu 5R,*
DrAF 1976, EncM&D, WrD 1976
Bloch-Michel, Jean 1912- *REn, WorAu*
Blocher, S J *BiDSA*
Blochin, Anne Elizabeth d1946 *DcNAA*
Blochman, Lawrence G 1900-1975 *ConAu 19,*
ConAu 53, EncM&D, WhWNAA,
WrD 1976
Block, Alexander *ChPo*
Block, Allan 1923- *ConAu 49, DrAP 1975*
Block, Eugene B 1890- *ConAu 5R*
Block, Herbert Lawrence 1909- *AmA&B*
Block, Irvin 1917- *ConAu 17R*
Block, Jack 1921- *ConAu 33*
Block, Jack 1931- *ConAu 53*
Block, Jean Libman *ConAu 5R*
Block, L J *Alli Sup*
Block, Lawrence 1938- *ConAu 1R*
Block, Libbie 1910?-1972 *ConAu 33*
Block, Louis James 1851-1927 *AmLY, DcAmA,*
DcNAA, WhWNAA
Block, Ralph 1889-1974 *ConAu 45*
Block, Rudolph Edgar 1870-1940 *AmA&B,*
AmLY, DcNAA
Block, Walter 1941- *ConAu 57*
Blockcolski, Lew *DrAP 1975*
Blocker, Clyde Edward 1918- *ConAu 33,*
IndAu 1917
Blocker, Hyacinth 1904- *BkC 5*
Blockinger, Betty *ConAu XR*
Blocklinger, Peggy O'More 1895- *ConAu 5R*
Blocksidge, Charles William *DcLEnL,*
Pen Eng
Blocksidge, Kathleen Mary 1904- *Au&Wr*
Blodget, Lorin 1823-1901 *Alli, Alli Sup,*
DcAmA, DcNAA
Blodget, Samuel 1757-1814 *DcNAA*
Blodgett, A C *ChPo S1*
Blodgett, Beverley 1926- *ConAu 57*
Blodgett, Geoffrey Thomas 1931- *ConAu 17R*
Blodgett, Harold William 1900- *AmA&B,*
ConAu 13R
Blodgett, Harriet Eleanor 1919- *ConAu 33*
Blodgett, Harriet Fairchild *ChPo*
Blodgett, Levi *OxAm*
Blodgett, Mabel Fuller 1869-1939 *AmA&B,*
AmLY, DcAmA
Blodgett, Richard 1940- *ConAu 49*
Blodgett, Ruth Robinson *AmA&B,*
WhWNAA
Blodgett, Samuel Haskell 1863-1940 *DcNAA*
Blodgett, Stephen Haskell 1862- *WhWNAA*
Bloede, Gertrude 1845-1905 *Alli Sup,*
AmA&B, BiD&SB, ChPo, DcAmA,
DcNAA
Bloede, Victor G *Alli Sup*
Bloem, Jakobus Cornelis 1887-1966 *CasWL,*
EncWL, Pen Eur
Bloem, Walter 1868-1951 *OxGer*
Bloemaert, Abraham 1564-1651 *AtlBL*
Bloembergen, Nicolaas 1920- *WrD 1976*
Bloemker, Albert William 1906- *IndAu 1917*
Bloesch, Donald George 1928- *ConAu 13R,*
IndAu 1917, WrD 1976
Bloesser, Robert 1930- *ConAu 37*
Blofeld, John Eaton Calthorpe 1913- *Au&Wr,*
ConAu 53, WrD 1976
Blok, Aleksandr Aleksandrovich 1880-1921
AtlBL, CasWL, ChPo S1, ClDMEuL,
CnMD, CnMWL, DcRusL, EncWL,
EvEuW, LongC, McGWD, ModSL 1,
ModWD, OxEng, Pen Eur, REn, TwCA,
TwCA Sup, TwCW, WhTwL
Bloke, Maurice *Alli Sup*
Blom, Eric Walter 1888-1959 *LongC*
Blom, Frans 1893- *WhWNAA*

Blom, Gaston ʟ 1920- *ConAu 25*
Blom-Cooper, Louis Jacques 1926- *Au&Wr,*
ConAu 5R
Blomberg, Barbara 1527?-1597 *OxGer*
Blomberg, Erik Axel 1894-1965 *CasWL,*
ClDMEuL, EncWL
Blomberg, Harry 1893- *ClDMEuL*
Blombery, W N *Alli*
Blome, Richard 1650?-1705 *Alli, Br&AmS,*
NewC
Blomefield, Francis *Alli*
Blomefield, Leonard *Alli Sup*
Blomefield, Miles 1525?- *DcEnL*
Blomefield, Robert Allan *Alli Sup*
Blomer, Ralph *Alli*
Blomfeld, Reginald 1856- *WhLA*
Blomfield, Adelaide *DrAP 1975*
Blomfield, Alfred 1833- *Alli Sup*
Blomfield, Barrington *Alli*
Blomfield, Charles James 1786-1857 *Alli,*
Alli Sup, BiDLA, BiDLA Sup, DcEnL
Blomfield, E V 1788-1816 *Alli*
Blomfield, Elsie *ChPo S1, ChPo S2*
Blomfield, Ezekiel 1778-1818 *ChPo*
Blomfield, Frederick George *Alli Sup*
Blomfield, George Becher *Alli*
Blomfield, James Charles *Alli Sup*
Blomfield, Joseph 1870- *WhLA*
Blomfield, Lewis S *Alli Sup*
Blomfield, William Ernest 1862- *WhLA*
Blomgren, Carl August 1865-1926 *DcNAA*
Blommaert, Philipp 1809-1871 *BiD&SB*
Blommel, Henry Howard 1924- *IndAu 1917*
Blondahl, Omar *OxCan Sup*
Blondal, Patricia *OxCan*
Blondel De Nesle *AtlBL, CasWL, EuA,*
EvEuW, NewC
Blondel, Elisabeth May *WhWNAA*
Blondel, James A d1734? *Alli*
Blondel, Maurice 1861-1949 *CatA 1952, OxFr*
Blood, Alison F *ChPo*
Blood, Benjamin Paul 1832-1919 *Alli Sup,*
AmA, AmA&B, DcNAA, OxAm,
REnAL
Blood, Henry Ames 1838?-1901? *ChPo,*
ChPo S2, DcNAA
Blood, Jerome W 1926- *ConAu 9R*
Blood, Marje *ConAu 41, WrD 1976*
Blood, Matthew *EncM&D*
Blood, Robert O, Jr. 1921- *ConAu 1R*
Blood, Thomas 1618?-1680 *NewC*
Blood, William *Alli Sup*
Bloodgood, Freeman A 1867- *DcAmA*
Bloodgood, John D d1915 *DcNAA*
Bloodgood, Simeon DeWitt 1799-1866 *Alli Sup,*
DcAmA, DcNAA
Bloodworth, Emma *Alli Sup, ChPo S1*
Bloody Claverse *NewC*
Bloody Mary *NewC*
Bloom, Alan Herbert 1906- *Au&Wr,*
ConAu 9R
Bloom, Edward Alan 1914- *ConAu 1R,*
IndAu 1917
Bloom, Erick Franklin 1944- *ConAu 57*
Bloom, Gordon F 1918- *ConAu 13R*
Bloom, Harold 1930- *AmA&B, ChPo,*
ConAu 13R, WrD 1976
Bloom, Harry 1913- *TwCW*
Bloom, Harry 1921- *WrD 1976*
Bloom, Hyman 1913- *REn*
Bloom, J H *Alli*
Bloom, Jack Don 1920- *Au&Wr*
Bloom, James Graver *ChPo*
Bloom, John Ernest George 1921- *Au&Wr,*
ConAu 5R
Bloom, John Porter 1924- *ConAu 49*
Bloom, Larry 1944- *AmSCAP 66*
Bloom, Lillian D 1920- *ConAu 17R*
Bloom, Lynn Marie Zimmerman 1934-
ConAu 13R, WrD 1976
Bloom, Lynn W 1882- *WhWNAA*
Bloom, Mary M Jones 1895- *IndAu 1917*
Bloom, Melvyn H 1938- *ConAu 45*
Bloom, Milton 1906- *AmSCAP 66*
Bloom, Murray 1889- *AmSCAP 66*
Bloom, Murray Teigh 1916- *ConAu 17R,*
WrD 1976
Bloom, Pauline *ConAu 41, WrD 1976*

ConAu 45, ConLC 2, ConP 1970,
ConP 1975, DcLEnL, EncWL, EvLB,
LongC, ModBL, ModBL Sup, NewC,
OxEng, Pen Eng, RAdv 1, REn, TwCA,
TwCA Sup, TwCW, WebEAL, WhTwL
Blunden, Margaret 1939- ConAu 23
Blundeville, Thomas Alli, DcEnL
Blunsden, John 1930- ConAu 57
Blunsdon, Norman 1915-1968 ConAu P-1
Blunt, Alfred Walter Frank 1879- WhLA
Blunt, Lady Anne Isabella 1837- Alli Sup
Blunt, Sir Anthony Frederick 1907- Au&Wr
Blunt, Arthur W Alli Sup
Blunt, Bruce ChPo S1
Blunt, Charles Alli, BiDLA
Blunt, Charles F Alli
Blunt, Don ConAu XR
Blunt, Mrs. E M Alli Sup
Blunt, Edmond March 1770-1862 DcAmA
Blunt, Edmund 1799- Alli
Blunt, Edmund M 1770-1862 Alli
Blunt, Edward NewC
Blunt, Fanny Alli Sup
Blunt, G Alli Sup
Blunt, George William 1802-1878 Alli,
Alli Sup, DcAmA, DcNAA
Blunt, H W Alli Sup
Blunt, Henry d1843 Alli, Alli Sup
Blunt, Hugh Francis 1877- AnMV 1926,
BkC 1, CatA 1947, WhWNAA
Blunt, Humphrey Alli Sup
Blunt, J Alli, BiDLA
Blunt, J K LongC
Blunt, John Alli
Blunt, John Henry 1823-1884 Alli Sup, DcEnL
Blunt, John James 1794-1855 Alli
Blunt, Joseph 1792-1860 Alli, DcAmA,
DcNAA
Blunt, Joyce Alli Sup
Blunt, Julia S Alli Sup
Blunt, Katharine 1876- WhWNAA
Blunt, Leonard Alli
Blunt, Nathaniel Bowditch 1804-1854 Alli
Blunt, R G Alli Sup
Blunt, Reginald 1856- ChPo S1, WhLA
Blunt, Richard Frederick Lefevre Alli Sup
Blunt, Stanhope English 1850-1926 Alli Sup,
DcAmA, DcNAA
Blunt, Thomas DcEnL
Blunt, Walter Alli
Blunt, Wilfred 1901- WrD 1976
Blunt, Wilfred Scawen 1840-1922 ChPo,
ChPo S1, DcLEnL, LongC
Blunt, Wilfrid Jasper Walter 1901- Au&Wr,
ConAu 21
Blunt, Wilfrid Scawen 1840-1922 Alli Sup,
BbD, BiD&SB, BrAu 19, Chmbr 3,
DcEnA, DcEnA Ap, EvLB, ModBL,
NewC, OxEng, Pen Eng, REn, WebEAL
Blunt, William Octavius Alli Sup
Blunt-Mackenzie, Sibell Lilian WhLA
Bluphocks, Lucien ConAu XR
Bluskov, Iliya 1839-1913 CasWL
Blust, Earl R IlBYP
Bluteau, Dom Raphael 1638-1734 Alli
Bluthgen, August Edward Viktor 1844-
BiD&SB
Bluthgen, Clara 1856- WhLA
Blutig, Eduard ConAu XR
Bluvstein, Rahel 1890-1931 Pen Cl, Pen Eur
Bly, Albert E 1892- AmSCAP 66
Bly, Myron T Alli Sup
Bly, Nellie 1867-1922 AmA, AmA&B,
CnDAL, DcNAA, OxAm, REn, REnAL
Bly, Robert 1926- AmA&B, ConAu 5R,
ConLC 1, ConLC 2, ConLC 5,
ConP 1970, ConP 1975, CrCAP,
DrAP 1975, ModAL Sup, Pen Am,
RAdv 1, WebEAL, WhTwL, WorAu,
WrD 1976
Blyden, Edward Wilmot 1832- Alli Sup, BbD,
BiD&SB
Blydenburgh, J W Alli
Blymyer, William H 1864-1939 OhA&B
Blyn, George 1919- ConAu 37
Blyth, Adam Alli Sup
Blyth, Alan Geoffrey 1929- ConAu 49,
WrD 1976

Blyth, Alexander Wynter Alli Sup
Blyth, Chay 1940- WrD 1976
Blyth, David Alli Sup
Blyth, Edward 1810-1873 Alli Sup
Blyth, Edward Egbert Alli Sup
Blyth, Edward Hamilton Alli Sup
Blyth, Emily May Estelle 1881- Au&Wr
Blyth, Frederick Cavan Alli Sup
Blyth, George Alli Sup
Blyth, George Francis Popham Alli Sup
Blyth, Harry 1852-1898 Alli Sup, EncM&D,
MnBBF, WhCL
Blyth, Henry Edward 1910- Au&Wr,
ConAu 21, WrD 1976
Blyth, J A OxCan Sup
Blyth, James N Alli Sup
Blyth, John WrD 1976
Blyth, M P Alli Sup
Blyth, P A Alli Sup, ChPo
Blyth, Reginald Horace ChPo S2
Blyth, Robert Alli, BiDLA
Blyth, S Alli
Blyth, Spencer R MnBBF
Blyth, Stephen Cleveland BbtC
Blyth, Thomas Allen Alli Sup
Blythe, Harry Randolph 1882-1913 ChPo S2
Blythe, Herbert 1847-1905 LongC
Blythe, J A St. John Alli Sup
Blythe, John Dean 1842-1869 Alli Sup
Blythe, LeGette 1900- AmA&B, ConAu 1R
Blythe, Ronald 1922- ConAu 5R, WrD 1976
Blythe, Samuel George 1868-1947 AmA&B,
DcNAA, REnAL
Blythe, Stuart Oakes 1890- AmA&B
Blythe, Vernon 1876- DcNAA, WhWNAA
Blythe, Walker Alli
Blythewood, W M And Jarman, T Alli Sup
Blyton, Carey 1932- ChPo S2, ConAu 49,
SmATA 9
Blyton, Emma Alli Sup
Blyton, Enid Mary 1898?-1968 AuBYP, ChPo,
ChPo S1, ChPo S2, ConAu 25, LongC,
WhCL
Blyton, William Joseph 1887-1944 CatA 1947
Boa, Kenneth 1945- ConAu 61
Boadella, David 1931- ConAu 53
Boaden, Caroline DcEnL
Boaden, James 1762-1839 Alli, BiDLA,
DcEnL, NewC
Boaden, John ChPo
Boag, John 1775-1863 Alli Sup
Boag, Thomas Alli Sup
Boag, William Alli
Boaistuau, Pierre d1566 OxFr
Boak, Arthur Edward Romilly 1888-1962
AmA&B, ConAu 5R
Boak, Denis 1932- Au&Wr, ConAu 13R
Boak, John Alli, BiDLA
Boake, Barcroft Henry 1866-1892 DcLEnL,
PoIre
Boake, Capel 1895-1945 DcLEnL
Boal, James PoIre
Boalch, Donald Howard 1914- Au&Wr,
ConAu 9R, WrD 1976
Boalt, Gunnar 1910- ConAu 57
Boar, Arthur ChPo
Board, C Stephen 1942- ConAu 57
Board, Joseph B, Jr. 1931- ConAu 29
Boardman, Anne Cawley MnnWr
Boardman, Arthur 1927- ConAu 61
Boardman, Charles C 1932- ConAu 29
Boardman, Eunice 1926- ConAu 9R
Boardman, Fon Wyman, Jr. 1911- ConAu 1R,
SmATA 6, WrD 1976
Boardman, George A BbtC
Boardman, George Dana 1828-1903 Alli Sup,
BiD&SB, DcAmA, DcNAA
Boardman, George Nye 1825-1915 DcAmA,
DcNAA
Boardman, Gwenn R 1924- ConAu 45
Boardman, Henry Augustus 1808-1880 Alli,
Alli Sup, CyAL 2, DcAmA, DcEnL,
DcNAA
Boardman, Horace Prentiss 1869- WhWNAA
Boardman, J Alli, BiDLA
Boardman, James Alli, Alli Sup, BiDLA
Boardman, John 1927- WrD 1976
Boardman, Mrs. M M Alli Sup

Boardman, Mabel Thorpe 1861?-1946 OhA&B,
WhWNAA
Boardman, Neil S 1907- ConAu P-1
Boardman, Richard J ArizL
Boardman, Ruby DeLongueville ChPo
Boardman, Samuel Lane 1836-1914 Alli Sup,
DcNAA
Boardman, Thomas Alli, BiDLA
Boardman, W E Alli Sup
Boardman, Mrs. W E Alli Sup
Boardman, William Alli, BiDLA
Boardman, William Edwin 1810-1886 DcNAA
Boardman, William Henry 1846-1914 DcAmA,
DcNAA
Boare, G Alli Sup
Boarino, Gerald L 1931- ConAu 23
Boarman, Patrick M 1922- ConAu 13R
Boas, F S 1862-1957 LongC
Boas, Franz 1858-1942 AmA&B, AmLY,
DcAmA, DcNAA, OxAm, OxCan,
OxCan Sup, REnAL, TwCA Sup,
WhWNAA
Boas, Frederick S 1862-1957 NewC
Boas, George 1891- WhWNAA
Boas, Guy 1896-1966 ChPo, ChPo S1,
ConAu P-1
Boas, Louise Schutz 1885- ChPo, ConAu 5R
Boas, Ludwig Gottfried Eduard 1868- WhLA
Boas, Marie ConAu XR
Boas, Maurits Ignatius 1892- ConAu 1R
Boas, Ralph Philip 1887-1945 DcNAA
Boase, Alan Martin 1902- Au&Wr,
ConAu 5R
Boase, Charles William 1804-1872 Alli Sup
Boase, Charles William 1828- Alli Sup
Boase, George Clement 1810-1880 Alli Sup,
ChPo
Boase, George Clement 1829- Alli Sup
Boase, H S Alli
Boase, Henry Alli, BiDLA
Boase, Henry Samuel 1799-1883 Alli Sup
Boase, Paul Henshaw 1915- ConAu 37,
IndAu 1917
Boase, Thomas Sherrer Ross 1898- ConAu 23
Boate, Gerard Alli
Boate, Greshon d1704 PoIre
Boate, Henrietta d1871 PoIre
Boateng, E A 1920- ConAu 23
Boatfield, Jeffrey Montagu 1924- Au&Wr
Boatman, Don Earl 1913- ConAu 1R
Boatner, Edward H 1898- AmSCAP 66
Boatner, Mark Mayo, III 1921- ConAu 21
Boatright, Mody Coggin 1896- ConAu 5R,
TexWr
Boatwright, Gertrude Floyd Harris WhWNAA
Boatwright, Howard 1918- AmSCAP 66,
ConAu 53
Boaz, Eliza Alli Sup
Boaz, Herman ChPo
Boaz, Martha Tearosse AmA&B, ConAu 9R
Bob, Brother ConAu XR
Bobart, Jacob Alli
Bobb, Bernard E 1917- ConAu 5R
Bobbe, Dorothie DeBear 1905-1975 ConAu 25,
ConAu 57, SmATA 1
Bobbett, Walter ChPo
Bobbin, Tim Alli
Bobbitt, Franklin 1876- WhWNAA
Bobbitt, John Franklin 1876- IndAu 1816
Bobby WhWNAA
Bober, Stanley 1932- ConAu 23
Bobin, Donald E M MnBBF
Bobin, John William d1935 MnBBF
Bobinski, George S 1929- ConAu 29,
WrD 1976
Bobker, Lee R 1925- ConAu 53
Boborykin, Peter Dmitriyevich 1836-1921?
CasWL, ClDMEuL, DcRusL, EvEuW
Bobri, V 1898- IlBYP, IlCB 1956, IlCB 1966
Bobrick, Sam 1932- AmSCAP 66
Bobritsky, Vladimir 1898- IlBYP, IlCB 1945,
IlCB 1956, IlCB 1966
Bobrov, Semyon Sergeyevich 1767-1810 CasWL,
DcRusL
Bobrow, Davis Bernard 1936- ConAu 57
Bobrow, Edwin E 1928- ConAu 23
Bobrowski, Johannes 1917-1965 CasWL,
EncWL, ModGL, OxGer, Pen Eur,

TwCW
Bobula, Ida *AmA&B*
Bocage, Manuel Maria Barbosa Du 1765-1805 *CasWL*, *EuA*, *EvEuW*, *Pen Eur*
Bocage, Pierre-Martinien Tousez 1797-1863 *OxFr*
Bocangel, Gabriel 1608-1658 *DcSpL*
Bocangel Y Unzueta, Gabriel 1608-1658 *CasWL*, *Pen Eur*
Bocca, Al *ConAu XR*
Boccaccio, Giovanni 1313-1375 *AtlBL*, *BbD*, *BiD&SB*, *CasWL*, *CyWA*, *DcBiA*, *DcEnL*, *DcEuL*, *EuA*, *EvEuW*, *NewC*, *OxEng*, *Pen Eur*, *RCom*, *REn*
Boccage, Marie Anne Fiquet Du 1710-1802 *EvEuW*
Boccalini, Traiano 1556-1613 *CasWL*, *DcEuL*, *EvEuW*, *Pen Eur*
Boccalini, Trajano 1556-1613 *REn*
Boccherini, Luigi 1743-1805 *AtlBL*
Bocchini, Phillip 1887- *WhWNAA*
Bochenski, Innocentius M *ConAu XR*
Bochenski, Joseph M 1902- *ConAu 5R*
Bocher, Maxime 1867-1918 *DcNAA*
Bochetel, Jean *OxFr*
Bochner, Salomon 1899- *ConAu 41*
Bock, Alan W 1943- *ConAu 41*
Bock, Alfred 1859-1932 *OxGer*
Bock, Carl *Alli Sup*
Bock, Carl H 1930- *ConAu 19*
Bock, Franz 1876- *WhLA*
Bock, Fred 1939- *AmSCAP 66*, *ConAu 25*
Bock, Frederick 1916- *ConAu 9R*
Bock, Hal *ConAu XR*, *SmATA XR*
Bock, Harold I 1939- *ConAu 29*, *SmATA 10*
Bock, Joanne 1940- *ConAu 57*
Bock, Joseph Carl 1884- *WhWNAA*
Bock, Kurt 1890- *WhLA*
Bock, Paul J 1922- *ConAu 53*
Bock, Peter Gidon 1934- *ConAu 17*
Bock, Philip Karl 1934- *ConAu 25*, *OxCan Sup*, *WrD 1976*
Bock, Vera *ChPo*, *ChPo S1*, *ChPo S2*, *ConICB*, *IlBYP*, *IlCB 1945*, *IlCB 1956*, *IlCB 1966*, *MorJA*
Bock, William Sauts *IlBYP*
Bockelman, Wilfred 1920- *ConAu 37*
Bockett, Benjamin Bradney *Alli Sup*
Bockett, J *Alli*
Bockl, George 1909- *ConAu 61*
Bocklin, Arnold 1827-1901 *AtlBL*, *OxGer*
Bockmon, Guy Alan 1926- *ConAu 5R*
Bockris, Victor *DrAP 1975*
Bockus, H William 1915- *ConAu 53*
Bocock, John Holmes 1813-1872 *BiDSA*, *DcNAA*
Bocock, John Paul 1856-1903 *BiDSA*, *ChPo*, *ChPo S1*, *DcNAA*
Bocock, Robert James 1940- *WrD 1976*
Bocock, Walter Kemper 1858-1904 *BiDSA*
Bocock, Willis Henry 1865- *BiDSA*
Boczek, Boleslaw Adam 1922- *ConAu 1R*
Bod, Peter 1911- *ConAu XR*
Bodansky, Meyer 1896-1941 *DcNAA*
Boddaert, Marie Agathe 1844-1914 *EvEuW*
Boddam-Whetham *Alli Sup*
Boddewyn, J 1929- *ConAu 25*
Boddie, Alexander *ChPo*
Boddie, Charles E 1911- *LivBA*
Boddington, Mrs. *Alli*
Boddington, Gracilla *Alli Sup*
Boddington, Harriet Olivia *Alli Sup*
Boddington, Mary 1776-1839? *PoIre*
Boddington, Reginald Stewart *Alli Sup*
Boddis, George 1886- *WhWNAA*
Boddy, A A *Alli Sup*
Boddy, Evan Marlett *Alli Sup*
Boddy, Frederick Arthur 1914- *ConAu 61*, *WrD 1976*
Boddy, Manchester 1891- *WhWNAA*
Boddy, Mary E *Alli Sup*
Boddy, Maurice George 1932- *Au&Wr*
Boddy, William Charles 1913- *Au&Wr*
Bode, Boyd Henry 1873-1953 *AmA&B*, *WhWNAA*
Bode, Carl 1854- *ChPo*
Bode, Carl 1911- *AmA&B*, *Au&Wr*, *ConAu 1R*, *DrAP 1975*, *WrD 1976*

Bode, Elroy 1931- *ConAu 25*
Bode, Mrs. J A *Alli Sup*
Bode, J E *Alli*
Bode, Johann Joachim 1720-1793 *OxGer*
Bode, Johann Joachim Christoph 1730-1797 *DcEuL*
Bode, John Ernest 1816-1874 *Alli Sup*
Bode, Rudolf 1881- *WhLA*
Bodecker, Carl Friedrich Wilhelm 1846- *DcAmA*
Bodecker, Nils Mogens 1922- *ChPo S1*, *ChPo S2*, *ConAu 49*, *IlBYP*, *IlCB 1956*, *IlCB 1966*, *SmATA 8*, *WrD 1976*
Bodeen, DeWitt 1908- *ConAu 25*
Bodel, Jean d1209? *CasWL*, *DcEuL*, *EvEuW*, *McGWD*, *OxFr*
Bodell, Mary *ConAu XR*
Bodelsen, Anders 1937- *Au&Wr*
Bodelsen, Merete 1907- *Au&Wr*
Boden, Mister *Alli*
Boden, Edward John *Alli Sup*
Boden, Frederick Cecil 1903- *ChPo S1*
Boden, G J *ChPo*
Boden, Hilda *ConAu XR*
Boden, James 1757-1841 *PoCh*
Boden, Jane *Alli Sup*, *ChPo S1*
Boden, Joseph *Alli*
Boden, Thomas *Alli Sup*
Bodenham, Countess E M De *Alli Sup*
Bodenham, Hilda Morris 1901- *ConAu 9R*
Bodenham, John 1558-1600? *Alli*, *CasWL*, *DcEnL*, *DcLEnL*, *EvLB*
Bodenhamer, William 1808-1905 *Alli Sup*, *DcNAA*
Bodenheim, Maxwell 1893?-1954 *AmA&B*, *CnDAL*, *ConAmL*, *DcLEnL*, *ModAL*, *OxAm*, *Pen Am*, *REn*, *REnAL*, *TwCA*, *TwCA Sup*
Bodenheimer, Edgar 1908- *ConAu 33*
Bodenstedt, Friedrich Martin Von 1819-1892 *BiD&SB*, *DcEuL*, *EvEuW*
Bodenstedt, Friedrich Von 1819-1892 *OxGer*
Bodenstein, Andreas *OxGer*
Bodet *DcSpL*
Bodey, Hugh 1939- *ConAu 61*, *WrD 1976*
Bodfan *WhLA*
Bodfish, George Madison 1841-1914 *DcNAA*
Bodger, Joan *ChPo S1*
Bodichon, Barbara Leigh 1827- *Alli Sup*
Bodie, Idella F 1925- *ConAu 41*
Bodin, Ed F 1894- *WhWNAA*
Bodin, Jean 1530-1596 *CasWL*, *DcEuL*, *EuA*, *EvEuW*, *OxFr*, *REn*
Bodine, George Imlay 1882-1947 *DcNAA*
Bodine, Helen Koues *WhWNAA*
Bodine, Richard C 1928- *IndAu 1917*
Bodine, William Budd 1841-1907 *DcNAA*
Bodington, John *Alli*
Bodington, Nancy H 1912- *ConAu 53*
Bodington, Nancy Hermione 1920- *Au&Wr*, *WrD 1976*
Bodington, Nicolas 1904- *Au&Wr*
Bodini, Vittorio 1914- *EncWL*
Bodius, Andrew *Alli*
Bodius, Marcus Alexander *Alli*
Bodius, Robert *Alli*
Bodius, Zacharias *Alli*
Bodker, Cecil Skaar 1927- *CasWL*
Bodkin, M McDonnell 1850-1933 *EncM&D*
Bodkin, Mathias McDonagh 1850- *PoIre*
Bodkin, Maud 1875- *ConAu P-1*, *REn*, *TwCA Sup*
Bodkin, Ronald G 1936- *ConAu 33*, *WrD 1976*
Bodkin, S S *PoIre*
Bodkin, Thomas 1887-1961 *Br&AmS*, *CatA 1952*, *LongC*
Bodle, Alan *OhA&B*
Bodle, Yvonne Gallegos 1939- *ConAu 33*, *WrD 1976*
Bodley, E W *Alli Sup*
Bodley, George Frederick *ChPo S1*
Bodley, J E C *Chmbr 3*
Bodley, James *Alli*
Bodley, John Edward Courtenay 1853- *DcEnA Ap*
Bodley, Josias *Alli*

Bodley, Josselin Reginald Courtenay 1893- *ChPo*
Bodley, Laurence 1546?-1615 *Alli*
Bodley, Rachel Littler 1831-1888 *OhA&B*
Bodley, Ronald Victor Courtenay 1892- *AmA&B*
Bodley, Temple 1852-1940 *AmA&B*, *DcNAA*, *WhWNAA*
Bodley, Sir Thomas 1545?-1613 *Alli*, *CasWL*, *ChPo*, *CrE&SL*, *DcEuL*, *DcLEnL*, *EvLB*, *NewC*
Bodman, Emanuel, Freiherr Von Und Zu 1874-1946 *OxGer*
Bodman, Ernest James 1875-1958 *IndAu 1917*
Bodmer, Johann Jakob 1698-1783 *BiD&SB*, *CasWL*, *DcEuL*, *EuA*, *EvEuW*, *OxGer*, *Pen Eur*, *REn*
Bodmershof, Imma Von 1895- *OxGer*
Bodner, Phil 1919- *AmSCAP 66*
Bodo, Murray 1937- *ConAu 57*
Bodoh, John J 1931- *ConAu 45*
Bodrugan, Adams *Alli*
Bodrugan, Nicholas *Alli*
Bodsworth, Fred 1918- *Au&Wr*, *ConAu 1R*, *ConNov 1972*, *ConNov 1976*, *OxCan*, *OxCan Sup*, *WrD 1976*
Bodtcher, Ludvig Adolph 1793-1874 *CasWL*, *Pen Eur*
Bodtcher, Ludwig Adolph 1793-1874 *BiD&SB*, *EvEuW*
Bodwell, Edith Perry *ChPo*
Bodwell, Richard *ConAu XR*
Body, Alfred H *ChPo S1*
Body, Charles William Edmund 1851-1912 *DcAmA*, *DcNAA*
Body, Geoffrey 1929- *Au&Wr*, *WrD 1976*
Body, George *Alli Sup*
Boece 480?-524? *OxEng*, *OxFr*
Boece SEE ALSO Boethius
Boece, Hector 1465?-1536? *Alli*, *BiD&SB*, *BrAu*, *CasWL*, *Chmbr 1*, *DcEnL*, *EvLB*, *NewC*, *OxEng*, *Pen Eng*
Boeck, Johann A 1917- *CrCD*
Boeckel, Florence Brewer 1885- *WhWNAA*
Boeckel, Richard Martin 1892- *AmA&B*
Boeckman, Charles 1920- *ConAu 13R*
Boecler, Otto C 1875- *WhWNAA*
Boedtcher, Ludvig Adolph 1793-1874 *DcEuL*
Boegehold, Betty *AuBYP*, *ChPo S1*
Boegehold, Erwin Julius Hans Karl 1876- *WhLA*
Boegner, Marc 1881-1970 *ConAu 29*
Boehlke, Frederick J, Jr. 1926- *ConAu 21*
Boehlke, Robert R 1925- *ConAu 5R*
Boehlow, Robert H 1925- *ConAu 53*
Boehm, Eric H 1918- *ConAu 13R*
Boehm, H R *ChPo*
Boehm, Henry 1775-1875 *Alli Sup*, *DcNAA*
Boehm, Max Hildebert 1891- *WhLA*
Boehm, Otto 1879- *WhLA*
Boehm, William D 1946- *ConAu 61*
Boehme, Jacob 1575-1624 *CasWL*, *DcEuL*, *OxEng*
Boehme, Jakob 1575-1624 *REn*
Boehme, Lillian R 1936- *ConAu 29*
Boehmer, Eduard *Alli Sup*
Boehmer, George H *Alli Sup*
Boehmer, Julius 1866- *WhLA*
Boehringer, C Louise *ArizL*
Boehringer, Robert 1885?-1974 *ConAu 53*, *OxGer*
Boeis, Hector 1470?-1550? *Alli*
Boekler, Johann Heinrich 1610-1672 *DcEuL*
Boelen, Bernard J 1916- *ConAu 41*
Boelsche, Wilhelm 1861-1939 *CIDMEuL*
Boendale, Jan Van 1280?-1352? *CasWL*, *DcEuL*
Boer, Charles 1939- *ConP 1970*, *ConP 1975*, *WrD 1976*
Boer, Dick 1906- *Au&Wr*
Boer, Harry R 1913- *ConAu 1R*
Boer, Richard Constant 1863- *WhLA*
Boer, Siebe De 1876- *WhLA*
Boericke, Felix Oriel 1857-1929 *DcNAA*
Boericke, William 1849-1929 *DcNAA*
Boericke, William And Dewey, W A *Alli Sup*
Boesch, Mark Joseph 1917- *ConAu 21*, *WhPNW*

Boese, Clifford *Alli Sup*
Boese, T *Alli Sup*
Boesel, David 1938- *ConAu 41*
Boesen, Victor 1908- *ConAu 37, IndAu 1917*
Boesiger, Willi 1904- *Au&Wr*
Boetcker, William John Henry 1873- *IndAu 1816*
Boethius, Anicius Manlus Severinus 480?-524? *AtlBL, BiD&SB, CasWL, CyWA, DcEnL, DcEuL, NewC, OxEng, Pen Cl, Pen Eur, RCom, REn*
Boethius SEE ALSO Boece
Boethius, Hector 1465?-1536 *Alli, BiD&SB, BrAu, CasWL, EvLB, NewC, Pen Eng*
Boetie, Dugmore 1920?-1966 *AfA 1*
Boetie, Etienne DeLa *OxFr*
Boetius A Bolswert 1580-1633 *CasWL*
Boetius, Anicius Manlius Torquatus S 470?-525? *BiD&SB*
Boetius, Hector 1465?-1536? *NewC*
Boettcher, Henry J 1893- *ConAu P-1*
Boeve, Edgar G 1929- *ConAu 21*
Boevey, Miss S M Crawley- *Alli Sup*
Boewe, Charles 1924- *ConAu 9R*
Boex, Justin *EvEuW*
Boezinger, Bruno 1859-1939 *DcNAA*
Boff, Charles *MnBBF*
Bofill I Mates, Jaume *CasWL*
Bogaduck *ConAu XR*
Bogaers, Adriaan 1795-1870 *BbD, BiD&SB*
Bogaers, Adrianus 1795-1870 *CasWL*
Bogan, Louise 1897-1970 *AmA&B, AuBYP, ChPo, CnDAL, CnE&AP, ConAmA, ConAu 25, ConLC 4, ConP 1970, DcLEnL, EncWL, ModAL, ModAL Sup, OxAm, Pen Am, RAdv 1, REn, REnAL, SixAP, TwCA, TwCA Sup, TwCW*
Bogan, Phebe M 1868-1927 *ArizL*
Bogan, Zachary 1625-1659 *Alli*
Bogardus, Adam H *Alli Sup*
Bogardus, Carl Robert 1906- *IndAu 1917*
Bogardus, Emory Stephen 1882- *AmA&B, WhWNAA*
Bogart, Alexander H 1804-1826 *Alli*
Bogart, Carlotta 1929- *ConAu 61*
Bogart, Elizabeth 1806?- *Alli, Alli Sup, ChPo S1, DcAmA, FemPA*
Bogart, Ernest Ludlow 1870- *AmLY, WhWNAA*
Bogart, Leo 1921- *ConAu 41*
Bogart, William Henry 1810-1888 *Alli Sup, AmA&B, BiD&SB, Br&AmS, DcAmA, DcNAA*
Bogatsky *DcEnL*
Bogdanov, A 1873-1928 *CasWL, DcRusL*
Bogdanovich, Ippolit Fyodorovich 1743?-1803 *BbD, BiD&SB, CasWL, DcRusL, EvEuW*
Bogdanovich, Maxim *DcRusL*
Bogdanovich, Modest Ivanovich 1805-1882 *BiD&SB*
Bogdanovich, Peter 1939- *ConAu 5R, WrD 1976*
Bogen, Boris D 1869-1929 *DcNAA, OhA&B*
Boger, Charlotte Gilson 1826- *Alli Sup*
Bogert, Beverley *ChPo*
Bogert, George Gleason 1884- *WhWNAA*
Bogert, L Jean 1888-1970 *ConAu P-1, WhWNAA*
Bogg, Carl Michael *ChPo*
Bogg, Edward *Alli*
Boggess, Arthur Clinton 1874-1955 *OhA&B, WhWNAA*
Boggess, Frank Austin 1872- *WhWNAA*
Boggess, Louise Bradford 1912- *ConAu 13R*
Boggett, William *Alli Sup*
Boggis, Doreen H *ChPo S1*
Boggis-Rolfe, Douglass Horace 1874- *WhLA*
Boggs, James *Alli Sup*
Boggs, James 1919- *LivBA*
Boggs, Lucinda Pearl 1874- *WhWNAA*
Boggs, Mrs. M L *Alli Sup*
Boggs, Ralph Steele 1901- *AnCL, AuBYP, ConAu P-1, DcSpL, IndAu 1917, SmATA 7, WhWNAA*
Boggs, Robert *Alli Sup*
Boggs, S E *Alli Sup*
Boggs, Thomas Kavanagh 1905-1952 *ChPo S2*
Boggs, Thomas Richmond 1875- *WhWNAA*
Boggs, Tom 1905- *AmA&B*

Boggs, W Arthur 1916- *ConAu 17R*
Boggs, Wade Hamilton, Jr. 1916- *ConAu 13R*
Boggs, William Bambrick 1842-1913 *DcNAA*
Boggs, William Robertson 1829-1911 *DcNAA*
Bogh, Erik 1822-1899 *BbD, BiD&SB*
Bogie, David James 1905- *Au&Wr, WrD 1976*
Bogle, C D *ChPo, ChPo S1*
Bogle, Donald *AuNews 1*
Bogle, Evelyn E *ChPo S1*
Bogner, Norman 1935- *AuNews 2, ConAu 5R, WrD 1976*
Bognini, Joseph Miezan 1936- *AfA 1*
Bogomil, Pop *CasWL*
Bogorov, Ivan 1818-1892 *CasWL*
Bogoslovsky, Christina Steel 1888?-1974 *ConAu 49*
Bogovic, Mirko 1816-1893 *BbD, BiD&SB*
Bogue, Mrs. A H *DcNAA*
Bogue, Benjamin Nathaniel 1882- *IndAu 1917*
Bogue, David 1750-1815? *Alli, BiDLA, DcEnL*
Bogue, James W *Alli Sup*
Bogue, Lilian *DcAmA*
Bogue, Lucile Maxfield 1911- *ConAu 37, WrD 1976*
Bogue, Max *ConAu XR*
Bogue, Robert H 1889- *WhWNAA*
Bogus, Diane *BlkAW*
Bogusch, Ronald A 1931- *AmSCAP 66*
Boguslavski, Adalbert 1759-1829 *BbD, BiD&SB*
Boguslawski, Wojciech 1757-1829 *CasWL*
Boguszewska, Helena 1886- *CasWL*
Bogza, George 1908- *CasWL*
Bohan, Elizabeth Baker 1849-1942? *ChPo, DcNAA*
Bohan, Peter *ConAu 33*
Bohanan, Wally *BlkAW*
Bohannan, Paul 1920- *ConAu 9R, WrD 1976*
Bohanon, Mary *BlkAW*
Bohanon, Otto Leland *BlkAW*
Bohatta, Hanus 1864- *WhLA*
Bohemian *WhLA*
Bohemus, Martinus *OxGer*
Bohen, Sister Marian 1930- *ConAu 5R*
Bohi, M Janette 1927- *ConAu 25*
Bohl, Franz Marius Theodor 1882- *WhLA*
Bohl DeFaber, Cecilia Francisca Hosefa 1796-1877 *CasWL, DcEuL, DcSpL*
Bohl DeFaber, Juan Nicholas 1770-1836 *DcEuL, DcSpL*
Bohl VonFaber, Johann Nikolaus 1770-1863 *DcSpL*
Bohlander, Jill 1936- *ConAu 37*
Bohlau, Helene 1859-1940 *BiD&SB, ClDMEuL, OxGer*
Bohle, Bruce 1918- *ConAu 21*
Bohle, Edgar 1909- *ConAu 1R*
Bohlen, Joe M 1919- *ConAu 5R*
Bohlman, Edna McCaull 1897- *ConAu P-1*
Bohlman, Herbert W 1896- *ConAu P-1*
Bohm, Elixe *ChPo*
Bohm, Wilhelm 1877- *WhLA*
Bohme, David M 1916- *AmSCAP 66*
Bohme, Franz Magnus 1827-1898 *OxGer*
Bohme, Jakob 1575-1624 *BbD, BiD&SB, CasWL, EuA, EvEuW, OxGer, Pen Eur, REn*
Bohme, Martin *OxGer*
Bohmer, Auguste 1785-1800 *DcEuL*
Bohmer, Gunter 1911- *WhGrA*
Bohmert, Wilhelm 1866- *WhLA*
Bohn, C F *ChPo*
Bohn, Eric *DcNAA*
Bohn, Frank 1878-1975 *ConAu 57, OhA&B*
Bohn, Henry George 1796-1884 *Alli, Alli Sup, BrAu 19, DcEnL, OxEng, REn*
Bohn, Ralph C 1930- *ConAu 17R*
Bohnenblust, Gottfried 1883- *WhLA*
Bohnstedt, John W 1927- *ConAu 33*
Bohomolec, Franciszek 1720-1784 *CasWL, EvEuW*
Bohr, Niels Henrik David 1885-1962 *OxEng*
Bohr, R L 1916- *ConAu 25*
Bohr, Theophilus 1914- *ConAu XR*
Bohrnstedt, George W 1938- *ConAu 33*
Bohrod, Aaron 1907- *ConAu 23*
Bohse, August 1661-1730 *OxGer*
Bohun, Edmund 1645-1699? *Alli, DcEnL,*

NewC
Bohun, R *Alli*
Bohun, William *Alli*
Boiardo, Matteo Maria 1441?-1494 *CasWL, CyWA, DcEnL, DcEuL, EuA, EvEuW, OxEng, Pen Eur, RCom, REn*
Boice, James Montgomery 1938- *ConAu 29, WrD 1976*
Boie, Heinrich Christian 1744-1806 *CasWL, DcEuL, EvEuW, OxGer*
Boie, Margarete 1880-1946 *OxGer*
Boieldieu, Francois-Adrien 1775-1834 *OxFr*
Boies, Henry Lamson 1830-1887 *DcNAA*
Boies, Henry Martyn 1837-1903 *DcAmA, DcNAA*
Boies, Lura Anna 1835-1859 *ChPo, DcNAA*
Boileau *DcEnL*
Boileau, D *Alli, BiDLA*
Boileau, Lady Ethel Mary Young 1882?-1942 *EvLB, TwCA, TwCA Sup*
Boileau, Etienne d1269? *OxFr*
Boileau, Gilles 1631-1669 *OxFr*
Boileau, Jacques 1635-1716 *OxFr*
Boileau, Lambert De *OxCan*
Boileau, Nicolas 1636-1711 *CasWL, DcEuL, OxEng, Pen Eur, RCom, REn*
Boileau, Pierre 1906- *WorAu*
Boileau-Despreaux, Nicolas 1636-1711 *AtlBL, BbD, BiD&SB, CyWA, EuA, EvEuW, OxFr*
Boillot, Felix 1880- *WhLA*
Boillot, Leon *OxCan*
Boily, Robert *OxCan Sup*
Boirac, Emile 1851-1917 *BiDPar*
Bois *Alli*
Bois, Hector *NewC*
Bois, J Samuel 1892- *ConAu 33, WrD 1976*
Bois, Louis Edouard 1813-1889 *DcNAA, OxCan*
Boisard, Francois Marie 1744-1833 *BiD&SB*
Boise, James Robinson 1815-1895 *Alli, Alli Sup, CyAL 2, DcAmA, DcNAA*
Boise, Otis Bardwell 1844- *DcAmA*
Boise, Otis Bardwell 1844-1912 *DcNAA*
Boisgelin, Louis *BiDLA*
Boisgobey, Fortune-Abraham Du 1821-1891 *BbD, BiD&SB*
Boisgobey, Fortune De 1824-1891 *EvEuW*
Boisguillebert, Pierre De 1646-1714 *OxFr*
Boishebert, Charles Deschamps De 1727-1797 *OxCan*
Boishebert, Henri-Louis Deschamps De 1679-1736 *OxCan*
Boisius *Alli*
Boisot, Louis 1856-1933 *DcNAA*
Boisrobert, Francois LeMetel, Sieur De 1589-1662 *CasWL, DcEuL, EvEuW, OxFr, Pen Eur, REn*
Boisrouvray, Bernard Du, Dom 1877- *WhLA*
Boisseree, Sulpiz 1783-1854 *OxGer*
Boissevain, Edna St. Vincent Millay *WhWNAA*
Boissevain, Jeremy 1928- *ConAu 57, WrD 1976*
Boissier, Gaston 1823-1908 *BiD&SB, DcEuL, OxFr*
Boissonnault, Charles-Marie 1902- *OxCan, OxCan Sup, WhWNAA*
Boissonnault, Marie D 1875- *WhWNAA*
Boiste, Pierre-Claude-Victoire *OxFr*
Boisvert, Abraham-Edmond *OxCan*
Boit, Robert Apthorp 1846-1919 *Alli Sup, DcNAA*
Boitard, Francois 1670?-1717? *BkIE*
Boitard, Louis Philippe d1760? *BkIE*
Boito, Arrigo 1842-1918 *AtlBL, BiD&SB, CasWL, ClDMEuL, EuA, EvEuW, Pen Eur, REn*
Boivin, Leonce *OxCan*
Bojardo, Matteo Maria 1441?-1494 *BbD, BiD&SB, REn*
Bojer, Johan 1872-1959 *CasWL, ClDMEuL, CyWA, DcBiA, EncWL Sup, EvEuW, LongC, OxAm, Pen Eur, REn, REnAL, TwCA, TwCA Sup, WhLA*
Bojesen, Maria *Alli Sup*
Bok, Bart J 1906- *ConAu 49*
Bok, Cary W 1905-1970 *ConAu 29*
Bok, Curtis 1897-1962 *AmA&B*

Bok, Edward William 1863-1930 *Alli Sup,*
AmA&B, BiD&SB, DcAmA, DcLEnL,
DcNAA, OxAm, REn, REnAL, TwCA,
TwCA Sup, WhWNAA
Bok, Priscilla F 1896- *ConAu 49*
Bokenam, Osbern 1393?-1447? *CasWL, NewC*
Bokenham, Osbern 1393?-1447? *CasWL,*
NewC
Boker, George Henry 1823-1890 *Alli, Alli Sup,*
AmA, AmA&B, BbD, BiD&SB, CasWL,
ChPo, Chmbr 3, CnDAL, CnThe,
CyAL 2, DcAmA, DcEnL, DcLEnL,
DcNAA, EvLB, McGWD, OxAm,
Pen Am, REnAL, REnWD
Boker, Irving *IlBYP*
Bokum, Fanny Butcher 1888- *ConAu 37*
Bokum, Hermann 1807-1878? *Alli Sup,*
DcNAA
Bokun, Branko 1920- *ConAu 45*
Bokwe, John Knox 1855-1922 *AfA 1*
Bol, Ferdinand 1616-1680 *AtlBL*
Bolaffey, H V *Alli, BiDLA*
Bolaine, N *Alli*
Bolamba, Antoine-Roger 1913- *AfA 1, Pen Cl*
Boland, Bertram John 1913- *Au&Wr*
Boland, Bridget 1913- *ConDr, WrD 1976*
Boland, Charles J *PoIre*
Boland, Charles Michael 1917- *ConAu 9R*
Boland, Clay A 1903-1963 *AmSCAP 66*
Boland, Clay A, Jr. 1931- *AmSCAP 66*
Boland, Daniel 1891- *ConAu P-1*
Boland, Eavan Aisling 1944- *ConP 1970*
Boland, Eleanor -1883 *PoIre*
Boland, Frank Kells 1875-1953 *IndAu 1917,*
WhWNAA
Boland, J M *Alli Sup*
Boland, John 1913- *ConAu 9R*
Boland, Lillian C 1919- *ConAu 29*
Boland, Margaret Limburg 1906-1966
IndAu 1917
Bolanden, Konrad Von 1828- *BiD&SB*
Bolar, Edith Dunn *ChPo S2*
Bolch, Ben W 1938- *ConAu 57*
Bold *ChPo, ChPo S1*
Bold, Alan 1943- *ConAu 25, ConP 1970,*
ConP 1975, WrD 1976
Bold, Henry *Alli*
Bold, John 1679-1757 *Alli*
Bold, Ralph *WrD 1976*
Bold, Samuel *Alli*
Bolde, Samuel *Alli*
Bolde, Thomas *Alli*
Bolden, Joseph *IlBYP*
Bolderwood, Rolf 1827- *BbD*
Bolding, Amy Agnes 1910- *ConAu 25,*
WrD 1976
Boldrewood, Ralph *BrAu 19*
Boldrewood, Rolf 1826-1915 *Alli Sup,*
BiD&SB, CasWL, ChPo, Chmbr 3,
DcLEnL, EvLB, LongC, NewC, OxEng,
Pen Eng, REn, WebEAL
Boldt, Herman St. John 1856- *WhWNAA*
Bolduc, Jean Baptiste Zacharie 1818-1889 *BbtC,*
DcNAA
Bole, Simeon James 1875- *WhWNAA*
Bolee, Harold *MnBBF*
Bolenius, Emma Miller *WhWNAA*
Boles, Donald Edward 1926- *ConAu 1R*
Boles, Gordon *Alli Sup*
Boles, H Leo 1874- *WhWNAA*
Boles, Hal *WrD 1976*
Boles, Harold Wilson 1915- *ConAu 17R,*
IndAu 1917, WrD 1976
Boles, Ina M *ChPo, ChPo S2*
Boles, J *PoIre*
Boles, James 1919- *LivBA*
Boles, John B 1943- *ConAu 37*
Boles, Katherine *Alli*
Boles, Paul Darcy 1919- *Au&Wr, ConAu 9R,*
IndAu 1917, SmATA 9
Boles, Robert E 1943- *BlkAW, DrAF 1976,*
LivBAA
Boleslavski, Richard 1887-1937 *AmA&B*
Boleslawita, B *EuA*
Boley, Jean 1914-1957 *AmA&B, AmNov*
Boley, William Henry 1883-1939 *DcNAA*
Boleyn, Anne 1507?-1536 *NewC, REn*
Bolgan, Anne C 1923- *ConAu 41*

Bolgar, Boyan 1910- *CasWL*
Bolger, Francis *OxCan*
Bolger, Francis Joseph 1914- *Au&Wr*
Bolger, Philip C 1927- *ConAu 57*
Boliac, Cezar 1813-1881 *CasWL*
Bolian, Polly 1925- *ConAu 33, IlBYP,*
SmATA 4
Bolieu *Alli*
Bolin, Luis 1894-1969 *ConAu 23*
Bolin, Mayne *MnBBF*
Bolin, Nicolai P 1908- *AmSCAP 66*
Bolina, Jack La 1842- *WhLA*
Boling, Katharine 1933- *ConAu 57*
Bolingbroke, Henry *Alli, BiDLA*
Bolingbroke, Henry St. John, Viscount 1678-1751
Alli, BbD, BiD&SB, BrAu, CasWL,
Chmbr 2, DcEnA, DcEnL, DcEuL,
DcLEnL, EvLB, NewC, OxEng, Pen Eng,
REn, WebEAL
Bolingbroke, William *MnBBF*
Bolinger, Dwight LeMerton 1907- *ConAu 13R,*
DcSpL, WrD 1976
Bolinger, Martha Louise 1917- *TexWr*
Bolino, August C 1922- *ConAu 1R,*
WrD 1976
Bolintineanu, Dimitrie 1819?-1872 *BiD&SB,*
CasWL, EvEuW
Bolio, Dolores 1882- *WhWNAA*
Bolitho, Archie A 1886- *ConAu P-1*
Bolitho, Henry Hector 1897?-1974 *Au&Wr,*
ConAu 53, ConAu P-1, DcLEnL, EvLB,
LongC, NewC, Pen Eng, TwCA,
TwCA Sup
Bolitho, William 1815-1895 *ChPo S2*
Bolitho, William 1890-1930? *DcLEnL, LongC,*
NewC, TwCA
Bolivar, Simon 1783-1830 *CasWL, DcSpL,*
Pen Am, REn
Boll, Carl R 1894- *ConAu P-1*
Boll, David 1931- *Au&Wr, ConAu 21,*
WrD 1976
Boll, Ernest *ConAu XR*
Boll, Heinrich 1917- *CasWL, ConAu 21,*
ConLC 2, ConLC 3, ConLC 6, EncWL,
EvEuW, ModGL, OxGer, Pen Eur, REn,
TwCW, WhTwL, WorAu
Boll, Jacob 1828-1880 *BiDSA*
Boll, Theo *ConAu XR*
Boll, Theophilus E M 1902- *ConAu 37,*
WrD 1976
Bollaert, William *Alli Sup*
Bollan, William d1776 *Alli, BbtC, DcAmA*
Bolland, Jean 1596-1665 *CasWL*
Bolland, John *Alli Sup*
Bolland, William *Alli, BiDLA*
Bolland, William Ernest *Alli Sup*
Bollard, Richard *Alli*
Bolle, Kees W 1927- *ConAu 25*
Bollen, Roger 1942?- *AuNews 1*
Bollens, John C 1920- *ConAu 1R*
Boller, Alfred Pancoast 1840-1912 *Alli Sup,*
DcAmA, DcNAA
Boller, Henry Augustus 1838-1902 *Alli Sup,*
DcNAA
Boller, Paul Franklin, Jr. 1916- *ConAu 1R*
Bolles, Albert Sidney 1846?-1939 *Alli Sup,*
DcAmA
Bolles, Alfred Sidney 1846?-1939 *DcNAA*
Bolles, Blair 1911- *AmA&B, ConAu 9R,*
WrD 1976
Bolles, Frank 1856-1894 *AmA&B, BiD&SB,*
ChPo, DcAmA, DcNAA
Bolles, J *ChPo*
Bolles, James Aaron 1810-1894 *Alli Sup,*
DcNAA, OhA&B
Bolles, John Augustus 1809-1878 *DcAmA,*
DcNAA
Bolles, John Rogers 1810-1895 *ChPo, DcNAA*
Bolles, Richard Nelson 1927- *ConAu 45*
Bolles, Robert C 1928- *ConAu 21*
Bolles, Sarah *ChPo*
Bolles, Simeon 1830- *DcNAA*
Bolles, William 1800-1883 *DcNAA*
Bolliac, Cezar 1813-1881 *CasWL*
Bolliger, Max 1929- *ConAu 25, SmATA 7*
Bolling, George Melville 1871- *WhWNAA*
Bolling, Richard 1916- *ConAu 17R,*
WrD 1976

Bolling, Robert *BiDSA*
Bollivar, Oliver *ChPo*
Bollman, Justus Erick 1769-1821 *DcNAA*
Bollman, Lewis 1811-1888 *IndAu 1816*
Bollo, Sarah *Au&Wr*
Bolls, Imogene L *DrAP 1975*
Bolmar, Antoine 1797-1861 *DcNAA*
Bolmer, William Brevoort *Alli Sup*
Bolner, James 1936- *ConAu 61*
Bolnest, Edward *Alli*
Bolo, Solomon *ConAu XR*
Bolognese, Donald Alan 1934- *ChPo S1,*
ChPo S2, IlBYP, IlCB 1966
Bolombo, G *AfA 1*
Bolron, R *Alli*
Bolsche, Wilhelm 1861-1939 *ClDMEuL,*
OxGer
Bolster, Sister M Angela 1925- *Au&Wr*
Bolster, William Wheeler 1823-1907 *DcAmA,*
DcNAA
Bolt, Carol *OxCan Sup*
Bolt, David Michael Langstone 1927- *Au&Wr,*
ConAu 1R
Bolt, Robert 1924- *CasWL, CnThe,*
ConAu 17R, ConDr, CrCD, McGWD,
ModWD, NewC, Pen Eng, REnWD,
TwCW, WebEAL, WorAu, WrD 1976
Bolt, Robert 1925- *LongC, ModBL Sup*
Bolte, Carl E, Jr. 1929- *AmSCAP 66*
Bolte, Charles Guy 1920- *AmA&B*
Bolte, Johannes 1858- *WhLA*
Bolte, John Willard 1884-1942 *DcNAA*
Bolten, Steven E 1941- *ConAu 37*
Bolton, A M *Alli Sup*
Bolton, A S *Alli Sup*
Bolton, Aquila Massey 1773-1857 *OhA&B*
Bolton, Carole 1926- *ConAu 49, SmATA 6*
Bolton, Charles *MnBBF*
Bolton, Charles Edward 1841-1901 *DcAmA,*
DcNAA, OhA&B
Bolton, Charles Knowles 1867-1950 *Alli Sup,*
AmA&B, BiD&SB, ChPo, DcAmA,
OhA&B, WhWNAA
Bolton, Cornelius Winter 1819- *Alli, Alli Sup*
Bolton, E C *BbtC*
Bolton, Edmund 1575?-1633? *Alli, CasWL,*
ChPo, DcEnL, DcLEnL, NewC
Bolton, Edmund And Webber, Horace Hervey
Alli Sup
Bolton, Ethel 1873-1954 *AmA&B, DcAmA*
Bolton, Evelyn 1928- *ConAu XR*
Bolton, F H *MnBBF*
Bolton, F T *MnBBF*
Bolton, Francis *Alli Sup*
Bolton, Sir Francis John d1887 *Alli Sup*
Bolton, Frederick Samuel *Alli Sup*
Bolton, George *Alli, BiDLA*
Bolton, Guy Reginald 1884- *AmA&B,*
AmSCAP 66, ConAu 5R, ConDr, LongC,
ModWD
Bolton, H W *Alli Sup*
Bolton, Hannah *Alli Sup*
Bolton, Henrietta d1930 *DcNAA*
Bolton, Henry *Alli Sup*
Bolton, Henry Carrington 1843-1903 *Alli Sup,*
BiD&SB, ChPo S1, DcAmA, DcNAA,
St&VC
Bolton, Herbert Eugene 1870-1953 *AmA&B,*
AmLY, OxAm, TexWr
Bolton, Horace Wilbert 1839- *DcNAA*
Bolton, Isabel *AmA&B, AmNov, ConAu XR,*
LongC, TwCA Sup
Bolton, Isobel 1883- *REnAL*
Bolton, Ivy May 1879- *AuBYP*
Bolton, James *Alli, BiDLA*
Bolton, James Jay 1824-1863 *Alli Sup*
Bolton, John *Alli, Alli Sup*
Bolton, John Robert Glorney 1901- *Au&Wr*
Bolton, Kenneth Ewart 1914- *Au&Wr,*
ConAu 9R
Bolton, M P W *Alli Sup*
Bolton, Maisie Sharman 1915- *ConAu 9R*
Bolton, Mother Margaret 1873-1943 *CatA 1947,*
DcNAA
Bolton, Nathaniel d1858 *IndAu 1816*
Bolton, Philip *Alli Sup*
Bolton, Mrs. R D *Alli Sup*
Bolton, Reginald Pelham 1856-1942 *DcNAA,*

Boner, Edmund d1569 *Alli*

Boner, Hieronymus *OxGer*

Boner, John Henry 1845-1903 *Alli Sup, AmA, AmA&B, BiD&SB, BiDSA, ChPo, ChPo S1, CnDAL, DcAmA, DcNAA*

Boner, Sally *TexWr*

Boner, Ulrich d1349 *CasWL, DcEuL, EvEuW, OxGer*

Bones, James *Alli*

Boness, A James 1928- *ConAu 37, WrD 1976*

Boness, Clarence M 1931- *AmSCAP 66*

Bonesteel, Mary 1864- *DcNAA*

Bonet, Honore 1345?-1406? *CasWL, EvEuW*

Bonett, Emery *ConAu XR, WrD 1976*

Bonett, John *ConAu XR, WrD 1976*

Bonett, John And Emery *EncM&D*

Boney, F N 1929- *ConAu 41*

Boney, William Jerry 1930- *ConAu 23*

Bonfils, Winifred Black *WhWNAA*

Bonfini, Antonio 1427?-1502? *CasWL*

Bonfons, Jean Carmine *OxCan*

Bongar, Emmet W 1919- *ConAu 33*

Bongard, Hermann 1921- *WhGrA*

Bongartz, Heinz *ConAu 49*

Bongartz, Roy 1924- *AmA&B, ConAu 13R*

Bonger, William Adriaan 1876- *WhLA*

Bonghi, Ruggero 1826-1895 *BiD&SB, CasWL*

Bongie, Laurence L 1929- *ConAu 61*

Bonham, Barbara Thomas 1926- *ConAu 17R, SmATA 7, WrD 1976*

Bonham, Frank 1914- *AuBYP, ConAu 9R, MorBMP, SmATA 1, ThBJA*

Bonham, Jeriah *Alli Sup*

Bonham, John 1907- *Au&Wr, WrD 1976*

Bonham, John M *Alli Sup*

Bonham, John Milton 1835-1897 *DcNAA*

Bonham, Milledge Louis 1880-1941 *AmA&B, DcNAA, WhWNAA*

Bonham, Thomas *Alli, ChPo*

Bonham Carter, Mark Raymond 1922- *Au&Wr*

Bonham-Carter, Victor 1913- *Au&Wr, ConAu 9R, WrD 1976*

Bonham Carter, Violet 1887- *ConAu 17, LongC*

Bonheim, Helmut 1930- *ConAu 1R*

Bonheur, Maria Rosa 1822-1899 *ChPo S1*

Bonhoeffer, Dietrich 1906-1945 *OxGer, WorAu*

Bonhome, Richard *Alli*

Bonhomme Richard *REn*

Bonhote, Elizabeth *Alli, BiDLA*

Bonhote, P L D *Alli, BiDLA*

Boni, Albert 1892- *AmA&B*

Boni, Margaret Bradford 1893?-1974 *AmA&B, ConAu 53*

Boni, Nazi 1910-1969 *AfA 1*

Boniface, Saint 680?-755 *Alli, BiB S, BiD&SB, CasWL, DcEnL, NewC, OxGer*

Bonifaci Calvo *CasWL*

Bonifacio Calvo *EvEuW*

Bonifacio DeAndrada Esilva, Jose 1765-1838 *Pen Am*

Bonile, L *Alli Sup*

Bonilla Y San Martin, Adolfo 1875-1926 *ClDMEuL, DcSpL*

Bonime, Florence 1907- *ConAu 49, DrAF 1976*

Bonime, Josef 1891-1959 *AmSCAP 66*

Bonime, Walter 1909- *ConAu 17*

Bonin, Daniel 1861- *WhLA*

Bonin, Joseph 1845-1917 *DcNAA*

Bonine, Gladys Nichols 1907- *ConAu P-1, IndAu 1917*

Bonington, Christian 1934- *ConAu 45, WrD 1976*

Bonington, Richard Parkes 1802-1828 *AtlBL*

Bonini, Charles P 1933- *ConAu 13R*

Bonivard, Francois De 1493?-1570 *NewC*

Bonjean, Charles M 1935- *ConAu 41*

Bonjour, Adrien 1912- *Au&Wr*

Bonjour, Edgar Conrad *Au&Wr*

Bonk, James *DrAP 1975*

Bonk, Wallace J 1923- *ConAu 9R*

Bonker, Frances 1895- *WhWNAA*

Bonn, John Louis 1906- *CatA 1947*

Bonn, M J 1873- *WhLA*

Bonnar, Alphonsus 1895-1968 *ConAu P-1*

Bonnar, John *Alli*

Bonnard, Isabel Stewart Way *WhWNAA*

Bonnard, Pierre 1867-1947 *AtlBL*

Bonnard, Sylvestre *OxFr*

Bonnault, Claude De *OxCan*

Bonne, Georg 1859- *WhLA*

Bonne, Nii Kwabena, III 1888-1960? *AfA 1*

Bonneau, Jacob d1786 *BkIE*

Bonnechose, Charles De *OxCan*

Bonnechose, Emile Boisnormand De 1801-1875 *BbD, BiD&SB*

Bonnefoy, Yves 1923- *Au&Wr, CasWL, EncWL Sup, Pen Eur, REn, WhTwL, WorAu*

Bonnekamp, Sonja Maria 1930- *Au&Wr*

Bonnel, James 1653-1699 *Alli*

Bonnell, Dorothy Haworth 1914- *ConAu 1R*

Bonnell, George *Alli*

Bonnell, Henry Houston 1859-1926 *DcNAA*

Bonnell, J M *BiDSA*

Bonnell, James 1653-1699 *Alli*

Bonnell, John Mitchell 1820-1871 *DcNAA*

Bonnell, John Sutherland 1893- *ConAu 5R*

Bonnelle, Frank J *ChPo S2*

Bonnelycke, Emil Christian Theodor 1893-1953 *CasWL*

Bonner, Carey 1859- *ChPo S1, WhLA*

Bonner, Charles 1896-1965 *AmA&B, AmNov*

Bonner, David Findley 1842- *OhA&B*

Bonner, Edmund d1569 *Alli*

Bonner, Gerald 1926- *ConAu 9R*

Bonner, Geraldine 1870-1930 *AmLY, DcNAA, WhWNAA*

Bonner, Hypatia Bradlaugh 1858- *WhLA*

Bonner, J *Alli, BiDLA*

Bonner, James *Alli*

Bonner, James Calvin 1904- *ConAu 9R, WrD 1976*

Bonner, John 1828-1899 *Alli, BbtC, CyAL 2, DcNAA*

Bonner, John Tyler 1920- *ConAu 49*

Bonner, Marita *BlkAW*

Bonner, Mary Graham 1890-1974 *AmA&B, AuBYP, CanNov, CarSB, ChPo, ConAu 49, WhWNAA*

Bonner, Michael *ConAu XR*

Bonner, Parker *ConAu XR, WrD 1976*

Bonner, Paul Hyde 1893-1968 *AmA&B, ConAu 1R*

Bonner, Raleigh *WhWNAA*

Bonner, Richard *Alli*

Bonner, Robert 1824-1899 *AmA&B*

Bonner, Ronnie 1920- *AmSCAP 66*

Bonner, Sherwood 1849-1883 *Alli Sup, AmA, AmA&B, BiDSA, DcAmA, DcNAA, OxAm, REnAL*

Bonner, Thomas N 1923- *ConAu 9R*

Bonner, William H 1924- *ConAu 53*

Bonnet, John *Alli*

Bonnet, Marie Marguerite 1865- *BiDSA*

Bonnet, Theodore F 1865-1920 *DcNAA*

Bonnetain, Paul *Alli Sup*

Bonnette, Jeanne 1907- *ConAu 41*

Bonnette, Victor *ConAu XR*

Bonneval, Claude-Alexandre, Comte De 1675-1747 *OxFr*

Bonneville, Benjamin Louis Eulalie De 1796-1878 *OxAm*

Bonneville, Douglas A 1931- *ConAu 21*

Bonney, Bill *ConAu XR*

Bonney, Callie L *ChPo*

Bonney, Catherine VanRensselaer *Alli Sup*

Bonney, Charles Carroll 1831-1903 *Alli Sup, DcAmA, DcNAA*

Bonney, Edward 1807-1864 *Alli Sup, AmA&B, DcNAA*

Bonney, Edwin Merl 1902- *WrD 1976*

Bonney, H Orrin 1903- *ConAu 9R*

Bonney, Lorriane G 1922- *ConAu 45*

Bonney, Merl E 1902- *ConAu 33*

Bonney, Mrs. P P *Alli Sup*

Bonney, S W *Alli Sup*

Bonney, Thomas *Alli*

Bonney, Thomas George 1833- *Alli Sup*

Bonney, William H *REnAL*

Bonnice, Joseph G 1930- *ConAu 49*

Bonnie, Richard J 1945- *ConAu 53*

Bonnieres, Robert De 1850- *BiD&SB*

Bonnifield, M S And Healy, T W *Alli Sup*

Bonnivard, Francois De 1493?-1570 *NewC, REn*

Bonnor, C *Alli, BiDLA*

Bonnor, Charles *Alli, BiDLA*

Bonnor, T *Alli*

Bonnor, Thomas *BkIE*

Bonnor, William Bowen 1920- *ConAu 9R, WrD 1976*

Bonny Dundee *NewC*

Bonny, Helen L 1921- *ConAu 49*

Bonny, Henry Kaye *Alli*

Bonnycastle, Charles 1792-1840 *Alli, DcNAA*

Bonnycastle, John d1821 *Alli, BiDLA*

Bonnycastle, R H *Alli*

Bonnycastle, Sir Richard Henry 1791-1847 *Alli, BbtC, DcLEnL, DcNAA, OxCan*

Bonnye, J H *Alli Sup*

Bonoeil, John *Alli*

Bonomi, J *Alli*

Bons, Jan 1918- *WhGrA*

Bonsal, Stephen 1865?-1951 *AmA&B, BiD&SB, BiDSA, DcAmA, OxAm, REnAL, TwCA Sup*

Bonsall, A J *ChPo*

Bonsall, Bartram L *Alli Sup*

Bonsall, Crosby Barbara Newell 1921- *IlBYP, IlCB 1966, ThBJA*

Bonsall, Elizabeth Hubbard 1890-1937 *DcNAA, WhWNAA*

Bonsels, Waldemar 1881-1952 *ClDMEuL, OxGer, TwCA, TwCA Sup*

Bonser, A E *MnBBF*

Bonser, Frederick Gordon 1875-1931 *DcNAA, WhWNAA*

Bonser, Thomas Athelstan 1860-1935 *OhA&B*

Bonshor, Frederick *ChPo S1*

Bonstetten, Charles-Victor De 1745-1832 *OxFr*

Bonstetten, Karl Viktor Von 1745-1832 *EvEuW, OxGer*

Bonte, George Willard 1873-1946 *DcNAA, OhA&B*

Bontekoe, Willem Ysbrandsz 1587-1630? *CasWL*

Bontempelli, Massimo 1878-1960 *CasWL, ClDMEuL, CnMD, EncWL, McGWD, ModWD, Pen Eur*

Bontempo, Charles J 1931- *ConAu 61*

Bontemps, Arna Wendell 1902-1973 *AmA&B, AmNov, AnMV 1926, Au&Wr, AuBYP, BkCL, BlkAW, ChPo S1, ConAu 1R, ConAu 41, ConLC 1, ConP 1970, JBA 1951, MorBMP, OxAm, REnAL, SmATA 2, St&VC, WebEAL*

Bontemps, Roger *OxFr*

Bontly, Thomas 1939- *ConAu 57, DrAF 1976*

Bontsema, Peter H 1897- *AmSCAP 66*

Bonus, Arthur 1864- *WhLA*

Bonus, Beate 1865- *WhLA*

Bonus, Daniel H 1887- *WhWNAA*

Bonus, John *Alli Sup*

Bonvesin Da La Riva 1240?-1315? *CasWL*

Bonwell, James *Alli*

Bonwick, James 1817-1906 *Alli Sup, DcLEnL*

Bonwick, T And Birch, J A *Alli Sup*

Bonwicke, Ambrose 1652- *Alli*

Bonx, Nathan J 1900-1950 *AmSCAP 66*

Bonynge, Robert W And Ward, Edwin C *Alli Sup*

Bonynge, Robert William 1863-1939 *DcNAA*

Bonzon, Paul Jacques 1908- *Au&Wr, AuBYP*

Boodin, John Elof 1869- *WhWNAA*

Boodle, Adelaide A *Alli Sup*

Boodle, Richard George *Alli Sup*

Boodman, David M 1923- *ConAu 23*

Boody, Emma Campbell *ChPo S2*

Boog, Carl Michel 1877- *ChPo*

Boog Watson, Elspeth Janet 1900- *Au&Wr, ConAu P-1*

Boojum *WhWNAA*

Book, John William 1850- *DcAmA, DcNAA, IndAu 1816*

Book, Martin Fredrik 1883-1961 *CasWL*

Book, William Frederick 1873-1940 *DcNAA, IndAu 1816, WhWNAA*

Book, William Henry 1863-1946 *DcNAA, IndAu 1816, WhWNAA*

Book-Senninger, Claude 1928- *ConAu 45*

Booker, Christopher *ChPo S2*

Booker, Daniel *Alli*
Booker, Edward *Alli Sup*
Booker, Ellen *Alli Sup*
Booker, Frank 1909- *Au&Wr*
Booker, John *Alli Sup*
Booker, John 1601-1667 *Alli*
Booker, John 1820-1895 *ChPo*
Booker, Luke 1762-1836 *Alli, BiDLA, ChPo S1*
Booker, Moore *PoIre*
Booker, More *Alli*
Booker, Simeon, Jr. *BlkAW*
Booker, Simeon Saunders 1918- *ConAu 9R, LivBAA*
Bookey, Sacheverell *Alli*
Bookie, Pede *WhWNAA*
Bookspan, Martin 1926- *ConAu 41*
Bookstaber, Philip David 1892- *WhWNAA*
Bookstein, Abraham 1940- *ConAu 53*
Bookwalter, John Wesley 1837-1915 *DcAmA, DcNAA, IndAu 1816, OhA&B*
Bookwalter, Lewis 1846-1935 *OhA&B*
Bool, A H *Alli Sup*
Boole, Ella Alexander 1858-1952 *OhA&B*
Boole, George 1815-1864 *Alli, Alli Sup, BrAu 19*
Boole, Mary *Alli Sup*
Boole, W H *Alli Sup*
Bools, Andrew *Alli Sup*
Boom, Alfred B 1928- *ConAu 25*
Boon, Francis *ConAu XR*
Boon, Louis Paul 1912- *CasWL, WhTwL*
Boon, Violet Mary *Au&Wr*
Boone, Charles Eugene *ConAu XR*
Boone, Charles Theodore 1838-1903 *Alli Sup, DcAmA, DcNAA*
Boone, Colin Campbell 1930- *Au&Wr*
Boone, Daniel 1734?-1820 *Alli, AmA&B, BiDSA, REn, REnAL*
Boone, Daniel R 1927- *ConAu 33, WrD 1976*
Boone, Henry Burnham 1872- *BiDSA*
Boone, James Shergold *Alli Sup*
Boone, Louis E 1941- *ConAu 41*
Boone, Pat 1934- *AmA&B, AmSCAP 66, ConAu 1R, SmATA 7, WrD 1976*
Boone, Richard Gause 1849-1923 *DcAmA, DcNAA, IndAu 1816, OhA&B*
Boone, Silas K *CarSB*
Boone, Stella A *TexWr*
Boone, T C *Alli*
Boone, Theodore Sylvester 1896- *WhWNAA*
Boone, William Jones 1811-1864 *BiDSA*
Booraem, H Toler *Alli Sup*
Booraem, John VanVorst 1838-1923 *DcNAA*
Boorde, Andrew 1490?-1549 *Alli, Chmbr 1, EvLB*
Boore, Walter Hugh 1904- *Au&Wr, ConAu 5R, WrD 1976*
Boorer, Wendy 1931- *ConAu 57*
Boorman, Henry Roy Pratt 1900- *Au&Wr*
Boorman, Howard L 1920- *ConAu 41*
Boorman, N *Alli*
Boorman, Scott A 1949- *ConAu 29*
Boorman, Sylvia *OxCan Sup*
Boorne, James *Alli Sup*
Boorstin, Daniel J 1914- *AmA&B, AuNews 2, ConAu 1R, WorAu, WrD 1976*
Boos, Frank Holgate 1893-1968 *ConAu 33*
Boos, Roman 1889- *WhLA*
Boos, William Frederick 1870-1949 *DcNAA*
Boosey, Thomas *Alli Sup*
Boot, John C G 1936- *ConAu 17R, WrD 1976*
Boot, W H J *ChPo, ChPo S1, ChPo S2*
Boote, Richard d1782 *Alli*
Booth, A *Alli*
Booth, Abraham 1734-1806 *Alli, DcEnL*
Booth, Alice *WhWNAA*
Booth, Amelia *REn*
Booth, Arthur Harold 1902- *Au&Wr*
Booth, Arthur John *Alli Sup*
Booth, Barbara *DrAP 1975*
Booth, Barton 1681-1733 *Alli, Chmbr 2, NewC*
Booth, Benjamin *Alli*
Booth, Bessie Walker *TexWr*
Booth, Bradford Allen 1909- *AmA&B*
Booth, Catherine *Alli Sup*
Booth, Charles 1840-1916 *BrAu 19, DcLEnL,*

LongC, OxEng
Booth, Charles Douglas Greaves 1887-1944 *DcNAA*
Booth, Charles Gordon 1896-1949 *AmA&B, WhWNAA*
Booth, Charles Octavius 1845- *DcNAA*
Booth, Charles Orrell 1918- *Au&Wr, ConAu 13R*
Booth, Christopher B *MnBBF*
Booth, Clarice Foster *ChPo*
Booth, Clifton Huey 1918- *ChPo*
Booth, D E *MnBBF*
Booth, David 1766-1846 *Alli, BiDLA*
Booth, Desmond John 1924- *Au&Wr*
Booth, E T *Alli Sup*
Booth, Edward C *ChPo*
Booth, Edwin *ConAu 17R*
Booth, Edwin Carton *Alli Sup*
Booth, Edwin Gillam 1810-1886 *DcNAA*
Booth, Edwin Prince 1898- *ChPo*
Booth, Edwin Thomas 1833-1893 *OxAm, REn, REnAL*
Booth, Eleanor Dixon *ChPo*
Booth, Eliza M J Von *Alli Sup*
Booth, Emma Scarr 1835-1927 *OhA&B*
Booth, Emmons Rutledge 1851-1934 *OhA&B*
Booth, Ernest Sheldon 1915- *ConAu 53*
Booth, Eva Gore *PoIre*
Booth, Felix *OxCan*
Booth, Franklin 1874-1948 *ChPo S1, IndAu 1917*
Booth, Frederick 1882-1948 *IndAu 1917*
Booth, Geoffrey *WrD 1976*
Booth, George *Alli, Alli Sup, BiDLA Sup*
Booth, George, Earl Of Warrington *Alli*
Booth, George C 1901- *ConAu P-1*
Booth, George Wilson 1844-1914 *DcNAA*
Booth, Gotthard 1899- *BiDPar*
Booth, Graham Charles 1935- *IlBYP, IlCB 1966*
Booth, H *Alli, BiDLA*
Booth, Harold Simmons 1891- *WhWNAA*
Booth, Harry John 1923- *Au&Wr*
Booth, Henry 1788-1869 *Alli Sup*
Booth, Henry, Earl Of Warrington 1651-1693 *Alli*
Booth, Henry Kendall 1876-1942 *DcNAA*
Booth, Henry Matthias 1843-1899 *Alli Sup, DcAmA, DcNAA*
Booth, Herbert 1862-1926 *DcNAA*
Booth, Hesketh *Alli Sup*
Booth, Irwin *ConAu XR*
Booth, James 1796-1880 *Alli Sup*
Booth, James 1806-1878 *Alli Sup*
Booth, James Curtis 1810-1888 *Alli, DcAmA, DcNAA*
Booth, John *Alli, Alli Sup, BiDLA*
Booth, John Bennion 1880-1961 *LongC*
Booth, John E 1919- *ConAu 9R*
Booth, John Wilkes 1838-1865 *OxAm, REn, REnAL*
Booth, Joseph *Alli*
Booth, Josiah 1852-1930 *ChPo*
Booth, Junius Brutus 1796-1852 *OxAm, REn, REnAL*
Booth, Martin 1944- *ConP 1970, ConP 1975, WrD 1976*
Booth, Mary H C 1831-1865 *Alli Sup, DcNAA*
Booth, Mary Josephine *WhWNAA*
Booth, Mary Louise 1831-1899 *Alli Sup, AmA&B, BiD&SB, CyAL 2*
Booth, Mary Louise 1831-1889 *DcAmA*
Booth, Mary Louise 1831-1899 *DcNAA*
Booth, Maud Ballington 1865-1948 *CarSB, DcAmA, NewC*
Booth, Ned *MnBBF*
Booth, Newton 1825-1892 *IndAu 1816*
Booth, Patrick *Alli Sup, MnBBF*
Booth, Patrick John 1929- *Au&Wr, ConAu P-1*
Booth, Peniston *Alli*
Booth, Philip 1907- *ChPo S1*
Booth, Philip 1925- *AmA&B, ConAu 5R, ConP 1970, ConP 1975, DrAP 1975, Pen Am, WorAu, WrD 1976*
Booth, Philip E *ChPo*
Booth, Pithie *Alli Sup*
Booth, Richard T *Alli Sup*

Booth, Robert *Alli*
Booth, Rosemary Frances 1928- *ConAu 53, WrD 1976*
Booth, S M *Alli Sup*
Booth, Samuel *Alli Sup*
Booth, Taylor L 1933- *ConAu 53*
Booth, W H *Alli Sup*
Booth, Walter S *Alli Sup*
Booth, Walter Sherman 1827-1901 *DcNAA*
Booth, Wayne Clayson 1921- *ConAu 1R, Pen Am, WrD 1976*
Booth, William *Alli Sup, ChPo S1*
Booth, William 1829-1912 *Alli Sup, LongC, NewC, REn*
Booth, William H, Goodman, J & Gregory,s *Alli Sup*
Booth, William Stone 1864-1926 *DcNAA*
Booth-Tucker, Frederick St. G DeLatour 1853- *BiD&SB, DcAmA, WhLA*
Boothby, B *Alli*
Boothby, Sir Brooke *Alli, BiDLA Sup*
Boothby, F *Alli*
Boothby, Frederick Lewis Maitland *WhLA*
Boothby, Guy Newell 1867-1905 *BrAu 19, Chmbr 3, EncM&D, EvLB, LongC, MnBBF*
Boothby, Josiah *Alli Sup*
Boothby, Richard *Alli*
Boothe, Clare 1903- *AmA&B, LongC, McGWD, ModWD, OxAm, REnAL, TwCA, TwCA Sup*
Boothe, Clare ALSO Luce, Clare Boothe
Boothe, James R 1917- *AmSCAP 66*
Boothe, N *Alli*
Boothhouse, Samuel *Alli*
Boothroyd, Basil 1910- *Au&Wr, ConAu 33, WrD 1976*
Boothroyd, Benjamin 1768-1836 *Alli, BiDLA*
Boothroyd, Geoffrey 1925- *Au&Wr*
Boothroyd, Samuel Latimer 1874- *WhWNAA*
Booton, Catherine Kage 1919- *Au&Wr, ConAu 61*
Booton, Harold William 1932- *Au&Wr, WrD 1976*
Booton, John Heiskell *BiDSA*
Boott, Francis 1792-1863 *Alli Sup*
Boott, William *Alli Sup*
Booty, Frederick *Alli Sup*
Booty, James Horatio *Alli Sup*
Booy, Theodoor De *DcNAA*
Boozer, H W *Alli Sup*
Bopp, Franz 1791-1867 *DcEuL*
Bopp, Raul 1898- *Pen Am*
Boppe, Meister *OxGer*
Boque, J Russell *MnBBF*
Bor, Matej 1913- *EncWL*
Bor, Matej 1913- *CasWL, ModSL 2*
Bor, Pieter 1559-1635 *CasWL*
Boraas, Julius 1871- *WhWNAA*
Boraas, Roger S 1926- *ConAu 33*
Borah, Leo Arthur 1889- *WhWNAA*
Borah, William Edgar 1865-1940 *DcNAA, REn*
Borah, Woodrow 1912- *ConAu 5R*
Boraischa, Menahem 1888-1949 *Pen Eur*
Boraston, George *Alli*
Boraston, William *Alli*
Boratynski *DcRusL*
Boratynsky, Yevgeny 1800-1844 *Pen Eur*
Borberg, Svend 1888-1947 *CasWL, CnMD, EvEuW*
Borbstaedt, A And Dwyer, Francis *Alli Sup*
Borch, Ole 1626-1690 *DcEuL*
Borch, Ted *ConAu XR*
Borchard, Edwin Montefiore 1884- *AmLY*
Borchard, Ruth 1910- *Au&Wr, ConAu 13R*
Borchardt, Bernard Fendig 1889- *WhWNAA*
Borchardt, Dietrich Hans 1916- *ConAu 23*
Borchardt, Frank L 1938- *ConAu 33, WrD 1976*
Borchardt, Georg *OxGer*
Borchardt, Hermann 1888-1951 *CatA 1952*
Borchardt, Ludwig 1863- *WhLA*
Borchardt, Rudolf 1877-1945 *CasWL, ClDMEuL, EncWL, ModGL, OxGer, Pen Eur*
Borchers, Eduard 1885- *WhLA*
Borchers, Gladys L 1891- *ConAu P-1*

Borchert, Gerald L 1932- *ConAu 37*
Borchert, Wolfgang 1921-1947 *CasWL, CnMD, CnThe, CrCD, EncWL, McGWD, ModGL, ModWD, OxGer, Pen Eur, REnWD, WorAu*
Borchgrevink, Carsten Egeberg 1864- *WhLA*
Borchsenius, Poul 1897- *Au&Wr*
Borck, Caspar Wilhelm Von 1704-1747 *CasWL, OxGer*
Borcke, Caspar Wilhelm Von 1704-1747 *OxGer*
Borcosque, Carlos 1894- *WhWNAA*
Borda, Jean-Charles 1733-1799 *OxFr*
Borde, Andrew 1500?-1549 *Alli, DcEnL, EvLB*
Bordeaux, Henry 1870-1963 *CasWL, CatA 1947, ClDMEuL, EncWL, EvEuW, LongC, OxFr, REn, TwCA, TwCA Sup*
Borden, Charles A 1912-1968 *AuBYP, ConAu 5R*
Borden, Henry 1901- *ConAu 41, OxCan Sup*
Borden, John 1825-1918 *DcNAA*
Borden, Lee *ConAu XR, WrD 1976*
Borden, Lizzie 1860-1927 *OxAm, REn, REnAL*
Borden, Lucille Papin 1873- *AmA&B, BkC 3, CatA 1947, WhWNAA*
Borden, M *ConAu XR*
Borden, Mary 1886-1968 *ConAu 25, ConAu P-1, EvLB, LongC, TwCA, TwCA Sup, WhWNAA*
Borden, Mattie Fuller *BiDSA*
Borden, Morton 1925- *ConAu 9R*
Borden, Neil Hopper 1895- *Au&Wr, ConAu 1R*
Borden, Norman E, Jr. 1907- *ConAu 17R*
Borden, Richard Carman 1900- *Au&Wr, ConAu P-1*
Borden, Sir Robert Laird 1854-1937 *DcNAA, OxCan, WhWNAA*
Borden, Simeon 1798-1856 *Alli, DcNAA*
Borden, William 1938- *ConAu 25, DrAF 1976*
Border, Dan *Alli*
Border, William Holmes *BlkAW*
Border Minstrel, The 1771-1832 *DcEnL*
Borderie, Bertrand DeLa *OxFr*
Borderieux, Carita 1874-1953 *BiDPar*
Borders, Cornelia *LivFWS*
Bordewijk, Ferdinand 1884-1965 *CasWL, EncWL, Pen Eur*
Bordin, Edward S 1913- *ConAu 57*
Bordin, Ruth B 1917- *ConAu 21*
Bording, Anders Christensen 1619-1677 *CasWL*
Bordley, John Beale 1727-1804 *Alli, BiDSA, DcNAA*
Borduas, Paul-Emile *OxCan, OxCan Sup*
Borea, Phyllis Gilbert 1924- *ConAu 29*
Boreham, Frank William 1871- *WhLA*
Boreham, Gordon F 1928- *ConAu 41*
Borel, Jacques 1925- *ConAu 33*
Borel, Petrus 1809-1859 *BiD&SB, CasWL, EuA, EvEuW, OxFr*
Borel, Pierre *OxFr*
Borel D'Hauterive, Petrus 1809-1859 *Pen Eur*
Boreman, Jean 1909- *ConAu 21*
Boreman, Richard *Alli*
Boreman, Robert d1675 *Alli*
Boreman, Thomas *Alli*
Boreman, Yokutiel 1825-1890 *Pen Eur*
Boren, Clifford J *ChPo S1*
Boren, Henry C 1921- *ConAu 17R*
Boren, James H 1925- *ConAu 41*
Borenius, Tancred 1885- *WhLA*
Borenstein, Audrey F *DrAF 1976*
Borenstein, Emily *DrAP 1975*
Borer, Mary Cathcart 1906- *Au&Wr, ConAu 9R, WrD 1976*
Boretz, Allen 1900- *AmSCAP 66*
Boretz, Alvin 1919- *AmSCAP 66*
Borfet, Abiel *Alli*
Borg, Dorothy 1902- *ConAu 23*
Borg, Inga *AuBYP*
Borg, Jack *MnBBF*
Borg, Selma And Brown, M A *Alli Sup*
Borg, Walter R 1921- *ConAu 33*
Borge, Victor 1909- *AmSCAP 66, WrD 1976*
Borgeaud, Charles 1861- *WhLA*
Borgedal, Paul 1888- *WhLA*
Borgen, Johan 1902- *CasWL, CnMD, EncWL,*

Pen Eur
Borger, Elias Anne 1784-1820 *CasWL*
Borger, Hans 1880- *WhLA*
Borgerhoff, Joseph Leopold 1868- *WhWNAA*
Borges, Jorge Luis 1899- *CasWL, ConAu 21, ConLC 1, ConLC 2, ConLC 3, ConLC 4, ConLC 6, DcCLA, DcSpL, EncWL, Pen Am, REn, TwCW, WhTwL, WorAu*
Borgese, Giuseppe Antonio 1882-1952 *CasWL, ClDMEuL, EncWL, Pen Eur, REn, TwCA, TwCA Sup*
Borget, Auguste *Alli*
Borget, Samuel *Alli*
Borghese, Junio Valerio 1906?-1974 *ConAu 53*
Borghi, Giuseppe 1790-1847 *CasWL, EvEuW*
Borghini, Raffaello 1541-1588? *CasWL, EvEuW*
Borghini, Vincenzo 1515-1580 *CasWL*
Borgia, Anthony V *ChPo*
Borgia, Cesare 1476?-1507 *NewC*
Borgia, Lucrezia 1480-1519 *NewC*
Borglum, Gutzon 1871?-1941 *OxAm, REn, REnAL*
Borgman, Albert Stephens 1890-1954 *AmA&B, WhWNAA*
Borgmann, Dmitri A 1927- *ConAu 17R*
Borgstrom, Georg A 1912- *ConAu 17R*
Borhegyi, Suzanne Catherine Sims De 1926- *AuBYP*
Borie, Lysbeth Boyd *ChPo*
Boring, Edwin Garrigues 1886- *AmA&B, ConAu 1R, WhWNAA*
Boring, Hazel *ChPo S2*
Boring, Phyllis Zatlin 1938- *ConAu 41*
Boringdon, Lord 1771- *BiDLA*
Boris, Joseph J *WhWNAA*
Boris And Gleb d1015 *Pen Eur*
Borja, Corinne And Robert *IlBYP*
Borja, Francisco De 1581-1658 *DcEuL*
Borja, Robert *IlBYP*
Borjesson, Johan 1790-1866 *CasWL, DcEuL*
Bork, Alfred M 1926- *ConAu 17R*
Borkenstein, Hinrich 1705-1777 *OxGer*
Borklund, C W 1930- *ConAu 21*
Borko, Harold 1922- *ConAu 13R*
Borkovec, Thomas D 1944- *ConAu 45*
Borlace, Edmond d1682 *Alli*
Borland, Barbara Dodge *ConAu P-1*
Borland, Beatrice 1906- *WhWNAA*
Borland, Hal 1900- *AmA&B, Au&Wr, ChPo, ConAu 1R, REnAL, SmATA 5, WorAu*
Borland, Harold Glen *ConAu XR, SmATA 5*
Borland, James Brown 1861-1939 *DcNAA*
Borland, John 1809-1888 *BbtC, DcNAA*
Borland, Kathryn Kilby 1916- *ConAu 53, IndAu 1917*
Borland, William Patterson 1867-1919 *DcNAA*
Borlase, Henry d1834 *Alli*
Borlase, James Skipp *Alli Sup*
Borlase, Skip *MnBBF*
Borlase, William 1696-1772 *Alli*
Borlase, William Copeland 1848- *Alli Sup*
Bormann, Charles *Alli Sup*
Bormann, Ernest G 1925- *ConAu 17R*
Bormeester, Abraham 1618-1645? *CasWL*
Born, Ann Rosemary 1924- *Au&Wr*
Born, Axel 1884- *WhLA*
Born, Bertran De *EuA*
Born, Max 1882-1970 *ConAu 5R, ConAu 25*
Born, Wolfgang 1893-1949 *DcNAA*
Borne, Dorothy *ConAu XR*
Borne, Hal 1911- *AmSCAP 66*
Borne, Ludwig 1786-1837 *BbD, BiD&SB, CasWL, DcEuL, EvEuW, OxGer, REn*
Borne, William *Alli*
Borneil, Giraut De *BiD&SB*
Bornemann, Ernest 1915- *Au&Wr, ConAu 9R, WrD 1976*
Borneman, H *ConAu XR*
Bornemann, Alfred H 1908- *ConAu 13R*
Bornemann, Felix 1861- *WhLA*
Bornemann, Johann Wilhelm Jakob 1766-1851 *OxGer*
Bornemann, Karl Georg 1855- *WhLA*
Bornemann, Wilhelm 1766-1851 *BiD&SB, CasWL*
Borner, Florence *ChPo S2*
Borner, Wilhelm 1882- *WhLA*

Bornet, Francois 1915- *AmSCAP 66*
Bornet, Vaughn Davis 1917- *ConAu 1R*
Bornhak, Conrad 1861- *WhLA*
Bornhausen, Karl 1882- *WhLA*
Bornier, Henri, Vicomte De 1825-1901 *BiD&SB, OxFr*
Borning, Bernard C 1913- *ConAu 1R*
Bornschein, Franz 1879-1948 *AmSCAP 66*
Bornschlegel, Ruth *IlBYP*
Bornstein, Diane 1942- *ConAu 57*
Bornstein, George 1941- *ConAu 29, WrD 1976*
Bornstein, Morris 1927- *ConAu 5R*
Bornstein, Ruth 1927- *ConAu 61*
Borntreger, John E 1837-1930 *IndAu 1816*
Borodin, Alexander Porfirevich 1833-1887 *AtlBL, REn*
Borodin, Sergey Petrovich 1902- *CasWL*
Borodkin, Abram E 1906- *AmSCAP 66*
Boroff, David 1917-1965 *ConAu 29, ConAu P-1*
Boron, Robert De *DcEuL, NewC, OxEng, OxFr*
Borooah, Anundoram 1850- *Alli Sup*
Boroson, Warren 1935- *ConAu 23*
Borough, Sir John *Alli*
Borough, Rube 1883- *WhWNAA*
Borough, Stephen 1525-1584 *NewC*
Borough, William *Alli*
Borovski, Conrad 1930- *ConAu 37*
Borovsky 1821-1856 *DcEuL*
Borowczyk, Walerian 1923- *WhGrA*
Borowitz, David *ChPo S2*
Borowitz, Eugene B 1924- *ConAu 49*
Borowski, Felix 1872-1956 *AmSCAP 66*
Borowski, Tadeusz 1922-1951 *CasWL, ModSL 2*
Borowy, Waclaw 1890-1950 *CasWL*
Borregaard, Ebbe 1933- *ConP 1970*
Borrell, D E 1928- *ConP 1970*
Borrell, Laura *PoIre*
Borrello, Alfred 1931- *ConAu 29*
Borrer, Dawson *Alli*
Borrett, George Tuthill *Alli Sup, BbtC*
Borrett, William C *OxCan*
Borrie, John 1915- *WrD 1976*
Borrie, Peter Forbes 1918- *Au&Wr*
Borringdon, Lord *Alli*
Borrmann, Martin 1895- *WhLA*
Borroff, Marie 1923- *ConAu 5R*
Borromini, Francesco 1599-1667 *AtlBL*
Borron, Robert De *OxEng, OxFr*
Borror, Donald J 1907- *ConAu 1R, WrD 1976*
Borrow, George Henry 1803-1881 *Alli, Alli Sup, AtlBL, BbD, BiD&SB, BrAu 19, CasWL, Chmbr 3, CyWA, DcBiA, DcEnA, DcEnL, DcEuL, DcLEnL, EvLB, MouLC 3, NewC, OxEng, Pen Eng, REn, WebEAL*
Borrows, G Mann *Alli*
Borrows, Stephen *NewC*
Borsch, Frederick Houk 1935- *ConAu 25*
Borsi, Giosue 1888-1915 *CasWL, ClDMEuL, EvEuW*
Borski, Lucia Merecka *AnCL*
Borsook, H *OxCan*
Borsselen, Philibert Van 1575-1627 *CasWL*
Borst, Beatrice West *AnMV 1926*
Borst, Max 1869- *WhLA*
Borst, Richard Warner 1885- *AnMV 1926*
Borten, Helen Jacobson 1930- *AuBYP, ChPo S2, ConAu 5R, IlCB 1966, SmATA 5, WrD 1976*
Borthwick, George *Alli, BiDLA*
Borthwick, J D *Alli Sup, OxCan*
Borthwick, J Douglas *BbtC*
Borthwick, Jane *Alli Sup, PoCh*
Borthwick, John *Alli*
Borthwick, John Douglas 1831?-1912 *ChPo S1, DcNAA*
Borthwick, Robert Brown *Alli Sup*
Borthwick, William *Alli, BiDLA*
Bortkiewicz, Ladislas Von 1868- *WhLA*
Bortner, Doyle M 1915- *ConAu 13R*
Bortner, Morton 1925- *ConAu 33*
Borton, Elizabeth *SmATA 1, ThBJA*
Borton, Hugh 1903- *AmA&B*

Borton, John C, Jr. 1938- *ConAu 29*
Borton, Terry *ConAu XR*
Borton DeTrevino, Elizabeth *NewbC 1966*
Bortstein, Larry 1942- *ConAu 33*
Bortz, Edward L 1896-1970 *ConAu P-1*
Boru, Brian *REn*
Borum, Joseph H d1893? *BiDSA*
Borup, George 1884-1912 *DcNAA*
Borup, Morten 1446?-1526 *CasWL, EvEuW*
Borus, Michael E 1938- *ConAu 37*
Borza, Eugene N 1935- *ConAu 25*
Bos, Charles Du 1882-1939 *CasWL, EvEuW, REn*
Bos, Lambert VanDen 1620?-1698? *CasWL*
Bosanketh, Edward *Alli Sup*
Bosanquet, Augustus Henry *Alli Sup*
Bosanquet, Bernard 1848-1923 *Alli Sup, LongC*
Bosanquet, Bernard Tindal *Alli Sup*
Bosanquet, Charles *Alli, BiDLA*
Bosanquet, Charles Bertie Pulleine 1834- *Alli Sup*
Bosanquet, Claude *Alli Sup*
Bosanquet, Edwin *Alli*
Bosanquet, F W *Alli Sup*
Bosanquet, George William *Alli Sup*
Bosanquet, J B And Puller, C *Alli*
Bosanquet, James Whatman 1804-1877 *Alli, Alli Sup*
Bosanquet, John Bernard *BiDLA*
Bosanquet, Mary *OxCan*
Bosanquet, R W *Alli*
Bosanquet, Robert Halford Macdowall *Alli Sup*
Bosanquet, Samuel Richard 1800-1882 *Alli, Alli Sup*
Bosanquet, W H *Alli*
Bosboom, Anna Louisa Gertrudia 1812-1886 *BbD, BiD&SB*
Bosboom-Toussaint, Anna Louisa G 1812-1886 *CasWL, EuA, EvEuW*
Bosboom-Toussaint, Anna Louise G 1812-1886 *Pen Eur*
Bosboon *Alli*
Bosc, Jean Maurice 1924- *WhGrA*
Boscan, Juan 1490?-1542? *DcEuL, DcSpL, OxEng*
Boscan Almogaver, Juan 1490?-1542? *BbD, BiD&SB, CasWL, EvEuW, Pen Eur, REn*
Boscawen, Benjamin *Alli Sup*
Boscawen, Edward 1711-1761 *OxCan*
Boscawen, Gertrude *Alli Sup*
Boscawen, M F E, Baroness LeDespencer 1822- *Alli Sup*
Boscawen, William 1752-1811 *Alli*
Boscawen, William St. Chad *Alli Sup*
Bosch, Bernardus 1746-1803 *CasWL*
Bosch, Hieronymus 1450?-1516 *AtlBL, REn*
Bosch, Jerome 1450?-1516 *REn*
Bosch, Jeronimo De 1740-1811 *CasWL*
Bosch, Juan 1909- *DcCLA*
Bosch, William Joseph 1928- *ConAu 29*
Bosch-Gimpera, Pedro 1891- *WhLA*
Bosco, Antoinette 1928- *ConAu 13R*
Bosco, Fernand-Marius-Joseph-Henri 1888- *EncWL*
Bosco, Henri 1888- *CasWL, EvEuW, OxFr, Pen Eur, REn, WorAu*
Bosco, Jack *ConAu XR*
Bosco, Monique 1927- *CanWr, OxCan, OxCan Sup*
Bose *DcOrL 2*
Bose, Bholanoth *Alli Sup*
Bose, Buddhadeva 1908- *Pen Cl, REn*
Bose, Chunilal 1861- *WhLA*
Bose, Irene Mott 1899?-1974 *ConAu 53*
Bose, N K 1901- *ConAu 23*
Bose, Shib Chunder *Alli Sup*
Bose, Tarun Chandra 1931- *ConAu 45*
Boserup, Ester 1910- *ConAu 57*
Boshaq, Ahmad Abu Eshaq Hallaj d1424? *DcOrL 3*
Boshell, Gordon *ChPo S2*
Boshelle, S E M *PoIre*
Bosher, Kate Lee Langley 1865-1932 *AmA&B, BiDSA, ChPo, DcNAA*
Boshinski, Blanche 1922- *ConAu 21, SmATA 10*

Bosio, Ferdinando 1829-1881 *BbD, BiD&SB*
Bosis, Adolfo De *CasWL*
Boskin, Joseph 1929- *ConAu 25*
Boskoff, Alvin 1924- *ConAu 13R, WrD 1976*
Bosland, Chelcie Clayton 1901- *ConAu 5R, WrD 1976*
Bosley, Harold A 1907-1975 *AmA&B, ConAu 49, ConAu 53*
Bosley, Keith 1937- *ConAu 57, ConP 1975, WrD 1976*
Bosmajian, Haig Aram 1928- *ConAu 17R, WrD 1976*
Bosman, Herman Charles 1905-1951 *CasWL, CnMWL, TwCW, WorAu*
Bosomworth, William Jackson *PoIre*
Bosper, Albert 1913- *CnMD*
Bosquet, Abraham *PoIre*
Bosquet, Alain 1919- *ConAu 13R, OxCan, OxCan Sup*
Bosquett, Abraham *Alli*
Boss, Andrew 1867- *WhWNAA*
Boss, Clara Pearce 1842-1899 *ChPo*
Boss, John *ChPo S2*
Boss, Judy 1935- *ConAu 57*
Bossange, Gustave *OxCan*
Bossard, James Herbert Siward 1888-1960 *AmA&B, WhWNAA*
Bosschere, Jean De 1878- *IlCB 1945*
Bossdorf, Hermann 1877-1921 *CasWL, OxGer*
Bosse, Abraham 1602-1676 *OxFr*
Bosse, E *OxCan Sup*
Bossewell, John *Alli*
Bosshart, Jakob 1862-1924 *CasWL*
Bossidy, John Collins *ChPo*
Bossone, Frank 1924- *AmSCAP 66*
Bossone, Richard M 1924- *ConAu 33, WrD 1976*
Bossu, M 1725?- *BiDSA*
Bossuet, Jacques Benigne 1627-1704 *AtlBL, BbD, BiD&SB, CasWL, DcEuL, EuA, EvEuW, OxEng, OxFr, Pen Eur, REn*
Bossut, M *BiDLA*
Bostelmann, Carl John 1905- *WhWNAA*
Bostelmann, Else *IlCB 1945*
Bosticco, Isabel Lucy Mary 1922- *WrD 1976*
Bosticco, Mary 1922- *Au&W, WrD 1976*
Bostick, Calvin T 1928- *AmSCAP 66*
Bostock, Donald Ivan 1924- *Au&Wr, WrD 1976*
Bostock, John 1773-1845 *Alli, BiDLA*
Bostock, John 1892- *Au&Wr*
Bostock, John Anthony *Au&Wr*
Bostock, Peter *Alli*
Bostock, Trevor 1933- *Au&Wr*
Boston, Charles K *ConAu XR, EncM&D*
Boston, John *Alli*
Boston, Leonard Napoleon 1874-1931 *DcNAA*
Boston, Lucy Maria 1892- *AnCL, Au&Wr, AuBYP, PiP, SenS, ThBJA, WhCL, WrD 1976*
Boston, Noel 1910-1966 *ConAu P-1*
Boston, Orlan William 1891- *Au&Wr*
Boston, Robert *Alli*
Boston, Stewart *OxCan Sup*
Boston, Thomas *Alli*
Boston, Thomas 1676?-1732 *Alli, CasWL, Chmbr 2, DcEnL, EvLB, NewC*
Boston Bard, The 1797-1857 *DcEnL*
Bostrom, Christopher Jacob 1797-1866 *CasWL, DcEuL*
Bostwick, Arthur Elmore 1860-1942 *AmA&B, AmLY, DcNAA, WhWNAA*
Bostwick, Charles Francis 1866-1923 *DcNAA*
Bostwick, David 1720?-1763 *Alli*
Bostwick, H *Alli*
Bostwick, Helen Louise 1826-1907 *Alli Sup, ChPo, ChPo S1, DcAmA, DcNAA, HsB&A, OhA&B*
Bostwick, Homer *DcNAA*
Bostwick, Lucy Standard 1832- *ChPo*
Bostwick, Mary E 1886-1959 *IndAu 1917*
Boswell *ConAu XR*
Boswell, Alexander 1706-1782 *NewC*
Boswell, Sir Alexander 1775-1822 *Alli, BiD&SB, BrAu 19, CasWL, ChPo, Chmbr 2, DcEnL, EvLB, NewC*
Boswell, Charles 1909- *ConAu 5R*
Boswell, Connee *AmSCAP 66*

Boswell, Della Hargrove 1888- *TexWr*
Boswell, Edward *Alli, BiDLA*
Boswell, George *Alli*
Boswell, H *Alli*
Boswell, Miss H *Alli, BiDLA*
Boswell, Hazel 1882- *IlCB 1945, OxCan Sup*
Boswell, Hilda *ChPo S2*
Boswell, J W *Alli*
Boswell, Jackson Campbell 1934- *ConAu 61*
Boswell, James *Alli*
Boswell, James 1740-1795 *Alli, AtlBL, BbD, BiD&SB, BrAu, CasWL, ChPo S2, Chmbr 2, CriT 2, CyWA, DcEnA, DcEnL, DcEuL, DcLEnL, EvLB, IlCB 1966, LongC, MnBBF, MouLC 2, NewC, OxEng, Pen Eng, RAdv 1, RCom, REn, WebEAL*
Boswell, James 1779-1822 *DcEnL*
Boswell, John *Alli*
Boswell, John Alexander Corrie *Alli Sup*
Boswell, Margie B 1875- *TexWr*
Boswell, Marvin *Alli Sup*
Boswell, P *Alli*
Boswell, Percy George Hamnall 1886- *WhLA*
Boswell, Peyton 1879-1936 *AmA&B*
Boswell, Robert Bruce *Alli Sup*
Boswell, Roger *Alli Sup*
Bosworth, Alfred Willson 1879- *WhWNAA*
Bosworth, Allan R 1901- *ConAu 1R*
Bosworth, Clifford Edmund 1928- *ConAu 13R*
Bosworth, David *Alli Sup*
Bosworth, Edward Increase 1861-1927 *DcNAA, OhA&B*
Bosworth, Francke Huntington 1843-1925 *DcAmA, DcNAA, OhA&B*
Bosworth, Frank *ConAu XR*
Bosworth, J Allan *AuBYP*
Bosworth, John *Alli Sup*
Bosworth, Joseph 1788?- *Alli, DcEnL*
Bosworth, Joseph S *Alli Sup*
Bosworth, Newton *Alli, BiDLA*
Bosworth, Newton 1776?-1848 *BbtC, DcNAA*
Bosworth, William *Alli, BlkAW*
Bosworth, William 1607-1650? *DcLEnL*
Bosworth Smith, Reginald 1839-1908 *BrAu 19*
Bote, Hermann d1520? *CasWL, OxGer*
Bote, Konrad *OxGer*
Botein, Bernard 1900-1974 *ConAu 45*
Boteler, Edward *Alli*
Boteler, Mattie M 1859-1929 *OhA&B*
Boteler, Nathaniel *Alli*
Botelho, Abel Acacio DeAlmeida 1856?-1917 *CasWL, ClDMEuL*
Botelho, Francis Martin 1893- *WhWNAA*
Botelho DeOliveira, Manuel 1636-1711 *CasWL*
Botelho Gosalvez, Raul 1917- *DcCLA*
Botero, Giovanni 1543?-1617 *CasWL, REn*
Botero, Giuseppe 1815-1885 *BiD&SB*
Botev, Christo 1847-1876 *EvEuW*
Botev, Hristo 1847-1876 *CasWL, Pen Eur*
Boteville, Francis *Alli*
Botez, Demostene 1893- *CasWL*
Botfield, Beriah 1807-1863 *Alli Sup*
Both, Carl *Alli Sup*
Botha, Colin Graham 1883- *Au&Wr, WhLA*
Botha, Dorothea Graham 1901- *WhLA, WhWNAA*
Bothamley, Westley 1861- *WhLA*
Bothams, W *ChPo S1*
Bothams, Walter *ChPo S2*
Bothelho DeOliveira, Manuel 1636-1711 *Pen Am*
Bothelho Gosalvez, Raul 1917- *Pen Am*
Bothmer, Countess M Von *Alli*
Bothwell, Earl Of 1536?-1578 *NewC*
Bothwell, Austin Macphail 1883- *WhWNAA*
Bothwell, Jean *AuBYP, ConAu 1R, JBA 1951, SmATA 2*
Botkin, Benjamin Albert 1901-1975 *AmA&B, Au&Wr, ConAu 57, ConAu P-1, REnAL, TwCA Sup*
Botkin, Charles Willoughby 1859-1927 *OhA&B*
Botkin, Perry 1907- *AmSCAP 66*
Boto, Eza *AfA 1, Pen Cl*
Botolph, Saint *NewC*
Botolphus, Saint *NewC*
Botomley, S *Alli*
Botoner, William Worcester 1415?-1490 *Alli*

Boulton, Edmund *NewC*
Boulton, G *EarAB*
Boulton, H J, Jr. *BbtC*
Boulton, Sir Harold Edwin 1859- *ChPo,*
ChPo S1
Boulton, Harry *ChPo*
Boulton, Henry John 1790-1870 *BbtC, OxCan*
Boulton, Hilda *ChPo*
Boulton, James Thompson 1924- *ConAu 29,*
WrD 1976
Boulton, Marjorie 1924- *Au&Wr*
Boulton, Richard *Alli*
Boulton, S B *Alli Sup*
Boulton, Samuel *Alli*
Boultwood, Emma *Alli Sup*
Boultwood, Harriet *Alli Sup*
Boulware, Marcus Hanna 1907- *ConAu 45,*
LivBAA
Bouma, Donald H 1918- *ConAu 41*
Bouman, Pieter M 1938- *ConAu 29*
Bouman, Walter Richard 1929- *ConAu 29*
Boumphrey, Chester M *ChPo S2*
Boun, Abraham *Alli*
Bouncher, Samuel *Alli*
Bound, Nic *Alli*
Bounden, Joseph *Alli*
Bounds, Edward McKendree 1835-1913 *DcNAA*
Bounds, S J *MnBBF*
Bouquet, Henry *Alli*
Bouquet, Michael Rome 1915- *Au&Wr*
Bour, Arthur *Alli*
Bourassa, Gustave 1860-1904 *DcNAA*
Bourassa, Henri 1868-1952 *AmLY, CanWr,*
OxCan
Bourassa, Joseph-Napoleon-Henri 1868-1952
CasWL
Bourassa, Napoleon 1827-1916 *BbtC, DcNAA,*
OxCan
Bourassa, Robert *OxCan Sup*
Bourbakis, Constantin J 1885- *WhWNAA*
Bourbon *NewC*
Bourbon, Ken *ConAu XR*
Bourbon, Nicolas 1503-1548? *CasWL, EvEuW*
Bourchier, Sir George 1821- *Alli Sup*
Bourchier, Lady Jane Barbara *Alli Sup*
Bourchier, Baron John Berners 1467-1533? *Alli,*
BrAu, CasWL, CrE&SL, DcEnL, NewC,
Pen Eng, REn
Bourchier, Thomas *Alli*
Bourdaloue, Louis 1632-1704 *DcEuL, OxFr,*
Pen Eur, REn
Bourdeaux, Michael Alan 1934- *Au&Wr,*
ConAu 33, WrD 1976
Bourdet, Edouard 1887-1945? *ClDMEuL,*
CnMD, EvEuW, McGWD, ModWD,
OxFr, Pen Eur
Bourdigne, Charles *OxFr*
Bourdillon, Francis *Alli Sup*
Bourdillon, Francis William 1852-1921 *Alli Sup,*
BiD&SB, ChPo, ChPo S1, DcEnA Ap,
NewC
Bourdon, David 1934- *ConAu 37*
Bourdon, Jean, Sieur De Saint-Francois
1601?-1668 *OxCan*
Bourdon, Rosario 1889-1961 *AmSCAP 66*
Bourdon D'Autray, Jacques 1652-1688 *OxCan*
Bourgeois, Emile 1857- *WhLA*
Bourgeois, Florence 1904- *IlCB 1945*
Bourgeois, M *BiDSA*
Bourgeois, Marguerite *BbtC*
Bourgeois, Phileas Frederic 1855-1913 *DcNAA*
Bourgeoys, Marguerite 1620-1700 *OxCan*
Bourges, Elemir 1852-1925 *CasWL, OxFr,*
Pen Eur
Bourget, Clermont *OxCan*
Bourget, Ignace 1799-1885 *BbtC, DcNAA,*
OxCan
Bourget, Paul 1852-1935 *BbD, BiD&SB,*
CasWL, CatA 1947, ClDMEuL, CyWA,
DcBiA, EncWL, EvEuW, LongC, OxEng,
OxFr, Pen Eur, REn, TwCA, TwCA Sup
Bourgholtzer, Frank 1919- *ConAu 25*
Bourignon, Antoinette 1616-1680 *PoCh*
Bourinot, Arthur Stanley 1893- *CanWr,*
DcLEnL, OxCan, REnAL
Bourinot, Arthur Stanley 1894- *ChPo,*
ChPo S1, WhWNAA
Bourinot, Sir John George 1837-1902 *Alli Sup,*

BbtC, BrAu 19, DcNAA, OxCan
Bourjaily, Barbara Webb *OhA&B*
Bourjaily, Monte Ferris 1894- *AmA&B*
Bourjaily, Vance 1922- *AmA&B, Au&Wr,*
ConAu 1R, ConNov 1972, ConNov 1976,
DrAF 1976, ModAL, OhA&B, OxAm,
Pen Am, REn, REnAL, WorAu,
WrD 1976
Bourke, Dermot R W, Earl Of Mayo 1851-
Alli Sup
Bourke, Hannah Maria *PoIre*
Bourke, J W *PoIre*
Bourke, James J 1837-1894 *PoIre*
Bourke, John Gregory 1846-1896 *Alli Sup,*
AmA, ArizL, DcAmA, DcNAA
Bourke, Joseph *Alli*
Bourke, Patrick Albert 1915- *WrD 1976*
Bourke, Sir Richard *Alli*
Bourke, Robert 1827- *Alli Sup*
Bourke, Thomas *Alli, BiDLA*
Bourke, Ulick J d1887 *Alli, Alli Sup*
Bourke, Vernon J 1907- *ConAu 9R,*
WrD 1976
Bourke, Walter M *Alli Sup*
Bourke-White, Margaret 1906?-1971 *AmA&B,*
ConAu 29, ConAu P-1, REn, REnAL
Bourlamaque, Francois-Charles De 1716-1764
OxCan
Bourland, Albert Pike 1861- *BiDSA*
Bourn, Abraham *Alli*
Bourn, Charles *Alli Sup*
Bourn, Henry H *Alli Sup*
Bourn, Immanuel 1590-1672 *Alli*
Bourn, Samuel *Alli*
Bourn, Thomas *Alli, BiDLA*
Bourne, A A *Alli Sup*
Bourne, Aleck William 1886?-1974 *Au&Wr,*
ConAu 53
Bourne, Alexander 1786-1849 *OhA&B*
Bourne, Benjamin *Alli*
Bourne, Benjamin Franklin *Alli Sup, DcNAA*
Bourne, C E *Alli Sup*
Bourne, C W *Alli Sup*
Bourne, Charles *Alli*
Bourne, Charles P 1931- *ConAu 9R*
Bourne, Charles R *Alli Sup*
Bourne, Dorothy D 1893- *ConAu 23*
Bourne, Edith Owen *Alli Sup*
Bourne, Edward Emerson 1797-1873 *Alli Sup,*
DcNAA
Bourne, Edward Gaylord 1860-1908 *Alli Sup,*
AmA, DcAmA, DcNAA
Bourne, Ella 1869-1947 *DcNAA, IndAu 1917*
Bourne, F W *Alli Sup*
Bourne, Frank Card 1914- *ConAu 17R,*
WrD 1976
Bourne, Geoffrey Howard 1909- *ConAu 33,*
WrD 1976
Bourne, George *MnBBF*
Bourne, George 1780-1845 *BbtC, DcAmA,*
DcNAA, OxCan
Bourne, George 1863-1927 *CnMWL, LongC,*
WebEAL, WhTwL, WorAu
Bourne, Gilbert Charles 1861- *WhLA*
Bourne, Henry *Alli*
Bourne, Henry Eldridge 1862-1946 *AmA&B,*
AmLY
Bourne, Henry Richard Fox 1837- *Alli Sup*
Bourne, Holly *Au&Wr*
Bourne, Hugh 1772-1852 *PoCh*
Bourne, Immanuel 1590-1672 *Alli*
Bourne, Isabella *Alli Sup, ChPo S2*
Bourne, J C *Alli*
Bourne, James R 1897- *ConAu 21*
Bourne, Jane *ChPo*
Bourne, John *Alli, Alli Sup*
Bourne, John Bury *Alli Sup*
Bourne, Kenneth 1930- *ConAu 25,*
OxCan Sup, WrD 1976
Bourne, Larry Stuart 1939- *ConAu 33,*
WrD 1976
Bourne, Lawrence *MnBBF*
Bourne, Lesley *ConAu XR*
Bourne, Lutwidge *Alli Sup*
Bourne, Lyle E, Jr. 1932- *ConAu 53*
Bourne, Margaret *ChPo*
Bourne, Miriam Anne 1931- *ConAu 21*
Bourne, Monica *ChPo S2*

Bourne, Nic *Alli*
Bourne, Peter *EncM&D*
Bourne, Peter Geoffrey 1939- *ConAu 57*
Bourne, Randolph Silliman 1886-1918 *AmA&B,*
AmWr, CasWL, CnDAL, DcLEnL,
DcNAA, ModAL, OxAm, Pen Am, REn,
REnAL, TwCA, TwCA Sup, WebEAL
Bourne, Robert 1769-1830 *Alli, BiDLA*
Bourne, Roy 1925- *Au&Wr*
Bourne, Ruth M *ConAu 33*
Bourne, S K *ChPo*
Bourne, Stephen *Alli Sup*
Bourne, Thomas *Alli Sup*
Bourne, Vincent 1695-1747 *Alli, BiDLA,*
BiDLA Sup, ChPo, ChPo S1, DcEnL,
NewC, OxEng, Pen Eng
Bourne, William *Alli*
Bourne, William Oland *Alli Sup, CarSB,*
ChPo, ChPo S1, ChPo S2, DcNAA
Bourneuf, Roland *OxCan Sup*
Bourns, Charles *Alli*
Bourque, Gilles *OxCan Sup*
Bourquin, Paul Henry James 1916- *Au&Wr,*
WrD 1976
Bourricaud, Francois 1922- *ConAu 29*
Bourrienne, Louis Antoine Fauvelet De
1769-1834 *DcEuL, REn*
Boursault, Edme 1638-1701 *CasWL, DcEuL,*
EvEuW, McGWD, OxFr, Pen Eur
Bouscaren, Anthony Trawick 1920- *ConAu 1R*
Bouscaren, T Lincoln 1884- *ConAu P-1*
Bouse, Henry *Alli*
Bousell, John *Alli*
Bousfield, Benjamin *Alli, BiDLA*
Bousfield, Charles *Alli Sup*
Bousfield, George *Alli Sup*
Bousfield, H Mary *ChPo S1*
Bousfield, Henry Brougham 1832- *Alli Sup*
Bousfield, John *Alli Sup*
Bousfield, William 1842- *Alli Sup*
Bousfield, William Robert 1854- *Alli Sup*
Bousono, Carlos 1923- *CasWL, Pen Eur,*
WorAu
Boussard, Jacques Marie 1910- *ConAu 29*
Boutcher, William *Alli*
Boutelje, Phil 1895- *AmSCAP 66*
Boutell, Charles 1812-1877 *Alli, Alli Sup*
Boutell, Clarence Burley 1908- *AmA&B*
Boutell, Henry Sherman 1905-1931 *ChPo,*
DcNAA
Boutell, Lewis Henry 1826-1899 *DcAmA,*
DcNAA
Boutell, Mary Elizabeth Chavallier *Alli Sup*
Boutelle, John Alonzo *Alli Sup*
Boutelle, Mary Keely *ChPo*
Boutelleau, Jacques *ClDMEuL, EvEuW, REn*
Boutens, Peter Cornelis 1870-1943 *CasWL,*
EvEuW, Pen Eur
Boutens, Petrus Cornelis 1870-1943 *ChPo*
Boutens, Pieter Cornelis 1870-1943 *ClDMEuL,*
EncWL
Boutet DeMonvel, L M 1850-1913 *JBA 1934,*
JBA 1951
Boutflower, Cecil Henry *Alli Sup*
Bouthillier, Jean Antoine *BbtC*
Boutier, Pierre *CasWL*
Boutnikoff, Ivan 1893- *AmSCAP 66*
Bouton, Archibald Lewis 1872-1941 *AmA&B,*
DcNAA
Bouton, Elizabeth *ChPo*
Bouton, Emily St. John 1837-1927 *AmLY,*
OhA&B
Bouton, John Bell 1830-1902 *Alli Sup, AmA,*
AmA&B
Bouton, John Bell 1830-1892 *BiD&SB*
Bouton, John Bell 1830-1902 *DcAmA, DcNAA,*
OhA&B
Bouton, Josephine *ChPo*
Bouton, Miles 1876- *WhWNAA*
Bouton, Nathaniel 1797-1878 *Alli Sup,*
DcAmA, DcNAA
Boutroux, Emile 1845-1921 *ClDMEuL, OxFr*
Bouts, Dierik 1410?-1475 *AtlBL*
Bouts, Dirk 1410?-1475 *AtlBL*
Bouts, Thierry 1410?-1475 *AtlBL*
Boutwell, George Sewall 1818-1905 *Alli Sup,*
BiD&SB, DcAmA, DcNAA
Boutwell, John Mason 1874- *WhWNAA*

Bouvard, Marguerite Anne 1937- *ConAu 37*
Bouve, Edward Tracy *DcAmA*
Bouve, Pauline Carrington d1928 *DcAmA*, *DcNAA*
Bouve, Thomas Tracy 1815-1896 *Alli Sup*, *ChPo*, *DcNAA*
Bouverie, Bertrand Pleydell- 1845- *Alli Sup*
Bouverie, Edward Oliver Pleydell- *Alli Sup*
Bouverie, Frederick William Byron *Alli Sup*
Bouverie, J Fortrey *Alli Sup*
Bouverie, Sophia *Alli*, *BiDLA*
Bouvet, Marie Marguerite 1865-1915 *AmA*, *AmA&B*, *BiD&SB*, *CarSB*, *DcAmA*, *DcNAA*
Bouvet, T *Alli*
Bouvier, Emile 1906- *ConAu 37*
Bouvier, Hannah M 1811-1870 *Alli*, *DcAmA*
Bouvier, John 1787-1851 *Alli*, *DcAmA*, *DcNAA*
Bouyer, Louis Jean 1913- *Au&Wr*
Bova, Basil 1919- *AmSCAP 66*
Bova, Ben W 1932- *ConAu 1R*, *ConAu 5R*, *SmATA 6*, *WrD 1976*
Bovard, John Freeman 1881- *WhWNAA*
Bovard, William Sherman 1864-1936 *DcNAA*, *IndAu 1917*
Bovasso, Julie 1930- *ConAu 25*, *ConDr*, *WrD 1976*
Bovee, Christian Nestell 1820-1904 *Alli Sup*, *DcAmA*, *DcNAA*
Bovee, Courtland Lowell 1944- *ConAu 49*
Bovee, John Wesley 1861-1927 *DcNAA*
Bovee, Marvin H *Alli Sup*
Bovee, Ruth *ConAu XR*
Bovell, James 1817-1880 *BbtC*, *DcNAA*
Bovenschen, Albert 1864- *WhLA*
Bovet, Richard *Alli*
Bovey, Henry Taylor 1852-1912 *DcNAA*
Bovey, Wilfrid *OxCan*
Bovill, Charles Henry 1873- *ChPo S1*
Bovis, H Eugene 1928- *ConAu 29*
Bovyer, R G *Alli*
Bow, Frank Townsend 1901- *OhA&B*
Bow, Jonathan Gaines 1850?- *DcNAA*
Bow, Robert Henry *Alli Sup*
Bow, Ross *MnBBF*
Bow, Russell 1925- *ConAu 23*
Bowack, John *Alli*
Bowater, John *Alli*
Bowber, Thomas *Alli*
Bowchier, Josh *Alli*
Bowchier, Richard *Alli*
Bowd, Douglas Gordon 1918- *WrD 1976*
Bowden, A *Alli*, *BiDLA Sup*
Bowden, Christine M 1908- *AmSCAP 66*
Bowden, Claude Evelyn *Au&Wr*
Bowden, Edwin T 1924- *ConAu 13R*
Bowden, Elbert Victor 1924- *ConAu 41*
Bowden, Gregory Houston 1948- *ConAu 41*
Bowden, Guy Arthur George 1909- *Au&Wr*
Bowden, Henry Sebastian *Alli Sup*
Bowden, Henry Warner 1939- *ConAu 49*
Bowden, J J 1927- *ConAu 29*
Bowden, James 1811- *Alli*, *Alli Sup*
Bowden, Jean 1925- *Au&Wr*, *ConAu 53*, *WrD 1976*
Bowden, Jim *WrD 1976*
Bowden, John *Alli*, *Alli Sup*, *BiDLA*
Bowden, John 1751-1817 *Alli*, *CyAL 1*, *DcAmA*, *DcNAA*
Bowden, John Edward *Alli Sup*
Bowden, John William 1798-1844 *Alli*, *BrAu 19*
Bowden, Joseph 1869- *Alli*, *BiDLA*, *WhWNAA*
Bowden, Leonard 1933- *ConAu 17R*
Bowden, Roland Heywood 1916- *Au&Wr*, *WrD 1976*
Bowden, Ruth Elizabeth Mary 1915- *Au&Wr*
Bowden, Thomas *Alli*
Bowden, Thomas Adolphus *Alli Sup*
Bowdich, Thomas Edward 1790-1824 *Alli*
Bowditch, Charles Pickering 1842-1921 *AmLY*, *DcNAA*
Bowditch, Henry Ingersoll 1808-1892 *Alli Sup*, *DcAmA*, *DcNAA*
Bowditch, Henry Pickering 1840-1911 *BiDPar*, *DcNAA*

Bowditch, Nathaniel 1773-1838 *Alli*, *AmA*, *CyAL 1*, *DcAmA*, *DcNAA*, *OxAm*, *REnAL*
Bowditch, Nathaniel Ingersoll 1805-1861 *Alli*, *CyAL 2*, *DcNAA*
Bowditch, Samuel *Alli*
Bowditch, Vincent Yardley 1852-1929 *Alli Sup*, *DcNAA*
Bowditch, William Ingersoll 1819-1909 *Alli Sup*, *DcNAA*
Bowdith, William Renwick *Alli Sup*
Bowdle, Donald N 1935- *ConAu 49*
Bowdler, Charles *Alli Sup*
Bowdler, Miss E *Alli*
Bowdler, Mrs. H *BiDLA*
Bowdler, Mrs. H M *Alli*
Bowdler, Jane 1743-1784 *ChPo S1*
Bowdler, John *Alli*, *BiDLA*
Bowdler, John 1783-1815 *Alli*, *ChPo*
Bowdler, Thomas 1754-1825 *Alli*, *BiDLA*, *BiDLA Sup*, *BrAu*, *CasWL*, *Chmbr 2*, *DcEnL*, *DcLEnL*, *EvLB*, *NewC*, *OxEng*
Bowdler, Thomas 1782-1857 *Alli*
Bowdoin, James 1726?-1790 *Alli*, *AmA&B*, *CyAL 1*
Bowdoin, James 1752-1811 *Alli*, *CyAL 1*
Bowdoin, Virginia *ChPo*
Bowdoin, William Goodrich 1860-1947 *AmA&B*, *AmLY*, *DcAmA*, *DcNAA*, *WhWNAA*
Bowduoin, William *WrD 1976*
Bowe, Gabriel P 1923- *ConAu 23*
Bowe, Laura *ChPo*
Bowe, Obadiah A 1807- *ChPo*
Bowell, Sir Mackenzie 1823-1917 *OxCan*
Bowen, Captain *Alli*, *BiDLA*
Bowen, Mrs. *Alli*
Bowen, Abel 1790-1850 *AmA&B*, *ChPo*, *DcNAA*, *EarAB*, *EarAB Sup*
Bowen, Anna Cornelia *WhWNAA*
Bowen, Barbara C 1937- *ConAu 37*, *WrD 1976*
Bowen, Benjamin F *Alli Sup*
Bowen, Benjamin Lester 1860-1920 *DcNAA*
Bowen, Betty Morgan 1921- *AuBYP*, *ConAu XR*
Bowen, Mrs. C E *Alli Sup*, *ChPo*
Bowen, Catherine Drinker 1897-1973 *AmA&B*, *ConAu 5R*, *ConAu 45*, *OxAm*, *REn*, *REnAL*, *SmATA 7*, *TwCA Sup*
Bowen, Sir Charles Christopher 1830-1917 *WebEAL*
Bowen, Charles Hartpole *Alli Sup*, *PoIre*
Bowen, Charles J *Alli Sup*
Bowen, Sir Charles Synge Christopher 1835-1896 *Alli Sup*, *PoIre*
Bowen, Christopher *Alli Sup*
Bowen, Clarence Winthrop 1852-1935 *Alli Sup*, *DcAmA*, *DcNAA*
Bowen, Clayton Raymond 1877-1934 *DcNAA*, *WhWNAA*
Bowen, Croswell 1905-1971 *ConAu 33*
Bowen, Dana Thomas 1896- *OhA&B*
Bowen, Desmond 1921- *ConAu 33*, *WrD 1976*
Bowen, Earl Kenneth 1918- *ConAu 5R*
Bowen, Edward Ernest 1836-1901 *Alli Sup*, *ChPo*, *ChPo S1*, *EvLB*, *PoIre*
Bowen, Edwin Winfield 1866-1953 *AmA&B*, *AmLY*, *BiDSA*, *WhWNAA*
Bowen, Elbert Russell 1918- *ConAu 13R*, *IndAu 1917*
Bowen, Eli 1824-1880? *Alli*, *Alli Sup*, *DcAmA*, *DcNAA*
Bowen, Eliza Andrews 1828-1898 *Alli Sup*, *BiDSA*, *DcAmA*, *DcNAA*
Bowen, Elizabeth 1899-1973 *Au&Wr*, *AuBYP*, *CasWL*, *ConAu 17*, *ConAu 41*, *ConLC 1*, *ConLC 3*, *ConLC 6*, *ConNov 1972*, *CyWA*, *DcLEnL*, *EncWL*, *EvLB*, *LongC*, *ModBL*, *ModBL Sup*, *NewC*, *OxEng*, *Pen Eng*, *RAdv 1*, *REn*, *TwCA*, *TwCA Sup*, *TwCW*, *WebEAL*, *WhTwL*
Bowen, Emanuel *Alli*
Bowen, Euros 1904- *Au&Wr*
Bowen, Ezra 1891-1945 *DcNAA*
Bowen, Francis *Alli Sup*
Bowen, Francis 1811-1890 *Alli*, *Alli Sup*, *AmA*, *AmA&B*, *CyAL 2*, *DcAmA*, *DcEnL*, *DcNAA*

Bowen, George 1816-1888 *Alli Sup*, *DcNAA*
Bowen, Sir George Ferguson 1821- *Alli Sup*
Bowen, Haskell L 1929- *ConAu 41*
Bowen, Herbert Courthope *Alli Sup*
Bowen, Herbert Wolcott 1856-1927 *Alli Sup*, *AmA&B*, *AmLY*, *DcAmA*, *DcNAA*
Bowen, Howard Rothmann 1908- *AmA&B*, *ConAu 23*, *WrD 1976*
Bowen, Irene *AuBYP*
Bowen, J Donald 1922- *ConAu 17R*
Bowen, James *Alli*
Bowen, James Keith 1932- *ConAu 37*
Bowen, James L 1842-1919 *HsB&A*
Bowen, John *Alli Sup*
Bowen, John 1924- *CnThe*, *ConAu 1R*, *ConDr*, *ConNov 1972*, *ConNov 1976*, *CrCD*, *REn*, *TwCW*, *WorAu*, *WrD 1976*
Bowen, John Eliot 1858-1890 *Alli Sup*, *ChPo S1*, *DcAmA*, *DcNAA*
Bowen, John G 1896- *AmSCAP 66*
Bowen, John Griffith 1924- *Au&Wr*, *NewC*
Bowen, John Wesley Edward 1855- *BiDSA*, *DcAmA*
Bowen, Joshua David 1930- *AuBYP*
Bowen, L P *Alli Sup*
Bowen, Littleton Purnell 1833-1933 *DcNAA*
Bowen, Louise DeKoven 1859- *WhWNAA*
Bowen, Malcolm *Alli*, *BiDLA*
Bowen, Margaret Barber *ChPo*
Bowen, Marjorie 1886-1952 *DcLEnL*, *EvLB*, *LongC*, *NewC*, *REn*, *TwCA*, *TwCA Sup*, *TwCW*, *WhLA*
Bowen, Mary M 1932- *ChPo*, *ConAu 23*
Bowen, Muriel 1926- *Au&Wr*
Bowen, Nathaniel 1779-1839 *DcNAA*
Bowen, Nettie Stephenson 1866- *WhWNAA*
Bowen, Noel H *BbtC*
Bowen, Norman Levi 1887- *WhWNAA*
Bowen, Olwen *WhCL*
Bowen, Pardon 1757-1826 *Alli*
Bowen, Peter 1939- *ConAu 57*
Bowen, Richard M 1928- *ConAu 23*, *WrD 1976*
Bowen, Robert Adger 1868- *BlkAW*, *ChPo*, *WhWNAA*
Bowen, Robert Cole *Alli Sup*
Bowen, Robert O 1920- *ConAu 9R*, *ConNov 1972*, *ConNov 1976*, *WrD 1976*
Bowen, Robert Sidney 1900- *AuBYP*
Bowen, Samuel *Alli*
Bowen, Sue Petigru 1824-1875 *AmA&B*, *BiD&SB*, *DcAmA*, *DcNAA*
Bowen, T J *Alli*, *Alli Sup*
Bowen, Thomas Jefferson 1814-1875 *Alli*, *BiDSA*, *DcNAA*
Bowen, W H *Alli Sup*
Bowen, Wilbur Pardon 1864-1928 *DcNAA*, *WhWNAA*
Bowen, William Abraham 1856-1921 *AmLY*, *DcNAA*
Bowen, William Alvin 1877-1937 *DcNAA*
Bowen, William Henry 1836-1915 *DcNAA*
Bowen, Zack 1934- *ConAu 29*, *WrD 1976*
Bowen-Judd, Sara 1922- *ConAu 9R*
Bowen-Rowlands, Ernest Bowen Brown *WhLA*
Bower, A A *Alli Sup*
Bower, Adelaide Howell 1889- *WhWNAA*
Bower, Alexander *Alli*, *BiDLA*
Bower, Amy 1881- *WhWNAA*
Bower, Archibald 1686-1766 *Alli*, *Chmbr 2*, *EvLB*
Bower, B M 1871-1940 *AmA&B*, *DcNAA*, *LongC*, *REnAL*, *TwCA*, *WhWNAA*
Bower, D H B *Alli Sup*
Bower, David A 1945- *ConAu 37*
Bower, E T C *Alli Sup*
Bower, Edward *Alli*
Bower, Elizabeth G *ChPo*
Bower, F LeN *ChPo*
Bower, Fay Louise 1929- *ConAu 53*
Bower, Frederic Orpen *Alli Sup*
Bower, George *Alli Sup*
Bower, George Henry Ker *Alli Sup*
Bower, George Spencer 1854- *Alli Sup*
Bower, Gordon H 1932- *ConAu 17R*
Bower, Sir Graham John 1848- *WhLA*
Bower, Hubert *Alli Sup*
Bower, J *Alli Sup*

Bower, John *Alli, Alli Sup*
Bower, John, Jr. *Alli*
Bower, John A *Alli Sup*
Bower, Julia Wells 1903- *ConAu 41*
Bower, Louise 1900- *ConAu 21*
Bower, Mark Noble *Alli Sup*
Bower, Maurice L 1922- *AmSCAP 66, ChPo*
Bower, Muriel 1921- *ConAu 49*
Bower, Neal Monroe 1906- *IndAu 1917*
Bower, Robert *Alli Sup*
Bower, Robert T 1919- *ConAu 49*
Bower, Selina A *Alli Sup*
Bower, Thomas *Alli*
Bower, Walter 1385-1449 *Alli, Chmbr 1, EvLB*
Bower, Warren 1898- *IndAu 1917*
Bower, William *Alli*
Bower, William Clayton 1878- *Au&Wr, ConAu 5R, IndAu 1917, WhWNAA, WrD 1976*
Bowerbank, E M *ChPo S2*
Bowerbank, James Scott 1797-1877 *Alli Sup*
Bowerbank, John *Alli, BiDLA Sup*
Bowerbank, John Scott 1797-1877 *Alli*
Bowerbank, T F *Alli, BiDLA Sup*
Bowering, George 1935- *ConAu 21, OxCan, OxCan Sup*
Bowering, George 1938- *ConNov 1972, ConP 1970, ConP 1975, WrD 1976*
Bowerman, George Franklin 1868-1960 *AmA&B, WhWNAA*
Bowerman, Paul 1898- *WhWNAA*
Bowers, A W *OxCan*
Bowers, Alexander *Alli Sup*
Bowers, Barbara Euphan *ChPo*
Bowers, C A 1935- *ConAu 29*
Bowers, Charles William *BiDSA*
Bowers, Claude Gernade 1878-1958 *AmA&B, IndAu 1816, OxAm, REn, REnAL, TwCA, TwCA Sup*
Bowers, Edgar 1924- *AmA&B, ChPo S1, ConAu 5R, ConP 1970, ConP 1975, Pen Am, WorAu, WrD 1976*
Bowers, Fanny *ChPo S1*
Bowers, Faubion 1917- *AmA&B, ConAu 5R, WrD 1976*
Bowers, Frederick V 1874-1961 *AmSCAP 66*
Bowers, Fredson Thayer 1905- *AmA&B, ChPo, ConAu 5R*
Bowers, George Ballard 1876-1944 *IndAu 1917*
Bowers, George K 1916- *ConAu 1R*
Bowers, Georgina 1830?- *Alli Sup, Br&AmS*
Bowers, John 1928- *ConAu 33, DrAF 1976, WrD 1976*
Bowers, John Hugh 1875-1923 *DcNAA*
Bowers, John Oliver 1860- *IndAu 1917*
Bowers, John Waite 1935- *ConAu 41*
Bowers, Lassie *BlkAW*
Bowers, Margaretta Keller 1908- *ConAu 5R, WrD 1976*
Bowers, Mildred *ChPo*
Bowers, Paul Eugene 1886-1938 *IndAu 1917*
Bowers, Peter Meiere *WhPNW*
Bowers, Q David 1938- *ConAu 41*
Bowers, Robert Hood 1877-1941 *AmSCAP 66*
Bowers, Ronald 1941- *ConAu 41*
Bowers, Santha Rama Rau 1923- *ConAu 1R*
Bowers, Thomas *Alli*
Bowers, Warner Fremont 1906- *ConAu 61*
Bowers, William Gray 1879- *WhWNAA*
Bowersox, Charles A 1846-1921 *OhA&B*
Bowes, Anne LaBastille *ConAu 57*
Bowes, Edward *ChPo S2*
Bowes, George Seaton *Alli Sup*
Bowes, Gordon E *OxCan*
Bowes, James Lord *Alli Sup*
Bowes, Sir Jerome *Alli*
Bowes, John *Alli Sup*
Bowes, John 1804-1874 *Alli Sup*
Bowes, John L *Alli Sup*
Bowes, Paul *Alli*
Bowes, Thomas *Alli*
Bowes-Lyon, Lilian Helen 1895-1949 *ChPo, ChPo S1, Chmbr 3, DclEnL*
Bowett, Derek William 1927- *Au&Wr, ConAu 9R*
Bowick, J *Alli Sup*
Bowick, Thomas *Alli Sup*

Bowick, William *Alli*
Bowie, Augustus J, Jr. *Alli Sup*
Bowie, Janetta 1907- *WrD 1976*
Bowie, Jim *ConAu XR, WrD 1976*
Bowie, Norman E 1942- *ConAu 33, WrD 1976*
Bowie, Robert R 1909- *ConAu P-1*
Bowie, Sam *ConAu XR, WrD 1976*
Bowie, Walter Russell 1882-1969 *AmA&B, ConAu 5R, WhWNAA*
Bowie, Walter Worthington *BiDSA*
Bowie, William 1872-1941 *DcNAA, WhWNAA*
Bowker, Francis E 1917- *ConAu 41*
Bowker, George *Alli Sup*
Bowker, Gordon Philip 1934- *Au&Wr*
Bowker, James *Alli Sup*
Bowker, John Westerdale 1935- *ConAu 25, WrD 1976*
Bowker, Margaret 1936- *ConAu 25, WrD 1976*
Bowker, Richard Rogers 1848-1933 *Alli Sup, AmA&B, BbD, BiD&SB, DcAmA, DcNAA, WhWNAA*
Bowker, Robin Marsland 1920- *Au&Wr, WrD 1976*
Bowland *ChPo*
Bowlby, Anthony A *Alli Sup*
Bowlby, John 1907- *ConAu 49*
Bowlby, Richard *Alli Sup*
Bowle, John *Alli*
Bowle, John 1725-1788 *Alli*
Bowle, John Edward 1905- *Au&Wr, ConAu 1R*
Bowlend, George B *EarAB*
Bowler, Mabel 1868- *WhWNAA*
Bowler, Metcalf 1726-1789 *DcNAA*
Bowler, R Arthur 1930- *ConAu 57*
Bowler, Stanley William 1907- *Au&Wr*
Bowles *Alli*
Bowles, Caroline Anne 1786-1854 *Alli, BrAu 19, ChPo, ChPo S1, Chmbr 3, DcEnL*
Bowles, Charles *Alli Sup*
Bowles, Chester 1901- *AmA&B, Au&Wr, REnAL*
Bowles, D Richard 1910- *ConAu 33*
Bowles, Edmund A 1925- *ConAu 33*
Bowles, Edward *Alli*
Bowles, Ella Shannon 1886-1975 *AmA&B, ConAu 57, WhWNAA*
Bowles, Emily *Alli Sup*
Bowles, Frances *ChPo S2*
Bowles, Frank H 1907-1975 *ConAu 13R, ConAu 57*
Bowles, Frederick G *ChPo*
Bowles, G J *BbtC*
Bowles, Mrs. George Cranley *Alli Sup*
Bowles, Gordon Townsend 1904- *ConAu P-1*
Bowles, Henry *Alli Sup*
Bowles, Jane 1917-1973 *Au&Wr, ConAu 19, ConAu 41, ConNov 1972, ModAL, Pen Am, WhTwL, WorAu*
Bowles, Janet Payne *IndAu 1816*
Bowles, John *Alli, BiDLA, BiDLA Sup*
Bowles, John 1833-1900 *DcNAA*
Bowles, Joseph Moore 1860-1934 *DcNAA*
Bowles, Michael Andrew 1909- *Au&Wr*
Bowles, Minna *Alli Sup*
Bowles, Oliver d1674 *Alli*
Bowles, Paul 1910- *AmA&B, AmSCAP 66, Au&Wr, ConAu 1R, ConLC 1, ConLC 2, ConNov 1972, ConNov 1976, DrAF 1976, ModAL, ModAL Sup, OxAm, Pen Am, RAdv 1, REnAL, TwCA Sup, TwCW, WhTwL, WrD 1976*
Bowles, Ralph Hartt 1870-1919 *DcNAA*
Bowles, Richard W 1918- *AmSCAP 66*
Bowles, Samuel 1797-1851 *AmA&B, REnAL*
Bowles, Samuel 1826-1878 *Alli Sup, AmA&B, BbD, BbtC, BiD&SB, DcAmA, DcNAA, OxAm, REnAL*
Bowles, Samuel 1851-1915 *AmA&B*
Bowles, Thomas *Alli*
Bowles, Thomas Gibson *Alli Sup*
Bowles, W *BbtC*
Bowles, W R *Alli, BiDLA, BiDLA Sup*
Bowles, William *Alli*

Bowles, William Augustus 1744-1805 *BiDSA, DcNAA*
Bowles, William Lisle 1762-1850 *Alli, BbD, BiD&SB, BiDLA, BiDLA Sup, BrAu 19, CasWL, ChPo, ChPo S1, ChPo S2, Chmbr 2, DcEnL, DcLEnL, EvLB, NewC, OxEng, Pen Eng, WebEAL*
Bowley, Arthur Lyon 1869- *WhLA*
Bowley, Marian E A 1911- *Au&Wr, WrD 1976*
Bowley, May *ChPo, ChPo S1, ChPo S2*
Bowley, Rex Lyon 1925- *Au&Wr, WrD 1976*
Bowlin, William Ray *ChPo S1*
Bowling, Edward Woodley *ChPo*
Bowling, Jackson M 1934- *ConAu 5R*
Bowling, John *Alli Sup*
Bowling, W K 1808- *Alli*
Bowlker, Charles *Alli*
Bowmaker, Walter *EvLB*
Bowman *Alli*
Bowman, Albert Elijah 1881- *WhWNAA*
Bowman, Albert Hall 1921- *ConAu 41*
Bowman, Alice Bertha *MnBBF*
Bowman, Anne *Alli Sup, CarSB, ChPo S1, DcEnL*
Bowman, Benjamin Allen 1902- *IndAu 1917*
Bowman, Brooks 1913-1937 *AmSCAP 66*
Bowman, Charles A *OxCan Sup*
Bowman, David J 1919- *ConAu 9R*
Bowman, Derek 1931- *WrD 1976*
Bowman, E Q *Alli Sup*
Bowman, Eddowes *Alli Sup*
Bowman, Edward Morris 1848-1913 *DcAmA, DcNAA*
Bowman, Euday L 1887-1949 *AmSCAP 66*
Bowman, Frank Paul 1927- *ConAu 33*
Bowman, Frederick H *Alli Sup*
Bowman, Frederick H U 1894- *MnBBF*
Bowman, Gerald d1967 *MnBBF*
Bowman, H L 1889- *WhWNAA*
Bowman, Harold Martin 1876-1949 *DcNAA*
Bowman, Heath 1910- *AmA&B, IndAu 1917*
Bowman, Henry *Alli*
Bowman, Henry A 1903- *ConAu P-1*
Bowman, Hetty 1838-1872 *Alli Sup, ChPo, ChPo S1, ChPo S2*
Bowman, Hildebrand *Alli*
Bowman, Howard Hiestand M 1886- *WhWNAA*
Bowman, Isa *ChPo S1, ChPo S2*
Bowman, Isaiah 1878-1950 *AmA&B, AmLY*
Bowman, J F *Alli Sup*
Bowman, Jacob L *Alli Sup*
Bowman, James Cloyd 1880-1961 *AmA&B, AnCL, AuBYP, JBA 1951, OhA&B, St&VC, WhWNAA*
Bowman, Jeanne *ConAu XR*
Bowman, John E *Alli*
Bowman, John Stewart 1931- *Au&Wr, ConAu 9R*
Bowman, John Wick 1894- *AmA&B, ConAu 1R*
Bowman, Karl M 1888-1973 *ConAu 41*
Bowman, LeRoy 1887-1971 *ConAu 33*
Bowman, Locke E, Jr. 1927- *ConAu 5R*
Bowman, Louise Morey 1882-1944 *ChPo, ChPo S1, DcNAA, WhWNAA*
Bowman, Marcelle 1914- *ConAu 25*
Bowman, Mary D 1924- *ConAu 25*
Bowman, Mary Jean 1908- *ConAu 33*
Bowman, Milo Jesse 1874-1948 *IndAu 1917*
Bowman, Ned A 1932- *ConAu 41*
Bowman, Paul Hoover 1914- *ConAu 33*
Bowman, Phila Butler *ChPo S1*
Bowman, Robert Mackenzie 1928- *ConAu 25, WrD 1976*
Bowman, Roland Claude 1870-1903 *ChPo*
Bowman, Samuel M And Irwin, Richard B *Alli Sup*
Bowman, Samuel Millard 1815-1885 *DcNAA*
Bowman, Shadrach Laycock 1829-1906 *DcNAA*
Bowman, Sylvia Edmonia 1914- *ConAu 1R, IndAu 1917, WrD 1976*
Bowman, Thomas *Alli Sup*
Bowman, Thomas d1792 *Alli, BiDLA, BiDLA Sup*
Bowman, Thomas 1817-1914 *DcNAA*
Bowman, Ward S, Jr. 1911- *ConAu 49*

Bowman, William *Alli, Alli Sup*
Bowman, William Ernest 1911- *Au&Wr*
Bowman-Porter, Arthur *ChPo S2*
Bowmans, Godfried J A 1913- *ConAu 29*
Bownd, Nic *Alli*
Bowne, Borden Parker 1847-1910 *Alli Sup,
   AmA, AmA&B, BiD&SB, DcAmA,
   DcNAA, OxAm*
Bowne, Eliza Soughgate 1783-1809 *CarSB*
Bowne, Ford *ConAu 49*
Bowne, P H *ChPo S2*
Bownes, James *Alli Sup*
Bownes, William E *MnBBF*
Bowness, William 1809-1867 *Alli Sup*
Bowneus, Peter *Alli*
Bownocker, John Adams 1865- *WhWNAA*
Bowood, Richard *ConAu XR*
Bowra, Harriette *Alli Sup*
Bowra, Sir Cecil Maurice 1898-1970 *Au&Wr,
   ConAu 1R, ConAu 29, DcLEnL, EvLB,
   LongC, ModBL, NewC, REn,
   TwCA Sup*
Bowra, Thomas *BiDLA, BiDLA Sup*
Bowran, John George 1839- *WhLA*
Bowrey, Thomas *Alli*
Bowring, Benjamin *OxCan*
Bowring, Bernard *ChPo S1*
Bowring, Edgar Alfred *Alli*
Bowring, Sir John 1792-1872 *Alli, Alli Sup,
   BbD, BiD&SB, BrAu 19, CarSB,
   CasWL, ChPo, ChPo S1, ChPo S2,
   Chmbr 3, DcEnL, DcLEnL, EvLB, PoCh*
Bowring, Lewin Bentham *Alli Sup*
Bowser, Edward Albert 1837?-1910 *Alli Sup,
   DcAmA, DcNAA*
Bowser, Frederick P 1937- *ConAu 49*
Bowser, Joan *ConAu XR*
Bowser, Laura Adah 1924?- *IndAu 1917*
Bowser, Pearl 1931- *ConAu 33*
Bowsfield, Colvin Cullen 1855-1940 *DcNAA*
Bowsfield, Hartwell *OxCan Sup*
Bowstead, John *Alli Sup*
Bowtell, John *Alli*
Bowyer, Sir George *Alli*
Bowyer, Sir George 1811-1883 *Alli, Alli Sup,
   BiDLA*
Bowyer, Howard K 1924- *IndAu 1917*
Bowyer, John W 1921- *ConAu 37,
   IndAu 1917*
Bowyer, John Wilson 1901- *TexWr*
Bowyer, Laura Ruth 1907- *Au&Wr*
Bowyer, Mathew Justice 1926- *ConAu 37,
   WrD 1976*
Bowyer, Reynold Gideon *Alli, BiDLA*
Bowyer, Thomas *Alli*
Bowyer, William 1699-1777 *Alli, BrAu,
   DcEnL, NewC, OxEng*
Bowyer-Yin, Leslie C *ChPo*
Box, Charles *Alli Sup*
Box, Edgar 1925- *ConAu XR, EncM&D,
   WrD 1976*
Box, G *Alli*
Box, George Herbert 1869- *WhLA*
Box, John *Alli Sup*
Box, Michael James *Alli Sup*
Box, Muriel Violette 1905- *Au&Wr,
   WrD 1976*
Box, Sydney 1907- *Au&Wr*
Box, Thomas *Alli Sup*
Boxall, Ernest *MnBBF*
Boxall, Sir William 1800-1879 *ChPo S1*
Boxer, Arabella *WrD 1976*
Boxer, Devorah *AuBYP*
Boxer, Edward Mourrier *Alli Sup*
Boxer, Emily Hahn 1905- *Au&Wr*
Boxer, F N *BbtC*
Boxerman, David Samuel 1945- *ConAu 61*
Boy *CasWL, ClDMEuL, EvEuW*
Boy-Ed, Ida 1852-1928 *OxGer*
Boyajian, Aram *DrAP 1975*
Boyars, Arthur 1925- *ConP 1970*
Boyarsky, Bill 1934- *ConAu 25*
Boycatt, W *Alli*
Boyce, A P *Alli Sup*
Boyce, Augustus Anson 1813-1909 *Alli Sup,
   DcNAA*
Boyce, Benjamin 1903- *AmA&B*
Boyce, Burke 1901- *AmA&B, AmNov*

Boyce, Edward Jacob *Alli Sup*
Boyce, Ella Ruth 1875-1943 *DcNAA*
Boyce, Florence Josephine *ChPo*
Boyce, George A 1898- *ConAu 53*
Boyce, George Walter *Alli Sup*
Boyce, Gray Cowan 1899- *ConAu 5R,
   WrD 1976*
Boyce, Hector *BrAu, NewC*
Boyce, James Pettigru 1827-1888 *Alli Sup,
   BiDSA, DcNAA*
Boyce, John *Alli Sup*
Boyce, John 1810-1864 *DcNAA*
Boyce, John Cox *Alli Sup*
Boyce, Neith *AmA&B*
Boyce, Ronald R 1931- *ConAu 9R*
Boyce, S S *Alli Sup*
Boyce, Samuel *Alli*
Boyce, Samuel d1775 *ChPo*
Boyce, Sarah A *ChPo*
Boyce, Thomas *Alli*
Boyce, William *Alli, PoIre*
Boyce, William 1710-1779 *Alli*
Boyce, William Binnington 1804- *Alli Sup*
Boyce, William Dickson 1848-1929 *DcNAA*
Boyce, William H *ChPo S2*
Boychuk, Bohdan 1927- *ModSL 2*
Boyd, A *Alli Sup*
Boyd, A J *Alli Sup*
Boyd, A S *ChPo, ChPo S1*
Boyd, Alamo *ConAu XR*
Boyd, Albert Truman 1901- *WhWNAA*
Boyd, Alexander *PoIre*
Boyd, Alexander Charles 1852- *Alli Sup*
Boyd, Andrew *Alli Sup*
Boyd, Andrew 1920- *ConAu 1R*
Boyd, Andrew Kennedy 1825-1899 *Alli Sup,
   BrAu 19, CasWL, Chmbr 3, DcEnA,
   DcEnA Ap, DcEnL, EvLB*
Boyd, Archibald *Alli Sup*
Boyd, Archibald 1803-1883 *Alli, Alli Sup*
Boyd, Barbara *AmA&B, WhWNAA*
Boyd, Belle 1843-1900 *Alli Sup, AmA&B,
   DcNAA*
Boyd, C *ChPo S2*
Boyd, C And Meara, W G *Alli Sup*
Boyd, C R *Alli Sup, BiDSA*
Boyd, Catharine S *ChPo*
Boyd, Charles d1857 *PoIre*
Boyd, Charles Arthur 1878- *WhWNAA*
Boyd, Charles Newell 1875-1937 *DcNAA*
Boyd, Clarence Eugene 1878- *WhWNAA*
Boyd, D C *Alli Sup*
Boyd, D R *Alli Sup*
Boyd, David *PoIre*
Boyd, David 1833- *PoIre*
Boyd, Dean *ConAu 5R*
Boyd, Don *MnBBF*
Boyd, E *Alli*
Boyd, E 1904?-1974 *ConAu 53*
Boyd, Mrs. E E *Alli Sup*
Boyd, E W *Alli Sup*
Boyd, Edna McGuire 1899- *IndAu 1917*
Boyd, Elisse *AmSCAP 66*
Boyd, Elizabeth *PoIre*
Boyd, Elizabeth Orr 1912- *Au&Wr*
Boyd, Ellen B 1855-1922 *OhA&B*
Boyd, Ellen Wright 1833- *DcAmA*
Boyd, Elsie Thompson 1904- *AmSCAP 66*
Boyd, Ernest Augustus 1887-1946 *AmA&B,
   DcNAA, LongC, OxAm, REnAL, TwCA,
   TwCA Sup*
Boyd, Erskine *HsB&A*
Boyd, Francis A 1844- *BlkAW*
Boyd, Frank *ConAu XR*
Boyd, Frank 1863- *WhLA*
Boyd, Frank 1893- *ConICB*
Boyd, Halbert Johnston 1872- *WhLA*
Boyd, Hannah Villiers *Alli Sup*
Boyd, Harper W, Jr. 1917- *ConAu 13R*
Boyd, Harriet Repplier *ChPo*
Boyd, Henry *PoIre*
Boyd, Henry 1756?-1832 *Alli, BiDLA, PoIre*
Boyd, Hugh *DcEnL*
Boyd, Hugh Alexander 1907- *WrD 1976*
Boyd, Hugh Fenwick 1852- *Alli Sup*
Boyd, Hugh Macauley 1746-1791? *Alli, PoIre*
Boyd, Hugh S 1781-1848 *Alli, BiDLA,
   BiDLA Sup, PoIre*

Boyd, Jack 1932- *ConAu 49*
Boyd, Jackson 1861-1920 *DcNAA,
   IndAu 1816*
Boyd, James *Alli*
Boyd, James 1858-1929 *DcNAA*
Boyd, James 1888-1944 *AmA&B, CnDAL,
   ConAmA, ConAmL, CyWA, DcLEnL,
   DcNAA, LongC, OxAm, Pen Am,
   REnAL, TwCA, TwCA Sup, WhWNAA*
Boyd, James Ellsworth 1863- *WhWNAA*
Boyd, James M 1919- *ConAu 33, WrD 1976*
Boyd, James Oscar 1874- *WhWNAA*
Boyd, James P *Alli Sup*
Boyd, James Penny 1836-1910 *DcNAA*
Boyd, James Robert 1804-1890 *Alli, Alli Sup,
   DcAmA, DcNAA*
Boyd, James Shield *ChPo S1*
Boyd, James Sterling 1917- *ConAu 49*
Boyd, John *Alli Sup, BlkAW, ConAu XR,
   OxCan, WrD 1976*
Boyd, John 1827?- *BbtC*
Boyd, John 1864-1933 *DcNAA*
Boyd, Sir John Alexander 1837-1916 *Alli Sup,
   BbtC, DcNAA*
Boyd, John D 1916- *ConAu 25*
Boyd, John Edward 1843-1912 *DcNAA*
Boyd, John Francis 1910- *Au&Wr, ConAu 5R*
Boyd, John MacNeill *Alli Sup*
Boyd, John Maxwell 1927- *Au&Wr*
Boyd, John P d1830 *Alli, BbtC*
Boyd, Julia *Alli Sup*
Boyd, Julian Parks 1903- *AmA&B, REnAL*
Boyd, Louise Arner 1887- *AmA&B*
Boyd, Louise Esther Vickroy 1827-1909 *Alli Sup,
   ChPo, ChPo S1, IndAu 1816, OhA&B*
Boyd, Madeleine Elsie *AmA&B*
Boyd, Malcolm 1923- *AmA&B, Au&Wr,
   ConAu 5R, WrD 1976*
Boyd, Margaret 1913- *Au&Wr, WrD 1976*
Boyd, Marion Margaret *ChPo, WhWNAA*
Boyd, Mark 1805?-1879 *Alli Sup*
Boyd, Mark Alexander 1562?-1601 *Alli,
   DcEnL, Pen Eng*
Boyd, Mark Frederick 1889- *WhWNAA*
Boyd, Martin A'Beckett 1893-1972 *Au&Wr,
   CasWL, ConAu P-1, ConNov 1972,
   DcLEnL, LongC, Pen Eng, TwCW*
Boyd, Mary D R *Alli Sup*
Boyd, Mary Stuart 1860- *WhLA*
Boyd, Maurice 1921- *AmA&B, ConAu 9R*
Boyd, Melba 1950- *BlkAW*
Boyd, Mildred Worthy 1921- *ConAu 17R*
Boyd, Minnie R *ChPo S1*
Boyd, Myron F 1909- *ConAu 41*
Boyd, Nancy *ConAmA, LongC, REn,
   REnAL*
Boyd, Olivia A *Alli Sup*
Boyd, Osborne *Alli Sup*
Boyd, Palmer *Alli Sup*
Boyd, Paul Prentice 1877- *WhWNAA*
Boyd, Percy -1876 *PoIre*
Boyd, Pliny Steele *Alli Sup*
Boyd, R *Alli Sup*
Boyd, R L F 1922- *ConAu 57*
Boyd, R Nelson *Alli Sup*
Boyd, Raven Freemont *BlkAW*
Boyd, Richard Henry 1843-1922 *DcNAA*
Boyd, Robert *Alli*
Boyd, Robert 1578-1627 *Alli, DcEnL*
Boyd, Robert 1792-1880 *OhA&B*
Boyd, Robert 1816-1879 *Alli Sup, DcNAA*
Boyd, Robert H 1912- *ConAu 53*
Boyd, Robert S 1928- *ConAu 13R*
Boyd, Robin 1919- *ConAu 17R*
Boyd, Samuel *BlkAW*
Boyd, Shylah 1945- *ConAu 61*
Boyd, Stephen Gill *Alli Sup*
Boyd, Sue Abbott *DrAP 1975*
Boyd, Theodore C *EarAB, EarAB Sup*
Boyd, Thomas 1867- *ChPo, PoIre*
Boyd, Thomas Alexander 1898-1935 *AmA&B,
   ConAmA, ConAmL, DcLEnL, DcNAA,
   LongC, OhA&B, OxAm, REnAL, TwCA,
   WhWNAA*
Boyd, Thomas C *EarAB Sup*
Boyd, Thomas Duckett 1854- *BiDSA*
Boyd, Thomas J *Alli Sup*
Boyd, Thomas J L Stirling 1886- *Au&Wr*

Boyd, Vaida Stewart *AnMV 1926*
Boyd, W P *Alli Sup*
Boyd, Waldo T 1918- *ConAu 29, WrD 1976*
Boyd, Walter *Alli, BiDLA, BiDLA Sup*
Boyd, Sir William 1812- *Alli*
Boyd, William 1874- *WhLA*
Boyd, William 1885- *ConAu 41*
Boyd, William Carr *PoIre*
Boyd, William Kenneth 1879-1938 *BiDSA, DcNAA*
Boyd, William Waddell 1862- *WhWNAA*
Boyd, Woodward 1898- *AmA&B, WhWNAA*
Boyd, Wynn Leo 1902- *AmSCAP 66*
Boyd, Zachary 1585?-1653? *Alli, CasWL, ChPo, Chmbr 1, DcEnL, EvLB, Pen Eng*
Boyd-Carpenter *WhWNAA*
Boyd-Orr, Lord 1880- *Au&Wr*
Boyde, H *Alli*
Boyde, Zachary *Alli*
Boydell, James *Alli*
Boydell, John *Alli*
Boydell, John d1739 *EarAB Sup*
Boydell, John 1719-1804 *ChPo S1*
Boydell, Josiah *Alli, BiDLA*
Boyden, Albert Gardner 1827-1915 *Alli Sup, DcNAA*
Boyden, Anna L *Alli Sup*
Boyden, Arthur Clarke 1852-1933 *DcNAA, WhWNAA*
Boyden, Edward Allen 1886- *WhWNAA*
Boyden, Henry *Alli Sup*
Boyden, Polly Chase *ChPo*
Boyden, Wallace Clarke 1858- *WhWNAA*
Boydston, Jo Ann 1924- *ConAu 29*
Boye, Inger *ChPo*
Boye, Karin Maria 1900-1941 *CasWL, ClDMEuL, EncWL, Pen Eur, WhTwL*
Boye, Kaspar Johan 1791-1853 *BiD&SB*
Boye, Martin Hans 1812-1909 *DcNAA*
Boyer, Abel 1667-1729 *Alli, BrAu, NewC, OxEng, OxFr*
Boyer, Brian D 1939- *ConAu 45*
Boyer, C Valentine 1880- *WhWNAA*
Boyer, Charles Clinton 1860-1932 *DcNAA*
Boyer, Charles Shimer 1869-1636 *DcNAA*
Boyer, Charles Sumner 1856-1928 *DcNAA*
Boyer, Charles W *Alli Sup*
Boyer, Claude 1618-1698 *CasWL, EvEuW, OxFr*
Boyer, Emanuel Roth 1857-1900 *DcAmA, DcNAA*
Boyer, Harold W 1908- *ConAu 1R*
Boyer, Jill Witherspoon *BlkAW*
Boyer, Nathalie 1861-1940 *DcNAA*
Boyer, Paul Samuel 1935- *ConAu 49*
Boyer, Richard Edwin 1932- *ConAu 23*
Boyer, Richard O 1903-1973 *ConAu 45*
Boyer, Robert *WrD 1976*
Boyer, Robert E 1929- *ConAu 41*
Boyer, Sophia Ames 1907?-1972 *ConAu 37*
Boyer, Walter E *ChPo S1*
Boyer, William W, Jr. 1923- *ConAu 13R*
Boyers, D *Alli, BiDLA*
Boyers, Robert 1942- *ConAu 53*
Boyes, Abel *Chmbr 2*
Boyes, Howard C *MnBBF*
Boyes, J *Alli Sup*
Boyes, John Frederick 1811-1879 *Alli, Alli Sup*
Boyes, Megan 1923- *Au&Wr, WrD 1976*
Boyesen, Hjalmar Hjorth 1848-1895 *Alli Sup, AmA, AmA&B, BbD, BiD&SB, CarSB, ChPo, ChPo S1, DcAmA, DcBiA, DcLEnL, DcNAA, JBA 1934, OhA&B, OxAm, REnAL*
Boyington, Gregory 1912- *AmA&B*
Boyis, Hector *NewC*
Boykin, Edward M *Alli Sup*
Boykin, James H 1914- *ConAu 5R*
Boykin, Samuel 1829-1899 *Alli Sup, BiDSA, DcNAA*
Boykowycz, Katherine *ChPo S1*
Boyl Vives DeCanesma, Carlos 1577-1618 *CasWL*
Boylan, Boyd *ConAu XR*
Boylan, Eugene 1904- *CatA 1952*
Boylan, Grace Duffie 1861?-1935 *AmA&B, DcAmA, DcNAA*
Boylan, James 1927- *ConAu 1R*

Boylan, John *WhWNAA*
Boylan, Leona Davis 1910- *ConAu 61*
Boylan, Lucile 1906- *ConAu P-1*
Boylan, Marguerite Theresa 1887- *OhA&B*
Boylan, Patrick *CatA 1947*
Boylan, R Dillon *PoIre*
Boylan, Teresa C 1868- *PoIre*
Boylan, William Aloysius 1869-1940 *DcNAA*
Boyland, Eric 1905- *WrD 1976*
Boyland, George H 1845-1919 *Alli Sup, DcAmA, OhA&B*
Boyland, Grace Duffie 1861?-1935 *ChPo*
Boyle, Andrew *ChPo S1*
Boyle, Andrew 1923- *ConAu 5R*
Boyle, Andrew Philip More 1919- *WrD 1976*
Boyle, Andrew Philip More 1922- *Au&Wr*
Boyle, Ann 1916- *ConAu 29, SmATA 10, WrD 1976*
Boyle, Charles 1676-1731 *Alli, DcEnL, NewC*
Boyle, Charles Cumberson 1854-1931 *DcNAA*
Boyle, Charles John *Alli Sup*
Boyle, David 1842-1911 *DcNAA*
Boyle, Sir Edward 1878- *WhLA*
Boyle, Edward Colquhoun *Alli Sup*
Boyle, Eleanor Vere 1825-1916 *Alli Sup, ChPo, ChPo S1*
Boyle, Emily Charlotte *Alli Sup, PoIre*
Boyle, Esmeralda 1840- *Alli Sup, BiDSA, DcAmA, PoIre*
Boyle, Francis *PoIre*
Boyle, Frederick 1841- *Alli Sup, MnBBF*
Boyle, G *PoIre*
Boyle, George 1902- *OxCan*
Boyle, George David 1828- *Alli Sup*
Boyle, George F 1886-1948 *AmSCAP 66*
Boyle, Hamilton *Alli*
Boyle, Harry Joseph 1915- *ConAu 13R*
Boyle, Henry *Alli*
Boyle, Henry Edmund Gaskin 1875- *WhLA*
Boyle, Herbert Edward *Alli Sup*
Boyle, J A 1916- *ConAu 61*
Boyle, Jack *EncM&D*
Boyle, James 1853-1939 *DcNAA, OhA&B*
Boyle, James Ernest 1873-1938 *DcNAA*
Boyle, James Thompson 1849- *ChPo, ChPo S1*
Boyle, John 1707-1762 *Alli, DcEnL, NewC, OxEng, PoIre*
Boyle, John 1822?-1885 *PoIre*
Boyle, John Andrew 1916- *Au&Wr, WrD 1976*
Boyle, John Hunter 1930- *ConAu 41*
Boyle, Joseph Barnes Swift 1845- *Alli Sup*
Boyle, Joyce 1901- *ConAu P-1*
Boyle, Kay 1903- *AmA&B, AmNov, CasWL, CnDAL, ConAmA, ConAu 13R, ConLC 1, ConLC 5, ConNov 1972, ConNov 1976, ConP 1970, ConP 1975, DcLEnL, DrAF 1976, DrAP 1975, EncWL, LongC, ModAL, OxAm, Pen Am, RAdv 1, REn, REnAL, TwCA, TwCA Sup, WhTwL, WrD 1976*
Boyle, Margaret 1862- *PoIre*
Boyle, Mary *ChPo*
Boyle, Mary 1882?-1975 *ConAu 53*
Boyle, Mary E *ChPo*
Boyle, Mary Louisa 1810?-1890 *Alli, Alli Sup, ChPo, PoIre*
Boyle, Murrough d1712 *PoIre*
Boyle, Oswald *Alli Sup*
Boyle, Peter *Alli Sup*
Boyle, R F *Alli Sup*
Boyle, R V *Alli Sup*
Boyle, Richard 1566-1644 *Alli*
Boyle, Robert *Alli, Chmbr 1, MnBBF*
Boyle, Robert 1627-1691 *Alli, CasWL, CyAL 1, DcEnL, EvLB, REn*
Boyle, Robert 1915- *ConAu 13R*
Boyle, Robert H 1928- *ConAu 17R*
Boyle, Robert Whelan d1889 *Alli Sup, PoIre*
Boyle, Roger 1621-1679 *Alli, BrAu, CasWL, Chmbr 1, DcEnL, DcLEnL, EvLB, NewC, OxEng, PoIre*
Boyle, Sarah Patton 1906- *ConAu P-1*
Boyle, Sarah Roberts 1812-1869 *ChPo*
Boyle, Stanley E 1927- *ConAu 41*
Boyle, Ted Eugene 1933- *ConAu 23*
Boyle, Virginia Frazer 1863-1938 *AmA&B, AmLY, BiD&SB, BiDSA, ChPo S1,*

Boyle, W R *Alli*
Boyle, William 1853-1923 *ChPo S2, McGWD, PoIre*
Boyle, William Robert Augustus *Alli Sup*
Boylen, Margaret Currier 1921- *ConAu 1R*
Boyles, C S, Jr. 1905- *AmA&B, ConAu 1R*
Boyles, Mary Lenora Mauch *IndAu 1917*
Boyles, Virgil Dillin 1872- *IndAu 1816*
Boyleston, Peter 1812-1894 *AmA*
Boylesve, Rene 1867-1926 *CasWL, ClDMEuL, EvEuW, OxFr, TwCA, TwCA Sup*
Boylston, Helen Dore 1895- *AuBYP, JBA 1951, WhCL*
Boylston, Peter *AmA&B, DcNAA*
Boylston, Zabdiel 1680-1766 *Alli*
Boyne, Donald Arthur Colin Aydon 1921- *Au&Wr*
Boyne, J *Alli, BiDLA*
Boyne, L S *Alli*
Boyne, Phyllis *Alli Sup*
Boyne, William *Alli Sup*
Boynton, Anna *ChPo*
Boynton, Charles Brandon 1806-1883 *Alli Sup, DcAmA, DcNAA, OhA&B*
Boynton, Edward Carlisle 1825-1893 *Alli Sup, DcAmA*
Boynton, Frank David 1863-1930 *DcNAA*
Boynton, George Mills 1837-1908 *DcNAA*
Boynton, Henry Cook 1874- *WhWNAA*
Boynton, Henry VanNess 1835-1905 *Alli Sup, DcAmA, DcNAA, OhA&B*
Boynton, Henry Walcott 1869-1947 *AmA&B, AmLY, DcAmA, DcNAA, REnAL, WhWNAA*
Boynton, Howard M *HsB&A*
Boynton, J *Alli Sup*
Boynton, Jeremy 1824-1883 *DcNAA*
Boynton, Julia Holmes *Alli Sup*
Boynton, Julia P *Alli Sup*
Boynton, Lewis Delano 1909- *ConAu 5R, WrD 1976*
Boynton, Luella 1906- *TexWr*
Boynton, Nehemiah 1856-1933 *DcNAA*
Boynton, Percy Holmes 1875-1946 *AmA&B, DcNAA, OxAm, REnAL, TwCA, TwCA Sup, WhWNAA*
Boyrie, Arthur *Alli Sup*
Boys, Mrs. *Alli*
Boys, Charles Vernon *WhLA*
Boys, Edward *Alli, Alli Sup*
Boys, Ernest *Alli Sup*
Boys, Florence Riddick 1875- *WhWNAA*
Boys, Henry *Alli*
Boys, James *Alli*
Boys, John *Alli, BiDLA*
Boys, John 1560-1643 *Alli*
Boys, John 1571-1625 *Alli*
Boys, Samuel Evan 1871-1966 *IndAu 1917*
Boys, T S *Alli*
Boys, Thomas 1792-1880 *Alli, Alli Sup*
Boys, William 1735-1803 *Alli*
Boys, William Fuller Alves 1833-1914 *Alli Sup, BbtC, DcNAA*
Boyse, E C *Alli Sup*
Boyse, John *Alli, PoIre*
Boyse, Joseph 1660-1728 *Alli*
Boyse, Samuel *Alli*
Boyse, Samuel 1708-1749? *Alli, PoIre*
Boyse, Thomas d1854 *PoIre*
Boysen, Johann Wilhelm 1834-1870 *CasWL*
Boyston *Alli*
Boyten, H E *MnBBF*
Boyton, Neil 1884-1956 *AmA&B, AuBYP, BkC 1, CatA 1947, WhWNAA*
Boyton, Paul 1848-1924 *DcNAA*
Boyton, Peggy *Au&Wr*
Boyum, Joy Gould 1934- *ConAu 33*
Boz 1812-1870 *DcEnL, NewC, OxEng*
Bozdech, Emanuel 1841-1889 *BiD&SB*
Boze, Arthur Phillip 1945- *BlkAW, ConAu 57*
Boze, Calvin *IIBYP*
Bozeman, Adda VonBruemmer 1908- *ConAu 5R, WrD 1976*
Bozic, Mirko 1919- *CasWL, ModSL 2, Pen Eur*
Bozman, John Leeds 1757-1823 *Alli, AmA&B, BiDSA, DcAmA, DcNAA*

Bozman, Mildred *ChPo*
Bozun *Alli, BiB N*
Bozveli, Neofit 1785?-1848 *CasWL*
Bozzo, Frank *IlBYP*
Bozzy *DcEnL*
Braak, Ivo 1906- *CasWL*
Braak, Menno Ter 1902-1940 *CasWL, Pen Eur*
Braasch, William Frederick 1878- *ConAu 29*
Braaten, Oskar Alexander 1881-1939 *CasWL*
Brabant, Auguste Joseph 1845-1912 *DcNAA, OxCan*
Brabant, F G *Alli Sup*
Brabant, Jan, Duke Of 1254?-1294 *CasWL*
Brabazon, Elizabeth Jane *Alli Sup*
Brabazon, Luke Brabazon- 1834-1860 *Alli Sup*
Brabazon, Mary J, Countess Of Meath *Alli Sup*
Brabazon, Reginald 1841- *Alli Sup*
Brabb, George J 1925- *ConAu 41*
Brabourne, Baron 1829-1893 *NewC*
Brabourne, Lord Edward Huggessen K-H
    1829-1893 *Alli Sup, BiD&SB, WhCL*
Brabourne, Theoph *Alli*
Brabrooke, Edward William 1839- *Alli Sup*
Brabson, George Dana 1900- *ConAu P-1*
Bracciolini, Francesco 1566-1645 *CasWL*
Bracciolini, G F Poggio 1380-1459 *DcEuL, REn*
Bracciolini-Poggio, Gian Francesco 1380-1459
    CasWL, EvEuW
Bracco, Roberto 1861?-1943 *CasWL, ClDMEuL, CnThe, EncWL, McGWD, ModWD, REnWD*
Brace, Arthur William 1923- *Au&Wr*
Brace, Benjamin *AmA&B, DcNAA*
Brace, Charles Loring 1826-1890 *Alli, Alli Sup, AmA&B, BbD, BiD&SB, CyAL 2, DcAmA, DcEnL, DcNAA*
Brace, David Kingsley 1891- *TexWr, WhWNAA*
Brace, DeWitt Bristol 1859-1905 *DcAmA, DcNAA*
Brace, Donald Clifford 1881-1955 *AmA&B*
Brace, Dudley *MnBBF*
Brace, Gerald Warner 1901- *AmA&B, AmNov, Au&Wr, ConAu 13R, OxAm, REnAL, TwCA, WrD 1976*
Brace, John Pierce 1793-1872 *Alli, AmA&B, DcAmA, DcNAA*
Brace, Jonathan 1810-1877 *Alli, DcNAA*
Brace, Maria Porter *DcNAA*
Brace, Richard Munthe 1915- *ConAu 1R*
Brace, Timothy *AmA&B, AmNov XR*
Bracebridge, Charles Holte *Alli Sup, ChPo*
Bracegirdle, Anne 1663?-1748 *NewC, REn*
Bracegirdle, Brian 1933- *Au&Wr, WrD 1976*
Bracegirdle, Cyril 1920- *Au&Wr, ConAu 45, WrD 1976*
Bracewell, Ronald N 1921- *ConAu 57*
Bracewell-Milnes, Barry 1931- *ConAu 33, WrD 1976*
Bracey, Howard E 1905- *ConAu 13R*
Bracey, John H, Jr. 1941- *ConAu 29, LivBA*
Bracher, Karl Dietrich 1922- *ConAu 45*
Bracher, Marjory Louise Scholl 1906-
    ConAu P-1, IndAu 1917
Brachmann, Karoline Luise 1777-1822 *BiD&SB*
Brachmann, Luise 1777-1822 *OxGer*
Brachvogel, Albert Emil 1824-1878 *BiD&SB, EvEuW, OxGer*
Brachvogel, Udo 1835- *BiD&SB*
Brack, Harold Arthur 1923- *ConAu 17R, WrD 1976*
Brack, Jessie Wanless *ChPo S1*
Brack, O M, Jr. 1938- *ConAu 41*
Brackbill, Yvonne 1928- *ConAu 23*
Bracke, Ole Olafson *ChPo S1*
Brackeen, L O 1902- *WhWNAA*
Brackel, Baroness Ferdinande Von 1835-
    BiD&SB
Bracken, Dorothy K *ConAu 23*
Bracken, Edward *Alli*
Bracken, Henry *Alli*
Bracken, Henry Martyn 1854-1938 *DcNAA*
Bracken, Joseph Andrew 1930- *ConAu 37*
Bracken, Peg 1920- *ConAu 1R*
Bracken, Thomas 1843-1898 *Alli Sup, ChPo, ChPo S1, Chmbr 3, PoIre*
Brackenbury, Augustus *Alli Sup*

Brackenbury, Charles Booth 1831-1890 *Alli Sup*
Brackenbury, Edward *Alli, BiDLA*
Brackenbury, Mrs. F *Alli Sup*
Brackenbury, George *Alli Sup*
Brackenbury, Henry 1837- *Alli Sup*
Brackenbury, Hilda *ChPo S1*
Brackenbury, Joseph *Alli, BiDLA*
Brackenridge, Henry Marie 1786-1871 *Alli, AmA, AmA&B, BbD, BbtC, BiD&SB, BiDSA, CyAL 1, DcAmA, DcNAA, OxAm*
Brackenridge, Hugh Henry 1748-1816 *Alli, AmA, AmA&B, BiD&SB, BiDSA, CasWL, CnDAL, CyAL 1, CyWA, DcAmA, DcLEnL, DcNAA, OxAm, OxEng, Pen Am, REn, REnAL, WebEAL*
Brackenridge, William *Alli*
Bracker, Charles Eugene 1895- *IlCB 1945*
Bracker, Jon 1936- *ConAu 17R*
Bracker, Milton *ChPo S1*
Brackett, Albert Gallatin 1829-1896 *Alli Sup, DcAmA, DcNAA*
Brackett, Anna Callender 1836-1911 *Alli Sup, ChPo, DcAmA, DcNAA*
Brackett, Charles 1892-1969 *AmA&B, REnAL, WhWNAA*
Brackett, Charles Albert 1856-1927 *DcNAA*
Brackett, Edward Augustus 1818-1908?
    AmA&B, DcAmA, DcNAA, OhA&B
Brackett, George E *Alli Sup*
Brackett, Jeffrey Richardson 1860-1949 *DcNAA*
Brackett, Leigh Douglas 1915- *ConAu 1R, OhA&B, WrD 1976*
Brackfield, Peter 1922- *Au&Wr*
Brackman, Arnold C 1923- *Au&Wr, AuNews 1, ConAu 5R*
Braconnet, Henry *Alli*
Bracq, Jean Charlemagne 1853-1934 *DcNAA, OxCan*
Bracque, Georges 1882-1963 *AtlBL*
Bracton, Henry De d1268 *Alli, BrAu, Chmbr 1, DcEnL, NewC, OxEng*
Bracy, William 1915- *ConAu 61*
Bradberry, David *Alli, BiDLA*
Bradbrook, Muriel Clara 1909- *ConAu 13R, WrD 1976*
Bradburn, Eliza Weaver *Alli Sup, ChPo*
Bradburn, Mrs. Frances H *Alli Sup*
Bradburn, James Denham *Alli Sup*
Bradburn, Norman M 1933- *ConAu 37*
Bradburne, E S 1915- *ConAu 25*
Bradbury, Ammi Ruhamah 1810-1899 *DcNAA*
Bradbury, Bianca 1908- *AmA&B, AuBYP, ConAu 13R, SmATA 3*
Bradbury, Charles 1798-1864 *DcNAA*
Bradbury, E P *ConAu XR*
Bradbury, Edward *Alli Sup*
Bradbury, George Ambrose *Alli Sup*
Bradbury, Harriet Bowker 1863-1945 *OhA&B*
Bradbury, Harry Bower 1863-1923 *DcNAA*
Bradbury, James *Alli Sup*
Bradbury, John *Alli, Alli Sup*
Bradbury, John Buckley *Alli Sup*
Bradbury, John M 1908-1969 *ConAu P-1*
Bradbury, Joseph *Alli Sup*
Bradbury, Louisa B *ChPo*
Bradbury, Malcolm 1932- *Au&Wr, ConAu 1R, ConNov 1972, ConNov 1976, ConP 1970, ModBL, ModBL Sup, NewC, TwCW, WrD 1976*
Bradbury, Marcia C *ChPo, ChPo S1*
Bradbury, Osgood *Alli Sup, AmA&B, DcNAA*
Bradbury, Parnell 1904- *Au&Wr, ConAu 13R, WrD 1976*
Bradbury, Ray 1920- *AmA&B, Au&Wr, AuNews 1, AuNews 2, CasWL, CnMWL, ConAu 1R, ConLC 1, ConLC 3, ConNov 1972, ConNov 1976, DrAF 1976, LongC, OxAm, Pen Am, REn, REnAL, TwCA Sup, TwCW, WrD 1976*
Bradbury, Robert H 1870- *WhWNAA*
Bradbury, S H *DcEnL*
Bradbury, S J *ChPo S2*
Bradbury, Samuel 1883-1947 *DcNAA, WhWNAA*
Bradbury, Stephen Henry *Alli Sup*

Bradbury, Thomas *Alli Sup*
Bradbury, Thomas 1677-1759 *Alli*
Bradbury, William Batchelder 1816-1868 *Alli, AmA&B, ChPo S1, DcNAA*
Bradbury, William Frothingham 1829-1914 *DcNAA*
Bradbury, Woodman 1866- *WhWNAA*
Bradby, Ann *LongC*
Bradby, Anne *REn*
Bradby, Edward Henry *Alli Sup*
Bradby, Godfrey Fox 1863-1847 *ChPo, ChPo S1, ChPo S2, LongC, MnBBF*
Bradby, James *Alli, BiDLA*
Bradby, M K *ChPo S2*
Bradby, Rachel 1943- *WrD 1976*
Braddick, John *Alli*
Braddock, Edward 1695-1755 *OxCan, REn*
Braddock, Emily A *ChPo, ChPo S1*
Braddock, Joseph Edward 1902- *Au&Wr, ChPo, ChPo S2*
Braddock, Richard R 1920- *ConAu 1R*
Braddon, Miss 1837-1915 *LongC*
Braddon, Edward *Alli Sup*
Braddon, Sir Henry Yule 1863- *WhLA*
Braddon, Lawrence *Alli*
Braddon, Mary Elizabeth 1837-1915 *Alli Sup, BbD, BiD&SB, BrAu 19, CasWL, Chmbr 3, DcBiA, DcEnA, DcEnA Ap, DcEnL, DcLEnL, EncM&D, EvLB, HsB&A, NewC, OxEng, REn*
Braddon, Russell Reading 1921- *Au&Wr, ConAu 1R, WrD 1976*
Braddord, Gamaliel 1863-1932 *REn*
Braddy, Haldeen 1908- *ConAu 17R, TexWr*
Braddy, Nella 1894- *AuBYP, ChPo S1*
Brade, William *Alli Sup*
Brade-Birks, Stanley Graham 1887- *Au&Wr, ConAu P-1, WrD 1976*
Braden, Alta Taylor *OhA&B*
Braden, Anne McCarty 1924- *AmA&B*
Braden, Charles Samuel 1887- *AmA&B, ConAu 5R, WhWNAA*
Braden, Clark 1831-1915 *OhA&B*
Braden, Irene A *ConAu XR*
Braden, James Andrew 1872-1954? *AmA&B, DcAmA, OhA&B*
Braden, Samuel Ray 1888- *WhWNAA*
Braden, Waldo W 1911- *ConAu 5R, WrD 1976*
Braden, William *Alli Sup*
Braden, William 1930- *ConAu 23*
Bradey, Barney *Alli Sup, PoIre*
Bradfield, James McComb 1917- *ConAu 5R*
Bradfield, Jolly Roger *ConAu XR*
Bradfield, Nancy 1913- *ConAu 29, WrD 1976*
Bradfield, Richard 1896- *ConAu 23*
Bradfield, Roger 1924- *ConAu 17R*
Bradfield, Thomas *Alli Sup, ChPo S1*
Bradfield, William *Alli Sup*
Bradford, A W *Alli*
Bradford, Adam *AuBYP, ConAu XR*
Bradford, Alden 1765-1843 *Alli, AmA&B, BiD&SB, DcAmA, DcNAA*
Bradford, Alexander Warfield 1815-1867
    Alli Sup, DcAmA, DcNAA
Bradford, Amory Howe 1846-1911 *Alli Sup, AmA&B, DcAmA, DcNAA*
Bradford, Andrew 1686-1742 *AmA&B, REn*
Bradford, Annie Chambers 1828- *Alli*
Bradford, Charles Barker 1862-1917 *DcNAA*
Bradford, Clara *Alli Sup, ChPo*
Bradford, Douglas *ChPo*
Bradford, Duncan d1887 *DcNAA*
Bradford, Ebenezer 1746-1801 *DcNAA, OxAm*
Bradford, Edward Hickling 1848-1926 *DcNAA*
Bradford, Edwin Emmanuel 1860- *MnBBF, WhLA*
Bradford, Ernest Smith 1877- *WhWNAA*
Bradford, Ernle 1922- *WorAu*
Bradford, Frederick Charles 1887- *WhWNAA*
Bradford, Gamaliel 1795-1839 *DcNAA*
Bradford, Gamaliel 1831-1911 *DcAmA, DcNAA*
Bradford, Gamaliel 1863-1932 *AmA&B, AmLY, AnMV 1926, CasWL, CnDAL, ConAmA, ConAmL, DcLEnL, DcNAA, OxAm, REnAL, TwCA, TwCA Sup, WhWNAA*

Bradford, George Partridge 1807-1890 *AmA*
Bradford, George Winthrop 1895-1960 *OhA&B*
Bradford, Gertrude Yergin 1881-1930 *OhA&B*
Bradford, J S *Alli Sup*
Bradford, James C 1885-1941 *AmSCAP 66*
Bradford, John *Alli, Alli Sup, BbtC, BiDLA,*
ChPo S1
Bradford, John d1555 *DcEnL*
Bradford, John 1749-1830 *AmA&B, DcNAA,*
OxAm
Bradford, John Stricker *ChPo*
Bradford, Joseph 1843-1886 *AmA, AmA&B,*
BiD&SB, BiDSA, DcAmA, DcNAA
Bradford, L *MnBBF*
Bradford, Leland Powers 1905- *ConAu 13R,*
WrD 1976
Bradford, Lydia Allen DeVilbiss 1882-
IndAu 1917
Bradford, Mrs. Marshall *AmNov XR*
Bradford, Mary *Alli Sup*
Bradford, Mary F *BiDSA*
Bradford, Mary Norton *ChPo*
Bradford, Nellie Knight *Alli Sup*
Bradford, Patience Andrewes 1918- *ConAu 33*
Bradford, Perry 1893- *AmSCAP 66*
Bradford, Peter Amory 1942- *ConAu 61,*
WrD 1976
Bradford, Ralph 1892- *AmA&B, ChPo*
Bradford, Reed H 1912- *ConAu 49*
Bradford, Richard 1932- *ConAu 49*
Bradford, Roark 1896-1948 *AmA&B,*
AmSCAP 66, ChPo, CnDAL, DcNAA,
LongC, OxAm, REn, REnAL, TwCA,
TwCA Sup
Bradford, Samuel 1652-1731 *Alli*
Bradford, Samuel Dexter *Alli*
Bradford, Sarah Elizabeth Hopkins 1818-
Alli Sup, AmA&B, DcNAA
Bradford, Sax 1907-1966 *ConAu 1R*
Bradford, Sylvester 1937- *AmSCAP 66*
Bradford, Thomas 1745-1838 *AmA&B*
Bradford, Thomas Lindsley 1847?-1918 *AmLY,*
DcNAA
Bradford, Walter 1937- *BlkAW, LivBA*
Bradford, Ward 1809- *OhA&B*
Bradford, Will *ConAu XR*
Bradford, William *Alli, Alli Sup, BiDLA*
Bradford, William 1590?-1657 *Alli, AmA,*
AmA&B, BbD, BiD&SB, CasWL,
CyAL 1, DcAmA, DcLEnL, DcNAA,
EvLB, MouLC 1, OxAm, Pen Am, REn,
REnAL, WebEAL
Bradford, William 1663-1752 *AmA&B, OxAm,*
REnAL
Bradford, William 1722-1791 *AmA&B, OxAm,*
REnAL
Bradford, William 1755-1795 *Alli, DcNAA*
Bradford, William C 1910- *ConAu 9R*
Bradford, William John Alden 1797-1858
DcNAA
Bradford, William Wills *WhWNAA*
Brading, Helen *Alli Sup*
Bradish, J S *MnBBF*
Bradlaugh, Charles 1833-1891 *Alli Sup,*
OxEng, REn
Bradlee, Benjamin C 1921- *AuNews 2,*
ConAu 61
Bradlee, Caleb Davis 1831-1897 *Alli Sup,*
ChPo, DcAmA, DcNAA
Bradlee, Frederic 1920- *ConAu 21*
Bradley *Alli*
Bradley, A C *ChPo S1*
Bradley, A G *BiDSA*
Bradley, Albert W *MnBBF*
Bradley, Alice 1875- *WhWNAA*
Bradley, Andrew Cecil 1851-1935 *Chmbr 3,*
DcLEnL, EvLB, LongC, NewC, OxEng,
Pen Eng, TwCA, TwCA Sup
Bradley, Arthur *Alli Sup*
Bradley, Arthur Granville 1850-1943 *NewC,*
OxCan, WhLA
Bradley, B *Alli Sup*
Bradley, Basil 1842-1904 *ChPo*
Bradley, Bert E 1926- *ConAu 41*
Bradley, Brigitte L 1924- *ConAu 37*
Bradley, C *Alli*
Bradley, C A M *BiDLA*
Bradley, Cahal *ChPo S1*

Bradley, Carolyn Gertrude 1898-1954
IndAu 1917
Bradley, Charles 1789-1871 *Alli, Alli Sup*
Bradley, Charles Edward 1874- *WhWNAA*
Bradley, Christine *ChPo*
Bradley, Christopher *Alli*
Bradley, Concho *ConAu XR*
Bradley, Cornelius Beach 1843-1936 *DcNAA*
Bradley, Cuthbert 1860?-1941 *Br&AmS*
Bradley, Cyrus Parker 1818-1838 *DcNAA*
Bradley, Daniel 1852- *PoIre*
Bradley, Daniel B *Alli Sup*
Bradley, David G 1916- *ConAu 13R*
Bradley, Duane 1914- *AuBYP, ConAu XR*
Bradley, E Sculley 1897- *AmA&B*
Bradley, Edson P 1907- *AmSCAP 66*
Bradley, Edward 1827-1889 *Alli Sup, BiD&SB,*
BrAu 19, CasWL, ChPo S2, Chmbr 3,
DcEnL, DcLEnL, EvLB, NewC, OxEng,
REn
Bradley, Edward Sculley 1897- *WhWNAA*
Bradley, Erwin S 1906- *ConAu 33*
Bradley, F *Alli*
Bradley, Francis Herbert 1846-1924 *Alli Sup,*
BrAu 19, CasWL, Chmbr 3, DcEuL,
DcLEnL, EvLB, LongC, NewC, OxEng
Bradley, G S *Alli Sup*
Bradley, George Edgar 1924- *IndAu 1917*
Bradley, George Granville 1821- *Alli Sup*
Bradley, George Kitching 1930- *IndAu 1917*
Bradley, Gertrude M *ChPo, ChPo S2*
Bradley, Gladys Lilian 1900- *Au&Wr,*
WrD 1976
Bradley, Glenn Danford 1884-1930 *DcNAA,*
OhA&B, WhWNAA
Bradley, H Dennis 1878- *WhLA*
Bradley, Harold Whitman 1903- *ConAu 33*
Bradley, Harry Cyrus 1871- *WhWNAA*
Bradley, Henriette Mary *Alli Sup*
Bradley, Henry *Alli*
Bradley, Henry 1845-1923 *Alli Sup, DcLEnL,*
EvLB, LongC, NewC, OxEng
Bradley, Henry Stiles 1869- *BiDSA*
Bradley, Henry T *BlkAW*
Bradley, Herbert Wild *ChPo*
Bradley, Ian Roberts Ambrose 1900- *Au&Wr,*
WrD 1976
Bradley, Isaac Samuel 1853-1912 *DcNAA*
Bradley, J Chester 1884- *WhWNAA*
Bradley, J J G *MnBBF*
Bradley, Mrs. J S *Alli Sup*
Bradley, James 1692-1762 *Alli*
Bradley, James Vandiver 1924- *ConAu 37,*
WrD 1976
Bradley, Jay D 1881- *WhWNAA*
Bradley, John *Alli, Alli Sup*
Bradley, John 1930- *ConAu 25*
Bradley, John Edwin 1839-1912 *DcAmA,*
DcNAA
Bradley, John Hodgdon, Jr. 1898-1962 *AmA&B,*
TwCA, TwCA Sup
Bradley, John Lewis 1917- *ConAu 29,*
WrD 1976
Bradley, John William *Alli Sup*
Bradley, Joseph F 1917- *ConAu 23*
Bradley, Joseph P 1813-1892 *DcNAA*
Bradley, Joshua 1773-1855 *DcNAA*
Bradley, Katharine Harris 1848?-1914 *BrAu 19,*
ChPo, ChPo S1, Chmbr 3, EvLB, LongC,
NewC, Pen Eng
Bradley, Sir Kenneth Granville 1904- *Au&Wr,*
ConAu P-1
Bradley, Lonsdale *Alli Sup*
Bradley, Manson J 1887- *WhWNAA*
Bradley, Marion Zimmer 1930- *ConAu 57*
Bradley, Marjorie D 1931- *ConAu 25*
Bradley, Mary *ChPo*
Bradley, Mary Emily 1835-1898 *Alli Sup,*
AmA&B, BiDSA, ChPo, DcAmA,
DcNAA
Bradley, Mary Hastings *AmA&B, AmLY,*
WhWNAA
Bradley, Michael *ConAu XR*
Bradley, Milton 1836-1911 *AmA&B, DcNAA*
Bradley, Nellie H *Alli Sup*
Bradley, O W *Alli*
Bradley, Preston 1888- *AmA&B*
Bradley, R *Alli*

Bradley, R C 1929- *ConAu 33, WrD 1976*
Bradley, Ramona Kaiser 1909- *OhA&B,*
WrD 1976
Bradley, Richard d1732 *Alli*
Bradley, Ritamary 1916- *ConAu 49*
Bradley, Robert A 1917- *ConAu 21*
Bradley, Robert Henry Augustus *Alli Sup*
Bradley, Robert M *Alli Sup*
Bradley, S *Alli*
Bradley, Sam 1917- *ConAu 21, ConP 1970,*
WrD 1976
Bradley, Samuel *Alli*
Bradley, Samuel Carlyle 1842- *DcNAA*
Bradley, Samuel Messenger *Alli Sup*
Bradley, Shelland 1874- *WhLA*
Bradley, Stephen Row 1754-1830 *Alli, DcNAA*
Bradley, T Waldron *Alli Sup*
Bradley, Theodore James 1874-1936 *DcNAA*
Bradley, Thomas *Alli*
Bradley, Thomas d1813 *Alli, BiDLA,*
BiDLA Sup
Bradley, Thomas Bibb 1830-1855 *BiDSA,*
DcNAA
Bradley, Van Allen 1913- *AmA&B, ConAu 37*
Bradley, Virginia 1912- *ConAu 61*
Bradley, W *Alli Sup*
Bradley, Walter Parke 1862-1947 *DcNAA*
Bradley, Walter Wadsworth 1878- *WhWNAA*
Bradley, Warren Ives 1847-1868 *Alli Sup,*
AmA&B, DcAmA, DcNAA
Bradley, Will H 1868-1962 *AmA&B*
Bradley, William *Alli Sup*
Bradley, William 1934- *ConAu 45*
Bradley, William Aspenwall 1878-1939 *AmA&B,*
AmLY, ChPo, DcNAA
Bradley, William H *Alli Sup*
Bradley, William H d1825 *Alli*
Bradley, William H 1868- *ChPo, IlCB 1945*
Bradley, William Joseph 1857- *ChPo S1*
Bradley, William L 1918- *ConAu 23*
Bradley, William O'Connell 1847-1914 *DcNAA*
Bradley-Birt, Francis Bradley *WhLA*
Bradlow, Edna Rom *ConAu P-1*
Bradlow, Frank Rosslyn 1913- *Au&Wr,*
ConAu P-1, WrD 1976
Bradly, John *Alli, BiDLA*
Bradman, William Albert George 1913- *Au&Wr*
Bradner, Enos 1892- *ConAu 57*
Bradner, Lester 1867-1929 *DcNAA*
Bradney, Joseph *Alli, BiDLA*
Bradnum, Frederick *ConDr*
Bradshaigh, Thomas *Alli*
Bradshaw *Alli*
Bradshaw, Ann Douglas *TexWr*
Bradshaw, Annie *Alli Sup*
Bradshaw, B *Alli Sup*
Bradshaw, Elizabeth Mahan 1874-1932
IndAu 1917
Bradshaw, George 1801-1853 *NewC*
Bradshaw, George 1907- *Au&Wr*
Bradshaw, George 1909?-1973 *ConAu 45*
Bradshaw, George Butler d1901 *Alli Sup,*
PoIre
Bradshaw, Henry *Alli Sup*
Bradshaw, Henry 1450-1513 *Alli, DcEnL,*
NewC
Bradshaw, Henry 1831-1886 *Alli Sup, NewC,*
OxEng
Bradshaw, James d1702 *Alli*
Bradshaw, John *Alli, Alli Sup*
Bradshaw, Mrs. John *Alli Sup*
Bradshaw, Julian Watson *Alli Sup*
Bradshaw, Leslie Havergal 1892- *AmA&B,*
WhWNAA
Bradshaw, Marion John 1886- *AmA&B,*
OhA&B
Bradshaw, Mary Ann Cavendish *Alli, BiDLA*
Bradshaw, Maude *Alli Sup*
Bradshaw, Percy V *ChPo, MnBBF*
Bradshaw, Samuel Alexander *Alli Sup*
Bradshaw, Sergeant *Alli*
Bradshaw, Sidney Ernest 1869-1938 *BiDSA,*
DcNAA, WhWNAA
Bradshaw, Silas *Alli Sup*
Bradshaw, Thomas 1868-1939 *Alli, DcNAA,*
PoIre
Bradshaw, W S *Alli Sup*
Bradshaw, Wellesley *DcNAA*

Bradshaw, Wesley *Alli Sup, AmA&B*
Bradshaw, William d1732 *Alli*
Bradshaw, William 1571-1618 *Alli*
Bradshaw, William Richard 1851?-1927 *BbD, DcNAA*
Bradshawe, Isabella *Alli Sup*
Bradsher, Earl L 1881- *WhWNAA*
Bradstreet, Anne *Alli*
Bradstreet, Anne 1612?-1672 *Alli, AmA, AmA&B, BiD&SB, CasWL, ChPo, ChPo S2, CnDAL, CnE&AP, CyAL 1, DcAmA, DcEnL, DcLEnL, DcNAA, EvLB, OxAm, OxEng, Pen Am, RAdv 1, REn, REnAL, WebEAL*
Bradstreet, Dudley *Alli*
Bradstreet, John 1711-1774 *OxCan*
Bradstreet, Robert *Alli, BiDLA*
Bradstreet, Simon d1741 *Alli*
Bradstreet, Simon d1771 *Alli*
Bradstreet, Simon 1603-1697 *OxAm*
Bradt, A Gordon 1896- *ConAu 57*
Bradt, Charles Edwin 1863-1922 *DcNAA, IndAu 1917*
Bradwardin, Thomas 1290?-1349 *Alli*
Bradwardine, Thomas 1290?-1349 *Alli, CasWL, DcEnL, EvLB*
Bradway, John S 1890- *ConAu 33*
Bradwell, James *Alli Sup*
Bradwell, James B *WrD 1976*
Bradwell, Myra *Alli Sup*
Bradwell, Stephen *Alli*
Bradwood, Wat *Alli Sup*
Brady, Alexander *OxCan*
Brady, Sir Antonio 1811-1881 *Alli Sup*
Brady, C *Alli Sup*
Brady, Charles *Alli Sup, PoIre*
Brady, Charles Andrew 1912- *BkC 6, CatA 1952, ConAu 5R*
Brady, Charlotte Westropp *PoIre*
Brady, Cyrus Townsend 1861-1920 *AmA&B, AmLY, BiD&SB, CarSB, DcAmA, DcNAA, OhA&B, OxAm, REn, REnAL*
Brady, Edwin James 1869- *ChPo S1, PoIre, WhLA*
Brady, Frank 1924- *ConAu 13R*
Brady, Frank 1934- *ConAu 61*
Brady, George Stewardson 1832- *Alli Sup*
Brady, Gerald Peter 1929- *ConAu 5R*
Brady, Gerard K 1929- *Au&Wr*
Brady, H Christine 1933- *Au&Wr*
Brady, Henry Bowman 1835-1891 *Alli Sup*
Brady, Irene 1943- *ConAu 33, SmATA 4*
Brady, J H *Alli*
Brady, J P *PoIre*
Brady, James Boyd 1845-1912 *DcNAA*
Brady, James Topham 1815-1869 *Alli Sup, DcNAA*
Brady, John d1814 *Alli, BiDLA, BiDLA Sup*
Brady, John Everett 1860-1941 *Alli Sup, DcNAA*
Brady, John Leeford 1866- *WhWNAA*
Brady, John Paul 1928- *ConAu 13R*
Brady, Leo 1917- *CatA 1952*
Brady, Mathew B 1823?-1896 *AmA&B, OxAm, REn, REnAL*
Brady, Maurice 1916- *Au&Wr*
Brady, Sir Maziere 1796-1871 *PoIre*
Brady, Muriel *AmA&B*
Brady, Nicholas *Alli*
Brady, Nicholas 1659-1726 *Alli, ChPo S1, Chmbr 2, DcEnL, EvLB, NewC, PoCh, PoIre*
Brady, Pearl Schilling 1903- *IndAu 1917*
Brady, Rita G *AuBYP*
Brady, Robert d1700 *Alli*
Brady, Samuel *Alli*
Brady, Terence *Alli*
Brady, Thomas John Bellingham 1841-1910 *PoIre*
Brady, William *Alli Sup, WhWNAA*
Brady, William Maziere 1825- *Alli Sup*
Brady, William N d1887 *DcNAA*
Brae, Andrew Edmund *Alli Sup*
Braekstad, H L *Alli Sup*
Braeme, Charlotte Monica *Alli Sup, NewC*
Braenne, Berit 1918- *ConAu 21*
Braescu, Gheorghe 1871-1949 *CasWL*
Braeuning-Oktavio, Hermann 1888- *WhLA*

Braga, Alberto 1851-1911 *ClDMEuL*
Braga, Joaquim Teofilo 1843-1924 *EvEuW*
Braga, Rubem 1913- *Pen Am*
Braga, Teofilo 1843-1924 *CasWL, ClDMEuL*
Braga, Theophilo 1843-1924 *BbD, BiD&SB*
Bragdon, Claude Fayette 1866-1946 *AmA&B, AmLY, ChPo, DcNAA, OhA&B, REnAL, WhWNAA*
Bragdon, Clifford R 1940- *ConAu 57*
Bragdon, Elspeth MacDuffie 1897- *ConAu 5R, SmATA 6*
Bragdon, Henry Wilkinson 1906- *ConAu 5R, WrD 1976*
Bragdon, Lillian Jacot *AuBYP*
Bragdon, Olive Evelyth 1858-1915 *DcNAA*
Bragg, Arthur N 1897- *ConAu P-1*
Bragg, Charles *IlBYP*
Bragg, Jane *Alli Sup*
Bragg, John *Alli Sup*
Bragg, Laura M 1881- *WhWNAA*
Bragg, Sir Lawrence 1890- *DcLEnL*
Bragg, Melvyn 1939- *ConAu 57, ConNov 1972, ConNov 1976, WrD 1976*
Bragg, William Chittenden 1845- *DcAmA*
Bragg, Sir William Henry 1862-1942 *DcLEnL*
Bragge, Francis *Alli*
Bragge, J *Alli, BiDLA*
Bragge, Mrs. M F *Alli Sup*
Bragge, Robert 1665-1737? *Alli*
Bragge, William *Alli Sup*
Bragge-Bathurst, William Hiley 1796-1877 *PoCh*
Braggiotti, Mario 1909- *AmSCAP 66*
Braham, A B *ChPo*
Braham, Allan John Witney 1937- *Au&Wr, WrD 1976*
Braham, Randolph Lewis 1922- *ConAu 1R*
Brahe, Tycho 1546-1601 *REn*
Brahm, Otto 1856-1912 *ClDMEuL, OxGer*
Brahm, W G De *Alli*
Brahman 1574-1662 *DcOrL 2*
Brahms, Caryl 1901- *ConDr, LongC, TwCW*
Brahms, Johannes 1833-1897 *AtlBL, NewC, OxGer, REn*
Brahs, Stuart J 1940- *ConAu 57*
Braid, James 1795-1860 *Alli, Alli Sup, BiDPar*
Braider, Donald 1923- *ConAu 33, WrD 1976*
Braidwood, Messrs. *Alli*
Braidwood, James *Alli Sup*
Braidwood, John *Alli Sup*
Braidwood, Peter Murray *Alli Sup*
Braidwood, W Baptist *Alli*
Braille, Louis 1809-1852 *OxFr, REn*
Brailsford, Edward J *Alli Sup*
Brailsford, Frances Wosmek 1917- *ConAu 29, WrD 1976*
Brailsford, Henry Noel 1873-1958 *LongC, NewC, TwCA, TwCA Sup*
Brailsford, J *Alli*
Brailsford, William *Alli Sup, ChPo*
Braim, Thomas Henry *Alli, Alli Sup*
Braimah, Joseph Adam 1916- *ConAu 61*
Brain, Belle Marvel 1859-1933 *DcAmA, DcNAA, OhA&B, WhWNAA*
Brain, George B 1920- *ConAu 41*
Brain, H D *MnBBF*
Brain, Joseph J 1920- *ConAu 13R*
Brain, Russell *ChPo*
Brainard, Charles H *Alli Sup*
Brainard, Charles Rollin *Alli Sup*
Brainard, Daniel 1812-1866 *Alli Sup*
Brainard, David Legge 1856-1946 *AmA&B, DcNAA*
Brainard, Franklin *DrAP 1975*
Brainard, Harry Gray 1907- *ConAu 1R*
Brainard, Joe *DrAP 1975*
Brainard, John Gardiner Calkins 1796-1828 *Alli, AmA, AmA&B, BiD&SB, ChPo, ChPo S1, CyAL 1, DcAmA, DcEnL, DcLEnL, DcNAA, OxAm, REnAL*
Braine, John 1922- *Au&Wr, CasWL, ConAu 1R, ConLC 1, ConLC 3, ConNov 1972, ConNov 1976, LongC, ModBL, ModBL Sup, NewC, Pen Eng, RAdv 1, REn, TwCW, WebEAL, WorAu, WrD 1976*
Braine, Robert D 1861-1943 *DcAmA, OhA&B*

Braine, Sheila E *ChPo, ChPo S1, ChPo S2*
Brainerd, Barron 1928- *ConAu 33*
Brainerd, Cephas 1831-1910 *DcNAA*
Brainerd, Charles N *Alli Sup*
Brainerd, Chauncey Corey 1874-1922 *DcNAA*
Brainerd, David 1718-1747 *Alli, AmA, AmA&B, CyAL 1, DcAmA, DcNAA, OxAm, REnAL*
Brainerd, Edith Rathbone d1922 *DcNAA*
Brainerd, Eleanor Hoyt 1868-1942 *AmA&B, DcNAA*
Brainerd, Erastus 1855-1922 *AmA&B, DcNAA*
Brainerd, Ethel M 1890- *WhWNAA*
Brainerd, Ezra 1844-1924 *DcNAA*
Brainerd, Henry Clark 1845-1930 *DcNAA*
Brainerd, Ira Hutchinson 1861-1935 *DcNAA*
Brainerd, Mrs. J G *ChPo S2*
Brainerd, Jehu *Alli Sup*
Brainerd, John W 1918- *ConAu 57*
Brainerd, Mary *Alli Sup*
Brainerd, Norman *AmA&B*
Brainerd, Thomas 1804-1866 *Alli Sup, DcNAA, OhA&B*
Brainin, Jerome 1916- *AmSCAP 66*
Brainin, Joseph 1895- *WhWNAA*
Brainin, Reuben 1862-1940? *CasWL, Pen Eur*
Brainthwait, William *Alli*
Braithwait, Gulielmus *Alli*
Braithwait, Richard 1588-1673 *Alli, CrE&SL*
Braithwaite *CasWL*
Braithwaite, Adeline *Alli Sup*
Braithwaite, Coulton *MnBBF*
Braithwaite, E R 1912- *ConNov 1972, WrD 1976*
Braithwaite, Eustace Edward Ricardo 1920- *Au&Wr, LongC, TwCW*
Braithwaite, George *Alli Sup*
Braithwaite, Henry Thomas *Alli Sup*
Braithwaite, John *Alli*
Braithwaite, Joseph Bevan 1818- *Alli Sup*
Braithwaite, Martha *Alli Sup*
Braithwaite, Max *OxCan Sup*
Braithwaite, Richard 1588-1673 *Alli, EvLB*
Braithwaite, Robert *Alli Sup*
Braithwaite, Thomas Wolfe *Alli Sup*
Braithwaite, William *Alli Sup*
Braithwaite, William Clark 1862-1922 *ChPo S1*
Braithwaite, William Stanley Beaumont 1878-1962 *AmA&B, BlkAW, ChPo, ChPo S1, ChPo S2, OxAm, REn, REnAL, TwCA, TwCA Sup*
Braithwayte, Richard 1588-1673 *Alli, DcEnL*
Brakel, Samuel J 1943- *ConAu 33*
Brakelond, Jocelin De *NewC*
Braken, Henry *Alli*
Braker, Ulrich 1735-1798 *CasWL, OxGer, Pen Eur*
Brakhage, Stan 1933- *AmA&B, ConAu 41, WrD 1976*
Bralesford, Humphrey *Alli*
Braley, Berton 1882-1966 *AmA&B, AnMV 1926, ChPo, ChPo S1, WiscW*
Braley, Evelyn Foley 1890- *WhLA*
Braling, Tom *ChPo S2*
Brallier, Floyd 1875- *WhWNAA*
Braly, Malcolm 1925- *ConAu 17R*
Bram, Israel 1883- *WhWNAA*
Bramah, Ernest 1868-1942 *DcLEnL, EncM&D, EvLB, LongC, NewC, REn, TwCA, TwCA Sup, TwCW*
Bramah, Joseph 1749-1815 *Alli, BiDLA, BiDLA Sup*
Bramall, Eric 1927- *Au&Wr, ConAu 9R*
Bramall, Henry *Alli Sup*
Bramante 1444?-1514 *AtlBL, REn*
Bramberg, Lars 1920- *WhGrA*
Brambeus, Baron *CasWL*
Bramble, Forbes 1939- *WrD 1976*
Bramble, Robert *Alli*
Brambleby, Ailsa 1915- *Au&Wr*
Bramblett, Agnes Cochran *ChPo S1*
Bramblett, Ella *ChPo S1*
Brame, Charlotte M 1836-1884 *HsB&A*
Brame, Terence *ChPo S2*
Brame, W B *Alli Sup*
Brameld, George William *Alli Sup, ChPo S1*

Brandt, Joseph August 1899- *AmA&B,*
IndAu 1917, WhWNAA
Brandt, Kaspar *CasWL*
Brandt, Leslie F 1919- *ConAu 23, WrD 1976*
Brandt, Lucile 1900- *ConAu 61*
Brandt, Margaret *REn*
Brandt, Matteo *Alli Sup*
Brandt, Olaf Elias 1862-1940 *DcNAA*
Brandt, Otto 1892- *WhLA*
Brandt, R A *ChPo S1*
Brandt, Rex 1914- *ConAu 13R*
Brandt, Richard *MnBBF*
Brandt, Richard Booker 1910- *AmA&B*
Brandt, Richard M 1922- *ConAu 33, WrD 1976*
Brandt, Sebastian 1458-1521 *BbD, BiD&SB, DcEnL*
Brandt, Sue R 1916- *ConAu 25*
Brandt, Tom *ConAu XR, EncM&D*
Brandt, Vincent S R 1924- *ConAu 37*
Brandt, William *Alli Sup*
Brandt, William E 1920- *ConAu 5R*
Brandwein, Chaim N 1920- *ConAu 23*
Brandwynne, Nat 1910- *AmSCAP 66*
Brandys, Kazimierz 1916- *CasWL, EncWL, ModSL 2*
Brandys, Marian 1912- *ConAu 57*
Branen, Jeff T 1872-1927 *AmSCAP 66*
Branfield, John Charles 1931- *Au&Wr, ConAu 41, WrD 1976*
Branford, Frederick Victor 1892- *ChPo S2, NewC*
Branford, Victor Veracis 1863- *WhLA*
Brangwyn, Frank *ChPo S2*
Branham, Adelia Pope 1861-1917 *IndAu 1816*
Branham, Charles Allen 1904- *OhA&B*
Branham, Grace Bagnall *ChPo*
Branigan, Keith 1940- *WrD 1976*
Branigin, Elba L 1870- *IndAu 1816*
Branks, William *Alli Sup*
Branley, Franklyn M 1915- *Au&Wr, AuBYP, BkP, ConAu 33, MorJA, REnAL, SmATA 4*
Brann, Esther *AuBYP, ConICB, JBA 1934, JBA 1951*
Brann, Henry Athanasius 1837-1921 *Alli Sup, DcNAA, PoIre*
Brann, William Cowper 1855-1898 *AmA, AmA&B, DcNAA, OxAm, REnAL*
Brannan, John *BbtC*
Brannan, Joseph Doddridge 1848-1930 *DcNAA*
Brannan, Robert Louis 1927- *ConAu 21*
Brannan, William Penn 1825-1866 *Alli Sup, ChPo, DcAmA, DcNAA, OhA&B, PoIre*
Brannen, Claude O 1884- *WhWNAA*
Brannen, Noah S 1924- *ConAu 25*
Brannen, Ted R 1924- *ConAu 17R*
Branner, Hans Christian 1903-1966 *CasWL, CnMD, EncWL, EvEuW, Pen Eur, TwCW, WorAu*
Branner, John Casper 1850-1922 *DcNAA*
Branner, R 1927-1973 *ConAu 5R, ConAu 45*
Brannon, Donn *DrAP 1975*
Brannon, Emma Collins *TexWr*
Brannon, Henry 1837-1914 *DcAmA, DcNAA*
Brannon, Melvin Amos 1865- *IndAu 1816*
Brannon, Peter Alexander 1882-1967 *AmA&B*
Brannon, Philip *Alli Sup*
Brannon, William T 1906- *ConAu P-1, WrD 1976*
Brannt, William T *Alli Sup*
Branom, Frederick K 1891- *WhWNAA*
Bransby, Emma Lindsay Squier 1892- *IndAu 1917*
Bransby, James Hews *Alli, BiDLA, ChPo*
Bransby, John *BiDLA*
Branscomb, Bennett Harvie 1894- *WhWNAA*
Branscombe, Gina 1881- *AmSCAP 66*
Branscombe, Mrs. Graham *Alli Sup*
Branscum, Robbie 1937- *ConAu 61*
Bransley, John *Alli*
Bransom, Paul 1885- *ChPo, ConICB, IlBYP, IlCB 1945, IlCB 1956, MorJA*
Branson, Anna J *ChPo S2*
Branson, David 1909- *ConAu 41*
Branson, Edward Regnier 1875-1937 *DcNAA*
Branson, Edwin Bayer 1877- *WhWNAA*

Branson, Eugene Cunningham 1861-1933 *BiDSA, DcNAA, WhWNAA*
Branson, H C *EncM&D*
Branson, Margaret Stimmann 1922- *ConAu 49*
Branson, Paul 1884- *ChPo S1*
Branson, Reginald Montague Auber *Alli Sup*
Bransten, Ruth McKenney 1911- *IndAu 1917*
Branston, Brian 1914- *ConAu 53*
Branston, F *ChPo*
Brant, Charles S 1919- *ConAu 25*
Brant, Ira 1921- *AmSCAP 66*
Brant, Irving Newton 1885- *AmA&B, ConAu 9R, REnAL, TwCA Sup*
Brant, J *Alli*
Brant, John *OxCan*
Brant, Joseph 1742-1807 *Alli, BbtC, OxAm, OxCan, REn, REnAL*
Brant, Lewis *ConAu XR*
Brant, Mary 1736-1796 *OxCan*
Brant, Sebastian 1458?-1521 *BiD&SB, CasWL, DcEuL, EuA, EvEuW, OxGer, Pen Eur, REn*
Branthwayt, Edward J *Alli Sup*
Brantley, William Theophilus 1852-1945 *DcAmA*
Brantly, William Theophilus 1850-1945 *Alli Sup, DcNAA*
Brantome, P DeBourdeilles, Seigneur De 1540?-1614 *BbD, BiD&SB, CasWL, DcEuL, EuA, EvEuW, OxEng, OxFr, Pen Eur, REn*
Branwhite 1745-1794 *Alli*
Braque, Georges 1881?-1963 *REn, WhGrA*
Bras Croche, Le *OxCan*
Brasbridge, Joseph *Alli*
Brasbridge, Thomas 1537- *Alli*
Brasch, Charles Orwell 1909- *Au&Wr, CasWL, ConP 1970, LongC, Pen Eng, TwCW, WebEAL*
Brasch, H D 1892- *WhLA*
Brasch, Ila Wales 1945- *ConAu 57*
Brasch, Rudolph 1912- *Au&Wr, ConAu 21, WrD 1976*
Brasch, Walter Milton 1945- *ConAu 57*
Braschi, Wilfredo 1918- *PueRA*
Brase, Paul *DrAP 1975*
Brasenose, Buller Of *DcEnL*
Brash, Edward *DrAP 1975*
Brash, James 1758-1835 *ChPo*
Brash, John *Alli Sup*
Brash, M M *MnBBF*
Brash, Marguerite McKie *ChPo S1*
Brash, Richard Rolt *Alli Sup*
Brashear, John Alfred 1840-1920 *DcNAA*
Brashears, Noah *DcNAA*
Brasher, Alfred *Alli Sup*
Brasher, Christopher William 1928- *ConAu 5R, WrD 1976*
Brasher, Nell 1912- *ConAu 61*
Brasher, Norman Henry 1922- *Au&Wr, ConAu 25, WrD 1976*
Brasher, Rex 1869- *WhWNAA*
Brashers, H C 1930- *ConAu 5R*
Brashler, William 1947- *ConAu 45*
Brasier, Richard *Alli*
Brasier, Virginia Rossmore 1910- *ConAu 61, St&VC, WrD 1976*
Brasier-Creagh, Patrick *ConAu XR*
Brasillach, Robert 1909-1945 *EncWL, Pen Eur*
Brasol, Boris 1885- *AmA&B*
Brass, Alister John Douglas 1937- *Au&Wr, WrD 1976*
Brass, John *BbtC*
Brass, Paul Richard 1936- *ConAu 17R*
Brasse, John d1833 *Alli*
Brasse, Samuel *Alli*
Brasselle, Keefe 1923- *AmSCAP 66*
Brasseur, Pierre *ConAu XR*
Brasseur DeBourbourg, Charles-E *BbtC, OxCan*
Brassey, Lady Anna 1840?-1887 *BrAu 19*
Brassey, Lady Anne 1840?-1887 *Alli Sup, BbD, BiD&SB*
Brassey, Robert Bingham 1875- *Br&AmS*
Brassey, Sir Thomas, Baron Brassey 1836- *Alli Sup*
Brasted, Fred *TexWr*
Brastow, Lewis Orsmond 1834-1912 *DcNAA*

Braswell, S N *Alli Sup*
Bratby, John Randall 1928- *Au&Wr, WrD 1976*
Bratescu-Voinesti, Ioan Alexandru 1868-1946 *CasWL*
Brath, Cecil E *BlkAW*
Brathwait, Richard 1588?-1673 *NewC*
Brathwaite, DcEnL
Brathwaite, Edward 1930- *ConAu 25, DrAP 1975, LongC, WebEAL, WrD 1976*
Brathwaite, Errol Freeman 1924- *Au&Wr, ConAu 57, ConNov 1972, ConNov 1976, WrD 1976*
Brathwaite, Lawson Edward 1930- *CasWL, ConP 1970, ConP 1975*
Brathwaite, Richard 1588?-1673 *Alli, CasWL, Chmbr 1, EvLB, NewC*
Brathwaite, Sheila R 1914- *ConAu 25*
Brathwaite, Thomas *Alli*
Brathwayte, Richard 1588?-1673 *NewC*
Bratt, Elmer Clark 1901- *ConAu 1R*
Bratt, John H 1909- *ConAu 17R*
Bratter, Charles Adolph 1861- *WhLA*
Brattgarg, Helge 1920- *ConAu 5R*
Brattle, Thomas 1657?-1713 *Alli, DcAmA, REnAL*
Brattle, William 1662-1717? *Alli, DcNAA*
Bratton, Fred Gladstone 1896- *ConAu P-1*
Bratton, Helen 1899- *ConAu 23, SmATA 4*
Bratton, Henry De d1268 *BrAu, NewC*
Bratton, John W 1867-1947 *AmSCAP 66*
Bratton, Karl H 1906- *AuBYP*
Bratton, Samuel Tilden 1878-1940 *DcNAA*
Bratton, Theodore DuBose 1862- *WhWNAA*
Brattstrom, Bayard H 1929- *ConAu 57*
Brau, Alexis 1921- *AmSCAP 66*
Brau, Salvador 1842-1912 *PueRA*
Brauckmann, Karl 1862- *WhLA*
Braude, Jacob M 1896- *ConAu 5R*
Braude, Michael 1936- *ConAu 17R*
Braude, William Gordon 1907- *ConAu 33*
Braudes, Avraham 1907- *CasWL*
Braudes, Reuben Asher 1851-1902 *CasWL*
Braudy, Leo 1941- *ConAu 37, WrD 1976*
Brauer, Jerald Carl 1921- *AmA&B, ConAu 33, WrD 1976*
Brauer, Kinley J 1935- *ConAu 21*
Brauer, Oscar Leo 1884- *WhWNAA*
Brauer, Theodor 1880-1942 *CatA 1952*
Brauer-Tuchorze, Johann Ernst 1863- *WhLA*
Brault, Gerard Joseph 1929- *ConAu 5R*
Brault, Jacques 1933- *CasWL, OxCan Sup*
Brault, Mrs. Richard *AmNov XR*
Braun *CarSB*
Braun Von Braunthal 1802-1866 *BbD, BiD&SB*
Braun, Antoine Nicolas 1815-1885 *DcNAA*
Braun, Edward 1936- *Au&Wr*
Braun, Felix 1885-1973 *CnMD, CrCD, EncWL, OxGer*
Braun, Gustav 1881- *WhLA*
Braun, Henry 1930- *ConAu 25, ConP 1970, DrAP 1975*
Braun, Hugh 1902- *Au&Wr, ConAu 25*
Braun, J Werner 1914-1972 *ConAu 37*
Braun, John R 1928- *ConAu 33*
Braun, Josef 1857- *WhLA*
Braun, Karl 1822-1893 *BiD&SB*
Braun, Kathy *AuBYP*
Braun, Kurt 1899- *AmA&B*
Braun, Lev 1913- *ConAu 41*
Braun, Lili 1865-1916 *OxGer*
Braun, Mattias 1933- *CnMD*
Braun, Oscar C 1859-1945 *OhA&B*
Braun, P A *BbtC*
Braun, Richard Emil 1934- *ConAu 9R, WrD 1976*
Braun, Saul M *AuBYP*
Braun, Theodore E D 1933- *ConAu 13R*
Braun, Volker 1939- *CrCD*
Braun, Wernher Von 1912- *AuBYP*
Braun, Wilhelm Von 1813-1860 *BiD&SB*
Braun-Vogelstein, Julie 1883- *WhLA*
Braund, Hal *ConAu XR*
Braund, Harold 1913- *ConAu 61*
Braund, James H *Alli Sup*
Braune, George Martin *Alli Sup*
Braungart, Richard *ChPo S2*

Braunholtz, Eugen Gustav Wilhelm 1859- *WhLA*
Braunholtz, Mary Antonie Beatrice 1889- *Au&Wr*
Braunlich, Erich 1892- *WhLA*
Brauns, Reinhard 1861- *WhLA*
Braunthal, Gerard 1923- *ConAu 13R, WrD 1976*
Braunthal, Julius 1891- *ConAu 23*
Brausewetter, Artur 1864- *WhLA*
Brautigan, Richard 1935?- *AmA&B, ConAu 53, ConLC 1, ConLC 3, ConLC 5, ConNov 1972, ConNov 1976, ConP 1970, ConP 1975, DrAF 1976, DrAP 1975, ModAL Sup, Pen Am, WrD 1976*
Brautlacht, Erich 1902-1957 *OxGer*
Brautlecht, Charles Andrew *WhWNAA*
Brav, Stanley R 1908- *ConAu 25*
Bravender, Frederick *Alli Sup*
Braverman, Harry 1920- *ConAu 53*
Braverman, Libbie Levin 1900- *OhA&B*
Brawe, Joachim Wilhelm Von 1738-1758 *DcEuL, OxGer*
Brawer, Florence B 1922- *ConAu 37*
Brawern, Henry *Alli*
Brawley, Benjamin Griffith 1882-1939 *AmA&B, AmLY, BlkAW, DcNAA, REnAL, TwCA, TwCA Sup, WhWNAA*
Brawley, Ernest 1937- *ConAu 53, DrAF 1976, WrD 1976*
Brawn, Dympna 1931- *ConAu 25*
Brawn, Max *Alli Sup*
Braxton, Allen Caperton 1862-1941 *DcNAA*
Braxton, Joanne M *BlkAW, DrAP 1975*
Bray, Mrs. *Chmbr 3*
Bray, Alfred James *Alli Sup*
Bray, Alison *ConAu XR*
Bray, Allen Farris, III 1926- *ConAu 9R*
Bray, Anna Eliza 1790-1883 *Alli, Alli Sup, BbD, BiD&SB, BrAu 19, CasWL, DcEnL, DcLEnL, EvLB, NewC*
Bray, Caroline *Alli Sup*
Bray, Charles 1811-1884 *Alli, Alli Sup*
Bray, Sir Denys 1875- *WhLA*
Bray, Douglas W 1918- *ConAu 13R*
Bray, E A *Alli*
Bray, Edward 1849- *Alli Sup*
Bray, Edward Atkyns 1778-1857 *Alli Sup, BiDLA*
Bray, Emily Octavia *Alli Sup*
Bray, Frank Chapin 1866-1949 *AmA&B, DcNAA, OhA&B*
Bray, Henry Truro 1846-1922 *Alli Sup, DcNAA*
Bray, Jeremiah Wesley *IndAu 1816*
Bray, John Jefferson 1912- *ChPo S2, WrD 1976*
Bray, Mabel E *ChPo S2*
Bray, Mary 1837- *DcNAA*
Bray, Robert L *BlkAW*
Bray, Roger *Alli*
Bray, Thomas *Alli*
Bray, Thomas 1656-1730 *Alli, AmA&B, ChPo S1*
Bray, Thomas John 1911- *Au&Wr*
Bray, Thomas Wells 1738-1808 *DcNAA*
Bray, Warwick 1936- *ConAu 25*
Bray, William *Alli*
Bray, William 1736-1832 *Alli, BiDLA*
Bray, William Gilmer 1903- *IndAu 1917*
Braybrooke, Lord 1783-1858 *Alli*
Braybrooke, David 1924- *ConAu 9R*
Braybrooke, Neville Patrick Bellairs 1928?- *Au&Wr, ConAu 5R, WrD 1976*
Braybrooke, Patrick 1894- *ChPo S1, WhLA*
Braybrooke, Baron Richard G Neville 1783-1858 *DcEnL*
Braybrooke, William L *Alli Sup*
Brayce, William *ConAu XR*
Braye, Lord *Alli Sup*
Brayley, Ann M *Alli Sup*
Brayley, Arthur Wellington 1863-1919 *DcNAA*
Brayley, Edward Wedlake 1773-1854 *Alli, BiDLA*
Brayley, Edward William *Alli*
Brayley, Leonard *MnBBF*
Brayman, Harold 1900- *ConAu 23*

Brayman, James O 1815-1887 *Alli, HsB&A, HsB&A Sup*
Brayman, Mason 1813-1895 *DcNAA*
Braymer, Daniel Harvey 1883-1932 *DcNAA, WhWNAA*
Braymer, Marguerite *ConAu XR*
Braymer, Marjorie Elizabeth 1911- *AnCL, ConAu 1R, SmATA 6*
Braynard, Frank O 1916- *ConAu 17R*
Brayne, *Alli*
Brayton, Alembert Winthrop 1848-1926 *DcAmA, DcNAA, IndAu 1816*
Brayton, Mary C And Terry, Ellen F *Alli Sup*
Brayton, Matthew 1818-1862 *OhA&B*
Brayton, Teresa *ChPo, ChPo S1*
Braza, Jacque *ConAu XR*
Brazell, Karen 1938- *ConAu 45*
Brazelton, Ethel M Colson *ChPo S2, WhWNAA*
Brazenor, Mrs. H *Alli Sup*
Brazer, John 1789-1846 *DcNAA*
Braziel, Arthur *BlkAW*
Brazier, Arthur M *LivBA*
Brazier, G W 1921- *Au&Wr*
Brazier, Marion Howard 1850-1925? *DcNAA, WhWNAA*
Brazil, Angela 1868-1947 *DcLEnL, EvLB, LongC, WhCL, WhLA*
Brazill, William J, Jr. 1935- *ConAu 53*
Brazleton, Julian *ChPo*
Brazza, Countess Cora Di 1862- *DcAmA*
Breach, Robert Walter 1927- *Au&Wr, ConAu 13R*
Bready, John Wesley 1887- *WhWNAA*
Breake, Thomas *Alli*
Breakenridge, John 1820-1854 *BbtC, DcNAA, OxCan*
Breakenridge, William M 1846-1931 *ArizL*
Breakey, J J C *Alli Sup*
Breakspear *OhA&B*
Breakspear, Nicholas *Alli*
Breakspear, Norman *MnBBF*
Breal, Michel-Jules-Alfred 1832-1915 *OxFr*
Brealey, George *Alli Sup*
Brealey, Richard A 1936- *ConAu 53*
Brean, Herbert 1907-1973 *ConAu 41, EncM&D, WorAu*
Brearey, Charles Benson *Alli Sup*
Brearley, Denis 1940- *ConAu 37*
Brearley, Harry Chase 1870-1940 *DcNAA*
Brearley, John *MnBBF*
Brearley, William Henry 1846-1909 *DcAmA, DcNAA*
Brears, Peter C D 1944- *WrD 1976*
Breasted, James Henry 1865-1935 *AmA&B, AmLY, DcLEnL, DcNAA, EvLB, LongC, OxAm, REn, REnAL, TwCA, TwCA Sup, WhWNAA*
Breathett, George 1925- *ConAu 13R*
Breatnac, Padraic *ChPo S1*
Breau, Louis 1893-1928 *AmSCAP 66*
Breault, William 1926- *ConAu 57*
Breaux, Daisy *DcNAA*
Breaux, Joseph A 1838-1926 *DcNAA*
Breazeale, J W M *BiDSA*
Brebeuf, Georges De 1618-1661 *CasWL, OxFr*
Brebeuf, Guillaume 1618-1661 *DcEuL*
Brebeuf, Jean De 1593-1649 *OxCan*
Brebner, John Bartlet 1895-1957 *AmA&B, OxCan*
Brecher, Charles Martin 1945- *ConAu 53*
Brecher, Edward M 1911- *ConAu 13R*
Brecher, Michael 1925- *ConAu 1R, WrD 1976*
Brecher, Ruth E 1911-1966 *ConAu P-1*
Brechin, Bishop Of *DcEnL*
Brechin, George *ChPo S1*
Brecht, Arnold 1884- *AmA&B*
Brecht, Bertolt 1898-1956 *AtlBL, CasWL, CIDMEuL, CnMD, CnMWL, CnThe, CrCD, CyWA, EncWL, EvEuW, LongC, McGWD, ModGL, ModWD, OxEng, OxGer, Pen Eur, RCom, REn, REnWD, TwCA, TwCA Sup, TwCW, TwTwL*
Brecht, Edith 1895- *ConAu 25, SmATA 6, WrD 1976*
Brecht, George *ConDr*
Breck, Alan *MnBBF*

Breck, Allen DuPont 1914- *ConAu 13R*
Breck, Carrie Ellis 1855-1934 *AmSCAP 66, ChPo*
Breck, Charles *Alli Sup*
Breck, Edward 1861-1929 *AmLY, DcNAA, WhWNAA*
Breck, George William 1863-1920 *ChPo S1*
Breck, James Lloyd 1818-1876 *Alli Sup, DcNAA*
Breck, Joseph 1794-1873 *Alli Sup, DcNAA*
Breck, Robert *Alli*
Breck, Samuel 1771-1862 *DcNAA*
Breck, Samuel 1834-1918 *DcNAA*
Breck, Vivian 1895- *AmA&B, AuBYP, ConAu XR, MorJA, SmATA 1*
Breckenfeld, Vivian Gurney 1895- *AmA&B, AuBYP, ConAu 5R, SmATA 1*
Breckenridge, Adam Carlyle 1916- *ConAu 29, WrD 1976*
Breckenridge, James d1879 *BbtC, DcNAA*
Breckenridge, John 1797-1841 *Alli*
Breckenridge, Robert Jefferson 1800- *Alli*
Breckenridge, Roeliff Morton 1870-1914 *DcNAA*
Breckinridge, John 1760-1806 *BiDSA*
Breckinridge, John 1797-1841 *BiDSA, DcAmA, DcNAA*
Breckinridge, John Cabell *BiDSA*
Breckinridge, Julia *Alli Sup*
Breckinridge, Robert Jefferson 1800-1871 *BiD&SB, BiDSA, DcAmA, DcNAA*
Breckinridge, Scott Dudley 1882-1941 *DcNAA*
Breckinridge, Sophonisba Preston 1866-1948 *DcNAA*
Breckinridge, William Campbell Preston 1837- *BiDSA*
Breckling, Grace Jamison 1900- *OhA&B*
Brecknock, T *Alli*
Brecourt, Guillaume Marcoureau, Sieur De 1637?-1685 *OxFr*
Breda, Tjalmar *ConAu XR, SmATA XR*
Bredahl, Christian Hviid 1784-1860 *CasWL, DcEuL*
Bredel, Willi 1901-1964 *CasWL*
Bredemeier, Harry Charles 1920- *ConAu 1R, ConAu 5R*
Bredemeier, Herbert G 1911- *IndAu 1917*
Breden, Christiane *BiD&SB, OxGer*
Bredero, Gerbrand A 1585-1618 *CnThe, DcEuL, EuA, Pen Eur, REnWD*
Brederode, Gerbrand A 1585-1618 *CasWL, ChPo, ChPo S1*
Brederoo, Gerbrand Adrianensz 1585-1618 *EvEuW*
Brederoo, Gerbrant Adriaenszoon 1585-1618 *BbD, BiD&SB*
Bredig, Georg 1868- *WhLA*
Bredin, Anthony *PoIre*
Bredin, Thomas *OxCan Sup*
Bredius, Abraham 1855- *WhLA*
Bredon, John *MnBBF*
Bredow, Miriam *ConAu XR*
Bredsdorff, Elias Lunn 1912- *Au&Wr, ConAu P-1, WrD 1976*
Bredsdorff, Jan 1942- *ConAu 21*
Bredvold, Louis I 1888- *ConAu 1R*
Bredwell, S *Alli*
Bree, Charles Robert *Alli Sup*
Bree, Frances Elizabeth *Alli Sup*
Bree, Germaine 1907- *ConAu 1R, WorAu, WrD 1976*
Bree, John d1786 *Alli*
Bree, Martin *Alli, BiDLA*
Bree, Robert *Alli, BiDLA*
Bree, S C *Alli*
Bree, W T *Alli*
Breed, David Riddle 1848-1931 *Alli Sup, DcAmA, DcNAA, WhWNAA*
Breed, Frederick Stephen 1876- *WhWNAA*
Breed, George J *ChPo S1*
Breed, Gertrude *ChPo S1*
Breed, Paul F 1916- *ConAu 33*
Breed, Robert Stanley 1877- *WhWNAA*
Breed, William Denison 1876-1931 *DcNAA*
Breed, William Pratt 1816-1889 *Alli Sup, DcAmA, DcNAA*
Breede, Adam 1897-1928 *DcNAA*
Breeden, Kay 1939- *Au&Wr*

Breeden, Marshall *WhWNAA*
Breeden, Stanley 1938- *Au&Wr, WrD 1976*
Breedlove, Joseph Penn 1874- *WhWNAA*
Breeks, James Wilkinson 1830-1872 *Alli Sup*
Breen, Andrew Edward 1863-1938 *DcNAA*
Breen, Dana 1946- *WrD 1976*
Breen, Henry Hegart 1805-1882 *Alli, Alli Sup, DcEnL, PoIre*
Breen, James 1826-1866 *Alli Sup*
Breen, Jon L 1943- *EncM&D*
Breen, May Singhi *AmSCAP 66*
Breen, P C T *PoIre*
Breen, Quirinus 1896- *ConAu 33*
Breere, Richard *Alli*
Brees, Bud 1921- *AmSCAP 66*
Brees, Orlo Marion *ChPo*
Breese, Burtis Burr 1867-1939 *DcNAA, WhWNAA*
Breese, Edward *Alli Sup*
Breese, Gerald 1912- *ConAu 41*
Breese, Sidney 1800-1878 *Alli Sup, DcNAA*
Breese, Zona *DcNAA*
Breeskin, Adelyn Dohme 1896- *ConAu 33*
Breeskin, Barnee 1910- *AmSCAP 66*
Breetveld, Jim Patrick 1925- *AuBYP, ConAu 1R*
Breeze, Rita Green 1879- *WhWNAA*
Breffort, Alexandre 1901-1971 *ConAu 29*
Bregendahl, Marie 1867-1940 *CasWL, ClDMEuL, EncWL, Pen Eur, REn*
Bregg, Dorothy *ChPo S1*
Bregman, Adolph 1890- *WhWNAA*
Bregman, Elsie Oschrin 1896- *WhWNAA*
Bregman, Jacob I 1923- *ConAu 41*
Bregy, Katherine Marie Cornelia 1888-1967 *AmA&B, BkC 2, CatA 1947, WhWNAA*
Brehaut, Mary *OxCan .*
Brehaut, Thomas Collings *Alli Sup*
Brehm, Alfred Edmund 1829-1884 *BiD&SB, OxGer*
Brehm, Bruno Von 1892-1974 *CasWL, OxGer*
Breidenbaugh, Edward Swayer 1849-1926 *DcNAA*
Breidenbaugh, Edward Swoyer 1849-1926 *Alli Sup, DcAmA*
Breidfjord, Sigurdur Eiriksson 1798-1846 *CasWL, EuA*
Breig, Joseph Anthony 1905- *BkC 6, CatA 1952, ConAu 5R*
Breihan, Carl William 1916- *Au&Wr, ConAu 1R*
Breillat, Catherine 1950- *ConAu 33*
Breimyer, Harold F 1914- *ConAu 17R, WrD 1976*
Breinburg, Petronella Alexandrina 1927- *ConAu 53, WrD 1976*
Breines, Paul 1941- *ConAu 61*
Breinlinger, Alice Berend *WhLA*
Breintnall, Joseph *Alli*
Breirly, Roger *Alli*
Breisach, Ernst Adolf 1923- *ConAu 1R*
Breisky, William J 1928- *ConAu 53*
Breit, Harvey 1913?-1968 *ConAu 5R, ConAu 25, WorAu*
Breit, Marquita E 1942- *ConAu 57*
Breit, William 1933- *ConAu 33*
Breitbach, Joseph 1903- *OxGer*
Breitenkamp, Edward Carlton 1913- *ConAu 25, IndAu 1917*
Breitenstein, Heinrich 1848- *WhLA*
Breitfuss, Leonid 1864- *WhLA*
Breithaupt, Rudolf Maria 1873- *WhLA*
Breitinger, Johann Jakob 1701-1776 *CasWL, DcEuL, EuA, EvEuW, OxGer, Pen Eur*
Breitkreuz, Horst 1925- *WhGrA*
Breitman, George 1916- *ConAu 61*
Breitman, Hans 1824-1903 *DcAmA, DcEnL, DcNAA*
Breitmann, Hans 1824-1903 *AmA, Chmbr*
Breitner, Erhard 1884- *WhLA*
Breitner, I Emery 1929- *ConAu 57*
Breitscheid, Rudolf 1874- *WhLA*
Breitwieser, Joseph Valentine 1884- *IndAu 1816*
Breitzke, Charles Frederick 1884- *WhWNAA*
Brekell, John d1775? *Alli*
Breland, Osmond Philip 1910- *ConAu 9R, WrD 1976*

Brelis, Dean 1924- *ConAu 9R*
Brelis, Nancy 1929- *ConAu 21*
Brelsford, William Vernon 1907- *Au&Wr, ConAu P-1*
Brem, Walter Vernon 1875- *WhWNAA*
Breman, Paul 1931- *ConAu 21*
Brembeck, Cole Speicher 1917- *IndAu 1917*
Brembeck, Winston Lamont 1912- *IndAu 1917*
Breme, Thomas *Alli*
Bremer, Beitrage 1744-1748 *DcEuL*
Bremer, Claus 1924- *CasWL*
Bremer, Frederika 1801-1865 *CasWL, DcEnL, DcEuL*
Bremer, Fredrika 1801-1865 *BbD, BiD&SB, ChPo, DcBiA, EuA, EvEuW, HsB&A, OxAm, Pen Eur, REnAL*
Bremer, John Lewis 1874- *WhWNAA*
Buemmer, Benjamin 1851-1938 *OxCan*
Bremner, Archibald 1849-1901 *DcNAA*
Bremner, Benjamin 1851-1938 *DcNAA*
Bremner, Blanche Irbe *ChPo*
Bremner, David *Alli Sup*
Bremner, Kate F *ChPo S1*
Bremner, Robert *Alli*
Bremner, Robert H 1917- *ConAu 23*
Bremner, W Leith *Alli Sup*
Bremner, W W *Alli Sup*
Bremond, Andre 1872- *CatA 1947*
Bremond, Henri 1865-1933 *CasWL, CatA 1947, ClDMEuL, OxFr, Pen Eur, REn*
Bremont, Anna Dumphy, Comtesse De *ChPo, ChPo S2*
Brems, Hans 1915- *ConAu 25*
Bremser, Ray 1934- *AmA&B, ConAu 17R, ConP 1970, ConP 1975, DrAP 1975, WrD 1976*
Bremyer, Jayne Dickey 1924- *ConAu 61*
Brenainn, Saint 484-577 *NewC*
Brenan, Daniel *BbtC*
Brenan, Gerald 1894- *ConAu 1R, LongC, TwCA Sup, WrD 1976*
Brenan, John *Alli, BiDLA Sup*
Brenan, John 1768?-1830 *PoIre*
Brenan, John Churchill *Alli Sup, ChPo, ChPo S1, PoIre*
Brenan, Joseph 1828-1857 *PoIre*
Brenan, Justin *Alli*
Brenan, M J *Alli*
Brenan, Robert Hardy *Alli Sup*
Brenchley, Julius Lucius d1873 *Alli Sup*
Brenchley, Winifred Elsie 1883- *WhLA*
Brend, William Alfred 1873- *WhLA*
Brendan, Saint 484-577 *NewC, OxFr*
Brende, John *Alli*
Brendel, Martin 1862- *WhLA*
Brender A Brandis, Gerrit 1751-1802 *CasWL*
Brendle, D F *Alli Sup*
Brendon, Piers 1940- *WrD 1976*
Brendtro, Lawrence K 1940- *ConAu 29*
Brene, Jose R 1927- *DcCLA*
Breneman, William Raymond 1907- *IndAu 1917*
Brener, Milton E 1930- *ConAu 29*
Brengelmann, Johannes Clemens 1920- *Au&Wr, ConAu 5R*
Brengle, Samuel Logan 1860-1935 *IndAu 1816*
Brenke, William Charles 1874- *WhWNAA*
Brenn, George J 1888- *WhWNAA*
Brennan, Alfred Laurens 1853-1921 *ChPo, ChPo S1*
Brennan, Bernard P 1918- *ConAu 5R*
Brennan, Blodgett E 1935-1970 *IndAu 1917*
Brennan, Christopher 1917- *ConAu XR, WrD 1976*
Brennan, Christopher John 1870-1932 *CasWL, ChPo, DcLEnL, Pen Eng, PoIre, TwCW, WebEAL, WorAu*
Brennan, Dan *MnnWr*
Brennan, Daniel Joseph 1929- *IndAu 1917*
Brennan, Edward John 1845- *Alli Sup, ChPo S1, PoIre*
Brennan, Elizabeth 1922- *CatA 1952*
Brennan, Frederick Hazlitt 1901-1962 *AmA&B*
Brennan, Gerald *ChPo S2*
Brennan, Gerald Thomas 1898- *BkC 1, CatA 1952*
Brennan, J *Alli Sup*

Brennan, J Fletcher *Alli Sup*
Brennan, J Keirn 1873-1948 *AmSCAP 66*
Brennan, James Alexander 1885-1956 *AmSCAP 66*
Brennan, James M *ChPo S1*
Brennan, John N H 1914- *Au&Wr, ConAu 1R*
Brennan, John Patrick 1866-1932 *OhA&B*
Brennan, Joseph 1829- *BiDSA*
Brennan, Joseph Gerard *AuBYP, ConAu 1R*
Brennan, Joseph Lomas 1903- *ConAu 5R, SmATA 6*
Brennan, Joseph Payne 1918- *ChPo S1, ConAu 1R, EncM&D, WrD 1976*
Brennan, Julia Sullivan *ChPo S1, PoIre*
Brennan, Lawrence D 1915- *ConAu 5R*
Brennan, Louis A 1911- *ConAu 17R*
Brennan, Maeve 1917- *ConLC 5, DrAF 1976*
Brennan, Martin Stanislaus 1845-1927 *Alli Sup, DcNAA*
Brennan, Maynard J 1921- *ConAu 13R*
Brennan, Michael Joseph, Jr. 1928- *ConAu 13R*
Brennan, Neil F 1923- *ConAu 37, WrD 1976*
Brennan, Niall 1918- *Au&Wr, ConAu 13R*
Brennan, Ray 1908?-1972 *ConAu 37*
Brennan, Richard 1833?-1893 *DcNAA*
Brennan, Robert *Alli Sup*
Brennan, Robert Edward 1897- *CatA 1947*
Brennan, Tim *ConAu XR*
Brennan, Will *ConAu XR*
Brennand, Frank *ConAu XR*
Brennecke, John H 1934- *ConAu 37*
Brenneman, Daniel 1834-1919 *IndAu 1816*
Brenneman, G W *ChPo S1*
Brenneman, Helen Good 1925- *ConAu 23, WrD 1976*
Brenneman, Henry B 1831-1887 *IndAu 1816, OhA&B*
Brenneman, Jesse LaMar 1886- *IndAu 1917, WhWNAA*
Brenner, Alfred *BlkAW*
Brenner, Anita 1905-1974 *AnCL, ConAu 49, ConAu 53, TexWr*
Brenner, Barbara Johnes 1925- *AuBYP, ConAu 9R, SmATA 4*
Brenner, Clarence Dietz 1892- *WhWNAA*
Brenner, Eduard Johannes Wilhelm 1888- *WhLA*
Brenner, Fred *IlBYP*
Brenner, Henry 1881- *IndAu 1917*
Brenner, Joseph Hayyim 1881-1921 *Pen Cl, Pen Eur*
Brenner, Raymond 1927- *AmSCAP 66*
Brenner, Robert William 1904-1959 *OhA&B*
Brenner, Selma Hautzik 1912- *AmSCAP 66*
Brenner, Sofia Elisabet 1659-1730 *CasWL, EvEuW*
Brenner, Summer 1945- *ConAu 61*
Brenner, Walter 1906- *AmSCAP 66*
Brenner, Yehojachin Simon 1926- *ConAu 21, WrD 1976*
Brenner, Yoseph Chaim 1881-1921 *CasWL*
Brenner-Eglinger, Hans 1873- *WhLA*
Brennglas, Adolf *OxGer*
Brenni, Vito J 1923- *ConAu 49*
Brennus 409?BC- *NewC*
Brenriker, C *Alli Sup*
Brent Of Bin Bin *CasWL, DcLEnL, TwCW*
Brent, B P *Alli Sup*
Brent, Berel *WhWNAA*
Brent, C F *ChPo*
Brent, Carl *ChPo*
Brent, Charles *Alli*
Brent, Mrs. Charles *Alli Sup*
Brent, Charles Henry 1862-1929 *DcAmA, DcNAA, WhWNAA*
Brent, Charlton *MnBBF*
Brent, Daniel *Alli Sup*
Brent, Earl Karl 1914- *AmSCAP 66*
Brent, Ernest *MnBBF*
Brent, Francis *MnBBF*
Brent, Frank Pierce 1852- *BiDSA*
Brent, Hally Carrington *ChPo*
Brent, Harold Patrick 1943- *ConAu 33*
Brent, Harry 1904- *AmSCAP 66, ConAu XR*
Brent, Henry Johnson 1811-1880 *Alli Sup, AmA&B, BiDSA, DcAmA, DcNAA*
Brent, J *Alli*
Brent, Jim 1898- *Au&Wr, WrD 1976*

Brent, John 1808-1882? *Alli Sup, ChPo S1*
Brent, Joseph Lancaster 1826-1905 *DcNAA*
Brent, Loring *AmA&B, OhA&B*
Brent, Sir Nathaniel 1573-1652 *Alli*
Brent, Peter 1931- *WrD 1976*
Brent, Stuart *AuBYP*
Brent, William *Alli*
Brent-Dyer, Elinor Mary *WhCL*
Brentano, Arthur 1858-1944 *AmA&B*
Brentano, Bernard Von 1901- *WhLA*
Brentano, Bettina *OxGer*
Brentano, Clemens Maria 1778-1842 *BbD, BiD&SB, CasWL, ChPo S1, DcEuL, EuA, EvEuW, OxGer, Pen Eur, REn*
Brentano, Elizabeth 1785-1859 *BbD, BiD&SB*
Brentano, Lowell 1895-1950 *AmA&B, REnAL*
Brentano, Lujo *Alli Sup*
Brentano, Robert 1926- *ConAu 23, IndAu 1917*
Brenten, John H *Alli Sup*
Brentford, Burke *DcNAA, HsB&A, OhA&B*
Brentjes, Burchard 1929- *Au&Wr*
Brenton, Edward Pelham 1774-1839 *Alli, DcEnL*
Brenton, Emily E *IndAu 1917*
Brenton, Howard 1942- *ConDr, WrD 1976*
Brenton, Sir Jahleel 1770-1844 *Alli*
Brereley, Roger 1586-1637 *NewC*
Brerely, John *Alli*
Brereton, Austin *Alli Sup*
Brereton, C D *Alli*
Brereton, Charles *Alli Sup*
Brereton, Cloudesley Shovell Henry 1863- *ChPo, WhLA*
Brereton, Emily *Alli Sup*
Brereton, Ethel C *ChPo, ChPo S1*
Brereton, Frederick Sadler 1872-1957 *ChPo S1, SixAP, WhCL*
Brereton, Geoffrey 1906- *Au&Wr, ConAu 25*
Brereton, Henry *Alli*
Brereton, Jane 1685-1740 *Alli, DcEnL*
Brereton, John *Alli, OxAm, REnAL*
Brereton, John LeGay 1828-1886 *Alli Sup*
Brereton, John LeGay, Jr. 1871?-1933 *ChPo, ChPo S2, DcLEnL, WhLA*
Brereton, Joseph Lloyd *Alli Sup*
Brereton, Owen Salisbury 1715-1798 *Alli*
Brereton, Robert Maitland *Alli Sup*
Brereton, Thomas *Alli*
Brereton, William *Alli*
Brereton, Sir William 1789-1864 *Alli Sup*
Brereton, William H *Alli Sup*
Brerewood, Edward 1565-1615 *Alli*
Brerewood, Thomas *Alli*
Breri *CasWL*
Bresher, M R *Alli Sup*
Bresky, Dushan *ConAu 53*
Breslauer, George W 1946- *ConAu 29*
Breslaw, Marcus Heinrich *Alli Sup*
Bresler, Fenton Shea 1929- *Au&Wr*
Bresler, Jerry *AmSCAP 66*
Breslich, Arthur Louis 1873-1924 *DcNAA*
Breslin, Herbert H 1924- *ConAu 53*
Breslin, Howard 1912- *AmA&B*
Breslin, James E 1935- *ConAu 33*
Breslin, Jimmy 1930- *AmA&B, AuNews 1, ConLC 4, WrD 1976*
Breslove, David 1891- *ConAu 9R*
Bresnan, Catharine Mary 1904- *WhWNAA*
Bressani, Francesco Giuseppe 1612-1672 *OxCan*
Bressler, Leo A 1911- *ConAu 57*
Bressler, Marion Ann 1921- *ConAu 57*
Brest, Vincent *Alli*
Brestowski, Carl August 1861- *WhLA*
Bretagne, Breton *DcEuL*
Bretel, Jacques *CasWL, EvEuW*
Bretel, Jean d1272 *CasWL*
Bretherton, Cyril Herbert Emmanuel 1878-1939 *ChPo, ChPo S1*
Bretherton, Edward *Alli Sup*
Bretland, Joseph 1742-1819 *Alli*
Bretnall, G H 1881- *WhWNAA*
Breton, Albert 1929- *ConAu 61*
Breton, Andre 1896-1966 *AtlBL, CasWL, ClDMEuL, ConAu 19, ConAu 25, ConLC 2, EncWL, EvEuW, LongC, ModRL, ModWD, OxFr, Pen Eur, RCom, REn, REnWD, TwCA Sup,*

TwCW, WhTwL
Breton, Edwin James 1828-1895 *MnBBF*
Breton, Guy *MnBBF*
Breton, John *Alli*
Breton, John d1275 *Alli*
Breton, Nicholas 1545?-1626? *Alli, BiD&SB, BrAu, CasWL, ChPo, ChPo S1, Chmbr 1, CnE&AP, CrE&SL, DcEnL, DcLEnL, EvLB, NewC, OxEng, Pen Eng, REn, WebEAL*
Breton, Pierre Napoleon 1858-1917 *DcNAA, MnBBF*
Breton, Virginie Demont 1859- *WhLA*
Breton, W L *EarAB*
Breton, William *Alli*
Breton, William Henry *Alli*
Breton DeLosHerreros, Manuel 1796?-1873 *BbD, BiD&SB, CasWL, DcSpL, EvEuW, McGWD, Pen Eur, REn*
Breton-Smith, Clare 1906- *Au&Wr*
Bretscher, Paul G 1921- *ConAu 17R*
Bretschneider, E *Alli Sup*
Bretschneider, Heinrich Gottfried Von 1739-1810 *BiD&SB*
Brett, Arthur *Alli*
Brett, Bruce Y 1922- *AmA&B*
Brett, David *ConAu XR*
Brett, Dorothy 1891- *REn*
Brett, Edward *ChPo S2*
Brett, Edwin *Alli Sup*
Brett, George Platt 1858-1936 *AmA&B*
Brett, George Platt, Jr. 1893- *AmA&B*
Brett, George Sidney 1879-1944 *CanWr, DcNAA, WhWNAA*
Brett, Grace Neff 1900- *ConAu 9R*
Brett, Harold *ConICB*
Brett, Harold M 1880?- *ChPo, IlCB 1945*
Brett, Hawksley *MnBBF*
Brett, Helena *Alli Sup*
Brett, John *Alli*
Brett, Mrs. John *Alli Sup*
Brett, John Watkins 1805-1863 *Alli Sup*
Brett, Joseph *Alli*
Brett, K B *OxCan Sup*
Brett, Sister M *PoIre*
Brett, Mary Elizabeth *Au&Wr, ConAu 9R, WrD 1976*
Brett, Michael *ConAu XR*
Brett, Molly *ConAu XR, WrD 1976*
Brett, Oliver 1881- *WhLA*
Brett, Peter *PoIre*
Brett, Raymond Laurence 1917- *Au&Wr, ConAu 1R, WrD 1976*
Brett, Reginald Baliol *NewC*
Brett, Richard 1561-1637 *Alli*
Brett, Robert 1808-1874 *Alli Sup*
Brett, Samuel *Alli*
Brett, Thomas 1667-1743 *Alli, Alli Sup, BbtC*
Brett, William *Alli Sup*
Brett, William Henry *Alli, Alli Sup*
Brett, William Howard 1846-1918 *AmA&B*
Brett-James, Antony 1920- *Au&Wr, ConAu 5R, WrD 1976*
Brett-Smith, Herbert Francis Brett *ChPo*
Brett-Smith, John Ralph Brett 1917- *AmA&B*
Brett-Smith, Richard 1923- *Au&Wr, ConAu 21*
Brett Young, Francis 1884-1954 *LongC, TwCA, TwCA Sup, TwCW*
Brett-Young, Jessica 1883-1970 *ConAu P-1*
Brettell, Mrs. *ChPo S1*
Brettell, Jacob 1793-1862 *ChPo S2*
Brettell, Noel Harry 1908- *ConP 1970*
Brettingham, Matthew *Alli*
Bretton, Henry De *BrAu, NewC*
Bretton, Henry L 1916- *ConAu 5R*
Brettschneider, Bertram D 1924- *ConAu 33*
Bretz, J Harlen 1882- *WhWNAA*
Bretzner, Christian Friedrich 1748-1807 *BiD&SB*
Bretzner, Christoph Friedrich 1748-1807 *OxGer*
Breuder, W Edward 1911- *AmSCAP 66*
Breuer, Bessie 1893-1975 *AmA&B, ConAu 17, ConAu 61, REnAL*
Breuer, Elizabeth 1892- *OhA&B, TwCA, TwCA Sup*
Breuer, Ernest 1886- *AmSCAP 66*
Breuer, Ernest Henry 1902- *ConAu 19*

Breuer, Hermann 1878- *WhLA*
Breuer, Marcel 1902- *ConAu 5R*
Breuer, Samson 1891- *WhLA*
Breues, John *Alli*
Breughel, Gerrit Henricksz Van 1573?-1635 *CasWL*
Breugle, George Swift *ChPo S1*
Breuil, Henri 1877-1961 *LongC*
Breul, Karl Hermann 1860- *WhLA*
Breunig, Jerome Edward 1917- *ConAu 13R*
Breunig, Leroy C 1915- *ConAu 61*
Breur, Leo William 1897- *WhWNAA*
Breval, Doctor *Alli*
Breval, John Durant De 1680?-1738 *Alli, NewC*
Brevannes, Maurice 1904- *IlBYP, IICB 1956*
Brevard, Caroline Mays 1860-1920 *DcNAA*
Brevard, Carolyn Mays 1860-1920 *BiDSA*
Brevard, Ephraim 1750?-1783 *BiDSA*
Brevard, Joseph *Alli*
Brevint, Daniel 1616-1695 *Alli*
Brevior, Thomas *Alli Sup*
Brevoort, Elias *Alli Sup*
Brevoort, Henry *CyAL 1*
Brevoort, James Carson 1818-1887 *Alli Sup, DcAmA, DcNAA*
Brevoort, James Renwick 1832-1918 *EarAB*
Brew, J O 1906- *ConAu 61*
Brew, Kwesi 1928- *Pen Cl*
Brew, Miss M W *Alli Sup, PoIre*
Brew, Osborne Henry Kwesi 1928- *AfA 1, ConP 1970, ConP 1975, WrD 1976*
Breward, Ian 1934- *WrD 1976*
Brewbaker, Charles Warren 1869- *OhA&B*
Brewer, Mrs. *Alli Sup*
Brewer, A T And Laubscher, G A *Alli Sup*
Brewer, Abraham Titus 1841-1933 *DcNAA, OhA&B*
Brewer, Anne *ChPo*
Brewer, Annette Fitch 1870-1960 *OhA&B*
Brewer, Anthony *Alli, ChPo, DcEnL*
Brewer, Antony *BbD, BiD&SB, NewC*
Brewer, Bertha E *ChPo, ChPo S1*
Brewer, Clifton Hartwell 1876-1947 *DcNAA*
Brewer, Daniel Chauncey 1861-1932 *Alli Sup, DcAmA, DcNAA, WhWNAA*
Brewer, David Josiah 1837-1910 *DcAmA, DcNAA*
Brewer, Derek Stanley 1923- *Au&Wr, ConAu 1R*
Brewer, Dorcas Irene Rock 1904- *IndAu 1917*
Brewer, Ebenezer Cobham 1810-1897 *Alli, Alli Sup, BiD&SB, ChPo, DcEnL, EvLB, NewC*
Brewer, Edward S 1933- *ConAu 33*
Brewer, Emil 1910- *TexWr*
Brewer, Emma *Alli Sup*
Brewer, Frances Joan 1913-1965 *ConAu P-1*
Brewer, Fredric Aldwyn 1921- *ConAu 17R, IndAu 1917*
Brewer, Garry Dwight 1941- *ConAu 33, WrD 1976*
Brewer, George *WhWNAA*
Brewer, George 1766- *Alli, BiDLA*
Brewer, George Emerson 1861-1939 *DcNAA, WhWNAA*
Brewer, Gil *AmA&B*
Brewer, Harriet *ChPo*
Brewer, Henry *Alli*
Brewer, Isaac William 1867- *WhWNAA*
Brewer, J F *Alli Sup*
Brewer, J Mason 1896- *BlkAW, ConAu 25, TexWr*
Brewer, Jack A 1933- *ConAu 23*
Brewer, James *Alli*
Brewer, James H Fitzgerald 1916- *ConAu 9R*
Brewer, James Norris *Alli, BiDLA*
Brewer, John M And Mayer, L *Alli Sup*
Brewer, John Marks *WhWNAA*
Brewer, John Mason 1896- *ChPo S1, LivBA*
Brewer, John Sherren 1810?-1879 *Alli, Alli Sup, BrAu 19, NewC*
Brewer, Josiah 1796-1872 *Alli, DcNAA*
Brewer, Kate *BiDSA*
Brewer, Leighton *OxCan*
Brewer, Luther Albertus 1858-1933 *AmA&B, AmLY, DcNAA, WhWNAA*
Brewer, Margaret L 1929- *ConAu 29*
Brewer, N *Alli Sup*

Brewer, Nicholas Richard 1857-1949 *AmA&B,*
 DcNAA
Brewer, Robert Frederick *Alli Sup*
Brewer, Robert K *Alli Sup*
Brewer, Mrs. Robert K *Alli Sup*
Brewer, Teresa 1931- *AmSCAP 66*
Brewer, Thomas *Alli, Alli Sup, CasWL*
Brewer, Thomas B 1932- *ConAu 21*
Brewer, Thomas Mayo 1814?-1880 *Alli Sup,*
 BbtC, DcAmA, DcNAA
Brewer, W *Alli Sup*
Brewer, William *Alli Sup*
Brewer, William A *Alli Sup*
Brewer, William C 1897?-1974 *ConAu 53*
Brewer, William Henry 1828-1910 *DcAmA,*
 DcNAA
Brewer, Willis 1844-1912 *BiDSA, DcNAA*
Brewer, Wilmon 1895- *Au&Wr, ChPo S1,*
 ConAu 5R, WrD 1976
Brewerton, George Douglas 1820-1901 *Alli Sup,*
 DcAmA, DcNAA
Brewerton, T LeGay *Alli*
Brewin, Andrew *OxCan Sup*
Brewin, Robert *Alli Sup*
Brewington, Marion Vernon 1902-1974
 ConAu 5R, ConAu 53
Brewsher, Mrs. M E *Alli Sup*
Brewster, Anne Maria Hampton 1818-1892
 Alli Sup, DcAmA, DcNAA
Brewster, Benjamin *AuBYP, ConAu XR,*
 SmATA 2, SmATA 5, WrD 1976
Brewster, Bess E *BlkAW*
Brewster, Celestia A 1812- *Alli*
Brewster, Charles Warren 1812-1868 *Alli Sup,*
 DcAmA, DcNAA
Brewster, Chauncey Bunce 1848-1941 *DcAmA,*
 DcNAA
Brewster, Sir David 1781-1868 *Alli, BiDLA,*
 BrAu 19, CasWL, Chmbr 3, DcEnA,
 DcEnL, EvLB
Brewster, Dorothy 1883- *AmA&B, Au&Wr,*
 ConAu 1R
Brewster, Edward 1886- *DcNAA*
Brewster, Edwin Tenney 1866- *AmLY*
Brewster, Eliot *AmA&B*
Brewster, Elizabeth 1922- *Au&Wr, CanWr,*
 ConAu 25, ConP 1970, ConP 1975,
 OxCan, OxCan Sup, WrD 1976
Brewster, Emma E *ChPo, ChPo S1*
Brewster, Eugene Valentine 1871-1939 *AmA&B,*
 DcNAA
Brewster, Frances S 1860- *WhWNAA*
Brewster, Sir Francis *Alli*
Brewster, Frederick Carroll 1825-1898 *Alli Sup,*
 DcAmA, DcNAA
Brewster, George 1800-1865 *Alli Sup, DcNAA,*
 OhA&B
Brewster, Harold Pomeroy 1831-1906 *DcNAA,*
 OhA&B
Brewster, Henry B 1850-1908 *Alli Sup, OxAm*
Brewster, J M *Alli Sup*
Brewster, James *Alli, BiDLA*
Brewster, James Henry 1856-1920 *DcNAA*
Brewster, John *Alli, BiDLA*
Brewster, Jonathan McDuffee 1835-1882
 DcNAA
Brewster, Joseph S *Alli Sup*
Brewster, Lillian *AmLY*
Brewster, Lyman Denison 1832- *ChPo*
Brewster, M E *Alli Sup*
Brewster, Margaret M *Alli Sup*
Brewster, Mary Shaw *Alli Sup*
Brewster, Osmyn 1797-1889 *AmA&B*
Brewster, Paul G 1898- *IndAu 1917*
Brewster, Richard *Alli*
Brewster, Samuel *Alli*
Brewster, Stanley Farrar 1889- *OhA&B*
Brewster, William *Alli, BiDLA*
Brewster, William 1851-1919 *AmA, DcNAA*
Brewster, William Nesbitt 1862-1916 *DcNAA,*
 OhA&B
Brewster, William Tenney 1869-1961 *AmA&B*
Brewtnall, E F *ChPo S1*
Brewtnall, R W S *ChPo, ChPo S1*
Brewton, John Edmund 1898- *ChPo, ChPo S1,*
 ChPo S2, ConAu 5R, SmATA 5
Brewton, Sara W And John E *BkP*
Brey, Charles *IlBYP*

Breyer, Frank Gottlob 1886- *WhWNAA*
Breyer, N L 1942- *ConAu 49*
Breyfogel, W L *Alli Sup*
Breynat, Gabriel-Joseph-Elie 1867-1954 *OxCan*
Breytenbach, Breyten 1939- *CasWL*
Breza, Tadeusz 1905-1970 *CasWL, ConAu 29*
Brezina, Jan 1917- *CasWL*
Brezina, Otokar 1868-1929 *CasWL, ClDMEuL,*
 EncWL, ModSL 2, Pen Eur, WorAu
Brezovacki, Tito 1757-1805? *CasWL, Pen Eur*
Brfwin, R *ChPo S1*
Brian *ConAu XR*
Brian Boroimhe 926-1014 *NewC, REn*
Brian Boru 926-1014 *NewC, REn*
Brian Borumha 926-1014 *NewC, REn*
Brian, Mrs. *Alli Sup*
Brian, Denis 1923- *ConAu 25*
Brian, James 1923- *ConAu XR, LongC*
Brian, Thomas *Alli*
Briand, Paul L, Jr. 1920- *ConAu 1R*
Briand, Rena 1935- *ConAu 29, WrD 1976*
Briant, Alexander 1557-1581 *Alli*
Briarly, Mary *WhWNAA*
Bribner, Francis *Alli*
Briccetti, Thomas B 1936- *AmSCAP 66*
Brice, Father *BkC 4*
Brice, Alexander *Alli*
Brice, Andrew *Alli*
Brice, Douglas Francis Aloysius 1916- *ChPo S2,*
 ConAu 21, WrD 1976
Brice, Edward Cowell *Alli Sup*
Brice, Germain 1500?-1538 *CasWL*
Brice, J *Alli, BiDLA*
Brice, John *Alli*
Brice, Marshall Moore 1898- *ConAu 17R,*
 WrD 1976
Brice, Seward William 1846- *Alli Sup*
Brice, Thomas *Alli*
Brichan, David d1814 *Alli, BiDLA,*
 BiDLA Sup
Brichant, A *OxCan Sup*
Brichant, Colette Dubois 1926- *ConAu 13R*
Brick *AmA&B*
Brick, Abraham Lincoln 1860-1908 *DcNAA,*
 IndAu 1917
Brick, John 1922-1973 *AmA&B, AuBYP,*
 ConAu 45, ConAu P-1, SmATA 10
Brick, Michael 1922- *ConAu 13R*
Brick, Titus A *Alli Sup*
Brickdale, Charles Fortescue 1857- *Alli Sup*
Brickdale, Eleanor Fortescue *ChPo S1,*
 IlCB 1945
Brickell, C W *ChPo S2*
Brickell, Henry Herschel 1889-1952 *AmA&B*
Brickell, John *Alli*
Brickell, Robert C *Alli Sup*
Brickenden, Catherine *OxCan*
Bricker, Garland Armor 1881- *OhA&B,*
 WhWNAA
Bricker, Victoria Reifler 1940- *ConAu 53*
Brickhill, Paul Chester Jerome 1916- *Au&Wr,*
 ConAu 9R, EvLB, TwCW
Brickington, Stephen *Alli*
Brickman, William Wolfgang 1913- *ConAu 1R,*
 WrD 1976
Bricknell, John *BiDSA*
Bricknell, W S *Alli*
Brickner, Richard P 1933- *ConAu 5R,*
 DrAF 1976
Brickner, Walter Max 1875-1930 *DcNAA,*
 WhWNAA
Bricktop *DcNAA*
Brickwood, Edwin Dampier *Alli Sup*
Brickwood, Latham C N Percy 1841- *Alli Sup*
Bricstan *BiB S*
Bricuth, John 1940- *ConAu XR*
Bridaine, Jacques 1701-1767 *OxFr*
Bridall, John *Alli*
Bride, Saint *NewC*
Bridecake, Ralph *Alli*
Bridecake, T *Alli, BiDLA*
Bridel, Arleville *BiDLA*
Bridel, Bedrich 1619-1680 *CasWL*
Bridel, Edmund Philip d1815 *BiDLA,*
 BiDLA Sup
Bridel, Philippe 1757-1845 *CasWL, EvEuW*
Bridenbaugh, Carl 1903- *AmA&B, ConAu 9R*
Bridferth *Alli, BiB S*

Bridgart, Charles W *Alli Sup*
Bridge, Ann 1891?-1974 *Au&Wr, CatA 1952,*
 ConAu 49, LongC, NewC, TwCA,
 TwCA Sup
Bridge, Arthur *Alli Sup*
Bridge, Bewick *Alli, BiDLA*
Bridge, Christiana *Alli Sup*
Bridge, Donald Ulysses 1894- *IndAu 1917*
Bridge, Francis *Alli*
Bridge, Franklin Morton 1915- *IndAu 1917*
Bridge, Gerard 1873- *ChPo S2, WhWNAA*
Bridge, Henry M *Alli Sup*
Bridge, Horatio 1806-1893 *AmA, DcAmA,*
 DcNAA, OxAm
Bridge, J *Alli Sup*
Bridge, J D *ChPo S2*
Bridge, James Howard 1856?-1939 *AmA&B,*
 DcAmA, DcNAA
Bridge, John *Alli Sup*
Bridge, John Frederick 1844- *Alli Sup*
Bridge, Josiah d1801 *Alli*
Bridge, Norman 1844-1925 *DcAmA, DcNAA*
Bridge, Samuel *Alli, BiDLA*
Bridge, T W *Alli Sup*
Bridge, Thomas 1657-1715 *Alli, DcNAA*
Bridge, William 1600-1690 *Alli*
Bridgecross, Peter *ConAu XR*
Bridgeforth, Med *BlkAW*
Bridgeman *Alli*
Bridgeman, G *Alli, BiDLA*
Bridgeman, George Thomas Orlando 1823-
 Alli Sup
Bridgeman, Helen Diana *ChPo*
Bridgeman, Raymond Landon 1848- *AmLY*
Bridgeman, R L ALSO Bridgman, Raymond
Bridgeman, Richard *ConAu XR*
Bridgeman, S C *Alli Sup*
Bridgeman, Thomas d1850 *Alli, DcNAA*
Bridgeman, William *Alli, BiDLA*
Bridgeman, William Barton 1916- *ConAu 9R*
Bridgen, R *Alli*
Bridgen, William *Alli*
Bridger, A E *Alli Sup*
Bridger, Charles *Alli Sup*
Bridger, Gordon 1928- *Au&Wr*
Bridger, James 1804-1881 *OxAm, REnAL*
Bridges, Miss *Alli Sup*
Bridges, Albert Fletcher 1853-1926 *IndAu 1816*
Bridges, Calvin Blackman 1889-1938 *DcNAA*
Bridges, Charles 1794-1869 *Alli, Alli Sup,*
 ChPo
Bridges, Edward Smith *Alli Sup*
Bridges, Elizabeth 1887- *ChPo S2*
Bridges, Emma A *Alli Sup*
Bridges, Ethel 1897- *AmSCAP 66*
Bridges, Mrs. F D *Alli Sup*
Bridges, Frederick *Alli Sup*
Bridges, George d1677 *Alli*
Bridges, Hal 1918- *ConAu 1R*
Bridges, Horace James 1880-1955 *AmA&B,*
 AmLY, WhWNAA
Bridges, James *Alli*
Bridges, Jeremiah *Alli*
Bridges, Sir John *Alli*
Bridges, John d1590 *Alli*
Bridges, John d1618 *Alli*
Bridges, John 1666?-1724 *Alli*
Bridges, John Affleck 1833- *ChPo*
Bridges, John George d1841 *BbtC*
Bridges, John Gourlay 1901- *Au&Wr*
Bridges, John Henry 1832-1906 *Alli Sup,*
 BrAu 19
Bridges, Lou 1917- *AmSCAP 66*
Bridges, Madeleine *ChPo*
Bridges, Madeline *AmA&B, DcAmA*
Bridges, Matthew 1800- *Alli, PoCh*
Bridges, Milton Arlanden 1894-1939 *DcNAA*
Bridges, Noah *Alli*
Bridges, Otis C 1916- *AmSCAP 66*
Bridges, Ralph *Alli*
Bridges, Ralph Waldo 1883-1946 *IndAu 1917*
Bridges, Robert *Alli, Chmbr 3*
Bridges, Robert 1858-1941 *AmA&B, AmLY,*
 BbD, BiD&SB, ChPo, DcAmA, DcNAA,
 WhWNAA
Bridges, Robert Seymour 1844-1930 *Alli Sup,*
 AnCL, AtlBL, CasWL, ChPo, ChPo S1,
 ChPo S2, CnE&AP, DcEnA, DcEnA Ap,

DcLEnL, EncWL, EvLB, LongC, ModBL,
NewC, OxEng, Pen Eng, REn, TwCA,
TwCA Sup, TwCW, WebEAL, WhTwL
Bridges, Roy 1885-1952 *DcLEnL, EvLB,*
WhLA
Bridges, Sallie *Alli Sup*
Bridges, Sarah *Alli Sup*
Bridges, Thomas *Alli, BiDLA*
Bridges, Thomas Charles 1868-1944 *MnBBF,*
WhCL
Bridges, Victor *MnBBF*
Bridges, Walter *Alli*
Bridges, William *Alli*
Bridges, William 1933- *ConAu 33*
Bridges, William Andrew 1901- *AmA&B,*
AuBYP, ConAu 33, IndAu 1917,
SmATA 5, WrD 1976
Bridges, William B *ChPo*
Bridges, William Thomas *Alli Sup*
Bridges, Yseult Lechmere *Au&Wr*
Bridges-Adams, William 1889-1965 *ConAu P-1*
Bridget, Mrs. *Alli*
Bridget, Saint *NewC*
Bridget, Saint 1302?-1373 *CasWL, EuA*
Bridget, Bride 1302?-1373 *EvEuW*
Bridgett, Thomas E *Alli Sup*
Bridgewater, Benjamin *DcEnL*
Bridgewater, B ALSO Bridgwater, B
Bridgewater, Francis H Egerton, Earl Of
1756?-1829 *Alli, DcEnL*
Bridgewater, John d1600? *Alli*
Bridgewater, Sarah *Alli Sup*
Bridgford, Samuel Hulme *ChPo S2*
Bridgham, Lillian Clisby *ChPo S2*
Bridgman *Alli*
Bridgman, Amy Sherman *AnMV 1926, ChPo*
Bridgman, Charles *Alli Sup*
Bridgman, Cunningham V *Alli Sup*
Bridgman, Elijah Cole 1801-1861 *DcAmA*
Bridgman, Eliza J Gillett *Alli Sup*
Bridgman, F M *ChPo*
Bridgman, Frederic Arthur 1847-1928 *BiDSA,*
DcAmA, DcNAA
Bridgman, Helen Bartlett 1855-1935 *AmA&B,*
DcNAA, WhWNAA
Bridgman, Herbert Lawrence 1844-1924
DcNAA
Bridgman, Howard Allen 1860-1929 *DcNAA*
Bridgman, Sir John *Alli*
Bridgman, Laura 1831-1931 *ChPo S2*
Bridgman, Lewis Jesse 1857-1931 *CarSB, ChPo,*
ChPo S1, ChPo S2, DcAmA
Bridgman, Marcus Fayette 1824-1899 *Alli Sup,*
ChPo S1, DcAmA, DcNAA
Bridgman, Mary *Alli Sup*
Bridgman, Sir Orlando *Alli*
Bridgman, Percy Williams 1882- *AmA&B,*
WhWNAA
Bridgman, Raymond L 1848-1925 *Alli Sup,*
DcNAA
Bridgman, R L ALSO Bridgeman, Raymond
Bridgman, Richard Whalley *Alli, BiDLA*
Bridgman, Sarah Atherton 1889?-1975
ConAu 57
Bridgman, Thomas 1795- *Alli, DcNAA*
Bridgwater, Benjamin *Alli*
Bridgwater, B ALSO Bridgewater, B
Bridgwater, Patrick 1931- *ConAu 5R*
Bridie, James 1888-1951 *CasWL, ChPo S1,*
Chmbr 3, CnMD, CnThe, CrCD,
DcLEnL, EncWL, EvLB, LongC,
McGWD, ModBL, ModWD, OxEng,
Pen Eng, REn, REnWD, TwCW,
WebEAL, WhLA, WhTwL, WorAu
Bridil, E P *Alli*
Bridle, Augustus 1869-1952 *CanNov, OxCan*
Bridlington, John Of *DcEnL*
Bridson, D G *ChPo*
Bridwell, Norman Ray 1928- *ConAu 13R,*
IndAu 1917, SmATA 4, WrD 1976
Bried, Hedi *DrAF 1976*
Briefs, Goetz Antony 1889-1974 *CatA 1952,*
ConAu 21, ConAu 49
Briegel, Ann C 1915- *ConAu 33*
Briegel, George F 1890- *AmSCAP 66*
Brien, Edward Henry *Alli Sup*
Brien, Raley *AmA&B, WhWNAA*
Brien, Roger 1910- *CanWr, OxCan*

Brientnall, Joseph *CyAL 1*
Brier, Howard Maxwell 1903-1969 *AuBYP,*
ConAu P-1, MorJA, SmATA 8,
WhPNW
Brier, Royce 1894- *AmA&B*
Brier, Warren Judson 1850- *AmLY*
Brier, Warren Judson 1931- *ConAu 25*
Briercliffe, Harold 1910- *Au&Wr*
Brierley, Benjamin 1825-1896 *Alli Sup,*
BiD&SB, NewC
Brierley, Joseph *Alli Sup*
Brierley, Marjorie Flowers 1893- *Au&Wr*
Brierley, Roger *NewC*
Brierley, Thomas *Alli Sup, ChPo S1*
Brierley, Wilfrid Gordon 1885- *WhWNAA*
Brierly, James Leslie 1881- *WhLA*
Brierre, Jean *BlkAW*
Brierre, Jean-Fernand 1909- *DcCLA*
Brierton, John 1572?-1619? *OxAm, REnAL*
Brierwood, Frank *Alli Sup*
Brieux, Eugene 1858-1932 *CasWL, ClDMEuL,*
CnMD, CnThe, EvEuW, LongC,
McGWD, ModWD, NewC, OxEng, OxFr,
Pen Eur, REn, REnWD, TwCA,
TwCA Sup
Brifaut, Charles 1781-1857 *OxFr*
Briffault, Robert Stephen 1876-1948 *LongC,*
NewC, REn, TwCA, TwCA Sup
Brigadere, Anna 1869-1933 *CasWL, EncWL*
Brigance, William Norwood 1896-1960 *AmA&B,*
IndAu 1917, WhWNAA
Briganti, Joseph E *Alli*
Brigden, Susan Jane 1938- *Au&Wr*
Briget, Elia *NewC*
Brigg, A *Alli Sup*
Brigg, Ethel M *ChPo S1*
Brigg, John Edwin *Alli Sup*
Brigg, Julius *ChPo, ChPo S1*
Briggs, Anna Beecroft 1864- *WhWNAA*
Briggs, Asa 1921- *Au&Wr, ConAu 5R,*
LongC, WrD 1976
Briggs, Austin, Jr. 1931- *ConAu 29*
Briggs, Barbara *AuBYP, BlkAW*
Briggs, Caroline Atherton *ChPo*
Briggs, Charles Augustus 1841-1913 *Alli Sup,*
AmA&B, BiD&SB, DcAmA, DcNAA,
WhWNAA
Briggs, Charles Frederick 1804-1877 *Alli,*
Alli Sup, AmA, AmA&B, BbD,
BiD&SB, CyAL 2, DcAmA, DcEnL,
DcNAA, OxAm, REnAL
Briggs, Charlie 1927- *ConAu 49*
Briggs, Clara A 1875-1930 *DcNAA*
Briggs, Clare A 1875-1930 *ChPo, ChPo S1*
Briggs, Clark Arthur 1883- *WhWNAA*
Briggs, Dorothy Corkille 1924- *ConAu 29*
Briggs, Emily 1831-1910 *DcNAA*
Briggs, Erasmus 1818- *DcNAA*
Briggs, Everett Francis 1908- *CatA 1952*
Briggs, F Allen 1916- *ConAu 33*
Briggs, Frank A 1872- *TexWr*
Briggs, Frederick W *Alli Sup*
Briggs, G W *WebEAL*
Briggs, G Wright 1916- *AmSCAP 66*
Briggs, George Edward 1893- *WrD 1976*
Briggs, George M 1919- *ConAu 33*
Briggs, George Waverley 1883- *Alli Sup,*
TexWr, WhWNAA
Briggs, Henry *Alli Sup*
Briggs, Henry 1556-1630 *Alli*
Briggs, Henry George *Alli Sup*
Briggs, Henry Perronet 1791-1844 *ChPo*
Briggs, Isabella McKelvey *ChPo*
Briggs, J *Alli*
Briggs, J P *Alli Sup*
Briggs, James *Alli, BiDLA*
Briggs, Jean 1925- *WrD 1976*
Briggs, Jimuel *DcNAA*
Briggs, John *ChPo S1*
Briggs, John 1785-1875 *Alli, Alli Sup*
Briggs, John Ely 1890- *WhWNAA*
Briggs, John Joseph 1819-1876 *Alli Sup*
Briggs, Joseph *Alli*
Briggs, Katharine Mary 1898- *Au&Wr,*
ChPo S2, ConAu 9R, WrD 1976
Briggs, Kenneth R 1934- *ConAu 33,*
WrD 1976
Briggs, L Cabot 1909-1975 *ConAu 5R,*

ConAu 57
Briggs, LeBaron Russell 1855-1934 *AmA&B,*
ChPo, DcAmA, DcNAA, OxAm, REnAL
Briggs, Lloyd Vernon 1863-1941 *AmA&B,*
DcNAA, WhWNAA
Briggs, M C *Alli Sup*
Briggs, Margaret Perkins *AnMV 1926*
Briggs, Marvin O *TexWr*
Briggs, Mary B *Alli Sup*
Briggs, Michael Harvey 1935- *Au&Wr*
Briggs, Milton *Alli Sup*
Briggs, Mitchell Pirie 1892- *AmA&B*
Briggs, Olive M 1873- *WhWNAA*
Briggs, Peter 1921-1975 *ConAu 25, ConAu 57*
Briggs, R C 1915- *ConAu 37*
Briggs, Raymond Redvers 1934- *Au&Wr, BkP,*
ChPo, ChPo S1, ChPo S2, IlBYP,
IlCB 1966, ThBJA
WhCL
Briggs, Richard *Alli*
Briggs, Robert *Alli*
Briggs, S R *Alli Sup*
Briggs, Sam *ChPo S2*
Briggs, T R Archer *Alli Sup*
Briggs, Thomas *Alli Sup, BbtC*
Briggs, Thomas Henry 1877- *REnAL,*
WhWNAA
Briggs, William *Alli Sup*
Briggs, William 1650?-1704 *Alli*
Briggs, William Harlowe 1876-1952 *AmA&B*
Briggs, William M *ChPo, ChPo S1*
Brigham, A *Alli Sup*
Brigham, Albert Perry 1855-1932 *DcNAA,*
WhWNAA
Brigham, Amariah 1798-1849 *Alli, DcAmA,*
DcNAA
Brigham, Besmilr 1923- *ConAu 29,*
DrAF 1976, DrAP 1975, WrD 1976
Brigham, Carl Campbell 1890-1943 *DcNAA,*
WhWNAA
Brigham, Charles Henry 1820-1879 *Alli,*
DcNAA
Brigham, Clarence Saunders 1877-1963
AmA&B, ChPo, WhWNAA
Brigham, Gershom Nelson 1820-1886 *Alli Sup,*
DcAmA, DcNAA
Brigham, Gertrude Richardson *AmA&B,*
AmLY, WhWNAA
Brigham, Grace *IlBYP*
Brigham, Harold Frederick 1897- *WhWNAA*
Brigham, Henry Randolph 1880- *WhWNAA*
Brigham, John C 1942- *ConAu 41*
Brigham, Johnson 1846-1936 *AmLY, DcNAA*
Brigham, Nicholas d1559 *Alli*
Brigham, Reed O 1888- *WhWNAA*
Brigham, Sarah Jeannette 1835-1929 *Alli Sup,*
ChPo, ChPo S1, DcAmA, DcNAA
Brigham, Sarah Prentice 1833- *Alli Sup,*
DcAmA
Brigham, Willard Irving Tyler 1859-1904
DcNAA
Brigham, William Tufts 1841-1926 *Alli Sup,*
DcAmA, DcNAA, WhWNAA
Brighouse, Harold 1882-1958 *CnMD, CnThe,*
DcLEnL, LongC, McGWD, ModWD,
NewC, TwCA, TwCA Sup, TwCW,
WebEAL, WhLA
Brighouse, J H *Alli Sup*
Bright, A W And Medd, G P *Alli Sup*
Bright, Amanda M *Alli Sup, BiDSA,*
LivFWS
Bright, Mrs. Augustus *Alli Sup*
Bright, Bruce Norman Francis 1919- *Au&Wr*
Bright, C A *MnBBF*
Bright, Charles *Alli Sup*
Bright, Edward Brailsford *Alli Sup*
Bright, Florence E *ChPo S1*
Bright, George *Alli*
Bright, Hazel *BlkAW*
Bright, Henry *Alli*
Bright, Henry Arthur 1830-1884 *Alli Sup*
Bright, Henry S *Alli Sup*
Bright, Houston 1916- *AmSCAP 66*
Bright, J H 1804-1837 *Alli, ChPo S1*
Bright, J M *Alli Sup*
Bright, J S *Alli Sup*
Bright, Jacob 1821- *Alli Sup*
Bright, James *Alli Sup, MnBBF*

Bright, James Franck 1832- *Alli Sup*
Bright, James Wilson 1852-1926 *AmA&B, DcNAA*
Bright, John *Alli Sup, Chmbr 3*
Bright, John 1811-1889 *Alli Sup, BbD, BiD&SB, NewC, REn*
Bright, John 1908- *AmA&B, ConAu 5R*
Bright, Jonathan Brown 1800-1879 *Alli Sup, CyAL 2, DcNAA*
Bright, Leonore *ChPo*
Bright, Mary Chavelita 1860-1945 *EvLB, LongC, TwCA, TwCA Sup*
Bright, Matilda A *Alli Sup*
Bright, Mynors 1818-1883 *Alli Sup*
Bright, Pamela 1914- *WrD 1976*
Bright, Richard 1789-1858 *Alli, Alli Sup*
Bright, Robert 1902- *AmA&B, AmNov, IlBYP, IlCB 1956, IlCB 1966, MorJA*
Bright, Ronnell L 1930- *AmSCAP 66*
Bright, Ruth Williams 1895?- *IndAu 1917*
Bright, Sol Kekipi 1919- *AmSCAP 66*
Bright, T *Alli Sup*
Bright, Timothy d1615? *Alli, DcEnL*
Bright, Verne 1893- *AnMV 1926, WhPNW, WhWNAA*
Bright, William *Alli Sup*
Bright, William 1824-1901 *Alli Sup, BrAu 19, ChPo S1, ChPo S2*
Bright, William 1928- *ConAu 33*
Brightbill, Charles K 1910- *ConAu 1R*
Brightland, John *Alli*
Brightley, Charles *Alli*
Brightly, Ben *MnBBF*
Brightly, Charles *BiDLA*
Brightly, Francis Frederick 1845-1920 *Alli Sup, DcAmA*
Brightly, Frank Frederick 1845-1920 *DcNAA*
Brightly, Frederick Charles 1812-1888 *Alli, Alli Sup, DcAmA, DcNAA*
Brightly, Joseph H 1818- *EarAB, EarAB Sup*
Brightman, Edgar Sheffield 1884-1953 *AmA&B, WhWNAA*
Brightman, Thomas 1557-1607 *Alli*
Brighton, Howard 1925- *ConAu 57*
Brighton, John George *Alli Sup*
Brighton, Wesley, Jr. *ConAu 57*
Brightwell, Cecilia Lucy 1811-1875 *Alli Sup, ChPo S1*
Brightwell, Leonard Robert 1889- *IlCB 1945, MnBBF*
Brightwell, Richard *Alli*
Brightwen, Eliza d1883 *Alli Sup*
Brightwen, Eliza 1830-1906 *BrAu 19*
Brigid, Saint 451?-525 *NewC*
Brignall, Edith *ChPo S1, ChPo S2*
Brignall, James *ChPo S2*
Brignano, Russell C 1935- *ConAu 57*
Brigola, Alfredo L 1923- *ConAu 41*
Brigstocke, Thomas d1881 *Alli Sup*
Brik, Osip Maximovich 1888- *CasWL*
Briley, Alice 1914- *ChPo*
Briley, John Richard 1925- *Au&Wr, WrD 1976*
Brilhart, John K 1929- *ConAu 23*
Brill, Abraham Arden 1874-1948 *AmA&B, DcNAA, REnAL, TwCA Sup, WhWNAA*
Brill, Alexander 1842- *WhLA*
Brill, Earl H 1925- *ConAu 17R*
Brill, Ethel C 1877- *AmA&B*
Brill, Francis *Alli Sup*
Brill, George Reiter 1867-1918 *ChPo S1, DcNAA*
Brill, Harvey Clayton 1881- *WhWNAA*
Brill, Reginald 1902- *Au&Wr*
Brillant, Jacques *OxCan Sup*
Brillat-Savarin, Anthelme 1755-1826 *AtlBL, BbD, BiD&SB, CasWL, EuA, EvEuW, NewC, OxEng, OxFr, REn*
Brilliant, Alan 1936- *ConP 1970, ConP 1975, WrD 1976*
Brilliant, Richard 1929- *ConAu 33, WrD 1976*
Briloff, Abraham J 1917- *ConAu 61*
Brim, Orville G, Jr. 1923- *ConAu 5R*
Brimberg, Stanlee 1947- *ConAu 49, SmATA 9, WrD 1976*
Brimble, William *Alli*

Brimfield, H *Alli Sup*
Brimhall, Dean R 1886- *WhWNAA*
Brimhall, John 1928- *AmSCAP 66*
Briminstool, E A *ChPo*
Brimley, George 1819-1857 *Alli Sup, BrAu 19, DcEnL*
Brimmer, Martin 1829-1896 *DcAmA, DcNAA*
Brimsmead, William *Alli*
Brin, Alexander 1895- *WhWNAA*
Brin, Herb 1915- *ConAu 49*
Brin, Ruth Firestone 1921- *ConAu 17R*
Brincken, Baroness Gertrud VonDen 1892- *WhLA*
Brinckerhoff, Isaac W 1821-1910 *DcNAA*
Brinckerinck, Johannes 1359-1419 *CasWL*
Brinckle, Joshua Gordon d1880 *Alli Sup, DcNAA*
Brinckle, William Draper 1798- *Alli*
Brinckloe, Julie *IlBYP*
Brinckloe, William Draper 1872-1933 *DcNAA*
Brinckmair, L *Alli*
Brinckman, Arthur *Alli Sup*
Brinckman, John 1814-1870 *CasWL, EuA, OxGer*
Brinckman, Rosemary *ChPo*
Brinckmann, Albert Erich 1881- *WhLA*
Brindel, June Rachuy 1919- *ConAu 49, SmATA 7*
Brindle, Ernest *MnBBF*
Brindle, Reginald Smith 1917- *WrD 1976*
Brindley, James 1716-1772 *Alli*
Brindley, James 1860?- *Br&AmS*
Brindley, Louis H *PoIre*
Brindley, R Baldwin *Alli Sup*
Brindley, Thomas Bardel *Alli Sup*
Brindley, Walter F *Alli Sup*
Brindze, Ruth 1903- *AuBYP, MorJA*
Brine, Bessie *ChPo S2*
Brine, Emily *Alli Sup*
Brine, Frederic 1829- *Alli Sup*
Brine, John 1703-1765 *Alli*
Brine, Lindesay 1834- *Alli Sup*
Brine, Louie *ChPo S1*
Brine, Mary Dow 1838-1925 *Alli Sup, AmA&B, ChPo, ChPo S1, ChPo S2, DcAmA, DcNAA*
Briney, John Benton 1839- *DcNAA*
Briney, Robert E 1933- *ConAu 53, EncM&D*
Bringhurst, Isaac *Alli*
Bringhurst, J *Alli*
Bringhurst, Nettie Houston *BiDSA*
Bringhurst, Nettie Power 1852-1932 *ChPo S1*
Bringhurst, Robert 1946- *ConAu 57*
Bringhurst, Thomas H And Swigart, Frank *Alli Sup*
Bringhurst, Thomas Hall 1819-1899 *IndAu 1816*
Brinig, Myron 1900- *AmA&B, AmNov, OxAm, REnAL, TwCA, TwCA Sup*
Brinin, John Malcolm 1916- *ChPo S2*
Brininstool, Earl Alonzo 1870-1957 *AmA&B, ChPo S1, WhWNAA*
Brinitzer, Carl 1907-1974 *ConAu 5R, ConAu 53*
Brink, Andre Philippe 1935- *CasWL, Pen Cl*
Brink, Carol Ryrie 1895- *AmA&B, AnCL, Au&Wr, AuBYP, ChPo S1, ConAu 1R, JBA 1951, MnnWr, MorBMP, Newb 1922, REnAL, SmATA 1, St&VC, WhPNW, WrD 1976*
Brink, Jan Ten 1834-1901 *BbD, BiD&SB, CasWL*
Brink, Raymond Woodard 1890- *WhWNAA*
Brinker, Martin *WhWNAA*
Brinker, Paul A 1919- *ConAu 25*
Brinkerhoff, H R *Alli Sup*
Brinkerhoff, Henry B 1836- *OhA&B*
Brinkerhoff, Robert Moore 1880-1958 *OhA&B, WhWNAA*
Brinkerhoff, Roeliff 1828-1911 *Alli Sup, DcNAA, OhA&B*
Brinkley, George A 1931- *ConAu 17R*
Brinkley, John 1763-1836 *Alli, BiDLA*
Brinkley, May 1898- *AnMV 1926*
Brinkley, William 1917- *AmA&B, Au&Wr, ConAu 21*
Brinkman, Gabriel 1924- *IndAu 1917*
Brinkman, George L 1942- *ConAu 53*

Brinkmann, Carl 1885- *WhLA*
Brinkmann, Ludwig 1880- *WhLA*
Brinkmann, Rolf Dieter 1940- *ModGL*
Brinks, Herbert J 1935- *ConAu 29*
Brinley, Bertrand R 1917- *ConAu 29*
Brinley, Charles Augustus 1847-1919 *DcNAA*
Brinley, Francis 1800-1889 *Alli Sup, CyAL 2, DcNAA*
Brinley, Gordon *OxCan*
Brinley, John *Alli*
Brinley, Kathrine Gordon Sanger d1966 *AmA&B*
Brinnin, John Malcolm 1916- *AmA&B, Au&Wr, ChPo, ConAu 1R, ConP 1970, ConP 1975, DrAP 1975, OxAm, Pen Am, REn, REnAL, TwCA Sup, WhTwL, WrD 1976*
Brinsley, John *Alli*
Brinsley, John 1600-1665 *Alli*
Brinsley, William *Alli*
Brinsley-Richards *Alli Sup*
Brinsmade, Robert Bruce 1873-1936 *DcNAA, WhWNAA*
Brinsmead, Edgar *Alli Sup*
Brinsmead, Hesba Fay 1922- *ConAu 21, SenS, WrD 1976*
Brinson, Rosemary Greene 1917- *AmSCAP 66*
Brinton, Christian 1870-1942 *AmA&B, DcNAA*
Brinton, Clarence Crane 1898- *TwCA, TwCA Sup*
Brinton, Crane 1898-1968 *AmA&B, ConAu 5R, ConAu 25, REn, REnAL*
Brinton, Daniel Garrison 1837-1899 *Alli Sup, AmA, AmA&B, BiD&SB, CyAL 2, DcAmA, DcNAA, OxAm*
Brinton, Edward 1924- *IndAu 1917*
Brinton, Henry 1901- *Au&Wr, ConAu 1R*
Brinton, Howard Haines 1884- *Au&Wr, ConAu 5R, REnAL*
Brinton, John Hill 1832-1907 *DcNAA*
Brinton, Selwyn 1860- *WhLA*
Brinton, Willard Cope 1880- *WhWNAA*
Brinton, William 1823-1867 *Alli Sup*
Brinvilliers, Marie-M, Marquise De 1630-1676 *OxFr, REn*
Brioche, Jean *OxFr*
Brion, Friederike 1752-1813 *OxGer*
Brion, Guy *ConAu XR*
Brion, John M 1922- *ConAu 23*
Brion, Marcel 1895- *Au&Wr*
Brisbane, Abbott Hall 1800?-1861 *BiDSA*
Brisbane, Albert 1809-1890 *AmA, AmA&B, DcNAA, OxAm, REnAL*
Brisbane, Albert Hall 1800?-1861 *DcNAA*
Brisbane, Arthur 1864-1936 *AmA&B, DcNAA, OxAm, REnAL, TwCA*
Brisbane, Coutts *MnBBF*
Brisbane, Emily *Alli Sup*
Brisbane, Holly E 1927- *ConAu 33*
Brisbane, John *Alli*
Brisbane, Robert Hughes 1913- *LivBA*
Brisbane, Sir Thomas *Alli*
Brisbane, William Henry 1803?-1878 *Alli Sup, DcNAA*
Brisbin, James Sanks 1837-1892 *Alli Sup, DcAmA, DcNAA*
Brisco, Norris Arthur 1875-1944 *DcNAA*
Brisco, Patricia 1927- *ConAu 29*
Brisco, Patty *ConAu XR*
Briscoe, Mrs. *Alli Sup*
Briscoe, Charles Francis 1868- *WhWNAA*
Briscoe, Chesley 1900- *AmSCAP 66*
Briscoe, D Stuart 1930- *ConAu 17R*
Briscoe, Ernest Edward 1882- *MnBBF*
Briscoe, Herman Thompson 1893-1960 *IndAu 1917*
Briscoe, Jill 1935- *ConAu 61*
Briscoe, John Daly 1827- *Alli Sup*
Briscoe, John Potter 1848-1926 *Alli Sup, ChPo S1*
Briscoe, Margaret Sutton *AmA&B, BiDSA, DcNAA*
Brisebarre, Edouard Louis 1818-1871 *BiD&SB*
Briskin, Jacqueline 1927- *ConAu 29*
Brisley, Joyce Lankester 1896- *Au&Wr, ChPo, ChPo S1, WrD 1976*
Brisman *Alli*

Brisman, Leslie 1944- *ConAu 61*
Briss, Vida *ChPo, ChPo S2*
Brissaud, E *Alli Sup*
Brissenden, Paul Frederick 1885-1974 *ConAu 17, ConAu 53, WhWNAA*
Brissenden, R F 1928- *ConAu 23*
Brissot, Jacques Pierre 1754-1793 *REn*
Brissot, Jean-Pierre 1754-1793 *OxFr*
Bristead, John *Alli*
Bristed, Charles Astor 1820-1874 *Alli, Alli Sup, AmA&B, BiD&SB, CyAL 2, DcAmA, DcNAA*
Bristed, Ezekiel *Alli*
Bristed, John 1778-1855 *Alli, AmA, AmA&B, BiDLA, CyAL 1, DcAmA, DcNAA*
Brister, C W 1926- *ConAu 13R*
Brister, Iola M *BlkAW*
Brister, Richard 1915- *ConAu 13R, WrD 1976*
Bristol, Bishop Of *BiDLA*
Bristol, Earl Of 1612-1677 *DcEnL*
Bristol, Earls Of *Alli*
Bristol, Augusta Cooper 1835-1910 *Alli Sup, ChPo S1, ChPo S2, DcAmA, DcNAA*
Bristol, Elias Leroy Macomb 1852?-1929 *Alli Sup, DcNAA*
Bristol, Frank Milton 1851-1932 *DcAmA, DcNAA*
Bristol, George Digby, Earl Of 1612-1677 *BrAu, DcEuL*
Bristol, John Isaac Devoe 1845-1932 *DcNAA*
Bristol, Bishop John Of *Alli*
Bristol, Julius *ConAu XR*
Bristol, Lee H, Jr. 1923- *ConAu 5R*
Bristol, Margaret *AmSCAP 66*
Bristol, Mary C *Alli Sup*
Bristol, R S *Alli Sup*
Bristol, Mrs. S A *Alli Sup*
Bristol, Sherlock 1815-1906 *DcNAA*
Briston, Mrs. A *Alli*
Bristow, Helen *Alli Sup*
Bristow, Mrs. A *BiDLA, PoIre*
Bristow, Allen P 1929- *ConAu 21*
Bristow, Gwen 1903- *AmA&B, AmNov, Au&Wr, ConAu 17R, EncM&D, REnAL, TwCA, TwCA Sup, WhWNAA, WrD 1976*
Bristow, Henry William 1817- *Alli Sup*
Bristow, J A *Alli, BiDLA*
Bristow, J C *Alli*
Bristow, James *Alli, BiDLA*
Bristow, James Francis 1918- *Au&Wr*
Bristow, John *Alli Sup*
Bristow, Richard 1538-1581 *Alli*
Bristow, Robert O'Neil 1926- *ConAu 25, WrD 1976*
Bristow, W *Alli, BiDLA*
Bristow, Whiston *BiDLA*
Bristow, Whitsen *Alli*
Bristow, William 1808- *BbtC*
Bristowe, Anthony 1921- *ConAu P-1*
Bristowe, Beatrice *Alli Sup*
Bristowe, John Syer *Alli Sup*
Bristowe, Samuel Boteler 1822- *Alli Sup*
Bristowe, Sibyl *ChPo S2*
Bristowe-Noble, J C *MnBBF*
Britain, Dan *ConAu XR*
Britain, Jonathan *Alli*
Britain, Radie 1904- *AmSCAP 66*
Britaine, William De *Alli*
Britan, Halbert Hains 1874-1945 *DcNAA, IndAu 1816, WhWNAA*
Britannicus 041?-055 *OxCan, REn*
Britcher, Phyllis 1900- *ChPo*
Britindian 1904- *ConAu XR, WrD 1976*
British Jeremiah, The *DcEnL*
British Pausanias, The *DcEnL*
British Settler, A *OxCan*
Britnell, G E *OxCan*
Brito, Bernardo De 1568-1617 *CasWL*
Brito, Phil 1915- *AmSCAP 66*
Briton, E Vincent *Alli Sup*
Briton, F *Alli Sup*
Britt, Addy 1891-1938 *AmSCAP 66*
Britt, Alan *DrAP 1975*
Britt, Albert 1874- *AmA&B, ConAu 5R*
Britt, Dell 1934- *ConAu 25, SmATA 1*
Britt, Elton 1913- *AmSCAP 66*

Britt, George 1895- *AmA&B*
Britt, Matthew 1872- *CatA 1952*
Britt, Nellie *BlkAW*
Britt, Sappho Henderson *AmA&B*
Britt, Steuart Henderson 1907- *ConAu 1R*
Britt, Thomas A *Alli Sup*
Brittain, Alfred 1867-1943 *DcNAA*
Brittain, Benjamin Edward 1913- *ChPo S1*
Brittain, C *Alli Sup*
Brittain, Carlo Bonaparte 1867-1920 *DcNAA*
Brittain, Frank Smith *Alli Sup*
Brittain, Frederick *Alli Sup, ChPo, ConAu 5R*
Brittain, Sir Harry 1873- *Au&Wr*
Brittain, Joan Tucker 1928- *ConAu 37*
Brittain, John 1849-1913 *DcNAA*
Brittain, Marion Luther 1866- *WhWNAA*
Brittain, Robert E *ChPo*
Brittain, Thomas 1806-1884 *Alli Sup*
Brittain, Vera Mary 1896-1970 *ChPo, ConAu 25, ConAu P-1, DcLEnL, EvLB, LongC, NewC, Pen Eng, REn, TwCA, TwCA Sup, TwCW*
Brittain, William Harold 1889- *WhWNAA*
Brittain, William James 1905- *Au&Wr*
Brittaine, Nicholas *NewC*
Brittan, Belle *Alli Sup, DcNAA*
Brittan, Charles Edward 1870- *IICB 1945*
Brittan, Harriette G 1823-1897 *Alli Sup, DcAmA, DcNAA*
Brittan, S B *Alli Sup*
Brittan, Samuel 1933- *ConAu 29*
Brittan, Samuel Byron d1883 *DcNAA*
Brittany, Louis *MnBBF*
Britten, Bashley *Alli Sup*
Britten, David Abbott 1912- *Au&Wr*
Britten, Edward Benjamin 1913- *ChPo S2*
Britten, Emma *Alli Sup*
Britten, F J *Alli Sup*
Britten, Frank Curzon *ChPo, MnBBF*
Britten, James *Alli Sup*
Britten Austin, Paul 1922- *ConAu 23*
Brittenden, Richard Trevor 1919- *Au&Wr*
Brittin, Norman Aylsworth 1906- *ConAu 17R, WrD 1976*
Britting, Georg 1891-1964 *EncWL, ModGL, OxGer, Pen Eur*
Brittle, Emily *Alli*
Brittle, Gath *ChPo S1*
Brittlebank, William *Alli Sup*
Britton, Alexander T *Alli Sup*
Britton, Dorothea S 1922- *ConAu 45*
Britton, Henry *Alli Sup*
Britton, Herbert *MnBBF*
Britton, Isaac W *EarAB*
Britton, James *ChPo*
Britton, Jessie L *ChPo S1*
Britton, John 1771-1857 *Alli, BiDLA, BiDLA Sup, DcEnL*
Britton, John J *Alli Sup*
Britton, Karl 1909- *ConAu 29, WrD 1976*
Britton, Mattie Lula Cooper 1914- *ConAu 5R*
Britton, Maxwell Edwin 1912- *IndAu 1917*
Britton, Nancy Pence *Au&Wr*
Britton, Nathaniel Lord 1859?-1934 *Alli Sup, BiD&SB, DcAmA, DcNAA*
Britton, Nicholas *Alli, NewC*
Britton, Rollin John 1863?-1931 *OhA&B, WhWNAA*
Britton, Thomas Allen *Alli Sup*
Britton, Thomas Hopkins 1817-1880 *Alli, Alli Sup*
Britton, Wiley *Alli Sup*
Britton, William Everett 1887- *WhWNAA*
Britton, Wilton Everett 1868-1939 *DcNAA*
Britts, Mattie Dyer 1842- *Alli Sup, DcAmA, DcNAA, IndAu 1816*
Britzius, Oscar 1906- *Au&Wr*
Briusov *TwCA, TwCA Sup*
Brixius *CasWL*
Brizeux, Auguste 1803-1858 *OxFr*
Brizeux, Julien Auguste Pelage 1803-1858 *BiD&SB, ChPo, EvEuW*
Brkic, Jovan 1927- *ConAu 41*
Bro, Harmon Hartzell 1919- *BiDPar, ConAu 25*
Bro, Marguerite 1894- *MorJA*
Broackes, William *Alli*

Broad, C E *Alli Sup*
Broad, Charles Lewis 1900- *ConAu 5R*
Broad, Charlie Dunbar 1887-1971 *Au&Wr, BiDPar, WhLA, WorAu*
Broad, Eric *ChPo S2*
Broad, George *Alli Sup*
Broad, Harold Peter 1909- *Au&Wr*
Broad, John *Alli Sup*
Broad, Thomas 1577-1639 *Alli*
Broad, Thomas D 1893- *TexWr*
Broadbeck, Captain *OhA&B*
Broadbent, *Alli*
Broadbent, Abel *MnBBF*
Broadbent, Adah L 1901-1970 *IndAu 1917*
Broadbent, Albert *ChPo S1*
Broadbent, D R *ChPo S2*
Broadbent, David *MnBBF*
Broadbent, Donald Eric 1926- *Au&Wr*
Broadbent, Edward 1936- *ConAu 45*
Broadbent, Henry *Alli Sup*
Broadbent, Joseph And Campin, Francis *Alli Sup*
Broadbent, William *Alli*
Broadbent, William Henry *Alli Sup*
Broadbottom, Geffery *NewC*
Broaddus, Andrew 1770-1848 *DcAmA, DcNAA*
Broaddus, Andrew 1818-1900 *Alli Sup, DcNAA*
Broaddus, J Morgan, Jr. 1929- *ConAu 21*
Broaddus, John 1770-1846 *BiDSA*
Broadfield, Aubrey Alfred 1910- *Au&Wr, WrD 1976*
Broadfoot, William *Alli Sup*
Broadhead, Garland Carr 1827- *BiDSA*
Broadhouse, John *Alli Sup*
Broadhurst, Alan Bagnall 1917- *Au&Wr, WrD 1976*
Broadhurst, Allan R 1932- *ConAu 5R*
Broadhurst, Cecil 1908- *AmSCAP 66*
Broadhurst, Edward *Alli*
Broadhurst, George Howells 1866-1952? *AmA&B, BiD&SB, DcNAA, ModWD, NewC, REnAL, TwCA, TwCA Sup*
Broadhurst, Henry 1840- *Alli Sup*
Broadhurst, Jean 1873- *WhWNAA*
Broadhurst, John *Alli Sup, BiDLA Sup*
Broadhurst, Ronald Joseph Callender 1906- *Au&Wr, ConAu P-1*
Broadhurst, Thomas *Alli, BiDLA*
Broadhurst, Thomas William 1857-1936 *DcNAA*
Broadley, Alexander Meyrick 1847- *Alli Sup*
Broadley, J *Alli Sup*
Broadley, John *Alli, BiDLA*
Broadley, Robert *Alli*
Broadley, Thomas *Alli, BiDLA*
Broadluck, Cephas *Alli Sup*
Broadribb, Violet *ConAu 41*
Broadus, Catherine 1929- *ConAu 37*
Broadus, Edmund Kemper 1876-1936 *DcLEnL, DcNAA, OxCan, WhWNAA*
Broadus, Eleanor H *OxCan*
Broadus, John Albert 1827-1895 *Alli Sup, BiDSA, DcAmA, DcNAA*
Broadus, Loren, Jr. 1928- *ConAu 37*
Broadus, Robert Deal *BlkAW*
Brobeck, Florence 1895- *OhA&B, WhWNAA*
Broby-Johansen, R 1900- *ConAu 25*
Brocardus, Francis *Alli*
Brocas, J *Alli, BiDLA*
Brocense, El *CasWL, DcSpL*
Broch, Hermann 1886-1951 *AmA&B, CasWL, ClDMEuL, CnMWL, CyWA, EncWL, ModGL, OxGer, Pen Eur, REn, TwCA, TwCA Sup, TwCW, WhTwL*
Broch, Hjalmar 1882- *WhLA*
Brochu, Andre 1942- *OxCan, OxCan Sup*
Brochu, Michel *OxCan Sup*
Brock, Alice May 1941- *ConAu 41*
Brock, Betty Carter 1923- *ConAu 29, SmATA 4, SmATA 7, WrD 1976*
Brock, Blanche Kerr 1888-1958 *AmSCAP 66*
Brock, C M *ChPo*
Brock, Mrs. Carey *ChPo, ChPo S1, DcEnL*
Brock, Charles Edmond 1870-1938 *ChPo, ChPo S1, JBA 1934, JBA 1951, WhCL*
Brock, Clutton- *TwCA, TwCA Sup*

Brokamp, Marilyn 1920- *ConAu 49,* *SmATA 10*
Brokamp, Ruth 1920- *IndAu 1917*
Brokaw, Clare Boothe *AmA&B*
Brokaw, Irving 1869-1939 *DcNAA*
Broke, Arthur d1563 *Alli, CasWL, Chmbr 1,* *EvLB, NewC*
Broke, John Gardener *Alli*
Broke, Sir P B V 1776-1840 *BbtC*
Broke, Sir Robert *Alli*
Broke, Thomas *Alli*
Brokensha, David W 1923- *ConAu 25*
Brokesby, Francis 1637-1715 *Alli*
Broket, John *Alli*
Brokhin, Yuri 1934- *ConAu 57*
Brokhoff, John R 1913- *ConAu 61*
Brokis, James *Alli*
Brokmeyer, Henry Conrad 1828-1906 *AmA&B,* *DcNAA*
Brokor, Gulabdas *DcOrL 2*
Brom *AmA&B*
Bromage, James Gosling *Alli Sup*
Bromage, Mary Cogan 1906- *ConAu P-1*
Brombart, Marcel 1907- *Au&Wr*
Bromberg, Walter 1900- *AmA&B*
Bromberger, Serge Paul 1912- *ConAu 29*
Brombert, Victor Henri 1923- *AmA&B,* *ConAu 13R*
Bromby, Charles Henry 1814- *Alli Sup*
Bromby, J H *Alli, BiDLA*
Bromby, W M *Alli Sup*
Brome, Alexander 1620-1666 *Alli, BiD&SB,* *CasWL, DcEnL, NewC, REn*
Brome, Edmund *Alli*
Brome, James *Alli*
Brome, Richard 1590-1652 *Alli, BiD&SB,* *BrAu, CasWL, ChPo, Chmbr 1, CnThe,* *CrE&SL, CriT 1, CyWA, DcEnL, EvLB,* *McGWD, NewC, OxEng, Pen Eng, REn,* *REnWD, WebEAL*
Brome, Vincent *Au&Wr, WrD 1976*
Brome, William *Alli*
Bromehead, Alexander Crawford *Alli Sup*
Bromehead, Elizabeth A *Alli Sup*
Bromehead, Joseph *Alli*
Bromehead, William Crawford- *Alli Sup*
Bromell, Henry 1942- *ConLC 5*
Bromell, Henry 1947- *ConAu 53, DrAF 1976,* *WrD 1976*
Bromesgrove, Samuel *Alli*
Bromfield, Annette Maria Coulton 1863-1947 *OhA&B*
Bromfield, Elizabeth *Alli Sup*
Bromfield, James *Alli Sup*
Bromfield, Louis 1896-1956 *AmA&B, AmNov,* *CnDAL, ConAmA, ConAmL, CyWA,* *DcBiA, DcLEnL, EncWL, EvLB, LongC,* *OhA&B, OxAm, Pen Am, REn, REnAL,* *TwCA, TwCA Sup, TwCW, WhWNAA*
Bromfield, Mary E *Alli Sup*
Bromfield, William *Alli*
Bromfield, Sir William 1712-1792 *Alli*
Bromfield, William Arnold *Alli Sup*
Bromhall, Thomas *Alli*
Bromhall, Winifred *ChPo, ConICB, IlBYP,* *IlCB 1945, IlCB 1956, MorJA*
Bromhead, E F *Alli*
Bromhead, Peter Alexander 1919- *ConAu 61,* *WrD 1976*
Bromige, David Mansfield 1935- *ConAu 25,* *ConP 1970, ConP 1975, DrAF 1976,* *DrAP 1975, WrD 1976*
Bromige, Iris Amy Edna 1910- *Au&Wr*
Bromiley, Geoffrey William 1915- *Au&Wr,* *ConAu 5R, WrD 1976*
Bromke, Adam 1928- *ConAu 13R, WrD 1976*
Bromley, Clara Fitzroy *Alli Sup*
Bromley, David G 1941- *ConAu 41*
Bromley, Eliza Nugent *Alli, BiDLA*
Bromley, Sir George *Alli*
Bromley, Gordon 1910- *WrD 1976*
Bromley, Henry *Alli, Alli Sup, BiDLA,* *BiDLA Sup*
Bromley, Henry Walter 1879- *WhWNAA*
Bromley, Isaac Hill 1833-1898 *AmA&B, ChPo*
Bromley, John d1717 *Alli*
Bromley, John Carter 1937- *ConAu 33*
Bromley, M I *Alli Sup*
Bromley, Robert Anthony d1806 *Alli*

Bromley, Samuel *Alli Sup*
Bromley, Thomas *Alli*
Bromley, Walter *Alli, BbtC, BiDLA,* *BiDLA Sup*
Bromley, William *Alli*
Bromley-Davenport *Alli Sup*
Bromme, *BbtC*
Brompton, John *Alli*
Bromwell, Henry Pelham Holmes 1823-1903 *DcNAA*
Bromwich *Alli*
Bromwich, Bryan J *Alli, BiDLA*
Bromwich, Thomas J I'A 1875- *WhLA*
Bromyard, Dorothy *Alli Sup*
Bromyard, John Of d1419 *DcEnL*
Bromyarde, John De d1419 *CasWL*
Brondgeest, J T *BbtC*
Brondsted, Holger Valdemar 1893- *Au&Wr*
Broner, E M *ConAu 17R, WrD 1976*
Bronfenbrenner, Martha 1878-1915 *DcNAA*
Bronfenbrenner, Martin 1914- *ConAu 13R*
Broniewski, Wladyslaw 1898?-1962 *CasWL,* *EncWL, ModSL 2*
Bronin, Andrew 1947- *ConAu 45*
Bronk, Isabelle 1858-1934 *DcNAA,* *WhWNAA*
Bronk, Mitchell 1862- *WhWNAA*
Bronk, William *DrAP 1975*
Bronkhurst, H V P *Alli Sup*
Bronnen, Arnolt 1895-1959 *CnMD, CrCD,* *McGWD, ModWD, OxGer, REn*
Bronner, Augusta F 1881- *WhWNAA*
Bronner, Edwin Blaine 1920- *ConAu 5R,* *WrD 1976*
Bronner, Ferdinand 1867- *WhLA*
Bronner, Franz Xaver 1758-1850 *OxGer*
Bronner, Leonard, Jr. 1902- *ChPo*
Bronowski, Jacob 1908-1974 *AmA&B, AnCL,* *ConAu 1R, ConAu 53, DcLEnL, WorAu*
Bronsen, David 1926- *ConAu 37*
Bronson, Asa 1798-1866 *DcNAA*
Bronson, Benjamin 1896- *AmSCAP 66*
Bronson, Bertrand Harris 1902- *AmA&B,* *ConAu 61*
Bronson, Carrie Waterman *ChPo*
Bronson, Edgar Beecher 1856-1917 *DcNAA*
Bronson, Enos *ChPo S1*
Bronson, Francis Woolsey 1901-1966 *AmA&B*
Bronson, Harry G 1898- *WhWNAA*
Bronson, Henry 1804-1893 *Alli Sup, DcNAA*
Bronson, Howard Logan 1878- *WhWNAA*
Bronson, Jessica *TexWr*
Bronson, Lita *ConAu XR*
Bronson, Lynn *AuBYP, ConAu XR, MorJA,* *SmATA 4*
Bronson, Miles *Alli Sup*
Bronson, Oliver *ConAu XR*
Bronson, Sherlock Anson 1807-1890 *Alli Sup,* *DcNAA, OhA&B*
Bronson, Thomas Bertrand 1857- *WhWNAA*
Bronson, Walter Cochrane 1862-1928 *AmA&B,* *DcAmA, DcNAA*
Bronson, Wilfred Swancourt 1894- *AmA&B,* *AuBYP, IlCB 1945, IlCB 1956,* *JBA 1934, JBA 1951, St&VC*
Bronson, William 1926- *ConAu 41*
Bronson, William White 1816-1900 *Alli Sup,* *DcNAA*
Bronson-Howard, George Fitzalan 1884-1922 *DcNAA, EncM&D*
Bronsted, P O *Alli*
Bronstein, Arthur J 1914- *ConAu 9R,* *WrD 1976*
Bronstein, Lev Davidovich *DcRusL, REn*
Bronstein, Yetta *ConAu XR*
Bronston, William *WrD 1976*
Bronte, Anne 1820-1849 *BbD, BiD&SB,* *BrAu 19, CasWL, ChPo, ChPo S1,* *Chmbr 3, CyWA, DcBiA, DcEnA,* *DcEnA Ap, DcEnL, DcEuL, DcLEnL,* *EvLB, OxEng, Pen Eng, RAdv 1,* *WebEAL*
Bronte, Anne, Charlotte, And Emily *PoIre*
Bronte, Charlotte 1816-1855 *Alli, AtlBL, BbD,* *BiD&SB, BrAu 19, CasWL, ChPo,* *ChPo S1, ChPo S2, Chmbr 3, CriT 3,* *CyWA, DcBiA, DcEnA, DcEnA Ap,* *DcEnL, DcEuL, DcLEnL, EvLB,*

HsB&A, MouLC 3, OxEng, Pen Eng, *RAdv 1, RCom, WebEAL*
Bronte, Emily Jane 1818-1848 *AtlBL, BbD,* *BiD&SB, BrAu 19, CasWL, ChPo,* *ChPo S1, ChPo S2, Chmbr 3, CnE&AP,* *CriT 3, CyWA, DcBiA, DcEnA,* *DcEnA Ap, DcEnL, DcEuL, DcLEnL,* *EvLB, MouLC 3, OxEng, Pen Eng,* *RAdv 1, RCom, WebEAL*
Bronte, Louisa *ConAu XR*
Bronte, Patrick 1777-1861 *Alli, BiDLA, PoIre*
Bronte, Patrick Branwell 1817-1848 *ChPo S1,* *DcEuL, PoIre*
Bronte Family *LongC, NewC, REn*
Bronte Sisters, The *RAdv 1*
Brontes, The *DcEnL, DcLEnL*
Brontius *Alli*
Bronwell, Arthur B 1909- *ConAu 33,* *WrD 1976*
Bronzino, Il 1503-1572 *AtlBL, REn*
Brood, Norman *MnBBF*
Brook, Abraham *Alli, BiDLA*
Brook, Mrs. Alexander *AmA&B*
Brook, Barry S 1918- *AmSCAP 66,* *ConAu 25*
Brook, Benjamin *Alli, BiDLA*
Brook, David 1932- *ConAu 13R, WrD 1976*
Brook, Eric *MnBBF*
Brook, George Leslie 1910- *Au&Wr,* *WrD 1976*
Brook, Henrietta R *ChPo S2*
Brook, John *Alli Sup*
Brook, Jonathan *Alli*
Brook, Leon *Alli Sup*
Brook, Leslie 1910- *ConAu 9R*
Brook, Nelsie *Alli Sup*
Brook, Peter 1925- *Au&Wr, CrCD*
Brook, Rachel *ChPo S1*
Brook, Richard *Alli Sup*
Brook, Sarah *Alli Sup*
Brook, Victor John Knight 1887- *Au&Wr,* *ConAu 1R*
Brook-Shepherd, Gordon 1918- *Au&Wr,* *ConAu 9R*
Brookbank, Joseph 1612- *Alli*
Brooke, Baron *CasWL, NewC*
Brooke, Lord *BrAu, Chmbr 1, DcEnL,* *WebEAL*
Brooke, Major *Alli*
Brooke, Miss *BiDLA, PoIre*
Brooke, A B *ConAu XR*
Brooke, Arthur *Alli, Alli Sup, CasWL,* *EvLB, MnBBF, NewC*
Brooke, Arthur d1563? *DcEnL*
Brooke, Arthur St. Clair *ChPo*
Brooke, Avery 1923- *ConAu 57*
Brooke, Brian 1889-1916 *ChPo S1, ChPo S2*
Brooke, Bryan Nicholas 1915- *ConAu 45,* *WrD 1976*
Brooke, C P *Alli Sup*
Brooke, Caris *ChPo S1*
Brooke, Carol *ConAu XR, WrD 1976*
Brooke, Charles *Alli Sup*
Brooke, Charles Frederick Tucker 1883-1946 *DcNAA, TwCA Sup*
Brooke, Charles Kennedy *Alli Sup*
Brooke, Charlotte *Alli*
Brooke, Charlotte 1740-1793 *CasWL,* *Chmbr 2, DcEnL, DcEuL, DcLEnL,* *EvLB, PoIre*
Brooke, Christopher d1627 *Alli, DcLEnL*
Brooke, Christopher Nugent Lawrence 1927- *Au&Wr, ConAu 5R, WrD 1976*
Brooke, Clara J *ChPo S1*
Brooke, DeCapell *Alli*
Brooke, Dinah 1936- *ConAu 49, WrD 1976*
Brooke, E Adveno *Alli Sup*
Brooke, E F *Alli Sup*
Brooke, Edward *Alli*
Brooke, Emma Frances d1926 *NewC*
Brooke, Frances 1724?-1789 *Alli, BbtC,* *CanWr, DcEnL, DcLEnL, NewC, OxCan,* *PoIre, REn, REnAL*
Brooke, Francis Taliaferro 1763-1851 *Alli,* *DcNAA*
Brooke, Baron Fulke Greville 1554-1628 *Alli,* *EvLB*
Brooke, Geoffrey 1884?- *Br&AmS, WhLA*

Brooke, Mrs. George *ChPo S1*
Brooke, Gilbert Edward 1873- *WhLA*
Brooke, Henry *Alli*
Brooke, Henry 1703-1783 *Alli, BiD&SB,*
  BrAu, CasWL, Chmbr 2, CyWA, DcEnL,
  DcEuL, DcLEnL, EvLB, NewC, OxEng,
  Pen Eng, PoIre, REn
Brooke, Henry James *Alli*
Brooke, Hilary *ChPo*
Brooke, James *Alli, Alli Sup*
Brooke, Sir James 1803- *Alli*
Brooke, James Mark Saurin 1842- *Alli Sup,*
  PoIre
Brooke, Jocelyn 1908-1956 *ConAu 5R, LongC,*
  ModBL, TwCA Sup
Brooke, John *Alli*
Brooke, John 1920- *Au&Wr, WrD 1976*
Brooke, John Arthur *ChPo S2*
Brooke, John Charles 1748-1794 *Alli*
Brooke, John Thompson 1800-1861 *OhA&B*
Brooke, Laurence *Alli Sup*
Brooke, Leonard Leslie 1862-1940 *AnCL,*
  ChPo, ChPo S1, ConICB, IlBYP,
  JBA 1934, JBA 1951, St&VC, WhCL
Brooke, Mary 1833-1917? *DcNAA*
Brooke, Mary Gould 1858-1946 *OhA&B*
Brooke, Maxey 1913- *ConAu 9R*
Brooke, N *Alli, BiDLA*
Brooke, Nicholas Stanton 1924- *ConAu 25*
Brooke, R *Alli*
Brooke, Ralph d1625 *Alli*
Brooke, Richard 1791-1861 *Alli, Alli Sup*
Brooke, Richard Sinclair d1882 *Alli Sup,*
  PoIre
Brooke, Sir Robert d1558 *Alli*
Brooke, Lord Robert Greville *Alli*
Brooke, Rupert 1887-1915 *AtlBL, CasWL,*
  ChPo, ChPo S2, Chmbr 3, CnE&AP,
  CnMWL, DcEuL, DcLEnL, EncWL,
  EvLB, LongC, ModBL, ModBL Sup,
  NewC, OxCan, OxEng, Pen Eng,
  RAdv 1, REn, TwCA, TwCA Sup,
  TwCW, WebEAL, WhTwL
Brooke, Rupert, Brown, J, And Browne, T
  DcEuL
Brooke, St. George Tucker 1844-1914 *BiDSA,*
  DcNAA
Brooke, Stopford Augustus 1832-1916 *Alli Sup,*
  BbD, BiD&SB, BrAu 19, ChPo,
  ChPo S1, ChPo S2, Chmbr 3,
  DcEnA Ap, DcEnL, DcEuL, DcLEnL,
  EvLB, LongC, NewC, Pen Eng, PoIre
Brooke, T *Alli*
Brooke, T H *Alli, BiDLA*
Brooke, Thomas *Alli, Alli Sup*
Brooke, Thomas Digby *Alli, BiDLA, PoIre*
Brooke, Tucker 1883-1946 *AmA&B, AmLY,*
  LongC, REnAL
Brooke, W B *Alli Sup*
Brooke, W H *Alli, BiDLA*
Brooke, Wesley *DcNAA*
Brooke, William *Alli, BiDLA*
Brooke, William G *Alli Sup*
Brooke, William T *Alli Sup*
Brooke, Z *Alli*
Brooke-Haven, P *ConAu XR*
Brooke-Little, John Philip Brooke 1927-
  Au&Wr, ConAu 23, WrD 1976
Brooke-Rose, Christine 1923- *ModBL,*
  ModBL Sup
Brooke-Rose, Christine 1926- *Au&Wr,*
  ConAu 13R, ConNov 1972, ConNov 1976,
  TwCW, WorAu, WrD 1976
Brooker, Bertram 1888-1955 *CanNov, DcLEnL,*
  OxCan
Brooker, Clark *ConAu XR, WrD 1976*
Brooker, Daniel *Alli*
Brooker, Louisa Jones 1869-1955 *OhA&B*
Brookes, C Bankes *Alli Sup*
Brookes, Calmer Frederick George 1820-
  Alli Sup
Brookes, E *Alli Sup*
Brookes, Edgar Harry 1897- *ConAu 1R,*
  WrD 1976
Brookes, Henry *Alli, Alli Sup*
Brookes, James Hall 1830-1897 *Alli Sup,*
  DcNAA
Brookes, John *Alli, Alli Sup*

Brookes, Joshua 1761-1833 *Alli*
Brookes, Kenneth Joseph Alban 1928- *Au&Wr*
Brookes, Matthew *Alli*
Brookes, Melanthe *Alli*
Brookes, Murray 1926- *Au&Wr, WrD 1976*
Brookes, Pamela 1922- *ConAu 25, WrD 1976*
Brookes, Reuben Solomon 1914- *Au&Wr,*
  ConAu P-1, WrD 1976
Brookes, Richard *Alli*
Brookes, Samuel *Alli, Alli Sup, BiDLA Sup*
Brookes, Sheridan *PoIre*
Brookes, Stella Brewer *LivBA*
Brookes, Thomas d1680 *Alli*
Brookes, Vincent Joseph 1906- *Au&Wr,*
  WrD 1976
Brookes, W M *Alli Sup*
Brookesbank, John *Alli*
Brookfield, Arthur Montagu *Alli Sup*
Brookfield, Charles 1857-1913 *LongC*
Brookfield, Charles H E *Alli Sup*
Brookfield, Jane Octavia *Alli Sup*
Brookfield, William Henry 1809-1874 *Alli Sup,*
  NewC
Brookhouse, Christopher 1938- *ConAu 29,*
  DrAF 1976, DrAP 1975
Brookhouser, Frank 1912?-1975 *ConAu 1R,*
  ConAu 61
Brooking, Charles 1723-1759 *BkIE*
Brookings, Robert Somers 1850-1932 *DcNAA*
Brookman, Denise Cass 1921- *ConAu 1R*
Brookman, Rosina Francesca 1932- *ConAu 61*
Brookover, Wilbur Bone 1911- *ConAu 33,*
  IndAu 1917, WrD 1976
Brooks, A Russell 1906- *ConAu 33,*
  WrD 1976
Brooks, Abbie M *Alli Sup*
Brooks, Albert Ellison 1908- *WrD 1976*
Brooks, Alden 1883- *OhA&B*
Brooks, Alfred Hulse 1871-1924 *DcNAA*
Brooks, Alfred Mansfield *AmLY*
Brooks, Amy d1931 *AmA&B, AmLY, CarSB,*
  DcNAA, WhWNAA
Brooks, Anita 1914- *AuBYP, ConAu 17R,*
  SmATA 5
Brooks, Anne Sooy 1911- *AmSCAP 66*
Brooks, Anne Tedlock 1905- *ConAu 1R*
Brooks, Arthur 1845-1895 *Alli Sup, DcAmA,*
  DcNAA
Brooks, Benjamin Talbott 1885- *WhWNAA*
Brooks, Bryant Butler 1861-1944 *DcNAA*
Brooks, Byron Alden 1845-1911 *Alli Sup,*
  DcNAA
Brooks, C *Alli Sup*
Brooks, C Carlyle 1888- *ConAu P-1*
Brooks, C P *Alli Sup*
Brooks, Charles 1795-1872 *Alli Sup, DcAmA,*
  DcNAA
Brooks, Charles 1872- *WhWNAA*
Brooks, Charles Alvin 1871-1936 *DcNAA,*
  WhWNAA
Brooks, Charles B 1921- *ConAu 1R*
Brooks, Charles E 1921- *ConAu 53*
Brooks, Charles Franklin 1891- *WhWNAA*
Brooks, Charles Stephen 1878-1934 *AmA&B,*
  ConAmL, DcNAA, OhA&B, TwCA,
  TwCA Sup, WhWNAA
Brooks, Charles Timothy 1813-1883 *Alli,*
  Alli Sup, AmA, AmA&B, BiD&SB,
  ChPo, ChPo S1, ChPo S2, CyAL 2,
  DcAmA, DcNAA, OxAm, PoCh
Brooks, Charles Walker 1912- *AmA&B*
Brooks, Charles Wesley 1836-1911 *DcNAA*
Brooks, Charles William Shirley 1816-1874 *Alli,*
  Alli Sup, BbD, BiD&SB, CasWL, ChPo,
  Chmbr 3, DcBiA, DcEnA Ap, DcEnL,
  DcLEnL, EvLB
Brooks, C W S ALSO Brooks, Shirley
Brooks, Charlotte K *AuBYP, LivBA*
Brooks, Chatty *OhA&B*
Brooks, Christopher Parkinson 1866-1909
  DcNAA
Brooks, Cleanth 1906- *AmA&B, CasWL,*
  ConAu 17R, DcLEnL, LongC, ModAL,
  OxAm, Pen Am, RAdv 1, REn, REnAL,
  TwCA Sup, WhTwL, WrD 1976
Brooks, Clyde 1881- *WhWNAA*
Brooks, Colin *MnBBF*
Brooks, Collin 1893- *ChPo S2*

Brooks, Constantina E *Alli Sup*
Brooks, D P 1915- *ConAu 25*
Brooks, David H 1929- *ConAu 61*
Brooks, Earl 1883-1968 *IndAu 1917*
Brooks, Edward 1831-1912 *Alli Sup, DcAmA,*
  DcNAA
Brooks, Edwin *BlkAW*
Brooks, Edwy Searles 1889-1965 *EncM&D,*
  MnBBF, WhCL
Brooks, Elbridge Gerry 1816-1878 *Alli Sup,*
  DcAmA
Brooks, Elbridge Streeter 1846-1902 *Alli Sup,*
  AmA, AmA&B, BbD, BiD&SB, CarSB,
  ChPo, DcAmA, DcNAA, JBA 1934,
  REnAL
Brooks, Eliphalet *OhA&B*
Brooks, Elisabeth Willard *DcNAA*
Brooks, Erastus 1815-1886 *DcNAA*
Brooks, Erica May *ChPo*
Brooks, Eugene Clyde 1871-1947 *AmA&B,*
  DcNAA
Brooks, F T *Alli Sup*
Brooks, Francis 1867-1898 *Alli, DcAmA,*
  DcNAA
Brooks, Fred Emerson 1850-1923? *AmA&B,*
  AmLY, ChPo, ChPo S1, DcAmA,
  DcNAA
Brooks, Fred Ernest 1868- *WhWNAA*
Brooks, Frederick 1842-1874 *Alli Sup*
Brooks, Gary D 1942- *ConAu 41*
Brooks, George *Alli Sup*
Brooks, George E, Jr. 1933- *ConAu 33,*
  WrD 1976
Brooks, George Sprague 1895- *WhWNAA*
Brooks, Geraldine 1875- *DcAmA*
Brooks, Glenn E, Jr. 1931- *ConAu 1R*
Brooks, Gwendolyn 1917- *AmA&B,*
  AuNews 01, BkCL, BlkAW, CasWL,
  ChPo, ChPo S1, ChPo S2, ConAu 1R,
  ConLC 1, ConLC 2, ConLC 4, ConLC 5,
  ConP 1970, ConP 1975, CrCAP,
  DrAP 1975, LivBA, ModAL,
  ModAL Sup, OxAm, Pen Am, RAdv 1,
  REnAL, SmATA 6, TwCA Sup,
  WrD 1976
Brooks, H *Alli Sup*
Brooks, Harlow 1879?-1936 *DcNAA,*
  WhWNAA
Brooks, Harry 1895- *AmSCAP 66*
Brooks, Harvey 1915- *ConAu 25*
Brooks, Harvey Oliver 1899- *AmSCAP 66*
Brooks, Harvey William *Alli Sup*
Brooks, Helen Morgan *BlkAW*
Brooks, Helena *Alli Sup*
Brooks, Henry *Alli Sup*
Brooks, Henry F *ChPo S2, PoIre*
Brooks, Henry James *Alli*
Brooks, Henry Mason *Alli Sup*
Brooks, Henry S 1830?-1910 *DcAmA, DcNAA*
Brooks, Henry Turner 1861-1946 *DcNAA*
Brooks, Hildegard 1875- *DcAmA*
Brooks, Hugh C 1922- *ConAu 29*
Brooks, Indiana *Alli*
Brooks, J F *Alli Sup*
Brooks, J P *Alli Sup*
Brooks, J S *Alli Sup*
Brooks, J T *Alli*
Brooks, J W *Alli*
Brooks, Jabez 1823-1910 *Alli Sup, DcNAA*
Brooks, Jack 1912- *AmSCAP 66*
Brooks, James *Alli*
Brooks, James 1810-1873 *Alli Sup, AmA&B,*
  DcNAA
Brooks, James Gordon 1801-1841 *Alli, AmA,*
  AmA&B, CyAL 2, DcEnL, DcNAA
Brooks, James J *Alli Sup*
Brooks, James Wilton 1853-1916 *DcNAA*
Brooks, Janet *BlkAW*
Brooks, Jennie 1853-1934 *DcNAA, OhA&B*
Brooks, Jeremy 1926- *Au&Wr, ConAu 5R,*
  ConNov 1972, ConNov 1976, WrD 1976
Brooks, Jerome 1931- *ConAu 49*
Brooks, John 1752-1825 *Alli*
Brooks, John 1920- *AmA&B, Au&Wr,*
  ConAu 13R
Brooks, John Benson 1917- *AmSCAP 66*
Brooks, John Graham 1846-1938 *BiD&SB,*
  DcAmA, DcNAA

Brooks, John P 1861- *WhWNAA*
Brooks, Jonathan *Alli, AmA&B*
Brooks, Jonathan Henderson 1904-1945 *BlkAW*
Brooks, Karen 1949- *ConAu 57*
Brooks, Kathleen Ida 1914- *Au&Wr*
Brooks, Keith 1923- *ConAu 17R*
Brooks, L *Alli Sup*
Brooks, Lake *OhA&B*
Brooks, Leonard 1911- *ConAu 13R*
Brooks, Leonard Harold d1950 *MnBBF*
Brooks, Lester 1924- *ConAu 33, SmATA 7*
Brooks, Lillie A 1874- *WhWNAA*
Brooks, Louis Thrush *ChPo S2*
Brooks, Louise *Alli Sup*
Brooks, Maria 1933- *ConAu 41*
Brooks, Maria Gowen 1795?-1845 *Alli, AmA, AmA&B, BiD&SB, ChPo S2, CnDAL, CyAL 1, DcAmA, DcEnL, DcNAA, EvLB, FemPA, OxAm, REnAL*
Brooks, Maria Sears d1893 *IndAu 1816*
Brooks, Martha *Alli Sup*
Brooks, Mary A *ChPo*
Brooks, Mary Elizabeth 1801-1841 *Alli, AmA, AmA&B, CyAL 2, FemPA*
Brooks, Mary Elizabeth 1925- *IndAu 1917*
Brooks, Matilda Moldenhauer *WhWNAA*
Brooks, Nathan Covington 1819?-1898 *Alli, BiDLA, CyAL 2, DcAmA, DcNAA*
Brooks, Nellie Sumner 1867- *OhA&B*
Brooks, Noah 1830-1903 *Alli Sup, AmA, AmA&B, BbD, BiD&SB, CarSB, DcAmA, DcNAA, JBA 1934, OxAm, REnAL*
Brooks, Pat 1931- *ConAu 57*
Brooks, Patricia 1926- *ConAu 25*
Brooks, Paul 1909- *ConAu 13R*
Brooks, Peter 1938- *ConAu 45*
Brooks, Peter Wright 1920- *Au&Wr, ConAu 9R, WrD 1976*
Brooks, Phillips 1835-1893 *Alli Sup, AmA&B, AnCL, BbD, BiD&SB, ChPo, ChPo S1, ChPo S2, Chmbr 3, DcAmA, DcNAA, OxAm, REnAL*
Brooks, Polly Schoyer 1912- *ConAu 1R*
Brooks, Ralph L 1901?-1965 *IndAu 1917*
Brooks, Richard 1912- *AmA&B, AmNov, ConDr*
Brooks, Robert Clarkson 1874-1941 *AmA&B, DcNAA, OhA&B*
Brooks, Robert Emanuel 1941- *ConAu 57*
Brooks, Robert Preston 1881- *WhWNAA*
Brooks, S H *Alli*
Brooks, Samuel *IndAu 1816*
Brooks, Samuel Palmer 1863- *BiDSA*
Brooks, Samuel Stevens 1890- *WhWNAA*
Brooks, Sarah Warner d1906 *AmA&B, ChPo S1, DcNAA*
Brooks, Shelton 1886- *AmSCAP 66*
Brooks, Shirley 1816-1874 *BrAu 19, ChPo S1*
Brooks, S ALSO Brooks, Charles W S
Brooks, Sidney 1892- *WhWNAA*
Brooks, Steve *DrAP 1975*
Brooks, Stewart M 1923- *ConAu 17R*
Brooks, Stratton D 1869- *WhWNAA*
Brooks, Sumner Cushing 1888- *WhWNAA*
Brooks, T B Harvey *Alli Sup*
Brooks, Thomas *Alli, Alli Sup*
Brooks, Thomas Benton 1836- *Alli Sup*
Brooks, Ulysses Robert 1846-1917 *BiDSA, DcNAA*
Brooks, Van Wyck 1886-1963 *AmA&B, AmLY, AmWr, AtlBL, CasWL, Chmbr 3, CnDAL, ConAmA, ConAmL, ConAu 1R, DcLEnL, EvLB, LongC, ModAL, OxAm, Pen Am, RAdv 1, REn, REnAL, TwCA, TwCA Sup, TwCW, WebEAL, WhWNAA*
Brooks, Vivian Collin 1922- *Au&Wr*
Brooks, W Hal 1933- *ConAu 57*
Brooks, Walter 1856-1933 *DcNAA*
Brooks, Walter Rollin 1886-1958 *AmA&B, ChPo, JBA 1951, WhWNAA*
Brooks, William Alexander *Alli Sup*
Brooks, William D 1929- *ConAu 33*
Brooks, William E 1875- *AnMV 1926, ChPo, ChPo S1, WhWNAA*
Brooks, William F *BlkAW*
Brooks, William Henry Salter *Alli Sup*

Brooks, William Keith 1848-1908 *Alli Sup, DcAmA, DcNAA, OhA&B*
Brooks, William Penn 1851-1938 *AmLY, DcNAA, WhWNAA*
Brooks, Winfield Sears 1902- *AmA&B*
Brooksbank, Joseph *Alli*
Brookshaw, George *Alli, BiDLA*
Brookshire, Elijah Voorhees 1856-1936 *DcNAA, IndAu 1917*
Brookter, Marie 1934?- *AuNews 1*
Broom, George J C *Alli Sup*
Broom, Herbert 1815-1882 *Alli, Alli Sup*
Broom, J E A *Alli Sup*
Broom, Leonard 1911- *AmA&B, ConAu 13R*
Broom, Thomas *Alli, BiDLA*
Broom, W W *Alli Sup*
Broome, Arthur *Alli, Alli Sup, BiDLA Sup*
Broome, Charles L 1925- *ConAu 41*
Broome, Edward W *Alli Sup*
Broome, Sir Frederick Napier 1842- *Alli Sup*
Broome, Isaac 1835-1922 *DcNAA*
Broome, Jack 1901- *Au&Wr*
Broome, John Egerton *ChPo S1*
Broome, John Henry *Alli Sup*
Broome, Lady Mary Ann d1911 *Alli Sup, CasWL, MnBBF*
Broome, Ralph *Alli, BiDLA*
Broome, Smith Sutton *WhWNAA*
Broome, William *Alli, Chmbr 2*
Broome, William 1689-1745 *Alli, CasWL, ChPo, DcEnL, EvLB, NewC*
Broomell, Isaac Norman 1861?-1941 *DcNAA, WhWNAA*
Broomell, Myron H 1906-1970 *ConAu P-1*
Broomfield, Gerald Webb 1895- *Au&Wr, ConAu 5R*
Broomfield, J H 1935- *ConAu 25*
Broomfield, James Polwarth *ChPo*
Broomfield, Robert 1930- *IlBYP, IlCB 1966*
Broomfield, William Robert *Alli Sup*
Broomhall, B *Alli Sup*
Broomsnodder, B MacKinley 1940- *ConAu 13R*
Broones, Martin *AmSCAP 66*
Brophy, Brigid 1929- *Au&Wr, CasWL, ConAu 5R, ConDr, ConLC 6, ConNov 1972, ConNov 1976, LongC, ModBL, ModBL Sup, NewC, TwCW, WhTwL, WorAu, WrD 1976*
Brophy, Donald F 1934- *ConAu 23*
Brophy, Dorothy Hall 1896- *WhWNAA*
Brophy, Elizabeth Bergen 1929- *ConAu 61*
Brophy, James David, Jr. 1926- *ConAu 1R*
Brophy, Jere 1940- *ConAu 45*
Brophy, John 1899-1965 *ConAu P-1, DcLEnL, EvLB, LongC, NewC, TwCA, TwCA Sup, TwCW*
Brophy, Liam 1910- *ConAu 9R*
Brophy, Liam 1916- *Au&Wr, BkC 6*
Brophy, Loire 1894-1947 *DcNAA*
Brophy, Robert J 1928- *ConAu 53*
Brophy, Truman William 1848-1928 *DcNAA*
Brorson, Hans Adolf 1694-1764 *CasWL, ChPo, DcEuL, Pen Eur*
Brosanus, Matthew *OhA&B*
Brosboll, Johan Carl Christian 1816-1900 *CasWL, EvEuW*
Brose, Olive J 1919- *ConAu 41*
Brosman, Catharine Savage 1934- *ConAu 61, DrAP 1975*
Brosnahan, Katherine Mary 1890-1940 *DcNAA, IndAu 1917*
Brosnahan, Leonard Francis 1922- *WrD 1976*
Brosnahan, Timothy 1856-1915 *DcNAA*
Brosnan, James Patrick 1929- *ConAu 1R*
Brosnan, Jim *ConAu XR*
Bross, Irwin D J 1921- *ConAu 37, WrD 1976*
Bross, William 1813-1890 *Alli Sup, AmA&B, BiD&SB, DcAmA, DcNAA*
Brossard, Chandler 1922- *AmA&B, ConAu 61, ConNov 1972, ConNov 1976, DrAF 1976, Pen Am, WrD 1976*
Brossard, Edgar Bernard 1889- *WhWNAA*
Brossard, Jacques *OxCan Sup*
Brossard, Nicole *OxCan Sup*
Brossard, Sebastien De *OxFr*
Brossboll, Johan Carl Christian *BiD&SB*
Brosses, Charles De 1709-1777 *EvEuW, OxFr*
Broster, Dorothy Kathleen 1877?-1950 *DcLEnL,*

JBA 1934, JBA 1951, TwCW, WhLA
Broster, Eric James 1904- *Au&Wr*
Broster, J *Alli*
Brosterhuysen, Johan Van 1596-1650 *CasWL*
Brostowin, Patrick Ronald 1931- *ConAu 13R*
Broszkiewicz, Jerzy 1922- *CrCD, ModWD*
Brotanek, Rudolf 1870- *WhLA*
Brothai, F *Alli*
Brother Antoninus *AmA&B*
Brother Eugene 1876- *WhWNAA*
Brotherhead, Alfred P *Alli Sup*
Brotherhead, William *Alli Sup, AmA&B, DcNAA*
Brothers, Abram 1861-1910 *DcNAA*
Brothers, Elmer Dewitt 1860-1937 *IndAu 1917, WhWNAA*
Brothers, Joyce 1927- *AuNews 1, ConAu 23*
Brothers, Richard *Alli, BiDLA*
Brotherston, Bruce Wallace 1877-1947 *DcNAA*
Brotherston, Gordon 1939- *ConAu 25, WrD 1976*
Brotherton, Alice Williams 1848-1930 *Alli Sup, AmA&B, AmLY, ChPo, ChPo S1, DcAmA, DcNAA, IndAu 1816, OhA&B*
Brotherton, Edward 1814-1866 *Alli Sup*
Brotherton, John Williams *OhA&B*
Brotherton, Mary *Alli Sup, ChPo S2*
Brotherton, Theodore Widney 1847-1915 *DcNAA*
Brotherton, Thomas *Alli*
Brotteaux, Pascal 1890- *BiDPar*
Brouard, Carl *CasWL*
Broucher, William E *ChPo*
Broudy, Harry S 1905- *ConAu 1R*
Brough, Mrs. *Alli Sup*
Brough, Anthony *Alli, BiDLA*
Brough, Bennett H *Alli Sup*
Brough, Charles Hillman 1876- *BiDSA, WhWNAA*
Brough, Francis *Alli Sup*
Brough, James Fox *Alli Sup*
Brough, John 1917- *WrD 1976*
Brough, John Cargill *Alli Sup*
Brough, Louisa *Alli Sup*
Brough, R Clayton 1950- *ConAu 57*
Brough, Robert Barnabas 1828-1860 *Alli Sup, ChPo, ChPo S1, NewC*
Brough, Walter W 1890- *ChPo*
Brough, William *Alli, ChPo S1*
Brough, William And Stokes, W *Alli Sup*
Broughall, Helen Katherine *WhWNAA*
Brougham, Lord 1778-1868 *BbtC, Chmbr 3*
Brougham, Catharine A M *Alli Sup*
Brougham, Henry *Alli*
Brougham, Lord Henry Peter 1778-1868 *Alli, Alli Sup, BbD, BiD&SB, BiDLA, BrAu 19, CasWL, DcLEnL, EvLB, NewC, OxEng, Pen Eng*
Brougham, John *Alli*
Brougham, John 1810?-1880 *Alli, Alli Sup, AmA, AmA&B, BbD, BiD&SB, ChPo S2, DcAmA, DcEnL, DcNAA, OxAm, PoIre, REnAL*
Brougham, Mary Elizabeth Storey *Alli Sup*
Brougham, Matthew Nixon *Alli Sup*
Brougham, R H V *ChPo*
Brougham, W E *Alli Sup*
Brougham and Vaux, Lord Henry Brougham 1778-1868 *DcEnL*
Brougher, Goldie Wade 1895- *IndAu 1917*
Broughton *Alli*
Broughton, A J *MnBBF*
Broughton, Arthur *Alli, BiDLA*
Broughton, Averell *ChPo S2*
Broughton, Bradford B 1926- *ConAu 21*
Broughton, Brian *Alli, BiDLA*
Broughton, Chara *ChPo S1*
Broughton, Charles *Alli, BiDLA Sup, ChPo*
Broughton, Clara *ChPo*
Broughton, Eliza *Alli*
Broughton, Frederic Claude *ChPo*
Broughton, Geoffrey 1927- *Au&Wr, WrD 1976*
Broughton, Herbert *Alli Sup*
Broughton, Hugh 1549-1612 *Alli*
Broughton, James 1913- *AmA&B, ChPo, ConAu 49, ConP 1970, ConP 1975, DrAP 1975, Pen Am, WrD 1976*

Broughton, John *Alli*
Broughton, Baron John Cam Hobhouse 1786-1869 *CasWL, DcEnL, EvLB, Pen Eng*
Broughton, Leonard Gaston 1865-1936 *BiDSA, DcNAA, WhWNAA*
Broughton, Leslie Hathan 1877-1952 *AmA&B*
Broughton, Lewis Price Delves 1836- *Alli Sup*
Broughton, Panthea Reid 1940- *ConAu 57*
Broughton, Philip F 1893- *AmSCAP 66*
Broughton, Rhoda 1840-1920 *Alli Sup, BbD, BiD&SB, BrAu 19, Chmbr 3, DcBiA, DcEnA, DcEnA Ap, DcEnL, DcLEnL, EvLB, HsB&A, LongC, NewC, OxEng*
Broughton, Richard d1634 *Alli*
Broughton, Rowlande *Alli*
Broughton, Samuel Daniel 1787-1837 *Alli, BiDLA Sup*
Broughton, T Alan 1936- *ConAu 45, DrAF 1976, DrAP 1975*
Broughton, Thomas *Alli*
Broughton, Thomas 1704-1774 *Alli, NewC*
Broughton, Thomas Duer *BiDLA, BiDLA Sup*
Broughton, Mrs. Vernon Delves *Alli Sup*
Broughton, William *Alli*
Broughton, William Robert *Alli, BiDLA*
Broughton DeGyfford, Baron *NewC*
Brouillan, Jacques-Francois De 1651-1705 *OxCan*
Brouillard, Carmel *OxCan*
Brouillette, Jeanne S *ConAu 1R*
Broun, Emily *ConAu XR*
Broun, Heywood Campbell 1888-1939 *AmA&B, CatA 1947, ConAmA, DcLEnL, DcNAA, OxAm, REn, REnAL, TwCA, TwCA Sup*
Broun, Heywood Hale 1918- *ConAu 17R*
Broun, Joannes *Alli*
Broun, John Allen *Alli Sup*
Broun, Sir R *BbtC*
Broun, William *Alli*
Brouncker, William, Viscount *Alli*
Brouse, Marian M *ChPo S2*
Broussard, James Francis 1881-1942 *DcNAA*
Broussard, Louis 1922- *ConAu 25*
Broussard, Vivian L *ConAu XR*
Brousseau, Kate 1862-1938 *DcNAA*
Broussel, Pierre *OxFr*
Brousel, Adriaen 1606?-1638 *AtlBL*
Brouwer, Petrus VanLimburg 1798-1847 *DcEuL*
Brow, Robert 1924- *ConAu 23*
Broward, Donn *ConAu XR*
Browder, Earl Russell 1891?-1973 *ConAu 45*
Browder, Lesley H, Jr. 1935- *ConAu 45*
Browder, Olin L, Jr. 1913- *ConAu 41*
Browder, Uriah Marion 1846-1907 *OhA&B*
Browder, Walter Everett 1939- *ConAu 53*
Browell, James *Alli, BiDLA*
Brower, Brock 1931- *AmA&B, ChPo S2, ConAu 25, DrAF 1976*
Brower, D H B *Alli Sup*
Brower, Daniel R 1936- *ConAu 41*
Brower, Daniel Roberts 1839-1909 *DcNAA*
Brower, David R 1912- *ConAu 61*
Brower, Harriette Moore 1869-1928 *DcNAA*
Brower, Jacob Vrandenberg 1844-1905 *AmA&B, DcAmA, DcNAA*
Brower, Kenneth 1944- *ConAu 25*
Brower, Linda A 1945- *ConAu 33*
Brower, Millicent *ConAu 41, SmATA 8*
Brower, Reuben Arthur 1908-1975 *ConAu 1R, ConAu 57*
Brower, Robert F *Alli Sup*
Brower, Robert H *ChPo S2*
Brower, William Leverich 1846-1940 *DcNAA*
Browere, John Henri Isaac 1790-1834 *EarAB Sup*
Browin, Frances Williams 1898- *AuBYP, ConAu P-1, SmATA 5*
Browing, Nellie *Alli Sup*
Browing SEE ALSO Browne
Brown *Alli*
Brown, Lord 1908- *Au&Wr*
Brown, Miss *Alli*
Brown, A *Alli Sup, ChPo*
Brown, A Curtis 1866-1945 *AmA&B*
Brown, A Henry *Alli Sup*
Brown, A J *BiDSA*

Brown, A M *Alli Sup*
Brown, A Seymour 1885-1947 *AmSCAP 66*
Brown, A W *Alli Sup*
Brown, Aaron Venable 1795-1859 *BiDSA, DcNAA*
Brown, Abbie Farwell 1872?-1927 *AmA&B, AmLY, AnCL, CarSB, ChPo, ChPo S1, ChPo S2, DcAmA, DcNAA, JBA 1934, TwCA, TwCA Sup, WhWNAA*
Brown, Abby Whitney *Alli Sup*
Brown, Abner William *Alli Sup*
Brown, Abram English 1849-1909 *DcAmA, DcNAA*
Brown, Addison 1830-1930 *DcNAA, OxCan Sup*
Brown, Adeline E *AmSCAP 66*
Brown, Al W 1884-1924 *AmSCAP 66*
Brown, Alan A 1929- *ConAu 25*
Brown, Albert Gallatin 1813-1880 *BiDSA, DcNAA*
Brown, Albert M 1901- *OhA&B*
Brown, Alberta L 1894- *ConAu P-1*
Brown, Alexander *Alli, Alli Sup, ChPo, ChPo S2*
Brown, Alexander 1775-1834 *ChPo S1*
Brown, Alexander 1823- *ChPo S1*
Brown, Alexander 1843-1906 *AmA&B, BiDSA, DcAmA, DcNAA*
Brown, Alexander 1905- *ConAu 1R*
Brown, Alexander Campbell *Alli, BiDLA*
Brown, Alexander Crum *Alli Sup*
Brown, Alexander M *Alli Sup*
Brown, Alexis *ConAu XR, SmATA XR*
Brown, Alfred *Alli Sup*
Brown, Alfred Barratt 1887- *WhLA*
Brown, Alfred J 1894- *CatA 1947*
Brown, Alfred Jerome 1878- *WhWNAA*
Brown, Alice 1857-1940 *Alli Sup, AmA&B, BbD, BiD&SB, ChPo, ChPo S2, ConAmL, DcAmA, DcLEnL, EvLB*
Brown, Alice 1857-1948 *OxAm, REnAL, TwCA, TwCA Sup*
Brown, Alice VanVechten 1862- *WhWNAA*
Brown, Allan *Alli Sup*
Brown, Allen 1926- *ConAu 13R*
Brown, Almedia Morton *Alli Sup*
Brown, Alonzo 1849- *IndAu 1917, WhWNAA*
Brown, Alonzo Leighton 1838-1904 *DcNAA*
Brown, Amy *ChPo*
Brown, Amyatt *Alli Sup*
Brown, Andrew *Alli, Alli Sup, BbtC*
Brown, Andrew Morton *Alli Sup*
Brown, Anna Muse *BiDSA*
Brown, Anna Robeson 1873- *ChPo, DcAmA*
Brown, Anna S *Alli*
Brown, Anne S K 1906- *ConAu 17R*
Brown, Annice Harris 1897- *ConAu 45*
Brown, Annie *Alli Sup*
Brown, Annie Johnson *Alli Sup*
Brown, Anthony *Alli, BiDLA, DcEnL*
Brown, Sir Anthony *Alli*
Brown, Archibald 1841- *Alli Sup*
Brown, Archibald G *Alli Sup*
Brown, Archibald Haworth 1938- *WrD 1976*
Brown, Arthur *Alli Sup*
Brown, Arthur Charles Lewis 1869-1946 *AmA&B, WhWNAA, DcNAA*
Brown, Arthur Judson 1856-1963 *AmA&B, AmLY, WhWNAA*
Brown, Arthur Wayne 1917- *ConAu 5R*
Brown, Ashley 1923- *ConAu 1R*
Brown, Ashmun 1872- *WhWNAA*
Brown, Athaleen 1908- *AmSCAP 66*
Brown, Audrey Alexandra 1904- *CanWr, DcLEnL, OxCan, REnAL*
Brown, B Frank 1917- *ConAu 9R*
Brown, B Katherine 1917- *ConAu 13R*
Brown, B R *Alli Sup*
Brown, Bailey E 1879- *WhWNAA*
Brown, Barnetta 1859-1938 *AmSCAP 66*
Brown, Barnum 1873- *WhWNAA*
Brown, Beatrice 1896- *TexWr*
Brown, Beatrice Bradshaw *CatA 1952*
Brown, Beatrice Curtis *ChPo, ChPo S1, ConAu XR*
Brown, Benjamin A *BlkAW*
Brown, Benjamin F *ChPo S1*
Brown, Benjamin F 1930- *ConAu 45*

Brown, Benjamin Gratz 1826-1885 *BiDSA*
Brown, Benjamin H 1866- *WhWNAA*
Brown, Bernard E 1925- *ConAu 1R*
Brown, Bert R 1936- *ConAu 41*
Brown, Bertrand 1888-1964 *AmSCAP 66, WhWNAA*
Brown, Beth *AmSCAP 66, ConAu 21*
Brown, Betty *ConAu XR*
Brown, Bill 1910-1964 *AuBYP, ConAu XR, SmATA 5*
Brown, Blanche Hodges *ChPo*
Brown, Blanche R 1915- *ConAu 13R, WrD 1976*
Brown, Bob 1886- *AmA&B, ConAu XR, WhWNAA*
Brown, Bob Burton 1925- *ConAu 23*
Brown, Bolton Coit 1864?-1936 *AmA&B, DcNAA*
Brown, Brodie Curtis *ChPo S1, ChPo S2*
Brown, Bruce 1903- *WhWNAA*
Brown, Buford Otis *WhWNAA*
Brown, Burdette Boardman 1871-1942 *DcNAA*
Brown, C *Alli Sup*
Brown, C O *Alli Sup*
Brown, Calvin Smith 1866-1945 *DcAmA, DcNAA*
Brown, Calvin Smith, Jr. 1909- *ConAu 49, WhWNAA*
Brown, Camille 1917- *ConAu 9R*
Brown, Campbell *MnBBF, WhLA*
Brown, Carl F 1910- *ConAu 41*
Brown, Carleton Fairchild 1869-1941 *AmA&B, DcNAA, WhWNAA*
Brown, Caroline *AmA&B, DcNAA*
Brown, Carrie L 1852- *ChPo*
Brown, Carroll Neide 1869-1938 *DcNAA*
Brown, Carter *ConAu XR*
Brown, Cassie 1919- *ConAu 45, OxCan Sup*
Brown, Cecil Kenneth 1900- *WhWNAA*
Brown, Cecil M *BlkAW, DrAF 1976, LivBA*
Brown, Charles *Alli*
Brown, Charles Armitage 1786-1842 *Alli, NewC*
Brown, Charles Barrington *Alli Sup*
Brown, Charles Brockden 1771-1810 *Alli, AmA, AmA&B, AtlBL, BbD, BiD&SB, CasWL, Chmbr 3, CnDAL, CriT 3, CyAL 1, CyWA, DcAmA, DcEnL, DcLEnL, DcNAA, EncM&D, EvLB, MouLC 2, OxAm, OxEng, Pen Am, RAdv 1, REn, REnAL, WebEAL*
Brown, Charles Carroll 1856- *WhWNAA*
Brown, Charles Ewing 1883- *IndAu 1917*
Brown, Charles H 1910- *ConAu 23*
Brown, Charles Hilton 1890- *ChPo S1*
Brown, Charles John *Alli Sup*
Brown, Charles O *ArizL*
Brown, Charles Perry *MnBBF*
Brown, Charles Philip 1798-1884 *Alli Sup*
Brown, Charles R *Alli Sup*
Brown, Charles Reynolds 1862-1950 *AmA&B, DcAmA, WhWNAA*
Brown, Charles Rufus 1849-1914 *Alli Sup, DcAmA, DcNAA*
Brown, Charles T 1912- *ConAu 41*
Brown, Charles Walter 1866-1934 *ChPo S1, DcNAA*
Brown, Charles William 1858-1928 *DcNAA*
Brown, Charlotte Hawkins 1882-1961 *BlkAW*
Brown, Christian Henry 1857-1933 *DcNAA, WhWNAA*
Brown, Christy 1932- *WrD 1976*
Brown, Clara Maude *AmA&B*
Brown, Clark 1935- *ConAu 25*
Brown, Claude 1937- *AmA&B, BlkAW, DrAF 1976, LivBA*
Brown, Clement 1928- *Au&Wr, WrD 1976*
Brown, Colin *Alli Sup*
Brown, Colin Rae *Alli Sup*
Brown, Conrad 1922- *AuBYP*
Brown, Constantine 1889-1966 *ConAu P-1*
Brown, Corinne *ChPo*
Brown, Cornelius *Alli Sup*
Brown, Curtis F 1925- *ConAu 61*
Brown, Cyril 1887-1949 *DcNAA*
Brown, Dale W 1926- *ConAu 37, WrD 1976*
Brown, Daniel G 1924- *ConAu 45*

Brown, David *Alli*
Brown, David d1812 *Alli*
Brown, David d1829 *Alli*
Brown, David 1803- *Alli Sup*
Brown, David 1916- *ConAu 13R*
Brown, David 1929- *ConAu 57*
Brown, David Arthur 1839-1903 *DcNAA*
Brown, David Boyer *Alli Sup*
Brown, David Grant 1936- *ConAu 13R*
Brown, David Leslie 1885- *OhA&B*
Brown, David Paul 1795-1872 *Alli, Alli Sup, AmA&B, BiD&SB, DcAmA, DcNAA*
Brown, David S 1915- *ConAu 29*
Brown, David Walter 1852-1920 *DcNAA*
Brown, Dee Alexander 1908- *ConAu 13R, SmATA 5, WrD 1976*
Brown, Delores A *BlkAW*
Brown, Demarchus Clariton 1857-1926 *IndAu 1816*
Brown, Demetra Vaka Kenneth 1877-1946 *AmA&B, BiDSA, DcNAA, WhWNAA*
Brown, Denise Scott 1931- *ConAu 41*
Brown, Dennis A 1926- *ConAu 61*
Brown, Derrick *ChPo S2*
Brown, Donald Eugene 1909- *ConAu P-1*
Brown, Donald Fowler 1909- *ConAu 41*
Brown, Donald Robert 1925- *ConAu 41*
Brown, Doris E 1910?-1975 *ConAu 61*
Brown, Douglas Frank Lambert 1907- *ConAu 25, WrD 1976*
Brown, Duane 1937- *ConAu 33*
Brown, Dugald Blair *Alli Sup*
Brown, Duncan *MnBBF*
Brown, E E *ChPo S1*
Brown, E Howard 1871-1944 *IndAu 1917*
Brown, E L *ChPo S1*
Brown, Earl Bigelow *ChPo S2*
Brown, Edgar S, Jr. 1922- *ConAu 9R*
Brown, Edith *ChPo*
Brown, Edmund Randolph 1845-1930 *IndAu 1917*
Brown, Edmund Woodward 1831-1902 *Alli Sup, DcNAA*
Brown, Edna *BlkAW*
Brown, Edna Adelaide 1875-1944 *AmA&B, DcNAA, JBA 1934, JBA 1951, WhWNAA*
Brown, Edward *Alli, Alli Sup*
Brown, Edward 1814- *OhA&B*
Brown, Edward J 1909- *ConAu 25*
Brown, Edward Killoran 1905-1951 *CanWr, CasWL, ChPo S1, DcLEnL, OxCan, OxCan Sup*
Brown, Edward Osgood 1847-1923 *DcNAA*
Brown, Edwin Arleigh 1857- *WhWNAA*
Brown, Edwin Tylor *DcLEnL*
Brown, Elaine *BlkAW*
Brown, Eleanor Frances 1908- *AuBYP, ConAu 29, SmATA 3*
Brown, Elinor Luella Baade 1915- *AmA&B*
Brown, Elizabeth B *Alli Sup*
Brown, Elizabeth Louise 1924- *ConAu 53*
Brown, Elizabeth Virginia 1866-1915 *DcNAA*
Brown, Ellen L *Alli Sup*
Brown, Ellen M *BlkAW*
Brown, Elmer Ellsworth 1861-1934 *AmA&B, DcAmA, DcNAA*
Brown, Emily *SmATA 6*
Brown, Emily Clara 1911- *ConAu 53*
Brown, Emma Alice *BiDSA, ChPo*
Brown, Emma B *ChPo*
Brown, Emma Elizabeth 1847- *Alli Sup, AmA&B, AmLY, BiD&SB, ChPo, ChPo S1, DcAmA*
Brown, Eric *MnBBF*
Brown, Ernest Faulkner 1854- *WhLA*
Brown, Ernest Henry Phelps 1906- *Au&Wr*
Brown, Ernest William 1866-1938 *DcAmA, DcNAA, WhWNAA*
Brown, Estelle Aubrey 1877-1958 *AmA&B, ArizL*
Brown, Ethel C *WhWNAA*
Brown, Eva *TexWr*
Brown, Eva P *ChPo*
Brown, Evelyn Marjorie 1911- *ConAu 21, WrD 1976*
Brown, Everett Thornton *ChPo S2*
Brown, Everit *Alli Sup*

Brown, F Andrew 1915- *ConAu 41*
Brown, F C *WhWNAA*
Brown, Fannie Carole *BlkAW*
Brown, Ford Keeler 1895- *WhWNAA*
Brown, Ford Madox 1821-1893 *REn*
Brown, Forman 1901- *AmSCAP 66*
Brown, Forrest *ConAu 49*
Brown, Fortune Charles 1813?-1888 *DcNAA*
Brown, Frances 1816-1879 *Alli, BbD, BiD&SB, ChPo, ChPo S1, PoIre*
Brown, Frances ALSO Browne, Frances
Brown, Frances Clifford *Alli Sup*
Brown, Frances Swan *ChPo*
Brown, Francis 1784-1820 *Alli, CyAL 1*
Brown, Francis 1849-1916 *Alli Sup, DcAmA, DcNAA*
Brown, Francis 1903- *AmA&B*
Brown, Francis Henry 1835-1917 *Alli Sup, DcNAA*
Brown, Francis James 1894- *WhWNAA*
Brown, Francis R 1914- *ConAu 41*
Brown, Frank Chouteau 1876-1947 *AmA&B, WhWNAA*
Brown, Frank Clyde 1870-1943 *DcNAA*
Brown, Frank Llewellyn 1862-1922 *DcNAA*
Brown, Frank Logan 1887- *WhWNAA*
Brown, Frank London 1927?-1962 *BlkAW*
Brown, Frederic 1906-1972 *ConAu 33, OhA&B*
Brown, Frederic Kenyon 1882-1935 *AmLY, DcNAA*
Brown, Frederick 1934- *ConAu 25*
Brown, Mrs. Frederick *Alli Sup*
Brown, Frederick G 1932- *ConAu 29, WrD 1976*
Brown, Frederick Kenyon 1882-1935 *WhWNAA*
Brown, Frederick M *Alli Sup*
Brown, Fredric 1906-1972 *AmA&B, Au&Wr, EncM&D, WorAu*
Brown, G Nelville 1932- *ConAu 17R*
Brown, G T *Alli Sup*
Brown, G W *MnBBF*
Brown, Gene 1928- *AmSCAP 66*
Brown, Geoff 1932- *ConAu 61*
Brown, George *Alli, Alli Sup*
Brown, George 1792-1871 *DcNAA, OhA&B*
Brown, George 1818-1880 *BbtC, OxCan*
Brown, George 1844- *Alli Sup*
Brown, George 1847- *WhLA*
Brown, George Douglas 1869-1902 *BrAu 19, CasWL, Chmbr 3, DcLEnL, EvLB, LongC, NewC, OxEng, Pen Eng*
Brown, George E *ChPo S1*
Brown, George Earl 1883-1964 *ConAu 5R*
Brown, George James Crowley *Alli Sup*
Brown, George Loring 1814-1889 *EarAB, EarAB Sup*
Brown, George Mackay 1921- *CasWL, ChPo S2, ConAu 21, ConLC 5, ConNov 1972, ConNov 1976, ConP 1970, ConP 1975, WrD 1976*
Brown, George Murray 1880-1960 *AmSCAP 66*
Brown, George Pliny 1836-1910 *DcNAA*
Brown, George R 1910- *AmSCAP 66*
Brown, George Rothwell d1960 *AmA&B*
Brown, George Shaw *Alli Sup*
Brown, George Stayley *Alli Sup*
Brown, George W *Alli Sup, OxCan Sup*
Brown, George Washington 1820-1915 *DcNAA*
Brown, George Washington 1828- *DcNAA*
Brown, George William 1812-1890 *Alli Sup, BiDSA*
Brown, George William 1812-1840 *DcNAA*
Brown, George William 1870-1932 *DcNAA*
Brown, George Williams *OxCan*
Brown, Gerald Saxon 1911- *ConAu 9R, OxCan*
Brown, Gerald W 1916- *ConAu 33*
Brown, Gerhard Baldwin- *Alli Sup*
Brown, Giles T 1916- *ConAu 17R*
Brown, Ginny *ConAu XR*
Brown, Glen Francis 1911- *IndAu 1917*
Brown, Glenn 1854-1932 *Alli Sup, BiDSA, DcAmA, DcNAA, WhWNAA*
Brown, Glenn J 1900-1960 *AmSCAP 66*
Brown, Goodwin 1852-1912 *DcNAA*
Brown, Goold 1791-1857 *Alli, AmA&B, CyAL 2, DcAmA, DcNAA, REnAL*

Brown, Grace *ChPo S1*
Brown, Grace Evelyn 1873- *AnMV 1926, WhWNAA*
Brown, Guy A *Alli Sup*
Brown, Gwethalyn Graham Erichsen d1965 *AmA&B*
Brown, Gwilym Slater 1928-1974 *ConAu 9R, ConAu 53*
Brown, H *ChPo S2*
Brown, H A *Alli Sup*
Brown, H Clark 1898- *WhWNAA*
Brown, H Clark ALSO Brown, Howard C
Brown, Mrs. H E *ChPo*
Brown, H Rap *LivBA*
Brown, H Rap ALSO Brown, Hubert Rap
Brown, H Rowland *ChPo S1*
Brown, H W *Alli Sup*
Brown, Hallie Quinn 1860-1949 *OhA&B*
Brown, Handy Nereus *BlkAW*
Brown, Harold Haven 1869-1932 *DcNAA*
Brown, Harold O J 1933- *ConAu 25*
Brown, Harper G *TexWr*
Brown, Harriet Grant *ChPo*
Brown, Harriett M 1897- *ConAu 5R*
Brown, Harrison Scott 1917- *AmA&B*
Brown, Harry Bates 1876-1962 *IndAu 1917*
Brown, Harry Fletcher 1867-1944 *ChPo S2*
Brown, Harry Gunnison 1880-1975 *ConAu 57, WhWNAA*
Brown, Harry Matthew 1921- *ConAu 25, OhA&B*
Brown, Harry O, Jr. 1919- *WrD 1976*
Brown, Harry Peter M'Nab 1917- *AmA&B, AmNov, OxAm, REnAL, TwCA Sup*
Brown, Harry Philip 1887- *WhWNAA*
Brown, Hattie *ChPo*
Brown, Hazel E 1893- *ConAu 57*
Brown, Helen *Alli Sup, AuBYP, ChPo S2*
Brown, Helen Dawes 1857-1941 *Alli Sup, AmA&B, DcAmA, DcNAA, WhWNAA*
Brown, Helen E *Alli Sup, ChPo S1*
Brown, Helen Gurley 1922- *AmA&B, ConAu 5R, WrD 1976*
Brown, Helen Keer *Alli Sup*
Brown, Henry *Alli, Alli Sup*
Brown, Henry 1789-1849 *DcNAA*
Brown, Henry Armitt 1846?-1879? *Alli Sup, DcAmA*
Brown, Henry B *EarAB*
Brown, Henry Billings 1836-1913 *Alli Sup, DcAmA, DcNAA*
Brown, Henry 'Box' 1816- *BlkAW*
Brown, Henry Collins 1863-1961 *AmA&B*
Brown, Henry D *Alli Sup*
Brown, Henry Harrison 1840-1918 *DcNAA*
Brown, Henry J *Alli Sup*
Brown, Henry Kirke 1814-1886 *EarAB, OxAm*
Brown, Henry T *Alli Sup*
Brown, Herbert Alfred 1905- *WrD 1976*
Brown, Herbert C 1912- *WrD 1976*
Brown, Herbert G *BlkAW*
Brown, Herbert Ross 1902- *ConAu P-1*
Brown, Hester Pierce *ChPo*
Brown, Hilary *ChPo, ChPo S1, ChPo S2*
Brown, Hilton 1890-1961 *LongC*
Brown, Hilton Ultimus 1859- *IndAu 1816*
Brown, Horatio Robert Forbes 1854- *Alli Sup*
Brown, Howard *MnBBF*
Brown, Howard Clark 1898- *AmA&B*
Brown, Howard C ALSO Brown, H Clark
Brown, Howard Mayer 1930- *ConAu 1R, WrD 1976*
Brown, Howard Nicholson 1849-1932 *Alli Sup, DcAmA, DcNAA*
Brown, Hubert Rap 1943- *AmA&B*
Brown, Hubert Rap ALSO Brown, H Rap
Brown, Hubert William 1858-1906 *DcAmA, DcNAA*
Brown, Hugh *Alli, ChPo*
Brown, Hugh Arbuthnot 1877- *WhWNAA*
Brown, Hugh Auchincloss 1879-1975 *ConAu 61*
Brown, Hugh Stowell 1823-1886 *Alli Sup*
Brown, Humphrey *Alli*
Brown, Huntington 1899- *ConAu P-1*
Brown, Ida *BiDSA*
Brown, Ida Mae *ConAu 29*
Brown, Ina Corinne 1896- *ConAu 5R, TexWr, WhWNAA*

Brown, Ina Ladd 1905- *ConAu P-1*
Brown, Ira Vernon 1922- *ConAu 5R*
Brown, Irene Bennett 1932- *ConAu 29,*
SmATA 3
Brown, Irving *AmA&B, DcNAA*
Brown, Irving 1835-1899 *DcNAA* .
Brown, Irving Henry 1888-1940 *AmA&B,*
DcNAA, WhWNAA
Brown, Isaac *Alli Sup, ChPo*
Brown, Isaac Baker *Alli, Alli Sup*
Brown, Isaac Hinton 1842-1889 *DcNAA*
Brown, Isaac VanArsdale 1784-1861 *DcNAA*
Brown, Isabella Marie 1917- *BlkAW*
Brown, Ivor John Carnegie 1891-1974 *Au&Wr,*
ConAu 9R, ConAu 49, DcLEnL, EvLB,
LongC, ModBL, NewC, Pen Eng,
SmATA 5, TwCA Sup
Brown, J *Alli, Alli Sup, BiDLA*
Brown, J A Hemingway *Alli Sup*
Brown, J Appleton *ChPo*
Brown, J B *Alli Sup*
Brown, J Campbell *Alli Sup*
Brown, J D *Alli Sup*
Brown, J E A *Alli Sup*
Brown, J Graham *Alli Sup*
Brown, J H *Alli, Alli Sup, ChPo S1*
Brown, J Holland *Alli Sup*
Brown, J J *OxCan Sup*
Brown, J Moray *Alli Sup*
Brown, J N E *OxCan*
Brown, J Newton 1803- *Alli*
Brown, J Newton ALSO Brown, John N
Brown, J P S 1930- *ConAu 61*
Brown, J T *Alli Sup*
Brown, J T T *Alli Sup*
Brown, J W *Alli Sup*
Brown, Mrs. J W *Alli Sup*
Brown, James *Alli, Alli Sup, BbtC, BiDLA,*
BlkAW, ChPo, DcNAA
Brown, James 1709-1787 *Alli*
Brown, James 1790-1870 *DcNAA*
Brown, James 1800-1855 *AmA&B*
Brown, James 1815-1890 *ChPo S2*
Brown, James 1834-1890 *Alli Sup*
Brown, James 1836- *ChPo S1*
Brown, James 1856- *ChPo*
Brown, James 1921- *ConAu 1R*
Brown, James Allen 1821-1883 *DcAmA*
Brown, James Baldwin 1781-1843 *Alli, BiDLA*
Brown, James Baldwin 1820-1884 *Alli Sup,*
DcEnL
Brown, James Bryce *Alli, BbtC, OxCan*
Brown, James Buchanan 1832?-1904 *ChPo,*
ChPo S1
Brown, James Cooke 1921- *ConAu 29*
Brown, James D *Alli Sup*
Brown, James E *Alli Sup*
Brown, James Fuller 1819-1901 *DcNAA*
Brown, James Goldie 1901- *WrD 1976*
Brown, James I 1908- *ConAu 17R, WrD 1976*
Brown, James Moore 1799-1862 *DcNAA*
Brown, James Nelson *BlkAW*
Brown, James Patrick 1948- *ConAu 29*
Brown, James Pennecock d1862 *ChPo S1*
Brown, James Scott *Alli Sup*
Brown, James Stephens 1828- *DcNAA*
Brown, James Wilson 1913- *ConAu 41*
Brown, Jane *ChPo*
Brown, Jeannette Perkins 1887- *ChPo*
Brown, Jeff *AuBYP*
Brown, Jefferson Beale 1857-1937 *DcNAA*
Brown, Jerry Wayne 1936- *ConAu 25*
Brown, Jessie Hunter *Alli Sup, OhA&B*
Brown, Jim *OxCan Sup*
Brown, Joe C *BlkAW*
Brown, Joe David 1915- *AmA&B, AmNov,*
ConAu 13R
Brown, Joe Evan 1892- *OhA&B*
Brown, John *Alli, Alli Sup, BiDLA, ChPo,*
ChPo S1, Chmbr 2, Chmbr 3, CyAL 1,
NewC
Brown, John d1679 *Alli*
Brown, John d1752 *Alli*
Brown, John d1766 *BbtC*
Brown, John d1808 *PoIre*
Brown, John d1858 *Alli Sup*
Brown, John 1715-1766 *BrAu, ChPo, EvLB*
Brown, John 1722-1787 *Alli, DcEnL*

Brown, John 1735-1788 *Alli*
Brown, John 1752-1787 *Alli*
Brown, John 1771-1850 *BiDSA*
Brown, John 1785- *Alli*
Brown, John 1797-1861 *Alli Sup*
Brown, John 1800-1859 *OxAm, REn, REnAL*
Brown, John 1810-1882 *Alli Sup, BiD&SB,*
BrAu 19, CarSB, CasWL, ChPo, DcEnA,
DcEnL, DcEuL, DcLEnL, EvLB, NewC,
OxEng, Pen Eng, REn
Brown, John 1812-1890 *ChPo S1*
Brown, John 1822- *ChPo*
Brown, John 1830-19?? *ChPo, ChPo S1*
Brown, John 1835-1859 *PoIre*
Brown, John 1887- *Au&Wr, ConAu P-1*
Brown, John 1920- *Au&Wr, ConAu 5R*
Brown, John 1934- *ConAu 25*
Brown, John, Of Haddington *Chmbr 2*
Brown, John Alexander Harvie- 1844- *Alli Sup*
Brown, John Allen *Alli Sup*
Brown, John Appleton 1844-1902 *EarAB*
Brown, John Aquila *Alli*
Brown, John Arthur 1914- *ConAu 17R,*
WhPNW
Brown, John Augustus 1857-1910 *DcNAA*
Brown, John Carter *ChPo, ChPo S1*
Brown, John Crombie d1885 *Alli Sup*
Brown, John Crosby 1838-1909 *DcNAA*
Brown, John Croumbie *Alli Sup*
Brown, John Davidson 1820?- *ChPo S1*
Brown, John E *Alli Sup*
Brown, John Edward 1908- *Au&Wr*
Brown, John Elward 1879- *WhWNAA*
Brown, John Franklin 1865-1940 *DcNAA,*
OhA&B, WhWNAA
Brown, John G 1831-1913 *EarAB, EarAB Sup*
Brown, John Henry *Alli Sup*
Brown, John Henry 1810-1905 *DcNAA*
Brown, John Henry 1820-1895 *BiDSA,*
DcNAA
Brown, John Henry 1859-1946 *DcNAA, PoIre*
Brown, John Howard 1840-1917 *DcAmA,*
DcNAA
Brown, John J 1916- *Alli Sup, ConAu 13R*
Brown, John L 1914- *Alli Sup, ConAu 49*
Brown, John Macmillan 1846- *WhLA*
Brown, John Mason *BiDSA*
Brown, John Mason 1837-1890 *DcNAA*
Brown, John Mason 1900-1969 *AmA&B,*
CnDAL, ConAu 9R, ConAu 25, LongC,
OxAm, Pen Am, REnAL, TwCA,
TwCA Sup
Brown, John Newton 1803-1868 *ChPo, DcAmA,*
DcNAA
Brown, John N ALSO Brown, J Newton
Brown, John Pairman 1923- *ConAu 33*
Brown, John Patrick 1839-1896 *Alli Sup,*
DcNAA, PoIre
Brown, John Pinkney 1842-1915 *DcNAA,*
IndAu 1917
Brown, John Porter 1814-1872 *Alli, Alli Sup,*
DcNAA, OhA&B
Brown, John Price 1844-1938 *DcNAA*
Brown, John Richard 1870-1926 *DcNAA*
Brown, John Russell 1923- *ConAu 21,*
WrD 1976
Brown, John Taylor *Alli Sup*
Brown, John Thomas Toshach 1854- *WhLA*
Brown, John Thompson *BiDSA*
Brown, John Walker 1814-1849 *Alli, ChPo,*
ChPo S2, CyAL 2, DcAmA, DcNAA
Brown, John William *Alli*
Brown, Jonathan 1805-1864 *DcNAA*
Brown, Joseph *Alli, Alli Sup*
Brown, Joseph 1784-1868 *Alli Sup*
Brown, Joseph 1837-1918 *DcNAA*
Brown, Joseph Brownlee 1824-1888 *BiDSA,*
DcAmA
Brown, Joseph C 1879-1945 *DcNAA,*
WhWNAA
Brown, Joseph E 1929- *ConAu 53*
Brown, Joseph Emerson 1821-1894 *BiDSA*
Brown, Joseph Epes d1937 *DcNAA*
Brown, Joseph G *ChPo, ChPo S2*
Brown, Joseph Henry 1831-1898 *DcNAA*
Brown, Joseph M 1851-1932 *BiDSA, DcNAA*
Brown, Josephine *Alli Sup*
Brown, Josiah d1793 *Alli*

Brown, Juanita *BlkAW*
Brown, Judith Gwyn 1933- *AuBYP, ChPo S1,*
IlCB 1966
Brown, Judith M 1944- *ConAu 41*
Brown, Julia *IndAu 1816*
Brown, Kate Louise 1857-1921 *ChPo, ChPo S1,*
ChPo S2, DcNAA
Brown, Katherine Holland d1931 *DcNAA*
Brown, Katherine Louise 1857- 192? *DcAmA*
Brown, Kathryn Lynch *TexWr*
Brown, Keith Crosby 1885-1948 *AmSCAP 66*
Brown, Kenneth 1868- *AmA&B, BiDSA,*
WhWNAA
Brown, Mrs. Kenneth *AmA&B, WhWNAA*
Brown, Kenneth H 1936- *AmA&B, Au&Wr,*
ConAu 13R, ConDr, DrAF 1976,
WrD 1976
Brown, Kenneth Irving 1896- *AmA&B,*
OhA&B
Brown, L *Alli Sup*
Brown, L B *Alli Sup*
Brown, Mrs. L D *Alli Sup*
Brown, L Guy 1895- *AmA&B*
Brown, L Q C *Alli Sup*
Brown, Ladbroke *LongC*
Brown, Lancelot 1715-1783 *AtlBL, NewC*
Brown, Lawrason 1871-1938 *DcNAA,*
WhWNAA
Brown, Lawrence Tracy 1894- *WhWNAA*
Brown, Lee Dolph 1890-1971 *AmA&B,*
ConAu 29
Brown, Leland 1914- *ConAu 1R, IndAu 1917,*
WrD 1976
Brown, Lennox John 1934- *BlkAW*
Brown, Leonard 1837-1914 *Alli Sup, ChPo,*
DcNAA, IndAu 1917
Brown, LeRoy Chester 1908- *ConAu P-1,*
IndAu 1917
Brown, Les 1912- *AmSCAP 66*
Brown, Les 1928- *ConAu 33*
Brown, Leslie Hilton 1917- *Au&Wr,*
ConAu 9R
Brown, Leslie Wilfrid 1912- *ConAu 17R*
Brown, Letitia J 1829-1887 *DcNAA*
Brown, Lew 1893-1958 *AmSCAP 66*
Brown, Lewis 1858-1930 *DcNAA*
Brown, Lillian Rowland *WhLA*
Brown, Linda 1939- *BlkAW*
Brown, Lionel 1888-1964 *LongC*
Brown, Littleton *Alli*
Brown, Lloyd Arnold 1907-1966 *AuBYP,*
ConAu P-1
Brown, Lloyd Louis 1913- *BlkAW*
Brown, Lloyd W *BlkAW*
Brown, Louis M 1909- *ConAu 49*
Brown, Lundin *BbtC*
Brown, Lyle C 1926- *ConAu 41*
Brown, M L T *ConAu 13R*
Brown, Mahlon A *AmA&B*
Brown, Major Dan *HsB&A*
Brown, Marc Tolon 1946- *SmATA 10*
Brown, Marcia 1918- *AmA&B, AnCL,*
AuBYP, BkP, Cald 1938, ChPo,
ChPo S2, ConAu 41, FamAI, IlBYP,
IlCB 1956, IlCB 1966, MorJA,
NewbC 1956, SmATA 7
Brown, Marcus Monroe 1855?-1915 *OhA&B*
Brown, Marel *WrD 1976*
Brown, Margaret Coote *ChPo S1*
Brown, Margaret Elizabeth 1899- *WrD 1976*
Brown, Margaret Wise 1910-1952 *AmSCAP 66,*
AuBYP, AuICB, ChPo, ChPo S1,
JBA 1951, REnAL
Brown, Margery *ConAu 25, SmATA 5*
Brown, Marie A *Alli Sup, ChPo*
Brown, Marie Adelaide *DcNAA*
Brown, Marion Francis *AnMV 1926*
Brown, Marion Marsh 1908- *AuBYP,*
ConAu 1R, SmATA 6
Brown, Mark Herbert 1900- *ConAu 21,*
WrD 1976
Brown, Marshall *Alli Sup*
Brown, Marshall L 1924- *ConAu 23*
Brown, Marshall R 1920- *AmSCAP 66*
Brown, Marshall Stewart 1875?-1948 *DcAmA,*
DcNAA
Brown, Martha *BlkAW*
Brown, Martha W *LivFWS*

Brown, Marvin L, Jr. 1920- *ConAu 53*
Brown, Mary 1913- *Au&Wr*
Brown, Mary Ann *ChPo, ChPo S1*
Brown, Mary-Anne 1812-1844 *ChPo S1*
Brown, Mary E And W A *Alli Sup*
Brown, Mary Elizabeth Adams 1842-1917
  ChPo S1, DcNAA, OhA&B
Brown, Mary Eugenia *Alli Sup*
Brown, Mary Hosmer 1856-1931 *DcNAA,*
  WhWNAA
Brown, Mary Jane 1895- *IndAu 1917*
Brown, Mary Josephine 1875-1912 *DcNAA*
Brown, Mary Mitchell *BiDSA*
Brown, Mary R *Alli Sup*
Brown, Mary Willcox *DcNAA*
Brown, Mather 1761-1831 *BkIE*
Brown, Matthew *Alli Sup*
Brown, Matthew 1776-1853 *DcNAA*
Brown, Mattye Jeanette *BlkAW*
Brown, Maurice 1881-1955 *LongC*
Brown, Maurice F 1928- *ConAu 41*
Brown, Maurice John Edwin 1906?-
  AmSCAP 66, Au&Wr
Brown, Merritt T 1913- *Au&Wr*
Brown, Michael 1931- *ConAu 33*
Brown, Michael B 1840- *PoIre*
Brown, Michael John 1932- *ConAu 29*
Brown, Middlemass *ChPo*
Brown, Milton Perry, Jr. 1928- *ConAu 9R*
Brown, Minna *ChPo*
Brown, Mister *NewC*
Brown, Morna Doris 1907- *ConAu 5R,*
  EncM&D
Brown, Morris Cecil 1943- *ConAu 37*
Brown, Moses 1703-1787 *Alli*
Brown, Moses True 1827-1900 *Alli Sup,*
  DcAmA, DcNAA, OhA&B
Brown, Muriel W 1892- *ConAu 23*
Brown, Murray 1929- *ConAu 37, WrD 1976*
Brown, Myra Berry 1918- *Au&Wr, AuBYP,*
  ConAu 1R, SmATA 6
Brown, Nacio, Jr. 1921- *AmSCAP 66*
Brown, Nacio Herb 1896-1964 *AmSCAP 66*
Brown, Nancy *AmA&B, WhWNAA*
Brown, Nathan *EarAB, EarAB Sup*
Brown, Neal 1856-1917 *DcNAA, WiscW*
Brown, Nelson *ChPo*
Brown, Nelson Courtlandt 1885- *WhWNAA*
Brown, Neville 1932- *ConAu 9R*
Brown, Nicholas *PoIre*
Brown, Nicholas 1769-1841 *CyAL 1*
Brown, Nigel 1907- *Au&Wr*
Brown, Norman D 1935- *ConAu 53*
Brown, Norman O 1913- *AmA&B, ConAu 21,*
  Pen Am, WorAu
Brown, Olive Stevens *ChPo*
Brown, Oliver M 1855-1874 *Alli Sup, BbD,*
  BiD&SB, BrAu 19, NewC
Brown, Oliver Phelps *Alli Sup*
Brown, Olympia 1835-1926 *DcNAA*
Brown, Oril 1908- *OhA&B*
Brown, Orlando *Alli Sup*
Brown, Orville Harry 1875- *WhWNAA*
Brown, Oscar, Jr. *BlkAW*
Brown, Oswald Eugene 1861-1939 *DcNAA*
Brown, Palmer 1919- *ChPo, IlBYP,*
  IlCB 1956, IlCB 1966
Brown, Pamela Beatrice 1924- *Au&Wr,*
  AuBYP, ConAu 13R, SmATA 5, WhCL
Brown, Parker B 1928- *ConAu 53*
Brown, Patricia L *LivBA*
Brown, Paul 1893- *AuBYP, BkCL, Br&AmS,*
  IlCB 1945, IlCB 1956, JBA 1951
Brown, Percy Whiting 1887- *OhA&B*
Brown, Peter *Alli*
Brown, Peter 1784?-1863 *BbtC, DcNAA*
Brown, Peter 1935- *ConAu 23*
Brown, Peter Arrell 1782-1860 *DcNAA*
Brown, P A ALSO Browne, Peter Arrell
Brown, Peter Douglas 1925- *ConAu 25,*
  WrD 1976
Brown, Peter Hume 1849-1918 *ChPo, Chmbr 3*
Brown, Peter Lancaster 1927- *ConAu 53*
Brown, Philip S *AuBYP*
Brown, Phoebe Allen Hinsdale 1783-1861
  AmA&B, ChPo S1, DcAmA, DcNAA,
  PoCh
Brown, R *Alli*

Brown, R 1928- *Au&Wr*
Brown, R Allen 1924- *Au&Wr, ConAu 5R*
Brown, R B *Alli*
Brown, R C *Alli Sup*
Brown, R Craig *OxCan Sup*
Brown, R G S 1929- *ConAu 29, WrD 1976*
Brown, R Warren *Alli Sup*
Brown, Rae *ConAu 49*
Brown, Ralph Adams 1908- *ConAu 33,*
  WrD 1976
Brown, Ralph Lawrence 1913- *WhWNAA*
Brown, Rawdon Lubbock 1803-1883 *Alli Sup*
Brown, Ray *ChPo*
Brown, Ray 1865-1944 *DcAmA, DcNAA*
Brown, Ray Andrews 1890- *WhWNAA*
Brown, Ray C B 1880- *WhWNAA*
Brown, Raymond Bryan 1923- *ConAu 17R*
Brown, Raymond Lamont 1939- *Au&Wr,*
  WrD 1976
Brown, Re Mona 1917- *ConAu 41*
Brown, Rebecca *DrAP 1975*
Brown, Regina Margaret *AuBYP*
Brown, Reginald Francis 1910- *Au&Wr*
Brown, Rex V 1933- *ConAu 53*
Brown, Richard *Alli, Alli Sup, BbtC,*
  BiDLA Sup, OxCan
Brown, Richard C 1919- *ConAu 5R*
Brown, Richard D 1939- *ConAu 53*
Brown, Richard H 1927- *ConAu 9R*
Brown, Richard Howard 1929- *ConAu 57*
Brown, Richard Maxwell 1927- *ConAu 17R*
Brown, Rita Mae 1944- *ConAu 45,*
  DrAF 1976, DrAP 1975
Brown, Robert *Alli, Alli Sup, BiDLA, ChPo,*
  ChPo S1
Brown, Robert 1549-1630 *Alli*
Brown, Robert ALSO Browne, Robert
Brown, Robert 1756-1831 *Alli*
Brown, Robert 1773-1858 *Alli, BrAu 19*
Brown, Robert 1844- *Alli Sup*
Brown, Robert 1921- *AmA&B*
Brown, Robert Carlton 1886- *WhWNAA*
Brown, Robert Christopher Lundin *Alli Sup,*
  OxCan
Brown, Robert E *Alli Sup*
Brown, Robert E 1907- *ConAu 5R*
Brown, Robert Elliott 1873-1938 *DcNAA*
Brown, Robert Goodell 1923- *ConAu 33,*
  WrD 1976
Brown, Robert H *BlkAW*
Brown, Robert H 1904- *WhWNAA*
Brown, Robert Hanbury 1916- *Au&Wr*
Brown, Robert Hewitt *Alli Sup*
Brown, Robert Joseph 1907- *ConAu P-1*
Brown, Robert L 1921- *ConAu 23, WrD 1976*
Brown, Robert Marshall 1870- *WhWNAA*
Brown, Robert McAfee 1920- *AmA&B,*
  ConAu 13R, WrD 1976
Brown, Robert N *Alli Sup*
Brown, Robert Neal Rudmose 1879- *WhLA*
Brown, Robert Raymond 1910- *AmA&B*
Brown, Robert Weir 1855- *Alli Sup*
Brown, Roger H 1931- *ConAu 9R*
Brown, Roger William 1925- *ConAu 13R*
Brown, Roland *ChPo*
Brown, Rollo Walter 1880-1956 *AmA&B,*
  ChPo S1, OhA&B, TwCA, TwCA Sup,
  WhWNAA
Brown, Rome Green 1862-1926 *DcNAA*
Brown, Rosalie Moore 1910- *ConAu 5R,*
  SmATA 9, WrD 1976
Brown, Roscoe C E 1867- *WhWNAA*
Brown, Rose 1883-1952 *AmA&B*
Brown, Rosellen *DrAF 1976, DrAP 1975*
Brown, Rowland *Alli Sup, ChPo S1,*
  ChPo S2
Brown, Roy Frederick 1921- *Au&Wr*
Brown, Roy Melton 1878- *WhWNAA*
Brown, Royal *WhWNAA*
Brown, Royston 1934- *Au&Wr*
Brown, Ruby Berkeley *BlkAW*
Brown, Ruth 1900- *WhWNAA*
Brown, Ruth Elizabeth Pemberton 1877-1944
  IndAu 1917
Brown, Ryland Thomas 1807-1890 *Alli Sup,*
  IndAu 1917
Brown, S *Alli, BiDLA*
Brown, Samn *BlkAW*

Brown, Samuel *Alli, Alli Sup*
Brown, Samuel 1768-1805 *Alli*
Brown, Samuel 1769-1834 *BiDSA*
Brown, Samuel 1817-1856 *Alli Sup*
Brown, Samuel Boardman 1860-1926 *DcNAA*
Brown, Samuel Borton *Alli Sup*
Brown, Samuel E *BlkAW*
Brown, Samuel E d1860 *EarAB, EarAB Sup*
Brown, Samuel Gilman 1813-1885 *Alli Sup,*
  CyAL 2, DcAmA, DcNAA
Brown, Samuel Horton 1878-1940 *DcNAA,*
  WhWNAA
Brown, Samuel R 1775-1817 *Alli, DcNAA*
Brown, Samuel Robbins 1810-1880 *DcNAA*
Brown, Samuel Sneade *Alli Sup*
Brown, Sanborn C 1913- *ConAu 17R,*
  WrD 1976
Brown, Sanford Miller 1855-1938 *DcNAA*
Brown, Sanger, II 1884- *WhWNAA*
Brown, Sara Lowe 1870-1957 *OhA&B*
Brown, Sarah *Alli*
Brown, Sarah Lee *BlkAW*
Brown, Sharon 1891- *ChPo S1, WhWNAA*
Brown, Sheldon S 1937- *ConAu 53*
Brown, Sidney DeVere 1925- *ConAu 33*
Brown, Simon *Alli*
Brown, Slater 1896- *AmA&B*
Brown, Solyman 1790-1876 *AmA, AmA&B,*
  ChPo, DcAmA, DcNAA, REnAL
Brown, Stafford *Alli*
Brown, Stanley 1914- *ConAu 49*
Brown, Stanley H 1927- *ConAu 45*
Brown, Stephen James Meredith 1881- *BkC 2,*
  CatA 1917, ChPo S1
Brown, Stephen W 1940- *ConAu 33*
Brown, Sterling Allen 1901- *AmA&B, BlkAW,*
  ConLC 1, DrAP 1975, LivBA, REnAL
Brown, Steven R 1939- *ConAu 49*
Brown, Stewardson *OxCan*
Brown, Stinson Joseph 1854-1923 *DcNAA*
Brown, Stuart C 1938- *ConAu 29*
Brown, Stuart Gerry 1912- *AmA&B,*
  ConAu 23
Brown, Susan Anna *Alli Sup*
Brown, Sydney MacGillvary 1895-1952
  AmA&B
Brown, T *Alli*
Brown, T Allston *Alli Sup*
Brown, T A ALSO Brown, Thomas Allston
Brown, T Craig- *Alli Sup*
Brown, T Merritt 1913- *ConAu 41*
Brown, T R *Alli Sup*
Brown, T Wesley *Alli Sup*
Brown, Tarleton 1754-1846 *DcNAA*
Brown, Tatton *Alli Sup*
Brown, Theo W 1934- *ConAu 61*
Brown, Theodore L 1928- *ConAu 33*
Brown, Theodore M 1925- *ConAu 33,*
  WrD 1976
Brown, Theophilus 1811-1879? *AmA, OxAm,*
  REnAL
Brown, Theron 1832-1914 *Alli Sup, AmA&B,*
  ChPo, ChPo S2, DcAmA, DcNAA
Brown, Thomas *Alli, Alli Sup, BiDLA,*
  Chmbr 2
Brown, Thomas 1663-1704 *Alli, BrAu, DcEnL,*
  DcLEnL, EvLB, NewC, OxEng, REn
Brown, Thomas 1778-1820 *Alli, BrAu 19,*
  DcEnL, EvLB, NewC
Brown, Thomas, The Younger 1779-1852 *ChPo,*
  DcEnL, NewC
Brown, Thomas Allston 1836-1918 *AmA&B,*
  DcNAA
Brown, Thomas Allston ALSO Brown, T A
Brown, Thomas B *Alli Sup*
Brown, Thomas Crowther *Alli Sup*
Brown, Thomas Edward 1830-1897 *Alli Sup,*
  BiD&SB, BrAu 19, ChPo, ChPo S2,
  Chmbr 3, DcEuL, DcLEnL, EvLB,
  NewC, OxEng
Brown, Thomas Edwin 1841-1924 *Alli Sup,*
  DcAmA, DcNAA
Brown, Thomas H 1930- *ConAu 57*
Brown, Thomas Kite 1885-1944 *DcNAA,*
  WhWNAA
Brown, Thomas Lloyd *Alli Sup*
Brown, Thomas N *Alli Sup*
Brown, Thomas Storrow 1803-1888 *BbtC,*

DcNAA, OxCan
Brown, Thomas Wemyss *Alli Sup*
Brown, Thurlow Weed d1866 *Alli Sup, DcAmA, DcNAA*
Brown, Tom *Chmbr 2*
Brown, Tom 1663-1704 *CasWL*
Brown, Truesdell S 1906- *ConAu 13R*
Brown, Tyki *BlkAW*
Brown, Valentine 1862- *ChPo, DcNAA*
Brown, Vandyke *Alli Sup, DcNAA, OhA&B*
Brown, Vinson 1912- *AuBYP, ConAu 1R*
Brown, Virginia Sharpe 1916- *Au&Wr, ConAu 13R*
Brown, Virginia Suggs 1924- *BlkAW, LivBA*
Brown, W Dawson *BbtC*
Brown, W Kennedy 1834-1915 *Alli Sup, DcNAA*
Brown, W K ALSO Brown, William K
Brown, W Martin *Alli Sup*
Brown, W Q *Alli Sup*
Brown, W S *Alli Sup*
Brown, W Wallace *Alli Sup, PoIre*
Brown, W Y *Alli Sup*
Brown, Waldo Franklin 1832- *Alli Sup, DcNAA*
Brown, Wallace 1933- *ConAu 17R*
Brown, Walter *Alli Sup*
Brown, Walter Earl 1928- *AmSCAP 66*
Brown, Walter Lee 1853-1904 *DcNAA*
Brown, Walter Lee 1924- *ConAu 33*
Brown, Walter R 1929- *ConAu 45*
Brown, Walter Wideman 1858- *BiDSA*
Brown, Warner *ConAu XR*
Brown, Warren Wilmer 1884- *WhWNAA*
Brown, Wayne 1944- *ConP 1975, WrD 1976*
Brown, Wenzell 1912- *AmA&B, Au&Wr, ConAu 1R*
Brown, Wesley 1945- *BlkAW, DrAF 1976, DrAP 1975*
Brown, Wilfred 1908- *ConAu 9R, WrD 1976*
Brown, Will C *AmA&B, ConAu XR*
Brown, William *Alli, Alli Sup, AuBYP, BiDLA, BiDLA Sup, ChPo S1, OxCan*
Brown, William 1738?-1789 *OxCan*
Brown, William 1808- *Alli Sup*
Brown, William 1835- *Alli Sup*
Brown, William 1836- *ChPo*
Brown, William 1881-1952 *BiDPar*
Brown, William Adams 1865-1943 *AmA&B, DcAmA, DcNAA, WhWNAA*
Brown, William B *BlkAW*
Brown, William Baker 1864- *WhLA*
Brown, William C *ChPo*
Brown, William Campbell 1928- *ConAu 57*
Brown, William Carlos 1853-1924 *DcNAA*
Brown, William Cullen *Alli, BiDLA*
Brown, William E 1907- *ConAu 29*
Brown, William Edgar *ChPo S1*
Brown, William F 1920- *ConAu 33*
Brown, William F 1928- *AmSCAP 66, ConAu 33*
Brown, William Garrott 1868-1913 *AmA&B, BiDSA, DcAmA, DcNAA*
Brown, William H 1748-1825 *BkIE*
Brown, William Haig 1823- *Alli Sup*
Brown, William Harvey 1862-1913 *DcNAA*
Brown, William Henry 1808-1883 *DcNAA*
Brown, William Henry 1884-1939 *DcNAA, WhWNAA*
Brown, William Hill 1765?-1793 *Alli, AmA, AmA&B, BiDSA, CnDAL, DcLEnL, DcNAA, OxAm, REn, REnAL*
Brown, William Horace 1855-1917 *DcNAA, IndAu 1917*
Brown, William James 1889- *Au&Wr, ConAu 5R*
Brown, William Kennedy 1834-1915 *OhA&B*
Brown, William K ALSO Brown, W K
Brown, William L 1910-1964 *ConAu 1R, SmATA 5*
Brown, William Laurence 1755-1830 *Alli, BiDLA*
Brown, William McEvery *OxCan*
Brown, William Montgomery 1855-1885 *BiDSA*
Brown, William Montgomery 1855-1937 *DcAmA, DcNAA, OhA&B, WhWNAA*
Brown, William Moseley 1894- *WhWNAA*
Brown, William Norman *Alli Sup,*
Brown, William Norman 1892- *AmA&B*

ConAu 57, ConAu 61
Brown, William Pennybrook *ChPo S1*
Brown, William Perry 1847-1923 *AmA&B, AmLY, BiDSA, DcNAA, HsB&A*
Brown, William Robert Henry *Alli, BiDLA*
Brown, William Wells 1816?-1884 *Alli Sup, AmA, AmA&B, BlkAW, DcNAA, REnAL*
Brown, William Young 1827-1914 *DcNAA*
Brown, Winifred M *ChPo S2*
Brown, Yeats- *TwCA, TwCA Sup*
Brown, Zaidee 1895- *WhWNAA*
Brown, Zenith Jones 1898- *AmA&B, ConAu 9R, EncM&D, TwCA, TwCA Sup, WhWNAA*
Brown And Jackson *Alli*
Brown-Azarowicz, Marjory F 1922- *ConAu 33*
Brown-Buck, Lillie 1860-1939 *DcNAA*
Brown-Potter, Cora *DcNAA*
Brownbill, John *Alli Sup*
Browne SEE ALSO Brown
Browne, Mrs. A C *Alli Sup*
Browne, A J *ChPo S1*
Browne, A M *ChPo S1*
Browne, Albert Gallatin 1835-1891 *Alli Sup, DcNAA*
Browne, Alexander *Alli, BiDSA*
Browne, Alfred Joseph Jukes- *Alli Sup*
Browne, Alice 1861-1925 *DcNAA*
Browne, Andrew *Alli*
Browne, Anita *AmA&B, WhWNAA*
Browne, Anna Maria 1938- *Au&Wr*
Browne, Annabella Maria *Alli Sup*
Browne, Annie Greene *BiDSA*
Browne, Arthur *Alli*
Browne, Arthur d1805 *Alli, PoIre*
Browne, Arthur 1699-1773 *Alli, CyAL 1*
Browne, Arthur H *Alli Sup*
Browne, Augusta *Alli Sup*
Browne, Benjamin A *BlkAW*
Browne, Benjamin Frederick 1793-1873 *AmA&B*
Browne, Bradford *AmSCAP 66*
Browne, C B *BiDLA Sup*
Browne, Calvin *BbtC*
Browne, Carmen L *ChPo S1*
Browne, Causten 1828-1909 *Alli Sup, DcAmA, DcNAA*
Browne, Charles *Alli*
Browne, Charles 1875-1947 *DcNAA*
Browne, Charles Farrar 1834-1867 *Alli Sup, AmA, AmA&B, BbD, BiD&SB, Chmbr 3, CnDAL, DcAmA, DcEnA Ap, DcEnL, DcLEnL, DcNAA, EvLB, OhA&B, OxAm, OxEng, Pen Am, REn, REnAL, WebEAL*
Browne, Charles Gordon *Alli Sup*
Browne, Charles Herbert 1881- *WhWNAA*
Browne, Charles Orde *Alli Sup*
Browne, Charles Thomas 1825-1868 *Alli Sup, PoIre*
Browne, Courtney 1915- *Au&Wr, ConAu 21*
Browne, Daniel Jay 1804- *Alli, DcNAA*
Browne, Dik 1917- *AuNews 1*
Browne, Dorothy Margaret Stuart *WhLA*
Browne, Dunn *AmA&B, DcNAA*
Browne, E Martin 1900- *Au&Wr, ConAu 25, LongC*
Browne, Edgar Athelstane *Alli Sup*
Browne, Edmond Charles *Alli Sup*
Browne, Edward *Alli*
Browne, Edward 1644-1708 *Alli*
Browne, Edward George Kirwan *Alli Sup*
Browne, Edward Granville *ChPo S2*
Browne, Edward Harold 1811- *Alli, Alli Sup, DcEnL*
Browne, Emily Bramhall *ChPo S1*
Browne, Emma Alice *LivFWS, PoIre*
Browne, Eppes Wayles 1879- *WhWNAA*
Browne, Ernest D 1900- *AmSCAP 66*
Browne, Felicia Dorothea *Alli, BiDLA*
Browne, Frances 1816-1879 *Alli Sup, BrAu 19, ChPo, DcEnL, DcLEnL, FamSYP, JBA 1934, St&VC, WhCL*
Browne, Frances ALSO Brown, Frances
Browne, Frances Elizabeth *ChPo*
Browne, Francis *Alli, PoIre*
Browne, Francis Fisher 1843-1913 *Alli Sup,*

AmA, AmA&B, ChPo, DcAmA, DcNAA
Browne, Francis James *WhLA*
Browne, Frederick George *Alli Sup*
Browne, G *ChPo*
Browne, G M *Alli Sup*
Browne, G Peter 1930- *ConAu 23, OxCan Sup, WrD 1976*
Browne, George *Alli Sup*
Browne, George d1560? *Alli*
Browne, George B *BlkAW*
Browne, George Earl *ChPo*
Browne, George Forrest 1833- *Alli Sup*
Browne, George H *Alli Sup*
Browne, George Henry 1857-1931 *DcNAA*
Browne, George Lathom 1815- *Alli Sup*
Browne, George Stephenson 1890- *ConAu 29*
Browne, George Waldo 1851-1930 *AmA&B, AmLY, DcAmA, DcNAA, HsB&A, WhWNAA*
Browne, George Walter *Alli Sup*
Browne, Gordon Frederick 1858-1932 *ChPo, ChPo S1, WhCL*
Browne, H H *ChPo*
Browne, Hablot Knight 1815-1882 *ChPo, ChPo S1, ChPo S2, HsB&A, NewC*
Browne, Harry *WrD 1976*
Browne, Harry 1918- *Au&Wr*
Browne, Harry 1933- *ConAu 49*
Browne, Henry *Alli, BbtC, BiDSA*
Browne, Henry 1918- *WrD 1976*
Browne, Henry H *Alli Sup*
Browne, Henry J 1853-1941 *CatA 1947*
Browne, Henry Joy *Alli Sup*
Browne, Henry Llewellyn *Alli Sup*
Browne, Herbert Janvrin *Alli Sup*
Browne, Howard 1908- *EncM&D*
Browne, Hugh Junor *Alli Sup*
Browne, Hyde Mathis *Alli, BiDLA*
Browne, I Henderson *Alli Sup*
Browne, Irving 1835-1899 *Alli Sup, AmA&B, BiD&SB, ChPo, DcAmA, DcNAA*
Browne, Isaac Hawkins 1705?-1760 *Alli, Chmbr 2, DcEnL, EvLB, NewC*
Browne, J *Alli, BiDLA*
Browne, J D *Alli*
Browne, Mrs. J D H *DcNAA*
Browne, J F *Alli Sup*
Browne, J H *Alli*
Browne, J Houston *Alli Sup*
Browne, J Jemmett 1832- *Alli Sup, PoIre*
Browne, J W *Alli Sup*
Browne, James *Alli, NewC*
Browne, Sir James *Alli, Alli Sup*
Browne, James Alexander *Alli Sup*
Browne, James Crichton *Alli Sup*
Browne, James P *Alli Sup*
Browne, Jeanetta *Alli Sup*
Browne, Jemmett *Alli Sup*
Browne, John *Alli, Alli Sup, BiDLA*
Browne, John 1823- *Alli Sup*
Browne, John 1838- *ChPo S1*
Browne, John Cave- *Alli Sup*
Browne, John Hutton Balfour *ChPo S1*
Browne, John Hutton Balfour 1845- *Alli Sup*
Browne, John Lewis 1866-1933 *AmSCAP 66*
Browne, John Ross 1821?-1875 *Alli, Alli Sup, AmA&B, ArizL, BbD, BiD&SB, CnDAL, CyAL 2, DcAmA, DcEnL, DcNAA, EarAB, EarAB Sup, OxAm, REnAL*
Browne, John Samuel 1782- *Alli, BiDLA*
Browne, Joseph *Alli, Alli Sup*
Browne, Joseph 1700-1767 *Alli*
Browne, Junius Henri 1833-1902 *Alli Sup, AmA&B, BbD, BiD&SB, DcAmA, DcNAA, OhA&B*
Browne, Katharine Maynadier *ChPo*
Browne, Laurence Edward 1887- *Au&Wr, WrD 1976*
Browne, Lena Griswold *ChPo*
Browne, Lennox *Alli Sup*
Browne, Leslie *MnBBF*
Browne, Lewis 1897-1949 *AmA&B, DcNAA, REnAL, TwCA, TwCA Sup, WhWNAA*
Browne, Lewis Allen 1876-1937 *AmA&B, DcNAA, REnAL*
Browne, Lewis G 1810- *ChPo S2*
Browne, M *BkIE*
Browne, Miss M A *ChPo S2*

ConP 1970, ConP 1975, DrAF 1976,
DrAP 1975, WrD 1976
Brownstein, Samuel C 1909- ConAu 5R,
WrD 1976
Brownswerd, John d1589 Alli
Brownswerd, John d1859 DcEnL
Brownswood, John Alli
Brownswood, William Alli
Broxis, Peter F 1936- Au&Wr
Broxoline, Charles Alli
Broxon, James William 1897- IndAu 1917
Broyles, J Allen 1934- ConAu 9R
Broyles, William Anderson 1879- WhWNAA
Brozek, Josef 1913- ConAu 45
Bru, Hedin 1901- CasWL
Brubacher, Abram R 1870-1939 DcNAA,
WhWNAA
Brubacher, John S 1898- AmA&B, ConAu 1R,
WrD 1976
Brubaker, Albert Philson 1852-1943 DcNAA
Brubaker, Dale L 1937- ConAu 53
Brubaker, Howard 1882-1957 AmA&B,
IndAu 1917
Brubaker, Joseph Daniel 1905- IndAu 1917
Brubaker, Sterling 1924- ConAu 21
Bruccoli, Matthew J 1931- ChPo S1,
ConAu 9R, WrD 1976
Bruce, Addington 1874- AmLY
Bruce, Alexander Alli, Alli Sup
Bruce, Alexander Balmain 1831- Alli Sup
Bruce, Alison Muriel 1929- Au&Wr
Bruce, Andrew Alexander 1866-1934 DcNAA
Bruce, Archibald 1777-1818 Alli
Bruce, Arthur Alli
Bruce, Arthur Loring AmA&B, DcNAA
Bruce, Basil Alli, BiDLA
Bruce, Ben F, Jr. 1920- ConAu 13R,
IndAu 1917
Bruce, C D 1862-1934 Br&AmS
Bruce, Charles Alli Sup
Bruce, Charles 1906-1971 CanWr, ConP 1970,
DcLEnL, OxCan, OxCan Sup, REnAL
Bruce, David MnBBF
Bruce, David 1860- ChPo
Bruce, Dickson Davies, Jr. 1946- ConAu 53,
WrD 1976
Bruce, Donald 1930- ConAu 17R
Bruce, Dorita M Fairlie ChPo S2
Bruce, Dwight Hall 1834-1908 DcNAA
Bruce, E BiDLA
Bruce, E And J Alli
Bruce, Mrs. E M Alli Sup
Bruce, Edward Alli
Bruce, Edward Caledon 1825- Alli Sup
Bruce, Eli Metcalf 1828-1866 BiDSA
Bruce, F J Alli Sup
Bruce, Francis Rosslyn Courtenay 1871-1956
ChPo
Bruce, Frederick Fyvie 1910- Au&Wr
Bruce, George 1909- CasWL, ChPo S1,
ChPo S2, ConP 1970, ConP 1975,
WrD 1976
Bruce, Gustav Marius 1879- WhWNAA
Bruce, Mrs. H Alli Sup
Bruce, H Addington 1874-1959 AmA&B,
BiDPar, WhWNAA
Bruce, Hamilton Alli Sup
Bruce, Harold Lawton 1887-1934 DcNAA,
WhWNAA
Bruce, Harry OxCan Sup
Bruce, Harry J 1931- ConAu 23
Bruce, Helm 1860-1927 DcNAA
Bruce, Henry DcAmA
Bruce, Henry Austin, Baron Aberdare 1815-
Alli Sup
Bruce, Henry J Alli Sup
Bruce, Herbert Alli Sup
Bruce, Irene ChPo S1
Bruce, J Alli Sup
Bruce, James Alli, Alli Sup, Chmbr 2
Bruce, James 1730-1794 Alli, BrAu, CasWL,
DcEnA, DcLEnL, EvLB, NewC, OxEng
Bruce, James 1808-1861 Alli Sup
Bruce, James Douglas 1862-1923 BiDSA,
DcNAA
Bruce, James E Brudenell Alli Sup
Bruce, Jeannette M 1922- ConAu 5R
Bruce, Jerome BiDSA

Bruce, John Alli, Alli Sup, BiDLA
Bruce, John d1866 BbtC
Bruce, John 1802-1869 Alli Sup
Bruce, John Collingwood 1805-1892 Alli,
Alli Sup, ChPo S1
Bruce, John Edward 1856-1924 BlkAW
Bruce, John Mitchell Alli Sup
Bruce, Josephine ChPo
Bruce, Kenneth 1876-1916 DcNAA
Bruce, L H ChPo S1
Bruce, Lennart 1919- ConAu 33, DrAP 1975,
WrD 1976
Bruce, Lenny 1925?-1966 AmA&B, ConAu 25
Bruce, Leo ConAu XR
Bruce, Lew Alli
Bruce, Mary 1927- ConAu 25, SmATA 1
Bruce, Mary B ChPo
Bruce, Mary Elizabeth Cumming Alli Sup
Bruce, Mary Lelia Hoge OhA&B
Bruce, Michael Alli
Bruce, Michael 1746-1767 Alli, CasWL, ChPo,
ChPo S1, ChPo S2, Chmbr 2, DcEnL,
EvLB, NewC, PoCh
Bruce, Michael And Logan, John Pen Eng
Bruce, Monica ConAu XR
Bruce, Norman ChPo S1
Bruce, Peter Henry Alli
Bruce, Philip Alexander 1856-1933 AmA&B,
BiDSA, DcAmA, DcNAA, OxAm,
WhWNAA
Bruce, Phyllis OxCan Sup
Bruce, Richard Alli
Bruce, Robert Alli, Alli Sup
Bruce, Robert 1274-1329 REn
Bruce, Robert 1599-1631 Alli
Bruce, Robert 1915- AmSCAP 66
Bruce, Robert 1927- Au&Wr, ConAu P-1,
WrD 1976
Bruce, Robert V 1923- ConAu 53
Bruce, Rosslyn 1871- ChPo, WhLA
Bruce, S Wakefield BiDLA
Bruce, Saunders Dewees 1825-1902 DcAmA
Bruce, Sylvia 1936- ConAu 33
Bruce, Thomas Alli Sup, BiDSA
Bruce, Titus Alli
Bruce, Violet R ConAu 29
Bruce, Virginia ChPo
Bruce, W Alli Sup
Bruce, W A MnBBF
Bruce, Wallace 1844-1914 Alli Sup, AmA&B,
BiD&SB, ChPo, ChPo S1, ChPo S2,
DcAmA, DcNAA
Bruce, Walter Alli
Bruce, William Alli, Alli Sup
Bruce, William 1824- Alli Sup
Bruce, William Cabell 1860-1946 AmA&B,
DcNAA, OxAm, REnAL, TwCA,
TwCA Sup, WhWNAA
Bruce, William George 1856- WhWNAA
Bruce, William H 1856- TexWr, WhWNAA
Bruce, Mrs. William Liddell BiDSA
Bruce, William Napier 1858- Alli Sup
Bruce, William Straton 1846- WhLA
Bruce, William U Alli
Bruce Lockhart, Sir Robert Hamilton 1887-1970
Au&Wr, LongC
Bruce Lockhart, Robin 1920- Au&Wr,
ConAu 25, WrD 1976
Bruce-Mitford, Rupert Leo Scott 1914- Au&Wr
Brucer, F F 1910- ConAu 1R
Bruch, Hilde 1904- AuNews 1, ConAu 53
Bruch, Richard Alli
Bruchac, Joseph, III 1942- ConAu 33,
DrAF 1976, DrAP 1975, WrD 1976
Bruchardt, Arno 1883- WhLA
Bruche, Countess Charles P De AmA&B
Bruchesi, Jean 1901- CanWr, CasWL,
CatA 1947, OxCan, WhWNAA
Bruchesi, Louis Joseph Paul Napoleon 1855-1939
DcNAA
Bruchey, Stuart 1917- ConAu 33
Bruck, Alfred 1865- WhLA
Bruck, Carl 1879- WhLA
Bruck, L Alli Sup
Bruckberger, Raymond-Leopold 1907-
CatA 1952
Brucke, Ernst Th Von 1880- WhLA
Brucker, Herbert 1898- AmA&B, ConAu 5R,

Brucker, Joseph Alli Sup
Brucker, Margaretta 1883-1958 OhA&B
Bruckner, Anton 1824-1896 AtlBL, OxGer,
REn
Bruckner, Arthur 1877- WhLA
Bruckner, Ferdinand 1891-1958 CnMD,
McGWD, ModGL, ModWD, OxGer
Bruckner, Friedrich 1891-1958 CrCD
Bruckner, John 1726-1804 Alli, BiDLA
Brucks, George Alexander Dunsterville Alli Sup
Bruckshaw, Samuel Alli
Brudenel, James T, Earl Of Cardigan 1797-1868
Alli Sup
Brudenell, Exton Alli
Bruder Klaus OxGer
Bruders, Henry 1869- WhLA
Brudi, Walter 1907- WhGrA
Brudno, Ezra Selig 1878-1954 AmA&B,
OhA&B, WhWNAA
Brueckmann, J George, Jr. 1904- AnMV 1926,
WhWNAA
Bruee, William BiDLA
Bruegel, Pieter 1525?-1569 AtlBL, REn
Brueggemann, Fritz 1876- WhLA
Brueghel, Pieter 1525?-1569 REn
Bruehl, Charles Paul 1876- BkC 2, CatA 1947,
WhWNAA
Bruel, Per Vilhelm 1915- Au&Wr
Bruemmer, Fred 1929- OxCan Sup,
WrD 1976
Bruen, Edward Tunis 1851-1889 Alli Sup,
DcNAA
Bruen, Lewis Alli
Bruen, Matthias 1793-1829 Alli, DcNAA
Bruen, Robert Alli
Bruening, J H 1929- BiDPar
Bruening, William H 1943- ConAu 57
Bruere, Henry 1882- WhWNAA
Bruere, Martha B ChPo, WhWNAA
Bruere, Robert W WhWNAA
Bruers, Antonio 188-?-1954 BiDPar
Bruerton, Courtney 1890- DcSpL
Brues, Otto 1897-1967 CnMD, ModWD,
OxGer
Bruess, Clint E 1941- ConAu 33
Bruestle, Beaumont 1905- AmA&B
Bruet, Edmond OxCan
Brueys, David-Augustin De 1640-1725 DcEuL,
McGWD, OxFr, REn
Bruff, Nancy 1909- AmNov, ConAu XR,
ConAu 41, WrD 1976
Bruff, Nancy 1915- AmA&B
Bruffee, Kenneth A 1934- ConAu 37
Bruford, Rose Elizabeth 1904- Au&Wr,
WrD 1976
Bruggen, Carry Van 1881-1932 CasWL
Bruggink, Donald J 1929- ConAu 13R
Bruggis, Thomas Alli
Brugman, Johannes 1400?-1473 CasWL
Brugmanns, Hajo 1868- WhLA
Brugmans, Henri J F W 1885-1961 BiDPar
Bruhl, Friedrich Alois, Graf Von 1739-1793
OxGer
Bruhl, Gustav CasWL
Bruhl, Gustavus 1829-1903 OhA&B
Bruhl, Heinrich, Graf Von 1700-1763 OxGer
Bruhn, Carl 1869- WhWNAA
Bruhns, George Frederick William 1874-1963
AmSCAP 66
Bruin, Claas 1671-1732 CasWL
Bruin, John ConAu 49, WrD 1976
Bruins, Elton J 1927- ConAu 53
Brulard, Henri OxFr
Brule, Etienne 1592?-1633 OxCan
Brulez, Raymond 1895- CasWL, EncWL
Bruller, Jean 1902- EvEuW, IlCB 1945,
LongC, ModRL, REn, TwCA Sup
Brulles Alli
Brulls, Christian EncM&D
Brulow, Caspar 1585-1627 CasWL
Brulow, Kaspar 1585-1627 DcEuL, OxGer
Brumbaugh, Martin Grove 1862-1930 DcNAA,
WhWNAA
Brumbaugh, Robert Sherrick 1918- ConAu 5R,
WrD 1976
Brumbaugh, Thomas B 1921- ConAu 49
Brumblay, Robert 1876- IndAu 1816

Brumfield, Louis Brucker *ConAmA*
Brumfield, W A 1875- *WhWNAA*
Brumhall *Alli*
Brumm, John Lewis 1878-1958 *AmA&B*
Brumm, Ursula 1919- *ConAu 29*
Brummell, George Bryan 1778-1840 *NewC*
Brummet, R Lee 1921- *ConAu 23*
Brummitt, Dan Brearley 1867-1939 *DcNAA*
Brummitt, Wyatt B 1897- *ConAu 9R*
Brumwell, William *Alli*
Brun Von Schonebeck *CasWL, OxGer*
Brun, Donald 1909- *WhGrA*
Brun, F Arthur 1896- *WhWNAA*
Brun, Friederike Sophie Christiane 1765-1835 *BiD&SB, OxGer*
Brun, Henri 1939- *ConAu 53, OxCan Sup*
Brun, Johan Nordal 1745-1816 *CasWL*
Brun, Nordahl 1745-1816 *DcEuL*
Brun, Pascal A 1889- *WhWNAA*
Brun, Samuel Jacques 1857-1908? *DcNAA*
Brun, Theodore 1898- *Au&Wr*
Bruncken, Ernest 1865- *WhWNAA*
Bruncken, Herbert 1896- *AmA&B*
Brundage, Albert Harrison 1862-1936 *DcNAA*
Brundage, Burr Cartwright 1912- *ConAu 41*
Brundage, Frances *ChPo S2*
Brundage, James A 1929- *ConAu 5R, WrD 1976*
Brundage, John Herbert 1926- *WrD 1976*
Brundage, William Milton 1857-1921 *DcNAA*
Brune, Clare *Alli Sup*
Brune, Guillaume-Marie-Anne *OxFr*
Brune, Joan De, The Elder 1588-1658 *CasWL*
Brune, Joan De, The Younger 1618-1649 *CasWL*
Brune, Lester H 1926- *ConAu 33*
Brune, T B And Curtis, H H *Alli Sup*
Bruneau, Charles *OxFr*
Bruneau, Jean *ConAu XR, OxCan*
Bruneau, Joseph 1866-1933 *DcNAA*
Bruneau, Mathurin 1784-1825? *OxFr*
Bruneau, Thomas C 1939- *ConAu 53*
Brunefille, G E *Alli Sup*
Brunel, Isambard 1837- *Alli Sup*
Brunelleschi, Filippo 1377-1446 *AtlBL, REn*
Brunelli, Louis Jean 1925- *AmSCAP 66*
Bruner, Frank G 1874- *WhWNAA*
Bruner, Henry Lane 1861- *WhWNAA*
Bruner, Herbert B 1894?-1974 *ConAu 53*
Bruner, James Dowden 1864- *BiDSA, WhWNAA*
Bruner, Jane Woodworth 1850?-1925? *Alli Sup, DcNAA*
Bruner, Jerome S 1915- *AmA&B, ConAu 45*
Bruner, Lawrence 1856-1937 *DcNAA, WhWNAA*
Bruner, Margaret E d1970? *AnMV 1926, ChPo, ChPo S1, ConAu P-1, IndAu 1917*
Bruner, Richard W 1926- *ConAu 49*
Bruner, Stephen C 1891- *WhWNAA*
Bruner, Wally 1931- *ConAu 49*
Brunet, Berthelot 1901-1948 *CanWr, OxCan*
Brunet, Jacques-Charles 1780-1867 *OxFr*
Brunet, Jean *OxFr*
Brunet, Louis Ovide 1826-1877 *DcNAA*
Brunet, Marta 1901-1966 *Pen Am*
Brunet, Michel 1917- *CanWr, OxCan, OxCan Sup*
Brunet, Ovide 1826-1877 *BbtC*
Brunet, Pierre-Gustave 1807-1896 *OxFr*
Brunetiere, Ferdinand 1849-1906 *BbD, BiD&SB, CIDMEuL, DcEuL, EuA, EvEuW, OxFr, Pen Eur*
Brunetiere, Vincent DeP Marie Ferdinand 1849-1906 *REn*
Brunetti, Cledo 1910- *ConAu 29*
Brunetto Latini *EuA*
Brunhoff, Jean De 1899-1937 *AuBYP, IlCB 1956, JBA 1951, WhCL*
Brunhoff, Laurent De 1925- *AuBYP, IlCB 1956, IlCB 1966, MorJA, WhCL*
Brunhouse, Robert Levere 1908- *ConAu 49*
Bruni, Leonardo 1370?-1444 *BiD&SB, CasWL, DcEuL, Pen Eur, REn*
Bruning, August Friedrich 1874- *WhLA*
Bruning, Heinrich 1885-1970 *OxGer*
Brunini, John Gilland 1899- *AmA&B, BkC 4, CatA 1947, ChPo S2*
Brunius, Bernardus *CasWL*

Brunken, Ernest 1865- *WhWNAA*
Brunn, Harry O, Jr. 1919- *Au&Wr, ConAu 1R, WrD 1976*
Brunn, Hermann 1862- *WhLA*
Brunn, Walter 1876- *WhLA*
Brunne, Robert ALSO Mannyng, Robert
Brunne, Robert De 1270?- *Alli, DcEnL*
Brunne, Robert Mannyng 1270?- *Alli*
Brunne, Robert Of 1270?- *EvLB*
Brunner, Arnold William 1857-1925 *DcNAA*
Brunner, David B 1835-1903 *DcNAA*
Brunner, Edmund DeSchweinitz 1889-1973 *ConAu 45, ConAu P-1, WhWNAA*
Brunner, Elizabeth 1920- *Au&Wr, WrD 1976*
Brunner, Emil 1889- *TwCA Sup*
Brunner, James A 1923- *ConAu 37*
Brunner, John 1934- *Au&Wr, ConAu 1R, WrD 1976*
Brunner, John Hamilton 1825- *BiDSA*
Brunner, Karl 1872- *WhLA*
Brunner, Karl 1887- *WhLA*
Brunner, Robert F 1938- *AmSCAP 66*
Brunner, Theodore F 1934- *ConAu 33*
Brunner, Thomas d1571 *OxGer*
Brunngraber, Rudolf 1900?-1960 *OxGer, TwCA, TwCA Sup*
Brunning, Benjamin *Alli*
Brunnmark, Gustavus *BiDLA*
Brunnow, Francis *Alli Sup*
Brunnow, Mrs. Francis *Alli Sup*
Bruno Von Hornberg *OxGer*
Bruno, Frank *ConAu XR*
Bruno, Giordano 1548-1600 *BiD&SB, CasWL, DcEuL, EuA, EvEuW, McGWD, Pen Eur, RCom, REn, REnWD*
Bruno, Guido 1884- *AmA&B, AmLY, REnAL*
Bruno, Harry A 1893- *WhWNAA*
Bruno, James 1917- *AmSCAP 66*
Bruno, James Edward 1940- *ConAu 41*
Bruno, Jean 1909- *BiDPar*
Bruno, Joann *BlkAW*
Bruno, Michael 1921- *ConAu 33*
Bruno, Richard M *Alli Sup*
Bruno, Vincent *ChPo*
Brunot, Ferdinand 1860-1938 *OxFr*
Brunowe, Marion J *Alli Sup, DcNAA*
Bruns, Professor *ChPo*
Bruns, Friedrich 1878- *WhWNAA*
Bruns, J Edgar 1923- *ConAu 5R*
Bruns, John Dickson 1836-1883 *BiDSA*
Bruns, William John, Jr. 1935- *ConAu 37, WrD 1976*
Brunschvicg, Leon 1869-1944 *OxFr*
Brunsell, Samuel *Alli*
Brunskill, Ronald William 1929- *WrD 1976*
Brunson, Alfred 1793-1882 *Alli Sup, DcNAA, OhA&B*
Brunson, Doris *BlkAW*
Brunson, Zoe *TexWr*
Brunswick, Duke Of *Alli*
Brunswick, Heinrich Julius, Duke Of 1564-1613 *DcEuL*
Brunton, Alex *Alli*
Brunton, Anna 1773?- *Alli, BiDLA*
Brunton, David W 1929- *ConAu 41*
Brunton, David William 1849-1927 *DcNAA, WhWNAA*
Brunton, George *Alli Sup*
Brunton, Louisa 1779-1860 *NewC*
Brunton, Mary 1778-1818 *Alli, BrAu 19, Chmbr 2, DcEnL, EvLB, NewC*
Brunton, Paul 1898- *Au&Wr*
Brunton, Thomas Lauder 1844- *Alli Sup*
Brunton, William 1850-1906 *BbtC, ChPo*
Brunton, William And Goodfellow, Robin *Alli Sup*
Bruntz, George G 1901- *ConAu 5R*
Brunwart Von Augheim *OxGer*
Brusasque, Elizabeth A *Alli*
Bruscambille *OxFr*
Brusch, Caspar 1518-1557 *OxGer*
Brush, Albert Moorehead 1897-1954 *OhA&B*
Brush, Christine Chaplin 1842-1892 *Alli Sup, AmA&B, BiD&SB, ChPo, DcAmA, DcBiA, DcNAA*
Brush, Craig B 1930- *ConAu 21*
Brush, Dorothy Hamilton 1894- *OhA&B*

Brush, Douglas Peirce 1930- *ConAu 57*
Brush, Edmund Cone 1852- *OhA&B*
Brush, Edward Nathaniel 1852- *WhWNAA*
Brush, Frederick Louis 1871- *ChPo, ChPo S2*
Brush, George Jarvis 1831-1912 *Alli Sup, DcAmA, DcNAA*
Brush, Joel *ChPo*
Brush, John E 1919- *ConAu 33, WrD 1976*
Brush, Judith M 1938- *ConAu 57*
Brush, Katharine 1902?-1952 *AmA&B, AmNov, OhA&B, REn, REnAL, TwCA, TwCA Sup, WhWNAA*
Brush, Mary Elizabeth 1857- *Alli Sup, DcNAA*
Brush, Ruth J 1910- *AmSCAP 66*
Brushingham, John Patrick 1855-1927 *DcNAA*
Brushwood, John S 1920- *ConAu 21*
Brusiloff, Phyllis 1935- *ConAu 57*
Brussel, James Arnold 1905- *Au&Wr, ConAu 1R*
Brussel-Smith, Bernard 1914- *IlBYP, IlCB 1956*
Brust, Alfred 1891-1934 *ModWD*
Brustein, Robert 1927- *AmA&B, Au&Wr, ConAu 9R, WorAu*
Brustlein, Daniel 1904- *AmA&B, IlBYP, IlCB 1966*
Brustlein, Janice Tworkov *AuBYP, ConAu 9R*
Brut, The *DcEnL*
Bruteau, Beatrice 1930- *ConAu 57, WrD 1976*
Bruton, Edward G *Alli Sup*
Bruton, Eric Moore *Au&Wr, ConAu 13R, WrD 1976*
Bruton, Henry J 1921- *ConAu 23*
Bruton, J G 1914- *ConAu 9R*
Bruton, William *Alli*
Brutten, Gene J 1928- *ConAu 37*
Brutten, Milton 1922- *ConAu 45*
Brutus *DcNAA*
Brutus 1789-1854 *AmA*
Brutus, Dennis 1924- *AfA 1, CasWL, ConAu 49, ConP 1970, ConP 1975, Pen Cl, RGAfl, TwCW, WrD 1976*
Brutus, Lucius Junius *NewC, REn*
Brutus, Marcus Junius 085?BC-042BC *NewC, REn*
Bruun, Bertel 1937- *Au&Wr, ConAu 45*
Bruun, Erik 1926- *WhGrA*
Bruun, Geoffrey 1898- *AmA&B, ConAu 1R, TwCA Sup*
Bruun, Malthe Conrad 1775-1826 *CasWL, DcEuL*
Bruun Olsen, Ernst 1923- *CasWL, CrCD*
Bruyas, James *BbtC*
Bruyas, S J *Alli Sup*
Bruyere, Jean DeLa *EvEuW*
Bruyn, Kathleen 1903- *ConAu 33*
Bry, Adelaide 1920- *ConAu 33*
Bry, Gerhard 1911- *ConAu 41*
Bry, Theodor De 1528-1598 *OxAm*
Bryan, Alfred 1871-1958 *AmSCAP 66, ChPo S1*
Bryan, Augustine *Alli*
Bryan, Augustine d1726 *Alli*
Bryan, C D B 1936- *AmA&B, DrAF 1976*
Bryan, Carter R 1911- *ConAu 33*
Bryan, Catherine 1907- *AnCL*
Bryan, Charles Faulkner 1911-1955 *AmSCAP 66*
Bryan, Charlotte Augusta Lowe 1867-1948 *IndAu 1816*
Bryan, Clark W 1824-1899 *Alli Sup, DcNAA*
Bryan, Daniel *Alli Sup, BiDSA*
Bryan, Daniel 1795-1866 *DcNAA*
Bryan, Dorothy M *CatA 1952*
Bryan, Ella Howard *BiDSA*
Bryan, Elmer Burritt 1865-1934 *DcNAA*
Bryan, Emma Lyon *BiDSA*
Bryan, Enoch Albert 1855-1941 *DcNAA, IndAu 1816*
Bryan, Sir Francis d1550 *Alli, DcEnL, DcEuL, NewC, OxEng*
Bryan, G McLeod 1920- *ConAu 1R*
Bryan, George 1860-1930 *DcNAA, WhWNAA*
Bryan, George Sands 1879-1943 *AmA&B, AnMV 1926, ChPo, ChPo S1, DcNAA, WhWNAA*

Bryan, Golda Moses *TexWr*
Bryan, Guy M *BiDSA*
Bryan, Hanna M *ChPo S1*
Bryan, Harrison 1923- *WrD 1976*
Bryan, Mrs. J M *Alli Sup*
Bryan, J Wallace 1884- *WhWNAA*
Bryan, J Y 1907- *ConAu 17*
Bryan, James 1810-1881 *DcNAA*
Bryan, Jennie Moore 1854-1931 *OhA&B*
Bryan, John *Alli*
Bryan, John 1853-1918 *OhA&B*
Bryan, John E 1931- *ConAu 53*
Bryan, John Stewart 1871-1944 *AmA&B*
Bryan, Joseph, III 1904- *AmA&B, AuBYP, ConAu 61, REnAL*
Bryan, Julian Scott *ChPo S2*
Bryan, Julien 1899-1974 *ConAu 53*
Bryan, Kirk 1888- *WhWNAA*
Bryan, Louise Chilton 1877- *TexWr*
Bryan, M T *ChPo*
Bryan, Margaret *Alli, BiDLA*
Bryan, Marian K 1900?-1974 *ConAu 53*
Bryan, Martin 1908- *ConAu 1R*
Bryan, Mary Edwards 1842?-1913 *Alli Sup, AmA, AmA&B, BiDSA, DcAmA, DcNAA, LivFWS*
Bryan, Matthew *Alli*
Bryan, Mavis 1915- *ConAu XR*
Bryan, Michael 1757-1821 *Alli, BiDLA, DcEnL*
Bryan, Philip *Alli*
Bryan, Ralph 1892- *TexWr*
Bryan, Ralph Burgess 1899- *WhWNAA*
Bryan, Robert *BlkAW*
Bryan, Ruth *Alli Sup*
Bryan, Sam *ChPo S1*
Bryan, Stanton Pierce 1827- *ChPo S2*
Bryan, Thomas E *Alli Sup*
Bryan, William *Alli, BiDLA*
Bryan, William Jennings 1860-1925 *AmA&B, DcAmA, DcNAA, OxAm, REn, REnAL*
Bryan, William Lowe 1860-1955 *AmA&B, IndAu 1816*
Bryan, William Smith 1846- *BiDSA*
Bryan, William Swan Plumer 1856-1925 *DcNAA*
Bryan, Wilmot Guy *Alli Sup*
Bryan, Worcester Allen 1873-1940 *DcNAA, WhWNAA*
Bryans, Clement And Hendy, F J R *Alli Sup*
Bryans, James William *Alli Sup*
Bryans, John Kennedy 1872- *ChPo S2*
Bryans, Robert Harbinson 1928- *Au&Wr, ConAu 5R*
Bryans, Robin 1928- *ConAu XR, WrD 1976*
Bryans, Sibella E *Alli Sup*
Bryanston, John *Alli*
Bryant, Alfred 1807-1881 *Alli, DcNAA*
Bryant, Anna Burnham 1860?- *ChPo, ChPo S1, DcAmA*
Bryant, Arthur *ChPo S1, ChPo S2*
Bryant, Arthur 1803-1883 *DcNAA*
Bryant, Arthur Herbert 1917- *AmA&B, AmNov*
Bryant, Sir Arthur Wynne Morgan 1899- *Au&Wr, DcLEnL, EvLB, LongC, NewC, TwCA, TwCA Sup, WrD 1976*
Bryant, Bernice 1908- *ConAu P-1*
Bryant, Beth Elaine 1936- *ConAu 13R*
Bryant, Bruce *MnBBF*
Bryant, Charles *Alli, BiDLA*
Bryant, Charles S 1808-1885 *DcNAA*
Bryant, Charles S And Murch, Abel B *Alli Sup*
Bryant, Charles William *ChPo S2*
Bryant, Cyril E 1917- *ConAu 61*
Bryant, Donald C 1905- *ConAu 13R*
Bryant, Dorothy 1930- *ConAu 53*
Bryant, Edgar Eugene 1861- *BiDSA*
Bryant, Edward 1928- *ConAu 9R*
Bryant, Edward 1945- *ConAu 45*
Bryant, Edwin 1805-1869 *AmA&B, BiDSA, DcNAA, OxAm*
Bryant, Edwin Eustace 1835-1903 *DcNAA*
Bryant, Frank Augustus 1851-1921 *DcNAA*
Bryant, Franklin Henry *BlkAW*
Bryant, Frederick James, Jr. 1942- *BlkAW, DrAP 1975*
Bryant, Gertrude Thomson *AuBYP*

Bryant, Gilmore Ward 1859- *WhWNAA*
Bryant, Hallman Bell 1936- *ChPo S2*
Bryant, Harold Child 1886- *WhWNAA*
Bryant, Hazel *BlkAW*
Bryant, Henry *Alli, BbtC*
Bryant, Henry A, Jr. 1943- *ConAu 53*
Bryant, Henry Edward Cowan 1873- *WhWNAA*
Bryant, Henry Grier 1859-1932 *DcNAA*
Bryant, Howard 1861- *WhWNAA*
Bryant, J C *Alli Sup*
Bryant, Jacob 1715-1804 *Alli, Chmbr 2*
Bryant, James C, Jr. 1931- *ConAu 49*
Bryant, James Henry *Alli Sup*
Bryant, Jerry H 1928- *ConAu 33, WrD 1976*
Bryant, Joel 1813-1868 *DcNAA*
Bryant, John Delavan 1811-1877 *Alli Sup, DcNAA*
Bryant, John Frederick 1753-1791 *Alli, ChPo S1*
Bryant, John Howard 1807-1902 *Alli, ChPo S1, CyAL 1, DcAmA, DcNAA*
Bryant, John Myron 1877- *WhWNAA*
Bryant, Joseph Allen, Jr. 1919- *ConAu 5R, WrD 1976*
Bryant, Joseph Decatur 1845-1914 *DcNAA*
Bryant, Katherine Cliffton 1912- *ConAu 13R*
Bryant, Keith L, Jr. 1937- *ConAu 49*
Bryant, L A 1927- *LivBA*
Bryant, Laura 1881-1961 *IndAu 1917*
Bryant, Lemuel d1754 *Alli*
Bryant, Leslie *ChPo S2*
Bryant, Lorinda Munson 1855-1931? *DcNAA, OhA&B, WhWNAA*
Bryant, Louise 1890-1936 *DcNAA*
Bryant, Margaret M 1900- *AmA&B, ConAu 1R*
Bryant, May *ChPo*
Bryant, Michael *PoIre*
Bryant, Ralph Clement 1877-1939 *DcNAA, WhWNAA*
Bryant, Robert Harry 1925- *ConAu 23, WrD 1976*
Bryant, Samuel Wood, Jr. 1908- *AmA&B*
Bryant, Sara Cone 1873- *AmA&B*
Bryant, Shasta M 1924- *ConAu 41*
Bryant, Sophie *Alli Sup*
Bryant, T Alton 1926- *ConAu 25*
Bryant, Thomas *Alli Sup*
Bryant, Verda E 1910- *ConAu 21*
Bryant, Mrs. W Hickes *Alli Sup*
Bryant, W J *Alli Sup*
Bryant, Wilbur F *Alli Sup*
Bryant, William Charles *Alli Sup*
Bryant, William Cullen 1794-1878 *Alli, Alli Sup, AmA, AmA&B, AtlBL, BbD, BiD&SB, CarSB, CasWL, ChPo, ChPo S1, ChPo S2, Chmbr 3, CnDAL, CnE&AP, CriT 3, CyAL 1, CyWA, DcAmA, DcEnL, DcLEnL, DcNAA, EvLB, MouLC 3, OxAm, OxEng, Pen Am, PoCh, RAdv 1, REn, REnAL, St&VC, WebEAL*
Bryant, William David 1917- *Au&Wr*
Bryant, William M *Alli Sup*
Bryant, William McKendree 1843-1919 *DcAmA, DcNAA, IndAu 1816*
Bryant, William Sohier 1861- *WhWNAA*
Bryant, Willie 1908-1964 *AmSCAP 66*
Bryant, Willis Rooks 1892- *ConAu 5R*
Bryanton, Robert Crowe *PoIre*
Bryar, Greta *ChPo*
Bryars, John *Alli*
Bryce, Lord *Chmbr 3*
Bryce, Charles *Alli Sup*
Bryce, Clarence Archibald 1849-1928 *DcNAA*
Bryce, Eric Albert 1932- *Au&Wr*
Bryce, George 1844-1931 *Alli Sup, Chmbr 3, DcNAA, OxCan*
Bryce, James *Alli, Alli Sup, BiDLA, PoIre*
Bryce, James 1806-1877 *Alli Sup*
Bryce, James 1838-1922 *Alli Sup, BbD, BiD&SB, BrAu 19, DcEnA, DcEnA Ap, EvLB, LongC, NewC, OxEng, Pen Am, Pen Eng, REn*
Bryce, Joseph W *ChPo*
Bryce, Lloyd Stephens 1851-1917 *AmA&B, BiD&SB, DcAmA, DcNAA*

Bryce, Murray D 1917- *ConAu 13R*
Bryce, Ronald *DcNAA*
Bryce, T T *Alli Sup*
Bryce, William Alexander 1886- *MnBBF*
Bryce Echenique, Alfredo 1939- *DcCLA*
Bryckinton, Stephen *Alli*
Brydall, John 1635- *Alli*
Bryde, John F 1920- *ConAu 33, WrD 1976*
Bryden, A P *Alli Sup*
Bryden, Henry Anderson 1854-1937 *Br&AmS, WhLA*
Bryden, John Marshall 1941- *ConAu 49*
Bryden, John R 1913- *ConAu 33*
Bryden, William *Alli*
Brydges, Sir Grey d1621 *Alli*
Brydges, Sir Harford Jones *Alli*
Brydges, Harold *Alli Sup, DcAmA, DcNAA*
Brydges, Henry *Alli*
Brydges, Sir Samuel Egerton 1762-1837 *Alli, BiDLA, CasWL, ChPo, Chmbr 2, DcEnL, DcLEnL, EvLB, NewC, OxEng, Pen Eng*
Brydie, Andrew *Alli Sup*
Brydie, Matthew *Alli Sup*
Brydon, Wilson P 1918- *AmSCAP 66*
Brydone, James Marr *BbtC, OxCan*
Brydone, Patrick 1743?-1818 *Alli, BiDLA*
Brydson, Thomas *Alli, BiDLA, ChPo S1*
Bryennius, Nicephorus 1062-1138 *CasWL, Pen Cl*
Bryer, Jackson R 1937- *ConAu 9R*
Bryer, James *Alli, BiDLA Sup*
Bryer, James T 1828-1895 *IndAu 1816*
Bryher 1894- *ConNov 1972, ConNov 1976, LongC, ModBL, RAdv 1, REn, WrD 1976*
Bryher, Winifred 1894- *TwCA Sup*
Brylka, Andreas 1931- *WhGrA*
Brylka-Thieme, Gertraud 1933- *WhGrA*
Brymer, Thomas Parr *Alli*
Brymn, J Tim 1881-1946 *AmSCAP 66*
Brymner, Alex *Alli*
Bryn, M Lafayette *Alli*
Bryner, Edna 1886- *WhWNAA*
Bryner-Schwab, Edna *WhWNAA*
Brynjolf Sweynsson 1605-1675 *DcEuL*
Brynjulfsson, Gisli 1827-1888 *EuA, EvEuW*
Brynolf Algotsson 1250?-1317 *CasWL*
Bryskett, Lewis 1545?-1612? *NewC*
Bryskett, Lodowick 1545?-1612? *Alli, CrE&SL, NewC*
Bryson, Alexander *Alli Sup*
Bryson, Bernarda 1903- *ChPo, IlBYP, IlCB 1956, IlCB 1966, ThBJA*
Bryson, Bernarda 1905- *ConAu 49, SmATA 9*
Bryson, Charles 1887- *CatA 1947*
Bryson, Charles Lee 1868-1949 *AmA&B, WhWNAA*
Bryson, Edgar L 1907- *TexWr*
Bryson, J *Alli Sup*
Bryson, James *Alli*
Bryson, John *Alli Sup, PoIre*
Bryson, Lyman 1888-1959 *AmA&B, REnAL, TwCA Sup, WhWNAA*
Bryson, Mrs. M I *Alli Sup*
Bryson, Mary Isabella *ChPo*
Bryson, T *Alli*
Bryson, Thomas H 1880-1943 *DcNAA*
Bryson, William A d1814 *PoIre*
Brysson-McKinlay, William Archibald 1862- *ChPo S1*
Bryton, Anne *Alli*
Bryusov, Valery Yakovlevich 1873-1924 *CasWL, ClDMEuL, DcRusL, EncWL, ModSL 1, Pen Eur, REn, TwCA, TwCA Sup, TwCW*
Brzekowski, Jan 1903- *CasWL*
Brzezinski, Zbigniew K 1928- *AmA&B, ConAu 1R*
Brzozowski, Leopold Stanislaw Leon 1878-1911 *CasWL, ModSL 2*
Buarque DeHolanda, Sergio 1902- *Pen Am*
Buba, Joy Flinsch *IlBYP, IlCB 1956*
Bubb, Mel *ConAu 57*
Bube, Adolf 1802-1873 *BiD&SB*
Bube, Richard H 1927- *ConAu 23, WrD 1976*
Bubeck, Mark I 1928- *ConAu 61*
Buber, Martin 1878-1965 *ConAu 25, EncWL,*

ModGL, OxGer, REn, TwCA Sup, WhTwL

Bubier, Edward Trevert 1858-1904 *DcNAA*
Bubier, G B *Alli Sup*
Buc, Sir George d1623 *Alli*
Buccellati, Giorgio 1937- *ConAu 41*
Bucchieri, Theresa F 1908- *ConAu 21*
Buccleugh, Duke Of *Alli*
Bucco, Martin 1929- *ConAu 29*
Bucer, Martin *OxGer*
Buch, C W *Alli*
Buchan, Alastair 1918- *Au&Wr, WrD 1976*
Buchan, Alexander *Alli Sup*
Buchan, Alexander Peter d1824 *Alli, BiDLA*
Buchan, Alexander Winton *Alli Sup*
Buchan, Anna d1948 *ChPo S2, Chmbr 3, DcLEnL, EvLB*
Buchan, Charles *MnBBF*
Buchan, Charles Forbes *Alli Sup*
Buchan, Christiana *Alli*
Buchan, David 1780-1838 *OxCan*
Buchan, David 1933- *ÇonAu XR*
Buchan, David Stewart Erskine, Earl Of 1742-1829 *Alli, BiDLA*
Buchan, John *Chmbr 3*
Buchan, John N S *OxCan*
Buchan, Baron John Tweedsmuir 1875-1940 *CasWL, ChPo, ChPo S1, ChPo S2, CnMWL, CyWA, DcLEnL, EncM&D, EvLB, JBA 1934, LongC, MnBBF, ModBL, NewC, OxCan, OxEng, Pen Eng, REn, TwCA, TwCA Sup, TwCW, WebEAL*
Buchan, Patrick d1881 *Alli Sup, ChPo, ChPo S1*
Buchan, Perdita 1940- *ConAu 21*
Buchan, Peter 1780-1834 *Alli, ChPo S1*
Buchan, Peter 1790-1854 *NewC*
Buchan, Stuart 1942- *ConAu 57*
Buchan, Thomas Buchanan 1931- *ConAu 25*
Buchan, Tom 1931- *ChPo S1, ConAu XR, ConP 1970, ConP 1975, WrD 1976*
Buchan, William 1729-1805 *Alli, DcEnL*
Buchan, William Paton *Alli Sup*
Buchanan, A Grahame *ChPo*
Buchanan, Miss A M F *ChPo S1*
Buchanan, A Russell 1906- *ConAu 13R*
Buchanan, Alexander Carlisle *BbtC, OxCan*
Buchanan, Allan d1749 *Alli*
Buchanan, Andrew *Alli, Alli Sup, ChPo S1*
Buchanan, Andrew Hays 1828-1914 *DcNAA*
Buchanan, Angus *OxCan*
Buchanan, Annabel Morris 1888- *AmSCAP 66, WhWNAA*
Buchanan, Arthur William Patrick 1870-1939 *DcNAA*
Buchanan, Benjamin Franklin *IndAu 1816*
Buchanan, Carl *MnBBF*
Buchanan, Charles *Alli*
Buchanan, Charles Milton 1868-1920 *DcNAA*
Buchanan, Chuck *ConAu XR*
Buchanan, Claudius 1766-1815 *Alli, BiDLA, BiDLA Sup, DcEnL*
Buchanan, Colin Ogilvie 1934- *ConAu 25, WrD 1976*
Buchanan, Cynthia 1942- *ConAu 45, DrAF 1976*
Buchanan, Cynthia D 1937- *ConAu 5R*
Buchanan, D *Alli Sup*
Buchanan, Daniel 1880- *WhWNAA*
Buchanan, Daniel C 1892- *ConAu 17R*
Buchanan, David *Alli*
Buchanan, David 1933- *ConAu 57*
Buchanan, David Wills 1844- *ChPo*
Buchanan, Donald W 1908- *ConAu P-1*
Buchanan, Dorothy Jacobs *ChPo S1*
Buchanan, Dugald 1716-1768 *ChPo, ChPo S1, ChPo S2, NewC*
Buchanan, E S *ChPo S1*
Buchanan, Ebenezer John 1844- *Alli Sup*
Buchanan, Francis *Alli Sup*
Buchanan, Francis 1825- *Alli, BiDLA, ChPo S1*
Buchanan, George *Alli, Alli Sup*
Buchanan, George 1506-1582 *Alli, BrAu, CasWL, Chmbr 1, CrE&SL, DcEnA, DcEnL, DcEuL, EvLB, NewC, OxEng, OxFr, Pen Eng*

Buchanan, George 1904- *Au&Wr, ConAu 9R, ConNov 1972, ConNov 1976, ConP 1970, ConP 1975, WrD 1976*
Buchanan, George Wesley 1921- *ConAu 37*
Buchanan, Harry *Alli Sup*
Buchanan, Herbert Earle 1881- *WhWNAA*
Buchanan, Isaac 1810-1883 *BbtC, DcNAA*
Buchanan, James *Alli, BbtC*
Buchanan, James 1791-1868 *Alli Sup, AmA&B, DcAmA, OxAm, REnAL*
Buchanan, James 1804-1870 *Alli Sup*
Buchanan, James J 1925- *ConAu 33, WrD 1976*
Buchanan, James McGill 1919- *ConAu 5R, WrD 1976*
Buchanan, James Robert *Alli Sup*
Buchanan, James Shannon 1864-1930 *DcNAA*
Buchanan, John *Alli, Alli Sup*
Buchanan, John Cross 1803-1839 *ChPo*
Buchanan, John Jenkins 1855-1937 *DcNAA, OhA&B*
Buchanan, John L *Alli, BiDLA*
Buchanan, Joseph 1785-1829 *BiDSA, DcAmA, DcNAA*
Buchanan, Joseph Ray 1851-1924 *DcNAA*
Buchanan, Joseph Rodes 1814-1899 *Alli Sup, BiDSA, DcAmA, DcNAA, OhA&B*
Buchanan, Keith 1919- *ConAu 23*
Buchanan, Madeleine d1940 *DcNAA*
Buchanan, Marion 1840- *ChPo S1*
Buchanan, Milton A 1878- *WhWNAA*
Buchanan, Pegasus 1920- *ConAu 9R*
Buchanan, Phyllis *Au&Wr*
Buchanan, Roberdeau 1839-1916 *Alli Sup, DcNAA*
Buchanan, Robert *Alli Sup, Chmbr 3*
Buchanan, Robert 1785-1873 *Alli Sup*
Buchanan, Robert 1797-1879 *OhA&B*
Buchanan, Robert 1802-1875 *Alli, Alli Sup*
Buchanan, Robert 1835-1875 *ChPo*
Buchanan, Robert Angus 1930- *ConAu 17R, WrD 1976*
Buchanan, Robert Earle 1883- *WhWNAA*
Buchanan, Robert Williams 1841-1901 *Alli Sup, BbD, BiD&SB, BrAu 19, CasWL, ChPo, ChPo S1, ChPo S2, DcBiA, DcEnA, DcEnA Ap, DcEnL, DcEuL, DcLEnL, EvLB, LongC, MouLC 4, NewC, OxEng, Pen Eng, REn*
Buchanan, Robertson *Alli, BiDLA, BiDLA Sup*
Buchanan, Roy G *ChPo S1*
Buchanan, Mrs. S E *TexWr*
Buchanan, Scott 1895-1968 *AmA&B*
Buchanan, T B *Alli Sup*
Buchanan, Thomas G 1919- *ConAu 1R*
Buchanan, Thompson 1877-1937? *AmA&B, DcNAA*
Buchanan, W B *Alli Sup*
Buchanan, W M *Au&Wr*
Buchanan, Walter 1865?- *ChPo S1*
Buchanan, William *Alli, BiDLA*
Buchanan, William 1781-1863 *Alli Sup*
Buchanan, William 1821-1868 *ChPo*
Buchanan, William 1930- *AuBYP, ConAu XR, WrD 1976*
Buchanan-Jardine, Sir John 1900- *Br&AmS*
Buchard, Robert 1931- *ConAu 33*
Bucharoff, Simon 1881-1955 *AmSCAP 66*
Buchberger, Michael 1874- *WhLA*
Buchdahl, Gerd 1914- *Au&Wr, ConAu 57, WrD 1976*
Buchegger, Erich 1924- *WhGrA*
Buchel, Carl *Alli Sup*
Buchele, William Martin 1895- *ConAu 57*
Buchen, Irving H 1930- *ConAu 25*
Buchenau, Arthur 1879- *WhLA*
Bucher, Bradley 1932- *ConAu 37*
Bucher, Charles A 1912- *ConAu 9R*
Bucher, Francois 1927- *ConAu 5R, WrD 1976*
Bucher, Glenn R 1940- *ConAu 57*
Bucher, Magnus 1927- *ConAu 41*
Bucher, Walter H 1888- *WhWNAA*
Bucherer, Fritz 1868- *WhLA*
Bucherer, Hans Theodor 1869- *WhLA*
Buchez, Philippe Benjamin Joseph 1796-1865 *BiD&SB*

Buchez, Philippe-Joseph-Benjamin 1796-1866 *OxFr*
Buchheim, Emma S *Alli Sup*
Buchheim, Lothar-Gunther 1918- *ConLC 6*
Buchheimer, Naomi Barnett 1927- *ConAu 5R*
Buchholtz, Andreas Heinrich 1607-1671 *CasWL, EvEuW, OxGer*
Buchholtz, Johannes 1882-1940 *CasWL, EncWL, EvEuW, TwCA, TwCA Sup*
Buchholz, Heinrich Ewald 1879-1955 *AmA&B, BiDSA*
Buchinskaya, Nadezhda A 1876-1952 *CasWL, DcRusL*
Buchkremer, Joseph 1864- *WhLA*
Buchler, Adolph 1867- *WhLA*
Buchler, Franz 1904- *OxGer*
Buchler, Justus 1914- *AmA&B, ConAu 5R*
Buchman, Dian Dincin *ConAu 61*
Buchman, Frank N D 1878-1961 *AmA&B, LongC*
Buchman, Herman 1920- *ConAu 41*
Buchman, Randall L 1929- *ConAu 45*
Buchman, Sidney 1902-1975 *ConAu 61*
Buchmann, Georg 1822-1884 *OxGer*
Buchner, Alexander 1827- *BbD*
Buchner, Augustus 1591-1661 *CasWL, OxGer*
Buchner, Edward Franklin 1868-1929 *BiDSA, DcNAA, WhWNAA*
Buchner, Ernst Hendrik 1880- *WhLA*
Buchner, Georg 1813-1837 *AtlBL, BiD&SB, CnThe, CyWA, EuA, McGWD, OxGer, Pen Eur, REn, REnWD*
Buchner, George 1813-1837 *BbD*
Buchner, Gladys Close *TexWr*
Buchner, Karl Georg 1813-1837 *CasWL, EvEuW*
Buchner, Ludwig 1824-1899 *BiD&SB, OxGer*
Buchner, Luise 1821-1877 *BiD&SB, OxGer*
Buchner, Max 1881- *WhLA*
Bucholz, John Theodore 1888- *WhWNAA*
Buchta, R *Alli Sup*
Buchtel, Forrest L 1899- *AmSCAP 66*
Buchwald, Art 1925- *AmA&B, AuNews 1, ConAu 5R, Pen Am, SmATA 10, WorAu, WrD 1976*
Buchwald, Emilie 1935- *ConAu 49, SmATA 7*
Buchwald, Georg 1859- *WhLA*
Buck, Mrs. *Alli Sup*
Buck, Adam *Alli*
Buck, Alan Michael *CatA 1947*
Buck, Albert Henry 1842-1922 *Alli Sup, DcAmA, DcNAA*
Buck, Anna Shaw *ChPo S1*
Buck, Arthur Eugene 1888- *WhWNAA*
Buck, Benjamin *Alli Sup*
Buck, Carl Darling 1866- *WhWNAA*
Buck, Carlton C 1907- *AmSCAP 66*
Buck, Charles 1771-1815 *Alli, BiDLA, BiDLA Sup*
Buck, Charles 1915- *ConAu 33*
Buck, Charles Neville 1879- *AmA&B, WhWNAA*
Buck, Charles Stary 1928- *AmSCAP 66*
Buck, Charles William 1849-1930 *BiDSA, DcNAA*
Buck, Daniel 1829-1905 *DcNAA*
Buck, Daniel Dana 1814-1895 *Alli, Alli Sup, ChPo S1, DcNAA*
Buck, Dudley 1839-1909 *Alli Sup, BbD, BiD&SB, DcAmA, DcNAA*
Buck, Edward *Alli Sup*
Buck, Edward 1814-1876 *DcNAA*
Buck, Sir Edward John 1862- *WhLA*
Buck, Frank 1882?-1950 *AmA&B, MnBBF, REnAL*
Buck, Frederick *Alli Sup*
Buck, Frederick Silas *ConAu 5R*
Buck, Gene 1885-1957 *AmA&B, AmSCAP 66, REnAL*
Buck, Sir George *Alli*
Buck, Gertrude 1871-1922 *AmLY, DcNAA*
Buck, Glenn 1905- *WhWNAA*
Buck, Gurdon 1807-1877 *Alli Sup, DcAmA, DcNAA*
Buck, Harry M 1921- *ConAu 33, WrD 1976*
Buck, Henry *Alli Sup*
Buck, Howard *ChPo S2*
Buck, Howard Swazey 1894- *AnMV 1926*

Buck, Irving A *BiDSA*
Buck, J H *Alli Sup*
Buck, J H Watson *Alli Sup*
Buck, J W *Alli*
Buck, Jacob R 1870- *BkC 3*
Buck, James *Alli*
Buck, James Smith 1812-1852 *Alli Sup, DcNAA*
Buck, Jirah Dewey 1838-1916 *DcAmA, DcNAA, OhA&B*
Buck, John Lossing 1890-1975 *ConAu 45, ConAu 61*
Buck, John N 1906- *ConAu 29*
Buck, Laura A *Alli Sup*
Buck, Lillie 1860-1939 *DcNAA*
Buck, Margaret Waring 1910- *AuBYP, ConAu 5R, SmATA 3, WrD 1976*
Buck, Marion A 1909- *ConAu P-1*
Buck, Mary K *ChPo S1, ChPo S2*
Buck, Maximilian *Alli*
Buck, N K 1875- *WhWNAA*
Buck, Nathaniel *Alli*
Buck, Oscar MacMillan 1885-1941 *DcNAA, WhWNAA*
Buck, Paul Herman 1899- *AmA&B, OhA&B, OxAm, TwCA, TwCA Sup*
Buck, Pearl S 1892-1973 *AmA&B, AmNov, Au&Wr, AuBYP, AuNews 1, CasWL, CnDAL, ConAmA, ConAu 1R, ConAu 41, ConNov 1972, CyWA, DcLEnL, EncWL, EvLB, LongC, ModAL, OxAm, Pen Am, REn, REnAL, SmATA 1, TwCA, TwCA Sup, TwCW, WhWNAA*
Buck, Philo Melvin, Jr. 1877-1950 *AmA&B, WhWNAA*
Buck, Richard Henry 1870?-1956 *AmSCAP 66, ChPo*
Buck, Richard Hugh Keats *Alli Sup*
Buck, Robert *Alli*
Buck, Robert M 1882- *WhWNAA*
Buck, Ruth *Alli Sup*
Buck, Samuel *Alli*
Buck, Solon Justus 1884-1962 *AmA&B, AmLY*
Buck, Stratton 1906- *ConAu 17*
Buck, T F *Alli Sup*
Buck, Tim *OxCan, OxCan Sup*
Buck, Vernon Ellis 1934- *ConAu 37, WrD 1976*
Buck, William E, Buck, Mrs. And Major, H *Alli Sup*
Buck, William Joseph 1825- *Alli Sup, DcNAA*
Buck, William Ray 1930- *AuBYP, ConAu 1R, WrD 1976*
Buckalew, Charles Rollin 1821-1899 *Alli Sup, DcAmA, DcNAA*
Bucke, Charles 1781-1847 *Alli*
Bucke, James *Alli*
Bucke, Richard Maurice 1837-1902 *Alli Sup, BbtC, DcNAA, OxAm, REnAL*
Buckels, Alec *ChPo, ChPo S2, IlCB 1945*
Buckeridge, Anthony Malcolm 1912- *ConAu 49, SmATA 6, WhCL*
Buckeridge, John d1631 *Alli, DcEnL*
Buckeye, Donald A 1930- *ConAu 49*
Buckham, J *Alli Sup*
Buckham, James 1858-1908 *ChPo, ChPo S2, DcAmA, DcNAA*
Buckham, John Wright 1864-1945 *AmA&B, DcNAA*
Buckham, Matthew Henry 1832-1910 *CyAL 1, DcNAA*
Buckham, P W *Alli*
Buckham, T R *Alli Sup*
Buckholtz, L Von *Alli Sup*
Buckhout, Mrs. Byron M 1836-1914 *DcNAA*
Buckhout, Robert 1935- *ConAu 45*
Buckhurst *Alli*
Buckhurst, Baron *NewC*
Buckhurst, Lord *DcEnL, OxEng*
Bucking, Hugo 1851- *WhLA*
Buckingham, Duke Of *Chmbr 1, Chmbr 2*
Buckingham, Duke Of 1592-1628 *NewC*
Buckingham, Duke Of 1628-1687 *Alli, BrAu, NewC, Pen Eng*
Buckingham, B R 1876- *WhWNAA*

Buckingham, Catherine Putman 1808-1888 *Alli Sup*
Buckingham, Catherine Putnam 1808-1888 *DcNAA*
Buckingham, Clyde E 1907- *ConAu P-1*
Buckingham, Edgar 1867-1940 *DcNAA, WhWNAA*
Buckingham, Emma May *Alli Sup, DcNAA*
Buckingham, George Tracy 1864-1940 *IndAu 1917*
Buckingham, George Villiers, Duke Of 1628-1687 *AtlBL, DcEnL, DcLEnL, EvLB, REn, REn*
Buckingham, Henry Stafford, Duke Of 1454-1483 *REn*
Buckingham, James 1932- *ConAu 29*
Buckingham, James Silk 1786-1855 *Alli, BbtC, BrAu 19, Chmbr 3, DcEnL, EvLB, NewC, OxAm, OxCan, OxEng*
Buckingham, Jamie 1932- *Au&Wr, ConAu XR*
Buckingham, Jane W *Alli Sup*
Buckingham, Joseph Tinker 1779-1861 *Alli, AmA&B, CyAL 2, DcAmA, DcNAA*
Buckingham, Leicester Silk 1825-1867 *Alli Sup*
Buckingham, Samuel Giles 1812-1898 *DcNAA*
Buckingham, Thomas d1731 *Alli*
Buckingham, Walter S, Jr. 1924- *ConAu 1R*
Buckingham, William 1832-1915 *BbtC, DcNAA, OxCan*
Buckingham, Willis J 1938- *ConAu 29*
Buckingham And Chandos, Duke Of *Alli, Alli Sup*
Buckingham And Normanby, John S, Duke Of 1648-1721 *BrAu, CasWL, EvLB, NewC*
Buckinghamshire, John Sheffield, Duke Of 1649-1721 *ChPo, DcEnL*
Buckinx, Pieter Geert 1903- *CasWL*
Buckland, A C *Alli*
Buckland, A R *ChPo S2*
Buckland, A W *Alli Sup*
Buckland, Anna Jane 1827- *Alli Sup*
Buckland, Charles Thomas *Alli Sup*
Buckland, Francis Trevelyan 1826-1880 *Alli, Alli Sup, BbD, BiD&SB, BrAu 19, Chmbr 3, DcEnL, EvLB, NewC, OxEng*
Buckland, John *Alli*
Buckland, Ralph 1564?-1611 *Alli*
Buckland, W Frank *Alli Sup*
Buckland, William 1784-1856 *Alli, DcEnL*
Buckland-Wright, Mary Elizabeth *Au&Wr*
Buckle, A *Alli Sup*
Buckle, E *Alli Sup*
Buckle, Fleetwood *Alli Sup*
Buckle, George Earle 1854-1935 *LongC, NewC*
Buckle, Henry Thomas 1821-1862 *Alli, Alli Sup, BiD&SB, BrAu 19, CasWL, Chmbr 3, DcEnA, DcEnA Ap, DcEnL, DcEuL, EvLB, NewC, OxEng, Pen Eng, REn*
Buckle, J G *Alli Sup*
Buckle, John *BbtC*
Buckle, Matthew Hughes George *Alli Sup*
Buckle, Mrs. Matthew Hughes George *Alli Sup*
Buckle, R Bentley *Alli*
Buckle, Richard 1916- *Au&Wr, WrD 1976*
Buckle, William *Alli, BiDLA*
Bucklee, Brookes *Alli Sup*
Buckler, Alexander *Alli Sup*
Buckler, Benjamin 1716-1780 *Alli*
Buckler, Charles And John Chessel *Alli Sup*
Buckler, E H *Alli*
Buckler, Edward *Alli*
Buckler, Edward H *Alli Sup*
Buckler, Ernest 1908- *Au&Wr, CanWr, CasWL, ConAu P-1, ConNov 1972, ConNov 1976, OxCan, OxCan Sup, TwCW, WrD 1976*
Buckler, George *Alli Sup*
Buckler, John C *Alli, Alli Sup*
Buckler, John Findlay *Alli Sup*
Buckler, Thomas Hepburn 1812-1901 *Alli, DcNAA*
Buckler, William Earl 1924- *ConAu 1R*
Bucklew, John 1914- *IndAu 1917*
Buckley, Albert Coulson 1873-1939 *DcNAA*
Buckley, Arabella Burton *Alli Sup*
Buckley, C F *Alli Sup*

Buckley, Eunice 1890- *Au&Wr*
Buckley, F *MnBBF*
Buckley, Fergus Reid 1930- *ConAu 21*
Buckley, Francis *Alli*
Buckley, Francis Joseph 1928- *ConAu 33, WrD 1976*
Buckley, Helen E 1918- *ConAu 5R, SmATA 2*
Buckley, Henry Burton 1845- *Alli Sup*
Buckley, J W *Alli*
Buckley, James Lane 1923- *ConAu 61*
Buckley, James Monroe 1836-1920 *Alli Sup, AmA&B, BbD, BiD&SB, DcAmA, DcNAA*
Buckley, Jerome Hamilton 1917- *AmA&B, ChPo, ConAu 1R*
Buckley, John *Alli Sup*
Buckley, John Peter 1873-1942 *IndAu 1917*
Buckley, Joseph *Alli Sup*
Buckley, Julian Gerard 1905- *ConAu 41*
Buckley, Loretta Bauer 1905- *ArizL*
Buckley, Mary L *ConAu 53*
Buckley, Michael Bernard 1831-1872 *Alli Sup, PoIre*
Buckley, Nancy *AnMV 1926, CatA 1947*
Buckley, Patrick J 1844?- *PoIre*
Buckley, Richard *MnBBF*
Buckley, Richard Wallace *BiDSA*
Buckley, Robert Burton *Alli Sup*
Buckley, Robert William 1840?-1897 *Alli Sup, PoIre*
Buckley, Samuel *Alli*
Buckley, Theodore William Alois 1825-1856 *Alli*
Buckley, Thomas H 1932- *ConAu 29, WrD 1976*
Buckley, Vincent 1925- *ConP 1970, ConP 1975, Pen Eng, WrD 1976*
Buckley, William Edward *Alli Sup*
Buckley, William F, Jr. 1925- *AmA&B, AuNews 1, ConAu 1R, WorAu, WrD 1976*
Bucklin, Sophronia E *Alli Sup*
Buckman, Benjamin E *Alli Sup*
Buckman, E *ChPo*
Buckman, James 1816-1884 *Alli, Alli Sup*
Buckman, James 1858-1908 *ChPo S1*
Buckman, John Wright 1864- *WhWNAA*
Buckman, Mrs. L G *Alli Sup*
Buckman, Peter Michael Amiel 1941- *WrD 1976*
Buckman, Rebecca T *ChPo*
Buckmaster, Henrietta *AmA&B, AmNov, Au&Wr, ConAu XR, OhA&B, SmATA 6, WorAu*
Buckmaster, John Charles *Alli Sup*
Buckmaster, Martin A 1862- *WhLA*
Buckmaster, Owen Stanley, Viscount 1890- *Au&Wr*
Buckminster, Joseph d1792 *Alli*
Buckminster, Joseph 1751-1812 *Alli, DcNAA*
Buckminster, Joseph Stevens 1784-1812 *Alli, AmA, AmA&B, CyAL 1, DcAmA, OxAm, REnAL*
Buckminster, Thomas *Alli*
Bucknall, Barbara Jane 1933- *ConAu 33, WrD 1976*
Bucknall, Benjamin *Alli Sup*
Bucknall, Hamilton Lindsay *Alli Sup*
Bucknall, Thomas *Alli*
Buckner, Elijah D 1843-1907 *DcNAA*
Buckner, G Davis 1885- *WhWNAA*
Buckner, J P *Alli Sup*
Buckner, Bishop John *Alli, BiDLA, BiDLA Sup*
Buckner, R A *Alli Sup*
Buckner, Mrs. R T *BiDSA*
Buckner, Richard *ChPo*
Buckner, Robert 1906- *ConAu 1R*
Buckner, Sally Beaver 1931- *ConAu 61, DrAP 1975*
Buckner, W P *Alli Sup*
Bucknill, John Charles 1817- *Alli Sup*
Buckridge, Thomas *Alli*
Buckridys *Alli*
Buckrose, J E *WhLA*
Buckskin Sam *HsB&A*
Buckstead, Richard C 1929- *ConAu 49*
Buckstone, John Baldwin 1802-1879 *BbD,*

Buhler, Curt Ferdinand 1905- *AmA&B,*
ChPo S1, ConAu 1R
Buhler, Cyril 1923- *Au&Wr*
Buhler, Fritz 1909- *WhGrA*
Buhler, Johann Georg *Alli Sup*
Buhler, Karl 1879- *WhLA*
Buhler, Mary Edith 1864- *ChPo, WhWNAA*
Buhlmann, Manfred 1885- *WhLA*
Buhrer, Albert *ChPo, ChPo S2*
Buhrman, Albert John, Jr. 1915- *AmSCAP 66*
Buhry, Hemedi Bin Abdalla Bin Saidi Al d1922
CasWL
Buhturi, Al- 821-897 *CasWL, DcOrL 3*
Buice, W Alfred 1895- *WhWNAA*
Buick, George d1904 *PoIre*
Buies, Arthur 1840-1901 *CanWr, CasWL,*
DcNAA, OxCan
Buirgy, Mary Higgins 1911- *ChPo S2*
Buissieres, Arthur De *OxCan*
Buist, Alexander *ChPo*
Buist, Charlotte 1942- *ConAu 29*
Buist, E G *ChPo S2*
Buist, George 1770-1808 *Alli, BiDSA*
Buist, John B *Alli Sup*
Buist, K A *Alli Sup*
Buist, Robert 1805-1880 *Alli, DcNAA*
Buist, Robert Cochrane 1868- *ChPo S1*
Buitenhuis, Elspeth *OxCan Sup*
Buitenhuis, Peter M 1925- *ConAu 25,*
OxCan Sup, WrD 1976
Bujold, Francoise *OxCan*
Bukalski, Peter J 1941- *ConAu 41*
Bukenya, Augustine S 1944- *AfA 1*
Buker, George E 1923- *ConAu 53*
Bukerji, Dhan Gopal *ChPo*
Bukharin, Nikolai Ivanovich 1888-1939 *REn*
Bukowski, Charles 1920- *AmA&B,*
ConAu 17R, ConLC 2, ConLC 5,
ConP 1970, ConP 1975, DrAF 1976,
DrAP 1975, ModAL Sup, Pen Am,
RAdv 1, WhTwL, WrD 1976
Buktenica, Norman A 1930- *ConAu 33*
Bulatkin, Eleanor Webster 1913- *ConAu 33*
Bulatovic, Miodrag 1930- *Au&Wr, CasWL,*
ConAu 5R, EncWL Sup, ModSL 2,
Pen Eur, TwCW
Bulbeck, Lord *NewC*
Bulens, Alexis *Alli Sup*
Buley, Bernard *MnBBF*
Buley, E C 1869- *MnBBF*
Buley, R Carlyle 1893-1968 *AmA&B,*
ConAu 21, ConAu 25, IndAu 1917,
OxAm, TwCA Sup
Bulfern, W P *Alli Sup*
Bulfinch, Charles 1763-1844 *AtlBL, OxAm,*
REnAL
Bulfinch, Ellen Susan 1844- *DcAmA*
Bulfinch, F V *ChPo*
Bulfinch, Maria H *Alli Sup*
Bulfinch, Stephen Greenleaf 1809-1870 *Alli,*
Alli Sup, AmA&B, ChPo S1, ChPo S2,
CyAL 2, DcAmA, DcNAA, PoCh
Bulfinch, Thomas 1796-1867 *Alli, Alli Sup,*
AmA, AmA&B, BiD&SB, CarSB, ChPo,
DcAmA, DcNAA, OxAm, REn, REnAL
Bulgakov, Mikhail Afanasyevich 1891-1940
CasWL, ClDMEuL, CnMD, CnThe,
DcRusL, EncWL Sup, EvEuW, McGWD,
ModSL 1, ModWD, Pen Eur, REn,
REnWD, TwCW, WhTwL, WorAu
Bulgakov, Sergey Nikolayevich 1871-1944
CasWL, DcRusL
Bulgarin, Faddey Venediktovich 1789-1859
CasWL, DcRusL, EvEuW
Bulgarin, Thaddeus 1789-1859 *DcEuL*
Bulger, George Ernest *Alli Sup, OxCan*
Buliard, Roger 1909- *CatA 1952, OxCan*
Bulien, Bernard *OxCan Sup*
Bulkeley, Benjamin *Alli*
Bulkeley, Christy C *AuNews 2*
Bulkeley, Edward *Alli*
Bulkeley, Henry J *Alli Sup*
Bulkeley, J Cummins *Alli*
Bulkeley, John *Alli*
Bulkeley, Lucius Duncan 1845-1928 *DcAmA*
Bulkeley, L D ALSO Bulkley, Lucius
Bulkeley, Richard George *Alli, Alli Sup*
Bulkley *BbtC*

Bulkley, Charles 1719-1797 *Alli*
Bulkley, Charles Henry Augustus 1819-1893
Alli Sup, ChPo, DcNAA
Bulkley, Edward *Alli, CyAL 1*
Bulkley, J Cummins *Alli*
Bulkley, John *Alli*
Bulkley, John 1679-1731 *Alli, DcNAA*
Bulkley, Lorenzo Hill 1856-1949 *OhA&B*
Bulkley, Lucius Duncan 1845-1928 *Alli Sup,*
DcNAA, WhWNAA
Bulkley, L D ALSO Bulkeley, Lucius
Bulkley, Peter 1583-1659 *Alli, CyAL 1,*
DcAmA
Bulkley, Sir Richard *Alli*
Bulkley, Robert J, Jr. *ChPo S1*
Bull *Alli*
Bull, Albert E *ChPo, MnBBF*
Bull, Angela 1936- *ConAu 21*
Bull, Augustine Howie *Alli Sup*
Bull, Carroll Gideon 1884- *WhWNAA*
Bull, Charles Livingston 1874-1932 *ConICB,*
DcNAA
Bull, Charles Stedman 1846- *DcAmA*
Bull, Coates Preston, Sr. 1872- *WhWNAA*
Bull, Digby *Alli*
Bull, G S *Alli*
Bull, Geoffrey Taylor 1921- *Au&Wr,*
ConAu 9R
Bull, George 1634-1710 *Alli, DcEnL, EvLB*
Bull, George Anthony 1929- *Au&Wr*
Bull, Gerald *ChPo S1*
Bull, Guyon Boys Garrett 1912- *Au&Wr,*
ConAu 5R, WrD 1976
Bull, H *Alli Sup*
Bull, Hedley Norman 1932- *ConAu 5R,*
WrD 1976
Bull, Henry *Alli*
Bull, J *Alli, BiDLA*
Bull, John *BlkAW*
Bull, John 1563?-1622? *Alli, NewC*
Bull, John Wrathall *Alli Sup*
Bull, Joseph *Alli, BiDLA*
Bull, Josiah *Alli Sup*
Bull, L *Alli Sup*
Bull, Lucy Catlin 1861-1903 *ChPo, ChPo S1*
Bull, Mary *ChPo*
Bull, Michael *Alli*
Bull, Nicholas *Alli*
Bull, Norman John 1916- *Au&Wr, WrD 1976*
Bull, Olaf Jacob Martin Luther 1883-1933
CasWL, ClDMEuL, EncWL, Pen Eur,
REn
Bull, Ole 1810-1880 *OxAm, REnAL*
Bull, Paul Bertie 1864- *WhLA*
Bull, Peter Cecil 1912- *Au&Wr, ConAu 25,*
WrD 1976
Bull, Prescott Bailey *ChPo*
Bull, Robert *Alli*
Bull, Roger *Alli*
Bull, Sara Chapman 1850-1911 *Alli Sup,*
DcAmA, DcNAA
Bull, Sidney Augustus 1847-1944 *DcNAA*
Bull, Sleeter 1887- *WhWNAA*
Bull, Storm 1913- *ConAu 9R*
Bull, Thomas *Alli, Alli Sup*
Bull, W And A H *Alli*
Bull, Sir William 1863- *WhLA*
Bull, William E 1909-1972 *ConAu P-1*
Bull, William Perkins 1870-1948 *DcNAA*
Bulla, Charles Dehaven 1862-1932 *DcNAA*
Bulla, Clyde Robert 1914- *AuBYP, AuICB,*
BkP, ConAu 5R, MorJA, SmATA 2
Bullant, Jean 1510-1578 *OxFr*
Bullar, Anne *Alli Sup*
Bullar, Henry *Alli*
Bullar, J F *Alli Sup*
Bullar, John *Alli, BiDLA*
Bullar, Joseph *Alli, Alli Sup*
Bullar, Mary And J F *Alli Sup*
Bullar, William *Alli Sup*
Bullard *Alli*
Bullard, Anna T J *Alli Sup*
Bullard, Arthur 1879?-1929 *AmLY, DcNAA,*
WhWNAA
Bullard, Asa 1804-1888 *Alli Sup, ChPo S1,*
DcAmA, DcNAA
Bullard, E John, III 1942- *ConAu 33*
Bullard, Frank Dearborn 1860-1936 *DcNAA*

Bullard, Fred Mason 1901- *ConAu 25*
Bullard, Frederic Lauriston 1866-1952 *AmA&B,*
OhA&B, REnAL
Bullard, Helen 1902- *ConAu 17R, WrD 1976*
Bullard, Henry Adams 1788-1851 *Alli, BiDSA*
Bullard, J Curry *Alli*
Bullard, Laura Curtis And Herzog, Emma
Alli Sup
Bullard, Marion *ConICB*
Bullard, Oral 1922- *ConAu 61*
Bullard, Robert Lee 1861-1947 *DcNAA,*
WhWNAA
Bullard, Roger A 1937- *ConAu 33*
Bullard, Washington Irving 1881- *WhWNAA*
Bullard, William Hannum Grubb 1866-1927
DcNAA
Bullard, William Norton 1853-1931 *DcNAA*
Bullard, William Ralph 1892- *WhWNAA*
Bulleid, Henry A V 1912- *Au&Wr,*
ConAu P-1, WrD 1976
Bullein, William d1576 *Alli, NewC*
Bullen, Arthur Henry 1857-1920 *Alli Sup,*
BrAu 19, ChPo, ChPo S1, Chmbr 3,
LongC, NewC
Bullen, Frank Thomas 1857-1915 *BiD&SB,*
Chmbr 3, CyWA, DcEnA Ap, EvLB,
JBA 1934, LongC, TwCA
Bullen, George *Alli, Alli Sup*
Bullen, Henry Lewis 1857-1938 *DcNAA*
Bullen, Henry St. John *Alli, BiDLA*
Bullen, Keith Edward 1906- *WrD 1976*
Bullen, M And A H *Alli Sup*
Bullen, Mary Swinton Legare *BiDSA*
Bullen, N Ravenor H *MnBBF*
Bullen, Thomas Joseph 1845- *Alli Sup*
Bullen Bear *WrD 1976*
Bullens, Denison K *WhWNAA*
Buller Of Brasenose *DcEnL*
Buller, Arthur Henry Reginald 1874-1944
DcNAA, WhWNAA
Buller, Charles 1806-1848 *Alli, BbtC, OxCan*
Buller, F H E 1926- *Au&Wr*
Buller, Sir Francis 1745-1800 *Alli*
Buller, Herman 1923- *ConAu 61*
Buller, Herman 1927- *OxCan, WrD 1976*
Buller, James 1812-1884 *Alli Sup*
Buller, Marguerite *ChPo*
Buller, W *Alli*
Buller, Sir Walter Lawry 1838- *Alli Sup*
Bullett, Gerald William 1893?-1958 *ChPo,*
ChPo S1, ChPo S2, DcLEnL, EvLB,
LongC, NewC, TwCA, TwCA Sup,
TwCW
Bulley, Agnes Amy *Alli Sup*
Bulley, Eleanor *Alli Sup*
Bulley, Frederick *Alli*
Bulley, John Francis 1843- *Alli Sup*
Bulleyn, William 1500?-1576 *Alli*
Bullhe Sah 1680-1758 *DcOrL 2*
Bullhe Shah 1680-1758 *CasWL*
Bulliard, Pierre *OxFr*
Bulliet, Clarence Joseph 1883-1952 *IndAu 1917*
Bulliet, Richard W 1940- *ConAu 57*
Bullingbroke, Edward *Alli*
Bullingbroke, Jonah Bilcher *Alli*
Bullinger, Ethelbert William *Alli Sup*
Bullinger, Heinrich 1504-1575 *CasWL, OxGer*
Bullingham, John *Alli*
Bullingham, Rodney *ConAu XR*
Bullins, Ed 1935?- *BlkAW, ConAu 49,*
ConDr, ConLC 1, ConLC 5, CrCD,
LivBAA, ModAL Sup, WrD 1976
Bullions, Peter 1791-1864 *Alli, DcAmA,*
DcNAA
Bullis, Harry Amos 1890- *ConAu 17*
Bullis, Jerald 1944- *ConAu 49, DrAP 1975*
Bullitt, Orville H 1894- *ConAu 33, WrD 1976*
Bullitt, William C 1891- *REn, REnAL*
Bullitt, William Marshall 1873- *WhWNAA*
Bullivant, Benjamin *Alli*
Bullivant, Cecil Henry 1882- *EncM&D,*
MnBBF
Bullivant, Daniel *Alli*
Bullivant, Garland 1920?- *Br&AmS*
Bullman *Alli*
Bullman, E *BiDLA*
Bullmer, Jerce *ChPo S2*
Bullocar *Alli*

Bulloch, James Dunwody 1824-1901 *Alli Sup,*
BiDSA, DcNAA
Bulloch, John *Alli Sup*
Bulloch, John 1805-1882 *Alli Sup*
Bulloch, John 1928- *Au&Wr*
Bulloch, John Malcolm 1867- *ChPo, ChPo S2,*
WhLA
Bulloch, Joseph Gaston Baillie 1852-
WhWNAA
Bulloch, Mary 1917- *Au&Wr*
Bullock, A *Alli Sup*
Bullock, Alan Louis Charles 1914- *Au&Wr,*
ConAu 1R, LongC
Bullock, Alexander Hamilton 1816-1882
Alli Sup, DcAmA, DcNAA
Bullock, Charles 1829- *Alli Sup, ChPo S1,*
ChPo S2
Bullock, Charles Jesse 1869-1941 *DcAmA,*
DcNAA
Bullock, Charles S, III 1942- *ConAu 33*
Bullock, Cynthia 1821- *ChPo, ChPo S2,*
DcNAA
Bullock, Francis And Thomas Austin *Alli Sup*
Bullock, Frederick William Bagshawe 1903-
Au&Wr, ConAu 5R, WrD 1976
Bullock, H A *Alli*
Bullock, Harry *OxCan Sup*
Bullock, Helen Eloise *ChPo*
Bullock, Henry *Alli*
Bullock, Henry 1907?-1973 *ConAu 41*
Bullock, Henry Allen 1906- *LivBA*
Bullock, J Lloyd *Alli*
Bullock, James Dempsey 1863- *WhWNAA*
Bullock, James George *Alli Sup*
Bullock, James Trower *Alli Sup*
Bullock, Jeffrey *Alli*
Bullock, L G *AuBYP*
Bullock, Lotte 1918- *Au&Wr*
Bullock, Michael Hale 1918- *Au&Wr,*
ChPo S2, ConAu 17R, ConP 1970,
ConP 1975, WrD 1976
Bullock, Paul 1924- *ConAu 29*
Bullock, R *Alli, BiDLA*
Bullock, Richard *Alli*
Bullock, Roger 1943- *Au&Wr*
Bullock, Shan F 1865- *BbD*
Bullock, Thomas *Alli*
Bullock, Thomas Austin *Alli Sup*
Bullock, W A C *Au&Wr*
Bullock, W F *Alli Sup*
Bullock, W J *Alli Sup*
Bullock, Walter 1907-1953 *AmSCAP 66*
Bullock, William *Alli*
Bullock, William 1797-1874 *BbtC, DcNAA*
Bullock, William Henry *Alli Sup*
Bullock, William Thomas 1818-1879 *Alli Sup*
Bullock-Webster, Llewelyn 1879- *WhWNAA*
Bullokar *Alli*
Bullokar, John *Alli*
Bullokar, William 1566?- *Alli, NewC*
Bullough, Donald Auberon 1928- *Au&Wr*
Bullough, Geoffrey 1901- *Au&Wr, ConAu 1R*
Bullough, Vern L 1928- *ConAu 9R,*
WrD 1976
Bullough, William Sydney 1914- *Au&Wr*
Bullow, Karl Eduard Von *BbD*
Bullowa, Ferdinand Ezra M d1919 *DcNAA*
Bullowa, Jesse Godfrey Moritz 1879-1943
DcNAA
Bullrich, Silvina 1915- *DcCLA*
Bullus, Eric E 1906- *WrD 1976*
Bullwinkle, Christine Wood *ChPo*
Bulman, Alfred *Alli Sup*
Bulman, B H *MnBBF*
Bulman, E *Alli*
Bulman, Joan Carroll Boone 1904- *Au&Wr*
Bulman, John *Alli, BiDLA*
Bulman, Oliver Meredith Boone 1902-1974
Au&Wr, ConAu 49
Bulmar, John *Alli*
Bulmer, Agnes 1775-1836 *Alli*
DcNAA
Bulmer, Henry Kenneth 1921- *Au&Wr,*
ConAu 13R, WrD 1976
Bulmer, Peter *Alli, BiDLA*
Bulmer, Thomas S *Alli Sup*
Bulmer-Thomas, Ivor 1905- *Au&Wr,*
ConAu P-1, WrD 1976

Bulosan, Carlos 1914-1956 *DcOrL 2,*
TwCA Sup
Bulow, Bernhard, Furst Von 1849-1929 *OxGer*
Bulow, Bertha Von *BiD&SB*
Bulow, Carl 1857- *WhLA*
Bulow, Karl Eduard Von 1803-1853 *BiD&SB*
Bulow, Margarete Von 1860-1885 *BiD&SB*
Buloz, Francois 1803-1877? *BiD&SB, OxFr*
Bulpin, Thomas Victor 1918- *Au&Wr,*
ConAu 9R, WrD 1976
Bulstrode, Edward 1588-1659 *Alli*
Bulstrode, George *Alli Sup*
Bulstrode, Sir Richard 1610-1711 *Alli, NewC*
Bulstrode, Whitelocke d1724 *Alli*
Bulteal, John *Alli*
Bulteel, John *Alli, DcEnL*
Bulthaupt, Heinrich Alfred 1849-1905 *BbD,*
BiD&SB, OxGer
Bultmann, Frederick *Alli Sup*
Bultmann, Rudolf Karl 1884- *ConAu 5R,*
OxGer, WorAu
Bulwer, Lady *Alli*
Bulwer, Sir Edward George Earle Lytton *Alli,*
BrAu 19, Chmbr 3, DcEnL, EvLB
Bulwer, Edward Robert *BrAu 19*
Bulwer, Sir Henry Lytton Earle 1801-1872 *Alli,*
BiD&SB, BrAu 19, Chmbr 3, DcEnL
Bulwer, John 1644?- *Alli, DcEnL*
Bulwer, Sir William H L E 1801-1872 *Alli Sup,*
EvLB
Bulwer-Lytton *Alli Sup, CasWL, ChPo*
Bulwer-Lytton, Edward George E Lytton
1803-1873 *AtlBL, BiD&SB, BrAu 19,*
CyWA, DcBiA, HsB&A, McGWD,
MouLC 3, NewC, Pen Eng, RAdv 1,
REn
Bulwer-Lytton, Edward Robert Lytton *NewC*
Bumke, Erwin 1874- *WhLA*
Bumke, Oswald 1877- *WhLA*
Bump. Charles Weathers 1872-1908 *DcNAA*
Bump, Franklin E, Jr. 1898- *WhWNAA*
Bump, Orlando Franklin 1841-1881? *Alli Sup,*
DcAmA, DcNAA
Bumpfield, W R *Alli*
Bumpus, Cora Hood *ChPo S1*
Bumpus, Hermon Carey 1862-1943 *DcAmA,*
DcNAA, WhWNAA
Bumpus, Jerry *DrAF 1976*
Bumstead, Eudora S 1860- *ChPo, ChPo S1*
Bumstead, Freeman Josiah 1826-1879 *Alli Sup,*
DcAmA, DcNAA
Bumstead, J *Alli Sup*
Bumstead, Josiah F 1797- *Alli*
Bumsted, Eudora S 1860- *ChPo S2*
Bumsted, J M 1938- *ConAu 41, OxCan Sup,*
WrD 1976
Bunao, G Burce 1926- *ConP 1970*
Bunbury *Alli, BbtC*
Bunbury, Miss *Alli*
Bunbury, C J F *Alli*
Bunbury, Sir Edward Herbert 1811- *Alli Sup*
Bunbury, Sir Henry *Alli*
Bunbury, Henry *Alli*
Bunbury, Henry William 1750-1811 *BkIE,*
OxEng
Bunbury, Selina *Alli, Alli Sup, DcEnL*
Bunbury, Thomas *Alli Sup*
Bunbury, William *Alli*
Bunbury, Sir William Henry 1750-1811
Br&AmS
Bunce *ChPo*
Bunce, Daniel *Alli Sup*
Bunce, Frank David 1905- *WhWNAA*
Bunce, Frank David 1907- *ConAu P-1*
Bunce, John *Alli*
Bunce, John Thackray *Alli Sup*
Bunce, Oliver Bell 1828-1890 *Alli Sup, AmA,*
AmA&B, BbD, BiD&SB, DcAmA,
DcNAA, OxAm, REnAL
Bunce, William Harvey 1903- *AuBYP,*
WhWNAA
Bunch, Mother *DcEnL*
Bunch, Boyd 1889- *AmSCAP 66*
Bunch, Clarence *ConAu 53*
Bunch, David R *ConAu 29*
Bunche, Ralph Johnson 1904-1971 *ConAu 33,*
REnAL
Buncle, John *Alli*

Buncombe, Samuel *Alli*
Bund *ChPo*
Bund, John William Bund Willis- 1843-
Alli Sup
Bundukhari, El *ConAu XR*
Bundy, Charles S *Alli Sup*
Bundy, Elizabeth Roxana 1850-1919 *DcNAA*
Bundy, Eve M 1910- *AmSCAP 66*
Bundy, John *Alli*
Bundy, Jonas Mills 1835-1891 *Alli Sup,*
AmA&B, BiD&SB, DcAmA, DcNAA
Bundy, Richard d1739? *Alli*
Bundy, Roy Dalton 1887- *OhA&B*
Bundy, Ruth Lashorne *ChPo*
Bundy, Walter Ernest 1889- *IndAu 1917*
Bung, Klaus 1935- *Au&Wr*
Bungakkai *DcOrL 1*
Bungay, E Newton *MnBBF*
Bungay, George Washington 1818?-1892
Alli Sup, AmA&B, BbD, BiD&SB, ChPo,
ChPo S1, ChPo S2, DcAmA, DcNAA
Bungay, Thomas 1270?- *NewC*
Bunge, Mario A 1919- *ConAu 9R*
Bunge, Rudolf 1836- *BbD, BiD&SB*
Bunge, Walter R 1911- *ConAu 25*
Buni, Andrew 1931- *ConAu 21*
Bunic-Vucicevic, Ivan 1597-1658 *CasWL*
Bunin, Ivan Alekseyevich 1870-1953 *CasWL,*
ClDMEuL, CnMWL, CyWA, DcRusL,
EncWL, EvEuW, LongC, ModSL 1,
Pen Eur, REn, TwCA, TwCA Sup,
TwCW, WhLA, WhTwL
Buning, Johan Willem Frederik Werumeus
1891-1958 *CasWL*
Bunke, H Charles 1922- *ConAu 9R*
Bunker, Alonzo 1837-1912 *DcNAA*
Bunker, Edward 1933- *ConAu 41*
Bunker, Gerald Edward 1938- *ConAu 37*
Bunker, John 1884- *AmA&B, CatA 1947,*
ChPo, OhA&B, WhWNAA
Bunker, John Wymond Miller 1886- *WhWNAA*
Bunker, Robert Emmet 1848-1931 *DcNAA*
Bunkley, Josephine M *Alli Sup*
Bunn, Alfred 1796-1860 *Alli, ChPo*
Bunn, Charles Wilson 1855-1941 *DcNAA*
Bunn, Henry *Alli Sup*
Bunn, John T 1924- *ConAu 37*
Bunn, John W 1898- *ConAu 23*
Bunn, Ronald F 1929- *ConAu 21*
Bunnell, Lafayette Houghton 1824-1903
DcNAA
Bunnell, Peter C 1937- *ConAu 33*
Bunnell, William S 1925- *ConAu P-1*
Bunner, E *BiDSA*
Bunner, Henry Cuyler 1855-1896 *Alli Sup,*
AmA, AmA&B, BbD, BiD&SB, ChPo,
ChPo S1, ChPo S2, Chmbr 3, CnDAL,
DcAmA, DcLEnL, DcNAA, EvLB,
OxAm, REn, REnAL
Bunner, Rudolph F *ChPo*
Bunnett, Fanny Elizabeth *Alli Sup*
Bunney, Edmund 1540-1617 *Alli*
Bunney, Edward *Alli*
Bunney, Francis 1543-1617 *Alli*
Bunning, Charles *Alli, BiDLA*
Bunning, J J And Sands, G *Alli Sup*
Bunny *DcNAA*
Bunny, Edmund 1540-1617 *Alli*
Bunny, Edward *Alli*
Bunny, Francis 1543-1617 *Alli*
Bunow, E J *Alli*
Bunseki, A Fukiau Kia 1934- *AfA 1*
Bunsen, Ernst Von *Alli Sup*
Bunsen, Baroness Frances 1791-1876 *Alli Sup*
Bunsen, Henry George d1885 *Alli Sup*
Bunsen, Robert Wilhelm 1811-1899 *OxGer,*
REn
Buntain, Ruth Jaeger *AuBYP*
Bunte, Karl 1878- *WhLA*
Bunting, A E 1928- *ConAu XR*
Bunting, Anne Evelyn 1928- *ConAu 53*
Bunting, Bainbridge 1913- *ConAu 61*
Bunting, Basil 1900- *ConAu 53, ConP 1970,*
ConP 1975, ModBL Sup, WhTwL,
WorAu, WrD 1976
Bunting, Daniel George *ChPo, LongC*
Bunting, Edward *Alli*
Bunting, Eve 1928- *ConAu XR*

Bunting, Henry Stanhope 1869-1948 *Alli,
DcNAA*
Bunting, Jabez 1778-1858 *Alli, BiDLA*
Bunting, Josiah 1939- *ConAu 45*
Bunting, Thomas Percival 1810- *Alli Sup*
Bunting, William *Alli Sup*
Buntlin, Henry T *Alli Sup*
Buntline, Ned 1823?-1886 *Alli Sup, AmA,
AmA&B, DcAmA, DcNAA, HsB&A,
MnBBF, OhA&B, OxAm, REn, REnAL*
Bunton, Frederica Katheryne *BlkAW*
Bunts, Frank Emory 1861-1928 *DcNAA,
OhA&B*
Bunuan, Josefina S 1935- *ConAu 33*
Bunworth, Richard *Alli*
Bunya, Yasuhide *DcOrL 1*
Bunyan, Humphrey *Alli*
Bunyan, John 1628-1668 *Alli, AtlBL, BbD,
BiD&SB, BrAu, CarSB, CasWL, ChPo,
ChPo S1, ChPo S2, Chmbr 1, CrE&SL,
CriT 2, CyWA,· DcEnA, DcEnL, DcEuL,
DcLEnL, EvLB, MouLC 1, NewC,
OxEng, Pen Eng, RAdv 1, RCom, REn*
Bunyan, John 1628-1688 *WebEAL*
Bunyan, John, Jr. *Alli Sup*
Bunyanus *DcNAA*
Bunyard, George *Alli Sup*
Bunyon, Charles John 1821- *Alli, Alli Sup*
Bunzel, John H 1924- *ConAu 17R*
Bunzel, Julius 1873- *WhLA*
Buol, S W 1934- *ConAu 49*
Buonarotti, Michel *OxFr*
Buonarotti, Michelangelo 1475-1564 *CasWL,
EvEuW*
Buonarotti, Michelangelo, The Younger
1568-1642 *CasWL, McGWD, Pen Eur*
Buoncompagno Da Segna d1240? *CasWL*
Buoy, Charles Wesley 1841-1887 *DcNAA*
Buoy, Katherine Maude 1872- *WhWNAA*
Burack, Abraham S 1908- *AmA&B,
ConAu 9R*
Burack, Elmer H 1927- *ConAu 37*
Burack, Sylvia 1916- *ConAu 21*
Buraeus, Johannes 1568-1652 *DcEuL*
Buralk, Elmer H 1927- *WrD 1976*
Buranelli, Vincent 1919- *ConAu 9R,
WrD 1976*
Burba, George Francis 1865-1920 *OhA&B*
Burbage, Cuthbert *REn*
Burbage, James d1597 *NewC, REn*
Burbage, Richard 1567?-1619 *NewC, REn*
Burbank, Addison Bushnell 1895- *CatA 1947,
IlCB 1945, IlCB 1956, JBA 1951*
Burbank, Luther 1849-1926 *DcNAA, REn*
Burbank, Natt B 1903- *ConAu 25*
Burbank, Nelson L 1898- *ConAu P-1*
Burbank, Rex James 1925- *ConAu 1R*
Burbank, W H *Alli Sup*
Burbidge, Edith Lucy *Au&Wr*
Burbidge, Edward *Alli Sup*
Burbidge, F W *Alli Sup*
Burbidge, George Wheelock 1847-1908 *DcNAA*
Burbidge, John *Alli Sup*
Burbidge, Thomas 1816- *Alli Sup, ChPo*
Burbridge, Edward *BlkAW*
Burbury, Mrs. *Alli*
Burbury, Frances E *Alli Sup*
Burbury, John *Alli*
Burby, William E 1893- *ConAu P-1*
Burch, Dallas S 1887- *WhWNAA*
Burch, Edward P 1870- *WhWNAA*
Burch, Ernest Ward 1875-1933 *DcNAA*
Burch, Florence E *Alli Sup*
Burch, Francis 1932- *ConAu 29*
Burch, Gladys 1899- *AuBYP*
Burch, Harriette E *Alli Sup*
Burch, N P *Alli Sup*
Burch, Pat 1944- *ConAu 57*
Burch, Robert Joseph 1925- *AuBYP,
ConAu 5R, MorBMP, SmATA 1, ThBJA,
WrD 1976*
Burch, Thomas *Alli*
Burch, Thomas Ross *Alli Sup*
Burch, William *Alli Sup*
Burchall, James *Alli*
Burcham, William Ernest 1913- *WrD 1976*
Burchard, Ernest Francis 1875- *WhWNAA*
Burchard, John Ely 1898-1975 *AmA&B,*

ConAu 1R, ConAu 61
Burchard, Max N 1925- *ConAu 23*
Burchard, O R *Alli Sup*
Burchard, Peter Duncan 1921- *Au&Wr,
AuBYP, ConAu 5R, IlCB 1956,
IlCB 1966, SmATA 5, ThBJA*
Burchard, Rachael C 1921- *ConAu 33*
Burchard, Samuel Dickinson 1812-1891 *ChPo,
DcNAA*
Burchard, Sue 1937- *ConAu 53*
Burchardt, Nellie 1921- *ConAu 21, SmATA 7,
WrD 1976*
Burchell, Mrs. E *Alli Sup*
Burchell, Joseph *Alli, BiDLA*
Burchell, Mary *Au&Wr*
Burchell, Old 1810-1879 *DcEnL*
Burchell, William J *Alli*
Burchenal, Elizabeth 1877- *IndAu 1816,
WhWNAA*
Burches, George *Alli*
Burchett, E S *Alli Sup*
Burchett, Godfrey *Alli Sup*
Burchett, Josiah *Alli*
Burchett, Randall E *ConAu 1R*
Burchett, Wilfred Graham 1911- *Au&Wr,
ConAu 49, WrD 1976*
Burchfield, Robert William 1923- *ConAu 41*
Burchiello, Domenico DaGiovanni 1404-1449?
CasWL, DcEuL, EvEuW, REn
Burchwood, Katharine T *ConAu 57*
Burchyer, Henry *Alli*
Burckett, Florence *BiDSA, LivFWS*
Burckhard, Max 1854-1912 *OxGer*
Burckhardt, Carl Jacob 1891-1974 *ConAu 49,
EncWL, OxGer*
Burckhardt, Georg 1881- *WhLA*
Burckhardt, Jacob Christoph 1818-1897 *AtlBL,
OxGer*
Burckhardt, Jakob Christoph 1818-1897 *CasWL,
EuA, EvEuW, REn*
Burckhardt, John L 1784-1817 *Alli, BrAu 19,
Chmbr 3, EvLB*
Burckmyer, Elizabeth *IlBYP*
Burd, Clara Miller *ChPo, ChPo S2, ConICB*
Burd, Henry Alfred *WhWNAA*
Burd, Richard *Alli*
Burd, Van Akin 1914- *ConAu 41*
Burd, William *Alli*
Burdach, Konrad 1859- *WhLA*
Burde, Andrew *Alli*
Burden *BiDLA*
Burden, E R *Alli Sup*
Burden, George *Alli Sup*
Burden, J *Alli*
Burden, Jean 1919- *ConAu 9R, ConP 1970,
DrAP 1975*
Burden, Jean 1914- *WrD 1976*
Burden, W *Alli*
Burder, George 1752-1832 *Alli, BiDLA, ChPo,
ChPo S1, PoCh*
Burder, George Bernard d1881 *Alli Sup*
Burder, Henry Forster *Alli*
Burder, Henry Foster *BiDLA*
Burder, John *Alli*
Burder, John 1940- *WrD 1976*
Burder, Samuel *Alli, BiDLA*
Burder, William *Alli*
Burdett, Mrs. *Alli*
Burdett, C A M *Alli Sup*
Burdett, Charles *Alli*
Burdett, Charles 1815- *Alli, Alli Sup,
AmA&B, BiD&SB, DcAmA, DcNAA,
EncM&D*
Burdett, Constance *Alli Sup*
Burdett, Everett Watson 1854-1925 *Alli Sup,
DcNAA*
Burdett, Sir Francis *Alli, BiDLA*
Burdett, Henry C *Alli Sup*
Burdett, Osbert 1885- *WhLA*
Burdett, Winston 1913- *ConAu 29*
Burdette, Eugene 1900- *AmSCAP 66*
Burdette, Franklin 1911-1975 *ConAu 61*
Burdette, Robert Jones 1844-1914 *Alli Sup,
AmA, AmA&B, BbD, BiD&SB, ChPo,
ChPo S1, ChPo S2, DcAmA, DcNAA,
OhA&B, OxAm, REnAL*
Burdge, Franklin *Alli Sup*

Burdge, Gordon 1906- *AmSCAP 66*
Burdick, Arthur Jerome 1858- *ChPo*
Burdick, Austin C *DcNAA*
Burdick, Charles Kellogg 1883-1940 *DcNAA,
WhWNAA*
Burdick, Charles Rollin 1826-1897 *DcNAA*
Burdick, Donald W 1917- *ConAu 53*
Burdick, Eric 1934- *ConAu 29*
Burdick, Eugene 1918-1965 *AmA&B,
ConAu 5R, ConAu 25, TwCW, WorAu*
Burdick, Francis Marion 1845-1920 *DcAmA,
DcNAA*
Burdick, Jennie Ellis *WhWNAA*
Burdick, Joel Wakeman 1853-1925 *DcNAA*
Burdick, Lewis Dayton *Alli Sup*
Burdick, Loraine 1929- *ConAu 57*
Burdick, Mary Livingston *ChPo*
Burdick, William Livesey 1860-1946 *DcNAA,
WhWNAA*
Burdin *Alli*
Burdon, Miss *Alli*
Burdon, Randal Mathews 1896- *Au&Wr,
ConAu P-1, DcLEnL*
Burdon, William 1764- *Alli, BiDLA*
Burdsall, Richard 1735-1824 *PoCh*
Burdy, Samuel d1820 *Alli, BiDLA, PoIre*
Bureau, James *Alli*
Bureau, Joseph *BbtC*
Buren, Martha Margareta Elisabet 1910-
ConAu P-1
Burenin, Viktor Petrovich 1841-1926 *CasWL*
Burette, Henry A *Alli Sup*
Burfield, Henry John *Alli Sup*
Burford, Eleanor *ConAu XR, EncM&D,
SmATA 2, WorAu, WrD 1976*
Burford, John *Alli*
Burford, Lolah 1931- *ConAu 41, WrD 1976*
Burford, Roger L 1930- *ConAu 41*
Burford, Samuel *Alli*
Burford, William 1927- *ConAu 5R,
ConP 1970, ConP 1975, DrAP 1975,
WrD 1976*
Burg, David 1933- *Au&Wr, ConAu 33*
Burg, Marie *Au&Wr*
Burgan, John D 1913-1951 *AmA&B, AmNov*
Burge, Lorenzo *Alli Sup*
Burge, Milward Rodon Kennedy *EncM&D*
Burge, William d1850 *Alli*
Burgeff, Hans 1883- *WhLA*
Burgeon, G A L *ConAu XR*
Burger *ChPo*
Burger, Albert E 1941- *ConAu 37*
Burger, Carl Victor 1888-1967 *ConAu 19,
IlCB 1966, SmATA 9*
Burger, Chester 1921- *ConAu 9R*
Burger, George V 1927- *ConAu 57*
Burger, Gottfried August 1747-1794 *BbD,
BiD&SB, CasWL, ChPo S1, DcEuL,
EuA, EvEuW, OxGer, Pen Eur, REn*
Burger, Henry G 1923- *ConAu 41*
Burger, Hugo *OxGer*
Burger, Jack 1925- *AmSCAP 66*
Burger, John *ConAu XR*
Burger, Nash K 1908- *ConAu 23*
Burger, Robert S 1913- *ConAu 29*
Burger, Ruth 1917- *ConAu 17R*
Burger, T H *Alli Sup*
Burgermyer, Catherine 1893- *IndAu 1917*
Burgersdijk, Leendert Alexander Johannes
1828-1900 *CasWL*
Burges *Alli*
Burges, Anthony *Alli*
Burges, Arnold *Alli Sup*
Burges, Cornelius d1665 *Alli*
Burges, Ellen *Alli Sup*
Burges, Francis *Alli*
Burges, G H *Alli*
Burges, George *Alli, BiDLA*
Burges, James *Alli*
Burges, Sir James Bland 1752- *Alli, BiDLA*
Burges, Norman Alan 1911- *WrD 1976*
Burges, Samuel *Alli*
Burges, Tristram 1770-1853 *DcNAA*
Burges, William 1827-1881 *Alli Sup*
Burgess, Mrs. *Alli, BiDLA*
Burgess, A F 1873- *WhWNAA*
Burgess, Alexander 1819-1901 *Alli Sup,
DcNAA*

Burgess, Anthony *Alli*
Burgess, Anthony 1917- *Au&Wr, AuNews 1, CasWL, ConAu 1R, ConLC 1, ConLC 2, ConLC 4, ConLC 5, ConNov 1972, ConNov 1976, DrAF 1976, EncWL Sup, LongC, ModBL, ModBL Sup, NewC, Pen Eng, RAdv 1, TwCW, WebEAL, WhTwL, WorAu, WrD 1976*
Burgess, Charles 1932- *ConAu 33, WrD 1976*
Burgess, Chester F 1922- *ConAu 21, WrD 1976*
Burgess, Christopher Victor 1921- *Au&Wr, ConAu 9R*
Burgess, Cornelius d1665 *Alli*
Burgess, Dale W 1910- *IndAu 1917*
Burgess, Daniel *Alli*
Burgess, Daniel 1645-1712 *Alli*
Burgess, Dorothy *ChPo*
Burgess, Ebenezer 1790-1870 *Alli Sup, DcNAA*
Burgess, Edward 1848-1891 *Alli Sup, DcAmA*
Burgess, Edward Sandford 1855-1928 *DcNAA, WhWNAA*
Burgess, Em *ConAu XR*
Burgess, Eric 1912- *Au&Wr*
Burgess, Eric 1920- *Au&Wr, ConAu 5R*
Burgess, Ernest Watson 1886- *WhWNAA*
Burgess, F F R *Alli Sup*
Burgess, Francis Henry 1884- *WhLA*
Burgess, Gelett 1866-1951 *AmA&B, AmLY, AnMV 1926, BiD&SB, ChPo, ChPo S1, CnDAL, ConAmL, ConICB, DcAmA, EncM&D, EvLB, IlCB 1945, IlCB 1956, LongC, OxAm, REn, REnAL, TwCA, TwCA Sup, TwCW, WhWNAA*
Burgess, George 1809-1866 *Alli, AmA&B, ChPo, ChPo S2, CyAL 2, DcAmA, DcNAA*
Burgess, George Kimball 1874-1932 *DcNAA, WhWNAA*
Burgess, Henry 1808-1886 *Alli, Alli Sup*
Burgess, Isaac Bronson 1858-1933 *DcNAA*
Burgess, J *Alli, Alli Sup*
Burgess, J J Haldane *Alli Sup, ChPo*
Burgess, Jackson 1927- *Au&Wr, ConAu 9R*
Burgess, James 1832- *Alli Sup, BbtC*
Burgess, Sir James Bland *DcEnL*
Burgess, James W *Alli Sup*
Burgess, John *Alli*
Burgess, John Cart *Alli, BiDLA*
Burgess, John H 1923- *ConAu 33*
Burgess, John L *Alli Sup*
Burgess, John William 1844-1931 *Alli Sup, BiDSA, DcAmA, DcNAA, WhWNAA*
Burgess, Joseph *Alli Sup*
Burgess, Joseph Tom d1886 *Alli Sup*
Burgess, Joshua *Alli Sup*
Burgess, Laurie Lorne 1882- *WhWNAA*
Burgess, Lucy M *Alli Sup*
Burgess, M Elaine *ConAu 13R*
Burgess, Marie Louis *BlkAW*
Burgess, Margaret Beatrice 1841- *ChPo S1*
Burgess, Mary 1909- *WrD 1976*
Burgess, Mary Wyche 1916- *ConAu 61*
Burgess, Norman 1923- *ConAu 25, WrD 1976*
Burgess, Otis Asa And Underwood, B F *Alli Sup*
Burgess, Paul 1886- *WhWNAA*
Burgess, Perry 1886-1962 *AmA&B, OhA&B, TwCA Sup*
Burgess, Philip M 1939- *ConAu 25*
Burgess, Richard 1786-1881 *Alli, Alli Sup*
Burgess, Robert F 1927- *ConAu 25, SmATA 4*
Burgess, Robert Herrmann 1913- *ConAu 9R, WrD 1976*
Burgess, Robert L 1938- *ConAu 29*
Burgess, Sally *WrD 1976*
Burgess, Stella Fisher 1881- *ChPo S2*
Burgess, Theodore Chalon 1859-1925 *DcNAA*
Burgess, Thomas 1755?-1837 *Alli, BiDLA, BiDLA Sup*
Burgess, Thornton Waldo 1874-1965 *AmA&B, AuBYP, CarSB, ChPo, JBA 1934, JBA 1951, OxAm, REn, REnAL, WhCL, WhWNAA*
Burgess, Trevor *ConAu XR*

Burgess, Tristam *Alli*
Burgess, Tristram *BbtC*
Burgess, W Randolph 1889- *ConAu 29, WhWNAA*
Burgess, W Starling *ChPo S2*
Burgess, Warren E 1932- *WrD 1976*
Burgess, William *Alli*
Burgess, William 1843-1922 *DcNAA*
Burgess, William Roscoe *Alli Sup*
Burgesse, John *Alli*
Burget, G E 1889- *WhWNAA*
Burgett, Arthur Edward 1870- *WhWNAA*
Burgett, Donald R 1925- *ConAu 21*
Burggraf, Waldfried *McGWD, OxGer*
Burgh, A *Alli, BiDLA*
Burgh, Benedict d1488 *Alli, DcEnL*
Burgh, Jacob VanDer 1600-1659 *CasWL*
Burgh, James 1714-1775 *Alli, NewC*
Burgh, Nicholas Procter *Alli Sup*
Burgh, R *Alli*
Burgh, Sydenham *Alli*
Burgh, Thomas *Alli*
Burgh, Walter *PoIre*
Burgh, Walter Hussey 1742-1783 *PoIre*
Burgh, William *Alli*
Burgh, William 1741-1808 *Alli*
Burghalter, Daniel 1867- *IndAu 1816*
Burghard, August 1901- *AuNews 2, ConAu 17R*
Burghardt, Andrew Frank 1924- *ConAu 5R*
Burghardt, Arthur *BlkAW*
Burghardt, Henry Dwight d1949 *DcNAA*
Burghardt, Walter J 1914- *ConAu 1R*
Burghclere, Lady *Chmbr 3*
Burgheim, Max 1848-1918 *OhA&B*
Burghers, Michael 1653?-1727 *BkIE*
Burghill, Robert 1572-1641 *Alli*
Burghley, Lord *Alli*
Burghley, Baron William Cecil 1520-1598 *NewC, REn*
Burghope, George *Alli*
Burghope, M *Alli*
Burgie, Irving 1924- *AmSCAP 66*
Burgin, George Brown 1856-1944 *Chmbr 3, LongC, NewC*
Burgin, Richard 1947- *ConAu 25*
Burgkmair, Hans 1473-1531 *OxGer*
Burglon, Nora *JBA 1951*
Burgon, John William 1813?-1888 *Alli, Alli Sup, BrAu 19, DcEnL, EvLB*
Burgos, Francisco Javier De 1778-1845 *BiD&SB*
Burgos, Francisco Javier De 1842-1902 *CasWL, EvEuW*
Burgos, Julia 1914-1953 *PueRA*
Burgoyne, General *Chmbr 2*
Burgoyne, Arthur Gordon d1914 *DcNAA*
Burgoyne, Elizabeth 1902- *Au&Wr, ConAu XR, WrD 1976*
Burgoyne, Sir John 1722-1792 *Alli, BbtC, BrAu, ChPo, DcEnL, DcLEnL, NewC, OxAm, OxEng, REn, REnAL*
Burgoyne, John Charles *Alli Sup*
Burgoyne, Sir John Fox 1782-1871 *Alli Sup*
Burgoyne, Sir John Montague 1832- *Alli Sup*
Burgoyne, Leon E 1916- *AuBYP*
Burgoyne, Montagu *Alli, BiDLA*
Burgoyne, Roderick Hamilton *Alli Sup*
Burguignon, Hubert Francois *BkIE*
Burgunder, Rose *ChPo*
Burgwyn, Collinson Pierrepont Edwards 1852-1915 *BiDSA, DcNAA*
Burgwyn, Mebane Holoman 1914- *ConAu 49, SmATA 7*
Burgwyn, William Hyslop Sumner 1845- *Alli Sup, BiDSA*
Burhaneddin, Kadi Ahmed 1344-1398 *DcOrL 3*
Burhans, Viola 1892- *WhWNAA*
Burhill, Robert 1572-1641 *Alli*
Burhoe, Ralph Wendell 1911- *ConAu 17R*
Burhop, Eric Henry Stoneley 1911- *WrD 1976*
Buri, Fritz 1907- *ConAu 17R*
Burian, Jarka M 1927- *ConAu 33, WrD 1976*
Burich, Nancy J 1943- *ConAu 29*
Buridan, Jean 1300?-1358? *CasWL, OxFr*
Burk Mangold *OxGer*
Burk, A F *Alli Sup*
Burk, Bruce 1917- *ConAu 61*
Burk, Edward *PoIre*

Burk, Frederic Lister 1862-1924 *DcNAA*
Burk, J H *Alli Sup*
Burk, James H *IndAu 1816*
Burk, John *Alli*
Burk, John Daly 1775?-1808 *AmA, AmA&B, BiDSA, DcAmA, DcNAA, OxAm, PoIre, REnAL*
Burk, Mrs. M B *ChPo*
Burk, Robert 1908-1940 *AmSCAP 66*
Burk, William Herbert 1867-1933 *DcNAA*
Burkam, Elzey Gallatin 1872-1940 *AmA&B*
Burke, Miss *PoIre*
Burke, Mrs. *Alli, BiDLA*
Burke, A D 1893- *WhWNAA*
Burke, Aedanus 1743-1802 *Alli, DcNAA*
Burke, Anna Christian *Alli Sup*
Burke, Arvid James 1906- *ConAu 23, WrD 1976*
Burke, B W *Alli, BiDLA*
Burke, Sir Bernard *Alli*
Burke, C A *ChPo S1*
Burke, C J 1917-1973 *ConAu 45*
Burke, C M *Alli Sup*
Burke, Carl F 1917- *ConAu 25*
Burke, Charles *PoIre*
Burke, Charles E And French, Charles W *Alli Sup*
Burke, Christian *Alli Sup, ChPo, ChPo S1, ChPo S2*
Burke, David 1927- *Au&Wr*
Burke, E P *Alli*
Burke, Edmund *Chmbr 2, PoIre*
Burke, Edmund 1729?-1797 *Alli, AtlBL, BbD, BiD&SB, BrAu, CasWL, CyWA, DcEnA, DcEnL, DcEuL, DcLEnL, EvLB, MouLC 2, NewC, OxAm, OxEng, Pen Eng, PoIre, REn, WebEAL*
Burke, Edmund 1753-1820 *DcNAA, OxCan*
Burke, Edmund J 1858-1941 *DcNAA*
Burke, Edmund M 1928- *ConAu 9R*
Burke, Fielding *AmA&B, AmNov, OxAm, TwCA, TwCA Sup*
Burke, Finley 1855-1903 *Alli Sup, DcNAA*
Burke, Fred George 1926- *AmA&B, ConAu 13R*
Burke, George *PoIre*
Burke, Gerald 1914- *ConAu 45*
Burke, Harry Eugene 1878- *WhWNAA*
Burke, J Bruce 1933- *ConAu 37*
Burke, J Francis 1914- *AmSCAP 66*
Burke, Jack *MnBBF*
Burke, James 1819- *Alli Sup*
Burke, James 1834-1904 *PoIre*
Burke, James 1917- *WrD 1976*
Burke, James Henry 1816-1882 *Alli, PoIre*
Burke, James Lee 1936- *ConAu 13R*
Burke, James Wakefield 1916- *ConAu 45*
Burke, John *Alli, Alli Sup, ConAu XR, PoIre*
Burke, John d1873 *ChPo S1, DcNAA*
Burke, John 1787?-1848 *DcEnL, NewC*
Burke, John Benjamin Butler 1873- *WhLA*
Burke, Sir John Bernard 1815- *Alli, Alli Sup, DcEnL, PoIre*
Burke, John Emmett 1908- *ConAu 37*
Burke, John Frederick 1922- *Au&Wr, ConAu 5R*
Burke, John French *Alli*
Burke, John Joseph 1875-1936 *DcNAA*
Burke, John W *BiDSA*
Burke, Johnny 1908-1964 *AmSCAP 66*
Burke, Jonathan *ConAu XR, MnBBF*
Burke, Joseph A 1884-1950 *AmSCAP 66*
Burke, Kenneth 1897- *AmA&B, AmWr, Au&Wr, CasWL, CnDAL, ConAmA, ConAu 5R, ConLC 2, ConNov 1972, ConNov 1976, ConP 1970, ConP 1975, DcLEnL, EvLB, ModAL, ModAL Sup, OxAm, Pen Am, RAdv 1, REn, REnAL, TwCA, TwCA Sup, WebEAL, WhTwL, WrD 1976*
Burke, Mrs. L *Alli*
Burke, Leda *ConAu XR, WrD 1976*
Burke, Luke *BbtC*
Burke, Lynn *AuBYP*
Burke, Mary Catherine 1834- *PoIre*
Burke, Norah Aileen 1907- *Au&Wr*
Burke, Oliver J *Alli Sup*

Burke, Pauline Wilcox 1884- *CatA 1947*
Burke, Peter 1811-1881 *Alli, Alli Sup, DcEnL*
Burke, Peter 1937- *ConAu 25*
Burke, Richard *Alli*
Burke, Richard C 1932- *ConAu 53*
Burke, Richard O'S *PoIre*
Burke, Robert Belle 1868-1944 *DcNAA*
Burke, Robert E 1921- *ConAu 21*
Burke, Russell 1946- *ConAu 33*
Burke, S Hubert *Alli Sup*
Burke, S M 1906- *ConAu 49*
Burke, Sarah J *ChPo, ChPo S1*
Burke, Shifty *ConAu 49, WrD 1976*
Burke, Thomas *PoIre*
Burke, Thomas 1867- *MnBBF*
Burke, Thomas 1886?-1945 *ChPo, ChPo S1,
    ChPo S2, EncM&D, EvLB, LongC,
    NewC, REn, TwCA, TwCA Sup*
Burke, Thomas A 1828- *Alli*
Burke, Thomas Nicholas 1830-1883 *Alli Sup,
    PoIre*
Burke, Thomas Travers *Alli, PoIre*
Burke, Ulick John 1843- *Alli Sup*
Burke, Ulick Peter 1937- *Au&Wr, WrD 1976*
Burke, Ulick Ralph 1845- *Alli Sup*
Burke, Vee 1921- *ConAu XR*
Burke, Velma Whitgrove 1921- *ConAu 53*
Burke, Victor 1882- *WhWNAA*
Burke, Virginia M 1916- *ConAu 45*
Burke, W *Alli, BiDLA*
Burke, W Talbot *Alli Sup*
Burke, W Warner 1935- *ConAu 37*
Burke, William *Alli, BiDLA, PoIre*
Burke, William 1792-1829 *NewC*
Burke, William Thomas 1926- *IndAu 1917*
Burked, S G *Alli Sup*
Burkert, Nancy Ekholm 1933- *ChPo S1,
    IlBYP, IlCB 1966, ThBJA*
Burkett, Albert Delson 1879-1946 *IndAu 1917*
Burkett, Charles William 1873- *AmLY,
    DcAmA, OhA&B, WhWNAA*
Burkett, Eva M 1903- *ConAu 33*
Burkett, Molly 1932- *ConAu 53*
Burkhalter, Barton R 1938- *ConAu 25*
Burkhard Von Hohenfels *CasWL*
Burkhard, Leonard A 1911- *AmSCAP 66*
Burkhardt, Franklin Alphus 1872-1945 *OhA&B*
Burkhardt, Georg *OxGer*
Burkhardt, Jakob 1818-1897 *DcEuL*
Burkhardt, Richard Wellington 1918-
    ConAu 1R
Burkhardt, Wilbur Neil 1889- *WhWNAA*
Burkhart Von Hohenfels *OxGer*
Burkhart, Charles 1924- *ConAu 13R*
Burkhart, James A 1914- *ConAu 9R*
Burkhart, Kathryn Watterson 1942- *ConAu 45*
Burkhart, Kitsi *ConAu XR*
Burkhart, Robert E 1937- *ConAu 29*
Burkhart, Roy Abram 1895-1962 *AmA&B,
    OhA&B*
Burkhead, Henry *Alli*
Burkhead, Jesse 1916- *ConAu 1R*
Burkholder, L J *OxCan*
Burkholder, Mabel *OxCan*
Burkholder, Walter H 1891- *WhWNAA*
Burkholz, Herbert 1932- *ConAu 25*
Burkholz, Herbert 1935- *Au&Wr*
Burkill, Tom Alec 1912- *ConAu 33,
    WrD 1976*
Burkitt, Francis Crawford 1864- *WhLA*
Burkitt, Lemuel 1750-1806? *BiDSA, DcNAA*
Burkitt, Miles Crawford 1890- *Au&Wr*
Burkitt, William 1650-1703 *Alli*
Burkley, Francis Joseph 1857-1940 *DcNAA*
Burkman, Ella Benedict *ChPo*
Burkman, Katherine H 1934- *ConAu 29*
Burkowsky, Mitchell R 1931- *ConAu 29*
Burks, Arthur W 1915- *ConAu 49*
Burks, David D 1924- *ConAu 33*
Burks, Gordon Engledow 1904- *ConAu 1R*
Burks, Martin Parks 1851-1928 *DcNAA*
Burla, Yehuda 1886-1969 *CasWL*
Burlace, Edmund *Alli*
Burlage, Henry Matthew 1897- *IndAu 1917*
Burlamaqui, Jean-Jacques 1694-1748 *OxFr*
Burland, Brian Berkeley 1931- *AuBYP,
    ConAu 13R, DrAF 1976, WrD 1976*
Burland, Cottie Arthur 1905- *Au&Wr, AuBYP,*

ConAu 5R, SmATA 5
Burleigh *DcNAA*
Burleigh, Baron *NewC*
Burleigh, Lord *Alli, DcEnL*
Burleigh, Anne Husted 1941- *ConAu 29*
Burleigh, Bennet G *Alli Sup*
Burleigh, Benny *BlkAW*
Burleigh, Cecil 1885- *AmSCAP 66*
Burleigh, Charles *Alli Sup*
Burleigh, Charles Calistus 1810-1878 *DcNAA*
Burleigh, Clarence Blendon 1864-1910 *DcNAA*
Burleigh, David Robert 1907- *ConAu 1R*
Burleigh, Donald Quimby 1894- *WhWNAA*
Burleigh, Edwin Clarence 1891- *WhWNAA*
Burleigh, Elmer *Alli Sup*
Burleigh, George Shepard 1821-1903 *Alli Sup,
    AmA, AmA&B, BiD&SB, ChPo,
    ChPo S1, ChPo S2, DcAmA, DcNAA*
Burleigh, Harry T 1886-1949 *AmSCAP 66*
Burleigh, J B *Alli*
Burleigh, Richard *Alli*
Burleigh, Walter 1275- *Alli*
Burleigh, Baron William Cecil 1520-1598 *REn*
Burleigh, William Grant 1866- *WhWNAA*
Burleigh, William Henry 1812-1871 *Alli, AmA,
    AmA&B, BiD&SB, ChPo, ChPo S1,
    CyAL 2, DcAmA, DcNAA*
Burlen, May Gibson *ChPo*
Burlend, Edward *Alli Sup*
Burles, William *Alli*
Burleson, Hugh Latimer 1865-1933 *ChPo S2,
    DcNAA*
Burley, John *Alli Sup*
Burley, Kevin H *OxCan Sup*
Burley, Walter 1275- *Alli*
Burley, William John 1914- *Au&Wr,
    ConAu 33*
Burlin, Natalie Curtis 1875-1921 *AmA&B,
    DcNAA, REnAL*
Burling, John *Alli Sup*
Burling, Lancaster Demorest 1882- *WhWNAA*
Burling, Robbins 1926- *ConAu 17R*
Burlingame, A W 1920- *ChPo S1*
Burlingame, Anne Elizabeth *WhWNAA*
Burlingame, Edward Livermore 1848-1922
    Alli Sup, AmA&B, DcNAA
Burlingame, Eugene Watson 1876-1932 *DcNAA*
Burlingame, Leonas Lancelot 1876- *WhWNAA*
Burlingame, M F *ChPo*
Burlingame, Merrill Gildea 1901- *WhPNW*
Burlingame, Roger 1889-1967 *AmA&B,
    ConAu 5R, REn, REnAL, SmATA 2,
    TwCA, TwCA Sup*
Burlingame, Sheila *ChPo S1*
Burlingame, Virginia 1900- *ConAu 23*
Burlingham, Dorothy 1891- *Au&Wr*
Burlingham, Gertrude Simmons 1872-
    WhWNAA
Burlingham, Hannah K d1901 *ChPo S1*
Burlinson, Harrison And Simpson, William
    Alli Sup
Burlison, William L 1882- *WhWNAA*
Burlyuk, David Davidovich 1882- *DcRusL*
Burlz, Thomas *Alli*
Burma, John H 1913- *ConAu 1R*
Burman, Ben Lucien 1895- *AmA&B, AmNov,
    Au&Wr, ConAu 5R, OxAm, REnAL,
    SmATA 6, TwCA, TwCA Sup,
    WhWNAA, WrD 1976*
Burman, Charles *Alli*
Burman, Ellen Elizabeth *Alli Sup*
Burman, Jose Lionel 1917- *Au&Wr,
    WrD 1976*
Burman, Petrus, Jr. 1713-1778 *CasWL*
Burmeister, Edwin 1939- *ConAu 29*
Burmeister, Eva 1899- *ConAu P-1*
Burmeister, Hermann 1807-1892 *BiD&SB*
Burmeister, Jon 1932- *Au&Wr*
Burmeister, Jon 1933- *ConAu 29, WrD 1976*
Burmeister, Lou E 1928- *ConAu 45*
Burmeister, Richard 1860- *WhLA*
Burmester, Heinrich 1839-1889 *CasWL, OxGer*
Burn, Lieutenant Colonel *Alli*
Burn, Mrs. *Alli Sup*
Burn, Andrew d1814 *Alli, BiDLA,
    BiDLA Sup*
Burn, Andrew Robert 1902- *Au&Wr,
    ConAu 1R, WrD 1976*

Burn, Belle Sumner Angier *WhWNAA*
Burn, Boris 1923- *IlCB 1966*
Burn, Charles *Alli Sup*
Burn, David *BbtC*
Burn, David William Murray 1862- *ChPo*
Burn, Doris 1923- *ConAu 29, SmATA 1,
    WhPNW*
Burn, Edward *Alli, BiDLA, BiDLA Sup*
Burn, J Harold 1892- *ConAu P-1*
Burn, James Dawson 1802- *Alli Sup*
Burn, John *Alli, BiDLA*
Burn, John Henry 1858- *ChPo*
Burn, John Ilderton *Alli, BiDLA*
Burn, John Southerden *Alli, Alli Sup*
Burn, Joshua Harold 1892- *Au&Wr*
Burn, Michael Clive 1912- *Au&Wr, ChPo S2*
Burn, Peter *Alli Sup, ChPo S1*
Burn, Richard 1720-1785 *Alli, Alli Sup*
Burn, Robert *Alli Sup*
Burn, Robert Scott *Alli Sup*
Burn, Samuel *Alli Sup*
Burn, Walter Adam And Raymond, William T
    Alli Sup
Burnaby, Andrew 1732-1812 *Alli, BbtC*
Burnaby, C A *Alli Sup*
Burnaby, E A *Alli, BiDLA*
Burnaby, E S *Alli Sup*
Burnaby, Frederick Gustavus 1842-1885
    Alli Sup, BiD&SB, NewC, OxEng
Burnaby, Mrs. Frederick Gustavus *Alli Sup*
Burnaby, John 1891- *Au&Wr, ConAu P-1*
Burnam, John Miller 1864-1921 *DcNAA*
Burnam, Tom 1913- *ConAu 61*
Burnand, Sir Francis Cowley 1836-1917
    *Alli Sup, BiD&SB, BrAu 19, ChPo,
    ChPo S2, Chmbr 3, DcEnL, EvLB,
    LongC, NewC, OxEng, REn*
Burnap, George 1885- *WhWNAA*
Burnap, George Washington 1802-1859 *Alli,
    CyAL 2, DcAmA, DcNAA*
Burnap, Jacob 1748-1821 *Alli*
Burnap, Naneen 1908- *AnMV 1926*
Burnap, Uzziah Cicero 1794-1854 *DcNAA*
Burnby, John *Alli*
Burncoat, Nancy *WhWNAA*
Burne, Charlotte Sophia *Alli Sup*
Burne, Dorothy *ChPo S1*
Burne, Evelyne *Alli Sup*
Burne, F S Janet *Alli Sup, ChPo S2*
Burne, Glen 1906- *ConAu XR*
Burne, Glenn S 1921- *ConAu 21*
Burne, James *Alli*
Burne, Kevin G 1925- *ConAu 13R*
Burne, Nicholas *Alli*
Burne, Ralph *ConAu XR*
Burne-Jones, Sir Edward Coley 1833-1898
    AtlBL, ChPo, ChPo S2, NewC, REn
Burnel, Henry *Alli*
Burnell, Arthur Coke 1840-1882 *Alli Sup,
    NewC*
Burnell, Fritz S *ChPo S1*
Burnell, George Rowdon *Alli Sup*
Burnell, Henry *PoIre*
Burnell, Henry Blomfield 1854- *Alli Sup*
Burnell, Maud M *ChPo*
Burnell, William Percival 1857- *OhA&B*
Burner, David 1937- *ConAu 25*
Burnes, Sir Alexander 1805-1841 *Alli*
Burnes, Ed Gaines *HsB&A*
Burnes, James *Alli*
Burness, Alexander G And Mavor, F J *Alli Sup*
Burness, W, Morton, J C And Murray, G
    Alli Sup
Burnet *Alli*
Burnet, Alexander 1614-1684 *Alli*
Burnet, Dana 1888-1962 *AmA&B, ChPo,
    ChPo S2*
Burnet, Elizabeth 1661-1709 *Alli*
Burnet, Frank Dana 1888-1962 *OhA&B*
Burnet, Sir Frank Macfarlane 1899- *Au&Wr,
    WrD 1976*
Burnet, George Bain 1894- *ConAu 23*
Burnet, Gilbert *Alli*
Burnet, Gilbert d1746 *Alli*
Burnet, Gilbert 1643-1715 *Alli, BrAu, CasWL,
    Chmbr 2, DcEnA, DcEnL, DcLEnL,
    EvLB, NewC, OxEng, Pen Eng, REn,
    WebEAL*

Burnet, Jacob 1770-1853 *Alli, DcNAA, OhA&B*

Burnet, James, Lord Monboddo 1714-1799 *Alli, DcEnL*

Burnet, James ALSO Burnett, James

Burnet, Jean *OxCan, OxCan Sup*

Burnet, John *BiDLA*

Burnet, John 1784- *Alli*

Burnet, Mary E 1911- *ConAu 53*

Burnet, Mary Quick 1863-1938 *IndAu 1917*

Burnet, Matthias d1806 *Alli*

Burnet, Percy Bentley 1861- *WhWNAA*

Burnet, Thomas *BiDLA, Chmbr 2*

Burnet, Thomas d1750? *Alli*

Burnet, Thomas d1753? *Alli*

Burnet, Thomas 1635?-1715 *Alli, BrAu, CasWL, DcEnL, DcLEnL, EvLB, NewC, OxEng, Pen Eng, REn*

Burnet, W *Alli Sup*

Burnet, Whittier 1876-1945 *OhA&B*

Burnet, William *Alli*

Burnet, William 1688-1729 *Alli*

Burnett, Alexander *Alli Sup*

Burnett, Alfred 1824-1884 *OhA&B*

Burnett, Alfred David 1937- *WrD 1976*

Burnett, Andrew *Alli*

Burnett, Athole *Alli Sup*

Burnett, Avis 1937- *ConAu 41*

Burnett, B L *Alli Sup*

Burnett, Ben George 1924- *ConAu 1R, WrD 1976*

Burnett, Calvin 1921- *ConAu 33*

Burnett, Charles C 1843-1898 *OhA&B*

Burnett, Charles H *Alli Sup*

Burnett, Charles M *Alli*

Burnett, Charles Theodore 1873-1946 *DcNAA, WhWNAA*

Burnett, Chester Henry 1842-1902 *DcNAA*

Burnett, Clough Turrill 1883- *WhWNAA*

Burnett, Collins W 1914- *ConAu 9R, IndAu 1917*

Burnett, Constance Buel 1893- *AuBYP, ConAu 5R*

Burnett, David 1931-1971 *ConAu 9R, ConAu 33*

Burnett, David Staats 1808-1867 *OhA&B*

Burnett, Dorothy Kirk 1924- *ConAu 5R*

Burnett, Edmund Cody 1864-1949 *AmLY, DcNAA, WhWNAA*

Burnett, Ernie 1884-1959 *AmSCAP 66*

Burnett, Frances Eliza Hodgson 1849-1924 *Alli Sup, AmA&B, AuBYP, BbD, BiD&SB, BiDSA, CarSB, ChPo, ChPo S2, Chmbr 3, ConAmL, DcAmA, DcBiA, DcLEnL, DcNAA, EvLB, FamSYP, JBA 1934, LongC, OxAm, OxEng, Pen Am, Pen Eng, REn, REnAL, TwCA, TwCA Sup, WhCL*

Burnett, Frank 1852- *WhWNAA*

Burnett, George *Alli, BiDLA*

Burnett, George d1811 *Alli*

Burnett, George 1822-1890 *Alli Sup*

Burnett, George 1918- *Au&Wr, WrD 1976*

Burnett, Gilbert T *Alli*

Burnett, Hallie Southgate *AmA&B, ConAu 13R, TwCA Sup, WrD 1976*

Burnett, Henry Lawrence 1838-1916 *OhA&B*

Burnett, Ivy Compton *LongC*

Burnett, James, Lord Monboddo 1714-1799 *EvLB, NewC, Pen Eng*

Burnett, James ALSO Burnet, James

Burnett, James Compton *Alli Sup*

Burnett, James G 1868-1894 *ChPo, DcAmA*

Burnett, Mrs. James G *ChPo*

Burnett, Janet 1915- *ConAu 49*

Burnett, Jean LaRue *ChPo*

Burnett, Joe Ray 1928- *ConAu 17R*

Burnett, John *Alli*

Burnett, John 1764-1810 *Alli*

Burnett, John 1925- *ConAu 57, WrD 1976*

Burnett, John Franklin 1851-1929 *DcNAA*

Burnett, June 1914- *AmSCAP 66*

Burnett, Laurence 1907- *ConAu 49*

Burnett, Miss M A *Alli*

Burnett, Myrtle Redwine *TexWr*

Burnett, Peter Hardeman 1807-1895 *Alli Sup, BiDSA, DcAmA, DcNAA*

Burnett, R Will 1912- *AmA&B*

Burnett, Richard *BiDLA*

Burnett, Ruth Griffith 1902- *IndAu 1917*

Burnett, Swan Moses 1847-1906 *Alli Sup, DcNAA*

Burnett, Theodore C 1861- *WhWNAA*

Burnett, Thomas *Alli*

Burnett, Verne Edwin 1896- *AmA&B*

Burnett, Virgil *ChPo S1*

Burnett, Vivian 1876-1937 *DcNAA*

Burnett, W H *Alli Sup*

Burnett, Waldo Irving 1828-1854 *Alli, DcAmA*

Burnett, Whit 1899-1973 *AmA&B, ConAu 13, ConAu 41, REnAL, TwCA, TwCA Sup*

Burnett, William Green 1833-1906 *IndAu 1816*

Burnett, William Riley 1899- *AmA&B, AmNov, CnDAL, ConAmA, ConAu 5R, DcLEnL, EncM&D, LongC, OhA&B, OxAm, Pen Am, REn, REnAL, TwCA, TwCA Sup, TwCW, WhWNAA*

Burnette, O Lawrence, Jr. 1927- *ConAu 33, WrD 1976*

Burney, Anton *ConAu XR*

Burney, Caroline *Alli*

Burney, Charles *Alli Sup*

Burney, Charles 1726-1814 *Alli, BiD&SB, BiDLA, BiDLA Sup, CasWL, DcEnA, DcEnL, DcEuL, DcLEnL, OxEng*

Burney, Charles, Jr. 1757-1817 *Alli, BiDLA*

Burney, Charles Parr *Alli*

Burney, Edward Francesco 1760-1848 *BkIE*

Burney, Elizabeth 1934- *ConAu 23*

Burney, Ethel R *ChPo S1*

Burney, Eugenia 1913- *ConAu 29*

Burney, Fanny 1752-1840 *AtlBL, BrAu 19, CasWL, Chmbr 2, CyWA, EvLB, NewC, Pen Eng, RAdv 1, REn*

Burney, Frances 1752-1840 *Alli, BbD, BiD&SB, BiDLA, DcBiA, DcEnA, DcEnA Ap, DcEnL, DcEuL, DcLEnL, EvLB, MouLC 3, OxEng, WebEAL*

Burney, James 1739-1821 *Alli, BiDLA, DcEnL*

Burney, James 1750-1821 *BrAu 19*

Burney, Leroy Edgar 1906- *IndAu 1917*

Burney, Richard *Alli*

Burney, Sarah Harriet 1770?-1844 *Alli, BiDLA, DcEnL, DcEuL, NewC*

Burney, Stanford Guthrie 1814- *Alli Sup, BiDSA, DcAmA*

Burney, William 1762-1832 *Alli, BiDLA*

Burnford, S D *ConAu XR, SmATA 3*

Burnford, Sheila 1918- *Au&Wr, AuBYP, BkCL, ChLR 2, ConAu 1R, OxCan, SmATA 3, WrD 1976*

Burnham, Baron 1833-1916 *NewC*

Burnham, Viscount 1862-1933 *NewC*

Burnham, Alan 1913- *ConAu 13R*

Burnham, Anna F *Alli Sup, ChPo, ChPo S1, ChPo S2*

Burnham, Benjamin Franklin 1831?-1898 *Alli Sup, DcAmA, DcNAA*

Burnham, Charles Guilford 1803-1866 *DcNAA*

Burnham, Clara Louise 1854-1927 *Alli Sup, AmA&B, AmLY, BbD, BiD&SB, ChPo, DcAmA, DcNAA, TwCA, WhWNAA*

Burnham, David 1907- *CatA 1952*

Burnham, Dorothy K *OxCan Sup*

Burnham, Eliza A *Alli Sup*

Burnham, Frederick Russell *BlkAW*

Burnham, Frederick Russell 1861?-1947 *AmA&B, ArizL, DcNAA*

Burnham, George Pickering 1814-1902 *Alli Sup, DcNAA*

Burnham, Harold B *OxCan Sup*

Burnham, J And Mitchell, W *Alli Sup*

Burnham, James 1905- *AmA&B, Pen Am, TwCA Sup*

Burnham, John *ChPo, ConAu XR*

Burnham, John Bird 1869-1939 *AmA&B, DcNAA*

Burnham, John C 1929- *ConAu 33*

Burnham, John Hampden 1860-1940 *DcNAA, WhWNAA*

Burnham, Maud *ChPo*

Burnham, R G *Alli*

Burnham, Richard 1749-1810 *Alli, PoCh*

Burnham, Robert Ward, Jr. 1913- *ConAu 17R*

Burnham, Roderick H *Alli Sup*

Burnham, Samuel 1833-1873 *ChPo*

Burnham, Sarah Maria 1818-1901 *Alli Sup, DcAmA, DcNAA*

Burnham, Smith 1866-1947 *AmA&B, DcNAA*

Burnham, Sophy 1936- *AuNews 1, ConAu 41*

Burnham, William Henry 1855-1941 *DcNAA, WhWNAA*

Burnham, William Power 1860-1930 *DcNAA*

Burnie, Robert William 1851- *Alli Sup*

Burnim, Kalman A 1928- *ConAu 1R*

Burningham, Helen Oxenbury *ThBJA*

Burningham, John Mackintosh 1936- *Au&Wr, IlBYP, IlCB 1966, ThBJA, WhCL*

Burnley, James 1842- *Alli Sup*

Burnouf, Eugene 1801-1852 *OxFr*

Burns, Alan 1929- *Au&Wr, ConAu 9R, ConNov 1972, ConNov 1976, WrD 1976*

Burns, Sir Alan Cuthbert 1887- *Au&Wr, WrD 1976*

Burns, Allan *Alli, BiDLA, BiDLA Sup*

Burns, Annelu 1889-1942 *AmSCAP 66*

Burns, Arthur *Alli*

Burns, Arthur Edward 1908- *Au&Wr*

Burns, Arthur F 1904- *AmA&B, ConAu 13R, WrD 1976*

Burns, Aubrey *TexWr*

Burns, Bernard 1915- *WrD 1976*

Burns, Betty 1909- *ConAu 19*

Burns, Bobby *ConAu XR*

Burns, Carol 1934- *ConAu 29, WrD 1976*

Burns, Cecil Delisle *WhLA*

Burns, Collette Marie 1898- *ChPo*

Burns, David 1848- *ChPo S1*

Burns, Dawson *Alli Sup*

Burns, E A *Alli Sup*

Burns, E Bradford 1932- *ConAu 17R*

Burns, Edward *Alli Sup*

Burns, Edward Francis *ChPo S2*

Burns, Edward McNall 1897- *AmA&B, ConAu 1R*

Burns, Eedson Louis Millard 1897- *ConAu 5R, OxCan Sup*

Burns, Eliza Bardman *Alli Sup*

Burns, Elizabeth Rollit *ChPo*

Burns, Elmer Ellsworth 1868- *WhWNAA*

Burns, George 1790- *Alli Sup, BbtC*

Burns, George C *Alli Sup*

Burns, George Plumer 1871- *WhWNAA*

Burns, Gerald P 1918- *ConAu 17R*

Burns, H *Alli Sup*

Burns, Hobert Warren 1925- *ConAu 1R*

Burns, Irene *IlBYP*

Burns, Islay 1817-1872 *Alli Sup*

Burns, Isobel 1772-1858 *ChPo S2*

Burns, J R *Alli Sup*

Burns, Jabez 1805-1876 *Alli, Alli Sup, AmA&B, BbtC, DcNAA*

Burns, James *Alli Sup*

Burns, James Aloysius 1867-1940 *AmLY, DcNAA, IndAu 1816*

Burns, James Drummond 1823-1864 *Alli Sup, ChPo, PoCh*

Burns, James F 1898-1960 *AmSCAP 66*

Burns, James Jesse 1838-1911 *DcNAA, OhA&B*

Burns, James MacGregor 1918- *AmA&B, Au&Wr, ConAu 5R, WorAu*

Burns, James W 1937- *ConAu 33*

Burns, Jim 1936- *ConP 1970, ConP 1975, WrD 1976*

Burns, Joan Simpson 1927- *WrD 1976*

Burns, Jock *MnBBF*

Burns, John *Alli, Alli Sup, BiDLA*

Burns, John D *ChPo S1*

Burns, John Horne 1916-1953 *AmA&B, AmNov, EvLB, ModAL, OxAm, Pen Am, REn, REnAL, TwCA Sup, TwCW, WebEAL*

Burns, John V 1907- *ConAu 33*

Burns, Keivin 1881- *WhWNAA*

Burns, Lee 1872-1957 *IndAu 1917*

Burns, Louisa 1869- *IndAu 1917*

Burns, M J *ChPo*

Burns, P *ChPo*

Burns, P 1938- *Au&Wr*

Burns, Paul C *ConAu 1R, SmATA 5*

Burns, Pearl Robison *TexWr*

Burns, R M *OxCan Sup*

Burns, Ralph 1922- *AmSCAP 66*
Burns, Ralph J 1901- *ConAu 25*
Burns, Ray *SmATA XR*
Burns, Raymond 1924- *SmATA 9*
Burns, Richard Dean 1929- *ConAu 17R*
Burns, Robert *Alli, BiDLA, Chmbr 2*
Burns, Robert 1759-1796 *Alli, AtlBL, BiD&SB, BrAu, CasWL, ChPo, ChPo S1, ChPo S2, CnE&AP, CriT 2, CyWA, DcEnA, DcEnA Ap, DcEnL, DcEuL, DcLEnL, EvLB, FamAYP, MouLC 2, NewC, OxEng, Pen Eng, RAdv 1, RCom, REn, WebEAL*
Burns, Robert 1789- *BbtC*
Burns, Robert Ferrier 1826-1896 *Alli Sup, BbtC, DcNAA*
Burns, Robert Grant 1938- *ConAu 25, DrAP 1975*
Burns, Robert Ignatius 1921- *ConAu 17R*
Burns, Robert Whitehall *WrD 1976*
Burns, Ruel Fox *IndAu 1917*
Burns, Sheila *ConAu XR, WrD 1976*
Burns, Tex *ConAu XR, WrD 1976*
Burns, Thomas *Alli, BiDLA*
Burns, Thomas 1848- *ChPo S1*
Burns, Thomas 1853- *WhLA*
Burns, Thomas 1928- *ConAu 41*
Burns, Thomas Stephen 1927- *ConAu 49*
Burns, Tom 1913- *ConAu 5R*
Burns, Vincent Godfrey 1893- *AmA&B, Au&Wr, AuNews 2, ConAu 41*
Burns, W Scott *BbtC*
Burns, Walter Noble 1872-1932 *AmA&B, ArizL, DcNAA*
Burns, Wayne 1918- *ConAu 1R*
Burns, William *Alli, Alli Sup, BiDLA, PoIre*
Burns, William A 1909- *ConAu P-1, SmATA 5*
Burns, William Henry 1840-1916 *DcNAA*
Burns, William John 1861-1932 *DcNAA, OhA&B*
Burns, Zed H 1903- *ConAu 33*
Burns-Ncamashe, Sipo Mangindi 1920- *AfA 1*
Burnshaw, Stanley 1906- *AmA&B, AnMV 1926, ConAu 9R, ConLC 3, ConP 1970, ConP 1975, DrAP 1975, REnAL, WorAu, WrD 1976*
Burnside, A W *Alli*
Burnside, Ambrose Everett 1824-1881 *IndAu 1917*
Burnside, Dora *ChPo*
Burnside, Helen *Alli Sup*
Burnside, Helen Marion 1844-1923 *Alli Sup, ChPo, ChPo S1, ChPo S2*
Burnside, R *Alli*
Burnside, R H 1870-1952 *AmSCAP 66*
Burnside, Robert *Alli*
Burnside, Thomas 1822-1879 *ChPo*
Burnside, William Smyth *Alli Sup*
Burnside, William Snow And Panton, A W *Alli Sup*
Burnstead, E S *ChPo S1*
Burnyeat, John *Alli*
Burow, Daniel R 1931- *ConAu 29*
Burpee, Charles Winslow 1859-1945 *DcNAA, WhWNAA*
Burpee, Lawrence Johnston 1873-1946 *AmLY, DcLEnL, DcNAA, OxCan, WhWNAA*
Burque, Francois Xavier 1851-1923 *DcNAA*
Burr, Aaron 1716-1757 *Alli, CyAL 1, DcAmA, DcNAA*
Burr, Aaron 1756-1836 *Alli, AmA&B, DcNAA, OxAm, REn, REnAL*
Burr, Aaron Ainsworth *DcNAA*
Burr, Agnes Rush *AmA&B, WhWNAA*
Burr, Alfred Edmund 1815-1900 *AmA&B*
Burr, Alfred Gray 1919- *ConAu 25*
Burr, Amelia Josephine 1878- *AmA&B, ChPo, ChPo S1, ChPo S2*
Burr, Anna Robeson 1873-1941 *AmA&B, ChPo S2, DcNAA, TwCA, WhWNAA*
Burr, Anne 1937- *ConAu 25, ConLC 6*
Burr, Aril Bond 1880-1955 *OhA&B*
Burr, Bell 1856-1931 *DcNAA*
Burr, Charles Chauncey 1817-1883 *Alli Sup, AmA&B, ChPo, DcNAA*
Burr, Dorothy Young 1912- *WrD 1976*
Burr, Ebenezer *Alli Sup*

Burr, Enoch Fitch 1818-1907 *Alli Sup, BiD&SB, DcAmA, DcNAA*
Burr, Fearing, Jr. *Alli Sup*
Burr, Frank A 1843-1894 *DcNAA*
Burr, Frank A And Hinton, Richard J *Alli Sup*
Burr, G D *Alli*
Burr, George Lincoln 1857-1938 *AmA&B, BiD&SB, DcAmA, DcNAA, WhWNAA*
Burr, Gray *DrAP 1975*
Burr, H S 1889- *WhWNAA*
Burr, Hanford Montrose 1864-1941 *DcNAA, WhWNAA*
Burr, Mrs. Higford *Alli*
Burr, Jane *AmA&B, ChPo*
Burr, Jennie M *ChPo, ChPo S1*
Burr, John R 1933- *ConAu 45*
Burr, Katherine Douglas d1901 *DcNAA*
Burr, Laura Boyle *ChPo*
Burr, Major Dangerfield *HsB&A*
Burr, S D V *Alli Sup*
Burr, Thomas Benge *Alli*
Burr, Wesley R 1936- *ConAu 37, WrD 1976*
Burr, William Henry *EarAB*
Burr, William Henry 1819-1908 *DcAmA, DcNAA*
Burr, William Hubert 1851-1934 *Alli Sup, DcAmA, DcNAA*
Burr, William Morris *ChPo, ChPo S1*
Burr, William Wesley 1880- *WhWNAA*
Burrage, Alfred McLelland 1889-1956? *MnBBF*
Burrage, Alfred Sherrington *MnBBF*
Burrage, Athol Harcourt 1899- *MnBBF*
Burrage, E H *Alli Sup*
Burrage, Edwin Harcourt 1839-1916 *MnBBF*
Burrage, Henry Sweetser 1837-1926 *Alli Sup, DcAmA, DcNAA*
Burrage, Walter Lincoln 1860-1935 *DcNAA*
Burrall, F A *Alli Sup*
Burrard, Sidney *Alli Sup*
Burrard, W Dutton *Alli Sup*
Burrel, Alexander *Alli*
Burrel, Andrew *Alli*
Burrel, George *Alli*
Burrel, J *Alli*
Burrel, John *Alli*
Burrell, A B *Alli Sup*
Burrell, A M *Alli Sup*
Burrell, Abram Bogart 1827-1872 *ChPo*
Burrell, Angus 1890-1957 *AmA&B*
Burrell, Benjamin Ebenezer 1892- *BlkAW*
Burrell, Berkeley G 1919- *ConAu 33*
Burrell, Caroline Benedict *WhWNAA*
Burrell, Charles Edward 1870- *WhWNAA*
Burrell, David B 1933- *ConAu 33*
Burrell, David James 1844?-1926 *Alli Sup, DcAmA, DcNAA*
Burrell, Edward J *Alli Sup*
Burrell, Evelyn Patterson *ConAu 53*
Burrell, George Arthur 1882-1957 *OhA&B*
Burrell, Herbert Leslie 1856-1910 *DcNAA*
Burrell, J *BiDLA*
Burrell, Joseph Dunn 1858-1930 *DcNAA, WhWNAA*
Burrell, Kenny 1931- *AmSCAP 66*
Burrell, Louis V *BlkAW*
Burrell, Martin 1858-1938 *CanWr, DcNAA, OxCan, WhWNAA*
Burrell, Orin Kay 1899-1964 *WhPNW*
Burrell, Percival *Alli*
Burrell, Percy Jewett 1877- *WhWNAA*
Burrell, Roy E C 1923- *ConAu 33*
Burrell, Lady Sophia 1760?-1802 *Alli, PoIre*
Burrell, Thomas William 1923- *Au&Wr, WrD 1976*
Burrell, William *Alli*
Burrell, William Palfrey 1843- *Alli Sup*
Burrhus *Alli*
Burridge, Ezekiel *Alli*
Burridge, Richard *Alli*
Burridge, S R *ChPo*
Burriel-Marti, Fernando 1905- *Au&Wr*
Burrill, A C 1881- *WhWNAA*
Burrill, Alexander Mansfield 1807-1869 *Alli, Alli Sup, DcAmA, DcNAA*
Burrill, Thomas Jonathan 1839-1916 *DcAmA, DcNAA*
Burrin, Frank Kleiser 1920- *ConAu 25, WrD 1976*

Burrington, George *Alli*
Burrington, Gilbert *Alli*
Burris, B C 1924- *ConAu 21*
Burris, Burmah *IlBYP*
Burris, F H *Alli Sup*
Burris, Marcus Lindsay 1872-1934 *OhA&B*
Burris, William Paxton 1865?-1946 *DcNAA, IndAu 1917*
Burris-Meyer, Harold 1902- *ConAu 41*
Burrish, Onslow *Alli*
Burritt, Burton Turrell 1899- *WhWNAA*
Burritt, Edwin C *WhWNAA*
Burritt, Eldon Grant 1868-1927 *DcNAA*
Burritt, Elihu 1810?-1879 *Alli, Alli Sup, AmA, AmA&B, BbD, BiD&SB, CyAL 2, DcAmA, DcEnL, DcNAA, OxAm, REnAL*
Burritt, Elijah Hinsdale 1794-1838 *Alli, DcNAA*
Burrough, Edward 1634-1668 *Alli*
Burrough, Edwin *ChPo S2*
Burrough, G F *Alli*
Burrough, Henry *Alli*
Burrough, James *Alli*
Burrough, John *Alli*
Burrough, Stephen *NewC*
Burrough, Thomas Hedley Bruce 1910- *Au&Wr*
Burroughes, Edward *Alli*
Burroughes, Jeremiah 1599-1646 *Alli*
Burroughes, Thomas *Alli*
Burroughs, Alathea S *ChPo*
Burroughs, Ben 1918- *ChPo, ChPo S2*
Burroughs, Bob 1937- *AmSCAP 66*
Burroughs, Charles 1787-1868 *DcNAA*
Burroughs, Dorothy *ChPo*
Burroughs, E H *Alli*
Burroughs, Edgar Rice 1875-1950 *AmA&B, AmLY, EvLB, LongC, MnBBF, OxAm, Pen Am, REn, REnAL, TwCA, TwCA Sup, TwCW*
Burroughs, Ellen *AmA&B*
Burroughs, Prince Emmanuel 1871- *WhWNAA*
Burroughs, Francis *Alli, BiDLA, PoIre*
Burroughs, H B Gresson *Alli*
Burroughs, Henry Colclough *Alli Sup*
Burroughs, Jack *ChPo*
Burroughs, James *Alli*
Burroughs, Jeremiah *Alli*
Burroughs, John *Alli*
Burroughs, Sir John d1643 *Alli*
Burroughs, John 1837-1921 *Alli Sup, AmA, AmA&B, AmLY, AnCL, BbD, BiD&SB, CarSB, ChPo, Chmbr 3, ConAmL, DcAmA, DcEnA Ap, DcLEnL, DcNAA, EvLB, JBA 1934, OxAm, Pen Am, REn, REnAL*
Burroughs, Joseph 1684?-1761 *Alli*
Burroughs, Lewis d1786 *PoIre*
Burroughs, Margaret Taylor Goss 1917- *BlkAW, ConAu 23, LivBA*
Burroughs, Newburgh *PoIre*
Burroughs, Peter *OxCan Sup*
Burroughs, Polly 1925- *ConAu 25, SmATA 2*
Burroughs, Samuel *Alli*
Burroughs, Stephen 1765?-1840 *Alli, DcAmA, DcNAA*
Burroughs, Thomas *Alli*
Burroughs, W H *Alli Sup*
Burroughs, W K *Alli*
Burroughs, Wilbur Greeley 1886- *WhWNAA*
Burroughs, William S 1914- *AmA&B, Au&Wr, AuNews 2, CasWL, ConAu 9R, ConLC 1, ConLC 2, ConLC 5, ConNov 1972, ConNov 1976, DrAF 1976, EncWL Sup, ModAL, ModAL Sup, OxAm, Pen Am, RAdv 1, REn, REnAL, TwCW, WebEAL, WhTwL, WorAu, WrD 1976*
Burroughs, William S, Jr. *DrAF 1976*
Burrow, Diana Wynne 1934- *WrD 1976*
Burrow, Edward J *Alli*
Burrow, Sir James 1701-1782 *Alli*
Burrow, James Gordon 1922- *ConAu 5R*
Burrow, John Anthony 1932- *Au&Wr*
Burrow, John Holme *Alli Sup*
Burrow, John W 1935- *ConAu 21*
Burrow, Reuben d1791 *Alli*

Burrow, Robert *Alli*
Burrow, Trigant 1875- *WhWNAA*
Burroway, Janet Gam 1936- *Au&Wr,*
ConAu 21, ConNov 1976
Burroway, Janet Gay 1936- *WrD 1976*
Burrowe, Stephen *NewC*
Burrowes, Amyas *Alli*
Burrowes, Elizabeth Haven *ChPo*
Burrowes, George 1811-1894 *Alli, Alli Sup,*
DcAmA, DcNAA
Burrowes, Hal *ChPo*
Burrowes, J F *Alli*
Burrowes, Katherine d1939 *DcNAA*
Burrowes, Michael Anthony Bernard 1937-
WrD 1976
Burrowes, Mike *WrD 1976*
Burrowes, Peter Edward 1844- *DcNAA*
Burrowes, Robert 1756?-1841 *Alli, PoIre*
Burrowes, Rose *Alli Sup*
Burrows, A J *Alli Sup*
Burrows, Abe 1910- *AmA&B, AmSCAP 66,*
ChPo S1, ConDr, ModWD, OxAm,
WrD 1976
Burrows, Angie M H 1860-1944 *DcNAA*
Burrows, David J 1936- *ConAu 41*
Burrows, Eric Norman Bromley 1882-1938
CatA 1952
Burrows, Francis *ChPo S1*
Burrows, Fredrika Alexander 1908- *ConAu 57*
Burrows, Harold *MnBBF*
Burrows, Henry William *Alli Sup*
Burrows, Hermann 1896- *Au&Wr*
Burrows, J *Alli*
Burrows, James *Alli Sup*
Burrows, James C 1944- *ConAu 29*
Burrows, Sir John C *Alli Sup*
Burrows, Lansing 1843-1919 *DcNAA*
Burrows, Leonard Ranson 1921- *Au&Wr,*
WrD 1976
Burrows, Mary *Alli Sup, ChPo S1*
Burrows, Miles James Edwin 1936- *Au&Wr,*
ConAu 21, ConP 1970, WrD 1976
Burrows, Millar 1889- *AmA&B, Au&Wr,*
OhA&B, WrD 1976
Burrows, Montagu 1819- *Alli Sup*
Burrows, Montrose T 1884- *WhWNAA*
Burrows, Roger 1935- *Au&Wr*
Burrows, William *Alli Sup*
Burrup, Percy E 1910- *ConAu 1R, WrD 1976*
Burruss, Julian Ashby 1876- *WhWNAA*
Burry, B Pullen *Alli Sup*
Burscough, Robert *Alli*
Burscough, William d1755 *Alli*
Bursk, Edward C 1907- *ConAu 1R*
Burslem, Rollo *Alli*
Burslem, Willoughby M *Alli*
Bursley, Joseph Aldrich 1877-1950 *IndAu 1917,*
WhWNAA
Burson, Elbert E 1903- *WhWNAA*
Burson, William 1833-1880 *OhA&B*
Burssens, Gaston 1896-1965 *CasWL*
Burstal, E Kynaston *Alli Sup*
Burstall, Aubrey F 1902- *Au&Wr*
Burstall, Sara Annie 1859- *WhLA*
Burstein, Abraham 1863- *ChPo S1*
Burstein, Abraham 1893- *OhA&B*
Burstenbinder, Elisabeth *OxGer*
Burstyn, Harold L 1930- *ConAu 9R*
Burt, Adam *Alli, BiDLA*
Burt, Al 1927- *ConAu 25*
Burt, Alfred LeRoy 1888- *ConAu P-1, OxCan*
Burt, Armistead 1802-1883 *BiDSA, DcNAA*
Burt, B C *Alli Sup*
Burt, Benjamin Chapman 1852-1915 *DcNAA*
Burt, Benjamin Hapgood 1882-1950
AmSCAP 66
Burt, Charles H *Alli Sup*
Burt, Clarence Edward 1886-1971 *Au&Wr*
Burt, Sir Cyril Lodowic 1883-1971 *BiDPar,*
ConAu 33, ConAu P-1, WhLA,
WhWNAA
Burt, Edward *Alli*
Burt, Emily Rose *ChPo*
Burt, Henry Jackson 1873-1928 *DcNAA*
Burt, Isabella *Alli Sup*
Burt, Jesse Clifton 1921- *ConAu 9R*
Burt, John J 1934- *ConAu 29*

Burt, John P *Alli Sup*
Burt, John Struthers 1880- *OhA&B*
Burt, John T *Alli*
Burt, John Thomas *Alli Sup*
Burt, Katharine Newlin 1882- *AmA&B,*
AmNov, REnAL, TwCA, TwCA Sup,
WhWNAA
Burt, Llewelyn Charles *Alli Sup*
Burt, Mary Elizabeth 1850-1918 *Alli Sup,*
AmA&B, AmLY, DcNAA
Burt, Maxwell Struthers 1882-1954 *ChPo,*
ChPo S2, TwCA, TwCA Sup
Burt, Michael 1900- *CatA 1947*
Burt, Nathaniel 1913- *AuBYP, ConAu 17R,*
WrD 1976
Burt, Nathaniel Clark 1825-1874 *Alli Sup,*
DcAmA, DcNAA, OhA&B
Burt, Olive Woolley 1894- *AuBYP, ChPo S2,*
ConAu 5R, SmATA 4
Burt, Pitts Harrison 1837-1906 *DcNAA,*
OhA&B
Burt, Richard *Alli, BiDLA*
Burt, Richard Welling 1823-1911 *OhA&B*
Burt, Samuel M 1915- *ConAu 23*
Burt, Stephen Smith 1850-1932 *DcNAA*
Burt, Struthers 1882-1954 *AmA&B, AmNov,*
CnDAL, ConAmA, ConAmL, OxAm,
REn, REnAL, WhWNAA
Burt, Thomas Seymour *Alli Sup*
Burt, William *Alli, BiDLA*
Burt, William 1852-1936 *DcNAA*
Burt, William Austin 1792-1858 *DcNAA*
Burt, William H *Alli Sup*
Burtchaell, Clara Grace d1940 *DcNAA*
Burtchaell, James Tunstead 1934- *ConAu 25*
Burte, Hermann 1879-1960 *ClDMEuL,*
ModWD, OxGer, WhLA
Burtenshaw *Alli*
Burthogge, Richard *Alli*
Burtin, Nicholas Victor 1828-1902 *DcNAA*
Burtin, Will 1908- *WhGrA*
Burtis, C Edward 1907- *ConAu 41*
Burtis, Thomson 1896- *AmA&B*
Burtis, W R M *BbtC*
Burtness, Paul Sidney 1923- *ConAu 17R*
Burtnett, Earl 1896-1936 *AmSCAP 66*
Burtoft, Lavina A Hollingsworth Judkins
1849-1929 *OhA&B*
Burton, Mrs. *Alli, BiDLA*
Burton, A *ChPo*
Burton, A E *ChPo*
Burton, Abigail Williams *ChPo*
Burton, Alan *MnBBF*
Burton, Alberta L *ChPo S2*
Burton, Alfred *BrAu 19*
Burton, Alma Holman 1855- *IndAu 1816*
Burton, Anthony 1933- *ConAu 61*
Burton, Arthur 1914- *ConAu 21*
Burton, Asa 1752-1836 *DcAmA, DcNAA*
Burton, B *Alli*
Burton, Bella F *Alli Sup*
Burton, Brian Keith 1931- *Au&Wr*
Burton, C E *ChPo S1*
Burton, Carl D 1913- *ConAu 1R*
Burton, Charles *Alli, BiDLA, EarAB Sup*
Burton, Charles 1793-1866 *Alli, Alli Sup*
Burton, Charles Emerson 1869-1940 *DcNAA,*
OhA&B
Burton, Mrs. Charles Henry *Alli Sup*
Burton, Charles James d1887 *Alli, Alli Sup*
Burton, Charles Pierce 1862-1947 *AmA&B,*
DcNAA, IndAu 1816
Burton, Clara May *ChPo S2*
Burton, Clarence Monroe 1853-1932 *DcNAA,*
WhWNAA
Burton, David H 1925- *ConAu 49*
Burton, Dolores Marie 1932- *ConAu 25*
Burton, Doris *BkC 6, CatA 1952*
Burton, Dwight L 1922- *ConAu 61*
Burton, Edmond Francis 1820- *Alli Sup*
Burton, Edmund *Alli, BiDLA, BiDLA Sup,*
MnBBF
Burton, Edward *Alli Sup*
Burton, Edward 1794-1836 *Alli*
Burton, Edward J 1917- *ConAu 23*
Burton, Eldin 1913- *AmSCAP 66*
Burton, Eli Franklin 1879-1948 *DcNAA*
Burton, Elizabeth *Au&Wr, AuBYP*

Burton, Ella *Alli Sup*
Burton, Ella 1845- *ChPo S1*
Burton, Ernest DeWitt 1856-1925 *DcAmA,*
DcNAA, OhA&B
Burton, Ernest James 1908- *Au&Wr*
Burton, Francis *Alli*
Burton, Sir Francis *OxCan*
Burton, Frederick Russell 1861-1909 *AmA&B,*
DcNAA
Burton, G R *ChPo S1*
Burton, Gabrielle 1939- *ConAu 45*
Burton, Genevieve 1912- *ConAu 33*
Burton, George *Alli*
Burton, George H *Alli Sup*
Burton, Gideon 1811-1903 *OhA&B*
Burton, Gustavus Matthew 1824- *Alli Sup*
Burton, Harold Hitz 1888- *OhA&B*
Burton, Harry Edwin 1868-1945 *DcNAA,*
WhWNAA
Burton, Harry McGuire 1898- *Au&Wr*
Burton, Henry *Alli, ChPo S1*
Burton, Henry 1579?-1648 *Alli*
Burton, Henry Bindon *Alli Sup, PoIre*
Burton, Henry R *Alli Sup*
Burton, Hester 1913- *Au&Wr, ChLR 1,*
ConAu 9R, SmATA 7, ThBJA, WhCL,
WrD 1976
Burton, Hezekiah d1681 *Alli*
Burton, Ian 1935- *ConAu 17R*
Burton, Lady Isabel 1831-1896 *Alli Sup,*
DcEuL, NewC
Burton, Ivor Flower 1923- *Au&Wr, WrD 1976*
Burton, J *Alli*
Burton, J Bloundelle *Alli Sup*
Burton, J E *BbtC*
Burton, J M *Alli Sup*
Burton, James R *EarAB*
Burton, Jennie Davis *HsB&A*
Burton, Joe Wright 1907- *AmA&B*
Burton, John *Alli, Alli Sup, Au&Wr*
Burton, John 1696-1771 *Alli*
Burton, John 1697-1771 *Alli*
Burton, John 1773-1822 *PoCh*
Burton, John 1834-1897 *DcNAA*
Burton, John 1894- *WhWNAA*
Burton, John, Jr. 1803- *ChPo S1, PoCh*
Burton, John Andrew 1944- *WrD 1976*
Burton, John E *Alli Sup*
Burton, John Henry 1809- *Au&Wr*
Burton, John Hill 1809-1881 *Alli, Alli Sup,*
BiD&SB, BrAu 19, CasWL, Chmbr 3,
DcEnL, DcLEnL, EvLB, NewC, OxEng,
Pen Eng
Burton, Mrs. John Hill *Alli Sup*
Burton, Joseph *Alli Sup*
Burton, Juliette T *Alli Sup*
Burton, Katharine *ChPo*
Burton, Katherine 1884- *CatA 1947*
Burton, Katherine 1887- *BkC 3, OhA&B*
Burton, Katherine 1890- *AuBYP*
Burton, Lewis William 1852- *WhWNAA*
Burton, Lindy 1937- *ConAu 25*
Burton, Lloyd E 1922- *ConAu 53*
Burton, Margaret Ernestine 1885- *WhWNAA*
Burton, Marion LeRoy 1874-1925 *AmA&B,*
AmLY, DcNAA
Burton, Mary Josephine 1903- *Au&Wr*
Burton, Maud R *ChPo*
Burton, Maurice 1898- *Au&Wr*
Burton, Miles *EncM&D*
Burton, Myron Garfield 1880-1923 *IndAu 1917*
Burton, Nat 1901-1945 *AmSCAP 66*
Burton, Nathan Smith 1821-1909 *DcNAA*
Burton, Nathaniel Judson 1824-1887 *Alli Sup,*
BiD&SB, DcAmA, DcNAA
Burton, Nelson, Jr. 1942- *ConAu 57*
Burton, Nic *Alli*
Burton, Philip d1792 *Alli*
Burton, Philip 1904- *ConAu 25*
Burton, Philippiana *Alli*
Burton, R T *Alli Sup*
Burton, R W *Alli Sup*
Burton, Reginald George 1864- *WhLA*
Burton, Richard 1861?-1940 *AmA&B,*
AnMV 1926, BbD, BiD&SB, ChPo,
ChPo S1, DcAmA, DcNAA, REnAL,
WhWNAA
Burton, Richard 1925- *NewC*

Burton, Sir Richard Francis 1821-1890 *Alli,*
Alli Sup, AtlBL, BbD, BiD&SB,
BrAu 19, CasWL, ChPo, ChPo S2,
Chmbr 3, DcEnA, DcEnA Ap, DcEnL,
DcEuL, DcLEnL, MouLC 4,
NewC, OxEng, Pen Eng, PoIre, REn,
WebEAL
Burton, Robert *Alli*
Burton, Robert 1577-1639? *Alli, AtlBL, BbD,*
BiD&SB, BrAu, CasWL, Chmbr 1,
CrE&SL, CriT 1, CyWA, DcEnA,
DcEnL, DcEuL, DcLEnL, EvLB,
MouLC 1, NewC, OxEng, Pen Eng,
RAdv 1, REn, WebEAL
Burton, Robert 1941- *ConAu 45*
Burton, Robert E 1927- *ConAu 61*
Burton, Robert H 1939- *ConAu 37*
Burton, Robert Wellesley 1941- *Au&Wr*
Burton, Roger V 1928- *ConAu 45*
Burton, Samuel *Alli*
Burton, Theodore Elijah 1851-1929 *DcAmA,*
DcNAA, OhA&B, WhWNAA
Burton, Thomas *Alli, AmA&B, ConAu XR,*
OxCan Sup, TwCA Sup, WrD 1976
Burton, Thomas Of *DcEnL*
Burton, Thomas Rudall *ChPo S1*
Burton, Thomas William 1860-1939 *OhA&B*
Burton, Val 1899- *AmSCAP 66*
Burton, Virginia Lee 1909-1968 *AmA&B,*
AnCL, AuBYP, AuICB, Cald 1938,
ConAu 25, ConAu P-1, IlBYP,
IlCB 1945, IlCB 1956, IlCB 1966,
JBA 1951, SmATA 2
Burton, W *Alli, Alli Sup*
Burton, Mrs. W Dinzey *Alli Sup*
Burton, W H *Alli*
Burton, W Henry *Alli Sup*
Burton, W K *Alli Sup*
Burton, W P *ChPo*
Burton, Mrs. W S *Alli Sup*
Burton, W W *Alli*
Burton, Warney *Alli Sup*
Burton, Warren 1800-1866 *Alli Sup, AmA&B,*
CyAL 2, DcAmA, DcNAA
Burton, William *Alli*
Burton, William d1667 *Alli*
Burton, William 1575-1645 *DcEnL*
Burton, William 1575-1681 *Alli*
Burton, William Evans 1804-1860 *Alli, AmA,*
AmA&B, DcAmA, DcNAA, OxAm,
REnAL
Burton, William George 1774- *Alli*
Burton, William H 1890-1964 *ConAu 1R*
Burton, William L 1928- *ConAu 21*
Burton-Fanning, Frederick William 1863-
WhLA
Burton-Opitz, Russell 1875-1954 *IndAu 1917*
Burtschi, Mary Pauline 1911- *ConAu 9R,*
WrD 1976
Burtt, Edwin Arthur 1892- *AmA&B, Au&Wr,*
ConAu 5R, WhWNAA, WrD 1976
Burtt, Everett Johnson, Jr. 1914- *ConAu 9R*
Burtt, George 1914- *ConAu 61*
Burtt, Harold Ernest 1890- *ConAu 17,*
WhWNAA
Burtt, John 1789-1866 *ChPo, DcNAA*
Burtt, T *Alli Sup*
Burwash, Edward Moore Jackson 1873- *AmLY*
Burwash, Nathanael 1839-1918 *Alli Sup,*
DcNAA, OxCan
Burwell, Adam Hood 1790?-1849 *DcNAA,*
OxCan
Burwell, Clifford R 1898- *AmSCAP 66*
Burwell, Letitia M *BiDSA, DcNAA*
Burwell, Lettie M *Alli Sup*
Burwell, William MacCreary 1809-1888
DcNAA
Burwell, William McCreery 1809-1888 *BiDSA*
Burwood, Jane *Alli*
Bury, Viscount *Alli Sup*
Bury, Adrian 1895- *ChPo S2*
Bury, Arthur *Alli*
Bury, Charles Kenneth Howard 1883- *WhLA*
Bury, Lady Charlotte Susan Maria 1775-1861
Alli, BrAu 19, Chmbr 2, DcEnL,
DcLEnL, EvLB
Bury, Edward *Alli*
Bury, Elizabeth d1720 *Alli*

Bury, H *Alli Sup*
Bury, James *Alli, Alli Sup*
Bury, John *Alli*
Bury, John Bagnell 1861-1927 *Chmbr 3,*
DcEnA Ap, EvLB, LongC, Pen Eng,
PoIre, TwCA
Bury, John Patrick Tuer 1908- *Au&Wr,*
ConAu 17R, WrD 1976
Bury, Judson Sykes 1852- *WhLA*
Bury, Richard De 1287?-1345 *Alli, BrAu,*
CasWL, Chmbr 1, DcEuL, EvLB, NewC,
OxEng
Bury, Richard Of 1287?-1345 *DcEnL*
Bury, Samuel *Alli*
Bury, Talb *Alli*
Bury, William *Alli Sup*
Bus, Gervais Du d1339? *CasWL, EvEuW*
Busbee, Charles Manly 1845-1909 *DcNAA*
Busbee, Fabius Hayward 1848-1908 *DcNAA*
Busbee, Perrin *Alli Sup*
Busbey, Hamilton 1840-1924 *DcNAA, OhA&B*
Busbey, L White 1852-1925 *DcNAA, OhA&B*
Busby, C A *Alli, BiDLA*
Busby, Edith *AuBYP*
Busby, Edith A Lake d1964 *IndAu 1917*
Busby, James *Alli Sup*
Busby, Richard 1606-1695 *Alli, NewC*
Busby, Thomas 1755-1838 *Alli, BiDLA,*
DcEnL
Busch, Bonnie 1884- *AmA&B*
Busch, Briton Cooper 1936- *ConAu 23,*
WrD 1976
Busch, Francis Xavier 1879-1975 *AmA&B,*
ConAu 61, ConAu P-1
Busch, Frederick 1941- *ConAu 33,*
ConNov 1976, DrAF 1976, WrD 1976
Busch, Frederick Carl 1873-1914 *DcNAA*
Busch, Fritz-Otto 1890- *Au&Wr*
Busch, Hans 1884- *WhLA*
Busch, Harald 1904- *Au&Wr*
Busch, Hermann VonDem 1468-1534 *CasWL*
Busch, Julia 1940- *ConAu 57*
Busch, Max Guston Reinhold 1865- *WhLA*
Busch, Niven 1903- *AmA&B, AmNov,*
Au&Wr, ConAu 13R, REn, REnAL,
TwCA Sup
Busch, Noel Fairchild 1906- *AmA&B,*
ConAu 49
Busch, Peter *Alli*
Busch, Philip Maxwell 1916- *IndAu 1917*
Busch, Wilhelm 1832-1908 *BiD&SB, CasWL,*
ChPo, ChPo S1, ChPo S2, ClDMEuL,
EuA, EvEuW, OxGer, Pen Eur, REn
Buschan, Georg Herman Theodor 1863- *WhLA*
Buschlen, John Preston *OxCan*
Busck, August 1870- *WhWNAA*
Busey, Bernice Bland 1918- *AmSCAP 66*
Busey, James L 1916- *ConAu 5R*
Busey, Samuel Clagett 1828?-1901 *Alli Sup,*
DcAmA, DcNAA
Busfield, Johnson Atkinson 1775-1849 *Alli,*
BiDLA
Bush, Adelaide *ChPo S1*
Bush, Belle *Alli Sup, ChPo S1*
Bush, Bertha Evangeline 1866- *ChPo*
Bush, Charles G *EarAB Sup*
Bush, Charles Peck 1813-1880 *Alli Sup,*
DcNAA
Bush, Christopher 1888?-1973 *EncM&D*
Bush, Clifford L 1915- *ConAu 33*
Bush, David Van 1882- *ChPo S1*
Bush, Douglas 1896- *AmA&B, CanWr,*
ConAu 37, DcLEnL, LongC, RAdv 1,
TwCA Sup, WrD 1976
Bush, Edward *Alli*
Bush, Edward Arthur *Alli, BiDLA*
Bush, Mrs. Edward G W *OhA&B*
Bush, Eliza C *Alli Sup*
Bush, Emma Florence *ChPo S2*
Bush, Eric Wheler 1899- *Au&Wr*
Bush, Mrs. Forbes *Alli*
Bush, Francis *Alli*
Bush, George 1796-1859 *Alli, Alli Sup,*
BiD&SB, CyAL 1, DcAmA, DcEnL,
DcNAA
Bush, George Cary *BiDSA*
Bush, George Gary 1843-1898 *Alli Sup,*
DcNAA

Bush, George P 1892- *ConAu 17R*
Bush, Gordon Kenner 1903- *WhWNAA*
Bush, Grace E 1875- *WhWNAA*
Bush, Grace E 1884- *AmSCAP 66*
Bush, Grace Elizabeth 1885- *ChPo S1*
Bush, Harold Montfort 1871-1945 *OhA&B*
Bush, Harold Richard *Alli Sup*
Bush, Henry Biddulph *Alli Sup*
Bush, Irving T 1869-1948 *DcNAA*
Bush, J *Alli*
Bush, Mrs. J Stafford *ChPo S1*
Bush, James S *Alli Sup*
Bush, Jim 1926- *ConAu 57*
Bush, John Nash Douglas 1896- *Au&Wr*
Bush, John W 1917- *ConAu 33*
Bush, Joseph *Alli, Alli Sup*
Bush, Joseph Bevans d1968 *BlkAW*
Bush, Lewis William *Au&Wr*
Bush, Louis F 1910- *AmSCAP 66*
Bush, Margaret *ChPo S2*
Bush, Martin H 1930- *ConAu 29, WrD 1976*
Bush, Norton 1834-1894 *EarAB*
Bush, Olivia Ward 1869- *BlkAW*
Bush, Paul 1490-1558 *Alli*
Bush, Raymond Gordon Wheeler 1885- *Au&Wr*
Bush, Richard James *Alli Sup, DcNAA*
Bush, Robert 1920-1972 *ConAu 33*
Bush, Robert Wheler *Alli Sup*
Bush, Stephen Hayes 1878- *WhWNAA*
Bush, Ted J 1922- *ConAu 17R*
Bush, Vannevar 1890-1974 *AmA&B,*
ConAu 53, REnAL, WhWNAA
Bush, W P D *Alli Sup*
Bush, Wendell T 1866-1941 *AmA&B*
Bush, Wesley Amos 1915- *Au&Wr*
Bush, William *Alli, Alli Sup*
Bush, William 1929- *ConAu 37*
Bush, William B *ChPo S1*
Bush, William Craddock *BiDLA*
Bush-Brown, James 1892- *ConAu 5R*
Bush-Brown, Louise 1896?-1973 *AuBYP,*
ConAu 49
Bush-Fekete, Ladislas 1898- *CnMD*
Busha, Charles Henry 1931- *ConAu 53*
Bushby, Anna S *Alli Sup*
Bushby, D Maitland 1900- *AmA&B, ArizL,*
WhWNAA
Bushby, E *Alli*
Bushby, Henry Jeffreys 1820- *Alli Sup*
Bushe, Amyas d1773 *Alli, PoIre*
Bushe, Charles Kendal 1767-1843 *PoIre*
Bushe, Gervaise Parker d1793 *Alli, PoIre*
Bushe, Henry Amyas d1837? *PoIre*
Bushe, Mary C *Alli Sup*
Bushe, Paul 1490-1558 *Alli*
Bushee, Alice Huntington 1867- *WhWNAA*
Bushee, Frederick Alexander 1872- *WhWNAA*
Bushel, Seth *Alli*
Bushel, Thomas 1594-1674 *Alli*
Bushell, Raymond 1910- *ConAu 13R,*
WrD 1976
Bushell, Thomas 1594-1674 *Alli*
Busher, Leon *Alli*
Bushkin, Joseph 1916- *AmSCAP 66*
Bushman, Richard Lyman 1931- *ConAu 21,*
WrD 1976
Bushmiller, Ernest Paul 1905- *AuNews 1,*
ConAu 29
Bushmiller, Ernie *ConAu XR*
Bushnan, John Stevenson 1808?-1884 *Alli,*
Alli Sup
Bushnell, Adelyn 1894- *AmNov*
Bushnell, Charles Ira 1826-1883 *Alli Sup,*
DcAmA, DcNAA
Bushnell, Charles J *CyAL 2*
Bushnell, Curtis Clark 1870-1936 *DcNAA*
Bushnell, David S 1927- *ConAu 41*
Bushnell, Edmond *Alli*
Bushnell, Edward 1865-1944 *OhA&B*
Bushnell, Faith *ChPo S2*
Bushnell, Frances Louisa *ChPo S2*
Bushnell, Geoffrey Hext Sutherland 1903-
Au&Wr, WrD 1976
Bushnell, George Ensign 1853-1924 *DcNAA*
Bushnell, George Herbert 1896- *WhLA*
Bushnell, Henry 1824-1905 *OhA&B*
Bushnell, Horace 1802?-1876 *Alli, Alli Sup,*
AmA&B, BbD, BiD&SB, CyAL 2,

DcAmA, DcEnL, DcLEnL, DcNAA,
OxAm
Bushnell, John Edward 1858- DcNAA
Bushnell, Joseph Platt 1842-1922? DcNAA
Bushnell, William H 1823-1909? Alli Sup,
DcAmA, HsB&A, HsB&A Sup
Bushrui, S B 1929- ConAu 17R
Busia, Kofi Abrefa 1913?- AfA 1
Busiri, Al- 1213-1296 CasWL
Busk, Mrs. Alli
Busk, George Alli
Busk, H W Alli Sup
Busk, Hans 1772-1862 ChPo
Busk, Hans 1815-1882 Alli Sup, DcEnL
Busk, M M Alli Sup
Busk, Rachel Harriette Alli Sup
Buske, Morris Roger 1912- ConAu 13R
Busken Huet, Coenraad 1826-1886 ClDMEuL,
EuA
Buskett, William C ChPo S2
Buskirk, Clarence Augustus 1842- IndAu 1816
Buskirk, Richard Hobart 1927- ConAu 1R,
IndAu 1917
Buskirk, Samuel Hamilton 1820-1879 DcNAA
Buslayev, Fedor Ivanovich 1818-1897 CasWL
Buson, Yosa 1716-1784 CasWL, ChPo,
DcOrL 1
Busoni, Ferruccio Benvenuto 1866-1924 AtlBL
Busoni, Rafaello 1900- AmA&B, AuBYP,
IlCB 1945, IlCB 1956, IlCB 1966,
JBA 1951
Buss, Arnold H 1924- ConAu 1R
Buss, Frances Mary LongC
Buss, Kate 1884- WhWNAA
Buss, Kate Meldrum ChPo
Buss, Martin J 1930- ConAu 33
Buss, Robert William 1804-1875 Alli Sup
Bussard, Paul 1904- BkC 3, CatA 1947
Busschbach, J G Van 1896- BiDPar
Bussche, Henri O A VanDen 1920- ConAu 5R
Busse, Carl 1872-1918 ClDMEuL, OxGer
Busse, Fritz 1903- WhGrA
Busse, Hans Hr 1894- WhLA
Busse, Henry 1894-1955 AmSCAP 66
Busse, Hermann Eris 1891-1947 OxGer
Busse, Karl 1872- BiD&SB
Bussell, Chase IndAu 1917
Bussell, Euphemia E G Alli Sup
Bussell, Frederick William Alli Sup
Bussell, William Alli Sup
Bussenius, Luellen Teters 1872- OhA&B
Busser, Ralph Cox 1875- WhWNAA
Busser, Samuel Edwin 1850-1926 DcNAA
Bussey, Ellen M 1926- ConAu 49
Bussey, George Moir Alli, ChPo
Bussey, Gertrude C 1888- WhWNAA
Bussey, Harry Findlater And Reid, T W
Alli Sup
Bussey, Hope 1916- TexWr
Bussey, William Henry 1879- WhWNAA
Bussi, Giovanni Andrea De 1417-1475 DcEuL
Bussiere, Paul Alli
Bussieres, Arthur De 1877-1913 CanWr
Bussieres, Simone 1918- ConAu 53
Bussing, Irwin 1898- IndAu 1917
Bussy, Dorothy Strachey d1960 ChPo S1,
LongC
Bussy, Roger DeRabutin, Comte De 1618-1693
DcEuL
Bussy D'Amboise, Louis DeClermont De OxFr
Bussy-Rabutin, R DeR, Comte De Bussy
1618-1693 EvEuW, OxFr, REn
Busta, Christine 1915- EncWL, ModGL,
OxGer, Pen Eur
Bustamante, A Jorge 1938- ConAu 33
Bustamante, Calixto DcSpL
Bustani, Butrus Al- 1819-1883 DcOrL 3
Busteed, Henry Elmsley Alli Sup
Busteed, Marilyn 1937- ConAu 61
Busteed, N William 1814-1872 HsB&A
Busteed, Thomas M Alli Sup
Buster Greene BlkAW
Buster, Maude Cummins TexWr, WhWNAA
Bustos Domecq, H ConAu XR
Busvine, James Ronald 1912- WrD 1976
Buswell, Arthur Moses 1888- WhWNAA
Buswell, Sir George Alli
Buswell, Henry Foster 1842-1919 DcNAA

Buswell, Henry Frederick Alli Sup
Buswell, J Oliver, Jr. 1895- ConAu 5R,
WrD 1976
Buswell, John Alli
Buswell, Leslie 1889- WhWNAA
Buswell, William Alli
Busybody, The NewC
Butchart, Isabel ChPo
Butcher, Dwight 1911- AmSCAP 66
Butcher, Earl Orlo 1903- IndAu 1917
Butcher, Edmund Alli, BiDLA
Butcher, Fanny 1888- AmA&B, WhWNAA
Butcher, George Alli, BiDLA
Butcher, Grace 1934- ConAu 25, DrAP 1975
Butcher, Harold John 1920- Au&Wr,
ConAu 23
Butcher, Harry C 1901- REnAL
Butcher, Henry William Alli Sup
Butcher, James Neal 1933- ConAu 33
Butcher, James W, Jr. BlkAW
Butcher, James Williams ChPo S1
Butcher, John Alli
Butcher, John Henry Alli Sup
Butcher, Judith 1927- ConAu 57
Butcher, M P Alli Sup
Butcher, Margaret Just 1913- LivBA
Butcher, Philip 1918- BlkAW, ConAu 1R
Butcher, Phillip 1918- LivBA
Butcher, Richard Alli
Butcher, Richard George H Alli Sup
Butcher, Russell Devereux 1938- ConAu 61
Butcher, Samuel 1811-1876 Alli Sup
Butcher, Samuel Henry 1850-1910 Alli Sup,
BiDPar, BrAu 19, DcEnA, DcEnA Ap,
LongC, NewC
Butcher, Thomas Kennedy 1914- Au&Wr,
ConAu P-1, WrD 1976
Butcher, William BiDLA
Butchvarov, Panayot K 1933- ConAu 33
Butck, Zulie 1947- ConAu XR
Bute, Marquis Of Alli Sup, NewC
Bute, John Stuart 1713-1792 Alli
Butel-Dumont, George Marie BbtC
Butera, Mary C 1925- ConAu 21
Butin, Romain Francois 1871-1937 DcNAA
Butina, F Alli Sup
Butkov, Yakov Petrovich 1815-1856 CasWL,
DcRusL
Butland, Gilbert James 1910- ConAu 21,
WrD 1976
Butler, Mrs. DcEnL
Butler, Reverend PoIre
Butler, A PoIre
Butler, A W ChPo S1
Butler, Alban 1710?-1773 Alli, DcEnL, NewC,
OxEng
Butler, Albert 1923- ConAu 13R
Butler, Alexander Hume Alli Sup
Butler, Alford Augustus 1845-1920 DcNAA
Butler, Alfred Johnson 1850- ChPo
Butler, Alfred Joshua Alli Sup
Butler, Amos William 1860-1937 DcAmA,
IndAu 1816
Butler, Anna Alli Sup
Butler, Anna Land 1901- BlkAW
Butler, Annie L 1920- ConAu 33
Butler, Annie Robina Alli Sup
Butler, Arthur D 1923- ConAu 1R
Butler, Arthur Gardiner Alli Sup
Butler, Arthur Gray Alli Sup, ChPo S1
Butler, Arthur John 1844-1910 Alli Sup,
BrAu 19, NewC
Butler, Arthur Richard 1925- Au&Wr
Butler, Audrey ChPo S2
Butler, B C Alli Sup
Butler, B Christopher 1902- ConAu 1R
Butler, Benjamin Franklin 1795-1858 DcNAA
Butler, Benjamin Franklin 1818-1893 DcAmA,
DcNAA
Butler, Bert S 1879- WhWNAA
Butler, Beverly Kathleen 1932- AuBYP,
ChPo S2, ConAu 1R, SmATA 7
Butler, Bill 1934- ConAu 57, Pen Am,
WrD 1976
Butler, Bion H 1857-1935 DcNAA
Butler, C Alli, BiDLA
Butler, Mrs. C ChPo S1
Butler, Caleb 1776-1854 DcNAA

Butler, Caroline H Alli Sup, ChPo
Butler, Charles Alli, BiDLA, BiDLA Sup
Butler, Charles 1559-1647 Alli, DcEnL
Butler, Charles 1750-1832 Alli, BiDLA,
BiDLA Sup, DcEnL
Butler, Charles Edward 1909- AmA&B,
CatA 1952
Butler, Charles Ewart Alli Sup
Butler, Charles George Alli Sup
Butler, Charles Henry 1859-1940 DcAmA,
DcNAA
Butler, Charles Henry 1894- ConAu 23
Butler, Charles R 1879- WhWNAA
Butler, Charles William Alli Sup
Butler, Clement Moore 1810-1890 Alli,
Alli Sup, DcAmA, DcNAA
Butler, Colin G 1913- WrD 1976
Butler, Cora C 1881- WhWNAA
Butler, Cuthbert 1858-1934 CatA 1947
Butler, D Alli
Butler, D P Alli Sup
Butler, David Edgeworth 1924- Au&Wr,
ConAu 5R
Butler, David Francis 1928- ConAu 41
Butler, E A Alli Sup
Butler, Edward Dundas Alli Sup
Butler, Edward Harry 1913- Au&Wr,
ConAu 13R
Butler, Eliza Marian 1885- TwCA Sup
Butler, Ellen Hamlin 1860- ChPo, ChPo S1
Butler, Ellis Parker 1869-1937 AmA&B, ChPo,
DcNAA, EncM&D, JBA 1934, OxAm,
REnAL, TwCA, WhWNAA
Butler, Erica Bracher 1905- ConAu 17
Butler, Ernest Alton 1926- ConAu 33
Butler, F E 1853- TexWr
Butler, F K ChPo S2
Butler, Francelia McWilliams 1913- ChPo,
ConAu 19
Butler, Frances Anne Alli, BrAu 19, ChPo,
REnAL
Butler, Francis 1810-1874 Alli Sup, DcNAA
Butler, Francis Gould Alli Sup
Butler, Frederick 1766-1843 CyAL 2, DcAmA,
DcNAA
Butler, Frederick Guy 1918- CasWL, Pen Eng
Butler, G Montague 1881- WhWNAA
Butler, G Paul 1900- ConAu 17
Butler, George Alli
Butler, George 1819- Alli Sup
Butler, George Cooper Alli Sup
Butler, George D 1893- ConAu 17R,
WrD 1976
Butler, George Frank 1857-1931 DcNAA
Butler, George Grey 1852- WhLA
Butler, George O ChPo
Butler, George Slade 1821-1882 Alli Sup
Butler, George Vincent 1904- WhWNAA
Butler, George William Alli Sup
Butler, Glen Anthony BlkAW
Butler, Glentworth Reeve 1855-1926 DcNAA
Butler, Guy 1918- Au&Wr, ConP 1970,
ConP 1975, TwCW, WrD 1976
Butler, Gwendoline Williams 1922- Au&Wr,
ConAu 9R, WrD 1976
Butler, Mrs. H Alli, BiDLA
Butler, Hal 1913- AuBYP, ConAu 57
Butler, Harriet DeWitt ChPo
Butler, Lady Harriot Alli
Butler, Henry Alli, BiDLA
Butler, Henry A 1872-1934 OhA&B
Butler, Henry D Alli Sup
Butler, Henry Montagu 1833- Alli Sup
Butler, Hiram Erastus 1841-1916 DcNAA
Butler, Hood C BlkAW
Butler, Horacio 1897- IlCB 1945
Butler, Howard Crosby 1872-1922 AmA&B,
AmLY, DcAmA, DcNAA
Butler, Howard Russell 1856-1934 DcNAA
Butler, Iris Mary 1905- Au&Wr, ConAu 21,
WrD 1976
Butler, Ivan 1909- Au&Wr
Butler, J Alli, Alli Sup, BiDLA
Butler, J Donald 1908- ConAu 1R
Butler, J M ChPo S1
Butler, Jack 1924- AmSCAP 66
Butler, James Alli, BiDLA
Butler, James 1755?-1842 OxAm

Byrne, James Patrick *Alli Sup*
Byrne, Jane *ChPo*
Byrne, Janet *Alli Sup*
Byrne, John *PoIre*
Byrne, John Francis *PoIre*
Byrne, John Keyes 1926- *WrD 1976*
Byrne, John Rice *Alli Sup*
Byrne, Johnny 1937- *Au&Wr*
Byrne, Joseph Grandson 1870-1945 *DcNAA,*
  WhWNAA
Byrne, Julia Clara 1819-1894 *Alli Sup,*
  BiD&SB
Byrne, M *Alli*
Byrne, Mary *PoIre*
Byrne, May *Alli Sup*
Byrne, Muriel St. Clare 1895- *Au&Wr,*
  ConAu P-1, WhLA, WhWNAA
Byrne, Nora C *ChPo S1*
Byrne, Oliver *Alli Sup*
Byrne, P E *PoIre*
Byrne, Patrick *PoIre*
Byrne, Richard Hill 1915- *ConAu 21*
Byrne, Robert 1930- *WrD 1976*
Byrne, Stephen *Alli Sup*
Byrne, Thomas Edgar Dickson *Alli Sup*
Byrne, Thomas Sebastian 1842?-1924 *Alli Sup,*
  BiDSA, OhA&B
Byrne, William *Alli Sup, PoIre*
Byrne, William 1836- *DcAmA*
Byrne, William A *PoIre*
Byrnes, Charles Metcalfe 1881- *WhWNAA*
Byrnes, Edward T 1929- *ConAu 53*
Byrnes, Esther F 1866- *WhWNAA*
Byrnes, Eugene F 1890?-1974 *ConAu 49*
Byrnes, James Francis 1879- *AmA&B*
Byrnes, Jane Luelling 1892- *WhWNAA*
Byrnes, M J *PoIre*
Byrnes, Michael *PoIre*
Byrnes, Robert F 1917- *ConAu 25*
Byrnes, Thomas *Alli Sup*
Byrnes, Thomas Edmund 1911- *ConAu 13R*
Byrnes, Thomas F 1842-1910 *DcNAA*
Byrom, Helen A *ChPo*
Byrom, James 1911- *Au&Wr, ConAu XR,*
  WrD 1976
Byrom, John *Alli*
Byrom, John 1692?-1763 *Alli, BrAu, ChPo,*
  Chmbr 2, DcEnA, DcEnL, DcLEnL,
  EvLB, NewC, OxEng, Pen Eng, PoCh
Byrom, Michael 1925- *ConAu 5R*
Byrom, William *Alli Sup*
Byron, Miss *Alli, BiDLA*
Byron, Mrs. *Alli, BiDLA*
Byron, Al 1932- *AmSCAP 66*
Byron, Asaman B W *BlkAW*
Byron, Augusta Ada *NewC*
Byron, Lord George Anson *Alli*
Byron, Lord George Gordon Noel 1788-1824 *Alli,*
  AtlBL, BbD, BiD&SB, BiDLA,
  BiDLA Sup, BrAu 19, CasWL, ChPo,
  ChPo S1, ChPo S2, Chmbr 3, CnE&AP,
  CnThe, CyWA, DcEnA, DcEnL, DcEuL,
  DcLEnL, EvLB, HsB&A, McGWD,
  NewC, OxEng, Pen Eng, RAdv 1, RCom,
  REn, REnWD, WebEAL
Byron, Gilbert 1903- *ConAu 17R*
Byron, Henry James 1834-1884 *Alli Sup, BbD,*
  BiD&SB, BrAu 19, Chmbr 3, DcEnL,
  EvLB
Byron, John *ConAu XR*
Byron, John 1723-1786 *Alli, NewC, OxEng*
Byron, Lionel Dawson *Alli Sup*
Byron, M *Alli Sup*
Byron, Mary *ChPo S2*
Byron, May Charissa d1936 *ChPo S1,*
  ChPo S2
Byron, Richard 1908- *AmSCAP 66*
Byron, Robert 1905-1941 *DcLEnL, EvLB,*
  LongC
Byron, Ronald 1918- *Au&Wr*
Byron, Stuart *DrAP 1975*
Byros, D B *Alli Sup*
Byrrne, E Fairfax *Alli Sup, PoIre*
Byrt, Edwin Andrew 1932- *Au&Wr,*
  WrD 1976
Byrum, Enoch Edwin 1861- *DcAmA,*
  IndAu 1816, WhWNAA
Byrum, Isabel Coston 1870-1938 *IndAu 1816,*

WhWNAA
Byrum, Russell R 1888- *WhWNAA*
Bysset, Abakuk *Chmbr 1*
Bysshe, Edward *Alli*
Bysshe, Edward 1615-1679 *Alli*
Bystander, A *OxCan*
Bythewood, W M *Alli*
Bythner, Victorinus *Alli*
Bywater, Hector Charles 1884-1940 *NewC*
Bywater, Ingram 1840-1914 *Alli Sup, BrAu 19,*
  LongC, NewC, OxEng
Bywater, John *Alli, BiDLA*
Bywater, John C *Alli Sup*
Bywater, William G, Jr. 1940- *ConAu 61*
Bywater, Witham Matthew *Alli Sup*
Bywaters, Jerry 1906- *TexWr*
Bzowiecki, Alfred N W 1899- *Au&Wr*

C

C, A *PoIre*
C, A S M *ChPo*
C, C *ChPo S1*
C, H M *PoIre*
C, J K *PoIre*
C, M A *ChPo S2*
C, M C *ChPo S1*
C, M S *ChPo*
C, O'B *PoIre*
C, S C *ChPo S1*
C A B *WhLA*
C K *WhWNAA*
C V T *WhWNAA*
C W B *BkIE*
Cababe, Michael 1855- *Alli Sup*
Caballero, Ann Mallory 1928- *ConAu 17R*
Caballero, Fernan 1796-1877 *BbD, BiD&SB, CasWL, EuA, EvEuW, Pen Eur, REn*
Caballero Calderon, Eduardo 1910- *DcCLA, Pen Am*
Caballero Del Milagro *DcSpL*
Caballero Zifar, Libro Del *CasWL*
Cabanel, Daniel *Alli, BiDLA*
Cabanillas, Ramon *Pen Eur*
Cabanis, Georges 1757-1808 *OxFr*
Cabanis, Jean Louis 1816- *BiD&SB*
Cabanis, Pierre Jean Georges 1757-1808 *BbD, BiD&SB*
Cabanis, Richard Schmidt *ChPo*
Cabaniss, Alice *DrAP 1975*
Cabaniss, H H And Harrison, W H *Alli Sup*
Cabaniss, J Allen 1911- *ConAu 1R*
Cabanyes, Manuel De 1808-1833 *DcEuL*
Cabaret, Jean *OxFr*
Cabarrus, Theresa *OxFr*
Cabassa, Victoria 1912- *ConAu 49*
Cabbell, Paul 1942- *ConAu 53*
Cabeen, David Clark 1886- *ConAu P-1*
Cabell, Branch *ConAmA*
Cabell, Edward Carrington 1816- *BiDSA*
Cabell, Mrs. I C *BiDSA*
Cabell, Isa Carrington *BiD&SB*
Cabell, James Alston *BiDSA*
Cabell, James Branch 1879-1958 *AmA&B, AmLY, AmNov, BiDSA, CasWL, Chmbr 3, CnDAL, CnMWL, ConAmA, ConAmL, CyWA, DcAmA, DcBiA, DcLEnL, EncWL, EvLB, LongC, ModAL, OxAm, OxEng, Pen Am, RAdv 1, REn, REnAL, TwCA, TwCA Sup, TwCW, WebEAL, WhWNAA*
Cabell, James Laurence 1813-1889 *Alli Sup, BiDSA*
Cabell, James Lawrence 1813-1889 *DcAmA, DcNAA*
Cabell, Julia Mayo 1800?-1850? *Alli Sup, BiDSA, DcAmA*
Cabell, Margaret Couch Anthony 1814-1883 *BiDSA*
Cabell, Nathaniel Francis 1807-1891 *AmA&B,*

DcNAA
Cabet, Etienne 1785?-1856 *OxAm, OxFr*
Cabeza DeVaca, Alvar Nunez 1490?-1557? *BiDSA, EuA, OxAm, REn*
Cabibi, John F J 1912- *ConAu 53*
Cable, Boyd 1878- *DcLEnL, WhLA*
Cable, Daniel *Alli*
Cable, George Washington 1844-1925 *Alli Sup, AmA, AmA&B, AmLY, AtlBL, BbD, BiD&SB, BiDSA, CasWL, ChPo, ChPo S1, Chmbr 3, CnDAL, CriT 3, CyWA, DcAmA, DcBiA, DcEnA Ap, DcLEnL, DcNAA, EvLB, OxAm, OxEng, Pen Am, RAdv 1, REn, REnAL, WebEAL, WhWNAA*
Cable, John Levi 1884- *OhA&B*
Cable, Lucy Leffingwell 1875- *ChPo*
Cable, Mary 1920- *ConAu 25, DrAF 1976, SmATA 9*
Cabot, A T *Alli Sup*
Cabot, Blake 1905?-1974 *ConAu 53*
Cabot, Carolyn Sturgis 1846-1917 *DcNAA*
Cabot, Ella Lyman 1866-1934 *DcNAA, WhWNAA*
Cabot, Hugh 1872-1945 *DcNAA*
Cabot, James Elliot 1821-1903 *Alli, DcAmA, DcNAA, OxCan*
Cabot, John 1450-1498 *NewC, OxCan, REn, REnAL*
Cabot, John M 1901- *AmA&B*
Cabot, Louis *Alli Sup*
Cabot, Lucia *ChPo*
Cabot, Philip 1872-1941 *DcNAA*
Cabot, Richard Clarke 1868-1939 *AmA&B, DcNAA*
Cabot, Robert Moors 1924- *ConAu 29, WrD 1976*
Cabot, Sebastian 1476?-1557 *Alli, NewC, OxCan, REn*
Cabot, William Brooks 1858-1949 *DcNAA, OxCan*
Cabral, Manuel Del 1907- *DcCLA*
Cabral, Olga 1909- *ConAu 25, DrAP 1975*
Cabral DeMelo Neto, Joao 1920- *CasWL, Pen Am*
Cabrera, Alonso De 1546?-1598? *CasWL*
Cabrera, C A De *DcEuL*
Cabrera, Infante Guillermo 1929- *CasWL*
Cabrera, Lydia 1900- *DcCLA*
Cabrera, Paul F *Alli*
Cabrera, Raimundo 1852- *AmLY*
Cabrera, Sarandy 1923- *DcCLA*
Cabrera DeCordoba, Luis 1559-1623 *CasWL*
Cabrera Infante, Guillermo 1929- *ConLC 5, DcCLA, EncWL Sup, Pen Am*
Cabrol, Fernand 1855-1937 *CatA 1947*
Cacavas, John 1930- *AmSCAP 66*
Caccia, Angela 1935- *Au&Wr*
Caccia-Dominioni, Paolo 1896- *ConAu 21*
Caccianiga, Antonio 1823-1903 *BiD&SB*
Cacciatore, Vera 1911- *Au&Wr, ConAu 5R,*

WrD 1976
Caccini, Giulio 1546-1618 *REn*
Cacella, Joseph 1882- *CatA 1952*
Cachapero, Emilya *DrAP 1975*
Cachemaille, Ernest Peter *Alli Sup*
Cachia, Pierre Jacques Elie 1921- *ConAu 25, WrD 1976*
Cackler, Christian 1791-1878 *OhA&B*
Cadahalso, Don Jose De 1741-1782 *BbD, BiD&SB*
Cadalso, Jose De 1741-1782 *BiD&SB, DcSpL, EvEuW, Pen Eur*
Cadalso, Josef 1741-1782 *DcEuL*
Cadalso Y Vazquez, Jose De 1741-1782 *CasWL, EuA, REn*
Cadbury, Elizabeth Mary 1858- *WhLA*
Cadbury, Henry Joel 1883-1974 *AmA&B, ConAu 53, ConAu P-1, WhWNAA*
Cadbury, James *Alli Sup*
Caddell, Cecilia Mary 1814-1877 *Alli Sup, PoIre*
Caddell, Henry *Alli*
Caddick, Richard *Alli, BiDLA*
Caddigan, Jack J 1879-1952 *AmSCAP 66*
Caddy, Alice *IlCB 1956*
Caddy, Elizabeth Alice *ChPo*
Caddy, Florence 1837- *Alli Sup*
Caddy, John *DrAP 1975*
Caddy, N Ward *Alli*
Caddy, William *Alli*
Cade, Anthony *Alli*
Cade, Jack d1450 *REn*
Cade, John *Alli*
Cade, John d1450 *NewC*
Cade, John Mills *Alli*
Cade, Peter *ConNov 1976*
Cade, Robin *WrD 1976*
Cade, Toni *BlkAW*
Cade, William *Alli*
Cadell, Mrs. Alexander *Alli Sup*
Cadell, Elizabeth 1903- *Au&Wr, ConAu 57, WrD 1976*
Cadell, Henry Moubray 1860- *WhLA*
Cadell, Mrs. Jessie 1844-1884 *Alli Sup*
Cadell, W A *Alli*
Cademan, Thomas *Alli*
Cadenhead, Ivie E, Jr. 1923- *ConAu 41*
Cadenhead, William 1819-1904 *Alli Sup, ChPo S2*
Cadenus *DcEnL*
Caderas, Gian F 1830-1891 *BiD&SB, CasWL*
Cadett, Thomas *Alli Sup*
Cadge *Alli*
Cadieux, Charles L 1919- *ConAu 57*
Cadieux, Lorenzo 1903- *ConAu 49*
Cadieux, Louis Marie 1783-1838 *BbtC, DcNAA*
Cadignan, Diane De *REn*
Cadilla DeMartinez, Maria 1886-1951 *PueRA*
Cadilla DeRuibal, Carmen Alicia 1908- *PueRA*
Cadillac, Antoine DeLaMothe 1658-1730 *OxCan,*

R*EnAL*

Cadiot, Clara *Alli Sup*
Cadle, Dean 1920- *ConAu 25*
Cadle, Emmett Howard 1884-1942 *IndAu 1917*
Cadman, Charles Wakefield 1881-1946 *AmSCAP 66, OxAm, REnAL*
Cadman, H W *Alli Sup*
Cadman, James Piper 1842- *Alli Sup, WhWNAA*
Cadman, Paul Fletcher 1889-1946 *DcNAA*
Cadman, Samuel Parkes 1864-1936 *AmA&B, DcNAA, WhWNAA*
Cadmus 1820-1898 *AmA, OhA&B*
Cadogan, Lady Adelaide *Alli Sup*
Cadogan, George *Alli*
Cadogan, William d1797 *Alli*
Cadogan, William Bromley 1751-1797 *Alli*
Cadol, Victor Edouard 1831-1898 *BbD, BiD&SB*
Cadoret, Remi Jere 1928- *BiDPar*
Cadou, Rene Guy 1920-1951 *CasWL, REn, WorAu*
Cadoudal, Georges 1771-1804 *OxFr*
Cadoudal, Louis Georges De 1823- *BiD&SB*
Cadoudal, Louis Georges De 1831-1898 *BbD*
Cadoux, Cecil John 1883- *WhLA*
Cadwalader d664? *NewC*
Cadwalader, John 1742-1786 *DcNAA*
Cadwalader, John L *Alli Sup*
Cadwalader, Richard McCall 1839- *Alli Sup*
Cadwalader, Thomas 1708-1799 *DcNAA*
Cadwallader, Clyde T 1898- *ConAu 5R*
Cadwallader, John d1786 *Alli*
Cadwallader, Richard McCall 1839- *DcAmA*
Cadwallader, Sharon 1936- *ConAu 49, SmATA 7*
Cadwallader, Thomas d1779 *Alli*
Cadwell, Clara Gertrude *OhA&B*
Cady, Daniel Leavens 1861-1934 *AmA&B, ChPo, ChPo S1, ChPo S2, DcNAA*
Cady, Edwin Harrison 1917- *AmA&B, ConAu 1R*
Cady, Edwin Welling 1873-1939 *DcNAA*
Cady, Gilbert H 1882- *WhWNAA*
Cady, H Emilie 1848-1941 *DcNAA*
Cady, Mrs. H N *Alli Sup*
Cady, H P 1874- *WhWNAA*
Cady, Harrison 1879- *WhWNAA*
Cady, Howard Stevenson 1914- *AmA&B*
Cady, Jack *DrAF 1976*
Cady, John Frank 1901- *AmA&B, ConAu 1R, IndAu 1917, WrD 1976*
Cady, John Henry 1846-1927 *ArizL, OhA&B*
Cady, Leo Isaac 1931- *Au&Wr*
Cady, Steve 1927- *ConAu 45*
Cady, Walter G 1874- *WhWNAA*
Cady, Walter Harrison 1877- *ChPo, ChPo S1, IlCB 1945*
Cady, Wilhelmina W *Alli Sup*
Caecilius 219?BC-168BC *CasWL, CnThe, Pen Cl, REnWD*
Caedmon 650?-680? *Alli, BbD, BiB S, BiD&SB, BrAu, CasWL, Chmbr 1, CriT 1, DcEnL, EvLB, MouLC 1, NewC, OxEng, Pen Eng, REn, WebEAL*
Caedmon, Father *ConAu XR*
Caefer, Raymond J 1926- *ConAu 17R*
Caelius Rufus, Marcus 083BC-048BC *Pen Cl*
Caemmerer, Richard R 1904- *ConAu 1R*
Caen, Herb 1916- *AuNews 1, ConAu 1R*
Caesar *NewC, OxEng*
Caesar, Caius Julius 100BC-044BC *BbD, BiD&SB*
Caesar, Dick 1905- *Au&Wr*
Caesar, Gaius Julius 100BC-044BC *CasWL, CyWA, Pen Cl, RCom*
Caesar, Gene 1927- *ConAu 1R*
Caesar, Irving 1895- *AmSCAP 66, Au&Wr, ChPo, REnAL*
Caesar, J James *Alli*
Caesar, John *Alli*
Caesar, Julius 100BC-044BC *REn*
Caesar, Sir Julius 1557-1636 *Alli*
Caesar, Julius P *Alli Sup*
Caesar, Philip *Alli*
Caesar, Sid 1922- *AmSCAP 66*
Caesarion 047BC-030BC *NewC*

Caesarius Of Heisterbach 1180?-1240? *CasWL, Pen Eur*
Caetani, Princess Marguerite 1880-1963 *LongC*
Cafferty, Bernard 1934- *ConAu 41*
Cafferty, James H 1819-1869 *EarAB*
Caffey, David L 1947- *ConAu 45*
Caffgn, Matthew *Alli*
Caffieri, Hector 1847-1932 *ChPo*
Caffin, Charles Henry 1854-1918 *AmA&B, AmLY, DcAmA, DcNAA*
Caffin, George Crawford *Alli Sup*
Caffrey, John G 1922- *ConAu 17R*
Caffrey, Kate *ConAu 49, WrD 1976*
Caffrey, Nancy *AuBYP*
Caffrey, William Robert *PoIre*
Caffyn, Kathleen Mannington *Chmbr 3*
Caflisch, Artur 1893-1971 *CasWL*
Caflisch, Max 1916- *WhGrA*
Cagan, Phillip D 1927- *ConAu 17R, WrD 1976*
Cagan, Sermet 1929- *CnThe, REnWD*
Cage, John 1912- *AmA&B, AmSCAP 66, ConAu 13R, ConDr, Pen Am, WrD 1976*
Cage, Thornton *Alli*
Cagiati, Mrs. Gaetano *AmA&B, DcNAA*
Cagliostro, Count Alessandro Di 1743-1795 *NewC, OxGer, REn*
Cagliostro, Giuseppe Balsamo 1743-1795 *OxFr*
Cagney, Charles Francis *Alli Sup*
Cagney, Peter 1918- *Au&Wr, ConAu XR*
Cagua, John *Alli*
Cahalane, Victor H 1901- *ConAu 23*
Cahan, Abraham 1860-1951 *AmA&B, BbD, BiD&SB, CasWL, ConAmL, DcAmA, EncWL Sup, ModAL, OxAm, Pen Am, REn, REnAL, TwCA, TwCA Sup, WhWNAA*
Cahan, Yaakov 1881-1960 *CasWL*
Cahen, Alfred B 1932- *ConAu 17R*
Cahen, Isidore 1826- *BiD&SB*
Cahen, Samuel 1796-1862 *BiD&SB*
Cahid Sidki Taranci 1910-1956 *CasWL*
Cahill *MnBBF*
Cahill, Alice M *ChPo*
Cahill, Audrey Fawcett 1929- *ConAu 23, WrD 1976*
Cahill, Daniel William 1796-1864 *Alli Sup*
Cahill, Holger 1893-1960 *AmA&B, AmNov*
Cahill, James C 1885- *WhWNAA*
Cahill, James F 1926- *ConAu 1R*
Cahill, James Semple 1881- *WhWNAA*
Cahill, Jane 1901- *ConAu 23*
Cahill, Mary F *WhWNAA*
Cahill, Patrick *ChPo S1*
Cahill, Robert S 1933- *ConAu 13R*
Cahill, Susan Neunzig 1940- *ConAu 37*
Cahill, Thomas 1940- *ConAu 49*
Cahill, Tom *ConAu 49*
Cahill, William *PoIre*
Cahn, Edgar S 1935- *ConAu 29*
Cahn, Edmond 1906-1964 *AmA&B*
Cahn, Ernst 1875- *WhLA*
Cahn, Harold A 1922- *BiDPar*
Cahn, Sammy 1913- *AmSCAP 66*
Cahn, Steven M 1942- *ConAu 21*
Cahn, William 1912- *ConAu 23*
Cahn, Zvi 1896- *ConAu 23*
Cahnman, Werner J 1902- *ConAu 49*
Cahoon, Grace W *WhWNAA*
Cahoon, Herbert 1918- *ChPo, ChPo S1*
Caiado, Henrique d1508? *CasWL*
Caiani, Joe 1929- *AmSCAP 66*
Caiden, Gerald E 1936- *Au&Wr, ConAu 29*
Caidin, Martin 1927- *AmA&B, AuNews 2, ConAu 1R*
Caie, J M *ChPo*
Caiger-Smith, Alan 1930- *ConAu 13R*
Caillard, Emma Marie *Alli Sup*
Caillavet, Gaston Arman De 1869-1915 *ClDMEuL, EvEuW, McGWD, OxFr*
Caille, Augustus 1854- *IndAu 1917, WhWNAA*
Caille, Rene 1799-1838 *OxFr*
Cailliet, Emile 1894- *AmA&B*
Cailliet, Lucien 1897- *AmSCAP 66*
Caillieu, Colijn d1484? *CasWL*
Caillois, Roger 1913- *ConAu 25, EncWL*
Cain, Brother *BlkAW*

Cain, Arthur H 1913- *ConAu 1R, SmATA 3*
Cain, Christopher *ConAu XR, SmATA 8*
Cain, George *BlkAW, LivBA*
Cain, Glen G 1933- *ConAu 21*
Cain, James Mallahan 1892- *AmA&B, AmNov, AuNews 1, CnDAL, CnMWL, ConAu 17R, ConLC 3, ConNov 1972, ConNov 1976, DcLEnL, EncM&D, LongC, ModAL, OxAm, Pen Am, REn, REnAL, TwCA, TwCA Sup, TwCW, WebEAL, WhWNAA, WrD 1976*
Cain, John 1805-1867 *IndAu 1816*
Cain, Johnnie Mae *BlkAW*
Cain, Kate Rohrer *ChPo*
Cain, Mildred Palmer 1902- *WhWNAA*
Cain, Neville d1935 *ChPo*
Cain, Noble 1896- *AmSCAP 66*
Cain, S C *ChPo S1*
Cain, Stanley Adair 1902- *IndAu 1917*
Cain, Timothy John 1907- *Au&Wr*
Cain, William 1847-1930 *Alli Sup, BiDSA, DcAmA, DcNAA, WhWNAA*
Caine, Sir Hall 1853-1931 *Chmbr 3, LongC, ModBL, NewC, REn, TwCA, TwCA Sup, TwCW*
Caine, Mark *ConAu XR*
Caine, Stanley P 1940- *ConAu 41*
Caine, Sydney 1902- *ConAu 25*
Caine, Sir Thomas Henry Hall 1853-1931 *Alli Sup, BbD, BiD&SB, DcBiA, DcEnA, DcEnA Ap, DcLEnL, EvLB, OxEng*
Caine, William *Alli Sup*
Caine, William Ralph Hall 1865-1939 *ChPo, ChPo S1, ChPo S2, NewC, WhLA*
Caine, William Sproston 1842- *Alli Sup*
Caines, Clement *Alli, BiDLA*
Caines, George 1771-1825 *Alli, DcAmA, DcNAA*
Caines, Jeannette *BlkAW*
Caiola, Al 1920- *AmSCAP 66*
Caird, Alexander MacNeel d1880 *Alli Sup*
Caird, Alice Mona 1858-1932 *NewC*
Caird, Edward 1835-1908 *Alli Sup, BrAu 19, CasWL, Chmbr 3, DcEuL, EvLB, NewC, OxEng*
Caird, George Bradford 1917- *Au&Wr, ConAu 61, WrD 1976*
Caird, Sir James 1816- *Alli, Alli Sup, BbtC*
Caird, Janet Hinshaw 1913- *Au&Wr, ConAu 49, WrD 1976*
Caird, John 1820-1898 *Alli, Alli Sup, BiDLA, BrAu 19, Chmbr 3, DcEnL, DcEuL, EvLB, NewC, OxEng*
Caird, Mona Hector 1858-1932 *BbD, BrAu 19, Chmbr 3*
Cairncross, Alec *ConAu XR*
Cairncross, Sir Alexander Kirkland 1911- *Au&Wr, ConAu 61, WrD 1976*
Cairncross, Andrew *Alli*
Cairncross, David *Alli Sup*
Cairncross, Frances 1944- *ConAu 57*
Cairncross, Thomas Scott *ChPo*
Cairnes, John Elliott 1823-1875 *Alli Sup, BrAu 19, NewC*
Cairnes, W W *Alli Sup*
Cairney, John 1930- *Au&Wr*
Cairns, Adam *Alli Sup*
Cairns, Christiana Victoria *Alli Sup, PoIre*
Cairns, David 1904- *Au&Wr, ConAu 61, WrD 1976*
Cairns, Dorian 1901-1972 *ConAu 37*
Cairns, Earle E 1910- *ConAu 1R, WrD 1976*
Cairns, Elizabeth *Alli*
Cairns, F A *Alli Sup*
Cairns, Grace Edith 1907- *ConAu 1R*
Cairns, Huntington 1904- *AmA&B, Au&Wr, ConAu 53*
Cairns, James Ford 1914- *Au&Wr, WrD 1976*
Cairns, John 1818- *Alli, Alli Sup*
Cairns, John C 1924- *ConAu 13R*
Cairns, Kate *DcNAA*
Cairns, Thomas W 1931- *ConAu 23*
Cairns, Trevor 1922- *ConAu 33, WrD 1976*
Cairns, William *Alli, Alli Sup, ChPo S1*
Cairns, William B 1867-1932 *AmA&B, DcNAA, WhWNAA*
Cairns, William DeWeese 1871- *WhWNAA*
Cairo, Jon *ConAu XR*

Caissa *ConAu XR*
Caithness, Countess Of *Alli Sup*
Caithness, Earl Of *Alli Sup*
Caithness, James Balharrie *ChPo*
Caius *NewC*
Caius, John *Alli*
Caius, John 1510-1573 *Alli*
Caius, Thomas d1572 *Alli*
Cajak, Jan 1863-1944 *CasWL*
Cajati, Mario 1902- *AmSCAP 66*
Cajori, Florian 1859-1930 *DcNAA,*
 WhWNAA
Cakrabarti, Amiya 1901- *DcOrL 2*
Caks, Aleksandrs *Pen Eur*
Calabrella, Baroness De *Alli*
Calabrese, Chaim Vital *CasWL*
Calabresi, Aldo 1930- *WhGrA*
Calabresi, Guido 1932- *ConAu 41*
Calabro, Louis 1926- *AmSCAP 66*
Calaferte, Louis 1928- *ConAu 45*
Calamari, John D 1921- *ConAu 37*
Calaminus, Georg 1545-1595 *OxGer*
Calamy, Benjamin d1686 *Alli, DcEnL*
Calamy, Edmund 1600?-1666 *Alli, Chmbr 1,*
 DcEnL, EvLB
Calamy, Edmund 1671-1732 *Alli*
Calamy, James d1714 *Alli*
Calapai, Letterio 1903- *IICB 1956*
Calas, Jean 1698-1762 *OxFr*
Calavera, Ferran Sanchez De *DcSpL*
Calbris, B *Alli*
Calcagnini, Celio 1479-1541 *CasWL*
Calcar, Elisa Carolina Ferdinanda Van
 1822-1904 *CasWL*
Calcaskie, John *Alli*
Calcott, Berkeley *PoIre*
Calcott, J *ChPo*
Calcott, John Wall *Alli, BiDLA*
Calcott, M E Berkeley *Alli Sup*
Calcott, Wellins *Alli*
Calcraft, Henry George 1836- *Alli Sup*
Calcraft, John William 1793?-1870 *NewC,*
 PoIre
Caldas *AfA 1*
Caldas Pereira DeSouza, Antonio 1762-1814
 BiD&SB
Caldbeck, Mary Costello *Alli Sup*
Caldcleugh, Alexander *Alli*
Caldecott, C *ChPo*
Caldecott, Marian *Alli Sup*
Caldecott, R M *Alli*
Caldecott, Randolph 1846-1886 *AnCL, CarSB,*
 ChPo, ChPo S1, ChPo S2, IlBYP,
 JBA 1934, JBA 1951, St&VC, WhCL
Caldecott, Thomas *Alli, BiDLA*
Caldecott, W S *Alli Sup*
Caldeleugh, W G *Alli Sup*
Calder, Alexander *Alli Sup*
Calder, Alexander 1898- *ChPo, REn*
Calder, Alma *Alli Sup, BiDSA*
Calder, Angus 1942- *Au&Wr, ConAu 29,*
 WrD 1976
Calder, Charles *Alli Sup*
Calder, Frederick *Alli, Alli Sup*
Calder, J E *Alli Sup*
Calder, James *Alli*
Calder, James Tait 1794?-1864 *Alli Sup*
Calder, Jenni 1941- *ConAu 45*
Calder, John 1733-1815 *Alli, BiDLA,*
 BiDLA Sup
Calder, Matthew Lewis 1919- *WrD 1976*
Calder, Nigel David Ritchie 1931- *Au&Wr,*
 ConAu 21, WrD 1976
Calder, Ritchie 1906- *AmA&B, Au&Wr,*
 ConAu 1R, LongC, OxCan, WorAu
Calder, Robert 1658- *Alli*
Calder, Robert Hogg 1844- *ChPo, ChPo S1*
Calder, Robert McLean 1841-1895 *ChPo S1*
Calder-Marshall, Arthur 1908- *Au&Wr,*
 ConAu 61, ConNov 1972, ConNov 1976,
 DcLEnL, WorAu, WrD 1976
Calderon, Fernando Juan Iglesias 1856- *AmLY*
Calderon, George 1868-1915 *LongC, NewC,*
 OxEng
Calderon, Serafin Estebanez 1801?-1867
 BiD&SB, EvEuW
Calderon DeLaBarca, Frances Erskine 1804-1882
 Alli, DcNAA

Calderon DeLaBarca, Pedro 1600-1681 *AtlBL,*
 BbD, BiD&SB, CasWL, CnThe, CyWA,
 DcEuL, DcSpL, EuA, EvEuW, McGWD,
 NewC, OxEng, Pen Eur, RCom, REn,
 REnWD
Calderon Y Beltran, Fernando 1809-1845
 BiD&SB
Calderone, Mary Steichen 1904- *AuNews 1*
Calderwood, David 1575-1650? *Alli, CasWL,*
 Chmbr 1, DcEnL, EvLB
Calderwood, Henry 1830-1897 *Alli Sup,*
 BiD&SB
Calderwood, Ivan E 1899- *ConAu 57*
Calderwood, James D 1917- *ConAu 5R*
Calderwood, James Lee 1930- *ConAu 21,*
 WrD 1976
Calderwood, Robert *Alli*
Calderwood, William *Alli Sup*
Calderwood, William Leadbetter 1865- *WhLA*
Caldicott, John William *Alli Sup*
Caldicott, Thomas Ford *Alli Sup*
Caldor, M T *Alli Sup, ChPo*
Caldwall, Richard 1513?-1585 *Alli*
Caldwall, Thomas *BiDLA*
Caldwell, Adelbert Farrington *ChPo*
Caldwell, Andrew 1752-1808 *Alli*
Caldwell, Anne 1867-1936 *AmSCAP 66*
Caldwell, Anne Marsh 1791-1874 *BrAu 19*
Caldwell, Augustine *Alli Sup*
Caldwell, Ben *BlkAW, DrAP 1975*
Caldwell, C Edson 1906- *ConAu 29*
Caldwell, Charles 1772-1853 *Alli, BiDSA,*
 CyAL 1, DcAmA, DcNAA
Caldwell, D *Alli Sup*
Caldwell, David S 1820-1889 *OhA&B*
Caldwell, Dennis 1919- *Au&Wr*
Caldwell, Erskine 1903- *AmA&B, AmNov,*
 AmWr, Au&Wr, AuNews 1, CasWL,
 CnDAL, ConAmA, ConAu 1R, ConLC 1,
 ConNov 1972, ConNov 1976, CyWA,
 DcLEnL, DrAF 1976, EncWL, EvLB,
 LongC, ModAL, ModAL Sup, OxAm,
 Pen Am, RAdv 1, REn, REnAL, TwCA,
 TwCA Sup, TwCW, WebEAL, WhTwL,
 WhWNAA, WrD 1976
Caldwell, Evantha *TexWr, WhWNAA*
Caldwell, Francis Cary 1868- *WhWNAA*
Caldwell, Frank 1867- *IndAu 1816,*
 WhWNAA
Caldwell, Gaylon L 1920- *ConAu 33*
Caldwell, George Chapman 1834-1907 *Alli Sup,*
 DcAmA, DcNAA
Caldwell, George Walter 1866-1946 *ChPo,*
 DcNAA
Caldwell, Gwendolyn D *BlkAW*
Caldwell, Halwin *Alli Sup*
Caldwell, Harry B 1935- *ConAu 37*
Caldwell, Henry *BbtC*
Caldwell, Howard Clay 1893- *IndAu 1917*
Caldwell, Howard Hayne 1831-1858 *Alli,*
 BiDSA, DcNAA
Caldwell, Howard Walter 1853?-1927 *AmA&B,*
 DcNAA, OhA&B
Caldwell, Hugh 1867- *ChPo*
Caldwell, Inga Gilson 1897- *ConAu 61*
Caldwell, Irene Catherine 1908- *ConAu 9R*
Caldwell, J H *BiDSA*
Caldwell, J R *HsB&A*
Caldwell, James *ConAu XR*
Caldwell, Sir James 1720?-1784 *Alli, PoIre*
Caldwell, James Fitz-James *BiDSA*
Caldwell, James Stamford *Alli*
Caldwell, Janet Taylor 1900- *TwCA,*
 TwCA Sup
Caldwell, John *Alli*
Caldwell, John Cope 1913- *AuBYP, ConAu 23,*
 SmATA 7
Caldwell, John H *Alli Sup*
Caldwell, John R *Alli Sup*
Caldwell, Joseph *Alli*
Caldwell, Joseph 1773-1835 *BiD&SB, BiDSA,*
 CyAL 1, DcAmA, DcNAA
Caldwell, Joseph H 1934- *ConAu 23*
Caldwell, Joshua William 1856-1909 *BiDSA,*
 DcAmA, DcNAA
Caldwell, Katherine M 1899- *WhWNAA*
Caldwell, Lewis A H *BlkAW*
Caldwell, Linus Boues 1834- *DcAmA*

Caldwell, Lisle Boues 1834- *Alli Sup, BiDSA,*
 DcNAA
Caldwell, Lynton 1913- *ConAu 29*
Caldwell, Mack M 1896- *WhWNAA*
Caldwell, Malcolm 1931- *ConAu 25*
Caldwell, Margaret F *ChPo*
Caldwell, Mary Elizabeth 1909- *AmSCAP 66*
Caldwell, Mary Townsend 1901- *TexWr*
Caldwell, Merritt 1806-1848 *Alli Sup, DcAmA,*
 DcNAA
Caldwell, Morgan *BbtC*
Caldwell, Oliver Johnson 1904- *ConAu 37*
Caldwell, Orestes H 1888- *WhWNAA*
Caldwell, Otis William 1869- *IndAu 1816,*
 WhWNAA
Caldwell, Peggy 1909- *TexWr*
Caldwell, Robert *Alli Sup*
Caldwell, Robert 1817- *Alli Sup*
Caldwell, Robert C *Alli Sup*
Caldwell, Robert Graham 1904- *ConAu 17R,*
 WrD 1976
Caldwell, Robert Granville 1882- *TexWr,*
 WhWNAA
Caldwell, Samuel Lunt 1820-1889 *DcAmA,*
 DcNAA
Caldwell, Taylor 1900- *AmA&B, AmNov,*
 Au&Wr, ConAu 5R, ConLC 2, LongC,
 OxAm, REn, REnAL, WrD 1976
Caldwell, Thomas *Alli, ChPo S2*
Caldwell, W H *Alli Sup*
Caldwell, Wallace Everett 1890- *AmA&B*
Caldwell, William C 1925- *IndAu 1917*
Caldwell, William Warner 1823-1908 *Alli,*
 ChPo, CyAL 2, DcAmA, DcNAA
Caldwell, William Warren 1823-1908 *BiD&SB*
Caldwell, Mrs. Willie Walker *BiDSA*
Cale, Johnny 1909- *AmSCAP 66*
Cale, Walter 1881-1904 *OxGer*
Calecas *CasWL*
Calef, Robert 1648?-1719 *Alli, AmA,*
 AmA&B, BbD, BiD&SB, CnDAL,
 DcAmA, DcNAA, OxAm, Pen Am,
 REnAL
Calef, Wesley 1914- *ConAu 13R*
Calemard DeLaFayette, Charles 1815- *BbD,*
 BiD&SB
Calentius d1503 *BiD&SB*
Calenzio d1503 *BiD&SB*
Calenzoli, Giuseppe 1815-1882 *BiD&SB*
Calep, Ralph *Alli*
Calepino, Ambrogio 1435-1511 *NewC, OxFr*
Calepino, Ambrosio 1435-1511 *OxEng*
Cales, Thomas *Alli*
Caley, J C *Alli Sup*
Caley, John 1763-1834 *Alli*
Caley, Robert *Alli Sup*
Caley, Rod *ConAu XR*
Calfa, Ambroise 1830- *BiD&SB*
Calfa, Corene 1835- *BiD&SB*
Calfa, V *Alli Sup*
Calfee, John Edward 1875-1940 *DcNAA,*
 WhWNAA
Calfhill, James 1530-1570 *Alli*
Calfill, James 1530-1570 *Alli*
Calhane, D Frank 1869- *WhWNAA*
Calhoon, Richard P 1909- *ConAu 57*
Calhoon, Robert M 1935- *ConAu 53*
Calhoun, Alfred R *Alli Sup*
Calhoun, Alice J *BiDSA*
Calhoun, Arthur Wallace 1885- *WhWNAA*
Calhoun, Calfrey C 1928- *ConAu 37*
Calhoun, Cornelia Donovan 1864-1949 *DcNAA*
Calhoun, D T *Alli Sup*
Calhoun, Eric *ConAu XR*
Calhoun, Fred Harvey Hall 1874- *WhWNAA*
Calhoun, George Miller 1886- *WhWNAA*
Calhoun, John Caldwell 1782-1850 *Alli, AmA,*
 AmA&B, BbD, BiD&SB, BiDSA,
 CyAL 1, DcAmA, OxAm, REn, REnAL
Calhoun, John William 1871- *TexWr,*
 WhWNAA
Calhoun, Joseph Gilbert 1856-1932 *DcNAA*
Calhoun, Mary Huiskamp 1926- *AuBYP,*
 ConAu 5R, SmATA 2, ThBJA
Calhoun, Newell Meeker 1847-1932 *DcNAA*
Calhoun, Philo Clarke 1889-1964 *AmA&B,*
 ChPo
Calhoun, Richard James 1926- *ConAu 33,*

WrD 1976
Calhoun, Robert Lowry 1896- *AmA&B*
Calia, Vincent F 1926- *ConAu 53*
Calian, Carnegie Samuel 1933- *ConAu 25,*
WrD 1976
Caliban *ConAu XR*
Califano, Joseph A, Jr. 1931- *ConAu 45*
Califf, Joseph M *Alli Sup*
Caliga, Isaac Henry 1857- *ChPo*
Caligan, Woodrow W 1913- *AmSCAP 66*
Caligula 012-041 *NewC, REn*
Calin, William 1936- *ConAu 21*
Calinescu, George 1899-1965 *CasWL*
Calisch, Edmund Nathaniel 1865-1946 *DcNAA,*
OhA&B, WhWNAA
Calish, Edward N 1865- *BiDSA*
Calisher, Hortense 1911- *AmA&B, Au&Wr,*
ConAu 1R, ConLC 2, ConLC 4,
ConNov 1972, ConNov 1976, DrAF 1976,
ModAL Sup, OxAm, Pen Am, TwCW,
WorAu, WrD 1976
Calitri, Charles J 1916- *ConAu 5R,*
WrD 1976
Calitri, Princine *ConAu 33*
Calker, Darrell W 1905-1964 *AmSCAP 66*
Calker, Wilhelm 1869- *WhLA*
Calkin, Homer Leonard 1912- *ConAu 41*
Calkin, J B *BbtC*
Calkin, John Burgess 1829-1918 *DcNAA*
Calkins, Alonzo *Alli Sup*
Calkins, Clinch *ChPo*
Calkins, Earnest Elmo 1868-1964 *AmA&B,*
ChPo, REnAL, WhWNAA
Calkins, Fay *ConAu XR*
Calkins, Franklin *ConAu XR*
Calkins, Franklin Welles 1857-1928 *AmA&B,*
DcNAA, MnBBF, WhWNAA
Calkins, Gary Nathan 1869-1943 *DcNAA,*
IndAu 1917, WhWNAA
Calkins, H A *OxCan*
Calkins, Harvey Reeves 1866-1941 *DcNAA,*
IndAu 1816
Calkins, Marshall 1828- *Alli Sup*
Calkins, Mary Whiton 1863-1930 *Alli Sup,*
ChPo, DcNAA, WhWNAA
Calkins, N A *ChPo S2*
Calkins, Norman Allison 1822-1895 *AmA,*
DcAmA, DcNAA
Calkins, Phineas Wolcott 1831-1924 *DcNAA*
Calkins, Raymond 1869- *WhWNAA*
Calkins, Wolcott *Alli Sup*
Call, Alice E LaPlant 1914- *ConAu 13R*
Call, Annie Payson 1853-1919? *AmLY,*
DcAmA, DcNAA
Call, Arthur Deerin 1869- *AmLY, WhWNAA*
Call, Daniel 1765?-1840 *Alli, BiDSA,*
ChPo S1
Call, Frank Oliver 1878- *ChPo, DcLEnL,*
OxCan, WhWNAA
Call, Hughie Florence 1890-1969 *ConAu 5R,*
SmATA 1, WhPNW
Call, Wathen Mark Wilks 1817-1890 *Alli Sup,*
BrAu 19
Call, Wilkinson 1834- *BiDSA*
Call, William Timothy 1856-1917 *DcNAA*
Callaert, Vrancke *CasWL*
Callaghan, Doctor *Alli*
Callaghan, Barry *OxCan Sup*
Callaghan, Catherine A 1931- *ConAu 33*
Callaghan, Gertrude *CatA 1947, ChPo,*
ChPo S2
Callaghan, J Dorsey 1895- *OhA&B*
Callaghan, James F 1839-1899 *OhA&B*
Callaghan, Mary Lloyd 1903- *IndAu 1917*
Callaghan, Morley Edward 1903- *CanNov,*
CanWr, CasWL, CatA 1947, ConAu 9R,
ConLC 3, ConNov 1972, ConNov 1976,
DcLEnL, EncWL Sup, LongC, NewC,
OxAm, OxCan, OxCan Sup, Pen Eng,
REn, REnAL, TwCA, TwCA Sup,
TwCW, WebEAL, WhTwL, WrD 1976
Callahan, Adalbert John 1905- *CatA 1947*
Callahan, Charles C 1910- *ConAu 17*
Callahan, Claire Wallis 1890- *AuBYP,*
ConAu 5R
Callahan, Daniel 1930- *ConAu 21*
Callahan, Dorothy *AuBYP*
Callahan, J Will 1874-1946 *AmSCAP 66*

Callahan, James Morton 1864- *AmLY, BiDSA,*
DcAmA, IndAu 1816, WhWNAA
Callahan, Jennie Waugh 1907- *Au&Wr*
Callahan, John F 1912- *ConAu 33, WrD 1976*
Callahan, Marie J *AmSCAP 66*
Callahan, Nelson J 1927- *ConAu 33,*
WrD 1976
Callahan, North 1908- *AmA&B, Au&Wr,*
ConAu 1R, WrD 1976
Callahan, Sidney Cornelia 1933- *ConAu 17R*
Callahan, Sterling G 1916- *ConAu 21*
Callam, James *Alli, BiDLA*
Callam, Tex *MnBBF*
Callan, Charles Jerome 1877- *BkC 2,*
CatA 1947
Callan, Edward T 1917- *ConAu 17R*
Callan, Hugh *Alli Sup*
Callan, John F *Alli Sup*
Callan, Mary Catherine *ChPo, ChPo S1*
Callan, Norman *ChPo S1*
Callan, Richard J 1932- *ConAu 53*
Callanan, Helena 1864?- *PoIre*
Callanan, James Joseph 1795-1829 *Alli, CasWL*
Callanan, Jeremiah John *ChPo, ChPo S1*
Callanan, Jeremiah Joseph 1795-1829 *CasWL,*
PoIre
Callander, James *Alli, BiDLA*
Callander, John *Alli, BiDLA*
Callander, John d1789 *Alli*
Callander, Thomas 1877- *WhWNAA*
Callander-Rice, Margie *ChPo S1*
Callant, A G *Alli Sup, ChPo S2*
Callard, Maurice Frederic Thomas 1912-
Au&Wr, ConAu 1R, WrD 1976
Callard, Thomas Henry 1912- *Au&Wr,*
ConAu 9R
Callard, Thomas Karr *Alli Sup*
Callas, Theo *ConAu XR*
Callaway, Dorothy *TexWr*
Callaway, Frances Bennett d1905 *DcNAA*
Callaway, Henry *Alli Sup*
Callaway, John *Alli*
Callaway, Morgan, Jr. 1862-1936 *BiDSA,*
DcNAA, TexWr, WhWNAA
Callbeck, Lorne C *OxCan*
Callcott, Lady 1788-1843 *DcEnL*
Callcott, Sir Augustus Wall 1779-1844 *Alli,*
ChPo
Callcott, George H 1929- *ConAu 29*
Callcott, J G *ChPo S1*
Callcott, John Wall 1766-1821 *Alli*
Callcott, Margaret Law 1929- *ConAu 61*
Callcott, Lady Maria 1788-1843 *Alli, NewC*
Callcott, Maria Hutchins *Alli, Alli Sup*
Callcott, William Hutchins 1807-1882 *Alli Sup*
Callen, William B 1930- *ConAu 23*
Callenbach, Ernest 1929- *ConAu 57*
Callendar, H L *Alli Sup*
Callender, Charles 1928- *ConAu 41*
Callender, E B *Alli Sup*
Callender, Edward Belcher 1851-1917 *ChPo,*
DcAmA, DcNAA
Callender, George 1918- *AmSCAP 66*
Callender, George William 1830-1878 *Alli Sup*
Callender, Guy Stevens 1865-1915 *DcAmA,*
DcNAA
Callender, Harold 1892-1959 *AmA&B,*
WhWNAA
Callender, Henry *Alli Sup*
Callender, James Thomas 1758-1803 *Alli,*
BiD&SB, BiDSA, DcAmA
Callender, James Thomson 1758-1803 *DcNAA*
Callender, John 1706-1748 *Alli, AmA&B,*
BbD, BiD&SB, CyAL 1, DcAmA,
DcNAA
Callender, Julian *ConAu XR*
Callender, Morgan 1862-1936 *DcNAA*
Callender, Romaine 1857-1930 *DcNAA,*
WhWNAA
Callender, Wesley P, Jr. 1923- *ConAu 17R*
Callender, William Romaine *Alli Sup*
Calleo, David P 1934- *ConAu 17R*
Caller, Mary Alice *BiDSA*
Callias, Nina De *OxFr*
Callicot, Theophilus Carey 1826- *Alli*
Callieres, Louis-Hector, Chevalier De 1646-1703
OxCan
Calligan, Hannah *Alli Sup*

Callihan, E L 1903- *ConAu 25*
Callihan, E Lee 1906- *WrD 1976*
Callihan, Elmer L *TexWr*
Callihou, James *WhWNAA*
Callimachus 305?BC-240?BC *AtlBL, BbD,*
BiD&SB, CasWL, CasEng, Pen Cl
Callimachus 310?BC- *REn*
Callinan, Bernard J 1913- *WrD 1976*
Callingham, James *Alli Sup*
Callinicos, Constantine 1913- *AmSCAP 66*
Callinus 675?BC- *CasWL, Pen Cl*
Callis, F *Alli Sup*
Callis, Helmut G 1906- *ConAu 53*
Callis, Robert *Alli*
Callis, Robert 1920- *ConAu 37*
Callison, Brian Richard 1934- *Au&Wr,*
ConAu 29, WrD 1976
Callister, Christian *ChPo*
Callister, Frank 1916- *Au&Wr, ConAu 13R,*
WrD 1976
Callisthenes 360?BC-328?BC *NewC, Pen Cl*
Callistratus *BbD*
Callon, Milton W 1906- *IndAu 1917*
Callot, Jacques 1592?-1635 *AtlBL, OxFr*
Callow, Alexander B, Jr. 1925- *ConAu 21*
Callow, Edward *Alli Sup*
Callow, Frances E And Alice M *Alli Sup*
Callow, James T 1928- *ConAu 41*
Callow, Philip Kenneth 1924- *ConAu 13R,*
ConNov 1976, WrD 1976
Calloway, Cab 1907- *AmSCAP 66*
Calloway, Doris Howes 1923- *ConAu 21*
Callum, Myles 1934- *ConAu 9R*
Callwell, J M *Alli Sup*
Callwood, June 1924- *Au&Wr*
Calman, A L *Alli Sup*
Calman, E S *Alli*
Calman, Montague 1917- *Au&Wr*
Calmann, John 1935- *ConAu 21*
Calmes, Albert 1881- *WhLA*
Calmes, Neville *WhWNAA*
Calmet, Augustine 1672-1757 *DcEuL, OxFr*
Calmo, Andrea 1510-1571 *CasWL*
Calmour, Alfred C *Alli Sup*
Calmour, Alfred Cecil 1857?-1912 *ChPo*
Calmus, Bernard Leon 1915- *Au&Wr*
Calnan, Thomas Daniel 1915- *ConAu 29,*
WrD 1976
Calne, Roy Yorke 1930- *ConAu 61*
Calnek, William Arthur 1822-1892 *DcNAA,*
OxCan
Calogero, Lorenzo 1910-1961 *EncWL*
Calomee, Lindsay *BlkAW*
Calonne, Charles-Alexandre De 1734-1802 *OxFr*
Calonne, Ernest De 1822-1877 *BiD&SB, OxFr*
Calprenede, Gautier DesCostes DeLa 1614-1663
EvEuW, NewC, OxEng
Calpurnia *REn*
Calpurnius Siculus, Titus 030?-080? *BbD,*
BiD&SB, CasWL, Pen Cl
Calter, Paul 1934- *ConAu 41*
Calthorp, John *BiDLA*
Calthorpe, Somerset John Gough 1831- *Alli Sup*
Calthrop, Annette *Alli Sup*
Calthrop, Charles *Alli*
Calthrop, George *Alli Sup, ChPo S1*
Calthrop, Gordon *Alli Sup*
Calthrop, Sir Harry *Alli*
Calthrop, Henry Calthrop Hollway- 1856-
Alli Sup
Calthrop, John *Alli*
Calthrop, Samuel Robert 1829-1917 *BiD&SB,*
ChPo, DcAmA, DcNAA
Calton, Robert Bell *Alli Sup*
Caluza, Reuben Tolakele 1900?-1965 *AfA 1*
Calvard, J L *ChPo S2*
Calver, Edward *Alli*
Calver, Edward Killwick *Alli Sup*
Calver, Gordon Anthony 1921- *Au&Wr*
Calverley, Charles Stuart 1831-1884 *Alli Sup,*
AtlBL, BbD, BiD&SB, BrAu 19, ChPo,
ChPo S1, ChPo S2, Chmbr 3, DcEnA,
DcEnL, DcEuL, DcLEnL, EvLB, OxEng,
Pen Eng, REn, WebEAL
Calverley, Henry Calverley *Alli Sup*
Calverley, William Slater *Alli Sup*
Calverly, Charles Stuart 1831-1884 *NewC*
Calverly, William *Alli*

Calvert, A K *Alli Sup*
Calvert, Augustus *PoIre*
Calvert, Barry George 1930- *WrD 1976*
Calvert, Bruce T 1866-1940 *DcNAA*
Calvert, Caroline Louisa Waring 1834-1872
 Alli Sup
Calvert, Cecilius, Lord Baltimore *Alli*
Calvert, Charles *Alli Sup*
Calvert, Charles 1785-1852 *ChPo*
Calvert, Elinor H 1929- *ConAu 5R*
Calvert, Frederick *Alli*
Calvert, Frederick 1806- *Alli Sup*
Calvert, Frederick, Lord Baltimore 1731-1771
 Alli
Calvert, Frederick B *Alli Sup*
Calvert, Frederick Crace 1819-1873 *Alli Sup*
Calvert, G H *BbtC*
Calvert, George *Alli Sup*
Calvert, George, Lord Baltimore 1582?-1632 *Alli,*
 OxCan
Calvert, George Henry 1803-1889 *Alli,*
 Alli Sup, AmA, AmA&B, BbD,
 BiD&SB, BiDSA, CyAL 2, DcAmA,
 DcEnL, DcLEnL, DcNAA, OxAm,
 REnAL
Calvert, George S *ChPo*
Calvert, Hubert 1875- *WhLA*
Calvert, James *AuBYP*
Calvert, James d1698 *Alli*
Calvert, James Michael 1913- *Au&Wr*
Calvert, John *Alli, Alli Sup, TwCA Sup*
Calvert, John W *Alli Sup*
Calvert, Laura D 1922- *ConAu 37*
Calvert, Luta Lorine *ChPo*
Calvert, Mary 1941- *WrD 1976*
Calvert, Monte A 1938- *ConAu 21*
Calvert, Sir Pet *Alli*
Calvert, Peter 1936- *Au&Wr, ConAu 25,*
 WrD 1976
Calvert, Philip Powell 1871- *WhWNAA*
Calvert, Robert *Alli*
Calvert, Robert, Jr. 1922- *ConAu 25*
Calvert, Sidney 1868- *WhWNAA*
Calvert, Thomas 1606-1679 *Alli*
Calvert, William *Alli Sup*
Calvert, William 1819-1880 *ChPo*
Calvert, William Robinson 1882- *MnBBF*
Calverton, Victor Francis 1900-1940 *AmA&B,*
 DcLEnL, DcNAA, OxAm, Pen Am,
 REnAL, TwCA
Calvez, Jean-Yves 1927- *ConAu 57*
Calvi, Count Felice 1822- *BiD&SB*
Calvin, Delano Dexter 1881-1948 *DcNAA,*
 OxCan
Calvin, Mrs. Frederick *AmA&B*
Calvin, Henry *ConAu XR, ConNov 1972,*
 ConNov 1976, WrD 1976
Calvin, Henry Kauffman 1869- *WhWNAA*
Calvin, Jean 1509-1564 *CasWL, EuA, EvEuW,*
 OxEng, OxFr
Calvin, Johannes 1509-1564 *DcEuL*
Calvin, John 1509-1564 *BbD, BiD&SB, NewC,*
 RCom, REn
Calvin, Joseph K 1895- *WhWNAA*
Calvin, V *Alli Sup*
Calvino, Italo 1923- *CasWL, ConLC 5,*
 EncWL Sup, ModRL, Pen Eur, TwCW,
 WhTwL, WorAu
Calvo, Carlo 1824-1893 *BiD&SB*
Calvo Sotelo, Joaquin 1905- *CrCD, McGWD,*
 ModWD
Calvus, Gaius Licinius Macer 082BC-047BC
 CasWL, Pen Cl
Calzabigi, Ranieri De' 1714-1795 *CasWL,*
 EvEuW
Cam 1913- *IlCB 1956*
Cam, Helen Maud 1885-1968 *ConAu P-1*
Cam, Joseph *Alli*
Cam, T C *Alli*
Camac, Charles Nicoll Bancker 1868-1940
 DcNAA, WhWNAA
Camara, Helder Pessoa 1909- *ConAu 61*
Camara, Joao Da 1852-1908 *ClDMEuL*
Camara, Juan Rodriguez DeLa *CasWL*
Camara, Laye 1928- *AfA 1, CasWL,*
 EncWL Sup
Camarata, Salvador 1913- *AmSCAP 66*
Camargo, Marie-Anne Cuppi 1710-1770 *OxFr*

Camba, Julio 1884-1962 *CasWL, ClDMEuL,*
 EvEuW
Cambaceres, Eugenio De 1843-1888 *CasWL,*
 DcSpL, Pen Am
Cambaceres, Jean-Jacques Regis De 1755-1824
 OxFr
Cambden, John *Alli*
Cambel, Lord Of Lorne *Alli*
Cambell, Sylvia *Alli Sup*
Cambern, May Hogan *AmSCAP 66*
Cambiaire, Celestin Pierre 1882- *WhWNAA*
Camblak, Gregory 1364- *Pen Eur*
Camblak, Grigorije 1364- *CasWL*
Cambon, Glauco 1921- *ConAu 17R*
Cambon, J J *BiDLA*
Cambreleng, Churchill Caldom 1786-1863
 DcNAA
Cambrensis, Giraldus *Alli, NewC, OxEng*
Cambridge, Ada 1844-1926 *Alli Sup, BbD,*
 BrAu 19, ChPo, ChPo S1, Chmbr 3,
 DcBiA, DcLEnL
Cambridge, Elizabeth 1893-1949 *LongC,*
 TwCA, TwCA Sup
Cambridge, George Owen *BiDLA*
Cambridge, Octavius Pickard- 1835- *Alli Sup*
Cambridge, Richard Owen 1717-1802 *Alli,*
 BiD&SB, DcEnL, EvLB, NewC, REn
Cambridge, William G *Alli Sup*
Cambyses II d522BC *REn*
Camden, Lord *Alli*
Camden, Charles *Alli Sup*
Camden, Richard *MnBBF*
Camden, William 1551-1623 *Alli, BiD&SB,*
 BrAu, CasWL, Chmbr 1, DcEnA,
 DcEnL, DcEuL, DcLEnL, EvLB, NewC,
 OxEng, Pen Eng
Came, A B *ChPo*
Camell, Robert *Alli*
Camell, Thomas *Alli*
Camelli, G J *Alli*
Cameniates, John *Pen Cl*
Camerarius, David *Alli*
Camerarius, Gul *Alli*
Camerarius, Ja *Alli*
Camerarius, Joachim 1500-1574 *DcEuL,*
 OxGer
Cameron, Mrs. *Alli*
Cameron, A *Alli Sup*
Cameron, Agnes Deans *OxCan*
Cameron, Alan 1900- *AmSCAP 66*
Cameron, Alan 1938- *ConAu 61*
Cameron, Alexander *Alli*
Cameron, Alexander Mackenzie *Alli Sup*
Cameron, Allan Gillies 1930- *Au&Wr,*
 WrD 1976
Cameron, Allan W 1938- *ConAu 33*
Cameron, Andrew *ChPo S2*
Cameron, Anthony *PoIre*
Cameron, Archibald 1771?-1836 *Alli Sup,*
 DcAmA, DcNAA
Cameron, Arnold Guyot 1864-1947 *DcNAA,*
 WhWNAA
Cameron, Brian *MnBBF*
Cameron, Bruce 1913- *ConAu 1R*
Cameron, Mrs. C *ChPo S2*
Cameron, C R *Alli*
Cameron, Captain *MnBBF*
Cameron, Charles *Alli, Alli Sup*
Cameron, Charles 1740?-1812 *AtlBL, BiDLA*
Cameron, Charles 1841- *Alli Sup*
Cameron, Sir Charles Alexander 1830- *Alli Sup,*
 PoIre
Cameron, Charles Hay 1795-1880 *Alli Sup*
Cameron, Charles Innes 1837-1879 *DcNAA*
Cameron, Charles Richard *BiDLA*
Cameron, Charlotte *OxCan*
Cameron, Clifford *MnBBF*
Cameron, Constance Carpenter 1937-
 ConAu 49
Cameron, D A *ConAu XR*
Cameron, D Ewen 1901-1967 *AmA&B*
Cameron, D Y *WrD 1976*
Cameron, Donald *WrD 1976*
Cameron, Donald Allan 1937- *ConAu 23,*
 WrD 1976
Cameron, Duncan *Alli*
Cameron, E T 1879- *WhWNAA*
Cameron, Edna M 1905- *ConAu P-1,*

 SmATA 3
Cameron, Edward Herbert 1875-1938 *DcNAA*
Cameron, Edward Robert 1857-1931 *DcNAA,*
 OxCan
Cameron, Eleanor 1912- *AuBYP, ChLR 1,*
 ChPo, ConAu 1R, SmATA 1, ThBJA
Cameron, Elizabeth *ConAu XR*
Cameron, Elizabeth Jane 1910- *ConAu 1R,*
 WrD 1976
Cameron, Ellen Gordon 1905- *WhWNAA*
Cameron, Emily *Alli Sup*
Cameron, Ewen *BiDLA*
Cameron, Ewin *Alli*
Cameron, Mrs. Finlay *Alli Sup*
Cameron, Florence Robertson *ChPo S2*
Cameron, Francis Marten *Alli Sup*
Cameron, Frank T 1909- *ConAu P-1*
Cameron, G Poulett 1806-1882 *Alli*
Cameron, George Fenton *Alli Sup*
Cameron, George Frederick 1854-1885 *Alli Sup,*
 CanWr, ChPo, ChPo S2, Chmbr 3,
 DcLEnL, DcNAA, OxCan, REnAL
Cameron, George G 1905- *AmA&B*
Cameron, George Poulett 1806-1882 *Alli Sup*
Cameron, H Lovett *BiD&SB*
Cameron, Henry Clay 1827- *Alli Sup, BiDSA,*
 DcAmA
Cameron, Henry P *Alli Sup*
Cameron, Hugh 1835-1918 *ChPo*
Cameron, Ian *ConAu XR, WrD 1976*
Cameron, Isabel *ChPo S1*
Cameron, J *Alli Sup, BbtC*
Cameron, J M 1910- *ConAu 5R*
Cameron, James *Alli Sup*
Cameron, James 1911- *Au&Wr, ConAu 23,*
 WrD 1976
Cameron, James R 1929- *ConAu 33*
Cameron, John *Alli, Alli Sup, BiDLA, ChPo,*
 ChPo S1, LongC
Cameron, John 1580?-1625 *Alli*
Cameron, John 1873- *WhWNAA*
Cameron, John 1914- *ConAu 29*
Cameron, John Hillyard 1817- *Alli Sup, BbtC*
Cameron, Kate *ChPo, ChPo S1*
Cameron, Katharine *IlCB 1945*
Cameron, Katherine *ChPo S2*
Cameron, Kenneth 1922- *Au&Wr*
Cameron, Kenneth Neill 1908- *ChPo S2,*
 ConAu 9R
Cameron, Kenneth Walter 1908- *ConAu 21*
Cameron, Lou 1924- *ConAu 1R*
Cameron, Ludovick Charles Richard 1866-
 Br&AmS
Cameron, M G *Alli Sup*
Cameron, Malcolm 1808- *BbtC*
Cameron, Malcolm Graeme 1857-1925 *DcNAA*
Cameron, Margaret 1867-1947 *AmLY XR,*
 DcNAA
Cameron, Marie *Alli Sup*
Cameron, Mary Emily *Alli Sup*
Cameron, Mary Lovett *Alli Sup*
Cameron, Mary Owen 1915- *ConAu 13R*
Cameron, Meribeth E 1905- *ConAu 1R*
Cameron, Norman 1905-1953 *ChPo, CnE&AP,*
 CnMWL, TwCW, WhTwL, WorAu
Cameron, Paul *Alli Sup*
Cameron, Peter Hay *Alli Sup*
Cameron, Polly 1928- *AuBYP, ChPo,*
 ConAu 17R, IlCB 1966, SmATA 2
Cameron, Richard d1680 *NewC*
Cameron, Robert 1839- *BbtC*
Cameron, Rod Rupert Edwin 1933- *IndAu 1917*
Cameron, Roderick 1913- *Au&Wr, WrD 1976*
Cameron, Rondo E 1925- *ConAu 1R,*
 WrD 1976
Cameron, Thomas *Alli*
Cameron, Thomas Wright Moir 1894- *WhLA*
Cameron, V Lovett *MnBBF*
Cameron, Verney Lovett 1844-1894 *Alli Sup,*
 BbD, BiD&SB
Cameron, Viola *WhWNAA*
Cameron, William *Alli*
Cameron, William 1751-1811 *ChPo, ChPo S1*
Cameron, William Bleasdell 1862-1951 *OxCan*
Cameron, William Bruce 1920- *ConAu 37*
Cameron, William C 1822-1889 *Alli Sup, ChPo,*
 ChPo S1
Cameron, William Evelyn 1842-1927 *BiDSA,*

DcNAA
Cameron, William Gordon *Alli Sup*
Cameron, William Macdonald 1923- *Au&Wr*
Cameron, William Norwood *Alli*
Cameron Of Lochiel, Donald 1695?-1748 *NewC*
Cameron-Price, George William James *Au&Wr*
Camfield, Benjamin *Alli*
Camfield, Francis *Alli*
Camidge, Charles Edward *Alli Sup*
Camillo *EuA*
Camillus 1758-1808 *AmA, OxCan*
Camilo *CasWL*
Camilo Sarmiento *PueRA*
Camilo, Don *ConAu XR*
Camino, Leon Felipe 1884- *CasWL, ClDMEuL, DcSpL, EvEuW*
Camino Galicia, Leon Felipe 1884- *REn*
Camisards *NewC*
Camlan, Goronva *Alli*
Camm, Bede, Dom 1864-1942 *CatA 1947*
Cammack, Floyd M 1933- *ConAu 9R*
Cammaerts, Emile Leon 1878-1953 *CarSB, ChPo, ChPo S1, ChPo S2, DcLEnL, EvEuW, LongC, TwCA Sup, WhLA*
Cammaerts, Tita *CarSB*
Cammann, Henry J And Camp, Hugh N *Alli Sup*
Cammann, Schuyler VanRensselaer 1912- *AmA&B, ConAu 9R*
Cammell, Charles Richard *ChPo, ChPo S2*
Camoens, Louis De 1524?-1580 *BbD*
Camoens, Luis De 1524?-1580 *AtlBL, ChPo S1, ChPo S2, CyWA, DcEuL, OxEng, RCom, REn*
Camoens, Luiz De 1524?-1580 *BiD&SB, DcBiA*
Camoes, Luis De 1524?-1580 *AtlBL, CasWL, EvEuW, Pen Eur, REn, REnWD*
Camoes, Luiz De 1524?-1580 *EuA, NewC*
Camoin, Francois Andre 1939- *ConAu 61*
Camp, Blanche Hammond *IndAu 1917*
Camp, Burton H 1880- *WhWNAA*
Camp, C C *Alli Sup*
Camp, Charles L 1893-1975 *ConAu 61*
Camp, Charles Wadsworth 1879-1936 *AmA&B, DcNAA*
Camp, Dalton Kingsley 1920- *ConAu 61, OxCan Sup*
Camp, David Nelson 1820-1916 *DcNAA*
Camp, Edgar Whittlesey 1860- *WhWNAA*
Camp, Fred V 1911- *ConAu 49*
Camp, George King 1851- *BiDSA*
Camp, James 1923- *ConAu 33, DrAP 1975*
Camp, John 1915- *WrD 1976*
Camp, Kate McKellar 1871- *TexWr*
Camp, Norman M *Alli Sup*
Camp, Pauline Frances *ChPo, ChPo S2*
Camp, Phineas *Alli Sup, ChPo*
Camp, T Edward 1929- *ConAu 13R*
Camp, Wadsworth *DcNAA*
Camp, Walter Chauncey 1859-1925 *AmA&B, AmLY, BiD&SB, ChPo, DcAmA, DcNAA, JBA 1934, JBA 1951, REnAL, WhWNAA, YABC 1*
Camp, Wesley D 1915- *ConAu 17R*
Camp, William Newton Alexander 1926- *Au&Wr, ConAu 61*
Campa, Arthur L 1905- *ConAu 17*
Campaigne, Jameson Gilbert 1914- *ConAu 1R*
Campan, Jeanne Louise Henriette 1752-1822 *BiD&SB, OxFr*
Campana, Dino 1885-1932 *CasWL, ClDMEuL, CnMWL, EncWL, ModRL, Pen Eur, WhTwL, WorAu*
Campanella, Francis B 1936- *ConAu 53*
Campanella, Giuseppe Maria *Alli Sup*
Campanella, Tommaso 1568-1639 *BbD, BiD&SB, CasWL, DcEuL, EuA, EvEuW, Pen Eur, REn*
Campanile, Achille 1900- *ClDMEuL*
Campanius, John 1601-1683 *REnAL*
Campantar *DcOrL 2*
Campardon, Emile 1834- *BiD&SB*
Campaspe *REn*
Campbell, Lady *Alli Sup*
Campbell, Lord *Alli Sup, Chmbr 3*
Campbell, Miss *Alli*
Campbell, A *Alli*

Campbell, A C *Alli, BiDLA, BiDLA Sup*
Campbell, A D *Alli*
Campbell, A Digby *BbtC*
Campbell, Ada P *ChPo S1*
Campbell, Alan K 1923- *ConAu 5R*
Campbell, Alexander *Alli, BiDLA, BiDSA, OxCan*
Campbell, Alexander 1788-1866 *Alli, Alli Sup, AmA&B, BbD, BiD&SB, DcAmA, DcNAA, OxAm*
Campbell, Alexander 1912- *ConAu 61*
Campbell, Alexander Augustus 1789-1846 *BiDSA, DcAmA, DcNAA*
Campbell, Alexander James 1839?- *Alli Sup, DcAmA, DcNAA*
Campbell, Alfred Gibbs *BlkAW*
Campbell, Alice B *ChPo*
Campbell, Alistair *ChPo S2*
Campbell, Alistair 1907-1974 *Au&Wr, ConAu P-1*
Campbell, Alistair 1925- *ChPo S1, ConP 1970, ConP 1975, WrD 1976*
Campbell, Amy *Alli Sup, ChPo S1, WhWNAA*
Campbell, Angus *ConAu XR*
Campbell, Angus 1910- *IndAu 1917*
Campbell, Ann R 1925- *ConAu 21*
Campbell, Anne 1888- *ChPo, REnAL*
Campbell, Anne Marsh *ChPo*
Campbell, Arabella Georgina *Alli Sup*
Campbell, Archibald *Alli, Alli Sup, ChPo S1, ChPo S2*
Campbell, Archibald d1513 *NewC*
Campbell, Archibald 1598-1661 *Alli*
Campbell, Lord Archibald 1846- *Alli Sup*
Campbell, Archibald Alexander *Alli Sup*
Campbell, Archibald Bruce 1881- *ConAu P-1*
Campbell, Archibald Young 1885- *ChPo, ChPo S1, WhLA*
Campbell, Arthur A 1924- *ConAu 1R*
Campbell, Austin 1884- *CanNov*
Campbell, Barbara *IlCB 1956*
Campbell, Bartley 1843-1888 *AmA, AmA&B, BiD&SB, DcAmA, DcNAA, HsB&A, OxAm, REnAL*
Campbell, Beatrice Murphy 1908- *ConAu XR*
Campbell, Bernard G 1930- *ConAu 23*
Campbell, Beth 1908- *WhWNAA*
Campbell, Big Bill *MnBBF*
Campbell, Blanche 1902- *ConAu 5R*
Campbell, Blanche Bingham *ChPo S1*
Campbell, Bridget *WrD 1976*
Campbell, Bruce *AuBYP, ConAu XR, MorJA, OxCan, SmATA 1*
Campbell, Bruce 1912- *Au&Wr*
Campbell, Mrs. C 1844- *ChPo*
Campbell, Mrs. C C *Alli Sup*
Campbell, C D N *Alli Sup*
Campbell, C J *Alli Sup*
Campbell, C Samuel 1900- *WhWNAA*
Campbell, Calder *Alli, ChPo S1*
Campbell, Camilla 1905- *ConAu 25*
Campbell, Charles *Alli, Alli Sup, BiDLA Sup*
Campbell, Charles 1807-1876 *Alli, Alli Sup, AmA, AmA&B, BiD&SB, BiDSA, DcAmA, DcNAA*
Campbell, Charles Arthur 1897-1974 *ConAu 49*
Campbell, Charles Diven 1877-1919 *IndAu 1917*
Campbell, Charles Milton 1852-1940 *DcNAA*
Campbell, Lady Charlotte *Alli, BiDLA*
Campbell, Clarence Gordon 1868-1956 *IndAu 1917*
Campbell, Clive *ConAu XR*
Campbell, Colin *Alli Sup*
Campbell, Colin d1729 *AtlBL, BkIE*
Campbell, Colin d1734 *Alli*
Campbell, Lord Colin 1853- *Alli Sup*
Campbell, Colin 1937- *Au&Wr*
Campbell, Colin Dearborn 1917- *ConAu 33*
Campbell, Mrs. Colin G *Alli Sup*
Campbell, Crichton *Alli Sup*
Campbell, D C *Alli Sup*
Campbell, D Charles D *Alli Sup*
Campbell, D Forbes *Alli*
Campbell, Daisy Rhodes 1854-1927 *AmLY, OhA&B, WhWNAA*
Campbell, David *Alli, BiDLA*

Campbell, David 1915- *CasWL, ConP 1970, ConP 1975, WorAu, WrD 1976*
Campbell, David A 1927- *ConAu 25*
Campbell, David P 1934- *ConAu 23*
Campbell, Dawson *Alli Sup*
Campbell, Doak S 1888- *WhWNAA*
Campbell, Don 1922- *ConAu 17R*
Campbell, Donald *Alli, Alli Sup, BiDLA, ChPo S2, ConAu XR, MnBBF*
Campbell, Donald 1940- *ConP 1975, WrD 1976*
Campbell, Donald Francis 1867- *WhWNAA*
Campbell, Donald Gordon 1925- *Au&Wr*
Campbell, Donald Guy 1922- *IndAu 1917*
Campbell, Donald Malcolm *ChPo*
Campbell, Dorcas Elizabeth 1896?-1959 *IndAu 1917*
Campbell, Dorothea Primrose *Alli*
Campbell, Douglas *Alli Sup, ChPo S1*
Campbell, Douglas 1839?-1893 *BiD&SB, DcAmA, DcNAA*
Campbell, Douglas Houghton 1859- *DcAmA, WhWNAA*
Campbell, Dudley 1833- *Alli Sup*
Campbell, Dugald *Alli Sup*
Campbell, Duncan *Alli, Alli Sup, PoIre*
Campbell, Duncan 1819?-1866 *DcNAA*
Campbell, Duncan 1819?-1886 *OxCan*
Campbell, E 1932- *Au&Wr*
Campbell, E A *Alli Sup*
Campbell, Mrs. Edmund *Alli Sup*
Campbell, Edward F, Jr. 1932- *ConAu 13R*
Campbell, Edward L *Alli Sup*
Campbell, Edward R 1787-1857 *ChPo*
Campbell, Edwin R 1787-1857 *OhA&B*
Campbell, Elizabeth *Alli Sup*
Campbell, Elizabeth, Countess Of Cawdor *Alli Sup*
Campbell, Elizabeth A *AuBYP*
Campbell, Elizabeth Anne *Alli Sup*
Campbell, Elizabeth McClure 1891- *ConAu 37, WrD 1976*
Campbell, Elsie Jane Cosler 1887- *OhA&B*
Campbell, Emma F R *Alli Sup*
Campbell, Ernest Q 1926- *ConAu 37*
Campbell, Erving *DcNAA*
Campbell, Etta *ChPo*
Campbell, Eugene Edward 1915- *ConAu 23*
Campbell, Eugene Miller 1922- *Au&Wr*
Campbell, Evelyn *Alli Sup*
Campbell, F A *Alli Sup*
Campbell, F R *Alli Sup*
Campbell, F W *BbtC*
Campbell, F W Groves *PoIre*
Campbell, Flann Canmer 1919- *Au&Wr*
Campbell, Florence M *Alli Sup*
Campbell, Floy 1873- *DcAmA*
Campbell, Frances Elizabeth *ChPo S1*
Campbell, Francis Stuart *ConAu XR, WrD 1976*
Campbell, Frank *Alli Sup*
Campbell, Frank 1880-1964 *IndAu 1917*
Campbell, Frederick Gordon Bluett *Alli Sup*
Campbell, G *Alli Sup*
Campbell, G L *Alli*
Campbell, G Wells *MnBBF*
Campbell, Gabrielle Margaret Vere *LongC*
Campbell, George *Alli, Alli Sup, Chmbr 2, ConP 1970*
Campbell, George 1719-1796 *Alli, BiD&SB, ChPo, DcEnL, EvLB*
Campbell, Sir George 1824-1892 *Alli Sup, BiD&SB*
Campbell, Lord George 1850- *Alli Sup*
Campbell, George Alexander 1869-1943 *DcNAA*
Campbell, George Archibald 1900- *Au&Wr*
Campbell, George D, Duke Of Argyll 1823- *Alli Sup*
Campbell, George Douglas *BrAu 19*
Campbell, George Frederick 1915- *WrD 1976*
Campbell, George Graham *OxCan*
Campbell, George John Douglas 1823- *Alli*
Campbell, Gertrude E, Lady Colin *Alli Sup*
Campbell, Sir Gilbert *MnBBF*
Campbell, Sir Gilbert Edward 1838- *Alli Sup*
Campbell, Gladys 1892- *IndAu 1917*
Campbell, Gordon *ChPo*
Campbell, Grace 1895-1963 *CanNov, CanWr,*

OxCan
Campbell, Mrs. Graham *Alli Sup*
Campbell, H *Alli Sup*
Campbell, H F *Alli Sup*
Campbell, Hannah *ConAu 9R*
Campbell, Hardy Webster *AmLY*
Campbell, Harry *MnBBF*
Campbell, Harvey B 1887- *WhWNAA*
Campbell, Hector *Alli, BiDLA*
Campbell, Helen Stuart 1839-1918 *Alli Sup, AmA&B, BbD, BiD&SB, DcAmA, DcNAA*
Campbell, Henry C 1926- *AmSCAP 66*
Campbell, Henry Colin 1862-1923 *DcNAA*
Campbell, Herbert *BlkAW*
Campbell, Herbert James 1925- *WrD 1976*
Campbell, Hope *ConAu 61*
Campbell, Howard E 1925- *ConAu 57*
Campbell, Hugh *Alli, Alli Sup*
Campbell, Sir Hugh *Alli*
Campbell, Hugh F *Alli Sup*
Campbell, Ian 1899- *ConAu 53*
Campbell, Ian 1942- *WrD 1976*
Campbell, Ian Barclay 1916- *Au&Wr, WrD 1976*
Campbell, Ian D *ChPo S1*
Campbell, Ignatius Roy Dunnachie 1901-1957 *CasWL, DcLEnL, EvLB*
Campbell, Isabel 1895- *WhWNAA*
Campbell, Isabella *BbtC*
Campbell, Ivar 1891?-1916 *ChPo*
Campbell, Ivie *Alli*
Campbell, J *Alli, Alli Sup*
Campbell, J A *ChPo S1*
Campbell, J A P *Alli Sup*
Campbell, J A R *Alli Sup*
Campbell, J Arthur 1916- *ConAu 53*
Campbell, J Gounod *OxCan*
Campbell, J H *Alli Sup*
Campbell, J L *Alli Sup*
Campbell, J R *Alli Sup, ChPo*
Campbell, J Ramsey 1946- *ConAu 9R*
Campbell, Jack K 1927- *ConAu 23*
Campbell, Jacob 1760-1788 *Alli, CyAL 1*
Campbell, James *Alli, Alli Sup, BiDLA*
Campbell, James 1758-1818 *PoIre*
Campbell, James 1920- *ConAu 57, WrD 1976*
Campbell, James Argyll 1884- *WhLA*
Campbell, James Dykes 1838-1895 *BrAu 19, ChPo, ChPo S2, Chmbr 3, NewC*
Campbell, James E *BlkAW*
Campbell, James Edwin 1867-1896? *BlkAW, OhA&B*
Campbell, James Joseph *Au&Wr*
Campbell, James Mann 1840-1926 *DcAmA, DcNAA*
Campbell, James Mason *Alli Sup*
Campbell, James R *Alli Sup*
Campbell, James Thomas *Alli Sup*
Campbell, James Valentine 1823-1890 *Alli Sup, DcAmA, DcNAA*
Campbell, James William *Alli Sup*
Campbell, Jane *Alli Sup, ChPo, ConAu XR, SmATA XR*
Campbell, Jane 1934- *ConAu 41*
Campbell, Jane C *Alli Sup*
Campbell, Jane Montgomery *ChPo*
Campbell, Jeff H 1931- *ConAu 41*
Campbell, Jesse H 1807-1881 *BiDSA, DcNAA*
Campbell, Joan *ChPo, ChPo S1*
Campbell, John *Alli, Alli Sup, BiDLA, BiDLA Sup, ChPo S1, Chmbr 2, OxCan*
Campbell, John 1653-1728 *REnAL*
Campbell, John 1708-1775 *Alli, BiD&SB, DcEnL*
Campbell, John 1766-1840 *Alli*
Campbell, Baron John 1779-1861 *Alli, Alli Sup, BbD, BiD&SB, BrAu 19, CasWL, DcEnL, EvLB*
Campbell, John 1794-1867 *Alli Sup*
Campbell, Sir John 1802-1877 *Alli Sup*
Campbell, John 1810-1874 *AmA&B, DcNAA*
Campbell, John 1839- *DcAmA*
Campbell, John 1840-1904 *DcNAA*
Campbell, John 1846- *ChPo*
Campbell, John, Earl Of London *Alli*
Campbell, John A *Alli Sup*
Campbell, John Archibald 1811-1889 *BiDSA,*

DcNAA
Campbell, John B T 1880- *WhWNAA*
Campbell, John Beautiste 1848- *WhWNAA*
Campbell, John Bunyan 1820-1904 *OhA&B*
Campbell, John Charles 1867-1919 *IndAu 1917, REnAL*
Campbell, John Coert 1911- *ConAu 1R*
Campbell, Sir John Douglas Sutherland *BiD&SB*
Campbell, John F V, Earl Cawdor 1817- *Alli Sup*
Campbell, John Francis 1822-1885 *Alli Sup, BiD&SB, BrAu 19, Chmbr 3, EvLB*
Campbell, John Franklin 1940?-1971 *ConAu 33*
Campbell, John George, Marquis Of Lorne 1845- *Alli Sup*
Campbell, John Kerr *Alli Sup*
Campbell, Sir John Logan 1817-1912 *DcLEnL*
Campbell, John Lorne 1845- *DcAmA*
Campbell, John Lorne 1906- *Au&Wr, ConAu 29*
Campbell, John Lyle 1818-1886 *Alli Sup, BiDSA, DcAmA, DcNAA*
Campbell, John Lyle 1827-1904 *DcNAA, IndAu 1917*
Campbell, John McLeod 1800-1872 *Alli Sup*
Campbell, John Menzies 1887- *Au&Wr*
Campbell, John P *ChPo S2*
Campbell, John Poage 1767-1814 *Alli, BiDSA, DcAmA, DcNAA, OhA&B*
Campbell, John R 1933- *ConAu 53*
Campbell, John Ramsey 1946- *WrD 1976*
Campbell, John Robert *Alli Sup*
Campbell, John TenBrook 1833-1911 *DcAmA, DcNAA*
Campbell, John W 1910-1971 *ConAu 21, ConAu 29, WorAu*
Campbell, John Wilson *Alli, BiDSA*
Campbell, John Wilson 1782-1833 *BiDSA, OhA&B*
Campbell, John Wood 1910- *AmA&B*
Campbell, Joseph *Alli Sup*
Campbell, Joseph 1879-1944 *CasWL, CatA 1947, ChPo, ChPo S1, EvLB, NewC, REn*
Campbell, Joseph 1904- *AmA&B, ConAu 1R, REnAL, TwCA Sup*
Campbell, Joseph M *PoIre*
Campbell, Judith 1914- *ConAu XR, WrD 1976*
Campbell, Juliet Hamersley Lewis 1823-1898 *Alli, ChPo, FemPA*
Campbell, Kareen Fleur *ConP 1970*
Campbell, Karlyn Kohrs 1937- *ConAu 53*
Campbell, Mrs. Kemper *ConAu XR*
Campbell, Kenneth *MnBBF*
Campbell, Killis 1872-1937 *AmA&B, DcNAA, TexWr*
Campbell, L M E *Alli Sup*
Campbell, Lachlan *DcNAA*
Campbell, Laura *ChPo, ChPo S1*
Campbell, Laurence R *ChPo S2*
Campbell, Lawrence Dundas *Alli*
Campbell, Lawrence James 1931- *Au&Wr, WrD 1976*
Campbell, Lewis 1830-1908 *Alli Sup, BrAu 19, ChPo S2, Chmbr 3, EvLB, NewC*
Campbell, Lily Bess 1883-1967 *AmA&B, OhA&B*
Campbell, Litta Belle 1886- *ConAu 5R*
Campbell, Loomis Joseph 1831-1896 *Alli Sup, BbD, BiD&SB, ChPo S2, DcNAA*
Campbell, Lorn, Jr. 1891- *WhWNAA*
Campbell, Louis Walter 1899- *OhA&B*
Campbell, Luke *ConAu 57*
Campbell, M A *ChPo S1*
Campbell, Miss M Montgomery *Alli Sup*
Campbell, Macy 1879- *WhWNAA*
Campbell, Sir Malcolm *MnBBF*
Campbell, Malcolm J 1930- *ConAu 57*
Campbell, Margaret *DcLEnL*
Campbell, Margaret 1916- *WrD 1976*
Campbell, Margaret Olympia *Alli Sup*
Campbell, Marion d1944 *OhA&B*
Campbell, Marius Robinson 1858- *WhWNAA*
Campbell, Marjorie Freeman *ChPo, OxCan*
Campbell, Marjorie Wilkins 1901- *OxCan, OxCan Sup*

Campbell, Mark *Alli Sup*
Campbell, Mary *REn*
Campbell, Mary Elizabeth 1903- *IndAu 1917, OhA&B*
Campbell, Mary Maxwell d1886 *ChPo S1*
Campbell, Mary Rebecca 1881-1939 *OhA&B*
Campbell, Michael Mussen 1924- *Au&Wr*
Campbell, Minnie Spence d1940 *DcNAA*
Campbell, Nancy *ChPo, ChPo S1*
Campbell, Nev 1883- *WhWNAA*
Campbell, Norman Robert 1880- *WhLA*
Campbell, Oscar James 1879-1970 *AmA&B, ChPo, ConAu 29, OhA&B*
Campbell, P *BbtC*
Campbell, Patricia Piatt 1901- *Au&Wr, ConAu 25, WhPNW*
Campbell, Patrick *OxCan*
Campbell, Patrick 1921- *WrD 1976*
Campbell, Mrs. Patrick 1865-1940 *LongC, NewC, REn*
Campbell, Paul Andrew 1902- *IndAu 1917*
Campbell, Paul Newell 1923- *ConAu 21, WrD 1976*
Campbell, Penelope 1935- *ConAu 33*
Campbell, Peter *Alli*
Campbell, Peter 1926- *Au&Wr, ConAu P-1*
Campbell, Peter Anthony 1935- *ConAu 21*
Campbell, Peter Colin *Alli Sup*
Campbell, Peter Walter 1926- *WrD 1976*
Campbell, Quintin *Alli Sup*
Campbell, R *Alli*
Campbell, R J 1867-1956 *LongC*
Campbell, R T *WrD 1976*
Campbell, R W *ConAu XR, SmATA 1*
Campbell, R Wright 1927- *ConAu 57*
Campbell, Ralph *BlkAW*
Campbell, Ramsey 1946- *ConAu 57*
Campbell, Randolph 1940- *ConAu 41*
Campbell, Rex R 1931- *ConAu 41*
Campbell, Richard *BiDSA*
Campbell, Richard Vary *Alli Sup*
Campbell, Rita Ricardo 1920- *ConAu 57*
Campbell, Robert *Alli, Alli Sup, NewC*
Campbell, Robert d1868 *PoCh*
Campbell, Robert 1808-1894 *OxCan*
Campbell, Robert 1832- *Alli Sup*
Campbell, Robert 1835-1921 *DcNAA*
Campbell, Robert 1922- *ConAu 53*
Campbell, Robert 1926- *WrD 1976*
Campbell, Robert Allen *Alli Sup*
Campbell, Robert C 1924- *ConAu 49*
Campbell, Robert Calder *ChPo S1*
Campbell, Robert Calder 1798-1857 *Alli Sup*
Campbell, Robert Dale 1914- *ConAu 9R*
Campbell, Robert E *OxCan*
Campbell, Robert Fishburne 1858-1947 *DcNAA, WhWNAA*
Campbell, Robert Granville 1879-1932 *DcNAA*
Campbell, Robert L 1880- *AnMV 1926*
Campbell, Robert Wellington 1926- *ConAu 1R*
Campbell, Roderick 1842- *OxCan*
Campbell, Rodolphus *ChPo S1*
Campbell, Rollo 1803-1871 *BbtC, DcNAA*
Campbell, Ronald *Alli Sup*
Campbell, Rosemae Wells 1909- *AuBYP, ConAu 13R, SmATA 1*
Campbell, Ross Turner 1863- *WhWNAA*
Campbell, Roy 1901?-1957 *CatA 1947, ChPo, CnE&AP, CnMWL, EncWL, LongC, ModBL, ModBL Sup, OxEng, Pen Eng, REn, TwCA, TwCA Sup, TwCW, WebEAL, WhTwL*
Campbell, Roy Dunnachie *Chmbr 3*
Campbell, Roy Hutcheson *Au&Wr*
Campbell, Ruth *ChPo S1*
Campbell, Ruth Ramsdell 1888- *AmA&B*
Campbell, S M *Alli Sup*
Campbell, Samuel Arthur 1895-1962 *AmA&B*
Campbell, Samuel Miner 1823-1892 *DcNAA*
Campbell, Sarah M, Countess Of Cawdor d1881 *Alli Sup*
Campbell, Scott *AmA&B, DcNAA*
Campbell, Scott 1858-1933 *ChPo*
Campbell, Selina H *Alli Sup*
Campbell, Sheldon 1919- *ConAu 41*
Campbell, Stanley W 1926- *ConAu 49*
Campbell, Stephen K 1935- *ConAu 49*
Campbell, Stewart *Alli Sup*

Campbell, Sydney G *MnBBF*
Campbell, T Beverly 1892- *WhWNAA*
Campbell, T Bowyer *BkC 5*
Campbell, T Moody 1879- *WhWNAA*
Campbell, Theophilus 1810?-1894 *Alli Sup, PoIre*
Campbell, Thomas *Alli, BiDLA, Chmbr 2, PoIrc, REnAL*
Campbell, Thomas 1733-1795 *PoIre*
Campbell, Thomas 1777-1844 *Alli, BbD, BiD&SB, BiDLA, BrAu 19, CasWL, ChPo, ChPo S1, ChPo S2, CriT 2, DcEnA, DcEnA Ap, DcEuL, DcLEnL, EvLB, MouLC 3, NewC, OxAm, OxEng, Pen Eng, PoCh, REn, WebEAL*
Campbell, Thomas A *PoIre*
Campbell, Thomas F 1924- *ConAu 21*
Campbell, Thomas Jefferson 1864- *WhWNAA*
Campbell, Thomas Joseph 1848-1925 *DcNAA, OxCan*
Campbell, Thomas M 1936- *ConAu 49*
Campbell, Thomasina M A F *Alli Sup*
Campbell, Valeria J *Alli Sup*
Campbell, Virginia 1914- *ChPo, IlBYP, IlCB 1956*
Campbell, W A *Alli Sup*
Campbell, W D C *BbtC*
Campbell, W Graham *Alli Sup*
Campbell, Walter *Alli Sup*
Campbell, Walter Frederick *Alli Sup*
Campbell, Walter L 1842-1905 *Alli Sup, OhA&B*
Campbell, Walter Stanley 1887-1957 *AmA&B, CnDAL, OxAm, REn, REnAL, TwCA, TwCA Sup, WhWNAA*
Campbell, Wanda Jay *AuBYP*
Campbell, Webster Duyckinck *ChPo*
Campbell, Wilfred 1861?-1918? *CanWr, OxCan, REn*
Campbell, Wilfred SEE Campbell, Wm W
Campbell, Will D 1924- *ConAu 5R*
Campbell, William *Alli, Alli Sup, BiDLA*
Campbell, William d1886 *Alli Sup*
Campbell, William Alexander 1881- *WhWNAA*
Campbell, William D *Alli Sup*
Campbell, William Edward 1875- *CatA 1952*
Campbell, William Edward March 1893-1954 *AmA&B, AmNov XR, ConAmA, REn, REnAL, TwCA Sup*
Campbell, Lord William Frederick 1824- *Alli Sup*
Campbell, William H *CyAL 1*
Campbell, William Henry 1808-1890 *BiDSA, DcAmA, DcNAA*
Campbell, William J 1850-1931 *AmA&B*
Campbell, William Rose *Alli Sup*
Campbell, William W 1806-1881 *Alli, BiD&SB, DcAmA, DcNAA*
Campbell, William Wallace 1862-1938 *DcNAA, WhWNAA*
Campbell, William Wilfred 1861?-1918? *BbD, BiD&SB, BrAu 19, ChPo, ChPo S1, Chmbr 3, DcLEnL, DcNAA, EvLB, REnAL*
Campbell, Wm W SEE Campbell, Wilfred
Campbell-Johnson, Alan 1913- *Au&Wr*
Campbell-Johnston *Alli Sup*
Campbell-Johnston, May Isabel 1885- *WhWNAA*
Campbell-Praed *Alli Sup*
Campbell-Purdie, Wendy 1925- *ConAu 21*
Campbell-Watson, Frank 1898- *AmSCAP 66*
Campbellton, N B *OxCan*
Campden, Hugh *DcEnL*
Campe, Joachim Heinrich 1746-1818 *BiD&SB, CarSB, DcEuL*
Campe, Johann Heinrich 1746-1818 *OxGer*
Campeau, Lucien *OxCan Sup*
Camper, Shirley *ConAu XR*
Campert, Remco Wouter 1929- *CasWL*
Campesino, Un *PueRA*
Camphuysen, Dirck Rafaelsz 1586-1627 *CasWL, Pen Eur*
Camphuysen, Dirk Rafaelszoon 1586-1627 *DcEuL, EuA*
Campian, Edmond 1540-1581 *Alli*
Campian, Edmund 1540-1581 *BbD*

Campian, Thomas *NewC*
Campin, F W *Alli Sup*
Campin, Francis *Alli Sup*
Campin, Robert 1378?-1444 *AtlBL*
Campion, Abraham *Alli*
Campion, Charles Heathcote *Alli Sup*
Campion, Donald John Martin 1930- *Au&Wr*
Campion, Edmond 1540-1581 *Alli*
Campion, Edmund 1540-1581 *NewC*
Campion, J S *Alli Sup*
Campion, John Thomas *Alli Sup*
Campion, John Thomas 1814- *PoIre*
Campion, Katherine *WhWNAA*
Campion, Mary C *ChPo S1*
Campion, Nardi Reeder 1917- *AuBYP, ConAu 1R*
Campion, Samuel S *Alli Sup*
Campion, Sarah *DcLEnL*
Campion, Sidney Ronald 1891- *Au&Wr, ConAu P-1, WrD 1976*
Campion, Thomas 1567?-1619? *Alli, AtlBL, BbD, BiD&SB, BrAu, CasWL, ChPo, ChPo S1, ChPo S2, Chmbr 1, CnE&AP, CrE&SL, CriT 1, DcEnL, DcEuL, DcLEnL, EvLB, NewC, OxEng, Pen Eng, RAdv 1, REn, WebEAL*
Campion, William Magan *Alli Sup*
Campistron, Jean Galbert De 1656?-1723? *BiD&SB, CasWL, CnThe, DcEuL, EvEuW, OxFr, REn, REnWD*
Campkin, Henry 1815?-1890 *ChPo S1*
Campkin, James *Alli Sup*
Camplin, John *Alli*
Camplin, John Mussendine *Alli Sup*
Campling, Christopher Russell 1925- *Au&Wr, WrD 1976*
Campling, F Knowles d1940 *MnBBF*
Campo, Estanislao Del 1834-1880 *CasWL, DcSpL, Pen Am*
Campo, Hubert A 1884- *WhWNAA*
Campoamor, Ramon De 1817-1901 *CasWL, ClDMEuL, DcEuL, DcSpL, EvEuW, Pen Eur, REn*
Campoamor Y Campoosorio, Don Ramon De 1817-1901 *BbD, BiD&SB*
Campoamor Y Camposorio, Ramon De 1817-1901 *EuA*
Campomanes, Pedor Rodriguez 1723-1803 *DcEuL*
Camprodon, Francisco 1816-1870 *BiD&SB*
Camprubi, Zenobia *DcSpL*
Camps, Francis Edward 1905-1972 *ConAu 37*
Camps, William *Alli Sup*
Camps, Mrs. William *Alli Sup*
Campson, Kaye *MnBBF*
Campton, David 1924- *Au&Wr, ConAu 5R, ConDr, CrCD, McGWD, WrD 1976*
Camsell, Charles 1876-1958 *OxCan, WhWNAA*
Camus, Albert 1913-1960 *AtlBL, CasWL, ClDMEuL, CnMD, CnMWL, CnThe, ConLC 1, ConLC 2, ConLC 4, CrCD, CyWA, EncWL, EvEuW, LongC, McGWD, ModRL, ModWD, OxEng, OxFr, Pen Eur, RCom, REn, REnWD, TwCA Sup, TwCW, WhTwL*
Camus, Jean-Pierre 1582?-1652? *CasWL, DcEuL, EvEuW, OxFr*
Can Grande *NewC*
Canaday, John E 1907- *AmA&B, ConAu 13R, EncM&D, WorAu*
Canadian, A *OxCan*
Canadien M P P, Un *OxCan*
Canakya *DcOrL 2*
Canale, Antonio 1697-1768 *REn*
Canales, Nemesio R 1878-1923 *PueRA*
Canaletto 1697-1768 *AtlBL*
Canaletto, Antonio 1697-1768 *REn*
Canan, James William 1929- *ConAu 61*
Canan, Keith 1895-1959 *IndAu 1917*
Canant, Edith Rayner 1901- *ChPo S2*
Canaries, James *Alli*
Canary *ConAu 57*
Canary, Robert H 1939- *ConAu 29*
Canavesio, Orlando 1916-1957 *BiDPar*
Canaway, Bill *WrD 1976*
Canaway, William Hamilton 1925- *Au&Wr, ConNov 1972, ConNov 1976, WrD 1976*

Canby, Henry Seidel 1878-1961 *AmA&B, AmLY, ChPo S1, CnDAL, ConAmA, ConAmL, DcLEnL, LongC, OxAm, REn, REnAL, TwCA, TwCA Sup, WhWNAA*
Canby, Margaret T *Alli Sup*
Canby, Marion G *ChPo S2*
Canceller, James *Alli*
Cancelmo, Joe 1897- *AmSCAP 66*
Cancer Y Velasco, Geronimo De 1600?-1665 *DcEuL*
Cancer Y Velasco, Jeronimo De 1600?-1655 *CasWL*
Cancian, Francesca M 1937- *ConAu 57*
Cancian, Francis Alexander 1934- *ConAu 53*
Cancian, Frank 1934- *ConAu XR*
Cand Bardai *DcOrL 2*
Candamo, F A 1661?-1704 *DcSpL*
Candamo, Francisco Antonio Bances 1661?-1704 *DcEuL*
Candar, Krisan *DcOrL 2*
Candaules *NewC*
Candee, Alexander M *WhWNAA*
Candee, Annie Chunn *ChPo*
Candee, Helen 1858-1949 *DcNAA*
Candee, Helen Churchill 1861- *DcAmA*
Candee, Helen Churchill 1868- *WhWNAA*
Candelaria, Frederick 1929- *ConAu 17R*
Candell, Victor G 1903- *ConICB*
Candida *ConAu XR*
Candidas *DcOrL 2*
Candidius, George *Alli*
Candido, Antonio 1918- *Pen Am*
Candidus *Alli*
Candilis, Wray O 1927- *ConAu 25, WrD 1976*
Candish, Thomas *Alli, NewC*
Candland, Douglas Keith 1934- *ConAu 5R, WrD 1976*
Candler, Allen Daniel 1834-1910 *BiDSA, DcNAA*
Candler, Beatrice Post *ChPo*
Candler, C *Alli Sup*
Candler, Chris 1905- *Au&Wr*
Candler, Howard *Alli Sup*
Candler, Warren Akin 1857-1941 *BiDSA, DcNAA, WhWNAA*
Candler, William Fulbright 1894- *WhWNAA*
Candlin, Edwin Frank 1911- *Au&Wr*
Candlin, Enid Saunders 1909- *ConAu 45*
Candlish, James S *Alli Sup*
Candlish, Robert Smith 1806-1873 *Alli, Alli Sup*
Candlish, Robert Smith 1807-1873 *DcEnL*
Candlyn, T Frederick H 1892-1964 *AmSCAP 66*
Candragomin *DcOrL 2*
Candy, Albert Luther 1857-1947? *DcNAA*
Candy, Edward *ConAu XR*
Candy, George 1841- *Alli Sup*
Candy, Hugh Charles Herbert *WhLA*
Candy, Mrs. M M *Alli Sup*
Candy, Robert 1920- *AuBYP, IlCB 1956*
Candy, Thomas Henry *Alli Sup*
Cane, Bevis *Alli Sup*
Cane, Henry *Alli*
Cane, John Vincent d1672 *Alli*
Cane, Melville Henry 1879- *AmA&B, AnMV 1926, ChPo, ChPo S1, ChPo S2, ConAu 1R, REnAL*
Cane, Miguel 1851-1905 *CasWL*
Cane, Robert *PoIre*
Cane, Robert 1807-1858 *Alli Sup*
Caner, Henry 1700-1792 *Alli*
Caner, Mary Paul 1893- *ConAu 21*
Canete, Manuel 1822-1891 *BbD, BiD&SB*
Canetti, Elias 1905- *CasWL, CnMD, CnMWL, ConAu 21, ConLC 3, CrCD, EncWL, ModGL, OxGer, Pen Eur, TwCW, WorAu*
Canfield, Arthur Graves 1859-1947 *DcNAA, WhWNAA*
Canfield, Cass 1897- *AmA&B, ConAu 41, WrD 1976*
Canfield, Delos Lincoln 1903- *ConAu 25, DcSpL*
Canfield, Donald T 1895- *WhWNAA*
Canfield, Dorothy 1879-1958 *AmA&B, AmNov, Chmbr 3, CnDAL, ConAmA, ConAmL, DcBiA, DcLEnL, JBA 1934, LongC, OxAm, REn, REnAL, TwCA,*

TwCA Sup, WhWNAA, YABC 1

Canfield, Dwight R 1872-1956 *OhA&B*
Canfield, Flavia A Camp 1844-1930 *DcNAA, OhA&B*
Canfield, Francesca Anna 1803-1823 *Alli*
Canfield, Gertrude A *LivFWS*
Canfield, Henry Judson 1789-1856 *Alli, DcAmA, DcNAA*
Canfield, James Hulme 1847-1909 *Alli Sup, DcAmA, DcNAA, OhA&B*
Canfield, James K 1925- *ConAu 25*
Canfield, John A 1941- *ConAu 37*
Canfield, Kenneth French 1909- *ConAu P-1*
Canfield, Leon Hardy 1886- *AmA&B, ConAu 1R*
Canfield, Mary Grace Webb 1864-1946 *OhA&B*
Canfield, Silas Sprague 1824-1902 *OhA&B*
Canfield, William Walker 1857-1937 *AmA&B, DcNAA*
Cang, Joel 1899- *ConAu 29*
Cangemi, Sister Marie Lucita 1920- *ConAu 21*
Canham, Doris *ChPo S1, ChPo S2*
Canham, Erwin Dain 1904- *AmA&B, ConAu P-1*
Canham, Kingsley 1945- *ConAu 57*
Canham, P *Alli*
Canidia *NewC*
Caniff, Milton Arthur 1907- *AuNews 1, OhA&B, REnAL*
Canini, Marco Antonio 1822-1891 *BiD&SB*
Canis, Jean 1840- *BiD&SB*
Canitz, Friedrich Rudolf, Freiherr Von 1654-1699 *CasWL, OxGer*
Canitz, Rudolf Von 1654-1699 *DcEuL*
Canivet, Charles Alfred 1839- *BbD, BiD&SB*
Canizares, Jose De 1676-1750 *BbD, BiD&SB, CasWL, DcEuL, EvEuW, McGWD*
Cankar, Ivan 1876-1918 *CasWL, CnMD, EncWL, EuA, EvEuW, ModSL 2*
Cankar, Izidor 1886-1958 *CasWL*
Canmore, Malcolm *NewC*
Cann, Jessie Yereance 1883- *WhWNAA*
Cannam, Peggie 1925- *AuBYP, ConAu 13R*
Cannan, Denis 1919- *Au&Wr, ConAu 57, ConDr, CrCD, LongC, WrD 1976*
Cannan, Doris *ChPo*
Cannan, Edwin 1862- *Alli Sup, WhLA*
Cannan, Gilbert 1884-1955 *Chmbr 3, DcLEnL, EvLB, LongC, ModBL, NewC, TwCA, TwCA Sup*
Cannan, Joanna 1898-1961 *LongC, TwCA, TwCA Sup, WhCL*
Canne, John *Alli*
Cannell, Joseph *Alli*
Canney, Maurice A 1872- *WhLA*
Canniff, William 1830-1910 *Alli Sup, BbtC, DcNAA, OxCan*
Canning, Albert Stratford George 1832- *Alli Sup*
Canning, Charles J S G, Baron Garvagh 1852- *Alli Sup*
Canning, Charlotte *Alli Sup, PoIre*
Canning, Dan 1851- *ChPo S1*
Canning, George *BiDLA, Chmbr 2*
Canning, George d1771 *Alli, PoIre*
Canning, George 1770-1827 *Alli, BiD&SB, BrAu 19, CasWL, ChPo, DcEnL, DcEuL, DcLEnL, EvLB, NewC, OxEng, PoIre*
Canning, Josiah Dean 1816-1892 *Alli Sup, AmA&B, ChPo, ChPo S1, DcNAA*
Canning, Pat *ChPo*
Canning, Ray R 1920- *ConAu 41*
Canning, Richard *Alli*
Canning, Stratford, Viscount Stratford 1786-1880 *Alli Sup, PoIre*
Canning, T *Alli*
Canning, Thomas *PoIre*
Canning, Victor 1911- *Au&Wr, ConAu 13R, EncM&D, LongC, MnBBF, WorAu, WrD 1976*
Canning, William *Alli Sup*
Cannings, Thomas *PoIre*
Cannock, D G *ChPo S1*
Cannock, Miss F *ChPo S1*
Cannon, Bill *ConAu XR*
Cannon, C E *BlkAW, LivBA*

Cannon, Carl Leslie 1888- *ChPo*
Cannon, Charles James 1800-1860 *Alli Sup, AmA, AmA&B, BiD&SB, DcAmA, DcNAA, OxAm, PoIre, REnAL*
Cannon, Cornelia James 1876- *AmA&B, JBA 1934, TwCA, TwCA Sup, WhWNAA*
Cannon, Curt *EncM&D*
Cannon, David Wadsworth, Jr. 1911-1938 *BlkAW*
Cannon, Edward *ChPo*
Cannon, Fanny Venable 1876- *AmA&B, AmLY, WhWNAA*
Cannon, Francis d1880? *PoIre*
Cannon, Garland Hampton 1924- *Au&Wr, ConAu 33, WrD 1976*
Cannon, George Lyman 1860-1918 *DcAmA, DcNAA*
Cannon, George Q *Alli Sup*
Cannon, Gertrude Morton *ChPo*
Cannon, Grace A *ChPo S1*
Cannon, Mrs. Grant *AmNov XR*
Cannon, Harold C 1930- *ConAu 45*
Cannon, Henry Lewin 1871-1919 *DcNAA*
Cannon, James Graham 1858-1916 *DcNAA*
Cannon, James Monroe, III 1918- *ConAu 1R*
Cannon, James P 1890?-1974 *ConAu 53*
Cannon, James Spencer 1776-1852 *Alli, DcAmA, DcNAA*
Cannon, Jimmy 1909-1973 *REnAL*
Cannon, John *Alli Sup*
Cannon, John 1918- *Au&Wr, ConAu 49*
Cannon, LeGrand, Jr. 1899- *AmA&B, AmNov, Au&Wr, CnDAL, REnAL, TwCA Sup*
Cannon, Lou 1933- *ConAu 29*
Cannon, Mark W 1928- *ConAu 13R*
Cannon, Nathaniel *Alli*
Cannon, Robert *Alli*
Cannon, Sarah Jane *ChPo*
Cannon, Steve 1935- *BlkAW, DrAF 1976*
Cannon, T *Alli*
Cannon, Walter Bradford 1871-1945 *DcNAA, WhWNAA*
Cannon, William 1918- *ConAu 29, WrD 1976*
Cannon, William Ragsdale 1916- *AmA&B, ConAu 1R*
Cano, Edward, Jr. 1927- *AmSCAP 66*
Cano-Ballesta, Juan 1932- *ConAu 49*
Cano Y Masas, Leopoldo 1844- *BbD, BiD&SB*
Canoll, John E Henry *ChPo*
Canon, John d1340? *Alli*
Canon, Lance Kirkpatrick 1939- *ConAu 45*
Canonchet d1676 *OxAm*
Canonge, Jules 1812-1870 *BbD, BiD&SB*
Canonge, Louis Placide 1822-1893 *AmA&B, BiDSA, DcNAA*
Canonicus, John d1340? *Alli*
Canontas, Seraphim George 1874-1944 *DcNAA*
Canosa, Michael Raymond 1920- *AmSCAP 66*
Canossa, Count Ludovico Of 1476-1532 *REn*
Canova, Antonio 1757-1822 *AtlBL*
Canovan, Margaret Evelyn 1939- *WrD 1976*
Canovas DelCastillo, Antonio 1826-1897 *BbD, BiD&SB*
Canovas DelCastillo, Antonio 1828-1897 *CasWL*
Canright, Dudley Marion 1840-1919 *Alli Sup, DcNAA*
Canrobert, Certain 1809-1895 *OxFr*
Cansdale, George Soper 1909- *Au&Wr, ConAu 9R*
Canse, John Martin 1869- *IndAu 1917*
Cansever, Edip 1928- *DcOrL 3*
Cansford, John *MnBBF*
Cansick, Frederick Teague *Alli Sup*
Cansinos-Assens, Rafael 1883- *ClDMEuL*
Cant *Alli*
Cant, Andrew d1728 *Alli*
Cant-Wall *Alli Sup*
Cantacuzene, Madam 1876- *WhWNAA*
Cantacuzene, Princess 1876- *AmA&B*
Cantacuzene, Julia 1876-1975 *ConAu 61*
Cantacuzenus, John d1355? *BiD&SB*
Cantacuzenus, John, VI d1382 *Pen Cl*
Cantacuzino, Constantin Stolnicul 1650-1716 *CasWL*
Cantaeus, Andreas *Alli*
Cantarella, Michele Francesco 1899- *AmA&B*

Cantelon, John E 1924- *ConAu 9R*
Cantemir, Antioch *EuA*
Cantemir, Prince Antiochus *BiD&SB*
Cantemir, Dimitrie 1673-1723 *CasWL, EuA*
Canter, Willem 1542-1575 *DcEuL*
Canterbery, E Ray 1935- *ConAu 41*
Canterbury, Archbishop Of *ChPo S1*
Canterbury, Dean Of *ChPo S1*
Canth, Minna 1844-1897 *CasWL, EvEuW, Pen Eur, REn*
Cantillon, Philip *Alli*
Cantin, Eileen 1931- *ConAu 53*
Cantin, Eugene Thorpe 1944- *ConAu 45*
Cantinat, Jean 1902- *ConAu 29*
Cantlay, A S *Alli Sup*
Cantle, G H *MnBBF*
Cantlie, James *Alli Sup*
Cantlon, Maurice 1926- *WrD 1976*
Canton, Alfred *Alli Sup*
Canton, Cal *BlkAW*
Canton, Don 1915- *AmSCAP 66*
Canton, Edwin *Alli Sup*
Canton, J *Alli, BiDLA*
Canton, John *Alli, BiDLA*
Canton, John 1718-1772 *Alli*
Canton, R *Alli Sup*
Canton, Rosado Licenciado Francisco 1867- *WhWNAA*
Canton, S Ruth *ChPo S1*
Canton, William 1845-1926 *Alli Sup, ChPo, ChPo S1, ChPo S2, NewC*
Cantoni, Alberto 1841-1904 *CasWL, ClDMEuL, EvEuW*
Cantoni, Carlo 1840- *BiD&SB*
Cantor, Arthur 1920- *ConAu 29*
Cantor, Eddie 1892-1964 *AmSCAP 66*
Cantor, Louis 1934- *ConAu 29*
Cantor, Muriel G 1923- *ConAu 33*
Cantor, Nathaniel Freeman 1898-1957 *IndAu 1917*
Cantori, Louis J 1934- *ConAu 29*
Cantova, Anthony *Alli*
Cantrell, Henry *Alli*
Cantrell, Mrs. John Blackwell *Alli Sup*
Cantrell, R J 1895- *TexWr*
Cantril, Hadley 1906- *AmA&B*
Cantu, Cesare 1804?-1895 *BiD&SB, CasWL, DcBiA, EuA, EvEuW*
Cantu Menon, O 1846-1899 *Pen Cl*
Cantu Menon, Oyyarattu 1847-1899 *DcOrL 2*
Cantwell, Andrew d1761 *Alli*
Cantwell, Dennis P 1940- *ConAu 57*
Cantwell, John Simon 1837-1907 *OhA&B*
Cantwell, Robert Emmett 1908- *AmA&B, Au&Wr, ConAmA, ConAu 5R, ConNov 1972, ConNov 1976, OxAm, REnAL, TwCA, TwCA Sup, TwCW, WrD 1976*
Cantwell, Virginia *ChPo S2*
Canty, Cathal *WhWNAA*
Canty, Emma *BlkAW*
Canty, Michael *Alli Sup*
Cantzlaar, George LaFond 1906-1967 *ConAu P-1*
Cantzler, Otto A R 1876- *WhLA*
Canuck, Janey *CanWr, DcNAA, OxCan, WhWNAA*
Canusi, Jose *ConAu XR, SmATA XR, WrD 1976*
Canute 994?-1035 *NewC, REn*
Canvane, Peter *Alli*
Canz, Wilhelmine 1815-1901 *OxGer*
Canziani, Estell Louise Starr 1887- *ChPo S2*
Canziani, Estella L M 1887- *ChPo S1, IlCB 1945*
Canzoneri, Robert 1925- *AmA&B, ConAu 17R, DrAF 1976, DrAP 1975*
Caouette, Jean Baptiste 1864-1922 *DcNAA*
Caouette, Real *OxCan Sup*
Capa Y Espada, Comedias De *DcEuL*
Capadose, Lieutenant Colonel *Alli*
Capaldi, Nicholas 1939- *ConAu 21*
Capano, Frank 1899-1956 *AmSCAP 66*
Caparn, William Barton *Alli Sup*
Capdevila, Arturo 1889- *EncWL*
Cape, George A *Alli Sup*
Cape, Judith *CanNov, CanWr, ConAu XR, OxCan, WrD 1976*

Cape, Peter Irwin 1929- *WrD 1976*
Cape, Thomas *Alli Sup*
Cape, William H 1920- *ConAu 9R*
Capecelatro, Cardinal Alphonse 1824- *BbD, BiD&SB*
Capeele, Russell Beckett 1917- *WrD 1976*
Capefigue, Baptiste Honore Raymond 1802-1872 *BiD&SB*
Capek, Josef 1887-1945 *CasWL, ClDMEuL, CnThe, REnWD*
Capek, Karel 1890-1938 *CasWL, ClDMEuL, CnMD, CnThe, CyWA, EncWL, EvEuW, LongC, McGWD, ModSL 2, ModWD, Pen Eur, REn, REnWD, TwCA, TwCA Sup, TwCW, WhTwL*
Capek, Milic 1909- *ConAu 1R*
Capek, Thomas 1861- *WhWNAA*
Capek-Chod, Karel Matej 1860-1927 *CasWL, ClDMEuL, EvEuW, ModSL 2, Pen Eur*
Capel, Arthur d1638 *Alli*
Capel, Lord Arthur d1649 *Alli*
Capel, Charles C *Alli Sup*
Capel, Charlotte Eliza *Alli Sup*
Capel, Daniel d1679 *Alli*
Capel, Hyde A *Alli Sup*
Capel, Richard 1586-1656 *Alli*
Capel, Roger *ConAu XR*
Capel, Sharon *BlkAW*
Capel, Thomas John 1836- *Alli Sup, BbD*
Capelin, George *Alli*
Capell, Brooke A De *Alli*
Capell, E E *Alli Sup*
Capell, Edward 1713-1781 *Alli, OxEng*
Capellanus, Andreas *EuA*
Capelle, Russell B 1917- *ConAu 5R*
Capellen Tot DenPol, Joan Derk VanDer 1741-1784 *CasWL*
Capen, E H *Alli Sup*
Capen, Elmer Hewitt 1838-1905 *DcNAA*
Capen, Joseph d1725 *Alli*
Capen, Nahum 1804-1886 *Alli, Alli Sup, AmA, BiD&SB, DcAmA, DcNAA*
Capen, Oliver Bronson 1878-1953 *AmA&B*
Capen, Samuel Paul 1878- *WhWNAA*
Capern, David *Alli Sup*
Capern, Edward 1819-1894 *Alli Sup, BbD, BiD&SB, ChPo, ChPo S1, DcEnL, NewC*
Capern, Thomas *Alli Sup*
Capers, Ellison 1837-1907 *BiDSA*
Capers, Gerald Mortimer, Jr. 1909- *ConAu 5R*
Capers, Henry D 1830- *Alli Sup, BiDSA*
Capers, William 1790-1855 *BiDSA, DcAmA, DcNAA*
Capes, Bernard *BiD&SB, Chmbr 3*
Capes, Bernard Edward Joseph d1918 *ChPo S1*
Capes, John Moore 1813-1889 *Alli Sup*
Capes, M Harriet M *Alli Sup*
Capes, Molly *ChPo*
Capes, Mrs. Robert *CatA 1952*
Capes, William P 1881- *WhWNAA*
Capes, William Wolfe *Alli Sup*
Capetanakis, Demetrios 1912-1944 *CnMWL, Pen Eur*
Capgrave, John 1393-1464 *BrAu, CasWL, Chmbr 1, DcEnL, EvLB, NewC, OxEng*
Capgravius, John d1464 *Alli*
Capitan, William H 1933- *ConAu 29, WrD 1976*
Capitein, Jacobus Elisa Joannes 1717-1745? *AfA 1*
Capizzi, Michael 1941- *ConAu 41*
Caplan, Edwin H *ConAu 41*
Caplan, Gerald 1917- *Au&Wr, ConAu 25*
Caplan, Harry 1896- *AmA&B, ConAu 23*
Caplan, Lionel *ConAu 33*
Caplan, Ralph 1925- *ConAu 13R*
Caples, John 1900- *AmA&B, ConAu 23*
Capli, Erdogan 1926- *AmSCAP 66*
Caplin, Alfred Gerald 1909- *ConAu 57*
Caplin, Roxey A *Alli Sup*
Caplovitz, David 1928- *ConAu 41*
Caplow, Theodore 1920- *AmA&B, ConAu 1R*
Cap'n Bill *WhWNAA*
Capon, Anthony 1926- *Au&Wr*
Capon, Paul 1912- *ConAu 5R*
Capon, Peter *ConAu XR*
Capon, William Albert 1860-1947 *DcNAA*

Caponigri, A Robert 1915- *Au&Wr, ConAu 37*
Caporale, Rocco 1927- *ConAu 37*
Caporali, Cesare 1531-1601 *CasWL*
Capote, Truman 1924- *AmA&B, AmNov, AmSCAP 66, Au&Wr, CasWL, CnDAL, CnMD, ConAu 5R, ConDr, ConLC 1, ConLC 3, ConNov 1972, ConNov 1976, DrAF 1976, EncWL, LongC, ModAL, ModAL Sup, ModWD, OxAm, Pen Am, RAdv 1, REn, REnAL, TwCA Sup, TwCW, WebEAL, WhTwL, WrD 1976*
Capouya, Emile *AmA&B*
Capp, Al 1909- *AmA&B, ConAu 57, REnAL*
Capp, Glenn Richard 1910- *ConAu 1R*
Capp, Mary Elizabeth *Alli, BiDLA*
Cappe, Catherine *Alli, BiDLA, BiDLA Sup*
Cappe, Newcome 1732-1800 *Alli*
Cappelli, Amy Spencer 1904- *AmSCAP 66*
Cappelluti, Frank Joseph 1935-1972 *ConAu 37*
Capper, Arthur 1865-1951 *AmA&B, WhWNAA*
Capper, Benjamin P *Alli, BiDLA*
Capper, Cecil *MnBBF*
Capper, Charles *Alli Sup*
Capper, Douglas Parode *ConAu 9R*
Capper, E N *Alli Sup*
Capper, Edmund *Alli Sup*
Capper, Henry *Alli Sup*
Capper, James *Alli, BiDLA*
Capper, Jasper *Alli Sup*
Capper, John *Alli Sup*
Capper, John Brainerd 1855- *WhLA*
Capper, Louisa *Alli, BiDLA*
Capper, Richard *Alli Sup*
Capper, Samuel James *Alli Sup*
Cappie, James *Alli Sup*
Cappleman, Josie Frazee *BiDSA*
Cappon, Alexander P 1900- *AmA&B*
Cappon, Daniel 1921- *ConAu 17R, WrD 1976*
Cappon, James 1854-1939 *Alli Sup, CanWr, DcLEnL, DcNAA, OxCan*
Cappon, Lester Jesse 1900- *AmA&B*
Capponi, Gino 1350?-1421 *CasWL, DcEuL*
Capponi, Gino, Marchese 1792-1876 *BiD&SB, CasWL, EuA*
Capps, Benjamin 1922- *ConAu 5R, SmATA 9, WrD 1976*
Capps, Clifford Lucille Sheats 1902- *ConAu 37*
Capps, Donald E 1939- *ConAu 29*
Capps, Edward 1866-1950 *AmA&B, DcAmA, WhWNAA*
Capps, Jack Lee 1926- *ConAu 23*
Capps, Joseph Almarin 1872- *WhWNAA*
Capps, Stephen Reid 1881-1949 *DcNAA, WhWNAA*
Capps, Walter Holden 1934- *ConAu 29*
Capra, Frank 1897- *ConAu 61, REnAL*
Capretta, Patrick J 1929- *ConAu 21*
Caprivi DeCaprera DeMontecuccoli, G L 1831-1899 *OxGer*
Capron, Carrie *Alli Sup*
Capron, E W *Alli Sup*
Capron, Elisha S 1806- *Alli*
Capron, Frederick Hugh 1857- *WhLA*
Capron, J Rand *Alli Sup*
Capron, Jean F 1924- *ConAu 21*
Capron, Louis 1891- *ConAu P-1*
Capron, Louis B *ChPo*
Capron, Mary J *Alli Sup*
Capron, Walter Clark 1904- *ConAu P-1*
Capron, William M 1920- *ConAu 29*
Capsadell, Louisa *DcNAA*
Capsadell, Louise *Alli Sup*
Capstaff, J S *Alli Sup*
Captain, The *MnBBF*
Captain Jack 1847-1917 *AmA*
Capuana, Luigi 1839-1915 *BbD, BiD&SB, CasWL, ClDMEuL, EuA, EvEuW, McGWD, Pen Eur, REn*
Capus, Alfred 1858-1922 *ClDMEuL, CnMD, EvEuW, McGWD, ModWD, OxFr*
Caputi, Anthony 1924- *ConAu 1R, WrD 1976*
Carabas, Marquis De *OxFr*
Carabetta, Frank 1944- *AmSCAP 66*
Carabine, Dennis *ChPo S2*
Caracalla 188-217 *REn*
Caractacus 030?- *NewC*

Caradoc Of Lancarvan d1154? *Alli, BiB N*
Caradog d1154? *Alli, NewC*
Caradon, Lord *ConAu XR*
Caragiale, Ion Luca 1852-1912 *CasWL, ClDMEuL, CnMD, EncWL, EuA, EvEuW, McGWD, Pen Eur*
Caragiale, Mateiu 1885-1936 *CasWL*
Caraher, Hugh *Alli Sup*
Caraman, Philip 1911- *Au&Wr, ConAu 9R*
Caran D'Ache 1858-1909 *NewC, OxFr*
Caranda, Michael J 1918- *AmSCAP 66*
Carano, Paul 1919- *ConAu 17R*
Caras, Roger A 1928- *AmA&B, ConAu 1R, WrD 1976*
Carasso, Katharine Valentine 1923- *ChPo*
Caratacus 030?- *NewC*
Caravaggio, Michelangelo Merisi Da 1569?-1609? *AtlBL, REn*
Caravan, Candie *ConAu XR*
Carawan, Carolanne M 1939- *ConAu 17R*
Carawan, Guy H, Jr. 1927- *ConAu 17R*
Carayon, Auguste 1813-1874 *BiD&SB, OxCan*
Carayon, P Auguste *BbtC*
Carazo, Castro 1895- *AmSCAP 66*
Carb, David *TexWr*
Carballido, Emilio 1925- *ConAu 33, CrCD, DcCLA*
Carballo, Emmanuel 1929- *DcCLA*
Carberry, Ethna *ChPo S1*
Carberry, H D 1921- *ConP 1970*
Carbery, Thomas F 1925- *ConAu 29*
Carbonara, Gerard 1886-1959 *AmSCAP 66*
Carbonaro *NewC*
Carbonell, Reyes 1917- *ConAu 9R*
Carboni, Erberto 1899- *WhGrA*
Carboni, Paolo 1912- *Au&Wr*
Carbonnier, Jeanne *ConAu 33, SmATA 3*
Carbotte, Gabrielle *CanWr*
Carbotte, Mrs. Marcel *CatA 1952*
Carboy, John *Alli Sup*
Carby, Dan *WrD 1976*
Carcano, Giulio 1812-1884 *BbD, BiD&SB, CasWL, ChPo, DcBiA*
Carcano, Giulio 1812-1882 *EvEuW*
Carcinus *CasWL*
Carco, Francis 1886-1958 *CasWL, ClDMEuL, EncWL, EvEuW, LongC, OxFr, Pen Eur, REn, TwCA, TwCA Sup*
Carcopino, Jerome 1881- *OxFr*
Carcopino-Tussoli, Francois Marie *LongC*
Card, Fred Wallace 1863- *WhWNAA*
Card, Henry 1779- *Alli, BiDLA, BiDLA Sup*
Card, Leslie Ellsworth 1893- *WhWNAA*
Card, Raymond 1893- *OxCan, WhWNAA*
Card, Virginia 1918- *AmSCAP 66*
Card, W *BiDLA*
Card, William *Alli*
Cardale, Edward Thomas *Alli Sup*
Cardale, George *Alli*
Cardale, John Bate 1802-1877 *Alli Sup*
Cardale, Paul *Alli*
Cardale, R *Alli*
Cardall, William *Alli Sup*
Cardano, Girolamo 1501-1576 *REn*
Cardarelli, Vincenzo 1887-1959 *CasWL, ClDMEuL, EncWL, EvEuW, Pen Eur*
Cardell, John *Alli*
Cardell, William S d1828 *Alli, ChPo S1*
Cardelle, Cora *Alli Sup*
Carden, A *Alli Sup*
Carden, J *Alli*
Carden, Karen W 1946- *ConAu 49*
Carden, Maren Lockwood *ConAu 53*
Carden, Patricia 1935- *ConAu 41*
Carden, Priscilla *AuBYP*
Carden, R A *BbtC*
Cardena, Clement 1914- *Au&Wr*
Cardenal, Ernesto 1925- *CasWL, ConAu 49, DcCLA, Pen Am, WhTwL*
Cardenas, A De *BiDSA*
Cardenas, Daniel N 1917- *ConAu 45*
Cardenas Y Rodriguez, Jose M De 1812-1882 *BbD, BiD&SB*
Cardenas Y Rodriguez, Nicolas De 1814-1868 *BiD&SB*
Carder, Leigh *AmA&B*
Cardew, Cornelius *Alli, BiDLA*
Cardew, Michael 1901- *ConAu 49*

Cardiff, Gladys H *DrAP 1975*
Cardigan, Earl Of *Alli Sup*
Cardijn, Joseph 1882- *BkC 5*
Cardinal, Harold *OxCan Sup*
Cardinal, J C *OxCan Sup*
Cardinal, John C *MnBBF*
Cardinal, Roger 1940- *ConAu 45*
Cardinal Wolsey *NewC*
Cardini, George 1913- *AmSCAP 66*
Cardon, Guy *MnBBF*
Cardona-Hine, Alvaro 1926- *ConAu 9R,*
  DrAP 1975
Cardona Torrico, Alcira 1926- *DcCLA*
Cardone, Samuel S 1938- *ConAu 17R*
Cardoni, Frank 1940- *AmSCAP 66*
Cardoni, Mary 1938- *AmSCAP 66*
Cardonnel, Adam De *Alli*
Cardoso, Antonio 1933- *AfA 1*
Cardoso, Pedro Monteiro 1890?-1942 *AfA 1*
Cardoza Y Aragon, Luis 1904- *DcCLA,*
  Pen Am
Cardozo, Benjamin Nathan 1870-1938 *AmA&B,*
  DcLEnL, DcNAA, OxAm, REn, REnAL,
  WhWNAA
Cardozo, Isaac N 1784-1850 *BiDSA*
Cardozo, J N *BiDSA*
Cardozo, Jacob Newton 1786-1873 *DcNAA*
Cardozo, Lois *AuBYP*
Cardozo, Lois S 1934- *ConAu 1R*
Cardozo, Michael H 1910- *ConAu 33*
Cardozo, Peter 1916- *ConAu 61*
Carducci, Giosue 1835-1907 *AtlBL, BbD,*
  BiD&SB, CasWL, ClDMEuL, CyWA,
  DcEuL, EuA, EvEuW, LongC, NewC,
  OxEng, Pen Eur, RCom, REn, WhTwL
Cardui, Van *ConAu XR*
Cardus, Sir Neville 1889-1975 *Au&Wr,*
  ConAu 57, ConAu 61, DcLEnL, LongC
Cardwell, Edward *Alli*
Cardwell, Francis *Alli Sup*
Cardwell, Guy Adams 1905- *AmA&B,*
  ChPo S2, ConAu 13R
Care, George *Alli*
Care, Henry *Alli*
Care, Norman S 1937- *ConAu 25*
Carel, John *Alli*
Carel DeSainte-Garde, Jacques *OxFr*
Careles, John *Alli*
Careless, Franck *Alli*
Careless, J M S 1919- *OxCan, OxCan Sup*
Careless, John *Alli, ChPo S2*
Careless, Thomas *Alli*
Carelesse, John *Alli*
Carell, Paul *Au&Wr*
Carellis, Edward *Alli Sup*
Careme *OxFr*
Careme, Marie-Antoine 1784-1833 *OxFr*
Careme, Maurice 1899- *CasWL*
Carens, James Francis 1927- *ConAu 61*
Carens, Thomas Henry 1893-1960 *AmA&B*
Cares, Paul B 1911- *ConAu 9R*
Carette, Louis *McGWD, WorAu*
Carette, Louis-Albert 1913- *Au&Wr*
Carew, Abel *Alli*
Carew, Sir Alexander *Alli*
Carew, Bamfylde Moore 1693-1770? *NewC*
Carew, Burleigh *MnBBF*
Carew, Conway *MnBBF*
Carew, Dorothy 1910?-1973 *ConAu 41*
Carew, Lady Elizabeth *Alli, ChPo, DcEnL*
Carew, George *Alli, Alli Sup*
Carew, Sir George *Alli*
Carew, Harold David 1890-1943 *AmA&B,*
  WhWNAA
Carew, Jack *MnBBF*
Carew, Jan Rynveld Alwin 1925- *CasWL,*
  ConNov 1972, ConNov 1976, WrD 1976
Carew, John Mohun 1921- *Au&Wr,*
  ConAu 13R
Carew, Laura A S *Alli Sup*
Carew, Rachel *Alli Sup*
Carew, Richard *Alli, Chmbr 1*
Carew, Richard 1555-1620 *Alli, BrAu,*
  CasWL, EvLB, NewC
Carew, Rivers Vervain 1935- *ConP 1970*
Carew, Sidney *MnBBF*
Carew, Singleton *MnBBF*
Carew, Thomas *Alli*

Carew, Thomas 1595?-1639 *Alli, AtlBL, BbD,*
  BiD&SB, BrAu, CasWL, ChPo,
  Chmbr 1, CnE&AP, CrE&SL, CriT 1,
  DcEnA Ap, DcEnL, DcEuL, DcLEnL,
  EvLB, MouLC 1, NewC, OxEng,
  Pen Eng, REn, WebEAL
Carew, Tim *ConAu XR*
Carew-Slater, Harold James 1909- *Au&Wr,*
  WrD 1976
Carey, PoIre
Carey, Lieutenant-Colonel *Alli Sup*
Carey, Aimee *Alli Sup*
Carey, Albert *Alli Sup*
Carey, Mrs. Albert *Alli Sup*
Carey, Alice 1820- *Alli, DcEnL, FemPA*
Carey, Angeline Parmenter 1854-1934
  IndAu 1816
Carey, Annie *Alli Sup*
Carey, Arthur Astor 1857- *AmLY*
Carey, Bill 1916- *AmSCAP 66*
Carey, Cartelet Priaulx *Alli Sup*
Carey, Charles *OhA&B*
Carey, Charles Henry 1857-1941 *Alli Sup,*
  DcNAA, OhA&B, WhWNAA
Carey, Charles M *ChPo S2*
Carey, Charles Stokes *Alli Sup*
Carey, Daniel *Alli Sup, BbtC*
Carey, David *Alli, BiDLA*
Carey, David 1782-1824 *ChPo*
Carey, David 1926- *AmSCAP 66*
Carey, Eben James 1889-1947 *DcNAA,*
  WhWNAA
Carey, Edward *Alli*
Carey, Edward L *ChPo S1*
Carey, Lady Elizabeth *Chmbr 1*
Carey, Elizabeth Sheridan *PoIre*
Carey, Emily J *Alli Sup*
Carey, Ernestine Gilbreth 1908- *Au&Wr,*
  ConAu 5R, SmATA 2, WrD 1976
Carey, Esther *Alli Sup*
Carey, Gary 1938- *ConAu 57*
Carey, George *Alli, BiDLA Sup*
Carey, George Saville 1743-1807 *Alli, DcEnL,*
  NewC
Carey, Harriet Mary *Alli Sup, ChPo*
Carey, Harry Wardwell 1875-1935 *DcNAA*
Carey, Henry *Alli, Alli Sup, Chmbr 2*
Carey, Henry 1596-1661 *Alli, DcEnL*
Carey, Henry 1687?-1743 *Alli, BiD&SB,*
  BrAu, CasWL, ChPo, ChPo S1, DcEnL,
  DcLEnL, EvLB, NewC, OxEng, Pen Eng,
  REn
Carey, Henry Charles 1793-1879 *Alli, Alli Sup,*
  AmA, AmA&B, BbD, BiD&SB,
  Chmbr 3, CyAL 1, DcAmA, DcEnL,
  DcNAA, OxAm, REnAL
Carey, Henry Lucius d1663 *DcEnL*
Carey, James *WrD 1976*
Carey, James, Jr. And Carey, Francis K
  Alli Sup
Carey, James Charles 1915- *ConAu 13R*
Carey, James P *Alli Sup*
Carey, Jane Perry Clark *AmA&B*
Carey, John *Alli, BiDLA*
Carey, John d1829 *Alli*
Carey, John 1934- *ConAu 57*
Carey, John Howard *Alli Sup*
Carey, Josie 1930- *AmSCAP 66*
Carey, Mrs. M *Alli Sup*
Carey, M L M *Alli Sup*
Carey, M R *Alli Sup*
Carey, Mother Marie Aimee 1931- *ConAu 13R*
Carey, Mary Josephine 1903-1947 *IndAu 1917*
Carey, Mathew 1760-1839 *Alli, AmA,*
  BiD&SB, CyAL 1, DcLEnL, OxAm,
  PoIre, REn, REnAL
Carey, Matthew 1760-1839 *AmA&B, BbD,*
  DcAmA, DcEnL, DcNAA
Carey, Michael *ConAu XR*
Carey, Omer L 1929- *ConAu 23*
Carey, Patrick 1623-1657 *Alli, CasWL, ChPo*
Carey, Peter *PoIre*
Carey, Sir Peter Stafford 1803-1886 *Alli Sup*
Carey, Phoebe 1825- *Alli, FemPA*
Carey, Richard John 1925- *ConAu 53*
Carey, Robert, Earl Of Monmouth 1560?-1639
  Alli, Chmbr 1, CrE&SL
Carey, Rosa Nouchette 1840-1909 *Alli Sup,*

  BbD, ChPo S1, LongC, NewC
Carey, Miss Sheridan *ChPo*
Carey, Thomas Joseph 1853- *DcNAA*
Carey, W *BiDLA*
Carey, W H *Alli Sup*
Carey, W R *ChPo*
Carey, Walter *Alli, Alli Sup*
Carey, Will Gage 1877- *BiDSA*
Carey, William *Alli, BiDLA*
Carey, William 1761-1834 *Alli*
Carey, William P 1768?-1839 *Alli, PoIre*
Carey-Hobson *Alli Sup*
Carey-Jones, N S 1911- *ConAu 21*
Carfagne, Cyril *ConAu XR*
Carfagno, Vincent R 1935- *ConAu 41*
Carfax, Catherine 1928- *ConAu XR,*
  WrD 1976
Carfrae, Eileen *ChPo S1, ChPo S2*
Cargas, Harry J 1932- *ConAu 13R*
Cargill, A B 1877- *WhWNAA*
Cargill, Alexander *Alli Sup*
Cargill, John *Alli Sup*
Cargill, Oscar 1898-1972 *AmA&B, ConAu 1R,*
  ConAu 33, REnAL
Cargill, Robert L 1929- *ConAu 25*
Cargill, Thomas *Alli Sup*
Cargo, David N 1932- *ConAu 57*
Cargoe, Richard *AmA&B, ConAu XR*
Carhart, Arthur Hawthorne 1892- *AmA&B,*
  ConAu P-1, WhWNAA
Carhart, Daniel 1839-1926 *Alli Sup, DcNAA*
Carhart, Edith Beebe *IndAu 1917*
Carhart, Ellen Soule *ChPo, ChPo S2*
Carhart, George S *ChPo*
Carhart, Henry Smith 1844-1920 *DcAmA,*
  DcNAA
Carhart, John Wesley *Alli Sup*
Carhart, Margaret Sprague 1877- *ChPo*
Caribe, El *PueRA*
Caridi, Ronald J 1941- *ConAu 25*
Carie, Walter *Alli*
Carier, Benjamin *Alli*
Carigiet, Alois 1902- *IlBYP, IlCB 1956,*
  IlCB 1966, ThBJA, WhGrA
Carignan, Oliver *OxCan*
Carin, Arthur A 1928- *ConAu 29*
Carin, Victor 1933- *Au&Wr*
Carington, W Whately 1884-1947 *BiDPar*
Carini, Edward 1923- *ConAu 61, SmATA 9*
Carins, Dixon *MnBBF*
Carion, John *Alli*
Caritat, Hocquet 1797?-1807? *AmA&B*
Caritat, Marie Jean Antoine Nicolas *NewC*
Cariteo, Benedicto Gareth 1450?-1514 *REn*
Cariteo, Gareth Benedetto 1450?-1514 *CasWL*
Cariveau, Robert Edward *WhWNAA*
Carkeet, Samuel *Alli*
Carkesse, Charles *Alli*
Carkesse, James *Alli*
Carl, Beverly May 1932- *ConAu 53*
Carl, Karl 1789-1854 *OxGer*
Carlander, Kenneth Dixon 1915- *IndAu 1917*
Carle, Eric 1929- *ChPo S2, ConAu 25,*
  IlBYP, SmATA 4
Carle, Frankie 1903- *AmSCAP 66*
Carle, Richard *AmA&B*
Carlell, Lodowick 1602-1675 *Alli, BrAu,*
  NewC
Carlen, Emilia Flygare 1807-1892 *BbD,*
  BiD&SB
Carlen, Emilie Flygare 1807-1892 *CasWL, EuA,*
  HsB&A
Carlen, Rosa 1836-1883 *BiD&SB*
Carles, William Richard 1848- *Alli Sup,*
  WhLA
Carleson, Rolf Alfred Douglas 1910- *BiDPar*
Carless, L M *Alli Sup*
Carleton *Alli, AmA&B, DcNAA*
Carleton 1823-1896 *AmA*
Carleton, Captain *Alli*
Carleton, Mrs. *Alli Sup*
Carleton, Ada *ChPo*
Carleton, Barbee Oliver 1917- *ConAu 23*
Carleton, Bukk G 1856-1914 *DcNAA*
Carleton, Captain Latham C *HsB&A,*
  YABC 1
Carleton, Cousin May *DcNAA, HsB&A,*
  OxCan

Carleton, Sir Dudley 1573-1631 *Alli*
Carleton, Fannie E *Alli Sup*
Carleton, George *Alli*
Carleton, George d1628 *Alli*
Carleton, George W *Alli Sup, EarAB, EarAB Sup*
Carleton, George Washington 1822-1902 *DcNAA*
Carleton, Gerald 1844- *PoIre*
Carleton, Baron Guy Dorchester 1724-1808 *OxCan*
Carleton, Henry 1785-1863 *Alli Sup, AmA, BiDSA, DcNAA*
Carleton, Henry Guy 1856-1910 *AmA, AmA&B, BbD, BiD&SB, BiDSA, DcAmA, DcNAA, OxAm, REnAL*
Carleton, Hiram *Alli Sup*
Carleton, Hugh *Alli Sup*
Carleton, James George *Alli Sup*
Carleton, James Henry 1814-1873 *DcNAA*
Carleton, John William 1800?- *Alli Sup, Br&AmS*
Carleton, Lancelot *Alli*
Carleton, Mark Thomas 1935- *ConAu 33, WrD 1976*
Carleton, Mary 1642?-1673 *NewC*
Carleton, Monroe Guy 1833-1918 *DcNAA*
Carleton, Osgood 1742-1816 *DcAmA, DcNAA*
Carleton, Robert Louis 1896-1956 *AmSCAP 66*
Carleton, T W *ChPo*
Carleton, Thomas *OxCan*
Carleton, Thomas Compton *Alli*
Carleton, W *Alli Sup*
Carleton, Will 1845-1912 *Alli Sup, AmA, AmA&B, BbD, BiD&SB, ChPo, ChPo S1, ChPo S2, CyAL 2, DcNAA, EvLB, OxAm, REnAL*
Carleton, William *Alli, AmA&B, Chmbr 3, WhWNAA*
Carleton, William 1794-1869 *Alli, Alli Sup, BbD, BiD&SB, BrAu 19, CasWL, CyWA, DcBiA, DcEnA, DcEnA Ap, DcEnL, DcLEnL, EvLB, HsB&A, NewC, OxEng, PoIre*
Carleton, William 1829-1897 *PoIre*
Carleton, William 1845-1912 *DcAmA, DcLEnL*
Carleton, William C 1827-1885 *PoIre*
Carleton, William Graves 1903?- *ConAu 25, IndAu 1917, WrD 1976*
Carletti, Ercole 1877-1946 *CasWL*
Carletti, J T *Alli Sup*
Carley, Karleen *AmSCAP 66*
Carley, Kenneth A *MnnWr*
Carley, Royal V 1906- *WrD 1976*
Carley, V Royal 1906- *ConAu 29*
Carli, Angelo 1937- *ConAu 49*
Carliell, Robert d1622? *Alli, OxEng*
Carlier, A G *Alli Sup*
Carlier, Anthony W *Alli Sup*
Carlile, Alexander 1788-1860 *Alli Sup, ChPo*
Carlile, Bess Howell 1890?-1969 *IndAu 1917*
Carlile, Christopher *Alli*
Carlile, Clark S 1912- *ConAu 41*
Carlile, Henry *ConAu 33, DrAP 1975*
Carlile, James *Alli, Alli Sup*
Carlile, John Charles *WhLA*
Carlile, Richard 1790-1843 *BrAu 19, NewC*
Carlile, Warrand *Alli Sup*
Carlile, William O And Martindale, B H *Alli Sup*
Carlin X *BlkAW*
Carlin, Francis 1881-1945 *AmA&B, CatA 1947, ChPo, ChPo S1, DcNAA*
Carlin, Gabriel S 1921- *ConAu 1R*
Carlin, Michel *Alli Sup*
Carlin, Thomas W 1918- *ConAu 25*
Carling, Foster G 1898- *AmSCAP 66*
Carling, Francis 1945- *ConAu 25*
Carlingford, Lord *Alli Sup*
Carlino, Lewis John 1932- *ConDr, WrD 1976*
Carlinsky, Dan 1944- *ConAu 21*
Carlisle, Bishop Of *BiDLA*
Carlisle, Earl Of *Alli Sup*
Carlisle, Earl Of 1748- *BiDLA*
Carlisle, Earl Of 1802-1864 *ChPo S1*
Carlisle, Mrs. *Alli Sup*
Carlisle, Sir Anthony 1768-1840 *Alli, BiDLA*

Carlisle, Arthur Drummond *Alli Sup*
Carlisle, Carol Jones 1919- *ConAu 29*
Carlisle, Charles Howard d1738 *Alli*
Carlisle, Christopher *Alli*
Carlisle, Clark *ConAu XR*
Carlisle, Clark, Jr. *SmATA 3*
Carlisle, D *Alli*
Carlisle, Douglas H 1921- *ConAu 45*
Carlisle, E Fred 1935- *ConAu 53*
Carlisle, Frederick Howard, Earl Of 1748-1825 *Alli, BrAu*
Carlisle, Frederick Howard, Earl Of 1748-1826 *DcEnL*
Carlisle, Frederick Howard, Earl Of 1748-1825 *OxEng*
Carlisle, George *Alli*
Carlisle, George James Howard, Earl 1843-1911 *ChPo*
Carlisle, George William Frederick H 1802- *Alli*
Carlisle, Helen Grace 1898- *AmA&B, ConAmA, WhWNAA*
Carlisle, Henry 1926- *ConAu 13R, DrAF 1976*
Carlisle, Henry E *Alli Sup*
Carlisle, Irene Jones *TexWr*
Carlisle, Isabella Byron, Countess Of 1721-1795 *Alli*
Carlisle, Countess Isabella Howard 1721-1795 *ChPo*
Carlisle, James *Alli*
Carlisle, James, Jr. *Alli*
Carlisle, James Henry 1825-1909 *BiDSA*
Carlisle, John Griffin 1835- *BiDSA*
Carlisle, Laura Mae *ChPo*
Carlisle, Lilian Baker 1912- *ConAu 53*
Carlisle, Nicholas *Alli, BiDLA*
Carlisle, Olga Andreyev 1930- *ConAu 13R*
Carlisle, R H 1865- *Br&AmS*
Carlisle, Rodney P 1936- *ConAu 45*
Carlisle, Thomas *Alli Sup*
Carlisle, Thomas 1944- *ConAu 53*
Carlisle, Thomas John *ChPo*
Carlisle, Walter Ewing 1877-1956 *OhA&B*
Carll, Lewis Buffett *Alli Sup*
Carll, M M *Alli Sup*
Carlo, Monte 1883- *AmSCAP 66*
Carlock, John R 1921- *ConAu 33*
Carloman 751-771 *OxFr*
Carloman 865-884 *OxFr*
Carlon, Patricia Bernardette *ConAu 13R*
Carloni, Giancarlo *IlBYP, IlCB 1966*
Carlos, Don 1545-1568 *NewC, REn*
Carlos, Edward Stafford *Alli Sup*
Carlos, Faya 1905- *TexWr*
Carlos, James *Alli*
Carlota 1840-1927 *REn*
Carlova, Vasile 1809-1831 *CasWL*
Carlquist, Sherwin 1930- *ConAu 13R*
Carls, Norman 1907- *ConAu 17*
Carlsen, G Robert 1917- *ConAu 17R, WrD 1976*
Carlsen, James C 1927- *ConAu 25*
Carlsen, Ruth Christoffer 1918- *ConAu 17R, SmATA 2, WrD 1976*
Carlson, Al *IlBYP*
Carlson, Andrew R 1934- *ConAu 29, WrD 1976*
Carlson, Anton Julius 1875- *WhWNAA*
Carlson, Arthur E 1923- *ConAu 37*
Carlson, Bernice Wells 1910- *AuBYP, ConAu 5R, SmATA 8, WrD 1976*
Carlson, Betty 1919- *ConAu 1R*
Carlson, Carl Walter 1907- *ConAu 49*
Carlson, Dale Bick 1935- *ConAu 9R, SmATA 1*
Carlson, E Leslie 1893- *AmA&B*
Carlson, Edgar Magnus 1908- *AmA&B*
Carlson, Elof Axel 1931- *ConAu 45*
Carlson, Eric W 1910- *ConAu 25*
Carlson, Esther Elisabeth 1920- *AuBYP, ConAu 5R*
Carlson, Evans Fordyce 1896-1947 *DcNAA*
Carlson, Fredrik Ferdinand 1811-1887 *BiD&SB*
Carlson, George *ChPo S2*
Carlson, Harry A 1904- *AmSCAP 66*
Carlson, John A 1933- *ConAu 29*
Carlson, John Roy *AmA&B, TwCA Sup*
Carlson, Kenneth S 1904- *Au&Wr*

Carlson, Leland Henry 1908- *AmA&B, ConAu 17R*
Carlson, Lewis H 1934- *ConAu 41*
Carlson, Loraine 1923- *ConAu 37, WrD 1976*
Carlson, Marvin 1935- *ConAu 23*
Carlson, Natalie Savage 1906- *AmA&B, AnCL, Au&Wr, AuBYP, AuICB, ConAu 1R, MorBMP, MorJA, REnAL, SmATA 2, WrD 1976*
Carlson, Oliver 1899- *WhWNAA*
Carlson, Reynold Edgar 1901- *ConAu 1R*
Carlson, Richard Stocks 1942- *ConAu 57*
Carlson, Robert E 1922- *ConAu 41*
Carlson, Ronald L 1934- *ConAu 33, WrD 1976*
Carlson, Roy L 1930- *ConAu 41*
Carlson, Ruth Kearney 1911- *ConAu 29, WrD 1976*
Carlson, Stan W *MnnWr*
Carlson, Theodore L 1905- *ConAu 45*
Carlson, Vada F 1897- *ConAu 23*
Carlson, William Hugh 1898- *ConAu 23, WhPNW*
Carlson, William S 1905- *ConAu 1R*
Carlston, Kenneth S 1904- *ConAu 5R*
Carlton, Alva *ConAu XR*
Carlton, Carrie *Alli Sup*
Carlton, Charles 1941- *ConAu 53*
Carlton, Charles Merritt 1928- *ConAu 45*
Carlton, David 1938- *Au&Wr, WrD 1976*
Carlton, Effie Canning *ChPo*
Carlton, Frank Tracy 1873- *OhA&B, WhWNAA*
Carlton, Gerald *HsB&A*
Carlton, Grace 1878- *Au&Wr*
Carlton, Henry F 1893?-1973 *ConAu 41*
Carlton, Lessie 1903- *ConAu 49*
Carlton, Lewis 1886- *MnBBF*
Carlton, Lillian E *ChPo S1*
Carlton, Osgood d1816 *Alli*
Carlton, Robert *AmA&B, DcNAA*
Carlton, Robert G 1927- *ConAu 17R*
Carlton, S P And Moore, W D *Alli Sup*
Carlton, William Newnham Chattin 1873-1943 *AmA&B, DcNAA*
Carlu, Jean Georges Leon 1900- *WhGrA*
Carlyle, Aileen *AmSCAP 66*
Carlyle, Alexander 1722-1805 *Alli, Chmbr 2, EvLB, NewC, OxEng, Pen Eng*
Carlyle, Alexander James 1861- *WhLA*
Carlyle, Benjamin F And Haynes, William *Alli Sup*
Carlyle, Emily Ruth Bull 1893- *WhWNAA*
Carlyle, Gavin *Alli Sup*
Carlyle, J E *Alli Sup*
Carlyle, Jane Baillie 1801-1866 *Alli Sup, NewC*
Carlyle, Jane Welsh 1801-1866 *BiD&SB*
Carlyle, John *Chmbr 3*
Carlyle, John Aitken 1801-1877 *Alli Sup, ChPo*
Carlyle, Joseph Dacre 1759?-1804 *Alli, PoCh*
Carlyle, Robert *Alli*
Carlyle, Rosa *ChPo S1*
Carlyle, Russ 1914- *AmSCAP 66*
Carlyle, Thomas *Alli, Chmbr 3*
Carlyle, Thomas 1795-1881 *Alli, Alli Sup, AtIBL, BbD, BiD&SB, BrAu 19, CasWL, ChPo, ChPo S1, ChPo S2, CriT 3, CyWA, DcEnA, DcEnL, DcEuL, DcLEnL, EvLB, FamAYP, MouLC 3, NewC, OxEng, Pen Eng, RAdv 1, RCom, REn, WebEAL*
Carlyle, Thomas 1803-1855 *Alli Sup*
Carlyon, Clement 1777-1864 *Alli Sup*
Carlyon, Edward Augustus 1823-1874 *Alli Sup*
Carlyon, Ellen *Alli Sup*
Carlyon, Philip 1811- *Alli Sup*
Carm Mac *ConAu XR*
Carmack, Edward Ward 1858-1908 *BiDSA, DcNAA*
Carmack, George Washington *OxCan*
Carmack, Robert M 1934- *ConAu 45*
Carmalt, William H *Alli Sup*
Carman, Albert Richardson 1865-1939 *DcNAA*
Carman, Bliss 1861-1929 *BbD, BiD&SB, CanWr, ChPo S2, CnDAL, ConAmL, DcAmA, DcEnA Ap, DcLEnL, DcNAA, LongC, OxAm, OxCan, OxEng, Pen Am,*

Pen Eng, REn, REnAL, TwCA,
TwCA Sup, WebEAL, WhWNAA
Carman, Dorothy Walworth 1900- *WhWNAA*
Carman, Dulce *ConAu XR*
Carman, Harry James 1884-1964 *AmA&B*
Carman, J Ernest 1882- *WhWNAA*
Carman, J Neale 1897-1972 *ConAu P-1*
Carman, John Walmsley 1834- *BbtC*
Carman, Robert A 1931- *ConAu 57*
Carman, W C *Alli Sup*
Carman, William Bliss 1861-1929 *CasWL,
ChPo, ChPo S1, Chmbr 3, EvLB*
Carman, William Young 1909- *Au&Wr,
ConAu 13R, WrD 1976*
Carmarthen, Marquis Of *Alli*
Carmen Sylva 1843-1916 *BiD&SB, DcEuL,
EuA, EvEuW, LongC, OxGer*
Carmen, Felix 1860-1916 *AmA, OxAm*
Carmen, Sister Joann 1941- *ConAu 21*
Carmer, Carl Lamson 1893- *AmA&B,
Au&Wr, AuBYP, ChPo, ChPo S1,
ChPo S2, ConAu 5R, OxAm, REn,
REnAL, St&VC, TwCA, TwCA Sup*
Carmer, Elizabeth Black 1904- *AuBYP,
IlCB 1956*
Carmey *Alli*
Carmi, T *ConAu XR*
Carmichael, A N *Alli*
Carmichael, Alexander 1832-1912 *Alli, ChPo*
Carmichael, Alfred *OxCan*
Carmichael, Andrew *Alli*
Carmichael, Andrew Blair 1780-1854? *PoIre*
Carmichael, Ann *ConAu XR*
Carmichael, Calum M 1938- *ConAu 53*
Carmichael, D R 1941- *ConAu 33*
Carmichael, Daniel 1826- *ChPo S1*
Carmichael, David Freemantle *Alli Sup*
Carmichael, Fred Walker 1924- *ConAu 17R,
WrD 1976*
Carmichael, Frederick 1708-1751 *Alli*
Carmichael, Frederick Falkiner *Alli Sup*
Carmichael, Harry *ConAu XR, WrD 1976*
Carmichael, Hartley James *Alli Sup*
Carmichael, Hoagland Howard 1899-
IndAu 1917
Carmichael, Hoagy 1899- *AmSCAP 66*
Carmichael, James *Alli, BiDLA*
Carmichael, James Wilson 1800-1868 *Alli Sup*
Carmichael, Jennings *ChPo*
Carmichael, Joel 1915- *ConAu 1R*
Carmichael, John *ChPo*
Carmichael, Leonard 1898-1973 *ConAu 41,
ConAu 45*
Carmichael, Marie *WhLA*
Carmichael, Mary D I *Alli Sup, ChPo S1*
Carmichael, Montgomery 1857-1936 *CatA 1947*
Carmichael, Norma Alexina 1888- *WhWNAA*
Carmichael, Oliver Cromwell 1891-1966
ConAu P-1, WhWNAA
Carmichael, Peter *Alli Sup, ChPo*
Carmichael, Peter A 1897- *ConAu 17*
Carmichael, Richard *Alli, BiDLA*
Carmichael, Robert Bell Booth *Alli Sup*
Carmichael, Robert Daniel 1879- *WhWNAA*
Carmichael, Roy *MnBBF*
Carmichael, Sara Anne *Alli Sup*
Carmichael, Stokely 1941- *AmA&B,
ConAu 57*
Carmichael, Thomas N 1919- *ConAu 29*
Carmichael, Waverley Turner *BlkAW*
Carmichael, William Edward 1922- *ConAu 37,
WrD 1976*
Carmiggelt, Simon Johannes 1913- *CasWL*
Carmilly, Moshe 1908- *ConAu 41*
Carmin, Robert Leighton 1918- *IndAu 1917*
Carmody, Jay 1900?-1973 *ConAu 41*
Carmontel, Louis Carrogis 1717-1806 *BiD&SB*
Carmontelle, Louis Carrogis 1717-1806 *OxFr*
Carmony, Donald Francis 1910- *IndAu 1917*
Carnac, Carol *EncM&D*
Carnac, John Henry Rivett- 1839- *Alli Sup*
Carnahan, David Hobart 1874- *WhWNAA*
Carnahan, James Richards 1840-1905 *CyAL 1,
IndAu 1816*
Carnahan, Marjorie R *AuBYP*
Carnahan, Walter Hervey 1891- *ConAu P-1,
IndAu 1917*
Carnall, Geoffrey Douglas 1927- *ConAu 13R,*

WrD 1976
Carnap, Rudolf P 1891-1970 *AmA&B,
ConAu 29, ConAu P-1, WorAu*
Carnarvon, Earl Of *Alli Sup, BbtC*
Carnarvon, Lord *Alli*
Carne, Elizabeth Catherine Thomas 1817-1873
Alli Sup
Carne, John *Alli*
Carne, Marcel 1906- *REn*
Carne, Robert H *Alli*
Carne, W *Alli Sup*
Carne-Ross *Alli Sup*
Carnegie, Alexander S 1869- *ChPo*
Carnegie, Andrew 1835?-1919 *Alli Sup,
AmA&B, BbD, BiD&SB, DcAmA,
DcNAA, LongC, OxAm, Pen Am, REn,
REnAL*
Carnegie, Dale 1888-1955 *LongC, Pen Am,
REnAL*
Carnegie, David *Alli Sup*
Carnegie, Dorothy Vanderpool *AuNews 1*
Carnegie, Georgina, Countess Of Northesk
Alli Sup
Carnegie, Sir James 1827- *Alli Sup, ChPo,
ChPo S1*
Carnegie, Raymond Alexander 1920- *ConAu 23*
Carnegie, Sacha *ConAu XR*
Carnegie, William *Alli Sup*
Carnegy, Patrick *Alli Sup*
Carneiro, Mario DeSa 1890-1916 *EvEuW*
Carnell, E J 1919-1967 *ConAu XR*
Carnell, Edward John 1919-1967 *AmA&B,
ConAu P-1*
Carnell, John 1912- *ConAu 25*
Carnell, P P *BiDLA Sup*
Carnelley, Thomas *Alli Sup*
Carner, Josep 1884-1971 *CasWL, ClDMEuL,
EncWL, EvEuW, Pen Eur*
Carner, Mosco 1904- *Au&Wr, ConAu P-1*
Carneri, Bartholomaus Von 1821- *BiD&SB*
Carnes, Captain *Alli Sup*
Carnes, Hannah *Alli Sup*
Carnes, J A *Alli Sup*
Carnes, Josef R 1903- *AmSCAP 66*
Carnes, Ralph L 1931- *ConAu 33*
Carnes, Sidney Cecil 1909-1953 *OhA&B*
Carnes, Valerie Bohanan 1940- *ConAu 33*
Carnett, P P *Alli*
Carney, Aubrey Toulmin 1921- *OhA&B*
Carney, James 1914- *ConAu 21*
Carney, John Otis 1922- *ConAu 1R*
Carney, Julia Fletcher 1823-1908 *ChPo*
Carney, Richard *BbtC*
Carney, Richard E 1923- *AmSCAP 66*
Carney, Richard Edward 1929- *ConAu 37,
WrD 1976*
Carney, T F 1931- *ConAu 49*
Carney, Mrs. T J *ChPo S1*
Carney, W Alderman 1922- *ConAu 25*
Carnicelli, D D 1931- *ConAu 61*
Carnie 1824- *ChPo*
Carnie, Ethel *ChPo S2*
Carnie, William 1824- *ChPo S1*
Carnochan, Janet 1839-1926 *DcLEnL, DcNAA,
OxCan*
Carnochan, John Murray 1817-1887 *Alli Sup,
DcAmA, DcNAA*
Carnochan, W B 1930- *ConAu 33, WrD 1976*
Carnot, Joseph B 1941- *ConAu 45*
Carnot, Maurus 1865-1935 *CatA 1952*
Carnota, J Athelstane Smith, Conde Da
Alli Sup
Caro, Annibale 1507-1566 *CasWL, DcEuL,
McGWD, Pen Eur, REn*
Caro, Jose Eusebio 1817-1853 *CasWL, DcSpL,
Pen Am*
Caro, Joseph 1488-1575 *CasWL, EuA*
Caro, Miguel Antonio 1843- *BiD&SB*
Caro, Robert A *WrD 1976*
Caro, Rodrigo 1573-1647 *CasWL, DcEuL,
Pen Eur*
Caroe, Sir Olaf Kirkpatrick 1892- *Au&Wr*
Caroe, William Douglas 1857- *WhLA*
Carol, Bill J *AmA&B, ConAu XR,
SmATA 3, WrD 1976*
Carolan *PoIre*
Carolan, Patrick 1766- *Alli, BiDLA, PoIre*
Carolan, T *Pen Eng*

Carolan, Turlough O' 1670-1738 *DcEnL*
Carolides, Paul 1843- *WhLA*
Caroline Of Anspach 1683-1737 *NewC*
Caroline Of Brunswick 1768-1821 *NewC*
Caroll, Evelyn *AmSCAP 66*
Caroll, Martha *Alli Sup*
Caroll, William *Alli*
Carolus-Duran 1837-1917 *OxFr*
Caron, Ivanhoe *OxCan*
Caron, Joseph William Ivanhoe 1875-1941
DcNAA
Caron, Pierre Augustin 1875-1952 *McGWD,
OxFr, REn*
Caron, R P *Alli*
Carona, Philip Ben 1925- *AuBYP, ConAu 1R*
Carossa, Hans 1878-1956 *CasWL, CatA 1952,
ClDMEuL, EncWL, EvEuW, ModGL,
OxGer, Pen Eur, TwCA, TwCA Sup,
TwCW*
Carosso, Vincent Phillip 1922- *ConAu 9R*
Carothers, E Eleanor 1882- *WhWNAA*
Carothers, J Edward 1907- *ConAu 41*
Carothers, Robert Lee 1942- *ConAu 45,
DrAP 1975*
Carozzi, Albert V 1925- *ConAu 53*
Carp, Frances Merchant 1918- *ConAu 23*
Carpaccio, Vittore 1450?-1526? *AtlBL, REn*
Carpelan, Bo 1926- *ConAu 49, Pen Eur,
SmATA 8*
Carpenter, Agricola *Alli*
Carpenter, Alexander *CasWL*
Carpenter, Alfred 1825- *Alli Sup*
Carpenter, Allan 1917- *ConAu 9R, SmATA 3,
WrD 1976*
Carpenter, Anna May d1900 *DcNAA*
Carpenter, Benjamin *Alli, Alli Sup, BiDLA*
Carpenter, C E *Alli Sup*
Carpenter, Carleton 1926- *AmSCAP 66*
Carpenter, Chapin Howard 1835-1887 *Alli Sup,
DcNAA*
Carpenter, Charles A 1929- *ConAu 33*
Carpenter, Charles E 1912- *AmSCAP 66*
Carpenter, Clarence Ray 1905-1975 *ConAu 57*
Carpenter, Clarence Willard 1888- *WhWNAA*
Carpenter, Cyrus C *Alli Sup*
Carpenter, Daniel *Alli, BiDLA*
Carpenter, Don 1931- *AmA&B, ConAu 45,
DrAF 1976*
Carpenter, Edmund Janes 1845-1924 *AmA&B,
AmLY, DcAmA, DcNAA, OxCan*
Carpenter, Edward *Alli Sup, Chmbr 3*
Carpenter, Edward 1844-1929 *BrAu 19, ChPo,
EvLB, LongC, ModBL, NewC, Pen Eng,
REn, WhTwL*
Carpenter, Edward Childs 1872?-1950 *AmA&B,
REnAL, WhWNAA*
Carpenter, Elias *Alli, BiDLA*
Carpenter, Elizabeth Sutherland 1920- *ChPo,
ConAu 21*
Carpenter, Elliot J 1894- *AmSCAP 66*
Carpenter, Ernest Charles 1865-1942 *DcNAA*
Carpenter, Esther Bernon 1848-1893 *Alli Sup,
BiD&SB, DcAmA, DcNAA*
Carpenter, Flora Leona 1877- *OhA&B*
Carpenter, Ford Ashman 1868- *AmLY,
WhWNAA*
Carpenter, Frances 1890-1972 *AmA&B,
Au&Wr, AuBYP, ConAu 5R, ConAu 37,
MorJA, SmATA 3*
Carpenter, Francis Bicknell 1830-1900 *Alli Sup,
DcAmA, DcNAA*
Carpenter, Frank DeYeaux *Alli Sup*
Carpenter, Frank George 1855-1924 *AmA&B,
DcNAA, OhA&B*
Carpenter, Frank Oliver 1858-1913 *DcAmA,
DcNAA*
Carpenter, Fred *ConAu XR*
Carpenter, Frederic Ives 1903- *ConAu 5R*
Carpenter, G J *Alli Sup*
Carpenter, G T *Alli Sup*
Carpenter, Lord George *Alli*
Carpenter, George B *ChPo*
Carpenter, George Rice 1863-1909 *AmA&B,
DcAmA, DcNAA*
Carpenter, George Washington 1802-1860
DcNAA
Carpenter, Gerald Leon 1924- *IndAu 1917*
Carpenter, Gladys Peet *ChPo S2*

Carpenter, H *ChPo S2*
Carpenter, H S *Alli Sup*
Carpenter, Harvey *Alli Sup*
Carpenter, Henry *Alli*
Carpenter, Henry Bernard 1840-1890 *DcAmA, DcNAA, PoIre*
Carpenter, Henry James 1839-1890 *Alli Sup*
Carpenter, Howard *BlkAW*
Carpenter, Hubert Vinton 1875- *WhWNAA*
Carpenter, Hugh Smith *Alli Sup*
Carpenter, Imogen 1919- *AmSCAP 66*
Carpenter, J *Alli, BiDLA*
Carpenter, J G *Alli Sup*
Carpenter, J H *Alli Sup*
Carpenter, J P *Alli Sup*
Carpenter, Jacobus *Alli*
Carpenter, James A 1928- *ConAu 37*
Carpenter, James M *Alli Sup*
Carpenter, John *Alli*
Carpenter, John 1370?-1441? *OxEng*
Carpenter, John A 1921- *ConAu 9R*
Carpenter, John Alden 1876-1951 *AmSCAP 66, ChPo S1, OxAm*
Carpenter, John Melvin 1910- *IndAu 1917*
Carpenter, John S 1860- *WhWNAA*
Carpenter, Joseph Edward *Alli*
Carpenter, Joseph Edwards 1813-1885 *ChPo, ChPo S1, PoIre*
Carpenter, Joseph Estlin *Alli Sup*
Carpenter, Joyce Frances *ConAu 33*
Carpenter, L P 1940- *WrD 1976*
Carpenter, Lant 1780-1840 *Alli, BiDLA*
Carpenter, Levy Leonidas 1891- *WhWNAA*
Carpenter, Liz *ConAu XR*
Carpenter, Mabel A *ChPo*
Carpenter, Marcus T *Alli Sup*
Carpenter, Margaret Haley *AmA&B, ChPo S1, ConAu 5R*
Carpenter, Marjorie 1896- *ConAu 45*
Carpenter, Mary 1807-1877 *Alli Sup*
Carpenter, Mary Haufle 1879- *WhWNAA*
Carpenter, Matilda Gilruth 1831-1923 *OhA&B*
Carpenter, Matthew T *BiDSA*
Carpenter, Maurice 1911- *WrD 1976*
Carpenter, Miles *ChPo S1*
Carpenter, Nan Cooke 1912- *ConAu 25, WrD 1976*
Carpenter, Nathaniel 1588-1628? *Alli*
Carpenter, Norma Lucile 1903- *WhWNAA*
Carpenter, P H *Alli Sup*
Carpenter, Patricia 1920- *ConAu 29*
Carpenter, Patrick *PoIre*
Carpenter, Pete *BlkAW*
Carpenter, Peter 1922- *ConAu 13R*
Carpenter, Philip Pearsall 1819-1877 *Alli Sup, BbtC*
Carpenter, R A *MnBBF*
Carpenter, Rhys 1889- *AmA&B, ConAu 57*
Carpenter, Richard *Alli*
Carpenter, Richard d1627 *Alli*
Carpenter, Richard C 1916- *ConAu 13R*
Carpenter, Rolla Clinton 1852-1919 *DcAmA, DcNAA*
Carpenter, Rue W *ChPo S1*
Carpenter, Russell Lant *Alli Sup*
Carpenter, S S *Alli Sup*
Carpenter, Samuel Warner *Alli, Alli Sup, BiDLA*
Carpenter, Sarah Osmond *Alli Sup*
Carpenter, Stephen Cullen d1820 *Alli, AmA&B, BbD, BiD&SB, DcAmA, DcNAA*
Carpenter, Stephen D *Alli Sup*
Carpenter, Stephen Haskins 1831-1878 *Alli Sup, DcAmA, DcNAA*
Carpenter, Stephen T d1820 *BiDSA*
Carpenter, Thomas *Alli, BiDLA*
Carpenter, Thorne M 1878- *WhWNAA*
Carpenter, W *Alli Sup*
Carpenter, Wesley M *Alli Sup*
Carpenter, William *Alli, Alli Sup*
Carpenter, William 1797-1874 *Alli Sup*
Carpenter, William 1830-1896 *DcAmA*
Carpenter, William Benjamin 1813-1885 *Alli, Alli Sup, BbD, DcEnL*
Carpenter, William Boyd 1841- *Alli Sup*
Carpenter, William H *ChPo S1*
Carpenter, William Henry *Alli Sup*

Carpenter, William Henry 1813-1899 *AmA&B, BiDSA, DcAmA, DcNAA*
Carpenter, William Henry 1853- *WhWNAA*
Carpenter, William Hookham 1792-1866 *Alli Sup*
Carpenter, William Lant *Alli Sup*
Carpentier, Alejo 1904- *CasWL, DcCLA, EncWL, Pen Am, TwCW, WorAu*
Carpentier, Georges *MnBBF*
Carper, Jean Elinor 1932- *ConAu 17R*
Carper, L Dean 1931- *ConAu 49*
Carpio, Bernardo Del *NewC*
Carpmael, A *Alli Sup*
Carpmael, Ernest *Alli Sup*
Carpmeal, W *Alli*
Carpozi, George, Jr. 1920- *ConAu 13R*
Carpue, J S *Alli*
Carpue, Joseph Constantine *BiDLA*
Carr, A *Alli Sup*
Carr, A A *ChPo S1*
Carr, A B *ChPo*
Carr, A H Z 1902-1971 *ConAu XR, EncM&D*
Carr, Adams *MnBBF*
Carr, Addis Emmet *Alli Sup*
Carr, Agnes *ChPo*
Carr, Alaric *Alli Sup*
Carr, Albert Z 1902-1971 *AmA&B, ConAu 1R, ConAu 33*
Carr, Alice H *ChPo S2*
Carr, Alice Vansittart 1850- *Alli Sup*
Carr, Allan *Alli*
Carr, Andrew *MnBBF*
Carr, Archie F 1909- *ConAu 13R*
Carr, Arthur *Alli Sup*
Carr, Arthur C 1918- *ConAu 37*
Carr, Arthur Japheth 1914- *ConAu 57*
Carr, Benjamin 1769-1831 *DcNAA*
Carr, Beryl *Alli Sup*
Carr, Catharine *ConAu XR, WrD 1976*
Carr, Charles Carl 1884-1952 *IndAu 1917, WhWNAA*
Carr, Christopher *Alli Sup*
Carr, Clarence R 1880- *BlkAW*
Carr, Clark Ezra 1836-1919 *DcNAA*
Carr, Daniel L And Brown, Joseph P *Alli Sup*
Carr, David William 1911- *ConAu 37*
Carr, Mrs. Donald *AmA&B*
Carr, Donald Eaton 1903- *ConAu 13R*
Carr, Dorothy Stevenson Laird 1912- *ConAu 9R*
Carr, E H 1892- *LongC*
Carr, E J *Alli Sup*
Carr, Edmund Donald *Alli Sup*
Carr, Edward *Alli Sup*
Carr, Edward Hallet 1892- *ConAu 61*
Carr, Edward Hallett 1892- *TwCA Sup*
Carr, Edward Henry *Alli Sup*
Carr, Edwin George 1937- *ConAu 61*
Carr, Edwin Hamlin 1865-1945 *DcNAA, IndAu 1917*
Carr, Ellis *Alli Sup*
Carr, Emily 1871-1945 *DcNAA, LongC, OxCan, REnAL*
Carr, Esther *Alli Sup*
Carr, Ezra S *Alli Sup*
Carr, Francis *Alli Sup*
Carr, Francis 1924- *Au&Wr, WrD 1976*
Carr, Francis Culling *Alli Sup*
Carr, Francis Howard 1874- *WhLA*
Carr, Frank *Alli Sup, MnBBF*
Carr, G P *Alli Sup*
Carr, G Ridley *Alli Sup*
Carr, G S *Alli Sup*
Carr, Gabrielle *Alli Sup*
Carr, Gene 1881-1959 *REnAL*
Carr, George 1704-1776 *Alli, MnBBF*
Carr, Glyn *ConAu XR, SmATA XR*
Carr, Gordon *MnBBF*
Carr, Gwen B 1924- *ConAu 41*
Carr, Hamzeh *ChPo S2*
Carr, Harriett Helen 1899- *Au&Wr, AuBYP, ConAu P-1, MorJA, SmATA 3*
Carr, Harry 1877-1936 *DcNAA*
Carr, Harvey *WhWNAA*
Carr, Helen *Alli Sup*
Carr, Herbert Wildon 1857- *WhWNAA*
Carr, Howard *MnBBF*
Carr, J H *Alli*

Carr, James *Alli Sup*
Carr, James Lloyd 1912- *Au&Wr, WrD 1976*
Carr, Jess 1930- *ConAu 29, WrD 1976*
Carr, Jo *Alli*
Carr, Jo Crisler 1926- *ConAu 21, WrD 1976*
Carr, John 1732-1807 *Alli*
Carr, Sir John 1772-1832 *Alli, BiDLA, ChPo S1, DcEnL*
Carr, John 1878- *BkC 5, CatA 1952*
Carr, John C 1929- *ConAu 53*
Carr, John Dickson 1905?- *AmA&B, Au&Wr, ConAu 49, ConLC 3, DcLEnL, EncM&D, EvLB, LongC, NewC, Pen Eng, REn, REnAL, TwCA, TwCA Sup, TwCW*
Carr, John Foster 1869- *AmLY*
Carr, John Geoffrey 1927- *WrD 1976*
Carr, John Laurence 1916- *ConAu 49*
Carr, John Rodham *Alli Sup*
Carr, John Walter 1862- *WhLA*
Carr, John Wesley 1859- *IndAu 1816, WhWNAA*
Carr, Joseph William Comyns 1849- *Alli Sup, Chmbr 3*
Carr, Kent *MnBBF*
Carr, Lascelles Robert *Alli, BiDLA*
Carr, Laura Garland 1835- *ChPo, ChPo S2*
Carr, Leon 1910- *AmSCAP 66*
Carr, Lisle *Alli Sup*
Carr, Lois Green 1922- *ConAu 61*
Carr, Lucien 1829-1915 *Alli Sup, BiD&SB, BiDSA, DcAmA, DcNAA*
Carr, Luella Bender *MnnWr*
Carr, Margaret 1935- *Au&Wr*
Carr, Margie 1900- *AmSCAP 66*
Carr, Mark William *Alli Sup*
Carr, Mary Jane 1899- *AuBYP, BkC 1, CatA 1952, ChPo S2, ConAu P-1, JBA 1951, SmATA 2*
Carr, Melton *MnBBF*
Carr, Michael W 1851-1922 *IndAu 1816, OhA&B*
Carr, Nicholas *Alli*
Carr, Philippa *WrD 1976*
Carr, R H 1878- *WhWNAA*
Carr, Ralph *Alli, Alli Sup*
Carr, Raymond 1919- *ConAu 17R*
Carr, Raymond Norman 1890- *IndAu 1917*
Carr, Richard *Alli*
Carr, Robert *Alli, Alli Sup, BiDLA, PoIre*
Carr, Robert Kenneth 1908- *AmA&B*
Carr, Robert Spencer 1909- *AmA&B, AmNov, OhA&B*
Carr, Robert V *ArizL*
Carr, Roberta *ConAu XR, WrD 1976*
Carr, S *WhWNAA*
Carr, Samuel *Alli*
Carr, Sarah 1850-1943? *DcNAA*
Carr, Stephen J *WhWNAA*
Carr, Stephen L *ConAu 57*
Carr, T S *Alli*
Carr, Thomas Henry 1905- *Au&Wr*
Carr, Victor P *ChPo S2*
Carr, Virginia Spencer 1929- *ConAu 61*
Carr, Wallace 1890- *MnBBF*
Carr, Warren Tyree 1917- *ConAu 5R*
Carr, William *Alli, Alli Sup, PoIre*
Carr, William George 1901- *AmA&B, ConAu 53, WrD 1976*
Carr, William H A 1924- *ConAu 13R*
Carr, William Windle *Alli, BiDLA*
Carr-Clements, J *MnBBF*
Carr-Gomm *Alli Sup*
Carr-Harris, Bertha Wright 1863-1949 *DcNAA, OxCan, WhWNAA*
Carr-Saunders, Alexander Morris 1886- *ConAu 1R, WhLA*
Carra, Emma *AmA&B*
Carracci, Agostino 1557-1602 *AtlBL*
Carracci, Annibale 1560-1609 *AtlBL, REn*
Carracci, Lodovico 1555-1619 *AtlBL*
Carracci Family *AtlBL*
Carranco, Lynwood 1922- *ConAu 57*
Carranza, Eduardo 1913- *DcCLA*
Carranza, Venustiano 1859-1920 *REn*
Carras, Nicholas S 1922- *AmSCAP 66*
Carrasquilla, Tomas 1858-1940 *CasWL, Pen Am*
Carraway, Gertrude S 1896- *WhWNAA*

Carre, Henry Beach 1871-1928 *DcNAA, WhWNAA*
Carre, Thomas d1674 *Alli*
Carre, Walter Riddell 1807-1874 *Alli Sup*
Carreau, Margaret 1899- *AmSCAP 66*
Carrel, Alexis 1873-1944 *CatA 1947, TwCA Sup, WhWNAA*
Carrel, Armand N 1800-1836 *Alli, OxFr*
Carrel, Cora Gaines 1860-1927 *OhA&B*
Carrel, Frank 1870-1940 *DcNAA, WhWNAA*
Carrel, Mark *ConAu XR*
Carrel, Minnie E Butler 1862-1938 *OhA&B*
Carrell, Alexis 1873-1944 *TwCA*
Carrell, Frank *OxCan*
Carrell, Lenore Kathrin Cary Gregory 1859-1911 *IndAu 1917*
Carrell, Norman Gerald 1905- *ConAu 25, WrD 1976*
Carrer, Luigi 1801-1850 *BiD&SB, EvEuW*
Carrera, Valentino 1834- *BiD&SB*
Carrera Andrade, Jorge 1903?- *CasWL, DcCLA, EncWL, Pen Am, TwCA Sup*
Carreras, Carlos N 1895-1959 *PueRA*
Carreras, T *ChPo S1*
Carrere, Emilio 1880-1947 *CasWL, EvEuW*
Carrere, John Merven 1858-1911 *DcNAA*
Carrere, Mentis *BlkAW*
Carretta, Jerry 1915- *AmSCAP 66*
Carreyett, T W 1927- *Au&Wr*
Carrick, A *Alli, BiDLA*
Carrick, A B *ConAu XR*
Carrick, Alice VanLeer 1875- *ChPo, ChPo S1, WhWNAA*
Carrick, Andrew *Alli Sup*
Carrick, Carol 1935- *ConAu 45, SmATA 7*
Carrick, Charles *ChPo S2*
Carrick, Donald 1929- *ConAu 53, IlBYP, SmATA 7*
Carrick, Edward *ChPo, ConAu XR, WrD 1976*
Carrick, George L *Alli Sup*
Carrick, J M *ChPo*
Carrick, John *ConAu XR*
Carrick, John Donald *Alli, ChPo*
Carrick, Malcolm 1945- *WrD 1976*
Carrick, T *ChPo*
Carrick, Valerie 1869-1948 *ChPo S2*
Carrick, Valery 1869-1948 *AnCL, ChPo, ConICB, IlCB 1945, JBA 1934, JBA 1951*
Carrie, John *Alli Sup*
Carrier *Alli*
Carrier, Augustus Stiles 1857-1923 *DcAmA, DcNAA*
Carrier, Constance 1908- *ConAu 33, ConP 1970, DrAP 1975, WrD 1976*
Carrier, Else Haydon 1879- *ChPo S2*
Carrier, Esther Jane 1925- *ConAu 17R*
Carrier, Louis Napoleon 1837-1912 *DcNAA*
Carrier, Lyman 1877- *WhWNAA*
Carrier, Roch 1937- *OxCan Sup*
Carrier, Warren 1918- *ConAu 9R, ConP 1970, DrAP 1975, OhA&B, WrD 1976*
Carriere, Eugene 1849-1906 *OxFr*
Carriere, Gaston 1913- *BkC 6, OxCan Sup*
Carrigan, Andrew G 1935- *ConAu 45, DrAP 1975*
Carrigan, D Owen 1933- *ConAu 25, OxCan Sup*
Carrigan, M J *OhA&B*
Carrigan, Nettie W *BlkAW*
Carrigan, Philip *Alli*
Carrighan, Terentius *PoIre*
Carrighar, Sally *AnCL, OhA&B*
Carrillo, Lawrence W 1920- *ConAu 13R, WrD 1976*
Carrillo DeSotomayor, Luis 1583-1610 *CasWL*
Carrillo Y Sotomayor, Luis De 1583-1610 *DcEuL, DcSpL, Pen Eur, REn*
Carrington, Lord *BiDLA*
Carrington, Mrs. *Alli Sup*
Carrington, Benjamin *Alli Sup*
Carrington, Charles Edmund 1897- *Au&Wr, ConAu 5R, WrD 1976*
Carrington, Edmund *Alli Sup*
Carrington, Emily *Alli Sup, ChPo S1, ChPo S2*
Carrington, F A *Alli*

Carrington, Fitzroy 1869-1954 *AmA&B, ChPo, WhWNAA*
Carrington, Frank G 1936- *ConAu 57*
Carrington, George *Alli Sup*
Carrington, Harold *BlkAW, LivBA*
Carrington, Henry *Alli Sup*
Carrington, Henry Beebe 1824-1912 *BiD&SB, DcAmA, DcNAA*
Carrington, Henry Beebee 1824-1912 *Alli Sup, AmA, AmA&B, ChPo, OhA&B*
Carrington, Hepworth *MnBBF*
Carrington, Hereward 1880-1958 *AmA&B, AmLY, BiDPar, WhWNAA*
Carrington, J K *MnBBF*
Carrington, James Beebee *Alli, WhWNAA*
Carrington, Kate *Alli Sup*
Carrington, Margaret Irvin 1831-1870 *Alli Sup, DcNAA, OhA&B*
Carrington, Mary Coles *ChPo, WhWNAA*
Carrington, Molly *ConAu XR*
Carrington, Noel Lewis 1894- *Au&Wr*
Carrington, Noel Thomas 1777-1830 *Alli, ChPo, ChPo S1, Chmbr 2, DcEnL*
Carrington, Norman Thomas 1905- *Au&Wr*
Carrington, Paul Dewitt 1931- *ConAu 29, WrD 1976*
Carrington, Richard 1921- *Au&Wr, ConAu 9R*
Carrington, Richard Christopher *Alli Sup*
Carrington, Robert Edmund *Alli Sup*
Carrington, Lord Robert Smith *Alli*
Carrington, S *Alli*
Carrington, Susanna *Alli*
Carrington, T J *Alli Sup*
Carrington, W *Alli*
Carrington, William John 1884-1947 *DcNAA*
Carrington, William Langley 1900-1970 *Au&Wr, ConAu P-1*
Carrington, William Thomas 1854-1937 *DcNAA*
Carrio DeLaVandera 1715?-1778? *Pen Am*
Carrion, Alejandro 1915- *DcCLA*
Carrion, Benjamin 1898- *DcCLA*
Carrion Maduro, Tomas 1870-1920 *PueRA*
Carrison, Daniel J 1917- *ConAu 37*
Carrithers, Gale H, Jr. 1932- *ConAu 41*
Carrithers, Wallace M 1911- *ConAu 25*
Carrithers, Walter A, Jr. 1924- *BiDPar*
Carritt, E F 1876-1964 *LongC*
Carrol, J Halstead *Alli Sup*
Carrol, John 1735-1817 *DcAmA*
Carroll, A B *ChPo S1*
Carroll, Adam 1897- *AmSCAP 66*
Carroll, Alexander Mitchell 1870-1925 *AmA&B, DcNAA*
Carroll, Alice VanBrook 1879-1958 *ChPo*
Carroll, Anna Ella 1815-1894 *Alli Sup, BiD&SB, BiDSA, DcAmA, DcNAA*
Carroll, Archer Latrobe 1894- *SmATA 7*
Carroll, B D 1940- *ConAu 53*
Carroll, B R *Alli*
Carroll, Barbara 1925- *AmSCAP 66*
Carroll, Benajah Harvey, Sr. 1843-1914 *BiDSA, DcNAA*
Carroll, Berenice A 1932- *ConAu 41*
Carroll, C Edward 1923- *ConAu 29, WrD 1976*
Carroll, Carroll 1902- *AmSCAP 66*
Carroll, Charles 1737-1832 *BiDSA*
Carroll, Charles 1876-1936 *DcNAA, WhWNAA*
Carroll, Charles Francis 1936- *ConAu 53*
Carroll, Consolata 1892- *AmA&B, AmNov*
Carroll, Curt *AuBYP, ConAu XR, SmATA 6*
Carroll, Daniel B 1928- *ConAu 41*
Carroll, Dixie *DcNAA*
Carroll, Donald K 1909- *ConAu 17*
Carroll, Earl 1893-1948 *AmA&B, AmSCAP 66*
Carroll, Ellen M *ChPo S1*
Carroll, Ellen Magrath 1878- *AnMV 1926, WhWNAA*
Carroll, Emily B *ChPo S1*
Carroll, Faye 1937- *ConAu 23*
Carroll, Gene 1898- *AmSCAP 66*
Carroll, George *ChPo S1*
Carroll, George D *Alli Sup*
Carroll, Georgia Lillian 1914- *AmSCAP 66*

Carroll, Gladys Hasty 1904- *AmA&B, AmNov, Au&Wr, ConAu 1R, OxAm, REnAL, TwCA, TwCA Sup, WhWNAA, WrD 1976*
Carroll, Gordon 1903- *AmA&B*
Carroll, Harry 1892-1962 *AmSCAP 66*
Carroll, Henry King 1847-1931 *Alli Sup, DcAmA, DcNAA*
Carroll, Herbert A 1897- *ConAu P-1*
Carroll, Howard 1854-1916 *Alli Sup, AmA&B, DcNAA*
Carroll, Irv 1907- *AmSCAP 66*
Carroll, James Milton 1852-1931 *DcNAA*
Carroll, Jessie *ChPo S1*
Carroll, Jim 1951- *ConAu 45, DrAP 1975*
Carroll, Jimmy 1913- *AmSCAP 66*
Carroll, John *Alli Sup, BbtC, PoIre*
Carroll, John 1735-1815? *AmA&B, BiDSA, DcNAA*
Carroll, John 1809?-1894? *DcNAA, OxCan*
Carroll, John 1892- *ChPo S1*
Carroll, John 1944- *ConAu 57*
Carroll, John B 1916- *ConAu 1R*
Carroll, John Charles 1885-1939 *DcNAA*
Carroll, John J 1924- *ConAu 13R*
Carroll, John Joseph 1856-1917 *DcAmA, DcNAA*
Carroll, John M 1928- *ConAu 37*
Carroll, John Millar 1925- *ConAu 5R*
Carroll, John Wallace 1906- *AmA&B*
Carroll, Joseph T 1935- *Au&Wr*
Carroll, June *AmSCAP 66*
Carroll, Kathleen Mary 1896- *ChPo S2, WhLA*
Carroll, Kenneth Lane 1924- *ConAu 37, WrD 1976*
Carroll, Latrobe 1894- *ConAu 1R, MorJA*
Carroll, Laura *ConAu XR, SmATA XR*
Carroll, Lewis 1832-1898 *Alli Sup, AnCL, AtlBL, AuBYP, BbD, BiD&SB, BrAu 19, CasWL, ChLR 2, ChPo, ChPo S1, ChPo S2, Chmbr 3, CnE&AP, CriT 3, CyWA, DcEnA, DcEnL, DcEuL, DcLEnL, EvLB, FamAYP, JBA 1934, NewC, OxEng, Pen Eng, RAdv 1, REn, St&VC, WebEAL, WhCL*
Carroll, Loren 1904- *AmA&B*
Carroll, Malachy Gerald *BkC 6*
Carroll, Mother Mary Gerald 1913- *ConAu 23*
Carroll, Mitchell 1885- *WhWNAA*
Carroll, Nicholas 1916- *Au&Wr*
Carroll, Patrick Joseph 1876- *BkC 1, CatA 1947, IndAu 1816, WhWNAA*
Carroll, Paul 1927- *ConAu 25, ConP 1970, ConP 1975, CrCAP, DrAP 1975, WrD 1976*
Carroll, Paul Vincent 1900-1968 *CasWL, CatA 1947, CnMD, CnThe, ConAu 9R, ConAu 25, DcLEnL, EncWL, LongC, McGWD, ModBL, ModBL Sup, ModWD, NewC, REnWD, TwCA, TwCA Sup*
Carroll, Phil 1895-1971 *ConAu P-1*
Carroll, Raymond G *AmA&B*
Carroll, Robert *ConAu XR*
Carroll, Robert Sproul 1869- *WhWNAA*
Carroll, Ruth Robinson 1899- *ConAu 1R, IlBYP, IlCB 1956, IlCB 1966, MorJA*
Carroll, St. Thomas Marion 1950- *ConAu XR*
Carroll, Stephen J, Jr. 1930- *ConAu 41*
Carroll, Ted *ConAu XR*
Carroll, Teresa Austin 1829-1909 *DcNAA*
Carroll, Thomas J 1909- *ConAu 1R*
Carroll, Thomas Theodore, Jr. 1925- *ConAu 9R*
Carroll, Tom M 1950- *ConAu 53*
Carroll, Vern 1933- *ConAu 57*
Carroll, Vinnette *BlkAW*
Carroll, W R *Alli Sup*
Carroll, William *Alli*
Carroll, William George *Alli Sup*
Carroll Of Carrolton, Charles 1737-1832 *BbtC*
Carrothers, Alfred William Rooke 1924- *WrD 1976*
Carrothers, George Ezra 1880-1966 *IndAu 1917*
Carrothers, Julia D *Alli Sup*
Carrothers, W *OxCan*
Carrow, Milton M 1912- *ConAu 25*
Carruth, Arthur Jay, Jr. 1887- *WhWNAA*
Carruth, Estelle 1910- *ConAu 9R*

Carruth, Frances Weston 1867- *DcAmA, DcNAA*
Carruth, Fred Hayden 1862-1932 *DcAmA, DcNAA*
Carruth, Gorton Veeder *ChPo*
Carruth, Gorton Veeder 1888- *WhWNAA*
Carruth, Gorton Veeder 1925- *ConAu 57*
Carruth, Hayden 1862-1932 *AmA&B, AmLY, CarSB, ChPo, ChPo S1, ChPo S2, REnAL*
Carruth, Hayden 1921- *AmA&B, ConAu 9R, ConLC 4, ConP 1970, ConP 1975, DrAP 1975, RAdv 1, REnAL, WorAu, WrD 1976*
Carruth, William Herbert 1859-1924 *AmA&B, ChPo, ChPo S1, ChPo S2, DcNAA, WhWNAA*
Carruthers, Miss *Alli Sup*
Carruthers, Alexander *ChPo S2*
Carruthers, C E *OxCan*
Carruthers, Clive Harcourt *ChPo S1*
Carruthers, George 1869-1947 *DcNAA*
Carruthers, J *BbtC*
Carruthers, Mrs. James *WhLA*
Carruthers, James E 1848- *WhLA*
Carruthers, John *Alli Sup*
Carruthers, John d1866 *DcNAA*
Carruthers, John Hector Macdonald 1902- *WhWNAA*
Carruthers, Sir Joseph Hector 1856- *WhLA*
Carruthers, M I K *ChPo S1*
Carruthers, Malcolm Euan 1938- *WrD 1976*
Carruthers, Matthew 1840- *ChPo*
Carruthers, Pat *MnBBF*
Carruthers, Peter Ambler 1935- *IndAu 1917*
Carruthers, Richard *ChPo S1*
Carruthers, Robert 1799-1878 *Alli Sup, BrAu 19, Chmbr 3, DcEnL, EvLB, NewC*
Carruthers, William *Alli*
Carruthers, William A 1800?-1850? *AmA&B, BiD&SB, BiDSA, CyAL 2, DcNAA*
Carry, John *BbtC*
Carry, Mary Jane *ChPo S1*
Carryl, Charles Edward 1841?-1920 *AmA, AmA&B, AnCL, BiD&SB, CarSB, ChPo, ChPo S2, DcAmA, DcNAA, EvLB, JBA 1934, OxAm, REn, REnAL, St&VC, TwCA*
Carryl, Guy Wetmore 1873-1904 *AmA&B, BiD&SB, ChPo, ChPo S1, ChPo S2, DcAmA, DcNAA, OxAm, REnAL*
Carryle, Charles Edward 1841- *Alli Sup*
Carsberg, Bryan Victor 1939- *ConAu 29*
Carse, David Bradley 1862- . *WhWNAA*
Carse, James P 1932- *ConAu 23*
Carse, Robert 1902-1971 *ConAu 1R, ConAu 29, SmATA 5*
Carshore, Joseph James *Alli Sup*
Carshore, Mrs. W S *Alli Sup*
Carslaw, W H *Alli Sup*
Carson, Alexander *Alli*
Carson, Alice Lovett *ChPo*
Carson, Anthony *Au&Wr*
Carson, Christopher 1809-1868 *REn*
Carson, Dwight *BlkAW*
Carson, Eva F Lovett *ChPo, ChPo S1, ChPo S2*
Carson, F L *Alli Sup*
Carson, Gerald 1899- *AmA&B, ConAu 1R*
Carson, Hampton L 1914- *ConAu 5R*
Carson, Hampton Lawrence 1852-1929 *DcAmA, DcNAA*
Carson, Harriet *Alli Sup*
Carson, Herbert L 1929- *ConAu 29, WrD 1976*
Carson, J G *Alli Sup*
Carson, James *Alli, BbtC, BiDLA, ConAu XR*
Carson, James Crawford Ledlie *Alli Sup*
Carson, James M 1887- *WhWNAA*
Carson, John Franklin 1920- *AuBYP, ConAu 9R, ConAu 13R, IndAu 1917, SmATA 1*
Carson, John Renshaw 1887-1940 *DcNAA*
Carson, Joseph 1808-1876 *Alli, Alli Sup, DcAmA, DcNAA, PoIre*
Carson, Julia Margaret Hicks 1899- *AuBYP,*

OhA&B
Carson, Kit 1910- *ConAu 57*
Carson, Kit 1809-1868 *LongC, MnBBF, OxAm, REnAL*
Carson, L B *MnBBF*
Carson, Lettie Gay *WhWNAA*
Carson, Luella Clay 1856- *WhWNAA*
Carson, Lular L 1921- *BlkAW, LivBA*
Carson, Major Lewis W *HsB&A*
Carson, Mary 1934- *ConAu 41*
Carson, Matt *MnBBF*
Carson, Norma Bright 1888- *ChPo S1, WhWNAA*
Carson, Rachel Louise 1907-1964 *AmA&B, AnCL, EvLB, LongC, OxAm, REn, TwCA Sup, TwCW*
Carson, Ray F 1939- *ConAu 61*
Carson, Robert 1909- *AmA&B, Au&Wr, ConAu 21*
Carson, Robert B 1934- *ConAu 57*
Carson, Robert C 1930- *ConAu 29*
Carson, Robert H *Alli Sup*
Carson, Ruby Leach 1894- *WhWNAA*
Carson, Ruth *ConAu XR*
Carson, Sylvia *EncM&D*
Carson, W B *Alli Sup*
Carson, William 1770-1843 *OxCan*
Carson, William Glasgow Bruce 1891- *ConAu 5R*
Carson, William Henry 1859- *DcAmA, DcNAA*
Carson, William James 1892- *WhWNAA*
Carson, Xanthus 1910- *ConAu 57*
Carss, Adam *ChPo*
Carstairs, Carroll *ChPo S2*
Carstairs, J *Alli, BiDLA Sup*
Carstairs, John Paddy *Au&Wr*
Carstairs, Kathleen *ConAu XR*
Carstairs, Rod *MnBBF*
Carstairs, William *Alli*
Carstares, William *Alli*
Carsten, Francis Ludwig 1911- *ConAu 13R, WrD 1976*
Carstens, Grace Pearce *ConAu 1R*
Carstensen, Roger Norwood 1920- *ConAu 5R, WrD 1976*
Carstone, Sydney *Alli Sup*
Carswell, Catherine Roxburgh 1879-1946 *ChPo S2, EvLB, LongC, NewC, Pen Eng, REn, TwCA, TwCA Sup*
Carswell, Donald 1882-1940 *ChPo, NewC*
Carswell, Doreen Erna 1927- *Au&Wr*
Carswell, Edward *Alli Sup, ChPo, ChPo S1*
Carswell, Evelyn M 1919- *AuBYP, ConAu 57*
Carswell, Francis *Alli*
Carswell, John Patrick 1918- *Au&Wr, ConAu 9R, WrD 1976*
Cartagena, Alfonso De 1385?-1456 *CasWL*
Cartan, Joseph 1811-1891 *PoIre*
Cartan, William *Alli Sup*
Carte, Gene E 1938- *ConAu 61*
Carte, Richard D'Oyly 1844-1901 *LongC*
Carte, Samuel *Alli*
Carte, Samuel 1653-1740 *Alli*
Carte, Thomas 1686-1754 *Alli, CasWL, Chmbr 2, DcEnL, EvLB, NewC*
Cartellieri, Otto 1872- *WhLA*
Cartellieri-Schroeter, Eva 1892- *WhLA*
Carten, Laura Paty *WhWNAA*
Carter *Alli*
Carter, Mrs. *Alli Sup*
Carter Dickson *DcLEnL*
Carter, A *Alli Sup*
Carter, A B *MnBBF*
Carter, A Forbes *ChPo S1*
Carter, A L *Alli Sup*
Carter, Adam *Alli Sup*
Carter, Agnes Louisa *Alli Sup, ChPo*
Carter, Agnes P *Alli Sup*
Carter, Alan 1936- *ConAu 33, WrD 1976*
Carter, Albert *Alli Sup*
Carter, Albert Howard 1913- *ConAu 25*
Carter, Alec *MnBBF*
Carter, Alfred Edward 1914- *ConAu 33*
Carter, Alfred George Washington 1819-1885 *Alli Sup, OhA&B*
Carter, Alfred Henry *Alli Sup*
Carter, Alice P *ChPo S1*

Carter, Aline B *ChPo S2*
Carter, Andrew *Alli Sup*
Carter, Angela 1940- *ConAu 53, ConLC 5*
Carter, Ann Alice 1880-1920 *ChPo*
Carter, Ann Augusta *Alli Sup*
Carter, Anna Alice *DcNAA*
Carter, Anne *ConAu XR*
Carter, Anthony L *OxCan Sup*
Carter, Avis Morton *WrD 1976*
Carter, Barbara 1925- *ConAu 53*
Carter, Barbara Barclay 1900- *BkC 3, CatA 1947, WhWNAA*
Carter, Benjamin *Alli*
Carter, Bennett Lester 1907- *AmSCAP 66*
Carter, Bernard M *BiDSA*
Carter, Beryl *ChPo S1*
Carter, Betty Landon *ChPo S2*
Carter, Bezoleel *Alli*
Carter, Boake 1898-1944 *DcNAA*
Carter, Boyd 1908- *ConAu 13R*
Carter, Bruce *AuBYP, ConAu XR*
Carter, Bryan 1917- *Au&Wr*
Carter, Byron L 1924- *ConAu 23*
Carter, Byrum Earl 1922- *IndAu 1917*
Carter, C R *Alli Sup*
Carter, Cedric Oswald 1917- *Au&Wr, WrD 1976*
Carter, Charles *Alli*
Carter, Charles Frederick 1863- *AmLY*
Carter, Charles Frederick 1919- *ConAu 1R, WrD 1976*
Carter, Charles H 1927- *ConAu 9R*
Carter, Charles Henry *Alli Sup*
Carter, Charles Webb 1905- *ConAu 21, IndAu 1917*
Carter, Charlotte Osgood *ChPo*
Carter, Clarence Edwin 1881-1961 *AmA&B, WhWNAA*
Carter, Clive 1941- *Au&Wr*
Carter, Coral Courtney 1883- *WhWNAA*
Carter, D *ChPo*
Carter, D P *Alli Sup*
Carter, David C 1946- *ConAu 45*
Carter, Dorothy Sharp 1921- *ConAu 49, SmATA 8*
Carter, Dyson 1910- *CanNov*
Carter, E *Alli*
Carter, E Lawrence 1910- *ConAu 25*
Carter, Edmund *Alli*
Carter, Edward 1902- *BbtC, ConAu 5R*
Carter, Elizabeth 1717-1806 *Alli, BiD&SB, BrAu, CasWL, ChPo, Chmbr 2, DcEnL, DcLEnL, EvLB, NewC, OxEng, WebEAL*
Carter, Emily *ChPo*
Carter, Emma Smuller d1928 *ChPo, DcNAA, WhWNAA*
Carter, Enid I *ChPo S2*
Carter, Ernest Frank 1899- *Au&Wr*
Carter, Ernestine Marie *Au&Wr, WrD 1976*
Carter, Everett 1919- *ConAu 13R, WrD 1976*
Carter, Feleciana *BiDSA*
Carter, Felicity Winifred *EncM&D*
Carter, Frances Monet 1923- *WrD 1976*
Carter, Frances Tunnell 1921?- *ConAu 37, WrD 1976*
Carter, Francis *Alli, BiDLA*
Carter, Francis d1783 *Alli*
Carter, Francis Edward 1851- *WhLA*
Carter, Franklin 1837-1919 *Alli Sup, DcAmA, DcNAA*
Carter, Frederick *ChPo, ChPo S2*
Carter, Frederick Albert 1893- *ChPo S1*
Carter, Sir Frederick Bowker Terrington 1819-1900 *OxCan*
Carter, G *Alli Sup*
Carter, George *Alli, BbtC*
Carter, George F 1912- *ConAu 5R*
Carter, George R *ChPo S1*
Carter, George William 1867-1930 *DcNAA*
Carter, Gwendolen Margaret 1906- *AmA&B, Au&Wr, WrD 1976*
Carter, Gwendolyn Margaret 1906- *ConAu 1R*
Carter, H Everett 1919- *AmSCAP 66*
Carter, H W *Alli Sup*
Carter, Harold 1925- *ConAu 33, WrD 1976*
Carter, Harry W *Alli*
Carter, Harvey Lewis 1904- *ConAu 23,*

IndAu 1917
Carter, Helene 1887-1960 *IlCB 1945, IlCB 1956, MorJA*
Carter, Henry *AmA&B*
Carter, Henry Hare 1905- *ConAu 41*
Carter, Henry John *Alli Sup*
Carter, Henry Vandyke *Alli Sup*
Carter, Henry Y *Alli*
Carter, Herbert S *MnBBF*
Carter, Herman J *BlkAW*
Carter, Hodding 1907-1972 *AmA&B, AmNov, AuBYP, ConAu 33, ConAu P-1, SmATA 2, TwCA Sup*
Carter, Horace E *Alli Sup*
Carter, Howard 1874-1939 *LongC*
Carter, Hugh 1895- *ConAu 37*
Carter, J Anthony 1943- *ConAu 61*
Carter, James *Alli Sup, AuBYP*
Carter, James 1853-1944 *AmA&B, DcNAA, WhWNAA*
Carter, James Cedric 1905- *IndAu 1917*
Carter, James Coolidge 1827-1905 *DcAmA, DcNAA*
Carter, James E 1935- *ConAu 57*
Carter, James G 1854- *ChPo S1*
Carter, James Gordon 1795-1849 *DcAmA, DcNAA*
Carter, James Madison Gore 1843-1919 *DcNAA*
Carter, James Puckette 1933- *ConAu 33*
Carter, James Richard 1940- *ConAu 33, WrD 1976*
Carter, Jean *BlkAW*
Carter, Jeff 1928- *Au&Wr*
Carter, Jesse Benedict 1872-1917 *DcNAA*
Carter, Jessie Benedict 1872-1917 *AmA&B*
Carter, Jessie E *Alli Sup*
Carter, John *Alli, BiDLA, ChPo, ChPo S1*
Carter, John 1745-1814 *AmA&B*
Carter, John 1748-1817 *Alli, BkIE*
Carter, John 1905-1975 *ChPo, ChPo S1, ChPo S2, ConAu 5R, ConAu 57, LongC*
Carter, John Corrie 1839- *Alli Sup*
Carter, John D *BlkAW*
Carter, John Franklin 1897-1967 *AmA&B, ConAu 25, EncM&D, REnAL, TwCA, TwCA Sup*
Carter, John Hanson *Alli Sup*
Carter, John Henton d1882 *DcNAA*
Carter, John Henton 1832-1910 *OhA&B*
Carter, John Mack 1928- *AmA&B*
Carter, John Pym *Alli Sup*
Carter, John Stewart 1912-1965 *AmA&B, ConAu P-1*
Carter, John Thomas 1921- *ConAu 33, WrD 1976*
Carter, Joseph 1912- *ConAu 49*
Carter, Karl W 1944- *BlkAW*
Carter, Katharine J 1905- *ConAu 5R, SmATA 2*
Carter, Landon *Alli*
Carter, Lee *ChPo*
Carter, Lief Hastings 1940- *ConAu 57*
Carter, Lillie Mae *BlkAW*
Carter, Lily *Alli Sup*
Carter, Lin 1930- *ConAu 41*
Carter, Lonnie 1942- *ConDr, WrD 1976*
Carter, Luther J 1927- *ConAu 57*
Carter, Mrs. M *Alli Sup*
Carter, M L 1948- *ConAu 33*
Carter, Martin Wylde 1927- *ConP 1970, ConP 1975, WrD 1976*
Carter, Mary 1923- *ConAu 9R*
Carter, Mary Elizabeth 1836- *DcNAA*
Carter, Mary Ellen 1923- *ConAu 25, WrD 1976*
Carter, Mary Hamilton *ChPo S1*
Carter, Mary Kennedy 1934- *LivBA*
Carter, Matthew *Alli*
Carter, Nathaniel Franklin 1830-1915 *DcAmA, DcNAA*
Carter, Nathaniel Hazeltine 1787-1830 *Alli, ChPo, CyAL 1, DcAmA, DcNAA*
Carter, Neil 1913- *ConAu 17R*
Carter, Nellie M *Alli Sup*
Carter, Nevada *ConAu XR*
Carter, Nicholas *Alli, AmA&B, DcNAA*
Carter, Nick *DcNAA*
Carter, Paul A 1926- *ConAu 33*

Carter, Paul J, Jr. 1912- *ConAu 21*
Carter, Peter 1825-1900 *Alli, Alli Sup, DcAmA, DcNAA*
Carter, Philip Youngman *EncM&D*
Carter, Phyllis Ann *AuBYP, ConAu XR, SmATA 2*
Carter, Ralph *Alli, ConAu XR*
Carter, Randolph 1914- *WrD 1976*
Carter, Ray 1908- *AmSCAP 66*
Carter, Richard *Alli, AmSCAP 66*
Carter, Richard 1918- *AmA&B, ConAu 61*
Carter, Robert 1807-1889 *AmA&B*
Carter, Robert 1819-1879 *Alli Sup, AmA, AmA&B, BiD&SB, DcAmA, DcNAA*
Carter, Robert A 1923- *ConAu 33*
Carter, Robert Brudenell *Alli Sup*
Carter, Robert M 1925- *ConAu 33*
Carter, Robert S *Alli Sup*
Carter, Russel Kelso 1849-1928 *Alli Sup, BiDSA, DcAmA*
Carter, Russell Gordon 1892-1957 *AmA&B, WhWNAA*
Carter, Russell Kelso 1849-1928 *DcNAA*
Carter, Ruth *Alli Sup, DcNAA*
Carter, S E *Alli Sup*
Carter, Samuel *Alli, Alli Sup*
Carter, Samuel, III 1904- *ConAu 57*
Carter, Sarah C *ChPo S2*
Carter, Simeon 1824- *ChPo S1*
Carter, St. Leger Landon *BiDSA, ChPo S2*
Carter, Steve *BlkAW*
Carter, Susan *Alli Sup*
Carter, Thomas *Alli, Alli Sup*
Carter, Thomas d1867 *Alli Sup*
Carter, Thomas 1768-1800 *Alli*
Carter, Thomas Fortescue *Alli Sup*
Carter, Thomas John Proctor *Alli Sup*
Carter, Thomas Sarsfield *Alli Sup, PoIre*
Carter, Thomas Thellson *Alli*
Carter, Thomas Thellusson *Alli Sup*
Carter, Val *MnBBF*
Carter, Victor Albert 1902- *Au&Wr, ConAu P-1*
Carter, Walter S *Alli Sup*
Carter, William *Alli, Alli Sup*
Carter, William 1868-1949 *DcNAA, WhWNAA*
Carter, William 1912- *Au&Wr*
Carter, William 1934- *ConAu 33*
Carter, William Allan *Alli Sup*
Carter, William Ambrose 1899- *ConAu P-1*
Carter, William B *Alli Sup*
Carter, William E 1926?- *AuBYP, ConAu 17R, SmATA 1*
Carter, William Giles Harding 1851-1925 *DcNAA*
Carter, William Lee 1925- *ConAu 1R*
Carter, William Lorenzo *ChPo S2*
Carter, William Page *BiDSA*
Carter, William R 1908- *AmSCAP 66*
Carter, Mrs. William S *ChPo S1*
Carter, William Samuel *Alli Sup*
Carter, William Spencer 1869-1944 *DcNAA*
Carter, William W *ChPo*
Carter, Wilmoth A *LivBA*
Carter, Wooll *Alli*
Carter, Worrall Reed 1885?-1975 *ConAu 57*
Carteret, A E *Alli Sup*
Carteret, Antoine Alfred Desire 1813-1889 *BiD&SB*
Carteret, John 1690-1763 *Alli*
Carteret, Philip 1639-1682 *Alli, REn*
Carterette, Edward C 1921- *ConAu 41*
Carthew, George Alfred 1807-1882 *Alli Sup*
Carthew, Thomas *Alli*
Carthy, Charles *PoIre*
Carthy, John Dennis 1923- *Au&Wr*
Carthy, Mother Mary Peter 1911- *ConAu 13R*
Cartier, Sir George-Etienne 1814-1873 *BbtC, OxCan*
Cartier, Georges 1929- *CanWr*
Cartier, Jacques 1491?-1557 *OxCan, OxFr, REn, REnAL*
Cartier, Steve *ConAu XR*
Cartland, Barbara 1904- *Au&Wr, ConAu 9R, LongC, TwCW, WrD 1976*
Cartland, Gertrude W *Alli Sup*
Cartledge, Groves Howard 1891- *WhWNAA*

Cartledge, Samuel Antoine 1903- *ConAu 1R*
Cartlich, George L *ChPo, ChPo S2*
Cartmell, Margaret R *Alli Sup*
Carton, James *Alli Sup*
Carton, Lonnic C *ChPo*
Carton, R C 1856-1928 *BrAu 19, Chmbr 3, LongC*
Carton DeWiart, Comte Henry 1869- *WhLA*
Cartouche, L D *Alli*
Cartouche, Louis-Dominique Bourguignon 1693-1721 *OxFr*
Cartter, Allan Murray 1922- *ConAu 5R*
Cartwright, Mrs. *Alli*
Cartwright, A *MnBBF*
Cartwright, Albert 1868- *WhLA*
Cartwright, Anson William Henry *Alli Sup*
Cartwright, Bruce 1882- *WhWNAA*
Cartwright, C E *OxCan*
Cartwright, Charles *Alli, BiDLA*
Cartwright, Christopher 1602-1658 *Alli*
Cartwright, Conway Edward 1837-1920 *DcNAA, PoIre*
Cartwright, Edmund 1743-1823 *Alli, BiDLA, DcEnL*
Cartwright, Eliza *Alli*
Cartwright, Elizabeth *ChPo*
Cartwright, F L *Alli Sup*
Cartwright, Frances D *Alli*
Cartwright, Francis *Alli*
Cartwright, George *Alli*
Cartwright, George 1739-1819 *Alli, BbtC, BiDLA, OxCan*
Cartwright, J *Alli, Alli Sup*
Cartwright, James Ellis *Alli Sup*
Cartwright, James Joel *Alli Sup*
Cartwright, James McGregor *ConAu XR*
Cartwright, John *Alli, BbtC*
Cartwright, John 1740-1824 *Alli, BiDLA*
Cartwright, Joseph *Alli Sup*
Cartwright, Joseph, Jr. *Alli Sup*
Cartwright, Julia *Alli Sup, Chmbr 3*
Cartwright, Mary J 1856- *IndAu 1917*
Cartwright, Nathaniel *Alli Sup*
Cartwright, Otho Grandford 1869-1943 *DcNAA*
Cartwright, Peter 1785-1872 *Alli Sup, AmA&B, BiD&SB, BiDSA, DcAmA, DcNAA, OhA&B, OxAm, Pen Am, REnAL*
Cartwright, R J *BbtC*
Cartwright, Richard *OxCan*
Cartwright, Sir Richard John 1835-1912 *DcNAA, OxCan*
Cartwright, Robert *Alli Sup*
Cartwright, Mrs. Robert *Alli Sup*
Cartwright, Sally 1923- *ConAu 49, SmATA 9*
Cartwright, T *Alli Sup*
Cartwright, Thomas *Alli*
Cartwright, Thomas 1535-1603 *Alli, CasWL*
Cartwright, Thomas 1634-1689 *Alli*
Cartwright, William *Alli, Alli Sup, Chmbr 1*
Cartwright, William 1611-1643 *Alli, BbD, BiD&SB, CasWL, ChPo, ChPo S1, CrE&SL, DcEnL, EvLB, NewC, OxEng, Pen Eng, REn, REnWD*
Cartwright, William Cornwallis 1826- *Alli Sup*
Cartwright, William H 1915- *AmA&B, ConAu 9R*
Carty, J S *PoIre*
Carty, James William, Jr. 1925- *ConAu 53*
Carty, Leo *IlBYP*
Carus, Paul 1852-1919 *Alli Sup, AmA&B, CasWL, DcAmA, DcNAA, REnAL, TwCA*
Carus, William *Alli, Alli Sup*
Carus-Wilson, Eleanora Mary 1897- *Au&Wr, ConAu 5R, WrD 1976*
Caruso, Bruno 1927- *WhGrA*
Caruso, Enrico 1873?-1921 *ChPo S1, NewC, REn*
Caruso, John Anthony 1907- *ConAu 33, WrD 1976*
Caruth, Donald L 1935- *ConAu 29*
Caruthers, Abraham *Alli Sup*
Caruthers, Eli Washington 1793-1865 *BiDSA, DcAmA, DcNAA*
Caruthers, Jeannette *BiDSA*
Caruthers, Mazie V *ChPo*

Case, William Scoville 1863-1928 *DcAmA, DcNAA*

Casebier, Virginia 1918- *ConAu 41*

Caseleyr, Camille Auguste Marie 1909- *Au&Wr, ConAu P-1*

Casella, Albert 1891- *McGWD*

Casely-Hayford, Adelaide 1868-1959 *AfA 1*

Casely-Hayford, Gladys May 1904-1950 *AfA 1, Pen Cl*

Casely-Hayford, Joseph Ephraim 1886-1930 *AfA 1*

Casement, Christina 1933- *Au&Wr*

Casement, Dan Dillon 1868- *WhWNAA*

Caserio, Jesse 1918- *AmSCAP 66*

Casewit, Curtis 1922- *ConAu 13R, SmATA 4*

Casey Jones d1900 *LongC*

Casey, Bernie *BlkAW*

Casey, Bill H 1930- *ConAu 1R*

Casey, Brigid 1950- *ConAu 49, SmATA 9*

Casey, Charles *Alli Sup, PoIre*

Casey, Claude 1912- *AmSCAP 66*

Casey, Daniel *PoIre*

Casey, Daniel A 1886- *BkC 4*

Casey, Daniel J 1937- *ConAu 57*

Casey, Elizabeth 1848- *Alli Sup*

Casey, Elizabeth Owens Blackburne 1845-1894 *PoIre*

Casey, Gavin S 1907- *TwCW*

Casey, Henry James *Alli Sup*

Casey, J K *Alli Sup*

Casey, James 1824-1909 *Alli Sup, PoIre*

Casey, James Joseph *Alli Sup*

Casey, John *Alli Sup, McGWD*

Casey, John E 1876- *WhWNAA*

Casey, John Harold 1897- *WhWNAA*

Casey, John Keegan 1846-1870 *ChPo S1, PoIre*

Casey, Joseph *Alli Sup*

Casey, Juanita 1925- *ConAu 49, WrD 1976*

Casey, Kathleen Aston *AmA&B*

Casey, Kenneth, Sr. 1899-1965 *AmSCAP 66*

Casey, Kevin 1940- *Au&Wr, ConAu 25, WrD 1976*

Casey, Leo J *ChPo S1*

Casey, Mart *ConAu XR*

Casey, Maurice William 1859- *PoIre*

Casey, Michael 1947- *ConLC 2, ConP 1975, DrAP 1975, WrD 1976*

Casey, Michael T 1922- *ConAu 21*

Casey, Ralph Droz 1890-1962 *AmA&B, ChPo S2*

Casey, Raymond O *BlkAW*

Casey, Richard Gardiner 1890- *ConAu 61, WrD 1976*

Casey, Robert Joseph 1890-1962 *AmA&B, CatA 1947, REnAL*

Casey, Rosemary Alice 1922- *ConAu 5R*

Casey, Silas 1807-1882 *Alli Sup, DcAmA, DcNAA*

Casey, Thomas Francis 1923- *ConAu 13R*

Casey, Wesley Eugene 1933- *AmSCAP 66*

Casey, William J 1861- *WhWNAA*

Casey, William VanEtten 1914- *ConAu 57*

Casgrain, Henry Raymond 1831-1904 *BbD, BiD&SB*

Casgrain, Henri-Raymond 1831-1904 *BbtC, CanWr, CasWL, DcNAA, OxCan*

Casgrain, Philippe Baby 1826-1917 *DcNAA*

Casgrain, Rene Edouard 1839-1917 *DcNAA*

Casgrain, Therese F *OxCan Sup*

Cash, Agnes E *ChPo S2*

Cash, Anthony 1933- *Au&Wr, WrD 1976*

Cash, Arthur Hill 1922- *IndAu 1917*

Cash, Grace 1915- *ChPo, ConAu 23, WrD 1976*

Cash, Grady *ConAu XR*

Cash, James *Alli Sup*

Cash, James Allan 1901- *Au&Wr, ConAu 5R*

Cash, Joseph H 1927- *ConAu 41*

Cash, Sebastian *ConAu XR*

Cash, Wilbur Joseph 1901-1941 *AmA&B, DcNAA, WorAu*

Cashin, Edward L 1927- *ConAu 21*

Cashin, James A 1911- *ConAu 17R, WrD 1976*

Cashin, T F *Alli Sup*

Cashman, D B *PoIre*

Cashman, Nellie *ArizL*

Cashman, Paul Harrison 1924- *ConAu 13R*

Cashman, Tony *OxCan Sup*

Casia *Pen Cl*

Casiano, Americo *DrAP 1975*

Casilear, John William 1811-1893 *EarAB*

Casimir Dren *WhWNAA*

Casimir, Paul 1922- *ChPo*

Casino *Alli*

Casis, Lilia Mary *TexWr*

Caskey, John L 1908- *ConAu 13R*

Caskey, Lacey Davis 1880-1944 *DcNAA*

Caskoden, Edwin *DcAmA, DcNAA*

Casler, John Overton 1838- *DcAmA, DcNAA*

Casler, John Overton 1866- *BiDSA*

Casler, Lawrence 1932- *ConAu 49*

Casley, David *Alli*

Caslon, William 1692-1766 *NewC*

Casmier, Adam A 1934- *ConAu 33*

Casmir, Fred L 1928- *ConAu 37*

Casner, A James 1907- *ConAu 5R*

Caso, Adolph 1934- *ConAu 57*

Cason, Edmond *Alli*

Cason, Hulsey 1893- *WhWNAA*

Cason, Mabel Earp 1892-1965 *ConAu P-1, SmATA 10*

Cason, P Martin *BlkAW*

Casona, Alejandro 1903-1965 *CasWL, CnMD, CrCD, EncWL, EvEuW, McGWD, ModWD, Pen Eur, REn, TwCW*

Caspar, C A And Patmore, E M *Alli Sup*

Caspar, Carl N *Alli Sup*

Caspar, Max 1880- *WhLA*

Caspari, Ernest W 1909- *ConAu 41*

Caspari, F A *Alli Sup*

Caspari, Wilhelm 1872- *WhLA*

Caspary, Vera 1904?- *AmA&B, Au&Wr, ConAu 13R, EncM&D, LongC, REnAL, TwCA Sup, WrD 1976*

Casper Von Lohenstein *CasWL, EvEuW*

Casper, Henry W 1909- *ConAu 37*

Casper, Jonathan D 1942- *ConAu 53*

Casper, Leonard Ralph 1923- *ConAu 1R, WrD 1976*

Caspipine, T *AmA&B*

Casque, Sammy *ConAu XR*

Casriel, H Daniel 1924- *ConAu 13R*

Cass, Carl Bartholomew 1901- *ConAu P-1*

Cass, Emily Elizabeth 1905- *Au&Wr*

Cass, Frederick Charles *Alli Sup*

Cass, Joan Evelyn *Au&Wr, AuBYP, ConAu 1R, SmATA 1, WrD 1976*

Cass, John A *Alli Sup*

Cass, Lewis 1782-1866 *Alli, AmA&B, BiD&SB, CyAL 1, DcAmA, DcNAA, OhA&B*

Cass, Thomas 1931- *Au&Wr, WrD 1976*

Cass-Beggs, Barbara *OxCan Sup*

Cassady, Ralph, Jr. 1900- *ConAu 1R*

Cassan, Stephen Hyde 1789-1841 *Alli*

Cassandra 1909-1967 *ConAu XR, LongC*

Cassandre, A M 1901- *WhGrA*

Cassara, Ernest 1925- *ConAu 41*

Cassard, George C *ChPo*

Cassard, Mabel Matheson *ChPo*

Cassatt, Mary 1845-1926 *AtlBL, OxAm, REn*

Cassavetes, John *ConDr*

Casseday, Benjamin *Alli Sup*

Casseday, Davis B *Alli Sup*

Cassedy, B *Alli Sup*

Cassedy, James H 1919- *ConAu 1R, WrD 1976*

Cassedy, Sylvia *ChPo S2*

Cassegrain, Arthur 1835-1868 *BbtC, DcNAA*

Cassel, Daniel Kalb 1820-1898 *DcNAA*

Cassel, Irwin M 1886- *AmSCAP 66*

Cassel, James *Alli*

Cassel, Lili 1924- *ChPo, IlCB 1956, SmATA XR*

Cassel, Russell N 1911- *ConAu 37, WrD 1976*

Casselberry, Evans *BiDSA*

Cassell, Frank A 1941- *ConAu 33*

Cassell, Frank Hyde 1916- *ConAu 37*

Cassell, John 1817-1865 *Alli Sup, ChPo S2, NewC*

Cassell, Richard A 1921- *ConAu 23*

Cassell, Sylvia 1924- *ConAu 5R*

Casselle, Corene Flowerette 1943- *BlkAW*

Cassells, James Patterson *Alli Sup*

Cassells, John *ConAu XR, WrD 1976*

Casselman, Alexander Clark 1852-1940 *DcNAA*

Casselman, Arthur Vale 1874-1957 *OhA&B*

Casselman, Warren Gottlieb Bruce 1921- *Au&Wr*

Cassels, Alan 1929- *ConAu 33, WrD 1976*

Cassels, Louis 1922-1974 *ConAu 9R, ConAu 45*

Cassels, Robert *Alli Sup*

Cassels, Samuel Jones 1806-1853 *AmA&B, DcNAA*

Cassels, Walter Richard 1826- *Alli Sup*

Casseres *TwCA, TwCA Sup*

Casserley, Anne *JBA 1934, JBA 1951*

Casserley, Julian Victor Langmead 1909- *ConAu 9R*

Cassey, Charles R 1933- *AmSCAP 66*

Cassiday, Bruce 1920- *ConAu 1R*

Cassidy, Charles Michael Ardagh 1936- *WrD 1976*

Cassidy, Claude *ConAu XR*

Cassidy, Claudia *AmA&B*

Cassidy, Francis Patrick 1895- *AmA&B*

Cassidy, Frederic Gomes 1907- *ConAu 1R, WrD 1976*

Cassidy, Gerald *ChPo*

Cassidy, Harold G 1906- *ConAu 25*

Cassidy, Henry Clarence 1910- *AmA&B*

Cassidy, John A 1908- *ConAu 33*

Cassidy, Martin *MnBBF*

Cassidy, Mary *ChPo S1*

Cassidy, Morley Franklin 1900- *AmA&B*

Cassidy, Patrick 1790?-1890? *PoIre*

Cassidy, Patrick Sarsfield 1852- *Alli Sup, PoIre*

Cassidy, Rosalind Frances 1895- *WhWNAA*

Cassidy, Vincent H 1923- *ConAu 21*

Cassie, R L *ChPo S2*

Cassie, William Fisher 1905- *Au&Wr, WrD 1976*

Cassilis, Ina Leon *Alli Sup, MnBBF*

Cassill, R V 1919- *AmA&B, ConAu 9R, ConLC 4, ConNov 1972, ConNov 1976, DrAF 1976, OxAm, RAdv 1, REnAL, WorAu, WrD 1976*

Cassilly, Francis 1860- *WhWNAA*

Cassils, Peter *ConAu XR*

Cassin, John 1813-1869 *Alli, BiD&SB, DcAmA, DcNAA*

Cassinari, John 1920- *AmSCAP 66*

Cassinelli, C W 1925- *ConAu 1R*

Cassino, Samuel E *Alli Sup*

Cassinone, Heinrich 1858- *WhLA*

Cassiodorus, Flavius Magnus Aurelius 485?-580? *CasWL, OxEng, Pen Cl, Pen Eur*

Cassirer, Ernst 1874-1945 *DcNAA, Pen Eur, TwCA Sup, WhLA*

Cassity, Turner 1929- *ConAu 17R, ConLC 6, DrAP 1975, WrD 1976*

Cassius d042BC *REn*

Cassius Dio Cocceianus 155?-235? *CasWL*

Cassius Hemina, Lucius 165?BC- *Pen Cl*

Casso, Evans J 1914- *ConAu 57*

Cassola, Albert Maria 1915- *Au&Wr, ConAu P-1*

Cassola, Carlo 1917- *Au&Wr, EncWL Sup, ModRL, Pen Eur, REn, TwCW, WorAu*

Cassoli, Piero 1918- *BiDPar*

Casson, Edmund *ChPo S2*

Casson, Frederick Ronald Christopher 1910- *Au&Wr*

Casson, Lionel 1914- *Au&Wr, ConAu 9R*

Casson, Margaret *Alli Sup*

Casson, R T *MnBBF*

Cassou, Jean 1897- *CasWL, EncWL, EvEuW*

Casstevens, Thomas William 1937- *ConAu 17R, WrD 1976*

Cassyere, Jacob Jacobsoon *CasWL*

Castagna, Edwin 1909- *ConAu 17*

Castagnier, Georges 1850- *DcAmA*

Castagno, Andrea Del 1423?-1457 *AtlBL*

Castagnola, Lawrence A 1933- *ConAu 29*

Castaldo, Joseph F 1927- *AmSCAP 66*

Castamore *Alli*

Castaneda, Carlos 1931- *ConAu 25, WrD 1976*

Castaneda, Carlos Eduardo 1896-1958 *BkC 3, REnAL, TexWr, WhWNAA*

Castaneda, Hector-Neri 1924- *ConAu 5R*

Castaneda, James A 1933- *ConAu 41*
Castaneda, Pedro De *ArizL*
Castanheda, Fernao Lopes De 1500?-1559 *BiD&SB, CasWL, Pen Eur*
Castberg, Leila *WhWNAA*
Casteel, John Laurence 1903- *AmA&B*
Castejon DeMenendez, Luz 1916- *DcCLA*
Castel, Albert 1928- *ConAu 1R*
Castel, J G 1928- *ConAu 21*
Castel, Jean d1476 *OxFr*
Castelao, Alfonso R *Pen Eur*
Castelar, Emilio 1832-1899 *BbD, BiD&SB, CasWL, ClDMEuL, DcSpL, REn*
Castelar Y Ripoll, Emilio 1832-1899 *EuA*
Castelein, Matthew De 1485-1550 *DcEuL*
Castelein, Matthijs De 1485-1550 *BiD&SB, CasWL*
Castelhun, Dorothea 1889- *WhWNAA*
Castell, Alburey 1904- *AmA&B*
Castell, Edmund 1606-1685 *Alli*
Castell, Merlyn *Alli Sup*
Castell, Robert *Alli*
Castell, William *Alli*
Castella, Hubert De *Alli Sup*
Castellan, N John, Jr. 1939- *ConAu 37*
Castellaneta, Carlo 1930- *Au&Wr, ConAu 13R*
Castellani, Count Aldo Of Chisimaio 1879- *Au&Wr*
Castellano, Juan Rodriguez 1900- *DcSpL*
Castellanos, Henry C *BiDSA*
Castellanos, Jane Mollie Robinson 1913- *ConAu 9R, SmATA 9*
Castellanos, Juan De 1522-1607? *CasWL, DcEuL, Pen Am*
Castellanos, Rosario 1915-1974 *ConAu 53*
Castellanos, Rosario 1925-1974 *CasWL, Pen Am*
Castelli, Ignaz Franz 1781-1862 *BiD&SB, OxGer*
Castellio, Sebastien 1515-1563 *OxFr*
Castellion, Sebastien 1515-1563 *OxFr*
Castello-Branco, Camillo 1826-1890 *BbD, BiD&SB, EuA*
Castellon, Federico 1914- *IlCB 1956*
Castelnau, Michel De 1520-1592 *OxFr*
Castelnovo, Leo Di 1835- *BiD&SB*
Castelnuovo, Enrico 1839- *BiD&SB*
Castelnuovo-Tedesco, Mario 1895- *AmSCAP 66*
Castelnuovo-Tedesco, Pietro 1925- *ConAu 21, WrD 1976*
Castelo Branco, Camilo 1825-1890 *CasWL, ClDMEuL, EvEuW*
Castelo Branco, Camilo 1825-1895 *Pen Eur*
Castelo Branco, Camilo 1825-1890 *REn*
Castelvecchio, Riccardo *BiD&SB*
Castelvetro, Lodovico 1505-1571 *CasWL, DcEuL, EuA, Pen Eur, REn*
Castetter, William Benjamin 1914- *ConAu 1R*
Casti, Giambattista 1721?-1803 *BbD, BiD&SB, CasWL, ChPo S1, EvEuW*
Casti, Giovanni Battista 1721?-1803 *DcEuL*
Castiello, Jaime 1898- *ChPo*
Castiglione *DcSpL*
Castiglione, Baldassare 1478-1529 *AtlBL, BbD, BiD&SB, CasWL, CrE&SL, DcEuL, EuA, EvEuW, NewC, OxEng, Pen Eur, RCom, REn*
Castildine *Alli*
Castilho, Antonio Feliciano De 1800-1875 *BiD&SB, CasWL, Pen Eur*
Castillejo, Christoval De 1490-1556 *BbD, BiD&SB*
Castillejo, Cristobal De 1490?-1550 *CasWL, DcEuL, DcSpL, Pen Eur, REn*
Castillo, Abelardo 1935- *DcCLA*
Castillo, Diego Enriquez De *DcEuL*
Castillo, Edmund Luis 1924- *AuBYP, ConAu 29, SmATA 1, WrD 1976*
Castillo, Hernando De 1490?- *DcEuL, DcSpL*
Castillo, John 1792-1845 *Alli Sup, ChPo, PoIre*
Castillo, Michel Del 1934- *ModRL, TwCW, WorAu*
Castillo Andraca Y Tamayo, Francisco Del 1716-1770 *Pen Am*
Castillo Solorzano, Alonso De 1584-1648? *BbD,*

BiD&SB, CasWL, DcEuL, DcSpL, Pen Eur
Castillo Y Solorzano, Alonso De 1584-1648? *REn*
Castle, Agnes d1922 *LongC, NewC*
Castle, Cassius Augustus 1822-1908 *ChPo, ChPo S1*
Castle, Charles 1939- *ConAu 33, WrD 1976*
Castle, Coralie 1924- *ConAu 57*
Castle, Eduard Friedrich Ferdinand 1875- *WhLA*
Castle, Edward James 1842- *Alli Sup*
Castle, Egerton 1858-1920 *Alli Sup, BbD, BiD&SB, Chmbr 3, DcEnA Ap, EvLB, LongC, NewC, REn, TwCA*
Castle, Emery N 1923- *ConAu 1R*
Castle, Frances *ConAu XR*
Castle, George *Alli*
Castle, Harold George 1907- *Au&Wr*
Castle, Henry Anson 1841-1916 *DcNAA*
Castle, Henry James 1811- *Alli Sup*
Castle, Mrs. J H *Alli Sup*
Castle, Jeffery Lloyd 1898- *Au&Wr*
Castle, Lee *ConAu XR*
Castle, Lewis *Alli Sup*
Castle, Marian Johnson 1898- *AmA&B, AmNov, ConAu 17*
Castle, Melissa Allen *TexWr*
Castle, Molly 1908- *Au&Wr*
Castle, Nicholas 1837-1922 *IndAu 1917*
Castle, Nicholas 1910- *AmSCAP 66*
Castle, Robert W, Jr. 1929- *ConAu 25*
Castle, Stanley *AmA&B*
Castle, Vernon Blythe 1887-1918 *DcNAA*
Castle, William *Alli*
Castleberry, John Jackson 1877-1937 *DcNAA*
Castleden, George *Alli Sup*
Castlehaven, James Touchet, Earl Of *Alli*
Castlemain, Roger Palmer, Earl Of *Alli*
Castlemaine, Earl Of *NewC*
Castleman, John *Alli*
Castleman, Josiah Hamilton 1873- *IndAu 1917, WhWNAA*
Castleman, Richard *Alli*
Castleman, Virginia Carter 1864- *AmA&B, AmLY, BiDSA, WhWNAA*
Castlemon, Alfred A *Alli Sup*
Castlemon, Harry 1842-1915 *Alli Sup, AmA, AmA&B, BiD&SB, DcAmA, DcNAA, OxAm, REnAL*
Castlen, Eppie Bowdre *Alli Sup, ChPo S1, LivFWS*
Castlereagh, Marquis Of Londonderry *Alli*
Castlereagh, Viscount 1769-1822 *BiDLA, NewC*
Castlereagh, Lord Robert Stewart 1769-1822 *Alli*
Castles, Clea *ChPo S2*
Castles, Francis G 1943- *ConAu 25*
Castles, John *Alli*
Castles, Lance 1937- *ConAu 25*
Castleton, A G *MnBBF*
Castleton, Virginia 1925- *ConAu 49*
Casto, Julius *Alli Sup*
Caston, M *Alli Sup*
Castor, Grahame 1932- *ConAu 13R*
Castor, Henry 1909- *AuBYP, ConAu 17R*
Castres, Abraham *Alli*
Castro, Agustin 1728-1790 *BiD&SB*
Castro, Americo 1885-1972 *ClDMEuL, ConAu 37, DcSpL*
Castro, Antonio 1946- *ConAu 53*
Castro, Armando 1904-1961 *AmSCAP 66*
Castro, Chris *Alli*
Castro, Eugenio De 1869-1944 *CasWL, ClDMEuL, EncWL, EvEuW, Pen Eur*
Castro, Francisco De *Pen Am*
Castro, Guillen De 1569-1631 *DcSpL, Pen Eur*
Castro, Ines De 1310?-1355 *DcSpL, REn*
Castro, Jose Maria Ferreira De 1898-1974 *CasWL, ConAu 53, EvEuW, ModRL*
Castro, Rosalia De 1837-1885 *CasWL 6, ClDMEuL, DcSpL, EuA, EvEuW, Pen Eur*
Castro, Tomas DeJesus 1902- *PueRA*
Castro, Tony 1946- *ConAu XR, WrD 1976*
Castro Alves, Antonio De 1847-1871 *CasWL, Pen Am, REn*

Castro-Klaren, Sara 1942- *ConAu 61*
Castro Quesada, Americo 1885- *CasWL, EvEuW*
Castro Y Bellvis, Guillen De 1569-1631 *CasWL, DcEuL, EuA, EvEuW, McGWD, REn*
Castruccio, Peter A 1925- *BiDPar*
Casty, Alan Howard 1929- *ConAu 1R, WrD 1976*
Casus, John *Alli*
Caswall, Edward 1814-1878 *Alli, Alli Sup, ChPo S1, PoCh*
Caswall, George *Alli*
Caswall, Henry 1810-1870 *Alli, Alli Sup, DcAmA, DcNAA*
Caswall, Isaac *WebEAL*
Caswall, John Edward *OxCan*
Caswell, Albert Edward 1884- *WhWNAA*
Caswell, Alexis 1799-1877 *Alli Sup, DcAmA, DcNAA*
Caswell, Anne *ConAu XR*
Caswell, Edward S *OxCan*
Caswell, Edward T *Alli Sup*
Caswell, Furman *ChPo*
Caswell, Mrs. George A *Alli Sup*
Caswell, Helen 1923- *ConAu 33, OxCan Sup*
Caswell, John *Alli*
Caswell, John Edgar 1905- *WhWNAA*
Caswell, Mary Woodbury *ChPo*
Caswell, Oscar Charles 1913- *AmSCAP 66*
Caswell, Robert Gamble 1892- *WhWNAA*
Caswell, Wilbur Larremore 1883- *WhWNAA*
Catafago, Joseph *Alli Sup*
Catala, Rafael E *DrAF 1976, DrAP 1975*
Catala, Victor 1873- *CasWL, ClDMEuL*
Catalano, Donald B 1920- *ConAu 57*
Catalano, Thomas J 1933- *AmSCAP 66*
Catalogne, Gedeon 1662-1729 *OxCan*
Catanese, Anthony James 1942- *ConAu 29, WrD 1976*
Catania, A Charles 1936- *ConAu 37*
Catao, Francisco Xavier Gomes 1896- *WrD 1976*
Catcheside, F L *Alli Sup*
Catchings, Waddill 1879-1967 *AmA&B*
Catchpole, Nathaniel 1904- *Au&Wr*
Catchpole, William Leslie 1900?- *MnBBF*
Catchpool, William *Alli Sup*
Catcombe, George *MnBBF*
Catcott, A S *Alli*
Catcott, Alexander *Alli*
Catcott, George J *Alli*
Cate, Claud Gibson *TexWr*
Cate, Curtis Wilson 1924- *Au&Wr, ConAu 53, WrD 1976*
Cate, Curtis Wolsey 1884-1976 *ConAu 61*
Cate, Eliza Jane 1812-1884? *DcAmA, DcNAA*
Cate, James Lea 1899- *AmA&B*
Cate, Laura *ChPo*
Cate, William Burke 1924- *ConAu 13R*
Cate, Wirt Armistead 1900- *AmA&B*
Cateline, Jeremy *Alli*
Cateora, Philip Rene 1932- *ConAu 5R*
Cater, Catherine 1917- *BlkAW*
Cater, Donald Brian 1908- *Au&Wr*
Cater, Douglass 1923- *AmA&B, ConAu 1R, WrD 1976*
Cater, Philip *Alli Sup*
Cater, Samuel *Alli*
Caterina Da Siena 1347-1380 *CasWL, EuA, EvEuW*
Cates, George 1911- *AmSCAP 66*
Cates, Ray A, Jr. 1940- *ConAu 29*
Cates, William Leist Redwin *Alli Sup*
Catesby, Lady Juliet *Alli*
Catesby, Mark 1679-1749 *Alli, CyAL 1, OxAm, REnAL*
Catfield, George *Alli Sup*
Catharine Of Genoa, Saint 1447- *OxEng*
Cathcart, Lord *OxCan*
Cathcart, Charles W And Caird, F M *Alli Sup*
Cathcart, Charlotte 1877-1964 *IndAu 1917*
Cathcart, George 1794- *Alli*
Cathcart, Helen *Au&Wr, ConAu 5R, WrD 1976*
Cathcart, John *Alli*
Cathcart, Noble Aydelotte 1898- *AmA&B*
Cathcart, Robert 1817-1870 *ChPo, ChPo S1*
Cathcart, Wallace Hugh 1865-1942 *OhA&B*

Cathcart, William 1826-1908 *Alli Sup, DcAmA, DcNAA*
Cathel, E E *MnBBF*
Cathell, Daniel Webster 1839-1925 *Alli Sup, BiDSA, DcAmA, DcNAA*
Cather, Carolyn *IlBYP*
Cather, George R *Alli Sup*
Cather, John *Alli Sup*
Cather, Katherine d1926 *DcNAA*
Cather, Willa Sibert 1873?-1947 *AmA&B, AmWr, AtlBL, CasWL, ChPo, ChPo S1, Chmbr 3, CnDAL, ConAmA, ConAmL, CyWA, DcBiA, DcLEnL, DcNAA, EncWL, EvLB, JBA 1934, LongC, ModAL, ModAL Sup, OxAm, OxCan, OxEng, Pen Am, RAdv 1, RCom, REn, REnAL, TwCA, TwCA Sup, TwCW, WebEAL, WhTwL, WhWNAA*
Catherall, Arthur 1906- *Au&Wr, AuBYP, ConAu 5R, MnBBF, SmATA 3, WrD 1976*
Catherall, Samuel *Alli*
Catherine II 1729-1796 *CasWL, DcEuL, EvEuW, OxFr, REn*
Catherine De Medicis 1519-1589 *OxFr, REn*
Catherine Of Alexandria, Saint *NewC*
Catherine Of Siena, Saint 1347-1380 *CasWL*
Catherine Parr 1509?-1548 *Alli, DcEnL, REn*
Catherine, Saint Of Siena 1347-1380 *BiD&SB, DcEuL*
Catherine, Saint ALSO Caterina
Catherine, Sister Mary *CatA 1947*
Catherine The Great 1729-1796 *DcRusL, REn*
Catherwood *ChPo*
Catherwood, Frederick 1925- *WrD 1976*
Catherwood, John *Alli*
Catherwood, Mary Hartwell 1847-1902 *Alli Sup, AmA, AmA&B, BbD, BiD&SB, DcAmA, DcBiA, DcLEnL, DcNAA, IndAu 1816, JBA 1934, OhA&B, OxAm, REnAL*
Cathey, Cornelius Oliver 1908- *ConAu 1R*
Cathie, Cameron *ChPo S2*
Cathill, James *Alli Sup*
Cathode Ray 1901- *WrD 1976*
Catholic Priest, A *PoIre*
Cathon, Laura E 1908- *ConAu 5R*
Cathrall, Isaac 1764-1819 *Alli, DcNAA*
Cathrall, William *Alli Sup*
Cathrein, Victor 1845- *WhLA*
Catiline d062BC *REn*
Catinat, Nicolas De 1637-1712 *OxFr*
Catizone, Joseph 1902- *AmSCAP 66*
Catledge, Turner 1901- *AmA&B, AuNews 1, ConAu 57*
Catlew, Samuel *Alli*
Catley, Ann *Alli*
Catley, Elaine Maud 1889- *WhWNAA*
Catlin, Esther Trowbridge *ChPo*
Catlin, George *Alli*
Catlin, George 1796-1872 *Alli Sup, AmA, AmA&B, AtlBL, BbD, BiD&SB, CasWL, DcAmA, DcEnL, DcLEnL, DcNAA, EvLB, OxAm, REn, REnAL*
Catlin, George 1896- *WrD 1976*
Catlin, Mrs. George *CatA 1947*
Catlin, George Byron 1857-1934 *DcNAA*
Catlin, Sir George Edward Gordon 1896- *Au&Wr, ConAu 13R, WhWNAA*
Catlin, George Lynde 1840-1896 *Alli Sup, ChPo, ChPo S1, ChPo S2, DcAmA, DcNAA*
Catlin, Henry Guy 1843- *DcAmA*
Catlin, J J d1826 *Alli*
Catlin, L R *ChPo*
Catlin, Louise 1861- *DcAmA*
Catlin, Warren Benjamin 1881- *ConAu 1R*
Catling, Darrel 1909- *Au&Wr, ConAu 5R*
Catling, G *MnBBF*
Catling, Patrick Skene *WrD 1976*
Catling, Thomas G *MnBBF*
Catlow, Agnes *Alli, Alli Sup*
Catlow, Joan 1911- *Au&Wr*
Catlow, Joanna 1911- *ConAu XR, WrD 1976*
Catlow, Joseph Peel *Alli Sup*
Catlow, Maria E *Alli Sup*
Catlow, Samuel *BiDLA*
Catlyn, John *Alli*
Catnach, James *ChPo S1*

Cato *ConAu XR, DcNAA, OxAm*
Cato, Dionysius *CasWL, DcEnL, NewC*
Cato, Marcus Porcius, The Elder 234BC-149BC *BiD&SB, CasWL, NewC, Pen Cl, REn*
Cato, Marcus Porcius, The Younger 095BC-046BC *CasWL, REn*
Cato, Marcus Porcius Priscus 234BC-149BC *BbD*
Cato, Nancy Fotheringham 1917- *ChPo S2, ConAu P-1, ConP 1970, TwCW*
Catoir, John T 1931- *ConAu 25*
Caton, Charles E 1928- *ConAu 9R*
Caton, Hiram 1936- *ConAu 53*
Caton, John Dean 1812-1895 *Alli Sup, BiD&SB, DcAmA, DcNAA*
Caton, T Motte *Alli, BiDLA*
Caton, William *Alli*
Caton-Thompson, Gertrude 1888- *WrD 1976*
Cator, Peter *Alli Sup*
Catron, John H 1916- *AmSCAP 66*
Catron, Louis E 1932- *ConAu 45*
Cats, Jacob 1577-1660 *BbD, BiD&SB, CasWL, EuA, EvEuW, Pen Eur*
Cats, Jakob 1577-1660 *DcEuL*
Cattan, Henry 1906- *ConAu 29, WrD 1976*
Cattanach, Christopher John *Au&Wr*
Cattanar *DcOrL 2, Pen Cl*
Cattaui, Georges 1896- *ConAu 25*
Cattell, C C *Alli Sup*
Cattell, Edward James 1856-1938 *DcNAA*
Cattell, Everett L 1905- *ConAu 1R*
Cattell, Henry Ware 1862- *WhWNAA*
Cattell, Jacques 1904-1960 *AmA&B*
Cattell, James McKeen 1860-1949? *AmA&B, DcNAA*
Cattell, Joseph *Alli*
Cattell, Psyche 1893- *ConAu 41*
Cattell, Raymond Bernard 1905- *AmA&B, Au&Wr, ConAu 5R, WrD 1976*
Cattell, Thomas *Alli*
Catterall, G C *Alli Sup*
Catterall, Ralph Charles Henry 1866-1914 *DcNAA*
Cattermole, George 1800-1868 *ChPo, ChPo S1, NewC*
Cattermole, L *Alli Sup*
Cattermole, Richard *Alli*
Cattermole, William *BbtC, OxCan*
Cattley, Stephen *Alli*
Cattlin, F Fisher *Alli Sup*
Cattlin, Thomas Magnus *Alli Sup*
Catto, Edward 1849- *ChPo S2*
Catto, Max 1909- *Au&Wr*
Catton, Bruce 1899- *Alli Sup, AmA&B, AuNews 1, ConAu 5R, OxAm, Pen Am, REn, REnAL, SmATA 2, TwCA Sup, WrD 1976*
Catton, Charles 1756-1819 *BkIE*
Catton, Charles, Jr. *Alli*
Catton, J Morris *Alli Sup*
Catton, William Bruce 1926- *ConAu 1R*
Cattopadhyay, Bankimcandra 1838-1894 *DcOrL 2*
Cattopadhyay, Saratcandra 1876-1937 *DcOrL 2*
Catty, C *Alli Sup*
Catty, Lewis *Alli, BiDLA*
Catullus, Caius Valerius 084?BC-054?BC *BbD, BiD&SB, DcEnL*
Catullus, Gaius Valerius 084?BC-054?BC *AtlBL, CasWL, CyWA, NewC, OxEng, Pen Cl, RCom, REn*
Catulus, Quintus Lutatius d087BC *Pen Cl*
Caturce, Jean De d1532 *OxFr*
Catz, Max *ConAu XR*
Cau, Jean 1925- *CnMD, TwCW, WorAu*
Cauble, Commodore Wesley 1874-1935 *IndAu 1917*
Cauchon, Joseph Edouard 1816-1885 *BbtC, DcNAA, OxCan*
Caudhari, Raghuvir *DcOrL 2*
Caudill, Harry Monroe 1922- *AmA&B, ConAu 33*
Caudill, Rebecca 1899- *AmA&B, AuBYP, ChPo S1, ConAu 5R, MorJA, SmATA 1, WrD 1976*
Caudry, Thomas *Alli*
Caudwell, Christopher 1907-1937 *DcLEnL, EncM&D, LongC, ModBL, Pen Eng,*

REn, TwCA, TwCA Sup, WebEAL
Cauffman, Stanley Hart 1880-1947 *DcNAA, WhWNAA*
Caughey, James 1810?-1892 *DcAmA, DcNAA*
Caughey, John Walton 1902- *AmA&B*
Caughey, LaRee Pfeiffer *TexWr*
Caulaincourt, Armand-A-L, Marquis De 1773-1827 *OxFr*
Cauldwell, Frank *ConAu XR, NewC, WrD 1976*
Cauldwell, H T *MnBBF*
Cauley, Terry *ConAu XR*
Cauley, Troy Jesse 1902- *ConAu 1R*
Caulfeild, A H W 1879- *WhWNAA*
Caulfeild, Edward Houston *PoIre*
Caulfeild, J *PoIre*
Caulfeild, James 1728-1799 *PoIre*
Caulfeild, John *PoIre*
Caulfeild, Sophia F A *PoIre*
Caulfield, Bishop Of Wexford *BiDLA*
Caulfield, D D *Alli*
Caulfield, E W *Alli Sup*
Caulfield, J *Alli*
Caulfield, James *Alli, BiDLA*
Caulfield, Peggy F 1926- *ConAu 5R*
Caulfield, Richard 1823-1871 *Alli Sup*
Caulfield, Sophia Frances Anne *Alli Sup, ChPo S1*
Cauliflower, Sebastian *ConAu XR*
Caulkins, Daniel 1824-1902 *OhA&B*
Caulkins, Frances Mainwaring 1796-1869 *Alli, Alli Sup, DcAmA, DcNAA*
Caulton, Isabella *Alli Sup, ChPo S2*
Cauman, Sam 1910- *ConAu 23*
Caumont, Mary *Alli Sup*
Caundishe, Richard *Alli*
Caunter, G H *Alli*
Caunter, Hobart *Alli*
Caunter, John Hobart 1794-1852 *Alli*
Caunter, Mary *Alli Sup*
Caunter, Violet Sibyl *Alli Sup*
Caurvana, Philippo *Alli*
Causey, Gilbert 1907- *WrD 1976*
Causley, Charles 1917- *Au&Wr, AuBYP, ChPo, ChPo S1, ChPo S2, CnE&AP, ConAu 9R, ConP 1970, ConP 1975, LongC, NewC, SmATA 3, WebEAL, WorAu, WrD 1976*
Caustic, Christopher 1771-1837 *AmA, AmA&B, DcEnL, DcNAA*
Causton, Henry Kent Staple *Alli Sup*
Causton, Mrs. S M *Alli Sup*
Caute, David 1936- *Au&Wr, ConAu 1R, ConDr, ConNov 1972, ConNov 1976, NewC, WrD 1976*
Cauthen, W Kenneth 1930- *ConAu 5R, WrD 1976*
Cauthorn, Henry Sullivan 1828-1905 *IndAu 1816*
Cautley, George Spencer d1880 *Alli Sup, ChPo*
Cautley, Sir Proby Thomas 1802-1871 *Alli Sup*
Cauty, Henry Evans *Alli Sup*
Cauty, W *Alli*
Cauvin, Jean *REn*
Cauvin, Joseph *Alli, Alli Sup*
Cava, Esther Laden 1916- *ConAu 37*
Cavacchioli, Enrico 1885-1954 *McGWD*
Cavada, F F *Alli Sup*
Cavafy, Constantine P 1863-1933 *AtlBL, CasWL, CnMWL, EncWL, EvEuW, LongC, OxEng, Pen Eur, REn, TwCA Sup, TwCW, WhTwL*
Cavaiani, Mabel 1919- *ConAu 57*
Cavalca, Domenico 1270?-1342 *CasWL*
Cavalcanti, Bartolomeo 1503-1562 *CasWL*
Cavalcanti, Giovanni *DcEuL*
Cavalcanti, Guido 1255?-1300 *AtlBL, BiD&SB, CasWL, EuA, EvEuW, Pen Eur, REn*
Cavalcaselle, Giovanni Battista 1820-1897 *BiD&SB*
Cavalier, Jean *OxFr, REn*
Cavalier, Julian 1931- *ConAu 49*
Cavallari, Alberto 1927- *ConAu 23*
Cavallaro, Ann 1918- *ConAu 5R*
Cavallaro, Carmen 1913- *AmSCAP 66*
Cavallini, Pietro 1250?-1330? *AtlBL*
Cavallo, Diana 1931- *AmA&B, ConAu 1R,*

Chadwick, Owen 1916- *WrD 1976*
Chadwick, Raymond Dean 1887- *IndAu 1917*
Chadwick, Ruth R *ChPo S1*
Chadwick, Samuel *Alli Sup*
Chadwick, Shelden *ChPo, ChPo S1, ChPo S2*
Chadwick, Sheldon *Alli Sup*
Chadwick, St. John *OxCan Sup*
Chadwick, W *Alli Sup*
Chadwick, W J *Alli Sup*
Chadwick, William *Alli Sup*
Chadwick, William Arthur *Alli Sup*
Chadwick, William Owen 1916- *Au&Wr,
    ConAu 1R*
Chadwin, Mark Lincoln 1939- *ConAu 25*
Chafa, Sara Genevra *ChPo S2*
Chafe, Levi G *OxCan*
Chafe, Wallace L 1927- *ConAu 29,
    WrD 1976*
Chafe, William H 1942- *ConAu 49*
Chafee, Zechariah, Jr. 1885-1958 *REnAL*
Chafee, Zechariah, Jr. 1885- *WhWNAA*
Chafer, Lewis Sperry 1871-1952 *OhA&B*
Chafetz, Henry 1916- *AuBYP, ConAu 1R*
Chafetz, Morris E 1924- *ConAu 13R*
Chaffee, Allen *AmA&B, ConAu P-1,
    MnBBF, SmATA 3, WhWNAA,
    WrD 1976*
Chaffee, Eleanor Alletta *ChPo*
Chaffee, Emory Leon 1885- *WhWNAA*
Chaffee, Harold Leland *ChPo*
Chaffee, Helen *ChPo*
Chaffee, J G *ChPo S1*
Chaffee, Zechariah 1885-1957 *AmA&B*
Chaffer, Richard *Alli Sup*
Chaffers, William 1811- *Alli Sup*
Chaffey, Susan *ChPo S1*
Chaffin, George *Alli Sup*
Chaffin, J W *Alli Sup*
Chaffin, Lillie D 1925- *ConAu 33, DrAF 1976,
    SmATA 4, WrD 1976*
Chaffin, Lucien Gates 1846-1927 *DcNAA*
Chaffin, William Ladd 1837-1922 *Alli Sup,
    DcAmA, DcNAA*
Chaffin, Yule M 1914- *ConAu 23*
Chafie, *Alli*
Chafin, Andrew 1937- *ConAu 53*
Chafin, Eugene Wilder 1852-1920 *DcNAA*
Chafin, William *Alli*
Chafulumira, English William 1930?- *AfA 1*
Chafy, John *Alli*
Chafy, William *Alli, BiDLA*
Chagall, David 1930- *ConAu 9R*
Chagall, Marc 1889?- *REn, WhGrA*
Chagas, Antonio Das 1631-1682 *CasWL,
    Pen Eur*
Chagla, Mahommedali Currim 1900- *Au&Wr*
Chagnon, Godfrey *BbtC*
Chahoon, Mary *ChPo*
Chai, Chen Kang 1916- *ConAu 21*
Chai, Ch'u 1906- *ConAu 9R*
Chai, Hon-Chan 1931- *ConAu 23*
Chai, Winberg 1934- *ConAu 5R*
Chaij, Fernando 1909- *ConAu 21*
Chaille, Stanford Emerson 1830-1911 *Alli Sup,
    BiDSA, DcAmA, DcNAA*
Chaille-Long, Charles 1842?-1917 *AmA&B,
    BbD, BiD&SB, DcNAA*
Chaillu, Paul Belloni Du 1829- *Chmbr 3,
    DcEnL, JBA 1934*
Chainey, George *Alli Sup*
Chairil Anwar 1922-1949 *CasWL, DcOrL 2,
    Pen Cl*
Chajes, Julius 1910- *AmSCAP 66*
Chakerian, Charles 1904- *ConAu 45*
Chakhrukhadze *DcOrL 3*
Chakour, Charles M 1929- *ConAu 33*
Chakravarty *DcOrL 2*
Chakravarty, Amiya 1901- *ConAu 1R*
Chalcocondylas, Laonicus 1432?-1490? *EvEuW*
Chalcocondyles, Laonicus 1432?-1490? *CasWL,
    Pen Cl*
Chalcondyles, Demetrius 1424-1511 *DcEuL,
    REn*
Chalenor, Mary *Alli*
Chalfaut, Mary Scott *ChPo*
Chalfin, M Mabel 1877- *WhWNAA*
Chalfont, Peter *MnBBF*
Chalford, K *Alli*

Chaliapin, Feodor Ivanovitch 1873-1938 *REn*
Chalieu, Guillaume Amfrye, Abbe De 1636-1720
    DcEuL
Chalk, Elizabeth *Alli*
Chalk, John Allen 1937- *ConAu 57*
Chalk, Ocania 1927- *ConAu 45, LivBA*
Chalk, Ronald Jack 1915- *Au&Wr*
Chalke, Herbert Davis 1897- *Au&Wr,
    WrD 1976*
Chalker, Dorothy *ChPo S2*
Chalkey, Thomas d1749 *Alli*
Chalkhill, John *Alli, BrAu, CasWL, ChPo,
    ChPo S1, Chmbr 1, DcEnL, DcLEnL,
    EvLB, NewC, OxEng*
Chalkley, Thomas 1675-1741 *BiD&SB,
    CyAL 1, DcAmA, DcNAA, OxAm,
    REnAL*
Chall, Jeanne S 1921- *ConAu 25*
Challans, Mary *NewC, WorAu, WrD 1976*
Challemel-Lacour, Paul Armand 1827-1896
    BiD&SB
Challen, James 1802-1878 *Alli, Alli Sup,
    ChPo, ChPo S1, DcAmA, DcNAA,
    OhA&B*
Challener, T *Alli Sup*
Challice, A E *Alli*
Challice, Annie Emma 1821-1875 *Alli Sup*
Challice, John 1815-1863 *Alli Sup*
Challice, Kenneth *WrD 1976*
Challis, George *Alli Sup*
Challis, Gordon 1932- *ConP 1970, WrD 1976*
Challis, H *ChPo*
Challis, Henry William 1841- *Alli Sup*
Challis, James 1803-1882 *Alli Sup*
Challis, R *Alli Sup*
Challiss, James Courtney 1860- *ChPo,
    WhWNAA*
Challoner, Richard 1691-1781 *Alli*
Challoner, Robert *Alli Sup*
Chalmers *Alli*
Chalmers, Adam *Alli Sup*
Chalmers, Alexander 1759-1834 *Alli, BiD&SB,
    BiDLA, BiDLA Sup, DcEnL, NewC*
Chalmers, Allan Knight 1897- *AmA&B,
    OhA&B*
Chalmers, Andrew C *Alli Sup*
Chalmers, Audrey 1899?-1957 *AuBYP,
    IlCB 1945, IlCB 1956*
Chalmers, Charles *Alli, Alli Sup*
Chalmers, David *Alli*
Chalmers, David 1530-1592 *Alli*
Chalmers, David Mark 1927- *ConAu 25*
Chalmers, Eric Brownlie 1929- *Au&Wr,
    WrD 1976*
Chalmers, Floyd S 1898- *ConAu 25,
    OxCan Sup, WhWNAA*
Chalmers, George 1742-1825 *Alli, BbD, BbtC,
    BiD&SB, BiDLA, CasWL, ChPo,
    Chmbr 2, DcEnL, EvLB, OxAm*
Chalmers, Grace Pratt 1819-1851 *Alli Sup,
    ChPo S1*
Chalmers, Harvey 1890-1971 *Au&Wr,
    ConAu 33*
Chalmers, James *Alli, Alli Sup*
Chalmers, James 1859- *WhWNAA*
Chalmers, James B *Alli Sup*
Chalmers, Jean d1939 *OhA&B*
Chalmers, John *Alli Sup*
Chalmers, John A *Alli Sup*
Chalmers, John W *OxCan Sup*
Chalmers, Lionel 1715-1777 *Alli, BiDSA,
    CyAL 1, DcAmA, DcNAA*
Chalmers, Mackenzie D E Stewart 1847-
    Alli Sup
Chalmers, Mary Eileen 1927- *AuBYP, ChPo,
    ConAu 5R, IlCB 1956, IlCB 1966,
    SmATA 6, ThBJA*
Chalmers, Patrick *Alli Sup*
Chalmers, Patrick Reginald 1872-1942 *Br&AmS,
    ChPo, ChPo S1, ChPo S2, WhLA*
Chalmers, Peter *Alli Sup*
Chalmers, Randolph Carleton 1908- *Au&Wr,
    WrD 1976*
Chalmers, Robert *Alli*
Chalmers, Stephen 1880-1935 *AmA&B, ChPo,
    DcNAA, WhWNAA*
Chalmers, Thomas 1780-1847 *Alli, BbD,
    BiD&SB, BiDLA, BiDLA Sup, BrAu 19,*

**Chmbr 3, DcEnL, DcLEnL, EvLB,
    OxEng**
Chalmers, W A d1798? *BkIE*
Chalmers, William d1792 *Alli*
Chalmers, William Scott 1888- *Au&Wr*
Chalon, Alfred Edward 1780-1860 *ChPo,
    ChPo S1*
Chalon, John *WrD 1976*
Chaloner, Edward 1590-1625 *Alli*
Chaloner, James d1661 *Alli*
Chaloner, John Seymour 1924- *Au&Wr*
Chaloner, Philip *Alli Sup*
Chaloner, Thomas *Alli*
Chaloner, Sir Thomas *Chmbr 1*
Chaloner, Sir Thomas 1515?-1565 *Alli, DcEnL*
Chaloner, Sir Thomas 1559-1615 *Alli*
Chaloner, William Henry 1914- *Au&Wr*
Chalout, Remi *OxCan Sup*
Chalupka, Jan 1791-1871 *CasWL*
Chalupka, Samo 1812-1883 *CasWL*
Cham 1819-1879 *OxFr*
Cham, The Great, Of Literature *DcEnL*
Chamales, Thomas T 1924-1960 *AmA&B*
Chamber *WhLA*
Chamber, John d1549 *Alli*
Chamberlain, Alexander Francis 1865-1914
    AmA&B, DcAmA, DcNAA
Chamberlain, Allen 1867- *AmA&B,
    WhWNAA*
Chamberlain, Arthur Henry 1872?-1942
    AmA&B, ChPo, WhWNAA
Chamberlain, Basil Hall 1850- *Alli Sup,
    WhLA*
Chamberlain, Betty 1908- *ConAu 33,
    WrD 1976*
Chamberlain, Brenda Irene 1912- *ConP 1970*
Chamberlain, C *Alli Sup*
Chamberlain, C, Jr. *Alli Sup*
Chamberlain, Cator *Alli Sup*
Chamberlain, Charles Joseph 1863- *WhWNAA*
Chamberlain, Christopher 1918- *IlCB 1966*
Chamberlain, Clark Wells 1870- *WhWNAA*
Chamberlain, Daniel Henry 1835-1907 *DcNAA*
Chamberlain, David *Alli*
Chamberlain, Edith L *Alli Sup*
Chamberlain, Elinor 1901- *AuBYP,
    ConAu P-1*
Chamberlain, Emily Hall d1916 *ChPo*
Chamberlain, Ernest Barrett 1883- *OhA&B*
Chamberlain, Ernest Noble 1899- *Au&Wr*
Chamberlain, George Agnew 1879-1966
    AmA&B, REnAL, WhWNAA
Chamberlain, H B *Alli Sup*
Chamberlain, Henry Richardson 1859-1911
    DcAmA, DcNAA
Chamberlain, Houston Stewart 1855-1927
    LongC, OxGer, REn
Chamberlain, Hugh 1664-1728 *Alli*
Chamberlain, Jacob 1835-1908 *Alli Sup,
    DcAmA, DcNAA, OhA&B*
Chamberlain, James Franklin 1869- *AmLY,
    WhWNAA*
Chamberlain, John *Alli*
Chamberlain, John 1553-1627 *CrE&SL*
Chamberlain, John Rensselaer 1903- *AmA&B,
    ConAu 57, OxAm, REnAL, TwCA,
    TwCA Sup*
Chamberlain, Joseph 1836- *Alli Sup*
Chamberlain, Joshua Lawrence 1828-1914
    DcAmA, DcNAA
Chamberlain, Julian Ingersoll 1873- *Br&AmS*
Chamberlain, Lawrence 1878- *AmLY,
    WhWNAA*
Chamberlain, Lawrence H 1906- *AmA&B*
Chamberlain, Leander Trowbridge 1837-1913
    DcNAA
Chamberlain, Mrs. M H *Alli Sup*
Chamberlain, Mason *Alli, BiDLA*
Chamberlain, Mellen 1821-1900 *Alli Sup,
    AmA, DcAmA, DcNAA*
Chamberlain, Montague 1844-1924 *Alli Sup,
    DcAmA, DcNAA*
Chamberlain, Narcisse 1924- *AmA&B,
    ConAu 13R*
Chamberlain, Nathan Henry 1830?-1901
    Alli Sup, BiD&SB, DcAmA, DcNAA
Chamberlain, Neil Wolverton 1915- *AmA&B,
    ConAu 13R*

Chamberlain, Neville 1869-1940 *REn*
Chamberlain, Parthene B *Alli Sup*
Chamberlain, Robert *Alli*
Chamberlain, Robert 1607- *Alli*
Chamberlain, Robert Lyall 1923- *ConAu 13R*
Chamberlain, Roy S 1907- *AmSCAP 66*
Chamberlain, Samuel 1895-1975 *AmA&B,*
Au&Wr, ConAu 23, ConAu 53,
WhWNAA
Chamberlain, Thomas *Alli, Alli Sup*
Chamberlain, Walter 1820- *Alli Sup*
Chamberlain, William 1619-1689 *Alli*
Chamberlain, William Isaac 1837-1920 *OhA&B*
Chamberlain, William Isaac 1862-1937 *DcNAA*
Chamberlain, William Mellen d1887 *Alli Sup*
Chamberlain, Winthrop Burr 1864- *WhWNAA*
Chamberlaine, Alexander Francis *OxCan*
Chamberlaine, Edward 1616-1703 *Alli*
Chamberlaine, Henry *Alli*
Chamberlaine, James *Alli*
Chamberlaine, John *Alli*
Chamberlaine, John d1723 *Alli*
Chamberlaine, Joseph *Alli*
Chamberlaine, Maud L *ChPo*
Chamberlaine, Nathaniel *Alli*
Chamberlaine, Richard *Alli*
Chamberlaine, Walter 1708?- *PoIre*
Chamberlaine, William 1752- *Alli, BiDLA*
Chamberland, J B E *BbtC*
Chamberland, Paul 1939- *CanWr, CasWL,*
OxCan, OxCan Sup
Chamberlane, William 1619-1689 *Alli*
Chamberlayne, Bartholomew *Alli*
Chamberlayne, Churchill Gibson 1876- *BiDSA*
Chamberlayne, Edward 1616-1703 *Alli, BrAu,*
NewC, OxEng
Chamberlayne, Israel 1795-1875 *Alli, Alli Sup,*
DcAmA
Chamberlayne, John 1666-1723 *Alli, NewC*
Chamberlayne, S E *Alli, BiDLA*
Chamberlayne, Tankerville *Alli Sup*
Chamberlayne, William 1619-1689 *Alli, BrAu,*
CasWL, ChPo, Chmbr 1, DcEnL,
DcLEnL, EvLB, NewC, OxEng
Chamberlen, Hugh *Alli*
Chamberlen, Paul *Alli*
Chamberlin, Brown 1827- *BbtC*
Chamberlin, Edward Hastings 1899- *AmA&B*
Chamberlin, Edwin M *Alli Sup*
Chamberlin, Eric Russell 1926- *Au&Wr*
Chamberlin, Everett *Alli Sup*
Chamberlin, Franklin *Alli Sup*
Chamberlin, Frederick 1870-1942 *AmA&B,*
AmLY
Chamberlin, Georgia Louise 1862-1943 *DcNAA*
Chamberlin, Harry D 1887-1944 *Br&AmS*
Chamberlin, Henry Harmon 1873-1951 *AmA&B,*
WhWNAA
Chamberlin, J Gordon 1914- *ConAu 1R*
Chamberlin, Jo Hubbard *AuBYP*
Chamberlin, Joseph Edgar 1851-1935 *AmA&B,*
BiD&SB, DcAmA, DcNAA
Chamberlin, Kate *Alli Sup*
Chamberlin, Leslie J 1926- *ConAu 53*
Chamberlin, Lily Pearl *TexWr*
Chamberlin, M Hope 1920-1974 *ConAu 45,*
ConAu 49
Chamberlin, Mary 1914- *Au&Wr, ConAu 45,*
WrD 1976
Chamberlin, Ralph Vary 1879- *WhWNAA*
Chamberlin, Rollin Thomas 1881- *WhWNAA*
Chamberlin, Thomas Chrowder 1843-1928
Alli Sup, AmA&B, DcAmA, DcNAA
Chamberlin, William Fosdick 1870-1943
OhA&B
Chamberlin, William Henry *OxCan*
Chamberlin, William Henry 1833-1912 *OhA&B*
Chamberlin, William Henry 1897-1969 *AmA&B,*
ConAu 5R, OxAm, REnAL, TwCA,
TwCA Sup
Chamberlon, Peter *Alli*
Chambers, Miss A C *Alli Sup*
Chambers, Aidan 1934- *Au&Wr, ChPo S2,*
ConAu 25, SmATA 1
Chambers, Anne *Alli Sup*
Chambers, Augusta *Alli Sup, ChPo S1*
Chambers, Bertram Mordaunt 1866- *WhLA*
Chambers, Bettie Keyes *BiDSA*

Chambers, C *Alli Sup*
Chambers, C Bosseron *ConICB*
Chambers, C E S 1859- *WhLA*
Chambers, C H *Alli*
Chambers, Charles *Alli, Alli Sup*
Chambers, Charles Haddon 1860-1921 *Chmbr 3,*
EvLB, LongC, REn, TwCA, TwCA Sup
Chambers, Charles Harcourt *Alli Sup*
Chambers, Charles Julius 1850- *Alli Sup, BbD,*
BiD&SB, DcAmA
Chambers, Clarke A 1921- *ConAu 41*
Chambers, David 1530-1592 *Alli*
Chambers, David Laurance 1879-1963 *AmA&B,*
IndAu 1816
Chambers, David Ware 1921- *IndAu 1917*
Chambers, Derek *MnBBF*
Chambers, Dewey W 1929- *ConAu 29*
Chambers, E K *ModBL*
Chambers, Sir Edmund Kerchever 1866-1954
CasWL, DcLEnL, EvLB, LongC, NewC,
OxEng, Pen Eng, REn, TwCA,
TwCA Sup
Chambers, Edward J 1925- *ConAu 17R*
Chambers, Edward Kerchever 1866- *ChPo*
Chambers, Edward Thomas Davies 1852-1931
DcNAA
Chambers, Ephraim 1680?-1740 *Alli, BrAu,*
DcEnL, NewC
Chambers, Ernest A 1928- *AmSCAP 66*
Chambers, Ernest J *OxCan*
Chambers, Ernest John 1862-1925 *DcNAA*
Chambers, Frank P 1900- *ConAu P-1*
Chambers, George *Alli, Alli Sup, DrAF 1976,*
DrAP 1975
Chambers, George 1786-1866 *DcNAA*
Chambers, George Frederick 1841- *Alli Sup*
Chambers, George Gailey 1873- *WhWNAA*
Chambers, George H *Alli Sup*
Chambers, Henry E 1860- *BiDSA*
Chambers, Howard V *ConAu 49*
Chambers, Humphrey *Alli*
Chambers, J *Alli*
Chambers, J D *Alli*
Chambers, James 1748- *ChPo*
Chambers, James Floyd, Jr. 1913- *AmA&B*
Chambers, James Julius 1850-1920 *DcNAA,*
OhA&B
Chambers, Jim Bernard 1919- *WrD 1976*
Chambers, John *Alli, BiDLA Sup*
Chambers, John Charles 1817-1874 *Alli Sup*
Chambers, John David 1805- *Alli Sup, PoCh*
Chambers, John Peter *Alli Sup*
Chambers, John Sharpe 1889- *WhWNAA*
Chambers, Jonathan David 1898- *ConAu 1R*
Chambers, Julius 1850-1920 *AmA&B*
Chambers, M M 1899- *ConAu 9R*
Chambers, Margaret Ada Eastwood 1911-
ConAu 9R, SmATA 2
Chambers, Maria Cristina *CatA 1947*
Chambers, Mariana *Alli*
Chambers, Marianne *BiDLA*
Chambers, Mary Catherine Elizabeth *Alli Sup*
Chambers, Mary Davoren *WhWNAA*
Chambers, Merritt Madison 1899- *AmA&B,*
OhA&B, WrD 1976
Chambers, Mortimer Hardin, Jr. 1927-
ConAu 9R
Chambers, Osborne William Samuel *Alli Sup*
Chambers, Peggy 1911- *Au&Wr, ConAu XR,*
SmATA 2
Chambers, Peter *Alli, ConAu XR*
Chambers, Philip 1936- *MnBBF*
Chambers, R *Alli Sup*
Chambers, R J 1917- *ConAu 17R*
Chambers, R W 1865-1933 *LongC*
Chambers, R W 1874-1942 *LongC*
Chambers, Raymond John 1917- *WrD 1976*
Chambers, Rex *MnBBF*
Chambers, Richard *Alli, BiDLA*
Chambers, Robert *Alli*
Chambers, Robert d1888 *Alli Sup*
Chambers, Sir Robert 1737-1803 *Alli*
Chambers, Robert 1802-1871 *Alli, Alli Sup,*
BbD, BiD&SB, BrAu 19, CasWL, ChPo,
ChPo S1, ChPo S2, DcEnA, DcEnL,
DcEuL, DcLEnL, EvLB, NewC, OxEng,
Pen Eng
Chambers, Robert 1881- *WhWNAA*

Chambers, Robert Warner *AuBYP*
Chambers, Robert William 1865-1933 *AmA&B,*
BbD, BiD&SB, CarSB, ChPo, ChPo S2,
Chmbr 3, DcAmA, DcBiA, DcLEnL,
DcNAA, OxAm, REnAL, TwCA
Chambers, S Francis *ChPo*
Chambers, Sabin *Alli*
Chambers, Sherman Daniel 1881- *IndAu 1917*
Chambers, Stephen A *BlkAW*
Chambers, Sydney *MnBBF*
Chambers, T And G Tattersall *Alli*
Chambers, Talbot Wilson 1819-1896 *Alli Sup,*
DcAmA, DcNAA
Chambers, Thomas King *Alli Sup*
Chambers, Violet *Alli Sup*
Chambers, W Walker 1913- *ConAu 29*
Chambers, Whittaker 1901-1961 *AmA&B,*
LongC, WorAu
Chambers, William *Alli, Alli Sup, BbtC,*
Pen Eng
Chambers, William 1800-1883 *Alli, Alli Sup,*
BiD&SB, CasWL, ChPo, ChPo S2,
DcEnA, DcEnL, DcEuL, EvLB
Chambers, Sir William 1726?-1796 *Alli, AtlBL*
Chambers, William And Robert *Chmbr 3*
Chambers, William Davis 1856- *IndAu 1917*
Chambers, William Nisbet 1916- *ConAu 5R*
Chambers, William Trout 1896- *ConAu P-1,*
IndAu 1917
Chambers, William Walker 1913- *WrD 1976*
Chambers-Ketchum, Annie 1874-1904 *ChPo S1*
Chambertin, Ilya 1931- *ConAu XR*
Chambliss, A W *Alli Sup*
Chambliss, Alexander Wilds 1812-1893 *DcNAA*
Chambliss, Charles Edward 1871- *WhWNAA*
Chambliss, J E *Alli Sup*
Chambliss, William C 1908?-1975 *ConAu 57*
Chambliss, William J 1923- *ConAu 13R*
Chambord, Comte De 1820-1883 *OxFr*
Chambray, Georges, Marquis De 1783-1848
BiD&SB
Chambre, Alan *Alli Sup*
Chambre, Albert Saint John *DcAmA*
Chambre, David 1530-1592 *Alli*
Chambre, Richard *Alli*
Chambre, Rowland *Alli*
Chambre, Willelmus De *Alli*
Chambres, Charles *Alli*
Chambrun, Clara Longworth, Comtesse De
1873-1954 *AmA&B*
Chameatus *CasWL*
Chamerovzow, Louis Alexis *Alli Sup*
Chametzky, Jules 1928- *ConAu 33*
Chamfort, Nicholas 1741-1794 *DcEuL*
Chamfort, Nicolas-Sebastien Roch 1741-1794
OxFr
Chamfort, Sebastien Roch Nicolas 1741-1794
AtlBL, BbD, BiD&SB, CasWL, EuA,
EvEuW, Pen Eur
Chamier, Frederick 1796-1870 *Alli, Alli Sup,*
BiD&SB, BrAu 19, Chmbr 3, DcEnL,
DcLEnL, EvLB, NewC
Chamier, George 1842-1915? *CasWL,*
WebEAL
Chamier, John *Alli, BiDLA*
Chamisso, Adalbert Von 1781-1838 *CasWL,*
DcBiA, EvEuW, Pen Eur, REn
Chamisso, Adelbert Von 1781-1838 *BbD,*
BiD&SB, ChPo, DcEuL, EuA, OxEng,
OxFr, OxGer
Chamnitzer, Ivan Ivanovich 1745-1784 *BiD&SB*
Chamot, Emile Monnin 1868- *WhWNAA*
Champ, Tom *MnBBF*
Champagne, Antoine *OxCan Sup*
Champagne, Marian 1915- *ConAu 5R*
Champagne, Maurice *OxCan Sup*
Champagne, Philippe De 1602-1674 *OxFr*
Champaigne, Philippe De 1602-1674 *OxFr*
Champcenetz, De 1759-1794 *DcEuL*
Champeaux, Guillaume De *NewC*
Champfleury 1821-1889 *BbD, BiD&SB,*
CasWL, OxFr, Pen Eur
Champfleury, Jules 1821-1889 *EvEuW*
Champier, Symphorien 1472?-1540? *BiD&SB,*
CasWL, OxFr
Champigny, Chevalier De *BiDSA*
Champigny, Jean Bochart, Chevalier De d1720
OxCan

Champigny, Robert J 1922- *ConAu 33*
Champion, Anthony 1724?-1801 *Alli*
Champion, Ellen Porter *ChPo*
Champion, Frederick Alfred 1908- *Au&Wr*
Champion, Harold 1902- *Au&Wr*
Champion, Helen Jean *OxCan*
Champion, J *Alli*
Champion, John Benjamin 1868-1948 *DcNAA*
Champion, John C 1923- *ConAu 17R*
Champion, John E 1922- *ConAu 13R*
Champion, John George *Alli Sup*
Champion, Joseph 1709- *Alli*
Champion, Larry S 1932- *ConAu 23, WrD 1976*
Champion, R A 1925- *ConAu 29*
Champion, Richard *Alli, BbtC*
Champion, Roland *DcNAA*
Champion, William *Alli Sup*
Champion, William James *Alli Sup*
Champion, William Scott *Alli Sup*
Champkin, Peter 1918- *ChPo S2, ConAu 5R, WrD 1976*
Champlain, Samuel De 1567?-1635 *OxAm, OxCan, OxFr, REn, REnAL*
Champley, James *Alli Sup*
Champlin, Edwin Ross 1854-1928 *Alli Sup, AmA&B, DcNAA, WhWNAA*
Champlin, Henry L *Alli Sup*
Champlin, James R 1928- *ConAu 21*
Champlin, James Tift 1811-1882 *Alli, Alli Sup, BiD&SB, DcAmA, DcNAA*
Champlin, John Denison 1834-1915 *Alli Sup, AmA&B, BiD&SB, DcAmA, DcNAA*
Champlin, Joseph M 1930- *ConAu 49*
Champlin, Virginia *Alli Sup, DcNAA*
Champmesle, Marie Desmares 1642-1698 *OxFr*
Champneis, John *Alli*
Champness, Thomas *Alli Sup*
Champness, William Swain *Alli Sup*
Champney, Anthony *Alli*
Champney, Elizabeth Williams 1850-1922 *AmA&B, BbD, BiD&SB, CarSB, ChPo, ChPo S1, DcAmA, DcNAA, OhA&B*
Champney, Freeman 1911- *ConAu 25*
Champney, H N *Alli Sup*
Champney, James Wells 1843-1903 *AmA&B*
Champney, John *Alli*
Champney, Lizzie J 1850- *Alli Sup*
Champney, T *Alli, BiDLA*
Champney, W L *ChPo, EarAB, EarAB Sup*
Champneys, Basil 1842- *Alli Sup, ChPo, ChPo S1, WhLA*
Champneys, Francis Henry 1848- *Alli Sup*
Champneys, William Weldon 1807-1875 *Alli Sup*
Champollion, Jean Francois 1790-1832 *BbD, OxFr, REn*
Champris, Gaillard De *OxCan*
Chamson, Andre 1900- *CasWL, CIDMEuL, ConAu 5R, EncWL, OxFr, Pen Eur, REn, TwCA, TwCA Sup*
Chamson, Andre Jules Louis 1900- *WhLA*
Ch'an, Chu 1913- *ConAu XR*
Chan, Jeffrey Paul *DrAF 1976*
Chan, Loren Briggs 1943- *ConAu 57*
Chan, Plato 1931- *IlCB 1945*
Chan, Shau Wing 1907- *AmA&B*
Chan, Sui Wesley *ChPo*
Chan, Wing-Tsit 1901- *AmA&B*
Chanaidh, Fear *ConAu XR*
Chanakya *ConAu XR, REn*
Chanan, Gabriel 1942- *ConAu 57*
Chance, Edward John *Alli Sup*
Chance, Frank 1826- *Alli Sup*
Chance, Henry *Alli*
Chance, John Newton 1911- *MnBBF*
Chance, Julie Grinnell *AmA&B, DcNAA*
Chance, Michael R A 1915- *Au&Wr*
Chance, Norman A *OxCan Sup*
Chance, Richard Newton d1957 *MnBBF*
Chance, Sir Roger 1893- *Au&Wr*
Chancel, A D *Alli*
Chancellor, Charles Williams 1833-1915 *Alli Sup, BiDSA, DcAmA, DcNAA*
Chancellor, Edwin Beresford 1868- *Alli Sup, WhLA*
Chancellor, Eustathius 1854- *BiDSA, DcAmA*
Chancellor, Frank *Alli Sup*

Chancellor, John *Au&Wr, AuNews 1, MnBBF*
Chancellor, John 1900- *ConAu 23*
Chancellor, Paul 1900-1975 *ConAu 57*
Chancellor, Richard d1556 *NewC*
Chancellor, Valerie Edith 1936- *Au&Wr*
Chancellor, William Estabrook 1867- *OhA&B*
Chancy, Charles *Alli*
Chand, Prem 1880-1936 *REn*
Chand Bardai *CasWL*
Chanda, Asok Kumar 1902- *ConAu 17R*
Chandar, Krishan 1914- *DcOrL 2*
Chandar Bhan *DcOrL 2*
Chandidas 1417-1477 *CasWL*
Chandler *Alli*
Chandler, A Bertram 1912- *ConAu 21, WrD 1976*
Chandler, Albert Richard 1884-1957 *OhA&B*
Chandler, Alfred D *Alli Sup*
Chandler, Alfred D, Jr. 1918- *ConAu 9R*
Chandler, Alfred L 1852- *Alli Sup*
Chandler, Alice 1931- *ConAu 53*
Chandler, Allison 1906- *ConAu P-1*
Chandler, Amos Henry *ChPo*
Chandler, Anna Curtis *ChPo*
Chandler, Arthur Bertram 1912- *Au&Wr*
Chandler, Asa Crawford *TexWr, WhWNAA*
Chandler, Augustus B 1839- *BiDSA*
Chandler, B *Alli*
Chandler, B J 1921- *ConAu 1R*
Chandler, Benjamin *Alli*
Chandler, Bessie 1856- *ChPo, ChPo S1, DcAmA*
Chandler, Blanche Mary 1863-1902 *ChPo*
Chandler, C F *CyAL 1*
Chandler, Caroline Augusta 1906- *AmA&B, AuBYP, BkC 4, CatA 1947, ConAu 17R*
Chandler, Caroline H *Alli*
Chandler, Carrie B *ChPo*
Chandler, Charles DeForest 1878-1939 *DcNAA, OhA&B*
Chandler, Charles Henry 1840-1885 *DcNAA*
Chandler, Daniel 1805-1866 *BiDSA*
Chandler, Daniel H *Alli Sup*
Chandler, David Geoffrey 1934- *ConAu 25, WrD 1976*
Chandler, David Leon *ConAu 49*
Chandler, David Porter 1933- *ConAu 45*
Chandler, Edna Walker 1908- *AuBYP, ConAu 1R*
Chandler, Edward d1750 *Alli*
Chandler, Edward Barron 1800-1880 *OxCan*
Chandler, Elizabeth Margaret 1807-1834 *Alli, AmA, AmA&B, BbD, BiD&SB, ChPo, ChPo S1, CyAL 2, DcAmA, DcNAA, FemPA, OxAm*
Chandler, Ellen Louise 1835- *Alli*
Chandler, Elsie Williams *ChPo*
Chandler, Francis Ward 1844-1926 *DcNAA*
Chandler, Frank *ConAu 57*
Chandler, Frank Wadleigh 1873-1947 *AmA&B, DcAmA, DcNAA, OhA&B*
Chandler, Mrs. G W *Alli Sup, DcNAA*
Chandler, Geoffrey 1922- *Au&Wr*
Chandler, George *Alli*
Chandler, George 1806-1893 *DcNAA*
Chandler, George 1915- *Au&Wr, ConAu 9R, WrD 1976*
Chandler, George Fletcher 1872- *WhWNAA*
Chandler, Henry *Alli*
Chandler, Henry William 1828-1889 *Alli Sup*
Chandler, Izora Cecilia d1906 *DcNAA*
Chandler, J V *ChPo S2*
Chandler, Jeff 1918-1961 *AmSCAP 66*
Chandler, John *Alli, ChPo*
Chandler, John 1806-1876 *Alli Sup, EvLB, PoCh*
Chandler, John Scudder 1849-1934 *DcNAA*
Chandler, John Westbrook *BiDLA*
Chandler, Joseph Ripley 1792-1880 *Alli, AmA&B, DcAmA, DcNAA*
Chandler, Julia *Alli Sup*
Chandler, Julian Alvin Carroll 1872-1934 *BiDSA, DcNAA*
Chandler, Katherine d1930 *DcNAA*
Chandler, Len 1935- *BlkAW*
Chandler, Louisa *ChPo*
Chandler, Mrs. M T W *FemPA*

Chandler, Margaret *ChPo S2*
Chandler, Margaret Kueffner 1922- *ConAu 17R*
Chandler, Mary 1687-1745 *Alli*
Chandler, Mary Greene 1818- *Alli, DcNAA*
Chandler, Olive *ChPo S1*
Chandler, Pat 1922- *AmSCAP 66*
Chandler, Peleg Whitman 1816-1889 *DcAmA, DcNAA*
Chandler, Peleg Whitmore 1816-1889 *Alli, Alli Sup*
Chandler, Pretor Whitty 1858- *WhLA*
Chandler, Raymond 1888-1959 *AmA&B, CasWL, CnMWL, DcLEnL, EncM&D, LongC, ModAL, ModAL Sup, OxAm, OxEng, Pen Am, REn, REnAL, TwCA Sup, TwCW, WebEAL, WhTwL*
Chandler, Reuben *Alli Sup*
Chandler, Richard *Alli Sup*
Chandler, Richard 1738-1810 *Alli*
Chandler, Richard Eugene 1916- *ConAu 5R*
Chandler, Ruth Forbes 1894- *AuBYP, ConAu 1R, SmATA 2, WrD 1976*
Chandler, S Bernard 1921- *ConAu 21, WrD 1976*
Chandler, Samuel *Alli*
Chandler, Samuel 1693-1756 *Alli*
Chandler, Stanley Cecil 1905- *Au&Wr*
Chandler, Stewart Curtis 1889- *WhWNAA*
Chandler, Sue Pinkston *LivBA*
Chandler, T H *Alli Sup*
Chandler, Thomas *Alli*
Chandler, Thomas 1911- *AuBYP*
Chandler, Thomas Bradbury 1728-1790 *Alli, CyAL 1, DcNAA*
Chandler, Thomas H *Alli Sup*
Chandler, Tony John 1928- *Au&Wr*
Chandler, W A *Alli Sup*
Chandler, Will H *ChPo*
Chandler, William *Alli*
Chandler, William Eaton 1835- *Alli Sup*
Chandler, William Henry 1878-1939 *DcNAA, WhWNAA*
Chandler-Newsom, Minnie *TexWr*
Chandler-Tucker, Gertrude Lee 1872-1953 *OhA&B*
Chandless, William *Alli Sup*
Chandola, Anoop C 1937- *ConAu 37*
Chandonnet, Ann 1943- *ConAu 61*
Chandonnet, Thomas Aime *BbtC*
Chandor, Anthony 1932- *ConAu 29*
Chandos, Viscount 1893- *Au&Wr*
Chandos, Dane *Au&Wr*
Chandos, Fay *ConAu XR, WrD 1976*
Chandos, Herbert *MnBBF*
Chandos, John 1918- *ConAu XR*
Chandra, Sharat *DrAP 1975*
Chandron, Mrs. A DeV *Alli Sup*
Chandu Menon *DcOrL 2*
Chaneles, Sol 1926- *ConAu 41*
Chaner, William Astor 1867- *DcAmA*
Chaney, George Leonard 1836-1922 *Alli Sup, BiD&SB, DcAmA, DcNAA*
Chaney, George R *Alli Sup*
Chaney, Henry A *Alli Sup*
Chaney, Jill 1932- *ConAu 25, WrD 1976*
Chaney, Lucian West 1857-1935 *DcNAA, WhWNAA*
Chaney, Lucien West 1857-1935 *Alli Sup, DcAmA*
Chaney, Newcomb K 1883- *WhWNAA*
Chaney, Otto Preston, Jr. 1931- *ConAu 33*
Chaney, William A 1922- *ConAu 33*
Chang, Ai-Ling 1920?- *DcOrL 1*
Chang, C Isabelle 1924- *ConAu 21*
Chang, Chen-Chi 1920- *BiDPar*
Chang, Chi 768?-830? *CasWL*
Chang, Chiu-Ling *DcOrL 1*
Chang, Constance D 1917- *ConAu 61*
Chang, Dae H 1928- *ConAu 57*
Chang, Diana *DrAF 1976, DrAP 1975*
Chang, Eileen 1920- *DcOrL 1, WorAu*
Chang, Garma Chen-Chi 1920- *Au&Wr*
Chang, Heng 078-139 *CasWL, DcOrL 1*
Chang, Hsien *DcOrL 1*
Chang, Hsien 990-1078 *DcOrL 1*
Chang, Hsin-Hai 1900?- *AmA&B, Au&Wr, ConAu 5R, WhLA*

Chapman, Edward Arnold 1906- *IndAu 1917*
Chapman, Edward Charles 1880- *WhWNAA*
Chapman, Edward J *Alli Sup, BbtC*
Chapman, Edward Mortimer 1862- *AmA&B*
Chapman, Edwin N *Alli Sup*
Chapman, Elizabeth 1919- *ConAu P-1, SmATA 10, WrD 1976*
Chapman, Elizabeth Rachel 1850-1897? *Alli Sup, ChPo*
Chapman, Elwood N 1916- *ConAu 37*
Chapman, Emily D *ChPo*
Chapman, Ervin S 1838-1921 *OhA&B*
Chapman, Ethel *CanNov, OxCan*
Chapman, Ethelyn Bryant *WhWNAA*
Chapman, F A 1818-1891 *ChPo S2, EarAB, EarAB Sup*
Chapman, F W *Alli*
Chapman, Francis 1869-1939 *DcNAA*
Chapman, Frank Michler 1864-1945 *AmA&B, DcAmA, DcNAA, JBA 1934, REnAL, TwCA, TwCA Sup*
Chapman, Frederic *ChPo*
Chapman, Sir Frederick Revans 1849- *WhLA*
Chapman, Frederick T *ChPo*
Chapman, Frederick Trench 1887- *IlCB 1956*
Chapman, G H Murray *MnBBF*
Chapman, G W Vernon 1925- *ConAu 29*
Chapman, George *Alli Sup, Chmbr 1*
Chapman, George 1559?-1634 *Alli, AtlBL, BbD, BiD&SB, BrAu, CasWL, ChPo, CnE&AP, CnThe, CrE&SL, CriT 1, CyWA, DcEnA, DcEnL, DcEuL, DcLEnL, EvLB, McGWD, MouLC 1, NewC, OxEng, Pen Eng, REn, REnWD, WebEAL*
Chapman, George 1723-1806 *Alli*
Chapman, George 1907- *ChPo*
Chapman, George Thomas 1786-1872 *Alli, Alli Sup, DcAmA, DcNAA*
Chapman, George W *Alli Sup*
Chapman, Guy Patterson 1889-1972 *Au&Wr, WorAu*
Chapman, H S 1803- *BbtC*
Chapman, H T *Alli*
Chapman, Harry Grafton *ChPo*
Chapman, Harvey Wood 1875-1941 *DcNAA*
Chapman, Helen E *Alli Sup*
Chapman, Henry *Alli*
Chapman, Henry Cadwalader 1845-1909 *Alli Sup, DcAmA, DcNAA*
Chapman, Henry Cleaver *Alli Sup*
Chapman, Henry Palmer 1865- *WhLA*
Chapman, Henry Samuel 1803-1881 *Alli Sup*
Chapman, Henry Smith 1871-1936 *DcNAA*
Chapman, Henry Thomas *Alli Sup*
Chapman, Hester W 1899- *Au&Wr, ConAu 9R*
Chapman, Hugh Boswell *Alli Sup*
Chapman, Isaac *Alli*
Chapman, J *Alli Sup*
Chapman, J Dudley 1928- *ConAu 23, WrD 1976*
Chapman, J G *Alli*
Chapman, Jacob And Lapham, W B *Alli Sup*
Chapman, James *Alli, Alli Sup, BiDLA*
Chapman, James 1799-1879 *Alli Sup*
Chapman, James 1919- *ConAu 41*
Chapman, James Crosby 1889-1925 *DcNAA*
Chapman, Jane Frances *Alli*
Chapman, John *Alli, Alli Sup, REn, WhWNAA*
Chapman, John 1704-1784 *Alli*
Chapman, John 1775?-1847 *AmA&B, OxAm*
Chapman, John 1865-1933 *CatA 1947*
Chapman, John 1900-1972 *AmA&B, ConAu 33*
Chapman, John 1927- *Au&Wr*
Chapman, John Abney 1821-1906 *Alli Sup, BiDSA, DcAmA, DcNAA*
Chapman, John Alexander 1875- *ChPo, ChPo S2*
Chapman, John Gadsby 1808-1889 *ChPo, EarAB, EarAB Sup*
Chapman, John Jay 1862-1933 *AmA&B, AtlBL, ChPo S1, CnDAL, DcAmA, DcNAA, OxAm, Pen Am, RAdv 1, REnAL, TwCA, TwCA Sup, WhWNAA*
Chapman, John Kemble *Alli Sup*

Chapman, John L 1920- *ConAu 1R*
Chapman, John Stanton Higham 1891- *AmA&B, AuBYP, TwCA, TwCA Sup, WhWNAA*
Chapman, John Wilbur 1859-1918 *DcNAA, IndAu 1816*
Chapman, Joseph Irvine 1912- *ConAu 61*
Chapman, Joseph Thomas *Alli Sup, ChPo S2*
Chapman, Joseph Warren 1855-1909 *ChPo S1*
Chapman, Julia B *ChPo*
Chapman, June R 1918- *ConAu 5R*
Chapman, Katharine Hopkins *BiDSA*
Chapman, Kenneth Francis 1910- *Au&Wr, ConAu P-1*
Chapman, Kenneth G 1927- *ConAu 13R*
Chapman, Kenneth Milton 1875- *AmA&B*
Chapman, L L *Alli Sup*
Chapman, Lee Jackson 1867-1953 *OhA&B*
Chapman, Loren J 1927- *ConAu 53*
Chapman, Lucie 1895- *AmA&B*
Chapman, Margaret Garner *Au&Wr*
Chapman, Maria Weston 1806-1885 *DcNAA, OxAm*
Chapman, Marie M 1917- *ConAu 61*
Chapman, Maristan *AmA&B, AmNov, AuBYP, REnAL, TwCA, TwCA Sup, WhWNAA*
Chapman, Mary *Alli Sup*
Chapman, Mary Francis 1838-1884 *Alli Sup*
Chapman, Mary Hamilton Illsley 1895- *AmA&B, AmNov XR, AuBYP, WhWNAA*
Chapman, Matthew James *Alli Sup*
Chapman, Michael Andrew 1884-1960 *CatA 1947, IndAu 1917*
Chapman, Nathaniel 1780-1853 *Alli, BiDSA, CyAL 1, DcAmA, DcNAA*
Chapman, Nell *BlkAW*
Chapman, Norton Everett *ChPo*
Chapman, Peggy *IlBYP*
Chapman, R W 1881-1960 *LongC*
Chapman, Raymond 1924- *Au&Wr, ConAu 5R*
Chapman, Richard *Alli*
Chapman, Richard Arnold 1937- *Au&Wr*
Chapman, Rick M 1943- *ConAu 49*
Chapman, Robert *Alli Sup, ChPo S2*
Chapman, Robert Barclay 1829- *Alli Sup*
Chapman, Robert C *Alli Sup*
Chapman, Robert William 1881-1960 *DcLEnL, EvLB, WhLA*
Chapman, Roger E 1916- *ConAu 23*
Chapman, Ronald George 1917- *Au&Wr, ConAu 5R, WrD 1976*
Chapman, Rose Woodallen 1875-1923 *DcNAA, OhA&B*
Chapman, Royal Norton 1889-1939 *DcNAA*
Chapman, Samuel *Alli*
Chapman, Samuel Greeley 1929- *ConAu 17R, WrD 1976*
Chapman, Stanley David 1935- *Au&Wr, ConAu 21, WrD 1976*
Chapman, Stanton *AmNov XR*
Chapman, Stephen *Alli*
Chapman, Steven *ConAu 41*
Chapman, Sydney 1888- *WhLA*
Chapman, Theodosia Spring *Alli Sup*
Chapman, Thomas *Alli*
Chapman, Thomas 1717-1760 *Alli*
Chapman, Thomas 1844- *ChPo S1*
Chapman, Thomas Jefferson *Alli Sup*
Chapman, Valentine Jackson 1910- *Au&Wr, WrD 1976*
Chapman, Victoria L 1944- *ConAu 57*
Chapman, W *Alli*
Chapman, W C *Alli Sup*
Chapman, Walker *ConAu XR, ThBJA*
Chapman, Walter Lynn 1913- *AmSCAP 66*
Chapman, Wendell 1895- *AmA&B*
Chapman, William *Alli, Alli Sup, BiDLA*
Chapman, Sir William *Alli*
Chapman, William 1850-1917 *CanWr, DcNAA, OxCan*
Chapman, William Gerard 1877-1945 *DcNAA, WhWNAA*
Chapman, William Stacey *Alli Sup*
Chapman, Woodallen 1875- *AmLY*
Chapman-Huston, Desmond 1884- *ChPo*

Chapman-Mortimer, William Charles 1907- *ConAu 13R, WrD 1976*
Chapone, Hester 1727-1801 *Alli, BiD&SB, BrAu, CarSB, CasWL, ChPo, Chmbr 2, DcEnL, DcLEnL, EvLB, NewC, WebEAL*
Chappel, Barth *Alli*
Chappel, R *Alli*
Chappel, Samuel *Alli*
Chappel, William 1582-1649 *Alli*
Chappell, Absalom Harris 1801-1878 *BiDSA, DcNAA*
Chappell, Clovis Gillham 1882- *AmA&B*
Chappell, Edward 1792-1861 *Alli, BbtC, OxCan*
Chappell, Fred 1936- *AmA&B, Au&Wr, ConAu 5R, DrAF 1976, DrAP 1975*
Chappell, Frederick Patey And Shoard, J *Alli Sup*
Chappell, George C *ChPo*
Chappell, George Shepard 1877-1946 *AmA&B, ChPo, DcNAA, REnAL*
Chappell, Gordon 1939- *ConAu 57*
Chappell, Helen F *BlkAW*
Chappell, J Harris 1849-1906 *BiDSA*
Chappell, Jennie *Alli Sup*
Chappell, Mollie *WrD 1976*
Chappell, Pearl Wallace *ChPo S2, TexWr*
Chappell, Philip E *Alli Sup*
Chappell, Vere Claiborne 1930- *ConAu 5R*
Chappell, Warren 1904- *ConAu 17R, IlBYP, IlCB 1945, IlCB 1956, IlCB 1966, SmATA 6, ThBJA, WhGrA*
Chappell, William 1582-1649 *DcEnL*
Chappell, William 1810?-1888 *Alli Sup, DcEnL*
Chappelou, John *Alli*
Chappelow, Allan *Au&Wr, ConAu 53, WrD 1976*
Chappelow, Leonard 1683-1768 *Alli*
Chapple, Edward *Alli Sup*
Chapple, Eliot Dismore 1909- *Au&Wr, ConAu 41*
Chapple, Joe Mitchell 1867-1950 *AmA&B, AmLY*
Chapple, John Alfred Victor 1928- *Au&Wr, ConAu 21, WrD 1976*
Chapple, John E *Alli Sup*
Chapple, Joseph Mitchell 1867- *ChPo, DcAmA*
Chapple, William *BiDLA*
Chapple, William d1781 *Alli*
Chapple, William d1784 *BiDLA Sup*
Chaput, Marcel *OxCan*
Chaput-Rolland, Solange *OxCan Sup*
Chapygin, Alexey Pavlovich 1870-1937 *CasWL, ClDMEuL, DcRusL, EvEuW*
Char, Rene 1907- *CasWL, CnMWL, ConAu 13R, EncWL, EvEuW, ModRL, OxFr, Pen Eur, REn, TwCW, WhTwL, WorAu*
Char, Tin-Yuke 1905- *ConAu 57*
Charanis, Peter 1908- *ConAu 37*
Charasha, Tembot 1902- *DcOrL 3*
Charbonneau, Jean 1875-1960 *CanWr, OxCan*
Charbonneau, Robert 1911-1967 *CanWr, CasWL, OxCan, OxCan Sup*
Chard, Leslie Frank, II 1934- *ConAu 33, WrD 1976*
Chard, Thomas S *Alli Sup*
Chardin, Jean 1643-1713 *OxFr, REn*
Chardin, Jean Baptiste Simeon 1699-1779 *AtlBL, OxFr, REn*
Chardin, Sir John 1643-1713 *Alli*
Chardon De Croisilles *CasWL*
Chardon De Reims *CasWL*
Chardon, John *Alli*
Chardon, M *BiDLA*
Chardonne, Jacques 1884-1968 *CasWL, ClDMEuL, EncWL, EvEuW, Pen Eur, REn, TwCA, TwCA Sup*
Chardry *CasWL*
Chareh Sultan El Osman *WhWNAA*
Chares, Henry *WrD 1976*
Chargin, Madeleine *ChPo*
Charhadi, Driss Ben Hamed *ConAu 13R*
Chari, C T K 1909- *BiDPar*
Chari, V Krishna 1924- *ConAu 17R*

Charier, B *Alli*
Charig, Phil 1902-1960 *AmSCAP 66*
Charik, Izy 1898-1937 *CasWL*
Charinho, Payo Gomes *CasWL*
Charisi, Jehuda Ben Salomo 1190?-1235 *BiD&SB*
Charitas, Sister M 1888- *BkC 5*
Charke, Charlotte d1760 *Alli*
Charke, Ezechiel *Alli*
Charke, William *Alli*
Charkovsky, Willis 1918- *AmSCAP 66*
Charland, Paul Victor 1858-1939 *DcNAA*
Charlap, Morris 1928- *AmSCAP 66*
Charldon, John *Alli*
Charle, Will *WrD 1976*
Charlemagne 742-814 *DcEuL, DcSpL, NewC, OxFr, REn*
Charlemont, James Caulfield, Earl Of 1728-1799 *Alli, PoIre*
Charles SEE ALSO Karl
Charles VII 1403-1461 *REn*
Charles IX 1550-1574 *OxFr*
Charles X 1757-1836 *OxFr*
Charles, Duke Of Orleans 1394?-1465 *AtlBL, CasWL, DcEuL, EuA, EvEuW, OxFr, Pen Eng, REn*
Charles IV, Holy Roman Emperor 1316-1378 *CasWL*
Charles V, Holy Roman Emperor 1500-1558 *DcEuL, REn*
Charles Julius *NewC*
Charles I, King Of England 1600-1649 *Alli, ChPo, DcEnL, NewC, REn*
Charles II, King Of England 1630-1685 *Alli, DcEnL, NewC, REn*
Charles I, King Of Spain *DcEuL*
Charles VIII, L'Affable 1470-1498 *OxFr*
Charles IV, Le Bel 1294-1328 *OxFr*
Charles VI, Le Bien-Aime 1368-1422 *OxFr*
Charles II, Le Chauvre 823-877 *OxFr*
Charles Le Gros 839-888 *OxFr*
Charles V, Le Sage 1337-1380 *OxFr*
Charles III, Le Simple 879-929 *OxFr*
Charles Le Temperaire 1433-1477 *OxFr*
Charles VII, Le Victorieux 1403-1461 *OxFr*
Charles Martel 714?-741 *OxFr, REn*
Charles The Bold 1433-1477 *NewC*
Charles The Great 742-814 *OxGer, REn*
Charles The Hammer 689?-741 *REn*
Charles, A O *Alli Sup*
Charles, C M 1931- *ConAu 49*
Charles, Charles Mitchell *Alli Sup*
Charles, Dick 1919- *AmSCAP 66*
Charles, Don C 1918- *ConAu 9R*
Charles, Donald *IlBYP*
Charles, Elizabeth Rundle 1828-1896 *Alli Sup, BbD, ChPo, ChPo S1, DcBiA, NewC*
Charles, Emily Thornton 1845-1890? *Alli Sup, ChPo, ChPo S1, DcAmA, DcNAA, IndAu 1816*
Charles, Ernest 1895- *AmSCAP 66*
Charles, Frances 1872- *DcAmA*
Charles, Francis 1872- *AmA&B*
Charles, Fred 1869- *WhLA*
Charles, George Drummond *Alli Sup*
Charles, George E *Alli Sup*
Charles, Gerda *Au&Wr, ConAu 1R, ConNov 1972, ConNov 1976, WorAu, WrD 1976*
Charles, H Frederick *Alli Sup*
Charles, Helen Dorothea White 1888- *IndAu 1917*
Charles, James Edward *Alli, IndAu 1816*
Charles, Joan 1914- *AmA&B, AmNov, OhA&B*
Charles, Joseph *Alli*
Charles, Louis *ConAu XR*
Charles, Mark *ConAu XR*
Charles, Martha Evans *BlkAW*
Charles, Maurice *EarAB Sup*
Charles, Nicholas *ThBJA*
Charles, Pierre 1883- *CatA 1952*
Charles, Ray 1918- *AmSCAP 66*
Charles, Richard *Alli*
Charles, Richard 1929- *Au&Wr, WrD 1976*
Charles, Robert H *ChPo*
Charles, Robert Henry *Alli Sup, WhLA*
Charles, Rollin L 1885- *WhWNAA*

Charles, Mrs. Rundle *ChPo S1*
Charles, Sam *ChPo S1*
Charles, Sascha 1896?-1972 *ConAu 37*
Charles, Searle F 1923- *ConAu 9R, WrD 1976*
Charles, T Cranstoun *Alli Sup*
Charles, Theresa *Au&Wr, ConAu XR, WrD 1976*
Charles, Thomas Edmonston *Alli Sup*
Charles, Will *ConAu XR*
Charles-Edwards, Thomas 1902- *Au&Wr*
Charless, Joseph 1772-1834 *AmA&B*
Charleston, Robert Jesse 1916- *Au&Wr, WrD 1976*
Charlesworth, Arthur Riggs 1911- *ConAu 53*
Charlesworth, Beedam *Alli Sup*
Charlesworth, Edward Gomersall *Alli Sup*
Charlesworth, Florence M 1885- *AmSCAP 66*
Charlesworth, Grace 1906- *Au&Wr, WrD 1976*
Charlesworth, Hector Willoughby 1873-1945 *DcNAA, OxCan*
Charlesworth, James Clyde 1900-1974 *AmA&B, ConAu 9R, ConAu 45*
Charlesworth, John Kaye 1889- *Alli, Au&Wr, BiDLA, ConAu P-1*
Charlesworth, Maria Louisa 1819-1880 *Alli Sup*
Charlesworth, Maria Louisa 1830- *DcEnL*
Charlesworth, Marie Louisa 1819-1880 *WhCL*
Charlesworth, Maxwell John 1925- *ConAu 1R*
Charlesworth, Ruby Hughes 1905- *OhA&B*
Charlesworth, Samuel Beddome *Alli Sup*
Charlesworth, Vernon J *Alli Sup*
Charlet, Arthur *Alli*
Charleton, Arthur G *Alli Sup*
Charleton, George *Alli*
Charleton, R J *Alli Sup*
Charleton, Rice *Alli*
Charleton, Robert 1809-1872 *Alli Sup*
Charleton, Walter 1619-1707 *Alli, Chmbr 1, DcEnL, EvLB*
Charleville, Countess Of *PoIre*
Charlevoix, Pierre Francois Xavier De 1682-1761 *BiDSA, OxCan*
Charley, Helen G 1909- *IndAu 1917*
Charley, William *Alli Sup*
Charley, Sir William Thomas 1833- *Alli Sup*
Charlie *MnBBF*
Charlier, Patricia Simonet 1923- *ConAu 37*
Charlier, Roger Henri 1921- *ConAu 37, WrD 1976*
Charlip, Remy 1929- *AuBYP, ChPo S1, ConAu 33, IlCB 1956, IlCB 1966, SmATA 4, ThBJA, WrD 1976*
Charlot, Andre Eugene Maurice 1882-1956 *REn*
Charlot, F *Alli Sup*
Charlot, Gaston *Au&Wr*
Charlot, Jean 1898- *CatA 1952, ConAu 5R, IlBYP, IlCB 1945, IlCB 1956, IlCB 1966, MorJA, SmATA 8, WrD 1976*
Charlotte Elizabeth 1792-1846 *DcEnL*
Charlotte, Elizabeth *Alli*
Charlson, David *ConAu XR*
Charlton *MnBBF*
Charlton, Charles *Alli*
Charlton, Charlie *Alli Sup*
Charlton, Donald Geoffrey 1925- *ConAu 1R*
Charlton, Edward *Alli Sup*
Charlton, Edwin A *Alli Sup*
Charlton, H B 1890-1961 *LongC*
Charlton, James *WhWNAA*
Charlton, John *ConAu XR*
Charlton, John 1840?- *Br&AmS*
Charlton, John Moon *Alli Sup*
Charlton, Lionel *Alli*
Charlton, Mary *Alli, BiDLA*
Charlton, Robert Foster 1911- *Au&Wr, WrD 1976*
Charlton, Robert Milledge 1807-1854 *Alli, AmA&B, BiDSA, ChPo, ChPo S1, CyAL 2, DcNAA*
Charlton, Samuel *Alli*
Charlton, Thomas Usher Pulaski 1781-1835 *Alli, BiDSA*
Charlton, Walter *Alli*
Charlton, Walter 1619-1707 *Alli*
Charlton, Walter Glasco 1854- *BiDSA*
Charlton, William Henry 1787-1866 *Alli Sup,*

ChPo S1
Charlus, Baron Palamede De *OxFr, REn*
Charlwood, Donald Ernest Cameron 1915- *Au&Wr, ConAu 23, WrD 1976*
Charmatz, Bill 1925- *ConAu 29, SmATA 7*
Charnance, L P *ConAu XR*
Charney, George 1905?-1975 *ConAu 61*
Charney, Hanna K 1931- *ConAu 49*
Charney, Maurice 1929- *ConAu 9R*
Charnin, Martin 1934- *AmSCAP 66*
Charnley, Mitchell Vaughn 1898- *AmA&B, IndAu 1917, WhWNAA*
Charnock, G F *Alli Sup*
Charnock, Joan Paget 1903- *Au&Wr, ConAu 33, WrD 1976*
Charnock, John H 1756-1807 *Alli, BbtC*
Charnock, Mary Anna E *ChPo*
Charnock, Richard *Alli*
Charnock, Richard Stephen 1820- *Alli Sup*
Charnock, Stephen 1628-1680 *Alli, DcEnL*
Charnock, Thomas *Alli*
Charnock, William Whytehead *Alli Sup*
Charnwood, Baron Godfrey Rathbone Benson 1864-1945 *EncM&D, LongC, REn, REnAL, TwCA, TwCA Sup*
Charny, Carmi 1925- *ConAu 13R*
Charny, Israel W 1931- *ConAu 37, ConAu 57, WrD 1976*
Charon *ClDMEuL*
Charosh, Mannis 1906- *ConAu 29, SmATA 5*
Charot, Mikhas 1896- *DcRusL*
Charpentier, Francois 1620-1702 *OxFr*
Charpentier, Gustave 1860-1956 *OxFr, REn*
Charpentier, Marc Antoine 1634-1704 *REn*
Charques, Dorothy 1899- *Au&Wr*
Charras, Jean Baptiste Adolphe 1810-1865 *BiD&SB*
Charrier, S J *Alli*
Charriere, Madame De 1740-1805 *OxEng, OxFr*
Charriere, Henri 1907?-1973 *ConAu 45*
Charriere, Isabelle De 1740?-1805 *BiD&SB, CasWL, EvEuW, REn*
Charriere DePenthaz, Isabella De 1740?-1805 *DcEuL*
Charron, Pierre 1541-1603 *CasWL, DcEuL, OxFr, Pen Eur*
Charsley, Fanny Anne *Alli Sup*
Charsley, W *Alli*
Charter, John *ChPo*
Charteris, Archibald Hamilton 1835- *Alli Sup*
Charteris, Sir Evan 1864-1940 *NewC, WhLA*
Charteris, F C *MnBBF*
Charteris, F W, Earl Of Wemyss & March 1818- *Alli Sup*
Charteris, Hugo 1922-1970 *WorAu*
Charteris, Leslie 1907- *AmA&B, Au&Wr, ConAu 5R, EncM&D, EvLB, LongC, MnBBF, NewC, REn, REnAL, TwCA, TwCA Sup, TwCW, WrD 1976*
Charteris, Leslie K *MnBBF*
Charteris, Matthew *Alli Sup*
Charters, Ann 1936- *ConAu 17R, WrD 1976*
Charters, Mark *PoIre*
Charters, Samuel *Alli*
Charters, Samuel 1929- *ConAu 9R*
Charters, Werrett Wallace 1875- *WhWNAA*
Chartham, Will *Alli*
Chartier, Alain 1390?-1440? *BiD&SB, CasWL, DcEuL, EuA, EvEuW, OxFr, Pen Eur, REn*
Chartier, Emile 1868-1951 *ClDMEuL, EvEuW, OxCan, OxFr, REn, WhWNAA*
Chartier, Jean d1464 *CasWL*
Chartok, Shepard *ChPo S1*
Chartrand, Joseph Demers 1852-1905 *DcNAA*
Chartres, Mark *PoIre*
Chartres, Samuel *BiDLA*
Charushin, Evgeny Ivanovich 1901- *WhGrA*
Charvat, Frank John 1918- *ConAu 1R*
Charvat, William 1905- *ChPo*
Charvet, Patrice Edouard 1903- *Au&Wr*
Chary, Frederick B 1939- *ConAu 49*
Charyk, John C *OxCan Sup*
Charyn, Jerome 1937- *AmA&B, ConAu 5R, ConLC 5, ConNov 1972, ConNov 1976, DrAF 1976, WrD 1976*
Chasan, Daniel Jack 1943- *ConAu 29*

Chase, A Elizabeth 1906- *ConAu P-1*
Chase, A W *Alli Sup*
Chase, Adam *ConAu XR*
Chase, Agnes 1869- *WhWNAA*
Chase, Alan L 1929- *ConAu 1R*
Chase, Alice *ConAu XR, SmATA 4*
Chase, Alice Elizabeth 1906- *Au&Wr, AuBYP*
Chase, Alston Hurd 1906- *ConAu 5R,
     WrD 1976*
Chase, Alvin Wood 1817-1885 *DcNAA*
Chase, Arthur Minturn 1873-1947 *AmA&B,
     DcNAA*
Chase, B W *Alli Sup*
Chase, Benjamin 1799-1889 *Alli Sup*
Chase, Borden *AmA&B, AmNov*
Chase, Burr Linden 1891- *AmA&B*
Chase, C H *Alli Sup*
Chase, C Thurston *Alli Sup*
Chase, Charles Frederic *Alli Sup*
Chase, Chris *AuNews 1*
Chase, Cleveland Bruce 1904?-1975 *ConAu 53,
     IndAu 1917*
Chase, Cora G 1898- *ConAu 61*
Chase, Daniel 1890- *AmA&B*
Chase, Donald 1943- *ConAu 53*
Chase, Dormer Augustus *Alli Sup*
Chase, Drummond Percy *Alli Sup*
Chase, Miss E A *Alli Sup*
Chase, E B *Alli Sup*
Chase, Edna Woolman *REnAL*
Chase, Eleanor Sawyer 1903- *WiscW*
Chase, Eliza Brown *Alli Sup, OxCan*
Chase, Eliza E *Alli Sup*
Chase, Elizabeth *ChPo*
Chase, Ellen E *ChPo*
Chase, Emma Lester *ChPo*
Chase, Francis *Alli Sup*
Chase, Francis Edward *Alli Sup*
Chase, Frank Eugene 1857-1920 *ChPo S2,
     DcNAA*
Chase, Frank Herbert 1870-1930 *DcNAA*
Chase, Franklin Henry 1864-1940 *DcNAA*
Chase, Frederic Henry *Alli Sup*
Chase, George 1849-1924 *Alli Sup, DcAmA,
     DcNAA*
Chase, George B *Alli Sup*
Chase, George Davis 1867- *WhWNAA*
Chase, George Millet 1873-1938 *DcNAA,
     WhWNAA*
Chase, George Wingate 1826-1867 *Alli Sup,
     DcAmA, DcNAA*
Chase, Gilbert 1906- *ConAu 17R*
Chase, Mrs. Hamilton Mercer *AmNov XR*
Chase, Harold W 1922- *ConAu 9R*
Chase, Harry Woodburn 1883- *WhWNAA*
Chase, Harvey Stuart 1861- *AmLY*
Chase, Heber *Alli*
Chase, Helen M *ChPo*
Chase, Henry S *Alli Sup*
Chase, Herbert E *Alli Sup*
Chase, Horace *Alli Sup*
Chase, Ilka 1905?- *AmA&B, Au&Wr,
     ConAu 61, REnAL*
Chase, Ira J 1793-1864 *Alli Sup*
Chase, Irah 1793-1864 *DcAmA, DcNAA*
Chase, Isaac McKim 1837-1903 *DcNAA*
Chase, J Newell 1904-1955 *AmSCAP 66*
Chase, Jackson H *Alli Sup*
Chase, James Compigne *Alli Sup*
Chase, James Hadley 1906- *Au&Wr,
     EncM&D, REn, TwCW*
Chase, Jason Franklin 1872-1926 *DcNAA*
Chase, Jessie MacMillan Anderson 1865-1949
     AmA&B, DcAmA, OhA&B, WhWNAA
Chase, John 1810-1879 *Alli Sup*
Chase, John A 1828?-1907 *OhA&B*
Chase, Joseph Cummings 1878-1965 *AmA&B,
     WhWNAA*
Chase, Judith Wragg 1907- *ConAu 41*
Chase, Leon Wilson 1877- *WhWNAA*
Chase, Lew Allen 1879- *WhWNAA*
Chase, Mrs. Lewis 1872- *AmLY*
Chase, Lewis Nathaniel 1873-1937 *AmA&B,
     AmLY, DcNAA, WhWNAA*
Chase, Loring D 1916- *ConAu 25*
Chase, Lucien B 1817-1864 *Alli Sup, BiDSA,
     DcAmA, DcNAA*
Chase, March F 1876- *WhWNAA*

Chase, Martin R 1886- *WhWNAA*
Chase, Mary Coyle 1907- *AmA&B, AuBYP,
     CnDAL, CnMD, ConDr, DcLEnL,
     LongC, McGWD, ModWD, OxAm, REn,
     REnAL, TwCA Sup, WrD 1976*
Chase, Mary Ellen 1887-1973 *AmA&B,
     AmNov, AuBYP, ChPo, ConAmA,
     ConAu 41, ConAu P-1, ConLC 2,
     DcLEnL, LongC, OxAm, Pen Am, REn,
     REnAL, SmATA 10, TwCA, TwCA Sup,
     WhWNAA*
Chase, Mary Granger *Alli Sup*
Chase, Mary M 1822-1852 *AmA&B*
Chase, Otta Louise 1909- *ConAu 49*
Chase, P E *Alli Sup*
Chase, Philander 1775-1852 *Alli, CyAL 1,
     DcAmA, DcNAA, OhA&B*
Chase, Phyllis *ChPo*
Chase, Pliny Earle 1820-1886 *Alli Sup,
     DcAmA, DcNAA*
Chase, Polly 1898- *AnMV 1926, ChPo*
Chase, Powell *ChPo, MnBBF*
Chase, Rhoda *ChPo S2, ConICB*
Chase, Richard *ChPo S1*
Chase, Richard 1904- *AmA&B, AnCL, BkCL,
     ConAu 61, MorJA*
Chase, Richard Volney 1914-1962 *AmA&B,
     Pen Am, REnAL, TwCA Sup*
Chase, Robert Greene *Alli Sup*
Chase, S B *Alli Sup*
Chase, S C *Alli Sup*
Chase, Salmon Portland 1808-1873 *AmA&B,
     BbD, BiD&SB, DcNAA, OhA&B*
Chase, Samuel *Alli, BiDLA Sup*
Chase, Samuel B, Jr. 1932- *ConAu 5R*
Chase, Sidney M *ChPo*
Chase, Squire 1802-1843 *DcNAA*
Chase, Stephen 1813-1851 *Alli*
Chase, Stuart 1888- *AmA&B, ChPo S2,
     ConAmA, DcLEnL, LongC, OxAm, REn,
     REnAL, TwCA, TwCA Sup, WhWNAA*
Chase, Theodore R *Alli Sup*
Chase, Thomas 1827-1892 *Alli Sup, BiD&SB,
     DcAmA, DcNAA*
Chase, Virginia 1902- *WrD 1976*
Chase, Virginia B *ChPo*
Chase, Virginia Lowell *ConAu XR*
Chase, W I *Alli Sup*
Chase, W S *Alli Sup*
Chase, Warren 1813-1891 *Alli Sup, DcNAA*
Chase, William Ingraham 1852-1889 *DcNAA*
Chase, William Merritt 1849-1916 *OxAm*
Chase, William Sheafe 1858-1940 *DcNAA*
Chasefield, H Carlton *MnBBF*
Chasemore, A *Alli Sup, ChPo*
Chaseton *MnBBF*
Chasin, Helen *AmA&B, ConP 1970,
     DrAP 1975*
Chasins, Abram 1903- *AmA&B, AmSCAP 66,
     ConAu 37*
Chaskell *AmLY XR*
Chasles, Philarete 1798-1873 *BiD&SB, OxFr*
Chasse, General *NewC*
Chasseaud, George Washington *Alli Sup*
Chasseriau, Theodore 1819-1856 *AtlBL*
Chassevant, Allyre 1865- *WhLA*
Chassignet, Jean-Baptiste 1571?-1635? *CasWL,
     Pen Eur*
Chastain, Madye Lee 1908- *AmA&B,
     ConAu 5R, IlCB 1956, MorJA,
     SmATA 4*
Chastain, Thomas *BlkAW*
Chasteen, Edgar R 1935- *ConAu 33*
Chastel, Andre 1912- *Au&Wr*
Chastelain, Georges 1405?-1475? *OxFr*
Chastelain, John Baptiste 1710-1771 *BkIE*
Chastelain De Couci, Le d1203 *CasWL*
Chastelard, Pierre DeBoscosel De 1540-1564
     OxFr
Chastellain, Georges 1405?-1475? *CasWL,
     OxFr, REn*
Chastellain, Pierre 1408?- *CasWL*
Chastellux, Francois Jean, Marquis De
     1734-1788 *OxAm, OxFr, REnAL*
Chasuble, Archdeacon, D D *Alli Sup*
Chatain, Robert *DrAF 1976, DrAP 1975*
Chatard, Francis Silas Marean 1834-1918
     Alli Sup, DcAmA, DcNAA, IndAu 1816

Chatburn, George Richard 1863-1940 *DcNAA,
     WhWNAA*
Chateaubriand, Francois Rene, Vicomte De
     1768-1848 *AtlBL, BbD, BiD&SB,
     BiDLA Sup, CasWL, CyWA, DcBiA,
     DcEuL, EuA, EvEuW, NewC, OxAm,
     OxEng, OxFr, Pen Eur, RCom, REn,
     REnAL*
Chateaubriant, Alphonse De 1877?-1951
     ClDMEuL, Pen Eur
Chateaubrun, Jean Baptiste Vivien 1686-1775
     BiD&SB
Chateauclair, Wilfred *Alli Sup, OxCan*
Chatel, Ferdinand-Francois 1795-1857 *OxFr*
Chatelain, Clara De 1807-1876 *Alli Sup,
     CarSB*
Chatelain, Ida *TexWr*
Chatelaine, Clara 1807-1876 *ChPo*
Chatelaine, John Baptiste 1710-1771 *BkIE*
Chatelet, Marquise Du 1706-1749 *OxFr*
Chatelet, Albert 1928- *ConAu 13R*
Chatelet, G E LeT DeB, Marquise Du 1706-1749
     REn
Chater, James *Alli*
Chater, Lucy *ChPo*
Chater, Melville 1878- *ChPo, WhWNAA*
Chater, Thomas *Alli, BiDLA*
Chatfield, Allen William *Alli Sup*
Chatfield, C *Alli*
Chatfield, Caroline 1889- *WhWNAA*
Chatfield, Charles 1934- *ConAu 37*
Chatfield, E Charles 1934- *WrD 1976*
Chatfield, Hale 1936- *ConAu 33, DrAP 1975*
Chatfield, Herbert Walter 1910- *Au&Wr*
Chatfield, John *Alli*
Chatfield, Michael 1934- *ConAu 25*
Chatfield, Paul *ChPo*
Chatfield, Robert *Alli, BiDLA*
Chatfield, Sara M *ChPo*
Chatfield-Taylor, Hobart Chatfield 1865-1945
     *AmA&B, AmLY, BbD, BiD&SB,
     DcAmA, DcNAA, WhWNAA*
Chatham, Earl Of 1708-1778 *Chmbr 2, NewC*
Chatham, Doug M 1938- *ConAu 61*
Chatham, Frank *MnBBF*
Chatham, James R 1931- *ConAu 33*
Chatham, Josiah G 1914- *ConAu 49*
Chatham, William Pitt, Earl Of 1708-1778 *Alli*
Chatillon, Pierre *OxCan Sup*
Chatillon, Walter Of 1135?-1184? *CasWL*
Chatman, Seymour B 1928- *ConAu 37,
     WrD 1976*
Chatrian, Alexandre 1826-1890 *CasWL, EuA,
     EvEuW, OxFr*
Chatrian, Louis Gratien C Alexandre 1826-1890
     DcBiA, NewC
Chatt, Orville K 1924- *ConAu 53*
Chattaway, E D *Alli Sup*
Chattaway, Thurland 1872-1947 *AmSCAP 66*
Chatterbox, Charles *AmA&B*
Chatterje, Bankim Chandra 1838-1894 *CasWL*
Chatterje, Sarat Chandra 1876-1936 *CasWL*
Chatterjee, Sir Abdul *WhLA*
Chatterjee, Margaret 1925- *ConAu 5R*
Chatterji *DcOrL 2*
Chatterji, Bankimchandra 1838-1894 *Pen Cl*
Chatterji, Saratchandra 1876-1938 *EncWL Sup*
Chatterton, Lady 1806-1876 *Alli*
Chatterton, A *BiDSA*
Chatterton, Edward Keble 1878-1944 *EvLB,
     NewC, WhLA*
Chatterton, George J *Alli Sup*
Chatterton, Lady Georgiana 1806-1876 *DcEnL*
Chatterton, Lady Henrietta G M Lascelles
     1806-1876 *Alli Sup*
Chatterton, Mason Daniel 1833-1903 *DcNAA*
Chatterton, Ruth 1893-1961 *AmA&B*
Chatterton, Thomas 1752-1770 *Alli, AtlBL,
     BbD, BiD&SB, BrAu, CasWL, ChPo,
     ChPo S1, Chmbr 2, CnE&AP, CriT 2,
     DcEnA, DcEnL, DcEuL, DcLEnL, EvLB,
     MouLC 2, NewC, OxEng, Pen Eng,
     RCom, REn, WebEAL*
Chatterton, Wayne 1921- *ConAu 37*
Chatto, Mrs. *Alli Sup*
Chatto, William Andrew *Alli*
Chattock, Christopher *Alli Sup*

Chattock, Richard S *Alli Sup*
Chatton, Stacy *WhWNAA*
Chattopadhyay, Harindranath 1898- *DcOrL 2*
Chattopadhyaya, Harindranath 1898- *DcLEnL*
Chattuck, E S *ChPo S1*
Chattuck, R S *ChPo S1*
Chauber, Theobald *OxGer*
Chaucer, Daniel *LongC*
Chaucer, Geoffrey 1340?-1400? *Alli, AnCL,
   AtlBL, BbD, BiD&SB, BrAu, CasWL,
   ChPo, ChPo S1, ChPo S2, Chmbr 1,
   CnE&AP, CriT 1, CyWA, DcEnA,
   DcEnL, DcEuL, DcLEnL, EvLB,
   MouLC 1, NewC, OxEng, Pen Eng,
   PoLE, RAdv 1, RCom, REn, WebEAL*
Chauchard, Captain *Alli*
Chaudet, Mary 1920- *AmSCAP 66*
Chaudhuri, Haridas 1913- *ConAu 5R*
Chaudhuri, Nirad Chandra 1897- *Au&Wr,
   CasWL, DcOrL 2, NewC, Pen Eng*
Chaudhuri, Sukanta 1950- *ConAu 57,
   ConP 1970*
Chaudon, Dom Louis-Mayeul *OxFr*
Chaudron, Adelaide DeVondel *BiDSA,
   LivFWS*
Chaudron, Louis DeVendel *BiDSA*
Chauffard, Rene-Jacques 1920?-1972 *ConAu 37*
Chaulieu, Guillaume Amfrye, Abbe De
   1639-1720 *BiD&SB, OxFr*
Chaumeix, Abraham-Joseph De 1730?-1790
   OxFr
Chaumonot, Pierre-Joseph-Marie 1611-1693
   OxCan
Chaumont, Francis Stephen B F De *Alli Sup*
Chauncey, Charles 1592-1672 *DcNAA*
Chauncey, Charles 1705-1787 *CnDAL, DcEnL,
   DcNAA, REn*
Chauncey, Shelton *DcNAA*
Chauncey, W S *Alli Sup*
Chauncy, Angel *Alli*
Chauncy, Charles 1592-1672 *Alli, CyAL 1,
   DcAmA*
Chauncy, Charles 1705-1787 *Alli, AmA,
   DcAmA, OxAm, REnAL*
Chauncy, Helen *ChPo*
Chauncy, Sir Henry 1632-1719 *Alli*
Chauncy, Isaac d1712 *Alli*
Chauncy, Isaac d1745 *Alli*
Chauncy, Maurice d1581 *Alli*
Chauncy, Nan Masterman 1900-1970 *AuBYP,
   ConAu 1R, SmATA 6, ThBJA*
Chauncy, Nathaniel *Alli*
Chauncy, William *Alli*
Chaundler, Christine 1887- *Au&Wr, ChPo,
   ChPo S1, ChPo S2, ConAu 29,
   SmATA 1, WhCL*
Chaundler, E *Alli*
Chaundler, Thomas *Alli*
Chaussard, Pierre Jean Baptiste 1766-1823
   BiD&SB
Chausse, Alcide 1868- *WhWNAA*
Chausson, Ernest 1855-1899 *AtlBL*
Chauveau, Charles Auguste 1877-1940 *DcNAA*
Chauveau, Paul 1898- *WhLA*
Chauveau, Pierre Joseph Olivier 1820-1890 *BbtC,
   BiD&SB, CanWr, DcNAA, OxCan*
Chauvel, R A *Alli*
Chauvenet, Regis 1842-1920 *DcNAA*
Chauvenet, William 1820-1870 *Alli, Alli Sup,
   DcAmA, DcNAA*
Chauvin, Nicolas 1770?- *NewC, OxFr*
Chauvin, Pierre, Sieur De Tonnetuit d1603
   OxCan
Chauvin, Remy 1913- *BiDPar*
Chaval *WhGrA*
Chavannes *AtlBL*
Chavannes, Mary Charlotte *Alli Sup*
Chavarie, Robert *OxCan Sup*
Chavasse, Pye Henry *Alli Sup*
Chavasse, William *Alli*
Chavchavadze, Aleksander 1786-1846 *DcOrL 3*
Chavchavadze, Ilia 1837-1907 *DcOrL 3,
   Pen Cl*
Chavchavadze, Paul 1899-1971 *ConAu 25,
   ConAu 29*
Chave, Gloria Maria *Au&Wr*
Chave, William *Alli Sup*
Chavel, Charles Ber 1906- *ConAu 49*

Chavernac, T *Alli, BiDLA*
Chaverton, Bruce *MnBBF*
Chavez, Angelico 1910- *BkC 2, CatA 1947,
   ChPo S1, ChPo S2*
Chavez, Carlos 1899- *AmSCAP 66, REn*
Chawner, Edward *Alli Sup*
Chawner, G *Alli Sup*
Chawner, Rosa A *Alli Sup*
Chawner, William *Alli Sup*
Chayefsky, Paddy 1923- *AmA&B,
   AmSCAP 66, CnMD, CnThe, ConAu 9R,
   ConDr, CrCD, McGWD, ModWD,
   OxAm, Pen Am, REnAL, WhTwL,
   WorAu, WrD 1976*
Chaytor, Henry *Alli Sup*
Chaytor, Henry John 1871- *MnBBF, WhLA*
Chazal, Malcolm De 1902- *Pen Eur*
Chazanof, William 1915- *ConAu 33,
   WrD 1976*
Chazelle, Pierre *OxCan*
Chazey, E Ligeret De *BiDSA*
Cheadle, Walter Butler 1835-1910 *BrAu 19,
   OxCan*
Cheales, Alan Benjamin *Alli Sup*
Cheare, Abraham *Alli*
Cheaste, Thomas *Alli*
Cheatham, Catharine Smiley Bugge *WhWNAA*
Cheatham, Katharine Smiley *ChPo*
Cheatham, Kitty *WhWNAA*
Cheatham, Modell *BlkAW*
Cheavens, Frank 1905- *ConAu 33, WrD 1976*
Cheavens, Martha Louis 1898-1975 *ConAu 57*
Checker, Chubby 1941- *AmSCAP 66*
Checkland, S G 1916- *ConAu 17R*
Checkley, John 1680?-1753 *Alli, DcAmA,
   DcNAA*
Checkley, Samuel d1769 *Alli*
Checus, Sir John *Alli*
Chedid, Andree 1921- *CasWL*
Chedsey, William *Alli*
Chedworth, Lord John *Alli*
Cheek, Frances Edith 1923- *ConAu 41*
Cheek, John *Alli Sup*
Cheeke, Henry *Alli*
Cheem, Aliph *Alli Sup*
Cheere, Edward *Alli Sup*
Cheesborough, Essie B *BiDSA, FemPA,
   LivFWS*
Cheese, Edmund H *Alli Sup*
Cheese, John Edmund *Alli Sup*
Cheeseman, Clara *Alli Sup*
Cheeseman, Lewis *Alli*
Cheeser, B *Alli Sup*
Cheesman, Abraham *Alli*
Cheesman, Christopher *Alli*
Cheesman, Paul R 1921- *ConAu 49*
Cheesman, Thomas *Alli*
Cheetham, Henry *Alli Sup*
Cheetham, James 1772-1810 *Alli, AmA,
   CyAL 1, DcAmA, DcNAA, OxAm,
   REnAL*
Cheetham, James Harold 1921- *Au&Wr*
Cheetham, John *Alli Sup*
Cheetham, Robert Clifford 1909- *Au&Wr*
Cheetham, Robert Farren *Alli*
Cheetham, Tom *MnBBF*
Cheever, David Williams 1831-1915 *Alli Sup,
   DcNAA*
Cheever, Ezekiel 1614?-1708 *Alli, AmA,
   AmA&B, CyAL 1, DcAmA, DcNAA,
   REnAL*
Cheever, George Barrell 1807-1890 *Alli,
   Alli Sup, BbD, BiD&SB, ChPo S1,
   ChPo S2, DcAmA, DcEnL, DcNAA*
Cheever, George D *Alli Sup*
Cheever, George R 1807- *CyAL 2*
Cheever, Harriet Anna 1870?- *AmA&B,
   DcNAA*
Cheever, Henry P *AmA&B*
Cheever, Henry Theodore 1814-1897 *Alli,
   Alli Sup, AmA&B, BiD&SB, CyAL 2,
   DcAmA, DcNAA*
Cheever, John 1912- *AmA&B, CasWL,
   ConAu 5R, ConLC 3, ConNov 1972,
   ConNov 1976, DrAF 1976, EncWL Sup,
   ModAL, ModAL Sup, OxAm, Pen Am,
   RAdv 1, REn, REnAL, TwCW,
   WebEAL, WhTwL, WorAu, WrD 1976*

Cheever, Nathaniel *Alli*
Cheever, Noah Wood 1839-1905 *Alli Sup,
   DcNAA*
Cheever, Samuel d1724 *Alli*
Cheever, William Maxen 1818-1878 *Alli Sup,
   IndAu 1816*
Cheeves, Mrs. E W Foote *BiDSA*
Cheeves, Langdon 1776-1857 *BiDSA*
Cheffey, Jessie Ann 1895- *OhA&B*
Cheffins, Ronald I 1930- *ConAu 45*
Chegwidden, Maud *ChPo S1*
Chegwidden, T C *Alli Sup*
Cheifetz, Dan *DrAF 1976*
Cheifetz, Philip M 1944- *ConAu 53*
Cheiffetz, Hyman 1901- *AmSCAP 66*
Cheiro *ChPo S1, WhWNAA*
Cheisley, John *Alli*
Cheisholm, Guil *Alli*
Chejne, Anwar G 1923- *ConAu 25, WrD 1976*
Chek Sorat *DcOrL 2*
Cheke, Sir John 1514-1557 *Alli, BrAu,
   CasWL, Chmbr 1, DcEnL, DcLEnL,
   EvLB, NewC, OxEng, Pen Eng*
Cheke, William *Alli*
Chekenian, Jane Gerard *ConAu XR*
Chekhov *LongC*
Chekhov, Anton Pavlovich 1860-1904 *AtlBL,
   CasWL, ClDMEuL, CnMD, CnThe,
   CyWA, DcEuL, DcRusL, EncWL, EuA,
   EvEuW, McGWD, ModSL 1, ModWD,
   NewC, OxEng, Pen Eur, RCom, REn,
   REnWD*
Chekhov, Anton ALSO Tchekhov, Anton
Chekki, Dan A 1935- *ConAu 61*
Chelcicky, Petr 1390?-1460? *CasWL, Pen Eur*
Chelczicky, Petr 1390?-1460? *DcEuL*
Cheley, Frank Howbert 1889-1941 *AmA&B,
   WhWNAA*
Chelf, Carl P 1937- *ConAu 37, WrD 1976*
Chelidonius, Benedictus *OxGer*
Chellappa, C S *DcOrL 2*
Chellis, Mary Dwinell *Alli Sup, DcAmA*
Chelsea, Sage Of *NewC*
Chelsum, James 1740-1801 *Alli*
Cheltnam, Charles Smith *Alli Sup*
Chelton, John *ConAu XR*
Chemery, V L *Alli Sup*
Chemnitz, Matthaus Friedrich 1815-1870
   BiD&SB, OxGer
Chemnitzer *ChPo S1*
Chemnizer, Ivan 1744-1784 *DcEuL*
Chen, Anthony 1929- *WrD 1976*
Chen, Chung-Hwan 1906- *ConAu 45*
Ch'en, Hung *DcOrL 1*
Ch'en, Hwei *ConAu XR*
Ch'en, I *DcOrL 1*
Chen, Jack 1908- *ConAu 41*
Ch'en, Jerome 1921- *ConAu 13R*
Chen, Joseph Tao 1925- *ConAu 37,
   WrD 1976*
Chen, Kan 1928- *ConAu 49*
Chen, Kenneth K S 1907- *ConAu 17R*
Chen, King C 1926- *ConAu 53*
Chen, Kuan I 1926- *ConAu 41*
Chen, Lincoln C 1942- *ConAu 49*
Ch'en, Meng-Chia *DcOrL 1*
Ch'en, Ming *DcOrL 1*
Chen, Nai-Ruenn 1927- *ConAu 23*
Chen, Philip S 1903- *ConAu 9R*
Ch'en, Po-Yu *DcOrL 1*
Chen, Samuel Shih-Tsai 1915- *ConAu 41*
Ch'en, Shih-Tao 1053-1102 *CasWL*
Chen, Ta 1892- *WhLA*
Chen, Theodore Hsi-En 1902- *ConAu 1R*
Chen, Tony 1929- *ConAu 37, SmATA 6*
Ch'en, Tu-Hsiu 1879-1942 *CasWL, DcOrL 1*
Ch'en, Tzu-Ang 661-702 *CasWL, DcOrL 1*
Chen, Vincent 1917- *ConAu 37*
Chenault, John *BlkAW*
Chenault, Lawrence R 1897- *ConAu 17*
Chenault, Nell *ConAu XR, SmATA 2*
Chenedolle, Charles-Julien De 1769-1833
   CasWL, OxFr, Pen Eur
Chenery, Thomas 1826-1884 *Alli Sup*
Chenery, William Ludlow 1884-1974 *ConAu 53,
   REnAL, WhWNAA*

Chenette, Edward Stephen 1895-1963
AmSCAP 66
Cheneviere, Jacques 1886- *CasWL*
Chenevix, Richard 1774-1830 *Alli, BiDLA, NewC, PoIre*
Chenevix-Trench *Alli Sup*
Chenevix Trench, Charles Pocklington 1914-
Au&Wr, ConAu 9R, ConAu 13R
Cheney, Anne Cleveland 1944- *ChPo, ConAu 61*
Cheney, Annie Elizabeth 1847-1916 *ChPo, DcNAA*
Cheney, Brainard 1900- *ConAu 25, WrD 1976*
Cheney, Charles Edward 1836-1916 *Alli Sup, DcAmA, DcNAA*
Cheney, Christopher Robert 1906- *Au&Wr*
Cheney, Clara Emma *Alli Sup*
Cheney, Cora 1916- *AuBYP, ConAu 1R, SmATA 3*
Cheney, Ednah Dow 1824-1904 *Alli Sup, AmA, AmA&B, BiD&SB, ChPo, ChPo S1, DcAmA, DcNAA*
Cheney, Frances Neel 1906- *ConAu 33*
Cheney, Frank J 1851-1919 *OhA&B*
Cheney, Harriet Vaughan 1815- *Alli, BbtC, DcAmA, DcNAA, OxCan*
Cheney, Harriet Vaughan Foster 1796- *AmA&B*
Cheney, John *Alli*
Cheney, John Vance 1848-1922 *Alli Sup, AmA, AmA&B, AmLY, BbD, BiD&SB, ChPo, ChPo S1, DcAmA, DcNAA, OxAm, REnAL*
Cheney, Lellen Sterling 1858- *WhWNAA*
Cheney, Lois A 1931- *ConAu 29*
Cheney, Mary *Alli Sup*
Cheney, Orion Howard 1869-1939 *DcNAA*
Cheney, Peter 1896-1951 *LongC*
Cheney, R H *Alli*
Cheney, Ralph *ChPo S1*
Cheney, Mrs. Ralph *WhWNAA*
Cheney, Seth Wells 1810-1856 *ChPo, EarAB*
Cheney, Sheldon 1886- *AmA&B, Au&Wr, REnAL, TwCA, TwCA Sup*
Cheney, Simeon Pease 1818-1890 *DcAmA, DcNAA*
Cheney, Ted *ConAu XR*
Cheney, Theodore Albert 1928- *ConAu 61*
Cheney, Theseus Apoleon 1830-1878 *Alli Sup, BiD&SB, DcAmA, DcNAA*
Cheney, Thomas E 1901- *ConAu 41*
Cheney, Warren 1855?-1921 *AmLY, ChPo S1, DcNAA*
Cheng, Bin 1921- *Au&Wr*
Ch'eng, Chang-Keng *DcOrL 1*
Cheng, Chen-To 1898-1958 *DcOrL 1*
Cheng, Ch'iao *DcOrL 1*
Cheng, Ch'ien *DcOrL 1*
Cheng, Chu-Yuan 1927- *ConAu 13R*
Ch'eng, Feng-Wu *DcOrL 1*
Ch'eng, Hao 1032-1085 *CasWL*
Cheng, Hsi-Ti *DcOrL 1*
Ch'eng, I 1033-1107 *CasWL, DcOrL 1*
Cheng, J Chester 1926- *ConAu 9R, WrD 1976*
Cheng, James K C 1936- *ConAu 25, WrD 1976*
Cheng, Pan-Ch'iao 1693-1766 *CasWL*
Cheng, Po-Ch'i *DcOrL 1*
Cheng, Ronald Ye-Lin 1933- *ConAu 41*
Cheng, Shih-Fa SEE Shih-Fa Cheng
Cheng, T'ien-Hsi *OxCan*
Cheng, Yi Kuo-Chiang *WrD 1976*
Cheng, Ying-Wan *ConAu 41*
Chenier, Andre Marie De 1762-1794 *AtlBL, BiD&SB, CasWL, DcEuL, EuA, EvEuW, OxEng, OxFr, Pen Eur, REn*
Chenier, Jean-Olivier 1806-1837 *OxCan*
Chenier, Joseph 1764-1811 *DcEuL*
Chenier, Marie-Andre 1762-1794 *BbD*
Chenier, Marie-Joseph De 1764-1811 *BbD, BiD&SB, CasWL, EvEuW, OxFr, Pen Eur*
Chennault, Anna Chan 1925?- *AmA&B, ConAu 61*
Chennault, Claire Lee 1890-1958 *AmA&B*
Chenneviere, Daniel *ConAu XR*
Chenneviere, Georges 1884-1929 *OxFr*

Chenoweth, Caroline VanDusen 1846- *Alli Sup, DcAmA, IndAu 1816*
Chenoweth, D *OxCan Sup*
Chenoweth, Vida S 1928- *ConAu 25*
Chenoweth, Wilbur 1899- *AmSCAP 66*
Chenu, Marcel Marie-Dominique 1895- *Au&Wr*
Cheny, Laurence *Alli Sup*
Chepmell, C W *Alli Sup*
Chepmell, Edward Charles *Alli Sup*
Chepmell, Havilland LeMesurier *Alli Sup*
Cher, Marie *AmA&B*
Cheragh Ali *Alli Sup*
Cheraskin, Emanuel 1916- *ConAu 53*
Cheraskoff, Michail Matvejevich 1733-1807 *BiD&SB*
Cherbonnier, Edmond LaBeaume 1918- *AmA&B*
Cherbuliez, Charles Victor 1829-1899 *BbD, BiD&SB, DcBiA, EuA, EvEuW, OxFr*
Cherbury, Lord *CnE&AP*
Cherdak, Jeanne 1915- *AmSCAP 66*
Cheret, Jules 1836- *ChPo*
Cherim, Stanley M 1929- *ConAu 53*
Cherington, Viscount *Alli*
Cherington, Paul Terry 1876- *WhWNAA*
Cherington, Paul Whiton 1918-1974 *ConAu 1R, ConAu 53*
Cheriot, Henri *BlkAW*
Cheriton, Odo Of d1247 *CasWL*
Chermayeff, Ivan 1932- *ChPo, IlCB 1966*
Chermayeff, Serge 1900- *ConAu 21*
Chermside, Mrs. Henry Lowther *Alli Sup*
Chermside, Richard Seymour Conway *Alli Sup*
Chernaik, Judith 1934- *ConAu 61*
Cherne, Leo M 1912- *AmA&B*
Cherney, Boris E 1921- *AmSCAP 66*
Cherniack, Louis 1908- *BiDPar*
Cherniavsky, Josef 1895-1959 *AmSCAP 66*
Cherniavsky, Michael 1923?-1973 *ConAu 41*
Chernier, Andre 1762-1794 *ChPo*
Chernis, Jay 1906- *AmSCAP 66*
Cherniss, Michael D 1940- *ConAu 37*
Chernocke, Robert *Alli*
Chernoff, Dorothy A *ConAu XR*
Chernoff, Goldie Taub 1909- *ConAu 33, SmATA 10*
Chernoff, Lewis H 1890- *WhWNAA*
Chernow, Carol 1934- *ConAu 57*
Chernow, Fred B 1932- *ConAu 57*
Cherny, Sasha 1880- *CasWL, DcRusL*
Chernyshevsky, Nikolay Gavrilovich 1828-1889 *CasWL, DcEuL, DcRusL, EuA, Pen Eur, REn*
Chernyshevsky, N ALSO Tchernyshevsky
Cheron, Louis 1655-1735 *BkIE*
Cherouny, Henry W *Alli Sup*
Cherpillourd, J *Alli*
Cherrett, J M 1935- *Au&Wr*
Cherrie, George Kruck 1865-1948 *AmA&B*
Cherrier, C S *BbtC*
Cherriman, John Bradford *Alli Sup, BbtC*
Cherrington, Ben Mark 1885- *AmA&B*
Cherrington, Ernest H, Jr. 1909- *Au&Wr, ConAu 33, WrD 1976*
Cherrington, Ernest Hurst 1877-1950 *OhA&B*
Cherrington, Leon G 1926- *ConAu 33*
Cherry, A *Alli*
Cherry, Andrew 1762-1812 *ChPo, ChPo S2, Chmbr 2, DcEnL, EvLB, PoIre*
Cherry, Caroline L 1942- *ConAu 57*
Cherry, Charles Conrad 1937- *ConAu 23, WrD 1976*
Cherry, Charles L 1942- *ConAu 57*
Cherry, George Loy 1905- *ConAu 5R*
Cherry, Gwendolyn *LivBA*
Cherry, Henry C *Alli*
Cherry, Henry Hardin 1864- *WhWNAA*
Cherry, J L *Alli Sup*
Cherry, John *Alli*
Cherry, Kelly *AuNews 1, ConAu 49, DrAF 1976, DrAP 1975, WrD 1976*
Cherry, Peter Patterson 1848-1937 *OhA&B*
Cherry, Sheldon H 1934- *ConAu 49*
Cherry, Thomas Crittenden 1862- *WhWNAA*
Cherryholmes, Anne *AuBYP, ConAu XR, SmATA 8*
Chertsey, Andrew *Alli*
Cherub, The *MnBBF*

Cherubini, Luigi 1760-1842 *AtlBL, REn*
Cherubini, Salvatore 1760-1842 *OxFr*
Cherville, Gaspard Georges, Marquis De 1821-1898 *BiD&SB*
Chervin, Ronda 1937- *ConAu 57*
Cherwinski, Joseph 1915- *ConAu 13R*
Chesbrough, Ellis S *Alli Sup*
Chesebro, Caroline 1825?-1873 *Alli, Alli Sup, BiD&SB, CyAL 2, DcAmA, DcNAA*
Chesebrough, Amos S *Alli Sup*
Chesebrough, Caroline 1825-1873 *AmA, AmA&B*
Cheselden, William 1688-1752 *Alli*
Cheseldine, Raymond Minshall 1892-1954 *OhA&B*
Chesen, Eli S 1944- *ConAu 37, WrD 1976*
Chesham, Henry *ConAu XR*
Chesham, Sallie *ConAu 29, WrD 1976*
Chesher, Kim 1955- *WrD 1976*
Cheshire, Clive *MnBBF*
Cheshire, David 1935- *Au&Wr*
Cheshire, Edward *Alli Sup*
Cheshire, Frank R *Alli Sup*
Cheshire, Geoffrey Leonard 1917- *Au&Wr, ConAu P-1*
Cheshire, John *Alli*
Cheshire, Joseph Blount 1850-1932 *BiDSA, DcNAA, WhWNAA*
Cheshire, Neil M *OxCan Sup*
Cheshire, Thomas *Alli, Alli Sup*
Chesire, Gifford Paul 1905- *WhPNW*
Cheskin, Louis 1909- *Au&Wr, ConAu 5R*
Chesler, Bernice 1932- *ConAu 25*
Chesler, Phyllis 1940- *ConAu 49*
Chesley, Lois Cameron 1906- *TexWr*
Chesley, Martin *OhA&B*
Cheslock, Louis 1898- *ConAu P-1, WrD 1976*
Chesney, Charles Cornwallis 1826-1876 *Alli Sup*
Chesney, Francis Rawdon 1789-1872 *Alli, Alli Sup*
Chesney, Sir George Tomkyns 1830-1895 *Alli Sup, BrAu 19, Chmbr 3, DcLEnL, NewC, OxEng*
Chesney, Inga L 1928- *ConAu 45*
Chesney, J *Alli Sup*
Chesney, J Portman *Alli Sup*
Chesney, Kathleen 1899- *Au&Wr, WrD 1976*
Chesney, Kellow 1914- *Au&Wr, ConAu 29*
Chesney, Louisa And O'Donnell, Jane *Alli Sup*
Chesnoff, Richard Z 1937- *ConAu 25*
Chesnut, J Stanley 1926- *ConAu 23*
Chesnut, Mary Boykin 1823-1886 *OxAm, REnAL*
Chesnutt, Charles Waddell 1858-1932 *AmA&B, AmLY, BlkAW, CasWL, CnDAL, CyWA, DcAmA, DcNAA, OhA&B, OxAm, Pen Am, REn, REnAL, TwCA, TwCA Sup, WhWNAA*
Chesnutt, Edgar B 1906- *WhWNAA*
Chess, Victoria *ChPo S1*
Chesser, Eustace 1902-1973 *Au&Wr, ConAu 9R, ConAu 45*
Chesshyre, Henry T Newton *Alli Sup, BbtC*
Chessler, Deborah *AmSCAP 66*
Chessman, Caryl 1921-1960 *AmA&B*
Chessman, G Wallace 1919- *ConAu 13R*
Chessman, Ruth 1910- *ConAu 17*
Chesson, F W *Alli Sup*
Chesson, Nora Hopper 1871-1906 *ChPo, ChPo S1, ChPo S2, NewC*
Chester *DcEnL*
Chester, Bishop Of *BiDLA*
Chester, Albert Huntington 1843-1903 *Alli Sup, DcAmA, DcNAA*
Chester, Alden 1848-1934 *DcNAA*
Chester, Alfred 1928?-1971 *Au&Wr, ConAu 33*
Chester, Annie M *Alli Sup*
Chester, Anson G *ChPo S2*
Chester, Colby Mitchell 1844- *WhWNAA*
Chester, Daniel Norman 1907- *Au&Wr*
Chester, Edward W 1935- *ConAu 23*
Chester, Eliza *ChPo*
Chester, Frederick Dixon Walthall 1861- *DcAmA, WhWNAA*
Chester, George Randolph 1869-1924 *AmA&B, DcNAA, EncM&D, MnBBF, OhA&B, OxAm, REn, REnAL, TwCA*

Chester, Gilbert *MnBBF*
Chester, Greville John 1830-1892 *Alli Sup, ChPo, PoIre*
Chester, Harriet Mary 1830?- *PoIre*
Chester, Harry Seward 1862-1906 *IndAu 1917*
Chester, Henrietta M *Alli Sup*
Chester, John *Alli Sup, DcNAA*
Chester, Joseph Lemuel 1821-1882 *Alli Sup, CyAL 2, DcAmA, DcNAA*
Chester, Laura *DrAP 1975*
Chester, Michael 1928- *AuBYP, ConAu 1R*
Chester, Norley *ChPo*
Chester, Norman 1907- *WrD 1976*
Chester, Peter *ConAu XR*
Chester, Richard d1883 *PoIre*
Chester, Robert *Alli*
Chester, Sir Robert 1566-1640 *CasWL*
Chester, Robert T 1908- *AmSCAP 66*
Chester, Samuel Hall 1851-1940 *DcNAA, WhWNAA*
Chester, Sarah E *Alli Sup*
Chester, Thomas *DcEnL, NewC*
Chester, W D *Alli Sup*
Chester, Wayland Morgan 1870- *WhWNAA*
Chester, William Bennett 1820-1893 *PoIre*
Chesterfield, Earl Of 1694-1773 *ChPo S1, Chmbr 2, DcEuL, NewC, RAdv 1*
Chesterfield, Hugh 1884- *ChPo*
Chesterfield, Philip D Stanhope, Earl Of 1694-1773 *Alli, AtlBL, BbD, BiD&SB, BrAu, CasWL, CyWA, DcEnA, DcEnL, DcLEnL, EvLB, OxEng, Pen Eng, REn, WebEAL*
Chesterfield, Ruth *Alli Sup, ChPo*
Chesterfield, Thomas De *Alli*
Chesterman, Hugh 1884- *ChPo S1, ChPo S2*
Chesterman, Jean 1920- *WrD 1976*
Chesterman, W D *Alli Sup*
Chesterton, Ada Elizabeth 1888- *NewC*
Chesterton, Arthur Kenneth 1899- *Au&Wr, ConAu P-1*
Chesterton, Mrs. Cecil 1870-1962 *LongC*
Chesterton, Cecil Edward 1879-1918 *ChPo*
Chesterton, Frances Alice 1875- *ChPo*
Chesterton, G K 1874-1936 *CnE&AP, CnMWL, CyWA, EncM&D, EncWL, LongC, ModBL, ModBL Sup, NewC, RAdv 1, REn, WebEAL, WhTwL*
Chesterton, George Laval *Alli, Alli Sup*
Chesterton, Gilbert Keith 1874-1936 *AnCL, AtlBL, BkC 6, CasWL, CatA 1947, ChPo, ChPo S1, ChPo S2, Chmbr 3, DcLEnL, EvLB, OxEng, Pen Eng, TwCA, TwCA Sup, TwCW, WhLA*
Chesterton, Rupert *MnBBF*
Chestnut, Mary Boykin *BiDSA*
Chestnut, Victor King 1867- *WhWNAA*
Chestnutt, Charles Waddell 1858-1932 *BiD&SB, DcLEnL*
Chestnutt, Edgar B 1906- *WhWNAA*
Cheston, Charles *Alli Sup*
Cheston, R B *Alli*
Chestor, Rui *ConAu XR*
Chestre, Thomas 1410?- *NewC, OxEng*
Chesworth, Frank *ChPo*
Chetham, James *Alli*
Chetham, John *Alli*
Chetham-Strode, Warren 1897?- *Au&Wr, ConAu P-1, LongC*
Chethimattam, John B 1922- *ConAu 25*
Chetin, Helen 1922- *ConAu 29, SmATA 6*
Chetkin, Leonard 1928- *AmSCAP 66*
Chetlain, Augustus Louis 1824-1914 *DcNAA*
Chettle, E M *ChPo S1*
Chettle, Henry 1560?-1607? *Alli, BiD&SB, BrAu, CasWL, Chmbr 1, CnThe, CrE&SL, DcEnL, DcLEnL, EvLB, NewC, OxEng, Pen Eng, REn, REnWD*
Chetwind, Charles *Alli*
Chetwind, Edward *Alli*
Chetwind, John *Alli*
Chetwind, Philip *Alli*
Chetwode, Alice Wilmot *Alli Sup*
Chetwode, Penelope 1910- *WrD 1976*
Chetwood, Knightly 1652-1720 *Alli*
Chetwood, William Rufus d1766 *Alli, DcEnL, NewC, PoIre*
Chetwynd, A B *Alli Sup*

Chetwynd, Berry *ConAu XR*
Chetwynd, D *ChPo S2*
Chetwynd, Mrs. Henry *Alli Sup*
Chetwynd, James *Alli*
Chetwynd, John 1623-1692 *Alli*
Chetwynd, Julia Bosville *Alli Sup*
Chetwynd, Thomas Henry *ChPo S1*
Chetwynd, Tom 1938- *ConAu 45*
Chetwynd-Hayes, R 1919- *ConAu 61*
Chetwynd-Stapylton *Alli Sup*
Cheung, Steven N S 1935- *ConAu 25*
Cheuse, Alan 1940- *ConAu 49*
Chevaillier, Faith *WhWNAA*
Chevalier, The Young *NewC*
Chevalier, Albert 1861-1923 *ChPo S1*
Chevalier, Elizabeth Pickett 1896- *AmA&B, AmNov, Au&Wr*
Chevalier, Emile 1828-1879 *DcNAA, OxCan*
Chevalier, H Emile *BbtC, DcNAA*
Chevalier, Haakon 1902- *AmA&B, Au&Wr, ConAu 61, WrD 1976*
Chevalier, Marie George 1889- *BiDPar*
Chevalier, Maurice 1888-1972 *ConAu 33*
Chevalier, Michel *OxAm*
Chevalier, Paul Eugene George 1925- *Au&Wr*
Chevalier, Temple *Alli*
Chevalier, Thomas d1824 *Alli, BiDLA*
Chevalier, W *ChPo*
Chevalier, W A *Alli Sup*
Chevalier, William Alfred Cramer *Alli Sup*
Chevalier De Saint George *NewC*
Chevalley, Abel 1868- *WhLA*
Chevallier, Charles Henry 1824-1885 *Alli Sup*
Chevallier, Gabriel 1895-1969 *CasWL, EvEuW, REn, TwCW*
Chevers, Christopher d1785 *PoIre*
Chevers, Norman 1818-1886 *Alli Sup*
Cheverton, George *Alli Sup*
Cheverton, Henry *Alli Sup*
Cheves, Langdon 1776-1857 *CyAL 2*
Chevigny, Bell Gale 1936- *ConAu 57*
Chevigny, Hector 1904-1965 *AmA&B, CatA 1947, REnAL, TwCA Sup, WhWNAA*
Cheviot, Andrew *ChPo*
Cheviot Of The Field *WhLA*
Chevreul, Leon Marie Martial 1852-1939 *BiDPar*
Chevreuse, Marie DeRohan, Duchesse De 1600-1679 *OxFr*
Chevrier, Lionel *OxCan*
Chevrillon, Andre 1864-1957 *OxFr*
Chevrotiere, Hector Chevigny DeLa *WhWNAA*
Chew, Allen F 1924- *ConAu 33, WrD 1976*
Chew, Beverly 1850-1924 *AmA&B, ChPo, ChPo S2*
Chew, Birdell *BlkAW*
Chew, Peter 1924- *ConAu 57*
Chew, Richard *Alli Sup*
Chew, Ruth 1920- *ConAu 41, SmATA 7*
Chew, Mrs. S J *Alli Sup*
Chew, Samuel *Alli Sup*
Chew, Samuel d1744 *Alli*
Chew, Samuel Claggett 1888-1960 *AmA&B, WhWNAA*
Chewett, Phyllida *ChPo S1*
Chewett, W C *BbtC*
Chewney, Nicholas *Alli*
Cheyfitz, Edward Theodore 1913- *OhA&B*
Cheyfitz, Eric *DrAP 1975*
Cheyn, William *Alli*
Cheyne *Alli*
Cheyne, A Bonar *Alli*
Cheyne, Alexander *Alli Sup*
Cheyne, Andrew *Alli Sup*
Cheyne, Charles Hartwell Horne *Alli Sup*
Cheyne, Elizabeth Gibson *ChPo*
Cheyne, George 1671-1743 *Alli*
Cheyne, James d1602 *Alli, ChPo S2*
Cheyne, John 1777-1836 *Alli, BiDLA*
Cheyne, Sir Joseph Lister Watson 1914- *Au&Wr*
Cheyne, Patrick *Alli Sup*
Cheyne, R M *Alli*
Cheyne, Thomas Kelly 1841-1915 *Alli Sup, BrAu 19, Chmbr 3*
Cheyne, William Watson *Alli Sup*
Cheynell, Francis 1608-1665 *Alli*

Cheyney, Arnold B 1926- *ConAu 23*
Cheyney, Edward Gheen 1878- *AmA&B*
Cheyney, Edward Potts 1861-1947 *Alli Sup, DcAmA, DcNAA*
Cheyney, Edward Ralph 1896- *AnMV 1926*
Cheyney, Lucia Trent 1897- *WhWNAA*
Cheyney, Peter 1896-1951 *DcLEnL, EncM&D, EvLB, MnBBF, REn, TwCW*
Cheyney, Ralph *WhWNAA*
Cheyney, Reginald Southouse d1951 *MnBBF*
Cheyney-Coker, Syl 1945- *ConP 1975, WrD 1976*
Chezy, Antoine Leonard De 1773-1832 *BbD, BiD&SB*
Chezy, Helmina Christiane Von 1783-1856 *BiD&SB*
Chezy, Wilhelm Von 1806-1865 *BiD&SB*
Chezy, Wilhelmine Christiane Von 1783-1856 *OxGer*
Chi, K'ang 223-262 *DcOrL 1*
Chi, Richard See Yee 1918- *ConAu 37, WrD 1976*
Chi, Wen-Shun 1910- *ConAu 13R*
Chi, Yun 1724-1805 *CasWL, DcOrL 1*
Chi-K'ung-Kuan Chu-Jen *DcOrL 1*
Chi-Wei *ConAu XR*
Chia, I 201?BC-169?BC *CasWL, DcOrL 1*
Chia-Hsuan Chu-Shih *DcOrL 1*
Chiabrera, Gabriello 1552-1638 *BbD, BiD&SB, CasWL, DcEuL, EuA, EvEuW, Pen Eur, REn*
Chiado, Antonio Ribeiro d1591 *CasWL*
Chiaffarelli, Alberte 1884-1945 *AmSCAP 66*
Chiampel, Durich 1510?-1582 *CasWL*
Chianese, Merle Molofsky *BlkAW, DrAF 1976*
Chiang, Ch'ing *DcOrL 1*
Chiang, Fang *DcOrL 1*
Chiang, Hai-Ch'eng *DcOrL 1*
Chiang, Kai-Shek 1886- *REn*
Chiang, Kuang-Tz'u 1901-1931 *DcOrL 1*
Chiang, K'uei 1155?-1221? *CasWL*
Chiang, Mei-Ling 1898- *REn*
Chiang, Pai-Shih 1155?-1230? *DcOrL 1*
Chiang, Ping-Chih *DcOrL 1*
Chiang, Shih-Ch'uan 1725-1785 *CasWL*
Chiang, Yee 1903- *IlCB 1945, IlCB 1956, LongC, TwCA Sup*
Ch'iao, Chi 1280-1345 *CasWL*
Chiappelli, Aldo 1907- *WhGrA*
Chiara, Piero 1913- *ConAu 53*
Chiarelli, Luigi 1880?-1947 *ClDMEuL, CnMD, McGWD, ModWD, REnWD*
Chiari, Joseph 1911- *Au&Wr, ConAu 5R*
Chiari, Pietro 1711-1785 *CasWL, DcEuL*
Chiarini, Giuseppe 1833-1908 *BiD&SB, CasWL*
Chiasson, Anselme *OxCan Sup*
Chiasson, Warren 1934- *AmSCAP 66*
Chiavacci, Vincenz 1847-1916 *BiD&SB, OxGer*
Chibald, William *Alli*
Chibnall, Marjorie McCallum 1915- *ConAu 29, WrD 1976*
Chicanot, Eugene Louis *OxCan*
Chichele, Mary *Alli Sup*
Chichester, Sir Alexander Palmer Bruce d1881 *Alli Sup*
Chichester, Charles Raleigh *Alli Sup*
Chichester, Edward *Alli*
Chichester, Sir Francis 1901-1972 *Au&Wr, ConAu 37, ConAu P-1*
Chichester, Frederick R, Earl Of Belfast 1827-1853 *Alli Sup, PoIre*
Chichester, Jane *ConAu XR*
Chick, Edson M 1924- *ConAu 23*
Chick, M P *ChPo*
Chickering, Arthur Merton 1887- *WhWNAA*
Chickering, Arthur W 1927- *ConAu 29*
Chickering, Frances E *Alli Sup*
Chickering, Geraldine Jencke *ChPo S1*
Chickering, Jesse 1797-1855 *DcAmA, DcNAA*
Chickering, John W *Alli Sup*
Chickering, John W, Jr. *Alli Sup*
Chickering, John White 1808-1888 *DcAmA, DcNAA*
Chickering, William Henry 1916-1945 *DcNAA*
Chickos, James Speros 1941- *ConAu 49*
Chideckel, Maurice 1880- *WhWNAA*

Chidester, Ann 1919- *AmA&B, AmNov, TwCA Sup*
Chidester, Floyd Earle 1884-1947 *DcNAA, WhWNAA*
Chidester, L W 1906- *AmSCAP 66*
Chidester, Nell *ChPo*
Chidlaw, Benjamin Williams 1811-1892 *OhA&B*
Chidley, Catherine *Alli*
Chidley, Samuel *Alli*
Chidsey, Donald Barr 1902- *AmA&B, AmNov, Au&Wr, ConAu 5R, REnAL, SmATA 3, TwCA Sup*
Chidyausiku, Paul 1935?- *AfA 1*
Chidzero, Bernard Thomas Gibson 1927- *ConAu 1R*
Chielens, Edward E 1943- *ConAu 53*
Chien De Montargis *OxFr*
Ch'ien, Chi-Po *DcOrL 1*
Ch'ien, Ch'ien-I 1582-1664 *CasWL, DcOrL 1*
Ch'ien, Chung-Shu *DcOrL 1*
Ch'ien, Hsing-Ts'un *DcOrL 1*
Ch'ien, Hsuan-T'ung *DcOrL 1*
Ch'ien, Ts'un-Hsun *ConAu XR*
Chiene, John *Alli Sup*
Chiera, Edward 1885-1933 *DcNAA*
Chiesa, Francesco 1871- *CasWL, ClDMEuL, EncWL, EvEuW*
Chifney *Alli*
Chignon, Niles *ConAu XR*
Chigounis, Evans 1931- *ConAu 45, DrAP 1975*
Chikamatsu Monzaemon 1653-1725 *CasWL, CnThe, CyWA, DcOrL 1, McGWD, Pen Cl, REn, REnWD*
Chikovani, Svimon 1902- *DcOrL 3*
Chiladze, Tamaz 1931- *DcOrL 3*
Chilcot, Harriet *Alli*
Chilcot, William d1711 *Alli*
Chilcote, Ronald H 1935- *ConAu 21*
Chilcott, John H 1924- *ConAu 41*
Child, Miss *Alli*
Child, A B *Alli Sup*
Child, A W *Alli Sup*
Child, Asaph Bemis 1813-1879? *ChPo S1, DcNAA*
Child, Charles *ChPo*
Child, Charles B 1903- *EncM&D*
Child, Charles Jesse 1901- *IlCB 1945*
Child, Charles Manning 1869- *WhWNAA*
Child, Clement Dexter 1868-1933 *DcNAA, WhWNAA*
Child, David Lee 1794-1874 *DcNAA*
Child, Elias *Alli Sup*
Child, Francis James 1825-1896 *Alli, Alli Sup, AmA, AmA&B, BiD&SB, ChPo, ChPo S1, CnDAL, CyAL 1, DcAmA, DcLEnL, DcNAA, EvLB, NewC, OxAm, OxEng, REn, REnAL*
Child, Frank Samuel 1854-1922 *Alli Sup, AmA&B, DcAmA, DcNAA*
Child, George Chaplin *Alli*
Child, Gilbert William *Alli Sup*
Child, H H 1869-1945 *LongC*
Child, Harry *Alli Sup*
Child, Heather 1912- *ConAu 9R*
Child, Henry *Alli Sup*
Child, Irvin L 1915- *ConAu 41*
Child, Isabella *ChPo*
Child, Jacob *BiDSA*
Child, James Erwin 1833-1912 *DcNAA*
Child, James T *Alli Sup*
Child, John *Alli*
Child, John 1922- *WrD 1976*
Child, Sir Josiah 1630-1699 *Alli, DcEnL*
Child, Julia 1912- *AmA&B, ConAu 41*
Child, Lydia Maria 1802-1880 *Alli, Alli Sup, AmA, AmA&B, BbD, BiD&SB, CarSB, CasWL, ChPo, ChPo S1, ChPo S2, Chmbr 3, CyAL 2, DcAmA, DcEnL, DcLEnL, DcNAA, EvLB, OxAm, REnAL, St&VC*
Child, Philip Albert 1898- *Au&Wr, CanNov, CanWr, CasWL, ConAu P-1, ConP 1970, DcLEnL, OxCan*
Child, Richard Washburn 1881-1935 *AmA&B, DcNAA, EncM&D, MnBBF, WhWNAA*
Child, Roderick 1949- *ConAu 25, WrD 1976*
Child, S *BiDLA*

Child, Samuel *Alli*
Child, Stephen 1866- *WhWNAA*
Child, T S *Alli Sup*
Child, W Stanley 1865- *WhWNAA*
Child, William 1607-1697 *Alli*
Childar, Catharine *Alli Sup*
Childe, Miss A F *Alli Sup*
Childe, C F *Alli*
Childe, Charles Frederick *Alli Sup*
Childe, E N *Alli*
Childe, F V *Alli*
Childe, Frances C *Alli Sup*
Childe, George Frederick *Alli Sup*
Childe, Henry Langdon 1892- *Au&Wr*
Childe, McAlpine *BbtC*
Childe, Vere Gordon 1892- *TwCA Sup*
Childe, Wilfred Rowland 1890- *CatA 1947, ChPo, ChPo S1, ChPo S2*
Childe-Pemberton, Harriet L *Alli Sup, ChPo S1*
Childerhose, R J *OxCan*
Childers, Charles *Alli Sup*
Childers, Erskine 1870-1922 *EncM&D, LongC, REn, TwCA, TwCW*
Childers, James Saxon 1899-1965 *AmA&B, ChPo, ChPo S1, REnAL, WhWNAA*
Childers, Robert Caesar 1838-1876 *Alli Sup*
Childers, Robert Erskine 1870-1922 *DcLEnL, EvLB*
Childers, Thomas 1940- *ConAu 37*
Children, John *Alli*
Children, John G *Alli*
Childress, Alice 1920- *BlkAW, ConAu 45, LivBAA, SmATA 7*
Childress, Alvin *BlkAW*
Childress, Edmund Howard 1873- *WhWNAA*
Childress, William 1933- *ConAu 41, DrAP 1975*
Childrey, Joshua 1623-1670 *Alli*
Childs, A P *Alli Sup*
Childs, Barney 1926- *ConAu 23*
Childs, C Sand *ConAu XR*
Childs, David Haslam 1933- *Au&Wr, ConAu 37, WrD 1976*
Childs, Edmund Burton 1887- *MnBBF*
Childs, Eleanor Stuart 1876- *AmA&B*
Childs, Emery E *Alli Sup*
Childs, Fay 1890- *SmATA 1*
Childs, Frank Hall 1859- *WhWNAA*
Childs, G B 1816- *Alli*
Childs, George Borlase 1816- *Alli Sup*
Childs, George William 1829-1894 *AmA&B, BbD, BiD&SB, ChPo S1, DcAmA, DcNAA*
Childs, H Fay 1890-1971 *ConAu P-1*
Childs, Harwood Lawrence 1898-1972 *Au&Wr, ConAu 25, ConAu 37*
Childs, J J *Alli*
Childs, James Bennett 1896- *AmA&B*
Childs, James Rives 1893- *AmA&B*
Childs, John Farnsworth *AuBYP*
Childs, John Lawrence 1899- *AmA&B*
Childs, Leroy 1888- *WhWNAA*
Childs, Lucy M *ChPo*
Childs, M Anna *Alli Sup*
Childs, Marilyn Grace Carlson 1923- *ConAu 9R*
Childs, Marquis William 1903- *AmA&B, ConAu 61, OxAm, REn, REnAL, TwCA Sup*
Childs, Mary Fairfax *ChPo*
Childs, Maryanna 1910- *ConAu 9R*
Childs, Richard *Alli*
Childs, Richard S 1882- *AmA&B, WhWNAA*
Childs, Robert Walker *Alli Sup*
Childs, Thomas 1825?-1899 *PoIre*
Childs, Thomas Spencer 1825-1914 *Alli Sup, DcAmA, DcNAA*
Childs, Mrs. Thomas Spencer *Alli Sup*
Childs-Clarke, Septimus John 1876- *WhLA*
Chiles, Mary Eliza 1820- *BiD&SB, DcAmA*
Chiles, Robert E 1923- *ConAu 17R*
Chiles, Rosa Pendleton 1866- *WhWNAA*
Chilingirov, Stiliyan 1881-1962 *CasWL*
Chillester, James *Alli*
Chillinden, Edmund *Alli*
Chillingsworth, William 1602-1644 *REn*
Chillingworth, J J *Alli Sup, PoIre*

Chillingworth, William 1602-1644 *Alli, BiD&SB, BrAu, Chmbr 1, DcEnL, EvLB, NewC, OxEng*
Chillman, James, Jr. 1891- *TexWr, WhWNAA*
Chilman, Eric 1893- *Au&Wr, ChPo, ChPo S1, ChPo S2, WrD 1976*
Chilmead, Edward 1610-1653 *Alli*
Chilson, Richard William 1943- *ConAu 57*
Chiltern, Faith *Alli Sup, ChPo S1, ChPo S2*
Chilton, Charles Frederick William 1917- *Au&Wr*
Chilton, Eleanor Carroll 1898-1949 *AmA&B, DcNAA, TwCA, TwCA Sup*
Chilton, John *Alli*
Chilton, John 1932- *ConAu 61*
Chilton, Richard *Alli*
Chilton, Robert Smythe *ChPo, ChPo S1*
Chilton, Thomas *Alli Sup*
Chilton, W E, Jr. 1893- *WhWNAA*
Chilton, W P *Alli Sup*
Chilver, Peter 1933- *ConAu 25, WrD 1976*
Chimaera *ConAu XR, SmATA 2*
Chimbamul *BlkAW*
Chin, Chuan *ConAu XR*
Chin, Frank 1940- *ConAu 33, DrAF 1976, DrAP 1975*
Chin, Robert 1918- *ConAu 61*
Chin, Sheng-T'an *DcOrL 1*
Chin, Yang Li *WorAu*
Chinaka, B A *AfA 1*
Chinard, Gilbert 1881- *AmA&B, OxAm, WhWNAA*
Chinery, Michael 1938- *WrD 1976*
Ching, James C 1926- *ConAu 37*
Chiniquy, Charles Paschal Telesphore 1809-1899 *Alli Sup, BbtC, DcNAA, OxCan*
Chinitz, Benjamin 1924- *ConAu 9R*
Chinmoy *ConAu 49*
Chinn, Ellen Purdy *TexWr*
Chinn, Laurene Chambers 1902- *ConAu 1R*
Chinn, Samuel *Alli Sup*
Chinn, William G 1919- *ConAu 33*
Chinnery, Ernest William Pearson 1887- *WhLA*
Chinnock, E J *Alli Sup*
Chinnubbie, Harjo *AmA&B*
Chinoy, Ely 1921-1975 *ConAu 1R, ConAu 57*
Chinoy, Helen Krich 1922- *ConAu 17R*
Chintamon, Hurrychund *Alli Sup*
Chipasula, Frank *BlkAW*
Chipley, W S *Alli Sup*
Chipman, Bruce Lewis 1946- *ConAu 37, WrD 1976*
Chipman, Daniel 1765-1850 *Alli, AmA, AmA&B, DcNAA*
Chipman, Donald E 1928- *ConAu 29, WrD 1976*
Chipman, George Ernest 1868-1916 *DcNAA*
Chipman, H G 1827-1852 *OhA&B*
Chipman, Herbert Lawrence 1866- *WhWNAA*
Chipman, Nathaniel 1752-1843 *Alli, BiDLA, DcAmA, DcNAA*
Chipman, Norton Parker 1838-1924 *OhA&B*
Chipman, R Manning *Alli Sup*
Chipman, Ward 1787-1851 *DcNAA*
Chipman, Warwick Fielding 1880- *WhWNAA*
Chipman, William Pendleton 1854-1937 *AmA&B, DcNAA*
Chipp, Elinor 1898- *AnMV 1926, ChPo*
Chipp, Herschel B 1913- *ConAu 25*
Chippendale, Annie E *ChPo*
Chippendale, George McCartney 1921- *WrD 1976*
Chippendale, Thomas 1718?-1779 *Alli, NewC*
Chipperfield, Joseph Eugene 1912- *Au&Wr, AuBYP, ConAu 9R, MorJA, SmATA 2*
Chipperfield, Robert Orr *DcNAA*
Chiri, Ruwa *BlkAW*
Chirico, Giorgio Di 1888- *REn*
Chirikov, Evgeny Nikolayevich 1864-1932 *CasWL*
Chirikov, Yevgeni Nikolayevich 1864-1932 *ClDMEuL, DcRusL*
Chirnside, Andrew *Alli Sup*
Chirol, J L *Alli, BiDLA*
Chirol, M Valentine *Alli Sup*
Chirol, Sir Valentine 1852-1929 *LongC, NewC*
Chirovsky, Nicholas L 1919- *ConAu 53*
Chisenhale, Sir Edward *Alli*

Chisenhale-Marsh *Alli Sup*
Chisholm, Mrs. A L *Alli Sup*
Chisholm, A R 1888- *ConAu 5R*
Chisholm, Adam Stuart Muir 1855-1931
  DcNAA
Chisholm, Alan Rowland 1888- *WrD 1976*
Chisholm, Alec H 1890- *ChPo, DcLEnL*
Chisholm, Belle V 1843- *Alli Sup, OhA&B*
Chisholm, Caroline 1810- *Alli*
Chisholm, Colin *Alli, BiDLA*
Chisholm, Earle *BlkAW*
Chisholm, Edwin *ChPo S1*
Chisholm, George C *Alli Sup*
Chisholm, George Goudie 1850- *WhLA*
Chisholm, Henry William *Alli Sup*
Chisholm, Hugh 1866-1924 *LongC, NewC*
Chisholm, Hugh J, Jr. 1913-1972 *ConAu 37*
Chisholm, J *ChPo*
Chisholm, K Lomneth 1919- *ConAu 61*
Chisholm, Lilian Mary 1906- *Au&Wr*
Chisholm, Louey *ChPo, ChPo S1*
Chisholm, Mary K 1924- *ConAu 37,
  WrD 1976*
Chisholm, Michael 1931- *ConAu 37,
  WrD 1976*
Chisholm, Myra Augur *ChPo S2*
Chisholm, R F 1904- *ConAu 29*
Chisholm, Roger K 1937- *ConAu 33*
Chisholm, Sam Whitten 1919- *ConAu 5R*
Chisholm, Shirley 1924- *AmA&B, ConAu 29,
  LivBAA, WrD 1976*
Chisholm, Thomas O *ChPo S1*
Chisholm, Walter 1856-1877 *Alli Sup, ChPo*
Chisholm, William B *ChPo S2*
Chisholm, William Mason *BlkAW*
Chisholm, William S, Jr. 1931- *ConAu 49*
Chisholm-Batten *Alli Sup*
Chisholme, David 1796?-1842 *BbtC, DcNAA*
Chishull, Edmund d1733 *Alli*
Chishull, John *Alli*
Chislett, Joseph *Alli Sup*
Chislett, William, Jr. 1884- *WhWNAA*
Chisman, Chris *Alli*
Chisolm, J B And Hyde, S, Jr. *Alli Sup*
Chisolm, J Julian *Alli Sup*
Chisolm, Lawrence W 1929- *ConAu 9R*
Chissell, Joan Olive *Au&Wr, ConAu 61,
  WrD 1976*
Chitepo, Herbert Wiltshire Pfumaindini 1923-
  AfA 1
Chitham, Edward 1932- *WrD 1976*
Chittenden, Albert Jerome *Alli Sup*
Chittenden, Brace 1864- *WhWNAA*
Chittenden, E W 1885- *WhWNAA*
Chittenden, Elizabeth F 1903- *ConAu 61,
  SmATA 9*
Chittenden, Ezra Porter 1851-1917 *DcNAA*
Chittenden, Frederick James 1873- *WhLA*
Chittenden, G B *Alli Sup*
Chittenden, Hiram Martin 1858-1917 *AmA&B,
  DcAmA, DcNAA, OxAm*
Chittenden, Miss L A *Alli Sup*
Chittenden, L E *ChPo, ChPo S2*
Chittenden, Larry *DcNAA, WhWNAA*
Chittenden, Lucius Eugene 1824-1900 *Alli Sup,
  BiD&SB, DcAmA, DcNAA*
Chittenden, Margaret 1935- *ConAu 53*
Chittenden, Newton H *Alli Sup*
Chittenden, Richard Handy 1836-1911 *DcNAA*
Chittenden, Russell Henry 1856-1943 *DcAmA,
  DcNAA, WhWNAA*
Chittenden, Thomas 1730-1797 *Alli*
Chittenden, William Lawrence 1862-1934
  *AmA&B, BiDSA, ChPo, ChPo S1,
  DcAmA, DcNAA, WhWNAA*
Chittick, Conrad *BlkAW*
Chittick, Victor Lovitt Oakes 1882- *OxCan,
  WhWNAA*
Chittick, William O 1937- *ConAu 41*
Chittum, Ida 1918- *ConAu 37, SmATA 7,
  WrD 1976*
Chitty, Arthur Benjamin 1914- *ConAu 53*
Chitty, Derwas James 1901- *Au&Wr*
Chitty, Edward *Alli, Alli Sup*
Chitty, Henry *Alli*
Chitty, Joseph 1776-1841 *Alli, BiDLA*
Chitty, Joseph, Jr. *Alli*
Chitty, R H *ChPo S1*

Chitty, Simon Casie *Alli Sup*
Chitty, Susan Elspeth 1929- *Au&Wr,
  ConAu P-1, WrD 1976*
Chitty, T *Alli*
Chitty, Thomas Willes 1855- *Alli Sup*
Chitty, Sir Thomas Willes 1926- *ConAu 5R,
  NewC, WorAu, WrD 1976*
Chitty, Thompson And Temple, Leofric
  Alli Sup
Chitty, W *Alli Sup*
Chitwood, Mabelle 1892- *IndAu 1917*
Chitwood, Marie Downs 1918- *ConAu 9R*
Chitwood, Mary Louisa 1832-1855 *IndAu 1816*
Chitwood, Oliver Perry 1874-1971 *AmA&B,
  ConAu P-1, WhWNAA*
Chitwood, William Hankins 1893-1965
  IndAu 1917
Chiu, Hong-Yee 1932- *ConAu 53*
Chiu, Hungdah 1936- *ConAu 37, WrD 1976*
Chivers, Thomas Holley 1809?-1858 *Alli Sup,
  AmA, AmA&B, BiD&SB, BiDSA,
  CasWL, ChPo, ChPo S2, CnDAL,
  DcAmA, DcNAA, OxAm, Pen Am, REn,
  REnAL*
Chlumberg, Hans 1897-1930 *CnMD, McGWD,
  ModWD, OxGer*
Chmelnizkij, Nikolaj Ivanovich 1789-1846 *BbD,
  BiD&SB*
Chmielewski, Edward 1928- *ConAu 13R*
Chmielovski, Peter 1848- *BiD&SB*
Cho, Ki-Cho'on 1913-1951 *DcOrL 1*
Cho, Yong Sam 1925- *ConAu 5R*
Choate, Agnes M *ChPo*
Choate, Ernest A 1900- *ConAu 49*
Choate, Florence *ConICB*
Choate, Gwen Peterson 1922- *ConAu 1R*
Choate, Isaac Bassett 1833-1917 *Alli Sup,
  ChPo, DcAmA, DcNAA*
Choate, J E 1916- *ConAu 33*
Choate, Joseph Hodges 1832-1917 *AmA&B,
  DcNAA, REnAL*
Choate, Lowell *Alli Sup*
Choate, R G *ConAu XR*
Choate, Rufus 1799-1859 *Alli, Alli Sup, AmA,
  AmA&B, BbD, BiD&SB, CyAL 2,
  DcAmA, DcNAA, REnAL*
Chocano, Jose Santos 1875-1934 *CasWL,
  DcSpL, EncWL, Pen Am, REn*
Chochlik *ConAu XR, WrD 1976*
Choderlos DeLaclos, Pierre Ambroise F
  1741-1803 *CasWL, EuA, EvEuW, OxFr*
Chodes, John 1939- *ConAu 61*
Chodorov, Edward 1904- *AmA&B, CnMD,
  ModWD, OxAm, REnAL*
Chodorov, Jerome 1911- *AmA&B, ConDr,
  McGWD, ModWD, REnAL, WrD 1976*
Chodorov, Stephan 1934- *ConAu 17R*
Chodos, Robert *OxCan Sup*
Chodowiecki, Daniel Nikolaus 1726-1801 *OxGer*
Chodzko, Alexander 1804-1891 *BiD&SB*
Chodzko, Ignacy 1795-1861 *BiD&SB*
Ch'oe, Ch'i-Won 857- *DcOrL 1*
Ch'oe, Nam-Son 1890-1957 *DcOrL 1*
Choirosphactes *CasWL*
Choiseul, Tristan *OxCan*
Choisy, Francois-Timoleon, Abbe De 1644-1724
  OxFr
Choleric, Brother *ConAu XR*
Cholieres, Nicolas, Sieur De *OxFr*
Cholmeley, Isobel C *Alli Sup*
Cholmley, Hugh *Alli*
Cholmondeley *Alli*
Cholmondeley, Alice *LongC*
Cholmondeley, Charles *Alli Sup*
Cholmondeley, Henry Pitt 1820- *Alli Sup*
Cholmondeley, Mary 1859-1925 *BbD, Chmbr 3,
  DcBiA, DcEuL, DcLEnL, EvLB, LongC,
  NewC, TwCA*
Cholmondeley, Thomas *Alli Sup*
Cholmondely-Pennell *Alli Sup*
Chomei *CasWL, DcOrL 1*
Chomet, Seweryn 1930- *Au&Wr*
Chomjakoff, Alexej Stepanovich 1804-1860 *BbD,
  BiD&SB*
Chommie, John C 1914- *ConAu 29*
Chomsky, Noam 1928- *AmA&B, ConAu 17R,
  Pen Am, WrD 1976*
Chonel, Charlotte *ConAu XR*

Chong, Chi-Yong 1903- *DcOrL 1*
Chong, Ch'ol 1536-1593 *CasWL, DcOrL 1*
Chong, Kug-In *DcOrL 1*
Chong, Kyong-Jo *ConAu XR*
Chong, Peng-Khuan *ConAu 25*
Chong, Yag-Yong 1762-1836 *DcOrL 1*
Choniates *CasWL*
Choniates, Michael 1138?-1222? *Pen Cl*
Choniates, Nicetas 1150?-1213 *Pen Cl*
Chope, Richard Robert *Alli Sup*
Choper, Jesse H 1935- *ConAu 13R*
Chopin, Frederic Francois 1810-1849 *AtlBL,
  NewC, OxFr, REn*
Chopin, Kate 1851-1904 *AmA, AmA&B, BbD,
  BiDSA, CasWL, CnDAL, DcAmA,
  DcLEnL, DcNAA, ModAL, ModAL Sup,
  OxAm, Pen Am, REn, REnAL*
Chopin, Rene 1885-1953 *CanWr, OxCan*
Choquette, Adrienne 1915- *CanWr, OxCan*
Choquette, Charles-Phillipe *WhWNAA*
Choquette, Ernest 1862-1941 *DcNAA, OxCan*
Choquette, Robert 1905- *CanWr, CasWL,
  OxCan, OxCan Sup, REn, REnAL*
Chorafas, Dimitris N 1926- *ConAu 5R,
  WrD 1976*
Chorao, Kay 1936- *ConAu 49, IlBYP,
  SmATA 8*
Chordal *DcNAA*
Chorell, Walentin 1912- *CrCD, EncWL Sup,
  Pen Eur, REnWD*
Chorley, Edward Clowes 1865-1949 *DcNAA*
Chorley, Henry Fothergill 1808-1872 *Alli,
  Alli Sup, BiD&SB, BrAu 19, ChPo,
  ChPo S1, ChPo S2, Chmbr 3, DcEnL,
  EvLB, NewC*
Chorley, John Rutter 1807?-1867 *Alli Sup*
Chorley, Joseph *Alli*
Chorley, Katharine *ChPo S2*
Chorley, William Brownsword 1800?- *Alli,
  Alli Sup, ChPo S1*
Chorlton, Mark *Alli Sup*
Chorlton, Thomas *Alli*
Chorlton, William *Alli Sup*
Chorny, Merron 1922- *ConAu 41*
Chorny, Sasha *ChPo, DcRusL*
Choromanski, Michal 1904-1972 *CasWL,
  EncWL, EvEuW, ModSL 2, Pen Eur,
  TwCW*
Choron, Jacques 1904-1972 *AuBYP,
  ConAu 33, ConAu P-1*
Chortatzis, Georgios *BiD&SB*
Chotenovsky, Zdenek 1929- *WhGrA*
Chotjewitz, Peter 1934- *ModGL*
Chou, Ch'i-Ying *DcOrL 1*
Chou, En-Lai 1898- *REn*
Chou, Li-Po 1908- *CasWL, DcOrL 1*
Chou, Pang-Yen 1056-1121 *CasWL, DcOrL 1*
Chou, Shu-Jen 1881-1936 *DcOrL 1, Pen Cl,
  REn*
Chou, Tso-Jen 1885-1966 *CasWL, DcOrL 1*
Chou, Tun-I 1017-1073 *CasWL*
Chou, Ya-Luu 1923- *ConAu 41*
Chou, Yang 1908- *DcOrL 1*
Choudhury, G W 1926- *ConAu 25*
Chouinard, Carroll 1907- *AmA&B*
Chouinard, Ephrem 1854-1918 *DcNAA*
Chouinard, Ernest 1856-1924 *DcNAA*
Chouinard, Honore Julien Jean Baptiste
  1850-1928 *DcNAA*
Choukas, Michael 1901- *ConAu 17*
Choules, John Overton 1801-1856 *Alli,
  ChPo S1, CyAL 2, DcAmA, DcNAA*
Chouteau, Auguste 1739-1829 *BiDSA*
Chovenus, Thomas *Alli*
Chow, Chung-Cheng 1908- *Au&Wr*
Chow, Gregory C 1929- *ConAu 13R*
Chow, Yung-Teh 1936- *ConAu 37*
Chowdhary, Savitri Devi 1907- *Au&Wr,
  ConAu P-1, WrD 1976*
Chown, Alice Amelia 1866-1949 *DcNAA*
Chown, Francis H *Alli Sup*
Chown, Joseph Parbery *Alli Sup*
Chown, Samuel Dwight 1853-1933 *DcNAA*
Choyce, A Newberry *ChPo*
Choyce, Patrick *ChPo*
Choynowski, Mieczyslaw 1909- *BiDPar*
Choynowski, Piotr 1885-1935 *EvEuW, Pen Eur*
Chrabr *CasWL*

Chraibi, Driss 1926- *DcOrL 3*
Chrest, C *Alli Sup*
Chrestien, Florent 1541-1596 *DcEuL*
Chretien De Troyes 1130?-1190? *AtlBL, BbD,
   BiD&SB, CasWL, CyWA, DcEuL, EuA,
   EvEuW, NewC, OxEng, OxFr, OxGer,
   Pen Eur, RCom, REn*
Chretien Li Gois *CasWL*
Chretien, Charles Peter *Alli Sup*
Chrimes, Stanley Bertram 1907- *Au&Wr,
   WrD 1976*
Chrislock, Carl H 1917- *ConAu 45*
Chrisman, Arthur Bowie 1889-1953 *AmA&B,
   AnCL, AuBYP, JBA 1934, JBA 1951,
   Newb 1922, REnAL, YABC 1*
Chrisman, Harry E 1906- *ConAu 1R*
Chrisman, Lewis Herbert 1883-1966 *AmA&B*
Chrisman, Oscar 1855-1929 *IndAu 1917*
Chrisp, John 1908- *Au&Wr*
Christ, Carl F 1923- *ConAu 21*
Christ, Henry I 1915- *ConAu 5R, WrD 1976*
Christ, Johann Friedrich 1700-1756 *DcEuL*
Christ, Lena 1881-1920 *OxGer*
Christ, Ronald 1936- *ConAu 25, WrD 1976*
Christ-Janer, Albert William 1910-1973
   AmA&B, ConAu 45
Christabel *PoIre*
Christen, Ada 1844-1901 *BiD&SB, CasWL,
   EvEuW, OxGer*
Christensen, Alberta Huish 1900- *ChPo S1*
Christensen, Asher Norman 1903-1961 *AmA&B*
Christensen, Clyde M 1905- *ConAu 53*
Christensen, David E 1921- *ConAu 13R*
Christensen, Edward L 1913- *ConAu 25*
Christensen, Eleanor Ingalls 1913- *ConAu 53*
Christensen, Erwin Ottomar 1890- *AmA&B,
   ConAu P-1*
Christensen, F W 1879- *WhWNAA*
Christensen, Francis 1902- *ConAu 23*
Christensen, Gardell Dano 1907- *AuBYP,
   ConAu 9R, IlCB 1956, SmATA 1*
Christensen, Haaken 1886- *IlCB 1956*
Christensen, Harold T 1909- *ConAu 45*
Christensen, J A 1927- *ConAu 53, WrD 1976*
Christensen, Jo Ippolito *ConAu 57*
Christensen, Otto Henry 1898- *ConAu 33,
   WrD 1976*
Christensen, Yolanda Maria Ippolito 1943-
   ConAu 57
Christenson, Carroll Lawrence 1902-
   IndAu 1917
Christenson, Cornelia Vos 1903- *ConAu 33,
   IndAu 1917, WrD 1976*
Christenson, Larry 1928- *ConAu 57*
Christenson, Reo M 1918- *ConAu 37*
Christesen, Clement Byrne 1911?- *Au&Wr,
   ConP 1970, DcLEnL*
Christgau, Alice Erickson 1902- *ConAu 17*
Christgau, Ferdinand G *ChPo*
Christian *CasWL*
Christian, Bertram *WhLA*
Christian, Bobby 1911- *AmSCAP 66*
Christian, C Russell *BiDSA*
Christian, C W 1927- *ConAu 21*
Christian, Carol Cathay 1923- *Au&Wr,
   ConAu 53, WrD 1976*
Christian, Edgar *OxCan*
Christian, Edmund V B *Alli Sup*
Christian, Edward *Alli, BiDLA*
Christian, Edward d1823 *Alli*
Christian, Mrs. Edward *Alli Sup*
Christian, Eugene 1860- *WhWNAA*
Christian, Fletcher 1730?- *NewC*
Christian, Frederick *ConAu XR*
Christian, Garth Hood 1921-1967 *ConAu P-1*
Christian, George Llewellyn 1841- *BiDSA*
Christian, Princess Helena A Victoria 1846-
   Alli Sup
Christian, Henry A 1876- *WhWNAA*
Christian, Henry A 1931- *ConAu 33*
Christian, J *Alli Sup*
Christian, James L 1927- *ConAu 57*
Christian, Jill *WrD 1976*
Christian, John *WrD 1976*
Christian, John 1930- *ConAu XR*
Christian, John Edward 1917- *IndAu 1917*
Christian, John Tyler *BiDSA*
Christian, John Wyrill 1926- *Au&Wr,*

Christian, L H *Alli Sup*
Christian, Marcus Bruce 1900- *BlkAW,
   LivBAA*
Christian, Mary Blount 1933- *ConAu 45,
   SmATA 9, WrD 1976*
Christian, Obadiah *BiDLA, BiDLA Sup*
Christian, Owen *Alli Sup, PoIre*
Christian, Peggy *ChPo S1*
Christian, Reginald Frank 1924- *Au&Wr,
   ConAu 5R*
Christian, Roy Cloberry 1914- *WrD 1976*
Christian, T P *Alli, BiDLA*
Christian, Theoph *Alli*
Christian, Viktor 1885- *WhLA*
Christian, William Gay 1862- *WhWNAA*
Christiani, Adolph F *Alli Sup*
Christiani, Dounia Bunis 1913- *ConAu 13R*
Christiani, Maud *ChPo*
Christiansen, Arne Einar 1861-1939 *BbD,
   BiD&SB, CasWL*
Christiansen, Arthur 1904-1963 *ConAu 1R,
   LongC*
Christiansen, F M 1871- *WhWNAA*
Christiansen, Harley Duane 1930- *ConAu 53*
Christiansen, Rex Samuel 1930- *Au&Wr*
Christiansen, Sigurd Wesley 1891-1947 *CasWL,
   EncWL, EvEuW, Pen Eur, TwCA,
   TwCA Sup*
Christianson, John 1934- *ConAu 23*
Christianson, Theodore 1883-1948 *DcNAA*
Christie, A J *BbtC*
Christie, Agatha 1890?-1976 *Au&Wr, AuBYP,
   AuNews 1, AuNews 2, CasWL, CnThe,
   ConAu 17R, ConAu 61, ConDr,
   ConLC 1, ConLC 6, ConNov 1972,
   ConNov 1976, DcLEnL, EncM&D, EvLB,
   LongC, MnBBF, NewC, OxEng,
   Pen Eng, REn, TwCA, TwCA Sup,
   TwCW, WrD 1976*
Christie, Albany James *Alli Sup*
Christie, Alex *Alli*
Christie, Alexander Graham 1880- *WhWNAA*
Christie, Alexander James d1843 *DcNAA*
Christie, Alice M *Alli Sup*
Christie, Ann Philippa *WrD 1976*
Christie, Annie Rothwell 1837-1927 *DcNAA*
Christie, Arthur William 1892- *WhWNAA*
Christie, Campbell 1893-1963 *LongC*
Christie, Dorothy *LongC*
Christie, Dugald 1855- *WhLA*
Christie, Francis Albert 1858- *WhWNAA*
Christie, Fyfe *Alli Sup*
Christie, George *BbtC*
Christie, George C 1934- *ConAu 37*
Christie, Hugh 1730-1774 *Alli*
Christie, Hugh 1913- *ConAu XR*
Christie, Ian Ralph 1919- *Au&Wr, ConAu 5R,
   WrD 1976*
Christie, J *Alli, Alli Sup*
Christie, J Knox 1877- *ChPo*
Christie, J Traill *Alli*
Christie, James *Alli, Alli Sup, BiDLA Sup*
Christie, James 1730-1803 *NewC*
Christie, James 1773-1831 *Alli, BiDLA,
   NewC*
Christie, James 1827-1900? *ChPo*
Christie, James Robert *Alli Sup*
Christie, Jane Johnstone 1860- *AmLY*
Christie, John 1848- *ChPo*
Christie, John 1882-1962 *LongC*
Christie, Keith *ConAu XR*
Christie, Lindsay H 1906?-1976 *ConAu 61*
Christie, Mary Elizabeth *Alli Sup*
Christie, Milton 1921- *ConAu 17R*
Christie, Nimmo *ChPo S2*
Christie, Peter *Alli Sup*
Christie, R M *Alli Sup*
Christie, Richard Copley 1830- *Alli Sup*
Christie, Robert *Chmbr 3*
Christie, Robert 1788-1856 *BbtC, DcNAA,
   OxCan*
Christie, Stephen *MnBBF*
Christie, Thomas *Alli, BiDLA*
Christie, Thomas 1761-1796 *Alli*
Christie, Thomas William *Alli Sup*
Christie, Trevor L 1905- *ConAu 21*
Christie, W D *Alli*

Christie, William *Alli Sup, BiDLA, ChPo S2*
Christie, William 1710-1744 *Alli*
Christie, William Dougal 1816-1874 *Alli Sup*
Christie, William Henry Mahoney 1845-
   Alli Sup
Christie-Murray, David Hugh Arthur 1913-
   Au&Wr, ConAu 53, WrD 1976
Christien, John *Alli Sup*
Christina 1626-1689 *DcEuL, REn*
Christina De Pisan 1364?-1430? *REn*
Christine De Pisan 1364?-1430? *CasWL, EuA,
   EvEuW, OxFr, Pen Eur*
Christine, Charles T 1936- *ConAu 33*
Christine, Dorothy Weaver 1934- *ConAu 33*
Christison, Alex *Alli*
Christison, John *Alli, BiDLA*
Christison, Robert *Alli, Alli Sup*
Christison, Sir Robert 1797-1882 *Alli Sup*
Christlieb, Emily *Alli Sup*
Christman, Bernice Bunn 1912- *IndAu 1917*
Christman, Don R 1919- *ConAu 17R*
Christman, Henry Clinton *ChPo S1*
Christman, Marion H 1902- *AmSCAP 66*
Christman, William Weaver 1865-1937 *AmA&B,
   DcNAA*
Christmas, Edwin *ChPo S1*
Christmas, Henry 1811-1868 *Alli, Alli Sup,
   BbtC, DcEnL, OxCan*
Christmas, Jane *Alli Sup*
Christmas, Joseph S *Alli*
Christmas, R A *DrAP 1975*
Christoforov, Assen 1910-1970 *CasWL*
Christol, Carl 1872- *WhWNAA*
Christol, Carl Quimby 1914- *ConAu 5R*
Christoph, James Bernard 1928- *Au&Wr,
   ConAu 5R, WrD 1976*
Christophe, Henri 1767-1820 *REn*
Christopher North *DcEuL, OxEng*
Christopher Of Mytilene 1000?-1050 *CasWL,
   Pen Cl*
Christopher, Saint 230?- *NewC, REn*
Christopher, Alfred Millard William *Alli Sup*
Christopher, E Earl 1872- *DcAmA*
Christopher, Fanny H *Alli Sup*
Christopher, James *BlkAW*
Christopher, Joe R 1935- *ConAu 53*
Christopher, John 1922- *ChLR 2, SenS,
   WorAu*
Christopher, John B 1914- *ConAu 13R*
Christopher, Louise *ConAu XR*
Christopher, M *Alli Sup*
Christopher, Matthew F 1917- *AuBYP,
   ConAu 1R, MorBMP, SmATA 2,
   WrD 1976*
Christopher, May 1912- *AmSCAP 66*
Christopher, Robin *ChPo*
Christopher, S *Alli Sup*
Christopher, T Hudson *WhWNAA*
Christopher, W S *Alli Sup*
Christophers, John Crowch *Alli Sup*
Christophers, Joseph S *Alli Sup*
Christophers, Sir Samuel R Christophers 1873-
   Au&Wr
Christophers, Samuel Woolcock 1810- *Alli Sup*
Christophersen, Paul Hans 1911- *Au&Wr,
   ConAu 57, WrD 1976*
Christopherson, Henry *Alli Sup*
Christopherson, John d1558 *Alli*
Christopulos, Athanasios 1772?-1847 *BiD&SB*
Christowe, Stoyan 1898- *AmA&B, Au&Wr,
   REnAL*
Christus, Petrus 1420?-1472? *AtlBL*
Christy, Betty 1924- *ConAu 57*
Christy, David 1802- *Alli, AmA&B, DcAmA,
   DcNAA, OhA&B*
Christy, Edwin Byron *Alli Sup*
Christy, Edwin P 1815-1862 *OxAm, REnAL*
Christy, George *ConAu 9R*
Christy, George W *BiDSA*
Christy, Henry 1810-1865 *Alli Sup*
Christy, Howard Chandler 1873?-1952 *AmA&B,
   ChPo, ChPo S2, IlCB 1945*
Christy, Joe *ConAu XR*
Christy, Joseph M 1919- *ConAu 29*
Christy, Miller *Alli Sup*
Christy, Robert *Alli Sup*
Christy, Thomas *Alli Sup*
Christy, Wilbur A 1845-1928 *OhA&B*

Churchman, David C 1933- *IndAu 1917*
Churchman, John d1805 *Alli*
Churchman, Michael 1929- *ConAu 37,*
WrD 1976
Churchman, Philip Hudson 1874- *WhWNAA*
Churchman, Theophilus *Alli*
Churchman, Walter *Alli*
Churchward, James 1852-1936 *AmA&B,*
DcNAA
Churchward, Lloyd Gordon 1919- *WrD 1976*
Churchward, William B *Alli Sup*
Churchy, G *Alli*
Churchyard, Thomas 1520?-1604 *Alli, BrAu,*
CasWL, Chmbr 1, CrE&SL, DcEnL,
DcLEnL, EvLB, NewC, OxEng, Pen Eng,
REn
Churi, Joseph H *Alli Sup*
Churton, Edward *Alli*
Churton, Edward 1800-1874 *Alli Sup, ChPo,*
ChPo S2
Churton, H B Whitaker *Alli*
Churton, Henry 1838-1905 *Alli Sup, AmA,*
DcNAA, OhA&B
Churton, Ralph 1754-1831 *Alli, BiDLA,*
BiDLA Sup
Churton, William Ralph *Alli Sup*
Chute, Anthony *Alli*
Chute, Arthur Hunt 1890- *WhWNAA*
Chute, B J *MnBBF*
Chute, B J 1913- *AmA&B, ConAu 1R,*
MorJA, SmATA 2, WrD 1976
Chute, Chaloner Wiggett *Alli Sup*
Chute, Chaloner William 1838- *Alli Sup*
Chute, Horatio Nelson 1847-1928 *DcAmA,*
DcNAA, WhWNAA
Chute, Joy *MnnWr*
Chute, Mary *MnnWr*
Chute, Rupert *ConAu XR*
Chute, William J 1914- *ConAu 9R*
Chwalek, Henryka C 1918- *ConAu 17R*
Chwast, Jacqueline 1932- *ChPo, ChPo S2,*
ConAu 49, IlBYP, IlCB 1966, SmATA 6
Chwast, Seymour *IlBYP*
Chwostoff, Count Dmitrij Ivanovich 1757-1835
BiD&SB
Chyet, Stanley F 1931- *ConAu 33*
Chynoweth, James B And Bruckner, W H
Alli Sup
Chynoweth, W Harris *Alli Sup*
Chytraeus, Nathan 1543-1598 *OxGer*
Cialente, Fausta 1900- *ConAu XR, TwCW*
Ciampi, Ignazio 1824-1880 *BiD&SB*
Ciampoli, Domenico 1855- *BiD&SB*
Cianciolo, Patricia Jean 1929- *ChPo S2,*
ConAu 37
Ciani, C *ChPo*
Ciarcia, John 1940- *AmSCAP 66*
Ciardi, John 1916- *AmA&B, AuBYP, BkCL,*
BkP, CasWL, ChPo, ChPo S1, ChPo S2,
CnDAL, ConAu 5R, ConP 1970,
ConP 1975, DrAP 1975, ModAL, OxAm,
Pen Am, RAdv 1, REn, REnAL,
SmATA 1, St&VC, ThBJA, TwCA Sup,
WebEAL, WrD 1976
Cibber, Colley 1671-1757 *Alli, BbD, BiD&SB,*
BrAu, CasWL, ChPo, Chmbr 2, CnThe,
CriT 2, CyWA, DcEnA, DcEnL, DcEuL,
DcLEnL, EvLB, McGWD, NewC,
OxEng, Pen Eng, PoLE, REn, REnWD,
WebEAL
Cibber, Susanna Maria 1714-1766 *Alli*
Cibber, Susannah Maria 1714-1766 *NewC*
Cibber, Theophilus 1703-1758 *Alli, DcEnL,*
DcEuL, NewC
Cibdareal, Fernan Gomez De *DcEuL*
Cicalello, Joseph 1908- *AmSCAP 66*
Cicci, Maria Luigia 1760-1794 *BiD&SB*
Cicellis, Catherine-Mathilda 1926- *ConAu 1R*
Cicellis, Kay 1926- *Au&Wr, ConAu XR,*
ConNov 1972, ConNov 1976, WrD 1976
Cicero, Marcus Tullius 106BC-043BC *AtlBL,*
BbD, BiD&SB, CasWL, CyWA, DcEuL,

NewC, OxEng, Pen Cl, RCom, REn
Cicero, Quintus Tullius 102BC-043BC *Pen Cl*
Cicognani, Cardinal Amleto Giovanni 1883-1973
CatA 1947, ConAu 45
Cicognani, Bruno 1879- *CasWL, ClDMEuL,*
Pen Eur
Ciconi, Teobaldo 1824-1863 *BiD&SB*
Cicourel, Aaron V 1928- *ConAu 53*
Cid, El 1040?-1099 *DcSpL, NewC, RCom*
Cid Perez, Jose 1906- *ConAu 53*
Ciechanowski, Jan 1888?-1973 *ConAu 41*
Cieco Da Ferrara *BiD&SB*
Cieco Di Ferrara, Il *CasWL*
Cielo, Astra *WhWNAA*
Cienfuegos, Nicasio Alvarez De 1764-1809 *BbD,*
BiD&SB, DcEuL, EvEuW, Pen Eur
Cieslewicz, Roman 1930- *WhGrA*
Cieza DeLeon, Pedro 1518?-1560 *CasWL*
Cifre DeLoubriel, Estela *PueRA*
Cilento, Ruth Yolanda 1925- *Au&Wr*
Ciletti, James *DrAP 1975*
Cilies Von Seyn *OxGer*
Cilley, Gordon Harper 1874-1938 *DcNAA*
Cilley, Jonathan Prince, Jr. 1835-1920 *DcNAA,*
OxCan
Cilliers, Charl Jean Francois 1941- *ConP 1970*
Cimabue, Giovanni 1240?-1302? *AtlBL, NewC,*
REn
Cimarosa, Domenico 1749-1801 *AtlBL*
Cimbollek, Robert 1937- *ConAu 57*
Ciminelli, Serafino De' 1466-1500 *CasWL,*
Pen Eur
Cimino, Harry *ChPo S2*
Cimino, Maria Pia *ChPo*
Cimon, Henri 1855-1927 *DcNAA*
Cina, Albert I 1896- *AmSCAP 66*
Cinaethon *Pen Cl*
Cincinnatus *DcNAA*
Cincinnatus, Lucius Quinctius 519?BC- *NewC*
Cincinnatus, Titus Quinctius 519?BC- *NewC*
Cingo, Zivko 1936- *ModSL 2*
Cingoli, Giulio *IlBYP, IlCB 1966*
Cingria, Charles-Albert 1883-1954 *CasWL*
Cini, Giovanni Battista d1586 *McGWD*
Cinna *ConAu XR*
Cinna, C Helvius *BiD&SB*
Cinna, Gaius Helvius 070?BC-044BC *CasWL,*
Pen Cl
Cinnamond, H P *MnBBF*
Cinnamus, John 1144?-1203? *CasWL, Pen Cl*
Cino Da Pistoia 1270?-1337 *CasWL, EuA*
Cino Da Pistoja 1270?-1337 *BiD&SB*
Cino De'Sigisbuldi Da Pistoia 1270?-1339
EvEuW
Cinthio, Giambattista Giraldi 1504-1573 *CasWL,*
DcEuL, EuA, McGWD, NewC, OxEng
Cintio *BiD&SB, EuA, NewC*
Cinzio *BiD&SB, EuA, EvEuW*
Cioffari, Vincenzo 1905- *ConAu 17R*
Cioran, E M 1911- *ConAu 25, WorAu*
Cipalunkar, Visnusastri 1850-1882 *DcOrL 2*
Cipes, Robert M 1930- *ConAu 23*
Cipico, Ivo 1869-1933 *EncWL*
Ciplijauskaite, Birute 1929- *ConAu 37*
Ciplunkar, Visnu Sastri 1850-1882 *CasWL*
Cipolla, Carlo Manlio 1922- *ConAu 5R,*
WrD 1976
Cipolla, Joan Bagnel *ConAu 49*
Cipriani, Giovanni Battista 1727-1785 *BkIE*
Ciraci, Norma 1922- *OhA&B*
Circuit Breaker *WrD 1976*
Circus, Jim *ConAu 9R*
Cire *ConAu XR*
Cirencester, Richard Of d1401? *Alli, OxEng*
Ciriaco D'Ancona 1391-1455? *CasWL, REn*
Ciriaco Of Ancona 1391?-1450? *DcEuL*
Cirino, Robert 1937- *ConAu 61*
Cirkel, Fritz 1863-1914 *DcNAA*
Cirlova, Vasile *CasWL*
Cismaru, Alfred 1933- *ConAu 61*
Cisneros, Antonio 1942- *DcCLA, DcSpL*
Cisse, Emile 1930?- *AfA 1*
Cissell, Eldrew Donald 1893?-1972 *IndAu 1917*
Cissell, Robert 1913- *IndAu 1917*
Cissoko, Siriman *AfA 1*
Cist, Charles 1738-1805 *AmA&B*
Cist, Charles 1793-1868 *AmA&B, DcNAA,*
OhA&B

Cist, Henry Martyn 1839-1902 *Alli Sup,*
AmA&B, DcAmA, DcNAA, OhA&B
Cist, Lewis Jacob 1818-1885 *ChPo, ChPo S1,*
DcAmA, DcNAA, OhA&B
Ciszek, Walter 1904- *ConAu P-1*
Citashe, I W W 1845?-1930? *AfA 1*
Citati, Pietro 1930- *ConAu 53*
Citovich, Enid Sarah Kortright 1902- *Au&Wr,*
WrD 1976
Cittafino, Ricardo *ConAu XR*
Ciuba, Edward J 1935- *ConAu 61*
Civasaqui, Jose 1916- *ConP 1970*
Civavakkiyar *DcOrL 2*
Civis *AmLY XR*
Cjis Maun *DcOrL 2*
Claassen, Harold 1905- *ConAu 19*
Claassen, P W 1886- *WhWNAA*
Clabon, John Moxon *Alli Sup*
Clack, J M *Alli*
Clack, Louise *Alli Sup, LivFWS*
Clack, Marie Louise *BiDSA*
Clack, Thomas Edward *Alli Sup*
Clacy, Mrs. Charles *Alli*
Clacy, Ellen *Alli Sup*
Clad, Noel Clovis 1924?-1962 *AmA&B,*
Au&Wr
Cladel, Leon 1835-1892 *BiD&SB, OxFr*
Cladet, Leon 1835-1892 *EvEuW*
Claerbaut, David 1946- *ConAu 45*
Claes, Ernest Andre Jozef 1885-1968 *CasWL,*
EncWL
Claffey, William J 1925- *ConAu 23*
Claflin, Mary Bucklin 1825-1896 *AmA&B,*
BiD&SB, DcAmA, DcNAA
Claflin, Sumner Franklin 1862- *ChPo S1*
Claflin, Tennessee Celeste 1838-1927 *AmA,*
OxAm
Claflin, Miss Tennie C 1838-1927 *Alli Sup,*
OhA&B
Clagett, John 1916- *AmA&B, AuBYP,*
ConAu 5R
Clagett, Marshall 1916- *AmA&B, ConAu 1R*
Clagett, Nicholas d1746 *Alli*
Clagett, Nicholas 1607-1663 *Alli*
Clagett, Nicholas 1654-1726 *Alli*
Clagett, William 1646-1688 *Alli*
Claggett, John *Alli*
Claggett, Sue Harry *Alli Sup*
Claghorn, Charles Eugene 1911- *ConAu 57*
Claghorn, Kate Holladay 1864-1938 *AmLY,*
DcAmA, DcNAA, WhWNAA
Clague, Ewan 1896- *ConAu 29*
Claiborne, Andrew *Alli Sup*
Claiborne, Craig 1920- *AmA&B, ConAu 1R*
Claiborne, F *Alli Sup, BiDSA*
Claiborne, Helen *ChPo S2*
Claiborne, John Francis Hamtramck 1809-1884
Alli Sup, AmA&B, BiDSA, DcAmA,
DcNAA
Claiborne, John Herbert 1828-1905 *Alli Sup,*
BiDSA, DcAmA, DcNAA
Claiborne, Martha J *BiDSA*
Claiborne, Nathaniel Herbert 1777-1859
AmA&B, BiDSA, DcAmA, DcNAA
Claiborne, Robert 1919- *ConAu 29*
Clain, Samuil 1745-1806 *CasWL*
Clair, Andree *ConAu 29*
Clair, Aston *Alli Sup*
Clair, Rene 1898- *REn*
Clair, Shirley *ChPo*
Clairant *Alli*
Claire, Keith *Au&Wr, ConAu XR*
Claire, Leon *ChPo S2*
Claire, William Francis 1935- *ConAu 57,*
DrAP 1975
Clairi, Robert De *OxFr*
Clairmont, Clara Mary Jane 1798-1879 *NewC,*
REn
Clairmont, Robert *ChPo*
Clairon, Claire Legris DeLatude 1723-1803
OxFr
Clairville, Louis Francois 1811-1879 *BiD&SB*
Clajus, Johannes 1535-1592 *OxGer*
Clamp, Helen Mary Elizabeth *Au&Wr*
Clampett, Bob *AuNews 1*
Clancey, John Charles 1854- *WhLA*
Clancy, Daniel Francis 1918- *IndAu 1917*
Clancy, James J *Alli Sup*

Clancy, John Gregory 1922- *ConAu 13R*
Clancy, Louise Breitenbach *WhWNAA*
Clancy, Michael -1780? *PoIre*
Clancy, Thomas H 1923- *ConAu 13R,*
WrD 1976
Clanes, Thomas *Alli, BiDLA*
Claney, M *Alli*
Clanmorris, Lord *Au&Wr*
Clanny, William Reid *Alli, BiDLA*
Clanricarde, Ulick, Marquis Of *Alli*
Clanton, Gene 1934- *ConAu 41*
Clanton, Gordon 1942- *ConAu 57*
Clanvowe, Sir John 1341-1391 *CasWL*
Clanvowe, Sir Thomas d1410? *CasWL,*
Chmbr 1
Clap, Nathaniel 1669-1745 *Alli, DcAmA,*
DcNAA
Clap, Roger 1609-1691 *Alli, CyAL 1,*
DcAmA, DcNAA
Clap, Thomas 1703-1767 *Alli, CyAL 1,*
DcAmA, DcNAA
Clapesattle, Helen 1908- *Au&Wr*
Clapham, Henoche *Alli*
Clapham, John *Alli*
Clapham, John 1908- *Au&Wr, ConAu 25,*
WrD 1976
Clapham, John Peele *ChPo S1*
Clapham, Jonathan *Alli*
Clapham, Richard 1878- *Br&AmS*
Clapham, Samuel 1755-1830 *Alli, BiDLA,*
BiDLA Sup
Clapin, Sylva 1853-1928 *DcNAA, OxCan*
Clapman, Sidney Walter 1912- *WrD 1976*
Clapp, Anna W P *ChPo*
Clapp, Mrs. C A *Alli Sup*
Clapp, Charles 1899-1962 *AmSCAP 66*
Clapp, Earle Hart 1877- *WhWNAA*
Clapp, Ebenezer *Alli Sup*
Clapp, Edwin Jones 1881-1930 *DcNAA*
Clapp, Eva Catherine *Alli Sup*
Clapp, Eva Katherine *AmA&B*
Clapp, Frank Leslie 1877-1937 *IndAu 1917*
Clapp, Frank Leslie 1877- *WhWNAA*
Clapp, Frederick Gardner 1879- *WhWNAA*
Clapp, Frederick Mortimer 1879- *AmA&B,*
ChPo, WhWNAA
Clapp, Henry, Jr. 1814-1875 *AmA, AmA&B,*
OxAm, Pen Am
Clapp, Henry Austin 1841-1904 *AmA,*
AmA&B, DcAmA, DcNAA
Clapp, Herbert C *Alli Sup*
Clapp, James Gordon 1909-1970 *ConAu P-1*
Clapp, John *Alli*
Clapp, Margaret Antoinette 1910-1974 *AmA&B,*
ConAu 49, OxAm, REnAL, TwCA Sup
Clapp, Mary Brennan 1884- *AnMV 1926,*
ChPo
Clapp, Mary Wolcott Welles 1879- *WhWNAA*
Clapp, Patricia 1912- *ConAu 25, SmATA 4,*
WrD 1976
Clapp, R M *Alli Sup*
Clapp, Susan Frances *ChPo S1*
Clapp, Theodore 1792-1866 *Alli Sup, BiDSA,*
DcAmA, DcNAA
Clapp, Verner W 1901-1972 *ConAu 37*
Clapp, William H *Alli Sup*
Clapp, William Warland, Jr. 1826-1891 *Alli Sup,*
AmA&B, DcNAA
Clappe, Ambrose *Alli*
Clappe, Louise Amelia Knapp Smith 1819-1906
AmA&B, OxAm
Clappen, John 1901- *Au&Wr*
Clapper, Raymond 1892-1944 *AmA&B,*
WhWNAA
Clapperton, Hugh 1788-1827 *Alli*
Clapperton, Jane Hume *Alli Sup*
Clapperton, Richard 1934- *Au&Wr,*
ConAu 25
Clapperton, William *Alli*
Clapthorne, Henry *Alli*
Clar, Arden 1915- *AmSCAP 66*
Clar, C Raymond 1903- *ConAu 37*
Clara Augusta *DcNAA, HsB&A*
Claramont, C *Alli*
Clardy, J V 1929- *ConAu 33*
Clare, Ada 1836-1874 *Alli Sup, AmA&B,*
OxAm, Pen Am, REnAL
Clare, Austin *Alli Sup*

Clare, Edward *Alli Sup*
Clare, Elizabeth *WrD 1976*
Clare, Frances *Alli Sup*
Clare, Francis D *ConAu XR*
Clare, Helen *AuBYP, ConAu XR,*
SmATA 3, ThBJA, WhCL
Clare, Israel Smith 1847-1924 *Alli Sup,*
AmA&B, AmLY, DcNAA
Clare, John 1793-1864 *Alli, AtlBL, BbD,*
BiD&SB, BrAu 19, CasWL, ChPo,
ChPo S1, ChPo S2, Chmbr 3, CnE&AP,
DcEnL, DcLEnL, EvLB, NewC, OxEng,
Pen Eng, REn, WebEAL
Clare, John Fitz-Gibbon, Earl Of 1749-1802 *Alli*
Clare, John Hollis, Earl Of *Alli*
Clare, Josephine *DrAP 1975*
Clare, Kittie *ChPo S1*
Clare, Margaret *ConAu XR*
Clare, Martin *Alli*
Clare, Mary Frances *Alli Sup*
Clare, Maurice *ChPo S2*
Clare, Peter *Alli*
Clare, R *Alli*
Clare, R A *Alli*
Clare, Ronald *MnBBF*
Clare, Sidney 1892- *AmSCAP 66*
Clare, Thomas Truitt 1924- *AmSCAP 66*
Clare, Vincent *MnBBF*
Clare, William *Alli*
Clarek, Timothy *Alli*
Claremon, Neil *DrAP 1975*
Clarence, Duke Of *Alli*
Clarence, A F *Alli Sup*
Clarence, George, Duke Of 1449-1478 *REn*
Clarence, S *Alli Sup*
Clarendon, Edward Hyde, Earl Of 1609?-1674
Alli, AtlBL, BiD&SB, BrAu, CasWL,
Chmbr 1, DcEnA, DcEnL, DcLEnL,
EvLB, NewC, OxEng, Pen Eng, REn,
WebEAL
Clarendon, George W F Villiers, Earl Of 1800-
Alli
Clarendon, Henry Hyde, Earl Of 1638-1709 *Alli*
Clarendon, R V *Alli, BiDLA*
Clarendon, Thomas *Alli*
Clarens, Carlos 1936- *ConAu 21*
Clareson, Thomas D 1926- *ConAu 1R*
Claret, G *Alli Sup*
Claretie, Jules Arsene Arnaud 1840-1913 *BbD,*
BiD&SB, DcBiA, EvEuW, OxFr, REn
Clarges, Kathleen Isabelle *Alli Sup*
Clari, Robert De d1217? *CasWL*
Claribel *BrAu 19, DcEnL, NewC, PoIre*
Clarida, Orville Clifton 1910- *AmSCAP 66*
Claridge, Gordon S 1932- *Au&Wr, ConAu 21*
Claridge, John *Alli, DcEnL*
Claridge, Joseph H 1870- *ArizL*
Claridge, R T *Alli*
Claridge, Richard 1649-1723 *Alli*
Clarin 1852-1901 *CasWL, ClDMEuL, DcSpL,*
EuA, EvEuW
Clarinda *DcEnL, NewC*
Clarizio, Harvey F 1934- *ConAu 33*
Clark *Alli*
Clark, A L *Alli Sup*
Clark, Absalom *Alli Sup*
Clark, Admont Gulick 1919- *ConAu 53*
Clark, Alan 1928- *ConAu 13R*
Clark, Alexander *Alli Sup*
Clark, Alexander 1834-1879 *Alli Sup,*
AmA&B, BiD&SB, ChPo, DcAmA,
DcNAA, OhA&B
Clark, Alexander Frederick Bruce 1884-
WhWNAA
Clark, Alexander Melville And William
Alli Sup
Clark, Alfred *MnBBF*
Clark, Alfred Alexander Gordon *EncM&D,*
LongC
Clark, Alfred Corning *Alli Sup*
Clark, Alice L *ChPo*
Clark, Alice P *ChPo S1*
Clark, Alice S 1922- *ConAu 41*
Clark, Allan 1907- *AmSCAP 66*
Clark, Allen Culling 1858-1943 *AmA&B,*
DcNAA
Clark, Alonzo Howard 1850-1918 *Alli Sup,*
DcAmA, DcNAA

Clark, Amy Ashmore 1882-1954 *AmSCAP 66*
Clark, Andrew *Alli Sup*
Clark, Andrew Hill 1911- *ConAu 25,*
OxCan Sup, WrD 1976
Clark, Ann 1898- *ChPo*
Clark, Ann L 1913- *ConAu 17R*
Clark, Ann Nolan 1898- *AmA&B, AnCL,*
AuBYP, AuICB, ConAu 5R, JBA 1951,
MorBMP, Newb 1922, SmATA 4,
St&VC
Clark, Anne 1909- *ConAu 29*
Clark, Anne 1921- *ChPo*
Clark, Annie E *Alli Sup*
Clark, Annie M L 1835-1920 *AmA&B*
Clark, Annie Maria 1835-1912 *DcNAA*
Clark, Arthur B *Alli Sup*
Clark, Arthur Bridgman 1866- *WhWNAA*
Clark, Arthur Hamilton 1841-1922 *AmA&B,*
DcNAA
Clark, Arthur Henry 1868-1951 *AmA&B*
Clark, Arthur Henry 1868- *WhWNAA*
Clark, Arthur Melville 1895- *ConAu 9R*
Clark, B F *Alli Sup*
Clark, Badger 1883-1957 *ArizL, ConAmL,*
OxAm, WhWNAA
Clark, B ALSO Clark, Charles Badger
Clark, Barrett Harper 1890-1953 *AmA&B,*
OxAm, REnAL, TwCA, TwCA Sup,
WhWNAA
Clark, Barzilla Worth 1881-1943 *IndAu 1917*
Clark, Ben T 1928- *ConAu 53*
Clark, Benjamin C *Alli Sup*
Clark, Benjamin P *BlkAW*
Clark, Bennett Champ 1890-1954 *AmA&B*
Clark, Bill *ConAu XR*
Clark, Billy C 1928- *ConAu 1R*
Clark, Blake Everett 1900- *WhWNAA*
Clark, Bracy *Alli, BiDLA*
Clark, Brian 1932- *ConAu 41*
Clark, Bruce Lawrence 1880- *WhWNAA*
Clark, C Dunning *Alli Sup*
Clark, C E *Alli Sup*
Clark, C E Frazer, Jr. 1925- *ConAu 33*
Clark, C F G *Alli Sup*
Clark, C H Douglas 1890- *ConAu 23*
Clark, Calvin Montague 1862-1947 *DcNAA*
Clark, Carl 1932- *BlkAW*
Clark, Carol 1948- *ConAu 57*
Clark, Catherine Anthony 1892- *ConAu P-1*
Clark, Catherine Pickens *DcNAA*
Clark, Champ 1850-1921 *BiDSA, DcNAA*
Clark, Charles *Alli, Alli Sup, HsB&A Sup*
Clark, Charles Badger 1883-1957 *AmA&B,*
ChPo, ChPo S1, DcLEnL, REnAL
Clark, Chas Badger ALSO Clark, Badger
Clark, Charles Cotesworth Pinckney 1822-1899
Alli Sup, DcAmA, DcNAA
Clark, Charles Dunning 1843-1892 *AmA&B,*
DcNAA, HsB&A
Clark, Charles E 1929- *ConAu 29*
Clark, Charles Edwin 1929- *WrD 1976*
Clark, Charles Heber 1841-1915 *Alli Sup,*
AmA, AmA&B, BiD&SB, BiDSA, ChPo,
Chmbr 3, DcAmA, DcNAA, EvLB,
OxAm, REnAL
Clark, Charles Manning Hope 1915- *Au&Wr*
Clark, Charles Tallifero 1917- *ConAu 13R*
Clark, Charles Theodore 1845-1911 *OhA&B*
Clark, Charles Upson 1875-1960 *AmA&B,*
WhWNAA
Clark, Charlotte Moon 1829-1895 *Alli Sup,*
AmA&B, DcNAA
Clark, China Debra 1950?- *BlkAW, ConAu 45,*
DrAP 1975
Clark, Colin 1905- *ConAu 61*
Clark, Cumberland 1862- *ChPo S2*
Clark, Curt *WrD 1976*
Clark, Cynthia Charlotte Moon 1829-1895
OhA&B
Clark, D *Alli Sup*
Clark, Mrs. D O *Alli Sup*
Clark, D W 1812- *Alli*
Clark, Daniel 1766-1813 *BiDSA, DcNAA*
Clark, Daniel 1835-1912 *DcNAA*
Clark, Daniel 1840?- *ChPo S1*
Clark, Daniel Atkinson 1779-1840 *DcNAA*
Clark, Daniel Kinnear *Alli Sup*
Clark, David *WrD 1976*

Clark, David Allen *ConAu XR*
Clark, David Gillis 1933- *ConAu 53*
Clark, David Lee *TexWr*
Clark, David Ridgley 1920- *Au&Wr,*
ConAu 17R, WrD 1976
Clark, Davis Wasgatt 1812-1871 *Alli Sup,*
DcAmA, DcNAA, OhA&B
Clark, Davis Wasgatt 1849-1935 *OhA&B*
Clark, Denis d1950? *AuBYP*
Clark, Dennis E 1916- *ConAu 29*
Clark, Dennis J 1927- *ConAu 1R*
Clark, Dian Manners *AmSCAP 66*
Clark, Don 1925- *ConAu 57*
Clark, Don 1930- *ConAu 29*
Clark, Donald E 1933- *ConAu 23*
Clark, Donald Lemen 1888-1966 *AmA&B,*
IndAu 1917
Clark, Dora Mae 1893- *ConAu 41*
Clark, Dorothy Park 1899- *AmA&B,*
AmNov XR, ConAu 5R
Clark, Dougan *Alli Sup*
Clark, E *Alli Sup*
Clark, E Warren *Alli Sup*
Clark, Edgar Frederick 1835-1914 *DcNAA*
Clark, Edna Maria 1874-1961 *OhA&B*
Clark, Edson Lyman 1827-1913 *Alli Sup,*
DcAmA, DcNAA
Clark, Edward 1878-1954 *AmSCAP 66*
Clark, Edward Gordon *Alli Sup*
Clark, Edward H G *Alli Sup*
Clark, Edward Lord 1834-1910 *Alli Sup,*
DcNAA
Clark, Edwin *Alli Sup*
Clark, Edwin Charles 1836- *Alli Sup*
Clark, Edwin Kitson 1866- *WhLA*
Clark, Eleanor 1913- *AmA&B, ConAu 9R,*
ConLC 5, ConNov 1972, ConNov 1976,
DrAF 1976, REnAL, TwCA Sup,
WrD 1976
Clark, Eleanor Grace 1895- *CatA 1947*
Clark, Electa Carter 1910- *IndAu 1917*
Clark, Eliot Candee 1883- *WhWNAA*
Clark, Elisha Lorenzo *Alli Sup*
Clark, Elizabeth J H *Alli Sup*
Clark, Ella Elizabeth 1896- *OxCan, WhPNW*
Clark, Ellery Harding 1874-1949 *AmA&B,*
WhWNAA
Clark, Elmer Talmage 1886-1966 *AmA&B,*
ConAu 5R, WhWNAA
Clark, Emily 1893-1953 *Alli, AmA&B,*
BiDLA
Clark, Emma E 1883-1930 *ChPo*
Clark, Emmons *Alli Sup*
Clark, Eric 1911- *Au&Wr, ConAu 13R,*
WrD 1976
Clark, Eric E 1937- *WrD 1976*
Clark, Eugenie 1922- *ConAu 49*
Clark, Eva Lee 1871-1947 *DcNAA*
Clark, Evert Mordecai 1879- *TexWr*
Clark, Ewan *Alli, BiDLA*
Clark, F W *Alli Sup*
Clark, Fannie Hunter *AnMV 1926*
Clark, Felicia Buttz 1862-1931 *AmA&B,*
DcNAA
Clark, Floyd Barzilla 1886- *TexWr*
Clark, Frances *Alli Sup*
Clark, Frances Elliott *ChPo*
Clark, Francis 1919- *ConAu 17R*
Clark, Francis B *Alli Sup*
Clark, Mrs. Francis E *WhWNAA*
Clark, Francis Edward 1851-1927 *AmLY,*
DcAmA, DcNAA, WhWNAA
Clark, Francis Foreman *Alli Sup*
Clark, Francis William *Alli Sup*
Clark, Frank 1922- *AuBYP*
Clark, Frank E *Alli Sup*
Clark, Frank J 1922- *AmSCAP 66,*
ConAu 13R
Clark, Frank Lowry 1869- *WhWNAA*
Clark, Frank Pinkney *Alli Sup*
Clark, Fred Emerson 1890-1948 *DcNAA,*
WhWNAA
Clark, Fred George 1890-1972 *ConAu 37,*
OhA&B
Clark, Frederick LeGros *Alli Sup*
Clark, Frederick Stephen 1908- *ConAu 21,*
WrD 1976
Clark, Frederick Thickstun 1858- *Alli Sup,*

DcAmA
Clark, G F *Alli Sup*
Clark, G N 1890- *LongC*
Clark, G Orr *ChPo*
Clark, Gavin Brown 1846- *Alli Sup*
Clark, Gene Emmet 1910- *AmSCAP 66*
Clark, Geoffrey H *MnBBF*
Clark, George *Alli, BiDLA*
Clark, George E *Alli Sup*
Clark, George Edward *Alli Sup, EarAB Sup*
Clark, George Faber 1813-1883 *Alli Sup*
Clark, George Gerlaw 1857-1931 *OhA&B*
Clark, George H *Alli*
Clark, George Henry 1819-1906 *DcNAA*
Clark, George Hunt 1809-1881 *AmA&B,*
BiD&SB, CyAL 2, DcAmA, DcNAA
Clark, George Huntington 1859-1941 *DcNAA*
Clark, George Larkin 1849-1919 *DcNAA*
Clark, George Lindenberg 1892- *IndAu 1917*
Clark, George Luther 1877- *WhWNAA*
Clark, Sir George Norman 1890- *Au&Wr,*
WhLA
Clark, George Ramsey 1857-1945 *OhA&B,*
WhWNAA
Clark, George Rogers 1752-1818 *DcAmA,*
OxAm, REn, REnAL
Clark, George Sidney Roberts Kitson
ConAu XR
Clark, George Thomas 1809- *Alli Sup*
Clark, George Thomas 1862-1940 *DcNAA*
Clark, George W *BlkAW*
Clark, George Whitfield 1831-1911 *Alli Sup,*
AmA&B, DcAmA, DcNAA
Clark, Georgiana Charlotte *Alli Sup*
Clark, Gerald *OxCan*
Clark, Gerald 1918- *ConAu 13R*
Clark, Gerald Roy 1911- *Au&Wr*
Clark, Gertrude Theresa 1868-1905 *OhA&B*
Clark, Gilbert *Alli, ChPo, ChPo S1*
Clark, Glenn 1882- *WhWNAA*
Clark, Gordon H 1902- *ConAu 1R*
Clark, Grahame 1907- *ConAu 5R*
Clark, Grover 1891-1938 *DcNAA, WhWNAA*
Clark, Gwenyth Lena 1910- *Au&Wr*
Clark, H *Alli Sup*
Clark, H A *Alli Sup*
Clark, H H *CarSB*
Clark, Mrs. H K W *Alli Sup*
Clark, H R D *MnBBF*
Clark, Hamlet *Alli Sup*
Clark, Harold Terry 1882- *OhA&B*
Clark, Harriet Elizabeth Abbott 1850-
WhWNAA
Clark, Harry 1885- *WhWNAA*
Clark, Harry 1917- *ConAu 61*
Clark, Harry Hayden 1901-1971 *AmA&B,*
ConAu 29
Clark, Helen S *OxCan Sup*
Clark, Helen Whitney *ChPo*
Clark, Henry *Alli, Alli Sup*
Clark, Mrs. Henry *MnBBF*
Clark, Henry B, II 1930- *ConAu 5R*
Clark, Henry Charles 1899- *WrD 1976*
Clark, Henry Howard *Alli Sup*
Clark, Henry James 1826-1873 *Alli Sup, AmA,*
BiD&SB, DcAmA, DcNAA
Clark, Henry Scott *DcAmA, DcNAA*
Clark, Henry Wadsworth 1899- *WhWNAA*
Clark, Henry William 1869- *WhLA*
Clark, Herma *ChPo*
Clark, Howard *ConAu XR, WrD 1976*
Clark, Howard Walton 1870-1941 *IndAu 1917*
Clark, Hugh *Alli, ChPo*
Clark, Imogen d1936 *AmA&B, BiD&SB,*
CarSB, DcAmA, DcNAA, WhWNAA
Clark, J *BiDLA, ChPo S1*
Clark, J A *Alli Sup*
Clark, J Desmond 1916- *WrD 1976*
Clark, J E *ChPo*
Clark, J H *Alli Sup*
Clark, J Paterson *Alli*
Clark, J Scott 1854- *Alli Sup, DcAmA*
Clark, J V H *Alli*
Clark, Jackie *AmSCAP 66*
Clark, James *Alli, Alli Sup, BiDLA*
Clark, Sir James 1788-1870 *Alli, Alli Sup*
Clark, James Bayard 1869-1947 *DcNAA,*
WhWNAA

Clark, James Beauchamp *DcNAA*
Clark, James Gowdy 1830-1897 *Alli Sup,*
BiD&SB, BiDSA, DcAmA, DcNAA
Clark, James H *Alli Sup*
Clark, James Henry 1814-1869 *DcAmA,*
DcNAA
Clark, James L 1855-1933 *IndAu 1816*
Clark, James M 1930- *ConAu 21*
Clark, James O A d1894 *BiDSA*
Clark, James V 1927- *ConAu 13R*
Clark, James Westfall *MnnWr*
Clark, Jane *OxCan Sup*
Clark, Jennifer *ChPo S2*
Clark, Jere Walton 1922- *ConAu 23*
Clark, Jeremiah Simpson 1872- *WhWNAA*
Clark, Jerome L 1928- *ConAu 37*
Clark, Joan *OhA&B*
Clark, John *Alli, Alli Sup, BlkAW, ChPo*
Clark, Sir John *Alli*
Clark, John d1734 *Alli*
Clark, John 1609-1676 *Alli*
Clark, John 1744-1805 *Alli*
Clark, John Abbot 1903- *WhWNAA*
Clark, John Alonzo 1801-1843 *Alli, ChPo S1,*
DcAmA, DcNAA
Clark, John Anthony 1890- *WhWNAA*
Clark, John Bates 1847-1938 *Alli Sup,*
AmA&B, AmLY, DcAmA, DcNAA,
WhWNAA
Clark, John Desmond 1916- *ConAu 61*
Clark, John Drury 1907- *ConAu 37*
Clark, John G 1932- *ConAu 17R*
Clark, John Goodrich 1867-1927 *IndAu 1917*
Clark, John Grahame Douglas 1907- *Au&Wr,*
WrD 1976
Clark, John Howard 1929- *Au&Wr*
Clark, John Jesse 1866-1939 *DcNAA*
Clark, John Maurice 1884-1963 *ConAu 5R*
Clark, John Murray 1860- *WhWNAA*
Clark, John Pepper 1935- *AfA 1, CasWL,*
ChPo S2, ConDr, ConP 1975,
EncWL Sup, LongC, ModWD, Pen Cl,
REnWD, RGAfl, TwCW, WebEAL,
WrD 1976
Clark, John R 1930- *ConAu 37*
Clark, John Scott 1854-1911 *DcNAA*
Clark, John Williams 1907- *Au&Wr,*
ConAu 13R
Clark, John Willis 1833-1910 *Alli Sup, OxEng*
Clark, Johnny *AmSCAP 66*
Clark, Jonas 1730-1805 *Alli, AmA&B,*
DcNAA
Clark, Joseph *ChPo S1*
Clark, Joseph, Jr. *Alli Sup*
Clark, Joseph Bourne 1836-1923 *DcNAA*
Clark, Joseph D 1893- *ConAu 33*
Clark, Joseph James 1893-1971 *ConAu 19,*
ConAu 29
Clark, Joseph L 1881- *ConAu 17*
Clark, Joseph Sylvester 1800-1861 *DcNAA*
Clark, Joshua *Alli*
Clark, Kate McIntosh *ChPo S2*
Clark, Kate Upson 1851-1935 *AmA&B, AmLY,*
ChPo, ChPo S1, ChPo S2, DcAmA,
DcNAA, WhWNAA
Clark, Kennedy *Alli, BiDLA*
Clark, Sir Kenneth 1903- *CasWL, LongC,*
TwCA Sup
Clark, Kenneth Bancroft 1914- *AmA&B,*
ConAu 33, LivBA
Clark, Kenneth Edward 1924- *Au&Wr*
Clark, Lord Kenneth McKenzie 1903- *Au&Wr*
Clark, Kenneth Sherman 1882-1943
AmSCAP 66
Clark, Kenneth Sherman 1882-1945 *DcNAA*
Clark, L D 1922- *ConAu 1R, DrAF 1976*
Clark, Latimer *Alli Sup*
Clark, Laurence 1914- *Au&Wr, ConAu 13R,*
WrD 1976
Clark, LaVerne Harrell 1929- *ConAu 13R,*
DrAF 1976, WrD 1976
Clark, Leon Pierce 1870-1943 *ChPo*
Clark, Leonard 1905- *Au&Wr, ChPo,*
ChPo S1, ChPo S2, ConAu 13R,
ConP 1970, ConP 1975, WrD 1976
Clark, Leonard H 1915- *ConAu 53*
Clark, Leroy D *ConAu 61*
Clark, Leslie Savage *ChPo*

Clark, Lewis Gaylord 1808-1873 *Alli, AmA, AmA&B, BbD, BiD&SB, ChPo, ChPo S2, CyAL 2, DcAmA, DcEnL, DcNAA, OxAm, REnAL*
Clark, Lindley Daniel 1862- *IndAu 1816*
Clark, Lovell C *OxCan Sup*
Clark, Luella *ChPo*
Clark, Lydia Ann d1933 *DcNAA, WhWNAA*
Clark, M *Alli*
Clark, Manning 1915- *ConAu 9R*
Clark, Marden J 1916- *ConAu 61*
Clark, Margaret *Alli*
Clark, Margaret 1924- *Au&Wr*
Clark, Margaret Goff 1913- *AuBYP, ConAu 1R, SmATA 8*
Clark, Margery *BkCL*
Clark, Marguerite Sheridan *AmA&B*
Clark, Maria Louisa Guidish 1926- *ConAu 5R, WrD 1976*
Clark, Marjorie Agnes 1911- *Au&Wr, ConAu 33, WrD 1976*
Clark, Martha Haskell *ChPo, ChPo S2*
Clark, Marvin R *Alli Sup*
Clark, Mary 1831- *DcAmA*
Clark, Mary Jane 1915- *ConAu 57*
Clark, Mary Lou *ConAu XR*
Clark, Mary Semour Cowles *ChPo*
Clark, Mary Senior *Alli Sup, ChPo*
Clark, Mary T *ConAu 37, WrD 1976*
Clark, Mary Wayne 1896- *AmA&B*
Clark, Mattie M *OxCan*
Clark, Maurine Doran 1892-1966 *IndAu 1917*
Clark, Mavis Thorpe *ConAu 57, SmATA 8*
Clark, Mazie Earhart 1874-1958 *BlkAW, OhA&B*
Clark, Melville 1883- *WhWNAA*
Clark, Merle *ConAu XR, WrD 1976*
Clark, Mildred E *ChPo S1*
Clark, Miles 1920- *ConAu 23*
Clark, Miriam S *ChPo, ChPo S1*
Clark, Muriel *ChPo S1*
Clark, N *Alli*
Clark, N G *CyAL 1*
Clark, Natalie Lord Rice 1867-1932 *OhA&B*
Clark, Nathaniel George 1825?-1896 *Alli Sup, DcAmA, DcNAA*
Clark, Neil McCullough 1890- *ConAu 5R, OhA&B, WhWNAA, WrD 1976*
Clark, Neville 1926- *Au&Wr*
Clark, Norman H 1925- *WhPNW*
Clark, Olynthus Burroughs 1864-1936 *DcNAA*
Clark, P H *Alli Sup*
Clark, Parlin *ConAu XR*
Clark, Patricia Finrow 1929- *ConAu 17R*
Clark, Pauline *ChPo S1*
Clark, Pepper 1935- *ConP 1970*
Clark, Perceval *Alli Sup*
Clark, Peter 1693?-1768 *Alli, DcNAA*
Clark, Peter E *AfA 1*
Clark, Peter Wellington *BlkAW*
Clark, Peyton Neale *BiDSA*
Clark, R *Alli*
Clark, Mrs. R E *ChPo*
Clark, R P *ChPo, ChPo S1*
Clark, Ramsey 1927- *AmA&B, ConAu 29*
Clark, Richard *Alli, BiDLA Sup*
Clark, Richard H 1824- *BiDSA*
Clark, Robert *Alli, Alli Sup, ChPo S2*
Clark, Robert 1911- *Au&Wr, ChPo S1, ConP 1970, WrD 1976*
Clark, Robert Carlton 1877-1939 *DcNAA*
Clark, Robert E 1912- *ConAu 41*
Clark, Robert E D 1906- *ConAu 5R*
Clark, Robert Hardy *WrD 1976*
Clark, Roberta Lewis *ChPo S1*
Clark, Rogie 1917- *AmSCAP 66*
Clark, Romane Lewis 1925- *ConAu 17R*
Clark, Ronald 1933- *AmSCAP 66*
Clark, Ronald Harry 1904- *Au&Wr, WrD 1976*
Clark, Ronald William 1916- *Au&Wr, AuBYP, ConAu 25, SmATA 2*
Clark, Roscoe Collins 1896- *IndAu 1917*
Clark, Rose B *WhWNAA*
Clark, Rose Cave Gould 1888- *IndAu 1917, WhWNAA*
Clark, Rufus Wheelwright 1813-1886 *Alli, Alli Sup, DcAmA, DcNAA*

Clark, S *Alli*
Clark, S D 1910- *OxCan Sup*
Clark, Mrs. S R Graham *Alli Sup*
Clark, Salter Storrs 1854-1935 *Alli Sup, DcNAA*
Clark, Samuel *Alli*
Clark, Samuel Adams 1822-1875 *Alli, DcNAA*
Clark, Samuel Delbert 1910- *ConAu P-1, OxCan*
Clark, Sarah D *ChPo*
Clark, Septima Poinsette 1898- *ConAu 5R*
Clark, Sereno Dickenson *Alli Sup*
Clark, Simeon Taylor 1836-1891 *DcAmA*
Clark, Simeon Tucker 1836-1891 *Alli Sup, ChPo, DcNAA*
Clark, Solomon Henry 1861-1927 *ChPo, WhWNAA*
Clark, Spencer Morton *ChPo S1*
Clark, Stephen Watkins 1810-1910 *Alli, DcNAA*
Clark, Stewart *Alli Sup*
Clark, Sue C 1935- *ConAu 41*
Clark, Susanna Rebecca Graham 1848- *DcAmA, DcNAA*
Clark, Sydney Aylmer 1890-1975 *AmA&B, Au&Wr, ConAu 5R, ConAu 57*
Clark, T *Alli*
Clark, T M *Alli Sup*
Clark, T Rutherford *Alli Sup*
Clark, Terry Nichols 1940- *ConAu 25, WrD 1976*
Clark, Theodore Minot 1845-1909 *DcAmA, DcNAA*
Clark, Thomas *Alli, Alli Sup, BbtC, BiDLA*
Clark, Thomas 1787-1866? *DcAmA, DcNAA*
Clark, Thomas A 1944- *ConP 1970*
Clark, Thomas Arkle 1862- *WhWNAA*
Clark, Thomas Curtis 1877-1954 *AmA&B, AnMV 1926, ChPo, IndAu 1816, WhWNAA*
Clark, Thomas Dionysius 1903- *AmA&B, ConAu 5R, WhWNAA*
Clark, Thomas Grieve *Alli Sup*
Clark, Thomas H *BiDSA*
Clark, Thomas Henry *Alli Sup*
Clark, Thomas March 1812-1903 *Alli, Alli Sup, DcAmA, DcNAA*
Clark, Tom 1941- *AmA&B, ConP 1970, ConP 1975, DrAP 1975, WrD 1976*
Clark, Truman R 1935- *ConAu 61*
Clark, Uriah *Alli Sup*
Clark, Ursula Mary 1940- *Au&Wr*
Clark, Valma *WhWNAA*
Clark, Van D 1909- *ConAu P-1, SmATA 2*
Clark, Victor 1908- *Au&Wr*
Clark, Victor Selden 1868- *AmLY, WhWNAA*
Clark, Vinnie B *WhWNAA*
Clark, Virginia *ConAu XR, SmATA 7*
Clark, W *Alli, Alli Sup*
Clark, W B *Alli*
Clark, W Fordyce 1865- *MnBBF*
Clark, W W *Alli Sup*
Clark, Walter 1846-1924 *BiDSA, DcAmA, DcNAA*
Clark, Walter A 1842- *BiDSA*
Clark, Walter Ernest 1873-1955 *OhA&B, WhWNAA*
Clark, Walter Houston 1902- *BiDPar, ConAu 37, WrD 1976*
Clark, Walter VanTilburg 1909-1971 *AmA&B, AmNov, CnDAL, ConAu 9R, ConAu 33, ConNov 1972, ConNov 1976, CyWA, ModAL, OxAm, Pen Am, RAdv 1, REn, REnAL, SmATA 8, TwCA Sup*
Clark, Wilfred *Alli*
Clark, Sir Wilfrid LeGros 1895- *Au&Wr*
Clark, William *Alli, Alli Sup, Pen Am*
Clark, William 1770-1838 *OxAm, REnAL*
Clark, William 1788-1869 *Alli Sup*
Clark, William 1821-1880 *Alli Sup*
Clark, William 1916- *ConAu 29*
Clark, William A 1931- *ConAu 33*
Clark, William Adolphus 1825-1906 *Alli Sup, DcNAA*
Clark, William C *Alli Sup*
Clark, William Donaldson 1916- *Au&Wr, WrD 1976*
Clark, William George 1821-1878 *Alli,*

Alli Sup, DcEnL, NewC
Clark, William Heaviside *Alli, BiDLA*
Clark, William J, Jr. 1840-1889 *Alli Sup*
Clark, William P d1884 *Alli Sup*
Clark, William Robinson 1829-1912 *Alli Sup, DcNAA*
Clark, William Russell 1900- *TexWr*
Clark, William Smith 1826-1886 *DcNAA*
Clark, William Smith, II 1900-1969 *AmA&B, ConAu 25*
Clark, William Tierney 1783-1852 *Alli*
Clark, Willis Gaylord 1808?-1841 *Alli, AmA, AmA&B, BbD, BiD&SB, ChPo, ChPo S1, ChPo S2, CyAL 2, DcAmA, DcNAA, REnAL*
Clark, Willis Gaylord 1827- *BiDSA*
Clark, Zachary *Alli*
Clark-Kennedy, Archibald Edmund 1893- *Au&Wr*
Clark Of Herriotshall, Arthur Melville 1895- *Au&Wr, WrD 1976*
Clarke, Adam 1760-1832 *Alli, BiDLA, DcEnL*
Clarke, Aidan *ChPo*
Clarke, Alexander *Alli*
Clarke, Alexander Ross *Alli Sup*
Clarke, Allen 1863- *ChPo*
Clarke, Alured 1690-1742 *Alli*
Clarke, Ambrose And Ross, Charles Henry *Alli Sup*
Clarke, Amy Key 1892- *Au&Wr, WrD 1976*
Clarke, Andrew *Alli*
Clarke, Anne *Alli, BiDLA Sup*
Clarke, Anthony *Alli*
Clarke, Anthony William *Alli Sup*
Clarke, Sir Arthur *Alli*
Clarke, Arthur Charles 1917- *Au&Wr, AuBYP, ConAu 1R, ConLC 1, ConLC 4, ConNov 1972, ConNov 1976, EvLB, LongC, NewC, TwCA Sup, TwCW, WebEAL, WrD 1976*
Clarke, Arthur Dawson *Alli Sup*
Clarke, Arthur G 1887- *ConAu 17*
Clarke, Mrs. Asia *Alli Sup*
Clarke, Austin 1896-1974 *Au&Wr, CasWL, ChPo S1, CnMD Sup, ConAu 29, ConAu 49, ConLC 6, ConP 1970, ConP 1975, LongC, ModBL, ModBL Sup, NewC, RAdv 1, REn, TwCA Sup, TwCW*
Clarke, Austin C 1934- *ConAu 25, ConNov 1972, ConNov 1976, OxCan, OxCan Sup, WrD 1976*
Clarke, Basil Fulford Lowther 1908- *Au&Wr, ConAu 5R, WrD 1976*
Clarke, Beaumaurice Stracey *Alli Sup*
Clarke, Benjamin *Alli Sup*
Clarke, Benjamin 1836- *Alli Sup*
Clarke, Benjamin Strettell 1823-1895 *Alli Sup, PoIre*
Clarke, Bernard *ChPo, PoIre*
Clarke, Brenda Margaret Lilian 1926- *Au&Wr, WrD 1976*
Clarke, C C *Alli Sup*
Clarke, C E *MnBBF*
Clarke, C L *Alli*
Clarke, Caroline Cowles Richard 1842-1913 *CarSB*
Clarke, Cecil *Alli Sup*
Clarke, Charles *Alli, Alli Sup, BbtC, BiDLA, DcNAA, OxCan*
Clarke, Mrs. Charles *Alli Sup*
Clarke, Charles Baron 1834- *Alli Sup*
Clarke, Charles C *Alli*
Clarke, Charles Cameron 1861-1935 *DcNAA*
Clarke, Charles Cowden 1787-1877 *Alli Sup, BbD, BiD&SB, CasWL, ChPo, ChPo S2, DcEnA, DcEnL, DcLEnL, EvLB, NewC, OxEng*
Clarke, Charles M *Alli*
Clarke, Charles Montague *Alli Sup*
Clarke, Mrs. Charles Montague *Alli Sup*
Clarke, Charles Pickering *Alli Sup*
Clarke, Charles William Barnett *Alli Sup*
Clarke, Clorinda 1917- *ConAu 25, SmATA 7, WrD 1976*
Clarke, Covington *AmA&B*
Clarke, Crichton 1882- *WhWNAA*
Clarke, Cuthbert *Alli*

Clarke, Cyril 1907- *WrD 1976*
Clarke, D A Hall *Alli*
Clarke, Mrs. D W C *Alli Sup*
Clarke, David E 1920- *ConAu 17R*
Clarke, David Waldo 1907- *Au&Wr, ConAu 9R*
Clarke, Derrick Harry 1919- *WrD 1976*
Clarke, Desmond 1907- *Au&Wr, WrD 1976*
Clarke, Donald Henderson 1887-1958 *AmA&B, AmNov*
Clarke, Dorothy Clotelle 1908- *WrD 1976*
Clarke, Dorothy Madeline *Au&Wr*
Clarke, Dorus 1797-1884 *Alli Sup, CyAL 2, DcAmA, DcNAA*
Clarke, Dudley Wrangel 1899-1974 *Au&Wr, ConAu P-1*
Clarke, Dwight Lancelot 1885- *ConAu 1R*
Clarke, E *Alli Sup*
Clarke, E F C *Alli Sup*
Clarke, E Lidner *MnBBF*
Clarke, Edith *Alli Sup*
Clarke, Edith Emily 1859-1932 *DcNAA, WhWNAA*
Clarke, Edmund William *Alli*
Clarke, Edward 1730-1786 *Alli*
Clarke, Edward Daniel 1769-1822 *Alli, BiD&SB, BiDLA, BrAu 19, Chmbr 2, DcEnL*
Clarke, Sir Edward George 1841- *Alli Sup*
Clarke, Edward Goodman *Alli, BiDLA*
Clarke, Edward Hammond 1820-1877 *Alli Sup, DcAmA, DcNAA*
Clarke, Edwin Leavitt 1888-1948 *DcNAA, OhA&B*
Clarke, Effie A *Alli Sup*
Clarke, Egerton 1899-1944 *CatA 1947*
Clarke, Eliot C *Alli Sup*
Clarke, Eliza *Alli Sup*
Clarke, Elizabeth Porter *WhWNAA*
Clarke, Ernest P 1859- *WhWNAA*
Clarke, F L *Alli Sup*
Clarke, Frances *ChPo*
Clarke, Frances E *Chmbr 3*
Clarke, Frances Elizabeth *AmA&B*
Clarke, Francis *Alli*
Clarke, Francis Coningsby Hannam *Alli Sup*
Clarke, Francis Devereux 1849-1913 *DcNAA*
Clarke, Francis F *Alli*
Clarke, Francis L *Alli, BiDLA*
Clarke, Frank Wigglesworth 1847-1931 *Alli Sup, DcAmA, DcNAA, WhWNAA*
Clarke, Frederick *Alli Sup*
Clarke, Frederick 1846- *Alli Sup*
Clarke, G R Lidner *MnBBF*
Clarke, George *Alli, BiDLA*
Clarke, George Frederick *OxCan*
Clarke, George Henry Vernon 1908- *Au&Wr*
Clarke, George Herbert 1873-1932 *ChPo, ChPo S1*
Clarke, George Herbert 1873-1953 *ChPo S2, DcLEnL, OxCan, REnAL, WhWNAA*
Clarke, George Kuhn *Alli Sup*
Clarke, George Rochfort *Alli Sup, PoIre*
Clarke, George Somers *Alli*
Clarke, George Sydenham 1848- *Alli Sup*
Clarke, George Timothy *ConAu 1R*
Clarke, Gertrude *WhWNAA*
Clarke, Gipsy 1888- *WhWNAA*
Clarke, Grace Giddings Julian 1865-1938 *IndAu 1816*
Clarke, Grant 1891-1931 *AmSCAP 66*
Clarke, H *Alli Sup, ChPo S2*
Clarke, H Conquest *Alli Sup*
Clarke, H E *Alli Sup*
Clarke, H Harrison 1902- *ConAu 1R, WrD 1976*
Clarke, H J *Alli*
Clarke, H R *Alli Sup*
Clarke, H W *Alli Sup*
Clarke, Hamilton *Alli Sup*
Clarke, Hans Thacher 1887-1972 *ConAu 37*
Clarke, Harry 1890- *ConICB*
Clarke, Harry Eugene, Jr. 1921- *ConAu 5R*
Clarke, Helen Alicia *AmLY*
Clarke, Helen Archibald 1860-1926 *AmA&B, BiD&SB, ChPo, ChPo S2, DcNAA, WhWNAA*
Clarke, Helen F *BlkAW*

Clarke, Helen T *ChPo*
Clarke, Henry *Alli, Alli Sup, BiDLA, PoIre*
Clarke, Henry 1745-1818 *Alli*
Clarke, Henry Butler 1863-1904 *BrAu 19*
Clarke, Henry James *Alli Sup*
Clarke, Henry Wilberforce *Alli Sup*
Clarke, Henry William *Alli Sup*
Clarke, Herbert Lincoln 1867-1945 *AmSCAP 66*
Clarke, Hermann Frederick 1882-1947 *DcNAA*
Clarke, Hewson 1787- *Alli, BiDLA, BiDLA Sup*
Clarke, Hockley *Au&Wr, WrD 1976*
Clarke, Howard William 1929- *ConAu 37*
Clarke, Hugh *BiDLA, PoIre*
Clarke, Hugh A *Alli Sup*
Clarke, Hugh Archibald 1839-1926 *DcNAA*
Clarke, Hugh Vincent 1919- *Au&Wr, WrD 1976*
Clarke, Hyde 1815-1895 *Alli, Alli Sup, BiD&SB*
Clarke, Ida Clyde 1878- *WhWNAA*
Clarke, Isaac Edwards 1830-1907 *Alli Sup, DcAmA, DcNAA*
Clarke, Isabel Constance *BkC 3, CatA 1947*
Clarke, J *Alli, Alli Sup*
Clarke, J A *Alli Sup*
Clarke, J B B *Alli*
Clarke, J F Gates 1905- *ConAu P-1*
Clarke, J F M *Alli Sup*
Clarke, J G *Alli Sup*
Clarke, J H *Alli*
Clarke, J Matt *BiDSA*
Clarke, J O A *Alli Sup*
Clarke, J Stirling *Alli Sup*
Clarke, J W *Alli, Alli Sup*
Clarke, Jack Alden 1924- *ConAu 29, WrD 1976*
Clarke, Jafah *ConAu XR*
Clarke, James *Alli, BiDLA*
Clarke, James 1934- *Au&Wr*
Clarke, James Edward *Alli*
Clarke, James Everitt 1868- *WhWNAA*
Clarke, James Fernandez 1812-1875 *Alli Sup*
Clarke, James Freeman 1810-1888 *Alli, Alli Sup, AmA, AmA&B, BbD, BbtC, BiD&SB, ChPo S1, ChPo S2, CyAL 2, DcAmA, DcLEnL, DcNAA, OxAm, REnAL*
Clarke, James Gowdy 1830- *Alli Sup*
Clarke, James H 1840- *IndAu 1917*
Clarke, James Paton *BbtC*
Clarke, James Stanier d1834 *Alli, BiDLA, BiDLA Sup*
Clarke, Jean *Alli Sup, DcNAA*
Clarke, Jennie G *ChPo*
Clarke, Jennie Thornley *BiDSA, ChPo*
Clarke, Jeremiah d1707 *Alli*
Clarke, Joan *WrD 1976*
Clarke, Joan Dorn 1924- *ConAu 9R*
Clarke, Joan L 1920- *WrD 1976*
Clarke, John *Alli, Alli Sup, BiDLA, ConAu XR, SmATA 5*
Clarke, John d1759 *Alli*
Clarke, John 1609-1676 *CyAL 1, OxAm, REnAL*
Clarke, John 1650-1721 *Alli*
Clarke, John 1755-1798 *Alli*
Clarke, John 1913- *ConAu P-1*
Clarke, John Algernon *Alli Sup*
Clarke, John Archer d1862 *BiDSA*
Clarke, John Bertridge d1824 *PoIre*
Clarke, John Caldwell Calhoun 1833-1915 *Alli Sup, DcNAA*
Clarke, John Digby 1901- *Au&Wr*
Clarke, John Edward *BiDLA Sup*
Clarke, John Erskine *Alli Sup, ChPo, ChPo S1, ChPo S2*
Clarke, John Henrik 1915- *AmA&B, AuNews 1, BlkAW, ConAu 53, LivBA*
Clarke, John Henry *Alli Sup*
Clarke, John Hessin 1857-1945 *OhA&B*
Clarke, John Joseph 1879- *ConAu 5R*
Clarke, John L *Alli*
Clarke, John Mason 1857-1925 *DcNAA, OxCan, WhWNAA*
Clarke, John Randall 1828?-1863 *Alli Sup*
Clarke, John Smith 1885- *ChPo S2*

Clarke, John Sutherland *Alli Sup*
Clarke, Joseph *Alli, Alli Sup*
Clarke, Joseph 1811?-1860 *Alli Sup*
Clarke, Joseph Ignatius Constantine 1846-1925 *Alli Sup, AmA&B, DcAmA, DcNAA, PoIre*
Clarke, Joseph Morison 1829-1899 *Alli Sup, DcAmA, DcNAA*
Clarke, Joseph Thacher *Alli Sup*
Clarke, Joseph Williams *Alli Sup*
Clarke, Joy Harold 1899- *IndAu 1917*
Clarke, Kamylla *WhWNAA*
Clarke, Kate Upson 1851- *BiDSA*
Clarke, Kenneth W 1917- *ConAu 17R*
Clarke, L *Alli*
Clarke, Lige 1942- *ConAu 41*
Clarke, Lilian Rebecca *Alli Sup*
Clarke, Louisa Lane *Alli Sup*
Clarke, Louise *ChPo*
Clarke, M A *Alli*
Clarke, Mrs. M G *Alli Sup*
Clarke, MacDonald 1798-1842 *AmA, DcAmA, DcLEnL, REnAL*
Clarke, Machael *ConAu 49*
Clarke, Marcus Andrew Hislop 1846?-1881 *Alli Sup, BbD, BiD&SB, BrAu 19, CasWL, ChPo S1, Chmbr 3, DcLEnL, EvLB, NewC, OxEng, Pen Eng, PoIre, WebEAL*
Clarke, Margaret Archibald 1901- *Au&Wr*
Clarke, Marion *PoIre*
Clarke, Marion Lucinda 1843- *ChPo*
Clarke, Martin Lowther 1909- *Au&Wr, ConAu 5R, WrD 1976*
Clarke, Mary 1793-1883 *OxFr*
Clarke, Mary 1923- *WrD 1976*
Clarke, Mary Ann *Alli*
Clarke, Mary Anne 1775?- *BiDLA*
Clarke, Mary Bayard 1827?-1886 *Alli Sup, AmA, AmA&B, BiD&SB, BiDSA, DcAmA, DcNAA, LivFWS*
Clarke, Mary E B *Alli Sup*
Clarke, Mary G *Alli Sup*
Clarke, Mary Gavin 1881- *Au&Wr, WhLA*
Clarke, Mary Latham *Alli Sup*
Clarke, Mary Stetson 1911- *ConAu 21, SmATA 5, WrD 1976*
Clarke, Mary Victoria Cowden 1809-1898 *Alli, Alli Sup, BbD, BiD&SB, ChPo, ChPo S1, DcEnA, DcEnA Ap, DcEnL, NewC, OxEng*
Clarke, Mary Washington 1913- *ConAu 25*
Clarke, Mary Whatley 1899- *ConAu 5R, WrD 1976*
Clarke, Matthew 1664-1726 *Alli*
Clarke, Matthew St. Clair *Alli*
Clarke, Maurice *MnBBF*
Clarke, McDonald 1798-1842 *AmA&B, BiD&SB, DcNAA, OxAm*
Clarke, M'Donald 1798-1842 *Alli, ChPo, CyAL 2*
Clarke, Michael *PoIre, SmATA 6*
Clarke, Mollie *ChPo S1*
Clarke, Montague *Alli Sup*
Clarke, N H Belden *Alli Sup*
Clarke, Neva Yvonne *Au&Wr, WrD 1976*
Clarke, Nina Grey *ChPo*
Clarke, Lady Olivia 1785?-1845 *PoIre*
Clarke, Pauline 1921- *AnCL, Au&Wr, AuBYP, ChPo, ConAu XR, SmATA 3, ThBJA, WhCL*
Clarke, Percy *Alli Sup*
Clarke, Percy A *MnBBF*
Clarke, Peter *ConP 1970*
Clarke, Peter H *OhA&B*
Clarke, Peter Hugh 1933- *Au&Wr*
Clarke, Phyllis Comyn *ChPo*
Clarke, Rebecca 1886- *AmSCAP 66*
Clarke, Rebecca Sophia 1833-1906 *Alli Sup, AmA, AmA&B, BiD&SB, CarSB, DcAmA, DcNAA*
Clarke, Reuben *Alli*
Clarke, Rev. C C 1768-1840 *DcEnL*
Clarke, Rev. Mr. 1779-1839 *DcEnL*
Clarke, Richard *Alli, BiDLA, ConAu XR*
Clarke, Richard E *ChPo S1*
Clarke, Richard F *Alli Sup*
Clarke, Richard Henry 1827-1911 *Alli Sup,*

BiD&SB, DcAmA, DcNAA
Clarke, Robert *Alli, Alli Sup, ConAu XR*
Clarke, Robert 1829-1899 *Alli Sup, DcNAA, OhA&B*
Clarke, Robert A *EarAB Sup*
Clarke, Robert Lowes *Alli Sup*
Clarke, Robin Harwood 1937- *Au&Wr, ConAu 13R*
Clarke, Ronald Francis 1933- *ConAu 21*
Clarke, Ruth 1914- *Au&Wr*
Clarke, Mrs. S *Alli Sup*
Clarke, S Dacre *MnBBF*
Clarke, Samuel *Alli, Chmbr 2*
Clarke, Samuel 1599-1682 *Alli, DcEnL*
Clarke, Samuel 1623-1669 *Alli*
Clarke, Samuel 1626-1700? *Alli*
Clarke, Samuel 1675-1729 *Alli, BiD&SB, BrAu, CasWL, DcEnL, EvLB, NewC, OxEng*
Clarke, Samuel A 1827-1909 *DcNAA*
Clarke, Samuel C *Alli Sup, ChPo*
Clarke, Samuel Childs 1821- *ChPo S1*
Clarke, Samuel Fessenden 1851-1928 *DcNAA*
Clarke, Samuel Robinson *Alli Sup*
Clarke, Sara J 1823-1904 *ChPo*
Clarke, Sara Jane *Alli*
Clarke, Sarah J 1840-1929 *AmA&B, DcNAA*
Clarke, Sarah M S *Alli Sup*
Clarke, Sebastian *BlkAW*
Clarke, Silvey *MnBBF*
Clarke, Stephen *Alli, Alli Sup, BiDLA*
Clarke, Sylvestre 1896-1932 *OxCan*
Clarke, T *Alli Sup*
Clarke, T E B *ConDr*
Clarke, Theodora M L Lane- *Alli Sup*
Clarke, Thomas *Alli, Alli Sup*
Clarke, Thomas B *Alli*
Clarke, Thomas Brooke *BiDLA*
Clarke, Thomas Curtis *Alli Sup*
Clarke, Thomas E 1918- *ConAu 53*
Clarke, Thomas Ernest Bennett 1907- *Au&Wr*
Clarke, Thomas Grey *Alli Sup*
Clarke, Thomas Joseph *Alli Sup*
Clarke, Thomas M *Alli Sup*
Clarke, Mrs. Thurston *AmNov XR*
Clarke, Tom *ConDr*
Clarke, Tom E 1915- *ConAu 5R, WhPNW*
Clarke, Vincent *MnBBF*
Clarke, W B *BbtC, ChPo, ChPo S1*
Clarke, W E And Roebuck, W D *Alli Sup*
Clarke, Mrs. W N *ChPo*
Clarke, Walter Irving 1868- *WhWNAA*
Clarke, William *Alli, Alli Sup, BiDLA*
Clarke, William 1696-1771 *Alli*
Clarke, William A *Alli*
Clarke, William Barker 1829-1905 *DcNAA*
Clarke, William Barnard *Alli Sup*
Clarke, William Branwhite 1798-1878 *Alli Sup*
Clarke, William Bruce *Alli Sup*
Clarke, William Dixon 1927- *ConAu 5R*
Clarke, William Fairlie 1833-1884 *Alli Sup*
Clarke, William Fayal 1855-1935 *AmA&B, ChPo, ChPo S2*
Clarke, William Fletcher 1824- *BbtC*
Clarke, William H *Alli Sup*
Clarke, William Harrison *Alli Sup*
Clarke, William Hawes Crichton 1882-1942 *DcNAA*
Clarke, William Horatio *Alli Sup*
Clarke, William Kemp Lowther 1879- *ChPo S1*
Clarke, William M 1922- *ConAu 41*
Clarke, William Newton 1841-1912 *DcAmA, DcNAA*
Clarke, William Thomas 1932- *ConAu 57*
Clarke, William Wilcox 1808-1881 *Alli Sup*
Clarkson, Adrienne 1939- *ConAu 49*
Clarkson, Anthony 1905- *Au&Wr*
Clarkson, Charles *Alli*
Clarkson, Christopher *Alli*
Clarkson, D A *Alli*
Clarkson, David 1622-1686 *Alli*
Clarkson, Douglas A *Alli Sup*
Clarkson, E Margaret 1915- *ConAu 1R, WrD 1976*
Clarkson, Ewan 1929- *ConAu 25, SmATA 9, WrD 1976*
Clarkson, Geoffrey 1914- *AmSCAP 66*
Clarkson, Geoffrey P E 1934- *ConAu 5R,*

WrD 1976
Clarkson, George Arthur *Alli Sup*
Clarkson, Harry F 1882-1959 *AmSCAP 66*
Clarkson, Henry Mazyck 1835-1915 *BiDSA, ChPo*
Clarkson, Jesse Dunsmore 1897-1973 *AmA&B, ConAu 5R, ConAu 45*
Clarkson, L *Alli Sup, DcAmA*
Clarkson, Lawrence *Alli*
Clarkson, Louise 1865-1928 *ChPo, ChPo S1, ChPo S2*
Clarkson, Paul S 1905- *ConAu 29*
Clarkson, Ruth Kelso *TexWr*
Clarkson, Samuel *Alli Sup*
Clarkson, Stephen *OxCan Sup*
Clarkson, Stephen 1937- *ConAu 41*
Clarkson, Thomas 1760-1846 *Alli, BiDLA, BrAu 19, DcEnL*
Clarkson, Thomas Streatfeild *Alli Sup*
Clarkson, Tom 1913- *WrD 1976*
Clarkson, William *Alli, Alli Sup*
Claro Oscuro *PueRA*
Claromont *Alli*
Clary, F A *Alli Sup*
Clary, Jack 1932- *ConAu 57*
Clase, John Mitchell *Alli Sup*
Clasen, Claus-Peter 1931- *ConAu 41*
Clason, A W *Alli Sup*
Clason, Isaac Starr 1789?-1834 *Alli, BiD&SB, CyAL 2, DcAmA, DcNAA*
Clasper, Paul Dudley 1923- *ConAu 1R*
Claspy, Everett M 1907?-1973 *ConAu 41*
Class, Heinrich 1868-1953 *OxGer*
Claster, Daniel S 1932- *ConAu 23*
Clater, Francis *Alli, BiDLA*
Clatworthy, Linda M *WhWNAA*
Claude 1499-1524 *OxFr*
Claude De Pontoux *OxFr*
Claude Gelee 1600-1682 *OxFr*
Claude Gellee 1600-1682 *OxFr*
Claude Le Lorrain 1600-1682 *OxFr*
Claude Lorrain 1600-1682 *AtlBL, NewC*
Claude, Jean 1619-1687 *DcEuL, OxFr*
Claude, Mary S *Alli Sup, ChPo, ChPo S2*
Claude, Richard Pierre 1934- *ConAu 29, WrD 1976*
Claudel, Alice Moser 1918- *ConAu 49, DrAP 1975*
Claudel, Paul 1868-1955 *AtlBL, CasWL, CatA 1947, ClDMEuL, CnMD, CnMWL, CnThe, EncWL, EvEuW, LongC, McGWD, ModRL, ModWD, OxEng, OxFr, Pen Eur, REn, REnWD, TwCA, TwCA Sup, TwCW, WhTwL, WhWNAA*
Claudet, M *BbtC*
Claudia, Sister Mary 1906- *ConAu P-1*
Claudian 370?-408? *CasWL, NewC, OxEng, Pen Cl*
Claudianus, Claudius *BiD&SB*
Claudius I 010BC-054AD *Pen Cl, REn*
Claudius, Hermann 1878- *CasWL, OxGer*
Claudius, Matthias 1740-1815 *BiD&SB, CasWL, ChPo S1, DcEuL, EuA, EvEuW, OxGer, Pen Eur, REn*
Claudius Quadrigarius, Quintus *CasWL, Pen Cl*
Claudy, Carl Harry 1879-1957 *AmA&B, AmLY, ChPo, ChPo S2, WhWNAA*
Clauert, Hans d1566 *OxGer*
Claughton, Piers Calveley 1814-1884 *Alli Sup*
Claughton, Thomas Legh *Alli Sup*
Clauren, Heinrich 1771-1854 *BiD&SB, OxGer*
Claus Narr *OxGer*
Claus, Hugo 1929- *CasWL, CnMD, EncWL, ModWD*
Claus, Marshall R 1936-1970 *ConAu 29*
Claus, Peter *REn*
Clausen, Aage R 1932- *ConAu 49*
Clausen, Agnes M *ChPo, ChPo S1*
Clausen, Bernard C 1892- *WhWNAA*
Clausen, Carl 1885- *WhWNAA*
Clausen, Connie 1923- *ConAu 1R*
Clausen, George 1852- *ChPo*
Clausen, Henrik Nicolai 1793-1877 *DcEuL*
Clausen, John Henry *ChPo S1*
Clausen, Mae Laura 1889- *WhWNAA*
Clausen, Roy Elwood 1891- *WhWNAA*
Clausen, Sven 1893-1961 *CasWL*

Clausen, Svend 1893-1961 *CnMD*
Clauser, Suzanne 1929- *ConAu 37*
Clausewitz, Karl Von 1780-1831 *OxGer*
Clauson, James Earl 1873-1937 *AmA&B, DcNAA, WhWNAA*
Claussen, Sophus Niels Christen 1865-1931 *CasWL, ClDMEuL, EncWL, EvEuW, Pen Eur, REn*
Clave, Antoni 1913- *WhGrA*
Clavel, Bernard 1923- *ConAu 45*
Clavel, Marcel 1894- *WhLA*
Clavel, Maurice 1918- *CnMD*
Clavel, Roger *Alli*
Clavell, James 1924- *ConAu 25, ConLC 6*
Clavell, John *Alli*
Clavell, John 1603-1642 *OxEng*
Clavell, Robert *Alli*
Clavell, Stauffer *WhLA*
Claveloux, Nicole *IlBYP*
Clavequin, E *Alli Sup*
Claver, Robert E 1928- *AmSCAP 66*
Claveret, Jean 1590-1666 *OxFr, REn*
Claverhouse, Joan Graham Of *NewC*
Claveria, Carlos 1909- *DcSpL*
Clavering, Henry *Alli*
Clavering, Robert *Alli*
Clavering, Robert d1747 *Alli*
Clavering, Vere *Alli Sup*
Clavers, Mary *Alli, AmA, AmA&B, DcNAA, OxAm, REn, REnAL*
Clavijo, Luy Gonzalez De d1412 *DcEuL*
Clavijo, Ruy Gonzalez De d1412 *CasWL*
Clavijo Y Fajardo, Jose 1730?-1806 *BiD&SB, CasWL, DcSpL*
Clavuot-Geer, Ursina *CasWL*
Clawson, Clayton Joseph 1916- *IndAu 1917*
Clawson, Marion 1905- *AmA&B*
Clawson, Mary 1910- *Au&Wr*
Claxton, Adelaide Amd Ross, C H *Alli Sup*
Claxton, Florence *Alli Sup*
Claxton, John *Alli*
Claxton, L *Alli*
Claxton, Laura *Alli Sup*
Claxton, Norah Mary *DcNAA*
Claxton, Sara *HsB&A*
Claxton, Timothy *Alli*
Claxton, William Rehn *Alli Sup*
Clay, Lady *Alli Sup*
Clay, Albert Tobias 1866-1925 *AmA&B, DcNAA*
Clay, Alexander Stephens 1853- *BiDSA*
Clay, Alice *Alli Sup*
Clay, Bertha M 1836-1884 *Alli Sup, AmA&B, NewC, REnAL*
Clay, Buriel, II 1943- *BlkAW, DrAF 1976, DrAP 1975*
Clay, C C *Alli*
Clay, Cassius Marcellus 1810-1903 *Alli, Alli Sup, BiD&SB, BiDSA, DcAmA, DcNAA*
Clay, Charles *Alli Sup, OxCan*
Clay, Charles M *Alli Sup, AmA&B, DcNAA, OhA&B*
Clay, Clement Claiborne 1816-1882 *BiDSA*
Clay, Clement Comer 1789-1866 *BiDSA*
Clay, Comer 1910- *ConAu 45*
Clay, Duncan *ConAu XR*
Clay, E, Jr. *BiDLA*
Clay, Edmund *Alli Sup*
Clay, Edward, Jr. *Alli*
Clay, Floyd M 1927- *ConAu 45*
Clay, Francis *Alli*
Clay, Henry *BiDSA*
Clay, Henry 1777-1852 *Alli, AmA, AmA&B, BbD, BiD&SB, CyAL 1, DcAmA, DcNAA, OxAm, REn, REnAL*
Clay, Henry 1883- *WhLA*
Clay, J *Alli, Alli Sup, BiDLA*
Clay, James 1805-1873 *Alli Sup*
Clay, James 1924- *ConAu 17R*
Clay, Jim *ConAu XR*
Clay, John *Alli, Alli Sup*
Clay, John, Jr. *Alli Sup*
Clay, John Cecil 1875-1930 *AmA&B, ChPo, DcNAA*
Clay, John Curtis *Alli*
Clay, John Gough 1809-1883 *Alli Sup*
Clay, Joseph 1764-1811 *Alli*

Clay, Josephine Russell *Alli Sup*
Clay, Katharine B *ChPo*
Clay, Marie M 1926- *ConAu 61*
Clay, Mary Rogers *BiDSA*
Clay, R Lomax *Alli*
Clay, Roberta L 1900- *ConAu 29, WrD 1976*
Clay, Sampson 1907- *Au&Wr*
Clay, Samuel *Alli*
Clay, Thomas *Alli*
Clay, Walter Lowe 1833-1875 *Alli*
Clay, William Keatinge 1797-1867 *Alli,
    Alli Sup*
Clay-Clopton, Virginia Carolina 1825- *BiDSA*
Claybaugh, Joseph *Alli Sup*
Clayden, Arthur *Alli Sup*
Clayden, Arthur William 1855- *WhLA*
Clayden, Peter William *Alli Sup*
Claydon, Charles Broadbent *Alli Sup*
Claydon, Leslie Francis 1923- *ConAu 53*
Clayes, Stanley A 1922- *ConAu 29*
Claypole, E W *Alli Sup*
Claypoole, Edward B 1883-1952 *AmSCAP 66*
Clayre, Alasdair 1935- *Au&Wr, ConP 1970,
    WrD 1976*
Clayton, A S *Alli*
Clayton, Alexander M d1889 *BiDSA*
Clayton, Augustin Smith 1783-1839 *BiDSA
    DcNAA*
Clayton, Barbara *ConAu XR*
Clayton, Benjamin *Alli Sup*
Clayton, Buck 1912- *AmSCAP 66*
Clayton, Cecil *Alli Sup*
Clayton, Charles *Alli Sup*
Clayton, Charles Curtis 1902- *AmA&B,
    ConAu 23*
Clayton, Edward Hyers 1886-1946 *DcNAA*
Clayton, Eleanor Creathorne *Alli Sup*
Clayton, Frank *ChPo S1*
Clayton, George *Alli, Alli Sup, BiDLA*
Clayton, Gyles *Alli*
Clayton, Henry Helm 1861- *WhWNAA*
Clayton, Howard 1918- *ConAu 29*
Clayton, J R *ChPo*
Clayton, James E 1929- *ConAu 9R*
Clayton, James L 1931- *ConAu 29*
Clayton, John *Alli, BiDLA, ConAu XR*
Clayton, John d1773 *Alli*
Clayton, John d1843 *Alli*
Clayton, John 1686- *BiDSA*
Clayton, John 1892- *ConAu 33*
Clayton, John, Jr. *BiDLA*
Clayton, John Jacob 1935- *ConAu 25,
    DrAF 1976*
Clayton, John William 1833- *Alli Sup*
Clayton, Joseph 1868-1943 *CatA 1947, WhLA*
Clayton, Keith 1928- *Au&Wr, ConAu 23*
Clayton, Louisa *Alli Sup*
Clayton, M *ChPo*
Clayton, Mary *Alli Sup*
Clayton, N *Alli*
Clayton, Paul C 1932- *ConAu 61*
Clayton, Prudence *Alli*
Clayton, Sir Richard *Alli, BiDLA*
Clayton, Richard Henry Michael 1907-
    ConAu 5R, EncM&D, WrD 1976
Clayton, Sir Robert *Alli*
Clayton, Robert 1695-1758 *Alli*
Clayton, Roberta Flake 1877- *ArizL*
Clayton, Stanley 1911- *WrD 1976*
Clayton, Susan *ConAu XR*
Clayton, Sylvia Ruth *Au&Wr, WrD 1976*
Clayton, Thomas *Alli, Alli Sup*
Clayton, Thomas 1932- *ConAu 41*
Clayton, Thompson B 1904- *ConAu 57*
Clayton, Victoria Virginia 1832-1908 *DcNAA*
Clayton, Virginia V *BiDSA*
Clayton, W C *Alli Sup*
Clayton, W H 1861- *WhWNAA*
Clayton, W W *ChPo S1*
Clayton, William *Alli, Alli Sup*
Claytor, Gertrude Boatright 1890?-1973 *ChPo,
    ChPo S2*
Claytor, Gertrude Boatwright 1890?-1973
    ConAu 45
Claytor, Graham 1852- *Alli Sup, BiDSA,
    ChPo*
Cleadon, Thomas *Alli*
Cleage, Albert B, Jr. 1911- *LivBA*

Cleage, Pearl *BlkAW*
Cleall, Charles 1927- *Au&Wr, ConAu 5R,
    WrD 1976*
Cleanth *ChPo*
Cleanthes Of Assos 331BC-232BC *BiD&SB,
    CasWL, Pen Cl*
Clear, Claudius *NewC*
Clear, Gwendolyn Frances *ChPo*
Clear, Hobart *OhA&B*
Clear, Val B 1915- *IndAu 1917*
Cleare, John 1936- *WrD 1976*
Clearidge, John *Alli*
Clearwater, Alphonse Trumpbour 1848-1933
    DcNAA
Cleary, Beverly 1916- *AmA&B, AuBYP,
    AuICB, ChLR 2, ConAu 1R, MorBMP,
    MorJA, SmATA 2, WrD 1976*
Cleary, James W 1927- *ConAu 17R*
Cleary, Jon 1917- *Au&Wr, ConAu 1R,
    ConNov 1972, ConNov 1976, WorAu,
    WrD 1976*
Cleary, Kate M *ChPo*
Cleary, Kathleen T M'Phelim 1863- *PoIre*
Cleary, Michael H 1902-1954 *AmSCAP 66*
Cleary, Robert *Alli Sup*
Cleary, Robert E 1932- *ConAu 41*
Cleary, Ruth *AmSCAP 66*
Cleary, Thomas Stanislaus 1851-1898 *Alli Sup,
    PoIre*
Cleave, Egbert *Alli Sup*
Cleaveland, Aaron *DcNAA*
Cleaveland, C H *Alli Sup*
Cleaveland, Charles H 1820-1863 *OhA&B*
Cleaveland, Mrs. E H J *Alli Sup*
Cleaveland, Elizabeth H Jocelyn *ChPo,
    ChPo S2*
Cleaveland, Ezra *Alli*
Cleaveland, George Aaron 1853-1922 *DcNAA*
Cleaveland, John *Alli Sup*
Cleaveland, John 1613-1659 *Alli*
Cleaveland, John 1722-1799 *DcAmA, DcNAA*
Cleaveland, John 1772-1815 *Alli*
Cleaveland, Kate *ChPo*
Cleaveland, Moses 1754-1806 *OhA&B*
Cleaveland, Nehemiah 1796-1877 *Alli Sup,
    DcAmA, DcNAA*
Cleaveland, Parker 1780-1858 *Alli, CyAL 1,
    DcAmA, DcNAA*
Cleaver, Carole 1934- *ConAu 49, SmATA 6*
Cleaver, Charles *Alli Sup*
Cleaver, Dale G 1928- *ConAu 17R,
    IndAu 1917*
Cleaver, Dudley *ChPo*
Cleaver, Eldridge 1935- *AmA&B, BlkAW,
    ConAu 21, LivBA, Pen Am, WebEAL,
    WrD 1976*
Cleaver, Elizabeth *OxCan Sup*
Cleaver, Hylton Reginald 1891-1961 *LongC,
    MnBBF, WhCL*
Cleaver, J Harvey *WhWNAA*
Cleaver, James 1911- *Au&Wr*
Cleaver, John *Alli*
Cleaver, Nancy *ConAu XR*
Cleaver, Percy D *ChPo S1*
Cleaver, Robert d1613 *Alli*
Cleaver, Vera *AuBYP*
Cleaver, William *Alli, AuBYP, BiDLA*
Cleaver, William 1742-1815 *Alli, BiDLA Sup*
Cleaver, William Henry *Alli Sup*
Cleaves, Anna *ChPo, ChPo S1*
Cleaves, Charles Poole 1869-1932 *ChPo S1*
Cleaves, E C *Alli Sup*
Cleaves, Emery N 1902- *ConAu 33*
Cleaves, Freeman 1904- *ConAu 1R*
Cleaves, Mary Wilkerson *BlkAW*
Clebanoff, Herman 1917- *AmSCAP 66*
Clebsch, William Anthony 1923- *ConAu 13R*
Clecak, Peter 1938- *ConAu 41*
Clee, John *ChPo S1*
Cleeton, Glen Uriel 1895- *AmA&B*
Cleeve, Alex *Alli*
Cleeve, Brian Brenden Talbot 1921- *Au&Wr,
    ConAu 49, WrD 1976*
Cleeve, J K *Alli, BiDLA*
Clegat, Nic *Alli*
Clegate *Alli*
Clegg, Annie *ChPo S2*
Clegg, Charles Myron, Jr. 1916- *AmA&B,*

ConAu 25
Clegg, Eric 1901- *WrD 1976*
Clegg, J *Alli Sup*
Clegg, James *Alli, Alli Sup*
Clegg, John *Alli*
Clegg, John 1909- *Au&Wr, WrD 1976*
Clegg, Reed K 1907- *ConAu P-1*
Clegg, William Paul 1936- *Au&Wr,
    WrD 1976*
Cleghorn, C A *MnBBF*
Cleghorn, David *Alli*
Cleghorn, George *Alli, Alli Sup*
Cleghorn, George 1716-1787 *Alli*
Cleghorn, Hugh *Alli Sup*
Cleghorn, James *Alli*
Cleghorn, Jane 1827- *ChPo S1*
Cleghorn, Reese 1930- *ConAu 25*
Cleghorn, Sarah Norcliffe 1876-1959 *AmA&B,
    ChPo, ChPo S1, ChPo S2, REnAL,
    TwCA, TwCA Sup, WhWNAA*
Cleghorn, Thomas *Alli, BiDLA*
Cleidemus 375?BC- *Pen Cl*
Cleife, Philip 1906- *Au&Wr*
Cleife, Virginia 1920- *Au&Wr*
Cleig, Charles *MnBBF*
Cleig, George *Alli*
Cleitarchus 300?BC- *Pen Cl*
Cleiveland, John *Alli, NewC*
Cleland, Archibald *Alli*
Cleland, Benjamin *Alli*
Cleland, Charles *Alli*
Cleland, Charles C 1924- *ConAu 41*
Cleland, David I 1926- *ConAu 25*
Cleland, Elizabeth *Alli*
Cleland, Emily Wadsworth *WhWNAA*
Cleland, Henry *Alli, BiDLA*
Cleland, Herdman Fitzgerald 1869-1935
    DcNAA, WhWNAA
Cleland, Hugh *ConAu XR*
Cleland, James *Alli*
Cleland, John *Alli Sup*
Cleland, John 1709-1789 *Alli, BiDSA, CasWL,
    NewC, OxEng*
Cleland, John Burton 1878- *WhLA*
Cleland, Mabel *ConAu XR, SmATA 5*
Cleland, Mabel Goodwin 1876- *WhWNAA*
Cleland, Mabel Ross *AmA&B*
Cleland, Morton *ConAu XR*
Cleland, Robert *Alli Sup*
Cleland, Robert Glass 1885-1957 *AmA&B,
    WhWNAA*
Cleland, Thomas 1778-1858 *Alli, BiDSA,
    DcAmA, DcNAA*
Cleland, W Wendell 1888-1972 *ConAu 37*
Cleland, William *Alli, ChPo, Chmbr 1,
    PoIre*
Cleland, William 1661?-1689 *DcEnL, NewC*
Clelland, Richard C 1921- *ConAu 17R*
Clem, Alan L 1929- *ConAu 9R, WrD 1976*
Clem, Charles Douglass 1876-1934 *BlkAW*
Clemance, Clement *Alli Sup*
Clemans, Sarah Isabella Chaffin 1840-1885
    OhA&B
Clemen, Wolfgang Hermann 1909- *ConAu 1R,
    WrD 1976*
Clemence *Alli*
Clemence, M *Alli, BiDLA*
Clemence, Richard V 1910- *ConAu 1R*
Clemenceau, Georges 1841-1929 *CIDMEuL,
    REn*
Clemens, Brackenridge *Alli Sup*
Clemens, Brian Horace 1931- *Au&Wr,
    WrD 1976*
Clemens, Cyril 1902- *AuNews 2, BkC 3,
    CatA 1947, REnAL, WhWNAA*
Clemens, Diane S 1936- *ConAu 29*
Clemens, E J M *Alli Sup*
Clemens, G C *Alli Sup*
Clemens, James R 1866- *ChPo*
Clemens, Jeremiah 1814-1865 *Alli, Alli Sup,
    AmA, AmA&B, BiD&SB, BiDSA,
    DcAmA, DcNAA, OxAm, REnAL*
Clemens, Samuel Langhorne 1835-1910 *Alli Sup,
    AmA, AmA&B, AnCL, ArizL, AuBYP,
    BbD, BiD&SB, BiDPar, BiDSA, CarSB,
    CasWL, ChPo, ChPo S1, Chmbr 3,
    CnDAL, CyAL 2, DcAmA, DcEnA,
    DcEnL, DcLEnL, DcNAA, EncM&D,*

EncWL, EvLB, JBA 1934, LongC,
OxAm, OxEng, Pen Am, RCom, REn,
REnAL, TwCA
Clemens, S L ALSO Mark Twain
Clemens, S L ALSO Twain, Mark
Clemens, Walter C 1933- *ConAu 17R,*
WrD 1976
Clemens, William Montgomery 1860-1931
Alli Sup, ChPo, DcAmA, DcNAA,
OhA&B, WhWNAA
Clement *Alli*
Clement I *OxEng*
Clement Of Alexandria 150?-214? *OxEng,*
Pen Cl
Clement Of Lanthony 1160?- *BiB N*
Clement Of Lathony 1160?- *Alli*
Clement Of Ochrida *CasWL*
Clement VII, Pope *REn*
Clement, Saint *Pen Eur*
Clement Smolyatich *DcRusL*
Clement, A *Alli*
Clement, Alfred John 1915- *ConAu 25,*
WrD 1976
Clement, Augustus Ward *Alli Sup*
Clement, Benjamin *Alli*
Clement, Charles 1921- *ChPo S1, IlCB 1956*
Clement, Clara Erskine 1834-1916 *Alli Sup,*
AmA&B, BiDSA, DcAmA, DcNAA
Clement, Clarence Elbert 1883- *WhWNAA*
Clement, Cora *Alli Sup*
Clement, E *Alli Sup*
Clement, Ernest Wilson 1860-1941 *AmLY,*
DcNAA, WhWNAA
Clement, Evelyn Geer 1926- *ConAu 53*
Clement, Gabriel *OxCan Sup*
Clement, George A *Alli Sup*
Clement, George C 1871- *WhWNAA*
Clement, George H 1909- *ConAu 29,*
WrD 1976
Clement, Gertrude *ChPo*
Clement, Hal *AmA&B, ConAu XR*
Clement, J *Alli Sup, ChPo S2*
Clement, Jacques *OxFr*
Clement, Jane Tyson 1917- *ConAu 25*
Clement, John *Alli Sup*
Clement, Kay *WhWNAA*
Clement, Margaret 1508-1570 *Alli*
Clement, Ora A 1883- *WhWNAA*
Clement, Richard 1937- *Au&Wr*
Clement, Roland C 1912- *ConAu 49*
Clement, Thomas *Alli, BiDLA*
Clement, Titus Flavius, Of Alexandria 150?-212?
CasWL
Clement, W H P *OxCan*
Clement, Will M *ChPo S2*
Clement, William *Alli Sup*
Clement, William d1799 *Alli*
Clement, William Henry Pope 1858-1922
DcNAA
Clementi, Vincent *BbtC*
Clementia, Sister Mary Edward 1878-
CatA 1947
Clementine *ChPo S1*
Clementis, Vladimir 1902-1952 *CasWL*
Clements, Arthur L 1932- *ConAu 29,*
WrD 1976
Clements, Bruce 1931- *ConAu 53*
Clements, Mrs. Colin *AmA&B, WhWNAA*
Clements, Colin Campbell 1894-1948 *AmA&B,*
DcNAA, REnAL, WhWNAA
Clements, E Catherine 1920- *ConAu 13R*
Clements, E H 1905- *ConAu P-1*
Clements, Edith S *WhWNAA*
Clements, Edward *Alli Sup*
Clements, Ellen Catherine 1920- *WrD 1976*
Clements, Frank *AuBYP*
Clements, Frederic Edward 1874-1945 *DcNAA,*
WhWNAA
Clements, George *Alli Sup*
Clements, George H *ChPo*
Clements, Guy L 1888- *WhWNAA*
Clements, Harry *MnBBF*
Clements, Henry George John *Alli Sup*
Clements, Hugh *Alli Sup*
Clements, J H *Alli Sup*
Clements, Jacob *Alli Sup*
Clements, James *Alli Sup*
Clements, Jonathan 1938- *Au&Wr*

Clements, Julia 1906- *Au&Wr, ConAu P-1*
Clements, Lewis *Alli Sup*
Clements, M E *Alli Sup*
Clements, Muriel *OxCan*
Clements, Noel Sanderson 1909- *WhWNAA*
Clements, Otis G, Jr. 1926- *AmSCAP 66*
Clements, R G *Alli Sup*
Clements, Robert John 1912- *ConAu 1R*
Clements, Roger Victor 1925- *Au&Wr*
Clements, Ronald Ernest 1929- *Au&Wr,*
ConAu 13R
Clements, Ruth S *ChPo*
Clements, Tad S 1922- *ConAu 25*
Clementson, W A B *MnBBF*
Cleminshaw, C G *Alli Sup*
Cleminshaw, G *Alli Sup*
Clemm, Virginia 1822-1847 *REnAL*
Clemmer, Mary 1839-1884 *Alli Sup, AmA,*
AmA&B, ChPo, DcAmA, DcNAA
Clemmons, Bob *BlkAW*
Clemmons, Carol Gregory 1945- *DrAP 1975*
Clemmons, Carole Gregory 1945- *BlkAW*
Clemmons, Francois 1945- *BlkAW, ConAu 41,*
DrAP 1975
Clemmons, Robert Starr 1910- *ConAu 21,*
WrD 1976
Clemmons, William 1932- *ConAu 57*
Clemo, Ebenezer 1831?-1860 *Alli Sup, BbtC,*
DcNAA
Clemo, Jack 1916- *ConAu XR, ConP 1970,*
ConP 1975, LongC, TwCW, WrD 1976
Clemo, Reginald John 1916- *Au&Wr,*
ConAu 13R
Clemons, Elizabeth *ConAu XR*
Clemons, Harry 1879- *ConAu P-1*
Clemons, Lulamae 1917- *LivBA*
Clemons, Walter, Jr. 1929- *ConAu 1R*
Clemson, Floride *LivFWS*
Clemson, Florine 1842-1871 *ChPo S1*
Clenardus, Nicolaus 1495-1542 *DcEuL*
Clenche, John *Alli*
Clendenen, Clarence Clemens 1899- *ConAu 1R*
Clendenin, Frank Montrose 1853-1930 *DcNAA,*
WhWNAA
Clendenin, John C 1903- *ConAu 17R*
Clendenin, William R 1917- *ConAu 13R*
Clendening, Logan 1884-1945 *AmA&B,*
DcNAA, TwCA, TwCA Sup
Clendenning, Sheila T 1939- *ChPo S1,*
ConAu 25
Clendinin, Frank Montrose 1853- *DcAmA*
Clendon, John *Alli*
Clendon, Thomas *Alli*
Clennel, John *BiDLA*
Clennell, Luke 1781-1840 *ChPo S1*
Clennil, John *Alli*
Cleobury, Miss *Alli*
Cleobury, Frank Harold 1892- *Au&Wr,*
ConAu P-1
Cleombrotus *Alli*
Cleon d422BC *NewC, REn*
Cleopatra 069BC-030BC *NewC, REn*
Clephan, James *Alli Sup*
Clephane *Alli*
Clephane, A *Alli, BiDLA Sup*
Clephane, Elizabeth Cecilia 1830-1869 *Alli Sup,*
ChPo, WebEAL
Clephane, Irene Amy *Au&Wr, ConAu 13R*
Clephane, Robert Douglas *Alli Sup*
Clephane, Walter C 1867- *WhWNAA*
Clepper, Henry 1901- *ConAu 45*
Clepper, Irene E *ConAu 53*
Clerc, Mrs. *Alli Sup*
Clerc, Charles 1926- *ConAu 37*
Clercq, Willem De 1795-1844 *CasWL*
Clere, Henry *Alli Sup*
Clere, Mrs. Henry *Alli Sup*
Clere, Vere *ChPo*
Clergue, Helen d1938 *DcNAA*
Clergyman, A *PoIre*
Clerici, Fabrizio 1913- *WhGrA*
Clerihew, Alexander *Alli Sup*
Clerinic *OhA&B*
Clerk *Alli*
Clerk Of Tranent *Chmbr 1, DcEnL*
Clerk, A *Alli Sup*
Clerk, Alice M *Alli Sup*
Clerk, Archibald *Alli Sup*

Clerk, Charles *Alli*
Clerk, David *Alli*
Clerk, Dugald *Alli Sup*
Clerk, Sir George Maxwell 1715-1784 *Alli*
Clerk, H Richardson *Alli Sup*
Clerk, John *Alli, Alli Sup*
Clerk, Sir John *Alli*
Clerk, John d1812 *Alli, DcEnL*
Clerk, K M *Alli Sup*
Clerk, M C *Alli Sup*
Clerk, Nellie S *Alli Sup*
Clerk, T *Alli*
Clerk, Thomas *BiDLA*
Clerk, W *Alli*
Clerk, William *Alli*
Clerk-Maxwell, James 1831-1879 *NewC,*
OxEng
Clerk Of Penicuik, Sir John 1684-1755 *NewC*
Clerk Of The 'California' *OxCan*
Clerke, Agnes Mary 1842-1907 *Alli Sup,*
BrAu 19
Clerke, Aubrey St. John *Alli Sup*
Clerke, Bartholomew *Alli*
Clerke, Charles Carr 1799-1877 *Alli, Alli Sup*
Clerke, Ellen Mary 1840-1906 *Alli Sup, PoIre*
Clerke, Francis *Alli*
Clerke, George *Alli*
Clerke, Gilbert *Alli*
Clerke, John *Alli, ChPo*
Clerke, John d1540 *Alli*
Clerke, Richard d1634 *Alli*
Clerke, Samuel *Alli*
Clerke, Thomas W *Alli*
Clerke, Tim *Alli*
Clerke, William *Alli*
Clerke, Sir William *Alli*
Clerke, Sir William Henry *BiDLA*
Clermont, Lord *Alli Sup*
Clermont, Emile 1880-1916 *OxFr*
Clery, Cornelius Francis *Alli Sup*
Clery, Michael *Alli*
Clery, Val 1924- *ConAu 49*
Cless, George Henry 1892- *OhA&B,*
WhWNAA
Clesse, Antoine 1816-1889 *BiD&SB*
Cleugh, Mary Frances 1913- *ConAu 1R,*
WrD 1976
Cleugh, Sophia 1887?- *TwCA, WhWNAA*
Cleve, John *ConAu XR*
Clevedon, John *WrD 1976*
Cleveland, Aaron 1744-1815 *Alli, AmA&B,*
BiD&SB, CyAL 2, DcAmA, DcNAA
Cleveland, Cecilia *Alli Sup*
Cleveland, Charles Dexter 1802-1869 *Alli,*
Alli Sup, AmA&B, DcAmA, DcNAA
Cleveland, Chester Wilson 1898-1961
IndAu 1917, WhWNAA
Cleveland, Cynthia Eloise 1845- *DcAmA,*
DcNAA, WhWNAA
Cleveland, E E *LivBA*
Cleveland, Ezra *Alli*
Cleveland, Frank *MnBBF*
Cleveland, Frederick Albert 1865-1946 *DcNAA,*
WhWNAA
Cleveland, George Bowen 1873- *WhWNAA*
Cleveland, Grace Elizabeth Matthews 1864-1933
OhA&B
Cleveland, Grover 1837-1908 *AmA&B,*
DcAmA, OxAm, REn, REnAL
Cleveland, Harlan 1918- *ConAu 1R,*
WrD 1976
Cleveland, Harold Van B 1916- *ConAu 23*
Cleveland, Helen M d1909 *DcNAA*
Cleveland, Henry *Alli Sup, BiDSA*
Cleveland, Henry Russell 1808?-1843 *Alli,*
AmA, BiDSA, DcAmA, DcNAA
Cleveland, Horace Gillette *Alli Sup*
Cleveland, Horace William Shaler 1814-1900
Alli Sup, AmA&B, DcAmA, DcNAA
Cleveland, John *Alli, Chmbr 1, ConAu XR,*
LongC
Cleveland, John 1613-1658 *BrAu, CasWL,*
ChPo, CnE&AP, CrE&SL, CriT 1,
DcEnL, EvLB, NewC, OxEng, Pen Eng,
REn, WebEAL
Cleveland, Kate *OhA&B*
Cleveland, Leslie 1921- *WrD 1976*
Cleveland, Libra Jan *IndAu 1917*

Cleveland, Parker *Alli*
Cleveland, Philip Jerome 1903- *ConAu 9R*
Cleveland, Ray L 1929- *ConAu 21, WrD 1976*
Cleveland, Richard Jeffrey 1773-1860 *Alli, DcAmA, DcNAA*
Cleveland, Rose Elizabeth 1846-1918 *Alli Sup, BbD, BiD&SB, DcAmA, DcNAA*
Cleveland, Sidney E 1919- *ConAu 9R*
Cleveland, Stephen Grover 1837-1908 *BiD&SB*
Cleveland, William Frederick *Alli Sup*
Cleveley, Robert d1809? *BkIE*
Clevely, Hugh *MnBBF*
Cleven, Cathrine *ConAu XR, SmATA 2*
Cleven, Kathryn Seward *ConAu 1R, SmATA 2*
Clevenger, Arthur Wilbur 1887- *IndAu 1917*
Clevenger, Ernest Allen, Jr. 1929- *ConAu 57*
Clevenger, Franklin Henry 1870-1940 *IndAu 1917*
Clevenger, Herbert Logan *ChPo S1*
Clevenger, Shobal Vail 1843-1920 *Alli Sup, DcAmA, DcNAA*
Clevenger, Theodore, Jr. 1929- *ConAu 41*
Clever, Charles P *Alli Sup*
Clever, Glenn 1918- *ConAu 57*
Clever, William *Alli*
Cleverdon, Douglas 1903- *Au&Wr, ChPo S2, ConAu 29*
Cleverley, G W *Alli Sup*
Cleverley Ford, D W 1914- *ConAu 25*
Clevin, Joergen 1920- *ConAu 29, SmATA 7*
Clevin, Jorgen *ConAu XR*
Clew, Jeffrey Robert 1928- *ConAu 57*
Clewe, Belle Ragnar Parsons 1878- *WhWNAA*
Clewell, John Henry 1855-1922 *BiDSA, DcNAA*
Clewes, Dorothy Mary 1907- *Au&Wr, AuBYP, ConAu 5R, SmATA 1*
Clewes, Howard 1912- *LongC*
Clewes, Howard 1916- *Au&Wr*
Clewes, Winston 1906- *LongC, TwCA Sup*
Clews, Henry 1834?-1923 *Alli Sup, AmA&B, DcNAA*
Clews, Henry E 1840- *BiD&SB, DcAmA*
Clibborn, Edward *PoIre*
Clibborn, John 1847- *WhLA*
Click, J W 1936- *ConAu 57*
Clieveland, John 1613-1658 *REn*
Cliff, Charles Joseph 1912- *AmSCAP 66*
Cliffe, Charles Frederick *Alli Sup*
Cliffe, Francis Henry *Alli Sup*
Cliffe, Gunton *MnBBF*
Cliffe, J T 1931- *Au&Wr*
Cliffe, John Henry *Alli Sup*
Cliffe, John Trevor 1931- *WrD 1976*
Clifford *Alli*
Clifford, Lady 1866-1945 *EvLB, LongC, NewC*
Clifford, Abraham *Alli*
Clifford, Albert Jerome 1918- *IndAu 1917*
Clifford, Anne 1589-1676 *Alli*
Clifford, Arthur *Alli, BiDLA Sup*
Clifford, Arthur Baldwin *Alli Sup*
Clifford, Sir Augustus William James 1788-1877 *Alli Sup*
Clifford, C H *Alli Sup*
Clifford, Carrie Williams *BlkAW*
Clifford, Charles *Alli, Alli Sup, BiDLA*
Clifford, Charles Cavendish 1821- *Alli Sup*
Clifford, Christopher *Alli*
Clifford, Cornelius Cyprian 1859-1938 *CatA 1947, DcNAA*
Clifford, Derek Plint 1917- *Au&Wr, ConAu 5R, WrD 1976*
Clifford, Ella *ChPo, DcNAA*
Clifford, Eth *ConAu XR, SmATA 3*
Clifford, Ethel *ChPo, WhLA*
Clifford, Frances *BiDLA*
Clifford, Francis *Alli*
Clifford, Francis 1917- *Au&Wr, ConAu XR, ConNov 1976*
Clifford, Frank S *Alli Sup*
Clifford, Fred H *ChPo*
Clifford, Frederick 1828- *Alli Sup*
Clifford, G A *Alli Sup*
Clifford, George *Alli, Alli Sup*
Clifford, Gordon 1902- *AmSCAP 66*
Clifford, H Dalton 1911- *ConAu 9R*

Clifford, Harold B 1893- *ConAu P-1, SmATA 10*
Clifford, Henry *Alli*
Clifford, Henry Dalton 1911- *Au&Wr*
Clifford, Henry De 1455?-1523 *NewC*
Clifford, Henry Marcus *Alli Sup*
Clifford, Sir Hugh 1866-1941 *CatA 1947*
Clifford, J B *Alli*
Clifford, J R S *Alli Sup*
Clifford, James *Alli*
Clifford, James Lowry 1901- *AmA&B, Au&Wr, ConAu 1R, IndAu 1917, WrD 1976*
Clifford, Jane *Alli Sup*
Clifford, Jeronimy *Alli*
Clifford, John *ConAu XR*
Clifford, John 1836- *Alli Sup*
Clifford, John Bryant *Alli Sup*
Clifford, John E 1935- *ConAu 37*
Clifford, John Garry 1942- *ConAu 53*
Clifford, John W 1918- *ConAu 17R*
Clifford, Lionel B *MnBBF*
Clifford, Lloyd *MnBBF*
Clifford, Lucy d1929 *Alli Sup, ChPo S2, NewC, REn, TwCA*
Clifford, M M *Alli, BiDLA*
Clifford, Margaret Cort 1929- *ConAu 25, SmATA 1*
Clifford, Margaret Rowe 1841-1926 *ArizL*
Clifford, Martin *LongC, MnBBF, WhCL*
Clifford, Martin d1677 *Alli*
Clifford, Martin 1910- *ConAu 25*
Clifford, Mary Louise Beneway 1926- *ConAu 5R, WrD 1976*
Clifford, Maurice *Alli Sup, ChPo, ChPo S1, ChPo S2*
Clifford, Nathan 1803-1881 *Alli Sup, DcAmA*
Clifford, Nicholas R 1930- *ConAu 21*
Clifford, Peggy *ConAu XR, SmATA 1*
Clifford, Philip Henry 1878-1942 *DcNAA*
Clifford, R Ad *MnBBF*
Clifford, Rob *Alli*
Clifford, Robert *BiDLA*
Clifford, Rosamond d1176? *NewC*
Clifford, Samuel *Alli, Alli Sup, PoIre*
Clifford, Sarah 1916- *ConAu 25*
Clifford, Sigerson 1913- *Au&Wr, ChPo S1*
Clifford, T R *Alli Sup*
Clifford, Theodore 1931- *ConAu XR*
Clifford, W *Alli*
Clifford, Mrs. W K *Chmbr 3*
Clifford, Mrs. W K d1929 *LongC*
Clifford, William *Alli*
Clifford, William Kingdon 1845-1879 *Alli Sup, BrAu 19, Chmbr 3, OxEng*
Clifford-Eskell *Alli Sup*
Cliffton, William 1772-1799 *Alli, AmA, CyAL 1, DcNAA, OxAm*
Clift, Betty *WhWNAA*
Clift, Denison Halley 1885- *AmA&B*
Clift, Henry *Alli*
Clift, Virgil Alfred 1912- *ConAu 9R, LivBA*
Clift, William *Alli, Alli Sup*
Clifton, Alice *Alli Sup*
Clifton, Bernice Marie *ConAu 5R*
Clifton, Baroness Elizabeth A M Bligh 1900- *ChPo S2*
Clifton, Francis *Alli*
Clifton, George H *Alli Sup*
Clifton, Harold Dennis 1927- *Au&Wr, WrD 1976*
Clifton, Harry Talbot DeVere *ChPo S1*
Clifton, Henry *MnBBF*
Clifton, J Colfort *Alli Sup*
Clifton, James A 1927- *ConAu 25*
Clifton, Jo *Alli*
Clifton, John Francis *Alli Sup*
Clifton, John Leroy 1881-1943 *OhA&B*
Clifton, L Colfort *Alli Sup*
Clifton, Lucille 1936- *BlkAW, ChPo S1, ConAu 49, ConP 1975, DrAP 1975, WrD 1976*
Clifton, Marguerite Ann 1925- *ConAu 13R*
Clifton, Oliver Lee *DcNAA*
Clifton, Richard *MnBBF*
Clifton, Robert Walker *Alli Sup*
Clifton, S *Alli Sup*
Clifton, Thomas A 1859-1935 *IndAu 1816*

Clifton, Tom *Alli Sup*
Clifton, Violet Mary Beauclerk 1883- *BkC 2, CatA 1947, ChPo, WhLA*
Clifton, William 1772-1799 *AmA&B, DcNAA*
Climacus *CasWL*
Climax, John *Pen Cl*
Climmons, Artie *BlkAW*
Clinard, Dorothy Long 1909- *ConAu 5R*
Clinard, Marshall B 1911- *ConAu 5R*
Clinard, Turner N 1911- *ConAu 37*
Clinch, Charles Powell 1797-1880 *AmA, AmA&B, BiD&SB, DcNAA*
Clinch, J B *Alli, BiDLA Sup*
Clinch, James Bernard 1770-1834 *PoIre*
Clinch, Joseph *OxCan*
Clinch, Joseph Hart 1806-1884 *BbtC, ChPo S1*
Clinch, William *Alli*
Clinche, Hugh d1847 *PoIre*
Clinchy, Everett Ross 1896- *AmA&B*
Clinchy, Russell James 1893- *AmA&B*
Cline, A J *Alli Sup*
Cline, C C *Alli Sup*
Cline, C Terry, Jr. 1935- *ConAu 61*
Cline, Catherine Ann 1927- *ConAu 17R*
Cline, Charles 1937- *ConAu 61*
Cline, Denzel C 1903- *ConAu 21*
Cline, Eileen Peck *WhWNAA*
Cline, G Griffen 1929- *ConAu 5R*
Cline, G S *Alli Sup*
Cline, Henry *Alli*
Cline, Leonard Lanson 1893-1929 *DcNAA*
Cline, Rodney 1903- *ConAu 61*
Cline, William Hamilton *ChPo*
Clinebell, Howard J, Jr. 1922- *ConAu 33, WrD 1976*
Clinedinst, Benjamin West 1859-1931 *ChPo*
Clingman, Nixon Poindexter *BiDSA*
Clingman, Thomas Lanier 1812-1897 *Alli Sup, BiDSA, DcAmA, DcNAA*
Clington, Allen H *Alli Sup*
Clinker, Humphrey *REn*
Clinkscales, John George 1855-1942 *DcNAA, WhWNAA*
Clint, H O'Reilly 1900-1961 *AmSCAP 66*
Clint, Mabel B d1939 *DcNAA*
Clinton, Althea L *OhA&B*
Clinton, C J F *Alli*
Clinton, C W *EarAB*
Clinton, D *DrAP 1975*
Clinton, Delores *BlkAW*
Clinton, DeWitt 1769-1828 *Alli, AmA&B, BiD&SB, CyAL 1, DcAmA, DcNAA, REnAL*
Clinton, Dorothy Randle *BlkAW*
Clinton, Eleanor E *ChPo S1*
Clinton, Garth *MnBBF*
Clinton, George *Alli Sup*
Clinton, George 1739-1812 *DcNAA, OxAm, REnAL*
Clinton, George Wylie 1859-1921 *BiDSA, DcNAA*
Clinton, Gloria *BlkAW*
Clinton, Harry *MnBBF*
Clinton, Henry *Alli Sup*
Clinton, Sir Henry 1738?-1795 *Alli, OxAm, REn, REnAL*
Clinton, Henry Fynes 1781-1852 *Alli, DcEnL, EvLB*
Clinton, Henry Laurens 1820-1899 *DcNAA*
Clinton, Herbert R *Alli Sup*
Clinton, Iris Annie 1901- *Au&Wr, ConAu P-1*
Clinton, Jeff *AmA&B, ConAu XR, WrD 1976*
Clinton, Kythe *Alli Sup*
Clinton, Larry 1909- *AmSCAP 66*
Clinton, Mabel A *ChPo S2*
Clinton, Mary E *ChPo S1*
Clinton, Richard Lee 1938- *ConAu 61*
Clinton, Ursula *BkC 3*
Clinton, W Henry *Alli, BiDLA*
Clinton, Walter *Alli Sup*
Clinton-Baddeley, Victor Clinton 1900- *ChPo S2*
Clio *DcEnL, NewC*
Clipper, Lawrence Jon 1930- *ConAu 49*
Clipperton, John *Alli*
Clippinger, Erle Elsworth 1875- *WhWNAA*
Clippinger, J A *Alli Sup*

Clippinger, Walter Gillan 1873-1948 *DcNAA*
Clipsham, Robert *Alli*
Clissold, Augustus 1797?-1882 *Alli, Alli Sup*
Clissold, Henry 1795-1867 *Alli, Alli Sup*
Clissold, John Stephen Hallett 1913- *Au&Wr*
Clithero, Myrtle E 1906- *ConAu 25*
Clithero, Sally *ConAu XR*
Clive, Archer 1801-1878 *Alli Sup*
Clive, Mrs. Archer 1801-1873 *ChPo S1, DcEnL*
Clive, Caroline Archer 1801-1873 *Alli Sup, BrAu 19, ChPo, NewC, OxEng*
Clive, Catherine 1711-1785 *Alli, NewC*
Clive, Clifford *MnBBF*
Clive, Geoffry 1927- *ConAu 33*
Clive, George *Alli Sup*
Clive, J H *Alli, BiDLA*
Clive, Katherine *Alli Sup*
Clive, Keith *MnBBF*
Clive, Mary 1907- *Au&Wr, ConAu 21*
Clive, Robert *Alli*
Clive, Baron Robert Clive Of Plassey 1725-1774 *Alli, NewC, REn*
Clive, William *WrD 1976*
Clive-Ross, F F 1921- *BiDPar*
Clodd, Edward 1840-1930 *Alli Sup, LongC, NewC*
Clode, Charles Matthew 1818- *Alli Sup*
Clode, Eliza *ChPo*
Clodfelter, Noah J 1853-1901 *Alli Sup, ChPo S2, IndAu 1816*
Clodius, John *Alli*
Clodius Licinus, Gaius 084?BC- *Pen Cl*
Clodius Pulcher, Publius d052BC *REn*
Cloeren, Hermann J 1934- *ConAu 41*
Cloete, Edward Fairly Stuart Graham 1897- *DcLEnL*
Cloete, Edward Fairlie Stuart Graham 1897- *Au&Wr*
Cloete, Stuart 1897- *AmA&B, CasWL, ConAu 1R, ConNov 1972, ConNov 1976, EncWL, LongC, REn, TwCA, TwCA Sup, TwCW, WhWNAA, WrD 1976*
Cloetta, Gian Gianet 1874-1965 *CasWL*
Clogan, Paul M 1934- *ConAu 33*
Clogie, Alexander *Alli*
Clok, Henry *Alli Sup*
Cloke, Harold Edward 1873- *WhWNAA*
Cloke, Thomas *Alli*
Clokey, Joseph Waddel 1890-1961 *AmSCAP 66, IndAu 1917*
Cloncurry, Lord *Alli Sup*
Cloninger, Margaret Theodora Deaver 1877- *WhWNAA*
Clonney, James Goodwin 1812-1867 *ChPo*
Cloots, Baron Jean-B DuVal DeGrace De 1755-1794 *OxFr*
Clopinel, Jean *Pen Eur*
Clopper, Edward Nicholas 1879-1953 *OhA&B*
Cloquet, Robert Louis Saurin *Alli Sup*
Clor, Harry M 1929- *ConAu 53*
Clore, Gerald L 1939- *ConAu 37*
Close, A Kathryn 1908?-1973 *ConAu 41*
Close, A P *EarAB, EarAB Sup*
Close, Charles William 1859-1915 *DcNAA*
Close, Eunice *ChPo*
Close, Francis 1797-1882 *Alli, Alli Sup*
Close, H P *MnBBF*
Close, Henry J *Alli*
Close, Henry T 1928- *ConAu 1R*
Close, John 1816-1891 *BrAu 19*
Close, John George *Alli Sup, PoIre*
Close, Kathleen *ChPo S1*
Close, Reginald Arthur 1909- *Au&Wr, ConAu 17R, WrD 1976*
Close, Samuel P *Alli Sup*
Close, Thomas 1796-1881 *Alli Sup*
Close, Upton 1894- *AmA&B, EvLB, TwCA, TwCA Sup, WhWNAA*
Close, William *Alli*
Closener, Fritsche d1373? *OxGer*
Closs, August 1898- *Au&Wr, ConAu 5R, WrD 1976*
Closs, Elizabeth *ConAu XR*
Closse, George *Alli*
Closson, Herman 1901- *ModWD*
Closson, W B *Alli Sup, ChPo, ChPo S1*

Clossy, Samuel *Alli*
Closterman, Pierre 1921- *REn*
Clostermann, Pierre 1921- *TwCW*
Clotfelter, Beryl E 1926- *ConAu 53*
Clotfelter, Cecil F 1929- *ConAu 53*
Clotilde De Surville *OxFr*
Cloud, Arthur David 1884-1966 *AmA&B*
Cloud, Mrs. C T *ChPo*
Cloud, D C *Alli Sup*
Cloud, Fred 1925- *ConAu 13R*
Cloud, John Hofer 1871- *WhWNAA*
Cloud, Virginia Woodward 1861-1938 *AmA&B, BiDSA, ChPo, ChPo S1, DcAmA*
Cloudsley-Thompson, J L 1921- *ConAu 17R*
Cloues, William Jacob 1860- *WhWNAA*
Clouet, Francois 1510?-1572? *AtlBL, REn*
Clouet, Jean 1485?-1540 *AtlBL*
Clough, Annie Crossley *Alli Sup*
Clough, Arthur Hugh 1819-1861 *Alli, Alli Sup, AtlBL, BiD&SB, BrAu 19, CasWL, ChPo, ChPo S1, ChPo S2, Chmbr 3, CnE&AP, CriT 3, DcEnA, DcEnL, DcEuL, DcLEnL, EvLB, MouLC 3, NewC, OxEng, Pen Eng, WebEAL*
Clough, B *Alli Sup*
Clough, Blanche *Alli Sup*
Clough, C *Alli Sup*
Clough, F Gardner 1895- *WhWNAA*
Clough, Francis Frederick 1912- *Au&Wr, ConAu P-1*
Clough, H G *BiDLA*
Clough, Henry J *Alli*
Clough, James *Alli, BiDLA*
Clough, James Cresswell *Alli Sup*
Clough, John E 1836- *Alli Sup*
Clough, Joseph W *Alli Sup*
Clough, Paul Wiswall 1882- *WhWNAA*
Clough, R L *Alli Sup*
Clough, R Stewart *Alli Sup*
Clough, Robert *ChPo S1*
Clough, Robert 1904- *Au&Wr*
Clough, Rosa Trillo 1906- *ConAu 13R*
Clough, Shepard Bancroft 1901- *AmA&B, Au&Wr, ConAu 1R, IndAu 1917, WrD 1976*
Clough, W O *Alli Sup*
Clough, William A 1899- *ConAu 21*
Clough, Wilson O 1894- *ConAu 17R*
Clouse, Robert Gordon 1931- *ConAu 29, WrD 1976*
Clouser, John William 1932- *ConAu 61*
Clouston, Charles *Alli Sup*
Clouston, Joseph Storer 1870-1944 *EvLB, Pen Eng, WhLA*
Clouston, Thomas Smith *Alli Sup*
Clouston, William Alexander 1843- *Alli Sup*
Clout, Colin *NewC*
Clout, Hugh Donald 1944- *ConAu 41*
Cloutier, Cecile 1930- *OxCan Sup*
Cloutier, David 1951- *ConAu 57, DrAP 1975*
Cloutier, Eugene 1921- *CanWr, OxCan, OxCan Sup*
Cloutier, Maurice E 1933- *AmSCAP 66*
Clouts, Sydney 1926- *ConP 1970, ConP 1975, WrD 1976*
Cloutt, Thomas *Alli, BiDLA*
Clover, Kitty *ChPo, ChPo S1*
Clover, Lewis P *BiDSA*
Clover, Samuel Travers 1859-1934 *AmA&B, DcNAA*
Clovis I 466?-511 *OxFr, REn*
Clow, Archie 1909- *Au&Wr*
Clow, Martha DeMey 1932- *ConAu 29, WrD 1976*
Clow, William McCullum 1853- *WhLA*
Cloward, Richard Andrew 1926- *ConAu 41*
Cloward, Robert Louis 1934- *AmSCAP 66*
Clowes, Anna *Alli Sup*
Clowes, Evelyn Mark *DcLEnL*
Clowes, Evelyn Mary *LongC*
Clowes, Frank *Alli Sup*
Clowes, James *BiDLA*
Clowes, John 1743-1831 *Alli, BiDLA Sup*
Clowes, W *Alli Sup*
Clowes, William *Alli*
Clowes, William Laird *Alli Sup*
Clowney, Edmund P 1917- *ConAu 5R*
Clubb, O Edmund 1901- *ConAu 37,*

WrD 1976
Clubb, Oliver E, Jr. 1929- *ConAu 5R*
Clubb, Miss S A *Alli Sup*
Clubbe, J *Alli*
Clubbe, John *Alli*
Clubbe, John L E 1938- *ConAu 25, WrD 1976*
Clubbe, William d1814 *Alli, BiDLA, BiDLA Sup, ChPo*
Clubon, John M *Alli Sup*
Cluff, Walter 1878-1943 *DcNAA*
Clugston, Katherine 1892- *IndAu 1917*
Clugston, Richard 1938- *ConAu 41*
Clugston, W G 1899- *WhWNAA*
Cluley, William *Alli Sup*
Clulow, William Benton 1802-1882 *Alli Sup*
Clum, Franklin D 1853-1925 *Alli Sup, DcNAA*
Clum, John P 1851-1932 *ArizL*
Clun, Arthur 1934- *ConAu XR*
Clune, Francis Patrick 1893-1971 *ConAu 23, ConAu 29*
Clune, Frank *ConAu XR*
Clune, Frank Patrick 1893- *DcLEnL*
Clune, Henry W 1890- *ConAu 1R, REnAL*
Clunes, G C *Alli Sup*
Cluney, Annie *ChPo*
Clunie, James *Alli*
Clunie, John *Alli*
Clunies Ross, Anthony 1932- *ConAu 53*
Cluny, Alexander *Alli, BbtC*
Clurman, Harold 1901- *AmA&B, Au&Wr, ConAu 1R, Pen Am, REnAL, WrD 1976*
Clute, Eugene 1878- *WhWNAA*
Clute, John Jacob *Alli Sup*
Clute, Morrel J 1912- *ConAu 13R*
Clute, Oscar 1873-1902 *Alli Sup, DcNAA*
Clute, Robert E 1924- *ConAu 41*
Clute, Willard Nelson 1869-1950 *AmA&B, AmL, DcAmA, WhWNAA*
Clutesi, George *OxCan Sup*
Clutha, Janet Paterson Frame 1924- *ConAu 1R*
Clutterbuck, Captain Cuthbert *NewC*
Clutterbuck, Henry *Alli, BiDLA*
Clutterbuck, J *Alli*
Clutterbuck, James Bennett *Alli Sup*
Clutterbuck, James Charles *Alli Sup*
Clutterbuck, Richard 1917- *ConAu 23, WrD 1976*
Clutterbuck, Robert 1772-1831 *Alli*
Clutterbuck, Thomas *Alli*
Clutton, Cecil 1909- *Au&Wr, WrD 1976*
Clutton, Henry *Alli Sup*
Clutton, John *Alli*
Clutton, Joseph *Alli*
Clutton-Brock, Arthur 1868-1924 *ChPo, EvLB, LongC, NewC, REn, TwCA*
Cluver, Eustace Henry 1894- *Au&Wr, ConAu P-1*
Cluvius *Pen Cl*
Cluysenaar, Anne Alice Andree 1936- *ConP 1970, ConP 1975, WrD 1976*
Clyde, Alton *Alli Sup*
Clyde, Bernard *HsB&A*
Clyde, James *Alli Sup*
Clyde, John Cunningham 1841-1915 *Alli Sup, DcAmA, DcNAA*
Clyde, Kate *ChPo*
Clyde, Kit *AmA&B*
Clyde, Norman Asa 1885- *ConAu 41*
Clyde, Paul Hibbert 1896- *AmA&B*
Clyde, William McCallum 1901- *Au&Wr*
Clyfton, Richard *Alli*
Clyfton, William *Alli*
Clyman, James 1792-1881 *OhA&B*
Clymer, Albert 1827-1897 *OhA&B*
Clymer, Eleanor 1906- *AuBYP, ConAu 61, SmATA 9, WrD 1976*
Clymer, Ella Dietz 1850?- *Alli Sup, BbD, BiD&SB*
Clymer, Ella Maria 1847- *DcNAA*
Clymer, Ella Maria 1856- *DcAmA*
Clymer, George *Alli Sup*
Clymer, Meredith 1817-1902 *Alli, Alli Sup, DcAmA, DcNAA*
Clymer, R Swinburne 1878- *AmA&B, WhWNAA*
Clymer, Reuben Swinburne 1878- *ConAu P-1*
Clymer, Theodore 1927- *ConAu 19*

Clymer, William Branford Shubrick 1855-1903 *DcNAA*
Clynder, Monica *ConAu XR*
Clyne, Douglas George Wilson 1912- *Au&Wr, WrD 1976*
Clyne, John *Alli Sup*
Clyne, Norval 1817-1889 *Alli Sup*
Clyne, Norval 1817-1888 *PoIre*
Clyne, Terence *ConAu XR*
Clynes, Solomon 1915- *Au&Wr*
Clytus, John 1929- *ConAu 29*
Cnudde, Charles F 1938- *ConAu 29*
Cnut *NewC*
Coachman, Robert *Alli*
Coad, Frederick Roy 1925- *Au&Wr, WrD 1976*
Coad, John *Alli*
Coad, Joseph *Alli, BiDLA*
Coad, Oral Sumner 1887- *ConAu 45*
Coady, Ida A And Ginn, F B *Alli Sup*
Coady, Moses Michael 1882- *CatA 1947, OxCan*
Coaker, Sir William Ford 1871-1938 *OxCan*
Coakley, Cornelius Godfrey 1862-1934 *DcNAA*
Coakley, John Lettsom *Alli*
Coakley, Mary Lewis 1907- *BkC 6, ConAu P-1, WrD 1976*
Coalbank, Susan *Alli Sup*
Coale, Charles B *Alli Sup*
Coalson, Alla *TexWr*
Coalson, Glo *IlBYP*
Coan, Charles Florus 1886-1928 *OhA&B*
Coan, Leander Samuel 1837-1879 *ChPo S2*
Coan, Lydia *Alli Sup*
Coan, Nonee Edward 1910- *AmSCAP 66*
Coan, Otis W 1895- *ConAu 33*
Coan, Richard W 1928- *WrD 1976*
Coan, Robert A *ChPo S1*
Coan, Titus 1801-1882 *Alli Sup, AmA, BiD&SB, DcAmA, DcNAA*
Coan, Titus Munson 1836-1921 *Alli Sup, AmLY, BbD, BiD&SB, DcAmA, DcNAA*
Coape, Henry Coe *Alli Sup*
Coar, John Firman 1863-1939 *DcNAA, WhWNAA*
Coasdell, Annie *ChPo*
Coaten, Arthur W 1872-1939 *Br&AmS*
Coates, Ainslie *Alli Sup*
Coates, Archie Austin 1891- *OhA&B*
Coates, Austin 1922- *Au&Wr, WrD 1976*
Coates, Belle 1896- *ConAu 5R, SmATA 2*
Coates, Benjamin *Alli Sup*
Coates, Benjamin H 1787- *Alli*
Coates, Charles *Alli, Alli Sup*
Coates, Digby *Alli*
Coates, Donald R 1922- *ConAu 49*
Coates, Doreen Frances 1912- *Au&Wr, WrD 1976*
Coates, Mrs. E *Alli Sup*
Coates, Florence Earle 1850-1927 *AmA&B, AmLY, BiD&SB, ChPo S1, ChPo S2, DcAmA, DcNAA, WhWNAA*
Coates, Geoffrey Edward 1917- *ConAu 37*
Coates, George Morrison 1874- *WhWNAA*
Coates, Grace Stone 1881- *AmA&B, ChPo S1, WhWNAA*
Coates, Henry Troth 1843-1910 *Alli Sup, AmA&B, ChPo, ChPo S1, DcNAA*
Coates, John *Alli Sup*
Coates, Joseph Hornor 1849-1930 *DcNAA*
Coates, Reynell 1802-1886 *Alli, ChPo S1*
Coates, Robert *OxCan Sup*
Coates, Robert Myron 1897-1973 *AmA&B, AmNov, Au&Wr, CnDAL, ConAu 5R, ConAu 41, ConNov 1972, DcLEnL, OxAm, Pen Am, REn, REnAL, TwCA, TwCA Sup*
Coates, Ruth Allison 1915- *ConAu 57*
Coates, W Burnett *Alli Sup*
Coates, Mrs. W H *ChPo*
Coates, Walter John 1880- *WhWNAA*
Coates, William Ames 1916- *ConAu 37*
Coates, William Martin *Alli Sup*
Coates, William R 1851-1935 *OhA&B*
Coates, Willson H 1899- *ConAu 37*
Coats, Alice M 1905- *Au&Wr, ConAu 53, IlCB 1945, WrD 1976*

Coats, George Wesley 1936- *ConAu 23, WrD 1976*
Coats, James *Alli*
Coats, Joseph *Alli Sup*
Coats, Peter 1910- *ConAu 49*
Coats, R H *OxCan*
Coats, R Roy 1898- *AmSCAP 66*
Coats, Robert Hamilton 1874- *WhWNAA*
Coats, W *BbtC*
Coats, William *OxCan*
Coatsworth, Edward *Alli*
Coatsworth, Elizabeth *AuICB, Newb 1922*
Coatsworth, Elizabeth Jane 1893- *AmA&B, AmNov, AnCL, AuBYP, BkCL, ChLR 2, ChPo, ChPo S1, ChPo S2, ConAu 5R, JBA 1934, JBA 1951, MorBMP, OxAm, REnAL, SmATA 2, St&VC, TwCA, TwCA Sup, WhCL*
Coatsworth, J *Alli Sup*
Coatsworth, W *Alli*
Cob, Chris *Alli*
Cob, S *Alli Sup*
Cobarruvias Orozco, Sebastian De d1613 *DcEuL*
Cobb, A B *Alli Sup*
Cobb, Alice 1909- *ConAu 5R, IndAu 1917*
Cobb, Ann 1873- *ChPo, ChPo S1, ChPo S2, WhWNAA*
Cobb, B F *Alli Sup*
Cobb, Bertha Browning 1868?-1951 *AmA&B, WhWNAA*
Cobb, Bessie A *BlkAW*
Cobb, Carl W 1926- *ConAu 21*
Cobb, Charlie 1944- *BlkAW, LivBA*
Cobb, Chester Francis 1899- *DcLEnL*
Cobb, Clarence F *Alli Sup*
Cobb, Cyrus 1834-1903 *DcAmA, DcNAA, EarAB Sup*
Cobb, Darius 1834-1919 *EarAB Sup*
Cobb, Emily C *ChPo S2*
Cobb, Ernest 1877-1964 *AmA&B, WhWNAA*
Cobb, Faye Davis 1932- *ConAu 9R*
Cobb, Frank Irving 1869-1923 *AmA&B*
Cobb, G Belton *MnBBF*
Cobb, George L 1886-1942 *AmSCAP 66*
Cobb, Gerard Francis *Alli Sup*
Cobb, Gershom 1780?-1824 *EarAB Sup*
Cobb, Henry Evertson *ChPo*
Cobb, Howell 1795- *BiDSA, DcAmA*
Cobb, Howell 1815-1868 *BiDSA, DcNAA*
Cobb, Humphrey 1899-1944 *AmA&B, DcNAA, LongC, REn, TwCA, TwCA Sup*
Cobb, Irvin S 1876-1944 *AmA&B, ChPo, CnDAL, ConAmL, DcNAA, EncM&D, EvLB, LongC, OxAm, REn, REnAL, TwCA, TwCA Sup, WhWNAA*
Cobb, Irwin 1876-1944 *TwCW*
Cobb, Isaac *ChPo S2*
Cobb, James 1756-1818? *Alli, BiDLA, NewC*
Cobb, James Francis 1829- *Alli Sup, ChPo*
Cobb, Janice 1952- *BlkAW*
Cobb, John *Alli, AmA&B, BiDLA*
Cobb, John 1921- *AmNov*
Cobb, John B, Jr. 1925- *ConAu 1R*
Cobb, John Nathan 1868- *WhWNAA*
Cobb, John Wolstenholme *Alli Sup*
Cobb, Jonathan Holmes 1799-1882 *DcAmA, DcNAA*
Cobb, Joseph Beckham 1819-1858 *Alli Sup, AmA&B, BiD&SB, BiDSA, DcAmA, DcNAA, OxAm, REnAL*
Cobb, Joyce *ChPo, ChPo S2*
Cobb, Levi Henry 1827- *Alli Sup*
Cobb, Lyman 1800-1864 *Alli, AmA, ChPo S1, DcAmA, DcNAA*
Cobb, M C 1932- *ConAu 29*
Cobb, Mary 1844-1927 *ChPo*
Cobb, Mary McKinley 1839- *BiDSA*
Cobb, Nathan Augustus 1859-1932 *AmLY, DcNAA, WhWNAA*
Cobb, Needham Bryan *BiDSA*
Cobb, Ruth *ChPo S1*
Cobb, Samuel d1713 *Alli, DcEnL*
Cobb, Sanford Hoadley 1838-1910 *DcAmA, DcNAA*
Cobb, Sophia Dickinson *Alli Sup*
Cobb, Stanwood 1881- *AmA&B, Au&Wr, ChPo, WhWNAA*
Cobb, Sylvanus 1799-1866 *Alli Sup, DcAmA,*

DcNAA
Cobb, Sylvanus, Jr. 1823-1887 *Alli, AmA, AmA&B, BiD&SB, CnDAL, DcAmA, DcBiA, DcNAA, EncM&D, HsB&A, HsB&A Sup, OxAm, REnAL*
Cobb, Thomas 1854- *Alli, MnBBF, WhLA*
Cobb, Thomas Read Rootes 1823-1862 *Alli Sup, BiDSA, DcAmA, DcNAA*
Cobb, Vicki 1938- *ChLR 2, ConAu 33, SmATA 8, WrD 1976*
Cobb, Weldon J *HsB&A*
Cobb, Will D 1876-1930 *AmSCAP 66*
Cobb, William Henry 1846-1923 *DcNAA*
Cobban, J Maclaren *Alli Sup*
Cobbe *Alli*
Cobbe, Frances Power 1822-1904 *Alli Sup, BiD&SB, BrAu 19, ChPo S1, Chmbr 3, DcEnL, DcLEnL, EvLB, NewC, OxEng, PoIre*
Cobbe, Lucie *Alli Sup*
Cobbe, Richard *Alli*
Cobbe, Thomas 1814-1882 *Alli Sup*
Cobbet, Thomas 1608-1685 *Alli*
Cobbett *ConAu XR*
Cobbett, Arthur *Alli Sup*
Cobbett, Mrs. E T *Alli Sup*
Cobbett, Richard *ConAu XR*
Cobbett, Richard Stuteley 1842-1877 *Alli Sup*
Cobbett, Susan d1889 *Alli Sup*
Cobbett, Thomas 1608-1685 *DcAmA, DcNAA*
Cobbett, Walter Willson 1847- *WhLA*
Cobbett, William 1762-1835 *Alli, AtlBL, BbD, BbtC, BiD&SB, BiDLA, BiDLA Sup, BrAu 19, CarSB, CasWL, Chmbr 2, CnDAL, DcEnA, DcEnL, DcEuL, DcLEnL, EvLB, MouLC 3, NewC, OxAm, OxEng, Pen Eng, REn, WebEAL*
Cobbett, William Pitt *Alli Sup*
Cobbin, Ingram *Alli, DcEnL*
Cobbin, John *BiDLA Sup*
Cobbin, Mary Eliza *Alli Sup*
Cobbing, Bob 1920- *ConP 1970, ConP 1975, WrD 1976*
Cobbleigh, Tom *WhLA*
Cobbold, Dorothy *Alli Sup*
Cobbold, Elizabeth 1767-1824 *Alli, ChPo S1*
Cobbold, George Augustus *Alli Sup*
Cobbold, Mrs. J *BiDLA Sup*
Cobbold, John Spencer *Alli, BiDLA, BiDLA Sup*
Cobbold, Richard 1797-1876? *Alli, DcEnL, DcLEnL, NewC*
Cobbold, Robert Henry *Alli Sup*
Cobbold, Thomas Spencer 1828-1886 *Alli Sup*
Cobbs, Nicholas Hamner 1796-1861 *BiDSA*
Cobbs, Price M 1928- *ConAu 23, LivBA*
Cobden, Edward d1764 *Alli*
Cobden, Halsted Elwin C *Alli Sup*
Cobden, J C *Alli Sup*
Cobden, Paul *Alli Sup*
Cobden, Richard 1804-1865 *Alli, Alli Sup, BiD&SB, BrAu 19, NewC, REn*
Cobden-Sanderson, T J 1840-1922 *ChPo S2, LongC*
Coben, Cy 1919- *AmSCAP 66*
Cober, Alan Edwin 1935- *IlBYP, IlCB 1966, SmATA 7*
Cobey, Louis 1897- *AmSCAP 66*
Cobham, Sir Alan *MnBBF*
Cobham, Sir Alan John 1894- *WhLA*
Cobham, Eleanor *NewC*
Cobham, Henry *ChPo S2*
Coble, Alice Marie Woolling 1914- *IndAu 1917*
Coble, Arthur Byron 1878- *WhWNAA*
Coble, John 1924- *ConAu 9R*
Coblentz, Catherine Cate 1897-1951 *AnMV 1926, ChPo, ChPo S1, JBA 1951*
Coblentz, David H *ChPo S2*
Coblentz, Edmond David 1882-1959 *AmA&B*
Coblentz, Stanton Arthur 1896- *AmA&B, AnMV 1926, Au&Wr, ChPo, ChPo S1, ChPo S2, ConAu 5R, REnAL, WhWNAA, WrD 1976*
Coblentz, Virgil 1862-1932 *DcAmA, DcNAA, WhWNAA*
Coblentz, William Weber 1873-1962 *AmA&B*
Cobley, Frederick *Alli Sup*
Cobley, John 1914- *ConAu 13R*

Cobrin, Harry Aaron 1902- *ConAu 29*
Coburn, Andrew 1932- *ConAu 53*
Coburn, F D *Alli Sup*
Coburn, Mrs. Fordyce *AmA&B, WhWNAA*
Coburn, Foster Dwight 1846-1924 *DcNAA*
Coburn, Frank Warren 1853-1923 *DcNAA*
Coburn, Frederick Simpson 1871- *ChPo, ChPo S1, ChPo S2, IlCB 1945*
Coburn, John *Alli Sup*
Coburn, John 1825-1908 *IndAu 1816*
Coburn, John Bowen 1914- *AmA&B, ConAu 1R*
Coburn, Kathleen 1905- *Au&Wr, OxCan*
Coburn, Oliver 1917- *Au&Wr*
Coburn, Richard 1886-1952 *AmSCAP 66*
Coburn, Stephen 1817-1882 *DcAmA*
Coburn, Walt 1889- *ArizL, ConAu P-1*
Coburn, Walter John 1889- *WhPNW*
Cocagnac, Augustin Maurice Jean 1924- *ConAu 25, SmATA 7*
Coccai, Merlin *OxEng*
Coccinus *CasWL*
Coccio, Marcantonio *CasWL*
Coccioli, Carlo 1920- *Au&Wr, ConAu 13R, EncWL, ModRL, REn, TwCW*
Coccola, Felix Raymond De *OxCan*
Coch-Y-Bonddhu *ConAu XR*
Cochard, Thomas S 1893- *ConAu 57*
Cochel, W A 1877- *WhWNAA*
Cochem, Martin Von 1633-1712 *DcEuL*
Cochet, Gabriel 1888-1973 *ConAu 45*
Cochin, Louis *OxCan*
Cochlaus, Johann 1479-1552 *OxGer*
Cochran, A W 1792-1849 *BbtC*
Cochran, B F *ChPo*
Cochran, Bert 1917- *ConAu 45*
Cochran, Charles L 1940- *ConAu 57*
Cochran, Fitzgerald *Alli Sup*
Cochran, Francis *Alli Sup*
Cochran, Hamilton 1898- *AmA&B, AmNov, Au&Wr, ConAu 1R, WrD 1976*
Cochran, Jacqueline *AmA&B*
Cochran, James C *BbtC*
Cochran, Jean Carter 1876- *AmA&B, WhWNAA*
Cochran, Jeff *ConAu XR*
Cochran, John *Alli Sup*
Cochran, John R 1937- *ConAu 41*
Cochran, John Salisbury 1841-1926 *OhA&B*
Cochran, Joseph Wilson 1867- *WhWNAA*
Cochran, Leslie H 1939- *ConAu 49*
Cochran, Louis 1899- *WhWNAA*
Cochran, Negley Dakin 1863-1941 *OhA&B*
Cochran, Thomas Childs 1902- *AmA&B, ConAu 61*
Cochran, Thomas Everette 1884- *WhWNAA*
Cochran, William *Alli, Alli Sup*
Cochran, William 1745?-1833 *BbtC*
Cochran, William C 1848-1936 *Alli Sup, OhA&B*
Cochrane, A Baillie *ChPo S1*
Cochrane, Alex Baillie *Alli*
Cochrane, Alexander D R W Baillie 1816- *DcEnL*
Cochrane, Alfred 1863- *ChPo S1*
Cochrane, Alfred Henry John 1865- *MnBBF, WhLA*
Cochrane, Archibald 1749-1831 *Alli*
Cochrane, Arthur C 1909- *ConAu 5R*
Cochrane, Basil *Alli, BiDLA*
Cochrane, Charles Henry 1856-1940 *DcNAA*
Cochrane, Charles Norris 1889-1945 *CanWr, DcNAA*
Cochrane, Charles Stuart *Alli*
Cochrane, Clark B 1843- *ChPo S1, ChPo S2*
Cochrane, Cyril 1902- *Au&Wr*
Cochrane, Elizabeth 1867-1922 *AmA, DcNAA, OxAm*
Cochrane, Eric 1928- *ConAu 49*
Cochrane, George *Alli Sup*
Cochrane, Glynn 1940- *ConAu 53*
Cochrane, James *Alli, Alli Sup*
Cochrane, James Athol *BiDLA*
Cochrane, James D 1938- *ConAu 29*
Cochrane, James Inglis *Alli Sup*
Cochrane, James L 1942- *ConAu 33*
Cochrane, John *Alli, Alli Sup, BiDLA*
Cochrane, John Dundas 1780-1825 *Alli*

Cochrane, John Henry *PoIre*
Cochrane, Louise Morley 1918- *ConAu 9R*
Cochrane, Mary *Alli Sup*
Cochrane, Robert *Alli Sup*
Cochrane, Robert 1854-1888 *ChPo*
Cochrane, Thomas *Alli, Alli Sup, BiDLA Sup, BrAu 19*
Cochrane, Lord Thomas *Alli*
Cochrane, Thomas, Earl Of Dundonald 1775-1860 *Alli Sup*
Cochrane, Thomas B, Earl Of Dundonald d1885 *Alli Sup*
Cochrane, Willard Wesley 1914- *AmA&B, ConAu 23*
Cochrane, William *OxCan*
Cochrane, William 1831-1898 *DcNAA*
Cochrane DeAlencar, Gertrude E Luise 1906- *Au&Wr, ConAu 5R*
Cochrane-Patrick *Alli Sup*
Cochrell, Boyd 1920- *Au&Wr*
Cochut, P A *Alli Sup*
Cock, Charles G *Alli*
Cock, David *Alli Sup*
Cock, Frederick William 1858- *WhLA*
Cock, John *Alli*
Cock, M R *Alli*
Cock, Oliver Jestie 1912- *Au&Wr, WrD 1976*
Cock, S *Alli, BiDLA*
Cock, Samuel *Alli*
Cock, Stanley *ChPo*
Cock, Thomas *Alli*
Cock, Thomas F *Alli Sup*
Cock, William *Alli*
Cockain, Sir Aston *DcEnL*
Cockaine, Sir Thomas 1519-1592 *Br&AmS*
Cockayne, Andreas Edward *Alli Sup*
Cockayne, George *Alli*
Cockayne, J *Alli*
Cockayne, M S *Alli Sup*
Cockayne, O *Alli*
Cockayne, Thomas Oswald 1807-1873 *Alli Sup*
Cockburn *BbtC*
Cockburn, Lieutenant-General *BiDLA Sup*
Cockburn, Mrs. d1794 *Chmbr 2, DcEnL*
Cockburn, Sir Alexander James Edmund 1802-1880 *Alli Sup*
Cockburn, Alexander Peter 1837-1905 *DcNAA*
Cockburn, Alicia 1713?-1794 *BrAu, EvLB, NewC, Pen Eng*
Cockburn, Alison 1713?-1794 *BrAu, ChPo, EvLB, Pen Eng*
Cockburn, Archibald *Alli*
Cockburn, Catherine 1679-1749 *Alli, DcEnL, NewC*
Cockburn, Claud 1904- *Au&Wr, WorAu*
Cockburn, George W *Alli Sup*
Cockburn, Henry *Chmbr 3*
Cockburn, Lord Henry Thomas 1779-1854 *Alli, Alli Sup, BrAu 19, CasWL, DcEnL, EvLB, OxEng, Pen Eng*
Cockburn, James *Alli, OxCan*
Cockburn, James Hutchison 1882- *Au&Wr*
Cockburn, James Seton *Alli Sup*
Cockburn, John *Alli*
Cockburn, John d1729 *Alli*
Cockburn, John 1897- *Au&Wr*
Cockburn, Sir John A 1850- *WhLA*
Cockburn, Patrick d1749 *Alli*
Cockburn, Patrick d1559 *Alli*
Cockburn, Robert *Alli, OxCan Sup*
Cockburn, Russell R *OxCan*
Cockburn, S *Alli Sup*
Cockburn, Samuel *Alli Sup*
Cockburn, Thomas *Alli*
Cockburn, Thomas Aiden 1912- *ConAu 9R*
Cockburn, William *Alli, BiDLA*
Cockburn, Sir William *Alli*
Cockcroft, James D 1935- *ConAu 25*
Cockcroft, John 1897-1967 *ConAu 21*
Cocke, Charles George *Alli*
Cocke, Emmanuel *OxCan Sup*
Cocke, J Z *Alli*
Cocke, James Richard 1863-1900 *DcAmA, DcNAA*
Cocke, Julia Zitella 1848?-1929 *ChPo, ChPo S1*
Cocke, Philip St. George 1808?-1861 *BiDSA, DcNAA*

Cocke, Sarah Cobb Johnson 1865- *BiDSA*
Cocke, Thomas *Alli*
Cocke, William Alexander *ChPo S1*
Cocke, William Archer *Alli, Alli Sup*
Cocke, Zitella 1831?-1929 *AmA&B, BiDSA, DcAmA, DcNAA*
Cockell, William *Alli, BiDLA*
Cocker, Benjamin Franklin 1821-1883 *Alli Sup, DcAmA, DcNAA*
Cocker, Edward 1631-1677? *Alli, BrAu, DcEnL, OxEng*
Cocker, John *Alli Sup*
Cocker, W J *Alli Sup*
Cocker, William Dixon *ChPo*
Cocker, William Johnson 1846-1901 *DcAmA, DcNAA*
Cockeram, Henry 1630?- *NewC*
Cockerell, Charles Robert 1788-1863 *Alli, Alli Sup*
Cockerell, Douglas Bennett 1870-1945 *LongC*
Cockerell, Hugh Anthony Lewis 1909- *Au&Wr, ConAu P-1*
Cockerell, Sir Sydney 1867-1962 *LongC*
Cockerell, Sydney Carlyle 1867-1962 *ChPo*
Cockerell, Sydney M *ChPo*
Cockerell, Sydney Morris 1906- *Au&Wr*
Cockerell, Theodore Dru Alison 1866- *WhWNAA*
Cockerham, Henry *Alli*
Cockes, Leonard *Alli*
Cockett, Mary 1915- *Au&Wr, ConAu 9R, SmATA 3*
Cockett, William *Alli Sup*
Cockin, Francis *Alli*
Cockin, Hereward Kirby 1854-1917 *DcNAA*
Cockin, Joseph *Alli, BiDLA Sup*
Cockin, William *Alli*
Cocking, John Martin 1914- *ConAu 53, WrD 1976*
Cocking, Matthew d1799 *OxCan*
Cocking, Walter Tusting 1907- *Au&Wr*
Cockings, George *Alli, BbtC, CyAL 1, OxCan*
Cockiolly Bird, The *ChPo*
Cockle, Mrs. *Alli, BiDLA*
Cockle, John *Alli Sup*
Cockle, Mary *ChPo, ChPo S1*
Cockle, Mrs. Moss *Alli Sup*
Cockloft, Jeremy *OxCan*
Cockman, Thomas *Alli*
Cockohan, Thomas *Alli*
Cockran, John *Alli Sup*
Cockran, William Bourke 1854-1923 *DcNAA*
Cockrell, Daisy Malone *TexWr*
Cockrell, Dura Brokaw 1877- *WhWNAA*
Cockrell, Francis Marion 1834- *BiDSA*
Cockrell, Marian 1909- *AmA&B, AmNov, ConAu 17*
Cockrell, Richard *BiDLA*
Cockrem, Edward *Alli Sup*
Cockrile, Richard *Alli*
Cockrum, William Monroe 1837-1924 *IndAu 1816*
Cocks *Alli*
Cocks, C *Alli*
Cocks, Henry Lawrence Somers 1862- *WhLA*
Cocks, John *Alli*
Cocks, John 1787-1861 *Alli Sup*
Cocks, John Somers *BiDLA*
Cocks, Myra *ConICB*
Cocks, Orrin Giddings 1877- *WhWNAA*
Cocks, Reginald S *BiDSA*
Cocks, Sir Richard *Alli*
Cocks, Sir Robert *Alli*
Cocks, Roger *Alli*
Cocks, Sampson *Alli Sup*
Cocks, W P *Alli*
Cockshut, Anthony Oliver John 1927- *ConAu 17R, WrD 1976*
Cockson, Edward *Alli*
Cockson, Thomas *Alli*
Cockson, W C *Alli Sup*
Cockton, Henry 1807-1853 *Alli, BrAu 19, Chmbr 3, DcBiA, DcEnL, MnBBF, NewC, WhCL*
Cocles, Bartholomew *Alli*
Coconas, Annibal, Comte De d1574 *OxFr*
CoConis, Ted *IlBYP*

Cocozzela, Peter 1937- *ConAu 37*
Cocteau, Jean 1889-1963 *AtlBL, CasWL, ClDMEuL, CnMD, CnMWL, CnThe, ConAu 25, ConLC 1, CyWA, EncWL, EvEuW, LongC, McGWD, ModRL, ModWD, OxEng, OxFr, Pen Eur, REn, REnWD, TwCA, TwCA Sup, TwCW, WhGrA, WhTwL*
Codax, Martin *CasWL*
Codd, Alfred *Alli Sup*
Codd, Edward Thornton *Alli Sup*
Codding, George A, Jr. 1923- *ConAu 33, WrD 1976*
Coddington, Charles E *Alli Sup*
Coddington, D *Alli Sup*
Coddington, Hanna *ChPo*
Coddington, William 1601-1678 *Alli, DcAmA, DcNAA*
Code, Grant Hyde 1896-1974 *ConAu 49*
Code, Henry Brereton d1830 *Alli, BiDLA, PoIre*
Code, John Marsden *Alli Sup*
Code, Joseph Bernard 1899- *CatA 1947, WhWNAA*
Codel, Martin 1903?-1973 *ConAu 41, WhWNAA*
Codemo, Luigia 1828-1898 *BiD&SB*
Coder, Samuel Maxwell 1902- *AmA&B, ConAu 37, WrD 1976*
Codere, Helen *OxCan Sup*
Coderre, Emile 1893- *CanWr, OxCan*
Coderre, J Emery *BbtC*
Codevilla, Angelo 1943- *ConAu 61*
Codian, Michael 1915- *AmSCAP 66*
Codinus *CasWL*
Codjoe, Thomas A 1925?- *AfA 1*
Codling, Bess *BlkAW*
Codman, John 1782-1847 *DcAmA, DcNAA*
Codman, John 1814-1900 *Alli Sup, AmA, AmA&B, BiD&SB, DcAmA, DcNAA*
Codman, John Sturgis 1868- *WhWNAA*
Codner, Elizabeth *PoCh*
Codrescu, Andrei 1946- *ConAu 33, DrAF 1976, DrAP 1975, WrD 1976*
Codrington, Christopher 1668-1710 *Alli*
Codrington, Kenneth DeBurgh 1899- *Au&Wr*
Codrington, Robert 1602-1665 *Alli*
Codrington, Robert Henry *Alli Sup*
Codrington, T *Alli*
Codrington, Thomas *Alli Sup*
Cody, Captain 1846-1917 *LongC*
Cody, Al *ConAu XR*
Cody, Alexander J *BkC 3*
Cody, C S 1923- *ConAu 61*
Cody, Claude Carr *BiDSA*
Cody, D Thane R 1932- *ConAu 57*
Cody, Hiram Alfred 1872-1948 *CanNov, ChPo, DcLEnL, DcNAA, OxCan, WhWNAA*
Cody, James R *WrD 1976*
Cody, John J 1930- *ConAu 29*
Cody, Martin L 1941- *ConAu 53*
Cody, Maxwell Bruce 1890- *WhWNAA*
Cody, S F 1862-1913 *LongC*
Cody, Sherwin 1868-1959 *AmA&B, AmLY, DcAmA, WhWNAA*
Cody, Stone *MnBBF*
Cody, Walt *ConAu XR, WrD 1976*
Cody, William Frederick 1846-1917 *AmA&B, DcNAA, HsB&A, OxAm, REn, REnAL*
Coe, Ada May 1890- *DcSpL*
Coe, Albert Buckner 1888- *WhWNAA*
Coe, Alice Rollit *ChPo*
Coe, Arthur 1897- *Au&Wr*
Coe, Benjamin H *Alli Sup*
Coe, C Norton 1915- *ConAu 1R*
Coe, Charles Clement *Alli Sup*
Coe, Charles Francis 1890-1956 *AmA&B, EncM&D, REnAL*
Coe, Charles H *BiDSA*
Coe, Douglas *AuBYP, ConAu XR, OhA&B, SmATA 1*
Coe, Edna Reilly 1888- *WhWNAA*
Coe, Edward Benton 1842-1914 *DcNAA*
Coe, Ernest Oswald *Alli Sup*
Coe, Fanny E *WhWNAA*
Coe, Francis *ChPo S2*
Coe, George Albert 1862- *BiD&SB, DcAmA, WhWNAA*

Coe, Katherine Hunter 1886-1950 *ChPo S2, IndAu 1917, OhA&B, WhWNAA*
Coe, Lloyd 1899- *IlCB 1956*
Coe, Michael Douglas 1929- *ConAu 1R, WrD 1976*
Coe, Mill L *ChPo*
Coe, Miriam 1902- *WrD 1976*
Coe, Miss R *Alli Sup*
Coe, Ralph T 1929- *ConAu 1R*
Coe, Richard *Alli*
Coe, Richard 1820?-1873 *ChPo, ChPo S1, CyAL 2*
Coe, Richard Livingston 1916- *AmA&B*
Coe, Richard Nelson Caslon 1923- *ConAu 25, WrD 1976*
Coe, Rodney Michael 1933- *ConAu 41*
Coe, Roland *ChPo*
Coe, Mrs. Spencer W *Alli Sup*
Coe, Thomas *Alli*
Coe, Tucker *EncM&D, WrD 1976*
Coe, William *Alli Sup*
Coe, William C 1930- *ConAu 37*
Coe, William C 1966- *WrD 1976*
Coe, William E *Alli Sup*
Coeffeteau, Nicolas 1574-1623 *DcEuL, OxFr*
Coelho, Francisco Adolfo 1847-1921 *EvEuW*
Coelho, George Victor 1918- *ConAu 45*
Coelho, Jose Francisco DeTrindade 1861-1908 *CasWL, ClDMEuL*
Coelho Neto, Henrique Maximiano 1864-1934 *Pen Am*
Coelius Antipater *CasWL*
Coelius Antipater, Lucius 140?BC- *Pen Cl*
Coello, Antonio 1605?-1653? *CasWL, DcEuL, EvEuW*
Coello Y Ochoa, Antonio 1611-1652 *McGWD*
Coelson, Launcelot *Alli*
Coen, John *PoIre*
Coen, Rena Neumann 1925- *ConAu 13R, WrD 1976*
Coenen, Frans 1886-1936 *CasWL*
Coens, Sister Mary Xavier 1918- *ConAu 21*
Coerne, Louis Adolphe 1870-1922 *DcNAA*
Coerr, Eleanor Beatrice 1922- *ConAu 25, SmATA 1, WrD 1976*
Cofer, Charles N 1916- *ConAu 37*
Cofer, M H *Alli Sup*
Coffee, Carrie *TexWr*
Coffeen, Henry Asa 1841-1912 *OhA&B*
Coffeen, Ruth Andrew 1897- *IndAu 1917*
Coffel, Clarence M 1900- *AmSCAP 66*
Coffey, Alan R 1931- *ConAu 33*
Coffey, Charles d1745 *Alli, Chmbr 2, DcEnL, PoIre*
Coffey, Charles Edward *Alli Sup*
Coffey, Dairine 1933- *ChPo S1, ConAu 21*
Coffey, Edward Hope, Jr. 1896-1958 *AmA&B*
Coffey, J I 1916- *ConAu 41*
Coffey, John *BlkAW*
Coffey, John W, Jr. 1925- *ConAu 45*
Coffey, Lorette *ChPo S1*
Coffey, Marilyn *ConAu 45*
Coffey, Walter Castella 1876?-1957 *IndAu 1917, WhWNAA*
Coffin, Addison 1822-1897 *IndAu 1917*
Coffin, Albert Isaiah *Alli Sup*
Coffin, Amary *Alli Sup*
Coffin, Arthur B 1929- *ConAu 29*
Coffin, Berton 1910- *ConAu 9R, IndAu 1917*
Coffin, Charles 1676-1749 *CasWL, Pen Eur, PoCh*
Coffin, Charles Carleton 1823-1896 *Alli Sup, AmA, AmA&B, BbD, BiD&SB, CarSB, DcAmA, DcNAA, OxAm, REnAL*
Coffin, Charles Emmet 1849-1934 *IndAu 1816, WhWNAA*
Coffin, Charles F *Alli Sup*
Coffin, Charles Fisher 1823-1916 *IndAu 1816*
Coffin, Charles Franklin 1856-1935 *IndAu 1816*
Coffin, David R 1918- *ConAu 5R, WrD 1976*
Coffin, Dean 1911- *ConAu 33*
Coffin, Elijah 1798-1862 *IndAu 1917*
Coffin, Elijah 1830-1910 *OhA&B*
Coffin, Frank Barbour 1871- *BlkAW*
Coffin, Frank M 1919- *ConAu 9R*
Coffin, Frederick M 1822- *EarAB, EarAB Sup*
Coffin, Geoffrey *AuBYP, ConAu XR, EncM&D, SmATA 3*

Coffin, George Sturgis 1903- *Au&Wr, ConAu 5R, WrD 1976*
Coffin, Henry Sloane 1877-1954 *AmA&B*
Coffin, Isaac Foster 1787-1861 *DcAmA, DcNAA*
Coffin, J G d1829 *Alli*
Coffin, James H *CyAL 2*
Coffin, James Henry 1806-1873 *Alli Sup, DcAmA, DcNAA*
Coffin, John Huntington Crane 1815-1890 *DcAmA, DcNAA*
Coffin, Joseph 1899- *ConAu 57*
Coffin, Joseph Herschel 1880- *IndAu 1917, WhWNAA*
Coffin, Joshua 1792-1864 *Alli, Alli Sup, DcAmA, DcNAA*
Coffin, Levi 1798-1877 *DcNAA, IndAu 1816, OhA&B*
Coffin, Lewis A, III 1932- *ConAu 61*
Coffin, Nathaniel W *Alli Sup*
Coffin, Patricia 1912-1974 *ConAu 33, ConAu 49*
Coffin, Peter *EncM&D*
Coffin, Pine *Alli, BiDLA*
Coffin, Robert Allen 1801-1878 *Alli Sup, DcAmA, DcNAA*
Coffin, Robert Aston 1819-1885 *Alli Sup*
Coffin, Robert Barry 1826-1886 *Alli Sup, AmA&B, BiD&SB, ChPo, DcAmA, DcEnL, DcNAA*
Coffin, Robert Peter Tristram 1892-1955 *AmA&B, AnMV 1926, ChPo, ChPo S1, ChPo S2, CnDAL, ConAmA, DcLEnL, LongC, OxAm, Pen Am, REn, REnAL, St&VC, TwCA, TwCA Sup, WhWNAA*
Coffin, Robert Stevenson 1797-1857 *Alli, AmA&B, BiD&SB, CyAL 2, DcAmA, DcEnL*
Coffin, Robert Stevenson 1797-1827 *DcNAA*
Coffin, Roland Folger 1826-1888 *Alli Sup, DcAmA, DcNAA*
Coffin, Sarah Taber *ChPo S2*
Coffin, Selden Jennings 1838-1915 *Alli Sup, DcAmA, DcNAA*
Coffin, Tristram 1912- *AmA&B, Au&Wr, ConAu 23, WrD 1976*
Coffin, Tristram Potter 1922- *AmA&B, ConAu 5R, WrD 1976*
Coffin, Victor *OxCan*
Coffin, William F *BbtC, OxCan*
Coffin, William Foster 1808-1878 *DcNAA*
Coffinberry, Andrew 1788-1856 *OhA&B*
Coffinet, Julien 1907- *ConAu 61*
Coffman, Barbara Frances 1907- *ConAu P-1, WrD 1976*
Coffman, Edward M 1929- *ConAu 33, WrD 1976*
Coffman, George Raleigh 1880-1958 *AmA&B*
Coffman, John S 1848-1899 *IndAu 1816*
Coffman, Lotus Delta 1875-1938 *AmA&B, IndAu 1816*
Coffman, Paul B 1900- *ConAu 21*
Coffman, Ramon P 1896- *AmA&B, Au&Wr, ConAu 17, IndAu 1917, SmATA 4*
Coffman, Steven *BlkAW*
Coffman, Virginia 1914- *ConAu 49*
Cogan, E *Alli, BiDLA*
Cogan, G *Alli*
Cogan, Henry *Alli*
Cogan, Thomas *BiDLA*
Cogan, Thomas d1607 *Alli*
Cogan, Thomas d1818 *Alli*
Cogane, Nelson 1902- *AmSCAP 66*
Coger, Leslie Irene 1912- *ConAu 21*
Cogerhall, Henry *Alli*
Coggan, Donald 1909- *Au&Wr, ConAu 17R, WrD 1976*
Coggan, G *BiDLA*
Cogger, Percy *MnBBF*
Coggeshall, C H *Alli Sup*
Coggeshall, George 1784-1861 *Alli, Alli Sup, AmA, AmA&B, DcAmA, DcNAA*
Coggeshall, Lilian *ChPo*
Coggeshall, Lowell Thelwell 1901- *IndAu 1917*
Coggeshall, William Turner 1824-1867 *Alli, Alli Sup, AmA, AmA&B, BiD&SB, DcAmA, DcNAA, OhA&B, OxAm*
Coggeshalle, Ralph d1228? *Alli, DcEnL*

Coggins, Herbert *AuBYP*
Coggins, Jack Banham 1911- *AuBYP, ConAu 5R, MorJA, SmATA 2, WrD 1976*
Coggins, Paschal Heston 1852-1917 *DcNAA*
Coggins, Ross 1927- *ConAu 13R*
Coggshall, William Turner *DcNAA*
Coghill, Anna Louisa 1836-1907 *ChPo*
Coghill, Donald Andrew Taylor *Alli Sup*
Coghill, George Ellet 1872-1941 *DcNAA*
Coghill, James H *BiDSA*
Coghill, James Henry *Alli Sup*
Coghill, Nevill 1899- *ConAu 13R, ConDr, NewC, REn, WrD 1976*
Coghill, Rhoda 1903- *ConP 1970*
Coghlan, Brian 1926- *ConAu 17R*
Coghlan, C L *Alli Sup*
Coghlan, Charles *Alli Sup*
Coghlan, Heber *PoIre*
Coghlan, Herbert *Alli Sup*
Coghlan, John *Alli Sup*
Coghlan, John Cole *Alli Sup*
Coghlan, Lucius *Alli, BiDLA*
Coghlan, R B *Alli*
Coghlan, William Edwin *Alli Sup*
Coghlan, William Mant *Alli Sup*
Cogie, Orgill *ChPo*
Coglan, John *Alli Sup*
Coglan, Thomas *Alli, BiDLA*
Cogley, John 1916- *ConAu 45*
Cogley, Thomas Sydenham 1840- *IndAu 1917*
Cogni, Giulio 1908- *BiDPar*
Cogswell, Charles *BbtC*
Cogswell, Coralie 1930- *ConAu 13R*
Cogswell, Elliott Colby 1814-1887 *Alli Sup, DcNAA*
Cogswell, Frederick Hull 1859-1907 *DcNAA*
Cogswell, Frederick William 1917- *Au&Wr, CanWr, CasWL, ConAu 5R, ConP 1970, ConP 1975, OxCan, OxCan Sup, WrD 1976*
Cogswell, Henry H *BbtC*
Cogswell, James 1720-1807 *Alli*
Cogswell, James A 1922- *ConAu 33*
Cogswell, Jonathan 1782-1864 *DcAmA, DcNAA*
Cogswell, Joseph Green 1786-1871 *Alli, AmA&B, CyAL 2, DcNAA*
Cogswell, Louise Trumbull *ChPo*
Cogswell, Theodora Bates *ChPo*
Cogswell, Theodore R 1918- *ConAu 1R, WrD 1976*
Cogswell, William *Alli*
Cogswell, William 1787-1850 *DcAmA, DcNAA*
Cogswell, William 1810-1847 *BbtC*
Cohan, Avery B 1914- *ConAu 61*
Cohan, George M 1878-1942 *AmA&B, AmSCAP 66, CnMD, LongC, McGWD, ModWD, OxAm, REn, REnAL*
Cohane, Tim 1912- *AmA&B, ConAu 9R*
Cohart, Mary 1911- *ConAu 57*
Cohcran, Martha C 1870- *ChPo*
Cohea, C May 1891- *TexWr*
Cohen, Abraham 1870- *WhWNAA*
Cohen, Albert Kircidel 1918- *ConAu 13R*
Cohen, Alfred J 1861-1928 *AmA&B, BiD&SB, DcAmA, DcNAA*
Cohen, Allan Y 1939- *ConAu 33*
Cohen, Anne Billings 1937- *ConAu 57*
Cohen, Armond E 1909- *OhA&B*
Cohen, Arthur A 1928- *ConAu 1R, DrAF 1976, WrD 1976*
Cohen, Arthur M 1927- *ConAu 33*
Cohen, Av Shalom 1928- *AmSCAP 66*
Cohen, B Bernard 1922- *ConAu 9R*
Cohen, Barbara 1932- *ConAu 53, SmATA 10*
Cohen, Ben 1907- *Au&Wr*
Cohen, Benjamin Victor 1894- *ConAu P-1, IndAu 1917*
Cohen, Bernard *Alli*
Cohen, Bernard Cecil 1926- *AmA&B*
Cohen, Bernard Lande 1902- *ConAu 29, WrD 1976*
Cohen, Bernard P 1930- *ConAu 45*
Cohen, Carl 1931- *ConAu 1R*
Cohen, D S And Sommer, H B *Alli Sup*
Cohen, Daniel 1936- *ConAu 45, SmATA 8*

Cohen, David 1882- *WhLA*
Cohen, David 1927- *AmSCAP 66*
Cohen, David 1930- *Au&Wr*
Cohen, David Steven 1943- *ConAu 53*
Cohen, E Yancy *Alli Sup*
Cohen, Edgar H 1913- *ConAu 29*
Cohen, Edmund D 1943- *ConAu 57*
Cohen, Edward M 1936- *ConAu 23*
Cohen, Elie Aron 1909- *Au&Wr, ConAu 53, WrD 1976*
Cohen, Florence Chanock 1927- *ConAu 5R*
Cohen, Fred 1939- *AmSCAP 66*
Cohen, G M *Alli Sup*
Cohen, Gary G 1934- *ConAu 57*
Cohen, Gerald *DrAF 1976*
Cohen, Gustavus *Alli Sup*
Cohen, Harry I *TexWr*
Cohen, Helen Louise 1882- *AmA&B, WhWNAA*
Cohen, Hennig 1919- *AmA&B, ChPo S2, ConAu 1R*
Cohen, Henry 1863- *BiDSA, TexWr, WhWNAA*
Cohen, Henry 1933- *ConAu 33, WrD 1976*
Cohen, I Bernard 1914- *AmA&B*
Cohen, Ira Sheldon 1924- *ConAu 5R*
Cohen, Israel *WhLA*
Cohen, J I And Lee, J F *Alli Sup*
Cohen, Jacob DaSilva Solis 1838?-1927 *Alli Sup, DcAmA, DcNAA*
Cohen, Jerome Alan 1930- *ConAu 49*
Cohen, Jerome B 1915- *ConAu 9R*
Cohen, Joan Lebold 1932- *ConAu 25, SmATA 4*
Cohen, John 1911- *Au&Wr, ConAu 13R, WrD 1976*
Cohen, John Michael 1903- *Au&Wr, ConAu 5R*
Cohen, Josef 1886- *WhLA*
Cohen, Joseph 1918- *AmSCAP 66*
Cohen, Joseph M 1917- *AmSCAP 66*
Cohen, Jozef 1921- *ConAu 29*
Cohen, Julius 1910- *AmA&B*
Cohen, Julius Berend 1859- *Alli Sup, WhLA*
Cohen, Julius Henry 1873- *WhWNAA*
Cohen, Kalman J 1931- *ConAu 13R*
Cohen, Kathleen Rogers 1933- *ConAu 53*
Cohen, L *Alli, BiDLA*
Cohen, Laurence Jonathan 1923- *Au&Wr, WrD 1976*
Cohen, Leonard 1934- *CanWr, CasWL, ChPo S1, ConAu 21, ConLC 3, ConNov 1972, ConNov 1976, ConP 1970, ConP 1975, OxCan, OxCan Sup, WebEAL, WrD 1976*
Cohen, Lester 1901-1963 *AmA&B, AmNov, WhWNAA*
Cohen, Louis 1876- *WhWNAA*
Cohen, Marshall 1929- *ConAu 45*
Cohen, Marvin 1931- *ConAu 25, DrAF 1976, DrAP 1975*
Cohen, Matt 1942- *ConAu 61, ConNov 1976, OxCan Sup, WrD 1976*
Cohen, Max *Alli Sup*
Cohen, Maxwell 1910- *WrD 1976*
Cohen, Mike *ConAu XR*
Cohen, Morris 1912- *ConAu 17R*
Cohen, Morris L 1927- *ConAu 49*
Cohen, Morris Raphael 1880-1947 *AmA&B, DcLEnL, DcNAA, OxAm, REnAL, TwCA, TwCA Sup*
Cohen, Morton H *ChPo S1*
Cohen, Morton Norton 1921- *Au&Wr, ConAu 1R, WrD 1976*
Cohen, Moses *Alli*
Cohen, Octavus Roy 1891-1959 *AmA&B, EncM&D, OxAm, REn, REnAL, TwCA, TwCA Sup, WhWNAA*
Cohen, Paul Pincus 1896- *WhWNAA*
Cohen, Percy 1891- *Au&Wr, WrD 1976*
Cohen, Peter Zachary 1931- *ConAu 33, SmATA 4, WrD 1976*
Cohen, Robert 1938- *ConAu 29*
Cohen, Robert Carl 1930- *ConAu 57, SmATA 8*
Cohen, Roberta G 1937- *ConAu 49*
Cohen, Ronald 1930- *ConAu 33, OxCan*
Cohen, Rosalyn *ConAu XR*

Cohen, Ruth Louisa 1906- *Au&Wr*
Cohen, S Alan 1933- *ConAu 29*
Cohen, S J *ChPo S1*
Cohen, Sanford 1920- *ConAu 1R*
Cohen, Selma Jeanne 1920- *ConAu 25, WrD 1976*
Cohen, Seymour Jay 1922- *AmA&B, ConAu 25*
Cohen, Sheldon *OxCan Sup*
Cohen, Sheldon 1933- *AmSCAP 66*
Cohen, Sheldon S 1931- *ConAu 25*
Cohen, Sidney 1910- *ConAu 13R*
Cohen, Sol B 1891- *AmSCAP 66*
Cohen, Solomon Solis 1857- *DcAmA*
Cohen, Stanley 1928- *ConAu 29*
Cohen, Stanley I 1928- *WrD 1976*
Cohen, Stephen F 1938- *ConAu 49*
Cohen, Stephen S 1941- *ConAu 33*
Cohen, Susan 1938- *ConAu 53*
Cohen, Victor 1896- *Au&Wr*
Cohen, Warren I 1934- *ConAu 21*
Cohen, Wilbur J 1913- *ConAu 25*
Cohen, William *Alli*
Cohen, William Benjamin 1941- *ConAu 37, WrD 1976*
Cohen, William Howard 1927- *ConAu 17R*
Cohen Of Birkenhead, Lord 1900- *Au&Wr*
Cohn, Adrian A 1922- *ConAu 25*
Cohn, Al 1925- *AmSCAP 66*
Cohn, Albert Mayer *ChPo, ChPo S1*
Cohn, Angelo 1914- *ConAu 5R*
Cohn, Arthur 1910- *AmSCAP 66*
Cohn, David L 1897-1961 *REnAL*
Cohn, David Lewis 1896-1960 *AmA&B*
Cohn, Gregory P 1919- *AmSCAP 66*
Cohn, Haim H 1911- *ConAu 45*
Cohn, Helen Desfosses 1945- *ConAu 41*
Cohn, James 1928- *AmSCAP 66*
Cohn, Jules 1930- *WrD 1976*
Cohn, Jules 1932- *ConAu 33*
Cohn, Maurice *Alli Sup*
Cohn, Morris M 1852-1922 *Alli Sup, IndAu 1816*
Cohn, Nik 1946- *Au&Wr*
Cohn, Norman 1915- *Au&Wr, ConAu 57, WrD 1976*
Cohn, Robert Greer 1921- *ConAu 9R*
Cohn, Rubin 1911- *ConAu 57*
Cohn, Stanley H 1922- *ConAu 29*
Cohn, Stewart 1921- *AmSCAP 66*
Cohn, Victor *MnnWr*
Cohoe, Grey *DrAF 1976, DrAP 1975*
Cohon, Barry *ConAu XR*
Cohon, Baruch J 1926- *ConAu 29*
Cohon, Beryl David *ConAu 1R*
Cohon, Samuel Solomon 1888-1959 *AmA&B, OhA&B*
Coignard, Jerome *OxFr*
Coigne, G *Alli Sup*
Coilzear, Rauf *Alli*
Coimin, Michael 1688-1760 *Pen Eng*
Coit, Charles Wheeler 1861- *WhWNAA*
Coit, Dorothy 1889- *AmA&B*
Coit, Henry Augustus 1830-1895 *DcNAA*
Coit, James Milnor 1845-1922 *Alli Sup, DcAmA, DcNAA*
Coit, Joseph Howland 1831-1906 *DcNAA*
Coit, Margaret Louise 1919?- *AmA&B, Au&Wr, AuBYP, ConAu 1R, OxAm, REnAL, SmATA 2, TwCA Sup*
Coit, Stanton 1857-1944 *DcAmA, OhA&B*
Coit, Thomas Winthrop 1803-1885 *Alli, Alli Sup, DcAmA, DcNAA*
Cojeen, Robert Henry 1920- *ConAu 37, WrD 1976*
Cokain, Sir Aston 1608-1684 *Alli*
Cokaine, Sir Aston 1608-1684 *Alli*
Cokaine, Sir Thomas *Alli*
Cokayne, Sir Aston 1608-1684 *CasWL, DcEnL, NewC*
Cokayne, George *Alli*
Cokayne, William *Alli*
Coke *Alli*
Coke, Charles Anthony *Alli Sup*
Coke, Desmond 1879-1940? *MnBBF, WhCL, WhLA*
Coke, E T *BbtC*
Coke, Sir Edward 1552?-1634? *Alli, BrAu,*

DcEnL, NewC, OxEng
Coke, Edward Thomas *OxCan*
Coke, Georgius Henricus *Alli*
Coke, Henry *Alli Sup*
Coke, Henry John 1827- *Alli Sup*
Coke, John *Alli*
Coke, John Talbot *Alli Sup*
Coke, Norma Nickell 1891- *TexWr*
Coke, Roger *Alli*
Coke, Thomas *Alli, BiDLA*
Coke, Thomas 1747-1814 *Alli, Alli, DcNAA*
Coke, Thomas W, Earl Of Leicester *Alli*
Coke, Thomas William *BiDLA*
Coke, Van Deren 1921- *ConAu 13R*
Coke, Zachary *Alli*
Coker, A M *Alli Sup*
Coker, C *Alli Sup*
Coker, Elizabeth Boatwright 1909- *ConAu 45*
Coker, Francis William 1878- *WhWNAA*
Coker, Jerry 1932- *ConAu 9R, IndAu 1917*
Coker, John *Alli, BiDLA*
Coker, Matthew *Alli*
Coker, N *Alli*
Coker, Thomas *Alli*
Coker, William Chambers 1872- *WhWNAA*
Coker, Wilson 1928- *AmSCAP 66*
Col, Gontier 1354?-1418 *CasWL*
Cola, P R *Alli Sup*
Colabella, Vincent *IlBYP*
Colaborador, El *PueRA*
Colacci, Mario 1910- *ConAu 5R*
Coladarci, Arthur Paul 1917- *ConAu 5R*
Colakovic, Rodoljub 1900- *Au&Wr*
Colamosca, Frank 1910- *AmSCAP 66*
Colange, Auguste Leon De 1819- *Alli Sup, CyAL 2*
Colanzi, Richard P 1929- *AmSCAP 66*
Colardeau, Charles Pierre 1732-1776 *BiD&SB, OxFr*
Colaw, Emerson S 1921- *ConAu 13R*
Colban, Adolphine Marie 1814-1884 *BbD, BiD&SB*
Colbatch *Alli*
Colbatch, John *Alli*
Colbeck, Alfred *Alli Sup, MnBBF*
Colbeck, Charles *Alli Sup*
Colbeck, Joseph, Jr. *Alli, BiDLA*
Colbeck, Maurice 1925- *Au&Wr, ConAu 13R, WrD 1976*
Colberg, Juan Enrique 1917-1964 *PueRA*
Colberg, Marshall Rudolph 1913- *ConAu 1R*
Colbert, Alison *DrAP 1975*
Colbert, Colin John 1924- *WrD 1976*
Colbert, Douglas A 1933- *ConAu 57*
Colbert, E *Alli Sup*
Colbert, Edwin Harris 1905- *ConAu 61, WrD 1976*
Colbert, Jean Baptiste 1619-1683 *OxFr, REn*
Colbert, Junior *Alli*
Colbert, Roman 1921- *ConAu 53*
Colbert, Roy Jefferson 1889- *IndAu 1917*
Colbert, Sybil *Alli Sup*
Colborne, Elizabeth A *ChPo*
Colborne, George *Alli Sup*
Colborne, Sir John 1778-1863 *OxCan*
Colborne, John 1833- *Alli Sup*
Colborne, Philip *Alli Sup*
Colborne, Rhoda E *Alli Sup*
Colborne, Robert *Alli*
Colborne-Veel, Annie *ChPo S1*
Colbourn, H Trevor 1927- *ConAu 33*
Colbran, St. John *Alli Sup*
Colbrath, M T *Alli Sup*
Colbron, Grace Isabel d1948 *AmA&B, WhWNAA*
Colburn, C William 1939- *ConAu 37*
Colburn, Dana Pond 1823-1859 *DcNAA*
Colburn, E *Alli Sup*
Colburn, Frona Eunice Wait 1859-1946 *DcNAA*
Colburn, George 1852- *ChPo S2*
Colburn, George A 1938- *ConAu 41*
Colburn, Jeremiah 1815- *CyAL 2*
Colburn, Warren 1793-1833 *DcAmA, DcNAA*
Colburn, Zerah 1804-1840 *DcNAA*
Colburn, Zerah 1832-1870 *Alli Sup, DcAmA, DcNAA*
Colburne *Alli*
Colby, Anita 1914- *AmA&B*

Colby, Averil 1900- *Au&Wr*
Colby, Benjamin N 1931- *ConAu 61*
Colby, Carroll Burleigh 1904- *AuBYP, ConAu 1R, MorJA, SmATA 3*
Colby, Celestia E *ChPo*
Colby, Charles Carlyle 1885- *WhWNAA*
Colby, Charles Carroll 1827-1907 *DcNAA*
Colby, Charles William 1867-1955 *OxCan*
Colby, Elbridge 1891- *AmA&B, CatA 1947, ConAu P-1, WrD 1976*
Colby, Frank Moore 1865-1925 *AmA&B, DcLEnL, DcNAA, OxAm, REnAL, TwCA, TwCA Sup*
Colby, Frederic Thomas *Alli Sup*
Colby, Frederick Myron 1848- *Alli Sup, DcAmA, DcNAA*
Colby, H G O *Alli*
Colby, Henry Francis 1842-1915 *Alli Sup, OhA&B*
Colby, J Rose 1856- *WhWNAA*
Colby, James Fairbanks 1850-1939 *DcNAA*
Colby, Jean Poindexter 1908?- *ChPo S1, ConAu 1R, WrD 1976*
Colby, John *Alli*
Colby, John 1787-1817 *DcNAA*
Colby, John H *Alli Sup*
Colby, John Stark 1851-1898 *Alli Sup, DcAmA, DcNAA*
Colby, June Rose 1856-1940? *DcNAA, OhA&B*
Colby, M F *BbtC*
Colby, Mary B *Alli Sup*
Colby, Merle Estes 1902- *AmA&B, AmNov*
Colby, Nathalie Sedgwick 1875-1942 *AmA&B, DcNAA, WhWNAA*
Colby, Robert *AmSCAP 66*
Colby, Robert A 1920- *ConAu 53*
Colby, Roy 1910- *ConAu 25*
Colby, Samuel *Alli*
Colby, Thomas *Alli, Alli Sup*
Colby, Vineta 1922- *ConAu 9R*
Colby, William Mudge *Alli*
Colchester, Bishop Of *ChPo S2*
Colchester, Lord *Alli, Alli Sup*
Colchester, Captain *MnBBF*
Colchester, Elizabeth Susan *Alli Sup*
Colclough, George *Alli*
Colcock, Annie T *BiDSA, ChPo*
Colcock, Erroll Hay *AmSCAP 66*
Colcord, Lincoln 1883-1947 *AmA&B, DcNAA, REnAL, WhWNAA*
Colcord, Millie *Alli Sup*
Colcraft, Henry Rowe *BiDSA*
Coldbeck, Mary C *Alli Sup*
Colden, Alexander *Alli, BiDLA*
Colden, Cadwallader 1688-1776 *Alli, AmA, AmA&B, CyAL 1, DcAmA, DcEnL, DcNAA, OxAm, OxCan, REnAL*
Colden, Cadwallader David 1769-1834 *Alli, DcAmA, DcNAA*
Coldham, James Desmond Bowden 1924- *Au&Wr, WrD 1976*
Coldstream, John Phillip *Alli Sup*
Coldwell, Albert Edward 1841-1916 *DcNAA*
Coldwell, Charles Simeon *Alli Sup*
Coldwell, David F C 1923- *ConAu 17R*
Coldwell, M J 1888-1974 *ConAu 53*
Coldwell, Thomas K *Alli Sup*
Coldwell, William Edward *Alli Sup*
Cole *Alli*
Cole, Abdiah *Alli*
Cole, Alan *MnBBF*
Cole, Alan Summerly 1846- *Alli Sup, WhLA*
Cole, Alfred Whaley *Alli Sup*
Cole, Alice Lena *ChPo*
Cole, Alice Vivian *BiDSA*
Cole, Allan *Alli Sup*
Cole, Ann Kilborn *ConAu XR*
Cole, Annie E *ChPo*
Cole, Arthur Charles 1886- *OhA&B, WhWNAA*
Cole, Arthur Raggett *Alli Sup*
Cole, Barry 1936- *Au&Wr, ConAu 25, ConNov 1972, ConNov 1976, ConP 1970, ConP 1975, WrD 1976*
Cole, Benjamin *Alli*
Cole, Caroline A E *Alli Sup*
Cole, Carter Stanard 1862- *ChPo S1*

Cole, Charles *Alli Sup*
Cole, Charles Augustus *Alli Sup*
Cole, Charles Nalson 1722-1804 *Alli*
Cole, Charles Woolsey 1906- *AmA&B*
Cole, Charlotte Druitt *ChPo, ChPo S1, ChPo S2*
Cole, Chester C *Alli Sup*
Cole, Christian *Alli*
Cole, Christopher Charles Harry 1916- *Au&Wr*
Cole, Clifford A 1915- *ConAu 13R*
Cole, Cyrenus 1863-1939 *AmA&B, DcNAA*
Cole, Dandridge MacFarlan 1921- *ConAu 13R*
Cole, Davis *AuBYP, ConAu XR, SmATA 2*
Cole, Donald Barnard 1922- *ConAu 5R*
Cole, Douglas 1934- *ConAu 5R*
Cole, E R 1930- *ConAu 53*
Cole, E W *Alli Sup*
Cole, Edmund Keith 1919- *WrD 1976*
Cole, Edna Lind *TexWr*
Cole, Edna Ritzenhaler *ArizL*
Cole, Edward C 1904- *ConAu 13R*
Cole, Edward Maule *Alli Sup*
Cole, Edward S *Alli Sup*
Cole, Edward William 1832-1918 *DcLEnL*
Cole, Elizabeth *ChPo*
Cole, Elsie *ChPo S1*
Cole, Eugene R 1930- *WrD 1976*
Cole, Fay-Cooper 1881-1961 *AmA&B, AmLY*
Cole, Francis *Alli*
Cole, Francis Edward Baston 1813-1878 *Alli Sup*
Cole, Francis Joseph 1872- *WhLA*
Cole, Francis Sewell *Alli Sup*
Cole, Franklin 1909- *AmSCAP 66*
Cole, Frederick Wing 1815-1845 *ChPo*
Cole, G Fitzroy *Alli Sup*
Cole, G Henry *Alli Sup*
Cole, George *Alli Sup*
Cole, George Douglas Howard 1889-1958 *ChPo, ChPo S2, DcLEnL, EncM&D, EvLB, LongC, NewC, TwCA, TwCA Sup, WhLA*
Cole, George R Fitz-Roy *Alli Sup*
Cole, George Watson 1850-1939 *DcNAA, WhWNAA*
Cole, Glenn Gates 1867- *WhWNAA*
Cole, Harry Ellsworth 1861-1928 *IndAu 1917, WhWNAA*
Cole, Helen Rosemary *TexWr*
Cole, Helen Wieand *ChPo*
Cole, Henry *Alli, Alli Sup*
Cole, Henry d1579 *Alli*
Cole, Sir Henry 1808-1882 *Alli Sup, BrAu 19, ChPo, ChPo S1, DcEnL*
Cole, Henry Hardy *Alli Sup*
Cole, Henry Warwick *Alli Sup*
Cole, Mrs. Henry Warwick *Alli Sup*
Cole, Howard C 1934- *ConAu 49*
Cole, Howard Norman 1911- *Au&Wr*
Cole, Hubert 1908- *Au&Wr, ConAu 5R*
Cole, Hylda C *ChPo*
Cole, Isaac John Cowden- *Alli Sup*
Cole, J Augustus *Alli Sup*
Cole, J E *Alli Sup*
Cole, J J *Alli Sup*
Cole, J R *Alli Sup*
Cole, Jack *ConAu XR*
Cole, Jackson 1901- *ConAu XR, MnBBF*
Cole, James E *Alli Sup*
Cole, James L d1823 *Alli*
Cole, Janet *ConAu XR*
Cole, John *Alli, Alli Sup, BiDLA*
Cole, John Alfred 1905- *ConAu P-1, WrD 1976*
Cole, John Peter 1928- *Au&Wr, ConAu 5R*
Cole, John Webb *Alli*
Cole, John William 1830?- *Alli Sup, NewC, PoIre*
Cole, Jonathan R 1942- *ConAu 53*
Cole, Josiah *Alli*
Cole, Miss L M *Alli Sup*
Cole, Larry 1936- *ConAu 45*
Cole, Lois Dwight 1902- *AmA&B, AuBYP, ConAu 1R, SmATA 10*
Cole, Luella 1893- *ConAu P-1*
Cole, M And Adeline *PoIre*
Cole, M D *ChPo*
Cole, M I 1893- *EncM&D*

Cole, Mabel Cook *AmA&B, WhWNAA*
Cole, Margaret Alice *ConAu 9R*
Cole, Margaret Isabel 1893- *Au&Wr,
    ConAu 5R, DcLEnL, LongC, NewC,
    TwCA, TwCA Sup, WhLA*
Cole, Marian Dairman 1811-1892 *ChPo S2*
Cole, Marion 1901- *Au&Wr*
Cole, Mary *Alli*
Cole, Mary 1853- *WhWNAA*
Cole, Maude E *TexWr, WhWNAA*
Cole, Merl Burke d1959 *OhA&B*
Cole, Michelle 1940- *ConAu 29*
Cole, Monica M 1922- *ConAu 1R*
Cole, Nat King 1919-1965 *AmSCAP 66*
Cole, Nathaniel *Alli, Alli Sup*
Cole, Nina *Alli Sup*
Cole, Owen Blayney 1808-1886 *PoIre*
Cole, Patience Bevier 1883- *WhWNAA*
Cole, Percival Richard 1879- *WhLA*
Cole, Ralph Dayton 1873-1932 *OhA&B*
Cole, Rex Vicat *ChPo S2*
Cole, Richard Henry 1851- *Alli Sup*
Cole, Richard John *Alli Sup*
Cole, Robert *Alli, Alli Sup*
Cole, Robert 1868-1911 *BlkAW*
Cole, Robert Andrew *Alli Sup*
Cole, Robert Eden George *Alli Sup*
Cole, Robert H 1918- *ConAu 33*
Cole, Robert L 1915- *AmSCAP 66*
Cole, Robert Wellesley 1907- *AfA 1*
Cole, Roger L 1933- *ConAu 25*
Cole, Rose Owen *Alli Sup*
Cole, Samuel Valentine 1851-1925 *AmLY,
    ChPo, ChPo S1, ChPo S2, DcNAA*
Cole, Sheila R 1939- *ConAu 53, WrD 1976*
Cole, Sonia 1918- *Au&Wr*
Cole, Stephen *ConAu XR*
Cole, Stephen 1941- *ConAu 29*
Cole, T *Alli*
Cole, Theodore Lee 1852- *WhWNAA*
Cole, Thomas *Alli, Alli Sup*
Cole, Thomas d1697 *Alli*
Cole, Thomas 1801-1847? *Alli, AmA&B,
    CyAL 2, OxAm*
Cole, Thomas 1933- *ConAu 33*
Cole, Timothy 1852- *WhWNAA*
Cole, Ulric 1905- *AmSCAP 66*
Cole, W H *Alli Sup*
Cole, Walter 1891- *IlCB 1945*
Cole, Wayne S 1922- *ConAu 23, WrD 1976*
Cole, Wendell 1914- *ConAu 23, WrD 1976*
Cole, William *Alli, Alli Sup, BkP,
    DrAP 1975*
Cole, William 1628-1662 *Alli*
Cole, William 1714-1782 *Alli*
Cole, William 1919- *AuBYP, ChPo, ChPo S1,
    ChPo S2, ConAu 9R, SmATA 9,
    WrD 1976*
Cole, William Earle 1904- *AmA&B,
    ConAu 17R*
Cole, William Graham 1917- *ConAu 17R*
Cole, William Morse 1866- *AmLY, DcAmA,
    WhWNAA*
Cole, William Robert *Alli Sup*
Colean, Miles Lanier 1898- *AmA&B,
    ConAu 21*
Colebatch, Sir Hal 1872- *WhLA*
Colebrook, Sir George *Alli*
Colebrook, Josiah *Alli*
Colebrooke, Henrietta *Alli, BiDLA*
Colebrooke, Henry Thomas 1765?-1837 *Alli,
    BiDLA*
Colebrooke, Robert *Alli*
Colebrooke, Sir Thomas Edward 1813- *Alli Sup*
Colebrooke, William *Alli Sup*
Coleburt, James Russell 1920- *Au&Wr,
    ConAu 13R, WrD 1976*
Coleeber *Alli*
Colegate, Isabel 1931- *ConAu 17R*
Colegrove, Chauncey Peter 1855- *WhWNAA*
Colegrove, Kenneth Wallace 1886-1975
    *AmA&B, ConAu 5R, ConAu 53,
    WhWNAA*
Colegrove, W *Alli Sup*
Coleire, Richard *Alli*
Coleman *Alli*
Coleman, Miss *Alli Sup*
Coleman, Albert Evander 1847- *WhWNAA*

Coleman, Alfred *Alli Sup*
Coleman, Algernon 1876-1939 *DcNAA,
    WhWNAA*
Coleman, Almand R 1905- *ConAu 29*
Coleman, Anita Scott *BlkAW, ChPo S1*
Coleman, Ann Mary *Alli Sup*
Coleman, Arthur *DrAF 1976*
Coleman, Arthur 1903- *TexWr*
Coleman, Arthur Philemon 1852-1939 *DcNAA,
    OxCan, WhWNAA*
Coleman, Mrs. Augustus T *OhA&B*
Coleman, Benjamin *Alli, Alli Sup*
Coleman, Bernard D 1919- *ConAu 25*
Coleman, Bruce P 1931- *ConAu 37*
Coleman, Carolyn *BlkAW*
Coleman, Caryl 1847-1928 *DcNAA*
Coleman, Mrs. Chapman *LivFWS*
Coleman, Charles *Alli, BiDLA*
Coleman, Charles John Darent Blake 1928-
    Au&Wr
Coleman, Charles Washington 1862- *BiDSA,
    ChPo*
Coleman, Christopher Bush 1875-1944 *AmA&B,
    DcNAA, IndAu 1816, WhWNAA*
Coleman, Clayton W 1901- *ConAu 29*
Coleman, Cy 1929- *AmSCAP 66*
Coleman, Cynthia Beverley Tucker 1832-
    BiDSA
Coleman, D C 1920- *ConAu 13R*
Coleman, E W *Alli Sup*
Coleman, Edmund T *Alli Sup*
Coleman, Edward *Alli, Alli Sup, BiDLA*
Coleman, Edward Davidson 1891-1939 *AmA&B,
    DcNAA*
Coleman, Elliott 1906- *ConAu 17R,
    ConP 1970, ConP 1975, WrD 1976*
Coleman, Emma Lewis *OxCan*
Coleman, Emmet G *ChPo S2*
Coleman, Ethel *BlkAW*
Coleman, Evans 1874- *ArizL*
Coleman, Evelyn Scherabon 1932- *ConAu 23*
Coleman, Francis 1913- *Au&Wr*
Coleman, Frank 1876- *WhLA*
Coleman, George W 1867- *WhWNAA*
Coleman, H *Alli Sup*
Coleman, Helena Jane 1860-1953 *DcLEnL*
Coleman, Henry *WhLA*
Coleman, Horace Wendell, Jr. 1943- *BlkAW,
    DrAP 1975*
Coleman, J *Alli Sup*
Coleman, J N *Alli*
Coleman, J Winston, Jr. 1898- *ConAu 49,
    WhWNAA*
Coleman, James *Alli Sup*
Coleman, James Andrew 1921- *Au&Wr,
    ConAu 5R, WrD 1976*
Coleman, James Covington 1914- *ConAu 1R*
Coleman, James Freeman *Alli Sup*
Coleman, James H *Alli Sup*
Coleman, James Melville 1859- *WhWNAA*
Coleman, James Nelson *BlkAW*
Coleman, James Samuel 1926- *ConAu 13R,
    IndAu 1917*
Coleman, James Smoot 1919- *ConAu 1R*
Coleman, Jamye H *BlkAW*
Coleman, John *Alli Sup*
Coleman, John 1803-1869 *Alli, DcNAA*
Coleman, John Noble 1793-1872 *Alli Sup*
Coleman, John R 1921- *AuNews 1,
    ConAu 1R*
Coleman, John Winston, Jr. 1898- *AmA&B*
Coleman, Kathleen Blake 1864-1915 *DcNAA*
Coleman, Kenneth 1916- *ConAu 23*
Coleman, Larry G 1946- *BlkAW*
Coleman, Laurence Vail 1893- *AmA&B*
Coleman, Leighton 1837-1907 *DcAmA,
    DcNAA*
Coleman, Lizzie Darrow *IndAu 1816*
Coleman, Lonnie William 1920- *AmA&B,
    AmNov*
Coleman, Lucile *ChPo S2*
Coleman, Lyman 1796-1882 *Alli, Alli Sup,
    DcAmA, DcNAA*
Coleman, Miss M *Alli Sup*
Coleman, Marion Moore 1900- *ConAu 17R*
Coleman, Mary Louise Randolph 1890- *OhA&B*
Coleman, Max *TexWr*
Coleman, Merton H 1889- *LivBA*

Coleman, Ornette 1930- *AmSCAP 66*
Coleman, Patrick James 1867- *PoIre*
Coleman, Pauline Hodgkinson *AuBYP*
Coleman, Peter J 1926- *ConAu 5R*
Coleman, Raymond James 1923- *ConAu 49*
Coleman, Raymond W 1901- *WrD 1976*
Coleman, Richard E 1933- *AmSCAP 66*
Coleman, Richard J 1941- *ConAu 41*
Coleman, Richard Patrick 1927- *ConAu 33*
Coleman, Robert E 1928- *ConAu 13R*
Coleman, Robert William Alfred 1916-
    ConAu 9R
Coleman, Roy Bennett 1889- *WhWNAA*
Coleman, Roy V 1885- *AmA&B*
Coleman, Satis N 1878- *WhWNAA*
Coleman, Shalom 1918- *WrD 1976*
Coleman, Terry 1931- *ConAu 13R, WrD 1976*
Coleman, Thaddeus *BiDSA*
Coleman, Thomas *Alli Sup*
Coleman, Thomas 1598-1647 *Alli*
Coleman, Thomas R 1942- *ConAu 57*
Coleman, Victor 1944- *OxCan Sup*
Coleman, W S *ChPo S2*
Coleman, Wanda *BlkAW*
Coleman, William 1766-1829 *Alli Sup,
    AmA&B, DcNAA*
Coleman, William Higgins d1863 *Alli Sup*
Coleman, William M *Alli Sup*
Coleman, William Stephen *Alli Sup*
Coleman, William Thomas *Alli Sup*
Coleman, William V 1932- *ConAu 57*
Coleman-Cooke, John 1914- *Au&Wr*
Coleman-Norton, P R 1898-1971 *ConAu 29*
Colenso, Bishop *Chmbr 3*
Colenso, Frances Ellen 1849-1887 *Alli Sup*
Colenso, John William 1814-1883 *Alli,
    Alli Sup, BiD&SB, BrAu 19, DcEnL,
    DcEuL, EvLB, OxEng, Pen Eng*
Coleny, Thomas *Alli*
Colepepper, J Spencer *Alli, BiDLA*
Colepepyr, Robert *Alli*
Colepresse, S *Alli*
Coler, Bird Sim 1867- *DcAmA*
Coler, Cyphron Seymour 1858-1944 *OhA&B*
Coler, Richard *Alli*
Coler, William N *Alli Sup*
Coleraine, Lord Henry Hare *Alli*
Colerick, Edward Fenwick 1822-1905 *Alli Sup,
    IndAu 1816, OhA&B*
Coleridge, Arthur Duke 1830- *Alli Sup*
Coleridge, Bernard John Seymour 1851-
    Alli Sup
Coleridge, Christabel Rose 1843- *Alli Sup,
    ChPo S1, ChPo S2*
Coleridge, David Hartley 1796-1849 *BrAu 19*
Coleridge, Derwent 1800-1883 *Alli, Alli Sup,
    ChPo, ChPo S1, DcEnL*
Coleridge, Derwent Moultrie 1831- *ChPo*
Coleridge, Edith *Alli Sup, ChPo S1*
Coleridge, Ernest Hartley 1846-1920 *BrAu 19,
    ChPo, Chmbr 3*
Coleridge, Lady Georgina 1916- *Au&Wr*
Coleridge, Gilbert 1859- *WhLA*
Coleridge, Hartley 1796-1849 *Alli, BiD&SB,
    CasWL, ChPo, ChPo S2, Chmbr 3,
    DcEnA, DcEnL, DcEuL, DcLEnL, EvLB,
    NewC, OxEng, Pen Eng*
Coleridge, Henry James 1823- *Alli Sup*
Coleridge, Henry Nelson 1800?-1843 *Alli,
    ChPo S1, DcEnL, NewC*
Coleridge, Herbert 1830-1861 *Alli Sup*
Coleridge, James Duke *Alli*
Coleridge, John *Alli, ConAu XR*
Coleridge, John Duke 1820?-1894 *Alli Sup,
    ChPo*
Coleridge, Sir John Taylor 1790-1876 *Alli,
    Alli Sup, DcEnL*
Coleridge, Mary Elizabeth 1861-1907 *BrAu 19,
    CasWL, ChPo, ChPo S1, Chmbr 3,
    DcLEnL, EvLB, LongC, NewC, OxEng*
Coleridge, Peter *Au&Wr*
Coleridge, Samuel Taylor 1772-1834 *Alli,
    AtlBL, BbD, BiD&SB, BiDLA, BrAu 19,
    CasWL, ChPo, ChPo S1, ChPo S2,
    Chmbr 3, CnE&AP, CriT 2, CyWA,
    DcEnA, DcEnL, DcEuL, DcLEnL, EvLB,
    MouLC 3, NewC, OxEng, Pen Eng,
    RAdv 1, RCom, REn, WebEAL*

Coleridge, Sara 1802-1852 *Alli, BiD&SB,*
BrAu 19, CasWL, ChPo, ChPo S1,
ChPo S2, Chmbr 3, DcEnL, DcLEnL,
EvLB, NewC, OxEng, St&VC
Coleridge, Stephen *WhLA*
Coleridge, Stephen William Buchanan 1854-
Alli Sup, ChPo S1
Coleridge, William Hart 1790-1850 *Alli*
Coles, Abraham 1813-1891 *Alli Sup, AmA&B,*
BiD&SB, ChPo S2, DcAmA, DcNAA
Coles, B *PoIre*
Coles, Charles Barwell *Alli Sup*
Coles, Charles Ernest 1876- *WhWNAA*
Coles, Charles Henry *Alli Sup*
Coles, Clara *Alli Sup, LivFWS*
Coles, Cowper Phipps *Alli Sup*
Coles, Cyril Henry 1899-1965 *ConAu P-1,*
EncM&D, LongC, TwCA Sup
Coles, Detective Inspector *MnBBF*
Coles, E Beatrice *Alli Sup*
Coles, Elisha d1688 *Alli*
Coles, Elisha 1640?- *Alli*
Coles, Emilie S *Alli Sup*
Coles, Flournoy, Jr. 1915- *ConAu 57*
Coles, George 1792-1858 *Alli Sup, DcAmA,*
DcNAA
Coles, George H 1810-1875 *OxCan*
Coles, Gilbert *Alli*
Coles, Harry L 1920- *ConAu 9R*
Coles, J M 1930- *Au&Wr*
Coles, James Oakley *Alli Sup*
Coles, John *Alli Sup*
Coles, John Morton 1930- *ConAu 29,*
WrD 1976
Coles, Joseph *Alli*
Coles, Kaines Adlard 1901- *Au&Wr,*
ConAu P-1
Coles, Manning *ConAu XR, EncM&D,*
LongC, TwCA Sup
Coles, Miriam *Alli Sup*
Coles, R *Alli*
Coles, Richard Bertram 1919- *Au&Wr*
Coles, Richard George *Alli Sup*
Coles, Robert 1929- *AmA&B, Au&Wr,*
ConAu 45
Coles, Sydney Frederick Arthur 1896- *Au&Wr,*
ConAu 5R
Coles, Thomas *Alli, BiDLA*
Coles, Vincent Stuckey Stratton *Alli Sup*
Coles, Walter *Alli Sup*
Coles, William *Alli*
Coles, William Allan 1930- *ConAu 33*
Coles, William E, Jr. 1932- *ConAu 61*
Colestock, Henry Thomas 1868- *WhWNAA*
Colesworthy, Daniel Clement 1810-1893
Alli Sup, ChPo, ChPo S1, CyAL 2,
DcAmA, DcNAA
Colet, John 1467?-1519 *Alli, CasWL,*
Chmbr 1, DcEnL, DcEuL, EvLB, NewC,
OxEng
Colet, John Annesley *Alli, BiDLA*
Colet, Louise Revoil 1810?-1876 *BiD&SB,*
OxFr
Coletta, Paolo Enrico 1916- *ConAu 41*
Colette, Sidonie Gabrielle 1873-1954 *AtlBL,*
CasWL, ClDMEuL, CnMWL, CyWA,
EncWL, EvEuW, LongC, ModRL,
OxEng, OxFr, Pen Eur, REn, TwCA,
TwCA Sup, TwCW, WhTwL
Colevenman, John *Alli*
Coley, Frederic C *Alli Sup*
Coley, Henry *Alli*
Coley, James *Alli Sup*
Coley, James Millman 1784- *Alli, BiDLA*
Coley, Rex 1898- *Au&Wr*
Coley, Samuel *Alli Sup*
Coley, William 1755- *Alli, BiDLA*
Colfax, Schuyler 1823-1885 *IndAu 1816*
Colford, William E 1908-1971 *ConAu 5R,*
ConAu 33
Colgan, John d1658 *Alli, DcEnL*
Colgan, William James *PoIre*
Colgrave, Bertram 1888-1968 *ConAu 25*
Colgrove, Chauncey Peter 1855-1936 *DcNAA*
Colgrove, R G P *OxCan Sup*
Colhouer, Thomas Henry 1829- *Alli Sup*
Colhoun, David *PoIre*
Colicchio, Ralph 1896- *AmSCAP 66*

Coligny, Gaspard De 1519-1572 *OxFr, REn*
Colimore, Vincent J 1914- *ConAu 37*
Colin Muset *CasWL, EvEuW, Pen Eur*
Colin, Alfred *Alli Sup*
Colin, Barthelemy Hardy *Alli Sup*
Colin, Galen C 1890- *WhWNAA*
Colin, Jean 1912- *ConAu 57, WhGrA,*
WrD 1976
Colin, John *Alli Sup*
Colin, Muret *DcEuL*
Colin, Paul 1892- *WhGrA*
Colin, Philipp *OxGer*
Colina, Jose DeLa 1934- *DcCLA*
Colina, Tessa Patterson 1915- *ConAu 17R*
Colinne, William *Alli*
Colinon, Maurice 1922- *BiDPar*
Colinski, A J *MnBBF*
Colinson, Robert *Alli*
Colinvaux, Paul 1930- *ConAu 41*
Colish, Marcia Lillian 1937- *ConAu 25,*
WrD 1976
Coll, Aloysius *ChPo, ChPo S2*
Coll Vidal, Antonio 1898- *PueRA*
Coll Y Toste, Cayetano 1850-1930 *PueRA*
Collado Martell, Alfredo 1900-1930 *PueRA*
Collamore, Edna A *ChPo, ChPo S2*
Colland, John *BiDLA, BiDLA Sup*
Collar, William Coe 1833-1916 *DcNAA*
Collard, Derek *IlBYP*
Collard, E A *OxCan*
Collard, Edwin Curwen *Alli Sup*
Collard, Elizabeth *OxCan Sup*
Collard, John *Alli*
Collard, Phyllis *ChPo S1*
Collard, Thomas *Alli*
Collazo, Bobby 1916- *AmSCAP 66*
Colle, Charles 1709-1783 *BiD&SB, OxFr*
Colledge, James Joseph 1908- *Au&Wr*
Colledge, Malcolm Andrew Richard 1939-
ConAu 25, WrD 1976
College, Stephen *Alli*
Collen, Neil *ConAu XR*
Collender, H W *Alli Sup*
Collender, Richard W 1841-1905 *PoIre*
Collens, John *Alli*
Collens, Thomas Wharton 1812-1879 *Alli Sup,*
AmA, AmA&B, BiDSA, DcAmA,
DcNAA
Collenuccio, Pandolfo 1444-1504 *CasWL*
Colleoni, Bartolommeo 1400-1475 *REn*
Coller, Edwin *Alli Sup*
Collerye, Roger De 1470?-1538? *OxFr*
Colles, Abraham *Alli, BiDLA*
Colles, Christopher 1738?-1816 *DcNAA*
Colles, Ramsay 1862-1919 *ChPo*
Colles, Richard *Alli, BiDLA*
Collester, C H *ChPo S1*
Collet, Fanny *Alli Sup*
Collet, Henry *Alli*
Collet, Jakobine Camilla 1813-1895 *BiD&SB*
Collet, John *Alli*
Collet, Joseph *Alli*
Collet, Samuel *Alli*
Collet, Sophia Dobson *Alli Sup*
Collet, Stephen *Alli*
Colletet, Francois 1628-1680? *OxFr*
Colletet, Guillaume 1598-1659 *BiD&SB,*
DcEuL, OxFr, REn
Colleton, John *Alli*
Collett, Beryl Bishop *WhWNAA*
Collett, Camilla 1813-1895 *CasWL, ClDMEuL,*
EuA
Collett, Charles 1826- *Alli Sup*
Collett, Edward *Alli Sup*
Collett, J *Alli*
Collett, J I *Alli Sup*
Collett, Jacobina Camilla 1813-1895 *DcEuL*
Collett, Jacobine Camilla 1813-1895 *EvEuW*
Collett, John *Alli, Alli Sup, BiDLA*
Collett, Mary Stokes Tibbals 1876-1933 *OhA&B*
Collett, William Reynolds *Alli Sup*
Collett-Sandars *Alli Sup*
Collette, Charles Hastings 1816- *Alli Sup*
Collette, William M 1921- *AmSCAP 66*
Colley, James *Alli Sup*
Colley, John *Alli*
Colley, William *Alli Sup*
Colliander, Tito 1904- *Pen Eur*

Collias, Joe G 1928- *ConAu 41*
Colliber, Samuel *Alli*
Collie, Alexander *Alli Sup*
Collie, J Norman *OxCan*
Collie, Michael 1929- *ConAu 49, ConP 1970,*
OxCan Sup
Collie, Ruth *LongC*
Collier, Mrs. *Alli Sup*
Collier, Ada 1843- *Alli Sup, BiD&SB,*
DcAmA, DcNAA
Collier, Arthur 1680-1732 *Alli, DcEnL*
Collier, Basil 1908- *Au&Wr, ConAu 5R*
Collier, Boyd D 1938- *ConAu 57*
Collier, Calhoun C 1916- *ConAu 25*
Collier, Charles *Alli Sup, ChPo S1, PoIre*
Collier, Charles Hale *Alli Sup*
Collier, Christopher 1930- *ConAu 33*
Collier, Coleman *Alli Sup*
Collier, Constance 1880?-1955 *NewC, REn*
Collier, David S 1923- *ConAu 21*
Collier, Douglas *ConAu XR*
Collier, Edmund *AuBYP*
Collier, Eric *OxCan*
Collier, Ethel *AuBYP*
Collier, Eugenia W 1928- *BlkAW, ConAu 49,*
LivBAA, WrD 1976
Collier, Frank Wilbur 1870-1845 *DcNAA*
Collier, Gaylan Jane 1924- *ConAu 37*
Collier, George Frederick *Alli Sup*
Collier, Giles *Alli*
Collier, Graham 1923- *ConAu 17R*
Collier, Graham 1937- *WrD 1976*
Collier, Helen *ChPo*
Collier, Henry Oswald Jackson *Au&Wr*
Collier, Hiram Price 1860-1913 *DcNAA*
Collier, James *Alli Sup*
Collier, James 1870- *WhLA*
Collier, James Lincoln 1928- *ConAu 9R,*
SmATA 8
Collier, Jane *Alli, ConAu XR, WrD 1976*
Collier, Jeremy 1650-1726 *Alli, BiD&SB,*
CasWL, Chmbr 1, DcEnA, DcEnL,
DcEuL, DcLEnL, EvLB, NewC, OxEng,
Pen Eng, REn, WebEAL
Collier, Joel *Alli*
Collier, John *Alli, ModBL*
Collier, John 1730?- *BiDLA*
Collier, John 1850-1934 *Alli Sup, ChPo*
Collier, John 1884-1968 *AmA&B, REnAL*
Collier, John 1901- *ConNov 1972,*
ConNov 1976, DcLEnL, EncM&D,
LongC, NewC, Pen Am, REn, REnAL,
TwCA, TwCA Sup, WrD 1976
Collier, John C *MnBBF*
Collier, John Dyer *Alli, BiDLA*
Collier, John Francis 1829- *Alli Sup*
Collier, John Payne 1789-1883 *Alli, Alli Sup,*
BiD&SB, CasWL, ChPo, ChPo S1,
ChPo S2, DcEnL, DcEuL, DcLEnL,
NewC, OxEng
Collier, John Samuel 1876- *IndAu 1816*
Collier, John T *Alli Sup*
Collier, Joseph Avery 1828-1864 *Alli, Alli Sup,*
DcAmA, DcNAA
Collier, Joshua *Alli, BiDLA*
Collier, Kenneth Gerald 1910- *WrD 1976*
Collier, Sir Laurence 1890- *Au&Wr,*
WrD 1976
Collier, Leonard Dawson 1908- *Au&Wr,*
ConAu 5R
Collier, Margaret *Alli Sup*
Collier, Mary A *Alli Sup*
Collier, Nathaniel *Alli*
Collier, Norman *MnBBF*
Collier, P *OxCan*
Collier, Peter 1835-1896 *Alli Sup, DcAmA,*
DcNAA
Collier, Peter Fenelon 1849-1909 *AmA&B*
Collier, Pope *TexWr*
Collier, Price 1860-1913 *AmA&B, ChPo,*
DcAmA, DcNAA
Collier, R P *Alli*
Collier, Richard 1924- *Au&Wr, ConAu 1R,*
WrD 1976
Collier, Robert, Baron Monkswell 1845-
Alli Sup
Collier, Robert Laird 1837-1890 *Alli Sup,*
BiD&SB, BiDSA, DcAmA, DcNAA

Collier, Sir Robert P, Baron Monkswell 1817-1886 *Alli Sup*
Collier, Simon 1938- *ConAu 23*
Collier, Simone *BlkAW*
Collier, Thomas *Alli*
Collier, Thomas Grey *Alli Sup*
Collier, Thomas Stephens 1842-1893 *AmA&B, ChPo, ChPo S1, DcAmA, DcNAA*
Collier, W d1803 *Alli*
Collier, William *Alli, PoIre*
Collier, William E 1924- *AmSCAP 66*
Collier, William Francis *Alli Sup*
Collier, William Miller 1867- *DcAmA, WhWNAA*
Collier, Zena 1926- *ConAu XR, WrD 1976*
Colligan, Francis J 1908- *ConAu 19*
Collignon, Charles d1785 *Alli*
Collignon, Jean Henri 1918- *ConAu 1R*
Collin, Frank *Alli Sup*
Collin, Hedvig *AuBYP, ConICB, IlCB 1956*
Collin, Heinrich Joseph Von 1771?-1811 *BiD&SB, CasWL, EvEuW, OxGer*
Collin, Marion 1928- *ConAu 9R*
Collin, Matthaus Von 1779-1824 *OxGer*
Collin, Nicholas *Alli*
Collin, Richard M *ChPo S1*
Collin, W E 1893- *CanWr, LongC, OxCan*
Collin-Barbie DuBocage, Louis *McGWD*
Collin D'Harleville, Jean Francois 1755-1806 *BiD&SB, DcEuL, EvEuW, OxFr*
Collinder, Per Arne 1890- *Au&Wr*
Colline *WhLA*
Colling, Elizabeth *Alli Sup*
Colling, James Kellaway *Alli, Alli Sup*
Collinge, John Gregory 1939- *Au&Wr, WrD 1976*
Collinges, Walter Edward *WhLA*
Collinges, John 1623-1690 *Alli*
Collingridge, William Hull *Alli Sup*
Collings, Arthur 1682-1760 *DcEnL*
Collings, Burton L 1880- *ChPo*
Collings, Edwin Geoffrey 1913- *Au&Wr, WrD 1976*
Collings, Ellsworth *AuBYP*
Collings, George *Alli Sup*
Collings, Gilbeart H 1895- *WhWNAA*
Collings, Harry Thomas 1880-1934 *DcNAA, WhWNAA*
Collings, J J *WrD 1976*
Collings, Jesse *Alli Sup*
Collings, Jillie *WrD 1976*
Collings, John *Alli*
Collings, John 1623-1690 *Alli, DcEnL*
Collings, Kenneth Brown 1898- *AmA&B*
Collings, S d1795? *BkIE*
Collingswood, Frederick *WrD 1976*
Collingwood, Charles 1917- *ConAu 29*
Collingwood, Charles Edward Stuart *Alli Sup*
Collingwood, Cuthbert 1826- *Alli Sup*
Collingwood, E W *Alli Sup*
Collingwood, F J W *Alli Sup*
Collingwood, Frances 1895- *Au&Wr*
Collingwood, Francis *Alli*
Collingwood, G L N *Alli*
Collingwood, Harry 1851-1920? *Alli Sup, MnBBF, WhCL*
Collingwood, Herbert Winslow 1857- *Alli Sup, AmLY, WhWNAA*
Collingwood, J Frederick *Alli Sup*
Collingwood, John *Alli*
Collingwood, Robin George 1889-1943 *CasWL, CnMWL, DcLEnL, LongC, OxEng, Pen Eng, REn, TwCA Sup*
Collingwood, Stuart Dodgson 1870- *ChPo, ChPo S1, ChPo S2*
Collingwood, Thomas *Alli*
Collingwood, W *Alli Sup*
Collingwood, William Gershom 1854-1932 *Alli Sup, ChPo, ChPo S1, ChPo S2, LongC, WhLA*
Collins *Alli*
Collins, A Keith *Alli Sup*
Collins, Abner M *Alli Sup*
Collins, Alice Roger *ChPo S1, WhWNAA*
Collins, Angelina Maria Lorraine 1820- *IndAu 1816*
Collins, Ann 1633?- *ChPo, ChPo S1*
Collins, Anna Church 1881- *IndAu 1917*

Collins, Anna Maria *Alli Sup*
Collins, Anne *Alli*
Collins, Anthony 1676-1729 *Alli, Chmbr 2, DcEnL*
Collins, Archie Frederick 1869- *IndAu 1816*
Collins, Arthur 1690?-1760 *Alli, DcLEnL, OxEng*
Collins, Barbara J 1929- *ConAu 57*
Collins, Barry E 1937- *ConAu 13R*
Collins, Bernard John 1909- *Au&Wr*
Collins, C, Jr. *Alli Sup*
Collins, C T *Alli*
Collins, Carvel 1912- *ConAu 17R, WrD 1976*
Collins, Charles *Alli, PoIre*
Collins, Charles 1813-1875 *Alli, BiDSA, DcAmA, DcNAA*
Collins, Charles Allston 1828-1873 *Alli Sup, BrAu 19, DcEnL*
Collins, Charles C 1919- *ConAu 25*
Cullins, Charles H 1832-1904 *Alli Sup, OhA&P*
Collins, Charles James 1820-1864 *Alli Sup*
Collins, Charles Macarthy *Alli Sup*
Collins, Charles Wallace 1879- *AmA&B*
Collins, Charles William 1880-1964 *AmA&B, IndAu 1816*
Collins, Christopher 1936- *ConAu 49*
Collins, Churton 1848-1908 *LongC*
Collins, Clarence B *BiDSA*
Collins, Clella Reeves 1893- *AmA&B*
Collins, Clem Wetzell 1883- *WhWNAA*
Collins, Clifton Wilbraham *Alli Sup*
Collins, Clinton 1863-1940 *OhA&B*
Collins, Colin *MnBBF*
Collins, Cuthbert Dale 1897-1956 *DcLEnL, EvLB*
Collins, D *ConAu XR*
Collins, Dale 1897- *TwCA, TwCA Sup*
Collins, David *PoIre*
Collins, David 1756-1810 *Alli*
Collins, David 1926- *Au&Wr*
Collins, David 1940- *ConAu 29, SmATA 7*
Collins, David A 1931- *ConAu 23*
Collins, David R 1940- *WrD 1976*
Collins, Denis B d1894 *PoIre*
Collins, Digby 1836- *Alli Sup*
Collins, Dorothea 1893-1948 *DcNAA*
Collins, Douglas 1912-1972 *ConAu 33*
Collins, Durward 1937- *BlkAW*
Collins, E *MnBBF*
Collins, Edward James Mortimer 1827-1876 *DcEnA*
Collins, Edward Treacher 1862- *WhLA*
Collins, Edwin R 1876- *WhWNAA*
Collins, Elijah Thomas 1818-1901 *OhA&B*
Collins, Elizabeth *Alli Sup*
Collins, Ernestine L B *ChPo S2*
Collins, F Herbert 1890- *ConAu P-1*
Collins, Fletcher, Jr. 1906- *ConAu 53*
Collins, Frances d1886 *Alli Sup*
Collins, Francis *BiDLA*
Collins, Francis 1801-1834 *BbtC, OxCan*
Collins, Francis Arnold 1873-1957 *AmA&B*
Collins, Francis C *Alli Sup*
Collins, Frank Shipley 1848-1920 *DcNAA*
Collins, Freda 1904- *ConAu XR, WrD 1976*
Collins, Frederica Joan Hale 1904- *ConAu P-1*
Collins, Frederick Lewis 1883-1950 *AmA&B*
Collins, G T *Alli Sup*
Collins, G W *Alli*
Collins, Gary 1934- *ConAu 57*
Collins, Geoffrey Morison 1923- *Au&Wr, WrD 1976*
Collins, George *Alli Sup*
Collins, George Edwin 1867- *Br&AmS*
Collins, George R 1917- *ConAu 1R*
Collins, George Wolseley *Alli Sup*
Collins, Greenville *Alli*
Collins, Harold Poulton *WhLA*
Collins, Harold Reeves 1915- *ConAu 25, WrD 1976*
Collins, Harry C *ConAu XR*
Collins, Harry Jones *BlkAW*
Collins, Helen Johnson 1918- *BlkAW*
Collins, Henrietta *ChPo*
Collins, Henry *Alli Sup, ChPo, PoCh*
Collins, Henry 1917- *ConAu 17R*
Collins, Henry B 1899- *AmA&B*

Collins, Henry Hill 1907-1961 *AuBYP*
Collins, Hercules *Alli*
Collins, Herman L 1865-1940 *AmA&B*
Collins, Hunt *ConAu XR, EncM&D, WorAu, WrD 1976*
Collins, J *Alli*
Collins, J D *ChPo S1*
Collins, J G *Alli Sup*
Collins, J L *Alli Sup*
Collins, Mrs. J S *Alli Sup*
Collins, J T *Alli Sup*
Collins, Jackie *WrD 1976*
Collins, Jacob C *BiDSA*
Collins, James *Alli Sup*
Collins, James 1904-1935 *DcNAA*
Collins, James Daniel 1917- *AmA&B, ConAu 1R*
Collins, James E *Alli Sup*
Collins, James H 1873- *WhWNAA*
Collins, James H 1904-1935 *OhA&B*
Collins, Jeffrey *ConAu XR*
Collins, Jennie *Alli Sup*
Collins, Joan 1921- *Au&Wr*
Collins, Joan Mary 1917- *Au&Wr*
Collins, John *Alli Sup, ChPo, Chmbr 2, PoIre*
Collins, John 1624-1683 *Alli*
Collins, John 1742-1808 *BiD&SB, EvLB, NewC*
Collins, John Churton 1848-1908 *Alli Sup, BrAu 19, CasWL, Chmbr 3, DcLEnL, EvLB, NewC, OxEng*
Collins, John H 1893- *ConAu 1R*
Collins, John M *Alli*
Collins, John M 1921- *ConAu 49*
Collins, John Philip 1870- *WhLA*
Collins, Joseph 1866- *AmA&B*
Collins, Joseph B 1898?-1975 *ConAu 53*
Collins, Joseph Edmund 1855-1892 *Alli Sup, DcNAA, OxCan*
Collins, Joseph Henry 1841- *Alli Sup*
Collins, Joseph Johnson, Jr. 1933- *ChPo S1*
Collins, Joseph Pullen *Alli Sup*
Collins, Joseph Victor 1858- *WhWNAA*
Collins, Joshua *Alli, BiDLA, BiDLA Sup*
Collins, Julius Lloyd 1889- *IndAu 1917*
Collins, June *ConAu XR*
Collins, L John 1905- *ConAu P-1*
Collins, Larry 1929- *AmA&B*
Collins, Laura G 1826- *BiDSA*
Collins, Laura J 1826-1912 *DcNAA*
Collins, Leslie Morgan 1914- *BlkAW*
Collins, Lewis 1797-1870 *Alli Sup, DcNAA*
Collins, Lewis John 1905- *Au&Wr, WrD 1976*
Collins, Lorraine 1931- *ConAu 57*
Collins, Louis 1797-1870 *Alli Sup, BiDSA, DcAmA*
Collins, Mabel *Alli Sup*
Collins, Marie 1935- *ConAu 53*
Collins, Mary 1895- *Au&Wr*
Collins, Mary Catherine Love 1882- *OhA&B*
Collins, Michael 1924- *ConAu XR, EncM&D*
Collins, Michael 1930- *ConAu 53*
Collins, Mortimer 1827-1876 *Alli Sup, BbD, BiD&SB, BrAu 19, ChPo, ChPo S2, Chmbr 3, DcEnL, EvLB, NewC*
Collins, Myron D 1901- *ConAu P-1*
Collins, Nicholas *Alli*
Collins, Norman Richard 1907- *Au&Wr, DcLEnL, EvLB, LongC, NewC, TwCA Sup, WrD 1976*
Collins, Pauline 1930- *BlkAW*
Collins, Pearl Valorous 1860-1931 *OhA&B*
Collins, Percy *DcNAA*
Collins, Perry McDonough *Alli Sup*
Collins, Peter 1920- *Au&Wr*
Collins, Peter Blumfield 1909- *Au&Wr*
Collins, Philip Arthur William 1923- *Au&Wr, ConAu 5R, WrD 1976*
Collins, R F *Alli Sup*
Collins, R N *Alli*
Collins, Rebecca *Alli Sup*
Collins, Richard *Alli, Alli Sup*
Collins, Robert Oakley 1933- *ConAu 1R, ConAu 9R*
Collins, Rowland Lee 1934- *ConAu 9R*
Collins, Ruth Philpott 1890-1975 *ConAu 1R, ConAu 53*

Colse, Peter *Alli*
Colson *Alli*
Colson, Charles *Alli*
Colson, Elizabeth Florence 1917- *AmA&B, Au&Wr, ConAu 1R, ConAu 53, WrD 1976*
Colson, Ethel Maud *ChPo, WhWNAA*
Colson, Francis Henry 1857- *WhLA*
Colson, Greta 1913- *Au&Wr, ConAu P-1*
Colson, H *Alli Sup*
Colson, Howard P 1910- *ConAu 29*
Colson, John d1760 *Alli*
Colson, John Henry Charles 1918- *Au&Wr, WrD 1976*
Colson, Nathaniel *Alli*
Colson, William *Alli*
Colston, Alexander *Alli Sup*
Colston, Henry *Alli Sup*
Colston, James *Alli Sup*
Colston, Launcelot *Alli*
Colston, Lowell G 1919- *ConAu 53*
Colston, Marianne *Alli*
Colston, R E *Alli Sup*
Colston-Baynes, Dorothy Julia *LongC*
Colt, Clem *ConAu XR, OhA&B*
Colt, Frederick Hoare *Alli Sup*
Colt, Martin *AuBYP, ConAu XR, SmATA 1*
Colt, S S *ChPo, ChPo S1*
Coltellacci, Giulio 1916- *WhGrA*
Colter, Cyrus 1910- *BlkAW, ConNov 1976, LivBAA, WrD 1976*
Colter, Mrs. J J *Alli Sup*
Colter, Shayne *ConAu XR, WrD 1976*
Coltharp, Jeannette Downs *BiDSA*
Coltharp, Lurline H 1913- *ConAu 17R, WrD 1976*
Coltheart, P *Alli*
Colthrop, Sir Henry *Alli*
Colthurst, Miss E *PoIre*
Coltman, Ernest Vivian *ConAu XR*
Coltman, Francis Joseph *Alli Sup*
Coltman, John *Alli Sup*
Coltman, John d1808 *Alli*
Coltman, N *Alli, BiDLA*
Coltman, Paul Curtis 1917- *ConP 1970*
Coltman, Will *ConAu XR*
Colton, Aaron Merrick 1809-1895 *DcNAA*
Colton, Arthur Willis 1868-1943 *AmA&B, AmLY, BiD&SB, ChPo, ChPo S1, DcAmA, DcNAA, WhWNAA*
Colton, Buel Preston 1852-1906 *Alli Sup, DcNAA*
Colton, C *BiDLA*
Colton, C E 1914- *ConAu 5R*
Colton, Caleb C 1780?-1832 *Alli*
Colton, Calvin 1789-1857 *Alli, AmA, AmA&B, CyAL 1, DcAmA, DcNAA*
Colton, Charles Caleb 1780?-1832 *BrAu 19, ChPo, Chmbr 3, DcEnL, EvLB, NewC*
Colton, Charles Henry 1848-1915 *DcNAA*
Colton, Charles J *BiDSA*
Colton, Charles Joseph 1868-1916 *ChPo S1*
Colton, Clarence Eugene 1914- *WrD 1976*
Colton, G Q *Alli Sup*
Colton, Gardner Quincy 1814-1898 *DcNAA*
Colton, George Hooker 1818-1847 *Alli, AmA&B, CyAL 2, DcAmA, DcNAA*
Colton, H E *Alli Sup*
Colton, Harold S 1881- *ConAu 1R*
Colton, Helen 1918- *ConAu 57*
Colton, J O *Alli*
Colton, James *ConAu XR*
Colton, James B, II 1908- *ConAu 37*
Colton, Joel 1918- *ConAu 1R, WrD 1976*
Colton, John 1889-1946 *DcNAA, McGWD, OxAm, REnAL, WhWNAA*
Colton, Julia M *DcAmA*
Colton, Julia Marie 1848- *ChPo*
Colton, Lizzie E *Alli Sup*
Colton, Mary J *ChPo*
Colton, Nea *ChPo*
Colton, Olive A 1873- *OhA&B*
Colton, T G *Alli Sup*
Colton, Thomas *Alli*
Colton, Walter 1797-1851 *Alli, AmA, AmA&B, BiD&SB, ChPo S1, CyAL 2, DcAmA, DcNAA, OxAm, REnAL*

Colum, Mary Gunning 1887?-1957 *CatA 1947, ChPo S1, LongC, NewC, REn, REnAL, TwCA, TwCA Sup*
Colum, Mary M 1887?-1957 *AmA&B, WhWNAA*
Colum, Padraic 1881-1972 *AmA&B, AmSCAP 66, AnCL, AuBYP, BkC 3, CarSB, CasWL, CatA 1947, ChPo, ChPo S1, ChPo S2, CnMD, ConAu 33, ConP 1970, DcLEnL, EncWL, EvLB, FamSYP, JBA 1934, JBA 1951, LongC, McGWD, ModBL, ModBL Sup, ModWD, NewC, Pen Eng, RAdv 1, REn, REnWD, St&VC, TwCA, TwCA Sup, TwCW, WebEAL*
Columba, Saint 521?-597 *CasWL, NewC, OxEng, Pen Eng, REn*
Columban, Saint 543?-615 *NewC*
Columbanus, Saint 543?-615 *Alli, BiB S, CasWL, DcEnL, NewC, Pen Eng, Pen Eur*
Columbus, Christopher 1451?-1506 *CasWL, DcEuL, EvEuW, NewC, OxAm, REn, REnAL*
Columbus, Samuel Jonae 1642-1679 *CasWL, DcEuL*
Columella, Lucius Junius Moderatus *BiD&SB, CasWL, OxEng, Pen Cl*
Colver, Alice Mary 1892- *AuBYP*
Colver, Alice Ross 1892- *AmA&B, AmNov, WhWNAA*
Colver, Anne 1908- *AmA&B, AuBYP, ConAu 45, OhA&B, SmATA 7*
Colvil, Edward *DcNAA*
Colvil, Samuel *Alli, BiDLA, DcEnL*
Colvile, Charles Frederick *Alli Sup*
Colvile, Charles Robert 1815-1886 *Alli Sup*
Colvile, Frederick Leigh 1819-1886 *Alli Sup*
Colvile, George *Alli*
Colvile, Henry Edward 1852- *Alli Sup*
Colville, John d1607 *Alli*
Colville, Mrs. John *Alli Sup*
Colville, John Rupert 1915- *ConAu 61, WrD 1976*
Colville, Margaret Agnes *Alli Sup*
Colville, Robert 1909- *Br&AmS*
Colville, W J *Alli Sup*
Colville, William *Alli*
Colvin, A *Alli Sup*
Colvin, Brenda 1897- *Au&Wr, WrD 1976*
Colvin, David Leigh 1880-1959 *OhA&B*
Colvin, David Leigh 1880- *WhWNAA*
Colvin, Fred Herbert 1867- *WhWNAA*
Colvin, Helen *Alli Sup*
Colvin, Howard Milton 1886-1956 *IndAu 1917*
Colvin, Howard Montagu 1919- *Au&Wr, ConAu 61*
Colvin, Ian Duncan *ChPo S1*
Colvin, Ian G 1912-1975 *ConAu 19, ConAu 57*
Colvin, James *ConAu XR*
Colvin, Mary Miles 1886-1956 *OhA&B*
Colvin, Sir Sidney 1845-1927 *Alli Sup, BiD&SB, ChPo S2, Chmbr 3, DcLEnL, EvLB, LongC, NewC, OxEng, TwCA, TwCA Sup*
Colvin, Stephen Sheldon 1869-1923 *DcNAA*
Colvin, Verplanck *Alli Sup*
Colvocoresses, George Musalas 1816-1872 *Alli, DcAmA, DcNAA*
Colwall, Daniel *Alli*
Colwell, C Carter 1932- *ConAu 41*
Colwell, Charles 1782-1860 *Alli Sup*
Colwell, Eileen 1904- *ChPo S1, ConAu 29, SmATA 2, WhCL*
Colwell, Ernest Cadman 1901-1974 *AmA&B, ConAu 5R, ConAu 53*
Colwell, John *Alli Sup*
Colwell, Lewis *Alli Sup*
Colwell, Robert 1931- *ConAu 33*
Colwell, Robert Forrest 1908- *Au&Wr*
Colwell, Stephen 1800-1871 *Alli, BiDSA, DcAmA, DcNAA, OhA&B*
Colwil, Alex 1620-1676 *Alli*
Colwin, Laurie 1945?- *ConLC 5*
Colyar, Arthur St. Clair 1818- *BiDSA*
Colyer, Frederick *Alli Sup*
Colyer, Thomas *Alli*
Colynet, Anthony *Alli*

Colyton, Henry John *OhA&B*
Coman, Edwin Truman, Jr. 1903- *ConAu 9R*
Coman, Katharine 1857-1915 *OhA&B*
Coman, Katherine 1857-1915 *DcAmA, DcNAA*
Comanche, El *AmA&B*
Combe, Andrew 1797-1847 *Alli*
Combe, Charles 1743-1817 *Alli, BiDLA*
Combe, Edward *Alli*
Combe, George 1788-1858 *Alli, BiD&SB, BrAu 19, Chmbr 3, DcEnL, EvLB*
Combe, Gordon Desmond 1917- *WrD 1976*
Combe, Marion *WrD 1976*
Combe, Martin And Lisle, Duncan *Alli Sup*
Combe, Taylor 1774-1826 *Alli, BiDLA*
Combe, William 1741-1823 *BiD&SB, BrAu 19, CasWL, ChPo, ChPo S2, Chmbr 2, DcLEnL, EvLB, NewC, OxEng, WebEAL*
Comben, John 1908- *Au&Wr*
Comber, Elizabeth *WorAu*
Comber, Lillian 1916- *Au&Wr, ConAu 9R*
Comber, Thomas *Alli*
Comber, Thomas d1778 *Alli*
Comber, Thomas 1644-1699 *Alli, DcEnL*
Comber, Thomas 1765- *BiDLA*
Comber, W T *Alli, BiDLA*
Comberbach, Roger *Alli*
Comberback, Silas Tomkyn *NewC*
Combermere, Viscountess *Alli Sup*
Combes, A *Alli*
Combes, Andre 1899- *CatA 1952*
Combes, Henry And Hines, Edwin *Alli Sup*
Combes, Luke M *Alli Sup*
Combrune, Michael *Alli*
Combs, A W 1912- *ConAu 17R*
Combs, Mrs. Fairfax *AmNov XR*
Combs, Josiah Henry 1886- *AmLY*
Combs, Richard Earl 1934- *ConAu 33*
Combs, Robert *ConAu XR*
Combs, Tram 1924- *ConAu 13R, DrAP 1975, Pen Am*
Combs, William Hobart 1896- *IndAu 1917*
Comden, Betty 1919- *AmA&B, AmSCAP 66, ConAu 49, ConDr*
Comeau, Arthur M 1938- *ConAu 61*
Comeau, Napoleon-Alexandre *OxCan*
Comeau, Robert *OxCan Sup*
Comeford, R E *Alli*
Comegys, Benjamin Bartis 1819-1901 *Alli Sup, BiD&SB, DcAmA, DcNAA*
Comegys, Charles George 1865-1943 *OhA&B*
Comegys, Cornelius George 1816-1896 *Alli, Alli Sup, OhA&B*
Comegys, Margaret Lewis *ChPo*
Comella, Lucian Francisco 1751-1812 *DcEuL*
Comella Y Villamitjana, Luciano F 1751-1812 *CasWL*
Comenius, Johann Amos 1592-1670? *BbD, BiD&SB, CarSB, CasWL, ChPo, ChPo S1, DcEuL, EuA, EvEuW, Pen Eur, St&VC*
Comer, Cornelia Atwood d1929 *DcNAA*
Comer, James P 1934- *ConAu 61*
Comer, Lee *WrD 1976*
Comerford, Felix *PoIre*
Comerford, Frank 1879- *WhWNAA*
Comerford, Michael *Alli Sup*
Comerford, Richard Esmond d1817 *PoIre*
Comerford, T *Alli*
Comes *DcNAA, WhWNAA*
Comestor, Petrus *OxEng*
Comey, Arthur Colman 1886- *WhWNAA*
Comey, Arthur M 1861- *WhWNAA*
Comfort, Alexander 1920- *Au&Wr, ConAu 1R, ConNov 1972, ConNov 1976, ConP 1970, ConP 1975, EncWL, EvLB, LongC, ModBL, Pen Eng, TwCA Sup, WrD 1976*
Comfort, Anna 1845-1931 *DcAmA, DcNAA*
Comfort, Barbara 1916- *IlCB 1956*
Comfort, Benjamin Freeman 1863- *WhWNAA*
Comfort, George Fisk 1833-1910 *Alli Sup, DcAmA, DcNAA*
Comfort, Howard 1904- *ConAu 37*
Comfort, Iris Tracy 1917- *ConAu 13R, WrD 1976*
Comfort, J W *Alli*

219

Comfort, Jane Levington 1903- *AuBYP,*
ConAu XR, SmATA 1
Comfort, John *MnBBF*
Comfort, Lucy Randall *Alli Sup*
Comfort, Mildred Houghton 1886- *ConAu 9R,*
MnnWr, SmATA 3
Comfort, Montgomery *ConAu 57*
Comfort, Richard *Alli Sup*
Comfort, Richard A 1933- *ConAu 21*
Comfort, Will Levington 1878-1932 *AmA&B,*
ConAmL, DcNAA, REnAL, TwCA,
TwCA Sup, WhWNAA
Comfort, William Wistar 1874-1955 *AmA&B,*
WhWNAA
Comines, Philippe De 1445?-1511 *BbD,*
BiD&SB, OxEng, REn
Comings, Benjamin Newton 1819-1899 *Alli,*
Alli Sup, DcNAA
Comings, Fowler *Alli, BiDLA*
Comini, Alessandra *WrD 1976*
Comini, Raiberto 1907- *AmSCAP 66*
Comins, Elizabeth Barker *ChPo S1*
Comins, Ethel M 1901- *ConAu 61*
Comins, Lizzie B *Alli Sup*
Comish, Newel Howland 1888- *WhWNAA*
Comisso, Giovanni 1895-1969 *CasWL,*
CIDMEuL, EncWL
Comley, James *Alli Sup*
Comly, John 1774-1850 *Alli, Alli Sup,*
DcAmA, DcNAA
Commager, Henry Steele 1902- *AmA&B,*
AuBYP, ChPo S1, ConAu 21, DcLEnL,
OxAm, Pen Am, REn, REnAL,
TwCA Sup, WrD 1976
Comment, Cuthbert 1705-1774 *DcEnL*
Commines, Philippe De 1445?-1511 *DcEuL,*
EvEuW, OxEng, Pen Eur
Commings, Robert *AmA&B*
Commins, Andrew 1832- *PoIre*
Commins, Dorothy Berliner *AuBYP*
Commins, John *Alli, BiDLA*
Commins, Saxe 1892?-1958 *AmA&B*
Commire, Anne *ChPo S2*
Commire, Jean 1626-1702 *CasWL*
Commodianus *BiD&SB, CasWL*
Commodus, Lucius Aelius Aurelius 161-192 *REn*
Commoner, Barry 1917- *AmA&B*
Commons, John Rogers 1862-1945? *AmLY,*
DcAmA, DcNAA, OhA&B, WhWNAA,
WiscW
Commynes, Philippe De 1445?-1511 *CasWL,*
EuA, Pen Eur
Comnena, Anna 1083-1148 *BiD&SB, EuA,*
NewC, Pen Cl
Comnena And Comnenus *OxEng*
Compagni, Dino 1255?-1324 *CasWL, DcEuL,*
EvEuW, Pen Eur
Comparette, Thomas Louis 1868-1922
IndAu 1816
Comparetti, Alice 1907- *ConAu 37*
Comparetti, Domenico 1835-1927 *CasWL*
Compeon, John *Alli*
Comper, John *Alli Sup*
Compere, Janet *IlBYP*
Compere, Mickie *ConAu XR*
Compiuta Donzella, La *CasWL*
Complo, Sister Jannita Marie 1935- *ConAu 57*
Comport, Brian 1938- *Au&Wr*
Comprone, Joseph J 1943- *ConAu 53*
Compston, H F B 1866- *WhLA*
Compston, J *Alli Sup*
Compton, Alfred Donaldson 1876-1949 *DcNAA*
Compton, Alfred G *Alli Sup*
Compton, Lord Alwyne 1825- *Alli Sup*
Compton, Ann *ConAu XR*
Compton, Arthur Holly 1892-1962 *AmA&B,*
OhA&B, REnAL, WhWNAA
Compton, Berdmore 1820- *Alli Sup*
Compton, Charles *Alli Sup*
Compton, Charles C 1898- *WhWNAA*
Compton, D A *Alli Sup*
Compton, D G 1930- *Au&Wr, ConAu 25*
Compton, David Rinaldo 1872-1926 *IndAu 1917*
Compton, Edward *Alli Sup*
Compton, Edward Montague *NewC*
Compton, Frances Snow *Alli Sup, OxAm*
Compton, Francis Snow *AmA&B, REnAL*
Compton, Guy *ConAu XR*

Compton, H K 1908- *Au&Wr*
Compton, Henry 1632-1713 *Alli*
Compton, Henry 1909- *ConAu 9R, WrD 1976*
Compton, Herbert *Alli Sup*
Compton, Herbert Eastwick *MnBBF*
Compton, James Vincent 1928- *ConAu 29,*
WrD 1976
Compton, Jemima *Alli Sup*
Compton, Joseph 1891-1964 *LongC*
Compton, Karl Taylor 1887-1954 *AmA&B,*
OhA&B
Compton, Margaret *DcNAA*
Compton, Sarah *Alli Sup*
Compton, Theodore *Alli Sup*
Compton, Thomas Armetriding *Alli Sup*
Compton, Virginia 1853-1940 *NewC*
Compton, Lord W *ChPo S1*
Compton, William Cookworthy 1854- *Alli Sup,*
WhLA
Compton, Wilson M 1890- *REnAL*
Compton, Wilson Martindale 1900- *OhA&B*
Compton-Burnett, Ivy 1892?-1969 *CasWL,*
CnMWL, ConAu 1R, ConAu 25,
ConLC 1, ConLC 3, DcLEnL, EncWL,
EvLB, LongC, ModBL, ModBL Sup,
NewC, OxEng, Pen Eng, RAdv 1, REn,
TwCA Sup, TwCW, WebEAL, WhTwL
Compton-Hall, Patrick Richard 1929- *Au&Wr*
Compton-Rickett, Arthur 1869- *WhLA*
Comrade, Robert W *MnBBF*
Comroe, Julius H 1882- *WhWNAA*
Comstock, Amy 1886- *WhWNAA*
Comstock, Andrew 1795-1864 *Alli, DcNAA*
Comstock, Anna Botsford 1854- *WhWNAA*
Comstock, Anthony 1844-1915 *Alli Sup,*
AmA&B, CnDAL, DcNAA, LongC,
OxAm, Pen Am, REnAL
Comstock, Augustus 1837- *HsB&A*
Comstock, Byron H *ChPo S1*
Comstock, Captain *HsB&A*
Comstock, Clarence Elmer 1866- *WhWNAA*
Comstock, Cyrus Ballou 1831-1910 *Alli Sup,*
DcAmA, DcNAA
Comstock, Daniel Webster 1840-1917
IndAu 1816, OhA&B
Comstock, Elizabeth A 1817-1860 *CyAL 2*
Comstock, Enos Benjamin 1879-1945 *ChPo S1,*
DcNAA
Comstock, Eunice E *ChPo*
Comstock, Frank 1922- *AmSCAP 66*
Comstock, Frank Mason 1855- *WhWNAA*
Comstock, Franklin G *Alli*
Comstock, G F *Alli*
Comstock, George Cary 1855-1934 *DcNAA,*
WhWNAA
Comstock, Harriet Theresa 1860- *AmA&B,*
AmLY, DcAmA, WhWNAA
Comstock, Helen 1893- *ConAu 5R*
Comstock, Henry B 1908- *ConAu 33*
Comstock, Howard Warren 1900-1938 *DcNAA*
Comstock, Jane *ChPo S2*
Comstock, John Adams, Jr. 1883- *WhWNAA*
Comstock, John Henry 1849-1931 *Alli Sup,*
DcAmA, DcNAA
Comstock, John Lee 1789-1858 *Alli, DcAmA,*
DcNAA
Comstock, John M *Alli Sup*
Comstock, Joseph E D *CyAL 2*
Comstock, Lucretia *ChPo*
Comstock, Mary Edgar 1897- *AnMV 1926*
Comstock, Sarah d1960 *AmA&B*
Comstock, Theodore Bryant 1849-1915 *Alli Sup,*
DcAmA, DcNAA
Comstock, Warren Ennis 1859- *ChPo,*
ChPo S1
Comstock, William *Alli Sup*
Comstock, William Collins 1924- *AmSCAP 66*
Comte, Auguste 1798-1857 *BbD, BiD&SB,*
CasWL, DcEuL, EuA, EvEuW, OxEng,
OxFr, REn
Comte, The Great *ConAu XR*
Comte De Paris *OxFr*
Comyn, Alice *Alli Sup*
Comyn, Angus *Alli Sup*
Comyn, D *Alli Sup*
Comyn, Emily H *Alli Sup*
Comyn, Henry *Alli Sup*
Comyn, John *ChPo S1*

Comyn, L N *Alli Sup*
Comyn, M *Pen Eng*
Comyn, R B *Alli*
Comyn, Samuel *Alli, BiDLA*
Comyns, Barbara *ConAu XR*
Comyns, Sir John d1740 *Alli, DcEnL*
Comyns, W H *Alli Sup*
Comyns-Carr, Barbara Irene Veronica 1912-
ConAu 5R
Conacher, D J 1918- *ConAu 25*
Conacher, J B 1916- *ConAu 25*
Conaeus, Georgius *Alli*
Conaire Mor 113?BC- *NewC*
Conan, Arthur Robert 1910- *Au&Wr*
Conan, Laure 1845-1924 *CanWr, DcNAA*
Conan Doyle *LongC, REn, TwCA,*
TwCA Sup
Conan Doyle, Adrian Malcolm 1910-1970
ConAu 5R, ConAu 29
Conan Doyle, Sir Arthur 1859-1930 *EncM&D*
Conanchet *OxAm*
Conant, A G *Alli Sup*
Conant, Alban Jasper 1821-1915 *BiDSA,*
DcAmA, DcNAA
Conant, Albert Jasper 1821-1915 *Alli Sup*
Conant, C B *ChPo S1*
Conant, Carlos Everett 1870-1925 *DcNAA*
Conant, Charles Arthur 1861-1915 *AmA&B,*
DcAmA, DcNAA
Conant, Eaton H 1930- *ConAu 53*
Conant, Edward 1829-1903 *DcNAA*
Conant, Frederick Odell *Alli Sup*
Conant, Hannah Chaplin 1809-1865 *CyAL 2*
Conant, Hannah O'Brien 1809-1865 *Alli Sup,*
ChPo, DcAmA, DcNAA
Conant, Helen Peters 1839-1899 *DcAmA,*
DcNAA
Conant, Helen S *ChPo S1*
Conant, Helen Stevens 1839- *Alli Sup*
Conant, Howard 1921- *ConAu 17R*
Conant, Isabel Fiske 1874- *AmA&B, ChPo,*
ChPo S1, WhWNAA
Conant, James Bryant 1893- *AmA&B,*
ConAu 13R, OxAm, REnAL
Conant, John *Alli*
Conant, John 1608-1693 *Alli*
Conant, Kenneth John 1894- *ConAu 1R,*
WrD 1976
Conant, Levi Leonard 1857-1916 *DcAmA,*
DcNAA
Conant, Ralph W 1926- *ConAu 29,*
WrD 1976
Conant, Robert Warren 1852-1930 *DcNAA*
Conant, Samuel Stillman 1831-1885 *Alli Sup,*
ChPo S1, DcAmA
Conant, T J *Alli*
Conant, Thomas 1842-1905 *DcNAA*
Conant, Thomas Jefferson 1802-1891 *Alli Sup,*
AmA&B, BiD&SB, CyAL 2, DcAmA,
DcNAA
Conant, Thomas Oakes *ChPo S1*
Conant, W C *Alli Sup*
Conard, Alfred Fletcher 1911- *ConAu 13R*
Conard, Howard Louis 1853-1925 *OhA&B*
Conard, Jesse *IndAu 1816*
Conard, Joseph W 1911- *ConAu 13R*
Conarroe, Joel 1934- *ConAu 29*
Conaty, Thomas James 1847-1915 *DcNAA*
Conaway, James 1941- *ConAu 33*
Concanen, Alfred *ChPo*
Concanen, Alfred Cottrell *Alli Sup*
Concanen, Edward *Alli Sup*
Concanen, G *Alli*
Concanen, Matthew 1701-1749 *Alli, BiDLA,*
DcEnL, PoIre
Concanen, Matthew, Jr. *Alli, PoIre*
Concannon, Helena 1878- *CatA 1947*
Concanon, George Blake *Alli Sup*
Concanon, Thomas *Alli*
Concha, Joseph L *DrAP 1975*
Conches, William De 1080?-1155? *BiB N*
Conchon, Georges 1925- *Au&Wr*
Concilio, Gennaro Luigi Vincenzo De 1835-1898
Alli Sup, DcAmA, DcNAA
Concini *OxFr*
Concino *OxFr*
Concolorcorvo 1715?-1778? *CasWL, DcSpL*
Conde, Prince Of *BiDLA*

Conde, Bertha *WhWNAA*
Conde, Jesse C 1912- *ConAu 57*
Conde, LeGrand 1621-1686 *OxFr*
Conde, Maria 1893- *WhWNAA*
Condee, Ralph Waterbury 1916- *ConAu 17R*
Condell, Henry d1627 *NewC*
Condell, Samuel *Alli Sup*
Condemine, Odette *OxCan Sup*
Conder, Alfred *Alli Sup*
Conder, Charles *ChPo S2*
Conder, Claude Reignier 1848- *Alli Sup*
Conder, E L *Alli Sup*
Conder, Eustace Rogers *Alli Sup*
Conder, Francis Roubillac *Alli Sup*
Conder, G W *Alli*
Conder, George *Alli Sup*
Conder, George William *Alli Sup*
Conder, James *Alli,* *BiDLA*
Conder, Joan Elizabeth *ChPo*
Conder, John 1714-1781 *Alli*
Conder, Josiah 1789-1855 *Alli,* *ChPo,*
  ChPo S1, *DcEnL,* *PoCh*
Condie, Daniel Francis 1796-1875 *Alli,* *DcAmA*
Condie, David Francis 1796-1875 *Alli Sup,*
  DcNAA
Condie, Ella G *ChPo*
Condillac, Etienne Bonnot DeMably De
  1715?-1780 *BiD&SB,* *CasWL,* *DcEuL,*
  EuA, *EvEuW,* *OxFr,* *Pen Eur,* *REn*
Condit, Blackford 1829-1906? *Alli Sup,*
  DcNAA, *IndAu 1816*
Condit, Carl Wilbur 1914- *ConAu 1R,*
  WrD 1976
Condit, Caroline Eaglesfield *ChPo*
Condit, Charles L *Alli Sup*
Condit, Ebenezer 1837-1913 *DcNAA*
Condit, I M *Alli Sup*
Condit, Jotham Halsey 1823-1909 *DcNAA*
Condit, Kenneth Hamilton 1888- *WhWNAA*
Condliffe, John Bell 1891- *AmA&B,*
  ConAu P-1, *WrD 1976*
Condo, A D *ChPo*
Condo, Samuel Salem *IndAu 1816*
Condom, Eveque De *OxFr*
Condon, Albert Edwin 1905-1973 *AmSCAP 66,*
  IndAu 1917
Condon, Charles T *ChPo*
Condon, Eddie 1905-1973 *ConAu 45*
Condon, Edward O'Meagher *Alli Sup*
Condon, Frank 1882-1940 *DcNAA,* *OhA&B*
Condon, George Edward 1916- *ConAu 45*
Condon, John C 1938- *ConAu 23*
Condon, Kevin 1921- *Au&Wr*
Condon, Lizzie G 1857- *Alli Sup,* *PoIre*
Condon, Michael E *OxCan*
Condon, Richard Thomas 1915- *AmA&B,*
  Au&Wr, *ConAu 1R,* *ConLC 4,* *ConLC 6,*
  ConNov 1972, *ConNov 1976,* *ModAL,*
  ModAL Sup, *Pen Am,* *WorAu,*
  WrD 1976
Condon, Robert 1921?-1972 *ConAu 37*
Condon, Thomas 1822-1907 *DcNAA*
Condon, Thomas 1834?-1864 *PoIre*
Condon, Thomas William *PoIre*
Condor, Gladyn *ConAu XR*
Condorcet, Marie-Jean-Antoine-Nicolas De
  1743-1794 *BbD,* *BiD&SB,* *CasWL,* *DcEuL,*
  EuA, *EvEuW,* *NewC,* *OxEng,* *OxFr,*
  REn
Condray, Bruno *WrD 1976*
Condry, William 1918- *WrD 1976*
Conduit, E W *Alli Sup*
Conduitt, John *Alli*
Condy, Henry Bollmann *Alli Sup*
Condy, Mrs. Nicholas Matthews *Alli Sup*
Cone *Alli*
Cone, Andrew And Johns, Walter R *Alli Sup*
Cone, C Edward *ChPo,* *ChPo S1*
Cone, Carl B 1916- *ConAu 9R,* *WrD 1976*
Cone, Edward Payson 1835-1905 *DcNAA*
Cone, Edward Winfield 1814-1871 *DcNAA*
Cone, George *Alli*
Cone, Helen Gray 1859-1934 *Alli Sup,*
  AmA&B, *AmLY,* *BbD,* *BiD&SB,* *ChPo,*
  ChPo S2, *DcAmA,* *DcNAA,* *WhWNAA*
Cone, James H 1938- *ConAu 33,* *LivBA*
Cone, Joe 1869- *ChPo,* *ChPo S1,* *ChPo S2*
Cone, John Albert 1859- *WhWNAA*

Cone, John F 1926- *ConAu 17R*
Cone, Mary *Alli Sup,* *OhA&B*
Cone, Molly Lamken 1918- *AuBYP,*
  ConAu 1R, *SmATA 1,* *ThBJA,*
  WrD 1976
Cone, Orello 1835-1905 *AmA,* *DcAmA,*
  DcNAA, *OhA&B*
Cone, Spencer Houghton 1785-1855 *DcNAA*
Cone, Spencer Wallace 1819-1888 *DcNAA*
Cone, Stephen Decatur 1840-1908 *OhA&B*
Cone, William F 1919- *ConAu 57*
Conerly, Perian Collier 1926- *ConAu 5R*
Cones, Francis Marion 1836-1917 *IndAu 1816*
Coney, John *Alli*
Coney, Thomas *Alli*
Confalonieri, Giulio 1926- *WhGrA*
Confalonieri E Negri *WhGrA*
Confer, Carl Vincent 1913- *IndAu 1917*
Confer, Robert 1931- *AmSCAP 66*
Confer, Vincent 1913- *ConAu 21*
Conford, Ellen 1942- *ConAu 33,* *SmATA 6,*
  WrD 1976
Confrey, Burton 1898- *AmA&B,* *BkC 1,*
  CatA 1947
Confrey, Edward E 1895- *AmSCAP 66*
Confucius *ConAu 57*
Confucius 551?BC-479BC *BbD,* *BiD&SB,*
  CasWL, *DcOrL 1,* *NewC,* *Pen Cl,*
  RCom, *REn*
Congdon, Carolyn M *ChPo,* *ChPo S1*
Congdon, Charles Taber 1821-1891 *Alli Sup,*
  AmA, *AmA&B,* *BiD&SB,* *ChPo,*
  DcAmA, *DcNAA*
Congdon, Clement Hillman 1868- *WhWNAA*
Congdon, H B *Alli Sup*
Congdon, Herbert Wheaton 1876-1965
  ConAu 5R
Congdon, James A *Alli Sup*
Congdon, James B *Alli Sup*
Congdon, Kirby 1924- *AmA&B,* *ConAu 13R,*
  Pen Am
Congdon, William Grosvenor 1912- *ConAu 17R*
Conger, A B *Alli Sup*
Conger, Arthur Latham 1872-1951 *OhA&B*
Conger, Emily Bronson 1843-1917 *OhA&B*
Conger, George Perrigo 1884-1960 *AmA&B*
Conger, George Perrigo 1884- *WhWNAA*
Conger, John 1921- *ConAu 13R*
Conger, Lesley *ConAu XR*
Conger, Marion 1915- *AuBYP,* *IndAu 1917*
Conger, Mary Josephine 1874- *WhWNAA*
Conger, Sarah Pike 1842- *OhA&B*
Congleton, Lord Henry Brooke Parnell *Alli*
Congrains Martin, Enrique 1932- *DcCLA,*
  Pen Am
Congreve, Charles W *Alli*
Congreve, Dora *Alli Sup*
Congreve, John *Alli Sup*
Congreve, Richard 1818-1899 *Alli Sup,*
  BiD&SB, *BrAu 19,* *DcEnL,* *NewC*
Congreve, Thomas *Alli*
Congreve, Willard J 1921- *ConAu 57*
Congreve, William 1670-1729 *Alli,* *AtlBL,*
  BbD, *BiD&SB,* *BiDLA,* *BrAu,* *CasWL,*
  ChPo S1, *Chmbr 2,* *CnThe,* *CriT 2,*
  CyWA, *DcEnA,* *DcEnA Ap,* *DcEnL,*
  DcEuL, *DcLEnL,* *EvLB,* *McGWD,*
  MouLC 2, *NewC,* *OxEng,* *Pen Eng,*
  RCom, *REn,* *REnWD,* *WebEAL*
Congreve, Sir William 1772-1828 *Alli,*
  BiDLA Sup
Conibear, Kenneth 1907- *CanNov*
Conibear, Kenneth And Frank *OxCan*
Coniers, John *Alli*
Conil, Jean 1917- *Au&Wr,* *ConAu 13R*
Coningesby, Fred *Alli*
Coningham, James *Alli*
Coningham, William *Alli Sup*
Coningsby, Christopher *DcNAA*
Coningsby, George *Alli*
Coningsby, Robert *Alli*
Coningsby, Thomas *Alli*
Coningsby, Thomas, Earl Of *Alli*
Conington, Francis Thirkill 1826-1863 *Alli Sup*
Conington, Henry *Alli Sup*
Conington, John 1825-1869 *Alli Sup,* *BrAu 19,*
  Chmbr 3, *DcEnA,* *DcEnL,* *EvLB,* *NewC*
Conkin, Paul K 1929- *ConAu 33*

Conkle, Ellsworth Prouty 1899- *AmA&B,*
  CnMD, *ModWD,* *OxAm,* *OxCan*
Conklin, Buel *Alli Sup*
Conklin, Carrie *Alli Sup*
Conklin, Coursen Baxter 1884- *WhWNAA*
Conklin, Mrs. E M *ChPo S1*
Conklin, Edmund Smith 1884-1942 *AmA&B,*
  DcNAA
Conklin, Edwin Grant 1863-1952 *OhA&B,*
  WhWNAA
Conklin, Gladys Plemon 1903- *AuBYP,*
  ConAu 1R, *SmATA 2*
Conklin, Groff 1904- *AmA&B,* *ConAu 1R*
Conklin, Jennie Maria Drinkwater 1841-1900
  Alli Sup, *AmA&B,* *DcAmA,* *DcNAA*
Conklin, John E 1943- *ConAu 37,* *WrD 1976*
Conklin, Julia Stout 1854- *IndAu 1816*
Conklin, Mrs. Nathaniel *DcNAA*
Conklin, Viola A 1849- *DcAmA,* *DcNAA*
Conkling, Alfred 1789-1874 *Alli,* *Alli Sup,*
  DcAmA, *DcNAA*
Conkling, Alfred Ronald 1850-1917 *Alli Sup,*
  DcAmA, *DcNAA*
Conkling, C *Alli Sup*
Conkling, Edgar Clark 1921- *IndAu 1917*
Conkling, Fleur *AuBYP*
Conkling, Grace Hazard 1878-1958 *AmA&B,*
  ConAmL, *OxAm,* *REnAL*
Conkling, Grace Walcott 1878-1958 *ChPo,*
  ChPo S1, *ChPo S2,* *TwCA,* *TwCA Sup*
Conkling, Hilda 1910- *AmA&B,* *AnCL,*
  BkCL, *ChPo,* *ConAmL,* *REnAL,* *St&VC,*
  TwCA, *TwCA Sup,* *WhWNAA*
Conkling, Howard *Alli Sup*
Conkling, Margaret Cockburn 1814-1890
  DcNAA
Conkling, Roscoe 1829-1888 *REnAL*
Conkling, Wallace Edmonds 1896- *AmA&B*
Conlay, Iris 1910- *ConAu P-1*
Conley, Cynthia *BlkAW*
Conley, Enid Mary 1917- *Au&Wr*
Conley, Everett Nathaniel 1949- *LivBA*
Conley, John 1912- *ConAu 61*
Conley, John Wesley 1852- *ChPo*
Conley, Larry 1895-1960 *AmSCAP 66*
Conley, Philip Mallory 1887- *AmA&B*
Conley, Robert J 1940- *ConAu 41,*
  DrAP 1975
Conlin, Bernard 1831-1891 *DcNAA*
Conlin, David A 1897- *ConAu 17R*
Conlin, Joseph R 1940- *ConAu 49*
Conlon, Denis J 1932- *ConAu 37*
Conly, Robert L 1918?-1973 *ConAu 41*
Conmee, James 1800?-1890? *PoIre*
Conmee, Robert *PoIre*
Conn, Canary Denise 1949- *ConAu 57*
Conn, Charles Paul 1945- *ConAu 57*
Conn, Charles William 1920- *ConAu 23*
Conn, Chester 1896- *AmSCAP 66*
Conn, Frances G 1925- *ConAu 33*
Conn, Herbert William 1859-1917 *Alli Sup,*
  DcAmA, *DcNAA*
Conn, Irving 1898-1961 *AmSCAP 66*
Conn, Peter J 1942- *ConAu 33*
Conn, Stetson 1908- *ConAu P-1*
Conn, Stewart 1936- *ConDr,* *ConP 1970,*
  ConP 1975, *WrD 1976*
Conn, William *Alli Sup*
Connak, Richard *Alli*
Connally, Tom 1877-1963 *AmA&B*
Connell, Arthur *Alli*
Connell, Arthur Knatchbull *Alli Sup*
Connell, Brian Reginald 1916- *Au&Wr,*
  ConAu 1R, *WrD 1976*
Connell, Charles Denys 1867- *PoIre*
Connell, Charles James *Alli Sup*
Connell, Evan S, Jr. 1924- *AmA&B,* *Au&Wr,*
  ConAu 1R, *ConLC 4,* *ConLC 6,*
  ConNov 1972, *ConNov 1976,* *DrAF 1976,*
  ModAL Sup, *OxAm,* *Pen Am,* *RAdv 1,*
  REnAL, *WhTwL,* *WorAu,* *WrD 1976*
Connell, F Norreys 1874-1948 *EvLB,* *LongC,*
  PoIre
Connell, Francis J 1888-1967 *AmA&B,*
  CatA 1947, *ConAu P-1*
Connell, Helen *TexWr*
Connell, Howard 1912- *AmSCAP 66*
Connell, Sir John *Alli*

Connell, John 1909-1965 *DcLEnL, LongC*
Connell, K H 1917- *ConAu 25*
Connell, Norreys 1874-1948 *REn, TwCA, TwCA Sup*
Connell, Philip *PoIre*
Connell, R *Alli Sup*
Connell, Richard Edward 1893-1949 *Alli, AmA&B, DcNAA, EncM&D, REnAL, TwCA, TwCA Sup, WhWNAA*
Connell, Sarah G *Alli Sup*
Connell, W F 1916- *Au&Wr*
Connellan, Leo *DrAP 1975*
Connellen, Mary *ConP 1970*
Connelley, Celia Logan 1837-1904 *OhA&B*
Connelley, William Elsey 1855-1930 *AmLY, BiDSA, DcAmA, DcNAA, WhWNAA*
Connelly, Celia Logan 1837-1904 *AmA&B, BiD&SB, DcAmA, DcNAA*
Connelly, Emma Mary d1900 *Alli Sup, AmA&B, AmLY, BiDSA, DcAmA, DcNAA*
Connelly, J M *Alli Sup*
Connelly, James H 1840-1903 *DcAmA, DcNAA*
Connelly, Marc 1890- *AmA&B, Chmbr 3, CnDAL, CnMD, CnThe, ConAmA, ConAmL, ConDr, DcLEnL, LongC, McGWD, ModAL, ModWD, OxAm, Pen Am, REn, REnAL, REnWD, WrD 1976*
Connelly, Marcus Cook 1890- *TwCA, TwCA Sup*
Connelly, Merval Hannah 1914- *ConP 1970*
Connelly, Owen 1924- *ConAu 17R*
Connelly, Pierce *Alli Sup*
Connelly, Thomas L 1938- *ConAu 17R*
Connelly, Thomas W 1839-1908 *OhA&B*
Connely, Louisa Fletcher 1878-1957 *IndAu 1917*
Connely, Willard 1888-1967 *AmA&B, ConAu 17*
Conner, Americus Wood 1854-1932 *IndAu 1917*
Conner, B H 1878- *WhWNAA*
Conner, Bonnie 1902- *TexWr*
Conner, Charles H 1864- *BlkAW*
Conner, Charlotte Barnes *REnAL*
Conner, Charlotte Mary Sanford *DcNAA*
Conner, Eliza Archard 1838-1912 *OhA&B*
Conner, Grace Brooks *ChPo*
Conner, Henry *MnBBF*
Conner, Jacob Elon 1861- *OhA&B*
Conner, James Ryan 1839-1930 *OhA&B*
Conner, Levietta Bartlett *Alli Sup*
Conner, Patrick Reardon 1907- *ConAu 5R*
Conner, Paul Willard 1937- *ConAu 17R*
Conner, Philip Syng Physick *Alli Sup*
Conner, Rachel A *ChPo S1*
Conner, Rearden 1907- *Au&Wr, ConAu XR, WrD 1976*
Conner, Reardon 1907- *LongC*
Conner, Sabra 1884- *AmA&B*
Conner, Walter Thomas 1877- *TexWr, WhWNAA*
Conners, Barry 1882-1933 *AmA&B*
Conners, Bernard F 1926- *ConAu 41*
Conners, Kenneth Wray 1909- *ConAu 29, WrD 1976*
Connery, David Pugsley 1895- *WhWNAA*
Connery, John *Alli Sup*
Connery, Robert Howe 1907- *AmA&B, ConAu 41*
Connery, Thomas Bernard Joseph 1838- *BiD&SB, DcAmA*
Connett, Eugene Virginius, III 1891-1969 *Br&AmS, ChPo S1, ConAu P-1, WhWNAA*
Connette, Earle 1910- *ConAu P-1*
Connick, C Milo 1917- *ConAu 1R, WrD 1976*
Conniff, James C G 1920- *BkC 6, ConAu 23*
Conning, John Stuart 1862-1946 *DcNAA*
Connington, J J 1880-1947 *EncM&D, EvLB, LongC, TwCA, TwCA Sup*
Connolly, Alonzo Putnam 1836-1915 *DcNAA*
Connolly, Charles Cashel *Alli Sup, PoIre*
Connolly, Cyril Vernon 1903-1974 *CasWL, CnMWL, ConAu 21, ConAu 53, ConNov 1972, DcLEnL, EncWL, EvLB, LongC, ModBL, NewC, OxEng, Pen Eng,*

RAdv 1, REn, TwCA Sup, TwCW, WebEAL
Connolly, Daniel 1836-1890 *Alli Sup, PoIre*
Connolly, Francis X 1909-1965 *AmA&B, CatA 1952, ConAu P-1*
Connolly, James 1829-1892 *Alli Sup, PoIre*
Connolly, James Brendan 1868-1957 *AmA&B, AmLY, BkC 3, CatA 1947, REnAL, TwCA, TwCA Sup*
Connolly, Jerome Patrick 1931- *IlBYP, IlCB 1966, SmATA 8*
Connolly, Louise 1862?-1927 *ChPo, DcNAA*
Connolly, Margaret Elizabeth *ConP 1970*
Connolly, Mary Hardinge *ChPo*
Connolly, Michael William 1853- *BiDSA*
Connolly, Paul *WrD 1976*
Connolly, Ray *WrD 1976*
Connolly, Terence Leo 1888-1961 *AmA&B, BkC 3, CatA 1947*
Connolly, Thomas Edmund 1918- *ConAu 1R*
Connolly, Thomas William J *Alli Sup*
Connolly, Vera L *WhWNAA*
Connolly, Vivian 1925- *ConAu 49*
Connoly, Theodore *Alli Sup*
Connop, Felix *ChPo S1*
Connor, Bernard 1666-1698 *Alli*
Connor, Carl Y *OxCan*
Connor, Eva G *ChPo*
Connor, Florence Griswold *ChPo S1*
Connor, George C *Alli Sup*
Connor, Henry Groves 1852-1924 *BiDSA, DcNAA*
Connor, J W *Alli Sup*
Connor, James Richard 1928- *IndAu 1917*
Connor, John *PoIre*
Connor, John Anthony 1930- *ConAu 13R*
Connor, Joyce Mary 1929- *WrD 1976*
Connor, Kate *Alli Sup*
Connor, Louis G 1883- *WhWNAA*
Connor, Louis T 1883- *WhWNAA*
Connor, Marie *Alli Sup*
Connor, Patricia 1943- *ConAu 25*
Connor, Pierre Norman 1895-1952 *AmSCAP 66*
Connor, Ralph 1860-1937 *CanWr, CasWL, ChPo, Chmbr 3, DcBiA, DcLEnL, DcNAA, EvLB, LongC, NewC, OxAm, OxCan, REnAL, TwCA, TwCA Sup, TwCW, WhWNAA*
Connor, Robert Digges Wimberley 1878- *AmLY, BiDSA*
Connor, Seymour V 1923- *ConAu 53*
Connor, T W *ChPo*
Connor, Terence d1748? *PoIre*
Connor, Thomas *PoIre*
Connor, Tony 1930- *ChPo S2, ConAu XR, ConP 1970, ConP 1975, WrD 1976*
Connor, W Robert 1934- *ConAu 41*
Connor, William 1909?-1967 *ConAu 25*
Connor, William L 1889-1946 *IndAu 1917*
Connor, Sir William Neil *LongC*
Connors, Bruton 1931- *ConAu XR, ConP 1970, WrD 1976*
Connors, Dorsey *ConAu 45*
Conny, Robert *Alli*
Conold, Robert *Alli*
Conolly, Arthur *Alli*
Conolly, Edward Tennyson *Alli Sup*
Conolly, James d1791 *PoIre*
Conolly, John 1794-1866 *Alli, Alli Sup*
Conolly, Joseph *Alli, BiDLA*
Conolly, Luke Aylmer d1833? *Alli, BiDLA, PoIre*
Conolly, Matthew Forster *Alli Sup*
Conon De Bethune 1150?-1220? *CasWL, OxFr, Pen Eur*
Conor, Glen *ConAu XR*
Conor, John R *Alli Sup*
Conot, Robert E 1929- *AmA&B, ConAu 45, WrD 1976*
Conover, C Eugene 1903- *ConAu 5R*
Conover, Charlotte Reeve 1855-1940 *OhA&B*
Conover, Elbert Moore 1885- *WhWNAA*
Conover, Frank 1853-1912 *OhA&B*
Conover, Hobart H 1914- *ConAu 13R*
Conover, J F *Alli*
Conover, Milton 1890- *WhWNAA*
Conover, O M *Alli Sup*
Conoway, Jane *Alli*

Conquest, Edwin Parker, Jr. 1931- *ConAu 29, WrD 1976*
Conquest, F *ChPo*
Conquest, George Robert Ackworth 1917- *Au&Wr*
Conquest, John Tricker 1789-1866 *Alli Sup*
Conquest, Ned *ConAu XR, WrD 1976*
Conquest, Owen *LongC, MnBBF, WhCL*
Conquest, Pleasanton Laws 1882-1938 *DcNAA*
Conquest, Robert 1917- *ConAu 13R, ConNov 1972, ConP 1970, ConP 1975, LongC, RAdv 1, TwCW, WorAu, WrD 1976*
Conquet, John H 1927- *AmSCAP 66*
Conrad Of Wurzburg d1287 *EvEuW*
Conrad, Andree 1945- *ConAu 29*
Conrad, Arcturus A 1855-1932 *DcNAA*
Conrad, Arcturus Z 1855-1937 *IndAu 1816, WhWNAA*
Conrad, Arthur S 1907- *IlCB 1956*
Conrad, Barnaby 1922- *AmA&B, ConAu 9R, REnAL, WorAu*
Conrad, Brenda *EncM&D*
Conrad, Carl Nicholas 1858-1932 *DcNAA, WhWNAA*
Conrad, Con 1891-1938 *AmSCAP 66*
Conrad, David Eugene 1928- *ConAu 17R*
Conrad, Earl 1912- *ConAu 1R*
Conrad, Edna 1893- *ConAu 33*
Conrad, Frederick William 1816-1898 *Alli Sup, DcAmA, DcNAA*
Conrad, Georg 1826-1902 *BiD&SB*
Conrad, Mrs. H D *Alli Sup*
Conrad, Harrison 1869-1930 *ArizL*
Conrad, Henry Clay 1852-1930 *DcNAA*
Conrad, Isaac John 1912- *Au&Wr*
Conrad, Jack 1923- *ConAu 9R*
Conrad, John W 1935- *ConAu 53*
Conrad, Joseph 1857-1924 *AtlBL, BbD, BiD&SB, CasWL, Chmbr 3, CnMD, CnMWL, CyWA, DcEnA Ap, DcEuL, DcLEnL, EncM&D, EncWL, EvLB, JBA 1934, LongC, ModBL, ModBL Sup, ModWD, NewC, OxEng, Pen Eng, RAdv 1, RCom, REn, TwCA, TwCA Sup, TwCW, WebEAL, WhTwL*
Conrad, Kenneth *ConAu XR*
Conrad, L K *ConAu XR*
Conrad, Lawrence Henry 1898- *ChPo S1, WhWNAA*
Conrad, Michael Georg 1846-1927 *BiD&SB, ClDMEuL, OxGer*
Conrad, Robert 1928- *ConAu 41*
Conrad, Robert Taylor 1810-1858 *Alli, AmA, AmA&B, BiD&SB, ChPo, ChPo S1, ChPo S2, CyAL 2, DcAmA, DcNAA, McGWD, OxAm, REnAL*
Conrad, Stephen *DcNAA*
Conrad, Sybil 1921- *AuBYP, ConAu 23*
Conrad, Thomas K *Alli Sup*
Conrad, Timothy Abbott 1803-1877 *Alli, Alli Sup, DcAmA, DcNAA*
Conrad, Tod *ConAu XR*
Conrad, William Chester 1882- *ConAu P-1, IndAu 1917*
Conradi, Hermann 1862-1890 *BiD&SB, CasWL, ClDMEuL, OxGer, REn*
Conradin *OxGer*
Conradis, Heinz 1907- *ConAu P-1*
Conrads, Ulrich 1923- *ConAu 9R*
Conran, Anthony 1931- *ConP 1970, ConP 1975, WrD 1976*
Conran, Mrs. E H I S *Alli Sup*
Conran, Henry Mascall *Alli Sup*
Conrard, George Harrison Aloysius 1869-1930 *OhA&B*
Conrart, Valentin 1603-1675 *CasWL, DcEuL, OxFr, REn*
Conron, Brandon 1919- *CanWr, ConAu 17R, OxCan, OxCan Sup*
Conrow, Robert W 1942- *ConAu 57, WrD 1976*
Conrow, Wilford S 1880- *WhWNAA*
Conroy, Charles Clifford 1881- *WhWNAA*
Conroy, Charles W 1922- *ConAu 13R*
Conroy, Frank 1936- *AmA&B*
Conroy, George *Alli Sup*
Conroy, J D *HsB&A*

Conroy, Jack 1899- *AmA&B, AmNov, ConAu XR, ConNov 1972, ConNov 1976, OhA&B, OxAm, WhWNAA, WrD 1976*
Conroy, John *Alli*
Conroy, John Wesley 1899- *ConAu 5R*
Conroy, Joseph Patrick 1869-1941 *DcNAA*
Conroy, Mary d1895 *Polre*
Conroy, Michael R 1945- *ConAu 53*
Conroy, Pat *AuNews 1*
Conroy, Peter V, Jr. 1944- *ConAu 53*
Conry, F *Pen Eng*
Conscience, Miss Blanche *Alli Sup*
Conscience, Hendrik 1812-1883 *BbD, BiD&SB, CasWL, ClDMEuL, CyWA, DcEuL, EuA, EvEuW, REn*
Conset, Henry *Alli*
Consett, Matthew *Alli, BiDLA*
Consett, Thomas *Alli*
Considerant, Victor Prosper 1809?-1893 *OxAm, OxFr*
Considine, Bob 1906- *AmA&B, AuNews 2, ConAu XR, REnAL*
Considine, Daniel 1849-1923 *DcNAA*
Considine, John Joseph 1897- *BkC 3, CatA 1947, ConAu 1R*
Considine, Robert Bernard 1906-1975 *CatA 1947, ConAu 61*
Consilvio, Thomas 1947- *ConAu 57*
Consolata, Sister Mary 1892- *AmA&B, AmNov XR, CatA 1952*
Consolo, Dominick P 1923- *ConAu 33*
Const, Francis *Alli, BiDLA*
Constable, C G And Stiffe, A W *Alli Sup*
Constable, C S *Alli*
Constable, Charles Stanley *BiDLA*
Constable, F *Alli*
Constable, F R A Brown *Alli Sup*
Constable, Henry *Alli, Alli Sup, Chmbr 1*
Constable, Henry 1562-1613 *BrAu, CasWL, ChPo, CrE&SL, DcEnL, DcLEnL, EvLB, NewC, OxEng, Pen Eng, REn*
Constable, Henry Strickland 1821- *Alli Sup*
Constable, J Goulton *Alli Sup*
Constable, John *Alli, Alli Sup*
Constable, John 1776-1837 *AtlBL, ChPo S1, NewC, REn*
Constable, Michael *Polre*
Constable, Thomas 1812-1881 *Alli Sup*
Constable, W G 1887- *ConAu 5R*
Constancio, F S *Alli*
Constanduros, Denis Stephanos 1910- *Au&Wr, WrD 1976*
Constanduros, Mabel *ChPo*
Constant, Alberta Wilson 1908- *ConAu 1R*
Constant, Alphonse-Louis 1810-1875 *OxFr*
Constant, Benjamin 1767-1830 *AtlBL, CyWA, Pen Eur*
Constant, Gustave Leon Marie 1869-1940 *CatA 1952*
Constant DeRebecque, Henri Benjamin 1767-1830 *BbD, BiD&SB, CasWL, DcEuL, EuA, EvEuW, OxEng, OxFr, REn*
Constantelos, Demetrios J 1927- *ConAu 21, WrD 1976*
Constantia *AmA&B*
Constantin, James A 1922- *ConAu 13R*
Constantin, Robert W 1937- *ConAu 25*
Constantin-Weyer, Maurice 1881- *OxCan, TwCA, TwCA Sup*
Constantine I 274?-337 *NewC, REn*
Constantine Manasses d1187? *CasWL, Pen Cl*
Constantine Of Preslav *CasWL, Pen Eur*
Constantine Of Rhodes *Pen Cl*
Constantine VII Porphyrogenitus 905-959 *CasWL, Pen Cl*
Constantine Presbyter *CasWL*
Constantine The Philosopher *CasWL*
Constantine The Priest *CasWL*
Constantine, Joseph *Alli Sup*
Constantine, William *Alli*
Constellano, Illion *HsB&A*
Contargyris, Ath 1892- *WhLA*
Contencin, J *ChPo*
Contessa, Karl Wilhelm 1777-1825 *OxGer*
Conteur *OhA&B*
Conti, Amelie Gabrielle S L, Princess Of *BiD&SB*
Conti, Antonio 1677-1749 *CasWL, EvEuW*

Conti, Clelia *OxFr*
Conti, Giusto De' 1389?-1449 *CasWL*
Conti, Oscar 1914- *WhGrA*
Conton, William 1925- *AfA 1, Au&Wr, ConAu 1R, Pen Cl, RGAfl, WrD 1976*
Contopoulos, N *Alli Sup*
Contoski, Victor 1936- *ConAu 25, DrAP 1975*
Contrecoeur, Claude-Pierre P, Sieur De *OxCan*
Contreras, Alonso De 1582-1640? *CasWL*
Contreras, Daniel 1926- *DcCLA*
Contreras, Francisco 1877-1933 *Pen Am*
Contreras, Heles 1933- *ConAu 37*
Contreras, Jeronimo *CasWL*
Contreras, Jerry *IlBYP*
Convenant, J *Alli*
Conversation Sharp *DcEnL*
Converse, Amassa 1795-1872 *BiDSA*
Converse, Charles Crozat 1832-1918 *DcNAA*
Converse, Florence 1871- *AmA&B, BiDSA, CarSB, ChPo, ChPo S1, ChPo S2, DcAmA, WhWNAA*
Converse, Frank H d1889 *Alli Sup*
Converse, Frederick Shepherd 1871-1940 *AmSCAP 66, OxAm, REnAL*
Converse, Harriet 1840?-1903 *Alli Sup, DcAmA, DcNAA*
Converse, Harriet Maxwell 1866-1903 *ChPo*
Converse, Henry D *Alli Sup*
Converse, James Booth 1844-1914 *Alli Sup, BiDSA, DcNAA*
Converse, James D *Alli Sup*
Converse, Josiah Holmes *Alli Sup*
Converse, Julius Orrin 1834-1902 *OhA&B*
Converse, Paul D 1889- *ConAu 17, WhWNAA*
Converse, Philip E 1928- *ConAu 13R*
Convict Writer, The *ConAu 49*
Conway *Alli*
Conway, Viscount *Alli*
Conway, Alan 1920- *ConAu 1R, WrD 1976*
Conway, Arlington B *ConAu XR*
Conway, B And Endean, J R *Alli Sup*
Conway, Bertrand 1872- *CatA 1947*
Conway, Charles 1885- *WhWNAA*
Conway, Clara *Alli Sup*
Conway, David 1939- *WrD 1976*
Conway, Denise *ConAu XR*
Conway, E Carolyn *WrD 1976*
Conway, Faulkner *AmA&B, AmLY XR*
Conway, Freda 1911- *ConAu 25, WrD 1976*
Conway, Frederick William *Polre*
Conway, Gilbert *Alli Sup*
Conway, Gordon *MnBBF*
Conway, Grace *ChPo, ChPo S1*
Conway, H D *Alli*
Conway, Harry Donald 1917- *Au&Wr, WrD 1976*
Conway, Helene *AuBYP*
Conway, Henry Seymour 1720-1795 *Alli, DcEnL*
Conway, Hugh *Alli Sup, BiD&SB, BrAu 19, NewC*
Conway, Hugh 1847-1885 *DcBiA*
Conway, Hugh Graham 1914- *Au&Wr*
Conway, J D 1905- *ConAu 1R*
Conway, J Gregory 1909?- *AmA&B, Au&Wr, WhWNAA*
Conway, James *Alli Sup*
Conway, Sir John *Alli*
Conway, John D *Alli Sup*
Conway, John Placid *Alli Sup*
Conway, John Seymour 1929- *ConAu 25*
Conway, Katherine Eleanor 1853-1927 *Alli Sup, AmA&B, BiD&SB, ChPo, DcAmA, DcNAA, Polre*
Conway, M M H *ChPo*
Conway, Margaret 1935- *ConAu 37*
Conway, Sir Martin 1856- *WhLA*
Conway, Moncure Daniel 1832-1907 *Alli Sup, AmA, AmA&B, BbD, BiD&SB, BiDSA, Chmbr 3, CyAL 2, DcAmA, DcLEnL, DcNAA, OhA&B, OxAm, Pen Am, REnAL*
Conway, Norman *ChPo*
Conway, R Seymour *Alli Sup*
Conway, Richard *MnBBF*
Conway, Thomas *REn*
Conway, Thomas D 1934- *ConAu 21*

Conway, Troy *WrD 1976*
Conway, Ward *ConAu XR*
Conway, William *Alli, Alli Sup*
Conway, Sir William Martin 1856- *Alli Sup, BiD&SB, Chmbr 3, DcEnA Ap*
Conwell, Eugene Alfred *Alli Sup*
Conwell, Hugh Earle 1893- *Au&Wr, WhWNAA*
Conwell, Russell Herman 1843-1925 *Alli Sup, AmA&B, AmLY, DcAmA, DcNAA, OxAm, OxCan, REnAL*
Conybeare, Charles Augustus *ConAu XR*
Conybeare, Charles Augustus Vansittart *Alli Sup*
Conybeare, Charles Frederick Pringle 1860-1927 *DcNAA*
Conybeare, John 1692-1755 *Alli, DcEnL*
Conybeare, John Josias 1779-1824 *Alli*
Conybeare, Mary Emily d1886 *Alli Sup*
Conybeare, W J d1857 *Alli, DcEnL*
Conybeare, William Daniel 1787-1857 *Alli, BrAu 19*
Conyers, Ansley *Alli Sup*
Conyers, Captain And Reginald Wray *MnBBF*
Conyers, Dorothea 1873- *Br&AmS*
Conyers, Frank 1905- *Au&Wr*
Conyers, James *Alli*
Conyers, James E 1932- *ConAu 41*
Conyers, Richard *Alli*
Conyers, Tobias *Alli*
Conyngham, Cuthbert *Alli Sup*
Conyngham, David Power 1840-1883 *Alli Sup, AmA&B, BbD, BiD&SB, DcAmA, DcNAA*
Conyngham, Elizabeth Emmet Lenox 1800- *Alli Sup, Polre*
Conyngham, William Joseph 1924- *ConAu 53*
Conyus 1942- *BlkAW*
Conyus, James *BlkAW*
Conz, Karl Philipp 1762-1827 *OxGer*
Conze, Edward J D 1904- *Au&Wr, ConAu 13R*
Coode, G *Alli, Alli Sup*
Coode, Helen H *Alli Sup*
Cooee *MnBBF*
Coogan, Daniel 1915- *ConAu 21*
Coogan, Joseph Patrick 1925- *ConAu 1R*
Cook *Alli*
Cook, Adrian 1940- *ConAu 49*
Cook, Alan Hugh 1922- *WrD 1976*
Cook, Albert John 1842-1916 *Alli Sup, DcAmA, DcNAA*
Cook, Albert Spaulding 1925- *ConAu 1R, WorAu*
Cook, Albert Stanburrough 1853-1927 *Alli Sup, AmA&B, DcAmA, DcNAA*
Cook, Alice Carter 1868- *AnMV 1926, WhWNAA*
Cook, Alice Rice 1899-1973 *ConAu 41*
Cook, Andrew 1836- *ChPo S1*
Cook, Arthur Bernard 1868- *ChPo S1*
Cook, Arthur Leroy 1878- *WhWNAA*
Cook, Aurelian *Alli*
Cook, Beverly Blair 1926- *ConAu 37*
Cook, Mrs. Bickersteth *Alli Sup*
Cook, Blanche Wiesen 1941- *ConAu 53*
Cook, Britton *OxCan*
Cook, Bruce 1932- *ConAu 33*
Cook, Carroll Blaine 1883-1922 *DcNAA*
Cook, Charles *Alli Sup*
Cook, Mrs. Charles *Alli Sup*
Cook, Charles F *ChPo S1, ChPo S2*
Cook, Charles Henry 1858-1933 *NewC, WhLA*
Cook, Charles Thomas 1886- *Au&Wr*
Cook, Chris 1945- *ConAu 57*
Cook, Christal 1940- *Au&Wr*
Cook, Clarence Chatham 1828-1900 *Alli Sup, AmA, AmA&B, BbD, BiD&SB, ChPo, DcAmA, DcNAA*
Cook, Daniel 1914- *ConAu 33*
Cook, Daniel J 1938- *ConAu 53*
Cook, David 1940- *WrD 1976*
Cook, David C, III 1912- *ConAu 57*
Cook, David C, Jr. 1881- *WhWNAA*
Cook, David Caleb 1850-1927 *DcNAA*
Cook, David J 1840-1907 *AmA&B, IndAu 1917*
Cook, Davidson *ChPo S1, WhLA*

Cook, Davidson 1874- *WhLA*
Cook, Don 1920- *ConAu 13R*, *WrD 1976*
Cook, Dorothy Mary *WrD 1976*
Cook, Douglas 1927- *BlkAW*
Cook, Dutton *DcEnL*
Cook, E C 1868- *WhWNAA*
Cook, E Fullerton 1879- *WhWNAA*
Cook, Mrs. E G *Alli Sup*
Cook, E H *Alli Sup*
Cook, Eben *BiDSA*
Cook, Ebenezer 1672?-1732 *Alli*, *AmA&B*,
    DcLEnL, *OxAm*, *Pen Am*, *REn*, *REnAL*
Cook, Ebenezer ALSO Cooke, Ebenezer
Cook, Eddie Gene 1911- *TexWr*
Cook, Edith W *ChPo*
Cook, Edmund Vance 1866- *WhWNAA*
Cook, Edward *Alli*
Cook, Edward Dutton 1829-1883 *Alli Sup*,
    NewC
Cook, Edward Richard *Alli Sup*
Cook, Edward Tyas 1857-1919 *Alli Sup*,
    DcEuL
Cook, Eliza 1818?-1889 *Alli*, *Alli Sup*, *BbD*,
    BiD&SB, *BrAu 19*, *ChPo*, *ChPo S1*,
    ChPo S2, *Chmbr 3*, *DcEnA*, *DcEnL*,
    DcLEnL, *EvLB*, *NewC*, *OxEng*
Cook, Elizabeth Christine 1876-1938 *DcNAA*
Cook, Ellen *Alli Sup*
Cook, Elsie Thornton *Au&Wr*
Cook, Eugene B, Henry, W And Gilberg, C
    Alli Sup
Cook, F C *Alli*
Cook, F Louise 1908- *ChPo*
Cook, Fannie 1893-1949 *AmA&B*, *AmNov*,
    DcNAA, *REnAL*
Cook, Flavel Smith 1827?-1900 *Alli Sup*, *PoIre*
Cook, Flavius Josephus 1838-1901 *AmA*,
    BiD&SB, *DcNAA*
Cook, Florence 1856-1904 *BiDPar*
Cook, Francis *Alli*
Cook, Frank Gaylord 1859- *WhWNAA*
Cook, Fred Gordon 1900- *MnBBF*
Cook, Fred James 1911- *AmA&B*, *AuBYP*,
    ConAu 9R, *DcAmA*
Cook, Frederick Albert 1865-1940 *DcAmA*,
    DcNAA, *OxCan*
Cook, Frederick Charles *Alli Sup*
Cook, G Ramsay *OxCan*
Cook, Gayla *BlkAW*
Cook, George *Alli*, *Alli Sup*, *BiDLA*
Cook, George Allan 1916- *ConAu 23*
Cook, George Cram 1873-1924 *AmA&B*,
    CnMD, *DcNAA*, *LongC*, *ModWD*,
    OxAm, *REn*, *REnAL*, *TwCA*,
    TwCA Sup
Cook, Mrs. George Cram *AmNov XR*
Cook, George Hammell 1818-1889 *Alli Sup*,
    DcAmA, *DcNAA*
Cook, George M *OxCan Sup*
Cook, George S 1920- *ConAu 49*
Cook, Gladys Emerson 1899- *AmA&B*,
    AuBYP, *ConAu 5R*, *IlCB 1956*
Cook, Gladys Moon 1907- *ConAu 33*
Cook, Glenn J 1913- *ConAu 25*
Cook, Grace Louise *DcAmA*
Cook, Grace Mabel 1889-1940 *IndAu 1917*
Cook, H B *Alli Sup*
Cook, Harold J *WhWNAA*
Cook, Harold Lewis *ChPo*, *ChPo S2*
Cook, Harold Reed 1902- *ConAu 13R*
Cook, Hartley Trevor Kemball *ChPo S1*
Cook, Henry *Alli Sup*, *ChPo*, *ChPo S1*
Cook, Henry Caldwell 1886-1939 *ChPo*
Cook, Howard 1901- *IlCB 1945*
Cook, Hugh C B 1910- *ConAu 57*
Cook, Ira 1916- *AmSCAP 66*
Cook, J *Alli*, *Alli Sup*
Cook, J F *BiDSA*
Cook, J Gordon 1916- *ConAu 9R*
Cook, Mrs. J T *ChPo S1*
Cook, Jack *ConAu XR*
Cook, James 1728-1779 *Alli*, *Alli Sup*, *BbD*,
    BbtC, *BrAu*, *ChPo S2*, *DcLEnL*, *NewC*,
    OxCan, *OxEng*, *REn*, *REnAL*
Cook, Mrs. James C *Alli Sup*
Cook, James Graham 1925- *ConAu 1R*
Cook, James Henry 1858-1942 *AmA&B*,
    DcNAA, *WhWNAA*

Cook, Jane E *ChPo S1*
Cook, Joan Marble 1920- *ConAu 57*
Cook, Joe 1890-1959 *IndAu 1917*
Cook, Joel 1842-1910 *Alli Sup*, *DcAmA*,
    DcNAA
Cook, John *Alli*, *Alli Sup*, *BbtC*
Cook, John 1773-1829 *Br&AmS*
Cook, John 1810- *Alli Sup*
Cook, John 1836- *Alli Sup*
Cook, John Atkins 1857- *WhWNAA*
Cook, John Augustine 1940- *ConAu 45*
Cook, John Douglas d1868 *DcEuL*
Cook, John Estes *ThBJA*
Cook, John H *ChPo*
Cook, John Mortimer Lennox 1923- *Au&Wr*
Cook, John T *Alli Sup*
Cook, John Williston 1844-1922 *DcNAA*
Cook, John Wilson *BbtC*
Cook, Joseph *DcNAA*
Cook, Joseph 1838-1901 *Alli Sup*, *AmA*,
    AmA&B, *BbD*, *DcAmA*
Cook, Joseph Jay 1924- *AuBYP*, *ConAu 1R*,
    SmATA 8
Cook, Joseph Simpson 1860-1933 *ChPo*
Cook, Keningale Robert 1845-1886 *Alli Sup*,
    PoIre
Cook, Kenneth Bernard 1929- *Au&Wr*
Cook, Lennox 1923- *WrD 1976*
Cook, Lloyd Allen 1899- *IndAu 1917*
Cook, Louisa S *Alli Sup*
Cook, Lucia B *ChPo S2*
Cook, Lyn *ConAu XR*, *OxCan Sup*,
    SmATA XR, *WrD 1976*
Cook, M *Alli*
Cook, Mabel *Alli Sup*
Cook, Mae Myrtle *ChPo*
Cook, Marc 1854-1882 *Alli Sup*, *DcAmA*,
    DcNAA
Cook, Marc E *ChPo S1*
Cook, Margaret G 1903- *ConAu 5R*
Cook, Marion Belden *AuBYP*
Cook, Mark 1942- *ConAu 37*
Cook, Martha Caverno *ChPo S1*
Cook, Martha Elizabeth Duncan Walker
    1806-1874 *Alli Sup*
Cook, Mary Larkin *ChPo S1*
Cook, Mary Louise d1891 *Alli Sup*, *BiDSA*,
    LivFWS
Cook, Mattie C *ChPo*
Cook, Melva Janice 1919- *ConAu 23*
Cook, Melville Thurston 1869- *WhWNAA*
Cook, Melvin A 1911- *ConAu 49*, *WrD 1976*
Cook, Mercer 1903- *BlkAW*, *LivBA*
Cook, Michael *OxCan Sup*
Cook, Mike 1939- *BlkAW*
Cook, Millicent Whiteside *Alli Sup*
Cook, Molly Connor *TexWr*
Cook, Moses *Alli*
Cook, Myra B 1933- *ConAu 23*
Cook, N M *ChPo*
Cook, Nancy Gwendolen 1902- *Au&Wr*
Cook, Neil E 1896- *ArizL*
Cook, Nina Hall *ChPo S1*
Cook, Olive 1916- *ConAu 5R*
Cook, Olive Rambo 1892- *AuBYP*,
    ConAu 13R
Cook, P Lesley 1922- *ConAu 13R*
Cook, Paul 1882- *TexWr*
Cook, R S *Alli Sup*
Cook, Ramona Graham *Au&Wr*, *ConAu 5R*
Cook, Ramsay 1931- *OxCan Sup*
Cook, Raymond Allen 1919- *ConAu 45*
Cook, Reginald Lansing 1903- *AnMV 1926*
Cook, Richard Briscoe 1838-1916 *Alli Sup*,
    BiDSA, *DcAmA*, *DcNAA*
Cook, Richard I 1927- *ConAu 23*
Cook, Robert *Alli Sup*
Cook, Robert Dane *ChPo S1*
Cook, Robert I 1920- *ConAu 33*
Cook, Robert William Arthur 1931- *Au&Wr*,
    ConAu 25
Cook, Robin 1931- *ConAu XR*, *WrD 1976*
Cook, Robley D *Alli Sup*
Cook, Roderick 1932- *ConAu 9R*
Cook, Roy Bird 1886-1961 *AmA&B*,
    WhWNAA
Cook, Roy J *ChPo S2*
Cook, Russell Sturgis 1811-1864 *PoCh*

Cook, S *Alli*
Cook, S E *Alli*
Cook, Sherman R *AuBYP*
Cook, Stanley 1922- *ConP 1975*, *WrD 1976*
Cook, Stuart W 1913- *ConAu 1R*
Cook, Sylvia 1938- *ConAu 49*
Cook, Tennessee Celeste Claflin 1845-1923
    OhA&B
Cook, Theodore A *ChPo*
Cook, Sir Theodore Andrea 1867-1928 *Br&AmS*
Cook, Theodore Pease 1844-1916 *Alli Sup*,
    DcAmA, *DcNAA*
Cook, Thomas *Alli*, *Alli Sup*, *BiDLA*
Cook, W H 1832- *Alli*
Cook, W Mercer 1903- *AmSCAP 66*
Cook, Walter *ChPo S2*
Cook, Walter Wheeler 1873-1943 *DcNAA*
Cook, Walter William Spencer 1888-
    WhWNAA
Cook, Warren Lawrence 1925- *ConAu 37*,
    WrD 1976
Cook, Webster 1854-1908 *DcNAA*
Cook, Will 1921- *AmA&B*
Cook, Will Marion 1869-1944 *AmSCAP 66*,
    BlkAW
Cook, William *Alli*, *Alli Sup*
Cook, William 1807- *EarAB*, *EarAB Sup*
Cook, William A 1881- *WhWNAA*
Cook, William Everett 1921- *IndAu 1917*
Cook, William Henry 1832-1899 *DcAmA*,
    DcNAA
Cook, William J, Jr. 1938- *ConAu 29*
Cook, William Wallace 1867-1933 *AmA&B*,
    DcNAA
Cook, William Wilson 1858-1930 *Alli Sup*,
    DcAmA, *DcNAA*
Cooke *Alli*
Cooke, A *Alli Sup*
Cooke, Miss A B *Alli Sup*
Cooke, A P *Alli Sup*
Cooke, A R *Alli Sup*
Cooke, Adelaide V *ChPo*
Cooke, Alexander *Alli*
Cooke, Alistair 1908- *AmA&B*, *AuNews 1*,
    ConAu 57, *LongC*, *OxAm*, *REnAL*,
    TwCA Sup, *WrD 1976*
Cooke, Anne *Alli*
Cooke, Anthony Charles 1826- *Alli Sup*
Cooke, Arthur Bledsoe 1869- *BiDSA*,
    WhWNAA
Cooke, Arthur Stanley *ChPo S1*
Cooke, Bancroft *Alli Sup*
Cooke, Barbara *AuBYP*, *ConAu 57*
Cooke, Bella *Alli Sup*
Cooke, Belle W *ChPo*, *ChPo S2*
Cooke, Benjamin *Alli*
Cooke, Benjamin d1793 *Alli*
Cooke, Bernard J 1922- *ConAu 13R*,
    WrD 1976
Cooke, Carrie Adelaide *Alli Sup*
Cooke, Sir Charles *Alli*
Cooke, Charles James *Alli Sup*
Cooke, Charles L 1891-1958 *AmSCAP 66*
Cooke, Charles Northcote *Alli Sup*
Cooke, Charles Wallwyn Radcliffe 1841-
    Alli Sup
Cooke, Christopher *Alli Sup*
Cooke, Clement Kinloch 1854- *Alli Sup*
Cooke, Colin Arthur 1903- *Au&Wr*
Cooke, Crawford B *Alli Sup*
Cooke, Croft- *TwCA*, *TwCA Sup*
Cooke, D W *Alli Sup*
Cooke, David Coxe 1917- *AuBYP*, *ConAu 1R*,
    SmATA 2
Cooke, Donald Ewin 1916- *AuBYP*,
    ConAu 1R, *SmATA 2*
Cooke, Douglas Hageman 1885- *WhWNAA*
Cooke, E *Alli*
Cooke, E W *Alli*
Cooke, Ebenezer 1672?-1732 *AmA&B*, *OxAm*,
    REn
Cooke, Ebenezer SEE Cook, Ebenezer
Cooke, Edith Helena *ChPo S1*
Cooke, Edmund Vance 1866-1932 *AmLY*,
    DcAmA, *DcNAA*, *OhA&B*
Cooke, Edna *ChPo*
Cooke, Edna A *ChPo*
Cooke, Edward *Alli*, *BiDLA*

Cooke, Sir Edward *NewC*
Cooke, Edward Alexander *Alli Sup*
Cooke, Edward F 1923- *ConAu 41*
Cooke, Edward William 1811-1880 *Alli Sup, ChPo*
Cooke, Edwin Oscar *ChPo*
Cooke, Elisha d1737 *Alli*
Cooke, Elizabeth *Alli*
Cooke, Elizabeth Harriet *Alli Sup*
Cooke, Emily A *ChPo S2*
Cooke, Ethel *ChPo S1, ChPo S2*
Cooke, F *Alli*
Cooke, F Sherman *ChPo S1*
Cooke, Flora Juliette d1953 *OhA&B*
Cooke, Frances E *Alli Sup*
Cooke, Francis Bernard 1872- *Au&Wr*
Cooke, Frederick Hale 1859-1912 *DcNAA*
Cooke, G Wingrove *Alli*
Cooke, Geoffrey Walter 1924- *Au&Wr*
Cooke, George *Alli*
Cooke, George 1773-1845 *DcEnL*
Cooke, Sir George *Alli*
Cooke, George Frederick 1756-1812 *NewC*
Cooke, George Willis 1848-1923 *Alli Sup, AmA&B, BiD&SB, DcAmA, DcNAA*
Cooke, George Wingrove 1814-1865 *Alli Sup*
Cooke, Gerald 1925- *ConAu 13R*
Cooke, Gilbert William 1899- *ConAu P-1*
Cooke, Grace MacGowan 1863-1944 *AmA&B, BiDSA, ChPo, ChPo S1, DcAmA, OhA&B*
Cooke, Greville 1894- *ConAu 13R*
Cooke, H *ChPo*
Cooke, Harriet B *Alli Sup*
Cooke, Helen M *ChPo*
Cooke, Henry *Alli, Alli Sup*
Cooke, Hereward Lester 1916-1973 *ConAu 1R, ConAu 45*
Cooke, Hugh And Harwood, Robert G *Alli Sup*
Cooke, J *Alli, BiDLA*
Cooke, J A *Alli*
Cooke, J Edmund Vance 1866-1932 *ChPo, ChPo S1*
Cooke, Jacob Ernest 1924- *AmA&B, ConAu 1R, WrD 1976*
Cooke, James *Alli, BiDLA*
Cooke, James Francis 1875-1960 *AmA&B, AmSCAP 66, WhWNAA*
Cooke, James Herbert *Alli Sup*
Cooke, James Samuel *Alli Sup*
Cooke, John *Alli, Alli Sup, BiDLA, CasWL, ChPo S1, DcEnL*
Cooke, John d1660 *BiDLA Sup*
Cooke, John 1594?- *NewC*
Cooke, Mrs. John *Alli Sup*
Cooke, John Conrade *Alli*
Cooke, John Esten 1783-1853 *DcNAA*
Cooke, John Esten 1830-1886 *Alli, Alli Sup, AmA, AmA&B, BbD, BiD&SB, BiDSA, CasWL, Chmbr 3, CyAL 2, CyWA, DcAmA, DcLEnL, DcNAA, EvLB, OxAm, Pen Am, REnAL*
Cooke, John Hunt *Alli Sup*
Cooke, Joseph *Alli, BiDLA*
Cooke, Josiah Parsons 1827-1894 *Alli Sup, BiD&SB, DcAmA, DcNAA*
Cooke, Laura S H *Alli Sup*
Cooke, Layton *Alli*
Cooke, LeBaron *AnMV 1926*
Cooke, Leslie Edward 1908-1967 *AmA&B*
Cooke, Marjorie Benton 1876-1920 *ChPo S1, DcNAA, IndAu 1816*
Cooke, Martin Warren 1840-1898 *Alli Sup, DcAmA, DcNAA*
Cooke, Marvin *ChPo*
Cooke, Mary Lu 1910- *TexWr*
Cooke, Matthew *Alli Sup*
Cooke, Mordecai Cubitt 1825- *Alli Sup*
Cooke, Morris Llewellyn 1872-1960 *AmA&B*
Cooke, N *BiDLA*
Cooke, Nathaniel *Alli, BiDLA Sup*
Cooke, Nicholas Francis 1829-1885 *Alli Sup, DcAmA, DcNAA*
Cooke, Parsons 1800-1864 *DcAmA, DcNAA*
Cooke, Philip Pendleton 1816-1850 *Alli, AmA, AmA&B, BiD&SB, BiDSA, ChPo S1, CyAL 2, DcAmA, DcNAA, OxAm, REnAL*

Cooke, Philip St. George 1809-1895 *Alli Sup, AmA, AmA&B, BiD&SB, BiDSA, DcAmA, DcNAA, OxAm*
Cooke, R *Alli Sup*
Cooke, R J *Alli Sup*
Cooke, R P *ChPo S1*
Cooke, Richard *Alli*
Cooke, Robert *Alli*
Cooke, Robert 1820-1882 *Alli Sup*
Cooke, Robert Humphrey *Alli Sup*
Cooke, Rose Terry 1827-1892 *Alli Sup, AmA, AmA&B, BbD, BiD&SB, ChPo, ChPo S2, CnDAL, DcAmA, DcLEnL, DcNAA, OxAm, REnAL*
Cooke, Samuel *Alli, Alli Sup*
Cooke, Shadrach *Alli*
Cooke, T *Alli Sup*
Cooke, T E Cozens *Alli Sup*
Cooke, Theodore *Alli Sup*
Cooke, Thomas *Alli, Alli Sup, Chmbr 2*
Cooke, Thomas 1702?-1756 *Alli, BiD&SB, DcEnL, NewC*
Cooke, Thomas Fothergill *Alli Sup*
Cooke, Thomas Weedon *Alli Sup*
Cooke, V M 1910- *WhWNAA*
Cooke, W *Alli, Alli Sup, BiDLA*
Cooke, W Bourne *MnBBF*
Cooke, W H *Alli Sup*
Cooke, William *Alli, Alli Sup, BiDLA, BiDLA Sup, ChPo S1*
Cooke, William d1814 *DcEnL*
Cooke, William 1740?-1824 *Alli, PoIre*
Cooke, William 1757-1832 *Alli*
Cooke, William 1806- *Alli Sup*
Cooke, William 1942- *ConAu 33, WrD 1976*
Cooke, William B *Alli*
Cooke, William Bryan *Alli Sup*
Cooke, Sir William Fothergill 1806-1879 *Alli Sup*
Cooke, William Henry 1812- *Alli Sup*
Cooke, William Smith *Alli Sup*
Cookesey, John *Alli*
Cookesley, William *Alli*
Cookesley, William G *Alli*
Cookesley, William Gifford *Alli Sup*
Cookman, A V 1894-1962 *LongC*
Cookman, Alfred 1828-1871 *Alli Sup, DcAmA, DcNAA*
Cookridge, E H 1908- *ConAu 25*
Cooks, Percival *MnBBF*
Cooksey, Richard *Alli, BiDLA*
Cooksley, Bert *ChPo*
Cooksley, S Bert 1903- *WhWNAA*
Cookson, A A *Alli Sup*
Cookson, Catherine 1906- *Au&Wr, ConAu 13R, SmATA 9, WrD 1976*
Cookson, Charles W 1861-1947 *OhA&B*
Cookson, Christopher 1824-1874 *Alli Sup*
Cookson, Christopher 1861- *ChPo, ChPo S1*
Cookson, Elizabeth *Alli Sup*
Cookson, George *ChPo S1*
Cookson, J *Alli*
Cookson, James *Alli, BiDLA*
Cookson, John Cookson Fife- 1844- *Alli Sup*
Cookson, Peter W 1913- *ConAu 49*
Cookson, Richard *Alli Sup*
Cookson, William 1939- *ConAu 49*
Cool, Harold 1890-1949 *AmSCAP 66*
Coolbrith, Ina Donna 1842-1928 *Alli Sup, AmA, AmA&B, AmLY, BbD, BiD&SB, ChPo, ChPo S1, DcAmA, DcNAA, OxAm, REnAL*
Coole, Benjamin *Alli*
Coole, W W *ConAu XR, WrD 1976*
Cooledge, Daniel *ChPo, ChPo S1*
Cooley, Ada E *ChPo*
Cooley, Adelaide I *Alli Sup*
Cooley, Alice Kingsbury *Alli Sup*
Cooley, Anna Maria 1874- *WhWNAA*
Cooley, Arnold James *Alli, Alli Sup*
Cooley, Charles Parsons 1867- *ChPo*
Cooley, DeWitt Clinton *Alli Sup*
Cooley, Edgar A *Alli Sup*
Cooley, Hattie *ChPo S1*
Cooley, James Avas 1901- *IndAu 1917*
Cooley, James Ewing 1802- *Alli, ChPo*
Cooley, John Kent 1927- *ConAu 13R, WrD 1976*

Cooley, Julia 1893- *ChPo, ChPo S1, ChPo S2*
Cooley, Lee Morrison 1919- *ConAu 9R*
Cooley, Leland Frederick 1909- *ConAu 5R*
Cooley, LeRoy Clark 1833-1916 *Alli Sup, DcAmA, DcNAA*
Cooley, Lydia *IlBYP*
Cooley, Lyman Edgar 1850-1917 *DcNAA*
Cooley, Marjorie L 1887- *WhWNAA*
Cooley, Peter *DrAP 1975*
Cooley, Richard A 1925- *ConAu 21*
Cooley, Thomas McIntyre 1824-1898 *Alli Sup, BiD&SB, DcAmA, DcNAA*
Cooley, William Desborough d1883 *Alli, Alli Sup*
Cooley, Winifred Harper *IndAu 1917, WhWNAA*
Coolidge, A J And Mansfield, J B *Alli Sup*
Coolidge, Algernon 1860- *WhWNAA*
Coolidge, Archibald C, Jr. 1928- *ConAu 37*
Coolidge, Archibald Cary 1866-1928 *AmA&B, DcNAA, WhWNAA*
Coolidge, Calvin 1872-1933 *AmA&B, DcNAA, OxAm, REn, REnAL*
Coolidge, Clarence Edwin 1870-1946 *DcNAA*
Coolidge, Clark 1939- *ConAu 33, ConP 1970, ConP 1975, DrAP 1975, WrD 1976*
Coolidge, Dane 1873-1940 *AmA&B, AmLY, ChPo, DcNAA, OxAm, WhWNAA*
Coolidge, Elizabeth Sprague *ChPo S1*
Coolidge, Emelyn Lincoln 1873-1949 *DcNAA, WhWNAA*
Coolidge, Fay Liddle *BlkAW*
Coolidge, Grace F 1850- *ChPo*
Coolidge, Grace Goodhue 1879- *WhWNAA*
Coolidge, John Gardner 1863-1936 *AmA&B, DcNAA, WhWNAA*
Coolidge, Louis Arthur 1861-1925 *AmLY, DcNAA*
Coolidge, Mary E Burroughs Roberts 1860-1945 *AmA&B, AmLY, DcNAA, IndAu 1816, WhWNAA*
Coolidge, Olivia Ensor 1908- *AuBYP, BkCL, ConAu 5R, MorJA, SmATA 1*
Coolidge, Peggy Stuart *AmSCAP 66*
Coolidge, Porter B 1865- *WhWNAA*
Coolidge, Richard H *Alli Sup*
Coolidge, Sarah E *Alli Sup*
Coolidge, Susan 1835-1905 *Alli Sup, AmA, AmA&B, BbD, BiD&SB, ChPo, ChPo S2, Chmbr 3, DcAmA, DcLEnL, DcNAA, EvLB, JBA 1934, OhA&B, REnAL, WhCL*
Cooling, Benjamin Franklin 1938- *ConAu 53*
Cooling, Dennis *Alli*
Coolus, Romain 1868-1952 *EvEuW, McGWD, OxFr*
Coolwater, John *ConAu XR*
Coolwell, R C *ChPo S1*
Coom, Charles Sleeman 1853-1930? *DcNAA*
Coomaraswamy, Ananda Kentish 1877-1947 *DcLEnL, DcNAA, WhWNAA*
Coombe, Charles George *Alli Sup*
Coombe, Thomas 1747-1822 *Alli, AmA, AmA&B, BiDLA, CyAL 1, DcNAA*
Coombe, Thomas 1758- *DcAmA*
Coombe, William 174!-1823 *Alli, BiD&SB, BiDLA, DcEnL*
Coombe-Tennant, Winifred M Serocold 1874-1956 *BiDPar*
Coombes, B L 1894?-1974 *ConAu 53*
Coombes, Henry 1909- *Au&Wr*
Coombes, Ian Ralph 1944- *Au&Wr*
Coombes, Josiah *Alli Sup*
Coombes, W *Alli, BiDLA*
Coombs, Annie Sheldon 1858-1890 *Alli Sup, AmA&B, BiD&SB, DcAmA, DcNAA*
Coombs, Charles Ira 1914- *AuBYP, ConAu 5R, SmATA 3*
Coombs, Charles Whitney 1859-1940 *AmSCAP 66*
Coombs, Chick *AuBYP, ConAu XR, SmATA 3*
Coombs, Douglas 1924- *ConAu 13R*
Coombs, J J *Alli Sup*
Coombs, James Vincent 1849-1920 *IndAu 1917*
Coombs, Jessie *Alli Sup*
Coombs, Joyce 1906- *Au&Wr, WrD 1976*

Coombs, Orde M *BlkAW, LivBA*
Coombs, Patricia 1926- *ConAu 1R, IlBYP, IlCB 1966, SmATA 3, WrD 1976*
Coombs, Philip H 1915- *ConAu 17R*
Coombs, Robert H 1934- *ConAu 41*
Coombs, Sarah 1868-1947 *DcNAA*
Coombs, W Bayley *Alli Sup*
Coombs, William *Alli Sup*
Coomer, George H *ChPo, ChPo S1*
Coomes, Martin F *Alli Sup*
Coomes, Oliver 1845-1921 *OhA&B*
Coomes, Oll 1845-1921 *HsB&A, OhA&B*
Coon, Carleton Stevens 1904- *AmA&B, Au&Wr, ConAu 5R, WorAu*
Coon, Charles Lee 1868- *BiDSA*
Coon, Gene L 1924- *ConAu 1R*
Coon, Horace C 1897-1961 *AmA&B*
Coon, Martha Sutherland 1884- *ConAu 25, WrD 1976*
Coon, Reune R *Alli Sup*
Coon, Stephen 1948- *ConAu 57*
Cooney, A W *ChPo S2*
Cooney, Barbara 1917- *AmA&B, AuBYP, BkP, ChPo, ConAu 5R, IlBYP, IlCB 1945, IlCB 1956, IlCB 1966, MorJA, NewbC 1956, SmATA 6, St&VC*
Cooney, David M 1930- *ConAu 17R*
Cooney, Eugene J 1931- *ConAu 45*
Cooney, John Michael 1874-1945 *DcNAA*
Cooney, John Michael 1874-1946 *IndAu 1816*
Cooney, Mary *PoIre*
Cooney, Michael 1921- *ConAu 25*
Cooney, Percival John 1871-1932 *CanNov, DcNAA, OxCan*
Cooney, Ray 1932- *Au&Wr*
Cooney, Robert 1800?-1870 *Alli Sup, BbtC, DcNAA, OxCan*
Cooney, Seamus 1933- *ConAu 53*
Coonley, Levi K *Alli Sup*
Coonley, Lydia Avery *ChPo, DcAmA, DcNAA*
Coons, Frederica Bertha 1910- *ConAu 17R*
Coons, William R 1934- *ConAu 41*
Coontz, Kathleen Read *ChPo*
Coontz, Robert Edward 1864-1935 *DcNAA*
Coop, Howard 1928- *ConAu 25*
Coope, Rosalys 1921- *ConAu 45*
Coope, William Jesser *Alli Sup*
Cooper *Alli*
Cooper, Mister *BiDLA*
Cooper, A *Alli*
Cooper, A B *ChPo, ChPo S1, ChPo S2*
Cooper, A N *Alli Sup*
Cooper, A R *Alli Sup*
Cooper, A W *ChPo, ChPo S1, ChPo S2*
Cooper, Abraham 1787-1868 *ChPo*
Cooper, Alexander *Alli*
Cooper, Alfred *Alli Sup*
Cooper, Alfred Benjamin 1863- *MnBBF, WhLA*
Cooper, Alfred Duff 1890-1954 *ChPo, DcLEnL, EvLB, NewC*
Cooper, Alfred Morton 1890- *ConAu P-1*
Cooper, Alvin Carlos 1925- *BlkAW*
Cooper, Andrew *Alli*
Cooper, Anna Julia 1859-1964 *BlkAW*
Cooper, Anthony Ashley *Alli, BrAu, Chmbr, DcEnL, DcLEnL, EvLB, NewC, REn*
Cooper, Anthony Ashley 1621-1683 *Alli*
Cooper, Anthony Ashley 1671-1713 *Alli, CasWL, MouLC 2*
Cooper, Anthony Ashley 1801-1885 *Alli Sup*
Cooper, Arnold Cook 1933- *ConAu 17R*
Cooper, Arthur *Alli Sup*
Cooper, Sir Astley Paston 1768-1841 *Alli, BiDLA*
Cooper, Barbara 1915- *Au&Wr*
Cooper, Barbara Ann 1929- *Au&Wr, ConAu 9R*
Cooper, Basil Henry 1819- *Alli Sup*
Cooper, Belle *AnMV 1926*
Cooper, Bernarr 1912- *ConAu 41*
Cooper, Bransby B *Alli*
Cooper, Brian Newman 1919- *Au&Wr, ConAu 1R, WrD 1976*
Cooper, Bruce M 1925- *ConAu 13R, WrD 1976*

Cooper, Bryan 1932- *Au&Wr, ConAu 25, WrD 1976*
Cooper, Bud 1899- *AmSCAP 66*
Cooper, C *Alli*
Cooper, Charles *ChPo S2*
Cooper, Charles B 1948- *BlkAW*
Cooper, Charles D *Alli, Alli Sup*
Cooper, Charles Edward *AfA 1*
Cooper, Charles Henry 1808-1866 *Alli Sup*
Cooper, Charles Henry St. John 1869-1926 *MnBBF*
Cooper, Charles M 1909- *ConAu 41*
Cooper, Charles Purton *Alli, Alli Sup*
Cooper, Charles W *BbtC, BiDSA*
Cooper, Charles W 1904- *ConAu 21*
Cooper, Charles W F *Alli Sup*
Cooper, Charles William *Alli Sup*
Cooper, Cheryl *AmSCAP 66*
Cooper, Chester L 1917- *ConAu 29*
Cooper, Chris *Alli*
Cooper, Christopher 1941- *WrD 1976*
Cooper, Christopher Donald Huntington 1942- *ConAu 29, WrD 1976*
Cooper, Clarence L, Jr. *BlkAW, LivBA*
Cooper, Clayton Sedgwick 1869-1936 *AmA&B, AmLY, DcNAA, WhWNAA*
Cooper, Mrs. Clayton Sedgwick *WhWNAA*
Cooper, Colin Symons 1926- *Au&Wr, WrD 1976*
Cooper, Courtney Ryley 1886-1940 *AmA&B, DcNAA, REnAL, TwCA, TwCA Sup*
Cooper, Darien B 1937- *ConAu 49*
Cooper, David E 1942- *ConAu 49*
Cooper, Derek Macdonald 1925- *WrD 1976*
Cooper, Lady Diana Duff 1892- *Au&Wr, LongC, NewC*
Cooper, Dorothy 1902-1939 *ChPo S2, OhA&B*
Cooper, Duff 1890-1954 *LongC*
Cooper, E *Alli, Alli Sup*
Cooper, E E *Alli Sup*
Cooper, E Fitzgerald *MnBBF*
Cooper, Edith Caskey 1873-1901 *IndAu 1917*
Cooper, Edith Emma 1862-1913 *BrAu 19, ChPo, Chmbr 3, EvLB, LongC, NewC, Pen Eng*
Cooper, Edmund 1926- *ConAu 33, WrD 1976*
Cooper, Edward *Alli, Alli Sup, BiDLA*
Cooper, Edward d1833 *Alli*
Cooper, Edward 1925- *AmSCAP 66*
Cooper, Edward Herbert *BbD*
Cooper, Edward J *Alli Sup*
Cooper, Elise *Alli Sup*
Cooper, Elizabeth *Alli, Alli Sup*
Cooper, Elizabeth 1877- *AmA&B, WhWNAA*
Cooper, Elizabeth Ann 1927- *ConAu 1R*
Cooper, Elizabeth Keyser 1910- *ConAu 1R*
Cooper, Ellwood 1829- *Alli Sup, DcAmA, DcNAA*
Cooper, Elsie Madeline *WhLA*
Cooper, Emily *Alli Sup*
Cooper, Emmanuel 1940- *ConAu 49*
Cooper, Esther *ConAu XR*
Cooper, Evelyne Love *AmSCAP 66*
Cooper, Francis *Alli Sup*
Cooper, Francis LeRoy 1884- *WhWNAA*
Cooper, Frank *Alli Sup, DcNAA, OxAm, REnAL*
Cooper, Mrs. Frank *Alli Sup*
Cooper, Frank E 1910-1968 *ConAu 21*
Cooper, Frank Irving 1867- *WhWNAA*
Cooper, Frederic DeBrebant *Alli Sup*
Cooper, Frederick Henry *Alli Sup*
Cooper, Frederick Taber 1864-1937 *AmA&B, ChPo S1, DcNAA*
Cooper, Freemont *MnBBF*
Cooper, G S *Alli Sup*
Cooper, George *Alli, BiDLA, ChPo, ChPo S1*
Cooper, George 1838-1927 *ChPo S2*
Cooper, George 1840-1927 *BkCL*
Cooper, George William Noel 1896- *WrD 1976*
Cooper, Giles 1918-1966 *CrCD, LongC*
Cooper, Gladys 1888-1971 *ConAu 33*
Cooper, Gordon John Llewellyn 1932- *ConAu 61, WrD 1976*
Cooper, Grace Rogers 1924- *ConAu 41*
Cooper, Sir Grey *Alli*
Cooper, H C *BbtC*

Cooper, H J *Alli Sup*
Cooper, H Stonehewer *Alli Sup*
Cooper, Harold E 1928- *ConAu 45*
Cooper, Henry Fox *Alli, BiDLA*
Cooper, Henry G *Alli Sup*
Cooper, Hermon Charles 1875- *WhWNAA*
Cooper, Homer H 1868- *IndAu 1816*
Cooper, Horatio C d1864 *IndAu 1816*
Cooper, Isaac Rhodes *Alli Sup*
Cooper, J G *Alli Sup*
Cooper, J Goldsmith *Alli Sup*
Cooper, J Lawrence *MnBBF*
Cooper, J T *Alli Sup*
Cooper, Jacob 1830-1904 *DcNAA, OhA&B*
Cooper, James *Alli, BiDLA, ChPo S1*
Cooper, James d1863 *Alli Sup*
Cooper, James Davis 1823-1904 *ChPo*
Cooper, James Fenimore 1728-1779 *CarSB*
Cooper, James Fenimore 1789-1851 *Alli, AmA, AmA&B, AmWr, AtlBL, AuBYP, BbD, BiD&SB, CasWL, Chmbr 3, CnDAL, CriT 3, CyAL 1, CyWA, DcAmA, DcBiA, DcEnA, DcEnL, DcLEnL, DcNAA, EvLB, HsB&A, MnBBF, MouLC 3, OxAm, OxEng, Pen Am, RAdv 1, RCom, REn, REnAL, WebEAL, WhCL*
Cooper, James Fenimore 1897?-1918 *ChPo S2, DcNAA*
Cooper, James L 1934- *ConAu 53*
Cooper, James M 1939- *ConAu 45*
Cooper, James R *ConAu XR*
Cooper, James Wesley 1842- *DcAmA*
Cooper, Jamie Lee *ConAu 9R, IndAu 1917*
Cooper, Jane 1924- *ConAu 25, ConP 1970, ConP 1975, DrAP 1975, WrD 1976*
Cooper, Jeff 1920- *ConAu 41*
Cooper, Jefferson *ConAu XR*
Cooper, Jeffrey 1943- *Au&Wr*
Cooper, Jennie *Alli Sup*
Cooper, Jeremy 1946- *WrD 1976*
Cooper, Jilly *WrD 1976*
Cooper, John *Alli, Alli Sup, BiDLA Sup*
Cooper, John 1810?-1870 *NewC*
Cooper, John 1825?- *Br&AmS*
Cooper, John C *ChPo S1*
Cooper, John Charles 1933- *Au&Wr, ConAu 23*
Cooper, John Cobb 1887- *ConAu 5R*
Cooper, John Cobb 1921- *AmA&B*
Cooper, John Craig 1925- *AmSCAP 66*
Cooper, John E 1922- *ConAu 25, WrD 1976*
Cooper, John Gilbert 1723-1769 *Alli, DcEnL*
Cooper, John H *Alli Sup*
Cooper, John Irwin 1905- *ConAu 41, OxCan, OxCan Sup*
Cooper, John L 1936- *BlkAW, ConAu 21*
Cooper, John M 1912- *ConAu 21*
Cooper, John Montgomery 1881- *CatA 1947*
Cooper, John R *ConAu 19, SmATA 1*
Cooper, John Ralph 1885- *WhWNAA*
Cooper, John Spencer *Alli Sup*
Cooper, Joseph *Alli Sup*
Cooper, Joseph 1635-1699 *Alli*
Cooper, Joseph Bonar 1912- *ConAu 17R, IndAu 1917, WrD 1976*
Cooper, Joseph D 1917-1975 *ConAu 5R, ConAu 57*
Cooper, Katherine *Alli Sup, ChPo S1*
Cooper, Kay 1941- *ConAu 45*
Cooper, Kenneth Ernest 1903- *Au&Wr*
Cooper, Kenneth Schaaf 1918- *ConAu 9R*
Cooper, Kent 1880-1965 *AmA&B, AmSCAP 66, DrAF 1976, IndAu 1917*
Cooper, Lane 1875-1959 *AmA&B, REnAL, WhWNAA*
Cooper, Lee Pelham 1926- *AuBYP, ConAu 5R, SmATA 5, WrD 1976*
Cooper, Leonard 1900- *Au&Wr*
Cooper, Leslie M 1930- *ConAu 41*
Cooper, Lettice 1897- *Au&Wr, ConAu 9R, ConNov 1972, ConNov 1976, WrD 1976*
Cooper, Lina Orman *Alli Sup*
Cooper, Louise Field 1905- *AmA&B, AmNov, ConAu 1R, REnAL, TwCA Sup*
Cooper, M *Alli Sup*
Cooper, Mae *ConAu 17R*
Cooper, Malcolm McGregor 1910- *Au&Wr*

Cooper, Margaret *ChPo S2*
Cooper, Maria Susanna *Alli*
Cooper, Mario 1905- *ConAu 23*
Cooper, Martha J *ChPo S1*
Cooper, Martin DuPre 1910- *WrD 1976*
Cooper, Mary Grace *Alli, Alli Sup*
Cooper, Sister Mary Ursula 1925- *ConAu 5R*
Cooper, Mattie Lula *ConAu XR*
Cooper, May *ChPo S2*
Cooper, Merian C 1893- *AmA&B*
Cooper, Michael 1930- *ConAu 13R*
Cooper, Morley *ConAu XR*
Cooper, Morris *Alli Sup*
Cooper, Myles 1735-1785 *Alli, CyAL 1,
DcAmA, DcNAA, OxAm, REnAL*
Cooper, Oliver St. John *Alli, BiDLA*
Cooper, Oscar Henry 1852-1932 *BiDSA,
DcNAA*
Cooper, Paul 1926- *ConAu 49*
Cooper, Paulette 1944- *ConAu 37, WrD 1976*
Cooper, Peter 1791-1883 *Alli Sup, AmA&B,
BbD, BiD&SB, DcAmA, DcNAA,
OxAm, REn, REnAL*
Cooper, Philip 1926- *ConAu 33*
Cooper, Phyllis 1939- *ConAu 53*
Cooper, R Bransby *Alli*
Cooper, Richard *Alli*
Cooper, Richard d1764 *BkIE*
Cooper, Richard, Jr. *BkIE*
Cooper, Richard Newell 1934- *ConAu 25,
WrD 1976*
Cooper, Robert *Alli Sup*
Cooper, Robert d1866 *BbtC*
Cooper, Robert Jermyn *Alli Sup*
Cooper, Robert Thomas *Alli Sup*
Cooper, Robert Ulsh 1898- *Au&Wr*
Cooper, Robert W 1925- *AmSCAP 66*
Cooper, Rose Marie 1937- *AmSCAP 66*
Cooper, Russell Morgan 1907- *AmA&B*
Cooper, S M *Alli*
Cooper, Samuel *Alli, BiDLA, CyAL 1*
Cooper, Samuel 1725-1783 *Alli, DcAmA,
DcNAA, REn*
Cooper, Samuel 1798-1876 *DcNAA*
Cooper, Samuel Williams 1860-1939 *Alli Sup,
DcNAA*
Cooper, Sandi E 1936- *ConAu 49*
Cooper, Sarah *Alli Sup*
Cooper, Saul 1934- *ConAu 1R*
Cooper, Sidney 1918- *AmSCAP 66*
Cooper, Signe Skott 1921- *ConAu 53*
Cooper, Susan 1935- *ConAu 29, SmATA 4*
Cooper, Susan Fenimore 1813-1894 *Alli, AmA,
AmA&B, BiD&SB, ChPo, CyAL 1,
DcAmA, DcEnL, DcLEnL, DcNAA,
OxAm, REnAL*
Cooper, Susan Mary 1935- *Au&Wr,
WrD 1976*
Cooper, Sylvia 1903- *ConAu 17*
Cooper, T *Alli Sup*
Cooper, T H *Alli, Alli Sup, BiDLA*
Cooper, T J *Alli Sup*
Cooper, Thomas *Alli, BiDLA, Chmbr 3*
Cooper, Thomas 1517?-1594 *Alli*
Cooper, Thomas 1759-1840? *Alli, AmA,
BiDSA, CyAL 2, DcAmA, DcNAA,
OxAm, REnAL*
Cooper, Thomas 1805-1892 *Alli Sup, BiD&SB,
BrAu 19, CasWL, DcEnL, EvLB, NewC*
Cooper, Thomas George *ChPo*
Cooper, Thomas N *Alli*
Cooper, Thomas Sidney 1803-1902 *ChPo S1*
Cooper, Thomas Thornville 1839-1878 *Alli Sup*
Cooper, Thomas William *Alli Sup*
Cooper, Thompson *Alli Sup*
Cooper, Vincent King *Alli Sup*
Cooper, Viola Irene 1894- *WhWNAA*
Cooper, W D *CarSB*
Cooper, W Dublin *BiDLA*
Cooper, W White *Alli*
Cooper, Wendy 1919- *Au&Wr, ConAu 13R,
WrD 1976*
Cooper, Wilbraham Villiers 1876- *WhLA*
Cooper, Willard 1890- *WhWNAA*
Cooper, William *Alli, Alli Sup, BiDLA,
BiDLA Sup, BlkAW, ConAu XR,
ModBL*
Cooper, William 1694-1743 *Alli, DcAmA,
DcNAA*
Cooper, William 1754-1809 *OxAm, REnAL*
Cooper, William 1910- *Au&Wr,
ConNov 1972, ConNov 1976, LongC,
NewC, Pen Eng, TwCW, WorAu,
WrD 1976*
Cooper, William Colby 1835-1914 *ChPo S2,
OhA&B*
Cooper, William Durrant 1812-1875 *Alli Sup*
Cooper, William Frierson *Alli Sup*
Cooper, William Heaton 1903- *Au&Wr*
Cooper, William Henry Hewlett *Alli Sup*
Cooper, William Hurlbert 1924- *ConAu 49*
Cooper, William John 1882-1935 *DcNAA*
Cooper, Rev. William M *Alli Sup*
Cooper, Sir William Mansfield 1903- *Au&Wr,
WrD 1976*
Cooper, William Ricketts 1843-1878 *Alli Sup*
Cooper, William Samuel *Alli Sup*
Cooper, William Temple *Alli Sup*
Cooper, William W 1914- *ConAu 13R*
Cooper, William White 1816-1886 *Alli Sup*
Cooper, Wyatt *AuNews 2*
Cooper, Zebina *Alli Sup*
Cooper Foster, Jeanne *Au&Wr, WrD 1976*
Cooper-Klein, Nina *ConAu XR*
Cooperman, Hasye 1909- *ConAu 37,
WrD 1976*
Cooperman, Stanley 1929- *ConAu 33,
ConP 1975, DrAP 1975, OxCan Sup,
WrD 1976*
Cooperrider, George T 1852-1916 *DcNAA,
OhA&B*
Coopersmith, Harry 1902?- *AmSCAP 66,
ConAu 21*
Coopersmith, Jacob Maurice 1903-
AmSCAP 66
Coopersmith, Stanley 1926- *ConAu 21*
Coopland, Mrs. R M *Alli Sup*
Cooplandt, A *CasWL*
Coore, Richard d1687 *Alli*
Coornhert, Dirck V 1522-1590 *BiD&SB,
CasWL, DcEuL, EuA, Pen Eur*
Coortresse, Richard *Alli*
Coote, Mrs. *Alli Sup*
Coote, Algernon C P *Alli Sup*
Coote, Brian 1929- *WrD 1976*
Coote, Charles *Alli, BiDLA*
Coote, Sir Charles d1661 *Alli*
Coote, Chilly *Alli*
Coote, Edward *Alli, ChPo*
Coote, H J *Alli*
Coote, Henry Charles 1815-1885 *Alli Sup*
Coote, Holmes 1817-1872 *Alli Sup*
Coote, J *Alli*
Coote, Jack Howard 1913- *Au&Wr*
Coote, R H *Alli*
Coote, Richard *Alli*
Coote, Robert *Alli, Alli Sup*
Coote, Walter *Alli Sup*
Coote, William *PoIre*
Cootner, Paul Harold 1930- *ConAu 9R,
IndAu 1917*
Coots, J Fred 1897- *AmSCAP 66*
Coover, James B 1925- *ConAu 57*
Coover, John Edgar 1872-1938 *DcNAA,
IndAu 1917, WhWNAA*
Coover, Melanchthon 1861- *WhWNAA*
Coover, Melanthane 1861- *WhWNAA*
Coover, Robert 1932- *AmA&B, ConAu 45,
ConLC 3, ConNov 1972, ConNov 1976,
DrAF 1976, ModAL Sup, Pen Am,
RAdv 1, WrD 1976*
Coox, Alvin D 1924- *ConAu 29, WrD 1976*
Copass, Blanche Collier *TexWr*
Copcutt, F *Alli Sup*
Cope *Alli*
Cope, Alan d1580? *Alli*
Cope, Alfred D *Alli*
Cope, Sir Anthony *Alli*
Cope, Charles Henry *Alli Sup*
Cope, Charles West 1811-1890 *ChPo, ChPo S2*
Cope, David 1941- *ConAu 33*
Cope, Edward Drinker 1840-1897 *Alli Sup,
DcAmA, DcNAA*
Cope, Edward Meredith 1818-1873 *Alli Sup*
Cope, Gilbert 1840-1928 *DcAmA, DcNAA*
Cope, Henry *Alli*

Cope, Horace *Alli Sup*
Cope, Jack 1913- *Au&Wr, CasWL,
ConAu XR, ConNov 1972, ConNov 1976,
ConP 1970, TwCW, WrD 1976*
Cope, Jackson Irving 1925- *IndAu 1917*
Cope, James, Marquis Biddle-Cope *Alli Sup*
Cope, John *Alli*
Cope, Sir John *Alli*
Cope, John Hautenville 1867- *WhLA*
Cope, Mabel R McNary 1896- *WhWNAA*
Cope, Margaret *ChPo S2*
Cope, Michael *Alli*
Cope, Millard Louis 1905- *TexWr*
Cope, Myron 1929- *ConAu 57*
Cope, Richard 1776-1856 *Alli Sup*
Cope, Robert Knox 1913- *ConAu 9R*
Cope, Robert L *Alli Sup*
Cope, Thomas Pym *Alli Sup*
Cope, W W *Alli Sup*
Cope, Sir William Henry 1811- *Alli Sup*
Cope, Sir Zachary 1881- *Au&Wr, ConAu P-1*
Copeau, Jacques 1879-1949 *CIDMEuL, CnMD,
McGWD, ModWD, OxFr, REn*
Copel, Sidney L 1930- *ConAu 23*
Copeland, Alfred James *Alli Sup*
Copeland, Allan 1926- *AmSCAP 66*
Copeland, Benjamin 1855-1940 *AmA&B,
DcNAA*
Copeland, Bill *ConAu XR*
Copeland, Charles Finney 1863- *AnMV 1926*
Copeland, Charles G 1858- *ChPo, ChPo S1,
ChPo S2*
Copeland, Charles Townsend 1860-1952
AmA&B, OxAm, REnAL, WhWNAA
Copeland, E Luther 1916- *ConAu 9R*
Copeland, Evelyn *ChPo S2*
Copeland, Frances Virginia *AuBYP*
Copeland, Fred 1884- *WhWNAA*
Copeland, George Dale *Alli Sup*
Copeland, Helen 1920- *ConAu 25, SmATA 4*
Copeland, J *Alli Sup*
Copeland, John *Alli, Alli Sup*
Copeland, John 1829- *ChPo S1*
Copeland, John 1934- *Au&Wr*
Copeland, Josephine *BlkAW*
Copeland, Julia Viola 1916- *AmSCAP 66*
Copeland, Margaret Scott *WhWNAA*
Copeland, Melvin T 1884-1975 *ConAu 21,
ConAu 57, WhWNAA*
Copeland, Miles 1916- *ConAu 29, WrD 1976*
Copeland, Morris A 1895- *ConAu P-1*
Copeland, Paul William 1917- *ConAu 25*
Copeland, Paul Worthington *AuBYP,
WhPNW*
Copeland, Robert Morris *Alli Sup*
Copeland, Ross H 1930- *ConAu 25*
Copeland, Royal Samuel 1868-1938 *DcAmA,
DcNAA*
Copeland, Thomas *Alli, BiDLA*
Copeland, Thomas Wellsted 1907- *Au&Wr,
ConAu 5R, OhA&B*
Copeland, Walter 1865-1929 *ChPo*
Copeland, William John *Alli Sup*
Copeland, William P *Alli Sup*
Copeman, E *Alli*
Copeman, Edward *Alli Sup*
Copeman, Fred 1907- *CatA 1952*
Copeman, George Henry 1922- *Au&Wr,
ConAu 5R, WrD 1976*
Copeman, S S *Alli Sup*
Coper, Rudolf 1904- *ConAu P-1*
Copernicus, Nicolaus 1473-1543 *BbD, BiD&SB,
CasWL, NewC, REn*
Copestick, Alfred *EarAB*
Copi, Irving M 1917- *ConAu 1R, WrD 1976*
Copic, Branko 1915- *CasWL, ModSL 2,
Pen Eur*
Copinger, Christopher *Alli Sup*
Copinger, Maurice *Alli, BiDLA*
Copinger, Walter Arthur 1847- *Alli Sup*
Copithorne, Judith *OxCan Sup*
Coplan, Kate M 1901- *ConAu 5R*
Copland, Aaron 1900- *AmA&B, AmSCAP 66,
Au&Wr, ConAu 5R, OxAm, REn,
REnAL*
Copland, Alexander *Alli*
Copland, Dudley *OxCan Sup*
Copland, Edward A *Alli Sup*

Copland, James *Alli, Alli Sup*
Copland, James 1791-1870 *Alli Sup*
Copland, John *Alli Sup*
Copland, Patrick *Alli*
Copland, Peter *Alli*
Copland, Robert *Alli*
Copland, Robert d1548? *Alli, CasWL*
Copland, Samuel *Alli, Alli Sup, BiDLA*
Copland, William *DcEuL, OxCan*
Coplen, Grace Wilson *ChPo*
Copleston, Edward *BiDLA, BiDLA Sup*
Copleston, Edward 1776-1849 *Alli, BrAu 19, DcEnL, NewC*
Copleston, Mrs. Edward *Alli Sup, BbtC*
Copleston, Edward Arthur *Alli Sup*
Copleston, Frederick Charles 1907- *Au&Wr, CatA 1952, ConAu 13R, WrD 1976*
Copleston, Henry Horace *Alli Sup*
Copleston, John *Alli*
Copleston, Reginald Stephen 1845- *Alli Sup*
Copleston, William James *Alli Sup*
Copley, Anthony *Alli*
Copley, Esther *Alli*
Copley, Heather 1920- *IlCB 1966*
Copley, J S *Alli, BiDLA*
Copley, John *Alli*
Copley, John Singleton 1738-1815 *AtlBL, OxAm, REn*
Copley, Josiah *Alli*
Copley, Josiah 1803-1884 *Alli Sup*
Coplin, William D 1939- *ConAu 23*
Copman, Louis 1934- *ConAu 57*
Copner, James *Alli Sup*
Copp, Andrew James, III *WrD 1976*
Copp, F S *ChPo*
Copp, Henry N *Alli Sup*
Copp, James 1916- *ConAu 25*
Copp, Jim *WrD 1976*
Copp, Theodore Bayard Fletcher 1902-1945 *DcNAA*
Coppa, Frank John 1937- *ConAu 33, WrD 1976*
Coppage, Lewellyn Jackson 1848-1933 *IndAu 1917*
Coppard, Alfred Edgar 1878-1957 *ChPo, ChPo S1, ChPo S2, DcLEnL, EvLB, LongC, NewC, OxEng, Pen Eng, REn, TwCA, TwCA Sup, TwCW, WhCL, WhTwL, YABC 1*
Coppard, Audrey 1931- *ConAu 29*
Coppard, S Selby *Alli Sup*
Coppe, Abiezer *Alli, ConAu XR*
Coppedge, Ruby Frazier Parsons 1892?-1970 *IndAu 1917*
Coppee, Francis Edouard Joachim 1842-1908 *DcBiA*
Coppee, Francis-Joachim-Edouard-Francois 1842-1907 *CasWL, EvEuW*
Coppee, Francois Edouard Joachim 1842-1908 *BbD, BiD&SB, ClDMEuL, CnMD, DcEuL, EuA, McGWD, ModWD, OxFr, Pen Eur, REn*
Coppee, Henry 1821-1895 *Alli, Alli Sup, AmA, AmA&B, BiD&SB, BiDSA, CyAL 2, DcAmA, DcNAA*
Coppel, Alec 1909?-1972 *ConAu 33*
Coppel, Alfred 1921- *ConAu 17R, DrAF 1976, WrD 1976*
Coppens, Charles 1835-1920 *Alli Sup, AmLY, OhA&B*
Copper, Basil 1924- *Au&Wr, WrD 1976*
Copper, Marcia S 1934- *ConAu 53*
Copperthwaite, R H *Alli Sup*
Copperud, Roy H 1915- *ConAu 9R, WrD 1976*
Coppi, Antonio 1782-1870 *BiD&SB*
Coppin, J Wylkyns *PoIre*
Coppin, John *PoIre*
Coppin, Levi J 1848- *DcAmA*
Coppin, Richard *Alli*
Copping, Arthur E *OxCan*
Copping, Edward 1828- *Alli Sup, DcEnL*
Copping, Harold *ChPo S2*
Copping, John *Alli*
Copping, Thomas *Alli*
Coppinger, J J 1813-1890 *PoIre*
Coppinger, Matthew *Alli*
Coppinger, Sir Nathaniel *Alli*

Coppinger, Richard William *Alli Sup*
Coppock, Charles 1906- *AuBYP*
Coppock, John Oates 1914- *ConAu 13R, IndAu 1917*
Coppock, Joseph David 1909- *AmA&B, ConAu 49, IndAu 1917*
Coppola, Carmine 1910- *AmSCAP 66*
Copway, George 1818-1863? *Alli, AmA&B, BiD&SB, DcAmA, DcNAA, OxAm, REnAL*
Coquelin, Benoit Constant 1841-1909 *BbD, BiD&SB*
Coquelin, Constant-Benoit 1841-1909 *OxFr*
Coquillart, Guillaume 1421?-1510 *DcEuL*
Coquillart, Guillaume 1450?-1510 *CasWL, OxFr*
Coquina *AmLY XR, DcNAA, OhA&B*
Coraes *EuA*
Coran, Charles 1814-1883 *OxFr*
Corathiel, Elisabethe Helene Christine 1893- *Au&Wr*
Corax *CasWL, Pen Cl*
Coray *CasWL, EuA*
Corazzini, Sergio 1886?-1907 *CasWL, ClDMEuL, Pen Eur*
Corb, Morty 1917- *AmSCAP 66*
Corbally, John Edward, Jr. 1924- *ConAu 5R*
Corbell, E T *ChPo S1*
Corben, T *ChPo*
Corbet, Edward *Alli*
Corbet, Henry *Alli Sup*
Corbet, Jeffray *Alli*
Corbet, John *Alli*
Corbet, John 1620-1680 *Alli*
Corbet, John Dryden *Alli Sup, PoIre*
Corbet, Mrs. M E *Alli Sup*
Corbet, Miles *Alli*
Corbet, Richard 1582-1635 *Alli, BiD&SB, CasWL, Chmbr 1, CnE&AP, CrE&SL, DcEnL, EvLB, NewC, Pen Eng, REn, WebEAL*
Corbet, Robert St. John *Alli Sup, DcEnL*
Corbet, Roger *Alli*
Corbet, Thomas *Alli*
Corbet, William John 1824-1909 *PoIre*
Corbett, Misses *Alli*
Corbett, A *Alli Sup*
Corbett, Alexander Frederic *Alli Sup*
Corbett, Arleigh Jean *WhWNAA*
Corbett, Bertha L *ChPo S1*
Corbett, Charles Henry *Alli Sup*
Corbett, E A *OxCan*
Corbett, Mrs. E J *ChPo S2*
Corbett, E K *Alli Sup*
Corbett, Mrs. E T *Alli Sup, ChPo, ChPo S1*
Corbett, Edmund Victor *Au&Wr, WrD 1976*
Corbett, Edward M *OxCan Sup*
Corbett, Edward P J 1919- *ConAu 17R, WrD 1976*
Corbett, Elizabeth Burgoyne 1846- *Alli Sup*
Corbett, Elizabeth Frances 1887- *AmA&B, AmNov, ConAu 5R, REnAL, TwCA, TwCA Sup, WhWNAA, WiscW*
Corbett, Frederick St. John 1862-1919 *ChPo S1, PoIre*
Corbett, Mrs. George *MnBBF*
Corbett, Harry *WhCL*
Corbett, J Elliott 1920- *ConAu 29*
Corbett, James Edward 1875- *AuBYP*
Corbett, Janice M 1935- *ConAu 37*
Corbett, Jim 1875-1955 *LongC*
Corbett, John Ambrose 1908- *Au&Wr, WrD 1976*
Corbett, Joseph Henry *Alli Sup*
Corbett, Julian *Alli Sup*
Corbett, L C *Alli Sup*
Corbett, Lee Cleveland 1867- *WhWNAA*
Corbett, M De *Alli*
Corbett, Maurice Nathaniel 1859- *BlkAW*
Corbett, Patrick 1916- *ConAu 17R*
Corbett, Pearson H 1900- *ConAu P-1*
Corbett, Percy E *OxCan*
Corbett, Richard 1582-1635 *ChPo, CrE&SL, OxEng, Pen Eng*
Corbett, Richmond McLain 1902- *ConAu P-1*
Corbett, Ruth 1912- *ConAu 29*
Corbett, Scott 1913- *Au&Wr, AuBYP, ChLR 1, ConAu 1R, SmATA 2*

Corbett, Sybil *ChPo*
Corbett, Thomas *Alli*
Corbett, Uvedale *Alli*
Corbett, Verna Margaret Greemore 1905- *IndAu 1917*
Corbett, William *DrAP 1975*
Corbett-Melcher, B *ChPo*
Corbett-Smith, A 1879- *MnBBF, WhLA*
Corbiere, Edouard 1793-1875 *BiD&SB*
Corbiere, Edouard Joachim 1845-1875 *CasWL, EuA, EvEuW, OxFr, Pen Eur, REn*
Corbiere, Tristan 1845-1875 *AtlBL, ClDMEuL*
Corbin, Alice 1881-1949 *AmA&B, ChPo S1, OxAm, REn, REnAL*
Corbin, Arnold 1911- *ConAu 9R*
Corbin, Arthur Linton 1874- *WhWNAA*
Corbin, Caroline Elizabeth 1835- *BiD&SB, DcAmA, DcNAA*
Corbin, Caroline Fairfield *Alli Sup*
Corbin, Charles B 1940- *ConAu 29*
Corbin, Charles L *Alli Sup*
Corbin, Charles Russell 1893-1950 *OhA&B*
Corbin, Claire 1913- *ConAu 41*
Corbin, Diana Fontaine Maury *Alli Sup, BiDSA*
Corbin, Donald A 1920- *ConAu 33*
Corbin, H Dan 1912- *ConAu 41*
Corbin, Iris *ConAu XR*
Corbin, J A *MnBBF*
Corbin, John *Alli Sup*
Corbin, John 1870-1959 *AmA&B, BiD&SB, CarSB, DcAmA, WhWNAA*
Corbin, John R *ChPo S1*
Corbin, Joseph Carter 1833- *BiDSA*
Corbin, Lloyd 1949- *BlkAW*
Corbin, Richard 1911- *ConAu 5R*
Corbin, William *Alli Sup, AuBYP, ConAu XR, SmATA 3*
Corbin, William 1916- *MorJA*
Corbishley, Thomas 1903- *Au&Wr, ConAu 13R, WrD 1976*
Corbitt, Helen Lucy 1906- *ConAu 5R*
Corbitt, John *Alli Sup*
Corbo, Dominic R, Jr. *BlkAW*
Corbould, A Chantrey 1870?- *Br&AmS, ChPo S2*
Corbould, Dorothea Mary *Alli Sup, ChPo S1*
Corbould, Edward *Alli*
Corbould, Edward Henry 1815-1905 *ChPo*
Corbould, Elvina *Alli Sup*
Corbould, H *ChPo*
Corbould, Henry 1787-1844 *ChPo S1*
Corbould, Richard 1757-1831 *BkIE*
Corbould, Walton *ChPo S1*
Corbridge, William *Alli Sup*
Corbusier *TwCA Sup*
Corbusier, Le 1887-1965 *LongC*
Corby, Dan *ConAu XR, SmATA 3, WrD 1976*
Corby, William 1833-1897 *AmA&B, DcNAA, IndAu 1816*
Corbyn, Benjamin *Alli*
Corbyn, Samuel *Alli*
Corchado, Manuel 1840-1884 *PueRA*
Corcoran, Barbara 1911- *ConAu 23, SmATA 3, WrD 1976*
Corcoran, Brewer 1877- *MnBBF, WhWNAA*
Corcoran, Gertrude B 1922?- *ConAu 29, WrD 1976*
Corcoran, Jean Kennedy 1926- *ConAu 1R*
Corcoran, Peter *PoIre*
Corcoran, Timothy 1872- *WhLA*
Corcos, Lucille 1908-1973 *AmA&B, AuBYP, ChPo, ConAu 21, IlCB 1956, IlCB 1966, SmATA 10*
Corcuera, Arturo 1935- *DcCLA*
Cord, Robert L 1935- *ConAu 33*
Cord, Steven Benson 1928- *ConAu 21*
Cord, William Harland *Alli Sup*
Cord, William O 1921- *ConAu 37*
Corda, Michael 1921- *AmSCAP 66*
Cordasco, Francesco 1920- *ConAu 13R*
Corday, Charlotte 1768-1793 *REn*
Corday, Leo 1902- *AmSCAP 66*
Corday D'Armont, Charlotte 1768-1793 *OxFr, OxGer*
Cordeaux, John *Alli Sup*
Cordeaux, William 1832- *Alli Sup*

Cordeiro, Joao Ricardo 1836-1881 *BiD&SB*
Cordell, Alexander 1914- *ConAu XR,*
  SmATA 7, WrD 1976
Cordell, Eugene Fauntleroy 1843- *BiDSA*
Cordell, Richard Albert 1896- *ConAu 1R,*
  IndAu 1917
Cordell, Stanley James 1925- *Au&Wr*
Corden, Warner Max 1927- *ConAu 33,*
  WrD 1976
Corder, Brice W 1936- *ConAu 53*
Corder, Jim 1929- *ConAu 17R*
Corder, Rosa *Alli Sup*
Corder, Susanna *Alli, Alli Sup*
Corderoy, Edward *Alli Sup*
Corderoy, Jeremy *Alli*
Cordery, Arthur 1847- *Alli Sup*
Cordery, Bertha Meriton *Alli Sup*
Cordery, John Graham *Alli Sup*
Cordier, Charles 1911- *CnMD*
Cordier, Mathurin 1479-1564 *CasWL*
Cordier, Ralph Waldo 1902- *ConAu 37*
Cordiner, Charles *Alli, BiDLA*
Cordiner, James *Alli, BiDLA*
Cordingley, John *ChPo*
Cordingly, David 1938- *WrD 1976*
Cordler, Maturin 1479-1564 *DcEuL*
Cordner, John *BbtC*
Cordoba, Martin Alfonso De d1476? *CasWL*
Cordonnier, Gerard Anatole F 1907- *BiDPar*
Cordry, Clem *MnBBF*
Cordry, Tom *ChPo S1*
Cordus, Euricius 1486-1535 *CasWL, OxGer,*
  Pen Cl
Cordwell, F C G *MnBBF*
Cordwell, J *Alli*
Core, Francis *Alli*
Core, Susie Pearl *ChPo S1*
Corelli, Archangelo 1653-1713 *AtlBL, REn*
Corelli, Marie 1855-1924 *BbD, BiD&SB,*
  ChPo, ChPo S1, Chmbr 3, DcEnA Ap,
  EvLB, LongC, ModBL, OxEng, Pen Eng,
  REn, TwCA, TwCA Sup, TwCW
Corelli, Marie 1864-1924 *Alli Sup, DcBiA,*
  DcLEnL, NewC
Coren, Alan 1938- *WrD 1976*
Coresi d1583? *CasWL*
Corey, A *Alli Sup*
Corey, A B *OxCan*
Corey, Charles Henry 1834-1899 *DcNAA*
Corey, Delorain P *Alli Sup*
Corey, Frank 1843-1934 *HsB&A*
Corey, Giles d1692 *OxAm*
Corey, Helen 1923- *IndAu 1917*
Corey, Henry B *Alli Sup*
Corey, Herbert 1872-1954 *OhA&B*
Corey, Kate T *ArizL*
Corey, Lewis 1894-1953 *AmA&B, OhA&B,*
  OxAm, TwCA, TwCA Sup
Corey, Mary *Alli Sup*
Corey, Paul 1903- *AmA&B, AmNov,*
  Au&Wr, ConAu 5R, REnAL, TwCA,
  TwCA Sup, WrD 1976
Corey, Robert *IlBYP*
Corey, Ruth Lechlitner 1901- *IndAu 1917*
Corey, Stephen Maxwell 1904- *WhWNAA*
Corey, William Alfred 1863- *WhWNAA*
Corf, Eliza *Alli Sup*
Corfe, George *Alli Sup*
Corfe, Joseph *Alli, BiDLA*
Corfe, Tom 1928- *Au&Wr*
Corfield, William Henry *Alli Sup*
Coriat, Junior *Alli*
Coriat, Isador H 1875- *WhWNAA*
Coriat, Thomas *Alli, OxEng*
Corigliano, John 1938- *AmSCAP 66*
Corina, Maurice 1936- *ConAu 57*
Corinna 500?BC- *BiD&SB, CasWL, DcEnL,*
  NewC, Pen Cl
Corinne *DcNAA, OhA&B*
Corinth, Lovis 1858-1925 *OxGer*
Coriolanus *WrD 1976*
Corippus, Flavius Cresconius *CasWL, Pen Eur*
Corita, Mary *AmA&B*
Cork, Earl Of *NewC*
Cork, Barry Joynson *MnBBF*
Cork, Nathaniel *Alli Sup*
Corke, Helen 1882- *Au&Wr, ConAu P-1*
Corke, Hilary 1921- *ConP 1970, ConP 1975,*

WrD 1976
Corker, Edward *Alli*
Corker, James *Alli*
Corker, Samuel *Alli*
Corkery, Daniel 1878-1964 *CasWL,*
  CatA 1947, NewC, TwCA Sup
Corkey, Alexander 1871-1914 *DcNAA*
Corkey, R 1881-1966 *ConAu P-1*
Corkling, Mary Anne Yates *Alli Sup*
Corkran, Alice Abigail d1916 *Alli Sup, ChPo,*
  ChPo S1
Corkran, David Hudson, Jr. 1902- *ConAu 5R*
Corkran, Henriette *Alli Sup*
Corkran, Herbert, Jr. 1924- *ConAu 29*
Corkran, J Fraser *ChPo, ChPo S1*
Corkran, John Frazer d1884 *Alli Sup, PoIre*
Corkran, Louise *Alli Sup*
Corkran, Sutton Fraser *Alli Sup*
Corlass, Reginald Walter *Alli Sup*
Corle, Edwin 1906-1956 *AmA&B, OxAm,*
  REnAL, TwCA Sup, WhWNAA
Corlett, John *Alli Sup*
Corlett, Wilfred John 1918- *Au&Wr*
Corlett, William Thomas 1854-1948 *OhA&B*
Corley, Anthony 1923- *ConAu 1R*
Corley, Donald *AmA&B*
Corley, Edwin 1931- *ConAu 25*
Corley, Ernest *ConAu XR, WrD 1976*
Corley, Robert N 1930- *ConAu 9R*
Corley, Thomas Anthony Buchanan 1923-
  Au&Wr, WrD 1976
Corley, William Laurence 1909- *Au&Wr*
Corliss, Allene 1898- *AmA&B*
Corliss, Anne Parrish *WhWNAA*
Corliss, Mrs. Charles Albert *AmA&B,*
  AmNov XR
Corliss, Charlotte N 1932- *ConAu 53*
Corliss, William R 1926- *ConAu 45*
Corlo, Bernardino *DcEuL*
Cormac 836-908 *DcEnL, NewC*
Cormack, Barbara Villy *OxCan*
Cormack, Bartlett 1898-1942 *DcNAA,*
  IndAu 1917
Cormack, C E *Alli Sup*
Cormack, James Maxwell Ross 1909- *Au&Wr,*
  ConAu P-1
Cormack, John *Alli, BiDLA*
Cormack, Sir John Rose 1815-1882 *Alli Sup*
Cormack, Margaret Grant 1913- *Au&Wr,*
  ConAu 1R
Cormack, Margaret Lawson 1912- *ConAu 1R*
Cormack, Maribelle 1902- *AuBYP, JBA 1951*
Cormack, W E *BbtC*
Cormack, William Epps 1796-1868 *OxCan*
Corman, Cid 1924- *ConP 1970, ConP 1975,*
  DrAP 1975, RAdv 1, WrD 1976
Cormenin, Louis-M DeLaHaye, Vicomte De
  1788-1868 *OxFr*
Cormick, C M *Alli*
Cormier, Frank 1927- *ConAu 23*
Cormier, Ramona 1923- *ConAu 49*
Cormier, Raymond J 1938- *ConAu 53*
Cormier, Robert Edmund 1925- *ConAu 1R,*
  SmATA 10
Cormouls, Thomas *Alli, BiDLA*
Corn-Law Rhymer, The *DcEnL, NewC*
Cornall, Richard *Alli Sup*
Cornaro, Luigi 1467-1566 *REn*
Cornazzano, Antonio 1429-1484 *CasWL*
Corncob, Jonathan *Alli*
Corne, Michele Felice 1752?-1845 *EarAB*
Corne, Molly E *OhA&B, WhPNW*
Corneau, Octavia Roberts *AmA&B,*
  WhWNAA
Corneille, Pierre 1606-1684 *AtlBL, BbD,*
  BiD&SB, CasWL, CnThe, CyWA,
  DcEuL, EuA, EvEuW, McGWD, NewC,
  OxEng, OxFr, Pen Eur, RCom, REn,
  REnWD
Corneille, Thomas 1625-1709 *BiD&SB,*
  CasWL, DcEuL, EuA, EvEuW, McGWD,
  OxFr, Pen Eur, REn, REnWD
Cornejo Polar, Antonio 1936- *DcCLA*
Cornelia 170?BC- *NewC*
Cornelisen, Ann 1926- *ConAu 25*
Cornelison, J A *Alli Sup*
Cornelius Gallus *CasWL, Pen Cl*
Cornelius Nepos 100?BC-025?BC *BiD&SB,*

CasWL, Pen Cl
Cornelius, Alberta *TexWr*
Cornelius, Charles Over 1890- *WhWNAA*
Cornelius, Charles S 1857- *WhWNAA*
Cornelius, Elias 1794-1852 *DcAmA*
Cornelius, Elias 1794-1832 *DcNAA*
Cornelius, Ellanor Frances 1869- *WhWNAA*
Cornelius, J W *Alli Sup*
Cornelius, Lucius *Alli*
Cornelius, Mary Ann 1829-1918 *DcNAA*
Cornelius, Mary Chilton Chase *AnMV 1926*
Cornelius, Mary H *Alli Sup*
Cornelius, Melissa Jeffras 1836-1924
  IndAu 1917
Cornelius, Peter *Alli*
Cornelius, Peter 1824-1874 *EvEuW*
Cornelius, Peter Von 1783-1867 *OxGer*
Cornelius, Temple H 1891-1964 *ConAu P-1*
Cornell, Mrs. *ChPo S2*
Cornell, A D 1923- *BiDPar*
Cornell, Adirenne *BlkAW*
Cornell, Alonzo Barton 1832-1904 *Alli Sup,*
  DcAmA, DcNAA
Cornell, Annette Patton *ChPo, ChPo S1,*
  OhA&B
Cornell, Beaumont Sandfield 1892-1958 *CanNov,*
  OxCan
Cornell, Ebenezer *Alli*
Cornell, Frederick Carruthers 1867-1921 *CasWL*
Cornell, George W 1920- *ConAu 9R*
Cornell, J F D *Alli Sup*
Cornell, Jean Gay 1920- *ConAu 45*
Cornell, John Henry 1828-1894 *DcAmA,*
  DcNAA
Cornell, John J *Alli Sup*
Cornell, John V *EarAB*
Cornell, Katharine 1898-1974 *ConAu 49,*
  OxAm
Cornell, Paul G *OxCan, OxCan Sup*
Cornell, S S *Alli*
Cornell, Sarah G *Alli Sup*
Cornell, Mrs. Stephen Webster *WhWNAA*
Cornell, W D *WiscW*
Cornell, William Mason 1802-1895 *Alli,*
  Alli Sup, DcAmA, DcNAA
Cornell, William N C *Alli Sup*
Corner, Miss *CarSB*
Corner, Caroline *Alli Sup*
Corner, George W 1889- *WhWNAA*
Corner, Horace Ranney *ChPo*
Corner, John 1788-1825 *ChPo*
Corner, Julia 1798-1875 *Alli, Alli Sup,*
  ChPo S2
Corner, Matthew *Alli Sup*
Corner, Philip 1933- *ConAu 23*
Corner, Sidney *Alli Sup*
Cornet Y Palau, Cayetano 1878- *WhLA*
Cornetet, Noah E 1867-1931 *OhA&B,*
  WhWNAA
Cornett, Alice 1911- *AmSCAP 66*
Cornett, Joe D 1935- *ConAu 53*
Cornett, R Orin 1913- *WrD 1976*
Cornewall-Jones *Alli Sup*
Corney, Bolton 1784-1870 *Alli, Alli Sup,*
  DcEnL
Cornfeld, Gaalyahu 1902- *ConAu 17*
Cornfield, John *Alli Sup*
Cornford, Christopher *ChPo S1*
Cornford, Frances Crofts 1886-1960 *ChPo,*
  ChPo S1, ChPo S2, DcLEnL, EvLB,
  LongC, NewC, Pen Eng, REn, TwCW
Cornford, Francis Macdonald 1874-1943 *LongC,*
  REn, TwCA Sup
Cornford, Leslie Cope 1867- *ChPo S1*
Cornford, Margaret *ChPo S1*
Cornford, Philip Henry *Alli Sup*
Cornford, Rupert John 1915-1936 *Pen Eng*
Cornforth, Edith *Alli Sup*
Cornforth, John 1937- *Au&Wr*
Cornforth, Maurice 1909- *Au&Wr,*
  ConAu 5R
Corngold, Stanley Alan 1934- *ConAu 37,*
  WrD 1976
Cornier, Vincent 1898- *EncM&D, MnBBF*
Cornificius *CasWL*
Cornificius, Quintus *Pen Cl*
Cornil, Georges 1863- *WhLA*

Cornillon, John Raymond Koppleman 1941-
ConAu 17R

Corning, Charles R Alli Sup
Corning, Howard McKinley 1896- AnMV 1926,
WhPNW, WhWNAA
Corning, J L Alli Sup
Corning, James Leonard 1828-1903 DcNAA
Corning, James Leonard 1855-1923 Alli Sup,
DcAmA, DcNAA
Corning, Kyle EncM&D
Corning, Mary Spring Alli Sup
Corning, W H Alli Sup
Cornings, Benjamin N 1817- Alli
Cornish, Miss Alli Sup
Cornish, Mrs. Alli Sup
Cornish, Daniel Alli Sup
Cornish, Dudley T 1915- ConAu 17R
Cornish, Francis Warre 1839- Alli Sup,
BiD&SB
Cornish, George Augustus 1874- WhWNAA
Cornish, George Henry 1834-1912 Alli Sup,
DcNAA
Cornish, George James Alli Sup
Cornish, Henry Alli Sup
Cornish, Hubert Ray 1878- WhWNAA
Cornish, John 1914- Au&Wr, ConAu 25,
OxCan, OxCan Sup
Cornish, Joseph Alli, BiDLA
Cornish, Kate BiDSA
Cornish, Katherine D Alli Sup, ChPo
Cornish, Mary 1897- Au&Wr
Cornish, Samuel James 1935?- BlkAW,
ConAu 41, ConP 1970, ConP 1975,
DrAP 1975, LivBA, WrD 1976
Cornish, Sidney William Alli Sup
Cornish, T H Alli
Cornish, Thomas 1830- Alli Sup
Cornish, Vaughan 1862- WhLA
Cornish, W H MnBBF
Cornish, W R 1937- Au&Wr, ConAu 29
Cornish, William ChPo
Cornish, William Floyer Alli, Alli Sup
Cornish, William Robert Alli Sup
Cornman, Oliver Perry 1866-1930 DcNAA
Corno DiBassetto LongC
Cornock, Stroud 1938- ConAu 25
Cornthwaite, Robert Alli
Cornuel, Anne-Marie Bigot 1605-1694 OxFr
Cornuelle, Richard C 1927- ConAu 17R,
IndAu 1917
Cornwall, Earl Of NewC
Cornwall, Barry Alli, BrAu 19, CasWL,
ChPo, ChPo S1, Chmbr 3, DcEnL,
DcEuL, DcLEnL, EvLB, NewC, OxEng
Cornwall, C M Alli Sup, DcNAA
Cornwall, E Judson 1924- ConAu 57
Cornwall, Ebenezer Alli Sup
Cornwall, Edward Everett 1866-1940 DcNAA
Cornwall, Frederic Alli Sup
Cornwall, Henry Alli
Cornwall, Henry Bedinger 1844-1917 Alli Sup,
DcAmA, DcNAA
Cornwall, Henry Sylvester 1831-1886 ChPo,
DcNAA
Cornwall, Ian Wolfran 1909- Au&Wr,
ConAu 9R
Cornwall, James Alli
Cornwall, Jim ConAu XR
Cornwall, John Alli
Cornwall, Martin ConAu XR
Cornwall, N E Alli
Cornwall, Nellie Alli Sup
Cornwall, Sarah Jerusha Alli Sup
Cornwall, Susan Peyton Alli Sup
Cornwall, Ursula ChPo, ChPo S2
Cornwalleys, Henry Alli
Cornwallis, Caroline Frances 1786-1858
Alli Sup
Cornwallis, Sir Charles d1630? Alli
Cornwallis, Charles, Marquis 1738-1805 Alli,
OxAm, REn, REnAL
Cornwallis, Edward 1713-1776 OxCan
Cornwallis, Frederick Alli
Cornwallis, James Alli
Cornwallis, Kinahan 1839-1917 Alli Sup, AmA,
AmA&B, BbtC, BiD&SB, DcAmA,
DcNAA, OxCan
Cornwallis, Mary Alli

Cornwallis, Sir William d1631 Alli, CrE&SL,
WebEAL
Cornwell, B M L Alli
Cornwell, David John Moore 1931- Au&Wr,
ConAu 5R, EncM&D, NewC, WorAu,
WrD 1976
Cornwell, Dorothea Graff 1925- OhA&B
Cornwell, Edward Lewis 1910- Au&Wr
Cornwell, Francis Alli
Cornwell, Henry Sylvester 1831-1886 Alli Sup,
AmA&B, BiD&SB, ChPo, ChPo S2,
DcAmA
Cornwell, James Alli
Cornwell, M S BiDSA
Cornwell, Smith ConAu 49
Cornyn, John Hubert 1875- AmA&B,
WhWNAA
Cornyn, John K Alli Sup
Cornyn, Stan 1933- AmSCAP 66
Corominas, John 1905- DcSpL
Coromines, Pere 1870-1939 ClDMEuL
Coronado, Carolina 1823-1911 BiD&SB,
CasWL, Pen Eur
Coronado, Francisco Vasquez De 1510-1554
REn, REnAL
Coronel Urtecho, Jose 1906- DcCLA
Corot, Jean Baptiste Camille 1796-1875 AtlBL,
NewC, OxFr, REn
Corp, Harriet Alli, BiDLA Sup
Corp, William Alli
Corpe, Henry Alli Sup
Corporal Trim ConAu 57
Corr, Lucinda H Alli Sup
Corr, Thomas John 1859-1885 Alli Sup, PoIre
Corradi, Gemma 1939- ConAu 23
Corradini, Enrico 1865-1931 ClDMEuL
Corral, Gabriel De 1588-1640 DcEuL
Corral, Pedro Del CasWL, DcEuL, EvEuW
Corrall, Alice Enid 1916- ConAu 5R
Corrance, Charles Thomas Alli Sup
Corre, Alan D 1931- ConAu 37
Correa, Gustavo 1914- ConAu 49
Correa, Judith Green ConAu XR
Correa DeAzevedo, Luiz Heitor 1905- Au&Wr
Correas, Gonzalo DcSpL
Corrector, Alexander The DcEnL
Correggio, Antonio Allegri Da 1494?-1534
AtlBL, ChPo, ChPo S1, REn
Correggio, Niccolo Da 1450-1508 CasWL
Correia, Gaspar 1496?-1561? CasWL, Pen Eur
Correia, Raimundo 1860-1911 Pen Am
Correia-Afonso, John 1924- ConAu 33
Correia DeOliveira, Antonio 1879- ClDMEuL
Correll, A Boyd EncM&D
Corren, Grace ConAu XR
Corresponsal, El PueRA
Corretjer, Juan Antonio 1908- DcCLA, PueRA
Correy, Lee SmATA XR
Corri, D Alli
Corrie, Archibald 1777-1857 Alli
Corrie, C J Alli Sup
Corrie, D Alli
Corrie, Edgar Alli, BiDLA
Corrie, George Elwes 1793-1885 Alli, Alli Sup
Corrie, James Alli
Corrie, Joe ChPo, ChPo S1
Corrie, John Alli, BiDLA
Corrie, Louisa Alli Sup
Corrie, Theodora Alli Sup
Corrie, William Alli Sup
Corrigan, Andrew Alli
Corrigan, Barbara 1922- ChPo, ConAu 57,
SmATA 8
Corrigan, Sir Dominic John 1802-1880 Alli Sup
Corrigan, Francis Joseph 1919- ConAu 5R
Corrigan, John D ConAu 41
Corrigan, P Alli Sup
Corrigan, Philip Richard Douglas 1942-
Au&Wr
Corrigan, Ralph L, Jr. 1937- ConAu 33
Corrigan, Robert A 1935- ConAu 9R
Corrigan, Robert Willoughby 1927- ConAu 5R,
WrD 1976
Corrington, John William 1932- AmA&B,
ConAu 13R, ConP 1970, ConP 1975,
DrAF 1976, WrD 1976
Corrington, Julian Dana 1891- AmA&B
Corriveau, Monique 1927- ConAu 61,

OxCan Sup
Corrodi, August 1826-1885 BbD, BiD&SB
Corrodi, Wilhelm August 1826-1885 OxGer
Corrothers, James David 1869-1917 AmA&B,
BlkAW, DcNAA
Corry, A C Alli Sup
Corry, Arthur PoIre
Corry, Bernard Alexander 1930- Au&Wr
Corry, Helen M PoIre
Corry, Henry Thomas Lowry- 1803-1873
Alli Sup
Corry, John Alli, BiDLA, PoIre
Corry, Joseph Alli, BiDLA
Corry, Percy 1894- Au&Wr
Corry, Sir Somerset Richard Lowry- 1835-
Alli Sup
Corry, Thomas Charles Stewart 1825-1896
Alli Sup, PoIre
Corry, Thomas H d1887? PoIre
Corsa, Helen Storm 1915- ConAu 17R
Corsan, George Hebden, Sr. 1867- WhWNAA
Corse, John Alli
Corsel, Ralph 1920- ConAu 25
Corsellis, Elizabeth ChPo S2
Corser, Harry Prosper 1864-1936 AmA&B,
DcNAA, WhWNAA
Corser, Thomas 1793-1876 Alli Sup
Corser, William Alli
Corsican, The NewC
Corsini, Raymond J 1914- ConAu 1R
Corso, Gregory 1930- AmA&B, CasWL,
ConAu 5R, ConLC 1, ConP 1970,
ConP 1975, CrCAP, DrAP 1975, OxAm,
Pen Am, RAdv 1, REn, REnAL, TwCW,
WebEAL, WrD 1976
Corson, Mrs. C R Alli Sup
Corson, Ella May Jacoby 1861-1953 OhA&B
Corson, Ellen Sherman ChPo
Corson, Eugene R 1855- WhWNAA
Corson, Fred Pierce 1896- Au&Wr, ConAu 23
Corson, Hazel W 1906- ConAu 1R
Corson, Hiram 1828-1911 Alli Sup, AmA,
AmA&B, BiD&SB, DcAmA, DcNAA,
REnAL
Corson, James Clarkson 1905- Au&Wr
Corson, John J 1905- ConAu 1R
Corson, John W Alli Sup
Corson, Juliet 1842-1897 Alli Sup, DcAmA,
DcNAA
Corson, Oscar Taylor 1857-1928 OhA&B
Corson, Richard ConAu 41, WrD 1976
Cort, David 1904- AmA&B, ConAu 9R
Cort, Mrs. David AmNov XR
Cort, Frans De 1834-1878 BiD&SB
Cort, Lillian Howard ChPo S1
Cort, M C ConAu XR, SmATA 1
Cort, Mary Lovina Alli Sup
Cort, William Walter 1887- WhWNAA
Cortada, Joan Pen Eur
Cortadillo PueRA
Cortambert, Louis Richard 1808-1881 AmA&B,
DcNAA
Cortazar, Julio 1914- CasWL, ConAu 21,
ConLC 2, ConLC 3, ConLC 5, DcCLA,
EncWL Sup, Pen Am, TwCW, WhTwL,
WorAu
Corte-Real, Gaspar OxCan
Corte Real, Jeronimo 1533?-1588? CasWL
Corteen, Wes ConAu XR, WrD 1976
Cortes, Carlos E 1934- ConAu 61
Cortes, Donoso DcSpL
Cortes, Fernando 1485-1547 NewC
Cortes, Hernan 1485-1547 CasWL, DcSpL,
Pen Am, REn
Cortes, Hernando 1485-1547 DcEuL, NewC,
OxAm, REn
Cortes, J D Alli Sup
Cortes, Juan B 1925- ConAu 37
Cortez, Fernando 1485-1547 NewC
Cortez, Hernan 1485-1547 REn
Cortez, Hernando 1485-1547 NewC, REn,
REnAL
Cortez, Jayne 1936?- BlkAW, DrAP 1975,
LivBAA
Corthell, Elmer Lawrence 1840-1916 Alli Sup,
DcAmA, DcNAA
Corti, Count Egon Caesar 1886- WhLA
Cortis, H L Alli Sup

Cortis, William *Alli Sup*
Cortis, William Smithson *Alli Sup*
Cortissoz, Ellen Mackay d1933 *AmA&B, DcAmA, DcNAA*
Cortissoz, Royal 1869-1948 *AmA&B, DcNAA, TwCA, TwCA Sup*
Corton, Antonio 1854-1913 *PueRA*
Cortona, Pietro Da 1596-1669 *AtlBL*
Cortright, David 1946- *ConAu 57*
Corty, Floyd L 1916- *ConAu 13R*
Corver, Marten 1727-1794 *CasWL*
Corvichen, Robert *Alli Sup*
Corvin, Eugen Alban 1886- *WhLA*
Corvin-Wiersbitski, Otto J Bernhard Von *Alli Sup*
Corvinus, Jakob *OxGer*
Corvo, Baron 1860-1913 *AtlBL, CasWL, ChPo S2, DcLEnL, EvLB, LongC, ModBL, NewC, OxEng, Pen Eng, REn, TwCA, TwCA Sup, TwCW*
Corwin, Betty L 1920- *AmSCAP 66*
Corwin, Edward Samuel 1878-1963 *AmA&B*
Corwin, Edward Tanjore 1834-1914 *Alli Sup, DcAmA, DcNAA*
Corwin, Jane Hudson 1809-1881 *OhA&B*
Corwin, Judith Hoffman 1946- *SmATA 10*
Corwin, June Atkin 1935- *IlCB 1966*
Corwin, Norman 1910- *AmA&B, AmSCAP 66, AuNews 2, CnDAL, ConAu 1R, OxAm, REnAL, TwCA Sup, WrD 1976*
Corwin, Robert Nelson 1865- *WhWNAA*
Corwin, Ronald Gary 1932- *ConAu 17R*
Corwin, Thomas 1794-1865 *Alli Sup, DcNAA, OhA&B*
Corwine, Richard M *Alli*
Cory, Adela Florence *LongC*
Cory, Arthur *Alli Sup*
Cory, Charles Barney 1857-1921 *Alli Sup, AmA, AmA&B, DcAmA, DcNAA*
Cory, Charles Henry 1834-1899 *DcAmA, DcNAA*
Cory, Corrine *ConAu 49*
Cory, Daniel 1904-1972 *ConAu 37*
Cory, David 1872-1966 *AmA&B, ConAu 25, WhWNAA*
Cory, Desmond 1928- *Au&Wr, ConAu XR*
Cory, E A *Alli*
Cory, Fannie Young *ChPo S1*
Cory, Fanny Young *ChPo*
Cory, Frederick William *Alli Sup*
Cory, George 1920- *AmSCAP 66*
Cory, Harry Thomas 1870- *IndAu 1816, WhWNAA*
Cory, Herbert Ellsworth 1883-1947 *CatA 1947, DcNAA, WhWNAA*
Cory, Howard L *ConAu XR*
Cory, Irene E 1910- *ConAu 49*
Cory, Isaac Preston *Alli*
Cory, Jean-Jacques 1947- *ConAu 57*
Cory, Ray *ConAu XR*
Cory, Thomas *Alli*
Cory, William Johnson 1823-1892 *Alli Sup, BrAu 19, CasWL, Chmbr 3, ChPo, ChPo S1, DcEuL, DcLEnL, EvLB, NewC, OxEng, REn*
Cory, Winifred Muriel *WhLA*
Corya, Florence *ChPo*
Corya, I E *ConAu 49*
Coryat, Junior *Alli*
Coryat, George d1606 *Alli, DcEnL*
Coryat, Thomas 1577-1617 *Alli, DcEnL, NewC, REn*
Coryate, George d1606 *Alli*
Coryate, Thomas 1577-1617 *Alli, BrAu, CasWL, Chmbr 1, DcEuL, DcLEnL, EvLB, NewC, OxEng, Pen Eng, REn*
Coryatt, Thomas 1577-1617 *CasWL, EvLB*
Corydon, Paul *MnBBF*
Corye, John *Alli*
Coryell, Horace Noble 1888-1965 *IndAu 1917*
Coryell, Hubert Vansant 1889- *WhWNAA*
Coryell, John Russell 1848?-1924 *AmA&B, DcNAA, EncM&D, OxAm, REn, REnAL*
Coryell, Russell Miers 1891- *WhWNAA*
Corymbaeus *Alli, NewC*
Coryn, H A W *Alli Sup*

Coryton, John 1826- *Alli, Alli Sup*
Cosbie, Arnold *Alli*
Cosbuc, Gheorghe 1866-1918 *CasWL, Pen Eur*
Cosby, Major *PoIre*
Cosby, Fortunatus 1802- *BiDSA, ChPo S1*
Coscia, Silvio 1899- *AmSCAP 66*
Cosel, Charlotte Von *BiD&SB*
Cosens, Mrs. E H F *ChPo*
Cosens, F W *Alli Sup*
Cosens, John *Alli*
Cosens, William Reyner *Alli Sup*
Cosenza, Mario Emilio 1880- *WhWNAA*
Coser, Lewis Alfred 1913- *AmA&B, ConAu 1R, WrD 1976*
Coser, Rose Laub 1916- *ConAu 13R*
Cosgrave, E Macdowell *Alli Sup*
Cosgrave, Jessica 1871-1949 *DcNAA*
Cosgrave, John O'Hara 1866-1947 *ChPo S2, DcNAA*
Cosgrave, John O'Hara, II 1908- *ConAu 1R, IlBYP, IlCB 1945, IlCB 1956, IlCB 1966, MorJA*
Cosgrave, Mary Dilva *ChPo S1*
Cosgrave, Patrick 1941- *ConAu 33, WrD 1976*
Cosgrove, Carol Ann 1943- *ConAu 29*
Cosgrove, Edmund *OxCan Sup*
Cosgrove, James M d1880? *PoIre*
Cosgrove, Margaret Leota 1926- *AuBYP, ConAu 9R, IlCB 1966*
Cosgrove, Maynard Giles 1895- *ConAu 57, OhA&B*
Cosgrove, Rachel *ConAu 49*
Cosgrove, Stephen *AuNews 1*
Cosh, Ethel Eleanor Mary 1921- *Au&Wr*
Cosh, Mary 1921- *ConAu 5R, WrD 1976*
Cosh, William *Alli*
Cosic, Bora 1932- *CasWL*
Cosic, Branimir 1901-1934 *CasWL*
Cosic, Dobrica 1921- *CasWL, EncWL Sup, ModSL 2, Pen Eur*
Cosimo *AtlBL*
Cosimo, Piero Di 1462-1521 *REn*
Cosin, James *Alli*
Cosin, John 1594-1672 *Alli, DcEnL*
Cosin, Richard *Alli*
Coskey, Evelyn 1932- *ConAu 41, SmATA 7*
Coslow, Sam 1902- *AmSCAP 66*
Cosmas Indicopleustes *CasWL, Pen Cl*
Cosmas Of Jerusalem *CasWL*
Cosmas Of Prague 1045?-1125 *CasWL, Pen Eur*
Cosmas, The Priest *CasWL, Pen Eur*
Cosneck, Bernard Joseph 1912- *ConAu 49*
Coss, Clay 1910- *AmA&B*
Coss, Thurman L 1926- *ConAu 13R*
Cossa, Pietro 1830-1881 *BiD&SB, CasWL, EvEuW, McGWD*
Cossar, John D *Alli Sup*
Cosseboom, Kathy Groehn *ConAu 57*
Cosserat, Jane G H *Alli Sup*
Cossett, Franceway Ranna 1790-1863 *BiDSA, DcAmA, DcNAA*
Cossham, J N *Alli, BiDLA*
Cossio, Jose Maria De 1895- *ClDMEuL*
Cossio, Manuel Bartolome 1858-1935 *CasWL, ClDMEuL, DcSpL*
Cossit, Charlotte *ChPo*
Cosslett, Mrs. *Alli Sup*
Cossman, E Joseph 1918- *ConAu 17R*
Cosson, Baron De And Burges, William *Alli Sup*
Cost, March *ConAu XR*
Costa, Albert Bernard 1929- *ConAu 13R*
Costa, Claudio Manuel Da 1729-1789 *Pen Am*
Costa, Emanuel M Da *Alli*
Costa, Gustavo 1930- *ConAu 37*
Costa, Isaac De *EuA*
Costa, Isaak Da 1798-1860 *BiD&SB*
Costa, Joaquin 1846-1911 *ClDMEuL*
Costa, Margaret Mary 1917- *Au&Wr*
Costa, Paolo 1771-1836 *CasWL*
Costa, Richard Hauer 1921- *ConAu 21*
Costa, S Mendes Da 1882- *WhLA*
Costa, William F 1920- *AmSCAP 66*
Costa Alegre, Caetano *AfA 1*
Costa I Llobera, Miquel 1854-1922 *CasWL, ClDMEuL, EvEuW, Pen Eur*

Costa Ricca, Lewis Da *WhLA*
Costa Y Martinez, Joaquin 1844?-1911 *CasWL, DcSpL, EvEuW, Pen Eur*
Costain, Thomas Bertram 1885-1965 *AmA&B, AmNov, AuBYP, CanWr, ConAu 5R, ConAu 25, DcLEnL, LongC, OxAm, OxCan, REn, REnAL, TwCA Sup, TwCW*
Costanso, Miguel *OxAm*
Costantin, M M 1935- *ConAu 45*
Costantini, Flavio 1926- *WhGrA*
Costanzo, Angelo De 1507-1591 *CasWL, DcEuL*
Costanzo, Gerald *DrAP 1975*
Costanzo, Jack *AmSCAP 66*
Costar, Pierre 1603-1660 *OxFr*
Costard, George 1710-1782 *Alli*
Costas, Procope 1900?-1974 *ConAu 53*
Coste, Peter *Alli*
Costeker *Alli*
Costello, Mrs. *Alli, BiDLA*
Costello, Augustine E *Alli Sup*
Costello, Bartley C 1871-1941 *AmSCAP 66*
Costello, Belle M *TexWr*
Costello, David Francis 1904- *ConAu 33, WhPNW, WrD 1976*
Costello, Donald P 1931- *ConAu 17R*
Costello, Dudley 1803-1865 *Alli, Alli Sup*
Costello, Edward *Alli*
Costello, Frederick Hankerson 1851-1921 *DcAmA, DcNAA*
Costello, Harry Todd 1885-1960 *IndAu 1917, WhWNAA*
Costello, John *PoIre*
Costello, Louisa Stuart 1799-1870 *Alli, Alli Sup, BrAu 19, ChPo S2, Chmbr 3, DcEnL, EvLB, NewC, PoIre*
Costello, Mark *DrAF 1976*
Costello, Michael *ConAu XR*
Costello, Patrick *Alli Sup*
Costello, Pierre *WhLA*
Costello, William Aloysious 1904- *ConAu 1R*
Costelloe, James C *Alli Sup, PoIre*
Costelloe, M Joseph 1914- *ConAu 41*
Costelloe, Mark *PoIre*
Coster, C Bernard *Alli Sup*
Coster, Charles Theodore Henri De 1827-1879 *ClDMEuL, CyWA, EuA, EvEuW, REn*
Coster, Dirk 1887-1956 *CasWL, EvEuW*
Coster, G T *ChPo S2*
Coster, George Thomas *Alli Sup*
Coster, Joan *ChPo*
Coster, Robert *Alli*
Coster, Samuel 1579-1665 *BiD&SB, CasWL, DcEuL*
Costetti, Giuseppe 1834- *BiD&SB*
Costigan, Arthur William *Alli, BiDLA*
Costigan, Daniel M 1929- *ConAu 33, WrD 1976*
Costigan, George Purcell 1870-1934 *DcNAA*
Costigan, George Purcell, Jr. 1879- *WhWNAA*
Costigan, Giovanni 1905- *ConAu P-1, WhPNW, WrD 1976*
Costigan, James 1926- *AmA&B*
Costikyan, Edward N 1924- *ConAu 17R*
Costill, O H *Alli*
Costin, Miron 1633-1691 *CasWL*
Costin, Nicolae 1660-1712 *CasWL*
Costin, Stanley Harry 1913- *Au&Wr*
Costis, Harry G 1928- *ConAu 45*
Costisella, Joseph *OxCan, OxCan Sup*
Costley, Thomas *PoIre*
Costley-White, Harold 1878- *WhLA*
Costley-White, Hope 1894- *Au&Wr, WrD 1976*
Coston, Martha J *Alli Sup*
Coston, William 1858-1942 *DcNAA*
Costonis, John J 1937- *ConAu 49*
Cosulich, Gilbert 1889- *WhWNAA*
Cosway, Mary d1804 *Alli*
Cota, Rodrigo d1504? *BiD&SB, CasWL*
Cota DeMaguaque, Rodrigo *DcEuL*
Cotarelo Y Mori, Emilio 1857-1936 *DcSpL*
Cotart, Jehan *OxFr*
Cote, Cyrille Hector Octave 1809-1850 *BbtC, OxCan*
Cote, Joseph Olivier 1820-1882 *BbtC, DcNAA*
Cote, M *Alli Sup*

Cote, Narcisse Omer 1859- *AmLY*, *WhWNAA*
Cote, Thomas 1869-1918 *DcNAA*
Cote, Wolfred Nelson *Alli Sup*
Cotes *Alli*, *BiDLA*
Cotes, Charles *Alli*
Cotes, Digby *Alli*
Cotes, E C And Swinhoe, Colonel *Alli Sup*
Cotes, Everard *DcNAA*
Cotes, Mrs. Everard 1861- *BbD*, *BiD&SB*, *Chmbr 3*
Cotes, Henry *Alli*, *BiDLA*, *ChPo*
Cotes, Hornor *DcNAA*
Cotes, J *Alli*, *BiDLA*
Cotes, Kenelm Digby *Alli Sup*
Cotes, Peter *Au&Wr*, *WrD 1976*
Cotes, Peter 1912- *ConAu 5R*
Cotes, Roger 1682-1716 *Alli*
Cotes, Sara Jeanette 1862-1922 *NewC*
Cotes, William *Alli*
Cotgrave, John *Alli*
Cotgrave, Randle d1634 *Alli*, *DcEuL*, *NewC*, *OxEng*, *OxFr*
Cotheal, Alexander Isaac 1840-1894 *DcAmA*
Cothern, Fayly H 1926- *ConAu 1R*, *WrD 1976*
Cothran, George W *Alli Sup*
Cothran, J Guy 1897- *ConAu 29*
Cothren, William 1819-1888 *Alli Sup*, *DcAmA*, *DcNAA*
Cotillo, Salvatore Albert 1886-1939 *DcNAA*
Cotin, Charles 1604-1682 *BiD&SB*, *OxFr*, *Pen Eur*
Cotlar, Mischa 1913- *BiDPar*
Cotler, Gordon 1923- *AmA&B*, *ConAu 1R*
Cotlow, Lewis N 1898- *AmA&B*
Cotman, John Sell 1780?-1842? *Alli*, *AtlBL*, *BiDLA*, *NewC*
Cotnam, Jacques *OxCan Sup*
Cotner, Robert Crawford 1906- *ConAu 37*
Cotner, Thomas E 1916- *ConAu 37*, *WrD 1976*
Cotrus, Aron 1891-1961 *CasWL*
Cotsell, George *Alli Sup*
Cott, Hugh Bamford 1900- *Au&Wr*, *WrD 1976*
Cott, Jonathan 1942- *ChPo S2*, *ConAu 53*
Cott, Ted 1917- *AmA&B*
Cotta, Johann Friedrich 1764-1832 *OxGer*
Cotta, John *Alli*
Cottam, Edward *Alli Sup*
Cottam, Samuel Elsworth 1863- *ChPo S2*
Cottam, Walter P 1894- *ConAu P-1*
Cottell, W H *Alli Sup*
Cotten, Nell Wyllie 1908- *ConAu 1R*
Cotten, Sallie Southall *BiDSA*, *ChPo*, *ChPo S1*
Cotter, Charles Henry 1919- *ConAu 13R*, *WrD 1976*
Cotter, Cornelius Philip 1924- *ConAu 1R*
Cotter, Edward F 1917- *ConAu 5R*
Cotter, George Sackville 1754?-1831 *Alli*, *PoIre*
Cotter, James *PoIre*
Cotter, James Finn 1929- *ConAu 33*, *WrD 1976*
Cotter, James Henry 1858-1947 *OhA&B*
Cotter, James Laurence 1782-1850 *PoIre*
Cotter, Janet M 1914- *ConAu 61*
Cotter, John R *Alli*
Cotter, Joseph Rogerson *Alli Sup*, *PoIre*
Cotter, Joseph Seaman 1861-1949 *AmA&B*, *BlkAW*, *ChPo*, *ChPo S1*, *WhWNAA*
Cotter, Joseph Seamon, Jr. 1895-1919 *BlkAW*
Cotter, Oliver *Alli Sup*
Cotter, R *PoIre*
Cotter, Richard V 1930- *ConAu 41*
Cotteral, Bonnie *TexWr*
Cotteral, Donnie *TexWr*
Cotterel, Sir Charles *Alli*
Cotterell, Sir Charles *DcEnL*
Cotterell, Edward *Alli Sup*
Cotterell, Geoffrey 1919- *Au&Wr*, *WorAu*, *WrD 1976*
Cotterell, George 1839- *ChPo S1*, *ChPo S2*
Cotterell, Peter 1930- *ConAu 49*
Cotteril, Grant *MnBBF*
Cotterill, C C And Little, E D *Alli Sup*
Cotterill, Charles Forster *Alli Sup*

Cotterill, Henry 1812-1886 *Alli Sup*, *DcEnL*
Cotterill, Henry Bernard *Alli Sup*
Cotterill, James H *Alli Sup*
Cotterill, Joseph Northland *Alli Sup*
Cotterill, Leonard *ChPo S1*
Cotterill, Robert Spencer 1884- *WhWNAA*
Cotterill, T *Alli*, *BiDLA*
Cotterill, Thomas 1779-1823 *PoCh*
Cottesford, S *Alli*
Cottesloe, Thomas Francis 1862- *ChPo S1*
Cottin, Marie 1770-1807 *BiD&SB*
Cottin, Sophie 1770-1807 *BbD*, *EvEuW*, *OxFr*
Cotting, Benjamin Eddy 1812-1897 *DcNAA*
Cotting, John Ruggles 1783-1867 *DcAmA*, *DcNAA*
Cottinger, H M *Alli Sup*
Cottingham, Harry *WhWNAA*
Cottingham, John *Alli*, *BiDLA*
Cottingham, L N *Alli*
Cottingham, Walter Horace 1866-1930 *OhA&B*
Cottle, Amos Simon 1768?-1800 *Alli*, *BiDLA*, *ChPo*, *NewC*
Cottle, Elizabeth *Alli Sup*
Cottle, Ernest Wyndham *Alli Sup*
Cottle, John *Alli*
Cottle, John Morford *Alli Sup*
Cottle, Joseph 1770-1853 *Alli*, *BiDLA*, *ChPo*, *DcEuL*, *NewC*
Cottle, Thomas J 1937- *BbtC*, *ConAu 33*, *WrD 1976*
Cottle, W C 1913- *ConAu 41*
Cottler, Joseph 1899- *ConAu 25*
Cottman, Evans W 1901- *IndAu 1917*
Cottman, George Streibe 1857-1941 *IndAu 1816*
Cotto Thorner, Guillermo 1916- *PueRA*
Cottom, Charles W *IndAu 1816*
Cotton, Alfred Johnson 1800-1858 *IndAu 1816*
Cotton, Amelia Lucy *Alli Sup*
Cotton, Sir Arthur Thomas 1803- *Alli Sup*
Cotton, Bartholomew De d1298? *Alli*
Cotton, Bartholomew De d1298? *NewC*
Cotton, Billy *WrD 1976*
Cotton, Charles 1630-1687? *Alli*, *BiD&SB*, *BrAu*, *CasWL*, *ChPo*, *ChPo S1*, *ChPo S2*, *Chmbr 1*, *CnE&AP*, *DcEnL*, *DcLEnL*, *EvLB*, *NewC*, *OxEng*, *Pen Eng*, *REn*, *WebEAL*
Cotton, Charles 1856- *WhLA*
Cotton, Charles P *Alli Sup*
Cotton, Clement *Alli*
Cotton, Edward *Alli*, *Alli Sup*
Cotton, Edward Howe 1881- *WhWNAA*
Cotton, Elizabeth Reid *Alli Sup*
Cotton, Ella Earls *BlkAW*
Cotton, F *Alli Sup*
Cotton, F Percy *ChPo S2*
Cotton, Fassett Allen 1862-1942 *IndAu 1816*
Cotton, Frederick 1848- *Br&AmS*
Cotton, George Edward Lynch 1813-1866 *Alli*, *Alli Sup*
Cotton, Gerald Brookes 1920- *Au&Wr*
Cotton, Henry *Alli*
Cotton, Henry John Stedman *Alli Sup*
Cotton, J D *Alli*
Cotton, James Harry 1896?- *AmA&B*, *OhA&B*
Cotton, James Sutherland 1847- *Alli Sup*
Cotton, John *Alli Sup*
Cotton, John d1757 *Alli*
Cotton, John d1789 *Alli*
Cotton, John 1584?-1652 *Alli*, *AmA*, *AmA&B*, *BiD&SB*, *CnDAL*, *CyAL 1*, *DcAmA*, *DcLEnL*, *DcNAA*, *OxAm*, *Pen Am*, *REn*, *REnAL*
Cotton, John 1640-1699 *Alli*
Cotton, John W 1925- *ConAu 33*, *ConP 1970*, *ConP 1975*, *WrD 1976*
Cotton, Josiah 1680-1756 *Alli*
Cotton, L T 1922- *Au&Wr*
Cotton, Lizzie E *Alli Sup*
Cotton, Mary Wooley Stapleton- *Alli Sup*
Cotton, Nathaniel 1705-1788 *Alli*, *BiDLA*, *BrAu*, *CarSB*, *ChPo S1*, *ChPo S2*, *Chmbr 2*, *EvLB*, *NewC*
Cotton, Nathaniel 1721-1788 *DcEnL*
Cotton, R P *Alli*
Cotton, Richard Lynch *Alli*
Cotton, Sir Robert Bruce 1571?-1631 *Alli*,

CasWL, *Chmbr 1*, *DcEnL*, *DcEuL*, *EvLB*, *NewC*, *OxEng*, *REn*
Cotton, Robert Turner *Alli Sup*
Cotton, Roger *Alli*
Cotton, Samuel George *Alli Sup*
Cotton, Sophia Anne *Alli Sup*
Cotton, Sir Sydney John 1792-1874 *Alli Sup*
Cotton, W C *Alli*
Cotton, W L *TexWr*
Cotton, Walter *BlkAW*
Cotton, Willia Dawson 1868-1942 *OhA&B*
Cotton, William *Alli Sup*
Cotton, William d1863 *Alli Sup*
Cotton, William A *Alli Sup*
Cotton, William Charles 1813-1879 *Alli Sup*, *ChPo*
Cotton, William James Richmond 1822- *Alli Sup*
Cottrell, Alan Howard 1919- *WrD 1976*
Cottrell, Byron E 1892- *WhWNAA*
Cottrell, C H *Alli*
Cottrell, Fred 1903- *ConAu 1R*
Cottrell, Geoffrey 1919- *ConAu 5R*
Cottrell, Mrs. Hugh *WhWNAA*
Cottrell, Ida Dorothy Ottley 1902- *EvLB*
Cottrell, John Michael 1930- *Au&Wr*
Cottrell, Leonard 1913- *Au&Wr*, *AuBYP*, *ConAu 5R*, *TwCW*, *WorAu*, *WrD 1976*
Cottrell, Leonard S, Jr. 1899- *AmA&B*
Cottrell, Robert D 1930- *ConAu 53*
Cottrell, William Frederick 1903- *AmA&B*
Coubertin, Baron Pierre De 1862- *WhLA*
Coubier, Heinz 1905- *CnMD*
Couch, *TwCA*, *TwCA Sup*
Couch, Sir Arthur Thomas Quiller *Alli Sup*, *ChPo*, *EvLB*, *JBA 1934*, *OxEng*
Couch, Edwardine Crenshaw 1894- *TexWr*
Couch, Enos *ChPo*
Couch, Helen F 1907- *ConAu 17*
Couch, James Fitton 1888- *WhWNAA*
Couch, John *Alli*
Couch, Jonathan 1789-1870 *Alli*, *Alli Sup*
Couch, Osma Palmer *ConAu XR*
Couch, Robert *Alli*
Couch, William, Jr. *BlkAW*, *LivBA*
Couch, William Terry 1901- *AmA&B*
Couchman, Giles *Alli*
Couchoro, Felix 1905?- *AfA 1*
Coucicault, Dion *HsB&A Sup*
Coucy, Gui, Chatelain De *OxFr*
Coudenhove, Ida Friedrike 1901- *CatA 1947*
Coudenhove-Kalergi, Count Richard N 1894-1972 *Au&Wr*, *ConAu 37*
Coudert, Frederic Rene 1832-1903 *DcNAA*
Coudert, Jo 1923- *Au&Wr*, *ConAu 17R*
Coudurier DeChassaigne, Joseph 1878- *WhLA*
Coue, Emile 1857-1926 *NewC*
Coues, Elliott 1842-1890 *Alli Sup*, *AmA&B*, *BbD*, *BbtC*, *BiD&SB*, *DcAmA*, *DcNAA*
Coues, Samuel Elliot *Alli*
Couet, Thomas Cyrille 1861-1931 *DcNAA*
Couet, Yvonne 1893- *WhWNAA*
Couffer, Jack C 1924- *Au&Wr*, *ConAu 1R*
Couger, J Daniel 1929- *ConAu 53*
Coughlan, John W 1927- *ConAu 21*
Coughlan, L *BbtC*
Coughlan, Maria 1895-1947 *DcNAA*
Coughlan, Robert 1914- *AmA&B*, *IndAu 1917*, *WrD 1976*
Coughlin, Bernard J 1922- *ConAu 13R*
Coughlin, Joseph Welter 1919- *ConAu 1R*
Coughlin, Margaret N *ChPo S2*
Coughlin, William J *Alli Sup*, *PoIre*
Coughran, Larry C 1925- *ConAu 21*
Couillard-Despres, Azarie 1876-1939 *OxCan*
Couissin, Paul Louis 1885- *WhLA*
Coulanges, Christophe De, Abbe De Livry d1687 *OxFr*
Coulanges, Fustel De 1830-1889 *DcEuL*
Coulanges, Philippe-Emmanuel, Marquis De 1633-1716 *OxFr*
Couldery, Fred A J 1928- *ConAu 9R*
Couldery, T W *ChPo S1*
Couldrey, Oswald Jennings *ChPo S1*, *ChPo S2*
Couleius, Abrahamus *Alli*
Coulet DuGard, Rene 1919- *ConAu 53*
Coulette, Henri 1927- *AmA&B*, *ConP 1970*, *ConP 1975*, *DrAP 1975*, *WrD 1976*

Cousteau, Jacques-Yves 1910- *AnCL, REn*
Cousteau, Philippe Pierre 1940- *ConAu 33*
Coustos, John *Alli*
Couteau, J B *Alli*
Couthon, Georges 1755-1794 *OxFr*
Coutie, George *Alli Sup*
Coutlee, L W P *Alli Sup*
Couto, Diogo Do 1542?-1616 *CasWL, Pen Eur*
Couto, Rui Ribeiro 1898-1963 *Pen Am*
Couton, John *Alli*
Coutsocheras, John P 1904- *Au&Wr*
Coutsoheras, John 1904- *Au&Wr*
Coutts, Francis *Alli Sup*
Coutts, Francis B Thomas Neville Money 1852- *Alli Sup, ChPo, ChPo S1*
Coutts, John *Alli Sup*
Coutts, Mrs. R B *PoIre*
Coutts, Robert 1803- *Alli*
Coutts, W G *ChPo*
Coutts-Smith, Kenneth 1929- *Au&Wr*
Couvreur, Jessie Catherine 1848-1897 *DcLEnL*
Couzyn, Jeni 1942- *ConP 1975, WrD 1976*
Covarrubias, Miguel 1905?-1958 *REnAL, IlCB 1945, IlCB 1956*
Covarrubias Y Orozco, Sebastian De 1539?-1613? *CasWL, DcSpL*
Covatta, Anthony Gallo 1944- *ConAu 53*
Cove, Augustus *Alli, BiDLA*
Cove, Morgan *Alli, BiDLA*
Covel, John 1638-1722 *Alli*
Covell, James 1796-1845 *DcAmA, DcNAA*
Covell, L T *Alli*
Covell, William *Alli*
Coven, Stephen *Alli*
Coveney, James 1920- *ConAu 41*
Coveney, Sister Mary *PoIre*
Coveney, Peter James 1924- *Au&Wr, ChPo S1*
Coventry, Countess Of *NewC*
Coventry, Lord *Alli*
Coventry, Andrew d1830 *Alli, BiDLA*
Coventry, Francis d1759? *Alli, NewC, OxEng*
Coventry, George *BbtC*
Coventry, Henry d1752 *Alli*
Coventry, John *Alli Sup, AmA&B, DcNAA*
Coventry, John 1825-1906 *AmA*
Coventry, John Seton 1915- *Au&Wr, CatA 1952*
Coventry, Richard George Temple *ChPo S1*
Coventry, Thomas *Alli*
Coventry, Sir William 1626-1686 *Alli*
Cover, Alan E *ChPo S2*
Cover, John Higson 1891- *AmA&B*
Cover, Robert M 1943- *ConAu 57*
Coverdale, Miles 1488-1568 *Alli, BbD, BiD&SB, BrAu, Chmbr 1, CasWL, DcEnL, DcEuL, DcLEnL, EvLB, NewC, OxEng, Pen Eng, REn, WebEAL*
Coverdale, R R *Alli Sup*
Coverley, Louise *ConP 1970*
Coverley, Sir Roger De *Alli*
Covert, James Thayne 1932- *ConAu 37*
Covert, John Cutler 1837-1919 *OhA&B*
Covert, Nicholas *Alli*
Covert, William Chalmers 1864-1942 *DcNAA, IndAu 1816, WhWNAA*
Coverte, Robert *Alli*
Covey, Mrs. Arthur S *AmA&B, ChPo, OhA&B, WhWNAA*
Covey, Cyclone 1922- *ConAu 21*
Covey, Leona *ChPo*
Covey, Stephen R 1932- *ConAu 33*
Covi, Madeline C *ChPo S2*
Covici, Pascal, Jr. 1930- *ConAu 1R*
Covil, George Smith *Alli Sup*
Coville, Cabot 1902- *Au&Wr*
Coville, Walter J 1914- *ConAu 1R, ConAu 5R*
Covin, Theron Michael 1947- *ConAu 57*
Covington, Chester *WhWNAA*
Covington, James W 1917- *ConAu 33, WrD 1976*
Covington, Martin Vaden 1936- *ConAu 37*
Covington, Phillip *ChPo S1*
Covington, Virginia Durant *LivFWS*
Covington, Warren 1921- *AmSCAP 66*
Covino, Frank 1931- *ConAu 57*
Cowan, Alan *ConAu XR*
Cowan, Andrew *Alli, BiDLA*
Cowan, Bertha Muzzy Sinclair 1875- *DcNAA, WhWNAA*

Cowan, C England *MnBBF*
Cowan, Charles *Alli, Alli Sup*
Cowan, Don F 1919- *WrD 1976*
Cowan, Edward *MnBBF*
Cowan, Edwina Abbott 1887- *WhWNAA*
Cowan, Esther Marshall 1886- *WhWNAA*
Cowan, F M *Alli Sup*
Cowan, Francis *MnBBF*
Cowan, Frank 1844-1905 *Alli Sup, AmA&B, BiD&SB, ChPo S2, DcAmA, DcNAA*
Cowan, G H 1917- *ConAu 17R*
Cowan, George D And Johnston, R L N *Alli Sup*
Cowan, George J 1877- *WhWNAA*
Cowan, Gordon 1933- *ConAu 25, WrD 1976*
Cowan, Helen I *OxCan*
Cowan, Henry 1884- *WhLA*
Cowan, Henry Jacob 1919- *Au&Wr, ConAu 53, WrD 1976*
Cowan, Hugh *Alli Sup*
Cowan, Ian Borthwick 1932- *ConAu 61*
Cowan, J B *Alli Sup*
Cowan, J L 1929- *ConAu 25*
Cowan, James 1738-1795 *Alli*
Cowan, James 1870-1943 *DcLEnL*
Cowan, James Allister 1901- *WhWNAA*
Cowan, James C 1927- *ConAu 29, WrD 1976*
Cowan, James Galloway *Alli Sup*
Cowan, John *Alli Sup, OxCan*
Cowan, John 1840- *ChPo*
Cowan, John Franklin 1854-1942 *AmA&B, DcNAA*
Cowan, Joseph Lloyd 1929- *WrD 1976*
Cowan, Louise Shillingburg 1916- *ConAu 1R*
Cowan, Lynn F 1888- *AmSCAP 66*
Cowan, Maurice Arthur *Au&Wr*
Cowan, Michael 1944- *AmSCAP 66*
Cowan, Michael H 1937- *ConAu 23*
Cowan, Peter *Alli Sup*
Cowan, Peter 1914- *ConAu 21, ConNov 1972, ConNov 1976, WrD 1976*
Cowan, Richard O 1934- *ConAu 53*
Cowan, Robert *Alli Sup*
Cowan, Mrs. Robert Ellsworth *WhWNAA*
Cowan, Robert Ernest 1862-1942 *AmA&B, DcNAA*
Cowan, Robert Granniss 1895- *ConAu P-1*
Cowan, Rubey 1891-1957 *AmSCAP 66*
Cowan, S Lloyd *TexWr*
Cowan, S R *ChPo S1*
Cowan, Sister St. Michael 1886- *CatA 1952*
Cowan, Sam K 1869- *WhWNAA*
Cowan, Samuel *Alli Sup*
Cowan, Samuel Kennedy 1850- *Alli Sup, ChPo S1, PoIre*
Cowan, Stanley Earl 1918- *AmSCAP 66*
Cowan, Ted *MnBBF*
Cowan, Thomas *Alli Sup*
Cowan, Thomas 1834- *ChPo S1*
Cowan, Thomas William *Alli Sup*
Cowan, Tom *ChPo, ChPo S1*
Cowan, Tom Keith 1916- *WrD 1976*
Cowan, William *Alli Sup, PoIre*
Cowan, William 1851-1929 *ChPo, ChPo S1, ChPo S2*
Coward, Edward Fales 1862-1933 *DcNAA*
Coward, George *Alli Sup*
Coward, John *Alli*
Coward, Noel 1899-1973 *Au&Wr, AuNews 1, CasWL, ChPo, ChPo S2, Chmbr 3, CnMD, CnThe, ConAu 17, ConAu 41, ConDr, ConLC 1, CrCD, CyWA, DcLEnL, EncWL, EvLB, LongC, McGWD, ModBL, ModBL Sup, ModWD, NewC, OxEng, Pen Eng, REn, REnWD, TwCA, TwCA Sup, TwCW, WebEAL*
Coward, Roger Vilven 1916- *Au&Wr, WrD 1976*
Coward, Thomas B 1896- *WhWNAA*
Coward, Thomas Ridgway 1896-1957 *AmA&B*
Coward, William *Alli, DcEnL*
Coward, William 1656-1725 *Alli*
Cowasjee, Saros 1931- *ConAu 9R, WrD 1976*
Cowdell, Thomas Daniel *BbtC, OxCan, PoIre*
Cowden, Dudley J 1899- *ConAu 41*
Cowden, Jasper Barnett *ChPo S2*
Cowden, Joanna Dunlap 1933- *ConAu 53*

Cowden, Robert 1833-1922 *OhA&B*
Cowden, Roy William *ChPo*
Cowden-Clarke, Charles *NewC*
Cowden-Clarke, Mary Victoria *NewC*
Cowden-Cole, Charlotte *Alli Sup*
Cowdery, Charlotte *Alli Sup*
Cowdery, Miss E *Alli Sup*
Cowdery, Jabez F *Alli Sup*
Cowdery, Jonathan 1767-1852 *DcNAA*
Cowdery, Mae V *BlkAW*
Cowdery, Mincy *BlkAW*
Cowdin, Jasper Barnett 1866?- *Alli Sup, AnMV 1926, DcAmA, DcNAA*
Cowdin, Mrs. V G *BiDSA*
Cowdrey, A E 1933- *ConAu 17R*
Cowdrey, Cecil *ChPo S1*
Cowdrey, Michael Colin 1932- *WrD 1976*
Cowdrick, Jesse C 1859-1899 *HsB&A, HsB&A Sup*
Cowdry, Richard *Alli*
Cowdy, Alan *MnBBF*
Cowdy, Samuel *Alli Sup*
Cowe, James *Alli, BiDLA*
Cowe, Robert *Alli Sup*
Cowee, Emma C D *ChPo*
Cowell, Benjamin 1781-1860 *DcAmA, DcNAA*
Cowell, Clara D *ChPo*
Cowell, Cyril 1888- *ChPo S2, ConAu 21*
Cowell, Edward Byles 1826- *Alli Sup*
Cowell, Sir Ernest Marshall 1886- *Au&Wr, WhLA*
Cowell, Frank Richard 1897- *Au&Wr, AuBYP, WrD 1976*
Cowell, George *Alli Sup*
Cowell, Henry Dixon 1897-1965 *REnAL, WhWNAA*
Cowell, Henry Von-Der-Heyde *Alli Sup*
Cowell, Herbert *Alli Sup*
Cowell, J W *Alli*
Cowell, John *Alli*
Cowell, John 1554-1611 *Alli*
Cowell, Joseph Leathley 1792-1863 *DcNAA, NewC*
Cowell, Richard 1897- *ConAu 53*
Cowell, William 1820-1868 *PoIre*
Cowen, Benjamin Rush 1831-1908 *DcNAA, OhA&B*
Cowen, David L 1909- *ConAu 13R*
Cowen, E *Alli*
Cowen, Elsa *Alli Sup*
Cowen, Esek 1787-1844 *DcNAA*
Cowen, Frances 1915?- *Au&Wr, ConAu XR, WrD 1976*
Cowen, Sir Frederic Hymen 1852- *ChPo, ChPo S2*
Cowen, Ida 1898- *ConAu 45*
Cowen, James *Alli Sup*
Cowen, Jane *Alli Sup*
Cowen, Patrick H *Alli Sup, DcAmA*
Cowen, Robert Churchill 1927- *ConAu 13R*
Cowen, Ron 1944- *ConDr, WrD 1976*
Cowen, Roy C 1930- *ConAu 33*
Cowen, Samuella *LivFWS*
Cowen, Sidney J *Alli, Alli Sup*
Cowen, Zelman 1919- *Au&Wr, ConAu 1R, WrD 1976*
Cowers, W R *Alli Sup*
Cowger, Roger R 1938- *AmSCAP 66*
Cowgill, Donald O 1911- *ConAu 37, WrD 1976*
Cowham, Hilda *ChPo S1*
Cowie, Alexander 1896- *AmA&B, ConAu 33, REnAL, WrD 1976*
Cowie, Benjamin Morgan 1816- *Alli Sup*
Cowie, D Murray 1872- *WhWNAA*
Cowie, Donald *ChPo, ChPo S1*
Cowie, Evelyn Elizabeth 1924- *Au&Wr, ConAu 13R, WrD 1976*
Cowie, George *BiDLA*
Cowie, Hamilton Russell 1931- *WrD 1976*
Cowie, Isaac 1848-1917 *DcNAA, OxCan*
Cowie, John Stewart 1898- *Au&Wr*
Cowie, Leonard Wallace 1919- *Au&Wr, ConAu 13R, SmATA 4, WrD 1976*
Cowie, Mervyn Hugh 1909- *Au&Wr, ConAu P-1, WrD 1976*
Cowie, Peter 1939- *ConAu 49*
Cowie, Robert 1842-1874 *Alli Sup*

Cox, Oliver Cromwell 1901- *Au&Wr,*
ConAu 1R
Cox, Ollie H *BlkAW*
Cox, Owen *Alli*
Cox, Palmer 1840-1924 *Alli Sup, AmA,*
AmA&B, BbD, BiD&SB, CarSB, ChPo,
ChPo S1, ChPo S2, DcAmA, DcNAA,
JBA 1934, MnBBF, OxAm
Cox, Patrick Brian 1914- *ConAu 45,*
WrD 1976
Cox, Philip W L 1883- *WhWNAA*
Cox, Ponsonby *Alli Sup*
Cox, R David 1937- *ConAu 29*
Cox, R K 1936- *Au&Wr*
Cox, R Merritt 1939- *ConAu 33, WrD 1976*
Cox, Rachel Dunaway 1904- *ConAu 33*
Cox, Ralph 1884-1941 *AmSCAP 66*
Cox, Reavis 1900- *ConAu P-1*
Cox, Reginald H W *MnBBF*
Cox, Richard *Alli*
Cox, Richard 1499-1581 *Alli, DcEnL*
Cox, Sir Richard 1650-1733 *Alli*
Cox, Richard 1931- *ConAu 21, WrD 1976*
Cox, Richard Alpha 1857-1939 *IndAu 1917*
Cox, Richard Howard 1925- *ConAu 13R,*
IndAu 1917
Cox, Richard Threlkeld 1898- *WhWNAA*
Cox, Robert 1810-1872 *Alli, Alli Sup, BiDLA*
Cox, Robert David 1937- *IndAu 1917*
Cox, Roger 1936- *PoIre, WrD 1976*
Cox, Rosalinda Alicia *Alli Sup*
Cox, Ross 1793-1853 *Alli, BbtC, OxCan*
Cox, Rowland *Alli Sup*
Cox, Mrs. S B *LivFWS*
Cox, S C *Alli, Alli Sup*
Cox, Samuel 1826- *Alli Sup*
Cox, Samuel Alfred *Alli Sup*
Cox, Samuel Compton *BiDLA*
Cox, Samuel Hanson 1793-1880 *Alli, DcAmA,*
DcNAA
Cox, Samuel O'Neil *Alli Sup*
Cox, Samuel Sullivan 1824-1889 *Alli, Alli Sup,*
AmA, AmA&B, BbD, BiD&SB, DcAmA,
DcNAA, OhA&B
Cox, Sandford C *IndAu 1816*
Cox, Sandra 1949- *BlkAW*
Cox, Sidney 1889- *ChPo S1, WhWNAA*
Cox, Susannah 1861-1923 *IndAu 1917*
Cox, Sydney *Alli Sup*
Cox, Syril *ChPo S1*
Cox, Thomas *Alli, Alli Sup*
Cox, Thomas R 1933- *ConAu 53*
Cox, W L P *Alli Sup*
Cox, Wallace Maynard *ConAu XR*
Cox, Wally 1924-1973 *ConAu 41*
Cox, Walter 1760?-1837 *PoIre*
Cox, Walter 1952- *BlkAW*
Cox, Walter S *Alli Sup*
Cox, Warren E 1895- *ConAu 33*
Cox, William *Alli Sup*
Cox, William d1851? *Alli, CyAL 2, DcNAA*
Cox, William 1805?-1847 *OxAm*
Cox, William Edward 1915- *BiDPar*
Cox, William Hamilton *Alli Sup*
Cox, William J 1851-1913 *Alli Sup, DcNAA*
Cox, William Junkin 1896- *WhWNAA*
Cox, William Lang Paige 1855- *WhLA*
Cox, Mrs. William N *Alli Sup*
Cox, William Robert 1901- *AuBYP,*
ConAu 9R
Cox, William Sands 1802-1875 *Alli Sup*
Cox, William Sebron 1939- *BiDPar*
Cox, William Trevor 1928- *ConAu 9R, NewC,*
WorAu, WrD 1976
Cox, William VanZandt 1852-1923 *DcNAA,*
OhA&B
Cox-George, Noah Arthur William 1915-
Au&Wr, ConAu 13R, WrD 1976
Cox-McCormack, Nancy 1885- *WhWNAA*
Coxe, Arthur Cleveland 1818-1896 *Alli,*
Alli Sup, AmA&B, BbD, BiD&SB,
ChPo, ChPo S1, ChPo S2, CyAL 2,
DcAmA, DcEnL, DcNAA, PoCh
Coxe, Benjamin *Alli*
Coxe, Brinton 1833-1892 *Alli Sup, DcNAA*
Coxe, Daniel *Alli, BiDSA*
Coxe, Eckley Brinton 1839-1895 *Alli Sup,*
DcAmA

Coxe, Edward d1814 *Alli, BiDLA,*
BiDLA Sup
Coxe, Eliza A *Alli, BiDLA*
Coxe, Francis *Alli*
Coxe, George Harmon 1901- *AmA&B,*
ConAu 57, EncM&D, MnBBF, REnAL,
WorAu
Coxe, Henry *Alli*
Coxe, Henry Carleton 1785-1840 *BiDSA*
Coxe, Henry Octavius *Alli Sup*
Coxe, Sir James *Alli Sup*
Coxe, John Redman 1773-1864 *Alli, DcAmA,*
DcNAA
Coxe, Leonard *Alli*
Coxe, Louis Osborne 1918- *AmA&B, ChPo,*
ChPo S1, ConAu 13R, ConP 1970,
ConP 1975, DrAP 1975, McGWD,
OxAm, WorAu, WrD 1976
Coxe, Macgrane 1859-1923 *DcNAA*
Coxe, Margaret 1800- *Alli, DcAmA, DcNAA,*
OhA&B
Coxe, Mary Amelia Choate *ChPo*
Coxe, Nehemiah *Alli*
Coxe, Nicholas 1625?- *Br&AmS*
Coxe, Peter *Alli*
Coxe, Richard Charles 1800-1865 *Alli,*
Alli Sup, ChPo, ChPo S1, ChPo S2
Coxe, Richard Smith 1792-1865 *Alli, AmA,*
BbtC, DcNAA
Coxe, Samuel H 1818- *CyAL 2*
Coxe, Tench 1755-1824 *Alli, BiDLA, DcAmA,*
DcNAA
Coxe, Thomas *Alli*
Coxe, William *Chmbr 2*
Coxe, William 1747-1828 *Alli, BiDLA,*
BiDLA Sup, BrAu 19, DcEnL, EvLB
Coxe, William 1762-1831 *DcNAA*
Coxen, Omer William 1866-1938 *IndAu 1917*
Coxeter, Harold Scott Macdonald 1907-
WrD 1976
Coxeter, Thomas 1689-1747 *Alli*
Coxey, Jacob Sechler 1854-1951 *OhA&B*
Coxey, Willard Douglas 1861-1943 *DcNAA*
Coxhead, E *ChPo*
Coxhead, Ethel *Alli Sup, ChPo S2*
Coxon, Ethel *Alli Sup*
Coxon, Herbert *Alli Sup*
Coxwell, Henry *Alli Sup*
Coy, Harold 1902- *AuBYP, ConAu 5R,*
SmATA 3, WrD 1976
Coy, Martin 1863-1949 *OhA&B*
Coy, Simeon 1851- *IndAu 1816*
Coykendall, Frederick 1872-1954 *AmA&B*
Coyle, Antony *PoIre*
Coyle, David Cushman 1887- *ConAu 1R*
Coyle, Edward *PoIre*
Coyle, Henry 1865?- *ChPo, PoIre*
Coyle, John Patterson 1852-1895 *DcAmA,*
DcNAA
Coyle, Kathleen 1886-1952 *NewC, REn,*
TwCA, TwCA Sup
Coyle, Lee 1925- *ConAu 41*
Coyle, Matthew 1862- *ChPo S1, PoIre*
Coyle, Robert Francis 1850-1917 *DcNAA*
Coyle, Robert McCurdy 1860-1936 *DcNAA,*
OhA&B
Coyle, William 1917- *ConAu 1R, PoIre*
Coyne, James Henry 1849-1942 *DcNAA,*
WhWNAA
Coyne, John R, Jr. 1935- *ConAu 37*
Coyne, Joseph 1839-1891 *PoIre*
Coyne, Joseph E 1918- *ConAu 13R*
Coyne, Joseph Sterling 1803-1868 *DcEnL,*
PoIre
Coyne, Joseph Stirling 1803-1868 *Alli Sup,*
BrAu 19, NewC
Coyner *BiDSA*
Coyner, Charles Luther 1853- *BiDSA, DcAmA,*
DcNAA
Coyner, J M *Alli Sup*
Coysh, Victor 1906- *ConAu 61*
Coyte, B *Alli*
Coyte, Joseph William *Alli, BiDLA*
Coyte, Tobias *Alli*
Coyte, William *Alli*
Cozart, Abram Whitenack 1870- *WhWNAA*
Coze, Paul 1903?-1974 *ConAu 53*
Cozens, Doctor *Alli*

Cozens, Alexander d1786 *Alli, BiDLA,*
BiDLA Sup
Cozens, Charles *Alli*
Cozens, E *Alli Sup*
Cozens, Frederick W 1890- *WhWNAA*
Cozens, Samuel *Alli, Alli Sup*
Cozens, Zachariah *Alli, BiDLA*
Cozzani, Ettore 1884- *CasWL*
Cozzens, Frederick Swartwout 1818-1869 *Alli,*
Alli Sup, AmA, AmA&B, BbD, BbtC,
BiD&SB, CyAL 2, DcAmA, DcNAA,
EarAB, OxAm, OxCan, REnAL
Cozzens, Issachar 1781-1865 *Alli, DcAmA,*
DcNAA
Cozzens, James Gould 1903- *AmA&B,*
AmNov, AmWr, CasWL, CnDAL,
ConAmA, ConAu 9R, ConLC 1,
ConLC 4, ConNov 1972, ConNov 1976,
CyWA, DcLEnL, DrAF 1976, EncWL,
LongC, ModAL, OxAm, Pen Am,
RAdv 1, REn, REnAL, TwCA,
TwCA Sup, TwCW, WebEAL,
WrD 1976
Cozzens, Samuel Woodworth 1834-1878
Alli Sup, AmA&B, DcAmA, DcNAA
Crabb, Alexander Richard 1911- *IndAu 1917*
Crabb, Alfred Leland 1884- *AmA&B, AmNov,*
ConAu P-1
Crabb, Cecil V, Jr. 1924- *ConAu 13R*
Crabb, Cecil VanMeter 1889- *WhWNAA*
Crabb, Edmond William 1912- *ConAu P-1,*
WrD 1976
Crabb, Edmund Williams 1912- *Au&Wr*
Crabb, George *Alli, BiDLA*
Crabb, George d1854 *Alli*
Crabb, Habakkuk 1750-1794 *Alli*
Crabb, Henry Stuart Malcolm 1922- *WrD 1976*
Crabb, John *Alli*
Crabb, Maria Josepha *Alli, BiDLA*
Crabb, Richard 1911- *ConAu 23*
Crabb, Roger *Alli*
Crabb, William Darwin *Alli Sup*
Crabbe, George 1754-1832 *Alli, AtlBL, BbD,*
BiD&SB, BiDLA, BiDLA Sup, BrAu 19,
CasWL, ChPo, ChPo S1, ChPo S2,
Chmbr 2, CnE&AP, CriT 2, CyWA,
DcEnA, DcEnL, DcEuL, DcLEnL, EvLB,
MouLC 3, NewC, OxEng, Pen Eng,
PoCh, RAdv 1, REn, WebEAL
Crabbe, William H *Alli Sup*
Crabites, Pierre 1877-1943 *CatA 1947,*
DcNAA
Crabshaw, Timothy 1790-1870 *AmA*
Crabtree, Arthur B 1910- *ConAu 17*
Crabtree, James William 1864-1945 *DcNAA,*
OhA&B
Crabtree, Lotta 1847-1924 *OxAm*
Crabtree, Paul 1918- *AmSCAP 66*
Crabtree, T T 1924- *ConAu 23*
Crabtree, William *Alli*
Crac, Monsieur De *OxFr*
Cracherode, Clayton Mordaunt 1729-1799 *Alli*
Crackanthorpe, Hubert Montague 1870-1896
BrAu 19
Crackel, Theodore Joseph 1938- *ConAu 33,*
WrD 1976
Cracklow, C *Alli*
Cracknell, Basil Edward 1925- *WrD 1976*
Cracknell, Benjamin *Alli, BiDLA*
Cracraft, J W *Alli Sup*
Cracraft, James 1939- *ConAu 53*
Cracroft, Bernard 1828- *Alli Sup*
Cracroft, Richard Holton 1936- *ConAu 53*
Craddock, Charles Egbert 1850-1922 *Alli Sup,*
AmA, AmA&B, BiD&SB, BiDSA,
Chmbr 3, DcAmA, DcLEnL, DcNAA,
OxAm, REn, REnAL
Craddock, Francis *Alli*
Craddock, Frederick Winston 1903- *Au&Wr*
Craddock, Patricia 1938- *ConAu 53*
Craddock, Thomas *Alli Sup*
Cradlebaugh, John Henry Rudy Ludwig 1850-
ChPo
Cradock, Fanny *Au&Wr*
Cradock, Mrs. H C *WhCL*
Cradock, Harriet *Alli Sup*
Cradock, John *Alli*
Cradock, Johnnie *Au&Wr*

Cradock, Joseph *Alli, BiDLA*
Cradock, Samuel 1620-1706 *Alli, CyAL 1*
Cradock, Thomas d1760 *Alli*
Cradock, Walter d1660 *Alli, CyAL 1*
Cradock, William *Alli*
Cradock, Zachary 1633-1695 *Alli*
Cradocke, Edward *Alli*
Cradocot *Alli*
Craf, John Riley 1911- *AmA&B*
Craford, Earl Of *Alli*
Crafordius, Matt *Alli*
Craft, Jessie *TexWr*
Craft, Michael 1928- *ConAu 25*
Craft, Robert 1923- *AmA&B, ConAu 9R,*
WrD 1976
Crafton, Allen 1890-1966 *AmA&B,*
WhWNAA
Crafton, Jessica Royer *WhWNAA*
Crafts, Annetta Stratford 1865- *ChPo,*
DcAmA
Crafts, Glenn Alty 1918- *ConAu 9R*
Crafts, James Mason 1839-1917 *Alli Sup,*
DcAmA, DcNAA
Crafts, Leo Melville 1863- *WhWNAA*
Crafts, Roger Conant 1911- *WrD 1976*
Crafts, Sara Jane d1930 *Alli Sup, OhA&B*
Crafts, Wilbur Fisk 1850-1922 *Alli Sup,*
ChPo S1, DcAmA, DcNAA
Crafts, Mrs. Wilbur Fisk *ChPo S1*
Crafts, William 1787-1826 *Alli, AmA,*
AmA&B, BiDSA, CyAL 1, DcAmA,
DcNAA, OxAm, REnAL
Crafts, William Augustus 1819-1906 *Alli Sup,*
DcAmA, DcNAA
Crafurdius, Thomas *Alli*
Crag, John *Alli*
Cragg, E H *Alli Sup*
Cragg, Gerald R 1906- *ConAu 61*
Cragg, Kenneth 1913- *ConAu 17R,*
WrD 1976
Cragg, Kenneth C 1904-1948 *DcNAA*
Cragge, John *Alli*
Craghan, John Francis 1936- *ConAu 53*
Craghead, Robert *Alli*
Cragin, Belle S *Alli Sup*
Cragin, Ethel Raymond *ChPo, WhWNAA*
Cragin, Louisa T *Alli Sup*
Cragin, Mary A *Alli Sup, ChPo*
Crago, Thomas Howard 1907- *Au&Wr,*
ConAu P-1, WrD 1976
Cragoe, Thomas Adolphus 1840- *Alli Sup*
Craig, A *Alli Sup*
Craig, A R *Alli, Alli Sup*
Craig, Abbie *ChPo*
Craig, Alain Tudor *Alli Sup*
Craig, Albert M 1927- *ConAu 37*
Craig, Alec 1897- *Au&Wr, ConAu XR*
Craig, Alexander *Alli, DcEnL*
Craig, Alexander 1567-1627 *ChPo*
Craig, Alexander 1923- *ConP 1970*
Craig, Alexander George 1897- *ConAu P-1*
Craig, Andrew *MnBBF*
Craig, Anna B *ChPo*
Craig, Archibald *Alli Sup*
Craig, Asa Hollister 1847- *WhWNAA*
Craig, Austin 1872- *AmLY, WhWNAA*
Craig, B F *Alli Sup*
Craig, Barbara M 1914- *ConAu 37*
Craig, Basil Tudor *Alli Sup*
Craig, Bill 1930- *ConAu 33*
Craig, Catharine Pringle 1826- *Alli Sup, ChPo*
Craig, Cecil Colvert 1898- *IndAu 1917*
Craig, Charles F 1872- *WhWNAA*
Craig, Clarence Tucker 1895-1953 *OhA&B*
Craig, Clifford 1896- *WrD 1976*
Craig, Daniel H *BbtC*
Craig, David 1929- *ConAu XR*
Craig, David 1932- *Au&Wr, ChPo S2,*
ConAu 41, WrD 1976
Craig, Denys *ConAu XR*
Craig, Dudley Peak 1890- *WhWNAA*
Craig, Duncan *Alli Sup*
Craig, E T *Alli Sup*
Craig, Edward *Alli*
Craig, Edward Anthony 1905- *Au&Wr,*
ConAu 13R, WrD 1976
Craig, Sir Edward Gordon 1872-1966 *ConAu 25,*
DcLEnL, Pen Eng

Craig, Edward Gordon 1872-1966 *WhLA*
Craig, Edward Hubert Cunningham 1874-
WhLA
Craig, Elisabeth May 1888- *WhWNAA*
Craig, Elizabeth Josephine 1883- *Au&Wr,*
ConAu 9R, WrD 1976
Craig, Eric *MnBBF*
Craig, Francis 1900- *AmSCAP 66*
Craig, Frank *ChPo*
Craig, G *Alli Sup*
Craig, G N *Alli Sup*
Craig, George 1920- *Au&Wr*
Craig, Georgia *ConAu XR*
Craig, Gerald M 1916- *ConAu 9R, OxCan,*
OxCan Sup
Craig, Gibson *Alli Sup*
Craig, Gordon 1872-1966 *LongC, REn, TwCA,*
TwCA Sup
Craig, Gordon Alexander 1913- *Au&Wr,*
ConAu 25
Craig, Hardin 1875-1968 *AmA&B, LongC,*
REnAL, TwCA Sup
Craig, Hazel Thompson 1904- *ConAu 1R*
Craig, Hugh *Alli Sup, ChPo S2*
Craig, Isa 1831-1903 *Alli Sup, AmA&B 19,*
ChPo, ChPo S2, HsB&A
Craig, J And Maule, W *Alli Sup*
Craig, J E *Alli Sup*
Craig, James *Alli Sup*
Craig, James 1682-1744 *Alli*
Craig, James Alexander 1855-1932 *DcAmA,*
DcNAA
Craig, James Alfred 1858- *WhLA*
Craig, James Chapman *ChPo S1*
Craig, Sir James Henry 1748-1812 *OxCan*
Craig, James Ireland 1868- *WhLA*
Craig, Jean Teresa 1936- *ConAu 5R,*
WrD 1976
Craig, John *Alli, Alli Sup, BiDLA,*
BiDLA Sup, Chmbr 1, OxCan Sup
Craig, John 1512?-1600 *Alli*
Craig, John 1800?-1870? *ChPo S1*
Craig, John 1852-1923 *DcNAA*
Craig, Sir John 1885- *Au&Wr*
Craig, John David 1903- *ConAu 17, OhA&B,*
WrD 1976
Craig, John Duncan d1909 *Alli Sup, ChPo,*
PoIre
Craig, John Eland *ConAu XR, SmATA 2*
Craig, John H 1885- *ConAu P-1*
Craig, John Kershaw *Alli Sup*
Craig, Jonathan *WrD 1976*
Craig, Joseph Edgar 1845-1925 *DcNAA*
Craig, Katherine L *WhWNAA*
Craig, Kenneth Macintosh *ChPo S2*
Craig, Larry *ConAu XR*
Craig, Laura 1860-1946 *DcNAA*
Craig, Lee *ConAu XR*
Craig, M Jean *AuBYP*
Craig, Margaret Maze 1911-1964 *ConAu 1R,*
MorJA, SmATA 9
Craig, Mary Francis 1923- *ConAu 1R,*
SmATA 6, ThBJA, WrD 1976
Craig, Matthew Robert Smith 1867-1921 *ChPo,*
ChPo S1
Craig, Maurice James 1919- *Au&Wr*
Craig, Neville B 1847-1926 *Alli Sup, DcNAA*
Craig, Oscar John 1846-1911 *IndAu 1917*
Craig, Peggy *ConAu XR*
Craig, Philip R 1933- *ConAu 25*
Craig, R D *Alli*
Craig, R S *ChPo S2*
Craig, Richard B 1935- *ConAu 53*
Craig, Richard Davis *Alli Sup*
Craig, Robert *Alli, Alli Sup*
Craig, Robert B 1944- *ConAu 49*
Craig, Robert Charles 1921- *ConAu 17R,*
WrD 1976
Craig, Robert Clark *Alli Sup*
Craig, Samuel G 1874-1960 *AmA&B,*
WhWNAA
Craig, Thomas *Alli, Alli Sup*
Craig, Sir Thomas 1548-1608 *Alli, DcEnL*
Craig, Thomas 1855-1900 *DcNAA*
Craig, W M *BiDLA*
Craig, William *Alli Sup*
Craig, William 1709-1783 *Alli*
Craig, William Alexander *PoIre*

Craig, William Marshall 1788-1828? *Alli, BkIE,*
ChPo
Craig-Brown *Alli Sup*
Craig-Knox, Isa 1831- *DcEnL*
Craige, Thomas *Alli Sup*
Craighead, Edwin Boone 1861- *BiDSA*
Craighead, Erwin 1852-1932 *DcNAA*
Craighead, Erwin 1852- *WhWNAA*
Craighead, James Geddes 1823-1895 *Alli Sup,*
DcNAA
Craighill, William Price 1833-1909 *Alli Sup,*
DcNAA
Craigie, Mrs. *Chmbr 3, LongC*
Craigie, Christopher *AmLY XR, DcAmA*
Craigie, David *Alli*
Craigie, Dorothy M 1908- *IlCB 1956*
Craigie, E Horne 1894- *ConAu 25, WrD 1976*
Craigie, J *Alli*
Craigie, Mary E *Alli Sup*
Craigie, Mrs. P M T 1867-1906 *DcLEnL*
Craigie, Pearl Mary Teresa 1867-1906 *AmA&B,*
BbD, BiD&SB, BrAu 19, DcEnA Ap,
EvLB, REn
Craigie, William 1790-1863 *BbtC*
Craigie, Sir William Alexander 1867-1957
DcLEnL, EvLB, LongC
Craigin, Louise T *ChPo*
Craigmyle, Lord Of *WhLA*
Craik, Mrs. *Chmbr 3, DcEnL, OxEng,*
WhCL
Craik, Arthur *ConAu XR*
Craik, David *Alli Sup*
Craik, Dinah Maria Mulock 1826-1887 *Alli Sup,*
AnCL, BbD, BiD&SB, BrAu 19, CarSB,
CasWL, ChPo, ChPo S1, ChPo S2,
DcEnA, DcEnA Ap, DcEuL, DcLEnL,
EvLB, FamSYP, HsB&A, JBA 1934,
NewC, REn, St&VC
Craik, Ellen S *Alli Sup*
Craik, George Lillie 1798-1866 *Alli, Alli Sup,*
BrAu 19, Chmbr 3, DcEnL, EvLB
Craik, Georgiana Marion 1831-1895 *Alli Sup,*
BiD&SB, CarSB, Chmbr 3, DcEnL,
NewC
Craik, Gladys Seton *ChPo S1*
Craik, Henry *Alli Sup*
Craik, Sir Henry 1846-1927 *Alli Sup, BrAu 19,*
Chmbr 3
Craik, James *Alli Sup*
Craik, Kenneth H 1936- *ConAu 45*
Craik, Wendy Ann 1934- *ConAu 25,*
WrD 1976
Craille, Wesley *ConAu XR*
Crain, Jeff *ConAu XR*
Crain, Robert L 1934- *ConAu 21*
Crain, Thomas Crowell Taylor 1860-1942
DcNAA
Craine, Eugene R 1917- *ConAu 33*
Crainic, Nichifor 1889- *CasWL*
Craith, E S *Alli Sup*
Crakanthorpe, Richard 1569-1624 *Alli*
Crake, Augustine David *Alli Sup*
Crakelt, W *Alli*
Cralle, Richard K *Alli, CyAL 1*
Cram, George Franklin 1842-1928 *DcAmA,*
DcNAA, WhWNAA
Cram, George F And Tenney, R A *Alli Sup*
Cram, James D 1931- *AmSCAP 66*
Cram, L D 1898- *IlCB 1956*
Cram, Mildred 1889- *ConAu 49*
Cram, Ralph Adams 1863-1942 *AmA&B,*
AmLY, BiD&SB, DcAmA, DcNAA,
OxAm, REnAL, WhWNAA
Cram, William Everett 1871- *AmLY, DcAmA,*
WhWNAA
Cramer, Clarence Henley 1905- *ConAu 13R*
Cramer, Edythe Stokes *TexWr*
Cramer, George H 1913- *ConAu 23*
Cramer, Harold 1927- *ConAu 29*
Cramer, J A *Alli*
Cramer, J S 1928- *ConAu 29*
Cramer, James 1915- *ConAu 23*
Cramer, Johann Andreas 1723-1788 *DcEuL,*
OxGer
Cramer, John Francis 1899-1967 *ConAu P-1*
Cramer, Julian *ChPo S1, DcNAA*
Cramer, Karl Friedrich 1752-1807 *DcEuL,*
OxGer

Cramer, Karl Gottlob 1758-1817 *BiD&SB,*
OxGer
Cramer, Michael John 1835-1898 *DcNAA,*
OhA&B
Cramer, Philibert And Gabriel *OxFr*
Cramer, Richard S 1928- *ConAu 29*
Cramer, Stanley H 1933- *ConAu 29,*
WrD 1976
Cramer, Stuart Warren 1868-1940 *DcNAA*
Cramer, William 1878-1945 *DcNAA*
Cramer, William Stuart 1873- *DcNAA,*
WhWNAA
Cramer, Zadok 1773-1813 *DcNAA*
Crammond, H *Alli*
Crammond, Hercules *BiDLA*
Crammond, Robert *Alli*
Cramp, John Mockett 1791?-1881 *Alli,*
Alli Sup, BbtC, DcNAA
Cramp, Thomas *ChPo S1*
Cramp, William *Alli Sup*
Crampton, C Ward 1877- *WhWNAA*
Crampton, Charles Gregory 1911- *AmA&B,*
ConAu 21
Crampton, G E E *Alli Sup*
Crampton, Georgia Ronan 1925- *ConAu 57*
Crampton, Henry Edward 1875- *WhWNAA*
Crampton, J N *Alli Sup*
Crampton, John Fiennes Twistleton *Alli Sup*
Crampton, Josiah *Alli Sup*
Crampton, Patricia Elizabeth 1925- *Au&Wr,*
ChPo S1
Crampton, Philip *Alli, BiDLA*
Crampton, Roland *ChPo S1*
Crampton, S R *Alli Sup*
Crampton, T *ChPo*
Cramton, Roger C 1929- *ConAu 33*
Cran, Mrs. George *OxCan*
Cran, Marion 1875-1942 *LongC, WhLA*
Cranach, Lucas 1472-1553 *AtlBL, REn*
Cranach, Lukas 1472-1553 *OxGer*
Cranage, David Herbert Somerset 1866- *WhLA*
Cranage, Joseph Edward *Alli Sup*
Cranborne, Viscount *Alli Sup*
Cranbrook, James *Alli Sup*
Cranbrook, James L *ConAu XR*
Cranc, Claus 1323?- *OxGer*
Cranch, Christopher Pearse 1813-1892 *Alli,*
Alli Sup, AmA, AmA&B, BbD,
BiD&SB, BiDSA, CasWL, ChPo,
ChPo S1, ChPo S2, Chmbr 3, CyAL 2,
DcAmA, DcNAA, EarAB, OxAm,
REnAL
Cranch, Jane Bowring *Alli Sup*
Cranch, John 1807-1891 *Alli, BiDLA,*
EarAB Sup
Cranch, Richard 1726-1811 *Alli, DcAmA*
Cranch, William 1769?-1855? *Alli, DcAmA,*
DcNAA
Crandall, Andrew Wallace 1894-1963
IndAu 1917
Crandall, Arthur F J *ChPo*
Crandall, Bruce Verne 1873-1945 *AmA&B,*
DcNAA
Crandall, Charles Henry 1858-1923 *Alli Sup,*
AmA&B, ChPo, ChPo S1, DcAmA,
DcNAA
Crandall, Charles Lee 1850-1917 *DcAmA,*
DcNAA
Crandall, Ernest L *ChPo*
Crandall, Floyd Milford 1858-1919 *DcNAA*
Crandall, Irving Bardshar 1890-1927 *DcNAA*
Crandall, James E 1930- *ConAu 41*
Crandall, John J *Alli Sup*
Crandall, Joy *ConAu 57*
Crandall, Lathan Augustus 1850-1923 *DcNAA*
Crandall, Lee Saunders 1887- *WhWNAA*
Crandall, Lucy S *Alli Sup*
Crandall, Norma 1907- *WrD 1976*
Crandall, William Lusk *Alli Sup*
Crandell, A B *ChPo*
Crandell, Helen Hopkins 1890- *WhWNAA*
Crandell, Richard F 1901-1974 *ConAu 53*
Crandolph, A J *Alli*
Crandon, John *Alli*
Crandon, LeRoi Goddard 1873-1939 *BiDPar,*
DcNAA
Crandon, Mina Stinson 1890?-1941 *BiDPar*
Crane, A Bromley *Alli Sup*

Crane, Aaron Martin 1839-1914 *DcNAA*
Crane, Alan 1901- *AuBYP*
Crane, Albert Loyal 1893- *WhWNAA*
Crane, Alex *ConAu XR*
Crane, Anne Moncure 1838?-1872 *Alli Sup,*
AmA, AmA&B, BiDSA, DcNAA,
LivFWS
Crane, B P *Alli Sup*
Crane, Bathsheba H 1811- *DcNAA*
Crane, Beatrice *ChPo S1, ChPo S2*
Crane, Berkeley *MnBBF*
Crane, Caroline 1858-1935 *DcNAA*
Crane, Caroline 1930- *ConAu 9R, WrD 1976*
Crane, Cephas Bennett 1833-1917 *Alli Sup,*
DcAmA, DcNAA
Crane, Charles Paston 1857- *WhLA*
Crane, Clarkson 1894- *AmA&B, AmNov*
Crane, Donald P 1933- *ConAu 61*
Crane, E J 1889- *WhWNAA*
Crane, Edgar *Alli Sup*
Crane, Edgar 1917- *ConAu 17R*
Crane, Edna Temple *ConAu XR*
Crane, Eleanor Maud *AmA&B*
Crane, Elizabeth Green *AmA&B, ChPo,*
DcAmA
Crane, Ellery Bicknell 1836-1925 *DcNAA*
Crane, Florence *AuBYP*
Crane, Frances 1896- *AmA&B, EncM&D*
Crane, Frank 1861-1928 *AmA&B, AmLY,*
ChPo, DcAmA, DcNAA, REnAL,
WhWNAA
Crane, G W *EarAB*
Crane, Gabriel 1783- *OhA&B*
Crane, George Washington, III 1901- *AmA&B,*
WhWNAA
Crane, Harold 1899-1932 *AmA&B, AmWr,*
AtlBL, CasWL, ChPo, ChPo S2,
CnDAL, CnE&AP, CnMWL, ConAmA,
CyWA, DcLEnL, DcNAA, EncWL,
EvLB
Crane, Hart 1899-1932 *LongC, ModAL,*
ModAL Sup, OhA&B, OxAm, OxEng,
Pen Am, RAdv 1, REn, REnAL, SixAP,
TwCA, TwCA Sup, TwCW, WebEAL,
WhTwL
Crane, Ichabod *DcNAA*
Crane, Irving *AuBYP*
Crane, Isaac M *Alli Sup*
Crane, J L *Alli Sup*
Crane, J Miriam *ChPo S1, ChPo S2*
Crane, James G 1927- *ConAu 13R*
Crane, Jane Miriam *Alli Sup*
Crane, Jim *ConAu XR*
Crane, Jimmie 1910- *AmSCAP 66*
Crane, John *Alli, Alli Sup*
Crane, Jonathan Townley 1819-1880 *Alli Sup,*
DcAmA, DcNAA
Crane, Julia G 1925- *ConAu 41*
Crane, Leo 1881- *AmA&B, ArizL,*
WhWNAA
Crane, Louis Burton 1869- *WhWNAA*
Crane, Lucy 1842-1882 *Alli Sup, ChPo S1*
Crane, Lydia *LivFWS*
Crane, Mary Campbell 1867-1943 *IndAu 1917*
Crane, Nathalia Clara Ruth 1913- *AmA&B,*
ChPo, ChPo S1, ChPo S2, ConAmL,
DcLEnL, OxAm, REnAL
Crane, Oliver 1822-1896 *Alli Sup, ChPo S1,*
DcAmA, DcNAA
Crane, Philip Miller 1930- *AmSCAP 66,*
ConAu 9R
Crane, R C *TexWr*
Crane, R S 1886-1967 *Pen Am*
Crane, Ralph *Alli*
Crane, Richard Teller 1832-1912 *DcNAA*
Crane, Robert *ConAu XR*
Crane, Ronald Salmon 1886-1967 *AmA&B,*
CasWL
Crane, Sibylla 1851-1902 *DcAmA, DcNAA*
Crane, Stephen *Alli Sup*
Crane, Stephen 1871-1900 *AmA, AmA&B,*
AmWr, AtlBL, BbD, BiD&SB, CasWL,
ChPo, Chmbr 3, CnDAL, CnE&AP,
CriT 3, CyWA, DcAmA, DcLEnL,
DcNAA, EvLB, LongC, ModAL, OxAm,
OxEng, Pen Am, RAdv 1, RCom, REn,
REnAL, WebEAL
Crane, Sylvia E 1918- *ConAu 33, WrD 1976*

Crane, T S *ChPo*
Crane, Theodore 1886- *WhWNAA*
Crane, Thomas *Alli, BiDLA*
Crane, Thomas 1843- *CarSB, ChPo*
Crane, Thomas And Houghton, Ellen E *Alli Sup*
Crane, Thomas Frederick 1844-1927 *Alli Sup,*
BiD&SB, DcAmA, DcNAA
Crane, Verner Winslow 1889- *AmA&B*
Crane, W J E *Alli Sup*
Crane, Walter 1845-1915 *Alli Sup, CarSB,*
ChPo, ChPo S1, ChPo S2, IlBYP,
JBA 1934, JBA 1951, NewC, St&VC,
WhCL
Crane, Warren Eugene 1889- *WhWNAA*
Crane, Wilder 1928- *ConAu 45*
Crane, William *Alli Sup*
Crane, William, Jr. *Alli*
Crane, William And Moses, Bernard *Alli Sup*
Crane, William Carey 1816-1885 *BiDSA,*
DcAmA, DcNAA
Crane, William D 1892- *ConAu 5R,*
SmATA 1
Crane, William Iler 1866-1924 *DcNAA*
Cranenburgh, D E *Alli Sup*
Craner, Henry *Alli*
Craner, Thomas *Alli*
Craney, Isabelle Ebbitt *ChPo S2*
Cranfield, Charles E B 1915- *ConAu 5R*
Cranfield, Geoffrey Alan 1920- *ConAu 5R*
Cranfield, R E *Alli Sup*
Cranfield, Thomas *Alli*
Cranfill, James Britton 1858- *TexWr,*
WhWNAA
Cranford, Clarence William 1906- *ConAu 1R*
Cranford, James *Alli*
Cranford, Robert J 1908- *ConAu 17*
Crank, W H *Alli*
Cranko, John 1927-1973 *ConAu 45*
Crankshaw, Edward 1909- *ConAu 25, LongC,*
TwCA Sup
Crankshaw, James 1844-1921 *DcNAA*
Cranley, Thomas *Alli*
Cranmer, George *Alli*
Cranmer, Gibson Lamb 1826-1903 *DcNAA,*
OhA&B
Cranmer, Thomas 1489-1556 *Alli, BrAu,*
CasWL, Chmbr 1, CrE&SL, DcEnL,
DcLEnL, EvLB, NewC, OxEng, Pen Eng,
REn, WebEAL
Cranmer-Byng, Lancelot Alfred 1872-1945 *ChPo,*
NewC
Crannell, Philip Wendell 1861- *WhWNAA*
Crannell Means, Florence 1891- *Au&Wr*
Cranny, Titus Francis 1921- *ConAu 25,*
WrD 1976
Cranston, Claudia 1892?-1947 *AmA&B,*
DcNAA, TexWr, WhWNAA
Cranston, David *Alli*
Cranston, Earl 1840-1932 *DcNAA, OhA&B*
Cranston, John *Alli Sup*
Cranston, Lucie Mason 1857-1937 *OhA&B*
Cranston, Maurice William 1920- *Au&Wr,*
ConAu 5R, WrD 1976
Cranston, Mechthild *ConAu 53*
Cranston, Robert *Alli Sup*
Cranston, William H *Alli Sup*
Cranstone, Mrs. L *Alli Sup*
Cranstoun, James *Alli Sup*
Cranstoun, Pauline Emily *Alli Sup, ChPo S1*
Cranswick, James M *Alli Sup*
Crantz, David *BbtC*
Cranwell, J *Alli*
Cranwell, John Philips 1904- *ConAu 61*
Cranwell, L *Alli*
Craon, Amauri *CasWL*
Craon, Maurice d1196 *CasWL*
Craon, Pierre d1216 *CasWL*
Crapanzano, Vincent 1939- *ConAu 53*
Crapol, Edward P 1936- *ConAu 45*
Crapps, Robert W 1925- *ConAu 53*
Craps, John *Alli Sup*
Crapsey, Adelaide 1878-1914 *AmA&B, ChPo,*
CnDAL, ConAmL, DcNAA, OxAm,
REn, REnAL, TwCA
Crapsey, Algernon Sidney 1847-1927 *AmA&B,*
DcNAA, OhA&B
Crapsey, Edward *Alli Sup*
Crary, C *Alli Sup*

Crary, Catherine S 1909- *ConAu P-1*
Crary, Christopher Gore 1806-1895 *OhA&B*
Crary, Margaret Coleman 1906- *AuBYP,*
ConAu 5R, SmATA 9
Cras, Herve *OxCan*
Crashaw *Alli*
Crashaw, H *Alli*
Crashaw, Richard 1612?-1649? *Alli, AtlBL,*
BiD&SB, BrAu, CasWL, ChPo,
ChPo S1, ChPo S2, Chmbr 1, CnE&AP,
CrE&SL, CriT 1, DcEnA, DcEnL,
DcEuL, DcLEnL, EvLB, MouLC 1,
NewC, OxEng, Pen Eng, RAdv 1, REn,
WebEAL
Crashaw, William 1572-1626 *Alli, NewC*
Crassett, J *Alli Sup*
Crassus, Lucius Licinius 140BC-091BC *Pen Cl*
Crassus, Marcus Licinius 115?BC-053BC *REn*
Crassweller, Robert D 1915- *ConAu 21*
Craster, Mrs. Edmond *ChPo S2*
Craster, John 1901- *WrD 1976*
Craster, Sir John Montagu 1901- *Au&Wr*
Cratchley, William Joseph 1908- *Au&Wr*
Crates *CasWL, Pen Cl*
Crates Of Thebes 365?BC-285BC *CasWL,*
Pen Cl
Crathorne, Arthur Robert 1875- *WhWNAA*
Cratinus 490?BC-423?BC *CasWL, Pen Cl*
Craton, Michael 1931- *ConAu 41*
Cratty, Bryant J 1929- *ConAu 25, WrD 1976*
Crauford, C *Alli*
Crauford, David 1665-1726 *Alli*
Crauford, George 1785-1809 *Alli*
Craufurd, Lieutenant Colonel *Alli*
Craufurd, A *Alli*
Craufurd, Alexander Henry Gregan *Alli Sup*
Craufurd, C W F *Alli Sup*
Craufurd, Charles *BiDLA*
Craufurd, Charles H *Alli*
Craufurd, George *Alli, BiDLA*
Craufurd, Harry James *Alli Sup*
Craufurd, John Lindesay, Earl Of *Alli*
Craufurd, Quintin *Alli, BiDLA*
Craufurd, Robert *BiDLA*
Craufurd, Thomas *Alli*
Cravath, Paul Drennan 1861-1940 *OhA&B*
Craveirinha, Jose 1922- *AfA 1*
Craven *Alli*
Craven, Lady *BiDLA*
Craven, Augustus 1808-1891 *Alli Sup,*
BiD&SB
Craven, Avery Odelle 1886- *AmA&B*
Craven, Braxton 1822-1882 *AmA&B, DcNAA*
Craven, Bruce 1881- *WhWNAA*
Craven, C W *Alli Sup*
Craven, Charles Audley Assheton *Alli Sup*
Craven, Lady Elizabeth Berkeley 1750-1828 *Alli,*
BiD&SB
Craven, Essex *MnBBF*
Craven, Frank d1945 *AmA&B*
Craven, George M 1929- *ConAu 61*
Craven, Henry And Barfield, John *Alli Sup*
Craven, Henry Thornton *Alli Sup*
Craven, Isaac *Alli*
Craven, J *Alli Sup*
Craven, James Brown *Alli Sup*
Craven, John J *Alli Sup*
Craven, John Vandegrift 1899- *WhWNAA*
Craven, M B *Alli Sup*
Craven, Margaret *WrD 1976*
Craven, R Keppel *Alli*
Craven, Scott *ChPo S2*
Craven, Thomas *Alli Sup*
Craven, Thomas 1889-1969 *AmA&B, AuBYP,*
REnAL, TwCA, TwCA Sup
Craven, Wesley Frank 1905- *AmA&B,*
ConAu 61
Craven, William 1731-1815? *Alli, BiDLA,*
BiDLA Sup
Craven, William George 1835- *Alli Sup*
Cravens, Gwen *DrAF 1976*
Cravens, Junius L *ChPo*
Cravens, Junius S *ChPo*
Cravens, Mary J 1825-1912 *OhA&B*
Craveri, Marcello 1914- *ConAu 21*
Cravioto, Alfonso 1884- *WhWNAA*
Craw, Freeman Godfrey Jerry 1917- *WhGrA*

Crawford *Alli*
Crawford, Captain *Alli, Alli Sup*
Crawford, Colonel *Alli*
Crawford, Earl Of *NewC*
Crawford, Mrs. *Alli*
Crawford, Mrs. And Barker, G *Alli Sup*
Crawford, A *Alli*
Crawford, Mrs. A *Alli Sup, PoIre*
Crawford, A Gordon *Alli Sup*
Crawford, A Maria 1884- *BiDSA*
Crawford, Adair d1795 *Alli*
Crawford, Alex *BbtC*
Crawford, Alexander Wellington 1866-1933
DcNAA, WhWNAA
Crawford, Alice Arnold 1850-1874 *Alli Sup,*
DcAmA, DcNAA, WiscW
Crawford, Allan *OxCan*
Crawford, Ann Fears 1932- *ConAu 21*
Crawford, Anna *ChPo*
Crawford, Annabella *Alli Sup*
Crawford, Archibald *Alli Sup, ChPo*
Crawford, Benjamin F 1881- *OhA&B*
Crawford, C Merle 1924- *ConAu 45*
Crawford, Caroline *WhWNAA*
Crawford, Char 1935- *ConAu 57*
Crawford, Charles *Alli*
Crawford, Charles 1763?- *DcNAA*
Crawford, Charles 1866-1945 *OhA&B*
Crawford, Charles O 1934- *ConAu 37*
Crawford, Charles P 1945- *ConAu 45*
Crawford, Charles W 1931- *ConAu 61*
Crawford, Charlotte Holmes *ChPo*
Crawford, Clan, Jr. 1927- *ConAu 57*
Crawford, David *ChPo S1*
Crawford, David 1666-1726 *ChPo*
Crawford, David L 1890?-1974 *ConAu 45*
Crawford, Deborah 1922- *ConAu 49,*
SmATA 6
Crawford, Donald W 1938- *ConAu 45*
Crawford, E *ChPo S1*
Crawford, Earl Stetson 1872- *ChPo*
Crawford, Earl Stetson 1877- *ChPo S1*
Crawford, Elizabeth *ChPo*
Crawford, Everett L 1879- *Br&AmS*
Crawford, Floretta S *ChPo*
Crawford, Frances *Alli Sup*
Crawford, Francis *Alli Sup*
Crawford, Francis J 1815?- *PoIre*
Crawford, Francis Marion 1854-1909 *Alli Sup,*
AmA, AmA&B, BbD, BiD&SB,
Chmbr 3, CnDAL, DcAmA, DcBiA,
DcEnA, DcEnA Ap, DcLEnL, DcNAA,
EvLB, LongC, OxAm, OxEng, Pen Am,
REn, REnAL
Crawford, Fred Roberts 1924- *ConAu 45*
Crawford, G *Alli, ChPo*
Crawford, George *Alli*
Crawford, George Arthur And Eberle, J A
Alli Sup
Crawford, George G 1898- *WhWNAA*
Crawford, George M *Alli*
Crawford, George W And Applewhite, J
Alli Sup
Crawford, Mrs. H L *Alli Sup*
Crawford, Hannah Louise 1879-1943 *DcNAA*
Crawford, Henry 1809- *ChPo S1*
Crawford, Iain 1922- *ConAu 1R*
Crawford, Isaac *BlkAW*
Crawford, Isabel Alice 1865- *WhWNAA*
Crawford, Isabella Valancy 1850-1887 *BrAu 19,*
CanWr, CasWL, ChPo, ChPo S1,
Chmbr 3, DcLEnL, DcNAA, NewC,
OxCan, OxEng, PoIre, REnAL
Crawford, J B *Alli Sup*
Crawford, J Marshall *Alli Sup, BiDSA*
Crawford, J W *Alli Sup*
Crawford, Jack 1847-1917 *AmA&B, DcNAA*
Crawford, Jack Randall 1878-1968 *AmA&B,*
WhWNAA
Crawford, James *Alli*
Crawford, James Coutts *Alli Sup*
Crawford, James Paul 1825- *ChPo*
Crawford, James Pyle Wickersham 1882-1939
AmA&B, DcNAA
Crawford, Jesse 1895-1962 *AmSCAP 66*
Crawford, Joanna 1941- *ConAu 9R*
Crawford, John *Alli, Alli Sup*
Crawford, John 1816-1873 *Alli Sup, ChPo*

Crawford, John 1851- *ChPo, ChPo*
Crawford, John E 1904-1971 *ConAu 17,*
SmATA 3
Crawford, John Howard *Alli Sup*
Crawford, John Lindesay, Earl Of *Alli*
Crawford, John Martin *Alli Sup*
Crawford, John Raymond 1886- *WhWNAA*
Crawford, John Richard 1932- *WrD 1976*
Crawford, John Robert *Alli Sup*
Crawford, John W 1894- *WhWNAA*
Crawford, John W 1914- *ConAu 1R*
Crawford, John W 1936- *ConAu 53*
Crawford, John Wallace 1838?-1896 *PoIre*
Crawford, John Wallace 1847-1917 *AmA,*
ChPo, ChPo S1, DcAmA, DcNAA,
OxAm, REnAL
Crawford, Joyce 1931- *ConAu 25*
Crawford, Kate *ChPo*
Crawford, Kenneth Bredin 1892- *Au&Wr*
Crawford, Kenneth Gale 1902- *AmA&B*
Crawford, Louisa Matilda Jane 1790?-1858
PoIre
Crawford, Louise Macartney 1808- *BiD&SB,*
ChPo
Crawford, Lydia Benedict *OhA&B*
Crawford, Mrs. M J E *Alli Sup*
Crawford, Mabel Sharman *Alli Sup*
Crawford, Marc *BlkAW*
Crawford, Margaret *Alli Sup*
Crawford, Martha F *Alli Sup*
Crawford, Marvin Howard 1894- *WhWNAA*
Crawford, Mary 1861-1946 *OhA&B*
Crawford, Mary 1908- *Au&Wr*
Crawford, Mary And Henry *REn*
Crawford, Mary Caroline 1874-1932 *AmA&B,*
AmLY, BiD&SB, DcAmA, DcNAA,
REnAL, WhWNAA
Crawford, Mary Mazeppa 1898- *IndAu 1917*
Crawford, Matsu W 1902- *ConAu 17*
Crawford, Max *DrAF 1976*
Crawford, Michael 1933- *Au&Wr*
Crawford, Nathaniel M 1811-1871 *BiDSA,*
DcAmA, DcNAA
Crawford, Nelson Antrim 1888-1963 *AmA&B,*
AnMV 1926, ChPo, ChPo S1,
WhWNAA
Crawford, Oswald *DcNAA*
Crawford, Patrick *Alli*
Crawford, Mrs. Penfound *Alli Sup*
Crawford, Phyllis 1899- *JBA 1951, SmATA 3*
Crawford, Richard 1935- *ConAu 57*
Crawford, Robert *Alli Sup, Chmbr 2,*
WrD 1976
Crawford, Robert d1733 *Alli, BrAu, DcEnL*
Crawford, Robert 1877- *WhLA*
Crawford, Robert M 1899-1961 *AmSCAP 66*
Crawford, Robert Platt 1893- *AmA&B,*
ConAu 17, WhWNAA
Crawford, Robert Wigram *Alli Sup*
Crawford, Roy Virgel 1897- *WhWNAA*
Crawford, Russell Tracy 1876- *WhWNAA*
Crawford, S Henry *Alli Sup*
Crawford, Sallie Wallace Brown 1915- *Au&Wr*
Crawford, Samuel Johnson 1835-1914? *DcNAA,*
IndAu 1917
Crawford, Samuel Wylie 1827-1892 *Alli Sup,*
DcAmA
Crawford, Samuel Wylie 1829-1892 *DcNAA*
Crawford, Stanley Gottlieb 1937- *Au&Wr,*
DrAF 1976
Crawford, T P *Alli Sup*
Crawford, T S 1945- *Au&Wr, ConAu 29*
Crawford, Thelmar Wyche 1905- *AuBYP,*
ConAu 1R
Crawford, Thomas *ChPo S1, ChPo S2*
Crawford, Thomas 1813-1857 *OxAm*
Crawford, Thomas Jackson 1812-1875 *Alli Sup*
Crawford, Thomas Robb 1821-1898 *OhA&B*
Crawford, Tom *DrAP 1976*
Crawford, W J 1880?-1920 *BiDPar*
Crawford, W N *BbtC*
Crawford, Will *ConICB*
Crawford, William *Alli, PoIre*
Crawford, William 1676-1742 *Alli, DcEnL*
Crawford, William 1929- *ConAu 1R*
Crawford, William H And Horatio Marbury *Alli*
Crawford, William Harris 1772-1834 *BiDSA*
Crawford, William Henry 1855-1944 *AmLY,*

DcNAA
Crawford And Balcarres, Earl Of 1812- *Alli Sup, DcEnL*
Crawford-Bromehead *Alli Sup*
Crawford-Frost, William Albert 1863-1936 *DcNAA, WhWNAA*
Crawfurd, Andrew *ChPo*
Crawfurd, Archibald *ChPo S1*
Crawfurd, Charles *Alli, BiDLA*
Crawfurd, David *Alli*
Crawfurd, George *Alli, Alli Sup*
Crawfurd, John 1780-1868 *Alli, Alli Sup*
Crawfurd, Oswald *DcEnL*
Crawfurd, Oswald John Frederick 1834- *Alli Sup*
Crawfurd, Thomas *Alli*
Crawhall, Joseph *Alli Sup*
Crawley, Captain *DcEnL*
Crawley, Aidan Merivale 1908- *Au&Wr, ConAu 61, WrD 1976*
Crawley, Alan *OxCan*
Crawley, Charles 1847- *Alli Sup*
Crawley, Edmund A *BbtC*
Crawley, Edwin Schofield 1862-1933 *DcNAA, WhWNAA*
Crawley, George John Lloyd *Alli Sup*
Crawley, Richard 1841-1898 *Alli Sup, ChPo*
Crawley, William John Chetwode *Alli Sup*
Crawley-Boevey *Alli Sup*
Crawshaw, John *Alli Sup*
Crawshaw, Nancy 1914- *Au&Wr*
Crawshaw, William Henry 1861-1940 *AmA&B, DcAmA, DcNAA, WhWNAA*
Crawshay, George *Alli Sup*
Crawshay, Mary *ChPo*
Crawshay, Rose Mary *Alli Sup*
Crawshay-Williams, Eliot 1879- *WhLA*
Crawshay-Williams, Rupert 1908- *Au&Wr*
Crawskey, John *Alli*
Cray, Edward 1933- *WrD 1976*
Cray, Julian *Alli Sup*
Crayder, Dorothy 1906- *ConAu 33, SmATA 7*
Crayder, Teresa *SmATA 1*
Craynecour, Marguerite De *WorAu*
Crayon, Geoffrey *Alli, AmA&B, CnDAL, DcEnL, OxAm, OxEng, REn, REnAL*
Crayon, Porte *DcAmA*
Crayton, Pearl *BlkAW*
Crayton, Sherman Gideon 1895- *IndAu 1917*
Craz, Albert G 1926- *AuBYP, ConAu 17R*
Crazy Horse 1849-1877 *OxAm*
Creager, Alfred L 1910- *ConAu 17R*
Creager, Charles E 1873- *OhA&B*
Creager, Eunice Whayne 1883-1948 *IndAu 1917*
Creager, William Pitcher 1878- *WhWNAA*
Creagh, James *Alli Sup*
Creagh, Sir Michael *PoIre*
Creagh, Patrick 1930- *ConAu 25*
Creagh-Osborne, Richard 1928- *ConAu 9R*
Creak, Albert *Alli Sup*
Creak, E W *Alli Sup*
Crealocke, Henry Hope *Alli Sup*
Creamer, David 1812-1887 *AmA&B, DcNAA*
Creamer, Edward Sherwood 1843?- *PoIre*
Creamer, H G *Alli Sup*
Creamer, Hannah G *Alli*
Creamer, Henry 1879-1930 *AmSCAP 66*
Creamer, Robert W 1922- *ConAu 21, WrD 1976*
Crean, John Edward, Jr. 1939- *ConAu 41*
Crean, Mary Walsingham *LivFWS*
Crean, Robert *AmA&B*
Creanga, Ioan 1837-1890 *EvEuW*
Creanga, Ion 1837-1889 *CasWL, ClDMEuL, Pen Eur*
Creange, Henry 1877-1945 *DcNAA*
Creany, William *PoIre*
Crease, J *Alli, BiDLA*
Crease, James *Alli, BiDLA*
Creaser, Thomas *Alli, BiDLA*
Creasey, Henry Alfred *Alli Sup*
Creasey, John 1908-1973 *Au&Wr, ConAu 5R, ConAu 41, EncM&D, LongC, MnBBF, REn, TwCW, WorAu*
Creasy, Sir Edward Shepherd 1812-1878 *Alli, Alli Sup, BrAu 19, CasWL, Chmbr 3, DcEnL, DcEuL, EvLB, REn*

Creatore, Luigi 1920- *AmSCAP 66*
Creber, J W Patrick 1930- *Au&Wr*
Crebillon, Claude Prosper Jolyot De 1707-1777 *BiD&SB, CasWL, DcEuL, EuA, EvEuW, OxFr, Pen Eur, REn*
Crebillon, Prosper Jolyot De 1674-1762 *AtlBL, BbD, BiD&SB, CasWL, CnThe, CyWA, DcEuL, EuA, EvEuW, McGWD, OxFr, Pen Eur, REn, REnWD*
Crechales, Anthony George 1926- *ConAu 29*
Crecine, John Patrick 1939- *ConAu 57*
Crecraft, Earl Willis 1886-1950 *IndAu 1816, OhA&B*
Crecy, Jeanne *ConAu XR, SmATA 5, WrD 1976*
Crecy, Odette De *OxFr*
Credle, Ellis 1902- *AuBYP, ConAu 13R, IlCB 1945, IlCB 1956, JBA 1951, SmATA 1, St&VC*
Cree, Edward David *Alli Sup*
Cree, Mary Crowther 1919- *Au&Wr*
Creech *BiDLA*
Creech, Thomas 1659-1700? *Alli, DcEnL, EvLB, NewC*
Creech, William 1745-1815 *Alli, BiDLA, BiDLA Sup, ChPo S1, NewC*
Creed, Cary E *Alli*
Creed, David *ConAu XR*
Creed, H Herries And Williams, W V V *Alli Sup*
Creed, Mrs. Warren *Alli Sup*
Creed, William *Alli*
Creegan, Charles Cole 1850-1939 *DcNAA*
Creek, Herbert LeSourd 1879- *IndAu 1917, WhWNAA*
Creekmore, Hubert 1907-1966 *AmA&B, AmNov, REnAL, TwCA Sup*
Creekmore, Raymond 1905- *IlCB 1956*
Creel, Cecil Willis 1889- *IndAu 1917*
Creel, George 1876-1953 *AmA&B, REnAL*
Creel, J Luke *MnnWr*
Creeley, Robert 1926- *AmA&B, Au&Wr, CasWL, ConAu 1R, ConLC 1, ConLC 2, ConLC 4, ConP 1970, ConP 1975, CrCAP, DrAF 1976, DrAP 1975, ModAL, ModAL Sup, Pen Am, RAdv 1, REnAL, WebEAL, WhTwL, WorAu, WrD 1976*
Creelman, Harlan 1864- *WhWNAA*
Creelman, James 1859-1915 *AmA&B, DcAmA, DcNAA*
Creelman, Marjorie B 1908- *ConAu 21*
Creeny, William Frederick *Alli Sup*
Creer, Edwin *Alli Sup*
Creery, Andrew Macreight *Alli Sup*
Creery, William Arthur *PoIre*
Creery, William Rufus 1824-1875 *BiDSA, DcNAA*
Crees, James Harold Edward 1882- *WhLA*
Creese, Bethea *Au&Wr, ConAu 9R, WrD 1976*
Creevey, Caroline Alathea 1843-1920 *DcNAA*
Creevey, Thomas 1768-1838 *BrAu 19, DcLEnL, EvLB, NewC, OxEng, REn*
Creffield, Edward *Alli*
Cregan, Beatrice *ChPo S1*
Cregan, C T *Alli Sup*
Cregan, David 1931- *Au&Wr, ConAu 45, ConDr, WrD 1976*
Cregan, Mairin *CatA 1947*
Creger, Ralph 1914- *ConAu 13R*
Crehan, Joseph Hugh 1906- *Au&Wr, WrD 1976*
Crehan, Thomas 1919- *Au&Wr, ConAu 5R*
Crehore, John D *Alli Sup*
Crehore, John Davenport 1891- *BiDPar*
Crehore, William Williams 1864-1918 *DcNAA, OhA&B*
Creichton, John *Alli*
Creigh, Alfred 1810- *Alli, Alli Sup*
Creighton, Alan B *OxCan*
Creighton, Charles *Alli Sup*
Creighton, Don *ConAu XR, WrD 1976*
Creighton, Donald Grant 1902- *Au&Wr, CanWr, DcLEnL, MnBBF, OxCan, OxCan Sup, WorAu*
Creighton, H *Alli*
Creighton, Helen *ChPo S1, OxCan,*

OxCan Sup
Creighton, Helen 1899- *ConAu 41*
Creighton, Helen 1914- *ConAu 33*
Creighton, J C *Alli*
Creighton, James *Alli, BiDLA, PoIre*
Creighton, James A 1901- *TexWr*
Creighton, James Edwin 1861-1924 *AmA&B, DcNAA*
Creighton, Jesse *WhWNAA*
Creighton, John *DrAP 1975*
Creighton, Louise 1850- *WhLA*
Creighton, Louise H *Alli Sup*
Creighton, Luella *OxCan, OxCan Sup*
Creighton, Luella Bruce 1901- *ConAu P-1*
Creighton, Mandell 1843-1901 *Alli Sup, BrAu 19, Chmbr 3, DcEuL, EvLB, NewC, OxEng*
Creighton, Bishop Mandell Of London 1843-1901 *DcEnA, DcEnA Ap*
Creighton, Mary Helen 1899- *Au&Wr*
Creighton, Robert 1593-1672 *Alli*
Creighton, Robert 1639-1736 *Alli*
Creighton, Thomas H 1904- *AmA&B, ConAu 5R*
Creighton, Trevor *Alli Sup*
Creighton, William Black 1864-1946 *DcNAA*
Creighton, William Henry 1859-1933 *DcNAA, WhWNAA*
Creitzburg, A M *BiDSA*
Crellin, Philip *Alli Sup*
Cremazie, Jacques *BbtC*
Cremazie, Joseph Jacques 1810-1872 *DcNAA*
Cremazie, Joseph Octave 1827-1879 *BbtC, CasWL, DcNAA*
Cremazie, Octave 1827-1879 *CanWr, OxCan, OxCan Sup*
Crembisceni, Giovanni Mario 1663-1728 *DcEuL*
Cremeans, Charles D 1915- *ConAu 5R*
Cremer, Frederic Daustini *Alli Sup*
Cremer, Jacobus Jan 1827-1880 *BiD&SB, CasWL*
Cremer, Jan 1940- *CasWL, ConAu 13R*
Cremer, Robert Roger 1947- *ConAu 61*
Cremer, William Henry *Alli Sup*
Cremin, Lawrence Arthur 1925- *AmA&B, ConAu 33*
Cremony, J C *Alli Sup*
Cremony, John C *ArizL*
Cremutius Cordus, Aulus d025 *Pen Cl*
Crena DeIongh, Daniel 1888-1970 *ConAu 25, ConAu 29*
Crenne, Helisenne De *CasWL, OxFr*
Crenner, James 1938- *ConAu 13R, ConP 1970, DrAP 1975*
Crenshaw, James L 1934- *ConAu 37, WrD 1976*
Crenshaw, Mary Ann *ConAu 57*
Crenshaw, R Parker, Jr. *ChPo*
Crequi, Renee-C DeFroullay, Marquise De 1714-1803 *OxFr*
Crerar, Duncan MacGregor 1837-1886 *ChPo*
Crerar, Thomas Alexander *OxCan*
Crerar, Thomas And Cusin, Alexander *Alli Sup*
Cresap, Mary *LivFWS*
Crescas, Hasdai 1340-1410 *CasWL, EuA, Pen Eur*
Cresner, A *Alli*
Crespel *BiDLA*
Crespi, Giuseppe Maria 1665-1747 *AtlBL*
Crespi, Juan 1721-1782 *REnAL*
Crespi, Pachita 1900- *AuBYP*
Crespigny, Mrs. Philip Champion De *WhLA*
Crespo, Antonio Candido Goncalves 1846-1883 *BiD&SB*
Cressac Bachelerie, Bertrande De 1899- *BiDPar*
Cressener, Drue *Alli*
Cresset, Edward d1754 *Alli*
Cressey, Donald R 1919- *ConAu 13R*
Cressey, E K *Alli Sup*
Cressey, George Babcock 1896-1963 *AmA&B, OhA&B*
Cressey, George Croswell 1856- *DcAmA, WhWNAA*
Cressey, Hugh Paulin De 1605-1674 *Alli*
Cressey, Serenus 1605-1674 *Alli*
Cressey, Tura Compton *TexWr*
Cressey, William W 1939- *ConAu 33*
Cressler, Alfred Miller 1877-1939 *OhA&B*

Cresson, Abigail *ChPo, ChPo S1*
Cresson, Bruce Collins 1930- *ConAu 45*
Cresson, Margaret French *AmA&B*
Cresson, William Penn 1873-1932 *DcNAA*
Cresswell, C *Alli*
Cresswell, Charles Neve 1828- *Alli Sup*
Cresswell, D *BiDLA*
Cresswell, Daniel 1776-1844 *Alli*
Cresswell, Mrs. Gerard *Alli Sup*
Cresswell, Helen 1936?- *Au&Wr, AuBYP,
ConAu 17R, SenS, SmATA 1,
WrD 1976*
Cresswell, Henry *Alli Sup*
Cresswell, Mrs. I S *Alli Sup*
Cresswell, Joseph *Alli*
Cresswell, Margaret R *Alli Sup*
Cresswell, Philip *Alli Sup*
Cresswell, R N *Alli*
Cresswell, Richard Henry *Alli Sup*
Cresswell, Ruth A *ChPo S2*
Cresswell, Thomas E *Alli*
Cresswell, Walter D'Arcy 1896- *DcLEnL*
Cresswick *Alli*
Cressy, H P De *Alli*
Cressy, Serenus 1605-1674 *Alli*
Cressy, Will Martin 1864- *AmLY*
Crestadoro, Andrea 1808-1879 *Alli Sup*
Creston *WhLA*
Creston, Dormer *LongC*
Creston, Paul 1906- *AmSCAP 66, REnAL*
Creswell, Frank O *Alli Sup*
Creswell, H B 1869-1960 *LongC*
Creswell, John A J 1828- *Alli Sup*
Creswell, Julia Pleasants 1827-1886 *BiDSA,
DcAmA, DcNAA, LivFWS*
Creswell, K A C 1879- *ConAu P-1*
Creswell, Robert *Alli Sup*
Creswell, Samuel Francis *Alli Sup*
Creswick, Margaret *Alli Sup*
Creswick, Maurice *MnBBF*
Creswick, Paul 1866- *MnBBF, WhLA*
Creswick, Thomas 1811-1869 *ChPo, ChPo S1*
Creswick, Wilfred *Alli Sup*
Cresy, Edward *Alli*
Cretan, Gladys 1921- *ConAu 29, SmATA 2*
Cretcher, Mack 1868-1946 *OhA&B,
WhWNAA*
Cretin, Guillaume 1465?-1525? *CasWL,
DcEuL, OxFr, Pen Eur*
Cretin, Roger Auguste *REn*
Cretzianu, Alexandre 1895- *Au&Wr*
Cretzmeyer, F X, Jr. 1913- *ConAu 13R*
Creutz, Count Gustaf Filip 1731?-1785 *CasWL,
DcEuL, EvEuW, Pen Eur*
Creuz, Baron Friedrich Karl Kasimir Von
1724-1770 *BiD&SB, DcEuL*
Creuze, A F B *Alli*
Creuzer, Georg Friedrich 1771-1858 *DcEuL,
OxGer*
Crevecoeur, Hector St. John De 1735-1813 *Alli,
CyAL 1, Pen Am*
Crevecoeur, Jean Hector St. John De 1735-1813
AtlBL, DcAmA, OxEng, WebEAL*
Crevecoeur, Michel-Guillaume Jean De
1735-1813 *AmA, AmA&B, CasWL,
CnDAL, CyWA, DcLEnL, DcNAA,
EvLB, OxAm, REn, REnAL, WebEAL*
Crevecoeur, St. John De 1735-1813 *AmA,
DcNAA*
Crever, Anna Rozilla *AnMV 1926*
Crevier, J A *BbtC*
Crew, Benjamin J d1885 *Alli Sup*
Crew, Fleming H 1882- *AmA&B, JBA 1951,
OhA&B*
Crew, Francis Albert Eley 1888- *ConAu 17*
Crew, Helen Coale 1866-1941 *AmA&B, ChPo,
ChPo S1, JBA 1934, JBA 1951*
Crew, Sir Thomas *Alli*
Crew, Tom *ChPo S2*
Crewdson, Isaac *Alli*
Crewdson, Jane Fox 1808-1863 *Alli Sup, ChPo,
ChPo S1, PoCh*
Crewdson, Mrs. T D *ChPo S2*
Crewe, Lord *ChPo*
Crewe, Annabel *Alli Sup*
Crewe, Charles H *Alli*
Crewe, Edward *Alli Sup*
Crewe, Mrs. Henry *ChPo*

Crewe, Henry Robert *Alli Sup*
Crewe, Thomas *Alli*
Crewe, Sir Thomas *Alli*
Crews, Donald *IlBYP*
Crews, Frederick C 1933- *AmA&B,
ConAu 1R*
Crews, Harry 1935- *AuNews 1, ConAu 25,
ConLC 6, DrAF 1976*
Crews, Judson 1917- *ConAu 13R, ConP 1970,
ConP 1975, DrAP 1975, WrD 1976*
Crews, Stella Louise 1950- *BlkAW*
Crews, William J 1931- *ConAu 25*
Crewson, Evander A 1849- *OhA&B*
Creyghton, Robert *Alli*
Creyton, Paul 1827-1916 *AmA, DcEnL,
DcNAA*
Cribari, Joe 1920- *AmSCAP 66*
Cribb, William *Alli, BiDLA*
Cribbet, John E 1918- *ConAu 17R*
Crichlow, Ernest T 1914- *IlBYP, IlCB 1966*
Crichton, The Admirable 1560-1583 *DcEnL*
Crichton, Sir A M *Alli*
Crichton, A W *Alli Sup*
Crichton, Alexander *Alli*
Crichton, Andrew *Alli*
Crichton, Anne 1920- *Au&Wr*
Crichton, Antoinette K *Alli Sup*
Crichton, Eleanor Moyra *Au&Wr*
Crichton, Hugh *Alli Sup*
Crichton, Jack *MnBBF*
Crichton, James 1560-1583 *Alli*
Crichton, James 1560-1583? *BrAu, NewC,
OxEng*
Crichton, James Dunlop 1907- *ConAu 13R,
WrD 1976*
Crichton, John *DcNAA, OxCan*
Crichton, John 1916- *ConAu 17R*
Crichton, Kate *Alli Sup*
Crichton, Kyle Samuel 1896-1960 *AmA&B,
Au&Wr, REnAL, TwCA, TwCA Sup*
Crichton, Lucilla Mathew *Au&Wr*
Crichton, Michael 1942- *AmA&B, Au&Wr,
AuNews 2, ConAu 25, ConLC 2,
ConLC 6, ConNov 1976, SmATA 9,
WrD 1976*
Crichton, Robert 1925- *AuNews 1,
ConAu 17R, WrD 1976*
Crichton, Ruth M 1914- *Au&Wr*
Crichton, Steve *MnBBF*
Crichton, William John *Alli Sup*
Crichton-Browne, James 1840- *WhLA*
Crichton-Stuart, John Patrick *NewC*
Crick, Bernard 1929- *Au&Wr, ConAu 1R,
WrD 1976*
Crick, Donald Herbert 1916- *Au&Wr,
WrD 1976*
Crick, S *ChPo S2*
Crick, Vernon *MnBBF*
Cricket *WhWNAA*
Crickmaur, Helen *Alli Sup*
Crickmay, Herbert John *Alli Sup*
Crickmer, William Burton *Alli Sup*
Crider, Harvey M 1839-1903 *ChPo S1*
Cridge, Alfred *Alli Sup*
Cridge, Annie Denton *Alli Sup*
Crighton, James 1560-1585 *DcEuL*
Crighton, James D 1847- *ChPo*
Crighton, John Clark 1903- *ConAu 33,
WrD 1976*
Crighton, Robert *Alli*
Crile, George Washington 1864-1943 *DcNAA,
OhA&B, WhWNAA*
Crile, Grace McBride 1876-1948 *OhA&B*
Crillon, Louis DesBalbis DeBerton De 1541-1615
REn*
Crilly, Daniel 1857- *PoIre*
Crim, Keith R 1924- *ConAu 29*
Crim, Matt *BiDSA*
Crim, Mort 1935- *ConAu 41*
Crimmin, D M *Alli*
Crimmin, Daniel Michael *BiDLA*
Crimmins, James Custis 1935- *ConAu 5R*
Crimmins, John Daniel 1844-1917 *DcNAA*
Crimmins, Martin L *TexWr*
Crimsall, Richard *Alli*
Crine *Alli*
Cringle, Tom *Alli Sup*
Crinkle, Nym *Alli Sup, BiD&SB, DcNAA*

Crinkley, Richard Dillard 1940- *WrD 1976*
Crinkley, Richmond 1940- *ConAu 29*
Cripe, Helen 1932- *ConAu 61*
Crippen, T G *Alli Sup*
Crippen, William G 1820-1863 *Alli Sup,
OhA&B*
Cripps, Anthony 1913- *ConAu 13R*
Cripps, Arthur S *Chmbr 3*
Cripps, Arthur Shearly 1869-1952 *ChPo S1,
DcLEnL, WhLA*
Cripps, Charles Alfred 1852- *Alli Sup*
Cripps, Henry W *Alli*
Cripps, John Stafford 1912- *Au&Wr*
Cripps, Matthew Anthony Leonard 1913-
Au&Wr*
Cripps, Reginald *ChPo, ChPo S1*
Cripps, Wilfred Joseph 1841- *Alli Sup*
Cripps, William Harrison *Alli Sup*
Crips, Robert *PoIre*
Cririe, James *Alli, BiDLA*
Crisinel, Edmond Henri 1897-1948 *CasWL*
Crisler, Lois *WhPNW*
Crisman, E B *Alli Sup*
Crisolora, Manuele 1350?-1415 *CasWL*
Crisp, Anthony Thomas 1927- *WrD 1976*
Crisp, C G 1936- *ConAu 37*
Crisp, Edwards *Alli Sup*
Crisp, Frank *Au&Wr*
Crisp, Frank R 1915- *ConAu 9R*
Crisp, Frederick Arthur *Alli Sup*
Crisp, J *Alli*
Crisp, John *Alli, Alli Sup, BiDLA*
Crisp, John Anthony *Alli Sup*
Crisp, Julia M *TexWr*
Crisp, Norman James 1923- *Au&Wr*
Crisp, Richard *Alli Sup*
Crisp, Robert *ConAu 1R*
Crisp, S E 1906- *Au&Wr*
Crisp, Samuel *Alli*
Crisp, Stephen *Alli*
Crisp, Thomas *BbtC*
Crisp, Tobias 1600-1642 *Alli*
Crisp, Tony *WrD 1976*
Crisp, William Finch *Alli Sup*
Crispe, Samuel *Alli*
Crispe, Thomas *Alli*
Crispin, Saint d285? *NewC*
Crispin, Edmund 1921- *Au&Wr, EncM&D,
WorAu*
Crispin, Gilbert d1114? *Alli*
Crispin, John 1936- *ConAu 53*
Crispin, S J *ChPo*
Crispin, William Frost 1833-1916 *OhA&B*
Crispinian, Saint d285? *NewC*
Crispo, John 1933- *ConAu 37, WrD 1976*
Crispo, John H G *OxCan Sup*
Crispo Acosta, Osvaldo 1884- *DcSpL*
Criss, Allie Toland *ChPo*
Criss, Mildred 1890- *AuBYP, BkC 3,
CatA 1947*
Crissey, Elwell 1899- *ConAu 23*
Crissey, Forrest 1864-1943 *AmA&B, ChPo,
DcNAA*
Crist, Bainbridge 1883- *AmSCAP 66,
IndAu 1917*
Crist, Eda 1909- *AuBYP*
Crist, Judith 1922- *AmA&B, AuNews 1,
WrD 1976*
Cristall, Ann Batten *Alli, BiDLA*
Cristiani, Richard S *Alli Sup*
Cristofilo Sardanapalo *PueRA*
Cristol, Vivian *ConAu 17R*
Cristy, George W *BiDSA*
Cristy, R J *ConAu XR*
Criswell, Cloyd M 1908- *ConAu P-1*
Criswell, R W *Alli Sup*
Criswell, Robert *Alli Sup*
Criswell, W A 1909- *AmA&B, ConAu 17R*
Criswick, H C *Alli Sup*
Critchell-Bullock, J C *OxCan*
Critchett, Charles *Alli Sup*
Critchett, Richard Claude *Chmbr 3*
Critchfield, Howard J 1920- *ConAu 53*
Critchfield, Leander J *Alli Sup*
Critchfield, Richard 1931- *ConAu 41*
Critchley, Edmund M R 1931- *ConAu 21*
Critchley, R *ChPo S2*

Critchley, Thomas Alan 1919- *Au&Wr,
ConAu 29, WrD 1976*
Critchlow, Dorothy 1904- *Au&Wr*
Crites, Stephen D 1931- *ConAu 41*
Critias Of Athens d403BC *CasWL*
Critic *ConAu XR*
Criticus *ConAu XR*
Critobulus *CasWL*
Critobulus, Michael 1400?-1467? *Pen Cl*
Criton *OxFr*
Crittenden, Annie R *BlkAW*
Crittenden, Christopher 1902- *AmA&B*
Crittenden, John Jordan 1787-1863 *BiDSA*
Crittenden, S W *Alli*
Crittenden, Wilma Ethel *TexWr*
Crittenton, Charles Nelson 1833-1909 *DcNAA*
Crivelli, Carlo 1430?-1493? *AtlBL*
Crnjanski, Milos 1893- *CasWL, ConAu P-1,
EncWL Sup, ModSL 2, Pen Eur*
Croal, D *Alli Sup*
Croal, George *Alli Sup*
Croal, Thomas A *Alli Sup*
Croarkin, Walter Elias 1899- *ChPo S1*
Croasdaile, Edward *Alli Sup*
Croasdell, Anne *ChPo*
Crobaugh, Emma *AuNews 2*
Crocchiola, Francis Stanley 1908- *CatA 1952*
Croce *DcEuL*
Croce, Benedetto 1866-1952 *AtlBL, CasWL,
ClDMEuL, DcEuL, EncWL, EvEuW,
LongC, NewC, OxEng, Pen Eur, REn,
TwCA, TwCA Sup, TwCW, WhLA*
Croce, Giovanni *Alli*
Croche, Monsieur *OxFr*
Crock, Clement H 1890- *CatA 1947*
Crockatt, Gilbert *Alli*
Crocker, Abraham *Alli, BiDLA*
Crocker, Bosworth *AmA&B, DcNAA,
WhWNAA*
Crocker, Charles W 1797-1861 *Alli Sup, ChPo,
ChPo S1, ChPo S2*
Crocker, Francis Bacon 1861-1921 *DcNAA*
Crocker, George Glover 1843-1913 *DcAmA,
DcNAA*
Crocker, H Radcliffe *Alli Sup*
Crocker, Hannah Mather 1752-1829 *Alli,
DcNAA, OxAm*
Crocker, Hannah Mather 1765-1847 *DcAmA*
Crocker, Harriet Francene *ChPo S1*
Crocker, Henry *Alli Sup, ChPo, ChPo S1*
Crocker, Henry 1845-1929 *DcNAA,
WhWNAA*
Crocker, Henry Graham 1868-1930 *DcNAA*
Crocker, Isaac *Alli Sup*
Crocker, James *Alli Sup*
Crocker, John G *Alli Sup*
Crocker, L B, Mourse, H S And Brown, J G
Alli Sup
Crocker, Lawton Vincent 1890- *WhWNAA*
Crocker, Lester G 1912- *ConAu 5R,
WrD 1976*
Crocker, Lionel George 1897- *AmA&B,
ConAu 25, WrD 1976*
Crocker, Lucretia *Alli Sup*
Crocker, Maria Briscoe *AnMV 1926*
Crocker, Mary Arnold Bosworth d1946
AmA&B, WhWNAA
Crocker, S R *Alli Sup*
Crocker, Uriah 1796-1887 *DcNAA*
Crocker, Uriah Haskell 1832-1902 *DcNAA*
Crocker, Uriel 1796-1887 *Alli Sup, AmA&B*
Crocker, Uriel Haskellu 1832-1902 *Alli Sup,
DcAmA*
Crocker, Walter Russell 1902- *ConAu 17R,
WrD 1976*
Crocker, William 1876- *WhWNAA*
Crocker, Zebulon *Alli*
Crocket, David *Alli Sup*
Crocket, G F H *Alli*
Crocket, James 1878- *WhLA*
Crocket, William Shillinglaw 1866- *ChPo*
Crockett, Albert Stevens 1873- *AmA&B,
ChPo S2, WhWNAA*
Crockett, Charles Winthrop 1862-1936 *DcNAA*
Crockett, Davy 1786-1836 *Alli, AmA&B,
BiD&SB, BiDSA, CyWA, DcAmA,
DcNAA, OxAm, Pen Am, REn, REnAL*
Crockett, George Louis 1861- *TexWr*

Crockett, George Ronald 1906- *Au&Wr,
ConAu P-1*
Crockett, H C *Alli*
Crockett, Ingram 1856- *AmA&B, BiDSA,
ChPo, ChPo S1, ChPo S2, DcAmA,
DcNAA*
Crockett, James Underwood 1915- *ConAu 33*
Crockett, Lindsay *MnBBF*
Crockett, Lucy Herndon 1914- *IlCB 1945,
IlCB 1956*
Crockett, Samuel Rutherford 1860-1914 *BbD,
BiD&SB, BrAu 19, CarSB, CasWL,
ChPo, Chmbr 3, DcBiA, DcEnA Ap,
DcLEnL, EvLB, LongC, NewC, Pen Eng,
REn, TwCA, TwCA Sup, WhCL*
Crockett, Sarah Murdock 1849-1937
IndAu 1917
Crockett, Vere Benard 1915- *Au&Wr*
Crockett, Walter Hill 1870-1931 *DcNAA,
WhWNAA*
Crockett, William Day 1869-1930 *DcNAA,
WhWNAA*
Crockett, William Shillinglaw 1866- *ChPo S1,
ChPo S2, WhLA*
Crockford, Dick *Alli Sup*
Crockford, Gertrude *Alli Sup*
Crocombe, Ronald Gordon 1929- *ConAu 13R,
WrD 1976*
Crocus, Cornelius 1500?-1558? *CasWL,
DcEuL*
Croesus 575?BC- *NewC, REn*
Croff, G B *Alli Sup*
Crofford, Lena H 1908- *ConAu P-1*
Croffut, William Augustus 1835-1915 *Alli Sup,
AmA&B, BiD&SB, ChPo, ChPo S1,
DcAmA, DcNAA*
Croft, Mrs. *Alli, BiDLA*
Croft, Aloysius 1906- *BkC 1*
Croft, Andrew 1906- *WrD 1976*
Croft, Cyrus W *Alli Sup*
Croft, G *Alli*
Croft, George 1747-1809 *Alli*
Croft, H Herbert S *Alli Sup*
Croft, H J *Alli Sup*
Croft, Henry *BbtC*
Croft, Herbert 1603-1691 *Alli, DcEnL*
Croft, Sir Herbert d1622 *Alli*
Croft, Sir Herbert 1751-1816 *Alli, BiDLA,
BiDLA Sup, DcEnL, NewC*
Croft, John *Alli, BiDLA*
Croft, John MacGrigor *Alli Sup*
Croft, John Michael 1922- *Au&Wr*
Croft, Noel Andrew Cotton 1906- *Au&Wr*
Croft, Robert *Alli*
Croft, Robert Charles *Alli Sup*
Croft, Roy *MnBBF*
Croft, Mrs. S *Alli Sup*
Croft, Thomas *Alli*
Croft, William 1677-1727 *Alli*
Croft-Cooke, Rupert 1903?- *Au&Wr,
CatA 1952, ChPo, ChPo S1, ConAu 9R,
LongC, NewC, TwCA, TwCA Sup,
WrD 1976*
Crofton, Dennis *Alli*
Crofton, Francis Blake 1841?-1912? *Alli Sup,
DcNAA, PoIre*
Crofton, Henry Thomas 1848- *Alli Sup*
Crofton, James *Alli Sup*
Crofton, M *Alli Sup*
Crofton, Morgan W *Alli Sup*
Crofton, Walter Cavendish 1806?-1870 *BbtC,
DcNAA*
Crofton, Sir Walter Frederick 1815- *Alli Sup*
Crofton, Zachary d1672? *Alli*
Crofts, Arthur H *ChPo S1*
Crofts, Ellen *Alli Sup*
Crofts, Frederick Sharer 1883-1951 *AmA&B*
Crofts, Freeman Wills 1879-1957 *DcLEnL,
EncM&D, EvLB, LongC, NewC,
Pen Eng, REn, TwCA, TwCA Sup,
TwCW*
Crofts, George Wallen 1842-1909 *ChPo,
ChPo S1*
Crofts, H *Alli Sup*
Crofts, Henry Olney *Alli Sup*
Crofts, James *Alli Sup*
Crofts, James Henry *Alli Sup*
Crofts, John *Alli, Alli Sup, BiDLA*

Crofts, John E V 1887- *ConAu 25*
Crofts, Robert *Alli*
Crofut, Marguerite *ChPo*
Crofut, William E, III 1934- *ConAu 25*
Crofutt, George A *Alli Sup*
Croger, F Julian *Alli Sup, ChPo*
Crogman, William Henry 1841-1931 *DcNAA*
Croil, James 1821-1916 *BbtC, DcNAA*
Croise, Jacques *ConAu XR*
Croiset, Marie-Joseph-Alfred 1845-1923 *OxFr*
Croisset, Francis De 1877-1937 *ClDMEuL,
EvEuW, McGWD, OxFr*
Croizier, Ralph 1935- *ConAu 61*
Croke, Alexander *Alli, BiDLA*
Croke, Sir Alexander *Alli*
Croke, Sir George 1559-1641 *Alli*
Croke, J Greenbag 1840- *Alli Sup, ChPo S2,
DcNAA*
Croke, J O'Byrne *PoIre*
Croke, John *Alli*
Croke, Richard d1558 *Alli*
Croker, Mrs. B M *Alli Sup, BbD*
Croker, Bertha M *BiD&SB*
Croker, Henry Temple *Alli*
Croker, John Wilson 1780-1857 *Alli, BiD&SB,
BiDLA, BrAu 19, CasWL, Chmbr 3,
DcEnA, DcEnL, DcEuL, DcLEnL, EvLB,
NewC, OxEng, Pen Eng, PoIre,
WebEAL*
Croker, Margaret Sarah *PoIre*
Croker, Richard *Alli, BiDLA*
Croker, Temple Henry 1729-1790? *PoIre*
Croker, Thomas *Alli*
Croker, Thomas Crofton 1798-1854 *Alli, BbD,
BiD&SB, BrAu 19, CasWL, ChPo,
ChPo S1, Chmbr 3, DcEnL, DcLEnL,
EvLB, NewC, OxEng, PoIre*
Croker, Thomas Francis Dillon 1831-1912
ChPo S1, PoIre
Croker, Walter *Alli*
Crole, Charles Stewart *Alli Sup*
Crole, Robert *Alli, Chmbr 1, NewC*
Croleus, Robert *Alli, NewC*
Croll, Alexander Angus *Alli Sup*
Croll, Edward Everett 1881- *WhWNAA*
Croll, J O'Byrne *Alli Sup*
Croll, James *Alli Sup*
Croll, James 1821-1890 *Alli Sup*
Croll, Morris William 1872- *WhWNAA*
Croll, Philip Columbus 1852-1949 *Alli Sup,
DcNAA, WhWNAA*
Croll, Robert Henderson 1869- *ChPo*
Croly, Miss *Alli Sup*
Croly, David Goodman 1829-1889 *Alli Sup,
AmA, AmA&B, BiD&SB, DcAmA,
DcNAA*
Croly, Elizabeth *ChPo*
Croly, George 1780-1860 *Alli, BbD, BiD&SB,
BrAu 19, ChPo, ChPo S1, Chmbr 3,
DcBiA, DcEnL, DcLEnL, EvLB, NewC,
OxEng, PoIre*
Croly, Herbert David 1869-1930 *AmA&B,
DcNAA, OxAm, TwCA, TwCA Sup*
Croly, J W *Alli Sup*
Croly, Jane Cunningham 1829?-1901 *Alli Sup,
AmA, AmA&B, BbD, BiD&SB, DcAmA,
DcNAA, OxAm*
Croly, Julian W *PoIre*
Croly, Richard *Alli Sup*
Croman, Dorothy Young *ConAu XR*
Cromar, Alexander *Alli Sup*
Cromar, James *ChPo S1*
Cromarhe, Hew *AmLY XR*
Cromartie, George, Earl Of *Alli*
Cromb, James *Alli Sup*
Crombie, Alexander 1760-1842 *Alli, BiDLA*
Crombie, Alistair Cameron 1915- *Au&Wr,
WrD 1976*
Crombie, Bunty *ChPo S1*
Crombie, Charles Mann *Alli Sup*
Crombie, Frances And Cusin, M D *Alli Sup*
Crombie, Frederick *Alli Sup*
Crombie, Helen *ChPo S1*
Crombie, J W *ChPo S2*
Crombie, James M *Alli Sup*
Crombie, John *Alli*
Crombie, John Mann *Alli Sup*
Crombie, William *Alli, DcEnL*

Crome, John 1768-1821 *Alli, AtlBL, NewC*
Cromek, Robert Hartley 1770-1812 *Alli, BrAu 19, ChPo*
Cromek, Thomas H *Alli Sup*
Cromer, Evelyn Baring, Earl 1841-1917 *ChPo, ChPo S2*
Cromerty *Alli*
Cromerty, Earl Of *Alli*
Cromie, Alice Hamilton 1914- *ConAu 9R*
Cromie, Robert 1909- *AmA&B, ConAu 1R*
Cromie, W James 1876- *WhWNAA*
Cromie, William J 1930- *ConAu 13R, SmATA 4*
Cromleich *PoIre*
Crommelin, L *Alli*
Crommelin, May DeLaCherois *BbD*
Crommelin, May DeLaChervis- *Alli Sup*
Crommelynck, Fernand 1885?-1970? *CasWL, ClDMEuL, CnMD, EncWL, EvEuW, McGWD, ModWD, Pen Eur, REn, REnWD, WorAu*
Crommelynck, Landa *IlBYP*
Crompe, John *Alli*
Cromptom, Margaret 1901- *ConAu P-1*
Crompton, Anne Eliot 1930- *ConAu 33*
Crompton, C *Alli*
Crompton, George *Alli*
Crompton, Henry 1836-1904 *Alli Sup, BrAu 19*
Crompton, Hugh *Alli*
Crompton, J *Alli, Alli Sup*
Crompton, James *Alli Sup*
Crompton, John *ConAu XR*
Crompton, Joshua *Alli*
Crompton, Louis 1925- *ConAu 33, WrD 1976*
Crompton, M W *Alli Sup*
Crompton, Margaret Norah 1901- *Au&Wr, WrD 1976*
Crompton, R S B *Alli Sup*
Crompton, Richard *Alli*
Crompton, Richmal 1890-1969 *ConAu XR, LongC, MnBBF, NewC, SmATA 5, WhCL*
Crompton, Robert *Alli Sup*
Crompton, Samuel *Alli Sup*
Crompton, Sarah *Alli Sup*
Crompton, Susan F *Alli*
Crompton, T *Alli Sup*
Crompton, William *Alli, ChPo, MnBBF*
Cromwell, Arthur Dayton 1869- *WhWNAA*
Cromwell, Emma Guy *WhWNAA*
Cromwell, Frederick 1899- *ArizL*
Cromwell, Gladys Louise Husted 1885-1919 *AmA&B, DcNAA, OxAm*
Cromwell, Harvey 1907- *ConAu 17R*
Cromwell, J Howard *Alli Sup*
Cromwell, John Gabriel *Alli Sup*
Cromwell, John Howard 1857-1937 *DcNAA*
Cromwell, Oliver 1599-1658 *Alli, NewC, REn*
Cromwell, Otelia *LivBA*
Cromwell, Richard Sidney 1925- *ConAu 53*
Cromwell, Samuel *Alli*
Cromwell, Sidney *Alli Sup*
Cromwell, Thomas *Alli*
Cromwell, Thomas, Earl Of Essex 1485?-1540 *DcEnL, NewC, REn*
Cromwell, Thomas Kitson 1792-1870 *ChPo*
Cromwell, Victor *MnBBF*
Cron, George *Alli Sup*
Cronau, Rudolf 1855-1939 *AmA&B, AmLY, DcNAA, WhWNAA*
Cronbach, Abraham 1882-1965 *ConAu 1R, IndAu 1917, OhA&B*
Crone, Anne 1915- *Au&Wr*
Crone, Kennedy 1883- *WhWNAA*
Crone, Rainer 1942- *ConAu 33*
Crone, Ruth 1919- *AuBYP, ConAu 9R, SmATA 4*
Cronegk, Johann Friedrich Von 1731-1758 *BiD&SB, CasWL, DcEuL, OxGer, Pen Eur*
Cronhelm, F W *Alli*
Cronhelm, Frederick William *Alli Sup*
Cronholm, Neander Nicholas 1843-1922 *DcNAA*
Cronin, A J 1896- *Au&Wr, CasWL, CatA 1947, Chmbr 3, ConAu 1R, ConNov 1976, DcLEnL, EncWL, EvLB,*

LongC, ModBL, NewC, Pen Eng, RAdv 1, REn, TwCA, TwCA Sup, TwCW, WhWNAA, WrD 1976
Cronin, Anthony 1926- *ConP 1970*
Cronin, Bernard *MnBBF*
Cronin, Bernard Charles 1884- *DcLEnL*
Cronin, Daniel *PoIre*
Cronin, David E *Alli Sup*
Cronin, Denis *Alli Sup*
Cronin, Edward 1840-1908 *PoIre*
Cronin, James E 1908- *ConAu 45*
Cronin, John F 1908- *CatA 1947, ConAu 37*
Cronin, Joseph M 1935- *ConAu 49*
Cronin, Michael *Au&Wr*
Cronin, Patrick 1835-1905 *PoIre*
Cronin, Vincent Archibald Patrick 1924- *Au&Wr, ConAu 9R, LongC*
Cronise, Titus Fay *Alli Sup*
Cronkite, Walter 1916- *AuNews 1, AuNews 2, ChPo S1, WrD 1976*
Cronne, Henry Alfred 1904- *Au&Wr*
Cronnelly, Richard Francis *Alli Sup*
Cronon, E David 1924- *ConAu 1R*
Cronus, Diodorus *ConAu XR*
Cronwright, Samuel Cron 1863- *WhLA*
Cronwright-Schreiner, S C *WhLA*
Cronyn, George William 1888- *AmA&B, IndAu 1917*
Cronyn, Mrs. Z R *ChPo*
Crook, Alja Robinson 1864-1930 *OhA&B*
Crook, Arthur Charles William 1912- *Au&Wr*
Crook, Fred *ChPo*
Crook, Sir George *Alli*
Crook, George 1829-1890 *OhA&B*
Crook, Henry T *Alli Sup*
Crook, Herbert Clifford 1882- *Au&Wr*
Crook, Isaac 1833-1916 *DcNAA, OhA&B*
Crook, J A 1921- *ConAu 23*
Crook, J Mordaunt 1937- *ConAu 41*
Crook, James Walter 1858-1933 *DcNAA, WhWNAA*
Crook, John *Alli*
Crook, John 1768- *BiDLA*
Crook, Margaret Brackenbury 1886- *ConAu P-1*
Crook, Mary B *Alli Sup*
Crook, Roger H 1921- *ConAu 1R*
Crook, W *Alli*
Crook, Welton Joseph 1886- *WhWNAA*
Crook, William *Alli Sup*
Crookall, Robert 1890- *ConAu 33*
Crooke, B *Alli*
Crooke, Charles Walter 1863- *IndAu 1816*
Crooke, Edmund Samuel *Alli Sup*
Crooke, George Alexander *Alli Sup*
Crooke, Helkiah *Alli*
Crooke, Henry *Alli*
Crooke, Samuel 1574-1649 *Alli*
Crooke, Unton *Alli*
Crooke, William *Alli*
Crooker, Earle T 1899- *AmSCAP 66*
Crooker, Joseph Henry 1850-1931 *Alli Sup, DcAmA, DcNAA*
Crookes, Sir William 1832-1919 *Alli Sup, BiDPar*
Crookham, Arthur L 1889- *WhWNAA*
Crooks, Florence Bingham 1875- *IndAu 1917*
Crooks, George Richard 1822-1897 *Alli, Alli Sup, DcAmA, DcNAA*
Crooks, James 1825-1908 *IndAu 1816, OhA&B*
Crooks, James B 1933- *ConAu 25*
Crookshank, Charles H *Alli Sup*
Crookshank, Edgar March *Alli Sup*
Crookshank, Harry *Alli Sup*
Crookshank, William d1769 *Alli*
Crookshanks *Alli*
Crookshanks, John *Alli*
Croom, David B *Alli Sup*
Croom, Joe N 1896- *WhWNAA*
Croom, John Halliday *Alli Sup*
Croome, William 1790-1860 *ChPo S1, EarAB, EarAB Sup*
Croon, William d1684 *Alli*
Cropley, Sir John *Alli*
Cropp, Ben 1936- *ConAu 33, WrD 1976*
Cropp, John *Alli Sup*
Cropper, Mrs. *Alli Sup*

Cropper, James *Alli Sup*
Cropper, Margaret *ChPo, ChPo S1, ChPo S2*
Cropper, Margaret Beatrice 1886- *Au&Wr*
Cropsey, Jasper F 1823-1900 *EarAB*
Crory, William Glenny *Alli Sup*
Cros, Charles 1842-1888 *CasWL, EvEuW, OxFr, Pen Eur*
Cros, Emile-Hortensius-Charles 1842-1888 *EuA*
Crosbie, Bartholomew F *Alli Sup*
Crosbie, Bligh Talbot *PoIre*
Crosbie, Hugh Provan 1912- *Au&Wr*
Crosbie, Marjorie *ChPo S2*
Crosbie, Provan 1912- *ConAu 9R*
Crosbie, Richard *Alli Sup*
Crosbie, W J *MnBBF*
Crosbie, William *Alli Sup*
Crosby, Alexander L 1906- *AuBYP, ConAu 29, MorBMP, SmATA 2*
Crosby, Alfred W, Jr. 1931- *ConAu 17R, WrD 1976*
Crosby, Allan James 1835-1881 *Alli Sup*
Crosby, Allen *Alli*
Crosby, Alpheus 1810-1874 *Alli, DcAmA, DcNAA*
Crosby, Bing 1904- *AmSCAP 66*
Crosby, Bob 1913- *AmSCAP 66*
Crosby, Caresse 1892-1970 *ConAu 25*
Crosby, Donald A 1932- *ConAu 53*
Crosby, Edward N *Alli*
Crosby, Ernest Howard 1856-1907 *AmA&B, ChPo S2, DcAmA, DcNAA*
Crosby, Everett Uberto 1871-1960 *AmA&B*
Crosby, Frances Jane VanAlstyne 1820-1915 *AmA&B, ChPo, ChPo S1, ChPo S2, DcAmA, DcNAA, REnAL, WebEAL*
Crosby, Franklin 1829-1898 *Alli Sup, DcNAA*
Crosby, G *ChPo*
Crosby, George S *Alli Sup*
Crosby, Harry 1897?-1929 *AmA&B, DcNAA, WhWNAA*
Crosby, Harry H 1919- *ConAu 13R*
Crosby, Henry Grew 1898-1929 *DcNAA*
Crosby, Howard 1826-1891 *Alli, Alli Sup, BbD, BiD&SB, CyAL 2, DcAmA, DcNAA*
Crosby, John Campbell 1912- *AmA&B, ConAu 1R, IlBYP, REnAL, WrD 1976*
Crosby, John F 1931- *ConAu 17R*
Crosby, Michael 1940- *ConAu 17R*
Crosby, Muriel 1908- *ConAu 17R*
Crosby, Nathan 1798-1885 *Alli Sup, DcAmA, DcNAA*
Crosby, Nicholas E *ChPo*
Crosby, Nora E *ChPo*
Crosby, Oscar Terry 1861- *WhWNAA*
Crosby, Percy Leo 1891- *AmA&B*
Crosby, Phoebe *AuBYP*
Crosby, Ruth 1897- *ConAu 49*
Crosby, Sumner McK 1909- *ConAu 13R*
Crosby, Sylvester Sage d1914 *Alli Sup, DcNAA*
Crosby, Thomas 1840-1914 *Alli, DcNAA*
Crosby, Thomas Boor *Alli Sup*
Crosby, Timothy *Alli Sup*
Crosby, Walter Wilson 1872- *WhWNAA*
Crosby, William Otis 1850-1925 *Alli Sup, DcAmA, DcNAA*
Crosdaile, H E *Alli Sup*
Crosfeild, Robert *Alli*
Crosfield, Miss A *Alli*
Crosfield, George *Alli, BiDLA*
Crosfield, H C *MnBBF*
Crosfield, R J *Alli, BiDLA*
Crosier, Alfred D *Alli Sup*
Croskery, Hugh *Alli Sup*
Croskery, Thomas 1830-1886 *Alli Sup*
Croskey, John Welsh 1858- *WhWNAA*
Croskill, John H 1810-1855 *BbtC, DcNAA*
Crosland, Andrew T 1944- *ConAu 53*
Crosland, Anthony Raven 1918- *Au&Wr*
Crosland, Camilla 1812-1895 *Alli Sup, ChPo*
Crosland, Margaret 1920- *Au&Wr, ChPo, ConAu 49, WrD 1976*
Crosland, Newton *Alli Sup*
Crosland, Mrs. Newton 1812-1895 *Alli, ChPo S1, DcEnL*
Crosland, Thomas William Hodgson 1863-1924 *ChPo, ChPo S1, ChPo S2*

Croslegh, Charles *Alli Sup*
Crosley, David *Alli*
Crosley, H *Alli*
Crosno, Manuela *ChPo*
Cross, A E *Alli Sup*
Cross, Albert Francis *Alli Sup*
Cross, Aleene Ann 1922- *ConAu 29*
Cross, Alexander Galbraith 1908- *Au&Wr*
Cross, Alfred Rupert Neale 1912- *Au&Wr*
Cross, Allen Eastman 1864- *ChPo, ChPo S1, ChPo S2*
Cross, Amanda *ConAu XR*
Cross, Andrew Jay 1855-1925 *DcNAA*
Cross, Anson Kent 1862- *WhWNAA*
Cross, Anthony Glenn 1936- *ConAu 37, MnBBF, WrD 1976*
Cross, Arthur Lyon 1873-1940 *AmA&B, DcNAA, WhWNAA*
Cross, Beverley 1931- *Au&Wr, ConDr, WrD 1976*
Cross, Brenda *WrD 1976*
Cross, C F And Bevan, E J *Alli Sup*
Cross, Charles Robert 1848-1921 *Alli Sup, DcAmA, DcNAA*
Cross, Charles Whitman 1854-1949 *DcNAA*
Cross, Claire 1932- *ConAu 23, WrD 1976*
Cross, Colin John 1928- *Au&Wr, ConAu 9R, WrD 1976*
Cross, Constance *Alli Sup, ChPo, ChPo S1*
Cross, Cora Melton *TexWr*
Cross, David Wallace 1814-1891 *Alli Sup, DcAmA, DcNAA, OhA&B*
Cross, Dennis *MnBBF*
Cross, Douglass 1920- *AmSCAP 66*
Cross, E A 1875- *WhWNAA*
Cross, Mrs. E J *Alli Sup*
Cross, Earle Bennett 1883-1946 *DcNAA*
Cross, Elizabeth D *Alli Sup, ChPo, ChPo S1*
Cross, Ella *Alli Sup*
Cross, Francis *Alli, Alli Sup*
Cross, Francis W And Hall, John R *Alli Sup*
Cross, Frank Clay 1893- *WhWNAA*
Cross, Frank Moore, Jr. 1921- *AmA&B*
Cross, George 1862-1929 *DcNAA, WhWNAA*
Cross, George N *Alli Sup*
Cross, Miss H *Alli Sup*
Cross, Henry *Alli Sup*
Cross, Herbert James 1934- *ConAu 45*
Cross, Ian 1925- *Au&Wr, ConNov 1972, ConNov 1976, Pen Eng, TwCW, WrD 1976*
Cross, Ira Brown 1880- *WhWNAA*
Cross, Mrs. J Taylor *ChPo, ChPo S1*
Cross, James *Alli Sup, AmA&B, ConAu XR, WrD 1976*
Cross, James C *Alli*
Cross, Jane Tandy 1817-1870 *BiDSA, DcAmA, DcNAA*
Cross, Jennifer 1932- *ConAu 29*
Cross, Jesse George 1835-1914 *DcNAA*
Cross, Jimmie *AmSCAP 66*
Cross, John *Alli, Alli Sup, MnBBF*
Cross, John Adam *Alli Sup*
Cross, John Edward *Alli Sup*
Cross, John Keir 1914-1967 *AuBYP, WhCL*
Cross, John Walter *Alli Sup*
Cross, Jonathan *Alli Sup*
Cross, Joseph 1813-1893 *Alli, Alli Sup, DcAmA, DcNAA*
Cross, K A *Alli Sup*
Cross, K G W 1927-1967 *ConAu P-1*
Cross, K Patricia 1926- *ConAu 33, WrD 1976*
Cross, Launcelot *Alli Sup*
Cross, Lucy Rogers 1834- *DcNAA*
Cross, M Claire *ConAu XR*
Cross, Marian *DcEnA*
Cross, Mary And Davidson, Anne J *Alli Sup*
Cross, Mary Ann 1819-1880 *Alli Sup, BrAu 19, EvLB, Pen Eng*
Cross, May *MnBBF*
Cross, Milton 1897-1975 *AmA&B, ConAu 53*
Cross, Nelson 1820-1897 *Alli Sup, OhA&B*
Cross, Nicholas *Alli*
Cross, Norman d1937 *ChPo S1*
Cross, Pennington *MnBBF*
Cross, Peter Brady *Alli, BiDLA*
Cross, R T *Alli Sup*
Cross, Richard *Alli Sup*

Cross, Sir Richard Assheton 1823- *Alli Sup*
Cross, Richard K 1940- *ConAu 33, WrD 1976*
Cross, Robert *Alli Sup*
Cross, Robert Brandt 1914- *ConAu 37*
Cross, Robert Dougherty 1924- *ConAu 1R*
Cross, Robert Singlehurst 1925- *Au&Wr, ConAu 5R, WrD 1976*
Cross, Roselle Theodore 1844-1924 *DcAmA, DcNAA, OhA&B*
Cross, Rupert 1912- *WrD 1976*
Cross, Ruth *TexWr, WhWNAA*
Cross, S T *Alli Sup*
Cross, Samuel Hazzard 1891-1946 *DcNAA*
Cross, Samuel S 1919- *ConAu 45*
Cross, Stewart *OhA&B*
Cross, Theodore L 1924- *ConAu 45*
Cross, Thomas *Alli Sup*
Cross, Thomas H *Alli Sup*
Cross, Thomas Uttermare *Alli Sup*
Cross, Thomson *MnBBF*
Cross, Tom Peete 1879- *AmA&B*
Cross, Trueman d1846 *BiDSA, DcNAA*
Cross, Victor *ConAu 49*
Cross, W *Alli Sup*
Cross, Walter d1701? *Alli*
Cross, Wilbur Lucius 1862-1948 *AmA&B, DcAmA, DcLEnL, DcNAA, OxAm, REnAL, TwCA, TwCA Sup*
Cross, Wilbur Lucius, III 1918- *Au&Wr, ConAu 1R, SmATA 2, WrD 1976*
Cross, William 1804-1886? *Alli, Alli Sup, ChPo, ChPo S1, ChPo S2*
Cross, Zora 1890- *ChPo, ChPo S1, ChPo S2, DcLEnL, WhLA*
Crosscountry *ConAu XR*
Crosse, Andrew F *Alli Sup*
Crosse, Charles Henry *Alli Sup*
Crosse, Cornelia A H 1784-1855 *Alli Sup*
Crosse, Gordon 1874- *ChPo S2*
Crosse, Henry *Alli*
Crosse, J H *Alli Sup*
Crosse, John *Alli, BiDLA*
Crosse, Peter *Alli*
Crosse, R S *Alli*
Crosse, Thomas Francis 1820-1888 *Alli Sup, BiDLA*
Crosse, William *Alli*
Crossen, Harry Sturgeon 1869- *WhWNAA*
Crossen, Kendell 1910- *ConAu 1R*
Crosser, Paul K 1902- *ConAu 1R*
Crossfield, R H 1868- *WhWNAA*
Crossing, William 1847-1928 *Alli Sup, ChPo S1*
Crossinge, Richard *Alli*
Crosskey, D *Alli Sup*
Crosskey, Henry William *Alli Sup*
Crossland, John Redgwick 1892- *ChPo, ChPo S1*
Crossley, Aaron *Alli*
Crossley, E, Gledhill, J And Nilson, J *Alli Sup*
Crossley, Hastings *Alli Sup*
Crossley, J T *Alli*
Crossley, James 1800-1883 *Alli Sup*
Crossley, M Louise *LivFWS*
Crossley, Thomas Hastings Henry 1846- *ChPo S2, PoIre*
Crossley-Holland, Kevin John William 1941- *ChPo S1, ConAu 41, ConP 1970, ConP 1975, SmATA 5, WrD 1976*
Crossman, Francis Geach 1788- *Alli, Alli Sup*
Crossman, Henry *Alli*
Crossman, Richard 1907-1974 *Au&Wr, ConAu 49, ConAu 61, REn, WorAu*
Crossman, Samuel *Alli*
Crosswell, Andrew *DcNAA*
Crosswell, Anne Pearson *AmSCAP 66*
Crosswell, Simon G *Alli Sup*
Crosswell, William 1804-1851 *Alli, BiD&SB, ChPo*
Crosswhite, E B 1897- *WhWNAA*
Crosthwaite, Charles *Alli, Alli Sup*
Crosthwaite, Charles Haukes Todd *Alli Sup*
Crosthwaite, J C *Alli*
Crosthwaite, J Fisher *Alli Sup*
Crosthwaite, John *Alli*
Crosthwaite, John Clarke *Alli Sup*
Croston, James 1830- *Alli Sup*
Croswell, Andrew 1709-1785 *Alli, DcAmA,*

DcNAA
Croswell, Edwin *Alli*
Croswell, Harry 1778-1858 *Alli, Alli Sup, CyAL 2, DcAmA, DcNAA*
Croswell, Sherman *Alli Sup*
Croswell, William d1834 *DcNAA*
Croswell, William 1804-1851 *Alli, AmA&B, ChPo S2, CyAL 2, DcAmA, DcNAA, PoCh*
Crotch, George Robert *Alli Sup*
Crotch, W Duppa *Alli Sup*
Crotch, William *Alli, BiDLA*
Croteau, John T 1910- *ConAu 9R, OxCan*
Crothers, Elizabeth 1882-1920 *DcNAA*
Crothers, George D 1909- *ConAu P-1*
Crothers, J Frances 1913- *ConAu 33, WrD 1976*
Crothers, Jessie F *ConAu XR*
Crothers, Rachel 1878-1958 *AmA&B, CnDAL, CnMD, CnThe, ConAmA, ConAmL, DcLEnL, EncWL Sup, LongC, McGWD, ModWD, OxAm, REn, REnAL, REnWD, TwCA, TwCA Sup, WhWNAA*
Crothers, Samuel 1783-1856 *OhA&B*
Crothers, Samuel Dickey 1883-1916 *OhA&B*
Crothers, Samuel McChord 1857-1927 *AmA&B, CarSB, ChPo S2, ConAmL, DcAmA, DcNAA, OxAm, REnAL, TwCA, TwCA Sup, WhWNAA*
Crothers, Sherman 1910- *AmSCAP 66*
Crothers, Thomas Davison 1842-1918 *DcAmA, DcNAA*
Crotty, William J 1936- *ConAu 21*
Crotus Rubeanus 1480-1539? *CasWL, OxGer*
Crotus Rubianus 1480-1539? *OxGer*
Crouch, Archer Philip *Alli Sup*
Crouch, Carrie J *TexWr*
Crouch, D *MnBBF*
Crouch, Edwin A *Alli*
Crouch, Frederick William Nicholls 1808-1896 *DcNAA*
Crouch, Gladys Sidney *ChPo S2*
Crouch, Henry *Alli*
Crouch, Humphrey *Alli*
Crouch, John *Alli*
Crouch, Julia *Alli Sup*
Crouch, Louisa J *Alli Sup*
Crouch, Marcus 1913- *Au&Wr, ChPo, ChPo S2, ConAu 9R, SmATA 4, WhCL, WrD 1976*
Crouch, Nathaniel *Alli*
Crouch, Pearl Riggs *ChPo*
Crouch, Richard Armstrong 1868- *WhLA*
Crouch, Stanley 1945- *BlkAW, DrAP 1975, LivBAA*
Crouch, Steve 1915- *ConAu 53*
Crouch, W George 1903- *ConAu 5R*
Crouch, Warwick Wyatt And Archer Philip *Alli Sup*
Crouch, William *Alli, Alli Sup*
Crouchback *NewC*
Croudace, Glynn 1917- *Au&Wr, ConAu 29*
Croudace, W C *Alli Sup*
Croughton, Thomas Hanmer *Alli Sup*
Crouleus, Robert *Alli*
Croune, William *Alli*
Crouse, Anna *AuBYP*
Crouse, David Eldridge 1882- *OhA&B*
Crouse, Nellis M *OxCan*
Crouse, Russel 1893-1966 *AmA&B, AuBYP, CnDAL, CnThe, ConAu 25, McGWD, ModWD, OhA&B, OxAm, REn, REnAL, TwCA Sup*
Crouse, William Harry 1907- *AuBYP, ConAu 5R, IndAu 1917, WrD 1976*
Crout, George C 1917- *ConAu 29*
Crouwel, Wim Hendrik 1928- *WhGrA*
Crouzet, Francois Marie-Joseph 1922- *ConAu 9R*
Croves, Hal *ConAu XR*
Crovitz, Herbert F 1932- *ConAu 29*
Crow, Mrs. d1895 *HsB&A*
Crow, Alice 1894-1966 *ConAu P-1*
Crow, Arthur H *Alli Sup*
Crow, Carl 1883-1945 *AmA&B, DcNAA, TwCA, TwCA Sup, WhWNAA*
Crow, Duncan 1920- *Au&Wr, WrD 1976*
Crow, Francis d1692 *Alli*

Crow, G *Alli Sup*
Crow, John Armstrong 1906- *AmA&B, ConAu 13R, DcSpL*
Crow, Leonard Roy 1893- *IndAu 1917*
Crow, Lester Donald 1897- *AmA&B, ConAu P-1*
Crow, Louisa A *Alli Sup*
Crow, Mark 1948- *ConAu 57*
Crow, Martha 1854-1924 *DcNAA*
Crow, Martin M 1901- *ConAu 19*
Crow, Sir Sackville *Alli*
Crow, Thomas *Alli Sup*
Crow, William Bernard 1895- *Au&Wr, ConAu P-1*
Crow, William H 1878- *WhWNAA*
Crowbate, Ophelia Mae *ConAu XR*
Crowberry, Daniel *Alli Sup*
Crowcroft, Andrew 1923- *ConAu 23*
Crowden, Charles *Alli Sup*
Crowder, John Hutton *Alli Sup*
Crowder, Michael 1934- *Au&Wr, ConAu 1R, WrD 1976*
Crowder, Richard Henry 1909- *ConAu P-1, IndAu 1917, WrD 1976*
Crowder, William 1882- *AmA&B*
Crowdy, E Percy 1850-1912 *Br&AmS*
Crowdy, John *Alli Sup*
Crowdy, W L *Alli Sup*
Crowe, Anna Mary *Alli*
Crowe, Anne Mary *BiDLA*
Crowe, Bettina Lum 1911- *AuBYP, Au&Wr, ConAu 9R, SmATA 6, WrD 1976*
Crowe, Catherine 1800-1876 *Alli, Alli Sup, BiD&SB, BrAu 19, CasWL, Chmbr 3, DcEnL, EvLB, NewC*
Crowe, Charles 1928- *ConAu 17R*
Crowe, Charles Monroe 1902- *ConAu 1R*
Crowe, Eyre Evans 1799-1868 *Alli, Alli Sup, BiD&SB, ChPo, EvLB, NewC, PoIre*
Crowe, F J 1929- *ConAu XR*
Crowe, Frederick *Alli Sup*
Crowe, Frederick Joseph William 1864- *WhLA*
Crowe, Henry *Alli*
Crowe, Jocelyn 1906- *IlCB 1945*
Crowe, John 1906- *ConAu P-1*
Crowe, John O'Beirne 1825?-1878? *Alli Sup, PoIre*
Crowe, John William *Alli Sup*
Crowe, Sir Joseph Archer 1825-1896 *Alli Sup, BiD&SB, EvLB*
Crowe, Martha Foote 1854-1924 *ChPo*
Crowe, Marygold Cecelia *ChPo*
Crowe, Nelson Kendall 1830- *IndAu 1816*
Crowe, Philip Kingsland 1908- *AmA&B, WrD 1976*
Crowe, Sir Sackville *Alli*
Crowe, Sylvia 1901- *Au&Wr, ConAu P-1*
Crowe, Thomas d1862 *Alli Sup*
Crowe, William 1745-1829 *Alli, BiD&SB, BiDLA, BrAu 19, Chmbr 2, EvLB, NewC, OxEng*
Crowe, Winfield Scott 1850- *DcAmA*
Crowell, Benedict 1869-1952 *OhA&B*
Crowell, Chester Theodore 1888-1941 *DcNAA, OhA&B, TexWr*
Crowell, Edward Payson 1830-1911 *Alli Sup, DcNAA*
Crowell, Edwin *OxCan*
Crowell, Elsinore Robinson *ChPo S1*
Crowell, Eugene 1817-1894 *Alli Sup, DcAmA, DcNAA*
Crowell, George H 1931- *ConAu 25*
Crowell, Grace Noll 1877-1969 *AmA&B, BkCL, ChPo, ChPo S1, ChPo S2, REnAL, TexWr, WhWNAA*
Crowell, James R 1893-1948 *DcNAA*
Crowell, Joan 1921- *ConAu 57*
Crowell, John 1814-1909 *Alli Sup, DcAmA, DcNAA*
Crowell, John 1823-1890 *ChPo S1*
Crowell, John Franklin 1857-1931 *DcAmA, DcNAA*
Crowell, Joshua F *ChPo*
Crowell, Mary Reed 1847-1934 *HsB&A*
Crowell, Merle 1888-1956 *AmA&B, WhWNAA*
Crowell, Mrs. Merle *AmNov XR*
Crowell, Muriel Beyea 1916- *ConAu 57*

Crowell, Norman Henry 1873- *TexWr, WhWNAA*
Crowell, Norton B 1914- *ConAu 9R, WrD 1976*
Crowell, Pers 1910- *ConAu 29, IlBYP, IlCB 1956, MorJA, SmATA 2, WhPNW*
Crowell, Robert 1787-1855 *Alli Sup, DcNAA*
Crowell, Thomas Irving, Jr. 1894-1960 *AmA&B*
Crowell, Thomas Young 1836-1915 *AmA&B, DcNAA*
Crowell, William 1806-1871 *Alli, DcAmA, DcNAA*
Crowen, Mrs. T J *Alli Sup*
Crowest, Frederick J *Alli Sup*
Crowfield, Christopher *DcEnL, DcNAA, OxAm, YABC 1*
Crowfoot 1830?-1890 *OxCan*
Crowfoot, John Rustat 1817-1875 *Alli Sup*
Crowfoot, William *Alli, BiDLA*
Crowley, Alastair 1875-1947 *PoIre*
Crowley, Aleister 1875-1947 *ChPo S1, LongC, REn*
Crowley, Christine 1922- *Au&Wr*
Crowley, Daniel J 1921- *ConAu 21*
Crowley, Denis O 1852- *PoIre*
Crowley, Desmond William 1920- *Au&Wr*
Crowley, Edward *Alli Sup*
Crowley, Frederick C J 1910- *Au&Wr*
Crowley, James *BiDLA*
Crowley, James B 1929- *ConAu 23*
Crowley, John *Alli, DcEnL*
Crowley, John 1942- *ConAu 61*
Crowley, John Edward 1943- *ConAu 53*
Crowley, Lilian Hall 1870- *WhWNAA*
Crowley, Mart 1935- *McGWD, WrD 1976*
Crowley, Mary Catherine d1920 *ChPo, DcAmA, DcNAA, PoIre*
Crowley, Robert 1518?-1588 *Alli, CasWL, Chmbr 1, CrE&SL, NewC*
Crowley, Thomas *Alli*
Crown, Abraham Wolf 1906- *Au&Wr*
Crown, David Allan 1928- *ConAu 25, WrD 1976*
Crown, John *Alli*
Crown, Paul 1928- *ConAu 17R*
Crowne, John 1640?-1703? *Alli, AmA&B, BiD&SB, BrAu, CasWL, Chmbr 2, DcEnL, EvLB, McGWD, NewC, OxEng, Pen Eng, REn, WebEAL*
Crowne, William *Alli*
Crownfield, Gertrude 1867-1945 *AmA&B, AuBYP, ChPo, ChPo S1, DcNAA, JBA 1934, JBA 1951, OhA&B, WhWNAA, YABC 1*
Crownfield, Henry *Alli*
Crowninshield, Bowdoin Bradlee 1867-1948 *DcNAA*
Crowninshield, Ethel *ChPo S1*
Crowninshield, Francis Welch 1872-1947 *DcNAA*
Crowninshield, Frank 1872-1947 *AmA&B, REn, REnAL*
Crowninshield, Frederic 1845-1918 *Alli Sup, AmA&B, DcNAA*
Crowninshield, Mary Bradford 1854-1913 *Alli Sup, BiD&SB, DcAmA, DcNAA*
Crowninshield, Mrs. Schuyler 1854-1913 *AmA&B, DcAmA, DcNAA*
Crowquill, Alfred 1804?-1872 *Alli, ChPo, ChPo S1, ChPo S2, DcEnL, NewC*
Crowsley, John *Alli*
Crowson, P S 1913- *ConAu 53*
Crowther, Alice *Alli Sup*
Crowther, Betty 1939- *ConAu 61*
Crowther, Bosley 1905- *AmA&B*
Crowther, Bryan d1815 *Alli, BiDLA, BiDLA Sup*
Crowther, Catherine E *Alli Sup*
Crowther, Doreen Stoddart 1926- *Au&Wr*
Crowther, Duane S 1934- *ConAu 25*
Crowther, Geoffrey 1907-1972 *ConAu 33*
Crowther, George *Alli Sup*
Crowther, George 1927- *Au&Wr, WrD 1976*
Crowther, George Francis *Alli Sup*
Crowther, George H *Alli Sup*
Crowther, Harold Francis 1920- *WrD 1976*
Crowther, J *Alli*
Crowther, J G 1899- *Au&Wr*

Crowther, James *Alli Sup*
Crowther, James Gerald 1899- *AuBYP, WrD 1976*
Crowther, K R *Alli Sup*
Crowther, M E *Alli Sup*
Crowther, P W *Alli*
Crowther, S *Alli*
Crowther, Samuel 1880-1947 *AmA&B, DcNAA, REnAL, WhWNAA*
Crowther, Samuel Adjai *Alli Sup*
Crowther, W E *Alli Sup*
Crowther, William Harding *Alli Sup*
Crowther, Wilma 1918- *ConAu 5R*
Croxall, James A *Alli Sup*
Croxall, James H *ChPo*
Croxall, Samuel 1690?-1752 *Alli, ChPo S1, DcEuL*
Croxford, Emily *Alli Sup*
Croxford, J C *Alli Sup*
Croxton, Anthony H 1902- *ConAu 61*
Croxton, Arthur Walley *WhLA*
Croxton, Frederick E 1899- *ConAu 23*
Croy, Count G De *Alli Sup*
Croy, Homer 1883-1965 *AmA&B, AmNov, REnAL, TwCA, TwCA Sup*
Crozer, Mrs. S A *Alli Sup*
Crozet, Charlotte 1926- *Au&Wr, ConAu 25*
Crozier, Ada B 1893-1934 *IndAu 1917*
Crozier, Alfred Owen 1863-1939 *OhA&B*
Crozier, Arthur Alger 1856-1899 *DcNAA*
Crozier, Brian 1918- *Au&Wr, ConAu 9R, WrD 1976*
Crozier, Eric John 1914- *Au&Wr, ChPo S2, LongC*
Crozier, Foster *Alli Sup*
Crozier, Francis Rawdon Moira 1796?-1848 *OxCan*
Crozier, Gladys Beattie *ChPo S1*
Crozier, H H *BiDSA*
Crozier, Harry Benge *TexWr*
Crozier, Henry Acheson *Alli Sup*
Crozier, Herbert *ChPo S2*
Crozier, John A *Alli Sup*
Crozier, John Beattie 1849-1921 *Alli Sup, Chmbr 3, TwCA, TwCA Sup*
Crozier, L S *Alli Sup*
Crozier, Mary 1908- *Au&Wr*
Crozier, O R L *Alli Sup*
Crozier, R H *Alli Sup*
Crozier, William And Henderson, Peter *Alli Sup*
Crozier, William Armstrong 1864-1913 *DcNAA*
Cru, Albert Louis 1881-1949 *DcNAA*
Cru, Robert L 1884- *WhLA*
Crucefix, R H *Alli Sup*
Crucelli, Father *Alli Sup*
Cruck-A-Leaghan *PoIre*
Cruden *Alli*
Cruden, Alexander 1701-1770 *Alli, BbD, BiD&SB, BrAu, DcEnL, DcLEnL, EvLB, NewC, OxEng, REn*
Cruden, John *Alli*
Cruden, R P *Alli*
Cruden, Robert 1910- *ConAu 33*
Cruess, William Vere 1886- *WhWNAA*
Cruger, Eliza 1848?- *Alli Sup, DcNAA*
Cruger, Henry 1739-1827 *CyAL 1*
Cruger, Johann 1598-1662 *OxGer, PoCh*
Cruger, Julia Grinnell d1920 *BbD, BiD&SB, DcAmA, DcNAA*
Cruger, Julie Grinnell d1920 *AmA&B*
Cruger, Mary 1834-1908 *Alli Sup, AmA&B, BiD&SB, DcAmA, DcNAA*
Cruice, James *Alli Sup, PoIre*
Cruickshank, Alexander 1900- *Au&Wr*
Cruickshank, Allan D 1907-1974 *ConAu 53*
Cruickshank, Brodie *Alli*
Cruickshank, Charles Greig 1914- *ConAu 23, WrD 1976*
Cruickshank, Helen 1907- *AuBYP*
Cruickshank, Helen Burness 1886- *ChPo S1, ChPo S2, ConP 1970, ConP 1975, WrD 1976*
Cruickshank, Helen Gere 1907- *ConAu P-1*
Cruickshank, James *BiDLA*
Cruickshank, John 1924- *ConAu 1R, WrD 1976*
Cruickshank, Marjorie 1920- *Au&Wr*

Cruickshank, Norah K *ChPo S1*
Cruickshank, Thomas *Alli*
Cruikshank, Ernest Alexander 1853-1939 *OxCan*
Cruikshank, George *Alli*
Cruikshank, George 1792-1878 *Alli, CarSB, ChPo, ChPo S1, ChPo S2, IlBYP, NewC, REn, St&VC*
Cruikshank, Helen B 1896- *ChPo, Pen Eng*
Cruikshank, Isaac 1756?-1810? *BkIE, ChPo*
Cruikshank, Isaac Robert 1789-1856 *ChPo*
Cruikshank, James *Alli*
Cruikshank, Robert *Alli*
Cruikshank, Robert 1789-1856 *ChPo, ChPo S1*
Cruikshank, Robert James *ChPo S1*
Cruikshank, William 1745-1800 *Alli*
Cruise, Francis Richard *Alli Sup*
Cruise, Richard *Alli Sup*
Cruise, Richard A *Alli*
Cruise, William *Alli, BiDLA*
Cruise-O'Brien, Conor 1917- *Au&Wr*
Crul, Cornelis 1500?-1550? *CasWL*
Crull, Adam Ullery d1915 *IndAu 1816*
Crull, Jodocus *Alli*
Crum, Bartley Cavanaugh 1900-1959 *AmA&B*
Crum, Lady Erskine *ChPo*
Crum, Howard Alvin 1922- *IndAu 1917*
Crum, Margaret *ChPo S2*
Crumbaugh, James C 1912- *BiDPar, ConAu 37*
Crumbley, D Larry 1941- *ConAu 29*
Crumit, Frank 1889-1943 *AmSCAP 66*
Crumley, James *DrAF 1976*
Crumley, John Jackson 1863-1952 *OhA&B*
Crumley, Thomas 1872- *WhWNAA*
Crummell, Alexander 1819-1898 *Alli Sup, AmA&B, DcAmA, DcNAA*
Crummey, Lawson Flick *Alli Sup*
Crummey, Robert O 1936- *ConAu 25*
Crump, Arthur *Alli Sup*
Crump, Barry John 1935- *Au&Wr, ConAu 13R, WrD 1976*
Crump, Charles C *Alli Sup*
Crump, Fred H, Jr. 1931- *ConAu 9R*
Crump, Frederick Octavius 1840- *Alli Sup*
Crump, Galbraith Miller 1929- *ConAu 57*
Crump, Geoffrey Herbert 1891- *Au&Wr, ConAu P-1, WrD 1976*
Crump, George Peter, Jr. *BlkAW*
Crump, Irving 1887- *AmA&B, AuBYP, JBA 1934, JBA 1951, MnBBF*
Crump, J *Alli, BiDLA*
Crump, James Irving 1887- *WhWNAA*
Crump, John *Alli*
Crump, Kenneth G, Jr. 1931- *ConAu 23*
Crump, Leslie Maurice 1875- *ChPo S2, WhLA*
Crump, Lucy *ChPo S1*
Crump, Paul *BlkAW*
Crump, Spencer 1923- *ConAu 23, WrD 1976*
Crump, Thomas 1929- *ConAu 49*
Crump, W H *Alli*
Crumpe, Miss *Alli Sup*
Crumpe, Samuel *Alli*
Crumpe, Thomas *Alli*
Crumpet, Peter *ConAu XR*
Crumpton, M Nataline 1857-1911 *DcNAA*
Crumpton, Washington Bryan 1842-1926 *DcNAA*
Crumrine, Boyd *Alli Sup*
Crumrine, N Ross, II 1934- *ConAu 13R*
Crundal, Anson *MnBBF*
Crunden, Reginald *MnBBF*
Crunden, Robert M 1940- *ConAu 29*
Crusader *WhLA*
Cruse, Christian Frederick 1794-1864 *DcAmA*
Cruse, David C *DrAP 1975*
Cruse, Francis *Alli Sup*
Cruse, Harold *AmA&B, BlkAW, LivBA*
Cruse, Heloise *AmA&B*
Cruse, Mary Anne *Alli Sup, BiDSA, DcAmA, LivFWS*
Cruse, Peter Hoffman 1793?-1832 *Alli, BiDSA*
Crusenstolpe, Magnus Jacob 1795-1865 *BiD&SB, CasWL*
Crusio, Cato *Alli*
Crusius, Johannes Paul 1588-1629 *OxGer*
Crusius, Lewis *Alli*
Cruso, Joh *Alli*
Cruso, Thalassa 1908- *AmA&B*

Cruso, Timothy 1657?-1697 *Alli*
Crust, Christie *Alli Sup*
Crutch, Denis *ChPo S2*
Crutchley, Hilda *ChPo S1*
Crutchley, John *Alli*
Crute, Sallie Spotswood *Alli Sup, LivFWS*
Cruttenden, Daniel Henry 1816-1874 *DcAmA, DcNAA*
Cruttenden, David H 1816- *Alli*
Cruttenden, Joseph *Alli*
Cruttenden, R *Alli*
Cruttwell, Alfred C *Alli Sup*
Cruttwell, C *Alli*
Cruttwell, C J *ChPo*
Cruttwell, Charles Thomas 1847- *Alli Sup*
Cruttwell, Richard *Alli, BiDLA*
Crutwell, Clement *Alli*
Crutwell, Richard *Alli*
Cruwys, H S *Alli*
Cruz, Agostinho Da 1540-1619 *CasWL*
Cruz, Juana Ines DeLa 1651-1695 *BiD&SB, DcSpL, McGWD*
Cruz, Ramon DeLa 1731-1794? *BiD&SB, DcSpL, McGWD*
Cruz, Ray 1933- *IlBYP, SmATA 6*
Cruz, San Juan DeLa 1542-1591 *BiD&SB, DcSpL*
Cruz, Sor Juana Ines DeLa 1648?-1695 *CasWL, CnThe, DcSpL, Pen Am, REnWD*
Cruz, Victor Hernandez 1949- *ConP 1970, ConP 1975, CrCAP, WrD 1976*
Cruz Cano Y Olmedilla, Ramon DeLa 1731-1794 *CasWL, EuA, EvEuW, Pen Eur, REn*
Cruz-Diez, Carlos 1923- *WhGrA*
Cruz E Silva, Antonio Dinis Da 1731-1799 *CasWL*
Cruz E Sousa, Joao De 1861-1898 *CasWL, Pen Am*
Cruz Monclova, Lidio 1899- *PueRA*
Cruz Varela, Juan 1794-1839 *DcSpL*
Cruz Y Nieves, Antonio 1907- *PueRA*
Cruzan, Rose Marie Brickler *IndAu 1917*
Cruzat, J W *BiDSA*
Cryan, Robert W W 1866?-1907 *PoIre*
Cryer, Gretchen *ConDr*
Cryer, James Wilfred *ChPo S2*
Cryer, Matthew Henry 1840-1921 *DcNAA*
Cryer, Neville Barker 1924- *Au&Wr*
Cryer, T And Jordan, H G *Alli Sup*
Cryer, William *ChPo S2*
Cryer, Willson *Alli Sup*
Crymes, Thomas *Alli*
Crynkle, Nym *DcAmA*
Crystal, David 1941- *ConAu 17R*
Crystal, H Y *MnBBF*
Csaszar, Ferencz 1807-1858 *BiD&SB*
Cseszmiczey, Janos 1434-1472 *CasWL*
Csicsery-Ronay, Istvan 1917- *ConAu 21*
Csiky, Gergely 1842-1891 *McGWD*
Csiky, Gregor 1841-1891 *BiD&SB*
Csokonai-Vitez, Mihaly 1773-1805 *CasWL, Pen Eur*
Csokonay, Vitez Mihaly 1773-1805 *BiD&SB*
Csokor, Franz Theodor 1885-1969 *CatA 1947, CnMD, CrCD, EncWL, McGWD, ModGL, ModWD, OxGer*
Ctesias *CasWL, Pen Cl*
Cua, Antonio S 1932- *ConAu 17R, WrD 1976*
Cuadra, Jose DeLa 1903-1941 *Pen Am*
Cuadra, Pablo Antonio 1912- *DcCLA, Pen Am*
Cuauhtemoc 1495?-1525 *REn*
Cuba, Ivan 1920- *WrD 1976*
Cuban, Larry 1934- *ConAu 29*
Cubas, Braz *ConAu XR*
Cubberley, Ellwood Patterson 1868-1941 *AmA&B, DcNAA, IndAu 1816, WhWNAA*
Cubberly, Fred 1869- *WhWNAA*
Cuber, John F 1911- *AmA&B, ConAu 9R*
Cubeta, Paul Marsden 1925- *ConAu 5R*
Cubillo, Alvaro *DcEuL*
Cubillo DeAragon, Alvaro 1596?-1661 *CasWL, McGWD*
Cubitt, George *Alli*
Cubley, Lucy Matilda *Alli Sup*
Cubley, W H *Alli Sup*
Cubranovic, Andrija 1480?-1520? *CasWL*
Cuchi Coll, Isabel 1904- *PueRA*
Cuchulain d002? *NewC*

Cuckow, J G *ChPo*
Cuckson, John 1846-1907 *DcAmA, DcNAA*
Cudahy, Brian J 1936- *ConAu 41*
Cudahy, John 1887-1943 *DcNAA*
Cudahy, Patrick 1849-1919 *DcNAA*
Cudahy, Sheila *ChPo S2*
Cuddehy, Mrs. *Alli Sup*
Cuddon, Eric 1905- *BiDPar*
Cuddon, James 1816- *Alli Sup*
Cuddon, John Anthony 1928- *Au&Wr, ConAu 5R, WrD 1976*
Cuddy, Lucy Alsanson *WhWNAA*
Cudlip, Annie Hall 1838- *Alli Sup, HsB&A*
Cudlip, Mrs. Pender *DcEnL, MnBBF*
Cudlipp, Edythe 1929- *ConAu 33*
Cudlipp, Hugh 1913- *Au&Wr*
Cudlipp, Percy *ChPo S1*
Cudlipp, Reginald 1910- *Au&Wr*
Cudlipp, Thelma *ChPo*
Cudmore, Daniel *Alli*
Cudmore, Patrick 1831- *Alli Sup, PoIre*
Cudworth, Angelina M *Alli Sup*
Cudworth, John *Alli*
Cudworth, John William *Alli Sup*
Cudworth, Ralph 1617-1688 *Alli, BrAu, CasWL, Chmbr 1, DcEnL, DcEuL, EvLB, NewC, OxEng, REn*
Cudworth, Warren H *Alli Sup*
Cudworth, William *Alli, Alli Sup*
Cue, Harold *ChPo S2*
Cuelho, Art 1943- *ConAu 61, DrAF 1976, DrAP 1975*
Cuellar, Jose T De 1835- *BbD, BiD&SB*
Cuervo, Rufino Jose *DcSpL*
Cuestas, Katherine L 1944- *BlkAW*
Cueva, Juan DeLa 1550?-1610? *BbD, BiD&SB, CasWL, DcEuL, DcSpL, EuA, EvEuW, McGWD, Pen Eur*
Cueva DeGaroza, Juan DeLa 1550?-1610? *REn*
Cuevas, Clara 1933- *ConAu 57*
Cuevas, Jose Luis 1933- *WhGrA*
Cuff, Henry 1560?-1601 *Alli*
Cuff, R D *OxCan Sup*
Cuffari, Richard 1925- *SmATA 6, ChPo S2, IlBYP*
Cuffe, Henry 1560?-1601 *Alli*
Cuffe, Maurice *Alli*
Cuffe, Robert *Alli Sup*
Cuffe, Lady Sybil Marjorie 1879-1943 *NewC*
Cuffe, Thomas Tenison *Alli Sup*
Cuffe, William O'Connor 1845-1898 *PoIre*
Cuffe, William U O, Earl Of Desart 1845-1898 *Alli Sup*
Cugnet, Francois Joseph 1720-1789 *BbtC, DcNAA*
Cugoana, Ottobah 1745?-1790? *AfA 1*
Cuidano, P *WhWNAA*
Cuillard, E M *Alli Sup*
Cuisenaire, Emile-Georges 1891?-1976 *ConAu 61*
Cuisinier, Jeanne A L 1890- *BiDPar*
Cuitt, George *Alli*
Cujas, Jacques 1522-1590 *DcEuL, OxFr*
Culberson, Charles A 1855- *BiDSA*
Culbert, Denny Cullingsworth 1892- *WhWNAA*
Culbertson, Anne Virginia 1864-1918 *ChPo, OhA&B*
Culbertson, Don S 1927- *ConAu 9R*
Culbertson, Earl 1897- *AmSCAP 66*
Culbertson, Ely 1891-1955 *AmA&B*
Culbertson, Henry Coe 1874-1933 *OhA&B*
Culbertson, Hugh Emmett 1882- *OhA&B*
Culbertson, J M 1921- *ConAu 9R*
Culbertson, James Coe 1840-1908 *OhA&B*
Culbertson, Manie 1927- *ConAu 49*
Culbertson, Matthew Simpson 1818-1862 *Alli Sup, DcAmA, DcNAA*
Culbertson, Michael Simpson *DcNAA*
Culbertson, Paul T 1905- *ConAu 37*
Culbertson, Robert *Alli*
Culbreth, David Marvel Reynolds 1855- *BiDSA, WhWNAA*
Cule, William Edward *ChPo, MnBBF*
Culham, B P *Alli*
Culham, R P *BiDLA*
Culhane, Mrs. *Alli Sup*
Culhane, Kate *PoIre*
Culin, Stewart 1858- *AmLY*

Culkin, Ann Marie 1918- *ConAu 9R*
Cull, David *OxCan Sup*
Cull, Francis *Alli*
Cull, John G 1934- *ConAu 41*
Cull, Mary *Alli Sup*
Cull, Richard *Alli*
Cullen, Miss *BiDLA*
Cullen, Archibald *Alli, BiDLA*
Cullen, C S *Alli*
Cullen, Charles *Alli, BiDLA, ChPo S1*
Cullen, Charles T 1940- *ConAu 53*
Cullen, Clarence Louis d1922 *DcNAA*
Cullen, Countee 1903-1946 *AmA&B, AnCL,
    AnMV 1926, BlkAW, CasWL, ChPo,
    ChPo S1, ConAmA, ConAmL, DcLEnL,
    DcNAA, ModAL, ModAL Sup, OxAm,
    Pen Am, RAdv 1, REn, REnAL, TwCA,
    TwCA Sup, WebEAL, WhWNAA*
Cullen, David *Alli Sup*
Cullen, E *PoIre*
Cullen, Edmund *Alli, BiDLA*
Cullen, Edward *Alli Sup*
Cullen, Frederick John 1888- *IndAu 1917*
Cullen, Gordon *WhGrA*
Cullen, J A *Alli Sup*
Cullen, J Howard *PoIre*
Cullen, John *Alli Sup, ChPo S1, PoIre*
Cullen, John 1837- *PoIre*
Cullen, Joseph P 1920- *ConAu 49*
Cullen, Margaret *Alli, BiDLA Sup*
Cullen, Michael *Alli*
Cullen, P J 1856- *PoIre*
Cullen, Patrick 1940- *ConAu 29*
Cullen, Paul *Alli*
Cullen, Stephen *Alli, BiDLA*
Cullen, Thomas Francis 1877-1945 *DcNAA*
Cullen, Thomas Gordon 1914- *WhGrA*
Cullen, Thomas Stephen 1868- *WhWNAA*
Cullen, William *Alli Sup*
Cullen, William 1712-1790 *Alli*
Culler, A Dwight 1917- *ConAu 17R*
Culler, Annette Lorena *ConAu XR*
Culler, Arthur Jerome 1883-1946 *OhA&B,
    WhWNAA*
Culler, Joseph Albertus 1858- *WhWNAA*
Culler, Lucy Yeend 1849-1924 *OhA&B*
Culley, Ellen *Alli Sup*
Culley, George 1734-1813 *Alli*
Culley, John J *MnBBF*
Culley, John L *Alli Sup*
Culley, Robert Spelman *Alli Sup*
Culley, Thomas R 1931- *ConAu 33*
Cullimore, Daniel Henry *Alli Sup*
Cullinan, Elizabeth 1933- *ConAu 25*
Cullinan, Gerald 1916- *ConAu 23*
Cullinan, Maxwell Cormac d1884 *Alli Sup,
    PoIre*
Cullingford, Cecil Howard Dunstan 1904-
    Au&Wr, ConAu 5R
Cullingworth, Charles James *Alli Sup*
Cullingworth, J *Alli Sup*
Cullingworth, J Barry 1929- *ConAu 1R,
    WrD 1976*
Cullison, Edwin *WhWNAA*
Cullman, Marguerite Wagner 1908- *ConAu 1R*
Cullmann, Oscar 1902- *Au&Wr*
Cullmer, William *Alli Sup*
Cullom, Shelby Moore 1829-1914 *DcNAA*
Cullop, Charles P 1927- *ConAu 25*
Cullum, Sir Dudley *Alli*
Cullum, George Washington 1809-1892 *Alli Sup,
    DcAmA, DcNAA*
Cullum, Sir John 1733-1785 *Alli*
Cullum, Ridgwell 1867-1943 *EvLB, LongC,
    MnBBF, OxCan, TwCA, TwCA Sup*
Cullum, Sir Thomas Gery *Alli, BiDLA*
Cullwick, Ernest Geoffrey 1903- *Au&Wr*
Cully, Iris V 1914- *ConAu 1R*
Cully, Kendig Brubaker 1913- *ConAu 1R,
    WrD 1976*
Cullyer, J *BiDLA*
Cullyer, John *Alli*
Culmer, Jethro Crooke 1855-1919 *IndAu 1917*
Culmer, John Wray *Alli Sup*
Culmer, Richard *Alli*
Culp, Delos Poe 1911- *ConAu 17R*
Culp, John H 1907- *ConAu 29*
Culp, Louanna McNary 1901-1965 *ConAu P-1,*

SmATA 2
Culp, Paula 1941- *ConAu 57*
Culpeper, Nicholas 1616-1654 *BrAu*
Culpeper, Nicolas 1616-1654 *DcLEnL*
Culpepper, Edward J 1903- *AmSCAP 66*
Culpepper, Sir John *Alli*
Culpepper, Nathaniel *Alli*
Culpepper, Nicholas 1616-1654 *Alli*
Culpepper, Sir Thomas *Alli*
Culros, Lady Elizabeth M *Alli*
Culross, James *Alli Sup*
Culross, Michael 1942- *ConAu 33,
    DrAP 1975*
Culsha, Edward Widt *Alli Sup*
Culsha, Mary *Alli Sup*
Culshaw, John 1924- *Au&Wr, ConAu 23,
    WrD 1976*
Culshaw, W J *MnBBF*
Culter, Horace M 1856- *WhWNAA*
Culter, Mary Nantz McCrae 1858- *IndAu 1816,
    WhWNAA*
Culver, C M *Alli Sup*
Culver, Dwight W 1921- *ConAu 9R*
Culver, Eloise Crosby 1915-1972 *BlkAW*
Culver, Elsie Thomas 1898- *ConAu 21*
Culver, Harold E 1883- *WhWNAA*
Culver, Henry Brundage 1869-1946 *DcNAA*
Culver, Miss J F *Alli Sup*
Culver, Kathryn *EncM&D*
Culver, Raymond Benjamin 1887-1938 *DcNAA*
Culver, Richard *Alli Sup*
Culver, S W *Alli Sup*
Culver, Timothy J *WrD 1976*
Culverhouse, C *Alli*
Culverwel, Nathanael d1651? *BrAu, OxEng,
    REn*
Culverwell, E P *Alli Sup*
Culverwell, Ezekiel *Alli*
Culverwell, Nathaniel *Alli*
Culverwell, Robert James *Alli Sup*
Culverwell, Thomas William *Alli Sup*
Culy, David *Alli*
Cumali, Necati 1921- *CasWL, REnWD*
Cumba *PueRA*
Cumback, Will 1829-1905 *DcNAA,
    IndAu 1816*
Cumberbatch, Elkin Percy 1880- *WhLA*
Cumberbatch, Lawrence S 1946- *BlkAW*
Cumberland, Bishop *Chmbr 2*
Cumberland, Duke Of *NewC*
Cumberland, Earls Of *Alli*
Cumberland, A M *MnBBF*
Cumberland, B *Alli Sup*
Cumberland, Charles *Alli Sup*
Cumberland, Charles C 1914- *ConAu 1R*
Cumberland, Denison *Alli*
Cumberland, Frederic Barlow 1846-1913
    DcNAA
Cumberland, George *Alli, BiDLA*
Cumberland, Guy *Alli Sup*
Cumberland, Kenneth Brailey 1913- *ConAu 53,
    WrD 1976*
Cumberland, Marten 1892-1972 *ConAu P-1*
Cumberland, Richard 1632-1718 *Alli, DcEnL*
Cumberland, Richard 1732-1811 *Alli, BiD&SB,
    BrAu, CasWL, Chmbr 2, DcEnA,
    DcEnL, DcLEnL, EvLB, McGWD,
    NewC, OxEng, Pen Eng, REn, WebEAL*
Cumberland, Stuart C *Alli Sup*
Cumberland, William Henry 1929- *ConAu 17R*
Cumberland Poet, The *DcEnL*
Cumberlege, Marcus Crossley 1938- *ConP 1970,
    ConP 1975, WrD 1976*
Cumbo, Kattie M 1938- *BlkAW, DrAP 1975,
    LivBAA*
Cumin, Patrick 1824- *Alli Sup*
Cuming, Edward William Dirom 1862-
    Br&AmS, WhLA
Cuming, Fortescue 1762-1828 *AmA&B,
    DcNAA*
Cuming, Geoffrey John 1917- *Au&Wr,
    ConAu 5R*
Cuming, Hugh Smith 1796-1859 *PoIre*
Cuming, Patrick *Alli*
Cuming, Ralph *Alli*
Cuming, William 1714-1788 *Alli*
Cumings, Elizabeth *ChPo*
Cumings, Henry *Alli*

Cumings, John Nathaniel 1905- *Au&Wr*
Cummin, Gaylord Church 1882- *WhWNAA*
Cummin, Joseph King *Alli Sup*
Cumming, A N *Alli Sup*
Cumming, Alexander d1814 *Alli, BiDLA,
    BiDLA Sup*
Cumming, Alexander 1726-1763 *Alli, DcNAA*
Cumming, Alexander 1883-1948 *DcNAA*
Cumming, Charles L B *Alli Sup*
Cumming, Constance Frederica Gordon 1837-
    Alli Sup
Cumming, Cosmo *Alli Sup*
Cumming, Elsa Gordon *ChPo*
Cumming, Henry Harford 1905-1945 *DcNAA*
Cumming, Hugh S 1869- *WhWNAA*
Cumming, J G 1863- *ChPo*
Cumming, James *Alli, BiDLA*
Cumming, James Elder *Alli Sup*
Cumming, Jane Eliza Gordon *Alli Sup*
Cumming, John 1810-1881 *Alli, Alli Sup,
    DcEnL*
Cumming, Joseph George *Alli Sup*
Cumming, Kate 1835- *Alli Sup, BiDSA,
    DcAmA, DcNAA, LivFWS*
Cumming, Linnaeus *Alli Sup*
Cumming, Marian 1896- *TexWr*
Cumming, Patricia 1932- *ConAu 61*
Cumming, Peter A *OxCan Sup*
Cumming, Preston *Alli*
Cumming, Primrose Amy 1915- *Au&Wr,
    ConAu 33, WrD 1976*
Cumming, R G *Alli*
Cumming, Richard 1928- *AmSCAP 66*
Cumming, Robert Dalziel 1871- *WhWNAA*
Cumming, W F *Alli Sup*
Cumming, William Gordon *Alli Sup*
Cumming, William P 1900- *ConAu 33,
    WrD 1976*
Cumming, William T And Bringhurst, J H
    Alli Sup
Cumming-Skinner, Dugald Matheson 1902-
    MnBBF
Cummings, A L T 1865- *WhWNAA*
Cummings, A W *Alli Sup*
Cummings, Abraham 1755-1827 *Alli*
Cummings, Amos Jay 1842?-1902 *DcAmA,
    DcNAA*
Cummings, Annie M *Alli Sup*
Cummings, Ariel Ivers 1823-1863 *ChPo S1,
    DcNAA*
Cummings, Arthur M *Alli Sup*
Cummings, Asa 1791-1856 *DcNAA*
Cummings, Bruce Frederick 1889-1919 *Chmbr 3,
    DcLEnL, EvLB, LongC, TwCA,
    TwCA Sup*
Cummings, Byron 1861- *ArizL*
Cummings, C C *BiDSA*
Cummings, Charles Amos 1833-1905 *DcAmA,
    DcNAA*
Cummings, E C *Alli Sup*
Cummings, E E 1894-1962 *AmA&B, AmWr,
    AnCL, AtlBL, AuBYP, CasWL, ChPo,
    CnDAL, CnE&AP, CnMD, CnMWL,
    ConAmA, ConAmL, ConLC 1, ConLC 3,
    CyWA, DcLEnL, EncWL, EvLB, LongC,
    McGWD, ModAL, ModAL Sup,
    ModWD, OxAm, OxEng, Pen Am,
    RAdv 1, REn, REnAL, SixAP, TwCA,
    TwCA Sup, TwCW, WebEAL, WhTwL*
Cummings, Emily *WhWNAA*
Cummings, Florence *ConAu 49*
Cummings, George *Alli*
Cummings, Hayman Alfred James *Alli Sup*
Cummings, Jacob Abbot 1773-1820 *Alli,
    DcNAA*
Cummings, Jean 1930- *ConAu 33*
Cummings, Jeremiah Williams 1823-1866
    *Alli Sup, BiDSA, ChPo, DcAmA,
    DcNAA, PoIre*
Cummings, John 1868-1936 *DcNAA*
Cummings, Joseph 1817-1890 *Alli Sup,
    DcNAA*
Cummings, Ken *MnBBF*
Cummings, Larry L 1937- *ConAu 53*
Cummings, M J *Alli Sup*
Cummings, Maria *Alli*
Cummings, Milton Curtis, Jr. 1933- *ConAu 13R,
    WrD 1976*

Cummings, Parke 1902- *AmA&B, ConAu P-1, SmATA 2*
Cummings, Patricia Hager 1924- *AmSCAP 66*
Cummings, Paul 1933- *ConAu 21*
Cummings, Preston 1800-1875 *DcNAA*
Cummings, R T *Alli*
Cummings, Richard *AuBYP, ConAu XR, OxCan Sup, WrD 1976*
Cummings, Richard LeRoy 1933- *ConAu 45*
Cummings, St. James 1858-1913 *BiDSA, DcNAA*
Cummings, Thomas Seir 1804-1894 *Alli Sup, DcAmA, DcNAA*
Cummings, Uriah d1910 *DcNAA*
Cummings, Violet M 1905- *ConAu 57*
Cummings, Virginia Macdonald *WhWNAA*
Cummings, W T 1933- *ConAu 1R*
Cummings, William Haymen *Alli Sup*
Cummings, Mrs. Wiloughby *WhWNAA*
Cummings-Bruce *Alli Sup*
Cummins, Adley H *Alli Sup*
Cummins, Alexandrine Macourt *Alli Sup*
Cummins, C *Alli Sup*
Cummins, Cecil *BlkAW*
Cummins, Cedric Clisten 1909- *IndAu 1917*
Cummins, D Duane 1935- *ConAu 37*
Cummins, E H 1790-1835 *BbtC*
Cummins, Earl Everett 1896-1938 *DcNAA*
Cummins, Ebenezer Harlow 1790-1835 *BiDSA, DcAmA, DcNAA*
Cummins, Edward *PoIre*
Cummins, Ella Sterling *Alli Sup, DcNAA*
Cummins, Francis 1732-1832 *BiDSA*
Cummins, George David 1822-1876 *Alli Sup, DcNAA*
Cummins, George Wyckhoff 1865-1942 *DcNAA*
Cummins, Geraldine Dorothy 1890-1969 *BiDPar, ConAu P-1*
Cummins, Harold 1893- *IndAu 1917, WhWNAA*
Cummins, John *Alli Sup*
Cummins, John James 1795-1867 *PoIre*
Cummins, John S *BbtC*
Cummins, Maria Susanna 1827-1866 *Alli Sup, AmA, AmA&B, BbD, BiD&SB, ChPo, Chmbr 3, DcAmA, DcBiA, DcLEnL, DcNAA, EvLB, OxAm, REn, REnAL, WhCL, YABC 1*
Cummins, Mary Francese *ChPo, ChPo S1*
Cummins, Mary Warmington 1923- *Au&Wr*
Cummins, P D *Au&Wr*
Cummins, Patrick 1880- *CatA 1952*
Cummins, Paul F 1937- *ConAu 33*
Cummins, Robert Constable 1887- *Au&Wr*
Cummins, Roger W *ChPo S2*
Cummins, Scott 1846-1928 *DcNAA*
Cummins, Walter 1936- *ConAu 41, DrAF 1976*
Cummying, Susannah 1780?- *Alli, BiDLA*
Cumont, Franz Valery Marie 1868- *WhLA*
Cumpston, Astrid Kate Oatelaye *IlBYP*
Cumpston, W H *Alli Sup*
Cunctator d203BC *REn*
Cundall, Frank 1858-1937 *Alli Sup, DcNAA*
Cundall, Frank 1858- *WhLA*
Cundall, James *Alli Sup*
Cundall, Joseph 1818-1895 *Alli Sup, CarSB*
Cundell, Henry *NewC*
Cundiff, B A *Alli Sup*
Cundiff, Edward William 1919- *ConAu 1R*
Cundy, Henry Martyn 1913- *ConAu 5R*
Cuneo, John R 1911- *ConAu 53*
Cuneo, Terrence *MnBBF*
Cuney, Waring 1906- *BlkAW*
Cuney-Hare, Maud 1874-1936 *BlkAW, DcNAA*
Cunha, Euclides Rodrigues Pimenta Da 1866-1909 *CasWL*
Cunha, Euclydes Da 1866-1909 *Pen Am*
Cunha, George Martin 1911- *ConAu 25*
Cunha, Jose Anastacio Da 1744-1787 *CasWL*
Cunha, Juan 1910- *DcCLA*
Cuninggim, Merrimon 1911- *AmA&B, ConAu 41*
Cuningham, James McNabb *Alli Sup*
Cuninghame, Alexander *Alli*
Cuninghame, David *Alli*
Cuninghame, James *Alli*

Cuninghame, Richard *Alli Sup*
Cuninghame, William *Alli*
Cunliffe, Barrington Windsor 1939- *ConAu 53*
Cunliffe, Barry 1939- *ConAu XR, WrD 1976*
Cunliffe, Elaine 1922- *Au&Wr, ConAu 33, WrD 1976*
Cunliffe, Henry *Alli Sup*
Cunliffe, John Arthur 1933- *Au&Wr, ConAu 61*
Cunliffe, John William 1865-1946 *AmA&B, ChPo, DcNAA, TwCA, TwCA Sup, WhWNAA*
Cunliffe, Marcus Falkner 1922- *AmA&B, Au&Wr, ConAu 21, WrD 1976*
Cunliffe, Mary H Pickersgill- *Alli Sup*
Cunliffe, R *Alli Sup*
Cunliffe, Richard R 1906- *AmSCAP 66*
Cunliffe, William Gordon 1929- *ConAu 25*
Cunliffe-Jones, Hubert 1905- *Au&Wr*
Cunliffe-Owen, Marguerite DeGodart 1861-1927 *DcNAA*
Cunliffe-Owen, Philip Frederick 1855-1926 *DcNAA*
Cunn, Samuel *Alli*
Cunningham, Albert Benjamin 1888-1962 *AmA&B, AmNov XR, OhA&B, TexWr, WhWNAA*
Cunningham, Alexander 1654-1737? *Alli*
Cunningham, Alexander 1763-1812 *ChPo S1*
Cunningham, Sir Alexander 1814- *Alli Sup, Chmbr 3*
Cunningham, Alexander W *Alli Sup*
Cunningham, Aline *ConAu 57*
Cunningham, Allan 1784-1842 *Alli, BbD, BiD&SB, BrAu 19, CasWL, ChPo, ChPo S1, ChPo S2, Chmbr 3, DcEnA, DcEnL, EvLB, NewC, OxEng, Pen Eng, REn*
Cunningham, Arthur 1928- *AmSCAP 66*
Cunningham, Auburn S 1884- *OhA&B, WhWNAA*
Cunningham, Mrs. B Sim *Alli Sup*
Cunningham, Brysson 1868- *WhLA*
Cunningham, C *Alli Sup*
Cunningham, C D And Abney, W DeW *Alli Sup*
Cunningham, Cathy *ConAu 49*
Cunningham, Charles *ChPo S2*
Cunningham, Chet 1928- *ConAu 49*
Cunningham, Cornelius Carman 1890-1958 *AmA&B*
Cunningham, Dale S 1932- *ConAu 13R*
Cunningham, Daniel John *Alli Sup*
Cunningham, David *Alli Sup*
Cunningham, Dellwyn *ChPo*
Cunningham, E *Alli Sup*
Cunningham, E V *AuBYP, ConAu XR, ConNov 1972, ConNov 1976, SmATA 7, WrD 1976*
Cunningham, Edward John *Alli Sup*
Cunningham, Eugene 1896-1957 *AmA&B, TexWr, WhWNAA*
Cunningham, F A *PoIre*
Cunningham, Floyd F 1899- *ConAu P-1, WrD 1976*
Cunningham, Francis 1820-1875 *Alli, Alli Sup, Chmbr 3*
Cunningham, Francois Aloysius 1862-1935 *DcNAA*
Cunningham, Frank *ConAu XR*
Cunningham, Frank H *Alli Sup*
Cunningham, G *Alli, Alli Sup, BiDLA*
Cunningham, G Watts 1881- *WhWNAA*
Cunningham, George *ChPo, ChPo S1*
Cunningham, George, Jr. 1927- *BlkAW*
Cunningham, George Godfrey *Alli*
Cunningham, Gustavus Watts 1881- *AmA&B*
Cunningham, H H 1913-1969 *ConAu P-1*
Cunningham, H S *Alli Sup*
Cunningham, Henry Duncan P *Alli Sup*
Cunningham, Sir Henry Stewart 1832?- *Alli Sup, BbD*
Cunningham, Holly Estil 1883-1952 *AmA&B, WhWNAA*
Cunningham, Horace Herndon 1913- *IndAu 1917*
Cunningham, Hugh *PoIre*
Cunningham, Isabella *Alli*
Cunningham, J A *Alli Sup*

Cunningham, J J *Alli Sup*
Cunningham, J V 1911- *AmA&B, ConAu 1R, ConLC 3, ConP 1970, ConP 1975, DrAP 1975, WorAu, WrD 1976*
Cunningham, J W *Alli, BiDLA, BiDLA Sup, ChPo*
Cunningham, James *Alli, BiDLA*
Cunningham, James 1936- *BlkAW*
Cunningham, James F 1901- *ConAu 19*
Cunningham, Jane *Alli Sup, PoIre*
Cunningham, John *Alli, Alli Sup, BiDLA, Chmbr 2*
Cunningham, Sir John *Alli*
Cunningham, John 1729-1773 *Alli, BrAu, ChPo, ChPo S1, DcEnL, DcLEnL, OxEng, PoIre*
Cunningham, John 1819- *Alli Sup*
Cunningham, John P *BbtC*
Cunningham, John William 1780-1861 *PoCh*
Cunningham, Joseph Davey *Alli, Chmbr 3*
Cunningham, Joseph Sandy 1928- *ConAu 61*
Cunningham, Joseph Thomas 1859- *WhLA*
Cunningham, Josh *Alli*
Cunningham, Josias *Alli*
Cunningham, Julia Woolfolk 1916- *AmA&B, AuBYP, ConAu 9R, MorBMP, SmATA 1, ThBJA*
Cunningham, Louis Arthur 1900- *CanNov, CanWr, OxCan, WhWNAA*
Cunningham, Louis Wyborn 1863- *WhWNAA*
Cunningham, Lyda Sue Martin 1938- *ConAu 17R*
Cunningham, Lady Margaret *Alli*
Cunningham, Margaret Essie *ConP 1970*
Cunningham, Mary *AuBYP*
Cunningham, Mary E *TexWr*
Cunningham, Merce *ConDr, WrD 1976*
Cunningham, Michael *ChPo S1*
Cunningham, Michael A 1945- *ConAu 41*
Cunningham, Minnie Fisher *TexWr*
Cunningham, Paul 1890-1960 *AmSCAP 66*
Cunningham, Peter *Alli*
Cunningham, Peter 1816-1869 *Alli, ChPo S2, Chmbr 3, DcEnL*
Cunningham, Robert Louis 1926- *ConAu 41*
Cunningham, Robert M, Jr. 1909- *ConAu 49*
Cunningham, Robert Oliver *Alli Sup*
Cunningham, Robert Stanley 1907- *ConAu 53*
Cunningham, Robert Sydney 1891- *WhWNAA*
Cunningham, Rosemary 1916- *ConAu 9R*
Cunningham, Mrs. Rudolph 1907- *AmSCAP 66*
Cunningham, Sumner Archibald 1843- *BiDSA*
Cunningham, Thomas Mounsey 1776-1834 *BrAu 19, Chmbr 3*
Cunningham, Timothy *Alli*
Cunningham, Virginia 1909- *AuBYP, OhA&B*
Cunningham, Wallace McCook 1881-1945 *OhA&B*
Cunningham, William *Alli, Alli Sup*
Cunningham, William 1781-1804 *PoIre*
Cunningham, William 1805-1861 *Alli Sup, ChPo, ChPo S1*
Cunningham, William 1849-1919 *BrAu 19*
Cunningham, William 1901-1967 *AmA&B*
Cunningham, William M 1829-1909 *Alli Sup, OhA&B*
Cunninghame *Alli*
Cunninghame, William *Alli, BiDLA*
Cunninghame Graham, Robert 1735?-1797? *NewC*
Cunninghame Graham, Robert Bontine 1852-1936 *CasWL, ChPo, Chmbr 3, DcLEnL, EvLB, LongC, ModBL, NewC, OxEng, REn, TwCA, TwCA Sup*
Cunnington, May *Alli Sup*
Cunnington, Phillis 1887-1974 *Au&Wr, ConAu 53*
Cunnington, Phillis 1887- *WrD 1976*
Cunninson, Ian 1923- *Au&Wr*
Cunnison, C V L *MnBBF*
Cuntaram Pillai, Alappurai Perumal 1855-1897 *DcOrL 2*
Cuntarar *DcOrL 2*
Cunynghame, Alexander *Alli*
Cunynghame, Arthur *OxCan*
Cunynghame, Sir Arthur Augustus Thurlow 1812-1884 *Alli Sup*

Cunynghame, Henry Hardinge Samuel 1848-
  Alli Sup
Cunz, Dieter 1910- *ConAu 19*
Cuoco, Vincenzo 1770-1823 *CasWL, EvEuW*
Cuomo, Edward A 1925- *AmSCAP 66*
Cuomo, George 1929- *ConAu 5R, DrAF 1976,
  DrAP 1975*
Cuomo, Mario Matthew 1932- *WrD 1976*
Cuoq, A *BbtC*
Cuoq, Jean Andre 1821-1898 *DcNAA*
Cuore, L B *DcNAA*
Cupitt, Don 1934- *ConAu 41*
Cupper, R A *Alli Sup*
Cupper, William *Alli*
Cuppett, Charles Harold 1894- *AmSCAP 66*
Cuppiramaniya Aiyar, Varakaneri V 1881-1925
  DcOrL 2
Cupples, Ann Jane *Alli Sup*
Cupples, George 1822-1891 *Alli Sup, BiD&SB*
Cuppurattinam, Kanaka 1891-1964 *DcOrL 2*
Cuppy, Hazlett Alva 1863-1934 *DcNAA*
Cuppy, Hazlitt Alva 1863-1934 *IndAu 1816,
  WhWNAA*
Cuppy, William Jacob 1884-1949 *AmA&B,
  DcNAA, IndAu 1816, REnAL, TwCA,
  TwCA Sup*
Cuptil, Arthur L *ChPo S2*
Curate Of Meudon *REn*
Curate, Jacob *Alli*
Curator *DcNAA*
Curbelo, Fausto 1911- *AmSCAP 66*
Cure, Edward Capel *Alli Sup*
Curel, Francois De 1854-1928 *CasWL,
  ClDMEuL, CnMD, EvEuW, McGWD,
  ModWD, OxFr, Pen Eur, REn, WhLA*
Cureton, William 1808-1864 *Alli Sup*
Curgenven, John Brendon 1831- *Alli Sup*
Curiatius Maternus *Pen Cl*
Curie, Eve 1904- *AmA&B, AnCL, Au&Wr,
  ConAu P-1, SmATA 1*
Curie, Marie Sklodowska 1867-1934 *REn*
Curie, Pierre 1859-1906 *OxFr*
Curioso Parlante, El *DcSpL*
Curl, Donald Walter 1935- *ConAu 33*
Curl, James Stevens 1937- *ConAu 37,
  WrD 1976*
Curle, Adam 1916- *ConAu 33*
Curle, Charles *Alli Sup*
Curle, Eric *ChPo S2*
Curle, James 1862- *WhLA*
Curle, Richard 1883-1968 *LongC*
Curley, Arthur 1938- *ConAu 21*
Curley, Charles 1949- *ConAu 57*
Curley, Daniel 1918- *ConAu 9R, DrAF 1976,
  WrD 1976*
Curley, Dorothy Nyren 1927- *ConAu 1R*
Curley, Edwin A *Alli Sup*
Curley, Michael J 1900-1972 *ConAu 37*
Curley, Thomas *DrAF 1976*
Curley, Walter J P 1922- *ConAu 53*
Curling, Audrey *Au&Wr, ConAu 61*
Curling, Bryan William Richard 1911- *Au&Wr,
  WrD 1976*
Curling, Henry 1803-1864 *Alli Sup*
Curling, James Bunce *Alli Sup*
Curling, John *Alli Sup*
Curling, Joseph James *Alli Sup*
Curling, Laura Jane *Alli Sup*
Curling, Thomas B *Alli*
Curling, William *Alli Sup*
Curll, Edmund 1675-1747 *Alli, BrAu, NewC,
  OxEng*
Curll, Walter *Alli*
Curme, George Oliver 1860-1948 *AmA&B,
  IndAu 1917, REnAL*
Curme, Thomas 1806-1884 *Alli Sup*
Curnock, Nehemiah *Alli Sup*
Curnow, Allen 1911- *CasWL, ChPo S2,
  ConDr, ConP 1970, ConP 1975, LongC,
  TwCW, WebEAL, WorAu, WrD 1976*
Curnow, Thomas Allen Monro 1911- *Pen Eng*
Curoe, Philip R V 1892- *WhWNAA*
Curphey, Edward George 1910- *Au&Wr*
Curr, Christian *ChPo, ChPo S1, ChPo S2*
Curr, Edward *Alli*
Curr, Edward M *Alli Sup*
Curr, John *Alli, BiDLA*
Curragh, Katharine 1909- *Au&Wr*

Curran, Charles A 1913- *ConAu 33*
Curran, Charles Courtney 1861- *ChPo*
Curran, Charles E 1934- *ConAu 23,
  WrD 1976*
Curran, Dale 1898- *AmA&B, AmNov*
Curran, Dolores 1932- *ConAu 57*
Curran, Donald J 1926- *ConAu 45*
Curran, Edwin 1892- *AmA&B*
Curran, Francis X 1914- *ConAu 17R,
  WrD 1976*
Curran, Garner 1870- *WhWNAA*
Curran, George Edwin 1892- *AmA&B,
  OhA&B*
Curran, Grace Wickman 1865-1946 *OhA&B*
Curran, Henry Grattan 1800-1876 *PoIre*
Curran, John Elliott 1818-1890 *Alli Sup,
  DcAmA, DcNAA*
Curran, John Joseph 1856- *DcNAA*
Curran, John Philpot 1750-1817 *Alli, BiDLA,
  ChPo, Chmbr 2, PoIre, REn*
Curran, Luella *ChPo*
Curran, Lulu *ChPo*
Curran, Mona *ConAu 5R*
Curran, Pauline Garner *WhWNAA*
Curran, Pearl Gildersleeve 1875-1941
  AmSCAP 66
Curran, Peter Malcolm 1922- *WrD 1976*
Curran, Robert Garner 1870- *WhWNAA*
Curran, Stuart 1940- *ConAu 29*
Curran, Thomas J 1929- *ConAu 45*
Curran, W Tees *OxCan*
Curran, Ward S 1935- *ConAu 41*
Curran, William Henry *Alli Sup*
Curray *Alli*
Currell, William Spencer 1858- *BiDSA*
Curren, Polly 1917- *ConAu 1R*
Current, Richard N 1912- *AmA&B,
  ConAu 1R*
Current-Garcia, Eugene 1908- *ConAu 17R*
Currer Bell *OxEng*
Currey, C *Alli*
Currey, Cecil B 1932- *ConAu 25*
Currey, Fanny W *Alli Sup*
Currey, Frederick 1819-1881 *Alli Sup*
Currey, George 1816-1885 *Alli, Alli Sup*
Currey, Josiah Seymour 1844-1928 *DcNAA*
Currey, R F 1894- *ConAu P-1*
Currey, Ralph Nixon 1907- *Au&Wr,
  ConP 1970, ConP 1975, WrD 1976*
Currey, Ronald Fairbridge 1894- *Au&Wr*
Currey, Seymour 1844- *AmLY*
Currie, A *Alli Sup*
Currie, Andrew S *Alli Sup*
Currie, Archibald Ernest *ChPo S1*
Currie, C L *Alli Sup*
Currie, David *ConAu XR, OxCan*
Currie, Duncan D *BbtC*
Currie, Fendall 1841- *Alli Sup*
Currie, George Graham 1867-1926 *ChPo,
  ChPo S1, DcNAA*
Currie, George Washington 1885- *IndAu 1917*
Currie, Gilbert Egleson *Alli Sup*
Currie, James *Alli Sup*
Currie, James 1756-1805 *Alli, ChPo, ChPo S1,
  ChPo S2, DcEnL*
Currie, James 1829- *ChPo S1*
Currie, James G *Alli Sup*
Currie, Jean 1919- *Au&Wr*
Currie, John Allister 1868?-1931 *ChPo,
  DcNAA*
Currie, John Ronald 1870- *WhLA*
Currie, Lauchlin 1902- *ConAu 21*
Currie, M A *Alli Sup*
Currie, Margaret Gill *BbtC, OxCan*
Currie, Lady Mary Montgomerie 1843-1905
  *BrAu 19, ChPo, ChPo S1, ChPo S2,
  Chmbr 3, NewC*
Currie, William *Alli*
Currie, William 1853- *ChPo S1*
Currie, William J *ChPo*
Currier And Ives *LongC, REn*
Currier, A H *Alli Sup*
Currier, Albert Henry 1837-1927 *OhA&B*
Currier, Alvin C 1932- *ConAu 23*
Currier, Celia *ChPo S1*
Currier, Charles Gilman 1855-1945 *DcNAA*
Currier, Charles Warren 1857-1918 *AmA&B,
  DcAmA, DcNAA*

Currier, Clinton Harvey 1876-1943 *DcNAA*
Currier, Emma C *Alli Sup*
Currier, John J *Alli Sup*
Currier, Mary Mehitabel 1869- *ChPo,
  ChPo S1*
Currier, Richard L 1940- *ConAu 57*
Currier, Sophronia *Alli Sup*
Currier, Thomas Franklin 1873-1946 *AmA&B,
  ChPo, DcNAA*
Currimbhoy, Asif 1928- *DcOrL 2*
Currington, Owen Josiah 1924- *WrD 1976*
Curris, Irwin *AmSCAP 66*
Curro, Evelyn Malone 1907- *ConAu 5R*
Curros Enriquez, Manuel 1851-1908 *ClDMEuL,
  Pen Eur*
Curry, Albert Bruce 1852-1939 *DcNAA*
Curry, Albert Bruce, Jr. 1887- *WhWNAA*
Curry, Andrew 1931- *BlkAW, ConAu 57*
Curry, Avon 1925- *ConAu XR, WrD 1976*
Curry, Charles Madison 1869-1944 *AmA&B,
  WhWNAA*
Curry, Daniel 1809-1887 *Alli Sup, DcAmA,
  DcNAA*
Curry, David *DrAP 1975*
Curry, Estell H 1907- *ConAu 23*
Curry, Eugene *Alli Sup*
Curry, G G *Alli*
Curry, Gladys 1931- *ConAu 29*
Curry, Jabez Lamar Monroe 1825-1903 *Alli Sup,
  AmA&B, BiDSA, DcAmA, DcNAA*
Curry, Jack A 1902- *AmSCAP 66*
Curry, James *Alli, BiDLA, BiDLA Sup*
Curry, James Bernard 1856-1932 *DcNAA*
Curry, Jane Louise 1932- *AuBYP, ConAu 17R,
  SmATA 1*
Curry, John *Alli*
Curry, John P *Alli Sup*
Curry, John Steuart 1897-1946 *IlCB 1945,
  OxAm, REn, REnAL*
Curry, Kenneth 1910- *ConAu 17R*
Curry, Leonard Preston 1929- *ConAu 29*
Curry, Lerond 1938- *ConAu 33, WrD 1976*
Curry, Lily *Alli Sup*
Curry, Linda 1953- *BlkAW*
Curry, Martha Mulroy 1926- *ConAu 61*
Curry, Otway 1804-1855 *Alli, AmA&B, ChPo,
  ChPo S1, DcAmA, DcNAA, OhA&B*
Curry, Paul 1917- *ConAu 49*
Curry, Peggy Simson 1911- *ConAu 33,
  DrAF 1976, SmATA 8*
Curry, R L *OxCan*
Curry, Richard Orr 1931- *AmSCAP 66,
  ConAu 13R, WrD 1976*
Curry, Samuel Silas 1847-1921 *ChPo S2,
  DcAmA, DcNAA*
Curry, T *Alli Sup*
Curry, Thomas And W B Miller *Alli*
Curry, W Lawrence 1906-1966 *AmSCAP 66*
Curry, Walter Clyde 1887- *WhWNAA*
Curry, William *Alli, BiDLA*
Curry, William Leontes 1839-1927 *OhA&B*
Curry, William Melville 1867-1935 *DcNAA,
  IndAu 1917, WhWNAA*
Curry-Lindahl, Kai 1917- *ConAu 49*
Curson, Henry *Alli*
Curson, John *Alli*
Curtayne, Alice 1898- *Au&Wr, BkC 6,
  CatA 1947, ConAu 53*
Curteis, Arthur Mapletoft *Alli Sup*
Curteis, Bessie C *Alli Sup*
Curteis, Mrs. E A *Alli Sup*
Curteis, George Herbert *Alli Sup*
Curteis, Ian 1935- *Au&Wr, WrD 1976*
Curteis, T J Horsley *BiDLA*
Curteis, Thomas *Alli*
Curteis, W C *Alli*
Curti, Merle 1897- *AmA&B, ConAu 5R,
  OxAm, REnAL, TwCA Sup*
Curties, Marianne *Alli, BiDLA*
Curties, T J Horseley *Alli*
Curties, Thomas Arthur *Alli Sup*
Curtin, D Thomas 1886-1963 *AmA&B*
Curtin, James R 1922- *ConAu 17R*
Curtin, Jeremiah 1840?-1906 *AmA, AmA&B,
  BiD&SB, DcAmA, DcNAA, REnAL*
Curtin, John C *PoIre*
Curtin, Mary Ellen 1922- *ConAu 57*
Curtin, Phillip D 1922- *ConAu 13R*

Curtin, Samuel *Alli*
Curtin, William M 1927- *ConAu 53*
Curtis *Alli*
Curtis, A W *ChPo*
Curtis, A W And D S *Alli Sup*
Curtis, Abel 1755-1783 *DcNAA*
Curtis, Alice 1860-1958 *AuBYP*
Curtis, Alice Bertha *AuBYP*
Curtis, Alice Turner *AmA&B, CarSB, ChPo, WhWNAA*
Curtis, Alva 1797-1881 *Alli, Alli Sup, DcAmA, DcNAA, OhA&B*
Curtis, Anna Louisa 1882- *OhA&B*
Curtis, Anne *Alli, BiDLA*
Curtis, Anthony 1926- *WrD 1976*
Curtis, Ariana 1833-1922 *DcNAA*
Curtis, Arnold 1917- *ConAu 29*
Curtis, Arthur B 1879- *WhWNAA*
Curtis, Arthur Gardiner 1907- *Au&Wr*
Curtis, Arthur Hale 1881- *WhWNAA*
Curtis, Benjamin Robbins 1809-1874 *Alli, Alli Sup, DcAmA, DcNAA*
Curtis, Benjamin Robbins, Jr. 1855-1891 *Alli Sup, DcAmA*
Curtis, Billy 1885-1954 *AmSCAP 66*
Curtis, Brian 1893- *WhWNAA*
Curtis, C H Octavius *Alli Sup*
Curtis, Caroline Gardiner 1827- *Alli Sup, BiD&SB, DcAmA, DcNAA*
Curtis, Chandler *Alli Sup*
Curtis, Charles *Alli, BiDLA*
Curtis, Charles Albert 1835-1907 *DcNAA*
Curtis, Charles Berwick *Alli Sup*
Curtis, Charles Boyd 1827-1905 *DcAmA, DcNAA*
Curtis, Charles E *Alli Sup*
Curtis, Charles J 1921- *ConAu 21*
Curtis, Charles Pelham 1891-1959 *AmA&B*
Curtis, Charles Ralph 1899- *Au&Wr, ConAu 5R*
Curtis, Charlotte *AuNews 2, ConAu 9R*
Curtis, Cyrus Hermann Kotzschmar 1850-1933 *AmA&B*
Curtis, David 1942- *ConAu 23*
Curtis, David A 1846-1923 *Alli Sup, AmLY, DcNAA*
Curtis, Douglas 1936- *WrD 1976*
Curtis, E A *Alli Sup*
Curtis, Eddie 1927- *AmSCAP 66*
Curtis, Edith Roelker 1893- *ConAu 1R, WrD 1976*
Curtis, Edmund *PoIre*
Curtis, Edward 1838-1912 *Alli Sup, DcAmA, DcNAA, OxCan Sup*
Curtis, Edward Lewis 1853-1911 *DcNAA*
Curtis, Edward S 1868-1952 *AmA&B*
Curtis, Elizabeth *ConICB*
Curtis, Elizabeth d1946 *DcNAA*
Curtis, Ella J *Alli Sup*
Curtis, Elnora Whitman *WhWNAA*
Curtis, Emma Ghent 1860-1918 *Alli Sup, ChPo, IndAu 1816*
Curtis, Eugene Newton 1880-1944 *DcNAA*
Curtis, Francis Day 1888- *WhWNAA*
Curtis, Francis Henry *Alli Sup*
Curtis, Frank B And Webster, William H *Alli Sup*
Curtis, G And Aldridge, T L *Alli Sup*
Curtis, George D *Alli Sup*
Curtis, Sir George Harold 1902- *Au&Wr*
Curtis, George Henry *Alli Sup*
Curtis, George Ticknor 1812-1894 *Alli, Alli Sup, AmA, AmA&B, BbD, BiD&SB, DcAmA, DcNAA, OxAm, REnAL*
Curtis, George William 1824-1892 *Alli, Alli Sup, AmA, AmA&B, BbD, BiD&SB, CasWL, ChPo, Chmbr 3, CyAL 2, DcAmA, DcBiA, DcEnL, DcLEnL, DcNAA, EvLB, OxAm, REn, REnAL*
Curtis, Georgina 1859-1922 *AmLY, DcNAA*
Curtis, Grace Stone *ChPo*
Curtis, H P *Alli Sup*
Curtis, H Pelham *ChPo*
Curtis, Harold 1897- *WhWNAA*
Curtis, Harriot 1817-1907 *AmA*
Curtis, Harriot F 1813-1889 *DcAmA*

Curtis, Heber D 1872- *WhWNAA*
Curtis, Henry *Alli*
Curtis, Henry Holbrook 1856-1920 *DcNAA*
Curtis, Henry Stoddard 1870- *AmLY, WhWNAA*
Curtis, Howard J 1906-1972 *ConAu 37*
Curtis, Hubert *Alli Sup*
Curtis, Isabel 1863-1915 *DcNAA*
Curtis, J C *Alli Sup*
Curtis, J S *Alli Sup*
Curtis, Jackie 1947- *ConDr, WrD 1976*
Curtis, James *Alli, BiDLA*
Curtis, James Wylie 1913- *IndAu 1917*
Curtis, Jean-Louis 1917- *CasWL, EncWL, Pen Eur, REn*
Curtis, Jessie *Alli Sup*
Curtis, John *Alli, Alli Sup, ConAu XR*
Curtis, John Charles *Alli Sup*
Curtis, John H *Alli*
Curtis, L A B *ChPo*
Curtis, Laura J *Alli Sup*
Curtis, Lewis Perry 1900- *ConAu 23*
Curtis, Lindsay R 1916- *ConAu 41*
Curtis, Loyal 1877-1947 *AmSCAP 66*
Curtis, Lynn A 1943- *ConAu 61*
Curtis, Mann 1911- *AmSCAP 66*
Curtis, Margaret James 1897- *ConAu 1R*
Curtis, Marion *BiDSA*
Curtis, Marjorie *ConAu XR*
Curtis, Mark H 1920- *ConAu 5R*
Curtis, Mary *Alli Sup*
Curtis, Mary E *ChPo*
Curtis, Mary Frazier *Alli Sup*
Curtis, Mary I *WhWNAA*
Curtis, Mattoon Monroe 1858-1934 *DcAmA, OhA&B*
Curtis, Moses Ashley 1808-1872 *BiDSA, DcAmA, DcNAA*
Curtis, Newton Mallory d1849 *Alli Sup, AmA&B, HsB&A*
Curtis, Newton Martin 1835-1910 *DcNAA*
Curtis, Norman 1917- *ConAu 45*
Curtis, Olin Alfred 1850-1918 *DcNAA*
Curtis, Orson Blair 1841-1901 *DcNAA*
Curtis, Otis Freeman 1888-1949 *DcNAA*
Curtis, Paul Allan, Jr. 1889-1943 *AmA&B, WhWNAA*
Curtis, Peter *ConAu XR, LongC, SmATA 8*
Curtis, R *Alli*
Curtis, R Farquhar *Alli Sup*
Curtis, Richard *Alli*
Curtis, Richard James Seymour 1900- *Au&Wr*
Curtis, Richard Kenneth 1924- *ConAu 1R*
Curtis, Robert *Alli Sup*
Curtis, Roger *Alli, BbtC*
Curtis, Rosemary Ann 1935- *ConAu 9R*
Curtis, Russell H *Alli Sup*
Curtis, Mrs. S B *ChPo S1*
Curtis, Samuel *Alli*
Curtis, Samuel Ives 1844- *DcAmA*
Curtis, Thomas *Alli, OxCan*
Curtis, Thomas Bradford 1911- *ConAu 61*
Curtis, Thomas Fenner 1815-1872 *Alli Sup, DcAmA, DcNAA*
Curtis, Tom *ConAu XR, WrD 1976*
Curtis, Wardon Allan 1867-1940 *DcNAA*
Curtis, Will *ConAu XR, WrD 1976*
Curtis, William *Alli, BiDLA, PoIre*
Curtis, William 1746-1799 *Alli*
Curtis, William E *OxCan*
Curtis, William Eleroy 1850-1911 *Alli Sup, AmA&B, BbD, BiD&SB, DcAmA, DcNAA, OhA&B*
Curtis, William O'Leary 1868- *PoIre*
Curtis, Winterton Conway 1875- *WhWNAA*
Curtis Brown, Beatrice 1901- *ConAu 25*
Curtiss, Abby 1820- *DcAmA, DcNAA*
Curtiss, Abby Allin *ChPo S2*
Curtiss, D S *Alli Sup*
Curtiss, Fred Hull *ChPo S1*
Curtiss, Frederic H 1869- *Br&AmS*
Curtiss, George Boughton 1852-1920 *DcNAA*
Curtiss, George Lewis 1835-1898 *IndAu 1816, OhA&B*
Curtiss, Hariette Augusta 1856?-1932 *DcNAA, WhWNAA*
Curtiss, John S 1899- *ConAu 19*

Curtiss, Mina 1896- *Au&Wr*
Curtiss, N M *Alli*
Curtiss, Percy *Alli Sup*
Curtiss, Phebe A 1856-1936 *OhA&B*
Curtiss, Philip *AmLY XR*
Curtiss, Philip Everett 1885-1964 *AmA&B, AmLY, WhWNAA*
Curtiss, Samuel Ives 1844-1904 *Alli Sup, DcAmA, DcNAA*
Curtiss, Ursula Reilly 1923- *AmA&B, Au&Wr, ConAu 1R, EncM&D*
Curtius *DcNAA*
Curtius, Ernst 1814-1896 *BbD, BiD&SB*
Curtius, Ernst Robert 1886-1956 *EncWL, WorAu*
Curtius Rufus, Quintus 030?- *CasWL, Pen Cl*
Curtman, Charles O *Alli Sup*
Curto, Josephine 1929- *WrD 1976*
Curto, Josephine J 1927- *ConAu 17R*
Curtois, John *Alli*
Curtois, M A *Alli Sup*
Curtwright, Wesley 1910- *BlkAW*
Curvers, Alexis-Theophile 1906- *Au&Wr*
Curwen, Annie 1857- *ChPo S2*
Curwen, B *Alli, BiDLA*
Curwen, Henry 1845-1892 *Alli Sup, BrAu 19, ChPo S1*
Curwen, J *Alli Sup*
Curwen, John 1816-1880 *Alli Sup*
Curwen, John Christian *Alli, BiDLA*
Curwen, John Spencer *Alli Sup*
Curwen, Maskell E 1825-1868 *Alli Sup, OhA&B*
Curwen, Samuel 1715-1802 *CyAL 1, DcAmA*
Curwin, M *Alli Sup*
Curwood, James Oliver 1878-1927 *AmA&B, DcNAA, LongC, MnBBF, OxAm, OxCan, REnAL, TwCA, TwCA Sup, WhWNAA*
Curzon, Lord *Chmbr 3*
Curzon, Fre *Alli*
Curzon, G *Alli Sup*
Curzon, George Nathaniel 1859-1925 *ChPo S1, DcEuL, NewC*
Curzon, John Henry Roper d1886 *Alli Sup*
Curzon, Robert 1810-1873 *Alli, Alli Sup, BrAu 19, OxEng*
Curzon, Sam *ConAu XR*
Curzon, Sarah Anne 1833-1898 *DcNAA*
Curzon, Virginia *ConAu XR*
Curzon Of Kedleston, G N Curzon, Marquis 1859-1925 *LongC, OxEng, TwCA, TwCA Sup*
Curzon-Siggers, William 1860- *WhLA*
Cusa, Nicholas Of 1401-1464 *REn*
Cusac, Marian H 1932- *ConAu 33*
Cusack, Alice M 1879- *WhWNAA*
Cusack, Dymphna 1902- *ConAu 9R, TwCW*
Cusack, Ellen Dymphna 1902- *Au&Wr, DcLEnL, WrD 1976*
Cusack, Lawrence X 1919- *ConAu 5R*
Cusack, Mary Frances 1830-1899 *Alli Sup, PoIre*
Cusanus *OxGer*
Cusdin, John Arthur 1919- *Au&Wr*
Cusenza, Frank Jerome 1899- *AmSCAP 66*
Cusenza, John *ChPo S1*
Cushing, Mrs. *Alli*
Cushing, Abel *Alli*
Cushing, Barry E 1945- *ConAu 53*
Cushing, Caleb 1800-1879 *Alli, Alli Sup, AmA, AmA&B, BiD&SB, CyAL 2, DcAmA, DcNAA*
Cushing, Mrs. Caleb *Alli*
Cushing, Caroline Elizabeth 1802-1832 *DcNAA*
Cushing, Catherine C 1874-1952 *AmSCAP 66*
Cushing, Charles Cyprian Strong 1879-1941 *AmA&B, DcNAA*
Cushing, Charles Phelps 1884-1960 *AmA&B*
Cushing, E L *OxCan*
Cushing, Mrs. E L *BbtC*
Cushing, Eliza Lanesford Foster 1794- *AmA&B, DcNAA*
Cushing, Frank Hamilton 1857-1900 *AmA, AmA&B, BiD&SB, DcAmA, DcNAA, OxAm, REnAL*
Cushing, George Holmes 1873-1953 *OhA&B, WhWNAA*

Cushing, Harry Alonzo 1870- *DcAmA*
Cushing, Harry Cooke 1869-1933 *DcNAA*
Cushing, Harry H *ChPo*
Cushing, Harvey Williams 1869-1939 *AmA&B,*
　DcNAA, LongC, OhA&B, OxAm,
　REnAL, WhWNAA
Cushing, Helen Grant 1896- *ChPo*
Cushing, Henriette *ChPo*
Cushing, J N *Alli Sup*
Cushing, Jacob d1809 *Alli*
Cushing, Jane 1922- *ConAu 29*
Cushing, John *Alli, BiDLA*
Cushing, Joseph R *ChPo S1*
Cushing, Josiah Nelson 1840-1905 *DcNAA*
Cushing, Luther Stearns 1803-1856 *Alli, AmA,*
　DcAmA, DcNAA
Cushing, Marshall Henry 1860-1915 *DcNAA*
Cushing, Mary Gertrude 1870-1945 *DcNAA*
Cushing, Mary W 189-?-1974 *ConAu 53*
Cushing, Paul *Alli Sup, Chmbr 3, DcNAA*
Cushing, Thomas 1821- *DcNAA*
Cushing, Tom 1874-1941 *AmA&B, DcNAA*
Cushing, William 1811-1895 *Alli Sup, DcAmA,*
　DcNAA
Cushman, Allerton Seward 1867-1930 *DcNAA,*
　WhWNAA
Cushman, Charlotte 1816-1876 *FemPA, OxAm,*
　REnAL
Cushman, Clara 1827-1863 *AmA*
Cushman, Clarissa White Fairchild 1889-
　AmA&B, OhA&B
Cushman, Corinne *HsB&A, OhA&B*
Cushman, Dan 1909- *ConAu 5R, WhPNW*
Cushman, David Quimby 1806-1889 *DcNAA*
Cushman, Evelyn *WhWNAA*
Cushman, Florence Evelyn *WhWNAA*
Cushman, Frederick E *Alli Sup*
Cushman, George H 1814-1876 *EarAB,*
　EarAB Sup
Cushman, George Henry 1859- *ChPo*
Cushman, Henry Wyles 1805-1863 *Alli Sup,*
　DcNAA
Cushman, Herbert Ernest 1865- *DcAmA,*
　WhWNAA
Cushman, Horatio Bardwell 1822- *DcNAA*
Cushman, Jerome 1914- *ConAu 1R,*
　SmATA 2, WrD 1976
Cushman, John F *Alli Sup*
Cushman, Ralph Spaulding 1879-1960 *AmA&B*
Cushman, Rebecca *ChPo*
Cushman, Robert d1626 *Alli*
Cushman, Robert W *Alli Sup*
Cushman, Robert Woodward 1800-1868 *ChPo*
Cushny, Arthur Robertson d1926 *DcNAA*
Cusick, David d1840? *DcNAA*
Cusin, Alexander *Alli Sup*
Cuskelly, Eugene James 1924- *ConAu 5R*
Cuskey, Walter 1934- *ConAu 41*
Cuspinian, Johannes 1443-1529 *OxGer*
Cussans, John Edwin *Alli Sup*
Cussell, W F *Alli Sup*
Cussler, Clive Eric 1931- *ConAu 45*
Cussons, John 1838-1912 *DcNAA*
Cust, Arthur Perceval Purey- 1828- *Alli Sup*
Cust, Sir Edward 1794-1878 *Alli Sup*
Cust, Emma Sophia, Countess Brownlow
　1791-1872 *Alli Sup*
Cust, Henry John Cockayne 1861-1917 *NewC*
Cust, Isabella *Alli Sup*
Cust, Lady Mary Anne d1882 *Alli Sup*
Cust, Nina *ChPo S1*
Cust, Sir Reginald John 1828-1915 *Alli Sup,*
　ChPo S1
Cust, Robert Needham 1821-1909 *Alli Sup,*
　ChPo S2
Custance, George *Alli, BiDLA*
Custance, Harry 1842?-1908 *Br&AmS*
Custance, Olive Eleanor 1874- *ChPo*
Custer, Chester Eugene 1920- *ConAu 41*
Custer, Claude *MnBBF*
Custer, Clint *ConAu XR*
Custer, Mrs. E S *Alli Sup*
Custer, Edgar A 1861-1937 *DcNAA*
Custer, Elizabeth Bacon 1842?-1933 *Alli Sup,*
　AmA&B, BiD&SB, DcAmA, DcNAA,
　REnAL
Custer, George Armstrong 1839-1876 *Alli Sup,*
　DcAmA, DcNAA, OhA&B, OxAm, REn

Custince, Louise C *ChPo*
Custine, Astolphe, Marquis De 1790-1857
　BiD&SB
Custis, George Washington Parke 1781-1857
　AmA, AmA&B, BbD, BiD&SB, BiDSA,
　DcAmA, DcLEnL, DcNAA, OxAm,
　REnAL
Custis, Vanderveer 1878- *WhWNAA*
Cutbill, Alfred *Alli Sup*
Cutbin, Thomas *Alli Sup*
Cutbush, Edward 1772-1843 *DcNAA*
Cutbush, James 1788-1823 *Alli, DcNAA*
Cutcheon, Byron Mac 1836-1908 *DcNAA*
Cutcliffe Hyne *LongC*
Cutforth, John Ashlin 1911- *Au&Wr,*
　ConAu 9R
Cutforth, Rene *Au&Wr*
Cuthbert *Alli*
Cuthbert Bede *OxEng*
Cuthbert, Father 1866-1939 *CatA 1947*
Cuthbert Of Canterbury d758 *Alli, BiB S*
Cuthbert, Saint d687 *NewC*
Cuthbert, A C *ChPo*
Cuthbert, Alexander *Alli Sup*
Cuthbert, Alexander A *Alli Sup*
Cuthbert, Alfred 1784?-1856 *BiDSA*
Cuthbert, C A *Alli Sup*
Cuthbert, Clifton 1907- *AmA&B, AmNov*
Cuthbert, Diana Daphne Holman-Hunt 1913-
　ConAu 1R
Cuthbert, Eleonora Isabel 1902- *ConAu P-1*
Cuthbert, G E *ChPo S2*
Cuthbert, James Hazard 1823-1893 *Alli Sup,*
　DcAmA
Cuthbert, James Hazzard 1823-1893 *BiDSA,*
　DcNAA
Cuthbert, John *HsB&A*
Cuthbert, John A 1788-1881 *BiDSA, DcNAA*
Cuthbert, Marion *ChPo S1*
Cuthbert, Marion Vera *BlkAW*
Cuthbert, R *Alli*
Cuthbert, Robert *BiDLA*
Cuthbert, Ross 1776-1861 *BbtC, DcNAA*
Cuthbert, W R *ChPo S1, ChPo S2*
Cuthbert Clutterbuck, Captain *NewC*
Cuthbertson, David *ChPo S1*
Cuthbertson, David Cunninghame 1881-
　ChPo S1
Cuthbertson, F *Alli Sup*
Cuthbertson, Francis *Alli Sup*
Cuthbertson, Gilbert Morris 1937- *ConAu 57*
Cuthbertson, James Lister 1851-1910 *DcLEnL*
Cuthbertson, John *Alli, Alli Sup, BiDLA*
Cuthbertson, Jona *Alli*
Cuthbertson, Stuart 1894- *DcSpL*
Cuthbertson, Tom 1945- *ConAu 45*
Cuthell, Edith E *Alli Sup, ChPo*
Cuthell, Edith F *ChPo S1, ChPo S2*
Cuthill, James *Alli Sup*
Cuthrell, Faith Baldwin 1893- *AmA&B, ChPo*
Cuthrell, Mrs. Hugh H *AmNov XR,*
　WhWNAA
Cutino, Salvatore *ChPo, ChPo S1*
Cutler, Ann *AuBYP*
Cutler, Benjamin Clarke 1798-1863 *Alli,*
　DcNAA
Cutler, Bruce 1930- *ConAu 1R, DrAP 1975*
Cutler, Carl C 1878- *AmA&B, ConAu 1R*
Cutler, Carroll 1829-1894 *DcNAA, OhA&B*
Cutler, Condict Walker 1859- *Alli Sup,*
　WhWNAA
Cutler, Donald R 1930- *ConAu 23*
Cutler, Ebbitt 1923- *ConAu 49, SmATA 9*
Cutler, Elbridge G *Alli Sup*
Cutler, Elbridge Jefferson 1831-1870 *Alli Sup,*
　AmA&B, BiD&SB, DcAmA, DcNAA
Cutler, Frederick Morse 1874- *WhWNAA*
Cutler, George O *Alli Sup*
Cutler, H A And Edge, F J *Alli Sup*
Cutler, Hannah Maria 1815-1896 *Alli Sup,*
　DcAmA, DcNAA
Cutler, Helen R *Alli Sup*
Cutler, Henry Stephen 1824-1902 *DcNAA*
Cutler, Irving H 1923- *ConAu 23*
Cutler, Ivor 1923- *Au&Wr, ConAu 5R,*
　ConP 1970, WrD 1976
Cutler, James Albert 1876- *OhA&B*
Cutler, James Elbert 1876- *WhWNAA*

Cutler, Jervis 1768-1844 *DcAmA, DcNAA,*
　OhA&B
Cutler, John 1839- *Alli Sup*
Cutler, Joseph 1815-1885 *Alli Sup, DcNAA*
Cutler, Julia Perkins 1815?-1904 *DcNAA,*
　OhA&B
Cutler, Julian S *ChPo S1*
Cutler, Katherine Noble 1905- *ConAu 5R*
Cutler, Lizzie Petit 1836?-1902 *AmA, AmA&B,*
　BiD&SB, BiDSA, DcAmA, DcNAA,
　LivFWS
Cutler, Manasseh 1742-1823 *Alli, DcAmA,*
　OhA&B
Cutler, Nahum Sawin 1837- *DcNAA*
Cutler, Nathaniel *Alli*
Cutler, Richard *Alli Sup*
Cutler, Robert 1895- *AmA&B*
Cutler, Samuel *Alli Sup, ConAu XR,*
　SmATA 5
Cutler, Samuel 1805-1880 *DcNAA*
Cutler, Thomas *Alli*
Cutler, Thomas William *Alli Sup*
Cutler, Timothy 1683-1765 *Alli, CyAL 1*
Cutler, U W *Alli Sup*
Cutler, William Parker 1813-1889 *DcNAA*
Cutler, William Parker And Julia Perkins
　Alli Sup
Cutliffe, H C *Alli Sup*
Cutliffe Hyne *TwCA, TwCA Sup*
Cutlip, Scott M 1915- *ConAu 5R*
Cutlore, Joseph *Alli*
Cutright, Phillips 1930- *ConAu 5R*
Cutshall, Alden 1911- *ConAu 9R*
Cutspear, W *Alli*
Cutsumbis, Michael N 1935- *ConAu 45*
Cutt, Margaret N *ChPo S2*
Cutt, Margaret Nancy 1913- *WrD 1976*
Cutt, W Towrie 1898- *OxCan Sup, WrD 1976*
Cutten, George Barton 1874-1962 *AmA&B,*
　AmLY, WhWNAA
Cutten, John H *BiDPar*
Cutter, Adaliza *ChPo S1*
Cutter, Benjamin *Alli Sup*
Cutter, Benjamin 1803-1864 *DcNAA*
Cutter, Benjamin 1857-1910 *DcNAA*
Cutter, Bloodgood Haviland 1817-1906 *AmA&B,*
　DcNAA
Cutter, C *Alli*
Cutter, Calvin d1880 *Alli Sup*
Cutter, Charles Ammi 1837-1903 *Alli Sup,*
　AmA&B, DcNAA
Cutter, Daniel Bateman 1808-1889 *DcNAA*
Cutter, Donald C 1922- *ConAu 33*
Cutter, Edward Francis 1810- *CyAL 2*
Cutter, Elizabeth H *Alli Sup*
Cutter, Elizabeth Reeve *AmA&B*
Cutter, Ephraim 1832-1917 *Alli Sup, DcNAA*
Cutter, Fred 1924- *ConAu 57*
Cutter, George R *Alli Sup*
Cutter, George W *Alli*
Cutter, George Washington 1801?-1865 *AmA,*
　AmA&B, BiDSA, ChPo S1, ChPo S2,
　DcAmA, DcNAA, IndAu 1917
Cutter, J E *Alli Sup*
Cutter, J S *ChPo*
Cutter, John Clarence *Alli Sup*
Cutter, Murray 1902- *AmSCAP 66*
Cutter, Orlando Phelps 1824-1884 *OhA&B*
Cutter, R H *Alli Sup*
Cutter, Robert Arthur 1930- *ConAu 57*
Cutter, William 1801-1867 *Alli, CyAL 2,*
　DcNAA
Cutter, William Parker 1867-1935 *DcNAA*
Cutter, William Richard 1847-1918 *DcNAA*
Cutting, Charles Latham 1914- *Au&Wr*
Cutting, Charles Suydam 1889- *AmA&B*
Cutting, Elisabeth Brown 1871-1946 *AmA&B,*
　DcNAA
Cutting, Hiram Adolphus 1832-1892 *Alli Sup,*
　DcAmA, DcNAA
Cutting, John H *Alli*
Cutting, Mary Stewart d1928 *DcNAA*
Cutting, Mary Stewart 1851-1924 *AmA&B,*
　ChPo, DcAmA, DcNAA
Cutting, Robert Fulton 1934- *DcNAA*
Cutting, Sewall Sylvester 1813-1882 *DcAmA,*
　DcNAA
Cutting, Starr Willard 1858-1935 *DcNAA*

Cutting, W A *Alli Sup*
Cuttino, G P 1914- *ConAu 23*
Cuttle, Evelyn Roeding *ConAu 57*
Cuttler, Charles D 1913- *ConAu 29*
Cutts, Edward Lewes *Alli, Alli Sup*
Cutts, James Madison 1805-1863 *Alli Sup, DcAmA, DcNAA*
Cutts, John *Alli*
Cutts, Lord John d1707 *Alli*
Cutts, John P 1927- *ConAu 45*
Cutts, Mary 1801-1882 *Alli Sup, DcNAA*
Cutts, Mary Pepperell Sparhawk 1809-1879
  Alli Sup, DcNAA
Cutts, Richard 1923- *ChPo S2, ConAu 33*
Cutwode, T *Alli*
Cuvaminata Aiyar, U Ve 1855-1942 *DcOrL 2*
Cuvier, Georges Leopold C F Dabobert
  1769-1832 *BiD&SB, OxFr, REn*
Cuyler, C C *Alli*
Cuyler, Cornelius C 1783-1850 *DcNAA*
Cuyler, Emily *Alli Sup*
Cuyler, Louise E 1908- *ConAu 23*
Cuyler, Stephen *ConAu XR*
Cuyler, Susanna 1946- *ConAu 61*
Cuyler, Theodore Ledyard 1822-1909 *Alli, Alli Sup, AmA&B, BiD&SB, DcAmA, DcNAA*
Cuyp, Aelbert Jacobsz 1620-1691 *AtlBL*
Cuyp, Albert 1620-1691 *NewC*
Cuzzani, Agustin 1917- *DcCLA*
Cvetaeva, Marina Ivanovna *EncWL*
Cvirka, Petras 1909-1947 *CasWL*
Cwojdzinski, Antoni 1896- *ModWD*
Cydones *CasWL*
Cydones, Demetrius 1324?-1397? *Pen Cl*
Cykler, Edmund A 1903- *ConAu 9R*
Cymon *AmA&B, DcNAA*
Cynaethus *Pen Cl*
Cynan *ConAu XR*
Cynddelw Brydydd Mawr 1155?-1200? *CasWL, Pen Eng*
Cynewulf *Alli, BiB S, BrAu, CasWL, Chmbr 1, CriT 1, DcEnL, EvLB, NewC, OxEng, Pen Eng, REn, WebEAL*
Cynicus 1854- *WhLA, WhWNAA*
Cynonfardd *AmLY XR*
Cynosuridis, Alphonse *BbtC*
Cynthia *AuNews 1*
Cynthius *EuA*
Cynwulf *REn*
Cyparissiotes *CasWL*
Cyples, William 1831-1882 *Alli Sup*
Cypress, J, Jr. *DcNAA*
Cyprian, Saint 200?-258 *CasWL, NewC, OxEng, Pen Cl, REn*
Cyr, Ellen M *DcNAA*
Cyr, Narcisse 1823-1894 *Alli Sup, BbtC, DcNAA*
Cyrano, Savinien De 1619-1655 *Pen Eur*
Cyrano DeBergerac, Savinien 1619-1655
  BiD&SB, CasWL, EuA, EvEuW, OxFr, Pen Eur, REn
Cyriax, James Henry 1904- *Au&Wr, WrD 1976*
Cyril, Bishop Of Turov *CasWL*
Cyril Of Alexandria d444 *CasWL*
Cyril Of Jerusalem 313?-386 *CasWL*
Cyril Of Scythopolis 524?-560? *CasWL, Pen Cl*
Cyril Of Turov *DcRusL*
Cyril, Saint 826?-869 *CasWL*
Cyrus d529BC *NewC*
Cyrus The Great d529BC *REn*
Cyveiliog, Owain *NewC*
Czaczkes, Shmuel Yosef *ConAu XR*
Czaja, Michael 1911- *ConAu 57*
Czajkovski, Michael 1808-1876 *BbD*
Czajkovski, Michal 1808-1876 *BiD&SB*
Czajkowski, Michal 1804-1886 *CasWL*
Czaplinski, Suzanne 1943- *ConAu 61*
Czartoryski, Prince Adam Jerzy 1770-1861
  CasWL
Czaszka, Tomasz *CasWL*
Czech, Svatopluk 1846-1908 *DcEuL*
Czechowicz, Jozef 1903-1939 *CasWL, ModSL 2, Pen Eur*
Czechowski, Michal B *Alli Sup*
Czepko, Daniel 1605-1660 *OxGer*

Czepko VonReigersfeld, Daniel 1605-1660
  CasWL
Czerniawski, Adam 1934- *ConAu 37*
Czerwonky, Richard Rudolph 1886-1949
  AmSCAP 66
Czobor, Agnes 1920- *ConAu 37*
Czuczor, Gergely 1800-1866 *BiD&SB*
Czyzewski, Tytus 1885-1945 *ModSL 2*

D

D, A *ChPo*
D, E L *PoIre*
D, F W *PoIre*
D, G W *PoIre*
D, H *ConAmL*
D, R D *ChPo S1*
D D *WhWNAA*
Da Ponte *AmA&B*
Daae, Ludvig 1834- *BbD, BiD&SB*
Daalberg, Bruno 1758-1818 *CasWL*
Daane, Calvin J 1925- *ConAu 41*
Daane, James 1914- *ConAu 23*
D'Abbes, Ingram 1900- *Au&Wr*
Dabbs, Jack Autrey 1914- *ConAu 17R*
Dabbs, James McBride 1896-1970 *ConAu P-1*
D'Abernon, Viscount 1857- *WhLA*
Dabit, Eugene 1898-1936 *ClDMEuL, EncWL, OxFr, REn*
Dabit, Eugene 1908-1936 *CasWL, EvEuW*
Dablon, Claude 1619?-1697 *OxCan*
Dabney, Charles William 1855-1945 *BiDSA, DcNAA, OhA&B, WhWNAA*
Dabney, Dick *DrAF 1976*
Dabney, Ford T 1883-1958 *AmSCAP 66*
Dabney, J P *Alli*
Dabney, Jonathan Peele *ChPo S1*
Dabney, Joseph Earl 1929- *ConAu 49, WrD 1976*
Dabney, Julia Parker 1850- *DcAmA*
Dabney, Lucy Jane 1880- *TexWr*
Dabney, Richard 1787-1825 *Alli, AmA, AmA&B, BiDSA, CyAL 1, DcAmA, DcNAA*
Dabney, Richard Heath 1860-1947 *Alli Sup, AmA&B, AmLY, BiDSA, DcAmA, DcNAA, WhWNAA*
Dabney, Robert Lewis 1820-1898 *Alli Sup, AmA&B, BbD, BiD&SB, BiDSA, DcAmA, DcNAA*
Dabney, Ross H 1934- *Au&Wr, ConAu 23*
Dabney, Virginius 1835-1894 *Alli Sup, AmA, AmA&B, BiD&SB, BiDSA, DcAmA, DcNAA*
Dabney, Virginius 1901- *AmA&B, ConAu 45, REnAL, TwCA Sup, WrD 1976*
Dabney, Walter Davis 1853-1899 *DcNAA*
Dabney, Wendell Phillips 1865-1952 *OhA&B*
Dabney, William Henry 1817-1888 *DcNAA*
Dabney, William M 1919- *ConAu 9R*
Daboll, Nathan 1750-1818 *AmA&B, BiD&SB, DcAmA, DcNAA*
Daboll, Nathan 1782-1863 *BiD&SB, DcAmA*
Daboll, Sherman B 1844-1910 *DcNAA*
Daborn, Robert d1628 *PoIre*
Daborne, Robert *Alli*
D'Abreu, Gerald Joseph 1916- *ConAu 19*
Dabrowska, Maria 1889-1965 *CasWL, ClDMEuL, EncWL, ModSL 2, Pen Eur*
DaCal, Ernesto Guerra 1911- *ConAu 5R*
Daccord, M *Alli Sup*
Dace, Wallace 1920- *ConAu 61*

Dacey, Norman F 1908- *ConAu 5R*
Dacey, Philip 1939- *ConAu 37, DrAP 1975*
Dach, Simon 1605-1659 *BbD, BiD&SB, CasWL, ChPo, DcEuL, OxGer, Pen Eur*
Dachsberg, Augustinus *OxGer*
Dacier, Madame 1654?-1720 *OxFr*
Dacier, Andre 1651-1722 *OxFr*
Dacier, Anne Lefevre 1654-1720 *DcEuL, EvEuW*
DaCosta, D A *Alli Sup*
DaCosta, Emanuel Mendez d1788? *Alli*
DaCosta, Isaac 1798-1860 *CasWL, DcEuL, EuA*
DaCosta, Isaak 1798-1860 *EvEuW*
DaCosta, Izaak 1798-1860 *BbD, BiD&SB*
DaCosta, J *Alli*
DaCosta, Jacob M 1833-1900 *Alli Sup, DcAmA, DcNAA*
Dacosta, John *Alli Sup*
DaCosta, John Chalmers 1863-1910 *DcAmA, DcNAA*
DaCosta, Maria Fatima Velho *AuNews 1*
DaCosta Andrade, Fernando *AfA 1*
DaCosta Pereira Furtado DeMendoca, H J *BiDLA*
Dacquin, Jeanne-Francoise 1811-1895 *OxFr*
Dacre, Lady *Alli, Chmbr 2, DcEnL, PoIre*
Dacre, B *Alli*
Dacre, Lady Barbarina Brand 1768-1854 *BbD, BiD&SB*
Dacre, Captain Stanley *MnBBF*
Dacre, Charlotte 1783?- *Alli, BiDLA, BiDLA Sup*
Dacres, William *Alli*
DaCruz, Daniel 1921- *ConAu 5R, WrD 1976*
DaCruz, Viriato 1928- *AfA 1*
DaCunha, J Gerson *Alli Sup*
Dacus, J A *Alli Sup*
Dadant, Camille P 1851- *WhWNAA*
Dadant, Marguerite George 1886- *WhWNAA*
Dadby, Joseph *Alli*
Dadd, F *ChPo S1*
Dadd, Frank 1851-1929 *ChPo*
Dadd, George H 1813- *Alli, DcAmA, DcNAA*
Dadd, Richard 1817-1887 *ChPo*
Daddi, Bernardo 1290?-1348? *AtlBL*
Daddow, Daniel *Alli Sup*
Daddow, Samuel H And Bannan, Benjamin *Alli Sup*
Dade, C *BbtC*
Dade, John *Alli*
Dade, William *Alli*
Dade, William d1790 *Alli*
Dadie, Bernard Binlin 1916- *AfA 1, CasWL, ConAu 25, EncWL Sup, Pen Cl, RGAfl*
Dadmun, J W *ChPo S1*
Dadson, A J *Alli Sup*
Dadu 1544-1603 *CasWL*
Daehlin, Reidar A 1910- *ConAu P-1*
Daem, Thelma Bannerman 1914- *ConAu 5R*

Daemmrich, Horst S 1930- *ConAu 45*
Daems, Servaas Domien 1838-1903 *BiD&SB*
Daenzer, Bernard John 1916- *ConAu 53, WrD 1976*
Daffan, Katie *AmA&B, BiDSA, TexWr*
Daffinger, Moritz Michael 1790-1849 *OxGer*
Daffner, Hugo 1882- *WhLA*
Dafforne, James d1880 *Alli Sup*
Dafforne, Richard *Alli*
Dafoe, John Wesley 1866-1944 *DcLEnL, DcNAA, OxCan*
Dafora, Asadata *BlkAW*
Dafydd Ab Edmwnd *CasWL*
Dafydd Ap Gwilym 1340?-1370? *CasWL, Pen Eng*
Dafydd Nanmor 1420?-1485? *CasWL, Pen Eng*
Dagan, Avigdor 1912- *ConAu 33*
Dagenais, James J 1928- *ConAu 41*
Dagenais, Pierre *OxCan*
Dager, Edward Z 1921- *ConAu 61*
Dagerman, Stig 1923-1954 *CasWL, CnMD, CnThe, CrCD, EncWL, EvEuW, McGWD, ModWD, Pen Eur, REnWD, WhTwL*
Dagg, John Leadley 1794-1884 *Alli Sup, BiDSA, DcAmA, DcNAA*
Dagge, Henry *Alli*
Dagge, Jonathan *Alli*
Dagge, Robert *Alli*
Daggett, Aaron Simon 1837- *WhWNAA*
Daggett, Mrs. Charles Stewart *DcNAA*
Daggett, James Lothian 1908- *IndAu 1917*
Daggett, John 1805-1885 *DcNAA*
Daggett, Mrs. L H *Alli Sup*
Daggett, Mabel Potter 1871-1927 *AmLY, DcNAA, WhWNAA*
Daggett, Mary Stewart 1856-1922 *AmLY, DcAmA, DcNAA, OhA&B*
Daggett, Naphtali d1780 *Alli, CyAL 1*
Daggett, Oliver Ellsworth 1810-1880 *DcNAA*
Daggett, R M *Alli Sup*
Daggett, Rollin Mallory 1831-1901 *DcNAA*
Daggett, Stuart 1881- *WhWNAA*
Dagh Dihlavi, Navab Mirza Khan 1831-1905 *DcOrL 2*
Daglarca, Fazil Husnu 1914- *DcOrL 3*
Dagleish, William *Alli*
Dagley, Helen *Alli Sup*
Dagley, Richard d1841 *Alli, BiDLA, ChPo S2*
Daglish, Alice *ChPo*
Daglish, Eric Fitch 1892- *ConICB, IlCB 1945, IlCB 1956, JBA 1934, LongC, TwCA, TwCA Sup*
Dagnall, J Deveral *MnBBF*
Dagnall, John Malone 1818-1917 *Alli Sup, DcNAA*
Dagnaud, Pierre-Marie *OxCan*
Dagobert *OxFr*
Dagonet *NewC*

D'Agostino, Angelo 1926- *ConAu 17R*
D'Agostino, Giovanna P 1914- *ConAu 57*
D'Agostino, Guido 1906- *AmNov*
D'Agostino, Guido 1910- *AmA&B*
D'Agostino, Joseph D 1929- *AmSCAP 66*
Dagoun Taya *DcOrL 2*
DaGraca, Jose Veira Mateus *AfA 1*
Dagrada, Mario 1934- *WhGrA*
Daguerre, Louis Jacques Mande 1787?-1851
  NewC, OxFr
Daguesseau, Henri-Francois 1668-1751 *DcEuL,
  OxFr*
Daguilar, Rose *Alli, BiDLA*
Dahl, Borghild 1890- *AuBYP, ConAu 1R,
  MnnWr, SmATA 7, ThBJA, WrD 1976*
Dahl, Curtis 1920- *ConAu 1R, WrD 1976*
Dahl, Francis W 1907- *AmA&B, REnAL*
Dahl, George 1881- *WhWNAA*
Dahl, Gordon J 1932- *ConAu 49*
Dahl, Ingolf 1912- *AmSCAP 66*
Dahl, J A *Alli Sup*
Dahl, Johan A *ChPo S2*
Dahl, Joseph Oliver 1893-1942 *DcNAA*
Dahl, Knut 1871- *WhLA*
Dahl, Konrad Neuman Hjelm 1843- *BiD&SB*
Dahl, Murdoch Edgcumbe 1914- *ConAu P-1,
  WrD 1976*
Dahl, Otto Gustav Colbiornsen 1893-
  WhWNAA
Dahl, Roald 1916- *Au&Wr, AuBYP,
  ChLR 1, ConAu 1R, ConLC 1,
  ConLC 6, ConNov 1972, ConNov 1976,
  DrAF 1976, MorBMP, NewC, PiP,
  RAdv 1, REn, REnAL, SmATA 1,
  ThBJA, WorAu, WrD 1976*
Dahl, Robert Alan 1915- *AmA&B*
Dahl, Ronald Albin 1938- *ConP 1970*
Dahl, Vladimir Ivanovich 1801-1872 *BiD&SB,
  CasWL, DcRusL*
Dahlberg, Arthur Chester 1896- *WhWNAA*
Dahlberg, Edward 1900- *AmA&B, ConAu 9R,
  ConLC 1, ConNov 1972, ConNov 1976,
  DrAF 1976, ModAL, ModAL Sup,
  OxAm, Pen Am, TwCA Sup, TwCW,
  WrD 1976*
Dahlberg, Edwin T 1892- *ConAu 17*
Dahlberg, Jane S 1923- *ConAu 23*
Dahlgren, Charles Bunker 1839- *DcAmA*
Dahlgren, Fredrik August 1816-1895 *BbD,
  BiD&SB, CasWL*
Dahlgren, John Adolph 1809-1870 *Alli Sup,
  DcAmA, DcNAA*
Dahlgren, Karl Fredrik 1791-1844 *BbD,
  BiD&SB*
Dahlgren, Madeleine Vinton 1835?-1898
  *Alli Sup, AmA&B, BbD, BiD&SB,
  DcAmA*
Dahlgren, Sarah Madeleine Vinton Goddard
  1835?-1898 *AmA, DcNAA, OhA&B*
Dahlgren, Ulric 1870-1946 *DcNAA*
Dahlie, Hallvard *OxCan Sup*
Dahlmann, Friedrich Christoph 1785-1860 *BbD,
  BiD&SB, DcEuL, OxGer*
Dahlstedt, Marden 1921- *ConAu 45,
  SmATA 8, WrD 1976*
Dahlstierna, Gunno 1661-1709 *CasWL*
Dahlstjerna, Gunno 1661-1709 *Pen Eur*
Dahlstrom, Earl C 1914- *ConAu 17R*
Dahme *Alli*
Dahms, Alan M 1937- *ConAu 49*
Dahmus, Joseph Henry 1909- *ConAu 21,
  IndAu 1917*
Dahn, Felix 1834-1912 *BbD, BiD&SB,
  CasWL, OxGer, REn*
Dahn, Julius Sophus Felix 1834-1912 *EvEuW*
Dahood, Mitchell 1922- *ConAu 25*
Dahrendorf, Ralf 1929- *ConAu 1R*
Dahyabhai, Dalapatram *DcOrL 2*
Daiches, David 1912- *Au&Wr, ChPo S1,
  ConAu 5R, DcLEnL, EvLB, LongC,
  ModBL, RAdv 1, REn, TwCA Sup,
  WrD 1976*
Daie, John 1522-1584 *CrE&SL*
Daigon, Arthur 1928- *ConAu 33*
Daiken, Leslie Herbert 1912- *ChPo S1,
  ChPo S2, ConAu 1R*
Dail, C C *ChPo S2*
Dailey, Virginia Poe *IndAu 1917*

Dailey, William Mitchell 1812-1877 *OhA&B*
Daily, Jay E 1923- *ConAu 33*
Daily, William Mitchell 1812-1877 *Alli Sup,
  IndAu 1816*
Daim, Wilfried 1923- *BiDPar*
Dain, Martin J 1924- *ConAu 13R*
Dain, Norman 1925- *ConAu 9R*
Daingerfield, Elliott 1859-1932 *DcNAA,
  WhWNAA*
Daingerfield, Foxhall Alexander 1887-1933
  DcNAA
Daingerfield, Henrietta Gray *BiDSA*
Daini, Sammi *DcOrL 1*
Dainton, Courtney 1920- *ConAu 9R,
  ConAu 13*
Dainton, Frederick 1914- *WrD 1976*
Dainton, William Courtney 1920- *Au&Wr*
Daintrey, Adrian Maurice 1902- *Au&Wr*
Dainty, Evelyn *ChPo*
Dainville, D *BbtC, OxCan*
Daish, John Broughton 1867-1918 *DcNAA*
Daisne, Johan 1912- *CasWL, EncWL,
  ModWD*
Daiute, Robert James 1926- *ConAu 9R,
  ConAu 13R*
Daivs, John Merrill 1846- *AmLY*
Dake, Charles Laurence 1883- *WhWNAA*
Dake, Laura M *ChPo*
Dake, O C *Alli Sup*
Dakers, Elaine *LongC*
Dakers, Manton *MnBBF*
Dakeyne, John Osmond *Alli Sup*
Dakhau *CasWL*
Dakin, David Martin 1908- *Au&Wr,
  WrD 1976*
Dakin, Florence 1869- *WhWNAA*
Dakin, Henry J *Alli Sup*
Dakin, Julian 1939- *ConAu 25*
Daking, William *Alli*
Dakins, William d1607 *Alli*
Dakins, William Whitfield *BiDLA,
  BiDLA Sup*
Dakotah *WhWNAA*
Dal, Erik 1922- *Au&Wr*
Dal, Vladimir Ivanocich 1801-1872 *BiD&SB,
  CasWL*
Daladier, Edouard 1884-1970 *REn*
Daland, Katharine Manaydier Browne *ChPo*
Daland, Robert T 1919- *ConAu 21*
Dalberg, John Emerich Edward *BrAu 19*
Dalberg, Karl T, Reichsfreiherr Von 1744-1817
  OxGer
Dalberg, Rudolf 1885- *WhLA*
Dalberg, Wolfgang Heribert Von 1750-1806
  DcEuL, OxGer
Dalberg-Acton, John Emerich Edward *NewC*
Dalbiac, James Charles *Alli, BiDLA*
Dalbor, John B 1929- *ConAu 17R*
Dalby, Isaac 1744-1824 *Alli, BiDLA*
Dalby, J Arnold *Alli Sup*
Dalby, John *Alli Sup*
Dalby, John Watson *Alli Sup*
Dalby, Joseph *Alli*
Dalby, Martha *Alli Sup*
Dalby, Sir William Bartlett 1840- *Alli Sup*
D'Alcamo, Cielo *CasWL*
Dalcho, Frederick 1770?-1836 *Alli, BiDSA,
  CyAL 1, DcAmA, DcNAA*
Dalcourt, Gerald Joseph 1927- *ConAu 33*
Dalcourt, Gerard Joseph 1927- *WrD 1976*
Dalcroze, Emile Jaques 1865-1951 *LongC*
Daldy, Thomas Mee *Alli Sup*
Dale, A W W *Alli Sup*
Dale, Adrian *WhWNAA*
Dale, Alan *Alli Sup, AmA&B, DcAmA,
  DcNAA*
Dale, Alfred *Alli Sup*
Dale, Alice *HsB&A*
Dale, Allen 1923- *IndAu 1917*
Dale, Annan *DcNAA*
Dale, Antony 1912- *Au&Wr, WrD 1976*
Dale, Austin *MnBBF*
Dale, B *Alli Sup*
Dale, Bryan *Alli Sup*
Dale, Cecil Clare Marston 1845- *Alli Sup*
Dale, Celia Marjorie 1912- *Au&Wr,
  ConAu 5R*
Dale, Charles William 1851- *Alli Sup*

Dale, Charles William Mitcalfe 1857- *Alli Sup*
Dale, Christopher 1917- *OhA&B*
Dale, D M C 1930- *ConAu 23*
Dale, Darley 1848- *Alli Sup, WhLA,
  WhWNAA*
Dale, Edgar 1900- *OhA&B*
Dale, Edward Everett 1879- *ConAu 5R,
  TexWr, WhWNAA*
Dale, Edwin *MnBBF*
Dale, Ernest 1917- *ConAu 13R*
Dale, Estil *AmA&B*
Dale, Frank Q 1911- *AmSCAP 66*
Dale, G P *Alli Sup*
Dale, George Williams Melville 1848- *Alli Sup*
Dale, Harrison 1898- *WhLA*
Dale, Harrison Clifford 1885- *OhA&B,
  WhWNAA*
Dale, Henley *ChPo S2*
Dale, Henry *Alli Sup*
Dale, J D Hilarius *Alli Sup*
Dale, Jack *ConAu XR*
Dale, James 1886- *ConAu 33*
Dale, James Murray *Alli Sup*
Dale, James Wilkinson 1812-1881 *Alli Sup,
  CyAL 2, DcAmA, DcNAA*
Dale, Jan VanDen 1460?-1522 *CasWL*
Dale, Jean 1904- *AmSCAP 66*
Dale, Jimmie 1917- *AmSCAP 66*
Dale, Jimmy 1901- *AmSCAP 66*
Dale, John *Alli*
Dale, John B 1905- *ConAu 13R*
Dale, Joseph *Alli Sup*
Dale, LaAfrique *BlkAW*
Dale, Laura A 1919- *BiDPar*
Dale, Leonard *MnBBF*
Dale, Magdalene L 1904- *ConAu 13R*
Dale, Margaret Jessy Miller 1911- *Au&Wr,
  ConAu 5R*
Dale, Martin *ChPo, MnBBF*
Dale, Nellie *ChPo*
Dale, Nelson C 1880- *WhWNAA*
Dale, Paul Worthen 1923- *ConAu 25,
  WrD 1976*
Dale, Peter 1938- *Au&Wr, ConAu 45,
  ConP 1970, ConP 1975, WrD 1976*
Dale, R *Alli Sup*
Dale, Mrs. R J *OxCan*
Dale, Rebecca VanHamm 1894?-1948 *OhA&B*
Dale, Reginald Rowland 1907- *ConAu 21,
  WrD 1976*
Dale, Richard 1932- *ConAu 33, WrD 1976*
Dale, Robert *Alli*
Dale, Robert William 1829- *Alli Sup, DcEnL*
Dale, Roland *MnBBF*
Dale, Rowland *MnBBF*
Dale, Ruth Bluestone *AuBYP*
Dale, Samuel 1659-1739 *Alli*
Dale, Sophia Dana 1853-1932 *OhA&B*
Dale, T Nelson 1845- *Alli Sup, WhWNAA*
Dale, Thomas *Alli*
Dale, Thomas 1797-1870 *Alli, ChPo, ChPo S1,
  ChPo S2*
Dale, Thomas F d1923 *Br&AmS*
Dale, Thomas Nelson 1845-1937 *DcAmA,
  DcNAA*
Dale, Thomas Pelham *Alli Sup*
Dale, Victor *MnBBF*
Dale, Vikki 1931- *AmSCAP 66*
Dale, William *Alli Sup*
Dale, William Kelynack 1833- *Alli Sup*
Dale, Winston *MnBBF*
Dalechamp, Caleb *Alli*
D'Alelio, Ellen F 1938- *ConAu 17R*
D'Alembert, Jean LeRond D' 1717-1783
  BiD&SB, DcEuL, EuA, EvEuW, OxFr
Dalencour, Francois *WhWNAA*
Dales, George S 1879- *OhA&B*
Dales, John Blakely 1815-1893 *DcAmA,
  DcNAA*
Dales, Richard C 1926- *ConAu 45*
Dales, Samuel *Alli, BiDLA*
Daleski, H M 1926- *Au&Wr, ConAu 33,
  WrD 1976*
D'Alessandro, Robert 1942- *ConAu 61*
Daley, Arthur 1904-1974 *AmA&B, ConAu 23,
  ConAu 45*
Daley, Bill *ConAu XR*

Daley, C F PoIre
Daley, Edith 1876-1948 AnMV 1926, OhA&B, WhWNAA
Daley, George William ChPo
Daley, Helen S ChPo
Daley, Joseph PoIre
Daley, Joseph A 1927- ConAu 53
Daley, Robert 1930- ConAu 1R
Daley, Victor James William Patrick 1858-1905 Chmbr 3, DcLEnL, PoIre
Dalfin D'Alvernha 1167?-1235 CasWL
Dalfiume, Richard Myron 1936- ConAu 25
D'Alfonso, John 1918- ConAu 29
Dalgairns, John Dabree 1818-1876 Alli Sup
Dalgarno, George 1627-1687 Alli
Dalgity, Isa ChPo S1
Dalgity, John ChPo S1
Dalgleish, John Alli
Dalgleish, Maisie Landels ChPo S2
Dalgleish, Walter Scott Alli Sup
Dalgleish, William Alli
Dalgliesh, Alice 1893- AmA&B, AnCL, AuBYP, ChPo, JBA 1934, JBA 1951, St&VC, WhWNAA
Dalgliesh, William BiDLA
Dalglish, Edward Russell 1913- ConAu 37, WrD 1976
Dalhousie, Dowager Countess Of Alli Sup
Dalhousie, Lord 1770-1838 OxCan
Dalhousie, N B OxCan
Dalhusius, J H Alli
Dali, Salvador 1904- AmA&B, REn, WhGrA
Dalin, M Alli Sup
Dalin, Olof Von 1708-1763 BbD, BiD&SB, CasWL
Dalin, Olof Von 1708-1763 EuA, EvEuW, DcEuL, Pen Eur
Dalison, Gulielme Alli
Dalitz, Richard Henry 1925- WrD 1976
Dalj, Vladimir Ivanovitch 1801-1872 BiD&SB
Dalkeith, Ferguson Summerville Alli Sup
Dall, Caroline Wells 1822-1912 Alli Sup, AmA&B, BiD&SB, ChPo S1, DcAmA, DcNAA
Dall, Charles Henry Appleton 1816-1886 Alli Sup, ChPo S1, DcAmA, DcNAA
Dall, Ian ChPo
Dall, James Alli Sup
Dall, William Healey 1845-1927 Alli Sup, BiD&SB, DcAmA, DcNAA
D'Allaire, M OxCan Sup
Dallam, Helen AmSCAP 66
Dallam, James Wilmer 1818-1847 Alli, AmA&B, DcNAA
D'Allard, Hunter ConAu XR, WrD 1976
Dallas, A G Alli Sup
Dallas, Alexander James 1759-1817 Alli, DcAmA, DcNAA
Dallas, Alexander Robert Charles d1869 Alli, Alli Sup
Dallas, Mrs. Alexander Robert Charles Alli Sup
Dallas, Angus BbtC
Dallas, E S 1828-1879 Alli, WebEAL
Dallas, E W Alli
Dallas, Elmslie William Alli Sup
Dallas, Eneas Sweetland 1828-1879 Alli Sup, BrAu 19, LongC
Dallas, George Alli
Dallas, Sir George 1758-1833 Alli, BiDLA
Dallas, George Mifflin 1792-1864 Alli, Alli Sup, DcAmA, DcNAA
Dallas, Helen Alexandria 1856-1944 BiDPar
Dallas, Jacob A 1825-1857 EarAB, EarAB Sup
Dallas, John ChPo S1
Dallas, Justina D Alli Sup
Dallas, Mary 1830-1897 DcAmA, DcNAA
Dallas, Mitzi 1928- AmSCAP 66
Dallas, Oswald MnBBF
Dallas, Philip 1921- ConAu 61
Dallas, Richard DcNAA, OhA&B
Dallas, Robert BiDLA
Dallas, Robert Charles 1754-1824 Alli, BbD, BiD&SB, BiDLA, NewC
Dallas, Ruth 1919- ChPo S2, ConP 1970, ConP 1975, LongC, WrD 1976
Dallas, Sandra ConAu XR
Dallas, Thomas Alli

Dallas, Vincent ConAu XR, WrD 1976
Dallas, W S Alli
Dallas, William Sweetland Alli Sup
Dallaway, Harriet Alli
Dallaway, J J Alli
Dallaway, James 1763-1834 Alli, BiDLA
Dallaway, R C Alli
Dalldorf, Gilbert 1900- WrD 1976
Dallek, Robert 1934- ConAu 25
Dalley, John Bede 1878-1935 DcLEnL
Dalliba, Gerda 1890-1913 ChPo
Dallin, Alexander 1924- ConAu 1R
Dallin, David Julievich 1889-1962 AmA&B, Au&Wr, TwCA Sup
Dallin, Leon 1918- AmSCAP 66, ConAu 1R
Dalling And Bulwer, Baron William Lytton 1801?-1872 Alli Sup, DcEnL, EvLB, Pen Eng
Dallinger, Frederick William 1871- DcAmA, WhWNAA
Dallinger, William Henry 1841- Alli Sup
Dallington, Sir Robert d1637 Alli
Dallmann, Charles Frederick William 1862- WhWNAA
Dallmann, Martha Elsie 1904- ConAu 1R
Dallmann, William 1862-1952 AmA&B
Dallmayr, Fred R 1928- ConAu 49
Dall'Ongaro, Francesco 1808-1873 BbD, BiD&SB, CasWL, EvEuW
Dallowe, Timothy Alli
Dallwitz-Wegner, Richard Von 1873- WhLA
Dally, Ann 1926- Au&Wr, ConAu 5R, WrD 1976
Dally, Frank Fether Alli
Dally, John Frederick Halls 1877- WhLA
Dalman, Gustaf 1855- WhLA
Dalmau Carnet, Sebastian 1884-1937 PueRA
D'Almeida, Anna Alli Sup
D'Almeida, William Barrington Alli Sup
Dalmiro DcSpL
Dalmon, Charles William 1872- ChPo, ChPo S1
D'Alonzo, C Anthony 1912-1972 ConAu 37
Dalphin, Marcia ChPo
DalPoggetto, Newton Francis 1922- ConAu 61
Dalrymple, Alexander 1737-1808 Alli, BbtC
Dalrymple, Byron W 1910- ConAu 57
Dalrymple, Campbell Alli
Dalrymple, Sir Charles 1839- Alli Sup
Dalrymple, Sir David 1726-1792 Alli, BiD&SB, DcEnL, EvLB
Dalrymple, Donald Alli Sup
Dalrymple, G A E Alli Sup
Dalrymple, George Elphinstone- Alli Sup
Dalrymple, Gwynne Weston Laidlaw 1903- WhWNAA
Dalrymple, Sir Hew 1652-1737 Alli
Dalrymple, Sir Hew Whiteford 1750-1830 Alli
Dalrymple, Mrs. J Elphinstone- Alli Sup
Dalrymple, Sir James Alli
Dalrymple, James 1619-1695 Alli
Dalrymple, Jean 1910- ConAu 5R, WrD 1976
Dalrymple, John d1789 Alli
Dalrymple, Sir John 1726-1810 Alli
Dalrymple, John 1804-1852 Alli
Dalrymple, Leona 1884- AmA&B, WhWNAA
Dalrymple, Willard 1921- ConAu 23, WrD 1976
Dalrymple, William Alli, BiDLA
Dalrymple, William d1813 Alli, BiDLA Sup
Dalrymple-Hay, Barbara Au&Wr
Dalrymple-Hay, John Au&Wr
Dalseme, Achille 1840- BiD&SB
Dalsheimer, Alice 1845-1880 BiDSA, LivFWS
Dalton ChPo
Dalton, A Forbes ChPo S1
Dalton, Alene ChPo
Dalton, Annie Charlotte 1865-1938 ChPo, DcLEnL, DcNAA, WhWNAA
Dalton, Brian James 1924- WrD 1976
Dalton, Charles Alli Sup
Dalton, Clive ConAu XR, WrD 1976
Dalton, Cornelius Neale 1842- Alli Sup
Dalton, Dennis Morgan 1929- Au&Wr
Dalton, Dorothy ConAu XR
Dalton, Douglas Alli Sup
Dalton, Edward Alli, Alli Sup, PoIre
D'Alton, Edward Alfred 1860- WhLA

Dalton, Edward Tuite d1822 Alli Sup, PoIre
Dalton, Frederic Thomas Alli Sup
Dalton, Gene W 1928- ConAu 25
Dalton, George William Alli Sup
Dalton, Gilbert MnBBF
Dalton, Grace E Alli Sup
Dalton, Henry Alli Sup
Dalton, Henry G Alli Sup
Dalton, Henry Robert Samuel Alli Sup
Dalton, J Alli
Dalton, James Alli, Alli Sup
Dalton, James Cecil 1848- WhLA
Dalton, James Forbes Alli Sup
Dalton, John 1709-1763 Alli, ChPo, NewC
Dalton, John 1766?-1844 Alli, BiDLA, BrAu 19
D'Alton, John 1792-1867 PoIre
D'Alton, John 1814-1874 Alli Sup
D'Alton, John 1882- CatA 1952
Dalton, John 1924- WrD 1976
Dalton, John Call 1825-1889 Alli Sup, DcAmA, DcNAA
Dalton, John Neale 1839- Alli Sup
Dalton, John Paul 1869- PoIre
Dalton, Joseph G Alli Sup
Dalton, Kit ChPo, ChPo S1
Dalton, L H ChPo S1
Dalton, Maria Regina Alli, BiDLA
Dalton, Mary Lee ChPo
Dalton, Melville IndAu 1917
Dalton, Michael 1554-1620 Alli
Dalton, Philip John Morgan 1923- Au&Wr
Dalton, Priscilla ConAu XR, WrD 1976
Dalton, R Alli
Dalton, Richard d1791 Alli
Dalton, Richard 1930- ConAu 57
Dalton, Roy C OxCan Sup
Dalton, Test 1875?-1945 AmA&B, AmLY, DcNAA, WhWNAA
Dalton, Thomas d1840 Alli Sup, BbtC
Dalton, VanBroadus 1885- OhA&B
Dalton, William 1821- Alli Sup, BbtC
Dalven, Rae 1904- ConAu 33
Dalvimart, M Alli
D'Alwis, James 1823-1878 Alli Sup, DcLEnL
Daly, Anne 1896- ConAu 29
Daly, Arnold 1875-1927 REn
Daly, Augustin 1838-1899 Alli Sup, AmA, AmA&B, BbD, CnDAL, CnThe, DcNAA, HsB&A, McGWD, ModWD, OxAm, REnAL, REnWD
Daly, Augustus A Alli Sup
Daly, Brian PoIre
Daly, Cahal Brendan 1917- WrD 1976
Daly, Carroll John 1889-1958 AmA&B, EncM&D, MnBBF, WhWNAA
Daly, Charles Patrick 1816-1899 Alli, Alli Sup, AmA, AmA&B, BbD, BiD&SB, CyAL 2, DcAmA, DcNAA
Daly, Cyril 1933- Au&Wr
Daly, Daniel Alli, BiDLA
Daly, Daniel 1595-1662 Alli
Daly, David Bingham Alli Sup
Daly, Mrs. Dominic D Alli Sup
Daly, Dominick 1798-1868 OxCan
Daly, Elizabeth 1878-1967 AmA&B, ConAu 23, ConAu 25, EncM&D, REnAL, TwCA Sup
Daly, Emily Joseph 1913- ConAu 9R
Daly, Eugene P 1860- PoIre
Daly, F Alli Sup
Daly, Frederic Alli Sup
Daly, George Thomas 1872- BkC 4
Daly, Guy D Alli Sup
Daly, J Bowles Alli Sup
Daly, James Jeremiah 1872- BkC 2, CatA 1947, ChPo S2
Daly, Jim ConAu XR
Daly, John Alli Sup
Daly, John Augustin 1838-1899 AmA, BiD&SB, BiDSA, DcAmA, DcNAA
Daly, Joseph 1891- AmSCAP 66
Daly, Joseph Francis 1840-1916 DcNAA
Daly, June ChPo
Daly, Lowrie John 1914- ConAu 13R, WrD 1976
Daly, Mary 1928- ConAu 25, WrD 1976
Daly, Sister Mary Virginia 1925- ConAu 17R

Daly, Maureen 1921- *AmA&B, AmNov, AuBYP, BkC 4, CatA 1947, ConAu XR, MorJA, REnAL, SmATA 2*
Daly, May Palmer *ChPo*
Daly, Myrtilla N *Alli Sup*
Daly, Nicholas 1863?- *ChPo S1, PoIre*
Daly, Patrick MacHale 1858- *Alli Sup, ChPo, PoIre*
Daly, Reginald Aldworth 1871- *OxCan, WhWNAA*
Daly, Robert Welter 1916- *ConAu 9R*
Daly, Saralyn R 1924- *ConAu 57*
Daly, Sheila John 1927?- *AuBYP, CatA 1952*
Daly, Thomas Augustine 1871-1948 *AmA&B, AmLY, BkC 1, CatA 1947, ChPo, ChPo S2, CnDAL, ConAmL, DcNAA, OxAm, REn, REnAL, TwCA, TwCA Sup, WhWNAA*
Daly, Victor *BlkAW*
Daly, William *Alli Sup*
Dalyell, Sir John Graham d1851 *Alli, BiDLA, DcEnL*
Dalyell, Robert Anstruther *Alli Sup*
Dalzel, Andrew 1750?-1806 *Alli*
Dalzel, Archibald *Alli, BiDLA*
Dalzel, James *Alli*
Dalzel, Peter *ConAu XR*
Dalzel Job, P 1913- *ConAu 13R*
Dalzell, Andrew *BiDLA*
Dalzell, James McCormick 1838-1924 *Alli Sup, OhA&B*
Dalzell, Kathleen Elizabeth 1919- *WrD 1976*
Dalzell, William Ronald 1910- *Au&Wr*
Dalzell-Ward, Arthur James 1914- *Au&Wr*
Dalziel, Alexander *Alli Sup*
Dalziel, Edith Margaret 1916- *Au&Wr*
Dalziel, Edward 1817- *ChPo, ChPo S1, ChPo S2*
Dalziel, Gavin 1764?- *ChPo*
Dalziel, George 1815-1902 *ChPo*
Dalziel, Gilbert 1853- *ChPo, WhLA*
Dalziel, Hugh *Alli Sup*
Dalziel, John Sanderson 1839-1937 *AmA&B*
Dalziel, Thomas B 1823- *ChPo, ChPo S1, ChPo S2*
Dam, Albert 1880- *Pen Eur*
Dam, Hari N 1921- *ConAu 57*
Dam, Jan 1896- *WhLA*
Dam, Niels Albert 1880- *CasWL*
Damachi, Ukandi 1942- *ConAu 45*
Daman, Miss *ChPo S1*
Daman, William *Alli*
Damant, Mary *Alli Sup*
Damas, David *OxCan Sup*
Damas, Leon-Gontran 1912- *CasWL, DcCLA*
Damascene, John *Pen Cl*
Damascenus *CasWL*
Damascius *Pen Cl*
Damasus I 366-381 *Pen Cl*
D'Amato, Anthony A 1937- *ConAu 29, WrD 1976*
D'Amato, Janet 1925- *ConAu 49, SmATA 9*
DaMatta, Joaquim Dias Cordeiro 1857-1894 *AfA 1*
Damaz, Paul F 1917- *ConAu 5R, WrD 1976*
Damberger, C F *Alli*
Dambourges, Francois 1742-1798 *BbtC, OxCan*
D'Ambra, Francesco 1499-1558 *CasWL*
D'Ambra, Lucio 1880-1940? *CasWL, EvEuW*
D'Ambrosio, Charles A 1932- *ConAu 23*
D'Ambrosio, Vinnie-Marie 1928- *ConAu 45, DrAP 1975*
Damdinsuren, Tsendiin 1908- *DcOrL 1*
Dame, Arthur Kent 1860- *WhWNAA*
Dame, Jean *ChPo S1*
Dame, Lawrence 1898- *Au&Wr, ConAu P-1*
Dame, Lorin Low And Collins, Frank S *Alli Sup*
D'Amelio, Dan 1927- *ConAu 33*
Damer, Mrs. *Alli*
Dameron, J Lasley 1925- *ConAu 53*
Dameron, Tadley 1917-1965 *AmSCAP 66*
Damerst, William A 1923- *ConAu 17R, WrD 1976*
Damets, Juan *Alli*
Damiani, Bruno Mario 1942- *ConAu 57*
Damiano, Laila *ConAu XR*
Damiao De Gois 1501-1574 *Pen Eur*
Damien, Father 1840-1888? *NewC, OxAm*

Damien DeVeuster, Joseph 1840-1889 *REn*
Damiens, Robert Francois 1714?-1757 *NewC, OxFr*
Damle, Krsnaji Kesav *DcOrL 2*
Damm, Christian Tobias 1699-1778 *DcEuL*
Damm, John S 1926- *ConAu 37*
Dammast, Jeanie Selina *Alli Sup*
Damnar, A D *Alli Sup*
Damocles 370?BC- *NewC*
Damodaragupta *DcOrL 2*
Damon *OxGer*
Damon And Pythias 370?BC- *NewC*
Damon, Howard Franklin 1833-1884 *Alli Sup, DcAmA, DcNAA*
Damon, Lindsay 1871-1940 *AmA&B, DcNAA, WhWNAA*
Damon, Robert *Alli Sup*
Damon, Samuel Chenery 1815-1885 *DcNAA*
Damon, Samuel Foster 1893-1971 *AmA&B, ChPo, ChPo S1, ChPo S2, REnAL, TwCA, TwCA Sup, WhWNAA*
Damon, Sophia M 1836-1888 *DcNAA*
Damon, Sophie M *Alli Sup*
Damon, Virgil Green 1895-1972 *ConAu 37, ConAu P-1*
Damon, William *Alli*
Damon, William Emerson 1838-1911 *Alli Sup, DcAmA, DcNAA*
Dampier, George *Alli*
Dampier, Thomas *Alli*
Dampier, William 1652-1715 *Alli, BrAu, Chmbr 2, DcLEnL, EvLB, NewC, OxEng, Pen Eng, REn*
Dampier, Sir William Cecil 1867-1952 *TwCA Sup*
Dampier, William James *Alli Sup*
Damrong, Prince *DcOrL 2*
Damrosch, Helen Therese *SmATA XR*
Damrosch, Leopold 1832-1885 *OxAm*
Damrosch, Leopold, Jr. 1941- *ConAu 45*
Damrosch, Walter Johannes 1862-1950 *AmSCAP 66, OxAm, REn, REnAL*
Damtoft, Walter A 1922- *ConAu 57*
Dan, Archdeacon *Alli*
Dan, Uncle *MnBBF*
Dana, Alexander Hamilton 1807-1887 *Alli Sup, DcAmA, DcNAA*
Dana, Amber *ConAu XR*
Dana, Arnold Guyot 1862-1947 *DcNAA*
Dana, Barbara 1940- *ConAu 17R*
Dana, Bill 1924- *AmSCAP 66*
Dana, Charles Anderson 1819-1897 *Alli, Alli Sup, AmA, AmA&B, BbD, BiD&SB, ChPo, CnDAL, DcAmA, DcNAA, OxAm, REn, REnAL*
Dana, Charles Edmund 1843-1914 *DcNAA*
Dana, Charles L 1852-1935 *DcAmA, DcNAA*
Dana, David D *Alli Sup*
Dana, E *Alli*
Dana, Edward Salisbury 1849-1935 *Alli Sup, DcAmA, DcNAA, WhWNAA*
Dana, Eliza A *Alli Sup*
Dana, Ethel Nathalie 1878- *WhWNAA*
Dana, Francis *ChPo S2, CyAL 1*
Dana, Francis d1811 *Alli*
Dana, Harvey Eugene 1888-1945 *AmA&B, DcNAA, TexWr, WhWNAA*
Dana, Henry Wadsworth Longfellow 1881-1950 *REnAL*
Dana, J F *BbtC*
Dana, J J *Alli Sup*
Dana, James 1735-1812 *Alli, DcAmA, DcNAA*
Dana, James Dwight 1813-1895 *Alli, Alli Sup, AmA, BbD, BiD&SB, CyAL 1, DcAmA, DcNAA, OxAm, REnAL*
Dana, James Freeman 1793-1827 *Alli, DcAmA, DcNAA*
Dana, James G *Alli*
Dana, John Cotton 1856-1929 *AmA&B, DcNAA, OxAm, WhWNAA*
Dana, Joseph 1742-1827 *Alli*
Dana, Julia M *ChPo, ChPo S1*
Dana, Julian *AmA&B*
Dana, Katharine Floyd 1835-1886 *Alli Sup, DcAmA, DcNAA*
Dana, Malcolm McGregor 1838-1897 *Alli Sup, DcNAA*

Dana, Marshall Newport 1885-1966 *WhPNW*
Dana, Marvin 1867- *AmA&B, DcAmA*
Dana, Mary *BiD&SB, DcAmA*
Dana, Mary Stanley Bunce 1810-1883 *AmA&B, ChPo, ChPo S1, DcNAA, FemPA*
Dana, Mercedes Cumming *TexWr*
Dana, Richard *ConAu XR, CyAL 1*
Dana, Richard Henry *Chmbr 3*
Dana, Richard Henry 1851-1931 *DcNAA, WhWNAA*
Dana, Richard Henry, Jr. 1815-1882 *Alli, Alli Sup, AmA, AmA&B, BbD, BiD&SB, CarSB, CasWL, Chmbr 3, CnDAL, CriT 3, CyAL 2, CyWA, DcAmA, DcEnL, DcLEnL, DcNAA, EvLB, MouLC 4, OxAm, OxEng, Pen Am, REn, REnAL, WebEAL*
Dana, Richard Henry, Sr. 1787-1879 *Alli, AmA, AmA&B, BbD, BiD&SB, ChPo, ChPo S1, CnDAL, CyAL 1, DcAmA, DcEnL, DcLEnL, DcNAA, EvLB, OxAm, Pen Am, REn, REnAL*
Dana, Richard Turner 1876- *WhWNAA*
Dana, Robert 1929- *ConAu 33, ConP 1970, ConP 1975, DrAP 1975, WrD 1976*
Dana, Samuel Luther 1795-1868 *Alli, DcAmA, DcNAA*
Dana, Samuel Worcester 1828-1921 *DcNAA*
Dana, Stephen Winchester 1840-1910 *DcNAA*
Dana, William B *Alli Sup*
Dana, William Coombs 1810-1873 *BiDSA, DcAmA, DcNAA*
Dana, William F *Alli Sup*
Dana, William Henry 1846-1916 *DcNAA*
Dana, Mrs. William Starr *DcAmA*
Danagher, Edward F 1919- *ConAu 9R*
Danaher, Franklin M *Alli Sup*
Danaher, Kevin 1913- *ConAu 33*
Danby, Francis 1793-1861 *ChPo S1*
Danby, Frank 1864-1916 *Alli Sup, BiD&SB, LongC*
Danby, Hope 1899- *Au&Wr, ConAu P-1*
Danby, John F 1911- *Au&Wr*
Danby, Mary *WrD 1976*
Danby, Miles William 1925- *ConAu 13R*
Danby, Thomas Osborne, Earl Of *Alli*
Danby, Thomas William *Alli Sup*
Dance, Charles Daniel *Alli Sup*
Dance, Edward Herbert 1894- *ConAu 37, WrD 1976*
Dance, F E X 1929- *ConAu 1R*
Dance, George d1824 *Alli, BiDLA*
Dance, Stanley Frank 1910- *Au&Wr, ConAu 17R, WrD 1976*
Dancer *Alli*
Dancer, John 1630?-1700? *Alli, PoIre*
Dancer, Thomas *Alli, BiDLA*
Dancer, William E *BlkAW*
Danchell, Frederick Hahn *Alli Sup*
Dancing Chancellor, The *NewC*
Danckwortt, Peter 1876- *WhLA*
D'Ancona, Alessandro 1835-1914 *CasWL*
D'Ancona, Mirella Levi 1919- *ConAu 53*
Dancourt, Florent Carton 1661-1725 *BiD&SB, CasWL, CnThe, DcEuL, EuA, EvEuW, McGWD, OxFr, REn, REnWD*
Dancy, Elizabeth 1509- *Alli*
Dancy, John Christopher 1920- *Au&Wr, WrD 1976*
Dancy, M M *WhWNAA*
Dancy, Walter 1946- *BlkAW*
Dandieu, Arnaud 1897- *WhLA*
Dandin 650?- *CasWL, DcOrL 2, Pen Cl*
Dandliker, Karl 1849- *BiD&SB*
Dandridge, Bartholomew 1691-1763? *BkIE*
Dandridge, Mrs. Danske 1858- *Alli Sup, AmA&B, BiDSA, DcAmA*
Dandridge, Raymond Garfield 1882-1930 *BlkAW, OhA&B*
Dandurand, Albert *OxCan*
Dandurand, Raoul *OxCan Sup*
Dandy, Walter Edward 1886-1946 *DcNAA, WhWNAA*
Dane, Arnold *MnBBF*
Dane, Carl *ConAu XR*
Dane, Clemence 1888-1965 *Chmbr 3, CnMD, DcLEnL, EncM&D, EvLB, LongC, McGWD, ModBL, ModWD, NewC,*

REn, TwCA, TwCA Sup, TwCW, WhLA
Dane, Coventry *Alli Sup*
Dane, Donald *MnBBF*
Dane, Herbert *ChPo*
Dane, James *Alli Sup*
Dane, John *Alli*
Dane, Lawrence *MnBBF*
Dane, Mark *ConAu XR, WrD 1976*
Dane, Mary 1905- *ConAu XR*
Dane, Merton *MnBBF*
Dane, Nathan 1752-1834? *Alli, DcAmA*
Dane, Richard *MnBBF*
Dane, Rupert *MnBBF*
Dane, Susan Martha 1849-1896 *ChPo S1*
Danelley, Elizabeth Otis 1838- *BiDSA*
Danelski, David J 1930- *ConAu 13R*
Danelson, Effa Eliza 1860- *WhWNAA*
Danenhower, John Wilson 1849-1887 *Alli Sup, DcAmA, DcNAA*
Daneo, Giovanni 1824- *BbD, BiD&SB*
Danes, John *Alli*
Danes, Pierre 1497-1577 *DcEuL*
Danesford, Earle *MnBBF*
Danesh, Ahmad *DcOrL 3*
Danesport, Lord 1853- *WhLA*
D'Anethan, Baroness E Mary *WhLA*
Danett, Thomas *Alli*
Danford, Harry Edmund 1879- *OhA&B*
Danford, Howard G 1904- *ConAu P-1*
Danforth, Eleanor Rinn 1883- *WhWNAA*
Danforth, Elizabeth Hanly *ChPo S2*
Danforth, H G *Alli Sup*
Danforth, Harry *HsB&A Sup*
Danforth, Henry Gold 1854-1918 *DcNAA*
Danforth, John 1660-1730 *Alli, DcAmA, DcNAA*
Danforth, Joshua Noble 1798-1861 *Alli Sup, BiDSA, DcAmA, DcNAA*
Danforth, Keyes 1822-1897 *DcNAA*
Danforth, Sister Maria Del Rey *BkC 5*
Danforth, Parke *Alli Sup*
Danforth, Paul M *WrD 1976*
Danforth, Samuel 1626-1674 *Alli, DcAmA, DcNAA*
Danforth, Samuel 1666-1727 *Alli, BiD&SB, DcAmA, DcNAA*
Danforth, Thomas *Alli*
Dangar, James George *Alli Sup*
Dange, Henri *DcAmA*
Dangeau, P DeCourcillon, Marquis De 1638-1720 *BiD&SB, DcEuL, OxFr, REn*
D'Angelo, Edward 1932- *ConAu 37*
D'Angelo, Lou *ConAu XR*
D'Angelo, Luciano 1932- *ConAu 33*
D'Angelo, Pascal 1894- *ChPo S1*
Dangerfield, Abner Walker 1883- *BlkAW*
Dangerfield, Balfour *ConAu XR, SmATA 2*
Dangerfield, Captain *MnBBF*
Dangerfield, Clint *ConAu XR, WrD 1976*
Dangerfield, Clinton *BiDSA, ChPo*
Dangerfield, Elma Tryphosa Birkett 1917- *Au&Wr*
Dangerfield, George Bubb 1904- *AmA&B, ConAu 9R, OxAm, PoIre, WorAu, WrD 1976*
Dangerfield, J *Alli*
Dangerfield, John *Alli Sup*
Dangerfield, Margaret S *ChPo*
Dangerfield, Robert George 1824-1858 *Alli Sup*
Dangerfield, Stanley William 1911- *Au&Wr*
Dangerfield, Thomas *Alli*
Dangle *WhLA*
Danhof, Clarence H 1911- *ConAu 37*
Dani, Ahmad Hasan 1920- *ConAu 13R*
Danican, Francois-Andre 1727-1795 *OxFr*
Daniel d745 *BiB S*
Daniel Adam Z Veleslavina *CasWL*
Daniel Church *BiB N*
Daniel De Merlai 1155?- *BiB N*
Daniel, The Well-Languaged *DcEnL*
Daniel Von Soest 1490?-1539? *CasWL, OxGer*
Daniel, Anita *AuBYP*
Daniel, Antoine 1601-1648 *OxCan*
Daniel, Arnaut *AtlBL, EuA, REn*
Daniel, Charles 1592-1661 *OxCan*
Daniel, Charles Floyd 1901- *WhWNAA*
Daniel, Charles Henry Olive 1856-1909 *ChPo*

Daniel, Edward Morton 1848- *Alli Sup*
Daniel, Eliza Farnsworth *Alli Sup*
Daniel, Evan *Alli Sup*
Daniel, Ferdinand Eugene 1839-1914 *BiDSA, DcNAA*
Daniel, Francois 1820-1908 *DcNAA*
Daniel, G *Alli Sup*
Daniel, George *Alli, BiDLA*
Daniel, George 1616-1657 *CasWL*
Daniel, George 1789-1864 *Alli Sup*
Daniel, George Bernard, Jr. 1927- *ConAu 13R*
Daniel, Gloria *BlkAW*
Daniel, Glyn E 1914- *Au&Wr, ConAu 57, EncM&D, TwCW*
Daniel, Godfrey *Alli*
Daniel, Guy 1912- *Au&Wr*
Daniel, Hawthorne 1890- *AmA&B, Au&Wr, ConAu 5R, JBA 1934, JBA 1951, SmATA 8, WhWNAA, WrD 1976*
Daniel, Henry John 1818- *Alli Sup*
Daniel, James Walter 1856- *BiDSA, DcNAA*
Daniel, Jerry C 1937- *ConAu 33*
Daniel, John *Alli*
Daniel, John Franklin 1873-1942 *DcNAA, WhWNAA*
Daniel, John Moncure 1825-1865 *Alli Sup, BiDSA, DcAmA, DcNAA*
Daniel, John T *DrAP 1975*
Daniel, John Warwick 1842-1910 *Alli Sup, BiDSA, DcAmA, DcNAA*
Daniel, Lewis C 1901- *ChPo S1*
Daniel, Mrs. Mackenzie *Alli*
Daniel, Martha Ann *ChPo S1*
Daniel, Mary Samuel *ChPo S2*
Daniel, Norman 1919- *ConAu 57*
Daniel, Pete 1938- *ConAu 37, WrD 1976*
Daniel, Peter Augustin *Alli Sup*
Daniel, Portia Bird *BlkAW*
Daniel, Ralph T 1921- *ConAu 53*
Daniel, Richard *Alli, PoIre*
Daniel, Robert L 1923- *ConAu 33*
Daniel, Mrs. Robert Mackenzie *Alli Sup*
Daniel, Robert Thomas *BiDSA*
Daniel, Robert W 1915- *ConAu 25*
Daniel, Roland *MnBBF, WhLA*
Daniel, Royal 1870- *BiDSA*
Daniel, Samuel *Alli*
Daniel, Samuel 1562-1619 *Alli, AtlBL, BbD, BiD&SB, BiDLA, BrAu, CasWL, ChPo, ChPo S1, Chmbr 1, CnE&AP, CrE&SL, CriT 1, DcEnA, DcEnL, DcEuL, DcLEnL, EvLB, MouLC 1, NewC, OxEng, Pen Eng, PoLE, REn, REnWD, WebEAL*
Daniel, T *Alli*
Daniel, W L 1876- *WhWNAA*
Daniel, William *Alli, BiDLA Sup*
Daniel, William Barker 1753-1833 *Alli, BiDLA, Br&AmS*
Daniel, William Thomas Shave 1806- *Alli Sup*
Daniel, Yuri 1926- *TwCW*
Daniel-Rops, Henry 1901-1965 *BkC 6, CatA 1952, EncWL*
Daniell, Albert Scott 1906-1965 *ConAu 5R*
Daniell, Alfred *Alli Sup*
Daniell, Charles Addison *Alli Sup*
Daniell, Clarmont John *Alli Sup*
Daniell, David Scott *ConAu XR*
Daniell, E R *Alli*
Daniell, Miss G F S *Alli Sup*
Daniell, Jere Rogers 1932- *ConAu 29*
Daniell, John Frederick 1790-1845 *Alli, DcEnL*
Daniell, John Jeremiah 1819- *Alli Sup*
Daniell, John Mortlock *Alli Sup*
Daniell, Moses Grant 1836-1909 *DcNAA*
Daniell, Rosemary *DrAP 1975*
Daniell, Samuel *Alli*
Daniell, Thomas 1750-1840 *Alli, BiDLA*
Daniell, W *ChPo*
Daniell, W H *Alli Sup*
Daniell, William D 1769-1837 *Alli, BiDLA*
Daniello, Bernardino d1565 *REn*
Daniells, Roy 1902- *Au&Wr, CanWr, ConAu 57, ConP 1970, ConP 1975, OxCan, OxCan Sup, WrD 1976*
Danielou, Alain 1907- *Au&Wr*
Danielou, Jean 1905-1974 *Au&Wr, CatA 1952, ConAu 23, ConAu 49*

Daniels, Anna Kleegman 1893-1970 *ConAu 29*
Daniels, Arlene Kaplan 1930- *ConAu 29*
Daniels, Arthur James 1863- *MnBBF*
Daniels, C G *Alli Sup*
Daniels, Cora 1852- *BbD, BiD&SB, BiDSA, DcAmA*
Daniels, David 1933- *ConAu 53*
Daniels, Draper 1913- *ConAu 53*
Daniels, Elizabeth Adams 1920- *ConAu 37, WrD 1976*
Daniels, Farrington 1889-1972 *Au&Wr, ConAu 5R, ConAu 37*
Daniels, Francis Potter 1869- *WhWNAA*
Daniels, Frederick Edward 1908- *Au&Wr*
Daniels, George Fisher 1820- *Alli Sup, DcAmA*
Daniels, George H 1935- *ConAu 25*
Daniels, George M 1927- *ConAu 29*
Daniels, Gertrude *DcAmA*
Daniels, Guy 1919- *ChPo S1, ConAu 21, SmATA 7*
Daniels, Harold R 1919- *ConAu 17R*
Daniels, Ionia *BlkAW*
Daniels, J W *Alli Sup*
Daniels, Jeffery Arthur 1932- *Au&Wr*
Daniels, John 1881- *WhWNAA*
Daniels, John Clifford 1915- *ConAu 13R*
Daniels, John S *ConAu XR*
Daniels, Jonathan 1902- *AmA&B, Au&Wr, AuBYP, CnDAL, ConAu 49, OxAm, REn, REnAL, TwCA, TwCA Sup*
Daniels, Josephus 1862-1948 *AmA&B, BiDSA, DcNAA, OxAm, REn, REnAL*
Daniels, Julia *ChPo*
Daniels, Lilla Wood *Au&Wr*
Daniels, Mabel E *ChPo*
Daniels, Mabel Wheeler 1879- *AmSCAP 66, WhWNAA*
Daniels, Mary 1937- *WrD 1976*
Daniels, Mose *ChPo S1*
Daniels, R Balfour 1900- *ConAu 49*
Daniels, Robert V 1926- *ConAu 1R*
Daniels, Roger 1927- *ConAu 5R, MnBBF*
Daniels, Sally 1931- *ConAu 1R*
Daniels, Steven Lloyd 1945- *ConAu 33*
Daniels, William Haven 1836- *Alli Sup, BiD&SB, DcAmA*
Daniels, William Henry *Alli Sup*
Daniels, Winthrop More 1867-1943? *DcAmA, DcNAA, OhA&B*
Daniels, Wylie Johnston 1888-1951 *IndAu 1917*
Danielson, Barbara *ChPo*
Danielson, Frances Weld *ChPo S2*
Danielson, J D *ConAu 57*
Danielson, Mrs. Jacques S *AmNov XR*
Danielson, Michael N 1934- *ConAu 33*
Danielson, Richard Ely 1885-1957 *AmA&B, Br&AmS*
Danielsson, Bengt Emmerik 1921- *Au&Wr*
Daniere, Andre L 1926- *ConAu 9R*
Daniil *CasWL*
Daniil The Exile *CasWL*
Daniil The Pilgrim *DcRusL*
Daniil The Prisoner *DcRusL, Pen Eur*
Danilevsky, Grigory Petrovich 1829-1890 *BbD, BiD&SB, CasWL, DcRusL, EvEuW*
Danilevsky, Nikolay Yakovlevich 1822-1885 *CasWL, DcRusL*
Danilo *Pen Eur*
Danilov, Kirsha *CasWL*
Danilov, Victor J 1924- *ConAu 13R*
Danis, H H *Alli*
Danish, Barbara 1948- *ConAu 57*
Danker, Frederick William 1920- *ConAu 13R*
Danker, William John 1914- *ConAu 13R, WrD 1976*
Danks, Heart Pease 1834-1903 *DcNAA*
Danks, William *Alli Sup*
Dann, Hollis Ellsworth 1861-1939 *DcNAA, WhWNAA*
Dann, Jack 1945- *ConAu 49, DrAF 1976*
Dann, Uriel 1922- *ConAu 25*
Dannatt, James Trevor 1920- *Au&Wr*
Dannay, Frederic 1905- *AmA&B, AuBYP, ConAu 1R, DcLEnL, EncM&D, EvLB, LongC, Pen Am, REn, TwCA,*

Darling, Flora Adams 1840-1910 *Alli Sup, AmA&B, BiD&SB, DcAmA, DcNAA*
Darling, Frank Clayton 1925- *ConAu 17R*
Darling, Frank Fraser 1903- *OxEng*
Darling, Fraser 1903- *LongC*
Darling, George *Alli Sup*
Darling, Grace *OxCan*
Darling, Grace Horsley 1815-1842 *NewC*
Darling, Henry 1823-1891 *Alli Sup, DcAmA, DcNAA*
Darling, Hope *AmLY XR*
Darling, Isabella Fleming 1861-1903 *ChPo, ChPo S1, ChPo S2*
Darling, J J *Alli*
Darling, James *Alli*
Darling, Jay Norwood 1876-1962 *AmA&B, WhWNAA*
Darling, John *Alli, Alli Sup*
Darling, Joseph Robinson 1872- *WhWNAA*
Darling, Kathy 1943- *ConAu XR, SmATA XR*
Darling, Lilian *ChPo*
Darling, Lois MacIntyre 1917- *AmA&B, AuBYP, ConAu 5R, IlCB 1966, SmATA 3, WrD 1976*
Darling, Louis 1916-1970 *AmA&B, AuBYP, ConAu 5R, IlCB 1956, IlCB 1966, MorJA, SmATA 3*
Darling, Mary Greenleaf 1848- *Alli Sup, AmA&B, ChPo, DcAmA, DcNAA*
Darling, Mary Kathleen 1943- *ConAu 53, SmATA 9*
Darling, Peter Middleton *Alli, BiDLA*
Darling, Richard L 1925- *ChPo S1, ConAu 23*
Darling, Samuel Boyd 1873-1948 *DcNAA*
Darling, T *Alli Sup*
Darling, W Stewart *BbtC*
Darling, William 1815-1884 *Alli Sup, DcAmA, DcNAA*
Darling, William Stewart 1818-1886 *DcNAA*
Darling, Sir William Young 1885- *ChPo S1, WhLA*
Darlinghurst, Daniel *Alli Sup*
Darlington, Alice B 1906-1973 *ConAu 25, ConAu 41*
Darlington, Charles F 1904- *ConAu 25*
Darlington, Cyril Dean 1903- *Au&Wr, ConAu 9R*
Darlington, George E d1901? *Br&AmS*
Darlington, H A *Alli Sup*
Darlington, James Henry 1856-1930 *AnMV 1926, ChPo, ChPo S1, DcNAA, WhWNAA*
Darlington, Marwood *ChPo*
Darlington, Mary *OxCan*
Darlington, Oscar Gilpin 1909- *Au&Wr*
Darlington, T *Alli Sup*
Darlington, Thomas 1858-1945 *Alli Sup, DcNAA*
Darlington, W A 1890- *LongC, WhLA*
Darlington, William 1782-1863 *Alli, BiD&SB, DcAmA, DcNAA*
Darlington, William Aubrey 1890- *Au&Wr, ConAu P-1, DcLEnL*
Darlton, Clark *ConAu XR*
Darmesteter, Madame *Chmbr 3*
Darmesteter, Agnes Mary Frances 1857- *Alli Sup, BbD, BiD&SB*
Darmesteter, Arsene 1846-1888 *DcEuL, OxFr*
Darmesteter, James 1849-1894 *Alli Sup, BbD, BiD&SB, OxFr*
Darmesteter, Mary 1857- *NewC*
Darmstaedter, Paul 1877- *WhLA*
Darnall, Frank Mauzy 1882- *TexWr*
Darnall, Marcy Bradshaw 1872- *WhWNAA*
Darnell, Henry Faulkner 1831-1915? *Alli Sup, BbtC, ChPo S1, DcAmA, DcNAA*
Darnell, Lilian Mabel 1912- *Au&Wr*
Darnell, W N *Alli*
Darnley, Lord Henry Stuart 1545-1567 *NewC, REn*
Darnton, Peter William *Alli Sup*
Darr, Ann 1920- *ConAu 57, DrAP 1975*
Darracott, R W *Alli*
Darragh, Darrash *WhWNAA*
Darrah, David Harley 1894- *OhA&B*
Darrah, William C 1909- *ConAu 57*
Darran, Mark *MnBBF*

Darrash Darragh *WhWNAA*
Darrell, Guy *MnBBF*
Darrell, John *Alli*
Darrell, John Harvey *Alli Sup*
Darrell, Joyce *Alli Sup*
Darrell, Margery *ChPo S2*
Darrell, Robery Donaldson 1903- *AmA&B*
Darrell, Walter *MnBBF*
Darrich, Sybah *WrD 1976*
Darroch, John *BbtC*
Darroch, Maurice A 1903- *ConAu 19*
Darrow, Benjamin Harrison 1889-1950 *OhA&B*
Darrow, Clarence R *ChPo S2*
Darrow, Clarence Seward 1857-1938 *AmA&B, DcLEnL, DcNAA, OhA&B, OxAm, REn, REnAL, TwCA, TwCA Sup, WhWNAA*
Darrow, Floyd Lavern 1880- *WhWNAA*
Darrow, Jason 1787-1868 *OhA&B*
Darrow, Karl X 1891- *WhWNAA*
Darrow, Ralph C 1918- *ConAu 61*
Darrow, Richard W 1915- *ConAu 21*
Darrow, Whitney 1881-1970 *AmA&B*
Darrow, Whitney, Jr. 1909- *AmA&B, ConAu 61*
Darsie, Charles 1872-1948 *DcNAA, OhA&B*
Darst, Lillie C 1846-1883 *OhA&B*
Darst, W Glen 1896- *AmSCAP 66*
Dart *Alli*
Dart, J H *Alli*
Dart, John *Alli, Alli Sup*
Dart, Joseph Henry 1817-1887 *Alli Sup*
Dart, Raymond Arthur 1893- *Au&Wr, ConAu P-1, WhLA*
Dart, Rufus, II *WhWNAA*
D'Artega, Alfonso 1907- *AmSCAP 66*
Dartnall, Henry *Alli Sup*
Dartnell, G E *Alli Sup*
Dartnell, George H *BbtC*
Darton, A W *WhWNAA*
Darton, Frederick Joseph Harvey d1936 *CarSB, ChPo*
Darton, J M *Alli Sup*
Darton, John *Alli Sup*
Darton, Margaret E *Alli Sup*
Darton, Nelson Horatio 1865-1948 *DcNAA, WhWNAA*
Darton, Nicholas *Alli*
Darton, Thomas Gates *Alli Sup*
Dartt, Mary *Alli Sup*
Daru, Count Pierre Antoine 1767-1829 *BiD&SB, OxFr*
D'Arusmont, Frances 1795-1852 *Alli, BiD&SB, DcAmA, OhA&B*
Daruwalla, Keki Nasserwanji 1937- *ConP 1970*
Darvas, Arpad 1927- *WhGrA*
Darvas, Jozsef 1912- *CrCD*
Darvas, Nicholas 1920- *ConAu 61*
Darveau, Louis Michel 1883-1875 *BbtC, DcNAA, OxCan*
Darvill, Fred T, Jr. 1927- *ConAu 57*
Darwall, Mrs. E *Alli*
Darwall, Elizabeth *BiDLA*
Darwall, John *Alli, BiDLA*
Darwin, B And E *ChPo S1*
Darwin, Beatrice *IlBYP*
Darwin, Bernard Richard Meirian 1876-1961 *ChPo, LongC, WhLA*
Darwin, Charles 1758-1778 *Alli*
Darwin, Charles Robert 1809-1882 *Alli, Alli Sup, AtlBL, BbD, BiD&SB, BrAu 19, CarSB, CasWL, Chmbr 3, CyWA, DcEnA, DcEnA Ap, DcEnL, DcEuL, DcLEnL, EvLB, MouLC 4, NewC, OxEng, Pen Eng, RCom, REn, WebEAL*
Darwin, Desmond *MnBBF*
Darwin, Edward Levett *Alli Sup*
Darwin, Elinor May d1954 *ChPo, ConICB, IlCB 1945, IlCB 1956*
Darwin, Erasmus 1731-1802 *Alli, BbD, BiD&SB, BrAu, CasWL, ChPo, ChPo S1, Chmbr 2, DcEnA, DcEnL, DcEuL, DcLEnL, EvLB, NewC, OxEng, Pen Eng, REn, WebEAL*
Darwin, Francis 1848-1925 *Alli Sup, DcEuL*
Darwin, George Henry *Alli Sup*
Darwin, George Howard 1845- *Alli Sup*

Darwin, Leonard 1850- *IlBYP, WhLA*
Darwin, Robert Waring *Alli, BiDLA*
Dary, David Archie 1934- *ConAu 29, WrD 1976*
Dary, Michael *Alli*
Daryl, A J *Alli Sup, MnBBF*
Daryl, Philippe *Alli Sup*
Daryl, Sidney *Alli Sup, ChPo*
Daryll, A B *ChPo S1*
Daryush, Elizabeth Bridges 1887- *ChPo, ChPo S2, ConAu 49, ConLC 6*
Das, Deb Kumar 1935- *ConP 1970, ConP 1975, REn, WrD 1976*
Das, Durga 1900-1974 *ConAu 29, ConAu 49*
Das, Gurcharan 1943- *ConAu 33*
Das, Jagannath Prasad 1931- *ConAu 57*
Das, Jibanananda 1899-1954 *DcOrL 2*
Das, Kamala 1934- *CasWL, ConP 1970, ConP 1975, WrD 1976*
Das, Manmath Nath 1929- *ConAu 13R*
Das, Prafulla Chandra 1927- *Au&Wr*
Das, Ranendra Kumar 1901- *IndAu 1917*
Das, Sarala *DcOrL 2*
Dascalos, Alexandre Mendonca DeOliveira *AfA 1*
Dasent, Sir George Webbe 1817-1896 *Alli Sup, AnCL, BbD, BiD&SB, BrAu 19, Chmbr 3, DcEnA, DcEnL, DcEuL, EvLB, NewC, OxEng, St&VC, WhCL*
DasGupta, Jyotirindra 1933- *ConAu 53*
DasGupta, Narendra Kumar 1910- *BiDPar*
Dash, Countess 1804-1872 *BbD, BiD&SB, OxFr*
Dash, Joan 1925- *ConAu 49*
Dash, Julian 1916- *AmSCAP 66*
Dash, Paul R *DcNAA*
Dash, Thomas R 1897- *AmA&B*
Dash, Tony 1945- *ConAu 33*
Dashiell, Alfred Sheppard 1901-1970 *AmA&B, WhWNAA*
Dashiell, John Frederick 1888- *IndAu 1917*
Dashiell, Margaret *ChPo S1*
Dashiell, T G *Alli Sup*
Dashkova, Ekaterina Romanovna 1743?-1810 *CasWL, DcEuL, EvEuW*
Dashmore, Frederick *Alli Sup*
Dashti 'Ali 1901?- *CasWL, DcOrL 3*
Dashwood, Edmee Elizabeth Monica *LongC*
Dashwood, Elizabeth Monica 1890-1943 *NewC, REn, WhLA*
Dashwood, George Henry 1802-1869 *Alli Sup*
Dashwood, J B *Alli Sup*
Dashwood, James *Alli, BiDLA*
Dashwood, Percy *MnBBF*
Dashwood, Richard Lewes *Alli Sup, OxCan*
Dashwood, Robert Julian 1899- *ConAu P-1*
DaSilveira, Onesimo 1935- *AfA 1*
Daskalos, Alexandre 1924-1961 *AfA 1*
Daskam, Josephine Dodge 1876- *AmA&B, BiD&SB, ChPo, ChPo S2, DcAmA*
Dasmann, Raymond 1919- *ConAu 5R*
Dass, Petter 1647-1707? *CasWL, DcEuL, EuA, EvEuW, Pen Eur*
Dassin, Jules *ConDr*
Dassler, C F W *Alli Sup*
Dassonville, Michel *OxCan Sup*
D'Assoucy, Charles Coippeau 1605-1679 *BbD, BiD&SB*
Dassy, G F *Alli Sup*
Dastur, Jahangir Fardunji 1886- *Au&Wr*
Date, Henry *ChPo S2*
Dater, Henry M 1909?-1974 *ConAu 49*
Dates, Henry Baldwin 1869- *WhWNAA*
Dathenus, Petrus 1531?-1588 *CasWL*
Dathorne, O R 1934- *ConAu 57, ConNov 1972, ConNov 1976, ConP 1970, WrD 1976*
Dati, Giuliano d1524 *CasWL*
Dati, Goro 1363-1465 *DcEuL*
Dati, Gregorio 1362-1435 *CasWL*
Dati, Leonardo DiPiero 1408-1472 *CasWL*
Datskevich, Sergei Ignatievich 1919- *WhGrA*
Datta, Michael Madhusudan 1824-1873 *DcOrL 2*
Datta, Sudhindranath 1901-1960 *DcOrL 2, REn*
D'Attilio, Anthony *IlBYP*
Datzell, Kathleen E *OxCan Sup*

Dau, Frederick W 1880- *WhWNAA*
Dau, William Herman Theodore 1864-1944 *DcNAA*
Daube, David 1909- *Au&Wr, ConAu 1R, WrD 1976*
Daubeney, Charles *BiDLA, BiDLA Sup*
Daubenton, Louis Jean Marie 1716-1799 *BiD&SB, OxFr*
Daubeny, Charles *BbtC*
Daubeny, Charles 1744-1827 *Alli*
Daubeny, Charles Giles Bridle 1795-1867 *Alli, Alli Sup*
Daubeny, E Clayton *Alli Sup*
Daubeny, Henry *Alli Sup*
Daubeny, Peter 1921-1975 *ConAu 61*
Dauber, Samuel 1882-1965 *ChPo*
D'Auberteuil, Hilliard *BbtC*
D'Aubigne *EvEuW*
D'Aubigne, Jean Henri Merle 1794-1872 *BbD, BiD&SB*
D'Aubigne, Theodore Agrippa 1552-1630 *Pen Eur*
Daubigny *Alli*
Daubigny, Charles Francois 1817-1878 *AtlBL*
Daubler, Theodor 1876-1934 *ClDMEuL, EncWL, ModGL, OxGer, Pen Eur*
Daubon, Jose Antonio 1840-1922 *PueRA*
Dauborne, Robert *Alli*
Daubuz, Charles 1670?-1740? *Alli*
Dauby And Leng *Alli*
Daucet, N B *Alli*
Dauchy, George K *Alli Sup*
Daudet, Alphonse 1840-1897 *AtlBL, BbD, BiD&SB, ChPo, ChPo S2, ClDMEuL, CyWA, DcBiA, DcEuL, EvEuW, McGWD, NewC, OxEng, OxFr, Pen Eur, RCom, REn*
Daudet, Alphonse Marie Leon 1867-1942 *EvEuW*
Daudet, Ernest 1837- *BbD, BiD&SB*
Daudet, Leon 1867?-1942 *CasWL, ClDMEuL, EncWL, NewC, OxFr, REn*
Daudet, Louis Marie Alphonse 1840-1897 *CasWL, EuA*
Dauenhauer, Richard L 1942- *ConAu 61*
Dauer, Dorothea 1917- *ConAu 37*
Dauer, Victor Paul 1909- *ConAu 17R, IndAu 1917*
Dauge, Henri *DcNAA*
Daugert, Stanley M 1918- *ConAu 17R*
Daughdrill, James H, Jr. 1934- *ConAu 41*
Daughen, Joseph R 1935- *ConAu 33*
Daugherty, Carroll Roop 1900- *AmA&B*
Daugherty, Charles Michael 1914- *AuBYP, IlCB 1956*
Daugherty, Edgar Fay 1874-1957 *IndAu 1917*
Daugherty, H H *Alli Sup*
Daugherty, Harry Micajah 1860-1941 *OhA&B*
Daugherty, Harry R 1883- *IlCB 1956*
Daugherty, Harvey Harrison 1841-1919 *IndAu 1816*
Daugherty, James Henry 1889-1974 *AmA&B, AmLY, AuBYP, BkP, ChPo, ChPo S1, ConAu 49, IlCB 1945, IlCB 1956, IlCB 1966, JBA 1934, JBA 1951, Newb 1922, St&VC*
Daugherty, Robert Long 1885- *IndAu 1917, WhWNAA*
Daughters, Charles G 1897- *OhA&B*
Daughters, Freeman 1873- *IndAu 1816*
Daughtrey, Anne Scott 1920- *ConAu 17R, WrD 1976*
Daughty, Stella *ChPo*
Dauguet, Marie 1865- *OxFr*
D'Aulaire, Edgar Parin 1898- *AmA&B, AnCL, AuBYP, BkCL, ConAu 49, ConICB, IlBYP, IlCB 1945, IlCB 1956, IlCB 1966, JBA 1951, SmATA 5, St&VC*
D'Aulaire, Ingri 1904- *AmA&B, AnCL, AuBYP, BkCL, ConAu 49, IlBYP, IlCB 1945, IlCB 1956, IlCB 1966, JBA 1951, SmATA 5, St&VC*
D'Aulaire, Ingri And Edgar Parin *BkP, Cald 1938, ChPo S2, JBA 1934*
Daulat Kazi *DcOrL 2*
Daulby, Daniel *Alli, BiDLA*
D'Aulnoy, Countess 1650?-1705 *St&VC, WhCL*

Daulton, Agnes Warner McClelland 1867-1944 *AmA&B, DcNAA, OhA&B, WhWNAA*
Daulton, George 1861-1913 *DcNAA*
Daumal, Rene 1908-1944 *EncWL, Pen Eur*
Daumer, Georg Friedrich 1800-1875 *BbD, BiD&SB, OxGer*
Daumier, Honore 1808-1879 *AtlBL, OxFr, REn*
Daun, Leopold, Graf Von 1705-1766 *OxGer*
Daunce, Edward *Alli*
Dauncey, John *Alli*
Daunch, Virginia Obenchain 1919- *AmSCAP 66*
Dauney, William *Alli*
Daunou, Pierre-Claude-Francois 1761-1840 *OxFr*
Daunt, Achilles *Alli Sup*
Daunt, Achilles 1832-1878 *Alli Sup*
Daunt, Atherley *MnBBF*
Daunt, Edward Synge Townsend *Alli Sup*
Daunt, John *Alli Sup*
Daunt, William Joseph O'Neill 1807- *Alli Sup*
Dauphin *OxFr*
Dauphin D'Auvergne *CasWL*
Dauphin, Roma *OxCan Sup*
Daurat, Jean *OxFr*
D'Aurevilly, B *Pen Eur*
D'Aurevilly, Jules Amedee Barbey *EuA*
Dauster, Frank 1925- *ConAu 53*
Dauten, Carl Anton 1913- *ConAu 5R*
Dauthendey, Max 1867-1918 *ClDMEuL, EncWL, EvEuW, ModGL, OxGer, Pen Eur*
Dautzenberg, Johan Michel 1808-1869 *CasWL*
D'Auvergne, Edward *Alli*
D'Auvergne, Muriel Nelson *ChPo*
Dauw, Dean C 1933- *ConAu 53*
Davall, Peter d1768 *Alli*
Davalos, Marcelino 1879- *AmLY*
Davan, Kingsmill *Alli, BiDLA*
Davanzati, Bernardo 1529-1606 *CasWL*
Davanzati, Chiaro 1230?-1303? *CasWL*
D'Avanzo, Mario Louis 1931- *ConAu 41*
Dave, Haribhadra *DcOrL 2*
Dave, Narmadasankar *DcOrL 2*
Dave, Shyam *ConAu XR*
Daveiss, Joseph Hamilton 1774-1811 *DcNAA*
Daveiss, Maria 1814-1896 *DcAmA*
Davelcourt, D *Alli*
Daveluy, Paule Cloutier 1919- *ConAu 9R, OxCan Sup*
Davenant, Charles 1656-1714 *Alli, NewC*
Davenant, Francis *Alli Sup*
Davenant, John 1576-1641 *Alli*
Davenant, William *Alli*
Davenant, Sir William 1606-1668 *Alli, BbD, BiD&SB, BrAu, CasWL, ChPo, ChPo S1, Chmbr 1, CnE&AP, CnThe, CrE&SL, CyWA, DcEnA, DcEnL, DcEuL, EvLB, McGWD, NewC, OxEng, Pen Eng, PoLE, REn, REnWD, WebEAL*
Daveney, Mrs. Burton *Alli Sup*
Daveney, Thomas Beevor *Alli Sup*
Davenport, Adelaide *HsB&A*
Davenport, Alfred *Alli Sup*
Davenport, Amzi Benedict *Alli Sup*
Davenport, Arthur *Alli Sup*
Davenport, Audrey 1920- *Au&Wr*
Davenport, Baylis *WhWNAA*
Davenport, C A *ChPo S1*
Davenport, Carrie *Alli Sup*
Davenport, Charles 1895-1955 *AmSCAP 66*
Davenport, Charles Benedict 1866-1944 *AmLY, DcAmA, DcNAA, WhWNAA*
Davenport, Charlotte C *ChPo S2*
Davenport, Christopher 1598-1680 *Alli*
Davenport, Cyril James 1848- *WhLA*
Davenport, D E *Alli Sup*
Davenport, David N 1925- *AmSCAP 66*
Davenport, E *ChPo S1*
Davenport, E M *Alli Sup*
Davenport, Elvia Wiggins *TexWr*
Davenport, Emma Anne Georgina *Alli Sup*
Davenport, Eugene 1856-1941 *AmA&B, AmLY, DcNAA, WhWNAA*
Davenport, F *Alli Sup, ChPo S2*
Davenport, Frances Gardiner 1870-1927 *DcNAA*

Davenport, Frances Helen *HsB&A*
Davenport, Francine *ConAu XR*
Davenport, Francis *Alli*
Davenport, Francis William *Alli Sup*
Davenport, Gene L 1935- *ConAu 33*
Davenport, George Devereux *Alli Sup*
Davenport, Guy, Jr. 1927- *ConAu 33, ConLC 6, DrAF 1976*
Davenport, Gwen 1910- *AmA&B, Au&Wr, ConAu 9R*
Davenport, Henry *ChPo S2*
Davenport, Herbert Joseph 1861-1931 *DcAmA, DcNAA*
Davenport, Homer Calvin 1867-1912 *AmA&B, DcAmA, DcNAA*
Davenport, Humphrey *Alli*
Davenport, J B *Alli Sup*
Davenport, J W *Alli Sup*
Davenport, James 1716-1757 *DcNAA*
Davenport, Jennette *BlkAW*
Davenport, John *Alli, Alli Sup*
Davenport, John 1597-1670 *Alli, BiD&SB, CyAL 1, DcAmA, DcNAA, OxAm*
Davenport, John Gaylord 1840-1922 *DcNAA*
Davenport, John I *Alli Sup*
Davenport, John Marriott d1882 *Alli Sup*
Davenport, John Sidney *Alli Sup*
Davenport, Marcia 1903- *AmA&B, AmNov, AuBYP, ConAu 9R, DcLEnL, LongC, OxAm, REn, REnAL, TwCA Sup*
Davenport, Marianna Bonnell *ChPo S2*
Davenport, Millia 1895- *Au&Wr*
Davenport, Montague *Alli Sup*
Davenport, Mrs. N *OxCan*
Davenport, Pembroke M 1911- *AmSCAP 66*
Davenport, R A *Alli*
Davenport, Reuben Briggs 1852-1932 *Alli Sup, DcNAA, WhWNAA*
Davenport, Richard *Alli*
Davenport, Robert *Alli, BrAu, DcEnL*
Davenport, Robert d1651? *BiD&SB*
Davenport, Robert 1624?-1640 *BbD*
Davenport, Robert 1624?-1640? *Pen Eng*
Davenport, Russell 1899-1954 *AmA&B, REnAL*
Davenport, Samuel *Alli Sup*
Davenport, Samuel Thomas *Alli Sup*
Davenport, Selina *Alli, BiDLA Sup*
Davenport, Spencer *ConAu XR*
Davenport, Tex *MnBBF*
Davenport, Walter Rice 1855- *DcNAA, WhWNAA*
Davenport, William Bromley 1821-1884 *Alli Sup, Br&AmS*
Davenport, William Edwards 1862-1944 *DcNAA*
Davenport, William Henry 1908- *Au&Wr, ConAu 1R, WrD 1976*
Daventer, Henry *Alli*
Daventry, Leonard John 1915- *ConAu 17R*
D'Averanches *DcEnL*
Daves, Francis Marion 1903- *ConAu 45*
Daves, Jessica 1898?-1974 *ConAu 53*
Daves, Michael 1938- *ConAu 9R*
Davey, Annette L *Alli Sup*
Davey, Cyril James 1911- *Au&Wr, ConAu 5R*
Davey, Evelyn *ChPo S2*
Davey, Frank 1940- *ConP 1970, OxCan, OxCan Sup*
Davey, Gilbert 1913- *Au&Wr, ConAu P-1, WrD 1976*
Davey, Henry *Alli Sup*
Davey, Henry Norman 1888- *ChPo S1*
Davey, James George *Alli Sup*
Davey, John *Alli, ConAu 57*
Davey, John 1846-1923 *DcNAA, OhA&B*
Davey, Mary *Alli Sup*
Davey, Norman 1900- *Au&Wr*
Davey, R *Alli Sup*
Davey, Samuel *Alli Sup, PoIre*
Davey, William *Alli Sup*
Davey, William Harrison *Alli Sup*
Davezac, Auguste *CyAL 1*
D'Avezac, Auguste Genevieve Valentin 1777-1851 *BiDSA*
Daviault, Pierre 1899-1964 *CanWr, WhWNAA*
Davico, Oskar 1909- *Au&Wr, CasWL, EncWL Sup, ModSL 2, Pen Eur*
David *BiB N*

David 1000?BC-960?BC *DcOrL 3, NewC*
David 1340?-1400? *NewC*
David D'Angers, Pierre-Jean 1783-1856 *OxFr*
David Grayson *DcLEnL*
David Of Bangor *BiB N*
David, Saint 495?-589? *Alli, NewC, REn*
David Von Augsberg 1210?-1272? *DcEuL,*
OxGer
David, A H *BbtC*
David, Anne 1924- *ConAu 29*
David, Ap Gwillum *Alli*
David, Ben *Alli*
David, Benjamin 1896- *AmSCAP 66*
David, C *Alli Sup*
David, C G *Alli Sup*
David, Charles Alexander 1855- *WhWNAA*
David, Eduard Heinrich Rudolf 1863- *WhLA*
David, Elizabeth *Au&Wr*
David, Emily *ConAu XR*
David, Eugene *AuBYP*
David, Evan John 1881- *AmA&B*
David, Florence Nightingale 1909- *Au&Wr*
David, Gerard 1450?-1523 *AtlBL*
David, Hal 1921- *AmSCAP 66*
David, Heather M 1937- *ConAu 37,*
WrD 1976
David, Henry 1907- *AmA&B*
David, Henry P 1923- *ConAu 13R*
David, Ismar *ChPo S1*
David, Jacques Louis 1748-1825 *AtlBL, OxFr*
David, Jay *ConAu XR*
David, Jean 1908- *WhGrA*
David, Jean Baptiste 1761-1841 *BiDSA,*
DcAmA, DcNAA
David, Job *Alli*
David, Jonathan *SmATA 3*
David, Laurent Olivier 1840-1926 *DcNAA*
David, Laurent Olivier 1840-1925 *OxCan*
David, Lee 1891- *AmSCAP 66*
David, Lester 1914- *ConAu 37*
David, Louis 1748-1825 *REn*
David, M *Alli*
David, Mack 1912- *AmSCAP 66*
David, Martin H 1935- *ConAu 37*
David, Maurice R 1893- *AmA&B*
David, Michael *Alli*
David, Michael Robert 1932- *ConAu 53*
David, Nicholas *ConAu XR*
David, Paul T 1906- *ConAu 5R*
David, R *Alli*
David, S S *EarAB*
David, Stephen M 1934- *ConAu 33*
David, T W Edgeworth *Alli Sup*
David, Urbain *BiDSA*
David, Vincent 1924- *AmSCAP 66*
David, W L *Alli Sup*
David, William *ConAu XR*
David, Worton *ChPo*
David-Darnac, Maurice 1913- *Au&Wr*
David-Neel, Alexandra 1868-1969 *ConAu 25*
Davidescu, Nicolae 1888-1954 *CasWL*
Davidge, J B F And Kimball, J G *Alli Sup*
Davidge, John *Alli Sup*
Davidge, John Beale 1768-1829 *DcNAA*
Davidge, Marion *ChPo*
Davidge, William *Alli Sup*
Davidge, William Pleater 1814-1888 *DcNAA*
Davidoff, M *Alli Sup*
Davidow, Mike 1913- *ConAu 57*
Davids, Anthony 1923- *ConAu 41*
Davids, C J *ChPo*
Davids, Jennifer 1945- *ConP 1970*
Davids, Lewis Edmund 1917- *ConAu 37*
Davids, Thomas William *Alli Sup*
Davids, Thomas William Rhys 1843- *Alli Sup,*
BbD, BiD&SB
Davidsohn, Alfred Samuel 1912- *Au&Wr*
Davidsohn, Georg 1872- *WhLA*
Davidson *Alli*
Davidson, A J K *Alli Sup*
Davidson, Abraham A 1935- *ConAu 53*
Davidson, Alan Eaton 1924- *WrD 1976*
Davidson, Alastair 1939- *ConAu 29*
Davidson, Alexander And Stuve, Bernard
Alli Sup
Davidson, Alexander Dyce 1807-1872 *Alli Sup*
Davidson, Alfred *Alli Sup*
Davidson, Andrew Bruce 1831?-1902 *Alli Sup,*

BrAu 19
Davidson, Angus Henry Gordon 1898- *Au&Wr,*
ChPo, ConAu 25
Davidson, Anstruther 1860-1932 *DcNAA*
Davidson, Anthony *Alli, BiDLA*
Davidson, Basil 1914- *AmA&B, Au&Wr,*
ConAu 1R, WorAu, WrD 1976
Davidson, Benjamin *Alli Sup*
Davidson, Bill *AuBYP*
Davidson, Carter 1905-1965 *AmA&B*
Davidson, Chalmers Gaston 1907- *AmA&B,*
ConAu 29, WrD 1976
Davidson, Chandler 1936- *ConAu 45*
Davidson, Charles *Alli*
Davidson, Charles 1852-1919 *DcAmA, DcNAA*
Davidson, Charles 1858- *AmLY*
Davidson, Charles 1929- *AmSCAP 66*
Davidson, Charles I C *Alli Sup*
Davidson, Sir Charles Peers 1841-1929 *DcNAA*
Davidson, Clara D 1874- *ChPo*
Davidson, Clarissa Start *ConAu 49*
Davidson, Clifford 1932- *ConAu 45*
Davidson, David *Alli*
Davidson, David 1908- *AmA&B, AmNov,*
ConAu 49, ConAu 57, TwCA Sup,
WrD 1976
Davidson, Diane 1924- *ConAu 29*
Davidson, Donald 1893-1968 *AmA&B, ChPo,*
ChPo S1, ConAmA, ConAu 5R,
ConAu 25, ConLC 2, DcLEnL, OxAm,
Pen Am, REnAL, SixAP, TwCA,
TwCA Sup, WhWNAA
Davidson, Donald H 1917- *ConAu 45*
Davidson, Doris *ChPo S1*
Davidson, E *Alli Sup*
Davidson, Mrs. E 1828-1873 *ChPo S1*
Davidson, E E 1923- *ConAu 33*
Davidson, E H *ChPo S2*
Davidson, Edith Bowker *AmA&B*
Davidson, Edna *TexWr*
Davidson, Edward 1827- *Alli Sup*
Davidson, Ellen Prescott *ConAu 49*
Davidson, Ellis A *Alli Sup*
Davidson, Eugene 1902- *Au&Wr, ConAu 1R,*
WrD 1976
Davidson, Eva Rucker 1894?-1974 *ConAu 53*
Davidson, Frank *ChPo*
Davidson, Frank Geoffrey 1920- *ConAu 29,*
WrD 1976
Davidson, G *Alli, Alli Sup*
Davidson, G C *OxCan*
Davidson, G F *Alli*
Davidson, G M *BbtC*
Davidson, G Ronald 1899- *Au&Wr*
Davidson, George *Alli Sup*
Davidson, George 1806-1872 *ChPo S2*
Davidson, George 1825- *DcAmA*
Davidson, George Trimble 1863- *DcAmA*
Davidson, Gladys *ChPo S1*
Davidson, Glen W 1936- *ConAu 61*
Davidson, Gordon Charles 1884-1922 *DcNAA*
Davidson, Gustav 1895-1971 *AmA&B,*
Au&Wr, ChPo, ConAu 29
Davidson, H C *Alli Sup*
Davidson, H M *Alli Sup*
Davidson, H R Ellis 1914- *ConAu 17R*
Davidson, Hannah Amelia 1852-1932 *DcNAA,*
WhWNAA
Davidson, Harold P 1908- *AmSCAP 66*
Davidson, Harriet Miller 1839-1883 *Alli Sup,*
ChPo S1
Davidson, Harry Carter 1905-1965 *AmA&B*
Davidson, Henry *Alli, Alli Sup*
Davidson, Mrs. Henry *Alli Sup*
Davidson, Henry A 1905-1973 *ConAu 45*
Davidson, Henry M 1839?-1900 *OhA&B*
Davidson, Herbert A 1932- *ConAu 17R*
Davidson, Hilda Ellis 1914- *Au&Wr*
Davidson, Hugh Coleman 1852- *Alli Sup*
Davidson, Mrs. Hugh Coleman *Alli Sup*
Davidson, Irene Mary 1892- *ChPo S1*
Davidson, Isobel 1869- *WhWNAA*
Davidson, Israel 1870-1939 *AmA&B, DcNAA,*
WhWNAA
Davidson, J *Alli Sup*
Davidson, J Brownlee 1880- *WhWNAA*
Davidson, James *Alli, Alli Sup, BiDLA*
Davidson, James d1866 *Alli Sup*

Davidson, James Bridge *Alli Sup*
Davidson, James Leigh Strachan- *Alli Sup*
Davidson, James Wheeler 1872-1933 *AmLY,*
DcAmA, DcNAA, WhWNAA
Davidson, James Wood 1829-1905 *Alli Sup,*
AmA, AmA&B, BiDSA, DcAmA,
DcNAA
Davidson, Jay Hartwell *WhWNAA*
Davidson, Jessica 1915- *ConAu 41, SmATA 5*
Davidson, Jo 1883-1952 *OxAm, REn, REnAL*
Davidson, John *Alli, Alli Sup, Chmbr 3*
Davidson, John 1549?-1603 *BrAu*
Davidson, John 1857-1909 *AtlBL, BbD,*
BiD&SB, BrAu 19, CasWL, ChPo,
ChPo S1, ChPo S2, CnE&AP, DcEnA,
DcEnA Ap, DcEuL, DcLEnL, EvLB,
LongC, ModBL, NewC, OxEng, Pen Eng,
REn, WebEAL
Davidson, John 1869-1905 *DcNAA*
Davidson, John Best *Alli Sup*
Davidson, John Morrison *Alli Sup*
Davidson, John Nelson *ChPo S1*
Davidson, John Thain *Alli Sup*
Davidson, Jonas Pascal Fitzwilliam *Alli Sup*
Davidson, Kate *Alli Sup*
Davidson, Lawrence H *LongC, REn*
Davidson, Lillian C *ChPo S1*
Davidson, Lionel 1922- *Au&Wr, ConAu 1R,*
WrD 1976
Davidson, Lucretia Maria 1808-1825 *Alli,*
AmA&B, BiD&SB, ChPo, CyAL 2,
DcAmA, DcEnL, DcNAA, FemPA
Davidson, M M *Alli Sup*
Davidson, Margaret *ConAu XR, PoIre*
Davidson, Margaret 1936- *ConAu 25,*
SmATA 5
Davidson, Margaret M *Alli, FemPA*
Davidson, Margaret Miller *FemPA*
Davidson, Margaret Miller 1787-1844 *AmA&B*
Davidson, Margaret Miller 1823-1838 *Alli,*
AmA&B, ChPo, ChPo S2, CyAL 2,
DcAmA, DcEnL
Davidson, Marshall B 1907- *AmA&B, Au&Wr,*
ConAu 33
Davidson, Mary R 1885-1973 *ConAu 5R,*
SmATA 9
Davidson, Michael Childers 1897- *Au&Wr,*
ConAu 29
Davidson, Mickie 1936- *ConAu 9R*
Davidson, Mildred *WrD 1976*
Davidson, Morrey 1899- *AmSCAP 66*
Davidson, Norbert R, Jr. 1940- *BlkAW*
Davidson, Paul 1930- *ConAu 13R*
Davidson, Peter *Alli Sup*
Davidson, R *Alli Sup*
Davidson, Randall Thomas *Alli Sup*
Davidson, Robert *Alli*
Davidson, Robert 1750-1812 *BiDSA, DcAmA,*
DcNAA
Davidson, Robert 1777- *ChPo*
Davidson, Robert 1808-1876 *Alli Sup, DcAmA*
Davidson, Robert And David Douglass *Alli*
Davidson, Robert F 1902- *ConAu 49*
Davidson, Roger H 1936- *ConAu 21,*
WrD 1976
Davidson, Samuel 1807- *Alli, Alli Sup,*
DcEnL
Davidson, Sandra Calder 1935- *ConAu 41*
Davidson, Sol M 1924- *ConAu 17R,*
WrD 1976
Davidson, T W *Alli Sup*
Davidson, Thomas *Alli*
Davidson, Thomas 1817-1885 *Alli Sup*
Davidson, Thomas 1838-1870 *ChPo S2*
Davidson, Thomas 1840-1900 *Alli Sup, AmA,*
AmA&B, BbD, BiD&SB, BrAu 19,
DcAmA, DcNAA, OxAm, REnAL
Davidson, Thomas F *Alli Sup*
Davidson, Virginia E *LivFWS*
Davidson, W *Alli Sup*
Davidson, Wilbur Leroy 1853-1912 *OhA&B*
Davidson, William *Alli, BiDLA*
Davidson, William F *BlkAW*
Davidson, William L *Alli Sup*
Davidson, William Mehard 1863-1930 *DcNAA*
Davidson, William Robert 1919- *ConAu 17R*
Davidson-Houston, J Vivian 1901-1965
ConAu 5R

Davidsone, David *Alli*
Davidsone, John *Alli*
Davie, Adam 1312?- *DcEnL*
Davie, Cedric Thorpe 1913- *Au&Wr*
Davie, Charles H *Alli*
Davie, Donald 1922- *CasWL, ChPo, ConAu 1R, ConLC 5, ConP 1970, ConP 1975, LongC, ModBL, ModBL Sup, NewC, REn, TwCW, WhTwL, WorAu, WrD 1976*
Davie, Elizabeth *Alli Sup*
Davie, Emily 1915- *Au&Wr*
Davie, George Scott *Alli Sup*
Davie, Ian 1924- *Au&Wr, WrD 1976*
Davie, John C *Alli*
Davie, Maurice Rea 1893-1964 *AmA&B, ConAu 5R, WhWNAA*
Davie, Michael 1924- *ConAu 57*
Davie, Oliver 1857-1911 *Alli Sup, OhA&B*
Davie, Owen Hosmer 1916- *Au&Wr, WrD 1976*
Davie, Robert Worthington 1897- *WhWNAA*
Davie, Sampson *Alli*
Davie, W Galsworthy *Alli Sup*
Davied, Camille *ConAu XR*
Davies *Alli, MnBBF*
Davies, Mrs. *Alli Sup*
Davies, A E 1867- *WhWNAA*
Davies, A Mervyn 1899- *ConAu 17R*
Davies, A W *MnBBF*
Davies, Acton 1870-1916 *DcNAA*
Davies, Ada Hilton 1893- *ConAu 17*
Davies, Alan T 1933- *ConAu 33*
Davies, Albert Emil 1875- *WhLA*
Davies, Alfred T 1930- *ConAu 13R*
Davies, Aneirin Talfan 1909- *Au&Wr, ChPo*
Davies, Anthony *Alli*
Davies, Arabella *Alli, BiDLA*
Davies, Arthur *Alli*
Davies, Arthur Bowen 1862-1928 *ChPo, OxAm*
Davies, Arthur Ernest 1867-1954 *OhA&B*
Davies, Arthur Llewelyn 1884- *WhLA*
Davies, Augustus Morse *Alli Sup*
Davies, B *Alli, BbtC*
Davies, Benjamin *Alli Sup*
Davies, Blodwen 1897-1966 *CanNov, OxCan, WhWNAA*
Davies, C A *Alli Sup*
Davies, C M *Alli*
Davies, C N *Alli*
Davies, Charles 1798-1876 *Alli, DcAmA, DcNAA*
Davies, Charles D *Alli Sup*
Davies, Charles G *Alli*
Davies, Charles Greenall *Alli Sup*
Davies, Charles Maurice *Alli Sup*
Davies, Charles Norman 1910- *Au&Wr*
Davies, Christie 1941- *WrD 1976*
Davies, Christina Jane d1887 *Alli Sup*
Davies, Clement *Alli Sup*
Davies, Colliss 1912- *ConAu P-1*
Davies, Cuthbert Collin 1896- *Au&Wr*
Davies, D *Alli, BiDLA*
Davies, Mrs. D *Alli Sup*
Davies, D Jacob 1916- *ConAu 5R*
Davies, D W *Alli, BiDLA*
Davies, Daniel R 1911- *ConAu 37, WrD 1976*
Davies, David *Alli, Alli Sup, BiDLA, DcLEnL, LongC*
Davies, David 1893-1951 *EvLB*
Davies, David Christopher 1827-1885 *Alli Sup*
Davies, David Ivor *McGWD*
Davies, David Jacob 1916- *Au&Wr*
Davies, David John 1879- *WhLA*
Davies, David Jones *Alli Sup*
Davies, David Margerison 1923- *Au&Wr, ConAu 5R, WrD 1976*
Davies, David Michael 1929- *Au&Wr*
Davies, David Peter *Alli, BiDLA*
Davies, David W 1908- *ConAu 9R*
Davies, Denis 1889-1900 *ChPo S2*
Davies, E *Alli, Alli Sup*
Davies, E T 1903- *WrD 1976*
Davies, E W L 1840?- *Br&AmS*
Davies, Ebenezer *Alli, Alli Sup*
Davies, Ebenezer Thomas 1903- *Au&Wr, ConAu P-1*
Davies, Edgar William *Alli Sup*

Davies, Edward *Alli Sup, BiDLA*
Davies, Edward 1756-1831 *Alli*
Davies, Edward C *MnBBF*
Davies, Edward Tegla 1880-1967 *Au&Wr, CasWL*
Davies, Edward William Lewis *Alli Sup*
Davies, Edwin *Alli Sup*
Davies, Eileen Winifred 1910- *ConAu P-1*
Davies, Lady Eleanor 1603-1652 *Alli*
Davies, Eliza Rhyl *Alli Sup*
Davies, Emily 1830-1921 *Alli Sup, BrAu 19*
Davies, Ernest Albert John 1902- *Au&Wr*
Davies, Evan *Alli, Alli Sup, OxCan*
Davies, Evan Thomas 1878- *Au&Wr*
Davies, Evan Y *ChPo*
Davies, Evelyn 1924- *ConAu 61*
Davies, Evelyn A 1915- *ConAu 61*
Davies, Franc *Alli*
Davies, Frederick *Alli Sup*
Davies, Frederick Herbert 1916- *Au&Wr*
Davies, G *Alli, BiDLA*
Davies, G C *Alli Sup*
Davies, George *Alli Sup, ChPo S2*
Davies, George Christopher 1849- *Alli Sup*
Davies, George Colliss Boardman 1912- *Au&Wr, WrD 1976*
Davies, George Harley *Alli*
Davies, George Jennings 1826-1884 *Alli Sup*
Davies, George R 1876- *WhWNAA*
Davies, Gerald Stanley *Alli Sup*
Davies, Griffith *Alli, BiDLA Sup*
Davies, Gwendoline Elizabeth 1880-1951 *LongC*
Davies, H C *ChPo S2*
Davies, Henry *Alli*
Davies, Henry And Laurent, Emile *Alli Sup*
Davies, Henry D *Alli Sup*
Davies, Henry William 1834-1895 *DcNAA*
Davies, Herbert 1818-1885 *Alli, Alli Sup*
Davies, Horton Marlais 1916- *ConAu 5R, WrD 1976*
Davies, Hubert Henry 1876-1917 *Chmbr 3, DcLEnL*
Davies, Hugh *Alli, BiDLA Sup*
Davies, Hugh Sykes 1909- *WorAu*
Davies, Hunter 1936- *ConAu 57, WrD 1976*
Davies, Ioan 1936- *ConAu 21*
Davies, Ivor K 1930- *ConAu 53*
Davies, Ivor Roland Morgan 1915- *Au&Wr*
Davies, J *Alli, Alli Sup*
Davies, J A *ChPo*
Davies, J Alford *ChPo S1*
Davies, J Clarence, III 1937- *ConAu 29*
Davies, J Dickenson *Alli Sup*
Davies, J Kenneth 1925- *ConAu 57*
Davies, J Trevor *Alli Sup*
Davies, Jack 1913- *Au&Wr*
Davies, James *Alli, Alli Sup*
Davies, James 1786-1881 *Alli Sup*
Davies, James 1820-1883 *Alli Sup*
Davies, James A *Alli Sup*
Davies, James Boyd *Alli Sup*
Davies, James Chowning 1918- *ConAu 45*
Davies, James Seymour *Alli, BiDLA*
Davies, James William Frederick 1878- *WhWNAA*
Davies, Jasper *WrD 1976*
Davies, Joan Howard *Au&Wr, WrD 1976*
Davies, John *Alli, Alli Sup, BiDLA, Chmbr 1, MnBBF*
Davies, Sir John *Chmbr 1*
Davies, John 1565?-1618 *BrAu, CasWL, DcEuL, DcLEnL, EvLB, OxEng, Pen Eng*
Davies, Sir John 1569-1626 *Alli, BbD, BiD&SB, BrAu, CasWL, DcEnL, ChPo S1, CnE&AP, CrE&SL, DcEnL, DcEuL, DcLEnL, EvLB, NewC, OxEng, Pen Eng, REn, WebEAL*
Davies, John 1625-1693 *Alli*
Davies, John 1679-1732 *Alli*
Davies, John Christopher Hughes *WrD 1976*
Davies, John David *Alli Sup*
Davies, John Fletcher d1889 *Alli Sup, PoIre*
Davies, John Gordon 1919- *Au&Wr, ConAu 5R, WrD 1976*
Davies, John Hamilton *Alli Sup*
Davies, John Henry *Alli Sup*
Davies, John Llewelyn 1826- *Alli Sup, DcEnL*

Davies, John Ogmore *Alli Sup*
Davies, John Paton, Jr. 1908- *ConAu 9R*
Davies, John Sylvester *Alli Sup*
Davies, John T 1869-1953 *OhA&B*
Davies, John Tasman 1924- *WrD 1976*
Davies, John Trevor 1907- *Au&Wr*
Davies, Joseph *Alli*
Davies, Joseph E 1876-1958 *AmA&B*
Davies, Julien T *Alli Sup*
Davies, Kenneth Gordon 1923- *Au&Wr*
Davies, Laurence 1926- *Au&Wr, ConAu 57*
Davies, Leslie Purnell 1914- *ConAu 21, WrD 1976*
Davies, Lester Lloyd 1922- *Au&Wr*
Davies, Lewis A 1911- *AmSCAP 66*
Davies, Louisa Alicc *Alli Sup*
Davies, Lucian *MnBBF*
Davies, Lady Lucy Clementina 1795-1879 *Alli Sup*
Davies, M C D *MnBBF*
Davies, Mansel Morris 1913- *Au&Wr, ConAu 9R, WrD 1976*
Davies, Margaret Constance 1923- *Au&Wr, ConAu 9R, WrD 1976*
Davies, Margaret Sidney 1885-1963 *LongC*
Davies, Martin Brett 1936- *WrD 1976*
Davies, Mary *Alli Sup*
Davies, Mary Carolyn *AmA&B, AmSCAP 66, ChPo, ChPo S1, ChPo S2, ConAmL, WhWNAA*
Davies, Maurice *ChPo S2*
Davies, Morton Rees 1939- *ConAu 37*
Davies, Myles *Alli*
Davies, Nathaniel 1809-1887 *Alli Sup*
Davies, Nathaniel Edward *Alli Sup*
Davies, Naunton Wingfield *Alli Sup*
Davies, Nigel 1920- *WrD 1976*
Davies, Norman 1939- *ConAu 41*
Davies, Oliver 1905- *ConAu 25, WrD 1976*
Davies, P M *BbtC*
Davies, Paul Mervyn 1914- *Au&Wr*
Davies, Pennar 1911- *Au&Wr, ConAu 13R*
Davies, Peter 1937- *ConAu 53*
Davies, Philip John *Alli Sup*
Davies, Piers Anthony David 1941- *WrD 1976*
Davies, R E G 1921- *ConAu 17R*
Davies, R N *Alli Sup*
Davies, R Rice *Alli Sup*
Davies, R T 1923- *ConAu 9R*
Davies, R W 1925- *ConAu 33*
Davies, Randall Robert Henry 1866- *ChPo, WhLA*
Davies, Rhys 1903- *Au&Wr, CasWL, ChPo S1, ConAu 9R, ConNov 1972, ConNov 1976, DcLEnL, EvLB, LongC, ModBL, Pen Eng, TwCA Sup, WrD 1976*
Davies, Richard *Alli*
Davies, Richard O 1937- *ConAu 17R*
Davies, Robert *Alli Sup*
Davies, Robert 1770-1836 *Alli*
Davies, Robert 1793-1875 *Alli Sup*
Davies, Robert William 1925- *WrD 1976*
Davies, Robertson 1913- *Au&Wr, CanWr, CasWL, CnThe, ConAu 33, ConDr, ConLC 2, ConNov 1972, ConNov 1976, DcLEnL, LongC, McGWD, OxCan, OxCan Sup, Pen Eng, REnAL, REnWD, TwCW, WorAu, WrD 1976*
Davies, Rod 1941- *ConAu 61*
Davies, Roger *Alli*
Davies, Rosemary Reeves 1925- *ConAu 49*
Davies, Rowland Lyttleton Archer *Alli Sup*
Davies, Rupert Eric 1909- *Au&Wr, ConAu 5R, WrD 1976*
Davies, Ruth A 1915- *ConAu 29*
Davies, S J 1918- *Au&Wr*
Davies, Samuel *Alli, Alli Sup*
Davies, Samuel 1723-1761 *Alli, CyAL 1, DcAmA, DcNAA, PoCh*
Davies, Samuel D *BiDSA*
Davies, Samuel J *Alli Sup*
Davies, Sarah *Alli Sup*
Davies, Sneyd d1769 *Alli, ChPo*
Davies, Thomas *Alli, Alli Sup, BbtC, BiDLA*
Davies, Thomas 1712?-1785 *Alli, DcLEnL, NewC*

Davies, Thomas Alfred 1809-1899 *Alli Sup, BiD&SB, DcAmA, DcNAA*
Davies, Thomas Frederick 1872-1936 *DcNAA*
Davies, Thomas Hart *Alli Sup*
Davies, Thomas Lewis Owen *Alli Sup*
Davies, Thomas M, Jr. 1940- *ConAu 57*
Davies, Thomas Owen Silvester *Alli Sup*
Davies, Thomas S *Alli*
Davies, Trefor Rendall 1913- *Au&Wr, ConAu P-1*
Davies, Uriah *Alli Sup*
Davies, Valentine 1905-1961 *AmA&B, AmNov*
Davies, W *Alli Sup*
Davies, W E *Alli Sup*
Davies, W H 1871-1940 *CasWL, CnE&AP, CnMWL, EncWL, LongC, ModBL, Pen Eng, REn, TwCW, WebEAL, WhLA, WhTwL*
Davies, W H A d1867 *BbtC*
Davies, Walter *Alli, BiDLA*
Davies, Walter Merlin 1910- *WrD 1976*
Davies, William *Alli, Alli Sup, BiDLA, BiDLA Sup, ChPo, ChPo S1*
Davies, Sir William 1863- *WhLA*
Davies, William David 1911- *ConAu 1R*
Davies, William George *Alli Sup*
Davies, William H A *OxCan*
Davies, William Henry 1871-1940 *AtlBL, ChPo, ChPo S1, ChPo S2, Chmbr 3, DcLEnL, EvLB, NewC, OxEng, TwCA, TwCA Sup*
Davies, William Kevill *Alli Sup*
Davies, William P 1862- *WhWNAA*
Davies, William Stearns 1877- *AmLY*
Davies, William Walter 1848-1922 *AmLY, DcNAA*
Davies, William Watkin 1891- *Au&Wr, WhLA*
Davies, Wyndham 1926- *ConAu 25*
Davies Of Hereford, John 1565?-1618 *NewC*
Davies-Woodrow, Constance Isabel 1899- *WhWNAA*
Daviess, Joseph Hamilton 1774-1811 *Alli, BiDSA, DcNAA*
Daviess, Maria Thompson 1814-1896 *BiDSA, DcNAA*
Daviess, Maria Thompson 1872-1924 *AmA&B, DcNAA*
Daviess, Marie T *LivFWS*
Davila, Alexandru 1862-1929 *CasWL*
Davila, Arrigo Caterino 1576-1631? *BiD&SB*
Davila, Arturo V *PueRA*
Davila, Enrico Caterino 1576-1631 *CasWL, EvEuW*
Davila, Jose Antonio 1898-1941 *PueRA*
Davila, Virgilio 1869-1943 *PueRA*
Davila Garibi, Jose Ignacio 1888- *WhWNAA*
Daville, John *Alli*
Davin, D M 1913- *ConAu 9R*
Davin, Dan 1913- *Au&Wr, ConNov 1972, ConNov 1976, LongC, Pen Eng, TwCW, WebEAL, WorAu, WrD 1976*
Davin, M B *Alli Sup*
Davin, Nicholas Flood 1843-1901 *Alli Sup, DcLEnL, DcNAA, OxCan, PoIre*
DaVinci ALSO Leonardo ALSO Vinci
DaVinci, Leonardo 1452-1519 *Pen Eur*
Davinson, Donald E 1932- *ConAu 5R, WrD 1976*
Daviot, Gordon 1897-1952 *Chmbr 3, DcLEnL, EncM&D, EvLB, LongC, NewC, Pen Eng, REn, TwCA Sup, TwCW*
Davis *Alli*
Davis, A C *ChPo*
Davis, A H *ChPo S1*
Davis, A I *BlkAW*
Davis, Achilles Edward 1866- *AmLY*
Davis, Adelle 1904-1974 *ConAu 37, ConAu 49, REnAL*
Davis, Alastair Jeffreys *ChPo S2*
Davis, Alec 1912- *Au&Wr*
Davis, Alexander *Alli Sup*
Davis, Alexander H *Alli Sup*
Davis, Alexander Jackson 1803-1892 *DcNAA, EarAB Sup*
Davis, Allan 1885- *AnMV 1926*
Davis, Allan 1922- *AmSCAP 66*
Davis, Allen F 1931- *ConAu 23, WrD 1976*

Davis, Allison 1902- *LivBA*
Davis, Andrew Jackson 1826-1910 *Alli, Alli Sup, BbD, BiD&SB, ChPo S1, DcAmA, DcNAA, OxAm*
Davis, Andrew McFarland 1833-1920 *DcAmA, DcNAA*
Davis, Angela 1944- *ConAu 57*
Davis, Anne Pence *TexWr*
Davis, Annie C *ChPo*
Davis, Annie Osborne 1842-1882 *PoIre*
Davis, Arnold *MnBBF*
Davis, Arthur G 1915- *ConAu 13R, WrD 1976*
Davis, Arthur Henderson 1882-1960 *IndAu 1917*
Davis, Arthur Hoey *DcLEnL*
Davis, Arthur Kennard 1910- *ConAu P-1*
Davis, Arthur Kyle 1867- *AmLY*
Davis, Arthur Kyle, Jr. 1897- *AmA&B, ConAu 17*
Davis, Arthur Newton 1879- *OhA&B*
Davis, Arthur P 1904- *BlkAW, ConAu 61, LivBAA*
Davis, Arthur Powell 1861-1933 *AmLY, DcNAA, WhWNAA*
Davis, Asahel 1791- *Alli, DcAmA, DcNAA*
Davis, Athie Sale 1885- *ChPo S2, WhWNAA*
Davis, Audrey *ConAu XR*
Davis, Augusta Cordelia 1839- *ChPo, DcAmA*
Davis, Barbara 1949- *BlkAW*
Davis, Beale 1884?-1929 *DcNAA, WhWNAA*
Davis, Ben Wood *ChPo*
Davis, Benjamin Marshall 1867-1953 *AmLY, IndAu 1917, WhWNAA*
Davis, Benny 1895- *AmSCAP 66*
Davis, Bernard George 1906- *AmA&B*
Davis, Bert H 1896- *WhWNAA*
Davis, Bertram H 1918- *ConAu 1R*
Davis, Bertram R *ChPo S2*
Davis, Bette *IlBYP*
Davis, Bette 1908- *ConAu 61*
Davis, Bob 1909- *AmSCAP 66, WhWNAA*
Davis, Boothe Colwell 1863-1942 *DcAmA, DcNAA*
Davis, Bradley Moore 1871- *WhWNAA*
Davis, Britton *ArizL*
Davis, Burke 1913- *AmA&B, AuBYP, ConAu 1R, SmATA 4, WrD 1976*
Davis, Burton *TexWr*
Davis, Buster 1920- *AmSCAP 66*
Davis, C J *Alli Sup*
Davis, C O *Alli Sup*
Davis, Calvin DeArmond 1927- *ConAu 5R, IndAu 1917*
Davis, Calvin Olin 1871- *WhWNAA*
Davis, Carl Henry 1883- *WhWNAA*
Davis, Caroline E 1831- *Alli Sup, CarSB, DcAmA*
Davis, Catherine Snodgrass *WhWNAA*
Davis, Charles *Alli Sup, BlkAW*
Davis, Charles 1923- *Au&Wr, ConAu 5R*
Davis, Charles Augustus 1795-1867 *AmA&B, DcNAA, OxAm, REnAL*
Davis, Charles Belmont 1866-1926 *DcAmA, DcNAA*
Davis, Charles Edward *Alli Sup*
Davis, Charles Gideon *Alli Sup*
Davis, Charles Gilbert 1849-1928 *DcNAA*
Davis, Charles H And Rae, Frank B *Alli Sup*
Davis, Charles Henry *Alli Sup*
Davis, Charles Henry 1807-1877 *Alli Sup, DcAmA*
Davis, Charles Henry 1845-1921 *DcAmA, DcNAA*
Davis, Charles Henry Stanley 1840-1917 *Alli Sup, AmA, DcAmA, DcNAA*
Davis, Charles T *ChPo*
Davis, Charles T 1929- *ConAu 37*
Davis, Charles Thomas *Alli Sup*
Davis, Cheryl *BlkAW*
Davis, Christine K *ChPo*
Davis, Christopher 1928- *Au&Wr, ConAu 9R, DrAF 1976, SmATA 6, WrD 1976*
Davis, Clara Hemphill *ChPo*
Davis, Clare Ogden *TexWr*
Davis, Clarkson 1833-1883 *IndAu 1816*
Davis, Clive Edward 1914- *AuBYP, ConAu 17R*

Davis, Clyde Brion 1894-1962 *AmA&B*
Davis, Clyde Brion 1894- *AmNov, CnDAL, ConAu 5R, OxAm, REn, REnAL, TwCA, TwCA Sup*
Davis, Cora M A d1885 *Alli Sup*
Davis, Creath 1939- *ConAu 57*
Davis, Crusoe R *Alli*
Davis, Curtis Carroll 1916- *ChPo S2, ConAu 9R, WrD 1976*
Davis, Cushman Kellogg 1838-1900 *Alli Sup, DcAmA, DcNAA*
Davis, D *BiDLA*
Davis, D Evan 1923- *ConAu 17R*
Davis, Daniel 1762?-1835 *Alli, DcAmA, DcNAA*
Davis, Daniel, Jr. *Alli*
Davis, Mrs. Daniel A *AmNov XR*
Davis, Daniel S 1936- *ConAu 45*
Davis, Daniel Webster 1862-1913 *BlkAW*
Davis, Danny 1930- *AmSCAP 66*
Davis, David Brion 1927- *AmA&B, ConAu 17R, WrD 1976*
Davis, David C L 1928- *ConAu 33*
Davis, David D 1854- *Alli, DcAmA*
Davis, David Howard 1941- *ConAu 53*
Davis, Dennis J 1933- *Au&Wr*
Davis, Denys 1921- *Au&Wr*
Davis, Derek Russell 1914- *Au&Wr*
Davis, Dimitris 1905- *IlCB 1966*
Davis, Don *EncM&D*
Davis, Donald Gordon, Jr. 1939- *ConAu 53*
Davis, Dorothy R *ChPo S1*
Davis, Dorothy Salisbury 1916- *AmA&B, Au&Wr, ConAu 37, EncM&D, WorAu, WrD 1976*
Davis, Dudley Hughes 1834- *BiDSA, DcNAA*
Davis, E Adams *ConAu XR*
Davis, E S *Alli Sup*
Davis, Edith 1859-1917 *DcNAA*
Davis, Edith Vezolles 1889- *WhWNAA*
Davis, Edna Cruger *ChPo*
Davis, Edward *Alli*
Davis, Edward, Oviatt, A G & Clark, E B *Alli Sup*
Davis, Edward Everett 1881- *TexWr, WhWNAA*
Davis, Edward Parker 1856-1937 *DcNAA*
Davis, Edward Zeigler 1878-1924 *ChPo S1*
Davis, Edwin *Alli Sup*
Davis, Edwin A *Alli Sup*
Davis, Edwin Adams 1904- *ConAu 25*
Davis, Edwin Hamilton 1811-1888 *Alli, BiD&SB, DcAmA, OhA&B*
Davis, Edwin John *Alli Sup*
Davis, Eliel 1803-1849 *PoCh*
Davis, Elisabeth Switzer *WhWNAA*
Davis, Eliza B *Alli Sup*
Davis, Elizabeth A *Alli Sup, ChPo, ChPo S1, ChPo S2*
Davis, Elizabeth G 1910?-1974 *ConAu 53*
Davis, Elizabeth Joy 1886- *TexWr*
Davis, Elizabeth Littlejohn *TexWr*
Davis, Ella May *ChPo S1*
Davis, Ellen Louisa *Alli Sup*
Davis, Ellery William 1857-1918 *DcNAA*
Davis, Ellis J *Alli Sup*
Davis, Elmer Holmes 1890-1958 *AmA&B, IndAu 1816, OxAm, REn, REnAL, TwCA, TwCA Sup, WhWNAA*
Davis, Elnathan *ChPo S1*
Davis, Elwood Craig 1896- *ConAu 1R*
Davis, Emerson 1798-1866 *Alli Sup, DcAmA, DcNAA*
Davis, Esther Eugenia 1897- *ChPo*
Davis, Eugene 1857-1897 *PoIre*
Davis, F James 1920- *ConAu 1R*
Davis, Fannie Stearns 1884- *ChPo, ChPo S1, ChPo S2, ConAmL*
Davis, Fitzroy 1912- *ConAu 49, WrD 1976*
Davis, Fletcher 1874- *TexWr*
Davis, Florence Boyce 1873-1938 *ChPo*
Davis, Forest K 1918- *ConAu 41*
Davis, Francis 1810-1885 *Alli, Alli Sup, BrAu 19, ChPo, ChPo S1, ChPo S2, PoIre*
Davis, Frank 1892- *Au&Wr*
Davis, Frank 1894- *AmSCAP 66*
Davis, Frank Marshall 1905- *AmA&B, BlkAW*

Davis, Franklin M, Jr. 1918- *ConAu 1R*
Davis, Franklyn Pierre 1868-1932 *ChPo S2,*
WhWNAA
Davis, Fred 1925- *ConAu 13R*
Davis, Frederick *Alli Sup*
Davis, Frederick 1909- *AmSCAP 66*
Davis, Frederick Barton 1909- *ConAu 1R*
Davis, Frederick Clyde 1902- *AmA&B,*
MnBBF
Davis, Frederick I *Alli Sup*
Davis, Frederick William 1858-1933 *AmA&B,*
ChPo, ChPo S2, DcNAA
Davis, Mrs. G S *ChPo S1*
Davis, Garold N 1932- *ConAu 41*
Davis, Garrett Morrow 1851- *BiDSA, DcNAA*
Davis, Gene *BlkAW*
Davis, Genevieve 1889-1950 *AmSCAP 66*
Davis, George *Alli, Alli Sup, BiDSA*
Davis, George B *Alli Sup, BlkAW,*
DrAF 1976, LivBA
Davis, George Breckenridge 1847-1914 *DcAmA,*
DcNAA
Davis, George Collin 1867-1929 *AmSCAP 66*
Davis, George E *Alli Sup*
Davis, George Henry *Alli Sup*
Davis, George Jesson *Alli Sup*
Davis, George L *Alli Sup*
Davis, George L, Sr. 1921- *ConAu 57*
Davis, George L L *BiDSA*
Davis, George Lynn Lachlan *Alli Sup*
Davis, George Theron 1899-1944 *DcNAA*
Davis, George Thomas 1810-1877 *DcAmA,*
DcNAA
Davis, George W *Alli Sup*
Davis, Geri Turner *BlkAW*
Davis, Gil *ConAu XR*
Davis, Gilbert Asa 1835- *DcNAA*
Davis, Gloria *BlkAW*
Davis, Godfrey Rupert Carless 1917- *Au&Wr*
Davis, Gordon *ConAu XR, EncM&D*
Davis, Gordon B 1930- *ConAu 53*
Davis, Grace Emeline 1876-1945 *DcNAA*
Davis, Grant Miller 1937- *ConAu 29*
Davis, Gustavus Fellowes 1797-1836 *ChPo S1*
Davis, Gwen 1936- *AmA&B, AuNews 1,*
ConAu 1R
Davis, H *Alli*
Davis, H Grady 1890- *ConAu 21*
Davis, H J 1866- *WhLA*
Davis, H L 1896-1960 *AmNov, CnDAL,*
CyWA, OxAm, REn, REnAL
Davis, H N 1881- *WhWNAA*
Davis, Hallam Walker 1884- *IndAu 1917,*
WhWNAA
Davis, Hannah E Brown 1841-1898 *IndAu 1816*
Davis, Harold Eugene 1902- *AmA&B,*
ConAu 1R, OhA&B, WrD 1976
Davis, Harold Lenoir 1896-1960 *AmA&B,*
ChPo S1, DcLEnL, TwCA, TwCA Sup
Davis, Harold S 1919- *ConAu 57*
Davis, Harriet *Alli Sup*
Davis, Harriet Eager 1892?-1974 *ConAu 49*
Davis, Harriet Riddle 1849-1938 *OhA&B*
Davis, Harriet Winton *ChPo, ChPo S1,*
WhWNAA
Davis, Harry E 1882-1955 *OhA&B*
Davis, Harry James And Owston, Hiram A
Alli Sup
Davis, Harry Rex 1921- *ConAu 1R*
Davis, Hassoldt 1907-1959 *AmA&B*
Davis, Hazel 1907- *AmSCAP 66*
Davis, Hazel Griffith *ChPo S1*
Davis, Helen Bayley d1965 *ChPo*
Davis, Helene *DrAP 1975*
Davis, Henry *Alli Sup*
Davis, Henry 1771-1852 *CyAL 2, DcNAA*
Davis, Henry 1866-1952 *CatA 1952*
Davis, Henry Edwards 1756-1784 *Alli*
Davis, Henry Frederick Alexander *Alli Sup*
Davis, Henry G *Alli Sup*
Davis, Henry George 1830-1857 *Alli Sup*
Davis, Henry Lyon *CyAL 1*
Davis, Henry Winter 1817-1865 *Alli, Alli Sup,*
BbD, BiD&SB, BiDSA, DcAmA,
DcNAA
Davis, Herbert John 1893-1967 *AmA&B,*
ConAu 1R
Davis, Herman Stearns 1868-1933 *DcNAA*

Davis, Hewlett *Alli*
Davis, Hope Hale *ConAu 25, DrAF 1976*
Davis, Horace 1831-1916 *Alli Sup, DcAmA,*
DcNAA
Davis, Horace Bancroft 1898- *ConAu 23,*
WhWNAA, WrD 1976
Davis, Howard V 1915- *ConAu 25*
Davis, Hugh *Alli*
Davis, I M 1926- *ConAu 61*
Davis, Irenaeus P *Alli Sup*
Davis, Isabella M *ChPo*
Davis, Israel *Alli Sup*
Davis, J *Alli, Alli Sup, ChPo*
Davis, J A *Alli Sup*
Davis, J B *Alli, BiDLA*
Davis, J C B *Alli*
Davis, J Cary 1905- *ConAu 41*
Davis, J Frank 1870- *AmA&B, DcNAA,*
TexWr, WhWNAA
Davis, J P *Alli Sup, ChPo S1*
Davis, J R A *Alli Sup*
Davis, J S *ChPo*
Davis, J Thomas 1880- *TexWr, WhWNAA*
Davis, Mrs. J W *Alli Sup*
Davis, J Walton *ChPo S2*
Davis, Jack, Jr. *ChPo S1*
Davis, Jackson 1882-1947 *DcNAA*
Davis, Jackson 1920- *AmSCAP 66*
Davis, James *Alli Sup, ChPo S2*
Davis, James 1854?-1907 *PoIre*
Davis, James Allan 1929- *ConAu 1R*
Davis, James D *Alli Sup*
Davis, James Davidson *Alli Sup*
Davis, James Edward 1817- *Alli Sup*
Davis, James Francis 1870-1942 *DcNAA*
Davis, James W 1935- *ConAu 29*
Davis, James W And Lees, F A *Alli Sup*
Davis, Jane *Alli Sup*
Davis, Jane S *ChPo S1*
Davis, Jean Reynolds 1927- *AmSCAP 66,*
ConAu 61
Davis, Jean Walton 1909- *WhPNW*
Davis, Jed H 1921- *ConAu 17R*
Davis, Jefferson 1808-1889 *Alli Sup, AmA&B,*
BbD, BiD&SB, BiDSA, DcAmA
Davis, Jefferson 1808-1899 *DcNAA*
Davis, Jefferson 1808-1889 *OxAm, REn,*
REnAL
Davis, Jerome 1891- *AmA&B, ConAu 5R,*
WhWNAA, WrD 1976
Davis, Jerome Dean 1838-1910 *DcNAA*
Davis, Jesse Buttrick 1871- *WhWNAA*
Davis, Jessica *AmA&B*
Davis, Jo *Alli*
Davis, Joe Lee 1906- *ConAu 5R*
Davis, Johanna 1937-1974 *ConAu 41,*
ConAu 53
Davis, John *Alli, Alli Sup, BiDLA, BiDSA,*
ChPo S2, Chmbr 1, CyAL 1, NewC
Davis, Sir John *Alli*
Davis, John 1550-1605 *Alli, DcEnL, EvLB,*
OxCan
Davis, John 1761-1847 *ChPo S1, DcNAA*
Davis, John 1774-1854 *AmA&B, DcNAA,*
OxAm, REnAL
Davis, John 1834- *Alli Sup*
Davis, John 1917- *Au&Wr, WrD 1976*
Davis, John A 1840?-1897 *DcAmA, DcNAA*
Davis, John A G 1801-1840 *Alli, BiDSA,*
DcAmA, DcNAA
Davis, John Carlyle 1878-1948 *AmSCAP 66*
Davis, John Chandler Bancroft 1822-1907
Alli Sup, BiD&SB, DcAmA, DcNAA
Davis, John David 1854-1926 *AmLY, DcAmA,*
DcNAA, WhWNAA
Davis, John David 1937- *ConAu 29,*
WrD 1976
Davis, John Ford *Alli, BiDLA*
Davis, Sir John Francis 1795-1890 *Alli,*
Alli Sup, BbD
Davis, John Gilbert 1904- *Au&Wr, WrD 1976*
Davis, John H 1904- *ConAu 29*
Davis, John H 1929- *ConAu 25*
Davis, John Hall *Alli Sup*
Davis, John J 1936- *ConAu 33*
Davis, John King 1884-1967 *ConAu P-1*
Davis, John McCan 1866-1916 *DcNAA*
Davis, John P *BlkAW*

Davis, John Patterson 1862-1903 *DcAmA,*
DcNAA
Davis, John Staige 1872-1946 *DcNAA*
Davis, John Woodbridge 1854-1902 *Alli Sup,*
DcAmA, DcNAA
Davis, Joseph *Alli, Alli Sup*
Davis, Joseph A 1919- *BlkAW*
Davis, Joseph Baker 1845-1920 *DcNAA*
Davis, Joseph Barnard *Alli Sup*
Davis, Joseph L *IndAu 1917*
Davis, Joseph M 1896- *AmSCAP 66*
Davis, Joseph Stancliffe 1885-1975 *ConAu 57,*
WhWNAA
Davis, Julia 1900- *AmA&B, ConAu 1R,*
JBA 1951, SmATA 6, WrD 1976
Davis, Julia Johnson *AnMV 1926, ChPo,*
WhWNAA
Davis, Julian 1902?-1974 *ConAu 53*
Davis, K 1918- *ConAu 1R*
Davis, Kary Cadmus 1867-1936 *AmLY,*
DcNAA, WhWNAA
Davis, Katharine Bement 1860-1935 *DcNAA*
Davis, Katharine DeFord *ChPo*
Davis, Katherine *ChPo S1*
Davis, Katherine K 1892- *AmSCAP 66*
Davis, Keith 1918- *WrD 1976*
Davis, Ken 1906- *ConAu 49*
Davis, Kenneth R 1921- *ConAu 17R*
Davis, Kenneth S 1912- *AmA&B, AmNov,*
ConAu 13R
Davis, Kingsley 1908- *ConAu 13R*
Davis, L *Alli Sup*
Davis, L A *Alli Sup*
Davis, L Clarke 1835- *Alli Sup*
Davis, L J 1940- *ConAu 25, DrAF 1976*
Davis, Lance E 1928- *ConAu 53*
Davis, Lanny J 1945- *ConAu 57*
Davis, Lavinia Riker 1909-1961 *AmA&B,*
AuBYP, JBA 1951, WhWNAA
Davis, Lawrence B 1939- *ConAu 45*
Davis, Lemuel A 1914- *AmSCAP 66*
Davis, Lemuel Clarke 1835-1904 *AmA&B,*
DcAmA, DcNAA, OhA&B
Davis, Lenwood G 1939- *ConAu 25, LivBA*
Davis, Leopold *Alli Sup*
Davis, LeRoy G *AnMV 1926, ChPo S2*
Davis, Leslie G 1887- *AnMV 1926*
Davis, Lew A 1930- *ConAu 21*
Davis, Lewis S *Alli Sup*
Davis, Lillian Burroughs 1896- *WhWNAA*
Davis, Lois Carlile 1921- *ConAu 13R*
Davis, Lou 1881-1961 *AmSCAP 66*
Davis, Louis *ChPo*
Davis, Louis E 1918- *ConAu 53*
Davis, Louisa I *Alli Sup*
Davis, Louise Taylor *ChPo S2*
Davis, Lucius Daniel 1826-1900 *Alli Sup,*
DcNAA
Davis, Lyman Edwyn 1854-1930 *Alli Sup,*
DcNAA, OhA&B
Davis, M *Alli, BiDLA*
Davis, M D *Alli Sup*
Davis, M Edward 1899- *ConAu 5R*
Davis, M S *Alli, Alli Sup*
Davis, Mack 1898-1947 *AmSCAP 66*
Davis, Maggie *ConAu 13R*
Davis, Maralee G *ConAu XR*
Davis, Marc 1934- *ConAu 29*
Davis, Marcus *Alli Sup*
Davis, Margaret Banfield 1903- *ConAu P-1*
Davis, Margaret Ellen O'Brien 1870-1898
BiDSA, DcAmA
Davis, Margaret Enid 1908- *Au&Wr*
Davis, Margaret Thomson *WrD 1976*
Davis, Marguerite 1889- *ChPo, ChPo S2,*
ConICB, IICB 1945, IICB 1956
Davis, Marilyn K 1928- *ConAu 5R*
Davis, Martha 1942- *ConAu 49*
Davis, Martha Ann *BiDSA*
Davis, Martyn P 1929- *WrD 1976*
Davis, Mary *ChPo S1*
Davis, Mary A 1836- *DcNAA*
Davis, Mary Anne *Alli, BiDLA, ChPo,*
ChPo S2
Davis, Mary Boyce *ChPo*
Davis, Mary Elizabeth Moragne 1815- *Alli Sup,*
ChPo S1
Davis, Mary Evelyn 1852-1909 *AmA, AmA&B,*

BiD&SB, BiDSA, ChPo, ChPo S1,
ChPo S2, DcAmA, DcNAA
Davis, Mary Gould 1882-1956 *AmA&B, AnCL,*
AuBYP, ChPo, ChPo S1, JBA 1934,
JBA 1951
Davis, Mary L 1935- *ConAu 49, SmATA 9*
Davis, Mary Lee *AmA&B, WhWNAA*
Davis, Mary Margaret 1834-1870 *Alli Sup*
Davis, Mary Octavia 1901- *ConAu 25,*
SmATA 6, TexWr
Davis, Matilda Louisa *Alli Sup*
Davis, Matthew Livingston 1766-1850 *Alli,*
DcAmA, DcNAA
Davis, Maxine *AmA&B, WrD 1976*
Davis, Melton S 1910- *ConAu 41*
Davis, Michael 1940- *ConAu 33*
Davis, Milburn *BlkAW*
Davis, Mildred Ann 1916- *ConAu 5R*
Davis, Minnie S 1835- *Alli Sup, BiDSA,*
DcNAA
Davis, Miriam K *Alli Sup*
Davis, Mollie E *Alli Sup*
Davis, Morris 1933- *ConAu 61*
Davis, Moshe 1916- *ConAu 9R*
Davis, Murray S 1940- *ConAu 53*
Davis, Natalie Zemon 1928- *ConAu 53*
Davis, Nathan 1812-1882 *Alli Sup*
Davis, Nathan Smith 1817-1904 *Alli Sup,*
DcAmA, DcNAA
Davis, Nathan Smith, Jr. 1858-1920 *AmLY,*
DcAmA, DcNAA
Davis, Nelson 1896- *Au&Wr*
Davis, Nicholas A *Alli Sup*
Davis, Nicholas Darnell *Alli Sup*
Davis, Nina *ChPo S2*
Davis, Noah 1818-1902 *DcNAA*
Davis, Noah Knowles 1830-1910 *Alli Sup,*
AmA&B, BiDSA, DcAmA, DcNAA
Davis, Nolan 1942- *BlkAW, ConAu 49*
Davis, Norah 1878- *AmA&B*
Davis, Norbert *EncM&D*
Davis, Norman 1913- *Au&Wr*
Davis, Nuel Pharr 1915- *Au&Wr, ConAu 29*
Davis, O W *Alli Sup*
Davis, Olin William 1904- *IndAu 1917*
Davis, Opal Evelyn Hoffert 1906-1971
IndAu 1917
Davis, Oscar King 1866-1932 *DcAmA, DcNAA*
Davis, Ossie 1917- *AmA&B, BlkAW, ConDr,*
LivBAA, WrD 1976
Davis, Owen 1874-1956 *AmA&B, CnDAL,*
CnMD, McGWD, ModWD, OxAm, REn,
REnAL, TwCA, TwCA Sup
Davis, Ozora Stearns 1866-1931 *AmLY,*
DcNAA, WhWNAA
Davis, P O 1890- *WhWNAA*
Davis, Patrick 1925- *WrD 1976*
Davis, Paulina 1813-1876 *DcNAA*
Davis, Paxton 1925- *ConAu 9R*
Davis, Peter Seibert 1828-1892 *Alli Sup,*
DcAmA, DcNAA
Davis, Philip *MnBBF*
Davis, Philip 1876- *WhWNAA*
Davis, Philip E 1927- *ConAu 49*
Davis, Philip L 1911- *AmSCAP 66*
Davis, Phoebe B *Alli Sup*
Davis, R C *Alli Sup*
Davis, R G 1933- *ConAu 57*
Davis, Ralph C 1894- *ConAu 33*
Davis, Ralph Henry Carless 1918- *Au&Wr,*
ConAu 5R, WrD 1976
Davis, Raymond Cazallis 1836-1919 *AmLY,*
DcAmA, DcNAA
Davis, Rebecca Blaine Harding 1831-1910
Alli Sup, AmA, AmA&B, BbD, BiD&SB,
DcAmA, DcBiA, DcLEnL, DcNAA,
OxAm, REn, REnAL
Davis, Rebecca Ingersoll 1828- *Alli Sup,*
ChPo S1, DcNAA
Davis, Reda *AuBYP*
Davis, Reuben 1813-1890 *BiDSA, DcAmA,*
DcNAA
Davis, Rex D 1924- *ConAu 9R*
Davis, Richard *Alli, Au&Wr, ConAu 53,*
WrD 1976
Davis, Richard 1649-1741 *Alli*
Davis, Richard Beale 1907- *AmA&B,*
ConAu 5R

Davis, Richard Bennett 1782-1854 *ChPo*
Davis, Richard Bingham 1771-1799 *Alli, ChPo,*
CyAL 2, DcAmA
Davis, Richard Harding 1864-1916 *AmA&B,*
BbD, BiD&SB, CarSB, CasWL,
Chmbr 3, CnDAL, DcAmA, DcBiA,
DcEnA Ap, DcLEnL, DcNAA, EncM&D,
EvLB, JBA 1934, LongC, OxAm,
Pen Am, REn, REnAL, TwCA,
TwCA Sup, WebEAL
Davis, Richard Whitlock 1935- *Au&Wr,*
ConAu 33, WrD 1976
Davis, Robert *BbtC, OxCan*
Davis, Robert 1881-1949 *AmA&B, AnCL,*
DcNAA, JBA 1951, YABC 1
Davis, Robert A 1917- *BlkAW*
Davis, Robert G *Alli Sup*
Davis, Robert Hobart 1869-1942 *AmA&B,*
DcNAA, REnAL, WhWNAA
Davis, Robert Means 1849-1904 *BiDSA*
Davis, Robert Murray 1934- *ConAu 33*
Davis, Robert Prunier 1929- *ConAu 5R,*
WrD 1976
Davis, Robert Ralph, Jr. 1941- *ConAu 37*
Davis, Robert S *Alli Sup*
Davis, Rocky 1927- *ConAu 61*
Davis, Roland Parker 1884- *WhWNAA*
Davis, Ronald L 1936- *ConAu 37*
Davis, Ronda Marie 1940- *BlkAW,*
DrAP 1975
Davis, Rosalind *Alli Sup*
Davis, Rosemary *Au&Wr, ConAu 5R*
Davis, Rosemary L *ConAu XR*
Davis, Roy Eugene 1931- *ConAu 9R*
Davis, Royal Jenkins 1878-1934 *DcNAA,*
WhWNAA
Davis, Russell F *BlkAW*
Davis, Russell Gerard 1922- *ConAu 5R,*
SmATA 3
Davis, Mrs. S M Henry *Alli Sup*
Davis, Samuel 1930- *ConAu 29*
Davis, Samuel Post 1850-1918 *DcNAA*
Davis, Samuel T 1838-1908 *DcNAA, OxCan*
Davis, Sarah Matilda *Alli Sup*
Davis, Sheila 1927- *AmSCAP 66*
Davis, Sheldon *ChPo*
Davis, Sheldon Emmor 1876- *WhWNAA*
Davis, Slack *ChPo*
Davis, Stephen Brooks 1874-1933 *DcNAA*
Davis, Stephen J *Alli Sup*
Davis, Stratford 1915- *Au&Wr, ConAu XR*
Davis, Stuart 1894-1964 *OxAm, REn*
Davis, Sturgiss Brown 1877- *WhWNAA*
Davis, Sydney Brian 1842- *IndAu 1816*
Davis, Sydney Charles Houghton 1887- *Au&Wr,*
ConAu 5R
Davis, T Frederick 1877- *WhWNAA*
Davis, Tamar *Alli Sup*
Davis, Terence 1924- *ConAu 21*
Davis, Theodore P 1855-1907 *IndAu 1816*
Davis, Thomas *Alli, Alli Sup*
Davis, Thomas 1804- *PoCh*
Davis, Thomas 1823-1848 *ChPo S2*
Davis, Thomas A *Alli*
Davis, Thomas J *Alli Sup*
Davis, Thomas J 1946- *ConAu 53*
Davis, Thomas Kirby 1826-1918 *DcNAA,*
OhA&B
Davis, Thomas Osborne 1814-1845 *BbD,*
BiD&SB, BrAu 19, CasWL, ChPo,
ChPo S1, Chmbr 3, EvLB, NewC,
Pen Eng, PoIre, REn
Davis, Thomas Robert Alexander 1917- *Au&Wr*
Davis, Thurston N 1913- *AmA&B*
Davis, Titus Elwood 1851- *AmLY*
Davis, Valentine D *Alli Sup*
Davis, Varina 1826-1906 *DcNAA*
Davis, Varina Anne Jefferson 1864-1898
Alli Sup, AmA&B, BiDSA, DcAmA,
DcNAA
Davis, Varina Howell 1826-1906 *AmA&B,*
BiDSA
Davis, Verne Theodore 1889-1973 *ConAu 1R,*
SmATA 6
Davis, Vincent 1930- *ConAu 17R, WrD 1976*
Davis, Virgil Earl 1903- *IndAu 1917*
Davis, W *Alli, Alli Sup*
Davis, W H *Alli Sup*

Davis, W Hawley 1880- *WhWNAA*
Davis, W J *Alli Sup*
Davis, W Jefferson 1885- *ConAu 29*
Davis, W M *ChPo*
Davis, W S *Alli Sup*
Davis, Wallace Clyde 1866- *WhWNAA*
Davis, Walter Bickford And Durrie, D *Alli Sup*
Davis, Watson 1896- *WhWNAA*
Davis, Wayne Harry 1930- *ConAu 33,*
WrD 1976
Davis, Webster 1861- *DcAmA*
Davis, Wiley H 1913- *ConAu 25*
Davis, Will A 1857- *IndAu 1917*
Davis, William *Alli, BiDLA*
Davis, William 1933- *Au&Wr*
Davis, William Bramwell 1832-1893 *DcAmA,*
DcNAA, OhA&B
Davis, William C 1946- *ConAu 61*
Davis, William F *Alli Sup*
Davis, William H 1939- *ConAu 33*
Davis, William Heath 1822-1909 *AmA&B,*
DcNAA
Davis, William Holmes 1873- *WhWNAA*
Davis, William Morris 1815?-1890? *DcNAA*
Davis, William Morris 1850-1934 *Alli Sup,*
AmLY, DcAmA, DcNAA
Davis, William Smith *Alli Sup*
Davis, William Stearns 1822-1907 *REnAL*
Davis, William Stearns 1877-1930 *AmA&B,*
CarSB, DcAmA, DcNAA, JBA 1934,
OxAm, TwCA, WhWNAA
Davis, William Thomas 1822-1907 *Alli Sup,*
AmA&B, DcAmA, DcNAA
Davis, William Virgil *DrAP 1975*
Davis, William Watts Hart 1820-1910 *Alli Sup,*
AmA&B, DcAmA, DcNAA
Davis, Winnie 1864-1898 *AmA&B, DcNAA*
Davis, Winnie McClanahan 1877- *TexWr*
Davis, Woodbury 1818-1871 *DcNAA*
Davis-Weyer, Caecilia 1929- *ConAu 41*
Davison *Alli, BiDLA*
Davison, Ada Clark 1882- *WhWNAA*
Davison, Albert Watson 1888- *WhWNAA*
Davison, Alex *Alli*
Davison, Alexander *BiDLA*
Davison, Alvin 1868-1915 *DcNAA*
Davison, Archibald T 1883-1961 *AmA&B*
Davison, Arthur B *Alli Sup*
Davison, C *Alli Sup*
Davison, Charles 1858- *WhLA*
Davison, Charles Frederic *Alli Sup*
Davison, Charles Stewart 1855-1942 *DcNAA,*
WhWNAA
Davison, D *Alli*
Davison, Dorothy *Au&Wr*
Davison, Edward 1789-1863 *Alli Sup*
Davison, Edward Lewis 1898-1970 *AmA&B,*
ChPo, CnDAL, ConAu 29
Davison, Francis 1575?-1619? *Alli, BrAu,*
ChPo, DcEnL, OxEng, WebEAL
Davison, Frank Cyril 1893- *AmA&B*
Davison, Frank Dalby 1893-1970 *CasWL,*
DcLEnL, TwCW
Davison, Frank Elon 1887-1960 *IndAu 1917*
Davison, Geoffrey 1927- *WrD 1976*
Davison, Gertrude Carr *Alli Sup*
Davison, Gideon Miner 1791?-1869 *DcNAA,*
OxCan
Davison, Gladys Patton 1905- *ConAu P-1*
Davison, H And Merivale, H *Alli*
Davison, Henry *Alli Sup*
Davison, Henry Pomeroy 1867-1922 *DcNAA*
Davison, Hilkiah *Alli*
Davison, James *Alli Sup*
Davison, John *Alli, Alli Sup*
Davison, John 1777-1834 *Alli*
Davison, Kenneth E 1924- *ConAu 9R*
Davison, Lesley *AmSCAP 66*
Davison, Mary *Alli Sup*
Davison, Ned J 1926- *ConAu 45*
Davison, Peter Hubert 1928- *AmA&B,*
ConAu 9R, ConP 1970, ConP 1975,
DrAP 1975, WrD 1976
Davison, Roderic H 1916- *ConAu 37*
Davison, Simpson *Alli Sup*
Davison, T Raffles *Alli Sup*
Davison, Thomas *Alli, Alli Sup*
Davison, W T *Alli Sup*

Davison, Wayne Marshall 1916- *AmSCAP 66*
Davison, Wilburt C 1892- *WhWNAA*
Davison, William *Alli*
Davisson, Charles Nelson 1917- *ConAu 25, IndAu 1917*
Davisson, John *Alli*
Davisson, William I 1929- *ConAu 17R*
Davitt, Arthur *Alli Sup*
Davitt, Michael 1846-1906 *Alli Sup, PoIre*
Davitt, Thomas E 1904- *ConAu 25*
Davol, Ralph 1874- *AmLY, WhWNAA*
Davors, Jo *Alli*
Davout, Louis-Nicolas *OxFr*
Davoyan, Razmik 1940- *DcOrL 3*
D'Avray, J Marshall *BbtC*
Davson, Harry Miller 1872- *WhLA*
Davy, Charles *Alli*
Davy, Chris *Alli*
Davy, Colin Kayser 1896- *Au&Wr*
Davy, Mrs. E M *Alli Sup*
Davy, Edmond *Alli*
Davy, Edmund William *Alli Sup*
Davy, Francis X 1916- *ConAu 29*
Davy, Henry *Alli*
Davy, Mrs. Herbert *Alli Sup*
Davy, Sir Humphry 1778-1829 *Alli, BbD, BiD&SB, BiDLA, BrAu 19, ChPo, ChPo S1, Chmbr 2, DcEnL, EvLB, NewC, OxEng*
Davy, John *Alli*
Davy, John d1824 *Alli*
Davy, John 1790-1868 *Alli Sup*
Davy, John Charles 1927- *Au&Wr*
Davy, John Tanner *Alli Sup*
Davy, Margaret E 1932- *Au&Wr*
Davy, Marian *Alli Sup*
Davy, Michael *Alli*
Davy, Richard *Alli Sup*
Davy, Robert Harry *Alli Sup*
Davy, William d1826 *Alli, BiDLA*
Davydov, Denis Vasilyevich 1784-1839 *BbD, BiD&SB, CasWL, DcRusL*
Davyes, Hatton *Alli*
Davyes, Thomas *Alli*
Davys, Edward *PoIre*
Davys, John *Alli, EvLB*
Davys, Sir John *Alli*
Davys, John 1550?-1605 *DcLEnL, NewC, OxEng*
Davys, Mary *Alli, PoIre*
Daw, John Ward 1907- *Au&Wr*
Dawbarn, Mrs. *BiDLA*
Dawbarn, Elizabeth *Alli Sup*
Dawbarn, R H M *Alli Sup*
Dawbarn, William *Alli Sup*
Dawbeny, H *Alli*
Dawber, Alfred 1908- *Au&Wr*
Dawborn, Mrs. *Alli*
Dawdy, Doris Ostrander *ConAu 53*
Dawe, Bruce 1930- *ConP 1970, ConP 1975, WebEAL, WrD 1976*
Dawe, Charles Joseph Sherwill 1835- *Alli Sup*
Dawe, Donald G 1926- *ConAu 33*
Dawe, Frances *Alli Sup, ChPo S1*
Dawe, G *BiDLA*
Dawe, George d1829 *Alli*
Dawe, George Grosvenor 1863-1948 *DcNAA*
Dawe, J M *ChPo S1*
Dawe, Margaret *ChPo S1*
Dawe, Roger David 1934- *ConAu 9R*
Dawe, T L *Alli Sup*
Dawe, W *Alli Sup*
Dawe, W H *Alli Sup*
Dawe, William *Alli Sup*
Dawes *Alli*
Dawes, Angela Kathleen 1911- *WhWNAA*
Dawes, Anna Laurens 1851-1938 *Alli Sup, AmA&B, BiD&SB, DcAmA, DcNAA, WhWNAA*
Dawes, Ben 1902- *Au&Wr, WrD 1976*
Dawes, Charles Gates 1865-1951 *AmA&B, OhA&B*
Dawes, Chester L 1886- *WhWNAA*
Dawes, Edward Naasson 1914- *WrD 1976*
Dawes, F J *Alli Sup*
Dawes, Jack *Alli*
Dawes, John *Alli, BiDLA*
Dawes, Lancelot 1580-1633 *Alli*

Dawes, M *Alli*
Dawes, Matthew *Alli, BiDLA, BiDLA Sup*
Dawes, Nathaniel Thomas, Jr. 1937- *ConAu 49*
Dawes, Neville Augustus 1926- *Au&Wr, ConAu 13R, ConP 1970*
Dawes, Richard 1708-1766 *Alli*
Dawes, Richard 1793-1867 *Alli Sup*
Dawes, Robyn M 1936- *ConAu 37*
Dawes, Rufus 1803-1859 *Alli, AmA&B, BiD&SB, ChPo, CyAL 2, DcAmA, DcNAA, OxAm*
Dawes, Rufus Cutler 1867-1940 *DcNAA, OhA&B*
Dawes, Rufus Robinson 1838-1899 *Alli Sup, OhA&B*
Dawes, Mrs. S E *Alli Sup*
Dawes, Sir Thomas *Alli*
Dawes, Thomas 1757-1825 *Alli, CyAL 2*
Dawes, William *Alli, Alli Sup*
Dawes, Sir William 1671-1724 *Alli*
Dawes, William Matthias *Alli Sup*
Dawidowicz, Lucy S *ConAu 25*
Dawis, Rene V 1928- *ConAu 45*
Dawkes, Thomas *Alli*
Dawkins, Cecil 1927- *ConAu 5R, DrAF 1976*
Dawkins, Henry *EarAB Sup*
Dawkins, Julia Dalrymple 1932- *Au&Wr*
Dawkins, William Boyd 1838- *Alli Sup*
Dawkins, William Gregory 1825- *Alli Sup*
Dawley, David 1941- *ConAu 45*
Dawley, Jack H *BlkAW*
Dawley, Powel Mills 1907- *ConAu 57*
Dawley, Thomas Robinson 1832-1904 *DcNAA*
Dawley, Thomas Robinson, Jr. 1862-1930 *DcAmA, DcNAA, WhWNAA*
Dawlish, John *MnBBF*
Dawn, C Ernest 1918- *ConAu 61*
Dawn, Dolly *AmSCAP 66*
Dawnay, Archibald Davis *Alli Sup*
Dawne, Derby *Alli*
Dawney, Benjamin *Alli*
Dawood, N J 1927- *ConAu 49*
Dawson *Alli*
Dawson, A *Alli Sup*
Dawson, A J 1872?-1951 *BbD, BiD&SB, NewC, WhCL*
Dawson, A W *MnBBF*
Dawson, Abraham *Alli, BiDLA*
Dawson, Aeneas MacDonnell 1810-1894 *Alli Sup, BbtC, DcNAA, OxCan*
Dawson, Alec John 1872- *WhLA*
Dawson, Alfred *Alli Sup*
Dawson, Mrs. Alfred *PoIre*
Dawson, Ambrose *Alli*
Dawson, Arnold H *MnBBF*
Dawson, Arthur 1695?-1775 *PoIre*
Dawson, Arthur Altham *Alli Sup*
Dawson, Arthur John Eardley *ChPo S2*
Dawson, Augusta L *Alli Sup*
Dawson, Benjamin d1814 *Alli, BiDLA, BiDLA Sup*
Dawson, Benjamin Elisha 1852-1922 *DcNAA*
Dawson, Birket *Alli*
Dawson, Birkett *BiDLA*
Dawson, Bully 1650?- *NewC*
Dawson, C A *OxCan*
Dawson, C T *MnBBF*
Dawson, Carl 1938- *ConAu 45*
Dawson, Charles *Alli, ChPo*
Dawson, Charles 1842- *PoIre*
Dawson, Charles Carroll 1833- *Alli Sup, DcAmA*
Dawson, Christopher *ChPo, PoIre*
Dawson, Christopher 1826- *ChPo S1*
Dawson, Christopher Henry 1889-1970 *CatA 1947, ConAu 1R, ConAu 29, TwCA Sup*
Dawson, Colin *MnBBF*
Dawson, Coningsby William 1883-1959 *AmA&B, ChPo S1, REnAL, TwCA, TwCA Sup, WhWNAA*
Dawson, Daniel Lewis 1855-1893 *DcAmA, DcNAA, PoIre*
Dawson, Digby D *Alli Sup*
Dawson, E *ChPo S1*
Dawson, Edgar 1872-1946 *BiDSA, DcNAA, WhWNAA*
Dawson, Edward Walter *Alli Sup*

Dawson, Edwin Collas *Alli Sup*
Dawson, Eli 1880-1960 *Alli, AmSCAP 66*
Dawson, Elizabeth 1910- *Au&Wr*
Dawson, Elizabeth 1914- *Au&Wr*
Dawson, Elizabeth 1930- *WrD 1976*
Dawson, Elmer A *ConAu 19, SmATA 1*
Dawson, Emma Frances 1851-1926 *DcNAA*
Dawson, F Morton *MnBBF*
Dawson, F Warrington 1878- *WhWNAA*
Dawson, Fawcett *Alli Sup*
Dawson, Fielding 1930- *ConLC 6, DrAF 1976*
Dawson, Flora *Alli Sup*
Dawson, Florence *Alli Sup*
Dawson, Francis Dennis Massy *Alli Sup*
Dawson, Francis Warrington 1840-1889 *BiDSA*
Dawson, Frederick *Alli Sup*
Dawson, Frederick Ackers *Alli Sup*
Dawson, G A R *Alli Sup*
Dawson, G P *BiDLA*
Dawson, G Pearson *Alli*
Dawson, Geoffrey 1874-1944 *ChPo S2, LongC*
Dawson, George *Alli*
Dawson, George 1813-1883 *Alli Sup, DcAmA, DcNAA*
Dawson, George 1821-1876 *Alli, Alli Sup*
Dawson, George Ellsworth 1861-1936 *DcNAA*
Dawson, George Francis *Alli Sup*
Dawson, George Glenn 1925- *ConAu 37, WrD 1976*
Dawson, George Mercer 1849-1901 *Alli Sup, Chmbr 3, DcNAA, OxCan*
Dawson, Giles E 1903- *ConAu 19*
Dawson, Grace Strickler 1891- *ChPo, ConAu 17R, WhWNAA*
Dawson, Gregory *ChPo*
Dawson, Henry Barton 1821-1889 *Alli, Alli Sup, AmA&B, CyAL 2, DcAmA, DcNAA*
Dawson, Hugh *MnBBF*
Dawson, J A *Alli Sup*
Dawson, J H *Alli*
Dawson, J T *Alli Sup*
Dawson, James *Alli Sup*
Dawson, James 1717?-1746 *NewC*
Dawson, James 1799-1878 *Alli Sup*
Dawson, James Hooper *Alli Sup*
Dawson, Jennifer *ConAu 57, ConNov 1972, ConNov 1976, WrD 1976*
Dawson, Jerry F 1933- *ConAu 33*
Dawson, John *Alli, Alli Sup*
Dawson, John 1734-1820 *Alli, BiDLA*
Dawson, John B 1915- *ConAu 13*
Dawson, John Charles 1876- *WhWNAA*
Dawson, John Frederic *Alli Sup*
Dawson, Sir John William 1820-1899 *Alli Sup, BbD, BbtC, BiD&SB, Chmbr 3, DcLEnL, DcNAA*
Dawson, Joseph *ChPo*
Dawson, Joseph Martin 1879- *TexWr*
Dawson, Lemuel Orah 1865-1938 *DcNAA*
Dawson, Lionel 1885- *Br&AmS*
Dawson, Llewellyn Stiles *Alli Sup*
Dawson, Miss M L *PoIre*
Dawson, M Phelps *ChPo S1*
Dawson, Mary *ChPo S1*
Dawson, Mary d1922 *DcNAA*
Dawson, Mary 1919- *ConAu 21*
Dawson, Mary Isabella *Alli Sup*
Dawson, Mildred A 1897- *ConAu 17R*
Dawson, Miles Menander 1863-1942 *AmLY, DcNAA, WhWNAA*
Dawson, Mitchell 1890- *AuBYP*
Dawson, Moses 1768-1844 *OhA&B*
Dawson, Nell 1870-1923 *DcNAA*
Dawson, Niles Menander 1863-1942 *DcAmA*
Dawson, Nora *OxCan Sup*
Dawson, Oliver 1908- *Au&Wr*
Dawson, Percy M 1873- *WhWNAA*
Dawson, Sir Philip 1867- *WhLA*
Dawson, Philip 1928- *ConAu 21*
Dawson, R MacGregor *OxCan*
Dawson, Ray *MnBBF*
Dawson, Robert 1941- *AmA&B, ConAu 21*
Dawson, S E *Alli Sup, OxCan*
Dawson, S J *Alli Sup, BbtC*
Dawson, Samuel Edward 1833-1916 *DcLEnL, DcNAA*
Dawson, Sea-Flower White Cloud *DrAP 1975*

D'Azeglio, Massimo Taparrelli, Marchese 1798-1866 *BiD&SB, CasWL, EvEuW, REn*
Dazey, Agnes J *ConAu 23, SmATA 2*
Dazey, Charles Turner 1855-1938 *AmA&B, DcNAA, WhWNAA*
Dazey, Frank M *ConAu 23, SmATA 2*
De, Bisnu 1909- *DcOrL 2*
De-Graft-Johnson, John Coleman 1919- *Au&Wr*
De-La-Noy, Michael 1934- *Au&Wr*
DeA, E I *PoIre*
Deacon *BiDLA*
Deacon, Augustus *Alli*
Deacon, D D, Jr. *Alli*
Deacon, E E *Alli*
Deacon, George Edward 1810-1886 *Alli Sup*
Deacon, H *Alli, BiDLA*
Deacon, Henry d1876 *Alli Sup*
Deacon, John *BiDLA*
Deacon, Lois 1899- *Au&Wr, WrD 1976*
Deacon, Mary Connor 1907- *AmSCAP 66*
Deacon, Richard *ConAu XR, WrD 1976*
Deacon, Thomas *Alli*
Deacon, W F *Alli, BbtC*
Deacon, William *Alli, BiDLA*
Deacon, William Arthur 1890-1964 *CanWr, DcLEnL, OxCan, WhWNAA*
Deacon, William Frederick 1799-1845 *ChPo*
DeAcosta, Mercedes 1898- *AnMV 1926, WhWNAA*
DeActon, Eugenia *BiDLA*
Deaderick, William Heiskell 1876- *WhWNAA*
Deadman, Ronald 1919- *Au&Wr*
Deadrick, William 1876- *AmLY*
Deady, John Christmas 1849-1884 *PoIre*
Deady, Matthew P *Alli Sup*
Deagon, Ann 1930- *ConAu 57, DrAP 1975*
DeAinslie, Charles Philip *Alli Sup*
Deak, Edward Joseph, Jr. 1943- *ConAu 53*
Deak, Francis 1899-1972 *ConAu 33*
Deak, Istvan 1926- *ConAu 25, WrD 1976*
Deakin, Alfred 1856-1919 *DcLEnL*
Deakin, Edward *Alli Sup*
Deakin, Frederick William Dampier 1913- *Au&Wr, ConAu 5R*
Deakin, Guy *MnBBF*
Deakin, H C *ChPo, ChPo S2*
Deakin, James 1929- *ConAu 21*
Deakin, Phyllis Annie *Au&Wr*
Deakin, Richard *Alli, Alli Sup*
Deakin, Rupert *Alli Sup*
Deakins, Roger Lee 1933- *ConAu 61*
Deal, Babs H 1929- *AmA&B, ConAu 1R*
Deal, Borden 1922- *AmA&B, Au&Wr, ConAu 1R, REnAL, WrD 1976*
Deal, Charles Henry 1903- *IndAu 1917*
Deal, William S 1910- *ConAu 5R*
Deale, Kenneth Edwin Lee 1907- *Au&Wr, ConAu 5R*
DeAlencar, Jose Marttiniano 1829-1877 *ChPo S2*
Dealey, E M 1892- *ConAu 23, TexWr*
Dealey, George Bannerman 1859-1946 *AmA&B*
Dealey, James Quayle 1861-1937 *AmLY, DcNAA, TexWr, WhWNAA*
Dealey, Ted *ConAu XR*
Dealing, Lilian *ChPo*
DeAlmeida, Jose Maria, And F Viana 1903- *AfA 1*
Dealtry, R B *Alli*
Dealtry, Robert *Alli, BiDLA*
Dealtry, William 1775-1847 *Alli, BiDLA Sup, BiDLA Sup*
Dealy, Jane M *ChPo*
Deam, Charles Clemons 1865-1953 *IndAu 1917*
Deam, Thomas Marion 1882- *IndAu 1917*
Deamer, Dulcie 1890- *DcLEnL*
DeAmicis, Edmondo 1846-1908 *CasWL, ClDMEuL, DcBiA, EuA, EvEuW, Pen Eur, REn*
Deams, S *Alli Sup*
Dean, Abner 1910- *AmA&B*
Dean, Agnes Louise *ChPo, ChPo S1, ChPo S2*
Dean, Alexander 1893-1939 *DcNAA, WhWNAA*
Dean, Alfreda Joan 1925- *Au&Wr*
Dean, Amber 1902- *ConAu 5R, WrD 1976*

Dean, Amos 1803-1868 *Alli, Alli Sup, DcAmA, DcNAA*
Dean, Anabel 1915- *ConAu 37, WrD 1976*
Dean, Arthur Davis 1872-1949 *DcNAA, WhWNAA*
Dean, Barbara J *BlkAW*
Dean, Bashford 1867-1928 *DcNAA*
Dean, Basil 1888- *ModWD*
Dean, Beryl 1911- *Au&Wr, ConAu 9R, WrD 1976*
Dean, Burton V 1924- *ConAu 45*
Dean, Charles Kilshaw *Alli Sup*
Dean, Charlotte *Alli Sup*
Dean, Corinne *BlkAW, OhA&B*
Dean, Donald *MnBBF*
Dean, Dwight G 1918- *ConAu 17R, WrD 1976*
Dean, E H *Alli Sup*
Dean, Edwin Frederick James 1907- *Au&Wr*
Dean, Edwin Robinson 1933- *ConAu 17R, IndAu 1917*
Dean, Ellet *ChPo S1*
Dean, Eric Douglas 1916- *BiDPar*
Dean, Francis M *Alli Sup, PoIre*
Dean, George Alfred *Alli, Alli Sup*
Dean, Graham M 1904- *AmA&B, AuBYP*
Dean, Howard E 1916- *ConAu 41*
Dean, James 1776-1849 *DcNAA*
Dean, Jeffrey S 1939- *ConAu 37*
Dean, Joel 1906- *ConAu 33*
Dean, John 1831-1888 *Alli, Alli Sup, DcAmA*
Dean, John A 1921- *ConAu 53*
Dean, John Marvin 1875-1935 *DcNAA*
Dean, John Ward 1815-1902 *Alli Sup, BiD&SB, CyAL 2, DcAmA, DcNAA*
Dean, Joseph Jolyon 1921- *Au&Wr*
Dean, Joseph Joy *Alli Sup*
Dean, Leon W 1889- *MnBBF, WhWNAA*
Dean, M S *Alli Sup*
Dean, Marguerite Mooers Marshall *WhWNAA*
Dean, Mary 1923- *Au&Wr*
Dean, Michael *BlkAW*
Dean, Nell Marr 1910- *AuBYP, ConAu 21*
Dean, Paul 1789-1860 *DcAmA, DcNAA*
Dean, Peter *Alli*
Dean, Phillip Hayes *BlkAW*
Dean, Reginald Scott 1897- *WhWNAA*
Dean, Richard *Alli*
Dean, Roy 1925- *ConAu 57*
Dean, S *Alli, Alli Sup*
Dean, Sidney 1818-1901 *DcNAA*
Dean, Mrs. Sidney Wallace *AmA&B*
Dean, Silas 1737-1789 *DcNAA*
Dean, Vera Micheles 1903-1972 *AmA&B, ConAu 37, REnAL, TwCA Sup*
Dean, Warren 1932- *ConAu 29*
Dean, William *Alli Sup*
Dean, William Denard 1937- *ConAu 37, WrD 1976*
Dean, Winton 1916- *Au&Wr*
Dean, Yetive H 1909- *ConAu P-1*
DeAnda, Peter *BlkAW*
DeAndrade, Mario Coelho Pinto 1928- *AfA 1*
Deane, Agnes Trevor *Alli Sup*
Deane, Alva *ChPo, ChPo S1*
Deane, Annie *ChPo*
Deane, Anthony Charles 1870- *ChPo, ChPo S1, ChPo S2, WhLA*
Deane, C P *Alli Sup*
Deane, Charles *Alli Sup*
Deane, Charles 1813-1889 *Alli Sup, AmA&B, CyAL 2, DcAmA, DcNAA*
Deane, Christopher Page *Alli Sup*
Deane, David J *Alli Sup*
Deane, Dorothy *ChPo*
Deane, Eddie V 1929- *AmSCAP 66*
Deane, Edmond 1572- *Alli*
Deane, Elsie *ChPo, ChPo S1*
Deane, F A *Alli Sup*
Deane, Fannie A *CarSB*
Deane, Henry *Alli, Alli Sup*
Deane, Henry Bargrave Finnelly 1846- *Alli Sup*
Deane, Henry Charles 1840- *Alli Sup*
Deane, Herbert Andrew 1921- *ConAu 1R*
Deane, Inigo Patrick 1860-1894 *PoIre*
Deane, J *Alli Sup*
Deane, James *Alli Sup*
Deane, Sir James Parker 1812- *Alli Sup*

Deane, John *Alli, Alli Sup*
Deane, John Bathurst *Alli Sup*
Deane, Leslie D 1926- *IndAu 1917*
Deane, Llewellyn *Alli Sup*
Deane, Lorna 1909- *Au&Wr, ConAu XR*
Deane, Margery 1850-1888 *Alli Sup, ChPo, DcAmA*
Deane, Mary *Alli Sup*
Deane, Milly *Alli Sup*
Deane, Nancy H 1939- *ConAu 29*
Deane, Norman *ConAu XR, EncM&D, LongC*
Deane, Richard Burton 1848-1930 *Alli, DcNAA, OxCan*
Deane, Samuel 1733-1814 *Alli, AmA, CyAL 1, DcNAA*
Deane, Samuel 1784-1834 *DcAmA, DcNAA*
Deane, Shirley Joan 1920- *AmA&B, Au&Wr, ConAu 1R, WrD 1976*
Deane, Silas 1737-1789 *BiD&SB, DcAmA*
Deane, Vesey *MnBBF*
Deane, Wallace *MnBBF*
Deane, William John 1823- *Alli Sup*
Deane, William Reed 1809-1871 *CyAL 2, DcAmA, DcNAA*
Deane-Drummond, Anthony 1917- *WrD 1976*
Deanesly, Margaret 1885- *Au&Wr*
DeAngeli, Marguerite Lofft 1889- *AmA&B, Au&Wr, AuBYP, AuICB, AuNews 2, BkCL, ChLR 1, ChPo, ChPo S1, ConAu 5R, ConICB, IlCB 1945, IlCB 1956, IlCB 1966, JBA 1951, MorBMP, Newb 1922, SmATA 1*
DeAngelis, Alberto 1885- *WhLA*
DeAngelis, Peter 1929- *AmSCAP 66*
DeAngelis, Thomas Jefferson 1859-1933 *DcNAA*
Deans, Mrs. Alexander *ChPo*
Deans, Harris 1886- *WhLA*
Deans, James Douglas *ChPo*
Deans, William *Alli Sup*
DeAparicio, Vibiana Chamberlin *DrAF 1976*
Dear, H C *Alli Sup*
Dearborn, Andrew *HsB&A*
Dearborn, George VanNess 1869-1938 *AmLY, DcNAA*
Dearborn, Henry *BbtC*
Dearborn, Henry Alexander Scammell 1783-1851 *Alli, CyAL 1, DcAmA, DcNAA*
Dearborn, Jeremiah Wadleigh *Alli Sup*
Dearborn, Nathaniel 1786-1852 *DcNAA, EarAB, EarAB Sup*
Dearborn, Ned 1865- *WhWNAA*
Dearborn, Ned Harland 1893-1962 *AmA&B*
Dearden, Harold 1883-1962 *LongC*
Dearden, James A 1924- *ConAu 33*
Dearden, James Shackley 1931- *ConAu 25, WrD 1976*
Dearden, John 1919- *ConAu 33*
Dearden, William *ChPo S1, ChPo S2*
Deardorff, Neva Ruth 1887-1958 *IndAu 1917*
Deardorff, Robert 1912- *ConAu 61*
Deare, James R *Alli, BiDLA*
Dearing, Sir Edward *Alli*
Dearle, Edward *Alli*
DeArmand, Frances Ullmann *AuBYP, ConAu 5R, SmATA 10*
DeArmas, Frederick A 1945- *ConAu 37*
Dearmer, Geoffrey 1893- *Au&Wr, ChPo, ChPo S1, ChPo S2, ConAu 23*
Dearmer, Mabel *ChPo S1*
Dearmer, Percy 1867-1936 *ChPo, ChPo S1, WhLA*
Dearmin, Jennie Tarascou 1924- *ConAu 5R*
Dearn, T D W *Alli, BiDLA*
Dearness, John 1852- *WhWNAA*
Dearsly, Henry Richard *Alli, Alli Sup*
Deas, Anne Izard *BiDSA*
Deas, Christie *ChPo*
Deas, F T R *Alli Sup*
Deas, Fanny M P *LivFWS*
Deas, Francis *Alli Sup*
Deas, George And James Anderson *Alli*
Deas, James *Alli Sup*
Deas, Katherine *BlkAW*
Dease, Edmund F 1856- *Br&AmS*
Dease, J R *PoIre*
Dease, Peter Warren *OxCan*

DeCoster, Cyrus C 1914- *ConAu 49*
DeCostobadie, F Palliser 1855- *Br&AmS*
Decourcelle, Pierre 1856- *BbD, BiD&SB*
DeCourcelles, James Hector *Alli Sup*
DeCourcy, F *Alli Sup*
DeCourcy, Richard 1743-1803 *Alli, PoIre*
DeCourcy-Parry, Charles Norman 1899-
  Br&AmS
DeCoursey, Russell Myles 1900- *IndAu 1917*
DeCourtenay, J M *BbtC*
DeCoy, Robert H, Jr. 1920- *BlkAW,
  ConAu 25, LivBA*
DeCrescenzo, Vincenzo 1875-1964 *AmSCAP 66*
DeCrespigny, Caroline *Alli*
DeCrespigny, Mrs. Champion *Alli*
DeCrespigny, Sir Claude Champion 1847-1935
  Br&AmS
DeCrespigny, Eyre Ch *Alli Sup*
DeCrespigny, Rafe 1936- *ConAu 57*
DeCrespigny, Rose Champion 1860-1935 *BiDPar*
DeCristoforo, Romeo John 1917- *ConAu 9R,
  WrD 1976*
DeCrow, Karen 1937- *ConAu 33*
Decrow, W E *Alli Sup*
Decrow, William Emery 1853-1905 *DcNAA*
Decter, Midge 1927- *ConAu 45, WrD 1976*
Dede, James *Alli, BiDLA*
Dede, Louis 1884- *WhLA*
Dedeaux, Richard A 1940- *BlkAW*
DeDecker, Jeremias 1610-1666 *ChPo*
Dedek, John F 1929- *ConAu 33*
Dedekind, Alexander 1856- *WhLA*
Dedekind, Friedrich 1525-1598 *BiD&SB,
  CasWL, DcEuL, OxGer*
Dederer, Pauline Hamilton 1878- *WhWNAA*
Dederick, Robert 1919- *ConP 1970,
  WrD 1976*
Dedham, Richard *MnBBF*
DeDiego, Jose 1868- *AmLY*
DeDienes, Andre 1913- *Au&Wr, ConAu 41*
DeDiesbach, Count Ghislain 1931- *Au&Wr*
Dedijer, Vladimir 1914- *Au&Wr, ConAu 1R*
Dedina, Michel Jean Bernard 1933- *Au&Wr,
  ConAu 33*
Dedman, S C *ChPo S1*
Dedmon, Emmett 1918- *AmA&B, Au&Wr,
  ConAu 9R, WrD 1976*
DeDunstanville And Basset, Lord 1753?- *BiDLA*
Dee, Arthur *Alli*
Dee, Dare *MnBBF*
Dee, Henry *ConAu XR*
Dee, John 1527-1608 *Alli, BrAu, CrE&SL,
  NewC, OxEng, REn*
Dee, Josephine *ChPo*
Dee, Minnie Roof 1866-1940 *DcNAA,
  WhWNAA*
Dee, Ruby 1923- *BlkAW, ChPo S2*
Dee, Sylvia 1914- *AmA&B, AmNov,
  AmSCAP 66*
Deeble, Joseph Harry 1819- *Alli Sup*
Deeble, R J *ConP 1970*
Deeble, William *Alli*
Deedes, Cecil *Alli Sup*
Deedes, Henry *Alli Sup*
Deedy, John 1923- *ConAu 33*
Deegener, Paul Johannes B 1875- *WhLA*
Deeley, Peter Alan 1934- *Au&Wr*
Deeley, Roger 1944- *Au&Wr, ConAu 53,
  WrD 1976*
Deelman, Christian Felling 1937-1964
  ConAu P-1
Deemer, Bill 1945- *ConAu 17R, ConP 1970*
Deemer, Charles *DrAF 1976*
Deemer, Horace Emerson 1858-1917 *DcNAA,
  IndAu 1917*
Deems, Charles Force 1820-1893 *Alli, Alli Sup,
  BiD&SB, BiDSA, DcAmA, DcNAA*
Deems, Edward Mark 1852-1929 *AmLY,
  BiDSA, ChPo S2, DcNAA, WhWNAA*
Deems, Frederick M *Alli Sup*
Deems, James Harry 1848-1931 *AmLY,
  DcNAA, WhWNAA*
Deen, Edith Alderman 1905- *ConAu 5R*
Deener, David R 1920- *ConAu 17R*
Deeping, Warwick 1877-1950 *DcLEnL, EvLB,
  LongC, NewC, Pen Eng, REn, TwCA,
  TwCA Sup, TwCW, WhLA*
Deer, Irving 1924- *ConAu 17R*

Deere, Alan Christopher 1917- *Au&Wr,
  WrD 1976*
Deering, Charles *Alli*
Deering, Sir Edward *Alli*
Deering, Edward d1576 *Alli*
Deering, F P *Alli Sup*
Deering, Fremont B *DcNAA*
Deering, Ivah Everett 1889- *OhA&B*
Deering, James H *Alli Sup*
Deering, John R *BiDSA*
Deering, Mary S *Alli Sup*
Deering, Nathanael *CyAL 2*
Deering, Nathaniel 1791-1881 *Alli, AmA,
  AmA&B, DcAmA, DcNAA, OxAm*
Deering, Richard *Alli*
Deering, Robert Waller 1865- *WhWNAA*
Deering, Thomas W *Alli Sup*
Deering, Tommy 1938- *AmSCAP 66*
Dees, R D *Alli*
Dees, W *ChPo*
Deese, James 1921- *ConAu 1R*
Deeter, Allen C 1931- *ConAu 45*
Deevers, W J *PoIre*
Deevy, Teresa 1894- *CatA 1952*
DeFaber, A *Alli Sup*
DeFalco, Joseph Michael 1931- *ConAu 13R,
  WrD 1976*
DeFazio, Marjorie *DrAP 1975*
DeFelice, Louise P 1945- *ConAu 61*
DeFelitta, Frank 1921- *ConAu 61*
DeFenouillet, Joseph Emile 1806-1859 *BbtC*
Defensor *DcNAA*
Deferrari, Roy Joseph 1890-1969 *AmA&B,
  CatA 1947, ConAu P-1*
DeFerrari, Sister Teresa Mary 1930- *ConAu 9R*
DeFerrariis, Antonio 1444-1517 *CasWL*
Deffand, Marie DeVichy-Chamrond Du
  1697-1780 *BbD, BiD&SB, DcEuL, NewC,
  OxFr, REn*
Deffner, Donald L 1924- *ConAu 17R*
Deffoux, Leon *OxFr*
Deffry, Frank 1938- *ConP 1970*
DeField, Edward *WhWNAA*
DeFilippi, Amedeo 1900- *AmSCAP 66*
DeFilippi, Filippo 1869- *WhLA*
DeFilippo, Eduardo 1900- *CnMD, CnThe,
  CrCD, McGWD, ModWD, REnWD*
DeFletin, P *ConAu XR*
DeFleury, Maria *PoCh*
DeFlori, C *ChPo, ChPo S1*
Defoe, Daniel 1660?-1731 *Alli, AtlBL, BbD,
  BiD&SB, BrAu, CarSB, CasWL,
  ChPo S1, Chmbr 2, CriT 2, CyWA,
  DcBiA, DcEnA, DcEnL, DcEuL,
  DcLEnL, EvLB, HsB&A, MnBBF,
  MouLC 2, NewC, OxEng, Pen Eng,
  RAdv 1, RCom, REn, WebEAL, WhCL*
Defoe, Ethellyn Brewer *ChPo*
DeFonblanque, Albany DeGrenier *Alli Sup*
DeFonblanque, Caroline Alicia *Alli Sup*
DeFonblanque, Edward Barrington *Alli Sup*
DeFonblanque, Ethel Maud *Alli Sup*
DeFonseka, Joseph Peter 1897- *CatA 1947*
DeFontaine, F G *Alli Sup*
DeFontaine, Felix Gregory 1834-1896 *AmA,
  AmA&B, BiD&SB, DcAmA, DcNAA*
DeFontaine, Wade Hampton 1893- *ConAu 5R*
DeFoor, John W 1929- *AmSCAP 66*
DeForbes *ConAu XR*
Deford, Frank 1938- *ConAu 33, WrD 1976*
DeFord, Miriam Allen 1888-1975 *AmA&B,
  ConAu 1R, EncM&D, REnAL, TwCA,
  TwCA Sup, WhWNAA*
DeFord, Sara Whitcraft 1916- *ConAu 25,
  OhA&B*
DeForest, Barry *HsB&A*
DeForest, Charles 1928- *AmSCAP 66*
DeForest, Charles Mills 1878-1947 *DcNAA*
DeForest, Charlotte B 1879- *ConAu 25,
  WhWNAA*
DeForest, Charlotte R *ChPo S1*
DeForest, Henry Pelouze 1864-1948 *AmA&B,
  DcNAA*
DeForest, J W *Alli*
DeForest, John Kinne Hyde 1844-1911 *DcNAA*
DeForest, John William 1826-1906 *Alli Sup,
  AmA, AmA&B, BbD, BiD&SB, CasWL,
  ChPo, CnDAL, CyWA, DcAmA,*

  *DcLEnL, DcNAA, EncM&D, EvLB,
  OxAm, Pen Am, REn, REnAL,
  WebEAL*
DeForest, Julia B *Alli Sup*
DeForest, Marian d1935 *DcNAA*
DeForest, Robert Weeks 1848- *DcAmA*
DeForrest, Virginia *ChPo S1*
DeForris, Ross *ChPo, ChPo S1*
DeFossard, Esta Harriet 1934- *Au&Wr*
DeFossard, R A 1929- *ConAu 41*
DeFraga, Geoff 1913- *Au&Wr*
DeFraine, John *Alli Sup*
DeFrancesco, Louis E 1888- *AmSCAP 66*
DeFranco, Boniface 1923- *AmSCAP 66*
DeFrees, Sister Madeline 1919- *ConAu 9R,
  DrAF 1976, DrAP 1975, WhPNW,
  WrD 1976*
DeFrees, Mary Madeline 1919- *ConP 1970*
Defresne, August 1893- *CnMD*
Defries, Amelia *WhLA*
Defries, R D *OxCan Sup*
DeFriese, Annie E *ChPo*
DeFuniak, William Q 1901- *ConAu 33*
DeGaris, Charles Francis 1886- *WhWNAA*
DeGarmo, Charles 1849-1934 *DcAmA,
  DcNAA*
DeGarmo, William Burton 1849-1936 *Alli Sup,
  AmLY, DcNAA, WhWNAA*
Degas, Edgar 1834-1917 *AtlBL, OxFr, REn*
Degas, Hilaire Germain Edgar 1834-1917 *NewC*
DeGaspe, Philippe Aubert 1786- *BbtC*
DeGaspe, Philippe Aubert, Jr. d1841 *BbtC*
DeGastyne, Serge 1930- *AmSCAP 66*
DeGaulle, Charles 1890-1970 *REn*
DeGaury, Gerald 1897- *ConAu 13R,
  WrD 1976*
DeGaztold, Carmen Bernos *ChPo S1*
Degee, Olivier *REn*
Degeer, I Vern 1902- *WhWNAA*
Degener, Hermann A L 1874- *WhLA*
Degenfeld-Schonburg, Ferdinand, Graf Von 1882-
  WhLA
DeGenlis, S DeSaint Aubin, Comtesse 1746-1830
  DcBiA
DeGennaro, Angelo Anthony 1919- *ConAu 13R*
DeGeorge, Richard T 1933- *ConAu 5R,
  WrD 1976*
DeGering, Etta Fowler 1898- *AuBYP,
  ConAu P-1, SmATA 7*
Degetau, Federico 1862-1914 *PueRA*
DeGex, Sir John Peter 1809-1887 *Alli Sup*
Degg, Simon *Alli*
Degge, Sir Simon *Alli*
DeGhelderode, Michel *ModRL, WorAu*
Deghy, Guy 1912- *Au&Wr, ConAu P-1,
  WrD 1976*
Degler, Carl N 1921- *ConAu 5R*
Degler, Howard Edward 1893- *WhWNAA*
Degler, Stanley E 1929- *ConAu 25*
Degnan, James Philip 1933- *ConAu 41*
DeGoesbriand, Louis 1816-1899 *DcNAA*
Degols, Gerard *Alli*
DeGoncourt, Edmond Louis Antoine Huot
  1822-1896 *DcBiA*
DeGoncourt, Jules Alfred Huot 1830-1870
  DcBiA
DeGongora, Luis *ChPo S1*
DeGourmont *TwCA*
DeGourmont, Remy *ModRL*
DeGouy, Louis Pullig 1875-1947 *DcNAA*
DeGracia Concepcion, Marcelo 1895-
  WhWNAA
DeGraeff, Allen *WrD 1976*
DeGraff, Lawrence 1871-1934 *DcNAA*
DeGraff, Lulu Hamilton *WhLA*
DeGraff, Robert 1909- *AmSCAP 66*
DeGraffenreidt, Baron Christopher *BiDSA*
DeGraft, Joe *ConDr, WrD 1976*
DeGraft, Joe Coliman 1932?- *AfA 1*
DeGraft-Johnson, John Coleman 1919-
  ConAu 21, WrD 1976
DeGramont, Sanche 1932- *AmA&B,
  ConAu 45*
DeGrasse, Will *Alli Sup*
Degravere, J *Alli*
DeGrazia, Alfred 1919- *AmA&B, ConAu 13R*
DeGrazia, Ettore 1909- *ConAu 61*
DeGrazia, Sebastian 1917- *AmA&B*

Deland, Margaret Wade 1857-1945 *Alli Sup, AmA&B, BbD, BiD&SB, ChPo, ChPo S1, ChPo S2, Chmbr 3, ConAmL, DcAmA, DcBiA, DcLEnL, DcNAA, LongC, OxAm, REn, REnAL, TwCA, TwCA Sup, WhWNAA*
DeLand, Tracy *WhWNAA*
Delandine, Antoine-Joseph *OxFr*
Delane, John Thaddeus 1817-1879 *Alli, DcLEnL, NewC, OxEng*
Delane, W F A *Alli*
Delaney SEE ALSO Delany
Delaney, Bud *ConAu 57*
Delaney, C F 1938- *ConAu 25*
DeLaney, Charles 1925- *AmSCAP 66*
Delaney, Daniel J 1938- *ConAu 41*
Delaney, Denis *ConAu XR, WrD 1976*
Delaney, Edmund T 1914- *ConAu 13R*
Delaney, Francis, Jr. 1931- *ConAu 57*
Delaney, Franey *ConAu XR*
Delaney, Harry 1932- *ConAu 25, SmATA 3*
Delaney, Jack J 1921- *ConAu 21*
Delaney, John Joseph 1910- *ConAu 1R*
Delaney, Lolo M 1937- *ConAu 57*
Delaney, Mary Murray 1913- *ConAu 53, WrD 1976*
Delaney, Norman Conrad 1932- *ConAu 37, WrD 1976*
Delaney, Oliver *Alli*
DeLaney, Paul 1865- *WhWNAA*
Delaney, Robert Finley 1925- *ConAu 1R*
Delaney, Samuel R 1942- *AmA&B, WrD 1976*
Delaney, Selden Peabody 1874- *AmLY*
Delaney, Shelagh 1939- *CnMD, ConAu 17R, ConDr, CrCD, LongC, McGWD, ModWD, NewC, Pen Eng, REn, TwCW, WorAu, WrD 1976*
Delaney, Theresa *OxCan*
DeLange, Edgar 1904-1949 *AmSCAP 66*
Delanglez, Jean *OxCan*
Delanne, Gabriel 1857-1926 *BiDPar*
Delano, Aline *Alli Sup*
Delano, Alonzo 1806?-1874 *AmA, AmA&B, DcNAA, OxAm, REnAL*
Delano, Amasa 1763-1823 *AmA&B, DcAmA, DcNAA, OxAm, REnAL*
Delano, Charles G *Alli Sup*
Delano, Edith Barnard 1875-1946 *AmA&B, DcNAA, WhWNAA*
Delano, Frances Jackson 1857- *DcAmA*
Delano, Isaac O 1904- *ConAu 25*
Delano, Jane Arminda 1862-1919 *DcNAA*
Delano, Kenneth J 1934- *ConAu 57*
Delany SEE ALSO Delaney
Delany, Clarissa Scott 1901-1927 *BlkAW*
Delany, Martin Robinson 1812-1885 *Alli Sup, AmA, BlkAW, DcNAA*
Delany, Mary 1700-1788 *Alli, BrAu, DcLEnL, NewC, OxEng*
Delany, Patrick 1685?-1768 *Alli, NewC, PoIre*
Delany, Paul 1937- *ConAu 29*
Delany, Ralph *PoIre*
Delany, Samuel R 1942- *BlkAW, ConNov 1976, DrAF 1976, LivBA*
Delany, Selden Peabody 1874-1935 *CatA 1947, DcNAA, WhWNAA*
Delany, William J 1844- *PoIre*
Delap, J *Alli*
Delap, John *Alli*
DeLaPaix, Jack *ChPo*
DeLaPasture *TwCA, TwCA Sup*
DeLaPasture, Edmee Elizabeth Monica 1890-1943 *EvLB*
DeLaPasture, Elizabeth Monica *DcLEnL*
DeLaPasture, Mrs. Henry 1866-1945 *EvLB, LongC*
Delaplaine, Edward Schley 1893- *Au&Wr, ChPo*
Delaplaine, Joseph 1777-1824 *AmA&B*
Delaplane, Stanton Hill 1907- *ConAu 25*
DeLaPoer, May *Alli Sup*
DeLaPonterie, Ferdinand *BbtC*
Delaporte, Michel 1806-1872 *BiD&SB*
Delaporte, Theophile *ConAu XR*
DeLaPortilla, Marta 1927- *ConAu 61*
DeLaPryme, Alexander George 1870- *WhLA*
Delapryme, Charles *Alli Sup*

DeLara, D E *Alli*
DeLaRame, Louisa 1840-1908 *Alli Sup*
DeLaRamee, Louise 1840-1908 *BrAu 19, CarSB, JBA 1934*
DeLaRamee, Marie Louise *OxEng*
Delaroche, Hippolyte 1797-1856 *OxFr*
DeLaRoche, Mazo 1885-1961 *CanNov, CanWr, CasWL, Chmbr 3, ConAmL, CyWA, DcLEnL, EvLB, JBA 1934, LongC, OxAm, OxCan, OxEng, Pen Eng, REn, REnAL, TwCA, TwCA Sup, TwCW*
Delaroche, Peter *BbtC*
DeLarrea, Victoria *IlBYP*
Delarue-Mardrus, Lucie 1880-1945 *EvEuW, OxFr*
Delasanta, Rodney 1932- *ConAu 33*
DeLasCuevas, Ramon *ConAu XR*
DeLaSerna *TwCA, TwCA Sup*
DeLaSerna, Ramon Gomez *ModRL*
DeLaspee, H *Alli Sup*
DeLaTaille, Maurice 1872-1933 *CatA 1952*
DeLaTorre, Lillian 1902- *AmA&B, AuBYP, ConAu XR, EncM&D, REnAL, TwCA Sup, WrD 1976*
DeLaTouche, Janet *Alli Sup*
Delatour, Georges *AtlBL*
DeLaubenfels, David J 1925- *ConAu 53*
DeLaunay, Mademoiselle *OxFr*
DeLaunay, Jacques F 1924- *ConAu 9R*
Delaunay, Robert 1885-1941 *AtlBL*
Delaune, Henry *Alli*
Delaune, Jewel Lynn DeGrummond *SmATA 7*
Delaune, Lynn *AuBYP, ConAu 1R*
Delaune, Thomas *Alli*
Delaune, Thomas 1667-1728 *Alli*
Delaune, William *Alli*
DeLaura, David Joseph 1930- *ConAu 23, WrD 1976*
DeLaurentis, Louise Budde 1920- *ConAu 5R*
Delaval, Barclay *Alli Sup*
Delaval, Edward Hussey 1729-1814 *Alli, BiDLA, BiDLA Sup*
Delavan, David Bryson 1850-1942 *DcNAA*
Delavan, Edward Cornelius 1793-1871 *Alli Sup, DcAmA, DcNAA*
DeLaVergne, George H 1868- *AmA&B*
Delavigne, Casimir 1793-1843 *DcEuL, McGWD, OxFr*
Delavigne, Jean Francois Casimir 1793-1843 *BbD, BiD&SB, CasWL, EuA, EvEuW*
Delavoye, Alexander Marin *Alli Sup*
DeLaVoye, G M *Alli Sup*
Delavrancea, Barbu 1858-1918 *CasWL, McGWD*
Delaware, Lord d1618 *BiDSA*
DeLaWarr, Countess *Alli Sup*
DeLaWarr, George Walter 1904-1969 *ConAu P-1*
DeLaWarr, Baron Thomas West 1577-1618 *OxAm, REnAL*
DeLaWarre *Alli*
Delay-Baillen, Claude 1934- *ConAu 53*
DeLaZouche, Lord *BrAu 19*
Delbanco, Nicholas F 1942- *ConAu 17R, ConLC 6, DrAF 1976, WrD 1976*
DelBarco, Lucy Salamanca *ConAu 17R*
DelBene, Bartolomeo 1514-1587 *CasWL*
DelBoca, Angelo 1925- *ConAu 25*
Delbos, Leon *Alli Sup*
DelCastillo, Michel 1933- *Au&Wr, ModRL, WorAu*
Delderfield, Eric Raymond 1909- *Au&Wr, ConAu 53, WrD 1976*
Delderfield, Ronald Frederick 1912-1972 *Au&Wr, ConAu 37, WhCL*
Delear, Frank J 1914- *ConAu 21, WrD 1976*
DeLeath, Vaughn 1896-1943 *AmSCAP 66*
Deledda, Grazia 1871-1936 *CasWL, ClDMEuL, CyWA, EncWL, EvEuW, ModRL, Pen Eur, REn, TwCA, TwCA Sup, TwCW, WhTwL*
DeLee, Joseph Bolivar 1869-1942 *AmLY, DcNAA, WhWNAA*
DeLeeuw, Adele Louise 1899- *AmA&B, AuBYP, ChPo S1, ConAu 1R, JBA 1951, OhA&B, SmATA 1, WhWNAA, WrD 1976*
DeLeeuw, Cateau Wilhelmina 1903- *Au&Wr,*

AuBYP, ConAu 1R, JBA 1951, OhA&B
DeLeeuw, Hendrik 1896- *AmA&B*
DeLegall, Walter 1936- *BlkAW*
Delehanty, W H *ChPo*
Delehaye, Hippolyte 1859-1941 *CatA 1947*
DeLeine, M A *Alli Sup*
DeLeon, Daniel 1852-1914 *DcNAA, OxAm*
DeLeon, Edwin 1828-1891 *Alli Sup, BbD, BiD&SB, BiDSA, DcAmA, DcNAA*
DeLeon, Edwin Warren 1868-1918 *DcNAA*
DeLeon, Nephtali *DrAF 1976*
DeLeon, Robert 1904-1961 *AmSCAP 66*
DeLeon, Stuart *Alli Sup*
DeLeon, Thomas Cooper 1839-1914 *Alli Sup, AmA, AmA&B, BiDSA, ChPo S1, DcAmA, DcNAA, REnAL*
DeLeone, Francesco Bartolomeo 1887-1948 *AmSCAP 66*
Delepierre, Joseph Octave 1802-1879 *Alli, Alli Sup*
DeLerma, Dominique-Rene 1928- *ConAu 45, IndAu 1917*
Delery, Francois Charles 1815-1880 *BiD&SB, BiDSA*
Delery, Francois Charles 1815-1858 *DcAmA*
Delery, Francois Charles 1815-1880 *DcNAA*
Delessert *BbtC*
Delessert, Etienne 1941- *ConAu 21, IlBYP*
DeLestry, Edmond Louis 1860-1933 *DcNAA, WhWNAA*
DeLestry, Louis Edmund 1860-1933 *DcAmA*
Deletanville, Thomas *Alli*
DeLevante, E R *Alli Sup*
DeLey, Herbert 1936- *ConAu 21*
Delf, Dirc Van 1365?- *CasWL*
Delf, Mrs. H F *Alli Sup*
Delf, Harry 1892-1964 *AmSCAP 66*
Delf, Thomas *Alli Sup*
Delf, William Herbert *ChPo S1*
Delfgaauw, Bernard 1912- *ConAu 23*
Delgado, Abelardo *DrAP 1975*
Delgado, Alan George 1909- *Au&Wr, ConAu 9R, WrD 1976*
Delgado, Emilio 1904-1967 *PueRA*
Delgado, Francisco *Pen Eur*
Delgado, Isaac *Alli*
Delgado, Jose M 1915- *ConAu 29*
Delgado, Washington 1927- *DcCLA*
DelGrande, Louis *OxCan Sup*
DeL'Horbe, Augusta Kirch *ChPo S1*
DeL'Hoste, Edward Paterson *Alli Sup*
D'Elia, Donald John 1933- *ConAu 57*
DeLiancourt, Raoul *ConAu XR*
Delibes, Leo 1836-1891 *AtlBL, OxFr, REn*
Delibes, Miguel 1920- *CasWL, ConAu XR, EncWL, TwCW*
Delibes Setien, Miguel 1920- *ConAu 45*
Delicado, Francisco *CasWL, DcSpL, Pen Eur*
Deliee, Felix J *Alli Sup*
Deligiorgis, Stavros 1933- *ConAu 61*
Deligny, Louis *WhWNAA*
DeLiguori, St. Alphonsas *ChPo S1*
Delilez, Francis *Alli Sup*
Delille, Henry A *Alli Sup*
Delille, J Douglas *Alli Sup*
Delille, Jacques 1738-1813 *BbD, CasWL, DcEuL, EvEuW, OxFr, Pen Eur*
Delillo, Don *DrAF 1976*
DeLima, Agnes 1887?-1974 *ConAu 53*
DeLima, Clara Rosa 1922- *ConAu 57*
DeLima, Sigrid 1921- *ConAu 25, DrAF 1976, WorAu, WrD 1976*
DeLisle, Claude Joseph Rouget *ChPo*
DeLisle, Edwin *Alli Sup*
DeLisle, Emma *BiDLA*
DeL'Isle, F Louis Jaquerod *Alli Sup*
Delisle, Francoise 1886?-1974 *ConAu 53*
Delisle, Harcourt *MnBBF*
DeLisle, Hirzel Carey *Alli Sup*
Delisle, Leopold-Victor 1826-1910 *OxFr*
Delisle DeSales, Jean-Claude Izouard 1741-1816 *OxFr*
DeLisser, Herbert George 1878-1944 *CasWL, DcLEnL, WebEAL*
Delisser, Richard L 1820- *Alli*
Delitzsch, Franz 1813-1890 *BiD&SB*
Delius, Anthony Ronald St. Martin 1916- *CasWL, ConAu 17R, ConP 1970,*

ConP 1975, Pen Eng, TwCW, WrD 1976
Delius, Frederick 1862-1934 AtlBL
Delk, Robert Carlton 1920- ConAu 45
Dell, Barton Alli Sup
Dell, Belinda 1925- ConAu XR, WrD 1976
Dell, Draycot Montagu 1888- ChPo S1, ChPo S2, MnBBF
Dell, E T, Jr. 1923- ConAu 13R
Dell, Edmund 1921- WrD 1976
Dell, Ethel Mary 1881-1939 EvLB, NewC, REn, TwCW
Dell, Floyd 1887-1969 AmA&B, AnMV 1926, CnDAL, ConAmA, ConAmL, DcLEnL, LongC, ModAL, OxAm, Pen Am, REn, REnAL, TwCA, TwCA Sup, WhWNAA
Dell, George Alli
Dell, J H Alli Sup
Dell, John d1810 Alli, BiDLA, BiDLA Sup
Dell, Jonas Alli
Dell, Robert Alli Sup
Dell, Sidney 1918- ConAu 5R, WrD 1976
Dell, William Alli
Della Crusca NewC
Della Cruscans DcEnL
DellaCasa, Giovanni 1503-1556 CasWL, Pen Eur, REn
DellaPorta, Giambattista 1535-1615 CasWL, McGWD, REn
Dellaripa, Dominic J 1921- AmSCAP 66
DellaRobbia AtlBL
DellaValle, Federico 1560?-1628 CasWL, McGWD, Pen Eur
DelleGrazie, Marie Eugenie OxGer
Dellenbaugh, Frederick Samuel 1853-1935 AmA&B, AmLY, DcAmA, DcNAA, OhA&B, WhWNAA
Dellin, Lubomir, A D 1920- ConAu 45
Dellinger, Dave AmA&B
Dellinger, John Howard 1886- WhWNAA
Delloff, Irving Arthur 1920- ConAu 13R
Dellquest, Augustus Wilfrid 1901- WhWNAA
Delman, David 1924- Au&Wr
DelMar, Alexander 1836-1926 Alli Sup, AmLY, BiD&SB, DcAmA, DcNAA
DelMar, Algernon 1870- AmLY, WhWNAA
Delmar, Dezso 1891- AmSCAP 66
DelMar, Eugene 1864- WhWNAA
DelMar, Frances WhWNAA
Delmar, Vina 1905- AmA&B, CnDAL, OxAm, REnAL, TwCA, TwCA Sup
DelMar, Walter 1862-1944 DcNAA, WhWNAA
DelMar, William Arthur 1880- WhWNAA
Delmard, Sophia Duberly Alli Sup
Delmas, Delphin Michael 1844-1928 DcNAA
Delmer, Denis Sefton 1904- Au&Wr, ConAu 5R
Delmere, F MnBBF
Delmonico, Andrea ConAu XR, WrD 1976
Delmonte, Felix Maria 1810?- BiD&SB
DelMonte, Louis J 1912- AmSCAP 66
Delmonte Y Tejada, Antonio 1783-1861 BiD&SB
Delmote, P Alli
DeLoach, Allen DrAP 1975
DeLoach, Charles F 1927- ConAu 37, WrD 1976
DeLoach, Clarence, Jr. 1936- ConAu 57
DelOccidente, Maria AmA&B
DeLoi, Raimon WhWNAA
DeLoier, Peter Alli
DeLolme, Jean Louis Chmbr 2
DeLolme, John Louis 1740?-1807 Alli, CasWL, DcEuL, EvEuW, EvLB
Delon, George And Rhodes, James F Alli Sup
DeLone, Ruth ConAu XR
Delone, Thomas ChPo
Delone, Thomas 1543?-1607? NewC
Deloney, Thomas 1543?-1600? Alli, AtlBL, BiD&SB, BrAu, CasWL, ChPo, Chmbr 1, CrE&SL, CriT 1, CyWA, DcEnL, DcLEnL, EvLB, NewC, OxEng, Pen Eng, REn, WebEAL
DeLong, Arthur Hamilton 1862-1919 OhA&B
DeLong, Emma J 1851-1940 DcNAA
DeLong, Emma W 1851-1940 AmA&B, WhWNAA

DeLong, George Washington 1844-1881 Alli Sup, AmA&B, BbD, BiD&SB, DcAmA, DcNAA
DeLong, Irwin Hoch 1873- WhWNAA
DeLong, John Alli Sup
DeLong, Leo Ray 1894- IndAu 1917
DeLong, Russell Victor 1901- AmA&B
DeLongchamps, Joanne 1923- ConAu 9R, DrAP 1975, WrD 1976
DeLora, Joann S 1935- ConAu 53
Delord, Taxile 1815-1877 BbD, BiD&SB
Deloria, Vine, Jr. 1933- AmA&B, ConAu 53
DeLorimier, Charles C BbtC
Delorme, Marion 1611?-1650 OxFr
Delorme, Michele ConAu XR
Delorme, Philibert 1510?-1570 AtlBL, OxFr
DeLorncourt, Oliver Alli Sup
DeLory, Alfred V 1930- AmSCAP 66
DeLosReyes, Gabriel ConAu 45
Deloughery, Grace L 1933- ConAu 33, WrD 1976
Delp, Irwin W 1889- OhA&B
Delpar, Helen 1936- ConAu 53
Delphi WhLA
Delpit, Albert 1849-1893 BbD, BiD&SB, BiDSA
DelRey, Lester 1915- AmA&B, AuBYP, ThBJA
DelRio, Angel DcSpL
Delta ConAu XR, DcEnL
Delta 1798-1851 Alli, CasWL, ChPo, DcEnL, NewC, Pen Eng
Delton, Judy 1931- ConAu 57
DeLubac, Henri Au&Wr, CatA 1952
DeLuc, J R 1726- BiDLA
DeLuca, A Michael 1912- ConAu 21
DeLuca, Angelo ChPo S2
DeLucca, John 1920- ConAu 41
Delugg, Anne Renfer 1922- AmSCAP 66
Delugg, Milton 1918- AmSCAP 66
DeLulion, John IlBYP
DeLuscar, Horace 1850?- ChPo S2
DelValle Inclan, Ramon ModRL, TwCA, TwCA Sup
Delvau, Alfred 1825-1867 BiD&SB
DelVecchio, Thomas ChPo S1
Delver, A Alli Sup
Delves-Broughton Alli Sup
Delves-Broughton, Jo 1916- Au&Wr
DelVicario, Silvio P 1921- AmSCAP 66
Delvig, Baron Anton Antonovich 1798-1831 CasWL, DcRusL, EuA
Delvin, George Alli
Delving, Michael AmA&B, SmATA 3, WorAu, WrD 1976
Delwig, Baron Anton Antonovich 1798-1831 BbD, BiD&SB
DeLys, J G M BiDLA
Delzell, Charles F 1920- ConAu 1R, WrD 1976
DeMadariaga LongC, TwCA, TwCA Sup
DeMadariaga, Don Salvador 1886- Au&Wr
Demades CasWL
DeMadina, Francisco 1907- AmSCAP 66
Demage, G MnBBF
Demaine, Don ConAu XR
DeMajo, W M 1917- WhGrA
Deman, E F Alli, Alli Sup
Demangeon, Albert 1872- WhLA
DeManio, Jack 1914- ConAu 61
Demant, Vigo Auguste Au&Wr
DeMar, Esmeralda ConAu XR
Demaray, Donald E 1926- ConAu 1R, WrD 1976
DeMarchi, Emilio 1851-1901 CasWL, CIDMEuL, EuA, EvEuW, Pen Eur, REn
DeMarco, Angelus A 1916- ConAu 9R
DeMarco, Arlene AuNews 1
DeMarco, Donald 1937- ConAu 61
DeMarconnay, Leblanc BbtC
DeMare, Eric Samuel 1910- Au&Wr, ConAu 9R
DeMare, George 1912- ConAu 23
DeMare, Jehanne 1919- ChPo
Demaree, Doris Clore 1903- IndAu 1917
Demarest, Abraham Jay 1858- ChPo S1
Demarest, David D 1819-1898 Alli Sup, DcAmA, DcNAA

Demarest, Doug ConAu XR, SmATA 8
Demarest, John Terhune 1813-1897 Alli Sup, DcAmA, DcNAA
Demarest, M L ChPo
Demarest, Mary Augusta 1838-1888 Alli, DcAmA, DcNAA
Demarest, T F C Alli Sup
Demarest, William H S 1863- WhWNAA
Demaret, Pierre 1943- ConAu 61
DeMarinis, Rick 1934- ConAu 57
Demaris, Ovid 1919- AmA&B, ConAu XR, WrD 1976
DeMartelly, John Stockton 1903- IlCB 1945
DeMartino, Manfred Frank 1924- Au&Wr
Demarville Alli
Demas, Vida 1927- ConAu 49, SmATA 9
DeMasi, Joseph 1904- AmSCAP 66
DeMasi, Joseph Anthony 1935- AmSCAP 66
DeMassa, Alexander P Regnier, Marquis 1831- DcBiA
DeMatteo, Donna 1941- ConAu 25
DeMauny, Erik 1920- ConAu 33
DeMaupassant, Guy EuA
DeMaupassant, Henri Rene Albert Guy 1850-1893 DcBiA
Demaus, Robert Alli Sup
DeMayo, F Alli Sup
Dembele, Sidiki 1930?- AfA 1
Dember, Harry 1882- WhLA
Dember, Jean Wilkins 1930- LivBA
Dembitz, Lewis Naphtali 1833- DcAmA
Dembo, Lawrence Sanford 1929- AmA&B, Au&Wr, ConAu 1R
Dembry, R Emmett 1850-1922 AmA
Demby, William 1922- BlkAW, LivBA, Pen Am
Demedts, Andre 1906- CasWL
DeMendelssohn, Hilde Maria 1911- Au&Wr
DeMendoza Rios, J BiDLA
DeMenil, Alexander Nicolas 1849-1928 BiDSA, DcNAA, WhWNAA
Dement, Merritt H Alli Sup
Dement, R S Alli Sup
DeMent, Roy Edward 1906- TexWr
DeMente, Boye 1928- ConAu 23
DeMenton, Francisco ConAu XR
Demers, Albert Fox 1863-1943 AmA&B, DcNAA
Demers, Benjamin 1848-1919 DcNAA
Demers, Hector 1878-1917 DcNAA
Demers, Jerome 1774?-1853 BbtC, DcNAA
DeMesne, Eugene ConAu 41
Demeter, Dimitrija 1811-1872 BiD&SB, CasWL
Demetillo, Ricardo 1920- ConP 1970, ConP 1975, WrD 1976
Demetra Vaka WhWNAA
Demetrius CasWL
Demetrius Cydones d1400 CasWL, Pen Cl
Demetrius Of Phaleron 350?BC-283BC Pen Cl
Demetrius Of Phalerum 350?BC- CasWL
Demetrius Of Rostov CasWL
Demetrius The Cynic Pen Cl
Demetrius Triclinius 1280?-1340? Pen Cl
Demetrius, Charles Alli
Demetrius, James Kleon 1920- ConAu 21
Demetrius, Lucia 1910- CasWL
DeMetz, V Alli Sup
DeMeza, W ChPo
DeMeza, Walter ChPo S1
DeMichele, Leopold John Manners Alli Sup
Demijohn, Thom ConAu XR
DeMilan, Sister Jean ConAu XR
Demill BbtC
DeMille, Agnes 1905- AmA&B, REnAL
DeMille, Alban Bertram 1873- ChPo
DeMille, Cecil B 1881-1959 AmA&B, REn, REnAL
Demille, Darcy 1929- LivBA
DeMille, Henry Churchill 1850-1893 AmA, AmA&B, BbD, BiD&SB, BiDSA, DcAmA, DcNAA
DeMille, James 1833?-1880 Alli Sup, BbD, BiD&SB, BrAu 19, CanWr, CyAL 2, DcBiA, DcLEnL, DcNAA, OxAm, OxCan
DeMille, Nelson 1943- ConAu 57
DeMille, Richard 1922- ConAu 23,

WrD 1976
DeMille, William Churchill 1878-1955 *AmA&B,*
ChPo S2, REnAL, WhWNAA
DeMilly, Augusta *LivFWS*
Deming, Alhambra G *WhWNAA*
Deming, Clarence 1848- *Alli Sup, DcAmA*
Deming, Dorothy 1893- *AuBYP*
Deming, Edwin Willard 1860- *ConICB*
Deming, Henry Champion 1815-1872 *Alli Sup,*
DcAmA, DcNAA
Deming, Horace Edward 1850-1930 *DcNAA*
Deming, Horace Grove 1885- *WhWNAA*
Deming, Kirk *OhA&B*
Deming, Leonard 1787-1853 *Alli Sup, DcNAA*
Deming, Louise Macpherson 1916-1976
ConAu 61
Deming, Norma Helen *WhWNAA*
Deming, P 1829-1915 *AmA&B, OxAm*
Deming, Paul *Alli Sup*
Deming, Philander 1829-1915 *BbD, BiD&SB,*
DcAmA, DcNAA, REnAL
Deming, Richard 1915- *ConAu 9R,*
WrD 1976
Deming, Robert H 1937- *ConAu 21,*
WrD 1976
Deming, Therese Osterheld 1874-1945 *AmA&B,*
DcNAA, WhWNAA
Deming, William Chapin 1869-1949 *OhA&B,*
WhWNAA
DeMirjian, Arto, Jr. 1931- *ConAu 57*
Demirtchian, Derenik 1877-1956 *DcOrL 3*
DeMiskey, Julian 1908- *IlCB 1966*
Deml, Jakob 1878-1961 *CasWL*
Demmel, Karl 1893- *WhLA*
Demming, Lanson F 1902- *AmSCAP 66*
Demmler, Franz C F *Alli Sup*
Demmon, Elwood Leonard 1892- *IndAu 1917*
Democrito *PueRA*
Democritus 460?BC-370?BC *CasWL, NewC,*
Pen Cl, REn
Democritus Junior 1576-1639 *Alli, DcEnL,*
NewC
Democritus Secundus *Alli*
Demodocus *REn*
Demogeot, Jacques Claude 1808-1894 *BiD&SB*
Demoivre, Abraham 1667-1757 *Alli*
Demolder, Eugene 1862-1919 *CasWL,*
ClDMEuL, OxFr
DeMolen, Richard Lee 1938- *ConAu 45*
DeMoleville, Bertrand *BiDLA*
Demonax *Pen Cl*
Demone, Harold W, Jr. 1924- *ConAu 5R*
DeMonfried, Henri 1879?-1974 *ConAu 53*
DeMontebello, Guy-Philippe Lannes 1936-
ConAu 45
DeMontfort, Guy *ConAu XR*
DeMontherlant *TwCA, TwCA Sup*
DeMontherlant, Henry *ModRL*
DeMontmorency, Hervey Of Edward 1868-
WhLA
DeMontreville Polak, Doris 1904?-1974
ConAu 49
DeMorat, A J And Pierce, J N *Alli Sup*
DeMordaunt, Walter Julius 1925- *ConAu 33,*
WrD 1976
Demorest, Dana James 1882- *WhWNAA*
Demorest, Mrs. H H *ChPo*
Demorest, Jean-Jacques 1920- *ConAu 5R*
Demorest, W Jennings *ChPo*
Demoret, Alfred 1843-1931 *OhA&B*
DeMorgan, Augustus 1806-1871 *Alli, Alli Sup,*
BrAu 19, ChPo, Chmbr 3, DcEnL,
DcEuL, EvLB
DeMorgan, Campbell Greig 1811-1876 *Alli Sup*
DeMorgan, John *Alli Sup*
DeMorgan, Mary *Alli Sup*
DeMorgan, Sophia Elizabeth *Alli Sup*
DeMorgan, William Frend 1839-1917 *CasWL,*
Chmbr 3, CyWA, DcBiA, DcEuL,
DcLEnL, EvLB, JBA 1934, LongC,
NewC, ModBL, OxEng, Pen Eng, REn,
TwCA, TwCA Sup, TwCW
DeMorny, Peter *ConAu XR*
DeMosenthal, J And Harting, J E *Alli Sup*
Demosthenes 384?BC-322BC *BbD, BiD&SB,*
CasWL, CyWA, DcEnL, NewC, OxEng,
Pen Cl, RCom, REn
DeMott, Benjamin 1924- *AmA&B, ConAu 5R,*

DrAF 1976, WorAu
DeMott, Donald W 1928- *ConAu 61*
DeMott, Josie *WhWNAA*
DeMotte, John Brewer 1848-1907 *IndAu 1816*
DeMourgues, Odette 1914- *ConAu 5R*
Dempewolff, Richard F 1914- *ConAu 1R*
Dempsey, David Knapp 1914- *ConAu 5R,*
REnAL, WrD 1976
Dempsey, Elam Franklin 1878- *WhWNAA*
Dempsey, G Drysdale *Alli*
Dempsey, Hugh A *OxCan Sup*
Dempsey, J J *Alli Sup*
Dempsey, James E 1876-1918 *AmSCAP 66*
Dempsey, Martin 1903- *CatA 1952*
Dempsey, Paul K 1935- *ConAu 25*
Dempsey, Richard *BbtC*
Dempsey, Richard A 1932- *ConAu 61*
Dempster, Charles Louisa Hawkins 1835- *BbD*
Dempster, Charlotte Louisa Hawkins 1835-
Alli Sup, BiD&SB
Dempster, Derek David 1924- *Au&Wr,*
ConAu 13R
Dempster, F P *ChPo S1*
Dempster, George 1736?-1818 *Alli, BiDLA,*
ChPo
Dempster, Henry *Alli Sup*
Dempster, John 1794-1863 *Alli Sup, DcAmA,*
DcNAA
Dempster, Roland Tombekai 1910-1965 *AfA 1,*
Pen Cl
Dempster, Ryland Newman 1895- *WhWNAA*
Dempster, Thomas 1579-1625 *Alli*
Demske, James Michael 1922- *ConAu 29*
DeMuldor, Carl *Alli Sup, DcNAA*
Demura, Fumio 1940- *ConAu 61*
DeMusset, Alfred 1810-1857 *DcBiA*
DeMusset, Paul *ChPo S2*
DeMuth, Flora Nash 1888- *IlCB 1956*
Demuth, Norman 1898-1968 *ConAu P-1*
Den, Petr *ConAu XR*
DeNahlik, Andrew John *Au&Wr*
Denaisius, Petrus 1560-1610 *OxGer*
Denali, Peter *ConAu XR*
DeNaut, George Matthews 1915- *AmSCAP 66*
DeNavarro, J M And D M *ChPo*
Denbeaux, Fred J 1914- *AmA&B, ConAu 5R*
Denbie, Roger 1906- *ConAu XR*
Denbigh, Kenneth George 1911- *WrD 1976*
Denbigh, Maurice *MnBBF*
DenBoer, James D 1937- *ConAu 23,*
ConP 1970, ConP 1975, DrAP 1975,
WrD 1976
Denby, Charles 1830-1904 *DcNAA,*
IndAu 1816
Denby, Edwin Orr 1903- *AmA&B, ConP 1970*
Dench, Ernest Alfred 1895- *WhWNAA*
Denck, Hans *OxGer*
Dender, Jay *ConAu XR*
Dendy, Edward *Alli*
Dendy, Marshall Coleman 1902- *ConAu 17*
Dendy, Walter Cooper 1794-1871 *Alli, Alli Sup*
Dene, Alan *MnBBF*
Dene, Edewaerd De 1505-1578? *CasWL*
Dene, Hampton *MnBBF*
Dene, Willemus De *Alli*
Deneen, James R 1928- *ConAu 45*
DeNeergaard, Virginia *AmSCAP 66*
Denenberg, Herbert S 1929- *ConAu 37,*
WrD 1976
DeNeufville, Richard 1939- *ConAu 53*
Denevan, William M 1931- *ConAu 41*
DeNevers, Edmond 1862-1906 *CanWr*
DeNevers, Noel 1932- *ConAu 37*
DeNevi, Donald P 1937- *ConAu 37*
Denevi, Marco 1922- *Pen Am*
Denewulf d897? *BiB S*
Denfeld, D 1939- *ConAu 41*
Deng, William 1929- *ConAu 13R*
Denham *Alli, BiDLA*
Denham, Captain *Alli*
Denham, Alice 1933- *ConAu 23*
Denham, Dixon *Alli*
Denham, Edward *Alli Sup*
Denham, H G 1880- *WhLA*
Denham, H M 1897- *Au&Wr, ConAu 61*
Denham, J F *Alli*
Denham, Sir James Steuart *Alli, OxEng*
Denham, Sir John 1615-1669 *Alli, BiD&SB,*

BrAu, CasWL, ChPo, ChPo S1,
Chmbr 1, CnE&AP, CrE&SL, DcEnA
Denham, Sir John 1615-1668 *DcEnL*
Denham, Sir John 1615-1669 *DcEuL, DcLEnL,*
EvLB, NewC, OxEng, Pen Eng, PoIre,
REn, WebEAL
Denham, John E *Alli*
Denham, Joseph *Alli*
Denham, Mary Orr *ConAu 1R*
Denham, Michael Aislobie d1859 *Alli Sup*
Denham, N *Alli*
Denham, Reginald 1894- *ConAu P-1*
Denham, Robert D 1938- *ConAu 53*
Denham, William *Alli*
DenHartog, Jacob P 1901- *WrD 1976*
Denholm, David 1924- *WrD 1976*
Denholm, James *Alli, BiDLA*
Denholm, Therese Mary Zita White 1933-
ConAu 9R
Denhurst, W W *BiDSA*
Deniehy, Daniel Henry 1828-1865 *Chmbr 3,*
DcLEnL, PoIre
Denier, Maurice *OxFr*
Denier, Tony *Alli Sup*
Denikin, Anton Ivanovich 1872-1947 *REn*
Dening, Mrs. E G H H *Alli Sup*
Dening, Thomas Henry *Alli Sup*
Denio, Elizabeth H *Alli Sup*
Denio, Francis Brigham 1848- *AmLY, DcAmA,*
WhWNAA
Denio, Hiram 1799-1871 *Alli, DcAmA*
Denious, Jess C 1879- *WhWNAA*
Denis, King Of Portugal 1261-1325 *CasWL*
Denis, Saint *OxFr*
Denis, Alfred Lewis Pinneo 1874-1930 *DcNAA*
Denis, Henry *Alli Sup*
Denis, Jean Ferdinand 1798-1890 *BiD&SB*
Denis, Johann Nepomuk Cosmas Michael
1729-1800 *CasWL, OxGer*
Denis, Lorimer 1904-1957 *BiDPar*
Denis, Louise 1710?-1790 *OxFr*
Denis, Michael 1729-1800 *DcEuL*
Denis, Michaela Holdsworth *Au&Wr,*
ConAu 13R
Denis, Paul 1909- *ConAu 21*
Denisoff, R Serge 1939- *ConAu 33,*
WrD 1976
Denison, Alfred *Alli Sup*
Denison, Barbara 1926- *ConAu 13R*
Denison, Carol *AuBYP*
Denison, Charles 1845-1909 *Alli Sup, DcAmA,*
DcNAA
Denison, Charles Marsh *Alli Sup*
Denison, Charles Wheeler 1809-1881 *Alli,*
Alli Sup, AmA&B, BiD&SB, ChPo,
DcAmA, DcNAA
Denison, Christine *ChPo S1, ChPo S2*
Denison, Daniel 1613-1682 *Alli, DcAmA,*
DcNAA
Denison, Dulcie Winifred Catherine *Au&Wr*
Denison, Edward 1840-1870 *Alli, Alli Sup*
Denison, Edward B *Alli*
Denison, Edward Fulton 1915- *ConAu 23,*
WrD 1976
Denison, Eliza Freeman *Alli Sup*
Denison, Elizabeth W *ChPo*
Denison, Frederic 1819-1901 *DcAmA, DcNAA*
Denison, Frederick 1819- *Alli Sup*
Denison, Frederick Charles 1846-1896 *Alli Sup,*
DcNAA, OxCan
Denison, George Anthony 1805- *Alli, Alli Sup*
Denison, George Taylor 1839-1925 *Alli Sup,*
BbtC, DcNAA, OxCan
Denison, Grace Elizabeth d1914 *DcNAA*
Denison, H M *Alli Sup*
Denison, J P *ChPo*
Denison, J W *ChPo S2*
Denison, John d1628? *Alli*
Denison, John Henry 1841-1924 *DcAmA,*
DcNAA
Denison, John Hopkins 1870-1936 *DcNAA*
Denison, John Ledyard 1826-1906 *Alli Sup,*
BiD&SB, DcAmA, DcNAA
Denison, Mary Andrews 1826-1911 *Alli,*
Alli Sup, AmA&B, BiD&SB, ChPo,
ChPo S1, DcAmA, DcNAA, HsB&A,
HsB&A Sup
Denison, Merrill 1893- *CanWr, DcLEnL,*

McGWD, OxCan, OxCan Sup, REnWD,
WhWNAA
Denison, Muriel *AuBYP*
Denison, Noel *Alli Sup*
Denison, Septimus Julius Augustus 1859-1937
DcNAA
Denison, Stephen *Alli*
Denison, T S *Alli Sup*
Denison, Thomas Stewart 1848-1911 *AmA&B,
DcNAA*
Denison, Sir William Thomas 1804-1871
Alli Sup
Denisot, Nicolas 1515-1559 *DcEuL*
Denk, Hans 1495?-1527 *OxGer*
Denkam, Mark *WhWNAA*
Denker, Henry 1912- *AmA&B, AmNov,
AuNews 1, CnMD Sup, ConAu 33*
Denkler, Horst 1935- *ConAu 53*
Denman, Clarence Phillips 1897- *WhWNAA*
Denman, Donald Robert 1911- *Au&Wr,
ConAu 61, WrD 1976*
Denman, Frank *AuBYP*
Denman, George *MnBBF*
Denman, Jacob S 1814- *Alli*
Denman, James Lemoine *Alli Sup*
Denman, Joseph *Alli*
Denman, Thomas *Alli, BiDLA*
Denmark, Alex *Alli*
Denmark, Harrison *ConAu XR*
Denne, Henry *Alli, BiD&SB*
Denne, John *Alli*
Denne, John 1693-1767 *Alli*
Denne, Samuel 1730-1799 *Alli*
Denne-Baron, Pierre Jacques Rene 1780-1854
BiD&SB
Dennehy, H E *Alli Sup*
Dennen, Ernest Joseph 1866-1937 *DcNAA,
WhWNAA*
Dennen, Grace Atherton 1874-1927
AnMV 1926, ChPo, DcNAA, WhWNAA
D'Ennery, Adolphe Philippe 1811-1899 *BbD,
BiD&SB, EvEuW, HsB&A*
Dennes, William Ray 1898- *AmA&B*
Denneston, E *Alli*
Dennett *BiDLA*
Dennett, Edward *Alli Sup*
Dennett, Herbert Victor 1893- *Au&Wr,
ConAu 5R*
Dennett, R E *Alli Sup*
Dennett, Roger Herbert 1876-1935 *AmLY,
DcNAA, WhWNAA*
Dennett, Tyler 1883-1949 *AmA&B, ChPo S2,
OxAm, REnAL, TwCA, TwCA Sup,
WhWNAA*
Denney, A H 1918- *Au&Wr*
Denney, Diana Patience 1910- *Au&Wr*
Denney, Joseph Villiers 1862-1935 *AmLY,
DcNAA*
Denney, Reuel Nicholas 1913- *AmA&B,
ConAu 1R, ConP 1970*
Denney, Ruell Nicholas 1913- *DrAP 1975*
Denni, Gwynne 1882-1949 *AmSCAP 66*
Denni, Lucien 1886-1947 *AmSCAP 66*
Dennie, Joseph 1768-1812 *Alli, AmA,
AmA&B, BiD&SB, CasWL, CyAL 1,
DcAmA, DcEnL, DcLEnL, OxAm,
Pen Am, REnAL*
Dennie, William H d1842 *Alli*
Denniker, Paul 1897- *AmSCAP 66*
Denning, Basil W 1928- *ConAu 33*
Denning, Elizabeth d1920 *ChPo*
Denning, Frank 1909- *AmSCAP 66*
Denning, J R *Alli Sup*
Denning, John Renton *ChPo S2*
Denning, Melita *ConAu XR*
Denning, Patricia *ConAu XR*
Denning, W F 1848- *WhLA*
Denning, Wade F, Jr. 1922- *AmSCAP 66*
Denning, William F *Alli Sup*
Dennis, Ada *ChPo S1*
Dennis, Alfred Lewis Pinneo 1874-1930 *DcNAA*
Dennis, Benjamin G 1929- *ConAu 45*
Dennis, C *Alli*
Dennis, C J 1876-1938 *LongC, TwCW*
Dennis, Charles 1844-1919 *IndAu 1816*
Dennis, Charles Henry 1860-1943 *AmA&B,
DcNAA*
Dennis, Clara *OxCan*

Dennis, Clarence Michael James 1876-1938
CasWL, ChPo, DcLEnL, EvLB
Dennis, David Worth 1849-1916 *DcNAA,
IndAu 1816*
Dennis, Everette E 1942- *ConAu 41*
Dennis, Frederic Shepard 1850-1934 *DcNAA*
Dennis, Geoffrey Pomeroy 1892-1963 *LongC,
NewC, TwCA, TwCA Sup*
Dennis, George *WhWNAA*
Dennis, George Palmer 1877- *WhWNAA*
Dennis, Ginny Maxey 1923- *AmSCAP 66*
Dennis, Henry Arnold 1891- *WhWNAA*
Dennis, Henry C 1918- *ConAu 41*
Dennis, Hugh *MnBBF*
Dennis, J *Alli*
Dennis, J Morley *Alli Sup*
Dennis, James Blatch Piggot 1816-1861 *Alli Sup*
Dennis, James Clarence 1876- *ChPo S1,
ChPo S2*
Dennis, James Morgan 1891- *ChPo*
Dennis, James Shepard 1842-1914 *DcNAA*
Dennis, James Teackle 1865-1918 *AmLY,
BiDSA, DcNAA*
Dennis, John *Alli Sup, ChPo, Chmbr 2*
Dennis, John 1657-1734 *Alli, BiD&SB, BrAu,
CasWL, ChPo, DcEnL, DcEuL, DcLEnL,
EvLB, NewC, OxEng, Pen Eng,
WebEAL*
Dennis, John H *Alli Sup*
Dennis, John Stoughton 1820-1885 *OxCan*
Dennis, Jonas *Alli*
Dennis, Joyce *ChPo S1*
Dennis, Lawrence 1893- *AmA&B*
Dennis, Lottie Mary *ChPo S1*
Dennis, Louis Munroe 1863-1936 *DcNAA*
Dennis, Martha Curl d1897 *IndAu 1816*
Dennis, Matt 1914- *AmSCAP 66*
Dennis, Morgan 1892?-1960 *AmA&B, AuBYP,
IlCB 1945, IlCB 1956, MorJA*
Dennis, Nigel 1912- *Au&Wr, CnMD,
CnMWL, CnThe, ConAu 25, ConDr,
ConNov 1972, ConNov 1976, CrCD,
ModBL, ModBL Sup, ModWD, NewC,
Pen Eng, RAdv 1, REn, TwCW,
WebEAL, WorAu, WrD 1976*
Dennis, Patrick *AmA&B, WorAu,
WrD 1976*
Dennis, Peter 1945- *ConAu 41*
Dennis, R Lloyd *Alli*
Dennis, R M *BlkAW*
Dennis, Ralph *AuNews 1*
Dennis, Richard Molesworth *ChPo*
Dennis, Robert *Alli Sup*
Dennis, Samuel *Alli, ChPo S1*
Dennis, Suzanne Easton 1922- *ConAu 25*
Dennis, T *Alli*
Dennis, Thomas *Alli, BiDLA*
Dennis, Walter Henry 1876-1956 *IndAu 1917*
Dennis, Wayne 1905- *ConAu 17R, WrD 1976*
Dennis, Wesley 1903-1966 *AuBYP, IlCB 1945,
IlCB 1956, IlCB 1966, MorJA*
Dennis, William *PoIre*
Dennis, William Henry *Alli Sup*
Dennis, William Herbert 1908- *Au&Wr*
Dennis-Jones, Harold 1915- *Au&Wr,
ConAu 57, WrD 1976*
Dennison, A Dudley, Jr. 1914- *ConAu 57*
Dennison, George 1925- *AmA&B*
Dennison, George Ambrose *Alli Sup, ChPo,
ChPo S2*
Dennison, George M 1935- *ConAu 53*
Dennison, Henry Sturgis 1877- *WhWNAA*
Dennison, J *Alli*
Dennison, Walter Traill *Alli Sup*
Dennison, William *Alli, BiDLA*
Denniston, Goldsmith *Alli Sup*
Denniston, J M *Alli Sup*
Denniston, John *Alli Sup*
Denniston, Robin Alastair 1926- *Au&Wr*
Dennistone, Walter *Alli*
Dennistoun, Aubrey S G *ChPo*
Dennistoun, George *Alli*
Dennistoun, James 1803-1855 *Alli Sup*
Denny, Sir Cecil Edward 1850-1928 *DcNAA,
OxCan*
Denny, Christopher Columbus *Alli Sup*
Denny, Collins 1854-1943 *DcNAA, WhWNAA*
Denny, E *Alli*

Denny, Sir Edward 1796-1889 *Alli, ChPo S2,
PoCh, PoIre*
Denny, Eleanor Mattie *ChPo S2, WhWNAA*
Denny, George Hutcheson 1870- *BiDSA,
WhWNAA*
Denny, Grace Goldena 1883- *WhPNW,
WhWNAA*
Denny, Harold Norman 1889-1945 *AmA&B,
DcNAA*
Denny, Henry *Alli*
Denny, Sir Henry Lyttelton Lyster 1878- *WhLA*
Denny, John *Alli, BiDLA*
Denny, John Howard 1920- *Au&Wr,
ConAu P-1, WrD 1976*
Denny, Ludwell 1894-1970 *AmA&B,
ConAu 29, IndAu 1917*
Denny, Marie Louise *BiDSA*
Denny, Martin 1911- *AmSCAP 66*
Denny, Maurice Ray 1918- *ConAu 41,
IndAu 1917*
Denny, Norman George 1901- *Au&Wr,
MnBBF*
Denny, Walter Bell 1882-1937 *DcNAA*
Denny, Sir William *Alli, DcEnL*
Denny, William Henry *Alli Sup*
Dennys, Edward Nichols *Alli Sup*
Dennys, N B *BbtC*
Dennys, Nicholas Belfield *Alli Sup*
Denoeu, Francois 1898-1975 *ConAu 53*
Denoff, Samuel 1928- *AmSCAP 66*
Denomme, Robert T 1930- *ConAu 25*
Denonville, J-R DeBrisay, Marquis De 1642-1710
OxCan
DeNoon, David 1928- *AmSCAP 66*
DeNoronha, Leslie 1926- *ConP 1970*
DeNoronha, Rui 1909-1943 *AfA 1*
DeNovo, John A 1916- *ConAu 9R*
Denroche, Edward *PoIre*
Densel, Mary *Alli Sup*
Densell *Alli*
Densen-Gerber, Judianne 1934- *ConAu 37,
WrD 1976*
Denslow, Ray Vaughn 1885- *WhWNAA*
Denslow, VanBuren 1833-1902 *Alli Sup,
DcNAA*
Denslow, William Wallace 1856-1915 *AmA&B,
ChPo, ChPo S1, ChPo S2, DcNAA*
Densmore, Frances 1867-1957 *REnAL,
WhWNAA*
Densmore, G B *Alli Sup*
Densmore, Hiram Delos 1862-1940 *DcNAA,
WhWNAA*
Densmore, John H 1880-1943 *AmSCAP 66*
Densmore, Lyman Willard *Alli Sup*
Denson, A C *Alli Sup*
Denson, Alan *ChPo S2*
Denson, John 1905- *AmA&B*
Denston, B L *Alli, BiDLA*
Dent, Alan Holmes 1905- *Au&Wr, ChPo S2,
ConAu 9R, LongC, WrD 1976*
Dent, Anthony Austen 1915- *Au&Wr,
ConAu 25*
Dent, Arthur *Alli*
Dent, Barbara Patricia 1919- *WrD 1976*
Dent, Lady Beaujolais Eleonora 1824- *Alli Sup*
Dent, C H *MnBBF*
Dent, Caroline *Alli Sup*
Dent, Charles *Alli Sup*
Dent, Clinton *Alli Sup*
Dent, Clinton Thomas *Alli Sup*
Dent, Colin 1921- *ConAu 13R, WrD 1976*
Dent, Denis *MnBBF*
Dent, Edward *Alli*
Dent, Emma *Alli Sup*
Dent, Frederick *Alli Sup*
Dent, G M *Alli Sup*
Dent, Giles *Alli*
Dent, Harold Collett 1894- *Au&Wr,
ConAu 5R, WrD 1976*
Dent, Hastings Charles *Alli Sup*
Dent, J C *Chmbr 3*
Dent, J M 1849-1926 *LongC, NewC*
Dent, John *Alli*
Dent, John 1911- *Au&Wr*
Dent, John Charles 1841-1888 *DcNAA, OxCan*
Dent, Robert K *Alli Sup*
Dent, Ronald 1904- *Au&Wr*
Dent, Thomas C *BlkAW*

Dent, Tom *LivBA*
Dent, William *Alli Sup*
Dentan, Robert Claude 1907- *AmA&B,*
ConAu 1R, IndAu 1917
Dentinger, Stephen *ConAu XR*
Dentler, Robert A 1928- *ConAu 1R*
Denton, Charles Frederick 1942- *ConAu 37,*
WrD 1976
Denton, Clara Janetta *ChPo, ChPo S1,*
ChPo S2
Denton, Daniel d1696 *Alli, AmA, OxAm*
Denton, Eardley Fraser Bailey *Alli Sup*
Denton, Franklin Evert 1859-1947 *Alli Sup,*
DcAmA, OhA&B
Denton, George *MnBBF*
Denton, H M 1882- *ConAu P-1*
Denton, J H 1939- *ConAu 41*
Denton, John 1625-1708 *Alli*
Denton, John Bailey *Alli, Alli Sup*
Denton, Lyman W *Alli Sup*
Denton, Matthew *Alli Sup*
Denton, Pem *TexWr*
Denton, Pete *MnBBF*
Denton, Sherman Foote 1856-1937 *OhA&B*
Denton, Thomas 1724-1777 *Alli*
Denton, Vernon Llewellyn 1881-1944 *DcNAA*
Denton, Wallace 1928- *ConAu 1R*
Denton, William 1605-1691 *Alli*
Denton, William 1815-1888 *Alli Sup*
Denton, William 1823-1883 *Alli Sup, OhA&B*
Denues, Celia 1915- *ConAu 41*
Denver, Athol *MnBBF*
Denver, Boone *ConAu XR*
Denver, Bruce *MnBBF*
Denver, Drake C *ConAu XR, OhA&B*
Denver, James William 1817-1892 *OhA&B*
Denver, Jane Campbell 1821-1847 *OhA&B*
Denver, John *ChPo S2*
Denver, Mary Caroline 1821-1860 *OhA&B*
Denver, Rod *ConAu XR*
Denvers, Jake *MnBBF*
Denville, Hugh *MnBBF*
Denyer, A *Alli Sup*
Denyer, James Charles 1915- *Au&Wr*
Denys, Jean *OxCan*
Denys, Nicolas 1598-1688 *OxAm, OxCan*
Denzel, Justin F 1917- *ConAu 53*
Denzer, Peter W 1921- *ConAu 5R*
Denzil *Alli*
Denzin, Norman K 1941- *ConAu 29*
DeOliveiro, M A F *AfA 1*
Deon, Michel 1919- *ConAu 37*
DeOsma, Lupe *AuBYP*
DeOtero, Blas *ModRL*
Deotyma 1830- *BiD&SB*
DeOvies, Raimundo 1877- *WhWNAA*
DePackh, Maurice 1896-1960 *AmSCAP 66*
Depalaine *Alli*
DePaola, Thomas Anthony 1934- *ConAu 49*
DePaola, Tomie *ConAu 49, IlBYP,*
IlCB 1966
DePaor, Risteard *ConAu XR*
DePaul, Gene 1919- *AmSCAP 66*
DePaur, Leonard *AmSCAP 66*
DePauw, Linda Grant 1940- *ConAu 21*
DePearsall, Robert Lucas *Alli Sup*
DePembroke, Morgan *Alli Sup*
DePenning, George A *Alli Sup*
DePereda, Prudencio 1912- *AmA&B, AmNov,*
ConAu 1R
Depestr, Michel Edouard *WhWNAA*
Depestre, Rene 1926- *CasWL, DcCLA*
Depew, Arthur M *ConAu 41*
Depew, Chauncey Mitchell 1834-1928 *AmA&B,*
BbD, BiD&SB, DcAmA, DcNAA,
REnAL, WhWNAA
Depew, Wally *ConAu XR, DrAP 1975*
Depew, Walter Westerfield 1924- *ConAu 5R*
DePeyster, John Watts 1821-1907 *Alli Sup,*
AmA, AmA&B, BbD, BiD&SB, DcAmA,
DcNAA
D'Epinay, Madame *OxFr*
DePolman, Willem *ConAu XR*
DePolnay, Peter 1906- *Au&Wr, LongC,*
TwCA Sup, WrD 1976
DePorte, Michael V 1939- *ConAu 49*
DePowis, T J *Alli Sup*
DePowis, Thomas Jones *ChPo S2*

Deppen, Jessie L 1881-1956 *AmSCAP 66*
Depping, J B *Alli*
DePre, Jean-Anne *WrD 1976*
Deprez, Paul *OxCan Sup*
Depta, Victor M 1939- *ConAu 49*
Deputy, Malcolm 1937- *IndAu 1917*
DePuy, E Cora *WhWNAA*
DePuy, Henry Walter 1820-1876 *Alli, BiD&SB,*
CarSB, DcAmA, DcNAA
DePuy, William Harrison 1821-1901 *Alli Sup,*
BiD&SB, DcAmA, DcNAA
DeQuen, Jean 1603-1659 *OxCan*
DeQuetteville, Philip Winter *Alli Sup*
DeQuille, Dan 1829-1898 *DcNAA, OhA&B,*
OxAm
DeQuille, Daniel *Alli Sup*
DeQuincey, F H *PoIre*
DeQuincey, J *PoIre*
DeQuincey, Thomas 1785-1859 *Alli, AtlBL,*
BbD, BiD&SB, BrAu 19, CasWL,
Chmbr 3, CriT 2, CyWA, DcBiA,
DcEnA, DcEnL, DcEuL, DcLEnL, EvLB,
MouLC 3, NewC, OxEng, Pen Eng,
RAdv 1, RCom, REn, WebEAL
Dequir, Fred *Alli*
DeRada, J *Pen Eur*
Derain, Andre 1880-1954 *AtlBL, REn*
DeRamus, Betty *BlkAW*
DeRan, Edna Smith 1870- *OhA&B,*
WhWNAA
DeRance, Charles E *Alli Sup*
Derante, P *Alli*
DeRas, Charles Stanton *Alli Sup*
Derber, Milton 1915- *Au&Wr*
Derby, Countess Of *Alli Sup*
Derby, Lord 1799-1869 *BrAu 19*
Derby, Alexander *Alli Sup*
Derby, Alice Crittenden *ChPo*
Derby, Alured *Alli Sup*
Derby, Charles Stanley, Earl Of *Alli*
Derby, E H *BbtC*
Derby, Edward G S Stanley, Earl Of 1799-1869
BbD, DcEnL
Derby, Elias Hasket 1803-1880 *Alli Sup,*
DcAmA, DcNAA
Derby, Ferdinando Stanley *Alli*
Derby, G H *DcEnL*
Derby, George 1819-1874 *Alli Sup, DcAmA,*
DcNAA
Derby, George Horatio 1823-1861 *AmA,*
AmA&B, BiD&SB, CnDAL, DcAmA,
DcLEnL, DcNAA, EarAB, OxAm,
REnAL
Derby, James Cephas 1818-1892 *Alli Sup,*
AmA&B, BiD&SB, DcAmA, DcNAA
Derby, James Stanley d1651 *Alli*
Derby, John *Alli*
Derby, John Barton 1792-1867 *DcAmA,*
DcNAA
Derby, John S *Alli Sup*
Derby, Perley *Alli Sup*
Derby, Richard *Alli*
Derby, Roswell, Jr. 1854-1927 *OhA&B*
Derbyshire, Alexander *BbtC*
Derbyshire, George *Alli Sup*
Dercum, Francis X 1856- *WhWNAA*
DeReeder, Pierre 1887-1966 *AmSCAP 66,*
ChPo S2
DeRegniers, Beatrice Schenk 1914- *AmA&B,*
Au&Wr, AuBYP, BkP, ChPo, ChPo S1,
ConAu 13R, IndAu 1917, MorJA,
SmATA 2, WrD 1976
D'Eremas, J P Val *Alli Sup*
Dereme, Tristan 1889-1942 *OxFr*
Derenberg, Walter J 1903-1975 *ConAu 61*
DeReneville, Mary Margaret Motley S 1912-
ConAu 5R, WrD 1976
Dereney, Thomas *Alli*
DeRenne, Wymberly Jones 1853-1916 *AmA&B*
DeRenzy, George Webb *PoIre*
Derenzy, Margaret Graves *PoIre*
DeRenzy, S S *BiDLA*
DeReyna, Rudy 1914- *ConAu 57*
Derfflinger, Georg Von 1606-1695 *OxGer*
Derfler, Leslie 1933- *ConAu 5R, WrD 1976*
Derham, Arthur Morgan 1915- *WrD 1976*
DeRham, Edith 1933- *ConAu 13R*

Derham, Enid *ChPo S1*
Derham, Morgan 1915- *ConAu 13R*
Derham, Robert *Alli*
Derham, Samuel *Alli*
Derham, William 1657-1735 *Alli*
Deric, Arthur J 1926- *ConAu 23*
DeRicci, James Herman 1847- *Alli Sup*
DeRiencourt, Amaury *Au&Wr*
DeRienzo, Silvio 1909- *AmSCAP 66*
Derin, P I *CasWL*
Dering, Cini Willoughby *WhLA*
Dering, E C *Alli Sup*
Dering, Edward *Alli*
Dering, Sir Edward *Alli*
Dering, Edward Heneage 1827- *Alli Sup*
Dering, Joan 1917- *Au&Wr, ConAu 9R,*
WrD 1976
Dering, Richard *MnBBF*
Dering, Mrs. Robert *Alli Sup*
Derington, Thomas Jones *Alli Sup*
DeRisi, William J 1938- *ConAu 53*
DeRivera, Joseph H 1932- *ConAu 41*
Derkar, Thomas *Alli*
Derleth, August 1909-1971 *AmA&B, AmNov,*
AuBYP, BkC 6, ChPo, ChPo S2,
CnDAL, ConAu 1R, ConAu 29,
ConNov 1972, DcLEnL, EncM&D,
OxAm, REn, REnAL, SmATA 5, TwCA,
TwCA Sup, WhWNAA
Derleth, Ludwig 1870-1948 *EncWL, OxGer*
Derman, Sarah Audrey 1915- *ConAu 1R*
Dermer, Edward Conduitt *Alli Sup*
Dermid, Jack 1923- *ConAu 49*
Dermody, Thomas 1775-1802 *Alli, CasWL,*
Chmbr 2, EvLB, NewC, PoIre
Dermott, L *Alli*
Dermott, Laurence 1720-1791 *PoIre*
Dermout, Maria 1888-1962 *CasWL, EncWL,*
WorAu
Dern, Karl L 1894- *ConAu 57*
Dern, Peggy Gaddis 1895?-1966 *AmA&B,*
ConAu 1R, ConAu 25
Dernburg, Friedrich 1833- *BiD&SB*
Dernburg, Thomas F 1930- *ConAu 1R*
DeRobeck, Nesta 1886- *ConAu 25*
DeRobertis, Giuseppe 1888-1963 *CasWL*
DeRoberto, Federico 1866-1927 *CasWL,*
ClDMEuL, EvEuW, Pen Eur, REn
Derodon, David *Alli*
Derok, M *Alli*
DeRomaszkan, Gregor 1894- *ConAu 13R*
Derome, Francois Magloire 1821- *BbtC,*
OxCan
Derome, Gilles *OxCan Sup*
DeRomestin, Augustus Henry Eugene 1830-
Alli Sup
DeRoo, Peter 1839-1926 *DcNAA*
DeRoos, F F *Alli*
DeRoos, Frederick Fitzgerald *BbtC*
DeRoos, Robert 1912- *ConAu 9R*
DeRoos, Sjoerd Hendrik 1877- *WhGrA*
DeRopp, Robert Sylvester 1913- *Au&Wr,*
ConAu 17R
Deror, Yehezkel *ConAu XR*
DeRos, Lord *Alli*
DeRos, W F *Alli*
DeRosa, Carmella Millie 1914- *AmSCAP 66*
DeRosa, Peter 1932- *ConAu 21*
DeRose, Peter 1900-1953 *AmSCAP 66*
Derosier, Arthur H, Jr. 1931- *ConAu 29*
DeRosny, Leon 1837- *BiD&SB*
De'Rossi, Azariah 1513-1578 *CasWL*
DeRossi, Claude J 1942- *ConAu 53*
DeRottenburg, Baron George *BbtC*
DeRottermund, Count Edouard Sylvestre
1813-1858 *BbtC*
Deroulede, Paul 1846-1914 *BbD, BiD&SB,*
CasWL, EvEuW, OxFr, Pen Eur
Derounian, Avodis Arthur 1909- *AmA&B,*
TwCA Sup
DeRoussy DeSales, Raoul J J Francois 1896-1942
DcNAA
Derozio, Henry Louis Vivian 1809-1831
DcLEnL, WebEAL
Derr, Homer Munro 1877- *WhWNAA*
Derr, Louis 1868-1923 *DcNAA*
Derr, Richard L 1930- *ConAu 53*
Derr, Thomas Sieger 1931- *ConAu 53*

Derrett, John Duncan Martin 1922- *Au&Wr,*
ConAu 13R, WrD 1976
Derrick *NewC*
Derrick, Charles *Alli, BiDLA*
Derrick, Francis *Alli Sup*
Derrick, Michael 1915- *CatA 1952*
Derrick, Paul 1916- *Au&Wr, CatA 1952,*
ConAu P-1
Derrick, Samuel 1724?-1769 *Alli, PoIre*
Derrick, Thomas *ChPo S1, IlCB 1945*
Derricke, John *Alli*
Derriman, James Parkyns 1922- *Au&Wr,*
WrD 1976
Derring, Edward *Alli*
Derry, Ebenezer *Alli Sup*
Derry, Ellen *Alli Sup*
Derry, John Wesley 1933- *Au&Wr,*
ConAu 5R
Derry, Joseph T *Alli Sup*
Derry, Joseph Tyrone 1841- *BiDSA*
Derry, Thomas Kingston 1905- *Au&Wr,*
ConAu 1R, WrD 1976
Derry, Vida *Au&Wr*
Derry And Raphoe, Bishop Of *DcEnL*
Dershowitz, Alan M 1938- *ConAu 25*
Dertouzos, Michael L 1936- *ConAu 23*
Derum, Jmaes Patrick 1893- *ConAu P-1*
DeRupe *PoIre*
DeRuth, Jan 1922- *ConAu 33, WrD 1976*
Dervin, Brenda 1938- *ConAu 29*
Dervin, Daniel A 1935- *ConAu 57*
Derwent, John *ChPo*
Derwent, Leith 1855- *Alli Sup*
Derwent, Vernon *MnBBF*
Derwentwater, Amelia Matilda Radclyffe d1880
Alli Sup
Derwin, Jordan 1931- *ConAu 13R*
Derwin, Marion *ChPo S1*
Derwood, Gene 1909-1954 *AmA&B*
Dery, Desiderius George 1867-1942 *DcNAA*
Dery, Tibor 1894- *CasWL, CrCD, EncWL,*
Pen Eur, TwCW, WorAu
DeRycke, Laurence Joseph 1907- *IndAu 1917*
Derzhavin, Gavriil Romanovich 1743-1816 *BbD,*
BiD&SB, CasWL, DcEuL, DcRusL, EuA,
EvEuW, Pen Eur, REn
DeSaavedra, Guadalupe *BlkAW*
DesAdrets, Baron F DeBeaumanoir 1513-1587
OxFr
Desaguliers, J H *Alli*
Desaguliers, John *Alli*
Desai, Anita 1937- *CasWL, ConNov 1972,*
ConNov 1976, REn, WrD 1976
Desai, Jhinabhai *DcOrL 2*
Desai, P B 1924- *ConAu 29*
Desai, R V *DcOrL 2*
Desai, Ram 1926- *ConAu 5R*
Desai, Rashmi H 1928- *ConAu 13R*
Desai, Rupin W 1934- *ConAu 45*
DeSaint Exupery, Antoine *ModRL*
DeSaint Jorre, John *WrD 1976*
DeSaint-Luc, Jean *WrD 1976*
DeSaint Phalle, Therese 1930- *ConAu 29*
DeSaint-Pierre, Jacques Henri Bernardin
1737-1814 *DcBiA*
DeSales, Raoul DeRoussy 1896-1942
CatA 1947
DeSalis, Harriet Anne *Alli Sup*
DeSalvo, Joseph S 1938- *ConAu 45*
Desan, Wilfrid 1908- *ConAu 61*
DeSanctis, Francesco 1817-1883 *BiD&SB,*
CasWL, ClDMEuL, DcEuL, EuA,
EvEuW, Pen Eur, REn
Desani, G V 1909- *CasWL, ConAu 45,*
ConNov 1972, ConNov 1976, WebEAL,
WrD 1976
DeSantillana, Giorgio Diaz 1902- *AmA&B,*
ConAu P-1
DeSantis, Emidio 1893- *AmSCAP 66*
DeSantis, Mary Allen 1930- *ConAu 9R*
DeSantis, Vincent P 1916- *ConAu 9R,*
WrD 1976
Desart, Earl Of *Alli Sup*
Desart, Lord *PoIre*
Desatnick, Robert L 1931- *ConAu 41*
Desaugiers, Marc Antoine Madeleine 1772-1827
BbD, BiD&SB, DcEuL, OxFr

Desaulniers, Francois Sever Lesieur 1850-1913
DcNAA
Desaulniers, Gonzalve 1863-1934 *CanWr,*
OxCan, WhWNAA
DeSausmarez, Maurice 1915-1969 *ConAu P-1*
Desaussure, H W 1775-1839 *Alli*
DeSaussure, Henry William 1763-1839 *BiDSA,*
DcAmA
DeSaussure, Wilmot Gibbes 1822-1886 *BiDSA*
DesAutels, Guillaume 1529-1581 *CasWL, OxFr*
Desautels, Joseph 1814-1881 *BbtC, DcNAA*
DeSauze, Emile Blais 1878- *WhWNAA*
DeSavistzky, Isabel *ChPo*
Desbarats, George E, Jr. *BbtC*
Desbarats, Peter 1933- *ConAu 17R, OxCan*
DesBarreaux, Jacques Vallee, Sieur 1599-1673
OxFr
DesBarres *Alli*
DesBarres, Joseph F W 1722-1824 *Alli, BbtC*
Desbiens, Albert *OxCan Sup*
Desbiens, Jean-Paul *OxCan Sup*
Desbordes-Valmore, Marceline 1786-1859
BiD&SB, CasWL, ChPo S1, EuA, OxFr,
Pen Eur
Desbordes-Valmore, Marceline Felicite
1817-1883 *EvEuW*
Desborough, Vincent Robin D'Arba 1914-
Au&Wr
Desbrisay, Charles Masse 1805-1847 *BbtC*
DesBrisay, Mather Byles *OxCan*
DesBrisay, William A *Alli Sup*
Desbrosses, Nelson *BlkAW*
Descalzi, Ricardo 1912- *DcCLA*
Descalzo, Martin *TwCW*
Descargues, Pierre 1925- *ConAu 37*
Descartes, Rene 1596-1650 *BbD, BiD&SB,*
CasWL, DcEuL, EuA, EvEuW, NewC,
OxEng, OxFr, Pen Eur, REn
Descaves, Lucien 1861-1949 *ClDMEuL,*
EvEuW, McGWD, OxFr
Deschamps *DcEuL*
Deschamps, Antoine Francois Marie 1800-1869
EvEuW, OxFr
Deschamps, Antony 1800-1869 *DcEuL,*
Pen Eur
Deschamps, Emile 1791-1871 *CasWL, DcEuL,*
EuA, EvEuW, OxFr, Pen Eur
Deschamps, Eustache 1346?-1406? *BbD,*
BiD&SB, CasWL, EuA, EvEuW, NewC,
OxEng, OxFr, Pen Eur, REn
Deschamps DeSaint Amand, Antony 1800-1869
BiD&SB
Deschamps DeSaint Amand, Emile 1791-1871
BbD, BiD&SB
Deschampsneufs, Henry Pierre Bernard 1911-
Au&Wr, ConAu 5R
DeSchanschieff, Juliet Dymoke 1919-
WrD 1976
Deschenaux, Jacques 1945- *ConAu 61*
Descherny, David *Alli*
Deschner, Donald 1933- *ConAu 21*
Deschner, Guenther 1941- *ConAu 41*
DeSchweinitz, Edmund Alexander 1825-1887
DcNAA, OhA&B
DeSchweinitz, Karl 1887-1975 *ConAu 57,*
ConAu 61
Desclot, Bernat *CasWL*
Desdunes, P A *BlkAW*
DesEcorres, Charles *DcNAA*
DesEcotais, Lewis *Alli*
DeSelincourt, Anne *WhWNAA*
DeSelincourt, Aubrey 1894-1962 *DcLEnL,*
LongC, WhCL
DeSelincourt, Mrs. Basil *ConAmA*
DeSelincourt, Ernest 1870-1943 *DcLEnL,*
EvLB, LongC, ModBL, TwCA,
TwCA Sup
DeSelincourt, Hugh 1878- *DcLEnL*
Deseret, Phineas *Alli Sup*
DeSerna, Concha Espina *ModRL*
DeSerna, Espina *TwCA, TwCA Sup*
DeSeverskey, Alexander Procofieff 1894-1974
AmA&B, ConAu 53
Desewo, P M 1925?- *AfA 1*
DeSeyn, Donna E 1933- *ConAu 21,*
WrD 1976
Desfontaines, Pierre Francois Guyot 1685-1745
OxFr, Pen Eur

DesGrieux, Chevalier *OxFr*
DeShands, Lottie Belle *BlkAW*
DeShazo, Edith K 1920- *ConAu 61*
DeShazo, Elmer Anthony 1924- *ConAu 37*
Deshen, Shlomo 1935- *ConAu 57*
DeShields, James Thomas 1891- *TexWr*
Deshler, Charles Dunham 1863-1943 *Alli,*
Alli Sup, DcNAA
Deshler, G Byron 1903- *ConAu 53*
Deshon, George 1823-1903 *Alli Sup, DcAmA,*
DcNAA
Deshoulieres, Antoinette 1638-1694 *BiD&SB,*
CasWL, DcEuL, OxFr
Deshpande, Gauri 1942- *ConP 1970*
DeSica, Vittorio 1902- *REn*
Desiderato, Otello 1926- *ConAu 37*
Desilets, Andre *OxCan Sup*
DeSimone, Daniel V 1930- *ConAu 25*
Desjardins, Alphonse *OxCan*
Desjardins, E *OxCan Sup*
Desjardins, Louis Georges 1849-1928 *DcNAA*
Desjardins, Paul 1859-1940 *BbD, BiD&SB,*
ClDMEuL, OxFr
DesLonde, Marie *BiDSA*
Deslonde, Mary D *Alli Sup*
DeSloovere, Frederick Joseph 1887-1945
DcNAA
Deslys, Charles 1821-1885 *BiD&SB, MnBBF*
DesMaiseaux, Peter 1666-1745 *Alli*
DesMaizeaux, Peter 1666-1745 *Alli*
Desmarais, Barbara G T 1942- *ConAu 25*
Desmarais, Ovide E 1919- *ConAu 1R*
Desmarchais, Rex 1908- *OxCan*
Desmarets DeSaint-Sorlin, Jean 1595-1676 *BbD,*
BiD&SB, CasWL, CnThe, EvEuW,
McGWD, OxFr, Pen Eur, REn, REnWD
DesMasures, Louis 1515?-1574? *CasWL,*
EvEuW, Pen Eur
Desmasures, Loys 1515?-1574? *OxFr*
Desmazures, Adam Charles Gustave 1818-1891
DcNAA, OxCan
DeSmet, Peter John 1801-1872 *DcAmA*
DeSmet, Pierre Jean 1801-1873 *DcNAA,*
OxAm, REnAL
DeSmith, Stanley Alexander 1922- *Au&Wr*
Desmond, Adrian J 1947- *ConAu 61*
Desmond, Alice Curtis 1897- *AmA&B,*
AuBYP, ConAu 1R, SmATA 8
Desmond, Frank *MnBBF*
Desmond, Humphrey Joseph 1858?-1932
DcAmA, DcNAA
Desmond, J Patrick 1910- *ConAu 9R*
Desmond, Johnny 1925- *AmSCAP 66*
Desmond, Robert William 1900- *Au&Wr*
Desmond, Shaw 1877-1960 *BiDPar, NewC*
Desmond, W *Alli, BiDLA*
Desmonde, William H 1921- *ConAu 1R*
Desmoulins, Camille 1760-1794 *DcEuL,*
EvEuW, OxFr, REn
Desmus, R *Alli*
Desnica, Vladan 1905-1967 *CasWL, ModSL 2,*
Pen Eur
Desnoes, Edmundo 1930- *DcCLA, Pen Am*
Desnoiresterres, Gustave 1817-1892 *BiD&SB*
Desnos, Robert 1900-1945 *CasWL, EncWL,*
ModRL, Pen Eur, REn, WhTwL,
WorAu
Desnoyers, Louis 1805-1868 *BiD&SB*
DeSoissons, Maurice 1927- *Au&Wr*
DeSola, Abraham 1825-1882 *BbtC, DcNAA*
DeSola, D A L And Raphall, M J *Alli*
DeSola, Ralph 1908- *ConAu 53*
DeSolano, Maria A *WhWNAA*
DeSolla, J M *Alli Sup*
DeSoloveytchik, George Michael 1902- *Au&Wr*
Desorgues, Joseph-Theodore 1763-1808 *OxFr*
DesOrmes, Renee *WhWNAA*
DeSoto, Fernando 1500?-1542 *REn*
DeSoto, Hernando 1500?-1542 *REn, REnAL*
DeSousa, Noemia Carolina Abranches 1927-
AfA 1
Desoutter, Denis Marcel 1919- *Au&Wr*
DeSoyres, John *Alli Sup*
DeSpain, Jay Roderic *ChPo S1*
Despard, C *Alli Sup*
Despard, Mrs. C J *ChPo*
Despard, George Packenham *Alli Sup*
Despard, Mrs. M C *Alli Sup*

Despard, Matilda *Alli Sup*
Despaurrius, M *Alli*
DesPeriers, Bonaventure 1510?-1544 *BiD&SB, CasWL, DcEuL, EvEuW, OxFr, Pen Eur*
Desplaines, Baroness Julie *ConAu XR*
Despland, Michel 1936- *ConAu 49*
Desportes, Philippe 1546?-1606 *BiD&SB, CasWL, DcEuL, EuA, EvEuW, OxFr, Pen Eur, REn*
Despreaux *OxFr*
DesPres, Josquin 1445?-1521 *AtlBL*
Despres, Leo A 1932- *ConAu 25*
Desprez, F *Alli Sup*
Desprez, Frank *ChPo S2*
Desprez, Philip Charles Soulbien *Alli Sup*
D'Esque, Count Jean Louis *MnBBF*
DesRivieres, Madeleine M *OxCan Sup*
DesRochers, Alfred 1901- *CanWr, OxCan, OxCan Sup, WhWNAA*
Desrochers, Clemence *OxCan Sup*
DesRoches, Catherine Fradonnet 1547-1587 *EuA*
DesRoches, Francis 1895- *WhWNAA*
Desroches, J Israel 1850-1922 *DcNAA*
DesRoches, Madeleine Neveu 1520?-1587 *EuA, OxFr*
Desrosiers, Abbe Adelard 1873- *WhWNAA*
Desrosiers, Leo-Paul 1896-1967 *CanWr, OxCan, OxCan Sup, WhWNAA*
Desrosiers, Marie Antoinette Tardif *OxCan, WhWNAA*
Dessalines, Jean Jacques 1758-1806 *REn*
Dessar, Leo Charles 1847-1924 *OhA&B*
Dessau, Moses *EuA*
Dessau, Paul 1894- *OxGer*
Dessauer, John Paul 1924- *ConAu 53, WrD 1976*
Dessaules, Henriette *OxCan Sup*
Dessaulles, Louis Antoine 1819-1895 *BbtC, DcNAA, OxCan*
Dessel, Norman F 1932- *ConAu 61*
Dessian, J *Alli*
Dessiou, Joseph *BiDLA*
Dessommes, Edward 1845- *BiDSA*
Dessommes, George *BiDSA*
DeStael, Germaine Necker, Baronne 1766-1817 *DcBiA*
DeStein, E *ChPo S1*
D'Esterre-Keeling *Alli Sup*
DeSteuch, Harriet Henry 1897?-1974 *ConAu 49*
Desti, Mary d1931 *DcNAA*
D'Estimauville, Robert d1829? *BbtC*
Destin, Joan *ChPo*
Destler, Chester McArthur 1904- *ConAu 5R, WrD 1976*
Destouche, Paul Emile 1794-1874 *ChPo S1*
Destouches 1680-1754 *REnWD*
Destouches, Louis Ferdinand 1894- *LongC, REn, TwCA, TwCA Sup*
Destouches, Philippe Nericault 1680-1754 *BbD, BiD&SB, CasWL, CnThe, DcEuL, EvEuW, McGWD, OxFr, Pen Eur, REn*
Destree, Jules 1863-1936 *CasWL*
Destry, Vince *ConAu XR, WrD 1976*
Destutt DeTracy, Antoine-Louis-Claude 1754-1836 *BiD&SB, OxFr*
Desty, Robert *Alli Sup*
DeSua, William Joseph 1930- *ConAu 13R*
DesUrsins, Princess M DeLaTremoille 1642?-1722 *OxFr*
Desvignes, Thomas *Alli Sup*
Desvoeux, A V *Alli*
DesVoignes, Jules Verne 1886-1911 *DcNAA*
DeSylva, B G 1895-1950 *AmSCAP 66*
DeSylva, Donald Perrin 1928- *ConAu 53*
DeTabley, Lord John Byron L Warren 1835-1895 *BiD&SB, BrAu 19, ChPo, DcEnA, EvLB, OxEng, PoIre*
DeTarr, Francis 1926- *ConAu 17R*
DeTeissier, George Frederick *Alli Sup*
DeTeissier, Baron Philip A, Of France 1819- *Alli Sup*
Deter, Dean 1945- *ConAu 53, DrAP 1975*
Deterline, William A 1927- *ConAu 5R*
DeTerra, Rhoda Hoff 1901- *ConAu 1R*
Detherage, May 1908- *ConAu 23*
Dethick, Henry *Alli*
Dethick, Sir William *Alli*

Dethier, Vincent G 1915- *WrD 1976*
Dethloff, Henry C 1934- *ConAu 23*
DeThoren, Alice *Alli Sup*
Dethridge, Frank *Alli Sup*
Dethycke *Alli*
Detine, Padre *ConAu 49, SmATA 6*
Detjen, Ervin W *ConAu 19*
Detjen, Louis Reinhold 1884- *WhWNAA*
Detjen, Mary Ford 1904- *ConAu P-1*
Detlef, Karl 1836-1876 *BiD&SB*
Detmold, Christian Edward 1810- *Alli Sup*
Detmold, Edward J 1883?- *ChPo S1, ConICB*
DeTocqueville, Alexis *OxAm, REnAL*
DeTodany, James *ConAu XR*
DeToledano, Ralph 1916- *AmA&B, AuNews 1*
DeTolnay, Charles Erich 1899- *AmA&B*
DeTournemir *DcRusL*
DeTrafford, Sir Humphrey F 1862-1929 *Br&AmS*
DeTrevino, Elizabeth Borton 1904- *AuICB, MorBMP, NewbC 1966*
Detro, Gene 1935- *ConAu 61*
DeTrobriand, Philip Regis 1816-1897 *DcAmA*
Dett, Robert Nathaniel 1882-1943 *AmA&B, AmSCAP 66, BlkAW*
Detter, Thomas *BlkAW*
DeTurk, Ernest E 1887- *WhWNAA*
Detweiler, Frederick German 1881- *OhA&B*
Detweiler, Robert 1932- *ConAu 33, WrD 1976*
Detwiler, Donald S 1933- *ConAu 37*
Detz, Phyllis 1911- *ConAu 33*
Detzer, Dorothy 1900- *IndAu 1917*
Detzer, Karl 1891- *AmA&B, ConAu P-1, IndAu 1917, WhWNAA*
Detzer, Laura Goshorn 1862-1954 *IndAu 1917*
Detzler, Jack J 1922- *ConAu 33, IndAu 1917*
Deuchar, A *Alli*
Deuchar, Robert *Alli Sup*
Deucher, Sybil *MorJA*
DeUnamuno, Miguel *ModRL, TwCA, TwCA Sup*
Deus, Joao De 1830-1896? *BiD&SB, Pen Eur*
Deus Ramos, Joao De 1830-1896 *CIDMEuL*
Deusbery, William *Alli*
Deutrich, Mabel E 1915- *ConAu 5R*
Deutsch, Adolph 1897- *AmSCAP 66*
Deutsch, Albert 1905-1961 *AmA&B*
Deutsch, Alex Tom *OhA&B*
Deutsch, Babette 1895- *AmA&B, AnCL, Au&Wr, ChPo, ChPo S1, ChPo S2, ConAmL, ConAu 1R, ConP 1970, ConP 1975, DcLEnL, DrAP 1975, EvLB, LongC, MorJA, OxAm, Pen Am, RAdv 1, REn, REnAL, SmATA 1, TwCA, TwCA Sup, TwCW, WhWNAA, WrD 1976*
Deutsch, Bernard Francis 1925- *ConAu 13R*
Deutsch, Emanuel Oscar Menahem 1829-1873 *Alli Sup, DcEnL, DcEuL*
Deutsch, Emery 1907- *AmSCAP 66*
Deutsch, Gotthard 1859-1921 *AmLY, DcAmA, DcNAA, OhA&B*
Deutsch, Gregory Paul 1952- *AmSCAP 66*
Deutsch, Harold C 1904- *ConAu 21*
Deutsch, Helen *AmSCAP 66*
Deutsch, Karl W 1912- *ConAu 41*
Deutsch, Monroe Emanuel 1879- *WhWNAA*
Deutsch, Morton 1920- *ConAu 1R*
Deutsch, Niklas Manuel *OxGer*
Deutsch, Ronald M 1928- *ConAu 1R*
Deutsch, Solomon 1816-1897 *Alli Sup, DcAmA*
Deutscher, Irwin 1923- *ConAu 25, WrD 1976*
Deutscher, Isaac 1907-1967 *ConAu 5R, ConAu 25, WorAu*
Deutschkron, Inge 1922- *ConAu 29*
Deutzman, Lawrence F 1880- *WhWNAA*
Deuwes, Giles *Alli*
Dev *DcOrL 2*
Devadutt, Vinjamuri E 1908- *ConAu 23*
DeVaere, Ulric Josef 1932- *ConAu 1R*
Devahuti, D 1929- *ConAu 45*
Deval, Govind Ballal 1855-1916 *DcOrL 2*
Deval, Jacques 1894?-1972 *CnMD, ConAu XR, EvEuW, McGWD, ModWD, Pen Eur, REn, TwCA, TwCA Sup*

DeValera, Eamon 1882- *ChPo S1, REn*
DeValera, Sinead 1879?-1975 *CatA 1952, ConAu 53*
DeValois, Ninette 1898- *Au&Wr*
DeVane, William Clyde 1898-1965 *AmA&B*
Devaney, James Martin 1890- *DcLEnL*
Devaney, John 1926- *ConAu 17R*
Devaney, Pauline Margaret 1937- *Au&Wr*
Devara Dasimayya *DcOrL 2*
Devaraksita Jayabahu Dharmakirti *DcOrL 2*
Devarius, M *Alli*
Devas, Charles Stanton *Alli Sup*
Devas, Nicolette 1911- *ConAu 13R*
DeVasconcellos, Antonio, Jr. 1918- *Au&Wr*
DeVault, Marion Vere 1922- *ConAu 1R, IndAu 1917*
DeVaux, Roland 1903-1971 *ConAu 33*
DeVaynes, Julia Henrietta Louisa *Alli Sup*
DeVeaux, Alexis *DrAF 1976*
DeVeaux, Richard *DcNAA*
DeVega, Lope *ChPo*
DeVegh, Elizabeth 1911- *Au&Wr*
DeVeil, Charles Maria *Alli*
Deveil, Sir Thomas *Alli*
Develin, Dora d1940 *DcNAA*
DeVelling, Charles Theodore 1842-1923 *OhA&B*
D'Evelyn, Katherine E 1899- *ConAu 17R*
Devendra, N Das *Alli Sup*
Devenish, Dorothy Grace Whitty 1912- *Au&Wr*
Devenish, Thomas *Alli*
Devenport, Pat 1904- *Au&Wr*
Dever, Joseph 1919-1970 *CatA 1952, ConAu 19, ConAu 29*
Dever, Joseph Gerard *BkC 6*
DeVerdon, T K *Alli Sup*
DeVere, Aubrey *Chmbr 3*
DeVere, Sir Aubrey 1788-1846 *Alli, BbD, BiD&SB, BrAu 19, ChPo, ChPo S1, DcEuL, NewC, PoIre*
DeVere, Aubrey Thomas 1814-1902 *Alli Sup, BbD, BiD&SB, BrAu 19, CasWL, ChPo, ChPo S1, ChPo S2, DcEnA, DcEnA Ap, DcEnL, DcEuL, DcLEnL, EvLB, MouLC 4, NewC, OxEng, Pen Eng, PoIre, REn, WebEAL*
DeVere, Edward *Chmbr 1, EvLB*
DeVere, Florence *Alli Sup*
DeVere, Jane *ConAu XR, WrD 1976*
DeVere, Mary d1830 *PoIre*
DeVere, Mary Ainge 1850?- *Alli Sup, AmA&B, BiD&SB, ChPo, DcAmA, DcNAA, PoIre*
DeVere, Maximilian Schele 1820-1898 *Alli, Alli Sup, AmA&B, BiD&SB, DcAmA*
DeVere, Sir Stephen Edward 1812-1904 *Alli Sup, PoIre*
DeVere, William 1844-1904 *ChPo S1*
Deverel *Alli*
Deverell, F H *Alli Sup*
Deverell, Mary *Alli, BiDLA*
Deverell, Robert *Alli, BiDLA*
Deverell, William Trapnell *Alli Sup*
Devereux *Alli*
Devereux, Captain *Alli*
Devereux, Anthony John 1931- *Au&Wr*
Devereux, Edward James Pryce 1899- *Au&Wr*
Devereux, Frederick L, Jr. 1914- *ConAu 49, SmATA 9*
Devereux, George 1908- *BiDPar*
Devereux, George H *Alli Sup*
Devereux, George T 1810?- *EarAB, EarAB Sup*
Devereux, Hilary 1919- *ConAu 13R*
Devereux, J E *Alli, BiDLA*
Devereux, John C *Alli Sup*
Devereux, Lillie *HsB&A*
Devereux, Marion *PoIre*
Devereux, Mary d1914 *AmA&B, DcAmA, DcNAA*
Devereux, Robert 1592-1646 *Alli*
Devereux, Robert 1922- *ConAu 5R*
Devereux, Robert, Earl Of Essex 1567?-1601? *Alli, CasWL, NewC*
Devereux, Thomas Pollock 1793-1869 *Alli, BiDSA, DcAmA*
Devereux, Walter, Earl Of Essex 1540?-1576 *Alli, CasWL*
Devereux, Walter Bourchier 1810-1868 *Alli Sup*

Devereux, William Cope *Alli Sup*
Deveria, Achille Jacques Howell 1800?-1857
    ChPo S1, OxFr
Deveria, Eugene 1805-1865 *OxFr*
DeVericour, L R *Alli*
Devery, Elizabeth Coleman *WhWNAA*
Devey, Mrs. E C *Alli Sup*
Devey, F W *Alli Sup*
Devey, Joseph *Alli Sup*
Devey, Louisa *Alli Sup*
DeVeyrac, Robert 1901- *IlCB 1945*
Devi, Indra 1899- *ConAu P-1*
Devi, Srimati Maya 1893- *WhLA*
DeVigne, H Rosier *MnBBF*
DeVigny, Alfred, Comte 1797-1863 *ChPo,*
    DcBiA
Deville, Edouard Gaston 1849-1924 *DcNAA*
Deville, Edward Gaston 1849-1924 *Alli Sup*
DeVilliers, Francois Ebenezer Stead 1894-
    Au&Wr
DeVilliers, Gerard 1929- *ConAu 61*
DeVinck, Antoine 1924- *ConAu 53*
DeVinck, Catherine 1922- *ConAu 57*
DeVinck, Jose M G A 1912- *ConAu 17R,*
    WrD 1976
Devine, Alex 1865- *WhLA*
Devine, David Macdonald 1920- *Au&Wr,*
    ConAu 1R, EncM&D, WrD 1976
Devine, Dominic *EncM&D, WrD 1976*
Devine, Edward James 1860-1927 *DcNAA,*
    OxCan
Devine, Edward Thomas 1867-1948 *DcAmA,*
    DcNAA, WhWNAA
Devine, George 1910-1966 *CrCD*
Devine, George 1941- *ConAu 45*
Devine, George Burnett 1892- *ChPo, OhA&B*
Devine, James d1890 *PoIre*
Devine, Janice 1909?-1973 *ConAu 41*
Devine, Minos 1871- *WhLA*
Devine, Patrick K *OxCan*
Devine, Thomas *BbtC*
Devine, Thomas G 1928- *ConAu 17R*
DeVinne, Daniel 1793-1883 *Alli Sup, DcAmA,*
    DcNAA
DeVinne, Theodore Low 1828-1914 *Alli Sup,*
    AmA, AmA&B, DcAmA, DcNAA,
    OxAm, REn, REnAL
DeVinney, Richard 1936- *ConAu 45*
Devins, John Bancroft 1856-1911 *DcNAA*
Devins, Joseph H, Jr. 1930- *ConAu 21,*
    WrD 1976
Devirieux, C J *OxCan Sup*
Devis, Ellen *BiDLA*
Devis, Ellin *Alli*
Devis, James *Alli*
DeVitis, Michael Angelo 1890- *WhWNAA*
DeVito, Albert 1919- *AmSCAP 66*
DeVito, Joseph Anthony 1938- *ConAu 37,*
    WrD 1976
Devkota, Laksmi Prasad 1909-1959 *DcOrL 2*
Devlan, Eugene *TwCA Sup*
Devletoglou, Nicos E 1936- *ConAu 41*
Devlin, Lord 1905- *Au&Wr*
Devlin, Denis 1908-1959 *CasWL, ModBL Sup,*
    WorAu
Devlin, Harry *ChPo S2, IlBYP*
Devlin, J Dacres *Alli*
Devlin, John J, Jr. 1920- *ConAu 37*
Devlin, Joseph 1869- *PoIre*
Devlin, L Patrick 1939- *ConAu 61*
Devlin, Owen *WhWNAA*
Devlin, Robert T *Alli Sup*
Devlin, Wende 1918- *ConAu 61*
Devlin, Wende And Harry *IlBYP*
Devoe, Alan 1909-1955 *AmA&B*
DeVoe, Walter 1874- *AmLY*
Devol, C *Alli Sup*
DeVol, Frank 1911- *AmSCAP 66*
Devol, George H 1829- *BiDSA, OhA&B*
Devol, Kenneth S 1929- *ConAu 49*
DeVoll, Calvin Joseph 1886- *AmSCAP 66*
DeVomecourt, Philippe *Au&Wr*
Devon, Duchess Of *ChPo S1*
Devon, Albert *ChPo S1*
Devon, James 1866- *WhLA*
Devon, John Anthony *ConAu XR*
Devon, Sarah *WrD 1976*
Devon, W A *Alli Sup*

Devonshire, Elizabeth Hervey, Duchess Of
    1759-1824 *Alli, ChPo*
Devonshire, F *Alli Sup*
Devonshire, Georgiana, Duchess Of 1757-1806
    Alli
Devonshire Poet, The *DcEnL*
DeVoore, Ann *ChPo S1*
Devor, John W 1901- *ConAu P-1*
Devore, Irven 1934- *ConAu 23*
DeVore, Nicolas 1882- *WhWNAA*
DeVorsey, Louis, Jr. 1929- *ConAu 21,*
    WrD 1976
DeVos, A George 1922- *ConAu 21*
DeVosjoli, Philippe L Thyraud 1920- *ConAu 29*
DeVoss, James C 1884- *WhWNAA*
DeVoto, Bernard Augustine 1897-1955 *AmA&B,*
    AmNov, AuNews 1, CnDAL, ConAmA,
    DcLEnL, EncWL, LongC, ModAL,
    OxAm, Pen Am, RAdv 1, REn, REnAL,
    TwCA, TwCA Sup, WhWNAA
Devoto, James d1752? *BkIE*
Devoto, John d1752? *BkIE*
Devoy, John 1842-1928 *Alli Sup, DcNAA*
Devrient, Eduard 1801-1877 *OxGer*
DeVries, Carrow 1906- *ConAu 53, WrD 1976*
DeVries, Egbert 1901- *ConAu 61*
DeVries, Henri *WhWNAA*
DeVries, Herbert A 1917- *ConAu 33*
DeVries, Jan 1819-1855 *DcEuL*
DeVries, John 1915- *AmSCAP 66*
DeVries, John Hendrik 1859-1939 *DcNAA,*
    WhWNAA
DeVries, Leonard 1919- *Au&Wr, ChPo S1*
DeVries, Peter 1910- *AmA&B, Au&Wr,*
    CnDAL, ConAu 17R, ConLC 1,
    ConLC 2, ConLC 3, ConNov 1972,
    ConNov 1976, DrAF 1976, EncWL Sup,
    ModAL, ModAL Sup, OxAm, Pen Am,
    REnAL, WhTwL, WorAu, WrD 1976
DeVries, Simon J 1921- *ConAu 57*
DeVries, William Levering 1865-1937 *DcNAA*
Devron, Gustavus *BiDSA*
Dew, Charles B 1937- *ConAu 21*
Dew, Ingle *Alli Sup*
Dew, Louise E 1871- *WhWNAA*
Dew, Samuel *Alli*
Dew, Thomas *Alli*
Dew, Thomas Roderick 1802-1846 *Alli, BiDSA,*
    CyAL 1, DcAmA, DcNAA
DeWaal, Daphne *ChPo S2*
DeWaal, Ronald Burt 1932- *ConAu 37,*
    WrD 1976
DeWaal, Victor 1929- *ConAu 29*
DeWaal, Violet Mary *WhWNAA*
DeWaal Malefijt, Annemarie 1914- *ConAu 61*
DeWaard, Elliott John 1935- *ConAu 49,*
    SmATA 7
Dewald, Paul A 1920- *ConAu 17R, WrD 1976*
DeWalden, Thomas Blaides 1811-1873 *BiD&SB,*
    DcAmA
DeWalsh, Faust Charles 1882- *WhWNAA*
Dewane, E *ChPo*
Dewar, Alexander 1822-1883 *Alli Sup,*
    ChPo S1
Dewar, Archibald 1792-1855 *ChPo S1*
Dewar, Daniel *Alli, Alli Sup, BiDLA*
Dewar, David Ross 1913- *Au&Wr*
Dewar, Douglas 1875- *WhLA*
Dewar, Ed H *Alli*
Dewar, George Albemarle Bertie 1862- *WhLA*
Dewar, Henry *Alli, BiDLA*
Dewar, James d1877 *Alli Sup, ChPo S1*
Dewar, John *Alli Sup*
Dewar, Lindsay 1891- *Au&Wr*
Dewar, Mary 1921- *ConAu 13R*
Dewar, Michael James Steuart 1918-
    WrD 1976
Dewart, Edward Hartley 1828-1903 *BbtC,*
    ChPo S1, DcNAA, OxCan, OxCan Sup,
    PoIre
Dewart, Leslie 1922- *AmA&B, ConAu 9R,*
    WrD 1976
Dewart, William Thompson 1875-1944 *AmA&B*
DeWatteville, Armand *Alli Sup*
Dewdney, John Christopher 1928- *WrD 1976*
Dewdney, Selwyn *OxCan*
Dewe, Joseph Adelbert 1866-1935 *DcNAA,*
    WhWNAA

DeWeerd, Harvey A 1902- *ConAu 25*
Dewees, Francis Percival *Alli Sup*
Dewees, William Potts 1768-1841 *Alli, DcAmA,*
    DcNAA
DeWeese, Truman Armstrong 1860-1936
    OhA&B
Dewell, T *Alli, BiDLA*
DeWelt, Don Finch 1919- *ConAu 1R*
Dewes, Alfred *Alli Sup*
D'Ewes, J *Alli Sup*
D'Ewes, Sir Symonds 1602-1650 *Alli*
DeWette, H *BbtC*
Dewey, Albert Peter 1916-1945 *DcNAA*
Dewey, Ariane 1937- *ConAu 49, IlBYP,*
    SmATA 7
Dewey, Bradley R 1934- *ConAu 29*
Dewey, Byrd Spilman 1856- *AmA&B, BiDSA*
Dewey, Chester 1783-1867 *DcAmA*
Dewey, Davis Rich 1858-1942 *AmLY, DcNAA*
Dewey, Dellon M *Alli Sup*
Dewey, Donald O 1930- *ConAu 37,*
    WrD 1976
Dewey, Edward R 1895- *ConAu 41*
Dewey, Frederick H 1853-1913 *HsB&A,*
    HsB&A Sup
Dewey, George 1837-1917 *DcNAA, REn*
Dewey, George W 1818- *Alli*
Dewey, Godfrey 1887- *ConAu 29*
Dewey, Irene Sargent 1896- *ConAu 17*
Dewey, J *Alli Sup*
Dewey, James *AmA&B, AmNov XR*
Dewey, John 1859-1952 *Alli Sup, AmA&B,*
    CasWL, ConAmA, DcAmA, DcLEnL,
    EvLB, LongC, OxAm, OxEng, Pen Am,
    REn, REnAL, TwCA, TwCA Sup,
    WebEAL, WhTwL, WhWNAA
Dewey, Lyster H 1865- *WhWNAA*
Dewey, Mary Elizabeth 1821-1910 *Alli Sup,*
    DcAmA, DcNAA
Dewey, Melvil 1851-1931 *Alli Sup, AmA&B,*
    AmLY, DcAmA, DcNAA, OxAm, REn,
    REnAL, WhWNAA
Dewey, Orville 1794-1882 *Alli, Alli Sup,*
    AmA&B, BiD&SB, CyAL 1, DcAmA,
    DcEnL, DcNAA
Dewey, Richard S 1845- *WhWNAA*
Dewey, Robert D 1923- *ConAu 9R*
Dewey, Robert E 1923- *ConAu 13R*
Dewey, T Henry *Alli Sup*
Dewey, Thomas Blanchard 1915- *ConAu 1R,*
    EncM&D, IndAu 1917
Dewey, Thomas Emmet 1859-1906 *ChPo S1*
Dewey, Willis Alonzo 1858-1938 *DcNAA,*
    WhWNAA
Dewhirst, Charles *Alli, BiDLA*
Dewhirst, Ian 1936- *WrD 1976*
Dewhurst, E M *Alli Sup*
Dewhurst, E R *BbtC*
Dewhurst, Edward Bury 1870-1941 *DcNAA*
Dewhurst, Frederic Eli 1855-1906 *DcAmA,*
    DcNAA
Dewhurst, J Frederic 1895- *ConAu 17*
Dewhurst, Jane *Alli Sup*
Dewhurst, Keith 1931- *ConAu 61, ConDr,*
    WrD 1976
Dewhurst, Kenneth 1919- *Au&Wr, ConAu 5R*
Dewhurst, William W *Alli Sup, BiDSA*
Dewi, Saint *NewC*
Dewick, Edward Chisholm 1884- *WhLA*
DeWilde, George James 1804-1871 *Alli Sup,*
    ChPo S2
DeWindt, Hal *BlkAW*
Dewing, Arthur Stone 1880-1971 *AmA&B,*
    WhWNAA
Dewing, Elizabeth B *AmNov XR*
Dewing, H C *Alli*
Dewing, Maria Richards 1845-1927 *DcNAA*
Dewing, Mrs. T W 1855- *Alli Sup, ChPo S1*
DeWint, Mrs. J P *Alli*
Dewint, Peter 1784-1849 *ChPo S1*
DeWitt, Benjamin 1774-1819 *Alli, DcAmA,*
    DcNAA
Dewitt, Benjamin Parke 1889- *AmLY*
DeWitt, Cornelius Hugh 1905- *ChPo S1,*
    IlCB 1945, IlCB 1956
DeWitt, E L *Alli Sup*
DeWitt, Mrs. F H *ChPo S1*
DeWitt, James *AuBYP, ConAu XR*

DeWitt, Jennie *Alli Sup*
DeWitt, John 1821-1906 *Alli Sup, CyAL 1, DcAmA, DcNAA*
DeWitt, John 1842- *Alli Sup, DcAmA*
DeWitt, Julia A Woodhull d1906 *DcNAA*
DeWitt, Mary Brewerton *ChPo S1*
DeWitt, Norman Wentworth 1876- *WhWNAA*
DeWitt, Roscoe Plimpton 1894- *TexWr*
DeWitt, Simeon 1756-1834 *Alli, DcAmA, DcNAA*
DeWitt, Susan d1824 *Alli*
DeWitt, Wallace *Alli Sup*
Dewlen, Al 1921- *Au&Wr, ConAu 1R*
Dewnes, G *Alli Sup*
DeWohl, Louis 1903- *BkC 5, CatA 1952*
DeWolf, L E *Alli*
DeWolf, L Harold 1905- *AmA&B, ConAu 1R*
DeWolf, Lyman E *Alli Sup*
DeWolf, Philip 1880-1934 *DcNAA*
Dewolf, Rose 1934- *ConAu 29*
DeWolf, William P *Alli*
DeWolfe, Genie Griffin 1879- *TexWr, WhWNAA*
DeWolfers, Amelia *ChPo*
Dewrance, Sir John 1858- *WhLA*
Dews, Nathan *Alli Sup*
Dewsland, Edgar *Alli Sup*
Dewson, Francis A 1881- *TexWr, WhWNAA*
DeWulf, Maurice 1867-1947 *CatA 1952*
Dewy, Robert Cullen *Alli Sup*
Dexter, Mrs. *Alli Sup*
Dexter, Byron 1900- *AmA&B*
Dexter, Charles 1830-1893 *Alli Sup, OhA&B*
Dexter, D Gilbert *ChPo*
Dexter, Edwin Grant 1868-1938 *DcNAA*
Dexter, Franklin Bowditch 1842-1920 *Alli Sup, AmA, AmA&B, DcAmA, DcNAA*
Dexter, Henry M *ChPo*
Dexter, Henry Martyn 1821-1890 *Alli Sup, BiD&SB, CyAL 2, DcAmA, DcNAA*
Dexter, Henry Morton 1846-1910 *DcNAA*
Dexter, Henry V *Alli Sup*
Dexter, Janet *ChPo*
Dexter, John *ConAu XR*
Dexter, John Thomas *Alli Sup*
Dexter, Lewis Anthony 1915- *ConAu 9R, WrD 1976*
Dexter, Mark *MnBBF*
Dexter, Morton 1846- *DcAmA*
Dexter, Philip *MnBBF*
Dexter, Ralph *MnBBF*
Dexter, Ransom *Alli Sup*
Dexter, Samuel 1726-1810 *DcNAA*
Dexter, Samuel 1761-1816 *Alli, DcAmA, DcNAA*
Dexter, Seymour 1841-1904 *DcNAA*
Dexter, Thomas Edward *Alli Sup*
Dexter, Timothy 1747-1806 *AmA, AmA&B, CnDAL, DcLEnL, DcNAA, OxAm, REn, REnAL*
Dexter, Walter 1877-1950? *MnBBF*
Dexter, Will *HsB&A, OhA&B*
Dey, Agnes Christall 1861-1895 *ChPo S1*
Dey, Frederic VanRensselaer 1861?-1922 *ChPo S2, EncM&D*
Dey, Frederick VanRensselaer 1861?-1922 *AmA&B, DcNAA, HsB&A, REn*
Dey, Mrs. Haryot Holt 1857- *WhWNAA*
Dey, Joseph C, Jr. 1907- *ConAu P-1*
Dey, Larry 1910- *AmSCAP 66*
Dey, Marmaduke *HsB&A*
Dey, R *Alli*
Dey, Robert *ChPo S2*
Deyermond, Alan D 1932- *ConAu 13R*
Deymann, Clementius *Alli Sup*
D'Eyncourt, Charles Tennyson- 1784-1861 *Alli Sup*
Deyneka, Anita 1943- *ConAu 61*
Deyo, Felix *ChPo S2*
DeYoung, Henry C 1890- *WhWNAA*
Deyssel, Lodewijk Van 1864-1952 *CasWL, ClDMEuL, EncWL, Pen Eur*
Dez-Coll, Bernat *CasWL*
Deza, Ernest C 1923- *ConAu 53*
DeZavala, Adina *TexWr*
DeZilwa, Lucien 1875- *DcLEnL*
Dezobry, Charles-Louis, And Bachelet, T *OxFr*
Dhalla, Nariman K 1925- *ConAu 25,*

WrD 1976
D'Halmar, Augusto 1880-1950 *Pen Am*
Dhammaraja, Sri *DcOrL 2*
Dhananjaya *DcOrL 2*
Dhanika *DcOrL 2*
Dhar, N R 1892- *WhLA*
D'Harcourt, Marguerite *OxCan Sup*
D'Harcourt, Raoul *OxCan Sup*
Dharmaraksa *DcOrL 1*
Dharmasena *DcOrL 2*
D'Harnoncourt, Rene 1901- *IlCB 1945*
Dharta, A S 1924- *DcOrL 2*
Dhavamony, Mariasusai 1925- *ConAu 33, WrD 1976*
Dhiel, Myra *Alli Sup*
Dhlomo, Herbert Isaac Ernest 1905?-1957 *AfA 1, DcLEnL, Pen Cl, TwCW*
Dhlomo, R R R *DcLEnL, Pen Cl*
Dhlomo, Rolfus Reginald Raymond 1901- *AfA 1*
Dhokalia, Prasad 1925- *ConAu 41*
Dhotel, Andre 1900- *CasWL, EncWL, REn, WorAu*
Dhrymes, Phoebus J 1932- *ConAu 29*
Dhu, Helen *Alli Sup*
Dia, Dick 1917- *AmSCAP 66*
Diabolin *PueRA*
Diack, Hunter 1908- *ConAu 21*
Diack, Philip 1929- *Au&Wr*
Diaghilev, Sergei Pavlovitch 1872-1919 *DcRusL, REn*
Diagne, Ahmadou Mapate 1890?- *AfA 1*
Diakhate, Lamine 1928- *AfA 1*
Diallo, Assane Y 1940?- *AfA 1*
Diallo, Bakary 1892- *AfA 1*
Diamant, Lincoln 1923- *ConAu 33, WrD 1976*
Diamant, Rudolph Maximilian Eugen 1925- *Au&Wr, WrD 1976*
Diamante, Juan Bautista 1625?-1687? *BiD&SB, CasWL, DcEuL, EvEuW, McGWD*
Diamond, Arthur Sigismund 1897- *Au&Wr, ConAu P-1, WrD 1976*
Diamond, David Leo 1915- *AmSCAP 66, REnAL*
Diamond, Edwin 1925- *ConAu 13R*
Diamond, Leo *AmSCAP 66*
Diamond, Leo G 1907- *AmSCAP 66*
Diamond, Lucy *ChPo*
Diamond, Malcolm L 1924- *ConAu 25*
Diamond, Nellie *ChPo*
Diamond, Robert Mach 1930- *ConAu 9R*
Diamond, Sander A 1942- *ConAu 49*
Diamond, Sigmund 1920- *ConAu 1R*
Diane De Poitiers, Duchesse DeV 1499-1566 *OxFr, REn*
Diaper, William 1685?-1717 *Alli, CnE&AP, OxEng*
Diara, Schavi M 1948- *ConAu 61*
Dias, Antonio Goncalves 1823-1864? *BiD&SB*
Dias, Earl Joseph 1916- *ConAu 23*
Dias, Joao 1926-1949 *AfA 1*
Diaz, Mrs. A M 1821-1904 *CarSB*
Diaz, Abbey Morton 1821-1904 *Alli Sup, AmA, AmA&B, BbD, BiD&SB, ChPo, DcAmA, DcNAA*
Diaz, Antonio Goncalves 1823-1864? *BiD&SB*
Diaz, Janet W 1935- *ConAu 53*
Diaz, Jorge 1930- *CrCD, DcCLA*
Diaz, Jose Pedro 1921- *DcCLA*
Diaz, Porfirio 1830-1915 *REn*
Diaz Alfaro, Abelardo M 1920- *DcCLA, PueRA*
Diaz Arrieta, Hernan 1891- *Pen Am*
Diaz DeBivar, Rodrigo *REn*
Diaz DeBivar, Ruy *REn*
Diaz DeEscobar, Narciso 1860- *BiD&SB*
Diaz DelCastillo, Bernal 1492?-1581? *BbD, BiD&SB, CasWL, DcEuL, DcSpL, EuA, EvEuW, Pen Am, Pen Eur, REn*
Diaz DeToledo, Pero 1418?-1466 *CasWL*
Diaz Lozano, Argentina 1912- *DcCLA*
Diaz Machicao, Porfirio 1909- *DcCLA*
Diaz Miron, Salvador 1853-1928 *CasWL, DcSpL, EncWL, Pen Am*
Diaz Montero, Anibal 1911- *PueRA*
Diaz-Plaja, Guillermo 1909- *DcSpL*
Diaz Rodriguez, Manuel 1868-1927 *CasWL,*

DcSpL, EncWL, Pen Am
Diaz Soler, Luis M 1916- *PueRA*
Diaz Valcarcel, Emilio 1929- *DcCLA, PueRA*
Dib, Mohammed 1920- *CasWL, DcOrL 3, EncWL*
Dibb, Paul 1939- *ConAu 45*
Dibben, Thomas *Alli*
Dibbin, L O *ChPo S1*
Dibble, J Birney 1925- *ConAu 17R, WrD 1976*
Dibble, Roy Floyd 1887-1929 *AmA&B, DcNAA, WhWNAA*
Dibble, Sheldon 1809-1845 *DcAmA, DcNAA*
Dibby, Kenelm Henry 1800- *DcEnL*
Dibdin, Charles 1745-1814 *Alli, BbD, BiD&SB, BiDLA, BiDLA Sup, BrAu, CasWL, ChPo, ChPo S1, ChPo S2, Chmbr 2, DcEnL, DcEuL, DcLEnL, EvLB, NewC, OxEng, St&VC*
Dibdin, Charles, Jr. d1833 *Alli, BiDLA*
Dibdin, Charles Isaac Mungo 1768-1833 *NewC*
Dibdin, Emily *Alli Sup*
Dibdin, James C *Alli Sup*
Dibdin, Lewis Tonna 1852- *Alli Sup*
Dibdin, Robert William *Alli Sup*
Dibdin, Thomas 1771-1841 *Alli, BiDLA, DcEnL*
Dibdin, Thomas Frognall 1776?-1847 *Alli, BiD&SB, BiDLA, ChPo S1, DcEnL, DcEuL, DcLEnL, NewC, OxEng*
Dibdin, Thomas John 1771-1841 *BiD&SB, ChPo, ChPo S2, DcEuL, EvLB, NewC*
Dibelius, Martin 1883-1947 *OxGer*
Dibner, Martin 1911- *Au&Wr, ConAu 1R*
DiBonaventura, Sam 1923- *AmSCAP 66*
DiC *ChPo S2*
Dicaearchus 320?BC- *Pen Cl*
Dice, Charles Amos 1878- *OhA&B, WhWNAA*
Dice, F M *Alli Sup*
Dicenta, Joaquin 1863-1917 *CasWL, ClDMEuL, EvEuW*
Dicenta Y Benedicto, Joaquin 1863-1917 *McGWD*
DiCerto, J J 1933- *ConAu 23, WrD 1976*
DiCesare, Mario A 1928- *ConAu 5R, WrD 1976*
Diceto, Radulph De *Alli*
Dicey, Albert Venn 1835-1922 *Alli Sup, DcEuL, NewC, OxEng*
Dicey, Edward Stephen 1832-1911 *Alli Sup, BiD&SB, DcEnL, NewC*
Dicey, Thomas *Alli*
Dichter, Ernest 1907- *AmA&B, ConAu 17R*
Dick, Sir Alex 1703-1785 *Alli*
Dick, Alexander *BbtC*
Dick, Andrew Coventry *Alli, Alli Sup*
Dick, Bernard F 1935- *ConAu 21, WrD 1976*
Dick, Conzae And Cresswell, James *Alli Sup*
Dick, Cotsford 1846-1911 *ChPo S1*
Dick, Cuthbert *ChPo S1*
Dick, Daniel T 1946- *ConAu 61*
Dick, Dorothy 1900- *AmSCAP 66*
Dick, Everett 1898- *ConAu 25*
Dick, G H *Alli Sup*
Dick, George Frederick 1881-1967 *IndAu 1917*
Dick, Gertrude McConnell 1899- *OhA&B*
Dick, Harris St. John *Alli Sup*
Dick, Henry *Alli Sup, ChPo*
Dick, Henry N 1902-1960 *IndAu 1917*
Dick, Herbert George *Alli Sup*
Dick, Ignace 1926- *ConAu 25*
Dick, John *Alli Sup, BiDLA*
Dick, John 1764-1833 *Alli*
Dick, Kay 1915- *Au&Wr, ConAu 13R, WrD 1976*
Dick, Marcel 1898- *AmSCAP 66*
Dick, Margaret *Au&Wr*
Dick, Mary *Alli Sup*
Dick, Philip K 1928- *AmA&B, ConAu 49, ConNov 1976, DrAF 1976, WrD 1976*
Dick, Robert *Alli, Alli Sup, BbtC*
Dick, Robert Christopher 1938- *ConAu 37, WrD 1976*
Dick, Samuel Medary 1857-1938 *OhA&B*
Dick, T *Alli Sup*
Dick, Thomas 1772?-1857 *Alli, DcEnL*
Dick, Thomas Lauder *Alli*

Dick, Trella Lamson 1889-1974 *AuBYP,*
ConAu 5R, SmATA 9
Dick, William *Alli*
Dick, William d1866 *Alli Sup*
Dick, Sir William *Alli*
Dick, William Brisbane 1827-1901 *Alli Sup,*
ChPo S1, DcNAA
Dick, William M 1933- *ConAu 41*
Dick, William Robertson *Alli Sup*
Dick-Lauder, Sir George Andrew 1917- *Au&Wr,*
WrD 1976
Dickason, David Howard 1907- *ConAu 33,*
IndAu 1917
Dicke, Robert H 1916- *ConAu 53, WrD 1976*
Dickel, Conrad *ChPo*
Dicken, Alldersey *Alli*
Dicken, Charlotte H *Alli Sup*
Dicken, E W Trueman 1919- *ConAu 9R*
Dicken, Samuel Newton 1901- *WhPNW*
Dickens, Arthur Geoffrey 1910- *Au&Wr,*
ConAu 53, WrD 1976
Dickens, Charles *Alli*
Dickens, Charles 1812-1870 *Alli, Alli Sup,*
AtlBL, AuBYP, BbD, BiD&SB,
BrAu 19, CarSB, CasWL, ChPo,
ChPo S1, ChPo S2, Chmbr 3, CriT 3,
CyWA, DcBiA, DcEnA, DcEnA Ap,
DcEnL, DcEuL, DcLEnL, EncM&D,
EvLB, FamAYP, HsB&A, JBA 1934,
MnBBF, MouLC 3, NewC, OxAm,
OxEng, Pen Am, Pen Eng, RAdv 1,
RCom, REn, St&VC, WebEAL, WhCL
Dickens, Charles, Jr. 1837-1896 *Alli Sup, BbD,*
BiD&SB, ChPo S2
Dickens, Craven Hildesley *Alli Sup*
Dickens, Dorothy Lee *BlkAW*
Dickens, Francis Jeffrey 1844-1886 *OxCan*
Dickens, Frank 1899- *Au&Wr*
Dickens, Georgiana *HsB&A, HsB&A Sup*
Dickens, Helen *Alli Sup*
Dickens, John *Alli*
Dickens, Mary *Alli Sup*
Dickens, Mary Angela 1838-1896 *BiD&SB*
Dickens, Milton 1908- *ConAu 1R*
Dickens, Monica Enid 1915- *Au&Wr,*
CatA 1947, ConAu 5R, ConNov 1972,
ConNov 1976, DcLEnL, EvLB, LongC,
NewC, Pen Eng, REn, SmATA 4,
TwCW, WorAu, WrD 1976
Dickens, Peter 1917- *WrD 1976*
Dickens, Theodore Henry *Alli Sup*
Dickenson, Baxter 1795-1875 *DcAmA*
Dickenson, J *Alli Sup*
Dickenson, John *Alli, CasWL*
Dickenson, May Freud *WhWNAA*
Dickenson, Thomas *Alli*
Dickerman, C W And Flint, C L *Alli Sup*
Dickerman, Don *ChPo*
Dickerman, Edward Dwight 1827-1907 *DcNAA*
Dickerman, George Sherwood 1843-1937 *AmLY,*
DcNAA
Dickerson, Don *ChPo S2*
Dickerson, Edward Nicoll *Alli Sup*
Dickerson, F Reed 1909- *ConAu 17R*
Dickerson, Glenda *BlkAW*
Dickerson, Grace Leslie 1911- *ConAu 5R,*
IndAu 1917
Dickerson, John 1939- *ConAu 57, WrD 1976*
Dickerson, Juanita M *BlkAW*
Dickerson, Mary A *WhWNAA*
Dickerson, Mary Cynthia 1866-1923 *AmLY,*
DcNAA
Dickerson, Philemon 1788-1862 *DcNAA*
Dickerson, Roy Ernest 1877-1944 *DcNAA*
Dickerson, Roy Ernest 1886-1965 *AmA&B,*
Au&Wr, ConAu 5R, IndAu 1917,
OhA&B, WhWNAA
Dickerson, W R *Alli Sup*
Dickerson, William E 1897- *ConAu 21*
Dickert, D A *BiDSA*
Dickeson, Montroville Wilson *Alli Sup*
Dickey, Adam Herbert 1864-1925 *DcNAA*
Dickey, Fannie Porter *ChPo S2*
Dickey, Franklin M 1921- *ConAu 23*
Dickey, Glenn 1936- *ConAu 53*
Dickey, Herbert Spencer 1876-1948 *AmA&B*
Dickey, James 1923- *AmA&B, AnCL,*
AuNews 1, AuNews 2, ConAu 9R,

ConLC 1, ConLC 2, ConLC 4,
ConP 1970, ConP 1975, CrCAP,
DrAF 1976, DrAP 1975, EncWL,
ModAL, ModAL Sup, OxAm, Pen Am,
RAdv 1, WebEAL, WhTwL, WorAu,
WrD 1976
Dickey, James H 1780-1856 *OhA&B*
Dickey, John *PoIre*
Dickey, John McElroy 1789-1849 *DcNAA,*
IndAu 1816
Dickey, K S *Alli Sup*
Dickey, Lee *ConAu XR*
Dickey, Marcus 1859-1950 *AmA&B,*
IndAu 1917
Dickey, Paul 1885-1933 *DcNAA*
Dickey, R P 1936- *ConAu 29, ConP 1970,*
ConP 1975, DrAP 1975, WrD 1976
Dickey, Robert B *OxCan*
Dickey, Robert Livingston 1861- *ConICB*
Dickey, Samuel 1872- *WhWNAA*
Dickey, W Laurence 1894- *WhWNAA*
Dickey, William 1928- *ConAu 9R, ConLC 3,*
ConP 1970, ConP 1975, DrAP 1975,
WorAu, WrD 1976
Dickie, Donalda James 1888- *WhWNAA*
Dickie, Edgar Primrose 1897- *Au&Wr,*
ConAu P-1, WrD 1976
Dickie, Francis 1890- *CanNov, WhWNAA*
Dickie, George 1812-1882 *Alli Sup*
Dickie, George 1926- *ConAu 33*
Dickie, George William 1844-1918 *DcNAA*
Dickie, J *Alli*
Dickie, James Francis 1851-1933 *DcNAA*
Dickie, John 1823-1891 *ChPo S1*
Dickie, John 1875- *WhLA*
Dickie, John 1923- *ConAu 13R*
Dickie, Matthew *Alli Sup*
Dickie, Matthew 1815-1870 *ChPo S1*
Dickie-Clark, H F 1922- *ConAu 21*
Dickins, Clara Swain *Alli Sup*
Dickins, Fanny D *Alli Sup*
Dickins, Lady Frances Elizabeth *Alli Sup*
Dickins, Frederick Victor *Alli Sup*
Dickins, John *Alli*
Dickinson, A *BiDLA*
Dickinson, A T, Jr. 1925- *ConAu 5R*
Dickinson, Adam *Alli*
Dickinson, Alan Edgar Frederick 1899- *Au&Wr,*
WrD 1976
Dickinson, Andrew 1801-1883 *Alli, DcNAA*
Dickinson, Ann Hepple 1877- *ChPo S1*
Dickinson, Anna Elizabeth 1842-1932 *Alli Sup,*
AmA&B, BiD&SB, DcAmA, DcNAA
Dickinson, Asa Don 1876-1960 *AmA&B,*
REnAL, WhWNAA
Dickinson, Blanche Taylor 1896- *BlkAW*
Dickinson, C Roy 1888-1949 *REnAL*
Dickinson, Charles Henry 1857-1938 *AmLY,*
DcNAA
Dickinson, Charles Monroe 1842-1924 *AmA&B,*
ChPo, DcAmA, DcNAA
Dickinson, Clarence 1873- *AmSCAP 66,*
IndAu 1917, WhWNAA
Dickinson, Clinton Roy 1888-1943 *AmA&B,*
DcNAA
Dickinson, Cornelius Evarts 1835-1925 *DcNAA,*
OhA&B
Dickinson, Daniel Stevens 1800-1866 *Alli Sup,*
DcAmA
Dickinson, Donald C 1927- *ConAu 23*
Dickinson, Dorothy *ChPo, ChPo S1,*
ChPo S2
Dickinson, E *ChPo*
Dickinson, Edmund 1624-1707 *Alli*
Dickinson, Edward 1853-1946 *AmA&B,*
AmLY, DcAmA, DcNAA, OhA&B,
WhWNAA
Dickinson, Edward C 1938- *ConAu 61*
Dickinson, Edwin Dewitt 1887- *WhWNAA*
Dickinson, Eleanor *PoIre*
Dickinson, Ellen E *Alli Sup*
Dickinson, Emily 1830-1886 *AmA, AmA&B,*
AmWr, AnCL, AtlBL, BiD&SB, CasWL,
ChPo, ChPo S1, ChPo S2, Chmbr 3,
CnDAL, CnE&AP, CriT 3, CyWA,
DcAmA, DcLEnL, DcNAA, EvLB,
ModAL, ModAL Sup, OxAm, OxEng,
Pen Am, RAdv 1, RCom, REn, REnAL,

St&VC, WebEAL
Dickinson, Eric Charles d1951 *ChPo S2*
Dickinson, Francis Henry *Alli Sup*
Dickinson, Francisco *Alli*
Dickinson, Frankie 1944- *Au&Wr*
Dickinson, Gideon *Alli Sup*
Dickinson, Goldsworthy Lowes 1862-1932
DcLEnL, EvLB, LongC, NewC, REn,
TwCA, TwCA Sup
Dickinson, Grace *Alli Sup*
Dickinson, H *Alli, BiDLA*
Dickinson, Harold H, Jr. 1913- *AmSCAP 66*
Dickinson, Harry Thomas 1939- *Au&Wr,*
ConAu 33, WrD 1976
Dickinson, Helen Adell 1875-1957 *AmLY,*
AmSCAP 66
Dickinson, Helen Mary *Alli Sup*
Dickinson, Helena A 1875-1957 *AmA&B*
Dickinson, Hercules Henry *Alli Sup*
Dickinson, J *Alli Sup*
Dickinson, J And E And Dowd, S E *Alli Sup*
Dickinson, James Charles *Alli Sup*
Dickinson, James Taylor 1861-1929 *DcNAA*
Dickinson, John *Alli Sup*
Dickinson, John 1732-1808 *Alli, AmA,*
AmA&B, BiD&SB, ChPo S1, CyAL 1,
DcAmA, DcLEnL, DcNAA, OxAm,
Pen Am, REnAL
Dickinson, John 1815-1876 *Alli Sup*
Dickinson, John K 1918- *ConAu 25*
Dickinson, John Woodbridge 1825-1901 *DcNAA*
Dickinson, Jonathan d1722 *DcAmA, DcNAA*
Dickinson, Jonathan 1688-1747 *Alli, CyAL 1,*
DcAmA, DcNAA
Dickinson, Joseph d1865 *Alli Sup*
Dickinson, June McWade 1924- *AmSCAP 66*
Dickinson, L *Alli Sup*
Dickinson, Leon T 1912- *ConAu 13R*
Dickinson, Lucy *ChPo*
Dickinson, Margaret *WrD 1976*
Dickinson, Marquis Fayette 1840-1915 *DcNAA*
Dickinson, Martha Gilbert *AmA&B, DcAmA,*
WhWNAA
Dickinson, Mary 1839-1914 *ChPo, ChPo S1,*
DcAmA, DcNAA
Dickinson, Mary Lowe *Alli Sup*
Dickinson, Maude Elizabeth *WhPNW*
Dickinson, Patric Thomas 1914- *Au&Wr,*
ChPo S1, ChPo S2, ConAu 9R,
ConP 1970, ConP 1975, WrD 1976
Dickinson, Peter 1927- *Au&Wr, ConAu 41,*
EncM&D, SmATA 5, WrD 1976
Dickinson, Peter Malcolm DeBrissac 1927-
Au&Wr
Dickinson, R *Alli*
Dickinson, Reginald 1841- *Alli Sup*
Dickinson, Richard William 1804-1874 *Alli Sup,*
DcAmA, DcNAA
Dickinson, Robert *Alli, BiDLA*
Dickinson, Robert Eric 1905- *Au&Wr,*
ConAu 5R
Dickinson, Robert Latou 1861- *WhWNAA*
Dickinson, Rodolphus 1787-1863 *Alli, DcAmA,*
DcNAA
Dickinson, Roy *DcNAA*
Dickinson, Ruth F 1933- *ConAu 37*
Dickinson, S Meredith *Alli Sup*
Dickinson, Samuel *Alli*
Dickinson, Stirling 1909- *ConAu 33*
Dickinson, Susan 1931- *ConAu 57, SmATA 8*
Dickinson, Mrs. T P *Alli Sup*
Dickinson, Thomas Herbert 1877-1961 *AmA&B,*
REnAL, TwCA, TwCA Sup, WhWNAA
Dickinson, Thorold 1903- *ConAu 45*
Dickinson, William *Alli, Alli Sup, BiDLA*
Dickinson, William Croft 1897-1963?
ConAu 1R, WhCL
Dickinson, William Howship 1832- *Alli Sup*
Dickinson, William Leeson *Alli Sup*
Dickinson-Bianchi, Martha *WhWNAA*
Dickison, J J *BiDSA*
Dickison, Maria Bobrowska 1902- *AmSCAP 66*
Dickison, Mary Elizabeth *BiDSA*
Dickler, Gerald 1912- *ConAu 9R*
Dickman, Joseph Theodore 1857-1927 *DcNAA,*
OhA&B
Dickmann, Max 1902- *Pen Am*
Dickore, Marie 1883- *OhA&B*

Dicks, Henry V 1900- *WrD 1976*
Dicks, John *Alli*
Dicks, Russell Leslie 1906-1965 *ConAu P-1*
Dicks, Father S *Alli Sup*
Dicksee, Margaret Isabel 1859-1900 *ChPo*
Dickson, A E *Alli Sup*
Dickson, A F *Alli Sup*
Dickson, Adam *Alli*
Dickson, Alex *Alli*
Dickson, Alexander *Alli Sup*
Dickson, Alexander F *Alli Sup*
Dickson, Andrew Flinn 1825-1879 *BiDSA,*
DcAmA, DcNAA
Dickson, Annan 1893- *Au&Wr*
Dickson, Archibald *Alli Sup*
Dickson, Arthur Parkinson 1888-1940? *OhA&B*
Dickson, Caleb *Alli*
Dickson, Carr *AmA&B, ConAu 49,*
EncM&D, LongC, REn
Dickson, Carter *AmA&B, ConAu 49,*
DcLEnL, EncM&D, LongC, NewC, REn,
TwCA, TwCA Sup
Dickson, Charles W, Jr. 1926- *ConAu 25*
Dickson, D *Alli Sup*
Dickson, D M *Alli*
Dickson, David *Alli*
Dickson, David 1583-1663? *Alli, ChPo S1,*
PoCh
Dickson, David 1809-1885 *DcNAA*
Dickson, Emma Dodiemeade *Alli Sup,*
ChPo S1
Dickson, Ernest Charles 1881-1939 *DcNAA*
Dickson, Franklyn 1941- *ConAu 53*
Dickson, Frederick S *Alli Sup*
Dickson, Frederick Stoever 1850-1925 *DcNAA*
Dickson, G S *ChPo S2*
Dickson, George E 1918- *ConAu 49*
Dickson, Gordon R 1923- *ConAu 9R*
Dickson, Harris 1868- *AmA&B, AmLY,*
BiDSA, DcAmA, WhWNAA
Dickson, Helen *ConAu XR, WhWNAA*
Dickson, J *Alli*
Dickson, J A R *Alli Sup*
Dickson, James *Alli, Alli Sup, BiDLA,*
OxCan
Dickson, James d1822 *Alli*
Dickson, James 1834-1926 *OxCan*
Dickson, James Grierson *MnBBF*
Dickson, James Hill *Alli, Alli Sup*
Dickson, Jeanie A *LivFWS*
Dickson, John *Alli Sup*
Dickson, John 1783-1852 *DcAmA, DcNAA*
Dickson, John Bathurst 1823- *Alli Sup, ChPo*
Dickson, John Jacob 1826- *IndAu 1917*
Dickson, John Thompson *Alli Sup*
Dickson, LaRue 1901- *AmSCAP 66*
Dickson, Leonard Eugene 1874- *WhWNAA*
Dickson, Lilian 1901- *Au&Wr*
Dickson, Lovat 1902- *Au&Wr, CanNov,*
ChPo S2, ConAu 13R, WrD 1976
Dickson, M A *Alli Sup*
Dickson, Margarette Ball 1884- *AnMV 1926,*
ChPo S2, WhWNAA
Dickson, Marguerite 1873-1953 *AuBYP,*
MorJA
Dickson, Mora Agnes 1918- *Au&Wr,*
ConAu 13R, WrD 1976
Dickson, Naida 1916- *ConAu 37, SmATA 8,*
WrD 1976
Dickson, Nicholas *Alli Sup*
Dickson, Paul 1939- *ConAu 33, WrD 1976*
Dickson, Peter George Muir 1929- *ConAu 13R*
Dickson, R W *Alli, BiDLA*
Dickson, Richard *Alli*
Dickson, Robert *Alli Sup*
Dickson, Robert J 1919- *ConAu 21*
Dickson, Miss S O'H *BiDSA*
Dickson, Samuel 1802-1869 *Alli, Alli Sup*
Dickson, Samuel Henderson *ChPo S1*
Dickson, Samuel Henry 1798-1872 *Alli,*
Alli Sup, BiDSA, CyAL 2, DcAmA,
DcNAA
Dickson, Stanley 1927- *ConAu 53*
Dickson, Stephen *Alli, OxCan*
Dickson, Thomas *Alli, Alli Sup*
Dickson, Violet Penelope 1896- *Au&Wr*
Dickson, Walter *Alli Sup*
Dickson, Walter R *Alli*

Dickson, William *Alli, Alli Sup, BiDLA*
Dickson, William 1817- *ChPo S1*
Dickson, William Edward *Alli Sup*
Dickson, William Gillespie *Alli Sup*
Dickson, William Kirk 1860- *WhLA*
Dickson, William M *Alli Sup*
Dickson, William Purdie 1823- *Alli Sup*
DiCostanzo, Angelo 1507-1591 *REn*
Dictys Cretensis *CasWL, OxEng, REn*
Dicuil 755?-825? *Alli, BiB S, CasWL,*
DcEnL
Dicus, M E *OhA&B*
DiCyan, Erwin 1908- *ConAu 37*
DiCyan, Erwin 1918- *WrD 1976*
Didcoct, John Joseph 1882-1927 *DcNAA*
Didelot, Marie 1903- *WhWNAA*
Diderot, Denis 1713-1784 *AtlBL, BbD,*
BiD&SB, CasWL, CnThe, CyWA,
DcEuL, EuA, EvEuW, McGWD, NewC,
OxEng, OxFr, Pen Eur, RCom, REn,
REnWD
Didham, Richard Cunningham *Alli Sup*
Didier, Adolphe *Alli Sup*
Didier, Charles 1805-1864 *BiD&SB*
Didier, Eugene Lemoine 1838-1913 *Alli Sup,*
AmA, AmA&B, BiD&SB, BiDSA,
DcAmA, DcNAA
Didier, Franklin James 1794-1840 *BiDSA,*
DcAmA, DcNAA
Didion, Joan 1934- *AmA&B, AuNews 1,*
ConAu 5R, ConLC 1, ConLC 3,
ConNov 1976, DrAF 1976, ModAL Sup,
WrD 1976
DiDonato, Pietro 1911- *AmA&B, OxAm,*
REnAL, TwCA, TwCA Sup
Didring, Ernst 1868-1931 *ClDMEuL*
Didwin, Isaac *DcNAA*
Didymus *CasWL, NewC*
Didymus 080?BC-010?AD *Pen Cl*
Die, Countess Of *CasWL*
Diebold, Janet Hart 1917- *OhA&B*
Diebold, John 1926- *ConAu 45*
Diebold, William, Jr. 1918- *ConAu 13R*
Dieck, Herman L 1873- *WhWNAA*
Dieckelmann, Heinrich 1898- *CasWL*
Diedrichs, John *Alli Sup*
Diefenbach, Jean 1926- *ChPo*
Diefenbaker, John *OxCan Sup*
Diefendorf, Dorr Frank 1874- *WhWNAA*
Dieffenbach, Christian 1822-1901 *BiD&SB*
Dieffenbach, Ernest *Alli*
Diego, Eliseo 1920- *DcCLA*
Diego, Gerardo 1896- *ClDMEuL, DcSpL,*
Pen Eur, REn
Diego, Jose De 1866-1918 *PueRA*
Diego Cendoya, Gerardo 1896- *CasWL,*
EncWL, EvEuW
Diego Padro, Jose I De 1896- *PueRA*
Diehl, Alice Mangold *Alli Sup*
Diehl, Anna Randall *Alli Sup*
Diehl, Charles Sanford 1854-1946 *AmA&B,*
TexWr
Diehl, Digby 1940- *ConAu 53*
Diehl, Edna Groff *ChPo S1*
Diehl, H A *Alli Sup*
Diehl, Henry Archer 1876-1952 *OhA&B*
Diehl, Katharine Smith 1906- *ConAu P-1*
Diehl, Michael 1819-1869 *OhA&B*
Diehl, Samuel Willauer Black 1851-1909
DcNAA
Diehl, W W 1916- *ConAu 17R*
Diehnel, Ellie Tatum *WhWNAA*
Diehnel, Tabitha Ellen 1878- *WhWNAA*
Diekenga, I E *Alli Sup*
Diekhoff, John Siemon 1905- *AmA&B,*
ConAu 29
Diekmann, Godfrey 1908- *ConAu 1R*
Dielman, Frederick 1847-1935 *ChPo*
Diemar, E M *Alli*
Diemer, Emma Lou 1927- *AmSCAP 66*
Diemer, Hugo 1876-1937 *DcNAA, WhWNAA*
Dienes, Zoltan Paul 1916- *Au&Wr*
Dieni, John 1924- *AmSCAP 66*
Dieni, Joseph 1923- *AmSCAP 66*
Dienner, John Astor 1883- *IndAu 1917*
Dienst, Alex 1870- *TexWr*
Dienst, George Elias 1858-1932 *AmLY,*
DcNAA, IndAu 1917

Dienstein, William 1909- *ConAu P-1*
Dier, Henry *Alli Sup*
Dierenfield, Richard Bruce 1922- *ConAu 17R,*
WrD 1976
Diereville, Sieur De *OxCan*
Dierickx, C W 1921- *ConAu 61*
Dierks, Jack Cameron 1930- *ConAu 29,*
WrD 1976
Diers, Carol Jean 1933- *ConAu 33*
Diers, Theodore C 1880- *WhWNAA*
Dierx, Marais Victor Leon 1838-1912 *BiD&SB,*
CasWL, EuA, EvEuW, OxFr
Dies, Edward Jerome 1891- *AmA&B, Au&Wr*
Diesel, Rudolf 1858-1913 *OxGer*
Dieserud, Juul 1861-1947 *DcNAA*
Diesing, Paul R 1922- *ConAu 1R*
Dieska, L Joseph 1913- *ConAu 37*
Dieskau, Baron Jean-Harmann De 1701-1767
OxCan
Diespecker, Richard 1907- *CanWr*
Diesslin, Howard Gustaf 1921- *IndAu 1917*
Dieterle, Til *AmSCAP 66*
Dietl, Ulla 1940- *ConAu 33*
Dietmar Der Setzer *OxGer*
Dietmar Von Aist 1139?- *CasWL, OxGer,*
Pen Eur
Dietrich Of Bern *REn*
Dietrich Von Apolda *OxGer*
Dietrich Von Bern *OxGer*
Dietrich Von Der Glezze *OxGer*
Dietrich, John E 1913- *ConAu 17R*
Dietrich, John Hassler 1878- *AmA&B,*
WhWNAA
Dietrich, Noah 1889- *ConAu 45*
Dietrich, R F 1936- *ConAu 23*
Dietrich, Richard V 1924- *ConAu 53*
Dietrich, Robert *ConAu XR, EncM&D*
Dietrich, Robert S 1928- *ConAu 1R*
Dietrich, Waldemar Fenn 1892- *WhWNAA*
Dietrich, Wilson G 1916- *ConAu 25*
Dietrick, Laurabelle *ChPo*
Dietrickson, Lorents Henrik Segelcke 1834-
BiD&SB
Diettert, Reuben Arthur 1901- *IndAu 1917*
Diettrich, Fritz 1902-1964 *OxGer*
Dietz, Betty Warner *AuBYP, ConAu XR*
Dietz, David Henry 1897- *Au&Wr,*
ConAu 1R, OhA&B, REnAL,
SmATA 10
Dietz, Elisabeth H 1908- *ConAu 29*
Dietz, Ella *Alli Sup, DcNAA*
Dietz, Frederick Charles 1888- *AmA&B*
Dietz, Howard 1896- *AmA&B, AmSCAP 66,*
ChPo, ConAu 53, ConDr, ModWD,
REnAL
Dietz, Lew 1907- *AuBYP, ConAu 5R,*
WrD 1976
Dietz, Norman D 1930- *ConAu 23*
Dietz, Peter O 1935- *ConAu 33*
Dietze, Gottfried 1922- *ConAu 23*
Dietzel, Paul F 1924- *ConAu 21*
Dietzenschmidt, Anton 1893-1955 *CnMD*
Dieulafoy, Jeanne Rachel 1851- *BiD&SB*
Diez, Friedrich Christian 1794-1876 *BiD&SB*
Diez, Katharina 1809-1882 *BiD&SB*
Diez-Canedo, Enrique 1879-1944 *CasWL,*
ClDMEuL, DcSpL, EncWL, EvEuW
Diez DeGames, Gutierre 1378?-1448? *CasWL*
Diez DelCorral, Luis 1911- *ConAu 13R*
Dieze, Johann Andreas 1749-1785 *DcEuL*
Diffendorfer, Ralph Eugene 1879-1951 *AmA&B,*
OhA&B, WhWNAA
Diffin, Leslye T *ChPo S1*
DiFiori, Lawrence *IlBYP*
DiFranco, Fiorenza 1932- *ConAu 45*
Digan, G C *Alli Sup*
Digby, Everard d1592 *Alli*
Digby, Sir Everard 1581-1606 *Alli*
Digby, Francis *Alli*
Digby, George 1612-1676 *Alli, BrAu, DcEuL*
Digby, Mrs. J D Wingfield *Alli Sup*
Digby, Lord John *Alli*
Digby, Sir John *Alli*
Digby, John 1580-1653 *Alli*
Digby, John A *Alli Sup*
Digby, Sir Kenelm 1603-1665 *Alli, BrAu,*
Chmbr 1, CrE&SL, DcEnA, DcEnL,
DcEuL, EvLB, NewC, OxEng, Pen Eng,

R*En*
Digby, Kenelm Edward 1836- *Alli Sup*
Digby, Kenelm Henry 1800-1880 *Alli, Alli Sup, BrAu 19, NewC, OxEng, PoIre*
Digby, R *Alli Sup*
Digby, Ronald Yarham 1900- *Au&Wr*
Digby, William *Alli, Alli Sup*
Digby, William 1849- *Alli Sup*
Digby-Beste *Alli Sup*
Digenis Akrites Basileios *Pen Eur*
Digennaro, Joseph 1939- *ConAu 53*
Digges, Sir Dudley 1583-1639 *Alli*
Digges, Dudley 1612?-1643 *Alli*
Digges, Edward *Alli*
Digges, Jeremiah *AmA&B, ConAu XR*
Digges, Sister Laurentia 1910- *ConAu 21*
Digges, Leonard d1573? *Alli*
Digges, Leonard 1588-1635 *Alli, CasWL, DcEuL*
Digges, Thomas d1595 *Alli*
Digges, Thomas Atwood 1741?-1821? *OxAm, REnAL*
Digges, West *Alli Sup*
Diggins, John P 1935- *ConAu 37*
Diggins, Julia E *AuBYP*
Diggle, James 1944- *ConAu 61*
Diggle, John William *Alli Sup*
Diggle, Roland 1887-1954 *AmSCAP 66*
Diggory, James C 1920- *ConAu 23*
Diggs, Annie 1853-1916 *DcNAA*
Diggs, Arthur *BlkAW*
Diggs, D William *Alli Sup*
Dighton, John 1909- *Au&Wr*
Dighton, Robert 1752-1814 *BkIE*
Dighton, T *Alli*
DiGiacomo, Salvatore 1860-1934 *CasWL, CIDMEuL, EncWL, EvEuW, McGWD*
DiGirolamo, Vittorio 1928- *ConAu 45*
Dignaga *DcOrL 2*
Dignam, C B *MnBBF*
Dignan, Browne *Alli*
DiGrazia, Thomas *IlBYP*
Dihati *CasWL*
Dihigo, John M 1866- *AmLY*
Dihkhuda, 'Ali Akbar 1880-1956 *CasWL*
Dihoff, Gretchen 1942- *ConAu 41*
Dijkstra, Bram 1938- *ConAu 37*
DiJulio, Max 1919- *AmSCAP 66*
Dik Keam *DcOrL 2*
Dike, Samuel Fuller 1815- *Alli Sup*
Dikeman, May *DrAF 1976*
Dikes, T *Alli*
Dikes, Thomas *BiDLA*
Diktonius, Elmer Rafael 1896-1961 *CasWL, EncWL Sup, EvEuW, Pen Eur*
Dil, Zakhmi *ConAu XR*
DiLampedusa, Giuseppe *ModRL*
Dilcock, Noreen 1907- *Au&Wr, WrD 1976*
DiLella, Alexander Anthony 1929- *ConAu 23, WrD 1976*
DiLello, Richard 1945- *ConAu 41*
DiLeo, Joseph H 1902- *ConAu 33, WrD 1976*
Diles, Dave 1931- *ConAu 57*
Dilherr, Johann Michael 1604-1669 *OxGer*
Diligent, J *Alli*
Dilke, Lady 1840-1904 *BrAu 19*
Dilke, Annabel 1942- *ConAu P-1*
Dilke, Ashton Wentworth 1850-1883 *Alli Sup*
Dilke, Charles Wentworth 1789-1864 *Alli, Alli Sup, BiD&SB, CasWL, Chmbr 3, DcEnL, DcEuL, EvLB, NewC*
Dilke, Sir Charles Wentworth 1843-1911 *Alli Sup, BbD, BiD&SB, BrAu 19, Chmbr 3, DcEnL, DcEuL, NewC, OxEng*
Dilke, Christopher Wentworth 1913- *Au&Wr*
Dilke, Lady Emilia Frances 1840-1904 *Alli Sup, BiD&SB, NewC*
Dilke, Margaret Mary 1857- *Alli Sup*
Dilke, Oswald Ashton Wentworth 1915- *WrD 1976*
Dilke, Thomas *Alli*
Dilks, David 1938- *ConAu 61*
Dilks, T Bruce *ChPo S2*
Dill, Alonzo T 1914- *ConAu 37*
Dill, Bessie *ChPo S2*
Dill, E M *Alli*
Dill, E Millard 1895-1961 *IndAu 1917*

Dill, Edward Marcus *Alli Sup*
Dill, James Brooks 1854-1910 *DcNAA*
Dill, Marshall, Jr. 1916- *AmA&B, ConAu 1R*
Dill, Mary *ChPo*
Dill, Peter M 1852-1929 *IndAu 1917*
Dill, Richard *Alli Sup*
Dill, W S *OxCan*
Dill, William L 1913- *AmSCAP 66*
Dillard, Annie 1945- *ConAu 49, DrAP 1975, SmATA 10, WrD 1976*
Dillard, Douglas F 1937- *AmSCAP 66*
Dillard, Dudley 1913- *ConAu 25*
Dillard, Emil L 1921- *ConAu 57*
Dillard, Hardy Cross 1902- *WrD 1976*
Dillard, J L 1924- *ConAu 41*
Dillard, James Hardy 1856-1940 *AmLY, BiDSA, DcNAA, WhWNAA*
Dillard, Jean *ChPo*
Dillard, Polly Hargis 1916- *ConAu 9R*
Dillard, R H W 1937- *AmA&B, ConAu 21, ConLC 5, ConP 1975, DrAF 1976, DrAP 1975, WrD 1976*
Dillavou, Essel B 1893- *WhWNAA*
Dillaway, Charles Knapp 1804-1889 *Alli, DcNAA*
Dillaye, Blanche *ChPo*
Dillaye, Stephen Devalson 1820-1884 *Alli Sup, DcAmA, DcNAA*
Dille, John M 1921?-1971 *ConAu 33*
Dillehay, Ronald C 1935- *ConAu 23*
Dillenbach, Hiram P *Alli Sup*
Dillenbeck, Marsden V *ConAu 25*
Dillenberger, Jane 1916- *ConAu 17R*
Dillenberger, John 1918- *AmA&B, ConAu 1R, WrD 1976*
Dillenius, John James 1687-1747 *Alli*
Diller, Angela *AuBYP*
Diller, Elliot VanNostrand 1904- *AmA&B*
Diller, John Irving *ChPo S2*
Diller, Joseph Silas 1850-1928 *DcNAA*
Diller, Marion E Thorpe *ChPo*
Diller, Theodore 1863- *AmLY, WhWNAA*
Dilles, James 1923- *Au&Wr, ConAu 1R*
Dilley, Edgar Peck 1874- *ChPo S1*
Dilley, Frank B 1931- *ConAu 13R*
Dilliard, Irving 1904- *ConAu 21*
Dilling, Walter James 1886- *WhLA*
Dillingham *AmLY XR*
Dillingham, Beth 1927- *ConAu 53*
Dillingham, Charles B 1868-1934 *AmA&B*
Dillingham, Frances Bent *AmA&B, ChPo, DcNAA*
Dillingham, Francis *Alli*
Dillingham, John Hoag 1839-1910 *DcNAA*
Dillingham, Pauline *TexWr*
Dillingham, William *Alli*
Dillingham, William B 1930- *ConAu 13R, WrD 1976*
Dillingham, William H 1790-1854 *Alli*
Dillistone, Frederick William 1903- *Au&Wr, ConAu 1R*
Dillman, Willard 1872- *DcAmA*
Dillon, Lord *Alli*
Dillon, Viscount *BiDLA*
Dillon, Allie *ChPo*
Dillon, Anna Hood *WhWNAA*
Dillon, Arthur *Alli, Alli Sup, ChPo S2, PoIre*
Dillon, Arthur E *ChPo S1*
Dillon, Arthur Orison 1873- *ChPo, WhWNAA*
Dillon, Augustus *Alli Sup*
Dillon, Brian d1872 *PoIre*
Dillon, Charles 1819-1881 *NewC*
Dillon, Charles 1873-1942 *AmA&B, WhWNAA*
Dillon, Conley Hall 1906- *ConAu 1R*
Dillon, Corinne Boyd *IlBYP, IlCB 1956*
Dillon, Dixie *MnBBF*
Dillon, Edmond *PoIre*
Dillon, Edward *PoIre*
Dillon, Eilis 1920- *Au&Wr, AuBYP, ConAu 9R, SmATA 2, ThBJA*
Dillon, Fannie Charles 1881-1947 *AmSCAP 66, WhWNAA*
Dillon, George 1906-1968 *AmA&B, ChPo, ChPo S1, ConAmA, DcLEnL, OxAm, REn, REnAL, TwCA, TwCA Sup*
Dillon, George F *Alli Sup*

Dillon, George H 1906- *AnMV 1926*
Dillon, Henry Augustus 1777-1832 *Alli, PoIre*
Dillon, J *Alli Sup*
Dillon, Sir J *Alli*
Dillon, J T 1940- *ConAu 33*
Dillon, John *PoIre*
Dillon, John Brown 1808?-1879 *AmA&B, DcAmA, DcNAA, IndAu 1816, OhA&B, PoIre*
Dillon, John Forrest 1831-1914 *Alli Sup, DcAmA, DcNAA*
Dillon, John Jeffcott *Alli Sup*
Dillon, John Joseph *Alli, BiDLA*
Dillon, John Milton 1868-1911 *DcNAA*
Dillon, John T *Alli*
Dillon, Lawrence S 1910- *ConAu 45*
Dillon, Lin 1847- *Alli Sup*
Dillon, Marjorie *ChPo S2*
Dillon, Martin 1949- *ConAu 61*
Dillon, Mary *BiDSA*
Dillon, Mary C d1923 *DcNAA*
Dillon, Merton L 1924- *ConAu 13R*
Dillon, Millicent G *DrAF 1976*
Dillon, Mrs. O'Shea *Alli Sup*
Dillon, Patrick 1848?-1909 *PoIre*
Dillon, Philip Robert 1868- *AmA&B*
Dillon, R C *Alli*
Dillon, Richard Hugh 1924- *AmA&B, ConAu 17R*
Dillon, T *ChPo S1*
Dillon, Theobald *Alli, BiDLA*
Dillon, Thomas d1852 *PoIre*
Dillon, Thomas J 1878-1949 *AmA&B*
Dillon, W E *PoIre*
Dillon, Wallace Neil 1922- *ConAu 1R*
Dillon, Wentworth 1633?-1684 *Alli, BrAu, CasWL, Chmbr 1, DcEnL, DcLEnL, NewC, OxEng, PoIre*
Dillon, William *Alli Sup, PoIre*
Dillon, William A 1877-1966 *AmSCAP 66*
Dillon, Wilton Sterling 1923- *ConAu 37, WrD 1976*
Dillwyn, Miss E A *Alli Sup*
Dillwyn, Lewis Weston *Alli, BiDLA*
Dilly, Charles 1739-1807 *NewC*
Dilly Tante *ConAu XR*
Dilmen, Gungor 1930- *REnWD*
Dilnot, George 1883-1951 *MnBBF*
Dilsner, Laurence *AmSCAP 66*
Dilson, Jesse 1914- *ConAu 25, WrD 1976*
Dilthey, Wilhelm 1833-1911 *CasWL, OxGer, Pen Eur*
Dilts, Jerome J 1890-1961 *IndAu 1917*
Diltz, Hanson Penn *Alli*
Dilworth, Hiram Powers 1878- *OhA&B*
Dilworth, Thomas d1780 *Alli*
Dilworth-Harrison, Talbot 1886- *Au&Wr*
Diman, Jeremiah Lewis 1831-1881 *Alli Sup, AmA, DcAmA, DcNAA*
DiMarco, Luis Eugenio 1937- *ConAu 45*
Dimberg, Ronald G 1938- *ConAu 61*
Dimbleby, J B *Alli Sup*
Dimick, Elisabeth *ChPo*
Dimick, Kenneth M 1937- *ConAu 29*
DiMinno, Daniel 1911- *AmSCAP 66*
Dimitri Rostovski, Saint 1651-1709 *DcRusL*
Dimitrova, Blaga 1922- *CasWL*
Dimitry, Alexander 1805-1883 *BiDSA*
Dimitry, Charles Patton 1837-1910 *Alli Sup, AmA&B, BbD, BiDSA, DcAmA, DcNAA*
Dimitry, John Bull Smith 1835-1901 *Alli Sup, BiDSA, DcAmA, DcNAA*
Dimmette, Celia Puhr 1896- *ConAu 29, OhA&B*
Dimmick, Charles *Alli Sup*
Dimmick, Forrest Lee 1893- *WhWNAA*
Dimmick, Luther F 1790-1860 *DcNAA*
Dimmick, Ruth Crosby *ChPo*
Dimmitt, Richard Bertrand 1925- *ConAu 17R*
Dimmock, Charles H *Alli Sup*
Dimmock, Frederick Hayden 1895-1955 *MnBBF, WhCL*
Dimmock, George 1852-1930 *Alli Sup, DcAmA, DcNAA*
Dimmock, Peter 1920- *Au&Wr*
Dimnet, Ernest 1866-1954 *CatA 1947, TwCA, TwCA Sup, WhLA*

Dimock, Anthony Weston 1842-1918 *AmLY, DcNAA*

Dimock, Gladys Ogden 1908- *ConAu 5R*

Dimock, Hedley G 1928- *ConAu 5R*

Dimock, Henry *Alli*

Dimock, James Francis *Alli Sup*

Dimock, Julian Anthony 1873-1945 *DcNAA, WhWNAA*

Dimock, Marshall Edward 1903- *ConAu 1R, WrD 1976*

Dimock, Nathaniel *Alli Sup*

Dimond, Mary B *Alli Sup, ChPo*

Dimond, S J 1938- *Au&Wr*

Dimond, Stanley E 1905- *ConAu 13R*

Dimond, Stuart John 1938- *ConAu 33, WrD 1976*

Dimond, William 1780?- *Alli, BiDLA, ChPo, ChPo S2*

Dimondstein, Geraldine 1926- *ConAu 33*

Dimont, Charles Tunnacliff 1872- *WhLA*

Dimont, Madelon 1938- *ConAu 41*

Dimont, Max I 1912- *ConAu 17R*

Dimont, Penelope *ConAu 57, WrD 1976*

Dimov, Dimitur 1909-1966 *CasWL*

Dimple, John *ChPo S2*

Dimsdale, Mrs. *Alli Sup*

Dimsdale, Helen Easdale 1907- *Au&Wr*

Dimsdale, Thomas 1718-1800 *Alli*

Dimson, Theo Aeneas 1930- *IlCB 1966, WhGrA*

Dimson, Wendy *ConAu XR*

DiNapoli, Mario 1914- *AmSCAP 66*

Dinarchus 360?BC-292?BC *CasWL, Pen Cl*

DiNardo, Nicholas 1906- *AmSCAP 66*

DiNardo, Thomas C 1905- *AmSCAP 66*

Dinarte, Sylvio 1843-1899 *DcBiA*

Dincklage-Campe, Emmy Von 1825-1891 *BiD&SB*

D'Indy, Vincent *AtlBL*

Dine, Jim *ConDr*

Dine, S S Van *EvLB, LongC, TwCA, TwCA Sup*

Dine, William *Alli*

Dineen, Joseph F 1897- *WhWNAA*

Dinekov, Petur 1910- *CasWL*

Dinely, Sir John *Alli*

Diner, Hasia R 1946- *ConAu 61*

Dinerman, Beatrice 1933- *ConAu 13R, WrD 1976*

Dinerman, Helen Schneider 1921?-1974 *ConAu 53*

Dines, Cora Pritchard *TexWr*

Dines, Glen 1925- *AuBYP, ConAu 9R, IlCB 1956, IlCB 1966*

Dines, Harry Glen 1925- *SmATA 7*

Dines, Michael *Au&Wr*

Dinesen, Isak 1885-1962 *AtlBL, CasWL, ConAu XR, CyWA, EncWL, EvEuW, LongC, Pen Eur, REn, TwCA, TwCA Sup, TwCW*

Dinesen, Thomas 1892- *Au&Wr*

Ding, J N *AmA&B, WhWNAA*

Dingane *BlkAW*

Dingelstedt, Baron Franz Von 1814-1881 *BiD&SB, EvEuW, OxGer*

Dingle, Aylward Edward 1876- *MnBBF*

Dingle, Edward 1814- *Alli Sup*

Dingle, Herbert 1890- *Au&Wr, ConAu 13R*

Dingle, John 1812- *Alli Sup*

Dingle, Reginald James 1889- *Au&Wr*

Dingley, Edward Nelson 1862-1930 *DcNAA*

Dingley, Robert *Alli*

Dingley, Robert 1619-1659 *Alli*

Dingley, Somerville *Alli*

Dingley, William *Alli*

Dingman, B S *Alli Sup*

Dingman, Charles Francis 1885- *WhWNAA*

Dings, John 1939- *ConAu 41*

Dingwall, Eric J *BiDPar*

Dingwall, W Orr 1934- *ConAu 21*

Dinhofer, A 1928- *ConAu 25*

Dinhofer, Alfred D 1930- *WrD 1976*

Dinis, Julio 1839-1871 *CasWL, Pen Eur*

Dinitz, Simon 1926- *ConAu 37*

Diniz 1261-1325 *EvEuW*

Diniz, Julio 1839-1871 *BiD&SB*

Diniz DaCruz E Silva, Antonio 1731-1799 *BiD&SB*

Dinkar 1908- *DcOrL 2*

Dinkins, Charles R *BiDSA, BlkAW*

Dinkins, James 1845-1939 *AmLY, BiDSA, DcNAA*

Dinkmeyer, Don C 1924- *ConAu 41*

Dinmore, Richard *Alli, BiDLA*

Dinneen, Betty 1929- *ConAu 57*

Dinneen, Joseph *PoIre*

Dinner, William *Au&Wr*

Dinnerstein, Leonard 1934- *ConAu 23, WrD 1976*

Dinnie, Robert 1808- *ChPo S1*

Dinnies, Anna Peyre 1816-1886 *Alli, BiD&SB, BiDSA, DcAmA, DcNAA, FemPA, LivFWS*

Dinning, John G *BbtC*

Dinnis, Enid Maud 1873-1942 *BkC 1, CatA 1947, ChPo, ChPo S2*

Dino *ConAu XR*

DiNovi, Eugene 1928- *AmSCAP 66*

Dinsdale, Caroline M *Alli Sup*

Dinsdale, Frederick d1872 *ChPo*

Dinsdale, Joshua *Alli*

Dinsdale, Richard Lewis 1907- *Au&Wr*

Dinsdale, Tim 1924- *ConAu 1R, WrD 1976*

Dinsdale, Walter Arnold 1905- *Au&Wr*

Dinshah Ardeshir, Taleyarkhan *Alli Sup*

Dinsmoor, M M F *ChPo*

Dinsmoor, Robert 1757-1836 *AmA, AmA&B, CyAL 1, DcNAA, PoIre*

Dinsmore, Arthur Morris 1892?-1947 *IndAu 1917*

Dinsmore, Charles Allen 1860-1941 *AmA&B, AmLY, DcAmA, DcNAA, WhWNAA*

Dinsmore, John *Alli Sup*

Dinsmore, John Walker 1839-1922 *DcNAA*

Dinsmore, Julia Stockton *ChPo*

Dinsmore, Robert 1757-1836 *Alli, DcAmA*

Dinsmore, Silas *ChPo*

Dinsmore, Violet E *ChPo*

Dintenfass, Mark 1941- *ConAu 25, WrD 1976*

Dintiman, George B 1936- *ConAu 53*

Dinu, Robert A 1928- *AmSCAP 66*

Dinwiddie, Alvin 1887- *TexWr*

Dinwiddie, Courtenay 1882-1943 *DcNAA*

Dinwiddie, Elizabeth McMurtie 1886- *OhA&B*

Dinwiddie, Robert 1690?-1770 *BiDSA*

Dinwiddie, William 1867-1934 *Alli Sup, BiDSA, DcAmA, DcNAA*

Dinwooddie, Robertus *Alli*

Dio Cassius 155?-235? *CasWL, Pen Cl*

Dio Chrysostom 040?-115? *CasWL, Pen Cl*

Diocletian 245-313 *NewC, REn*

Diodati, Charles 1608?-1638 *DcEuL, NewC*

Diodorus *NewC*

Diodorus Siculus 060?BC- *CasWL, OxEng, Pen Cl*

Diogenes *PueRA*

Diogenes 412?BC-323BC *NewC, REn*

Diogenes 1809-1887 *AmA*

Diogenes Junior *WhLA*

Diogenes Laertius 200?-250 *BiD&SB, CasWL, NewC, OxEng, Pen Cl, REn*

Diogenes Of Apollonia 460?BC- *Pen Cl*

Diogenes Of Oenoanda *Pen Cl*

Diogenes The Cynic *Pen Cl*

Diole, Philippe V 1908- *ConAu 53*

Diole, Phillippe 1908- *Au&Wr*

Dion, Carmen *AmSCAP 66*

Dion, Gerard 1912- *ConAu 41, OxCan Sup*

Dion, Sister Raymond DeJesus 1918- *ConAu 5R*

Dion-Levesque, Rosaire *WhWNAA*

Dion-Levesque, Rosario *OxCan*

Dione, Robert L 1922- *ConAu 57*

Dionisopoulos, P Allan 1921- *ConAu 29*

Dionisotti-Casalone, Carlo 1908- *Au&Wr*

Dionne, Charles Eusebe 1846-1925 *DcNAA*

Dionne, Narcisse Eutrope 1848-1917 *DcNAA, OxCan*

Dionysius Of Halicarnassus 030?BC-007?BC *CasWL, NewC, Pen Cl*

Dionysius The Areopagite 050?- *CasWL, NewC, Pen Cl*

Dionysius The Carthusian 1402-1471 *CasWL*

Dionysius The Elder 430?BC-367BC *NewC*

Dionysius The Younger 395?BC-343?BC *NewC*

Dionysius Thrax 150?BC-090?BC *CasWL, Pen Cl*

Diop, Anta, Sheikh 1923- *Pen Cl*

Diop, Birago Ismail 1906- *AfA 1, CasWL, EncWL Sup, Pen Cl, RGAfl*

Diop, David Mandessi 1927-1960 *AfA 1, Pen Cl, RGAfl*

Diop, Massyla 1886?-1932 *AfA 1*

Diop, Ousmane Soce *AfA 1*

DiOrio, Al 1950- *ConAu 57*

Dios Peza, Juan Dc 1852-1910 *DcSpL*

Dioscordies Of Anabarzus *Pen Cl*

Dioscorides *CasWL*

Diotima *ConAu XR*

DiPalma, Raymond 1943- *ConAu 29, DrAP 1975*

DiPasquale, Dominic 1932- *ConAu 57*

DiPeso, Charles C 1920- *ConAu 57*

Diphilus 350?BC-225?BC *CasWL, Pen Cl*

DiPietro, Robert Joseph 1932- *ConAu 17R, WrD 1976*

DiPirani, Eugenio 1852?-1939 *AmLY, AmSCAP 66*

Diplomat *TwCA, TwCA Sup, WhWNAA*

Dipoko, Mbella Sonne 1936- *AfA 1, ConP 1970, RGAfl*

Dipper, Alan 1922- *Au&Wr, ConAu 49*

Dipple, Elizabeth 1937- *ConAu 33, WrD 1976*

Dippold, George Theodore *Alli Sup*

DiPrima, Diane 1934- *ConAu 17R, ConP 1970, ConP 1975, DrAF 1976, DrAP 1975, WrD 1976*

Diprose, John *Alli Sup*

Dirck, Cornelius Lansing 1785-1857 *DcAmA*

Dircks, Henry 1806-1873 *Alli Sup*

DiRenzo, Gordon J 1934- *ConAu 53*

Diringer, David 1900-1975 *ConAu 1R, ConAu 57*

Dirix, M E *Alli Sup*

Dirk, R 1924- *ConAu XR*

Dirksen, Charles J 1912- *ConAu 5R*

DiRoccaferrera Ferrero, Giuseppe M 1912- *ConAu 13R*

Dirom, Alexander *Alli, BiDLA*

Dirrill, Charles *Alli, BiDLA*

Dirrim, Allen Wendell 1929- *ConAu 23*

Dirscherl, Denis 1934- *ConAu 21*

Dirvin, Joseph I 1917- *ConAu 5R*

Disbrowe, Charlotte Anne Albinia *Alli Sup*

Disbrowe, J *Alli*

Discant, Mack 1916-1961 *AmSCAP 66*

Disch, Thomas M 1940- *ConAu 23*

Disengomoko, A Emile 1915-1965 *AfA 1*

Disher, Maurice Willson 1893-1969 *ConAu P-1, WhLA*

Disher, Willson 1893-1969 *LongC*

Dishman, Pat 1939- *ConAu 17R*

Dismond, Henry Binga 1891- *BlkAW*

Disney, Mrs. *Alli Sup*

Disney, Alex *Alli*

Disney, David *Alli*

Disney, Doris Miles 1907-1976 *AmA&B, Au&Wr, ConAu 5R, EncM&D*

Disney, Dorothy Cameron 1903- *EncM&D*

Disney, Henry P *OxCan*

Disney, John *Alli, BiDLA*

Disney, John 1677-1730 *Alli*

Disney, John 1746-1816 *Alli*

Disney, Samuel *Alli*

Disney, W *Alli*

Disney, Walt 1901-1966 *ChPo, ChPo S1, ChPo S2, LongC, OxAm, REn, REnAL, WhCL, WhGrA*

Disney, William *Alli Sup*

Disney, William Henry *Alli Sup*

Dison, Norma 1928- *ConAu 53*

Disosway, E *Alli Sup*

Disosway, E T *Alli Sup*

Disosway, Gabriel Poillon 1798-1868 *Alli Sup, DcAmA, DcNAA*

Disraeli, Benjamin 1804-1881 *Alli, Alli Sup, AtlBL, BiD&SB, BrAu 19, CasWL, Chmbr 3, CyWA, DcBiA, DcEnA, DcEnA Ap, DcEnL, DcEuL, DcLEnL, EvLB, MouLC 3, NewC, OxEng, Pen Eng, RAdv 1, REn, WebEAL*

Disraeli, B ALSO Beaconsfield Earl Of

D'Israeli, Isaac 1766-1848 *Alli, BbD, BiD&SB,*

BrAu 19, CasWL, ChPo, Chmbr 2,
DcEnA, DcEnL, DcEuL, DcLEnL, EvLB,
NewC, OxEng, Pen Eng, REn
D'Israeli, J BiDLA
Disraeli, Robert 1903- ConAu P-1
Dissette, T K Alli Sup
Disston, Harry 1899- ConAu 41
Distant, William Lucas Alli Sup
Distefano, Juan Carlos 1933- WhGrA
Distin-Maddick Alli Sup
Distler, Paul Francis 1911- ConAu 5R
Disturnell, John 1801-1877 Alli Sup, AmA&B,
DcAmA, DcNAA
Disturnell, Josiah Alli
Ditcher, Selina Alli Sup
Ditchfield, Peter Hampson 1854- WhLA
Dithmar, Edward Augustus 1854-1917 AmA,
AmA&B, DcNAA
Ditlevsen, Tove Irma Margit 1918- CasWL,
EncWL, Pen Eur
Ditman, Norman Edward 1877-1944 DcNAA
Ditmars, Raymond Lee 1876-1942 AmA&B,
AuBYP, DcNAA, JBA 1934, JBA 1951,
REnAL, TwCA, TwCA Sup, WhWNAA
Ditmas, Francis Ivan Leslie WhLA
Ditrichstein, Leo 1865-1928 DcNAA
Ditsky, John DrAF 1976, DrAP 1975
Ditson, George Leighton 1812-1895 Alli Sup,
AmA&B, BiD&SB, DcAmA, DcNAA
Ditson, Oliver 1811-1888 AmA&B
Dittemore, John Valentine 1876-1937
IndAu 1917
Dittenhaver, Sarah L 1901- AmSCAP 66
Ditterich, Keith 1913- WrD 1976
Dittes, James E 1926- ConAu 61
Dittmar, William Alli Sup
Ditto, Margaret Emma ChPo S1
Ditto, Roy Waymon 1895- TexWr
Ditton, Humphrey 1675-1715 Alli
Dittrick, Howard 1877-1954 OhA&B
Ditzel, Paul C 1926- ConAu 41
Ditzen, Lowell Russell 1913- ConAu 17R
Ditzen, Rudolf LongC, REn
Ditzen, Rudolph 1893-1947 TwCA, TwCA Sup
Ditzion, Sidney 1908-1975 ConAu 41,
ConAu 57
Divale, William Tulio 1942- ConAu 33,
WrD 1976
DiValentin, Maria Messuri 1911- ConAu 5R,
SmATA 7
Divall, Edith Hickman ChPo
Divatia, Narasimharao DcOrL 2
Diven, Robert Joseph 1869- WhWNAA
Diver, Ebenezer Alli Sup
Diver, Katherine Helen Maud 1867- WhLA
Diver, Maud 1867?-1945 EvLB, LongC,
TwCA, TwCA Sup, TwCW
D'Ivernois, Sir Francis BiDLA
Diverres, Armel Hugh 1914- Au&Wr,
ConAu 9R
Divine, Arthur Durham 1904- Au&Wr,
DcLEnL
Divine, Charles 1889- AmA&B, AnMV 1926,
ChPo S2, WhWNAA
Divine, Charles 1889- ChPo
Divine, David DcLEnL
Divine, Robert A 1929- ConAu 5R, WrD 1976
Divine, S R Alli Sup
Divine, Thomas Francis 1900- ConAu 37,
WrD 1976
Divine Sarah NewC
Divino Lodovico NewC
Divoire, Fernand 1883-1951 OxFr
Divoky, Diane 1939- ConAu 33
Divoll, W Alli Sup
Dix, Beulah Marie 1876- AmA&B, CarSB,
DcAmA, JBA 1934, JBA 1951, REnAL
Dix, Charles T 1840-1873 EarAB
Dix, Dorothea Lynde 1802-1887 Alli, AmA,
AmA&B, BiD&SB, DcAmA, DcNAA,
OxAm
Dix, Dorothy 1870?-1951 AmA&B, BiDSA,
OxAm, REn, REnAL, WhWNAA
Dix, Edgar Hutton, Jr. 1892- WhWNAA
Dix, Edwin Asa 1860-1911 AmA&B, ChPo,
DcAmA, DcNAA
Dix, Fred Keller 1891-1944 OhA&B,
WhWNAA

Dix, H L Alli Sup
Dix, Henry Alli
Dix, James Alli Sup
Dix, John Alli, Alli Sup
Dix, John Adams 1798-1879 Alli, Alli Sup,
BbD, BiD&SB, CyAL 2, DcAmA,
DcNAA
Dix, John Homer 1810?-1884 Alli, DcAmA,
DcNAA
Dix, Maurice Buxton 1889-1957 CanNov,
MnBBF
Dix, Morgan 1827-1908 Alli Sup, AmA&B,
BiD&SB, DcAmA, DcNAA
Dix, Robert H 1930- ConAu 23
Dix, Thomas Alli, BiDLA
Dix, William Chatterton 1837-1898 Alli Sup,
ChPo, ChPo S1, ChPo S2, PoCh
Dix, William Giles 1821-1898 Alli Sup,
DcAmA
Dix, William S Alli, ChPo
Dixelius-Brettner, Hildur 1879- TwCA,
TwCA Sup
Dixey, Frank 1892- Au&Wr
Dixey, Giles ChPo
Dixey, Harold Giles ChPo S1
Dixey, Wolstan ChPo, ChPo S1
Dixie AmLY XR, WhWNAA
Dixie, Lady Florence Caroline 1858- Alli Sup
Dixie, Marmaduke ChPo
Dixon, Amzi Clarence 1854-1925 AmLY,
BiDSA, DcNAA
Dixon, Arthur 1921- Au&Wr, ChPo S1
Dixon, Asher Hooper WhWNAA
Dixon, Beaufort Harkness Alli Sup
Dixon, Benjamin Homer 1819-1899 DcNAA
Dixon, Bernard Homer Alli Sup
Dixon, Cecilia Maria Alli Sup, ChPo S1
Dixon, Charles Alli Sup
Dixon, Charles George Alli Sup
Dixon, Clarice Madeleine 1889-1945 DcNAA
Dixon, Cliff 1889- AmSCAP 66
Dixon, Conrad 1927- WrD 1976
Dixon, Cross MnBBF
Dixon, D B Alli Sup
Dixon, Don MnBBF
Dixon, Edith Helen Alli Sup
Dixon, Edmund Saul 1809- Alli, Alli Sup
Dixon, Edward H Alli Sup
Dixon, Edwina BlkAW
Dixon, Ella Nora Hepworth WhLA
Dixon, F E BbtC
Dixon, Fletcher 1743- Alli, BiDLA
Dixon, Francis B Alli Sup
Dixon, Frank Haigh 1869- DcAmA
Dixon, Franklin W CarSB, ConAu 17R,
EncM&D, SmATA 1, SmATA 2
Dixon, Frederick Alli
Dixon, Frederick Augustus 1843-1919 ChPo,
DcNAA
Dixon, G K ChPo S1
Dixon, George Alli, BbtC, BiDLA
Dixon, George d1800? OxCan
Dixon, George Washington 1808?-1861
AmA&B
Dixon, Harry Vernor 1908- AmA&B,
ConAu P-1
Dixon, Henry Alli
Dixon, Henry Hall 1822-1870 Alli Sup,
Br&AmS, BrAu 19, NewC
Dixon, Henry Horatio 1869- WhLA
Dixon, Henry John Alli Sup
Dixon, J ChPo
Dixon, J M 1820?- OhA&B
Dixon, Jacob 1793-1849 Alli Sup, OhA&B
Dixon, James Alli Sup, BbtC, MnBBF
Dixon, James 1814-1873 BiD&SB
Dixon, James D Alli Sup
Dixon, James Henry 1803?-1876 Alli Sup,
ChPo S1
Dixon, James Main 1856-1933 AmA&B,
AmLY, DcAmA, DcNAA, WhWNAA
Dixon, Jeane AmA&B
Dixon, John Alli, Alli Sup, BbtC, BiDLA
Dixon, John H Alli Sup
Dixon, John W, Jr. 1919- ConAu 9R
Dixon, Joseph Alli, Alli Sup
Dixon, Joseph 1824- Alli Sup
Dixon, Joseph Kossuth 1856-1926 DcNAA

Dixon, Joseph L 1896- ConAu 61
Dixon, Joshua Alli, BiDLA
Dixon, Lucy Alli Sup
Dixon, Margaret ChPo
Dixon, Marjorie 1887- AuBYP, ConAu 23
Dixon, Melvin BlkAW
Dixon, Mort 1892-1956 AmSCAP 66
Dixon, Olive K TexWr
Dixon, Paige ConAu XR, WrD 1976
Dixon, Peter L 1931?- ConAu 45, SmATA 6
Dixon, Pierson 1904-1965 ConAu P-1
Dixon, R Alli
Dixon, R J Alli Sup
Dixon, Reginald Arthur Norton 1910- Au&Wr
Dixon, Richard Alli, BiDLA
Dixon, Richard Watson 1833-1900 Alli Sup,
BiD&SB, BrAu 19, CasWL, ChPo,
ChPo S1, Chmbr 3, DcLEnL, EvLB,
NewC, OxEng, WebEAL
Dixon, Robert Alli
Dixon, Robert B Alli Sup
Dixon, Robert W MnBBF
Dixon, Roger Alli
Dixon, Roger 1930- ConAu 53, WrD 1976
Dixon, Roland Burrage 1875-1934 AmA&B,
DcNAA
Dixon, Royal 1885-1962 AmA&B, TexWr,
WhWNAA
Dixon, Ruth ConAu XR
Dixon, S F Alli Sup
Dixon, Sam BlkAW
Dixon, Sam Houston TexWr
Dixon, Samuel Gibson 1851- AmLY
Dixon, Stephen DrAF 1976
Dixon, Susan 1829-1907 DcAmA, DcNAA
Dixon, Susan Bullett 1827- BiDSA
Dixon, Susan Houston BiDSA
Dixon, Thomas Alli, Alli Sup
Dixon, Thomas 1864-1946 AmA&B, BiD&SB,
BiDSA, CasWL, CnDAL, DcAmA,
DcLEnL, DcNAA, OxAm, REnAL,
TwCA, TwCA Sup, WebEAL,
WhWNAA
Dixon, Thomas Aloysius Alli Sup
Dixon, Tom MnBBF
Dixon, Walter Ernest 1871- WhLA
Dixon, William Alli, BiDLA
Dixon, William Gray Alli Sup
Dixon, William Henry 1783-1854 Alli Sup
Dixon, William Hepworth 1821-1879 Alli,
Alli Sup, BbD, BiD&SB, BrAu 19,
CasWL, Chmbr 3, DcEnA, DcEnL,
DcEuL, EvLB, NewC
Dixon, William John 1848- Alli Sup
Dixon, William MacNeile 1866- ChPo,
ChPo S2, PoIre, WhLA
Dixon, William Scarth 1848-1933 Br&AmS
Dixon, Wilmott d1915 Br&AmS
Dixon, Winifred Hawkridge WhWNAA
Dixon, Zella Allen 1858-1924 AmA&B, AmLY,
DcNAA
Dixwell, George B Alli Sup
Dizard, Wilson P 1922- ConAu 17R
Dizdar, Mak 1917- CasWL
Dizenzo, Charles 1938- ConAu 25, ConDr,
WrD 1976
DiZerega, K B ChPo
Dizney, Henry 1926- ConAu 33
Dizzy NewC
Djalski, Ksaver Sandor 1854-1935 CasWL,
Pen Eur
Djanetjo Ma Ma Lei DcOrL 2
Djang, Yuan Shan 1892- WhLA
Djangatolum BlkAW
Djeddah, Eli 1911- ConAu 37
Djilas, Milovan 1911- Au&Wr, WorAu
Djoleto, Amu 1929- AfA 1
Djordjic, Ignjac Pen Eur
Djordjic, Ignjat 1675-1737 CasWL
Djorup, Christian 1880- WhWNAA
D'Joseph, Jac 1919- AmSCAP 66
Djurdjevic, Ignjat 1675-1737 CasWL
Djurdjevic, Stijepo 1579-1632 CasWL
Djwa, Sandra OxCan Sup
D'Lower, I Del 1912- AmSCAP 66
D'Lugoff, Burton C 1928- AmSCAP 66
Dlugosz, Jan 1415-1480 CasWL
Dluhosch, Eric 1927- ConAu 25

Dmitriyev, Ivan Ivanovich 1760-1837 *BbD,*
BiD&SB, CasWL, DcEuL, DcRusL
Dmitry Rostovsky 1651-1709 *CasWL*
Dmochowski, Franciszek Ksawery 1762-1808
CasWL
Dmytryshyn, Basil 1925- *ConAu 21*
Dnyandev *DcOrL 2*
Doak, Margaret *PoIre*
Doak, Wade Thomas 1940- *Au&Wr,*
ConAu 57, WrD 1976
Doake, Margaret *Alli Sup*
Doan, Edward Newell 1904- *OhA&B*
Doan, Eleanor Lloyd *ConAu 1R, WrD 1976*
Doan, Frank Carleton 1877-1927 *DcNAA,*
OhA&B
Doan, Thi Diem 1705-1746 *DcOrL 2, Pen Cl*
Doane, Alfred *OxCan*
Doane, Augustus Sidney 1808-1852 *Alli*
Doane, Dorothy *AmSCAP 66*
Doane, Duane Howard 1883- *WhWNAA*
Doane, George Hobart 1830-1905 *Alli Sup,*
DcAmA, DcNAA
Doane, George Washington 1799-1859 *Alli,*
AmA&B, BiD&SB, ChPo, ChPo S1,
CyAL 2, DcAmA, DcNAA, PoCh,
REnAL, WebEAL
Doane, Gilbert Harry 1897- *ConAu P-1,*
WhWNAA
Doane, Marion S *ConAu XR*
Doane, Nehemiah 1820- *Alli Sup*
Doane, Pelagie 1906-1966 *AuBYP, ChPo,*
ConAu 1R, IlCB 1945, IlCB 1956,
MorJA, SmATA 7
Doane, Robert Rutherford 1889-1960 *OhA&B*
Doane, W Howard 1831- *ChPo S1*
Doane, William Croswell 1832-1913 *Alli Sup,*
AmA&B, BiD&SB, ChPo, ChPo S1,
DcAmA, DcNAA
Doane, William Howard 1831-1915 *AmA&B*
Dobb, Maurice Herbert 1900- *Au&Wr,*
ConAu 9R, WrD 1976
Dobbie, J Frank 1888- *CnDAL*
Dobbin, Elizabeth *PoIre*
Dobbin, John E 1914- *ConAu 9R*
Dobbin, Orlando Thomas 1807-1891 *Alli,*
Alli Sup, PoIre
Dobbins, Austin C 1919- *ConAu 57*
Dobbins, Charles G 1908- *ConAu P-1*
Dobbins, Douglas 1860-1927 *IndAu 1816*
Dobbins, Frank Stockton 1855-1916 *Alli Sup,*
DcNAA
Dobbins, Gaines Stanley 1886- *ConAu 1R,*
WhWNAA
Dobbins, Harry Thompson 1865- *WhWNAA*
Dobbins, Marybelle King 1900- *ConAu 41,*
IndAu 1917
Dobbins, Natalia 1894- *WhWNAA*
Dobbs, Arthur 1684?-1765 *Alli, BiDSA,*
OxCan
Dobbs, Catherine Rose Biggs 1908- *OhA&B*
Dobbs, Farrell 1907- *ConAu 49*
Dobbs, Francis 1750-1811 *Alli, BiDLA, PoIre*
Dobbs, Hoyt McWhorter 1878- *WhWNAA*
Dobbs, Kildare 1923- *OxCan, OxCan Sup*
Dobbs, Richard *Alli*
Dobbs, Richard Stewart 1808- *Alli Sup*
Dobbs, Rose *AuBYP*
Dobbyn, John F 1937- *ConAu 53*
Dobel, D *Alli*
Dobell, Bertram 1842-1914 *ChPo, ChPo S1,*
ChPo S2, LongC, TwCA, TwCA Sup
Dobell, Byron 1927- *AmA&B*
Dobell, Clarence *ChPo S2*
Dobell, Elizabeth Mary *Alli Sup*
Dobell, Eva *ChPo*
Dobell, Horace 1828- *Alli Sup*
Dobell, I M B 1909- *ConAu P-1*
Dobell, John 1757-1840 *Alli, PoCh*
Dobell, Joseph *BiDLA*
Dobell, Peter *Alli*
Dobell, Peter C *OxCan Sup*
Dobell, Sidney Thompson 1824-1874 *Alli Sup,*
BbD, BiD&SB, BrAu 19, CasWL, ChPo,
ChPo S1, ChPo S2, Chmbr 3, DcEnA,
DcEnA Ap, DcEnL, DcEuL, DcLEnL,
EvLB, NewC, OxEng, Pen Eng, REn,
WebEAL
Dober, Anna 1713-1739 *PoCh*

Dober, Richard P *ConAu 9R*
Dobereiner, Peter Arthur 1925- *Au&Wr*
Dobias, Frank 1902- *ConICB, IlCB 1945*
Dobie, A *Alli*
Dobie, Armistead Mason 1881- *WhWNAA*
Dobie, Bertha McKee 1890?-1974 *ConAu 53*
Dobie, Charles Caldwell 1881-1943 *AmA&B,*
DcNAA, OxAm, REnAL, TwCA,
TwCA Sup, WhWNAA
Dobie, David *Alli Sup*
Dobie, Edith 1894-1975 *ConAu 23, ConAu 57*
Dobie, Frank 1888- *WhWNAA*
Dobie, George *ChPo, ChPo S1*
Dobie, J Frank 1888-1964 *AmA&B,*
ConAu 1R, DcLEnL, OxAm, REn,
REnAL, TexWr, TwCA Sup
Dobie, John Shedden *Alli Sup*
Dobie, William Wilson *Alli Sup*
Dobin, Abraham 1907- *ConAu 53*
Dobkin, Alexander 1908-1975 *ChPo S1,*
ConAu 57, IlCB 1956
Dobkin DeRios, Marlene 1939- *ConAu 61*
Dobkins, J Dwight 1943- *ConAu 49*
Dobler, Bruce 1939- *ConAu 53*
Dobler, Lavinia G 1910- *ConAu 1R, MorBMP,*
SmATA 6
Dobles, Fabian 1918- *DcCLA*
Doblin, Alfred 1878-1957 *CasWL, CatA 1952,*
ClDMEuL, EncWL, EvEuW, ModGL,
OxGer, Pen Eur, REn, TwCA,
TwCA Sup, WhTwL
Dobner, Maeva Park 1918- *ConAu 29*
Dobney, Fredrick J 1943- *ConAu 53*
Dobney, H H *Alli Sup*
Dobney, J T *Alli*
Dobraczynski, Jan 1910- *Au&Wr, ConAu P-1,*
Pen Eur
Dobree, Arthur *Alli Sup*
Dobree, Bonamy 1891-1974 *Au&Wr, ChPo,*
ChPo S1, ConAu 5R, ConAu 53,
DcLEnL, ModBL, NewC, REn
Dobree, Louisa Emily *Alli Sup*
Dobree, Valentine 1894- *NewC*
Dobrentey, Gabriel 1796-1851 *BbD, BiD&SB*
Dobriansky, Lev Eugene 1918- *AmA&B,*
ConAu 1R
Dobrin, Arnold Jack 1928- *ConAu 25,*
IlCB 1966, SmATA 4
Dobrin, Arthur 1943- *ConAu 61*
Dobrogeanu-Gherea, Constantin 1855-1920
CasWL, ClDMEuL
Dobrolyubov, Aleksandr Mikhaylovich 1876-
DcRusL, Pen Eur
Dobrolyubov, Nikolai Aleksandrovich 1836-1861
BiD&SB, CasWL, DcEuL, DcRusL, EuA,
EvEuW, Pen Eur, REn
Dobrovolsky, Sergei P 1908- *ConAu 33,*
WrD 1976
Dobrovsky, Josef 1753-1829 *BiD&SB, CasWL,*
DcEuL, EvEuW, Pen Eur
Dobson, Alban *ChPo S1*
Dobson, Augusta Mary Rachel 1872-1923
ChPo S1, ChPo S2
Dobson, Austin 1840-1921 *BiD&SB, BrAu 19,*
DcEnL, DcEuL, LongC, MouLC 4,
NewC, WebEAL
Dobson, Barrie 1931- *ConAu 33*
Dobson, E Philip 1910- *ConAu P-1*
Dobson, Edward *Alli Sup*
Dobson, Eric John 1913- *Au&Wr, ConAu 13R*
Dobson, Frances Mary *ChPo*
Dobson, George Edward *Alli Sup*
Dobson, Henry Austin 1840-1921 *Alli Sup,*
BbD, CasWL, ChPo, ChPo S1, ChPo S2,
Chmbr 3, DcEnA, DcEnA Ap, DcLEnL,
EvLB, OxEng, Pen Eng
Dobson, Mrs. Henry Austin *Alli Sup*
Dobson, Henry Walker 1899- *Au&Wr*
Dobson, James A C 1833-1896 *IndAu 1917*
Dobson, James C, Jr. 1936- *ConAu 29,*
WrD 1976
Dobson, John *Alli*
Dobson, John M 1940- *ConAu 37*
Dobson, Joseph R *Alli Sup*
Dobson, Joshua *Alli*
Dobson, Kenneth Austin 1907- *Au&Wr,*
WrD 1976
Dobson, Margaret 1888- *ChPo S1*

Dobson, Margaret J 1931- *ConAu 53*
Dobson, Matthew d1784 *Alli*
Dobson, Richard Barrie 1931- *WrD 1976*
Dobson, Robert *Alli*
Dobson, Rosemary 1920- *ChPo, ConP 1970,*
ConP 1975, WhTwL, WrD 1976
Dobson, Susannah *Alli*
Dobson, Thomas *Alli Sup*
Dobson, W H *MnBBF*
Dobson, W S *Alli*
Dobson, William *Alli*
Dobson, William 1820-1884 *Alli Sup*
Dobson, William Arthur Charles Harvey 1913-
ConAu 13R, WrD 1976
Dobson, William Clarke Thomas 1817-1898
ChPo
Dobson, William T *Alli Sup, ChPo S1*
Dobuzhinskii, Mstislav Valerianovich 1875-
IlCB 1945
Doby, Tibor 1914- *ConAu 5R*
Dobyns, Fletcher 1872-1942 *OhA&B*
Dobyns, Henry F 1925- *ConAu 37, WrD 1976*
Dobyns, John *Alli*
Dobyns, Stephen 1941- *ConAu 45,*
DrAP 1975, WrD 1976
Dobyns, William Ray 1861-1932 *AmLY,*
DcNAA
Dobzhansky, Theodosius 1900-1975 *AmA&B,*
ConAu 61, ConAu P-1
Dochant, George *Alli*
Docharty, G B *Alli*
Docherty, James L *EncM&D, WrD 1976*
Dock, George 1860- *WhWNAA*
Dock, Lavinia L 1858- *DcNAA*
Dockeray, J C 1907- *ConAu 45*
Dockery, Eva Hunt *WhWNAA*
Dockham, Reuben Edson 1879- *AnMV 1926*
Docking, James Tippet 1861-1916 *DcNAA*
Dockirray, Thomas *Alli*
Dockrell, William Bryan 1929- *ConAu 37*
Dockstader, Cornelia I *ArizL*
Dockstader, Frederick J 1919- *ConAu 13R*
Docktor, Irv 1918- *IlCB 1956*
Doctor A *ConAu 49, SmATA 8*
Doctor Invincibilis *NewC*
Doctor Mirabilis *NewC*
Doctor Ordinatissimus d1347 *DcEnL*
Doctor Quad *AmLY XR*
Doctor Sangredo *PueRA*
Doctor Seuss *ConAu XR*
Doctor Slop 1773-1856 *DcEnL*
Doctor Subtilis *NewC*
Doctor Syntax *AmLY XR*
Doctorow, E L 1931- *AuNews 2, ConAu 45,*
ConLC 6, DrAF 1976, ModAL Sup
Doctors, Samuel I 1936- *ConAu 53*
Docultree, Amoo *Alli*
Docura, Ann *Alli*
Docwra, Mary E *Alli Sup*
Doczy, Ludwig Von 1845- *BiD&SB*
Dod, Albert Baldwin 1805-1845? *CyAL 1,*
DcAmA, DcNAA
Dod, Charles Roger 1793-1855 *Alli, DcEnL*
Dod, H *Alli*
Dod, John *Alli*
Dod, John 1547-1645 *Alli, DcEnL*
Dod, Marcus *Alli*
Dod, Pierce *Alli*
Dod, Samuel *Alli*
Dod, Thomas *Alli*
Dodd, A Charles *Alli*
Dodd, Anna Bowman 1855?-1929 *Alli Sup,*
BiD&SB, DcAmA, DcNAA
Dodd, Arthur Edward 1913- *Au&Wr,*
ChPo S2, ConAu 9R, WrD 1976
Dodd, Arthur Herbert 1891?-1975 *ConAu 57,*
WrD 1976
Dodd, C E *Alli*
Dodd, Catherine Filene *WhWNAA*
Dodd, Catherine Isabel *WhLA*
Dodd, Charles d1745? *Alli, DcEnL*
Dodd, Charles Harold 1884-1973 *Au&Wr,*
ConAu 45, WhLA
Dodd, Daniel d1793? *BkIE*
Dodd, Derrick *ChPo S1, DcNAA*
Dodd, Donald B 1940- *ConAu 57*
Dodd, Ed Benton 1902- *ConAu 25, SmATA 4*
Dodd, Edward *ConAu 49*

Doggett, C B *Alli Sup*
Doggett, Daniel Seth 1810-1880 *Alli Sup, BiDSA, DcNAA*
Doggett, David Seth 1810-1880 *DcAmA*
Doggett, Frank 1906- *ConAu 21*
Doggett, Henry S 1837-1885? *Alli Sup, OhA&B*
Doggett, John d1852 *CyAL 1*
Doggett, Kate 1835?- *Alli Sup*
Doggett, Lawrence Locke 1864-1957 *OhA&B*
Doggett, P D *Alli Sup*
Doggett, Thomas d1721 *NewC*
Dogherty, Mrs. *Alli*
Dogherty, Hugh *Alli*
Dogherty, Thomas d1805 *Alli*
Dogood, Henry John 1813-1869 *Alli Sup*
Dohan, Edith 1877-1943 *DcNAA*
Dohan, Mary Helen 1914- *WrD 1976*
Dohen, Dorothy 1923- *CatA 1952*
Doheny, Michael 1805-1863 *Alli Sup, PoIre*
Doherty, Lady *Alli Sup*
Doherty, Mrs. 1790?- *BiDLA*
Doherty, A *Alli Sup*
Doherty, Austin *PoIre*
Doherty, Charles Hugh 1913- *Au&Wr, ConAu 9R, SmATA 6*
Doherty, Mrs. Edward *CatA 1952*
Doherty, Edward J 1890-1975 *AmA&B, BkC 3, CatA 1947, ConAu 57*
Doherty, Francis Malcolm *Alli Sup, ChPo, PoIre*
Doherty, Henry Latham 1870-1939 *OhA&B*
Doherty, Herbert J, Jr. 1926- *ConAu 1R*
Doherty, Hugh *Alli Sup, BiDLA*
Doherty, Ivy R Duffy 1922- *ConAu 9R*
Doherty, J J *Alli Sup*
Doherty, J M *Alli Sup*
Doherty, John *Alli Sup, PoIre*
Doherty, John 1786?-1850 *PoIre*
Doherty, John Stephen *AuBYP*
Doherty, Len 1930- *Au&Wr*
Doherty, Malcolm *Alli Sup*
Doherty, Martin W 1899- *CatA 1947*
Doherty, Mary Lee 1904- *ChPo*
Doherty, P I *Alli Sup*
Doherty, P J *MnBBF*
Doherty, Patrick 1838-1872 *DcNAA*
Doherty, Philip Joseph 1856-1928 *DcNAA*
Doherty, Robert R *Alli Sup*
Doherty, Robert W 1935- *ConAu 21*
Doherty, William Butler *Alli Sup*
Doherty, William J *Alli Sup*
Doherty, William Thomas, Jr. 1923- *ConAu 53*
Dohm, Ernst 1819-1883 *BiD&SB*
Dohna, Abraham, Burggraf Und Herr Zu 1579-1631 *OxGer*
Dohna, Fabian, Burggraf Und Herr Zu 1550-1621 *OxGer*
Dohne, J L *Alli Sup*
Dohony, E L *Alli Sup*
Dohrenwend, Barbara Snell 1927- *ConAu 25*
Dohring, Fritz *OxGer*
Doi, Kochi 1886- *WhLA*
Doig, Mrs. Charles *Alli Sup*
Doig, David *Alli, BiDLA*
Doig, David d1800 *Alli*
Doig, Jameson W 1933- *ConAu 37*
Doig, Mary *Alli Sup*
Doin, Ernest 1809-1891 *DcNAA*
Doisy, Louisa *Alli Sup*
Dok Mai Sot 1906-1963 *Pen Cl*
Doke, Clement Martyn 1893- *Au&Wr*
Dokenfeld, H *Alli Sup*
Dokey, Richard *DrAF 1976*
Dokmai Sot 1906-1962 *DcOrL 2*
Dolan, Albert Harold 1892- *BkC 3, CatA 1947*
Dolan, Edward F, Jr. 1924- *ConAu 33*
Dolan, Harry *BlkAW*
Dolan, John 1929- *AmSCAP 66*
Dolan, John Patrick 1923- *ConAu 5R*
Dolan, John Richard 1893- *ConAu 9R*
Dolan, Josephine A 1913- *ConAu 49*
Dolan, Lida 1912- *AmSCAP 66*
Dolan, Paul 1910- *ConAu 9R*
Dolan, Robert Emmett 1906- *AmSCAP 66*
Dolan, Thomas Michael *Alli Sup*
Dolan, Winthrop W 1909- *ConAu 57*

Dolbear, Amos Emerson 1837-1910 *Alli Sup, BiD&SB, DcAmA, DcNAA*
Dolben, Digby Mackworth 1848-1867 *BrAu 19, ChPo, OxEng*
Dolben, Sir John *Alli*
Dolben, John 1625-1686 *Alli*
Dolberg, Alexander 1933- *Au&Wr*
Dolbey, Robert Valentine 1878- *WhLA*
Dolbier, Maurice 1912- *AmA&B, AuBYP, MorJA*
Dolby, Anastasia *Alli Sup*
Dolby, George *Alli Sup*
Dolby, James L 1926- *ConAu 45*
Dolby, John *Alli Sup*
Dolby, Richard *Alli*
Dolby, Thomas *Alli*
Dolby, William *Alli Sup*
Dolce, Carlo 1616-1686 *ChPo*
Dolce, Lodovico 1508-1568 *BiD&SB, CasWL, McGWD, REn*
Dolce, Philip C 1941- *ConAu 57*
Dolch, Edward William 1889- *WhWNAA*
Dolci, Danilo 1924- *Au&Wr, TwCW, WorAu*
Dole, Charles Fletcher 1845-1927 *Alli Sup, AmLY, BiD&SB, DcAmA, DcNAA, WhWNAA*
Dole, Edmund Pearson 1850-1928 *Alli Sup, DcAmA, DcNAA*
Dole, George Henry 1857-1942 *DcNAA*
Dole, Gertrude E *ConAu 41*
Dole, Helen James Bennett d1944 *Alli Sup, AmA&B, WhWNAA*
Dole, Jeremy H 1932- *ConAu 17R*
Dole, Margaret A *ChPo*
Dole, Nathan Haskell 1852-1935 *Alli Sup, AmA&B, AmLY, BbD, BiD&SB, ChPo, ChPo S1, ChPo S2, DcAmA, DcBiA, DcLEnL, DcNAA, OxAm, REnAL, TwCA, TwCA Sup, WhWNAA*
Doleman, John *Alli*
Doleman, Nic *Alli*
Doleman, Robert *Alli*
Doler, Sir Daniel *Alli*
Dolet, Etienne 1509-1546 *DcEuL, EvEuW, OxFr, REn*
Dolezal, Carroll *IlBYP*
Dolezel, Lubomir 1922- *ConAu 45*
Dolge, Alfred 1848- *AmLY*
Dolgoff, Ralph L 1932- *ConAu 33*
Dolgorukova, Princess Natalia Borisovna 1714-1771 *CasWL*
Doliber, Earl L 1947- *ConAu 49*
Dolim, Mary Nuzum 1925- *AuBYP, ConAu 17R*
Dolin, Edwin 1928- *ConAu 45*
Dolin, Patrick *ChPo S2*
Doliner, Roy 1932- *ConAu 1R*
Dolinin, A 1883- *CasWL*
Dolinsky, Meyer 1923- *ConAu 57*
Dolinsky, Mike *ConAu 57*
Dolit, Alan 1934- *ConAu 61*
Dolitzki, Menachem Mendel 1856-1931 *Pen Eur*
Doll, Richard 1912- *WrD 1976*
Doll, Ronald C 1913- *ConAu 13R, WrD 1976*
Doll, William 1897- *WhWNAA*
Dollar, Robert 1844-1932 *DcNAA*
Dollard, James B 1872-1946 *ChPo, ChPo S1, DcLEnL, DcNAA, PoIre*
Dollard, John 1900- *AmA&B*
Dollard, William 1861- *PoIre*
Dollard DesOrmeaux, Adam 1635-1660 *OxCan*
Dollen, Charles Joseph 1926- *ConAu 5R*
Dolley, Charles S *Alli Sup*
Dollfuss, Engelbert 1892-1934 *OxGer, REn*
Dollier DeCasson, Francois 1636-1701 *OxCan*
Dollinger, Ignaz Von 1799-1890 *OxGer*
Dollinger, John Joseph Ignatius 1809?-1890 *BbD, BiD&SB*
Dolliver, Barbara Babcock 1927- *ConAu 5R*
Dolliver, Clara G *Alli Sup, ChPo, ChPo S1, ChPo S2*
Dollman, Francis T *Alli, Alli Sup*
Dolloff, Eugene Dinsmore 1890- *ConAu 1R*
Dollond, John 1706-1761 *Alli*
Dollond, Peter 1730-1820 *Alli, BiDLA*
Dolman, Bernard Frederick Joseph 1903- *Au&Wr*

Dolman, Nic *Alli*
Dolman, Robert *Alli*
Dolmatch, Theodore B 1924- *ConAu 41*
Dolmatovsky, Yevgeni Aronovich 1915- *CasWL, DcRusL*
Dolmetsch, Carl Frederick 1911- *WrD 1976*
Dolmetsch, Carl R 1924- *ChPo S1, ConAu 21*
Dolopathos *CasWL*
Dolores, Sister Marian *ConAu XR*
Dolph, John M 1895-1962 *AmSCAP 66*
Dolphin, Rex *MnBBF*
Dolphin, Robert, Jr. 1935- *ConAu 29*
Dolsen, Harriet *Alli Sup*
Dolson, Clara A Matson *ChPo S2*
Dolson, Cora A Matson *ChPo*
Dolson, Hildegarde 1908- *ConAu 5R, SmATA 5*
Doman, Glenn J 1919- *ConAu 61*
Doman, Henry *Alli Sup*
Doman, J *Alli Sup*
Domanovic, Radoje 1873-1908 *ModSL 2, Pen Eur*
Domanska, Janina *AuBYP, AuNews 1, ChPo S2, ConAu 17R, IlCB 1966, SmATA 6, ThBJA*
Domar, Evsey D 1914- *WrD 1976*
Domaradzki, Theodore F 1910- *ConAu 45*
Domat, Jean 1625-1696 *OxFr*
Dombey *ChPo S1*
D'Ombrain, Henry Honywood *Alli Sup*
D'Ombrain, Nicholas 1944- *WrD 1976*
Dombrowski, Gerard *DrAP 1975*
Dombrowski, Kathe Schonberger Von 1881- *IlCB 1945*
Domecq H Bustos *ConAu XR*
Domeier, William d1815 *BiDLA, BiDLA Sup*
Domekins, George Peter *Alli*
Domelt, Philobeth *Alli*
Domenchina, Juan Jose 1898- *CIDMEuL*
Domencich, Thomas A *ConAu 29*
Domenichetti, Richard Hippisley *Alli Sup*
Domenichi, Ludovico 1515-1564 *CasWL*
Domenichino, Il 1581-1641 *AtlBL, REn*
Domenico Veneziano *AtlBL*
Domentijan *Pen Eur*
Domergue, Maurice 1907- *ConAu 25*
Domerham, Adam De *Alli*
Domett, Alfred 1811-1887 *Alli Sup, BiD&SB, BrAu 19, CasWL, ChPo, Chmbr 3, DcEnL, DcLEnL, NewC, OxEng, WebEAL*
Domett, Henry W *Alli Sup*
Domhoff, G William 1936- *ConAu 45*
Domier, William *Alli*
Domin, Hilde 1912- *ModGL, OxGer*
Domingues, Mario 1899- *AfA 1*
Dominguez Bastida *DcSpL*
Dominguez, Jose DeJesus 1843-1898 *PueRA*
Dominguez DeCamargo, Hernando d1657 *Pen Am*
Domini, Jon *ConAu XR*
Domini, Rey *ConAu XR*
Dominian, Jack 1929- *WrD 1976*
Dominic, Saint 1170-1221 *REn*
Dominic, Sister Mary *ConAu XR, WrD 1976*
Dominic, R B *EncM&D*
Dominicet, R *Alli*
Dominici, Giovanni 1356?-1419 *CasWL*
Dominick, Andrew *Alli*
Dominie, The *WrD 1976*
Dominie, Otis G *BlkAW*
Domino *OxCan*
Dominowski, Roger L 1939- *ConAu 45*
Dominy, Eric Norman 1918- *Au&Wr, ConAu 9R, WrD 1976*
Domitius Marsus 054?BC-004?BC *Pen Cl*
Domjan, Joseph 1907- *AuBYP, ConAu 9R*
Domke, Helmut George 1914-1974 *Au&Wr, ConAu P-1*
Domke, Martin 1892- *ConAu P-1, WrD 1976*
Dommen, Arthur J 1934- *ConAu 9R*
Dommermuth, William P 1925- *ConAu 17R, WrD 1976*
Dommett, Alfred 1811-1887 *ChPo S1*
Dommeyer, Frederick Charles 1909- *BiDPar, ConAu 37*
Domvile, Sir Barry Edward *Au&Wr*
Domvile, Lady Margaret 1840- *Alli Sup*

Domville, Edward James *Alli Sup*
Domville, Eric 1929- *ConAu 41*
Don Carlos *NewC*
Don Jose *WhWNAA*
Don Quixote *WhWNAA*
Don Raimundo d1150 *DcSpL*
Don Tomasito *ConAu XR*
Don, David *Alli*
Don, George *Alli*
Don, Isabel *Alli Sup*
Don, James *Alli*
Don, Lina *Alli Sup*
Don-Carlos, Cooke 1874- *WhWNAA*
Don-Carlos, Lulu Cooke *ChPo*
Don Leavy, Kathleen *BiDSA*
Donagan, Alan 1925- *ConAu 5R*
Donagan, Barbara 1927- *ConAu 17R*
Donaghe, M Virginia *Alli Sup*
Donaghey, Frederick 1865?-1937 *AmA&B*
Donaghey, George W 1856-1937 *DcNAA*
Donaghue, Derek *MnBBF*
Donaghy, Henry J 1930- *ConAu 53*
Donaghy, Thomas J 1928- *ConAu 21*
Donaghy, William A 1910?-1975 *ConAu 53*
Donahey, James Harrison 1875-1949 *AmA&B,*
    OhA&B
Donahey, Mary Dickerson 1876-1962 *AmA&B,*
    ChPo, OhA&B, WhWNAA
Donahey, Vic 1873-1946 *OhA&B*
Donahey, William 1883?-1970 *AuBYP,*
    ChPo S2, OhA&B, WhWNAA
Donahoe, Bernard 1932- *ConAu 17R*
Donahoe, Daniel Joseph 1853-1930 *DcNAA,*
    PoIre
Donahoe, Patrick 1811-1901 *AmA&B*
Donahoe, Thomas J 1862- *PoIre*
Donahue, Daniel Joseph 1853- *AmLY*
Donahue, Francis James 1917- *ConAu 17R,*
    WrD 1976
Donahue, George T 1911- *ConAu 17R*
Donahue, Jack Clifford 1917- *AmA&B*
Donahue, Lester Bernard 1880-1941 *DcNAA*
Donahue, Ralph James 1897- *WhWNAA*
Donald, Aida DiPace 1930- *ConAu 21*
Donald, David 1920- *AmA&B, Au&Wr,*
    ConAu 9R, OxAm, WorAu
Donald, Elijah Winchester 1848-1904 *DcAmA,*
    DcNAA
Donald, G W 1820- *Alli Sup, ChPo, ChPo S1*
Donald, George 1800-1851 *ChPo*
Donald, Ian 1910- *Au&Wr, WrD 1976*
Donald, James *Alli, Alli Sup, ChPo S2*
Donald, Maxwell Bruce 1897- *WrD 1976*
Donald, Robert *Alli*
Donald, Vivian *ConAu XR*
Donald, Walter *ChPo S2*
Donald, William *ChPo S1*
Donald, William Spooner 1910- *Au&Wr,*
    WrD 1976
Donalds, Gordon *AuBYP, ConAu XR,*
    WrD 1976
Donaldson *Alli*
Donaldson, Mrs. *Alli Sup*
Donaldson, Alexander 1851- *ChPo*
Donaldson, Alfred Lee 1866-1923 *DcNAA*
Donaldson, Augustus Blair *Alli Sup*
Donaldson, Carolyn A *ChPo S2*
Donaldson, Duncan *ChPo S1*
Donaldson, E Talbot 1910- *ConAu 49*
Donaldson, Elvin F 1903- *ConAu 1R*
Donaldson, Frances 1907- *ConAu 61,*
    WrD 1976
Donaldson, Francis 1823-1891 *DcNAA*
Donaldson, Frank 1822-1891 *Alli Sup, DcAmA*
Donaldson, Frank, Jr. *Alli Sup*
Donaldson, Gordon 1913- *Au&Wr,*
    ConAu 13R, OxCan Sup, WrD 1976
Donaldson, Henry Herbert 1857-1938 *AmLY,*
    DcNAA
Donaldson, Herbert 1918- *AmSCAP 66*
Donaldson, J A *BbtC*
Donaldson, James *Alli, Alli Sup*
Donaldson, James 1831- *Alli Sup*
Donaldson, James Lowry 1814-1885 *BiDSA,*
    DcAmA, DcNAA
Donaldson, Jean Chalmers *WhPNW*
Donaldson, John *Alli, Alli Sup*
Donaldson, John 1737-1801 *Alli*

Donaldson, John 1892- *WhWNAA*
Donaldson, John William 1811-1861 *Alli,*
    Alli Sup, BrAu 19, DcEuL
Donaldson, Joseph *Alli, Alli Sup*
Donaldson, Major *MnBBF*
Donaldson, Malcolm 1884- *Au&Wr,*
    ConAu P-1
Donaldson, Norman 1922- *ConAu 33,*
    WrD 1976
Donaldson, Paschal *Alli Sup, ChPo S1*
Donaldson, Robert A *ChPo S2*
Donaldson, S J *Alli Sup*
Donaldson, S James *Alli Sup*
Donaldson, Scott 1928- *ConAu 25, WrD 1976*
Donaldson, T L *Alli*
Donaldson, Thomas *Alli, Alli Sup, ChPo*
Donaldson, Thomas Corwin 1843-1898 *DcAmA,*
    DcNAA, OhA&B
Donaldson, Thomas Leverton 1795-1885
    Alli Sup
Donaldson, Walter *Alli, Alli Sup*
Donaldson, Walter 1893-1947 *AmSCAP 66*
Donaldson, Will 1891-1954 *AmSCAP 66*
Donaldson, William *Alli, Alli Sup*
Donaldus *WhWNAA*
Donalitius, Christian *CasWL*
Donart, Arthur C 1936- *ConAu 37*
Donat, Mrs. And Mrs. Hudson *Alli*
Donat, Anton *ConAu XR*
Donat, John 1933- *ConAu 13R*
Donatello 1386-1466 *AtlBL, REn*
Donati, Alesso *DcEuL*
Donato *TwCA, TwCA Sup*
Donato, Anthony 1909- *AmSCAP 66,*
    ConAu P-1, WrD 1976
Donatus, Aelius 330?- *CasWL, NewC, OxEng,*
    Pen Cl
Donau, P *Alli Sup*
Donavan, John 1905- *ConAu XR*
Donavin, Simpson K 1831-1902 *OhA&B*
Donbavand, B *Alli Sup*
Donceel, Joseph F 1906- *Au&Wr, ConAu 1R*
Doncevic, Ivan 1909- *CasWL*
Donchess, Barbara 1922- *ConAu 57*
Dondey, Theophile *OxFr*
Dondo, Mathurin 1884- *AmA&B, WhWNAA*
Done, William Edward Pears 1883- *Au&Wr*
Done, William Stafford *Alli*
Donegan, Michael *PoIre*
Donegan, Pamela *BlkAW*
Donegan, Sylvia E *ChPo S1*
Donehoo, George Patterson 1862-1934 *DcNAA*
Donelaitis, Kristijonas 1714-1780 *CasWL,*
    Pen Eur
Donelan, A M *Alli Sup*
Donelan, John P *Alli Sup*
Donelson, Andrew Jackson 1800-1871 *BiDSA*
Donelson, Irene W 1913- *ConAu 17R*
Donelson, Kenneth W 1910- *ConAu 17R*
Donenfeld, James 1917- *AmSCAP 66*
Doner, Mary Frances 1893- *AmA&B, AmNov,*
    ConAu 13R, WrD 1976
Doney, Carl G 1867-1955 *AmLY, OhA&B*
Doney, Willis 1925- *ConAu 21*
Donez, Ian 1891- *AmSCAP 66*
Dong-Ho *DcOrL 2*
Dongmo, Jean Louis 1945?- *AfA 1*
Dongo, Malika *BlkAW*
Dongworth, Richard *Alli*
Donheiser, Alan D 1936- *ConAu 37*
Doni, Anton Francesco 1513-1574 *CasWL,*
    EvEuW, Pen Eur, REn
Donian, Mitchell *ChPo*
Donici, Alexandru 1806-1866 *EvEuW*
Donington, Robert 1907- *Au&Wr, ConAu 33*
Doniphan, Alexander 1808-1887 *AmA&B*
Donis, Miles 1937- *ConAu 29*
Donish, Ahmad 1827-1897 *DcOrL 3*
Donisthorpe, George T *Alli Sup*
Donisthorpe, Ida M Loder *LongC*
Donisthorpe, Wordsworth 1847- *Alli Sup*
Donizetti, Gaetano Maria 1797-1848 *AtlBL,*
    REn
Donker, Anthonie 1902-1965 *CasWL*
Donkersley, R *Alli Sup*
Donkin, Major *Alli*
Donkin, Arthur Scott *Alli Sup*
Donkin, Mrs. Charles T B *CatA 1952*

Donkin, John George *OxCan*
Donkin, T C *Alli Sup*
Donkin, William Fishburn 1814-1869 *Alli Sup*
Donleavy, J P 1926- *AmA&B, Au&Wr,*
    AuNews 2, CnMD, ConAu 9R, ConDr,
    ConLC 1, ConLC 4, ConLC 6,
    ConNov 1972, ConNov 1976, DrAF 1976,
    ModAL, ModWD, OxAm, Pen Am,
    RAdv 1, TwCW, WebEAL, WhTwL,
    WorAu, WrD 1976
Donlevy, Alice *Alli Sup*
Donlevy, Harriet 1817-1907 *ChPo, DcAmA,*
    DcNAA
Donlevy, J T *PoIre*
Donlevy, John *Alli Sup*
Donmall, S E *ChPo*
Donn, Abraham 1718-1746 *Alli*
Donn, Benjamin 1729-1798 *Alli*
Donn, James *Alli*
Donn, Rob 1714-1778 *Pen Eng*
Donn-Byrne, Brian Oswald 1889-1928 *AmA&B,*
    NewC, OxAm, REn, REnAL, TwCA,
    TwCA Sup
Donna, Natalie 1934- *AuBYP, ConAu 9R,*
    SmATA 9, WrD 1976
Donnachie, Ian L 1944- *Au&Wr, WrD 1976*
Donnadieu, Marguerite *WorAu*
Donnan, George R *Alli Sup*
Donnan, Laura 1854-1930 *IndAu 1816*
Donnan, Mary Winters 1859-1913 *IndAu 1816*
Donnars, Jacques 1919- *BiDPar*
Donnavan, Corydon 1816?- *OhA&B*
Donnay, Maurice 1859-1945 *ClDMEuL,*
    CnMD, EvEuW, McGWD, ModWD,
    OxFr, Pen Eur, REn
Donne, Alicia *ChPo S1, ChPo S2*
Donne, Alphonse *Alli Sup*
Donne, B *Alli*
Donne, Benjamin *Alli, BiDLA Sup*
Donne, Charles Edward *Alli Sup*
Donne, Daniel *Alli*
Donne, J P *ChPo S1*
Donne, John 1571?-1631 *Alli, AtlBL,*
    BiD&SB, BrAu, CasWL, ChPo,
    ChPo S1, ChPo S2, Chmbr 1, CnE&AP,
    CrE&SL, CriT 1, CyWA, DcEnA,
    DcEnA Ap, DcEnL, DcEuL, DcLEnL,
    EvLB, MouLC 1, NewC, OxEng,
    Pen Eng, RAdv 1, RCom, REn,
    WebEAL
Donne, John 1604-1662 *Alli, NewC*
Donne, M A *Alli Sup*
Donne, M F H *ChPo, ChPo S1, ChPo S2*
Donne, M H P *ChPo S1*
Donne, Maxim *ConAu 57*
Donne, William *Alli Sup*
Donne, William Bodham 1807-1882 *Alli,*
    Alli Sup, BrAu 19
Donne-Byrne, Brian Oswald *DcLEnL*
Donneau DeVise, Jean 1638-1710 *CasWL*
Donnegan, James *Alli*
Donnel, J A *Alli*
Donnell, Annie Hamilton 1862- *AmLY, ChPo,*
    DcNAA, WhWNAA
Donnell, E J *Alli Sup*
Donnell, Emma Amanda 1861-1937 *IndAu 1917*
Donnell, Jess F 1906- *WhWNAA*
Donnell, John C 1919- *ConAu 41*
Donnell, John D 1920- *ConAu 53*
Donnell, R W *ChPo S2*
Donnell, Robert *Alli Sup*
Donnell, Robert 1784-1855 *DcNAA*
Donnellan, Michael Thomas 1931- *ConAu 37,*
    WrD 1976
Donnelly, A *MnBBF, PoIre*
Donnelly, Alton S 1920- *ConAu 23*
Donnelly, Andrew 1893-1955 *AmSCAP 66*
Donnelly, Augustine Stanislaus 1923- *Au&Wr*
Donnelly, Austin Stanislaus *WrD 1976*
Donnelly, Charles Francis 1836-1909 *DcNAA*
Donnelly, Desmond L 1920- *ConAu 13R*
Donnelly, Dorothy *ChPo, ChPo S1*
Donnelly, Dorothy 1880-1928 *AmSCAP 66*
Donnelly, Dorothy Marie 1903- *Au&Wr,*
    CatA 1947, ConAu 5R, WrD 1976
Donnelly, Edward *Alli Sup*
Donnelly, Eleanor C 1818- *PoIre*
Donnelly, Eleanor Cecilia 1838-1917 *Alli Sup,*

AmA&B, BiD&SB, ChPo S1, DcAmA,
DcNAA
Donnelly, Eliza A *Alli Sup*
Donnelly, Francis Patrick 1869- *BkC 1,*
CatA 1947
Donnelly, Sister Gertrude Joseph 1920-
ConAu 13R
Donnelly, Harold Irvin 1892-1937 *DcNAA,*
WhWNAA
Donnelly, Ignatius 1831-1901 *Alli Sup, AmA,*
AmA&B, BbD, BiD&SB, CasWL,
DcAmA, DcEnA Ap, DcLEnL, DcNAA,
OxAm, Pen Am, PoIre, REnAL,
WebEAL
Donnelly, James 1824-1868 *PoIre*
Donnelly, James H, Jr. 1941- *ConAu 29*
Donnelly, James S, Jr. 1943- *WrD 1976*
Donnelly, John Fritcheville Dykes 1834-
Alli Sup
Donnelly, Joseph Gordon 1856-1915 *DcNAA*
Donnelly, Joseph P *OxCan Sup*
Donnelly, Michael Joseph *AnMV 1926*
Donnelly, Murray *OxCan Sup*
Donnelly, P *PoIre*
Donnelly, R *Alli*
Donnelly, Robert *PoIre*
Donnelly, William *BbtC*
Donnelly, William M 1856-1885 *PoIre*
Donnely, Eleanor Cecilia 1838-1917 *ChPo*
Donner, Jorn 1933- *ConAu 13R*
Donner, Stanley T 1910- *ConAu 61*
Donnet, Jacques 1917- *AmSCAP 66*
Donnison, David Vernon 1926- *Au&Wr,*
WrD 1976
Donnison, Frank Siegfried Vernon 1898-
Au&Wr, ConAu 1R, WrD 1976
Donnithorne, Audrey Gladys 1922- *Au&Wr,*
ConAu 17R, WrD 1976
Donno, Elizabeth Story 1921- *ConAu 1R*
Donnollon, John P *Alli Sup*
Donoghoe, J *PoIre*
Donoghue, Alli
Donoghue, David 1891- *TexWr*
Donoghue, Denis 1928- *ConAu 17R*
Donoghue, Dennis *BlkAW*
Donoghue, J *BiDLA*
Donoghue, Mildred R 1929- *ConAu 25,*
WrD 1976
Donoho, Thomas Seton *PoIre*
Donohoe, Thomas 1917- *ConAu 53*
Donohue, John K 1909- *ConAu P-1*
Donohue, John W 1917- *ConAu 5R*
Donohue, Mark 1937- *ConAu 57*
Donoso, Jose 1924- *ConLC 4, DcCLA,*
EncWL Sup, Pen Am
Donoso Cortes, Juan 1809-1853 *CasWL, EuA*
Donoughmore, Earl Of 1756- *Alli, BiDLA*
Donoughue, A *PoIre*
Donoughue, Bernard 1934- *ConAu 17R,*
WrD 1976
Donovan, Cornelius *Alli Sup*
Donovan, Corydon *OhA&B*
Donovan, D J *ChPo S2*
Donovan, Denis *PoIre*
Donovan, Dick 1843-1934 *Alli Sup, EncM&D,*
MnBBF, NewC
Donovan, E *BiDLA*
Donovan, Edward *Alli*
Donovan, Edward Frances d1943 *AmA&B*
Donovan, Edward J 1904- *ConAu 5R*
Donovan, Frank 1906- *ConAu 1R*
Donovan, Frank 1919-1975 *ConAu 61*
Donovan, Frank Pierce, Jr. *MnnWr*
Donovan, Frank Robert 1906- *AuBYP*
Donovan, H L 1887- *WhWNAA*
Donovan, Henry *PoIre*
Donovan, J W *Alli Sup*
Donovan, James A, Jr. 1917- *ConAu 23*
Donovan, James Britt 1916- *ConAu 9R*
Donovan, John *Alli*
Donovan, John 1861-1933 *CatA 1952*
Donovan, John 1919- *ConAu 1R, WrD 1976*
Donovan, John Alexander 1871- *WhWNAA*
Donovan, John C 1920- *ConAu 37*
Donovan, Joseph Wesley 1839-1933 *DcNAA,*
OhA&B
Donovan, Michael *Alli*
Donovan, Patrick *Alli*

Donovan, Peter 1884- *CanNov, OxCan*
Donovan, Robert Alan 1921- *ConAu 17R*
Donovan, Robert John 1912- *AmA&B,*
Au&Wr, ConAu 1R
Donovan, Timothy Paul 1927- *ConAu 53*
Donovan, Walter 1888-1964 *AmSCAP 66*
Donovan, William *ConAu XR*
Dons, Aage 1903- *CasWL, EvEuW, Pen Eur*
Donson, Cyril 1919- *ConAu 23*
Doob, Anthony N 1943- *ConAu 33*
Doob, Leonard W 1909- *AmA&B, ConAu 5R,*
SmATA 8, WrD 1976
Doob, Penelope Billings Reed 1943- *ConAu 53*
Doody, Francis Stephen 1917- *ConAu 13R*
Doody, W H *Alli Sup*
Doog, K Caj *ConAu XR*
D'Ooge, Benjamin Leonard 1860-1940 *AmA&B,*
DcNAA, WhWNAA
D'Ooge, Martin Luther 1839-1915 *AmA&B,*
DcNAA
Dooley, A H d1903 *IndAu 1816*
Dooley, Arch R 1925- *ConAu 13R*
Dooley, Channing Rice 1878-1956 *IndAu 1917*
Dooley, D J 1921- *ConAu 25*
Dooley, Edna Mohr 1907- *AmSCAP 66*
Dooley, George B 1867- *ChPo*
Dooley, Howard J 1944- *ConAu 53*
Dooley, John Henry 1866-1934 *DcNAA*
Dooley, Martin *ConAmL, DcLEnL*
Dooley, Mister *EvLB, TwCA, TwCA Sup*
Dooley, Patrick K 1942- *ConAu 53*
Dooley, Peter C 1937- *ConAu 49*
Dooley, Roger Burke 1920- *BkC 6, CatA 1952,*
ConAu 1R
Dooley, Thomas 1927-1961 *AmA&B*
Dooley, Tom *BlkAW*
Dooley, William G 1905?-1975 *ConAu 57*
Dooley, William Henry 1880- *WhWNAA*
Doolin, Dennis James 1933- *ConAu 13R*
Doolittle, Benjamin 1695-1748? *DcAmA,*
DcNAA
Doolittle, Charles Leander 1843-1919 *Alli Sup,*
DcNAA, IndAu 1917
Doolittle, Eric C E 1869-1920 *AmLY, DcNAA*
Doolittle, Esther Hull *ChPo*
Doolittle, Hilda 1886-1961 *AmA&B, AtlBL,*
CasWL, ChPo S2, Chmbr 3, CnDAL,
ConAmA, ConAmL, DcLEnL, EncWL,
EvLB, LongC, ModAL, ModAL Sup,
OxAm, Pen Am, REn Am, REnAL,
TwCA, TwCA Sup, TwCW, WebEAL
Doolittle, James C *Alli Sup*
Doolittle, Jerome 1933- *ConAu 53*
Doolittle, Justus 1824-1880 *Alli Sup, DcNAA*
Doolittle, Mark 1781- *Alli*
Doolittle, Mary Antoinette 1810-1886 *DcNAA*
Doolittle, Samuel d1717 *Alli*
Doolittle, Theodore Sandford 1836-1893
DcNAA
Doolittle, Thomas 1630-1707 *Alli*
Dooly, Isma *BiDSA*
Doone, Jice *ConAu XR*
Dooner, William Toke *Alli Sup*
Doorly, Ruth K 1919- *ConAu 25*
Doornkamp, John Charles 1938- *ConAu 57*
Dopp, Katharine Elizabeth 1863-1944 *AmA&B,*
DcNAA, WhWNAA
Dopp, Katherine Elizabeth 1863- *AmLY*
Doppelt, Frederic Aubrey 1906-1972
IndAu 1917
Dopping, Doctor *Alli*
Doppo *DcOrL 1*
Dopuch, Nicholas 1929- *ConAu 61*
Dor, Ana *ConAu XR, SmATA XR*
Dor, Georges *OxCan Sup*
Dora D'Istria 1828?-1888? *BbD, BiD&SB*
Doran, Alban Henry Griffiths *Alli Sup*
Doran, Charles Guilfoyle d1909 *PoIre*
Doran, Elsa 1915- *AmSCAP 66*
Doran, George Henry 1869- *ChPo*
Doran, J *ChPo*
Doran, James 1837-1917 *DcNAA*
Doran, James Ewen 1923- *Au&Wr*
Doran, John 1807-1878 *Alli, Alli Sup, BbD,*
BiD&SB, BrAu 19, Chmbr 3, DcEnA,
DcEnL, EvLB, NewC, PoIre
Doran, Joseph Ingersoll *Alli Sup*
Dorant, Gene *ConAu XR*

Dorat, Claude Joseph 1734-1780 *ChPo S2,*
DcEuL, OxFr
Dorat, Jean 1502?-1588 *DcEuL, OxFr*
Doray, Maya 1922- *ConAu 45*
Dorcaster, Nicholas *Alli*
Dorchester, Lord 1876- *Br&AmS, OxCan*
Dorchester, Daniel 1827-1907 *Alli Sup,*
DcAmA, DcNAA
Dorchester, Daniel 1851-1944 *DcNAA*
Dorchester, Frank E 1880- *WhWNAA*
Dorcy, Sister Mary Jean 1914- *BkC 6,*
ConAu 9R
Dore, Anita 1914- *ConAu 29*
Dore, Claire 1934- *ConAu 9R*
Dore, Gabriel *WhWNAA*
Dore, Gustave 1832-1883 *AtlBL, ChPo,*
ChPo S1, ChPo S2, IlBYP, OxFr, REn
Dore, J R *ChPo S2*
Dore, James *Alli, BiDLA*
Dore, John Read *Alli Sup*
Doree, Charles 1875- *Au&Wr*
Doreian, Patrick 1942- *ConAu 45*
Doremus, Jennie Brown *IndAu 1816*
Doremus, Robert *IlBYP*
Doremus, S D *Alli Sup*
Doremus, Thomas Edmund 1922-1962
ConAu 1R
Doren *TwCA, TwCA Sup*
Dorer-Egloff, Eduard 1807-1864 *BiD&SB*
Doreski, William 1946- *ConAu 45,*
DrAP 1975
Doresse, Jean 1917- *Au&Wr*
Dorety, Sister Helen Angela 1870- *WhWNAA*
Dorey, Milnor 1876- *WhWNAA*
Dorey, T A 1921- *ConAu 17R*
Dorfler, Peter 1878-1955 *ClDMEuL, OxGer*
Dorfman, Eugene 1917- *ConAu 29*
Dorfman, Joseph 1904- *AmA&B, ConAu 45*
Dorfman, Nancy S 1922- *ConAu 53*
Dorfman, Robert 1916- *ConAu 17R*
Dorfsman, Louis 1918- *WhGrA*
Dorgan, John Aylmer 1836-1867 *Alli Sup,*
BiD&SB, DcAmA, DcNAA, PoIre
Dorgan, Thomas Aloysius 1877-1929 *AmA&B*
Dorge, Jeanne Emilie Marie *ConAu XR*
Dorgeles, Roland 1886-1973 *CasWL,*
ClDMEuL, ConAu XR, EncWL, EvEuW,
OxFr
Doria, Adair Andrew 1811- *Alli Sup*
Doria, Andrea 1468?-1560 *REn*
Doria, Samuel *Alli Sup*
Dorian, Edith M 1900- *ConAu P-1, SmATA 5*
Dorian, Frederick 1902- *ConAu P-1*
Dorian, Marguerite *ConAu 17R, SmATA 7*
Dorida Mesenia *PueRA*
Doring, E Duncan *ChPo*
Dorion, Sir Antoine-Aime 1818-1891 *OxCan*
Dorion, E P *BbtC*
Dorion, Eric 1826-1866 *OxCan*
Dorion, Jacques Edmond 1827- *BbtC*
Dorion, Jean Baptiste Eric 1826-1866 *BbtC*
Dorion, V P W 1827- *BbtC*
Doris, Lillian 1899- *ConAu 5R*
Dorislaus, Jo J C *Alli*
Dorkinfield, H *Alli Sup*
Dorland, Arthur Garratt 1887- *WhWNAA*
Dorland, Pieter 1454-1507 *DcEuL*
Dorland, William Alexander Newman
WhWNAA
Dorlant, Pieter 1454-1507 *CasWL*
Dorliae, Saint 1935- *ConAu XR*
Dorliae, Peter Gondro 1935- *ConAu 29*
Dorling, Henry Taprell *DcLEnL, LongC,*
MnBBF
Dorling, William *Alli Sup, ChPo*
Dorman *Alli*
Dorman, Mrs. C T *BiDSA*
Dorman, Kathleen *WhWNAA*
Dorman, Michael 1932- *ConAu 13R,*
SmATA 7, WrD 1976
Dorman, Rushton M *Alli Sup*
Dorman, Sonya *DrAF 1976, DrAP 1975*
Dorman, Thomas d1572? *Alli*
Dorman, William *Alli*
Dorman, William H *Alli Sup*
Dormandy, Clara 1902?- *Au&Wr, ConAu P-1*
Dormer *PoIre*
Dormer, Daniel *Alli Sup*

Dougherty, Celius 1902- *AmSCAP 66*
Dougherty, Ching-Yi 1915- *ConAu 5R*
Dougherty, Dan 1897-1955 *AmSCAP 66*
Dougherty, Jennie 1888- *AmSCAP 66*
Dougherty, Joanna Foster *ConAu XR*
Dougherty, John Edwin 1887- *WhWNAA*
Dougherty, John Hampden 1849-1918 *DcNAA*
Dougherty, Jude P 1930- *ConAu 45*
Dougherty, Raymond Philip 1877-1933 *DcNAA*
Dougherty, Richard 1921- *AmA&B*,
    ConAu 1R
Dougherty, Richard M 1935- *ConAu 33*
Dougherty, Richard Martin 1935- *IndAu 1917*
Doughtie, Charles *AuBYP*
Doughtie, Edward 1935- *ConAu 45*
Doughty *Alli*
Doughty, Arthur *Chmbr 3*
Doughty, Sir Arthur George 1860-1936 *DcLEnL*,
    DcNAA, OxCan
Doughty, Charles Montagu 1843-1926 *Alli Sup*,
    AtlBL, BrAu 19, CasWL, ChPo,
    Chmbr 3, CnE&AP, CyWA, DcLEnL,
    EncWL, EvLB, LongC, ModBL, NewC,
    Pen Eng, REn
Doughty, Gregory *Alli*
Doughty, Henry Montagu 1841- *Alli Sup*
Doughty, John *Alli*
Doughty, John 1598?-1672 *Alli*
Doughty, John Franklin 1909- *TexWr*
Doughty, Leonard 1865- *TexWr*
Doughty, Nina Beckett 1911- *ConAu 53*
Doughty, Oswald 1889- *ConAu P-1*,
    WrD 1976
Doughty, Sarah P *Alli Sup, ChPo S2*
Doughty, Thomas *Alli*
Doughty, Thomas 1793-1856 *OxAm*
Doughty, Wayne Dyre 1929-1968 *IndAu 1917*
Doughty, William Ellison 1873- *WhWNAA*
Doughty, William Henry *BiDSA*
Douglas *Alli*
Douglas, Doctor *Alli*
Douglas Marg *MnBBF*
Douglas, Mister *Alli, BiDLA*
Douglas, Mrs. *Alli*
Douglas, A B *Alli Sup*
Douglas, A F *Alli Sup*
Douglas, A G *BbtC*
Douglas, Aaron 1898- *ChPo S1*
Douglas, Al 1907- *AmSCAP 66*
Douglas, Albert *ConAu XR*
Douglas, Alex *Alli*
Douglas, Lord Alfred Bruce 1870-1945
    CatA 1947, ChPo, ChPo S2, DcLEnL,
    EvLB, LongC, NewC, OxEng, Pen Eng,
    REn, WhLA
Douglas, Alice C *ChPo S2*
Douglas, Alice May 1865-1943 *AmA&B*,
    AmLY, BiD&SB, ChPo, DcAmA,
    DcNAA, WhWNAA
Douglas, Alison *ChPo S1*
Douglas, Amanda Minnie 1837?-1916 *Alli Sup*,
    AmA, AmA&B, BbD, BiD&SB, CarSB,
    ChPo S1, ChPo S2, DcAmA, DcNAA
Douglas, Andrew *Alli*
Douglas, Ann C *ConAu XR*
Douglas, Archibald *Alli*
Douglas, Archibald 1328?-1400? *NewC*
Douglas, Archibald 1449?-1514 *NewC*
Douglas, Archibald A H *ChPo*
Douglas, Archibald Alexander *Alli Sup*
Douglas, Arthur *WrD 1976*
Douglas, Aubrey Augustus 1887- *WhWNAA*
Douglas, Augusta Anne *Alli Sup*
Douglas, Bert 1900-1958 *AmSCAP 66*
Douglas, Bessie *PoIre*
Douglas, C H *WrD 1976*
Douglas, C Home *Alli Sup*
Douglas, Caroline Margaret 1821- *Alli Sup*
Douglas, Carstairs *Alli Sup*
Douglas, Charles *Alli*
Douglas, Charles A *Alli*
Douglas, Charles Edward *Alli Sup*
Douglas, Charles Henry 1861-1954 *AmA&B*,
    WhWNAA
Douglas, Charles Henry James 1865-1931
    DcNAA
Douglas, Charles Noel 1863-1920 *ChPo*
Douglas, Charles Winfred 1867-1944 *AmA&B*,

DcNAA
Douglas, Christina Jane *Alli Sup*
Douglas, Clarence Brown 1864- *AmA&B*
Douglas, Clifford Hugh *LongC, OxCan*
Douglas, David *Alli, MnBBF*
Douglas, David 1799-1834 *OxCan*
Douglas, David Charles 1898- *Au&Wr*
Douglas, Dick, Jr. 1912- *WhWNAA*
Douglas, E *Alli Sup*
Douglas, Edith *Alli Sup, DcNAA*
Douglas, Lady Eleanor *Alli*
Douglas, Elizabeth *Alli Sup*
Douglas, Lady Elizabeth K 1821- *Alli Sup*
Douglas, Ellen *ConAu XR, DrAF 1976*
Douglas, Elroy *BlkAW*
Douglas, Ernest 1888- *ArizL*
Douglas, Evelyn *Alli Sup*
Douglas, F Dwen *ChPo S1*
Douglas, Francis *Alli*
Douglas, Francis Archibald Kelhead 1896- *ChPo*
Douglas, Frank William 1878- *WhWNAA*
Douglas, Fred *ChPo S1*
Douglas, Frederic Sylvester North 1791-1819
    Alli, BiDLA
Douglas, Gavin 1474?-1522 *Alli, BiD&SB*,
    BrAu, CasWL, Chmbr 1, CnE&AP,
    CriT 1, DcEnA, DcEuL, DcLEnL, EvLB,
    NewC, OxEng, Pen Eng, REn, WebEAL
Douglas, Gawain 1474?-1522 *REn*
Douglas, Gawen 1475-1522 *Alli*
Douglas, Gawin 1474?-1522 *Alli, AtlBL*,
    BrAu, DcEnL, DcLEnL, EvLB,
    MouLC 1, NewC, OxEng
Douglas, George *Alli, Alli Sup, BrAu 19*,
    CasWL, Chmbr 3, DcLEnL, EvLB,
    NewC
Douglas, George 1869-1902 *CyWA, LongC*,
    Pen Eng
Douglas, George A H *ChPo S1*
Douglas, Sir George Brisbane 1863-1920 *ChPo*
Douglas, Sir George Buchanan Scott 1856-1935
    ChPo S2, WhLA
Douglas, George Cuningham Monteath 1826-
    Alli Sup
Douglas, George M *OxCan*
Douglas, George Norman 1868-1952 *EvLB*
Douglas, George William 1850-1926 *AmLY*,
    ChPo
Douglas, George William 1863-1945 *AmA&B*,
    DcNAA, WhWNAA
Douglas, Lady Gertrude Georgina *Alli Sup*
Douglas, Glenn *ConAu XR*
Douglas, Helen *ChPo S1*
Douglas, Henry Alexander *Alli Sup*
Douglas, Henry Russell 1925- *Au&Wr*
Douglas, Herman *Alli Sup*
Douglas, Hope *ChPo S1*
Douglas, Sir Howard 1776-1861 *Alli, Alli Sup*,
    BbtC
Douglas, Hudson *AmA&B*
Douglas, Ian 1881- *WhLA*
Douglas, J B *Alli Sup*
Douglas, J D 1922- *ConAu 13R*
Douglas, J P *Alli Sup, ChPo*
Douglas, J S *Alli Sup*
Douglas, J W B 1914- *Au&Wr*
Douglas, James *Alli, Alli Sup, BbtC, BiDLA*,
    ChPo S2, Chmbr 3, MnBBF, OxCan
Douglas, Sir James 1286?-1330 *NewC, REn*
Douglas, James 1675-1742 *Alli*
Douglas, Sir James 1803-1877 *OxCan*
Douglas, James 1837?-1918 *AmLY, ArizL*,
    DcNAA
Douglas, James 1869- *PoIre*
Douglas, James And Martin Laycock *Alli*
Douglas, James Dixon 1922- *Au&Wr*,
    WrD 1976
Douglas, Lord James Edward Sholto 1855-
    Alli Sup
Douglas, James John *Alli Sup*
Douglas, James McM *SmATA 5*
Douglas, James William Bruce 1914-
    WrD 1976
Douglas, Jane *Alli*
Douglas, Jame *ChPo*
Douglas, Lady Jane *Alli*
Douglas, Janet Mary *Alli Sup*
Douglas, John *Alli, Alli Sup, BbtC*,

ConAu XR
Douglas, John 1721-1807 *Alli*
Douglas, John Christie *Alli Sup*
Douglas, John Roy *ChPo*
Douglas, John Scott 1905- *AuBYP*,
    WhWNAA
Douglas, John Sholto *NewC*
Douglas, John William *Alli Sup*
Douglas, Katharine Waldo *DcNAA*
Douglas, Kathryn *ConAu XR*
Douglas, Keith 1920-1944 *LongC*,
    ModBL Sup, OxEng, Pen Eng, WebEAL,
    WhTwL, WorAu
Douglas, L G *Alli Sup*
Douglas, Larry 1917- *AmSCAP 66*
Douglas, Leonard *MnBBF*
Douglas, Leonard M 1910- *ConAu 23*
Douglas, Lloyd Cassel 1877-1951 *AmA&B*,
    AmNov, CyWA, EvLB, IndAu 1917,
    LongC, OhA&B, OxAm, Pen Am, REn,
    REnAL, TwCA, TwCA Sup, TwCW,
    WhWNAA
Douglas, Lloyd Virgil 1902- *Au&Wr*
Douglas, Louis H 1907- *ConAu 21*
Douglas, M *Alli Sup*
Douglas, Mack R 1922- *ConAu 21*
Douglas, Malcolm *ChPo*
Douglas, Margaret *ChPo S1*
Douglas, Marian *Alli Sup, AmA&B*,
    DcAmA, DcNAA
Douglas, Marian 1842- *ChPo, ChPo S1*,
    ChPo S2
Douglas, Marjory Stoneman 1890- *AmA&B*,
    AuNews 2, ConAu 1R, SmATA 10
Douglas, Mary 1921- *Au&Wr*
Douglas, Mary Butler d1858 *OhA&B*
Douglas, Maud Isidore *ChPo*
Douglas, Michael *WrD 1976*
Douglas, Minnie *Alli Sup*
Douglas, Niel *Alli, BiDLA*
Douglas, Noel *ChPo*
Douglas, Norman 1868-1952 *AtlBL, CasWL*,
    ChPo, ChPo S1, Chmbr 3, CnMWL,
    CyWA, DcLEnL, LongC, ModBL, NewC,
    OxEng, Pen Eng, RAdv 1, REn, TwCA,
    TwCA Sup, TwCW, WebEAL, WhTwL
Douglas, Olive *DcLEnL, EvLB*
Douglas, Lady Oliver Eleanor Custance 1874-
    ChPo
Douglas, Paul Howard 1892- *AmA&B*
Douglas, Prentice Perry *BlkAW*
Douglas, R *OxCan*
Douglas, Robert *Alli, Alli Sup, BiDLA*,
    ConAu XR
Douglas, Sir Robert *Alli, DcEnL*
Douglas, Robert Kennaway 1838- *Alli Sup*,
    BiD&SB
Douglas, Robert Martin 1849- *BiDSA*
Douglas, Robert R *Alli Sup*
Douglas, Robert W *ChPo S2*
Douglas, Rodney K *BlkAW*
Douglas, Sarah Parker 1824-1881 *ChPo S1*
Douglas, Shane *ConAu XR*
Douglas, Silas Hamilton 1816-1890 *Alli Sup*,
    DcAmA, DcNAA
Douglas, Stair *Alli Sup*
Douglas, Stephen Arnold 1813-1861 *AmA&B*,
    OxAm, REn, REnAL
Douglas, Sylvester *BiDLA*
Douglas, Sylvester, Lord Glenbervie 1747-1823
    Alli
Douglas, Theodore Wayland 1897-1961
    AmA&B
Douglas, Thomas *Alli, Alli Sup*
Douglas, Thomas 1790-1855 *BiDSA*
Douglas, William *Alli, Alli Sup, BiDLA*,
    ChPo S1
Douglas, William d1752 *Alli*
Douglas, William 1724-1810 *NewC*
Douglas, William A 1934- *ConAu 45*
Douglas, William Archer Sholto 1886-
    WhWNAA
Douglas, William Orville 1898- *AmA&B*,
    Au&Wr, AuBYP, ConAu 9R, MnnWr,
    OxAm, REn, REnAL, TwCA Sup,
    WhPNW, WrD 1976
Douglas, William Scott 1815-1883 *Alli Sup*,
    DcEuL

Down, C Maurice *MnBBF*
Down, Eliza *Alli Sup, ChPo S1*
Down, Goldie 1918- *ConAu 25*
Down, John Langdon Haydon 1828- *Alli Sup*
Down, Richard *Alli Sup*
Downame, George d1634 *Alli*
Downame, John d1644 *Alli*
Downard, E N *ChPo S1*
Downard, William L 1940- *ConAu 49*
Downe, B *Alli, BiDLA*
Downe, Darby *Alli*
Downe, John *Alli*
Downer, Alan Seymour 1912-1970 *AmA&B, ConAu 33, ConAu P-1*
Downer, Arthur Cleveland 1847- *WhLA*
Downer, Arthur G *ChPo S2*
Downer, Charles Alfred 1866-1930 *AmLY, DcNAA*
Downer, George *Alli Sup*
Downer, James Walker 1864-1932 *DcNAA*
Downer, Marion 1892?-1971 *AuBYP, ConAu 33*
Downes *Alli, TwCA, TwCA Sup*
Downes, Captain *PoIre*
Downes, Alfred *Alli Sup*
Downes, Alfred Michael 1862-1907 *DcNAA*
Downes, Andrew 1550?-1627 *Alli*
Downes, Anne Miller d1964 *AmA&B, AmNov, WhWNAA*
Downes, Arthur Henry *Alli Sup*
Downes, Bryan Trevor 1939- *ConAu 33, WrD 1976*
Downes, Charles *Alli Sup*
Downes, David Anthony 1927- *ConAu 33, WrD 1976*
Downes, Francis *Alli Sup*
Downes, George 1790?-1846 *Alli, PoIre*
Downes, Henry *Alli, BiDLA*
Downes, J *EarAB, EarAB Sup*
Downes, John *Alli, Alli Sup, PoIre*
Downes, John 1799-1882 *Alli, DcAmA, DcNAA*
Downes, Joseph *Alli, BiDLA, PoIre*
Downes, Kerry 1930- *Au&Wr*
Downes, Louise 1857-1940 *DcNAA*
Downes, Marion *ChPo*
Downes, Olin 1886-1955 *AmA&B*
Downes, Olinthus Gregory *Alli Sup*
Downes, P G *OxCan*
Downes, Quentin *EncM&D*
Downes, Randolph Chandler 1901-1975 *ConAu 49, ConAu 61, OhA&B*
Downes, Robert *Alli*
Downes, Robert P *ChPo S2*
Downes, Samuel *Alli*
Downes, Theop *Alli*
Downes, Thomas *Alli*
Downes, William Howe 1854-1941 *Alli Sup, AmA&B, AmLY, BiD&SB, DcAmA, DcNAA, WhWNAA*
Downes, William Macnamara *PoIre*
Downey, Alan 1889- *CatA 1952*
Downey, Augustine Francis 1865?- *PoIre*
Downey, David George 1858-1935 *DcNAA*
Downey, Edmund *Alli Sup, WhLA*
Downey, Edmund 1856- *PoIre*
Downey, Fairfax Davis 1893- *AmA&B, AmSCAP 66, AuBYP, ChPo, ConAu 1R, OxCan, REnAL, SmATA 3, WhWNAA, WrD 1976*
Downey, Glanville 1908- *ConAu 1R*
Downey, Hal *WhWNAA*
Downey, Harris *ConAu 13R*
Downey, John Florian 1846-1939 *DcNAA*
Downey, Joseph d1870 *PoIre*
Downey, June Etta 1875?-1932 *ChPo, DcNAA, WhWNAA*
Downey, Lawrence William 1921- *ConAu 17R*
Downey, Morton 1901- *AmSCAP 66*
Downey, Murray William 1910- *ConAu 1R*
Downey, Raymond Joseph 1914- *AmSCAP 66*
Downey, Richard 1859-1898 *PoIre*
Downey, Richard 1881- *CatA 1947*
Downey, Samuel R *Alli Sup*
Downey, Sean Morton 1933- *AmSCAP 66*
Downey, Thomas *Alli, BiDLA, ChPo, MnBBF, PoIre*
Downham, Eric 1921- *Au&Wr*

Downham, G *Alli*
Downham, George d1634 *Alli*
Downiche, Anne *Alli*
Downie, David 1838-1927 *DcAmA, DcNAA*
Downie, J And Bird, D J *Alli Sup*
Downie, John *OxCan Sup*
Downie, Leonard, Jr. 1942- *ConAu 49, WrD 1976*
Downie, Mary Alice 1934- *ConAu 25, OxCan Sup, WrD 1976*
Downie, Murdo *Alli, BiDLA*
Downie, N M 1910- *ConAu 17R*
Downie, Thomas *Alli Sup*
Downie, William *OxCan*
Downing, A *Alli Sup*
Downing, A B 1915- *ConAu 29*
Downing, Andrew 1838-1917 *ArizL, ChPo*
Downing, Andrew Jackson 1815-1852 *Alli, AmA, AmA&B, BiD&SB, CyAL 2, DcAmA, DcNAA*
Downing, Bladen *Alli*
Downing, C T *Alli*
Downing, Calybute 1606-1644 *Alli*
Downing, Charles 1802-1885 *DcNAA*
Downing, Charles Toogood *Alli Sup*
Downing, Chris 1931- *ConAu 57*
Downing, Clement *Alli*
Downing, Denis J d1909 *PoIre*
Downing, E H *Alli Sup*
Downing, Edward Collins 1862-1948 *OhA&B, WhWNAA*
Downing, Ellen Mary Patrick 1828-1869 *PoIre*
Downing, Fanny Murdaugh 1835?-1894 *Alli Sup, AmA&B, BiD&SB, BiDSA, DcNAA, LivFWS*
Downing, Frances 1835?-1894 *DcAmA, DcNAA*
Downing, George *Alli, PoIre*
Downing, Sir George 1623-1684 *NewC*
Downing, Sir George 1684?-1749 *NewC*
Downing, Henry 1817-1871 *Alli Sup*
Downing, Henry Francis 1851- *BlkAW*
Downing, J *AmA&B, BiDLA*
Downing, J Hyatt 1888- *WhWNAA*
Downing, Jack *CnDAL, DcAmA, DcNAA*
Downing, Jack 1792-1868 *AmA*
Downing, John *Alli, BiDLA*
Downing, John Allen 1922- *ConAu 53, WrD 1976*
Downing, Joseph *Alli*
Downing, Laura Case 1843-1914 *ArizL, OhA&B*
Downing, Lester N 1914- *ConAu 25*
Downing, Major Jack 1792-1868 *DcEnL, DcNAA, OxAm*
Downing, Mary 1815?-1881 *PoIre*
Downing, Mary A *Alli Sup*
Downing, Olive Inez 1888?-1961 *IndAu 1917*
Downing, Richard Ivan 1915- *Au&Wr*
Downing, Mrs. S E C *Alli Sup*
Downing, Samuel *Alli Sup*
Downing, Todd 1902- *AmA&B*
Downing, Warwick 1931- *ConAu 53*
Downing, William *Alli Sup*
Downinge, Sir George *Alli*
Downman, Hugh 1740-1809 *Alli*
Downs, A *BbtC*
Downs, Annie Sawyer *ChPo*
Downs, Anthony 1930- *ConAu 49*
Downs, Brian Westerdale 1893- *Au&Wr*
Downs, Charles Algernon 1823-1906 *DcNAA*
Downs, Edward 1829?-1884 *OhA&B*
Downs, Elizabeth *Alli Sup*
Downs, Mrs. Georgie *DcNAA*
Downs, Harold *ChPo S2*
Downs, Harriet Street *ChPo*
Downs, Hugh 1921- *ConAu 45*
Downs, Hunton 1918- *ConAu 1R, ConAu 5R*
Downs, Jacques M 1926- *ConAu 37*
Downs, Lenthiel H 1915- *ConAu 25*
Downs, Norton 1918- *ConAu 1R*
Downs, Robert Bingham 1903- *AmA&B, ConAu 1R*
Downs, Robert C S 1937- *ConAu 45, DrAF 1976*
Downs, Sarah Elizabeth 1843- *AmA&B, DcNAA*
Downs, W Scott *OxCan*

Downs, William Andrew 1890- *AmSCAP 66*
Downs, Winfield Scott 1895- *WhWNAA*
Downton, Henry *Alli Sup, ChPo, ChPo S1*
Dows, Henry A *Alli Sup*
Dowse, Robert Edward 1933- *ConAu 21, WrD 1976*
Dowse, Thomas Stretch *Alli Sup*
Dowsett, C F *Alli Sup*
Dowsett, Joseph Morewood 1864- *WhLA*
Dowsing, William *Alli, Alli Sup*
Dowsing, William 1868- *ChPo S1, ChPo S2*
Dowson, Alfred C *Alli Sup*
Dowson, Ernest Christopher 1867-1900 *AtlBL, BrAu 19, CasWL, ChPo, ChPo S1, ChPo S2, Chmbr 3, CnE&AP, DcLEnL, EvLB, MouLC 4, NewC, OxEng, Pen Eng, REn, WebEAL*
Dowson, Henry *Alli Sup*
Dowson, J Emerson And Alfred *Alli Sup*
Dowson, James *Alli*
Dowson, John *Alli Sup*
Dowson, John 1810-1881 *Alli Sup*
Dowson, Joseph Emerson 1844- *WhLA*
Dowson, Thomas *Alli Sup*
Dowst, Henry Payson 1876-1921 *DcNAA*
Dowst, Somerby Rohrer 1926- *ConAu 33*
Dowton, William 1764-1851 *NewC*
Dowty, A A *Alli Sup*
Doxey, Roy W 1908- *ConAu 41*
Doxiadis, Constantinos Apostolos 1913-1975 *ConAu 41, ConAu 57*
Doxopatres *CasWL*
Doxtater, Lee Walter 1885-1935 *DcNAA*
Doyle, Major *Alli*
Doyle, Adrian M C *ConAu XR*
Doyle, Sir Arthur Conan 1859-1930 *Alli Sup, AtlBL, AuBYP, BbD, BiD&SB, BiDPar, CarSB, CasWL, ChPo, ChPo S1, Chmbr 3, CyWA, DcBiA, DcEnA Ap, DcLEnL, EncM&D, EvLB, JBA 1934, LongC, MnBBF, ModBL, NewC, OxEng, Pen Eng, PoIre, RAdv 1, REn, TwCA, TwCA Sup, TwCW, WebEAL, WhCL, WhTwL*
Doyle, Brian 1930- *Au&Wr, ChPo S1, ConAu 53*
Doyle, C A *ChPo*
Doyle, Camilla *ChPo S2*
Doyle, Charles 1928- *ConAu 25, ConP 1970, ConP 1975, WrD 1976*
Doyle, Charles Anthony 1867- *PoIre*
Doyle, Charles Hugo 1904- *CatA 1947*
Doyle, Charles William 1852-1903 *DcAmA, DcNAA*
Doyle, Darley *Alli Sup*
Doyle, David *ConAu XR*
Doyle, Drac *MnBBF*
Doyle, E D'Alton *PoIre*
Doyle, E L *PoIre*
Doyle, Edward *Alli Sup, PoIre*
Doyle, Edward 1854- *AmA&B, DcNAA*
Doyle, Edwin Adams 1867-1941 *OhA&B*
Doyle, Esther M 1910- *ConAu 45*
Doyle, Francis Cuthbert *Alli Sup*
Doyle, Sir Francis Hastings Charles 1810-1888 *Alli Sup, BiD&SB, Br&AmS, BrAu 19, ChPo, ChPo S1, ChPo S2, DcEnA, DcEnL, DcEuL, DcLEnL, EvLB, NewC, OxEng, PoIre*
Doyle, Francis Xavier 1886-1928 *DcNAA*
Doyle, Gerald S *OxCan, OxCan Sup*
Doyle, Hannah *Alli Sup*
Doyle, Henry Grattan 1889-1964 *AmA&B, DcSpL, WhWNAA*
Doyle, J B *Alli Sup*
Doyle, J E *MnBBF*
Doyle, J E P *Alli Sup*
Doyle, James d1834 *Alli*
Doyle, James E *Alli Sup*
Doyle, James Warren *Alli Sup*
Doyle, James Warren 1786-1834 *PoIre*
Doyle, Janet *ChPo S1*
Doyle, John *ChPo*
Doyle, John A *Chmbr 3*
Doyle, John Andrew 1844-1907 *Alli Sup, BrAu 19, NewC*
Doyle, John Hardy 1844-1919 *OhA&B*
Doyle, John M 1884-1940 *DcNAA*

Doyle, John P *Alli Sup*
Doyle, John Robert, Jr. 1910- *ConAu 25*
Doyle, Joseph Beatty 1849-1927 *DcNAA,
OhA&B*
Doyle, Lynn 1873-1961 *CasWL, LongC,
NewC*
Doyle, Lynne 1940?- *IndAu 1917*
Doyle, M M'Donald *PoIre*
Doyle, Marion *AmA&B, ChPo, WhWNAA*
Doyle, Marion Wade 1844- *ChPo S2*
Doyle, Martha Claire MacGowan 1869-
AmA&B, DcAmA
Doyle, Martin *Alli, Alli Sup, BbtC, OxCan,
PoIre*
Doyle, Matthew *PoIre*
Doyle, Michael *PoIre*
Doyle, Michael Joseph 1850- *DcNAA*
Doyle, Mike *OxCan Sup, WrD 1976*
Doyle, Monte 1926- *Au&Wr*
Doyle, Patrick *Alli Sup*
Doyle, Paul A 1925- *ConAu 13R, WrD 1976*
Doyle, Pearla May *TexWr*
Doyle, Phyllis 1901- *Au&Wr*
Doyle, Richard 1824-1883 *Alli Sup, ChPo,
ChPo S1, ChPo S2, DcEuL, NewC*
Doyle, Stanton *MnBBF*
Doyle, Terence *Alli Sup*
Doyle, W *BiDLA*
Doyle, Walter 1899-1945 *AmSCAP 66*
Doyle, William *Alli, BbtC*
Doyle, William A 1820?-1867 *PoIre*
Doyle, William F *Alli Sup*
D'Oyley, Catherine *Alli*
D'Oyley, Charles *Alli, BiDLA*
D'Oyly, Charles John *Alli Sup*
D'Oyly, George 1778-1846 *Alli, BiDLA*
D'Oyly, Robert *Alli*
Doylye, Doctor *Alli*
Doyne, Philip 1733-1765 *PoIre*
Doyne, William Thomas *Alli Sup*
Doyno, Victor A 1937- *ConAu 37*
Doyon, Constant 1875-1927 *DcNAA*
Dozer, Donald Marquand 1905- *ConAu 1R*
Dozier, Arthur, Jr. *BlkAW*
Dozier, Craig Lanier 1920- *ConAu 41*
Dozier, Edward P 1916-1971 *ConAu 29*
Dozier, Orion Theophilus 1848-1925 *BiDSA,
ChPo, ChPo S1, DcNAA*
Drabble, Margaret 1939- *Au&Wr,
ConAu 13R, ConLC 2, ConLC 3,
ConLC 5, ConNov 1972, ConNov 1976,
LongC, ModBL Sup, RAdv 1, TwCW,
WhTwL, WrD 1976*
Drabble, Phil 1914- *Au&Wr*
Drabek, Thomas E 1940- *ConAu 45*
Drabkin, Yakov Davidovich *TwCA,
TwCA Sup*
Drach, Ivan 1936- *ModSL 2*
Drache, Daniel *OxCan Sup*
Drachkovitch, Milorad M 1921- *ConAu 17R*
Drachler, Jacob 1909- *ConAu 61*
Drachler, Rose 1911- *ConAu 53, DrAP 1975*
Drachman, Bernard 1861-1945 *AmA&B,
DcNAA*
Drachman, Edward Ralph 1940- *ConAu 29*
Drachman, Holger 1846-1908 *REn*
Drachman, Julian Moses 1894- *AnMV 1926,
ChPo S1, ConAu 61*
Drachmann, Holger Henrik Herholdt 1846-1908
*BbD, BiD&SB, CasWL, ClDMEuL,
DcEuL, EuA, EvEuW, Pen Eur*
Drachsler, Julius 1889-1927 *DcNAA*
Drackett, Phil 1922- *Au&Wr, ConAu 9R,
WrD 1976*
Draco *NewC, REn*
Draco, F *ConAu XR, SmATA 6, WrD 1976*
Dracon *NewC*
Dracontius, Blossius Aemilius *CasWL, Pen Cl,
Pen Eur*
Draffin, Jasper Owen 1884- *WhWNAA*
Drage, Charles Hardinge 1897- *Au&Wr,
ConAu 5R, WrD 1976*
Drage, Geoffrey *Alli Sup*
Drage, Theodore Swaine *OxCan*
Drage, William *Alli*
Dragge, William *Alli*
Drago, G *Alli Sup*
Drago, Harry Sinclair 1888- *AmA&B,*

OhA&B
Drago, Sinclair *OhA&B*
Dragojevic, Danijel 1934- *CasWL*
Dragon, Carmen 1914- *AmSCAP 66*
Dragonet, Edward *ConAmA, TwCA,
TwCA Sup*
Dragonette, Ree *DrAP 1975*
Dragoo, Don Wayne 1925- *IndAu 1917*
Dragoumis, Ion 1878-1920 *CasWL*
Dragoumis, Julia D 1858- *WhLA*
Dragun, Osvaldo 1929- *CrCD, DcCLA*
Drain, Brooks D 1891- *WhWNAA*
Drainie, John *OxCan*
Drakard, John *Alli, BiDLA*
Drake *Alli*
Drake, Mrs. *Alli*
Drake, Alan *MnBBF*
Drake, Alan Davis 1945- *AmA&B*
Drake, Albert Dee 1935- *ConAu 33,
DrAF 1976, DrAP 1975, WrD 1976*
Drake, Alexander Wilson 1843-1916? *AmA&B,
DcNAA*
Drake, Alice Hutchins 1889?-1975 *ConAu 61*
Drake, Antoinette *ChPo*
Drake, B *BbtC*
Drake, B M *BiDSA*
Drake, Barbara 1939- *ChPo S2, ConAu 33,
DrAF 1976, DrAP 1975*
Drake, Benjamin 1795?-1841 *Alli, AmA,
AmA&B, BiD&SB, BiDSA, CyAL 1,
DcAmA, DcNAA, OhA&B*
Drake, Benjamin M 1800-1860 *BiDSA*
Drake, Charles Bernard *Alli Sup*
Drake, Charles D 1924- *WrD 1976*
Drake, Charles Daniel 1811-1892 *Alli, Alli Sup,
CyAL 1, DcAmA, DcNAA, OhA&B*
Drake, Charles Francis Tyrwhitt 1846-1874
Alli Sup
Drake, Daniel 1785-1852 *Alli, AmA&B,
BiDSA, CyAL 1, DcAmA, DcNAA,
OhA&B, OxAm, REnAL*
Drake, Deamor R 1874- *IndAu 1816*
Drake, Dick *MnBBF*
Drake, Durant 1878-1933 *AmLY, DcNAA,
WhWNAA*
Drake, Edward Cavendish *Alli*
Drake, Emily Hopkins 1877- *OhA&B,
WhWNAA*
Drake, Emma Frances 1849- *DcNAA*
Drake, Ervin M *AmSCAP 66*
Drake, Francis d1770 *Alli*
Drake, Sir Francis 1540?-1596? *Alli, NewC,
REn, REnAL*
Drake, Francis E *Alli Sup*
Drake, Francis Samuel 1828-1885 *Alli Sup,
AmA, AmA&B, BiD&SB, CyAL 2,
DcAmA, DcNAA*
Drake, Frank *MnBBF*
Drake, Frank D 1930- *ConAu 17R*
Drake, Gaston V *ChPo, ChPo S1*
Drake, H W *ChPo*
Drake, Henry Holman *Alli Sup*
Drake, James 1667-1707 *Alli*
Drake, James Frederick 1863-1933 *AmA&B*
Drake, James Madison 1837-1913 *Alli Sup,
DcAmA, DcNAA*
Drake, Jeanie *BiDSA, DcAmA*
Drake, Jim 1935- *AmSCAP 66*
Drake, Joan *Alli, WrD 1976*
Drake, Joan Howard 1924- *Au&Wr,
ConAu 13R*
Drake, John *MnBBF*
Drake, John 1846- *ChPo S1*
Drake, Joseph Rodman 1795-1820 *Alli, AmA,
AmA&B, BbD, BiD&SB, ChPo,
ChPo S2, Chmbr 3, CnDAL, CyAL 1,
DcAmA, DcLEnL, DcNAA, EvLB,
OxAm, Pen Am, REn, REnAL*
Drake, L H *ChPo S1*
Drake, Leah Bodine 1914- *ChPo, ChPo S1*
Drake, Lisl *ConAu XR*
Drake, Maria Upham *ChPo*
Drake, Mary 1913- *TexWr*
Drake, Michael 1935- *ConAu 25*
Drake, Milton 1916- *AmSCAP 66*
Drake, Nathan *Alli, BiDLA*
Drake, Nathan 1766-1836 *Alli, DcEnL*
Drake, Nicholas *ChPo S1*

Drake, O T *Alli Sup*
Drake, R *Alli*
Drake, Richard Bryant 1925- *ConAu 37*
Drake, Robert 1930- *ConAu 17R*
Drake, Rodney *MnBBF*
Drake, Roger *Alli*
Drake, Rupert *MnBBF*
Drake, St. Clair 1911- *AmA&B, LivBA*
Drake, Samuel Adams 1833-1905 *Alli,
Alli Sup, AmA, AmA&B, BbD,
BiD&SB, ChPo S1, CyAL 2, DcAmA,
DcNAA*
Drake, Samuel Gardner 1798-1875 *Alli,
Alli Sup, AmA, AmA&B, BiD&SB,
CyAL 1, DcAmA, DcNAA, OxCan*
Drake, Sandra *BlkAW*
Drake, Stillman 1910- *ConAu 41*
Drake, Thomas Edward 1907- *IndAu 1917*
Drake, W *Alli*
Drake, W Magruder 1914- *ConAu 41*
Drake, W Raymond 1913- *Au&Wr,
ConAu 53, WrD 1976*
Drake, William *Alli, Alli Sup*
Drake, Sir William *Alli*
Drake, William A 1899-1965 *AmA&B,
OhA&B*
Drake, William D 1922- *ConAu 21*
Drake, William Earle 1903- *ConAu P-1,
WrD 1976*
Drake, William Henry 1856-1927 *ChPo*
Drake, Sir William Richard 1817- *Alli Sup*
Drake-Brockman, Henrietta Frances York 1918-
DcLEnL
Drake-Brockman, Ralph E 1875- *WhLA*
Drakeford, I *Alli Sup*
Drakeford, John W 1914- *ConAu 1R*
Dralle, Elizabeth Mary 1910- *ConAu 1R*
Dralloc, John *Alli, BiDLA Sup*
Dralloc, N *BiDLA*
Drane, Augusta T 1823- *Alli Sup, ChPo S1*
Drane, J W C *Alli Sup*
Drane, James 1930- *ConAu 13R*
Dranfield, Charles And Halifax, G D *Alli Sup*
Drange, Theodore M 1934- *ConAu 37*
Dranmor 1823-1888 *BiD&SB, OxGer*
Dransfeld, Jane 1875- *AmA&B, ChPo,
WhWNAA*
Dransfield, Michael Pender 1948- *ConAu 37*
Dransfield, William *Alli, Alli Sup*
Drant, Thomas *Alli*
Drant, Thomas d1578? *Alli, CrE&SL*
Drapeau, Stanislas 1821-1893 *BbtC, OxCan*
Drapeau, Stanislaus 1821-1893 *DcNAA*
Draper, Alfred Ernest 1924- *Au&Wr,
ConAu 33, WrD 1976*
Draper, Andrew Sloan 1848-1913 *AmA&B,
ChPo, DcAmA, DcNAA, OhA&B*
Draper, Arthur Stimson 1882- *WhWNAA*
Draper, Ben *MnBBF*
Draper, Bourne Hall *ChPo S1*
Draper, Canyon *ConAu XR*
Draper, Cena Christopher 1907- *ConAu 17R,
WrD 1976*
Draper, Charles *Alli*
Draper, Charles Hiram 1888- *WhWNAA*
Draper, Charles Robert 1914- *Au&Wr*
Draper, E *ChPo*
Draper, E A *Alli*
Draper, Earle Sumner 1893- *WhWNAA*
Draper, Edgar 1926- *ConAu 13R*
Draper, Edgar Marian 1894- *WhWNAA*
Draper, Edward Alured *BiDLA*
Draper, Edythe Squier 1883- *WhWNAA*
Draper, Elizabeth Fowler *TexWr*
Draper, Ellinor Elizabeth Nancy 1915-
ConAu 17R, WrD 1976
Draper, Francis 1832- *Alli Sup, ChPo S1*
Draper, G *Alli Sup*
Draper, George *Alli Sup*
Draper, Hal 1914- *ConAu 17R, WrD 1976*
Draper, Harry Napier *Alli Sup*
Draper, Hastings *ChPo, MnBBF*
Draper, Henry *Alli, BiDLA, CyAL 2*
Draper, Henry 1837-1882 *Alli Sup, BiDSA,
DcAmA, DcNAA*
Draper, James *OxCan Sup*
Draper, John *Alli Sup*
Draper, John 1702-1762 *AmA&B*

Draper, John Christopher 1835-1885 *Alli Sup,*
BiDSA, CyAL 2, DcAmA, DcNAA
Draper, John William 1811-1882 *Alli, Alli Sup,*
AmA, AmA&B, BbD, BiD&SB,
Chmbr 3, CyAL 2, DcAmA, DcEnL,
DcNAA, EvLB, REnAL
Draper, John William 1893- *AmA&B,*
ConAu P-1, WhWNAA
Draper, Lyman Copeland 1815-1891 *Alli,*
Alli Sup, AmA, AmA&B, BiD&SB,
BiDSA, DcAmA, DcNAA
Draper, M L Y *Alli Sup*
Draper, Nancy *AuBYP*
Draper, Norman R 1931- *ConAu 53*
Draper, Peter *Alli Sup*
Draper, Richard 1726?-1774 *AmA&B*
Draper, Ruth 1884-1956 *REnAL*
Draper, Theodore 1912- *AmA&B,*
ConAu 13R
Draper, W *BiDLA*
Draper, W H *Alli, BbtC*
Draper, Warren F *Alli Sup*
Draper, William *Alli*
Draper, Sir William 1721-1787 *Alli, CyAL 1*
Draper, William Columbus 1850- *IndAu 1816*
Draper, William Franklin 1842-1910 *DcNAA*
Draper, William George 1825-1868 *BbtC,*
DcNAA
Draper, William Henry 1801-1877 *OxCan*
Draper, William Henry 1855- *ChPo, ChPo S2*
Drapes, Edward *Alli*
Drapes, John Lamphier *Alli Sup*
Drapkin, Herbert 1916- *ConAu 33*
Drapkin, Israel 1906- *ConAu 57*
Drave, Winston *MnBBF*
Drawbaugh, Jacob W, Jr. 1928- *AmSCAP 66*
Drawbell, James Wedgwood 1899- *Au&Wr*
Drawbridge, Cyprian Leycester 1868- *WhLA*
Drawcansir, Sir Alexander 1707-1754 *DcEnL,*
OxEng
Draxe, Thomas *Alli*
Draxler-Mandred, Karl Ferdinand 1806-1879
BiD&SB
Dray, Thomas *Alli*
Dray, William H 1921- *ConAu 33*
Drayer, Adam Matthew 1913- *ConAu 9R*
Drayne, George *AmA&B, WhWNAA*
Drayson, A W *MnBBF*
Drayson, Alfred Wilkes 1827- *Alli Sup*
Drayson, Caroline Agnes *Alli Sup*
Drayson, Dorothy Dyott *ChPo*
Drayson, Phyllis *ChPo*
Drayson, R A *MnBBF*
Drayton, Charles Geoffrey 1924- *Au&Wr*
Drayton, Geoffrey *WebEAL*
Drayton, Grace Gebbie 1877-1936 *AmA&B,*
AmLY, ChPo, WhWNAA
Drayton, Henry Shipman 1840?-1923 *Alli Sup,*
AmLY, DcNAA
Drayton, J B *Alli, BiDLA*
Drayton, John 1766-1822 *Alli, AmA, BiDSA,*
CyAL 1, DcAmA, DcNAA
Drayton, Joseph *EarAB*
Drayton, Lillian R *DcNAA*
Drayton, Michael 1563-1631 *Alli, AtlBL, BbD,*
BiD&SB, BrAu, CasWL, ChPo,
ChPo S1, Chmbr 1, CnE&AP, CrE&SL,
CriT 1, CyWA, DcEnA, DcEnL, DcEuL,
DcLEnL, EvLB, McGWD, MouLC 1,
NewC, OxEng, Pen Eng, REn, WebEAL
Drayton, Ronald *BlkAW*
Drayton, Thomas *Alli, BlkAW*
Drayton, William Henry 1742-1779 *Alli,*
BiDSA
Drayton, William Henry 1742-1778 *CyAL 1*
Drayton, William Henry 1742-1779 *DcAmA,*
DcNAA, OxAm
Drda, Jan 1915-1970 *CasWL, ModSL 2,*
Pen Eur
Drea, E V *PoIre*
Dreamer *ConAmA*
Drebel, Cornelius 1572-1634 *Alli*
Dredge, James *Alli Sup*
Dreer, Herman 1889- *BlkAW*
Drees, Charles William 1851-1926 *OhA&B*
Dreesen, Minnie Roberts 1886?- *TexWr,*
WhWNAA
Dreher, E S *ChPo S1*

Dreher, William Counts 1856- *WhWNAA*
Dreier, Frederik Henrik Hennings 1827-1853
CasWL
Dreier, Thomas 1884- *AmA&B, WhWNAA*
Dreifort, John E 1943- *ConAu 45*
Dreifus, Claudia 1944- *ConAu 45*
Dreifuss, Kurt 1897- *ConAu 1R*
Dreikurs, Rudolf 1897- *AmA&B, ConAu 1R*
Dreikurs, Rudolph 1897-1972 *ConAu 33*
Dreiser, Paul *AmA&B*
Dreiser, Theodore 1871-1945 *AmA&B, AmLY,*
AmWr, AtlBL, CasWL, Chmbr 3,
CnDAL, CnMD, CnMWL, ConAmA,
ConAmL, CyWA, DcAmA, DcBiA,
DcLEnL, DcNAA, EncM&D, EncWL,
EvLB, IndAu 1816, LongC, ModAL,
ModAL Sup, ModWD, OxAm, OxEng,
Pen Am, RAdv 1, RCom, REn, REnAL,
TwCA, TwCA Sup, TwCW, WebEAL,
WhTwL, WhWNAA
Dreitzel, Hans Peter 1935- *ConAu 41*
Drekmeier, Charles 1927- *ConAu 1R*
Drelincourt, P *Alli*
Drennan, John Swanwick 1809-1893 *PoIre*
Drennan, Marie 1890-1950 *AnMV 1926,*
OhA&B, WhWNAA
Drennan, William *Alli, BiDLA, Chmbr 3*
Drennan, William 1754-1820 *BbD, BrAu 19,*
ChPo, PoIre, DcEnL
Drennan, William, Jr. 1802-1873 *PoIre*
Drennen, D A 1925- *ConAu 1R*
Drenova, A S *Pen Eur*
Dresbach, Glenn Ward 1889-1968 *AmA&B,*
ChPo, ChPo S1, ChPo S2, ConAu 5R,
REnAL, TexWr, WhWNAA
Drescher, John M 1928- *ConAu 49*
Drescher, Martin 1863-1920 *CasWL*
Drescher, Seymour 1934- *ConAu 9R*
Dreschfeld, Julius *Alli Sup*
Dresner, Hal 1937- *ConAu 13R*
Dresner, Samuel 1925- *WrD 1976*
Dresner, Samuel H 1923- *ConAu 5R*
Dressel, DeWitt Ewing *WhWNAA*
Dressel, Paul L 1910- *ConAu 9R*
Dresser, Christopher *Alli Sup*
Dresser, Davis 1904- *AmA&B, EncM&D,*
WorAu
Dresser, Helen McCloy 1904- *Au&Wr,*
ConAu XR
Dresser, Henry Eeles *Alli Sup*
Dresser, Horace E 1803-1877 *Alli Sup,*
ChPo S1, DcNAA
Dresser, Horatio Willis 1866-1954 *AmA&B,*
AmLY, BiD&SB, DcAmA
Dresser, Julius A 1838-1893 *AmA*
Dresser, Lawrence *IlBYP*
Dresser, Paul 1857-1906 *AmA&B,*
AmSCAP 66, IndAu 1917, OxAm,
REnAL
Dresslar, Fletcher Bascom 1858-1930 *DcNAA,*
IndAu 1917
Dressler, Marie 1873-1934 *AmA&B, DcNAA,*
REn
Dretske, Frederick I 1932- *ConAu 25*
Dreux, Albert 1887-1949 *CanWr, OxCan*
Drew *TwCA, TwCA Sup*
Drew, Alfred *ChPo S1*
Drew, Andrew 1792-1878 *Alli Sup, OxCan*
Drew, Benjamin 1812-1903 *Alli Sup, BbtC,*
DcNAA
Drew, Bernard *ChPo S1*
Drew, Bess Murphy *TexWr*
Drew, Catherine *Alli Sup*
Drew, Charles Edward 1890- *WhWNAA*
Drew, Columbus *BiDSA*
Drew, Donald J 1920- *ConAu 57*
Drew, Dorothy A H *ChPo S1*
Drew, Dwight Chandler 1878-1932 *DcNAA*
Drew, Edward *Alli, BiDLA*
Drew, Edwin *Alli Sup*
Drew, Elizabeth 1887-1965 *ChPo, ConAu 5R*
Drew, Francis Browning Drew Bickerstaffe 1858-
Alli Sup
Drew, Francis Robert *Alli Sup*
Drew, Fraser 1913- *ConAu 13R, WrD 1976*
Drew, Frederic *Alli Sup*
Drew, G S *Alli*
Drew, George Smith 1819-1880 *Alli Sup*

Drew, Gilman Arthur 1868-1934 *DcNAA*
Drew, Gordon *MnBBF*
Drew, James B C *Alli Sup*
Drew, John *Alli, Alli Sup*
Drew, John 1827-1862 *OxAm*
Drew, John 1853-1927 *AmA&B, DcNAA*
Drew, John G *Alli Sup*
Drew, Joseph *Alli Sup*
Drew, Katherine Fischer 1923- *ConAu 9R*
Drew, Mary Frances *Alli Sup*
Drew, Melville *MnBBF*
Drew, Michael *MnBBF*
Drew, Morgan *ConAu XR*
Drew, Reginald *MnBBF*
Drew, Richard *Alli*
Drew, Robert *Alli*
Drew, Samuel 1765-1833 *Alli, BiDLA*
Drew, Sidney *MnBBF*
Drew, Thomas 1800-1870 *PoIre*
Drew, Vaughan *MnBBF*
Drew, W B *Alli Sup*
Drew, William *Alli, BiDLA*
Drew, William A 1798- *Alli*
Drew, William Henry *Alli Sup*
Drew-Bear, Robert 1901- *ConAu 33*
Drewe, Edward *Alli*
Drewe, Elizabeth Duncan d1879 *Alli Sup*
Drewery, Mary 1918- *ConAu 25, SmATA 6,*
WrD 1976
Drewett, Mrs. E *Alli Sup*
Drewitt, Thomas d1803 *Alli, BiDLA,*
BiDLA Sup
Drewry, A Hill *Alli Sup*
Drewry, C S *Alli*
Drewry, Carleton 1901- *AmA&B*
Drewry, Charles Stewart *Alli Sup*
Drewry, Edith Stewart *Alli Sup*
Drewry, George Overend *Alli Sup*
Drewry, Guy Carleton 1901- *Au&Wr,*
ConAu 5R
Drewry, John Eldridge 1902- *AmA&B,*
WhWNAA, WrD 1976
Drewry, P H 1875- *WhWNAA*
Drewry, William Sidney *BiDSA*
Drexel, Jay B *ConAu XR*
Drexler, J F *ConAu XR*
Drexler, Rosalyn 1926- *AmA&B, ConDr,*
ConLC 2, ConLC 6, DrAF 1976,
ModAL Sup, WrD 1976
Drey, S *Alli Sup*
Dreyer, Dave 1894- *AmSCAP 66*
Dreyer, Edward C 1937- *ConAu 21*
Dreyer, Max 1862-1946 *CIDMEuL, ModWD,*
OxGer
Dreyer, Peter Richard 1939- *Au&Wr*
Dreyfus, Abraham 1847- *BiD&SB*
Dreyfus, Alfred 1859-1935 *NewC, REn*
Dreyfus, Edward A 1937- *ConAu 37,*
WrD 1976
Dreyfus, Fred *ConAu XR*
Dreyfus, Hubert Lederer 1929- *ConAu 33,*
IndAu 1917
Dreyfus, Lilian Gertrude *ChPo*
Dreyfus, Stuart E 1931- *IndAu 1917*
Dreyfuss, Henry 1904-1972 *ConAu 37,*
ConAu 45
Dreyspring, Adolphe 1835-1907 *Alli Sup,*
DcNAA
Drezen, Youenn *Pen Eur*
Dribben, Judith Strick 1923- *ConAu 37*
Driberg, Thomas Edward Neil 1905- *Au&Wr*
Driberg, Tom 1905- *WrD 1976*
Driesch, Hans 1867-1941 *BiDPar*
Drieu LaRochelle, Pierre 1893-1945 *CasWL,*
CIDMEuL, EncWL, EvEuW, OxFr,
Pen Eur
Driftwood, Penelope *ConAu 57*
Driggs, Collins H 1911- *AmSCAP 66*
Driggs, Frank Howard 1895- *WhWNAA*
Driggs, George W *Alli Sup*
Driggs, Howard Roscoe 1873-1963 *AmA&B,*
WhWNAA
Driggs, Laurence LaTourette 1876-1945
AmA&B, DcNAA, WhWNAA
Drille, Hearton *Alli Sup*
Drimmer, Frederick 1916- *ConAu 61*
Drinan, Adam 1903- *ChPo S1, ConP 1970,*
ConP 1975, WrD 1976

Drinan, Robert F 1920- *ConAu 9R*
Dring, Nathaniel *ConAu XR*
Drinkall, Gordon Spencer 1927- *Au&Wr,*
ConAu 9R
Drinker, Anne 1827- *Alli, AmA&B, BiD&SB,*
DcAmA, DcNAA
Drinker, Cecil Kent 1887- *WhWNAA*
Drinker, Henry Sturgis 1850-1937 *Alli Sup,*
AmLY, DcNAA, WhWNAA
Drinkrow, John *ConAu 49, WrD 1976*
Drinkwater, Albert E *Alli Sup*
Drinkwater, C H *BbtC*
Drinkwater, Francis Harold 1886- *Au&Wr,*
BkC 2, CatA 1952, ConAu 1R,
WrD 1976
Drinkwater, Harry *Alli Sup*
Drinkwater, Hartley *MnBBF*
Drinkwater, Jennie Maria *Alli Sup, AmA&B,*
DcNAA
Drinkwater, John 1882-1937 *Alli, BiDLA,*
CasWL, ChPo, ChPo S1, ChPo S2,
Chmbr 3, CnMD, CnThe, DcLEnL,
EvLB, JBA 1934, LongC, McGWD,
ModBL, ModWD, NewC, OxEng,
Pen Eng, REn, St&VC, TwCA,
TwCA Sup, WebEAL, WhLA
Drinkwater, Penny 1929- *WrD 1976*
Drinnon, Richard 1925- *ConAu 13R*
Dripps, Robert Dunning *ChPo S2*
Driscoll, Annette Sophia 1857- *WhWNAA*
Driscoll, Barry *IlCB 1966*
Driscoll, Charles Benedict 1885-1951 *AmA&B,*
REnAL, WhWNAA
Driscoll, Clara 1881-1945 *AmA&B, DcNAA*
Driscoll, Dennis 1912- *Au&Wr*
Driscoll, Frederick 1830- *BbtC, DcNAA*
Driscoll, Gertrude 1898?-1975 *ConAu 61*
Driscoll, Joseph 1902-1954 *AmA&B*
Driscoll, Louise 1875-1957 *AmA&B, AmLY,*
AnMV 1926, ChPo, WhWNAA
Driscoll, Peter 1942- *ConAu 49*
Drisler, Henry 1818-1897 *Alli, CyAL 1,*
DcAmA, DcNAA
Drive, G J *Alli Sup*
Driver, Abraham *Alli*
Driver, Charles Jonathan 1939- *Au&Wr,*
ConAu 29, ConNov 1976, ConP 1970,
WrD 1976
Driver, Christopher Prout 1932- *Au&Wr,*
ConAu 57, WrD 1976
Driver, Donald *ConDr*
Driver, Godfrey Rolles 1892-1975 *ConAu 21,*
ConAu 57
Driver, Harold Edson 1907- *ConAu 1R*
Driver, Henry Austen *ChPo S1*
Driver, James *Alli Sup*
Driver, Leeotis Lincoln 1867- *IndAu 1816*
Driver, S P *ChPo*
Driver, Samuel Rolles 1846-1914 *Alli Sup,*
BiD&SB, BrAu 19
Driver, Tom 1925- *ConAu 1R*
Driver, Vincent *Alli Sup*
Driver, William *Alli*
Driving Hawk, Virginia *ConAu 49*
Drobisch, Gustav Theodor 1811-1882 *BiD&SB*
Droch *AmA&B, AmLY XR, ChPo,*
DcAmA, WhWNAA
Droege, John Albert 1861- *WhWNAA*
Droescher, Vitus B 1925- *ConAu 33*
Droguett, Carlos 1915- *DcCLA*
Drohan, Neville Thomas 1931- *Au&Wr*
Droit, Michael 1923- *Au&Wr*
Droit, Michel 1923- *ConAu 5R*
Droke, Maxwell 1896-1959 *IndAu 1917*
Drolet, Antonio *OxCan*
Drolet, Gustave Adolphe 1844-1904 *DcNAA*
Drollinger, Karl Friedrich 1688-1742 *DcEuL,*
OxGer
Dromgoole, J P *Alli Sup*
Dromgoole, Miss Will Allen 1860-1934 *AmA&B,*
BiD&SB, BiDSA, ChPo, ChPo S1,
DcAmA, DcNAA, WhWNAA
Dron, R W 1869- *WhLA*
Drone, Eaton Sylvester 1842-1917 *Alli Sup,*
DcAmA, DcNAA
Dronke, Ernst 1822- *OxGer*
Droogenbroeck, Jan Van 1835-1902 *BiD&SB*
Droop, Henry Richmond *Alli Sup*

Drop Shot *AmA&B*
Drope, Francis *Alli*
Drope, John *Alli*
Droppers, Carl Hyink 1918- *ConAu 5R,*
WrD 1976
Droppers, Garrett 1860-1927 *DcNAA*
Droppers, Garrett And Dachsel, C A P *Alli Sup*
Dropsie, Moses Aaron 1821-1905 *DcNAA*
Dror, Yehezkel 1928- *ConAu 21, WrD 1976*
Drossaart Lulofs, H J 1906- *ConAu 13R*
Drossinis, Georg 1859- *BiD&SB*
Drost, Aarnout 1810-1834 *CasWL, Pen Eur*
Droste, Coenraat 1642-1734 *CasWL*
Droste, Georg 1866-1935 *CasWL*
Droste-Hulshoff, Annette Von 1797-1848 *BbD,*
BiD&SB, CasWL, DcEuL, EuA, EvEuW,
OxGer, Pen Eur, REn
Droste ZuVischering, K A, Freiherr Von
1773-1845 *OxGer*
Drotning, Phillip T 1920- *ConAu 25*
Drouart La Vache *CasWL*
Drouet, Bessie 1879?-1940 *DcNAA*
Drouet, Juliette 1806-1883 *OxFr*
Drouet, Minou 1947- *ChPo*
Drouet, Robert 1870- *DcAmA*
Drought, Charles Edward *Alli Sup*
Drought, E D *Alli Sup*
Drought, James 1931- *AmA&B, ConAu 5R*
Drought, Robert *Alli, BiDLA*
Drouin, Francis M 1901- *ConAu 37*
Drouville, J B *Alli, BiDLA*
Drower, Lady Ethel Stefana 1879-1972 *Au&Wr,*
ConAu P-1
Drower, Margaret Stefana 1911- *WrD 1976*
Drown, Daniel Augustus 1823-1900 *Alli Sup,*
ChPo, ChPo S2, DcNAA
Drown, Edward Staples 1861-1936 *DcNAA,*
WhWNAA
Drown, Harold J 1904- *ConAu 49*
Drowne, Tatiana B 1913- *ConAu 17R*
Droysen, Johann Gustav 1808-1884 *BiD&SB*
Droz, Antoine-Gustave 1832-1895 *OxFr*
Droz, Gustave 1832-1895 *BiD&SB*
Droze, Wilmon Henry 1924- *ConAu 17R*
Drozhzhin, Spiridon Dmitrievich 1848-1930
CasWL, DcRusL
Drubert, John H 1925- *ConAu 45*
Druce, Christopher *ChPo S2, ConAu XR*
Druce, Clifford John 1886- *ChPo S1*
Druce, G C 1850- *Alli Sup, WhLA*
Druce, Robert 1929- *Au&Wr*
Drucker, A P R 1876- *WhWNAA*
Drucker, Andre 1909- *Au&Wr*
Drucker, Daniel Charles 1918- *WrD 1976*
Drucker, H M 1942- *WrD 1976*
Drucker, Peter F 1909- *AmA&B, ConAu 61*
Drucker, Peter Ferdlinand *Au&Wr*
Drucker, Phillip *OxCan XR*
Drueck, Charles John 1873-1945 *IndAu 1917*
Druery, Charles T *Alli Sup*
Druery, Charles Thomas *ChPo S1*
Druery, J H *Alli*
Druid, The *BrAu 19, NewC*
Druid, David *HsB&A*
Druillettes, Gabriel 1610-1681 *OxCan*
Druitt, George *PoIre*
Druitt, Robert 1814-1883 *Alli, Alli Sup*
Druker, Philip *OxCan*
Drukker, J *ConAu XR*
Drukker, Sara Tobias 1852-1914 *OhA&B*
Druks, Herbert 1937- *ConAu 21, WrD 1976*
Drum, Bob *ConAu XR*
Drum, Robert F 1918- *ConAu 5R*
Drum, Walter 1870- *AmLY*
Drumev, Vassil 1840-1901 *CasWL*
Drumheller, Sidney J 1923- *ConAu 53*
Drumm, George 1874-1959 *AmSCAP 66*
Drummond *Alli, BiDLA*
Drummond, Mrs. *ChPo*
Drummond, A J *Alli Sup*
Drummond, A T *BbtC*
Drummond, Abernethy *Alli*
Drummond, Alex *Alli*
Drummond, Alex M *Alli*
Drummond, Alison 1903- *WrD 1976*
Drummond, David *Alli Sup*
Drummond, David Thomas Kerr d1876 *Alli,*
Alli Sup, PoCh

Drummond, Donald F 1914- *ConAu 1R*
Drummond, Dorothy W 1928- *ConAu 41*
Drummond, E A H 1758-1830 *Alli*
Drummond, E Hay *BiDLA*
Drummond, Edith Marie Dulce 1883-1970
Au&Wr, ConAu P-1
Drummond, Edward *Alli*
Drummond, Ellen Lane 1897- *ConAu 1R*
Drummond, G M *Alli Sup*
Drummond, George H *Alli*
Drummond, George William Auriole Hay
1761-1807 *ChPo*
Drummond, Sir Gordon 1771-1854 *OxCan*
Drummond, Mrs. H *Alli*
Drummond, Hamilton *Alli Sup, PoIre*
Drummond, Harold D 1916- *ConAu 33*
Drummond, Harriet *Alli*
Drummond, Henry *Chmbr 3*
Drummond, Henry 1786-1860 *Alli, Alli Sup*
Drummond, Henry 1851-1897 *Alli Sup, BbD,*
BiD&SB, BrAu 19, EvLB, NewC,
OxEng
Drummond, Henry Home *Alli, BiDLA*
Drummond, Humphrey 1922- *Au&Wr*
Drummond, Ian M 1933- *ConAu 37,*
WrD 1976
Drummond, Isabel *WhWNAA*
Drummond, Ivor *WrD 1976*
Drummond, J *ChPo S2*
Drummond, James *Alli Sup*
Drummond, James 1835- *Alli Sup, BiD&SB*
Drummond, James 1869- *WhLA*
Drummond, James L *Alli*
Drummond, John *Alli, Alli Sup, MnBBF*
Drummond, Lord John *Alli*
Drummond, John Dorman 1915- *Au&Wr*
Drummond, Josiah Hayden 1827-1902 *Alli Sup,*
DcAmA, DcNAA
Drummond, June 1923- *ConAu 13R*
Drummond, Kenneth H 1922- *ConAu 17R*
Drummond, Lewis Henry 1848-1929 *DcNAA*
Drummond, M *Alli Sup*
Drummond, Patrick Hamilton 1857- *WhLA*
Drummond, Peter Robert 1802-1879 *Alli Sup*
Drummond, R *Alli*
Drummond, Richard H 1916- *ConAu 41*
Drummond, Robert Blackley *Alli Sup*
Drummond, Robert Hay 1711-1776 *Alli*
Drummond, Robert J 1858- *WhLA*
Drummond, Sara King 1871-1909 *DcNAA*
Drummond, T *Alli, BiDLA*
Drummond, T B *Alli*
Drummond, Thomas *Alli*
Drummond, Violet Hilda 1911- *Au&Wr,*
ConAu 13R, IlBYP, IlCB 1956,
IlCB 1966, SmATA 6, ThBJA,
WrD 1976
Drummond, W H *Chmbr 3*
Drummond, W V *Alli Sup*
Drummond, Walter *AuBYP, ConAu XR,*
ThBJA
Drummond, Sir William d1828 *Alli, BiDLA*
Drummond, William, Earl Of Hawthornden
1585-1649 *Alli, BbD, BiD&SB, CasWL,*
ChPo, ChPo S1, Chmbr 1, CnE&AP,
CrE&SL, DcEnA, DcEnL, DcEuL, EvLB,
Pen Eng, WebEAL
Drummond, William Hamilton 1778-1865 *Alli,*
BiDLA, PoIre
Drummond, William Henry 1845-1879 *Alli Sup*
Drummond, William Henry 1854-1907 *CanWr,*
CasWL, ChPo, ChPo S1, ChPo S2,
DcLEnL, DcNAA, EvLB, NewC, OxCan,
OxEng, PoIre, REn Sup, REnAL, TwCA,
TwCA Sup
Drummond DeAndrade, Carlos 1902- *CasWL,*
EncWL, Pen Am, TwCW, WhTwL
Drummond Of Hawthornden, William 1585-1649
BrAu, DcLEnL, NewC, OxEng, REn
Drumont, Edouard 1844-1917 *OxFr*
Druon, Maurice Samuel Roger Charles 1918-
Au&Wr, CasWL, ConAu 13R, EncWL,
Pen Eur, REn, WorAu
Drury *Alli*
Drury, Allen 1918- *AmA&B, ConAu 57,*
ConNov 1972, ConNov 1976, OxAm,
REnAL, TwCW, WorAu, WrD 1976
Drury, Anna Harriet *Alli, Alli Sup, ChPo,*

Polre
Drury, Augustus Waldo 1851-1935 *Alli Sup,*
DcAmA, DcNAA, IndAu 1816, OhA&B,
WhWNAA
Drury, Miss B Paxson *Alli Sup*
Drury, C W C *MnBBF*
Drury, Charles *Alli*
Drury, Charles 1890- *AmSCAP 66*
Drury, Clare Marie *ConAu XR*
Drury, Clifford Merrill 1897- *AmA&B,*
ConAu 9R, WhPNW, WhWNAA
Drury, Drew *Alli*
Drury, E C *OxCan*
Drury, Edward *Alli*
Drury, Edward James *Alli Sup*
Drury, Francis Keese Wynkoop 1878-1954
AmA&B, WhWNAA
Drury, Heber *Alli Sup*
Drury, Honor *ChPo S1*
Drury, James Westbrook 1919- *ConAu 5R*
Drury, John 1898-1972 *Au&Wr, ConAu 5R,*
ConAu 33
Drury, John Benjamin 1838-1909 *Alli Sup,*
DcAmA, DcNAA
Drury, Margaret Josephine 1937- *ConAu 53*
Drury, Marion Richardson 1849-1939 *Alli Sup,*
DcAmA, IndAu 1816
Drury, Maxine Cole 1914- *ConAu 5R,*
WrD 1976
Drury, Michael *ConAu 49*
Drury, O'Brien *Alli*
Drury, R *BiDLA*
Drury, Robert *Alli*
Drury, Samuel Smith 1878- *WhWNAA*
Drury, Tresa Way 1937- *ConAu 53*
Drury, W *Alli Sup*
Drury, W B *Alli*
Drury, Wells 1851-1932 *AmLY, DcNAA*
Drury, William *Alli*
Drury, William Vallancy *Alli Sup*
Drushinin, Alexander Vassilyevitch 1824-1864
BiD&SB
Druten *TwCA, TwCA Sup*
Drutman, Irving 1910- *AmSCAP 66*
Druxman, Michael Barnett 1941- *ConAu 49*
Druyanov, Alter 1870-1938 *CasWL, Pen Eur*
Druzbacka, Elzbieta 1695-1765 *CasWL*
Druzhina-Osor'in, Callistratus *Pen Eur*
Druzhinin, Alexander Vasilyevich 1824-1864
CasWL, DcRusL
Drvota, Mojmir 1923- *ConAu 57*
Dryander *CasWL*
Dryander, Jonas 1748-1810 *Alli*
Dryansky, G Y *ConAu 49*
Dryasdust, The Rev. Dr. *DcEnL*
Drych, Theophilus Evans *Alli*
Dryden, A A *Alli Sup*
Dryden, Adam *Alli Sup*
Dryden, Cecil Pearl 1887- *ConAu 25,*
WhPNW
Dryden, Charles d1704 *Alli*
Dryden, Sir Henry Edward Leigh 1818-
Alli Sup
Dryden, John *Alli, ConAu XR*
Dryden, John 1631-1700 *Alli, AtlBL, BbD,*
BiD&SB, BrAu, CasWL, ChPo,
ChPo S1, Chmbr 1, CnE&AP, CnThe,
CriT 2, CyWA, DcEnA, DcEnL, DcEuL,
DcLEnL, EvLB, McGWD, MouLC 1,
NewC, OxEng, Pen Eng, PoCh, PoLE,
RAdv 1, RCom, REn, REnAL, WebEAL
Dryden, John 1668?-1701 *Alli*
Dryden, John Fairfield 1839-1911 *DcNAA*
Drydog, Doggrel *DcEnL*
Dryer, Charles Redway Wilmarth 1850?-927
AmLY, DcNAA, IndAu 1917
Dryerre, Henry 1848- *ChPo*
Dryerre, Henry 1881- *WhLA*
Drysdale, A H *Alli Sup*
Drysdale, Alexander H *ChPo S1*
Drysdale, Alfred E *Alli Sup*
Drysdale, Charles Robert *Alli Sup*
Drysdale, Charles Vickery 1874- *WhLA*
Drysdale, John 1718-1788 *Alli*
Drysdale, John James *Alli Sup*
Drysdale, William *Alli*

Drysdale, William 1852-1901 *Alli Sup,*
BiD&SB, BiDLA, CarSB, DcAmA,
DcNAA
Drysen, Paul *Alli Sup*
Dryswich, Ambrose *Alli*
Drzazga, John 1907- *ConAu P-1*
Drzic, Djore *Pen Eur*
Drzic, Dzore 1461-1501 *CasWL*
Drzic, Marin 1508?-1567 *CasWL, Pen Eur*
D'Souza, C T *Alli Sup*
D'Souza, Jerome 1897- *CatA 1952*
Dua, R P 1930- *ConAu 25*
Dua, Ramparkash 1931- *WrD 1976*
Du'aji, 'Ali Ad- 1909-1949 *DcOrL 3*
Duane, Alexander 1858-1926 *DcNAA,*
WhWNAA
Duane, James d1797 *Alli*
Duane, James Chatham 1824-1897 *Alli Sup,*
DcAmA
Duane, Jim *ConAu XR*
Duane, L Ray 1897- *AmSCAP 66*
Duane, Matthew *Alli*
Duane, Richard B *Alli Sup*
Duane, W N *Alli Sup*
Duane, William *Alli Sup, BbtC*
Duane, William 1760-1835 *Alli, AmA&B,*
CyAL 1, DcAmA, DcNAA, OxAm
Duane, William 1808-1882 *Alli, DcAmA,*
DcNAA
Duane, William 1872- *WhWNAA*
Duane, William John 1780-1865 *Alli, DcAmA,*
DcNAA
Duane, William N *ChPo*
Duarte, King Of Portugal 1391-1438 *CasWL*
Duarte, Dom 1391-1438 *Pen Eur*
Duarte, Fausto Castilho 1903-1953 *AfA 1*
Duarte, Joseph S 1913- *ConAu 57*
DuBarry, Comtesse 1746-1793 *NewC*
DuBarry, Camille *WhWNAA*
DuBarry, Edmond L *Alli*
DuBarry, Jeanne Becu, Comtesse 1743-1793
OxFr
DuBarry, Mari Jeanne Becu, Comtesse
1743-1793 *REn*
DuBartas, Guillaume DeSalluste 1544-1590
CasWL, ChPo, DcEuL, EuA, EvEuW,
NewC, OxEng, OxFr, Pen Eur
Dubay, Thomas Edward 1921- *ConAu 1R*
DuBay, William H 1934- *ConAu 17R*
Dubbs, Joseph Henry 1838-1910 *Alli Sup,*
ChPo, DcAmA, DcNAA
Dube, Jean Claude *OxCan Sup*
Dube, John *Pen Cl*
Dube, John Langalibalele 1871-1946 *AfA 1*
Dube, Marcel 1930- *CanWr, CasWL, CnThe,*
McGWD, OxCan, OxCan Sup, REnWD
Dube, Rodolphe 1905- *CanWr, OxCan*
Dube, Violet *AfA 1*
DuBellay, Guillaume 1491-1543 *CasWL,*
DcEuL, OxFr
DuBellay, Jean 1492-1560 *DcEuL, OxFr*
DuBellay, Joachim 1522?-1560 *AtlBL, CasWL,*
ChPo, DcEuL, EuA, EvEuW, OxFr,
Pen Eur, REn
DuBellay, Martin d1559 *DcEuL*
Dubensky, Arcady 1890- *AmSCAP 66*
Dubensky, Leo 1914- *AmSCAP 66*
Duberly, Frances Isabella *Alli Sup*
Duberman, Martin B 1930- *AmA&B, Au&Wr,*
ConAu 1R, ConDr, CrCD, WrD 1976
Duberstein, Helen Laura 1926- *ConAu 45,*
DrAF 1976, DrAP 1975, WrD 1976
Dubey, Matt 1928- *AmSCAP 66*
Dubh, Cathal O 1928- *ConAu XR*
Dubh, Scian *Alli Sup*
Dubie, Norman *DrAP 1975*
Dubillard, Roland 1923- *CnMD Sup, CrCD,*
ModWD, Pen Eur, REnWD
Dubin, Al 1891-1945 *AmSCAP 66*
Dubin, Robert 1916- *ConAu 45*
Dubin, Samuel Sanford 1914- *ConAu 37*
Dubinsky, David Alexandrovich 1920- *WhGrA*
Dubkin, Lois Knudson 1911- *ConAu 5R*
DuBlane, Daphne *ConAu XR, SmATA XR*
Dublin, Archibishop Of *DcEnL*
Dublin, Conrad Padraic 1905- *WhWNAA*
Dublin, Jack 1915- *ConAu 23*
Dublin, Louis I 1882- *WhWNAA*

Duboc, Charles Edouard *BiD&SB*
Duboc, Julius 1829-1903 *BiD&SB*
DuBoccage, Marie Anne Fiquet 1710-1802
BiD&SB
Duboff, Al 1909- *AmSCAP 66*
Dubofsky, Melvyn 1934- *ConAu 49*
Dubois, Alan *WhWNAA*
Dubois, Augustus Jay 1849-1915 *Alli Sup,*
DcAmA, DcNAA
DuBois, Burghardt 1868- *AmLY*
DuBois, Constance Goddard 1855?-1911?
AmA&B, DcAmA, OhA&B
Dubois, Dick *WhWNAA*
Dubois, Lady Dorothea 1728-1774 *Polre*
Dubois, E C *Alli Sup*
Dubois, Edward *Alli, BiDLA, DcEnL*
Dubois, Elfrieda Theresa 1916- *Au&Wr,*
ConAu 9R, WrD 1976
DuBois, Eugene Floyd 1882- *WhWNAA*
DuBois, F R *ChPo S1*
DuBois, Frances Hulme 1889- *OhA&B*
DuBois, Gaylord 1899- *WhWNAA*
DuBois, Cardinal Guillaume 1656-1723 *OxFr*
DuBois, Gussie Packard *ChPo*
DuBois, Guy Pene 1884-1958 *AmA&B*
Dubois, Hamilton Graham 1885- *ChPo*
Dubois, J A *Alli*
Dubois, Jacques 1912- *WhGrA*
Dubois, James T 1851-1920 *DcNAA*
DuBois, M *WrD 1976*
DuBois, Mary Constance 1879-1959 *AmA&B,*
AmLY
Dubois, P B *Alli*
DuBois, Patterson 1847-1917 *ChPo S1,*
DcNAA
Dubois, Paul-Francois 1793-1784 *OxFr*
Dubois, Peter *Alli*
DuBois, Shirley Graham 1907- *BlkAW,*
IndAu 1917, WrD 1976
DuBois, Theodora McCormick 1890- *AmA&B,*
AuBYP
DuBois, W E B 1868-1963 *AmA&B, ConLC 1,*
ConLC 2
DuBois, William Ben *ChPo S2*
DuBois, William Edward Burghardt 1868-1963
BiDSA, BlkAW, CasWL, ConAmL,
DcAmA, DcLEnL, LongC, OxAm,
Pen Am, REn, REnAL, TwCA,
TwCA Sup, WebEAL, WhWNAA
DuBois, William Ewing 1810-1881 *Alli Sup,*
DcAmA, DcNAA
DuBois, William Pene 1916- *AmA&B, AuBYP,*
ChLR 1, ChPo S1, ConAu 5R,
IlCB 1945, IlCB 1956, IlCB 1966,
JBA 1951, Newb 1922, SmATA 4,
St&VC, WhCL
DuBois-Reymond, Emil 1818-1896 *BiD&SB*
DuBoisgobey, Fortune Hippolyte Auguste
1821?-1891 *BiD&SB, DcBiA, EncM&D,*
OxFr
Dubonee, Ylessa *BlkAW*
DuBos, Charles 1882-1939 *CatA 1947,*
CIDMEuL, OxFr, Pen Eur, REn
Dubos, Jean Baptiste 1670-1742 *BiD&SB,*
DcEuL, OxFr
Dubos, Rene 1901- *AmA&B, ConAu 5R*
Duboscq DeBeaumont, Gaston *OxCan*
DuBose, Mrs. C W *FemPA*
DuBose, Catherine Anne 1826-1906 *Alli,*
Alli Sup, BiDSA, DcAmA
DuBose, Hampden C *Alli Sup*
DuBose, Horace Mellard 1858-1941 *BiDSA,*
DcNAA
DuBose, Joel Campbell 1855- *BiDSA*
DuBose, John Witherspoon 1836- *BiDSA*
DuBose, Kate A *LivFWS*
DuBose, LaRocque 1926- *ConAu 23,*
SmATA 2
DuBose, Louise Jones 1901- *ConAu P-1*
DuBose, William Porcher 1836-1918 *AmA&B,*
BiDSA, DcAmA, DcNAA
Dubost *Alli, BiDLA*
Dubost, Christopher *Alli, BiDLA*
DuBoulay, John 1811- *Alli Sup*
DuBoulay, Thomas *Alli Sup*
Dubourdieu, Francis *Polre*
Dubourdieu, John *Alli, BiDLA*
Dubourg, Augustus W *Alli Sup*

DuBow, Fredric L 1944- *ConAu 25*
Dubric, Saint *NewC*
Dubricus, Saint *NewC*
DuBridge, Lee Alvin 1901- *IndAu 1917*
DuBrin, Andrew J 1935- *ConAu 41*
DuBroff, Sidney 1929- *Au&Wr, ConAu 21*
Dubrovin, Vivian 1931- *ConAu 57*
Dubruck, Alfred J 1922- *ConAu 37*
DuBruck, Edelgard E 1925- *ConAu 17R, WrD 1976*
Dubs, Homer H 1892-1969 *ConAu P-1*
Dubthach, MacLughair 448?- *DcEnL*
Dubue, M *Alli*
Dubus, Andre 1936- *ConAu 21*
DuCalvet, Pierre *BbtC*
DuCamp, Maxime 1822-1894 *BiD&SB, OxFr*
DuCane, Sir Charles 1825- *Alli Sup*
DuCane, Sir Edmund Frederick 1830- *Alli Sup*
DuCane, Peter 1901- *Au&Wr*
DuCange, Charles DuFresne, Sieur 1610-1688 *BbD, BiD&SB, CasWL, DcEuL, EvEuW, NewC, OxEng, OxFr*
Ducange, Victor Henri Joseph Brahain 1783-1833 *BiD&SB*
DuCann, Charles Garfield Lott *Au&Wr*
Ducarel, Andrew Coltee 1713-1785 *Alli*
Ducarel, P J *Alli, BiDLA*
Ducas 1400?-1470 *CasWL*
Ducas 1400?-1470? *Pen Cl*
Ducas, Dorothy 1905- *AuBYP, ConAu 5R*
Ducasse, C J 1881- *BiDPar, ConAu 1R*
Ducasse, Isidore Lucien 1847-1870 *ClDMEuL, EuA, EvEuW, OxFr*
Ducat, Arthur C *Alli Sup*
Ducatel, Julius Timoleon 1796-1849 *DcAmA, DcNAA*
Duccio Di Buoninsegna 1255?-1318? *AtlBL, REn*
Ducdame *OhA&B*
Duce, Robert 1908- *Au&Wr, ConAu 5R, WrD 1976*
DuCerceau, Jacques Androuet 1510?- *OxFr*
Duchacek, Ivo D 1913- *ConAu 1R, WrD 1976*
DuChaillu, Paul Belloni 1835-1903 *Alli Sup, AmA, AmA&B, BbD, BiD&SB, BiDSA, CarSB, Chmbr 3, DcAmA, DcEnL, DcNAA, JBA 1934, OxAm, REnAL*
Duchal, James 1697-1761 *Alli*
Duchamp, Marcel 1887-1968 *AtlBL, REn*
Ducharme, Jacques 1910- *CatA 1947*
Ducharme, Rejean 1942?- *CasWL, OxCan Sup*
Duchatel, Pierre 1480-1552 *OxFr*
DuChatelet, Gabrielle-Emilie, Marquise 1706-1749 *OxFr*
Duchaussois, Pierre Jean Baptiste 1878-1940 *DcNAA, OxCan*
Duche, Jacob 1737?-1798 *Alli, AmA, AmA&B, BiDLA, CyAL 1, DcAmA, DcNAA, OxAm*
Duche, Jean 1915- *Au&Wr, ConAu 9R*
Duchene, Louis-Francois 1927- *WrD 1976*
Duchesne, A E *ChPo*
Duchesne, Antoinette *ConAu XR*
Duchesne, Jacques *ConAu XR, OxCan Sup*
Duchesne, Janet 1930- *IICB 1966*
Duchesne, Louis 1843-1922 *OxFr*
Duchess, The *BiD&SB, BrAu 19, NewC*
Ducic, Jovan 1871?-1943 *CasWL, ClDMEuL, EncWL, ModSL 2, Pen Eur*
Ducie, Earl Of *Alli Sup*
DuCille, Ann 1949- *BlkAW*
Ducis, Jean-Francois 1733-1816 *BiD&SB, CasWL, DcEuL, EvEuW, OxFr*
Duck, Arthur 1580-1649 *Alli*
Duck, Leonard William 1916- *Au&Wr*
Duck, Stephen 1705-1756 *Alli, ChPo, ChPo S1, DcEnL, OxEng*
Duckat, Walter Benjamin 1911- *ConAu 29*
Ducker, Robert *Alli Sup*
Duckert, Mary 1929- *ConAu 53*
Duckett, Alfred 1917?- *BlkAW, ConAu 45*
Duckett, Sir George Floyd 1811- *Alli, Alli Sup*
Duckett, Thomas *Alli*
Duckett, William 1768-1841 *PoIre*
Duckham, Alec Narraway 1903- *Au&Wr, WrD 1976*
Duckham, Baron Frederick 1933- *Au&Wr,*

WrD 1976
Ducksbury, Sally *ChPo*
Duckworth, Alistair M 1936- *ConAu 41*
Duckworth, Allen Oliver 1910- *TexWr*
Duckworth, Dyce *Alli Sup*
Duckworth, George E 1903-1972 *ConAu 1R, ConAu 33*
Duckworth, Leslie Blakey 1904- *WrD 1976*
Duckworth, Sophie Hagemann 1870-1951 *AnMV 1926, OhA&B*
Duckworth, William *Alli Sup*
Duckworth, Willie Lee 1924- *AmSCAP 66*
Duclaux, Madame *Chmbr 3*
Duclaux, Agnes Mary Frances Robinson 1857-1944 *ChPo, ChPo S1, ChPo S2, WhLA*
Duclos, Charles Pinot 1704-1772 *BiD&SB, CasWL, EvEuW, OxFr, Pen Eur, REn*
Ducloux, Walter 1913- *AmSCAP 66*
Ducornet, Erica 1943- *ConAu 37, SmATA 7*
Ducoudray-Holstein, H Lafayette Villaume 1763-1839 *DcNAA*
Ducray-Duminil, Francois-Guillaume 1761-1819 *OxFr*
DuCreux, Francois *OxCan*
Ducy, Sir Simon *Alli*
Duczynska, Ilona *OxCan Sup*
Duda, Stanislav 1921- *WhGrA*
Duddell, Benjamin *Alli*
Dudden, Arthur P 1921- *ConAu 5R*
Duddington, Charles Lionel 1906- *Au&Wr*
Duddy, John H 1904- *AmSCAP 66*
Duddy, Lyn *AmSCAP 66*
DuDeffand, Marie, Marquise 1697-1780 *OxFr*
Dudek, Louis 1918- *CanWr, CasWL, ConAu 45, ConP 1970, ConP 1975, DcLEnL, OxCan, OxCan Sup, WebEAL, WrD 1976*
Dudeney, Mrs. Henry 1866-1945 *NewC*
Dudeney, Henry Ernest 1857- *WhLA*
Dudevant, Madame *BiD&SB, EuA*
Dudgeon, Florence E *Alli Sup*
Dudgeon, G *Alli*
Dudgeon, John Hepburn *Alli Sup*
Dudgeon, Muriel Ann *WhPNW*
Dudgeon, Robert Charles *Alli Sup*
Dudgeon, Robert Ellis *Alli Sup*
Dudgeon, William *Alli*
Dudintsev, Vladimir Dmitriyevich 1918- *ModSL 1, Pen Eur, REn, TwCW, WorAu*
Dudleigh, Agnes *Alli Sup*
Dudley *Alli*
Dudley, Albertus True 1886-1955 *AmA&B*
Dudley, B J 1931- *ConAu 25*
Dudley, Bide 1877- *AmA&B, WhWNAA*
Dudley, C W *Alli*
Dudley, Charles And Forsyth, Frank *Alli Sup*
Dudley, Dean 1823-1906 *Alli, Alli Sup, CyAL 2, DcAmA, DcNAA*
Dudley, Donald Reynolds 1910- *Au&Wr, ConAu 5R*
Dudley, Dud *Alli*
Dudley, E Lawrence 1879- *WhWNAA*
Dudley, Earl *Alli*
Dudley, Edgar Swartwout 1845-1911 *DcNAA*
Dudley, Edmund 1462-1510 *Alli*
Dudley, Edward 1926- *ConAu 45*
Dudley, Elizabeth *Alli Sup*
Dudley, Emelius Clark 1850-1928 *DcNAA, WhWNAA*
Dudley, Ernest 1908?- *Au&Wr, ConAu 13R, MnBBF*
Dudley, F *Alli, BiDLA*
Dudley, Frank *AmNov XR, MnBBF, TwCA, TwCA Sup*
Dudley, G M *Alli*
Dudley, Sir Gamaliel *Alli*
Dudley, Geoffrey Arthur 1917- *Au&Wr, ConAu 13R, WrD 1976*
Dudley, Guilford, Jr. 1907- *ConAu 19*
Dudley, Guilford A 1921-1972 *ConAu 41*
Dudley, Sir Henry Bate 1745-1824 *Alli, BiDLA*
Dudley, Homer Price 1855-1928 *ChPo S1*
Dudley, Howard *Alli*
Dudley, J G *Alli Sup*
Dudley, J L *Alli Sup*
Dudley, Lady Jane *Alli*
Dudley, Jane *ChPo S1*

Dudley, Jay *ConAu XR*
Dudley, John *Alli, BiDLA*
Dudley, John, Duke Of Northumberland 1502?-1553 *Alli, REn*
Dudley, Joshua *Alli*
Dudley, Lavinia Pratt *AmA&B*
Dudley, Louise 1884- *ConAu 23*
Dudley, Lucy May Bronson 1848-1920 *DcAmA, DcNAA, OhA&B*
Dudley, M E *PoIre*
Dudley, Marion Vienna *Alli Sup*
Dudley, Sir Matthew *Alli*
Dudley, Myron Samuel 1837-1905 *DcNAA*
Dudley, Nancy *AuBYP, ConAu XR, SmATA XR*
Dudley, Owen Francis 1882- *BkC 2, CatA 1947*
Dudley, Paul 1675-1751 *Alli, CyAL 1*
Dudley, Peter *ChPo S2*
Dudley, Robert *ChPo*
Dudley, Robert 1532?-1588 *Alli, NewC, REn*
Dudley, Sir Robert 1573-1639 *Alli*
Dudley, Ruth H 1905- *ConAu 61*
Dudley, S H *BlkAW*
Dudley, Thomas *CyAL 1*
Dudley, Thomas Underwood 1837-1904 *Alli Sup, BiDSA, DcAmA, DcNAA*
Dudley, Walter Bronson 1877-1944 *AmA&B, AmSCAP 66, WhWNAA*
Dudley, Sir William *Alli*
Dudley, William Bruce 1891- *WhWNAA*
Dudley, William Russell 1849-1911 *Alli Sup, DcAmA, DcNAA*
Dudley-Smith, Timothy 1926- *Au&Wr, WrD 1976*
Dudley-Smith, Trevor *EncM&D*
Dudman, Richard 1918- *ConAu 45*
Dudney, Sara Stead 1872- *TexWr*
Dudok, Gerard Anton 1887- *WhLA*
Duek, Charles C *Alli Sup*
Dueker, Christopher W 1939- *ConAu 57*
Dueker, Joyce S 1942- *ConAu 57*
Duell, Holland Sackett 1881-1942 *DcNAA*
Duell, Prentice 1894-1960 *ArizL, IndAu 1917*
Duemichen, Anna *Alli Sup*
Duenas, Juan De d1460? *CasWL*
Duer, Alice *ChPo, DcAmA*
Duer, Caroline King 1865- *ChPo*
Duer, Catherine King *DcAmA*
Duer, Douglas *ChPo*
Duer, Edward Louis 1836- *DcAmA*
Duer, John 1782-1858 *Alli, DcAmA, DcNAA*
Duer, William Alexander 1780-1858 *Alli, AmA&B, CyAL 1, DcAmA, DcNAA*
Duerk, Hilarion 1883- *BkC 3*
Duerr, Alvan Emile 1872-1947 *DcNAA*
Duerrenmatt, Friedrich 1921- *ConAu 17R*
Duey, Philip Alexander 1901- *AmSCAP 66, IndAu 1917*
DuFail, Noel 1520?-1591 *CasWL, OxFr*
Dufault, Peter Kane 1923- *ConAu 33, DrAP 1975, WrD 1976*
DuFaur DePibrac, Guy *OxFr*
Dufay *Alli*
Dufay, Guillaume 1400?-1474 *AtlBL, REn*
Dufay, Pierre *OxFr*
Duff, A *Alli*
Duff, A H *ChPo S1*
Duff, Alexander 1806-1878 *Alli, Alli Sup, DcEnL*
Duff, Andrew Halliday 1830-1877 *Alli Sup, DcEnL*
Duff, Anne Jane Wharton *Alli Sup*
Duff, Annis *ChPo*
Duff, Archibald 1845- *WhLA*
Duff, Charles 1894- *ConAu 1R*
Duff, Clayton *ChPo*
Duff, Mrs. David *OhA&B*
Duff, David Skene 1912- *Au&Wr, WrD 1976*
Duff, Douglas Valder 1901- *Au&Wr, CatA 1952*
Duff, Edward Gordon 1863-1924 *ChPo S2*
Duff, Emma Lorne d1935 *DcNAA*
Duff, Ernest A 1929- *ConAu 25*
Duff, Esther Lilian *ChPo*
Duff, Gerald 1938- *ConAu 45*
Duff, Harry 1855- *Alli Sup*
Duff, Sir Hector Livingston 1872- *WhLA*

Duff, Henrietta Anne 1842-1879 *Alli Sup,*
  ChPo, PoIre
Duff, James Grant 1789-1858 *Alli, OxEng*
Duff, John B 1931- *ConAu 45*
Duff, John Robert Keitley 1862- *WhLA*
Duff, John Wight 1866- *WhLA*
Duff, Maggie *ConAu XR*
Duff, Margaret K *ConAu 37*
Duff, Sir Mountstuart Elphinstone Grant
  1829-1906 *Alli Sup, BiD&SB, BrAu 19,*
  Chmbr 3, DcEnL, EvLB
Duff, P *Alli*
Duff, Patrick William 1901- *Au&Wr*
Duff, Peter 1802-1869 *DcAmA, DcNAA*
Duff, Raymond S 1923- *ConAu 23*
Duff, Robert Ffrench *Alli Sup*
Duff, U Francis *ChPo*
Duff, W *Alli, BiDLA*
Duff, William *Alli*
Duff, William Alexander 1872-1950 *OhA&B*
Duff-Gordon, Lady Lucie 1821-1869 *BrAu 19,*
  DcEuL
Duffee, Mary Gordon 1840- *BiDSA*
Duffee, May Margaretta *OhA&B*
Duffel, Mary Gordon 1840?- *DcAmA*
Duffell, Annie *Alli Sup*
Dufferin, Countess Of *Chmbr 3*
Dufferin, Lord 1826-1902 *Alli, Chmbr 3,*
  BrAu 19, OxCan
Dufferin, Frederick T Blackwood, Earl Of
  1826-1902 *BbD, BiD&SB, DcEnL*
Dufferin, Lady Helen Selina 1807-1867 *Alli,*
  BbD, BiD&SB, BrAu 19, ChPo,
  ChPo S1, ChPo S2, EvLB, PoIre
Dufferin, Helen ALSO Sheridan, Helen
Dufferin And Ava, Marquis Of 1826-1903
  Alli Sup, PoIre
Duffett, Thomas *Alli, CasWL, PoIre*
Duffey, Mrs. E B *Alli Sup*
Duffey, Eliza Bisbee d1898 *DcAmA, DcNAA*
Duffey, J B *ChPo S1*
Duffey, John B *Alli Sup*
Duffie, C R *Alli*
Duffield, Alexander James 1821-1890 *Alli Sup*
Duffield, Anne 1893- *Au&Wr, ConAu P-1*
Duffield, Divie Bethune 1821-1891 *DcNAA*
Duffield, George 1732-1790 *Alli*
Duffield, George 1794-1869? *Alli, DcAmA,*
  DcNAA
Duffield, George 1818-1888 *Alli Sup, DcAmA,*
  PoCh
Duffield, Gervase E 1935- *WrD 1976*
Duffield, Grace H *ChPo*
Duffield, John *Alli*
Duffield, John Thomas 1823-1901 *Alli Sup,*
  DcAmA, DcNAA
Duffield, Nina Hatchett *ChPo*
Duffield, Pitts 1869-1938 *AmA&B*
Duffield, Samuel Augustus Willoughby
  1843-1887 *Alli Sup, AmA, AmA&B,*
  BiD&SB, ChPo, DcAmA, DcNAA
Duffield, William Ward 1823-1907 *Alli Sup,*
  DcAmA, DcNAA
Duffin, Celia And Ruth *ChPo*
Duffin, Felix *Alli Sup*
Duffin, Henry Charles 1884- *Au&Wr,*
  ConAu P-1
Duffin, Ruth And Celia *ChPo S1*
Duffin, William *Alli Sup*
Duffus, Robert Luther 1888-1972 *AmA&B,*
  AmNov, Au&Wr, ChPo, ConAu 37,
  REnAL, TwCA, TwCA Sup
Duffy, Annie V *Alli Sup, BiDSA*
Duffy, Bella *Alli Sup*
Duffy, Bernard 1882- *Au&Wr*
Duffy, Bernard C 1902-1972 *ConAu 37*
Duffy, Sir Charles Gavan 1816-1903 *Alli Sup,*
  BrAu 19, ChPo S1, Chmbr 3, EvLB,
  NewC, OxEng, Pen Eng, PoIre
Duffy, Dennis *OxCan Sup*
Duffy, Edmund 1899-1962 *AmA&B*
Duffy, Elizabeth 1904- *ConAu 19*
Duffy, Essie Phelps *ChPo*
Duffy, Francis Patrick 1871-1932 *DcNAA*
Duffy, Francis R 1915- *ConAu 49*
Duffy, Helene 1926- *ConAu 17R*
Duffy, Herbert Smith 1900-1956 *OhA&B*
Duffy, James Oscar Greeley 1864-1933 *AmLY,*

DcAmA, DcNAA, PoIre
Duffy, James William *Alli Sup*
Duffy, John *ChPo S1*
Duffy, John 1915- *ConAu 17R*
Duffy, John 1926- *Au&Wr*
Duffy, John J 1934- *ConAu 57*
Duffy, Maureen 1933- *Au&Wr, ConAu 25,*
  ConDr, ConNov 1972, ConNov 1976,
  TwCW, WhTwL, WrD 1976
Duffy, Michael Francis 1906- *MnBBF*
Duffy, Nona Keen *ChPo*
Duffy, Patrick Lawrence 1879- *BiDSA*
Duffy, Richard 1873-1949 *DcNAA*
Duffy, Robert *Alli Sup, PoIre*
Duffy, T And Cummings, T J *Alli Sup*
Duffy, Thomas Gavan 1888-1942? *BkC 3,*
  CatA 1947
Dufief, N G *Alli*
Dufour, Alexander *Alli, BiDLA*
Dufour, Cyprien *BiDSA*
Dufour, John James 1763-1827 *IndAu 1816*
Dufour, Perret 1807-1884 *IndAu 1917*
Dufour, W *Alli*
Dufrenoy, Adelaide-Gilberte Billet 1765-1825
  OxFr
DuFresne, Charles *NewC*
Dufresne, Frank 1895- *WhWNAA*
Dufresne, Guy *OxCan Sup*
Dufresnoy, Charles Alphonse 1611-1655 *OxFr*
Dufresny, Charles DeLaRiviere 1648?-1724 *BbD,*
  BiD&SB, DcEuL, OxFr
Dufresny, Charles Riviere 1648?-1724 *McGWD,*
  OxFr, REn
D'Ufrey, Thomas 1650-1723 *BbD*
Dufton, Henry *Alli Sup*
Dufton, William *Alli, Alli Sup*
Dufty, Joseph *Alli Sup*
Dufy, Raoul 1877-1953? *AtlBL, REn*
Dugall, George d1850 *PoIre*
Dugan, Alan 1923- *AmA&B, ConLC 2,*
  ConLC 6, ConP 1970, ConP 1975,
  CrCAP, DrAP 1975, ModAL,
  ModAL Sup, OxAm, Pen Am, RAdv 1,
  REnAL, WorAu, WrD 1976
Dugan, Caro Atherton *ChPo, ChPo S1*
Dugan, Caro Atkinson *ChPo S2*
Dugan, Mrs. George E *BiDSA*
Dugan, James *Alli Sup*
Dugan, James 1912- *AnCL, ConAu 5R*
Dugan, Raymond Smith 1878-1940 *DcNAA*
Duganne, Augustine Joseph Hickey 1823-1884
  Alli, Alli Sup, AmA, AmA&B, BiD&SB,
  DcAmA, DcNAA, HsB&A, OxAm,
  REnAL
Dugard, Augustus John *ChPo*
DuGard *TwCA, TwCA Sup*
DuGard, Roger Martin *AtlBL, EncWL,*
  ModRL
Dugard, Samuel *Alli*
Dugard, Thomas *Alli*
Dugard, William 1605-1662 *Alli*
Dugas, Alphonse Chartes 1858-1924 *DcNAA*
Dugas, Emma L N *AmSCAP 66*
Dugas, Georges 1833-1928 *DcNAA, OxCan*
Dugas, Louis Alexander 1806-1884 *BiDSA*
Dugas, Marcel-Henri 1883-1947? *CanWr,*
  DcNAA, OxCan
Dugast, Georges *OxCan*
Dugat, Gentry 1895- *TexWr, WhWNAA*
Dugdale, Gilbert *Alli*
Dugdale, Sir John *Alli*
Dugdale, Kathleen 1897- *IndAu 1917*
Dugdale, Norman 1921- *WrD 1976*
Dugdale, Richard Louis 1841-1883 *Alli,*
  Alli Sup, DcAmA, DcNAA
Dugdale, Stephen *Alli*
Dugdale, Sir William 1605-1686 *Alli, BiD&SB,*
  BrAu, CasWL, Chmbr 1, DcEnA
Dugdale, Sir William 1605-1685 *DcEnL*
Dugdale, Sir William 1605-1686 *DcLEnL,*
  EvLB, NewC, OxEng
Dugdale, William Stratford *Alli Sup*
Dugdale, Mrs. Z *Alli Sup*
Dugey, Mattie Belle *TexWr*
Duggan, Alfred Leo 1903-1964 *AnCL, AuBYP,*
  LongC, ModBL, TwCA Sup, TwCW
Duggan, Bernard *PoIre*
Duggan, Denise Valerie *Au&Wr*

Duggan, Eileen May *CatA 1947, ChPo,*
  ChPo S1, ConP 1970, DcLEnL
Duggan, George Henry 1912- *ConAu 17R,*
  WrD 1976
Duggan, Janie Pritchard *BiDSA*
Duggan, Joseph J 1938- *ConAu 29*
Duggan, Joseph Jenkins 1874- *WhWNAA*
Duggan, Mary M 1921- *ConAu 25*
Duggan, Maurice Noel 1922-1975 *CasWL,*
  ConAu 53, ConNov 1972, ConNov 1976,
  WebEAL
Duggan, Peter Paul d1861 *EarAB, EarAB Sup*
Duggan, Thomas Stephen 1850-1945 *DcNAA*
Duggar, Benjamin Minge 1872- *AmLY*
Dugger, Ronnie 1930- *ConAu 21*
Dugger, Sheperd M 1854- *AmA&B*
Dugger, Shepherd Monroe 1854- *BiDSA*
Duggins, James, Jr. 1933- *ConAu 37*
Dughi, Nancy *ConAu 1R*
Dugmore, Clifford William 1909- *Au&Wr,*
  ConAu 13R
Dugmore, Ernest Edward *Alli Sup*
Dugmore, Thomas *Alli*
Dugonics, Andras 1740-1818 *CasWL*
Duguay, Raoul 1939- *OxCan Sup*
Duguay-Trouin, Rene 1673-1736 *BiD&SB,*
  OxFr
Dugud, Patrick *Alli*
Dugue, Charles Oscar 1821-1872 *Alli, AmA&B,*
  BiDSA, CyAL 2, DcNAA
DuGuesclin, Bertrand 1320?-1380 *OxFr*
Duguid, A F *OxCan*
Duguid, Charles 1884- *WrD 1976*
Duguid, J E *Alli Sup*
Duguid, Julian 1902- *TwCA, TwCA Sup*
Duguid, Robert *ConAu XR*
DuGuillet, Pernette 1520?-1545 *CasWL, EuA,*
  OxFr, Pen Eur
DuHaillan, Bernard Pirard, Seigneur 1535-1610
  OxFr
Duhamel, Georges 1884-1966 *CasWL,*
  ClDMEuL, ConAu 25, EncWL, EvEuW,
  LongC, ModRL, ModWD, OxFr,
  Pen Eur, REn, TwCA, TwCA Sup,
  TwCW, WhTwL
Duhamel, P Albert 1920- *ConAu 5R*
Duhamel, Roger 1916- *CanWr, CasWL,*
  OxCan, OxCan Sup
Duhamel, Vaughn L *DrAP 1975*
DuHamel, William 1866- *DcAmA*
DuHausset, Madame *OxFr*
Duhigg, Bartholomew *Alli, BiDLA*
Duhl, Leonard J 1926- *ConAu 13R,*
  WrD 1976
Duhring, Henry *Alli*
Duhring, Julia 1836-1892 *Alli Sup, BiD&SB,*
  DcAmA, DcNAA
Duhring, Louis Adolphus 1845-1913 *Alli Sup,*
  DcAmA, DcNAA
Duigan, James *PoIre*
Duigenan, Patrick 1735-1816 *Alli, BiDLA*
Duignan, Michael George *Alli Sup*
Duignan, Peter 1926- *ConAu 13R*
Duignan, W H *Alli Sup*
Duillier, N F *Alli*
Duim, Frederik 1674-1750? *CasWL*
Duinkerken, Anton Van 1903-1968 *CasWL*
Dujardin, Edouard 1861-1949 *LongC, NewC,*
  OxFr, REn
DuJardin, Rosamond Neal 1902-1963 *AmA&B,*
  ConAu 1R, MorJA, REnAL, SmATA 2
DuJon, Francois *BrAu, NewC*
Duka, Ivo *WrD 1976*
Duka, Theodore *Alli Sup*
Dukas, Paul-Abraham 1865-1935 *OxFr*
Duke, The Iron *NewC*
Duke, Alexander *PoIre*
Duke, Alvah 1908- *ConAu 45*
Duke, Anita *WrD 1976*
Duke, Basil Wilson 1838-1916 *Alli Sup,*
  BiDSA, ChPo S2, DcNAA
Duke, Benjamin 1931- *ConAu 49*
Duke, Bill *BlkAW*
Duke, Billy 1927- *AmSCAP 66*
Duke, Derek *MnBBF*
Duke, Donald Norman 1929- *ConAu 17R,*
  WrD 1976
Duke, Edward *Alli, Alli Sup*

Duke, Francis *Alli*
Duke, George *Alli*
Duke, Henry Hinxman *Alli Sup*
Duke, Herbert C *Alli Sup*
Duke, John *ConAu XR*
Duke, John 1899- *AmSCAP 66*
Duke, John Kline 1844-1903 *OhA&B*
Duke, Joshua *Alli Sup*
Duke, Madelaine *Au&Wr, ConAu 57, WrD 1976*
Duke, Neville Frederick 1922- *Au&Wr*
Duke, R T W, Jr. 1853- *BiDSA*
Duke, R T W And Francis H Smith *Alli*
Duke, Richard *Chmbr 2*
Duke, Richard d1711 *Alli*
Duke, Richard DeLaBarre 1930- *ConAu 57*
Duke, Valentine *Alli Sup*
Duke, Vernon 1903- *AmSCAP 66, ConAu XR*
Duke, Will *ConAu 49*
Duke, William 1757-1840 *Alli, BiDSA, DcAmA, DcNAA*
Duke, William Waddell 1882-1946 *DcNAA*
Duke, Winifred d1962 *EncM&D, WhLA*
Duke Coombe *DcEnL*
Duke-Elder, Sir Stewart 1898- *Au&Wr, WrD 1976*
Duke Of Barre *WhWNAA*
Duke Of Xensi *WhLA*
Dukelsky, Vladimir 1903-1969 *ConAu 29*
Duker, Abraham G 1907- *ConAu 53*
Duker, Sam 1905- *ConAu 13R*
Dukert, Joseph Michael 1929- *AuBYP, ConAu 5R, WrD 1976*
Dukes, Ashley 1885-1953? *DcLEnL, NewC, WhLA*
Dukes, Clement *Alli Sup*
Dukes, Cuthbert 1890- *Au&Wr, WhLA*
Dukes, D *ChPo*
Dukes, Edwin Joshua *Alli Sup*
Dukes, Harriet Elizabeth Gross 1855-1939 *OhA&B*
Dukes, Sir Paul 1889- *WhLA*
Dukes, Paul 1934- *ConAu 23*
Dukes, Philip *ConAu XR*
Dukinfield, Jane *Alli Sup*
Dukore, Bernard F 1931- *ConAu 25*
Dulac, Edmund 1882-1953 *CarSB, ChPo, ChPo S2, ConICB, IlCB 1945, JBA 1951, WhCL*
Dulac, George *OhA&B*
Dulack, Thomas 1935- *ConAu 25*
Dulaney, Benjamin Lewis 1857-1930 *DcNAA*
Dulaney, Daniel *Alli*
Dulany, Daniel 1685-1753 *DcNAA*
Dulany, Daniel 1722?-1797 *AmA, BiDSA, DcAmA, DcNAA, OxAm*
Dulany, Harris 1940- *ConAu 33, DrAF 1976*
Dulaurens, Henri Joseph 1719-1787? *BiD&SB*
Dulberg, Joseph *Alli Sup*
Dulcken, Augustus *ChPo S2*
Dulcken, Henry William 1832-1894 *Alli Sup, ChPo, ChPo S2*
Duley, Margaret 1894- *OxCan*
Dulhut, Daniel Greysolon 1639-1710 *OxCan*
Dulieu, Jean *ConAu XR*
Dulk, Albert Friedrich Benno 1819-1884 *BiD&SB, CasWL*
Dull, Charles Elwood 1878-1947 *DcNAA*
Dull, Paul Phellis 1907- *OhA&B*
Dullaert, Heiman 1636-1684 *CasWL*
Dullea, Owen J *Alli Sup*
Duller, Eduard 1809-1853 *BiD&SB, OxGer*
Dulles, Allen 1893-1969 *AmA&B*
Dulles, Allen Macy 1854-1930 *DcNAA, WhWNAA*
Dulles, Allen W 1893-1969 *ConAu 23*
Dulles, Avery Robert 1918- *CatA 1952, ConAu 9R, WrD 1976*
Dulles, Charles Winslow 1850-1921 *Alli Sup, AmLY, DcAmA, DcNAA*
Dulles, Eleanor Lansing 1895- *ConAu 9R*
Dulles, Foster Rhea 1900-1970 *AmA&B, ConAu 29, ConAu P-1, OhA&B, TwCA Sup*
Dulles, John Foster 1888-1959 *AmA&B*
Dulles, John W F 1913- *ConAu 1R*
Dulles, John Welsh 1823-1887 *Alli Sup,*

BiD&SB, DcAmA, DcNAA
Dullin, Charles 1885-1949 *ClDMEuL, OxFr, REn*
Dulmage, Will E 1883-1953 *AmSCAP 66*
Dulock, Jerre A *BlkAW*
Dulsey, Bernard M 1914- *ConAu 9R*
Duly, Sidney John 1891- *Au&Wr, WhLA*
Dum Dum 1869- *ChPo, ChPo S1, ChPo S2, WhLA*
DuMaine, Duchesse *OxFr*
Dumanoir, Philippe 1806-1865 *BiD&SB*
Dumarchais, Pierre 1882-1970 *ConAu 29, TwCA, TwCA Sup*
Dumarchey, Pierre *ConAu XR*
Dumarsais, Cesar Chesneau 1676-1756 *OxFr*
Dumas, Aaron *BlkAW*
Dumas, Alexandre, Fils 1824-1895 *AtlBL, BbD, BiD&SB, CasWL, CnThe, CyWA, DcBiA, DcEuL, EuA, EvEuW, HsB&A, McGWD, NewC, OxEng, OxFr, Pen Eur, RCom, REn, REnWD*
Dumas, Alexandre, Pere 1802-1870 *AtlBL, BbD, BiD&SB, CarSB, CasWL, CnThe, CyWA, DcEuL, EuA, EvEuW, HsB&A, McGWD, MnBBF, NewC, OxEng, OxFr, Pen Eur, RCom, REn, REnWD, WhCL*
Dumas, Andre A 1908- *BiDPar*
Dumas, Evelyn *OxCan Sup*
Dumas, Gerald J 1930- *BlkAW, ConAu 25, DrAP 1975*
Dumas, Henry L 1934-1968 *BlkAW, ConLC 6*
Dumas, Roger *OxCan Sup*
Dumas, William Thomas 1858- *BiDSA, ChPo, DcAmA*
Dumas Davy DeLaPailleterie, Alexandre 1802-1870 *DcBiA*
Dumas-Renan, Auguste 1881- *WhLA*
DuMaurier, Angela 1904- *Au&Wr*
DuMaurier, Daphne 1907- *Au&Wr, ConAu 5R, ConLC 6, ConNov 1972, ConNov 1976, CyWA, DcLEnL, EncM&D, EvLB, LongC, ModBL, NewC, Pen Eng, RAdv 1, REn, TwCA, TwCA Sup, TwCW, WrD 1976*
DuMaurier, George Louis Palmella Busson 1834-1896 *BbD, BiD&SB, BrAu 19, CasWL, ChPo, ChPo S2, Chmbr 3, CyWA, DcBiA, DcEuL, DcLEnL, EvLB, MouLC 4, NewC, OxEng, Pen Eng, RAdv 1, REn*
DuMaurier, Sir Gerald 1873-1934 *NewC*
Dumb Ox *NewC*
Dumbell, John *Alli*
Dumble, Edwin Theodore 1852-1927 *IndAu 1917*
Dumbledore, Richard *Alli Sup*
Dumbleton, Edgar Norris *Alli Sup*
Dumbleton, William A 1927- *ConAu 37*
Dumbrille, Dorothy Martha 1897?- *Au&Wr, CanNov, WrD 1976*
Dumergue, Edward *Alli Sup*
Dumeril, Edelestand Pontus 1801-1871 *OxFr*
Dumerque, Edward *Alli Sup*
Dumersan, Theophile Marion 1780-1849 *BiD&SB*
Dumesnil, Clement *BbtC*
DuMitand, M *BiDLA*
Dumitriu, Petru 1924- *Au&Wr, CasWL, ModRL, TwCW, WorAu*
Dummer, Jeremiah 1679?-1739 *Alli, AmA, AmA&B, CyAL 1, DcAmA, OxAm*
Dumon, William *Alli*
Dumond, Annie Nelles *BiDSA*
Dumond, Dwight Lowell 1895- *AmA&B, OhA&B*
Dumond, H V *ChPo*
DuMond, Joseph H 1898- *AmSCAP 66*
Dumont, Daniel Boone *HsB&A*
Dumont, Fernand 1927- *CanWr, OxCan Sup*
Dumont, Frank 1848-1919 *HsB&A*
Dumont, Gabriel 1838-1906 *OxCan*
Dumont, Henrietta *ChPo S2*
Dumont, Henry 1878- *WhWNAA*
Dumont, Julia Louisa Corry 1794-1857 *Alli Sup, BiD&SB, DcAmA, DcNAA, OhA&B*
Dumont, Laura Louisa Cory 1794-1857 *IndAu 1816*

Dumont, Pierre Etienne Louis 1759-1829 *EvEuW*
Dumont, Rene *Au&Wr*
Dumoulin, Heinrich 1905- *ConAu 5R*
Dumouriez, Charles-Francois 1739-1823 *OxFr*
Dumphie, Charles J *ChPo S2*
Dumpleton, John LeFevre 1924- *Au&Wr, ConAu 13R*
Dumpty, Humpty S *ConAu XR*
Dun, Lord *Alli*
Dun, Angus 1892-1972 *ConAu 33*
Dun, Barclay *Alli*
Dun, Finlay *Alli Sup*
Dun, James *Alli*
Dun, John *Alli, Alli Sup*
Dun, John Davis 1891- *OhA&B*
Dun, P *Alli Sup*
Dun Karm *CasWL, Pen Cl*
Dunas, Joseph C 1900- *ConAu 17R*
Dunash Ben Labrat 920?-980? *CasWL*
Dunathan, Arni T 1936- *ConAu 53*
Dunaway, Maude Edwin 1882-1934 *DcNAA*
Dunaway, Thomas Sanford 1872-1932 *DcNAA*
Dunbabin, Robert Leslie 1869- *WhLA*
Dunbabin, Thomas 1883- *Au&Wr*
Dunbar, Agnes 1312?-1369 *NewC*
Dunbar, Aldis *ChPo, ChPo S2*
Dunbar, Charles Franklin 1830-1900 *DcAmA, DcNAA*
Dunbar, Charles Stuart 1900- *Au&Wr, WrD 1976*
Dunbar, David *Alli, Alli Sup*
Dunbar, Dorothy 1923- *ConAu 9R*
Dunbar, Edward Dunbar *Alli Sup*
Dunbar, Edward E *Alli Sup*
Dunbar, Ernest 1927- *ConAu 25*
Dunbar, George 1774-1851 *Alli, BiDLA*
Dunbar, Helen Flanders 1902-1959 *AmA&B*
Dunbar, Henry d1883 *Alli Sup*
Dunbar, J Rimell *Alli Sup*
Dunbar, James 1833- *Alli, Alli Sup, BbtC*
Dunbar, Jane Thorpe 1861- *WhWNAA*
Dunbar, Janet 1901- *Au&Wr, ConAu 9R*
Dunbar, Jennie *ChPo*
Dunbar, John *Alli, Alli Sup*
Dunbar, John Greenwell 1930- *Au&Wr, ConAu 23*
Dunbar, John Orval 1920- *IndAu 1917*
Dunbar, M C *Alli Sup*
Dunbar, Margaret Juliana Maria *Alli Sup*
Dunbar, Mary F P *Alli Sup*
Dunbar, Newell 1845-1925 *DcNAA*
Dunbar, Noel *HsB&A*
Dunbar, Paul Laurence 1872-1906 *AmA, AmA&B, BiD&SB, BkCL, BlkAW, CasWL, ChPo, ChPo S1, ChPo S2, Chmbr 3, CnDAL, DcAmA, DcNAA, OhA&B, OxAm, Pen Am, RAdv 1, REn, REnAL, WebEAL*
Dunbar, Robert Nugent d1866 *Alli Sup, PoIre*
Dunbar, Seymour 1866-1947 *DcNAA, OhA&B*
Dunbar, Lady Sophia *Alli Sup*
Dunbar, Sydney *Alli Sup*
Dunbar, T J *PoIre*
Dunbar, Tony 1949- *ConAu 33*
Dunbar, Wallace *ChPo*
Dunbar, William d1810 *Alli*
Dunbar, William 1460?-1530? *Alli, AtlBL, BbD, BiD&SB, BrAu, CasWL, ChPo, ChPo S2, Chmbr 1, CnE&AP, CriT 1, DcEnA, DcEnL, DcEuL, DcLEnL, EvLB, MouLC 1, NewC, OxEng, Pen Eng, REn, WebEAL*
Dunbar, William B *Alli Sup*
Dunbar, Willis F 1902- *ConAu 5R*
Dunbar-Nelson, Alice Moore 1875-1935 *BlkAW*
Dunbaugh, Frank Montgomery 1895- *ConAu 45*
Dunboyne, Lady *Alli Sup*
Dunboyne, Lord 1917- *WrD 1976*
Duncalf, Frederic 1882-1963 *AmA&B, TexWr*
Duncan d1040? *NewC*
Duncan, Professor *ChPo S1*
Duncan, A D 1930- *ConAu 33*
Duncan, A H *Alli Sup*
Duncan, Alastair R C 1915- *WrD 1976*
Duncan, Alex *ConAu 57, WrD 1976*
Duncan, Alexander *Alli, BiDLA*
Duncan, Alistair 1927- *ConAu 61*

Duncan, Andrew *Alli, Alli Sup, BiDLA*
Duncan, Andrew 1745-1828 *Alli*
Duncan, Andrew, Jr. *Alli, BiDLA*
Duncan, Archibald *Alli*
Duncan, Ardinelle Bean 1913- *ConAu 1R*
Duncan, Ben 1927- *Au&Wr, WrD 1976*
Duncan, Bowie 1941- *ConAu 33*
Duncan, C J 1916- *ConAu 25*
Duncan, Charles *Alli Sup*
Duncan, Charles T 1914- *ConAu 17R*
Duncan, Charles William *Alli Sup*
Duncan, Clyde H 1903- *ConAu 17R*
Duncan, Daniel d1761 *Alli*
Duncan, Daniel 1649-1735 *Alli*
Duncan, David *Alli Sup*
Duncan, David 1900- *Au&Wr*
Duncan, David 1913- *AmA&B, AmNov, Au&Wr, ConAu 5R, WhPNW*
Duncan, David Douglas 1916- *AuNews 1*
Duncan, Delbert J 1895- *ConAu 41*
Duncan, Dorothy 1903-1957 *OxCan*
Duncan, Duke *DcNAA*
Duncan, Edmonstoune 1866-1920 *ChPo S1, ChPo S2*
Duncan, Edward 1804-1882 *ChPo, ChPo S1*
Duncan, F *BbtC*
Duncan, Florence I *Alli Sup*
Duncan, Frances *WhWNAA*
Duncan, Francis *Alli, BiDLA Sup, MnBBF, OxCan*
Duncan, Francis 1836-1888 *Alli Sup*
Duncan, G P *Alli Sup*
Duncan, George *Alli Sup*
Duncan, Gregory *ConAu XR, SmATA 3*
Duncan, Handasyde *Alli Sup*
Duncan, Hazel *ChPo S2*
Duncan, Henry *Alli*
Duncan, Herman Cope *Alli Sup*
Duncan, Hugh Dalziel 1909- *ConAu 23*
Duncan, Irma 1897- *ConAu 49*
Duncan, Isabella *Alli Sup*
Duncan, Isadora 1878-1927 *AmA&B, OxAm, REn, REnAL*
Duncan, Mrs. J C Lundie *ChPo*
Duncan, James *Alli, MnBBF*
Duncan, James 1857-1928 *DcNAA*
Duncan, James Foulis *Alli, Alli Sup*
Duncan, James Matthews 1826- *Alli Sup*
Duncan, James S *OxCan Sup*
Duncan, Jane *Au&Wr, ConAu XR, WrD 1976*
Duncan, Jimmy 1935- *AmSCAP 66*
Duncan, John *Alli, BiDLA, ChPo S2*
Duncan, John d1814 *BiDLA Sup*
Duncan, John Allison 1903- *OhA&B*
Duncan, John Brown 1883-1945 *OhA&B*
Duncan, John Charles 1882- *IndAu 1917, WhWNAA*
Duncan, John M *Alli, BbtC, OxCan*
Duncan, John Morison *Alli Sup*
Duncan, John Paul 1909- *IndAu 1917*
Duncan, John Shute *Alli*
Duncan, John Spenser Ritchie 1921- *Au&Wr*
Duncan, Jonathan *Alli*
Duncan, Joseph *Alli Sup*
Duncan, Joseph E 1921- *ConAu 5R*
Duncan, Julia K *AmNov XR, ConAu 19, SmATA 1*
Duncan, Kathleen Mary 1907- *Au&Wr*
Duncan, Kenneth Sandilands 1912- *Au&Wr, ConAu 9R*
Duncan, Kunigunde 1886- *AmA&B, ChPo S1, ChPo S2, ConAu 5R, WhWNAA*
Duncan, Leslie *MnBBF*
Duncan, Lindsay *ChPo*
Duncan, Lois 1934- *AuBYP, ConAu XR, SmATA 1, WrD 1976*
Duncan, Mrs. M G L *Alli*
Duncan, Malcolm C *Alli Sup*
Duncan, Marion Herbert 1896- *OhA&B*
Duncan, Mark d1640 *Alli*
Duncan, Mark d1648 *Alli*
Duncan, Mary Bell M *Alli Sup*
Duncan, Mary Lundie 1814-1840 *Alli, ChPo*
Duncan, Norman 1871-1916 *AmA&B, CanWr, DcAmA, DcLEnL, DcNAA, JBA 1934, JBA 1951, OhA&B, OxCan, REnAL,*

YABC 1
Duncan, Otis Dudley 1921- *ConAu 13R*
Duncan, Pam 1938- *ConAu 37*
Duncan, Peter Collin 1895- *Au&Wr*
Duncan, Peter Martin 1836- *Alli Sup*
Duncan, Pope A 1920- *ConAu 13R*
Duncan, R S *Alli Sup, BiDSA*
Duncan, Robert *Alli Sup, ChPo, ChPo S2*
Duncan, Robert 1699-1729 *Alli*
Duncan, Robert 1919- *AmA&B, CasWL, ConAu 9R, ConLC 1, ConLC 2, ConLC 4, ConP 1970, ConP 1975, CrCAP, DrAP 1975, ModAL, ModAL Sup, Pen Am, RAdv 1, REn, REnAL, WebEAL, WorAu, WrD 1976*
Duncan, Robert Dick *Alli Sup*
Duncan, Robert F 1890?-1974 *ConAu 53*
Duncan, Robert Kennedy 1868-1914 *DcNAA*
Duncan, Robert Moore 1900-1938 *DcNAA*
Duncan, Ronald 1914- *Au&Wr, CnMD, CnThe, ConAu 5R, ConDr, ConP 1970, ConP 1975, CrCD, EvLB, ModBL, ModWD, TwCW, WrD 1976*
Duncan, Rosetta 1900-1959 *AmSCAP 66*
Duncan, Sara Jeannette 1862-1922 *CanWr, Chmbr 3, DcLEnL, DcNAA, OxCan*
Duncan, Sinclair Thomson *Alli Sup*
Duncan, Sylvia 1916- *Au&Wr*
Duncan, T C *Alli Sup*
Duncan, Thelma *BlkAW*
Duncan, Thomas Watson *Alli Sup*
Duncan, Thomas William 1905- *AmA&B, AmNov, ConAu 1R, REnAL*
Duncan, Vivian 1902- *AmSCAP 66*
Duncan, W B *BiDSA*
Duncan, W J *Alli Sup*
Duncan, W Murdoch 1909- *ConAu 13R*
Duncan, W P *Alli*
Duncan, W Raymond 1936- *ConAu 41*
Duncan, W Stewart *Alli Sup*
Duncan, W W *Alli Sup, ChPo S2*
Duncan, Walter Jack 1881-1941 *ChPo S2, IndAu 1917*
Duncan, Walter Wofford Tucker 1869-1945 *DcNAA, OhA&B*
Duncan, Watson Boone 1867-1930 *DcNAA, WhWNAA*
Duncan, William *Alli*
Duncan, William 1717-1760 *Alli*
Duncan, William 1832-1918 *OxCan*
Duncan, William Cary 1874-1945 *AmA&B, AmSCAP 66, DcNAA, WhWNAA*
Duncan, William Cecil 1824-1864 *Alli Sup, BiDSA, DcAmA, DcNAA*
Duncan, William Murdoch 1909- *Au&Wr, MnBBF*
Duncan, William P *ChPo*
Duncan, William Stevens 1834-1892 *DcAmA, DcNAA*
Duncan, William Wallace *Alli Sup*
Duncan-Clark, Samuel John 1875-1938 *DcNAA*
Duncan-Kemp, Alice Monkton 1901- *Au&Wr*
Duncanson, John *Alli Sup*
Duncanson, Michael E 1948- *ConAu 57*
Duncker, Dora 1855- *BiD&SB*
Duncker, Max Wolfgang 1811-1886 *BiD&SB*
Dunckley, Henry 1823- *Alli Sup*
Dunckley, James *Alli Sup*
Duncombe, Mrs. *BiDLA*
Duncombe, Charles 1794-1875 *DcNAA*
Duncombe, David C 1928- *ConAu 29*
Duncombe, Frances 1900- *ConAu 25*
Duncombe, Giles *Alli*
Duncombe, Henry J *Alli*
Duncombe, John *Alli*
Duncombe, John 1730?-1785? *Alli, BkIE*
Duncombe, Mrs. John d1812 *Alli*
Duncombe, Thomas S *Alli Sup*
Duncombe, William 1690-1769 *Alli*
Duncon, Eleaz *Alli*
Duncon, John *Alli*
Duncon, Samuel *Alli*
Duncumb, John *Alli, BiDLA*
Dundas, Sir David 1735?-1820 *Alli, BiDLA*
Dundas, Henry, Viscount Melville 1741?-1811 *Alli*
Dundas, James *Alli*
Dundas, John *Alli*

Dundas, Louisa Mary *Alli Sup*
Dundas, Robert *Alli Sup*
Dundass, Samuel Rutherford 1820-1850 *OhA&B*
Dundee, Viscount *NewC*
Dundee, Douglas *MnBBF*
Dundee, Robert *ConAu XR*
Dundes, Alan 1934- *ConAu 23*
Dundonald, Earl Of *Alli, Alli Sup, BiDLA*
Dundonald, Lord 1775-1860 *BrAu 19*
Dundonald, Mona *ChPo S2*
Dundonald, Thomas Cochrane 1775-1862 *BbtC*
Dundy, Elaine 1937?- *Au&Wr, ConNov 1976, TwCW, WrD 1976*
Dunford, Emilie *Alli Sup*
Dungal *Alli*
Dungan, David Roberts 1837-1920 *Alli Sup, AmLY, DcNAA, IndAu 1816*
Dungan, James M 1851-1925 *IndAu 1917*
Dungan, Olive 1903- *AmSCAP 66*
Dungey, J W *Alli Sup*
Dungleson, Richard James 1834-1901 *Alli Sup, BiDSA*
Dunglison, Richard James 1834-1901 *DcAmA, DcNAA*
Dunglison, Robley 1798-1869 *Alli, DcAmA, DcNAA*
Dunham, Aileen *OxCan*
Dunham, Arthur 1893- *ConAu 33*
Dunham, Barrows 1905- *ConAu 5R*
Dunham, Bertha Mabel *WhWNAA*
Dunham, Carroll 1828-1877 *Alli Sup, DcAmA, DcNAA*
Dunham, Chester Forrester 1891-1959 *OhA&B*
Dunham, Donald Carl 1908- *ConAu 1R*
Dunham, Elizabeth M 1872- *WhWNAA*
Dunham, H Warren 1906- *ConAu 13R, WrD 1976*
Dunham, Henry Morton 1853-1929 *DcNAA*
Dunham, James Henry 1870-1953 *AmA&B*
Dunham, John L 1939- *ConAu 29*
Dunham, Katherine 1910- *AmSCAP 66, BlkAW, LivBA, REnAL*
Dunham, Kingsley Charles 1910- *Au&Wr, WrD 1976*
Dunham, Lowell 1910- *ConAu 37*
Dunham, Mabel 1881-1957 *CanNov, CanWr, OxCan*
Dunham, Montrew Goetz 1919- *ConAu 17R, IndAu 1917*
Dunham, Moses Earle 1825-1898 *DcAmA*
Dunham, Robert Carr *Alli Sup*
Dunham, S Astley d1858 *Alli*
Dunham, Samuel 1835-1936 *DcNAA*
Dunham, Samuel Clarke 1855-1920 *ChPo, DcNAA*
Dunham, William D 1910- *AmSCAP 66*
Dunham, William Huse, Jr. 1901- *ConAu 49*
Dunham, William Russell 1833?-1911 *Alli Sup, DcAmA, DcNAA*
Dunhill, Thomas Frederick 1877- *WhLA*
Dunin-Martsinkevich, Vikenti 1807-1884 *DcRusL*
Duning, George 1908- *AmSCAP 66*
Duniway, A J 1834-1915 *Alli Sup*
Duniway, Abigail Jane Scott 1834-1915 *Alli Sup, AmA, AmA&B, DcNAA*
Duniway, Clyde Augustus 1866-1944 *DcNAA, WhWNAA*
Dunjee, Roscoe 1883- *BlkAW*
Dunkel, Harold Baker 1912- *ConAu 5R*
Dunkel, Wilbur Dwight 1901- *IndAu 1917*
Dunkelgrafin, Die 1800?-1837 *OxGer*
Dunkerley, Gregor Hamilton 1927- *Au&Wr*
Dunkerley, Roderic 1884- *Au&Wr, ConAu P-1*
Dunkerley, William Arthur 1852-1941 *EvLB, NewC, TwCA, TwCA Sup*
Dunkin, Alfred John 1812-1870 *Alli, Alli Sup*
Dunkin, Christopher 1812-1881 *BbtC, OxCan*
Dunkin, Edwin 1821- *Alli Sup*
Dunkin, Edwin Hadlow Wise 1849- *Alli Sup*
Dunkin, John *Alli*
Dunkin, Paul Shaner 1905- *ConAu 33, IndAu 1917, WrD 1976*
Dunkin, William 1709?-1765 *Alli, PoIre*
Dunkle, William F, Jr. 1911- *ConAu 53*

Dunkley, Ferdinand Luis 1869-1956
    AmSCAP 66
Dunkman, William E 1903- *ConAu 25*
Dunlap, Andrew 1794-1835 *Alli, DcAmA*
Dunlap, Aurie N 1907- *ConAu 37*
Dunlap, Colonel Walter B *DcNAA, HsB&A*
Dunlap, E K 1853-1885 *OhA&B*
Dunlap, Frederick 1881- *WhWNAA*
Dunlap, G D 1923- *ConAu 49*
Dunlap, George T 1864-1956 *AmA&B*
Dunlap, Hope 1880- *ChPo, ConICB,*
    IlCB 1945
Dunlap, J D *Alli*
Dunlap, Jane *ConAu 49*
Dunlap, John 1747-1812 *AmA&B*
Dunlap, John A 1793?-1858? *Alli, DcAmA*
Dunlap, Knight 1875-1949 *AmA&B,*
    WhWNAA
Dunlap, Laura 1855-1947 *DcNAA*
Dunlap, Leslie W 1911- *ConAu 37, WrD 1976*
Dunlap, Lon *ConAu XR*
Dunlap, Louis M 1911- *AmSCAP 66*
Dunlap, M E *Alli Sup*
Dunlap, Maurice Pratt 1882- *OhA&B*
Dunlap, Orrin Elmer, Jr. 1896-1970 *AmA&B,*
    ConAu P-1
Dunlap, Samuel Fales 1825?-1905 *Alli,*
    DcAmA, DcNAA
Dunlap, William 1766-1839 *Alli, AmA,*
    AmA&B, BbD, BiD&SB, BiDLA,
    CasWL, CnDAL, CnThe, CyAL 1,
    DcAmA, DcNAA, EvLB, McGWD,
    OxAm, Pen Am, REnAL, REnWD,
    WebEAL
Dunleavy, Gareth W 1923- *ConAu 33*
Dunleavy, Janet Egleson 1928- *ConAu 57*
Dunlevy, A H *Alli Sup*
Dunlevy, Anthony Howard 1793-1881 *OhA&B*
Dunlevy, William 1769-1826 *OhA&B*
Dunlop, Mrs. *Alli Sup*
Dunlop, Agnes Mary Robinson *Au&Wr,*
    AuBYP, ConAu 13R, SmATA 3,
    WrD 1976
Dunlop, Alexander *Alli, Alli Sup*
Dunlop, Alexander 1684-1742 *Alli*
Dunlop, Alexander Graham *Alli Sup*
Dunlop, Alison May 1835-1888 *ChPo S1*
Dunlop, Bell *Alli*
Dunlop, Douglas Morton 1909- *Au&Wr*
Dunlop, Durham *Alli Sup*
Dunlop, E S *OxCan*
Dunlop, Geoffrey *PoIre*
Dunlop, Geoffrey A *ChPo S2*
Dunlop, George Howard 1868-1941 *IndAu 1917*
Dunlop, Ian Geoffrey David 1925- *Au&Wr,*
    ConAu 9R, WrD 1976
Dunlop, James 1795-1856 *Alli, DcAmA,*
    DcNAA
Dunlop, John *Chmbr 2*
Dunlop, John 1755-1820 *BiD&SB*
Dunlop, John B 1942- *ConAu 57*
Dunlop, John Colin 1785?-1842 *Alli, BiD&SB,*
    BiDLA Sup, BrAu 19, Chmbr 3, DcEnL,
    EvLB, NewC
Dunlop, John Thomas 1914- *ConAu 13R*
Dunlop, M P *MnBBF*
Dunlop, Madeline Anne Wallace *Alli Sup*
Dunlop, Margaret J *ChPo S1*
Dunlop, Murray *Alli*
Dunlop, Richard 1921- *ConAu 17R,*
    WrD 1976
Dunlop, Robert Glasgow *Alli*
Dunlop, Robert Henry Wallace *Alli Sup*
Dunlop, Robert Vetch *Alli Sup*
Dunlop, Ronald Ossory 1894- *Au&Wr*
Dunlop, Thomas 1839-1915 *Alli Sup, ChPo S1,*
    ChPo S2
Dunlop, W S *BiDSA*
Dunlop, William 1692-1720 *Alli*
Dunlop, William 1768-1821 *PoIre*
Dunlop, William 1792?-1848 *BbtC, CanWr,*
    DcLEnL, OxCan
Dunman, Thomas 1849-1882 *Alli Sup*
Dunmore, John 1923- *WrD 1976*
Dunmore, Spencer S 1928- *ConAu 33,*
    WrD 1976
Dunn *Alli*
Dunn, Lady *Alli, BiDLA*

Dunn, Alan 1900-1974 *AmA&B, ConAu 33,*
    ConAu 49
Dunn, Amy E *ChPo*
Dunn, Amy Talbot *ChPo*
Dunn, Andrew Hunter *Alli Sup*
Dunn, Ann And Catherine H *Alli Sup*
Dunn, Archibald J *Alli Sup*
Dunn, Arthur Wallace 1859-1926 *DcNAA*
Dunn, Arthur William 1868-1927 *DcNAA*
Dunn, Ballard S 1829-1897 *Alli Sup, BiDSA,*
    DcNAA
Dunn, Bonnie 1920- *AmSCAP 66*
Dunn, Byron Archibald 1842-1923? *AmA&B,*
    AmLY, DcAmA, DcNAA
Dunn, Caleb 1834- *ChPo, ChPo S1*
Dunn, Catherine H *Alli Sup*
Dunn, Catherine M 1930- *ConAu 37*
Dunn, Catherine Tate 1859-1940 *IndAu 1917*
Dunn, Charles W 1915- *ConAu 49, WrD 1976*
Dunn, Charles William *OxCan*
Dunn, Christopher Blencowe *Alli Sup*
Dunn, Delmer D 1941- *ConAu 25*
Dunn, Donald H 1929- *ConAu 33*
Dunn, Douglas 1942- *Au&Wr, ConAu 45,*
    ConLC 6, ConP 1970, ConP 1975,
    WrD 1976
Dunn, Dyrus George *Alli Sup*
Dunn, Edgar S, Jr. 1921- *ConAu 9R*
Dunn, Edward *Alli, BiDLA*
Dunn, Eliza *DcNAA, WhWNAA*
Dunn, Elizabeth Hammond *Alli Sup*
Dunn, Esther Cloudman 1891- *AmA&B*
Dunn, Ethel 1932- *ConAu 23*
Dunn, Fannie Wyche 1879-1946 *DcNAA*
Dunn, Florence E *ChPo*
Dunn, Gwen *ChPo S2*
Dunn, H Percy *Alli Sup*
Dunn, Halbert Louis 1896-1975 *ConAu 61*
Dunn, Hampton 1916- *ConAu 57*
Dunn, Harold 1929- *ConAu 9R*
Dunn, Harris *ConAu XR*
Dunn, Harvey T 1884- *IlCB 1945*
Dunn, Henry *Alli, Alli Sup*
Dunn, Hugh Patrick 1916- *WrD 1976*
Dunn, J B *ChPo S2*
Dunn, Jacob Piatt 1855-1924 *Alli Sup, AmLY,*
    DcAmA, DcNAA, IndAu 1816
Dunn, James *ConAu XR*
Dunn, James B *Alli Sup*
Dunn, James Philip 1884-1936 *AmSCAP 66*
Dunn, James Taylor 1912- *ConAu 5R*
Dunn, Jerry G 1916- *ConAu 23*
Dunn, John *Alli, Alli Sup, BbtC*
Dunn, John Frederick 1905- *Au&Wr,*
    WrD 1976
Dunn, John Gilding 1938- *Au&Wr*
Dunn, Joseph Allan Elphinstone 1872-1941
    AmA&B, AmLY, DcNAA, MnBBF
Dunn, Joseph Bragg *BiDSA*
Dunn, Judith F *ConAu 57*
Dunn, Judy *ConAu XR, SmATA 5*
Dunn, Julia E *Alli Sup*
Dunn, Katherine 1945- *ConAu 33*
Dunn, L A *Alli Sup*
Dunn, Laurence Theodore 1910- *Au&Wr*
Dunn, Leslie C 1893- *WhWNAA*
Dunn, Lewis Romaine 1822-1876 *Alli Sup,*
    DcAmA, DcNAA
Dunn, Lloyd W 1906- *ConAu 57*
Dunn, Marion Herndon 1920- *ConAu 29*
Dunn, Martha 1848-1915 *ChPo, DcNAA*
Dunn, Martha Baker *DcAmA*
Dunn, Marty *OxCan Sup*
Dunn, Mary Alice 1897- *Au&Wr*
Dunn, Mary Lois 1930- *ConAu 61, SmATA 6*
Dunn, Matthias *Alli Sup*
Dunn, Michael 1918- *AmSCAP 66*
Dunn, N J *Alli Sup*
Dunn, Nathaniel 1800-1889 *Alli Sup, DcNAA,*
    PoIre
Dunn, Nell 1936- *ConNov 1976, WrD 1976*
Dunn, Oscar 1844-1885 *DcNAA, OxCan*
Dunn, Patience Louise 1922- *Au&Wr,*
    ConAu 5R
Dunn, Sir Patrick *Alli*
Dunn, Peter Norman 1926- *Au&Wr,*
    WrD 1976
Dunn, Rebecca Welty 1890- *AmSCAP 66*

Dunn, Robert 1877-1955 *AmA&B*
Dunn, Robert William *Alli Sup*
Dunn, Robinson Potter 1825-1867 *PoCh*
Dunn, S *Alli*
Dunn, S P *ChPo S2*
Dunn, Samuel *Alli*
Dunn, Samuel 1798- *Alli Sup*
Dunn, Samuel Watson 1918- *ConAu 1R,*
    WrD 1976
Dunn, Sarah Jane *Alli Sup, ChPo*
Dunn, Stanley Gerald 1879- *WhLA*
Dunn, Stephen 1939- *ConAu 33, DrAP 1975,*
    WrD 1976
Dunn, Stuart 1900- *ConAu 57*
Dunn, Thomas S *Alli Sup*
Dunn, Waldo Hilary 1882-1969 *AmA&B,*
    ConAu 21, OhA&B, WhWNAA
Dunn, William J 1906- *ConAu 33,*
    IndAu 1917
Dunn, William L 1924- *ConAu 37*
Dunn, William Meese *Alli Sup*
Dunnahoo, Terry 1927- *ConAu 41, SmATA 7*
Dunne, Charles *Alli, BiDLA*
Dunne, Edward Fitzsimons 1853-1937 *DcNAA*
Dunne, Finley Peter 1867-1936 *AmA&B,*
    BiD&SB, CatA 1947, Chmbr 3,
    ConAmL, DcAmA, DcLEnL, DcNAA,
    EvLB, LongC, OxAm, OxEng, Pen Am,
    REn, REnAL, TwCA, TwCA Sup
Dunne, Francis William Bradney *Alli Sup*
Dunne, George H 1905- *ConAu 1R,*
    WrD 1976
Dunne, Gerald T 1919- *ConAu 45*
Dunne, Gerald W E 1886-1953 *BkC 2, ChPo,*
    OhA&B
Dunne, J W 1875-1949 *BiDPar, LongC*
Dunne, Jacob Thompson 1798?- *PoIre*
Dunne, John *Alli*
Dunne, John Gregory 1932- *AuNews 1,*
    ConAu 25
Dunne, John Hart *Alli Sup*
Dunne, John S 1929- *ConAu 13R, WrD 1976*
Dunne, John William 1875-1949 *DcLEnL,*
    EvLB, REn
Dunne, L *Alli Sup*
Dunne, Mary Chavelita *LongC*
Dunne, Mary Collins 1914- *ConAu 41*
Dunne, Peter Finlay 1867-1936 *TwCW*
Dunne, Peter Masten 1889- *BkC 3, CatA 1947*
Dunne, Philip 1908- *ConAu P-1*
Dunnel, Henry Gale *Alli Sup*
Dunner, Joseph 1908- *AmA&B, Au&Wr,*
    ConAu 21
Dunnett, Alastair MacTavish 1908- *Au&Wr*
Dunnett, Dorothy 1923- *Au&Wr, ConAu 1R,*
    WrD 1976
Dunnett, Margaret Rosalind 1909- *Au&Wr,*
    WrD 1976
Dunnett, R F *MnBBF*
Dunnicliff, H B 1885- *WhLA*
Dunnicliffe, Henry *Alli Sup*
Dunning, Captain *Alli*
Dunning, Albert Elijah 1844-1923 *Alli Sup,*
    AmA&B, DcAmA, DcNAA
Dunning, Annie Ketchum 1831- *Alli Sup,*
    BiD&SB, DcAmA, DcNAA
Dunning, Charlotte *Alli Sup, AmA&B,*
    DcAmA, DcNAA
Dunning, Dan *HsB&A*
Dunning, Edwin James 1821-1901 *DcAmA,*
    DcNAA
Dunning, John *Alli Sup*
Dunning, John 1731-1783 *Alli*
Dunning, John Harry 1927- *Au&Wr*
Dunning, M O B *Alli Sup*
Dunning, Philip 1890?-1957 *AmA&B, CnMD,*
    McGWD, ModWD, REnAL
Dunning, R *Alli Sup*
Dunning, R W *OxCan*
Dunning, Richard *Alli, BiDLA*
Dunning, Robert William 1938- *ConAu 53*
Dunning, Stephen 1924- *ChPo S1, ConAu 25*
Dunning, T J *Alli Sup*
Dunning, William Archibald 1857?-1922
    AmA&B, DcAmA, DcNAA
Dunnington, Hazel Brain 1912- *ConAu 21*
Dunnington, Tom *IlBYP*
Dunois, Jean 1402-1468 *OxFr*

DuNouy, Pierre Lecomte 1883-1947 *CatA 1952*
Dunovant, R G M *Alli Sup*
Dunoyer, Maurice *ConAu XR*
Dunoyer DeSegonzac, Andre 1884-1974 *ConAu 53, WhGrA*
Dunphie, Charles James 1820?-1908 *Alli Sup, ChPo, PoIre*
Dunphy, Jack 1914- *ConAu 25*
Dunphy, Thomas And Cummins, Thomas J *Alli Sup*
Dunraven, Wyndham Wyndham-Quin, Earl Of 1841-1926 *BbD, BiD&SB, OxCan*
Dunraven And Mount Earl, Earl Of *Alli Sup*
Dunroy, William Reed Hopper 1869- *ChPo*
Duns, Joannes Scotus 1265?-1308? *BrAu*
Duns, John 1820- *Alli Sup*
Duns Scotus, Joannes 1265?-1308? *BbD, BiD&SB, CasWL, DcEuL, EvLB, OxEng*
Duns Scotus, John 1265?-1308 *Alli, NewC, REn*
Dunsany, Baron Edward J M Prax Plunkett 1878-1957 *Alli Sup, AtlBL, CasWL, ChPo, ChPo S1, ChPo S2, CnMD, CnThe, DcLEnL, EncM&D, EvLB, JBA 1934, LongC, McGWD, ModBL, ModWD, NewC, OxEng, Pen Eng, REn, REnWD, TwCA, TwCA Sup, TwCW*
Dunscomb, J W *BbtC*
Dunscomb, Samuel Whitney, Jr. 1868- *WhWNAA*
Dunscombe, T *Alli*
Dunsford, Martin d1807 *Alli, BiDLA, BiDLA Sup*
Dunsheath, Joyce 1902- *Au&Wr, ConAu 5R*
Dunsheath, Percy 1886- *Au&Wr*
Dunshee, Henry Webb *Alli Sup*
Dunshunner, Augustus 1813-1865 *DcEnL*
Dunsmore, William *Alli Sup*
Dunsmuir, Amy *Alli Sup*
Dunson, Josh 1941- *ConAu 25*
Dunstable, John 1370?-1458? *Alli, AtlBL, REn*
Dunstable, Robert *DcEnL*
Dunstan, Saint 925?-988 *Alli, BiB S, DcEnL, NewC*
Dunstan, Andrew *ConAu XR*
Dunstan, Gregory *MnBBF*
Dunstan, H Mainwaring *Alli Sup*
Dunstan, James *Alli Sup*
Dunstan, Ralph *Alli Sup*
Dunstan, Reginald 1914- *ConAu 21*
Dunstanville, Francis, Lord De *Alli*
Dunstar, Samuel *Alli*
Dunstedter, Eddie 1897- *AmSCAP 66*
Dunster, Charles *Alli, BiDLA, BiDLA Sup*
Dunster, D *Alli*
Dunster, Dave Francis Thomas 1926- *Au&Wr, WrD 1976*
Dunster, H P *Alli*
Dunster, Henry 1609-1659 *Alli, AmA&B, CyAL 1*
Dunster, Henry Peter *Alli Sup*
Dunster, Mark *BlkAW*
Dunster, Samuel *Alli*
Dunstervill, Edward *Alli*
Dunsterville, Edward 1796-1873 *Alli Sup*
Dunsterville, Galfrid Clement Keyworth 1905- *Au&Wr, ConAu P-1*
Dunsterville, Lionel Charles 1866-1946 *ChPo S1, LongC*
Dunsterville, P C *ChPo*
Dunston, Arthur John 1922- *WrD 1976*
Dunstone, Maxwell Frederick 1915- *Au&Wr*
Dunthorne, John d1792? *BkIE*
Dunthorne, Richard 1711-1775 *Alli*
Dunton, Edith Kellogg 1875-1944 *AmA&B, WhWNAA*
Dunton, James Gerald 1899- *AmA&B, OhA&B*
Dunton, John *Alli*
Dunton, John 1659-1733 *Alli, BrAu, Chmbr 2, CyAL 1, DcEnL, DcNAA, NewC, OxAm, OxEng, REnAL*
Dunton, Mary Jane *ChPo S1*
Dunton, Samuel Cady 1910?-1975 *ConAu 61*
Dunton, William Herbert 1878-1936 *AmA&B*
Dunville, Sir Robert Grimshaw d1910 *PoIre*
Dunwell, Francis Henry 1819-1880 *Alli Sup*

Dunwoodie, Dominick *PoIre*
Dunworth, Grace *AmA&B*
Duodu, Cameron 1937- *AfA 1*
Duonelaitis, Kristijonas *CasWL*
DuPage, Florence *AmSCAP 66*
DuPage, Richard 1908- *AmSCAP 66*
Dupanloup, Felix Antoine Philippe 1802-1878 *BbD, BiD&SB, DcEuL, OxFr*
Dupaty, Emmanuel 1775-1851 *BiD&SB*
Dupee, Frederick Wilcox 1904- *AmA&B, ConAu P-1, TwCA Sup*
Dupee, Louise *ChPo*
Duperier, Charles 1622-1692 *CasWL*
Duperier, Francois *OxFr*
DuPerrier, Edmond 1900- *WhWNAA*
DuPerron, Jacques Davy 1556-1618 *BiD&SB, CasWL, DcEuL, OxFr*
Dupin, Amantine Aurore Lucile *EuA*
Dupin, August Dupont *ConAu XR*
Dupin, Aurore *OxFr*
Dupin, Jacques 1927- *WorAu*
Dupin, Jean-Henri 1787-1887 *OxFr*
Dupin, Louis-Ellies 1657-1719 *OxFr*
Dupleix, Joseph-Francois 1697-1763 *OxFr*
Duplessis, Francois Xavier 1694- *BbtC*
DuPlessis, Izak Dawid 1900- *CasWL*
Duplessis, Marie 1824-1847 *OxFr*
Duplessis, Maurice LeNoblet 1890-1959 *OxCan*
Duplessis, Yves *ConAu XR*
Duplessis-Mornay, Philippe De 1549-1623 *DcEuL, OxFr*
DuPlessys, Maurice 1864-1924 *OxFr*
Duplex, George *Alli Sup*
Dupon, Aurore Amantine Lucille *REn*
DuPonceau, Peter S 1760-1844 *Alli, CyAL 1*
DuPonceau, Pierre Etienne 1760-1844 *AmA, AmA&B, DcAmA, DcNAA, OxAm, REnAL*
DuPont, Bessie 1864-1949 *DcNAA*
Dupont, C V *OxCan*
DuPont, Eleuthere Irenee 1771-1834 *REn*
DuPont, Henry Algernon 1838-1926 *DcAmA, DcNAA*
Dupont, John *Alli, BbtC*
DuPont, Marcella Miller *ChPo S1*
Dupont, Paul *ConAu XR, WrD 1976*
DuPont, Philip Francis 1878- *ChPo S2*
Dupont, Pierre 1821-1870 *BiD&SB, EvEuW, OxFr*
Dupont DeNemours, Pierre Samuel 1739-1817 *BiD&SB, OxFr, REn*
Dupont-Sommer, Andre 1900- *Au&Wr*
DuPontet, C *ChPo*
Duport, J H A *Alli Sup*
Duport, James 1606-1679 *Alli*
Duport, John d1617 *Alli*
Duppa, Brian 1588-1662 *Alli*
Duppa, Richard d1831 *Alli, BiDLA, BiDLA Sup*
Duprat, Alphonse *AmA&B*
DuPratz, Antoine Simon LePage 1689-1775 *AmA&B, BiDSA*
DuPratz, M LePage *Alli*
Dupre, Catherine *Au&Wr, ConAu 25, WrD 1976*
DuPre, Charles C *Alli Sup*
Dupre, Edward *Alli*
Dupre, Ferdinand *Alli Sup*
Dupre, Hope *WhWNAA*
Dupre, Jimmy R 1906- *AmSCAP 66*
Dupre, John d1835 *Alli, BiDLA*
Dupre, Louis Karel 1925- *ConAu 9R, WrD 1976*
Dupre, William *Alli*
Dupree, A Hunter 1921- *ConAu 9R*
Dupree, Grace *WhWNAA*
Dupree, Harry 1911- *AmSCAP 66*
Dupree, Katharine *ChPo S1*
Dupree, Louis 1925- *ConAu 41*
Dupree, Morrison *WhWNAA*
Duprey, Henri *ConAu XR*
Duprey, Richard A 1929- *ConAu 5R*
DuPuget, Louis Albert *Alli Sup*
DuPui, James *Alli Sup*
Dupuis, Adrian M 1919- *ConAu 9R, WrD 1976*
Dupuis, Hanmer Lewis *Alli Sup*
Dupuis, Joseph *Alli*

Dupuis, Nathan Fellowes 1836-1917 *DcNAA*
Dupuis, Theodore Crane *Alli Sup*
Dupuis, Thomas S 1733-1796 *Alli*
Dupuy, Ann Eliza 1814-1881 *BiDSA*
Dupuy, Eliza Ann 1814-1881 *Alli, AmA, AmA&B, BiD&SB, DcAmA, DcNAA, LivFWS, OxAm, REnAL*
Dupuy, F *Alli Sup*
Dupuy, Mollie Jeannette 1872- *ChPo*
Dupuy, Pierre 1896- *OxCan, WhWNAA*
Dupuy, Richard Ernest 1887-1975 *AmA&B, ConAu 1R, ConAu 57*
Dupuy, Trevor Nevitt 1916- *AuBYP, ConAu 1R, SmATA 4, WrD 1976*
DuPuy, William Atherton 1876-1941 *AmA&B, AmLY, DcNAA, WhWNAA*
Duque De Rivas *DcSpL*
Duque Job, El *DcSpL*
Duquery, Henry *Alli, BiDLA*
Duquesa De Soma *DcSpL*
Duquesne, M *Alli*
Duquesne DeMenneville, Ange, Marquis 1702?-1778 *OxCan*
Duquet, Joseph Norbert 1828-1891 *BbtC, DcNAA, OxCan*
Durack, Mary 1913- *Au&Wr, WrD 1976*
Duram, James C 1939- *ConAu 53*
Duran, Agustin 1789?-1862 *BiD&SB, DcSpL*
Duran, Manuel E 1925- *ConAu 25*
Duran, Simeon Ben Zemah 1361-1444 *CasWL*
Durand, Mrs. Albert C *AmA&B, WhWNAA*
Durand, Alice *BiD&SB, EvEuW*
Durand, Asher Brown 1796-1886 *AmA&B, EarAB, OxAm*
Durand, Charles 1811-1905 *DcLEnL, DcNAA*
Durand, David 1679-1763 *Alli*
Durand, Edward Dana 1871- *AmLY, WhWNAA*
Durand, Lady Emily Augusta *Alli Sup*
Durand, Evelyn 1870-1900 *DcNAA*
Durand, Sir Henry Marion 1812-1871 *Alli Sup*
Durand, Sir Henry Mortimer 1850- *Alli Sup, BbD*
Durand, John 1822-1908 *Alli Sup, DcNAA*
Durand, John Dana 1913- *ConAu 61*
Durand, Loyal, Jr. 1902- *ConAu 21*
Durand, Oswald *CasWL*
Durand, Robert 1944- *ConAu 57*
Durand, Wade Hampton 1887-1964 *AmSCAP 66*
Durand, William Frederick 1859- *DcAmA*
Durandeaux, Jacques 1926- *ConAu 25*
Durandi, Jacopo 1737-1817 *BiD&SB*
Durang, Christoph *ChPo S1*
Durant, Ariel K 1898- *ConAu 9R*
Durant, Asher *REn*
Durant, Charles *Alli Sup, ChPo*
Durant, Charles Ferson 1805-1873 *DcNAA*
Durant, E Elliott *BlkAW*
Durant, Estienne 1585-1618 *OxFr*
Durant, Ghislani *Alli Sup*
Durant, Gilles 1550?-1615? *BiD&SB, DcEuL, OxFr*
Durant, Gladys May 1899- *Au&Wr, WrD 1976*
Durant, Heloise *Alli Sup*
Durant, Henry Fowle 1822-1881 *AmA&B*
Durant, J *Alli*
Durant, John *Alli*
Durant, John 1620- *Alli*
Durant, John 1902- *AmA&B, AuBYP, ConAu 9R*
Durant, Mrs. Kenneth *AmA&B*
Durant, Samuel W *Alli Sup*
Durant, Will 1885- *AmA&B, ConAu 9R, DcLEnL, EvLB, LongC, OxAm, REn, REnAL, TwCA, TwCA Sup, WhWNAA*
Durante, Jimmy 1893- *AmSCAP 66*
Duranti, Count Durante 1718-1780 *BiD&SB*
Duranti, Samuel *Alli*
Duranty, Louis Emile Edmond 1833-1880 *EvEuW, OxFr*
Duranty, Walter 1884-1957 *AmA&B, OxAm, REnAL, TwCA, TwCA Sup*
Durao, Jose DeSanta Rita, Frei 1702?-1784 *CasWL*
Duras, Claire L DeKersaint, Duchess Of 1777?-1828 *BiD&SB, OxFr*

Duras, Marguerite 1914- *CasWL, CnMD Sup, CnThe, ConAu 25, ConLC 3, ConLC 6, CrCD, EncWL, EvEuW, McGWD, ModRL, ModWD, Pen Eur, REn, REnWD, TwCW, WhTwL, WorAu*
Duratschek, M Claudia 1894- *ConAu 37*
Duratschek, Sister Mary Claudia 1894- *ConAu XR*
Durayd B As-Simma 530-630 *DcOrL 3*
D'Urban, William Stewart M *BbtC*
Durband, Alan 1927- *Au&Wr, ConAu 5R, WrD 1976*
Durbin, Harriet Whitney *ChPo*
Durbin, John Price 1800-1876 *Alli, AmA&B, BiD&SB, BiDSA, DcAmA, DcNAA*
Durbin, Mary Lou 1927- *ConAu 21*
Durbin, Richard Louis 1928- *ConAu 53*
Durbridge, Francis 1912- *Au&Wr, EncM&D*
Durcan, Paul 1944- *ConP 1970*
Durch, Der Verein *ClDMEuL*
Durden, Robert Franklin 1925- *ConAu 9R, WrD 1976*
Durel, John 1625-1683 *Alli*
Durell, Ann *AuBYP*
Durell, David 1728-1775 *Alli*
Durell, Fletcher 1859-1946 *DcNAA, WhWNAA*
Durell, Philip *Alli*
Durell, Thomas Jackson 1866- *WhWNAA*
Durem, Ray 1915-1963 *BlkAW*
Duren, George Bancroft *ChPo*
Duren, William Larkin 1870- *AmA&B*
Durer, Albrecht 1471-1528 *AtlBL, NewC, OxGer, REn*
D'Urfe, Honore 1567-1625 *Pen Eur*
Durfee, Calvin *Alli Sup*
Durfee, Charles A *Alli Sup*
Durfee, David A 1929- *ConAu 29, WrD 1976*
Durfee, Job 1790-1847 *Alli, AmA, AmA&B, CyAL 1, DcAmA, DcNAA*
Durfee, Thomas 1826-1907 *Alli Sup*
Durfee, Thomas 1826-1901 *ChPo, DcAmA, DcNAA*
Durfee, William Pitt 1855-1941 *DcNAA*
D'Urfey, Thomas 1653-1723 *Alli, BiD&SB, BrAu, CasWL, ChPo, Chmbr 1, DcEnA, DcEnL, EvLB, NewC, OxEng, Pen Eng, REn*
D'Urfey, Tom 1653-1723 *REn*
Durgin, George Francis *OxCan*
Durgnat, Raymond Eric 1932- *Au&Wr, ConAu 17R, WrD 1976*
Durham, Bishop Of *BiDLA*
Durham, Earl Of 1792-1840 *BbtC, OxCan*
Durham, Anne *WrD 1976*
Durham, Cecile E *ChPo S2*
Durham, David *EncM&D*
Durham, E Samuel 1853-1944 *OhA&B*
Durham, Eddie 1909- *AmSCAP 66*
Durham, Elizabeth Malcolm *AnMV 1926*
Durham, Frances R *ChPo S1*
Durham, George R 1888-1902 *ChPo S1*
Durham, James *Alli*
Durham, James 1622?-1658 *Alli*
Durham, James Andrew Cuninghame 1879- *WhLA*
Durham, James George *Alli, BiDLA*
Durham, John *ConAu XR*
Durham, John I 1933- *ConAu 29*
Durham, John Stephens 1861-1919 *BlkAW*
Durham, Mae J *AnCL, ConAu 57*
Durham, Marilyn 1930- *ConAu 49, DrAF 1976*
Durham, Mary Edith 1863- *WhLA*
Durham, Philip 1912- *ConAu 9R*
Durham, Richard V 1817- *BlkAW*
Durham, Robert Lee 1870-1949 *DcNAA*
Durham, Simeon Of *Alli*
Durham, Thomas J, Sr. 1924- *AmSCAP 66*
Durham, William 1611-1868? *Alli, Alli Sup*
Durian, Petros 1852-1872 *DcOrL 3*
Durie, Anna *OxCan*
Durie, James 1823- *ChPo S1*
Durinc, Der *OxGer*
Duringsfeld, Ida Von 1815-1876 *BiD&SB*
Duris 340?BC-260BC *CasWL, Pen Cl*
Durivage, Francis Alexander 1814-1881 *Alli, Alli Sup, AmA, AmA&B, BiD&SB,*

ChPo S1, ChPo S2, DcAmA, DcNAA
Durkan, Patrick Francis d1910 *PoIre*
Durkee, J Stanley 1866- *AmA&B*
Durkee, Mary C 1921- *ConAu 13R*
Durkee, Silas *Alli Sup*
Durkheim, Emile 1858-1917 *ClDMEuL, OxFr*
Durkin, Mrs. Douglas *AmNov XR*
Durkin, Douglas Leader 1884- *CanNov, ChPo S1, OxCan*
Durkin, Henry P 1940- *ConAu 53*
Durkin, Joseph Thomas 1903- *ConAu P-1*
Durlacher, Ed *AuBYP*
Durland, Kellogg 1881-1911 *DcNAA*
Durland, William R 1931- *ConAu 57*
Durnbaugh, Donald F 1927- *ConAu 21, WrD 1976*
Durnford, Charles, And E H East *Alli*
Durnford, Edward *Alli Sup*
Durnford, Mary *BbtC*
Durnford, W *Alli, BiDLA*
Duroche, Leonard L 1933- *ConAu 37*
Durocher, Olivier *OxCan Sup*
Durocher, R *OxCan Sup*
DuRose, William Porcher 1836-1918 *AmLY*
Duroselle, Jean-Baptiste Marie Lucien C 1917- *ConAu 9R*
Durr, Fred 1921- *ConAu 37*
Durr, William Kirtley 1924- *ConAu 13R, WrD 1976*
Durrad, A J *ChPo*
Durrah, Jim *BlkAW*
Durrak, Jam d1706 *DcOrL 2*
Durrani, Mahmood Khan 1914- *ConAu P-1*
Durrani, Mahmundkhan 1914- *Au&Wr*
Durrant, Digby 1926- *ConAu 21*
Durrant, J C B *ChPo S1*
Durrant, Philip John 1901- *Au&Wr, WrD 1976*
Durrant, R G *Alli Sup*
Durrant, Sheila 1945- *WrD 1976*
Durrant, Valentine *Alli Sup*
Durrell, Ann *ChPo*
Durrell, Donald D 1903- *ConAu 17R*
Durrell, Gerald Malcolm 1925- *Au&Wr, AuBYP, ConAu 5R, LongC, NewC, REn, SmATA 8, TwCW, WorAu, WrD 1976*
Durrell, Jacqueline Sonia Rasen 1929- *ConAu 23*
Durrell, Jacquie *ConAu XR*
Durrell, Lawrence 1912- *Au&Wr, CasWL, ChPo, CnE&AP, CnMD, CnMWL, ConAu 9R, ConDr, ConLC 1, ConLC 4, ConLC 6, ConNov 1972, ConNov 1976, ConP 1970, ConP 1975, DcLEnL, EncWL, EvLB, LongC, ModBL, ModBL Sup, ModWD, NewC, OxEng, Pen Eng, RAdv 1, REn, TwCA Sup, TwCW, WebEAL, WhTwL, WrD 1976*
Durrenberger, Robert Warren 1918- *ConAu 23*
Durrenmatt, Friedrich 1921- *Au&Wr, CasWL, CnMD, CnThe, ConLC 1, ConLC 4, CrCD, EncWL, EvEuW, McGWD, ModGL, ModWD, OxGer, Pen Eur, REn, REnWD, TwCW, WhTwL, WorAu*
Durrett, Idell *TexWr*
Durrett, Reuben Thomas 1824-1913 *Alli Sup, AmA, AmA&B, BiDSA, DcAmA, DcNAA*
Durrie, Daniel Steele 1819-1892 *Alli Sup, AmA&B, CyAL 2, DcAmA, DcNAA*
Durst, Charles Elmer 1884- *WhWNAA*
Durst, Paul 1921- *Au&Wr, ConAu 23*
Durst, Simon *ChPo S2*
D'Urstelle, Pierre *ConAu XR*
Durstine, Roy Sarles 1886-1962 *AmA&B*
Durston, Georgia Roberts *ChPo*
Durston, William *Alli*
Durtain, Luc 1881- *OxFr*
Duruy, Georges 1853- *BiD&SB*
Duruy, Victor 1811-1894 *BiD&SB, OxFr*
Durville, Hector 1849-1923 *BiDPar*
Durville, Henri 1888- *BiDPar*
Durward, Bernard Isaac 1817-1902 *ChPo, WiscW*
Dury, Alex *Alli*
Dury, John *Alli*
Durych, Jaroslav 1886-1962 *CasWL, ClDMEuL, EncWL, ModSL 2, Pen Eur,*

TwCW
Duryea, J B 1864- *WhWNAA*
Duryea, Joseph T *Alli Sup*
Duryea, Nina Larrey 1874-1951 *AmA&B*
Duryee, Mary Ballard *ChPo, ChPo S2*
Duryee, S *Alli Sup*
Duryee, William Rankin 1838-1897? *DcAmA, DcNAA*
DuRyer, Pierre 1600?-1658 *CasWL, DcEuL, EuA, EvEuW, McGWD, OxFr, REn*
Durzak, Manfred 1938- *ConAu 49*
Dusany, Lord 1878- *WhLA*
Dusautoy, Frederick *Alli*
Dusautoy, J A *Alli*
DuSautoy, Peter 1921- *ConAu 5R*
Duse, Eleonora 1859-1924 *REn*
Dusenberry, William Howard 1908- *ConAu P-1*
Dusenbery, Gail 1939- *ConP 1970*
Dusenbury, Winifred L *ConAu XR*
DuShane, Donald 1885-1947 *IndAu 1917*
Dushman, Saul 1883- *WhWNAA*
Dushnitzky-Shner, Sara 1913- *ConAu 29*
DuSoe, Robert C 1892-1958 *MorJA, WhWNAA*
Dussauce, Hippolyte d1869 *DcNAA*
Dussault, Francois-Joseph 1769-1824 *OxFr*
Dussek, O B *ChPo*
Dussieux, L *BbtC*
Dussieux, Louis-Etienne *OxCan*
Dust 1937- *BlkAW*
Duster, A Gentleman With A *NewC*
Duster, Alfreda M Barnett 1904- *LivBA*
Duster, Troy 1936- *ConAu 29, LivBA*
Dustin, Charles *AmA&B, OhA&B*
Dusty Waters *WhWNAA*
Dutch, George Sheldon 1891- *WhWNAA*
Dutch, J S *Alli Sup*
Dutcher, Addison Porter 1818-1884 *Alli Sup, DcAmA, DcNAA, OhA&B*
Dutcher, Andrew *Alli Sup*
Dutcher, George Matthew 1874-1959 *AmA&B, WhWNAA*
Dutcher, Jacob Conkling 1820?-1888 *DcAmA, DcNAA*
Dutcher, Salem *Alli Sup*
Dutens, Lewis 1729-1812 *Alli*
Dutfield, James *Alli*
Duthie, Charles S 1911- *ConAu 29*
Duthie, David Wallace *OxCan*
Duthie, James *Alli Sup*
Duthie, Jane Allardice Farquhar 1845- *ChPo*
Duthie, Robert 1826-1865 *ChPo S1*
Duthie, William *Alli Sup*
Duthoit, David *Alli Sup*
Duthy, John *Alli, BiDLA*
DuToit, Jacob Daniel *CasWL*
Dutourd, Jean 1920- *Au&Wr, CasWL, McGWD, ModRL, REn, TwCA Sup*
Dutra E Mello, Antonio Francisco 1823-1843 *BiD&SB*
Dutt *DcOrL 2*
Dutt, Greece C *Alli Sup*
Dutt, Michael Madhusudan 1824?-1873 *Alli Sup, CasWL, DcLEnL, WebEAL*
Dutt, Rajani Palme 1896-1974 *Au&Wr, ConAu 53, ConAu P-1, DcLEnL*
Dutt, Romesh Chunder 1848-1909 *Alli Sup, BrAu 19, CasWL, DcLEnL*
Dutt, Satyen *CasWL*
Dutt, Shoshee Chunder, Rai Bahadar *Alli Sup*
Dutt, Toru 1856-1877 *Alli Sup, BbD, BiD&SB, CasWL, ChPo, ChPo S1, DcLEnL, Pen Eng, WebEAL*
Dutt, Udoy Chand *Alli Sup*
Dutta, Michael Madhusudan 1824-1873 *CasWL*
Dutta, Reginald 1914- *ConAu 61*
Dutta, Rex *ConAu XR*
Dutta, Romesh Chandra 1848-1909 *CasWL*
Dutta, Satyen *CasWL*
Dutton, Amy *Alli Sup*
Dutton, Charles 1842- *Alli Sup*
Dutton, Charles Judson 1888-1964 *AmA&B, WhWNAA*
Dutton, Clarence Edward 1841-1912 *Alli Sup, DcAmA, DcNAA*
Dutton, Edward Payson 1831-1923 *AmA&B, ChPo*
Dutton, Emily Helen 1870-1947 *DcNAA*

Dutton, Francis *Alli*
Dutton, Geoffrey Piers Henry 1922- *Au&Wr,*
CasWL, ConAu 45, ConNov 1972,
ConNov 1976, ConP 1970, ConP 1975,
WrD 1976
Dutton, George *Alli Sup*
Dutton, George Burwell 1881- *WhWNAA*
Dutton, H F *Alli, BiDLA*
Dutton, H Mary *ChPo S1*
Dutton, H P 1885- *WhWNAA*
Dutton, Hely *Alli, BiDLA*
Dutton, Henry 1796-1869 *Alli, DcAmA*
Dutton, Isabella *Alli Sup*
Dutton, Joan Parry 1908- *ConAu 9R*
Dutton, John *Alli*
Dutton, John M 1926- *ConAu 41*
Dutton, M R 1783-1825 *Alli*
Dutton, Mary 1922- *Au&Wr, ConAu 33*
Dutton, Matthew *Alli*
Dutton, Maude Barrows 1880- *CarSB*
Dutton, Ralph 1898- *Au&Wr, ConAu 13R*
Dutton, Reginald George *Alli Sup*
Dutton, Mrs. S E T *ChPo*
Dutton, Samuel Train 1849-1919 *DcAmA,*
DcNAA
Dutton, Samuel William Southmayd 1814-1866
DcNAA
Dutton, Thomas 1767?- *Alli, BiDLA*
Dutton, Thomas, Guy Nott, & John Glover *Alli*
Dutton, William Elliott *Alli Sup*
Dutton, William S 1893- *WhWNAA*
Dutz *ConAu XR, SmATA 6*
Duuh, Ali 1850?-1910? *AfA 1*
Duun, Olav 1876-1939 *ClDMEuL, CyWA,*
EncWL, Pen Eur, REn, TwCA,
TwCA Sup
Duun, Ole Julius 1876-1939 *CasWL, EvEuW*
Duus, Peter 1933- *ConAu 25*
DuVair, Guillaume 1556-1621 *CasWL, OxFr,*
Pen Eur
Duval *Alli*
Duval, Alexandre 1767-1842 *BiD&SB, OxFr*
DuVal, Charles *Alli Sup*
Duval, Charles H d1906 *PoIre*
Duval, Claude 1643-1670 *NewC, REn*
Duval, Delphine 1837-1906 *DcNAA*
DuVal, F Alan 1916- *ConAu 33*
Duval, Francis *Alli*
Duval, J C *Alli Sup*
Duval, Jeanne *OxFr*
Duval, John Crittenden 1816-1897 *AmA&B,*
DcNAA
Duval, John Edward *PoIre*
Duval, John Pope 1790-1855 *BiDSA*
Duval, John Pope 1790-1855? *DcAmA*
Duval, Kulgan D *ChPo, ChPo S2*
Duval, Lucien *BiDSA*
Duval, M *Alli*
Duval, Mary Fisher *BiDSA*
Duval, Mary W 1850- *BiDSA*
DuVal, Michael *Alli*
Duval, Paul *OxCan Sup, OxFr*
Duval, Paul Alexandre 1855-1906 *EuA*
Duval, Philip Snaith *Alli Sup*
Duvall, Charles Thomas 1863- *ChPo*
Duvall, Evelyn Millis 1906- *AmA&B,*
ConAu 1R, SmATA 9, WrD 1976
Duvall, Richard M 1934- *ConAu 45*
Duvall, Trumbull Gillette 1861-1951
IndAu 1917, OhA&B
Duvall, W Clyde 1917- *ConAu 17R*
Duvar, John Hunter *BbtC, BiD&SB*
DuVaul, Virginia C *ConAu 49*
Duveen, Geoffrey 1883-1975 *ConAu 61*
Duveneck, Frank 1848-1919 *OxAm, REn*
DuVerdier, Antoine 1544-1600 *OxFr*
Duverger *Alli*
Duverger, J *BiDLA*
DuVergier DeHauranne, Jean 1581-1643 *OxFr,*
REn
Duvergier DeHauranne, Louis-P-E *OxCan*
Duvergier D'Hauranne, Prosper 1798-1881
BiD&SB
Duvernay, Ludger 1799-1852 *OxCan*
Duvernois, Henri 1875-1937 *McGWD, OxFr*
Duveyrier, Charles 1803-1866 *BiD&SB*
DuVivier, Joseph Dupont, Sieur 1707-1760
OxCan

Duvoisin, Roger Antoine 1904-1968 *AmA&B,*
Au&Wr, AuBYP, AuICB, BkP,
Cald 1938, ChPo, ChPo S1, ChPo S2,
ConAu 13R, IlBYP, IlCB 1945,
IlCB 1956, IlCB 1966, JBA 1951,
SmATA 2, St&VC, WhCL, WhGrA,
WrD 1976
DuWors, Richard E 1914- *ConAu 45*
Dux, Adolf 1822-1881 *BiD&SB*
Duxbury, Arthur 1903- *Au&Wr*
Duxbury, C *Alli Sup*
Duy, Pham 1927- *ConAu 61*
Duyckinck, Evert Augustus 1816-1878 *Alli,*
Alli Sup, AmA, AmA&B, BbD,
BiD&SB, CyAL 2, DcAmA, DcEnL,
DcNAA, OxAm, Pen, REnAL
Duyckinck, George Long 1823-1863 *Alli,*
Alli Sup, AmA, AmA&B, BbD,
BiD&SB, CyAL 2, DcAmA, DcNAA,
Pen Am, REnAL
Duyckinck, Whitehead Cornell 1843-1936
DcNAA
Duym, Jonkheer Jacob 1547-1624? *CasWL*
Duyse, Prudens Van 1804-1859 *BiD&SB,*
CasWL, EuA
Dvarakanatha Raya *Alli Sup*
Dvivedi, Mahavirprasad 1864-1938 *DcOrL 2*
Dvorak, Antonin 1841-1904 *AtlBL, OxAm,*
REn, REnAL
Dvoretzky, Edward 1930- *ConAu 37,*
WrD 1976
Dvornik, Francis 1893-1975 *ConAu 1R,*
ConAu 61
D'vys, George Whitefield 1860-1941 *AmLY,*
CarSB, WhWNAA
Dwarris, F *Alli, BiDLA*
Dweck, Susan 1943- *ConAu 33*
Dwiggins, Clare Victor *ChPo*
Dwiggins, Don 1913- *ConAu 17R, SmATA 4*
Dwiggins, William Addison 1880-1956 *AmA&B,*
IlCB 1945, IlCB 1956, OhA&B, OxAm,
REnAL
Dwight, Allan *ConAu XR, SmATA XR*
Dwight, Benjamin Woodbridge 1816-1889
Alli Sup, DcAmA, DcNAA
Dwight, Charles Abbott Schneider 1860- *ChPo*
Dwight, Charles P *OxCan*
Dwight, Edwin Welles 1789-1841 *DcAmA,*
DcNAA
Dwight, Elizabeth Amelia *Alli Sup*
Dwight, Harrison Gray Otis 1803-1862 *Alli,*
DcAmA, DcNAA
Dwight, Harrison Griswold 1875-1959 *AmA&B,*
WhWNAA
Dwight, Henry C d1832 *Alli*
Dwight, Henry E *Alli Sup, CyAL 1*
Dwight, Henry Edwin 1797-1832 *DcAmA,*
DcNAA
Dwight, Henry Otis 1843-1917 *Alli Sup,*
AmA&B, DcAmA, DcNAA
Dwight, Herbert Bristol 1885- *WhWNAA*
Dwight, James *Alli Sup*
Dwight, James McLaren Breed 1825-1897
DcNAA
Dwight, John Sullivan 1813-1893 *Alli, Alli Sup,*
AmA, AmA&B, BbD, BiD&SB, ChPo,
ChPo S1, DcAmA, DcNAA, OxAm,
REnAL
Dwight, Margaret D 1883-1946 *DcNAA*
Dwight, Marianne 1816-1901 *AmA, OxAm*
Dwight, Mary Ann 1806-1858 *Alli, Alli Sup,*
DcAmA, DcNAA
Dwight, Melatia Everett *ChPo*
Dwight, Nathaniel 1770-1831 *Alli, DcAmA,*
DcNAA
Dwight, Samuel *Alli*
Dwight, Sereno Edwards 1786-1850 *Alli,*
CyAL 2, DcAmA, DcNAA
Dwight, Theodore 1764-1846 *Alli, AmA,*
AmA&B, BiD&SB, ChPo, CyAL 1,
DcAmA, DcNAA, OxAm, REn, REnAL
Dwight, Theodore, Jr. 1796-1866 *Alli, Alli Sup,*
AmA, AmA&B, BbtC, BiD&SB,
CyAL 1, DcAmA, DcNAA, OxCan
Dwight, Theodore William 1822-1892 *Alli Sup,*
AmA, DcAmA, DcNAA
Dwight, Thomas 1843-1911 *Alli Sup, DcAmA,*
DcNAA

Dwight, Tilton *DcNAA*
Dwight, Timothy 1752-1817 *Alli, AmA,*
AmA&B, BiD&SB, BiDLA, CasWL,
ChPo, ChPo S1, CnDAL, CyAL 1,
DcAmA, DcEnL, DcNAA, EvLB, OxAm,
Pen Am, PoCh, REn, REnAL, WebEAL
Dwight, Timothy 1828-1916 *Alli Sup, BiD&SB,*
Chmbr 3, DcAmA, DcNAA
Dwight, William Buck 1833- *DcAmA*
Dwinell, Melvin 1825-1887 *DcNAA*
Dwinelle, John W *Alli Sup*
Dwinger, Edwin Erich 1898- *ClDMEuL,*
OxGer
Dworkin, Gerald 1937- *ConAu 53*
Dworkin, Martin S *DrAF 1976, DrAP 1975*
Dworkin, Rita 1928- *ConAu 23*
Dworzan, Helene *DrAF 1976*
Dwoskin, Stephen 1939- *WrD 1976*
Dwyer, Anthony *PoIre*
Dwyer, Charles P *Alli Sup*
Dwyer, Edward 1821- *Alli Sup*
Dwyer, Francis *Alli Sup*
Dwyer, Ion E 1870- *WhWNAA*
Dwyer, James Francis 1874- *AmA&B*
Dwyer, John *Alli Sup*
Dwyer, John Hanbury *ChPo S1*
Dwyer, John William 1865- *DcAmA*
Dwyer, P W *Alli, BiDLA, PoIre*
Dwyer, Richard 1919- *Au&Wr*
Dwyer, Walter W 1894- *BiDPar*
Dwyer-Jones, Alice Louise 1913- *WrD 1976*
Dwyer-Joyce, Alice 1913- *Au&Wr, ConAu 53*
Dyagilev, S P *DcRusL*
Dyak, Miriam *DrAP 1975*
Dyal, James A 1928- *ConAu 5R*
Dyal, William M, Jr. 1928- *ConAu 21*
Dyall, Charles *Alli Sup*
Dyall, Valentine 1908- *Au&Wr*
Dyar, Harrison Gray 1866-1929 *DcNAA*
Dyar, Muriel Campbell 1876- *OhA&B*
Dyason, William *Alli*
Dyatt, Thomas W 1771-1861 *DcNAA*
Dybek, Stuart *DrAF 1976, DrAP 1975*
Dyce 1806-1864 *ChPo*
Dyce, Alexander 1798-1869 *Alli, BiD&SB,*
BrAu 19, CasWL, ChPo, ChPo S1,
ChPo S2, Chmbr 3, DcEnL, DcEuL,
EvLB, NewC
Dyce, E Archer *MnBBF*
Dyce, Gilbert *Alli Sup*
Dyce, W C *Alli Sup*
Dychard, James *Alli Sup*
Dyche, Thomas *Alli, ChPo*
Dyck *AtlBL*
Dyck, Anni 1931- *ConAu 25*
Dyck, Harvey L *OxCan Sup*
Dyck, J William 1918- *ConAu 57*
Dyck, Martin 1927- *ConAu 41*
Dyckman, Jacob 1788-1822 *Alli, DcAmA*
Dyckman, John William 1922- *ConAu 1R*
Dyckman, Thomas Richard 1932- *ConAu 33*
Dyde, Rowland *BiDLA*
Dyde, Samuel Walters 1862-1947 *DcNAA*
Dyde, W *Alli, BiDLA*
Dye, Charity 1849-1921 *ChPo S1, DcNAA,*
IndAu 1816
Dye, Charles *ConAu XR*
Dye, David L 1925- *ConAu 23*
Dye, Deacon *Alli Sup*
Dye, Eva Emery 1855-1947 *AmLY, DcAmA,*
DcNAA, WhWNAA
Dye, F *Alli Sup*
Dye, Harold E 1907- *ConAu 29*
Dye, J H *Alli Sup*
Dye, James W 1934- *ConAu 23*
Dye, John Smith *Alli Sup*
Dye, John T 1835-1913 *IndAu 1816*
Dye, Thomas R 1935- *ConAu 33*
Dye, William McEntyre 1831-1899 *Alli Sup,*
DcNAA, DcAmA
Dye, William Seddinger, Jr. 1880- *WhWNAA*
Dyen, Isidore 1913- *ConAu 53, WrD 1976*
Dyer, Ada May 1876- *OhA&B*
Dyer, Adelina F *ChPo*
Dyer, Alexander Brydie 1852-1920 *DcNAA*
Dyer, Alfred Saunders *Alli Sup*
Dyer, Alfred Stace *Alli Sup*
Dyer, Arthur Reginald 1877- *WhLA*

Dyer, Beverly 1921- *ConAu 61*
Dyer, Brian *WrD 1976*
Dyer, C Raymond *ConAu XR*
Dyer, Catherine Cornelia 1817-1903 *Alli Sup,*
DcAmA, DcNAA
Dyer, Charles 1928- *Au&Wr, ConAu 21,*
ConDr, CrCD, WrD 1976
Dyer, Christopher 1935- *Au&Wr, WrD 1976*
Dyer, David *Alli Sup*
Dyer, David Patterson 1838-1924 *DcNAA*
Dyer, Ebenezer Porter 1813-1882 *Alli Sup,*
ChPo S2, ChPo S1, DcNAA
Dyer, Sir Edward 1543?-1607 *Alli, BiD&SB,*
BrAu, CasWL, Chmbr 1, CnE&AP,
CrE&SL, DcEuL, EvLB, NewC, OxEng,
REn
Dyer, Edward 1645- *ChPo S2*
Dyer, Edward Oscar 1853-1914 *DcNAA*
Dyer, Elizabeth 1890- *WhWNAA*
Dyer, F J *Alli Sup*
Dyer, Frances J *ChPo S1*
Dyer, Frank Lewis 1870-1941 *DcNAA*
Dyer, Frederick C 1919?- *ConAu 17R,*
WrD 1976
Dyer, Frederick N *Alli Sup*
Dyer, George *Alli*
Dyer, George 1755-1841 *Alli, BiDLA, BrAu,*
DcEnL, DcLEnL, NewC, OxEng
Dyer, George 1903- *AmA&B, WhWNAA*
Dyer, George E 1928- *ConAu 37*
Dyer, George J 1927- *ConAu 13R*
Dyer, Gertrude P *Alli Sup*
Dyer, H McNeile *Alli Sup*
Dyer, Heman 1810-1900 *Alli Sup, DcAmA,*
DcNAA
Dyer, Henry *Alli Sup*
Dyer, Isaac Watson 1855-1937 *Alli Sup,*
DcNAA, WhWNAA
Dyer, Isadore 1865-1920 *DcNAA*
Dyer, J M *Alli Sup*
Dyer, Sir James 1511-1582 *Alli*
Dyer, James 1934- *WrD 1976*
Dyer, John 1699?-1758? *Alli, BiD&SB, BrAu,*
CasWL, ChPo, ChPo S1, Chmbr 2,
CnE&AP, DcEnL, DcEuL, DcLEnL,
EvLB, NewC, OxEng, Pen Eng, REn,
WebEAL
Dyer, John Lewis 1812-1901 *OhA&B*
Dyer, John Martin 1920- *ConAu 13R,*
WrD 1976
Dyer, John Percy 1902- *ConAu 1R*
Dyer, John Thomas 1918- *Au&Wr, WrD 1976*
Dyer, Joseph Chessborough 1780-1871 *Alli Sup*
Dyer, Kate Gambold 1880?- *IndAu 1917*
Dyer, Lewis *Alli Sup*
Dyer, Louis 1851-1908 *AmA, AmA&B,*
DcAmA, DcNAA
Dyer, Mary 1780- *DcNAA*
Dyer, Oliver 1824-1907 *DcAmA, DcNAA*
Dyer, Raymond *ConAu XR*
Dyer, Richard *Alli*
Dyer, Ruth Omega 1885- *AmA&B, ChPo,*
WhWNAA
Dyer, Samuel 1725?-1772 *Alli, DcEuL*
Dyer, Sidney 1814-1898 *Alli Sup, AmA&B,*
BiD&SB, BiDSA, ChPo S1, DcAmA,
DcNAA, IndAu 1816
Dyer, Susan Hart *ChPo*
Dyer, Sydney 1819-1898 *ChPo S2*
Dyer, Thomas Firminger Thiselton- 1848-
Alli Sup, ChPo S1
Dyer, Thomas Henry 1804-1888 *Alli, Alli Sup,*
BiD&SB, DcEnL
Dyer, W E *ChPo*
Dyer, W Lincoln *IndAu 1816*
Dyer, Walter Alden 1878-1943 *AmA&B,*
AmLY, DcNAA, WhWNAA
Dyer, William d1696 *Alli*
Dyer, William B *ChPo*
Dyer, William G 1925- *ConAu 41*
Dyer, William Henry *Alli Sup*
Dyess, Tony R Q 1910- *AmSCAP 66*
Dygasinski, Adolf 1839-1902 *BiD&SB,*
ClDMEuL
Dygasinski, Tomasz Adolf 1839-1902 *CasWL*
Dygat, Stanislaw 1914- *CasWL, EncWL*
Dyherrn, Baron George Von 1848-1878 *BiD&SB*
Dyk, Viktor 1877-1931 *CasWL, ClDMEuL,*

EncWL, ModSL 2
Dyk, Walter 1899-1972 *ConAu 37*
Dyke *TwCA, TwCA Sup*
Dyke, Cornelius Gysbert 1900-1943 *DcNAA*
Dyke, Daniel d1614? *Alli*
Dyke, E *ChPo*
Dyke, Elizabeth d1926 *ChPo S1, ChPo S2*
Dyke, Henry Van *Chmbr 3, JBA 1934*
Dyke, Jeremiah d1620 *Alli*
Dyke, John 1935- *ConAu 25*
Dyke, Sidney Campbell 1886- *Au&Wr*
Dyke, T Webb *Alli, BiDLA*
Dyke, Thomas Jones *Alli Sup*
Dykema, Karl W 1906- *ConAu 25*
Dykema, Peter W 1873- *WhWNAA*
Dykeman, Carl *ChPo*
Dykeman, Wilma *ConAu XR, WrD 1976*
Dyker, Bob *OxCan*
Dykes *Alli*
Dykes, Archie R 1931- *ConAu 17R*
Dykes, Jack 1929- *ConAu 33, WrD 1976*
Dykes, James *BlkAW*
Dykes, James Oswald 1835- *Alli Sup*
Dykes, James William Ballantine *Alli Sup*
Dykes, Jeff C 1900- *ConAu 5R*
Dykes, Oswald *Alli*
Dykes, Thomas *Alli Sup*
Dykhuizen, George 1899- *ConAu 49*
Dykstra, Clarence Addison 1883-1950 *OhA&B*
Dykstra, Gerald 1922- *ConAu 45*
Dykstra, Gerald Oscar 1906- *OhA&B*
Dykstra, Leslie 1897- *WhWNAA*
Dykstra, Robert R 1930- *ConAu 25*
Dykstra, Waling 1821-1914 *CasWL*
Dylan, Bob 1941- *AmA&B, AmSCAP 66,*
ConAu 41, ConLC 3, ConLC 4,
ConLC 6, ConP 1970, ConP 1975,
WrD 1976
Dylan, Robert 1941- *AmSCAP 66*
Dylander, John 1709?-1741 *DcNAA*
Dyllingham, Francis *Alli*
Dymally, Mervyn M 1926- *ConAu 41*
Dyment, Clifford 1914-1971 *Au&Wr, ChPo,*
ChPo S2, ConAu 33, ConAu P-1,
ConP 1970
Dymock, John *Alli, BiDLA*
Dymoke, Juliet 1919- *Au&Wr, WrD 1976*
Dymond, Alfred Hutchinson 1827- *Alli Sup*
Dymond, Henry *Alli Sup*
Dymond, Jonathan 1796-1828 *Alli, NewC*
Dymond, Robert *Alli Sup*
Dymov, Ossip 1878-1959 *CnMD, ModWD*
Dymsza, William A 1922- *ConAu 49*
Dynely, James *AuBYP*
Dynes, Russell R 1923- *ConAu 9R*
Dyos, John *Alli*
Dyott, George M 1883-1972 *AmA&B,*
ConAu 37
Dyrness, William A 1943- *ConAu 33,*
WrD 1976
Dyroff, Jan Michael 1942- *ConAu 61*
Dysart, Earl Of *Alli*
Dysart, E J 1900- *TexWr*
Dysart, Ferne Cabot *TexWr*
Dyson, Mrs. *Alli Sup*
Dyson, Anne Jane 1912- *ConAu 21*
Dyson, Anthony Edward 1928- *Au&Wr,*
ConAu 57
Dyson, C E *Alli Sup*
Dyson, Charles Wilson 1861-1930 *DcNAA*
Dyson, Edward George 1865-1931 *Chmbr 3,*
DcLEnL, TwCW
Dyson, Hal 1884- *AmSCAP 66*
Dyson, Humphrey *Alli*
Dyson, Jeremiah *Alli*
Dyson, John B *Alli Sup*
Dyson, Richard R *Alli, BiDLA*
Dyson, Samuel *Alli Sup*
Dyson, Theophilus *Alli*
Dyson, Verne 1879- *AmA&B*
Dyve, Sir Lewis *Alli*
Dywasuk, Colette Taube 1941- *ConAu 45*
Dzanayty, Ivan *DcOrL 3*
Dzhubin, E Georgievich *EncWL*
Dzhugashvili, Iosef Visarionovich *DcRusL,*
REn
Dzierzkovski, Joseph 1807-1865 *BbD, BiD&SB*
Dziewanowski, M Kamil 1913- *ConAu 29*

Dzovo, Emmanuel Victor Kwame 1915?- *AfA 1*
Dzyuba, Ivan 1931- *CasWL*
Dzyubin, Eduard Georgievich 1895-1934
DcRusL

E

E, A *PoIre*
E A *WhLA*
E A B *WhLA*
E C M *WhLA*
E D M 1801-1880 *AmA*
E F C *WhWNAA*
E K *WhLA*
E P *ConAmA*
E P H *HsB&A*
Eaborn, Colin 1923- *WrD 1976*
Eachard, John *Alli*
Eachard, John 1636-1697 *Alli, NewC*
Eaches, Owen Philips 1840-1930 *DcNAA, WhWNAA*
Eade, Sir Peter 1825- *Alli Sup*
Eades, Christopher *Alli Sup*
Eades, John *Alli*
Eadfrith d721 *BiB S*
Eadfrith, Bishop *DcEnL*
Eadie, Donald 1919- *ConAu 33, WrD 1976*
Eadie, John 1810-1876 *Alli, Alli Sup, BbD, BiD&SB, DcEnL*
Eadie, Thomas Michael 1941- *ConP 1970*
Eadmer 1060?-1124? *Alli, BiB N, BiD&SB, BrAu, CasWL, DcEnL, EvLB, NewC, OxEng*
Eadmer Of Canterbury *Chmbr 1*
Eadmund *NewC*
Eadon, A *Alli Sup*
Eadon, Edward *Alli Sup*
Eadon, John *Alli, BiDLA*
Eadon, Samuel *Alli Sup*
Eadred *NewC*
Eads, H L *Alli Sup*
Eads, James Buchanan 1820-1887 *Alli Sup, DcAmA, DcNAA, IndAu 1917*
Eadward *NewC*
Eadwig *NewC*
Eady, K M And R *MnBBF*
Eady, L G *ChPo S1*
Eagar, Alexander Richard d1909 *Alli Sup, PoIre*
Eagar, Frances 1940- *ConAu 61*
Eagar, Frederick John *Alli Sup*
Eager, Cora M *ChPo S1*
Eager, Edward 1911-1964 *AmSCAP 66, AnCL, AuBYP, ChPo, MorJA, WhCL*
Eager, George *ChPo*
Eager, Mary Ann *AmSCAP 66*
Eager, Patrick Henry 1852- *BiDSA*
Eager, Samuel W 1900- *WhWNAA*
Eagle, Chester 1933- *ConAu 57*
Eagle, Cornelia *ChPo S2*
Eagle, Dorothy 1912- *ConAu 23*
Eagle, F K And E Younge *Alli*
Eagle, Fra *Alli*
Eagle, Joanna 1934- *ConAu 25*
Eagle, John *Alli Sup*
Eagle, P A *Alli*
Eagle, Robert H 1921- *ConAu 21*
Eagle, Solomon *Chmbr 3, LongC, NewC*

Eagle, William *Alli*
Eagles, John 1783-1855 *Alli, BiD&SB, DcEnL*
Eagles, Thomas *Alli*
Eagles, Thomas Henry *Alli Sup*
Eaglesfield, Carina Campbell 1856-1925 *IndAu 1816*
Eaglesfield, Francis *WrD 1976*
Eagleson, Hodge MacIlvain 1895- *OhA&B*
Eagleson, John 1941- *ConAu 53*
Eagleston, J H *Alli Sup*
Eaglestone, C R *Alli Sup*
Eagleton, Clyde 1891- *TexWr, WhWNAA*
Eagleton, Terence Francis 1943- *Au&Wr, ConAu 57, WrD 1976*
Eagleton, Terry *ConAu 57*
Eagly, Robert V 1933- *ConAu 49*
Eahfrith *NewC*
Eaker, Ira C 1896- *AmA&B*
Eakes, Mildred 1894- *OhA&B*
Eakin, Frank Edwin, Jr. 1936- *ConAu 53*
Eakin, Mary K 1917- *ConAu 1R*
Eakin, Richard M 1910- *ConAu 61*
Eakin, Vera 1900- *AmSCAP 66*
Eakins, David W 1923- *ConAu 49*
Eakins, Thomas 1844-1916 *AtlBL, OxAm, REn, REnAL*
Eakle, Arthur Starr 1862-1931 *DcNAA*
Ealdfrith *NewC*
Ealdhelm *Chmbr 1, NewC*
Eales, John R 1910- *ConAu 9R*
Eales, Samuel John *Alli Sup*
Ealhwine *EvLB, NewC*
Ealred *Alli*
Ealwhine *BrAu, Pen Eng*
Ealy, Lawrence Orr 1915- *ConAu 33, OhA&B*
Eames, Edwin 1930- *ConAu 41*
Eames, Elizabeth Jessup *Alli, ChPo, FemPA*
Eames, Genevieve Torrey *AuBYP*
Eames, Hugh 1917- *ConAu 45*
Eames, Jane A 1816-1894 *Alli, Alli Sup, DcAmA, DcNAA*
Eames, John d1744 *Alli*
Eames, Juanita *AmSCAP 66*
Eames, Richard *Alli Sup*
Eames, Roscoe L *Alli Sup*
Eames, S Morris 1916- *ConAu 57*
Eames, T W *Alli Sup*
Eames, Wilberforce 1855-1937 *AmA&B, ChPo, ChPo S1, DcNAA, OxAm, REnAL*
Eannes DeAzurara, Gomes *EuA*
Earbery, Matthias *Alli*
Eardley, George C 1926- *ConAu 57*
Eardley-Wilmot *Alli Sup*
Eardley-Wilmot, Sir John Eardley 1821-1896 *Br&AmS*
Earee, Robert Brisco *Alli Sup*
Earhart, Amelia 1898-1937 *ChPo, DcNAA, REn*
Earhart, H Byron 1935- *ConAu 37, WrD 1976*

Earhart, Lida Belle *WhWNAA*
Earhart, Will 1871-1960 *AmSCAP 66, OhA&B*
Earl, David M 1911- *ConAu 13R*
Earl, Donald 1931- *ConAu 57*
Earl, Frank *MnBBF*
Earl, George W *Alli*
Earl, Henry Hilliard 1842-1927 *Alli Sup, DcNAA*
Earl, Herbert P *Alli Sup*
Earl, I P *ChPo*
Earl, Jabez 1676?-1768 *Alli*
Earl, John Prescott *AmA&B*
Earl, Lawrence 1915- *Au&Wr, ConAu 9R*
Earl, Paul Hunter 1945- *ConAu 49*
Earl, Ralph 1751-1801 *OxAm*
Earle, A B *Alli Sup*
Earle, Abraham L *Alli Sup*
Earle, Alfred *Alli Sup*
Earle, Alice Morse 1853?-1911 *AmA&B, BbD, BiD&SB, ChPo S1, DcAmA, DcLEnL, DcNAA, OxAm, REnAL*
Earle, Ambrose *MnBBF*
Earle, Augustus *Alli*
Earle, E Lyall *ChPo S2*
Earle, Edward Mead 1894-1954 *AmA&B*
Earle, Eyvind 1916- *IlCB 1956*
Earle, Ferdinand 1878- *ChPo, ChPo S1*
Earle, Franklin Sumner 1856-1929 *DcNAA, WhWNAA*
Earle, G W *Alli Sup*
Earle, George *ChPo S2*
Earle, Horace *Alli Sup*
Earle, J C *Alli Sup*
Earle, J Lumley *Alli Sup*
Earle, Sir James *Alli, BiDLA*
Earle, John *Alli, BiDLA, Chmbr 1*
Earle, John 1601?-1665 *Alli, BbD, BiD&SB, BrAu, CasWL, CrE&SL, DcEnL, DcLEnL, EvLB, MouLC 1, NewC, OxEng, Pen Eng, REn, WebEAL*
Earle, John 1824-1903 *Alli Sup, NewC*
Earle, John Charles 1850- *Alli Sup*
Earle, Kathleen Jean *Au&Wr*
Earle, Mrs. L B *Alli Sup*
Earle, Lisette *Alli Sup*
Earle, Mabel *ChPo*
Earle, Mabel Lavinia 1873- *WhWNAA*
Earle, Mary Tracy 1864- *DcAmA*
Earle, Melanie Tracy *ChPo*
Earle, Michael *MnBBF*
Earle, Mortimer Lamson 1864-1905 *DcNAA*
Earle, Olive Lydia *Au&Wr, ConAu 23, IlBYP, IlCB 1956, IlCB 1966, MorJA, SmATA 7*
Earle, Peter G 1923- *ConAu 17R*
Earle, Pliny 1809-1892 *Alli Sup, DcAmA, DcNAA*
Earle, Ralph 1874-1939 *DcNAA*
Earle, Ralph 1907- *ConAu 1R*
Earle, Samuel Thomas 1849-1931 *DcNAA,*

WhWNAA
Earle, Sarah Brown *ChPo*
Earle, Sullivan *Alli Sup*
Earle, Swepson 1879-1943 *DcNAA,
WhWNAA*
Earle, Thomas 1796-1849 *Alli Sup, DcAmA,
DcNAA*
Earle, Thomas And Congdon, Charles T
Alli Sup
Earle, Vana 1917- *IlCB 1956*
Earle, Victoria *BlkAW*
Earle, W J *AmA&B*
Earle, Walter *ChPo S1*
Earle, Waring *Alli Sup*
Earle, William, Jr. *Alli, BiDLA*
Earle, William Benson 1740-1796 *Alli*
Earles, John 1601-1665 *Alli*
Earley, Jackie *DrAP 1975*
Earley, Jacqueline 1939- *BlkAW*
Earley, Martha *ConAu XR*
Earley, Tom 1911- *ConAu 33, ConP 1970,
WrD 1976*
Earley, William *Alli Sup*
Earlie, Miss M A *Alli Sup*
Earlie, May Agnes *HsB&A*
Earlom, Richard 1742-1822 *Alli*
Earls, Michael 1873-1937 *CatA 1947, ChPo,
ChPo S1, DcNAA, PoIre*
Earlston, Thomas Of *NewC*
Early, Eleanor d1969 *AmA&B, CatA 1952,
TwCA Sup, WhWNAA*
Early, James 1923- *ConAu 45*
Early, John 1786-1873 *BiDSA*
Early, Jubal Anderson 1816-1894 *Alli Sup,
BbD, BiD&SB, BiDSA, DcAmA,
DcNAA*
Early, Mary Washington Cabell 1846- *BiDSA*
Early, Robert 1940- *ConAu 49*
Early, Samuel Stockwell 1827- *IndAu 1816*
Earnest, Ernest Penney 1901- *AmA&B,
ChPo S2, ConAu 33, WrD 1976*
Earnest, Joseph William *ChPo*
Earnest, Mary 1908- *TexWr*
Earnest, Robert *Alli, BiDLA*
Earney, Fillmore C F 1931- *ConAu 57*
Earnhart, Myron L 1913- *AmSCAP 66*
Earnshaw, Anthony 1924- *Au&Wr, ConAu 53,
WrD 1976*
Earnshaw, Brian 1929- *ConAu 25*
Earnshaw, C *Alli, BiDLA*
Earnshaw, Catherine *REn*
Earnshaw, Harold *ChPo*
Earnshaw, James *Alli, BbtC*
Earnshaw, L *Alli Sup*
Earnshaw, Patricia 1922- *Au&Wr*
Earnshaw, Samuel *Alli Sup*
Earnshaw, Thomas *Alli, BiDLA*
Earnshaw, Walter John 1918- *Au&Wr*
Earnshaw, William *Alli, BbtC*
Earnulph *Alli*
Earp, Edwin Lee 1867- *WhWNAA*
Earp, Frank Russell 1871- *WhLA*
Earp, George Butler *Alli Sup*
Earp, James William 1888- *WhWNAA*
Earp, John *Alli Sup*
Earp, Virgil *ConAu XR*
Earps, Joseph *Alli Sup*
Earsden, John *Alli*
Earwaker, John Parsons *Alli Sup*
Easby-Smith, James Stanislaus 1870- *BiDSA*
Easdale, John Adeney 1903- *ChPo*
Eash, John Trimble 1906- *IndAu 1917*
Easmon, Raymond Sarif 1925- *AfA 1, ConDr,
RGAfL, WrD 1976*
Easmon, Sarif *LongC*
Eason, Alex *Alli*
Eason, Charles *Alli Sup*
Eason, L *Alli*
Eassie, P B *Alli Sup*
Eassie, W *Alli Sup*
Easson, D E *ChPo S2*
Easson, James 1895- *ConAu 5R, WrD 1976*
East, Anna Merritt *WhWNAA*
East, Ben 1898- *ConAu 33*
East, C Earl 1890- *IndAu 1917*
East, Cecil James *Alli Sup*
East, Charles 1924- *ConAu 17R, DrAF 1976*
East, Clyde H 1899- *WhWNAA*

East, D J *Alli*
East, Ed 1894-1952 *AmSCAP 66*
East, Edward *Alli Sup*
East, Sir Edward Hyde *Alli, BiDLA*
East, Edward Murray 1879-1938 *DcNAA,
WhWNAA*
East, Henry *Alli Sup*
East, John *Alli, PoCh*
East, John Marlborough 1932- *ConAu 21*
East, John Marlborough 1936- *WrD 1976*
East, John Porter 1931- *ConAu 17R,
WrD 1976*
East, John R 1845-1907 *IndAu 1917*
East, Michael *ConAu XR, WorAu,
WrD 1976*
East, P D 1921- *ConAu 1R*
East, Thomas *Alli*
East, Timothy *Alli Sup*
East, Wilfrid *Alli Sup*
East, William Gordon 1902- *Au&Wr,
WrD 1976*
Eastaway, Edward *EvLB, LongC*
Eastburn, James Wallis 1797-1819 *Alli, AmA,
AmA&B, DcAmA, DcNAA, OxAm,
PoCh, REnAL*
Eastburn, Manton 1801-1872 *Alli, DcAmA,
DcNAA*
Eastcott, Richard 1740?-1828 *Alli, BiD&SB,
BiDLA*
Easter, DeLaWarr Benjamin 1867- *AmLY*
Easter, John D *Alli Sup*
Easter, Marguerite Elizabeth 1839-1894
*AmA&B, BiDSA, ChPo, DcAmA,
DcNAA*
Easterbrook, Joseph *Alli*
Easterbrook, William Thomas 1907- *Au&Wr,
OxCan*
Easterby, W *Alli Sup*
Easterfield, Thomas Hill 1866- *WhLA*
Eastes, Helen M 1892- *AmSCAP 66*
Eastham, Jack Kenneth 1901- *Au&Wr*
Easther, Alfred *Alli Sup*
Easthope, Lady Elizabeth d1865 *Alli Sup*
Eastin, Roy B 1917- *ConAu 41*
Eastlake, Lady 1816?- *Chmbr 3, DcEnL*
Eastlake, A V R *ChPo*
Eastlake, C E *ChPo S1*
Eastlake, C R *ChPo*
Eastlake, Charles Lock *Alli Sup*
Eastlake, Sir Charles Lock 1793-1865 *Alli,
Alli Sup, BiD&SB, DcEnL, NewC, REn*
Eastlake, Lady Elizabeth 1809-1893 *Alli Sup,
BrAu 19, EvLB*
Eastlake, William 1917- *AmA&B, Au&Wr,
ConAu 5R, ConNov 1972, ConNov 1976,
DrAF 1976, ModAL Sup, OxAm,
Pen Am, REnAL, WorAu, WrD 1976*
Eastlund, Madelyn *WrD 1976*
Eastman, Alexander F *AmLY XR*
Eastman, Alfred C *ChPo*
Eastman, Arthur Andrew 1893- *IndAu 1917*
Eastman, Arthur M 1918- *ConAu 23*
Eastman, Aurelia Mae *ChPo*
Eastman, Barrett 1869- *DcAmA*
Eastman, Charles Alexander 1858-1939
*AmA&B, AmLY, ConAmL, DcAmA,
JBA 1934, JBA 1951, OxAm, REnAL,
YABC 1*
Eastman, Charles Gamage 1816-1860 *Alli,
AmA&B, BbD, BiD&SB, ChPo,
ChPo S2, CyAL 2, DcAmA, DcNAA,
REnAL*
Eastman, Charles Rochester 1868- *DcAmA*
Eastman, Edward Roe 1885- *ConAu P-1,
WhWNAA*
Eastman, Elaine Goodale 1863-1948 *AmA&B,
AmLY, ChPo, DcAmA, WhWNAA*
Eastman, Elizabeth 1905- *AmA&B, AmNov*
Eastman, Ephraim Richard 1854-1931 *OhA&B*
Eastman, Frances Whittier 1915- *ConAu 1R,
IndAu 1917*
Eastman, Francis Smith 1800?-1847? *DcNAA*
Eastman, Fred 1886-1963 *AmA&B, OhA&B,
WhWNAA*
Eastman, G Don *ConAu 49*
Eastman, G W And Fulton, Levi S *Alli*
Eastman, Harrison 1823?- *EarAB, EarAB Sup*
Eastman, Joel Webb 1939- *ConAu 13R*

Eastman, Julia Arabella 1837-1911 *Alli Sup,
AmA&B, BiD&SB, DcAmA, DcNAA*
Eastman, Linda Anne 1867- *OhA&B,
WhWNAA*
Eastman, Lucius Root 1809-1892 *DcNAA*
Eastman, Mary Henderson 1818-1880? *Alli,
AmA&B, BiD&SB, BiDSA, ChPo,
DcAmA, DcEnL, DcNAA, OxAm,
REnAL*
Eastman, Max 1883-1969 *AmA&B, AmLY,
CasWL, ChPo, CnDAL, ConAmA,
ConAmL, ConAu 9R, ConAu 25,
DcLEnL, LongC, OxAm, Pen Am, REn,
REnAL, TwCA, TwCA Sup*
Eastman, P D 1909- *IlCB 1966*
Eastman, P M *Alli Sup*
Eastman, Philip 1799-1869 *Alli, DcAmA*
Eastman, Philip D *AuBYP*
Eastman, Richard M 1916- *ConAu 17R*
Eastman, Roger 1931- *ConAu 53*
Eastman, Samuel C *Alli Sup*
Eastman, Samuel Mack *OxCan*
Eastman, Sarah E *ChPo S1*
Eastman, Seth 1808-1875 *Alli, AmA&B,
DcAmA, DcNAA, REnAL*
Eastman, Sophie E *ChPo S1*
Eastman, Young *ChPo*
Eastmead, William *Alli*
Eastment, Winifred 1899- *Au&Wr, WrD 1976*
Eastmond, Claude T *BlkAW*
Easton, Alexander *Alli Sup*
Easton, Allan 1916- *ConAu 49*
Easton, Burton Scott 1877- *WhWNAA*
Easton, David *Alli Sup*
Easton, David 1917- *ConAu 33, WrD 1976*
Easton, Edward *ConAu XR, WrD 1976*
Easton, George *Alli Sup, OxCan*
Easton, James *Alli*
Easton, James George *Alli Sup*
Easton, Loyd D 1915- *ConAu 21, WrD 1976*
Easton, M G *Alli, Alli Sup*
Easton, Mary *ChPo S2*
Easton, Peter Z *Alli Sup*
Easton, Robert 1915- *ConAu 13R, WrD 1976*
Easton, Samuel *Alli*
Easton, Sidney *BlkAW*
Easton, Sidney 1896- *AmSCAP 66*
Easton, Stewart Copinger 1907- *ConAu 1R*
Easton, Thomas *Alli*
Easton, William *Alli Sup*
Easton, William Edgar *BlkAW*
Easton, William Heyden 1916- *IndAu 1917*
Eastwick, Edward Backhouse 1814-1883 *Alli,
Alli Sup, BbD, BiD&SB*
Eastwick, Ivy Olive 1905- *AuBYP, BkCL,
ChPo, ChPo S1, ConAu 5R, SmATA 3,
WrD 1976*
Eastwick, William Joseph *Alli Sup*
Eastwick-Field, John Charles 1919- *Au&Wr*
Eastwood, B *Alli Sup*
Eastwood, Benjamin 1825-1899 *DcAmA*
Eastwood, C Cyril 1916- *ConAu 5R*
Eastwood, Frances *Alli Sup*
Eastwood, Francis *ChPo S1*
Eastwood, Frederick *Alli Sup*
Eastwood, Helen 1892- *Au&Wr*
Eastwood, Helen J *Alli Sup*
Eastwood, J Herbert *ChPo*
Eastwood, J R *Alli Sup, ChPo, ChPo S1,
ChPo S2*
Eastwood, Jonathan 1824-1864 *Alli Sup*
Eastwood, Marvin *Alli Sup*
Eaton, A *Alli*
Eaton, Amasa Mason 1841-1914 *DcNAA*
Eaton, Amos 1776-1842 *DcAmA, DcNAA*
Eaton, Anne Thaxter 1881-1971 *AmA&B,
ChPo, ChPo S1*
Eaton, Arthur Wentworth Hamilton 1849-1937
*Alli Sup, AmA&B, BiD&SB, ChPo,
DcAmA, DcNAA, OxCan, WhWNAA*
Eaton, Asa 1778-1858 *DcNAA*
Eaton, Brevet *EarAB Sup*
Eaton, Charles Edward 1916- *ConAu 5R,
ConP 1970, ConP 1975, DrAF 1976,
DrAP 1975, WrD 1976*
Eaton, Charlotte Ann *Alli Sup*
Eaton, Charlotte E *Alli*
Eaton, Clement 1898- *AmA&B, ConAu 1R,*

WrD 1976

Eaton, Cyrus 1784-1875 Alli, Alli Sup, CyAL 1, DcAmA, DcNAA
Eaton, Cyrus Stephen 1883- AmA&B
Eaton, Daniel C 1834-1895 Alli Sup, DcAmA, DcNAA
Eaton, Daniel C 1837-1912 DcAmA, DcNAA
Eaton, Daniel Isaac d1814 Alli, BiDLA, BiDLA Sup
Eaton, David Alli, Alli Sup, BiDLA
Eaton, Dorman Bridgman 1823-1899 Alli Sup, DcAmA, DcNAA
Eaton, Earle Hooker ChPo
Eaton, Edith 1867-1914 DcNAA
Eaton, Edna Aurelia 1879- WhWNAA
Eaton, Edward Byrom Alli Sup
Eaton, Edward Dwight 1851-1942 AmA&B, DcNAA, WhWNAA
Eaton, Elon Howard 1866-1934 DcNAA
Eaton, Emily Lovett ChPo
Eaton, Estelle Atley BlkAW
Eaton, Evelyn Sybil Mary 1902- AmA&B, AmNov, Au&Wr, CanNov, CanWr, ConAu 53, OxCan, REnAL, TwCA Sup
Eaton, F B Alli Sup
Eaton, Flora Alli Sup
Eaton, Florence Taft 1857- WhWNAA
Eaton, Francis Alli Sup
Eaton, Frank Herbert 1851-1908 DcNAA
Eaton, Frederick A Alli Sup
Eaton, George L AuBYP, ConAu XR, WrD 1976
Eaton, Helen Slocomb WhWNAA
Eaton, Herbert N Alli Sup
Eaton, Hugh M 1865- ChPo, ChPo S1
Eaton, J H 1927- ConAu 1R
Eaton, James Robert 1902- IndAu 1917
Eaton, James Webster 1856-1901 DcNAA
Eaton, Jeanette 1885-1968 AmA&B, AnCL, JBA 1934, JBA 1951, OhA&B, St&VC
Eaton, Jimmy 1906- AmSCAP 66
Eaton, John 1575-1641 Alli, DcEnL
Eaton, John 1829-1906 DcNAA, OhA&B
Eaton, John 1942- IlBYP
Eaton, John C 1935- AmSCAP 66
Eaton, John Henry 1790-1856 Alli, BiDSA, DcAmA, DcNAA
Eaton, John Herbert 1927- WrD 1976
Eaton, John Matthews Alli Sup
Eaton, John Richard Turner Alli Sup
Eaton, Joseph Alli
Eaton, Joseph W 1919- ConAu 1R
Eaton, Leonard K 1922- ConAu 21
Eaton, Lilley Alli Sup
Eaton, Mabel Leta ChPo
Eaton, Malcolm 1914- AmSCAP 66
Eaton, Margaret ChPo
Eaton, Margaret 1796-1879 REn
Eaton, Marquis 1876-1925 DcNAA
Eaton, Morton Monroe Alli Sup
Eaton, Myron Luther 1857- WhWNAA
Eaton, Nathaniel Alli
Eaton, Peggy O'Neale 1796-1879 AmA&B, REn
Eaton, Richard Alli
Eaton, Richard Behrens 1914- WrD 1976
Eaton, Roy Wesley 1878- WhWNAA
Eaton, S E ChPo S1
Eaton, Samuel Alli
Eaton, Samuel John Mills 1820-1899 Alli Sup, DcAmA, DcNAA
Eaton, Seymour ChPo
Eaton, Seymour 1859-1916 DcNAA
Eaton, Theodore H, Jr. 1907- ConAu 53
Eaton, Theodore Hildreth 1877- WhWNAA
Eaton, Thomas Damant Alli Sup
Eaton, Thomas Ray Alli Sup
Eaton, Thomas Treadwell 1845-1907 Alli Sup, BiDSA, DcAmA, DcNAA
Eaton, Tom 1940- ConAu 41, IlBYP
Eaton, Trevor Michael William 1934- ConAu 23, WrD 1976
Eaton, Virginia ChPo S1, ChPo S2
Eaton, W Alli
Eaton, W A ChPo S1
Eaton, W E A ChPo S1
Eaton, Walter Prichard 1878-1957 AmA&B, CarSB, ChPo, ChPo S2, ConAmL,

REnAL, TwCA, TwCA Sup, WhWNAA
Eaton, Wyatt 1849-1896 ChPo
Eaves, James Clifton 1912- ConAu 13R
Eaves, Lucile 1869- AmLY, WhWNAA
Eavey, Charles B 1889- ConAu 5R
Eavey, Louise Bone 1900- ConAu 5R
Eayrs, Hugh Smithurst 1894-1940 DcNAA
Eayrs, James 1926- OxCan, OxCan Sup
Eban, Abba 1915- ConAu 57
Eban, Aubrey ConAu 57
Ebbesen, Ebbe B 1944- ConAu 49
Ebbett, Eve 1925- WrD 1976
Ebbins, Milton Keith 1914- AmSCAP 66
Ebbutt, Percy G 1858?- Alli Sup
Ebejer, Francis 1925- ConAu 29
Ebel, Henry 1938- ConAu 53
Ebeling, Adolf 1823-1896 BiD&SB
Ebeling, Christoph Daniel 1741?-1817 BiD&SB
Ebeling, Gerhard 1912- ConAu 9R
Eben, C T Alli Sup
Ebenstein, William 1910- AmA&B, ConAu 1R, WrD 1976
Eber, Dorothy Harley 1930- ConAu 41
Eberhard, Priester OxGer
Eberhard Of Bethune Pen Eur
Eberhard Of Bourges Pen Eur
Eberhard Von Cersne CasWL, OxGer
Eberhard Von Gandersheim CasWL
Eberhard Von Sax OxGer
Eberhard Von Wampen OxGer
Eberhard, August Gottlob 1769-1845 EvEuW
Eberhard, Christian August Gottlob 1769-1845 BiD&SB
Eberhard, Ernst 1839- DcAmA
Eberhard, Ernst Hans 1866- WhLA
Eberhard, Frederick George 1889- IndAu 1917, WhWNAA
Eberhard, Gustav 1867- WhLA
Eberhard, Johann August 1739-1809 BiD&SB, DcEuL
Eberhard, M Alli Sup
Eberhard, Otto Glaubrecht Karl Theodor 1875- WhLA
Eberhard, Wolfram 1909- ConAu 49
Eberhardt, Ernest Godlove 1864-1953 IndAu 1917
Eberhardt, John J 1869- WhWNAA
Eberhardt, John T ChPo S1
Eberhardt, Newman Charles 1912- ConAu 1R, IndAu 1917
Eberhart, Mignon Good 1899- AmA&B, AuNews 2, EncM&D, LongC, REnAL, TwCA, TwCA Sup, WhWNAA
Eberhart, Nelle Richmond 1871-1944 AmA&B, AmSCAP 66, DcNAA, REnAL, WhWNAA
Eberhart, Perry 1924- ConAu 17R
Eberhart, Richard 1904- AmA&B, AmWr, CasWL, ChPo, CnE&AP, ConAu 1R, ConLC 3, ConP 1970, ConP 1975, DrAP 1975, DcLEnL, LongC, ModAL, ModAL Sup, OxAm, Pen Am, RAdv 1, REn, REnAL, SixAP, TwCA Sup, TwCW, WebEAL, WhTwL, WrD 1976
Eberharter, Andreas 1865- WhLA
Eberle, Edith 1889- OhA&B
Eberle, Eliza ChPo
Eberle, Irmengarde 1898- AmA&B, AuBYP, BkCL, ConAu 1R, JBA 1951, SmATA 2
Eberle, J Alli
Eberle, John 1787-1838 DcAmA, DcNAA
Eberle, Josef 1901- EncWL
Eberlein, Harold Donaldson d1964 AmA&B
Eberlein, Harold Donaldson WhWNAA
Eberlein, Kurt Karl 1890- WhLA
Eberlin, Johann VonGunzburg 1465?-1530? OxGer
Eberlin VonGuntzburg, Johann 1465?-1530? CasWL
Eberling, Ernest Jacob 1894- WhWNAA
Eberman, Willis Gilbert 1917- ConAu 9R, WhPNW
Ebernand Von Erfurt OxGer
Ebers, Georg Moritz 1837-1898 BbD, BiD&SB, CasWL, DcBiA, EuA, EvEuW, OxGer, REn
Ebers, John Alli
Ebersole, A V, Jr. 1919- ConAu 37

Ebersole, E C Alli Sup
Ebersole, Ezra Christian 1840-1919 DcAmA, DcNAA
Ebersole, John Franklin 1884-1945 DcNAA
Ebersole, William Stahl 1862- WhWNAA
Eberstadt, Charles F 1914?-1974 ConAu 53
Eberstadt, Frederick AuBYP
Eberstadt, Isabel 1934?- AuBYP
Eberstadt, Isabel And Frederick ChPo
Ebert, Arthur Frank 1902- ConAu 5R
Ebert, Friedrich 1871-1925 OxGer, REn
Ebert, James D 1921- WrD 1976
Ebert, Johann Arnold 1723-1795 BiD&SB, CasWL, DcEuL, OxGer
Ebert, Justus 1869-1946 DcNAA
Ebert, Karl Egon 1801-1882 BiD&SB, DcEuL, EvEuW
Ebert, Karl Egon Von 1801-1882 OxGer
Eblana, Sister 1907- ConAu P-1
Eble II De Ventadorn CasWL
Eble, Gui, Peire And Elias D'Ussel CasWL
Eble, Kenneth Eugene 1923- ConAu 1R, WrD 1976
Eblen, Jack Ericson 1936- ConAu 33
Eblis, J Philip ConAu XR
Ebne Sina DcOrL 3
Ebne Yamin 1286-1368 DcOrL 3
Ebner, Christine 1277-1355 OxGer
Ebner, Margareta 1291-1351 OxGer
Ebner, Margarethe 1291-1351 CasWL
Ebner-Eschenbach, Baroness Marie Von 1830-1916 BbD, BiD&SB, CasWL, ClDMEuL, EncWL, EuA, EvEuW, OxGer, Pen Eur
Ebon 1942- BlkAW
Ebon, Martin 1917- ConAu 23
Ebrard, Johannes Heinrich August 1818-1888 BbD, BiD&SB
Ebreo, Leone EvEuW
Ebright, Frederick ChPo S1
Ebright, Homer Kingsley 1878- WhWNAA
Ebsen, Buddy 1908- AmSCAP 66
Ebstein, Erich Hugo 1880- WhLA
Ebsworth, John Alli Sup
Ebsworth, Joseph 1788-1868 BiD&SB
Ebsworth, Joseph Woodfall Alli Sup
Ebsworth, Raymond 1911- ConAu 1R
Eburne, Richard Alli
Eburne, William Hawthorne Alli Sup
Eby, Cecil DeGrotte 1927- ConAu 1R, WrD 1976
Eby, Frederick 1874-1968 AmA&B, TexWr
Eby, Lois Christine 1908- AuBYP, IndAu 1917
Eby, Louise Saxe 1902-1948 DcNAA
Eca DeQueiros, Jose Maria De 1845-1900 CasWL, EuA, EvEuW, Pen Eur
Eca DeQueiroz, Jose Maria 1845-1900 BbD, BiD&SB, ClDMEuL, REn
Eccarius, Johann Georg 1818- Alli Sup
Eccles, Alfred Alli Sup
Eccles, Ambrose d1809 Alli
Eccles, Charlotte O'Conor d1911 PoIre
Eccles, David 1904- ConAu 53
Eccles, Ellen Ann Shove Alli Sup
Eccles, Frank 1923- WrD 1976
Eccles, Henry E 1898- ConAu P-1, WrD 1976
Eccles, James Alli
Eccles, John d1735 Alli
Eccles, Marriner Stoddard 1890- AmA&B
Eccles, Robert Gibson 1848?-1934 DcNAA, WhWNAA
Eccles, Samuel Alli
Eccles, Seth 1800-1884 Alli Sup
Eccles, William J 1917- ConAu 9R, OxCan, OxCan Sup
Ecclesine, Joseph B Alli Sup
Eccleston, James Alli
Eccleston, Theodore Alli
Ecclestone, Arthur 1892- Au&Wr
Ecclestone, Edward Alli
Egberht NewC
Echard, Laurence 1670?-1730 Alli, BiD&SB, Chmbr 2, DcEnL, EvLB
Echegaray, Jose 1832-1916 BbD, BiD&SB, ClDMEuL, CnMD, DcSpL, McGWD, ModRL, ModWD, Pen Eur, REn, TwCW

Echegaray Y Eizaguirre, Jose 1832-1916 *CasWL, EuA, EvEuW*
Echeruo, Kevin 1946-1969 *AfA 1*
Echeruo, Michael J C 1937- *AfA 1, ConAu 57, ConP 1970, ConP 1975, WrD 1976*
Echeverria, Durand 1913- *ConAu 9R, WrD 1976*
Echeverria, Esteban 1805?-1851 *BbD, BiD&SB, CasWL, DcSpL, Pen Am, REn*
Echeverria, Manuel Gonzales *Alli Sup*
Echezabal, F T And J R *BiDSA*
Echlin, David *PoIre*
Echlin, Edward Patrick 1930- *ConAu 23, WrD 1976*
Echlin, John *Alli*
Echlin, John Robert *Alli Sup*
Echols, Carl *BlkAW*
Echols, John M 1913- *ConAu 5R*
Echols, Ula Waterhouse *WhWNAA*
Echols, William Holding 1858-1934 *DcNAA*
Eck, Johann 1486-1543 *OxGer*
Eckard, Frederick S *ChPo*
Eckard, James Read 1805-1887 *DcAmA*
Eckardt, A Roy 1918- *ConAu 37, WrD 1976*
Eckardt, Alice L 1923- *ConAu 37*
Eckardt, Arthur Roy 1918- *AmA&B*
Eckardt, Johannes 1260?-1328? *NewC*
Eckardt, Ludwig 1827-1871 *BiD&SB*
Eckart, Meister *OxGer*
Eckart, Dietrich 1868-1923 *OxGer*
Eckart, Johannes 1260?-1328? *NewC*
Eckaus, Richard S 1926- *ConAu 45*
Eckehard *DcSpL*
Eckehart Von Hochheim, Meister 1260?-1327 *OxGer*
Eckel, Lizzie St. John *Alli Sup, DcNAA*
Eckel, Malcolm W 1912- *ConAu 61*
Eckelberry, Grace Kathryn 1902- *ConAu 33*
Eckels, Jon *BlkAW, ConAu 49, DrAP 1975, LivBAA, WrD 1976*
Eckenrode, Hamilton James 1881- *AmA&B*
Eckenstein, Lina d1931 *ChPo S1*
Ecker, H Paul 1922- *ConAu 29*
Ecker, Judith K 1933- *AmSCAP 66*
Ecker, Thomas R 1935- *AmSCAP 66*
Ecker-Racz, L Laszlo 1906- *ConAu 49*
Eckermann, Johann Peter 1792-1854 *BiD&SB, CasWL, EuA, EvEuW, NewC, OxGer, REn*
Eckersley, Hampson S *Alli Sup*
Eckersley, Thomas 1914- *WhGrA*
Eckerson, Margaret H *Alli Sup*
Eckerson, Olive Taylor 1901- *ConAu 1R*
Eckerson, Theodore John *Alli Sup, DcNAA*
Eckert, Allan W 1931- *ConAu 13R*
Eckert, Christian 1874- *WhLA*
Eckert, Horst 1931- *ConAu 37, SmATA 8*
Eckert, Josephine Pauline *OhA&B*
Eckert, Robert P, Jr. 1903- *WhWNAA*
Eckert, Ruth E 1905- *ConAu 13R*
Eckert-Lawrence, Ida *WhWNAA*
Eckes, Alfred Edward, Jr. 1942- *ConAu 61*
Eckford, James Christie 1840- *ChPo*
Eckford, Thomas *ChPo S1*
Eckhardt, Eduard 1864- *WhLA*
Eckhardt, Tibor 1888-1972 *ConAu 37*
Eckhart 1260?-1327 *DcEuL*
Eckhart, Meister 1260?-1327 *CasWL, EuA, OxGer*
Eckhart, Johannes 1260?-1327 *EvEuW, NewC, Pen Eur*
Eckholm, Erik P 1949- *ConAu 57*
Ecking, Samuel 1757-1785 *Alli*
Eckleberry, Roscoe Huhn 1891- *WhWNAA*
Eckles, Clarence Henry 1875-1933 *DcNAA*
Eckley, Grace 1932- *ConAu 45*
Eckley, Joseph 1750-1811 *Alli*
Eckley, Sophia May *Alli Sup*
Eckley, William Thomas 1855-1908 *DcNAA*
Eckley, Wilton Earl, Jr. 1929- *ConAu 49*
Eckman, Frederick 1924- *ConAu 33, DrAP 1975*
Eckman, George Peck 1860-1920 *DcNAA*
Eckman, Lester S 1937- *ConAu 49*
Eckmar, F R *ConAu XR*

Eckoff, William Julius 1853-1908 *DcNAA*
Eckstein, Alexander 1915- *ConAu 1R, WrD 1976*
Eckstein, Carl 1859- *WhLA*
Eckstein, Ernst 1845-1900 *BbD, BiD&SB, OxGer*
Eckstein, George Frederick *Alli Sup*
Eckstein, Gustav 1890- *AmA&B, ConAu 57, OhA&B, TwCA Sup, WhWNAA*
Eckstein, Harry *ConAu 1R*
Eckstein, Maxwell 1905- *AmSCAP 66*
Eckstein, Otto 1927- *ConAu 13R*
Eckstorm, Fannie Hardy 1865-1946 *AmA&B, ChPo S2, DcNAA*
Eckstrom, Fannie Hardy 1865-1946 *DcAmA, WhWNAA*
Eclair, Lyden *OhA&B*
Eclov, Shirley *ConAu XR*
Economakis, Olga *AuBYP*
Economo, Constantin, Baron Of San Serff 1876- *WhLA*
Economou, George 1934- *ConAu 25, ConP 1970, ConP 1975, DrAP 1975, WrD 1976*
Ecrevisse, Peter 1804-1879 *BbD, BiD&SB*
Ecritt, W H *Alli Sup*
Ecroyd, Donald H 1923- *ConAu 1R*
Ecroyd, William Farrer 1827- *Alli Sup*
Ecton, John *Alli*
Ed, Carl Frank Ludwig 1890-1959 *AmA&B*
Edalji, Shapurji *Alli Sup*
Edda *CasWL*
Eddington, Sir Arthur Stanley 1882-1944 *Chmbr 3, DcLEnL, EvLB, LongC, NewC, OxEng, TwCA, TwCA Sup, WhLA*
Eddins, A W *TexWr*
Eddins, Dwight L 1939- *ConAu 33, WrD 1976*
Eddis, Arthur Clement 1849- *Alli Sup*
Eddis, Arthur Shelly *Alli Sup*
Eddis, William *Alli*
Eddison, Edwin *Alli Sup*
Eddison, Eric Rucker 1882-1945 *DcLEnL, WhLA, WorAu*
Eddison, John 1916- *ConAu 61*
Eddison, Roger 1916- *ConAu P-1*
Eddius Stephanus d721? *BiB S*
Eddius, Stephanus 634?-709? *DcEnL*
Eddleman, H Leo 1911- *ConAu 13R*
Eddowes, John *Alli Sup*
Eddrup, Edward Paroissien *Alli Sup*
Eddy, A D *Alli Sup*
Eddy, Ansel Doane 1798-1875 *DcAmA*
Eddy, Arthur Jerome 1859-1920 *DcNAA*
Eddy, Brayton 1901-1950 *AmA&B, WhWNAA*
Eddy, C W *Alli Sup*
Eddy, Charles *Alli Sup*
Eddy, Charles Brayton 1902- *WhWNAA*
Eddy, Clarence 1851-1937 *Alli Sup, DcAmA, DcNAA*
Eddy, Daniel Clarke 1823-1896 *Alli, Alli Sup, AmA&B, BiD&SB, CarSB, DcAmA, DcNAA*
Eddy, David Brewer 1877-1946 *DcNAA*
Eddy, David Manton 1928- *AmSCAP 66*
Eddy, Elizabeth M 1926- *ConAu 21*
Eddy, George Sherwood 1871-1963 *AmA&B, ChPo, TwCA, TwCA Sup*
Eddy, Harrison Prescott 1870-1937 *DcNAA*
Eddy, Henry Turner 1844-1921 *Alli Sup, DcAmA, DcAmA, DcNAA*
Eddy, Isaac 1776?- *EarAB Sup*
Eddy, J H 1784-1817 *Alli*
Eddy, John *ChPo*
Eddy, John 1932- *ConAu 61*
Eddy, John Percy 1881-1975 *Au&Wr, ConAu 61*
Eddy, Lefa Morse *ChPo*
Eddy, Mary Baker 1821-1910 *Alli Sup, AmA, AmA&B, BiD&SB, CasWL, ChPo, ChPo S1, ChPo S2, DcAmA, DcLEnL, DcNAA, LongC, OxAm, OxEng, REn, REnAL*
Eddy, Richard 1828-1906 *Alli Sup, CyAL 2, DcAmA, DcNAA*
Eddy, Roger Whittlesey 1920- *Au&Wr, ConAu 17R*

Eddy, Samuel 1769-1839 *Alli, DcNAA*
Eddy, Samuel 1897- *MnnWr*
Eddy, Samuel K 1926- *ConAu 1R*
Eddy, Sarah J 1851-1945 *DcNAA*
Eddy, Sherwood 1871-1963 *OxAm, REnAL, WhWNAA*
Eddy, Ted 1904- *AmSCAP 66*
Eddy, Thomas 1758-1827 *DcAmA, DcNAA*
Eddy, Thomas Mears 1823-1874 *Alli Sup, DcAmA, DcNAA, OhA&B*
Eddy, William Alfred 1896-1962 *AmA&B*
Eddy, William Holden *ChPo*
Eddy, Zachary 1815-1891 *Alli Sup, DcAmA, DcNAA*
Ede, Charles *Alli Sup*
Ede, Detective Inspector *MnBBF*
Ede, George *Alli Sup*
Ede, James *Alli, BiDLA*
Ede, Joseph *Alli Sup*
Ede, William Moore 1848- *WhLA*
Edeer, B *Alli Sup*
Edel, Abraham 1908- *ConAu 1R, WrD 1976*
Edel, Joseph Leon 1907- *Au&Wr, REnAL*
Edel, Leon 1907- *AmA&B, ConAu 1R, OxAm, RAdv 1, REn, WorAu, WrD 1976*
Edel, Matthew 1941- *ConAu 29*
Edelen, Philip *Alli*
Edelheit, Harry 1891-1955 *AmSCAP 66*
Edelin, Benedict 1900- *WhWNAA*
Edell, Celeste *ConAu 1R*
Edelman, Elaine *DrAP 1975*
Edelman, H And Dukes, L *Alli Sup*
Edelman, Katherine *ChPo S1, WhWNAA*
Edelman, Lily 1915- *AuBYP, ConAu 61*
Edelman, Maurice 1911-1975 *Au&Wr, ConAu 61, ConNov 1972, ConNov 1976, LongC, TwCW, WorAu*
Edelman, Maurice 1911- *WrD 1976*
Edelman, Murray J 1919- *ConAu 33, WrD 1976*
Edelman, Paul S 1926- *ConAu 9R*
Edelman, Philip E 1894- *WhWNAA*
Edelman, W *Alli*
Edelmann, Richard 1861- *WhLA*
Edelson, Edward 1929- *AmSCAP 66*
Edelson, Edward 1932- *ConAu 17R*
Edelstein, David S 1913- *ConAu 61*
Edelstein, J M 1924- *ConAu 53*
Eden, Alvin N 1926- *ConAu 61*
Eden, Charles H *MnBBF*
Eden, Charles Henry *Alli Sup*
Eden, Charles Page 1807-1885 *Alli, Alli Sup*
Eden, Dorothy 1912- *WrD 1976*
Eden, Eleanor *Alli Sup*
Eden, Emily 1797-1869 *Alli Sup, BbD, BiD&SB, DcLEnL, NewC, OxEng*
Eden, Frederick *Alli, Alli Sup*
Eden, Sir Frederick Morton 1766-1809 *Alli, BiD&SB, DcEnL*
Eden, Guy Ernest Morton *ChPo S1*
Eden, Helen Josephine Parry 1885- *CatA 1947*
Eden, Helen Parry *ChPo, ChPo S2*
Eden, Horatia K F *ChPo S1*
Eden, Janet *Alli Sup*
Eden, Lizzie Selina *Alli Sup*
Eden, Mary 1919- *Au&Wr*
Eden, Morton Robert *Alli Sup*
Eden, Patience *ChPo S2*
Eden, R C *Alli Sup*
Eden, Richard 1521?-1576 *Alli, BrAu, NewC, OxEng*
Eden, Robert *Alli, Alli Sup*
Eden, Robert Henley *Alli*
Eden, William *Alli*
Edenborough, A *ChPo S1*
Edens, J *Alli*
Edens, Roger 1905- *AmSCAP 66*
Eder, Josef Maria 1855- *WhLA*
Eder, Phanor James 1880- *WhWNAA*
Ederer, Bernard Francis *MnnWr, OxCan*
Edersheim, Alfred 1825-1889 *Alli Sup, BbD, BiD&SB*
Edersheim, E W *Alli Sup*
Edes *Alli*
Edes, Benjamin 1732-1803 *AmA&B*
Edes, Henry Herbert 1849-1922 *Alli Sup, AmA&B, DcAmA, DcNAA*

Edes, Richard Sullivan 1810-1877 *Alli Sup*
Edes, Robert Thaxter 1838-1913? *Alli Sup,*
AmA&B, DcAmA, DcNAA
Edey, Maitland A 1910- *ConAu 57*
Edey, Marion *ChPo*
Edfelt, Johannes 1904- *CasWL, EncWL*
Edgar, Alfred 1896- *MnBBF*
Edgar, Andrew *Alli Sup*
Edgar, Cornelius Henry 1811-1884 *Alli Sup,*
DcAmA
Edgar, David 1948- *ConAu 57, WrD 1976*
Edgar, J *Alli Sup*
Edgar, James *BbtC*
Edgar, James Clifton 1859-1939 *DcNAA*
Edgar, Sir James David 1841-1899 *Alli Sup,*
BbtC, DcNAA, OxCan
Edgar, James Pitt *Alli Sup*
Edgar, John *Alli*
Edgar, Sir John *Alli, DcEnL, NewC*
Edgar, John Faris 1814-1905 *OhA&B*
Edgar, John George 1834-1864 *Alli Sup, BbD,*
BiD&SB, EvLB
Edgar, Joseph Haythorne *Alli Sup*
Edgar, Josephine 1907- *ConAu XR*
Edgar, Ken 1925- *ConAu 49*
Edgar, Kenneth 1924- *IndAu 1917*
Edgar, Lewis *MnBBF*
Edgar, Louise *ChPo*
Edgar, Madalen G *ChPo, ChPo S1*
Edgar, Marriott *ChPo S1*
Edgar, Lady Matilda 1844-1910 *DcNAA,*
OxCan
Edgar, Oscar Pelham 1871-1948 *CasWL,*
DcLEnL
Edgar, Pelham 1871-1948 *CanWr, DcNAA,*
OxCan
Edgar, R H *Alli Sup*
Edgar, Randolph 1884-1931 *DcNAA,*
WhWNAA
Edgar, Robert MacCheyne *Alli Sup*
Edgar, Samuel *Alli*
Edgar, William *Alli*
Edgar, William Crowell 1856-1932 *ChPo S2,*
DcNAA
Edgarton, James Arthur 1869-1938 *ChPo*
Edgarton, Miss S C 1819-1848 *CarSB*
Edgarton, Sarah Carter Mayo 1819-1848 *Alli,*
AmA, ChPo, ChPo S1, ChPo S2
Edgarton, W P *Alli Sup*
Edgcome, Libella B *Alli Sup*
Edgcumbe, Edward Robert Pearce- 1851-
Alli Sup
Edgcumbe, Lady Ernestine Emma Horatia 1843-
Alli Sup
Edgcumbe, Richard *Alli Sup*
Edgcumbe, Richard 1716-1761 *BiD&SB*
Edgcumbe, Richard 1843- *WhLA*
Edgcumbe, Sir Robert P *ChPo S2*
Edge, Findley B 1916- *ConAu 5R, WrD 1976*
Edge, Frederick Milnes *Alli Sup*
Edge, James Broughton *Alli Sup*
Edge, Selwyn Francis 1868- *WhLA*
Edge, William John *Alli, Alli Sup*
Edgecumbe, James *Alli*
Edgecumbe, Lord Mountmorres *Alli*
Edgell, Alfred Wyatt *Alli Sup*
Edgell, Edgell Wyatt- *Alli Sup*
Edgell, Miss H J *Alli Sup*
Edgelow, George *Alli Sup*
Edger, Henry *Alli Sup*
Edger, Samuel *Alli Sup*
Edgerley, John Torriano 1904- *Au&Wr*
Edgerly, Webster 1852-1926 *DcNAA*
Edgerton, A J *Alli Sup*
Edgerton, Alice Craig 1874-1946 *AmA&B,*
WhWNAA
Edgerton, Frank Eugene 1875- *WhWNAA*
Edgerton, Franklin 1885-1963 *AmA&B,*
WhWNAA
Edgerton, Harold Eugene 1903- *ConAu 53,*
WrD 1976
Edgerton, James Arthur 1869-1938 *AmLY,*
ChPo S2, DcAmA, DcNAA, OhA&B
Edgerton, Jesse 1845-1929 *OhA&B*
Edgerton, Robert B 1931- *ConAu 53*
Edgerton, Swartout 1870- *WhWNAA*
Edgerton, Walter 1806-1879 *Alli Sup,*
IndAu 1816, OhA&B

Edgerton, Wealthy Rowena 1840- *ChPo*
Edgerton, William B 1914- *ConAu 29*
Edgerton, William Franklin 1893- *AmA&B*
Edgett, Edward Francis 1867- *ChPo S1*
Edgett, Edwin Francis 1867-1948 *AmA&B,*
DcAmA, DcNAA
Edgeworth, C Sneyd *Alli*
Edgeworth, Frances Anne *Alli Sup*
Edgeworth, Francis Beaufort d1846 *PoIre*
Edgeworth, Francis Ysidro 1845- *Alli Sup*
Edgeworth, Maria 1767-1849 *Alli, AtlBL,*
BbD, BiD&SB, BiDLA, BrAu 19, CarSB,
CasWL, ChPo, Chmbr 2, CriT 2, CyWA,
DcBiA, DcEnA, DcEnL, DcEuL,
DcLEnL, EvLB, MouLC 3, NewC,
OxEng, Pen Eng, PoIre, RAdv 1, REn,
WebEAL, WhCL
Edgeworth, Mary L *Alli Sup*
Edgeworth, Michael Pakenham 1812-1881
Alli Sup
Edgeworth, Richard Lovell 1744-1817 *Alli,*
BiDLA, ChPo, Chmbr 2, DcEnA, DcEnL,
DcEuL
Edgeworth, Roger d1560? *Alli*
Edgeworth, Miss Temple *PoIre*
Edgeworth, Theodore *Alli*
Edghill, Mary *ChPo S1*
Edgington, Eugene Sinclair 1924- *ConAu 25,*
WrD 1976
Edgington, Thomas Benton 1837-1929 *DcNAA*
Edginton, George William *Alli Sup*
Edgley, Charles K 1943- *ConAu 57*
Edgley, John C *Alli Sup*
Edgley, Roy 1925- *ConAu 29, WrD 1976*
Edgley, Samuel *Alli*
Edgren, Anne Charlotte 1849-1892 *BiD&SB,*
CasWL, EvEuW
Edgren, August Hjalmar 1840-1903 *Alli Sup,*
AmA&B, BbD, BiD&SB, DcAmA,
DcNAA
Edgren, Harry D 1899- *ConAu 33*
Edgren, John Alexis 1839-1908 *DcAmA,*
DcNAA
Edgren-Leffler, Anne Charlotte 1849-1892 *BbD*
Edguardus, Dav *Alli*
Edgun 1913- *IlBYP, IlCB 1956*
Edgworth, Robert *Alli*
Edgworth, Roger d1560? *Alli*
Edib, Adivar Halide *DcOrL 3*
Edib, Halide *EncWL Sup*
Edidin, Ben M 1900-1948 *DcNAA*
Edie, George *Alli*
Edie, James M 1927- *ConAu 9R*
Edie, Lionel Danforth 1893- *WhWNAA*
Ediger, Peter J 1926- *ConAu 33*
Ediger, Theodore Allan 1905- *WhWNAA*
Edinborough, Arnold 1922- *Au&Wr*
Edinburgh, Bishop Of *DcEnL*
Edinburgh, Duke Of *Alli Sup*
Edinburgh, Prince Philip, Duke Of *Au&Wr*
Edinger, Ray William 1888- *WhWNAA*
Edington, Arlo Channing 1890-1953 *AmA&B,*
WhWNAA
Edington, Carmen Ballen 1894- *AmA&B*
Edington, Robert *Alli, BiDLA*
Edis, Arthur Wellesley *Alli Sup*
Edis, Emily *ChPo S2*
Edis, Mary *Alli Sup*
Edis, Robert William 1839- *Alli Sup*
Edison, Charles 1890- *ChPo*
Edison, Harry 1915- *AmSCAP 66*
Edison, John Sibbald *Alli Sup*
Edison, Judith *ConAu XR*
Edison, Julian T *ChPo*
Edison, Thomas Alva 1847?-1931 *LongC, REn,*
REnAL
Edith Swan-Neck *NewC*
Edith, Stevenson *Alli Sup*
Edkins, Diana M 1947- *ConAu 41*
Edkins, Jane Rowbotham *Alli Sup*
Edkins, Joseph 1823- *Alli Sup*
Edkins, Joshua *Alli, BiDLA, PoIre*
Edler, Karl Erdmann 1844- *BiD&SB*
Edleston, R *Alli Sup*
Edlin, A *Alli, BiDLA*
Edlin, Herbert Leeson 1913- *Au&Wr,*
ConAu 61, WrD 1976
Edlin, Rosabelle Alpern 1914- *ConAu 9R*

Edlyn, Richard *Alli*
Edman, David 1930- *ConAu 37*
Edman, Irwin 1896-1954 *AmA&B, REnAL,*
TwCA, TwCA Sup
Edman, Marion 1901- *ConAu P-1*
Edman, Victor Raymond 1900-1967 *AmA&B,*
ConAu 1R
Edmands, Jane Loring *Alli Sup*
Edmands, John 1820-1915 *Alli Sup, AmA&B,*
DcNAA
Edmead, William *Alli*
Edmed, John *Alli Sup*
Edmer *EvLB, NewC*
Edmeston, James 1791-1867 *Alli, ChPo,*
ChPo S1, ChPo S2, PoCh
Edmiston, Dorothy *TexWr*
Edmiston, Earle Robert 1904- *WhWNAA*
Edmiston, Helen Jean Mary 1913- *Au&Wr*
Edmiston, Homer 1872- *WhWNAA*
Edmiston, Jean 1913- *ConAu 13R*
Edmond, Amanda M *Alli, Alli Sup, ChPo*
Edmond, James 1859-1933 *DcLEnL*
Edmond, John 1816- *Alli Sup*
Edmond, John Philip *Alli Sup*
Edmondes, Sir Clement 1566-1622 *Alli*
Edmondes, Sir Thomas 1563-1639 *Alli*
Edmonds, Mrs. *Alli Sup*
Edmonds, Albert Sydney 1897- *WhWNAA*
Edmonds, Ann C *ConAu XR*
Edmonds, Cecil John 1889- *Au&Wr,*
ConAu P-1, WrD 1976
Edmonds, Charles *Alli, Alli Sup, ConAu XR,*
WrD 1976
Edmonds, Sir Clement 1566-1622 *Alli*
Edmonds, Cyrus R *Alli, Alli Sup*
Edmonds, E *Alli Sup*
Edmonds, Elizabeth Mayhew *Alli Sup*
Edmonds, Francis W *Alli Sup*
Edmonds, Frank *MnBBF*
Edmonds, Franklin Spencer 1874- *DcAmA,*
WhWNAA
Edmonds, Fred *ChPo, ChPo S2*
Edmonds, George *Alli Sup, DcNAA*
Edmonds, Harry 1891- *Au&Wr, MnBBF*
Edmonds, Helen 1904-1968 *ConAu 5R,*
ConAu 25
Edmonds, Helen G 1911- *LivBA*
Edmonds, Henry *Alli Sup*
Edmonds, Herbert *Alli Sup*
Edmonds, I G 1917- *ConAu 33, SmATA 8*
Edmonds, J *Alli Sup*
Edmonds, John *Alli*
Edmonds, John W, And George T Dexter *Alli*
Edmonds, John Worth 1799-1874 *Alli Sup,*
DcAmA, DcNAA
Edmonds, Mary *Alli Sup*
Edmonds, Paul *ChPo, ChPo S2*
Edmonds, Percy *MnBBF*
Edmonds, Randolph 1900- *BlkAW*
Edmonds, Richard 1801-1886 *Alli Sup*
Edmonds, Richard Hathaway 1857-1930 *BiDSA,*
DcNAA, WhWNAA
Edmonds, Richard W *AuBYP*
Edmonds, S Emma E *Alli Sup*
Edmonds, Shepard N 1876-1957 *AmSCAP 66*
Edmonds, T *Alli, BiDLA*
Edmonds, Thomas 1826- *Alli Sup*
Edmonds, Thomas Rowe *Alli Sup*
Edmonds, Vernon H 1927- *ConAu 37*
Edmonds, W A *Alli Sup*
Edmonds, W Lambert *Alli Sup*
Edmonds, Walter Dumaux 1903- *AmA&B,*
AmNov, AuBYP, CnDAL, ConAmA,
ConAu 5R, CyWA, DcLEnL, ModAL,
MorBMP, MorJA, Newb 1922, OxAm,
Pen Am, REn, REnAL, SmATA 1,
TwCA, TwCA Sup, WrD 1976
Edmondson, Christopher *Alli Sup*
Edmondson, Edna Hatfield 1886- *IndAu 1917*
Edmondson, Edward *Alli Sup*
Edmondson, G C 1922- *ConAu 57*
Edmondson, Henry 1607-1659 *Alli*
Edmondson, J *Alli*
Edmondson, James *Alli Sup*
Edmondson, Joseph *Alli Sup*
Edmondson, Joseph d1786 *Alli*
Edmondson, Sybil 1898- *Au&Wr*
Edmondson, Thomas *Alli Sup*

Edmondson, Thomas William 1859-1938 *DcNAA*
Edmons, Thomas *Alli*
Edmonson, Harold A 1937- *ConAu 41*
Edmonson, James Bartlett 1882- *WhWNAA*
Edmonson, Jonathan *Alli*
Edmonson, Joseph d1786 *Alli*
Edmonson, Munro Sterling 1924- *ConAu 33, WrD 1976*
Edmonston, Biot And Saxby, Jessie M *Alli Sup*
Edmonston, Eliza d1867? *Alli Sup*
Edmonston, Jesse 1858- *TexWr*
Edmonstone, Sir Archibald 1795-1871 *Alli, Alli Sup, BiD&SB*
Edmonstone, Arthur *Alli, BiDLA*
Edmonstone, E *ChPo S1*
Edmonstone, William *Alli, BiDLA*
Edmund I 922?-946 *NewC*
Edmund De Hadenham *Alli*
Edmund, Saint 840?-870 *NewC*
Edmund, Saint d1242 *Alli*
Edmund, Sean *SmATA 4*
Edmunds, Albert Joseph 1857-1941 *AmA&B, AmLY, ChPo S2, DcNAA, WhWNAA*
Edmunds, Charles Wallis 1873-1941 *DcNAA*
Edmunds, Sir Clement 1566-1622 *Alli*
Edmunds, David *Alli Sup*
Edmunds, Mrs. E L *Alli Sup*
Edmunds, Flavell *Alli Sup*
Edmunds, James *Alli Sup*
Edmunds, John *Alli, Alli Sup*
Edmunds, John 1913- *AmSCAP 66*
Edmunds, Murrell 1898- *ConAu 1R, WhWNAA*
Edmunds, Pocahontas Wight 1904- *WhWNAA*
Edmunds, Richard *Alli, BiDLA*
Edmunds, Robert Charles 1906- *Au&Wr*
Edmunds, Simeon 1917- *BiDPar, ConAu 17R*
Edmunds, Sterling Edwin 1880-1944 *DcNAA*
Edmunds, T Murrell 1898- *WrD 1976*
Edmundsen, George 1848- *WhLA*
Edmundson, Garth 1900- *AmSCAP 66*
Edmundson, George *Alli Sup*
Edmundson, Joseph 1909- *Au&Wr*
Edmundson, W G *BbtC*
Edmundson, William *Alli*
Edmunston, J *Alli Sup*
Ednyfed, J G Pym Ap *Alli Sup*
Edogawa, Rampo 1894- *Pen Cl*
Edouart, Alexander 1818-1892 *EarAB Sup*
Edqvist, Dagmar 1903- *CasWL, EvEuW*
Edred d955 *NewC*
Edridge, Rebecca *Alli, BiDLA*
Edridge-Green *Alli Sup*
Edridge-Green, Frederick William 1863- *WhLA*
Edsall, Florence Small *ChPo*
Edsall, Marian S 1920- *ConAu 49, SmATA 8*
Edschmid, Kasimir 1890-1966 *CasWL, ClDMEuL, EncWL, ModGL, OxGer, Pen Eur*
Edskog, Ebba Frideborg 1903- *Au&Wr*
Edson, Charles Farwell 1861?-1936 *AnMV 1926, ChPo*
Edson, Charles Powell 1861?-1936 *ChPo S1*
Edson, Gus 1901-1966 *AmA&B*
Edson, Hanford A 1837-1920 *IndAu 1816*
Edson, J T 1928- *ConAu 29*
Edson, N I *Alli Sup*
Edson, Obed 1832-1919 *DcNAA*
Edson, Russell 1935- *ConAu 33, ConP 1975, DrAP 1975, WrD 1976*
Edstrom, David 1873-1938 *AmA&B, DcNAA*
Eduardi, Guillermo *ConAu XR*
Edward I 1239-1307 *NewC*
Edward II 1284-1327 *NewC, REn*
Edward III 1312-1377 *NewC*
Edward IV 1442-1483 *NewC*
Edward V 1470-1483 *NewC*
Edward VI 1537-1553 *Alli, BbD, BiD&SB, DcEnL, NewC, REn*
Edward VII 1841-1910 *NewC*
Edward VIII 1894-1972 *ConAu 33, NewC, REn*
Edward, Duke Of York 1373?-1415 *Br&AmS, CasWL*
Edward The Confessor 1004?-1066 *NewC*
Edward The Elder d924 *NewC*
Edward The Martyr 963-978 *NewC*

Edward, Bowyer *Alli*
Edward, Catherine *Alli Sup*
Edward, Daniel *Alli Sup*
Edward, Eliza *Alli Sup*
Edward, Grey Of Fallodon, Viscount 1862- *WhLA*
Edward, J *Alli*
Edward, Thomas *Alli Sup*
Edwardes, Alice *ChPo*
Edwardes, Allen *ConAu XR*
Edwardes, Annie *Alli Sup, DcEnL*
Edwardes, Charles *Alli Sup, MnBBF*
Edwardes, Miss E C Hope- *Alli Sup*
Edwardes, Edward *ChPo S2*
Edwardes, Edward J *Alli Sup*
Edwardes, Lady Emma *Alli Sup*
Edwardes, Sir Herbert Benjamin 1819-1868 *Alli, Alli Sup, NewC*
Edwardes, Michael F H 1923- *Au&Wr, ConAu 57*
Edwardes-Trevor *Alli Sup*
Edwards *Alli*
Edwards, Archdeacon *Alli*
Edwards, Miss *BiDLA*
Edwards, A M, Johnston, C And Smith, H *Alli Sup*
Edwards, Adeline *Alli Sup*
Edwards, Agnes *ChPo*
Edwards, Al *ConAu XR*
Edwards, Alan *MnBBF*
Edwards, Alan W *MnBBF*
Edwards, Albert *AmLY XR, DcNAA*
Edwards, Allen Jack 1926- *ConAu 33, WrD 1976*
Edwards, Allen L 1914- *ConAu 25*
Edwards, Amelia Ann Blandford 1831-1892 *Alli Sup, BbD, BiD&SB, BrAu 19, ChPo S1, Chmbr 3, DcBiA, DcEnA, DcEnL, DcEuL, HsB&A, NewC*
Edwards, Anna Maria *PoIre*
Edwards, Anne 1927- *Au&Wr, ConAu 61, WrD 1976*
Edwards, Annie *BbD*
Edwards, Anthony David 1936- *ConAu 13R*
Edwards, Arthur M *Alli Sup*
Edwards, Arthur Robin 1867-1936 *DcNAA, WhWNAA*
Edwards, Austin Southwick 1885- *WhWNAA*
Edwards, B A *Alli Sup*
Edwards, Basil *Alli Sup, ChPo*
Edwards, Bela Bates 1802-1852 *Alli, AmA&B, CyAL 2, DcAmA, DcNAA*
Edwards, Bertram *ConAu XR*
Edwards, Bickerton Augustus *Alli Sup*
Edwards, Boyd 1876-1944 *DcNAA*
Edwards, Bronwen Elizabeth 1948- *ConAu XR*
Edwards, Bruce *Alli Sup*
Edwards, Bryan 1743-1800 *Alli, DcEnL*
Edwards, C A *Alli Sup*
Edwards, C L *HsB&A*
Edwards, Mrs. C M *Alli Sup*
Edwards, Carl N 1943- *ConAu 57*
Edwards, Carolus *Alli*
Edwards, Cecil 1903- *WrD 1976*
Edwards, Cecile Pepin 1916- *AuBYP, ConAu 5R*
Edwards, Charles *WrD 1976*
Edwards, Charles 1628-1691? *CasWL*
Edwards, Charles 1797-1868 *Alli, Alli Sup, ChPo S1, DcAmA, DcNAA*
Edwards, Charles Edward 1930- *ConAu 17R*
Edwards, Charles Johnston 1855- *Alli Sup*
Edwards, Charles Lincoln 1863-1937 *DcNAA*
Edwards, Charles Mundy, Jr. 1903- *ConAu 45*
Edwards, Charles William 1873- *WhWNAA*
Edwards, Charleszime Spears 1907- *LivBA*
Edwards, Charlotte *ConAu 29*
Edwards, Christine 1902- *ConAu P-1*
Edwards, Clara *AmSCAP 66*
Edwards, Clara McKinney 1888- *WhWNAA*
Edwards, Clifford D 1934- *ConAu 61*
Edwards, Corwin D 1901- *ConAu 17R, WrD 1976*
Edwards, D *Alli*
Edwards, D C *Alli Sup*
Edwards, D H *Alli Sup, ChPo*
Edwards, David *Alli Sup*
Edwards, David C 1937- *ConAu 41*

Edwards, David Herschell 1846- *ChPo S1*
Edwards, David Lawrence 1929- *Au&Wr, ConAu 5R*
Edwards, Donald 1904- *WrD 1976*
Edwards, Donald Earl 1916- *ConAu XR, OhA&B*
Edwards, Dorothy *Au&Wr, ConAu 25, SmATA 4, WrD 1976*
Edwards, Dorothy 1902- *WhLA*
Edwards, E *Alli*
Edwards, E J *BkC 4*
Edwards, E M *Alli Sup*
Edwards, E Price *Alli Sup*
Edwards, Edgar O 1919- *ConAu 1R*
Edwards, Edward *Alli, BiDLA*
Edwards, Edward 1738-1806 *Alli, BkIE*
Edwards, Edward 1812-1886 *Alli Sup, BiD&SB, DcEnL*
Edwards, Edward Bartholomew 1873-1948 *AmA&B, DcNAA*
Edwards, Edward E *ChPo*
Edwards, Edward Everett 1908- *IndAu 1917*
Edwards, Edward J 1904- *CatA 1952*
Edwards, Edwin 1823-1879 *Alli Sup*
Edwards, Edwin B 1891-1963 *AmSCAP 66*
Edwards, Eleanor Lee *HsB&A, OhA&B*
Edwards, Eliezer *Alli Sup*
Edwards, Elisha Jay 1847-1924 *DcNAA*
Edwards, Elizabeth *ConAu 49*
Edwards, Elwyn Hartley 1927- *ConAu 61*
Edwards, Emory 1841- *Alli Sup, DcAmA*
Edwards, Enid 1914- *Au&Wr*
Edwards, Eric Graeme 1927- *Au&Wr*
Edwards, Evan *Alli Sup*
Edwards, F E *ConAu XR*
Edwards, F G *Alli Sup*
Edwards, F J *Alli Sup*
Edwards, F W *Alli Sup*
Edwards, Frank Allyn 1908- *ConAu 1R*
Edwards, Frederic *Alli*
Edwards, Frederick *Alli Sup*
Edwards, Frederick 1863-1948 *DcNAA*
Edwards, Frederick 1868- *AnMV 1926*
Edwards, Frederick E *Alli Sup*
Edwards, Frederick Yeats *Alli Sup*
Edwards, G C *Alli*
Edwards, G N *ChPo S1*
Edwards, G Sutherland *Alli Sup*
Edwards, George *Alli, BbtC, BiDLA*
Edwards, George 1694-1773 *Alli*
Edwards, George 1752-1823 *BbD, BiD&SB*
Edwards, George 1914- *ConAu 53*
Edwards, George Cunningham 1787-1837 *DcNAA*
Edwards, George Cunningham 1852-1930 *DcNAA*
Edwards, George Graveley 1896- *Au&Wr*
Edwards, George Nelson 1830-1868 *Alli Sup*
Edwards, George Thornton 1868-1932 *DcNAA*
Edwards, George Wharton 1859?-1950 *Alli Sup, AmA&B, AmLY, BbD, BiD&SB, ChPo, ChPo S2, DcAmA, WhWNAA, IlCB 1945*
Edwards, Gerard Noel *BiDLA*
Edwards, Gillian Mary 1918- *Au&Wr, ConAu 25, WrD 1976*
Edwards, Gordon 1899- *WrD 1976*
Edwards, Griffith *Alli Sup*
Edwards, Gus 1879-1945 *AmA&B, AmSCAP 66, REnAL*
Edwards, Harry *BlkAW, LivBA*
Edwards, Harry 1893- *BiDPar*
Edwards, Mrs. Harry Bennett- 1835- *Alli Sup*
Edwards, Harry Stillwell 1855-1938 *AmA&B, BiD&SB, BiDSA, ChPo S1, DcAmA, DcNAA, OxAm, REn, REnAL, WhWNAA*
Edwards, Harvey 1929- *ConAu 25, SmATA 5, WrD 1976*
Edwards, Henry *Alli, Alli Sup*
Edwards, Henry 1871- *TexWr, WhWNAA*
Edwards, Henry James 1893- *Au&Wr, ConAu 13R*
Edwards, Henry Sutherland 1828- *Alli Sup, BbD, BiD&SB, DcEnL*
Edwards, Henry Thomas 1837-1884 *Alli Sup*
Edwards, Herbert Charles 1912- *Au&Wr, ConAu 9R*

Egan, Lavinia *BiDSA*
Egan, Lesley *ConAu XR*
Egan, Leslie *EncM&D*
Egan, Maurice Francis 1852-1924 *Alli Sup,
AmA&B, AmLY, BbD, BiD&SB, BkC 4,
ChPo S1, ChPo S2, DcAmA, DcNAA,
PoIre*
Egan, Michael 1941- *ConAu 45*
Egan, P M *Alli Sup*
Egan, Patrick 1837-1869 *PoIre*
Egan, Philip S 1920- *ConAu 1R*
Egan, Pierce 1772-1849 *BbD, BiD&SB,
Br&AmS, BrAu 19, CasWL, ChPo,
ChPo S1, Chmbr 3, CyWA, DcEnA,
DcEnL, DcEuL, DcLEnL, EvLB, NewC,
OxEng, PoIre*
Egan, Pierce 1814-1880 *Alli Sup, BbD,
BiD&SB, Chmbr 3, DcEnA, DcEnL,
HsB&A, MnBBF, NewC, OxEng*
Egan, Raymond B 1890-1952 *AmSCAP 66*
Egan, Richard Whittington 1924- *Au&Wr*
Egan, Robert *Alli*
Egan, Thomas *Alli*
Egan, Thomas Selby *Alli Sup, ChPo S2,
PoIre*
Egan, William Constantine 1841-1930 *DcNAA*
Egar, John Hodson 1832-1942 *Alli Sup,
DcAmA, DcNAA*
Egbert 639-729 *BiB S*
Egbert 775?-839 *NewC*
Egbert, Archbishop Of York 678?-766 *Alli*
Egbert Of York 678?-766 *BiB S*
Egbert, Donald Drew 1902-1973 *ConAu 23,
ConAu 37*
Egbert, H, Jr. 1826-1900 *EarAB, EarAB Sup*
Egbert, James Chidester 1859-1948 *AmLY,
DcNAA, WhWNAA*
Egbert, Seneca 1863-1939 *DcNAA*
Egbert, Virginia Wylie 1912- *ConAu 21*
Egbuna, Obi Benue 1938- *AfA 1, ConDr,
TwCW, WrD 1976*
Egelhaaf, Gottlieb 1848- *BiD&SB*
Egelshem, Wells *Alli*
Egen Von Bamberg, Meister *CasWL, OxGer*
Egenolf Von Staufenberg *OxGer*
Eger, Karl 1864- *WhLA*
Eger, Paul 1881- *WhLA*
Egerer, J W *ChPo S1*
Egeria *Pen Eur*
Egermeier, Elsie E 1890- *ChPo S1, ConAu 5R,
WhWNAA*
Egerton *Alli*
Egerton, Lady Alix *ChPo S1*
Egerton, Charles *Alli, ChPo*
Egerton, D T *Alli*
Egerton, Lady Frances *Alli*
Egerton, Francis *BiD&SB, Chmbr 2*
Egerton, Francis 1824- *Alli Sup*
Egerton, Francis, Earl Of Ellesmere 1800-1857
Alli
Egerton, Francis Henry *Alli, BiDLA, DcEnL*
Egerton, George 1860-1945 *Chmbr 3, EvLB,
LongC, TwCA, TwCA Sup*
Egerton, Helen Merrill *ChPo*
Egerton, Henry *Alli*
Egerton, John *Alli*
Egerton, John Coker d1888 *Alli Sup*
Egerton, Lady M *Alli Sup*
Egerton, Sir Philip DeMalpas Grey- 1806-1881
Alli Sup
Egerton, Philip Henry 1824- *Alli Sup*
Egerton, Reginald Ansell Day 1925- *Au&Wr*
Egerton, Stephen *Alli*
Egerton, Thomas *Alli*
Egerton, Sir Thomas 1540?-1617 *Alli, NewC,
OxEng*
Egerton, Thomas, Earl Of Wilton 1799-
Alli Sup
Egerton, William *Alli*
Egerton-Warburton, Rowland Eyles *DcLEnL*
Egg, Edward T *Alli Sup*
Egg, Maria 1910- *ConAu 29*
Egg-Benes, Maria *ConAu XR*
Egge, Peter 1869-1959 *BiD&SB, CasWL,
ClDMEuL, CnMD, EncWL, Pen Eur,
TwCA, TwCA Sup*
Eggeling, Hans Friedrich 1878- *ConAu 1R*
Eggeling, Julius 1842- *Alli Sup, BbD,*

BiD&SB
Eggenberger, David 1918- *ConAu 9R,
SmATA 6*
Eggenhofer, Nicholas *IlBYP*
Eggenschwiler, David 1936- *ConAu 37*
Egger, Carl 1892- *WhLA*
Egger, Emile 1813-1885 *BiD&SB*
Egger, M David 1936- *ConAu 57*
Egger, Max 1863- *WhLA*
Egger, Rowland Andrews 1908- *Au&Wr,
ConAu 5R*
Eggers, J Philip 1940- *ConAu 33*
Eggers, Melvin Arnold 1916- *IndAu 1917*
Eggers, William T 1912- *ConAu 29*
Eggert Olafsson 1726-1768 *DcEuL*
Eggert, Charles Augustus 1853-1931 *DcNAA*
Eggert, Gerald G 1926- *ConAu 21*
Eggleston, Benjamin 1747-1832 *OhA&B*
Eggleston, Cary 1884- *WhWNAA*
Eggleston, Edward 1837-1902 *Alli Sup, AmA,
AmA&B, BbD, BiD&SB, CarSB,
CasWL, ChPo, ChPo S1, Chmbr 3,
CnDAL, CyAL 2, CyWA, DcAmA,
DcBiA, DcRusL, DcNAA, EvLB,
IndAu 1816, JBA 1934, OxAm, OxEng,
Pen Am, REn, REnAL, WebEAL*
Eggleston, Emma *ChPo*
Eggleston, Frederic William 1875- *WhLA*
Eggleston, George Cary 1839-1911 *Alli Sup,
AmA, AmA&B, BbD, BiD&SB, BiDSA,
CyAL 2, DcAmA, DcBiA, DcLEnL,
DcNAA, IndAu 1816, OxAm, REnAL*
Eggleston, Joseph DuPuy, Jr. 1867- *BiDSA,
WhWNAA*
Eggleston, Joseph W *BiDSA*
Eggleston, Wilfrid 1901- *CanNov, ConAu 23,
OxCan, OxCan Sup, WrD 1976*
Eggleston, William *Alli Sup*
Egglestone, William Morley *Alli Sup*
Egharevba, Jacob Uwadiaf, Chief 1920?- *AfA 1*
Egill, Skallagrimsson *BbD, BiD&SB, CasWL*
Egilsson, Sveinbjorn 1791-1852 *BbD, BiD&SB,
DcEuL*
Eginhard 770-840 *BbD, BiD&SB, NewC,
OxEng, OxFr, Pen Eur*
Egle, William Henry 1830-1901 *Alli Sup,
AmA&B, DcAmA, DcNAA*
Egler, Frank E 1911- *ConAu 29, WrD 1976*
Eglesfield, Fr *Alli*
Eglesfield, James *Alli*
Egleson, Janet F *ConAu 57*
Egleston, G W *Alli Sup*
Egleston, Melville *Alli Sup*
Egleston, Nathaniel Hillyer *Alli Sup*
Egleston, Thomas 1832-1900 *Alli Sup,
DcAmA, DcNAA*
Egleton, John *Alli*
Eglington, Charles 1918- *ConP 1970*
Eglinton, Sir Hugh Of *Chmbr 1*
Eglinton, John 1868-1961 *ChPo S1, LongC,
ModBL, NewC*
Eglisem, George *Alli*
Eglisemmius, George *Alli*
Eglisham, George *Alli*
Egliston, E H *MnBBF*
Eglitis, Anslavs *Pen Eur*
Egmont 1522-1568 *OxGer*
Egmont, Earls Of *Alli*
Egnatzik, Joseph 1920- *AmSCAP 66*
Egner, Philip 1870-1956 *AmSCAP 66*
Egner, Thorbjorn 1912- *WhGrA*
Egremont, Earl Of *OxCan*
Egremont, Godfrey *Alli Sup*
Egremont, John *Alli, BiDLA*
Egremont, Michael *EncM&D*
Egudu, Romanus N 1940?- *AfA 1, ConP 1970*
Eguilaz, Luis 1830-1878 *BiD&SB*
Eguren, Jose Maria 1882-1942 *CasWL, EncWL,
Pen Am*
Egwin Of Worcester d718? *Alli, BiB S,
DcEnL*
Egypt, Ophelia Settle 1903- *LivBA*
Ehinger, Ella M *ChPo S2*
Ehle, John 1925- *AmA&B, Au&Wr,
ConAu 1R, ConAu 9R, DrAF 1976,
WrD 1976*
Ehler, Annette Blackburn 1864- *WhWNAA*
Ehlers, Friedrich Robert *WhLA*

Ehlers, Henry James 1907- *ConAu 13R,
WrD 1976*
Ehlert, Lois Jane 1934- *IlCB 1966*
Ehlert, Louis 1825-1884 *BiD&SB*
Ehmcke, Fritz Helmut 1878- *WhGrA*
Ehninger, Douglas Wagner 1913- *ConAu 5R,
IndAu 1917*
Ehninger, John W 1827-1889 *ChPo, ChPo S1,
EarAB, EarAB Sup*
Ehre, Edward 1905- *ConAu 9R*
Ehre, Milton 1933- *ConAu 53*
Ehrenbaum, Ernst M E 1861- *WhLA*
Ehrenberg, Paul 1875- *WhLA*
Ehrenberg, Victor Leopold 1891- *Au&Wr,
ConAu 5R, WrD 1976*
Ehrenberg, Wolfgang 1909- *BiDPar*
Ehrenbourg, Ilya 1891-1967 *TwCA,
TwCA Sup*
Ehrenburg *Pen Eur*
Ehrenburg, Ilya Grigoryevich 1891-1967 *CasWL,
ClDMEuL, ConAu 25, DcRusL, EncWL,
EvEuW, LongC, ModSL 1, REn, TwCW*
Ehrencron-Kidde, Astrid Margrethe 1874-1960
CasWL
Ehrenfried, Georg *OxGer*
Ehrenhaft, Felix 1897- *WhLA*
Ehrenpreis, Anne Henry 1927- *ConAu 53*
Ehrenreich, Max 1864- *WhLA*
Ehrensperger, Harold Adam 1897- *IndAu 1917*
Ehrenstein, Albert 1886-1950 *EncWL, ModGL,
OxGer, Pen Eur*
Ehrensvaerd, Geesta 1910- *ConAu 49*
Ehrensvard, Count Carl August 1745-1800
CasWL
Ehrenwald, Jan 1900- *BiDPar, ConAu 49*
Ehrenzweig, Albert A 1906- *ConAu 29,
WrD 1976*
Ehrenzweig, Armin 1864- *WhLA*
Ehresmann, Julia M 1939- *ConAu 33*
Ehret, Christopher 1941- *ConAu 37,
WrD 1976*
Ehret, G D *Alli*
Ehret, Walter 1918- *AmSCAP 66*
Ehrhardt, John Christian *OxCan*
Ehrhardt, Reinhold 1900- *ConAu 29*
Ehrhart, W D 1948- *ConAu 61*
Ehrich, Lewis Rinaldo 1849- *DcAmA*
Ehrke, Hans 1898- *CasWL*
Ehrler, Hans Heinrich 1876-1951 *OxGer*
Ehrlich, Alfred Heinrich 1822-1899 *BiD&SB*
Ehrlich, Amy 1942- *ConAu 37*
Ehrlich, Anne Howland 1933- *ConAu 61*
Ehrlich, Arnold 1923- *ConAu 33*
Ehrlich, Bettina Bauer 1903- *AuBYP,
ConAu P-1, IlCB 1956, IlCB 1966,
MorJA, SmATA 1*
Ehrlich, Eugene H 1922- *ConAu 1R,
WrD 1976*
Ehrlich, Howard J 1932- *ConAu 17R*
Ehrlich, Jack *ConAu XR*
Ehrlich, Jacob Wilburn 1900-1971 *ConAu 33*
Ehrlich, Jake *ConAu XR*
Ehrlich, John Gunther 1930- *ConAu 1R*
Ehrlich, Leonard 1905- *AmA&B, TwCA*
Ehrlich, Max 1909- *ConAu 1R, WrD 1976*
Ehrlich, Nathaniel J 1940- *ConAu 53*
Ehrlich, Paul 1932- *WrD 1976*
Ehrlich, Robert S 1935- *ConAu 23*
Ehrlich, Sam 1872-1927 *AmSCAP 66*
Ehrlich, Walter 1921- *ConAu 9R*
Ehrman, John Patrick William 1920- *Au&Wr,
ConAu 5R, WrD 1976*
Ehrmann, Bertha Pratt King 1879- *IndAu 1917*
Ehrmann, Bess Virginia Hicks 1879-
IndAu 1917
Ehrmann, Herbert B 1891- *ConAu 25*
Ehrmann, Mary Bartholomew d1939 *DcNAA*
Ehrmann, Max 1872-1945 *AmA&B, AmLY,
ChPo S2, DcNAA, IndAu 1816,
WhWNAA*
Ehrsam, Theodore George 1909- *ConAu 45*
Eibl-Eibesfeldt, Irenaus 1928- *Au&Wr,
ConAu 9R*
Eibling, Harold Henry 1905- *ConAu 37*
Eiby, George 1918- *ConAu 53*
Eich, Gunter 1907-1972 *CasWL, EncWL,
ModGL, OxGer, Pen Eur, TwCW,
WhTwL, WorAu*

Eichelbaum, Samuel 1894-1967 *ModWD*
Eichelberger, Clayton L 1925- *ConAu 41*
Eichelberger, S *Alli*
Eichelberger, W S 1865- *WhWNAA*
Eichenbaum, Boris Mikhaylovich 1886- *CasWL*
Eichenberg, Fritz 1901- *AnCL, ChPo S2,
ConAu 57, IlBYP, IlCB 1945, IlCB 1956,
IlCB 1966, MorJA, SmATA 9, St&VC,
WhGrA*
Eichendorff, Joseph, Freiherrr Von 1788-1857
*AtlBL, BbD, BiD&SB, CasWL, DcBiA,
DcEuL, EuA, EvEuW, McGWD, OxFr,
OxGer, Pen Eur, RCom, REn*
Eichenlaub, John Ellis 1922- *ConAu 1R*
Eicher, Elizabeth *ConAu 17R*
Eicher, Joanne B 1930- *ConAu 49*
Eichhorn, C *BiDLA*
Eichhorn, David Max 1906- *ConAu P-1*
Eichhorn, Douglas *DrAP 1975*
Eichhorn, Hermene Warlick 1906-
AmSCAP 66
Eichhorn, Johann Gottfried 1752-1827 *BiD&SB*
Eichhorn, Werner 1899- *ConAu 29*
Eichinger, Hubert 1926- *Au&Wr*
Eichler, Albert 1879- *WhLA*
Eichler, Julian 1910- *AmSCAP 66*
Eichmann, Adolf 1906-1962 *REn*
Eichner, Alfred S 1937- *ConAu 13R*
Eichner, Hans 1921- *Au&Wr, ConAu 5R,
WrD 1976*
Eichner, James A 1927- *ConAu 13R,
SmATA 4*
Eichner, Maura *ConAu XR*
Eichorn, Charles *Alli*
Eichorn, Dorothy H 1924- *ConAu 49*
Eichrodt, Ludwig 1827-1892 *BbD, BiD&SB,
OxGer*
Eichtal, Gustave D' 1804-1886 *BiD&SB*
Eicke, Edna *ChPo, IlBYP*
Eicke, J *Alli Sup*
Eickhoff, Andrew R 1924- *ConAu 21,
WrD 1976*
Eide, Arthur Hansin 1886- *WhWNAA*
Eidelberg, Ludwig 1898-1970 *ConAu 29,
ConAu P-1*
Eidelberg, Paul 1928- *ConAu 23*
Eidenbenz, Hermann 1902- *WhGrA*
Eidlitz, Leopold 1823-1896 *Alli Sup, DcAmA*
Eidmann, Frank Lewis 1887-1941 *DcNAA*
Eidom, Rudolph *TexWr*
Eidt, Robert C 1923- *ConAu 33*
Eiduson, Bernice Tabackman 1921- *ConAu 1R*
Eielson, Jorge Eduardo 1921- *DcCLA*
Eifert, Virginia Snider 1911-1966 *AmA&B,
Au&Wr, AuBYP, ConAu 1R, SmATA 2*
Eiffe, P *PoIre*
Eifion Wyn 1867-1926 *CasWL*
Eigenmann, Carl H 1863-1927 *DcNAA*
Eigerman, Hyman *ChPo*
Eigner, Edwin M 1931- *ConAu 21*
Eigner, Larry 1927- *ConAu XR, ConP 1970,
ConP 1975, WrD 1976*
Eigner, Laurence 1927- *ConAu 9R*
Eike Von Repgau 1189?-1233? *OxGer*
Eike Von Repgowe *CasWL*
Eikenberry, Dan Harrison 1888-1963
IndAu 1917
Eikenberry, William Lewis 1871- *WhWNAA*
Eikenhorst, L Van *DcEuL*
Eiker, Mathilde 1893- *AmA&B, TwCA,
TwCA Sup, WhWNAA*
Eiler, Homer 1868- *WhWNAA*
Eilers, Hazel Kraft 1910- *WrD 1976*
Eilhart Von Oberg *CasWL, OxGer, Pen Eur*
Eiloart, Mrs. 1830- *DcEnL, MnBBF*
Eiloart, A B *Au&Wr*
Eiloart, Elizabeth 1830- *Alli Sup*
Eiloart, Ernest 1854- *Alli Sup*
Eilon, Samuel 1923- *ConAu 5R, WrD 1976*
Eilshemius, Louis Michel 1864-1941 *AmA&B,
AnMV 1926, AtlBL, DcNAA*
Eimer, D Robert 1927- *ConAu 13R*
Eimerl, Sarel 1925- *ConAu 21*
Einarsson, Indridi 1851-1939 *CasWL, EncWL,
EvEuW*
Einbond, Bernard Lionel 1937- *ConAu 37,
WrD 1976*
Einem, Gottfried Von 1918- *OxGer*

Einenkel, Eugen *Alli Sup*
Eingman, William F *ChPo S1*
Einhard 770?-840 *CasWL, NewC, OxEng,
OxFr, OxGer, Pen Eur*
Einhart *OxGer*
Einhorn, Max 1862- *WhWNAA*
Einion Ap Gwalchmai *DcEnL*
Einsel, Mary E 1929- *ConAu 29, WrD 1976*
Einsel, Naiad *SmATA 10*
Einsel, Walter 1926- *AuBYP, SmATA 10*
Einselen, Anne F 1900- *AmA&B, AmNov XR*
Einsiedel, Friedrich Hildebrand Von 1750-1828
OxGer
Einsiedel, R V *WhLA*
Einstein, Albert 1879-1955 *AmA&B, CasWL,
DcLEnL, LongC, OxAm, OxEng, REn,
REnAL, WhLA, WhWNAA*
Einstein, Alfred 1880-1952 *AmA&B, LongC,
TwCA Sup*
Einstein, Carl 1885-1940 *OxGer*
Einstein, Lewis 1877- *ChPo S1, WhWNAA*
Einstein, Stanley 1934- *ConAu 53*
Einzig, Paul 1897- *Au&Wr, ConAu 9R*
Einzig, Susan 1922- *IlCB 1966*
Eipper, Paul 1891- *JBA 1934, JBA 1951*
Eirionnach *PoIre*
Eisdell, J S *Alli*
Eisdorfer, Carl 1930- *ConAu 41*
Eisele, Albert A 1936- *ConAu 41*
Eiselen, Frederick Carl 1872-1937 *AmLY,
DcNAA, WhWNAA*
Eiseley, Loren Corey 1907- *AmA&B, Au&Wr,
ConAu 1R, REnAL, WorAu*
Eisen, Carol G *ConAu 49*
Eisen, Franz 1695-1777 *BkIE*
Eisen, Gustavus Augustus 1847-1940 *AmA&B,
AmLY, DcNAA, WhWNAA*
Eisen, Mathias Johannes 1857- *WhLA*
Eisenbart, Johann Andreas 1661-1727 *OxGer*
Eisenberg, Azriel Louis 1903- *AuBYP,
ConAu 49*
Eisenberg, Daniel Bruce 1946- *ConAu 57*
Eisenberg, Dennis Harold 1929- *ConAu 25,
WrD 1976*
Eisenberg, Larry 1919- *ConAu 33, WrD 1976*
Eisenberg, Lee 1946- *ConAu 61*
Eisenberg, Maurice 1902-1972 *ConAu 37*
Eisenberg, Ralph 1930-1973 *ConAu 5R,
ConAu 45*
Eisenbud, Jule 1908- *Au&Wr, BiDPar,
ConAu 49*
Eisendrath, Blanche Goodman *WhWNAA*
Eisendrath, Craig R 1936- *ConAu 49*
Eisendrath, Daniel Nathan 1867-1939 *DcNAA*
Eisenhauer, William G 1925- *AmSCAP 66*
Eisenhower, Dwight David 1890-1969 *AmA&B,
OxAm, REn, REnAL*
Eisenhower, John S D 1922- *ConAu 33*
Eisenmenger, Robert Waltz 1926- *ConAu 37*
Eisenreich, Herbert 1925- *ModGL, OxGer*
Eisenschiml, Otto 1880-1963 *AmA&B,
ConAu 1R*
Eisenson, Jon 1907- *Au&Wr, ConAu 17R,
WrD 1976*
Eisenstadt, A S 1920- *ConAu 9R*
Eisenstadt, E And Whitmore, C J *Alli Sup*
Eisenstadt, Shmuel Noah 1923- *ConAu 25,
WrD 1976*
Eisenstat, Jane Sperry 1920- *ConAu 1R*
Eisenstein, Alfred *AmSCAP 66*
Eisenstein, Ira 1906- *ConAu 21*
Eisenstein, Sam A 1932- *ConAu 61,
DrAF 1976, DrAP 1975*
Eisenstein, Sergei M 1898-1948 *REn*
Eisgruber, Elsa *ChPo S1, IlCB 1945*
Eisinger, Chester E 1915- *ConAu 23*
Eisler, Hanns 1898-1962 *OxGer*
Eisler, Paul 1922- *ConAu 61*
Eisler, Robert I 1882- *WhLA*
Eismann, Bernard N 1933- *ConAu 1R*
Eisner, Betty Grover 1915- *ConAu 29,
WrD 1976*
Eisner, Gisela 1925- *Au&Wr, ConAu P-1,
WrD 1976*
Eisner, Kurt 1867-1919 *OxGer*
Eisner, Lotte Henriette *ConAu 45*
Eisner, Robert 1922- *WrD 1976*
Eisner, Victor 1921- *ConAu 53*

Eisner, Will 1917- *AmA&B*
Eissenstat, Bernard W 1927- *ConAu 45*
Eister, Allan W 1915- *ConAu 45*
Eitan, Israel 1885-1935 *DcNAA, WhWNAA*
Eitel, Edmund Henry *ChPo S1*
Eitel, Ernest John *Alli Sup*
Eiteman, David 1930- *ConAu 45*
Eiteman, Wilford J 1902- *ConAu 1R*
Eitner, Lorenz E A 1919- *ConAu 1R,
WrD 1976*
Eitzen, Allan 1928- *IlBYP, SmATA 9*
Eitzen, D Stanley 1934- *ConAu 53*
Eitzen, Ruth 1924- *ConAu 41, SmATA 9*
Eiximenis, Francesc 1340?-1409 *CasWL,
EvEuW*
Eizaguirre, Jose Echegaray Y 1833-1916 *CyWA*
Ejima, Ichiroemon 1667-1736 *CasWL*
Ejima, Kiseki 1667-1736 *CasWL, DcOrL 1*
Ejima, Shigetomo 1667-1736 *CasWL*
Ekblaw, Sidney E 1903- *ConAu 37*
Ekblaw, W Elmer 1882- *WhWNAA*
Eke, G S *MnBBF*
Ekeblad, Frederick A 1917- *ConAu 5R*
Ekeley, John Bernard 1869- *WhWNAA*
Ekeloef, Gunnar 1907-1968 *ConAu 25*
Ekelof, Bengt Gunnar 1907-1968 *EncWL*
Ekelof, Gunnar 1907-1968 *CasWL,
ConAu XR, Pen Eur, WhTwL, WorAu*
Ekelund, Vilhelm 1880-1949 *CasWL,
CIDMEuL, EncWL, Pen Eur*
Ekert-Rotholz, Alice Maria Augusta *Au&Wr*
Ekhof, Konrad 1720-1778 *OxGer*
Ekins, Bishop *ChPo*
Ekins, Charles *Alli*
Ekins, H R 1901-1963 *AmA&B*
Ekins, Jeffrey d1791 *Alli*
Ekirch, Arthur A, Jr. 1915- *Au&Wr,
ConAu 5R, WrD 1976*
Ekkehard *OxGer*
Ekkehart *OxGer*
Ekkehart I 900?-973 *CasWL, Pen Eur*
Ekkehart IV 980?-1060? *CasWL, Pen Eur*
Ekker, Charles 1930- *ConAu 37*
Eklund, Gordon 1945- *ConAu 33, WrD 1976*
Eklund, Jane Mary *ConAu XR*
Eklund, John M 1909- *WrD 1976*
Ekman, Paul 1934- *ConAu 37*
Ekman, Rosalind 1933- *ConAu 33*
Eknath 1548?-1608? *CasWL*
Ekola, Giles C 1927- *ConAu 17R*
Ekrem Recaizade 1847-1914 *DcOrL 3*
Eksell, Olle 1918- *WhGrA*
Ekstein, Rudolf 1912- *Au&Wr, ConAu 5R*
Ekstrand, Ray 1917- *AmSCAP 66*
Ekulona, Ademola *BlkAW*
Ekvall, Robert Brainerd 1898- *ConAu 1R,
WrD 1976*
Ekwall, Eldon E 1933- *ConAu 29*
Ekwell, Eilert 1877-1964 *LongC*
Ekwensi, C O D 1921- *ConAu XR*
Ekwensi, Cyprian 1921- *AfA 1, Au&Wr,
CasWL, ConAu 29, ConLC 4,
ConNov 1972, ConNov 1976, EncWL Sup,
LongC, Pen Cl, RGAfl, TwCW,
WebEAL, WhTwL, WorAu, WrD 1976*
Ekwere, John 1930?- *AfA 1*
El, Leatrice *BlkAW*
El-Aref, Aref d1973 *ConAu 41*
El-Ayouty, Yassin 1928- *ConAu 29*
El-Baz, Farouk 1938- *ConAu 25*
El Divino *DcSpL*
El Greco *NewC*
El Hardallo *AfA 1*
El Inca *DcSpL*
El-Meligi, A Moneim 1923- *ConAu 17R*
El-Messidi, Kathy Groehn 1946- *ConAu 57*
El-Nil, Ebn *ConAu XR*
El Sabio *DcSpL*
El Solitario *DcSpL, EuA*
El Uqsor *ConAu XR*
El-Yezdi, Haji Abdu *ChPo*
Elagabalus 205-222 *NewC*
Elam, Charles *Alli Sup*
Elam, Charles Milton 1882-1944 *OhA&B*
Elam, Dorothy Allen Conley 1904- *LivBA*
Elam, Richard M 1920- *ConAu 61, SmATA 9*
Elam, Shelby S 1878- *WhWNAA*
Eland, William *Alli*

Eliot, William G 1811-1887 *Alli*
Eliot, William G C, Earl Of St. Germans
  1829-1881 *Alli Sup*
Eliot, William Granville *Alli, BiDLA*
Eliot, William Greenleaf 1811-1887 *Alli Sup,
  DcAmA, DcNAA*
Eliot, William Horace 1824-1852 *DcNAA*
Eliot Hurst, M E 1938- *ConAu 57*
Eliott, Miss *Alli*
Eliovson, Sima Benveniste 1919- *Au&Wr,
  ConAu 13R*
Elis, Islwyn Ffowc 1924- *Au&Wr*
Elis, John *Alli*
Elisabeth SEE ALSO Elizabeth
Elisabeth Christine, K Von Preussen 1715-1797
  OxGer
Elisabeth, Countess Of Nassau-Saarbr.
  1397-1456 *CasWL*
Elisabeth, Heilige 1207-1231 *OxGer*
Elisabeth, Kaiserin Von Osterreich 1837-1898
  OxGer
Elisabeth, Queen Consort 1843-1916 *EuA*
Elisabeth, Queen Of Romania *EvEuW, OxGer*
Elisabeth Von Nassau-Saarbrukken 1397-1456
  OxGer
Elisabeth Von Schonau 1129?-1164 *OxGer*
Eliscu, Edward *AmSCAP 66*
Eliscu, Frank 1912- *ConAu 57*
Elisio, Filinto 1734-1819 *Pen Eur*
Elisofon, Eliot 1911-1973 *AmA&B, ConAu 41*
Elison, George 1937- *ConAu 53*
Elissamburu, Jean-Baptiste *Pen Eur*
Elitos *Alli*
Eliza 1717-1806 *DcEnL*
Elizabeth SEE ALSO Elisabeth
Elizabeth 1866-1941 *EvLB, LongC, NewC,
  REn, TwCA, TwCA Sup*
Elizabeth II 1926- *REn*
Elizabeth Marie, Sister 1914- *ConAu 9R*
Elizabeth Of Hungary, Saint d1231 *REn*
Elizabeth Ottilia Louisa 1843-1916 *DcEuL*
Elizabeth, Princess 1770- *Alli, BiDLA*
Elizabeth, Queen *Chmbr 1*
Elizabeth I, Queen Of England 1533-1603 *Alli,
  CasWL, DcEnL, EvLB, NewC, REn*
Elizabeth, Queen Of Roumania *BiD&SB,
  ChPo, LongC*
Elizabeth, Charlotte *Alli*
Elizondo, Salvador 1932- *DcCLA*
Elizondo, Sergio D *DrAP 1975*
Eljon, Pat *ChPo S2*
Elke Von Repgowe *DcEuL*
Elkes, Richard *Alli*
Elkholy, Abdo A 1925- *ConAu 23*
Elkin, Benjamin *Alli*
Elkin, Benjamin 1911- *Au&Wr, AuBYP,
  ConAu 1R, SmATA 3, WrD 1976*
Elkin, Frederick 1918- *ConAu 41*
Elkin, Judith Laikin 1928- *ConAu 53*
Elkin, Rosie Helen *ChPo*
Elkin, Stanley 1930- *AmA&B, ConAu 9R,
  ConLC 4, ConLC 6, ConNov 1972,
  ConNov 1976, DrAF 1976, EncWL Sup,
  Pen Am, WrD 1976*
Elkin, William Baird 1863- *WhWNAA*
Elkind, David 1931- *ConAu 45*
Elking, Henry *Alli*
Elkington, Joseph *Alli*
Elkington, W M *MnBBF, OxCan*
Elkins, Dov Peretz 1937- *AuBYP, ConAu 29,
  SmATA 5, WrD 1976*
Elkins, Ella Ruth 1929- *ConAu 25*
Elkins, Felton Broomall 1889-1944 *DcNAA*
Elkins, Hervey *Alli Sup*
Elkins, T H 1926- *Au&Wr*
Elkins, William Lewis 1855- *BiDSA*
Elkins, William R 1926- *ConAu 33*
Elkinton, Joseph *OxCan*
Elkon, Juliette *ConAu 57*
Elkon-Hamelecourt, Juliette 1912- *ConAu 57*
Elkus, Albert 1884-1946 *AmSCAP 66*
Elkus, Jonathan 1931- *AmSCAP 66*
Ella, John *Alli Sup*
Ellaby, Francis *Alli*
Ellaby, James And Thelwall, A S *Alli*
Ellacombe, Henry Nicholson *Alli Sup*
Ellacombe, Henry Thomas 1790-1885 *Alli Sup*
Ellacott, Samuel Ernest 1911- *Au&Wr,*

ConAu 5R, WrD 1976
Ellam, Mrs. *ChPo S1*
Ellard, Gerald 1894- *BkC 1, CatA 1947*
Ellard, Harry G 1864-1913 *OhA&B*
Ellard, Virginia G 1839-1912 *OhA&B*
Ellbar, George *MnBBF*
Elledge, W Paul 1938- *ConAu 25*
Ellegood, J *BbtC*
Ellemjay, Louise *BiDSA*
Ellen, Barbara 1938- *AuBYP, ConAu 5R*
Ellen, The Late Henry *AmA&B*
Ellen Alleyne *OxEng*
Ellenberger, Bertha E *ChPo S2*
Ellenberger, Henri F 1905- *ConAu 29*
Ellenborough, Edward Law, Earl Of *Alli Sup*
Ellende Knabe, Der *OxGer*
Ellender, Raphael 1906-1972 *ConAu 37*
Ellens, J Harold 1932- *ConAu 57*
Ellenson, Gene 1921- *ConAu 57*
Ellenwood, Frank Oakes 1878- *WhWNAA*
Ellenwood, March *Alli Sup*
Eller, George *Alli Sup*
Eller, Homer C 1845-1896 *Alli Sup, DcNAA*
Eller, Meredith Freeman 1912- *IndAu 1917*
Eller, Vernard 1927- *ConAu 23, WrD 1976*
Ellerbe, Alma Martin Estabrook 1871-
  IndAu 1816, WhWNAA
Ellerbe, Paul *WhWNAA*
Ellerbe, Rose Lucille 1861-1929 *DcNAA,
  WhWNAA*
Ellerker, Marie St. S *BkC 1*
Ellerman, Annie Winifred *LongC, WrD 1976*
Ellerman, Charles F *Alli Sup*
Ellerton, Alf *ChPo*
Ellerton, Edward *Alli Sup*
Ellerton, F G *ChPo S1*
Ellerton, John 1826-1893 *Alli Sup, ChPo,
  ChPo S1, WebEAL*
Ellerton, John Lodge *Alli Sup*
Ellery, Eloise 1874- *WhWNAA*
Ellery, John Blaise 1920- *ConAu 9R*
Ellery-Anderson, William MacMahon 1919-
  Au&Wr
Ellesby, James *Alli*
Ellesmere, Baron *Alli, NewC*
Ellesmere, Countess Of *Alli*
Ellesmere, Earl Of *Chmbr 2*
Ellesmere, Francis Egerton, Earl Of 1800-1857
  Alli, BiD&SB, DcEnL
Ellet, Charles 1810-1862 *Alli, Alli Sup, AmA,
  DcAmA, DcNAA*
Ellet, Elizabeth Fries 1818-1877 *Alli, Alli Sup,
  AmA, AmA&B, BbD, BiD&SB,
  ChPo S1, CyAL 2, DcAmA, DcNAA,
  FemPA, HsB&A*
Elletson, Sara C B *Alli Sup*
Ellett, M Deborah 1949- *BlkAW*
Ellett, Marcella Howard 1931- *ConAu 23,
  IndAu 1917*
Elley 1904- *DcOrL 3*
Ellfeldt, Lois 1910- *ConAu 33*
Ellia, Felix *Alli*
Ellice, Edward 1781-1863 *DcNAA, OxCan*
Ellice, James 1787-1856 *Alli Sup*
Ellice, Jane *Alli Sup*
Ellice, Robert *Alli Sup, ChPo, ChPo S1*
Ellicott, Andrew 1754?-1820 *Alli, CyAL 1,
  DcNAA*
Ellicott, Charles John 1819- *Alli, Alli Sup,
  BbD, DcEnL*
Ellicott, John *Alli*
Ellicott, John Morris 1859- *BiDSA, DcAmA,
  WhWNAA*
Ellin, E M 1905- *ConAu 29*
Ellin, Stanley 1916- *AmA&B, Au&Wr,
  ConAu 1R, EncM&D, REnAL, WorAu,
  WrD 1976*
Elling, Karl A 1935- *ConAu 25*
Elling, Ray H 1929- *ConAu 33*
Ellinger, John Henry 1919- *Au&Wr,
  WrD 1976*
Ellingford, Herbert Frederick *WhLA*
Ellinghoe, John *ChPo*
Ellingsworth, Huber W 1928- *ConAu 21*
Ellington, Duke 1899-1974 *AmSCAP 66,
  ConAu 49*
Ellington, Edward *Alli*

Ellington, Edward Kennedy 1899-1974
  ConAu 49
Ellington, George *Alli Sup*
Ellington, James W 1927- *ConAu 37*
Ellington, Mercer 1919- *AmSCAP 66*
Ellingwood, Albert Russell 1887-1934 *DcNAA,
  WhWNAA*
Ellingwood, Finley 1852-1920 *DcNAA,
  IndAu 1917*
Ellingwood, Lena B 1866- *WhWNAA*
Ellinwood, Frank F 1826-1908 *Alli Sup,
  BiD&SB, DcAmA, DcNAA*
Ellinwood, Leonard 1905- *ConAu 1R*
Ellinwood, Ralph Everett 1893-1930 *DcNAA*
Elliot *Alli*
Elliot, Miss *BiDLA*
Elliot, A J *OxCan*
Elliot, Adam *Alli*
Elliot, Alexander *Alli Sup*
Elliot, Anne *PoIre*
Elliot, Arthur Ralph Douglas 1846- *Alli Sup*
Elliot, Benjamin 1786-1836 *DcAmA*
Elliot, Charles 1792- *Alli*
Elliot, Charles Burke 1861- *AmLY*
Elliot, Charles Gilbert John Brydone 1818-
  Alli Sup
Elliot, Charles H *Alli*
Elliot, Lady Charlotte d1880 *Alli Sup*
Elliot, Daniel Giraud 1835-1915 *Alli Sup,
  DcAmA, DcNAA*
Elliot, E *Alli, BiDLA*
Elliot, Ebenezer *Chmbr 3*
Elliot, Edith M 1912- *ConAu 23*
Elliot, Elisabeth 1926- *Au&Wr, ConAu 5R*
Elliot, Frances *Alli Sup*
Elliot, Frank M *Alli Sup*
Elliot, George *Alli, OxCan*
Elliot, Sir George Augustus 1812- *Alli Sup*
Elliot, George Henry 1831-1900 *Alli Sup,
  DcAmA, DcNAA*
Elliot, George T 1827-1871 *Alli Sup, DcNAA*
Elliot, Sir Gilbert 1722-1777 *Alli, BiD&SB,
  Chmbr 2*
Elliot, Gilbert 1800- *Alli, Alli Sup*
Elliot, Gordon *OxCan*
Elliot, Sir Henry Miers 1808-1853 *Alli Sup*
Elliot, Henry Rutherford 1849-1906 *Alli Sup,
  AmA&B, BiD&SB, DcAmA, DcNAA*
Elliot, Hugh Frederick Hislop 1848- *Alli Sup*
Elliot, James *Alli, Alli Sup*
Elliot, James 1775-1839 *DcNAA*
Elliot, Jane 1727-1805 *Alli, BbD, BiD&SB,
  EvLB, NewC, OxEng, Pen Eng*
Elliot, Jean 1727-1805 *Chmbr 2, EvLB,
  NewC, Pen Eng*
Elliot, Sir John *Alli*
Elliot, John d1786 *Alli*
Elliot, Sir John 1898- *Au&Wr*
Elliot, John 1918- *Au&Wr, WrD 1976*
Elliot, John Harold 1900- *Au&Wr*
Elliot, John Lettsom *Alli Sup*
Elliot, Jonathan 1784-1846 *AmA, REnAL*
Elliot, Leo *EarAB Sup*
Elliot, Margaret *Alli Sup*
Elliot, Mary A Lattin 1903- *ArizL*
Elliot, Maud Howe 1854-1948 *DcLEnL*
Elliot, R d1788 *Alli*
Elliot, R W *Alli Sup*
Elliot, Richard d1788 *PoCh*
Elliot, Robert *Alli*
Elliot, Robert Henry 1837- *Alli Sup*
Elliot, Robert Henry 1864- *WhLA*
Elliot, Russel *Alli Sup*
Elliot, Samuel 1777-1845 *DcNAA*
Elliot, Samuel Hayes 1809-1869 *Alli, Alli Sup,
  AmA&B, DcAmA, DcNAA*
Elliot, T F *BbtC*
Elliot, Thomas *Alli, BiDLA*
Elliot, Thomas 1820- *PoIre*
Elliot, Thomas John *Alli Sup*
Elliot, Sir Walter 1803-1887 *Alli Sup*
Elliot, William *Alli Sup*
Elliot And Strobel *Alli*
Elliotson, John 1791-1868 *Alli, BiDPar*
Elliott, Alexander *ChPo S1*
Elliott, Alfred *Alli Sup*
Elliott, Alonzo 1891-1964 *AmSCAP 66*
Elliott, Anne *REn*

Elliott, Arthur H *Alli Sup*
Elliott, Arthur Henry d1918 *DcNAA*
Elliott, Benjamin 1786?-1836 *BiDSA, DcNAA*
Elliott, Blanche 1890-1959 *ChPo, OhA&B*
Elliott, Brian Robinson 1910- *ConAu 25, WrD 1976*
Elliott, Bruce 1915?-1973 *ConAu 41*
Elliott, Byron K And Elliott, William F *Alli Sup*
Elliott, Byron Kosciusko 1835-1913 *DcAmA, DcNAA, IndAu 1917*
Elliott, C B *Alli*
Elliott, C Orville 1913- *ConAu 33, WrD 1976*
Elliott, Charles 1792-1869 *Alli Sup, BiDSA, DcAmA, DcNAA, OhA&B*
Elliott, Charles 1815-1892 *Alli Sup, DcAmA, DcNAA*
Elliott, Sir Charles Alfred 1835- *Alli Sup*
Elliott, Charles B *Alli*
Elliott, Charles Burke 1861-1935 *Alli Sup, DcAmA, DcNAA, OhA&B*
Elliott, Charles Gleason 1850-1926 *DcNAA*
Elliott, Charles John *Alli Sup*
Elliott, Charles Loring 1812-1868 *EarAB*
Elliott, Charles Wyllys 1817-1883 *Alli Sup, BbD, BiD&SB, DcAmA, DcNAA*
Elliott, Charlotte 1789-1871 *Alli Sup, BiD&SB, ChPo, ChPo S1, ChPo S2, DcEnL, NewC, PoCh*
Elliott, Chip *ConAu XR*
Elliott, Christopher Robin 1929- *Au&Wr, WrD 1976*
Elliott, David W 1939- *ConAu 45*
Elliott, E *Alli Sup*
Elliott, E E, III 1945- *ConAu 29*
Elliott, Ebenezer 1781-1849 *Alli, BbD, BiD&SB, BrAu 19, CasWL, ChPo, ChPo S1, ChPo S2, DcEnA, DcEnL, DcLEnL, EvLB, NewC, OxEng, Pen Eng, REn, WebEAL*
Elliott, Edward 1874- *WhWNAA*
Elliott, Edward Bishop 1793-1875 *Alli, Alli Sup*
Elliott, Edward Charles 1874- *WhWNAA*
Elliott, Edward King *Alli Sup*
Elliott, Edwin Bailey 1851- *WhLA*
Elliott, Elizabeth *ChPo*
Elliott, Elizabeth Shippen Green *IlCB 1945*
Elliott, Emilia *DcNAA*
Elliott, Emily *BlkAW*
Elliott, Emily Elizabeth Steele 1836-1897 *ChPo, ChPo S1*
Elliott, Emily Steele *Alli Sup*
Elliott, Ernest Eugene 1878-1941 *DcNAA, IndAu 1816, WhWNAA*
Elliott, Ezekiel Brown 1823-1888 *Alli Sup, DcAmA*
Elliott, F Ann *ChPo*
Elliott, F G *ChPo*
Elliott, Francis Perry 1861-1924 *DcNAA*
Elliott, Frank R 1817-1878 *Alli*
Elliott, Franklin Reuben 1817-1878 *Alli Sup, DcAmA, DcNAA, OhA&B*
Elliott, G Maurice 1883-1959 *BiDPar*
Elliott, George *Alli Sup*
Elliott, George 1851-1930 *AmLY, DcNAA, OhA&B, WhWNAA*
Elliott, George 1861- *Alli Sup*
Elliott, George 1918- *RAdv 1, WorAu*
Elliott, George Henry *Alli Sup*
Elliott, George M *Alli Sup*
Elliott, George P 1918- *AmA&B, ConAu 1R, ConLC 2, ConNov 1972, ConNov 1976, ConP 1970, ConP 1975, DrAF 1976, DrAP 1975, IndAu 1917, ModAL, ModAL Sup, OxAm, WrD 1976*
Elliott, George Percy *Alli*
Elliott, George Roy 1883-1963 *AmA&B, WhWNAA*
Elliott, Gertrude *ChPo*
Elliott, Sir Gilbert *DcEnL*
Elliott, H M *Alli*
Elliott, Mrs. H V *ChPo*
Elliott, Harley 1940- *ConAu 49, DrAP 1975*
Elliott, Harrison Sacket 1882-1951 *OhA&B*
Elliott, Sir Henry Miers 1808-1853 *BiD&SB*
Elliott, Henry Rutherford 1849- *DcAmA*
Elliott, Henry Venn 1792-1865 *Alli, Alli Sup*
Elliott, Henry Wood 1846-1930 *Alli Sup,*

BiD&SB, DcAmA, DcNAA, OhA&B*
Elliott, Hettie 1865-1926 *IndAu 1917*
Elliott, Howard 1860-1928 *DcNAA*
Elliott, J A *ChPo*
Elliott, J Arthur *MnBBF*
Elliott, J M K 1830?- *Br&AmS*
Elliott, James 1775-1839 *DcAmA*
Elliott, James Rupert *OxCan*
Elliott, James William 1890- *IndAu 1917*
Elliott, Jan Walter 1939- *ConAu 37, WrD 1976*
Elliott, Jane *ChPo, DcEnL*
Elliott, Janice 1931- *ConAu 13R, WrD 1976*
Elliott, Jean L *OxCan Sup*
Elliott, John 1768-1824 *DcAmA*
Elliott, John 1938- *ConAu 25*
Elliott, John Arthur *ChPo S2*
Elliott, John B 1907- *AmSCAP 66*
Elliott, John B 1911- *IndAu 1917*
Elliott, John E 1931- *ConAu 1R*
Elliott, John H 1930- *ConAu 5R, WrD 1976*
Elliott, John M 1914- *AmSCAP 66*
Elliott, John R, Jr. 1937- *ConAu 25*
Elliott, Jonathan 1784-1846 *Alli, DcAmA*
Elliott, Joseph Davenport *Alli Sup*
Elliott, Joseph Dwight 1927-1956 *IndAu 1917*
Elliott, Joseph Peter 1815- *IndAu 1816*
Elliott, Joseph Taylor 1837-1916 *IndAu 1816, OhA&B*
Elliott, Julia Anne d1841 *PoCh*
Elliott, Kathleen 1897-1940 *DcNAA*
Elliott, Kit 1936- *ConAu 29*
Elliott, Lawrence 1924- *ConAu 5R*
Elliott, Leo 1814- *EarAB*
Elliott, Leonard M 1902- *ConAu P-1*
Elliott, Lewis 1921- *AmSCAP 66*
Elliott, Lillian Elwyn *AmA&B*
Elliott, Lydia Landon *IndAu 1816*
Elliott, M L *ChPo, ChPo S2*
Elliott, Madge *ChPo, ChPo S2*
Elliott, Margaret *ChPo S1*
Elliott, Mary *Alli, CarSB, ChPo, ChPo S1, ChPo S2*
Elliott, Maud Howe 1854-1948 *Alli Sup, AmA&B, AmLY, BbD, BiD&SB, ChPo S1, ChPo S2, DcAmA, DcNAA, OxAm, REnAL, WhWNAA*
Elliott, Michael *MnBBF*
Elliott, N *Alli Sup*
Elliott, Neil 1938- *ConAu 25*
Elliott, Norabelle Camp *ChPo*
Elliott, Orrin Leslie 1860-1940 *DcNAA*
Elliott, Osborn 1924- *AmA&B, ConAu 1R*
Elliott, R *Alli Sup, BiDLA*
Elliott, Ralph H 1925- *ConAu 1R*
Elliott, Ralph Warren Victor 1921- *Au&Wr*
Elliott, Raymond Pruitt 1904- *ConAu 17R*
Elliott, Richard d1788 *BiDLA Sup*
Elliott, Richard Smith *Alli Sup, BiDSA*
Elliott, Richard V 1935- *ConAu 33*
Elliott, Robert *ChPo S2, ConAu XR*
Elliott, Robert d1910 *PoIre*
Elliott, Robert Carl 1914- *ConAu 1R, IndAu 1917*
Elliott, Robert Cowell *MnBBF*
Elliott, Robert G 1874-1939 *DcNAA*
Elliott, Rowland *Alli Sup*
Elliott, Ruth *Alli Sup*
Elliott, Ruth 1888- *WhWNAA*
Elliott, Sarah A *Alli Sup, LivFWS*
Elliott, Sarah Barnwell 1848-1928 *Alli Sup, AmA, AmA&B, BbD, BiD&SB, BiDSA, CnDAL, DcAmA, DcNAA, OxAm*
Elliott, Sarah M 1930- *ConAu 41*
Elliott, Sheldon D 1906-1972 *ConAu 33*
Elliott, Simon Bolivar 1830-1917 *DcNAA*
Elliott, Sophronia Maria 1854-1942 *DcNAA*
Elliott, Spencer Hayward 1883-1967 *ConAu P-1, WhLA*
Elliott, Stephen 1771-1830 *Alli, CyAL 1, DcAmA, DcNAA*
Elliott, Stephen 1806-1866 *Alli, Alli Sup, BiDSA, DcNAA*
Elliott, Steven 1771-1830 *BiDSA*
Elliott, Sumner Locke 1917- *Au&Wr, ConAu 5R*
Elliott, Sydney Robert 1902- *Au&Wr*
Elliott, T C 1862- *WhWNAA*

Elliott, Thomas *Alli Sup*
Elliott, Thomas Joseph 1941- *ConAu 49*
Elliott, W *Alli Sup*
Elliott, W J *Alli Sup*
Elliott, Walter Hackett Robert 1842-1928 *AmA&B, DcNAA, OhA&B*
Elliott, Washington L *Alli Sup*
Elliott, William *Alli Sup, BiDSA*
Elliott, William 1761-1808 *CyAL 1*
Elliott, William 1788-1863 *Alli, AmA&B, BbD, BiD&SB, CyAL 1, DcAmA, DcNAA*
Elliott, William Douglas *DrAF 1976, DrAP 1975*
Elliott, William Frederick 1859-1927 *DcNAA, IndAu 1917*
Elliott, William James *MnBBF*
Elliott, William Marion 1903- *ConAu P-1, IndAu 1917*
Elliott, William Rowcliffe 1910- *WrD 1976*
Elliott, William S 1877- *WhWNAA*
Elliott, William Yandell 1896- *AmA&B*
Elliott-Bateman, Michael Robert 1928- *Au&Wr*
Elliott-Binns, Michael 1923- *Au&Wr*
Elliott-Burns, Michael Ferrers 1923- *WrD 1976*
Elliott-Cannon, Arthur Elliott 1919- *Au&Wr*
Ellis *Alli*
Ellis, Doctor *Alli*
Ellis, Miss *Alli Sup*
Ellis, A *Alli Sup*
Ellis, A Caswell 1871- *WhWNAA*
Ellis, A Montgomery *Alli Sup*
Ellis, A Raymond *WhWNAA*
Ellis, Albert 1913- *AmA&B, ConAu 1R, WrD 1976*
Ellis, Alec 1932- *ConAu 45, WrD 1976*
Ellis, Alexander John 1814-1890 *Alli Sup*
Ellis, Alexander Robert 1903- *Au&Wr*
Ellis, Alfred Burdon *Alli Sup*
Ellis, Alfred Shelley *Alli Sup*
Ellis, Alston 1847-1920 *OhA&B*
Ellis, Amanda M 1898- *ConAu 23*
Ellis, Amory *Alli Sup*
Ellis, Anne 1875-1938 *AmA&B, DcNAA*
Ellis, Anne Weir 1931- *Au&Wr, WrD 1976*
Ellis, Annie Raine *Alli Sup*
Ellis, Arthur *Alli Sup*
Ellis, Arthur Blake 1854-1923 *Alli Sup, DcNAA*
Ellis, Arthur Mackay *Alli Sup*
Ellis, Arthur Thomas 1892- *WhLA*
Ellis, Audrey *WrD 1976*
Ellis, B Robert 1940- *ConAu 53*
Ellis, Benjamin 1798-1831 *Alli, DcNAA*
Ellis, C M *Alli Sup*
Ellis, Carleton 1876-1941 *DcNAA*
Ellis, Carolyn *ChPo*
Ellis, Carrie *ChPo*
Ellis, Catherine Ruth *ChPo*
Ellis, Charles *Alli*
Ellis, Mrs. Charles *Alli Sup*
Ellis, Charles H Fairfax *Alli Sup*
Ellis, Charles Howard 1895- *ConAu P-1*
Ellis, Charles Mayo 1818-1878 *Alli Sup, DcAmA, DcNAA*
Ellis, Charles Thomas *Alli, BiDLA*
Ellis, Clara Spalding *WhWNAA*
Ellis, Clement 1630-1700 *Alli*
Ellis, Clyde T 1908- *ConAu 23*
Ellis, Conyngham *Alli Sup*
Ellis, Mrs. Conyngham *Alli Sup*
Ellis, Cuthbert Hamilton 1909- *Au&Wr, ConAu 13R*
Ellis, Daniel *Alli, Alli Sup, BiDLA*
Ellis, David 1874- *WhLA*
Ellis, David 1918- *Au&Wr*
Ellis, David Maldwyn 1914- *ConAu 9R*
Ellis, Dom *Alli*
Ellis, Don Carlos 1883- *WhWNAA*
Ellis, Dorothea Mary 1913- *Au&Wr*
Ellis, E E *Alli Sup*
Ellis, E M *Alli Sup*
Ellis, Edgar William 1864- *OhA&B*
Ellis, Edith 1876-1960 *AmA&B, WhWNAA*
Ellis, Edmund *Alli*
Ellis, Edward *Alli, Alli Sup*
Ellis, Edward Robb 1911- *ConAu 25, WrD 1976*

Ellis, Edward Sylvester 1840-1916 *Alli Sup,
    AmA, AmA&B, BbD, BiD&SB, CarSB,
    DcAmA, DcNAA, HsB&A, OhA&B,
    OxAm, REnAL, WhCL, YABC 1*
Ellis, Edwin J *Alli Sup*
Ellis, Ella Thorp 1928- *ConAu 49, SmATA 7,
    WrD 1976*
Ellis, Ellen E *Alli Sup*
Ellis, Elmer 1901- *AmA&B*
Ellis, Elmo I 1918- *ConAu 33*
Ellis, Erastus Ranney 1832-1914 *Alli Sup,
    DcNAA*
Ellis, Ethel E *Alli Sup*
Ellis, F S *Alli Sup*
Ellis, Florence Hawley 1906- *ConAu 61*
Ellis, Frank *ChPo, ChPo S1, ChPo S2,
    MnBBF*
Ellis, Frank K 1933- *ConAu 25*
Ellis, Franklin 1828-1885 *Alli Sup, DcNAA*
Ellis, Frederick Starbridge 1830-1901 *ChPo,
    ChPo S2*
Ellis, G *BiDLA*
Ellis, George *Alli Sup, Chmbr 2*
Ellis, George 1753?-1815 *Alli, BiD&SB,
    BiDLA, BiDLA Sup, BrAu, CasWL,
    ChPo, DcEnL, DcEuL, DcLEnL, EvLB,
    NewC, OxEng, Pen Eng*
Ellis, George A *Alli Sup*
Ellis, George E R *Alli Sup*
Ellis, George Edward 1814-1894 *Alli, Alli Sup,
    AmA&B, BbD, BiD&SB, CyAL 2,
    DcAmA, DcNAA,
    DcEnL*
Ellis, George James W Agar 1797-1833 *Alli,
    DcEnL*
Ellis, George Viner *Alli, Alli Sup*
Ellis, George Washington 1875-1919 *AmA&B,
    AmLY, BlkAW, DcNAA*
Ellis, Grace A *Alli Sup*
Ellis, Griffith Ogden 1869-1948 *AmA&B,
    REnAL, WhWNAA*
Ellis, H *Alli*
Ellis, Harold 1926- *WrD 1976*
Ellis, Harold Milton 1885-1947 *AmA&B,
    DcNAA, WhWNAA*
Ellis, Harriet Warner *Alli Sup*
Ellis, Harry Bearse 1921- *AmA&B, AuBYP,
    ConAu 1R, SmATA 9, WrD 1976*
Ellis, Havelock 1859-1939 *AtlBL, ChPo,
    LongC, ModBL, NewC, REn, TwCA,
    TwCA Sup, WhLA*
Ellis, Sir Henry d1855 *Alli*
Ellis, Henry 1721-1806 *Alli, OxCan*
Ellis, Sir Henry 1777-1869 *Alli, BbD, BiDLA,
    ChPo, DcEnL*
Ellis, Henry Havelock 1859-1939 *CasWL,
    DcLEnL, EvLB, OxEng*
Ellis, Henry T *Alli Sup*
Ellis, Hercules 1810?-1879 *Alli Sup, PoIre*
Ellis, Howard *Alli Sup*
Ellis, Howard S 1898- *ConAu 49*
Ellis, Howard Woodrow 1914- *ConAu 1R,
    IndAu 1917*
Ellis, Humphrey *Alli*
Ellis, Humphry Francis 1907- *Au&Wr,
    ConAu 5R, WrD 1976*
Ellis, J *Alli*
Ellis, J E *Alli Sup*
Ellis, J H S 1893- *ConAu 23*
Ellis, J V *Alli Sup, BbtC*
Ellis, Jack 1908- *AmSCAP 66*
Ellis, James *Alli, Alli Sup*
Ellis, James 1935- *ConAu 37*
Ellis, James Tandy *BiDSA*
Ellis, James Whitcomb 1848-1929 *DcNAA,
    IndAu 1917*
Ellis, Jeffrey Hardy 1912- *Au&Wr*
Ellis, Job Bicknell 1829-1905 *DcNAA*
Ellis, Jody 1925- *ConAu 57*
Ellis, John *Alli, Alli Sup*
Ellis, John 1698-1791 *Alli, DcEnL*
Ellis, John 1710?-1776 *Alli*
Ellis, John 1812-1894 *OhA&B*
Ellis, John 1815-1896 *DcNAA*
Ellis, John, Jr. *Alli*
Ellis, John B *Alli Sup*
Ellis, John Breckenridge 1870-1956 *AmA&B,*

AmLY, BiDSA, DcAmA, WhWNAA*
Ellis, John Eimeo *Alli Sup*
Ellis, John Harvard 1841-1870 *Alli Sup, ChPo,
    DcNAA*
Ellis, John M 1936- *ConAu 49*
Ellis, John Marion 1917- *ConAu 49*
Ellis, John Rathbone *Alli Sup*
Ellis, John Tracy 1905- *AmA&B, Au&Wr,
    BkC 5, CatA 1952, ConAu 1R*
Ellis, John W *ChPo*
Ellis, John William 1839-1910 *DcNAA*
Ellis, Joseph *Alli Sup, ChPo S1*
Ellis, Joseph J 1943- *ConAu 53*
Ellis, Katharine Ruth 1879- *AmA&B*
Ellis, Keith Stanley 1927- *Au&Wr, WrD 1976*
Ellis, Kenneth Leslie 1924- *Au&Wr*
Ellis, L And Lewis, M *Alli Sup*
Ellis, Leo R 1909- *ConAu 9R*
Ellis, Leonora Beck *BiDSA*
Ellis, Lewis Ethan 1898- *Au&Wr, ConAu 5R*
Ellis, Lady Louisa *Alli Sup*
Ellis, Louise *WrD 1976*
Ellis, M A *Alli Sup*
Ellis, M Leroy 1928- *ConAu 37*
Ellis, Mabel Farrar *TexWr*
Ellis, Malcolm Henry 1890- *WhLA*
Ellis, Margaret *Alli Sup*
Ellis, Mark Karl 1945- *WrD 1976*
Ellis, Mary *Alli Sup*
Ellis, Mary F *ChPo*
Ellis, Mary Jackson 1916- *ConAu 1R, MnnWr*
Ellis, Mary Leith 1921- *ConAu 23, WrD 1976*
Ellis, Mary W *Alli Sup*
Ellis, Max Mapes 1887-1953 *IndAu 1917*
Ellis, Melvin Richard 1912- *ConAu 13R,
    SmATA 7*
Ellis, Milton 1885-1947 *DcNAA, WhWNAA*
Ellis, Miriam Green 1879- *WhWNAA*
Ellis, Norman R 1924- *ConAu 13R*
Ellis, Octavius James *Alli Sup*
Ellis, Oliver C DeC 1889- *Au&Wr*
Ellis, Olivia *ConAu XR, WrD 1976*
Ellis, Paul Franklyn 1904- *WhWNAA*
Ellis, Philip *Alli*
Ellis, Phillis Marion *Alli Sup*
Ellis, Ray C 1898- *ConAu 21*
Ellis, Richard *Alli Sup*
Ellis, Sir Richard *Alli*
Ellis, Richard E 1937- *ConAu 61*
Ellis, Richard N 1939- *ConAu 33, WrD 1976*
Ellis, Richard White Bernard 1902- *ConAu P-1*
Ellis, Robert *Alli, Alli Sup*
Ellis, Robert d1875 *BiD&SB*
Ellis, Robert 1820?-1885 *Alli Sup, BiD&SB*
Ellis, Robert Leslie 1817-1859 *Alli, Alli Sup*
Ellis, Robert Stephenson *Alli Sup*
Ellis, Robert Walpole 1868-1937 *DcNAA*
Ellis, Robinson 1834-1913 *Alli Sup, BrAu 19*
Ellis, Roland *Alli Sup*
Ellis, Royston 1941- *Au&Wr, ConAu 5R,
    WrD 1976*
Ellis, Rush *Alli Sup*
Ellis, Samuel *Alli Sup*
Ellis, Sarah Stickney 1812-1872 *Alli, Alli Sup,
    BbD, BiD&SB, ChPo, ChPo S1,
    Chmbr 3, NewC*
Ellis, Seger 1904- *AmSCAP 66*
Ellis, Stewart Marsh *WhLA*
Ellis, Sumner 1828-1886 *Alli Sup, DcAmA,
    DcNAA*
Ellis, Sydney *Alli Sup*
Ellis, T F, And Adolphus, J S *Alli*
Ellis, Teresa *BlkAW*
Ellis, Theodore Gunville 1829-1883 *Alli Sup*
Ellis, Thomas *Alli*
Ellis, Thomas Evelyn 1880- *ChPo S2*
Ellis, Thomas T *Alli Sup*
Ellis, Tristram James *Alli Sup*
Ellis, Ulrich Ruegg 1904- *WrD 1976*
Ellis, Vivian 1904- *Au&Wr*
Ellis, Vivian Locke *ChPo, ChPo S1*
Ellis, W *Alli*
Ellis, Mrs. W H M 1886-1942 *Br&AmS*
Ellis, W Outram *Alli Sup*
Ellis, Wade Hampton 1866- *WhWNAA*
Ellis, William *Alli, Alli Sup, BiDLA*
Ellis, William 1794-1872 *Alli Sup, BbD,
    DcEnL*

Ellis, William 1800-1881 *Alli, Alli Sup,
    BiD&SB*
Ellis, William 1918- *ConAu 49*
Ellis, Mrs. William 1812- *DcEnL*
Ellis, Sir William C *Alli*
Ellis, William Donohue 1918- *ConAu 49*
Ellis, William Hodgson 1845-1921 *DcNAA*
Ellis, William R And Parker, J C *Alli Sup*
Ellis, William Ronald Archer 1913- *Au&Wr*
Ellis, William Smith *Alli Sup*
Ellis, William Thomas 1873- *WhWNAA*
Ellis, Wilmot Burrows Edward *Alli Sup*
Ellis-Fermor, Una Mary 1894-1958 *NewC*
Ellison, Alfred 1854-1934 *IndAu 1816*
Ellison, Alfred 1916- *ConAu 1R*
Ellison, Craig W 1944- *ConAu 57*
Ellison, Cuthbert *Alli*
Ellison, Dick *MnBBF*
Ellison, Edity Nicholl *ChPo*
Ellison, Edna Mae *ChPo*
Ellison, Ellis *MnBBF*
Ellison, Gerald Alexander 1910- *ConAu P-1*
Ellison, Harlan 1934- *ConAu 5R, ConLC 1,
    DrAF 1976, WrD 1976*
Ellison, Henry *Alli Sup*
Ellison, Henry 1811- *ChPo S1, ChPo S2*
Ellison, Henry 1931-1965 *ConAu 5R*
Ellison, Henry John *Alli Sup*
Ellison, Henry Leopold 1903- *Au&Wr,
    ConAu 5R, WrD 1976*
Ellison, Herbert J 1929- *ConAu 13R*
Ellison, James E 1927- *ConAu 13R,
    IndAu 1917*
Ellison, James Whitfield 1929- *ConAu 1R*
Ellison, Jerome 1907- *AmA&B, ConAu 29*
Ellison, Joan Audrey 1928- *Au&Wr,
    WrD 1976*
Ellison, John *Alli, Alli Sup, ChPo S2*
Ellison, John Malcus 1889- *ConAu 1R*
Ellison, Matthew 1804- *BiDSA*
Ellison, Max 1914- *AuNews 1, ConAu 57*
Ellison, Nathaniel *Alli*
Ellison, Norman Frederick 1893- *Au&Wr*
Ellison, R *Alli, BiDLA*
Ellison, Ralph Waldo 1914- *AmA&B, BlkAW,
    CasWL, CnDAL, ConAu 9R, ConLC 1,
    ConLC 3, ConNov 1972, ConNov 1976,
    DrAF 1976, EncWL, LivBA, ModAL,
    ModAL Sup, OxAm, Pen Am, RAdv 1,
    REn, REnAL, TwCW, WebEAL,
    WhTwL, WorAu, WrD 1976*
Ellison, Reuben Young 1907- *ConAu 13R*
Ellison, Robert Spurrier 1875-1945 *IndAu 1917*
Ellison, Seacome *Alli*
Ellison, Thomas *Alli Sup*
Ellison, Virginia Howell 1910- *ConAu 33,
    SmATA 4, WrD 1976*
Ellison, William Henry 1878- *WhWNAA*
Elliston, Bobbretta M *BlkAW*
Elliston, Fannie *ChPo S1*
Elliston, Miss George 1883-1946 *AmA&B,
    AnMV 1926, ChPo S1, ChPo S2,
    OhA&B*
Elliston, H B 1895- *WhWNAA*
Elliston, Maxine Hall *BlkAW*
Elliston, Robert William 1774-1831 *Alli,
    BiDLA*
Elliston, Valerie Mae 1929- *ConAu 9R*
Ellman, Michael 1942- *ConAu 45*
Ellmann, Richard 1918- *AmA&B, Au&Wr,
    ConAu 1R, RAdv 1, WorAu, WrD 1976*
Ellms, Charles *EarAB*
Ellowis, Sir Gervase *Alli*
Ells, Benjamin Franklin 1805-1874 *OhA&B*
Ells, Robert Wheelock 1845-1911 *DcNAA*
Ellsasser, Richard 1926- *AmSCAP 66*
Ellsberg, Edward 1891- *AmA&B, AmNov,
    Au&Wr, AuBYP, ConAu 5R, JBA 1934,
    JBA 1951, REnAL, SmATA 7, TwCA,
    TwCA Sup*
Ellson, Ellis *MnBBF*
Ellstein, Abraham 1907-1963 *AmSCAP 66*
Ellsworth, D A *ChPo S1*
Ellsworth, Mrs. E C *ChPo*
Ellsworth, Ephraim Elmer 1837-1861 *Alli Sup,
    DcNAA*
Ellsworth, Erastus Wolcott 1822-1902 *Alli,
    ChPo S1, CyAL 2, DcAmA, DcNAA*

Ellsworth, Etta D *ChPo*
Ellsworth, Henry Leavitt 1791-1858 *DcAmA*
Ellsworth, Henry William 1814-1864 *Alli, DcAmA, DcNAA, IndAu 1816*
Ellsworth, Henry William 1837-1924 *DcNAA*
Ellsworth, John Orval 1891- *Au&Wr*
Ellsworth, Lincoln 1880-1951 *AmA&B*
Ellsworth, Mary Wolcott 1830-1870 *Alli Sup, AmA&B, DcAmA, DcNAA*
Ellsworth, O *Alli Sup*
Ellsworth, Oliver *Alli*
Ellsworth, P T 1897- *ConAu 17R*
Ellsworth, Ralph Eugene 1907- *ConAu 1R, WrD 1976*
Ellsworth, Robert H 1895- *AmSCAP 66*
Ellsworth, S George 1916- *ConAu 45*
Ellsworth, Sallie Bingham 1937- *ConAu 1R*
Ellsworth, William Webster 1855-1936 *AmA&B, ChPo, DcNAA*
Ellul, Jacques 1912- *Au&Wr*
Ellwanger, George Herman 1848-1906 *AmA&B, BbD, BiD&SB, DcAmA, DcNAA*
Ellwanger, Henry Brooks 1851-1883 *Alli Sup, DcAmA, DcNAA*
Ellwanger, William DeLancey 1855-1913 *AmA&B, DcAmA, DcNAA*
Ellwood, Mrs. *Alli*
Ellwood, Mrs. A K *DcEnL*
Ellwood, Charles Abram 1873-1946 *AmLY, DcNAA, WhWNAA*
Ellwood, G Montague 1875- *WhLA*
Ellwood, Gracia Fay 1938- *ConAu 29, WrD 1976*
Ellwood, Marjorie Barker 1904- *WhWNAA*
Ellwood, Robert S, Jr. 1933- *ConAu 41*
Ellwood, Thomas 1639-1713 *Alli, BiD&SB, BrAu, ChPo, ChPo S1, ChPo S2, Chmbr 2, DcEnL, DcEuL, EvLB, NewC, REn*
Elly, Sandham *Alli Sup*
Ellyot, George *Alli*
Ellys, Anthony 1693-1761 *Alli, DcEnL*
Ellys, Sir Richard d1742 *Alli*
Ellys, Tobias *Alli*
Ellyson, Thomas *Alli*
Elman, Harry 1914- *AmSCAP 66*
Elman, Irving 1922- *AmSCAP 66*
Elman, Mischa 1891- *AmSCAP 66*
Elman, Richard 1934- *AmA&B, ConAu 17R, DrAF 1976*
Elman, Robert 1930- *ConAu 45*
Elmendorf, Dwight Lathrop 1859-1929 *DcNAA*
Elmendorf, Francis Littleton 1902- *IndAu 1917*
Elmendorf, John J 1827-1896 *Alli Sup, DcAmA, DcNAA*
Elmendorf, Mary J *AnMV 1926, WhWNAA*
Elmendorf, Mary Lindsay 1917- *ConAu 57*
Elmendorf, Theresa Hubbell 1855-1932 *ChPo, DcNAA*
Elmer, Cedric Nagel 1939- *AmSCAP 66*
Elmer, Herbert Charles 1860-1935 *DcNAA, WhWNAA*
Elmer, Irene 1937- *AuBYP, ConAu 1R*
Elmer, J *Alli*
Elmer, Jonathan *CyAL 2*
Elmer, Joseph *Alli*
Elmer, Laura *ChPo, ChPo S1*
Elmer, Lucius Quintius Cincinnatus 1793-1883 *Alli, Alli Sup, CyAL 2, DcAmA, DcNAA*
Elmer, Manuel Conrad 1886- *WhWNAA*
Elmer, Rachael Robinson *ChPo*
Elmer, Robert P 1877- *WhWNAA*
Elmes, James 1782-1862 *Alli, BiD&SB*
Elmes, Webster *Alli Sup*
Elmham, Thomas 1390?-1440? *Alli, BiD&SB, DcEnL*
Elmhirst, Edward Pennell 1845- *Alli Sup*
Elmi, Bownderi *AfA 1*
Elmi Bonderi *Pen Cl*
Elmlicht, Twinrock *Alli Sup*
Elmo *ChPo S1, ChPo S2*
Elmore, Mrs. A *ChPo S1*
Elmore, Alfred 1815-1881 *ChPo*
Elmore, Emily W *WhWNAA*
Elmore, H M *Alli, BiDLA*
Elmore, James Buchanan 1857-1942 *ChPo, IndAu 1816*
Elmore, Jefferson 1862-1935? *DcNAA, WhWNAA*

Elmore, Nellie Maie Moore *IndAu 1917*
Elmore, Robert 1913- *AmSCAP 66*
Elmore, Theda Mize *TexWr*
Elmore, Wilber Theodore 1871-1935 *DcNAA*
Elmquist, Axel Louis 1884- *AmLY*
Elmsley, Peter 1773-1825 *Alli, BiD&SB, DcEnL, DcEuL*
Elmslie, Kenward 1929- *AmA&B, AmSCAP 66, ConAu 21, ConP 1970, ConP 1975, DrAF 1976, DrAP 1975, WrD 1976*
Elmslie, W G *Alli Sup*
Elmslie, William Alexander Leslie 1885-1965 *ConAu P-1*
Elmslie, William Jackson *Alli Sup*
Elmstrom, George P 1925- *ConAu 5R*
Elmwood, Elnathan *DcNAA*
Elmwood, Rose *Alli Sup*
Elocution Walker 1732-1807 *DcEnL*
Eloi, Saint 588-659 *OxFr*
Elow, Lawrence 1927- *AmSCAP 66*
Elphege, Saint *NewC*
Elphick, Antony Charles 1927- *Au&Wr*
Elphick, E L *ChPo S1*
Elphinston, Lord Balmerino *Alli*
Elphinston, James *Alli*
Elphinston, James 1721-1809 *Alli, BbD, BiD&SB, DcEnL*
Elphinston, William 1431?-1514 *Alli*
Elphinstone, Francis *ConAu XR, WrD 1976*
Elphinstone, Sir Howard Craufurd 1830-1890 *Alli Sup*
Elphinstone, Howard Warburton 1830- *Alli Sup*
Elphinstone, Mountstuart 1779?-1859 *Alli, Alli Sup, BrAu 19, Chmbr 3, DcEnL, EvLB, NewC, OxEng*
Elphinstone, R *Alli Sup*
Elphinstone-Dalrymple *Alli Sup*
Elphinstone-Fyffe, John Macpherson 1913- *Au&Wr*
Elrington, Clement C *PoIre*
Elrington, H *Alli Sup, ChPo*
Elrington, John Battersby *Alli, BiDLA*
Elrington, M Pakenham *Alli Sup*
Elrington, Stephen Nolan 1820?-1890 *Alli Sup, PoIre*
Elrington, Thomas d1835 *Alli, BiDLA*
Elrod, M 1863- *WhWNAA*
Elsam, Richard *Alli, BiDLA*
Elsberg, Louis 1836-1885 *Alli Sup, DcAmA*
Elsberry, Terence 1943- *ConAu 45*
Elsbree, Langdon 1929- *ConAu 33*
Elsdale, Henry *Alli Sup*
Elsdale, Samuel *Alli, BiDLA*
Else, Anne *Alli, BiDLA*
Else, Gerald Frank 1908- *ConAu 61*
Else, Joseph *Alli*
Else, R *Alli, BiDLA*
Else-Mitchell, Rae 1914- *Au&Wr*
Elseffer, Amanda Shaw *ChPo, ChPo S1*
Elsen, Albert Edward 1927- *ConAu 5R, WrD 1976*
Elsensohn, Sister Mary Alfreda 1897- *CatA 1952, WhPNW*
Elser, Donald 1915- *OhA&B*
Elser, Frank B *ChPo*
Elser, Frank Ball 1885-1935 *AmA&B, DcNAA, TexWr*
Elsevier *NewC*
Elsheimer, Adam 1578-1610 *AtlBL*
Elshemus, Louis Michael 1864-1941 *ChPo S1, DcNAA*
Elsholtz, Franz Von 1791-1872 *BiD&SB*
Elsie-Jean *WhWNAA*
Elskamp, Max 1862-1931 *CasWL, ClDMEuL, EncWL*
Elsley, Charles Heneage *Alli Sup*
Elsley, J *Alli*
Elsly, William *Alli*
Elslyot, Thomas *Alli*
Elsmere, Jane Shaffer 1932- *ConAu 37, WrD 1976*
Elsmere, Sloane *Alli*
Elsmo, Ralph Norman 1919- *AmSCAP 66*
Elsmo, Sverre S 1910- *AmSCAP 66*
Elsna, Hebe *Au&Wr*
Elsner, Gisela 1937- *ConAu 9R, TwCW*
Elsner, Henry, Jr. 1930- *ConAu 21*

Elsner, Henry Leopold 1855-1916 *DcNAA*
Elsom, A *Alli Sup*
Elsom, John Edward *WrD 1976*
Elson, Arthur 1873-1940 *AmA&B, AmLY, DcAmA, DcNAA, WhWNAA*
Elson, Charles 1909- *AmA&B*
Elson, Edward L R 1906- *WrD 1976*
Elson, Eward L R 1906- *ConAu 5R*
Elson, F *Alli Sup*
Elson, George *OxCan*
Elson, Henry William 1857-1954 *AmA&B, BiD&SB, DcAmA, OhA&B, REnAL, WhWNAA*
Elson, Jane *Alli, BiDLA*
Elson, John Mebounre 1881?- *CanNov, OxCan, WhWNAA*
Elson, Lawrence M 1935- *ConAu 53*
Elson, Louis Charles 1848-1920 *Alli Sup, AmA, AmA&B, AmLY, BbD, BiD&SB, ChPo, ChPo S1, DcAmA, DcNAA, OxAm*
Elson, Ruth Miller 1917- *ConAu 13R*
Elson, William Harris 1856-1935 *DcNAA*
Elspeth *ConAu XR, SmATA 6*
Elsschot, Willem 1882-1960 *CasWL, ClDMEuL, EncWL, Pen Eur, WhTwL*
Elster, Kristian Mandrup 1841-1881 *CasWL, ClDMEuL*
Elstob *Alli, BiDLA*
Elstob, Elizabeth 1663?-1756 *Alli, CasWL*
Elstob, Peter 1915- *ConAu 1R, WrD 1976*
Elstob, William *Alli, BiDLA*
Elstob, William 1673-1714 *Alli*
Elstobb, W *Alli*
Elston, Allan Vaughan 1887- *AmA&B, Au&Wr, ConAu 1R, MnBBF, WrD 1976*
Elston, Charles Sidney 1899- *Au&Wr*
Elston, Gene 1922- *ConAu 33*
Elston, J *Alli*
Elstrack, R *Alli*
Elsum, John *Alli*
Elsy, Mary *Au&Wr, WrD 1976*
Elsynge, Henry 1598-1654 *Alli, DcEnL*
Elting, Mary 1906- *ConAu 9R, MorJA, SmATA 2*
Elting, Mary 1909- *AuBYP*
Eltinge, LeRoy 1872-1931 *DcNAA*
Eltoft, Thomas *Alli Sup*
Elton, Mrs. *Alli Sup*
Elton, Sir Abraham *Alli, BiDLA*
Elton, Sir Arthur Hallam 1818-1883 *Alli Sup, DcEnL*
Elton, Sir Charles Abraham 1778-1853 *Alli, BiD&SB, BiDLA, ChPo, ChPo S2*
Elton, Charles Isaac 1839- *Alli Sup*
Elton, Edward *Alli*
Elton, Edwin J 1939- *ConAu 53*
Elton, Geoffrey Rudolph 1921- *Au&Wr, ConAu 9R, LongC, WrD 1976*
Elton, Lord Godfrey 1892- *Au&Wr, ChPo S1, LongC*
Elton, James Frederick 1840-1877 *Alli Sup*
Elton, James Frederick And Bourdillon, L *Alli Sup*
Elton, John *ConAu XR, WrD 1976*
Elton, Maude Lay *ChPo*
Elton, Oliver 1861-1945 *ChPo S2, DcLEnL, EvLB, LongC, NewC, OxEng, TwCA, TwCA Sup, WhLA*
Elton, Richard *Alli*
Elton, Romeo 1790-1870 *Alli, CyAL 1, DcAmA*
Elton, W R 1921- *Au&Wr*
Eltringham, William *Alli*
Eltzholtz, Carl Frederick 1840-1929 *AmLY, DcNAA*
Eluard, Paul 1895-1952 *AtlBL, CasWL, ClDMEuL, CnMWL, EncWL, EvEuW, ModRL, OxEng, OxFr, Pen Eur, REn, TwCA Sup, TwCW, WhTwL*
Elvas, The Gentleman Of *BiDSA*
Elven, Cornelius 1797-1873 *PoCh*
Elven, J P *Alli*
Elvenich, Peter Joseph 1796-1886 *BiD&SB*
Elvey, Stephen 1805-1860 *Alli Sup*
Elviden, Edmund *Alli*
Elvidge, G H *Alli Sup*
Elvin, Anne Katharine Stevenson 1933- *ConAu 17R*

Elvin, Charles Norton *Alli Sup*
Elvin, Drake *ConAu XR*
Elvin, Harold 1909- *Au&Wr, ConAu 5R, WrD 1976*
Elvin, Herbert Lionel 1905- *Au&Wr, ConAu P-1*
Elvis, Sister Of Community Of Epiphany 1902- *Au&Wr*
Elvy, John Miller *Alli Sup*
Elward, James 1928- *ConAu 29*
Elwart, Joan Potter 1927- *ConAu 25, SmATA 2*
Elwell, Edward Henry 1825-1890 *Alli Sup, DcAmA, DcNAA*
Elwell, Edward Simeon *Alli Sup*
Elwell, Fayette Herbert 1885- *ConAu 5R, WhWNAA*
Elwell, Felicia Rosemary 1912- *Au&Wr, AuBYP*
Elwell, Herbert 1898- *AmSCAP 66*
Elwell, Jerry MacElroy 1922- *ConAu 57*
Elwell, John Johnson 1820-1900 *Alli Sup, DcNAA, OhA&B*
Elwell, Joseph Bowne 1874-1920 *DcNAA*
Elwell, Levi Henry 1854-1916 *DcNAA*
Elwell, Paul Bedford *Alli Sup*
Elwell, William Odell *Alli*
Elwell-Sutton, Laurence Paul 1912- *ConAu 5R, WrD 1976*
Elwes, A W *BiDSA*
Elwes, Alfred *Alli Sup*
Elwes, Alfred Thomas *ChPo, ChPo S2*
Elwes, Dudley George Cary- *Alli Sup*
Elwes, Henry John *Alli Sup*
Elwes, Hervey *ChPo S1*
Elwes, Richard *ChPo S1*
Elwes, Robert *Alli, Alli Sup*
Elwes, Robert Harvey Monro *Alli Sup*
Elwin, Fountain *Alli*
Elwin, J F *Alli Sup*
Elwin, Malcolm 1903- *Au&Wr, LongC, TwCA Sup*
Elwin, Verrier 1902-1964 *LongC*
Elwin, Warwick *Alli Sup*
Elwin, Whitwell 1816-1900 *BrAu 19, Chmbr 3, DcEnL, EvLB, NewC*
Elwood, Catharyn 1903?-1975 *ConAu 61*
Elwood, Mildred *ChPo S2*
Elwood, Muriel 1902- *AmA&B, ConAu P-1, REnAL*
Elwood, Robert Arthur 1873- *WhWNAA*
Elwood, Roger 1943- *ConAu 57*
Elwood, Rosalind 1930- *Au&Wr*
Elworthy, Albert Henry *Alli Sup*
Elworthy, Frederic Thomas *Alli Sup*
Elworthy, John *Alli*
Elwyn, Alfred Langdon 1804-1884 *Alli Sup, AmA&B, BiD&SB, DcAmA, DcNAA*
Ely, Alfred 1815-1892 *Alli Sup, DcNAA*
Ely, Alfred E *ChPo S1*
Ely, Charles Arthur 1829-1864 *OhA&B*
Ely, David 1927- *AmA&B, ConAu 53, ConNov 1972, ConNov 1976, DrAF 1976, WrD 1976*
Ely, Donald P 1930- *ConAu 29*
Ely, Mrs. E McKean *ChPo*
Ely, Edward T *Alli Sup*
Ely, Edward Talbot 1850-1885 *DcNAA*
Ely, Effie Smith *ChPo*
Ely, Ezra S 1786-1861 *Alli, DcAmA, DcNAA*
Ely, Frederick *ConAu XR*
Ely, G H *LongC*
Ely, George *MnBBF*
Ely, Helen Rutherford d1920 *DcNAA*
Ely, Henry *Alli*
Ely, Humphrey *Alli*
Ely, John *Alli*
Ely, Paul 1897-1975 *ConAu 53*
Ely, Richard Theodore 1854-1943 *Alli Sup, AmLY, BbD, BiD&SB, DcAmA, DcNAA, REnAL, WiscW*
Ely, Virginia Shackelford 1899- *ConAu 1R*
Ely, Zebulon d1824? *Alli*
Elyot, Sir Thomas 1490?-1546 *Alli, BiD&SB, BrAu, CasWL, Chmbr 1, CrE&SL, CriT 1, DcEnA, DcEnL, DcEuL, DcLEnL, EvLB, MouLC 1, NewC, OxEng, Pen Eng, REn, WebEAL*

Elys, Edmund *Alli*
Elysio, Filinto *EvEuW*
Elytis, Odysseus 1911- *WorAu*
Elytis, Odysseus 1912- *Pen Eur*
Elzaburu, Manuel 1851-1892 *PueRA*
Elzas, A *Alli Sup*
Elzas, Barnett Abraham 1867-1936 *BiDSA, DcNAA*
Elze, Karl 1821-1889 *BiD&SB*
Elzevier *NewC*
Elzevir *NewC*
Elzevir, Bonaventure 1583-1652 *NewC*
Elzevir, Gilles d1651 *NewC*
Elzevir, Joost 1575?-1617? *NewC*
Elzevir, Louis 1540?-1617 *NewC*
Elzevir, Louis 1566?-1621? *NewC*
Elzevir, Matthieu 1564?-1640 *NewC*
Elzinga, Kenneth G 1941- *ConAu 49*
Emans, Elaine V *ChPo*
Emans, Robert 1934- *ConAu 53*
Emants, Marcellus 1848-1923 *BbD, BiD&SB, CasWL, CIDMEuL*
Emanuel, Cedric 1906- *Au&Wr*
Emanuel, Harry *Alli Sup*
Emanuel, James 1923- *CrCAP*
Emanuel, James A 1921- *BlkAW, ConAu 29, ConP 1975, DrAP 1975, LivBA, WrD 1976*
Emanuel, Joseph George 1871- *WhLA*
Emard, Joseph Medard 1853-1927 *DcNAA*
Emberley, Barbara A 1932- *ConAu 5R, SmATA 8, ThBJA*
Emberley, Barbara And Ed *BkP, ChPo, ChPo S1*
Emberley, Ed 1931- *AuBYP, AuICB, ConAu 5R, IlBYP, IlCB 1966, NewbC 1966, SmATA 8, ThBJA*
Embey, Philip *ConAu XR, WrD 1976*
Embiricos, Andreas 1901- *EncWL Sup*
Embirikos, Andreas 1901- *Pen Eur*
Emblen, D L 1918- *ConAu 33*
Embler, Weller Beardsley 1906- *AmA&B*
Embleton, Dennis *Alli Sup*
Emboden, William A, Jr. 1935- *ConAu 41*
Embree, Ainslie Thomas 1921- *ConAu 1R*
Embree, Charles B, Jr. 1919- *AmSCAP 66*
Embree, Charles Fleming 1874-1905 *DcAmA, DcNAA, IndAu 1816*
Embree, Edwin Rogers 1883-1950 *AmA&B, REnAL, WhWNAA*
Embree, Emily Davant *TexWr*
Embree, Louise 1887-1972 *IndAu 1917, WhWNAA*
Embrey, Jacqueline *ChPo S2*
Embry, James Crawford 1834-1897 *DcNAA, IndAu 1917*
Embry, Margaret Jacob 1919- *ConAu 1R, SmATA 5*
Embury, Mrs. 1806-1863 *DcEnL*
Embury, Emma Catherine 1806-1863 *Alli, AmA, AmA&B, BbD, BiD&SB, ChPo, ChPo S1, CyAL 2, DcAmA, DcNAA, FemPA, OxAm*
Embury, Susan Pindar *ChPo*
Emch, Arnold 1871- *WhWNAA*
Emden, Alfred Charles Richard 1850- *Alli Sup*
Emecheta, Buchi 1944- *WrD 1976*
Emeneau, Murray Barnson 1904- *ConAu 1R, WrD 1976*
Emenhiser, JeDon 1933- *ConAu 37*
Emeny, Brooks 1901- *OhA&B*
Emerald, John *HsB&A*
Emerick, Kenneth F 1925- *ConAu 53*
Emerson, Adaline Talcott 1837-1915 *ChPo, DcNAA*
Emerson, Alfred 1859- *DcAmA*
Emerson, Alfred Edwards 1896- *Au&Wr*
Emerson, Alice B *AmA&B, CarSB, ConAu 19, SmATA 1*
Emerson, Alice Fernald d1941 *DcNAA, IndAu 1917*
Emerson, Benjamin Dudley 1781-1872 *ChPo, DcNAA*
Emerson, Benjamin Kendall 1843-1932 *DcNAA*
Emerson, Brownwood 1904- *TexWr*
Emerson, Caroline Dwight 1891-1973 *AuBYP, ChPo, ConAu 45, ConAu P-1*
Emerson, Charles Chauncy d1836 *CyAL 2*

Emerson, Charles Noble 1821-1869 *Alli Sup, DcAmA, DcNAA*
Emerson, Charles Phillips 1872-1938 *DcNAA*
Emerson, Charles Phillips 1912- *IndAu 1917*
Emerson, Charles Vincent *WhWNAA*
Emerson, Charles Wesley 1837-1908 *DcNAA*
Emerson, David 1900- *Au&Wr, ConAu 5R, WrD 1976*
Emerson, Donald 1913- *ConAu 21*
Emerson, Earl *ChPo*
Emerson, Edward Bliss 1804-1835 *ChPo*
Emerson, Edward Milton *Alli Sup*
Emerson, Edward Randolph 1856-1924 *DcNAA*
Emerson, Edward Waldo 1844-1930 *AmA&B, DcAmA, DcNAA*
Emerson, Edward Waldo 1856- *AmLY*
Emerson, Edwin *AmA&B, HsB&A, HsB&A Sup*
Emerson, Edwin 1823-1908 *DcNAA*
Emerson, Edwin 1869-1959 *AmA&B, BiD&SB, DcAmA, WhWNAA*
Emerson, Edwin L *ChPo, ChPo S1*
Emerson, Ellen Russell 1837-1907 *Alli Sup, AmA&B, BiD&SB, DcAmA, DcNAA*
Emerson, Eugenia O *ChPo S2*
Emerson, Everett Harvey 1925- *ConAu 13R*
Emerson, Florence *DcAmA*
Emerson, Frank C 1936- *ConAu 53*
Emerson, Frederick 1788-1857 *Alli, DcAmA, DcNAA*
Emerson, G R *ChPo S1*
Emerson, George Barrell 1797-1881 *Alli, Alli Sup, AmA&B, DcAmA, DcNAA*
Emerson, George Homer 1822?-1898 *Alli Sup, DcAmA, DcNAA*
Emerson, George Rose *Alli Sup*
Emerson, Gouverneur 1796-1874 *Alli, Alli Sup*
Emerson, H O 1893- *ConAu 23*
Emerson, Harrington 1853-1931 *AmLY, DcNAA*
Emerson, Henry P 1846-1930 *DcNAA, WhWNAA*
Emerson, J *ChPo S2, EarAB*
Emerson, James *Alli*
Emerson, James G, Jr. 1926- *ConAu 17R*
Emerson, Jesse Milton 1818-1898 *Alli Sup, DcAmA, DcNAA*
Emerson, John 1874-1956 *AmA&B, OhA&B*
Emerson, Mrs John *AmA&B*
Emerson, John Swift *Alli, BiDLA*
Emerson, Joseph 1700-1767 *Alli*
Emerson, Joseph 1777-1833 *Alli, DcAmA, DcNAA*
Emerson, Laura Salome 1907- *ConAu P-1, IndAu 1917*
Emerson, Lucy 1769?-1855 *DcNAA*
Emerson, Mrs. M Farley *OhA&B*
Emerson, Marion Winslow 1886- *WhWNAA*
Emerson, Mary S *Alli Sup*
Emerson, Mrs. N S *Alli*
Emerson, Nanette Snow 1802-1884 *ChPo*
Emerson, Nannette Snow 1840-1884 *DcNAA*
Emerson, Nathaniel Bright 1839-1915 *DcNAA*
Emerson, Nathaniel Waldo 1854-1930 *DcNAA*
Emerson, O B 1922- *ConAu 25*
Emerson, Oliver Farrar 1860-1927 *AmA&B, AmLY, DcNAA, OhA&B, WhWNAA*
Emerson, P H *Alli Sup*
Emerson, Paul 1887-1937 *DcNAA*
Emerson, Ralph 1787-1862 *DcAmA, DcNAA*
Emerson, Ralph Waldo 1803-1882 *Alli, Alli Sup, AmA, AmA&B, AmWr, AnCL, AtlBL, BbD, BiD&SB, CasWL, ChPo, ChPo S1, Chmbr 3, CnDAL, CnE&AP, CriT 3, CyAL 2, CyWA, DcAmA, DcEnA, DcEnA Ap, DcEnL, DcLEnL, DcNAA, EvLB, MouLC 4, OxAm, OxEng, Pen Am, RAdv 1, RCom, REn, REnAL, St&VC, WebEAL*
Emerson, Richard Wirtz 1925- *OhA&B*
Emerson, Ronald *ConAu XR*
Emerson, Rupert 1899- *AmA&B, ConAu 1R*
Emerson, Ruthven *PoIre*
Emerson, Samuel *Alli Sup*
Emerson, Samuel Franklin 1850-1939 *DcNAA*
Emerson, Sara Anna 1855-1939 *DcNAA*
Emerson, Sybil 1895- *IlCB 1945*
Emerson, T *Alli*

Emerson, Thomas I 1907- *ConAu 21,*
WrD 1976
Emerson, Walter Crane 1863-1929 *DcNAA*
Emerson, William *Alli Sup*
Emerson, William 1701-1782 *Alli, DcEnL*
Emerson, William 1769-1811 *Alli, DcNAA*
Emerson, William Andrew *Alli Sup*
Emerson, William Andrew 1851- *DcNAA*
Emerson, William Dana 1813-1891 *DcNAA,*
OhA&B
Emerson, William K 1925- *ConAu 41*
Emerson, William Robie Patten 1869-
WhWNAA
Emerson, Willis George 1856-1918 *Alli Sup,*
DcAmA, DcNAA
Emersone, John *Alli*
Emerton, Ephraim 1851-1935 *Alli Sup,*
AmA&B, BiD&SB, DcAmA, DcNAA
Emerton, James Alexander 1805-1869 *Alli Sup*
Emerton, James Henry 1847-1930 *Alli Sup,*
BiD&SB, DcAmA, DcNAA
Emerton, Wolseley Partridge 1843- *Alli Sup*
Emeruwa, Leatrice *BlkAW*
Emery, Alfred *Alli Sup*
Emery, Anne 1907- *AuBYP, ConAu 1R,*
MorJA, SmATA 1
Emery, C M *ChPo*
Emery, David A 1920- *ConAu 29*
Emery, Miss E B *Alli Sup*
Emery, Emma Wilson *TexWr*
Emery, Fred A 1875- *WhWNAA*
Emery, Fred Parker 1865-1927 *DcNAA*
Emery, G F *Alli Sup*
Emery, George Alexander 1821-1894 *DcNAA*
Emery, George Davis 1855- *DcNAA*
Emery, Gilbert 1875-1945 *OxAm*
Emery, Henry Crosby 1872-1924 *DcNAA*
Emery, Ina Capitola 1868-1941 *DcNAA,*
WhWNAA
Emery, J K *ChPo S2*
Emery, Lucilius Alonzo 1840-1920 *DcNAA*
Emery, Mabel Sarah 1859- *DcNAA*
Emery, Orman Chester 1860- *WhWNAA*
Emery, Philip Alfred 1830- *DcNAA*
Emery, Richard W *ChPo*
Emery, Robert *Alli Sup*
Emery, Robert Firestone 1927- *ConAu 37,*
WrD 1976
Emery, Rufus 1827- *DcNAA*
Emery, Russell Guy 1908- *AuBYP*
Emery, S I *Alli Sup*
Emery, S L *ChPo S2*
Emery, Samuel Hopkins 1815-1901 *Alli Sup,*
DcNAA
Emery, Sarah Anna 1821-1907 *Alli Sup,*
DcAmA, DcNAA
Emery, Stephen Albert 1841-1891 *DcNAA*
Emery, Susan L 1846-1917 *DcNAA*
Emery, Walter Byron 1907- *ConAu 1R*
Emery, William *Alli Sup*
Emes, Thomas *Alli*
Emett, Rowland 1906- *IlCB 1956, WhGrA*
Emin, Fyodor Alexandrovich 1735?-1770
CasWL, DcEuL, DcRusL
Emin, Gevorg 1919- *DcOrL 3*
Emine, Nikita Ossipovich 1815-1891 *BbD,*
BiD&SB
Eminence Rouge *NewC*
Eminescu, Michael 1850-1889 *BiD&SB*
Eminescu, Mihai 1850-1889 *CasWL, Pen Eur*
Eminescu, Mihail 1850-1889 *ClDMEuL, EuA,*
EvEuW
Eminson, E A *Alli Sup*
Emiot, Israel *DrAF 1976, DrAP 1975*
Emison, Emily Adams 1881-1963 *IndAu 1917*
Emlyn, Henry *Alli, BiDLA*
Emlyn, Thomas 1663-1743 *Alli*
Emma, Ronald David 1920- *ConAu 25*
Emmanuel, Emmanuel 1886- *WhLA*
Emmanuel, Philip D 1909- *ConAu P-1*
Emmanuel, Pierre 1916- *CasWL, EncWL,*
OxFr, REn, WorAu
Emme, Eugene M 1919- *ConAu 13R*
Emmens, S H *Alli Sup*
Emmeram, Heiliger *OxGer*
Emmerich, Andre 1924- *ConAu 9R,*
WrD 1976
Emmerich, Katharina d1824 *OxGer*

Emmerich, Robert D 1904- *AmSCAP 66*
Emmerick, A *Alli*
Emmerick, R E 1937- *ConAu 25*
Emmerson, H H *ChPo*
Emmerson, Sir Harold Corti 1896- *Au&Wr*
Emmerson, Henry Russell 1899- *ConAu 5R*
Emmerson, John *OxCan*
Emmerson, John K 1908- *ConAu 57*
Emmerson, Walter Leslie 1901- *Au&Wr*
Emmerton, Isaac *Alli*
Emmerton, James Arthur 1834-1888 *Alli Sup,*
DcAmA, DcNAA
Emmet SEE ALSO Emmett
Emmet, Alida Chanler *ChPo*
Emmet, Christopher Temple 1761-1788 *PoIre*
Emmet, Dorothy Mary 1904- *Au&Wr,*
ConAu 9R, NewC 1976
Emmet, Eric Revell 1909- *Au&Wr, WrD 1976*
Emmet, J K 1841-1891 *PoIre*
Emmet, Lydia F *ChPo S1*
Emmet, Robert 1778-1803 *PoIre, REn*
Emmet, Rosina 1854- *ChPo*
Emmet, Thomas Addis *BiDSA*
Emmet, Thomas Addis 1764-1827 *Alli, DcAmA,*
DcNAA
Emmet, Thomas Addis 1828-1919 *Alli Sup,*
AmA&B, DcAmA, DcNAA
Emmet, William LeRoy 1859-1941 *DcNAA,*
WhWNAA
Emmett SEE ALSO Emmet
Emmett, A D 1879- *WhWNAA*
Emmett, Alfred Snowdon *Alli Sup*
Emmett, Bruce 1949- *ConAu 57*
Emmett, Chris 1886- *AmA&B, TexWr*
Emmett, Daniel Decatur 1815-1904 *AmA,*
AmA&B, ChPo, ChPo S1, ChPo S2,
OxAm, REnAL
Emmett, F Rowland *ChPo*
Emmett, J B *Alli*
Emmett, J Filmer *Alli Sup*
Emmett, M *Alli Sup*
Emmett, Thomas Addis *BiDLA*
Emmett Brothers *MnBBF*
Emmitt, James 1806-1895 *OhA&B*
Emmitt, Robert 1925- *ConAu 29*
Emmons, Della Florence Gould 1890- *MnnWr,*
WhPNW
Emmons, Earl H *ChPo S1*
Emmons, Ebenezer 1799-1863 *Alli Sup,*
CyAL 1, DcAmA, DcNAA
Emmons, Elizabeth Wales 1867- *WhWNAA*
Emmons, G T *OxCan*
Emmons, George Foster 1811-1884 *Alli Sup,*
DcAmA, DcNAA
Emmons, Lloyd Clement 1887- *WhWNAA*
Emmons, Martha *TexWr*
Emmons, Nathanael 1745-1840 *CyAL 1,*
DcAmA, DcNAA
Emmons, Nathaniel 1745-1840 *Alli, BiDLA*
Emmons, Richard 1788-1837? *DcNAA*
Emmons, Ronald 1948- *BlkAW*
Emmons, S B *Alli Sup*
Emmons, Samuel Franklin 1841-1911 *Alli Sup,*
DcAmA, DcNAA
Emmot, G *Alli*
Emmrich, Curt 1897- *ConAu 29, EncWL*
Emmrich, Kurt *ConAu XR*
Emms, Robert *Alli*
Emorey, N *ConAu XR*
Emory, A M *Alli Sup*
Emory, Frederick 1853-1908 *DcAmA, DcNAA*
Emory, John 1789-1835 *BiDSA, DcAmA,*
DcNAA
Emory, Robert 1814-1848 *BiDSA, DcAmA,*
DcNAA
Emory, William Closson 1894- *WhWNAA*
Emory, William Helmsley 1811-1887 *Alli,*
Alli Sup, BiDSA, DcAmA, DcNAA
Emparan, Diego De 1718-1807? *BbD, BiD&SB*
Empedocles *BbD, BiD&SB, CasWL, NewC,*
Pen Cl
Empey, Arthur Guy 1883-1963 *AmA&B*
Empey, LaMar T 1923- *ConAu 29*
Empie, Adam *Alli Sup*
Empis, Adolphe 1795-1868 *BbD, BiD&SB*
Empsall, Edith *ChPo S2*
Empson, Charles Anglesey *Alli Sup*
Empson, William 1790-1852 *DcEnL*

Empson, William 1906- *CasWL, CnE&AP,*
CnMWL, ConAu 17R, ConLC 3,
ConP 1970, ConP 1975, DcLEnL,
EncWL, LongC, ModBL, NewC, OxEng,
Pen Eng, RAdv 1, REn, TwCA Sup,
TwCW, WebEAL, WhTwL, WrD 1976
Emra, J N *Alli Sup*
Emra, William Henry Atkinson *Alli Sup*
Emrich, Duncan 1908- *ChPo S1, ChPo S2,*
ConAu 61
Emrich, Marion Vallat *ChPo S2*
Emrys Ap Iwan 1851-1906 *CasWL*
Emser, Hieronymus 1477?-1527 *OxGer*
Emshwiller, Carol *ConAu 53, DrAF 1976*
Emsley, Clare *ConAu XR, WrD 1976*
Emslie, M L *ConAu XR*
Emson, Frank E *Alli Sup*
Emswiler, George P 1830- *IndAu 1816*
Emswiler, John Edward 1880-1940 *DcNAA*
Emtage, James Bernard DeCourcey *Au&Wr*
Emurian, Ernest K 1912- *AmSCAP 66*
Enamorado Cuesta, Jose 1892- *PueRA*
Enander, Johan Alfred 1842-1910 *DcNAA*
Enault, Louis 1822-1900 *BbD, BiD&SB*
Encausse, Gerard 1865-1916 *BiDPar*
Encina, Juan Del 1469?-1529? *BbD, BiD&SB,*
CasWL, DcSpL, EvEuW, McGWD,
Pen Eur, REn
Encisco, Diego Ximenez De *BiD&SB*
Enciso, Bartolome Lopez De *DcEuL*
Enciso, Diego Jimenez De *CasWL*
Enckell, Rabbe Arnfinn 1903- *CasWL, EncWL,*
Pen Eur
Encken, R *Alli Sup*
Endacott, G B 1901- *Au&Wr, ConAu 5R*
Endacott, M Violet 1915- *ConAu 9R*
Ende, Jean 1947- *ConAu 53*
Endean, James Russell 1826- *Alli Sup*
Endecott, John 1589?-1665 *OxAm, REn,*
REnAL
Enderbie, Percy *Alli, DcEnL*
Enderby, W D *MnBBF*
Enders, Harvey 1892-1947 *AmSCAP 66*
Endicott, Charles Moses 1793-1863 *Alli Sup,*
AmA&B, BbD, BiD&SB, DcAmA,
DcNAA
Endicott, Ellen Bellows *ChPo*
Endicott, John 1589?-1665 *REn*
Endicott, Robert Rantoul 1905- *AmA&B*
Endicott, William Crowninshield 1860-1936
DcNAA
Endler, Norman S 1931- *ConAu 23*
Endlich, Gustav Adolf 1856- *Alli Sup, DcAmA*
Endo, Shusaku 1923- *ConAu 29*
Endore, Guy 1900-1970 *AmA&B, AmNov,*
Au&Wr, ConAu 1R, ConAu 25,
WhWNAA
Endress, Doctor 1755-1827 *Alli*
Endress, Christian 1755-1827 *DcAmA*
Endrezze-Probst, Anita *DrAP 1975*
Enehjelm, Helen Margaret Mary Af 1909-
CatA 1952
Enelow, Allen J 1922- *ConAu 17R*
Enelow, H G *WhWNAA*
Enelow, Hyman Gerson 1877-1934 *DcNAA*
Enfantin, Barthelemy Prosper 1796-1864 *DcEuL,*
OxFr
Enfield, Viscountess *Alli Sup*
Enfield, Edward *Alli Sup*
Enfield, William *Alli, BiDLA*
Enfield, William 1741-1797 *Alli, ChPo,*
ChPo S1, DcEnL, NewC, PoCh
Engall, Thulia Susannah *Alli Sup*
Engberg, Edward 1928- *ConAu 21*
Engberg, Holger L 1930- *ConAu 37*
Engblom, Verne A 1919- *AmSCAP 66*
Engdahl, Sylvia Louise 1933- *ChLR 2,*
ConAu 29, SmATA 4, WrD 1976
Engebrecht, P A 1935- *ConAu 57*
Engel, Alan S 1932- *ConAu 37*
Engel, Bernard F 1921- *ConAu 13R,*
WrD 1976
Engel, Carl 1818-1882 *Alli Sup*
Engel, Carl 1883-1944 *AmSCAP 66,*
WhWNAA
Engel, Claire-Elaine *Au&Wr*
Engel, David 1894- *Au&Wr*
Engel, Eduard 1851- *BbD, BiD&SB*

Engel, Georg 1866-1931 *OxGer*
Engel, Gilson Colby 1898- *Au&Wr*
Engel, James F 1934- *ConAu 23*
Engel, Joachim Jakob 1741-1802 *DcEuL*
Engel, Johann Friedrich 1844- *ChPo*
Engel, Johann Jakob 1741-1802 *BiD&SB,*
OxGer
Engel, Lehman 1910- *AmA&B, ConAu 41*
Engel, Leo *Alli Sup*
Engel, Leonard 1916-1964 *AmA&B*
Engel, Louis *Alli Sup*
Engel, Louis Henry, Jr. 1909- *ConAu 21*
Engel, Marian 1933- *ConAu 25,*
ConNov 1976, OxCan Sup, WrD 1976
Engel, Monroe 1921- *ConAu 5R, WrD 1976*
Engel, Pauline Newton 1918- *ConAu 17R*
Engel, Salo 1908- *ConAu 33*
Engel, Srul Morris 1931- *ConAu 37,*
ConAu 53
Engelbach, Alfred H *Alli Sup*
Engelbach, Reinhard 1796?- *BiDLA*
Engelberg, Edward 1929- *ConAu 37*
Engelbrecht, Helmuth Carol 1895-1939 *DcNAA,*
WhWNAA
Engelbretsdatter, Dorothe 1634-1716 *CasWL*
Engelhardt, Charles Anthony *DcNAA*
Engelhardt, M Veronice 1912- *WrD 1976*
Engelhardt, N L 1882- *WhWNAA*
Engelhardt, Zephyrin 1851-1934 *CatA 1947,*
DcNAA
Engelhart, Max Dissette 1901- *WhWNAA*
Engelke, Gerrit 1890-1918 *EncWL, OxGer*
Engell, Dee *WhWNAA*
Engelman, Jan 1900- *CasWL*
Engelmann, George 1809-1884 *DcNAA*
Engelmann, George Julius 1847-1903 *Alli Sup,*
DcAmA, DcNAA
Engelmann, Hugo O 1917- *ConAu 41*
Engelmann, Michael 1928- *WhGrA*
Engelmann, Siegfried E 1931- *ConAu 23*
Engels, Friedrich 1820-1895 *OxGer, REn*
Engels, John David 1931- *ConAu 13R,*
ConP 1970, DrAP 1975, IndAu 1917
Engels, Norbert 1903- *AmA&B, BkC 5,*
ConAu 17, IndAu 1917, WrD 1976
Engeman, John T 1901- *AuBYP*
Enger, Norman L 1937- *ConAu 25*
Engerman, Stanley L 1936- *ConAu 53*
Engerrand, George C 1877- *TexWr*
Enggass, Robert 1921- *ConAu 13R*
Enghaus, Christine 1817-1910 *OxGer*
Enghien, Louis-A-H DeBourbon, Duc D'
1772-1804 *OxFr*
Engholm, Eva 1909- *Au&Wr*
Engl, Lieselotte 1918- *ConAu 49*
Engl, Theodor 1925- *ConAu 49*
Englaender, Sigmund *Alli Sup*
England, Allan *MnBBF*
England, Barry 1932- *Au&Wr, ConAu 25*
England, E M *ConAu XR, WrD 1976*
England, E Squires *ConAu 57*
England, Edith Mary 1899- *Au&Wr*
England, Edwin Bourdieu *Alli Sup*
England, George *Alli*
England, George Allan 1877-1936 *AmA&B,*
ChPo, DcNAA, OxCan, WhWNAA
England, Gordon Philip 1901- *WhWNAA*
England, Harry *ChPo*
England, Jay Raymond *BlkAW*
England, John *Alli, ChPo S2*
England, John 1786-1842 *Alli, AmA&B,*
BiDSA, CyAL 1, DcAmA, DcNAA,
PoIre
England, Martha Winburn 1909- *ChPo S1,*
ConAu P-1
England, Maurice Derrick 1908- *WrD 1976*
England, Thomas R *Alli*
England, Wilbur Birch 1903- *Au&Wr,*
ConAu 1R
Englander, Richard *EncWL*
Engle, Alice B *Alli Sup*
Engle, Eloise 1923- *ConAu 1R, SmATA 9,*
WrD 1976
Engle, John D, Jr. 1922- *ConAu 57*
Engle, Paul 1908- *AmA&B, ChPo, ChPo S1,*
ChPo S2, CnDAL, ConAmA, ConAu 1R,
ConP 1970, ConP 1975, DcLEnL,
DrAP 1975, OxAm, REnAL, SixAP,

WorAu, WrD 1976
Engle, Thelburn LaRoy 1901- *ConAu 13R,*
IndAu 1917, WrD 1976
Engle, Trall 1881- *OhA&B*
Engle, Washington Alvord d1907 *DcNAA*
Engle, William Clothier *ChPo S2*
Engle, Willis Darwin 1846-1925 *IndAu 1816*
Englebert, Omer 1893- *CatA 1952*
Englebert, Victor 1933- *ConAu 57, SmATA 8*
Englefield, Cicely 1893- *IlCB 1945*
Englefield, Sir Henry Charles 1752-1822 *Alli,*
BiDLA, DcEnL
Englehardt, Fred 1885-1944 *DcNAA*
Englehardt, Zephyrin 1851-1934 *OhA&B*
Engleheart, G D *BbtC*
Engleheart, John Gardner Dillman 1823-
Alli Sup
Engleheart, N B *Alli Sup*
Englekirk, John Eugene 1905- *DcSpL*
Engleman, Anna Ulen *ChPo S2*
Engleman, Finis E 1895- *ConAu 9R*
Engleman, James Ozro 1873-1943 *AmA&B,*
DcNAA, IndAu 1917, OhA&B,
WhWNAA
Engler, Larry 1949- *ConAu 53*
Engler, Markus 1898- *Au&Wr*
Engler, Richard E, Jr. 1925- *ConAu 37*
Engler, Robert *ConAu 1R*
Englert, Clement Cyril 1910- *ConAu 1R*
Engles, William Morrison 1797-1867 *Alli,*
Alli Sup, ChPo S2, DcAmA, DcNAA
English, Arnold 1920- *ConAu XR*
English, Arthur *OxCan*
English, Barbara 1933- *ConAu 33, WrD 1976*
English, Brenda H *WrD 1976*
English, Don *MnBBF*
English, Douglas 1870- *ChPo, ChPo S2*
English, E H *Alli*
English, E Schuyler 1899- *AmA&B*
English, Earl 1905- *ConAu 37*
English, Edward d1973 *ConAu 41*
English, Fenwick Walter 1939- *ConAu 45*
English, Frances Mary *Alli Sup*
English, George Bethune 1787-1828 *Alli, AmA,*
BiD&SB, CyAL 1, DcAmA, DcNAA
English, Granville 1900- *AmSCAP 66*
English, H S *Alli*
English, Henry Scales *Alli Sup*
English, Horace Bidwell 1892- *WhWNAA*
English, Isobel 1923- *ConNov 1976*
English, Isobel 1925- *ConAu 53, WrD 1976*
English, Isobel 1958- *Au&Wr*
English, Ivy *ChPo*
English, J *Alli*
English, James R *PoIre*
English, James W 1915- *ConAu 21*
English, Jean M 1937- *ConAu 29*
English, Jessie Millard *WhWNAA*
English, John *Alli, BiDLA*
English, John George *Alli, BiDLA*
English, John Mahan 1845-1927 *DcNAA*
English, Josiah Giberton 1833-1916 *OhA&B*
English, Maria *Alli Sup*
English, Maurice 1909- *AmA&B, ChPo S2,*
ConAu 9R, ConP 1970, ConP 1975,
WrD 1976
English, Michael *Alli*
English, Oliver Spurgeon 1901- *Au&Wr,*
ConAu 33
English, Peter *Alli*
English, Robert *Alli*
English, Ronald 1913- *Au&Wr, ConAu P-1,*
WrD 1976
English, Rubynn M, Sr. *BlkAW*
English, Thomas *Alli*
English, Thomas Alfred *Alli Sup*
English, Thomas Dunn 1819-1902 *Alli,*
Alli Sup, AmA, AmA&B, BbD,
BiD&SB, ChPo, ChPo S1, ChPo S2,
CnDAL, CyAL 2, DcAmA, DcLEnL,
DcNAA, OxAm, REnAL
English, Thomas Hopkins 1895- *Au&Wr,*
ChPo, ChPo S2, ConAu 5R
English, Walter 1889- *Au&Wr*
English, William d1778 *BbD, BiD&SB*
English, William B *AmA&B*
English, Mrs. William D *AmNov XR*
English, William Eastin 1854-1926 *DcNAA,*

IndAu 1816
English, William Hayden 1822-1896 *DcAmA,*
DcNAA, IndAu 1816
English, William Watson *Alli Sup*
English Aristophanes, The *DcEnL*
English Juvenal, The 1653-1684 *DcEnL*
English Mersenne, The 1624-1683 *DcEnL*
English Opium-Eater, The 1785-1859 *DcEnL*
English Petrarch, The *DcEnL*
English Rabelais, The *DcEnL*
English Sappho, The *DcEnL*
English Seneca, The 1574-1656 *DcEnL*
English Terence, The *DcEnL*
Englizian, H Crosby 1923- *ConAu 23*
Engquist, Richard 1933- *ConAu 29*
Engstrand, Stuart David 1905-1955 *AmA&B,*
AmNov, TwCA Sup
Engstrom, Albert 1869-1940 *CasWL,*
ClDMEuL, EncWL, EvEuW, REn
Engstrom, W A 1925- *ConAu 57*
Engvick, William *AuBYP, ChPo*
Enikel *OxGer*
Enis, Ben M 1942- *ConAu 57*
Enke, Stephen 1916?-1974 *Au&Wr, ConAu 53*
Enking, Ottomar 1867-1945 *CasWL, OxGer*
Enloe, Cynthia H 1938- *ConAu 37*
Enlow, David R 1916- *ConAu 5R*
Enn, C C *OhA&B*
Enneking, John J *ChPo*
Ennery, Adolphe-Philippe D' 1811-1899 *HsB&A,*
OxFr
Ennes, Antonio 1848- *BiD&SB*
Ennes, Harold E 1911- *IndAu 1917*
Ennever, William 1869-1947 *NewC*
Ennis, C W *Alli Sup*
Ennis, Jacob *Alli Sup*
Ennis, Laura 1870- *WhWNAA*
Ennis, Leroy Massey 1893- *WhWNAA*
Ennis, Luna May *IndAu 1917*
Ennis, Robert H 1927- *ConAu 25*
Ennis, William Duane 1877-1947 *DcNAA*
Ennis, Willie, Jr. *BlkAW*
Ennius, Quintus 239BC-169BC *BbD, BiD&SB,*
CasWL, OxEng, Pen Cl, REn
Enno, Ernst 1875-1934 *EncWL*
Ennodius, Magnus Felix 474?-521 *CasWL,*
Pen Eur
Eno, Henry Lane 1871-1928 *DcNAA*
Eno, Joel Nelson 1852-1937 *DcNAA*
Eno, William Phelps 1858-1945 *DcNAA*
Enoch, Frederick *Alli Sup, ChPo S1*
Enoch, Olive *ChPo*
Enoch, Richard *Alli*
Enock, C Reginald 1868- *WhLA*
Enomiya-Lassalle, Hugo M 1898- *ConAu 23*
Enomoto Kikaku *CasWL*
Enos, James Lysander 1825- *Alli*
Enright, Richard William *Alli Sup*
Enrick, Norbert Lloyd 1920- *ConAu 13R*
Enright, Dennis Joseph 1920- *Au&Wr,*
ChPo S2, ConAu 1R, ConLC 4,
ConNov 1972, ConNov 1976, ConP 1970,
ConP 1975, LongC, ModBL, ModBL Sup,
NewC, Pen Eng, TwCW, WhTwL,
WorAu, WrD 1976
Enright, Elizabeth 1909-1968 *AmA&B, AnCL,*
AuBYP, BkCL, ConAu 25, ConAu 61,
IlCB 1945, IlCB 1956, JBA 1951,
Newb 1922, SmATA 9
Enright, Walter J 1879- *AmA&B, ChPo*
Enrique *PueRA*
Enriqueta, Maria 1872- *WhWNAA*
Enriquez Gomez, Antonio 1600?-1660? *BiD&SB,*
CasWL, EvEuW, Pen Eur
Enroth, Clyde A 1926- *ConAu 37*
Enscoe, Gerald 1926- *ConAu 5R*
Ensell, Mrs. E J *Alli Sup*
Enser, A G S 1915- *Au&Wr*
Ensign, Hermon Lee *DcAmA*
Ensign, Newton Edward 1882- *WhWNAA*
Ensign, Samuel James Russell 1898- *OhA&B*
Ensley, Enoch 1836-1891 *DcNAA*
Ensley, Francis Gerald 1907- *ConAu P-1*
Ensley, Wilma Evangeline 1907- *IndAu 1917*
Enslin, Christian *BbtC*
Enslin, Morton Scott 1897- *Au&Wr,*
ConAu 17R
Enslin, Theodore 1925- *ConAu 53, ConP 1970,*

ConP 1975, DrAP 1975, Pen Am,
WrD 1976

Ensminger, Marion Eugene 1908- ConAu 49
Ensor, Alick Charles Davidson 1906- Au&Wr,
WrD 1976
Ensor, Allison 1935- ConAu 25
Ensor, F Sidney Alli Sup
Ensor, George Alli Sup, PoIre
Ensor, George 1769-1843 Alli, BiD&SB,
BiDLA
Ensor, James Dorant Alli Sup
Ensor, Baron James Sydney 1860-1949 AtlBL
Ensor, Laura Alli Sup
Ensor, Sir Robert Charles Kirkwood 1877-1950?
ChPo S2, DcLEnL, LongC
Ent, Sir George 1604-1689 Alli, DcEnL
Enteman, Willard F 1936 ConAu 33
Enten, Harry MnBBF
Enterline, James Robert 1932- ConAu 41
Enters, Angna 1907- AmA&B, Au&Wr,
WhWNAA
Enthoffer, Joseph Alli Sup
Enthoven, Alain C 1930- ConAu 49
Enthoven, Jacqueline WhPNW
Enthoven, Reginald Edward 1869- WhLA
Entick, John 1713-1773 Alli
Entinck, John 1713-1773 Alli
Entine, Alan D 1936- ConAu 23
Enton, Harry 1854-1927 HsB&A
Entrikin, Isabelle Webb ChPo
Entwisle, Doris R 1924- ConAu 5R
Entwisle, Edmund Alli
Entwisle, Eric Arthur 1900- Au&Wr,
WrD 1976
Entwistle, Harold 1923- ConAu 29
Entwistle, William James 1896?-1952 DcSpL,
WhLA
Enty, John Alli
Envallson, Carl Magnus 1756-1806 CasWL
Enz, Jacob J 1919- ConAu 41
Enzensberger, Hans Magnus 1929- CasWL,
EncWL, EvEuW, ModGL, OxGer,
Pen Eur, TwCW, WorAu
Enzina, Juan Del 1469-1530? DcEuL
Enzinas, Francisco De 1520?-1552 CasWL
Enzo 1220?-1272 CasWL
Eobanus Hessus, Helius 1488-1540 DcEuL
Eon DeBeaumont, Charles D' 1728-1810 NewC,
OxFr
Eorsi, Istvan 1931- CrCD
Eotvos, Baron Jozsef 1813-1871 BbD, BiD&SB,
CasWL, EvEuW, Pen Eur
Epafrodito ConAu XR
Epanya-Yondo, Elolongue 1930- AfA 1
Epee, Charles Michel DeL' 1712-1789 REn
Epernay, Mark ConAu XR
Ephesian 1894-1949 LongC
Ephorus 405?BC-330?BC CasWL, Pen Cl
Ephraem CasWL
Ephraim, Joseph L BlkAW
Ephrem The Syrian, Saint 306?-373 CasWL
Ephron, Nora AuNews 2
Ephron, Phoebe 1916-1971 ConAu 33
Ephros, Gershon 1890- AmSCAP 66
Epicharmos 530?BC-440?BC BiD&SB,
CasWL, Pen Cl
Epictetus 055?-135? BbD, BiD&SB, CasWL,
NewC, Pen Cl, RCom, REn
Epicure, An ChPo S1
Epicurus 340?BC-270?BC BbD, BiD&SB,
CasWL, NewC, OxEng, Pen Cl, RCom,
REn
Epifanov, Gennadi Dmitrievich 1900- WhGrA
Epimenides 630?BC- NewC, OxEng, REn
Epinay, Louise Florence Petronille D' 1726-1783
DcEuL, EvEuW, OxFr, REn
Epinay, Madame DeLaLive D' 1726-1783 BbD,
BiD&SB
Epler, Percy H 1872-1975 ConAu 57,
WhWNAA
Epp, Eldon Jay 1930- ConAu 17R, WrD 1976
Epp, Frank H 1929- ConAu 29
Epp, Margaret Agnes 1913- ConAu 9R,
WrD 1976
Epp, Peter 1894-1959 OhA&B
Eppens, Edward Henry 1873-1941 DcNAA
Epperson, Aloise Barbour BlkAW
Epperson, Gordon 1921- ConAu 25

Eppert, Carl 1882-1961 AmSCAP 66
Eppert, Josie ChPo
Eppinga, Jacob D 1917- ConAu 33
Eppink, Norman R 1906- ConAu 53
Epple, Anne Orth 1927- ConAu 33,
WrD 1976
Eppley, Garrett G 1896- IndAu 1917
Epps, Edgar G 1929- ConAu 49
Epps, Ellen 1809-1876 Alli Sup
Epps, Francis MnBBF
Epps, George Napoleon 1815-1874 Alli Sup
Epps, John 1805-1869 Alli Sup
Epps, Preston H 1888- ConAu 37
Epps, Richard Alli Sup
Epps, Robert L 1932- ConAu 17R
Epps, William OxCan Sup
Eppse, Merl R 1893- OhA&B
Epsilon ConAu XR, WrD 1976
Epstein, Abraham 1892-1942 DcNAA
Epstein, Abraham 1892- WhWNAA
Epstein, Arnold Leonard 1924- Au&Wr
Epstein, Benjamin Robert 1912- ConAu 45
Epstein, Beryl Williams 1910- AuBYP,
ConAu 5R, MorJA, OhA&B, SmATA 1
Epstein, Charlotte 1921- ConAu 61
Epstein, Cynthia Fuchs 1933- ConAu 29,
WrD 1976
Epstein, Daniel Mark 1948- ConAu 49,
DrAP 1975
Epstein, David M 1930- AmSCAP 66
Epstein, Dena J 1916- ConAu 41
Epstein, Donald K 1933- AmSCAP 66
Epstein, Edward Jay 1935- ConAu 17R
Epstein, Edwin M 1937- ConAu 25
Epstein, Erwin H 1939- ConAu 29, WrD 1976
Epstein, Howard M 1927- ConAu 23
Epstein, Sir Jacob 1880-1959 AtlBL, LongC,
OxAm, REn, REnAL
Epstein, Jason 1928- ConAu 57
Epstein, Judith Sue DrAP 1975
Epstein, Julius 1901-1975 ConAu 57
Epstein, June Sadie 1918- WrD 1976
Epstein, Leon D 1919- ConAu 13R
Epstein, Leslie DrAF 1976
Epstein, Morris 1921-1973 ConAu 45,
ConAu P-1
Epstein, Samuel 1909- AuBYP, ConAu 9R,
MorJA, SmATA 1
Epstein, Seymour 1917- AmA&B, Au&Wr,
ConAu 1R, DrAF 1976, WrD 1976
Epstein, William H 1944- ConAu 61
Epton, Nina Consuelo Au&Wr, ConAu 5R
Equiano, Africanus Olauda 1745?-1797 AfA 1,
BlkAW
Equiano, Olaudah 1745?-1797 CasWL
Equicola, Mario 1470?-1525 CasWL, REn
Equinox, Thomas Alli
Eramus, M Nott ConAu XR
'Eraqi, Fakhroddin Ebrahim B Shahryar d1289
DcOrL 3
Erasmus, Charles J 1921- ConAu 1R
Erasmus, Desiderius 1466?-1536 AtlBL, BbD,
BiD&SB, CasWL, CrE&SL, CyWA,
DcEnL, DcEuL, DcSpL, EuA, EvEuW,
NewC, OxEng, OxFr, OxGer, Pen Eur,
RCom, REn
Erasmus, M Nott ConAu XR
Erastus 1524-1583 DcEuL
Eratosthenes 275?BC-195?BC CasWL, Pen Cl
Erauso, Catalina De 1592-1650? CasWL
Erb, Alta Mae 1891- ConAu P-1
Erb, Emerson Clayton 1928- IndAu 1917
Erb, Lawrence 1877- WhWNAA
Erb, Paul 1894- ConAu 9R, WrD 1976
Erben, Karel Jaromir 1811-1870 BiD&SB,
CasWL, DcEuL, EuA, EvEuW, Pen Eur
Erbery, William Alli
Erceldoune, Thomas Of 1220?-1297 BiD&SB,
BrAu, CasWL, EvLB, NewC, OxEng
Erceldoun, Thomas Of 1220?-1297 BbD
Ercildoune, Thomas Of 1220?-1297 Chmbr 1
Ercilla, Alonso De 1533-1594? DcSpL,
Pen Eur
Ercilla Y Zuniga, Alonso De 1533-1594? BbD,
BiD&SB, CasWL, DcEuL, EuA, EvEuW,
REn
Erck, W Alli Sup
Erckmann, Emile 1822-1899 CasWL, DcBiA,

EuA, EvEuW, NewC
Erckmann-Chatrian 1822-1899 BbD, BiD&SB,
CasWL, DcEnL, DcEuL, EuA, EvEuW,
NewC, OxEng, OxFr
Ercole, Velia DcLEnL
Ercombert BiB S
Erdelyi, Gabor ChPo S1
Erdelyi, Janos 1814-1868 BbD, BiD&SB
Erdene, Sengiin 1929- DcOrL 1
Erdeswicke, Sampson d1603 Alli
Erdman SEE ALSO Erdmann
Erdman, Charles Rosenbury 1866-1960 AmA&B,
WhWNAA
Erdman, David V 1911- ChPo S1, ConAu 1R
Erdman, Ernie 1879-1946 AmSCAP 66
Erdman, Howard Loyd 1935- ConAu 23
Erdman, Johann Eduard 1805-1892 BbD
Erdman, Loula Grace AmA&B, AmNov,
AuBYP, ConAu 5R, MorJA, SmATA 1,
TexWr
Erdman, Nikolai Robertovich 1902?-1970
ConAu 29, ModWD, Pen Eur
Erdman, Paul E 1932- AuNews 1, ConAu 61,
WrD 1976
Erdman, Theodore John 1930- AmSCAP 66
Erdman, William Jacob 1834-1923 DcNAA
Erdmann SEE ALSO Erdman
Erdmann, Johann Eduard 1805-1892 BiD&SB
Erdmann, Myrtle Hill 1872-1949 OhA&B
Erdmann, Nikolai 1902-1936 CnMD
Erdmannsdorffer, Bernhard 1833-1901 BiD&SB
Erdody, Leo 1888-1949 AmSCAP 66
Erdoes, Richard 1912- IlBYP, IlCB 1966
Erdos, Paul L 1914- ConAu 29
Erduran, Refik 1928- REnWD
Erenburg, Ilya Grigoriyevich 1891-1967 CasWL,
ClDMEuL, DcRusL, Pen Eur, TwCA,
TwCA Sup
Erhard, Ludwig Au&Wr
Erhard, Thomas A 1923- ConAu 33,
WrD 1976
Erhard, Walter 1920- IlCB 1966
Erhardt, Eva Charles 1907- IndAu 1917
Eric The Red 950?-1000? OxCan, REn
Eric, Kenneth ConAu XR
Ericeira, Francisco DeMenezes, Count Of
1673-1743 BiD&SB
Erichsen, Hugo 1860- Alli Sup, AmLY,
WhWNAA
Erichsen, John Eric 1818- Alli, Alli Sup
Erick, Fred WhWNAA
Ericksen, Ephraim Gordon 1917- ConAu 5R
Ericksen, Gerald L 1931- ConAu 29
Ericksen, Kenneth J 1939- ConAu 37
Erickson, Arvel Benjamin 1905- ConAu 21
Erickson, Carl Gustav 1877-1936 DcNAA
Erickson, Charlotte Joanne 1923- Au&Wr
Erickson, D S Alli Sup
Erickson, Donald A 1925- ConAu 29
Erickson, E Walfred 1911- ConAu 5R
Erickson, Edsel L 1928- ConAu 53
Erickson, Erik Homburger 1902- Au&Wr
Erickson, Erling Arthur 1934- ConAu 33,
WrD 1976
Erickson, Frank 1923- AmSCAP 66
Erickson, Jack 1898- AmSCAP 66
Erickson, Keith V 1943- ConAu 29
Erickson, Lois J ChPo
Erickson, M E 1918- ConAu 9R
Erickson, Marion J 1913- ConAu 17R
Erickson, Phoebe 1907- AuBYP, ConAu 1R,
IlCB 1956
Erickson, Sabra Rollins 1912- ConAu 5R
Erickson, W Bruce 1938- ConAu 49
Erickson, Walter WrD 1976
Ericson, David ChPo
Ericson, Ian MnBBF
Ericson, Joe Ellis 1925- ConAu 41
Ericson, Leif 975?- NewC, REn, REnAL
Ericson, Walter AuBYP, ConAu XR,
SmATA 7, TwCA Sup
Ericsson, Henry 1861-1947 DcNAA
Ericsson, John 1803-1889 Alli Sup, BiD&SB,
DcAmA
Ericsson, Leif NewC, OxCan
Ericsson, Mary Kentra 1910- ConAu 1R
Ericsson, Olaf A Alli Sup
Erieus OxCan

Erigena, Johannes Scotus 810?-891? *Alli, NewC, REn*
Erigena, John *BrAu*
Erigena, John 810?-891? *EvLB, OxEng*
Erigena, John Scotus *DcEnL*
Erikson, Eric *MnBBF*
Erikson, Erik H 1902- *AmA&B, ConAu 25, WrD 1976*
Erikson, Henry Anton 1869- *WhWNAA*
Erikson, Mel *IIBYP*
Erikson, Stanley 1906- *ConAu 37*
Erikssen, Erik McKinley 1896-1941 *DcNAA, WhWNAA*
Eriksson, Marguerite A 1911- *ConAu 13R*
Erinna *CasWL, Pen Cl*
Erith, Francis Norton *Alli Sup*
Erith, John 1904- *Au&Wr, WrD 1976*
Erith, Lynn *Alli Sup*
Erlam, J S *Alli Sup*
Erlanger, Philippe 1903- *Au&Wr, ConAu 5R*
Erle, R *ChPo*
Erle, Talbot *Alli Sup, ChPo*
Erle, Thomas William *Alli Sup*
Erle, Sir William 1793-1880 *Alli Sup*
Erlich, Lillian 1910- *AuBYP, ConAu 1R, SmATA 10*
Erlich, Victor 1914- *ConAu 9R*
Erlingsson, Thorsteinn 1858-1914 *CasWL, ClDMEuL, EncWL*
Ermatinger, Charles Oakes Zaccheus 1851-1921 *Alli Sup, DcNAA, OxCan*
Ermatinger, Edward 1797-1876 *BbtC, DcNAA*
Ermine, Will *OhA&B*
Ermold The Black *Pen Eur*
Ernest, Brother 1897- *AuBYP, BkC 3, CatA 1947*
Ernest, Charles *Alli Sup*
Ernest, Victor 1911- *ConAu 33*
Ernest, William *ConAu XR*
Ernesti, Johann August 1707-1781 *DcEuL*
Ernharth, Ronald Louis 1936- *ConAu 45*
Erni, Hans 1909- *WhGrA*
Erni, Henry *Alli Sup*
Ernle, Lord *Chmbr 3*
Ernle, Baron Rowland Edmund Prothero 1851-1937 *NewC, TwCA, TwCA Sup*
Erno, Richard B 1923- *ConAu 13R*
Ernouf, Alfred Auguste 1817-1889 *BiD&SB*
Ernshaw, J *Alli Sup*
Ernst August, King Of Hanover 1771-1851 *OxGer*
Ernst, Doctor *Alli*
Ernst I, Herzog Von Bayern-Munchen 1771-1851 *OxGer*
Ernst, Alice Henson *WhPNW*
Ernst, Bernard Morris Lee 1879-1938 *DcNAA*
Ernst, Carl Henry 1938- *ConAu 45*
Ernst, Carl Wilhelm 1845-1919 *DcNAA*
Ernst, Clara *ConAu XR*
Ernst, Clayton Holt 1886-1945 *AmA&B, WhWNAA*
Ernst, Earle 1911- *Au&Wr, ConAu 5R*
Ernst, George Alexander Otis 1850-1912 *DcNAA*
Ernst, Harold Clarence 1856-1923 *DcNAA*
Ernst, John 1940- *ConAu 45*
Ernst, Kathryn 1942- *ConAu 61*
Ernst, Margaret Samuels 1894- *ConAu P-1*
Ernst, Margot Klebe 1939- *ConAu 23*
Ernst, Max 1891- *REn*
Ernst, Morris L 1888- *AmA&B, ConAu 5R, REnAL, WrD 1976*
Ernst, Oswald H 1842-1926 *Alli Sup, DcAmA, DcNAA*
Ernst, Otto 1862-1926 *CasWL, ModWD*
Ernst, Paul 1866-1933 *CasWL, ClDMEuL, CnMD, EncWL, EvEuW, McGWD, ModGL, ModWD, OxGer, Pen Eur, WhLA*
Ernst, Robert 1915- *ConAu 23, WrD 1976*
Ernst, William 1830- *Alli Sup*
Ernsting, Walter 1920- *ConAu 37*
Ernuin, E *ChPo*
Ernulf 1040-1124 *NewC*
Ernulph, Bishop Of Rochester 1040-1124 *Alli, BiB N*
Ernyei, Sandor 1924- *WhGrA*
Ero *WhWNAA*

Erostratus *REn*
Erra-Pater *OxEng, REn*
Erralt, Thomas *Alli*
Errante, Vincenzo 1813-1891 *BiD&SB*
Erratic Enrique 1838-1900? *AmA, DcNAA*
Errett, Isaac 1820-1888 *Alli Sup, AmA&B, DcAmA, DcNAA, OhA&B*
Errington, George *Alli Sup*
Errol, John *BlkAW*
Erroll, Henry *Alli Sup*
Errym, Malcolm J *HsB&A, MnBBF*
Ersch, Johann Samuel 1766-1828 *EvEuW*
Ershov, Peter Pavlovich 1815-1869 *CasWL*
Erskine, Lord *Chmbr 2*
Erskine, Albert Russel 1871-1933 *DcNAA*
Erskine, Alexander K *ChPo S1*
Erskine, Andrew 1739-1793 *Alli*
Erskine, Barbara Peattie 1885-1915 *ChPo S1*
Erskine, C M *Alli Sup*
Erskine, Charles *Alli, BiDLA*
Erskine, Charles Thomas *Alli Sup*
Erskine, David 1670-1755 *Alli*
Erskine, Sir David 1772-1837 *BbD, BiD&SB*
Erskine, David Stewart *Alli*
Erskine, Dorothy Bliss 1906- *AmA&B, AmNov, OhA&B*
Erskine, Dorothy Ward 1896- *Au&Wr*
Erskine, Ebenezer 1680-1754 *Alli*
Erskine, Emma 1854-1924 *DcNAA*
Erskine, Mrs. Esme Stewart *Alli*
Erskine, F J *Alli Sup*
Erskine, Sir Francis R, Earl Of Rosslyn 1833- *Alli Sup*
Erskine, Francis Robert *ChPo*
Erskine, George *Alli*
Erskine, Gladys Shaw 1895- *WhWNAA*
Erskine, H T *Alli*
Erskine, Henry *ChPo*
Erskine, Henry 1624-1696 *Alli*
Erskine, Henry 1746-1817 *Alli, NewC*
Erskine, James *Alli Sup*
Erskine, John 1508?-1591 *Alli*
Erskine, John 1695-1768 *Alli, DcEnL*
Erskine, John 1721-1803 *Alli*
Erskine, John 1879-1951 *AmA&B, AmLY, AmNov, ChPo, ChPo S1, CnDAL, ConAmA, ConAmL, DcLEL, LongC, OxAm, REnAL, TwCA, TwCA Sup, WhWNAA*
Erskine, John Elphinstone *Alli Sup*
Erskine, John Francis *Alli*
Erskine, Laurie York 1894- *AmA&B*
Erskine, Margaret *Au&Wr, ChPo, ChPo S2, ConAu XR*
Erskine, Payne 1854-1924 *Alli Sup, ChPo*
Erskine, Ralph 1685-1752 *Alli, ChPo S1, DcEnL, EvLB, NewC*
Erskine, Robert *Alli*
Erskine, Rosalind *ConAu XR, WrD 1976*
Erskine, Thomas *Alli Sup, Chmbr 3*
Erskine, Lord Thomas 1750-1823 *Alli, BiDLA*
Erskine, Thomas 1788-1870 *Alli Sup, BrAu 19, DcEnL, EvLB*
Erskine, Mrs. Thomas *Alli Sup*
Erskine, Walter C, Earl Of Kellie 1810-1872 *Alli Sup*
Erskine, William *Alli Sup*
Erskine, Wilson Fiske 1911- *ConAu 1R*
Erskine-Crum, Lady *ChPo*
Erskine-Lindop, Audrey Beatrice Noel *Au&Wr, TwCW*
Erskine Of Linlathen, Thomas 1788-1870 *NewC*
Erswicke, John *Alli*
Ertel, Aleksander Ivanovich 1855-1909 *CasWL, ClDMEuL, DcRusL, Pen Eur*
Ertel, James 1922- *ConAu 9R*
Erter, Isaac 1791-1851 *CasWL*
Ertl, Emil 1860-1935 *OxGer*
Ertz, Susan 1894?- *Au&Wr, Chmbr 3, ConAu 5R, LongC, NewC, TwCA, TwCA Sup*
Ervin, Janet Halliday 1923- *ConAu 29, SmATA 4*
Ervin, Patrick *WhWNAA*
Ervin, Susan 1927- *ConAu XR*
Ervin, Theodore Robert 1928- *ConAu 13R*
Ervin-Tripp, Susan Moore 1927- *ConAu 53*
Ervine, St. John 1883-1971 *CasWL, ChPo S1,*

Chmbr 3, CnMD, CnThe, ConAu 29, DcLEnL, EvLB, LongC, McGWD, ModBL, ModWD, NewC, Pen Eng, REnWD, TwCA, TwCA Sup, TwCW, WebEAL
Erving, Henry Wood 1851-1941 *DcNAA*
Erwin, A H *Alli Sup*
Erwin, Edward 1937- *ConAu 29*
Erwin, F Th *OxGer*
Erwin, Frank Alexander 1860-1930 *DcNAA*
Erwin, George 1913- *AmSCAP 66*
Erwin, Helen Blodgett *ChPo S1*
Erwin, James *Alli Sup*
Erwin, James Shrewsbury 1857-1918 *DcNAA*
Erwin, Lee 1908- *AmSCAP 66*
Erwin, Walter *ChPo S2*
Erzberger, Matthias 1875-1921 *OxGer*
Erzherzog Karl *OxGer*
Esarey, Logan 1873-1942 *DcNAA, IndAu 1816, WhWNAA*
Esau, Helmut 1941- *ConAu 57*
Escalera, Belen *BlkAW*
Escandon, Ralph 1928- *ConAu 37*
Escarpenter, Claudio 1922- *ConAu 17R*
Escarraz, Donald Ray 1932- *ConAu 21*
Eschelbach, Claire John 1929- *ConAu 1R*
Eschenbach, Wolfram Von d1218? *BbD, BiD&SB*
Eschenburg, Johann Joachim 1743-1820 *DcEuL, NewC*
Escher, Franklin 1881- *WhWNAA*
Escher, Franklin 1915- *ConAu 9R*
Escherich, Elsa Falk 1888- *ConAu 5R*
Escherny, D D *Alli*
Escherny, Francois Louis 1733-1815 *BiD&SB*
Eschholz, Paul A 1942- *ConAu 37*
Escholier, Raymond 1882- *WhLA*
Escobar, Alberto 1929- *DcCLA*
Escobar Y Mendoza, Antonio 1589-1669 *OxFr*
Escoiquiz, Juan De *DcEuL*
Escosura, Patricio DeLa 1807-1878 *BbD, BiD&SB, CasWL, REn*
Escott, Hay Sweet- *Alli Sup*
Escott, Mary Lois 1923- *Au&Wr*
Escott, Thomas Hay Sweet 1844- *Alli Sup, ChPo S2*
Escouchy, Mathieu D' 1420?-1482? *CasWL*
Escragnolle, Alfredo D' *REn*
Escritt, Leonard Bushby 1902- *Au&Wr*
Escriva, Bernat *CasWL*
Escriva, Josemaria *ConAu 57*
Escriva, Juan 1480?- *CasWL, DcEuL*
Escriva DeBalaguer, Josemaria 1902-1975 *ConAu 57*
Esdaile, Arundell James Kennedy 1880- *ChPo*
Esdaile, David *Alli Sup*
Esdaile, James 1808-1859 *Alli, BiDPar*
Esdaile, M M *Alli Sup*
Esegar *WhLA*
Esek, Uncle 1818-1885 *AmA*
Esenin, Sergei Aleksandrovich 1895-1925 *CasWL, ClDMEuL, CnMWL, EncWL, EvEuW, Pen Eur, REn, WhTwL, WorAu*
Esenwein, Joseph Berg 1867-1946 *AmA&B, ChPo, DcNAA, REnAL, WhWNAA*
Eseoghene *BlkAW*
Esfandiary, F M 1930- *Au&Wr, ConAu 17R, DrAF 1976, WrD 1976*
Eshag, Eprime 1918- *Au&Wr*
Eshelman, Byron E 1915- *ConAu 1R*
Eshelman, M M *Alli Sup*
Esher, Viscount 1852-1930 *NewC*
Esherick, Wharton S *ChPo*
Eshleman, Clayton 1935- *ConAu 33, ConP 1970, ConP 1975, DrAP 1975, IndAu 1917, Pen Am, WrD 1976*
Eshleman, Juliette Evelina 1875- *ChPo*
Eshleman, Lloyd Wendell 1902- *WhWNAA*
'Eshqi, Mohammad Reza 1893?-1924 *DcOrL 3*
Eskadale, Evan *AmLY XR*
Eskelin, Neil J 1938- *ConAu 33*
Eskell, Abraham Clifford- *Alli Sup*
Eskell, Frederick A *Alli Sup*
Eskell, Louis *Alli Sup*
Eskelund, Karl 1918- *Au&Wr, ConAu 23*
Eskenazi, Gerald 1936- *ConAu 61*
Eskie *WhWNAA*
Eskilson, Richard E 1923- *AmSCAP 66*

Eskin, Frada 1936- *ConAu 37*, *WrD 1976*
Eskow, John *DrAP 1975*
Eskow, Seymour 1924- *ConAu 9R*
Esler, Anthony James 1934- *ConAu 23*,
  WrD 1976
Esler, E Rentoul *Alli Sup*
Esler, William K 1930- *ConAu 53*
Eslie-Nelham *Alli Sup*
Esling, Catharine Harbeson 1812- *Alli*, *ChPo*,
  DcAmA, *DcNAA*, *FemPA*
Esling, Charles Henry Augustine 1845-1907
  BiD&SB, *DcAmA*, *DcNAA*
Esman, Aaron H 1924- *ConAu 61*
Esmark, Dorrien *MnBBF*
Esmein, Jean 1923- *ConAu 49*
Esmenard, Joseph Alphonse 1770-1811 *BiD&SB*
Esmenard, Joseph-Etienne 1769-1811 *OxFr*
Esmeralda, Aurora 1853- *DcNAA*, *WhWNAA*
Esmond, Henry *PoIre*
Esmond, Henry V *Chmbr 3*
Esmonde, T *Alli Sup*
Eson, Morris E 1921- *ConAu 13R*
Esop *NewC*
Espagne, John D' *Alli*
Esparbes, George-Thomas D' 1864-1944 *OxFr*
Espejo *CasWL*
Espejo, Antonio *ArizL*
Espenheim, Frank R *ChPo*
Espenshade, Edward B, Jr. 1910- *ConAu 1R*
Esper, Erwin A 1895- *ConAu P-1*
Espey, Clara Ewing *ChPo*
Espey, John 1913- *Au&Wr*, *ConAu 5R*,
  ConNov 1972, *ConNov 1976*, *DrAF 1976*,
  WrD 1976
Espin, Thomas Espinell *Alli Sup*
Espina, Antonio 1894?- *CasWL*, *ClDMEuL*,
  EvEuW
Espina, Concha 1877?-1955 *CasWL*, *DcSpL*,
  EncWL, *REn*, *TwCA*, *TwCA Sup*
Espina DeLaSerna, Concha 1877-1955 *EvEuW*
Espina DeSerna, Concha 1877-1955 *ClDMEuL*,
  ModRL
Espinasse, Mademoiselle De L' *BiD&SB*
Espinasse, Albert 1905-1972 *ConAu 37*
Espinasse, Bernard *MnBBF*
Espinasse, Francis *Alli Sup*
Espinasse, Isaac *Alli*, *BiDLA*
Espinasse, James *Alli*
Espinel, Vicente 1550-1624 *BiD&SB*, *DcEuL*,
  DcSpL, *EuA*, *Pen Eur*
Espinel Martinez, Vicente 1550-1624 *CasWL*
Espino, Federico 1939- *ConP 1970*,
  ConP 1975, *WrD 1976*
Espinosa, Aurelio Macedonio 1880- *DcSpL*,
  WhWNAA
Espinosa, Jose E 1900-1967 *ConAu 25*
Espinosa, Pedro 1578-1650 *CasWL*, *DcEuL*,
  DcSpL, *EvEuW*, *Pen Eur*
Espinosa, Rudy *DrAF 1976*
Espirito Santo, Alda De 1926- *AfA 1*
Esposito, John C 1940- *ConAu 33*
Esprit, Jacques 1611-1678 *OxFr*
Espriu, Salvador 1913- *CasWL*
Espronceda, Jose De 1808-1842 *BbD*, *BiD&SB*,
  CasWL, *DcEuL*, *EuA*, *EvEuW*, *Pen Eur*
Espronceda Y Delgado, Jose De 1808-1842
  DcSpL, *REn*
Espy, James Pollard 1785-1860 *Alli*, *DcAmA*,
  DcNAA, *OhA&B*
Espy, Willard R 1910- *ConAu 49*
Esquemeling, Alexander Olivier 1645?-1707
  OxEng, *REn*
Esquenazi-Mayo, Roberto 1920- *ConAu 45*
Esquilache, Prince Francisco DeB Y A De
  1581-1658 *CasWL*
Esquiros, Henri Alphonse 1814-1876 *BbD*,
  BiD&SB, *EvEuW*, *OxFr*
Esquivel Pren, Jose 1897- *WhWNAA*
Essame, Hubert 1896- *Au&Wr*, *ConAu 49*
Essary, Jesse Frederick 1881-1942 *AmLY*,
  DcNAA, *WhWNAA*
Esser, Robin 1933- *ConAu 29*
Essery, R J 1930- *Au&Wr*
Essery, Richard Aubrey *Alli Sup*
Essery, W A *ChPo S1*
Essery, William Alfred *Alli Sup*
Esses, Emma *MnBBF*
Essex, Earl Of *CasWL*, *NewC*

Essex, Arthur Capel, Earl Of *Alli*
Essex, Captain *MnBBF*
Essex, Harry J 1951- *ConAu 33*, *WrD 1976*
Essex, James 1723-1784 *Alli*
Essex, John *Alli*
Essex, Lewis *MnBBF*
Essex, Louis *MnBBF*
Essex, Mary *ConAu XR*, *WrD 1976*
Essex, Richard *MnBBF*
Essex, Robert Devereux, Earl Of *Alli*
Essex, Rosamund Sibyl 1900- *Au&Wr*
Essex, Walter Devereux, Earl Of *Alli*
Essex-Cater, Antony John 1923- *WrD 1976*
Essick, Robert N 1942- *ConAu 53*
Essig, Charles James 1841-1901 *DcNAA*
Essig, Edward Oliver 1884-1964 *IndAu 1917*,
  WhWNAA
Essig, Hermann 1878-1918 *CnMD*, *ModWD*,
  OxGer
Essington, Robert William *Alli Sup*
Esslemont, Peter *ChPo S2*
Esslinger, Dean R 1942- *ConAu 61*
Essoe, Gabe 1944- *ConAu 25*
Esson, George Auldjo *Alli Sup*
Esson, H *BbtC*
Esson, Louis 1879-1943 *ChPo S1*, *LongC*,
  ModWD
Esson, Thomas Louis Buvelot 1879-1943
  DcLEnL
Esson, W B *Alli Sup*
Est, William *Alli*
Estabrook, A H 1885- *WhWNAA*
Estabrook, Henry Dodge 1854-1917 *ChPo*,
  DcNAA
Estabrooks, George Hoben 1895?-1973 *Au&Wr*,
  BiDPar, *ConAu 45*
Estabrooks, Henry L *Alli Sup*
Estang, Luc 1911- *ConAu 61*, *EncWL*, *OxFr*,
  Pen Eur, *WorAu*
Estarellas, Juan 1918- *ConAu 45*
Estaunie, Edouard 1862-1942 *ClDMEuL*,
  EncWL, *EvEuW*, *OxFr*
Estcourt, Edgar Edmund 1816-1884 *Alli Sup*
Estcourt, Mary Jane *Alli Sup*
Estcourt, Richard 1668-1712? *Alli*, *BrAu*,
  DcEnL
Este, Charles 1753-1829 *Alli*, *BiDLA*
Este, Charles H *BlkAW*
Este, John *Alli*
Este, M L *Alli*, *BiDLA*
Este, Mary B *Alli Sup*
Este, Michael *Alli*
Estebanez Calderon, Serafin 1799-1867 *CasWL*,
  DcSpL, *EuA*, *EvEuW*, *Pen Eur*, *REn*
Estee, Charles F *Alli Sup*
Estee, Morris M d1903 *Alli Sup*, *DcNAA*
Estel, P G *MnBBF*
Estella, Diego De 1524-1578 *CasWL*, *DcEuL*,
  EvEuW
Estelle *ChPo S1*
Estelle, Sister Mary 1907- *ConAu P-1*
Estep, Irene Compton *ConAu 1R*, *SmATA 5*
Estep, W R, Jr. 1920- *ConAu 13R*
Esterbrook, William P And Monckton, J H
  Alli Sup
Estergreen, Marian Morgan 1917- *ConAu 17R*
Esterhazy, Marie C Ferdinand Walsin 1847-1923
  REn
Esterly, Glenn 1942- *ConAu 33*
Esterow, Milton 1928- *ConAu 17R*
Estes, Arthur Theodore 1868- *IndAu 1917*
Estes, Dana 1840-1909 *Alli Sup*, *AmA&B*,
  DcNAA
Estes, David Foster 1851-1926 *DcAmA*,
  DcNAA
Estes, Dena Elliott *ChPo S1*
Estes, Edith Perry *ChPo*
Estes, Eleanor 1906- *AmA&B*, *AmNov*,
  AnCL, *AuBYP*, *BkCL*, *ChLR 2*,
  ConAu 1R, *IlCB 1956*, *JBA 1951*,
  MorBMP, *Newb 1922*, *REnAL*, *SenS*,
  SmATA 4, *SmATA 7*, *St&VC*
Estes, Hiram Cushman 1823- *Alli Sup*,
  DcAmA
Estes, John E 1939- *ConAu 57*
Estes, Louise Reid *Alli Sup*
Estes, Matthew *BiDSA*
Estes, Rice 1907- *ConAu P-1*

Estes, William Lawrence 1855-1940 *DcNAA*
Estes, Winston M 1917- *ConAu 29*,
  WrD 1976
Esteven, John *AmNov XR*, *OhA&B*
Esteves, Jose DeJesus 1882-1918 *PueRA*
Esteves, Sandra Maria *DrAP 1975*
Estey, George *Alli*
Estey, George F 1924- *ConAu 33*
Estey, James Arthur 1886- *IndAu 1816*,
  WhWNAA
Estey, Stephen Sewall 1861-1932 *DcNAA*
Esthus, Raymond Arthur 1925- *ConAu 13R*
Estienne *OxFr*
Estienne, Charles 1504?-1564 *NewC*
Estienne, Henri 1531?-1598 *CasWL*, *DcEuL*,
  EuA, *EvEuW*, *REn*, *Pen Eur*
Estienne, Robert 1503-1559 *DcEuL*
Estill, Amanda Julia *TexWr*
Estill, Bonnie 1909- *TexWr*
Estill, Harry Fishburne 1861- *AmLY*, *TexWr*,
  WhWNAA
Estimauville, Robert Anne D' 1754-1831
  DcNAA, *OxCan*
Estlander, Carl Gustaf 1834-1910 *CasWL*
Estlin, John Prior *Alli*, *BiDLA*
Estock, Anne 1923- *ConAu 1R*
Eston, John *Alli*
Estoril, Jean *AuBYP*, *ConAu XR*,
  SmATA 5, *WrD 1976*
Estrada, Diego, Duque De 1589-1647? *CasWL*
Estrada, Doris 1923- *ConAu 17R*
Estrada, Jacquelyn 1946- *ConAu 29*
Estrada, Ricardo 1920- *DcCLA*
Estrees, Francois Annibal, Duke D' 1573-1670
  BiD&SB
Estrees, Gabrielle D' 1573-1599 *OxFr*, *REn*
Estrella, Joseph C 1908- *AmSCAP 66*
Estridge, Mary *Alli Sup*
Estrin, Herman A 1915- *ConAu 17R*
Estuniga, Lope Ortiz De 1407?-1477? *CasWL*
Estvan, B *Alli Sup*
Estvan, Mathilde *Alli Sup*
Estwick, Nicholas *Alli*
Estwick, Samuel *Alli*
Esty, Annette 1879-1948 *DcNAA*
Esty, Lucien Coy 1899-1929 *DcNAA*
Esty, Robert P *ChPo*, *ChPo S1*
Esty, Thomas Cushing 1870- *WhWNAA*
Esty, William 1868-1928 *DcNAA*
Eswarchandra Vidyasagar 1820-1891 *CasWL*
Etan, Raymond *OhA&B*, *WhWNAA*
Etaples, Jacques Lefevre D' 1453-1536 *REn*
Etchahoun *CasWL*
Etchahun *Pen Eur*
Etchell, Mabel *Alli Sup*
Etcheson, Warren W 1920- *ConAu 41*
Eterovich, Adam S 1930- *ConAu 49*
Eterovich, Francis Hyacinth 1913- *ConAu 37*
Ethelbert d797 *BiB S*
Ethelburga, Saint d676? *NewC*
Ethelfleda d918? *NewC*
Ethelnoth *BiB S*
Ethelred 1109?-1166 *Alli*, *BiD&SB*
Ethelred I d871 *NewC*
Ethelred II 968?-1016 *NewC*
Ethelred, Saint 1109-1116 *NewC*
Ethelston, Charles Wicksted *Alli*, *BiDLA*
Ethelwald d740 *BiB S*
Ethelward d998? *Alli*, *BiB S*
Ethelwerd d998? *NewC*
Ethelwold 925?-984 *Alli*, *BiB S*
Ethelwold, Saint 925?-984 *NewC*
Ethelwolf 770?- *Alli*, *BiB S*
Etheredge, Sir George 1635?-1691? *BrAu*,
  DcLEnL, *EvLB*, *OxEng*
Etherege, George 1514?-1588 *BiD&SB*, *NewC*
Etherege, Sir George 1635?-1691? *Alli*, *AtlBL*,
  BiD&SB, *BrAu*, *CasWL*, *Chmbr 2*,
  CnThe, *CriT 2*, *CyWA*, *DcEnA*, *DcEnL*,
  DcLEnL, *EvLB*, *McGWD*, *MouLC 1*,
  NewC, *OxEng*, *Pen Eng*, *REn*, *REnWD*,
  WebEAL
Etheridge *Alli*
Etheridge, Eugene Wesley 1925- *ConAu 5R*
Etheridge, John Wesley 1804-1866 *Alli Sup*
Etheridge, Kelsie *Alli Sup*
Etheridge, Robert *Alli Sup*
Etheridge, Robert, Jr. *Alli Sup*

Etherington, Charles Leslie 1903- *ConAu 5R, WrD 1976*
Etherington, George *Alli*
Etherington, George F *Alli*
Etherington, L N *Alli Sup*
Etherington, Thomas d1815 *Alli, BiDLA, BiDLA Sup*
Etherington, William *Alli Sup*
Etherton, P T 1879- *MnBBF, WhLA*
Ethier-Blais, Jean 1926- *OxCan Sup*
Ethridge, Willie Snow 1900- *AmA&B, AuNews 1, ConAu 17R, WhWNAA*
Ethryg 1514?-1588? *Alli*
Ethrygg, George 1514?-1588? *BiD&SB*
Etiemble, Rene Joseph Ernest 1909- *CasWL*
Etienne *ConAu XR*
Etienne De Bourbon 1190?-1261 *Pen Eur*
Etienne De Fougeres d1178 *CasWL*
Etienne, Charles 1504?-1564 *NewC*
Etienne, Charles Guillaume 1778-1845 *BbD, BiD&SB, OxFr*
Etienne, Lieutenant R N 1893- *ChPo S2*
Etlar, Carit 1816-1900 *BiD&SB, CasWL, EvEuW*
Etler, Charles *Alli Sup*
Etmekjian, James 1915- *WrD 1976*
Etmekjian, James 1916- *ConAu 5R*
Eton, William *Alli, BiDLA, DcEnL*
Etonian *ChPo*
Etough, Henry *Alli*
Ets, Marie Hall 1895- *AnCL, Au&Wr, AuBYP, AuICB, BkP, ChPo, ConAu 1R, FamAI, IlBYP, IlCB 1945, IlCB 1956, IlCB 1966, JBA 1951, NewbC 1956, SmATA 2, St&VC, WrD 1976*
Ets-Hokin, Judith Diane 1938- *ConAu 61*
Etsu *TwCA, TwCA Sup*
Etteldorf, Raymond P 1911- *ConAu 9R*
Etter, Dave 1928- *ConAu 17R, ConP 1970, DrAP 1975, WrD 1976*
Etter, John W 1846-1895 *Alli Sup, DcNAA*
Etter, Les 1904- *ConAu 25*
Etting, Frank Marx d1890 *Alli Sup, DcNAA*
Etting, Irving *Alli Sup*
Etting, Theodore M *Alli Sup*
Ettinger, Elzbieta 1925- *ConAu 29, WrD 1976*
Ettinger, Richard Prentice 1893-1971 *ConAu 29*
Ettinger, Robert C W 1918- *ConAu 13R*
Ettinger, Salomon 1799-1855 *Pen Eur*
Ettinger, Solomon 1800?-1856 *McGWD*
Ettinghausen, Maurice L 1883- *ChPo S1*
Ettingsall, Thomas d1850? *PoIre*
Ettleson, Abraham 1897- *ConAu 23*
Ettlinger, Gerard H 1935- *ConAu 61*
Ettlinger, Harold 1910?-1944 *DcNAA*
Ettmuller, Ludwig 1802-1877 *BiD&SB*
Ettore, Eugene 1921- *AmSCAP 66*
Ettrick, Henry *Alli*
Ettrick, W *Alli, BiDLA*
Ettrick Shepherd, The 1772-1835 *DcEnL, NewC*
Etty, William 1787-1849 *ChPo*
Etulain, Richard W 1938- *ConAu 45*
Etzel *OxGer*
Etzioni, Amitai Werner 1929- *ConAu 1R*
Etzkorn, K Peter 1932- *ConAu 49*
Etzkowitz, Henry 1940- *ConAu 25*
Euba, Femi 1935?- *AfA 1*
Eubank, Earle Edward 1887-1945 *AmA&B, DcNAA, OhA&B, WhWNAA*
Eubank, Jessie Burrall *WhWNAA*
Eubank, Keith 1920- *ConAu 5R*
Eubank, Kent 1877- *WhWNAA*
Eubank, Nancy 1934- *ConAu 41*
Eubanks, Ralph T 1920- *ConAu 17R*
Eubulus *CasWL*
Eucken, Rudolf 1846-1926 *OxGer*
Euclid 323?BC- *CasWL, NewC, OxEng, Pen Cl, REn*
Euclides Of Megara 450?BC-380?BC *CasWL*
Euderbie *Alli*
Eudes 858-898 *OxFr*
Eudoxus 408?BC-355BC *Pen Cl*
Euer, Sampson *Alli*
Eugammon *Pen Cl*
Eugen, Prinz Von Savoyen 1663-1736 *OxGer*
Eugene, Brother *WhWNAA*

Eugene Of Savoy, Prince 1663-1736 *REn*
Eugenianus *CasWL*
Eugenicus *CasWL*
Eugenie, Empress 1826-1920 *OxFr, REn*
Eugenius Of Palermo 1130?-1203 *Pen Cl*
Eugenius Of Toledo 600?-658 *Pen Eur*
Euhemerus 311BC-298BC *OxEng*
Euhemerus 370?BC- *NewC*
Eulalie *OhA&B*
Eulate Sanjurjo, Carmen 1871-1961 *PueRA*
Eulenberg, Herbert 1876-1949 *ClDMEuL, CnMD, ModWD, OxGer, WhLA*
Eulenspiegel, Till d1350 *NewC, REn*
Eulenspiegel, Tyll d1350 *REn*
Eulert, Don 1935- *ConAu 49*
Euller, John E 1926- *ConAu 9R*
Eumelus *Pen Cl*
Eunapius 345?-420? *CasWL*
Eunson, Dale 1904- *AmA&B, AmNov, ConAu 41, SmATA 5*
Eunson, G *Alli*
Eunson, Robert C 1912-1975 *ConAu 13R, ConAu 61*
Euphemides, Aristos *ConAu XR*
Euphorion 275?BC-200?BC *CasWL, NewC, Pen Cl*
Eupolis 446?BC-412?BC *BbD, BiD&SB, CasWL, Pen Cl*
Eurelius, Gunno 1658-1709 *DcEuL*
Eureti, J *Alli Sup*
Eurich, Alvin C 1902- *ConAu 17R*
Euringer, Richard 1891-1953 *ClDMEuL, OxGer*
Euripides 480?BC-406?BC *AtlBL, BbD, BiD&SB, CasWL, CnThe, CyWA, DcEnL, McGWD, NewC, OxEng, Pen Cl, RCom, REn, REnWD*
European *ConAu XR*
Eury, Catherine d1795 *PoIre*
Eusden, John 1922- *ConAu 45*
Eusden, Laurence 1688-1730 *Alli, BiD&SB, BrAu, ChPo, DcEnA, DcEnL, EvLB, NewC, OxEng, Pen Eng, PoIre, PoLE*
Eusebius 260?-340? *CasWL, OxEng*
Eusebius Of Caesarea 260?-340? *NewC, REn*
Eusebius Pamphili 260?-340? *BbD, BiD&SB, Pen Cl*
Eustace *NewC*
Eustace, Cecil John 1903- *BkC 3, CanNov, CatA 1947, ConAu 49, WhWNAA, WrD 1976*
Eustace, Evans *Alli*
Eustace, John Chetwode 1762?-1815 *Alli, BiDLA, BiDLA Sup, PoIre*
Eustace, John Skey d1805 *Alli*
Eustace, Sir Maurice *Alli*
Eustace, May 1904- *ConAu 5R*
Eustace, Robert *EncM&D*
Eustache *CasWL*
Eustache D'Amiens *CasWL*
Eustache Deschamps 1340?-1415 *DcEuL*
Eustacius *DcSpL*
Eustathius Of Thessalonica d1192? *CasWL, Pen Cl*
Eustis, Caroline *ChPo*
Eustis, Helen 1916- *EncM&D, OhA&B*
Eustis, Henry Lawrence 1819-1885 *DcNAA*
Eustis, James Biddle 1834- *BiDSA*
Euston, George *Alli Sup*
Euthymius Of Turnovo *CasWL*
Eutropius *BiD&SB, CasWL, Pen Cl*
Euwer, Anthony Henderson 1877- *ChPo, ChPo S2*
Evagrius Of Pontus 345?-399 *CasWL*
Evagrius Scholasticus 536?- *CasWL*
Evain, Elaine 1931- *ConAu 57*
Evan, Carol *ConAu XR*
Evan, William 1922- *ConAu 1R*
Evan Owen, Benjamin 1918- *Au&Wr*
Evance, Daniel *Alli*
Evance, Miss S *Alli, BiDLA*
Evander, John *Alli*
Evangelic Doctor, The *DcEnL*
Evangeline *OhA&B*
Evanier, David *DrAF 1976*
Evanke, George *Alli*
Evanoff, Vlad 1916- *ConAu 5R, WrD 1976*
Evans, Lord 1899- *Au&Wr*

Evans, Lord SEE ALSO Evans, B Ifor
Evans, A Eurule *MnBBF*
Evans, Abbie Huston 1881- *ChPo, ConAu 57, ConP 1970, ConP 1975, WorAu, WrD 1976*
Evans, Abel 1679-1737 *Alli, BiD&SB, EvLB*
Evans, Abigail A *Alli Sup*
Evans, Ada J *WhWNAA*
Evans, Ada Smith 1882- *TexWr, WhWNAA*
Evans, Alan *ConAu XR, WrD 1976*
Evans, Albert Eubule *Alli Sup*
Evans, Albert Owen 1864- *WhLA*
Evans, Albert S *Alli Sup*
Evans, Alcwyn C *Alli Sup*
Evans, Alfred Alexander 1905- *Au&Wr, ConAu P-1*
Evans, Alfred Bowen *Alli, Alli Sup*
Evans, Alice 1868-1946 *DcNAA*
Evans, Alice Lois *ChPo*
Evans, Allan Roy 1885- *CanNov*
Evans, Allen Roy 1885- *OxCan*
Evans, Alvin Eleazor 1878- *WhWNAA*
Evans, Anne *Alli Sup*
Evans, Anne 1820-1870 *Alli Sup, BrAu 19, ChPo S2*
Evans, Anthony 1922- *Au&Wr*
Evans, Anthony Walton White 1817-1886 *DcNAA*
Evans, Arise *Alli*
Evans, Arthur B *Alli*
Evans, Arthur Benoni 1781-1854 *NewC*
Evans, Arthur Bruce 1948- *ConAu 61*
Evans, Arthur Humble *Alli Sup*
Evans, Sir Arthur John 1851-1941 *Alli Sup, DcLEnL, EvLB, LongC, NewC, OxEng*
Evans, Arthur Maybury 1874- *WhWNAA*
Evans, Augusta Jane 1835-1909 *Alli Sup, AmA, AmA&B, BbD, BiD&SB, DcAmA, DcLEnL, DcNAA, LivFWS, OxAm, REnAL*
Evans, B *Alli Sup*
Evans, B E *MnBBF*
Evans, B Ifor 1899- *WhLA*
Evans, B Ifor SEE ALSO Evans, Lord
Evans, B J *MnBBF*
Evans, Bergen 1904- *AmA&B, Au&Wr, ConAu 5R, OhA&B*
Evans, C *Alli*
Evans, Mrs. C *Alli Sup*
Evans, C S *CarSB*
Evans, C Stephen 1948- *ConAu 33*
Evans, Caleb 1737-1791 *Alli*
Evans, Caradoc 1878-1945 *CasWL, CnMWL, DcLEnL, EvLB, LongC, ModBL, NewC, REn, TwCA, TwCA Sup, TwCW, WebEAL, WhLA, WhTwL*
Evans, Caroline *ChPo*
Evans, Cecily Louise *OxCan Sup*
Evans, Charles *Alli Sup, ChPo S2*
Evans, Charles 1802-1879 *Alli, DcNAA*
Evans, Charles 1850-1935 *AmA&B, CnDAL, DcNAA, OxAm*
Evans, Charles 1870- *WhWNAA*
Evans, Charles 1890- *IndAu 1917*
Evans, Charles H *Alli Sup*
Evans, Charles P *Alli Sup*
Evans, Charles Watkyns DeLacy *Alli Sup*
Evans, Charles Worthington 1812-1889 *DcNAA*
Evans, Cherry 1928- *ConAu P-1*
Evans, Chris d1924 *DcNAA*
Evans, Christmas *Alli*
Evans, Clement Anselm 1833-1911 *AmA&B, BiDSA, DcAmA, DcNAA*
Evans, Constance May 1890- *ConAu 9R, WrD 1976*
Evans, Conway *Alli Sup*
Evans, D L *Alli*
Evans, D M *Alli Sup*
Evans, Dale *AmSCAP 66*
Evans, Daniel 1792-1846 *BiD&SB*
Evans, Daniel Luther 1895- *OhA&B*
Evans, Daniel Silvan *Alli Sup*
Evans, David *Alli, Alli Sup, BiDLA*
Evans, David 1878-1945 *CasWL*
Evans, David Allan 1940- *ConAu 49, DrAP 1975*
Evans, David Ellis 1930- *ConAu 25, WrD 1976*

Evans, David Morier 1819-1874 *Alli Sup*
Evans, David R 1937- *ConAu 33*
Evans, David Stanley 1916- *Au&Wr,*
ConAu 41, WrD 1976
Evans, Della J d1960? *IndAu 1917*
Evans, Dilwen Mary 1916- *Au&Wr*
Evans, Don 1938- *BlkAW*
Evans, Donald 1884-1921 *AmA&B, DcNAA,*
OxAm, REnAL
Evans, Donald 1927- *ConAu 41*
Evans, Donald P 1930- *ConAu 57*
Evans, DuO Geredigion 1792-1846 *BiD&SB*
Evans, E J And Hurndall, William *Alli Sup*
Evans, E T *Alli Sup*
Evans, Edith 1888- *NewC*
Evans, Edmund 1826-1905 *CarSB, ChPo,*
ChPo S1, ChPo S2
Evans, Edmund C *Alli*
Evans, Edna 1913- *AuBYP*
Evans, Edward *Alli*
Evans, Edward 1716-1798 *BiD&SB*
Evans, Edward Benjamin *Alli Sup*
Evans, Edward G, Jr. 1916- *ConAu 45*
Evans, Edward Payson 1831-1917 *Alli Sup,*
AmA&B, BiD&SB, DcAmA, DcNAA
Evans, Eli N 1936- *AuNews 1, ConAu 45*
Evans, Elizabeth 1932- *ConAu 53*
Evans, Elizabeth Edson 1832?-1911 *Alli Sup,*
AmA&B, BiD&SB, DcAmA, DcNAA
Evans, Elizabeth Hewling 1818-1855 *Alli,*
DcNAA
Evans, Emma Cobb *TexWr*
Evans, Emmery 1943- *BlkAW*
Evans, Emyr Estyn 1905- *Au&Wr, ConAu 5R,*
WrD 1976
Evans, Eubule *MnBBF*
Evans, Eva Knox 1905- *AuBYP, MorJA*
Evans, Evan 1730?-1790 *Alli, BiD&SB*
Evans, F G M *WrD 1976*
Evans, F Gwynne *ChPo*
Evans, Fallon 1925- *ConAu 1R*
Evans, Florence Wilkinson *AmA&B, ChPo,*
ChPo S1, ChPo S2
Evans, Frances Monet Carter 1923- *ConAu 37,*
WrD 1976
Evans, Frank 1850- *Alli Sup*
Evans, Frank Edgar 1876-1941 *DcNAA*
Evans, Frank Howel *MnBBF*
Evans, Frankis Tilney 1900- *Au&Wr*
Evans, Sir Frederick John Owen 1815-1885
Alli Sup
Evans, Frederick Noble 1881-1946 *OhA&B*
Evans, Frederick William 1808-1893 *Alli Sup,*
AmA&B, BbD, BiD&SB, DcAmA,
DcNAA
Evans, G D'Arcy *Alli Sup*
Evans, G Edward 1937- *ConAu 33*
Evans, G N D 1935-1971 *ConAu 33,*
OxCan Sup
Evans, G T *ChPo*
Evans, G W D *Alli*
Evans, Gareth Lloyd 1923- *Au&Wr*
Evans, Geoffrey C 1901- *ConAu 17R,*
WrD 1976
Evans, George *Alli Sup, ChPo S2*
Evans, George 1844-1942 *DcNAA*
Evans, George Alfred 1850-1925 *Alli Sup,*
DcNAA
Evans, George Bird 1906- *ConAu 1R*
Evans, George David *Alli Sup*
Evans, George E *Chmbr 3*
Evans, George Essex 1863-1909 *ChPo,*
ChPo S1, DcLEnL
Evans, George Ewart 1909- *Au&Wr,*
ConAu 61, WrD 1976
Evans, George H *ChPo*
Evans, George Henry *Alli Sup*
Evans, George Henry 1805-1856 *OxAm*
Evans, George Hill 1872- *WhWNAA*
Evans, George Samuel 1876-1904 *DcNAA*
Evans, George W 1861- *WhWNAA*
Evans, George W, II 1920- *ConAu 21*
Evans, Gilmore *Alli Sup*
Evans, Gordon H 1930- *ConAu 13R*
Evans, Grose 1916- *WrD 1976*
Evans, Gwyn 1899-1938 *MnBBF*
Evans, Gwynfor 1912- *ConAu 61*
Evans, Mrs. H Lloyd *Alli Sup*

Evans, H T P 1928- *Au&Wr*
Evans, Harold Matthew 1928- *ConAu 41,*
WrD 1976
Evans, Harris *ConAu XR*
Evans, Harry *ChPo S1*
Evans, Harry Carroll 1885-1932 *DcNAA,*
WhWNAA
Evans, Henry Bentall *Alli Sup*
Evans, Henry Ridgley 1861-1949 *AmA&B,*
AmLY
Evans, Henry Smith *Alli Sup*
Evans, Hilary 1929- *ConAu 1R*
Evans, Howard *Alli Sup*
Evans, Howard Ensign 1919- *ConAu 5R*
Evans, Howard Heber *Alli Sup*
Evans, Hubert *MnBBF*
Evans, Hubert 1892- *OxCan*
Evans, Hugh *Alli*
Evans, Hugh Davy 1792-1868 *Alli, Alli Sup,*
BiDSA, DcAmA, DcNAA
Evans, Humphrey 1914- *ConAu 29*
Evans, Idella M 1924- *ConAu 29*
Evans, Idrisyn Oliver 1894- *Au&Wr,*
ConAu 13R, WrD 1976
Evans, Israel d1817 *Alli*
Evans, Ivor Burford Needham 1913- *Au&Wr*
Evans, J *Alli, ChPo S1*
Evans, J D *BbtC*
Evans, J E *Alli Sup*
Evans, Mrs. J G *AmA&B*
Evans, J N 1920- *ConAu 25*
Evans, J R *ChPo S2*
Evans, J Robert 1942- *ConAu 57*
Evans, Jacob A 1920- *ConAu 25*
Evans, James 1801-1846 *OxCan*
Evans, James Allan S 1931- *ConAu 37,*
WrD 1976
Evans, James F 1932- *ConAu 25*
Evans, James Harington 1785-1849 *Alli, PoCh*
Evans, Jay 1925- *ConAu 61*
Evans, Jean Bell Shaw 1910- *Au&Wr*
Evans, Jean Cherry 1928- *Au&Wr*
Evans, Jean Lorna 1922- *Au&Wr*
Evans, Joan 1893- *Au&Wr, ConAu 13R*
Evans, John *Alli, Alli Sup, BiD&SB,*
BiDLA, EncM&D
Evans, John 1680-1730 *Alli*
Evans, John 1767-1827 *Alli, BiDLA, ChPo,*
ChPo S1
Evans, John 1814-1897 *OhA&B*
Evans, John 1823-1908 *Alli Sup, BiD&SB,*
OxEng
Evans, John 1828- *Alli Sup*
Evans, John Davies 1925- *Au&Wr*
Evans, John Ellis 1882- *IndAu 1917*
Evans, John J, Sr. 1861- *WhWNAA*
Evans, John R d1973? *ChPo S2*
Evans, John Roberts 1914- *Au&Wr*
Evans, John W 1904- *ConAu 33*
Evans, John Wainwright 1883- *BiDPar*
Evans, John X 1933- *ConAu 37*
Evans, Jonathan 1749-1809 *PoCh*
Evans, Joseph *Alli Sup*
Evans, Joseph W 1921- *ConAu 23*
Evans, Julia 1913- *Au&Wr, AuBYP,*
ConAu 13R, WrD 1976
Evans, Katherine *Alli*
Evans, Katherine Floyd 1901-1964 *AuBYP,*
ConAu 5R, IlCB 1966, SmATA 5
Evans, Kathleen Marianne 1911- *Au&Wr,*
ConAu 9R, WrD 1976
Evans, Kay Harris 1906- *ConAu 1R*
Evans, Kenneth 1917- *Au&Wr, ConAu 53,*
WrD 1976
Evans, Larry d1925 *DcNAA*
Evans, Laurence 1923- *ConAu 37, WrD 1976*
Evans, Lawlor B *Alli Sup*
Evans, Lawrence Boyd 1870-1928 *DcAmA,*
DcNAA, OhA&B
Evans, Lawton Bryan 1862-1934 *AmLY,*
BiDSA, DcNAA, WhWNAA
Evans, Leo L 1927- *AmSCAP 66*
Evans, Lewis *Alli*
Evans, Lewis 1700?-1756 *Alli, DcAmA,*
DcNAA
Evans, Lizzie Phelps 1846- *DcAmA*
Evans, Llwellyn Ioan 1833-1892 *OhA&B*
Evans, Luther Harris 1902- *ConAu 17R*

Evans, Luther S *ChPo S1*
Evans, Madison 1834-1866 *Alli Sup,*
IndAu 1816
Evans, Margaret *Alli Sup, PoIre*
Evans, Margiad 1909- *CasWL*
Evans, Marguerite Florence Helene *NewC*
Evans, Mari 1923- *BlkAW, ConAu 49,*
ConP 1975, CrCAP, DrAP 1975,
LivBAA, SmATA 10, WrD 1976
Evans, Marian 1819-1880 *CasWL, DcEnA,*
DcEnL, EvLB
Evans, Marion 1926- *AmSCAP 66*
Evans, Mark *Alli Sup, ChPo S1*
Evans, Marvin R 1915- *ConAu 49*
Evans, Mary *ChPo*
Evans, Mary 1890- *WhWNAA*
Evans, Mary Ann 1819-1880 *BiD&SB,*
BrAu 19, CarSB, DcLEnL, EvLB, NewC,
OxEng, Pen Eng, REn
Evans, Mary Anna 1857- *DcNAA*
Evans, Mary Ellen *BkC 6*
Evans, Mary N *ChPo*
Evans, Sir Maurice 1901- *NewC, REn*
Evans, Maurice J *Alli Sup*
Evans, Max 1925- *Au&Wr, ConAu 1R*
Evans, Medford 1907- *ConAu 25, TexWr*
Evans, Melbourne G 1912- *ConAu 33*
Evans, Milton G 1862-1939 *DcNAA*
Evans, Morgan *Alli Sup, ConAu XR*
Evans, N Dean 1925- *ConAu 21*
Evans, Nathaniel 1742-1767 *Alli, AmA,*
AmA&B, CnDAL, CyAL 1, DcAmA,
DcLEnL, DcNAA, OxAm, REn, REnAL
Evans, Nelson Wiley 1842-1913 *DcNAA,*
OhA&B
Evans, Nevil Norton 1865-1948 *DcNAA,*
WhWNAA
Evans, Norman Carl 1891-1965 *IndAu 1917*
Evans, Oliver 1755-1819 *Alli, DcAmA,*
DcNAA
Evans, Oliver 1915- *ConAu 17R*
Evans, Patricia Healy 1920- *AuBYP,*
ConAu XR
Evans, Patrick Fleming 1851- *Alli Sup*
Evans, Paul 1938- *AmSCAP 66*
Evans, Paul 1945- *ConP 1970*
Evans, R H *Alli, BiDLA*
Evans, Raymond B 1915- *AmSCAP 66*
Evans, Rear Admiral *MnBBF*
Evans, Redd 1912- *AmSCAP 66*
Evans, Rhydwyn Harding 1900- *Au&Wr*
Evans, Richard Louis 1906- *AmA&B,*
ConAu 9R
Evans, Robert *Alli, BiDLA, ChPo*
Evans, Robert, Jr. 1932- *ConAu 17R*
Evans, Robert Charles 1918- *Au&Wr*
Evans, Robert F 1930- *ConAu 23*
Evans, Robert H *Alli*
Evans, Robert Henry 1937- *ConAu 23*
Evans, Robert L 1917- *ConAu 49*
Evans, Robert Maunsell *PoIre*
Evans, Robert Owen 1919- *ConAu 13R,*
WrD 1976
Evans, Robert P 1918- *ConAu 13R*
Evans, Robert Wilson *Alli*
Evans, Robley Dunglison 1846-1912 *AmA&B,*
DcAmA, DcNAA
Evans, Rodney E 1939- *ConAu 49*
Evans, Rowland, Jr. 1921- *ConAu 23,*
WrD 1976
Evans, Rupert Nelson 1921- *ConAu 37,*
IndAu 1917
Evans, Samuel *Alli Sup*
Evans, Samuel B 1837- *DcNAA*
Evans, Sebastian 1830-1909 *Alli Sup, BrAu 19,*
ChPo, ChPo S1, DcLEnL, NewC, OxEng
Evans, Shirlee 1931- *ConAu 61*
Evans, Silas 1876- *WhWNAA*
Evans, Simeon Adams 1837-1895 *DcNAA*
Evans, Smith *Alli*
Evans, Stanley G 1912-1965 *ConAu P-1*
Evans, T H *Alli Sup*
Evans, T Rhys *Alli Sup*
Evans, Taliesin 1843-1926 *DcNAA*
Evans, Telynog 1840-1865 *BbD, BiD&SB*
Evans, Theophilus 1693-1767 *Alli, CasWL,*
Pen Eng
Evans, Thomas *Alli, Alli Sup, BiDLA*

DcAmA, *DcNAA*

Evertts, Eldonna Louise Becker 1917-
ConAu 21, *IndAu 1917*

Everwine, Peter *DrAP 1975*

Every, George 1909- *Au&Wr*, *ConAu 13R*,
WrD 1976

Every, Philip Cochrane *AuBYP*

Eves, Mrs. *Alli*, *BiDLA*

Eves, George *Alli*

Eves, Reginald T *MnBBF*

Evetts, Basil Thomas Alfred *Alli Sup*

Evetts, Julia Anne 1944- *WrD 1976*

Evezard, Alice *Alli Sup*

Evill, William *Alli Sup*

Evins, Joseph Landon 1910- *ConAu 61*

Evison, Frances Millicent Marion 1880-
AmA&B

Evjen, John Oluf 1874-1942 *DcNAA*

Evlachow, Alexandre 1880- *WhLA*

Evliya Celebi B Dervis Muhammed Zilli
1611?-1683? *CasWL*, *DcOrL 3*, *Pen Cl*

Evoe *ConAu XR*, *LongC*, *NewC*, *TwCA*,
TwCA Sup

Evoy, John J 1911- *ConAu 5R*

Evrard The German *CasWL*

Evreinov, Nikolai Nikolayevich 1879-1953
CasWL, *ClDMEuL*, *CnMD*, *CnThe*

Evslin, Bernard 1922- *ConAu 23*

Evslin, Dorothy 1923- *ConAu 57*

Evtimy Of Turnovo 1330?-1395 *CasWL*

Evtushenko, Evgeniy Alexandrovich 1933-
CasWL, *ConLC 1*, *EncWL*, *EvEuW*,
Pen Eur, *WhTwL*, *WorAu*

Ewald, Alexander Charles 1842- *Alli Sup*

Ewald, Carl 1856-1908 *CasWL*, *EuA*, *EvEuW*

Ewald, Georg Heinrich August 1803-1875 *BbD*,
BiD&SB

Ewald, Herman Frederik 1821-1908? *BiD&SB*,
CasWL, *DcEuL*, *EvEuW*

Ewald, Johannes 1743-1781 *BbD*, *BiD&SB*,
CasWL, *CnThe*, *DcEuL*, *EuA*, *EvEuW*,
Pen Eur, *REn*, *REnWD*

Ewan, James *Alli Sup*

Ewan, William *Alli Sup*

Ewart, Alfred James 1872- *WhLA*

Ewart, Andrew 1911- *ConAu 17R*

Ewart, Ernest Andrew 1878-1943 *DcLEnL*,
WhLA

Ewart, Frank Carman 1871-1942 *DcNAA*,
OhA&B, *WhWNAA*

Ewart, Gavin B 1916- *Au&Wr*, *ChPo S1*,
ChPo S2, *ConP 1970*, *ConP 1975*,
WorAu, *WrD 1976*

Ewart, Henry C *Alli Sup*

Ewart, James Cossar *Alli Sup*

Ewarts, John *Alli*, *Alli Sup*

Ewart, John Alexander 1821- *Alli Sup*

Ewart, John Skirving 1849-1933 *Alli Sup*,
AmLY, *DcNAA*, *OxCan*

Ewart, Joseph *Alli Sup*

Ewart, William 1820-1873 *Alli Sup*

Ewart, William Dunlop 1923- *Au&Wr*

Ewbank, George *Alli*

Ewbank, Henry Lee 1893-1960 *IndAu 1917*

Ewbank, Louis Blaisdel 1864-1953 *IndAu 1917*

Ewbank, Thomas 1792-1870 *Alli*, *AmA&B*,
BbD, *BiD&SB*, *CyAL 2*, *DcAmA*,
DcNAA

Ewbank, Walter F 1918- *ConAu 25*

Ewbank, William Withers *Alli Sup*

Ewell, Alice Maude 1860-1946 *BiDSA*, *ChPo*,
DcAmA, *DcNAA*

Ewell, Arthur Woolsey 1873- *WhWNAA*

Ewell, James 1773-1832 *DcNAA*

Ewell, John Louis 1840-1910 *DcNAA*

Ewell, M L B *Alli Sup*

Ewell, Marshall Davis 1844-1928 *Alli Sup*,
DcAmA, *DcNAA*, *WhWNAA*

Ewell, Thomas 1785-1826 *DcNAA*

Ewen, David 1907- *AmA&B*, *Au&Wr*,
AuBYP, *ConAu 1R*, *REnAL*, *SmATA 4*,
WrD 1976

Ewen, Frederic 1899- *ConAu 23*, *WrD 1976*

Ewen, James *Alli*

Ewen, John 1741-1821 *BiD&SB*, *ChPo*

Ewen, Robert B 1940- *ConAu 37*

Ewen, W M *Alli*

Ewens, E W *PoIre*

Ewens, Gwendoline Wilson *WrD 1976*

Ewer, Bernard Capen 1877- *WhWNAA*

Ewer, Ferdinand Cartwright 1826-1883 *Alli Sup*,
DcAmA, *DcNAA*

Ewer, John *Alli*

Ewer, Monica d1964 *LongC*

Ewers, Hans Heinz 1871-1943 *OxGer*

Ewers, John C 1909- *ConAu 17R*, *OxCan*,
OxCan Sup

Ewers, Mary H *ChPo S2*

Ewes, Sir Symonds D' *Alli*

Ewing, Mrs. *DcEuL*

Ewing, A *Alli*, *Alli Sup*

Ewing, Alexander *Alli*

Ewing, Alexander d1804 *Alli*, *BiDLA*

Ewing, Alexander 1814-1873 *Alli Sup*, *DcEnL*

Ewing, Sir Alexander William Gordon 1896-
Au&Wr

Ewing, Alfred Cyril 1899- *Au&Wr*,
ConAu 5R

Ewing, Archibald d1804 *Alli*, *BiDLA Sup*

Ewing, Cortez Arthur Milton 1896-1962
IndAu 1917

Ewing, D D 1883- *WhWNAA*

Ewing, David Walkley 1923- *ConAu 1R*,
WrD 1976

Ewing, Edwin Evans 1824-1901 *HsB&A*

Ewing, Elbert William Robinson *BiDSA*

Ewing, Elizabeth 1904- *ConAu 41*

Ewing, Elizabeth Cameron 1906- *WrD 1976*

Ewing, Elmore Ellis 1840-1900 *DcNAA*,
OhA&B

Ewing, Emma P 1838- *Alli Sup*, *DcAmA*,
DcNAA

Ewing, Finis 1773-1841 *BiDSA*, *DcAmA*,
DcNAA

Ewing, George W 1923- *ConAu 45*

Ewing, Grenville 1767-1841 *BiDLA*

Ewing, Greville 1767-1841 *Alli*

Ewing, Hugh Boyle 1826-1905 *Alli Sup*,
AmA&B, *BbD*, *BiD&SB*, *DcAmA*,
DcNAA, *OhA&B*

Ewing, J A *Alli Sup*

Ewing, James *Alli*

Ewing, James 1866-1943 *DcNAA*

Ewing, James Cameron *ChPo*, *ChPo S1*

Ewing, Sir James Caruthers Rhea 1854-1925
DcNAA

Ewing, Jennie Pendleton *ChPo*

Ewing, John 1732-1802 *Alli*, *BiDSA*, *CyAL 1*,
DcAmA, *DcNAA*

Ewing, John Melvin 1925- *ConAu 53*

Ewing, John S 1916- *ConAu 13R*

Ewing, Joseph Grant 1866-1938 *DcNAA*

Ewing, Julia Horatia *Chmbr 3*

Ewing, Juliana Horatia 1841-1885 *Alli Sup*,
BbD, *BiD&SB*, *BrAu 19*, *CarSB*,
CasWL, *ChPo*, *ChPo S1*, *ChPo S2*,
DcLEnL, *EvLB*, *FamSYP*, *JBA 1934*,
NewC, *OxEng*, *St&VC*, *WhCL*

Ewing, Kathryn 1921- *ConAu 61*

Ewing, Max Anderson 1903-1934 *OhA&B*,
WhWNAA

Ewing, Peter *Alli*, *BiDLA*

Ewing, Presley Kittredge 1860-1927 *DcNAA*

Ewing, Quincy 1867- *WhWNAA*

Ewing, R K *Alli Sup*

Ewing, R L 1878- *WhWNAA*

Ewing, Sherman 1901-1975 *ConAu 57*

Ewing, Thomas *Alli*

Ewing, Thomas 1862-1942 *OhA&B*,
WhWNAA

Ewing, Thomas John d1906 *PoIre*

Ewing, William *Alli Sup*

Ewing, William 1857- *WhLA*

Ewing, William Maurice 1906- *Au&Wr*

Ewington, H *Alli*

Ewy, Donna 1934- *ConAu 33*

Ewy, Rodger 1931- *ConAu 33*

Ex - R S M *ConAu XR*

Ex Constable Y *MnBBF*

Ex Private *MnBBF*

Exall, Barry *ConAu XR*

Exall, Henry *TexWr*

Exall, J *Alli*

Exall, Joseph *Alli*

Exall, Joshua *Alli*

Exarchopoulos, Nicolaos 1874- *WhLA*

Excoffon, Roger 1910- *WhGrA*

Exelby, J A *Alli Sup*

Exell, Frank Kingsley 1902- *ConAu 5R*

Exell, Joseph Samuel 1849- *Alli Sup*

Exeter, Bishop Of *BiDLA*

Exeter, Joseph Of *DcEnL*

Eximinez, Francesch d1409 *DcEuL*

Exley, Frederick 1930- *AuNews 2*, *ConLC 6*,
DrAF 1976

Exley, Thomas *BiDLA*

Exline, Frank 1858- *IndAu 1917*

Exman, Eugene 1900-1975 *ConAu 61*,
ConAu P-1

Exner, Max Joseph 1871- *WhWNAA*

Exon, Francis *Alli Sup*

Expilly, Jean Charles Marie 1814-1886 *BiD&SB*

Expilly, Jean-Joseph D' *OxFr*

Exton, Brudenot *Alli*

Exton, Clive 1930- *ConAu 61*, *ConDr*,
WrD 1976

Exton, John *Alli*

Exton, Richard Brudenell *Alli*, *Alli Sup*

Exton, William, Jr. 1907- *ConAu 45*,
WrD 1976

Exton-Smith, Arthur Norman 1920- *Au&Wr*

Exupery, Antoine DeSaint *ModRL*

Eybers, Elisabeth 1915- *CasWL*, *EncWL*,
Pen Cl

Eyck, Frank 1921- *ConAu 25*, *WrD 1976*

Eyck, Hubert Van 1366?-1420 *AtlBL*, *NewC*,
REn

Eyck, Jan Van 1386?-1440 *NewC*

Eyck, Pieter Nicolaas Van 1887-1954 *CasWL*

Eycleshymer, Albert Chauncey 1867-1925
DcNAA

Eye, The *ChPo S2*

Eye, August Von 1825-1896 *BiD&SB*

Eye, Glen G 1904- *ConAu 49*

Eye Witness *AmA&B*, *OxCan*

Eyen, Tom 1940- *ConAu 25*, *ConDr*,
WrD 1976

Eyerly, Jeannette Hyde 1908- *ConAu 1R*,
SmATA 4

Eyerman, John 1867- *DcAmA*

Eyestone, Robert 1942- *ConAu 41*

Eykman, Christoph 1937- *ConAu 41*

Eyler, Ervan Charles 1900- *WhWNAA*

Eyles, Edward Wells *Alli Sup*

Eyles, Leonora 1889-1960 *LongC*

Eyles, Wilfred Charles 1891- *ConAu 17*

Eyma, Louis Xavier 1816-1876 *BbD*, *BiD&SB*

Eyre, Mrs. *Alli Sup*

Eyre, Annette *WrD 1976*

Eyre, Beebe *Alli Sup*

Eyre, Belle *ChPo*

Eyre, Christian *Alli Sup*

Eyre, Edmund John 1767-1816 *Alli*, *BiD&SB*,
BiDLA

Eyre, Edward *Alli*, *BiDLA*

Eyre, Francis d1804 *Alli*

Eyre, Frank 1862- *ChPo*, *ChPo S1*, *ChPo S2*

Eyre, George *Alli Sup*

Eyre, Sir James 1734-1799 *Alli*

Eyre, Sir James 1792-1857 *Alli Sup*

Eyre, John *Alli*, *BiDLA*

Eyre, Joseph *Alli*

Eyre, Katherine Wigmore 1901-1970 *AmA&B*,
MorJA

Eyre, Laurence 1881-1959 *AmA&B*,
WhWNAA

Eyre, Lora Alice Moore *IndAu 1917*

Eyre, Mary *Alli Sup*

Eyre, R H S *Alli Sup*

Eyre, Richard *Alli*

Eyre, Richard M 1944- *ConAu 61*

Eyre, Robert *Alli*

Eyre, Robert 1922- *WrD 1976*

Eyre, S R 1922- *ConAu 23*

Eyre, Selwyn *Alli Sup*

Eyre, Simon d1459 *REn*

Eyre, Sir Vincent 1811-1881 *Alli*, *Alli Sup*

Eyre, William *Alli*

Eyre, William d1670 *Alli*

Eyre-Todd, George 1862- *ChPo*, *ChPo S1*,
WhLA

Eyres, Joseph *Alli*

Eysenck, Hans Jurgen 1916- *Au&Wr*,
ConAu 9R, *WrD 1976*

Eyssen, Marguerite Folsom 1893- *OhA&B*
Eysteinn Asgrimsson d1361 *EuA*
Eyster, C William 1917- *ConAu 29*
Eyster, Mrs. John Augustine English
  WhWNAA
Eyster, Nellie 1831-1922 *Alli Sup, AmA&B,
  BbD, BiD&SB, BiDSA, DcAmA,
  DcNAA*
Eyster, Penelope A Margaretta Blessing
  1831?-1922 *AmA&B*
Eyster, William R 1841-1918 *Alli Sup,
  AmA&B, HsB&A*
Eytel, Lola *ChPo S2*
Eyth, Eduard 1809-1884 *BiD&SB*
Eyth, Julie *BbD, BiD&SB*
Eyth, Max Von 1836-1906 *CasWL, EvEuW,
  OxGer*
Eytinge, Margaret *Alli Sup, AmA&B, ChPo,
  ChPo S1*
Eytinge, Pearl *ChPo*
Eytinge, Rose 1835-1911 *AmA, AmA&B,
  DcNAA*
Eytinge, Sol, Jr. 1833-1905 *ChPo, EarAB,
  EarAB Sup*
Eyton, Charlotte *Alli Sup*
Eyton, John *Alli, BiDLA*
Eyton, R M *Alli Sup*
Eyton, Robert *Alli Sup*
Eyton, Robert William 1815-1881 *Alli,
  Alli Sup*
Eyton, Thomas Campbell 1809-1880 *Alli,
  Alli Sup*
Eyuboglu, Bedri Rahmi 1913- *CasWL*
Ezekiel *DcOrL 3, REn*
Ezekiel, H C *BiDSA*
Ezekiel, Mordecai J B 1899?-1974 *ConAu 53,
  WhWNAA*
Ezekiel, Moses 1844-1917 *REnAL*
Ezekiel, Nissim 1924- *CasWL, ConAu 61,
  ConP 1970, ConP 1975, REn, WebEAL,
  WrD 1976*
Ezekiel, Nizzim 1921- *DcOrL 2*
Ezekiel, Raphael S 1931- *ConAu 53*
Ezell, Anna C 1885- *WhWNAA*
Ezell, Harry E 1918- *ConAu 1R*
Ezell, Helen Ingle 1903- *AmSCAP 66*
Ezell, John Samuel 1917- *ConAu 1R*
Ezera, Kalu 1925- *ConAu 13R*
Ezhutchachan *DcOrL 2*
Ezilie *BlkAW*
Eznik Of Kolb *CasWL*
Ezra *DcOrL 3*
Ezuttacchan *Pen Cl*
Ezzo Of Bamberg *CasWL, EvEuW*

F

F, E L *ChPo*
F, L N *PoIre*
F, S H *ChPo S1*
F G R *WhLA*
F P A *AmA&B, ConAmA, OxAm, TwCA, TwCA Sup, WhWNAA*
Fa-Hsien d420? *CasWL, DcOrL 1*
Faarah, Nuur 1850?-1930? *AfA 1, Pen Cl*
Faas, Larry A 1936- *ConAu 29*
Faasen, Pieter Jacobus 1833- *BbD, BiD&SB*
Faasen, Rosier 1833- *BiD&SB*
Faba, Guido *CasWL*
Fabbri, Cora Randall 1871-1892 *BiD&SB, ChPo S1, DcAmA, DcNAA*
Fabbri, Diego 1911- *CasWL, CnMD, CnThe, EncWL, McGWD, ModWD*
Fabel, Peter *NewC*
Fabell, Walter C *AuBYP*
Fabens, A E *ChPo*
Fabens, Joseph Warren 1821-1875 *Alli Sup, BiD&SB, DcAmA, DcNAA*
Faber, Mrs. *Alli Sup*
Faber, Arthur DeD *Alli Sup*
Faber, Arthur Henry *Alli Sup*
Faber, Cecilia Bohl De *BiD&SB*
Faber, Charles F 1926- *ConAu 29*
Faber, Christine *Alli Sup*
Faber, Doris 1924- *AuBYP, ConAu 17R, SmATA 3*
Faber, Francis Atkinson 1805-1876 *Alli Sup*
Faber, Francis William 1815-1863 *DcEnL*
Faber, Frederick William 1814-1863 *Alli, Alli Sup, BbD, BiD&SB, BrAu 19, ChPo, ChPo S2, Chmbr 3, DcLEnL, EvLB, NewC, OxEng, PoCh, WebEAL*
Faber, Geoffrey Cust 1889-1961 *ChPo, ChPo S2, NewC*
Faber, George Louis *Alli Sup*
Faber, George Stanley 1773-1854 *Alli, BiDLA, DcEnL*
Faber, Goldschmidt *WhLA*
Faber, Harman 1832-1913 *EarAB Sup*
Faber, Harold 1919- *AuBYP, ConAu 13R, SmATA 5*
Faber, Hermann *WhLA*
Faber, Hermann 1888- *WhLA*
Faber, John, Sr. *Alli*
Faber, John Henry 1918- *ConAu 13R, WrD 1976*
Faber, M A *Alli Sup*
Faber, M D 1936- *ConAu 29*
Faber, Nancy W 1909- *ConAu 5R*
Faber, Nicholas *Alli*
Faber, Peter Christian Frederik 1810-1877 *CasWL*
Faber, Richard Stanley 1924- *Au&Wr, ConAu 61*
Faber, Walter 1857-1928 *Br&AmS*
Faber, William E 1902- *AmSCAP 66*
Faber, William Frederic 1860-1934 *AmLY, DcNAA*

Fabes, Gilbert H *ChPo, ChPo S2*
Fabian Montes *PueRA*
Fabian, Donald L 1919- *ConAu 23*
Fabian, Josephine C 1903- *ConAu P-1*
Fabian, Max *WhWNAA*
Fabian, Robert d1513? *Alli, DcEnL, OxEng*
Fabigan, Hans 1901- *WhGrA*
Fabilli, Mary 1914- *ConP 1970*
Fabio, Sarah Webster 1928- *BlkAW, DrAP 1975, LivBA*
Fabius 1732-1808 *AmA, AmA&B*
Fabius Maximus Verrucosus, Quintus d203BC *NewC*
Fabius Pictor, Quintus *CasWL, Pen Cl*
Fabius Rusticus 030?-110 *Pen Cl*
Fable, Francois Joseph 1846- *BiD&SB*
Fabra, Pompeu 1869-1951 *CasWL*
Fabre, Amant Joseph 1842?- *BiD&SB*
Fabre, Emile 1869-1955 *McGWD, OxFr, Pen Eur*
Fabre, Ferdinand 1830-1898 *BbD, BiD&SB, EvEuW, OxFr*
Fabre, Hector 1834-1910 *BbtC, DcNAA, OxCan*
Fabre, Jean Henri 1823-1915 *AnCL, JBA 1934, JBA 1951, LongC, OxFr, REn*
Fabre, Jean Raymond Auguste 1792-1839 *BiD&SB*
Fabre, Michel J 1933- *ConAu 45*
Fabre, Victorin 1785-1831 *BiD&SB*
Fabre D'Eglantine, Philippe Francois N 1755-1794 *BbD, BiD&SB, CasWL, DcEuL, EvEuW, OxFr*
Fabre D'Olivet, Antoine 1767?-1825 *BiD&SB, OxFr*
Fabres, Oscar 1900- *ChPo S1, IlBYP, IlCB 1956*
Fabri, Cora Randall 1871-1892 *ChPo*
Fabri, Pierre 1460?-1520? *CasWL*
Fabri, Ralph 1894-1975 *ConAu 19, ConAu 57*
Fabriano, Gentile Da 1370?-1428 *AtlBL, REn*
Fabricant, Solomon 1906- *AmA&B*
Fabricius, Gaius d270?BC *REn*
Fabricius, Johan Wigmore 1899- *Au&Wr, CasWL, ConAu 53, EvEuW, IlCB 1945, TwCA, TwCA Sup*
Fabricius, Johann Albert 1668-1736 *DcEuL, EvEuW*
Fabricius, Johannes *OxGer*
Fabricius, Sara 1880- *Au&Wr*
Fabricius, Wilhelm 1857- *WhLA*
Fabricius Luscinus, Gaius d250?BC *NewC*
Fabritius, Carel 1622?-1654 *AtlBL*
Fabrizi, Cinzio Aloise *CasWL*
Fabrizio, Ray 1930- *ConAu 33*
Fabrizius, Peter *ConAu XR, WrD 1976*
Fabry, Joseph B 1909- *ConAu 25, WrD 1976*
Fabry, M F *ChPo*
Fabry, Rudolf 1915- *CasWL*
Fabrycky, Wolter Joseph 1932- *ConAu 21*
Fabun, Don 1920- *ConAu 45*

Fabyan, Robert d1513? *Alli, BrAu, Chmbr 1, DcEnL, EvLB, NewC, OxEng*
Facey, James William *Alli Sup*
Fack, Caroline *WhLA*
Fack, Kathe *WhLA*
Fack, L 1846- *WhLA*
Fackenheim, Emil L 1916- *ConAu 23, WrD 1976*
Facklam, Margery Metz 1927- *ConAu 5R*
Fackler, D Parks *Alli Sup*
Fackler, David Morris *Alli*
Fackler, S A 1857- *BiDSA*
Fackre, Gabriel Joseph 1926- *ConAu 17R*
Facos, James F 1924- *ChPo S1, ConAu 41*
Facy, William *Alli*
Faddegon, Barend 1874- *WhLA*
Faden, William *Alli, BiDLA*
Faden, William G *Alli*
Fader, Daniel 1930- *ConAu 33*
Faderman, Lillian 1940- *ConAu 33*
Fadette *AmA&B, DcNAA*
Fadeyev, Aleksandr Aleksandrovich 1901-1956 *CasWL, DcRusL, EncWL, EvEuW, ModSL 1, Pen Eur, REn, TwCW*
Fadeyev, Rostislav Andreievitch 1824-1884 *BbD, BiD&SB*
Fadiman, Clifton 1904- *AmA&B, ChPo S2, ConAu 61, RAdv 1, REnAL, TwCA, TwCA Sup*
Fadiman, Edwin, Jr. 1925- *ConAu 29*
Fadiman, James 1939- *ConAu 33*
Fadner, Frank 1910- *ConAu 9R*
Faed, John *ChPo S2*
Faed, Thomas 1826-1890 *ChPo, ChPo S1*
Faerno, Gabriel d1561 *ChPo*
Faesi, Robert 1883-1972 *CnMD, EncWL, EvEuW, OxGer, WhLA*
Faessler, Shirley *OxCan Sup*
Fafunwa, Babs 1940?- *AfA 1*
Fag, Frederick *DcEnL*
Fagan, Brian Murray 1936- *ConAu 41, WrD 1976*
Fagan, Charles Gregory d1885 *PoIre*
Fagan, Edward R 1924- *ConAu 9R*
Fagan, James Bernard 1873- *PoIre*
Fagan, James Octavius 1858- *AmA&B*
Fagan, Louis Alexander *Alli Sup*
Fagan, Thomas d1883 *PoIre*
Fagan, William Long 1838- *BiDSA, ChPo S1*
Fagas, Jimmie 1924- *AmSCAP 66*
Fage, John *Alli*
Fage, John Donnelly 1921- *ConAu 5R, WrD 1976*
Fage, Mary *Alli*
Fage, Robert *Alli*
Fagella, Anthony 1899- *AmSCAP 66*
Fagen, Richard R 1933- *ConAu 17R*
Fager, Charles E 1942- *ConAu 21*
Fagerberg, Sven Gustaf 1918- *CasWL*
Fagerstrom, Stan 1923- *ConAu 57*
Fagg, John Gerardus 1860-1917 *DcNAA*

Fagg, Sidney Vernon 1918- *Au&Wr,*
WrD 1976
Fagge, Charles Hilton 1838-1883 *Alli Sup*
Faggett, H L *BlkAW*
Faghani, Baba d1519 *CasWL*
Fagin, Larry *DrAP 1975*
Fagin, N Bryllion 1892- *AnMV 1926*
Fagiuoli, Giambattista 1660-1742 *BiD&SB*
Fagley, Frederick Louis 1879-1958 *AmA&B,*
OhA&B
Fagley, Richard M 1910- *ConAu 1R*
Fagnani, Charles Prospero 1854-1940 *DcNAA,*
WhWNAA
Fagothey, Austin 1901- *ConAu P-1*
Faguet, Emile 1847-1916 *BbD, BiD&SB,*
ClDMEuL, EuA, EvEuW, OxFr,
Pen Eur, REn
Fagundes, Joao Alvares *OxCan*
Fagundes Varela, Luis Nicolau 1841-1875
Pen Am
Fagundo, Ana Maria 1938- *ConAu 37*
Fagunwa, Daniel O 1910?-1963 *AfA 1, CasWL,*
Pen Cl, TwCW, WhTwL
Fagus 1872-1933 *ClDMEuL, OxFr*
Fagyas, Maria *ConAu 33*
Faherty, William B 1914- *ConAu 5R*
Fahey, Denis 1883- *CatA 1952*
Fahey, James, Jr. *BbtC*
Fahey, James C 1903-1974 *ConAu 53*
Fahey, John *WhPNW*
Fahey, John H 1873-1950 *AmA&B*
Fahie, A *Alli Sup*
Fahie, J J *Alli Sup*
Fahlcrantz, Christian Erik 1790-1866 *BbD,*
BiD&SB
Fahlcrantz, Kristian Erik 1790-1866 *DcEuL*
Fahler, Jarl Ingmar 1925- *BiDPar*
Fahnestock, Ruth *ChPo S1*
Fahnestock, Zephine Humphrey 1874- *AmA&B,*
WhWNAA
Fahrenheit, Gabriel Daniel 1686-1736 *REn*
Fahrenkrog, Ludwig Carl Wilhelm 1867- *WhLA*
Fahrner, Ignace 1865- *WhLA*
Fahrni, Margaret Morton *OxCan*
Fahs, Charles Harvey 1872- *WhWNAA*
Fahs, Ivan J 1932- *ConAu 45*
Fahy, Francis Arthur 1854- *Alli Sup, ChPo,*
ChPo S1, PoIre
Faidit, Gaucelm *BbD, BiD&SB, EvEuW*
Faiko, Alexey Mikhailovich 1893- *CasWL*
Fail, Noel Du 1520?-1591 *DcEuL*
Failing, Ida C *ChPo*
Faillet, Georges *OxFr*
Faillon, Etienne Michel 1799-1870 *BbtC,*
DcNAA, OxCan
Faillon, Michel Etienne 1799-1870 *BbD,*
BiD&SB
Fain, Haskell 1926- *ConAu 33*
Fain, Sammy 1902- *AmSCAP 66*
Fain, William 1917-1961 *AmA&B*
Fainlight, Harry *ConP 1970*
Fainlight, Ruth 1931- *ConAu 17R,*
ConP 1970, ConP 1975, WrD 1976
Fainsod, Merle 1907-1972 *AmA&B,*
ConAu 33, ConAu P-1
Fainzilberg, Ilya Arnoldovich 1897-1937 *CasWL,*
DcRusL
Fair, A A *ConAu XR, EncM&D, EvLB,*
LongC, Pen Am, TwCA Sup
Fair, C A 1923- *ConP 1970*
Fair, Campbell *Alli Sup*
Fair, Charles B 1921- *AmSCAP 66*
Fair, Charles M 1916- *ConAu 13R*
Fair, Eugene 1877-1937 *DcNAA, WhWNAA*
Fair, F M *Alli*
Fair, George *Alli, BiDLA*
Fair, Gordon Maskew 1894- *WhWNAA*
Fair, J Murray *WhWNAA*
Fair, James R, Jr. 1920- *ConAu 29*
Fair, LeRoy 1885-1970 *IndAu 1917*
Fair, Ray C 1942- *ConAu 29*
Fair, Ronald L 1932- *AmA&B, BlkAW,*
DrAP 1976, LivBA
Fair Fax *PueRA*
Fair Rosamond, The *NewC*
Fairall, Herbert S 1858-1907 *Alli Sup,*
DcNAA
Fairbairn *Alli*

Fairbairn, Mrs. *Alli Sup*
Fairbairn, Alexander *OxCan*
Fairbairn, Andrew Martin 1838-1912 *Alli Sup,*
BrAu 19, Chmbr 3
Fairbairn, Angus *ChPo S1*
Fairbairn, Ann 1902?-1972 *AmA&B,*
ConAu XR
Fairbairn, Arthur Rex Dugard 1904-1957
TwCW
Fairbairn, Douglas 1926- *ConAu 33,*
WrD 1976
Fairbairn, Helen *ConAu XR*
Fairbairn, Ian J 1933- *ConAu 53*
Fairbairn, James *Alli Sup*
Fairbairn, Mrs. James Angus *ChPo S1*
Fairbairn, John *Alli*
Fairbairn, John C *Alli Sup*
Fairbairn, John Clarkson 1809-1873 *ChPo S1*
Fairbairn, John Sheilds 1868- *WhLA*
Fairbairn, Margaret Waters 1825- *ChPo*
Fairbairn, Patrick 1805-1874 *Alli, Alli Sup*
Fairbairn, Robert Brinckerhoff 1818-1899
Alli Sup, DcAmA, DcNAA
Fairbairn, Sir Thomas *DcEnL*
Fairbairn, Sir William 1789-1874 *Alli Sup,*
DcEnL
Fairbairns, Zoe 1948- *Au&Wr, ConAu 29,*
WrD 1976
Fairbank, Alfred John 1895- *Au&Wr,*
ConAu 5R, WhGrA, WrD 1976
Fairbank, Calvin 1816-1898 *DcAmA, DcNAA*
Fairbank, H W *Alli Sup*
Fairbank, Janet Ayer 1878?-1951 *AmA&B,*
OxAm, TwCA, TwCA Sup, WhWNAA
Fairbank, John King 1907- *AmA&B,*
ConAu 1R
Fairbanks, Arthur 1864-1944 *DcAmA,*
DcNAA, WhWNAA
Fairbanks, Cassie *BbtC*
Fairbanks, Charles B *Alli Sup*
Fairbanks, Constance 1866- *ChPo*
Fairbanks, Douglas *WhWNAA*
Fairbanks, Edward Taylor 1836-1919 *AmLY,*
DcNAA
Fairbanks, Ernest E 1897- *WhWNAA*
Fairbanks, George Rainsford 1820-1906 *Alli,*
Alli Sup, BiDSA, DcAmA, DcNAA
Fairbanks, H F *Alli Sup*
Fairbanks, Harold Wellman 1860- *DcAmA,*
WhWNAA
Fairbanks, Lorenzo Sayles 1825-1897 *Alli Sup,*
DcAmA, DcNAA
Fairbanks, Nat *MnBBF*
Fairbanks, Sabrina *WhWNAA*
Fairbridge, Dorothea 1862-1931 *DcLEnL*
Fairbridge, Kingsley Ogilvie 1885-1924 *CasWL,*
DcLEnL
Fairbrother, Fred 1894- *Au&Wr*
Fairbrother, Nan 1913-1971 *ConAu 5R,*
ConAu 33
Fairburn, Arthur Rex Dugard 1904-1957
CasWL, ChPo S2, DcLEnL, LongC,
Pen Eng, WebEAL, WorAu
Fairburn, Eleanor 1928- *Au&Wr, ConAu 61,*
WrD 1976
Fairchild, Arthur Henry Rolph 1875-
WhWNAA
Fairchild, Ashbel Green 1795-1864 *Alli,*
AmA&B, BbD, BiD&SB, DcAmA,
DcNAA
Fairchild, Charles Bryant *Alli Sup*
Fairchild, Clarence *AmA&B*
Fairchild, David 1869-1954 *AmA&B,*
WhWNAA
Fairchild, Mrs. E A *Alli Sup*
Fairchild, E R *Alli Sup*
Fairchild, Edgar 1898- *AmSCAP 66*
Fairchild, Edward Henry 1816-1889 *OhA&B*
Fairchild, Edwin H *Alli Sup*
Fairchild, Edwin Milton 1865- *DcAmA*
Fairchild, Fred Rogers 1877- *WhWNAA*
Fairchild, George Moore 1854-1912 *Alli Sup,*
DcNAA, OxCan
Fairchild, George Thompson 1838-1901 *BiDSA,*
DcNAA, OhA&B
Fairchild, Helen 1845-1931 *DcNAA*
Fairchild, Henry Pratt 1880-1956 *AmA&B,*
TwCA Sup, WhWNAA

Fairchild, Herman LeRoy 1850-1943 *Alli Sup,*
DcAmA, DcNAA, WhWNAA
Fairchild, Hoxie Neale 1894-1973 *AmA&B,*
ConAu 5R, ConAu 45
Fairchild, James Harris 1817-1902 *Alli Sup,*
AmA&B, BbD, BiD&SB, DcAmA,
DcNAA, OhA&B
Fairchild, Louis W 1901- *AmA&B*
Fairchild, Lucius 1831-1896 *OhA&B*
Fairchild, M Augusta *Alli Sup*
Fairchild, Mary Salome 1855-1921 *AmA&B,*
DcAmA, DcNAA
Fairchild, Milton 1865- *WhWNAA*
Fairchild, Queenie *OxCan*
Fairchild, Ruth Moncrief *TexWr*
Fairchild, Thomas *Alli*
Fairchild, William *Au&Wr*
Fairclough, Daniel *Alli, NewC*
Fairclough, Henry Rushton 1862-1938 *AmLY,*
DcNAA, WhWNAA
Fairclough, John *Alli*
Fairclough, Samuel *Alli*
Fairclough, Thomas H 1905- *AmSCAP 66*
Fairfax, B *Alli*
Fairfax, Beatrice 1878?-1945 *AmA&B,*
DcNAA, RENAL
Fairfax, Brian *Alli*
Fairfax, Bryan *Alli*
Fairfax, Edward 1580?-1635? *Alli, BbD,*
BiD&SB, BrAu, CasWL, Chmbr 1,
CnE&AP, DcEnL, EvLB, NewC, REn
Fairfax, Lord Ferdinando d1648 *Alli*
Fairfax, James Griffyth 1886- *ChPo S2,*
WhLA
Fairfax, John *Alli, Alli Sup*
Fairfax, John 1930- *ConP 1970, ConP 1975,*
WrD 1976
Fairfax, John 1937- *ConAu 49*
Fairfax, L *Alli Sup, AmA&B, DcNAA,*
OhA&B
Fairfax, Marion *AmA&B, WhWNAA*
Fairfax, Nathaniel *Alli*
Fairfax, Thomas *Alli*
Fairfax, Lord Thomas 1612-1671 *Alli, NewC,*
Pen Eng, REn
Fairfax, Virginia *ChPo*
Fairfax, William *Alli*
Fairfax-Blakeborough, John 1883- *Au&Wr,*
Br&AmS, WhLA
Fairfax-Brown, Hilda *ChPo*
Fairfax-Lucy, Brian 1898- *ConAu 29,*
SmATA 6
Fairfield, Arthur R *Alli Sup*
Fairfield, Caroline E *DcNAA*
Fairfield, Cecily Isobel 1892- *DcLEnL*
Fairfield, Charles *MnBBF*
Fairfield, Cicily Isabel 1892- *EvLB, LongC,*
NewC, Pen Eng
Fairfield, Clarence *WhWNAA*
Fairfield, Edmund Burke 1821-1904 *DcNAA,*
OhA&B
Fairfield, Francis Gerry 1844-1887 *Alli Sup,*
DcAmA, DcNAA
Fairfield, Genevieve Genevra 1832- *Alli,*
BiD&SB, DcAmA
Fairfield, Ida *ChPo S1*
Fairfield, Jane Frazee 1810?- *Alli, Alli Sup,*
DcAmA, DcNAA
Fairfield, John *Alli, ConAu XR, WrD 1976*
Fairfield, Richard 1937- *ConAu 41*
Fairfield, Roy P 1918- *ConAu 33*
Fairfield, Sumner Lincoln 1803-1844 *Alli,*
AmA, BiD&SB, ChPo, CyAL 2,
DcAmA, DcLEnL, DcNAA, OxAm,
REnAL
Fairfield, Wynn Cowan 1886- *WhWNAA*
Fairflay, Francis *BbtC*
Fairholme, Elisabeth Carola 1910- *Au&Wr*
Fairholme, George *Alli*
Fairholt, Frederick William 1818?-1866 *Alli,*
Alli Sup, DcEnL
Fairlamb, J Remington *ChPo S1*
Fairlamb, Marian *ChPo S1*
Fairleigh, Frank *DcEnL, NewC*
Fairless, Michael 1869-1901 *ChPo S2,*
DcLEnL, EvLB, LongC, TwCA,
TwCA Sup
Fairless, William Dean *Alli Sup*

Fairley, Barker 1887- *Au&Wr, ConAu 1R*
Fairley, Edwin 1864-1941 *DcNAA*
Fairley, Margaret *OxCan*
Fairley, Michael Charles 1937- *ConAu 37, WrD 1976*
Fairley, Peter 1930- *ConAu 29*
Fairley, Ruth Ann 1924- *BlkAW*
Fairley, W *Alli Sup*
Fairlie, Mrs. *Alli*
Fairlie, Frank *ChPo S1*
Fairlie, Gerard 1889- *Au&Wr, EncM&D, MnBBF*
Fairlie, John Archibald 1872-1947 *DcAmA, DcNAA, WhWNAA*
Fairlie, Robert F *Alli Sup*
Fairlie, Walter *Alli Sup*
Fairly, T S *MnBBF*
Fairman, Captain *Alli, BiDLA*
Fairman, Charles 1897- *ConAu 45*
Fairman, Edward St. John *Alli Sup*
Fairman, George 1881-1962 *AmSCAP 66*
Fairman, Henry Clay 1849- *BiDSA*
Fairman, Joan Alexandra 1935- *ConAu 33, SmATA 10, WrD 1976*
Fairman, Seibert 1896- *WhWNAA*
Fairman, Virgil B *CatA 1947*
Fairman, William *Alli, BiDLA*
Fairmann, John *Alli Sup*
Fairmont, Ethel *WhWNAA*
Fairn, Duncan 1906- *Au&Wr, WrD 1976*
Fairweather, Ernest Reginald 1910- *Au&Wr*
Fairweather, George W 1921- *ConAu 13R*
Fairweather, James *Alli Sup*
Fairweather, Mabel L *ChPo S1*
Fairweather, Virginia 1922- *ConAu 29*
Fairwheater, Thomas *Alli*
Faison, Mabel Hubbard 1884-1946 *OhA&B*
Faissler, Margareta 1902- *ConAu 5R*
Fait, Hollis F 1918- *ConAu 1R*
Faith, Percy 1908- *AmSCAP 66*
Faith, Russell 1929- *AmSCAP 66*
Faithfull, Emily 1835-1895 *Alli Sup, DcEnL, HsB&A*
Faithfull, Mrs. Francis G *Alli Sup*
Faithfull, Gail 1936- *ConAu 57, SmATA 8*
Faithfull, James Grantham 1818-1873 *Alli Sup*
Faithfull, Lilian Mary 1865- *WhLA*
Faithorn, John *Alli, BiDLA Sup*
Faithorn, William 1656-1701 *ChPo*
Faithorne, William 1616-1691 *Alli*
Faitinelli, Pietro De' 1280?-1349 *CasWL*
Faiz, Faiz Ahmad *CasWL*
Faiz Ahmad Faiz 1912- *DcOrL 2*
Faizi, Abu'l-Faiz Mubarak-Shah 1547-1595 *CasWL*
Faizi, Shaikh Abu'l-Faiz 1547-1595 *DcOrL 2*
Fajans, Kasimir *WhLA*
Fakhr-Al-Din Jurjani, As'ad *CasWL*
Fakhry, Majid 1923- *ConAu 29*
Fakhuri, 'Umar 1895-1946 *DcOrL 3*
Fakirmohan Senapati *DcOrL 2*
Falaguera, Shemtob 1225?-1295? *CasWL*
Falardeau, Jean Charles *OxCan, OxCan Sup*
Falcao, Cristovao 1515?-1553? *CasWL, Pen Eur*
Falch, Andrew Emil 1876- *WhWNAA*
Falch, N *Alli*
Falciglia, Patrick 1942- *AmSCAP 66*
Falck, Colin 1934- *ConP 1975, WrD 1976*
Falck, Richard 1873- *WhLA*
Falcke, Eugene *Alli Sup*
Falco, Anthony M 1923- *AmSCAP 66*
Falco, Maria J 1932- *ConAu 61*
Falcon, Pierre 1793-1876 *OxCan*
Falcon, Richard *ConAu XR*
Falcon, Thomas *Alli*
Falcon, William *Alli*
Falcon, William D 1932- *ConAu 17R*
Falcon-Barker, Ted 1923- *Au&Wr, ConAu 25*
Falconar, Harriet 1774- *Alli, BiDLA, ChPo, ChPo S1*
Falconar, Maria 1772- *Alli, BiDLA, ChPo*
Falconbridge *OhA&B*
Falconbridge, Alex *Alli*
Falconbridge, Anna Maria *Alli, BiDLA*
Falconbridge, John Delatre 1875- *WhWNAA*
Falconer, Agnes S *ChPo S1, ChPo S2*
Falconer, Allan A *ChPo*

Falconer, David *Alli*
Falconer, Sir David *Alli*
Falconer, E J *ChPo*
Falconer, Edmund 1814-1879 *Alli Sup, PoIre*
Falconer, Harriet *BlkAW*
Falconer, Helen *Alli Sup*
Falconer, Hugh 1808-1865 *Alli, Alli Sup, ChPo*
Falconer, Ion Grant Neville Keith- 1856-1887 *Alli Sup*
Falconer, James *ConAu XR*
Falconer, John *Alli*
Falconer, Lance *BrAu 19, NewC*
Falconer, Magnus *Alli*
Falconer, Marie *BlkAW*
Falconer, Pearl *IlCB 1966*
Falconer, Randle Wilbraham 1816-1881 *Alli Sup*
Falconer, Richard *Alli*
Falconer, Sir Robert Alexander 1867-1943 *DcNAA*
Falconer, Thomas *Alli, BiDLA, BiDSA*
Falconer, Thomas d1839 *Alli*
Falconer, Thomas 1736-1792 *Alli, DcEnL*
Falconer, Thomas 1805-1882 *Alli Sup*
Falconer, Thomas, And Fitzherbert, E H *Alli*
Falconer, William *Alli Sup, Chmbr 2*
Falconer, William 1732?-1769 *Alli, BbD, BiD&SB, BrAu, CasWL, ChPo, ChPo S1, ChPo S2, DcEnA, DcEnL, DcLEnL, EvLB, NewC, OxEng, Pen Eng, WebEAL*
Falconer, William 1743?-1824 *Alli, BiDLA, NewC*
Faldo, John *Alli*
Faldo, Thomas *Alli*
Fale, Robert *Alli*
Fale, Thomas *Alli*
Falenski, Felicyan 1825- *BiD&SB*
Falero, Frank, Jr. 1937- *ConAu 37*
Fales, Edward Lippitt *Alli Sup, DcAmA*
Fales, Fanny *Alli, FemPA*
Fales, William R *Alli Sup*
Fales, Winnifred 1875- *WhWNAA*
Falgate, Isaac *Alli*
Faliero, Marino *REn*
Falih Rifki Atay 1894- *CasWL*
Falk, Adalbert 1827-1900 *OxGer*
Falk, Charles John 1899- *ConAu 23, IndAu 1917*
Falk, Elsa *ConAu XR*
Falk, H E *Alli Sup*
Falk, Hans 1918- *WhGrA*
Falk, Irving A 1921- *ConAu 23*
Falk, Johannes Daniel 1768-1826 *BiD&SB, OxGer*
Falk, K George 1880- *WhWNAA*
Falk, Leslie A 1915- *ConAu 9R*
Falk, Myron Samuel 1878-1945 *DcNAA*
Falk, Richard A 1930- *ConAu 5R*
Falk, Robert And Phipson, T H *Alli Sup*
Falk, Signi Lenea 1906- *ConAu 5R, WrD 1976*
Falk, Stanley Lawrence 1927- *ConAu 1R, WrD 1976*
Falk, Ze'ev W 1923- *ConAu 21, WrD 1976*
Falk-Roenne, Arne 1920- *ConAu 23*
Falkberget, Johan Petter 1879-1967 *CasWL, ClDMEuL, EncWL, Pen Eur, REn*
Falke, Friedrich 1871- *WhLA*
Falke, Gustav 1853-1916 *OxGer*
Falke, Jacob Von 1825-1897 *BbD, BiD&SB*
Falke, Konrad 1880-1942 *OxGer*
Falke, Otto 1862- *WhLA*
Falkenburg, Francis E *ChPo*
Falkener *Alli*
Falkener, Edward *Alli, Alli Sup*
Falkener, William *Alli*
Falkenhayn, Erich Von 1861-1922 *REn*
Falkenheiner, Wilhelm 1858- *WhLA*
Falkiner, Sir Frederick R 1831-1908 *PoIre*
Falkiner, Robert Henry *PoIre*
Falkirk, Richard *WrD 1976*
Falkirke, John De *Alli*
Falkland *Alli*
Falkland, Lord *OxCan*
Falkland, Viscount *Alli, CasWL*
Falkland, Charles, Viscount *Alli*

Falkland, Henry Cary, Viscount *DcEnL*
Falkland, Henry Cary, Viscount 1576-1633 *DcEnL*
Falkland, Lucius Cary, Viscount 1610?-1643 *DcEnL, NewC*
Falkland, Samuel *CasWL, EuA*
Falkland, W *Alli, BiDLA*
Falkner, C Litton *ChPo*
Falkner, Frederic *Alli*
Falkner, George *Alli Sup*
Falkner, John Meade 1858-1932 *CnMWL, DcLEnL, EvLB, LongC, REn, WhCL, WorAu*
Falkner, Leonard 1900- *ConAu 23, MnBBF, OhA&B, WhWNAA*
Falkner, Murry 1899- *ConAu 23*
Falkner, R *Alli Sup*
Falkner, Rhoda Ann 1826-1863 *BbtC*
Falkner, Robert Henry *Alli Sup*
Falkner, Thomas d1780 *Alli*
Falkner, W C *Alli Sup, BiDSA*
Falkner, William *Alli, AmA&B, ConAmA*
Falkner, William Cuthbert 1825?-1879? *DcLEnL, DcNAA, OxAm, Pen Am*
Falkner, William Harrison *EvLB*
Falkonberg, B E *Alli Sup*
Fall, Bernard B 1926-1967 *AmA&B, ConAu 1R, ConAu 25, WorAu*
Fall, Charles Gershom 1845-1932 *Alli Sup, AmLY, ChPo, DcAmA, DcNAA*
Fall, Delos 1848-1921 *DcAmA, DcNAA*
Fall, Frank Andrews 1878- *AmLY, WhWNAA*
Fall, Frieda Kay 1913- *ConAu 41*
Fall, Henry Clinton 1862-1939 *DcNAA, WhWNAA*
Fall, Howard Alex *IndAu 1917*
Fall, James *Alli*
Fall, Marcus *Alli Sup*
Fall, Thomas *Alli, AuBYP*
Falla, Frank W 1911- *Au&Wr*
Falla, Manuel De 1876-1946 *AtlBL, REn*
Fallada, Hans 1893-1947 *CasWL, EncWL, EvEuW, LongC, ModGL, OxGer, Pen Eur, REn, TwCA, TwCA Sup, WhTwL*
Fallal, Ferdinando *Alli*
Fallaw, Lance *ChPo*
Fallaw, Wesner 1907- *ConAu 1R*
Falle, Philip 1655-1742 *Alli*
Faller, Kevin 1920- *ConAu 53, ConP 1970, WrD 1976*
Fallere, Felicia 1948- *ConAu XR*
Fallers, Lloyd A 1925-1974 *ConAu 9R, ConAu 49*
Fallersleben, Hoffmann Von *REn*
Falligant, Robert 1839-1902 *BiDSA*
Fallis, Edwina H *ChPo, ChPo S1*
Fallis, Laurence S *DrAP 1975*
Fallmerayer, Jacob Philipp 1790-1861 *BbD, BiD&SB*
Fallon, Carlos 1909- *ConAu 41*
Fallon, Eunice *ChPo*
Fallon, Frederic 1944-1970 *ConAu 41*
Fallon, Mrs. G *PoIre*
Fallon, George *ConAu XR*
Fallon, Martin *ConAu XR, WrD 1976*
Fallon, Padraic 1905- *ConP 1970, ConP 1975*
Fallon, Patricia Ely *ChPo S1*
Fallon, S W *Alli Sup*
Fallon, Susan Ann *PoIre*
Falloon, Daniel d1862 *BbtC, DcNAA*
Falloon, William Marcus d1891 *Alli Sup, PoIre*
Falloux, Alfred Frederic Pierre 1811-1886 *BiD&SB*
Fallow, Burnett *ChPo, MnBBF*
Fallow, T M *Alli*
Fallowes, Thomas *Alli*
Fallowfield, J *Alli*
Fallowfield, John *Alli*
Fallows, Alice Katharine 1872-1932 *ChPo, DcNAA, WhWNAA*
Fallows, Edward Huntington 1865-1940 *DcNAA*
Fallows, James M 1949- *ConAu 45*
Fallows, Samuel 1835-1922 *Alli Sup, AmA&B, AmLY, DcAmA, DcNAA*
Falls, Charles Buckles 1874-1960 *AuBYP,*

*ChPo, ChPo S2, ConICB, IlCB 1945,
IlCB 1956, IndAu 1917, JBA 1934,
JBA 1951*
Falls, Cyril Bentham 1888- *ConAu P-1*
Falls, DeWitt Clinton 1864-1937 *DcNAA*
Fallstaff, Sir John *Alli*
Fallstrom, Daniel 1858-1937 *ClDMEuL*
Falorp, Nelson P *ConAu 49*
Falsen, Enevold De 1755-1808 *BiD&SB*
Falsen, Envold De 1755-1808 *DcEuL*
Falstaff Fakir *CasWL*
Falstaff, Jake *AmA&B, ChPo, DcNAA,
OhA&B*
Falstein, Louis 1909- *AmA&B*
Falster, Christian 1690-1752 *BiD&SB, CasWL,
DcEuL*
Falt, Clarence Manning d1912 *ChPo*
Falta, Wilhelm 1875- *WhLA*
Faludy, George 1913- *ConAu 21*
Faludy, Gyorgy 1913- *Pen Eur*
Fambri, Paul 1827?- *BbD, BiD&SB*
Fame, V *ChPo*
Family Doctor *WrD 1976*
Famularo, Joseph John 1922- *ConAu 1R*
Fan, Ch'eng-Ta 1126-1193 *CasWL*
Fan, Chung-Yen 989-1052 *CasWL*
Fan, Kuang Huan 1932- *ConAu 23*
Fan-Fan *OxCan*
Fanch, James *Alli*
Fancher, Ewilda 1928- *ConAu 61*
Fancourt, Charles St. John *Alli Sup*
Fancourt, Mary St. John 1898- *Au&Wr,
WrD 1976*
Fancourt, Samuel 1678-1768 *Alli, DcEuL*
Fancutt, Frank 1897- *Au&Wr*
Fancutt, Walter 1911- *Au&Wr, ConAu P-1,
WrD 1976*
Fandel, John *DrAP 1975*
Fander, John *Alli Sup*
Fandly, Juraj 1750-1811 *CasWL*
Fane, Mrs. Cecil *Alli Sup*
Fane, Lady Elizabeth *Alli*
Fane, Essex *MnBBF*
Fane, Florence *Alli Sup*
Fane, Sir Francis *Alli*
Fane, Henry Edward *Alli*
Fane, Julian 1827-1870 *Alli, BbD, ChPo,
ChPo S1, DcEnL*
Fane, Julian C H And Lytton, Robert E
Alli Sup
Fane, Julian Charles 1927- *Au&Wr,
ConAu 13R, WrD 1976*
Fane, Mildmay, Earl Of Westmorland
1602-1664? *CasWL*
Fane, Rupert *MnBBF*
Fane, Violet 1843-1905 *Alli Sup, BrAu 19,
ChPo, ChPo S1, ChPo S2, NewC*
Fanfani, Pietro 1815-1879 *BbD, BiD&SB*
Fang, Hsiao-Ju 1357-1402 *CasWL*
Fang, Irving E 1929- *ConAu 49*
Fang, Pao *DcOrL 1*
Fangen, Ronald August 1895-1946 *CasWL,
EncWL, EvEuW, Pen Eur, REn*
Fanger, Donald 1929- *ConAu 13R*
Fangor, Wojciech 1922- *WhGrA*
Fani *DcOrL 3*
Fanita *BlkAW*
Fann, Al *BlkAW*
Fann, Ernie *BlkAW*
Fann, K T 1937- *ConAu 61*
Fann, William E 1930- *ConAu 49*
Fannant, Edward *Alli*
Fannant, Thomas *Alli*
Fannin, David 1754?-1825 *BiDSA*
Fannin, John *Alli*
Fanning, David 1756?-1825 *DcAmA*
Fanning, Edmund 1737-1818 *OxCan*
Fanning, Edmund 1769-1841 *DcNAA*
Fanning, Golbert d1810 *Alli*
Fanning, John Thomas 1837-1911 *Alli Sup,
DcAmA, DcNAA*
Fanning, Leonard M 1888-1967 *ConAu 5R,
SmATA 5*
Fanning, Michael *PoIre*
Fanning, Nathaniel 1755-1805 *DcNAA*
Fanning, Odom 1920- *ConAu 53, WrD 1976*
Fannius, Gaius 145?BC- *Pen Cl*
Fanny, Aunt *ChPo*

Fanny Fern 1811-1872 *CyAL 2*
Fanny Forester *CyAL 2*
Fanny, Lord *NewC*
Fanon, Frantz 1925-1961 *WorAu*
Fansen, B *WhLA*
Fanshaw, Catherine Maria 1765-1834 *ChPo S1*
Fanshaw, Cecil *MnBBF*
Fanshaw, Sir Richard 1608-1666 *Alli*
Fanshaw, Sir Thomas *Alli*
Fanshawe, Lady *Chmbr 1*
Fanshawe, Lady Anne Harrison 1625-1680 *Alli,
BiD&SB, BrAu, OxEng*
Fanshawe, Catherine Maria 1765-1834 *Alli,
BiD&SB, BrAu 19, ChPo, ChPo S2,
Chmbr 2, DcEnL, DcLEnL, EvLB,
NewC, OxEng*
Fanshawe, Cecil *MnBBF*
Fanshawe, Cyril Aston *Alli Sup*
Fanshawe, Sir Richard 1608-1666 *BrAu,
CasWL, ChPo, Chmbr 1, DcEnL, EvLB,
NewC, Pen Eng, WebEAL*
Fansler, Dean Spruill 1885- *WhWNAA*
Fansler, Harriott Ely *WhWNAA*
Fant, Erik Michael 1754-1817 *DcEuL*
Fant, Joseph Lewis, III 1928- *ConAu 13R*
Fant, Louis J, Jr. 1931- *ConAu 37*
Fanta, J Julius 1907- *ConAu 33*
Fantasio *WhWNAA*
Fante, John 1911- *AmA&B, OxAm, TwCA,
TwCA Sup*
Fantel, Hans 1922- *ConAu 49*
Fantham, Harold Benjamin *WhLA*
Fantin-Latour, Ignace Henri J T 1836-1904
AtlBL, OxFr
Fantl, Kurt 1914- *BiDPar*
Fantoni, Giovanni 1755-1807 *CasWL, EvEuW*
Fantosme, Jordan *OxFr*
Fantus, Bernard 1874- *WhWNAA*
Fanu, Joseph Sheridan Le *BrAu 19*
Farabee, Barbara 1944- *ConAu 57*
Farabee, William Curtis 1865-1925 *AmA&B,
DcNAA*
Farabi, Al- 870?-950 *CasWL*
Farabi, Abu Nasr Muhammad B M B T U Al-
870?-950 *DcOrL 3*
Faraday, Frederick J *Alli Sup*
Faraday, Michael 1791-1867 *Alli, Alli Sup,
BbD, BiD&SB, BrAu 19, Chmbr 3,
DcEnL, EvLB, NewC, OxEng, REn*
Faraday, Wilfred Barnard 1874- *WhLA*
Farago, Ladislas 1906- *AmA&B*
Farah, Caesar Elie 1929- *ConAu 41*
Farah, Nuruddin 1945- *AfA 1*
Farah, Theodore Khalil 1909- *WhWNAA*
Faralla, Dana 1909- *AmA&B, AmNov,
ConAu 49, SmATA 9*
Faralla, Dorothy W *ConAu 49, SmATA XR*
Faram, John *Alli Sup*
Farau, Alfred 1904-1972 *ConAu 37*
Faraud, Henri *OxCan*
Farazdaq, Al- *CasWL*
Farb, Peter 1929- *AmA&B, Au&Wr,
ConAu 13R*
Farber, Bernard 1922- *ConAu 23*
Farber, Burton A 1913- *AmSCAP 66*
Farber, Donald C *ConAu 29*
Farber, Edith A *ChPo*
Farber, John Clarke 1893- *IndAu 1917*
Farber, Joseph C 1903- *ConAu 33*
Farber, Marvin 1901- *AmA&B, ConAu 49*
Farber, Milton L 1902- *OhA&B*
Farber, Nathaniel C 1918- *AmSCAP 66*
Farber, Seymour M 1912- *ConAu 57*
Farber, William Sims 1885-1963 *IndAu 1917*
Farberman, Harold 1930- *AmSCAP 66*
Farberman, Harvey A 1939- *ConAu 45*
Farberow, Norman L 1918- *ConAu 17R*
Farbrick, Jonathan *DcNAA*
Farbrother, J C *Alli Sup*
Farbrother, Roger *Alli*
Farbstein, W E *ChPo*
Farca, Marie C 1935- *ConAu 37*
Fardd, Eben 1802-1863 *ChPo S1*
Fardely, William *BiDLA*
Fardley, William *Alli*
Fardo, George *ChPo*
Farebrother, A *Alli Sup*
Farel, Conrad *ConAu XR*

Farel, Guillaume 1489-1565 *OxFr*
Farely, Alison *WrD 1976*
Farer, Tom J 1935- *ConAu 17R*
Faret, Nicolas 1600?-1646 *OxFr*
Farewell *Alli*
Farewell, James *Alli, PoIre*
Farewell, Nina *ConAu XR*
Farey, John 1766-1826 *Alli, BiDLA*
Farge *TwCA, TwCA Sup*
Fargis, Paul 1939- *ConAu 21*
Fargo, Doone *ConAu XR, WrD 1976*
Fargo, Joe *ConAu XR*
Fargo, Lucille Foster 1880- *AuBYP, OhA&B*
Fargo, Ruth 1870- *WhWNAA*
Fargue, Leon-Paul 1876-1947 *CasWL,
ClDMEuL, EncWL, EvEuW, OxFr,
Pen Eur, REn, WorAu*
Fargus, Frederick John 1847-1885 *Alli Sup,
BbD, BiD&SB, BrAu 19, NewC*
Farhi, Musa Moris 1935- *Au&Wr, WrD 1976*
Faria, Fenasco *Alli*
Faria, Manoel Severim De 1583-1655 *BiD&SB*
Faria, Otavio De 1908- *Pen Am*
Faria E Sousa, Manuel 1590-1649 *CasWL*
Faria Y Sousa, Manoel De 1590-1649 *BiD&SB,
DcEuL*
Faribault, George Barthelemi 1789-1866 *BbtC,
DcNAA*
Faribault, Marcel *OxCan Sup*
Faricy, Robert L 1926- *ConAu 37, WrD 1976*
Farid *DcOrL 2*
Farid d1552 *DcOrL 2*
Faridi, S N *ConAu XR*
Faridi, Shah Nasir 1929- *ConAu 29,
WrD 1976*
Faries, Clyde J 1928- *ConAu 37*
Farigoule, Louis 1885-1972 *ConAu 37, LongC,
REn*
Farina, Richard 1936?-1966 *AmA&B,
ConAu 25*
Farina, Salvatore 1846-1918 *BbD, BiD&SB,
ClDMEuL*
Farindon, Anthony 1596-1658 *Alli*
Farinelli 1705-1782 *REn*
Faringdon, Anthony 1596-1658 *Alli*
Farington *Alli*
Farington, Miss And Raines, R F *Alli Sup*
Farington, Joseph 1747-1821? *Alli, BkIE,
Chmbr 3*
Farington, William *Alli*
Farini, Carlo Luigi 1812-1866 *BbD, BiD&SB*
Farini, G A *Alli Sup*
Faris, John Thomson 1871-1949 *AmA&B,
CarSB, DcNAA, WhWNAA*
Faris, Lillie Anne 1868-1945 *OhA&B*
Faris, Robert E L 1907- *ConAu 17R*
Faris, Selim *Alli Sup*
Faris, William W *Alli Sup*
Farish, Charles *Alli, BiDLA*
Farish, John *Alli, BiDLA*
Farish, Margaret Kennedy 1918- *ConAu 5R*
Farish, W B *BiDLA*
Farish, William *Alli, BiDLA Sup*
Faritius d1117 *BiB N*
Farjeon, Annabel 1919- *ConAu 53*
Farjeon, Benjamin Leopold 1838-1903 *Alli Sup,
BbD, BiD&SB, BrAu 19, Chmbr 3,
DcBiA, DcEnL, DcLEnL, EncM&D,
HsB&A, NewC*
Farjeon, Eleanor 1881-1965 *AnCL, AuBYP,
BkCL, CasWL, CatA 1952, ChPo,
ChPo S1, ChPo S2, ConAu P-1, DcLEnL,
JBA 1934, JBA 1951, LongC, NewC,
SmATA 2, St&VC, TwCA, TwCA Sup,
TwCW, WhCL*
Farjeon, Eve Annabel 1919- *Au&Wr*
Farjeon, Herbert 1887-1945 *DcLEnL, EvLB,
NewC, Pen Eng*
Farjeon, Herbert 1887-1946 *TwCW*
Farjeon, Joan Jefferson 1913- *IlCB 1956*
Farjeon, Joseph Jefferson 1883-1955 *MnBBF,
NewC, TwCA, TwCA Sup*
Farkas, Philip 1914- *ConAu 49*
Farleigh, John 1900-1965 *LongC*
Farler, John Prediger *Alli Sup*
Farley, C R L *MnBBF*
Farley, Carol 1936- *ConAu XR, SmATA 4,
WrD 1976*

Farley, Charles 1771-1859 *NewC*
Farley, Edward *Alli, BiDLA*
Farley, Edward 1929- *ConAu 61*
Farley, Edward J 1904- *AmSCAP 66*
Farley, Eugene J 1916- *ConAu 33*
Farley, Fawle Egbert Griffith 1922- *Au&Wr*
Farley, Frank Edgar 1868-1943 *AmA&B*
Farley, Frederick Augustus 1800-1892 *DcAmA,*
DcNAA
Farley, Harriet 1817-1907 *Alli, Alli Sup,*
AmA, AmA&B, BbD, BiD&SB, CarSB,
CyAL 2, DcAmA, DcNAA, OxAm,
REnAL
Farley, Henry *Alli, ChPo*
Farley, J *Alli*
Farley, James Aloysius 1888- *CatA 1952*
Farley, James Lewis 1823-1885 *Alli Sup,*
BiD&SB, NewC
Farley, Jean 1928- *ConAu 23, DrAP 1975*
Farley, John Murphy 1842-1918 *DcNAA*
Farley, Miriam Southwell 1907?-1975
ConAu 57
Farley, Philip *Alli Sup*
Farley, Ralph Milne *WorAu*
Farley, Rawle 1922- *ConAu 45, WrD 1976*
Farley, Robert *Alli, CasWL*
Farley, Robert E *ChPo*
Farley, Roland 1892-1932 *AmSCAP 66*
Farley, Walter 1915- *AuBYP, ConAu 17R,*
JBA 1951, MorBMP, SmATA 2
Farley, William Meymott *Alli Sup*
Farlie, Robert *Alli, CasWL*
Farlow, John Woodford 1853-1937 *DcNAA*
Farlow, William Gilson 1844-1919 *Alli Sup,*
BbD, BiD&SB, DcAmA, DcNAA
Farmacevten *ConAu XR*
Farman, Elbert Eli 1831-1911 *DcNAA*
Farman, Ella 1843-1907 *Alli Sup, AmA&B,*
BiD&SB, CarSB, ChPo, ChPo S1,
DcAmA
Farman, Samuel *Alli Sup*
Farmer, A W *Alli, DcNAA*
Farmer, Albert J 1894- *ConAu 23, WrD 1976*
Farmer, August Neustadt 1872- *WhWNAA*
Farmer, Bernard James 1902- *ConAu 5R,*
WhWNAA
Farmer, Bertram Hughes 1916- *Au&Wr,*
WrD 1976
Farmer, C M *BiDSA*
Farmer, Charles J 1943- *ConAu 57*
Farmer, Clarence *BlkAW*
Farmer, Edith *ChPo*
Farmer, Edward *ChPo*
Farmer, Elihu Jerome 1836-1900 *Alli Sup,*
DcAmA, DcNAA, OhA&B
Farmer, Ethel *ChPo*
Farmer, Fannie Merritt 1857-1915 *AmA&B,*
DcAmA, DcNAA, REnAL
Farmer, Frank Lethbridge *Alli Sup*
Farmer, Gary R 1923- *ConAu 57*
Farmer, Gene 1919-1972 *ConAu 37*
Farmer, Henry *MnBBF*
Farmer, Henry Tudor 1782-1828 *Alli, AmA&B,*
BiD&SB, BiDSA, CyAL 1, DcAmA,
DcNAA
Farmer, Herbert Henry 1892- *Au&Wr*
Farmer, Hugh 1714-1787 *Alli, NewC*
Farmer, Jacob *Alli*
Farmer, James 1920- *AmA&B*
Farmer, James Eugene 1867-1915 *AmA&B,*
DcAmA, DcNAA, OhA&B
Farmer, John *Alli, NewC*
Farmer, John 1789-1838 *Alli, AmA, AmA&B,*
CyAL 2, DcAmA, DcNAA
Farmer, John 1798-1859 *DcAmA, DcNAA*
Farmer, John S *Alli Sup*
Farmer, Lydia Hoyt 1842-1903 *Alli Sup,*
AmA&B, BiD&SB, DcAmA, DcNAA,
OhA&B
Farmer, Martha L 1912- *ConAu 23*
Farmer, Nell R 1876- *WhWNAA*
Farmer, Penelope 1939- *AuBYP, ConAu 13R,*
WrD 1976
Farmer, Peter *ConAu XR*
Farmer, Philip Jose 1918- *AmA&B,*
ConAu 1R, ConLC 1, DrAF 1976,
IndAu 1917
Farmer, R *Alli, BiDLA*

Farmer, R L *ConAu XR*
Farmer, Richard *Alli, Chmbr 2*
Farmer, Richard d1814 *Alli, BiDLA Sup*
Farmer, Richard 1735-1797 *Alli, DcEnL,*
EvLB, NewC, Pen Eng
Farmer, Richard Neil 1928- *ConAu 17R,*
WrD 1976
Farmer, Robert Allen 1938- *ConAu 23*
Farmer, Sarah Stock *Alli Sup*
Farmer, Silas 1839-1902 *Alli Sup, DcAmA,*
DcNAA
Farmer, Thomas *Alli*
Farmer, Wendell *AuBYP*
Farmer, William *Alli*
Farmer George 1738-1820 *NewC, REn*
Farmer Smith *WhWNAA*
Farmerie, William *Alli*
Farmers, Eileen Elizabeth 1918- *Au&Wr*
Farmiloe, Dorothy Alicia 1920- *ConAu 61,*
OxCan Sup, WrD 1976
Farmiloe, Edith *ChPo S1*
Farmlet, Charles *Alli Sup*
Farn, J C *Alli Sup*
Farnabie, Thomas 1575-1647 *Alli*
Farnaby, Giles *Alli*
Farnaby, Thomas 1575-1647 *Alli*
Farnam, Charles Henry 1846-1909 *Alli Sup,*
DcNAA
Farnam, Henry Walcott 1853-1933 *DcAmA,*
DcNAA
Farnash, Hugh *ConAu XR*
Farnborough, Baron *EvLB, NewC*
Farndale, James 1916- *ConAu 25, WrD 1976*
Farndale, W A J 1916- *WrD 1976*
Farnell, Charles Anson *Alli Sup*
Farnell, Frederic James 1885- *WhWNAA*
Farnell, Lewis Richard 1856- *Alli Sup, WhLA*
Farner, Donald S 1915- *ConAu 53*
Farneworth, Ellis d1762 *Alli*
Farnfield, William Henry *Alli Sup*
Farnham, Barry Maxwell *Alli*
Farnham, Burt *ConAu XR, SmATA XR*
Farnham, Charles Haight 1841-1929 *DcAmA,*
DcNAA
Farnham, Eliza Woodson 1815-1864 *Alli,*
Alli Sup, AmA, AmA&B, BbD,
BiD&SB, CyAL 2, DcAmA, DcNAA
Farnham, J J *Alli Sup*
Farnham, Jessie *ChPo S1*
Farnham, John Marshall Willoughby 1829-
DcAmA
Farnham, Luther 1816- *CyAL 2*
Farnham, M W *Alli Sup*
Farnham, Mateel Howe d1957 *AmA&B*
Farnham, Thomas J 1938- *ConAu 53*
Farnham, Thomas Jefferson 1804-1848 *AmA,*
AmA&B, DcAmA, DcNAA
Farnham, Willard Edward 1891- *AmA&B,*
Au&Wr
Farnie, Henry Brougham d1889 *Alli Sup,*
ChPo
Farnill, Barrie 1923- *WrD 1976*
Farningham, Marianne *Alli Sup, ChPo,*
ChPo S1, ChPo S2
Farnol, Jeffery 1878-1952 *NewC, REn, TwCA,*
TwCA Sup, WhLA
Farnol, Jeffrey 1878-1952 *LongC, TwCW*
Farnol, John Jeffrey 1878-1952 *Chmbr 3,*
DcLEnL, EvLB
Farnsworth, Charles Hubert 1859-1947 *AmA&B,*
DcNAA
Farnsworth, Dana 1905- *ConAu 61*
Farnsworth, Dorothy McPherson *ChPo*
Farnsworth, E Allan 1928- *ConAu 13R*
Farnsworth, F F 1869- *WhWNAA*
Farnsworth, Jerry 1895- *ConAu P-1*
Farnsworth, Lee W 1932- *ConAu 33*
Farnsworth, Paul Randolph 1899- *ConAu 29*
Farnsworth, Robert M 1929- *ConAu 53*
Farnum, Alexander 1830-1884 *Alli Sup,*
DcNAA
Farnum, Mabel Adelaide *BkC 1, CatA 1947*
Farnwald *CasWL*
Farnworth, Richard *Alli*
Farnworth, Warren 1935- *WrD 1976*
Farny, Henry F 1847-1916 *ChPo, OhA&B*
Farny, Margaret Withrow 1898- *OhA&B*
Faron, Louis C 1923- *ConAu 9R*

Farquar, Agnes Stephens *WhWNAA*
Farquhar, Arthur Briggs 1838-1925 *DcNAA*
Farquhar, B H *ChPo S2*
Farquhar, Barbara H *Alli Sup*
Farquhar, David *Alli*
Farquhar, Edward *ChPo S2*
Farquhar, Edward 1843-1905 *DcNAA*
Farquhar, Ferdinand *Alli*
Farquhar, Francis P 1887-1975 *ConAu 57,*
ConAu P-1
Farquhar, George 1678-1707 *Alli, AtlBL, BbD,*
BiD&SB, BrAu, CasWL, Chmbr 2,
CnThe, CriT 2, CyWA, DcEnA, DcEnL,
DcLEnL, EvLB, McGWD, MouLC 2,
NewC, OxEng, Pen Eng, PoIre, REn,
REnWD, WebEAL
Farquhar, George G *MnBBF*
Farquhar, George Taylor Shillito 1857-1927
ChPo S2
Farquhar, Henry 1851-1925 *DcNAA*
Farquhar, James Shaw 1890- *WhWNAA*
Farquhar, James Taylor Floyd 1858- *ChPo S1*
Farquhar, Jane Allardice 1845- *ChPo*
Farquhar, John *Alli*
Farquhar, John Nicol 1861- *WhLA*
Farquhar, Maria *Alli Sup*
Farquhar, R *Alli Sup*
Farquhar, Robert *OhA&B*
Farquhar, Robert Townsend *Alli, BiDLA*
Farquhar, Ross 1883-1938 *OhA&B*
Farquhar, William *Alli Sup*
Farquhar, William Henry *Alli Sup*
Farquhar-Bernard *Alli Sup*
Farquharson, Finlay 1810?- *ChPo S1*
Farquharson, George *Alli, BiDLA*
Farquharson, Martha 1828-1909 *Alli Sup,*
AmA, AmA&B, BiDSA, DcAmA,
DcNAA, OhA&B, OxAm, WhCL
Farquharson, Rica *OxCan*
Farquharson, Robert *Alli Sup*
Farquharson, T *BiDLA*
Farquharson, William *Alli*
Farr, Alfred Derek 1930- *Au&Wr, WrD 1976*
Farr, David M L 1922- *Au&Wr, ConAu 37,*
OxCan Sup
Farr, Diana Pullein-Thompson *ConAu 13R*
Farr, Douglas *ConAu XR*
Farr, Edward *Alli, Alli Sup*
Farr, Finis 1904- *ConAu 1R, SmATA 10*
Farr, Frederic William 1860-1939 *DcNAA*
Farr, Judith 1936- *ConAu 29*
Farr, Michael Bryant 1924- *Au&Wr,*
ConAu 29
Farr, Muriel *ChPo S2*
Farr, Roger C *ConAu 33*
Farr, Ronald Lewis *BlkAW*
Farr, Samuel 1741-1795 *Alli*
Farr, T J 1902-1962 *AmA&B*
Farr, William *Alli*
Farr, William 1807-1883 *Alli Sup*
Farra, Madame E *ConAu XR*
Farragher, Shaun *DrAP 1975*
Farragut, Jack *HsB&A*
Farragut, Loyall *Alli Sup*
Farrah, Mary J *ChPo S1, ChPo S2*
Farran, Don *ChPo S2*
Farran, Roy Alexander 1921- *Au&Wr,*
WrD 1976
Farrand, Banks *Alli Sup*
Farrand, Elizabeth Martha d1900 *Alli Sup,*
DcNAA
Farrand, Miss H A *Alli Sup*
Farrand, Livingston 1867-1939 *AmA&B,*
DcNAA
Farrand, Max 1869-1945 *AmA&B, AmLY,*
DcNAA, WhWNAA
Farrand, Sarah Ann *Alli Sup*
Farrant, Henry *Alli*
Farrant, Leda 1927- *ConAu 21*
Farrant, Richard d1585? *Alli*
Farrar, Adam Storey 1826- *Alli Sup*
Farrar, C C S *Alli Sup*
Farrar, C S *BiDSA*
Farrar, Charles Alden John d1893 *Alli Sup,*
BiD&SB, DcAmA, DcNAA
Farrar, Charles S *Alli Sup*
Farrar, E R *Alli Sup*
Farrar, E W *ChPo S2*

Farrar, Edgar Howard 1849-1922 *DcNAA*
Farrar, Eliza Ware 1791-1870 *Alli, Alli Sup,*
  AmA&B, BiD&SB, DcAmA, DcNAA
Farrar, F S *OxCan*
Farrar, Frank R d1897 *BiDSA*
Farrar, Frederick William 1831-1903 *Alli Sup,*
  BbD, BiD&SB, BrAu 19, CasWL, ChPo,
  Chmbr 3, DcEnA, DcEnA Ap, DcEnL,
  EvLB, NewC, Pen Eng, WhCL
Farrar, Geraldine 1882- *AmSCAP 66, REn*
Farrar, Irene *BiDSA*
Farrar, James McNall 1853-1921 *AmLY,*
  DcNAA
Farrar, John 1799-1853 *DcNAA*
Farrar, John 1802-1884 *Alli, Alli Sup*
Farrar, John Chipman 1896-1974 *AmA&B,*
  ChPo, ChPo S1, ChPo S2, ConAu 53,
  REnAL, St&VC
Farrar, John Martindale *Alli Sup*
Farrar, Joseph *Alli Sup*
Farrar, Lancelot Leighton, Jr. 1932- *ConAu 53*
Farrar, Larston Dawn 1915-1970 *ConAu 1R,*
  ConAu 29
Farrar, Mary J *ChPo*
Farrar, Maurice *Alli Sup*
Farrar, R Henry *Alli Sup*
Farrar, Richard *Alli*
Farrar, Ronald Truman 1935- *ConAu 33,*
  WrD 1976
Farrar, Thomas *Alli Sup*
Farrar, Thomas, Jr. *Alli Sup*
Farrar, Thomas James 1869- *WhWNAA*
Farrar, Timothy 1788-1874 *Alli, Alli Sup,*
  CyAL 2, DcAmA, DcNAA
Farrar, Walton T 1918- *AmSCAP 66*
Farrar-Hockley, Anthony Heritage 1924-
  Au&Wr
Farre, Gerard *Alli Sup*
Farre, John Richard 1775- *Alli, BiDLA,*
  BiDLA Sup
Farre, Rowena *Au&Wr*
Farre, Samuel *Alli, BiDLA Sup*
Farrel SEE ALSO Farrell
Farrel, Mrs. *Alli*
Farrel, Bryan Henry 1923- *Au&Wr*
Farrel, Charles *Alli*
Farrel, George *Alli*
Farrel, James A *Alli*
Farrel, John *Alli*
Farrel, R *Alli*
Farrell SEE ALSO Farrel
Farrell, Mrs. *BiDLA*
Farrell, Alan 1920- *Au&Wr, ConAu 13R*
Farrell, Andrew 1889-1938 *IndAu 1917*
Farrell, Anne A 1916- *ConAu 25*
Farrell, Barry *OxCan Sup*
Farrell, Ben *ConAu XR, SmATA XR,*
  WrD 1976
Farrell, Bryan Henry 1923- *ConAu 49*
Farrell, Catharine *ConAu XR*
Farrell, David *ConAu XR, WrD 1976*
Farrell, Desmond *ConAu XR*
Farrell, Gabriel 1886- *AmA&B*
Farrell, Hugh *PoIre*
Farrell, J *Alli Sup*
Farrell, J G 1935- *Au&Wr, ConLC 6,*
  ConNov 1972, ConNov 1976, WrD 1976
Farrell, J R *ChPo S2*
Farrell, James T 1904- *AmA&B, AmWr,*
  CasWL, CnDAL, ConAmA, ConAu 5R,
  ConLC 1, ConLC 4, ConNov 1972,
  ConNov 1976, CyWA, DcLEnL,
  DrAF 1976, EncWL, EvLB, LongC,
  ModAL, OxAm, Pen Am, RAdv 1, REn,
  REnAL, TwCA, TwCA Sup, TwCW,
  WebEAL, WhTwL, WrD 1976
Farrell, James T 1907- *AmNov*
Farrell, John *BiDLA, Chmbr 3*
Farrell, John 1851-1904 *DcLEnL, PoIre*
Farrell, John 1889- *Au&Wr*
Farrell, John T *BlkAW*
Farrell, Joseph 1841-1885 *Alli Sup, PoIre*
Farrell, Kathleen Amy 1912- *Au&Wr,*
  ConAu 5R
Farrell, Kirby 1942- *ConAu 33*
Farrell, M *PoIre*
Farrell, M J 1905- *Br&AmS*
Farrell, Matthew Charles 1921- *ConAu 49*

Farrell, Melvin L 1930- *ConAu 13R*
Farrell, Morgan 1885- *WhWNAA*
Farrell, Ned E *Alli Sup*
Farrell, Patricia *ConAu XR*
Farrell, R *BiDLA*
Farrell, Walter 1902- *CatA 1947*
Farrelly, M John 1927- *ConAu 13R*
Farren, Edwin James *Alli*
Farren, Elizabeth 1759-1829 *NewC*
Farren, F C *Alli Sup*
Farren, George *Alli*
Farren, Richard J *ConAu XR*
Farren, Richard M *WrD 1976*
Farren, Robert *Alli Sup*
Farren, Robert 1909- *BkC 4, CatA 1947,*
  ConP 1970
Farren, William 1786-1861 *NewC*
Farrens, Howard *TexWr*
Farrer, David 1906- *ConAu 25*
Farrer, E *Alli, BiDLA*
Farrer, Edmund *Alli Sup*
Farrer, Georgiana *Alli Sup*
Farrer, Henrietta Louisa *Alli Sup*
Farrer, Isaac *Alli*
Farrer, James *Alli Sup*
Farrer, James Anson 1849- *Alli Sup*
Farrer, John *Alli, BiDLA, BiDLA Sup*
Farrer, Katharine Dorothy 1911- *Au&Wr,*
  ConAu 5R
Farrer, Mary *Alli*
Farrer, Richard Ridley *Alli Sup*
Farrer, Sir Thomas Henry 1819-1899 *Alli Sup,*
  NewC
Farrer, William *Alli*
Farrere, Claude 1876-1957 *CasWL, EncWL,*
  EvEuW, OxFr
Farres, Captain *Alli*
Farresley, Thomas *Alli*
Farrien *ChPo*
Farrier, J *ChPo S1*
Farries, Francis Wallace 1840- *DcAmA*
Farries, Richard Spearman E *Alli Sup*
Farries, Thomas *Alli Sup*
Farrimond, John 1913- *Au&Wr, WrD 1976*
Farrington, Reverend *Alli*
Farrington, Alice M *ChPo*
Farrington, Benjamin 1891-1974 *Au&Wr,*
  ConAu 53
Farrington, Dora Davis 1880- *WhWNAA*
Farrington, Edward Holyoke 1860-1934 *DcNAA,*
  WhWNAA
Farrington, Fielden 1909- *IndAu 1917*
Farrington, Frank 1873- *AmLY, WhWNAA*
Farrington, Frederic Ernest 1872-1930 *DcNAA*
Farrington, Harry Webb 1880-1930 *ChPo*
Farrington, Harry Webb 1880-1931 *DcNAA*
Farrington, J *Alli*
Farrington, John *Alli*
Farrington, Margaret Vere *Alli Sup, DcAmA*
Farrington, Maude *WrD 1976*
Farrington, Oliver Cummings 1864-1933
  DcAmA, DcNAA, WhWNAA
Farrington, Richard *Alli*
Farrington, Selwyn Kip, Jr. 1904- *AmA&B,*
  AuBYP
Farrington, Wallace Rider 1871- *WhWNAA*
Farris, Herbert *MnBBF*
Farris, John *BlkAW, DrAP 1975*
Farris, Martin T 1925- *ConAu 21*
Farris, Paul L 1919- *ConAu 9R*
Farrison, William Edward 1902- *BlkAW,*
  ConAu 29
Farriss, Charles Sherwood 1856-1938 *AmA&B,*
  DcNAA
Farriss, N M 1938- *ConAu 25*
Farro, Daniel *Alli*
Farrokhi, Abu'l-Hasan 'Ali d1037 *DcOrL 3*
Farrokhzad, Forugh 1934-1967 *DcOrL 3*
Farrow, A M L *Alli*
Farrow, Edward Samuel 1855-1942 *Alli Sup,*
  DcAmA, DcNAA
Farrow, Edward Samuel 1855- *WhWNAA*
Farrow, George Edward 1866-1920? *ChPo,*
  ChPo S1, ChPo S2, MnBBF, WhCL
Farrow, J 1935- *ConAu XR*
Farrow, John G *ChPo S2*
Farrow, John Villiers 1906?-1963 *AmA&B,*
  BkC 5, CatA 1947, WhWNAA

Farrow, Johnny 1912- *AmSCAP 66*
Farrow, Morley *Alli Sup*
Farrow, R 1920- *Au&Wr*
Farrugia, Vincent Paul 1919- *Au&Wr*
Farrukhi, Abu'l-Hasan 'Ali Ibn Julugh d1038
  CasWL
Farrukhzad, Furugh 1935-1967 *CasWL*
Farson, Daniel Negley 1927- *WrD 1976*
Farson, Negley 1890-1960 *AmA&B, LongC,*
  TwCA, TwCA Sup
Farthing, Alison 1936- *WrD 1976*
Farthing, John *Alli*
Farthing, John C *OxCan*
Farthing, Ralph *Alli*
Farwell, Arthur 1872-1952 *AmSCAP 66*
Farwell, Byron E 1921- *ConAu 13R*
Farwell, Evelyn Michell *Alli Sup*
Farwell, George 1845- *Alli Sup*
Farwell, George Michell 1911- *Au&Wr,*
  ConAu 21
Farwell, John Villiers 1825-1903 *DcNAA*
Farwell, Mrs. M E C *Alli Sup*
Farwell, Parris Thaxter 1856-1930 *DcNAA*
Farwell, William W *Alli Sup*
Fary, John *Alli*
Farzad, Mas'ud 1906- *CasWL, DcOrL 3*
Farzan, Massud 1936- *ConAu 53*
Fasana, Paul James 1933- *ConAu 37*
Fascinato, Jack 1915- *AmSCAP 66*
Fasel, George W 1938- *ConAu 23*
Fasi, 'Allal Al- 1910- *DcOrL 3*
Fasold, Ralph W 1940- *ConAu 29*
Fasquelle, Jean Louis 1808-1862 *Alli, DcAmA,*
  DcNAA
Fassett, James 1904- *ConAu 49*
Fassett, James Hiram 1869-1930 *DcNAA*
Fassig, Oliver Lanard 1860- *WhWNAA*
Fassit, Margaret C *ChPo S2*
Fassler, Joan 1931- *ConAu 61*
Fast, Edward G *Alli Sup*
Fast, Howard 1914- *AmA&B, AmNov,*
  Au&Wr, AuBYP, CnDAL, ConAu 1R,
  ConNov 1972, ConNov 1976, DcLEnL,
  ModAL, OxAm, Pen Am, REn, REnAL,
  SmATA 7, TwCA Sup, TwCW,
  WebEAL, WrD 1976
Fast, Julius 1919- *ConAu 25*
Fastenrath, Johannes 1839- *BbD, BiD&SB*
Fasting, Claus d1791 *DcEuL*
Fastlife *ConAu XR*
Fastolf, Sir John 1378?-1459 *NewC*
Fastoul, Baude *CasWL*
Fastre, J A M *Alli Sup*
Fat Contributor, The *NewC*
Fatchen, Max 1920- *Au&Wr, ConAu 25*
Fath, Edward Arthur 1880- *WhWNAA*
Father Of Angling, The *DcEnL, NewC*
Father Of English Poetry, The *DcEnL*
Father Of English Prose, The *DcEnL*
Father Of History, The *NewC*
Father Of Jests, The 1684-1738 *DcEnL*
Father Of Medicine *NewC*
Father Of Moral Philosophy *NewC*
Father Of The English Detective Novel *NewC*
Father Prout *DcEnL, DcLEnL*
Fathers Of The Church *NewC*
Fatima 606?-632 *NewC*
Fatio, Louise 1904- *BkP, ConAu 37, MorJA,*
  SmATA 6, WrD 1976
Fatisha *BlkAW, DrAP 1975*
Fatouros, Arghyrios A 1932- *ConAu 13R,*
  WrD 1976
Fatout, Paul 1897- *ConAu 23, IndAu 1917*
Faubel, Arthur L 1896- *WhWNAA*
Faubion, Dorothy *ChPo*
Fauche-Borel, Louis *BiDLA*
Faucher, Albert-Maurice 1844-1897
  OxCan Sup
Faucher, Claire *CanWr, OxCan*
Faucher, W Thomas 1945- *ConAu 57*
Faucher DeSaint-Maurice, Narcisse H E
  1844-1897 *BbtC, CanWr, DcNAA, OxCan*
Fauchet, Claude 1529?-1601? *CasWL, DcEuL,*
  OxFr
Fauchois, Rene 1882-1962 *McGWD, ModWD*
Faucit, Helen 1817-1898 *NewC*
Faucitt, Helen *Alli Sup*
Fauconnier, Henri *TwCA, TwCA Sup*

Faugere, Prosper 1810-1887 *OxFr*
Faugeres, Margaretta 1771-1801 *Alli, CyAL 1, OxAm*
Faught, L Ashley *Alli Sup*
Faught, Millard C 1916- *AmA&B*
Faujas DeSaint-Fond, Barthelemy 1741-1819 *OxFr*
Faukner, Thomas *Alli Sup*
Faul, August *Alli Sup*
Faulding, Gertrude M *ChPo S1*
Faulds, Henry *Alli Sup*
Fauley, Wilbur Finley 1872-1942 *AmA&B, DcNAA, OhA&B*
Faulhaber, Charles Bailey 1941- *ConAu 53*
Faulhaber, Ludwig Joseph 1893- *WhLA*
Faulhaber, Martha 1926- *ConAu 33, SmATA 7*
Faulhaber, Cardinal Michael 1869- *CatA 1947*
Faulk, John Henry 1913- *AmA&B*
Faulk, Odie B 1933- *ConAu 25, WrD 1976*
Faulkener, Charles *Alli*
Faulkner, A B *Alli, BiDLA*
Faulkner, Alexander *Alli Sup*
Faulkner, Anne Irvin 1906- *AuBYP, ConAu 1R*
Faulkner, B *Alli*
Faulkner, Charles Herman 1937- *ConAu 25, IndAu 1917, WrD 1976*
Faulkner, Edward H 1886- *OhA&B*
Faulkner, Frank *Alli Sup, HsB&A*
Faulkner, Fred 1941- *AmSCAP 66*
Faulkner, George d1775 *Alli, DcEnL*
Faulkner, Georgene 1873- *AmA&B, AuBYP, WhWNAA*
Faulkner, H C *Alli Sup*
Faulkner, Harold Underwood 1890- *AmA&B, ConAu 1R, WhWNAA*
Faulkner, Henry *Alli Sup*
Faulkner, Herbert Waldron 1860-1940 *DcNAA, WhWNAA*
Faulkner, Jack 1918- *AmSCAP 66*
Faulkner, John *IlBYP*
Faulkner, John 1901-1963 *ConAu 1R*
Faulkner, John Alfred 1857-1931 *DcNAA, WhWNAA*
Faulkner, Joseph E 1928- *ConAu 45*
Faulkner, Joseph P *Alli Sup*
Faulkner, Nancy 1906- *Au&Wr, AuBYP, ConAu XR*
Faulkner, Nathan *Alli Sup*
Faulkner, Peter 1933- *Au&Wr, ConAu 5R*
Faulkner, Ray 1906- *ConAu 5R*
Faulkner, Richard Rowland *Alli Sup*
Faulkner, Rose E *Alli Sup*
Faulkner, Sarah E Sherwood *ChPo S1*
Faulkner, Thomas *Alli, BiDLA*
Faulkner, Virginia Louise 1913- *AmA&B*
Faulkner, W *Alli, BiDLA*
Faulkner, William 1897-1962 *AmA&B, AmNov, AmWr, AtlBL, AuNews 1, CasWL, Chmbr 3, CnDAL, CnMD, CnMWL, ConAmA, ConLC 1, ConLC 3, ConLC 6, CrCD, CyWA, DcLEnL, EncM&D, EncWL, LongC, ModAL, ModAL Sup, ModWD, OxAm, OxEng, Pen Am, RAdv 1, RCom, REn, REnAL, TwCA, TwCA Sup, TwCW, WebEAL, WhTwL*
Faulkner, William Harrison 1897- *EvLB*
Faulkner, William Humphrey *Alli, BiDLA*
Faulknor, Clifford Vernon 1913- *ConAu 17R, OxCan Sup, WrD 1976*
Faulks, Theodosia *DcNAA*
Faull, Lesley *WrD 1976*
Faulwasser, Carl Julius 1855- *WhLA*
Faunce, Daniel Worcester 1829-1911 *Alli Sup, DcNAA, DcAmA*
Faunce, Frances Avery *ChPo*
Faunce, Linus *Alli Sup*
Faunce, Roland Cleo 1905- *ConAu 1R*
Faunce, Sarah Avery *ChPo*
Faunce, William Alden 1928- *ConAu 25, WrD 1976*
Faunce, William Herbert Perry 1859-1930 *AmA&B, AmLY, DcNAA*
Faunt, Arthur *Alli*
Faunthorpe, John Pincher *Alli Sup*
Fauntleroy, Henry *Alli Sup*

Faupel, John F 1906- *ConAu 5R*
Fauquier, Francis 1720-1768 *Alli, BiDSA*
Fauquier, George Lillie Wodehouse *Alli Sup*
Faure, Elie 1873-1937 *CasWL, ClDMEuL, TwCA, TwCA Sup*
Faure, Gabriel Urbain 1845-1924 *AtlBL, OxFr, REn*
Faure, Raoul Cohen 1909- *AmA&B, AmNov, TwCA Sup*
Faure, William Caldwell *WrD 1976*
Fauriel, Claude 1772-1844 *BbD, BiD&SB, DcEuL, OxFr*
Faurot, Jean H 1911- *ConAu 29*
Fausboll, V *Alli Sup*
Fauset, Arthur Huff 1899- *BlkAW, ConAu 25, LivBAA, OxCan*
Fauset, Jessie Redmon 1884?-1961 *AmA&B, BlkAW, TwCA Sup, TwCA Sup*
Fausett, Sarah *ChPo, ChPo S2*
Fausold, Martin L 1921- *ConAu 23*
Fausset SEE ALSO Faussett
Fausset, Andrew Robert 1821- *Alli Sup*
Fausset, Godfrey *Alli*
Fausset, Hugh I'Anson 1895-1965 *LongC, ModBL, NewC, TwCA, TwCA Sup*
Fausset, Hugh L'Anson 1895-1965 *DcLEnL, EvLB*
Faussett SEE ALSO Fausset
Faussett, Alessie Bond 1841- *PoIre*
Faussett, Godfrey *BiDLA*
Faussett, Hugh I'Anson 1895- *WhLA*
Faussett, Robert Godfrey *Alli Sup*
Faussett, Thomas Godfrey Godfrey- 1829-1877 *Alli Sup*
Faussett, William *Alli Sup*
Faust, Albert Bernhardt 1870-1951 *AmA&B, AmLY, CasWL, WhWNAA*
Faust, Clarence H 1901-1975 *ConAu 57*
Faust, Frederick 1892-1944 *AmA&B, ChPo, DcLEnL, DcNAA, EncM&D, LongC, MnBBF, REn, REnAL, TwCA, TwCA Sup*
Faust, Georg 1480?-1539? *OxGer*
Faust, Henri *TexWr*
Faust, Irvin 1924- *AmA&B, ConAu 33, ConNov 1972, ConNov 1976, DrAF 1976, WrD 1976*
Faust, Johann *NewC*
Faust, Naomi F *BlkAW, ConAu 61*
Faust, Samuel D 1852-1929 *OhA&B*
Faust-Newton, Cosette *TexWr*
Fausti, Remo P 1917- *ConAu 41*
Faustus 390?- *Alli*
Faustus Of Byzantium *DcOrL 3*
Fauteux, Aegidius 1876-1941 *DcNAA, OxCan, WhWNAA*
Fauteux, Joseph-Noel *OxCan*
Fauth, Robert T 1916- *ConAu 1R*
Fauvel, Pierre 1866- *WhLA*
Fauvet, Jacques 1914- *Au&Wr*
Faux, W *Alli*
Fava, Guido *CasWL*
Fava, Onorato 1859- *BiD&SB*
Fava, Rita 1932- *ChPo, ChPo S1, IlCB 1956, IlCB 1966*
Favart, Charles Simon 1710-1792 *BbD, BiD&SB, CasWL, DcEuL, EvEuW, OxFr*
Favell *Alli*
Favell, Mister *BiDLA*
Favell, Charles *Alli*
Favell, James *Alli*
Favenc, Ernest 1846?-1908 *Alli Sup, DcLEnL*
Faverel, Arthur *DcNAA*
Faversham, Julie 1871-1921 *DcNAA*
Faverty, Frederic Everett 1902- *ChPo S1, ConAu 45*
Favetti, Carlo 1819-1892 *CasWL*
Favey, George *Alli Sup*
Favier, Jean-Louis 1720?-1784 *OxFr*
Favill, John 1847-1927 *DcNAA*
Favill, John 1886-1946 *DcNAA*
Faville, Curtis *DrAP 1975*
Faville, David Ernest 1899- *ConAu 1R*
Faville, John 1847- *DcAmA, WhWNAA*
Favorinus 080?-150? *Pen Cl*
Favorsky, Vladimir Andreyevich 1886- *WhGrA*
Favour, John d1623 *Alli*

Favret, Andrew G 1925- *ConAu 17R*
Favretti, Rudy J 1932- *ConAu 53*
Favrot, Henry L *BiDSA*
Fawcett, Mrs. *Chmbr 3*
Fawcett, Benjamin 1715-1780 *Alli*
Fawcett, Brian 1906- *Au&Wr, WrD 1976*
Fawcett, Captain *MnBBF*
Fawcett, Clara Hallard 1887- *ConAu P-1*
Fawcett, Claude W 1911- *ConAu 49*
Fawcett, Douglas 1866- *WhLA*
Fawcett, Edgar 1847-1904 *Alli Sup, AmA, AmA&B, BbD, BiD&SB, ChPo, ChPo S1, ChPo S2, DcAmA, DcEnA Ap, DcLEnL, DcNAA, OxAm, REnAL*
Fawcett, F Dubrez 1891-1968 *ConAu P-1, MnBBF*
Fawcett, George *Alli Sup*
Fawcett, Harold Pascoe 1894- *Au&Wr*
Fawcett, Henry *Alli Sup, Chmbr 3*
Fawcett, Henry 1833-1884 *Alli Sup, BbD, BiD&SB, BrAu 19, DcEnA, DcEnL, EvLB*
Fawcett, Howard Samuel 1877- *WhWNAA*
Fawcett, J *Alli, Alli Sup*
Fawcett, James *Alli, BiDLA*
Fawcett, John *Alli, Alli Sup*
Fawcett, John 1739-1817 *Alli, ChPo, ChPo S1, DcEnL, PoCh*
Fawcett, John 1768-1837 *BiDLA, NewC*
Fawcett, John, Jr. *BiDLA*
Fawcett, Sir John Henry 1831- *Alli Sup*
Fawcett, Joseph d1804 *Alli, BiDLA*
Fawcett, Joshua d1864 *Alli Sup*
Fawcett, Marion *ConAu XR*
Fawcett, Mary Huestis 1843- *OhA&B*
Fawcett, Millicent 1847-1929 *Alli Sup, BbD, BiD&SB, DcEnL, NewC*
Fawcett, Richard *Alli*
Fawcett, Samuel *Alli*
Fawcett, Sophia Alice *Alli Sup*
Fawcett, Thomas *Alli*
Fawcett, W J *PoIre*
Fawcett, W L *Alli Sup*
Fawcett, Sir William 1728-1804 *Alli*
Fawcett, William Claude 1902-1941 *Br&AmS*
Fawcett, William Mitchell 1839- *Alli Sup*
Fawconer, Samuel *Alli*
Fawcus, Arnold Douglas 1917- *Au&Wr*
Fawdry, Dallas Wood 1932- *Au&Wr*
Fawdry, Reginald Charles 1873- *WhLA*
Fawkes, Miss *Alli Sup*
Fawkes, Mrs. *Alli Sup*
Fawkes, Francis 1720?-1777 *Alli, BbD, BiD&SB, ChPo, Chmbr 2, DcEnL, EvLB, NewC*
Fawkes, Frank Attfield *Alli Sup*
Fawkes, Guy *NewC*
Fawkes, James *Alli*
Fawkes, Walter *Alli*
Fawkner, Anthony *Alli*
Fawler, John *Alli*
Fawley, Jude *REn*
Fawley, Wilbur *AmA&B, OhA&B*
Fawside, John *ChPo S1*
Fawsit, John *Alli Sup*
Fax, Elton Clay 1909- *ConAu 13R, LivBA*
Faxon, Arba D 1895?-1975 *ConAu 61*
Faxon, Florence R *ChPo*
Faxon, Frederick Winthrop 1866-1936 *AmLY, ChPo S2, DcNAA, WhWNAA*
Faxon, Henry W 1830-1864 *AmA&B*
Faxon, Lavinia *ConAu XR*
Faxon, Ralph Henry 1882- *WhWNAA*
Faxon, Walter 1848-1920 *DcNAA*
Fay, Albert Hill 1871-1937 *DcNAA, WhWNAA*
Fay, Alice *ChPo S2*
Fay, Amy 1844-1928 *Alli Sup, DcAmA, DcNAA, WhWNAA*
Fay, Andras 1786-1864 *CasWL, EvEuW*
Fay, Andreas 1786-1864 *BbD, BiD&SB*
Fay, Bernard 1893- *TwCA, TwCA Sup*
Fay, C R *OxCan*
Fay, Charles Ernest 1846-1931 *AmA&B*
Fay, Charles Norman 1848-1944 *DcNAA, WhWNAA*
Fay, Charles R 1867-1934 *DcNAA, WhWNAA*

Fay, Edward Allen 1843-1923 *Alli Sup, AmLY, DcNAA*
Fay, Edwin W *BiDSA*
Fay, Edwin Whitfield 1865-1920 *DcNAA*
Fay, Erica *ChPo*
Fay, Frederic L 1890- *ConAu 21*
Fay, Gaston *ChPo, ChPo S1, ChPo S2, EarAB, EarAB Sup*
Fay, Gerard 1913-1968 *ConAu P-1*
Fay, Gerda *Alli Sup, ChPo*
Fay, Gordon S 1912- *ConAu 53*
Fay, Heman Allen 1779-1865 *BbtC, DcNAA*
Fay, Henry 1868- *WhWNAA*
Fay, Ida *ChPo*
Fay, Irving Wetherbee 1861-1936 *DcNAA*
Fay, John 1921- *ConAu 57*
Fay, Jonas 1737-1818 *DcNAA*
Fay, Joseph D *Alli Sup*
Fay, Joseph Dewey 1779-1825 *AmA&B*
Fay, Julia Douglas *Alli Sup*
Fay, Leo 1920- *ConAu 13R*
Fay, Mary Helen *ConAu XR*
Fay, Peter Ward 1924- *ConAu 57*
Fay, Sidney Bradshaw 1876-1967 *AmA&B, TwCA, TwCA Sup, WhWNAA*
Fay, Stanley J *ChPo S1*
Fay, Stephen 1938- *ConAu 25*
Fay, Theodore Sedgwick 1807-1898 *Alli, Alli Sup, AmA, AmA&B, BbD, BiD&SB, ChPo, CnDAL, CyAL 2, DcAmA, DcEnL, DcLEnL, DcNAA, OxAm, REnAL*
Fayer, Mischa Harry 1902- *ConAu 1R*
Fayerman, Francis *Alli*
Fayerman, Richard *Alli*
Fayers, Thomas *Alli Sup*
Fayerweather, John 1922- *ConAu 1R*
Fayerweather, Margaret Doane *ChPo S2*
Fayko, Aleksey 1893- *Pen Eur*
Fayle, Joshua *Alli Sup*
Fayrer, Sir Joseph 1824- *Alli Sup*
Fayturi, Muhammad Miftah Al- 1930- *DcOrL 3*
Fayyazi *DcOrL 2*
Fazakerley, George Raymond 1921- *Au&Wr, ConAu 13R*
Fazakerly *Alli*
Fazal, Muhammad Abul 1939- *ConAu 29, WrD 1976*
Fazal Sah *DcOrL 2*
Fazekas, Mihaly 1766-1828 *Pen Eur*
Fazil, Maulana Muhammad *DcOrL 2*
Fazil Husnu Daglarca 1914- *CasWL*
Fazio Degli Uberti 1300?-1367? *BiD&SB, EuA*
Fazio, Bartolommeo d1457 *DcEuL*
Fazioli, Bernardo 1897-1942 *AmSCAP 66*
Fazioli, Billy 1898-1924 *AmSCAP 66*
Fazzano, Joseph E 1929- *ConAu 5R*
Fea, Allen 1860- *BiD&SB*
Fea, Henry Robert 1914- *WhPNW*
Fea, James *Alli, Alli Sup*
Fea, James Lyon 1937- *WrD 1976*
Fea, John W *Alli*
Feachem, Richard William DeFecamp 1914- *Au&Wr*
Feagans, Raymond 1953- *ConAu 57*
Feagin, Joe R 1938- *ConAu 37*
Feagles, Anita 1926- *AuBYP, ConAu 1R, SmATA 9*
Feagles, Elizabeth *ConAu XR*
Feague, Mildred H 1915- *ConAu 29*
Feake, Christopher *Alli*
Feake, John *Alli*
Feal-Deibe, Carlos 1935- *ConAu 37*
Fear, David E 1941- *ConAu 53*
Fear, Duncan *MnBBF*
Fear Chanaidh *ConAu XR*
Fearing, Alden *AmLY XR*
Fearing, Blanche *AmA&B*
Fearing, Kenneth 1902-1961 *AmA&B, AmNov, CnDAL, CnE&AP, ConAmA, DcLEnL, EncM&D, ModAL, OxAm, Pen Am, RAdv 1, REn, REnAL, SixAP, TwCA, TwCA Sup, WebEAL, WhTwL*
Fearing, Lilian Blanche 1863-1901 *AmA&B, DcAmA, DcNAA*
Fearing, Lillien Blanche 1863-1901 *Alli Sup, BiD&SB*

Fearn, Anne 1868-1939 *DcNAA*
Fearn, C Eaton *MnBBF*
Fearn, H N *Alli Sup*
Fearn, John *Alli, BiDLA*
Fearn, Joseph *Alli Sup*
Fearn, Mrs. Joseph *ChPo S2*
Fearn, Maggie *Alli Sup, ChPo S1*
Fearne, Charles *Alli*
Fearne, Charles 1749-1794 *Alli, DcEnL*
Fearne, Flora *ChPo*
Fearnley, F M *Alli Sup*
Fearnley, Frank *Alli Sup*
Fearnley, Thomas *Alli Sup*
Fearnley, William *Alli Sup*
Fearnox, Barry J *WhWNAA*
Fearon, Alec *Alli Sup*
Fearon, Daniel Robert 1835- *Alli Sup*
Fearon, Diana 1915- *Au&Wr*
Fearon, George Edward 1901- *Au&Wr, ConAu P-1*
Fearon, Henry *Alli Sup*
Fearon, Henry Bradshaw *Alli*
Fearon, James Peter *Alli, BiDLA*
Fearon, John D 1920- *ConAu 37*
Fearon, John Peter *Alli Sup*
Fearon, Joseph *Alli*
Fearon, Joseph F *Alli*
Fearon, Michael *ChPo S1*
Fearon, Peter 1942- *ConAu 29*
Fearon, William Robert 1892- *WhLA*
Feaser, Daniel David 1920- *IlBYP, IlCB 1966*
Feather, Leonard G 1914- *AmA&B, AmSCAP 66, ConAu 61*
Feather, William 1889- *AmA&B, Au&Wr, OhA&B*
Featherman, Americus 1822- *Alli Sup, DcAmA*
Feathers, J A 1916- *Au&Wr*
Featherstone, Donald Frederick 1918- *Au&Wr*
Featherstone, Joseph 1940- *ConAu 33*
Featherstone, Robert Marion 1914- *IndAu 1917*
Featherstonehaugh, Francis *ConAu XR*
Featherstonehaugh, George William *Alli*
Featherstonehaugh, H *Alli*
Featherstonhaugh, G W *BbtC*
Featley, Daniel 1582-1645? *Alli, DcEnL, NewC*
Featley, John d1666 *Alli*
Featley, Richard d1681 *Alli*
Featly, Daniel 1582-1644 *Alli*
Feaver, George Arthur 1937- *Au&Wr, ConAu 29*
Feaver, J Clayton 1911- *ConAu 25*
Febure, Mrs. *Alli*
Febvre, Lucien 1878- *OxFr*
Fecher, Constance 1911- *Au&Wr, ConAu 49, SmATA 7, WrD 1976*
Fechner, Gustav Theodor 1801-1887 *BbD, BiD&SB, OxGer*
Fechter, Alyce Shinn 1909- *ConAu P-1*
Feckenham, John De d1585 *Alli*
Fedde, Friedrich Karl Georg 1873- *WhLA*
Fedde, Norman A 1914- *ConAu 5R*
Fedden, Henry 1908- *ConAu 9R*
Fedden, Katharine Waldo Douglas d1939 *AmA&B, DcNAA, WhWNAA*
Fedden, Robin Romilly 1908- *Au&Wr, ConAu XR, ConP 1970*
Fedden, Mrs. Romilly d1939 *AmLY*
Fedder, Edwin H 1929- *ConAu 37*
Fedder, Norman Joseph 1934- *ConAu 21, WrD 1976*
Fedder, Ruth 1907- *ConAu 5R*
Feddoes, Sadie Clothil 1931- *BlkAW*
Fedelle, Estelle *WrD 1976*
Feder, Bernard 1924- *ConAu 33, WrD 1976*
Feder, Ernest 1913- *ConAu 37*
Feder, Ernst 1881- *WhLA*
Feder, Karah 1920- *ConAu 17R*
Feder, Lillian *ConAu 41*
Federer, Heinrich 1866-1928 *CasWL, ClDMEuL, EncWL, OxGer*
Federici, Camillo 1749-1802 *BiD&SB*
Federlein, Gottfried Harrison 1883-1952 *AmSCAP 66*
Federman, Raymond 1928- *ConAu 17R, ConLC 6, DrAF 1976, DrAP 1975, WrD 1976*

Federspiel, Jurg 1931- *ModGL*
Fedin, Konstantin Aleksandrovich 1892-1970 *CasWL, ClDMEuL, DcRusL, EncWL, EvEuW, ModSL 1, Pen Eur, REn, TwCW, WorAu*
Fedkovic, Joseph Horodencuk 1834-1888 *BiD&SB*
Fedoroff, Alexander 1927- *ConAu 1R*
Fedorov *DcRusL*
Fedrie, Francis *Alli Sup*
Fedyshyn, Oleh S 1928- *ConAu 49*
Fee, Benjamin J *DrAP 1975*
Fee, Chester Anders 1893-1951 *AmA&B, ChPo S1*
Fee, Harry Thomas 1871-1934? *DcNAA*
Fee, John Gregg 1816-1901 *Alli Sup, DcNAA*
Fee, Walter Ray 1902- *IndAu 1917*
Fee, William Ingram 1817-1900 *OhA&B*
Feeder, Frederick *Alli Sup*
Feegel, John R 1932- *ConAu 57*
Feehan, James *PoIre*
Feeley, Kathleen 1929- *ConAu 33*
Feelings, Muriel 1938- *BlkAW, LivBA*
Feelings, Thomas 1933- *ConAu 49, SmATA 8*
Feelings, Tom 1933- *BkP, ConAu 49, IlBYP, LivBAA, SmATA 8, ThBJA*
Feeman, Harlan Luther 1873- *WhWNAA*
Feeney, Leonard 1897- *AmA&B, Au&Wr, CatA 1947, ChPo, ChPo S1, ChPo S2, WrD 1976*
Feeney, Patrick d1900? *PoIre*
Feeney, Thomas Butler *CatA 1952, ChPo S1*
Feenstra, Henry John 1936- *ConAu 37*
Feerick, John David 1936- *ConAu 13R*
Feffer, Itzik 1900-1948? *CasWL, Pen Eur*
Fegan, Camilla 1939- *ConAu 21*
Fegiz, Rita Fava 1932- *IlBYP, IlCB 1966*
Fehl, Philipp P 1920- *ConAu 33, WrD 1976*
Fehlandt, August Frederick 1869-1939 *DcNAA, WhWNAA*
Fehr, Hans 1874- *WhLA*
Fehren, Henry 1920- *ConAu 21*
Fehrenbach, Theodore Reed 1925- *Au&Wr, ConAu 1R, WrD 1976*
Fehrenbacher, Don Edward 1920- *ConAu 1R, WrD 1976*
Fehrle, Eugen 1880- *WhLA*
Fehrs, Johann Hinrich 1838-1916 *CasWL, OxGer*
Feibel, Frederick 1906- *AmSCAP 66*
Feibes, Walter 1928- *ConAu 53*
Feibleman, James Kern 1904- *AmA&B 2, Au&Wr, AuNews 2, ConAu 5R, TwCA Sup*
Feibleman, Peter S 1930- *REnAL*
Feied, Frederick 1925- *ConAu 13R*
Feierman, Steven 1940- *ConAu 53*
Feiffer, Jules 1929- *AmA&B, Au&Wr, CnThe, ConAu 17R, ConDr, ConLC 2, CrCD, McGWD, SmATA 8, WrD 1976*
Feigelson, Naomi R 1932- *ConAu 33*
Feigenbaum, Lawrence H 1918- *ConAu 25*
Feigert, Frank B 1937- *ConAu 53*
Feigl, Herbert 1902- *ConAu P-1*
Feijo, Antonio Joaquim DeCastro 1862-1917 *ClDMEuL, EvEuW*
Feijoo, Benito Jeronimo 1676-1764 *Pen Eur*
Feijoo Y Montenegro, Benito Jeronimo 1676-1764 *CasWL, DcSpL, EuA, EvEuW*
Feikema, Feikenegro, Benito Jeronimo 1912- *AmA&B, AmNov, ConAu XR, OxAm, TwCA Sup, WrD 1976*
Feil, Hila 1942- *ConAu 37*
Feild, Edward *OxCan*
Feild, John *Alli*
Feilde, Anna *ChPo S1, ChPo S2*
Feilde, Matthew d1796 *Alli*
Feilden, Eliza Whigham *Alli Sup*
Feilden, Henry St. Clair *Alli Sup*
Feilden, J Leyland *Alli Sup*
Feilden, Phoebe M *Alli Sup*
Feilding, Viscount, And Kennedy, Captain *Alli*
Feilding, Charles 1902- *ConAu 25*
Feilding, Everard 1867-1936 *BiDPar*
Feiler, Arthur 1879- *WhLA*
Feiler, Max Christian 1904- *CnMD*
Feiler, Seymour 1919- *ConAu 41*
Feiling, Sir Keith Grahame 1884- *Au&Wr,*

NewC
Fein, Leah Gold *ConAu 49*
Fein, Leonard J 1934- *ConAu 13R*
Fein, Pearl *AmSCAP 66*
Fein, Richard J 1929- *AmA&B, ConAu 45*
Feinberg, Abraham L 1899- *Au&Wr, ConAu 9R*
Feinberg, Barry 1938- *ConAu 29, WrD 1976*
Feinberg, Gerald 1933- *ConAu 25, WrD 1976*
Feinberg, Hilda *ConAu 49*
Feinberg, Joel 1926- *ConAu 17R*
Feinberg, Leonard 1914- *ConAu 5R, WrD 1976*
Feinberg, Samuel Maurice 1895- *AmA&B*
Feinberg, Walter 1937- *ConAu 57*
Feingold, Eugene 1931- *ConAu 17R, WrD 1976*
Feingold, Gustave Alexander 1880-1948 *DcNAA*
Feingold, Henry L 1931- *ConAu 29*
Feingold, Jessica 1910- *ConAu 25*
Feingold, S Norman 1914- *ConAu 13R*
Feininger, Andreas 1906- *AmA&B*
Feininger, Lyonel 1871-1956 *AtlBL, OxGer, REn*
Feinman, Alvin *DrAP 1975*
Feinsilver, Alexander 1910- *ConAu 13R*
Feinsilver, Lillian Mermin 1917- *ConAu 29, WrD 1976*
Feinstein, Alan 1931- *ConAu 25*
Feinstein, Elaine 1930- *ConP 1975, WrD 1976*
Feinstein, Sherman C 1923- *ConAu 57*
Feirberg, Mordecai Z 1874-1899 *CasWL, Pen Eur*
Feirstein, Frederick 1940- *ConAu 45, DrAP 1975*
Feis, Herbert 1893-1972 *AmA&B, Au&Wr, ConAu 33, ConAu P-1, OxAm, WorAu*
Feis, Jacob 1842- *Alli Sup*
Feis, Jakob 1842- *BiD&SB*
Feis, Ruth 1892- *ConAu 19*
Feise, Ernst 1884-1966 *ConAu 17*
Feisi, Abul-Feis Ibn Mubarak 1547-1595 *BbD, BiD&SB, REn*
Feisilber, I *EvEuW*
Feist, Aubrey 1903- *Au&Wr, ConAu 41*
Feist, C *Alli*
Feist, Charles 1795- *Alli, BiDLA*
Feist, T M *Alli Sup*
Feit, E Edward 1924- *ConAu 5R*
Feitama, Sybrand 1694-1758 *BiD&SB, CasWL*
Feith, Herbert 1930- *ConAu 19*
Feith, Rhijnvis 1753-1824 *BbD, BiD&SB, CasWL, DcEuL, EuA, EvEuW*
Feitler, Bea 1938- *WhGrA*
Feiwel, George R 1929- *ConAu 17R*
Feiyasi, Abul Feis Ibn Mubarak 1547-1595 *REn*
Fejes, Claire 1920- *ConAu 21*
Fejes, Endre 1923- *ConAu 25*
Fejto, Francois 1909- *ConAu 29*
Feke, Robert 1705?-1750 *OxAm*
Fekete, Irene Anne Francis 1936- *Au&Wr*
Fekrat, M Ali 1937- *ConAu 45*
Felch, I K *Alli Sup*
Felch, William Farrand 1855-1930 *OhA&B*
Feld, Michael 1938- *Au&Wr, ConAu 33, WrD 1976*
Feld, Rose Caroline 1895- *AmA&B, WhWNAA*
Feld, Ross 1947- *ConAu 33, DrAF 1976, DrAP 1975*
Feld, Werner J 1910- *ConAu 21, WrD 1976*
Felder, Franz Michael 1839-1869 *BiD&SB, OxGer*
Felder, Raoul Lionel 1934- *ConAu 33*
Felderman, Eric 1944- *AmA&B*
Felderman, Leo 1890-1945 *DcNAA*
Feldman, Abraham J 1893- *AmA&B*
Feldman, Alan *DrAF 1976, DrAP 1975*
Feldman, Burton 1926- *ConAu 33*
Feldman, Edmund Burke 1924- *ConAu 33*
Feldman, Edwin Barry 1925- *ConAu 5R, WrD 1976*
Feldman, George J 1904- *ConAu P-1*
Feldman, Gerald D 1937- *ConAu 21, WrD 1976*
Feldman, Herbert 1910- *ConAu 29*
Feldman, Herman 1894-1947 *DcNAA*
Feldman, Irving 1928- *AmA&B, Au&Wr,*

ChPo S2, ConAu 1R, ConP 1970, ConP 1975, DrAP 1975, Pen Am, WrD 1976
Feldman, Kenneth A 1937- *ConAu 29*
Feldman, Leslie *AuNews 1*
Feldman, Lionel *OxCan Sup*
Feldman, Louis H 1926- *ConAu 53*
Feldman, M P 1933- *ConAu 41*
Feldman, Myer 1917- *WrD 1976*
Feldman, Samuel Nathan 1931- *ConAu 25*
Feldman, Sandor S 1891?-1973 *ConAu 41*
Feldman, Saul D 1943- *ConAu 41*
Feldman, Sol E 1933- *ConAu 25*
Feldman, William Hugh 1892- *WhWNAA*
Feldman, William Moses 1880- *WhLA*
Feldmann, Leopold 1802-1882 *BbD, BiD&SB*
Feldstein, Saul 1940- *AmSCAP 66*
Feldt, Allan Gunnar 1932- *ConAu 41*
Feldzamen, A N 1931- *ConAu 25*
Feletz, Charles Dorimond De 1767-1850 *BiD&SB, OxFr*
Felgate, Samuel *Alli*
Felheim, Marvin 1914- *ConAu 1R*
Feli, Monsieur *OxFr*
Felibien *OxFr*
Felices, Jorge 1917- *PueRA*
Feliciano Mendoza, Ester 1917- *PueRA*
Felinski, Alojzy 1771-1820 *CasWL, Pen Eur*
Felipe V *DcSpL*
Felipe Trigo *EuA*
Felipe, Leon 1884- *DcSpL, Pen Eur, REn*
Feliu Y Codina, Jose 1847-1897 *CasWL, EvEuW*
Felix Of Croyland *Alli, BiB S, DcEnL*
Felix, David 1921- *ConAu 45*
Felix, N *Alli*
Felix, Pastor *AmA&B, DcNAA*
Felkel, Henry L *BiDSA*
Felkel, Herbert *WhWNAA*
Felkenes, George T 1930- *ConAu 57*
Felker, Charles Aurand 1899- *IndAu 1917*
Felker, Evelyn H 1933- *ConAu 57*
Felker, Jere L 1934- *ConAu 23*
Felker, P H *Alli Sup*
Felkin, Alfred Laurence 1856- *CarSB, WhLA*
Felkin, Ellen Thorneycroft 1860-1929 *CarSB, NewC, WhLA*
Felkin, H M *Alli Sup*
Felkin, Mrs. John *Alli Sup*
Felkin, Mrs. R W *Alli Sup*
Felkin, William *Alli Sup*
Felknor, Bruce L 1921- *ConAu 21*
Fell, Doctor *REn*
Fell, Archie *Alli Sup*
Fell, Dora *Alli Sup*
Fell, Edgar Tremlett 1895- *WhWNAA*
Fell, Elizabeth *Alli*
Fell, Frederick *OhA&B*
Fell, H Granville 1872- *WhLA*
Fell, Howard Barraclough 1917- *Au&Wr, ConAu 33*
Fell, Hunter Francis *Alli*
Fell, J Weldon *Alli*
Fell, James B *ChPo S1*
Fell, John 1625-1686 *Alli, BrAu, DcEnL, NewC, OxEng, REn*
Fell, John 1735-1797 *Alli*
Fell, John Corry *Alli Sup*
Fell, John L 1927- *ConAu 53*
Fell, Joseph B *Alli Sup*
Fell, Joseph P, III 1931- *ConAu 13R*
Fell, Margaret *Alli*
Fell, R C *Alli*
Fell, Ralph d1814 *Alli, BiDLA, BiDLA Sup*
Fell, Samuel 1594-1649 *Alli*
Fell, Stephen *Alli*
Fell, Walter William *Alli, BiDLA*
Fell, William *BiDLA*
Fell, William Richmond 1897- *WrD 1976*
Felland, Ole Gunderson 1853-1938 *DcNAA*
Felleman, Hazel *ChPo S2*
Feller, Frank d1908 *ChPo*
Feller, Robert William Andrew 1918- *AuBYP*
Feller, Sherman 1918- *AmSCAP 66*
Fellinge, Harry Lee 1888- *WhWNAA*
Fellings, Henry *WhWNAA*
Fellini, Federico 1920- *REn*
Fellman, Gordon 1934- *ConAu 53*

Fellman, Michael 1943- *ConAu 45*
Fellmeth, Robert C 1945- *ConAu 49*
Fellner, Rudolph *AuBYP*
Fellner, William John 1905- *ConAu 1R*
Fellow, Henry Coffin 1856- *ChPo S1, IndAu 1816, WhWNAA*
Fellow, R *Alli Sup*
Fellowe, Henry *Alli, BiDLA*
Fellowes, Anne *ConAu XR, WrD 1976*
Fellowes, E J *Alli Sup*
Fellowes, Edmund Horace 1870-1951 *NewC, WhLA*
Fellowes, Edward Colton 1864-1928 *DcNAA*
Fellowes, Francis 1803-1888 *DcNAA*
Fellowes, Sir James *Alli*
Fellowes, Mary Elizabeth *ChPo S1*
Fellowes, Robert 1770-1847 *Alli, BiDLA, DcEnL*
Fellowes, William D *Alli*
Fellowes-Gordon, Ian Douglas 1921- *ConAu 5R, Au&Wr*
Fellows, Annie J *ChPo*
Fellows, Brian John 1936- *ConAu 25*
Fellows, Sir Charles 1799-1860 *Alli, BiD&SB, BrAu 19*
Fellows, Donald Keith 1920- *ConAu 41*
Fellows, Edward B *ChPo S1*
Fellows, Mrs. Frank P *Alli Sup*
Fellows, G S *Alli Sup*
Fellows, George Emory 1858-1942 *AmLY, DcAmA, DcNAA, WhWNAA*
Fellows, Henry Parker 1848-1927 *Alli Sup, DcNAA*
Fellows, Hugh P 1915- *ConAu 37*
Fellows, Jay 1940- *ConAu 61*
Fellows, John *Alli, Alli Sup, BiDLA, BiDLA Sup*
Fellows, John d1785 *ChPo, PoCh*
Fellows, John 1760-1844 *BiD&SB, DcAmA, DcNAA*
Fellows, Lawrence 1924- *ConAu 49*
Fellows, Lena Gilbert *Alli Sup*
Fellows, Malcolm Stuart 1924- *Au&Wr, ConAu 9R, WrD 1976*
Fellows, Muriel H *AuBYP, ConAu 53, SmATA 10*
Fellows, Otis 1908- *ConAu 1R*
Fellows, R B *Alli Sup*
Fellows, Robert *Alli*
Fellows, Sarah A W *Alli Sup*
Fellows, Thomas Howard *Alli Sup*
Fellows-Johnston, Annie *AmA&B*
Felltham, Owen 1602?-1668? *Alli, BrAu, CasWL, Chmbr 1, EvLB, NewC, OxEng, REn*
Fels, Rendigs 1917- *ConAu 37*
Felsen, Gregor 1916- *JBA 1951*
Felsen, Henry Gregor 1916- *AuBYP, ConAu 1R, SmATA 1*
Felsher, Howard D 1927- *ConAu 17R*
Felshin, Simon *ChPo S1*
Felsing, William August 1891- *TexWr, WhWNAA*
Felstein, Ivor 1933- *Au&Wr, ConAu 41, WrD 1976*
Felstiner, L John, Jr. 1936- *ConAu 45*
Felt, Ephraim Porter 1868-1943 *DcNAA, WhWNAA*
Felt, Jeremy P 1930- *ConAu 23*
Felt, Joseph Barlow 1789-1869 *Alli, Alli Sup, AmA, AmA&B, BiD&SB, DcAmA, DcNAA*
Felt, Margaret Elley 1917- *ConAu 9R, WhPNW*
Felt, Sue 1924- *IlCB 1956*
Felter, Emma K 1896- *ConAu P-1*
Felter, Harvey Wickes 1865-1927 *DcNAA, OhA&B*
Felter, Mrs. M A *ChPo S1*
Felter, William Landon 1862-1933 *DcNAA, WhWNAA*
Feltham, John *Alli*
Feltham, Owen 1602?-1668? *Alli, DcEnL, DcLEnL, NewC, REn*
Feltoe, Charles Lett *Alli Sup*
Felton, B *DrAF 1976, DrAP 1975, LivBA*
Felton, Cornelius Conway 1807-1862 *Alli, Alli Sup, AmA, AmA&B, BbD,*

BiD&SB, CyAL 1, CyAL 2, DcAmA, DcNAA
Felton, Cyrus 1815-1890 Alli Sup, DcNAA
Felton, Daniel Alli
Felton, Edmond Alli
Felton, Frederick A MnBBF
Felton, George Alli
Felton, Harold William 1902- AuBYP, ChPo S2, ConAu 1R, MorJA, SmATA 1
Felton, Henry Alli
Felton, Henry 1679-1740 Alli, DcEnL
Felton, James A BlkAW
Felton, James Lee 1874-1932 ArizL
Felton, John 1595?-1628 NewC, REn
Felton, John H Alli
Felton, Mary ChPo
Felton, Nicholas d1626 Alli
Felton, Rebecca Latimer 1835-1930 AmA&B, BiDSA, DcNAA, WhWNAA
Felton, Ronald Oliver 1909- Au&Wr, ConAu 9R, SmATA 3
Felton, S Alli
Felton, William Alli, BiDLA
Felton, William H 1823-1909 BiDSA
Feltre, Vittorino Da CasWL
Feltskog, E N 1935- ConAu 37
Feltus, Benjamin Bloomfield PoIre
Feltwell, R Alli
Felver, Charles Stanley 1916- ConAu 33, WrD 1976
Femiano, Samuel D 1932- ConAu 21
Fen, James Alli
Fen, John d1615 Alli
Fenby, Charles 1905- Au&Wr
Fenby, Eric 1906- ConAu 25, WrD 1976
Fenby, Thomas Alli
Fencer, James Alli
Fendall, James Alli Sup
Fendall, Percy Alli Sup
Fendell, Bob 1925- ConAu 57
Fendell, Stanton Jonathan Davidson 1895- AnMV 1926
Fenderson, Harold 1910- BlkAW
Fenderson, Mark ChPo
Fendler, Edvard AmSCAP 66
Fenelon, Francois DeSalignac DeLaM 1651-1715 AtlBL, BbD, BiD&SB, CasWL, ChPo S1, DcEuL, EuA, NewC, OxEng, OxFr, Pen Eur, REn
Fenelon, Timothy Brendan PoIre
Feneon, Felix 1861-1944 OxFr
Fenerty, Charles BbtC
Fenestella 052?BC-019?AD CasWL, Pen Cl
Fenety, George Edward 1812-1899 BbtC, DcNAA, OxCan
Feng, Chih 1905- CasWL
Feng, Hsueh-Feng 1904?- CasWL
Feng, Hsueh-Feng 1906- DcOrL 1
Feng, Kuei-Fen 1809-1874 CasWL
Feng, Meng-Lung 1574?-1646? CasWL, DcOrL 1
Feng, Nai-Ch'ao DcOrL 1
Feng, Tao 882-954 CasWL
Feng, Yen-Chi DcOrL 1
Feng, Yu-Lung DcOrL 1
Fenger, Frederic Abildgaard 1882- AmLY, WhWNAA
Feniger, Siegmund WrD 1976
Fenin, George N 1916- ConAu 9R
Fenlon, Paul Edward 1921- ConAu 13R
Fenn, Lady Alli
Fenn, Alice And Fenn, Louisa M Alli Sup
Fenn, Annie S Alli Sup
Fenn, Charles 1907- Au&Wr, ConAu 9R, WrD 1976
Fenn, Clive Robert 1870?- MnBBF
Fenn, Dan H, Jr. 1923- ConAu 1R
Fenn, Lady Eleanor 1743-1813 CarSB, ChPo, DcEnL
Fenn, Elizabeth Hawley ChPo
Fenn, George Manville 1831-1909 Alli Sup, BbD, BiD&SB, BrAu 19, ChPo, ChPo S2, Chmbr 3, DcBiA, DcEnL, EvLB, HsB&A, MnBBF, NewC, WhCL
Fenn, Harry 1845-1911 ChPo S1, ChPo S2, EarAB, EarAB Sup
Fenn, Harvey ChPo
Fenn, J E Alli Sup

Fenn, John d1615 Alli
Fenn, Sir John 1739-1794 Alli, DcEnL
Fenn, Joseph Alli
Fenn, Percy Thomas 1892- OhA&B
Fenn, R J Alli Sup
Fenn, R W 1867- WhWNAA
Fenn, Richard Alli
Fenn, W W MnBBF
Fenn, Warwell Alli
Fenn, William Wallace 1862-1932 DcAmA, DcNAA
Fenn, William Wilthew 1827?- Alli Sup
Fenne, John d1615 Alli
Fenne, Thomas Alli
Fennel, Charles T P Alli Sup
Fennel, James 1766-1816 Alli
Fennell, Charles Augustus Maude Alli Sup
Fennell, Hugh Wordsworth d1956 MnBBF
Fennell, J W Alli Sup
Fennell, James 1766-1816 AmA, AmA&B, BiDLA, CnDAL, DcNAA, NewC
Fennell, John 1918- Au&Wr
Fennell, John Greville 1807-1885 Alli Sup
Fennell, John Lister Illingworth 1918- ConAu 1R, WrD 1976
Fennell, Mark 1844-1931 OhA&B
Fennell, Patrick 1842- PoIre
Fennell, Samuel PoIre
Fennelly, Catherine 1918- ConAu 37
Fennelly, John F 1899-1974 ConAu 53
Fennema, Owen Richard 1929- ConAu 49
Fenneman, Nevin M 1865-1945 DcNAA, OhA&B, WhWNAA
Fenner, Ball Alli Sup
Fenner, Beatrice 1904- AmSCAP 66
Fenner, C G Alli Sup
Fenner, Carol Elizabeth 1929- ConAu 5R, IlCB 1966, SmATA 7, WrD 1976
Fenner, Charles E BiDSA
Fenner, Christopher Smith 1823-1879 DcNAA
Fenner, Cornelius George 1822-1847 ChPo S2, DcAmA, DcNAA, OhA&B
Fenner, Dudley d1587 Alli
Fenner, E D Alli Sup
Fenner, Erasmus Darwin 1807-1866 DcNAA
Fenner, Frank John 1914- WrD 1976
Fenner, H Wolcott 1911-1972 ConAu 33, ConAu 37
Fenner, James 1923- ConAu 37
Fenner, Mrs. Jesse A OhA&B
Fenner, John J, Jr. BlkAW
Fenner, Kay Toy ConAu P-1
Fenner, Lanon A, Jr. BlkAW
Fenner, Lud John Alli
Fenner, Marian Warner Wildman 1876- ChPo
Fenner, Martha Day ChPo
Fenner, Mildred Sandison 1910- ConAu 33
Fenner, Phyllis Reid 1899- AuBYP, ConAu 5R, SmATA 1
Fenner, Ralph MnBBF
Fenner, Theodore 1919- ConAu 37
Fenner, William 1600-1640? Alli
Fennes, Clinton MnBBF
Fennimore, Keith John 1917- ConAu 57
Fenning, Daniel Alli
Fenning, Frederick Alexander 1874- WhWNAA
Fenno, Ann M ChPo S2
Fenno, Cordelia Brooks ChPo
Fenno, Dick 1927- AmSCAP 66
Fenno, F H Alli Sup
Fenno, John 1751-1798 AmA&B, OxAm
Fenno, R Francis, Jr. 1926- ConAu 5R
Fenno, Sara Perry 1857- WhWNAA
Fennor, William Alli
Fenollosa, Ernest Francisco 1853-1908 AmA, BiDSA, CnDAL, DcAmA, DcLEnL, DcNAA, OxAm, REn, REnAL, WebEAL
Fenollosa, Mary McNeil d1954 AmA&B, BiDSA, ChPo, DcAmA, WhWNAA
Fensch, Edwin A 1903- ConAu P-1
Fensch, Thomas 1943- ConAu 25
Fensham, Frank Charles 1925- Au&Wr
Fenster, Harry 1919- AmSCAP 66
Fenstermaker, J Van 1933- ConAu 29
Fenstock, Belle AmSCAP 66
Fenteman, Cooper Alli Sup
Fenten, Barbara D 1935- ConAu 53

Fenten, D X 1932- ConAu 33, SmATA 4, WrD 1976
Fenton PoIre
Fenton, Carroll Lane 1900-1969 AmA&B, AuBYP, ConAu 1R, ConAu 29, MorJA, SmATA 5
Fenton, Charles A 1919-1960 AmA&B
Fenton, Charles Hamilton Alli Sup
Fenton, Edward d1603 Alli
Fenton, Edward 1917- Au&Wr, AuBYP, ConAu 9R, SmATA 7, ThBJA
Fenton, Edward Dyne d1880 Alli Sup
Fenton, Elijah 1683-1730 Alli, BiD&SB, BrAu, CasWL, ChPo S1, Chmbr 2, DcEnA, DcEnL, EvLB, NewC, Pen Eng
Fenton, Eva ChPo
Fenton, Farrar Alli Sup
Fenton, Francis Dart Alli Sup
Fenton, Frank 1903-1971 ConAu 33
Fenton, Frank E 1904- OhA&B
Fenton, Freda ConAu XR
Fenton, Frederick Enos Alli Sup
Fenton, Sir Geoffrey 1539?-1608 Alli, BrAu, CrE&SL, NewC
Fenton, George Livingstone ChPo S1
Fenton, Gertrude Alli Sup
Fenton, Gladys ChPo S1
Fenton, H J H Alli Sup
Fenton, Henry Albert Alli Sup
Fenton, Howard AmSCAP 66
Fenton, J Alli
Fenton, J D Alli Sup
Fenton, James Alli Sup
Fenton, James 1949- ConP 1975, WrD 1976
Fenton, Sir Jeffrey d1608 Alli
Fenton, Jessie Chase 1894- WhWNAA
Fenton, John Alli Sup
Fenton, John Charles 1921- Au&Wr, ConAu P-1, WrD 1976
Fenton, John H 1921- ConAu 37
Fenton, John Y 1933- ConAu 53
Fenton, Joseph Clifford 1906- Au&Wr, CatA 1947, ConAu 5R
Fenton, Kate ChPo
Fenton, Mildred Adams 1899- Au&Wr, MorJA
Fenton, Myfanwy Alli Sup
Fenton, Richard d1821 Alli, BiDLA
Fenton, Roderick MnBBF
Fenton, Roger Alli
Fenton, Sophia Harvati 1914- ConAu 33
Fenton, Thomas Alli, Alli Sup
Fenton, W N OxCan Sup
Fenton, William James 1868- WhLA
Fentress, John W BlkAW
Fenwick, Lieutenant Colonel Alli
Fenwick, Mrs. BiDLA
Fenwick, Andrew Alli Sup
Fenwick, Charles G 1880-1973 ConAu 41
Fenwick, Mrs. E Alli
Fenwick, E Hurry Alli Sup
Fenwick, Edward William Alli Sup
Fenwick, Elizabeth Au&Wr
Fenwick, Francis DeWolfe ChPo
Fenwick, G E BbtC
Fenwick, George Alli
Fenwick, Horace Alli Sup
Fenwick, John Alli, BiDLA
Fenwick, John Ralph Alli, BiDLA
Fenwick, Kay ConAu XR
Fenwick, Kenneth Au&Wr
Fenwick, R O Alli, BiDLA
Fenwick, Samuel Alli Sup
Fenwick, Stephen Alli Sup
Fenwick, T Fitz-Roy Alli Sup
Fenwick, Thomas Alli, BbtC, BiDLA
Fenwick, William Alli
Fenwick, William 1905- WhWNAA
Fenwick-Miller Alli Sup
Fenwick-Owen, Roderic Franklin Rawnsley 1921- Au&Wr
Fenwicke, John Alli
Feofan Prokopovich 1681-1736 DcRusL
Feola, Jose M 1926- BiDPar
Fer, James Alli Sup
Ferander, Elliot W 1938- ConAu 21
Feraoun, Mouloud 1913-1962 CasWL
Feraud, F G BiDLA

Feraud, Jean-Francois *OxFr*
Feravolo, Rocco Vincent 1922- *AuBYP,*
ConAu 1R, SmATA 10
Ferazani, Larry 1940- *ConAu 61*
Ferber, Adolph C 1916- *IndAu 1917*
Ferber, Andrew 1935- *ConAu 53*
Ferber, Edna 1887-1968 *AmA&B,*
AmNov, AuNews 1, Chmbr 3, CnDAL, CnMD,
CnThe, ConAmA, ConAmL, ConAu 5R,
ConAu 25, DcLEnL, EncWL, EvLB,
LongC, McGWD, ModAL, ModWD,
OxAm, Pen Am, REn, REnAL,
SmATA 7, TwCA, TwCA Sup, TwCW,
WhWNAA, WiscW
Ferber, Nat Joseph 1889-1945 *AmA&B,*
DcNAA
Ferber, Robert 1922- *ConAu 37, WrD 1976*
Ferdinand *PueRA*
Ferdinand I, Kaiser 1503-1564 *OxGer*
Ferdinand II, Kaiser 1578-1637 *OxGer*
Ferdinand III, Kaiser 1608-1657 *OxGer*
Ferdinand I, Kaiser Von Osterreich 1793-1875
OxGer
Ferdinand II Of Aragon 1452-1516 *REn*
Ferdinand V Of Castile 1452-1516 *REn*
Ferdinand Von Tirol, Erzherzog 1529-1595
OxGer
Ferdinand, Roger 1898- *CnMD, McGWD*
Ferdinand, Theodore Nichols 1929- *ConAu 23,*
IndAu 1917
Ferdinand, Val *BlkAW*
Ferdon, Edwin N, Jr 1913- *ConAu 21*
Ferdousi, Abolqasem Mansur B Hasan
940?-1020? *DcOrL 3*
Ferebe, George *Alli*
Fereira, Antonio 1528-1569 *DcEuL*
Fereira, Miguel Leitao *DcEuL*
Ferejohn, John A 1944- *ConAu 53*
Ferel, W *Alli Sup*
Ference, Michael 1911- *IndAu 1917*
Fergerson, William *ChPo*
Fergus, A Freeland *Alli Sup*
Fergus, Andrew *Alli Sup*
Fergus, Henry *Alli, BiDLA*
Fergus, John *ChPo*
Fergus, John F *ChPo S1*
Fergus, Mrs. M *Alli Sup*
Fergus, Patricia M 1918- *ConAu 53*
Ferguson SEE ALSO Fergusson
Ferguson *Alli*
Ferguson, A *MnBBF*
Ferguson, A M, Jr. *Alli Sup*
Ferguson, A M And John *Alli Sup*
Ferguson, Adam *Alli, Chmbr 2*
Ferguson, Adam 1723?-1816 *Alli, BbD,*
BiD&SB, CasWL, DcEnL, EvLB, NewC
Ferguson, Alfred Riggs 1915-1974 *ConAu 1R,*
ConAu 49, IndAu 1917
Ferguson, Allyn 1924- *AmSCAP 66*
Ferguson, Andrew *Alli, Alli Sup*
Ferguson, Archibald *Alli Sup*
Ferguson, Arthur B 1913- *ConAu 5R*
Ferguson, Bessie Gowan *WhWNAA*
Ferguson, Blanche Emanuel 1906- *BlkAW,*
IndAu 1917, LivBA
Ferguson, C A *ChPo*
Ferguson, C E 1928- *ConAu 17R*
Ferguson, Charles D 1832- *OhA&B*
Ferguson, Charles Pinckney 1824-1906
IndAu 1917
Ferguson, Charles W 1901- *AmA&B,*
ConAu 13R, REnAL, TexWr
Ferguson, Chris 1944- *ConAu 57*
Ferguson, Clarence Clyde, Jr. 1924- *ConAu 5R*
Ferguson, D *Alli Sup*
Ferguson, David *Alli*
Ferguson, Donald N 1882- *ConAu 5R*
Ferguson, Dugald 1940- *Alli Sup, ChPo S1p*
Ferguson, E James 1917- *ConAu 61*
Ferguson, Elizabeth Graeme 1739-1801 *Alli,*
AmA&B, ChPo S1, CyAL 1, DcAmA
Ferguson, Emily *OxCan*
Ferguson, Emma Henry 1840-1905 *BiDSA,*
DcNAA
Ferguson, Eugene Clay *ChPo S2*
Ferguson, Evelyn C 1910- *WhPNW,*
WrD 1976
Ferguson, Everett 1933- *ConAu 33,*

WrD 1976
Ferguson, Fergus *Alli Sup*
Ferguson, George *Alli Sup*
Ferguson, George Dalrymple 1829-1926 *DcNAA*
Ferguson, George Henry Hewitt Oliphant- 1817-
Alli Sup
Ferguson, H *Alli*
Ferguson, Henry 1848?-1917 *DcAmA, DcNAA*
Ferguson, Howard 1908- *ConAu P-1*
Ferguson, Hugh Henry *CyAL 1*
Ferguson, Ira Lunan 1904- *BlkAW*
Ferguson, J A *Alli Sup*
Ferguson, J Halcro 1920- *ConAu 1R*
Ferguson, James *Alli, Alli Sup*
Ferguson, Sir James *Alli*
Ferguson, James 1710-1776 *Alli, DcEnL*
Ferguson, James 1842- *ChPo*
Ferguson, James Haig 1862- *WhLA*
Ferguson, James M 1936- *ConAu 23*
Ferguson, Jan Helenus *Alli Sup*
Ferguson, Jesse Babcock d1870 *Alli Sup,*
DcNAA
Ferguson, John *Alli, Alli Sup, ChPo S2*
Ferguson, John 1850-1939 *DcNAA*
Ferguson, John 1881-1928 *ChPo*
Ferguson, John 1921- *Au&Wr, ConAu 5R*
Ferguson, John Bell *Au&Wr*
Ferguson, John Bohn 1879- *OhA&B*
Ferguson, John Calvin 1866- *WhLA,*
WhWNAA
Ferguson, John Charles *Alli Sup*
Ferguson, John Clarke *ChPo*
Ferguson, John Creery *Alli Sup*
Ferguson, John DeLancey 1888- *AmA&B,*
OhA&B
Ferguson, John Henry 1907- *ConAu 13R*
Ferguson, M Carr 1931- *ConAu 49*
Ferguson, Margaret C 1863- *WhWNAA*
Ferguson, Marilyn 1938- *ConAu 25*
Ferguson, Lady Mary Catherine *Alli Sup*
Ferguson, Max *OxCan Sup*
Ferguson, Mike 1934- *ConAu 25*
Ferguson, Milton James 1879-1954 *AmA&B,*
WhWNAA
Ferguson, N L *ChPo S1*
Ferguson, Olin Jerome 1875- *WhWNAA*
Ferguson, Oliver W 1924- *ConAu 5R*
Ferguson, Peter Roderick Innes 1933- *Au&Wr,*
ConAu 5R, WrD 1976
Ferguson, Richard Saul 1837- *Alli Sup*
Ferguson, Richard William *Alli Sup*
Ferguson, Robert *Alli, Alli Sup*
Ferguson, Robert d1714 *Alli, NewC*
Ferguson, Robert 1837- *Alli Sup*
Ferguson, Robert D 1921- *ConAu 17R*
Ferguson, Robert M *Alli Sup*
Ferguson, Robert W 1940- *ConAu 61*
Ferguson, Russell Jennings 1898-1955
IndAu 1917
Ferguson, Sir Samuel 1810-1886 *Alli Sup, BbD,*
BiD&SB, BrAu 19, CasWL, ChPo,
ChPo S1, Chmbr 3, EvLB, NewC,
OxEng, Pen Eng, PoIre
Ferguson, Suzanne 1939- *ConAu 57*
Ferguson, Thomas 1900- *Au&Wr*
Ferguson, Thomas Ewing *TexWr*
Ferguson, Thomas Owens *PoIre*
Ferguson, Thompson B 1857-1921 *DcNAA*
Ferguson, Tom *Alli Sup*
Ferguson, W H *Alli Sup*
Ferguson, W L *ChPo*
Ferguson, Walter W 1930- *IlBYP, IlCB 1956*
Ferguson, William *Alli, Alli Sup, ChPo*
Ferguson, William 1820-1887 *Alli Sup*
Ferguson, William 1823- *Alli Sup*
Ferguson, William 1943- *ConAu 49*
Ferguson, William Blair Morton 1881-1967
AmA&B
Ferguson, William Dwyer *Alli, Alli Sup*
Ferguson, William Porter Frisbee 1861-1929
AmLY, DcNAA, WhWNAA
Ferguson, William Scott 1875-1954 *AmA&B,*
WhWNAA
Ferguson And Vance *Alli*
Fergusone, David *Alli*
Furgusson SEE ALSO Furguson
Fergusson, A *Alli Sup*
Fergusson, Adam *Alli Sup*

Fergusson, Adam 1724- *BiDLA*
Fergusson, Adam 1782-1862 *BbtC, OxCan*
Fergusson, Alexander *Alli Sup, BiDLA*
Fergusson, Sir Bernard 1911- *Au&Wr,*
ConAu 9R, DcLEnL
Fergusson, Charles Bruce *OxCan*
Fergusson, David *Alli*
Fergusson, Edmund Morris 1864-1934 *DcNAA,*
WhWNAA
Fergusson, Elizabeth Graeme *AmA&B*
Fergusson, Erna 1888-1964 *AmA&B,*
ConAu P-1, SmATA 5
Fergusson, Francis 1904- *AmA&B, ConAu 9R,*
REnAL, TwCA Sup, WrD 1976
Fergusson, G Bruce *OxCan Sup*
Fergusson, Harvey 1890-1971 *AmA&B,*
AmNov, CnDAL, ConAu 33, OxAm,
REnAL, TwCA, TwCA Sup, WhWNAA
Fergusson, James *BiDLA*
Fergusson, James 1808-1886 *Alli, Alli Sup,*
BbD, BiD&SB, DcEnL, EvLB, NewC
Fergusson, Sir James 1904- *Au&Wr*
Fergusson, James R *Alli Sup*
Fergusson, John *Alli*
Fergusson, Robert *Alli, BiDLA, Chmbr 2*
Fergusson, Robert 1750-1774 *Alli, BbD,*
BiD&SB, BrAu, CasWL, ChPo,
ChPo S2, DcEnL, DcLEnL, EvLB,
NewC, OxEng, Pen Eng, WebEAL
Fergusson, Robert Menzies 1859- *Alli Sup,*
ChPo, ChPo S2
Fergusson, Samuel *ChPo S2*
Fergusson, Sir Samuel 1810-1886 *DcLEnL*
Fergusson, Thomas *ChPo S2*
Fergusson, W F *Alli Sup*
Fergusson, William *Alli, Alli Sup*
Fergusson, William 1806-1862 *ChPo*
Fergusson, Sir William 1808-1877 *Alli Sup*
Fergusson Hannay, Lady *Au&Wr, ConAu 9R*
Fergusson Hannay, Doris *WrD 1976*
Feriencik, Mikulas Stefan 1825-1881 *CasWL*
Ferkiss, Victor C 1925- *ConAu 21*
Ferland, Albert 1872-1943 *CanWr, OxCan*
Ferland, Jean Baptiste Antoine 1805-1864 *BbtC,*
CanWr, DcNAA, OxCan
Ferlin, Nils 1898-1961 *CasWL, EncWL,*
Pen Eur
Ferlinghetti, Lawrence 1919?- *ConAu 5R,*
ConDr, ConLC 2, ConLC 6, ConP 1970,
ConP 1975, CrCAP, CrCD, DrAP 1975,
ModAL, OxAm, Pen Am, RAdv 1, REn,
REnAL, TwCW, WebEAL, WhTwL,
WorAu, WrD 1976
Ferlinghetti, Lawrence 1920- *AmA&B,*
CasWL
Ferlita, Ernest 1927- *ConAu 29, WrD 1976*
Ferm, Betty 1926- *ConAu 23*
Ferm, Deane William 1927- *ConAu 33,*
WrD 1976
Ferm, Robert Livingston 1931- *ConAu 13R*
Ferm, Vergilius Ture Anselm 1896-1974
AmA&B, Au&Wr, ConAu 9R, ConAu 49,
OhA&B
Ferman, Joseph Wolfe 1906- *AmA&B*
Fermar, Henrietta Louisa *Alli*
Fermat, Pierre De 1595?-1665 *OxFr*
Ferme, Charles d1620? *Alli, DcEnL*
Ferme, George *Alli Sup*
Fermi, Laura Capon 1907- *AmA&B, AuBYP,*
ConAu 1R, SmATA 6, WrD 1976
Fermor, Arabella d1738 *NewC*
Fermor, Henrietta Louisa d1761 *NewC*
Fermor, Patrick Leigh 1915- *Au&Wr, LongC,*
TwCW, WorAu
Fermor, William *Alli, BiDLA*
Fermoy, W Lerwick *Alli Sup*
Fern, Doctor *Alli*
Fern, Alan M 1930- *ConAu 33*
Fern, Eugene A 1919- *ConAu 1R, SmATA 10*
Fern, Fanny 1811-1872 *Alli, AmA, AmA&B,*
BbD, BiD&SB, ChPo, DcAmA, DcBiA,
DcEnL, DcNAA, OxAm, REnAL
Fern, Robert *Alli*
Fern, Thomas *Alli*
Fernald, Mrs. Charles F *Alli Sup*
Fernald, Charles Henry 1838-1921 *Alli Sup,*
DcAmA, DcNAA
Fernald, Charles Henry 1894- *WhWNAA*

Fernald, Chester Bailey 1869-1938 *AmA&B,*
BiD&SB, DcAmA, DcNAA, OxAm,
REnAL, WhWNAA
Fernald, Hannah G *ChPo*
Fernald, James Champlin 1838-1918 *AmA&B,*
DcAmA, DcNAA, OhA&B
Fernald, John 1905- *ConAu 23*
Fernald, Merritt Caldwell 1838-1916 *DcNAA*
Fernald, Robert Heywood 1871-1937 *DcNAA*
Fernald, Woodbury M *Alli Sup*
Fernan Caballero 1796-1877 *CasWL, DcEuL,*
DcSpL, EuA
Fernan, E C *Alli Sup*
Fernandes, Joao *OxCan*
Fernandes, Millor 1924- *WhGrA*
Fernandez, Diego 1530?-1581 *BiD&SB*
Fernandez, E E And Smythies, A *Alli Sup*
Fernandez, Eleonora *Alli*
Fernandez, Geronimo *DcEuL*
Fernandez, Jose S 1893- *BiDPar*
Fernandez, Joseph *Alli Sup*
Fernandez, Joseph A 1921- *ConAu 37*
Fernandez, Juan Santos 1847- *AmLY*
Fernandez, Julio A 1936- *ConAu 33*
Fernandez, Lucas 1474?-1542 *BiD&SB,*
CasWL, DcEuL, McGWD, Pen Eur
Fernandez, Macedonio 1874-1952 *Pen Am*
Fernandez, Pablo Armando 1930- *Pen Am*
Fernandez, Ronaldo *BlkAW*
Fernandez Almagro, Melchor 1895- *ClDMEuL*
Fernandez Ardavin, Luis 1892- *McGWD*
Fernandez DeAvellaneda, Alonso *CasWL,*
DcSpL, REn
Fernandez DeHeredia, Juan 1310?-1396 *CasWL*
Fernandez DeJerena, Garci *Pen Eur*
Fernandez DeJerena ALSO Ferrandez
Fernandez DeLaReguera, Ricardo 1914-
Au&Wr, ConAu 5R
Fernandez DeLizardi, Jose Joaquin 1776-1827
CasWL, CyWA, DcSpL, Pen Am, REn
Fernandez DeLosRios, Angel 1821-1879
BiD&SB
Fernandez DeMoratin *DcSpL, EvEuW*
Fernandez DeMoratin, Leandro 1760-1828
CasWL, EuA, McGWD, REn
Fernandez DeMoratin, Nicolas 1737-1780
CasWL, McGWD
Fernandez DeOviedo, Gonzalo 1478-1557 *PueRA*
Fernandez DePiedrahita, Lucas 1624-1688 *BbD,*
BiD&SB
Fernandez DeRojas, Juan *DcSpL*
Fernandez DeVelasco Y Pimentel, B 1783-1851
CasWL, EvEuW
Fernandez Florez, Wenceslao 1885?-1964
CasWL, ClDMEuL, EncWL, EvEuW,
REn
Fernandez-Guerra Y Orbe, Aureliano 1816?-1894
BbD, BiD&SB
Fernandez-Guerra Y Orbe, Luis 1818-1894
BiD&SB
Fernandez Juncos, Manuel 1846-1928 *PueRA*
Fernandez-Lizardi, Jose Joaquin 1771-1827
BiD&SB
Fernandez MacGregor, Genaro 1883-
WhWNAA
Fernandez-Madrid, Jose 1789-1829 *BiD&SB*
Fernandez-Marina, R 1909- *ConAu 41*
Fernandez Mendez, Eugenio 1924- *PueRA*
Fernandez Moreno, Baldomero 1885-1950
Pen Am
Fernandez Moreno, Cesar 1919- *DcCLA*
Fernandez Pacheco *DcSpL*
Fernandez Retamar, Roberto 1930- *DcCLA,*
Pen Am
Fernandez Spencer, Antonio 1923- *DcCLA*
Fernandez Vanga, Epifanio 1880-1961 *PueRA*
Fernandez Y Gonzalez, Manuel 1821-1888 *BbD,*
BiD&SB, CasWL, ClDMEuL, DcSpL,
REn
Fernandis, Sarah Collins 1863- *BlkAW*
Fernando VII *DcSpL*
Fernando, Marian Frances *Alli Sup*
Fernando, Patrick 1931- *ConP 1970*
Ferne, Henry 1602-1661 *Alli*
Ferne, Sir John d1610? *Alli, DcEnL*
Ferne, Robert *Alli*
Ferne, William *Alli*
Fernea, Elizabeth Warnock 1927- *ConAu 13R*

Fernea, Robert Alan 1932- *ConAu 33*
Fernehough, William *Alli*
Fernel, John *Alli, BiDLA*
Fernett, Gene 1924- *ConAu 49*
Ferneyhough, Frank 1911- *Au&Wr*
Ferneyhough, Roger 1941- *Au&Wr*
Fernie, John *Alli, Alli Sup*
Fernie, William Thomas *Alli Sup*
Fernihough, John C *Alli Sup*
Fernleigh, Frederick *Alli Sup*
Fernow, Bernhard Edouard 1851-1923 *DcNAA*
Fernow, Berthold 1837-1908 *Alli Sup, AmA,*
AmA&B, DcAmA, DcNAA
Ferns, Henry Stanley 1913- *Au&Wr,*
ConAu 5R
Ferns, Ronald George 1925- *IlCB 1966*
Feron, John *Alli, BiDLA*
Ferra, Count Di *WhWNAA*
Ferracuti, Franco 1927- *ConAu 25*
Ferrall, Denis *Alli*
Ferrall, S A *Alli*
Ferran Degrie, Antonio 1877- *WhLA*
Ferrand, Eduard 1813-1842 *BiD&SB*
Ferrand, Mrs. William Robson *ChPo S1*
Ferrandez DeJerena, Garci *CasWL*
Ferrandez DeJerena ALSO Fernandez
Ferrante, Arthur 1921- *AmSCAP 66*
Ferrar, Harold 1935- *WrD 1976*
Ferrar, John *Alli, PoIre*
Ferrar, Nicholas 1592-1637 *Alli, BrAu, NewC,*
REn
Ferrar, Robert *Alli*
Ferrar, W J *MnBBF*
Ferrar, W M *Alli Sup*
Ferrar, William Hugh *Alli Sup*
Ferrara, Il Cieco Di *CasWL*
Ferrari, Giuseppe 1812-1876 *BbD, BiD&SB*
Ferrari, Mary Selby *DrAP 1975*
Ferrari, Paolo 1822-1889 *BiD&SB, EvEuW,*
McGWD
Ferrari, Severino 1856-1905 *BiD&SB,*
ClDMEuL
Ferraris, Richard 1922- *AmSCAP 66*
Ferrarius, James Alex *Alli*
Ferraro, Joseph 1895- *AmSCAP 66*
Ferrars, E X 1907- *ConAu XR, EncM&D*
Ferrars, Edward *REn*
Ferrars, Elizabeth 1907- *Au&Wr, ConAu XR,*
WrD 1976
Ferrater-Mora, Jose 1912- *ConAu 1R*
Ferraud, Jean-Francois *OxFr*
Ferrazzi, Giuseppe Jacopo 1813-1887 *BiD&SB*
Ferre, Clifford F 1920- *AmSCAP 66*
Ferre, Frederick 1933- *ConAu 13R,*
WrD 1976
Ferre, Gustave A 1918- *ConAu 1R*
Ferre, Nels Frederick Solomon 1908-1971
AmA&B, ConAu 29
Ferrebee, Michael *Alli*
Ferree, Abby M Laflin *Alli Sup*
Ferree, Barr 1864?-1924 *DcNAA*
Ferree, J W *Alli Sup*
Ferreira, Antonio 1528-1569 *BbD, BiD&SB,*
CasWL, CyWA, EuA, EvEuW, Pen Eur,
REnWD
Ferreira, Antonio Batica 1938?- *AfL 1*
Ferreira, Djalma 1913- *AmSCAP 66*
Ferreira, Jose DaSilva Maia 1825?- *AfL 1*
Ferreira DeCastro, Jose Maria 1898-1974
ConAu 49, EncWL, EvEuW, ModRL,
Pen Eur, TwCW, WhTwL
Ferreira DeVasconcellos, Jorge d1585 *BiD&SB,*
EuA
Ferrel, William 1817-1891 *Alli Sup, DcAmA,*
DcNAA
Ferrell, Chiles Clifton 1865- *BiDSA*
Ferrell, Mallory Hope 1935- *ConAu 33*
Ferrell, Robert H 1921- *ConAu 5R*
Ferrell, Robert W 1913- *ConAu 13R*
Ferrell, T *Alli Sup*
Ferreol, Marcel Auguste 1899-1974 *ConAu 53,*
McGWD
Ferrer, Aldo 1927- *ConAu 25*
Ferrer, Max *Alli Sup*
Ferrer Canales, Jose 1913- *PueRA*
Ferrer DelRio, Antonio 1814-1872 *CasWL*
Ferrer Hernandez, Gabriel 1847-1900 *PueRA*
Ferrer Otero, Rafael 1885-1951 *PueRA*

Ferreras, Juan De 1652-1735 *BiD&SB, DcSpL*
Ferrerius, Johannes *Alli*
Ferrero, Guglielmo 1871-1942 *BiD&SB,*
ClDMEuL, TwCA, TwCA Sup
Ferrero, Leo 1903-1933 *CnMD, McGWD*
Ferrers, Edward *Alli*
Ferrers, George 1512?-1579? *Alli, CasWL,*
DcEnL, NewC
Ferrers, Henry 1579-1663 *Alli*
Ferrers, Norman Macleod *Alli Sup*
Ferrers, Richard *Alli*
Ferres, James Moir *BbtC*
Ferres, John H 1932- *ConAu 41*
Ferrette, Jules *Alli Sup*
Ferrey, Benjamin *Alli*
Ferreyra DeLaCerda, Bernarda 1595-1644
BiD&SB
Ferriar, John 1764-1815 *Alli, BiDLA,*
BiDLA Sup, DcEnL, EvLB
Ferriby, John *Alli*
Ferrie, Adam d1864 *BbtC*
Ferrie, William 1815-1903 *BbtC, DcNAA*
Ferrier, Ben And Ferrier, Marion *OxCan*
Ferrier, David 1843- *Alli Sup*
Ferrier, E Eloise *IndAu 1917*
Ferrier, J T *Alli Sup*
Ferrier, James Frederick 1808-1864 *Alli,*
Alli Sup, BrAu 19, Chmbr 3, DcEnL,
EvLB, NewC, OxEng
Ferrier, James Walter *Alli Sup*
Ferrier, Janet Mackay 1919- *Au&Wr,*
ConAu 9R
Ferrier, John *Alli*
Ferrier, John Turing *Alli Sup*
Ferrier, Mary d1855 *Alli*
Ferrier, Paul 1843-1920 *EvEuW*
Ferrier, Robert *Alli, Alli Sup*
Ferrier, Susan E 1782-1854 *BbD, BiD&SB,*
BrAu 19, CasWL, ChPo S2, Chmbr 3,
DcBiA, DcEnA, DcEnL, DcEuL,
DcLEnL, EvLB, NewC, OxEng,
WebEAL
Ferrier, W *Alli, BiDLA*
Ferrier, William Warren 1855-1945 *DcNAA,*
IndAu 1917
Ferrigni, Piero Francesco L C 1836-1895
BiD&SB
Ferril, Helen Ray 1897- *OhA&B*
Ferril, Thomas Hornsby 1896- *AmA&B, ChPo,*
ChPo S1, ChPo S2, CnDAL, ConP 1970,
ConP 1975, OxAm, REnAL, TwCA Sup,
WrD 1976
Ferrin, Clark Ela 1818-1881 *DcNAA*
Ferrin, Dana Holman 1886-1960 *AmA&B*
Ferris, Anita Brockway 1881-1923 *DcNAA*
Ferris, Benjamin d1867 *Alli, DcNAA*
Ferris, Benjamin G *Alli, Alli Sup*
Ferris, Constance 1898- *WhWNAA*
Ferris, Daniel *Alli Sup*
Ferris, Don A 1919- *AmSCAP 66*
Ferris, Elizabeth *ChPo*
Ferris, Ezra 1783-1857 *IndAu 1816*
Ferris, George Hooper 1867-1917 *DcNAA*
Ferris, George Titus 1840- *Alli Sup, BiD&SB,*
DcAmA, DcNAA
Ferris, Helen Josephine 1890?-969 *AmA&B,*
AuBYP, ChPo, JBA 1934, JBA 1951,
REnAL, WhWNAA
Ferris, Henry Weybridge *Alli Sup*
Ferris, Isaac *CyAL 2*
Ferris, J F *Alli Sup*
Ferris, Jacob *Alli Sup*
Ferris, James *Alli, BiDLA*
Ferris, James Cody *AmNov XR, ConAu 19,*
SmATA 1
Ferris, John Alexander *Alli Sup*
Ferris, John Stephen 1937- *WrD 1976*
Ferris, Mary Lanman Douw 1855- *AmLY*
Ferris, Murray Whiting *ChPo*
Ferris, Paul Frederick 1929- *Au&Wr,*
ConAu 5R, WrD 1976
Ferris, Richard *PoIre*
Ferris, Robert *PoIre*
Ferris, Samuel *Alli, BiDLA*
Ferris, Sarah *Alli, BiDLA*
Ferris, Theodore N, Jr. 1920- *OhA&B*
Ferris, Theodore Parker 1908-1972 *AmA&B,*

Field, Benjamin *Alli Sup*
Field, Benjamin Franklin 1868- *AnMV 1926,*
 WhWNAA
Field, Benjamin Rush 1861-1935 *Alli Sup,*
 AmLY, DcNAA
Field, Caroline Leslie 1853-1902 *Alli Sup,*
 AmA&B, BiD&SB, ChPo, ChPo S1,
 DcAmA, DcNAA
Field, Carolyn W *ChPo S1*
Field, Charles *ConAu XR*
Field, Charles Dickinson 1836- *Alli Sup*
Field, Charles Kellogg 1873- *ChPo, ChPo S1,*
 ChPo S2
Field, Chester *Alli*
Field, David Dudley 1781-1867 *Alli Sup,*
 DcAmA, DcNAA
Field, David Dudley 1805-1894 *Alli Sup,*
 DcAmA, DcNAA
Field, Dawn Stewart 1940- *ConAu 57,*
 WrD 1976
Field, Dick 1912- *ConAu 57*
Field, E E *Alli Sup*
Field, Mrs. E M 1856- *Alli Sup, ChPo,*
 ChPo S1
Field, Edmund *Alli Sup*
Field, Edward *BbtC*
Field, Edward 1858-1928 *DcAmA, DcNAA*
Field, Edward 1924- *AmA&B, ConAu 13R,*
 ConP 1970, ConP 1975, CrCAP,
 DrAP 1975, SmATA 8, WrD 1976
Field, Edward Brenton 1903- *WhWNAA*
Field, Edward Salisbury 1878-1936 *DcNAA,*
 IndAu 1917
Field, Edwin Williams 1804-1871 *Alli, Alli Sup*
Field, Elinor Whitney 1889- *ChPo, ChPo S1*
Field, Ernest R 1925- *ConAu 5R*
Field, Eugene 1850-1895 *Alli Sup, AmA,*
 AmA&B, AmSCAP 66, AuBYP, BbD,
 BiD&SB, BiDSA, CarSB, CasWL, ChPo,
 ChPo S1, ChPo S2, Chmbr 3, CnDAL,
 DcAmA, DcLEnL, DcNAA, EvLB,
 JBA 1934, OxAm, OxEng, Pen Am,
 RAdv 1, REn, REnAL, St&VC
Field, F E *Alli Sup*
Field, Frank 1936- *ConAu 21*
Field, Frank Chester *ConAu XR*
Field, Frank McCoy 1887- *ConAu 45*
Field, Frederick *Alli, Alli Sup*
Field, Frederick 1801-1885 *Alli Sup*
Field, Frederick V 1905- *WhWNAA*
Field, G *Alli Sup, BiDLA*
Field, G d1859 *EarAB*
Field, G W 1914- *ConAu 37*
Field, George *Alli Sup*
Field, George 1777-1854 *Alli*
Field, George Purdey *Alli Sup*
Field, George Washington d1889 *Alli Sup,*
 DcAmA, DcNAA
Field, Gordon Lawrence 1939- *ConAu 17R*
Field, Grace Stone *ChPo*
Field, H A *ChPo S1*
Field, Hamilton Easter 1873- *AmLY*
Field, Hazel E 1891- *ConAu P-1*
Field, Henry *Alli*
Field, Henry 1902- *AmA&B, Au&Wr*
Field, Henry Martyn 1822-1907 *Alli, Alli Sup,*
 AmA&B, BbD, BiD&SB, DcAmA,
 DcNAA
Field, Henry Martyn 1837-1912 *Alli Sup,*
 DcAmA, DcNAA
Field, Mrs. Henry Martyn *Alli Sup*
Field, Hermann H 1910- *Au&Wr*
Field, Hope 1905- *OhA&B*
Field, Horace *Alli Sup*
Field, Mrs. Horace *Alli Sup*
Field, Irving M 1934- *ConAu 25*
Field, Isobel Osbourne Strong 1858-
 IndAu 1816
Field, James *Alli*
Field, Mrs. James A *ChPo, DcAmA*
Field, James A, Jr. 1916- *ConAu 25*
Field, James Alfred 1880-1927 *DcNAA*
Field, Jasper Newton 1855-1929 *OhA&B*
Field, Joanna *ConAu XR, WrD 1976*
Field, John *Alli*
Field, John 1813-1884 *Alli Sup*
Field, John 1910- *ConAu 33, WrD 1976*
Field, John 1928- *WrD 1976*

Field, John Edward *Alli Sup*
Field, John P 1936- *ConAu 37*
Field, Joseph M 1810-1856 *AmA&B, BiDSA,*
 DcAmA, DcNAA, OxAm, PoIre, REnAL
Field, Joshua Leslie 1857- *Alli Sup*
Field, Joyce W 1932- *ConAu 29*
Field, Kate 1838-1896 *Alli Sup, AmA&B,*
 BbD, BiD&SB, BiDSA, DcAmA,
 DcNAA
Field, Leon C *Alli Sup*
Field, Leonard And Dunn, Edward C *Alli Sup*
Field, Leslie A 1926- *ConAu 29*
Field, Lida Amanda d1908 *BiDSA*
Field, Lilian Dudley *Alli Sup*
Field, Louise A *OhA&B*
Field, Louise Maunsell *AmA&B*
Field, Lucy *Alli Sup*
Field, M J *Au&Wr*
Field, Marcus *MnBBF*
Field, Margaret *Alli Sup*
Field, Mark G 1923- *ConAu 37, WrD 1976*
Field, Martha Reinhard 1855- *BiDSA*
Field, Martin d1833 *Alli*
Field, Mary H *ChPo*
Field, Mary Katherine 1838-1896 *DcAmA,*
 DcNAA
Field, Matthew *Alli*
Field, Matthew C 1812-1844 *Alli, ChPo S1,*
 PoIre
Field, Maunsell Bradhurst 1822-1875 *Alli Sup,*
 AmA, AmA&B, BiD&SB, DcAmA,
 DcNAA
Field, Michael *Alli Sup, BrAu 19, ChPo,*
 ChPo S1, ChPo S2, Chmbr 3,
 DcEnA Ap, DcEuL, DcRusL, EvLB,
 LongC, ModBL, NewC, OxEng, Pen Eng,
 REn
Field, Michael 1915-1971 *ConAu 29*
Field, Mildred Fowler 1897- *AnMV 1926*
Field, Minna *ConAu 25*
Field, Nathan 1587-1620? *BrAu, CasWL,*
 CnThe, CrE&SL, EvLB, Pen Eng, REn,
 REnWD
Field, Nathaniel *Alli, Chmbr 1*
Field, Nathaniel 1587-1620? *DcEnA, DcEnL,*
 DcLEnL, NewC, OxEng, WebEAL
Field, Nathaniel 1805-1888 *BiDSA,*
 IndAu 1816
Field, Parker B *Alli Sup*
Field, Peter *MnBBF, WrD 1976*
Field, Peter 1876-1949 *DcNAA*
Field, R *Alli Sup*
Field, Rachel 1894-1942 *AmA&B, AnCL,*
 AuBYP, BkCL, CarSB, ChPo, ChPo S1,
 ChPo S2, CnDAL, ConAmA, ConICB,
 DcNAA, JBA 1934, JBA 1951, LongC,
 Newb 1922, OxAm, REnAL, St&VC,
 TwCA, TwCA Sup, TwCW
Field, Richard 1561-1616 *Alli, DcEnL*
Field, Richard Stockton 1803-1870 *Alli,*
 CyAL 2, DcNAA
Field, Rogers *Alli Sup*
Field, Roswell F *ChPo S1*
Field, Roswell Martin 1851-1919 *AmA,*
 AmA&B, BiD&SB, BiDSA, ChPo,
 ChPo S2, DcAmA, DcNAA
Field, Sara Bard 1882- *AmA&B, AnMV 1926,*
 ChPo, ChPo S1, ChPo S2, OhA&B,
 TwCA, TwCA Sup, WhWNAA
Field, Stanley 1911- *ConAu 21*
Field, Stephen Johnson 1816-1899 *DcNAA,*
 OxAm
Field, Theop *Alli*
Field, Thomas *Alli Sup*
Field, Thomas P 1914- *ConAu 9R*
Field, Thomas Warren 1821?-1881 *Alli Sup,*
 AmA, AmA&B, DcAmA, DcNAA
Field, W *Alli, BiDLA*
Field, Walter 1824-1876 *Alli Sup*
Field, Walter S 1899- *ConAu 49*
Field, Walter Taylor 1861-1939 *AmA&B,*
 AmLY, ChPo, DcNAA, WhWNAA
Field, Wilford E *MnBBF*
Field, William *Alli, BiDLA*
Field, William 1846- *WhLA*
Field, William Noe 1915- *CatA 1952*
Field, William Osgood *ChPo*
Field, Wright *AnMV 1926*

Fielde, Adele Marion 1839-1916 *DcAmA,*
 DcNAA
Fielden, Charlotte *OxCan Sup*
Fielden, Olga *Au&Wr*
Fielden, Thomas Perceval 1882- *Au&Wr,*
 ConAu 5R
Fielder, Charles N 1900- *AmSCAP 66*
Fielder, F *Alli Sup*
Fielder, Gertrude W *ChPo*
Fielder, Herbert *BiDSA*
Fielder, James *Alli Sup*
Fielder, John *Alli*
Fielder, Mildred 1913- *ConAu 13R,*
 WrD 1976
Fielder, Richard *Alli*
Fieldhouse, Charles Hubbard 1883-1969
 IndAu 1917
Fieldhouse, Murray Julian 1925- *Au&Wr*
Fieldhouse, Thomas *ChPo S1*
Fielding, A *LongC*
Fielding, A E *NewC, TwCA*
Fielding, A W *ConAu XR*
Fielding, Alexander Wallace 1918- *Au&Wr*
Fielding, Charles George *Alli*
Fielding, Copley *ChPo S1*
Fielding, Daphne Winifred Louise 1904-
 Au&Wr, ConAu 9R
Fielding, Gabriel 1916- *ConAu XR,*
 ConNov 1972, ConNov 1976, ModBL,
 ModBL Sup, NewC, RAdv 1, WorAu,
 WrD 1976
Fielding, George *Alli, BiDLA*
Fielding, Harry Lee *WhWNAA*
Fielding, Henry 1707-1754 *Alli, AtlBL, BbD,*
 BiD&SB, BrAu, CasWL, ChPo,
 ChPo S1, Chmbr 2, CnThe, CriT 2,
 CyWA, DcBiA, DcEnA, DcEnL, DcEuL,
 DcLEnL, EvLB, McGWD, MouLC 2,
 NewC, OxEng, Pen Eng, RAdv 1, RCom,
 REn, REnWD, WebEAL
Fielding, Howard *MnBBF*
Fielding, Hubert *WrD 1976*
Fielding, James Holyrod *Alli*
Fielding, Jerry 1922- *AmSCAP 66*
Fielding, John *Alli*
Fielding, Sir John d1780 *Alli*
Fielding, Joseph 1800- *Alli Sup*
Fielding, Joy 1945- *ConAu 49, OxCan Sup*
Fielding, Lee 1888-1963 *AmSCAP 66*
Fielding, Mantle 1865-1941 *DcNAA*
Fielding, Newton Smith 1799-1856 *Alli Sup*
Fielding, Raymond E 1931- *ConAu 17R,*
 WrD 1976
Fielding, Robert *Alli*
Fielding, Sarah 1710-1768 *Alli, BbD,*
 BiD&SB, BrAu, CarSB, CasWL,
 Chmbr 2, DcEnA, DcEnL, DcEuL,
 DcLEnL, EvLB, NewC Eng, OxEng,
 Pen Eng
Fielding, T *Alli*
Fielding, T H *Alli*
Fielding, Temple Hornaday 1913- *AmA&B,*
 ConAu 29
Fielding, Vernon *MnBBF*
Fielding, Waldo L 1921- *ConAu 45*
Fielding, William J 1886- *AmA&B,*
 ConAu 13R, WhWNAA
Fielding, Xan *ConAu XR, WrD 1976*
Fielding-Hall, Harold 1859-1917 *ChPo S1*
Fielding-Ould, Fielding *ChPo S2*
Fiedler, Leslie A 1917- *ConLC 4, ModAL*
Fieldmouse, Timon *DcEnL*
Fields, Adele M *Alli Sup*
Fields, Alan 1930- *Au&Wr*
Fields, Annie Adams 1834-1915 *Alli Sup,*
 AmA, AmA&B, BbD, BiD&SB, ChPo,
 ChPo S2, CnDAL, DcAmA, DcNAA
Fields, Arthur 1888-1953 *AmSCAP 66*
Fields, Arthur C 1926?-1974 *ConAu 49*
Fields, Beverly 1917- *ConAu 49*
Fields, Buddy 1889-1965 *AmSCAP 66*
Fields, Caroline C *Alli Sup*
Fields, Dorothy 1905-1974 *AmSCAP 66,*
 ConAu 49, ConDr
Fields, Florence *ChPo*
Fields, Irving 1915- *AmSCAP 66*
Fields, J C 1863- *WhWNAA*
Fields, James Thomas 1817?-1881 *Alli,*

Alli Sup, *AmA*, *AmA&B*, *BbD*,
BiD&SB, *ChPo*, *ChPo S1*, *ChPo S2*,
CnDAL, *CyAL 2*, *DcAmA*, *DcEnL*,
DcLEnL, *DcNAA*, *OxAm*, *REnAL*
Fields, Jeff *AuNews 2*
Fields, Joseph 1895-1966 *AmA&B*, *CnMD*,
ConAu 25, *McGWD*, *ModWD*
Fields, Julia 1938- *BlkAW*, *DrAP 1975*,
LivBAA
Fields, Lewis Maurice 1867-1941 *REnAL*
Fields, Maurice C *BlkAW*
Fields, Maurice C 1915-1938 *DcNAA*
Fields, Nora *ConAu 49*
Fields, Victor Alexander 1901- *Au&Wr*,
ConAu 5R, *WrD 1976*
Fields, Wilbert J 1917- *ConAu 13R*
Fields, William Claude 1880-1946 *DcNAA*
Fieler, Frank B 1935- *ConAu 41*
Fien, Lupin 1908- *AmSCAP 66*
Fiene, Ernest 1894-1965 *ConAu P-1*
Fiennes, Celia 1662-1741 *Alli Sup*, *OxEng*
Fiennes, Nathaniel 1608-1669 *Alli*
Fiennes, Ranulph 1944- *ConAu 45*
Fiennes, Richard N 1909- *ConAu 23*,
WrD 1976
Fiennes, William 1582-1662 *Alli*
Fierburtus, Nic *Alli*
Fiero, George William 1906- *WhWNAA*
Fiero, James Newton 1847-1931 *Alli Sup*,
DcNAA, *WhWNAA*
Fiery, Samuel M *BiDSA*
Fieschi, Joseph 1790-1836 *OxFr*
Fieser, Max 1930- *ConAu 13R*
Fiesole, Mino Da 1431-1484 *REn*
Fievee, Joseph 1767-1839 *BiD&SB*, *OxFr*
Fife, Lord *Alli*
Fife, Austin E 1909- *ConAu 53*
Fife, Duncan 1893- *Br&AmS*
Fife, George Buchanan 1869-1939 *AmA&B*,
DcNAA
Fife, J C *Alli Sup*
Fife, M B *Alli Sup*
Fife, Robert Herndon 1871-1958 *AmA&B*
Fife, Robert Oldham 1918- *ConAu 37*
Fife, W W *Alli Sup*
Fife-Cookson *Alli Sup*
Fifelfo, Francesco 1398-1481 *DcEuL*
Fifield, Lawrence Wendell 1891-1935 *DcNAA*
Fifield, William 1916- *Au&Wr*, *ConAu 13R*,
WrD 1976
Figaro 1809-1837 *DcSpL*
Figaro 1814-1875 *AmA*, *OxAm*
Figes, Eva 1932- *Au&Wr*, *ConAu 53*,
ConNov 1976, *WrD 1976*
Figg, James Carnegie 1857-1886 *ChPo S1*
Figg, R W *Alli Sup*
Figges, James *Alli*
Figgis, Darrell 1882-1925 *NewC*, *PoIre*
Figgis, John Benjamin *Alli Sup*
Figgs, Carrie Law Morgan *BlkAW*
Figh, Margaret Gillis 1896- *ConAu 29*
Fighter Pilot, A *ConAu XR*
Figueiredo, Fidelino DeSousa 1888- *ClDMEuL*
Figueiredo, Guilherme 1915- *CnThe*, *REnWD*
Figueiredo, Manuel De 1725-1801 *CasWL*
Figueiredo, Cristoval Suarez De *BiD&SB*
Figueroa, Diego De *DcEuL*
Figueroa, Edwin 1925- *PueRA*
Figueroa, Francisco 1730?-1800? *BiD&SB*
Figueroa, Francisco Acuna De 1791-1862 *BbD*,
BiD&SB
Figueroa, Francisco De 1540?-1620? *BbD*,
BiD&SB, *CasWL*, *DcEuL*, *Pen Eur*
Figueroa, John 1920- *ConP 1970*, *ConP 1975*,
WrD 1976
Figueroa, John L *DrAF 1976*
Figueroa, Jose *DcEuL*
Figueroa, Jose-Angel *BlkAW*, *DrAP 1975*
Figueroa, Loida *ConAu 57*
Figueroa, Pablo 1938- *ConAu 61*, *SmATA 9*
Figueroa, Sotero 1863-1923 *PueRA*
Figueroa-Chapel, Ramon 1935- *ConAu 45*,
DrAP 1975
Figueroa DeCifredo, Patria *PueRA*
Figueroa-Mercado, Loida 1917- *ConAu 57*
Figueroa Y Cordoba, Diego 1619- *CasWL*
Figueroa Y Cordoba, Jose 1625- *CasWL*
Figuerora, Cristoval Suarez De *BbD*

Figuier, Guillaume Louis 1819-1894 *BiD&SB*
Figuier, Louis Guillaume 1819-1894 *BbD*
Figuli, Margita 1909- *CasWL*
Figurito, Joseph 1922- *ConAu 29*
Fijan, Carol 1918- *ConAu 53*
Fikret, Tevfik 1867-1915 *CasWL*, *DcOrL 3*
Fikso, Eunice Cleland 1927- *ConAu 5R*
Filarete, Il 1400?-1470 *REn*
Filas, Francis Lad 1915- *Au&Wr*, *BkC 5*,
ConAu 5R
Filas, Thomas J 1908- *AmSCAP 66*
Filbey, Edward Joseph 1879- *WhWNAA*
Filby, P William 1911- *ChPo S2*, *ConAu 9R*,
WrD 1976
Fildes, Samuel Luke 1844-1927 *ChPo*
Filding, Ford *Alli*
Filelfo, Francesco 1398-1481 *CasWL*, *REn*
Filene, Catherine 1896- *WhWNAA*
Filene, Edward Albert 1860-1937 *DcNAA*
Filene, Peter G 1940- *ConAu 21*
Filep, Robert Thomas 1931- *ConAu 45*
Fileti-Ramondetta, Concettina 1830- *BbD*,
BiD&SB
Filewood, F R *Alli*
Filgate, Fitzherbert *Alli*
Filgate, James M 1911- *Au&Wr*
Filhive, Don Juan *BiDSA*
Filia *AmA&B*
Filiatrault, Jean 1919- *CanWr*, *OxCan*
Filicaia, Vincenzo Da 1642-1707 *CasWL*,
EvEuW, *Pen Eur*, *REn*
Filicaja, Vincenzo Da 1642-1707 *BbD*,
BiD&SB, *DcEuL*
Filimon, Nicolae 1819-1865 *CasWL*
Filinto Elysio *CasWL*, *EvEuW*
Filion, Jean-Paul *OxCan*
Filipowski, H E *Alli*
Filippo, Eduardo De 1900- *EncWL*
Filkes, John *Alli*, *BiDLA Sup*
Filkin, Walt 1876- *ChPo*, *ChPo S1*,
WhWNAA
Fillans, James 1808-1852 *ChPo*
Filleau, E A *ChPo S2*
Fillebrown, Charles Bowdoin 1842-1917 *DcNAA*
Fillebrown, Rebekah Huddell 1863- *ChPo*
Fillebrown, Thomas 1836-1908 *DcNAA*
Filler, Harry 1908- *AmSCAP 66*
Filler, Louis 1912- *ConAu 1R*, *OhA&B*
Fillery, William Edmund 1903- *AnMV 1926*
Filleul, Marianne 1828- *Alli Sup*
Filleul, Philip Valpy Mourant *Alli Sup*
Filley, Anna d1896 *DcNAA*
Filley, Mrs. C L *BiDSA*
Filley, Mrs. Chauncey I *Alli Sup*
Filley, Chauncey Ives 1829-1923 *DcNAA*
Filley, Horace Clyde 1878- *WhWNAA*
Fillmer, Henry Thompson 1932- *ConAu 23*
Fillmore, Augustus D 1823- *Alli*
Fillmore, Henry 1881-1956 *AmSCAP 66*
Fillmore, John Comfort 1843-1898 *Alli Sup*,
DcAmA, *DcNAA*, *OhA&B*
Fillmore, Lewis *ChPo S2*
Fillmore, Lowell 1882- *ConAu P-1*
Fillmore, Millard 1800-1874 *AmA&B*, *OxAm*,
REnAL
Fillmore, Parker Hoysted 1878-1944 *AmA&B*,
DcNAA, *JBA 1934*, *JBA 1951*, *OhA&B*,
YABC 1
Fillmore, Roscoe Alfred 1887- *ConAu 5R*
Fillmore, W Rickert *ChPo S1*
Fills, Robert *Alli*
Film *WhLA*
Filmer, Catherine *Alli Sup*
Filmer, Edward *Alli*
Filmer, Robert *CyAL 1*
Filmer, Sir Robert *Chmbr 1*
Filmer, Sir Robert d1647 *Alli*
Filmer, Sir Robert d1688 *DcEnL*
Filmer, Sir Robert 1590?-1653? *EvLB*, *NewC*
Filmore, Lewis *Alli Sup*
Filomena *WhLA*
Filomena Del Monte *PueRA*
Filon, Auguste 1800-1875 *BiD&SB*
Filsinger, Ernest B 1880- *WhWNAA*
Filson, Davidson 1829-1899 *OhA&B*
Filson, Floyd Vivian 1896- *AmA&B*,
ConAu 61
Filson, John 1747?-1788 *Alli*, *AmA*, *AmA&B*,

BiDLA, *BiDSA*, *DcAmA*, *DcNAA*,
OhA&B, *OxAm*, *REnAL*
Filteau, Gerard *OxCan*
Filumena, Saint *REn*
Fimberg, Harold Alfred 1907- *AmSCAP 66*
Fin-Bec *DcEnL*
Fina, Jack 1913- *AmSCAP 66*
Finality John *NewC*
Finberg, Franz A 1907- *TexWr*, *WhWNAA*
Finberg, Herbert Patrick Reginald 1900-1974
Au&Wr, *ConAu 53*, *ConAu P-1*
Finch, A C *ChPo S2*
Finch, A Elley *Alli Sup*
Finch, Amanda *BlkAW*
Finch, Anne 1661-1720 *Alli*, *BrAu*, *CasWL*,
ChPo, *ChPo S1*, *CnE&AP*, *DcEnL*,
EvLB, *NewC*
Finch, B *Alli*, *BiDLA*
Finch, Barbara Clay *Alli Sup*, *ChPo S1*
Finch, Bernard *MnBBF*
Finch, C *ChPo*, *ChPo S1*
Finch, Charles *Alli*
Finch, Christopher 1939- *WrD 1976*
Finch, Daniel 1647-1729? *Alli*
Finch, Dick 1898-1955 *AmSCAP 66*
Finch, Donald George 1937- *ConAu 53*
Finch, Mrs. E *Alli Sup*
Finch, Edward *Alli*
Finch, Frances E And Sibley, Frank J *Alli Sup*
Finch, Francis Miles 1827-1907 *AmA*,
AmA&B, *BbD*, *BiD&SB*, *ChPo*, *DcAmA*,
DcNAA, *OxAm*, *REnAL*
Finch, Francis Oliver *Alli Sup*
Finch, George *Alli*, *Alli Sup*
Finch, Gerard Brown 1835- *Alli Sup*
Finch, Harold Josiah 1898- *Au&Wr*,
WrD 1976
Finch, Heneage d1689 *Alli*
Finch, Heneage 1621-1682 *Alli*
Finch, Heneage Wynne *ChPo S1*
Finch, Henry *Alli*
Finch, Sir Henry 1558-1625 *Alli*, *NewC*
Finch, Henry Leroy 1918- *ConAu 41*
Finch, J *BbtC*
Finch, John *Alli*, *ConDr*
Finch, John Bird 1852-1887 *DcAmA*, *DcNAA*
Finch, John Lord *Alli*
Finch, Julia Neely *ChPo*
Finch, Marianne *Alli Sup*
Finch, Martin *Alli*
Finch, Matthew *ConAu XR*, *WrD 1976*
Finch, Merton *ConAu XR*, *WrD 1976*
Finch, Mildred Austin *ChPo*
Finch, Peter 1947- *ConP 1970*, *WrD 1976*
Finch, R *Alli*, *BiDLA*
Finch, Richard *Alli*
Finch, Robert 1783-1830 *Alli*
Finch, Robert Duer Claydon 1900- *CanWr*,
CasWL, *ConAu 57*, *ConP 1970*,
ConP 1975, *DcLEnL*, *LongC*, *OxCan*,
WrD 1976
Finch, Robert Poole *Alli*
Finch, Ruth Goddard 1906- *AmSCAP 66*
Finch, Ruy H 1890- *WhWNAA*
Finch, Thomas *Alli*, *BiDLA*
Finch, W *Alli*
Finch, William *Alli*
Finch, William Albert 1855-1912 *DcNAA*
Finch, William Stafford *Alli Sup*
Finch-Hatton *Alli Sup*
Fincham, J R S 1926- *Au&Wr*
Fincham, John *Alli Sup*
Fincher, Cameron Lane 1926- *ConAu 41*
Fincher, Ernest B 1910- *ConAu 53*
Fincher, Joseph *Alli*
Finck, Edward Bertrand 1870-1931 *BiDSA*,
DcNAA, *WhWNAA*
Finck, Furman J 1900- *ConAu 33*
Finck, Henry Theophilus 1854-1926 *Alli Sup*,
AmA&B, *AmLY*, *BbD*, *BiD&SB*,
BiDSA, *DcAmA*, *DcNAA*, *REnAL*
Fincke, Charles Louis 1873-1906 *DcNAA*
Fincke, Gary 1945- *ConAu 57*
Finckel, Edwin A 1917- *AmSCAP 66*
Finckelthaus, Gottfried 1610-1647? *OxGer*
Finckh, Ludwig 1876-1964 *OxGer*
Finden, W And E *Alli*
Findlater, Andrew 1810-1885 *NewC*

Findlater, Charles *Alli, BiDLA*
Findlater, Jane Helen 1866-1946 *LongC, NewC, WhLA*
Findlater, Mary 1865-1964 *LongC, WhLA*
Findlater, Richard 1921- *Au&Wr*
Findlay, A G *Alli*
Findlay, Alexander 1874- *WhLA*
Findlay, Bruce *Alli Sup*
Findlay, Bruce Allyn 1895-1972 *ConAu P-1*
Findlay, Cecilia *Alli Sup*
Findlay, David Kilpatrick 1901- *Au&Wr, ConAu P-1, OxCan*
Findlay, E B *ChPo*
Findlay, Hugh 1880- *ChPo, WhWNAA*
Findlay, J *Alli*
Findlay, James F, Jr. 1930- *ConAu 49*
Findlay, Jessie Patrick *Alli Sup*
Findlay, John K *Alli*
Findlay, John Niemeyer 1903- *Au&Wr, ConAu 5R*
Findlay, John Ritchie 1824-1898 *Alli Sup, NewC*
Findlay, Joseph John 1860- *WhLA*
Findlay, Philip *Alli Sup*
Findlay, Robert 1721-1814 *Alli, BiDLA, BiDLA Sup*
Findlay, Robert R 1932- *ConAu 45*
Findlay, William *ChPo S2*
Findley, Paul 1921- *ConAu 29*
Findley, Samuel 1818-1889 *Alli Sup, DcAmA, DcNAA, OhA&B*
Findley, Samuel 1831-1908 *DcNAA, OhA&B*
Findley, Timothy 1930- *ConAu 25, OxCan Sup*
Findley, William 1741?-1821 *Alli, DcAmA, DcNAA*
Fine, Benjamin 1905-1975 *AmA&B, ConAu 5R, ConAu 57*
Fine, Elsa Honig 1930- *ConAu 49*
Fine, Henry Burchard 1858-1928 *DcAmA, DcNAA*
Fine, I V 1918- *ConAu 17R*
Fine, Irving 1914-1962 *AmSCAP 66*
Fine, Jack Wolf 1922- *AmSCAP 66*
Fine, John *Alli Sup*
Fine, John 1794-1867 *DcNAA*
Fine, Ralph Adam 1941- *ConAu 29*
Fine, Reuben 1914- *ConAu 17R*
Fine, Sidney 1904- *AmSCAP 66*
Fine, Sidney 1920- *ConAu 1R, WrD 1976*
Fine, Sydney 1920- *AmA&B*
Fine, Sylvia *AmSCAP 66*
Fine, Warren 1943- *ConAu 21*
Fine, William Michael 1924- *ConAu 13R*
Fineberg, S Andhil 1896- *AmA&B, Au&Wr*
Finegan, J T *Alli*
Finegan, Jack 1908- *ConAu 1R, WrD 1976*
Finegan, James Emmet 1876-1940 *DcNAA*
Finegan, Thomas Edward 1866-1932 *DcNAA, WhWNAA*
Finegan, William J 1917- *AmSCAP 66*
Fineman, Irving 1893- *AmA&B, AmNov, Au&Wr, ConAu 1R, ConAu 5R, OxAm, REnAL, TwCA, TwCA Sup, WhWNAA, WrD 1976*
Finer, Herman 1898- *AmA&B*
Finer, Leslie 1921- *ConAu 13R*
Finer, Samuel Edward 1915- *Au&Wr, ConAu 41*
Finerty, John Frederick 1846-1908 *AmA&B, DcAmA, DcNAA*
Finestone, Harry 1920- *ConAu 45*
Finett, Sir John 1571-1640 *Alli*
Fingard, Judith *OxCan Sup*
Finger, Benjamin Sardon, Jr. 1914- *Au&Wr*
Finger, Charles Joseph 1869?-1941 *AmA&B, AnCL, AuBYP, BkCL, DcNAA, JBA 1934, Newb 1922, OhA&B, REnAL, TwCA, WebEAL*
Fingesten, Peter 1916- *ConAu 13R*
Finglass, Esther *Alli, BiDLA*
Finglass, John *Alli*
Fingleton, John Henry Webb 1908- *Au&Wr*
Finigan, J T *BiDLA*
Fink, Arthur Emil 1903- *ConAu 1R*
Fink, Augusta 1916- *ConAu 33, WrD 1976*
Fink, Brat *ConAu XR*
Fink, Bruce 1861-1927 *OhA&B*

Fink, Denman 1880- *ChPo, ChPo S1*
Fink, Edith 1918- *ConAu 61*
Fink, Gary M 1936- *ConAu 53*
Fink, Gottfried Wilhelm 1783-1846 *OxGer*
Fink, Henry 1893-1963 *AmSCAP 66*
Fink, Joseph 1915- *ConAu 57*
Fink, Leo Gregory *BkC 4*
Fink, Merton 1921- *Au&Wr, ConAu 9R, WrD 1976*
Fink, Michael 1939- *AmSCAP 66*
Fink, Mike 1770?-1823? *CnDAL, OxAm, REnAL*
Fink, Ollie E 1898- *OhA&B*
Fink, Paul Jay 1933- *ConAu 53*
Fink, Stevanne Auerbach *ConAu 57*
Fink, William B 1916- *ConAu 41*
Fink, William Wescott 1844- *ChPo, DcNAA*
Fink, Z S 1902- *ConAu P-1*
Finke, George 1869- *AmLY, WhWNAA*
Finke, John, Jr. 1898-1965 *AmSCAP 66*
Finkel, Benjamin Franklin 1865- *WhWNAA*
Finkel, Donald 1929- *AmA&B, ConAu 23, ConP 1970, ConP 1975, DrAP 1975, WrD 1976*
Finkel, George 1909-1975 *Au&Wr, ConAu 17, SmATA 8*
Finkel, Lawrence S 1925- *ConAu 13R*
Finkelhoffe, Fred L *REnAL*
Finkelnburg, Gustavus Adolphus 1837-1908 *DcNAA*
Finkelstein, Jacob Joel 1922-1974 *ConAu 53*
Finkelstein, Leonid Vladimirovitch 1924- *ConAu 23*
Finkelstein, Louis 1895- *AmA&B, ConAu 13R, OhA&B, WhWNAA*
Finkelstein, Marina S 1921?-1972 *ConAu 33*
Finkelstein, Sidney 1910?-1974 *ConAu 45*
Finkenbinder, Erwin Oliver 1884- *WhWNAA*
Finkle, Jason L 1926- *ConAu 23*
Finlason, W *Alli*
Finlason, William Francis *Alli Sup*
Finlay, Campbell K 1909- *Au&Wr, ConAu 5R*
Finlay, Dan *Alli Sup*
Finlay, David J 1934- *ConAu 25*
Finlay, David Lake *Alli Sup*
Finlay, Finona *ConAu XR*
Finlay, George 1799-1875 *Alli, Alli Sup, BbD, BiD&SB, BrAu 19, Chmbr 3, DcEnA, EvLB, NewC, OxEng*
Finlay, Sir Graeme Bell 1917- *Au&Wr*
Finlay, Ian 1906- *Au&Wr, WrD 1976*
Finlay, Ian F 1924- *Au&Wr*
Finlay, Ian Hamilton 1925- *ChPo S2, ConP 1970, ConP 1975, WebEAL, WorAu, WrD 1976*
Finlay, J R *Alli Sup*
Finlay, James Fairbairn *Alli Sup*
Finlay, John *Alli, ChPo S2*
Finlay, John 1782-1810 *Alli, NewC*
Finlay, John Alexander Robertson 1917- *Au&Wr*
Finlay, John W *Alli Sup, PoIre*
Finlay, Matthew Henderson 1916- *ConAu 13R*
Finlay, T *Alli Sup*
Finlay, T A *Alli Sup*
Finlay, Virgil *ChPo*
Finlay, William 1792-1847 *ChPo*
Finlay, William 1936- *ConAu XR, WrD 1976*
Finlay, Winifred Lindsay Crawford 1910- *Au&Wr, ConAu 9R, WrD 1976*
Finlayson, Ann 1925- *ConAu 29, SmATA 8*
Finlayson, Duncan *OxCan*
Finlayson, George *Alli*
Finlayson, Grace McConahy Reininger 1885- *OhA&B*
Finlayson, James *Alli, Alli Sup*
Finlayson, James d1872 *Alli Sup*
Finlayson, John *Alli*
Finlayson, John 1780-1826 *Alli*
Finlayson, Joseph Andrews *Alli*
Finlayson, Roderick David 1904- *ConNov 1976, DcLEnL, LongC, WebEAL, WrD 1976*
Finlayson, T Campbell *Alli Sup*
Finletter, Thomas K 1893- *AmA&B*
Finley, Mrs. C D *ChPo*
Finley, Catherine L *BlkAW*
Finley, David Dewees 1933- *IndAu 1917*

Finley, Elisabeth R *ChPo*
Finley, Eugenia Howard *BiDSA*
Finley, Glenna 1925- *AuNews 1, ConAu XR, WrD 1976*
Finley, Harold M 1916- *ConAu 17R*
Finley, Harriet *Alli Sup*
Finley, Irene 1880- *WhWNAA*
Finley, James Bradley 1781-1856 *Alli Sup, AmA&B, DcAmA, DcNAA, OhA&B*
Finley, Jean *OhA&B*
Finley, John 1797-1866 *Alli Sup, AmA&B, BbD, BiD&SB, BiDSA, ChPo, ChPo S1, DcAmA, DcNAA, IndAu 1816, OhA&B, PoIre, REnAL*
Finley, John, Jr. *ChPo S2*
Finley, John Huston 1863-1940 *AmA&B, ChPo, ChPo S1, DcNAA*
Finley, John Huston, Jr. 1904- *AmA&B*
Finley, John Park 1854- *Alli Sup, DcAmA*
Finley, Lewis M 1929- *ConAu 61*
Finley, Lorraine Noel 1899- *AmSCAP 66, AnMV 1926*
Finley, Martha Farquharson 1828-1909 *Alli Sup, AmA, AmA&B, BiD&SB, BiDSA, CarSB, CnDAL, DcAmA, DcNAA, IndAu 1816, OhA&B, OxAm, REnAL, WhCL*
Finley, Mike *DrAP 1975*
Finley, Moses I 1912- *AmA&B, ConAu 5R*
Finley, Robert 1772-1817 *Alli, CyAL 1, DcNAA*
Finley, Ruth Ebright 1884-1955 *AmA&B, OhA&B*
Finley, Samuel 1715-1766 *Alli, CyAL 1, DcNAA*
Finley, William L 1876- *AmLY, WhWNAA*
Finn, Alexander *Alli Sup*
Finn, Anna E *WhWNAA*
Finn, Dorothy Elizabeth *ConP 1970*
Finn, Edmund 1819-1898 *DcLEnL*
Finn, Elizabeth Anne *Alli Sup*
Finn, Eugenia Townsend 1887- *WhWNAA*
Finn, Francis James 1859-1928 *AmA&B, AmLY, BiD&SB, BiDSA, DcAmA, DcNAA, OhA&B, WhWNAA*
Finn, Frank 1868- *WhLA*
Finn, Frank S *ChPo, HsB&A*
Finn, Henry J 1782-1840 *Alli, BbtC, CyAL 1*
Finn, Henry James William 1787-1840 *AmA, AmA&B, DcNAA*
Finn, Hugh Lauder 1925- *ConP 1970*
Finn, Jack M *MnBBF*
Finn, James *Alli, Alli Sup*
Finn, James 1924- *IndAu 1917*
Finn, Jonathan 1884?-1971 *ConAu 29*
Finn, Sister Mary Paulina 1842-1935 *DcNAA*
Finn, R Welldon *ConAu XR*
Finn, Ralph Leslie 1912- *ConAu 5R*
Finn, Ralph Leslie 1922?- *Au&Wr, WrD 1976*
Finn, Reginald Patrick Arthur Welldon 1900- *Au&Wr, ConAu 13R*
Finn, Rex Welldon *ConAu XR*
Finn, William J 1881-1961 *AmSCAP 66*
Finnamore, John *Alli Sup, PoIre*
Finnegan, Ruth H *ConAu XR*
Finnelly, W *Alli*
Finnemore, Hilda 1891- *MnBBF*
Finnemore, John E *MnBBF*
Finneran, John *Alli Sup*
Finneran, Richard J 1943- *ConAu 29, WrD 1976*
Finnerty, Peter *Alli, BiDLA*
Finney, Ben R 1933- *ConAu 45*
Finney, Burnham 1899- *OhA&B*
Finney, Charles Grandison 1792-1875 *Alli, AmA&B, DcAmA, DcNAA, OhA&B*
Finney, Charles Grandison 1905- *AmA&B, ConAu 29, TwCA, TwCA Sup*
Finney, David John 1917- *Au&Wr*
Finney, Escott *MnBBF*
Finney, Frederick Norton 1832-1916 *DcNAA*
Finney, Gertrude Elva 1892- *AuBYP, ConAu P-1, IndAu 1917, WhPNW*
Finney, Gretchen Ludke 1901- *ConAu 9R*
Finney, Harry Anson 1886- *WhWNAA*
Finney, Jack 1911- *Au&Wr*
Finney, John *Alli*
Finney, Marian MacLean *WhWNAA*

Finney, Mark *ConAu XR*
Finney, Ross Lee 1875-1934 *DcNAA, WhWNAA*
Finney, Ross Lee 1906- *AmSCAP 66*
Finney, Roy P 1897- *WhWNAA*
Finney, S G *Alli Sup*
Finney, S J *Alli Sup*
Finney, Theodore Mitchell 1902- *AmA&B, ConAu 61*
Finney, William *Alli Sup*
Finnie, Richard 1906- *OxCan*
Finnie, Williamson Jackson 1913- *Au&Wr*
Finnigan, Joan 1923- *ConP 1970, ConP 1975*
Finnigan, Joan 1925- *ConAu 17R, WrD 1976*
Finnigan, Joan *OxCan Sup*
Finnigan, John 1925- *Au&Wr*
Finnin, Mary *ConP 1970, WrD 1976*
Finnis, B T *Alli Sup*
Finnur Jonsson 1704-1789 *DcEuL*
Finocchiaro, Mary 1913- *ConAu 29*
Finola *ChPo S1*
Finot, Louis-Jean 1898- *WhLA*
Finotti, Joseph Maria 1817-1879 *Alli Sup, AmA&B, BiD&SB, DcAmA, DcNAA*
Finstein, Max *ConP 1970*
Finston, Nat W *AmSCAP 66*
Finta, Alexander 1881- *IlCB 1945*
Finucane, Jack *DcEnL*
Finx, E *OxGer*
Finzgar, Franc Saleski 1871-1962 *CasWL, EncWL*
Fiofori, Tam *BlkAW*
Fiona Macleod *NewC, OxEng*
Fiore, Carmen Anthony *BlkAW*
Fiore, Michael V 1934- *ConAu 45*
Fiore, Peter Amadeus 1927- *ConAu 33, WrD 1976*
Fiore, Silvestro 1921- *ConAu 17R*
Fiorentino, Giovanni *REn*
Fiorino, A John 1926- *ConAu 29, WrD 1976*
Fiorino, Vincent C 1899- *AmSCAP 66*
Fiorio, Franco Emilio 1912-1975 *ConAu 61*
Fiorito, Ernest 1907-1960 *AmSCAP 66*
Fiorito, Ted 1900- *AmSCAP 66*
Fiott, John *Alli, BiDLA*
Fippin, Elmer Otterbein 1879-1949 *OhA&B, WhWNAA*
Firaq Gorakhpuri 1896- *DcOrL 2*
Firbank, Arthur Annesley Ronald 1886-1926 *TwCA, TwCA Sup*
Firbank, Ronald 1886-1926 *AtlBL, CasWL, CnMWL, DcLEnL, EncWL, LongC, ModBL, ModBL Sup, NewC, OxEng, Pen Eng, RAdv 1, REn, TwCW, WebEAL, WhTwL*
Firbank, Thomas 1910- *Au&Wr*
Firchow, Peter 1937- *ConAu 37, WrD 1976*
Firdausi 935?-1020? *AnCL, BiD&SB, NewC, REn*
Firdausi, Abul Kasim Mansur 935?-1020? *OxEng*
Firdausi, Abu'l-Qasim 935?-1020? *CasWL, RCom*
Firdausi, Mansur Abu'l-Qasim 935?-1020? *Pen Cl*
Firdousi 935?-1020? *AnCL, NewC, REn*
Firdusi 935?-1020? *AnCL, BbD, BiD&SB, NewC, REn*
Firdusi, Abdul Cassem 935?-1020? *ChPo S1*
Firdusi, Abul Kasim Mansur 935?-1020? *OxEng*
Firebrace, Sir Aylmer Newton George 1886- *Au&Wr, ConAu 5R*
Firebrace, John *Alli*
Firebrace, Roy Charles 1889- *BiDPar*
Firenzuola, Agnolo 1493-1543? *BbD, BiD&SB, CasWL, DcEuL, EuA, Pen Eur, REn*
Fireside, Harvey F 1929- *ConAu 29, WrD 1976*
Firestone, Clark Barnaby 1869-1957 *AmA&B, OhA&B, REnAL*
Firestone, Harvey Samuel 1868-1938 *DcNAA, OhA&B*
Firestone, Harvey Samuel, Jr. 1898-1973 *ConAu 41, OhA&B*
Firestone, Idabelle 1874-1954 *AmSCAP 66*
Firestone, May Elizabeth 1869-1909 *DcNAA*
Firestone, O J 1913- *ConAu 41, OxCan Sup, WrD 1976*

Firestone, Shulamith 1945- *ConAu 29, WrD 1976*
Firestone, Tom 1929- *ConAu XR*
Firey, Milton Jacob 1839-1908 *OhA&B*
Firey, Walter Irving 1916- *ConAu 1R, WrD 1976*
Firkins, Chester 1882-1915 *ChPo, DcNAA*
Firkins, Ina TenEyck 1866-1937 *DcNAA*
Firkins, Oscar W 1864-1932 *AmA&B, DcNAA, TwCA*
Firkins, Peter Charles 1926- *WrD 1976*
Firmage, George J 1928- *ConAu 9R*
Firmenich-Richartz, Johannes Matthias 1808-1889 *BiD&SB*
Firmicus Maternus, Julius *CasWL*
Firmin, Giles 1617-1697 *Alli*
Firmin, Thomas 1632-1697 *Alli*
Firminger, Thomas Augustus Charles *Alli Sup*
Firsoff, Val Axel 1910- *WrD 1976*
First, Ruth 1925- *Au&Wr, ConAu 53, WrD 1976*
Firth, Abraham *Alli Sup*
Firth, Sir Charles Harding 1857-1936 *Alli Sup, ChPo S1, Chmbr 3, DcLEnL, NewC, OxEng*
Firth, Edith G *OxCan, OxCan Sup*
Firth, Elizabeth *Alli Sup*
Firth, J C *Alli Sup*
Firth, John Benjamin 1868- *ChPo S1, ChPo S2*
Firth, Joseph Firth Bottomley- 1842-1889 *Alli Sup*
Firth, Julia *Alli Sup*
Firth, Norman Charles 1895- *WhWNAA*
Firth, Raymond William 1901- *Au&Wr*
Firth, Richard *Alli Sup*
Firth, William *Alli, BiDLA*
Fisch, Gerald G 1922- *ConAu 13R*
Fisch, Harold 1923- *ConAu 37, WrD 1976*
Fisch, Max H 1900- *ConAu 33*
Fischart, Johann 1546?-1589? *BbD, BiD&SB, CasWL, DcEuL, EuA, EvEuW, OxGer, Pen Eur*
Fischbach, Julius 1894- *ConAu 5R, SmATA 10*
Fischel, Walter Joseph 1902-1973 *AmA&B, ConAu 23, ConAu 41*
Fischer, Agnew *Alli Sup*
Fischer, Ann 1919- *ConAu 25*
Fischer, Ann A *IlBYP*
Fischer, Anton Otto 1882- *IlCB 1945, IlCB 1956*
Fischer, Carl H 1903- *ConAu 17R*
Fischer, Carl Theodore 1912-1954 *AmSCAP 66*
Fischer, David Hackett 1935- *ConAu 17R*
Fischer, Donald E 1935- *ConAu 41*
Fischer, Edna *AmSCAP 66*
Fischer, Edward Adam 1914- *ConAu 1R, IndAu 1917, WrD 1976*
Fischer, Ernst 1899-1972 *ConAu 37*
Fischer, Ernst Kuno Berthold 1824- *BbD*
Fischer, George 1923- *ConAu 53*
Fischer, George 1932- *ConAu 25*
Fischer, George Alexander d1922 *DcNAA*
Fischer, George William 1906- *IndAu 1917*
Fischer, Gerald C 1928- *ConAu 23*
Fischer, Gretl Kraus *ChPo S2*
Fischer, H Theodore 1901- *BiDPar*
Fischer, Hans Erich 1909-1958 *IlBYP, IlCB 1956, IlCB 1966, MorJA*
Fischer, J L 1923- *ConAu 17R*
Fischer, Joel 1939- *ConAu 25*
Fischer, Johann 1881- *WhLA*
Fischer, Johann Bernhard Von 1685-1772 *OxGer*
Fischer, Johann Georg 1816-1897 *BiD&SB, OxGer*
Fischer, John 1910- *AmA&B, ConAu 9R*
Fischer, Kuno 1824-1907 *BiD&SB*
Fischer, Leck 1904-1956 *CnMD, Pen Eur*
Fischer, LeRoy H 1917- *ConAu 17R*
Fischer, Louis 1864- *WhWNAA*
Fischer, Louis 1896-1970 *AmA&B, Au&Wr, ConAu 25, ConAu P-1, REn, REnAL, TwCA Sup*
Fischer, Louis Albert 1865-1921 *DcNAA*
Fischer, Marjorie 1903-1961 *AmA&B*
Fischer, Martin Henry 1879- *OhA&B, WhWNAA*

Fischer, Otokar 1883-1938 *CasWL, ClDMEuL*
Fischer, Otto Peter Leck 1904-1956 *CasWL*
Fischer, Robert H 1918- *ConAu 37*
Fischer, Vera Kistiakowsky 1928- *ConAu 23*
Fischer, Wilhelm 1846-1932 *OxGer*
Fischer, William Joseph 1879-1912 *DcNAA*
Fischer, Wolfgang Georg 1933- *ConAu 33*
Fischer VonErlach, Johann Bernhard 1656-1723 *AtlBL, OxGer*
Fischl, Viktor *ConAu XR*
Fischman, Leonard L 1919- *ConAu 13R*
Fischtrom, Harvey 1933-1974 *ConAu 53, ThBJA*
Fischtrom, Margot Zemach *ThBJA*
Fiset, Louis-Joseph-Charles *OxCan*
Fiset, Louis Joseph Cyprien 1825?-1898 *BbtC, DcNAA*
Fisgrave, Anthony *Alli, BiDLA*
Fisguill, Richard *AmA&B, DcNAA*
Fish, Asa Israel 1820-1879 *DcNAA*
Fish, Byron Morris 1908- *ConAu 45*
Fish, Byron Morris 1909- *WhPNW*
Fish, Carl Russell 1876-1932 *AmA&B, AmLY, DcNAA, WhWNAA, WiscW*
Fish, D T *Alli Sup*
Fish, Daniel 1848-1924 *DcNAA*
Fish, Daniel W 1820-1899 *DcNAA*
Fish, E J *Alli Sup*
Fish, Everett W 1845- *DcNAA*
Fish, Ezra Job 1828-1890 *DcNAA*
Fish, Fannie *ChPo*
Fish, Frank Leslie 1863-1927 *DcNAA*
Fish, Franklin W *Alli Sup*
Fish, George T *Alli Sup*
Fish, Helen Dean 1890-1953 *AmA&B, ChPo*
Fish, Henry *Alli, Alli Sup*
Fish, Henry Clay 1820-1877 *Alli, Alli Sup, DcAmA, DcNAA*
Fish, Horace 1885-1929 *DcNAA, WhWNAA*
Fish, Isabel Morton *ChPo*
Fish, Ishmael *Alli Sup*
Fish, J B *Alli Sup*
Fish, John Charles Lounsbury 1870- *WhWNAA*
Fish, Julian *ConAu XR*
Fish, Kenneth L 1926- *ConAu 29*
Fish, Miss L A *ChPo*
Fish, Lisbeth G *ChPo S1*
Fish, Margery 1892- *ConAu 5R*
Fish, Pierre Augustine 1865-1931 *DcAmA, DcNAA, WhWNAA*
Fish, Robert *Alli Sup*
Fish, Robert L 1912- *Au&Wr, ConAu 13R, EncM&D*
Fish, Simon d1531? *Alli, DcEnL*
Fish, Stanley Eugene 1938- *Au&Wr*
Fish, Tallu *ChPo S2*
Fish, Williston 1858-1939 *AmA&B, DcAmA, DcNAA, OhA&B, REnAL, WhWNAA*
Fishacre, Richard d1248 *Alli*
Fishback, L M *Alli Sup*
Fishback, Margaret 1904- *AmA&B, ChPo, ChPo S2*
Fishback, William Pinckney 1831-1901 *IndAu 1816, OhA&B*
Fishbein, Meyer H 1916- *ConAu 41*
Fishbein, Morris 1889- *AmA&B, ConAu 5R, WhWNAA*
Fishberg, Maurice 1872- *WhWNAA*
Fishbourne, Edmund Gardiner *Alli Sup*
Fishbourne, G W *Alli Sup*
Fishburn, Angela Mary 1933- *WrD 1976*
Fishburn, Hummel 1901- *ConAu P-1*
Fishburn, Josephine Redmond *ChPo S1*
Fishburn, Peter C 1936- *ConAu 45*
Fishel, Leslie H, Jr. 1921- *ConAu 23*
Fisher *Alli, BiDLA*
Fisher, Admiral *Alli*
Fisher, A *Alli*
Fisher, A E *WrD 1976*
Fisher, Aileen Lucia 1906- *AuBYP, BkCL, BkP, ChPo, ChPo S1, ChPo S2, ConAu 5R, MorJA, SmATA 1*
Fisher, Alan W 1939- *ConAu 53, WrD 1976*
Fisher, Albert Kendrick 1856- *DcAmA*
Fisher, Alden L 1928- *ConAu 25*
Fisher, Alexander *Alli, OxCan*
Fisher, Alexander 1864- *WhLA*
Fisher, Alexander Metcalf 1794-1822 *Alli,*

CyAL 1
Fisher, Alfred Hugh 1867- *ChPo S2,
WhWNAA*
Fisher, Alice *Alli Sup*
Fisher, Allan George Barnard 1895- *ConAu 33,
WhLA*
Fisher, Ambrose *Alli*
Fisher, Anne Benson 1898- *AmA&B, AmNov*
Fisher, Arabella Burton 1840- *Alli Sup*
Fisher, Arthur M 1886-1971 *IndAu 1917*
Fisher, Arthur Stanley Theodore 1906- *Au&Wr*
Fisher, Arthur William *ChPo*
Fisher, Arthur William 1872- *AnMV 1926*
Fisher, Bart 1943- *ConAu 45*
Fisher, Benjamin Franklin 1873-1916? *ChPo S1,
DcNAA, OhA&B*
Fisher, Bessie Lewis *ChPo S1*
Fisher, Blanche V *ChPo*
Fisher, Bud 1884-1954 *AmA&B*
Fisher, C *Alli Sup*
Fisher, C M *Alli Sup*
Fisher, C William 1916- *ConAu 5R*
Fisher, Caroline M 1812- *Alli, CyAL 2*
Fisher, Charles 1808-1880 *OxCan*
Fisher, Charles Alfred 1916- *Au&Wr*
Fisher, Charles Harold *Au&Wr, WrD 1976*
Fisher, Clarence Stanley 1876-1941 *DcNAA*
Fisher, Clay *AmA&B*
Fisher, Clyde Olin 1891- *WhWNAA*
Fisher, Cyrus *AmA&B, AmNov XR*
Fisher, Dan 1920- *AmSCAP 66*
Fisher, Daniel *Alli*
Fisher, Daniel Webster 1838-1913 *DcNAA,
IndAu 1816*
Fisher, David *AuBYP*
Fisher, David 1924- *Au&Wr*
Fisher, David E 1932- *ConAu 53, WrD 1976*
Fisher, David Theodore 1922- *IndAu 1917*
Fisher, Doris 1915- *AmSCAP 66*
Fisher, Dorothea Frances Canfield *WhWNAA*
Fisher, Dorothy Canfield 1879-1958 *AmA&B,
AmNov XR, CarSB, ChPo, ChPo S1,
ChPo S2, Chmbr 3, CnDAL, ConAmA,
ConAmL, LongC, ModAL, OhA&B,
OxAm, REn, REnAL, TwCA,
TwCA Sup, WhWNAA, YABC 1*
Fisher, Douglas George 1902- *Au&Wr*
Fisher, E Burke 1799?-1859? *OhA&B*
Fisher, Ebenezer 1815-1879 *DcAmA, DcNAA*
Fisher, Edmund Henry *Alli Sup*
Fisher, Edward *Alli, DcEnL*
Fisher, Edward 1902- *ConAu 1R, WrD 1976*
Fisher, Edward Thornton *Alli Sup*
Fisher, Edwin George 1909- *Au&Wr*
Fisher, Eivor Hilda 1884- *Au&Wr*
Fisher, Elizabeth Florette 1873-1941 *DcNAA,
WhWNAA*
Fisher, Ernest Arthur 1887- *Au&Wr,
ConAu 13R, WrD 1976*
Fisher, Ernest McKinley 1893- *WhWNAA,
WrD 1976*
Fisher, Fanny E *Alli Sup, PoIre*
Fisher, Frances Christine *Alli Sup, DcAmA,
DcNAA, LivFWS*
Fisher, Franklin M 1934- *ConAu 17R,
WrD 1976*
Fisher, Fred 1875-1942 *AmSCAP 66*
Fisher, Fred L 1911- *ConAu 1R*
Fisher, Frederic Henry *Alli Sup*
Fisher, Frederick Bohn 1882-1938 *DcNAA*
Fisher, Frederick Richard *Alli Sup*
Fisher, Galen Merriam 1873- *WhWNAA*
Fisher, Gene Harvey 1922- *ConAu 41,
IndAu 1917*
Fisher, George *Alli*
Fisher, George Adams 1835-1904 *Alli Sup,
OhA&B*
Fisher, George Battye *Alli Sup*
Fisher, George Clyde 1878-1949 *AmA&B,
OhA&B*
Fisher, George D *Alli Sup*
Fisher, George Egbert 1863-1920 *DcNAA*
Fisher, George Jackson 1825-1893 *Alli Sup,
DcAmA, DcNAA*
Fisher, George James Burns 1893- *WhWNAA*
Fisher, George John 1871- *OhA&B,
WhWNAA*
Fisher, George Park 1827-1909 *Alli Sup, AmA,*

*AmA&B, BbD, BiD&SB, DcAmA,
DcNAA*
Fisher, Gertrude Arquene *BlkAW*
Fisher, Glen Harry 1922- *IndAu 1917*
Fisher, Glenn W 1924- *ConAu 53*
Fisher, Grant S *DrAP 1975*
Fisher, H *Alli Sup*
Fisher, H L *Alli Sup*
Fisher, Hammond Edward 1900-1955 *AmA&B*
Fisher, Harold Henry 1890-1975 *AmA&B,
ConAu 61, WhWNAA*
Fisher, Harrison 1875?-1934 *AmA&B,
DcNAA*
Fisher, Harry Linn 1885- *WhWNAA*
Fisher, Havelock *Alli Sup*
Fisher, Henry *Alli, Alli Sup, BiDLA*
Fisher, Herbert Albert Laurens 1865-1940
*Chmbr 3, DcLEnL, EvLB, LongC, NewC,
TwCA, TwCA Sup*
Fisher, Herbert W *Alli Sup*
Fisher, Horace Newton 1836-1916 *DcNAA*
Fisher, Humphrey J 1933- *ConAu 33*
Fisher, Irene 1895- *WhWNAA*
Fisher, Irving 1867-1947 *AmA&B, AmLY,
DcAmA, DcNAA, WhWNAA*
Fisher, Isobel Hume *ChPo S1*
Fisher, J A *Alli Sup*
Fisher, J B *Alli, BiDLA*
Fisher, J F *Alli*
Fisher, J R 1943- *ConAu 45*
Fisher, J Randolph 1906- *BlkAW*
Fisher, J T *Alli, BiDLA*
Fisher, J Thomas 1936- *ConAu 33*
Fisher, James *Alli, BiDLA*
Fisher, James 1759?- *ChPo*
Fisher, James A, Jr. 1933- *BlkAW*
Fisher, James Maxwell McConnell 1912-
Au&Wr
Fisher, Jane Watts 1894-1968 *IndAu 1917*
Fisher, Jasper *Alli*
Fisher, Jessie 1909- *AmSCAP 66*
Fisher, John *Alli, Alli Sup, BiDLA,
Chmbr 1*
Fisher, John 1459-1535 *Alli, BbD, BrAu,
CasWL, DcEnL, EvLB*
Fisher, John 1748?-1825 *Alli, BiDLA*
Fisher, John 1909- *Au&Wr*
Fisher, John 1926- *Au&Wr, BlkAW*
Fisher, John C 1927- *ConAu 41*
Fisher, John Charlton 1794-1849 *BbtC*
Fisher, John Cowley 1807- *Alli Sup*
Fisher, John Dix 1797-1850 *DcNAA*
Fisher, John Francis *Alli Sup*
Fisher, John Hurt 1919- *Au&Wr, ConAu 21*
Fisher, Jonathan *Alli, BiDLA*
Fisher, Jonathan 1768-1847 *DcNAA, EarAB*
Fisher, Joseph *Alli, Alli Sup, BiDLA*
Fisher, Joseph R 1855- *WhLA*
Fisher, Joshua 1748-1833 *DcNAA*
Fisher, Joshua Francis 1807-1873 *Alli Sup,
DcAmA, DcNAA*
Fisher, K *ChPo*
Fisher, Kitty *Alli*
Fisher, Laine *ConAu XR*
Fisher, Laura Harrison 1934- *ConAu 13R,
SmATA 5*
Fisher, Laura Hope *Alli Sup*
Fisher, Laura Page *ChPo*
Fisher, Lawrence V 1923- *ConAu 17R,
WrD 1976*
Fisher, Lee 1908- *ConAu 33, IndAu 1917,
WrD 1976*
Fisher, Leland Milton 1875- *BlkAW*
Fisher, Lena Leonard 1870-1930 *OhA&B*
Fisher, Leonard Everett 1924- *AuBYP,
ConAu 1R, IlCB 1956, IlCB 1966,
MorBMP, SmATA 4, ThBJA, WrD 1976*
Fisher, Lewis Beals 1857-1936 *DcNAA*
Fisher, Lillian Estelle 1891- *ConAu P-1,
WrD 1976*
Fisher, Lois Jeannette 1909- *ConAu 5R*
Fisher, Louis 1934- *ConAu 37, WrD 1976*
Fisher, Lydia Jane 1800-1884 *PoIre*
Fisher, M *Alli Sup, MnBBF*
Fisher, M A *Alli Sup*
Fisher, M F K *DrAF 1976*
Fisher, Mahlon Leonard 1874-1947 *AmA&B,
ChPo*

Fisher, Margaret B 1918- *ConAu 17R*
Fisher, Margaret Hazard *ChPo S2*
Fisher, Margaret Trusler 1901- *IndAu 1917*
Fisher, Margery 1913- *Au&Wr, AuBYP,
ChPo, WhCL*
Fisher, Margot *ConAu XR*
Fisher, Marjorie Williams 1916- *AmSCAP 66*
Fisher, Marjory M *WhWNAA*
Fisher, Mark 1895-1948 *AmSCAP 66*
Fisher, Martin Luther 1871-1942 *IndAu 1917*
Fisher, Marve A 1907-1957 *AmSCAP 66*
Fisher, Marvin 1916- *AmSCAP 66*
Fisher, Marvin 1927- *ConAu 21, WrD 1976*
Fisher, Mary 1858- *DcAmA, DcNAA,
WhWNAA*
Fisher, Mary Ann 1839- *DcNAA*
Fisher, Mary L 1928- *ConAu 33*
Fisher, Michael John 1933- *Au&Wr,
ConAu 1R*
Fisher, Michael Montgomery 1834-1891
Alli Sup, DcAmA, DcNAA, IndAu 1917
Fisher, Miles Mark 1899-1970 *ConAu P-1*
Fisher, Miriam Louise Scharfe 1939-
ConAu 13R, IndAu 1917
Fisher, Morris 1922- *ConAu 21*
Fisher, Murray *MnBBF*
Fisher, Myles d1819 *Alli*
Fisher, Nathaniel 1742-1812 *Alli*
Fisher, Nicholas E 1894-1961 *AmSCAP 66*
Fisher, Nigel 1913- *WrD 1976*
Fisher, Norman George 1918- *Au&Wr*
Fisher, O *Alli Sup*
Fisher, Olive M *OxCan*
Fisher, Osmond *Alli Sup*
Fisher, Mrs. Paul E *Alli Sup*
Fisher, Paul Hawkins *Alli Sup*
Fisher, Payne 1616-1693 *Alli, DcEnL*
Fisher, Peter *Alli*
Fisher, Peter 1782-1848 *BbtC, DcNAA,
OxCan*
Fisher, Peter Jack 1923- *Au&Wr*
Fisher, Philip *Alli*
Fisher, Philip A 1907- *ConAu 61*
Fisher, R T *Alli*
Fisher, Ralph Talcott, Jr. 1920- *ConAu 41*
Fisher, Redwood S 1782-1856 *DcNAA*
Fisher, Reuben 1923- *AmSCAP 66*
Fisher, Richard *Alli Sup*
Fisher, Richard 1936- *ConAu 17R*
Fisher, Richard Barnard *Alli, BiDLA*
Fisher, Richard Trott 1805- *Alli Sup, ChPo*
Fisher, Robert *Alli*
Fisher, Robert 1840- *ChPo*
Fisher, Robert Alexander *Alli Sup*
Fisher, Robert C 1930- *ConAu 53*
Fisher, Robert H 1918- *WrD 1976*
Fisher, Robert J 1924- *ConAu 61*
Fisher, Robert Mackenzie 1840- *ChPo S2*
Fisher, Robert W 1883- *WhWNAA*
Fisher, Roger *Alli*
Fisher, Roger 1922- *ConAu 37*
Fisher, Roy 1930- *ConP 1970, ConP 1975,
WrD 1976*
Fisher, Rudolph 1897-1934 *BlkAW*
Fisher, Samuel *Alli*
Fisher, Samuel Reed 1810-1881 *DcAmA,
DcNAA*
Fisher, Samuel Sparks 1832-1874 *Alli Sup*
Fisher, Samuel Ware 1814-1874 *Alli Sup,
ChPo, CyAL 2, DcAmA, DcNAA,
OhA&B*
Fisher, Seymour 1922- *ConAu 33*
Fisher, Sidney George 1809-1871 *Alli Sup,
AmA&B, DcNAA*
Fisher, Sidney George 1856-1927 *BiD&SB,
WhWNAA*
Fisher, Sophie *AmA&B*
Fisher, St. John 1459-1535 *OxEng*
Fisher, Steve 1912- *EncM&D*
Fisher, Stokely S 1865-1924 *DcNAA, OhA&B*
Fisher, Sydney George 1809-1871 *DcAmA*
Fisher, Sydney George 1856-1927 *AmA&B,
AmLY, DcAmA, DcNAA*
Fisher, Theodore Willis 1837-1914 *Alli Sup,
DcAmA, DcNAA*
Fisher, Thomas *Alli, BiDLA*
Fisher, Thomas 1801-1856 *Alli Sup, ChPo,
DcAmA, DcNAA*

Fisher, Vardis 1895-1968 *AmA&B, AmNov, Au&Wr, CnDAL, ConAmA, ConAu 5R, ConAu 25, CyWA, DcLEnL, LongC, ModAL, OxAm, Pen Am, REn, REnAL, TwCA, TwCA Sup, WhWNAA*
Fisher, W *MnBBF*
Fisher, W D *ChPo S1*
Fisher, W L *Alli Sup*
Fisher, W W Caleo *Alli Sup*
Fisher, Wade *ConAu XR, WrD 1976*
Fisher, Wallace E 1918- *ConAu 23*
Fisher, Walter M *Alli Sup*
Fisher, Walter R 1931- *ConAu 13R*
Fisher, Walter William *Alli Sup*
Fisher, Wayne Benjamin 1915- *IndAu 1917*
Fisher, Welthy Honsinger 1880- *AmA&B, Au&Wr, ConAu 1R*
Fisher, William *Alli, Alli Sup*
Fisher, William 1909- *BlkAW*
Fisher, William Albert 1859-1944 *DcNAA*
Fisher, William Arms 1861-1948 *AmA&B, AmSCAP 66, DcNAA*
Fisher, William Bayne 1916- *Au&Wr, WrD 1976*
Fisher, William Hubbell 1837?-1909 *Alli Sup, DcNAA, OhA&B*
Fisher, William Richard 1824-1888 *Alli Sup*
Fishlake, J R *Alli*
Fishler, Mary Shiverick 1920- *ConAu 5R*
Fishlock, David Jocelyn 1932- *Au&Wr, WrD 1976*
Fishman, Betty G 1918- *ConAu 5R*
Fishman, Burton J 1942- *ConAu 45*
Fishman, Charles 1942- *ConAu 57, DrAP 1975*
Fishman, George Samuel 1937- *ConAu 25*
Fishman, Isidore 1908- *Au&Wr*
Fishman, Jack 1920- *ConAu 9R*
Fishman, Joshua A 1926- *ConAu 41*
Fishman, Leo 1914- *ConAu 17R*
Fishman, Lew 1939- *ConAu 61*
Fishman, Sterling 1932- *ConAu 45*
Fishman, William J 1921- *Au&Wr*
Fishta, G *Pen Eur*
Fishwick, Henry 1835- *Alli Sup*
Fishwick, Marshall William 1923- *ConAu 5R*
Fisk, Professor *Alli*
Fisk, Archie Campbell 1836- *DcNAA*
Fisk, Benjamin Franklin d1832 *DcNAA*
Fisk, Callene *DcNAA*
Fisk, Charles H *ChPo S2*
Fisk, Clinton Bowen 1822?-1890 *Alli Sup, DcNAA*
Fisk, Dorothy Mary *Au&Wr*
Fisk, E K 1917- *ConAu 17R*
Fisk, Earl E 1892- *WhWNAA*
Fisk, Emily O *ChPo S1*
Fisk, Eugene Lyman 1867-1931 *DcNAA, WhWNAA*
Fisk, Fidelia 1816-1864 *Alli Sup*
Fisk, Frances Battaile *TexWr*
Fisk, Franklin Woodbury 1820-1901 *Alli Sup, DcAmA, DcNAA*
Fisk, G W 1882- *BiDPar*
Fisk, George *Alli, Alli Sup*
Fisk, George Mygatt 1864-1910 *DcNAA, OhA&B*
Fisk, Mary Lee *ChPo*
Fisk, May Isabel *WhWNAA*
Fisk, McKee 1900- *ConAu 21*
Fisk, Nicholas *IlBYP*
Fisk, Otis Harrison 1870-1944 *DcNAA*
Fisk, Pliny 1792-1825 *Alli*
Fisk, Samuel 1828-1864 *Alli Sup, DcAmA*
Fisk, Samuel 1907- *ConAu 57*
Fisk, Wilbur 1792-1839 *Alli, AmA&B, BbD, DcAmA, DcNAA*
Fiske, Mrs. *Alli, BiDLA*
Fiske, A A *Alli Sup*
Fiske, Amos Kidder 1842-1921 *AmA&B, AmLY, BiD&SB, DcAmA, DcNAA*
Fiske, Annette 1873- *WhWNAA*
Fiske, Asa Severance 1833-1925 *AmLY, DcNAA, OhA&B*
Fiske, Bradley Allen 1854-1942 *Alli Sup, DcNAA, WhWNAA*
Fiske, Charles 1868-1942 *DcNAA, WhWNAA*
Fiske, Cyrus Hartwell 1890- *WhWNAA*

Fiske, Daniel T *Alli Sup*
Fiske, Daniel Willard 1831-1904 *Alli Sup, BiD&SB, DcNAA*
Fiske, David Lewis 1898- *WhWNAA*
Fiske, Fidelia 1816-1864 *DcNAA*
Fiske, George Converse 1872-1927 *DcNAA*
Fiske, George Walter 1872-1945 *AmA&B, AmLY, DcNAA, OhA&B, WhWNAA*
Fiske, Homer 1914- *AmSCAP 66*
Fiske, Horace Spencer 1859-1940 *AmA&B, AmLY, DcNAA, WhWNAA*
Fiske, Isabella Howe *AmA&B, ChPo S1*
Fiske, J S *Alli Sup*
Fiske, John 1601-1677 *Alli*
Fiske, John 1842-1901 *Alli Sup, AmA, AmA&B, BbD, BiD&SB, Chmbr 3, DcAmA, DcLEnL, DcNAA, EvLB, OxAm, OxCan, Pen Am, REnAL*
Fiske, Jonathan *Alli*
Fiske, Lewis Ransom 1825-1901 *DcAmA, DcNAA*
Fiske, Marjorie *ConAu XR*
Fiske, Mary H d1889 *DcNAA*
Fiske, Minnie Maddern 1865-1932 *BiDSA, OxAm*
Fiske, Nathan 1733-1799 *Alli, AmA&B, DcAmA, DcNAA, OxAm*
Fiske, Nathan Welby 1798-1847 *Alli, DcAmA, DcNAA*
Fiske, Oliver d1837 *Alli*
Fiske, Ralph Browning *DcAmA*
Fiske, Roger Elwyn 1910- *Au&Wr, ConAu 13R, WrD 1976*
Fiske, Samuel Wheelock 1828-1864 *AmA&B, DcNAA*
Fiske, Stephen Ryder 1840-1916 *Alli Sup, AmA, AmA&B, BiD&SB, DcAmA, DcNAA*
Fiske, W *EarAB, EarAB Sup*
Fiske, Willard 1831-1904 *AmA&B, CyAL 2, DcNAA*
Fiskin, A M I 1916- *ConAu 23*
Fisler, Miss A *Alli Sup*
Fison, David Charles 1908- *WrD 1976*
Fison, Joseph Edward 1906- *Au&Wr*
Fison, Lorimer And Howitt, Alfred W *Alli Sup*
Fison, Margaret *Alli Sup*
Fison, Roger *MnBBF*
Fissen, J P *Alli*
Fissenmeyer, J P *BiDLA*
Fiston, William *Alli*
Fiszel, Henryk 1910- *ConAu 29*
Fiszman, Joseph R 1921- *ConAu 41*
Fitch, A M B *Alli Sup*
Fitch, Adelaide C *ChPo S1*
Fitch, Albert Parker 1877-1944 *DcNAA, WhWNAA*
Fitch, Alger Morton, Jr. 1919- *ConAu 53*
Fitch, Anita *ChPo*
Fitch, Anna M *Alli Sup*
Fitch, Asa 1809-1878 *DcNAA*
Fitch, Asahel Norton 1847-1915 *DcNAA*
Fitch, Bob 1938- *ConAu 21*
Fitch, Charles Elliott 1835-1918 *DcNAA*
Fitch, Charles L *Alli Sup*
Fitch, Chauncey W *Alli Sup*
Fitch, Clarke *AuBYP, ConAmA, ConAu XR, SmATA XR*
Fitch, Clifford Penny 1884- *WhWNAA*
Fitch, Clyde 1865-1909 *AmA, AmA&B, CarSB, Chmbr 3, CnDAL, CnMD, CnThe, DcLEnL, DcNAA, McGWD, ModAL, ModWD, OxAm, Pen Am, REnAL, REnWD*
Fitch, Ebenezer 1756-1833 *ChPo, CyAL 1*
Fitch, Edwin M 1902- *ConAu 25*
Fitch, Eleazar Thompson 1791-1871 *Alli Sup, DcNAA, PoCh*
Fitch, Elijah 1745-1788 *Alli, CyAL 1, DcAmA, DcNAA*
Fitch, Ernest Robert 1878-1935 *DcNAA*
Fitch, Florence Mary 1875-1959 *AmA&B, AuBYP, MorJA, OhA&B*
Fitch, Frederic Brenton 1908- *Au&Wr*
Fitch, George Hamlin 1852-1915 *AmA&B, DcNAA*
Fitch, George Helgeson 1877-1915 *AmA&B, CarSB, DcNAA, REnAL*

Fitch, J *Alli*
Fitch, Jabez 1672-1746 *Alli*
Fitch, James 1622-1702 *DcNAA*
Fitch, James Marston, Jr. 1909- *AmA&B*
Fitch, James Monroe 1878-1942 *DcNAA*
Fitch, John *Alli Sup*
Fitch, John 1743-1798 *Alli*
Fitch, John, IV *SmATA XR*
Fitch, Sir Joshua Girling 1824-1903 *Alli Sup, BrAu 19*
Fitch, Kenneth 1929- *ConAu 49*
Fitch, Laura M *ChPo*
Fitch, Lyle C 1913- *ConAu 13R*
Fitch, Ralph *NewC*
Fitch, Robert Elliott 1902- *AmA&B*
Fitch, Samuel Sheldon *Alli Sup*
Fitch, Simon 1820-1905 *Alli Sup, DcNAA*
Fitch, Stanley K 1920- *ConAu 29*
Fitch, Theodore F 1900- *AmSCAP 66*
Fitch, Thomas 1700-1774 *DcNAA*
Fitch, Thomas 1906- *Au&Wr*
Fitch, Walter *ChPo S1*
Fitch, William Clyde 1865-1909 *AmA, BbD, BiD&SB, DcAmA, DcNAA*
Fitch, William Edward 1867- *WhWNAA*
Fitch, William Edwards *BiDSA*
Fitch-Brewer, Annette *OhA&B*
Fitchett, William Henry *Chmbr 3, MnBBF*
Fite, Emerson David 1874-1953 *AmA&B, AmLY, OhA&B, WhWNAA*
Fite, Gilbert C 1918- *ConAu 33*
Fite, Mack *ConAu XR*
Fite, Warner 1867-1955 *AmA&B*
Fite, William Benjamin 1869- *WhWNAA*
Fithian, Edward William 1845- *Alli Sup*
Fithian, Philip Vickers 1747-1776 *AmA&B*
Fitler, Mary Biddle 1878?-1966 *ConAu 25*
Fitrat, Abdurrauf 1884-1947? *DcOrL 3*
Fitt, J Nevill 1850?- *Alli Sup, Br&AmS*
Fitt, Mary 1897-1959 *LongC*
Fitter, Richard Sidney Richmond 1913- *Au&Wr, WrD 1976*
Fitting, James E 1939- *ConAu 45*
Fitting, Melvin 1942- *ConAu 29*
Fittis, Robert Scott *Alli Sup*
Fittler, James 1758-1835 *Alli, BiDLA, BkIE*
Fitton, Edward Brown *Alli Sup*
Fitton, James *Alli Sup*
Fitton, Sam *ChPo*
Fitton, Sarah Margaret *Alli Sup*
Fitton, William *Alli*
Fitts, Ada M 1869-1943 *DcNAA*
Fitts, Dudley 1903-1968 *AmA&B, ConAu 25, ModAL, OxAm, Pen Am, REnAL, TwCA, TwCA Sup*
Fitts, J H *Alli Sup*
Fitts, James Franklin 1840-1890 *AmA&B, BiD&SB, CarSB, DcAmA, DcNAA*
Fitts, William Howard 1918- *ConAu 21*
Fitz, A W, Sr. *BlkAW*
Fitz, Asa 1810- *Alli, ChPo S1*
Fitz, G W *Alli Sup*
Fitz, J W And Fitz, J *Alli Sup*
Fitz, James *BiDSA*
Fitz, Jean DeWitt 1912- *ConAu 29*
Fitz-Albion *Alli*
Fitz-Boodle, George Savage *Chmbr 3, NewC, OxEng*
Fitz-Brian, B *Alli*
Fitz-Cook, H *ChPo S1*
Fitz-Erin *PoIre*
Fitz-Geffrey, Henry *Alli*
Fitz-Geffry, Charles 1575?-1636 *Alli, CasWL, ChPo*
Fitz-Geoffry, Charles 1575?-1636 *Alli*
Fitz-Gerald, Carolyn 1932- *ConAu 41*
Fitz-Gerald, John Driscoll, II 1873-1946 *AmA&B, AmLY, DcNAA*
Fitz-Gerald, William Thomas 1759?-1829 *ChPo*
Fitz-Gibbon, John *Alli*
Fitz-Hardinge, George Charles Grantley *Alli Sup*
Fitz-Henry, Mary Christine 1893- *Au&Wr*
Fitz-Hugh, Thomas 1862- *AmLY*
Fitz-James, James *Alli*
Fitz-James, Oswald *Alli*
Fitz-John, Matilda *Alli, BiDLA*
Fitz-Patrick, Hugh Louis 1861-1921 *DcNAA*

Fitz-Simon, Ellen *ChPo S1*
Fitz-Stephen, William *BiB N*
Fitzachary, John Christopher 1840-1902
   Alli Sup, PoIre
Fitzadam, John Thompson 1833- *Alli Sup*
Fitzalan, Roger *ConAu XR, WrD 1976*
Fitzallen, Walter *Alli Sup*
Fitzball, Edward *Alli Sup, Chmbr 2*
Fitzclarence, Earl Of Munster *Alli*
Fitzclarence, Lord Frederick 1799-1854 *Alli Sup*
Fitzclarence, W, Countess Of Munster *Alli Sup*
Fitzcotton, Henry *Alli, PoIre*
Fitzell, John 1922- *ConAu 13R*
FitzGeorge, George William Adolphus *Alli Sup*
Fitzgeorge-Parker, Tim 1920- *WrD 1976*
Fitzgerald *PoIre*
Fitzgerald, Lord *Alli*
Fitzgerald, Anna A 1842- *PoIre*
Fitzgerald, Arlene J *ConAu 23*
Fitzgerald, Augustin *PoIre*
Fitzgerald, Barbara *WrD 1976*
Fitzgerald, Barry Charles 1939- *ConAu 37*
Fitzgerald, Brassil *BkC 1*
Fitzgerald, C P 1902- *ConAu 17R*
Fitzgerald, Captain Hugh *ThBJA*
Fitzgerald, Caroline *PoIre*
Fitzgerald, Cathleen 1932- *ConAu 33*
Fitzgerald, Charles d1908 *BiDSA*
Fitzgerald, Charles C P *Alli Sup*
Fitzgerald, Charles Edward *Alli Sup*
Fitzgerald, Charles Egerton *Alli Sup*
Fitzgerald, Charles Patrick 1902- *Au&Wr,*
   WrD 1976
Fitzgerald, Charles W, Duke Of Leinster
   1819-1887 *Alli Sup*
Fitzgerald, D *BbtC*
Fitzgerald, Desmond 1846-1928 *Alli Sup,*
   DcNAA
Fitzgerald, Edward *Alli, Alli Sup, BiDLA*
FitzGerald, Edward *Chmbr 3*
Fitzgerald, Edward d1823 *PoIre*
Fitzgerald, Edward 1809-1883 *Alli Sup, AtlBL,*
   BbD, BiD&SB, BrAu 19, CasWL, ChPo,
   ChPo S1, ChPo S2, CnE&AP, CriT 3,
   CyWA, DcEnA, DcEnA Ap, DcEuL,
   DcLEnL, EvLB, MouLC 4, NewC,
   OxEng, Pen Eng, PoIre, RCom, REn,
   WebEAL
Fitzgerald, Edward 1856-1928 *DcNAA*
Fitzgerald, Edward Ambrose *Alli Sup*
Fitzgerald, Edward Earl 1919- *AmA&B,*
   AuBYP
Fitzgerald, Edward Marlborough *PoIre*
Fitzgerald, Lady Elizabeth 1528?-1589 *NewC*
Fitzgerald, Ella 1918- *AmSCAP 66*
Fitzgerald, Ernest Abner 1925- *ConAu 29,*
   WrD 1976
Fitzgerald, F *Alli Sup*
Fitzgerald, F Scott 1896-1940 *AmA&B, AmWr,*
   AtlBL, AuNews 1, CasWL, Chmbr 3,
   CnDAL, CnMD, CnMWL, ConAmA,
   ConAmL, CyWA, DcLEnL, DcNAA,
   EncM&D, EncWL, EvLB, LongC,
   ModAL, ModAL Sup, OxAm, OxEng,
   Pen Am, RAdv 1, RCom, REn, REnAL,
   TwCA, TwCA Sup, TwCW, WebEAL,
   WhTwL, WhWNAA
Fitzgerald, Frances 1940- *ConAu 41*
Fitzgerald, Francis Alexander 1805-1897 *PoIre*
Fitzgerald, Frederick *WhWNAA*
Fitzgerald, G *Pen Eng, PoIre*
Fitzgerald, G M 1780-1850 *ChPo S1*
Fitzgerald, George Robert 1748?-1786 *Alli,*
   PoIre
Fitzgerald, Gerald *Alli, MnBBF, PoIre*
Fitzgerald, Gerald 1930- *ConAu 37*
FitzGerald, Gerald Augustus Robert 1844-
   Alli Sup
Fitzgerald, Gerald Beresford *Alli Sup*
Fitzgerald, Gerald E 1920- *ConAu 25*
Fitzgerald, Gerald M C 1894- *BkC 1,*
   CatA 1947, ChPo S1
FitzGerald, Gregory 1923- *ConAu 49,*
   DrAF 1976
Fitzgerald, Hal *ConAu XR*
Fitzgerald, Harrington 1847- *WhWNAA*
Fitzgerald, Henry Purefoy *Alli Sup*
Fitzgerald, Hugh Nugent *TexWr*

Fitzgerald, J *Alli Sup*
Fitzgerald, J D *Alli Sup, PoIre*
Fitzgerald, J E *Alli Sup*
Fitzgerald, Jack *ConAu XR*
Fitzgerald, James *Alli, BiDLA, PoIre*
Fitzgerald, James A *ConAu 1R*
Fitzgerald, James Anderson 1883- *TexWr,*
   WhWNAA
Fitzgerald, James Edward *BbtC*
Fitzgerald, Jane Bailey *TexWr*
Fitzgerald, John *Alli, ConAu XR*
Fitzgerald, John d1910 *PoIre*
Fitzgerald, John Charles *PoIre*
Fitzgerald, John D *DcSpL*
Fitzgerald, John D 1907- *ChLR 1*
Fitzgerald, John F G Purcell *Alli Sup*
Fitzgerald, John Foster Vesey *Alli Sup*
Fitzgerald, John Joseph 1928- *ConAu 37*
Fitzgerald, John Vesey Vesey 1848- *Alli Sup*
Fitzgerald, Joseph 1793-1856 *PoIre*
Fitzgerald, Keane *Alli*
Fitzgerald, Kevin 1902- *CatA 1952*
Fitzgerald, Laurine Elisabeth 1930- *ConAu 37*
Fitzgerald, Lawrence P 1906- *ConAu 1R*
Fitzgerald, M *ChPo*
Fitzgerald, M S *Alli Sup*
Fitzgerald, Marcella Agnes 1845- *Alli Sup,*
   PoIre
Fitzgerald, Mark James 1906- *IndAu 1917*
Fitzgerald, Mary Small 1875- *ChPo S2,*
   TexWr, WhWNAA
Fitzgerald, Maureen Elizabeth 1920- *Au&Wr*
Fitzgerald, Maurice Noel Purcell 1835-1878
   Alli Sup, PoIre
Fitzgerald, Maurice O'Regan 1881-1942
   DcNAA
Fitzgerald, Michael *PoIre*
Fitzgerald, Nigel 1906- *Au&Wr*
Fitzgerald, Oscar Penn 1829-1911 *Alli Sup,*
   AmA&B, BiDSA, DcAmA, DcNAA
Fitzgerald, P *Alli*
Fitzgerald, Mrs. P F *Alli Sup*
Fitzgerald, Patrick 1926- *ConAu 9R*
Fitzgerald, Percy Hetherington 1834- *Alli Sup,*
   BbD, BiD&SB, ChPo S2, DcEnL
Fitzgerald, Philip *Alli Sup*
Fitzgerald, Pitt Loofbourrow 1893- *OhA&B*
Fitzgerald, Preston *Alli, BiDLA, PoIre*
Fitzgerald, Richard *Alli Sup*
Fitzgerald, Richard 1938- *ConAu 45*
Fitzgerald, Robert Allan *Alli Sup*
FitzGerald, Robert David 1902- *Au&Wr,*
   CasWL, ChPo S2, ConAu 17R,
   ConP 1970, ConP 1975, DcLEnL,
   Pen Eng, REn, TwCW, WebEAL,
   WorAu, WrD 1976
Fitzgerald, Robert Stuart 1910- *AmA&B,*
   CatA 1952, ConAu 1R, ConP 1970,
   ConP 1975, DrAP 1975, ModAL, OxAm,
   Pen Am, REnAL, TwCA Sup,
   WrD 1976
Fitzgerald, Ruby *TexWr*
Fitzgerald, Samuel *Alli*
Fitzgerald, Sarah Jane *Alli Sup*
Fitzgerald, Shafto Justin Adair 1859- *ChPo,*
   ChPo S1, PoIre
Fitzgerald, Thomas d1752 *PoIre*
Fitzgerald, Thomas 1819-1891 *AmA, AmA&B*
FitzGerald, Thomas Austin 1889- *WhWNAA*
Fitzgerald, Walter *Alli Sup*
Fitzgerald, William *Alli, PoIre*
Fitzgerald, William 1814-1883 *Alli Sup,*
   DcEnL, PoIre
Fitzgerald, William, Jr. *PoIre*
Fitzgerald, William Foster Vesey *Alli Sup*
Fitzgerald, Sir William Robert Seymour
   1818-1885 *PoIre*
Fitzgerald, William Thomas 1759-1829 *Alli,*
   BiDLA, DcEnL, PoIre
Fitzgerald, Zelda Sayre 1900-1948 *AmA&B,*
   AuNews 1
Fitzgibbon, Constantine 1919- *AmA&B,*
   Au&Wr, ConAu 1R, WorAu, WrD 1976
Fitzgibbon, Edward 1803-1857 *Alli Sup*
Fitzgibbon, Gerald 1793-1882 *Alli Sup*
Fitzgibbon, Gerald 1837-1909 *PoIre*
Fitzgibbon, Henry Macaulay 1855- *Alli Sup,*
   WhLA

Fitzgibbon, James 1780-1863 *BbtC, OxCan*
Fitzgibbon, Joanne Eileen Theodora 1916-
   Au&Wr, ConAu 5R, WrD 1976
Fitzgibbon, Mary Agnes *OxCan*
FitzGibbon, Mary Agnes 1851-1915 *Alli Sup,*
   DcNAA, OxCan
Fitzgibbon, Russell Humke 1902- *IndAu 1917*
Fitzgibbon, William *Alli Sup*
Fitzgibbons, John *Alli*
Fitzhardinge, Joan Margaret 1912- *Au&Wr,*
   AuBYP, ConAu 13R, SmATA 2, ThBJA
Fitzhenry, James *Alli*
Fitzherbert, Sir Anthony d1538 *Alli, DcEnL*
Fitzherbert, E H *Alli*
Fitzherbert, Nicholas 1550?-1612 *Alli*
Fitzherbert, Thomas 1552-1640 *Alli*
Fitzherbert, Sir William 1748-1791 *Alli*
Fitzhugh, Carolyn Buck *ChPo*
Fitzhugh, Francis *Alli Sup*
Fitzhugh, George 1806?-1881 *Alli, Alli Sup,*
   AmA&B, BiDSA, DcAmA, DcNAA,
   OxAm
Fitzhugh, John *Alli Sup*
Fitzhugh, Louise 1928-1974 *AuBYP, ChLR 1,*
   ConAu 29, ConAu 53, SmATA 1,
   ThBJA
Fitzhugh, P K *ChPo S2*
Fitzhugh, Percy Keese 1876-1950 *AmA&B,*
   AmLY, WhWNAA
Fitzhugh, William 1651-1701 *BiDSA*
Fitzhugh, William Henry 1792-1830 *Alli,*
   BiDSA
Fitzhugh, William W *ChPo S2*
Fitzjames, James *OxCan*
Fitzlyon, Cecily April 1920- *Au&Wr,*
   ConAu 5R
Fitzlyon, Kyril 1910- *Au&Wr*
Fitzmaurice, Lord Edmund George 1846-
   Alli Sup, WhLA
Fitzmaurice, F *BkIE*
Fitzmaurice, Mrs. F M *Alli Sup*
Fitzmaurice, George 1877-1963 *CasWL, CnThe,*
   McGWD, ModWD, REnWD
Fitzmaurice, George W H, Earl Of Orkney 1827-
   Alli Sup
Fitzmaurice, James *PoIre*
Fitzmaurice-Kelly, James 1857?-1923 *DcSpL,*
   REn, TwCA, TwCA Sup
Fitzmyer, Joseph A 1920- *ConAu 9R*
Fitzneal, Richard d1198 *Chmbr 1, DcEuL*
Fitzneale, Richard d1198 *NewC*
Fitznigel, Richard d1198 *NewC*
Fitznoodle 1843-1926 *AmA*
Fitzosborne, Sir Thomas 1710-1799 *Alli,*
   DcEnL
Fitzpatrick *PoIre*
Fitzpatrick, Alfred 1862-1936 *DcNAA*
Fitzpatrick, B M *Alli Sup*
Fitzpatrick, Beatrice B *IndAu 1917*
Fitzpatrick, Bernard *Alli Sup*
Fitzpatrick, Edward Augustus 1884-1960
   AmA&B, WhWNAA
Fitzpatrick, Eleanor A T *ChPo*
Fitzpatrick, Francis Burke 1872- *WhWNAA*
Fitzpatrick, H *Alli*
Fitzpatrick, James Benedict 1881-1964 *AmA&B*
Fitzpatrick, Sir James Percy 1862-1931 *DcLEnL,*
   Pen Eng, WhCL
Fitzpatrick, Sir Jeremiah *Alli*
Fitzpatrick, John *Alli*
Fitzpatrick, John 1859- *PoIre*
Fitzpatrick, John Clement 1876-1940 *AmA&B,*
   DcNAA
Fitzpatrick, John Tracy 1878-1933 *DcNAA,*
   WhWNAA
Fitzpatrick, Joseph P 1913- *ConAu 17R*
Fitzpatrick, L *PoIre*
Fitzpatrick, Michael J 1863-1950 *AmSCAP 66*
Fitzpatrick, Nicholas Richard *Alli Sup*
Fitzpatrick, Patrick Vincent 1792-1865 *PoIre*
Fitzpatrick, Sir Percy 1862-1931 *Chmbr 3,*
   TwCW
Fitzpatrick, R *PoIre*
Fitzpatrick, R H *PoIre*
Fitzpatrick, R W *Alli*
Fitzpatrick, Richard *Chmbr 2*
Fitzpatrick, Sir Richard 1747-1813 *PoIre*
Fitzpatrick, T *Alli Sup*

Fitzpatrick, Thomas 1799?-1854 *OxAm*
Fitzpatrick, Walter *Alli Sup*
Fitzpatrick, William John 1830-1895 *Alli Sup*,
 BiD&SB, *DcEnL*
Fitzralph, Richard d1360 *BrAu*, *OxEng*
Fitzroy, Ernest James Augustus *Alli Sup*
Fitzroy, Robert 1805-1865 *Alli*, *Alli Sup*,
 NewC, *OxEng*
FitzRoy, Yvonne *OxCan*
Fitzroy-Somerset *Alli Sup*
Fitzsimmons, Cleo 1900- *ConAu 1R*
Fitzsimmons, Cortland 1893-1949 *AmA&B*,
 DcNAA
Fitzsimmons, Robert *AuBYP*
Fitzsimmons, Robert 1862-1917 *DcNAA*
Fitzsimmons, Thomas 1926- *ConAu 33*,
 DrAP 1975
FitzSimon, Ellen 1805-1883 *Alli Sup*, *PoIre*
Fitzsimon, Henry 1569-1644 *Alli*
Fitzsimons, Edward John *PoIre*
Fitzsimons, F W 1881- *WhLA*
Fitzsimons, Louise 1932- *ConAu 61*
Fitzsimons, Mathew Anthony 1912-
 ConAu 13R, *IndAu 1917*
Fitzsimons, Neal 1928- *ConAu 33*
Fitzsimons, Raymund *ConAu 33*, *WrD 1976*
FitzSimons, Ruth M *ConAu 53*
Fitzsimons, Vivian Frederick Maynard 1901-
 Au&Wr
Fitzsmith, Richard *Alli*
Fitzstephen, William d1190? *Alli*, *BrAu*,
 DcEnL, *EvLB*, *NewC*, *OxEng*
Fitzwater, Lily *ChPo S1*
Fitzwater, Perry Braxton 1871- *WhWNAA*
Fitzwaters, Colonel *Alli*
Fitzwilliam, Charles William, Earl *Alli*
Fitzwilliam, Edward 1833- *PoIre*
Fitzwilliam, G W *Alli*
Fitzwilliam, John *Alli*
Fitzwilliam, William *BbtC*
Fitzwilliam, William W, Viscount Milton
 1839-1877 *Alli Sup*
Fitzwilliam, William Wentworth, Earl 1748-1833
 Alli, *BiDLA*
Fitzwilliams, Duncan Campbell Lloyd 1877-
 WhLA
Fitzwygram, Sir Frederick Wellington 1823-
 Alli Sup
Fitzwygram, John *Alli Sup*
Fitzwygram, Loftus Adam 1832- *Alli Sup*
Fix, Betty S *ChPo S1*
Fix, Thomas Lewis *Alli Sup*
Fixel, Arthur Ellis 1885- *WhWNAA*
Fixel, Rowland W 1887- *WhWNAA*
Fixler, Michael 1927- *Au&Wr*, *ConAu 13R*
Fizer, John 1925- *ConAu 53*
Fizerburtus, Nic *Alli*
Fizes, M *Alli*
Fjelde, Rolf 1926- *ConAu 17R*, *WrD 1976*
Flaccus *OxEng*
Flaccus 1807-1873 *AmA*, *DcNAA*
Flaccus Horatius *DcNAA*
Flaccus, Bella *ChPo S1*
Flaccus, Gaius Valerius *NewC*
Flaccus, Kimball 1911- *ChPo S2*, *SixAP*
Flaccus, Louis W *ChPo S1*
Flaccus, Quintus Horatius *REn*
Flachsland, Caroline 1750-1809 *OxGer*
Flacius, Matthias 1520-1575 *DcEuL*
Flacius Illyricus, Matthias 1520-1575 *CasWL*,
 OxGer
Flack, Captain *Alli Sup*
Flack, Dora D 1919- *ConAu 57*
Flack, Elmer Ellsworth 1894- *ConAu 17R*
Flack, Horace Edgar 1879- *WhWNAA*
Flack, Marjorie 1897-1958 *AmA&B*, *AuBYP*,
 ChPo, *IlCB 1945*, *IlCB 1956*, *JBA 1934*,
 JBA 1951, *St&VC*
Flacks, Richard 1938- *ConAu 49*
Fladeland, Betty 1919- *ConAu 45*, *WrD 1976*
Flag *EarAB Sup*
Flagello, Nicholas 1928- *AmSCAP 66*
Flagg, Ann *BlkAW*
Flagg, Charles Allcott 1870-1920 *DcNAA*
Flagg, Charles Noel 1848-1916 *DcNAA*
Flagg, Edmund 1815-1890 *Alli*, *Alli Sup*,
 AmA, *AmA&B*, *BbD*, *BiD&SB*, *BiDSA*,
 CyAL 2, *DcAmA*, *DcEnL*, *DcNAA*

Flagg, Edward Octavius 1824-1911 *ChPo*,
 DcAmA, *DcNAA*
Flagg, Elizabeth E *Alli Sup*
Flagg, Ernest 1857-1947 *DcNAA*, *DcNAA*
Flagg, Francis 1898-1946 *ChPo*, *WhWNAA*
Flagg, Isaac 1843-1931 *DcAmA*, *DcNAA*
Flagg, Issac 1843-1931 *AmLY*
Flagg, James Montgomery 1877-1960 *AmA&B*,
 ChPo, *ChPo S2*, *OxAm*, *REnAL*
Flagg, Jared, Jr. *Alli Sup*
Flagg, Jared Bradley 1820-1899 *DcNAA*
Flagg, John Foster Brewster 1804-1872 *Alli*,
 DcAmA, *DcNAA*
Flagg, John Henry 1843-1911 *ChPo*, *ChPo S1*,
 ChPo S2, *DcNAA*
Flagg, Josiah 1737-1795? *DcNAA*
Flagg, Josiah Foster 1789-1853 *DcNAA*
Flagg, Josiah Foster 1835-1928 *DcNAA*
Flagg, Mildred Buchanan 1886- *AmA&B*
Flagg, Thomas Wilson 1805-1884 *AmA*,
 DcNAA
Flagg, William Joseph 1818-1898 *Alli Sup*,
 DcAmA, *DcNAA*, *OhA&B*
Flagg, Wilson 1805-1884 *Alli*, *Alli Sup*, *AmA*,
 AmA&B, *BiD&SB*, *ChPo*, *DcAmA*,
 DcNAA
Flagler, Robert S 1890-1935 *AmSCAP 66*
Flagstad, Kirsten 1895-1962 *REn*
Flaherty, David H 1940- *ConAu 25*
Flaherty, Douglas 1939- *ConAu 33*,
 ConP 1970, *DrAP 1975*
Flaherty, Frances Hubbard *AmA&B*
Flaherty, Joe *AmA&B*
Flaherty, Robert Joseph 1884-1951 *AmA&B*,
 OxCan, *REn*
Flaherty, Roderic *Alli*
Flaherty, W E *Alli Sup*
Flaiano, Ennio 1910-1972 *ConAu 37*
Flaig, Eleanore 1902-1954 *IndAu 1917*
Flaischlen, Casar 1864-1920 *OxGer*
Flaissier, Sabine 1906- *Au&Wr*
Flake, Arthur 1862- *WhWNAA*
Flake, Chad J 1929- *ConAu 29*
Flake, Otto 1880-1965 *EncWL*, *ModGL*,
 OxGer
Flamank, James *Alli Sup*
Flamant, Adolphe *Alli Sup*
Flamholtz, Eric 1943- *ConAu 57*
Flaminio, Marcantonio 1498-1550 *DcEuL*, *REn*
Flamm, Dudley 1931- *ConAu 25*, *WrD 1976*
Flammarion, Camille 1842-1925 *BbD*, *BiD&SB*,
 BiDPar, *DcEuL*
Flammer, Philip M 1928- *ConAu 45*
Flammonde, Paris *ConAu 17R*
Flamsteed, John 1646-1719 *Alli*
Flanagan, Charles 1830?-1856 *PoIre*
Flanagan, Dan Collins 1899-1960 *IndAu 1917*
Flanagan, Dorothy Belle *AmA&B*
Flanagan, Edward *PoIre*
Flanagan, Eileen C *OxCan Sup*
Flanagan, James *PoIre*
Flanagan, Jewel Mace *TexWr*
Flanagan, John *Alli Sup*
Flanagan, John C 1906- *ConAu 1R*
Flanagan, John F d1882? *PoIre*
Flanagan, John T 1906- *ConAu 17R*
Flanagan, Jonathan *PoIre*
Flanagan, Joseph David Stanislaus 1903-
 CatA 1952, *ConAu 13R*
Flanagan, Martin J *PoIre*
Flanagan, Neal M 1920- *ConAu 17R*
Flanagan, Patrick Joseph 1940- *Au&Wr*,
 WrD 1976
Flanagan, Ralph 1919- *AmSCAP 66*
Flanagan, Richard *DrAF 1976*
Flanagan, Robert 1941- *ConAu 33*,
 DrAF 1976, *DrAP 1975*, *OxCan Sup*
Flanagan, Roderick 1828-1861 *Alli Sup*, *PoIre*
Flanagan, Roger *PoIre*
Flanagan, S W And C Kelly *Alli*
Flanagan, Sylvia *ChPo*
Flanagan, T J *HsB&A*
Flanagan, Thomas *PoIre*
Flanagan, Thomas 1814-1865 *Alli Sup*
Flanagan, Thomas 1923- *EncM&D*
Flanagan, Thomas Jefferson 1890- *BlkAW*
Flanders, G T *Alli Sup*
Flanders, Helen Hartness 1890-1972 *AmA&B*,

ChPo S1, ChPo S2, ConAu 33,
 ConAu P-1
Flanders, Henry 1824?-1911 *Alli*, *Alli Sup*,
 AmA&B, *DcAmA*, *DcNAA*
Flanders, Henry Jackson, Jr. 1921- *ConAu 33*
Flanders, Louisa B *ChPo*
Flanders, Michael 1922-1975 *Au&Wr*, *AuBYP*,
 ChPo, *ChPo S1*, *ChPo S2*, *ConAu 5R*,
 ConAu 57
Flanders, Ned A 1918- *ConAu 37*, *WrD 1976*
Flanders, Ralph Edward 1880-1970 *ConAu P-1*
Flanders, Robert Bruce 1930- *ConAu 17R*
Flandrau, Charles Eugene 1828-1903 *AmA&B*,
 DcAmA, *DcNAA*
Flandrau, Charles Macomb 1871-1938 *AmA&B*,
 DcAmA, *DcNAA*, *OxAm*, *REnAL*,
 TwCA, *TwCA Sup*
Flandrau, Grace Hodgson *AmA&B*,
 WhWNAA
Flandre, Charles De *Alli Sup*
Flandreau, Charles Macomb 1871-1938
 BiD&SB
Flanery, E B 1932- *ConAu 61*
Flanigan, Lloyd A 1933- *ConAu 33*
Flanigan, Robert Lee 1926- *AmSCAP 66*
Flanigen, J R *Alli Sup*
Flanner, Hildegarde 1899- *AmA&B*
Flanner, Janet 1892- *AmA&B*, *IndAu 1917*,
 OxAm, *REnAL*, *WorAu*, *WrD 1976*
Flanner, Mary H *ChPo*
Flannery, Edward H 1912- *ConAu 13R*
Flannery, Harry W 1900-1975 *ConAu 57*
Flannery, Harry W 1900- *ConAu P-1*
Flannery, M Jay 1857-1920 *OhA&B*
Flannery, Thomas J 1840- *PoIre*
Flannery, William 1830- *PoIre*
Flasch, Joy 1932- *ConAu 37*
Flash, Henry Lynden 1835-1914 *Alli Sup*,
 BiD&SB, *BiDSA*, *ChPo S1*, *DcAmA*,
 DcNAA, *OhA&B*
Flash Flood *SmATA 6*
Flassan, Gaetan Raxis, Count De 1770-1845
 BiD&SB
Flaster, Karl 1905-1965 *AmSCAP 66*
Flather, John *Alli*
Flather, John Joseph 1862-1926 *DcAmA*,
 DcNAA
Flatley, Mary M *ChPo*
Flatman, Thomas 1637?-1688? *Alli*, *BrAu*,
 CasWL, *ChPo*, *ChPo S1*, *Chmbr 1*,
 DcEnL, *DcLEnL*, *EvLB*, *NewC*, *OxEng*
Flato, Ludwig 1911- *AmSCAP 66*
Flatow, Leon 1889-1944 *AmSCAP 66*
Flatt, Willa Mary 1882- *TexWr*
Flatters, J J *Alli*
Flattery, Maurice Douglas 1870-1925 *DcNAA*
Flaubert, Gustave 1821-1880 *AtlBL*, *BbD*,
 BiD&SB, *CasWL*, *CIDMEuL*, *CyWA*,
 DcBiA, *DcEuL*, *EuA*, *EvEuW*, *NewC*,
 OxEng, *OxFr*, *Pen Eur*, *RCom*, *REn*
Flavel, John *Alli*, *Chmbr 1*
Flavel, John 1627-1691 *Alli*, *DcEnL*, *EvLB*
Flavel, Phineas *Alli*
Flavell, Geoffrey 1913- *Au&Wr*
Flavell, John H 1928- *ConAu 17R*
Flavin, Martin 1883-1967 *AmA&B*, *AmNov*,
 CnMD, *ConAu 5R*, *ConAu 25*, *DcLEnL*,
 McGWD, *ModWD*, *OxAm*, *REnAL*,
 TwCA, *TwCA Sup*
Flavio, Biondo *DcEuL*
Flavius, Brother *ConAu XR*
Flavius, Snaeus *WhLA*
Flaxman, Arthur John *Alli Sup*
Flaxman, E *MnBBF*
Flaxman, John 1755-1826 *Alli*, *AtlBL*, *BiDLA*,
 BkIE, *ChPo*
Flaxman, Traudl 1942- *ConAu 25*
Flaxmer, Sarah *Alli*
Flayderman, Phillip C 1930- *ConAu 23*
Fleay, Frederick Gard 1831-1909 *Alli Sup*,
 NewC
Flebbe, Mrs. George H *AmA&B*
Fleche, Jesse d1611? *OxCan*
Flecher, Henry McDonald 1840?- *PoIre*
Flechier, Esprit 1632-1710 *BbD*, *BiD&SB*,
 DcEuL, *OxFr*, *Pen Eur*
Fleck, Betty *ConAu XR*
Fleck, Charles S 1916- *AmSCAP 66*

Fleck, Conrad *DcEuL*
Fleck, George Morrison 1934- *IndAu 1917*
Fleck, Konrad *CasWL, OxGer*
Flecker, Eliezer *Alli Sup*
Flecker, James Elroy 1884-1915 *CasWL, ChPo, ChPo S1, ChPo S2, Chmbr 3, CnE&AP, CnMWL, CnThe, DcEuL, DcLEnL, EvLB, LongC, McGWD, ModBL, NewC, OxEng, Pen Eng, REn, TwCA, TwCA Sup, TwCW, WebEAL*
Fleckie, Andrew *Alli, BiDLA*
Flecknoc, Richard *WhLA*
Flecknoe, Richard 1600?-1678? *Alli, BrAu, CasWL, Chmbr 1, DcEnL, EvLB, NewC, OxEng, Pen Eng, PoIre, REn*
Fleece, Jeffrey 1920- *ConAu 17R*
Fleege, Urban H 1908- *ConAu 45*
Fleeman, J D *ChPo*
Fleer, Jack D 1937- *ConAu 25*
Fleeson, Doris *WhWNAA*
Fleeson, Neville 1887-1945 *AmSCAP 66*
Fleet, Charles *Alli, Alli Sup, BiDLA*
Fleet, Edward *Alli*
Fleet, F R *Alli Sup*
Fleet, J G *Alli Sup*
Fleet, Maxwell *MnBBF*
Fleet, Thomas 1685-1758 *AmA&B*
Fleet, William Henry *BbtC, OxCan*
Fleeta *DcAmA*
Fleetwood, Mrs. *Alli*
Fleetwood, Charles *Alli*
Fleetwood, Everard *Alli*
Fleetwood, Frances 1902- *ConAu 45*
Fleetwood, Frank *ConAu XR*
Fleetwood, John *Alli, DcEnL*
Fleetwood, William *Alli*
Fleetwood, William d1603 *Alli*
Fleetwood, William 1656-1723 *Alli, DcEnL*
Fleharty, S F *Alli Sup*
Fleischbein, Sister M Catherine Frederic 1902- *ConAu 5R*
Fleischer, Anthony Charles 1928- *Au&Wr*
Fleischer, Charles 1871- *WhWNAA*
Fleischer, Dave *AmSCAP 66*
Fleischer, Gustav A 1863- *WhWNAA*
Fleischer, Manfred P 1928- *ConAu 29*
Fleischer, Nathaniel S 1888?-1972 *ConAu 37*
Fleischhacker, David 1933- *AmSCAP 66*
Fleischman, Albert Sidney 1920- *AuBYP, ConAu 1R*
Fleischman, David 1912- *AmSCAP 66*
Fleischman, Harry 1914- *ConAu 5R, WrD 1976*
Fleischman, Joseph *Alli Sup*
Fleischman, Sid 1920- *AnCL, ChLR 1, ConAu XR, SmATA 8, ThBJA*
Fleischmann, Glen H 1909- *ConAu 33*
Fleischmann, Harriet 1914- *ConAu 21*
Fleischmann, Julius 1900- *OhA&B*
Fleischmann, Maximilian Charles 1877-1951 *OhA&B*
Fleischmann, Raoul H 1885-1969 *AmA&B*
Fleisher, Frederic Elliott 1933- *ConAu 21, WrD 1976*
Fleisher, Mark 1907- *AmSCAP 66*
Fleisher, Martin 1925- *ConAu 45*
Fleisher, Michael 1942- *ConAu 25*
Fleisher, Wilfrid 1897- *WrD 1976*
Fleishman, Avrom 1933- *ConAu 21, WrD 1976*
Fleishman, Clara S *Alli Sup*
Fleishman, Edwin A 1927- *ConAu 21*
Fleishman, S L *Alli Sup*
Fleishman, Seymour 1918- *IlBYP, IlCB 1956, IlCB 1966*
Fleisser, Marieluise 1901-1974 *CnMD, ConAu 49, EncWL Sup, OxGer*
Fleitman, Lida L 1885?- *Br&AmS*
Flejsar, Josef 1922- *WhGrA*
Flekser, A L *CasWL*
Flemalle, Master Of *AtlBL*
Flemer, John Adolph 1859- *WhWNAA*
Flemer, William, III 1922- *ConAu 61*
Fleming, Abraham *Alli*
Fleming, Albert *Alli Sup*
Fleming, Alexander *Alli*
Fleming, Sir Alexander 1881-1955 *LongC*
Fleming, Alice Carew Mulcahey 1928- *AuBYP,*

ConAu 1R, SmATA 9, WrD 1976
Fleming, Alice Kipling 1868-1948 *BiDPar*
Fleming, Alice May *HsB&A*
Fleming, Allan Robb 1929- *WhGrA*
Fleming, Andrew G *Alli Sup*
Fleming, Ann Cuthbert d1860 *BbtC, DcNAA*
Fleming, Ann C ALSO Flemming, Ann C
Fleming, Archibald 1800-1875 *DcNAA*
Fleming, Archibald Lang 1883-1953 *OxCan*
Fleming, Berry 1899- *AmA&B, AmNov, Au&Wr, ConAu 1R, WrD 1976*
Fleming, Burton Percival 1881-1936 *DcNAA*
Fleming, C M 1894- *Au&Wr, ConAu 5R*
Fleming, Caleb 1698-1779 *Alli*
Fleming, Charles *ChPo*
Fleming, Charles Alexander 1916- *WrD 1976*
Fleming, Charles Francis 1912?- *IndAu 1917*
Fleming, Christopher 1599-1631 *Alli*
Fleming, Christopher 1800-1880 *Alli Sup*
Fleming, Clint *OxCan*
Fleming, Curtis *Alli*
Fleming, Daniel Johnson 1877- *OhA&B, WhWNAA*
Fleming, David Hay 1849- *WhLA*
Fleming, David James 1947- *Au&Wr*
Fleming, Denna Frank 1893- *AmA&B, ConAu 1R*
Fleming, Elizabeth *ChPo, ChPo S1, ChPo S2, St&VC*
Fleming, Elizabeth P *AuBYP*
Fleming, Emily *Alli Sup*
Fleming, Fletcher *Alli Sup*
Fleming, Francis P *BiDSA*
Fleming, George *Alli Sup, AmA&B, BiD&SB, DcAmA, DcNAA*
Fleming, George 1833- *Alli Sup*
Fleming, George 1858- *DcEnA Ap*
Fleming, George J 1917- *ConAu 37*
Fleming, George James 1904- *LivBA*
Fleming, George Thornton 1855-1928 *DcNAA*
Fleming, Gerald 1921- *Au&Wr, ConAu 53*
Fleming, Giles *Alli*
Fleming, H K 1901- *Au&Wr, ConAu 33*
Fleming, Harloe Robert *Alli Sup*
Fleming, Harold 1927- *ConAu 17R*
Fleming, Harold M 1900- *ConAu 21*
Fleming, Harriet S *ChPo*
Fleming, Howard *Alli Sup*
Fleming, Ian 1908-1964 *AuBYP, ConAu 5R, ConLC 3, EncM&D, LongC, NewC, Pen Eng, REn, SmATA 9, TwCW, WorAu*
Fleming, Isaac Plant *Alli Sup*
Fleming, J *Alli Sup*
Fleming, J A *Alli Sup*
Fleming, Miss J A *Alli Sup*
Fleming, James *Alli, Alli Sup*
Fleming, James 1817-1888 *PoIre*
Fleming, James 1830-1908 *ChPo*
Fleming, James C *BlkAW*
Fleming, James M *Alli Sup*
Fleming, James Simpson *Alli Sup*
Fleming, John *Alli Sup, ChPo*
Fleming, John 1785-1857 *Alli, Alli Sup*
Fleming, John 1786?-1832 *BbtC, DcNAA, OxCan*
Fleming, John 1919- *Au&Wr*
Fleming, John Adam 1877- *WhWNAA*
Fleming, John Chester 1906-1964 *IndAu 1917*
Fleming, John Dick 1863- *WhWNAA*
Fleming, John F *ChPo S1*
Fleming, Joy Amelia Blanche 1909- *Au&Wr*
Fleming, Laurence William Howie 1929- *WrD 1976*
Fleming, Lucy Ward Randolph 1847- *Alli Sup, ChPo, ChPo S1, ChPo S2*
Fleming, Malcolm *Alli*
Fleming, Margaret 1803-1811 *BrAu 19, DcLEnL, EvLB, NewC*
Fleming, Marjorie 1803-1811 *NewC*
Fleming, Marjory 1803-1811 *ChPo, ChPo S2, OxEng*
Fleming, Martin *PoIre*
Fleming, Martin J *PoIre*
Fleming, May Agnes 1840-1880 *Alli Sup, BbtC, BiD&SB, DcAmA, DcNAA, HsB&A, OxCan*
Fleming, Miles 1919- *ConAu 29, WrD 1976*

Fleming, Oliver *EncM&D, EvLB, LongC, NewC*
Fleming, Patrick 1599-1631 *Alli, DcEnL*
Fleming, Paul 1609-1640 *BbD, BiD&SB, CasWL, DcEuL, EuA, EvEuW, OxGer, Pen Eur, REn*
Fleming, Peter *Alli, BbtC*
Fleming, Peter 1907-1971 *Au&Wr, ConAu 33, EvLB, LongC, Pen Eng, REn, TwCA, TwCA Sup, TwCW*
Fleming, Ray 1945- *BlkAW*
Fleming, Robert 1630-1694 *Alli, DcEnL*
Fleming, Robert 1856- *ChPo, ChPo S1*
Fleming, Robert, Jr. d1716 *Alli*
Fleming, Robert Peter 1907-1971 *DcLEnL*
Fleming, Robins 1856-1942 *DcNAA*
Fleming, Ronald *MnBBF*
Fleming, S *Alli Sup*
Fleming, Samuel *Alli, BiDLA*
Fleming, Sir Sandford 1827-1915 *BbtC, DcNAA, OxCan*
Fleming, Sandford 1888- *ConAu P-1, WhWNAA*
Fleming, Sanford 1827-1915 *Alli Sup*
Fleming, Sarah Lee Brown *BlkAW*
Fleming, Sydney Hall *Alli Sup*
Fleming, T Q *Alli Sup*
Fleming, Theodore B, Jr. 1917- *ConAu 45*
Fleming, Thomas *Alli*
Fleming, Thomas J 1927- *AmA&B, ConAu 5R, SmATA 8*
Fleming, Thomas Kelman 1927- *Au&Wr*
Fleming, Tom *ChPo S2*
Fleming, W d1742 *Alli*
Fleming, W G *OxCan Sup*
Fleming, Waldo *ConAmA, TwCA, TwCA Sup*
Fleming, Wallace Bruce 1872-1952 *AmA&B, OhA&B, WhWNAA*
Fleming, Walter Lynwood 1874-1932 *BiDSA, DcNAA, WhWNAA*
Fleming, William *Alli, Alli Sup*
Fleming, William 1860- *ChPo*
Fleming, William 1909- *ConAu 17R*
Fleming, William Hansell 1844-1915 *AmA&B, DcAmA, DcNAA*
Fleming, William Henry 1856?- *AmLY, BiDSA, WhWNAA*
Fleming, William Kaye 1870- *ChPo*
Fleming, William Stuart 1816-1896 *DcNAA*
Fleming, Williamina Paton 1857-1911 *DcNAA*
Fleming And Tibbins *Alli*
Flemister, John T *BlkAW*
Flemming, Ann Cuthbert *OxCan*
Flemming, Ann C ALSO Fleming, Ann C
Flemming, D Lambden *Alli Sup*
Flemming, Francis *Alli*
Flemming, Harford *Alli Sup, DcNAA*
Flemming, Robert d1483 *Alli*
Flemmyng, Robert d1483 *CasWL*
Flemmynge, Robert d1483 *Alli*
Flemyng, Francis Patrick *Alli Sup*
Flemyng, Malcolm *Alli*
Flender, Harold 1924- *ConAu 49, DrAF 1976*
Flenley, Ralph *OxCan*
Flers, Robert DeLaMotte-Ango De 1872-1927 *CasWL, CIDMEuL, EvEuW, McGWD, ModWD, OxFr*
Flesch, Rudolf 1911- *AmA&B, ConAu 9R, WrD 1976*
Flescher, Irwin 1926- *ConAu 37, WrD 1976*
Flescher, Joachim 1906- *Au&Wr*
Flesher, John *Alli*
Flesher, Thomas *Alli*
Fleta *Alli*
Fletcher *Alli*
Fletcher d1844 *BbtC*
Fletcher, Baron 1903- *Au&Wr*
Fletcher, Miss A *Alli Sup*
Fletcher, Abraham 1714-1793 *Alli*
Fletcher, Adam *ConAu XR*
Fletcher, Adele Whitely 1898- *ConAu P-1, WhWNAA*
Fletcher, Alan 1931- *WhGrA*
Fletcher, Alan Mark 1928- *WrD 1976*
Fletcher, Alexander 1787-1860 *Alli, Alli Sup, DcEnL*

Fletcher, Alfred Charles Benson 1885-1928 *DcNAA*
Fletcher, Alfred Ewen *Alli Sup*
Fletcher, Alice Cunningham 1838-1923 *AmA&B, DcAmA, DcNAA*
Fletcher, Andrew *Chmbr 1, MnBBF*
Fletcher, Andrew 1653?-1716 *Alli, DcEnL, EvLB, Pen Eng*
Fletcher, Ann *BiDLA*
Fletcher, Anna *ChPo S1*
Fletcher, Anne *Alli*
Fletcher, Anthony *Alli*
Fletcher, Archibald *Alli*
Fletcher, Archie 1890- *AmSCAP 66*
Fletcher, Arnold Charles 1917- *ConAu 17R*
Fletcher, Banister *Alli Sup*
Fletcher, Basil Alais 1900- *Au&Wr, WrD 1976*
Fletcher, Beale *AuBYP*
Fletcher, Benjamin *Alli*
Fletcher, Bob 1938- *BlkAW*
Fletcher, C *Alli, Alli Sup*
Fletcher, C W *Alli Sup*
Fletcher, Charles *Alli, BiDLA*
Fletcher, Charles Robert Leslie *Alli Sup, LongC*
Fletcher, Charles Seton *MnBBF*
Fletcher, Charlie May Hogue 1897- *AuBYP, ConAu 9R, SmATA 3*
Fletcher, Christian *Alli*
Fletcher, Colin 1922- *AuNews 1, ConAu 13R, WrD 1976*
Fletcher, David 1940- *ConAu XR, WrD 1976*
Fletcher, E *Alli*
Fletcher, E B *Alli Sup*
Fletcher, Edith *Alli Sup*
Fletcher, Edward H *Alli Sup*
Fletcher, Edward Taylor 1816?-1897 *BbtC, DcNAA*
Fletcher, Eliza *Chmbr 3*
Fletcher, Eliza 1770-1858 *Alli Sup*
Fletcher, Frances 1894- *AnMV 1926, WhWNAA*
Fletcher, Francis *Alli*
Fletcher, Frank *ChPo S2*
Fletcher, G W H *Alli Sup*
Fletcher, George *Alli, ChPo S1, Chmbr 1*
Fletcher, Giles 1549?-1611 *Alli, BrAu, CasWL, CrE&SL, DcLEnL, NewC, Pen Eng, OxEng*
Fletcher, Giles 1588?-1623 *Alli, AtlBL, BbD, BiD&SB, BrAu, CasWL, ChPo, CnE&AP, CrE&SL, DcEnA, DcEnL, DcEuL, DcLEnL, EvLB, NewC, OxEng, Pen Eng, REn, WebEAL*
Fletcher, Grace Nies 1895- *AmA&B, Au&Wr, ConAu 5R*
Fletcher, Grant 1913- *AmSCAP 66*
Fletcher, Harris Francis 1892- *AmA&B, ConAu 1R, WhWNAA*
Fletcher, Harry Lutf Verne 1902- *Au&Wr, ConAu 9R*
Fletcher, Helen Jill 1911- *AuBYP, ConAu 9R*
Fletcher, Henry *Alli Sup*
Fletcher, Henry Charles *Alli Sup*
Fletcher, Horace 1849-1919 *DcNAA*
Fletcher, Horace 1869- *DcAmA*
Fletcher, Ian 1920- *ConP 1970, ConP 1975, WrD 1976*
Fletcher, Inglis 1888-1969 *AmA&B, AmNov, Au&Wr, AuNews 1, CnDAL, ConAu 5R*
Fletcher, James 1811-1832 *Alli*
Fletcher, James 1852-1908 *DcNAA*
Fletcher, James Cooley 1823-1901 *Alli, DcAmA, DcNAA, IndAu 1816*
Fletcher, Mrs. James Cooley *Alli Sup*
Fletcher, James Michael John 1852- *WhLA*
Fletcher, James Ogden *Alli Sup*
Fletcher, James Phillips *Alli, Alli Sup*
Fletcher, Jefferson Butler 1865-1946 *AmA&B, ChPo, DcNAA, REnAL*
Fletcher, Jesse C 1931- *ConAu 9R*
Fletcher, John *Alli, BbtC, BiDLA, Chmbr 1*
Fletcher, John 1579-1625 *AtlBL, BbD, BiD&SB, BrAu, CasWL, ChPo, ChPo S1, CnE&AP, CnThe, CrE&SL, CriT 1, CyWA, DcEnA, DcEnL, DcEuL, DcLEnL, EvLB, McGWD, MouLC 1,*

NewC, OxEng, Pen Eng, REn, REnWD, WebEAL
Fletcher, John 1791-1862 *DcNAA*
Fletcher, John Brunsdon *Alli Sup*
Fletcher, John Gould 1886-1950 *AmA&B, AmLY, AnCL, CasWL, ChPo, Chmbr 3, CnDAL, ConAmA, ConAmL, DcLEnL, EncWL, EvLB, LongC, ModAL, OxAm, Pen Am, REn, REnAL, SixAP, TwCA, TwCA Sup, WhWNAA*
Fletcher, Mrs. John Gould 1897- *AmA&B*
Fletcher, John James *Alli Sup*
Fletcher, John Madison 1873-1944 *DcNAA*
Fletcher, John Walter James 1937- *Au&Wr, WrD 1976*
Fletcher, John William *Alli Sup, ChPo S1*
Fletcher, John William 1729-1785 *Alli*
Fletcher, Joseph *Alli, Alli Sup, BiDLA*
Fletcher, Joseph 1784-1843 *Alli*
Fletcher, Joseph 1862- *ChPo S1*
Fletcher, Joseph 1905- *ConAu 21*
Fletcher, Joseph Francis 1905- *Au&Wr*
Fletcher, Joseph Moody 1828- *ChPo S2*
Fletcher, Joseph Smith 1863-1935 *Alli Sup, BbD, ChPo S2, EncM&D, EvLB, LongC, NewC, TwCA, WhLA*
Fletcher, Julia A *ChPo*
Fletcher, Julia Constance 1858?-1938 *Alli Sup, AmA&B, BbD, BiD&SB, DcAmA, DcEnA Ap, DcNAA*
Fletcher, L J *Alli Sup*
Fletcher, Lelih Gill 1880- *TexWr, WhWNAA*
Fletcher, Leon 1921- *ConAu 49*
Fletcher, Lisa A *ChPo S2*
Fletcher, Louisa *ChPo S2*
Fletcher, Lucille *ConAu XR*
Fletcher, Lucy *Alli Sup, ChPo S1*
Fletcher, Mabel Elizabeth Billings 1886- *ChPo*
Fletcher, Maria Jewsbury *ChPo S1*
Fletcher, Mary *AuNews 1*
Fletcher, Mary P *Alli Sup*
Fletcher, Matilda *Alli Sup*
Fletcher, Miriam *Alli Sup*
Fletcher, Orlin Ottman 1847-1937 *DcNAA, WhWNAA*
Fletcher, Philip *Alli*
Fletcher, Phineas 1582-1650 *Alli, AtlBL, BrAu, CasWL, ChPo, ChPo S1, Chmbr 1, CnE&AP, CrE&SL, DcEnA, DcEnL, DcEuL, DcLEnL, EvLB, NewC, OxEng, Pen Eng, REn, WebEAL*
Fletcher, R *Alli*
Fletcher, Mrs. R J 1880- *WhWNAA*
Fletcher, Ral *Alli*
Fletcher, Ralph Beaumont 1920- *Au&Wr*
Fletcher, Richard *Alli*
Fletcher, Robert *Alli, Alli Sup*
Fletcher, Robert 1823- *DcAmA*
Fletcher, Robert Henry 1885?-1972 *ConAu 37, WhPNW*
Fletcher, Robert Howe 1850-1936 *AmA&B, DcAmA, DcNAA, OhA&B*
Fletcher, Robert Huntington 1875-1919 *ChPo, DcNAA*
Fletcher, Robert Samuel 1900-1959 *OhA&B*
Fletcher, Ronald 1921- *Au&Wr, ConAu 33, WrD 1976*
Fletcher, Miss S *Alli*
Fletcher, Samuel *Alli, BiDLA*
Fletcher, Sedgley Bernice 1903- *Au&Wr*
Fletcher, Shepherd *Alli Sup*
Fletcher, Stevenson Whitcomb 1875- *WhWNAA*
Fletcher, Stoughton 'Bruz' 1907?-1941 *IndAu 1917*
Fletcher, Susan Willis *Alli Sup*
Fletcher, T Thomas Fortune *BlkAW*
Fletcher, Tex 1910- *AmSCAP 66*
Fletcher, Thomas *Alli*
Fletcher, Thomas C *Alli Sup*
Fletcher, W *CarSB, ChPo S1*
Fletcher, Walter *ChPo S2*
Fletcher, William *Alli, Alli Sup*
Fletcher, William Baldwin 1837-1907 *Alli Sup, DcAmA, DcNAA, IndAu 1917*
Fletcher, William C 1932- *ConAu 23*
Fletcher, William George Dimock *Alli Sup*
Fletcher, William Isaac 1844-1917 *DcNAA*

Fletcher, William Leslie *PoIre*
Fletcher, William Meade 1870-1943 *DcNAA, WhWNAA*
Fletcher, William Whigham 1918- *WrD 1976*
Fletcher-Cooke, Charles 1914- *Au&Wr*
Fletcher-Cooke, John 1911- *WrD 1976*
Flett, Sir John Smith 1869- *WhLA*
Fleur, Anne *IlBYP, IlCB 1956*
Fleur, Claude 1640-1723 *BiD&SB*
Fleur, William *WrD 1976*
Fleurange, R DeLaMarck, Seigneur De d1537 *OxFr*
Fleure, Herbert John 1877- *WhLA*
Fleuridas, Ellie Rae *ConAu XR*
Fleuron, Svend 1874- *EvEuW*
Fleury, Cardinal Andre-Hercule De 1653-1743 *OxFr*
Fleury, Charles Robert *Alli Sup*
Fleury, Claude 1640-1723 *DcEuL, OxFr*
Fleury, Delphine 1904- *ConAu XR, IndAu 1917*
Fleury, Jules *OxFr*
Fleury, L *Alli Sup*
Fleury, Maria De *Alli*
Fleury-Husson, Jules *BiD&SB*
Flew, Antony G N 1923- *Au&Wr, BiDPar, ConAu 5R, WrD 1976*
Flewelling, Ralph Tyler 1871- *AmA&B, WhWNAA*
Flewellyn, Juliette 1850- *DcAmA*
Flewker, W *Alli Sup*
Flex, Walter 1887-1917 *ClDMEuL, OxGer*
Flexer, Akim Lvovich 1863-1926 *DcRusL*
Flexman, Roger 1708-1795 *Alli*
Flexner, Abraham 1866-1959 *AmA&B, REnAL, TwCA, TwCA Sup*
Flexner, Anne Crawford 1874-1955 *AmA&B, REnAL, WhWNAA*
Flexner, Eleanor 1908- *ConAu 45*
Flexner, Hortense 1885- *AmA&B, AnMV 1926, ChPo, ChPo S1, ChPo S2*
Flexner, James Thomas 1908- *AmA&B, Au&Wr, ConAu 1R, SmATA 9, WhWNAA, WrD 1976*
Flexner, Jennie Maas 1882-1944 *DcNAA*
Flexner, Simon 1863-1946 *DcNAA*
Flexner, Stuart Berg 1928- *ConAu 13R*
Flick, Alexander Clarence 1869-1942 *AmA&B, AmLY, DcAmA, DcNAA, OhA&B, WhWNAA*
Flick, Ella Marie *CatA 1947*
Flick, Ella Mary Elizabeth *BkC 1*
Flick, Lawrence Francis 1856-1938 *CatA 1952, DcNAA, WhWNAA*
Flick, Oka Stanton 1890-1970 *IndAu 1917*
Flick-Flood, Dora *AmSCAP 66*
Flickinger, Daniel Krumler 1824-1911 *Alli Sup, DcAmA, DcNAA, OhA&B*
Flickinger, Junius Rudy *DcAmA*
Flickinger, Minnie Keys 1907- *IndAu 1917*
Flickinger, Robert Elliott 1848- *DcNAA*
Flickinger, Roy Caston 1876-1942 *AmA&B, DcNAA*
Fliegel, Frederick C 1925- *ConAu 49*
Fliegel, Hellmuth *OxGer*
Flieger, Wilhelm 1931- *ConAu 25*
Flier, Michael Stephen 1941- *ConAu 37, WrD 1976*
Fliess, Peter Joachim 1915- *ConAu 21, WrD 1976*
Flight *WhWNAA*
Flight, Claude 1881- *ChPo, ChPo S2*
Flight, Edward G *Alli Sup*
Flight, Walter *Alli Sup*
Flindall, John Morris *Alli, BiDLA*
Flinders, Matthew *Alli*
Flinders, Matthew d1814 *Alli*
Flinders, Neil J 1934- *ConAu 21, WrD 1976*
Fling, Fred Morrow 1860?-1934 *AmA&B, DcNAA*
Fling, Maude Hammond 1873- *WhWNAA*
Flink, Harvey Wagner 1902- *ChPo*
Flink, Salomon J 1906- *ConAu 1R*
Flinn, Andrew d1820 *Alli*
Flinn, David Edgar *Alli Sup*
Flinn, Frank M *Alli Sup*
Flinn, John Joseph 1851-1929 *DcNAA*
Flinn, M W 1917- *ConAu 17R*

Flint, Abel 1765-1825 *DcAmA, DcNAA*
Flint, Albert Stovell 1853-1923 *DcNAA*
Flint, Annie Johnson 1866-1931 *ChPo,*
ChPo S2
Flint, Austin 1812-1886 *Alli, Alli Sup,*
DcAmA, DcNAA
Flint, Austin 1836-1915 *Alli Sup, AmA&B,*
DcAmA, DcNAA
Flint, Betty Margaret 1920- *Au&Wr,*
ConAu 23, WrD 1976
Flint, Catherine S *Alli Sup*
Flint, Charles Louis 1824-1889 *Alli, DcAmA,*
DcNAA
Flint, Charles Ranlett 1850-1934 *DcNAA*
Flint, Cort Ray 1915- *ConAu 49, WrD 1976*
Flint, David *OxCan Sup*
Flint, E DeP *ConAu XR*
Flint, Francis Stewart 1885-1960 *NewC*
Flint, Frank Stewart 1885-1960 *DcLEnL, EvLB,*
LongC, ModBL, Pen Eng, REn, TwCA,
TwCA Sup, WebEAL
Flint, Frederic *Alli Sup*
Flint, George *Alli*
Flint, Grover 1867-1909 *DcAmA, DcNAA*
Flint, Henry d1760 *Alli*
Flint, Henry Martyn 1829-1868 *Alli Sup,*
DcAmA, DcNAA
Flint, Jacob 1767-1835 *DcNAA*
Flint, James *Alli*
Flint, John Edgar 1930- *ConAu 37,*
WrD 1976
Flint, Joshua Barker 1801-1864 *BiDSA,*
DcAmA
Flint, Larry *WhWNAA*
Flint, Leon Nelson 1875-1955 *AmA&B,*
WhWNAA
Flint, Martha Bockee d1900 *DcAmA, DcNAA*
Flint, Micah P 1807-1830 *Alli, ChPo S1,*
DcAmA, DcNAA, OhA&B
Flint, Robert 1838-1910 *Alli Sup, BrAu 19,*
Chmbr 3, NewC
Flint, Roland *DrAP 1975*
Flint, Sarah A *Alli Sup*
Flint, Sargent *Alli Sup*
Flint, Stamford Raffles *Alli Sup*
Flint, Susan C *Alli Sup*
Flint, Timothy 1780-1840 *Alli, AmA,*
AmA&B, BbD, BiD&SB, BiDSA,
CnDAL, CyAL 1, DcAmA, DcEnL,
DcLEnL, DcNAA, OhA&B, OxAm,
REnAL
Flint, Wesley Pillsbury 1882-1943 *DcNAA,*
WhWNAA
Flint, William *Alli*
Flint, William Russell 1881-1970 *ChPo S2*
Flint, William Ruthven 1875-1933 *DcNAA*
Flintoff, Kit H *MnBBF*
Flintoff, Owen *Alli*
Flinzer, Fedor 1832- *ChPo, ChPo S1*
Flipper, Henry Ossian *Alli Sup*
Flippin, Percy Scott 1874- *AmA&B,*
WhWNAA
Flippin, William Searcy *Alli Sup*
Flippo, Edwin B 1925- *ConAu 33*
Flisch, Julia A *Alli Sup, BiDSA*
Fliskin, David *ChPo*
Flitner, David Perkins 1949- *ConAu 45,*
SmATA 7
Flloyd, Thomas *Alli*
Floan, Howard R 1918- *ConAu 17R*
Flockhart, J L *PoIre*
Flockhart, James *Alli Sup*
Flockhart, Robert *Alli Sup*
Flocos, Nicholas *DrAP 1975*
Flodoard 894?-966 *NewC, OxEng, Pen Eur*
Floethe, Louise Lee 1913- *AuBYP, ConAu 1R,*
SmATA 4
Floethe, Richard 1901- *ChPo S2, ConAu 33,*
IlCB 1945, IlCB 1956, IlCB 1966,
MorJA, SmATA 4
Floherty, John Joseph 1882-1964 *AmA&B,*
AuBYP, JBA 1951
Flom, George Tobias 1871-1960 *AmA&B*
Flom, George Tobias 1871- *AmLY,*
WhWNAA
Flood, Charles Bracelen 1929- *ConAu 41*
Flood, Charles Bracelen 1930- *AmA&B*
Flood, Daniel J 1904- *AmA&B*

Flood, E Thadeus 1932- *ConAu 49*
Flood, Evadna 1894- *IndAu 1917*
Flood, Henry 1732-1791 *Alli, PoIre*
Flood, John Charles Henry *Alli Sup*
Flood, Kenneth Urban 1925- *ConAu 9R*
Flood, Paul *MnBBF*
Flood, Robert *Alli*
Flood, Theodore L *Alli Sup*
Flood, Walter Edgar 1908- *Au&Wr*
Flood, Warden Hatton *Alli Sup*
Floquet, Pierre Amable 1797-1881 *BbD,*
BiD&SB
Flora Del Valle *PueRA*
Flora, Charles Jerry 1928- *IndAu 1917*
Flora, Fletcher 1914- *ConAu 1R*
Flora, James 1914- *ConAu 5R, IlBYP,*
IlCB 1956, IlCB 1966, SmATA 1,
ThBJA
Flora, Jane *ChPo*
Flora, Joseph Martin 1934- *ConAu 13R,*
WrD 1976
Flora, Paul 1922- *WhGrA*
Floredice, H W *Alli Sup*
Floren, Lee 1910- *Au&Wr, ConAu 5R,*
WhPNW, WrD 1976
Floren, Myron 1919- *AmSCAP 66*
Florence *IlBYP*
Florence 1811-1850 *AmA&B, AmA*
Florence Of Worcester d1118 *Alli, BiB N,*
BrAu, CasWL, Chmbr 1, DcEnL, EvLB,
NewC, OxEng, Pen Eng
Florence, Mary Sargent *ChPo*
Florence, Percy *AmA&B*
Florence, Ronald 1942- *ConAu 33, WrD 1976*
Florence, William Jermyn 1831-1891 *DcNAA,*
PoIre
Florenski, Pavel Alexandrovich 1882-1938?
DcRusL
Florentin, Eddy 1923- *ConAu 49*
Florer, Warren Washburn 1869- *AmLY*
Flores, Angel 1900- *AmA&B, DcSpL*
Flores, Anton 1818-1865 *CasWL*
Flores, Ignacio F 1934- *AmSCAP 66*
Flores, Ivan 1923- *ConAu 17R, WrD 1976*
Flores, Jean De *DcEnL*
Flores, Juan De *CasWL, DcEuL, DcSpL*
Florescu, Radu R 1925- *ConAu 41*
Florete *PueRA*
Florez, Enrique 1702-1773 *DcEuL, DcSpL*
Florez, Henrique 1701-1773 *BiD&SB*
Florez DeSetien Y Huidobro, Enrique 1702-1773
CasWL
Flori, C De *Alli Sup*
Florian, Alphonse De *Alli Sup*
Florian, Jean Pierre Claris De 1755-1794 *BbD,*
BiD&SB, CasWL, ChPo, ChPo S1,
DcEuL, EuA, EvEuW, OxFr, REn
Florian, John *Alli*
Florian, Jolly B *BiDLA*
Florian, Mario 1917- *DcCLA*
Florian, Miroslav 1931- *ModSL 2*
Florilegus *Alli*
Florin, Lambert William 1905- *ConAu 17R,*
WhPNW
Florin, Theo H 1908- *CasWL*
Florinsky, Michael T 1894- *AmA&B,*
ConAu 1R, WrD 1976
Florio *AmA&B, CyAL 2*
Florio, Giovanni 1553?-1625 *CrE&SL,*
Pen Eng
Florio, John 1553?-1625 *Alli, BiD&SB, BrAu,*
CasWL, ChPo S1, Chmbr 1, CrE&SL,
DcEnL, DcEuL, DcLEnL, EvLB, NewC,
OxEng, Pen Eng, REn
Floriot, Rene 1902-1975 *ConAu 61*
Floris, Pet Williamson *Alli*
Florismart *NewC*
Florit, Eugenio 1903- *DcCLA, Pen Am*
Florsheim, Cecil *ChPo*
Florus, Annaeus *Pen Cl*
Florus, Lucius Annaeus *CasWL*
Flory, Aaron M 1833-1893 *IndAu 1816*
Flory, Charles D 1902- *ConAu 41*
Flory, Jane Trescott 1917- *ConAu 9R*
Flory, John Samuel 1866- *AmLY, BiDSA*
Flory, Julia McCune 1882-1971 *ConAu 21,*
ConAu 29
Flos Regum Arthurus *NewC*

Flotow, Baron Friedrich Von 1812-1883 *AtlBL*
Floud, Jean Esther 1915- *Au&Wr*
Floud, Roderick 1942- *ConAu 45*
Flourens, Marie Jean Pierre 1794-1867 *BiD&SB*
Flournoy, Parke Poindexter 1839-1935 *DcNAA*
Flournoy, Theodore 1854-1920 *BiDPar*
Flower *Alli*
Flower, Benjamin *Alli, BiDLA*
Flower, Benjamin Orange 1858?-1918 *AmA&B,*
BbD, BiD&SB, DcAmA, DcNAA
Flower, Christopher *Alli*
Flower, Dean S 1938- *ConAu 21*
Flower, Desmond John Newman 1907- *Au&Wr,*
ChPo, ChPo S2, ConAu 9R
Flower, Edward Fordham 1805-1883 *Alli Sup*
Flower, Elliott 1863-1920 *AmA&B, AmLY,*
ChPo S1, DcAmA, DcNAA
Flower, Frank Abial 1854-1911 *Alli Sup,*
BiD&SB, DcAmA, DcNAA
Flower, George 1788-1862 *DcNAA, OhA&B*
Flower, Harry Alfred 1901- *Au&Wr,*
ConAu P-1
Flower, Henry *Alli*
Flower, Isabel *Alli Sup*
Flower, Jake *WrD 1976*
Flower, James Howard 1883- *AmA&B,*
ChPo S1
Flower, John *Alli*
Flower, John 1936- *ConAu 37*
Flower, John Matthew 1929- *WrD 1976*
Flower, John Wickham *Alli Sup*
Flower, Lamdrack *Alli Sup*
Flower, Margaret 1907- *Au&Wr, ConAu 61,*
WrD 1976
Flower, Sir Newman 1879-1964 *LongC*
Flower, Pat 1914- *WrD 1976*
Flower, Philip William *Alli Sup*
Flower, Richard *Alli, BiDLA*
Flower, Robert *PoIre*
Flower, Robert T *Alli*
Flower, Robin Ernest William 1881-1946 *ChPo,*
EvLB, LongC
Flower, Sarah Fuller *DcLEnL*
Flower, Stephen *Alli Sup*
Flower, Thomas *Alli*
Flower, Valley *ChPo S1*
Flower, Sir Walter Newman 1897- *MnBBF*
Flower, William *Alli*
Flower, William Balmbro *Alli, Alli Sup*
Flower, Sir William Henry 1831-1899 *Alli Sup,*
BrAu 19
Flower Of Poets, The *DcEnL*
Flower Of Strathearn, The *NewC*
Flowerdew, A *Alli, BiDLA*
Flowerdew, Alice 1759-1830 *ChPo S1, PoCh*
Flowerdew, D C *Alli, BiDLA*
Flowerdew, Henry *Alli Sup*
Flowerdew, Herbert *MnBBF*
Flowerdew, Phyllis *WrD 1976*
Flowers, Ann Moore 1923- *ConAu 9R*
Flowers, Charles 1942- *ConAu 29*
Flowers, George French 1811-1872 *Alli Sup*
Flowers, Montaville 1868-1934 *DcNAA,*
OhA&B
Flowre, John *Alli*
Floy, Eugenia *ChPo*
Floy, James 1806-1863 *Alli Sup, DcAmA,*
DcNAA
Floyd, Barry Neil 1925- *ConAu 33*
Floyd, Calvin James 1931- *AmSCAP 66*
Floyd, Carlisle 1926- *AmSCAP 66*
Floyd, Cornelia *Alli Sup*
Floyd, David Bittle 1846-1922 *DcNAA*
Floyd, Edward *Alli*
Floyd, Gareth *ChPo S1, IlBYP*
Floyd, Gilbert *MnBBF*
Floyd, Grace C *ChPo S1*
Floyd, John *Alli*
Floyd, M *Alli Sup*
Floyd, May Elliott *ChPo*
Floyd, N J *Alli Sup, BiDSA*
Floyd, Nicholas Jackson 1828- *DcNAA*
Floyd, Robert *Alli Sup*
Floyd, Robert Mitchell 1849- *DcAmA,*
DcNAA
Floyd, Ronald *BlkAW*
Floyd, Silas Xavier 1869- *BlkAW*
Floyd, Thomas *Alli*

Floyd, Troy S 1920- *ConAu 37*
Floyd, W E G 1939- *ConAu 33*
Floyd, William 1871-1943 *DcNAA,*
  WhWNAA
Floyd, William Anderson 1928- *ConAu 29*
Floyd-Jones *Alli Sup*
Floyd-Jones, DeLancey 1826-1902 *DcAmA,*
  DcNAA
Floyer, A M *Alli Sup*
Floyer, E L *Alli Sup*
Floyer, Edith S *Alli Sup*
Floyer, Ernest Ayscoghe *Alli Sup*
Floyer, Sir John 1649-1734 *Alli, DcEnL*
Floyer, Phil *Alli*
Fluck, Reginald Alan Paul 1928- *Au&Wr,*
  ConAu 9R
Fluckiger, Adolf 1917- *WhGrA*
Fluckiger, Friedrich A And Hanbury, D
  Alli Sup
Flud, Robert 1574-1637 *NewC*
Fludd, Robert 1574-1637 *Alli, BrAu, DcEnL,*
  NewC, OxEng
Fludyer, John *Alli*
Fluegel, Maurice 1833-1911 *DcNAA*
Flugel, Ewald 1863-1914 *DcNAA*
Flugel, Felix 1892- *WhWNAA*
Flugel, Johann Gottfried 1788-1855 *BbD,*
  BiD&SB
Fluharty, Irwin A 1903- *WhWNAA*
Flumiani, Carlo M 1911- *ConAu 13R*
Flumiani, Carlo Maria 1902- *WhWNAA*
Fluno, Robert Y 1916- *ConAu 33*
Flutter, J *Alli*
Flux, William *Alli Sup*
Fly *Alli*
Fly, Elijah M *Alli Sup*
Fly, Henry *Alli, BiDLA Sup*
Flygare-Carlen, Emilie 1807-1892 *BiD&SB,*
  EuA
Flygt, Sten G 1911- *ConAu 9R*
Flying Bishop, The *OxCan*
Flynn, Allan 1894-1965 *AmSCAP 66*
Flynn, Barbara 1928- *SmATA 9*
Flynn, Charles F 1949- *ConAu 57*
Flynn, Clarence Edwin 1886- *ChPo S2,*
  IndAu 1917, WhWNAA
Flynn, Daniel *Alli Sup*
Flynn, Donald R 1928- *ConAu 29*
Flynn, Edward F 1913- *AmSCAP 66*
Flynn, Errol 1909-1959 *AmA&B*
Flynn, Frank 1900-1964 *AmSCAP 66*
Flynn, Frank 1906- *WrD 1976*
Flynn, George M *BlkAW*
Flynn, George Q 1937- *ConAu 25*
Flynn, Gerard 1924- *ConAu 41*
Flynn, Hamilton *MnBBF*
Flynn, J A *PoIre*
Flynn, Jackson *WrD 1976*
Flynn, James Joseph 1911- *ConAu 23*
Flynn, James Robert 1934- *ConAu 21,*
  WrD 1976
Flynn, John Joseph 1936- *ConAu 17R*
Flynn, John Thomas 1882-1964 *AmA&B,*
  TwCA, TwCA Sup
Flynn, Joseph Michael 1848-1910 *DcNAA*
Flynn, Leslie Bruce 1918- *ConAu 1R,*
  WrD 1976
Flynn, Mary Margaret 1915- *Au&Wr*
Flynn, Sister Maureen 1900- *BkC 6*
Flynn, P J *Alli Sup*
Flynn, Paul P 1942- *ConAu 37*
Flynn, Robert L 1932- *ConAu 29, DrAF 1976*
Flynn, Theodore Thomson 1883- *WhLA*
Flynt, Josiah 1869-1907 *DcAmA, DcNAA,*
  EncM&D, OxAm, REnAL, TwCA,
  TwCA Sup
Flynt, Larry *AuNews 2*
Flynt, Wayne 1940- *ConAu 37*
Fo, Dario 1926- *CrCD*
Foakes, Grace 1910- *WrD 1976*
Foakes, John Weston *Alli Sup*
Foakes-Jackson, Frederick John 1885-1941
  AmA&B
Foard, J F *Alli Sup*
Foard, James Thomas 1831- *Alli Sup*
Foat Tugay, Emine 1897- *ConAu P-1*
Fobes, Perez d1812 *Alli*
Fobes, Walter K *Alli Sup*

Foch, Ferdinand 1851-1929 *OxFr, REn*
Focht, Mildred *ChPo*
Focillon, Henri 1881-1943 *OxFr*
Fock, Gorch 1880-1916 *CasWL, OxGer*
Focke, Ernest Paul Walter 1896- *Au&Wr*
Focquenbroch, Willem Godschalk Van 1635-1675
  CasWL
Foda, Ann *WrD 1976*
Foda, Aun *ConAu XR*
Fodeba, Keita 1921- *AfA 1, Pen Cl*
Foden, James *Alli Sup*
Fodio, Usuman Dan *CasWL*
Fodor, Eugene 1905- *AmA&B, ConAu 21*
Fodor, Ladislaus 1898- *CnMD*
Fodor, Nandor 1895- *BiDPar*
Fody, Ilona 1920- *AmSCAP 66*
Foelber, Paul Frederick 1926- *IndAu 1917*
Foerster, Norman 1887- *AmA&B, ChPo,*
  CnDAL, ConAmA, ConAu 5R, DcLEnL,
  OxAm, Pen Am, REnAL, TwCA,
  TwCA Sup, WhWNAA
Foerster, Robert Franz 1883-1941 *DcNAA,*
  WhWNAA
Foeth, A A *DcRusL*
Fofanov, Konstantin Mikhailovich 1862-1911
  CasWL, ClDMEuL, DcRusL
Foff, Arthur R 1925- *ConAu 33*
Fogarty, J Paul 1893- *AmSCAP 66*
Fogarty, Jonathan Titulescu *ConAu XR,*
  WrD 1976
Fogarty, Michael Patrick 1916- *ConAu 21,*
  WrD 1976
Fogarty, Thomas 1873- *ChPo*
Fogarty, William Michael 1873-1936
  IndAu 1917
Fogazzaro, Antonio 1842-1911 *BbD, BiD&SB,*
  CasWL, ClDMEuL, CyWA, DcBiA,
  EuA, EvEuW, LongC, McGWD, ModRL,
  OxEng, Pen Eur, REn, TwCA,
  TwCA Sup
Fogdall, Sorenus P 1879- *WhWNAA*
Fogel, Aaron *DrAP 1975*
Fogel, David 1891-1944 *CasWL*
Fogel, Edwin Miller 1874-1949 *AmA&B*
Fogel, Ruby *ConAu 17R*
Fogelqvist, Torsten 1880-1941 *ClDMEuL*
Fogerty, Elsie 1865-1945 *LongC*
Fogerty, J *Alli Sup*
Fogg, A *Alli, BiDLA*
Fogg, Ellen M *Alli Sup*
Fogg, Ezekias *Alli*
Fogg, Fagin *OhA&B*
Fogg, George Gilman 1813- *Alli Sup*
Fogg, Gordon Elliott 1919- *Au&Wr,*
  WrD 1976
Fogg, Henry George Witham *Au&Wr*
Fogg, L M *ChPo S1*
Fogg, Laurence *Alli*
Fogg, Lawrence Daniel 1879-1914 *DcNAA*
Fogg, P M 1881- *WhWNAA*
Fogg, Peter W *Alli, BiDLA*
Fogg, William Perry 1826-1909 *Alli Sup,*
  OhA&B
Foggo, Algernon *Alli Sup*
Foggo, George 1793-1869 *Alli Sup*
Fogie, Francis, Sr. *DcNAA*
Foglar, Ludwig 1819-1889 *BiD&SB*
Fogle, French R 1912- *ConAu 37*
Fogle, Richard Harter 1911- *ConAu 5R,*
  OhA&B
Foglio, Frank 1921- *ConAu 57*
Fogo, A *BiDLA Sup*
Foik, Paul Joseph 1880-1941 *CatA 1947,*
  DcNAA, TexWr, WhWNAA
Foisel, John 1894- *OhA&B*
Foix, J V 1894- *CasWL, Pen Eur*
Fokke Simonsz, Arend 1755-1812 *BiD&SB,*
  CasWL
Fokkema, D W 1931- *ConAu 17R*
Folani, Femi *BlkAW*
Folcard *Alli*
Folch-Ribas, Jacques *OxCan Sup*
Folchard *Alli, BiB S*
Folco Of Marseilles *CasWL*
Foldes, Eugene 1891- *WhWNAA*
Foldes, Jolan 1903- *EvEuW, REn, TwCA,*
  TwCA Sup
Folejewski, Zbigniew 1910- *ConAu 17R*

Folengo, Giralomo 1491?-1544 *DcEuL, REn*
Folengo, Teofilo 1491?-1554 *BbD, BiD&SB,*
  CasWL, NewC, OxFr, Pen Eur, REn
Folengo, Teophilo 1491?-1554 *OxEng*
Foley, Allen Richard 1898- *ConAu 45*
Foley, Bernice Williams 1902- *ConAu 29*
Foley, Betty Smith *ChPo, ChPo S1*
Foley, Cedric John 1917- *Au&Wr*
Foley, Charles 1908- *Au&Wr, ConAu P-1*
Foley, Daniel 1815-1874 *Alli Sup*
Foley, Daniel Joseph 1913- *AuBYP,*
  ConAu 5R
Foley, Doug 1942- *ConAu 57*
Foley, E D *Alli Sup*
Foley, George Cadwalader 1851-1935 *DcNAA,*
  WhWNAA
Foley, H J *Alli Sup*
Foley, Helen *ConAu XR*
Foley, Helen 1896-1937 *ChPo, ChPo S1*
Foley, Henry *Alli Sup*
Foley, James *Alli*
Foley, James William 1874-1939 *ChPo,*
  ChPo S1, ChPo S2, DcNAA, WhWNAA
Foley, John 1917-1974 *ConAu 9R, ConAu 53*
Foley, John Henry 1818-1874 *PoIre*
Foley, John L *ChPo S1*
Foley, John Porter 1910- *IndAu 1917*
Foley, Louis 1892- *OhA&B*
Foley, Louise Munro 1933- *ConAu 37,*
  WrD 1976
Foley, Martha *AmA&B, REnAL*
Foley, Michael Hamilton 1819?- *BbtC*
Foley, Pearl *CanNov*
Foley, Patrick Kevin 1856-1937 *AmA&B,*
  DcNAA
Foley, Richard *Alli, BiDLA*
Foley, Robert *Alli*
Foley, Samuel *Alli*
Foley, Syd 1909- *AmSCAP 66*
Foley, Vincent D 1933- *ConAu 57*
Foley, Virginia J 1906- *AnMV 1926*
Foley, William E 1938- *ConAu 33*
Folger, Henry Clay 1857-1930 *DcNAA,*
  REnAL
Folger, John H *Alli Sup*
Folger, Peleg 1734-1789 *Alli, CyAL 1*
Folger, Peter 1617-1690? *Alli, AmA, AmA&B,*
  CyAL 1, DcAmA, DcNAA, OxAm,
  REnAL
Folger, Robert B *Alli Sup*
Folger, William C *Alli Sup*
Folgore, DaSan Gimignano 1270?-1330?
  CasWL, ChPo S1
Foli, R, Madame *Alli Sup*
Foligno, Cesare 1878- *WhLA*
Folin, Otto Knut Olof 1867-1934 *DcNAA*
Foliot, Gilbert d1188 *Alli*
Foliot, Robert d1186 *Alli*
Folk, Edgar Estes 1856-1917 *DcAmA, DcNAA*
Folkard, Charles James 1878-1963 *ChPo,*
  ChPo S1, ConICB, IlCB 1945, WhCL
Folkard, Charles Watson *Alli Sup*
Folkard, Henry Coleman 1827- *Alli Sup*
Folkard, Richard, Jr. *Alli Sup*
Folkard, W A *ChPo*
Folkers, George Fulton 1929- *ConAu 49*
Folkerts, George W 1938- *ConAu 53*
Folkerts, Hayo 1871- *WhLA*
Folkertsma, Eeltsje Boates 1893-1968 *CasWL*
Folkes, Martin 1690-1754 *Alli*
Folkingham, W *Alli*
Folkman, Jerome Daniel 1907- *ConAu 29,*
  WrD 1976
Folkmar, Daniel 1861-1932 *AmLY, DcAmA,*
  DcNAA
Folks, Homer 1867-1963 *AmA&B, WhWNAA*
Folland, H F 1906- *ConAu 49*
Follen, Adolf 1794-1855 *OxGer*
Follen, August 1794-1855 *BiD&SB, OxGer*
Follen, Mrs. Charles d1860 *CyAL 1*
Follen, Charles Theodore Christian 1796-1840
  Alli, AmA&B, CyAL 1, DcAmA,
  DcNAA, OxAm
Follen, Eliza Lee 1787-1860 *Alli, AmA,*
  AmA&B, BiD&SB, ChPo, ChPo S1,
  ChPo S2, DcAmA, DcNAA, FemPA,
  St&VC
Follen, Karl 1796-1840 *OxGer*

Follet, Margaret Whipple 1907- *OhA&B*
Follett, Barbara Newhall 1914-1939 *ChPo S1*
Follett, Eliza G Ward 1801-1876 *OhA&B*
Follett, Helen d1970 *AmA&B, AuBYP*
Follett, Mary Parker 1868-1933 *DcAmA, DcNAA*
Follett, Oran 1798-1894 *Alli Sup, OhA&B*
Follett, Robert J R 1928- *ConAu 21*
Follett, W W *Alli Sup*
Follett, Wilson 1887-1963 *AmA&B*
Folley, Terence T 1931- *ConAu 21*
Folley, Vern L 1936- *ConAu 49*
Folliard, Hugo *WhWNAA*
Follingham, W *Alli*
Folliot *Alli*
Folliott, Thomas *Alli Sup*
Follisius, Jacob *Alli*
Follmann, J F, Jr. 1908- *ConAu 17R*
Folly, Dennis Wilson 1954- *BlkAW*
Folmer, Henry Daniel 1852-1930 *OhA&B*
Folmsbee, Beulah *ChPo, ChPo S1*
Folmsbee, Stanley J 1899- *ConAu 29*
Folquet De Marseille 1160?-1231 *CasWL, EuA, Pen Eur*
Folsom, Benjamin 1790-1833 *DcNAA*
Folsom, Charles *Alli*
Folsom, Charles 1794-1872 *AmA&B*
Folsom, Charles Follen 1842-1907 *Alli Sup, DcAmA, DcNAA*
Folsom, E G *Alli Sup*
Folsom, Elizabeth Irons 1876- *WhWNAA*
Folsom, Florence *ChPo S1*
Folsom, Franklin 1907- *AuBYP, ConAu 1R, SmATA 5, WrD 1976*
Folsom, George 1802-1869 *Alli, AmA&B, DcAmA, DcNAA*
Folsom, Jack *ConAu XR*
Folsom, James Madison 1838- *BiDSA, DcNAA*
Folsom, John B 1931- *ConAu 45*
Folsom, John Dana 1842-1912 *DcNAA*
Folsom, Joseph P *BiDSA*
Folsom, Justus Watson 1871-1936 *DcNAA, WhWNAA*
Folsom, Kenneth E 1921- *ConAu 21*
Folsom, Marion Bayard 1893- *ConAu 17*
Folsom, Marvin Hugh 1929- *ConAu 57*
Folsom, Mary E *ChPo*
Folsom, Michael Brewster 1938- *AuBYP*
Folsom, Montgomery Morgan 1857-1898 *BiDSA, DcNAA*
Folsom, Nathaniel Smith 1806-1890 *Alli, DcNAA*
Folsom, William Henry Carman 1817-1900 *DcNAA*
Folta, Jeannette R 1934- *ConAu 25*
Foltin, Lore Barbara 1913- *ConAu 25*
Foltz, Charles Steinman 1859-1941 *AmA&B, DcNAA*
Foltz, Jonathan Messersmith 1810-1877 *DcNAA*
Foltz, William J 1936- *ConAu 9R*
Folupa, Frank *WhWNAA*
Folwell, Arthur Hamilton 1877-1962 *AmA&B*
Folwell, Arthur M *ChPo*
Folwell, William Watts 1833-1929 *AmA&B, AmLY, DcAmA, DcNAA, OhA&B, WhWNAA*
Folz, Hans 1450?-1515? *BbD, BiD&SB, CasWL, Pen Eur, OxGer*
Fombona *DcSpL*
Fomeen, Basil 1902- *AmSCAP 66*
Fomina, Iraida 1906- *WhGrA*
Fomon, Samuel J 1923- *ConAu 53*
Fon Eisen, Anthony T 1917- *ConAu 13R*
Fonarow, Jerry 1935- *ConAu 53*
Fonblanque *Alli Sup*
Fonblanque, Albany William 1793?-1872 *Alli, BrAu 19, Chmbr 3, DcEnA, DcEnL, EvLB, NewC*
Fonblanque, J S M *Alli*
Fonblanque, J W M *Alli*
Fonblanque, John DeGrenier 1759-1837 *Alli, BiDLA*
Fonck, Leopold 1865-1930 *CatA 1952*
Fond, John *Alli*
Fone, Byrne R S *ChPo S1*
Foner, Eric 1943- *ConAu 29, WrD 1976*
Foner, Nancy 1945- *ConAu 53*

Foner, Philip Sheldon 1910- *AmA&B, ConAu 9R*
Fonfrias, Ernesto Juan 1909- *PueRA*
Fonnereau, Thomas George *Alli Sup*
Fonseca, Aguinaldo Brito 1922- *AfA 1, Pen Cl*
Fonseca, Aloysius Joseph 1915- *ConAu 13R, WrD 1976*
Fonseca, Antonio Jose Branquinho Da 1905- *EncWL*
Fonseca, Cristobal De 1550?-1621 *CasWL, EvEuW*
Fonseca, John DosReis 1925- *ConAu 17R, WrD 1976*
Fonseca, Mario Alberto 1939- *AfA 1*
Font, Pedro d1781 *OxAm*
Fontainas, Andre 1865-1948 *CasWL, EvEuW, OxFr*
Fontaine, Andre 1921- *ConAu 25*
Fontaine, Arthur Benjamin 1876-1940 *DcNAA*
Fontaine, Charles 1513?-1587? *DcEuL, EuA, OxFr*
Fontaine, Edward *Alli Sup*
Fontaine, Edward 1814-1884 *DcNAA*
Fontaine, Francis *Alli Sup, DcAmA*
Fontaine, Francis 1844-1901 *BiDSA, DcNAA*
Fontaine, Jules *OxCan*
Fontaine, Lamar 1829- *BiDSA, ChPo, ChPo S1, DcNAA*
Fontaine, M B *ChPo*
Fontaine, Nicolas 1625-1709 *OxFr*
Fontaine, Robert *OxCan, REnAL*
Fontaine, William Morris 1835-1913 *Alli Sup, DcNAA*
Fontaines, Marie Louis Charlotte De d1730 *DcEuL, OxFr*
Fontan, Louis Marie 1801-1839 *BbD, BiD&SB*
Fontana, Bernard L 1931- *ConAu 17R*
Fontana, Ferdinand 1850- *BiD&SB*
Fontana, Gian 1897-1935 *CasWL*
Fontana, Vincent James 1923- *ConAu 13R*
Fontane, Theodor 1819-1898 *BiD&SB, CasWL, ChPo S2, ClDMEuL, CyWA, EuA, EvEuW, OxGer, Pen Eur, REn*
Fontane, Tony *AmSCAP 66*
Fontanella, Girolamo 1612?-1644? *Pen Eur*
Fontanes, Marquis Louis De 1757-1821 *BbD, BiD&SB, CasWL, DcEuL, OxFr, Pen Eur*
Fontaney, Antoine-Etienne 1803-1837 *OxFr*
Fontanges, Marie-Angelique, Duchesse De 1661-1681 *OxFr*
Fontanne, Lynne 1887?- *OxAm, REn*
Fonte, Bartholomew De *OxCan*
Fontenay, Charles Louis 1917- *ConAu 25, WrD 1976*
Fontenay, Guillaume De 1861-1914 *BiDPar*
Fontenay-Mareuil, F DuVal, Marquis De 1594?-1665 *OxFr*
Fontenelle, Bernard LeBovier De 1657-1757 *AtlBL, BbD, BiD&SB, CasWL, DcEuL, EuA, EvEuW, OxFr, Pen Eur, REn*
Fontenot, Mary Alice 1901- *WrD 1976*
Fontenot, Mary Alice 1910- *ConAu 37*
Fontenrose, Joseph 1903- *ConAu 5R, WrD 1976*
Fontes, Amando 1899-1967 *CasWL*
Fontes-Pereira, Jose De *AfA 1*
Fonvielle, Wilfried De 1828- *BiD&SB*
Fonvizin, Denis Ivanovich 1745-1792 *BiD&SB, CasWL, CnThe, DcRusL, EuA, McGWD, Pen Eur, REn, REnWD*
Foord, Anthony *Alli*
Foord, Archibald Smith 1914-1969 *ConAu P-1*
Foord, Edward *Alli*
Foord, Emanuel *DcEnL*
Foord, John *Alli*
Foord, John 1842-1922 *DcNAA*
Foord, Joseph *Alli*
Foot, Alicia Julia *Alli Sup*
Foot, Arthur Wynne *Alli Sup*
Foot, Charles H *Alli Sup*
Foot, Edward Edwin 1828- *Alli Sup, ChPo S2*
Foot, Hugh Mackintosh 1907- *Au&Wr, ConAu 9R*
Foot, James *Alli*
Foot, James Abraham *Alli Sup*
Foot, Jesse 1744?-1827 *Alli, BiDLA*

Foot, John *Alli*
Foot, John Vickars *Alli Sup*
Foot, Joseph Ives 1796-1840 *DcNAA*
Foot, Michael Mackintosh 1913- *Au&Wr, WrD 1976*
Foot, Michael Richard Daniell 1919- *Au&Wr, ConAu 5R, WrD 1976*
Foot, Paul Mackintosh 1937- *ConAu 17R*
Foot, Peter *Alli*
Foot, Rose *Alli Sup*
Foot, Samuel Alfred 1790-1878 *Alli Sup, DcNAA*
Foot, William *Alli*
Foote *BiDLA*
Foote, Agnes Cope *ChPo*
Foote, Albert E 1846-1895 *DcNAA*
Foote, Albertus B *ChPo*
Foote, Alexander L R *Alli Sup*
Foote, Alice G *ChPo*
Foote, Allen Ripley 1842-1921 *DcNAA, OhA&B*
Foote, Andrew Hull 1806-1863 *Alli, DcAmA, DcNAA*
Foote, Arthur William 1853-1937 *DcNAA, OxAm*
Foote, Darby Mozelle 1942- *ConAu 61*
Foote, Dorothy Norris 1908- *ConAu 21*
Foote, E J *Alli, BiDLA Sup*
Foote, E K *ChPo*
Foote, Edward Bliss 1829-1906 *Alli Sup, DcNAA, OhA&B*
Foote, Edward Bond 1854-1912 *Alli Sup, DcNAA, OhA&B*
Foote, Elizabeth Louisa 1866- *WhWNAA*
Foote, Francis Seeley 1883- *WhWNAA*
Foote, Gaston 1902- *OhA&B*
Foote, Gaston 1903- *AmA&B*
Foote, Mrs. Henry Grant *Alli Sup*
Foote, Henry Stuart 1800-1880 *Alli, Alli Sup, AmA&B, BiD&SB, BiDSA, DcAmA, DcNAA*
Foote, Henry Wilder 1838-1889 *Alli Sup, DcAmA, DcNAA*
Foote, Henry Wilder 1875-1964 *AmA&B, WhWNAA*
Foote, Horton 1916- *AmA&B, ConDr, WorAu*
Foote, James *Alli, Alli Sup*
Foote, James Stephen 1851-1925 *DcNAA*
Foote, John *Alli Sup*
Foote, John A *ChPo S1*
Foote, John Alderson 1849- *Alli Sup*
Foote, John Ambrose 1874-1931 *DcNAA*
Foote, John Parsons 1783-1865 *Alli Sup, DcNAA, OhA&B*
Foote, John Taintor 1881-1950 *AmA&B, OhA&B, REnAL*
Foote, Julia A J 1823- *OhA&B*
Foote, Lucius Harwood 1826-1913 *Alli Sup, AmA&B, DcAmA, DcNAA, OhA&B*
Foote, Marion F *TexWr*
Foote, Mary Hallock 1847-1938 *Alli Sup, AmA&B, BbD, BiD&SB, ChPo, ChPo S1, DcAmA, DcNAA, EarAB, EarAB Sup, OxAm, REnAL, WhWNAA*
Foote, Mary Selina 1887-1924 *DcNAA*
Foote, Robert Rowden 1901- *Au&Wr*
Foote, S A M *Alli Sup*
Foote, Samuel 1720?-1777 *Alli, AnCL, BiD&SB, BrAu, CasWL, ChPo, Chmbr 2, DcEnA, DcEnL, EvLB, McGWD, MouLC 2, NewC, OxEng, Pen Eng, REn, WebEAL*
Foote, Samuel, Jr. *Alli*
Foote, Shelby 1916- *AmA&B, ConAu 5R, ConNov 1972, ConNov 1976, DrAF 1976, REnAL, TwCA Sup, WrD 1976*
Foote, Wilder 1905-1975 *ConAu 57*
Foote, William C *Alli Sup*
Foote, William Henry 1794-1869 *Alli, Alli Sup, BiDSA, DcAmA, DcNAA*
Footman, David John 1895- *Au&Wr*
Footman, Henry 1831- *Alli Sup*
Footner, Hulbert 1879-1944 *AmA&B, AmLY, DcNAA, EncM&D, OxCan, WhWNAA*
Foott, Mary Hannay 1846-1918 *Alli Sup, ChPo*
Forain, Jean-Louis 1852-1931 *OxFr*

Foraker, Joseph Benson 1846-1917 *DcNAA,
OhA&B*
Foraker, Julia Bundy *OhA&B*
Foran, Donald J 1943- *ConAu 33*
Foran, Joseph Kearney 1857-1931 *Alli Sup,
BbD, BiD&SB, DcNAA, PoIre*
Foran, Martin Ambrose 1844-1921 *Alli Sup,
OhA&B*
Foran, Mary Frances 1931- *Au&Wr*
Forberg, Ati 1925- *AuBYP, ChPo, ChPo S1,
ChPo S2, IlCB 1966*
Forbes *Alli*
Forbes, Mrs. *PoIre*
Forbes, A K H *Alli Sup*
Forbes, Mrs. A S C *AmA&B*
Forbes, Aleck *DcNAA*
Forbes, Alexander *Alli, Alli Sup, ChPo,
OxCan*
Forbes, Alexander d1749 *Alli*
Forbes, Alexander 1678-1762 *DcEnL*
Forbes, Alexander Gruar *Alli Sup*
Forbes, Alexander Kinloch *Alli Sup*
Forbes, Alexander Penrose 1817-1875 *Alli,
Alli Sup, DcEnL*
Forbes, Allan 1874- *Br&AmS*
Forbes, Anita P *AmA&B, ChPo S1*
Forbes, Anna *Alli Sup*
Forbes, Archibald 1838-1900 *Alli Sup, BbD,
BiD&SB, BrAu 19, Chmbr 3, DcEnL*
Forbes, Arthur *Alli*
Forbes, Athol *MnBBF*
Forbes, Avary William Holmes- 1853- *Alli Sup*
Forbes, Bryan 1926- *ConDr, WrD 1976*
Forbes, C J F Smith d1880 *Alli Sup*
Forbes, Calvin 1945- *BlkAW, ConAu 49,
DrAP 1975*
Forbes, Charles Henry 1866-1933 *DcNAA,
WhWNAA*
Forbes, Sir Charles Stewart d1884 *Alli Sup*
Forbes, Colin 1923- *Au&Wr*
Forbes, Cornelia *ChPo*
Forbes, Daniel *Alli, WrD 1976*
Forbes, David *Alli*
Forbes, David 1828-1876 *BiD&SB*
Forbes, DeLoris Stanton 1923- *ConAu 9R*
Forbes, Duncan 1685-1747 *Alli*
Forbes, Duncan 1798-1868 *Alli, Alli Sup*
Forbes, Mrs. E A *Alli Sup*
Forbes, E Howard *MnBBF*
Forbes, E M *ChPo*
Forbes, Edgar Allen 1872- *AmA&B, AmLY*
Forbes, Edward *Chmbr 3*
Forbes, Edward 1815-1854 *Alli, BiD&SB,
BrAu 19*
Forbes, Edward Archibald 1869- *WhLA*
Forbes, Edwin 1839-1895 *Alli Sup, AmA&B,
DcNAA, EarAB, EarAB Sup*
Forbes, Eli 1726-1804 *Alli, DcNAA*
Forbes, Elisha *EarAB Sup*
Forbes, Ella C *ChPo*
Forbes, Elliot 1917- *ConAu 9R*
Forbes, Esther 1894?-1967 *AmA&B, AmNov,
AnCL, AuBYP, ChPo S2, ConAu 25,
ConAu P-1, CyWA, DcLEnL, MorJA,
Newb 1922, OxAm, REn, REnAL,
SmATA 2, TwCA, TwCA Sup*
Forbes, Ethel M Villiers *Alli Sup*
Forbes, Evelyn Michell *Alli Sup*
Forbes, F E *Alli*
Forbes, Francis *Alli*
Forbes, G F *Alli Sup*
Forbes, G H *Alli*
Forbes, George *Alli Sup*
Forbes, Sir George A H, Earl Of Granard 1833-
Alli Sup
Forbes, George Hay *Alli Sup*
Forbes, Gordon S *Alli Sup*
Forbes, Graham B *ConAu 19, SmATA 1*
Forbes, Grant *MnBBF*
Forbes, Granville Hamilton *Alli Sup*
Forbes, Guillaume 1865- *WhWNAA*
Forbes, H *Alli Sup*
Forbes, H Campbell *MnBBF*
Forbes, H Wilson *MnBBF*
Forbes, Harriette Merrifield 1856-1915
AmA&B, DcAmA
Forbes, Henry Ogg 1851- *Alli Sup, BbD,
BiD&SB, WhLA*

Forbes, Henry Prentiss 1849-1913 *DcNAA*
Forbes, Henry W 1918- *ConAu 1R*
Forbes, Baron Horace Courtenay *Alli Sup*
Forbes, Isabella *Alli Sup*
Forbes, J G *Alli*
Forbes, J V G 1916- *ConAu 9R*
Forbes, Jack D 1934- *ConAu 1R*
Forbes, James 1749-1819 *Alli, BiD&SB,
BiDLA*
Forbes, James 1871-1938 *AmA&B, DcNAA,
ModWD, OxAm*
Forbes, James David 1809-1868 *Alli, Alli Sup,
BiD&SB, BrAu 19, Chmbr 3, DcEnL,
EvLB*
Forbes, James Grant *Alli*
Forbes, Joan Rosita 1893- *EvLB*
Forbes, Joanne R 1930- *ConAu 37*
Forbes, John *Alli, CyAL 1*
Forbes, John 1570?-1634 *Alli*
Forbes, John 1593-1648 *Alli, DcEnL*
Forbes, Sir John 1787-1801 *Alli, DcEnL*
Forbes, John 1802- *Alli Sup*
Forbes, John Douglas 1910- *ConAu 53*
Forbes, John H, And John Jardine *Alli*
Forbes, John Murray 1813-1898 *DcNAA*
Forbes, John Thomas 1857- *WhLA*
Forbes, Katherine d1956 *AuBYP*
Forbes, Kathryn 1909-1966 *AmA&B, AmNov,
ConAu XR, REn, REnAL, SmATA XR*
Forbes, Leslie *Alli*
Forbes, Litton *Alli Sup*
Forbes, Lou 1902- *AmSCAP 66*
Forbes, Margaret *ChPo S1*
Forbes, Murray *Alli, BiDLA*
Forbes, Patrick *Alli*
Forbes, Patrick 1564-1635 *Alli, DcEnL*
Forbes, Patrick 1925- *ConAu 25*
Forbes, Robert *Alli, Alli Sup*
Forbes, Robert Bennet 1804-1889 *Alli Sup,
AmA&B, DcAmA, DcNAA*
Forbes, Rosita 1893-1967 *LongC, NewC,
TwCA, TwCA Sup, WhLA*
Forbes, S Russell *Alli Sup*
Forbes, Stanton 1923- *ConAu XR, EncM&D,
WrD 1976*
Forbes, Stephen Alfred 1844-1930 *Alli Sup,
DcAmA, DcNAA*
Forbes, Thomas Rogers 1911- *ConAu 41*
Forbes, Urquhart Atwell 1850- *Alli Sup*
Forbes, W B d1928 *Br&AmS*
Forbes, W Cameron 1870- *WhWNAA*
Forbes, William *Alli, Alli Sup, ChPo S1*
Forbes, William 1585-1634 *Alli, DcEnL*
Forbes, Sir William 1739-1806 *Alli*
Forbes, William Alexander 1855-1883 *Alli Sup*
Forbes, William G 1838-1884 *Alli Sup*
Forbes, William Hathaway 1840-1897 *ChPo*
Forbes-Boyd, Eric 1897- *ConAu 13R,
WrD 1976*
Forbes-Leith *Alli Sup*
Forbes-Leslie *Alli Sup*
Forbes-Robertson *Alli Sup*
Forbes-Robertson, Diana *NewC*
Forbes-Robertson, Sir Johnston 1853-1937
ChPo S2, LongC
Forbin, Claude, Comte De 1656-1733 *OxFr*
Forbis, William H 1918- *ConAu 37*
Forbus, Ina B *ConAu 1R, WrD 1976*
Forbush, Bliss 1896- *AmA&B*
Forbush, Edward Howe 1858-1929 *AmA&B,
DcNAA*
Forbush, William Byron 1868- *AmLY,
WhWNAA*
Forby, Robert *Alli, BiDLA Sup*
Force, Manning Ferguson 1824-1899 *Alli Sup,
AmA&B, BiD&SB, DcAmA, DcNAA,
OhA&B*
Force, Peter 1790-1868 *Alli, AmA, AmA&B,
BiD&SB, CyAL 2, DcAmA, DcNAA,
OxAm, REnAL*
Force, Roland W 1924- *ConAu 41*
Force, William M 1916- *ConAu 21*
Force, William Quereau 1820-1880 *DcAmA,
DcNAA*
Forcellini, Egidio 1688-1768 *BiD&SB, NewC,
OxEng*
Forcett, Charles Michell *BiDLA*
Forcey, Charles B 1925- *ConAu 1R*

Forchhammer, Peter Wilhelm 1801-1894
BiD&SB
Forchheimer, F *Alli Sup*
Forchheimer, Paul 1913- *ConAu 53*
Forcione, Alban Keith 1938- *ConAu 33,
WrD 1976*
Ford, Miss *Alli*
Ford, Agnes Gibbs 1902- *ConAu 21*
Ford, Alan Wayne 1926- *Au&Wr*
Ford, Albert Lee *ConAu XR*
Ford, Alec George 1926- *ConAu 5R,
WrD 1976*
Ford, Alfred E *Alli Sup*
Ford, Alice 1906- *ConAu P-1*
Ford, Amasa B 1922- *ConAu 21*
Ford, Anne Elizabeth 1875- *WhWNAA*
Ford, Anthony *Alli, MnBBF*
Ford, Arthur L 1937- *ConAu 57*
Ford, Arthur P *BiDSA*
Ford, Barry *MnBBF*
Ford, Boris 1917- *Au&Wr, WrD 1976*
Ford, Brian J 1939- *ConAu 41, WrD 1976*
Ford, Brinsley 1908- *Au&Wr*
Ford, Carl 1920- *AmSCAP 66*
Ford, Charles *Alli Sup*
Ford, Charles Henri 1908- *TexWr*
Ford, Charles Henri 1913- *AmA&B,
ConAu 25, ConP 1975*
Ford, Charles Henri 1919- *WrD 1976*
Ford, Charles Lawrence 1830- *Alli Sup,
ChPo S1*
Ford, Clara Anne 1893- *OhA&B*
Ford, Clellan Stearns 1909- *AmA&B*
Ford, Collier *ConAu XR*
Ford, Collin 1889-1924 *OhA&B*
Ford, Corey 1902-1969 *AmA&B, ConAu 25,
EncM&D, REnAL, WhWNAA*
Ford, Corydon La 1813-1894 *Alli Sup,
DcAmA, DcNAA*
Ford, Daniel 1931- *ConAu 17R, WrD 1976*
Ford, Daniel Sharp 1822-1899 *AmA&B*
Ford, David *Alli, ConAu 57*
Ford, David Barnes 1820-1903 *Alli Sup,
DcNAA*
Ford, David Everard *Alli, PoCh*
Ford, Donald Frank Williams 1924- *Au&Wr,
ConAu 5R*
Ford, Donald H 1926- *ConAu 41*
Ford, Douglas M *Alli Sup*
Ford, Douglas William Cleverley 1914- *Au&Wr,
ConAu 61, WrD 1976*
Ford, E *Alli Sup*
Ford, Edmund Bisco *Au&Wr*
Ford, Edsel 1928-1970 *AmA&B, ChPo S1,
ConAu 29, ConAu P-1*
Ford, Edward *Alli*
Ford, Sir Edward *Alli*
Ford, Edward 1813- *Alli Sup*
Ford, Elbur *ConAu XR, EncM&D,
SmATA 2, WrD 1976*
Ford, Elisabeth 1895?-1944 *DcNAA*
Ford, Elmer Ellsworth *ChPo S2*
Ford, Elsie *WhWNAA*
Ford, Emily C *ChPo*
Ford, Emily Ellsworth 1825?-1893 *Alli Sup,
DcAmA, DcNAA*
Ford, Ernest B 1916- *AmSCAP 66*
Ford, Ernest Jennings 1919- *AmSCAP 66*
Ford, Ford Madox 1873-1939 *AtlBL, CasWL,
ChPo, ChPo S1, CnMWL, CyWA,
DcLEnL, EncWL, EvLB, LongC, ModBL,
ModBL Sup, NewC, OxEng, Pen Eng,
RAdv 1, REn, REnAL, TwCA,
TwCA Sup, TwCW, WebEAL, WhTwL*
Ford, Franklin L 1920- *ConAu 17R*
Ford, Fred *ConAu XR*
Ford, Frederick Walter *Alli Sup*
Ford, George *Alli, ChPo S2*
Ford, George Burdett 1879-1930 *DcNAA*
Ford, George D 1880?-1974 *ConAu 53*
Ford, George H 1914- *ConAu 1R, WrD 1976*
Ford, George L 1914- *ConAu 5R*
Ford, Gordon Buell, Jr. 1937- *ConAu 21,
WrD 1976*
Ford, Guy B 1922- *ConAu 5R*
Ford, Guy Stanton 1873-1962 *AmA&B*
Ford, H *Alli Sup*
Ford, H J *ChPo, ChPo S1, ChPo S2*

Ford, Harriet 1868-1949 *AmA&B, DcNAA*
Ford, Harriott Anne *Alli Sup*
Ford, Helen J *Alli Sup, ChPo*
Ford, Henry 1863-1947 *AmA&B, REn*
Ford, Henry Allen d1894 *Alli Sup, DcNAA*
Ford, Henry Clinton 1867- *BiDSA*
Ford, Henry Jones 1851-1925 *AmA&B, AmLY, DcAmA, DcNAA, WhWNAA*
Ford, Herbert Paul 1927- *ConAu 17R, MnBBF, WrD 1976*
Ford, Hilary *WorAu*
Ford, Hildegarde *ConAu XR*
Ford, Horace A *Alli Sup*
Ford, Isaac Nelson 1848-1912 *DcAmA, DcNAA*
Ford, J *Alli*
Ford, J E 1880- *WhWNAA*
Ford, J Massingberd *ConAu XR*
Ford, James 1797-1877 *Alli, Alli Sup*
Ford, James 1884-1944 *DcNAA*
Ford, James Allan 1920- *Au&Wr, ConAu P-1, WrD 1976*
Ford, James L C 1907- *ConAu 29*
Ford, James Lauren 1854-1928 *AmA&B, BbD, BiD&SB, BiDSA, ChPo, ChPo S1, DcAmA, DcNAA*
Ford, Jeremiah Denis Mathias 1873-1958 *AmA&B, CatA 1947, DcSpL*
Ford, Jesse Hill 1928- *AmA&B, ConAu 1R, ConNov 1972, ConNov 1976, Pen Am, WrD 1976*
Ford, Joan 1921- *AmSCAP 66*
Ford, John *Alli Sup, Chmbr 1, WhWNAA*
Ford, Sir John *Alli*
Ford, John 1586-1640? *Alli, AtlBL, BbD, BiD&SB, BrAu, CasWL, ChPo, CnE&AP, CnThe, CrE&SL, CriT 1, CyWA, DcEnA, DcEnL, EvLB, McGWD, MouLC 1, NewC, Pen Eng, REn, REnWD, WebEAL*
Ford, John 1619?- *OxEng*
Ford, John 1639?- *DcLEnL*
Ford, John 1895-1973 *ConAu 45, REnAL*
Ford, John Donaldson 1840-1918 *DcNAA*
Ford, John Lane *Alli Sup*
Ford, Joseph Brandon 1918- *AmA&B*
Ford, Josephine Massyngberde *ConAu 41*
Ford, Julia Ellsworth 1859- *AmA&B*
Ford, Kate Brearly *ChPo*
Ford, Kathleen 1932- *ConAu 25*
Ford, Kirk *WrD 1976*
Ford, L *Alli Sup*
Ford, Lauren 1891- *AuBYP, IlCB 1945, IlCB 1956*
Ford, Lee 1936- *ConAu 25*
Ford, Lee Ellen 1917- *WrD 1976*
Ford, Leighton F S 1931- *Au&Wr, ConAu 17R*
Ford, Leonard A *MnnWr*
Ford, LeRoy 1922- *ConAu 9R*
Ford, Leslie 1898- *AmA&B, ConAu XR, EncM&D, TwCA, TwCA Sup, WhWNAA*
Ford, Lester R 1886- *TexWr*
Ford, Lewis B *ConAu XR*
Ford, Lori 1928- *AmSCAP 66*
Ford, Marcia *ConAu XR, SmATA 6*
Ford, Margaret 1927- *Au&Wr*
Ford, Margaret Patricia 1925- *ConAu 9R*
Ford, Marian *Alli Sup*
Ford, Mary Anne McMullen 1841-1876 *DcNAA, OhA&B, PoIre*
Ford, Mary Forker 1905- *ConAu 9R, IndAu 1917*
Ford, Melbourne H *Alli Sup*
Ford, Michael *Alli Sup*
Ford, Mina Conklin *Alli Sup*
Ford, Miriam Allen De *WhWNAA*
Ford, Nancy K *AuBYP*
Ford, Nick Aaron 1904- *BlkAW, ConAu 25*
Ford, Norman Dennis 1921- *ConAu 23*
Ford, Norrey *WrD 1976*
Ford, Patricia *BlkAW*
Ford, Patrick *ChPo, ChPo S1*
Ford, Patrick 1835-1913 *AmA, AmA&B, DcNAA*
Ford, Patrick 1914- *ConAu 23*
Ford, Paul Leicester 1865-1902 *Alli Sup, AmA,*

AmA&B, BbD, BiD&SB, CarSB, ChPo S1, Chmbr 3, CnDAL, DcAmA, DcBiA, DcLEnL, DcNAA, EvLB, JBA 1934, OxAm, REn, REnAL
Ford, Percy 1894- *Au&Wr, WrD 1976*
Ford, Phyllis M 1928- *ConAu 33*
Ford, Quentin *MnBBF*
Ford, Ranulph *Alli*
Ford, Richard *Alli, BiDLA, Chmbr 3*
Ford, Richard 1796-1858 *Alli, BrAu 19, DcEnL, DcLEnL, EvLB, NewC, OxEng*
Ford, Richard Brice 1935- *ConAu 37*
Ford, Richard Clyde 1870-1951 *AmA&B, WhWNAA*
Ford, Robert 1845-1905 *ChPo, ChPo S1, ChPo S2*
Ford, Robert A D *CanWr, ConP 1970, ConP 1975, OxCan, OxCan Sup, WrD 1976*
Ford, Robert E *ConAu 29*
Ford, Robert Edgar *BlkAW*
Ford, Robert N 1909- *ConAu 33, WrD 1976*
Ford, Mrs. Rochester *LivFWS*
Ford, Roland M *Alli Sup*
Ford, S Gertrude *ChPo, ChPo S2*
Ford, S P *BbtC*
Ford, Sallie Rochester 1828-1910 *Alli Sup, AmA&B, BbD, BiD&SB, BiDSA, DcAmA, DcNAA*
Ford, Samuel Howard 1819-1905 *DcAmA, DcNAA*
Ford, Samuel Howard 1823- *Alli Sup, BiDSA*
Ford, Sewell 1868-1946 *AmA&B, DcNAA, REnAL, WhWNAA*
Ford, Sheridan d1922 *DcNAA*
Ford, Sherman, Jr. 1929- *AmSCAP 66*
Ford, Simeon 1855-1933 *IndAu 1917*
Ford, Simon 1619-1699 *Alli*
Ford, Stephen *Alli*
Ford, Stephen VanRensselaer 1836?-1910 *ChPo S1, DcNAA*
Ford, T *Alli*
Ford, T Murray 1854- *MnBBF*
Ford, Theodosia *Alli Sup, LivFWS*
Ford, Thomas *Alli, Alli Sup, BiDLA*
Ford, Thomas 1800-1850 *DcAmA, DcNAA*
Ford, Thomas 1835- *Alli Sup*
Ford, Thomas B *BiDSA*
Ford, Thomas R 1923- *ConAu 49*
Ford, Thomas W 1924- *ConAu 21*
Ford, W *Alli*
Ford, W H *Alli Sup*
Ford, W Herschel 1900- *ConAu 9R*
Ford, Wally 1950- *BlkAW*
Ford, Walter Burton 1874- *WhWNAA*
Ford, Webster *ChPo, ConAmA*
Ford, William *Alli*
Ford, William Henry 1839-1897 *Alli Sup, DcAmA*
Ford, William Wilbraham 1846- *Alli Sup*
Ford, Worthington Chauncey 1858-1941 *Alli Sup, AmA&B, BiD&SB, DcAmA, DcNAA, OxAm, TwCA, TwCA Sup*
Fordcliffe, W G *MnBBF*
Forde, A N 1923- *ConP 1970*
Forde, Brownlow *BiDLA Sup, PoIre*
Forde, Gertrude *Alli Sup*
Forde, H A *Alli Sup*
Forde, Hugh 1847- *WhLA*
Forde, John 1813- *PoIre*
Forde, R Asheton *MnBBF*
Forde, William *Alli*
Forde-Johnston, James 1927- *Au&Wr, ConAu 9R, WrD 1976*
Forder, Anthony 1925- *WrD 1976*
Forder, Charles Robert 1907- *Au&Wr, WrD 1976*
Forder, Henry George 1889- *Au&Wr*
Forder, Walter *MnBBF*
Fordham, George *Alli Sup*
Fordham, Herbert George 1854- *WhLA*
Fordham, M C *ChPo S1*
Fordham, Mrs. M L *HsB&A*
Fordham, Mary Weston *BlkAW*
Fordham, Michael 1905- *Au&Wr*
Fordham, Peta *Au&Wr, WrD 1976*
Fordin, Hugh 1935- *ConAu 57, WrD 1976*
Fordun, John Of d1384? *Alli, CasWL,*

Chmbr 1, *DcEnL, EvLB, Pen Eng*
Fordwych, Jack *MnBBF*
Fordwych, John Edmund *MnBBF*
Fordyce, Charles *WhWNAA*
Fordyce, Claude P 1883- *WhWNAA*
Fordyce, David *Alli*
Fordyce, David 1711-1751 *Alli*
Fordyce, George 1736-1802 *Alli*
Fordyce, Henrietta *Alli*
Fordyce, James 1720-1796 *Alli, ChPo S1*
Fordyce, John *Alli, Alli Sup*
Fordyce, William *Alli, Alli Sup*
Fordyce, Sir William 1724-1792 *Alli*
Fore, William Frank 1928- *ConAu 5R*
Foree, Kenneth, Jr. 1895- *TexWr, WhWNAA*
Forell, George W 1919- *ConAu 1R*
Foreman, Carl 1914- *ConAu 41, ConDr*
Foreman, Dennis Walden 1900- *OhA&B*
Foreman, Edward Reuben 1868-1936 *DcNAA*
Foreman, Grant 1869-1953 *AmA&B*
Foreman, Harry 1915- *ConAu 33*
Foreman, John *Alli Sup*
Foreman, Kenneth Joseph 1891- *ConAu 33*
Foreman, Kent *BlkAW*
Foreman, L L 1901- *ConAu 5R*
Foreman, Lawton Durant 1913- *ConAu 9R*
Foreman, Michael 1938- *ConAu 23, SmATA 2*
Foreman, Paul *DrAP 1975*
Foreman, Richard 1937- *ConDr, WrD 1976*
Foreman, Russell Ralph 1921- *Au&Wr*
Foreman, Stephen *PoIre*
Foreness, E *Alli*
Forer, Lois G 1914- *ConAu 29*
Forer, Lucille K *ConAu 37*
Forer, Mort *OxCan Sup*
Fores, John 1914- *ConAu 25*
Foresman, Hugh Austin 1867-1960 *AmA&B*
Foresman, Rebecca B *ChPo S2*
Foresman, Robert *ChPo S1*
Forest, Antonia *WrD 1976*
Forest, Felix C *ConAu XR*
Forest, Frederick *HsB&A*
Forest, Ilse 1896- *ConAu 19*
Forest, Louis Effingham De *OxCan*
Forest, Mary *ChPo*
Forest, Neil *Alli Sup*
Forest, William Edward 1850-1903 *DcNAA*
Forest, William S *BiDSA*
Forester *OxAm*
Forester, Cecil Scott 1899-1966 *AmA&B, ConAu 25, CyWA, DcLEnL, EncM&D, EvLB, LongC, MnBBF, ModBL, NewC, RAdv 1, REn, REnAL, TwCA, TwCA Sup, TwCW, WebEAL, WhCL*
Forester, Fanny *Alli, AmA&B, DcNAA, OxAm*
Forester, Frank 1807-1858 *AmA, AmA&B, ChPo, DcAmA, DcEnL, DcLEnL, HsB&A, NewC, OxAm, REnAL*
Forester, Thomas *Alli*
Foresti, E Felix *Alli*
Forestier, Auber *Alli Sup, DcAmA, DcNAA*
Forez *ConAu XR*
Forfar, Elizabeth *ChPo S1*
Forfar, Robert *Alli Sup*
Forfar, William Bentinck *Alli Sup*
Forgan, James Berwick 1852-1924 *DcNAA*
Forgan, R *Alli Sup*
Forge, John *MnBBF*
Forges *Alli*
Forgus, Ronald 1928- *ConAu 41*
Forio, Robert *ConAu XR*
Forjett, Charles *Alli Sup*
Forjett, Ernest Houston *Alli Sup*
Forke, Robert *OxCan*
Forker, Olan Dean 1928- *IndAu 1917*
Forkner, John LaRue 1844-1926 *IndAu 1917*
Forkosch, Morris D 1908- *ConAu 41*
Forlong, Gordon *Alli Sup*
Forlong, James George Roche *Alli Sup*
Forma, Warren 1923- *ConAu 45*
Forman, Adam *Alli Sup*
Forman, Alfred *Alli Sup*
Forman, Brenda 1936- *ConAu 9R, SmATA 4*
Forman, Brenda-Lu 1936- *Au&Wr, AuBYP*
Forman, Charles *Alli*

REn

Forstman, H Jackson 1929- *ConAu 13R*
Forsyte, Charles 1920- *Au&Wr*
Forsyth, Alex *Alli*
Forsyth, Andrew Russel *Alli Sup*
Forsyth, Anne 1933- *ConAu 29*
Forsyth, Austin James Esslemont 1907- *Au&Wr*
Forsyth, C *Alli*
Forsyth, Cecil 1870-1941 *AmSCAP 66,*
  DcNAA
Forsyth, Charles Codrington *OxCan*
Forsyth, Chester Hume 1881- *IndAu 1917,*
  WhWNAA
Forsyth, David J C 1940- *ConAu 41*
Forsyth, David P 1930- *ConAu 9R*
Forsyth, Ebenezer *Alli Sup*
Forsyth, Ethel *Alli Sup*
Forsyth, Evelyn *Alli Sup*
Forsyth, F J *Alli Sup*
Forsyth, Frederick 1938- *ConLC 2, ConLC 5,*
  WrD 1976
Forsyth, George Alexander 1837-1915 *DcNAA*
Forsyth, George H, Jr. 1901- *ConAu 37*
Forsyth, Gloria *AuBYP*
Forsyth, Ilene 1928- *ConAu 37*
Forsyth, J S *Alli*
Forsyth, James *Alli*
Forsyth, James 1838-1871 *Alli Sup*
Forsyth, James 1913- *CnMD, ConDr,*
  ModWD, WrD 1976
Forsyth, James Bell 1803-1869 *Alli Sup, BbtC,*
  DcNAA
Forsyth, John 1780-1841 *BiDSA*
Forsyth, John 1811?-1886 *Alli Sup, DcNAA*
Forsyth, John 1881- *WhWNAA*
Forsyth, John Hamilton *Alli*
Forsyth, Joseph 1763-1815 *Alli, BiD&SB,*
  BiDLA
Forsyth, Robert *Alli, BiDLA*
Forsyth, Robert Bell 1879- *WhWNAA*
Forsyth, Thomas Miller 1871- *WhLA*
Forsyth, W E H *Alli Sup*
Forsyth, William *Alli*
Forsyth, William 1737-1804 *Alli*
Forsyth, William 1812- *Alli Sup, DcEnL*
Forsyth, William 1818-1879 *Alli Sup,*
  BiD&SB
Forsyth, William, Jr. *Alli, BiDLA*
Forsyth, William Douglass 1909- *Au&Wr*
Forsyth-Grant, Annie *WhLA*
Forsyth-Grant, Minnie Caroline d1923 *DcNAA*
Forsythe, Irene *ConAu 49*
Forsythe, James F *ChPo*
Forsythe, Mary Elizabeth *ChPo*
Forsythe, Robert 1896-1960 *AmA&B, TwCA,*
  TwCA Sup
Forsythe, Robert Stanley 1886- *WhWNAA*
Forsythe, Ronald *WrD 1976*
Forsythe, Sidney A 1920- *ConAu 41*
Fort, Mrs. C M *Alli Sup*
Fort, Charles 1874-1932 *AmA&B, DcNAA,*
  OxAm, REnAL, TwCA
Fort, Eleanor H 1914- *AmSCAP 66*
Fort, Francis *Alli*
Fort, Frank *HsB&A*
Fort, George Franklin 1809-1872 *Alli Sup,*
  DcAmA, DcNAA
Fort, Paul 1834-1902 *AmA*
Fort, Paul 1872-1960 *CasWL, ChPo,*
  ChPo S2, ClDMEuL, EncWL, EvEuW,
  OxFr, Pen Eur, REn, WorAu
Fort, Tomlinson 1787-1859 *BiDSA*
Fort, Williams Edwards, Jr. 1905- *ConAu 37*
Forte, Allen 1926- *ConAu 41*
Forte, Christine 1906- *BlkAW*
Forte, David F 1941- *ConAu 53*
Forteguerri, Giovanni 1508-1582 *BiD&SB*
Forteguerri, Niccolo 1674-1735 *DcEuL*
Forten, Charlotte L 1838-1914 *BlkAW*
Fortescue, C *Alli Sup*
Fortescue, Chichester, Baron Carlingford 1823-
  Alli Sup
Fortescue, Lady E *Alli*
Fortescue, Earl *Alli*
Fortescue, Edward Francis Knottesford *Alli Sup*
Fortescue, George 1578?-1659 *NewC*
Fortescue, George Knottesford *Alli Sup*
Fortescue, Granville Roland 1875-1952 *AmA&B*

Fortescue, Hugh, Earl Fortescue 1818- *Alli Sup*
Fortescue, J *Alli*
Fortescue, J F *Alli Sup*
Fortescue, John *Alli*
Fortescue, Sir John *Alli*
Fortescue, Sir John 1394?-1476? *Alli, BrAu,*
  CasWL, DcEnL, EvLB, NewC, OxEng
Fortescue, Sir John William 1859-1933 *Alli Sup,*
  Chmbr 3, DcLEnL, OxEng, WhLA
Fortescue, Thomas *Alli*
Fortescue, Thomas, Baron Clermont 1815-1887
  Alli Sup
Fortesque, Sir John 1394?-1476? *Chmbr 1,*
  BbD
Fortey, Emily C *ChPo S2*
Forth, Earl Of *Alli*
Forth, Agnes A *ChPo S2*
Forth, George 1856-1898 *AmA*
Forth, Henry *Alli*
Forth, William *Alli*
Forthhere d738? *BiB S*
Portier, Alcee 1856-1914 *AmA&B*
  BiD&SB, BiDSA,
  DcAmA, DcNAA
Fortier, Florent *BiDSA*
Fortier, Samuel 1855- *WhWNAA*
Fortiguerri, Niccolo 1674-1735 *BiD&SB*
Fortin, Gerald *OxCan Sup*
Fortin, Marie DesNeiges 1898- *WhWNAA*
Fortis, Giovanni Battista 1741-1803 *BiD&SB*
Fortis, Johnny 1913- *AmSCAP 66*
Fortlage, Karl 1806-1881 *BiD&SB*
Fortman, Edmund J 1901- *ConAu 21*
Fortnum, Mrs. *Alli, BiDLA*
Fortnum, Charles Drury Edward *Alli Sup*
Fortnum, Peggy 1919- *ChPo, IlBYP,*
  IlCB 1956, IlCB 1966
Fortrey, Samuel *Alli*
Fortson, Bettiola Heloise 1890- *BlkAW*
Fortt, Inez Julia Long 1902- *WrD 1976*
Fortunatus, Venantius Honorius C 530?-609?
  BiD&SB, CasWL, Pen Eur
Fortune, Alonza Willard 1873-1950 *OhA&B*
Fortune, E F T *Alli, BiDLA*
Fortune, Jan Isbelle 1892- *TexWr, WhWNAA*
Fortune, Neil *MnBBF*
Fortune, Robert 1813-1880 *Alli, Alli Sup,*
  BiD&SB
Fortune, Timothy Thomas 1856-1928 *Alli Sup,*
  AmA&B, BlkAW, DcNAA
Forwald, Haakon Gabriel 1897- *BiDPar*
Forward, Luke *ConAu XR*
Forwell, William *Alli Sup*
Forwood, William Stump 1830-1892 *Alli Sup,*
  BiDSA, DcAmA, DcNAA
Fory, W R *Alli Sup*
Forzano, Giovacchino 1884-1970 *ClDMEuL,*
  CnMD, ModWD
Fosbery, Thomas Vincent 1807-1875 *Alli Sup,*
  PoIre
Fosbroke, Gerald Elton 1876-1964 *AmA&B,*
  WhWNAA
Fosbroke, John Baldwin *Alli Sup*
Fosbroke, Thomas Dudley 1770-1842 *BiD&SB*
Fosbrooke, John *Alli*
Fosbrooke, Thomas Dudley 1770-1842 *Alli,*
  BiDLA, BiDLA Sup
Foscari, Francesco 1373-1457 *NewC, REn*
Foscolo, Niccolo Ugo 1778-1827 *BbD*
Foscolo, Ugo 1778-1827 *BiD&SB, CasWL,*
  DcEuL, EuA, EvEuW, McGWD,
  Pen Eur, REn
Foscue, Edwin Jay 1899- *ConAu 1R*
Fosdick, Charles *Alli*
Fosdick, Charles Austin 1842-1915 *Alli Sup,*
  AmA, AmA&B, BbD, BiD&SB, CarSB,
  DcAmA, DcNAA, OxAm, REnAL
Fosdick, H M *BbtC*
Fosdick, Harry Emerson 1878-1969 *AmA&B,*
  AuBYP, ConAu 25, REnAL, TwCA Sup,
  WhWNAA
Fosdick, James William 1858-1937 *DcNAA*
Fosdick, Raymond Blaine 1883-1972 *AmA&B,*
  AmLY, ConAu 37
Fosdick, William Whiteman 1825-1862 *Alli Sup,*
  AmA, AmA&B, BiD&SB, DcAmA,
  DcNAA, OhA&B
Fosgate, Blanchard *Alli Sup*

Fosket, Henry *Alli*
Foskett, Antony Charles 1926- *Au&Wr*
Foskett, Daphne 1911- *WrD 1976*
Foskett, Douglas John 1918- *Au&Wr,*
  ConAu 1R, WrD 1976
Foskett, Edgar *Alli Sup*
Foskett, Edward *Alli Sup*
Foskett, Henry *BiDLA*
Foskett, Reginald 1909- *ConAu 21*
Foskett, Thomas Moore *Alli Sup*
Foss, Claude William 1855-1935 *AmLY,*
  DcNAA
Foss, Cyrus David 1834-1910 *DcNAA*
Foss, Edward 1787-1870 *Alli, Alli Sup,*
  DcEnL
Foss, Hugh James 1868- *WhLA*
Foss, John *Alli*
Foss, Lukas 1922- *AmSCAP 66*
Foss, Martin Moore 1878- *AmA&B*
Foss, Phillip Oliver *ConAu 13R*
Foss, Sam Walter 1858-1911 *AmA, AmA&B,*
  ChPo, ChPo S1, ChPo S2, DcAmA,
  DcNAA, EvLB, OxAm, REnAL
Foss, William Otto 1918- *AuBYP,*
  ConAu 17R
Fossat, George *Alli, BiDLA*
Fossat, Thomas *Alli*
Fosse, Alfred *WrD 1976*
Fossett, Frank *Alli Sup*
Fossler, Laurence 1857-1933 *DcNAA*
Fossum, Paul Robert 1893- *WhWNAA*
Fossum, Robert H 1923- *ConAu 25,*
  WrD 1976
Foster *Alli*
Foster, Lieutenant *Alli*
Foster, Mrs. *Alli*
Foster, A *Alli Sup*
Foster, A F *Alli*
Foster, Mrs. A J *ChPo*
Foster, Abigail Adams *ChPo*
Foster, Agness Greene 1863-1933 *AmA&B,*
  AmLY, ChPo S1, DcNAA, WhWNAA
Foster, Al 1924- *AmSCAP 66*
Foster, Alan Dean 1946- *ConAu 53*
Foster, Alan S *ChPo*
Foster, Alfred Edye Manning *MnBBF, WhLA*
Foster, Allyn King 1868-1934 *DcNAA*
Foster, Ann *ChPo S1*
Foster, Anne H 1875- *WhWNAA*
Foster, Anthony 1785-1820 *Alli*
Foster, Ardeen 1862- *AmA&B*
Foster, Ardennes Jones *ChPo S2*
Foster, Arnold *ChPo*
Foster, Arthur *Alli*
Foster, Arthur H *Alli Sup*
Foster, Sir Augustus J *Alli*
Foster, Balthazar Walter *Alli Sup*
Foster, Mrs. Beauregard *WhLA, WhWNAA*
Foster, Benjamin *Alli Sup*
Foster, Benjamin 1750-1798 *Alli, DcNAA*
Foster, Birket 1825-1899 *Alli, ChPo, ChPo S1,*
  ChPo S2
Foster, Brian 1920- *Au&Wr, WrD 1976*
Foster, C J *Alli*
Foster, Carno A 1916- *ConAu 41*
Foster, Caroline Holcomb Wright 1864-1929
  OhA&B
Foster, Celeste K *MnnWr*
Foster, Chapin D 1887- *WhWNAA*
Foster, Charles *Alli Sup*
Foster, Charles Howell 1913- *ConAu 17R*
Foster, Charles Hubbs 1833-1895 *DcAmA*
Foster, Charles Irving 1898- *ConAu 1R*
Foster, Charles James 1820-1883 *Alli Sup,*
  AmA&B, DcNAA, OhA&B
Foster, Charles William 1939- *ConAu 57*
Foster, Clement LeNeve 1841- *Alli Sup*
Foster, Craig Curtis 1947- *LivBA*
Foster, David *Alli*
Foster, David Manning 1944- *ConNov 1976,*
  WrD 1976
Foster, David Skaats 1852?-1920 *Alli Sup,*
  AmA&B, DcAmA, DcNAA
Foster, David William 1940- *ConAu 21,*
  WrD 1976
Foster, Don 1948- *ConAu 33, WrD 1976*
Foster, Donald 1928- *ConAu 53*
Foster, Donald Abbotts 1904- *Au&Wr*

Fothergill, Philip G 1908- *ConAu 5R*
Fothergill, S *Alli Sup*
Fothergill, Samuel *Alli, Alli Sup, BiDLA*
Fothergill, Samuel d1773 *Alli*
Fothergill, Thomas *Alli*
Fothergill, William *Alli Sup*
Fotheringham, E M *MnBBF*
Fotheringham, James *Alli Sup*
Foti, Jacques 1924- *AmSCAP 66*
Fotin, Larry 1911- *AmSCAP 66*
Fottler, Myron David 1941- *ConAu 37,
    WrD 1976*
Fottrell, George *Alli Sup*
Fouche, Joseph, Duke Of Otranto 1759?-1820
    OxFr, REn
Fouche, L N *BiDSA*
Foucher, Adele 1803-1868 *OxFr*
Foucher, Paul 1810-1875 *BiD&SB*
Foucher DeCareil, Count Louis A 1826-1891
    BiD&SB
Foucquet, Jean 1416?-1480 *AtlBL, OxFr*
Foucquet, Nicolas 1615-1680 *OxFr, REn*
Foudras, C *BiDLA*
Fougasse *ConAu XR, LongC, WhLA*
Fougner, Baron *WhWNAA*
Fougner, Gustav Selmer 1884-1941 *AmA&B,
    DcNAA, WhWNAA*
Fouillee, Alfred 1838-1912 *OxFr*
Foul-Weather Jack *NewC*
Foulche-Delbosc, Raymond 1864-1929 *DcSpL*
Foulds, Andrew 1815-1841 *ChPo*
Foulds, Elfrida Vipont 1902- *ConAu 53,
    WrD 1976*
Fouler, William *Alli*
Foulface, Philip *Alli*
Foulis, Andrew 1712-1774? *Alli, DcEuL*
Foulis, Henry 1638?-1685 *Alli*
Foulis, Hugh *CasWL, Chmbr 3, Pen Eng*
Foulis, Sir James d1791 *Alli, BiDLA*
Foulis, Oliver *Alli*
Foulis, R *Alli Sup*
Foulis, Robert *Alli Sup*
Foulis, Robert 1707-1776 *Alli, DcEuL, NewC*
Foulk, Charles William 1869- *WhWNAA*
Foulke, Elizabeth Ellen *IndAu 1816*
Foulke, Robert 1930- *ConAu 45*
Foulke, Roy Anderson 1896- *ConAu 1R*
Foulke, William Dudley 1848-1935 *Alli Sup,
    AmA&B, AmLY, DcAmA, DcNAA,
    IndAu 1816*
Foulke, William Parker *Alli Sup*
Foulkes, A D *Alli Sup*
Foulkes, A Peter 1936- *ConAu 37*
Foulkes, E S *Alli*
Foulkes, Fred K 1941- *ConAu 33*
Foulkes, Martin *Alli*
Foulkes, Percy Hedworth 1871- *WhLA*
Foulkes, Peter *Alli*
Foulkes, Peter 1936- *WrD 1976*
Foulkes, Robert *Alli*
Foulkes, Thomas *Alli Sup*
Foulkes, William Decimus Inglett *Alli Sup*
Foulkes, William Hiram 1877- *WhWNAA*
Foulser, George James 1919- *Au&Wr*
Foulston, J *Alli*
Foulston, Pauline Heckard 1900- *WhWNAA*
Fountain, C R 1879- *WhWNAA*
Fountain, John *Alli*
Fountain, Leatrice 1924- *ConAu 23*
Fountain, Paul *OxCan*
Fountain, Peter *CyAL 1*
Fountain Of Life, The *DcEnL*
Fountaine, Sir Andrew 1680-1753 *Alli, DcEnL*
Fountaine, Henry Thomas *Alli Sup*
Fountaine, John *Alli*
Fountainhall, Lord *Alli*
Fountainhall, Sir John Lauder *Alli*
Fountayne, John *Alli*
Fouque, Friedrich Heinrich K DeLaMotte
    1777-1843 *BbD, BiD&SB, CarSB, CasWL,
    DcBiA, DcEuL, EuA, EvEuW, HsB&A,
    NewC, OxEng, OxGer, Pen Eur, REn,
    WhCL*
Fouque, Karoline DeLaMotte 1773-1831 *OxGer*
Fouqueray, Henri *OxCan*
Fouquet, Jean 1420?-1480? *AtlBL, OxFr,
    REn*
Fouquet, Nicolas 1615-1680 *OxFr, REn*

Fouquier, Jacques Francois Henri 1838-1901
    BiD&SB
Fouquier-Tinville, Antoine Quentin 1746-1795
    OxFr, REn
Four, Du, W *Alli*
Fouraker, Lawrence Edward 1923- *ConAu 1R*
Fourdrinier, Harriet Elizabeth *Alli Sup*
Fourdrinier, P *ChPo*
Fourdrinier, Paul d1758 *BkIE*
Fourdrinier, Paul d1769? *BkIE*
Foure, Helene Selter 1889- *OhA&B,
    WhWNAA*
Foure, Robert 1886- *WhWNAA*
Fourest, Georges *OxFr*
Fourest, Michel *ConAu XR*
Fourestier, James *Alli*
Fourestier, Paul *Alli*
Fourier, Charles 1772-1837 *OxFr, REnAL*
Fourier, Francois Marie Charles 1772-1837 *BbD,
    BiD&SB, CasWL, DcEuL, EuA, NewC*
Fourier, Baron Jean Baptiste Joseph 1768-1830
    BiD&SB
Fournel, Francois Victor 1829-1894 *BbD,
    BiD&SB*
Fournier, Alain 1886-1914 *CasWL, ClDMEuL,
    LongC, ModRL, TwCA, TwCA Sup*
Fournier, Alexis Jean 1865- *WhWNAA*
Fournier, August 1850- *BiD&SB*
Fournier, Daniel *Alli*
Fournier, Edouard 1819-1880 *BiD&SB*
Fournier, Henri Alban 1886-1914 *AtlBL,
    EvEuW, OxFr, REn*
Fournier, Jules 1884-1918 *BbtC, CanWr,
    DcNAA, OxCan*
Fournier, Marc Jean Louis 1818-1879 *BiD&SB*
Fournier, Pierre *REn, WorAu*
Fournier, Pierre-Sylvain *OxCan Sup*
Fournier, Roger *OxCan*
Fourquet, Nicholas 1615-1680 *DcEuL*
Fourth, Clifton *ConAu XR*
Fourth Brother, The *ConAu XR*
Fouse, Dorothea *ChPo S2*
Foust, Clement Edgar *WhWNAA*
Foust, Edmond C d1945 *IndAu 1917*
Foust, Paul J 1920- *ConAu 49*
Fouste, E Bonita Rutledge 1926- *ConAu 13R*
Fout, Henry Harness 1861-1947 *OhA&B*
Fout, John C 1937- *ConAu 57*
Fouts, Tom C 1918- *AmSCAP 66*
Fovargue, Stephen *Alli*
Fowell, Gertrude M *ChPo S2*
Fowell, Samuel *Alli Sup*
Fowey, Roger *MnBBF*
Fowke, Edith 1913- *ChPo S1, ChPo S2,
    ConAu 37, OxCan, OxCan Sup,
    WrD 1976*
Fowke, Frank Rede *Alli Sup*
Fowke, Gerard 1855-1933 *AmLY, BiDSA,
    DcNAA, OhA&B, WhWNAA*
Fowke, John *Alli*
Fowke, Ruth 1929- *Au&Wr*
Fowke, Vernon C *OxCan*
Fowkes, Thomas *Alli Sup*
Fowldes, William *Alli*
Fowle, Daniel 1715-1787 *AmA&B, DcNAA*
Fowle, Edmund *Alli Sup*
Fowle, Frank Fuller 1877- *WhWNAA*
Fowle, Fulmer William *Alli*
Fowle, Fulwar Craven *Alli Sup*
Fowle, James *Alli Sup*
Fowle, Nat C *Alli Sup*
Fowle, Otto 1852-1920 *DcNAA*
Fowle, T Lloyd *Alli Sup*
Fowle, Thomas *Alli*
Fowle, Thomas Welbank *Alli Sup*
Fowle, William *Alli, BiDLA*
Fowle, William Bentley 1795-1865 *DcNAA*
Fowle, William Henry *Alli Sup*
Fowler *Alli*
Fowler, A Z 1896- *TexWr*
Fowler, Alastair David Shaw 1930- *ConAu 13R,
    WrD 1976*
Fowler, Amy *Alli Sup*
Fowler, Austin 1928- *ConAu 23*
Fowler, C H *Alli Sup*
Fowler, Carl Hitchcock 1873- *AmLY*
Fowler, Charles Augustus *Alli Sup*
Fowler, Charles B 1931- *ConAu 57*

Fowler, Charles Evan 1867- *DcAmA,
    WhWNAA*
Fowler, Charles Henry 1837-1908 *AmA&B,
    DcNAA*
Fowler, Charles Newell 1852-1932 *DcNAA*
Fowler, Christopher 1611-1676 *Alli*
Fowler, David Burton *Alli, BiDLA*
Fowler, David Covington 1921- *ChPo S1,
    ConAu 1R, WhPNW*
Fowler, Don D 1936- *ConAu 33, WrD 1976*
Fowler, Douglas 1940- *ConAu 57*
Fowler, Edward 1632-1714 *Alli, DcEnL,
    NewC*
Fowler, Edward P *Alli Sup*
Fowler, Edward Parsons *Alli Sup*
Fowler, Egbert Willard d1901 *ChPo S2*
Fowler, Ellen Thorneycroft 1860-1929 *BiD&SB,
    ChPo, ChPo S1, ChPo S2, Chmbr 3,
    DcBiA, DcEnA Ap, NewC*
Fowler, Elsie Melchert *ChPo, ChPo S1*
Fowler, Ethel Louise *ChPo S1, ChPo S2*
Fowler, F W *Alli Sup*
Fowler, Mrs. F W *Alli Sup*
Fowler, Francis George 1870-1918 *DcLEnL,
    LongC, TwCA, TwCA Sup*
Fowler, Frank *ChPo S2*
Fowler, Frank 1833-1863 *Alli Sup*
Fowler, Frank 1852-1910 *DcAmA, DcNAA*
Fowler, Gene 1890-1960 *AmA&B, CatA 1952,
    REn, REnAL, TwCA, TwCA Sup*
Fowler, Gene 1931- *AmA&B, ConAu 53,
    ConP 1970, ConP 1975, DrAP 1975,
    WrD 1976*
Fowler, George *Alli, Alli Sup, DcNAA*
Fowler, George B *Alli Sup*
Fowler, George Little 1855-1926 *DcNAA*
Fowler, George P 1909- *ConAu 41*
Fowler, George Ryerson 1843-1906 *DcNAA*
Fowler, Guy 1893?-1966 *ConAu 25*
Fowler, H W 1858-1933 *LongC, Pen Eng*
Fowler, W H ALSO Fowler, Henry Watson
Fowler, H W And F G *OxEng*
Fowler, Hammond 1901- *WhWNAA*
Fowler, Harold North 1859- *AmLY,
    WhWNAA*
Fowler, Harriet P *Alli Sup*
Fowler, Harry 1934- *ConAu 45*
Fowler, Harry G *ChPo S1*
Fowler, Helen Rosa Huxley 1917- *Au&Wr,
    ConAu P-1*
Fowler, Henry 1824-1872 *Alli Sup, DcAmA,
    DcNAA*
Fowler, Henry Thatcher 1867-1948 *AmA&B,
    AmLY, DcNAA, WhWNAA*
Fowler, Henry Watson 1818- *ChPo*
Fowler, Henry Watson 1858-1933 *DcLEnL,
    EvLB, NewC, REn, TwCA, TwCA Sup*
Fowler, J *Alli*
Fowler, J A *Alli Sup*
Fowler, J C *Alli Sup*
Fowler, J H *Alli Sup*
Fowler, J Kingston *Alli Sup*
Fowler, James H 1812-1854 *DcNAA*
Fowler, Jessie Allen 1856-1932 *DcNAA*
Fowler, John *Alli, Alli Sup*
Fowler, John d1579 *Alli*
Fowler, John A d1911 *DcNAA*
Fowler, John Coke 1815- *Alli Sup*
Fowler, Joseph *BiDLA*
Fowler, Joseph Thomas *Alli Sup*
Fowler, Josiah 1800-1891 *OhA&B*
Fowler, Katherine *OxEng*
Fowler, Kenneth Abrams 1900- *Au&Wr,
    ConAu 5R, WrD 1976*
Fowler, Lorenzo Niles 1811-1896 *Alli Sup,
    DcAmA, DcNAA*
Fowler, Lydia 1823-1879 *Alli Sup, DcAmA,
    DcNAA*
Fowler, Mary Blackford 1892- *OhA&B*
Fowler, Mary Elizabeth 1911- *ConAu 29*
Fowler, Moses Field *Alli Sup*
Fowler, Nathaniel Clark 1858-1918 *AmLY,
    DcNAA*
Fowler, Orin 1791-1852 *DcAmA, DcNAA*
Fowler, Orrin S 1809-1887 *Alli*
Fowler, Orson Squire 1809-1887 *Alli Sup,
    DcAmA, DcNAA*
Fowler, Philemon Halstead 1814-1879 *Alli Sup,*

Fox, Vernon 1916- *ConAu 37*
Fox, Victor J *ConAu XR*
Fox, W J 1780- *BiDLA*
Fox, W J 1786- *Alli*
Fox, Walter Dennis 1867-1911? *AmA&B,*
BiDSA, DcNAA
Fox, Willard 1919- *ConAu 21*
Fox, William *Alli, Alli Sup, BiDLA*
Fox, Sir William 1812- *Alli Sup*
Fox, William, Jr. *Alli, BiDLA*
Fox, William Freeman 1840-1909 *DcNAA*
Fox, William Johnson d1864 *Alli Sup*
Fox, William Lloyd 1921- *ConAu 17R*
Fox, William McNair 1924- *ConAu 5R*
Fox, William Price, Jr. 1926- *ConAu 17R*
Fox, William Sherwood 1878- *CanWr,*
WhWNAA
Fox, William Tilbury 1836-1879 *Alli Sup*
Fox, William Wellington 1909- *AuBYP,*
ConAu 1R
Fox, Wilson 1831-1887 *Alli Sup*
Fox-Smith, Cicely *ChPo, ChPo S1, ChPo S2*
Foxall, Raymond 1916- *Au&Wr, ConAu 9R,*
WrD 1976
Foxcraft, Alexander *Alli*
Foxcroft, Alexander *BiDLA*
Foxcroft, Elizabeth Howard 1850-1888 *Alli Sup,*
ChPo, ChPo S1
Foxcroft, Frank 1850-1921 *Alli Sup, AmA&B,*
ChPo, ChPo S1, DcNAA
Foxcroft, Frank 1892- *WhWNAA*
Foxcroft, H C *WhLA*
Foxcroft, John *Alli*
Foxcroft, Thomas 1697-1769 *Alli, DcNAA*
Foxe, Arthur Norman 1902- *ConAu 9R,*
WrD 1976
Foxe, John 1516?-1587 *BbD, BiD&SB, BrAu,*
CasWL, Chmbr 1, CrE&SL, CriT 1,
DcEnL, DcEuL, DcLEnL, EvLB, NewC,
OxEng, Pen Eng, REn, WebEAL
Foxe, John SEE Also Fox, John
Foxe, Luke 1586-1635 *Alli, OxCan*
Foxell, John *Alli*
Foxell, Maurice *ChPo S2*
Foxell, Nigel 1931- *Au&Wr, OxCan Sup,*
WrD 1976
Foxell, William James *ChPo, ChPo S2*
Foxhall, George 1882- *WhWNAA*
Foxle, George *Alli*
Foxley, Joseph *Alli Sup*
Foxley, Thomas *Alli*
Foxon, William *Alli*
Foxton, E *DcAmA*
Foxton, Frederick Joseph *Alli, Alli Sup*
Foxton, Thomas *Alli*
Foxwell, E *Alli Sup*
Foxwell, Ivan Cottam 1914- *Au&Wr,*
WrD 1976
Foxwell, W *Alli*
Foxworth, Nilene Elizabeth 1936- *BlkAW*
Foxworthy, Frank W 1873- *WhWNAA*
Foxx, Jack *ConAu 49*
Foxx, Richard M 1944- *ConAu 45*
Foy, Eddie *DcNAA*
Foy, Kenneth R 1922- *ConAu 25*
Foy, Nancy 1934- *ConAu 45*
Foy, Peter *MnBBF*
Foye, James Clark 1841-1896 *Alli Sup,*
DcAmA, DcNAA
Foye, M W *Alli*
Foye, Wilbur Garland 1886-1935 *DcNAA*
Foyle, Christina Agnes Lilian 1911- *Au&Wr*
Foyle, Kathleen 1892- *Au&Wr*
Foyle, William A 1885-1963 *ChPo, LongC*
Foyster, J A *Alli Sup*
Foyster, J G *Alli*
Foyster, John Raymond 1907- *Au&Wr*
Fozdar, Jamshed K 1926- *ConAu 49*
Fra Elbertus *TwCA, TwCA Sup*
Fracastoro, Girolamo 1483?-1553 *CasWL,*
DcEuL, REn
Fracchia, Umberto 1889-1930 *CasWL, EvEuW*
Frace, Charles *IlBYP*
Frachtenberg, Leo Joachim 1883-1930 *DcNAA*
Frackenpohl, Arthur R 1924- *AmSCAP 66,*
ConAu 17R
Fracker, S B 1889- *WhWNAA*
Frackleton, Susan S 1848- *Alli Sup, DcAmA*

Frada, Johanna *WhWNAA*
Fraddle, Farragut *ConAu XR*
Fradenburgh, Adelbert Grant 1868-1936
DcNAA
Fradenburgh, Jason Nelson 1843- *Alli Sup,*
DcNAA
Fradkin, Elvira Kush 1890?-1972 *ConAu 37*
Fraelich, Richard O 1924- *ConAu 5R*
Fraenkel, Gerd 1919-1970 *ConAu P-1*
Fraenkel, Heinrich 1897- *Au&Wr,*
ConAu 13R, WrD 1976
Fraenkel, Jack R 1932- *ConAu 29, WrD 1976*
Fraenkel, Osmond K 1888- *ConAu 23*
Fraet, Frans d1558 *CasWL*
Fragonard, Alexander Evariste 1780-1850
ChPo S1
Fragonard, Jean Honore 1732-1806 *AtlBL,*
OxFr, REn
Frahm, Anne B Schwerdt 1927- *ConAu 9R*
Fraiberg, Louis Benjamin 1913- *ConAu 1R*
Frain, M Theo *WhWNAA*
Fraine, Harold George 1900- *ConAu 1R,*
WrD 1976
Fraire, Isabel 1934- *DcCLA*
Frakes, George Edward 1932- *ConAu 29,*
WrD 1976
Fraknoi, Wilhelm 1843- *BiD&SB*
Fraleck, Edison Baldwin 1841- *WhWNAA*
Fraley, Oscar 1914- *AmA&B*
Fram, Eugene Harry 1929- *ConAu 17R*
Frame, Mrs. Daniel *AmNov XR*
Frame, Donald Murdoch 1911- *ConAu 17R,*
WrD 1976
Frame, Elizabeth *Alli Sup, BbtC, OxCan*
Frame, Esther Gordon 1840-1920 *IndAu 1917*
Frame, James *Alli Sup*
Frame, Janet 1924- *CasWL, ConAu XR,*
ConLC 2, ConLC 3, ConLC 6,
ConNov 1972, ConNov 1976, ConP 1975,
LongC, NewC, Pen Eng, RAdv 1,
TwCW, WebEAL, WorAu, WrD 1976
Frame, Nathan T 1840-1915 *OhA&B*
Frame, Paul 1913- *IlBYP, IlCB 1966*
Frame, Robert *Alli Sup*
Frame, Thomas *ChPo*
Framer, Walter H 1908- *AmSCAP 66*
Framo, James L 1922- *ConAu 41*
Frampton, Algernon *Alli*
Frampton, G *BiDLA*
Frampton, H F *MnBBF*
Frampton, John *Alli*
Frampton, Louisa Charlotte *Alli Sup*
Frampton, Matthew *Alli*
Frampton, Merle E 1903- *ConAu 25*
Frampton, Th *Alli*
Frampton, Thomas Shipdem *Alli Sup*
Framton, G *Alli*
Franc, Marc *ChPo S2*
Franc, Maud Jeanne *Alli Sup*
Francaise *DcNAA*
Francatelli, Charles Elme 1805-1876 *Alli Sup,*
DcEnL
France, Anatole 1844-1924 *AtlBL, BbD,*
BiD&SB, CasWL, ClDMEuL, CyWA,
DcBiA, DcEuL, EncWL, EvEuW, LongC,
ModRL, NewC, OxEng, OxFr, Pen Eur,
RCom, REn, TwCA, TwCA Sup, TwCW,
WhTwL
France, Beulah Sanford 1891-1971 *ConAu 33*
France, Claire *ConAu XR, OxCan*
France, Evangeline *ConAu XR*
France, Francis *Alli Sup*
France, Harold L 1930- *ConAu 49*
France, Hector 1840- *BiD&SB*
France, Helena Ruth 1913- *Au&Wr*
France, L A *ChPo S1, ChPo S2*
France, Lewis Browne 1833-1907 *Alli Sup,*
AmA&B, DcAmA, DcNAA, OhA&B
France, Malcolm 1928- *Au&Wr, ConAu 23*
France, Martha C *Alli Sup*
France, Ruth 1913-1968 *LongC*
France, Victor *WhLA*
France-Hayhurst, Evangeline Chaworth 1904-
Au&Wr, ConAu P-1
Frances, Miss *ConAu XR*
Frances, Emily *Alli Sup*
Frances, Esteban 1915- *IlCB 1966*
Frances, Immanuel 1618-1710? *CasWL*

Frances, Mary *Alli Sup*
Frances, Paula 1924- *AmSCAP 66*
Francesca *AmA&B, AtlBL*
Francesca Da Rimini *NewC, REn*
Francesca, Piero Della 1420?-1492 *REn*
Francesca, Rosina *ConAu XR*
Francesco Da Barberino 1264-1348 *CasWL*
Franchere, Gabriel 1786-1863 *BbtC, DcNAA,*
OxAm, OxCan, OxCan Sup
Franchere, Hoyt Catlin *WhPNW*
Franchere, Ruth Myers *WhPNW*
Franchi, Ausonio 1821-1895 *BiD&SB*
Franchini, Anthony J 1898- *AmSCAP 66*
Franchore, Gabriel 1786- *Alli*
Franchot, Nicholas VanVranken 1855-1943
DcNAA
Francillon, F *Alli*
Francillon, James 1802-1866 *Alli Sup*
Francillon, John *Alli*
Francillon, Robert Edward 1841-1919 *Alli Sup,*
BbD, BiD&SB, ChPo, DcEnL
Francis *Alli*
Francis I 1494-1547 *DcEuL, REn*
Francis D'Assisi, Saint 1182?-1226 *BiD&SB*
Francis Ferdinand 1863-1914 *REn*
Francis Joseph I 1830-1916 *REn*
Francis, Miss *ConAu XR*
Francis Of Assisi, Saint 1182?-1226 *CasWL,*
EuA, EvEuW, NewC, RCom, REn
Francis, Saint 1182?-1226 *CarSB, NewC,*
Pen Eur
Francis Xavier 1885- *WhWNAA*
Francis Xavier, Saint 1506-1552 *NewC*
Francis, A D 1900- *ConAu 21*
Francis, A D ALSO Francis, David
Francis, Anne *ConAu XR, WrD 1976*
Francis, Anne d1800 *Alli*
Francis, Annette 1928- *AmSCAP 66*
Francis, B *Alli Sup*
Francis, Basil Hoskins 1906- *Au&Wr,*
ConAu P-1
Francis, Beata *Alli Sup, ChPo*
Francis, Benjamin 1734-1799 *Alli, PoCh*
Francis, Mrs. Blundell *BbD*
Francis, C *Alli*
Francis, C E *WrD 1976*
Francis, C M *Alli Sup*
Francis, Charles *Alli, BiDLA*
Francis, Charles Richard *Alli Sup*
Francis, Charles Spencer 1853-1911 *DcNAA*
Francis, Charles Stephen 1805-1887 *AmA&B*
Francis, Colin *ChPo*
Francis, Connie *AmSCAP 66*
Francis, Convers 1795-1863 *Alli, CyAL 1,*
DcAmA, DcNAA, OxAm
Francis, Daniel *ConAu XR*
Francis, David 1900- *WrD 1976*
Francis, David ALSO Francis, A D
Francis, David Noel 1904- *Au&Wr,*
ConAu 5R
Francis, David Rowland 1850-1927 *BiDSA,*
DcNAA
Francis, Dayrell Joseph Thackwell *Alli Sup*
Francis, Dee *ConAu XR*
Francis, Devon 1901- *ConAu 61*
Francis, Dick 1920- *Au&Wr, ConAu 5R,*
ConLC 2, ConNov 1976, EncM&D,
WrD 1976
Francis, Dorothy Brenner 1926- *ConAu 21,*
SmATA 10, WrD 1976
Francis, E K *OxCan*
Francis, E Warren *Alli Sup*
Francis, Eliza S *Alli*
Francis, Emma E *ChPo*
Francis, Emma S *ChPo, ChPo S2*
Francis, Ernest *Alli Sup*
Francis, F *Alli*
Francis, F J *Alli*
Francis, Francis 1822-1886 *Alli Sup, Br&AmS*
Francis, Francis, Jr. *Alli Sup*
Francis, Frank *ChPo S2*
Francis, Frank 1901- *WrD 1976*
Francis, Franz *BrAu*
Francis, Frederick John *Alli Sup*
Francis, George *Alli Sup*
Francis, George Grant 1814-1882 *Alli Sup*
Francis, George Hy *Alli*
Francis, George William 1800-1865 *Alli Sup*

Francis, H E 1924- *ConAu 25, WrD 1976*
Francis, Harold *Alli Sup*
Francis, Harriet B *ChPo*
Francis, Helen Dannefer 1915- *ConAu 13R, WrD 1976*
Francis, Henry *Alli*
Francis, Henry S 1925- *AuBYP*
Francis, Henry Thomas *Alli Sup*
Francis, J G *Alli, Alli Sup*
Francis, J T *Alli*
Francis, James Allan 1864-1928 *DcNAA*
Francis, James Bicheno 1815-1892 *Alli Sup, DcAmA, DcNAA*
Francis, Jean *Alli Sup*
Francis, John *Alli, Alli Sup*
Francis, John 1811-1882 *NewC*
Francis, John, Jr. 1875-1954 *AmA&B, WhWNAA*
Francis, John Collins *Alli Sup*
Francis, John Wakefield 1789-1861 *Alli, AmA&B, CyAL 1, DcAmA, DcNAA*
Francis, Joseph 1801-1893 *DcNAA*
Francis, Joseph Green 1849-1930 *AmA&B, ChPo, ChPo S1*
Francis, Joseph Greene 1849-1930 *DcNAA*
Francis, Laura *Alli Sup*
Francis, Marilyn 1920- *ConAu 5R, WrD 1976*
Francis, Mark *Alli Sup*
Francis, Mary C *BiDSA*
Francis, Mary E 1855?-1930? *LongC, NewC, PoIre*
Francis, Mary O *HsB&A Sup*
Francis, Michel *ConAu XR*
Francis, Nelle 1914- *ConAu 37*
Francis, Nina *Alli Sup*
Francis, Pamela 1926- *ConAu 29, WrD 1976*
Francis, Philip *Alli*
Francis, Philip 1708?-1773 *Alli, DcEnL, NewC, PoIre*
Francis, Sir Philip 1740-1818 *Alli, BbD, BiD&SB, BiDLA, BrAu, CasWL, DcEnL, DcEuL, EvLB, NewC*
Francis, Sir Philip 1822-1876 *Alli Sup*
Francis, Philip 1927- *ConAu XR, WrD 1976*
Francis, Philip S 1918- *ConAu 17R*
Francis, R Mabel 1880- *ConAu 25*
Francis, Richard *Alli*
Francis, Richard C *TexWr*
Francis, Robert 1901- *AmA&B, ChPo, ChPo S1, ConAu 1R, ConP 1970, ConP 1975, DrAP 1975, WrD 1976*
Francis, Roy G 1919- *ConAu 1R*
Francis, Ruth Garrison 1895- *AnMV 1926*
Francis, S *Alli Sup*
Francis, Samuel Ward 1835-1886 *Alli Sup, AmA&B, CyAL 2, DcAmA, DcNAA*
Francis, Seseen *AmSCAP 66*
Francis, Sophia L *Alli, BiDLA*
Francis, Stephen D *MnBBF*
Francis, T M *MnBBF*
Francis, Thomas *Alli Sup*
Francis, Valentine Mott 1834-1907 *Alli Sup, DcAmA, DcNAA*
Francis, W *Alli, BiDLA*
Francis, W Nelson 1910- *Au&Wr*
Francis, Wayne L 1935- *ConAu 41*
Francis, William 1922- *Au&Wr*
Francis Fytton, Charles Farid Bassili 1928- *Au&Wr*
Francis-Williams, Lord *ConAu XR*
Francisci, Erasmus 1627-1694 *OxGer*
Francison, Alfred *Alli Sup*
Franck, Adolphe 1809-1893 *BiD&SB, OxFr*
Franck, Cesar Auguste 1822-1890 *AtlBL, OxFr, REn*
Franck, Frederick Sigfred 1909- *AmA&B, Au&Wr, ConAu 1R, WrD 1976*
Franck, Hans 1879-1963? *EncWL, ModWD, OxGer*
Franck, Harry Alverson 1881-1962 *AmA&B, REnAL, TwCA, TwCA Sup, WhWNAA*
Franck, Johann 1618-1677 *BiD&SB, OxGer*
Franck, Phyllis 1928- *ConAu 53*
Franck, Richard *Alli*
Franck, Sebastian 1499-1542 *BiD&SB, CasWL, OxGer, Pen Eur*

Franck, Thomas Martin 1931- *ConAu 33, WrD 1976*
Francke, August Hermann 1663-1727 *DcEuL, OxGer*
Francke, Kuno 1855-1930 *AmA&B, BiD&SB, CasWL, DcAmA, DcNAA, WhWNAA*
Franckenberg, Abraham Von 1593-1652 *OxGer*
Franckenstein, Mrs. Joseph M *AmNov XR*
Francklin *Alli*
Francklin, Gracious *Alli*
Francklin, R *Alli*
Francklin, Thomas *Alli*
Francklin, Thomas 1721-1784 *Alli, DcEnL*
Francklin, William *Alli*
Francklyn, Gilbert *Alli, BiDLA*
Francklyn, Thomas *Alli*
Franco, Francisco 1892- *REn*
Franco, Harry 1804-1877 *AmA, AmA&B, DcEnL, OxAm, REnAL*
Franco, Jean 1914- *ConAu 25*
Franco, Jean 1924- *ConAu 23*
Franco, Matteo 1447-1494 *REn*
Franco, Niccolo 1515?-1570 *BiD&SB, CasWL, REn*
Franco, R Solomon *Alli*
Franco, Veronica 1546-1591 *CasWL*
Franco-Mendes, David 1713-1792 *CasWL*
Franco Oppenheimer, Felix 1912- *PueRA*
Francoeur, Anna K 1940- *ConAu 53*
Francoeur, Louis *OxCan*
Francoeur, Robert Thomas 1931- *ConAu 37, WrD 1976*
Francois I 1494-1547 *OxFr*
Francois II 1544-1560 *OxFr*
Francois De Sales, Saint 1567-1622 *CasWL, EuA, OxFr, Pen Eur*
Francois, Andre 1915- *Au&Wr, IlBYP, IlCB 1956, IlCB 1966, ThBJA, WhGrA*
Francois, Louise Von 1817-1893 *OxGer*
Francois, Luise Von 1817-1893 *BbD, BiD&SB*
Francois, Marie Louise Von 1817-1893 *CasWL, EvEuW*
Francois, Pierre 1932- *ConAu 17R*
Francois, Victor Emmanuel 1866-1944 *DcNAA*
Francois, William E 1924- *ConAu 13R*
Francois DeNeufchateau, Count Nicolas L 1750-1828 *BiD&SB*
Francoise 1900?-1961 *AnCL, IlBYP, IlCB 1956, IlCB 1966, MorJA*
Francq, Edward Nathaniel Lloyd 1934- *IndAu 1917*
Francq VanBerkhey, Johannes Le 1729-1812 *BiD&SB*
Franda, Marcus Francis 1937- *ConAu 23, WrD 1976*
Frandere *WhWNAA*
Frandsen, Arden N 1902- *ConAu 1R*
Frandsen, Maude Linstrom 1908- *WrD 1976*
Franes, S O *MnBBF*
Frangkiser, Carl 1894- *AmSCAP 66*
Frank 1814-1852 *AmA*
Frank, Father *ChPo*
Frank, Uncle *ChPo*
Frank, Andre Gunder 1929- *ConAu 21*
Frank, Anne 1929-1944 *REn, TwCW*
Frank, Benis M 1925- *ConAu 37*
Frank, Bruno 1887-1945 *AmA&B, ClDMEuL, CnMD, EncWL, McGWD, ModGL, ModWD, OxGer, REn, TwCA, TwCA Sup*
Frank, Camilla Mays 1899- *AmSCAP 66*
Frank, Charles E 1911- *ConAu 21, WrD 1976*
Frank, Charles Raphael 1937- *ConAu 37, WrD 1976*
Frank, Doctor *DcNAA*
Frank, Florence *ChPo*
Frank, Florence Kiper *WhWNAA*
Frank, G *Alli Sup*
Frank, Gerold 1907- *Au&Wr*
Frank, Glenn 1887-1940 *AmA&B, DcNAA, WiscW*
Frank, Goldalie 1908- *ConAu P-1*
Frank, H Eric 1921- *ConAu 49*
Frank, Harry Thomas 1933- *ConAu 53*
Frank, Helmut J 1922- *ConAu 17R, WrD 1976*
Frank, Henry 1854-1933 *Alli Sup, DcAmA, DcNAA, IndAu 1816*

Frank, Henry 1854- *WhWNAA*
Frank, Irving 1910- *ConAu 21*
Frank, Isaiah 1917- *ConAu 1R*
Frank, Jacob H *BbtC*
Frank, Janet *ConAu 57*
Frank, Jeffrey 1942- *ConAu 21*
Frank, Jerome D 1909- *ConAu 5R*
Frank, John *Alli*
Frank, Joseph *Alli, BiDLA*
Frank, Joseph 1916- *AmA&B, ConAu 1R, WorAu*
Frank, Joseph Otto 1885-1949 *IndAu 1917*
Frank, Josette 1893- *AuBYP, ChPo, ChPo S2, ConAu P-1, SmATA 10*
Frank, Lawrence K 1890- *ConAu 1R*
Frank, Lee *ConAu 49*
Frank, Leonhard 1882-1961 *ClDMEuL, CnMD, EncWL, McGWD, ModGL, ModWD, OxGer, Pen Eur, REn, TwCA, TwCA Sup*
Frank, Mabel Livingstone *ChPo*
Frank, Marcel Gustave 1909- *AmSCAP 66*
Frank, Mark 1613-1664 *Alli*
Frank, Mary *Alli Sup*
Frank, May *WhWNAA*
Frank, Murray 1908- *ConAu 37*
Frank, Nathalie D 1918- *ConAu 9R*
Frank, Pat 1907-1964 *AmNov, ConAu 5R*
Frank, Peter *DrAP 1975*
Frank, Philipp 1884-1966 *ConAu 25*
Frank, Rene 1910-1965 *AmSCAP 66*
Frank, Robert Glenn 1926- *Au&Wr*
Frank, Robert Tilden 1875-1949 *DcNAA*
Frank, Robert Worth 1914- *ConAu 13R, IndAu 1917*
Frank, Ronald E 1933- *ConAu 5R*
Frank, Ruth Verd 1899- *AmSCAP 66*
Frank, Sebastian 1499-1542 *OxGer*
Frank, Semen Lyudvigovich 1877-1950 *CasWL, EncWL*
Frank, Sheldon *DrAF 1976*
Frank, Simon Lyudvigovich 1877-1950 *DcRusL*
Frank, Stanley B 1908- *ConAu 5R*
Frank, Tenney 1876-1939 *AmA&B, DcNAA, WhWNAA*
Frank, Thomas *Alli*
Frank, Waldo 1889-1967 *AmA&B, AmNov, CnDAL, ConAmA, ConAmL, ConAu 25, DcLEnL, ModAL, OxAm, Pen Am, REn, REnAL, TwCA, TwCA Sup, WhWNAA*
Frankau, Gilbert 1884-1952 *ChPo S1, ChPo S2, DcLEnL, EncM&D, EvLB, LongC, NewC, REn, TwCA, TwCA Sup, WhLA*
Frankau, Joan *LongC*
Frankau, Mary Evelyn Atkinson 1899- *ConAu P-1, SmATA 4*
Frankau, Pamela 1908-1967 *AmA&B, CatA 1947, ConAu 25, DcLEnL, EvLB, LongC, NewC, Pen Eng, REn, TwCA, TwCA Sup, TwCW*
Frankau, Ronald *ChPo, ChPo S1*
Franke, Carl Wilfred 1928- *ConAu 23, WrD 1976*
Franke, David 1938- *ConAu 49*
Franke, Holly L 1943- *ConAu 49*
Franke, Sartorius Hermann *Alli Sup*
Frankel, A Steven 1942- *ConAu 53*
Frankel, Bernice *ConAu 61, SmATA 9*
Frankel, Charles 1917- *AmA&B, Au&Wr, ConAu 5R*
Frankel, Doris *ChPo S2*
Frankel, Edward *AuBYP*
Frankel, Emil 1886- *WhWNAA*
Frankel, Hans H 1916- *ConAu 61*
Frankel, Joseph 1913- *Au&Wr, ConAu 5R, WrD 1976*
Frankel, Julius *Alli Sup*
Frankel, Lee Kaufer 1867- *WhWNAA*
Frankel, Sally Herbert 1903- *Au&Wr*
Frankel, Sandor 1943- *ConAu 33, WrD 1976*
Frankel, Zygmunt 1929- *ConAu 41*
Franken, Rose 1898- *AmA&B, AmNov, Au&Wr, CnMD, ModWD, REn, REnAL, TwCA, TwCA Sup*
Frankena, William K 1908- *ConAu 17R*
Frankenberg, Celestine Gilligan *ConAu 9R*
Frankenberg, Lloyd 1907-1975 *AmA&B,*

ChPo S1, ConAu 1R, ConAu 57, REnAL, TwCA Sup

Frankenberg, Robert Clinton 1911- IlBYP, IlCB 1956, IlCB 1966

Frankenberg, Theodore Thomas 1877-1958 OhA&B, WhWNAA

Frankenburg, Abraham Von 1593-1652 DcEuL

Frankenburg, Charis Ursula 1892- Au&Wr, WrD 1976

Frankenburg, Robert ChPo S2

Frankenfield, Parke T 1929- AmSCAP 66

Frankenstein, Alfred Victor 1906- AmA&B, ConAu 1R

Frankenstein, Carl 1905- ConAu 9R

Frankenstein, Gustavus 1829?-1893 OhA&B

Frankenstein, John Peter 1816?-1881 OhA&B

Frankfort, Ellen 1936- ConAu 29

Frankfurt, Harry Gordon 1929- ConAu 41

Frankfurter, Felix 1882-1965 AmA&B, DcLEnL, OxAm, REn, REnAL, WhWNAA

Frankfurter, Glen 1918- Au&Wr, OxCan Sup

Frankfurter, Philip CasWL, OxGer

Frankfurter Gretchen OxGer

Frankhouser, Floyd Richard 1944- WrD 1976

Frankis, Geoffrey George Alfred 1919- Au&Wr

Frankl, Ludwig August 1810-1894 BiD&SB

Frankland, Mrs. Alli

Frankland, Benjamin 1819-1876 Alli, Alli Sup

Frankland, Charles Colville Alli

Frankland, E H A Alli Sup

Frankland, Edward 1825- Alli Sup

Frankland, Edward Percy 1884- NewC

Frankland, Noble 1922- WrD 1976

Frankland, Percy Faraday Alli Sup

Frankland, Sir Thomas Alli

Frankland, Thomas 1633-1690 Alli

Frankland, William Alli, BiDLA

Frankland, William Adolphus Alli Sup

Franklin Alli

Franklin, A ConAu XR

Franklin, Alexander John 1921- Au&Wr, ConAu 13R, WrD 1976

Franklin, Alfred White 1905- Au&Wr, ConAu 57

Franklin, Andrew d1845 Alli, BiDLA, PoIre

Franklin, Ann 1696-1763 REnAL

Franklin, B Alli Sup

Franklin, Benjamin Chmbr 3

Franklin, Benjamin 1706-1790 Alli, AmA, AmA&B, AmWr, AtlBL, BbD, BiD&SB, CasWL, ChPo, ChPo S1, ChPo S2, CnDAL, CriT 3, CyAL 1, CyWA, DcAmA, DcEnL, DcLEnL, DcNAA, EvLB, MouLC 2, NewC, OxAm, OxEng, Pen Am, RCom, REn, REnAL, WebEAL

Franklin, Benjamin 1812-1876? DcNAA, IndAu 1816

Franklin, Benjamin 1819-1898 Alli Sup, DcAmA, DcNAA

Franklin, Benjamin Alvey 1869- WhWNAA

Franklin, Bernard ChPo

Franklin, Billy J 1940- ConAu 33

Franklin, Burt 1903-1972 ConAu P-1

Franklin, Carl BlkAW

Franklin, Charles 1909- Au&Wr, ConAu XR

Franklin, Chester A 1880- WhWNAA

Franklin, Christine Ladd 1847-1930 DcNAA, WhWNAA

Franklin, Clarence 1932- BlkAW

Franklin, Dave AmSCAP 66

Franklin, Denson Nauls 1914- ConAu 1R

Franklin, Edward Carroll 1822-1885 Alli Sup, DcNAA

Franklin, Edward Earle 1898- WhWNAA

Franklin, Edward Herbert 1930- ConAu 13R

Franklin, Edward Zeus DcNAA

Franklin, Eleanor Ann 1795-1825 Alli, DcEnL, NewC

Franklin, Elizabeth ConAu XR

Franklin, Ethel Mary TexWr

Franklin, Eugene ConAu XR

Franklin, Fabian 1853-1939 AmLY, DcNAA

Franklin, Frank George 1861- WhWNAA

Franklin, George ChPo

Franklin, George Cory 1872- MorJA

Franklin, George E 1890-1971 ConAu P-1

Franklin, H Bruce 1934- ConAu 5R

Franklin, Harold 1920- ConAu 29

Franklin, Harold L 1934- ConAu 57

Franklin, Harry 1906- ConAu P-1, WrD 1976

Franklin, Henry 1906- Au&Wr

Franklin, Mrs. Hugh AmNov XR

Franklin, J Alli, BiDLA, ChPo

Franklin, J E 1937- BlkAW, ConAu 61

Franklin, Jacob Abraham Alli Sup

Franklin, James Alli

Franklin, James 1697-1735 AmA&B, CyAL 1, EarAB, OxAm, REnAL

Franklin, James Thomas BlkAW

Franklin, Jay ConAu XR, TwCA, TwCA Sup

Franklin, Jean Dwight 1865- ChPo, ChPo S2

Franklin, Jimmie 1909- AmSCAP 66

Franklin, Sir John 1786-1847 Alli, BrAu 19, NewC, OxCan, OxEng

Franklin, John Hope 1915- AmA&B, ConAu 1R, ConAu 5R, LivBA, WrD 1976

Franklin, Joseph And Headington, J A Alli Sup

Franklin, Josephine CarSB

Franklin, Josias CyAL 1

Franklin, Keith ConAu XR

Franklin, Leo Morris 1870-1948 DcNAA, IndAu 1917

Franklin, Miss M Alli Sup

Franklin, Malvin M 1889- AmSCAP 66

Franklin, Marc A 1932- ConAu 29

Franklin, Marshall 1929- ConAu 53

Franklin, Mary Lucretia Barker OhA&B

Franklin, Max ConAu XR, WrD 1976

Franklin, Michael ChPo

Franklin, Miles 1879-1954 CasWL, TwCW

Franklin, Nat ConAu XR

Franklin, Nellie Baker TexWr

Franklin, Olga 1912- Au&Wr, WrD 1976

Franklin, R W 1937- ConAu 23

Franklin, Richard Alli

Franklin, Richard 1918- ConAu 21

Franklin, Richard Langdon 1925- WrD 1976

Franklin, Robert Alli, Alli Sup

Franklin, Samuel Harvey 1928- WrD 1976

Franklin, Samuel Rhoades 1825-1909 DcAmA, DcNAA

Franklin, Stella Maria Sarah Miles 1879-1954 DcLEnL

Franklin, Steve ConAu XR, SmATA 6

Franklin, Thomas Alli

Franklin, Thomas Levering 1820-1899 DcAmA

Franklin, Viola Price 1855- AnMV 1926, WhWNAA

Franklin, W Alli Sup

Franklin, William Alli, BiDLA

Franklin, William 1730?-1813 DcNAA, OxAm

Franklin, William Suddards 1863-1930 DcNAA, WhWNAA

Franklin, William Temple d1823 Alli

Franklin Of Theology, The DcEnL

Frankly, Mister ChPo S2

Franklyn, Blanche 1895- AmSCAP 66

Franklyn, Cecil ChPo S1

Franklyn, Charles Aubrey Hamilton 1896- Au&Wr, ConAu 9R

Franklyn, Francis Alli

Franklyn, H Mortimer Alli Sup

Franklyn, Henry Bowles Alli Sup

Franklyn, Julian BiDPar

Franklyn, Milt J 1897-1962 AmSCAP 66

Franko, Ivan 1856-1916 CasWL, DcRusL, ModSL 2, Pen Eur

Franko, Lawrence G 1942- ConAu 37

Franks, Augustus Wollaston 1826- Alli Sup

Franks, Boyce T 1906- WhWNAA

Franks, Cyril Maurice 1923- ConAu 13R

Franks, George Alli Sup

Franks, James Alli, BiDLA

Franks, James Clarke Alli

Franks, John Alli, BiDLA

Franks, Lucinda 1946- ConAu 53

Franks, Margaret B Alli Sup

Franks, Sir Oliver 1905- NewC

Franks, Robert Sleightholme 1871-1963 ConAu 5R, WhLA

Franks, Thetta Quay 1867-1947 ChPo, DcNAA

Franks, Tillman B 1920- AmSCAP 66

Frankum, Richard Alli Sup, ChPo

Frankz, Thomas Alli

Franquet, Louis OxCan

Franquiz, Jose A 1906- PueRA

Fransella, Fay ConAu 25

Frants, Milton Newberry 1854- AnMV 1926

Frantz, Charles 1925- ConAu 5R

Frantz, George Arthur 1890?- IndAu 1917

Frantz, Joe Bertram 1917- AmA&B, ConAu 1R

Frantz, Virginia J Alli Sup, BiDSA

Franul VonWeissenthurn, Johanna 1773-1845 BiD&SB

Franz II 1768-1835 OxGer

Franz Ferdinand, Erzherzog 1863-1914 OxGer

Franz Joseph, Kaiser 1830-1916 OxGer

Franz I, Kaiser 1708-1765 OxGer

Franz, Shepherd Ivory 1874-1933 DcNAA

Franz, Willis Walton ChPo S1

Franz-Walsh, Joseph ChPo

Franzblau, Abraham N 1901- ConAu 29

Franzblau, Rose N 1905- ConAu 29

Franzen, Carl Gustave Frederick 1886-1966 IndAu 1917

Franzen, Frans Michael 1772-1847 BiD&SB

Franzen, Franz Michael 1772-1847 CasWL, DcEuL

Franzen, Gosta Knut 1906- ConAu 41

Franzen, Lavern G 1926- ConAu 61

Franzen, Nils-Olof 1916- ConAu 29, SmATA 10

Franzero, Carlo Maria 1892- ConAu 1R

Franzius, Enno 1901- ConAu 25, WrD 1976

Franzmann, Martin Hans 1907- ConAu 1R, WrD 1976

Franzos, Karl Emil 1848-1904 BiD&SB, EuA, EvEuW, OxGer

Franzwa, Gregory M 1926- ConAu 23

Frapan, Ilse 1852- BiD&SB

Fraprie, Frank Roy 1874- WhWNAA

Fraps, George Stronach 1876- TexWr, WhWNAA

Frasca, John 1916- ConAu 49

Frascatoro, Gerald ConAu XR

Frascino, Edward IlBYP

Frascona, Joseph Lohengrin 1910- ConAu 17R

Frasconi, Antonio 1919- AmA&B, AnCL, AuBYP, ConAu 1R, IlCB 1956, IlCB 1966, SmATA 6, ThBJA, WhGrA

Frase, Larry E 1945- ConAu 41

Frase, Robert W 1912- ConAu 33

Fraser, A Alli Sup, BiDLA

Fraser, Agnes Alli Sup

Fraser, Agnes Maude 1859- OxCan, WhLA

Fraser, Alex ConAu XR

Fraser, Alexander Alli, BiDLA

Fraser, Alexander 1860-1936 AmLY, DcNAA, OxCan

Fraser, Mrs. Alexander Alli Sup

Fraser, Alexander, Baron Saltoun 1820-1886 Alli Sup

Fraser, Alexander A Alli Sup

Fraser, Alexander Campbell 1819-1914 Alli Sup, BiD&SB, BrAu 19, Chmbr 3, DcEnL, OxEng

Fraser, Alexander Thomas Alli Sup

Fraser, Alice M ChPo

Fraser, Allan 1900- Au&Wr, ConAu 57

Fraser, Amy Stewart 1892- ConAu 49, WrD 1976

Fraser, Anne Ermatinger d1930 CanNov, DcNAA, OxCan

Fraser, Anthea 1930- WrD 1976

Fraser, Antonia 1932- WrD 1976

Fraser, Arthur Ronald 1888-1974 ConAu 53

Fraser, Arvonne S 1925- ConAu 33

Fraser, Beatrice AuBYP

Fraser, Betty ChPo S1

Fraser, Betty M 1928- IlBYP, IlCB 1966

Fraser, Blair 1909- ConAu 23, OxCan Sup

Fraser, Cecil Eaton 1895-1947 DcNAA

Fraser, Charles 1782-1860 BiDSA

Fraser, Chelsea Curtis 1876-1954 AmA&B, WhWNAA

Fraser, Claude Lovat 1890-1921 ChPo, ChPo S1, ChPo S2, JBA 1951

Fraser, Colin 1935- ConAu 21

Fraser, Conon 1930- Au&Wr, ConAu P-1,

WrD 1976
Fraser, D *Alli, Alli Sup*
Fraser, Daniel *Alli Sup*
Fraser, Dean 1916- *ConAu 45*
Fraser, Donald 1826-1892 *Alli Sup, BbtC,
DcNAA*
Fraser, Donald 1870- *WhLA*
Fraser, Donald Andrew 1875- *ChPo, ChPo S1,
WhWNAA*
Fraser, Dorothy *ChPo S2*
Fraser, Douglas 1910- *WrD 1976*
Fraser, Douglas Ferrar 1929- *ConAu 1R*
Fraser, E W *ChPo*
Fraser, Edith Emily Rose Oram 1903- *Au&Wr,
ConAu P-1*
Fraser, Edward *ChPo*
Fraser, Elise Parker 1903- *ConAu 1R*
Fraser, Elizabeth *WhWNAA*
Fraser, Ella J *MnBBF*
Fraser, Eric 1902- *IICB 1956*
Fraser, Esther *OxCan Sup*
Fraser, F A *ChPo, ChPo S1, ChPo S2*
Fraser, Ferrin *AuBYP*
Fraser, Frances *OxCan Sup*
Fraser, G G *Alli Sup*
Fraser, G S 1915- *ConP 1970, ConP 1975,
ModBL, Pen Eng, REn, WorAu*
Fraser, George MacDonald 1925- *Au&Wr,
ConAu 45, WrD 1976*
Fraser, George Sutherland 1915- *Au&Wr,
CasWL, ChPo, WrD 1976*
Fraser, Gordon *ChPo*
Fraser, Gordon Holmes 1898- *ConAu P-1*
Fraser, Grace *ChPo*
Fraser, Graham *OxCan Sup*
Fraser, Harry 1937- *WrD 1976*
Fraser, Hastings *Alli Sup*
Fraser, Henry *Alli, BiDLA*
Fraser, Herbert 1890-1953 *OhA&B*
Fraser, Hermia Harris 1902- *OxCan,
WhWNAA*
Fraser, Hugh *Alli Sup*
Fraser, Mrs. Hugh *BiD&SB*
Fraser, Hugh C *Alli Sup*
Fraser, Ian 1897-1974 *ConAu 53, OxCan,
WrD 1976*
Fraser, Ian Watson 1907- *WrD 1976*
Fraser, J T 1923- *ConAu 61*
Fraser, James *Alli, BiDLA, ConAu XR,
WrD 1976*
Fraser, James 1639- *Alli*
Fraser, James 1700-1769 *Alli*
Fraser, James 1818-1885 *Alli Sup*
Fraser, James Baillie 1783-1856 *Alli, Alli Sup,
BiD&SB, Chmbr 2, DcEnL, NewC*
Fraser, James Chalmers Dean 1850- *Alli Sup,
ChPo S1*
Fraser, Jane *ConAu 57, WrD 1976*
Fraser, Janet Hobhouse *ConAu 57*
Fraser, John *Alli, Alli Sup, ChPo, OxCan,
OxCan Sup*
Fraser, John 1745-1819 *Alli*
Fraser, John 1820-1899 *DcNAA*
Fraser, John 1931- *ConAu 29*
Fraser, John A 1838-1878 *ChPo S1*
Fraser, Sir John Foster 1868- *WhLA*
Fraser, John W 1840?- *ChPo, ChPo S2*
Fraser, Joshua *Alli Sup, OxCan*
Fraser, Kathleen 1937- *ConP 1970,
DrAP 1975*
Fraser, Lennox *ChPo S2*
Fraser, Lydia Falconer d1876 *ChPo S1*
Fraser, Malcolm d1815 *BbtC*
Fraser, Mary L *OxCan*
Fraser, Maxwell *Au&Wr*
Fraser, Morris 1941- *WrD 1976*
Fraser, Neil McCormick 1902- *ConAu 5R*
Fraser, Norman *Alli Sup*
Fraser, Olive *ChPo S2*
Fraser, P M *ChPo S2*
Fraser, Patrick *Alli, Alli Sup*
Fraser, Lord Patrick 1819-1880 *Alli Sup*
Fraser, Patrick Allan *Alli Sup*
Fraser, Peter 1928- *WrD 1976*
Fraser, Peter 1932- *ConAu 33*
Fraser, R *Alli*
Fraser, Robert *Alli, BiDLA*
Fraser, Robert S *ChPo S1*

Fraser, Robert William 1810-1876 *Alli,
Alli Sup*
Fraser, Ronald 1888-1974 *ConAu XR, LongC*
Fraser, Ronald 1901- *ConAu XR*
Fraser, Russell Alfred 1927- *AmA&B,
AmA&B, WrD 1976*
Fraser, Shirley *OxCan Sup*
Fraser, Simon *Alli, BiDLA*
Fraser, Simon 1667-1747 *Alli*
Fraser, Simon 1776-1862 *OxCan*
Fraser, Stewart Erskine 1929- *ConAu 13R*
Fraser, Susan *Alli, BiDLA*
Fraser, Sylvia 1935- *ConAu 45*
Fraser, T Mackenzie *Alli Sup*
Fraser, Thomas *Alli*
Fraser, Thomas 1840- *Alli Sup*
Fraser, Thomas Gamble 1807- *Alli Sup*
Fraser, Thomas M'Kenzie 1822- *ChPo S1*
Fraser, Thomas Roderick *Alli Sup*
Fraser, W *Alli, BiDLA*
Fraser, W A *MnBBF*
Fraser, W Alfred *BlkAW*
Fraser, W B 1905- *ConAu 25*
Fraser, W Hamish 1941- *WrD 1976*
Fraser, W Lionel d1965 *ConAu P-1*
Fraser, W W *Alli, BiDLA*
Fraser, Walter Ian Reid 1911- *Au&Wr,
WrD 1976*
Fraser, Wilber John 1869- *WhWNAA*
Fraser, William *ChPo S1*
Fraser, Sir William *Alli Sup*
Fraser, William 1817-1879 *Alli Sup*
Fraser, William 1824-1877 *Alli Sup*
Fraser, William Alexander 1859-1933 *CanNov,
DcNAA, OxCan, WhWNAA*
Fraser, Sir William Augustus 1826-1898
Alli Sup, ChPo, ChPo S1
Fraser, William Henry 1853-1916 *DcNAA*
Fraser, William Henry 1873- *WhWNAA*
Fraser, W H ALSO Frazer, William H
Fraser, William Kaspar 1884-1949 *DcNAA*
Fraser, William Ruxton *Alli Sup*
Fraser Darling, Frank 1903- *Au&Wr,
ConAu 61*
Fraser-Harris, David Fraser 1867- *WhLA*
Fraser Harris, Ida Mary Irene *Au&Wr*
Fraser Harrison, Brian 1918- *Au&Wr,
ConAu P-1*
Fraser-Simson, H *ChPo S1*
Fraser-Tytler, Christina Catherine *ChPo,
ChPo S1*
Frasheri, A *Pen Eur*
Frasheri, M *Pen Eur*
Frasheri, N *Pen Eur*
Frasheri, S *Pen Eur*
Frasier, George Willard 1890- *WhWNAA*
Frasier, James E 1923- *ConAu 17R*
Frasier, Scottie McKenzie *AnMV 1926,
WhWNAA*
Frassanito, William A 1946- *ConAu 57*
Frastick, Perry *WhWNAA*
Fratcher, William Franklin 1913- *Au&Wr,
ConAu 5R, WrD 1976*
Frater Jocundus *CasWL*
Fratti, Mario 1927- *ConDr, CrCD, ModWD,
WrD 1976*
Frau Aja *OxGer*
Frau Rat *OxGer*
Frauenlob 1250-1318 *BiD&SB, OxGer,
Pen Eur*
Frauenlob, Heinrich VonMeissen 1250-1318
CasWL, EuA
Fraunce, Abraham 1558?-1633? *Alli, BrAu,
CasWL, DcEnL, DcEuL, NewC*
Frautschi, R L 1926- *ConAu 17R*
Fray Justo *PueRA*
Fray Mocho *Pen Am*
Fraydas, Stan 1918- *ConAu 57*
Frayer, Ihna Thayer 1873- *OhA&B*
Frayn, Michael 1933- *Au&Wr, ConAu 5R,
ConDr, ConNov 1972, ConNov 1976,
ModBL Sup, NewC, WorAu, WrD 1976*
Frayssinous, Denis De 1765-1841 *OxFr*
Frazar, Douglas 1836-1896 *Alli Sup, CarSB,
DcAmA, DcNAA*
Frazee, Charles A 1929- *ConAu 37,
WrD 1976*
Frazee, Charles Stephen 1909- *Au&Wr*

Frazee, George 1821-1904 *DcNAA*
Frazee, John 1790-1852 *OxAm*
Frazee, Louis Jacob 1819-1905 *DcNAA*
Frazee, Steve 1909- *ConAu 5R*
Frazee-Bower, Helen 1896- *ChPo, ChPo S1*
Frazee-Wheeler, Nahda *ChPo*
Frazer, Mrs. *Alli*
Frazer, Alex *Alli*
Frazer, Andrew *AuBYP, ConAu XR,
WrD 1976*
Frazer, Daniel *Alli Sup*
Frazer, Elizabeth d1967 *AmA&B*
Frazer, Ephraim P 1829- *EarAB Sup*
Frazer, J F *Alli Sup*
Frazer, James *Alli*
Frazer, Sir James George 1854-1941 *Alli Sup,
AtlBL, CasWL, Chmbr 3, DcEnA Ap,
DcLEnL, EvLB, LongC, NewC, OxEng,
Pen Eng, REn, TwCA, TwCA Sup,
WebEAL*
Frazer, John *Alli*
Frazer, John DeJean 1813-1852 *PoIre*
Frazer, John Ernest Sullivan 1870- *WhLA*
Frazer, John William 1885- *WhWNAA*
Frazer, Martin *MnBBF*
Frazer, Perry D 1866-1943 *DcNAA*
Frazer, Persifor 1844-1909 *Alli Sup, DcAmA,
DcNAA*
Frazer, R H *MnBBF*
Frazer, R M *MnBBF*
Frazer, Robert Caine *EncM&D*
Frazer, Robert W 1911- *ConAu 17R*
Frazer, S *Alli*
Frazer, William *Alli Sup*
Frazer, William Henry 1873-1953 *AmA&B,
WhWNAA*
Frazer, William J, Jr. 1924- *ConAu 17R*
Frazer, William Robert 1933- *IndAu 1917*
Frazer, William Walter 1899- *IndAu 1917*
Frazer, Winifred Dusenbury 1916- *ConAu 25,
ConAu 13R*
Frazer-Hurst, Douglas 1883- *ConAu P-1*
Frazier, Arthur *WrD 1976*
Frazier, Charles Harrison 1870-1936 *DcNAA*
Frazier, Chester North 1882-1973 *IndAu 1917*
Frazier, Claude A 1920- *ConAu 29*
Frazier, Corinne Reid *WhWNAA*
Frazier, Edward Franklin 1894-1962 *AmA&B*
Frazier, George 1911-1974 *ConAu 25,
ConAu 49*
Frazier, Ida May Hedrick 1860-1943 *OhA&B*
Frazier, Levi, Jr. *BlkAW*
Frazier, Mark *Alli Sup*
Frazier, Max Yergan *BlkAW*
Frazier, Neta Lohnes 1890- *AuBYP,
ConAu 1R, SmATA 7, WhPNW,
WrD 1976*
Frazier, Ruby Primus *BlkAW*
Frazier, Scottie McKenzie *WhWNAA*
Frazier, Thomas R 1931- *ConAu 33*
Frazzini, Al 1890-1963 *AmSCAP 66*
Freake, A *Alli, BiDLA*
Freake, William *Alli*
Fream, W *Alli Sup*
Frear, Emma 1870- *ChPo*
Frearson, John *Alli Sup*
Freas, Lenwood *IlBYP*
Frease, Harry 1865-1953 *OhA&B*
Freberg, Stan 1926- *AmSCAP 66*
Frechette, Annie Thomas Howells 1844-1938
OhA&B
Frechette, Louis Honore 1839-1908 *BbD, BbtC,
BiD&SB, CanWr, CasWL, ChPo,
ChPo S1, DcNAA, OxAm, OxCan, REn,
REnAL*
Freck, Laura Faith 1890- *WhWNAA*
Frede, Richard 1934- *AmA&B*
Fredeman, William E 1928- *ChPo S2,
ConAu 33*
Fredenburgh, Franz A 1906- *ConAu 33*
Freder, Johannes 1510-1562 *OxGer*
Frederic De Ghyvelde 1838-1916 *DcNAA*
Frederic, Harold 1856-1898 *Alli Sup, AmA,
AmA&B, AmWr, BbD, BiD&SB,
CasWL, Chmbr 3, CnDAL, CyWA,
DcAmA, DcBiA, DcEnA Ap, DcLEnL,
DcNAA, EvLB, ModAL, ModAL Sup,*

OxAm, Pen Am, REn, REnAL, WebEAL
Frederic, Henrica　*Alli Sup*
Frederic, Sister M Catherine　*ConAu XR*
Frederick I 1123?-1190　*NewC*
Frederick Barbarossa　*NewC*
Frederick, Der Alte Fritz 1712-1786　*NewC*
Frederick II, Emperor 1194-1250　*CasWL*
Frederick II, King Of Prussia 1712-1786　*CasWL, DcEuL, NewC, REn*
Frederick Stead　*WhWNAA*
Frederick The First　*REn*
Frederick The Great 1712-1786　*NewC, OxFr, REn*
Frederick, Charles　*Alli*
Frederick, Sir Charles　*Alli*
Frederick, Christine 1883-　*WhWNAA*
Frederick, Dick　*ConAu XR*
Frederick, J George　*MnBBF*
Frederick, John　*MnBBF*
Frederick, John H 1896-　*ConAu 1R*
Frederick, John Towner 1893-　*AmA&B*
Frederick, Justus George 1882-　*AmA&B, WhWNAA*
Frederick, Oswald　*ConAu XR*
Frederick, Robert Allen 1928-　*ConAu 45*
Frederick, Robert Wendell 1899-　*IndAu 1917*
Frederick, Walter　*AmLY XR*
Fredericks, Alfred　*ChPo, ChPo S1, ChPo S2, EarAB, EarAB Sup*
Fredericks, Arnold　*AmA&B, AuBYP, DcNAA*
Fredericks, Carlton 1910-　*AuNews 1, ConAu 53*
Fredericks, Frank　*ConAu XR, WrD 1976*
Fredericks, Frohm　*ConAu XR*
Fredericks, L　*Alli Sup*
Fredericks, Marc 1927-　*AmSCAP 66*
Fredericks, Pierce Griffin 1920-　*ConAu 13R*
Fredericks, Vic　*ConAu XR*
Fredericks, William A 1924-　*AmSCAP 66*
Fredericq, Paul 1850-　*BiD&SB*
Frederiksen, Erik Ellegaard 1924-　*WhGrA*
Frederiksen, Johan Ditlev 1848-1926　*DcNAA*
Frederikson, Edna 1904-　*ConAu 49*
Fredet, Peter 1801-1856　*BiDSA, DcAmA, DcNAA*
Fredge, Frederique 1906-　*ConAu 21*
Fredman, Henry John 1927-　*ConAu 29*
Fredricks, Edgar J 1942-　*ConAu 25*
Fredrickson, George M 1934-　*ConAu 17R*
Fredrickson, Olive A 1901-　*ConAu 49*
Fredrickson, Thomas 1928-　*AmSCAP 66*
Fredro, Count Aleksander 1793-1876　*BiD&SB, CasWL, CnThe, EuA, EvEuW, McGWD, Pen Eur, REnWD*
Fredro, Andrzej Maksymilian 1620?-1679　*CasWL*
Fredro, Johann Alexander 1829-1891　*BiD&SB*
Free　*ConAu XR*
Free, Ann Cottrell　*ConAu 9R*
Free, B B　*Alli*
Free, Beckwith Dodwell　*BiDLA*
Free, Edward Elway 1883-1939　*DcNAA*
Free, George D 1863-　*BiDSA*
Free, John　*Alli*
Free, John d1465　*CasWL*
Free, Lloyd A 1908-　*ConAu 13R*
Free, Major Mickey　*HsB&A*
Free, Richard W　*Alli Sup*
Free, William Joseph 1933-　*ConAu 9R*
Free, William Norris 1933-　*ConAu 25*
Free John, Bubba　*WrD 1976*
Free Lance　*ChPo, ChPo S1*
Freebairn, James　*Alli*
Freebetter, Edmund　*AmA&B*
Freeborn, Richard H 1926-　*ConAu 1R*
Freeburg, Victor Oscar 1882-　*WhWNAA*
Freebury, Hugh Allen 1917-　*Au&Wr*
Freed, Alvyn M 1913-　*ConAu 61*
Freed, Arthur 1894-1973　*AmSCAP 66, ConAu 41*
Freed, Isadore 1900-1961　*AmSCAP 66*
Freed, Lewis 1913-　*IndAu 1917*
Freed, Louis Franklin 1903-　*Au&Wr, ConAu 5R*
Freed, Ralph 1907-　*AmSCAP 66*
Freed, Ruth　*AmSCAP 66*

Freed, Walter 1903-　*AmSCAP 66*
Freedberg, Sydney Joseph 1914-　*ConAu 1R, WrD 1976*
Freedgood, Lillian 1911-　*ConAu 13R*
Freedgood, Morton 1912?-　*AuNews 1, EncM&D*
Freedland, Michael 1934-　*ConAu 41, WrD 1976*
Freedley, Angelo Tillinghast 1850-1907　*Alli Sup, DcAmA, DcNAA*
Freedley, Edwin Troxell 1827-1904　*Alli, Alli Sup, DcAmA, DcNAA*
Freedley, George Reynolds 1904-1967　*AmA&B, ConAu 5R*
Freedman, Alfred M 1917-　*ConAu 49*
Freedman, Arthur M 1916-　*ConAu 41*
Freedman, Barnett 1901-　*IlCB 1945, IlCB 1956*
Freedman, Benedict 1919-　*AmA&B, AmNov*
Freedman, Daniel X 1921-　*ConAu 41, IndAu 1917*
Freedman, David Noel 1922-　*ConAu 1R*
Freedman, Florence B　*ChPo S2*
Freedman, Gerald 1927-　*AmSCAP 66*
Freedman, Guy L 1916-　*AmSCAP 66*
Freedman, Leonard 1924-　*ConAu 1R*
Freedman, M David 1938-　*ConAu 41*
Freedman, Marcia K 1922-　*ConAu 25*
Freedman, Maurice 1920-1975　*Au&Wr, ConAu 25, ConAu 61, WrD 1976*
Freedman, Max C 1893-1962　*AmSCAP 66*
Freedman, Mervin Burton 1920-　*ConAu 29, WrD 1976*
Freedman, Morris 1920-　*ConAu 5R*
Freedman, Nancy 1920-　*AmA&B, AmNov, ConAu 45*
Freedman, Robert 1934-　*AmSCAP 66*
Freedman, Robert Owen 1941-　*ConAu 33*
Freedman, Ronald 1917-　*ConAu 9R, WrD 1976*
Freedman, Russell 1929-　*AuBYP, ConAu 17R*
Freedman, Warren 1921-　*ConAu 17R*
Freehill, Maurice F 1915-　*ConAu 5R*
Freehoff, Joseph C 1864-1939　*DcNAA*
Freehoff, William A 1889-　*WhWNAA*
Freeke, William 1663-　*Alli*
Freeland, Carrie J　*Alli Sup*
Freeland, Daniel Niles 1825-1913　*DcNAA*
Freeland, Humphry William 1814-　*Alli Sup*
Freeland, John 1826-1888　*ChPo*
Freeland, John Maxwell 1920-　*Au&Wr, ConAu 13R, WrD 1976*
Freeland, Parker W　*Alli Sup*
Freeland, W H　*Alli*
Freeland, William 1828-1903　*Alli Sup, ChPo, ChPo S1*
Freeley, Austin J 1922-　*ConAu 5R*
Freeling, Nicolas 1927-　*ConAu 49, ConNov 1972, ConNov 1976, EncM&D, TwCW, WorAu, WrD 1976*
Freeman, Mrs.　*NewC*
Freeman, A C　*Alli Sup, ChPo*
Freeman, Mrs. A M　*Alli Sup*
Freeman, Abraham Clark 1843-1911　*DcNAA*
Freeman, Albert DuBois 1850-1943　*OhA&B*
Freeman, Alden 1862-　*AmLY*
Freeman, Alexander　*Alli Sup*
Freeman, Alexander Martin　*WhLA*
Freeman, Alfred S　*MnBBF*
Freeman, Anne Frances 1936-　*ConAu 1R*
Freeman, Annie F　*ChPo, ChPo S1, ChPo S2*
Freeman, Arthur　*ChPo, ChPo S1*
Freeman, Arthur 1938-　*ConAu 1R*
Freeman, Austin 1862-1943　*LongC, TwCA, TwCA Sup*
Freeman, Austin ALSO Freeman, Richard
Freeman, Barbara Constance 1906-　*Au&Wr, WrD 1976*
Freeman, Barnardus 1660-1743　*DcAmA*
Freeman, Bernard 1660-1743　*DcNAA*
Freeman, Bud 1915-　*AmSCAP 66*
Freeman, C Wade 1906-　*ConAu 5R*
Freeman, Carol S 1941-　*BlkAW*
Freeman, Carolyn R　*ChPo*
Freeman, Darlene 1934-　*ConAu 29*
Freeman, David 1922-　*Au&Wr, WrD 1976*
Freeman, David 1945-　*ConDr, OxCan Sup, WrD 1976*

Freeman, David Hugh 1924-　*ConAu 1R*
Freeman, Don 1908-　*AuBYP, BkP, IlCB 1956, IlCB 1966, MorJA*
Freeman, Donald Cary 1938-　*ConAu 53*
Freeman, Donald McKinley 1931-　*ConAu 37*
Freeman, Douglas Southall 1886-1953　*AmA&B, CyWA, OxAm, REn, REnAL, TwCA, TwCA Sup*
Freeman, Miss E　*MnBBF*
Freeman, Edward Augustus 1823-1892　*Alli, Alli Sup, BbD, BiD&SB, BrAu 19, CasWL, ChPo, ChPo S1, Chmbr 3, DcEnA, DcEnL, EvLB, NewC, OxEng, Pen Eng*
Freeman, Ella Vilosa　*TexWr*
Freeman, Ernest 1922-　*AmSCAP 66*
Freeman, Eugene　*AuBYP*
Freeman, Eugene 1906-　*ConAu 41*
Freeman, Francis　*Alli*
Freeman, Frank　*AmLY XR*
Freeman, Frank E 1908-　*IndAu 1917*
Freeman, Frank Nugent 1880-　*WhWNAA*
Freeman, Frederick 1800-1883　*Alli Sup, DcAmA, DcNAA*
Freeman, G　*Alli*
Freeman, G L 1904-　*ChPo, ConAu 13R*
Freeman, Gage Earle　*Alli Sup, ChPo S2*
Freeman, George　*Alli*
Freeman, George D 1937-　*AmSCAP 66*
Freeman, Gilbert 1893-　*WhWNAA*
Freeman, Gillian 1929-　*Au&Wr, ConAu 5R, ConNov 1972, ConNov 1976, WrD 1976*
Freeman, Godfrey　*AuBYP*
Freeman, Goodlove　*Alli*
Freeman, H W　*Alli Sup*
Freeman, Harold Webber 1899-　*Au&Wr, LongC, TwCA, TwCA Sup*
Freeman, Harriet Augusta　*Alli*
Freeman, Harriot Augusta　*BiDLA*
Freeman, Harrop A 1907-　*ConAu 13R*
Freeman, Harry Lawrence　*BlkAW*
Freeman, Henry　*Alli Sup*
Freeman, Henry Stanhope　*Alli Sup*
Freeman, Howard E 1929-　*ConAu 5R*
Freeman, Ira Henry 1906-　*ConAu P-1*
Freeman, Ira Maximilian 1905-　*AmA&B, AuBYP, MorJA*
Freeman, Irene　*TexWr*
Freeman, Ireneus　*Alli*
Freeman, J J　*Alli*
Freeman, Jack　*MnBBF*
Freeman, James 1759-1835　*Alli, DcAmA*
Freeman, James Dillet 1912-　*ChPo S1, ConAu 17R*
Freeman, James Edward 1866-1943　*AmLY, DcNAA, WhWNAA*
Freeman, James Edwards 1808-1884　*Alli Sup, AmA, DcNAA*
Freeman, James Midwinter 1827-1900　*Alli Sup, DcAmA, DcNAA*
Freeman, Jean Todd 1929-　*ConAu 25*
Freeman, Jessie Reed 1883-　*IndAu 1917*
Freeman, Jo 1945-　*ConAu 61*
Freeman, John　*Alli, Alli Sup, BiDLA*
Freeman, John 1880-1929　*ChPo, ChPo S2, DcLEnL, EvLB, LongC, ModBL, NewC, Pen Eng, TwCA*
Freeman, Mrs. John　*MnBBF*
Freeman, John Albert 1920-　*BiDPar*
Freeman, John Crosby 1941-　*ConAu 13R*
Freeman, John D　*Alli*
Freeman, John D, Jr. 1884-　*WhWNAA*
Freeman, John Henry Gordon 1903-　*MnBBF*
Freeman, Joseph 1897-1965　*AmA&B, AmNov, OxAm, TwCA, TwCA Sup*
Freeman, Joseph Elisha　*Alli, Alli Sup*
Freeman, Joseph John　*Alli Sup*
Freeman, Joshua　*Alli*
Freeman, Josiah Bumstead 1826-　*Alli*
Freeman, Julia Deane　*Alli Sup, AmA&B, ChPo, DcNAA*
Freeman, Julia Susan Wheelock 1833-1900　*Alli Sup, OhA&B*
Freeman, Kathleen 1879-1959　*LongC, WhLA*
Freeman, Kennet　*Alli*
Freeman, Larry　*ConAu XR*
Freeman, Lawrence 1906-　*AmSCAP 66*
Freeman, Leonard 1860-　*WhWNAA*

Freeman, Lewis Ransome 1878- *AmA&B, MnBBF, OxCan, WhWNAA*
Freeman, Lorrain *BlkAW*
Freeman, Lucy 1916- *AmA&B, ConAu 5R, WrD 1976*
Freeman, Lydia 1907- *MorJA*
Freeman, Lyon *Alli*
Freeman, Madeline A *OxCan Sup*
Freeman, Mae Blacker 1907- *MorJA*
Freeman, Margaret 1893- *ChPo, ConICB, IlCB 1945*
Freeman, Margaret B 1905- *AmA&B*
Freeman, Margaret C 1913- *ConAu 57*
Freeman, Margaret N 1915- *ConAu 9R*
Freeman, Marilla Waite *BiDSA*
Freeman, Martin J 1899- *OhA&B*
Freeman, Mary E Wilkins 1852-1930 *AmA&B, AmLY, CarSB, CasWL, ChPo, ChPo S1, ChPo S2, CnDAL, ConAmL, DcAmA, DcEnA Ap, DcLEnL, DcNAA, LongC, OxAm, OxEng, Pen Am, REn, REnAL, TwCA*
Freeman, Nathaniel Chapman *ChPo S2*
Freeman, Ned 1895- *AmSCAP 66*
Freeman, Norman L *Alli Sup*
Freeman, Patriot *PoIre*
Freeman, Philip 1818-1875 *Alli Sup*
Freeman, R *Alli*
Freeman, R T *Alli Sup*
Freeman, Richard *Alli*
Freeman, Richard Austin 1862-1943 *EncM&D, EvLB, NewC, REn, TwCA, TwCA Sup*
Freeman, Richard ALSO Freeman, Austin
Freeman, Richard Borden 1908- *ConAu 1R, WrD 1976*
Freeman, Richard S *Alli Sup*
Freeman, Robert 1878-1940 *ChPo S2, DcNAA, WhWNAA*
Freeman, Roger A 1904- *ConAu 25, WrD 1976*
Freeman, Rosemary 1913- *Au&Wr*
Freeman, Russell 1926- *AmSCAP 66*
Freeman, Ruth B 1906- *ConAu 41*
Freeman, Ruth L Sunderlin 1907- *ChPo S1, ConAu P-1*
Freeman, S *Alli, BiDLA*
Freeman, Samuel *Alli*
Freeman, Samuel 1743-1831 *Alli, DcAmA, DcNAA*
Freeman, Serge Herbert *AuBYP*
Freeman, Spencer 1892- *WrD 1976*
Freeman, Stan 1920- *AmSCAP 66*
Freeman, Stephen *Alli*
Freeman, Strickland *Alli, BiDLA*
Freeman, Mrs. T E *Alli Sup*
Freeman, Terence Reginald 1909- *IlCB 1956*
Freeman, Theophilus *Alli, BiDLA*
Freeman, Thomas *WrD 1976*
Freeman, Thomas 1590?- *Alli, DcEnL, EvLB*
Freeman, Thomas Matthew *Alli Sup*
Freeman, Thomas Walter 1908- *Au&Wr, ConAu 5R, WrD 1976*
Freeman, Ticker 1911- *AmSCAP 66*
Freeman, Tom Everman 1898- *TexWr, WhWNAA*
Freeman, W *Alli, BiDLA*
Freeman, Walter 1895-1972 *ConAu 33, ConAu P-1*
Freeman, Ward 1879-1943 *DcNAA*
Freeman, Warren S 1911- *ConAu 5R*
Freeman, William *Alli, ChPo S2, MnBBF*
Freeman, William A 1880- *OhA&B*
Freeman, Winfield 1848-1926 *DcNAA, OhA&B*
Freeman, Winifred Edith 1918- *WrD 1976*
Freeman-Grenville, Greville Stewart P 1918- *ConAu 5R, WrD 1976*
Freeman-Ishill, Rose 1895- *ConAu P-1*
Freeman-Mitford, Algernon Bertram 1837-1916 *NewC*
Freemantle, W R *Alli*
Freemon, Frank R 1938- *ConAu 45*
Freeport, Sir Andrew *BbtC, BiDLA, BiDLA Sup, DcEnL, NewC*
Freer, Adam *Alli*
Freer, Frederick Ashe *Alli Sup*
Freer, George *Alli, BiDLA*
Freer, Mrs. H *Alli Sup*

Freer, Harold Wiley 1906- *ConAu 21*
Freer, Martha Agnes d1939 *AmLY, DcNAA*
Freer, Martha Walker 1822- *DcEnL*
Freer, Mrs. Otto *WhWNAA*
Freer, Paul Caspar 1862-1912 *DcAmA, DcNAA*
Freer, William Thomas *Alli Sup*
Frees, Paul 1920- *AmSCAP 66*
Freese, Andrew 1816-1904 *OhA&B*
Freese, J H *Alli*
Freese, Jacob R 1826-1885 *Alli Sup, DcNAA*
Freese, John Henry *Alli Sup*
Freese, John Wesley 1840-1911 *DcNAA*
Freeston, Mrs. *Alli Sup*
Freeston, Charles Lincoln 1865- *WhLA*
Freeston, J H *Alli, BiDLA*
Freestone, Basil 1910- *Au&Wr*
Freestone, Brian Frank Ernest 1916- *Au&Wr*
Freestrom, Hubert J 1928- *ConAu 37*
Freeth, F *Alli Sup*
Freeth, John d1808 *BiDLA, BiDLA Sup*
Freeth, Lizzie A *Alli Sup*
Freeze, John Gosse 1825-1913 *DcNAA*
Fregault, Guy 1918- *CanWr, OxCan, OxCan Sup*
Fregly, Bert 1922- *ConAu 57*
Fregoso, Federico 1480-1541 *REn*
Freher, Philip *Alli*
Frei, Gebhard 1905- *BiDPar*
Freiberg, Albert Henry 1868- *WhWNAA*
Freiberg, Heinrich Von *OxGer*
Freid, Jacob 1913- *ConAu 1R*
Freidank *CasWL, DcEuL, OxGer*
Freidel, Frank Burt, Jr. 1916- *AmA&B, ConAu 1R*
Freides, Thelma K 1930- *ConAu 49*
Freidin, Seymour Kenneth 1917- *AmA&B, ConAu 1R*
Freidson, Eliot 1923- *ConAu 5R*
Freihofer, Lois Diane 1933- *ConAu 13R*
Freilich, Joan S 1941- *ConAu 57*
Freilich, Morris 1928- *ConAu 37*
Freiligrath, Ferdinand 1810-1876 *BbD, BiD&SB, ChPo S1, EuA, OxGer, REn*
Freiligrath, Hermann Ferdinand 1810-1876 *CasWL, DcEuL, EvEuW, Pen Eur*
Freiligrath-Kroeker *Alli Sup*
Freind, John 1675-1728 *Alli*
Freind, Robert 1667-1751 *Alli*
Freind, William *Alli*
Freinkel, Edna 1932- *Au&Wr*
Freire, Albuquerque 1935?- *AfA 1*
Freire-Maia, Newton 1918- *ConAu 29*
Freischutz *REn*
Freisler, Roland 1893-1945 *OxGer*
Freitag, George 1909- *OhA&B*
Freitag, Joseph Kendall *DcAmA*
Freitas, Margarete Elisabeth 1927- *ConAu 45*
Freitas, Richard 1915- *AmSCAP 66*
Freixedo, Salvador 1923- *ConAu 29*
Freize, James *Alli*
Freke, Edmund *Alli*
Freke, Henry *Alli Sup*
Freke, John *Alli*
Freke, Thomas *Alli*
Freke, William *Alli*
Freligh, Martin 1813-1889 *Alli, Alli Sup, DcNAA*
Frelinghuysen, Theodore 1787-1862 *CyAL 1, CyAL 2*
Frelinghuysen, Theodore 1787-1862 *CyAL 1, CyAL 2*
Fremantle, Anne 1910- *AmA&B, BkC 5, CatA 1952, ConAu 13R, LongC, REnAL, TwCA Sup*
Fremantle, Arthur James Lyon 1835- *Alli Sup*
Fremantle, William Henry 1831- *Alli Sup*
Fremantle, William Robert *Alli Sup*
Fremgen, James Morgan 1933- *ConAu 17R, WrD 1976*
Fremlin, Celia 1914- *AmA&B, Au&Wr, ConAu XR, WrD 1976*
Fremlin, R *Alli Sup*
Fremlin, Victor *MnBBF*
Fremont, Anne A *Alli Sup*
Fremont, Donatien 1881-1967 *OxCan, OxCan Sup*
Fremont, Jessie Benton 1824-1902 *Alli Sup, AmA, AmA&B, BiD&SB, BiDSA, DcAmA, DcNAA*

Fremont, John Charles 1813-1890 *Alli, Alli Sup, AmA, AmA&B, BbD, BiD&SB, BiDSA, CyAL 2, DcAmA, DcNAA, OxAm, REn, REnAL*
Fremont, Mrs. John Charles *AmA&B*
Fremont, Philip Richard *Alli*
Fremont, W B *ConAu XR*
Fremstad, Olive 1871-1951 *REn*
Frenaud, Andre 1907- *WorAu*
French *Alli*
French, Mrs. A M *Alli Sup*
French, Alfred 1916- *WrD 1976*
French, Alfred J *Alli Sup*
French, Alice 1850-1934 *Alli Sup, AmA, AmA&B, AmLY, BbD, BiD&SB, BiDSA, CarSB, DcAmA, DcNAA, LongC, OxAm, REn, REnAL*
French, Allen 1870-1946 *AmA&B, CarSB, ChPo, DcAmA, JBA 1934, JBA 1951, MnBBF, REnAL, YABC 1*
French, Alvah P 1867-1927 *DcNAA*
French, Anne Warner 1869-1913 *AmA&B, DcNAA*
French, Arthur Willard 1868- *WhWNAA*
French, Asel Belden 1838- *OhA&B*
French, Austa Malinda 1810-1880 *DcNAA*
French, Benjamin Franklin 1799-1877 *Alli, BiDSA, CyAL 2, DcAmA, DcNAA*
French, Burton Lee 1875-1954 *IndAu 1917*
French, Calvin L 1934- *ConAu 53*
French, Caroline *WhWNAA*
French, Charles E 1923- *ConAu 45*
French, Charles Sheldon 1855-1914 *ChPo S1, DcNAA*
French, Charles Wallace 1858-1920 *DcNAA*
French, Daniel *Alli, BiDLA, PoIre*
French, Daniel Chester 1850-1931 *OxAm, REnAL*
French, David *Alli, DrAP 1975, OxCan Sup*
French, Donald Graham *ChPo S1, OxCan*
French, Doris *OxCan Sup*
French, Dorothy Kayser 1926- *AuBYP, ConAu 9R, SmATA 5*
French, Edward L 1916- *ConAu 21*
French, Edwin M C 1870- *WhWNAA*
French, Elizabeth Wilmshurst *Alli Sup*
French, Elsie Janet 1861-1952 *OhA&B*
French, Ferdinand Courtney 1861-1927 *DcAmA, DcNAA*
French, Fiona 1944- *ConAu 29, SmATA 6*
French, Frances-Jane 1929- *Au&Wr*
French, Frank 1850-1933 *ChPo*
French, Frank John 1919- *Au&Wr*
French, G *Alli*
French, Gary *DrAP 1975*
French, George *Alli, Alli Sup*
French, George 1853-1935 *DcNAA*
French, George Hazen 1841-1935 *Alli Sup, DcNAA*
French, George Russell 1803-1881 *Alli, Alli Sup*
French, Gerald 1883- *Au&Wr*
French, Gilbert James 1804-1866 *Alli, Alli Sup*
French, Giles Leory 1894- *WhPNW*
French, Goldwin *OxCan*
French, H *ChPo, ChPo S2*
French, Henry Flagg 1813-1885 *Alli Sup, DcNAA*
French, Henry Willard 1854?- *Alli Sup, BiD&SB, DcAmA, DcNAA*
French, Herbert 1875- *WhLA*
French, Herbert E 1912- *ConAu 45*
French, Herbert Greer 1872-1942 *OhA&B*
French, Hollis 1868-1940 *DcNAA*
French, James Bogle *Alli*
French, James Branwhite *Alli Sup*
French, James Clark And Carey, Edward *Alli Sup*
French, James Edgar *BlkAW*
French, James Murphy *PoIre*
French, James Strange 1807-1886 *DcNAA*
French, John 1616-1657 *Alli*
French, John Calvin 1875- *WhWNAA*
French, John Homer 1824-1888 *DcNAA*
French, John McLean 1863-1940 *DcNAA*
French, John William 1809?-1871 *Alli Sup, DcAmA, DcNAA*
French, Jonathan 1740-1809 *Alli*

French, Joseph Lewis 1858-1936 *AmA&B,*
DcAmA, DcNAA
French, Joseph Milton 1895-1962 *AmA&B*
French, Kathryn *ConAu XR*
French, Lillie Hamilton 1854-1939 *AmA&B,*
DcAmA, DcNAA
French, Lucy Virginia 1830?-1881 *Alli Sup,*
AmA, AmA&B, BiD&SB, BiDSA,
ChPo S2, DcAmA, DcNAA, LivFWS
French, Miss M *Alli Sup*
French, Maida Parlow *OxCan*
French, Marion Flood 1920- *AuBYP,*
ConAu 33
French, Marion Leone 1899- *ChPo S1*
French, Matthew *Alli*
French, Maxwell *ChPo S2*
French, Nathaniel Stowers 1854-1905 *DcNAA*
French, Nicholas *Alli*
French, Nora May d1907 *ChPo S2*
French, Paul *AmA&B, AuBYP, ConAu XR,*
LongC, SmATA 1, ThBJA
French, Peter 1918- *Au&Wr, ConAu 1R*
French, Peter A 1942- *ConAu 45*
French, R B D 1904- *ConAu 25*
French, R N *Alli, BiDLA, PoIre*
French, Richard H *Alli Sup, PoIre*
French, Richard Valpy *Alli Sup*
French, Robert *Alli Sup*
French, Robert Jackson *Alli Sup*
French, Robert Warren 1911- *IndAu 1917*
French, Samuel *ChPo S1*
French, Samuel G 1818- *BiDSA*
French, Scott Robert 1948- *ConAu 57*
French, Susan *ChPo S2*
French, Thomas Ewing 1871-1944 *DcNAA*
French, Thomas Valpy *Alli Sup*
French, W H *Alli Sup*
French, W R *Alli Sup*
French, Warren G 1922- *ConAu 1R,*
WrD 1976
French, William *Alli, OxCan Sup*
French, William d1849 *Alli*
French, William Henry 1815-1881 *Alli Sup,*
DcAmA, DcNAA
French, William M 1817-1886 *IndAu 1816*
French, William Marshall 1907- *ConAu P-1*
French, William Percy 1854-1920 *ChPo S1,*
PoIre
Frend, A *ConAu XR*
Frend, H T, And T H Ware *Alli*
Frend, Henry Tyrwhitt 1819- *Alli Sup*
Frend, William 1757-1841 *Alli, BiDLA,*
NewC
Frend, William Hugh Clifford 1916- *Au&Wr,*
ConAu 21, WrD 1976
Frende, Gabriel *Alli*
Freneau, Peter d1813 *Alli, CyAL 1*
Freneau, Philip 1752-1832 *Alli, AmA,*
AmA&B, AtlBL, BiD&SB, CasWL,
ChPo, ChPo S1, Chmbr 3, CnDAL,
CriT 1, CyAL 1, CyWA, DcAmA,
DcLEnL, DcNAA, EvLB, MouLC 3,
OxAm, OxEng, Pen Am, REn, REnAL,
WebEAL
Frenkel, Richard E 1924- *ConAu 21*
Frenkiel, Zygmunt 1902- *Au&Wr*
Frenssen, Gustav 1863-1945 *ClDMEuL,*
EncWL, EvEuW, OxGer, TwCA,
TwCA Sup
Frenz, Horst 1912- *ConAu 29, IndAu 1917*
Frenzel, Karl Wilhelm 1827-1914 *BiD&SB,*
OxGer
Frenzeny, F *ChPo*
Frenzeny, Paul *EarAB Sup*
Frere, A F *Alli Sup, ChPo S1*
Frere, Alice M *Alli Sup*
Frere, B *Alli, BiDLA*
Frere, Charles *Alli, Alli Sup*
Frere, Elizabeth *Alli Sup*
Frere, Emile 1917- *ConAu 41*
Frere, Emily Temple *Alli Sup*
Frere, Sir Henry Bartle Edward 1815-1884
Alli Sup
Frere, James Arnold 1920- *Au&Wr,*
ConAu 5R
Frere, James Hatley *Alli, BiDLA Sup*
Frere, John Alexander *Alli Sup*
Frere, John Hookham 1769-1846 *Alli, BbD,*

BiD&SB, BrAu 19, CasWL, ChPo,
ChPo S1, ChPo S2, Chmbr 2, DcEnL,
DcEuL, EvLB, NewC, OxEng, Pen Eng,
REn, WebEAL
Frere, Mary *Alli Sup*
Frere, Paul 1917- *Au&Wr, ConAu 5R*
Frere, Sheppard 1916- *ConAu 21*
Frere, Thomas *Alli Sup*
Frere-Cook, Gervis 1928- *WrD 1976*
Freret, Nicolas 1688-1749 *OxFr*
Frerichs, A C 1910- *ConAu 25*
Freron, Elie Catherine 1718-1776 *DcEuL, OxFr,*
Pen Eur
Freschet, Berniece 1927- *ConAu 17R*
Frescobaldi, Dino 1270?-1316? *CasWL, EuA*
Frescobaldi, Girolamo 1583-1643 *AtlBL*
Frescobaldi, Leonardo 1350?-1420? *CasWL,*
EvEuW
Frescobaldi, Matteo 1297?-1348 *CasWL, EuA*
Frese, Dolores Warwick 1936- *ConAu 5R*
Frese, Jakob 1690?-1729 *CasWL, DcEuL*
Frese, James *Alli*
Fresenus, Fritz *CasWL*
Freshfield, Douglas William 1845- *Alli Sup*
Freshfield, Mrs. Henry *Alli Sup*
Freshman, Charles 1819-1875 *BbtC, DcNAA*
Freshwater, Douglas Hope 1876- *WhLA*
Fressant, Hermann *OxGer*
Fresselicque, John *Alli*
Freston, A *Alli, BiDLA*
Fretageot, Nora Chadwick 1858-1937
IndAu 1917
Fretheim, Terence E 1936- *ConAu 25*
Fretwell, Elbert Kirtley 1878- *WhWNAA*
Fretwell, Stephen DeWitt 1942- *ConAu 53*
Freuchen, Lorentz Peter Elfred 1886-1957
CasWL, EvEuW
Freuchen, Peter 1886-1957 *AuBYP, Pen Eur,*
TwCA, TwCA Sup
Freud, Anna 1895- *Au&Wr, WrD 1976*
Freud, Sigmund 1856-1939 *AtlBL, BiDPar,*
CasWL, ChPo S2, CyWA, EncWL,
EncWL Sup, LongC, NewC, OxGer,
Pen Eur, RCom, REn, TwCA,
TwCA Sup, TwCW, WhLA, WhTwL
Freudenberger, Herman 1922- *ConAu 13R,*
WrD 1976
Freudenheim, Yehoshua 1894- *ConAu 21*
Freudenthal, Hans 1905- *ConAu 25*
Freudenthal, Josef 1903-1964 *AmSCAP 66*
Freugon, Ruby *EncM&D*
Freund, E Hans 1905- *ConAu 1R*
Freund, Ernst 1864-1932 *DcNAA*
Freund, Gerald 1930- *ConAu 1R*
Freund, Gisele 1912- *ConAu 49*
Freund, John Christian *Alli Sup*
Freund, John E 1921- *ConAu 13R*
Freund, Paul A 1908- *ConAu 1R*
Freund, Philip 1909- *AmA&B, AmNov,*
ConAu 13R, WhWNAA, WrD 1976
Freund, Rudolf 1915- *IlBYP, IlCB 1945,*
IlCB 1957
Freundlich, August L 1924- *ConAu 49*
Freval, John Baptist De *Alli*
Frewen, Accepted *Alli*
Frewen, Hugh Moreton 1853- *ChPo, ChPo S1*
Frewen, John *Alli, Alli Sup*
Frewen, Moreton *Alli Sup*
Frewen, Thomas *Alli, Alli Sup*
Frewer, Ellen Elizabeth *Alli Sup*
Frewer, Glyn Mervyn Louis 1931- *Au&Wr,*
AuBYP, ConAu 13R, WrD 1976
Frewin, Leslie 1917- *Au&Wr, ConAu 5R*
Frewin, Leslie 1920- *WrD 1976*
Frewin, Richard, And William Sims *Alli*
Frey, Adolf 1855-1920 *BiD&SB, OxGer*
Frey, Albert Romer 1858-1926 *Alli Sup,*
DcAmA, DcNAA
Frey, Erich A 1931- *ConAu 45*
Frey, Frederick Ward 1929- *ConAu 53*
Frey, Friedrich Hermann *BiD&SB*
Frey, Helen Virginia *ChPo*
Frey, Henry A 1923- *ConAu 33*
Frey, Hugo 1873-1952 *AmSCAP 66*
Frey, Jakob 1500?-1562? *CasWL, OxGer*
Frey, Jakob 1824-1875 *BiD&SB, OxGer*
Frey, John Philip 1871-1957 *OhA&B*
Frey, John Philip 1871- *WhWNAA*

Frey, Joseph Samuel Christian Frederick
1771?-1850 *Alli, BiDLA, DcAmA, DcNAA*
Frey, Leonard H 1927- *ConAu 29*
Frey, Marlys 1931- *ConAu 25*
Frey, Shaney *AuBYP*
Frey, Sidney 1920- *AmSCAP 66*
Freybe, Heidi Huberta *EncM&D*
Freyberg, James *Alli Sup*
Freyer, Dermot *ChPo S2, PoIre*
Freyer, Frederic *ConAu XR, EncM&D,*
WrD 1976
Freyer, P Johnson *Alli Sup*
Freylinghausen, Johann Anastasius 1670-1739
BbD, BiD&SB, OxGer
Freyre *DcSpL*
Freyre, Gilberto DeMello 1900- *CasWL,*
EncWL Sup, Pen Am, REn, TwCW,
WorAu
Freytag, Gustav 1816-1895 *BbD, BiD&SB,*
CasWL, ClDMEuL, CyWA, DcBiA,
DcEuL, EuA, EvEuW, McGWD, OxGer,
Pen Eur, REn, REnWD
Frezzi, Federico 1346?-1416 *CasWL*
Friang, Brigitte Elizabeth 1924- *Au&Wr*
Friar, Kimon 1911- *AmA&B, WorAu*
Friar Bungay *NewC*
Frias, Duque De *CasWL*
Frias, Heriberto 1870-1928 *Pen Am*
Fribourg, Marjorie G 1920- *AuBYP,*
ConAu 1R
Fric, Joseph Vaclav 1829-1890 *BiD&SB*
Fricero, Kate *ChPo S1*
Friche, V F 1870-1929 *DcRusL*
Friche, Vladimir Maximovich 1870-1929
CasWL
Frick, C H *ConAu XR, SmATA 6,*
WrD 1976
Frick, Charles *Alli*
Frick, Charles 1823-1860 *DcNAA*
Frick, Constance *ConAu XR, SmATA 6*
Frick, George *Alli*
Frick, George 1793-1870 *DcNAA*
Frick, George F 1925- *ConAu 13R*
Frick, Harvey Lee 1906- *BiDPar*
Frick, Minnie DeMotte *WhWNAA*
Frick, William *Alli*
Frick, William Keller 1850-1918 *DcNAA*
Fricke, Cedric V 1928- *ConAu 13R*
Fricker, Anne *Alli Sup*
Fricker, H W *Alli Sup*
Fricks, Richard *DrAP 1975*
Frida, Emil *EuA*
Friday, David 1876-1945 *DcNAA, WhWNAA*
Fridegard, Jan 1897-1968 *CasWL, Pen Eur*
Fridegard, Johan Fridolf 1897- *EncWL*
Fridegode *BiB S*
Fridegorde *Alli*
Fridge, Susie *TexWr*
Fridjonsson, Guomundur 1869-1944 *EncWL*
Fridthjof Of Okland *WhLA*
Fridy, Wallace 1910- *ConAu 1R*
Fridy, William Wallace 1910- *WrD 1976*
Friebert, Stuart *DrAP 1975*
Fried, Barbara 1924- *ConAu 45*
Fried, Charles 1935- *ConAu 29*
Fried, Eleanor L 1913- *ConAu 29*
Fried, Erich 1921- *ModGL, OxGer, Pen Eur,*
WorAu
Fried, Gerald 1928- *AmSCAP 66*
Fried, John J 1940- *ConAu 33*
Fried, Joseph P 1939- *ConAu 37, WrD 1976*
Fried, Martin *AmSCAP 66*
Fried, Morton H 1923- *ConAu 21*
Fried, William 1945- *ConAu 57*
Friedan, Betty 1921- *AmA&B, WrD 1976*
Friedberg, Gertrude Tonkonogy *ConAu 21,*
WrD 1976
Friedberg, Martha *DrAP 1975*
Friedberg, Maurice 1929- *ConAu 1R,*
WrD 1976
Friedel, Francis Joseph 1897-1959 *OhA&B*
Friedelbaum, Stanley H 1927- *ConAu 37*
Friedell, Egon 1878-1938 *EncWL, OxGer*
Frieden, Bernard J 1930- *ConAu 13R,*
WrD 1976
Friedenberg, Edgar Z 1921- *AmA&B*
Friedenthal, Richard 1896- *OxGer*
Friedenwald, Harry 1864- *WhWNAA*

Friedenwald, Herbert 1870- *AmLY*
Friedenwald, Julius 1866- *WhWNAA*
Frieder, Emma 1891- *ConAu 33*
Friederich, Matthaus d1559 *OxGer*
Friederich, Werner Paul 1905- *AmA&B,*
  Au&Wr, ConAu 13R
Friederichsen, Kathleen 1910- *ConAu 17R*
Friedheim, Robert L 1934- *ConAu 21*
Friedl, Ernestine 1920- *ConAu 37*
Friedl, John 1945- *ConAu 53*
Friedlaender SEE ALSO Friedlander
Friedlaender, Israel 1876-1920 *DcNAA*
Friedlaender, V Helen *ChPo S2*
Friedland, Abraham Hyman 1892-1939 *OhA&B*
Friedland, Anatole 1881-1938 *AmSCAP 66*
Friedland, David Lionel 1936- *ConP 1970*
Friedland, Ronald Lloyd 1937-1975 *ConAu 33,*
  ConAu 57
Friedland, Seymour 1928- *ConAu 25*
Friedland, William H 1923- *ConAu 13R,*
  WrD 1976
Friedlander SEE ALSO Friedlaender
Friedlander, Der *OxGer*
Friedlander, Albert Hoschander 1927-
  ConAu 23, WrD 1976
Friedlander, Israel 1876-1920 *AmA&B*
Friedlander, Joanne K 1930- *ConAu 61,*
  SmATA 9
Friedlander, Ludwig 1824- *BiD&SB*
Friedlander, Michael 1833- *Alli Sup*
Friedlander, Stanley Lawrence 1938-
  ConAu 17R
Friedlander, V Helen *ChPo, ChPo S1*
Friedlander, Walter A 1891- *ConAu 37,*
  WrD 1976
Friedlander, William Barr 1899- *AmSCAP 66*
Friedman, Alan Warren 1939- *ConAu 25,*
  WrD 1976
Friedman, Albert B 1920- *ConAu 1R*
Friedman, Alice R 1900- *ConAu 41*
Friedman, Arnold P 1909- *ConAu 45*
Friedman, Avner 1932- *ConAu 53*
Friedman, B H 1926- *AmA&B, ConAu 1R,*
  DrAF 1976, WrD 1976
Friedman, Bruce Jay 1930- *AmA&B,*
  ConAu 9R, ConDr, ConLC 3, ConLC 5,
  ConNov 1972, ConNov 1976, DrAF 1976,
  McGWD, ModAL, ModAL Sup, Pen Am,
  RAdv 1, WorAu, WrD 1976
Friedman, Charles 1902- *AmSCAP 66*
Friedman, Edward Ludwig 1903- *ConAu 1R*
Friedman, Elias *WrD 1976*
Friedman, Elisha Michael 1889- *WhWNAA*
Friedman, Emanuel David 1884- *WhWNAA*
Friedman, Estelle Ehrenwald 1920- *AuBYP,*
  ConAu 5R, SmATA 7
Friedman, Eve Rosemary Tibber 1929- *Au&Wr,*
  ConAu 5R
Friedman, Frieda 1905- *MorJA*
Friedman, Ina R 1926- *ConAu 53*
Friedman, Irving 1903- *AmSCAP 66*
Friedman, Irving S 1915- *ConAu 45*
Friedman, Isaac Kahn 1870-1931 *AmA&B,*
  DcAmA, DcNAA
Friedman, Isaiah 1921- *ConAu 53*
Friedman, Jacob Horace 1916- *WrD 1976*
Friedman, Jerry 1938- *AmSCAP 66*
Friedman, John *ConP 1970, WrD 1976*
Friedman, Judi *AuNews 2*
Friedman, Ken *DrAP 1975*
Friedman, Kenneth 1939- *ConAu 25*
Friedman, Lawrence J 1940- *ConAu 53*
Friedman, Lawrence Meir 1930- *ConAu 13R,*
  WrD 1976
Friedman, Lenemaja 1924- *ConAu 61*
Friedman, Leo 1869-1927 *AmSCAP 66*
Friedman, Marcia 1925- *ConAu 57*
Friedman, Maurice Stanley 1921- *ConAu 13R*
Friedman, Melvin J 1928- *ConAu 21,*
  WrD 1976
Friedman, Milton 1912- *AmA&B, Au&Wr,*
  ConAu 1R, WrD 1976
Friedman, Murray 1926- *ConAu 57*
Friedman, Myles I 1924- *ConAu 57*
Friedman, Norman 1925- *ConAu 1R,*
  WrD 1976
Friedman, Paul *DrAF 1976*
Friedman, Paul 1899-1972 *ConAu 37*

Friedman, Richard *DrAP 1975*
Friedman, Richard H 1924-1954 *AmSCAP 66*
Friedman, Rosemary 1929- *WrD 1976*
Friedman, Roslyn Berger 1924- *ConAu 17R*
Friedman, Roy 1934- *ConAu 25*
Friedman, Samuel B 1919- *AmSCAP 66*
Friedman, Sanford *DrAF 1976*
Friedman, Saul S 1937- *ConAu 57*
Friedman, Sol 1920- *AmSCAP 66*
Friedman, Stanleigh P 1884-1961 *AmSCAP 66*
Friedman, Stuart 1913- *ConAu 1R,*
  IndAu 1917
Friedman, William Frederick 1891- *AmA&B*
Friedman, Winifred 1923?-1975 *ConAu 61*
Friedman, Wolfgang Gaston 1907- *Au&Wr*
Friedmann, Alfred 1845- *BiD&SB*
Friedmann, Arnold 1925- *ConAu 41*
Friedmann, Herbert 1900- *AmA&B*
Friedmann, Paul *Alli Sup*
Friedmann, Yohanan 1936- *ConAu 33,*
  WrD 1976
Friedrich III 1415-1493 *OxGer*
Friedrich Christian, Herzog Von A 1765-1814
  OxGer
Friedrich II, Der Grosse 1712-1786 *OxGer*
Friedrich Der Schone 1286?-1330 *OxGer*
Friedrich Der Streitbare 1370-1428 *OxGer*
Friedrich Der Weise 1463-1525 *OxGer*
Friedrich I, Kaiser 1122?-1190 *OxGer*
Friedrich II, Kaiser 1194-1250 *OxGer*
Friedrich III, Kaiser 1831-1888 *OxGer*
Friedrich, Kaiserin *OxGer*
Friedrich Koditz Von Saalfeld *OxGer*
Friedrich I, Konig In Preussen 1657-1713 *OxGer*
Friedrich II, Konig Von Preussen 1712-1786
  OxGer
Friedrich II, Kurfurst Von Brandenberg
  1413-1471 *OxGer*
Friedrich V Von Der Pfalz, Kurfurst 1596-1632
  OxGer
Friedrich Von Hausen d1190 *CasWL, DcEuL,*
  OxGer, Pen Eur
Friedrich Von Leiningen *OxGer*
Friedrich Von Sonnenburg *OxGer, Pen Eur*
Friedrich Wilhelm, Der Grosse Kurfurst
  1620-1688 *OxGer*
Friedrich Wilhelm I, Konig Von P 1688-1740
  OxGer
Friedrich Wilhelm II, Konig Von P 1744-1797
  OxGer
Friedrich Wilhelm III, Konig Von P 1770-1840
  OxGer
Friedrich Wilhelm IV, Konig Von P 1795-1861
  OxGer
Friedrich, Carl Joachim 1901- *AmA&B,*
  Au&Wr
Friedrich, Caspar David 1774-1840 *OxGer*
Friedrich, Friedrich 1828-1890 *BiD&SB*
Friedrich, Kaspar David 1774-1840 *AtlBL*
Friedrich, Otto Alva 1929- *AmA&B,*
  ConAu 5R
Friedrich, Paul 1927- *ConAu 29, WrD 1976*
Friedrich, Ralph 1913- *ChPo, OhA&B*
Friedrichs, Hermann 1854- *BiD&SB*
Friedrichs, Robert W 1923- *ConAu 49*
Friel, Arthur O 1885-1959 *AmA&B,*
  WhWNAA
Friel, Brian 1929- *Au&Wr, CnThe,*
  ConAu 21, ConDr, ConLC 5, McGWD,
  ModBL Sup, ModWD, REnWD, WorAu,
  WrD 1976
Friel, George 1910- *Au&Wr, WrD 1976*
Friel, Henry J *BbtC*
Frielink, A Barend 1917- *ConAu 21*
Friend, Cliff 1893- *AmSCAP 66*
Friend, Ellery *ChPo S1*
Friend, Hilderic *Alli Sup*
Friend, John Albert Newton 1881- *WhLA*
Friend, Joseph H 1909- *ConAu 25*
Friend, Ollivia Byrd *TexWr*
Friend, Oscar Jerome 1897-1963 *AmA&B,*
  AmA&B
Friend, Patrick *MnBBF*
Friend, Robert 1913- *ConAu 13R, WrD 1976*
Friend, Robert C *BlkAW*
Friend, Rose Cathay *Alli Sup*
Friendlich, Dick 1909- *AuBYP, ConAu XR*
Friendlich, Richard J 1909- *ConAu P-1*

Friendly, Aunt *DcAmA*
Friendly, Edwin S 1884- *WhWNAA*
Friendly, Fred W 1915- *AmA&B, ConAu 23*
Frier, David A 1931- *ConAu 29*
Friere, Edsard *WhLA*
Friermood, Elisabeth Hamilton 1903- *AuBYP,*
  ConAu 1R, IndAu 1917, MorJA,
  SmATA 5, WrD 1976
Friers, Rowel Boyd 1920- *IlCB 1956*
Frierson, Henry *Alli*
Fries, Adelaide Lisetta 1871-1949 *AmA&B,*
  BiDSA, DcNAA
Fries, Albert Charles 1908- *ConAu 1R*
Fries, Charles Carpenter 1887- *AmA&B*
Fries, Fritz Rudolf 1935- *ConAu 25*
Fries, J Elias 1876- *WhWNAA*
Fries, Jakob Friedrich 1773-1843 *BiD&SB*
Fries, Robert Francis 1911- *Au&Wr*
Friesen, J W *OxCan Sup*
Friesner, Isidore 1874-1945 *DcNAA*
Friess, Horace Leland 1900-1975 *ConAu 61*
Frieze, Henry Simmons 1817-1889 *Alli Sup,*
  CyAL 2, DcAmA, DcNAA
Friis, Babbis *ConAu XR, SmATA 7, ThBJA*
Friis, Erik Johan 1913- *WrD 1976*
Friis, Jens Andreas 1821-1896 *BiD&SB*
Friis-Baastad, Babbis Ellinor 1921-1970
  ConAu 17R, SmATA 7, ThBJA
Friis Moller, Kai 1888-1960 *CasWL, Pen Eur*
Frijling-Schreuder, E C M 1908- *ConAu 61*
Frik 1230?-1310 *DcOrL 3*
Frikart, Thuringen 1429-1519 *OxGer*
Frillman, Paul W 1911-1972 *ConAu 25,*
  ConAu 37
Friman, Klaus 1746-1829 *BiD&SB*
Friman, Peder Harboe 1752-1839 *BiD&SB*
Frimann, Claus 1746-1829 *DcEuL*
Friml, Rudolf 1879-1972 *AmSCAP 66*
Friml, Rudolph 1879-1972 *ConAu 37*
Friml, William 1921- *AmSCAP 66*
Frimmer, Steven 1928- *ConAu 33*
Frimoth, Lenore B 1927- *ConAu 5R*
Fringo, P *Alli*
Frings, Ketti 1915- *AmA&B, McGWD,*
  OhA&B, OxAm, REnAL
Frings, Manfred S 1925- *ConAu 17R*
Frink, Almira L Corey *ChPo S1*
Frink, Henry Allyn 1844-1898 *DcNAA*
Frink, Henry C *Alli Sup*
Frink, Maurice 1895-1972 *ConAu 25,*
  IndAu 1917
Frinta, Mojmir S 1922- *ConAu 25, WrD 1976*
Friojonsson, Guomundur 1869-1944 *ClDMEuL*
Frisbee, Lucy Post *AuBYP*
Frisbee, Alvah Lillie 1830-1917 *Alli Sup,*
  DcNAA
Frisbie, Barnes *Alli Sup*
Frisbie, H L *ChPo*
Frisbie, Levi 1748-1806 *Alli, DcAmA,*
  DcNAA
Frisbie, Levi 1783?-1822 *Alli, CyAL 1,*
  DcAmA, DcNAA
Frisbie, Louise K 1913- *ConAu 61*
Frisbie, Margery 1923- *ConAu 5R*
Frisbie, Richard P 1926- *ConAu 5R*
Frisbie, Robert Dean 1896-1948 *AmA&B,*
  DcNAA, OhA&B
Frisbie, William Albert 1867- *AmA&B, ChPo,*
  ChPo S1
Frisby, Terence 1932- *ConDr, WrD 1976*
Frisch, Albert T 1916- *ChPo S1*
Frisch, Anthony 1921- *ChPo S1*
Frisch, Billy 1882- *AmSCAP 66*
Frisch, Daniel 1897-1950 *IndAu 1917*
Frisch, Max 1911- *CasWL, CnMD, CnThe,*
  ConLC 3, CrCD, EncWL, EvEuW,
  McGWD, ModGL, ModWD, OxGer,
  Pen Eur, REn, REnWD, TwCW,
  WhTwL, WorAu
Frisch, Morton J 1923- *ConAu 33*
Frisch, Otto Robert 1904- *AuBYP, ConAu 9R,*
  WrD 1976
Frischauer, Willi 1906- *Au&Wr, ConAu 5R*
Frischlin, Nicodemus 1547-1590 *DcEuL,*
  OxGer, Pen Eur
Frischlin, Philipp Nicodemus 1547-1590 *CasWL*
Frishman, David 1862-1922 *CasWL, Pen Eur*

Friskey, Margaret Richards 1901- AuBYP,
ConAu 5R, SmATA 5
Frison, Theodore Henry 1895- WhWNAA
Frison-Roche, Roger 1906- REn
Frissell, Toni ChPo
Frisselle, Frank Monroe 1862-1925 DcNAA
Friswell, James Hain 1825?-1878 Alli Sup,
DcEnL
Friswell, Laura H Alli Sup
Fritchman, Stephen Hole 1902- OhA&B
Frith, Francis Alli Sup
Frith, Gilbert R Alli Sup
Frith, Harold James WrD 1976
Frith, Henry 1840- Alli Sup, CarSB,
ChPo S1, MnBBF
Frith, Miss I Alli Sup
Frith, J Alli Sup
Frith, John Alli
Frith, John d1533 Alli
Frith, Joseph Alli Sup
Frith, Mary 1585?-1660? NewC
Frith, Michael IlBYP
Frith, W Cockayne Alli, BiDLA
Frith, William Alli Sup
Frith, William Powell 1819-1909 Alli Sup,
ChPo
Frithwald d763 BiB S
Fritsch, Albert Joseph 1933- WrD 1976
Fritsch, Charles Theodore 1912- WrD 1976
Fritsch, Felix Eugene 1879- WhLA
Fritsch, William August 1841- IndAu 1816
Fritsche, Vladimir Maximovich CasWL
Fritschel, George John 1867- WhWNAA
Fritschel, Gottfried Leonhard Wilhelm
1836-1889 DcAmA
Fritschler, A Lee 1937- ConAu 33
Fritz ConAu XR, HsB&A, HsB&A Sup
Fritz, Emanuel 1886- WhWNAA
Fritz, Henry E 1927- ConAu 17R
Fritz, Jean Guttery 1915- AuBYP, ChLR 2,
ChPo S2, ConAu 1R, MorBMP,
SmATA 1, ThBJA
Fritz, John 1822-1913 DcNAA
Fritz, John Henry Charles 1874-1953 OhA&B,
WhWNAA
Fritz, Walter Helmut 1929- OxGer
Fritzsch, Gerhard 1924-1969 OxGer
Frizell, Joseph Palmer 1832-1910 DcNAA
Frizell, Martha G Sinks 1893-1956 OhA&B
Frizell, W Alli, BiDLA
Frizell, William Givens 1866-1943 OhA&B
Frizelle, Richard PoIre
Frizzle, Norman 1946- WrD 1976
Frobel, Friedrich 1782-1852 ChPo, ChPo S1,
ChPo S2, OxGer
Frobel, F ALSO Froebel, Friedrich
Froben, Johann 1460-1527 OxGer
Froben, Johannes 1460-1527 DcEuL
Frobenius, Doctor Alli
Frobisher, Joseph Edwin 1847?- Alli Sup,
DcNAA
Frobisher, Sir Martin 1535?-1594 Alli, NewC,
OxCan, REn
Froboess, Harry 1899- ConAu 17
Froding, Gustaf 1860-1911 CasWL, ChPo S1,
ClDMEuL, EuA, EvEuW, Pen Eur, REn
Frodoard NewC
Frodsham, George Horsfall 1863- ChPo S1
Froebel, Friedrich Wilhelm August 1782-1852
BbD, BiD&SB, LongC
Froebel, Julius 1805-1893 BiD&SB
Froeber, Richard R 1929- AmSCAP 66
Froelich, Robert E 1929- ConAu 45
Froggatt, William Alli Sup
Frohlich, Abraham Emanuel 1796-1865
BiD&SB, OxGer
Frohlich, Karl Hermann 1821-1898 BiD&SB
Frohlich, Katharine OxGer
Frohlich, Lorens 1820-1908 ChPo
Frohman, Charles 1860-1915 OxAm, REnAL
Frohman, Charles E 1901- ConAu 29,
WrD 1976
Frohman, Daniel 1851-1940 AmA&B, OhA&B,
OxAm, REnAL
Frohn, John C ChPo, ChPo S1
Frohock, Wilber Merrill 1908- AmA&B,
ConAu 25
Frohschammer, Jakob 1821-1893 BiD&SB

Froiseth, Jennie Anderson Alli Sup
Froissart, Jean 1337?-1410? AtlBL, BbD,
BiD&SB, CasWL, CyWA, DcEuL, EuA,
EvEuW, NewC, OxEng, OxFr, Pen Eur,
REn
Froissart, Sir John 1337?-1410? WhCL
Frokelewe, John De Alli
Frolich, L ChPo S1
Froman, Elizabeth Hull 1920-1975 ConAu 53,
ConAu P-1, SmATA 10
Froman, Lewis A, Jr. 1935- ConAu 5R
Froman, Robert 1917- AuBYP, ConAu 1R,
SmATA 8
Frome, David AmA&B, ConAu XR,
EncM&D, TwCA, TwCA Sup,
WhWNAA
Frome, John Sibree Alli, BiDLA
Frome, Michael 1920- ConAu 1R, WrD 1976
Frome, Samuel Blake Alli, BiDLA
Fromentin, Eugene 1820-1876 BiD&SB,
CasWL, CyWA, DcEuL, EuA, EvEuW,
OxFr, Pen Eur
Fromento, John F Alli
Fromm, Erich 1900- AmA&B, Au&Wr,
Pen Am, REn, REnAL, TwCA Sup,
WhTwL, WrD 1976
Fromm, Erika 1910- ConAu 9R
Fromm, Gary 1933- ConAu 17R
Fromm, Harold 1933- ConAu 23
Fromm, Herbert 1905- AmSCAP 66,
ConAu 49
Fromm, Lilo IlBYP
Frommel, Emil 1828-1896 BiD&SB
Frommenius, Andrew Alli
Fromondus Libertus Alli
Frondizi, Risieri 1910- ConAu 41
Fronius, Hans 1903- WhGrA
Fronsperger, Leonhard 1520?-1575 OxGer
Frontaura, Carlos 1834- BiD&SB
Frontenac, Louis DeBuade, Comte De
1622?-1698 OxAm, OxCan
Frontier, Tex ConAu XR
Frontinus, Sextus Julius 030?-104? BiD&SB,
CasWL, Pen Cl
Fronto, Marcus Cornelius 100?-166? BiD&SB,
CasWL, Pen Cl
Frooks, Dorothy 1899- ConAu 57
Froome, Keith Davy 1921- Au&Wr
Froomkin, Joseph 1927- ConAu 23
Froscher, Wingate 1918- ConAu 1R
Frosini, Pietro 1885-1951 AmSCAP 66
Frost, Mrs. Alli Sup
Frost, Arthur Burdett 1851-1928 AmA&B,
ChPo, ChPo S1, ChPo S2, DcAmA,
DcNAA, OxAm, REnAL, St&VC
Frost, B Alli
Frost, Barbara 1903- AnMV 1926
Frost, Brian Reginald Thomas 1926- Au&Wr
Frost, C Vernon EncM&D, MnBBF
Frost, Charles Alli
Frost, Charles Christopher 1806-1880 DcNAA
Frost, Charles William 1848- ChPo S1
Frost, Conrad MnBBF
Frost, Edwin Brant 1866-1935 DcNAA
Frost, Elizabeth Hollister 1887-1958 AmA&B,
AmNov, ChPo
Frost, Ernest 1918- Au&Wr, ConAu 9R,
WrD 1976
Frost, Frances Mary 1905-1959 AmA&B,
AmNov, BkCL, ChPo, ChPo S1,
ChPo S2, MorJA, REnAL, St&VC,
WhWNAA
Frost, Frederick EncM&D, OxCan
Frost, G Alli Sup
Frost, Gavin 1930- ConAu 45
Frost, Gerhard Emanuel 1909- ConAu P-1
Frost, Grace Ingles ChPo S1
Frost, Harold G 1893-1959 AmSCAP 66
Frost, Helen 1898- ConAu P-1
Frost, Henry Frederic Alli Sup
Frost, Henry W Alli Sup
Frost, Holloway Halstead 1889-1935 DcNAA
Frost, Honor Elizabeth 1918- Au&Wr
Frost, J Alli
Frost, Mrs. J Alli Sup
Frost, James A 1918- ConAu 37
Frost, James Marion 1849-1916 BiDSA,

DcNAA
Frost, Joe L 1933- ConAu 25
Frost, John Alli
Frost, John d1877 Alli Sup
Frost, John 1800-1859 Alli, AmA&B,
DcAmA, DcNAA
Frost, Joni ConAu XR
Frost, Josephine C 1864-1942 DcNAA
Frost, Mrs. L J H Alli Sup
Frost, Lesley ConAu 21
Frost, Leslie Miscampbell 1895-1973 ConAu 41,
OxCan Sup
Frost, Marguerite Scribner 1876-1944 ChPo,
DcNAA
Frost, Marjorie 1914- ConAu 25
Frost, Max Gilbert 1908- Au&Wr, ConAu P-1
Frost, Meigs Oliver 1882- TexWr, WhWNAA
Frost, Percival Alli Sup
Frost, Peter Kip 1936- ConAu 33, WrD 1976
Frost, Quintin Alli
Frost, Rex 1914- Au&Wr, OxCan,
WrD 1976
Frost, Richard d1778 Alli
Frost, Richard 1929- ConAu 33, DrAP 1975,
WrD 1976
Frost, Richard H 1930- ConAu 25
Frost, Richard T 1926-1972 ConAu 37,
ConAu P-1
Frost, Robert 1874?-1963 AmA&B, AmLY,
AmWr, AnCL, AtlBL, CasWL, ChPo,
ChPo S1, ChPo S2, Chmbr 3, CnDAL,
CnE&AP, CnMWL, ConAmA, ConAmL,
ConLC 1, ConLC 3, ConLC 4, CyWA,
DcLEnL, EncWL, EvLB, LongC,
ModAL, ModAL Sup, OxAm, OxEng,
Pen Am, RAdv 1, RCom, REn, REnAL,
SixAP, St&VC, TwCA, TwCA Sup,
TwCW, WebEAL, WhTwL, WhWNAA
Frost, Robert Carlton 1926- ConAu 53
Frost, Russell E 1900- WhWNAA
Frost, S E, Jr. 1899- ConAu 19, WrD 1976
Frost, Sarah Annie 1839?- Alli Sup, DcNAA
Frost, Sarah E A Alli Sup
Frost, Stanley 1881-1942 DcNAA, OhA&B
Frost, Stanley Brice 1913- ConAu 61,
WrD 1976
Frost, Thomas MnBBF
Frost, Thomas 1821-1908 Alli Sup, CarSB
Frost, Thomas Gold 1866-1948 DcNAA
Frost, Timothy Prescott 1850-1937 DcNAA
Frost, W C Alli Sup
Frost, Walter Archer 1876-1964 AmA&B,
WhWNAA
Frost, Wesley 1884- OhA&B
Frost, William 1917- ConAu 41
Frost, William Albert Crawford 1863-
WhWNAA
Frost, William Dodge 1867- WhWNAA
Frost, William Goodell 1854-1938 BiDSA,
DcAmA, DcNAA, WhWNAA
Frost, William Henry 1863-1904? CarSB,
DcNAA
Frostic, Gwen 1906- ChPo S2, ConAu 17R
Frostick, Michael 1917- ConAu 9R
Frothingham, Arthur Lincoln 1859-1923
AmA&B, DcAmA, DcNAA
Frothingham, Ellen 1835-1902 Alli Sup,
DcAmA, DcNAA
Frothingham, Ephraim L And Arthur L
Alli Sup
Frothingham, Eugenia Brooks 1874- AmA&B,
DcAmA
Frothingham, F E Alli Sup
Frothingham, Jessie Peabody 1862-1949
AmA&B, DcAmA, DcNAA
Frothingham, John B Alli Sup
Frothingham, Louis Adams 1871-1928 DcNAA
Frothingham, Nathaniel Langdon 1793-1870 Alli,
AmA&B, BiD&SB, ChPo, ChPo S1,
ChPo S2, CyAL 2, DcAmA, DcNAA
Frothingham, Octavius Brooks 1822-1895
Alli Sup, AmA, AmA&B, BbD, BiD&SB,
DcAmA, DcNAA, OxAm
Frothingham, Paul Revere 1864-1926 AmA&B,
AmLY, DcAmA
Frothingham, Richard 1812-1880 Alli, Alli Sup,
AmA, AmA&B, CyAL 2, DcAmA,
DcNAA

Frothingham, Robert 1865-1937 *AmA&B, DcNAA*
Frothingham, Thomas Goddard 1865-1945 *AmA&B, WhWNAA*
Frothingham, Washington 1822- *Alli Sup, DcAmA, DcNAA*
Froude, James Anthony 1818-1894 *Alli, Alli Sup, AtlBL, BbD, BiD&SB, BrAu 19, CasWL, Chmbr 3, DcEnA, DcEnA Ap, DcEnL, DcEuL, DcLEnL, EvLB, MouLC 4, NewC, OxEng, Pen Eng, REn, WebEAL*
Froude, Richard Hurrell 1803-1836 *Alli, BrAu 19, DcEuL, OxEng*
Froumund Of Tegernsee 960?-1008? *CasWL*
Frowd, E *Alli Sup*
Frowd, J G Pluyer *Alli Sup*
Frowde, Neville *Alli*
Frowde, Philip d1738 *Alli*
Frowen, Stephen Francis 1923- *Au&Wr*
Frowen, Trevor James 1919- *Au&Wr*
Froy, Herald *ConAu XR, WrD 1976*
Froysell, Thomas d1672 *Alli*
Frucht, Phyllis 1936- *ConAu 57*
Fruchtenbaum, Arnold G 1943- *ConAu 61*
Fruchter, Benjamin 1914- *Au&Wr, ConAu 1R, WrD 1976*
Fruchter, Norman 1937- *AmA&B*
Fruehling, Rosemary T 1933- *ConAu 33*
Fruer, Alfred W *ChPo S1*
Frug, Simon Samuel 1860-1916 *Pen Eur*
Frugoni, Carlo Innocenzio Maria 1692-1768 *BbD, BiD&SB*
Frugoni, Carlo Innocenzo Maria 1692-1768 *CasWL, EvEuW, Pen Eur*
Fruhan, William E, Jr. 1943- *ConAu 41*
Fruit, John Phelps 1855-1938 *BiDSA, DcAmA, DcNAA*
Frullani, Emilio 1808-1879 *BiD&SB*
Fruman, Norman 1923- *ConAu 37*
Frumkin, Gene 1928- *AmA&B, ConAu 9R, DrAP 1975, WrD 1976*
Frumkin, Robert M 1928- *ConAu 23*
Frundsberg, Georg Von 1473-1528 *OxGer*
Frutiger, Adrian 1928- *WhGrA*
Fruton, Joseph S 1912- *ConAu 49, WrD 1976*
Fruytiers, Jan d1580? *CasWL*
Fry, A A *BbtC*
Fry, Alan 1931- *Au&Wr, ConAu 45, OxCan Sup*
Fry, Alfred A *Alli*
Fry, Anna Ruth 1878- *WhLA*
Fry, Anne *Alli, BiDLA*
Fry, Augustin B *ChPo*
Fry, Barbarr 1932- *ConAu 25*
Fry, Benjamin St. James 1824-1892 *BiDSA, DcNAA, OhA&B*
Fry, Bernard Mitchell 1915- *IndAu 1917*
Fry, Bettine *ChPo*
Fry, C George 1936- *ConAu 37*
Fry, Carli 1897-1956 *CasWL*
Fry, Caroline 1787-1846 *Alli, BiDLA, ChPo, ChPo S1, ChPo S2*
Fry, Charles Burgess 1872-1956 *MnBBF*
Fry, Charles Luther 1894-1932 *DcNAA, WhWNAA*
Fry, Christopher 1907- *Au&Wr, AuBYP, CasWL, CnMD, CnMWL, CnThe, ConAu 17R, ConDr, ConLC 2, ConP 1970, ConP 1975, CrCD, CyWA, DcLEnL, EncWL, EvLB, LongC, McGWD, ModBL, ModBL Sup, ModWD, NewC, OxEng, Pen Eng, REn, TwCA Sup, TwCW, WebEAL, WrD 1976*
Fry, Clara W T *Alli Sup*
Fry, Danby Palmer 1818- *Alli, Alli Sup*
Fry, David *ConAu XR*
Fry, Donald K 1937- *ConAu 25*
Fry, Edmund *Alli, Alli Sup, BiDLA*
Fry, Edward *Alli Sup*
Fry, Sir Edward 1827- *Alli Sup*
Fry, Edward Alexander M *Alli Sup*
Fry, Edward Bernard 1925- *ConAu 9R, WrD 1976*
Fry, Edward Hogg *Alli Sup*
Fry, Elizabeth 1780-1845 *Alli, REn*
Fry, Francis 1803-1886 *Alli Sup, NewC*

Fry, G *Alli Sup*
Fry, George Gardiner *Alli Sup*
Fry, Guy *ChPo*
Fry, H P *Alli*
Fry, Henry *Alli Sup*
Fry, Henry Davidson 1853-1919 *Alli Sup, DcNAA*
Fry, Herbert Oswald *Alli Sup*
Fry, Hilary G 1922- *ConAu 17R*
Fry, Howard Massey 1889- *WhWNAA*
Fry, Howard T 1919- *ConAu 37*
Fry, J Reese *Alli*
Fry, J Reese ALSO Fry, Joseph Reese
Fry, Jacob 1834-1920 *AmLY, DcNAA*
Fry, James *Alli*
Fry, James Barnet 1827-1894 *Alli Sup, AmA&B, BiD&SB, DcAmA, DcNAA*
Fry, Jesse *BiDSA*
Fry, John *Alli, BiDLA*
Fry, John Hemming 1860-1946 *DcNAA, IndAu 1917*
Fry, Joseph Reese 1811-1865 *AmA&B, DcNAA, OhA&B*
Fry, Joseph Reese ALSO Fry, J Reese
Fry, Katharine 1801-1886 *Alli Sup*
Fry, Maggie Culver 1900- *AuNews 1*
Fry, Mattie B 1879- *IndAu 1917*
Fry, Reginald C *MnBBF*
Fry, Richard *Alli*
Fry, Roger Elliot 1866-1934 *LongC, ModBL, NewC, OxEng, REn, TwCA, TwCA Sup*
Fry, Ronald W 1949- *ConAu 57*
Fry, Rosalie Kingsmill 1911- *Au&Wr, AuBYP, ChPo S1, ConAu 9R, IlCB 1956, IlCB 1966, SmATA 3, ThBJA, WrD 1976*
Fry, Ruth 1878-1962 *LongC*
Fry, Samuel *Alli*
Fry, Sarah Maria *Alli Sup*
Fry, Susanna Margaret Davidson 1841-1920 *OhA&B*
Fry, Theodore *Alli Sup*
Fry, Sir Theodore Penrose 1892- *Au&Wr, CatA 1947*
Fry, Thomas *Alli, BiDLA*
Fry, Thomas Charles 1846- *WhLA*
Fry, W H *Alli Sup*
Fry, William *Alli*
Fry, William F 1924- *ConAu 5R*
Fry, William H *Alli*
Fry, William Henry 1815-1864 *AmA&B, DcNAA*
Fryar, Mark *Alli Sup*
Fryars, Austin 1865- *MnBBF*
Fryatt, Norma R *AuBYP, ConAu 57*
Fryberg, Mart 1890-1952 *AmSCAP 66*
Fryberger, Agnes Moore 1868- *IndAu 1816, WhWNAA*
Fryburger, Vernon R, Jr. 1918- *ConAu 1R*
Frydman, Szajko 1911- *ConAu 25*
Frye, Alexis Everett 1859-1936 *AmA&B, DcNAA*
Frye, Alton 1936- *ConAu 21, WrD 1976*
Frye, Burton James Conrad 1920- *ChPo S1, OhA&B*
Frye, C B *Alli*
Frye, Dean *AuBYP*
Frye, E F *ChPo*
Frye, Ellen 1940- *ConAu 49*
Frye, Herman Northop 1912- *CasWL, Pen Eng*
Frye, James Albert 1863-1933 *DcNAA*
Frye, John 1910- *ConAu 49*
Frye, Keith 1935- *ConAu 53*
Frye, Northrop 1912- *AmA&B, CanWr, ConAu 5R, EncWL Sup, NewC, OxCan, OxCan Sup, Pen Am, RAdv 1, WorAu, WrD 1976*
Frye, Pearl 1917- *AmA&B*
Frye, Prosser Hall 1866-1934 *DcNAA*
Frye, Richard Nelson 1920- *AmA&B, ConAu 5R, WrD 1976*
Frye, Roland Mushat 1921- *ConAu 9R*
Frye, Theodore Christian 1869- *WhWNAA*
Fryer, Alfred C *Alli Sup, ChPo S2*
Fryer, Colin Bernard 1933- *Au&Wr, WrD 1976*
Fryer, Donald S *ConAu XR*

Fryer, Eugenie M 1879- *WhWNAA*
Fryer, Henry *Alli*
Fryer, Holly C 1908- *ConAu P-1*
Fryer, Jane Eayre *ChPo, WhWNAA*
Fryer, John *Alli*
Fryer, John 1839-1928 *DcNAA*
Fryer, Peter James 1927- *Au&Wr*
Fryer, Phae Noble 1888-1956 *IndAu 1917*
Fryer, William J *Alli Sup*
Frykenberg, Robert Eric 1930- *ConAu 25, WrD 1976*
Fryklund, Verne C 1896- *ConAu 13R*
Frykman, John H 1932- *ConAu 33*
Frymier, Jack Rimmel 1925- *ConAu 17R, IndAu 1917*
Fryscak, Milan 1932- *ConAu 53*
Fryth, John *Alli*
Fryxell, Anders 1795-1881 *BbD, BiD&SB*
Fu, Hsuan *DcOrL 1*
Fu, Ssu-Nien *DcOrL 1*
Fua-Fusinato, Erminia 1834-1876 *BbD, BiD&SB*
Fuat, Memet 1926- *DcOrL 3*
Fuca, Juan De *OxCan*
Fuchs, Abraham Moses 1890- *CasWL*
Fuchs, Bruno Gunter 1928- *ModGL*
Fuchs, Charles Emilio 1907- *AmSCAP 66*
Fuchs, Daniel 1909- *AmA&B, ConNov 1972, ConNov 1976, DrAF 1976, ModAL, ModAL Sup, OxAm, Pen Am, RENAL, WebEAL, WhTwL, WrD 1976*
Fuchs, Daniel 1934- *ConAu 37*
Fuchs, Emil 1866-1929 *DcNAA*
Fuchs, Erich 1916- *ConAu 29, SmATA 6*
Fuchs, Estelle *ConAu 57*
Fuchs, Gertaut *ChPo S1*
Fuchs, Gunter Bruno 1928- *OxGer*
Fuchs, Jacob 1939- *ConAu 23*
Fuchs, Josef 1912- *ConAu 21*
Fuchs, Lawrence H 1927- *ConAu 1R*
Fuchs, Victor Robert 1924- *ConAu 1R*
Fuchs, Vivian 1905- *WrD 1976*
Fucik, Julius 1903-1943 *CasWL, Pen Eur*
Fucini, Renato 1843-1921 *CasWL, ClDMEuL, Pen Eur*
Fudge, Joanne Claire *ChPo S1*
Fuegi, John 1936- *ConAu 37, WrD 1976*
Fuentes, Carlos 1928- *AuNews 2, ConLC 3, DcCLA, EncWL Sup, WorAu*
Fuentes, Carlos 1929- *CasWL, Pen Am, TwCW, WhTwL*
Fuentes, Roberto 1934- *ConAu 57*
Fuerbringer, Ludwig Ernst 1864?-1947 *DcNAA, WhWNAA*
Fuerer-Haimendorf, Christoph Von 1909- *ConAu 13R, ConAu P-1*
Fuerst, Adrian 1916- *IndAu 1917*
Fuertes, James Hillhouse 1863-1932 *DcAmA, DcNAA*
Fuertes, Louis Agassiz 1874-1927 *DcNAA*
Fuess, Claude Moore 1885-1963 *AmA&B, OxAm, REnAL, TwCA, TwCA Sup, WhWNAA*
Fuessle, Newton Augustus 1883-1924 *DcNAA*
Fuetrer, Ulrich *CasWL, OxGer*
Fufuka, Karama *ConAu XR*
Fugard, Athol 1932- *CasWL, CnThe, ConDr, ConLC 5, TwCW, WhTwL, WrD 1976*
Fugate, Francis L 1915- *ConAu 25*
Fugate, Joe K 1931- *ConAu 23*
Fugate, Terence 1930- *ConAu 5R*
Fugger *OxGer*
Fugger, Andreas d1457 *NewC*
Fugger, Anton 1493-1560 *NewC*
Fugger, Georg 1453-1506 *NewC*
Fugger, Jakob d1469 *NewC*
Fugger, Jakob 1459-1525 *NewC*
Fugger, Johann d1408 *NewC*
Fugger, Johann 1300?- *NewC*
Fugger, Lukas *NewC*
Fugger, Raymund 1489-1535 *NewC*
Fugger, Ulrich 1441-1510 *NewC*
Fuhmann, Franz 1922- *ModGL*
Fuhr, Lulu 1864- *WhWNAA*
Fuhrmann, Franz 1922- *OxGer*
Fuhro, Wilbur J 1914- *ConAu 9R*
Fujikawa, Gyo *IlBYP, IlCB 1966*
Fujita, Tamao 1905- *ConAu 37, SmATA 7*

Fuller, William Wilson 1857-1912 *IndAu 1917*
Fuller-Maitland, John Alexander 1856-1936
  Chmbr 3, NewC, WhLA
Fullerton, Colonel *Alli*
Fullerton, Alex *Alli*
Fullerton, Alexander Fergus 1924- *Au&Wr,*
  ConAu 17R
Fullerton, Amy Fullerton- *Alli Sup*
Fullerton, Charles 1924- *WrD 1976*
Fullerton, Edith Loring 1876-1931 *DcNAA*
Fullerton, Eleanor *Alli Sup, LivFWS*
Fullerton, Gail Putney 1927- *ConAu 37,*
  WrD 1976
Fullerton, George *Alli Sup*
Fullerton, George S 1859-1925 *Alli Sup,*
  AmA&B
Fullerton, George Stuart 1859-1925 *DcAmA,*
  DcNAA
Fullerton, Lady Georgiana Charlotte 1812-1885
  Alli, Alli Sup, BbD, BiD&SB, BrAu 19,
  ChPo, ChPo S1, Chmbr 3, DcEnA,
  DcEnL, EvLB, NewC
Fullerton, Hubert *MnBBF*
Fullerton, Hugh *ChPo S1*
Fullerton, Hugh Stuart 1873-1945 *DcNAA,*
  OhA&B
Fullerton, John 1836-1904 *ChPo, ChPo S1*
Fullerton, John Charles Mark 1924- *Au&Wr*
Fullerton, Kemper 1865-1941? *DcNAA,*
  OhA&B, WhWNAA
Fullerton, Mary *ChPo S2*
Fullerton, William Morton 1865- *DcAmA*
Fullerton, William Young 1857- *Alli Sup,*
  WhLA
Fullilove, Maggie Shaw *BlkAW*
Fullmer, Daniel W 1922- *ConAu 33*
Fullmer, June Z 1920- *ConAu 25, WrD 1976*
Fullmer, Samuel *Alli*
Fullom, Stephen Watson *Alli, Alli Sup*
Fullwood, Anne Hunt 1906- *IndAu 1917*
Fullwood, Charles Trudeau 1866- *WhWNAA*
Fullwood, Francis *Alli*
Fullwood, William *Alli*
Fulman, William 1632-1688 *Alli*
Fulmer, Chesta Holt 1900-1957 *OhA&B*
Fulmer, Clark Adelbert 1867-1940 *DcNAA,*
  WhWNAA
Fulmer, Robert M 1939- *ConAu 57*
Fulmer, Samuel *Alli*
Fulmore, Zachary Taylor 1846-1923 *BiDSA,*
  DcNAA
Fulop-Miller, Rene 1891-1963 *AmA&B,*
  TwCA, TwCA Sup
Fulthrop, Christopher *Alli*
Fulton, A *Alli Sup*
Fulton, A R *Alli Sup*
Fulton, Albert Rondthaler 1902- *ConAu 1R,*
  IndAu 1917
Fulton, Alexander R 1825-1891 *DcNAA*
Fulton, Ambrose Cowperthwaite 1811-1903
  DcNAA
Fulton, Chandos 1839-1904 *Alli Sup, DcNAA*
Fulton, Charles Carroll *Alli Sup*
Fulton, David Bryant *BlkAW*
Fulton, George *Alli, BiDLA*
Fulton, Gere 1939- *ConAu 53*
Fulton, H *Alli*
Fulton, Henry *Alli Sup*
Fulton, J W *Alli, BiDLA*
Fulton, Jack 1903- *AmSCAP 66*
Fulton, James Alexander *Alli Sup*
Fulton, James Forest 1846- *Alli Sup*
Fulton, Jane *ChPo S1*
Fulton, John *Alli*
Fulton, John 1834-1907 *Alli Sup, DcAmA,*
  DcNAA
Fulton, Justin Dewey 1828-1901 *Alli Sup,*
  DcAmA, DcNAA, OhA&B
Fulton, Len 1934- *ConAu 57, DrAF 1976*
Fulton, Levi S *Alli*
Fulton, Maurice Garland 1877- *ChPo*
Fulton, Norman 1927- *ConAu 37*
Fulton, Paul C 1901- *ConAu P-1*
Fulton, R I And Trueblood, T C *Alli Sup*
Fulton, Reg 1924- *AmSCAP 66*
Fulton, Robert *Alli Sup*
Fulton, Robert 1765-1815 *Alli, BiDLA,*
  DcNAA, REn, REnAL

Fulton, Robert Burwell 1849- *BiDSA*
Fulton, Robert Irving 1855-1916 *DcNAA*
Fulton, Robin 1937- *ChPo S2, ConAu 33,*
  ConP 1970, ConP 1975, WrD 1976
Fulton, William 1876- *WhLA*
Fults, John Lee 1932- *ConAu 53*
Fultz, Dessa M *ChPo*
Fulvia d040BC *REn*
Fulwell, Ulpian 1530?-1585? *CasWL, DcEnL*
Fulwell, Ulpin 1556- *Alli*
Fulwood, Francis *Alli*
Fulwood, Peter *Alli*
Fulwood, William *Alli*
Fumento, Rocco 1923- *ConAu 1R, WrD 1976*
Fumet, Stanislas 1896- *CatA 1947*
Funai, Mamoru R 1932- *ChPo S1, IlCB 1966*
Funck-Brentano, Frantz 1862-1947 *OxFr*
Funck-Brentano, Theophile 1830- *BiD&SB*
Funckelin, Jakob 1520?-1565 *OxGer*
Fundaburk, Emma Lila 1922- *ConAu 41*
Funderburk, Guy B 1902- *ConAu 45*
Funderburk, Thomas Ray 1928- *ConAu 17R,*
  IndAu 1917
Fung, Hing Kwai *WhLA*
Fung, Yu-Lan 1895- *Au&Wr*
Funk, Annie Lee *TexWr*
Funk, Arthur Layton 1914- *ConAu 23*
Funk, Arville Lynn 1929- *IndAu 1917*
Funk, Charles Earle 1881-1957 *AmA&B,*
  OhA&B
Funk, D V K *TexWr*
Funk, Henry Daniel 1875-1925 *DcNAA*
Funk, Isaac Kauffman 1839-1912 *AmA&B,*
  DcAmA, DcNAA, OhA&B
Funk, John Clarence 1884- *WhWNAA*
Funk, John Fretz 1835-1930 *IndAu 1816*
Funk, Peter V K 1921- *ConAu 21*
Funk, Robert Walter 1926- *ConAu 33,*
  IndAu 1917
Funk, Thompson 1911- *ConAu 49, SmATA 7*
Funk, Tom *ConAu 49, IlBYP, SmATA 7*
Funk, Wilfred John 1883-1965 *AmA&B, ChPo,*
  ChPo S2
Funk, William R 1861-1935 *DcNAA*
Funke, Lewis 1912- *AmA&B, ConAu 49*
Funkhouser, George A 1841-1927 *OhA&B*
Funkhouser, William Delbert 1881-1948
  IndAu 1917, WhWNAA
Funkquist, Herman Peter Anton 1870- *WhLA*
Funnell, William *Alli*
Funston, Frederick 1865-1917 *DcNAA,*
  OhA&B
Funt, Allen 1914- *AmSCAP 66*
Fuqua, Stephen Ogden 1874-1943 *DcNAA*
Fur Trader, A *OxCan*
Furbank, P N 1920- *ConAu 21*
Furbay, Elizabeth Dearmin *IndAu 1917*
Furbay, John Harvey 1903- *AmA&B, OhA&B*
Furbee, Leonard J 1896?-1975 *ConAu 61*
Furber, George C *EarAB*
Furber, Robert *Alli*
Furbish, James *Alli Sup*
Furbish, Julia *Alli Sup*
Furbish, Julia Morton *Alli Sup*
Furer, Howard B 1934- *ConAu 33*
Furetiere, Antoine 1619-1688 *CasWL, DcEuL,*
  EuA, EvEuW, OxFr
Furey, Michael *EncM&D*
Furfey, Paul Hanly 1896- *BkC 1, CatA 1947,*
  ConAu 23
Furley, Lieutenant *Alli, BiDLA*
Furley, Catherine Grant *ChPo S1*
Furley, John *Alli Sup*
Furley, Robert *Alli Sup*
Furlong, Alice *ChPo, ChPo S1, PoIre*
Furlong, Atherton *Alli Sup*
Furlong, Charles Joseph *Alli Sup*
Furlong, Charles Wellington 1874- *REnAL,*
  WhWNAA
Furlong, Gordon *Alli Sup*
Furlong, J S *Alli*
Furlong, Mrs. Leigh *Alli Sup*
Furlong, Marianne *PoIre*
Furlong, Mary 1866-1898 *PoIre*
Furlong, Monica 1930- *Au&Wr*
Furlong, Norman 1907- *Au&Wr*
Furlong, Patrick M *PoIre*
Furlong, Thomas *Alli Sup*

Furlong, Thomas 1794-1827 *ChPo S1, PoIre*
Furlong, Vivienne Carole 1941- *Au&Wr*
Furlong, William *BbtC*
Furly, Samuel *Alli*
Furman, Alfred Antoine 1856-1940 *DcNAA*
Furman, Bess 1894- *AmA&B*
Furman, Charles Edwin 1801-1880 *ChPo,*
  DcNAA
Furman, Franklin DeRonde 1870-1943 *DcNAA,*
  WhWNAA
Furman, Gabriel 1800-1854 *DcNAA*
Furman, Garrit 1782-1848 *DcNAA*
Furman, Howard VanFleet d1902 *DcNAA*
Furman, James Clement 1809- *BiDSA*
Furman, Lucy d1958 *AmA&B, WhWNAA*
Furman, Nathaniel Howell 1892- *WhWNAA*
Furman, Richard 1755-1825 *Alli, BiDSA,*
  DcNAA
Furman, Richard 1816-1886 *BiDSA, DcNAA*
Furman, Roger *BlkAW*
Furman, S E *Alli Sup*
Furman, Sam H 1918- *AmSCAP 66*
Furmanov, Dmitri Andreyevich 1891-1926
  CasWL, ClDMEuL, DcRusL, EvEuW,
  REn, TwCW
Furnas, Boyd Edwin 1848-1897 *ChPo S2,*
  OhA&B
Furnas, Clifford Cook 1900-1969 *AmA&B,*
  Au&Wr, IndAu 1917
Furnas, Joseph Chamberlain 1905- *AmA&B,*
  Au&Wr, IndAu 1917, REnAL, WorAu
Furnas, Marthedith 1904- *AmA&B, AmNov*
Furnberg, Louis 1909-1957 *CnMD, EncWL,*
  OxGer
Furneaux, Henry 1829- *Alli Sup*
Furneaux, Philip 1726-1783 *Alli*
Furneaux, Rupert 1908- *ConAu 1R*
Furneaux, W S *Alli Sup*
Furnell, M C *Alli Sup*
Furness, Audrey 1911- *Au&Wr*
Furness, Caroline Ellen 1869-1936 *DcNAA*
Furness, Clifton Joseph 1898-1946 *DcNAA,*
  IndAu 1917
Furness, Edna L 1906- *ConAu 37, WrD 1976*
Furness, Helen Kate 1837-1883 *Alli Sup,*
  DcAmA, DcNAA
Furness, Horace Howard 1833-1912 *Alli Sup,*
  AmA&B, BbD, BiD&SB, Chmbr 3,
  CyAL 2, DcAmA, DcNAA, NewC,
  OxAm, REn, REnAL
Furness, Horace Howard 1865-1930 *ChPo,*
  DcNAA, WhWNAA
Furness, John *Alli, BiDLA*
Furness, John Hay *ChPo S1*
Furness, Richard 1791-1857 *Alli Sup*
Furness, William Henry 1802-1896 *Alli,*
  Alli Sup, AmA, AmA&B, BiD&SB,
  CyAL 2, DcAmA, DcNAA
Furness, William Henry 1866-1920 *DcAmA,*
  DcNAA
Furnish, Victor Paul 1931- *ConAu 23,*
  WrD 1976
Furniss, Beatrice 1885- *WhWNAA*
Furniss, Dorothy *ChPo S1, ChPo S2*
Furniss, Edgar Stephenson 1890-1972 *ConAu 37,*
  WhWNAA
Furniss, Grace Livingston 1864-1938 *AmA&B,*
  DcNAA
Furniss, Harry 1854-1925 *ChPo, ChPo S1,*
  ChPo S2, WhCL
Furniss, James J *Alli Sup*
Furniss, John Joseph 1809-1865 *Alli Sup*
Furniss, L M *MnBBF*
Furniss, Norman Francis 1922- *ConAu 1R*
Furniss, Ruth Pine 1893- *WhWNAA*
Furniss, W Todd 1921- *ConAu 57*
Furniss, William *Alli, Alli Sup*
Furniss, William 1820-1882 *DcNAA*
Furnivall, Frederick James 1825-1910 *Alli Sup,*
  BiD&SB, BrAu 19, ChPo S1, ChPo S2,
  Chmbr 3, DcEnA, DcEnA Ap, DcEnL,
  DcLEnL, EvLB, LongC, NewC, OxEng,
  REn
Furnivall, P *Alli Sup*
Furon, Raymond 1898- *Au&Wr*
Furphy, Joseph 1843-1912 *CasWL, DcLEnL,*
  EvLB, Pen Eng, REn, TwCW, WebEAL
Furqat, Zokirjon 1858-1909 *DcOrL 3*

Furry, William Davis 1874- *WhWNAA*
Furse, Barton *MnBBF*
Furse, Charles Wellington *Alli Sup*
Furse, George Armand 1834- *Alli Sup*
Furse, M *Alli Sup*
Furse, Margaret Cecelia *ChPo*
Furse, Ralph *ChPo*
Furse, Roger *ChPo*
Fursman, John *Alli*
Furst, A *Alli Sup*
Furst, Clyde Bowman 1873-1931 *DcNAA*
Furst, Herbert E A *ChPo S2*
Furst, Hugo *Alli Sup*
Furst, Julius 1805-1873 *BiD&SB*
Furstenburg, Gertrude 1881-1928 *DcNAA*
Furtado, Celso 1920- *ConAu 17R*
Furtado, John *Alli*
Furtado, R DeL 1922- *REn*
Furtado, Thomas A 1928- *AmSCAP 66*
Furth, George *ConDr*
Furth, Hans G 1920- *ConAu 45*
Furukawa Mokuami *CasWL*
Furukawa, Toshi 1924- *ConAu 45*
Fuseli, Henry 1741-1825 *Alli, AtlBL, BiDLA,*
  BkIE, CasWL, NewC
Fusely, Henry 1741-1825 *OxGer*
Fusfeld, Daniel R 1922- *ConAu 45*
Fush *OhA&B*
Fusinato, Arnaldo 1817-1888 *BiD&SB*
Fuson, Benjamin Willis 1911- *ConAu 37,*
  WrD 1976
Fuson, Henry Harvey 1876- *AnMV 1926*
Fuson, Robert Henderson 1927- *IndAu 1917*
Fuss, Peter 1932- *ConAu 23*
Fussell, Edwin 1922- *ConAu 53*
Fussell, George Edwin 1889- *Au&Wr,*
  ConAu 5R, WrD 1976
Fussell, Milton Howard 1855-1921 *DcNAA*
Fussell, Paul 1924- *ChPo S1, ConAu 17R*
Fussenegger, Gertrud 1912- *EncWL, Pen Eur*
Fussli, Hans Heinrich 1745-1832 *OxGer*
Fussli, Johann Heinrich 1741-1825 *CasWL,*
  EuA, OxGer
Fussner, Frank Smith 1920- *ConAu 1R,*
  WrD 1976
Fust, Johann 1400?-1466? *NewC, OxGer*
Fust, Milan 1888-1967 *CasWL, Pen Eur*
Fustel DeCoulanges, Numa Denis 1830-1889
  BiD&SB, EuA, EvEuW, OxFr
Futabatei, Shimei 1864-1909? *CasWL,*
  DcOrL 1, Pen Cl
Futhey, James L *Alli Sup*
Futhey, John Smith 1820-1888 *Alli Sup,*
  DcAmA, DcNAA
Futrelle, Jacques 1875-1912 *AmA&B, BiDSA,*
  DcNAA, EncM&D, TwCA
Futshane, Zora Z T *AfA 1*
Futvoye, George *BbtC*
Fuze, Magema Ka Magwaza 1845?-1922?
  AfA 1
Fuzelier, Louis 1672-1752 *OxFr*
Fuzuli, Mehmed Bin Suleyman 1494-1556?
  CasWL, DcOrL 3
Fyers, William Augustus *Alli Sup*
Fyfe *ChPo*
Fyfe, Andrew *Alli, BiDLA*
Fyfe, Archibald *Alli*
Fyfe, H Hamilton 1869-1951 *NewC*
Fyfe, James Hamilton 1837-1880 *Alli Sup*
Fyfe, Robert Alexander 1816-1878 *BbtC,*
  DcNAA
Fyfe, William Wallace *Alli Sup*
Fyffe, Charles Alan 1845-1892 *Alli Sup, BbD,*
  BiD&SB
Fyffe, Don 1925- *ConAu 25*
Fyleman, Rose 1877-1957 *AnCL, BkCL, ChPo,*
  ChPo S1, ChPo S2, EvLB, JBA 1934,
  JBA 1951, LongC, St&VC, TwCA,
  TwCA Sup, WhCL, WhLA
Fyler, Fanny *Alli Sup*
Fyler, Samuel *Alli*
Fyles, Franklin 1847-1911 *AmA&B, DcAmA,*
  DcNAA, REnAL
Fyloll, Jasper *Alli*
Fynch, Martin *Alli*
Fynes, Charles *Alli, BiDLA Sup*
Fynes-Clinton, Osbert Henry 1869- *WhLA*
Fynn, Arthur John 1857-1930 *DcNAA,*

WhWNAA
Fynn, Robert *Alli*
Fynney, Fielding Best *Alli*
Fyodorov, Innokenti Vasilievich 1836-1883
  DcRusL
Fysh, Frederic *Alli Sup*
Fysh, Henry *Alli*
Fysh, Thomas *Alli*
Fysh, Wilmot Hudson 1895- *ConAu 17R*
Fyshe, Thomas 1845-1911 *DcNAA*
Fysher, Robert *Alli*
Fyson, Jenny Grace 1904- *Au&Wr, ConAu 21*
Fyson, Thomas *Alli*
Fytche, Albert *Alli Sup*
Fytton, Francis 1928- *Au&Wr*
Fyvie, Isabella 1843- *ChPo, ChPo S1,*
  ChPo S2
Fyvie, J *ChPo S2*
Fyzee Rahamin, S 1880- *DcLEnL*

G

G, C C V *PoIre*
G, H *PoIre*
G, H W *PoIre*
G, J *PoIre*
G, M C *PoIre*
G, M E *ChPo S1*
G, S E *ChPo S1*
G, T *PoIre*
G B *ConAu XR*
G B S *LongC*
G D *PoIre*
G E X *OhA&B*
G F F *EarAB*
G J *WhLA*
G K C *LongC, WhLA*
G W M *WhWNAA*
Gaa, Charles J 1911- *ConAu 17R*
Gaal, Charles J 1893- *AmSCAP 66*
Gaard, David 1945- *ConAu 25*
Gaathon, A L 1898- *ConAu 49*
Gabb, James *Alli Sup*
Gabb, Thomas *Alli, BiDLA*
Gabb, William More 1839-1878? *Alli Sup,*
  DcAmA, DcNAA
Gabbett, Joseph *Alli, BiDLA*
Gabble, Gridiron *Alli*
Gabbler Gridiron *DcEnL*
Gabe, Dora 1886- *CasWL*
Gabe, Marie Rose *ChPo*
Gabel, Margaret 1938- *ConAu 33, WrD 1976*
Gabelein, Frank Ely 1899- *AmA&B*
Gabelentz, Hans 1872- *WhLA*
Gabell, Henry *Alli, BiDLA*
Gabelle, James 1874-1940 *DcNAA*
Gabirol, Solomon Ben Judah 1020?-1057?
  CasWL, EuA, Pen Eur
Gable, J Harris 1902- *AmA&B, WhWNAA*
Gable, Rufe 1892- *WhWNAA*
Gablehouse, Charles 1928- *ConAu 21*
Gabler, Milton 1911- *AmSCAP 66*
Gablik, Suzi 1934- *ConAu 33, WrD 1976*
Gabo, Naum 1890- *Au&Wr, ConAu 33*
Gabor, Dennis 1900- *Au&Wr, ConAu 17R*
Gaboriall, Emile 1833-1873 *MnBBF*
Gaboriau, Emile 1835?-1873 *BbD, BiD&SB,*
  CasWL, CyWA, DcBiA, EncM&D, EuA,
  EvEuW, HsB&A, NewC, OxEng, OxFr,
  Pen Eur, REn
Gabourel, Harriet *Alli Sup*
Gaboury, Antonio *ConAu 45*
Gabra, Egzi'abeher 1860?-1914? *AfA 1*
Gabre-Medhin, Tsegaye *AfA 1*
Gabriel, A L 1907- *ConAu 5R*
Gabriel, Ange Jacques 1698-1782 *AtlBL*
Gabriel, Charles H, Jr. 1892-1934 *AmSCAP 66*
Gabriel, Charles Hutchinson 1856-1932
  AmSCAP 66, ChPo, ChPo S1, DcNAA
Gabriel, Gilbert Wolf 1890-1952 *AmA&B,*
  AmNov, REnAL, WhWNAA
Gabriel, Jacques Ange 1698-1782 *AtlBL*
Gabriel, Joel C 1830-1891 *OhA&B*

Gabriel, John *Alli, MnBBF*
Gabriel, Juri Evald 1940- *Au&Wr, WrD 1976*
Gabriel, Luci 1597-1663 *CasWL*
Gabriel, Mari Cruz 1926- *ConP 1970*
Gabriel, Ralph Henry 1890- *AmA&B,*
  ConAu 13R, REnAL
Gabriel, Robert Burd d1804 *Alli*
Gabriel, Simbad Mgrditch *AmLY*
Gabriel, Steffan 1565?-1638 *CasWL*
Gabriel, Virginia *Alli Sup*
Gabriel-Robinet, Louis 1909-1975 *ConAu 61*
Gabriel Y Galan, Jose Maria 1870-1905 *CasWL,*
  ClDMEuL, Pen Eur
Gabrieli, Giovanni 1555?-1612 *AtlBL, REn*
Gabrielle, Helen *Alli Sup*
Gabrielli *BiDLA*
Gabrielson, Iran 1889- *ConAu P-1*
Gabrielson, James 1917- *ConAu 29*
Gabryella *CasWL*
Gabugah, O O 1945- *BlkAW*
Gaburo, Kenneth Louis 1926- *AmSCAP 66*
Gace Brule d1220? *CasWL, EvEuW, OxFr,*
  Pen Eur
Gace, Frederic Aubert *Alli Sup*
Gace, William *Alli*
Gachechiladze, D *DcOrL 3*
Gaches, Louis 1848- *Alli Sup*
Gadbury, Job d1715 *Alli*
Gadbury, John 1627-1692? *Alli*
Gadbury, Thomas *Alli*
Gadbury, Timothy *Alli*
Gadd, David 1912- *ConAu 57*
Gadd, Maxine *OxCan Sup*
Gadda, Carlo Emilio 1893-1973 *CasWL,*
  EncWL, ModRL, Pen Eur, TwCW,
  WhTwL, WorAu
Gaddes, Peter *ConAu XR*
Gaddes, Thomas *Alli Sup*
Gaddesby, Richard *Alli*
Gaddesden, John Of *Alli, DcEnL*
Gaddi, Agnolo 1345?-1396 *AtlBL*
Gaddi, Taddeo 1300?-1366 *AtlBL*
Gaddi Family *AtlBL*
Gaddis, Alfred *IndAu 1816*
Gaddis, Cyrus Jacob 1868- *WhWNAA*
Gaddis, J Wilson 1910?-1975 *ConAu 57*
Gaddis, John Lewis 1941- *ConAu 45*
Gaddis, Maxwell Pierson 1811-1888 *Alli Sup,*
  DcNAA, OhA&B
Gaddis, Peggy 1895-1966 *AmA&B,*
  ConAu XR, WhWNAA
Gaddis, Thomas E 1908- *ConAu 29*
Gaddis, Vincent Hayes 1913- *ConAu 13R,*
  WrD 1976
Gaddis, William 1922- *AmA&B, ConAu 17R,*
  ConLC 1, ConLC 3, ConLC 6,
  ConNov 1972, ConNov 1976, DrAF 1976,
  ModAL Sup, Pen Am, RAdv 1, WorAu,
  WrD 1976
Gaddo Di Zanobi *AtlBL*
Gaddy, C Welton 1941- *ConAu 61*

Gade, John Allyne 1875-1955 *AmA&B*
Gadesby, Richard *Alli*
Gadesden, Ellen *Alli Sup*
Gadgil, Dhananjaya Ramchandra 1901-
  Au&Wr
Gadgil, Gangadhar Gopal 1923- *DcOrL 2*
Gadifer De La Salle *CasWL*
Gadiyev, Taomek *DcOrL 3*
Gadkari, Ram Ganes 1885-1919 *DcOrL 2*
Gadney, Reg 1941- *ConAu 49*
Gado, Frank 1936- *ConAu 49*
Gadola, Guglielm 1902-1961 *CasWL*
Gadow, Hans *Alli Sup*
Gadpaille, Warren J 1924- *ConAu 61*
Gadsby, John *Alli Sup*
Gadsden *Alli*
Gadsden, Christopher Edwards 1785-1852
  BiDSA, DcNAA
Gadsden, Janice Marie 1952- *BlkAW*
Gadson, W H *MnBBF*
Gaebelein, Arno Clemens 1861-1945 *AmA&B,*
  DcNAA, WhWNAA
Gaebelein, Frank Ely 1899- *ConAu 1R,*
  ConAu 13R, WhWNAA
Gaeddart, Lou Ann *BkP*
Gaediaty, Taomaq 1882-1931 *DcOrL 3*
Gaehde, Christian 1875- *WhLA*
Gaekwar III, Sir Sayaji Rao 1863- *WhLA*
Gael, Samuel Higgs 1806- *Alli, Alli Sup*
Gaeng, Paul A 1924- *ConAu 37*
Gaer, Joseph 1897- *AmA&B, AuBYP,*
  ConAu 9R, MorJA
Gaer, Yossef *ConAu XR*
Gaeta, Francesco 1879-1927 *ClDMEuL*
Gaetz, Adolphus *OxCan*
Gaetz, Annie Louise *OxCan*
Gaffney, Bernard d1885 *PoIre*
Gaffney, Cornelia *AmA&B*
Gaffney, Floyd *BlkAW*
Gaffney, James 1931- *ConAu 57*
Gaffney, Mason 1923- *ConAu 49*
Gaffney, William S 1828- *PoIre*
Gag, Flavia 1907- *AuBYP, ConAu 5R,*
  IlCB 1945, IlCB 1956, MnnWr, MorJA
Gag, Wanda 1893-1946 *AmA&B, AnCL,*
  AuBYP, ChPo S2, ConICB, DcNAA,
  FamAI, IlCB 1945, JBA 1934, JBA 1951,
  REnAL, TwCA, TwCA Sup, YABC 1
Gagan, David P *OxCan Sup*
Gage, Viscount *Alli*
Gage, Alfred Payson 1836-1903 *Alli Sup,*
  DcAmA, DcNAA
Gage, Alvin Clifford 1870- *WhWNAA*
Gage, Emma d1925 *DcNAA*
Gage, F Benjamin *ChPo*
Gage, Frances Dana 1808-1884 *Alli Sup, AmA*
  AmA&B
  ChPo, ChPo S1,
  ChPo S2, DcAmA, DcNAA, OhA&B,
  REnAL
Gage, Hannah B *ChPo S1*

Gage, Hy 1878- *WhWNAA*
Gage, J A *Alli Sup*
Gage, John *Alli*
Gage, M *Alli, BiDLA*
Gage, Mary *ChPo*
Gage, Matilda Joslyn 1826-1898 *DcAmA, DcNAA*
Gage, Moses D 1828- *IndAu 1816*
Gage, Nicholas *ConAu 49*
Gage, Simon Henry 1851-1944 *DcAmA, DcNAA, WhWNAA*
Gage, Thomas 1596?-1656 *Alli, NewC, OxAm*
Gage, William 1915- *ConAu 25*
Gage, William Leonard 1832-1889 *Alli Sup, BiD&SB, DcAmA, DcNAA*
Gage, William W 1925- *ConAu 13R*
Gage, Wilson 1922- *AuBYP, ConAu XR, SmATA 3, ThBJA, WrD 1976*
Gager, Charles Stuart 1872-1943 *DcNAA, WhWNAA*
Gager, William 1555-1622 *Alli, BrAu, CasWL*
Gagern, Wilhelm Heinrich, Freiherr Von 1799-1880 *OxGer*
Gagg, John Colton 1916- *Au&Wr*
Gagliano, Frank 1931- *ConAu 45, ConDr, WrD 1976*
Gagliardo, John G 1933- *ConAu 23, WrD 1976*
Gagliardo, Ruth *AuBYP*
Gagneur, Louise 1832-1902 *BbD, BiD&SB*
Gagnon, Charles Alphonse Nathanael 1851-1932 *DcNAA*
Gagnon, David T *OxCan Sup*
Gagnon, Ernest 1834-1915 *BbtC, DcNAA, OxCan*
Gagnon, Jean-Louis 1913- *ConAu 23, OxCan, OxCan Sup*
Gagnon, John H 1931- *ConAu 33*
Gagnon, Marcel-Aime *OxCan Sup*
Gagnon, Maurice *OxCan Sup*
Gagnon, Phileas 1854-1915 *DcNAA, OxCan*
Gaguin, Robert 1433-1501 *OxFr*
Gahagan, Goliah *NewC*
Gahagan, Henry *PoIre*
Gahagan, John *Alli*
Gahagan, Matthias *Alli*
Gahagan, Usher *Alli, PoIre*
Gahan, Aloysius C 1861- *PoIre*
Gahan, B T *ChPo S1*
Gahan, James J 1841?- *PoIre*
Gahan, William *Alli*
Gaherty, Sherry 1951- *ConAu 57*
Gahm, Anna Higsbee *ChPo S1*
Gaida, Pr *OxCan Sup*
Gaige, Crosby 1882-1949 *DcNAA*
Gailey, Harry A 1926- *ConAu 45*
Gailey, James *Alli Sup*
Gailey, James Herbert, Jr. 1916- *ConAu 5R, WrD 1976*
Gailey, Matthew 1835- *Alli Sup, PoIre*
Gailhard, J *Alli*
Gaillard, Auger *CasWL*
Gaillard, Bulee 1916- *AmSCAP 66*
Gaillard DeChampris, H *OxCan*
Gailly DeTaurines, Charles *OxCan*
Gailor, Thomas Frank 1856-1935 *AmA&B, BiDSA, DcAmA, DcNAA, WhWNAA*
Gaimar *BiB N*
Gaimar, Geffrei *OxFr*
Gaimar, Geoffrey *Alli, BrAu, CasWL, Chmbr 1, EvLB*
Gaine, Hugh 1726?-1807 *AmA&B, CyAL 1, REnAL*
Gaines, Albert Cecil *HsB&A*
Gaines, Charles Kelsey 1854-1944? *AmA&B, DcNAA, WhWNAA*
Gaines, Diana 1912- *ConAu 1R*
Gaines, Ernest J 1933- *AuNews 1, BlkAW, ConAu 9R, ConLC 3, ConNov 1972, ConNov 1976, DrAF 1976, LivBA, WrD 1976*
Gaines, Francis Pendleton 1892-1963 *AmA&B*
Gaines, Fred *DrAP 1975*
Gaines, Garry *Alli Sup, DcNAA, HsB&A, HsB&A Sup, OhA&B*
Gaines, George Strother 1784-1873 *BiDSA*
Gaines, J E *BlkAW*
Gaines, John Wesley 1840- *DcAmA*

Gaines, Lee 1914- *AmSCAP 66*
Gaines, Marion Toulmin 1869- *ChPo S1*
Gaines, Mary *Alli Sup*
Gaines, Matthew John 1937- *Au&Wr*
Gaines, Morrell Walker 1875-1931 *DcNAA*
Gaines, Pierce Welch 1905- *ConAu 13R*
Gaines, Richard L 1925- *ConAu 49*
Gaines, Robert 1912- *Au&Wr*
Gaines, Ruth 1877- *AmA&B*
Gaines, Samuel Richards 1869-1945 *AmSCAP 66*
Gaines, Wesley John 1840-1912 *DcNAA*
Gainesforde, Thomas *Alli*
Gainham, Sarah Rachel 1922- *AmA&B, WrD 1976*
Gainsborough, Thomas 1727-1788 *AtlBL, BkIE, ChPo, NewC, REn*
Gainsbrugh, Glen M 1949- *ConAu 25*
Gainsburg, Joseph 1894- *ConAu 5R*
Gainsford, Thomas *Alli*
Gainsford, William Dunn 1843- *Alli Sup*
Gair, Malcolm *Au&Wr*
Gairden, George *Alli*
Gairdner, James 1828-1912 *Alli Sup, BiD&SB, BrAu 19, Chmbr 3, NewC, OxEng*
Gairdner, John 1790-1876 *Alli Sup*
Gairdner, John Smith *Alli Sup*
Gairdner, M S *Alli Sup*
Gairdner, Robert *Alli Sup*
Gairdner, William *Alli*
Gairdner, William Tennant *Alli Sup*
Gairy, Richardson A *BlkAW*
Gaiser, Gerd 1908- *CasWL, EncWL, ModGL, OxGer, Pen Eur, TwCW, WorAu*
Gaisford, Stephen *Alli, BiDLA*
Gaisford, Thomas 1780-1855 *Alli, BiDLA*
Gaite, Francis *ConAu XR, EncM&D*
Gaither, Frances Ormond Jones 1889-1955 *AmA&B, AmNov, TwCA Sup*
Gaither, Gant 1917- *ConAu 9R*
Gaithorne-Hardy, G M *ChPo S1*
Gaitskell, Charles D 1908- *ConAu 29*
Gaitskell, William *Alli*
Gaius 110?-180? *NewC, OxEng*
Gaj, Ljudevit 1808?-1872 *CasWL, Pen Eur*
Gajcy, Tadeusz 1922-1944 *CasWL*
Gajdusek, D Carleton 1923- *WrD 1976*
Gal, Allon 1934- *ConAu 45*
Gal, Hans 1890- *ConAu 5R, WrD 1976*
Galaal *AfA 1, Pen Cl*
Galabin, Alfred Louis *Alli Sup*
Galaction, Gala 1879-1961 *CasWL*
Galaher, George Fitzgerald *Alli Sup*
Galaida, Edward 1906- *OhA&B*
Galand, Rene 1923- *ConAu 45*
Galanos, Spyros 1896- *WhLA*
Galanoy, Terry 1927- *ConAu 45*
Galanskov, Yuri 1939?-1972 *ConAu 37*
Galante, Pierre 1909- *Au&Wr, ConAu 13R, WrD 1976*
Galanter, Eugene 1924- *ConAu 1R*
Galantiere, Lewis 1895- *AmA&B*
Galarneau, Claude *OxCan Sup*
Galatopoulos, Stelios 1932- *Au&Wr, WrD 1976*
Galba 005?BC-069AD *REn*
Galba, Marti Johan De *DcSpL*
Galbraith, Anna Mary 1859-1923 *AmLY, DcNAA*
Galbraith, Clare K 1919- *ConAu 33*
Galbraith, E *Alli Sup*
Galbraith, Georgie Starbuck 1909- *ConAu P-1*
Galbraith, Glen Williams 1889-1969 *IndAu 1917*
Galbraith, Helen J B *ChPo S2*
Galbraith, J F *OxCan*
Galbraith, James *Alli Sup*
Galbraith, Jean 1906- *ConAu 37, WrD 1976*
Galbraith, John B *Alli Sup*
Galbraith, John Kenneth 1908- *AmA&B, ConAu 21, LongC, REnAL, WorAu, WrD 1976*
Galbraith, John S 1916- *ConAu 5R, OxCan*
Galbraith, Joseph A, And Samuel Haughton *Alli*
Galbraith, Madelyn 1897- *ConAu 33*
Galbraith, Richard *Alli, Alli Sup*
Galbraith, Robert Christy 1833?-1916 *DcNAA, OhA&B*

Galbraith, T *Alli Sup*
Galbraith, Thomas *BbtC*
Galbraith, William *Alli*
Galbreath, Charles Burleigh 1858-1934 *AmA&B, DcNAA, OhA&B*
Galbreath, Robert 1938- *ConAu 41*
Galbreath, Thomas Crawford 1876-1916 *DcNAA*
Galczynski, Konstanty Ildefons 1905-1953 *CasWL, EncWL, ModSL 2, Pen Eur*
Galdone, Paul 1914- *AuBYP, BkP, ChPo, ChPo S1, ChPo S2, IlCB 1956, IlCB 1966, ThBJA*
Galdos *AtlBL, DcSpL, TwCA, TwCA Sup*
Galdos, Benito Perez 1845-1920 *BbD, BiD&SB, ClDMEuL, DcBiA, ModRL*
Galdos, Perez Benito 1845-1920 *Pen Eur*
Gale *Alli*
Gale, Alan *MnBBF*
Gale, Amory 1815-1874 *DcNAA*
Gale, Arthur James Victor 1895- *Au&Wr*
Gale, Arthur Sullivan 1877- *WhWNAA*
Gale, Benjamin 1715-1790 *Alli, DcNAA*
Gale, C J *Alli*
Gale, Daphne Frances Rumsey 1915- *Au&Wr*
Gale, David C *ChPo*
Gale, Donald Hawking 1908- *Au&Wr*
Gale, Dunstan *Alli*
Gale, E C *Alli Sup*
Gale, Edwin Oscar 1832-1916 *ChPo S1*
Gale, Elizabeth *WhWNAA*
Gale, Frederick 1823- *Alli Sup*
Gale, George 1816-1868 *Alli Sup, DcNAA*
Gale, George 1857-1944 *DcNAA, OxCan*
Gale, H Winter *MnBBF*
Gale, Henry Gordon 1874-1942 *DcNAA, WhWNAA*
Gale, Henry Stanley *Alli Sup*
Gale, Herbert M 1907- *ConAu P-1*
Gale, J T *Alli Sup*
Gale, John *ConAu XR, MnBBF*
Gale, John 1680-1721 *Alli*
Gale, John 1925- *Au&Wr*
Gale, John B *Alli Sup*
Gale, Levin 1824-1875 *Alli, DcNAA*
Gale, Martha T *Alli Sup*
Gale, Mary Elizabeth *AmA&B*
Gale, Nahum 1812-1876 *DcNAA*
Gale, Norman Rowland 1862-1942 *ChPo, ChPo S1, ChPo S2, Chmbr 3, DcEnA Ap, DcLEnL, EvLB, NewC*
Gale, Raymond F 1918- *ConAu 25*
Gale, Richard M 1932- *ConAu 25*
Gale, Robert L 1919- *ConAu 9R*
Gale, Roger 1672-1744 *Alli*
Gale, S *Alli, Alli Sup*
Gale, Samuel d1826 *BbtC*
Gale, Samuel 1682-1754 *Alli*
Gale, Samuel 1783-1865 *BbtC, DcNAA, OxCan*
Gale, Stanley 1902- *Au&Wr*
Gale, Theophilus 1628-1678 *Alli, CyAL 1, DcEuL, NewC*
Gale, Thomas 1507- *Alli*
Gale, Thomas 1636-1702 *Alli*
Gale, Vi *ConAu 33, ConP 1970, ConP 1975, DrAP 1975, WrD 1976*
Gale, W A A *Alli Sup*
Gale, William Daniel 1906- *WrD 1976*
Gale, Zale *WhWNAA*
Gale, Zona 1874-1938 *AmA&B, AmLY, AnMV 1926, ChPo, ChPo S2, CnDAL, CnMD, ConAmA, ConAmL, DcLEnL, DcNAA, EvLB, LongC, McGWD, ModWD, OxAm, Pen Am, REn, REnAL, TwCA, TwCA Sup, TwCW, WhWNAA, WiscW*
Galeano, Eduardo H 1940- *ConAu 29, DcCLA*
Galella, Ron 1931- *AuNews 1, ConAu 53, WrD 1976*
Galen 129?-199? *CasWL, NewC, Pen Cl*
Galen, Claudius 129?-199? *OxEng*
Galen, Cardinal Clemens August *OxGer*
Galen, Philipp 1813-1899 *BiD&SB*
Galenson, Walter 1914- *ConAu 25, WrD 1976*
Galentin, C B *Alli Sup*
Galenus, Claudius 129?-199 *OxEng*
Galeotti, Serio 1922- *Au&Wr*

Galer, Roger Sherman 1863- *WhWNAA*
Gales, Joseph 1761-1841 *AmA&B, REnAL*
Gales, Kathleen 1927- *Au&Wr*
Gales, Richard Lawson 1862-1927 *Alli Sup, ChPo, ChPo S1*
Galewitz, Herb 1928- *ConAu 41*
Galfo, Armand J 1924- *ConAu 17R*
Galfredus Monumetensis *Alli*
Galiani, Ferdinando 1728-1787 *CasWL, DcEuL, EuA, McGWD, OxFr*
Galib, Seyh 1757-1799 *CasWL*
Galib Dede, Seyh 1757-1799 *DcOrL 3*
Galich, Manuel 1913- *DcCLA*
Galiffe, James A *Alli*
Galignani, Giovanni Antonio d1821 *NewC, OxEng*
Galignani, John Anthony 1796-1873 *NewC*
Galignani, William 1798-1882 *NewC*
Galilei, Galileo 1564-1642 *CasWL, DcEuL, EuA, EvEuW, NewC, OxEng, Pen Eur, RCom, REn*
Galinas, Gratien 1909- *OxCan Sup*
Galindo, Mrs. *Alli, BiDLA*
Galindo, Sergio 1926- *DcCLA*
Galindus, Fortunius *Alli*
Galinee, Rene-Francois-Brehant De *OxCan*
Galinsky, G Karl 1942- *ConAu 33, WrD 1976*
Gall, Alice Crew 1878-1949 *AmA&B, AuBYP, JBA 1951, OhA&B*
Gall, Franz Joseph 1758-1828 *NewC, OxFr, REn*
Gall, H R *Alli Sup*
Gall, Isabella *Alli Sup*
Gall, James *Alli, Alli Sup*
Gall, James Hogg 1842-1878 *ChPo*
Gall, Meredith D 1942- *ConAu 53*
Gall, Morris 1907- *ConAu 45*
Gall, Richard 1776-1801 *Alli, BiD&SB, ChPo, ChPo S1, ChPo S2, Chmbr 2*
Gall, W G *Alli Sup*
Gall, William *Alli Sup*
Gall, Sir William 1777-1836 *BrAu 19*
Gallacher, Daniel W 1848?- *ChPo S1*
Gallacher, H G *ChPo S2*
Gallacher, Tom *ConDr*
Gallager, Gale *ConAu XR*
Gallagher, Art, Jr. 1925- *WrD 1976*
Gallagher, Bridget d1894 *PoIre*
Gallagher, Buell Gordon 1904- *AmA&B*
Gallagher, Charles A 1927- *ConAu 61*
Gallagher, Charles Wesley 1846-1916 *DcNAA*
Gallagher, David P 1944- *ConAu 45*
Gallagher, Edward A 1928- *AmSCAP 66*
Gallagher, Elizabeth Lucy 1870- *ChPo*
Gallagher, F O'Neill *ChPo, ChPo S1, PoIre*
Gallagher, Fannie H *Alli Sup*
Gallagher, James R 1943- *AmSCAP 66*
Gallagher, James Roswell 1903- *ConAu 57, WrD 1976*
Gallagher, James Thomas 1855-1936 *DcNAA*
Gallagher, James Thomas 1855- *PoIre*
Gallagher, John F 1936- *ConAu 17R*
Gallagher, Kent G 1933- *ConAu 33*
Gallagher, Louis Joseph 1885-1972 *CatA 1952, ConAu 37*
Gallagher, Mary Antonio *DcNAA*
Gallagher, Sister Mary Dominic 1917- *ConAu 17R*
Gallagher, Mason *Alli Sup*
Gallagher, Matthew *Alli, BiDLA*
Gallagher, Matthew P 1919- *ConAu 5R*
Gallagher, Patrick 1930- *ConAu 45*
Gallagher, Richard Farrington 1926- *ConAu 1R*
Gallagher, Robert E 1922- *ConAu 13R*
Gallagher, Sears 1869- *ChPo S1*
Gallagher, Tess *DrAP 1975*
Gallagher, Thomas *ConAu 1R*
Gallagher, William Davis 1808-1894 *Alli, Alli Sup, AmA, AmA&B, BbD, BiD&SB, BiDSA, ChPo, ChPo S1, CyAL 2, DcAmA, DcLEnL, DcNAA, OhA&B, OxAm, PoIre, REnAL*
Gallagher, William J *ChPo*
Gallaher, Art, Jr. 1925- *ConAu 1R*
Gallaher, F M *Alli Sup*
Gallaher, James 1792-1853 *DcNAA, OhA&B*
Gallaher, Wallace W 1861-1959 *OhA&B*
Galland, Antoine 1646-1715 *DcEuL, OxFr*

Galland, Isaac 1790-1858 *OhA&B*
Galland, Joseph Stanislaus 1882-1947 *DcNAA*
Gallant, Mavis 1922- *Au&Wr, ConNov 1972, ConNov 1976, DrAF 1976, NewC, OxCan, OxCan Sup, WorAu, WrD 1976*
Gallant, Roy Arthur 1924- *AuBYP, ConAu 5R, SmATA 4, WrD 1976*
Gallant, T Grady 1920- *ConAu 5R, WrD 1976*
Gallardo, Aurelio Luis 1831-1869 *BiD&SB*
Gallardo, Bartolome Jose 1776-1852 *DcSpL*
Gallardo Y Blanco, Bartolome Jose 1776-1852 *CasWL*
Gallati, Mary Ernestine *Au&Wr, ConAu 5R*
Gallati, Robert R J 1913- *ConAu 1R*
Gallatin, Abraham Alfonse Albert 1761-1849 *DcLEnL*
Gallatin, Albert 1761-1849 *Alli, AmA&B, BbtC, BiD&SB, CyAL 1, DcAmA, DcNAA, OxAm, REnAL*
Gallatin, Albert Eugene 1881-1952 *AmA&B*
Gallatin, James 1796-1876 *DcNAA*
Gallatley, W *Alli Sup*
Gallaudet, Edward Miner 1837-1917 *Alli Sup, DcAmA, DcNAA*
Gallaudet, Herbert Draper 1876-1944 *DcNAA*
Gallaudet, Herbert E *ChPo*
Gallaudet, Thomas Hopkins 1787-1851 *Alli, AmA&B, BbD, BiD&SB, DcAmA, DcNAA*
Gallaway, Edward 1869-1930 *DcNAA*
Gallaway, J C *Alli Sup*
Gallaway, W H *ChPo*
Gallaway, William *Alli*
Galle, Andreas Wilhelm Gottfried 1858- *WhLA*
Galle, F C 1919- *ConAu 61*
Gallegan, Peter d1850 *PoIre*
Gallegly, J S 1898- *ConAu 5R*
Gallego, Juan Nicasio 1777-1853 *BbD, BiD&SB, CasWL, DcEuL, EvEuW, Pen Eur*
Gallego, Laura 1924- *PueRA*
Gallegos, Charles B *AmSCAP 66*
Gallegos, Dora Marie *AmSCAP 66*
Gallegos, Romulo 1884-1968? *CasWL, CyWA, DcSpL, EncWL, Pen Am, REn, TwCW*
Gallenga, Antonio Carlo Napoleone 1810-1895 *Alli Sup, BiD&SB*
Galler, David 1929- *ConAu 25, ConP 1970, DrAP 1975*
Gallerite, The *ConAu XR*
Gallery, D *Alli Sup*
Gallery, Dan *ConAu XR*
Gallery, Daniel V 1901- *ConAu 13R*
Galletly, Alexander *Alli Sup*
Galletti DiCadilhac, Margaret Isabella *Alli Sup*
Galley, George *Alli*
Galleymore, Fanny 1946- *WrD 1976*
Galleymore, Frances 1946- *Au&Wr*
Galleze, Englebert *OxCan*
Galli DaBibiena *AtlBL*
Galliard *Alli*
Galliard, Bradshaw *Alli*
Gallichan, Walter M 1861- *WhLA*
Gallico, Grace Lane 1921- *AmSCAP 66*
Gallico, Paul 1897- *AmA&B, AmNov, Au&Wr, AuNews 1, ConAu 5R, ConLC 2, ConNov 1972, ConNov 1976, DcLEnL, EvLB, REnAL, TwCA Sup, TwCW, WrD 1976*
Gallie, Menna Humphreys 1920- *ConAu 1R*
Gallie, Walter Bryce 1912- *Au&Wr*
Gallienne *TwCA, TwCA Sup*
Gallienne, Richard Le *Chmbr 3*
Gallier, James 1798-1868 *DcNAA*
Gallimard, Gaston 1881-1975 *ConAu 61*
Gallimore, Francis *Alli*
Gallin, Sister Mary Alice 1921- *ConAu 13R*
Gallina, Giacinto 1852-1897 *CasWL*
Gallinger, Osma Couch *ConAu XR*
Gallison, John 1788-1820 *Alli*
Gallitzin, Prince Demetrius Augustine 1770-1841 *DcAmA*
Gallitzin, Furstin *OxGer*
Gallizier, Nathan 1866-1927 *DcNAA, OhA&B*
Gallman, Waldemar J 1899- *ConAu P-1*
Gallner, Sheldon M 1949- *ConAu 53*
Gallo, Jesus 1870- *WhWNAA*

Gallo, Louis *DrAP 1975*
Gallogly, J *Alli Sup*
Gallon, Arthur J 1915- *ConAu 57*
Gallon, Tom 1866- *BiD&SB*
Gallop, Sammy 1915- *AmSCAP 66*
Galloupe, Francis Ellis *Alli Sup*
Galloway, Lieutenant-Colonel *Alli*
Galloway, Allan Douglas 1920- *ConAu 25, WrD 1976*
Galloway, Beverly Thomas 1863-1939 *DcAmA, DcNAA, WhWNAA*
Galloway, Charles Betts 1849-1909 *BiDSA, DcAmA, DcNAA*
Galloway, Christian F J *OxCan*
Galloway, David D 1937- *ConAu 21*
Galloway, George *Alli, BiDLA, WhLA*
Galloway, George Barnes 1898- *AmA&B, ConAu 1R*
Galloway, Jesse James 1882-1962 *IndAu 1917*
Galloway, John C 1915- *ConAu 25*
Galloway, John Cole *Alli*
Galloway, Joseph 1731?-1803 *Alli, AmA, CyAL 1, DcAmA, DcNAA, OxAm*
Galloway, Joseph 1840- *IndAu 1917*
Galloway, Joseph D *Alli Sup*
Galloway, Julia Rebecca 1874-1955 *OhA&B*
Galloway, Lee 1872- *WhWNAA*
Galloway, Margaret Cecilia 1915- *Au&Wr, ConAu 13R*
Galloway, Patrick *Alli*
Galloway, Robert *Alli, Alli Sup*
Galloway, Robert L *Alli Sup*
Galloway, Thomas Walton 1866-1929 *AmLY, DcNAA, WhWNAA*
Galloway, Tod B 1863-1935 *AmSCAP 66*
Galloway, W *Alli Sup*
Galloway, William *Alli Sup*
Galloway, William Albert 1860-1931 *OhA&B*
Galloway, William Brown *Alli, Alli Sup*
Galloway Poet, The *DcEnL*
Gallu, Samuel *AuNews 2*
Gallucci, Robert L 1946- *ConAu 61*
Gallup, Anna Billings 1872- *WhWNAA*
Gallup, Dick 1941- *ConAu 33, DrAP 1975*
Gallup, Donald Clifford 1913- *AmA&B, Au&Wr, ConAu 25*
Gallup, Elizabeth 1846-1935 *DcNAA*
Gallup, George Horace 1901- *AmA&B, ConAu 13R, LongC, REn, REnAL*
Gallup, James *Alli*
Gallup, Joseph Adams 1769-1849 *DcAmA, DcNAA*
Gallup, Richard John 1941- *ConP 1970*
Gallus, Gaius Asinius d033 *Pen Cl*
Gallus, Gaius Cornelius 069?BC-026BC *CasWL, Pen Cl*
Gallus, Marcus Fadius 065?BC- *Pen Cl*
Gallwey, N Payne- *Alli Sup*
Gallwey, Peter *Alli Sup*
Gallwey, Sir Ralph William Payne- 1848- *Alli Sup*
Gallwey, Thomas *Alli Sup, PoIre*
Gallwey, W Timothy 1938- *ConAu 53*
Gally, Henry 1696-1769 *Alli*
Gally, James Wellesley 1828-1891 *Alli Sup, OhA&B*
Galotti, Emilia *REn*
Galouye, Daniel Francis 1920- *ConAu 9R*
Galoway, Patrick *Alli*
Galoway, Trevor *MnBBF*
Galpin, Brian John Francis 1921- *Au&Wr*
Galpin, Charles Josiah 1864- *WhWNAA*
Galpine, Calvin *Alli*
Galpine, John *Alli, BiDLA*
Galster, Karl Paul Hans 1851- *WhLA*
Galster, Robert Miller 1928- *IlBYP, IlCB 1966*
Galsworthy, John 1867-1933 *AtlBL, CasWL, ChPo, ChPo S1, ChPo S2, Chmbr 3, CnMD, CnMWL, CnThe, CyWA, DcBiA, DcLEnL, EncWL, EvLB, LongC, McGWD, ModBL, ModBL Sup, ModWD, NewC, OxEng, Pen Eng, RAdv 1, RCom, REn, REnWD, TwCA, TwCA Sup, TwCW, WebEAL, WhLA, WhTwL*
Galt, Sir Alexander Tilloch 1817-1893 *Alli Sup, BbtC, DcNAA, OxCan*
Galt, Edwin *Alli Sup*

Galt, John 1779-1839 *Alli, BbD, BbtC, BiD&SB, BiDLA, BrAu 19, CanWr, CasWL, ChPo, ChPo S2, Chmbr 3, CyWA, DcBiA, DcEnA, DcEnL, DcLEnL, EvLB, NewC, OxCan, OxEng, Pen Eng, WebEAL*
Galt, John Minson 1819-1862 *Alli Sup, DcNAA*
Galt, Matthew *Alli*
Galt, Thomas Franklin, Jr. 1908- *ConAu 5R, SmATA 5*
Galt, Tom 1908- *ConAu XR, SmATA 5, MorJA*
Galt, William *Alli Sup*
Galton *Alli*
Galton, Arthur *Alli Sup*
Galton, Sir Douglas Strutt 1823- *Alli Sup*
Galton, Sir Francis 1822-1911 *Alli Sup, BbD, BiD&SB, BrAu 19, Chmbr 3, DcEnL, DcLEnL, EvLB, LongC, NewC*
Galton, Frank Wallis 1869- *WhLA*
Galton, John C *Alli Sup*
Galton, John Lincoln 1807-1878 *Alli Sup*
Galton, Lawrence 1913- *ConAu 57*
Galton, Raymond Percy 1930- *Au&Wr*
Galton, S Tertius *Alli, BiDLA*
Galton, Samuel *Alli*
Galton, Theodore Howard *Alli Sup*
Galtrey, Albert Sidney 1878- *WhLA*
Galuppi, Baldassare 1706-1785 *REn*
Galus, Henry S 1923- *ConAu 5R*
Galvan, John *PoIre*
Galvan, Manuel DeJesus 1834-1910 *CasWL, Pen Am*
Galvan, Roberto A *DrAP 1975*
Galvani, Luigi 1737-1798 *NewC*
Galvao, Antonio 1490?-1557 *CasWL*
Galvao, Duarte *AfA 1*
Galvao, Henrique 1895- *TwCW*
Galvez, Manuel 1882-1962 *CasWL, DcSpL, EncWL, Pen Am, REn, TwCW*
Galvez DeMontalvo, Luis 1927- *ConAu XR*
Galvez DeMontalvo, Luis 1549?-1591? *CasWL*
Galvin, Brendan 1938- *ConAu 45, DrAP 1975*
Galvin, James Patrick 1914- *IndAu 1917*
Galvin, John R 1929- *ConAu 23*
Galvin, Patrick 1927- *ConP 1970*
Galvin, Thomas J 1932- *ConAu 13R*
Galvin, Tom *PoIre*
Galway, Viscount 1844-1931 *Br&AmS*
Galway, Norman *ConAu XR*
Galwey, Geoffrey Valentine 1912- *WrD 1976*
Galwey, I T *Alli Sup, PoIre*
Gam, David *Alli*
Gam, Rita 1927- *ConAu 45*
Gama, Jose Basilio Da 1740-1795 *BiD&SB, CasWL, Pen Am*
Gama, Vasco Da 1460?-1524 *NewC, REn*
Gamache, Louis-Olivier 1784-1854 *OxCan*
Gamage, G A *ChPo*
Gamage, William *Alli, DcEnL*
Gamaliel *NewC*
Gambado, Geoffrey *Alli, Br&AmS*
Gambara, Veronica 1485-1550 *CasWL, REn*
Gambaro, Griselda 1928- *DcCLA*
Gambart, Ernest *Alli Sup*
Gambeld, W *Alli*
Gambetta, Leon 1838-1882 *OxFr, REn*
Gambier, Sir E J *Alli*
Gambier, Mrs. J *Alli Sup*
Gambier, James Ed *Alli, BiDLA*
Gambier, James William *Alli Sup*
Gambier, Kenyon *OhA&B*
Gambier, Samuel James *Alli Sup*
Gamble, Andrew Michael 1947- *WrD 1976*
Gamble, Frederick John 1904- *Au&Wr, ConAu P-1*
Gamble, Henry John *Alli, Alli Sup, PoIre*
Gamble, J *BiDLA*
Gamble, J S *Alli Sup*
Gamble, John *Alli*
Gamble, John 1859- *WhLA*
Gamble, Quo Vadis Gex 1950- *BlkAW, LivBAA*
Gamble, Richard Wilson *Alli Sup*
Gamble, Samuel Walter 1852-1932 *DcNAA, WhWNAA*
Gamble, Sidney David 1890-1968 *ConAu P-1,*

OhA&B
Gamboa, Federico 1864-1939 *CasWL, DcSpL, Pen Am*
Gambold, John *Chmbr 2*
Gambold, John d1771 *Alli*
Gambrall, Theodore Charles 1842?-1897 *DcNAA*
Gambrell, Herbert Pickens 1898- *AmA&B, ConAu 1R, TexWr*
Gambrell, James Bruton 1841-1921 *BiDSA, DcNAA*
Gambrill, J Montgomery 1880-1953 *AmA&B, AmLY*
Gambrill, Richard V N 1890- *Br&AmS*
Gambs, John S 1899- *ConAu 13R*
Game, Josiah Bethea 1869-1935 *DcNAA, WhWNAA*
Gamertsfelder, Solomon Jacob 1851-1925 *DcNAA, OhA&B*
Games, Abram 1914- *WhGrA*
Games, John *Alli*
Gamez, Gutierre Diez De 1379?-1450 *DcEuL*
Gamgee, Arthur *Alli Sup*
Gamgee, John *Alli Sup*
Gamgee, Joseph *Alli Sup*
Gamgee, Joseph Sampson 1828-1886 *Alli Sup*
Gammack, Arthur James 1871-1927 *DcNAA*
Gammage, Allen Z 1917- *ConAu 5R*
Gammage, Mrs. Grady *ArizL*
Gammage, Robert G 1817-1888 *Alli Sup*
Gammage, William Leonard 1942- *ConAu 57*
Gammell, Isaac 1861?-1932 *DcNAA*
Gammell, William 1812-1889 *Alli, CyAL 1, DcAmA, DcNAA*
Gammon, D J *MnBBF*
Gammon, Frederic T *Alli Sup*
Gammon, John *Alli*
Gammon, Robert William 1867- *WhWNAA*
Gammon, Roland 1920- *ConAu 49*
Gammon, Samuel Rhea 1889- *TexWr, WhWNAA*
Gammond, W L *Alli Sup*
Gamon, Christofle De 1575-1621 *OxFr*
Gamon, Hannibal *Alli*
Gamon, John *Alli Sup*
Gamoran, Mamie 1900- *ConAu 5R*
Gamow, George 1904-1968 *AmA&B, REnAL, TwCA Sup*
Gamsakhurdia, Konstantine 1891- *DcOrL 3, Pen Cl*
Gamson, William Anthony 1934- *ConAu 33, WrD 1976*
Gamst, Frederick Charles 1936- *ConAu 29, WrD 1976*
Gamwell, S Clearstone *ChPo S2*
Gan, Peter 1894-1974 *OxGer*
Gan, Y A *DcRusL*
Gandalac, Lennard *ConAu XR*
Gandee, Lee R 1917- *ConAu 33*
Gander, Sir Gregory 1745-1815 *Alli, DcEnL*
Gander, Joseph *Alli*
Gander, Leonard Marsland 1902- *Au&Wr*
Ganders, Harry S 1894- *WhWNAA*
Gandevia, Bryan Harle 1925- *Au&Wr, WrD 1976*
Gandhi, Mohandas Karamchand 1869-1948 *CasWL, DcLEnL, OxEng, Pen Cl, REn*
Gandier, Alfred 1861-1932 *DcNAA, WhWNAA*
Gandolphy, Peter 1760?-1821 *Alli, BiDLA, BiDLA Sup*
Gandon, James 1760-1824 *Alli*
Gandy, Henry *Alli*
Gandy, Joseph *Alli, BiDLA*
Gane, Mrs. *ChPo*
Gane, Douglas M *Alli Sup*
Gane, John *Alli*
Gane, William Law 1815- *BbtC*
Ganelon *REn*
Gangel, Kenneth O 1935- *ConAu 25*
Gangemi, Kenneth 1937- *ConAu 29, DrAF 1976, DrAP 1975*
Gangesa *DcOrL 2*
Ganghofer, Ludwig Albert 1855-1920 *BiD&SB, OxGer*
Gangoly, Orun Coomar 1920- *WhGrA*
Gangooly, Jogut Chunder *Alli Sup*
Gangopadhyay, Narayan 1918-1970 *DcOrL 2*

Gangulee, Nagendra Nath 1889- *WhLA*
Ganguly, Sachindra Nath 1932- *BiDPar*
Ganivet, Angel 1865-1898 *CasWL, ClDMEuL, DcSpL, EuA, EvEuW, Pen Eur, REn*
Ganley, Albert Charles 1918- *ConAu 13R*
Ganly, T J *Alli*
Gann, Ernest Kellogg 1910- *AmA&B, AmNov, AuNews 1, ConAu 1R, TwCW, WhPNW, WorAu, WrD 1976*
Gann, Lewis Henry 1924- *Au&Wr, ConAu 5R, WrD 1976*
Gann, Thomas William Francis *WhWNAA*
Gannau *OxFr*
Ganneau *OxFr*
Gannet, Deborah 1760-1827 *DcNAA*
Gannett, Abbie M *Alli Sup*
Gannett, Caleb 1745-1818 *Alli*
Gannett, Ezra Stiles 1801-1871 *BbtC, DcAmA*
Gannett, Frank Ernest 1876-1957 *AmA&B, REnAL, WhWNAA*
Gannett, Henry 1846-1914 *Alli Sup, AmA&B, DcAmA, DcNAA, REnAL*
Gannett, Kent 1887- *AmSCAP 66*
Gannett, Lewis Stiles 1891-1966 *AmA&B, ChPo, REnAL, TwCA, TwCA Sup*
Gannett, Mabel Anstice d1933 *DcNAA, WhWNAA*
Gannett, Ruth Chrisman Arens 1896- *IlCB 1956, MorJA*
Gannett, Ruth Stiles 1923- *AuBYP, BkCL, ConAu 21, SmATA 3*
Gannett, William Channing 1840-1923 *Alli Sup, AmA&B, BiD&SB, ChPo, ChPo S1, DcAmA, DcNAA*
Gannino, Ruth Lillian 1916- *AmSCAP 66*
Gannon, Anna 1876- *ChPo, DcAmA*
Gannon, David 1904- *CatA 1952*
Gannon, E J *MnBBF*
Gannon, John P *PoIre*
Gannon, Kim 1900- *AmSCAP 66*
Gannon, Nicholas John 1829-1875 *Alli Sup, PoIre*
Gannon, Robert Haines 1931- *ConAu 9R, SmATA 8*
Gannon, Robert Ignatius 1893- *BkC 5, CatA 1952, ConAu P-1, WrD 1976*
Gannon, W G *Alli Sup*
Gano, John 1727-1804 *Alli, BiDSA, DcNAA*
Gano, Louise Heinke 1885-1949 *OhA&B*
Ganoe, William Addleman 1881- *AmA&B, WhWNAA*
Ganong, William Francis 1864-1941 *DcNAA, OxCan*
Ganor *REn*
Ganora *REn*
Ganpat *MnBBF*
Gans, Edgar H *Alli Sup*
Gans, Eric L 1941- *ConAu 33, WrD 1976*
Gans, Herbert J 1927- *Au&Wr, ConAu 1R*
Gans, Richard 1880- *WhLA*
Ganse, Hervey Doddridge 1822-1891 *DcAmA, DcNAA*
Gansfort, Wessel 1419?-1489 *CasWL*
Ganshof, Francois-Louis 1895- *ConAu 19*
Ganss, George Edward 1905- *ConAu 49*
Ganss, Henry George 1855-1912 *DcNAA*
Gant, Frederick James *Alli Sup*
Gant, Jonathan *ConAu XR*
Gant, Lisbeth A 1948- *BlkAW, LivBA*
Gant, Margaret *ChPo*
Gant, Phyllis 1922- *ConAu 57*
Gant, Roland *ChPo*
Gant, S C *Alli Sup*
Gantenbein, Winifred Watson *ChPo*
Ganter, Franz S *DcNAA*
Gantillon, Peter John Francis *Alli Sup*
Gantillon, Simon 1887-1961 *EvEuW, McGWD*
Gantner, Neilma Baillieu 1922- *Au&Wr, WrD 1976*
Gantor, Franz S *BiDSA*
Gantry, Susan Nadler 1947- *ConAu 61*
Gantt, Fred, Jr. 1922- *ConAu 9R*
Gantt, Henry Laurence 1861-1919 *DcNAA*
Gantt, Thomas T *Alli Sup*
Gantvoort, Arnold Johann 1857-1937 *DcNAA, OhA&B, WhWNAA*
Gantz, Charlotte Orr 1909- *ConAu 49*
Gantzer, Colleen *ConAu XR*

Gantzer, Hugh 1931- *ConAu 61*
Ganyard, A O *ChPo*
Ganz, Arthur 1928- *ConAu 49*
Ganz, Margaret 1927- *ConAu 45*
Ganz, Rudolph 1877- *AmSCAP 66*
Ganzel, Dewey Alvin, Jr. 1927- *ConAu 25*
Ganzglass, Martin Richard 1941- *ConAu 33*
Ganzo, Robert 1898- *WorAu*
Gaon Of Wilna, The *CasWL*
Gaona, Ralph Raymond, Sr. 1925-
   AmSCAP 66
Gaos, Vicente 1919- *Pen Eur*
Gapanov, Boris 1934?-1972 *ConAu 37*
Gapper, E P *Alli*
Gar, Bar *Alli*
Gara, Larry 1922- *ConAu 53*
Garabrant, Nellie M *ChPo, ChPo S1,*
   ChPo S2
Garamond, Claude d1561 *NewC, OxFr*
Garand, Edouard 1901- *WhWNAA*
Garasse, Francois 1585-1631 *OxFr*
Garat, Dominique-Joseph 1750?-1832 *OxFr*
Garatt, Arthur *ChPo S1*
Garay, Janos 1812-1853 *BbD, BiD&SB,*
   CasWL
Garay, Leslie Andrews 1924- *Au&Wr*
Garb, Solomon 1920- *ConAu 13R, WrD 1976*
Garbarino, Joseph W 1919- *ConAu 53*
Garbayo, Fermin Hernandez 1929- *WhGrA*
Garbe, Robert 1878-1927 *CasWL*
Garber, Clark McKinley 1891- *OhA&B*
Garber, Eugene K 1932- *ConAu 57*
Garber, Frederick 1929- *ConAu 53*
Garber, John Palmer 1858?-1936 *DcNAA,*
   WhWNAA
Garber, Lee O 1900- *ConAu 37*
Garber, Paul Neff 1899- *AmA&B*
Garber, Virginia *ChPo*
Garber, Virginia Armistead *BiDSA*
Garbett, Arthur Selwyn 1883- *WhWNAA*
Garbett, Colin 1881- *ConAu P-1*
Garbett, Cyril Forster 1875-1955 *NewC*
Garbett, Edward 1817-1887 *Alli Sup*
Garbett, Edward Lacey *Alli Sup*
Garbett, Isabel Charlotte *Alli Sup*
Garbett, James *Alli*
Garbini, Giovanni 1931- *ConAu 21*
Garbit, Frederick J *Alli Sup*
Garbo, Norman 1919- *ConAu 17R*
Garborg, Aadne 1851-1924 *CasWL*
Garborg, Arne 1851-1924 *BbD, BiD&SB,*
   CasWL, ClDMEuL, CnMD, EuA,
   Pen Eur
Garbutt, Bernard 1900- *IlCB 1956*
Garbutt, Douglas 1922- *Au&Wr, WrD 1976*
Garbutt, John L *MnBBF*
Garbutt, Richard *Alli*
Garcao, Pedro Antonio Correia 1724-1772 *BbD,*
   BiD&SB, CasWL, Pen Eur
Garceau, Oliver 1911- *ConAu 29, WrD 1976*
Garces, Francisco Tomas Hermenegildo
   1738-1781 *ArizL, OxAm*
Garcia, Albert Y 1938- *AmSCAP 66*
Garcia, Antonio Carlos 1925- *WhGrA*
Garcia, F Chris 1940- *ConAu 53*
Garcia, Felix 1906- *AmSCAP 66*
Garcia, Genaro 1867- *AmLY*
Garcia, Juan *OxCan Sup*
Garcia, Russell 1916- *AmSCAP 66*
Garcia Calderon, Francisco 1883-1953 *CasWL,*
   DcSpL, Pen Am
Garcia Calderon, Ventura 1886-1959 *CasWL,*
   EncWL, Pen Am
Garcia Castaneda, Salvador 1932- *ConAu 61*
Garcia DeCastrojeris *DcSpL*
Garcia DeLaHuerta, Vicente 1734-1787 *CasWL,*
   DcSpL, EvEuW, McGWD, Pen Eur,
   REn
Garcia DeLaHuerta Y Munoz, Vicente A
   1734-1787 *EuA*
Garcia DeQuevedo, Jose Heriberto 1819-1871
   BiD&SB
Garcia Gomez, Emilio 1905- *Pen Eur*
Garcia Gutierrez, Antonio 1813-1884 *BiD&SB,*
   CasWL, DcSpL, EuA, EvEuW, McGWD,
   Pen Eur, REn
Garcia Hortelano, Juan 1928- *TwCW*
Garcia Lorca, Federico 1898?-1936 *AtlBL,*

CasWL, ClDMEuL, CnMWL, CyWA,
   DcSpL, EncWL, EvEuW, McGWD,
   ModRL, ModWD, Pen Eur, RCom, REn,
   REnWL, TwCA, TwCA Sup, TwCW
Garcia Lorca, F ALSO Lorca, Federico
Garcia Marquez, Gabriel 1928- *CasWL,*
   ConAu 33, ConLC 2, ConLC 3, DcCLA,
   EncWL Sup, Pen Am, WhTwL, WorAu
Garcia Monge, Joaquin 1881- *DcSpL*
Garcia Morente, Manuel 1888-1941 *ClDMEuL*
Garcia Ponce, Juan 1932- *DcCLA*
Garcia Tassara, Gabriel 1817-1875 *CasWL,*
   Pen Eur
Garcia Terres, Jaime 1924- *Pen Am*
Garcia Y Tassara, Gabriel 1817-1875 *BiD&SB*
Garcilaso De La Vega 1503?-1536 *BbD,*
   BiD&SB, CasWL, DcSpL, EuA, EvEuW,
   Pen Eur, REn
Garcilaso De La Vega, El Inca 1539?-1616?
   CasWL, DcSpL, EuA, EvEuW, NewC,
   Pen Am, REn, REnAL
Garcilasso De La Vega 1503-1536 *DcEuL,*
   OxEng
Garcke, Emile And Fells, J M *Alli Sup*
Garczynski, Stephen 1806-1833 *BiD&SB*
Gard *TwCA, TwCA Sup*
Gard, Alison *Alli Sup*
Gard, Anson A *OxCan*
Gard, Elizabeth Barbara 1937- *Au&Wr*
Gard, Joyce 1911- *Au&Wr, AuBYP*
Gard, Lillian *ChPo, ChPo S1, ChPo S2*
Gard, Richard A 1914- *ConAu 1R*
Gard, Robert *REnAL*
Gard, Robert E *OxCan*
Gard, Robert Edward *AuBYP*
Gard, Roger Martin Du *ModRL*
Gard, Wayne 1899- *AmA&B, AnMV 1926,*
   ConAu 1R, TexWr, WhWNAA
Gardam, Jane 1928- *ConAu 49*
Garde, Evelina San *ChPo*
Garde, Richard *Alli*
Garden, Mrs. *Alli Sup*
Garden, Alex *Alli*
Garden, Alexander 1685?-1756 *Alli, AmA,*
   DcAmA, DcNAA
Garden, Alexander 1730?-1791 *Alli, BiDSA,*
   CyAL 1, DcAmA
Garden, Alexander 1757-1829 *BiDSA, DcAmA,*
   DcNAA
Garden, Alexander 1785-1856 *BiDSA*
Garden, Bruce 1936- *ConAu XR, WrD 1976*
Garden, Charles *Alli, BiDLA*
Garden, Edward James Clarke 1930- *ConAu 25,*
   WrD 1976
Garden, Francis 1721-1793 *Alli*
Garden, Francis 1810-1884 *Alli, Alli Sup*
Garden, George *Alli*
Garden, James *Alli, BiDLA*
Garden, John *ConAu XR*
Garden, Mary 1877- *REn*
Garden, Nancy 1938- *ConAu 33, WrD 1976*
Garden, William *ChPo S1*
Gardener, Helen Hamilton 1853-1925 *Alli Sup,*
   AmA&B, AmLY, DcAmA, DcNAA,
   OhA&B
Gardener, Thomas *Alli*
Gardenhire, Samuel Major 1855-1923 *DcAmA,*
   DcNAA
Gardenor, William *Alli*
Gardenstone, Lord *Alli*
Gardette, Charles Desmarais *Alli Sup, ChPo*
Gardette, E B *Alli Sup*
Gardiner, A F *Alli*
Gardiner, Alfred George 1865-1946 *DcLEnL,*
   EvLB, LongC, NewC, WhLA
Gardiner, Annie Walker *ChPo S1*
Gardiner, Asa Bird 1839-1919 *DcAmA,*
   DcNAA
Gardiner, Bertha Meriton *Alli Sup*
Gardiner, C Harvey 1913- *Au&Wr,*
   ConAu 1R
Gardiner, Catriona *ChPo*
Gardiner, Cecilia A *Alli Sup*
Gardiner, Charles Alexander 1855-1910 *DcNAA*
Gardiner, Charles Fox 1857-1947 *DcNAA*
Gardiner, Sir Christopher *OxAm*
Gardiner, Clarke *WhWNAA*
Gardiner, Dorothy 1894- *AmA&B, Au&Wr*

Gardiner, Edmund *Alli*
Gardiner, Frederick 1822-1889 *Alli Sup,*
   DcAmA, DcNAA, OhA&B, WhLA
Gardiner, Glenn Lion 1896-1962 *ConAu 1R*
Gardiner, H T *Alli Sup*
Gardiner, Harold Charles 1904-1969 *AmA&B,*
   BkC 6
Gardiner, Harry Norman 1855-1927 *DcNAA,*
   WhWNAA
Gardiner, Helen Hamilton *BiDSA*
Gardiner, Herbert Fairbairn 1849-1924 *DcNAA*
Gardiner, J *Alli, BiDLA*
Gardiner, James *Alli*
Gardiner, James 1688-1745 *NewC*
Gardiner, John *Alli, BiDLA, ChPo, ChPo S1*
Gardiner, John d1830 *CyAL 1*
Gardiner, John 1757- *BiDLA*
Gardiner, John Hays 1863-1913 *DcNAA*
Gardiner, John Smallman *Alli*
Gardiner, John Stanley 1872- *WhLA*
Gardiner, John Sylvester John 1765-1830 *Alli,*
   CyAL 1, DcNAA
Gardiner, Judy 1922- *ConAu 21*
Gardiner, Kathleen *ChPo S2*
Gardiner, Linda *Alli Sup*
Gardiner, Mary *Alli Sup*
Gardiner, Mary L *ChPo*
Gardiner, Matthew *PoIre*
Gardiner, Ner d1875? *Alli Sup*
Gardiner, Patrick Lancaster 1922- *Au&Wr,*
   ConAu 1R, WrD 1976
Gardiner, Persis *ChPo*
Gardiner, Peter *ChPo*
Gardiner, Ralph *Alli*
Gardiner, Richard *Alli, BbtC, BiDLA*
Gardiner, Richard 1591-1670 *Alli*
Gardiner, Robert Barlow *Alli Sup*
Gardiner, Robert K A 1914- *ConAu 21*
Gardiner, Robert W 1932- *ConAu 53,*
   WrD 1976
Gardiner, Sir Robert William 1782-1864
   Alli Sup
Gardiner, Rolf 1902- *Au&Wr*
Gardiner, Samuel *Alli*
Gardiner, Samuel Rawson 1829-1902 *Alli Sup,*
   BbD, BiD&SB, BrAu 19, CasWL,
   Chmbr 3, DcEnA, DcEnA Ap, EvLB,
   NewC, OxEng
Gardiner, Stephen 1483-1555 *Alli*
Gardiner, Susan H *ChPo*
Gardiner, W *Alli, Alli Sup, ChPo S2*
Gardiner, William *Alli, Alli Sup, BiDLA,*
   ChPo
Gardiner, William 1804- *ChPo S1*
Gardiner, Mrs. William *Alli Sup*
Gardiner, William Nelson 1766-1814 *BkIE*
Gardiner-Hill, Harold 1891- *Au&Wr*
Gardizi, Abu Sa'id 'Abd Al-Hayy *CasWL*
Gardner, A *Alli Sup*
Gardner, Alan 1925- *ConAu 21*
Gardner, Alexander 1821-1882 *DcNAA*
Gardner, Alice *Alli Sup*
Gardner, Anne *ConAu 49*
Gardner, Archibald *Alli Sup*
Gardner, Arthur *Alli Sup*
Gardner, Arthur 1878- *Au&Wr*
Gardner, Augustus Kinsley 1812-1876 *Alli,*
   Alli Sup, CyAL 1, DcAmA, DcNAA
Gardner, Augustus Peabody 1865-1918 *DcNAA*
Gardner, Benjamin Franklin 1900- *BlkAW*
Gardner, Brian 1931- *Au&Wr, ChPo S2,*
   ConAu 13R, WrD 1976
Gardner, Carl 1931- *BlkAW*
Gardner, Celia Emmeline 1884- *Alli Sup,*
   DcNAA
Gardner, Charles Joseph Thomas 1912- *Au&Wr,*
   WrD 1976
Gardner, Charles K 1787-1869 *Alli, DcAmA,*
   DcNAA
Gardner, D Bruce 1924- *ConAu 49*
Gardner, Daniel *Alli Sup*
Gardner, Daniel Pereira d1853 *Alli, DcNAA*
Gardner, David P 1933- *ConAu 21*
Gardner, Dennis Roy 1930- *Au&Wr*
Gardner, Dic *AuBYP, ConAu XR*
Gardner, Donald Robert Hugh 1938-
   ConP 1970
Gardner, Donald Yetter 1912- *AmSCAP 66*

Gardner, Dorothy E M 1900- *ConAu 23*
Gardner, Dorsey 1842-1894 *Alli Sup, BiD&SB, DcAmA, DcNAA*
Gardner, Douglas William 1909- *Au&Wr*
Gardner, E C *ChPo*
Gardner, Edmund Garratt 1869- *ChPo, WhLA*
Gardner, Edward *Alli, Alli Sup, BiDLA*
Gardner, Edward Clinton 1920- *ConAu 13R, WrD 1976*
Gardner, Edward Hall 1883- *WhWNAA*
Gardner, Eldon J 1909- *ConAu 41*
Gardner, Ella Waterbury 1893- *ChPo, ChPo S1*
Gardner, Emelyn Elizabeth *ChPo S1*
Gardner, Erle Stanley 1889-1970 *AmA&B, ConAu 5R, ConAu 25, EncM&D, EvLB, LongC, MnBBF, OxAm, Pen Am, REn, REnAL, TwCA, TwCA Sup, TwCW, WhWNAA*
Gardner, Ernest Arthur 1862- *WhLA*
Gardner, Eugene *ChPo S1*
Gardner, Eugene Clarence 1836-1915 *Alli Sup, DcAmA, DcNAA*
Gardner, F S *ChPo*
Gardner, Francis Peter Edmund 1928- *Au&Wr*
Gardner, Frank 1856-1922 *DcNAA*
Gardner, Frank Augustine 1861-1938 *DcNAA*
Gardner, Frank Duane 1864- *WhWNAA*
Gardner, Frank Matthias 1908- *Au&Wr, WrD 1976*
Gardner, Franklin B *Alli Sup*
Gardner, Frederick *ChPo S2*
Gardner, G Ray *BlkAW*
Gardner, George *Alli*
Gardner, George Henry *Alli Sup*
Gardner, George William 1888- *WhWNAA*
Gardner, Gerald 1929- *ConAu 1R*
Gardner, Gerard *OxCan*
Gardner, Gilbert J *Alli Sup*
Gardner, Gilson 1869-1935 *AmA&B, DcNAA, WhWNAA*
Gardner, Mrs. H C *Alli Sup, ChPo, ChPo S1*
Gardner, H P *ChPo S1*
Gardner, Helen Louise 1908- *Au&Wr, ChPo S2, WorAu, WrD 1976*
Gardner, Herbert *Alli Sup*
Gardner, Horace John 1896- *WhWNAA*
Gardner, Isabella Stewart 1915- *AmA&B, CnE&AP, ConP 1970, ConP 1975, CrCAP, DrAP 1975, WorAu, WrD 1976*
Gardner, J *Alli*
Gardner, J S *Alli Sup*
Gardner, James *Alli Sup, ChPo*
Gardner, Jani 1943- *ConAu 25*
Gardner, Jeanne LeMonnier 1925- *ConAu 17R, SmATA 5*
Gardner, Jeffrey *ConAu XR*
Gardner, John *Alli, Alli Sup*
Gardner, John 1804-1880 *Alli Sup*
Gardner, John 1933- *AuNews 1, ConLC 2, ConLC 3, ConLC 5, ConNov 1976, DrAF 1976, ModAL Sup, RAdv 1, WrD 1976*
Gardner, John Dunn *Alli Sup*
Gardner, John E 1917- *ConAu 17R*
Gardner, John Edmund 1926- *Au&Wr, WrD 1976*
Gardner, John Lane 1793-1869 *DcNAA*
Gardner, John William 1912- *AmA&B, ConAu 1R, ConAu 5R*
Gardner, John William 1919- *Au&Wr*
Gardner, Joseph L 1933- *ConAu 29*
Gardner, Julia Emily *Alli Sup*
Gardner, Laurence Panting *Alli, BiDLA*
Gardner, Lawrence *ConAu XR, WrD 1976*
Gardner, Leonard *DrAF 1976*
Gardner, Lewis J 1836-1909 *HsB&A*
Gardner, Lillian Soskin 1907- *AuBYP*
Gardner, Lloyd C 1934- *ConAu 9R*
Gardner, Lucile Blake *TexWr*
Gardner, M H 1857- *WhWNAA*
Gardner, Martin 1914- *AmA&B, ChPo, ChPo S1, ChPo S2*
Gardner, Mary Adelaide 1920- *ConAu 21, WrD 1976*
Gardner, Mary Peaslee *ChPo S1*
Gardner, Mary Russell *Alli Sup, ChPo*
Gardner, Matthew 1790-1873 *OhA&B*

Gardner, Maurice 1909- *AmSCAP 66*
Gardner, Michael 1920- *AmSCAP 66*
Gardner, Nancy Bruff 1915- *ConAu 13R, WrD 1976*
Gardner, Paul 1930- *WrD 1976*
Gardner, Percy 1846- *Alli Sup, WhLA*
Gardner, R H 1918- *ConAu 33*
Gardner, Ralph D 1923- *ConAu 13R, WrD 1976*
Gardner, Richard *Alli*
Gardner, Richard 1931- *AmA&B, ConAu 21, WrD 1976*
Gardner, Richard A 1931- *ConAu 33, WrD 1976*
Gardner, Richard Newton 1927- *AmA&B*
Gardner, Riley W 1921- *ConAu 13R*
Gardner, Robert 1911- *ConAu 61*
Gardner, Robert Edward 1891- *OhA&B*
Gardner, Robert Waterman 1866-1937 *DcNAA*
Gardner, S A *Alli Sup*
Gardner, S Ursula *Alli Sup*
Gardner, Samuel 1891- *AmSCAP 66*
Gardner, Samuel Jackson 1788-1864 *Alli, Alli Sup, CyAL 1, DcAmA, DcNAA*
Gardner, T C *Alli Sup*
Gardner, Thomas *Alli*
Gardner, Thurman C *TexWr*
Gardner, Victor Ray 1885- *WhWNAA*
Gardner, W *Alli*
Gardner, W Biscombe *ChPo*
Gardner, W H *Alli Sup*
Gardner, W W *Alli Sup*
Gardner, Wallace 1905?- *IndAu 1917*
Gardner, Walter M 1861- *WhLA*
Gardner, Warren Winslow 1909- *IndAu 1917*
Gardner, William *Alli*
Gardner, William Amory 1863- *ChPo S1*
Gardner, William Earl 1928- *ConAu 5R*
Gardner, William Edward 1872- *AmLY, WhWNAA*
Gardner, William H *ChPo*
Gardner, William Henry 1837- *DcNAA*
Gardner, William Henry 1865-1932 *AmLY, AmSCAP 66, DcAmA, DcNAA*
Gardner, William Henry 1902-1969 *ConAu P-1*
Gardner, William Sisson 1861- *WhWNAA*
Gardner, William W *Alli Sup*
Gardner-Sharp, Abbie *DcNAA*
Gardner-Smith, Percival 1888- *ConAu 17*
Gardnor, John *Alli*
Gardon, Margarita *PueRA*
Gardons, S S *WrD 1976*
Gardonyi, Geza 1863-1922 *CasWL, ClDMEuL, Pen Eur*
Gardyner, George *Alli*
Gare, Nene 1919- *Au&Wr*
Gareau, Etienne 1915- *ConAu 45*
Gareau, Frederick H 1923- *ConAu 5R*
Garelick, May 1910- *AuBYP, BkP*
Garell, Peter *ChPo S2*
Garencieres, Theophilus *Alli*
Garencieres, Theophilus De *Alli*
Garesche, Edward Francis 1876- *AnMV 1926, CatA 1947, WhWNAA*
Garey, Samuel *Alli*
Garey, Thomas Andrew 1830-1909 *OhA&B*
Garfias, Valentin R 1883- *WhWNAA*
Garfield, Brian 1939- *ConAu 1R, WrD 1976*
Garfield, Evelyn Picon 1940- *ConAu 57*
Garfield, J *Alli*
Garfield, James Abram 1831-1881 *Alli Sup, AmA&B, BiD&SB, DcAmA, OhA&B, OxAm, REnAL*
Garfield, James B 1881- *SmATA 6*
Garfield, Leon 1921- *Au&Wr, ConAu 17R, PiP, SenS, SmATA 1, WhCL, WrD 1976*
Garfield, Sol L 1918- *ConAu 29*
Garfield, Viola 1899- *WhPNW*
Garfin *DcSpL*
Garfinkel, Bernard 1929- *ConAu 25*
Garfinkel, Herbert 1920- *ConAu 1R*
Garfit, Arthur *Alli Sup*
Garfitt, Alan 1920- *Au&Wr*
Garfitt, Roger 1944- *ConAu 33, WrD 1976*
Garforth, Francis William 1917- *Au&Wr, ConAu 9R, WrD 1976*
Garfunkel, Louis X 1897?-1972 *ConAu 37*

Gargan, Denis *Alli Sup*
Gargot, Nicolas *OxCan*
Garibaldi, Giuseppe 1807-1882 *NewC, OxFr, REn*
Gariepy, Charles Napoleon 1868-1932 *DcNAA*
Gariepy, Henry 1930- *ConAu 49*
Garigue, Philippe *OxCan Sup*
Garin, N 1852-1906 *CasWL, DcRusL*
Garioch, George *Alli*
Garioch, Robert 1908- *CasWL*
Garioch, Robert 1909- *ConP 1970, ConP 1975, WrD 1976*
Garip, A *DcOrL 3*
Garis, Howard Roger 1873-1962 *AmA&B, CarSB, REnAL*
Garis, Lilian C 1873-1954 *AmA&B*
Garis, Lillian C 1873-1954 *CarSB, OhA&B*
Garis, Robert 1925- *ConAu 17R*
Garis, Roy Lawrence 1897- *WhWNAA*
Garland, Ailsa Mary *Au&Wr*
Garland, Alison L *Alli Sup*
Garland, Annie *ChPo S1*
Garland, Augustus Hill 1832-1899 *BiDSA, DcNAA*
Garland, Bennett *ConAu XR, WrD 1976*
Garland, Claude M 1880- *WhWNAA*
Garland, David John 1864- *WhLA*
Garland, Edward *Alli*
Garland, G M *Alli Sup*
Garland, George *ConAu XR*
Garland, George Minot 1848-1926 *DcNAA*
Garland, George Vallis *Alli Sup*
Garland, Gordon Willie 1919- *Au&Wr*
Garland, Hamlin 1860-1940 *AmA&B, AmLY, AtlBL, BbD, BiD&SB, BiDPar, CasWL, ChPo, Chmbr 3, CnDAL, ConAmA, ConAmL, CyWA, DcAmA, DcBiA, DcLEnL, DcNAA, EvLB, LongC, ModAL, OxAm, OxCan, OxEng, Pen Am, RAdv 1, REn, REnAL, St&VC, TwCA, TwCA Sup, WebEAL, WhWNAA, WiscW*
Garland, Harry Parsons 1859-1935 *DcNAA*
Garland, Helen C *Alli Sup*
Garland, Hugh A 1805-1854 *Alli, BiDSA, DcNAA*
Garland, James *Alli Sup*
Garland, James d1842? *PoIre*
Garland, James Albert 1870-1906 *DcNAA*
Garland, John *Alli, AmLY XR, CasWL, DcEnL, PoIre*
Garland, Joseph 1893- *AmA&B*
Garland, Joseph C 1903- *AmSCAP 66*
Garland, Landon Cabell 1810-1895 *BiDSA, DcAmA, DcNAA*
Garland, M J *ChPo S1*
Garland, Madge 1900- *ConAu 25*
Garland, Marie Tudor *AnMV 1926*
Garland, N Surrey *Alli Sup*
Garland, Patrick *Au&Wr*
Garland, Phyl 1935- *LivBA*
Garland, Richard *BbtC*
Garland, Robert 1895-1955 *AmA&B, REnAL*
Garland, Rosemary *Au&Wr*
Garland, Thomas C *Alli Sup*
Garland, Thomas Whale 1812- *Alli Sup*
Garlanda, Frederico *Alli Sup*
Garlandia, Joannes De *Alli*
Garle, Hubert 1856- *Br&AmS*
Garlich, Thomas *Alli*
Garlick, Mrs. A H *Alli Sup*
Garlick, Frederick Smith *Alli Sup*
Garlick, Peter C 1923- *ConAu 41*
Garlick, Phyllis L *ChPo, ChPo S1*
Garlick, Raymond 1926- *ConAu 53, ConP 1970, ConP 1975, WrD 1976*
Garlick, Theodatus 1805?-1884 *Alli, DcNAA, OhA&B*
Garlington, Ernest Albert *BiDSA*
Garlington, Warren K 1923- *ConAu 9R*
Garlock, Thomas M 1929- *AmSCAP 66*
Garman, Harrison 1858- *WhWNAA*
Garman, Samuel 1846?-1927 *Alli Sup, DcAmA, DcNAA*
Garmany, Jasper Jewett *Alli Sup*
Garmendia, Salvador 1928- *DcCLA*
Garmon, William S 1926- *ConAu 21*
Garmston, John *Alli*

Garmston, Shadrach *Alli*
Garnal, M *Alli Sup*
Garneau, Alfred 1836-1904 *BbtC, CanWr, OxCan*
Garneau, Francois-Xavier 1809-1866 *Alli, BbtC, CanWr, CasWL, DcNAA, OxCan, OxCan Sup, REn, REnAL*
Garneau, Hector 1871- *AmLY*
Garneau, Hector DeSaint-Denys 1912-1943 *CanWr, CasWL, DcNAA, OxCan, OxCan Sup*
Garneau, Michel *OxCan, OxCan Sup*
Garneau, Rene 1907- *CanWr*
Garneau, Sylvain 1930-1953 *CanWr, OxCan, OxCan Sup*
Garner, Adam 1898- *AmSCAP 66*
Garner, Alan 1935- *Au&Wr, CasWL, ChPo S1, PiP, SenS, ThBJA, WhCL, WrD 1976*
Garner, C H *BiDSA*
Garner, Claud Wilton 1891- *ConAu 9R*
Garner, Dwight L 1913- *ConAu 25*
Garner, Elvira 1895- *IlCB 1945*
Garner, Erroll 1923- *AmSCAP 66*
Garner, Harry Hyman 1910- *ConAu 17R*
Garner, Hugh 1913- *Au&Wr, CanWr, CasWL, ConNov 1972, ConNov 1976, OxCan, OxCan Sup, TwCW, WrD 1976*
Garner, J W *BiDSA*
Garner, James *Alli Sup*
Garner, James Wilford 1871-1938 *AmA&B, DcAmA, DcNAA, WhWNAA*
Garner, John *Alli, OxCan Sup*
Garner, John Leslie *Alli Sup*
Garner, Katherine Minta *ChPo S1*
Garner, Lewis *Alli Sup*
Garner, Linton S 1915- *AmSCAP 66*
Garner, Paul 1910- *ConAu 37*
Garner, Richard Lynch 1848-1920 *DcAmA, DcNAA*
Garner, Robert *Alli, Alli Sup*
Garner, Ross 1914- *ConAu 33*
Garner, Samuel *Alli Sup*
Garner, Wendell R 1921- *ConAu 5R*
Garner, William 1920- *Au&Wr, ConAu 29, WrD 1976*
Garner, William R 1936- *ConAu 21*
Garnet, Eldon 1946- *ConAu 61*
Garnet, Frances *WhLA*
Garnet, Henry 1555-1606 *Alli*
Garnett, Alexander Yelverton Peyton *BiDSA*
Garnett, Arthur Campbell 1894- *AmA&B, ConAu 1R*
Garnett, Betty 1893- *WhWNAA*
Garnett, Christopher Browne 1906-1975 *ConAu 61*
Garnett, Constance 1861-1946 *DcLEnL, LongC, NewC, OxEng, Pen Eng, REn*
Garnett, D J *Alli Sup*
Garnett, David 1891- *WrD 1976*
Garnett, David 1892- *Au&Wr, CasWL, ConAu 5R, ConLC 3, ConNov 1972, ConNov 1976, CyWA, DcLEnL, EncWL, EvLB, LongC, ModBL, NewC, Pen Eng, REn, TwCA, TwCA Sup, TwCW, WhLA*
Garnett, Edward *Alli Sup*
Garnett, Edward 1868-1937 *CasWL, DcLEnL, LongC, NewC, REn, TwCA, TwCA Sup*
Garnett, Elizabeth *Alli Sup*
Garnett, Eve C R *Au&Wr, AuBYP, ConAu 1R, IlCB 1945, IlCB 1956, SmATA 3, WhCL, WrD 1976*
Garnett, Henry 1905- *Au&Wr*
Garnett, J *Alli*
Garnett, James Mercer 1770-1843 *BiDSA, DcNAA*
Garnett, James Mercer 1840-1916 *Alli Sup, AmA&B, BiDSA, DcAmA, DcNAA*
Garnett, John *Alli, BiDLA Sup*
Garnett, John d1782 *Alli*
Garnett, Judith L C 1862- *WhWNAA*
Garnett, Louis Anacharsis 1821-1901 *Alli Sup, DcNAA*
Garnett, Louise Ayres d1937 *AmA&B, AmLY, AnMV 1926, ChPo, ChPo S1, ChPo S2, DcNAA, IndAu 1816, WhWNAA*
Garnett, Lucy Mary Jane d1934 *Alli Sup,*

ChPo, WhLA
Garnett, M A *Alli Sup*
Garnett, Maxwell 1880- *WhLA*
Garnett, Mayn Clew *DcNAA*
Garnett, Muscoe Russell Hunter 1821-1864 *DcNAA*
Garnett, Peter *MnBBF*
Garnett, Porter 1871-1951 *AmA&B, ChPo S1*
Garnett, Ray *ChPo S1*
Garnett, Reuben Broadie *ChPo S1*
Garnett, Richard *Chmbr 3*
Garnett, Richard 1789-1850 *Alli Sup*
Garnett, Richard 1835-1906 *Alli Sup, BbD, BiD&SB, BrAu 19, CasWL, ChPo, ChPo S1, DcEnA, DcEnA Ap, DcEnL, DcLEnL, EvLB, LongC, NewC, OxEng, Pen Eng, REn*
Garnett, Richard Duncan Carey 1923- *ConAu 5R, WrD 1976*
Garnett, Robert Singleton 1866-1932 *ChPo S1*
Garnett, Roger 1905- *ConAu XR*
Garnett, Theodore S *BiDSA*
Garnett, Thomas 1766-1802 *Alli*
Garnett, Thomas 1799-1878 *Alli Sup*
Garnett, William 1850- *Alli Sup, WhLA*
Garnham, L W *Alli Sup*
Garnham, Nicholas 1937- *ConAu 33*
Garnham, Percy Cyril Claude 1901- *WrD 1976*
Garnham, Robert E 1753-1802 *Alli*
Garnier *BiB N*
Garnier, Charles 1605?-1649 *OxCan*
Garnier, Charlotte Marie-Reine *Au&Wr*
Garnier, John *Alli Sup*
Garnier, John Hutchison 1810?-1898 *DcNAA*
Garnier, Robert 1534-1590 *BiD&SB, CasWL, CnThe, DcEuL, EuA, EvEuW, McGWD, NewC, OxFr, Pen Eur, REn, REnWD*
Garnier, Thomas *Alli*
Garnier, Thomas Parry *Alli Sup*
Garnier-De Pont-Sainte-Maxence *OxFr*
Garnons, John d1792? *Alli*
Garns, William Henry *ChPo*
Garnsey, Henry Edward Fowler *Alli Sup*
Garoian, Leon 1925- *ConAu 1R*
Garon, Yves *OxCan Sup*
Garrad, Larch S 1936- *ConAu 61*
Garraghan, Gilbert Joseph 1871?-1942 *BkC 1, CatA 1947, DcNAA*
Garrard, Edmund *Alli*
Garrard, Elizabeth *Alli, BiDLA*
Garrard, George *Alli*
Garrard, Lancelot Austin 1904- *Au&Wr, ConAu P-1, WrD 1976*
Garrard, Lewis Hector 1829-1887 *Alli Sup, DcNAA, OhA&B, OxAm, REnAL*
Garrard, Thomas *Alli Sup*
Garrard, Will *Alli*
Garrard, William *Alli, Alli Sup*
Garratt, Alfred Charles 1813?-1891 *Alli Sup, DcNAA*
Garratt, Alfred Charles 1896- *Au&Wr*
Garratt, Arthur John 1916- *Au&Wr*
Garratt, Evelyn R *Alli Sup*
Garratt, G *Alli Sup*
Garratt, J Hilary *MnBBF*
Garratt, Philip *Alli Sup*
Garratt, Samuel *Alli, Alli Sup*
Garratt, W A *Alli*
Garratt, W A J *Alli Sup*
Garraty, John A 1920- *ConAu 1R*
Garreau, Emile Henry 1891- *AmA&B*
Garreau, Louis-Armand 1817-1865 *REnAL*
Garret, Augusta Brown *Alli Sup*
Garrete, Walter *Alli*
Garretson, Arthur Samuel 1851-1917 *DcNAA, OhA&B*
Garretson, Ferdinand VanDerveer 1839-1919 *DcNAA*
Garretson, James E 1828-1895 *Alli Sup, AmA&B, DcAmA, DcNAA*
Garretson, Robert L 1920- *ConAu 17R*
Garrett, Alexander Charles 1832-1924 *Alli Sup, BiDSA, DcAmA, DcNAA*
Garrett, Alfred B 1906- *ConAu 5R*
Garrett, Alfred Cope 1867-1946 *DcNAA*
Garrett, Almeida 1799-1854 *CnThe, Pen Eur, REnWD*
Garrett, Barbara Semple *Alli Sup*

Garrett, Byron Oscar 1897- *WhWNAA*
Garrett, Charles *Alli Sup*
Garrett, Charles Bodenham *Alli Sup*
Garrett, Charlotte *DrAP 1975*
Garrett, Edmund Henry 1853-1929 *AmA&B, ChPo, ChPo S1, ChPo S2, DcAmA, DcNAA, WhWNAA*
Garrett, Edward *Alli Sup, ChPo S2, DcEnL*
Garrett, Eileen Jeanette 1893-1970 *AmA&B, BiDPar, ConAu 25*
Garrett, Elizabeth *Alli Sup*
Garrett, Erwin Clarkson 1879-1954 *AmA&B, ChPo, ChPo S1, ChPo S2, WhWNAA*
Garrett, F *Alli Sup*
Garrett, F V *OxCan Sup*
Garrett, Florence Rome 1912- *WrD 1976*
Garrett, Franklin M 1906- *ConAu 57*
Garrett, Garet 1878-1954 *AmA&B, TwCA, TwCA Sup*
Garrett, George Palmer 1929- *AmA&B, ConAu 1R, ConLC 3, ConNov 1972, ConNov 1976, ConP 1970, ConP 1975, DrAF 1976, DrAP 1975, OxAm, RAdv 1, REnAL, WorAu, WrD 1976*
Garrett, George W *Alli Sup*
Garrett, Helen 1895- *AuBYP*
Garrett, Howard 1931- *ConAu 61*
Garrett, James J 1837- *BiDSA*
Garrett, James Leo, Jr. 1925- *ConAu 33*
Garrett, James Oscar 1888- *TexWr*
Garrett, Jimmy *BlkAW*
Garrett, Joao Baptista DaSilva L DeA 1799-1854 *CasWL, EuA*
Garrett, John *Alli Sup*
Garrett, John 1920- *ConAu 33*
Garrett, Leonard J 1926- *ConAu 17R*
Garrett, Leslie 1931- *ConAu 17R*
Garrett, Lewis *BiDSA*
Garrett, Lewis 1773-1857 *DcNAA*
Garrett, Lillian 1914- *ConAu 29, WrD 1976*
Garrett, Lloyd Fry 1886- *AmSCAP 66*
Garrett, Mark *Alli Sup*
Garrett, Pat F 1850-1908 *DcNAA*
Garrett, Peter K 1940- *ConAu 25*
Garrett, Randall *ThBJA*
Garrett, Retta Scott 1888- *TexWr*
Garrett, Rhoda And Garrett, Agnes *Alli Sup*
Garrett, Romeo Benjamin 1910- *ConAu 37*
Garrett, S Raymond *PoIre*
Garrett, Samuel *Alli Sup*
Garrett, Samuel Bond 1844-1926 *IndAu 1917*
Garrett, Stephen 1922- *Au&Wr*
Garrett, Thomas E *Alli Sup, BiDSA*
Garrett, Thomas M 1924- *ConAu 1R*
Garrett, Thomas Samuel 1913- *ConAu 1R, WrD 1976*
Garrett, Tom 1913- *ConAu XR*
Garrett, Truman *ConAu XR*
Garrett, Wendell D 1929- *ConAu 9R*
Garrett, Willard Hayes 1873- *WhWNAA*
Garrett, William 1809- *BiDSA*
Garrett, William 1890-1967 *ConAu P-1*
Garrett, William Robertson 1839-1904 *BiDSA, DcNAA*
Garretto, Paolo Federico 1903- *WhGrA*
Garrettson, Freeborn 1752-1827 *DcNAA*
Garrick, David 1717-1779 *Alli, BrAu, CasWL, Chmbr 2, CriT 2, DcEnA, DcEnL, DcEuL, DcLEnL, EvLB, McGWD, MouLC 2, NewC, OxEng, Pen Eng, REn*
Garrick, H B W *Alli Sup*
Garrick, John *MnBBF*
Garrigan, Owen 1928- *ConAu 23*
Garrigou-Lagrange, Reginald Marie 1877- *CatA 1947*
Garrigue, Jean 1914-1972 *AmA&B, ConAu 5R, ConAu 37, ConLC 2, ConP 1970, ConP 1975, IndAu 1917, ModAL, ModAL Sup, OxAm, Pen Am, RAdv 1, REnAL, TwCA Sup*
Garrigues, Adele M *Alli Sup*
Garrigues, Fernando And Cayley, Charles *Alli Sup*
Garrigues, Henri Jacques 1831-1913 *DcNAA*
Garrigues, Henry Jacques 1831-1913 *Alli Sup, DcAmA*
Garrioch, Alfred Campbell 1848-1934 *DcNAA,*

OxCan
Garrish, Harold J d1956 *MnBBF*
Garrison, Curtis W 1901- *OhA&B*
Garrison, Edwin William 1805-1840 *DcNAA*
Garrison, Elisha Ely 1871-1935 *DcNAA,*
OhA&B
Garrison, Fielding Hudson 1870-1935 *AmA&B,*
DcNAA, WhWNAA
Garrison, Frederick *AuBYP, ConAmA,*
ConAu XR, SmATA XR
Garrison, George Pierce 1853-1910 *BiDSA,*
DcAmA, DcNAA
Garrison, I L 1868- *ArizL*
Garrison, James 1943- *ConAu 61*
Garrison, James H 1842-1931 *AmLY, DcAmA,*
DcNAA, WhWNAA
Garrison, Joan *ConAu XR*
Garrison, Joseph Fithian 1823-1892 *Alli Sup,*
DcAmA, DcNAA
Garrison, Karl C 1900- *ConAu 37*
Garrison, Lloyd McKim 1867-1900 *DcNAA*
Garrison, Omar V 1913- *ConAu 33,*
WrD 1976
Garrison, Peggy *DrAP 1975*
Garrison, Richard Benjamin 1926- *ConAu 13R,*
IndAu 1917
Garrison, Sidney Clarence 1887-1945 *DcNAA,*
WhWNAA
Garrison, Stephen Olin 1853-1900 *Alli Sup,*
DcNAA
Garrison, Theodosia Pickering 1874-1944
AmA&B, ChPo, ChPo S2, ConAmL,
DcNAA, REnAL, St&VC
Garrison, Webb B 1919- *ConAu 1R*
Garrison, Wendell Phillips 1840-1907 *Alli Sup,*
AmA&B, BiD&SB, ChPo, DcAmA,
DcNAA
Garrison, William Lloyd 1805-1879 *Alli, AmA,*
AmA&B, BiD&SB, ChPo, Chmbr 3,
DcAmA, DcEnL, DcLEnL, DcNAA,
EvLB, OxAm, REn, REnAL
Garrison, William Lloyd 1838-1909 *DcNAA*
Garrison, William Lloyd 1879- *BbD*
Garrison, Winfred Ernest 1874- *AmA&B,*
AmLY, ConAu 1R, WhWNAA
Garrity *ConAu XR*
Garrity, Devin Adair 1905- *AmA&B*
Garrity, Joan Theresa *AuNews 1*
Garro, Elena 1920- *DcCLA*
Garrod, Alfred B, And Edward Ballard *Alli*
Garrod, Sir Alfred Baring 1819- *Alli Sup*
Garrod, Alfred Henry 1846-1879 *Alli Sup*
Garrod, Archibald Edward 1858- *Alli Sup*
Garrod, Heathcote William 1878-1960 *ChPo,*
ChPo S1, NewC
Garros, Pey De *CasWL*
Garrott, Hal 1877- *WhWNAA*
Garrow, David William *Alli, BiDLA Sup*
Garrow, J *Alli, BiDLA*
Garroway, Alderman *Alli*
Garry, James *PoIre*
Garry, Nicholas 1782?-1856 *OxCan*
Garry, R *Alli Sup*
Garshin, Vsevolod Mikhailovich 1855-1888 *BbD,*
BiD&SB, CasWL, CIDMEuL, DcRusL,
EuA, EvEuW, Pen Eur
Garside, Alston Hill 1888-1946 *DcNAA*
Garside, Charles Brierley 1818-1876 *Alli Sup*
Garside, Edward Ballard 1907- *AmA&B*
Garside, Firth *Alli Sup*
Garside, Frances Leigh 1862- *WhWNAA*
Garson, Barbara 1942- *AmA&B, ConAu 33*
Garson, Eugenia *ChPo S1*
Garson, G David 1943- *ConAu 53*
Garson, Mort 1924- *AmSCAP 66*
Garson, Noel George 1931- *ConAu 29*
Garson, Paul 1946- *ConAu 49*
Garst, Doris Shannon 1894- *AuBYP,*
ConAu 1R, SmATA 1
Garst, John Fredric 1932- *ConAu 45*
Garst, Laura Delany 1861-1925 *OhA&B*
Garst, Shannon 1899- *AuBYP, ConAu XR,*
JBA 1951, SmATA 1
Garstang, Basil *WhLA*
Garstang, Jack 1927- *ConAu XR*
Garstang, James Gordon 1927- *ConAu 13R*
Garstang, John 1876- *WhLA*
Garstang, Stephen W 1933- *IndAu 1917*

Garstang, Walter *Alli Sup*
Garstein, Oskar Bernhard 1924- *ConAu 13R*
Garstin, A *MnBBF*
Garstin, Crosbie 1887- *ChPo, ChPo S1,*
ChPo S2
Garstin, John *Alli*
Garstin, John Ribton 1836- *Alli Sup*
Gart, Thiebold *CasWL*
Gart, Thiebolt *OxGer*
Garten, Hugh F 1904- *ConAu 5R*
Garten, Hugo F 1904- *Au&Wr, WrD 1976*
Garten, Jan *AuBYP*
Gartenberg, Egon 1911- *ConAu 57*
Gartenberg, Leo 1906- *ConAu 9R*
Garter, Barnard *Alli*
Garth, John *Alli*
Garth, John Goodall 1871- *WhWNAA*
Garth, Morris *ChPo S2*
Garth, Philip *Alli Sup*
Garth, Sir Richard 1820- *Alli Sup*
Garth, Sir Samuel 1661-1719 *Alli, BiD&SB,*
BrAu, CasWL, Chmbr 2, DcEnA,
DcEnL, DcEuL, EvLB, NewC, OxEng,
Pen Eng, REn, WebEAL
Garth, Thomas Russell 1872-1939 *DcNAA,*
WhWNAA
Garth, Will *AmA&B*
Garth-Thornton *Alli Sup*
Garthoff, Raymond Leonard 1929- *AmA&B,*
Au&Wr, ConAu 5R, WrD 1976
Garthshore, Maxwell 1732-1812 *Alli*
Garthwait, Henry *Alli*
Garthwaite, Malaby *ConAu XR*
Garthwaite, Marion Hook 1893- *AuBYP,*
ConAu 5R, SmATA 7
Garthwaite, Wymond Bradbury 1895- *ChPo,*
ConICB
Gartian, George H 1882-1963 *AmSCAP 66,*
ChPo S1
Gartland, Robert Aldrich 1927- *ConAu 17R*
Gartman, Louise 1920- *ConAu 17R*
Gartmann, Heinz 1917- *Au&Wr*
Gartner, Alan 1935- *ConAu 33*
Gartner, Chloe Maria 1916- *ConAu 1R,*
WrD 1976
Gartner, Karl Christian 1712-1791 *DcEuL,*
OxGer
Gartner, Lloyd P 1927- *ConAu 1R*
Gartny, T *DcRusL*
Garton, Charles 1926- *ConAu 45*
Garton, James *Alli*
Garton, Malinda Dean *ConAu 1R*
Garton, Nancy Wells 1908- *Au&Wr,*
ConAu 5R
Garton, Nina R 1905- *ConAu 21*
Garton, Ronald Verner 1899- *Au&Wr*
Gartside, M *Alli, BiDLA*
Gartside, Richard Nelson 1903- *WhWNAA*
Gartwood *Alli*
Garvagh, Lord *Alli Sup*
Garve, Andrew 1908- *ConAu XR, EncM&D,*
WorAu
Garve, Christian 1742-1798 *OxGer*
Garver, John Anson 1854-1936 *DcNAA*
Garver, Richard B 1934- *ConAu 33*
Garvey, Amy Jacques 1896?-1973 *ConAu 45*
Garvey, Edward B 1914- *ConAu 41*
Garvey, John F *ChPo*
Garvey, Mother Mary 1845-1932 *OhA&B*
Garvey, Maura *PoIre*
Garvey, Michael Angelo *Alli Sup*
Garvey, Mona 1934- *ConAu 29*
Garvice, Charles 1833-1920 *Alli Sup, NewC*
Garvie, Alexander Rae 1839-1875 *DcNAA,*
OxCan
Garvie, Alfred Ernest 1861- *WhLA*
Garvie, William *BbtC, OxCan*
Garvin, Amelia Beers 1878-1956 *ChPo, OxCan*
Garvin, Charles D 1929- *ConAu 57*
Garvin, Hugh Carson 1842-1918 *OhA&B*
Garvin, James Louis 1868-1947 *DcLEnL,*
LongC, NewC
Garvin, Mrs. John *WhWNAA*
Garvin, John William 1859-1935 *ChPo,*
ChPo S1, DcNAA, OxCan
Garvin, Katharine 1904- *ConAu 5R*
Garvin, Lawrence 1945- *ConAu 53*
Garvin, Margaret Root d1949 *AmA&B,*

AnMV 1926
Garvin, Paul L 1919- *ConAu 13R*
Garvin, Richard M 1934- *ConAu 49*
Garvin, Viola Girard *ChPo*
Garvin, William 1922- *ConAu 25*
Garvock, Blanche A L *Alli Sup*
Garwood *Alli*
Garwood, Darrell Nelson 1909- *ConAu 29,*
IndAu 1917
Garwood, Irving 1883-1957 *AmA&B, OhA&B*
Garwood, John *Alli, Alli Sup*
Garwood, Louise *TexWr*
Gary, Falkland L 1897- *Au&Wr*
Gary, G *Alli Sup*
Gary, John 1932- *AmSCAP 66*
Gary, Madeleine Sophie 1923- *BlkAW,*
LivBAA, WrD 1976
Gary, Romain 1914- *Au&Wr, CasWL,*
EncWL, ModRL, REn, TwCW, WorAu
Garza, Daniel *DrAP 1975*
Garzilli, Enrico 1937- *ConAu 41*
Gasc, Ferdinand E A *Alli Sup*
Gasc, Frederick *Alli Sup*
Gascar, Pierre 1916- *EncWL, ModRL, REn,*
WorAu
Gasch, Marie 1875-1945 *DcNAA*
Gascoigne, Arthur Bamber 1935- *Au&Wr*
Gascoigne, Bamber 1935- *ConAu 25,*
WrD 1976
Gascoigne, Caroline Leigh 1813-1883 *BiD&SB,*
DcEnL
Gascoigne, Sir Crisp *Alli*
Gascoigne, Eric *MnBBF*
Gascoigne, George 1525?-1577 *Alli, BbD,*
BiD&SB, BrAu, CasWL, ChPo,
ChPo S1, Chmbr 1, CnE&AP, CnThe,
CrE&SL, CriT 1, DcEnA, DcEnL,
DcEuL, DcLEnL, EvLB, McGWD,
MouLC 1, NewC, OxEng, Pen Eng,
REn, REnWD, WebEAL
Gascoigne, Henry B *Alli*
Gascoigne, Mrs. M A *Alli Sup*
Gascoigne, Noel Hamlyn 1910- *CatA 1952*
Gascoigne, Sir William 1350?-1419 *NewC*
Gascon, The *ConAu XR*
Gascoyn, Sir Bernard *Alli*
Gascoyne, A M *Alli Sup*
Gascoyne, David 1916- *ChPo, CnE&AP,*
ConP 1970, ConP 1975, EncWL, LongC,
ModBL, Pen Eng, TwCW, WebEAL,
WhTwL, WorAu, WrD 1976
Gascoyne, Richard *Alli Sup*
Gaselee, John Stephen 1933- *Au&Wr,*
WrD 1976
Gaselee, Stephen 1882- *WhLA*
Gash, Norman 1912- *Au&Wr, ConAu 1R,*
WrD 1976
Gask, Lillian *CarSB*
Gaskarth, John *Alli*
Gaskell, Mrs. *Alli Sup*
Gaskell, Mrs. 1810-1865 *Alli, Chmbr 3,*
DcEnL
Gaskell, Annie *Alli Sup*
Gaskell, Elizabeth Cleghorn 1810-1865 *Alli Sup,*
AtlBL, BbD, BiD&SB, BrAu 19, CasWL,
CriT 3, CyWA, DcBiA, DcEnA, DcEuL,
DcLEnL, EvLB, HsB&A, MouLC 3,
NewC, OxEng, Pen Eng, RAdv 1, REn,
WebEAL
Gaskell, George *Alli Sup*
Gaskell, Hugh Selwyn *ChPo S1*
Gaskell, Jane 1941- *ConAu 5R, WrD 1976*
Gaskell, John *Alli Sup*
Gaskell, Philip 1926- *Alli Sup, Au&Wr,*
ConAu 5R, WrD 1976
Gaskell, Thomas F 1916- *ConAu 17R*
Gaskell, Thomas Penn *Alli Sup*
Gaskell, W H *Alli Sup*
Gaskell Denvil, Jane 1941- *Au&Wr*
Gaskill, Clarence 1892-1947 *AmSCAP 66*
Gaskill, Harold V 1905-1975 *ConAu 57*
Gaskill, Joseph W 1843-1932 *OhA&B*
Gaskin, Mrs. Arthur *ChPo*
Gaskin, Catherine 1929- *AmA&B, Au&Wr,*
TwCW, WrD 1976
Gaskin, George *Alli, BiDLA, BiDLA Sup*
Gaskin, James J *Alli, Alli Sup*
Gaskin, John *Alli*

Gaskin, Robert Tate *Alli Sup*
Gaskoin, Charles Jacinth Bellairs *WhLA*
Gaskoin, George *Alli Sup*
Gaskoin, Mrs. Herman *Alli Sup*
Gaspar Molendo *PueRA*
Gaspar, Margit 1908- *CrCD*
Gasparain, Agenor Etienne, Comte De 1810-1871 *BbD*
Gasparin, Agenor Etienne, Comte De 1810-1871 *BiD&SB*
Gasparini, Graziano 1926- *ConAu 41*
Gasparini, Len *OxCan Sup*
Gasparino Of Barzizza 1370?-1431 *DcEuL*
Gasparotti, Elizabeth Seifert 1897- *Au&Wr, ConAu 1R*
Gasparotti, Mrs. John *AmNov XR*
Gaspe, Philippe-Joseph Aubert De 1786-1871 *BiD&SB, CasWL, REn*
Gasper, Louis 1911- *ConAu 13R*
Gaspey, Thomas 1788-1871 *Alli, Alli Sup, ChPo S1*
Gaspey, William 1812-1886 *Alli Sup*
Gaspine, John *Alli*
Gasquet, Francis 1846-1929 *Alli Sup, EvLB, NewC, OxEng*
Gass, Irene *AuBYP*
Gass, Joseph 1864- *WhLA*
Gass, Patrick 1771-1870 *Alli, AmA&B, BbtC, BiDLA, DcNAA*
Gass, Sherlock Bronson 1878-1945 *AmA&B, OhA&B, WhWNAA*
Gass, William H 1924- *AmA&B, Au&Wr, ConAu 17R, ConLC 1, ConLC 2, ConNov 1972, ConNov 1976, DrAF 1976, EncWL Sup, ModAL Sup, Pen Am, RAdv 1, WorAu, WrD 1976*
Gassaway, Frank Harrison d1923 *ChPo S1*
Gassaway, Franklin Harrison d1923 *DcNAA*
Gassaway, Katherine *ChPo*
Gassendi, Pierre 1592-1655 *BiD&SB, CasWL, DcEuL, NewC, OxEng, OxFr, REn*
Gassert, Robert G 1921- *ConAu 17R*
Gasset *CnMWL, TwCA, TwCA Sup*
Gassier, Pierre 1915- *ConAu 49*
Gassiot, M *BiDLA*
Gassner, Gustav 1881- *WhLA*
Gassner, Jerome Joseph 1901- *CatA 1952*
Gassner, John Waldhorn 1903-1967 *AmA&B, ConAu 1R, ConAu 25, REnAL, WhWNAA*
Gassner, Julius S 1915- *ConAu 37*
Gasso, Bernard 1926- *AmSCAP 66*
Gast, Johannes d1572 *OxGer*
Gast, John *Alli*
Gaster, M *Alli Sup*
Gaster, Theodore Herzl 1906- *AmA&B, ConAu 17*
Gastev, Alexey Kapitonovich 1882- *CasWL, DcRusL*
Gastil, Raymond D 1931- *ConAu 29*
Gastineau, Edward T *Alli Sup*
Gaston Phoebus, Count Of Foix 1331-1391 *CasWL*
Gaston, Mrs. A F *Alli Sup*
Gaston, Bill *WrD 1976*
Gaston, Charles Robert 1874- *WhWNAA*
Gaston, Edwin Willmer, Jr. 1925- *ConAu 1R, WrD 1976*
Gaston, H A *Alli Sup*
Gaston, Hugh *Alli*
Gaston, James McFadden 1824-1903 *BiDSA, DcNAA*
Gaston, Jerry 1940- *ConAu 45*
Gaston, Joseph 1833-1913 *DcNAA, OhA&B*
Gaston, Lyle R 1929- *AmSCAP 66*
Gaston, William James 1927- *Au&Wr, WrD 1976*
Gastrell, Francis 1662-1725 *Alli*
Gastrell, Peregrine *Alli*
Gaszynski, Konstantin 1809-1866 *BiD&SB*
Gat, Dimitri V 1936- *ConAu 29*
Gataker, Charles 1614?-1680 *Alli*
Gataker, Thomas *Alli*
Gataker, Thomas 1574-1654 *Alli*
Gatanyu, James 1945- *AfA 1*
Gatch, Milton McCormick, Jr. 1932- *ConAu 29, WrD 1976*
Gatchell, Charles 1851-1910 *Alli Sup, DcAmA,*

DcNAA, OhA&B
Gatchell, Fannie Kilbourne *WhWNAA*
Gatchell, Thomas *Alli*
Gatell, Frank Otto 1931- *ConAu 9R*
Gatenby, Rosemary 1918- *ConAu 21*
Gates, Arnold Francis 1914- *OhA&B*
Gates, Arthur Irving 1890-1972 *ConAu 37*
Gates, B Cecil 1877-1941 *AmSCAP 66*
Gates, Barrington *ChPo*
Gates, Betty *BlkAW*
Gates, C Ray 1885- *WhWNAA*
Gates, Caleb Frank 1857-1946 *DcNAA, WhWNAA*
Gates, Charles Marvin 1904-1963 *WhPNW*
Gates, Charles O *Alli Sup*
Gates, Clifford *MnBBF*
Gates, Crawford 1921- *AmSCAP 66*
Gates, Doris 1901- *AnCL, AuBYP, AuICB, ConAu 1R, JBA 1951, SmATA 1*
Gates, Eddie *BlkAW*
Gates, Eleanor 1875-1951 *AmA&B, CarSB, REnAL, WhWNAA*
Gates, Ellen Maria Huntington 1835-1920 *Alli Sup, ChPo, ChPo S1, DcAmA, DcNAA*
Gates, Elmer 1859-1923 *DcNAA, OhA&B*
Gates, Errett 1870-1951 *AmLY, OhA&B*
Gates, Gary Rickey 1934- *IndAu 1917*
Gates, Geoffrey *Alli*
Gates, George Augustus 1851-1912 *DcNAA*
Gates, Herbert Wright 1868- *WhWNAA*
Gates, Horatio 1728?-1806 *OxAm, REn, REnAL*
Gates, Isaac Edgar 1874-1933 *DcNAA*
Gates, J M 1924- *ConAu 57*
Gates, Jean Key 1911- *ConAu 33*
Gates, John A 1898- *ConAu 5R*
Gates, John Floyd 1915- *ConAu 1R*
Gates, John Howard 1865- *WhWNAA*
Gates, Josephine Scribner 1859-1930 *AmA&B, AmLY, DcNAA, OhA&B, WhWNAA*
Gates, Lawrence Gibson 1858-1939 *OhA&B*
Gates, Lewis Edwards 1860-1924? *DcAmA, DcNAA, OxAm, REnAL*
Gates, Lillian Francis 1901- *ConAu 25, OxCan Sup*
Gates, Mary G *ChPo*
Gates, Merrill Edwards 1848- *DcAmA*
Gates, Natalie *ConAu 23*
Gates, Paul Wallace 1901- *AmA&B, Au&Wr, ConAu 1R, WrD 1976*
Gates, Philip *Alli Sup*
Gates, R Ruggles 1882- *WhLA*
Gates, Robbins L 1922- *ConAu 13R*
Gates, Susa Young 1856-1933 *DcNAA, WhWNAA*
Gates, Theodore Burr 1824-1911 *DcNAA*
Gates, Willey Francis 1865-1941 *OhA&B*
Gates, William *OxCan*
Gates, William B 1917-1975 *ConAu 61, IndAu 1917*
Gates, William Edmond 1863-1940 *DcNAA*
Gatewood, Julia Greenleaf 1854- *BiDSA*
Gatewood, L A *BlkAW*
Gatewood, Willard B, Jr. 1931- *ConAu 17R*
Gatfield, George *Alli Sup*
Gatford, *Alli*
Gatford, Lionel *Alli*
Gath *AmA&B, DcAmA, OxAm*
Gathercole, Michael Augustus d1886 *Alli, Alli Sup*
Gatheru, Reuel John Mugo 1925- *AfA 1*
Gathorne-Hardy, Geoffrey M *OxCan*
Gathorne-Hardy, Jonathan G 1933- *Au&Wr, WrD 1976*
Gathorne-Hardy, Robert *OxCan*
Gatien, Felix 1776-1844 *DcNAA*
Gatineau, Felix 1857-1927 *DcNAA*
Gatisden *Alli*
Gatke, Robert Moulton 1896- *WhWNAA*
Gatland, Kenneth William 1924- *Au&Wr, WrD 1976*
Gatlin, Douglas S 1928- *ConAu 21*
Gatner, Elliott S M 1914- *ConAu 9R*
Gato, J A *ConAu XR*
Gato, Juan Alvarez 1430?-1496 *DcEuL*
Gaton Arce, Freddy 1920- *DcCLA*
Gator, E Z *BlkAW*

Gatschet, A S *BiDSA*
Gatschet, Albert Samuel 1832- *Alli Sup*
Gatsos, Nikos 1915- *WhTwL*
Gatterman, Eugen Ludwig 1886- *WhLA*
Gattey, Charles Neilson 1921- *Au&Wr, ConAu 13R, WrD 1976*
Gatti, Armand 1924- *CasWL, CnMD Sup, CnThe, CrCD, EncWL Sup, McGWD, ModWD, Pen Eur, REnWD*
Gatti, Attilio 1896- *AmA&B, AuBYP, JBA 1951*
Gatti, Daniel Jon 1946- *ConAu 45*
Gatti, Ellen Morgan *AuBYP*
Gatti, Enzo 1942- *ConAu 61*
Gatti, Richard DeY 1947- *ConAu 45*
Gattinger, Augustin 1825-1903 *DcNAA*
Gattmann, Eric 1925- *ConAu 49*
Gatto, Alfonso 1909- *Pen Eur*
Gatton, Benjamin *Alli*
Gatty, Alfred 1813-1903 *Alli, Alli Sup, ChPo, ChPo S1, DcEnL*
Gatty, Mrs. Alfred *Alli*
Gatty, Alfred Scott 1847-1918 *Alli Sup, ChPo, ChPo S1*
Gatty, Horatia Katharine Frances 1846- *Alli Sup, CarSB, ChPo, ChPo S1*
Gatty, Juliana Horatia 1841-1885 *DcEuL, NewC*
Gatty, Margaret Scott 1809-1873 *Alli Sup, BiD&SB, CarSB, ChPo, ChPo S1, ChPo S2, DcEnA, DcEnL, DcEuL, DcLEnL, EvLB, NewC, WhCL*
Gatty, Nicholas Comyn 1874-1946 *NewC*
Gatty, Reginald A *ChPo, ChPo S1*
Gatty, Stephen Herbert *ChPo*
Gatzke, Hans Wilheim 1915- *AmA&B, ConAu 1R, WrD 1976*
Gau, John *Chmbr 1*
Gaucelm Faidit 1185?-1220 *CasWL*
Gauch, Patricia Lee 1934- *ConAu 57*
Gauden, John 1605-1662 *Alli, BrAu, Chmbr 1, DcEnL, EvLB, NewC, OxEng, REn*
Gaudet, Frederick J 1902- *ConAu 5R*
Gaudet, Placide 1850-1930 *DcNAA, OxCan*
Gaudi Y Cornet, Antoni 1852-1926 *AtlBL*
Gaudon, Jean 1926- *Au&Wr*
Gaudy, Baron Franz Von 1800-1840 *BiD&SB, OxGer*
Gauer, Harold 1914- *ConAu 13R*
Gauguin, Paul 1848-1903 *AtlBL, LongC, NewC, OxFr, REn*
Gaul, Albro T *AuBYP*
Gaul, Avery 1886- *OhA&B, WhWNAA*
Gaul, George *ChPo S1*
Gaul, Harriette Lester Avery 1886- *OhA&B*
Gaul, Harvey Bartlett 1881-1945 *AmSCAP 66*
Gaul, William Gilbert 1855-1919 *ChPo, ChPo S1*
Gauld, Charles A 1911- *ConAu 13R*
Gauld, James *ChPo*
Gaulden, Ray 1914- *ConAu 17R*
Gauldie, Enid Elizabeth 1928- *WrD 1976*
Gauldie, William Sinclair 1918- *Au&Wr, ConAu 33*
Gaule, John *Alli*
Gaulle, General De *OxFr*
Gault, Franklin Benjamin 1851-1918 *OhA&B*
Gault, Mark *ConAu XR*
Gault, Robert *Alli Sup*
Gault, William Campbell 1910- *AuBYP, ConAu 49, EncM&D, SmATA 8*
Gaultier, Bon *BrAu 19, ChPo*
Gaultier-Garguille *OxFr*
Gaunt, Hardy *MnBBF*
Gaunt, Jeffrey *MnBBF*
Gaunt, John *Alli*
Gaunt, John Of *NewC*
Gaunt, Leonard 1921- *Au&Wr, ConAu 5R*
Gaunt, M B *MnBBF*
Gaunt, Mary *Chmbr 3, WhLA*
Gaunt, William 1900- *Au&Wr, ConAu 9R, LongC, TwCA Sup, WrD 1976*
Gaunt Wolf *MnBBF*
Gauntier, Gene *WhWNAA*
Gauntlett, Henry *BiDLA*
Gauntlett, Henry John 1805-1876 *Alli, Alli Sup*
Gauquelin, Michel 1928- *ConAu 57*
Gaus, George J *WhWNAA*

Gause, Frank Ales 1874- *AmLY*, *IndAu 1816*
Gause, Harry Taylor 1853-1925 *DcNAA*
Gause, Isaac 1843-1920 *OhA&B*
Gauss, Christian Frederick 1878-1951 *AmA&B*,
  AmLY, *ChPo*, *REnAL*
Gauss, Marianne 1885- *AmA&B*
Gaustad, Edwin Scott 1923- *ConAu 1R*
Gaut, John McReynolds 1841-1918 *DcNAA*
Gautama *NewC*
Gautama Buddha *NewC*
Gauthier, Louis *OxCan Sup*
Gauthier, Marguerite *REn*
Gauthier-Villars, Henri 1859-1931 *EvEuW*
Gautier D'Arras 1135-1198 *CasWL*, *OxFr*
Gautier De Chatillon *CasWL*
Gautier De Coinci d1236 *CasWL*
Gautier De Dargies *CasWL*
Gautier D'Epinal *CasWL*, *OxFr*
Gautier Le Leu *CasWL*
Gautier, Dick 1931- *AmSCAP 66*
Gautier, Judith 1850- *BbD*, *BiD&SB*, *OxFr*
Gautier, Leon 1832-1897 *BiD&SB*
Gautier, Marguerite *OxFr*
Gautier, Theophile 1811-1872 *AtlBL*, *BbD*,
  BiD&SB, *CasWL*, *CyWA*, *DcBiA*,
  DcEuL, *EuA*, *EvEuW*, *NewC*, *OxEng*,
  OxFr, *Pen Eur*, *RCom*, *REn*
Gautier Benitez, Jose 1851- *PueRA*
Gauust, Doscen *OxCan*
Gauvreau, Charles Arthur 1860-1924 *DcNAA*
Gauvreau, Claude *OxCan Sup*
Gauvreau, Emile 1894?-1956 *REnAL*,
  WhWNAA
Gavan, John *PoIre*
Gavarni 1804-1866 *AtlBL*, *OxFr*
Gaver, Jack 1906-1974 *AmA&B*, *ConAu 53*
Gaver, Jessyca 1915- *ConAu 53*
Gaver, Mary Virginia 1906- *ConAu 1R*
Gaveston, Piers d1312 *NewC*
Gavett, J William 1921- *ConAu 25*
Gavett, Thomas W 1932- *ConAu 13R*
Gavin *ConAu XR*
Gavin, Antony *Alli*
Gavin, Bill 1936- *Au&Wr*
Gavin, Catherine Irvine 1907- *AmA&B*,
  Au&Wr, *ConAu 1R*, *WrD 1976*
Gavin, D *BbtC*
Gavin, Eileen A 1931- *ConAu 45*
Gavin, Frank E 1854- *IndAu 1816*
Gavin, Frank Stanton Burns 1890-1938 *AmA&B*,
  DcNAA, *OhA&B*
Gavin, J And Hord, O B *Alli Sup*
Gavin, James M 1907- *AmA&B*, *ConAu P-1*
Gavin, Malcolm Ross 1908- *Au&Wr*
Gavin, Wilfred *MnBBF*
Gavin-Brown, Wilfred Arthur 1904- *Au&Wr*,
  ConAu P-1
Gavisk, Francis Henry 1856-1932 *IndAu 1917*
Gavit, John Palmer 1868-1954 *AmA&B*,
  WhWNAA
Gavitt, Elnathan Corrington 1808-1896 *DcNAA*
Gavner, John *Alli*
Gavron, Daniel 1935- *ConAu 29*
Gavronsky, Serge 1932- *ConP 1970*,
  DrAP 1975, *WrD 1976*
Gavshon, Arthur L 1916- *ConAu 5R*
Gaw, Allison 1877-1954 *AmA&B*
Gaw, Ethelean Tyson *AmA&B*, *AnMV 1926*,
  WhWNAA
Gaw, J Allison 1877-1954 *WhWNAA*
Gaw, Walter A 1904- *ConAu 1R*
Gawain Edwards *WhWNAA*
Gawain Poet, The *CriT 1*, *WebEAL*
Gawalowski, Karl Wilhelm 1861- *WhLA*
Gawen, Nicholas *Alli*
Gawler, John Cox *Alli Sup*
Gawler, William *Alli*
Gawsworth, John 1912- *Au&Wr*, *ChPo*,
  ChPo S1, *ChPo S2*, *ConAu XR*,
  ConP 1970, *EvLB*, *LongC*
Gawthrop, Hugh *Alli Sup*
Gawton, Richard *Alli*
Gaxotte, Pierre 1895- *OxFr*
Gay, Agnes *ChPo*
Gay, Byron 1886-1945 *AmSCAP 66*
Gay, Carl Warren 1877- *WhWNAA*
Gay, Carlo T E 1913- *ConAu 49*
Gay, Delphine 1804-1855 *BiD&SB*, *EvEuW*,

Gay, Eben Howard 1858- *DcAmA*
Gay, Ebenezer 1696-1787 *Alli*, *DcAmA*,
  DcNAA
Gay, Elinor *Alli Sup*, *OhA&B*
Gay, Frederick Parker 1874-1939 *DcNAA*
Gay, Harry Nelson 1870-1932 *AmLY*, *DcNAA*,
  WhWNAA
Gay, Henry A *BlkAW*
Gay, J Drew *Alli Sup*
Gay, James 1810-1891 *Alli Sup*, *DcNAA*
Gay, John *Alli*
Gay, John 1685?-1732 *Alli*, *AtlBL*, *BiD&SB*,
  BrAu, *CarSB*, *CasWL*, *ChPo*, *ChPo S1*,
  ChPo S2, *Chmbr 2*, *CnE&AP*, *CnThe*,
  CriT 2, *CyWA*, *DcEnA*, *DcEnA Ap*,
  DcEnL, *DcEuL*, *DcLEnL*, *EvLB*,
  McGWD, *MouLC 2*, *NewC*, *OxEng*,
  Pen Eng, *REn*, *REnWD*, *WebEAL*
Gay, John 1813-1885 *Alli Sup*
Gay, Joseph *Alli*, *NewC*
Gay, Kathleen Agnes Robson 1890- *BiDPar*
Gay, Kathlyn R 1930- *ConAu 21*, *SmATA 9*,
  WrD 1976
Gay, Laverne 1914- *CatA 1952*
Gay, Lettie 1901- *WhWNAA*
Gay, M A H *Alli Sup*
Gay, Marie Francois Sophie 1776-1852 *BbD*
Gay, Mary Ann Harris 1829- *BiDSA*, *ChPo S2*,
  DcNAA
Gay, Maurice *Alli Sup*
Gay, Minnie B *TexWr*
Gay, Nicholas *Alli*
Gay, Paul *OxCan Sup*
Gay, Peter 1923- *AmA&B*, *ConAu 13R*
Gay, Robert Malcolm 1879-1961 *AmA&B*
Gay, Romney *ChPo*
Gay, Sophie 1776-1852 *BiD&SB*, *OxFr*
Gay, Susan E *Alli Sup*
Gay, Sydney Howard 1814-1888 *Alli Sup*,
  AmA, *AmA&B*, *BiD&SB*, *DcAmA*,
  DcNAA
Gay, William *Alli*
Gay, Zhenya 1906- *AuBYP*, *BkCL*, *ChPo*,
  ChPo S2, *IlCB 1945*, *IlCB 1956*, *MorJA*
Gay-Crosier, Raymond 1937- *ConAu 41*
Gay-Kelly, Doreen 1952- *ConAu 61*
Gay-Lussac, Joseph Louis 1778-1850 *REn*
Gay Page *WhWNAA*
Gayangos, Pascual De 1809-1897 *DcSpL*
Gayangos Y Arce, Pascual De 1809-1897
  Alli Sup, *BiD&SB*, *CasWL*
Gayarre, Charles *BiDSA*
Gayarre, Charles Etienne Arthur 1805-1895 *Alli*,
  Alli Sup, *AmA*, *AmA&B*, *BbD*,
  BiD&SB, *CyAL 2*, *DcAmA*, *DcLEnL*,
  DcNAA, *OxAm*, *REnAL*
Gaydon, Alfred Gordon 1911- *Au&Wr*,
  WrD 1976
Gaydos, Michael J 1940- *ConAu 53*
Gaye, Phoebe Fenwick *Au&Wr*
Gaye, Selina *Alli Sup*
Gayer, Arthur Edward *Alli Sup*
Gayle, Addison, Jr. 1932- *BlkAW*, *ConAu 25*,
  LivBAA
Gayle, Newton *AmA&B*
Gayler, Charles 1820-1872 *Alli*, *Alli Sup*
Gayler, Charles 1820-1892 *AmA*, *AmA&B*,
  BiD&SB, *DcAmA*, *DcNAA*, *OhA&B*,
  REnAL
Gayles, Anne Richardson 1923- *ConAu 53*
Gayley, Charles Mills 1858-1932 *AmA&B*,
  DcAmA, *DcNAA*, *REnAL*, *WhWNAA*
Gaylin, Willard M 1925- *ConAu 23*,
  WrD 1976
Gaylord, Franklin Augustus 1856-1943 *DcNAA*
Gaylord, Glance *Alli Sup*, *AmA&B*, *DcAmA*,
  DcNAA
Gaylord, Harriet *WhWNAA*
Gaylord, Lewis And Tucker, Luther *Alli*
Gaylord, Timeus 1893- *ChPo*
Gaylord, Willis 1792-1844 *DcNAA*
Gaymar, Geffrei *OxFr*
Gaymar, Geoffrey *NewC*
Gaynor, Charles 1909- *AmSCAP 66*
Gaynor, Jessie Love 1863-1921 *AmLY*, *ChPo*
Gaynor, William Jay 1851-1913 *DcNAA*

Gayre Of Gayre And Nigg, Robert 1907-
  Au&Wr, *ConAu 5R*, *WrD 1976*
Gayton, Edmund *Alli*
Gaza, Theodore 1400-1475 *REn*
Gaza, Theodorus 1400-1475 *DcEuL*
Gazaway, Rena 1910- *ConAu 29*
Gazda, George M 1931- *ConAu 61*
Gazdag, Erzsi *ChPo S2*
Gaze, Harold *ChPo S2*
Gaze, Harry 1878-1959 *OhA&B*
Gaze, R Michael 1927- *WrD 1976*
Gaze, Richard 1917- *Au&Wr*, *ConAu 1R*
Gazell, James A 1942- *ConAu 49*
Gazes, Theodore *CasWL*, *Pen Cl*
Gazi, Stephen 1914- *ConAu 45*
Gazis, Denos C 1930- *ConAu 57*
Gazlay, Allen W *Alli Sup*, *OhA&B*
Gazlay, James William 1784-1874 *OhA&B*
Gazlay, S *Alli Sup*
Gazley, John G 1895- *ConAu 61*
Gazzam, Audley William 1836-1884 *Alli Sup*,
  DcNAA
Gazzam, Clara Griffith *ChPo S2*
Gazzo, Michael 1923- *McGWD*
Gazzoletti, Antonio 1813-1866 *BiD&SB*
Gbadamosi, Bakare A 1930- *AfA 1*
Geach, Christine 1930- *Au&Wr*, *ConAu 25*,
  WrD 1976
Geach, E F A *ChPo*
Geach, Francis d1798 *Alli*
Geach, Henry Harper *Alli Sup*
Geach, Patricia Sullivan 1916- *ConAu 29*
Geake, Charles *ChPo S2*
Geale, Hamilton *PoIre*
Geanakoplos, Deno John 1916- *ConAu 1R*
Geaney, Dennis Joseph 1914- *ConAu 5R*
Gear, C William 1935- *ConAu 53*
Gear, H L *Alli Sup*
Gear, Norman William 1920- *Au&Wr*
Geard, C *Alli Sup*
Geard, John *Alli*, *BiDLA*
Geare, Allen *Alli*
Geare, Edward *Alli*, *Alli Sup*
Geare, Edward Arundel 1844- *Alli Sup*
Gearey, Caroline *Alli Sup*
Gearey, John 1926- *ConAu 45*
Gearhart, Bill R 1928- *WrD 1976*
Gearhart, Ephriam Maclay, Sr. 1880-
  WhWNAA
Gearhart, Livingston 1916- *AmSCAP 66*
Gearhart, Sally Miller 1931- *ConAu 57*
Gearheart, B R 1928- *ConAu 23*
Gearing, Fred O 1922- *ConAu 29*
Gearing, William *Alli*
Gearing-Thomas, G *ConAu XR*, *WrD 1976*
Geary, Clifford N 1916- *IlBYP*, *IlCB 1956*
Geary, Douglas 1931- *Au&Wr*, *ConAu 13R*
Geary, Efton F 1940- *BlkAW*
Geary, Eleanor Margaret *Alli Sup*
Geary, Eleanor P *Alli Sup*
Geary, Elizabeth *PoIre*
Geary, Eugene 1863- *PoIre*
Geary, Grattan *Alli Sup*
Geary, Herbert Valentine 1894-1965 *ConAu P-1*
Geary, John F *Alli Sup*
Geary, L *Alli Sup*
Geary, Riley White 1888- *ArizL*
Geary, Stanley *MnBBF*
Geary, William Nevill Montgomerie 1859-
  Alli Sup
Geauque, Harry Aiman 1891- *WhWNAA*
Gebauer, Jan 1838-1907 *DcEuL*
Gebauer, Johannes 1868- *WhLA*
Geber *NewC*, *OxEng*, *REn*
Gebest, Charles J 1872-1937 *AmSCAP 66*
Gebhard, Truchsess Von Waldburg 1547-1600
  OxGer
Gebhard, Anna Laura Munro 1914- *ConAu 5R*
Gebhard, Elizabeth Louisa 1859-1924 *DcNAA*
Gebhard, Paul Henry 1917- *AmA&B*,
  ConAu 5R, *IndAu 1917*
Gebhardt, George Frederic 1874- *WhWNAA*
Gebhardt, Lola Gertrude 1880- *WhWNAA*
Gebhart, Benjamin 1923- *ConAu 53*
Gebhart, Emile 1839- *BiD&SB*
Gebler, Ernest 1915- *AmA&B*, *ConAu 5R*,
  WrD 1976

Gebler, Tobias Philipp, Freiherr Von 1726-1786 *OxGer*
Geck, Francis J 1900- *ConAu 23*
Gecys, Casimir C 1904- *ConAu 19*
Gedde, John *Alli*
Gedde, Walter *Alli*
Geddes, Alexander 1737-1802 *Alli, Chmbr 2, DcEnL, EvLB*
Geddes, Alexander Benjamin 1904- *Au&Wr*
Geddes, Arthur *ChPo S2*
Geddes, Charles L 1928- *ConAu 49*
Geddes, Gary *OxCan Sup*
Geddes, Gordon *ChPo S2*
Geddes, Henry 1912- *Au&Wr*
Geddes, J Gamble *BbtC*
Geddes, James *Alli Sup*
Geddes, James 1710-1749 *Alli*
Geddes, James, Jr. 1858-1948 *AmA&B, AmLY, DcNAA, WhWNAA*
Geddes, James Young 1850- *ChPo*
Geddes, Janet *NewC*
Geddes, Jenny *NewC*
Geddes, Joan Bel 1916- *ConAu 57*
Geddes, Michael d1715 *Alli*
Geddes, Norman Bel 1893-1958 *REn, REnAL*
Geddes, Patrick 1854-1932 *Alli Sup, BbD, BiD&SB, LongC, TwCA, TwCA Sup, WhLA*
Geddes, Virgil 1897- *AmA&B, REnAL, TwCA, TwCA Sup*
Geddes, William *Alli*
Geddes, William Duguid *Alli Sup*
Geddie, John *Alli Sup, BbtC, ChPo S2, OxCan*
Geddings, E *Alli Sup*
Geden, John Dury 1822-1886 *Alli Sup*
Gedge, G C *Alli Sup*
Gedge, John Wycliffe *Alli Sup*
Gedge, Johnson Hall *Alli Sup*
Gedge, W B *ChPo S1*
Gedney, C W *Alli Sup*
Gedney, Richard Solomon *Alli Sup*
Gedrut *OxGer*
Geduld, Harry M 1931- *ConAu 9R*
Gedye, George Eric Rowe 1890- *TwCA, TwCA Sup*
Gedye, W H *Alli Sup*
Gee, Alex *Alli*
Gee, Arthur Cecil 1912- *Au&Wr*
Gee, Edward *Alli*
Gee, Elizabeth Amelia *Alli Sup*
Gee, Ernest R 1878- *Br&AmS*
Gee, George *PoIre*
Gee, George E *Alli Sup*
Gee, Henry 1858-1938 *ChPo S1*
Gee, Herbert Leslie 1901- *Au&Wr, ConAu 9R*
Gee, Howard James 1884- *WhWNAA*
Gee, J *Alli*
Gee, Jeff *OxCan*
Gee, John *Alli Sup*
Gee, John d1639 *Alli*
Gee, John Archer 1894-1944 *DcNAA*
Gee, Joshua *Alli*
Gee, Joshua 1698-1748 *Alli, DcNAA*
Gee, Lethonia *BlkAW*
Gee, Maurice 1931- *ConNov 1976, WrD 1976*
Gee, Osman *MnBBF*
Gee, Pattie Williams *BiDSA*
Gee, Richard *Alli Sup*
Gee, Samuel Jones *Alli Sup*
Gee, W W Haldane *Alli Sup*
Gee, Wilson 1888-1961 *AmA&B*
Gee Double You *WhWNAA*
Geel, Jacob 1789-1862 *CasWL, DcEuL, Pen Eur*
Geen, Clifford 1891- *Au&Wr*
Geen, Maurice Steadman 1901- *Au&Wr*
Geer, Alpheus 1863-1941 *DcNAA*
Geer, Candy 1950- *ChPo*
Geer, Charles 1922- *IlBYP, IlCB 1956, IlCB 1966*
Geer, Curtis Manning 1864-1938 *DcNAA*
Geer, George Jarvis 1821-1885 *Alli Sup, DcAmA, DcNAA*
Geer, George P *Alli Sup*
Geer, John James 1833-1867 *Alli Sup, OhA&B*
Geer, Ney N 1895- *OhA&B*
Geer, Theodore Thurston 1851-1924 *DcNAA*

Geer, Walter 1857-1937 *AmA&B, DcNAA, WhWNAA*
Geer, William Chauncey 1876- *OhA&B*
Geere, John *Alli*
Geering, Ken 1925- *Au&Wr*
Geering, Thomas *Alli Sup*
Geersh, Eafim 1899- *AmSCAP 66*
Geertz, Clifford 1926- *ConAu 33*
Geeslin, A W *Alli Sup*
Geffe, Nicholas *Alli*
Geffen, Pauline Felix *ChPo, ChPo S1*
Geffen, Roger 1919- *ConAu 17R*
Geffroy, Gustave 1856-1926 *OxFr*
Geffroy, Mathieu Auguste 1820-1895 *BiD&SB*
Gefvert, Constance J 1941- *ConAu 53*
Gehman, Betsy Holland 1932- *ConAu 17R*
Gehman, Henry Snyder 1888- *ConAu 13R, WhWNAA, WrD 1976*
Gehman, Richard Boyd 1921-1972 *ConAu 1R, ConAu 33*
Gehri, Alfred 1896?-1972 *ConAu 33*
Gehring, Albert 1870-1926 *AmLY, DcNAA, OhA&B*
Gehring, F *Alli Sup*
Gehring, John George 1857-1932 *DcNAA, OhA&B*
Gehring, Mabel Grey 1882- *OhA&B*
Gehris, Paul 1934- *ConAu 45*
Gehrkens, Karl Wilson 1882- *WhWNAA*
Gehrs, John H 1882- *WhWNAA*
Geib, Warren J 1880- *WhWNAA*
Geibel, Adam 1855-1933 *AmLY, AmSCAP 66*
Geibel, Emanuel 1815-1884 *BiD&SB, CasWL, DcEuL, EuA, EvEuW, OxGer, Pen Eur, REn*
Geier, Arnold 1926- *ConAu 1R*
Geier, Woodrow A 1914- *ConAu 21*
Geigel Polanco, Vicente 1904- *PueRA*
Geiger, Don Jesse 1923- *ConAu 5R, WrD 1976*
Geiger, George 1905- *AmSCAP 66*
Geiger, George Lowell 1902- *WhWNAA*
Geiger, George Raymond 1903- *AmA&B, OhA&B*
Geiger, Homer Kent 1922- *ConAu 1R, WrD 1976*
Geiger, John Lewis *Alli Sup*
Geiger, Joseph Roy 1887- *WhWNAA*
Geiger, Louis G 1913- *ConAu 13R*
Geiger, O Frank 1864- *WhWNAA*
Geiger, Raymond Aloysius *AuNews 1*
Geiger, Wilhelm 1856- *WhLA*
Geijer, Erik Gustaf 1783-1847 *BbD, BiD&SB, CasWL, DcEuL, EuA, Pen Eur*
Geijerstam, Gosta Af 1888- *TwCA, TwCA Sup*
Geijerstam, Gustaf Af 1858-1909 *CasWL, ClDMEuL, EuA, EvEuW, REn*
Geikie, A Constable *BbtC*
Geikie, A Cunningham *Alli Sup*
Geikie, Archibald 1835-1924 *Alli, Alli Sup, BbD, BiD&SB, BrAu 19, Chmbr 3, DcEnL, NewC*
Geikie, Evelyn Cunningham *Alli Sup*
Geikie, James *Alli Sup*
Geikie, James 1839- *Alli Sup, BiD&SB*
Geikie, John Cunningham 1824- *Alli Sup, BbtC*
Geil, William Edgar 1865-1925 *AmA&B, AmLY, DcNAA*
Geiler, Johann Of Kaiserberg 1445-1510 *DcEuL*
Geiler VonKaiserberg, Johann 1445-1510 *CasWL, OxGer*
Geiregat, Pieter 1828-1902 *BiD&SB*
Geiringer, Karl 1899- *AmA&B, ConAu 13R*
Geironnydd, Ienen Glan 1765-1855 *ChPo*
Geis, Darlene Stern *AuBYP, ConAu 1R, SmATA 7*
Geis, Florence L 1933- *ConAu 57*
Geis, Gilbert 1925- *ConAu 9R*
Geise, Otto *WhLA*
Geisel, Theodor Seuss 1904- *AmA&B, AmSCAP 66, AuBYP, AuICB, ChLR 1, ChPo, ChPo S1, ChPo S2, ConAu 13R, FamAI, IlCB 1945, IlCB 1956, IlCB 1966, REn, REnAL, SmATA 1, TwCA, TwCA Sup*
Geiser, Karl Frederick 1869-1951 *AmLY,*

Geiser, Samuel Wood 1890- *TexWr*
Geisler, Mary Hibbs *ChPo S1*
Geisler, Norman Leo 1932- *ConAu 25, WrD 1976*
Geismar, Ludwig Leo 1921- *ConAu 25, WrD 1976*
Geismar, Maxwell 1909- *AmA&B, Au&Wr, ConAu 1R, RAdv 1, REnAL, TwCA Sup, WrD 1976*
Geissinger, James Allen 1873-1935 *DcNAA, OhA&B*
Geissler, Max 1868- *WhLA*
Geist, Edna Evelyn 1878-1953 *OhA&B*
Geist, Harold 1916- *ConAu 17R, WrD 1976*
Geist, Robert John 1912- *ConAu 41*
Geist, Valerius 1938- *ConAu 61*
Geisweiler, Maria *BiDLA*
Geitgey, Doris A 1920- *ConAu 53*
Geiwitz, P James 1938- *ConAu 29*
Gekiere, Madeleine 1919- *ChPo, ChPo S1, IlBYP, IlCB 1956, IlCB 1966, ThBJA*
Gelatt, Roland 1920- *ConAu 13R*
Gelb, Arthur 1924- *ConAu 1R*
Gelb, Barbara Stone 1926- *ConAu 1R*
Gelb, Ignace Jay 1907- *AmA&B, ConAu 9R*
Gelb, Joyce 1940- *ConAu 61*
Gelb, Philip *ChPo S1*
Gelbart, Dan 1918- *WhGrA*
Gelbart, Larry 1928- *AmA&B, AmSCAP 66*
Gelber, Harry Gregor 1926- *Au&Wr, ConAu 25*
Gelber, Jack 1926- *CnMD*
Gelber, Jack 1932- *AmA&B, CasWL, CnThe, ConAu 1R, ConDr, ConLC 1, ConLC 6, CrCD, McGWD, ModAL, ModWD, Pen Am, REn, REnAL, REnWD, TwCW, WebEAL, WorAu, WrD 1976*
Gelber, Lionel Morris 1907- *Au&Wr, ConAu 13R, WrD 1976*
Gelber, Stanley Jay 1936- *AmSCAP 66*
Gelber, Steven M 1943- *ConAu 53*
Geld, Ellen Bromfield 1932- *ConAu 37*
Geld, Gary 1935- *AmSCAP 66*
Geldard, Frank A 1904- *ConAu 41*
Geldard, John *Alli Sup*
Geldart, Edmund Martin 1844-1885 *Alli Sup*
Geldart, Ernest *Alli Sup*
Geldart, Hannah Ransome d1861 *Alli Sup*
Geldart, Peter *MnBBF*
Geldart, T C *Alli*
Geldart, Mrs. Thomas *Alli*
Geldenhauer, Gerardus 1482-1542 *CasWL*
Geldert, Grace *DcNAA*
Geldert, Mrs. Louis Napoleon *AmA&B*
Gelee, Claude *OxFr*
Gelee, Jacquemart *OxFr*
Gelegbalsang 1846-1923 *DcOrL 1*
Gelernt, Jules 1928- *ConAu 23*
Gelert 1800?- *Br&AmS*
Geley, Gustave 1868-1924 *BiDPar*
Gelfand, Lawrence Emerson 1926- *ConAu 5R*
Gelfand, Michael 1912- *Au&Wr, WrD 1976*
Gelfand, Morris Arthur 1908- *ConAu 49*
Gelfond, Rhoda 1946- *ConAu 49, DrAP 1975*
Gelinas, Andre *OxCan Sup*
Gelinas, Gratien 1909- *CanWr, CasWL, McGWD, OxCan, REnWD*
Gelinas, Gratien 1910- *CnThe*
Gelinas, Joseph Gerin 1874-1927 *DcNAA*
Gelinas, Paul J 1911- *ConAu 41, SmATA 10*
Gell, Edith Mary 1860- *WhLA*
Gell, Francis *Alli Sup*
Gell, Frank *ConAu 57*
Gell, H M *ChPo*
Gell, John *Alli, BiDLA*
Gell, John Philip *ChPo*
Gell, Philip *Alli, Alli Sup*
Gell, Robert d1665 *Alli*
Gell, Sir William 1777-1836 *Alli, BiDLA, DcEnL*
Gellee, Claude *OxFr*
Geller, Allen 1941- *ConAu 25*
Geller, Bruce 1930- *AmSCAP 66*
Geller, James Jacob 1893- *ChPo*
Gellerman, Saul W 1929- *ConAu 5R*
Gellert, Christian Furchtegott 1715-1769 *BbD, BiD&SB, CasWL, DcEuL, EuA, EvEuW,*

OxGer, Pen Eur

Gellert, Furchtegott 1715-1769 ChPo S1
Gellert, Judith 1925- ConAu 33
Gellert, Lawrence 1898- AmSCAP 66
Gellert, Leon 1892- Au&Wr
Gelles, Richard J 1946- ConAu 61
Gellhorn, Ernst 1893- ConAu 21
Gellhorn, Martha 1908- AmA&B, AmNov,
   Au&Wr, ConNov 1972, ConNov 1976,
   DrAF 1976, OxAm, REnAL, TwCA,
   TwCA Sup, WrD 1976
Gellhorn, Walter 1906- AmA&B, ConAu 13R
Gelli, Giambattista 1498-1563 BiD&SB,
   CasWL, EvEuW, REn
Gelli, Giovan Battista 1498-1563 Pen Eur
Gelli, Giovanni Battista 1498-1563 DcEuL
Gellibrand, Emma CarSB
Gellibrand, Henry 1597-1636 Alli
Gellibrand, Joseph Alli
Gellie, Mary E Alli Sup, ChPo S1
Gellinek, Christian 1930- ConAu 23,
   WrD 1976
Gellinek, Janis Little 1938- ConAu 41
Gelling, Peter 1925- Au&Wr
Gellis, Roberta L 1927- ConAu 5R
Gellius, Aulus 123?-165? BiD&SB, CasWL,
   NewC, OxEng, Pen Cl
Gellius, Gnaeus 175?BC- Pen Cl
Gellius, John Alli
Gellman, Estelle Sheila 1941- ConAu 53
Gellman, Irwin F 1942- ConAu 45
Gellman, James Alli
Gellner, Ernest Andre 1925- Au&Wr,
   ConAu 5R, WrD 1976
Gellner, John 1907- Au&Wr, ConAu 29,
   OxCan Sup
Gelman, Harold S 1912- AmSCAP 66
Gelman, Steve 1934- ConAu 25, SmATA 3
Gelmis, Joseph S 1935- ConAu 45
Gelpi, Albert 1931- ConAu 33, WrD 1976
Gelpi, Donald L 1934- ConAu 17R
Gelsted, Einar Otto 1888-1968 CasWL
Gelsted, Otto 1888-1968 Pen Eur
Geltar OxGer
Gelven, Michael 1937- ConAu 29, WrD 1976
Gelzer, Jay WhWNAA
Gelzer, Matthias 1886- ConAu 25
Gem, Harvey Alli Sup
Gem, Richard Alli
Gemelli, Agostino 1878- CatA 1952
Gemistos, Georgios Plethon 1356-1450 DcEuL
Gemistus Plethon, George CasWL, Pen Cl
Gemme, Francis Robert 1934- ConAu 23
Gemmel, John Alli Sup
Gemmell, Alan Robertson 1913- Au&Wr,
   WrD 1976
Gemmell, Constance ChPo S2
Gemmell, Ian Whitaker 1934- Au&Wr
Gemmell, John Alexander ChPo S1
Gemmell, Robert 1821- Alli Sup, ChPo S1
Gemmell, Thomas M Alli Sup
Gemmer, Caroline M Alli Sup, ChPo,
   ChPo S1, ChPo S2
Gemmett, Robert J 1936- ConAu 33
Gemmil, John Alli
Gemmill, Jane Brown 1898- ConAu 1R
Gemmill, Jane Wilson Alli Sup
Gemmill, John Alexander 1847-1905 DcNAA
Gemmill, William Nelson 1860-1930 DcNAA,
   WhWNAA
Gemmingen, Baron Otto Heinrich Von 1755-1836
   BiD&SB, DcEuL
Gemmingen-Hornberg, Otto Heinrich Von
   1755-1836 OxGer
Gemund, Wilhelm 1873- WhLA
Gemunder, George 1816-1899 Alli Sup,
   DcAmA, DcNAA
Genand, Joseph Auguste 1839- BbtC
Genast, Eduard 1797-1866 OxGer
Genast, Karl Albert Wilhelm 1822-1887
   BiD&SB
Gendell, Murray 1924- ConAu 9R
Genders, Roy Au&Wr
Gendlin, Eugene T 1926- ConAu 1R
Gendzier, Irene Lefel 1936- ConAu 23
Gendzier, Stephen J 1930- ConAu 33
Genee, Rudolf 1824- BbD, BiD&SB
Genella, Julian 1907- AmSCAP 66

Genesius, Joseph Pen Cl
Genest, John 1764-1839 DcEnA, OxEng
Genest, P Alli
Geneste, M Alli
Genestet, Petrus Augustus De 1829-1861 CasWL
Genet AmA&B, WorAu
Genet, Edmond Charles Edouard 1763-1834 REn
Genet, Jean 1909- CnThe, REnWD
Genet, Jean 1910- CasWL, CnMD, CnMWL,
   ConAu 13R, ConLC 1, ConLC 2,
   ConLC 5, CrCD, EncWL, EvEuW,
   LongC, McGWD, ModRL, ModWD,
   Pen Eur, REn, TwCW, WhTwL, WorAu
Genevais, J A Alli
Genevieve, Saint 422?-512 NewC, OxFr
Genevoix, Maurice 1890- CasWL, EncWL,
   EvEuW, OxCan
Gengembre, P W And Brown, J H Alli
Gengembre, Sophie EarAB
Gengenbach, Pamphilus 1480?-1524? CasWL,
   OxGer
Genger, Roger AmSCAP 66
Genghis Khan 1162-1227 NewC, REn
Genia 1930- IlBYP, IlCB 1966
Genin, John Nicholas 1819-1878 DcAmA,
   DcNAA
Genin, Sylvester 1822-1850 OhA&B
Genin, Thomas Hedges 1796-1868 AmA&B,
   DcNAA, OhA&B
Genings, J Alli
Genji Monogatari CasWL
Genlis, Brulart DeSillery BiDLA Sup
Genlis, Felicite DeSaint-Aubin, Mme De
   1746-1830 OxFr
Genlis, Stephanie Felicite, Comtesse De
   1746-1830 BbD, BiD&SB, EuA, EvEuW
Genn, Caroline Alli Sup
Genna, Mrs. E Alli Sup
Gennadius CasWL
Gennadius, John Alli Sup
Genne, William H 1910- ConAu 17R
Gennep, Jaspar Von 1515?-1580 CasWL,
   OxGer
Genone, Hudor DcNAA
Genovese, Eugene Dominick 1930- AmA&B
Genovese, Gen 1917- AmSCAP 66
Gensichen, Otto Fanz 1847- BiD&SB
Gensler, Kinereth DrAP 1975
Gensler, Lewis E 1896- AmSCAP 66
Gent Alli
Gent, George William Alli Sup
Gent, J B BiDLA
Gent, Peter AuNews 1
Gent, Peter A 1925- Au&Wr
Gent, Thomas 1693-1778 Alli, ChPo, ChPo S1,
   PoIre
Gent, Thomas 1780- Alli, BiDLA
Genth, Frederick A Louis Charles William
   1820-1893 Alli Sup, DcAmA
Genthe, Arnold 1869-1942 AmA&B, DcNAA
Genthe, Charles V 1937- ConAu 29,
   WrD 1976
Gentil Alli
Gentil, Richard 1917- WrD 1976
Gentil-Bernard, Pierre Joseph Bernard 1708-1775
   BbD, BiD&SB, OxFr
Gentile Da Fabriano 1370?-1427 AtlBL
Gentile, Giovanni 1875-1944 CasWL,
   CIDMEuL, EvEuW
Gentili, Alberico 1552?-1608? NewC
Gentilis, Albericus 1552?-1608? Alli, OxEng
Gentilis, Robert 1590-1654 Alli
Gentillet, Innocent d1595? DcEuL, OxFr
Gentleman, David William 1930- Au&Wr,
   ChPo S1, ConAu 25, IlBYP, SmATA 7,
   WhGrA, WrD 1976
Gentleman, Francis 1728-1784 Alli, NewC,
   PoIre
Gentleman, Robert Alli
Gentleman, Tobias Alli
Gentleman With A Duster, A NewC
Gentles, Frederick 1912- ConAu 29
Gentry, Byron B 1913- ConAu 13R
Gentry, Curt 1931- ConAu 9R
Gentry, Dwight L 1919- ConAu 1R
Gentry, Helen 1897- AmA&B
Gentry, Pearl Owen 1878- TexWr
Gentry, Thomas George 1843-1905 Alli Sup,

DcAmA, DcNAA
Gentry, William Daniel 1836- DcNAA
Gentz, Friedrich Von 1764-1832 BiD&SB,
   DcEuL, OxGer
Genung, George Frederick 1850-1935 AmLY,
   DcNAA, WhWNAA
Genung, John Franklin 1850-1919 Alli Sup,
   AmA&B, AmLY, ChPo S1, DcAmA,
   DcNAA
Geoffrey SEE ALSO Geofrey
Geoffrey Alli
Geoffrey, Abbot Of Saint Alban's d1146 BiB N
Geoffrey Crayon OxEng
Geoffrey De Vinesauf DcEnL
Geoffrey De Vinsauf Alli
Geoffrey Gaimar Alli, BiB N
Geoffrey Of Burton d1151 BiB N
Geoffrey Of Coldingham d1215? BiB N
Geoffrey Of Landaff BiB N
Geoffrey Of Monmouth 1100?-1154 Alli, BbD,
   BiB N, BiD&SB, BrAu, CasWL,
   Chmbr 1, DcEnL, EvLB, NewC, OxEng,
   OxFr, Pen Eng, REn, WebEAL
Geoffrey Of Vinsauf CasWL
Geoffrey The Grammarian DcEnL
Geoffrey, Charles ConAu XR
Geoffrey, Theodate CatA 1952, ConAu XR,
   WhWNAA
Geoffrin, Marie Therese Rodet 1699-1777
   DcEuL, OxFr
Geoffrion, Louis Philippe 1875-1942 OxCan,
   DcNAA, WhWNAA
Geoffroy De Paris OxFr
Geoffroy, Julien-Louis 1743-1814 OxFr
Geoffroy Saint-Hilaire, Etienne 1772-1844 OxFr
Geofrey SEE ALSO Geoffrey
Geofrey De Vinsauf BiB N
Geofrey Of Monmouth DcEuL
Geogehan, Thomas G Alli Sup
Geoghegan, Arthur Gerald 1810-1889 PoIre
Geoghegan, Sister Barbara 1902- ConAu P-1
Geoghegan, Edward Alli, BiDLA
Geoghegan, Joseph Bryan 1815-1889 PoIre
Geoghegan, Mary PoIre
Geoghegan, William 1844- ChPo S1, PoIre
Geometres CasWL
Georg Wilhelm, Kurfurst Von Brandenburg
   1595-1640 OxGer
Georgakas, Dan 1938- ConAu 45, DrAP 1975
George I 1660-1727 NewC
George II 1683-1760 NewC, OxGer
George III 1738-1820 NewC
George IV 1762-1830 NewC
George V 1865-1936 NewC
George VI 1895-1952 NewC
George Acropolites 1217-1282 CasWL, Pen Cl
George Cedrenus CasWL, Pen Cl
George Codinus Curopalates CasWL
George Gemistus Plethon 1355?-1452 CasWL,
   Pen Cl
George Monachus CasWL
George Of Pisidia Pen Cl
George Of Trebizond 1395-1484 CasWL,
   DcEuL
George Pachymeres 1242-1310? CasWL,
   Pen Cl
George Phrantzes 1401- CasWL
George Pisides CasWL
George, Saint NewC, REn
George Scholarius d1468? CasWL
George Sphrantzes Pen Cl
George Syncellus d810? Pen Cl
George The Monk Pen Cl
George The Syncellus CasWL
George, A C Alli Sup
George, A Robert ChPo S1
George, Albert Joseph 1913-1968 AmA&B
George, Alexander Lawrence 1920- ConAu 13R
George, Amara 1835- BiD&SB
George, Amos Alli Sup
George, Andrew Jackson 1854?-1907 ChPo S1,
   DcNAA
George, Andrew McIntyre 1857-1927 OhA&B
George, Anita Alli
George, Arial Wellington 1882-1948 DcNAA
George, Benjamin ChPo S1, ChPo S2
George, Charles B Alli Sup
George, Charles H 1922- ConAu 9R

George, Claude Swanson, Jr. 1920- *ConAu 13R,*
 WrD 1976
George, Daniel 1890-1967 *DcLEnL, LongC*
George, David *ConAu XR*
George, David Lloyd *Chmbr 3*
George, Don 1909- *AmSCAP 66*
George, Don R 1903- *AmSCAP 66*
George, Earl 1924- *AmSCAP 66*
George, Edgar Madison 1907- *ConAu 1R,*
 IndAu 1917
George, Edward Augustus 1865-1921 *DcNAA*
George, Eliot *WrD 1976*
George, Emery E 1933- *ConAu 41*
George, Ernest *Alli Sup, MnBBF*
George, F E *ChPo S2*
George, Fairfax *MnBBF*
George, Frank Honywill 1921- *Au&Wr*
George, George *Alli Sup*
George, Gertrude M *Alli Sup*
George, Graham Elias 1912- *WrD 1976*
George, Harold Coulter 1881-1937 *DcNAA*
George, Henry *Alli Sup, Chmbr 3*
George, Henry 1839-1897 *Alli Sup, AmA,*
 AmA&B, BbD, BiD&SB, CasWL,
 DcAmA, DcLEnL, DcNAA, EvLB,
 NewC, OxAm, OxEng, Pen Am, REn,
 REnAL, WebEAL
George, Henry 1862-1916 *AmA&B, DcNAA*
George, Henry Stephen *ChPo S2*
George, Hereford Brooke *Alli Sup, ChPo S2*
George, J *BbtC*
George, James 1801?-1870 *DcNAA*
George, James Zachariah 1826-1897 *Alli Sup,*
 BiDSA, DcNAA
George, Jean Craighead 1919- *AmA&B, AnCL,*
 Au&Wr, AuBYP, ChLR 1, ConAu 5R,
 IlCB 1956, MorBMP, MorJA,
 NewbC 1966, SmATA 2
George, John *Alli, AmA&B, BiDLA, ConDr*
George, Mrs. John *ChPo S2*
George, John E 1936- *ConAu 53*
George, John L 1916- *AnCL, AuBYP, BkCL,*
 ConAu 5R, SmATA 2
George, Julia W H *Alli Sup*
George, M Dorothy *ConAu P-1*
George, M Herbert *ChPo S1*
George, Malcom F 1930- *ConAu 57*
George, Margaret Gilman *ChPo*
George, Marian M *WhWNAA*
George, Marian M 1865- *AmLY, WhWNAA*
George, Marion E *ConAu XR*
George, Mary Yanaga 1940- *ChPo S2,*
 ConAu 29, WrD 1976
George, N L 1902- *ConAu 29*
George, Nathan Dow 1808-1896 *Alli Sup,*
 DcAmA, DcNAA
George, Peter 1924-1966 *ConAu 25*
George, Phil *DrAP 1975*
George, R D 1866- *WhWNAA*
George, Renee 1924- *IlCB 1956*
George, Robert Esmonde Gordon 1890-1969
 CatA 1947, ConAu P-1
George, Roy E 1923- *ConAu 37*
George, Sidney Charles 1898- *Au&Wr,*
 ConAu 53
George, Stefan Anton 1868-1933 *AtlBL,*
 CasWL, ChPo, ClDMEuL, CnMWL,
 CyWA, EncWL, EvEuW, LongC,
 ModGL, OxGer, Pen Eur, REn, TwCA,
 TwCA Sup, TwCW, WhTwL
George, Vesper Lincoln 1865-1934 *ChPo*
George, W Lloyd 1900?-1975 *ConAu 53*
George, Walter Lionel 1882-1926 *Chmbr 3,*
 LongC, NewC, TwCA
George, William *Alli, Alli Sup*
George, William Reuben 1866?-1936 *DcNAA,*
 WhWNAA
George, Wilma 1918- *Au&Wr, ConAu XR,*
 WrD 1976
Georgescu-Roegen, Nicholas 1906- *ConAu 23,*
 WrD 1976
Georgeson, Sir P *Alli*
Georgi, Charlotte *ConAu 1R*
Georgie, Leyla 1906-1945 *DcNAA*
Georgiev, Mihalaki 1854-1916 *CasWL*
Georgiou, Constance *ChPo S1*
Georgiou, Constantine 1927- *ConAu 13R,*
 SmATA 7

Georgius Continuatus *CasWL*
Georgius Tranoscius *CasWL*
Gephart, Joseph Curtin 1902- *AmA&B*
Gephart, William Franklin 1877- *WhWNAA*
Geppert, William L 1882- *WhWNAA*
Gerahty, James *Alli*
Gerahty, Laura *ChPo*
Gerald De Barri *NewC*
Gerald De Bary *Chmbr 1*
Gerald Of Barry *Pen Eng*
Gerald The Welshman *CasWL*
Gerald, Alexander 1728-1795 *EvLB*
Gerald, Carolyn Fowler 1937- *BlkAW*
Gerald, Florence *BiDSA*
Gerald, James Esward 1906- *Au&Wr,*
 ConAu 5R
Gerald, John Bart 1940- *ConAu 5R,*
 DrAF 1976
Gerald, Samuel J *TexWr*
Gerald, Ziggy *ConAu XR*
Geraldy, Paul 1885- *CasWL, ClDMEuL,*
 CnMD, McGWD, ModWD
Gerard, Archbishop Of York d1108 *BiB N*
Gerard De Montreal *OxFr*
Gerard De Nerval 1808-1855 *BbD, BiD&SB,*
 EuA, OxFr
Gerard, Albert S 1920- *ConAu 29*
Gerard, Alexander *Alli, Chmbr 2*
Gerard, Alexander 1728-1795 *Alli, Pen Eng*
Gerard, Charles 1914- *ConAu 29*
Gerard, Charles B *Alli Sup*
Gerard, Clinton W 1842?-1894 *OhA&B*
Gerard, Dave 1909- *ConAu 53*
Gerard, Dorothea 1855- *Alli Sup, BbD,*
 BiD&SB
Gerard, E D *Alli Sup*
Gerard, Francis *MnBBF*
Gerard, Baron Francois Pascal Simon 1770-1837
 AtlBL
Gerard, G *Alli Sup*
Gerard, Gaston *ConAu XR*
Gerard, Gilbert d1815 *Alli, BiDLA,*
 BiDLA Sup
Gerard, Helen Jane *Alli Sup*
Gerard, Ida Linn *Alli Sup*
Gerard, James *Alli*
Gerard, James Watson 1822?-1900 *Alli Sup,*
 ChPo, DcAmA, DcNAA
Gerard, James Watson 1867-1951 *AmA&B,*
 WhWNAA
Gerard, Jane *ConAu 1R*
Gerard, John *MnBBF*
Gerard, John 1545-1612 *BrAu, DcLEnL,*
 NewC, OxEng
Gerard, Ralph W 1900-1974 *ConAu 49*
Gerard, Richard 1876-1948 *AmSCAP 66,*
 REnAL
Gerard, William *Alli, Alli Sup, BiDLA*
Gerard-Libois, Jules C 1923- *ConAu 33*
Gerarde, John 1545-1607? *Alli*
Gerardo Alcides *PueRA*
Gerardot, J *Alli*
Gerasimov, Mikhail *DcRusL*
Gerassi, John 1931- *ConAu 5R*
Gerat, Barry *Alli*
Gerathy, James *Alli, BiDLA*
Geraud, Andre 1882-1974 *ConAu 53*
Geraud, Saint *AmA&B*
Gerbel, Nikolaus 1485?-1560 *OxGer*
Gerber, Albert B 1913- *ConAu 17R*
Gerber, Alex 1895- *AmSCAP 66*
Gerber, Dan 1940- *ConAu 33, DrAF 1976,*
 DrAP 1975
Gerber, Douglas E 1933- *ConAu 29,*
 WrD 1976
Gerber, Helmut E 1920- *ConAu 23*
Gerber, Merrill Joan 1938- *ConAu 13R*
Gerber, Sanford E 1933- *ConAu 49*
Gerber, William 1908- *ConAu 37, WrD 1976*
Gerberding, George Henry 1847-1927 *AmLY,*
 DcNAA
Gerbers, Teresa 1933- *ConAu 53*
Gerbert D'Aurillac 940-1003 *OxFr*
Gerbert De Montreuil *BiD&SB, CasWL,*
 EvEuW
Gerbert Of Aurillac 940-1003 *Pen Eur*
Gerbet, Philippe 1798-1864 *OxFr*
Gerbie, Frederic *OxCan*

Gerbier, Sir Balthasar 1591-1667 *Alli*
Gerbier, Charles *Alli*
Gerbier, George D'Ouvilly *Alli*
Gerbner, George 1919- *ConAu 45*
Gerboth, Walter W 1925- *ConAu 13R*
Gerchunoff, Alberto 1883-1950 *Pen Am*
Gerdes, Florence Marie 1919- *ConAu 25*
Gerdts, William H 1929- *ConAu 13R*
Gere, Charles March 1869- *IlCB 1945*
Gere, George Grant 1848- *DcAmA*
Gere, William *Alli*
Geree, John *Alli*
Geree, John 1600-1649 *Alli*
Geree, Stephen *Alli*
Geren, Paul Francis 1913- *AmA&B*
Gerena Bras, Gaspar 1909- *PueRA*
Gerengel, Simon *OxGer*
Gerfen, Ernest E d1944 *DcNAA*
Gergely, Tibor 1900- *IlBYP, IlCB 1945,*
 IlCB 1956
Gergen, Kenneth J 1934- *ConAu 33*
Gergory, Caspar Rene 1846- *Alli Sup*
Gerhard Von Minden *CasWL, OxGer*
Gerhard, Benjamin *Alli*
Gerhard, Frederick *Alli Sup*
Gerhard, George B 1916- *IndAu 1917*
Gerhard, Happy 1920- *ConAu 57*
Gerhard, William Paul 1854-1927 *Alli Sup,*
 DcAmA, DcNAA
Gerhard, William Wood 1809-1872 *Alli,*
 Alli Sup, DcAmA, DcNAA
Gerhardi, William Alexander 1895- *Au&Wr,*
 ConAu 25, ConLC 5, ConNov 1972,
 ConNov 1976, LongC, ModBL, NewC,
 OxEng, REn, TwCA, TwCA Sup,
 TwCW, WrD 1976
Gerhardt, Lydia A 1934- *ConAu 61*
Gerhardt, Paul 1607-1676 *BbD, BiD&SB,*
 CasWL, DcEuL, EuA, EvEuW, OxGer,
 Pen Eur, PoCh
Gerhardt, Paul 1847- *ChPo S1*
Gerhart, Emanuel Vogel 1817-1904 *Alli Sup,*
 DcAmA, DcNAA, OhA&B
Gerhart, Genevra 1930- *ConAu 57*
Gerhoh Von Reichersburg 1093-1169 *OxGer*
Gericault, Theodore 1791-1824 *AtlBL, OxFr,*
 REn
Gerich, Valentine 1898- *AmSCAP 66*
Gerig, Jared Franklin 1907- *IndAu 1917*
Gerig, John Lawrence 1878- *WhWNAA*
Gerig, Orie Benjamin 1894- *OhA&B*
Gerig, Reginald R 1919- *ConAu 57*
Gerin, Elzear *BbtC*
Gerin, Leon 1863-1951 *CanWr, OxCan*
Gerin, Winifred *ConAu 25*
Gerin-Lajoie, Antoine 1824-1882 *BbtC, CanWr,*
 CasWL, DcNAA, OxCan
Gerking, Shelby Delos 1918- *IndAu 1917*
Gerlach, Don R 1932- *ConAu 9R, WrD 1976*
Gerlach, Luther P 1930- *ConAu 41*
Gerlach, Vernon S 1922- *ConAu 61*
Gerlache DeGomery, Baron De 1866- *WhLA*
Gerland *Alli, BiB N, DcEnL*
Gerle, Wolfgang Adolf 1781-1846 *BiD&SB*
Gerloff, Hans 1887- *BiDPar*
Germacaw, Takla Hawaryat 1915- *AfA 1*
Germain, Jean-Claude *OxCan Sup*
Germain, Walter 1889-1962 *BiDPar*
Germain, William McKee 1892- *OhA&B*
Germains, Mrs. E A *Alli Sup*
German, Donald R 1931- *ConAu 57*
German, Gene Arlin 1933- *ConAu 45*
German, Joan W 1933- *ConAu 57*
German, Yuri Pavlovich 1910- *CasWL,*
 DcRusL, EvEuW
Germane, Gayton E 1920- *ConAu 1R*
Germani, Gino 1911- *ConAu 53*
Germanicus *ConAu XR, OxGer*
Germanicus Caesar 015BC-019AD *REn*
Germanicus, Julius Caesar 015BC-019AD
 Pen Cl
Germann, A C 1921- *ConAu 1R*
Germanus *CasWL*
Germar, Herb *ConAu XR*
Germar, William H 1911- *ConAu 23*
Germino, Dante 1931- *ConAu 53*
Gernert, Eleanor Towles 1928- *ConAu 37*
Gernon, William *Alli Sup*

Gernsback, Hugo 1884-1967 *AmA&B, WhWNAA*

Gernsheim, Helmut Erich Robert 1913- *Au&Wr, ChPo, ConAu 5R, WrD 1976*

Gerok, Friedrich Karl Von 1815-1890 *EvEuW, OxGer*

Gerok, Karl 1815-1890 *BiD&SB*

Gerold, Karl 1906-1973 *ConAu 41*

Gerold, William 1932- *ConAu 17R*

Geroldt, Fritz *Alli Sup*

Geronimo 1829-1909 *REn, REnAL*

Gerontius *NewC*

Gerould, Daniel C 1928- *ConAu 29*

Gerould, Gordon Hall 1877-1953 *AmA&B, ChPo, OxAm*

Gerould, James Thayer 1872-1951 *AmA&B*

Gerould, Katharine Fullerton 1879-1944 *AmA&B, ConAmA, ConAmL, DcLEnL, DcNAA, OxAm, REnAL, TwCA, TwCA Sup*

Gerould, Samuel Lankton 1834-1906 *DcNAA*

Gerov, Nayden 1823-1900 *CasWL*

Gerow, Edwin 1931- *ConAu 53*

Gerrald, Joseph *Alli*

Gerrans, B *Alli*

Gerrard, Miss d1807 *Alli*

Gerrard, Alfred W *Alli Sup*

Gerrard, Eleanor 1905?-1961 *IndAu 1917*

Gerrard, John *Alli, BiDLA*

Gerrard, Peter *MnBBF*

Gerrard, Philip *Alli*

Gerrard, Robert *MnBBF*

Gerrard, Samuel *Alli Sup*

Gerrard, William *Alli*

Gerring, Ray H 1926- *ConAu 13R*

Gerrish, Brian Albert 1931- *ConAu 5R, WrD 1976*

Gerrish, Frederic Henry 1845-1920 *Alli Sup, DcNAA*

Gerrish, George *MnBBF*

Gerrish, Theodore 1846-1923 *DcAmA, DcNAA*

Gerrity, David James 1923- *ConAu 1R*

Gerry, Charles Frederick 1823-1900 *Alli Sup, ChPo, DcNAA*

Gerry, Elbridge 1744-1814 *Alli, REnAL*

Gerry, Mrs. H B *Alli Sup*

Gerry, Margarita Spaulding 1870- *AmA&B, CarSB*

Gersaint, E F *Alli*

Gerschenkron, Alexander 1904- *AmA&B, ConAu 45*

Gersh, Harry 1912- *ConAu 1R*

Gershen, Martin 1924- *ConAu 33*

Gershenson, Daniel E 1935- *ConAu 5R*

Gershenzon, Mikhail Osipovich 1869-1925 *CasWL, ClDMEuL, DcRusL, EvEuW*

Gershman, Herbert S 1926-1971 *ConAu 25, ConAu 33*

Gershom Ben Judah, Me'or Hagolah 960?-1028 *CasWL*

Gershon, Karen Tripp 1923- *Au&Wr, ConAu XR, ConP 1970, ConP 1975, WrD 1976*

Gershoy, Leo 1897-1875 *AmA&B, Au&Wr, ConAu 57, ConAu P-1*

Gershwin, Arthur 1900- *AmSCAP 66*

Gershwin, George 1898-1937 *AmSCAP 66, AtlBL, McGWD, OxAm, REn, REnAL*

Gershwin, Ira 1896- *AmA&B, AmSCAP 66, DcLEnL, OxAm, REnAL*

Gerson, Felix Napoleon 1862- *AmLY, WhWNAA*

Gerson, Frederick H *Alli Sup*

Gerson, Jean Charlier De 1363-1429 *CasWL, DcEuL, EvEuW, OxFr, REn*

Gerson, Louis Leib 1921- *ConAu 17R*

Gerson, Noel Bertram 1914- *AmA&B, Au&Wr, AuBYP, WrD 1976*

Gerson, Thomas Isaac 1906- *WhWNAA*

Gerson, Virginia *Alli Sup, CarSB, ChPo, ChPo S1, IlCB 1945*

Gerson, Walter 1935- *ConAu 41*

Gerson, Wolfgang 1916- *ConAu 33*

Gersoni, Diane 1947- *ConAu 53*

Gersoni, Henry 1844-1897 *Alli Sup, DcNAA*

Gersoni-Stavn, Diane 1947- *ConAu XR*

Gersonides, Levi Ben Gerson 1288-1344 *CasWL, Pen Eur*

Gerstacker, Friedrich Wilhelm Christian 1816-1872 *BiD&SB, CasWL, EuA, EvEuW, HsB&A, OxAm, OxGer*

Gerstaecker, F *BiDSA*

Gerstenberg, Alice 1885- *AmA&B, AmLY, ChPo S2, WhWNAA*

Gerstenberg, Charles William 1882-1948 *DcNAA, WhWNAA*

Gerstenberg, Heinrich Wilhelm Von 1737-1823 *BiD&SB, CasWL, DcEuL, EuA, EvEuW, McGWD, OxGer, Pen Eur*

Gerstenberger, Donna Lorine 1929- *ConAu 5R, WrD 1976*

Gerster, Arpad Geyza Charles 1848-1923 *Alli Sup, DcNAA*

Gerster, Georg 1928- *ConAu 37*

Gerster, Patrick G 1942- *ConAu 57*

Gerstine, Jack *ConAu XR*

Gerstine, John 1915- *ConAu 5R*

Gerstl, Joel E 1932- *ConAu 21*

Gerstle, Edward G *Alli Sup*

Gerstle, Kurt H 1923- *ConAu 53*

Gerstner, Edna Suckau 1914- *ConAu 1R*

Gerstner, John H 1914- *ConAu 1R*

Gerstner, Karl 1930- *WhGrA*

Gert, Bernard 1934- *ConAu 29*

Gerteiny, Alfred G 1930- *ConAu 21*

Gerteis, Louis S 1942- *ConAu 45*

Gerth, Donald Rogers 1928- *ConAu 45*

Gertler, Menard M 1919- *ConAu 9R*

Gertman, Samuel 1915- *ConAu 1R*

Gertrud Von Hackeborn 1241-1298 *OxGer*

Gertrud Von Helfta 1256-1302 *OxGer*

Gertsen, Alexander Ivanovich *CasWL, DcRusL, EuA*

Gertz, Elmer 1906- *ConAu 13R, WrD 1976*

Gertzog, Irwin N 1933- *ConAu 29*

Geruzez, Eugene 1799-1865 *OxFr*

Gervais, C H *OxCan Sup*

Gervaise Of Tilbury d1235 *NewC*

Gervas, Thaurr *WhWNAA*

Gervase *Alli*

Gervase, Bishop Of Seez d1228 *BiB N*

Gervase Of Canterbury *BiB N*

Gervase Of Chichester *Alli, BiB N*

Gervase Of Tilbury *Alli, BiB N, CasWL, DcEnL, NewC*

Gervasi, Frank H 1908- *AmA&B, ConAu 13R, ConAu P-1*

Gervinus, Georg Gottfried 1805-1871 *BbD, BiD&SB, OxGer, Pen Eur*

Gervis, Henry *Alli*

Gervis, Ruth S 1894- *IlCB 1945*

Gerwig, Anna Mary 1907- *ConAu 17*

Gerwig, George William 1867-1950 *OhA&B*

Gerwig, George William 1867- *WhWNAA*

Gerwin, Donald 1937- *ConAu 25, WrD 1976*

Gery, Robert *Alli*

Gery, Thomas *Alli*

Gesch, Dorothy K 1923- *ConAu 29*

Gesch, Roy George 1920- *ConAu 23, WrD 1976*

Geschwender, James A 1933- *ConAu 41*

Gesell, Arnold Lucius 1880-1961 *AmA&B, REnAL, WhWNAA*

Gesensway, Louis 1906- *AmSCAP 66*

Geslin, Lucien *OxCan Sup*

Gesner, Abraham 1797-1864 *Alli, Alli Sup, BbtC, DcNAA, OxCan*

Gesner, Carol 1922- *ConAu 29, WrD 1976*

Gesner, Clark 1938- *AmSCAP 66*

Gesner, Conrad 1516-1565 *DcEuL*

Gesner, Elsie Miller 1919- *ConAu 17R, WrD 1976*

Gesner, Johann Matthias 1691-1761 *DcEuL, NewC, OxEng*

Gesner, Konrad 1516-1565 *OxGer*

Gesoff, Hilda I *AmSCAP 66*

Gessel, Gertrude *TexWr*

Gessler, Clifford Franklin 1893- *AmA&B, REnAL, WhWNAA*

Gessner, Lynne 1919- *ConAu 25, WrD 1976*

Gessner, Muriel M *ChPo*

Gessner, Robert 1907-1968 *AmA&B*

Gessner, Salomon 1730-1788 *CasWL, DcEuL, EvEuW, OxFr, OxGer, Pen Eur*

Gest, Edmund *Alli*

Gest, John Marshall 1859-1934 *DcNAA*

Gest, William Purves 1861-1939 *DcNAA*

Gestefeld, Ursula Newell 1845-1921 *DcNAA*

Gestie, Bernice Dainard 1899- *WhWNAA*

Gesualdo, Carlo 1560?-1613 *AtlBL, REn*

Geszner, Salomon 1730-1788 *BiD&SB*

Getchell, Alice McClure *ChPo*

Getchell, Frank H *Alli Sup*

Getchell, George H *Alli Sup*

Gethen-Richardson, Wilfred 1912- *Au&Wr*

Gethin, Lady Grace 1676-1697 *Alli*

Gething, Richard *Alli*

Gething, Thomas W 1939- *ConAu 41*

Getlein, Dorothy Woolen 1921- *ConAu 9R*

Getlein, Frank 1921- *AmA&B, ConAu 9R*

Getman, Frederick Hutton 1877- *WhWNAA*

Getseus, Daniel *Alli*

Gettell, Raymond Garfield 1881-1949 *AmA&B, WhWNAA*

Gettemy, Charles Ferris 1868-1939 *DcNAA, WhWNAA*

Gettemy, Mary Ellen 1839-1908 *DcNAA*

Gettens, Rutherford John 1900?-1974 *ConAu 49*

Getteridge, R S *Alli Sup*

Gettleman, Marvin E 1933- *ConAu 37*

Getty, Edmund *Alli Sup*

Getty, Gerald W 1913- *ConAu 57*

Getty, Hilda F 1938- *ConAu 61*

Getty, Jean Paul 1892- *Au&Wr*

Getty, Jennie Violet 1861-1913 *DcNAA*

Getty, John d1857 *PoIre*

Gettys, Warner Ensign *TexWr*

Getz, Gene Arnold 1932- *ConAu 29, IndAu 1917*

Getz, George *Alli*

Getzels, Jacob Warren 1912- *ConAu 45*

Getzoff, Carole 1943- *ConAu 61*

Getzov, Ramon M 1925- *AmSCAP 66*

Geudens, Martin *Alli Sup*

Gevaert, Francois Auguste 1828- *BiD&SB*

Gevers, Marie 1883- *CasWL*

Gewecke, Clifford George, Jr. 1932- *ConAu 23*

Gewehr, Wolf M 1939- *ConAu 45*

Gewirtz, Jacob L 1924- *ConAu 45*

Gewirtz, Leonard Benjamin 1918- *ConAu 1R*

Gex, Quo Vadis 1950- *BlkAW*

Geyelin, George Kennedy *Alli Sup*

Geyer, Alan 1931- *ConAu 9R*

Geyer, Eva Newcomer *ArizL*

Geyer, Florian 1490-1525 *OxGer*

Geyer, Georgie Anne 1935- *ConAu 29*

Geyer, H S *Alli*

Geyer, Henry Sheffie 1790-1859 *BiDSA*

Geyl, Pieter 1887-1966 *WhLA, WorAu*

Geyman, John P 1931- *ConAu 37, WrD 1976*

Geyter, Julius De 1830- *BiD&SB*

Gezelle, Guido 1830-1899 *CasWL, ClDMEuL, EuA, EvEuW, Pen Eur*

Gezi, Kalil I 1930- *ConAu 25*

Gfeller, S *Pen Eur*

Ghadimi, Hossein 1922- *ConAu 61*

Ghai, Dharam P 1936- *ConAu 21*

Ghalib, Asadullah Khan 1797-1869 *CasWL, Pen Cl*

Ghalib, Mirza Asadullah Khan 1797-1869 *DcOrL 2*

Ghani, S *DcOrL 3*

Ghavvasi *DcOrL 2*

Ghazali, Abu Hamid Muhammad 1058-1111 *CasWL*

Ghazali, Muhammad Ibn Muhammad Al-1059-1111 *Pen Cl*

Ghazaros Pharpetsi *DcOrL 3*

Ghazzali, Abu Hamid Muhammad Al- 1059-1111 *DcOrL 3*

Ghelderode, Michel De 1898-1962 *CasWL, CnMD, CnThe, ConLC 6, EncWL, McGWD, ModRL, ModWD, Pen Eur, REn, REnWD, TwCW, WhTwL, WorAu*

Ghent, William James 1866-1942 *AmLY, IndAu 1816*

Gheon, Henri 1875-1944 *CasWL, CatA 1947, ClDMEuL, CnMD, CnThe, EncWL, EvEuW, McGWD, ModWD, OxFr, Pen Eur, REn*

Gheorghiu, C Virgil 1905- *TwCW*

Gheorghiu, Constantin Virgil 1916- *ConAu 33, EncWL*

Gherardi, Gherardo 1891?-1949 *CnMD,*

Gibbs, Henry St. John Clair *ConAu 1R*
Gibbs, Isaac Ebenezer *Alli Sup*
Gibbs, James *Alli*
Gibbs, James 1682?-1754 *Alli, AtlBL*
Gibbs, James Atwood, Jr. *WhPNW*
Gibbs, Jeanne Osborne *ChPo*
Gibbs, Jeannette Phillips 1892- *AmA&B*
Gibbs, Joanifer 1947- *ConAu 57*
Gibbs, John *Alli, Alli Sup*
Gibbs, John G 1930- *ConAu 41*
Gibbs, Joseph *Alli Sup*
Gibbs, Josiah Francis 1845-1932 *DcNAA*
Gibbs, Josiah Willard 1790-1861 *Alli, Alli Sup,*
    AmA&B, CyAL 1, DcAmA, DcNAA,
    REnAL
Gibbs, Josiah Willard 1839-1903 *DcAmA,*
    DcNAA, OxAm, REnAL
Gibbs, Lincoln Robinson 1868- *WhWNAA*
Gibbs, Margaret E *ChPo, ChPo S2*
Gibbs, Mark 1920- *ConAu 5R*
Gibbs, Montgomery *Alli Sup*
Gibbs, Paul T 1897- *ConAu 9R*
Gibbs, Peter Bawtree 1903- *Au&Wr,*
    ConAu 1R
Gibbs, Philip *Alli*
Gibbs, Sir Philip Hamilton 1877-1962
    CatA 1947, Chmbr 3, DcLEnL, EvLB,
    LongC, ModBL, NewC, REn, TwCA,
    TwCA Sup, TwCW
Gibbs, R Darnley 1904- *WrD 1976*
Gibbs, Rafe *ConAu XR*
Gibbs, Raphael Sanford 1912- *ConAu 5R,*
    WhPNW
Gibbs, Richard *Alli*
Gibbs, Robert *Alli Sup, OxCan Sup*
Gibbs, Samuel *Alli*
Gibbs, T M *Alli*
Gibbs, Terry 1924- *AmSCAP 66*
Gibbs, Thomas F *Alli Sup*
Gibbs, Sir Vicary 1752-1820 *Alli, BiDLA*
Gibbs, W *Alli*
Gibbs, Willa 1917- *AmA&B, AmNov*
Gibbs, William *Alli*
Gibbs, William Alfred 1819- *Alli Sup,*
    ChPo S1, ChPo S2
Gibbs, William And Gibbs, Josiah Willard
    Alli Sup
Gibbs, William E 1936- *ConAu 21*
Gibbs, Winifred Stuart 1871-1928 *DcNAA,*
    WhWNAA
Gibbs, Wolcott 1822-1903 *CyAL 1, DcAmA*
Gibbs, Wolcott 1902-1958 *AmA&B, REnAL*
Gibbs-Smith, Charles Harvard 1909- *Au&Wr,*
    ConAu 9R, WrD 1976
Gibby, Robert Gwyn 1916- *ConAu 13R*
Giberne, Agnes 1845- *Alli Sup, ChPo,*
    ChPo S1, WhLA
Giberson, Dorothy *ConAu 1R*
Gibian, George 1924- *ConAu 1R*
Gibier, Paul 1851-1900 *DcNAA*
Giblett, Paul *Alli*
Giblin, Charles Homer 1928- *ConAu 41*
Gibney, John *Alli, BiDLA*
Gibney, Robert Dwarris *Alli Sup*
Gibney, Somerville *Alli Sup, ChPo, ChPo S2,*
    MnBBF
Gibney, Virgil Pendleton 1847-1927 *Alli Sup,*
    DcNAA
Gibran, Kahlil 1883-1931 *AmA&B, CasWL,*
    ChPo S1, DcNAA, TwCA, TwCA Sup
Gibson *Alli*
Gibson, A *ChPo S1*
Gibson, A M *Alli Sup*
Gibson, Abraham *Alli*
Gibson, Albert *Alli Sup*
Gibson, Albert Andrew 1913-1961 *AmSCAP 66*
Gibson, Sir Alexander *Alli*
Gibson, Alexander 1800-1867 *Alli Sup*
Gibson, Alexander And White, J F *Alli Sup*
Gibson, Alexander Craig 1813-1874 *Alli Sup*
Gibson, Alexander George 1875- *WhLA*
Gibson, Anna L 1875- *WhWNAA*
Gibson, Antony *Alli*
Gibson, Arnold Hartley 1878- *WhLA*
Gibson, Arrell Morgan 1921- *ConAu 41*
Gibson, Art *Alli*
Gibson, Arthur S *Alli Sup, ChPo S1*
Gibson, Benjamin *Alli, BiDLA*

Gibson, C *ChPo*
Gibson, Cecil 1923- *Au&Wr*
Gibson, Charles 1874-1954 *AmA&B*
Gibson, Charles 1920- *ConAu 21*
Gibson, Charles Bernard *Alli Sup*
Gibson, Charles Brockway *WhWNAA*
Gibson, Charles Dana 1867-1944 *AmA&B,*
    ChPo, DcAmA, DcNAA, OxAm, REn,
    REnAL
Gibson, Charles Donnel 1863- *DcAmA*
Gibson, Charles Edmund 1916- *Au&Wr,*
    ConAu 5R, WrD 1976
Gibson, Charles Hammond 1874- *DcAmA,*
    WhWNAA
Gibson, Charles Philip *Alli Sup*
Gibson, Charles R 1870- *WhLA*
Gibson, Charline 1937- *LivBA*
Gibson, Constance *ChPo S1*
Gibson, Dale *OxCan Sup*
Gibson, Derlyne 1936- *ConAu 23*
Gibson, Donald B 1933- *ConAu 25*
Gibson, Douglas *ChPo*
Gibson, E *ChPo S1*
Gibson, Edgar Charles Sumner *Alli Sup*
Gibson, Edmund 1669-1748 *Alli*
Gibson, Edmund P 1898-1961 *BiDPar*
Gibson, Edward Hay 1901- *Au&Wr*
Gibson, Elizabeth 1869-1931 *ChPo, ChPo S1,*
    ChPo S2
Gibson, Elsie 1907- *ConAu 61*
Gibson, Ernest Dana 1906- *ConAu 29,*
    WrD 1976
Gibson, Eva Katherine Clapp 1857-1916
    AmA&B, DcAmA, DcNAA
Gibson, Evelyn Helena 1910- *Au&Wr*
Gibson, F W *OxCan Sup*
Gibson, Francis *Alli, BiDLA*
Gibson, Frank K 1924- *ConAu 37*
Gibson, Frank Markey 1857-1929 *DcNAA*
Gibson, George Alexander *Alli Sup*
Gibson, George Alexander 1858- *WhLA*
Gibson, George Herbert Rae 1881-1932 *DcNAA*
Gibson, George Miles 1860-1932 *DcNAA*
Gibson, George Robert 1918- *Au&Wr*
Gibson, George Stacey *Alli Sup*
Gibson, Gertrude Hevener 1906- *ConAu 5R*
Gibson, Graeme 1934- *OxCan Sup*
Gibson, H *Alli Sup*
Gibson, H P 1867- *WhWNAA*
Gibson, Harry Clark *ConAu XR*
Gibson, Henry *Alli, Alli Sup*
Gibson, Henry Richard 1837- *WhWNAA*
Gibson, Hugh *ChPo*
Gibson, Ivor F *ChPo S2*
Gibson, J C *BbtC*
Gibson, J Harris *Alli Sup*
Gibson, J M *BiDSA*
Gibson, J S *Alli Sup*
Gibson, J Westby- *Alli Sup*
Gibson, James *Alli, Alli Sup, BbtC*
Gibson, James 1799-1871 *Alli Sup*
Gibson, James 1864- *WhLA*
Gibson, James Charles 1919- *Au&Wr*
Gibson, James Kimball 1836- *DcAmA*
Gibson, James L 1935- *ConAu 5R*
Gibson, James W 1932- *ConAu 41*
Gibson, James Young 1826-1886 *Alli Sup*
Gibson, Janice T 1934- *ConAu 41*
Gibson, John *Alli, Alli Sup, BbtC, BiDLA*
Gibson, John d1879 *Alli Sup*
Gibson, John d1887 *Alli Sup*
Gibson, John 1907- *ConAu 33*
Gibson, John M 1899- *ConAu 1R*
Gibson, John Monro 1838- *Alli Sup*
Gibson, John Westby- *Alli Sup*
Gibson, Joseph *Alli*
Gibson, Joseph Thompson 1844-1922 *DcNAA*
Gibson, Josephine *ConAu XR, SmATA 2,*
    ThBJA
Gibson, Juanita *TexWr*
Gibson, Katharine 1893- *AmA&B, JBA 1951,*
    OhA&B, St&VC
Gibson, Kennet *Alli*
Gibson, Lee *OxCan Sup*
Gibson, Leonard *Alli*
Gibson, Louis Henry 1854-1908 *DcAmA,*
    DcNAA, IndAu 1816
Gibson, Louisa *Alli Sup*

Gibson, Maralee G 1924- *ConAu 17R*
Gibson, Mary Stanley *HsB&A Sup*
Gibson, Matthew *Alli*
Gibson, Michael Dara 1922- *Au&Wr*
Gibson, Miles 1947- *WrD 1976*
Gibson, Morgan 1929- *ConAu 25, DrAP 1975*
Gibson, Nevin H 1915- *ConAu 49*
Gibson, O *Alli Sup*
Gibson, Ostorius 1871-1925 *ArizL*
Gibson, Powell Willard 1875- *BlkAW*
Gibson, Preston 1879-1937 *AmA&B, DcNAA*
Gibson, Quentin 1913- *WrD 1976*
Gibson, Randall Lee 1832-1892 *BiDSA*
Gibson, Raymond E 1924- *ConAu 23*
Gibson, Reginald Walter 1901- *ConAu P-1*
Gibson, Richard *Alli Sup*
Gibson, Richard 1931- *ConAu 41*
Gibson, Robert *Alli*
Gibson, Robert 1927- *WrD 1976*
Gibson, Robert Christopher 1826?- *Alli Sup*
Gibson, Robert Edward Lee 1864-1918 *BiDSA,*
    DcNAA
Gibson, Robert Lamplugh *Alli Sup*
Gibson, Robert Williams 1854-1927 *DcNAA*
Gibson, Rosemary *ConAu 49*
Gibson, Rufus *BlkAW*
Gibson, S *Alli Sup*
Gibson, Samuel *Alli*
Gibson, Stanley Taylor *Alli Sup*
Gibson, Stuart 1893- *WhWNAA*
Gibson, T *Alli*
Gibson, T A *Alli, BbtC*
Gibson, Thomas *Alli, Alli Sup*
Gibson, Thomas d1562 *Alli*
Gibson, Thomas Ellison 1822- *Alli Sup*
Gibson, W *Alli*
Gibson, W S *Alli*
Gibson, Walker 1919- *AmA&B, ConAu 1R*
Gibson, Walter Brown 1897- *EncM&D,*
    WhWNAA
Gibson, Walter M *Alli, Alli Sup*
Gibson, Walter Murray 1823-1888 *DcNAA*
Gibson, Westby *Alli*
Gibson, Wilfrid Wilson 1878-1962 *ChPo,*
    ChPo S1, ChPo S2, Chmbr 3, DcLEnL,
    EvLB, LongC, ModBL, NewC, Pen Eng,
    REn, TwCA, TwCA Sup, WebEAL,
    WhLA
Gibson, William *Alli, Alli Sup, BiDLA*
Gibson, William 1788-1868 *BiDSA, DcAmA,*
    DcNAA
Gibson, William 1826-1887 *BiDSA, ChPo S1,*
    DcAmA, DcNAA
Gibson, William 1858-1896 *ChPo*
Gibson, William 1914- *CnMD, ConAu 9R,*
    ConDr, McGWD, ModAL, ModWD,
    Pen Am, REnAL, WorAu, WrD 1976
Gibson, William 1915- *ChPo S2*
Gibson, William Carleton 1913- *ConAu 17R*
Gibson, William E 1944- *ConAu 33*
Gibson, William Hamilton 1850-1896 *Alli Sup,*
    AmA, AmA&B, BbD, BiD&SB, DcAmA,
    DcNAA
Gibson, William J *Alli Sup*
Gibson, William Ralph Boyce 1869- *WhLA*
Gibson, William Sidney 1814-1871 *Alli Sup*
Gibson, William W 1914- *AmA&B*
Gibson, William Walker *ChPo*
Gicaru, Muga 1920- *AfA 1, Pen Cl*
Gicovate, Bernard 1922- *ConAu 37*
Gidal, Sonia 1922- *Au&Wr, AuBYP,*
    ConAu 5R, SmATA 2
Gidal, Tim N 1909- *ConAu 5R, SmATA 2*
Gidde, Walter *Alli*
Giddens, Paul H *MnnWr*
Giddings, Franklin Henry 1855-1931 *AmA&B,*
    ChPo, DcAmA, DcNAA, REnAL
Giddings, Howard Andrus 1868-1949 *DcNAA*
Giddings, James Louis 1909-1964 *ConAu P-1,*
    OxCan Sup
Giddings, John Calvin 1930- *WrD 1976*
Giddings, Joshua Reed 1795-1864 *Alli,*
    Alli Sup, AmA&B, BiD&SB, DcAmA,
    DcNAA, OhA&B
Giddings, Luther 1823?- *Alli Sup, OhA&B*
Giddings, Nahum James 1883- *WhWNAA*
Giddings, Paula *BlkAW*
Giddings, Robert *ChPo S2*

Gilbert, George Blodgett 1871-1948 *DcNAA*

Gilbert, George Darcy *HsB&A*

Gilbert, George Holley 1854-1930 *DcAmA, DcNAA, WhWNAA*

Gilbert, Glenn Gordon 1936- *ConAu 33, WrD 1976*

Gilbert, Grove Karl 1843-1918 *Alli Sup, DcAmA, DcNAA*

Gilbert, H *MnBBF*

Gilbert, Harold 1912- *Au&Wr*

Gilbert, Harriet 1948- *ConAu 57, WrD 1976*

Gilbert, Helen Earle *AnMV 1926, AuBYP*

Gilbert, Mrs. Henry Abraham *Alli Sup*

Gilbert, Henry Franklin Belknap 1868-1928 *DcNAA*

Gilbert, Herbert *Alli Sup*

Gilbert, Herman Cromwell 1923- *BlkAW, ConAu 29*

Gilbert, Hiram T *Alli Sup*

Gilbert, Howard Worcester 1819-1894 *ChPo S1, DcAmA, DcNAA*

Gilbert, Sir Humphrey 1539?-1583 *Alli, CasWL, NewC, OxAm, OxCan, OxEng, REn, REnAL*

Gilbert, J H *Alli Sup*

Gilbert, J P *Alli Sup*

Gilbert, Jack Glenn 1925- *ConP 1970, DrAP 1975, Pen Am*

Gilbert, Jack Glenn 1934- *ConAu 25*

Gilbert, James *Alli*

Gilbert, James 1935- *ConAu 29*

Gilbert, James Eleazer 1839-1909 *DcNAA*

Gilbert, James Stanley 1855-1906 *ChPo, ChPo S1*

Gilbert, Jarvey 1917- *ConAu 33, WrD 1976*

Gilbert, Sir Jeffray 1674-1726 *Alli*

Gilbert, Joan 1931- *ConAu 21, SmATA 10*

Gilbert, John *Alli*

Gilbert, John d1761 *Alli*

Gilbert, Sir John 1817-1897 *ChPo, ChPo S1, ChPo S2*

Gilbert, John 1912- *Au&Wr*

Gilbert, John Raphael 1926- *Au&Wr, WrD 1976*

Gilbert, John Thomas 1829-1898 *Alli Sup, BbD, BiD&SB, BrAu 19*

Gilbert, Joseph *BiDLA*

Gilbert, Joseph d1852 *Alli*

Gilbert, Josiah 1814- *Alli Sup, BiD&SB*

Gilbert, Kenneth 1889- *AmA&B, WhPNW*

Gilbert, L Wolfe 1886- *AmSCAP 66*

Gilbert, Levi 1852-1917 *DcAmA, DcNAA, OhA&B*

Gilbert, Linda 1847-1895 *DcNAA*

Gilbert, Luther M *Alli Sup*

Gilbert, Marcel *OxCan Sup*

Gilbert, Martin 1936- *ConAu 9R*

Gilbert, Sister Mary *ConAu XR, ConP 1970, WrD 1976*

Gilbert, Mercedes d1952 *BlkAW*

Gilbert, Michael Francis 1912- *Au&Wr, ConAu 1R, EncM&D, WorAu, WrD 1976*

Gilbert, Miriam *ConAu XR, WrD 1976*

Gilbert, Nan *ConAu XR, SmATA 2, WrD 1976*

Gilbert, Nathaniel *Alli*

Gilbert, Nicolas Joseph Laurent 1751-1780 *BiD&SB, CasWL, DcEuL, EuA, EvEuW, OxFr, Pen Eur*

Gilbert, Mrs. R L *Alli Sup*

Gilbert, Ray 1912- *AmSCAP 66*

Gilbert, Richard E 1919- *AmSCAP 66*

Gilbert, Robert *Alli*

Gilbert, Robert E 1939- *ConAu 53*

Gilbert, Russell Wieder 1905- *ConAu 45*

Gilbert, Ruth 1917- *ChPo S1, ConP 1970, ConP 1975, WrD 1976*

Gilbert, Ruth Gallard Ainsworth 1908- *Au&Wr, ConAu 9R*

Gilbert, S R *OxCan Sup*

Gilbert, Samuel *Alli*

Gilbert, Sandra M 1936- *ConAu 41, DrAF 1976, DrAP 1975*

Gilbert, Sara 1943- *ConAu 57*

Gilbert, Simeon *Alli Sup*

Gilbert, Stephen 1912- *ConAu 25*

Gilbert, T *Alli Sup*

Gilbert, Thomas *Alli, Alli Sup, BiDLA*

Gilbert, Thomas 1613-1694 *Alli*

Gilbert, W *Alli, BiDLA*

Gilbert, William *Alli, BiDLA, DcEnL*

Gilbert, William 1540-1603 *Alli, BrAu, DcEnL, NewC, OxEng*

Gilbert, William 1804-1889? *Alli Sup, BiD&SB*

Gilbert, Sir William Schwenck 1836-1911 *Alli Sup, AtlBL, BbD, BiD&SB, BrAu 19, CasWL, ChPo, ChPo S1, ChPo S2, Chmbr 3, CnE&AP, CnThe, CyWA, DcEnA, DcEnA Ap, DcEnL, DcEuL, DcLEnL, EvLB, McGWD, ModWD, MouLC 4, NewC, OxEng, Pen Eng, REn, REnWD, St&VC, WebEAL*

Gilbert, Willie 1916- *ConAu 45*

Gilbert, Zack 1925- *BlkAW*

Gilberts, Helen Ilene 1909- *ConAu 29, WrD 1976*

Gilbertson, John D *Alli Sup*

Gilbertson, Merril Thomas 1911- *ConAu 9R*

Gilbertson, Mildred Geiger 1908- *ConAu 5R, SmATA 2, WrD 1976*

Gilbertson, Virginia M 1914- *AmSCAP 66*

Gilbertus Anglicus *Alli, BiB N*

Gilbertus Legleus *Alli*

Gilbey, Jack *ChPo, ChPo S1*

Gilbey, John Newman 1888- *ChPo S2*

Gilbey, Tresham 1862- *Br&AmS*

Gilbey, Sir Walter 1831-1914 *Br&AmS*

Gilboa, Amir 1917- *CasWL, WorAu*

Gilboa, Yehoshua A 1918- *ConAu 29, WrD 1976*

Gilborne, John *PoIre*

Gilbreath, Alice 1921- *ConAu 25*

Gilbreath, Kent 1945- *ConAu 45*

Gilbreth, Frank B, Jr. 1911- *AmA&B, ConAu 9R, SmATA 2*

Gilbreth, Frank Bunker 1868-1924 *DcNAA, REnAL*

Gilbreth, Lillian Evelyn Moller 1878-1972 *ConAu 33, REnAL, WhWNAA*

Gilbride, Claire 1919- *AmSCAP 66*

Gilby, Anthony *Alli*

Gilby, Goddred *Alli*

Gilby, Henry F *Alli Sup*

Gilby, W H *Alli*

Gilby, W O S *Alli Sup*

Gilby, William *Alli*

Gilcher, Edwin L 1909- *ConAu 29*

Gilchrist, Alan William 1913- *Au&Wr, ConAu 21*

Gilchrist, Alexander 1828-1861 *Alli, Alli Sup, ChPo, DcEnL, DcLEnL, OxEng*

Gilchrist, Alfred 1880?- *Alli Sup, ChPo, ChPo S1*

Gilchrist, Anne *ChPo S2*

Gilchrist, Anne 1828-1885 *Alli Sup, REnAL*

Gilchrist, Annie Somers 1864?- *Alli Sup, AmA&B, BiDSA, DcNAA*

Gilchrist, Beth Bradford 1879-1957 *AmA&B, WhWNAA*

Gilchrist, Christianna Glass 1862- *ArizL, ChPo*

Gilchrist, Ebenezer 1707-1774 *Alli*

Gilchrist, Fredericka Raymond 1846?- *DcAmA, DcNAA*

Gilchrist, Herbert Harlakenden *Alli Sup*

Gilchrist, I *Alli Sup*

Gilchrist, J 1927- *ConAu 25*

Gilchrist, J G *Alli Sup*

Gilchrist, James *Alli, BiDLA*

Gilchrist, James Grant d1906 *DcNAA*

Gilchrist, James P *Alli*

Gilchrist, John *Alli, BiDLA Sup, ChPo S2*

Gilchrist, John Borthwick 1759-1841 *Alli, BiDLA*

Gilchrist, Marie Emilie 1893- *AnMV 1926, ChPo, ChPo S2, OhA&B*

Gilchrist, May *ChPo S2*

Gilchrist, Octavius 1779-1823 *Alli, BiDLA*

Gilchrist, Paul *Alli*

Gilchrist, Peter *Alli*

Gilchrist, R R 1924- *Au&Wr*

Gilchrist, Robert *Alli Sup*

Gilchrist, Robert Murray 1868- *DcEnA Ap*

Gilchrist, Robert Niven 1888- *Au&Wr*

Gilchrist, Rosetta Luce 1851-1921 *OhA&B*

Gilchrist, S D *MnBBF*

Gilchrist, Thomas Caspar 1862-1927 *DcNAA*

Gildas 516?-570? *Alli, BiB S, BrAu, CasWL, Chmbr 1, DcEnL, EvLB, NewC, OxEng, Pen Eng, REn*

Gildea, J R *PoIre*

Gildehaus, Charles *Alli Sup*

Gildemeister, Otto 1823-1902 *OxGer*

Gilden, Bert 1915?-1971 *ConAu 29, ConAu P-1*

Gilden, K B *ConAu XR*

Gilden, Katya *ConAu 9R*

Gilder, George F 1939- *AuNews 1, ConAu 17R*

Gilder, Jeannette Leonard 1849-1916 *Alli Sup, AmA&B, BiD&SB, DcAmA, DcNAA*

Gilder, Joseph Benson 1858-1936 *AmA&B, ChPo, DcNAA*

Gilder, Richard Watson 1844-1909 *Alli Sup, AmA, AmA&B, BbD, BiD&SB, ChPo, ChPo S1, Chmbr 3, DcAmA, DcEnA Ap, DcLEnL, DcNAA, EvLB, OxAm, Pen Am, REn, REnAL*

Gilder, Rodman 1877-1953 *AmA&B*

Gilder, Rosamond DeKay *AmA&B, ConAu 1R*

Gilder, William Henry 1838-1900 *Alli Sup, BiD&SB, DcAmA, DcNAA, OxCan*

Gilderdale, John *Alli*

Gilderdale, John Smith *Alli Sup*

Gilderoy d1638? *NewC, REn*

Gilderoy, Roland *Alli Sup*

Gildersleeve, Basil Lanneau 1831-1924 *Alli Sup, AmA, AmA&B, BiD&SB, BiDSA, DcAmA, DcNAA, REnAL*

Gildersleeve, Mrs. C H 1834-1899 *Alli Sup, ChPo S2, DcNAA, HsB&A*

Gildersleeve, Charles H *Alli Sup*

Gildersleeve, Stewart *HsB&A*

Gildersleeve, Thomas R 1927- *ConAu 29, WrD 1976*

Gildersleeve, Virginia Crocheron 1877-1965 *AmA&B, WhWNAA*

Gilding, Elizabeth *Alli*

Gildner, Gary 1938- *ConAu 33, DrAF 1976, DrAP 1975, WrD 1976*

Gildon, Charles 1665-1724 *Alli, BiD&SB, CasWL, Chmbr 2, DcEnL, EvLB*

Gildus *Alli*

Gildzen, Alex 1943- *ConAu 41*

Gile, Louisa Boyd *ChPo, ChPo S1*

Giles SEE ALSO Gilles

Giles *Alli*

Giles, Blessed *NewC*

Giles De Paris d1141? *Pen Eur*

Giles, Saint *NewC, REn*

Giles, Albert 1885- *WhWNAA*

Giles, Alfred E *Alli Sup*

Giles, Anne H *Alli Sup*

Giles, Arthur Edward 1864- *WhLA*

Giles, Brian *ChPo*

Giles, Carl H 1935- *ConAu 29*

Giles, Carl Ronald 1916- *WhGrA*

Giles, Charles 1783-1867 *DcNAA, PoCh*

Giles, Chauncey 1813-1893 *Alli Sup, AmA&B, BiD&SB, DcAmA, DcNAA, OhA&B*

Giles, Edward *Alli Sup*

Giles, Ella Augusta 1851- *Alli Sup, DcAmA, DcNAA*

Giles, Frederick John 1928- *Au&Wr*

Giles, Frederick Reed 1864-1897 *IndAu 1816*

Giles, Frije Williams *Alli Sup*

Giles, Frye Williams 1819-1898 *DcNAA*

Giles, Gordon A *ConAu XR*

Giles, Henry 1809-1882 *Alli, Alli Sup, AmA&B, BiD&SB, DcAmA, DcNAA*

Giles, Herbert Allen *Alli Sup*

Giles, Hermann Harry 1901- *AmA&B*

Giles, J A *Alli*

Giles, James *Alli Sup, BiDLA*

Giles, Janice Holt 1905- *AmA&B, ConAu 1R*

Giles, Joanna Elder *WhLA*

Giles, John *Alli, Alli Sup*

Giles, John 1921- *WrD 1976*

Giles, John Allen 1808-1884 *Alli Sup*

Giles, John Douglas *Alli Sup*

Giles, Johnny 1911- *AmSCAP 66*

Giles, Joseph *Alli*

Giles, Kris *ConAu XR*
Giles, Lionel 1875- *WhLA*
Giles, Mascall *Alli*
Giles, Norman 1879-1947 *CasWL*
Giles, Oscar John Jennings *Alli Sup*
Giles, Peter 1860-1935 *ChPo*
Giles, Raymond *ConAu XR*
Giles, Robert Harris *Alli Sup*
Giles, Samuel *Alli Sup*
Giles, Verlie Story 1897- *AnMV 1926*
Giles, William *Alli*
Giles, William Branch 1762-1830 *Alli*, *BiDSA*, *DcNAA*
Gilfond, Edward S, Jr. 1906- *ConAu 57*
Gilfillan, George *Chmbr 3*, *WebEAL*
Gilfillan, George 1813-1878 *Alli*, *Alli Sup*, *BbD*, *BrAu 19*, *ChPo*, *ChPo S1*, *ChPo S2*, *DcEnL*, *EvLB*, *NewC*
Gilfillan, James *Alli Sup*
Gilfillan, James 1797-1874 *Alli Sup*
Gilfillan, Joseph Alexander 1838-1913 *DcNAA*
Gilfillan, Merrill *DrAP 1975*
Gilfillan, Robert 1798-1850 *Alli*, *BiD&SB*, *BrAu 19*, *ChPo*, *Chmbr 3*, *EvLB*, *NewC*
Gilfillan, Samuel *Alli*
Gilfond, Henry *ConAu 23*, *SmATA 2*
Gilford, C B 1920- *ConAu 17R*
Gilforde, Robert *MnBBF*
Gilgamesh *DcOrL 3*
Gilge, Jeanette 1924- *ConAu 61*
Gilgen, Albert R 1930- *ConAu 37*
Gilham, William *Alli Sup*
Gilhooley, Leonard 1921- *ConAu 37*
Gilhooley, Lord *DcNAA*
Gili, Elizabeth Helen 1913- *WrD 1976*
Gili Y Gaya, Samuel 1892- *DcSpL*
Gilien, Sasha 1925?-1971 *ConAu 33*
Gilkes, A H *Alli Sup*
Gilkes, A N 1900- *ConAu 5R*
Gilkes, Martin *ChPo S2*
Gilkey, Langdon 1919- *ConAu 17R*
Gilkie, James *Alli*
Gilkin, Iwan 1858-1924 *CasWL*, *ClDMEuL*, *EvEuW*
Gilkison, Grace *ConICB*
Gilkison, John 1844-1895 *ChPo*, *ChPo S1*
Gilkison, W S 1912- *Au&Wr*
Gilks *ChPo S2*
Gilks, Morton *Alli*
Gilks, Thomas *Alli Sup*
Gilkyson, Phoebe Hunter 1880- *WhWNAA*
Gilkyson, Phoebe Hunter 1893- *WhWNAA*
Gilkyson, Walter 1880- *AmA&B*, *WhWNAA*
Gilkyson, Mrs. Walter *AmA&B*, *WhWNAA*
Gill *Alli*, *MnBBF*
Gill, Alexander 1564-1635 *Alli*
Gill, Alexander 1597-1642 *Alli*
Gill, Andre 1840-1885 *OxFr*
Gill, Andrew J Mitchell *Alli Sup*
Gill, Augustus Herman 1864-1936 *DcAmA*, *DcNAA*, *WhWNAA*
Gill, Bob 1931- *ConAu 1R*
Gill, Brendan 1914- *AmA&B*, *ConNov 1972*, *ConNov 1976*, *DrAF 1976*, *Pen Am*, *REnAL*, *TwCA Sup*, *WrD 1976*
Gill, C Haughton *Alli Sup*
Gill, C O 1904- *TexWr*
Gill, Carolyn 1918- *AmSCAP 66*
Gill, Charles *Alli Sup*
Gill, Charles 1871-1918 *CanWr*
Gill, Charles Clifford 1885-1948 *DcNAA*, *WhWNAA*
Gill, Charles Ignace Adelard 1871-1918 *DcNAA*, *OxCan*
Gill, Corrington 1898-1946 *DcNAA*
Gill, Crispin 1916- *Au&Wr*, *ConAu 21*
Gill, David Lawrence William 1934- *ConAu 29*, *ConP 1970*, *ConP 1975*, *WrD 1976*
Gill, Delia Mary *ChPo*, *ChPo S1*
Gill, Derek L T 1919- *ConAu 49*, *SmATA 9*
Gill, Edward Anthony Wharton 1855-1944 *OxCan*
Gill, Eric 1882-1940 *BkC 5*, *CatA 1947*, *DcLEnL*, *LongC*, *TwCA Sup*
Gill, Evan Robertson 1892- *ConAu 9R*
Gill, Frances 1885-1937 *DcNAA*
Gill, Frederick 1898- *ConAu 5R*
Gill, George *ChPo S1*

Gill, George Creswell *BiDSA*
Gill, Henry *Alli Sup*
Gill, Henry Galloway *Alli Sup*
Gill, Henry Joseph d1903 *PoIre*
Gill, Henry M *ChPo S1*
Gill, Henry Vincent 1872- *WhLA*
Gill, Hugh *WrD 1976*
Gill, I K 1924- *ConAu 61*
Gill, Isobel Sarah *Alli Sup*
Gill, James *Alli Sup*
Gill, Jeremiah *Alli*, *BiDLA*
Gill, Jerry H 1933- *ConAu 33*, *WrD 1976*
Gill, John *Alli Sup*, *DrAP 1975*, *OxCan Sup*
Gill, John 1697-1771 *Alli*
Gill, John Beadnell *Alli Sup*
Gill, John C *Alli Sup*
Gill, Joseph *Alli*, *Alli Sup*
Gill, Joseph 1901- *Au&Wr*, *ConAu 9R*
Gill, Joseph 1908- *WrD 1976*
Gill, Josephine Pauline Eckert 1921- *OhA&B*
Gill, Julia 1820-1882 *ChPo*, *ChPo S1*, *ChPo S2*
Gill, Julia And Lee, Frances *Alli Sup*
Gill, Lawrence *MnBBF*
Gill, Leonard Upcott *Alli Sup*
Gill, M Park *ChPo*, *ChPo S2*
Gill, MacDonald *ChPo*, *ChPo S1*
Gill, Margery Jean 1925- *ChPo*, *ChPo S1*, *IlBYP*, *IlCB 1966*
Gill, Mary Harvey *Alli Sup*
Gill, May Terry *TexWr*, *WhWNAA*
Gill, Michael Bedford 1937- *Au&Wr*
Gill, Myrna Lakshmi 1943- *ConP 1970*, *OxCan Sup*, *WrD 1976*
Gill, Norman Thorpe 1909- *Au&Wr*
Gill, Peter 1939- *ConDr*, *WrD 1976*
Gill, R W And Johnson, J *Alli*
Gill, Ralph 1919- *AmSCAP 66*
Gill, Raymond Blackstone 1928- *Au&Wr*
Gill, Richard *Alli Sup*
Gill, Richard 1922- *ConAu 41*
Gill, Richard Cochran 1901-1958 *AmA&B*, *AuBYP*
Gill, Richard T 1927- *ConAu 23*
Gill, Robert Sutherland 1886- *AmA&B*
Gill, Ronald Crispin 1916- *WrD 1976*
Gill, Sidney Paul *ChPo*
Gill, Theodore Nicholas 1837-1914 *Alli Sup*, *BbtC*, *DcAmA*, *DcNAA*
Gill, Thomas *Alli*, *Alli Sup*, *BiDLA*
Gill, Thomas Hornblower 1819- *Alli Sup*, *PoCh*
Gill, Thomas Howard *Alli Sup*
Gill, Tom 1891- *AmA&B*, *WhWNAA*
Gill, Traviss 1891- *Au&Wr*, *ConAu P-1*
Gill, W *BbtC*, *ChPo*
Gill, Wilfrid Austin *ChPo*
Gill, William *Alli Sup*
Gill, William Fearing 1844-1917 *Alli Sup*, *ChPo S1*, *DcAmA*, *DcNAA*
Gill, William Henry 1910- *Au&Wr*, *WrD 1976*
Gill, William Hugh 1841-1904 *DcNAA*
Gill, William Icrin 1831-1902 *DcNAA*
Gill, William Ireland *Alli Sup*, *DcAmA*
Gill, William John 1843-1881 *Alli Sup*
Gill, William Wyatt *Alli Sup*
Gill, Wilson Lindsley 1851-1941 *DcNAA*, *OhA&B*
Gill, Winifred Ethel 1902- *Au&Wr*
Gillam, Benjamin And Gillam, Zachariah *OxCan*
Gillam, David S 1915- *AmSCAP 66*
Gillam, John Graham 1883- *WhLA*
Gillan, R *Alli*
Gillan, R D *ChPo*
Gillan, Robert 1800-1879 *Alli Sup*
Gilland, James d1811 *PoIre*
Gillander, H *MnBBF*
Gillanders, W R *MnBBF*
Gillane, John d1735 *Alli*
Gillard, John Thomas 1900-1942 *CatA 1947*, *DcNAA*
Gillchrest, Muriel Noyes 1905- *ConAu 25*
Gille, Philippe 1834-1901 *BiD&SB*
Gillelan, George Howard 1917- *AuBYP*, *ConAu 1R*
Gilleland, J C *BbtC*

Gilleland, William M *BiDSA*
Gillen, Henry *ChPo S1*
Gillen, Mollie 1908- *ConAu 41*
Gillenson, Lewis William 1918- *Au&Wr*, *ConAu 5R*
Gilles SEE ALSO Giles
Gilles De Paris *CasWL*
Gilles Le Vinier d1252 *CasWL*
Gilles, Albert S, Sr. 1888- *ConAu 57*
Gilles, Eloise 1929- *AmSCAP 66*
Gilles, Helen Illona Trybulowski 1901- *Au&Wr*
Gillese, John Patrick 1920- *Au&Wr*, *ConAu 13R*
Gillespie *Alli*
Gillespie, Alexander *Alli*, *BiDLA*
Gillespie, Charles Bancroft 1865-1915 *DcNAA*
Gillespie, Charles George Knox *Alli Sup*
Gillespie, Dizzy 1917- *AmSCAP 66*
Gillespie, Elizabeth *Alli Sup*
Gillespie, Elizabeth 1821-1901 *DcAmA*, *DcNAA*
Gillespie, Frances Elma 1895-1948 *DcNAA*
Gillespie, G K *ChPo*, *ChPo S1*
Gillespie, George *Chmbr 1*
Gillespie, George 1613-1648 *Alli*, *EvLB*, *NewC*
Gillespie, George 1683-1760 *DcAmA*, *DcNAA*
Gillespie, George Robertson *Alli Sup*
Gillespie, Gerald Ernest Paul 1933- *ConAu 25*, *WrD 1976*
Gillespie, Haven 1888- *AmSCAP 66*
Gillespie, Helena *BiDSA*
Gillespie, Howard C 1908- *IndAu 1917*
Gillespie, James *Alli*
Gillespie, James E, Jr. 1940- *ConAu 53*
Gillespie, James Edward 1887- *WhWNAA*
Gillespie, Janet Wicks 1913- *ConAu 5R*
Gillespie, Jean *ChPo*
Gillespie, Jessie *ChPo*, *ChPo S1*
Gillespie, John *Alli Sup*
Gillespie, John E 1921- *ConAu 17R*, *IndAu 1917*
Gillespie, Joseph *Alli Sup*
Gillespie, Joseph H *BiDSA*
Gillespie, Joseph H 1861-1889 *DcNAA*
Gillespie, Leonard *Alli*, *BiDLA*
Gillespie, Louis John 1886-1941 *DcNAA*
Gillespie, M *MnBBF*
Gillespie, Marcia Ann 1944- *AuNews 2*, *LivBAA*
Gillespie, Marian Evans 1889-1946 *AmSCAP 66*, *DcNAA*
Gillespie, Neal C 1933- *ConAu 33*
Gillespie, Richard Charles 1903- *TexWr*, *WhWNAA*
Gillespie, Samuel Lovejoy 1838-1909 *OhA&B*
Gillespie, Susan *ConAu XR*
Gillespie, Susan 1906- *Au&Wr*
Gillespie, Thomas *Alli*
Gillespie, W *Alli*
Gillespie, William *Alli*, *BiDLA*, *ChPo S1*
Gillespie, William Hewitt 1905- *BiDPar*
Gillespie, William Honyman *Alli Sup*
Gillespie, William Mitchell 1816-1868 *Alli*, *Alli Sup*, *CyAL 1*, *DcAmA*, *DcNAA*
Gillespie, Yetza 1903- *ChPo*
Gillespy, E *Alli*, *BiDLA*
Gillespy, George *DcNAA*
Gillespy, William 1824-1886 *BbtC*, *DcNAA*
Gillet, Eliphalet 1768-1848 *DcNAA*
Gillet, Joseph Anthony 1837-1908 *DcNAA*
Gillet, Joseph Eugene 1888- *DcSpL*
Gillet, Martin Stanislaus 1875-1951 *CatA 1952*
Gillet, R *Alli*
Gillet, Ransom Hooker 1800-1876 *Alli Sup*, *DcAmA*, *DcNAA*
Gillett, Charles Ripley 1855-1948 *AmA&B*, *AmLY*, *DcNAA*
Gillett, Charlie 1942- *ConAu 33*, *WrD 1976*
Gillett, Eric Walkey 1893- *Au&Wr*, *ConAu 5R*
Gillett, Ezra Hall 1823-1875 *Alli Sup*, *AmA&B*, *DcAmA*, *DcNAA*
Gillett, Frederick Huntington 1851-1935 *DcNAA*
Gillett, Henry Martin 1902- *CatA 1952*
Gillett, Henry Webster 1861-1943 *DcNAA*
Gillett, J A And Rolfe, W J *Alli Sup*

Gillett, J D 1913- *ConAu 49*
Gillett, J T *Alli*
Gillett, James Buchanan 1856- *TexWr*
Gillett, John H *Alli Sup*
Gillett, Margaret 1930- *ConAu 1R, WrD 1976*
Gillett, Mary Bledsoe *ConAu 25, SmATA 7*
Gillette, Mrs. A D *ChPo S2*
Gillette, Abram Dunn 1807-1882 *Alli, Alli Sup, DcNAA*
Gillette, Arnold S 1904- *ConAu 1R*
Gillette, Bob *WrD 1976*
Gillette, C P 1859- *WhWNAA*
Gillette, Don Carle *WhWNAA*
Gillette, Edward 1854-1936 *DcNAA*
Gillette, Fanny Lemira 1828-1926 *DcNAA*
Gillette, Halbert Powers 1869- *DcAmA*
Gillette, Henry Sampson 1915- *ConAu 5R, WrD 1976*
Gillette, John Morris 1866-1949 *AmLY, DcNAA, WhWNAA*
Gillette, King Camp 1855-1932 *DcNAA*
Gillette, Leland J 1912- *AmSCAP 66*
Gillette, Lucia Fidelia 1827- *DcAmA, DcNAA*
Gillette, Mary A *ChPo*
Gillette, Paul 1938- *ConAu 53*
Gillette, Virginia M 1920- *ConAu 57*
Gillette, William 1855-1937 *AmA&B, BbD, BiD&SB, Chmbr 3, DcAmA, DcLEnL, DcNAA, McGWD, ModWD, OxAm, REnAL*
Gillgren, May *ChPo S2*
Gillham, Charles Edward 1898- *AnCL*
Gillham, D G 1921- *ConAu 21*
Gilliam, Charles Frederick 1853-1915 *Alli Sup, DcNAA, OhA&B*
Gilliam, David Tod 1844-1923 *Alli Sup, AmLY, DcNAA, OhA&B*
Gilliam, Edward Winslow 1834-1925 *DcNAA*
Gilliams, Maurice 1900- *CasWL, EncWL*
Gilliard, Edmond 1875-1969 *CasWL*
Gilliat, Edward *Alli Sup*
Gilliatt, Penelope 1932- *AuNews 2, ConAu 13R, ConLC 2, ConNov 1972, ConNov 1976, DrAF 1976, WrD 1976*
Gillie, Christopher 1914- *Au&Wr, WrD 1976*
Gillieron, Jules 1854-1926 *OxFr*
Gillies, Alexander 1907- *Au&Wr*
Gillies, Andrew *ChPo S2*
Gillies, Andrew 1870- *WhWNAA*
Gillies, Archibald C 1834-1887 *BbtC, DcNAA*
Gillies, Donald 1899-1944 *ChPo S1*
Gillies, James B *Alli Sup*
Gillies, John *Chmbr 2*
Gillies, John 1712-1796 *Alli*
Gillies, John 1747-1836 *Alli, BiDLA, DcEnL, EvLB*
Gillies, Margaret 1803-1887 *ChPo S1*
Gillies, Mary *Alli Sup*
Gillies, Mary Davis 1900- *ConAu 25*
Gillies, N *Alli Sup*
Gillies, Robert Pierce *Alli, BiDLA, DcEnL*
Gillies, William *Alli Sup*
Gilliess, Charles *Alli Sup*
Gillig, Charles A *Alli Sup*
Gilligan, Edmund 1899-1973 *AmA&B, ConAu 45, REnAL, TwCA Sup*
Gilligan, Sonja Carl 1936- *ConAu 57*
Gillilan, James David 1858-1935 *OhA&B*
Gillilan, Strickland 1869-1954 *AmA&B, AmLY, ChPo, OhA&B, REnAL, WhWNAA*
Gilliland, A R 1887- *WhWNAA*
Gilliland, Hap 1918- *ConAu 53*
Gilliland, Thaddeus Stephens 1834-1909 *OhA&B*
Gilliland, Thomas *Alli, BiDLA*
Gillin, Caroline J 1932- *ConAu 45*
Gillin, Donald George 1930- *ConAu 33*
Gillin, John Lewis 1871-1958 *AmA&B, WhWNAA*
Gillin, John P 1907-1973 *AmA&B, ConAu 41, ConAu 45*
Gilling, Isaac *Alli*
Gillingham, B *Alli Sup*
Gillingham, George Thomas *Alli Sup*
Gillings, G W *Alli Sup*
Gillington, Alice E *ChPo S1*

Gillington, May C *ChPo S1, ChPo S2*
Gillingwater, Edmund *Alli, BiDLA*
Gillinson, Stanley 1920- *Au&Wr, WrD 1976*
Gilliom, Peter 1847-1934 *IndAu 1816*
Gillis, Adolph *ChPo*
Gillis, Andrew Colin 1879- *WhWNAA*
Gillis, Don 1912- *AmSCAP 66*
Gillis, Everett A 1914- *ConAu 41*
Gillis, James 1802-1864 *Alli Sup, BbtC*
Gillis, James Andrew 1829-1914 *DcNAA*
Gillis, James Martin 1876-1957 *AmA&B, BkC 6, CatA 1947, REnAL, WhWNAA*
Gillis, James P *OxCan*
Gillis, John R 1939- *ConAu 33*
Gillis, Sylvester 1899- *AmSCAP 66*
Gillis, William Robert 1840-1929 *DcNAA*
Gillison, Lenora *BlkAW*
Gillispie, Charles C 1918- *ConAu 13R*
Gilliss, James Melville 1811-1865 *Alli, DcAmA, DcNAA*
Gilliss, Walter 1855-1925 *AmA&B, ChPo S1, DcNAA, OxAm, REnAL*
Gillitt, J *Alli Sup*
Gillkrest, James *Alli Sup*
Gillman, Henry 1833-1915 *ChPo, DcAmA, DcNAA, PoIre*
Gillman, James *Alli, BiDLA*
Gillman, John *Alli*
Gillman, Olga Marjorie 1894- *Au&Wr, ConAu 5R*
Gillman, Richard 1929- *ConAu 17R*
Gillman, Webster *Alli, BiDLA*
Gillmer, Thomas C 1911- *ConAu 57*
Gillmer, Tom *ConAu 57*
Gillmor, C Stewart *ConAu 45*
Gillmor, Clotworthy 1938- *Alli, Alli Sup, PoIre*
Gillmor, Daniel S 1917?-1975 *ConAu 61*
Gillmor, Donald M 1926- *ConAu 41*
Gillmor, Frances 1903- *AmA&B, ArizL, ConAu 17, WhWNAA, WrD 1976*
Gillmore, David 1934- *Au&Wr, ConAu 23*
Gillmore, Parker *Alli Sup*
Gillmore, Quincy Adams 1825-1888 *Alli Sup, DcAmA, DcNAA, OhA&B*
Gillmore, Rufus Hamilton 1879-1935 *AmA&B, DcNAA*
Gillon, Adam 1921- *ConAu 5R, WrD 1976*
Gillon, Diana 1915- *Au&Wr, ConAu 13R*
Gillon, Joseph *Alli, BiDLA*
Gillon, Meir Selig 1907- *Au&Wr, ConAu 13R*
Gillon, Thomas *Alli*
Gillot, Jacques *DcEuL, OxFr*
Gillott, Honor Ross 1945- *WrD 1976*
Gillott, Jackie *WrD 1976*
Gillow, George *Alli Sup*
Gillow, Henry 1839- *Alli Sup*
Gillow, John 1814-1877 *Alli Sup*
Gillow, Joseph 1850- *Alli Sup*
Gillow, Thomas *BiDLA*
Gillquist, Peter E 1938- *ConAu 29*
Gillray, James 1757-1815 *Alli, BkIE, NewC*
Gillsater, Sven 1921- *Au&Wr*
Gillson, Edward *Alli*
Gillum, L G *Alli Sup*
Gillum, R *Alli, BiDLA*
Gillum, William d1797 *Alli*
Gilly, Sarah *Alli*
Gilly, W O S *Alli*
Gilly, William Stephen d1855 *Alli*
Gilm, Hermann Von 1812-1864 *EvEuW*
Gilm ZuRosenegg, Hermann Von 1812-1864 *BbD, BiD&SB, OxGer*
Gilman, Albert Franklin, Jr. 1900- *WhWNAA*
Gilman, Arthur 1837-1909 *Alli Sup, AmA&B, BbD, BiD&SB, DcAmA, DcNAA, REnAL*
Gilman, Benjamin Ives 1852-1933 *DcNAA*
Gilman, Bradley 1857-1932 *DcAmA, DcNAA*
Gilman, Caroline Howard 1794-1888 *Alli, AmA&B, BiD&SB, BiDSA, ChPo, ChPo S1, CyAL 1, DcAmA, DcNAA, FemPA, LivFWS, OxAm, REnAL*
Gilman, Chandler Robbins 1802-1865 *AmA&B, DcAmA, DcNAA, OhA&B*
Gilman, Charles *Alli*
Gilman, Charlotte Perkins 1860-1935 *AmA&B, AmLY, ChPo, DcAmA, DcNAA,*

WhWNAA
Gilman, Daniel Coit 1831-1908 *Alli Sup, AmA&B, BiD&SB, BiDSA, DcAmA, DcNAA, OxAm, REnAL*
Gilman, Dorothy 1923- *Au&Wr, ConAu XR, SmATA 5*
Gilman, Dorothy Foster 1891- *AmA&B*
Gilman, Dugan *DrAP 1975*
Gilman, George G *ConAu 57*
Gilman, George H *Alli Sup*
Gilman, J *EarAB, EarAB Sup*
Gilman, Jane *ChPo*
Gilman, John T *ChPo S2*
Gilman, Lawrence 1878-1939 *AmA&B, DcNAA, REnAL, TwCA, TwCA Sup*
Gilman, Margaret 1896-1958 *AmA&B*
Gilman, Maria *DcNAA*
Gilman, Mary Rebecca 1859- *DcAmA*
Gilman, Mildred Evans 1898- *WhWNAA*
Gilman, Nicholas Paine 1849-1912 *Alli Sup, AmA&B, DcAmA, DcNAA, OhA&B*
Gilman, R J *Alli Sup*
Gilman, Richard 1925- *ConAu 53*
Gilman, Robert Cham *WrD 1976*
Gilman, Samuel 1791-1858 *Alli, AmA&B, BiDSA, CyAL 1, DcAmA, DcNAA*
Gilman, Sander L 1944- *ConAu 53*
Gilman, Stella 1844- *Alli Sup, DcAmA*
Gilman, Theodore 1841-1930 *DcAmA, DcNAA*
Gilman, W *EarAB, EarAB Sup*
Gilman, Wenona *DcNAA*
Gilman, William 1909- *Au&Wr, ConAu 1R*
Gilman, William H 1911- *ConAu 17R*
Gilmer, Albert Hatton 1878-1950 *AmA&B*
Gilmer, Beverly Von Haller 1909- *ConAu 5R*
Gilmer, Elizabeth Meriwether 1870-1951 *AmA&B, BiDSA, REnAL, WhWNAA*
Gilmer, Francis Walker 1790-1826 *DcNAA, OxAm*
Gilmer, George Rockingham 1790-1859 *BiDSA, DcAmA, DcNAA*
Gilmer, John H *Alli Sup*
Gilmer, W *Alli*
Gilmer, Walker 1935- *ConAu 33*
Gilmor, Harry 1838-1883 *Alli Sup, BiDSA, DcNAA*
Gilmor, S A *ChPo*
Gilmore, Al-Tony 1946- *ConAu 57*
Gilmore, Albert Field *WhWNAA*
Gilmore, Anna Neil *ChPo*
Gilmore, Annella Slaughter *ChPo*
Gilmore, Charles L *ConAu 33*
Gilmore, Don 1930- *ConAu 29*
Gilmore, Eddy Lanier King 1907- *ConAu 5R*
Gilmore, Eddy Lanier King 1909- *Au&Wr*
Gilmore, Edith Spacil 1920- *ConAu 1R*
Gilmore, Elinor *ChPo S2*
Gilmore, Elizabeth McCabe 1874-1953 *AmSCAP 66, WhWNAA*
Gilmore, Elsie L 1869-1956 *OhA&B*
Gilmore, Emily *Alli Sup*
Gilmore, Ernest *Alli Sup*
Gilmore, Eugene Allen 1871- *WhWNAA*
Gilmore, Florence 1880-1945 *OhA&B*
Gilmore, Gene 1920- *ConAu 33*
Gilmore, George 1720?-1811 *BbtC*
Gilmore, George William 1858-1933 *AmLY, DcNAA, WhWNAA*
Gilmore, H *Alli Sup*
Gilmore, Harold L 1931- *ConAu 53*
Gilmore, Horace Herman 1903- *AuBYP*
Gilmore, Iris *AuBYP*
Gilmore, J A *Alli Sup*
Gilmore, J Herbert, Jr. 1925- *ConAu 33*
Gilmore, James Roberts 1823-1903 *Alli Sup, AmA&B, BbD, BiD&SB, DcAmA, DcEnL, DcNAA*
Gilmore, Jene Carlton 1933- *ConAu 33*
Gilmore, John *Alli Sup*
Gilmore, John 1937- *ConAu 25*
Gilmore, John Washington 1872- *WhWNAA*
Gilmore, Joseph Henry 1834-1918 *Alli Sup, AmA&B, DcAmA, DcNAA*
Gilmore, Maeve *Au&Wr, WrD 1976*
Gilmore, Mary 1865-1962 *CasWL, DcLEnL, LongC, TwCW*
Gilmore, Mary Louisa 1829- *PoIre*
Gilmore, Melvin Randolph 1868-1940 *DcNAA,*

WhWNAA

Gilmore, Minnie *Alli Sup, ChPo*
Gilmore, Myron Piper 1910- *Au&Wr*
Gilmore, Patrick Sarsfield 1829-1892 *ChPo*
Gilmore, Thomas H *PoIre*
Gilmore, William Edward 1824-1908 *OhA&B*
Gilmour, A *Alli Sup*
Gilmour, David *Alli Sup*
Gilmour, Edith 1896- *AmSCAP 66*
Gilmour, Garth Hamilton 1925- *Au&Wr,
ConAu P-1*
Gilmour, George P *OxCan*
Gilmour, James *Alli Sup*
Gilmour, John *Alli Sup, ChPo Sup*
Gilmour, Sir John *Alli*
Gilmour, John Scott Lennox 1906- *Au&Wr*
Gilmour, Richard 1824-1891 *DcNAA*
Gilmour, Robert *Alli, BiDLA Sup*
Gilpatric, Guy 1896-1950 *AmA&B, REnAL,
TwCA, TwCA Sup*
Gilpatrick, Eleanor G 1930- *ConAu 23*
Gilpatrick, Naomi 1918- *CatA 1947*
Gilpin, Alan 1924- *ConAu 25, WrD 1976*
Gilpin, Alec Richard 1920- *ConAu 45*
Gilpin, Alfred *BbtC*
Gilpin, Bernard *Alli*
Gilpin, Bernard 1517-1583 *Alli*
Gilpin, Mrs. C *Alli Sup*
Gilpin, Edward *Alli*
Gilpin, Edwin *Alli*
Gilpin, Edwin 1851-1907 *DcNAA*
Gilpin, Elizabeth *Alli Sup*
Gilpin, George *Alli*
Gilpin, Gilbert *Alli*
Gilpin, Henry *Alli*
Gilpin, Henry D 1801-1860 *Alli, AmA&B,
DcAmA, DcNAA*
Gilpin, J Bernard *BbtC*
Gilpin, Jeremiah *Alli*
Gilpin, John *Alli*
Gilpin, Joseph *Alli*
Gilpin, Joshua *Alli, BiDLA*
Gilpin, Joshua 1765-1840 *DcAmA, DcNAA*
Gilpin, Rand *Alli*
Gilpin, Richard *Alli*
Gilpin, Richard 1625-1699 *Alli*
Gilpin, Robert G, Jr. 1930- *ConAu 5R*
Gilpin, Sidney *Alli Sup*
Gilpin, Thomas *Alli, BiDLA*
Gilpin, Thomas 1776-1853 *DcNAA*
Gilpin, W B *Alli Sup*
Gilpin, William *Alli Sup, Chmbr 2*
Gilpin, William d1848 *Alli*
Gilpin, William 1724-1804 *Alli, BkIE, BrAu,
CasWL, DcLEnL, NewC, OxEng,
WebEAL*
Gilpin, William 1813?-1894 *AmA, DcNAA,
OxAm, REnAL*
Gilpin, William Sawrey d1843 *Alli*
Gilroy, C G *Alli*
Gilroy, Clinton G *Alli Sup*
Gilroy, Frank D 1925- *AmA&B, ConDr,
ConLC 2, CrCD, DrAF 1976, McGWD,
ModWD, OxAm, WrD 1976*
Gilroy, John 1872-1937 *AmSCAP 66*
Gilroy, William Edgar 1876- *WhWNAA*
Gilruth, James H *Alli Sup*
Gilson, Adrian *Alli Sup*
Gilson, Barbara *WhCL*
Gilson, Charles 1878-1943 *MnBBF, WhCL,
WhLA*
Gilson, David *Alli*
Gilson, E B *ChPo, ChPo S1*
Gilson, Etienne Henry 1884- *CatA 1947, OxFr,
TwCA, TwCA Sup*
Gilson, Goodwin Woodrow 1918- *ConAu 17R*
Gilson, Jewett Castello 1844-1926 *DcNAA*
Gilson, John H 1841-1916 *OhA&B*
Gilson, Roy Rolfe 1875-1933 *AmA&B,
DcAmA, DcNAA, WhWNAA*
Gilson, Thomas Q 1916- *ConAu 5R*
Gilstrap, Elizabeth Haigh 1822-1891 *ChPo S2*
Gilstrap, Opal *TexWr*
Gilstrap, Robert L 1933- *ConAu 9R*
Giltinan, Caroline 1884- *AnMV 1926,
CatA 1947, ChPo, ChPo S1*
Giltner, Leigh Gordon 1875- *ChPo, WhWNAA*
Giltner, Ward 1882- *WhWNAA*

Gilzean, Elizabeth Houghton Blanchet 1913-
Au&Wr, ConAu 9R
Gimbel, John 1922- *ConAu 1R, WrD 1976*
Gimber, Stephen Henry *EarAB Sup*
Gimbutas, Marija 1921- *ConAu 13R*
Gimenez, Joseph Patrick *BlkAW*
Gimenez Arnau Y Gran, Jose Antonio 1912-
McGWD
Gimenez Caballero, Ernesto 1899- *CasWL,
ClDMEuL, DcSpL, EvEuW, REn*
Gimingham, Miss A E *Alli Sup*
Gimmestad, Victor E 1912- *ConAu 57*
Gimpel, Herbert J 1915- *ConAu 17R*
Gimson, Alfred Charles 1917- *ConAu 5R,
WrD 1976*
Ginandes, Shepard 1928- *ConAu 41*
Gindely, Anton 1829-1892 *BiD&SB*
Gindhart, Thomas J 1908- *AmSCAP 66*
Gindin, James 1926- *ConAu 5R, WrD 1976*
Giner DeLosRios, Francisco 1839-1915 *CasWL,
ClDMEuL, DcSpL, EvEuW*
Gingell, Benjamin Broughton 1924- *ConP 1970,
WrD 1976*
Gingell, William Raymond *Alli Sup*
Ginger, Ann Fagan 1925- *ConAu 53*
Ginger, Helen 1916- *ConAu 17R*
Ginger, John 1933- *Au&Wr, ConAu 25,
WrD 1976*
Ginger, Samuel *IndAu 1816*
Ginger Jar *OhA&B*
Gingerich, Melvin 1902- *ConAu 25*
Gingerich, Owen 1930- *ConAu 53*
Ginglend, David R 1913- *ConAu 17R*
Gingold, Helene E A *Alli Sup*
Gingold, Hermione *ConAu 5R*
Gingras, Joseph Apollinaire 1847-1935 *DcNAA*
Gingras, Jules Fabian 1829?-1884 *DcNAA*
Gingras, Leon 1804?-1860 *BbtC, DcNAA*
Gingras, Ulric-L *OxCan*
Gingrich, Arnold 1903- *AmA&B, Au&Wr,
ConAu 13R, REnAL, WhWNAA,
WrD 1976*
Gingrich, Curvin Henry 1880- *WhWNAA*
Gingrich, F Wilbur 1901- *ConAu 17*
Ginguene, Pierre-Louis 1748-1816 *OxFr*
Giniger, Kenneth Seeman 1919- *Au&Wr,
ConAu 5R*
Ginn, Edwin 1838-1914 *AmA&B*
Ginner, Isaac B *Alli Sup*
Ginns, Ronald 1896- *ConAu P-1*
Ginott, Haim G 1922-1973 *AmA&B,
ConAu 45*
Ginquet, A J 1796-1846 *BbtC*
Ginsberg, Allen 1926- *AmA&B, AuNews 1,
CasWL, ConAu 1R, ConLC 1, ConLC 2,
ConLC 3, ConLC 4, ConLC 6,
ConP 1970, ConP 1975, CrCAP,
DrAP 1975, EncWL, LongC, ModAL,
ModAL Sup, OxAm, Pen Am, RAdv 1,
REn, REnAL, TwCW, WebEAL,
WhTwL, WorAu, WrD 1976*
Ginsberg, Louis 1895- *ConAu 13R,
ConP 1970*
Ginsberg, Louis 1896- *ChPo, DrAP 1975,
REnAL, WhWNAA*
Ginsberg, Robert 1937- *ConAu 25*
Ginsberg, Sol 1885-1963 *AmSCAP 66*
Ginsburg, Benedict William 1859- *WhLA*
Ginsburg, Christian David 1830-1914 *Alli Sup,
BiD&SB, BrAu 19*
Ginsburg, Mirra *ConAu 17R, SmATA 6*
Ginsburg, Ruth Bader 1933- *ConAu 53*
Ginsburg, Seymour 1927- *ConAu 21*
Ginsburgh, Robert N 1923- *ConAu 13R*
Ginsburgs, George 1932- *ConAu 53,
WrD 1976*
Ginsbury, Norman 1902- *Au&Wr, ConAu 5R,
DcLEnL, WrD 1976*
Ginter, Maria 1922- *Au&Wr, WrD 1976*
Ginther, Mrs. Pemberton d1959 *AmA&B*
Gintis, Herbert 1940- *ConAu 57*
Ginzberg, Asher *CasWL*
Ginzberg, Eli 1911- *AmA&B, ConAu 5R,
WrD 1976*
Ginzberg, Louis 1873-1953 *AmA&B, AmLY,
REnAL*
Ginzburg, Natalia Levi 1916- *CasWL,
ConLC 5, EncWL Sup, ModRL, WorAu*

Ginzburg, Ralph 1929- *Au&Wr, ConAu 21*
Ginzburg, Simeon 1890-1944 *CasWL*
Ginzkey, Franz Karl Von 1871-1963 *OxGer*
Gioberti, Vincenzo 1801-1852 *BiD&SB,
CasWL, EuA, Pen Eur*
Gioja, Melchiore 1767-1829 *BiD&SB*
Giono, Jean 1895-1970 *CasWL, ClDMEuL,
CnMD, CnMWL, ConAu 29, ConAu 45,
ConLC 4, CyWA, EncWL, EvEuW,
McGWD, ModRL, ModWD, OxFr,
Pen Eur, REn, TwCA, TwCA Sup,
TwCW, WhTwL*
Giordan, Alma Roberts 1917- *ConAu 57*
Giordani, Igino 1894- *CatA 1947*
Giordani, Pietro 1774-1848 *BiD&SB, CasWL,
DcEuL*
Giordano DaPisa 1260?-1311 *CasWL*
Giordano DaRivalto 1260?-1311 *CasWL*
Giorg, Kara *OhA&B*
Giorgione, Il 1478?-1510 *AtlBL, REn*
Giorno, John 1936- *ConAu 33, ConP 1970,
DrAP 1975*
Gioseffi, Daniela 1941- *ConAu 45,
DrAF 1976, DrAP 1975*
Giotto 1266?-1337 *NewC, REn*
Giotto Di Bondone 1266?-1337 *AtlBL*
Giovaninetti, Silvio 1901-1959 *McGWD*
Giovannetti, Alberto 1913- *ConAu 9R*
Giovannetti, Pericle Luigi 1916- *WhGrA*
Giovanni Fiorentino *CasWL, EvEuW*
Giovanni, Domenico Di *DcEuL*
Giovanni, Nikki 1943- *AuNews 1, BlkAW,
ChPo S2, ConAu 29, ConLC 2,
ConLC 4, ConP 1975, CrCAP,
DrAP 1975, LivBA, RAdv 1, WrD 1976*
Giovannini, Caesar 1925- *AmSCAP 66*
Giovannitti, Arturo 1884-1959 *AmA&B,
ConAmL, OxAm, REn, REnAL, TwCA*
Giovannitti, Len 1920- *ConAu 13R,
DrAF 1976*
Giovannone, Anthony J 1923- *AmSCAP 66*
Giovanopoulos, Paul Arthur 1939- *ChPo S1,
IlBYP, SmATA 7*
Giovio, Paolo 1483-1552 *CasWL, DcEuL,
REn*
Giozza, Pier Giacinto 1846- *BiD&SB*
Gipe, Spang *WhWNAA*
Gippius, Zinaida Nikolayevna 1869-1945
*CasWL, DcRusL, EncWL Sup, Pen Eur,
WhTwL*
Gipps, George *Alli*
Gipps, Henry *Alli*
Gipps, Thomas *Alli*
Gipson, Frederick Benjamin 1908-1973 *AmA&B,
AuBYP, ConAu 1R, ConAu 45,
SmATA 2, ThBJA*
Gipson, James Herrick 1885-1965 *AmA&B*
Gipson, John 1932- *ConAu 61*
Gipson, Lawrence Henry 1880-1971 *AmA&B,
Au&Wr, ConAu 5R, ConAu 33, OxAm,
OxCan, OxCan Sup, WhWNAA, WorAu*
Giraldi, Giambattista Cinzio 1504-1573 *CasWL,
EvEuW, REn*
Giraldi, Giglio Gregorio 1479-1552 *BiD&SB,
CasWL*
Giraldi, Giovanni Battista 1504-1573 *BbD,
BiD&SB, EuA, NewC*
Giraldi, Lilio Gregorio 1478-1552 *DcEuL*
Giraldi Cinthio, Giambattista 1504-1573
McGWD, Pen Eur
Giraldus Cambrensis 1146?-1220? *Alli, BiB N,
BrAu, CasWL, Chmbr 1, DcEnL,
DcEuL, NewC, Pen Eng*
Giraldus De Barri 1146?-1220? *EvLB, NewC,
OxEng*
Giralt Miracle, Ricardo 1911- *WhGrA*
Girard D'Amiens *CasWL*
Girard La Pucelle d1184 *BiB N*
Girard Of Cornwall *BiB N*
Girard, Alexandre *OxCan*
Girard, Alfred C *Alli Sup*
Girard, Charles Frederic 1822-1895 *Alli Sup,
DcAmA, DcNAA*
Girard, Gabriel *OxFr*
Girard, Henri *McGWD*
Girard, M D, Madame *BiDSA*
Girard, Pierre 1892-1956 *CasWL*
Girard, Rene N 1923- *ConAu 9R*

Girard, Rodolphe *OxCan*
Girardeau, John Lafayette 1825-1898 *BiDSA,*
DcAmA, DcNAA
Girardey, Ferreol 1839-1930 *DcNAA*
Girardin *OxFr*
Girardin, Delphine De 1804-1884 *BbD*
Girardin, Emile De 1806?-1881 *BbD, BiD&SB,*
EvEuW, OxFr
Girardin, Mme Emile De 1804-1855 *OxFr*
Girardin, Marie Alfred Jules De 1832-1888
BiD&SB
Girardin, Rene-Louis, Marquis De 1735-1808
OxFr
Girardon, Francois 1628-1715 *OxFr*
Girardot, Marion Reid *ArizL*
Giraud, Albert 1860-1929 *CasWL, ClDMEuL,*
EvEuW
Giraud, Count Giovanni 1776-1834 *BiD&SB,*
McGWD
Giraud, Marcel *OxCan, OxCan Sup*
Giraudoux, Jean 1882-1944 *AtlBL, Au&Wr,*
CasWL, ClDMEuL, CnMD, CnMWL,
CnThe, CyWA, EncWL, EvEuW, LongC,
McGWD, ModRL, ModWD, NewC,
OxEng, OxFr, Pen Eur, RCom, REn,
REnWD, TwCA, TwCA Sup, TwCW,
WhTwL
Giraut De Bornelh 1165?-1220 *EuA*
Girdler, J S *Alli, BiDLA*
Girdler, Tom Mercer 1877-1965 *IndAu 1917*
Girdleston, J L *Alli*
Girdlestone, Arthur Gilbert *Alli Sup*
Girdlestone, C A *Alli Sup*
Girdlestone, Charles 1797-1881 *Alli, Alli Sup*
Girdlestone, Cuthbert Morton 1895- *Au&Wr,*
ConAu 5R
Girdlestone, E D *Alli Sup*
Girdlestone, Edward 1805-1884 *Alli Sup*
Girdlestone, Henry *Alli Sup*
Girdlestone, J L *BiDLA*
Girdlestone, Robert Baker *Alli Sup*
Girdlestone, Thomas 1758-1822 *Alli*
Girdlestone, Thomas 1758- *BiDLA*
Girdlestone, William *Alli*
Girdlestone, William Harding *Alli Sup*
Girdner, John Harvey 1856- *WhWNAA*
Girdwood, Gilbert Finlay *Alli Sup*
Girdwood, William *Alli Sup*
Girhori, Makhdum 'Abdu'r-Rahim 1739-1778
DcOrL 2
Girle, S *Alli, BiDLA*
Girleanu, Emil 1878-1914 *CasWL*
Girling, Charles John 1897-1916 *ChPo S1*
Girling, Zoe 1907?- *NewC*
Girndt, Otto 1835- *BiD&SB*
Girod, Amury d1837 *BbtC, DcNAA, OxCan*
Girod, Gerald R 1939- *ConAu 53*
Girod, Gordon H 1920- *ConAu 1R*
Girodias, Maurice 1919- *Au&Wr*
Giron Cerna, Carlos 1904- *DcCLA*
Gironella, Jose Maria 1917- *EncWL, ModRL,*
REn, TwCA Sup, TwCW
Girouard, Desire 1836-1911 *BbtC, DcNAA*
Giroud, Francoise *AuNews 1*
Giroux, Andre 1916- *CanWr, OxCan*
Giroux, Maurice *OxCan Sup*
Giroux, Suzanne *OxCan Sup*
Girrard, J *Alli*
Girri, Alberto 1919- *DcCLA, Pen Am*
Girrieor, Elsie Dana *ChPo*
Girson, Rochelle *ConAu 23*
Girswold, Hattie 1842- *Alli Sup*
Girtin, James *Alli*
Girtin, Thomas *Alli*
Girtin, Thomas 1775-1802 *AtlBL*
Girtin, Thomas 1913- *Au&Wr, ConAu 9R*
Girton, Daniel *Alli*
Girty, George Herbert 1869-1939 *DcNAA*
Girty, Simon 1741-1818 *REn, REnAL*
Girun, Gian 1898- *CasWL*
Girvan, Alex *Alli*
Girvan, Helen 1891- *AuBYP, MorJA*
Girvin, John *Alli*
Giry, Arthur 1848-1899 *OxFr*
Girzaitis, Loretta 1920- *ConAu 49*
Gisborne, John *Alli, BiDLA*
Gisborne, L *Alli*
Gisborne, Thomas *Alli*

Gisborne, Thomas 1758-1846 *Alli, BiDLA,*
ChPo, ChPo S1, ChPo S2
Gisborne, William *Alli, Alli Sup, BiDLA*
Gisecke, Nikolaus Dietrich 1724-1765 *BiD&SB*
Giseke, Nikolaus Dietrich 1724-1765 *CasWL,*
OxGer
Giseke, Robert 1827-1890 *BiD&SB, OxGer*
Gish, Arthur G 1939- *ConAu 29, WrD 1976*
Gish, Lillian 1896?- *REn*
Gishford, Anthony 1908-1975 *ConAu 53*
Gismonde *OxFr*
Giso d1086 *BiB S*
Gisolfi, Anthony M 1909- *ConAu 17*
Gissing, Algernon *Alli Sup*
Gissing, George Robert 1857-1903 *Alli Sup,*
AtlBL, BbD, BiD&SB, BrAu 19, CasWL,
Chmbr 3, CyWA, DcEnA Ap, DcEuL,
DcLEnL, EvLB, LongC, ModBL, NewC,
OxEng, Pen Eng, RAdv 1, REn,
WebEAL
Gissing, T W *Alli Sup*
Gist, Christopher 1706?-1759 *OxAm, REnAL*
Gist, Nathan Howard 1885- *WhWNAA*
Gist, Noel Pitts 1899- *Au&Wr, ConAu 1R*
Gist, Ronald R 1932- *ConAu 23*
Gitchoff, G Thomas 1938- *ConAu 53*
Gitchoff, Tom 1938- *ConAu XR*
Githens, Charles *ChPo S1*
Githens, Harry W 1895- *WhWNAA*
Gitin, David 1941- *ConAu 49, DrAP 1975*
Gitin, Maria 1946- *ConAu 61*
Gitlin, Murray 1903- *ConAu 1R*
Gitlin, Todd 1943- *ConAu 29*
Gitlow, A Leo 1918- *ConAu 1R*
Gittell, Marilyn 1931- *ConAu 21*
Gittelsohn, Roland B 1910- *ConAu 5R,*
WrD 1976
Gittinger, J Price *ConAu 41*
Gittinger, Roy 1878- *WhWNAA*
Gittings, Christine *Au&Wr, WrD 1976*
Gittings, Dan *Alli*
Gittings, Ella Pamela Beecher 1852-1935
OhA&B
Gittings, Jo Manton 1919- *Au&Wr, AuBYP,*
ConAu 5R, SmATA 3
Gittings, John 1938- *ConAu 21*
Gittings, Robert William Victor 1911- *Au&Wr,*
ChPo S2, ConAu 25, ConP 1970,
ConP 1975, SmATA 6, WrD 1976
Gittins, Dan *Alli*
Gittleman, Edwin 1929- *ConAu 21*
Gittler, Joseph B 1912- *WrD 1976*
Gittler, Joseph B 1914- *ConAu 37*
Giuliotti, Domenico 1877- *CatA 1952,*
ClDMEuL
Giurlani, Aldo 1885-1974 *ConAu XR*
Giuseppi, John 1900- *ConAu 23*
Giusti, George 1908- *WhGrA*
Giusti, Giuseppe 1809-1850 *BiD&SB, CasWL,*
DcEuL, EvEuW, Pen Eur, REn
Giusti, Vincenzo 1532-1619 *McGWD*
Giustinian, Leonardo 1388?-1446 *CasWL, REn*
Giuttari, Theodore Richard 1931- *ConAu 29*
Given, Abraham 1825-1895 *IndAu 1816*
Given, Andrew *Alli Sup*
Given, John *PoIre*
Given, John James *Alli Sup*
Given, Patrick *PoIre*
Given, Samuel Fee 1845-1867 *PoIre*
Given, Thomas *ChPo S1, PoIre*
Given, Welker 1853-1938 *DcNAA, OhA&B*
Givens, Willard Earl 1886- *IndAu 1917*
Givins, Robert Cartwright 1845-1915 *DcNAA*
Givler, John Paul 1882- *WhWNAA*
Givler, Robert Chenault 1884- *AmA&B*
Gizycka, Eleanor M *AmA&B*
Gizycka, Felicia 1905- *AmA&B*
Gjallandi, Thorgils 1851-1915 *CasWL*
Gjalski, Ksaver Sandor 1854-1935 *ClDMEuL*
Gjellerup, Karl Adolph 1857-1919 *BiD&SB,*
CasWL, ClDMEuL, EncWL, EuA,
EvEuW, Pen Eur, REn, TwCW
Gjelsness, Barent *DrAP 1975*
Gjerset, Knut 1865-1936 *AmA&B, DcNAA,*
WhWNAA
Gjorgjic, Ignaz 1676-1737 *BiD&SB*
Gjorwell, Carl Christoffer 1731-1811 *CasWL*
Glaab, Charles N 1927- *ConAu 5R*

Glackemeyer, Charles 1820-1892 *DcNAA*
Glackemeyer, Edward Claude 1826-1910
DcNAA
Glackens, Ida Dimock *ChPo*
Glackens, Louise M *ChPo*
Glackens, William James 1870-1938 *AtlBL,*
OxAm
Glackmeyer, Edward *BbtC*
Glad, Betty 1929- *ConAu 21*
Glad, Donald 1915- *ConAu 13R*
Gladden, Edgar Norman 1897- *ConAu 21,*
WrD 1976
Gladden, Frank A *BlkAW*
Gladden, Thomas Luther 1861- *WhWNAA*
Gladden, Washington 1836-1918 *Alli Sup,*
AmA&B, BbD, BiD&SB, ChPo, DcAmA,
DcNAA, OhA&B, REnAL
Gladding, Mrs. E M *Alli Sup*
Gladding, Effie Price 1865-1947 *OhA&B*
Glade, William P, Jr. 1929- *ConAu 41*
Gladish, David F 1928- *ConAu 41*
Gladkov, Fyodor Vasilyevich 1883-1958 *CasWL,*
ClDMEuL, DcRusL, EncWL, EvEuW,
ModSL 1, REn, TwCA, TwCA Sup,
TwCW
Gladman, Frederick John *Alli Sup*
Gladman, George 1800-1863 *BbtC, OxCan*
Gladson, William Nathan 1866- *WhWNAA*
Gladstone, Alfred *Alli Sup*
Gladstone, Arthur 1861- *WhLA*
Gladstone, Gary 1935- *ConAu 29*
Gladstone, George *Alli Sup*
Gladstone, Herbert John, Viscount 1856- *WhLA*
Gladstone, J *Alli*
Gladstone, Jemima Compton *Alli Sup*
Gladstone, John Hall 1827-1902 *Alli Sup,*
NewC
Gladstone, M J 1923- *ConAu 53*
Gladstone, R J 1865- *WhLA*
Gladstone, Thomas H *Alli Sup*
Gladstone, William Ewart 1809-1898 *Alli,*
Alli Sup, BbD, BiD&SB, CasWL, ChPo,
Chmbr 3, DcEnA, DcEnA Ap, DcEnL,
EvLB, NewC, OxEng, REn
Gladstone, William Henry *Alli Sup*
Gladwell, Adolphus *Alli Sup*
Gladwell, Derek Channon 1925- *Au&Wr,*
WrD 1976
Gladwin, Francis *Alli, BiDLA Sup*
Gladwin, Mary Elizabeth 1861?-1939 *DcNAA,*
OhA&B
Gladwin, Peter *MnBBF*
Gladwin, William Zachary *ChPo, DcAmA,*
DcNAA
Gladych, B Michael 1910- *ConAu 5R*
Glaenzer, Richard Butler 1876-1937 *AmA&B,*
ChPo, ChPo S1, DcNAA
Glaeser, Ernst 1902-1962 *OxGer, TwCA,*
TwCA Sup
Glaessner, Verina 1942- *WrD 1976*
Glaettli, Walter E 1920- *ConAu 21*
Glahe, Fred R 1934- *ConAu 37, WrD 1976*
Glaisher, James 1809-1903 *Alli Sup, BiD&SB*
Glaister, Elizabeth *Alli Sup*
Glaister, John 1892- *Au&Wr*
Glaister, William *Alli Sup*
Glanckoff, Samuel 1894- *ChPo, ConICB,*
IlCB 1945
Glancy, Michael F *Alli Sup*
Glandore, Earl Of *Alli*
Glanius *Alli*
Glanvil ALSO Glanvill, Glanville
Glanvil, Bartholomew *Alli*
Glanvil, Sir John d1661 *Alli*
Glanvil, John 1664-1735 *Alli*
Glanvil, Joseph 1636-1680 *Alli*
Glanvil, Ranulph De d1190 *Alli, Chmbr 1*
Glanvill ALSO Glanvil, Glanville
Glanvill, Joseph 1636-1680 *Alli, BrAu, CasWL,*
DcLEnL, EvLB, NewC, OxEng, Pen Eng,
REn
Glanvill, Ranulph De d1190 *Alli*
Glanville ALSO Glanvil, Glanvill
Glanville, Brian Lester 1931- *Au&Wr,*
ConAu 5R, ConLC 6, ConNov 1972,
ConNov 1976, NewC, WorAu,
WrD 1976
Glanville, Ernest 1856-1925 *Alli Sup, CasWL,*

DcLEnL

Glanville, H L *MnBBF*
Glanville, Irene Macmillan *ChPo S1*
Glanville, John *Alli*
Glanville, Ranulph De d1190 *Alli, BiB N, DcEnL, OxEng*
Glanz, Edward C 1924- *ConAu 1R*
Glanz, Rudolf 1892- *ConAu 49*
Glanzman, Louis S 1922- *IlBYP, IlCB 1966*
Glapthorn, Henry *Alli*
Glapthorne, Henry 1610-1643? *Alli, BiD&SB, BrAu, CasWL, Chmbr 1, CrE&SL, DcEnL, DcLEnL, EvLB, NewC, Pen Eng, WebEAL*
Glareanus, Henricus 1488-1563 *OxGer*
Glarum, L Stanley 1908- *AmSCAP 66*
Glas, Adam *Alli*
Glas, George *Alli*
Glas, John 1635-1773 *Alli*
Glas, John 1725-1765 *Alli*
Glasby, John S 1928- *Au&Wr*
Glascock, Clyde Chew 1872- *TexWr*
Glascock, Mary W *Alli Sup*
Glascock, Will H 1857-1901 *IndAu 1816*
Glascock, William Nugent 1787-1847 *Alli, BiD&SB, BrAu 19, Chmbr 3, DcLEnL, EvLB*
Glascocke, T *Alli*
Glascott, Cradock *Alli*
Glasel, John 1930- *AmSCAP 66*
Glaser, Adolf 1829- *BiD&SB*
Glaser, Comstock *WrD 1976*
Glaser, Daniel 1918- *ConAu 61*
Glaser, E M 1913- *ConAu 23*
Glaser, Edward 1918-1972 *ConAu 37*
Glaser, Eleanor Dorothy 1918- *Au&Wr, ConAu XR, WrD 1976*
Glaser, Emil G 1903- *WhWNAA*
Glaser, Hy 1923- *AmSCAP 66*
Glaser, Isabel J *DrAF 1976*
Glaser, Kurt 1914- *ConAu 1R, WrD 1976*
Glaser, Lynn 1943- *ConAu 21*
Glaser, Milton 1929- *ChPo S2, ConAu 17R, IlBYP, IlCB 1966*
Glaser, Robert 1921- *ConAu 17R*
Glaser, Rollin Oliver 1932- *ConAu 25*
Glaser, Sam 1912- *AmSCAP 66*
Glaser, Sioma 1919- *AmSCAP 66*
Glaser, Victoria 1918- *AmSCAP 66*
Glaser, William Arnold 1925- *ConAu 1R, WrD 1976*
Glasgow, D *Alli Sup*
Glasgow, Ellen Anderson Gholson 1874-1945 *AmA&B, AmWr, AtlBL, BiD&SB, BiDSA, CasWL, ChPo, ChPo S1, Chmbr 3, CnDAL, ConAmA, ConAmL, CyWA, DcAmA, DcBiA, DcLEnL, DcNAA, EncWL, EvLB, LongC, ModAL, OxAm, OxEng, Pen Am, RAdv 1, REn, REnAL, TwCA, TwCA Sup, TwCW, WebEAL, WhWNAA*
Glasgow, G R *ChPo S1*
Glasgow, George 1891- *CatA 1952*
Glasgow, Gordon H H 1926- *ConAu 29*
Glasgow, J Ewing *Alli Sup*
Glasgow, James 1805-1890 *Alli Sup, PoIre*
Glasgow, Samuel McPheeters 1883- *WhWNAA*
Glasheen, Patrick 1897- *ConAu P-1*
Glasier, Hugh *Alli*
Glasier, Jessie 1865-1955 *OhA&B*
Glaskin, Gerald Marcus 1923- *Au&Wr, ConAu 53, WrD 1976*
Glaskowsky, Nicholas A, Jr. 1928- *ConAu 5R*
Glason, Billy 1904- *AmSCAP 66*
Glaspell, Susan 1882-1948 *AmA&B, AmNov, Chmbr 3, CnDAL, CnMD, ConAmA, ConAmL, DcLEnL, DcNAA, LongC, McGWD, ModWD, OxAm, REn, REnAL, TwCA, TwCA Sup, WhWNAA*
Glaspie, Nancy A *ChPo*
Glasrud, Bruce 1940- *ConAu 41*
Glass, C *Alli Sup*
Glass, Carter 1858-1946 *DcNAA*
Glass, Charles E *Alli Sup*
Glass, Chester d1921 *DcNAA*
Glass, David Victor 1911- *Au&Wr*
Glass, Dudley 1899- *Au&Wr, ChPo S1*
Glass, Francis 1790-1825 *Alli, CyAL 1,*

DcNAA, OhA&B

Glass, George *Alli*
Glass, H *Alli*
Glass, Henry Alexander *Alli Sup*
Glass, Hugh d1833? *OxAm, REnAL*
Glass, James *PoIre*
Glass, Joanna *DrAF 1976*
Glass, John 1635-1773 *Alli*
Glass, John 1725-1765 *Alli*
Glass, John F 1936- *ConAu 53*
Glass, Joseph *Alli Sup*
Glass, Justine Claire *Au&Wr, ConAu XR*
Glass, Sister M Fides 1889- *BkC 2, CatA 1952*
Glass, Malcolm *DrAP 1975*
Glass, Montague Marsden 1877-1934 *AmA&B, ChPo, DcNAA, REn, REnAL, TwCA*
Glass, Paul Eugene 1934- *AmSCAP 66*
Glass, Richard Aitken 1874- *ChPo*
Glass, Ruth *Au&Wr, WrD 1976*
Glass, Samuel *Alli*
Glass, Stanley Thomas 1932- *ConAu 21, WrD 1976*
Glass, Thomas *Alli*
Glassberg, B Y 1902- *ConAu P-1*
Glassbrenner, Adolf 1810-1876 *BiD&SB, EvEuW, OxGer*
Glassburner, Bruce 1920- *ConAu 33*
Glassco, John Stinson 1909- *Au&Wr, CasWL, ConAu 13R, ConNov 1972, ConNov 1976, ConP 1970, ConP 1975, OxCan, OxCan Sup, WrD 1976*
Glasscock, Anne Bonner 1924- *ConAu 1R*
Glasscock, Carl Burgess 1884-1942 *AmA&B, WhWNAA*
Glasscock, J L, Jr. *Alli Sup*
Glasse, Captain *Alli, BiDLA*
Glasse, Doctor *Alli*
Glasse, Mrs. *DcEnL*
Glasse, Hannah *NewC, OxEng*
Glasse, Henry George d1809 *Alli*
Glasse, John *Alli*
Glasse, Robert Marshall 1929- *ConAu 29*
Glasse, Samuel *Alli*
Glasser, Albert 1916- *AmSCAP 66*
Glasser, Allen 1918- *ConAu 9R*
Glasser, Otto 1895- *OhA&B*
Glasser, Paul H 1929- *ConAu 29*
Glasser, Ralph 1916- *Au&Wr*
Glasser, Stephen A 1943- *ConAu 53*
Glassey, Stanley Churchill 1888- *Au&Wr*
Glassford, James *Alli, BiDLA*
Glassie, Henry *OxCan Sup*
Glassley, Ray Hoard 1887- *IndAu 1917*
Glassman, Michael 1899- *ConAu 13R, WrD 1976*
Glassner, Martin Ira 1932- *ConAu 41*
Glasson, Thomas Francis 1906- *Au&Wr, ConAu P-1, WrD 1976*
Glasson, William Henry 1874- *BiDSA, DcAmA, DcNAA, WhWNAA*
Glassop, Lawson 1913-1966 *ConAu P-1*
Glatigny, Albert Joseph Alexandre 1839-1873 *EuA, OxFr*
Glatigny, Joseph Albert Alexandre 1839-1873 *EvEuW*
Glatstein, Jacob 1896-1971 *CasWL, ConAu 33*
Glattauer, Ned *IlBYP*
Glatthorn, Allan A 1924- *ConAu 13R*
Glatzer, Hal 1946- *ConAu 57*
Glatzer, Nahum Norbert 1903- *AmA&B, ConAu 13R*
Glauber, Uta 1936- *ConAu 29*
Glaucus *NewC*
Glauritz, Grace *ChPo*
Glaus, Marlene A 1933- *ConAu 23, WrD 1976*
Glavin, John P 1933- *ConAu 57*
Glazarova, Jarmila 1901- *CasWL, Pen Eur, TwCW*
Glaze, Andrew Louis 1920- *ConAu 17R, DrAP 1975, WrD 1976*
Glaze, Eleanor 1930- *AuNews 1, ConAu 49*
Glaze, Thomas E 1914- *ConAu 1R*
Glazebrook, G P DeT 1899- *OxCan Sup*
Glazebrook, G P DeT 1900- *OxCan*
Glazebrook, Harriet A *Alli Sup, ChPo S1*
Glazebrook, James 1744-1803 *Alli*

Glazebrook, Philip 1937- *ConAu 29*
Glazebrook, R T *Alli Sup*
Glazener, Mary U 1921- *ConAu 17R*
Glazer, Melvin 1931- *AmSCAP 66*
Glazer, Nathan 1923- *AmA&B, ConAu 5R, WrD 1976*
Glazer, Nona Y *ConAu XR*
Glazer, Sidney 1905- *ConAu 1R, WrD 1976*
Glazer, Tom 1914- *AmSCAP 66, ConAu 61, SmATA 9*
Glazer-Malbin, Nona 1932- *ConAu 33*
Glazier, Kenneth MacLean 1912- *ConAu 9R*
Glazier, Lyle 1911- *ChPo S1, ConAu 37*
Glazier, Willard 1841-1905 *Alli Sup, AmA&B, BiD&SB, DcAmA, DcNAA*
Glazier, William Belcher 1827?-1870 *Alli, DcNAA, OhA&B*
Glazunov, Alexander Konstantinovich 1865-1936 *AtlBL*
Gleadall, John William *Alli Sup*
Gleadow, Rupert Seeley 1909- *Au&Wr, ConAu 9R*
Gleadowe, Thomas Littlewood *Alli Sup*
Gleason, Arthur Huntington 1878-1923 *DcNAA*
Gleason, C W *Alli Sup*
Gleason, Christine *ChPo*
Gleason, Clarence Willard 1866- *AmLY*
Gleason, Edward Baldwin 1854-1934 *DcNAA, WhWNAA*
Gleason, Eugene Franklin 1914- *ConAu 1R*
Gleason, Fannie Matoon *WhWNAA*
Gleason, Frederick *AmA&B*
Gleason, Gene *ConAu XR*
Gleason, George W *HsB&A*
Gleason, Harold 1892- *ConAu P-1*
Gleason, Harold Willard *ChPo*
Gleason, J Paul 1902- *WhWNAA*
Gleason, Jackie 1916- *AmSCAP 66*
Gleason, Judith 1929- *ConAu 61*
Gleason, Lafayette Blanchard 1863-1937 *DcNAA*
Gleason, Madeline 1913- *ConP 1970*
Gleason, Mary M 1931- *AmSCAP 66*
Gleason, Oscar R *Alli Sup*
Gleason, Rachel Brooks 1820- *Alli Sup, DcAmA, DcNAA*
Gleason, Ralph Joseph 1917-1975 *ConAu 61*
Gleason, Robert Walter 1917- *ConAu 1R*
Gleason, Sarell Everett 1905-1974 *AmA&B, ConAu 53*
Gleason, Selina Gascoigne 1884-1957 *OhA&B*
Gleason, William J 1846-1905 *OhA&B*
Gleave, John Thomas 1917- *Au&Wr, WrD 1976*
Gleaves, Albert 1858-1937 *DcNAA, WhWNAA*
Gleaves, Robert M 1938- *ConAu 53*
Gleaves, Suzanne 1904- *ConAu 9R*
Glebov, Anatoli Glebovich 1899- *ModWD*
Gleckner, Robert Francis 1925- *ConAu 1R, WrD 1976*
Gledhill, Alan 1895- *Au&Wr, ConAu P-1, WrD 1976*
Gledstone, James Paterson *Alli Sup*
Gleed, Charles Sumner 1856-1920 *Alli Sup, DcNAA*
Gleed, James Willis 1859-1926 *DcNAA*
Gleeson, James Timothy 1915- *Au&Wr*
Gleeson, Joseph Michael 1861- *ChPo, ChPo S2*
Gleeson, Ruth 1925- *ConAu 9R*
Glehn, A A Von *Alli Sup*
Glehn, Miss M E Von *Alli Sup*
Gleich, Joseph Alois 1772-1841 *OxGer*
Gleichen, Count Albert Edward Wilfred *Alli Sup*
Gleichen, Lord Edward 1863- *WhLA*
Gleichen-Russwurm, Emilie Von 1804-1872 *OxGer*
Gleick, Beth Youman *AuBYP*
Gleig, Charles Edward Stuart *Alli Sup*
Gleig, George *Alli, BiDLA, BiDLA Sup*
Gleig, George Robert 1796-1888 *Alli, Alli Sup, BiD&SB, BrAu 19, Chmbr 3, DcEnL, EvLB, OxEng*
Gleim, Johann Wilhelm Ludwig 1719-1803 *BbD, BiD&SB, CasWL, DcEuL, EuA, EvEuW, OxGer, Pen Eur*
Gleiman, Lubomir 1923- *ConAu 41*

Gleisser, Marcus D 1923- *ConAu 17R*
Gleizes, Albert *REn*
Glemham, Charles *Alli*
Glemham, Henry *Alli Sup*
Glemser, Bernard 1908- *Au&Wr*
Glen, A *Alli*
Glen, Alexander 1850- *Alli Sup*
Glen, Catharine Young *ChPo*
Glen, Duncan Munro 1933- *Au&Wr, ChPo S2, ConAu 21, ConP 1975, WrD 1976*
Glen, Emilie *DrAP 1975*
Glen, Eugene *ConAu XR*
Glen, Frank Grenfell 1933- *WrD 1976*
Glen, Irma *AmSCAP 66*
Glen, J Stanley *ConAu P-1*
Glen, John *Alli, Alli Sup*
Glen, John King *Alli*
Glen, Reginald Cunningham *Alli Sup*
Glen, Robert S 1925- *ConAu 29*
Glen, Rowan *MnBBF*
Glen, William *Alli, Alli Sup, BiDLA*
Glen, William 1789-1826 *BiD&SB, BrAu 19, ChPo, ChPo S1, ChPo S1, EvLB*
Glen, William Cunningham *Alli, Alli Sup*
Glenbervie, Lord *Alli, BiDLA*
Glencairn, Countess Isabella *Alli, BiDLA*
Glenconner, Lady *ChPo*
Glenconner, Pamela Genevieve A Tennant 1871- *ChPo S1, ChPo S2*
Glenday, Alice 1920- *ConAu 57, WrD 1976*
Glendenning, Donn *ConAu XR*
Glendenning, John *Alli Sup*
Glendenning, Raymond Carl 1907- *Au&Wr*
Glendinning, Richard 1917- *ConAu 21*
Glendinning, Sally *ConAu 49*
Glendinning, Sara W 1913- *ConAu 49*
Glendon, Mary Ann 1938- *ConAu 41*
Glendower, Owen 1359?-1415? *NewC*
Glenie, James 1750?-1817 *Alli, BiDLA, OxCan*
Glenister, Sydney Haywood 1908- *Au&Wr*
Glenk, Robert 1870- *WhWNAA*
Glenn, Earl Rouse 1887-1962? *DcNAA, IndAu 1917, WhWNAA*
Glenn, Edwin Forbes 1857-1926 *DcNAA*
Glenn, Emma Lee Patterson 1869-1942 *OhA&B*
Glenn, Garrard 1878-1949 *DcNAA*
Glenn, Harold T 1910- *ConAu 5R*
Glenn, Isa 1888- *AmA&B, TwCA*
Glenn, Jacob B 1905-1974 *ConAu 9R, ConAu 49*
Glenn, James *BiDSA, ConAu XR*
Glenn, James Spahr 1875- *OhA&B*
Glenn, Jerry 1938- *ConAu 45*
Glenn, Jessie *Alli Sup*
Glenn, John H 1921- *AnCL*
Glenn, Lois 1941- *ConAu 61*
Glenn, Mary Wilcox 1869-1940 *DcNAA*
Glenn, Morton B 1922- *ConAu 61*
Glenn, Nanie Ashton *TexWr*
Glenn, Norval Dwight 1933- *ConAu 17R*
Glenn, Oliver Edmunds 1878- *IndAu 1917, WhWNAA*
Glenn, Paul Joseph 1893- *BkC 3, CatA 1947*
Glenn, Robert George 1843- *Alli Sup*
Glenn, S F *Alli Sup*
Glenn, Tyree 1912- *AmSCAP 66*
Glenn, W M 1888- *WhWNAA*
Glenn, William *Alli Sup, PoIre*
Glennie, John Stuart Stuart- *Alli Sup*
Glennon, James Aloysius 1900- *Au&Wr, ConAu 25, WrD 1976*
Glennon, Maurade 1926- *ConAu 25*
Glenny, George M F 1793-1874 *Alli Sup, ChPo S1*
Glenny, Lyman A 1918- *ConAu 17R*
Glenny, Michael Valentine 1927- *Au&Wr*
Glenorchy, Willielma, Viscountess 1741-1786 *Alli*
Glenthworth, Marguerite Linton 1881- *AmLY*
Glenton, Emily *ChPo S1, ChPo S2*
Glenton, Frederic *Alli, BiDLA*
Glentworth, Marguerite Linton 1881- *DcAmA*
Gles, Margaret Breitmaier 1940- *ConAu 57*
Glesener, Edmond 1874- *ClDMEuL*
Gleser, Goldine C 1915- *ConAu 17R*
Gless, Eleanor M 1908- *AmSCAP 66*
Glessing, Robert J 1930- *ConAu 29*

Glew, E L *Alli Sup*
Gliauda, Jurgis 1906- *ConAu 5R, WrD 1976*
Glick, Carl Cannon 1890- *AmA&B, Au&Wr, ConAu 5R, REnAL*
Glick, Edward Bernard 1929- *ConAu 23, WrD 1976*
Glick, G Wayne 1921- *ConAu 25*
Glick, Henry Robert 1942- *ConAu 29*
Glick, Jesse G M 1874-1938 *AmSCAP 66*
Glick, Paul Charles 1910- *ConAu 5R, IndAu 1917*
Glick, Thomas F 1939- *ConAu 29*
Glick, Virginia Kirkus 1893- *ConAu 21*
Glickman, Albert S 1923- *ConAu 53*
Glickman, Arthur P 1940- *ConAu 61*
Glickman, Fred 1903- *AmSCAP 66*
Glicksberg, Charles Irving 1900- *ConAu 1R, WrD 1976*
Glicksman, Abraham M 1911- *ConAu 5R*
Glidden, Frederick D 1908-1975 *ConAu 21, ConAu 61*
Glidden, Horace Knight 1901- *ConAu P-1*
Gliddon, George Robins 1801-1857 *Alli, CyAL 2*
Glidewell, John Calvin 1919- *ConAu 13R*
Glieg, Charles *MnBBF*
Gliers, Der Von *OxGer*
Gliewe, Unada G 1927- *ConAu 29, SmATA 3, WrD 1976*
Glikberg *DcRusL*
Glikes, Erwin 1937- *ConAu 13R*
Glines, Carroll V, Jr. 1920- *ConAu 1R*
Glingall, Richard Butler, Earl Of 1794-1858 *Alli*
Glinka, Avdotia Pavlovna 1795-1863 *BiD&SB*
Glinka, Fyodor Nikolayevich 1786?-1880 *BbD, BiD&SB, CasWL, DcRusL*
Glinka, Gregory Andreevich 1774-1818 *BiD&SB*
Glinka, Mikhail Ivanovich 1804-1857 *AtlBL, REn*
Glinka, Sergius Nicolaievich 1774?-1847 *BbD, BiD&SB*
Gliozzo, Charles 1932- *ConAu 45*
Glisan, Rodney 1827-1890 *Alli Sup, BiDSA, DcAmA, DcNAA*
Glisic, Milovan 1847-1908 *CasWL, Pen Eur*
Glissant, Edouard 1928- *DcCLA*
Glisson, Francis 1597-1677 *Alli*
Glisson, William, And Gulston, Ant *Alli*
Gloag, J A Lake *Alli Sup*
Gloag, John 1896- *Au&Wr, WrD 1976*
Gloag, Julian 1930- *AmA&B, AuNews 1, ConNov 1972, ConNov 1976, DrAF 1976, WrD 1976*
Gloag, Paton James 1823- *Alli Sup*
Globensky, Charles Auguste Maximilien 1830-1906 *DcNAA, OxCan*
Glocar, Emilian 1906- *OhA&B*
Glock, Charles Y 1919- *ConAu 53*
Glock, Marvin David 1912- *ConAu 23, WrD 1976*
Glocker, Theodore Wesley 1881- *WhWNAA*
Gloden, Marie *ChPo S1*
Glogau, Art 1922- *ConAu 53*
Glogau, Jack 1886-1953 *AmSCAP 66*
Gloger, Georg 1603-1631 *OxGer*
Gloomey Dean, The *NewC*
Glorfeld, Louis E 1916- *ConAu 53*
Glorious John *DcEnL*
Glos, Raymond E 1903- *ConAu 23*
Glossop, Reginald *MnBBF*
Glossy, Samuel *Alli*
Gloster, Arch *Alli*
Gloster, Hugh Morris 1911- *AmA&B, BlkAW, LivBAA*
Gloucester, Duke Of *NewC*
Gloucester, Robert Of *Alli, Chmbr 1, DcEnL*
Gloucester, Vernon *MnBBF*
Gloux, Olivier 1818-1883 *HsB&A*
Glovach, Linda 1947- *ConAu 37, SmATA 7, WrD 1976*
Glover *Alli*
Glover, Anna *Alli Sup*
Glover, Arnold *ChPo S2*
Glover, Arthur James 1873- *WhWNAA*
Glover, Bruce *MnBBF*
Glover, Caroline H 1823- *Alli, CyAL 1*
Glover, David Carr, Jr. 1925- *AmSCAP 66*
Glover, Denis James Matthews 1912- *CasWL,*

ChPo S1, ChPo S2, ConP 1970, ConP 1975, DcLEnL, LongC, Pen Eng, TwCW, WebEAL, WrD 1976
Glover, Edward 1888- *Au&Wr*
Glover, Elizabeth *DcAmA*
Glover, F R *OxCan*
Glover, Frank Graham 1894- *Au&Wr*
Glover, Frederick Robert Augustus *Alli, Alli Sup*
Glover, G Clabon d1934? *MnBBF*
Glover, George *Alli Sup*
Glover, Harry 1912- *WrD 1976*
Glover, Henry *Alli*
Glover, James *Alli Sup*
Glover, Janet Reaveley 1912- *Au&Wr, WrD 1976*
Glover, Janice 1919- *ConAu 17R, WrD 1976*
Glover, Jean *Chmbr 2*
Glover, Jeannie 1758-1801 *ChPo, ChPo S1*
Glover, Jimmy 1861- *WhLA*
Glover, Joe 1903- *AmSCAP 66*
Glover, John 1767-1849 *BkIE*
Glover, John D 1915- *ConAu 5R*
Glover, John Hulbert *Alli Sup*
Glover, Judith 1943- *WrD 1976*
Glover, Julia Lestarjette 1866- *AmA&B, ChPo S2, WhWNAA*
Glover, Leland E 1917- *ConAu 9R*
Glover, Leonard Horace *BlkAW*
Glover, Lizzie *Alli Sup*
Glover, Mark *MnBBF*
Glover, Mary Baker *Alli Sup*
Glover, Matthew *Alli Sup*
Glover, Michael 1922- *Au&Wr, ConAu 17R, WrD 1976*
Glover, Modwena 1916- *Au&Wr*
Glover, Octavius *Alli Sup*
Glover, P *Alli Sup*
Glover, Phillips *Alli*
Glover, Richard *Alli Sup, Chmbr 2*
Glover, Richard 1712-1785 *Alli, BbD, BiD&SB, BrAu, DcEnL, DcLEnL, EvLB, NewC, OxEng, REn*
Glover, Robert 1543-1588 *Alli*
Glover, Robert Hall 1871-1947 *DcNAA, WhWNAA*
Glover, Robert Mortimer *Alli Sup*
Glover, Serjt W *Alli*
Glover, Terrot Reaveley *Chmbr 3*
Glover, Thomas *Alli*
Glover, Tony Harp Dog 1939- *ConAu 13R*
Glover, W *Alli Sup*
Glover, W J *ChPo S2*
Glover, William *Alli, Alli Sup*
Glowacki, Aleksander *ClDMEuL*
Glowacki, Alexander *EuA*
Glubb, Sir John Bagot 1897- *Au&Wr, ConAu 9R, WrD 1976*
Glubb, Peter Southmead 1819- *Alli Sup*
Glubok, Shirley 1933- *AuBYP, ChLR 1, ConAu 5R, MorBMP, SmATA 6, ThBJA*
Gluck, Barbara Elisabeth *EuA, EvEuW*
Gluck, Christoph Willibald 1714-1787 *AtlBL, NewC, REn*
Gluck, Herb 1925- *ConAu 45*
Gluck, James Fraser 1852-1897 *DcNAA*
Gluck, Jay 1927- *ConAu 21*
Gluck, John 1925- *AmSCAP 66*
Gluck, Louise 1943- *ConAu 33, ConP 1970, ConP 1975, CrCAP, DrAP 1975, WrD 1976*
Gluckberg, Alexander Mikhaylovich 1880-1933 *DcRusL*
Gluckel Von Hameln 1645-1724 *EvEuW*
Gluckman, Bernard L 1909- *AmSCAP 66*
Gluckman, H Max 1911-1975 *WrD 1976*
Gluckman, Max 1911-1975 *Au&Wr, ConAu 9R, ConAu 57*
Glud, Don *WrD 1976*
Glueck, Eleanor Touroff 1898-1972 *AmA&B, ConAu 17, ConAu 37, WhWNAA*
Glueck, Nelson 1900-1971 *AmA&B, ConAu 17, OhA&B, REnAL*
Glueck, Sheldon 1896- *AmA&B, ConAu 5R, WhWNAA*
Glueck, William Frank 1934- *ConAu 33*
Glueckel Von Hameln 1645-1724 *Pen Eur*
Gluek, Alvin C, Jr. *OxCan*

Glum Eyjolfsson 940?-1003? *BiD&SB*
Glumer, Claire Von 1825- *BiD&SB*
Glustrom, Simon W 1924- *ConAu 21*
Glut, Donald F 1944- *ConAu 33, WrD 1976*
Glycas, Michael *CasWL, Pen Cl*
Glyde, John *Alli Sup*
Glyn, Anthony *MnBBF*
Glyn, Anthony 1922- *Au&Wr, ConAu 53, WrD 1976*
Glyn, Ashley Carr 1839-1875 *Alli Sup*
Glyn, Caroline 1947- *ConAu 9R*
Glyn, Clayton *BiD&SB*
Glyn, Elinor 1864-1943 *DcLEnL, EvLB, LongC, NewC, OxEng, REn, TwCA, TwCA Sup, TwCW*
Glyn, Sir George Lewen 1806-1885 *Alli Sup*
Glyn, Gerald *Alli Sup*
Glyn, Harrison *MnBBF*
Glyn, Herbert *Alli Sup*
Glyn, Lewis Edmund *Alli Sup*
Glyn, Thomas C And Jameson, Robert S *Alli*
Glyndon, Howard 1840-1929 *Alli Sup, AmA&B, ChPo, ChPo S1, DcAmA, DcEnL, DcNAA*
Glynes, Ella Maria *DcAmA, DcNAA*
Glynn, James A 1941- *ConAu 57*
Glynn, Jeanne Davis 1932- *ConAu 29*
Glynn, John *Alli*
Glynn, Joseph *Alli Sup*
Glynn, Joseph 1865-1907 *PoIre*
Glynn, Robert d1800 *Alli*
Glynn-Ward, H *OxCan*
Glynne, Sir Stephen Richard 1807-1874 *Alli Sup*
Glynne-Jones, William 1907- *Au&Wr, ConAu 5R*
Gmeiner, John 1847-1913 *DcAmA, DcNAA*
Gmelin, Otto 1886-1940 *OxGer*
Gnagey, Thomas D 1938- *ConAu 49*
Gnapheus, Guilhelmus 1493-1568 *CasWL*
Gnapheus, Gulielmus 1493-1568 *DcEuL*
Gnapheus, Wilhelm 1493-1568 *OxGer*
Gnarowski, Michael 1934- *Au&Wr, ConAu 41, ConP 1970, ConP 1975, OxCan Sup, WrD 1976*
Gnedich, Nicolai Ivanovich 1784-1833 *BbD, BiD&SB*
Gnedich, Nikolay Ivanovich 1784-1833 *CasWL, DcRusL*
Gneisenau, August W A Neithardt Von 1760-1831 *OxGer*
Gneist, Rudolph 1816-1895 *BiD&SB*
Gnessin, Uri-Nissan 1879-1913 *CasWL*
Gnoli, Count Domenico 1838-1915 *CasWL, ClDMEuL, IlCB 1966*
Gnosticus *ConAu XR*
Go, Puan Seng 1904- *ConAu 29*
Go-Kyogoku *DcOrL 1*
Go-Toba *DcOrL 1*
Goacher, Denis 1925- *ConP 1975, WrD 1976*
Goad, Christopher *Alli*
Goad, John 1615-1689 *Alli*
Goad, Thomas d1638 *Alli*
Goad, W Arthur *MnBBF*
Goadby, Edwin *Alli Sup*
Goadby, Henry *Alli*
Goadby, J *Alli, BiDLA*
Goadby, Joseph Jackson *Alli Sup*
Goadby, Robert d1778 *Alli*
Goadby, Thomas 1829- *Alli Sup*
Goalen, Alexander 1835-1872 *Alli Sup*
Goalen, Walter *Alli Sup*
Goaman, Muriel *Au&Wr, WrD 1976*
Goater, John H *EarAB, EarAB Sup*
Goater, Q H *ChPo*
Gobar, Ash 1930- *ConAu 41*
Gobat, Samuel *Alli*
Gobbato, Imero 1923- *IlBYP, IlCB 1966*
Gobelins *NewC*
Gobelins, Jean d1476 *NewC*
Gobetti, Piero 1901-1926 *ClDMEuL*
Gobind Singh *DcOrL 2*
Gobineau, Joseph Arthur, Comte De 1816-1882 *BbtC, BiD&SB, CasWL, ClDMEuL, EuA, EvEuW, OxFr, Pen Eur, REn*
Goble, George Washington 1887- *WhWNAA*
Goble, Neil 1933- *ConAu 29*
Goble, Warwick *ChPo S1, ConICB, IlCB 1945*

Goblet, H F *Alli Sup*
Gobrecht, Christian 1785-1844 *EarAB Sup*
Gobright, Lawrence Augustus 1816-1879 *Alli Sup, DcNAA*
Gocek, Matilda A 1923- *ConAu 49*
Gochhausen, Luise Von 1752-1807 *OxGer*
Gockel, Herman W 1906- *ConAu 1R*
Gockingk, Leopold Friedrich Gunther Von 1748-1828 *BiD&SB, DcEuL*
Goclenius, Rodolphus 1547-1628 *OxGer*
God, John *Alli*
Godard, John George *Alli Sup*
Godard, S A *Alli Sup*
Godbert, Geoffrey Harold 1937- *ConP 1970*
Godbey, John Emory 1839-1932 *DcNAA*
Godbey, William B 1833-1920 *DcNAA*
Godbold, Edward Stanly, Jr. 1942- *ConAu 37, WrD 1976*
Godbold, Mollie Moore 1877- *TexWr, WhWNAA*
Godbold, N *Alli*
Godbolt, John *Alli*
Godbout, Jacques 1933- *CanWr, CasWL, OxCan, OxCan Sup*
Godcharles, Frederic Antes 1872-1944 *AmA&B*
Godchaux, Elma d1941 *DcNAA*
Goddam, Adam *Alli*
Goddard, Mrs. *PoIre*
Goddard, Alfred *ConAu XR*
Goddard, Arthur *Alli Sup*
Goddard, Austin Parke *Alli*
Goddard, Burton L 1910- *ConAu 23*
Goddard, Charles *Alli*
Goddard, Charles W *Alli Sup*
Goddard, Charles William 1879?-1951 *AmA&B, REnAL*
Goddard, Cyril *ChPo S1*
Goddard, Delano A *Alli Sup*
Goddard, Donald 1934- *ConAu 17R*
Goddard, Dwight 1861-1939 *DcNAA*
Goddard, Edwin Charles 1865- *WhWNAA*
Goddard, Ernest Hope 1879-1939 *MnBBF*
Goddard, F W *Alli Sup*
Goddard, Frederick Bartlett 1834- *DcNAA*
Goddard, George Frederick *Alli Sup*
Goddard, Gladys Benjamin 1881?-1976 *ConAu 61*
Goddard, Glendon Boyce 1899- *AmSCAP 66*
Goddard, Gloria 1897- *AmA&B, AnMV 1926, WhWNAA*
Goddard, Henry Herbert 1866-1957 *OhA&B*
Goddard, J R 1930- *ConAu 29*
Goddard, James *Alli*
Goddard, John Calvin 1852-1945 *DcNAA, WhWNAA*
Goddard, John Leybourn 1840- *Alli Sup*
Goddard, Jonathan 1617-1674 *Alli*
Goddard, Joseph *Alli Sup*
Goddard, Julia L Bachope d1896 *Alli Sup, ChPo, ChPo S1, ChPo S2*
Goddard, Kate Cox *ChPo*
Goddard, Madeleine Vinton *Alli Sup*
Goddard, Morrill 1866-1937 *DcNAA*
Goddard, Nettye George 1923- *LivBA*
Goddard, Norman Molyneux 1881-1917 *MnBBF*
Goddard, O E 1867- *WhWNAA*
Goddard, Paul Beck 1811-1866 *Alli, BiDSA, DcNAA*
Goddard, Peter Stephen d1781 *Alli*
Goddard, Philip *Alli*
Goddard, Pliny Earle 1869-1928 *AmA&B, AmLY, DcNAA, OxCan, REnAL*
Goddard, Ralph Willis 1887-1929 *DcNAA*
Goddard, S A *Alli Sup*
Goddard, Thomas *Alli*
Goddard, Sir Victor 1897- *Au&Wr*
Goddard, William *Alli, DcLEnL*
Goddard, William 1740-1817 *Alli, DcNAA*
Goddard, William Giles 1794-1846 *Alli, CyAL 1*
Goddard, William Stanley 1757-1845 *Alli, BiDLA, BiDLA Sup*
Godden, Geoffrey Arthur 1929- *Au&Wr, WrD 1976*
Godden, Jon 1906- *Au&Wr, WorAu, WrD 1976*
Godden, Rumer 1907- *AnCL, Au&Wr, AuBYP, ChPo, ChPo S1, ChPo S2,*

ConAu 5R, ConNov 1972, ConNov 1976, DcLEnL, LongC, MorBL, NewC, PiP, RAdv 1, REn, SmATA 3, TwCA, TwCA Sup, TwCW, WhCL, WrD 1976
Godden, Thomas *Alli*
Godding, James *Alli Sup*
Godding, William Whitney 1831-1899 *Alli Sup, DcNAA*
Gode, Alexander *ConAu XR*
Gode, Marguerite *ChPo*
Gode VonAesch, Alexander 1906-1970 *ConAu P-1*
Godeau, Antoine 1605-1672 *DcEuL, OxFr*
Godecker, Helena Catherine 1888- *IndAu 1917*
Godefroi De Bouillon 1058-1100 *OxFr*
Godefroi De Leigni *CasWL*
Godefroi, Henry 1844- *Alli Sup*
Godefroy De Bouillon 1061?-1100 *NewC*
Godefroy, Frederic-Eugene 1826-1897 *BiD&SB, OxFr*
Godeman *NewC*
Godescalc 805?-869 *CasWL*
Godet, Gylles *Alli*
Godet, Philippe Ernest 1850-1922 *BiD&SB, CasWL*
Godet, Theodore L *Alli Sup*
Godey, John 1912- *AuNews 1, EncM&D*
Godey, Louis Antoine 1804-1878 *AmA, AmA&B, REn*
Godfray, Hugh *Alli Sup*
Godfrey *DcEnL*
Godfrey Of Bouillon 1061?-1100 *DcEuL, NewC*
Godfrey Of Viterbo 1120?-1191 *CasWL*
Godfrey Of Winchester d1107 *Alli, BiB N*
Godfrey, Ambrose And Godfrey, John *Alli*
Godfrey, Arthur 1903- *AmSCAP 66*
Godfrey, Arthur W *BbtC*
Godfrey, Benjamin *Alli Sup*
Godfrey, Boyly *Alli*
Godfrey, C B *Alli, BiDLA*
Godfrey, Caroline A *Alli Sup*
Godfrey, Charles G *Alli Sup*
Godfrey, Charles M *OxCan Sup*
Godfrey, Cuthbert John 1914- *ConAu 5R, WrD 1976*
Godfrey, Dave 1938- *ConNov 1972, ConNov 1976, OxCan, OxCan Sup, WrD 1976*
Godfrey, Edward K *Alli Sup*
Godfrey, Elizabeth *ChPo*
Godfrey, Emmeline Stuart 1861- *WhLA*
Godfrey, Ernest Gordon 1897- *Au&Wr*
Godfrey, Ernest Henry 1862- *WhLA*
Godfrey, Frederick M 1901-1974 *Au&Wr, ConAu P-1*
Godfrey, Mrs. G W *Alli Sup*
Godfrey, George F *Alli Sup*
Godfrey, Mrs. Henry *PoIre*
Godfrey, Henry F 1906- *ConAu 25*
Godfrey, Hollis 1874-1936 *DcNAA*
Godfrey, James Logan 1907- *Au&Wr*
Godfrey, Joe, Jr. *WhWNAA*
Godfrey, John *Alli, ChPo*
Godfrey, John A *Alli Sup*
Godfrey, John E *ChPo*
Godfrey, John R *WhWNAA*
Godfrey, John Thomas *Alli Sup*
Godfrey, Joyce *ChPo S1, ChPo S2*
Godfrey, Lionel Robert Holcombe 1932- *Au&Wr, WrD 1976*
Godfrey, Michael d1695 *Alli*
Godfrey, Nathaniel Stedman *Alli Sup*
Godfrey, Mrs. Nathaniel Stedman *Alli Sup*
Godfrey, Peter 1917- *Au&Wr*
Godfrey, Robert *Alli*
Godfrey, Robert H 1905- *AmSCAP 66*
Godfrey, Samuel *Alli, BiDLA*
Godfrey, Thomas *Alli*
Godfrey, Thomas 1736-1763 *Alli, AmA, AmA&B, BiD&SB, BiDSA, CasWL, CnDAL, CyAL 1, DcAmA, DcLEnL, DcNAA, EvLB, OxAm, Pen Am, REn, REnAL*
Godfrey, Vincent Hubbard 1894?-1975 *ConAu 57, WhWNAA*
Godfrey, Vivian 1921- *ConAu 61*
Godfrey, Wilfred *ChPo S2*

Goheen, Robert Francis 1919- *AmA&B, Au&Wr*
Gohman, Donald 1927- *AmSCAP 66*
Gohman, Fred Joseph 1918- *ConAu 5R*
Goines, Donald 1935?-1974 *AuNews 1, BlkAW*
Going, Charles Buxton 1863- *AmA&B, ChPo, DcAmA, REnAL, WhWNAA*
Going, E T R *ChPo*
Going, Ellen Maud 1859-1925 *DcAmA, DcNAA*
Going, Maud 1859-1925 *ChPo*
Going, V L *MnBBF*
Goins, Ellen H 1927- *ConAu 33*
Goiorani, Ciro 1834- *BiD&SB*
Gois, Damiao De 1502-1574 *CasWL*
Goist, Park Dixon 1936- *ConAu 37*
Goitein, S D 1900- *ConAu 61*
Goitein, Solomon Dob Fritz 1900- *ConAu XR*
Gojawiczynska, Apolonia 1896-1963 *CasWL*
Gojawiczynska, Pola 1896-1963 *CasWL, ClDMEuL*
Gokak, Vinayak Krishna 1909- *REn, WrD 1976*
Gokalp, Mehmed Ziya 1875-1924 *DcOrL 3*
Gokalp, Ziya 1875-1924 *CasWL*
Gokceli, Yasa Kemal *WorAu*
Gokhale, Aravind Visnu 1919- *DcOrL 2*
Gokhale, Balkrishna Govind 1919- *ConAu 1R*
Golann, Cecil Paige 1921- *ConAu 33*
Golann, Stuart E 1936- *ConAu 57*
Golant, William 1937- *WrD 1976*
Golay, Frank H 1915- *ConAu 1R*
Golborne, John *Alli*
Golburne, John *Alli*
Gold, Alan R 1948- *ConAu 45*
Gold, Anita 1932- *AmSCAP 66*
Gold, Bert 1917- *AmSCAP 66*
Gold, Don 1931- *ConAu 61*
Gold, Doris B 1919- *ConAu 23*
Gold, Douglas 1894- *ConAu P-1, IndAu 1917*
Gold, Edward *DrAP 1975*
Gold, Edwin Richard 1905- *WrD 1976*
Gold, Ernest 1921- *AmSCAP 66*
Gold, F *Alli, BiDLA*
Gold, Herbert 1924- *AmA&B, ConAu 9R, ConLC 4, ConNov 1972, ConNov 1976, DrAF 1976, ModAL, OxAm, Pen Am, RAdv 1, REnAL, TwCW, WorAu, WrD 1976*
Gold, Horace L 1914- *AmA&B, Au&Wr, WorAu*
Gold, Ivan 1932- *AmA&B, Au&Wr, ConAu 5R, ConNov 1972, ConNov 1976, DrAF 1976, WrD 1976*
Gold, Jacob 1921- *AmSCAP 66*
Gold, Joe 1894- *AmSCAP 66*
Gold, Joseph 1933- *ConAu 21*
Gold, Martin 1925- *AmSCAP 66*
Gold, Martin 1931- *ConAu 29*
Gold, Michael 1894-1967 *AmA&B, CnMD, ConAu XR, ModWD, OxAm, Pen Am, REn, REnAL, TwCA, TwCA Sup, WebEAL*
Gold, Milton J 1917- *ConAu 17R*
Gold, Phyllis *ConAu 57*
Gold, Robert S 1924- *ConAu 53*
Gold, Seymour M 1933- *ConAu 41*
Gold, Sharlya *ConAu 61, SmATA 9*
Gold, Theodore Sedgwick 1818-1906 *Alli Sup, DcNAA*
Gold, Victor 1922- *WrD 1976*
Gold, Victor Roland 1924- *ConAu 53*
Gold, Wally 1928- *AmSCAP 66*
Gold, William Jason 1845-1903 *DcNAA*
Goldammer, T S *Alli Sup*
Goldbarth, Albert 1948- *ConAu 53, ConLC 5, DrAP 1975*
Goldbeck, David M 1942- *ConAu 49*
Goldbeck, Frederick E 1902- *WrD 1976*
Goldbeck, Nikki 1947- *ConAu 49*
Goldbeck, Robert 1839-1908 *DcNAA*
Goldberg, Alvin Arnold 1931- *ConAu 41*
Goldberg, Arthur J 1908- *AmA&B*
Goldberg, Barney 1918- *ConAu 23*
Goldberg, Carl 1938- *ConAu 49*
Goldberg, Edward M 1931- *ConAu 53*
Goldberg, Gerald Jay 1929- *AmA&B,*

ConAu 49, DrAF 1976
Goldberg, Harry 1912- *AmSCAP 66*
Goldberg, Harvey E 1939- *ConAu 45*
Goldberg, Herb 1937- *ConAu 61*
Goldberg, Herman Raphael 1915- *ConAu 9R*
Goldberg, Isaac 1887-1938 *AmA&B, DcNAA, REn, REnAL, TwCA, WhWNAA*
Goldberg, Israel 1887-1964 *AmA&B*
Goldberg, Joseph P 1918- *ConAu 37*
Goldberg, Leah 1911-1970 *CasWL, ConAu 25*
Goldberg, Louis 1908- *Au&Wr, ConAu 13R, WrD 1976*
Goldberg, Louis 1943- *ConAu XR*
Goldberg, M A 1919- *ConAu 25*
Goldberg, Mark L 1927- *AmSCAP 66*
Goldberg, Martha 1907- *AuBYP*
Goldberg, Miriam Levin 1914- *ConAu 41*
Goldberg, P Selvin 1917- *ConAu 5R*
Goldberg, Phyllis 1941- *ConAu 57*
Goldberg, Ray A 1926- *ConAu 49*
Goldberg, Reuben Lucius 1883-1970 *AmA&B, AmSCAP 66, ConAu 5R, WhWNAA*
Goldberg, Rube 1883-1970 *ConAu XR*
Goldberg, Samual Louis 1926- *Au&Wr, WrD 1976*
Goldberg, Stan J 1939- *ConAu 49*
Goldberg, Steven 1941- *ConAu 53*
Goldberger, Arthur Stanley 1930- *ConAu 9R*
Goldberger, Henry Harold 1878- *WhWNAA*
Goldblatt, Harold M 1888- *AmSCAP 66*
Goldburgh, Stephen J 1935- *ConAu 21*
Golde, Peggy 1930- *ConAu 37*
Golde, Walter H 1887-1963 *AmSCAP 66*
Goldemberg, Rose Leiman *ConAu 49*
Golden, Arthur 1924- *ConAu 33*
Golden, Aubrey E *OxCan Sup*
Golden, Dorothy *Au&Wr*
Golden, Ernie 1890- *AmSCAP 66*
Golden, Grace Blaisdell 1899-1966 *IndAu 1917*
Golden, Harry 1902- *AmA&B, Pen Am, RAdv 1, REnAL, WorAu*
Golden, Harry 1903- *ConAu 1R*
Golden, J *Alli Sup*
Golden, Jeffrey S 1950- *ConAu 33*
Golden, John *PoIre*
Golden, John 1874-1955 *AmA&B, AmSCAP 66, OhA&B, REnAL*
Golden, L L L *ConAu 23*
Golden, Leon 1930- *ConAu 17R, WrD 1976*
Golden, Michael Joseph 1862-1918 *DcNAA*
Golden, Morris 1926- *ConAu 1R*
Golden, Ruth I 1910- *ConAu 17*
Golden, Sylvia *AmSCAP 66*
Golden, William *Alli, BiDLA*
Golden, William 1911- *WhGrA*
Golden Gorse *St&VC, WhCL*
Goldenberg, Herbert 1926- *ConAu 41*
Goldenberg, Marion Heather *ConP 1970*
Goldenberg, Morris 1911- *AmSCAP 66*
Goldenberg, William Leon 1936- *AmSCAP 66*
Goldenson, Daniel R 1944- *ConAu 25*
Goldenson, Robert M 1908- *ConAu 29, WrD 1976*
Goldenthal, Allan Benarria 1920- *ConAu 17R*
Goldenweiser, Alexander 1880-1940 *AmA&B, DcNAA*
Goldenweiser, Emanuel Alexander 1883- *WhWNAA*
Golder, Christian 1849-1922 *OhA&B*
Golder, Frank Alfred 1877-1909 *DcNAA*
Golder, S *Alli Sup*
Golder, William *Alli Sup*
Goldesborough, John *Alli*
Goldfaden, Abraham Haim Lipke 1840-1908 *CnThe, McGWD, ModWD, REnWD*
Goldfaden, Avraham 1840-1908 *Pen Eur*
Goldfader, Edward H 1930- *ConAu 29*
Goldfarb, Nathan 1913- *ConAu 13R, WrD 1976*
Goldfarb, Ronald Lawrence 1933- *ConAu 23, WrD 1976*
Goldfarb, Russell M 1934- *ConAu 37, WrD 1976*
Goldfarb, Sidney *DrAP 1975*
Goldfeder, Cheryl 1949- *ConAu 53*
Goldfeder, James 1943- *ConAu 53*
Goldfeder, Jim 1943- *ConAu XR*
Goldfein, Alan *DrAF 1976*

Goldfield, Mrs. Simon *AmNov XR*
Goldfinch, A O *TexWr*
Goldfinger, Erno 1902- *Au&Wr*
Goldfrank, Esther S 1896- *ConAu 61*
Goldfrank, Helen Colodny 1912- *AuBYP, ConAu 1R, SmATA 6*
Goldfrap, John Henry 1879-1917 *DcNAA*
Goldfried, Marvin R 1936- *ConAu 37*
Goldhaber, Gerald Martin 1944- *ConAu 57*
Goldhamer, Herbert 1907- *ConAu 45*
Goldhurst, Richard 1927- *ConAu 57*
Goldhurst, William 1929- *ConAu 5R*
Goldicult, John *Alli*
Goldie, Alexander 1841- *ChPo S1*
Goldie, Alexander Robert *Alli Sup*
Goldie, Francis And Scola, Father *Alli Sup*
Goldie, George 1748-1804 *Alli*
Goldie, James *ChPo*
Goldie, John *Alli*
Goldie, Mark H G *Alli Sup*
Goldie, T W *BbtC*
Goldin, Augusta 1906- *ConAu 17R, WrD 1976*
Goldin, Ezra 1867-1915 *Pen Eur*
Goldin, Judah 1914- *AmA&B, ConAu 33*
Goldin, Milton 1927- *ConAu 61*
Golding, Arthur 1536?-1605? *Alli, BrAu, CasWL, ChPo S2, Chmbr 1, CnE&AP, CrE&SL, DcEnL, DcEuL, EvLB, NewC, Pen Eng, WebEAL*
Golding, Benjamin 1793-1863 *Alli Sup*
Golding, Charles *Alli Sup*
Golding, Frederick Campbell 1901- *Au&Wr*
Golding, Godfrey *Alli Sup*
Golding, Harry *CarSB, ChPo S2*
Golding, J E *Alli Sup*
Golding, Lawrence A 1926- *ConAu 61*
Golding, Louis 1895-1958 *ChPo, ChPo S1, DcLEnL, EvLB, LongC, ModBL, NewC, REn, TwCA, TwCA Sup, TwCW*
Golding, Louis 1907- *ConAu P-1, WrD 1976*
Golding, Louise Sarah 1923- *Au&Wr*
Golding, Matilda Young *ChPo S1*
Golding, Morton J 1925- *ConAu 21*
Golding, P *Alli*
Golding, Peter 1947- *WrD 1976*
Golding, Raymund Marshall 1935- *WrD 1976*
Golding, Widdows *Alli*
Golding, William 1911- *CasWL, CnMWL, ConAu 5R, ConLC 1, ConLC 2, ConLC 3, ConNov 1972, ConNov 1976, EncWL, LongC, ModBL, ModBL Sup, ModWD, NewC, Pen Eng, RAdv 1, REn, TwCW, WebEAL, WhTwL, WorAu, WrD 1976*
Golding-Bird, Robert James *ChPo S2*
Goldingham, B *Alli*
Goldingham, Henry *Alli*
Goldini, Carlo 1707-1793 *CnThe*
Goldisborough, John *Alli*
Goldknopf, David 1918- *ConAu 53*
Goldman, A E O 1947- *ConAu 57*
Goldman, Albert 1927- *AmA&B, ConAu 17R*
Goldman, Alex J 1917- *ConAu 49*
Goldman, Alvin L 1938- *ConAu 45*
Goldman, Arnold 1936- *ConAu 17R, WrD 1976*
Goldman, Bernard 1922- *ConAu 53*
Goldman, Bruce 1942- *ConAu 61*
Goldman, Charles R 1930- *ConAu 53*
Goldman, Edward Alphonso 1873- *WhWNAA*
Goldman, Edwin Franko 1878- *AmSCAP 66*
Goldman, Emma 1869-1940 *DcNAA, OxAm, REnAL*
Goldman, Eric Frederick 1915- *AmA&B, ConAu 5R, WrD 1976*
Goldman, Irving 1911- *ConAu 29*
Goldman, James A 1927- *AmA&B, ConAu 45, ConDr, McGWD, WrD 1976*
Goldman, Lee A 1946- *ConAu 25*
Goldman, Lloyd *DrAP 1975*
Goldman, Marcus Selden 1894- *ConAu 41*
Goldman, Marshall Irwin 1930- *ConAu 9R, WrD 1976*
Goldman, Maurice *AmSCAP 66*
Goldman, Mayer C 1874- *WhWNAA*
Goldman, Merle 1931- *ConAu 33*
Goldman, Michael Paul 1936- *ConAu 17R,*

ConP 1970, DrAP 1975
Goldman, Peter L 1933- ConAu 21
Goldman, Phyllis W 1927- ConAu 29
Goldman, Raymond Leslie 1895- WhWNAA
Goldman, Richard Franko 1910- AmA&B,
AmSCAP 66, ConAu 9R, WrD 1976
Goldman, Robert 1932- AmSCAP 66
Goldman, Ronald ConAu 23
Goldman, Sheldon 1939- ConAu 23
Goldman, Sherli E 1930- ConAu 25
Goldman, Solomon 1893-1953 AmA&B
Goldman, William 1931- AmA&B, ConAu 9R,
ConDr, ConLC 1, ConNov 1972,
ConNov 1976, DrAF 1976, Pen Am,
WebEAL, WrD 1976
Goldmann, Lucien Serge 1913-1970 Au&Wr,
ConAu 25
Goldman, Sidney 1903- Au&Wr
Goldmark, Pauline Dorothea ChPo S2
Goldmark, Rubin 1872-1936 OxAm
Goldner, Bernard B 1919- ConAu 5R
Goldner, Jack 1900- ConAu 25
Goldner, Nancy 1943- ConAu 57
Goldner, Orville 1906- ConAu 53
Goldney, Edward, Sr. Alli
Goldney, G Alli Sup
Goldney, Kathleen M BiDPar
Goldoni, Carlo 1707-1793 AtlBL, BiD&SB,
CasWL, CyWA, DcEuL, EuA, EvEuW,
McGWD, OxEng, Pen Eur, RCom, REn,
REnWD
Goldrick, Michael OxCan Sup
Goldring, Douglas 1887-1960 ChPo, EvLB,
LongC, ModBL, NewC, TwCA,
TwCA Sup, WhLA
Goldring, Patrick Thomas Zachary 1921-
Au&Wr, ConAu 29, WrD 1976
Goldring, Winifred 1888- WhWNAA
Goldsack, R Alli Sup
Goldsborough, Charles Washington 1779-1843
Alli, BiDSA, DcNAA
Goldsborough, Edmund Kennedy 1844?-1912
DcNAA
Goldsborough, Robert OhA&B
Goldsborough, William Worthington 1831-1901
DcNAA
Goldsbury, John 1795-1890 ChPo S1
Goldsbury, Paul W 1869- WhWNAA
Goldscheider, Ludwig 1896- ConAu 5R
Goldschmidt, H E Alli Sup
Goldschmidt, Hans 1893- WhWNAA
Goldschmidt, Hermann 1860- WhLA
Goldschmidt, Meir A 1819-1887 BbD, BiD&SB,
CasWL, EuA, EvEuW, Pen Eur
Goldschmidt, Meyer A 1819-1887 DcEuL
Goldschmidt, Walter Rochs 1913- ConAu 9R
Goldschmidt, Yaaqov 1927- ConAu 29,
WrD 1976
Goldsen, Rose Kohn 1918- ConAu 1R
Goldsmid, Anna Maria 1806-1889 Alli,
Alli Sup
Goldsmid, Sir Frederic John 1818- Alli Sup,
BiD&SB
Goldsmid, Howard J Alli Sup
Goldsmid, Isabella Alli Sup
Goldsmid, Lionel F ChPo S2
Goldsmith, Alban Alli Sup
Goldsmith, Arnold L 1928- ConAu 41
Goldsmith, Arthur, Jr. 1926- ChPo,
ConAu 13R
Goldsmith, Barbara 1931- ConAu 53
Goldsmith, Carol Evan 1930- ConAu 29
Goldsmith, Christabel Alli Sup, DcNAA
Goldsmith, Francis Alli
Goldsmith, G Alli
Goldsmith, Glenn Warren 1886-1943 DcNAA
Goldsmith, Goldwin C 1871- ChPo, TexWr
Goldsmith, Ilse Sondra 1933- ConAu 37
Goldsmith, Immanuel 1921- Au&Wr,
WrD 1976
Goldsmith, J Alli
Goldsmith, J C Alli Sup
Goldsmith, Jack 1931- ConAu 57
Goldsmith, John Herman Thorburn 1903-
Au&Wr
Goldsmith, Lewis 1763- Alli, BiDLA
Goldsmith, Margaret E 1920- Au&Wr
Goldsmith, Mary Alli, BiDLA, ChPo S2

Goldsmith, Maurice 1913- Au&Wr
Goldsmith, Middleton 1818-1887 DcNAA
Goldsmith, Milton 1861- AmLY, WhWNAA
Goldsmith, Oliver Chmbr 2
Goldsmith, Oliver 1728?-1774 Alli, AtlBL,
BbD, BiD&SB, BrAu, CarSB, CasWL,
ChPo, ChPo S1, ChPo S2, CnE&AP,
CnThe, CriT 2, CyWA, DcBiA, DcEnA,
DcEnA Ap, DcEnL, DcEuL, DcLEnL,
EvLB, HsB&A, McGWD, MouLC 2,
NewC, OxEng, Pen Eng, PoIre, RAdv 1,
REn, REnWD, WebEAL
Goldsmith, Oliver 1794?-1861 BbtC, CanWr,
DcLEnL, DcNAA, OxCan, PoIre
Goldsmith, Peter ConAu XR, LongC, TwCA,
TwCA Sup
Goldsmith, Reuben ChPo S1
Goldsmith, Robert 1882-1924 DcNAA
Goldsmith, Robert Hillis 1911- ConAu 49
Goldsmith, Sharon S 1948- ConAu 57
Goldsmith, Wallace ChPo
Goldsmith, William 1910- ChPo S2
Goldson, Rae L Segalowitz 1893- ConAu 5R
Goldson, William BiDLA
Goldstein, Abraham S 1925- ConAu 33
Goldstein, Alvin H, Sr. 1902-1972 ConAu 33
Goldstein, Bernard R 1938- ConAu 57
Goldstein, David 1870- BkC 1, CatA 1947
Goldstein, David 1933- ConAu 17R
Goldstein, E D 1926- Au&Wr
Goldstein, E Ernest 1918- ConAu 9R
Goldstein, Edward 1923- ConAu 9R
Goldstein, Irwin L 1937- ConAu 41
Goldstein, Israel 1896- AmA&B, ConAu 53,
WrD 1976
Goldstein, Jonathan Amos 1929- ConAu 25,
WrD 1976
Goldstein, Joseph 1923- Au&Wr, ConAu 17R,
WrD 1976
Goldstein, Joseph M 1868-1939 DcNAA
Goldstein, Kenneth M 1940- ConAu 33
Goldstein, Laurence 1937?-1972 ConAu 33
Goldstein, Leo S 1924- ConAu 13R
Goldstein, Malcolm 1925- ConAu 49
Goldstein, Martin E 1939- ConAu 41
Goldstein, Max Aaron 1870-1941 DcNAA
Goldstein, Milton 1915- ConAu 45
Goldstein, Nathan 1927- ConAu 45, IlBYP
Goldstein, Philip 1910- ConAu 53
Goldstein, Rhoda L 1926- ConAu 57
Goldstein, Richard 1944- ConAu 25
Goldstein, Robert Gary 1938- AmSCAP 66
Goldstein, Roberta Butterfield 1917- ConAu 9R
Goldstein, Sidney 1927- ConAu 23, WrD 1976
Goldstein, Stephen R 1938- ConAu 61
Goldstein, William Isaac 1932- ConAu 13R
Goldstein, William S 1926- AmSCAP 66
Goldston, Robert Conroy 1927- AmA&B,
Au&Wr, ConAu 17R, SmATA 6
Goldstone, Aline Lewis WhWNAA
Goldstone, Lawrence A ConAu 49
Goldstone, Richard H 1921- ConAu 33
Goldstuecker, Theodor 1821-1872 Alli Sup
Goldsworthy, David 1938- ConAu 33
Goldsworthy, William Arthur 1878-
AmSCAP 66
Goldthorpe, J E 1921- ConAu 49
Goldthorpe, John Au&Wr
Goldthwait, James Walter 1880-1948 DcNAA,
WhWNAA
Goldthwaite, Eaton K 1907- ConAu 25
Goldthwaite, Stephen Grant 1868- WhWNAA
Goldwater, Barry M 1909- AmA&B,
ConAu 41, WrD 1976
Goldwater, John AuNews 1
Goldwater, Robert 1907-1973 ConAu 41
Goldwater, S S ChPo
Goldwell, Charles Alli
Goldwell, Henry Alli
Goldwin, William Alli
Goldwyn, Samuel 1882-1974 REnAL
Goldy DcEnL
Gole, Victor Leslie 1903- WrD 1976
Golembiewski, Robert T 1932- ConAu 5R
Golenbock, Peter 1946- ConAu 57
Golenishchev-Kutuzov, Arseny Arkadyevich
1848-1912? CasWL, DcRusL
Golf, Royal E 1926- ConAu 1R

Golffing, Barbara ConP 1970
Golffing, Francis 1910- AmA&B, ConAu 5R
Goliard, Roy WrD 1976
Golias DcEuL
Goligher, Kathleen BiDPar
Golightly, Bonnie H 1919- ConAu 1R
Golightly, Charles Pourtales 1807-1885 Alli Sup
Golitsyn, Prince Dmitri Petrovich 1860-1919
DcRusL
Goll, Ivan 1891-1950 OxGer
Goll, Iwan 1891-1950 CasWL, Pen Eur,
WhTwL
Goll, Jaroslav 1846- BiD&SB
Goll, Reinhold Weimar 1897- AuBYP,
ConAu 5R, WrD 1976
Goll, Yvan 1891-1950 CasWL, EncWL,
ModGL, ModWD, OxGer, Pen Eur,
WhTwL, WorAu
Gollahon, Gladys 1908- AmSCAP 66
Gollan, Robin 1917- ConAu 13R
Gollancz, Sir Israel 1863?-1930 Chmbr 3,
EvLB, WhLA
Gollancz, Sir Victor 1893-1967 ChPo S2,
LongC
Golledge, John Alli, BiDLA
Golledge, Reginald G 1937- ConAu 41
Goller, Celia 1914- ConAu 13R
Gollings, Franklin O A 1919- ConAu 23
Gollomb, Joseph 1881-1950 AmA&B, AnCL,
AuBYP, JBA 1934, JBA 1951, REnAL,
TwCA, TwCA Sup
Gollwitzer, Heinz 1917- ConAu 25
Golob, Zvonimir 1927- CasWL
Golobie, John d1927 DcNAA
Golombek, H Au&Wr
Golon, Sergeanne 1903-1972 Au&Wr,
ConAu 37, TwCW
Golovin, Ivan 1816- Alli
Golovine, Michael N 1903-1965 ConAu 5R
Golshan DcOrL 3
Golson, Benny 1929- AmSCAP 66
Golssenau TwCA, TwCA Sup
Golsworthy, Arnold MnBBF
Golt Alli
Golty, Richard Alli
Goltz, Bogumil 1801-1870 OxGer
Goltz, Joachim, Freiherr VonDer 1892-1972
OxGer
Golub, Jacob Solomon 1895- OhA&B
Golz, R Lud 1936- ConAu 13R
Gomara, F DeLopez De CasWL, DcEuL
Gombaud, Jean Ogier De 1570-1666 OxFr
Gombauld, Jean Ogier De 1570?-1666 CasWL,
DcEuL, OxFr
Gombault, Jean Ogier De 1570-1666 OxFr
Gomberg, Adeline Wishengrad 1915-
ConAu 17R
Gomberg, Vladimir Germanovich 1894- DcRusL,
TwCA, TwCA Sup
Gomberg, William 1911- ConAu 17R
Gomberville, Marin LeRoy 1600?-1674 BbD,
BiD&SB, CasWL, DcAmA, OxFr, REn
Gombrich, Ernst Hans Josef 1909- ConAu 53,
WorAu, WrD 1976
Gombrowicz, Witold 1904-1969 CasWL,
CnMD, ConAu 19, ConAu 25, ConLC 4,
CrCD, EncWL, McGWD, ModSL 2,
ModWD, Pen Eur, TwCW, WhTwL,
WorAu
Gomersal, Robert 1600-1646 Alli
Gomersall, Mrs. A Alli, BiDLA
Gomersall, Robert 1602?-1644? Alli, CasWL
Gomersall, William 1850?- Br&AmS
Gomery, Percy 1881- CanNov, OxCan,
WhWNAA
Gomes, Alair DeOliveira 1921- BiDPar
Gomes, Edwin H Alli Sup
Gomes, Joao Baptista 1775-1803 BiD&SB
Gomes DeAmorim, Francisco 1827-1891
BiD&SB
Gomes Leal, Antonio Duarte 1848-1921
BiD&SB, CasWL
Gomez, Antonio Enriquez 1602?-1662? DcEuL
Gomez, David F 1940- ConAu 49
Gomez, Estevan OxCan
Gomez, Rudolph 1930- ConAu 53
Gomez, Vicente 1911- AmSCAP 66
Gomez Costa, Arturo 1895- PueRA

Goodwin, Cardinal 1880-1944 *AmA&B*
Goodwin, Cardinal Lee 1880- *WhWNAA*
Goodwin, Caroline Georgiana *Alli Sup*
Goodwin, Charles *MnBBF*
Goodwin, Charles Carroll 1832-1917 *DcNAA*
Goodwin, Charles D 1929- *AmSCAP 66*
Goodwin, Charles H *Alli Sup*
Goodwin, Charles Jacques 1866-1935 *DcNAA*
Goodwin, Charles Jacques 1866- *WhWNAA*
Goodwin, Charles Wycliffe 1817-1878 *Alli Sup*
Goodwin, Christina *Alli Sup*
Goodwin, Christopher *Alli*
Goodwin, Craufurd D W 1934- *ConAu 37*
Goodwin, Daniel 1832-1901 *Alli Sup, DcAmA, DcNAA*
Goodwin, Daniel 1835-1922 *DcNAA*
Goodwin, Daniel Raynes 1811-1890 *Alli Sup, DcAmA, DcNAA*
Goodwin, David *MnBBF*
Goodwin, E S d1833 *Alli*
Goodwin, Edward *Alli Sup*
Goodwin, Edward B *Alli Sup*
Goodwin, Edwin W *Alli Sup*
Goodwin, Elijah 1807-1879 *DcNAA, IndAu 1917, OhA&B*
Goodwin, Eugene D 1938- *ConAu XR, WrD 1976*
Goodwin, Francis d1835 *Alli*
Goodwin, Frank 1841-1912 *DcNAA*
Goodwin, G M Colquitt *Alli Sup, ChPo S1*
Goodwin, Geoffrey Alfred 1921- *Au&Wr, WrD 1976*
Goodwin, George *Alli, BiDLA*
Goodwin, Grace Duffield 1869- *AmLY, ChPo S1*
Goodwin, H D *Alli Sup*
Goodwin, Hal *ConAu XR*
Goodwin, Hannah Elizabeth Bradbury 1827-1893 *Alli Sup, AmA&B, DcAmA, DcNAA*
Goodwin, Harold 1919- *ConAu 57, IlBYP*
Goodwin, Harold Leland 1914- *ConAu 1R*
Goodwin, Harry And Knight, William *Alli Sup*
Goodwin, Harvey 1818- *Alli, Alli Sup*
Goodwin, Helen Angell *ChPo*
Goodwin, Mrs. Henry *Alli Sup*
Goodwin, Henry Bedingfield *Alli Sup*
Goodwin, Henry M *Alli Sup*
Goodwin, Henry Martyn 1820-1893 *DcNAA*
Goodwin, Hermon Camp 1813-1891 *DcAmA, DcNAA*
Goodwin, Isaac 1786-1832 *Alli, DcAmA, DcNAA*
Goodwin, J *Alli Sup*
Goodwin, J Cheever 1850-1912 *AmA&B*
Goodwin, Joe 1889-1943 *AmSCAP 66*
Goodwin, John *Alli*
Goodwin, John 1593-1665 *Alli*
Goodwin, John Abbott 1824-1884 *Alli Sup, DcAmA, DcNAA*
Goodwin, Lavinia Stella 1833-1911 *Alli Sup, ChPo, ChPo S1, ChPo S2, DcAmA, DcNAA*
Goodwin, Leonard 1929- *ConAu 41*
Goodwin, LeRoy *BlkAW*
Goodwin, Mrs. M M B *Alli Sup*
Goodwin, Mark *ConAu XR*
Goodwin, Mary *ChPo S2*
Goodwin, Maud Wilder 1856-1935 *AmA&B, BiD&SB, CarSB, DcAmA, DcNAA, REnAL*
Goodwin, Nathaniel 1782-1855 *Alli, Alli Sup, DcAmA, DcNAA*
Goodwin, P A *Alli*
Goodwin, Peter *Alli*
Goodwin, Philip d1699? *Alli*
Goodwin, Richard M 1913- *ConAu 29, WrD 1976*
Goodwin, Ruby Berkley 1903- *BlkAW*
Goodwin, Simon *Alli*
Goodwin, Stephen 1943- *ConAu 57, DrAF 1976*
Goodwin, T *Alli, BiDLA*
Goodwin, Thomas *Alli, Alli Sup, BiDLA, Chmbr 1*
Goodwin, Thomas 1600-1680? *Alli, EvLB*
Goodwin, Thomas Aiken 1818-1906 *Alli Sup, IndAu 1816*
Goodwin, Thomas G *Alli Sup*

Goodwin, Thomas Shepard *Alli Sup*
Goodwin, Trevor Walworth 1916- *Au&Wr, WrD 1976*
Goodwin, Una M *Alli Sup*
Goodwin, Walter 1889- *AmSCAP 66*
Goodwin, William *Alli*
Goodwin, William Archer Rutherford 1869-1939 *DcNAA*
Goodwin, William Frederic 1823-1872 *DcNAA*
Goodwin, William Lawton 1856-1941 *DcNAA, WhWNAA*
Goodwin, William Watson 1831-1912 *Alli Sup, DcAmA, DcNAA*
Goodwin-Talcott, Hannah Elizabeth 1827-1893 *DcNAA*
Goodwyn, Alfred George *Alli Sup*
Goodwyn, Christopher *Alli*
Goodwyn, Edmund *Alli, BiDLA*
Goodwyn, Frank 1911- *TexWr*
Goodwyn, H *Alli*
Goodwyn, Henry *Alli Sup*
Goodwyn, John *Alli*
Goodwyn, Lawrence 1928- *ConAu 23*
Goodwyn, Thomas *Alli*
Goody, Joan Edelman 1935- *ConAu 17R*
Goodyear, Aaron *Alli*
Goodyear, Edith *ChPo*
Goodyear, Joseph 1797-1839 *ChPo*
Goodyear, Nolan A 1882- *WhWNAA*
Goodyear, Robert Arthur Hanson 1877?-1948 *MnBBF, WhCL, WhLA*
Goodyear, Stephen Frederick 1915- *Au&Wr, WrD 1976*
Goodyear, Watson Andrews 1838-1891 *Alli Sup, DcNAA*
Goodyear, William Henry 1846-1923 *Alli Sup, AmA, AmA&B, AmLY, BiD&SB, DcAmA, DcNAA, REnAL*
Goodyeare, William *Alli*
Goodykoontz, Colin Brummitt 1855?-1958 *AmA&B, IndAu 1917*
Googe, Barnabe 1540-1594 *BrAu, CasWL, ChPo, Chmbr 1, CrE&SL, DcEuL, DcLEnL, EvLB, NewC, OxEng, REn*
Googe, Barnaby 1540-1594 *Alli, DcEnL*
Gookin, Daniel 1612-1686 *Alli, AmA, AmA&B, BiD&SB, CyAL 1, DcAmA, DcNAA, OxAm, REn, REnAL*
Gookin, Frederick William 1853-1936 *DcNAA*
Gookin, M B *MnBBF*
Gookin, Nathaniel 1687-1734 *Alli, DcNAA*
Gookin, Vincent *Alli*
Gookins, Samuel Barnes 1809-1880 *IndAu 1816*
Goold, Marshall Newton 1881-1935 *DcNAA*
Goold, Nathan 1846-1914 *DcNAA*
Goold, Sam 1893-1931 *AmSCAP 66*
Goold, William 1809-1890 *DcNAA*
Goold, William H *Alli, Alli Sup*
Goold-Adams, Deenagh 1916- *Au&Wr*
Goold-Adams, Richard John Moreton 1916- *Au&Wr, ConAu 13R*
Goolden, Barbara *Au&Wr*
Goolden, Samuel *Alli*
Goolrick, John Tackett 1844-1925 *DcNAA*
Gooneratne, Yasmine 1935- *ConAu 29*
Gooneratne, Yasmine 1936- *ConP 1970*
Goossen, Agnes *ConAu XR*
Goossen, Eugene Coons 1920- *AmA&B*
Goossen, Irvy W 1924- *ConAu 37*
Gopal, Sarvepalli 1923- *WrD 1976*
Gopaleen, Myles Na *LongC, WorAu*
Gopp, C *Alli Sup*
Goran, 'Abdullah 1904-1962 *DcOrL 3*
Goran, Call *ConAu XR*
Goran, Lester 1928- *ConAu 45*
Goran, Morris 1918- *ConAu 1R*
Gorbatov, Alexander V 1891?-1973 *ConAu 45*
Gorbatov, Boris Leontievich 1908-1954 *CasWL, DcRusL, EvEuW, TwCW*
Gorbunov, Ivan Fyodorovich 1831-1895 *CasWL, DcRusL, EvEuW*
Gordan, John D *ChPo*
Gorden, Raymond L 1919- *ConAu 53*
Gordenker, Leon 1923- *ConAu 23*
Gordh, George 1912- *ConAu 13R*
Gordi, Toomi *ChPo*
Gordimer, Nadine 1923- *Au&Wr, CasWL, ConAu 5R, ConLC 3, ConLC 5,*

ConNov 1972, ConNov 1976, NewC, Pen Eng, TwCW, WhTwL, WorAu, WrD 1976
Gordin, Harry Mann 1855-1923 *DcNAA*
Gordin, Jacob 1853-1909 *AmA, CnThe, DcNAA, McGWD, ModWD, REnAL, REnWD*
Gordin, Morris 1893- *WhWNAA*
Gordin, Richard Davis 1928- *ConAu 53*
Gordis, Robert 1908- *AmA&B, Au&Wr, ConAu 13R, WrD 1976*
Gordon *Alli*
Gordon, Lieutenant-Colonel *Alli, BiDLA*
Gordon, Mrs. *BbtC*
Gordon Of Lochinvar *Alli*
Gordon, A H *BbtC*
Gordon, Abraham *Alli*
Gordon, Sir Adam *Alli, BiDLA, BiDLA Sup*
Gordon, Adam Lindsay 1833-1870 *Alli Sup, BiD&SB, Br&AmS, BrAu 19, CasWL, ChPo, ChPo S1, ChPo S2, Chmbr 3, DcLEnL, EvLB, NewC, OxEng, Pen Eng, WebEAL*
Gordon, Adoniram Judson 1836-1895 *Alli Sup, DcAmA, DcNAA*
Gordon, Aharon David 1856-1922 *CasWL*
Gordon, Albert I 1903-1968 *ConAu P-1*
Gordon, Alen 1932- *AmSCAP 66*
Gordon, Alex *ConAu XR*
Gordon, Alexander *Alli, Alli Sup, BiDLA*
Gordon, Alexander d1750 *Alli*
Gordon, Sir Alexander Duff *Alli*
Gordon, Alexander George *Alli*
Gordon, Sir Alexander Hamilton- 1817- *Alli Sup*
Gordon, Alexander McGregor Rose *ChPo S2*
Gordon, Alfred 1874- *WhWNAA*
Gordon, Alvin J 1912- *ConAu 33*
Gordon, Ambrose, Jr. 1920- *ConAu 33*
Gordon, Andrew 1712-1751 *Alli*
Gordon, Andrew 1828-1887 *DcNAA*
Gordon, Andrew Robertson *OxCan*
Gordon, Angela *ConAu XR*
Gordon, Angela 1880-1936 *ChPo S2*
Gordon, Ann 1885- *WhWNAA*
Gordon, Anna Adams 1853-1931 *DcNAA*
Gordon, Anthony *Alli, BiDLA*
Gordon, Antoinette K 1892?-1975 *ConAu 57*
Gordon, Archibald D 1848-1895 *BbD, BiD&SB, DcAmA*
Gordon, Armistead Churchill 1855-1931 *Alli Sup, AmA&B, AmLY, BiD&SB, BiDSA, ChPo, ChPo S1, DcAmA, DcNAA, WhWNAA*
Gordon, Armistead Churchill, Jr. 1897-1953 *AmA&B*
Gordon, Arthur 1912- *ConAu 5R*
Gordon, Arthur Hamilton 1829-1912 *OxCan*
Gordon, Bernard *Alli*
Gordon, Bernard Ludwig 1931- *ConAu 29*
Gordon, C A *Alli*
Gordon, C L *Alli Sup*
Gordon, Caroline 1895- *AmA&B, AmNov, AmWr, CasWL, CatA 1952, ConAu P-1, ConLC 6, ConNov 1972, ConNov 1976, CyWA, DrAF 1976, ModAL Sup, OxAm, Pen Am, RAdv 1, REn, REnAL, TwCA, TwCA Sup, WrD 1976*
Gordon, Charles *BlkAW*
Gordon, Sir Charles, Baron Meldrum 1847- *Alli Sup*
Gordon, Charles Alexander *Alli, Alli Sup*
Gordon, Charles George 1833-1885 *Alli Sup, NewC, REn*
Gordon, Charles S *ChPo S2*
Gordon, Charles William 1860-1937 *BiD&SB, CanNov, CanWr, Chmbr 3, DcLEnL, DcNAA, EvLB, LongC, NewC, OxAm, OxCan, REnAL, TwCA, TwCA Sup, WhWNAA*
Gordon, Clarence 1835-1920 *Alli Sup, BiD&SB, DcAmA, DcNAA*
Gordon, Colonel H R *AmA&B, YABC 1*
Gordon, Cosmo Reid *Alli Sup*
Gordon, Cyrus Herzel 1908- *ConAu 1R, WrD 1976*
Gordon, D *Alli*
Gordon, D I 1930- *Au&Wr*

Gordon, Dane R 1925- *ConAu 33*
Gordon, Daniel M 1845-1925 *Alli Sup,*
DcNAA, OxCan
Gordon, David 1820-1893 *PoIre*
Gordon, David Cole 1922- *ConAu 25*
Gordon, Diana R 1938- *ConAu 49*
Gordon, Donald *ConAu XR, WrD 1976*
Gordon, Donald Craigie 1911- *ConAu 17R,*
WrD 1976
Gordon, Donald Ramsay 1929- *ConAu 37,*
WrD 1976
Gordon, Dorothy 1893- *AmA&B, AuBYP,*
ChPo S1
Gordon, Lady Duff 1821-1869 *Chmbr 3,*
DcEnL
Gordon, Lady Duff ALSO Gordon, Lucie
Gordon, Duncan *Alli, BiDLA*
Gordon, Edmund Wyatt 1921- *ConAu 37,*
LivBAA
Gordon, Edwin 1927- *ConAu 17R*
Gordon, Edyth Mae *BlkAW*
Gordon, Eleanor Lytle 1835-1917 *DcNAA*
Gordon, Elizabeth 1866-1922 *AmLY, CarSB,*
ChPo, ChPo S1, DcNAA
Gordon, Elizabeth 1907- *AmA&B*
Gordon, Elizabeth Putnam 1851-1933 *DcNAA*
Gordon, Ernest 1916- *Au&Wr, ConAu 1R,*
WrD 1976
Gordon, Esther Saranga 1935- *ConAu 53,*
SmATA 10
Gordon, Ethel Edison 1915- *ConAu 53,*
WrD 1976
Gordon, Eugene 1890- *BlkAW, WhWNAA*
Gordon, Francis *Alli*
Gordon, Francis Hogg 1853- *ChPo*
Gordon, Francis S d1882 *PoIre*
Gordon, Frank *Alli Sup*
Gordon, Frederick *CarSB, ConAu 19,*
SmATA 1
Gordon, Frederick Charles 1856-1924 *ChPo*
Gordon, Fritz *ConAu XR, WrD 1976*
Gordon, Gary *ConAu XR*
Gordon, Geoffrey *MnBBF*
Gordon, George *Alli, Alli Sup, BiDLA,*
ChPo S2
Gordon, George A 1853-1929 *AmA&B,*
DcAmA, DcNAA, WhWNAA
Gordon, George Byron 1870-1927 *AmA&B,*
AmLY, DcNAA
Gordon, George Byron 1911- *ConAu 33*
Gordon, George Campbell *Alli*
Gordon, George Henry 1823-1886 *Alli Sup,*
DcAmA, DcNAA
Gordon, George N 1822-1861 *BbtC*
Gordon, George N 1926- *ConAu 1R,*
WrD 1976
Gordon, George Noel, Lord Byron 1788-1824
CriT 2, MouLC 2
Gordon, George Stuart 1881-1942 *ChPo*
Gordon, Georgina *Alli Sup*
Gordon, Georgina Jane *ChPo S1*
Gordon, Gerald 1909- *Au&Wr, CasWL,*
ConAu P-1
Gordon, Giles Alexander Esme 1940- *ConAu 41,*
ConP 1970, ConP 1975, WrD 1976
Gordon, Gordon 1912- *Au&Wr, ConAu 5R,*
EncM&D, IndAu 1917
Gordon, Grace *ChPo*
Gordon, Lord Granville Armyne 1856- *Alli Sup,*
ChPo
Gordon, Guanetta Stewart *ConAu 37*
Gordon, H *Alli Sup*
Gordon, Hal 1910- *AmSCAP 66*
Gordon, Hampden Charles 1885- *ChPo S1*
Gordon, Hanford Lennox 1836-1920 *Alli Sup,*
ChPo S2, DcNAA
Gordon, Harold J, Jr. 1919- *ConAu 33,*
WrD 1976
Gordon, Harry 1925- *ConAu XR*
Gordon, Harry Allen 1883-1947 *DcNAA*
Gordon, Hastings *Alli Sup*
Gordon, Henry *Alli Sup, BbtC*
Gordon, Henry Alfred 1925- *ConAu 53*
Gordon, Henry Doddridge *Alli Sup*
Gordon, Sir Henry William 1818-1887 *Alli Sup*
Gordon, Homer King 1896- *WhWNAA*
Gordon, Huntly 1898- *Au&Wr*
Gordon, Ian *ConAu XR*

Gordon, Ian Alistair 1908- *ConAu 25,*
WrD 1976
Gordon, Ida L 1904- *ConAu 33*
Gordon, Ida L 1907- *WrD 1976*
Gordon, Irving 1915- *AmSCAP 66*
Gordon, Irwin Leslie 1888-1954 *AmA&B*
Gordon, J *Alli, Alli Sup*
Gordon, J W *ChPo*
Gordon, James *Alli, Alli Sup, BiDLA,*
BiDSA
Gordon, James 1543-1620 *Alli*
Gordon, James 1553-1641 *Alli*
Gordon, James 1833-1912 *DcNAA*
Gordon, James 1918- *ConAu 61*
Gordon, James Bentley *Alli*
Gordon, James D d1872 *BbtC, DcNAA*
Gordon, James Edward *Alli Sup*
Gordon, James Edward Henry *Alli Sup*
Gordon, James Frederick Skinner *Alli Sup*
Gordon, James Lindsay 1860?-1904 *AmA&B,*
BiDSA, DcNAA
Gordon, James Logan 1858-1930 *DcNAA*
Gordon, Janet *Alli Sup, LongC, TwCA Sup*
Gordon, Jean *ChPo S1*
Gordon, Jessie *ChPo S1*
Gordon, John *Alli, Alli Sup, BiDLA,*
WhWNAA
Gordon, John d1793 *Alli*
Gordon, John 1850-1923 *DcNAA*
Gordon, John 1890- *Au&Wr*
Gordon, John 1925- *ConAu 25, SmATA 6*
Gordon, Mrs. John *Alli Sup*
Gordon, John Brown 1832-1904 *AmA&B,*
BiDSA, DcAmA, DcNAA
Gordon, John Fraser 1916- *Au&Wr,*
WrD 1976
Gordon, John Henry *Alli Sup*
Gordon, John M *Alli Sup*
Gordon, John Steele 1944- *ConAu 57*
Gordon, John William *WrD 1976*
Gordon, Jonathan W 1820-1887 *IndAu 1816,*
PoIre
Gordon, Joseph *Alli Sup*
Gordon, Joseph 1819-1858 *OhA&B*
Gordon, Joseph Claybaugh 1842-1903 *DcNAA*
Gordon, Judah Loeb 1830-1892 *EuA*
Gordon, Julien *AmA&B, BiD&SB, DcAmA,*
DcNAA
Gordon, Kate *Alli Sup*
Gordon, Katherine *ChPo*
Gordon, Ken *BlkAW*
Gordon, Laura DeForce 1838-1907 *DcNAA*
Gordon, Leland J 1897- *ConAu 41*
Gordon, Leonard 1935- *ConAu 53*
Gordon, Leonard A 1938- *ConAu 37*
Gordon, Leonard H D 1928- *ConAu 29*
Gordon, Leslie Howard *ChPo, ChPo S2*
Gordon, Lew *ConAu XR*
Gordon, Lewis *Alli*
Gordon, Lillian L 1925- *ConAu 29*
Gordon, Lois G 1938- *ConAu 33, WrD 1976*
Gordon, Loudon Harcourt *Alli*
Gordon, Loudoun Harcourt *BiDLA*
Gordon, Lady Lucie Duff 1821-1869 *Alli,*
Alli Sup
Gordon, Lucie ALSO Gordon, Lady Duff
Gordon, Lydia L *Alli Sup*
Gordon, M *Alli Sup*
Gordon, Mack 1904-1959 *AmSCAP 66*
Gordon, Margaret 1868- *AmA&B, WhWNAA*
Gordon, Margaret Anna 1939- *ChPo S2,*
IlBYP, IlCB 1966, SmATA 9
Gordon, Margaret Maria *Alli Sup*
Gordon, Margery *ChPo*
Gordon, Marquis Lafayette 1843-1900 *DcAmA,*
DcNAA
Gordon, May E 1840-1921 *OhA&B*
Gordon, Michael *PoIre*
Gordon, Michael 1940- *ConAu 41*
Gordon, Mildred 1912- *Au&Wr, ConAu 5R,*
EncM&D
Gordon, Mitchell 1925- *ConAu 5R,*
WrD 1976
Gordon, Myron J 1920- *ConAu 5R*
Gordon, N M d1871 *Alli, Alli Sup*
Gordon, Neal MacDougal d1871 *DcNAA*
Gordon, Neil *EvLB, LongC, TwCA,*
TwCA Sup

Gordon, Neil E 1886- *WhWNAA*
Gordon, Nina *ChPo*
Gordon, Noah 1926- *ConAu 17R*
Gordon, Oakley Junior 1922- *IndAu 1917*
Gordon, Oliver *ConAu XR*
Gordon, Patricia 1904- *AmA&B*
Gordon, Patricia 1909- *ConAu 21*
Gordon, Patrick *Alli*
Gordon, Patrick 1644-1736 *DcNAA*
Gordon, Percival Hector 1884- *ConAu 41*
Gordon, Percy *Alli Sup*
Gordon, Peter *ConAu XR*
Gordon, Philip 1894- *AmSCAP 66*
Gordon, Pryse Lockhart *Alli*
Gordon, Ralph 1863- *WhWNAA*
Gordon, Ray *WrD 1976*
Gordon, Rex *Au&Wr, ConAu XR,*
WrD 1976
Gordon, Richard 1921- *Au&Wr, MnBBF,*
TwCW
Gordon, Richard L 1934- *ConAu 29*
Gordon, Robert *Alli, Alli Sup*
Gordon, Robert d1650? *Alli*
Gordon, Sir Robert *Alli*
Gordon, Robert A 1908- *ConAu 5R*
Gordon, Robert C 1921- *ConAu 5R*
Gordon, Robert C 1941- *AmSCAP 66*
Gordon, Robert Hunter 1815?-1857 *PoIre*
Gordon, Robert J 1911- *AmSCAP 66*
Gordon, Ross *Alli Sup*
Gordon, Ruth 1896- *AmA&B*
Gordon, S S *MnBBF*
Gordon, Samuel *Alli Sup*
Gordon, Samuel Dickey 1859-1936 *AmLY,*
OhA&B
Gordon, Sanford D 1924- *ConAu 33*
Gordon, Selma *ConAu XR, SmATA 3*
Gordon, Seton 1886- *WhLA*
Gordon, Sol 1923- *ConAu 53*
Gordon, Stanley *MnBBF*
Gordon, Stewart *AuBYP, ConAu XR,*
WrD 1976
Gordon, Susan Joan 1942- *ChPo S2*
Gordon, Suzanne 1945- *ConAu 49*
Gordon, Sydney 1914- *Au&Wr, ConAu 29,*
WrD 1976
Gordon, T *Alli*
Gordon, Taylor 1893-1971 *BlkAW*
Gordon, Theodore J 1930- *ConAu 17R*
Gordon, Thomas *Alli, BiDLA*
Gordon, Thomas 1684?-1750 *Alli*
Gordon, Thomas 1918- *ConAu 29, WrD 1976*
Gordon, Thomas Edward *Alli Sup*
Gordon, Thomas F 1781-1860? *Alli, DcAmA,*
DcNAA
Gordon, Tom *ConAu XR, MnBBF*
Gordon, Violet *WhWNAA*
Gordon, W Ireland *Alli Sup*
Gordon, W J *Alli Sup, ChPo, MnBBF*
Gordon, W Murray *MnBBF*
Gordon, Walter Kelly 1930- *ConAu 33*
Gordon, Wendell 1916- *ConAu 17R*
Gordon, William *Alli, Alli Sup*
Gordon, William 1728-1807 *Alli, AmA&B,*
BiDLA, DcAmA, DcNAA, OxAm
Gordon, William 1801-1849 *Alli*
Gordon, William 1857- *ChPo, ChPo S1*
Gordon, William 1863- *WhLA*
Gordon, William Clark 1865-1936 *DcNAA*
Gordon, William Henry Barefield 1906- *BlkAW*
Gordon, William John *Alli Sup*
Gordon, William Robert 1811-1896? *Alli Sup,*
DcAmA, DcNAA
Gordon, William St. Clair 1858-1924 *DcNAA*
Gordon, William Steward 1868-1948 *OhA&B*
Gordon, William Thomas *Alli Sup*
Gordon, Wilmer Ingalls 1860-1943 *OhA&B*
Gordon, Yehuda Leib 1830-1892 *CasWL,*
Pen Eur
Gordon-Brown, Ian Selby 1925- *Au&Wr*
Gordon Clark, A A *LongC*
Gordon-Cumming, Constance Frederica 1837-
Alli Sup, BiD&SB
Gordon-Roby, Ola *ChPo*
Gordon-Stables, William 1840- *BiD&SB*
Gordon-Walker, Patrick Chrestien 1907-
Au&Wr, ConAu 29, WrD 1976
Gordone, Charles 1925- *AmA&B, BlkAW,*

ConDr, ConLC 1, ConLC 4, LivBA,
McGWD, WrD 1976
Gordons, The ConAu XR, EncM&D
Gordy, John Pancoast 1851-1908 Alli Sup,
DcAmA, DcNAA, OhA&B
Gordy, Wilbur Fisk 1854-1929 AmA&B,
AmLY, DcAmA, DcNAA
Gore, Albert Augustus Alli Sup
Gore, Anthony BlkAW
Gore, Catherine Grace Frances 1799-1861 Alli,
BbD, BiD&SB, BrAu 19, Chmbr 3,
DcEnA, DcEnL, DcLEnL, EvLB,
HsB&A, NewC, OxEng
Gore, Challiss 1887- WhWNAA
Gore, Charles Alli, Chmbr 3
Gore, Charles 1853-1932 Alli Sup, BiD&SB,
EvLB, LongC, NewC, OxEng, WhLA
Gore, Charles Frederick Alli Sup
Gore, Christopher 1758-1827 Alli, DcNAA
Gore, Constance Florence Margaret Teresa 1919-
Au&Wr
Gore, Francis 1769-1852 OxCan
Gore, Mrs. G ChPo
Gore, George Alli Sup
Gore, Graham OxCan
Gore, Henry Alli
Gore, James Howard 1856-1939 Alli Sup,
BiDSA, DcAmA, DcNAA, WhWNAA
Gore, John Alli, Alli Sup, PoIre
Gore, John Ellard Alli Sup
Gore, John Francis 1885- NewC
Gore, John M ChPo
Gore, Leslie Alli Sup
Gore, Montague Alli, BbtC
Gore, R T Alli
Gore, Russell 1881- WhWNAA
Gore, Thomas 1631-1684 Alli
Gore, Thomas Pryor 1870- BiDSA
Gore, Willard G ChPo S2
Gore, William PoIre
Gore, William Jay 1924- ConAu 9R
Gore-Booth, Constance LongC
Gore-Booth, Eva Selena 1870-1926 ChPo,
DcLEnL, EvLB, LongC, NewC, PoIre
Gore-Booth, Paul Henry 1909- WrD 1976
Gorecki, Jan 1926- ConAu 57
Goree, Father Alli
Goreh, Ellen Lakshmi Alli Sup
Goreh, Nehemiah Alli Sup
Gorelick, Molly C 1920- ConAu 23,
SmATA 9
Gorelik, Mordecai 1899- ConAu 23,
WrD 1976
Gorell, Ronald Gorell Barnes 1884- ChPo,
ChPo S1, ChPo S2, EvLB, WhLA
Gorell Barnes, William Lethbridge 1909-
WrD 1976
Goren, Charles H 1901- AmA&B
Goren, Judith 1933- ConAu 61
Gorenko, Anna Andreyevna 1888- ConAu XR,
DcRusL, EvEuW, WorAu
Gorer, Geoffrey Edgar 1905- Au&Wr,
TwCA Sup
Gores, Joe ConAu XR
Gores, Joseph N 1931- Au&Wr, ConAu 25
Gorey, Edward St. John 1925- ChPo, ChPo S1,
ConAu 5R, IlBYP, IlCB 1966
Gorey, Hays ConAu 57
Gorgani, Fakhroddin As'ad DcOrL 3
Gorgas, Ferdinand James Samuel 1834-1914
Alli Sup, DcAmA, DcNAA
Gorgas, William Crawford 1854-1920 DcNAA
Gorgen, Mary ChPo S2
Gorges, Sir Arthur d1625 Alli, NewC
Gorges, Ferdinando Alli
Gorges, Sir Ferdinando 1566?-1647 Alli, OxAm,
REnAL
Gorges, Grace ChPo, ChPo S1
Gorges, M Alli Sup
Gorges, Mary d1911 ChPo, ChPo S1, PoIre
Gorgey, Gabor 1929- CrCD
Gorgias 483?BC-375?BC CasWL, REn
Gorgias, Johann 1640-1684 OxGer
Gorham, Charles Alfred Alli Sup
Gorham, Charles Orson 1911-1975 AmA&B,
AmNov, ConAu 1R, ConAu 61
Gorham, Elsie Alli Sup, ChPo
Gorham, Francis ChPo S1

Gorham, Frederick Poole 1871-1933 DcNAA
Gorham, George Congdon 1832-1909 DcAmA,
DcNAA
Gorham, George Cornelius Alli
Gorham, George Martyn Alli Sup
Gorham, Henry Stephens Alli Sup
Gorham, Mrs. J C ChPo S2
Gorham, J U 1920- ConAu 53
Gorham, John Alli Sup
Gorham, John d1829 Alli
Gorham, Maurice Anthony Coneys 1902-
Au&Wr, CatA 1952, ConAu 9R
Gorham, Michael AuBYP, ConAu XR,
SmATA 5, WrD 1976
Gorham, Myrtle Campbell BlkAW
Gorham, William Alli
Gorin, Igor 1908- AmSCAP 66
Goring, Colonel Alli
Goring, C Alli, BiDLA
Goring, Hermann 1893-1946 OxGer
Goring, J H ChPo S1
Goring, Jack ChPo S1
Goris, Jan-Albert 1899- ClDMEuL
Gorkin, Jess 1913-1936 AmA&B
Gorky, Arshile 1904-1948 AtlBL, REn
Gorky, Maxim 1868-1936 AtlBL, BiD&SB,
CasWL, ClDMEuL, CnMD, CnMWL,
CnThe, CyWA, DcRusL, EncWL,
EvEuW, McGWD, ModSL 1, ModWD,
OxEng, Pen Eur, RCom, REn, REnWD,
TwCA, TwCA Sup, TwCW, WhTwL
Gorle, James Alli Sup
Gorling, Lars 1931-1966 ConAu 21, ConAu 25
Gorman, Beth ConAu XR
Gorman, Burton William 1907- ConAu 29,
IndAu 1917
Gorman, Ginny ConAu XR, WrD 1976
Gorman, Herbert Sherman 1893-1954 AmA&B,
AmNov, ChPo, ChPo S1, OxAm,
REnAL, TwCA, TwCA Sup, WhWNAA
Gorman, John Andrew 1938- ConAu 41
Gorman, John Berry 1793-1864 BiDSA,
DcNAA
Gorman, John Berry, Jr. 1839- BiDSA
Gorman, Katherine 1899- ConAu 29,
WhWNAA
Gorman, Ossian Daniel 1841- BiDSA
Gorman, Patrick E 1892- AmSCAP 66
Gorman, Ralph 1897-1972 ConAu 37
Gorman, T J MnBBF
Gorman, T Walter 1916?-1972 ConAu 37
Gorman, Terry IlBYP, IlCB 1956
Gorman, Thomas Murray Alli Sup
Gorman, W Gordon Alli Sup
Gormley, Jill Eileen Mary 1932- Au&Wr
Gormley, John J PoIre
Gorn, Janice L 1915- ConAu 53
Gorner, Karl August 1806-1884 BiD&SB
Gorney, Jay 1896- AmSCAP 66
Gorney, Sondra 1918- ConAu 45
Gornfeld, Arkady Georgievich 1867-1944
CasWL
Gornick, Vivian 1935- WrD 1976
Gornicki, Lukasz 1527-1603 CasWL
Gorodetski, Sergey Mitrofanovich 1884-1967
CasWL, DcRusL
Gorody, George 1914- AmSCAP 66
Gorostiza, Carlos 1920- DcCLA
Gorostiza, Jose 1901- CasWL, Pen Am
Gorostiza Y Cepeda, Don Manuel E De
1791-1851 BiD&SB
Gorrell, Robert Mark 1914- ConAu 1R,
IndAu 1917, WrD 1976
Gorres, Mrs. Carl CatA 1947
Gorres, Jakob Joseph Von 1776-1848 DcEuL,
EvEuW
Gorres, Johann Joseph Von 1776-1848 OxGer
Gorres, Joseph Von 1776-1848 BbD, BiD&SB,
CasWL, REn
Gorri, Tobia CasWL
Gorrie, Alexander BbtC
Gorrie, Daniel Alli Sup
Gorrie, David Alli Sup
Gorrie, John 1803-1855 DcNAA
Gorrie, Peter Douglas 1813-1884 Alli, DcAmA,
DcNAA
Gorringe, Henry Honeychurch 1841-1885
Alli Sup, DcAmA, DcNAA

Gorsline, Douglas Warner 1913- AmA&B,
ChPo S1, ConAu 61, IlBYP, IlCB 1956,
IlCB 1966
Gorst, Sir John Eldon 1835- Alli Sup
Gorter, Herman 1864-1927 CasWL, ClDMEuL,
Pen Eur, WorAu
Gorter, Simon 1838-1871 CasWL
Gortner, Ross A, Jr. 1912- ConAu 5R
Gorton, Benjamin 1757?-1836 DcNAA
Gorton, David Allyn 1832-1916 DcAmA,
DcNAA
Gorton, John Alli
Gorton, Mary Jane ChPo S2
Gorton, Richard A 1932- ConAu 57
Gorton, Samuel 1592?-1677 Alli, CyAL 1,
DcAmA, DcNAA, OxAm, REnAL
Goryan, Sirak ConAu XR, LongC
Goschen, Georg Joachim 1752-1828 OxGer
Goschen, George Joachim 1831-1907 Alli Sup,
BiD&SB
Gosdan Alli
Gosden BiDLA
Gosden, Peter Henry John Heather 1927-
Au&Wr
Gose, Elliot B, Jr. 1926- ConAu 33
Gosfield, H Heddingham MnBBF
Gosford, Lord 1776-1849 OxCan
Goshay, Robert C 1931- ConAu 13R
Goshen, Charles E 1916- ConAu 21
Goshorn, Elizabeth 1953- ConAu 61
Goslavski, Maurycy 1802-1834 BiD&SB
Goslicki, Wawrzyniec Grzymala 1530?-1607
CasWL
Goslin, David A 1936- ConAu 9R
Goslin, Omar Pancoast 1899-1942 DcNAA
Goslin, Samuel B Alli Sup
Gosling, J C B 1930- WrD 1976
Gosling, Jane Alli, BiDLA
Gosling, John Neville 1905- ConAu 5R
Gosling, Robert Alli
Gosling, William Flower 1901- Au&Wr,
ConAu 5R, WrD 1976
Gosling, William Gilbert 1863-1930 OxCan
Goslovich, Marianne ConAu XR
Gosman, Frederick Alli Sup
Gosnell, Betty 1921- ConAu XR, WrD 1976
Gosnell, Elizabeth Duke Tucker 1921-
ConAu 29
Gosnell, Harold Foote 1896- AmA&B,
ConAu 41
Gosnell, R E OxCan
Gosnell, R Edward 1860-1931 DcNAA
Gosnell, Samuel PoIre
Gosnell, Thomas Knolles Alli, BiDLA
Goss, Alexander 1814-1872 Alli Sup
Goss, Anthony 1922- Au&Wr
Goss, C C Alli Sup
Goss, Charles Frederic 1852-1930 DcAmA,
DcNAA, OhA&B
Goss, Clay 1946- BlkAW, ConAu 57
Goss, Dwight 1857-1909 DcNAA
Goss, Elbridge Henry 1830-1908 Alli Sup,
DcAmA, DcNAA
Goss, Fred 1873- Br&AmS
Goss, Herbert Alli Sup
Goss, L Allan Alli Sup
Goss, Linda BlkAW
Goss, Madeleine 1892- AmA&B
Goss, Prothesia S Alli
Goss, Robert Charles 1929- IndAu 1917
Goss, Warren Lee 1835-1925 Alli Sup,
AmA&B, AmLY, CarSB, DcAmA,
DcNAA, WhWNAA
Goss, William Calvin 1853?-1923 IndAu 1917
Goss, William Freeman Myrick 1859-1928
Alli Sup, DcNAA
Goss, William Henry Alli Sup
Goss, William Thompson BlkAW
Gossaert, Geerten 1884-1958 CasWL
Gossan, N I Alli Sup
Gosse, Sir Edmund William 1849-1928 Alli Sup,
BbD, BiD&SB, CarSB, CasWL, ChPo,
ChPo S1, ChPo S2, Chmbr 3, CnMWL,
DcEnA, DcEnA Ap, DcEnL, DcLEnL,
EvLB, LongC, ModBL, NewC, OxEng,
Pen Eng, TwCA, TwCA Sup, TwCW,
WebEAL
Gosse, Philip 1879- WhLA

Gosse, Philip Henry 1810-1888 *Alli, Alli Sup, BbD, BbtC, BiD&SB, DcEnL, OxCan*
Gosse, Robert Wilkes *Alli Sup*
Gossec, Francois-Joseph 1734-1829 *OxFr*
Gosselin, Amedee Edmond 1863-1941 *DcNAA*
Gosselin, Andre *OxCan Sup*
Gosselin, Auguste Honore 1843-1917 *DcNAA, OxCan*
Gosselin, Charles *BbtC*
Gosselin, David 1836-1926 *DcNAA*
Gosselin, Leon d1842 *BbtC*
Gosselin, Mary *BbtC*
Gosset, Adelaide L J *ChPo, ChPo S1*
Gosset, Arthur Henry 1854- *Alli Sup*
Gosset, J A *Alli Sup*
Gosset, J M *BiDLA*
Gosset-Tanner *Alli Sup*
Gossett, Margaret *AuBYP*
Gossett, Thomas F 1916- *ConAu 13R*
Gossip, Arthur John 1873- *WhLA*
Gossip, G H D *Alli Sup*
Gossip, John J *ChPo*
Gossip, Robert *Alli Sup*
Gossip, William *BbtC*
Gossman, Lionel 1929- *ConAu 17R*
Gosson, Stephen 1554-1624 *Alli, BiD&SB, BrAu, CasWL, Chmbr 1, CrE&SL, DcEnL, DcEuL, EvLB, NewC, OxEng, Pen Eng*
Gossouin De Metz *CasWL*
Gostelo, Walter *Alli*
Gostelow, Mary 1943- *ConAu 61*
Gostick, Jesse *Alli Sup*
Gosting, Richard 1941- *AmSCAP 66*
Gostling, William 1705-1777 *Alli*
Gostwick, Joseph d1887 *Alli Sup*
Gostwyke, Roger *Alli*
Gostwyke, William *Alli*
Gosvami, Hemcandra 1872-1928 *DcOrL 2*
Gosvenor, Edward *Alli Sup*
Goswell, John *Alli*
Goswold, Paul *Alli*
Gosynhyll, Edward *Alli*
Goszczynski, Severin 1803-1876 *BiD&SB*
Goszczynski, Seweryn 1801-1876 *CasWL*
Gotch, F *Alli Sup*
Gotch, Frederick William 1807- *Alli, Alli Sup*
Gotesky, Rubin 1906- *ConAu 45*
Gothard, Barbara Wallace *Alli Sup*
Gother, John d1704 *Alli*
Gotlieb, Phyllis 1926- *Au&Wr, CanWr, ConAu 13R, ConP 1970, ConP 1975, OxCan, OxCan Sup, WrD 1976*
Gotovac, Vlado 1930- *CasWL*
Gotselin d1098 *Alli, BiB S*
Gotshalk, D W 1901- *AmA&B, ConAu 1R*
Gotshall, William Charles 1870-1935 *DcNAA*
Gott, Charles 1887-1938 *DcNAA*
Gott, Emil 1864-1908 *ClDMEuL*
Gott, John *Alli Sup*
Gott, Richard Willoughby *Au&Wr, WrD 1976*
Gott, Samuel *Alli*
Gotta, Salvatore 1887- *CasWL, EvEuW*
Gottchalk, Laura Riding *ConAmA*
Gottehrer, Barry H 1935- *AmA&B, ConAu 13R*
Gotter, Friedrich Wilhelm 1746-1797 *BiD&SB, CasWL, DcEuL, EvEuW, OxGer*
Gotterer, Malcolm H 1924- *ConAu 37*
Gottesman, Irving I 1930- *ConAu 37*
Gottesman, Ronald 1933- *ConAu 23*
Gottfried Von Neifen *CasWL, OxGer, Pen Eur*
Gottfried Von Strassburg *BbD, BiD&SB, CasWL, CyWA, DcEuL, EuA, EvEuW, OxGer, Pen Eur, RCom, REn*
Gottfried, Alex 1919- *ConAu 1R*
Gottfried, Manfred 1900- *AmA&B*
Gottfried, Martin 1933- *ConAu 23*
Gottfried, Theodore Mark 1928- *ConAu 33*
Gottheil, Gustav 1827-1903 *DcNAA*
Gottheil, Richard James Horatio 1862-1936 *Alli Sup, AmA&B, DcNAA, WhWNAA*
Gotthelf, Jeremias 1797-1854 *BiD&SB, CasWL, EuA, EvEuW, OxGer, Pen Eur, REn*
Gottifredi, Bartolomeo *CasWL*

Gottler, Archie 1896-1959 *AmSCAP 66*
Gottler, Jerome 1915- *AmSCAP 66*
Gottlieb, Adolph 1903-1974 *ConAu 49*
Gottlieb, Bernhardt Stanley 1898- *ConAu 1R*
Gottlieb, Darcy *DrAP 1975*
Gottlieb, Elaine *ConAu 61, DrAF 1976*
Gottlieb, Gerald 1923- *AuBYP, ConAu 5R, SmATA 7*
Gottlieb, Jack 1930- *AmSCAP 66*
Gottlieb, Lois Davidson 1926- *ConAu 17R*
Gottlieb, Louis E 1923- *AmSCAP 66*
Gottlieb, Naomi R 1925- *ConAu 57*
Gottlieb, Robin 1928- *AuBYP, ConAu 1R*
Gottlieb, William P *AuBYP*
Gottliebsen, Ralph Joseph 1910- *Au&Wr*
Gottlober, Abraham 1811-1899 *CasWL, McGWD*
Gottschalk 808?-868? *Pen Eur*
Gottschalk, Alfred Louis Moreau 1873-1918 *DcNAA*
Gottschalk, Laura Riding *AmA&B, ChPo, ConAmA, ConAu XR, WhWNAA, WrD 1976*
Gottschalk, Louis 1899-1975 *AmA&B, Au&Wr, ConAu 13R, ConAu 57*
Gottschalk, Louis A 1916- *ConAu 53*
Gottschalk, Louis Moreau 1829-1869 *OxAm*
Gottschalk, Louis Reichenthal 1899- *TwCA Sup, WhWNAA*
Gottschalk, Paul A 1939- *ConAu 61*
Gottschall, Rudolf Von 1823-1909 *BiD&SB, EvEuW, OxGer*
Gottsched, Johann Christoph 1700-1766 *CasWL, CnThe, DcEuL, EuA, EvEuW, McGWD, OxGer, Pen Eur, REn, REnWD*
Gottsched, Luise Adelgunde 1713-1762 *CasWL, DcEuL, OxGer*
Gottshall, Franklin Henry 1902- *ConAu 5R, WrD 1976*
Gottuso, Tony 1916- *AmSCAP 66*
Gotwals, John W, III 1938- *AmSCAP 66*
Gotwals, Vernon 1924- *ConAu 5R*
Gotz, Ignacio L 1933- *ConAu XR, WrD 1976*
Gotz, Johann Nikolaus 1721-1781 *DcEuL, EvEuW, OxGer, Pen Eur*
Goucher, John Franklin 1847?-1922 *AmA&B, DcNAA*
Goud, Anne 1917- *ConAu 61*
Goudeau, Lee, Jr. 1936- *AmSCAP 66*
Goudelin, Pierre *CasWL*
Goudey, Alice E 1898- *AuBYP, ThBJA*
Goudge, Elizabeth 1900- *Au&Wr, AuBYP, ChPo, ConAu 5R, LongC, NewC, REn, SmATA 2, ThBJA, TwCA, TwCA Sup, TwCW, WhCL, WrD 1976*
Goudie, Andrew Shaw 1945- *ConAu 49*
Goudl, William M *Alli*
Goudy, Frederic William 1865-1947 *AmA&B, DcNAA, OxAm, REnAL, WhWNAA*
Goudy, Henry *Alli Sup*
Goue, August Siegfried Von 1742-1789 *OxGer*
Gouffe, Alphonse *Alli Sup*
Gougar, Helen Mar Jackson 1843-1907 *DcNAA, IndAu 1816*
Gougaud, Louis 1877-1941 *CatA 1947, WhLA*
Gouge, Alexander *Alli Sup*
Gouge, Henry Albert *Alli Sup*
Gouge, Orson *ConAu XR*
Gouge, Thomas 1605-1681 *Alli*
Gouge, William 1575-1653 *Alli*
Gouge, William M 1796-1863 *Alli, AmA, DcAmA, DcNAA*
Gouger, Henry *Alli Sup*
Gough, Alfred William 1862- *WhLA*
Gough, Archibald Edward *Alli Sup*
Gough, Barry Morton 1938- *ConAu 61, OxCan Sup*
Gough, Benjamin 1805-1877 *Alli Sup, ChPo, ChPo S1, ChPo S2, PoCh*
Gough, C *Alli Sup*
Gough, C J *Alli*
Gough, Catherine 1931- *ConAu 25*
Gough, Clement *PoIre*
Gough, Edward *Alli Sup*
Gough, Edward W *Alli Sup*
Gough, H T *PoIre*
Gough, Hazel Ketcham *WhWNAA*
Gough, Henry 1821- *Alli Sup*

Gough, Herbert *Alli Sup*
Gough, J *Alli, BiDLA*
Gough, John *Alli*
Gough, John B 1817-1886 *Alli, Alli Sup, AmA, AmA&B, BiD&SB, DcAmA, DcNAA, OxAm*
Gough, John Wiedhofft 1900- *Au&Wr, ConAu 13R, WrD 1976*
Gough, Kathleen *ConAu XR*
Gough, L *TexWr*
Gough, Philip 1908- *ChPo, IlCB 1956*
Gough, Richard 1735-1809 *Alli, CasWL, Chmbr 2, EvLB*
Gough, Strickland *Alli*
Gough, T T *Alli Sup*
Gough, Vera *ConAu 25*
Gough, William *Alli*
Goughe, Alex *Alli*
Goughe, Hugh *Alli*
Gougov, Nikola Delchev 1914- *ConAu 45*
Gouin, L F *BbtC*
Gouin, Sir Lomer 1861-1929 *OxCan*
Gouin, Paul-Neree 1898- *OxCan*
Gouinlock, G *BbtC*
Goujon, Jean 1510?-1565? *AtlBL, OxFr*
Gouland, Henry Godfrey *Alli Sup*
Goulart, Frances Sheridan 1938- *ConAu 57*
Goulart, Ron 1933- *ConAu 25, SmATA 6*
Goulbourn, Edward Meyrick 1818- *DcEnL*
Goulbourne, Carmin Auld 1912- *BlkAW*
Goulbourne, Edward *BiDLA*
Goulburn, Edward *Alli, Br&AmS*
Goulburn, Edward Meyrick 1818- *Alli, Alli Sup, BiD&SB*
Gould, A Pearce *Alli Sup*
Gould, Alan *EncM&D, WorAu*
Gould, Alfred Ernest 1909- *Au&Wr, ConAu 5R*
Gould, Alice Lawry *ChPo*
Gould, Augustus Addison 1805-1866 *Alli, Alli Sup, DcAmA, DcNAA*
Gould, Beatrice Blackmar 1898- *AmA&B, ConAu 25*
Gould, Benjamin Apthorp 1787-1859 *DcAmA, DcNAA*
Gould, Benjamin Apthorp 1824-1896 *Alli, Alli Sup, BiD&SB, DcAmA, DcNAA*
Gould, Benjamin Apthorp 1870-1937 *DcNAA*
Gould, Bernard *LongC*
Gould, Bruce *ChPo S1*
Gould, Bruce 1898- *WhWNAA*
Gould, Bruce Grant 1942- *ConAu 45*
Gould, Cecil 1918- *ConAu 21*
Gould, Charles *Alli Sup*
Gould, Charles Bruce 1898- *AmA&B*
Gould, Charles Newton 1868-1949 *OhA&B*
Gould, Charles Winthrop 1849-1931 *DcNAA*
Gould, Chester 1900- *EncM&D*
Gould, Clarence Pembroke 1884- *OhA&B, WhWNAA*
Gould, Cora Smith 1855-1945 *ChPo, DcNAA*
Gould, Daniel 1625?-1716 *DcNAA*
Gould, Danny 1921- *AmSCAP 66*
Gould, Dayton Thomas 1847-1943 *OhA&B*
Gould, Douglas Parsons 1919- *ConAu 1R*
Gould, E E *ChPo S2*
Gould, E W *BiDSA*
Gould, Edith Kingdon *ChPo*
Gould, Edward Baring- d1872 *Alli Sup*
Gould, Edward E 1911- *AmSCAP 66*
Gould, Edward Sherman 1808?-1885 *Alli, Alli Sup, AmA, AmA&B, BiD&SB, CyAL 2, DcAmA, DcNAA, OxAm*
Gould, Edward Sherman 1837-1905 *DcNAA*
Gould, Edwin *Alli Sup*
Gould, Elgin Ralston Lovell 1860-1915 *DcAmA, DcNAA*
Gould, Elizabeth 1904- *AmSCAP 66*
Gould, Elizabeth Lincoln d1914 *CarSB, ChPo, DcNAA*
Gould, Elizabeth Porter 1848-1906 *ChPo S1, ChPo S2, DcNAA*
Gould, Ezra Palmer 1841-1900 *Alli Sup, DcAmA, DcNAA*
Gould, Felix *ConAu P-1*
Gould, Florence *Alli Sup*
Gould, Francis Carruthers 1844-1925 *ChPo, ChPo S2, NewC*

Gould, Frederick James 1855- *WhLA*
Gould, G Lydia *ChPo*
Gould, George 1818-1882 *Alli Sup*
Gould, George Milbry 1848-1922 *AmA&B, DcAmA, DcNAA, OhA&B*
Gould, Gerald 1885-1936 *ChPo, ChPo S1, DcLEnL, EvLB, ModBL, NewC, WhLA*
Gould, Hannah Flagg 1789-1865 *Alli, AmA, AmA&B, BbD, BiD&SB, ChPo, ChPo S1, CyAL 2, DcAmA, DcNAA, FemPA*
Gould, Harris P 1871- *WhWNAA*
Gould, Harrison *MnBBF*
Gould, Jack 1914- *AmA&B*
Gould, Jack 1917- *AmSCAP 66*
Gould, James 1770-1838? *Alli, CyAL 2, DcAmA, DcNAA*
Gould, James 1922- *ConAu 33, WrD 1976*
Gould, James Warren 1924- *ConAu 5R*
Gould, Jay 1836-1892 *DcNAA*
Gould, Jay R 1906- *ConAu 45*
Gould, Jean Rosalind 1909- *AuBYP, OhA&B*
Gould, Jean Rosalind 1919- *ConAu 5R, WrD 1976*
Gould, Jeannie T *Alli Sup*
Gould, John 1804-1881 *Alli, Alli Sup, BiD&SB*
Gould, John 1908- *REnAL, TwCA Sup*
Gould, John 1936- *Au&Wr*
Gould, John A 1944- *ConAu 57*
Gould, John M *Alli Sup*
Gould, John Melville 1848-1909 *DcNAA*
Gould, John Thomas 1908- *AmA&B, ChPo S2*
Gould, John W 1814-1838 *Alli, BiD&SB, CyAL 2, DcAmA, DcNAA*
Gould, Joseph *Alli Sup, OxCan*
Gould, Joseph E 1912- *ConAu 9R*
Gould, Josiah *Alli Sup*
Gould, Josiah B 1928- *ConAu 45*
Gould, Julian 1915- *AmSCAP 66*
Gould, Kenneth Miller 1895-1969 *AmA&B*
Gould, Laura Stedman *AmA&B*
Gould, Lettie *ConAu XR*
Gould, Lewis L 1939- *ConAu 41*
Gould, Lilian 1920- *ConAu 49, SmATA 6*
Gould, Lois *AmA&B, ConLC 4, DrAF 1976, WrD 1976*
Gould, Lucius D 1814- *Alli, Alli Sup*
Gould, M T *Alli*
Gould, Marion K *WhWNAA*
Gould, Mark 1811-1896 *DcNAA*
Gould, Mary Earle 1885- *ConAu 5R*
Gould, Maurice M 1909- *ConAu 5R, WrD 1976*
Gould, Michael *ConAu XR*
Gould, Morton 1913- *AmSCAP 66*
Gould, Nathaniel *BbtC*
Gould, Nathaniel 1857-1919 *Br&AmS, DcLEnL, EvLB, MnBBF, OxEng*
Gould, Nathaniel Duren 1781-1864 *Alli, DcAmA, DcNAA*
Gould, Mrs. O F 1859- *WhWNAA*
Gould, Peter Robin 1932- *ConAu 1R, WrD 1976*
Gould, R DeTracy *Alli Sup*
Gould, Richard 1660?-1709 *CasWL*
Gould, Richard A 1939- *ConAu 53*
Gould, Robert *Alli*
Gould, Robert F 1836- *Alli Sup, BiD&SB*
Gould, Robert Howe *Alli Sup*
Gould, Ronald 1904- *WrD 1976*
Gould, Sabine Baring- 1834- *Alli Sup*
Gould, Sarah *Alli Sup*
Gould, Stephen *EncM&D*
Gould, Sylvester Clark 1840-1909 *DcNAA*
Gould, Theodore A *ChPo*
Gould, Thomas R *Alli Sup*
Gould, Thomas Ridgeway 1818-1881 *DcNAA*
Gould, Tracy *Alli Sup*
Gould, W T *Alli*
Gould, Wesley Larson 1917- *ConAu 1R*
Gould, William *Alli, Alli Sup*
Goulde, William *Alli*
Goulden, Joseph C 1934- *ConAu 17R, WrD 1976*
Goulden, Mark *Au&Wr*
Goulder, Grace *ConAu XR*
Goulding, Edmund 1891-1959 *AmSCAP 66*

Goulding, Francis Robert 1810-1881 *Alli, Alli Sup, AmA&B, BiD&SB, BiDSA, CarSB, DcAmA, DcNAA, REnAL*
Goulding, Laurence G 1838- *PoIre*
Goulding, Mina E *Alli Sup*
Gouldman, Francis *Alli*
Gouldner, Alvin Ward 1920- *ConAu 13R*
Gouldsborough, John *Alli*
Gouldsbury, Cullen *Chmbr 3*
Gouldsbury, Henry Cullen 1881-1916 *DcLEnL*
Gouled, Vivian G 1911- *ConAu 41*
Goulet, Denis A 1931- *ConAu 41*
Goulet, Robert 1924- *ConAu 1R, OxCan*
Goulett, Harlan M 1927- *ConAu 21*
Gouley, John William Severin 1832-1920 *Alli Sup, DcAmA, DcNAA*
Goulianos, Joan Rodman 1939- *ConAu 49*
Goullart, Peter 1902- *Au&Wr, ConAu P-1*
Goulson, Cary *OxCan Sup*
Goulson, Theodore d1632 *Alli*
Goulston, Theodore d1632 *Alli*
Goulstone, Mrs. S *Alli Sup*
Goulter, Eliza Eleanor *Alli Sup*
Gounod, Charles Francois 1818-1893 *AtlBL, NewC, OxFr, REn*
Goupil, Rene 1608-1642 *OxCan*
Goupy, Joseph 1680?-1763? *BkIE*
Goupy, Louis *BkIE*
Gouraud, Aimee Crocker 1863-1941 *DcNAA*
Gouraud, George Fauvel 1872- *ChPo S2, DcAmA*
Gourdie, Thomas 1913- *Au&Wr, ConAu 1R, WrD 1976*
Gourdon *Alli*
Gourdon, Sir Robert *Alli*
Gourevitch, Doris-Jeanne *ConAu 17R*
Gourgaud, Baron Gaspard 1783-1852 *OxFr*
Gourlay, John *Alli, BiDLA*
Gourlay, John Edgar Reginald 1854-1923 *DcNAA*
Gourlay, John Lowry 1821-1904 *DcNAA*
Gourlay, Robert Fleming 1778-1863 *Alli, BbtC, BiDLA, DcLEnL, DcNAA, OxCan*
Gourlay, William *Alli, BbtC, BiDLA*
Gourley, G Douglas 1911- *ConAu 1R*
Gourley, Joseph Harvey 1883- *WhWNAA*
Gourlie, John H, Jr. *Alli Sup*
Gourlie, Norah Dundas *Au&Wr, ConAu P-1*
Gourmont, Remy De 1858-1915 *AtlBL, CasWL, CIDMEuL, CyWA, EncWL, LongC, ModRL, OxFr, Pen Eur, REn, TwCA, TwCA Sup*
Gournay, Jean Claude Marie Vincent De 1712-1759 *DcEuL*
Gournay, Marie DeJars, Demoiselle De 1566-1645 *DcEuL, OxFr*
Gournay, Vincent De 1712-1759 *OxFr*
Gourville, Jean Herault De 1625-1703 *OxFr*
Gousha, Mrs. Joseph R *AmA&B, AmNov XR, OhA&B*
Goutard, Adolphe 1893- *Au&Wr*
Gouverneur, Marion d1913 *DcNAA*
Gouvion-Saint-Cyr, Laurent *OxFr*
Gouvy, Gertrude 1899-1960 *OhA&B*
Gouwens, Teunis E 1886- *WhWNAA*
Govan, Christine Noble 1897- *WrD 1976*
Govan, Christine Noble 1898- *AmNov, AuBYP, ConAu 1R, SmATA 9*
Govan, Donald D 1945- *BlkAW*
Govan, Mary Christine Noble 1897- *Au&Wr*
Govan, Mary Christine Noble 1898- *AmA&B*
Govan, Oswald *BlkAW*
Govan, Thomas P 1907- *ConAu 45*
Govan, William *Alli Sup*
Govan-Stewart, Isabel Rosie 1900- *Au&Wr*
Gove, Charles Augustus 1854-1933 *DcNAA*
Gove, Mary Sargeant *DcNAA*
Gove, Philip Babcock 1902-1972 *ConAu 37, ConAu P-1*
Gove, Richard *Alli*
Gove, Samuel K 1923- *ConAu 33*
Govean, Felice 1819- *BiD&SB*
Goveanus, Thomas *Alli*
Goveia, Elsa Vesta 1925- *ConAu 21, WrD 1976*
Goveneche, Gabriel *ConAu XR*
Gover, Charles E d1872 *Alli Sup*
Gover, E T *Alli Sup*

Gover, Robert 1929- *AmA&B, ConAu 9R, ConNov 1972, ConNov 1976, DrAF 1976, Pen Am, WhTwL, WorAu, WrD 1976*
Govern, Elaine 1939- *ConAu 53*
Govern, Rena Greenlee *BlkAW*
Govett, R *Alli*
Govett, R, Jr. *Alli*
Govett, Robert *Alli Sup*
Govett, Thomas Romaine 1837-1885 *Alli Sup*
Govinda, Anagarika 1898- *Au&Wr, ConAu 23*
Govindagraj *DcOrL 2*
Govoni, Albert P 1914- *ConAu 53*
Govoni, Corrado 1884-1965 *CasWL, Pen Eur, WhTwL*
Govoni, Laura E 1914- *ConAu 33*
Govorchin, Gerald Gilbert 1912- *ConAu 13R*
Govsky, John M 1921- *AmSCAP 66*
Gow, Alexander M *Alli Sup*
Gow, Andrew Sydenham 1886- *ChPo*
Gow, Donald 1920- *ConAu 41*
Gow, Elizabeth *Alli Sup*
Gow, George Coleman 1860-1938 *DcAmA, DcNAA*
Gow, Gordon *WrD 1976*
Gow, Gregson *Alli Sup*
Gow, Henry 1861- *WhLA*
Gow, James *Alli Sup*
Gow, James 1814- *ChPo S1*
Gow, James 1854-1923 *ChPo S1*
Gow, John *PoIre*
Gow, John Milne 1844-1898 *DcNAA, OxCan*
Gow, Margaret M 1920- *Au&Wr*
Gow, Mary L *ChPo*
Gow, Minnie M *ChPo*
Gow, Neil *Alli*
Gow, Ronald 1897- *Au&Wr, ChPo S2, ConAu 25, ConDr, DcLEnL, WrD 1976*
Gowa, Juliette *Alli Sup*
Gowan, A H P *Alli Sup*
Gowan, Elsie Park *OxCan*
Gowan, James R *BbtC*
Gowan, John Curtis 1912- *ConAu 13R, WrD 1976*
Gowan, Ogle Robert 1796-1876 *BbtC, DcNAA*
Gowan, Peter *Alli Sup*
Gowan, Walter Edward *Alli Sup*
Gowanlock, Theresa *OxCan*
Gowans, Alan 1923- *AmA&B, ConAu 1R*
Gowans, Sir James 1821- *Alli Sup*
Gowans, William 1803-1870 *Alli Sup, AmA&B, DcNAA*
Gowar, F R *Alli*
Goward, Gladys McFadden *BlkAW*
Gowen, Emmett 1902- *AmA&B, Au&Wr, ConAu P-1*
Gowen, Herbert Henry 1864- *AmLY, WhWNAA*
Gowen, James A 1928- *ConAu 17R*
Gowen, John Knowles, Jr. 1894- *WhWNAA*
Gower *Alli*
Gower, Alfred Rowland *Alli Sup*
Gower, Arthur Francis Gresham Leveson- 1851- *Alli Sup*
Gower, Bailey *Alli Sup*
Gower, Craven *MnBBF*
Gower, Foote *Alli*
Gower, Granville W G Leveson- 1838- *Alli Sup*
Gower, Herschel 1919- *ConAu 5R*
Gower, Humphrey *Alli*
Gower, John *Alli*
Gower, John 1330?-1408 *Alli, BiD&SB, BrAu, CanWr, Chmbr 1, CnE&AP, CriT 1, DcEnA, DcEnL, DcEuL, DcLEnL, EvLB, MouLC 1, NewC, OxEng, Pen Eng, PoLE, REn, WebEAL*
Gower, Moral *DcEnL*
Gower, Nathaniel *Alli*
Gower, Owen *Alli Sup*
Gower, Richard *Alli*
Gower, Richard Hall *Alli, BiDLA*
Gower, Sir Robert 1880- *WhLA*
Gower, Lord Ronald Sutherland 1845- *Alli Sup*
Gower, Stanley *Alli*
Gowers, Sir Ernest Arthur 1880-1966 *ChPo, LongC, NewC, WorAu*
Gowers, William R *Alli Sup*
Gowin, Enoch Burton *WhWNAA*
Gowing, Emilia Aylmer 1846-1905 *PoIre*

Gowing, Lawrence 1918- *ConAu 9R*
Gowing, Margaret Mary 1921- *WrD 1976*
Gowing, Peter Gordon 1930- *ConAu 53*
Gowing, Richard *Alli Sup*
Gowing, Sydney 1878- *MnBBF*
Gowing, T *Alli Sup*
Gowland, J E *Alli Sup*
Gowland, John Stafford *OxCan*
Gowland, Mariano E 1933- *ConAu 5R*
Gowring, Mrs. Aylmer *Alli Sup*
Gowring, George James *Alli Sup*
Gowring, H A *Alli Sup*
Gowring, T S *Alli Sup*
Goya, Francis Jose De 1746-1828 *ChPo*
Goya Y Lucientes, Francisco Jose De 1746-1828
    AtlBL, NewC, REn
Goyau, Georges-Pierre-Louis-Theophile-
    1869-1939 *CatA 1947*
Goyder, David George *Alli Sup*
Goyder, George Armin 1908- *Au&Wr,
    WrD 1976*
Goyen *AtlBL*
Goyen, William 1915- *AmA&B, Au&Wr,
    AuNews 2, ConAu 5R, ConLC 5,
    ConNov 1972, ConNov 1976, DrAF 1976,
    OxAm, Pen Am, REnAL, WorAu,
    WrD 1976*
Goyen, William 1918- *ModAL*
Goyer, Robert S 1923- *ConAu 41*
Goyne, Richard 1902-1957 *MnBBF*
Goytisolo, Juan 1931- *CasWL, ConLC 5,
    EncWL Sup, ModRL, TwCW, WorAu*
Gozlan, Leon 1803-1866 *BiD&SB, OxFr*
Gozzano, Guido 1883-1916 *CasWL, ClDMEuL,
    EncWL, EuA, Pen Eur, REn, WhTwL*
Gozzi, Carlo 1720-1806 *BiD&SB, CasWL,
    CnThe, DcEuL, EuA, EvEuW, McGWD,
    Pen Eur, REn, REnWD*
Gozzi, Gaspare 1713-1786 *DcEuL, EvEuW*
Gozzi, Gasparo 1713-1786 *BiD&SB, CasWL,
    Pen Eur*
Gozzoli, Benozzo 1420-1497 *AtlBL, REn*
Gpc *WhLA*
Gqoba, William Wellington 1840-1888 *AfA 1*
Graa *WhWNAA*
Graaf, Peter *WorAu*
Grabau, Mrs. Amadeus W *WhWNAA*
Grabau, Amadeus William 1870-1946 *DcNAA,
    WhWNAA*
Grabau, Mary Antin 1888?- *DcAmA*
Grabbe, Christian Dietrich 1801-1836 *BiD&SB,
    CasWL, CnThe, EuA, EvEuW, McGWD,
    OxGer, Pen Eur, REn, REnWD*
Graber, Alexander 1914- *ConAu 1R,
    SmATA 7*
Graber, Doris A 1923- *ConAu 33*
Grabfield, J P And Burns, P S *Alli Sup*
Grabham, Michael C *Alli Sup*
Grabianski, Janusz 1928- *ConAu 45*
Grabianski, Janusz 1929- *IlBYP, IlCB 1966,
    ThBJA*
Grabiel, Zephaniah Orland 1860-1902 *OhA&B*
Grabill, Joseph L 1931- *ConAu 29*
Grabmann, Martin 1875-1949 *CatA 1952*
Grabo, Carl Henry 1881- *AmA&B,
    WhWNAA*
Grabo, Norman Stanley 1930- *ConAu 1R*
Graboff, Abner 1919- *IlBYP, IlCB 1966*
Grabovski, Michael 1805-1863 *BiD&SB*
Grabowski, Count Stanislaus S Albert 1828-1874
    HsB&A Sup
Grabowski, Z Anthony 1903- *ConAu 5R*
Graburn, Nelson 1936- *ConAu 45,
    OxCan Sup*
Graca Aranha, Jose Pereira De 1868-1931 *REn*
Grace Greenwood *CyAL 2*
Grace, A F *Alli Sup*
Grace, Alfred Augustus 1867-1942 *DcLEnL*
Grace, Allen Zechariah *Alli Sup*
Grace, C W *ChPo*
Grace, Frank Devaney 1891- *AmSCAP 66*
Grace, Gerald R 1936- *ConAu 45*
Grace, Helen K 1935- *ConAu 53*
Grace, Henry *Alli*
Grace, Joan C 1921- *ConAu 61*
Grace, Job *Alli*
Grace, John Gladstone *WhWNAA*
Grace, Joseph *ConAu XR*

Grace, Sheffield *Alli, PoIre*
Grace, William *Alli Sup*
Grace, William Gilbert 1848-1915 *NewC*
Grace, William Joseph 1910- *CatA 1952,
    ConAu P-1*
Gracey, George Frederick Handel 1879- *WhLA*
Gracey, Harry L 1933- *ConAu 41*
Gracey, Hugh Kirkwood 1868- *WhLA*
Gracey, S L *Alli Sup*
Gracian, Baltasar 1601-1658 *REn*
Gracian Y Morales, Baltasar 1601-1658 *CasWL,
    DcEuL, DcSpL, EuA, EvEuW, Pen Eur*
Gracie, Archibald 1858-1912 *DcNAA*
Gracie, Charlie 1936- *AmSCAP 66*
Gracie, L C *MnBBF*
Gracin, M *Alli*
Gracq, Julien 1909- *ModRL*
Gracq, Julien 1910- *CasWL, CnMD, EncWL,
    Pen Eur, REn, TwCA Sup*
Gracy, David Bergen, II 1941- *ConAu 25,
    WrD 1976*
Gracza, Margaret Young 1928- *ConAu 13R*
Grad, Bernard 1920- *BiDPar*
Grad, Frank P 1924- *ConAu 33*
Graddon, John *ChPo S1*
Grade, Arnold 1928- *ConAu 29*
Grade, Chaim 1910- *CasWL*
Gradeley, Yorick *ChPo S2*
Gradle, Henry 1855-1911 *Alli Sup, DcAmA,
    DcNAA*
Gradnik, Alojz 1882-1967 *CasWL, EncWL,
    ModSL 2*
Gradon, Dorothy *ChPo*
Gradon, Pamela Olive Elizabeth 1915- *Au&Wr*
Graduate of Oxford, A *DcEnL*
Grady, Benjamin Franklin 1831-1914 *DcNAA*
Grady, Henry Woodfin 1850-1889 *AmA,
    BiDSA, DcLEnL, DcNAA, OxAm,
    REnAL*
Grady, Ronan Calistus, Jr. 1921- *ConAu 49*
Grady, Standish Grove 1815- *Alli, Alli Sup*
Grady, Thomas d1820 *PoIre*
Graebner, Alan 1938- *ConAu 61*
Graebner, August Lawrence 1849-1904 *DcAmA*
Graebner, Augustus Lawrence 1849-1904
    DcNAA
Graebner, Norman Arthur 1915- *AmA&B,
    ConAu 13R, WrD 1976*
Graebner, Theodore 1876- *WhWNAA*
Graebner, Walter A 1909- *ConAu P-1,
    OhA&B*
Graef, Hilda C 1907- *BkC 5, CatA 1952,
    ConAu 5R*
Graefe *TwCA, TwCA Sup*
Graeff, Grace M 1918- *ConAu 23*
Graeffer, John *BiDLA*
Graem, C Montis R *Alli*
Graeme, Bruce 1900- *Au&Wr, EncM&D,
    MnBBF, WrD 1976*
Graeme, David *EncM&D*
Graeme, Elliott *Alli Sup*
Graeme, John 1748-1772 *Alli*
Graeme, Lilias *Alli Sup*
Graeme, Roderic 1926- *Au&Wr, EncM&D*
Graeme, Sheila 1944- *ConAu 25*
Graeme, William *Alli*
Graevius, Johann Georg 1623?-1703 *DcEuL,
    NewC*
Graf, Arturo 1848-1913 *BbD, BiD&SB,
    CasWL, ClDMEuL*
Graf, Ernest 1879- *BkC 3, CatA 1947*
Graf, LeRoy Philip 1915- *ConAu 41*
Graf, Oskar Maria 1894-1967 *AmA&B,
    Au&Wr, EncWL, ModGL, Pen Eur,
    TwCA, TwCA Sup*
Graf, Rudolf F 1926- *ConAu 9R*
Graff, Anton 1736-1813 *OxGer*
Graff, E Jonny 1911- *AmSCAP 66*
Graff, George 1886-1973 *AmSCAP 66,
    ConAu 41*
Graff, Gerald 1937- *ConAu 29*
Graff, Henry Franklin 1921- *AmA&B, ChPo,
    ConAu 1R, WrD 1976*
Graff, John Franklin *Alli Sup*
Graff, Polly Anne *SmATA 7*
Graff, Mrs. S S *OhA&B*
Graff, S Stewart 1908- *AuBYP, ConAu 49,
    SmATA 9*

Graff, Sigmund 1898- *ModWD*
Graffan, Hugh *PoIre*
Graffigny, Francoise De 1695-1758 *BiD&SB,
    OxFr*
Graffis, Herbert Butler 1893- *IndAu 1917*
Grafflin, Margaret Johnston *ChPo S2*
Grafton, Augustus Henry Fitzroy, Duke Of
    1736-1811 *Alli*
Grafton, Carl 1942- *ConAu 53*
Grafton, Charles Chapman 1830?-1912 *Alli Sup,
    DcAmA, DcNAA*
Grafton, Garth *OxCan*
Grafton, H *Alli Sup*
Grafton, H D *Alli*
Grafton, James Douglas 1916- *Au&Wr*
Grafton, Mary *Alli*
Grafton, Richard d1572 *Alli, CasWL,
    Chmbr 1, DcEnL, EvLB*
Grafton, Samuel 1907- *AmA&B*
Gragg, Agnes *Alli Sup*
Graglia, C *Alli*
Graglia, G A *Alli*
Graham *Alli*
Graham, Doctor *Alli*
Graham, A M *ChPo*
Graham, Abbie 1889- *OhA&B, TexWr*
Graham, Ada 1931- *ConAu 29, WrD 1976*
Graham, Aelred 1907- *AmA&B, CatA 1952,
    ConAu 5R*
Graham, Al 1897- *AuBYP, ChPo, ChPo S1*
Graham, Albert Adams 1848-1896 *OhA&B*
Graham, Albert B 1868- *WhWNAA*
Graham, Alberta *AuBYP*
Graham, Alexander *Alli Sup*
Graham, Alexander And Ashbee, H S *Alli Sup*
Graham, Alexander J S *Alli Sup*
Graham, Alexander John 1930- *ConAu 13R,
    WrD 1976*
Graham, Alexis *MnBBF*
Graham, Alice Walworth 1905- *Au&Wr,
    ConAu 1R*
Graham, Alistair 1938- *ConAu 49*
Graham, Andrew Guillemard 1913- *Au&Wr*
Graham, Andrew Jackson 1830-1894 *Alli Sup,
    DcNAA*
Graham, Angus *OxCan*
Graham, Angus 1892- *Au&Wr*
Graham, Angus 1919- *ConAu 17R*
Graham, Angus A 1867- *WhWNAA*
Graham, Anne *Au&Wr*
Graham, Armitage *MnBBF*
Graham, Armytage *MnBBF*
Graham, Arthur *BlkAW*
Graham, Austyn *Alli Sup*
Graham, Bertie Neil Grant Gordon 1904-
    Au&Wr
Graham, Bessie 1883-1966 *AmA&B*
Graham, Billy *ChPo S1, ConAu XR*
Graham, Brother *WrD 1976*
Graham, C *Alli Sup*
Graham, C H And Lane, O F *Alli Sup*
Graham, Catherine *Alli*
Graham, Charles *Alli Sup, ChPo, ChPo S1*
Graham, Christopher Columbus 1784-1884
    DcNAA
Graham, Clara *OxCan*
Graham, Clarence H 1906-1971 *ConAu 33*
Graham, Clarence Reginald 1907- *AuBYP*
Graham, Constance *Alli Sup*
Graham, Courtenay P *DrAP 1975*
Graham, Cunninghame *TwCA, TwCA Sup*
Graham, D L 1944-1970 *BlkAW*
Graham, Daniel McBride 1817-1889 *DcNAA*
Graham, David *Alli Sup*
Graham, David 1808-1852 *DcAmA, DcNAA*
Graham, David, Jr. *Alli*
Graham, David Allan *Alli Sup*
Graham, Desmond 1940- *WrD 1976*
Graham, Donald W 1903- *ConAu 29*
Graham, Dorothy 1893-1959 *AmA&B, AmNov,
    TwCA, TwCA Sup, WhWNAA*
Graham, Dougal 1724-1779 *Alli, ChPo S1,
    Chmbr 2, NewC, Pen Eng*
Graham, Douglas *Alli Sup*
Graham, Douglas Cunninghame *Alli Sup*
Graham, Edward Harrison 1902- *Au&Wr*
Graham, Edward Kidder 1876-1918 *BiDSA,
    DcNAA*

Graham, Edward P 1862-1944 *OhA&B*
Graham, Eleanor 1896- *Au&Wr*, *ChPo*, *ChPo S1*, *ChPo S2*, *WhCL*
Graham, Emma d1922 *DcNAA*
Graham, Ennis *Alli Sup*, *Chmbr 3*, *DcLEnL*, *EvLB*, *LongC*, *NewC*
Graham, Evarts Ambrose 1883- *WhWNAA*
Graham, Frank 1894-1965 *AmA&B*
Graham, Frank 1913- *Au&Wr*
Graham, Frank, Jr. 1925- *AuBYP*, *ConAu 9R*, *WrD 1976*
Graham, Frank Dunstone 1890-1949 *DcNAA*
Graham, Fred P 1931- *ConAu 37*
Graham, Frederica *Alli Sup*
Graham, Gene S 1924- *ConAu 41*
Graham, George *Alli*, *Alli Sup*
Graham, George 1675-1751 *Alli*
Graham, George Adams 1904- *AmA&B*
Graham, George Farquhar *Alli*
Graham, George Farquhar Irving *Alli Sup*
Graham, George Frederick *Alli Sup*
Graham, George J, Jr. 1938- *ConAu 45*
Graham, George Rex 1813-1894 *AmA*, *AmA&B*, *REnAL*
Graham, George W *BiDSA*
Graham, George Washington 1847-1923 *DcNAA*
Graham, Sir Gerald 1830- *Alli Sup*
Graham, Gerald Sandford 1903- *Au&Wr*, *OxCan*
Graham, Gertrude *Alli Sup*
Graham, Grace *Alli Sup*
Graham, Grace 1910- *ConAu P-1*
Graham, Gwethalyn 1913-1965 *AmA&B*, *CanNov*, *CanWr*, *OxCan*, *REnAL*
Graham, Hannah Isabel *ChPo S1*, *WhWNAA*
Graham, Harold *MnBBF*
Graham, Harold L 1897- *AmSCAP 66*
Graham, Harry Edward 1940- *ConAu 29*
Graham, Harry Jocelyn Clive 1874-1936 *ChPo*, *ChPo S1*, *ChPo S2*, *CnMWL*, *EvLB*, *LongC*, *NewC*, *WhCL*, *WhLA*
Graham, Helen Holland *AuBYP*
Graham, Henry *Alli Sup*, *PoIre*
Graham, Henry 1930- *ConP 1970*, *ConP 1975*, *WrD 1976*
Graham, Henry Grey *Alli Sup*
Graham, Henry H *WhWNAA*
Graham, Henry Jocelyn Clive *WhLA*
Graham, Homer *WhWNAA*
Graham, Howard Jay 1905- *ConAu 33*
Graham, Hugh *ConAu XR*
Graham, Hugh 1758-1829 *BbtC*
Graham, Hugh Davis 1936- *ConAu 23*, *WrD 1976*
Graham, Ian 1923- *ConAu 45*
Graham, Ilse 1914- *ConAu 57*
Graham, Irvin 1909- *AmSCAP 66*
Graham, Isabella 1742-1814 *Alli*, *DcNAA*
Graham, J A *BiDLA*
Graham, J C *Alli Sup*
Graham, J D *BbtC*
Graham, J Walter 1906- *ConAu 1R*
Graham, James *Alli*, *Alli Sup*, *Chmbr 1*, *ConAu XR*, *WrD 1976*
Graham, James 1612-1650 *Alli*, *ChPo*, *EvLB*, *NewC*, *Pen Eng*
Graham, James Chandler 1868- *WhWNAA*
Graham, James John *Alli Sup*
Graham, James John George *Alli Sup*
Graham, Sir James Robert George 1792- *Alli*
Graham, John *Alli*, *Alli Sup*, *BiDLA*, *OhA&B*
Graham, John 1649?-1689 *NewC*
Graham, John 1694-1773 *Alli*
Graham, John 1754?-1817 *BkIE*
Graham, John 1774-1844 *PoIre*
Graham, John 1822-1879 *PoIre*
Graham, John 1926- *ConAu 33*, *WrD 1976*
Graham, John Alexander 1941- *ConAu 25*
Graham, John Andrew 1764-1841 *Alli*, *DcAmA*, *DcNAA*
Graham, John Charles Edward 1931- *Au&Wr*
Graham, John H *BbtC*
Graham, John Hamilton 1826-1900? *DcNAA*
Graham, John Lorimer *Alli*
Graham, John Murray 1809-1881 *Alli Sup*
Graham, John Remington 1940- *ConAu 33*

Graham, John Thomas 1928- *ConAu 53*
Graham, John W *Alli Sup*
Graham, John William 1859- *WhLA*
Graham, Johnny 1911- *AmSCAP 66*
Graham, Jory *ConAu 29*
Graham, Joseph A 1855- *BiDSA*
Graham, Katharine 1917- *AuNews 1*
Graham, Kenneth 1859-1932 *BiD&SB*, *ChPo S2*
Graham, Lawrence S 1936- *ConAu 45*
Graham, Le *BlkAW*, *LivBA*
Graham, Leonard *Alli Sup*
Graham, Lewis 1900- *AmSCAP 66*
Graham, Lillian S *MnnWr*
Graham, Linda 1958- *BlkAW*
Graham, Loren R 1933- *ConAu 21*, *IndAu 1917*
Graham, Lorenz B 1902- *BlkAW*, *ConAu 9R*, *LivBAA*, *MorBMP*, *SmATA 2*, *ThBJA*
Graham, Lorenz B 1908- *REnAL*
Graham, Lorraine *ChPo S1*
Graham, Lucile 1887- *OhA&B*
Graham, Sir Lumley 1828- *Alli Sup*
Graham, M F W *Alli Sup*
Graham, Mabel *Alli Sup*
Graham, Malbone Watson 1898-1965 *AmA&B*
Graham, Malcolm 1923- *ConAu 53*
Graham, Malcolm Kintner 1872-1941 *DcNAA*, *IndAu 1917*
Graham, Margaret 1850-1910 *DcAmA*, *DcNAA*
Graham, Margaret Althea 1924- *ConAu 9R*
Graham, Margaret Bloy 1920- *IlBYP*, *IlCB 1956*, *IlCB 1966*, *MorJA*
Graham, Maria *Alli*, *BiDLA*
Graham, Mary *Alli Sup*
Graham, Mary Jane 1803-1830 *Alli*
Graham, Matthew Moore 1805-1882 *PoIre*
Graham, Maud 1871- *PoIre*
Graham, Maude Fitzgerald Susan 1912- *Au&Wr*
Graham, Michael 1898- *Au&Wr*
Graham, Milton D 1916- *ConAu 45*
Graham, Myrtis 1892- *TexWr*
Graham, Neill *ConAu XR*
Graham, Nellie *BiD&SB*
Graham, Otis L, Jr. 1935- *ConAu 21*
Graham, Patricia Albjerg 1935- *ConAu 25*
Graham, Patrick *Alli*, *BiDLA*
Graham, Peter *AfA 1*
Graham, Peter Anderson *ChPo S1*
Graham, Philip 1894- *AmA&B*
Graham, Preston *HsB&A*
Graham, R P *ChPo*
Graham, Rachel 1895- *ConAu P-1*
Graham, Ramona *ConAu XR*
Graham, Sir Reginald 1835-1920 *Br&AmS*
Graham, Richard *Alli*
Graham, Richard 1934- *ConAu 29*
Graham, Robert *Alli*, *Alli Sup*, *BiDLA*, *ChPo S2*, *Chmbr 2*, *WhWNAA*
Graham, Robert 1735?-1797? *EvLB*, *NewC*
Graham, Robert 1943- *ConAu XR*
Graham, Robert Bontine Cunninghame 1852-1936 *Chmbr 3*, *EvLB*, *LongC*, *Pen Eng*
Graham, Robert G 1925- *ConAu 25*
Graham, Robert Hay *Alli*
Graham, Robert Hudson *Alli Sup*
Graham, Robert V 1912- *AmSCAP 66*
Graham, Robin Lee 1949- *ConAu 49*, *SmATA 7*
Graham, Roger *OxCan*
Graham, Roger 1885-1938 *AmSCAP 66*
Graham, Ronny 1919- *AmSCAP 66*
Graham, Rosa *ChPo*
Graham, Rudy Bee 1947- *BlkAW*
Graham, Ruth Morris *BlkAW*
Graham, S *Alli Sup*
Graham, Samuel James 1837- *Alli Sup*
Graham, Samuel L And Sawyer, Frank E *Alli Sup*
Graham, Scott *Alli Sup*
Graham, Sean 1920- *ConAu 21*
Graham, Sheilah 1908?- *AmA&B*, *AuNews 1*, *WrD 1976*
Graham, Shirley And Lipscomb, George D *BkCL*, *St&VC*

Graham, Shirley Lola 1906- *LivBA*
Graham, Shirley Lola 1907- *AmA&B*, *AuBYP*, *BlkAW*, *MorJA*, *TwCA Sup*
Graham, Stephen 1884- *Au&Wr*, *Chmbr 3*, *DcLEnL*, *EvLB*, *LongC*, *NewC*, *REn*, *TwCA*, *TwCA Sup*
Graham, Susan 1912- *ConAu 17R*
Graham, Sylvester 1794-1851 *DcAmA*, *DcNAA*
Graham, T J *Alli Sup*
Graham, Ted *ChPo S1*
Graham, Thomas *Alli Sup*
Graham, Thomas 1805- *Alli*
Graham, Thomas F 1923- *ConAu 23*
Graham, Thomas Forrest Harkness *ChPo S1*
Graham, Thomas J *Alli*
Graham, Thomas Ottiwell 1883- *WhLA*
Graham, Tom *AmNov XR*, *ConAmA*
Graham, Victor Ernest 1920- *WrD 1976*
Graham, Virginia Taylor 1897- *ChPo*, *ChPo S1*
Graham, W *Alli*
Graham, W B *Alli Sup*
Graham, W Fred 1930- *ConAu 33*, *WrD 1976*
Graham, Walter *Alli*, *Alli Sup*
Graham, William *Alli*, *Alli Sup*, *BiDLA*, *MnBBF*
Graham, William 1810-1883 *Alli Sup*, *PoIre*
Graham, William 1816- *PoIre*
Graham, William 1887- *WhLA*
Graham, William Alexander 1804-1875 *BiDSA*, *DcNAA*
Graham, William Franklin 1918- *AmA&B*, *ChPo S1*, *ConAu 9R*
Graham, William Hugh 1912- *WrD 1976*
Graham, William Sloan 1818-1847 *CyAL 2*
Graham, William Sydney 1918- *CasWL*, *ConP 1970*, *ConP 1975*, *ModBL*, *WorAu*, *WrD 1976*
Graham, Winifred *WhLA*
Graham, Winston Mawdsley 1910- *ConAu 49*
Graham, Winston Mawdsley 1911?- *Au&Wr*, *ConNov 1972*, *ConNov 1976*, *TwCW*, *WrD 1976*
Graham-Bonnalie, F E 1897- *Au&Wr*
Graham Of Claverhouse, John, Viscount 1649?-1689 *NewC*, *REn*
Graham-White, Anthony 1940- *ConAu 61*
Grahame, Agnes Vetch *Alli Sup*
Grahame, Arnold *MnBBF*
Grahame, Edith *Alli Sup*
Grahame, Elspeth 1862-1946 *ChPo*, *ChPo S1*
Grahame, F *ChPo S1*
Grahame, F R *Alli Sup*
Grahame, Frances *Alli Sup*
Grahame, Georgina S *Alli Sup*
Grahame, Gordon Hill *CanNov*
Grahame, James *Alli*, *Alli Sup*, *Chmbr 2*, *DcEnL*
Grahame, James 1765-1811 *Alli*, *BrAu 19*, *CasWL*, *ChPo*, *ChPo S1*, *ChPo S2*, *DcEnL*, *DcLEnL*, *EvLB*, *NewC*
Grahame, James 1790-1842 *OxAm*
Grahame, Kenneth 1859-1932 *AnCL*, *AtlBL*, *AuBYP*, *BkCL*, *CarSB*, *CasWL*, *ChPo*, *ChPo S1*, *Chmbr 3*, *CnMWL*, *CyWA*, *DcLEnL*, *EvLB*, *FamSYP*, *JBA 1934*, *LongC*, *ModBL*, *NewC*, *OxEng*, *Pen Eng*, *REn*, *St&VC*, *TwCA*, *TwCA Sup*, *TwCW*, *WhCL*, *YABC 1*
Grahame, Nellie *Alli Sup*, *DcAmA*
Grahame, Simeon *Alli*
Grahame, Simion 1570-1614 *Chmbr 1*, *EvLB*
Grahame, Simon 1570-1614 *EvLB*
Grahame, Walter *Alli Sup*
Grahm, Ruth Lillian 1924- *AmSCAP 66*
Graile, Edmund *Alli*
Graile, John *Alli*
Grain, Corney *Alli Sup*
Grain, William *Alli Sup*
Graindor De Brie d1189? *CasWL*
Graindor De Douai *CasWL*
Graindorge, M Frederic-Thomas *OxFr*
Grainge, William *Alli Sup*
Grainger, A J 1929- *ConAu 33*
Grainger, A M *Alli Sup*
Grainger, Arthur M *HsB&A*
Grainger, Edward *Alli*

Grainger, Francis Edward *EncM&D, MnBBF*
Grainger, James 1721?-1766? *Alli, BrAu, Chmbr 2, DcEnL, EvLB, NewC*
Grainger, James Moses 1879- *BiDSA*
Grainger, M Allerdale *OxCan*
Grainger, M D 1721?-1766 *ChPo*
Grainger, Percy Aldridge 1882-1961 *AmSCAP 66, OxAm*
Grainger, Porter *BlkAW*
Grainger, T B *Alli*
Grainger, William d1793? *BkIE*
Gralapp, Leland Wilson 1921- *ConAu 13R*
Gram, Hans 1685-1748 *DcEuL*
Gram, Harold A 1927- *ConAu 25*
Gramatky, Hardie 1907- *AmA&B, AnCL, AuBYP, AuNews 1, BkP, ConAu 1R, IlCB 1945, IlCB 1956, IlCB 1966, JBA 1951, SmATA 1, St&VC*
Gramatky, Hardy *AuICB*
Grambs, Jean D 1919- *ConAu 17R*
Gramet, Charles *AuBYP, ConAu 1R*
Gramiades *WhLA*
Gramko, Ida 1925- *DcCLA*
Gramm, Carl H 1879-1945 *DcNAA*
Gramm, William 1818-1901 *DcAmA*
Grammaticus *ConAu XR*
Grammaticus, Aelfric *BrAu*
Grammont, Antoine, Duc De 1604-1678 *OxFr*
Grammont, Philibert De 1621-1707 *DcEuL*
Gramont, Antoine, Duc De 1604-1678 *OxFr*
Grampp, William D 1914- *ConAu 33, WrD 1976*
Grams, Armin 1924- *ConAu 45*
Gramsbergen, Matthijs *CasWL*
Gramsci, Antonio 1891-1937 *CasWL*
Gramshaw, H *ChPo S1*
Gran, Haaken Hasberg 1870- *WhLA*
Gran, John M *MnnWr*
Granada, Luis De 1504-1588 *CasWL, DcSpL, EuA, EvEuW, Pen Eur*
Granados, Paul *WrD 1976*
Granan, Edward *Alli*
Granard, Earl Of *Alli Sup*
Granat, Robert 1925- *ConAu 1R, DrAF 1976, WrD 1976*
Granatstein, J L 1939- *ConAu 25, OxCan Sup*
Granberg, Wilbur J 1906- *ConAu 5R, WhPNW*
Granberry, Edwin Phillips 1897- *AmA&B, ConAu 21, REnAL, TwCA, TwCA Sup*
Granberry, Helen *ChPo S1*
Granbery, John Cowper 1829-1907 *Alli Sup, BiDSA, DcAmA, DcNAA*
Granbery, John Cowper 1874-1953 *AmA&B, TexWr, WhWNAA*
Granby, Marquis Of *NewC*
Granby, Phil *MnBBF*
Grand, Gordon 1883- *Br&AmS*
Grand, Murray 1919- *AmSCAP 66*
Grand, Sarah Frances Elizabeth 1862-1943 *BbD, BiD&SB, Chmbr 3, DcBiA, DcEnA Ap, DcLEnL, LongC, NewC, OxEng, TwCA, TwCA Sup*
Grand, William *Alli, BiDLA*
Grand-Carteret, John 1850?- *BiD&SB*
Grand Corrupter, The *NewC*
Grand Dauphin, Le 1661-1711 *OxFr*
Grand Monarque, Le *NewC*
Grand Old Man, The *NewC*
Granda, Julio *IlBYP*
Grandbois, Alain 1900- *CanWr, CasWL, OxCan, OxCan Sup, Pen Eng*
Grandbois, Madeleine *OxCan*
Grandchild, J A *Alli Sup*
Grande, Luke M 1922- *ConAu 5R*
Grande Mademoiselle, La *OxFr*
Grandfield, Raymond J 1931- *ConAu 53*
Grandfontaine, Hector D'A, Sieur De 1627-1696 *OxCan*
Grandgent, Charles Hall 1862-1939 *AmA&B, AmLY, DcNAA, REnAL, WhWNAA*
Grandi, S *Alli*
Grandin, Egbert Henry 1855- *DcAmA*
Grandin, Ruth T *OhA&B*
Grandjany, Marcel 1891- *AmSCAP 66*
Grand'Maison, Jacques *OxCan Sup*
Grandmont, Eloi De 1921-1971 *CanWr, OxCan Sup*

Grandmontagne, Francisco 1866-1936 *ClDMEuL*
Grandpre, Pierre De *OxCan Sup*
Grandville 1803-1847 *OxFr*
Grandville, J J *ChPo S1*
Grandy, Richard E *Alli Sup*
Granet, B *BbtC*
Graney, Maurice Richard 1907- *IndAu 1917*
Grange, Lady *Alli*
Grange, A Demain *ChPo*
Grange, Cyril 1900- *Au&Wr, ConAu P-1, WrD 1976*
Grange, Herbert *OxCan*
Grange, John *Alli, CasWL*
Grange, Peter *ConNov 1972, ConNov 1976, SmATA 5, WrD 1976*
Granger, Alfred Hoyt 1867-1939 *DcNAA, OhA&B*
Granger, Bruce Ingham 1920- *ConAu 1R, WrD 1976*
Granger, Clive W J 1934- *ConAu 9R*
Granger, Edith *ChPo*
Granger, Frank Butler 1875-1928 *DcNAA*
Granger, Gideon 1767-1822 *Alli, DcNAA*
Granger, James 1723-1776 *Alli, Chmbr 2, DcEnL, EvLB, NewC*
Granger, John Albert 1833-1906 *DcNAA*
Granger, Joseph *Alli*
Granger, Luc *OxCan Sup*
Granger, Mary Ethel *Alli Sup*
Granger, Moses Moorhead 1831-1913 *Alli Sup, DcAmA, DcNAA, OhA&B*
Granger, T C *Alli*
Granger, Thomas *Alli*
Granger, William Alexander 1850-1922 *DcNAA*
Granger, William D *Alli Sup*
Granich, Irving 1893?-1967 *AmA&B, ConAu 25, Pen Am, REn, REnAL*
Granich, Irwin 1893-1967 *ConAu 45*
Granick, David 1926- *ConAu 1R, WrD 1976*
Granite, Harvey R 1927- *ConAu 33*
Granite, Tony *ConAu XR, WrD 1976*
Grannan, Charles P 1846-1924 *DcNAA*
Grannatt, Harry Silleck *ChPo*
Grannell, Robert J *PoIre*
Grannis, Anna Jane 1856-1947 *AmLY, DcAmA, WhWNAA*
Granniss, Anna Jane 1856-1947 *AmA&B, ChPo S2, DcNAA*
Granniss, Ruth S *AmA&B*
Granovetter, Mark S 1943- *WrD 1976*
Granovski, Timofey Nikolayevich 1813-1855 *DcRusL*
Granovsky, Anatoli 1922-1974 *ConAu 53*
Granovsky, Timofey Nikolayevich 1813-1855 *CasWL*
Granowsky, Alvin 1936- *ConAu 21*
Granrud, John Evenson 1863-1920 *DcNAA*
Gransden, K W 1925- *ChPo S1, ConP 1970*
Granson, Oton De 1345?-1397 *CasWL*
Granstaff, Bill 1925- *SmATA 10*
Grant *Alli, BiDLA*
Grant, Mrs. *Alli, Alli Sup*
Grant, Mrs. 1755-1838 *BiDLA, CyAL 2*
Grant, A *Alli, BiDLA*
Grant, A C *Alli Sup*
Grant, A F *OhA&B*
Grant, A R *MnBBF*
Grant, A W *TexWr*
Grant, Alan *Alli Sup*
Grant, Albert Weston 1856-1930 *DcNAA*
Grant, Alex *Alli*
Grant, Alexander *BbtC*
Grant, Sir Alexander 1826-1884 *Alli, Alli Sup, BbD, BiD&SB*
Grant, Alexander Henley *Alli Sup*
Grant, Alexander Thomas Kingdom 1906- *Au&Wr, ConAu 53, WrD 1976*
Grant, Alfred J 1914- *AmSCAP 66*
Grant, Alison *ChPo*
Grant, Allan *Alli Sup, DcNAA*
Grant, Alma 1892- *AmSCAP 66*
Grant, Allen 1832-1914 *AmA*
Grant, Alta *ChPo*
Grant, Ambrose *EncM&D, WrD 1976*
Grant, Andrew *Alli*
Grant, Anne McVickar 1755-1838 *Alli, BiD&SB, BrAu 19, Chmbr 2, DcEnL,*

DcLEnL, EvLB, NewC, OxAm, REnAL
Grant, Annie *Alli Sup*
Grant, Anson *MnBBF*
Grant, Anthony *PoIre*
Grant, Anthony 1806-1883 *Alli, Alli Sup*
Grant, Arthur James 1862- *WhLA*
Grant, Asahel 1807-1844 *Alli, DcAmA, DcNAA*
Grant, Barbara M 1932- *ConAu 53*
Grant, Ben O 1901- *TexWr*
Grant, Benjamin *Alli Sup*
Grant, Bert 1878-1951 *AmSCAP 66*
Grant, Blanche C *ChPo*
Grant, Brewin *Alli Sup*
Grant, Brian 1939- *ConAu 57*
Grant, Bruce 1893- *AuBYP, ConAu 1R, SmATA 5*
Grant, Bruce Alexander 1925- *Au&Wr*
Grant, C H *Alli Sup*
Grant, Caroline, Countess Of Seafield 1830- *Alli Sup*
Grant, Charles *Alli, Alli Sup, AmA&B, BiDLA, WhWNAA*
Grant, Charles 1746-1823 *Alli*
Grant, Sir Charles 1836- *Alli Sup*
Grant, Charles, Viscount De Vaux *Alli, BbtC, BiDLA*
Grant, Charles Martin *Alli Sup*
Grant, Charles N 1887-1937 *AmSCAP 66*
Grant, Charles Rollin 1846-1933 *OhA&B*
Grant, Charles William *Alli Sup*
Grant, Claude D 1944- *BlkAW, DrAP 1975*
Grant, Colesworthey *Alli Sup*
Grant, Colin *Alli Sup*
Grant, Courteney *Alli Sup*
Grant, Cuthbert 1793-1854 *OxCan*
Grant, D *Alli*
Grant, Daniel *Alli Sup*
Grant, David *Alli, BiDLA*
Grant, David 1823-1886 *Alli Sup, ChPo, ChPo S1, ChPo S2*
Grant, David Ogilvie 1925- *Au&Wr*
Grant, Denby *MnBBF*
Grant, Don *ConAu XR*
Grant, Donald Chester Peter 1892- *IndAu 1917*
Grant, Dorothy Fremont 1900- *AmA&B, AmNov, BkC 3, CatA 1947, ConAu 23*
Grant, Douglas *AmA&B, ChPo, DcNAA, MnBBF*
Grant, Duncan *Alli*
Grant, E B *Alli Sup*
Grant, E Gordon *MnBBF*
Grant, Edward d1601 *Alli, DcEnL*
Grant, Eleanor *Alli Sup*
Grant, Elihu 1873-1942 *AmA&B, DcNAA, WhWNAA*
Grant, Elizabeth *Alli Sup, Chmbr 2*
Grant, Elliott Mansfield 1895- *ConAu 5R*
Grant, Ellsworth Strong 1917- *ConAu 57*
Grant, Ethel Watts Mumford 1878-1940 *AmA&B, AmLY, ChPo, DcNAA*
Grant, Eva 1907- *ConAu 49, SmATA 7*
Grant, F W *Alli Sup*
Grant, Mrs. Forrest *Alli Sup*
Grant, Francis 1660?-1726 *Alli*
Grant, Francis James 1863- *WhLA*
Grant, Frederick *Alli Sup*
Grant, Frederick Clifton 1891-1974 *AmA&B, ConAu 1R, ConAu 49, WhWNAA*
Grant, Frederick Richard Charles *Alli Sup*
Grant, George *Alli Sup*
Grant, George Barnard 1849-1917 *DcNAA*
Grant, George Hook 1896- *AmA&B*
Grant, George Monro 1835-1902 *Alli Sup, BbD, BbtC, BiD&SB, DcLEnL, DcNAA, OxCan*
Grant, George Parkin 1918- *OxCan, OxCan Sup*
Grant, Gerald *Alli Sup*
Grant, Gertrude Elizabeth *Alli Sup*
Grant, Gordon H 1875-1962 *AmA&B, IlCB 1956*
Grant, Harding *Alli*
Grant, Harry *MnBBF*
Grant, Harry 1922- *AmSCAP 66*
Grant, Harry Johnston 1881- *WhWNAA*
Grant, Hay Macdowall *Alli Sup*
Grant, Henry *Alli Sup*

Grant, Henry Clark 1810- *BbtC*
Grant, Henry H *PoIre*
Grant, Herbert *Alli Sup*
Grant, Hilda Kay *ConAu 1R, OxCan*
Grant, Howard *MnBBF*
Grant, Isabel Frances *Au&Wr*
Grant, J *Alli*
Grant, J B 1940- *ConAu 57*
Grant, J G *ChPo*
Grant, Miss J K *Alli Sup*
Grant, J M *Alli Sup*
Grant, Mrs. J P *BbtC*
Grant, James *Alli, BiDLA, Chmbr 3, MnBBF*
Grant, James 1802-1879? *Alli, Alli Sup, DcEnL*
Grant, James 1822-1887 *Alli, Alli Sup, BbD, BiD&SB, BrAu 19, DcBiA, DcEnA Ap, DcEnL, DcLEnL, EvLB, NewC, OxEng*
Grant, James 1840-1885 *Alli Sup*
Grant, Mrs. James 1755-1838 *ChPo, ChPo S2*
Grant, James Alexander 1829- *BbtC*
Grant, James Augustus 1827-1892 *Alli Sup, BiD&SB, Chmbr 3, EvLB*
Grant, James G *ChPo S2*
Grant, James J 1908- *OhA&B*
Grant, James M *Alli*
Grant, James Miller 1853-1940 *DcNAA, WhWNAA*
Grant, James P *Alli Sup*
Grant, James Richard 1880- *WhWNAA*
Grant, James Russell 1924- *Au&Wr, ChPo S2, WrD 1976*
Grant, Jane *ChPo S2, ConAu XR*
Grant, Jane 1895-1972 *ConAu 25, ConAu 33*
Grant, Jeremiah *Alli*
Grant, Jerome *ChPo S2*
Grant, Jerry 1923- *AmSCAP 66*
Grant, Jesse Root 1858-1934 *AmA&B, DcNAA*
Grant, Joan 1907- *Au&Wr, ConAu XR, TwCW*
Grant, John *Alli, Alli Sup, BiDLA*
Grant, John Cameron *Alli Sup, ChPo S2*
Grant, John Cameron 1934- *Au&Wr*
Grant, John Clark *ChPo S2*
Grant, John E 1925- *ConAu 41*
Grant, John J 1932- *ConAu 53*
Grant, John McBain 1923- *Au&Wr*
Grant, John Peter *Alli, BiDLA*
Grant, John Webster 1919- *ConAu 5R, OxCan Sup, WrD 1976*
Grant, John Wesley 1850- *BlkAW*
Grant, John Wynniatt *Alli Sup*
Grant, Johnson 1773-1845 *Alli, BiDLA*
Grant, Joseph 1805-1835 *ChPo*
Grant, Joy *ChPo S1*
Grant, Judith 1929- *ConAu 21*
Grant, Judith Towers *Alli Sup*
Grant, Julia Dent *AmA&B*
Grant, Julius 1901- *Au&Wr, WrD 1976*
Grant, K W *ChPo*
Grant, Kay *ConAu 23*
Grant, Klein *Alli*
Grant, Mrs. L *Alli Sup*
Grant, Landon *EncM&D*
Grant, Leigh 1947- *IlBYP, SmATA 10*
Grant, Leslie *MnBBF*
Grant, Lewis 1872- *ChPo S1*
Grant, Louis T 1943- *ConAu 53*
Grant, Louisa K *Alli, Alli Sup*
Grant, Madeleine Parker 1895- *AuBYP*
Grant, Madeline *OxCan Sup*
Grant, Madison 1865-1937 *AmA&B, DcNAA*
Grant, Margaret *AmA&B*
Grant, Maria M *Alli Sup*
Grant, Marshall 1926- *AmSCAP 66*
Grant, Mary *Alli Sup, ChPo S1*
Grant, Mary A 1890- *ConAu 25*
Grant, Maude Margaret *WhWNAA*
Grant, Maxwell *EncM&D, MnBBF*
Grant, Michael 1914- *Au&Wr, ConAu 1R, WrD 1976*
Grant, Micki *BlkAW*
Grant, Miles *Alli Sup*
Grant, Myrna 1934- *ConAu 53*
Grant, Neil 1938- *ConAu 33, WrD 1976*

Grant, Nigel Duncan Cameron 1932- *ConAu 17R, WrD 1976*
Grant, Ozro F 1908- *ConAu 21*
Grant, P *Alli*
Grant, P W *Alli Sup*
Grant, Patrick *Alli, Alli Sup*
Grant, Patrick 1698-1762 *Alli*
Grant, Percy Stickney 1860-1927 *AmA&B, AmLY, ChPo, ChPo S2, DcNAA, REnAL*
Grant, Peter *Alli Sup, ChPo, ChPo S1*
Grant, Raymond James *Alli*
Grant, Richard -1897 *PoIre*
Grant, Richard B 1925- *ConAu 1R*
Grant, Richard E 1949- *BlkAW*
Grant, Robert *Alli, Alli Sup, BiDLA*
Grant, Sir Robert 1785-1838 *ChPo, PoCh*
Grant, Robert 1797-1887 *Alli Sup*
Grant, Robert 1814- *Alli*
Grant, Robert 1818- *ChPo*
Grant, Robert 1852-1940 *Alli Sup, AmA&B, BiD&SB, ChPo S2, DcAmA, DcBiA, DcLEnL, DcNAA, OxAm, REnAL, TwCA, TwCA Sup, WhWNAA*
Grant, Robert 1862- *AmLY*
Grant, Robert B 1933- *ConAu 45*
Grant, Robert Edmund 1793-1874 *Alli, BiD&SB*
Grant, Robert M 1917- *AmA&B*
Grant, Roderick 1941- *Au&Wr, WrD 1976*
Grant, Roger *Alli*
Grant, Susan *ChPo S1*
Grant, Lady Sybil *ChPo*
Grant, T H *BbtC*
Grant, Thomas 1816-1870 *Alli Sup*
Grant, Thornley *Alli Sup*
Grant, Ulysses Sherman 1867-1932 *DcNAA, WhWNAA*
Grant, Ulysses Simpson 1882-1885 *Alli Sup, AmA&B, BbD, BiD&SB, DcAmA, DcNAA, OhA&B, OxAm, REn, REnAL*
Grant, Verne E 1917- *ConAu 53, WrD 1976*
Grant, Vernon W 1904- *ConAu 17R*
Grant, W *Alli Sup*
Grant, W Leonard 1914- *ConAu 17R*
Grant, Wilhelmina *ChPo*
Grant, William *Alli, Alli Sup*
Grant, William H *Alli Sup*
Grant, William Lawson 1872-1935 *DcNAA, OxCan*
Grant-Duff *Alli Sup*
Grant Duff, Douglas Ainslie *NewC*
Grant Duff, James *OxEng*
Grant Duff, Sir Mountstuart Elphinstone 1829-1906 *BrAu 19*
Grant Wallace, Lewis *ConAu XR*
Granter, Gratiana *ChPo S2*
Grantham, Alexander 1899- *ConAu 19*
Grantham, Dewey Wesley, Jr. 1921- *ConAu 1R*
Grantham, George Peirce *Alli Sup*
Grantham, Henry *Alli*
Grantham, John *Alli Sup*
Grantham, Thomas *Alli*
Grantham, Sir Thomas *Alli*
Grantland, Keith *ConAu XR*
Grantly, Archdeacon *REn*
Grantoff, C *Alli Sup*
Granville, Cardinal *Alli*
Granville, Agostino Bozzi 1783-1871 *Alli, Alli Sup*
Granville, Augustus Kerr Bozzi *Alli Sup*
Granville, Charles *Alli*
Granville, Denis *Alli*
Granville, F C *ChPo S2*
Granville, Mrs. Frederic *Alli Sup*
Granville, G *Chmbr 2*
Granville, George, Lord Landsdowne 1667?-1735? *Alli, CasWL, ChPo S1, DcEnL, NewC*
Granville, Joseph Mortimer *Alli Sup*
Granville, Paulina Bozzi *Alli Sup*
Granville, Sir Richard *Alli*
Granville, Wilfred 1905- *Au&Wr, ConAu P-1*
Granville, William Anthony 1863-1943 *DcNAA, WhWNAA*
Granville-Barker, George 1913- *DcLEnL*
Granville-Barker, Harley Granville 1877-1946 *CasWL, Chmbr 3, CnMD, CyWA,*

DcLEnL, EvLB, LongC, McGWD, ModBL, ModWD, NewC, OxEng, Pen Eng, REn, REnWD, TwCA, TwCA Sup, TwCW, WebEAL, WhLA, WhTwL
Granville-Barker, Helen *AmA&B*
Grapel, William 1822- *Alli Sup*
Grapho *ConAu XR, DcNAA, OhA&B*
Gras, Felix 1844-1901 *BiD&SB, ClDMEuL, DcBiA*
Gras, Norman Scott Brien *WhWNAA*
Grascome, Samuel *Alli*
Grases, Pedro 1909- *DcSpL*
Grasett, G R 1811-1847 *BbtC*
Grass, Frances *WhWNAA*
Grass, Guenter 1927- *ConAu 13R*
Grass, Gunter 1927- *CasWL, ConLC 1, ConLC 2, ConLC 4, ConLC 6, CrCD, EncWL, EvEuW, McGWD, ModGL, ModWD, OxGer, Pen Eur, REnWD, TwCA, WorAu*
Grass, Gunter 1928- *CnMD*
Grass, Gunther 1927- *CnThe, WhTwL*
Grasse, Francois-Joseph-Paul, Comte De 1722-1788 *OxFr*
Grassi, Angela 1826- *BiD&SB*
Grassineau, James *Alli*
Grasso, Ralph 1934- *AmSCAP 66*
Grasty, Charles Henry 1863-1924 *AmA&B, DcNAA*
Grasty, John S *Alli Sup, BiDSA*
Grasty, John Sharshall 1880-1930 *DcNAA*
Gratacap, Louis Pope 1850-1917 *Alli Sup, DcAmA, DcNAA*
Grathwohl, Susan *DrAP 1975*
Gratiant, Gilbert 1901- *DcCLA*
Gratius, Ortwin 1491-1541 *DcEuL*
Gratius, Ortwinus 1480?-1542 *OxGer*
Gratix, James *Alli Sup*
Grattan, C J *Alli Sup*
Grattan, Clinton Hartley 1902- *AmA&B, ConAu 1R, OxAm, REnAL, TwCA, TwCA Sup, WhWNAA, WrD 1976*
Grattan, Donald Henry 1926- *Au&Wr*
Grattan, H P *PoIre*
Grattan, Henry 1746?-1820 *Alli, BbD, BiD&SB, BiDLA, Chmbr 2, PoIre, REn*
Grattan, Lawrence 1870-1941 *DcNAA*
Grattan, Peachy R *Alli, Alli Sup*
Grattan, Richard *Alli Sup*
Grattan, Thomas Colley 1792-1864 *Alli, Alli Sup, BiD&SB, BrAu 19, Chmbr 3, DcEnA, DcEnL, EvLB, NewC, OxAm, PoIre*
Grattan, W H *Alli Sup*
Grattan, William *Alli*
Grattius *CasWL*
Gratton, Herbert J *MnBBF*
Gratton, Thomas Colley 1792-1864 *DcLEnL*
Gratus, Jack 1935- *WrD 1976*
Gratz, Rebecca 1781-1869 *AmA&B, REnAL*
Gratz, Simon 1838?-1925 *AmA&B, DcNAA*
Grau, Jacinto 1877-1958 *CasWL, ClDMEuL, ModWD, Pen Eur, REn*
Grau, Robert 1858-1916 *DcNAA*
Grau, Shirley Ann 1929- *AmA&B, Au&Wr, AuNews 2, ConAu 1R, ConLC 4, ConNov 1972, ConNov 1976, DrAF 1976, ModAL, OxAm, Pen Am, REn, REnAL, WorAu, WrD 1976*
Grau Delgado, Jacinto 1877-1958 *EncWL, McGWD*
Graubard, Mark A 1904- *ConAu 1R, WrD 1976*
Grauman, Lawrence, Jr. 1935- *ConAu 33, WrD 1976*
Graunn, G E *Alli Sup*
Graunt, Edward *Alli*
Graunt, John *Alli*
Graunt, John 1620-1674 *Alli*
Graupe, Daniel 1934- *ConAu 41*
Graupera, Carlos M 1915- *ConAu 49*
Graustein, William Caspar 1888-1941 *DcNAA, WhWNAA*
Gravatt, Glenn Gilmore 1899- *WhWNAA*
Grave, Christian *Alli*

Grave, George Ann *Alli*
Grave, John De *Alli*
Grave, S A 1916- *ConAu 5R*
Gravel, Mike 1930- *ConAu 41, WrD 1976*
Gravel, Pierre *OxCan Sup*
Gravelle, Barbara *DrAP 1975*
Gravelot 1669-1773 *BkIE*
Gravely, Ralph 1898- *WhWNAA*
Gravely, William B 1939- *ConAu 49*
Graven, Jack *DrAP 1975*
Gravener, George *Alli Sup*
Gravengaard, Hans Peter 1896- *OhA&B*
Gravenor, Benjamin *Alli*
Graveny, Cecil *MnBBF*
Graver, Lawrence Stanley 1931- *ConAu 25, WrD 1976*
Graver, Mary Byrd 1901- *IndAu 1917*
Gravere, Julius De *Alli*
Graves *ChPo S1*
Graves, Mrs. A J *Alli*
Graves, A P *Alli Sup*
Graves, Ada J *ChPo*
Graves, Adelia Cleopatra Spencer 1821-1895 *Alli Sup, BiDSA, DcAmA, DcNAA, LivFWS, OhA&B*
Graves, Alfred Perceval 1846-1931 *Alli Sup, BrAu 19, ChPo, ChPo S1, Chmbr 3, DcLEnL, EvLB, LongC, NewC, OxEng, PoIre, REn, WhLA*
Graves, Algernon *Alli Sup*
Graves, Alida W *Alli Sup*
Graves, Allen W 1915- *ConAu 17R*
Graves, Anson Rogers 1842-1932 *DcNAA, WhWNAA*
Graves, Arnold Felix 1847- *PoIre, WhLA*
Graves, Barbara Farris 1938- *ConAu 41*
Graves, Charles 1812-1899 *PoIre*
Graves, Charles Alfred 1850-1928 *DcNAA*
Graves, Charles Larcom 1856-1944 *Alli Sup, ChPo, ChPo S1, ChPo S2, PoIre, WhLA*
Graves, Charles Parlin 1911-1972 *AuBYP, ConAu 5R, ConAu 37, SmATA 4*
Graves, Charles Patrick Ranke 1899- *Au&Wr*
Graves, Clara 1808-1871 *PoIre*
Graves, Clotilde Inez Augusta Mary 1863?-1932 *Alli Sup, CatA 1947, Chmbr 3, LongC, NewC, PoIre, WhLA*
Graves, Frank Pierrepont 1869-1956 *AmA&B, AmLY, WhWNAA*
Graves, Frederick Wyatt *ChPo S1*
Graves, Gaylord Willis 1884- *WhWNAA*
Graves, George *Alli, BiDLA*
Graves, George Ann *Alli, BiDLA*
Graves, Gordon Harwood 1884- *IndAu 1816*
Graves, Gregory *Alli Sup*
Graves, H A *Alli Sup, BiDSA*
Graves, Henry Clinton 1830-1917 *Alli Sup, DcNAA*
Graves, Horace John Funge 1903- *Au&Wr*
Graves, Ida 1902- *NewC*
Graves, J P *Alli Sup*
Graves, Jackson Alpheus 1852-1933 *AmA&B, DcNAA*
Graves, James 1815-1886 *Alli Sup*
Graves, James Robinson 1820-1893 *Alli Sup, BiDSA, DcAmA, DcNAA*
Graves, John *Alli, BiDLA*
Graves, John Alexander 1920- *ConAu 13R, ConAu 1R*
Graves, John Temple 1856-1925 *BiDSA, DcNAA*
Graves, John Temple 1892-1961 *AmA&B, WhWNAA*
Graves, Joseph *PoIre*
Graves, Kersey 1815- *Alli Sup, IndAu 1816*
Graves, Leon B 1946- *ConAu 29*
Graves, Louis 1883- *BiDSA, WhWNAA*
Graves, Lulu Grace 1874-1949 *DcNAA*
Graves, Morris 1910- *REn*
Graves, Mortimer *MnBBF*
Graves, R And Graves, Ashton J *Alli*
Graves, Ralph 1924- *AmA&B*
Graves, Ralph A 1882- *WhWNAA*
Graves, Ralph Henry 1878-1939 *AmA&B, DcNAA*
Graves, Ralph Seaman, Jr. 1923- *AmSCAP 66*
Graves, Richard *Alli, BiDLA, BiDLA Sup, Chmbr 2*

Graves, Richard 1715-1804 *Alli, BrAu, CasWL, DcEnL, DcLEnL, NewC, OxEng, WebEAL*
Graves, Richard 1763-1829 *Alli, DcEnL*
Graves, Richard Hastings 1791-1877 *Alli Sup*
Graves, Richard L 1928- *ConAu 57*
Graves, Richard L 1931- *ConAu 53*
Graves, Robert *Alli, BiDLA, Chmbr 3*
Graves, Robert 1895- *AnCL, AuBYP, CnE&AP, CnMWL, ConAu 5R, ConLC 1, ConLC 2, ConLC 6, ConNov 1972, ConNov 1976, ConP 1970, ConP 1975, CyWA, EncWL, LongC, ModBL, ModBL Sup, NewC, RAdv 1, REn, TwCA, TwCA Sup, TwCW, WebEAL, WhTwL, WrD 1976*
Graves, Robert James 1796-1853 *Alli, Alli Sup*
Graves, Robert Perceval 1810-1893 *Alli Sup, PoIre*
Graves, Robert Ranke 1895- *Au&Wr, CasWL, ChPo, ChPo S1, ChPo S2, DcLEnL, EvLB, OxEng, Pen Eng*
Graves, Robert VonRanke 1895- *WhLA*
Graves, Rosewell Hobart 1833-1912 *DcNAA*
Graves, Roswell T 1833- *BiDSA*
Graves, Samuel *Alli*
Graves, Samuel Colleton 1788- *BiDLA Sup*
Graves, Samuel R *Alli Sup*
Graves, Susan B 1933- *ConAu 41*
Graves, W Brooke 1899- *ConAu P-1*
Graves, Wallace 1922- *Au&Wr, ConAu 33, WrD 1976*
Graves, William 1916- *AmSCAP 66*
Graves, William Lucius *ChPo*
Graves, William Phillips 1870-1933 *DcNAA, WhWNAA*
Graves, William Sidney 1865-1940 *DcNAA, WhWNAA*
Graves, William Whites 1871- *BkC 2, CatA 1947*
Gravier, Gabriel *BiDSA*
Graviere, Jean Pierre Edmond J DeLa 1812-1892 *BbD, BiD&SB*
Gravina, Gian Vincenzo 1664-1718 *CasWL, EvEuW*
Gravina, Giovanni Vincenzo 1664-1718 *DcEuL*
Gravlund, Thorkild Thastum 1879-1939 *CasWL*
Gray, Mrs. *FemPA*
Gray, Miss A A *CarSB, ChPo*
Gray, A C *BiDSA*
Gray, Abdon *ChPo*
Gray, Agnes *ChPo S2*
Gray, Agnes Kendrick 1894- *AnMV 1926, ChPo S1*
Gray, Agnes M *Alli Sup*
Gray, Alan Ware 1924- *Au&Wr*
Gray, Albert Zabriskie 1840-1889 *Alli Sup, ChPo S2, DcAmA, DcNAA*
Gray, Alexander *Alli*
Gray, Alexander 1882-1921 *DcNAA*
Gray, Sir Alexander 1882-1968 *CasWL, ChPo, ChPo S1, ChPo S2, ConAu 5R, WhLA*
Gray, Alfred Orrin 1914- *ConAu 17R, WrD 1976*
Gray, Alfred Rudolf, Jr. 1933- *BlkAW*
Gray, Alice *Alli Sup, AuBYP*
Gray, Alma *ChPo*
Gray, Alonzo 1808-1860 *Alli, DcNAA*
Gray, Amy *Alli Sup*
Gray, Andrew *Alli, Alli Sup, BbtC, BiDLA, MnBBF*
Gray, Ann Thomson *Alli*
Gray, Annabel *Alli Sup*
Gray, Annie *Alli Sup*
Gray, Archibald *BbtC*
Gray, Arnold *Alli Sup*
Gray, Arthur *ChPo*
Gray, Arthur Irving 1859- *AmA&B, DcAmA*
Gray, Asa 1810-1888 *Alli, Alli Sup, AmA, AmA&B, BbD, BiD&SB, CyAL 2, DcAmA, DcNAA, OxAm, REn, REnAL*
Gray, Austin Kayingham 1888-1945 *DcNAA*
Gray, B G *BbtC*
Gray, Barry 1826-1886 *Alli Sup, AmA&B, ChPo, ChPo S1, DcAmA, DcEnL, DcNAA*
Gray, Barry 1916- *ConAu 61*

Gray, Barton *BiDSA*
Gray, Basil 1904- *ConAu P-1*
Gray, Berkeley *EncM&D, MnBBF*
Gray, Bernard *PoIre*
Gray, Bernard E 1888- *WhWNAA*
Gray, Bertram *Alli Sup*
Gray, Beulah Brazelton 1882-1964 *IndAu 1917*
Gray, Bill *ConAu XR*
Gray, Bradford H 1942- *ConAu 57*
Gray, Carl *DcNAA*
Gray, Carolyn Elizabeth 1873-1938 *DcNAA*
Gray, Cecil *MnBBF*
Gray, Charles 1782-1851 *Alli, BiDLA, ChPo*
Gray, Charles Alden 1857-1933 *ChPo*
Gray, Charles Augustus 1938- *ConAu 17R, WrD 1976*
Gray, Charles Norris *Alli Sup*
Gray, Charles Wright *AmA&B*
Gray, Charlesworth *ChPo*
Gray, Charlotte Elvira 1873-1926 *AmLY, DcNAA*
Gray, Chauncey 1904- *AmSCAP 66*
Gray, Chris *Alli*
Gray, Clarence Truman 1877- *TexWr, WhWNAA*
Gray, Clayton 1918- *WrD 1976*
Gray, Clifford F 1930- *ConAu 25, IndAu 1917*
Gray, Clifton Daggett 1874-1948 *DcNAA*
Gray, Cora E 1883- *WhWNAA*
Gray, Dallas A 1898- *AmSCAP 66*
Gray, Dan T 1878- *WhWNAA*
Gray, Dane *MnBBF*
Gray, Darrell *DrAP 1975*
Gray, David *Chmbr 3*
Gray, David 1836-1888 *Alli Sup, BiD&SB, ChPo S2, DcAmA, DcNAA*
Gray, David 1838-1861 *Alli Sup, BiD&SB, BrAu 19, ChPo, ChPo S2, DcEnL, EvLB, NewC*
Gray, David 1870-1968 *AmA&B, AmLY, Br&AmS, DcAmA*
Gray, Dionis *Alli*
Gray, Don *MnBBF*
Gray, Dorothy Kate 1918- *Au&Wr, WrD 1976*
Gray, Dulcie *ConAu 5R, WrD 1976*
Gray, Dwight E 1903- *ConAu 23*
Gray, E Conder *Alli Sup*
Gray, E E *OxCan*
Gray, Edward Dundas McQueen 1854-1932 *ChPo S1, DcNAA*
Gray, Edward Whitaker 1748-1807 *Alli*
Gray, Edwyn A 1927- *ConAu 41*
Gray, Eleanor *ChPo S1*
Gray, Elisha 1835-1901 *Alli Sup, DcAmA, DcNAA, OhA&B*
Gray, Elizabeth Caroline *Alli Sup*
Gray, Elizabeth Janet 1902- *AmA&B, AnCL, AuBYP, ConAu XR, JBA 1934, JBA 1951, Newb 1922, SmATA 6*
Gray, Ellington *NewC*
Gray, Ellis *Alli Sup*
Gray, Ellis 1715-1753 *ChPo*
Gray, Ernest 1908- *WhWNAA*
Gray, Farnum 1940- *ConAu 49*
Gray, Floyd 1926- *ConAu 25*
Gray, Floyd F 1915- *IndAu 1917*
Gray, Francine DuPlessix 1930- *ConAu 61*
Gray, Francis Calley 1790-1856 *Alli, ChPo, DcAmA, DcNAA*
Gray, Francis W 1874- *WhLA*
Gray, Francis W 1877- *WhWNAA*
Gray, Frederick *Alli Sup*
Gray, G S *Alli Sup*
Gray, Genevieve S 1920- *ConAu 33, SmATA 4*
Gray, Geoffrey *MnBBF*
Gray, George *Alli Sup, PoIre*
Gray, George Godfrey 1854- *Alli Sup*
Gray, George Hugh 1922- *ConAu 17R*
Gray, George Robert 1808-1872 *Alli, Alli Sup*
Gray, George Seaman 1835-1885 *DcAmA, DcNAA*
Gray, George William 1886-1960 *AmA&B*
Gray, George Zabriskie 1838-1889 *Alli Sup, DcAmA, DcNAA*

Gray, Gibson 1922- *ConAu 33*
Gray, Gilbert *MnBBF*
Gray, Giles Wilkeson 1889- *ConAu 5R, IndAu 1917*
Gray, Greta *WhWNAA*
Gray, Mrs. Hamilton *Alli*
Gray, Harold 1894- *AmA&B, REnAL, WhWNAA*
Gray, Harold James 1907- *WrD 1976*
Gray, Harold St. George 1872- *WhLA*
Gray, Harriet *WrD 1976*
Gray, Henry *Alli, MnBBF*
Gray, Henry David 1873- *AmA&B, WhWNAA*
Gray, Henry Peters 1819-1877 *EarAB*
Gray, Herbert Branston 1851- *Alli Sup, WhLA*
Gray, Horace, Jr. *Alli*
Gray, Horatio 1828-1903 *Alli Sup, DcNAA*
Gray, Hugh *Alli, BbtC, BiDLA, OxCan*
Gray, I E *Alli Sup*
Gray, I W D *BbtC*
Gray, Isabella A *ChPo S1*
Gray, J A *MnBBF*
Gray, J E *ChPo S1*
Gray, J Glenn 1913- *ConAu 37, WrD 1976*
Gray, J M 1930- *ConAu 53*
Gray, J R *ChPo*
Gray, J Richard 1929- *ConAu 1R*
Gray, J Stanley 1894- *ConAu 17*
Gray, J T *Alli*
Gray, Jack 1927- *ConDr, OxCan Sup, WrD 1976*
Gray, James *Alli, Alli Sup*
Gray, James 1770-1824 *DcNAA*
Gray, James 1899- *AmA&B, AmNov, Au&Wr, ConAu 13R, MnnWr, REnAL, TwCA, TwCA Sup, WhWNAA, WrD 1976*
Gray, Mrs. James *Alli*
Gray, James A *Alli*
Gray, James Black *Alli Sup*
Gray, James Cowper *Alli Sup*
Gray, James H *OxCan Sup*
Gray, James Martin 1851-1935 *DcNAA*
Gray, James R 1921- *ConAu 33*
Gray, Jane *ConAu XR, WrD 1976*
Gray, Jane Lewers 1796-1871 *Alli, ChPo, PoCh, PoIre*
Gray, Jenny *ConAu XR, SmATA 4*
Gray, Jerry 1915- *AmSCAP 66*
Gray, John *Alli*
Gray, John 1866-1934 *ChPo, ChPo S1, ChPo S2, CnMWL*
Gray, John 1913- *Au&Wr, ConAu 9R*
Gray, John C *Alli*
Gray, John Chipman 1839-1915 *Alli Sup, DcAmA, DcNAA*
Gray, John Edward 1800-1875 *Alli, Alli Sup*
Gray, John H *Alli*
Gray, John Hamilton *OxCan*
Gray, John Hamilton 1814-1889 *Alli Sup, DcNAA, OxCan*
Gray, John Henry 1828-1890 *Alli Sup*
Gray, John Henry 1859-1946 *DcNAA*
Gray, Mrs. John Henry *Alli Sup*
Gray, John M *Alli Sup*
Gray, John Milner 1889-1970 *ConAu 29*
Gray, John Morgan *OxCan*
Gray, John Thompson *BiDSA*
Gray, John W 1935- *ConAu 17R*
Gray, John Y And Lowson, George *Alli Sup*
Gray, John Young 1846- *ChPo*
Gray, Johnnie *Alli Sup*
Gray, Jonathan *Alli*
Gray, Josceline *Alli Sup*
Gray, Joseph Henry 1856- *WhLA*
Gray, Joseph M M 1877-1957 *AmA&B, OhA&B, WhWNAA*
Gray, Joslyn *AmA&B, WhWNAA*
Gray, Joyce G 1933- *Au&Wr*
Gray, Juanita R 1918- *ConAu 61*
Gray, Kay *MnBBF*
Gray, Landon Carter 1850-1900 *DcNAA*
Gray, Laura 1885- *WhWNAA*
Gray, Lawrence *Alli Sup*
Gray, Leslie *OxCan*
Gray, Lewis Cecil 1881- *WhWNAA*

Gray, Louisa M *Alli Sup*
Gray, M C *Alli Sup*
Gray, M M *ChPo*
Gray, Malcolm *MnBBF*
Gray, Marian *ConAu XR*
Gray, Martin 1925- *AuNews 1, ChPo, ChPo S1*
Gray, Mary Agatha 1868- *CatA 1947*
Gray, Mary MacRae *ChPo*
Gray, Maxwell 1847-1923 *Alli Sup, ChPo S1, Chmbr 3, DcBiA*
Gray, Melville *Alli Sup*
Gray, Meredith *ChPo S1*
Gray, Michael 1932- *Au&Wr*
Gray, Millicent Ethelred 1873- *ChPo*
Gray, Milner 1899- *WhGrA*
Gray, Morris 1856-1931 *Alli Sup, ChPo, DcAmA, DcNAA, WhWNAA*
Gray, Murray *MnBBF*
Gray, Nicholas *Alli*
Gray, Nicholas Stuart 1922- *ConAu 21, SmATA 4, WrD 1976*
Gray, Nicholas Stuart 1923- *PiP*
Gray, Nicolete Mary 1911- *Au&Wr, WrD 1976*
Gray, Norah Neilson *ChPo*
Gray, Oliver Cromwell 1821-1871 *OhA&B*
Gray, Oscar S 1926- *ConAu 29*
Gray, Patricia Clark *AuBYP, ConAu 29, SmATA 7*
Gray, Patrick *BbtC*
Gray, Patrick W *DrAP 1975*
Gray, Patsey *ConAu XR, SmATA 7*
Gray, Paul *ChPo*
Gray, Peter 1908- *ConAu 41*
Gray, Peter And Woodward, B B *Alli Sup*
Gray, Philip Hayward 1906- *WrD 1976*
Gray, Professor *MnBBF*
Gray, R E *MnBBF*
Gray, Ralph D 1933- *ConAu 21*
Gray, Richard 1929- *WrD 1976*
Gray, Richard Butler 1922- *ConAu 1R, WrD 1976*
Gray, Robert *BiDLA, OxAm*
Gray, Robert 1762-1834 *Alli*
Gray, Robert 1809-1872 *Alli Sup*
Gray, Robert 1825-1887 *Alli Sup*
Gray, Robert F 1912- *ConAu 17R*
Gray, Robert Keith 1922- *Au&Wr*
Gray, Robert Keith 1923- *ConAu 1R*
Gray, Robert Mack 1922- *ConAu 13R*
Gray, Robertson *Alli Sup, DcNAA, OhA&B*
Gray, Roland *MnBBF*
Gray, Roland Palmer *ChPo, ChPo S1*
Gray, Ronald Douglas 1919- *ConAu 17R*
Gray, Ronald Francis 1918- *ConAu 5R*
Gray, Rosalie *Alli Sup, DcNAA*
Gray, Ruby Archer 1873- *WhWNAA*
Gray, Russell *Alli Sup*
Gray, Ruth Howard 1894- *WhWNAA*
Gray, S *Alli*
Gray, Samuel Frederick *Alli*
Gray, Samuel Octavus *Alli Sup*
Gray, Simon 1936- *Au&Wr, AuNews 1, CnThe, ConAu 23, ConDr, ConNov 1972, ConNov 1976, OxCan, OxCan Sup, WrD 1976*
Gray, Stedman H 1882- *WhWNAA*
Gray, Stephen *Alli, ChPo*
Gray, Susan Gale *ChPo*
Gray, T *ChPo S1*
Gray, Thomas *Alli, Alli Sup, Chmbr 2*
Gray, Sir Thomas d1369? *CasWL*
Gray, Thomas 1716-1771 *Alli, AtlBL, BbD, BiD&SB, BrAu, CasWL, ChPo, ChPo S1, ChPo S2, CnE&AP, CriT 2, CyWA, DcEnA, DcEnL, DcEuL, DcLEnL, EvLB, MouLC 2, NewC, OxEng, Pen Eng, RAdv 1, RCom, REn, WebEAL*
Gray, Thomas, Jr. 1803-1849 *ChPo S1, DcNAA*
Gray, Thomas J 1888-1924 *AmSCAP 66*
Gray, Timothy *AmSCAP 66*
Gray, Tony George Hugh 1922- *Au&Wr, ConAu XR, WrD 1976*
Gray, W *Alli Sup*
Gray, W Forbes *ChPo S2*

Gray, W R *Alli Sup*
Gray, Wade *BlkAW*
Gray, Walter *BiDLA, CasWL, MnBBF*
Gray, Walter Augustus *Alli Sup*
Gray, Walter T *Alli Sup, DcNAA*
Gray, Wellington B 1919- *ConAu 1R, WrD 1976*
Gray, Westmoreland 1896- *TexWr*
Gray, Whitley 1887- *WhWNAA*
Gray, William *Alli Sup*
Gray, William 1530?- *ChPo*
Gray, William And Gray, Dochard *Alli*
Gray, William A *Alli Sup*
Gray, William B *ChPo S2*
Gray, William Bittle 1891- *ConAu 13R*
Gray, William Cunningham 1830-1901 *Alli Sup, DcNAA, OhA&B*
Gray, William Dudley 1912- *IndAu 1917*
Gray, William H *Alli Sup*
Gray, William Henry 1810-1889 *Alli Sup, DcNAA*
Gray, William Scott 1885-1960 *AmA&B, WhWNAA*
Gray, Winifred *ChPo S2*
Gray-Stack, Charles Maurice 1912- *Au&Wr*
Gray-Wilson *Alli Sup*
Graybar, Lloyd J 1938- *ConAu 57*
Graybeal, David M 1921- *ConAu 17R*
Graybill, Ron 1944- *ConAu 33*
Graydon, Alexander 1752-1818 *Alli, AmA&B, CyAL 1, DcAmA, DcNAA, OxAm*
Graydon, Charles *PoIre*
Graydon, George *Alli*
Graydon, H Murray *MnBBF*
Graydon, Katharine Merrill 1858-1934 *IndAu 1816*
Graydon, Mark *MnBBF*
Graydon, Mary Merrill 1835-1917 *IndAu 1816*
Graydon, Robert Murray d1937 *MnBBF*
Graydon, Thomas Hetherington 1881-1949 *OhA&B*
Graydon, William 1759-1840 *Alli, DcAmA, DcNAA*
Graydon, William Murray 1864-1946 *CarSB, MnBBF*
Graye, John *Alli Sup*
Grayhurst, Thomas *Alli*
Grayl, D *Alli Sup*
Grayl, Druid *ChPo, ChPo S2*
Grayland, Eugene Charles *Au&Wr, ConAu P-1, WrD 1976*
Grayland, Valerie Merle *Au&Wr, ConAu 9R, SmATA 7, WrD 1976*
Grayling, W I *Alli Sup*
Graymont, Barbara *OxCan Sup*
Grayson, A K 1935- *ConAu 41*
Grayson, Alan 1930- *AmSCAP 66*
Grayson, Alice Barr *ConAu XR*
Grayson, Andrew Jackson 1838-1913 *IndAu 1917*
Grayson, Cary Travers, Jr. 1919- *ConAu 17R*
Grayson, Cecil 1920- *Au&Wr, ConAu 13R*
Grayson, Charles 1905-1973 *ConAu 41, WhWNAA*
Grayson, Charles Prevost 1859-1939 *DcNAA*
Grayson, David 1870-1946 *AmA&B, AmLY XR, ChPo S2, ConAmL, DcLEnL, DcNAA, EvLB, LongC, OxAm, REnAL, TwCA, TwCA Sup, WhWNAA*
Grayson, E *Alli, DcNAA*
Grayson, Eldred *AmA&B, DcNAA*
Grayson, Ethel Kirk 1890- *CanNov, ChPo, OxCan*
Grayson, Henry 1910- *ConAu 41*
Grayson, Hubert *MnBBF*
Grayson, James *Alli Sup*
Grayson, Janet 1934- *ConAu 53*
Grayson, L M *OxCan Sup*
Grayson, Marion F 1906- *AuBYP, ConAu 5R*
Grayson, Melvin J 1924- *ConAu 45*
Grayson, P W *Alli*
Grayson, Robert A 1927- *ConAu 33*
Grayson, William John 1788-1863 *Alli, Alli Sup, AmA&B, BiDSA, CnDAL, CyAL 1, DcAmA, DcNAA, OxAm, REnAL*
Grayson, William S *Alli Sup*
Graystands, Robert De *Alli*

Grayzel, Solomon 1896- *ConAu 1R*
Grazebrook, Henry *Alli Sup*
Grazebrook, Henry Sydney 1836- *Alli Sup*
Grazia, Thomas Di *IlBYP*
Graziani, Girolamo 1604-1675 *BiD&SB*
Graziano, Ann 1928- *AmSCAP 66*
Graziano, Caesar Frankie 1904- *AmSCAP 66*
Grazie, Marie Eugenie Delle 1864-1931 *OxGer*
Grazzini, Anton Francesco 1503-1584 *CasWL,*
  McGWD, Pen Eur, REn
Grazzini, Antonio Francesco 1503-1584
  BiD&SB
Grazzini, Antonio Francesco 1503-1583 *DcEuL*
Greacen, Robert 1920- *Au&Wr*
Gready, Edward *PoIre*
Greally, John 1934- *Au&Wr, WrD 1976*
Grean, Stanley 1920- *ConAu 29, WrD 1976*
Greane, David *BlkAW*
Great Cham Of Literature, The *DcEnL*
Great Commoner, The *NewC*
Great Comte, The *ConAu XR*
Great Earl, The *NewC*
Great Magician, The *DcEnL*
Great Merlini *ConAu XR*
Great Moralist, The *DcEnL*
Great Unknown, The *DcEnL*
Greatbach, John *Alli Sup*
Greated, Timothy *Alli*
Greathead, Henry 1757- *Alli, BiDLA*
Greathed, H H *Alli Sup*
Greatheed, Bertie d1804 *Alli, BiDLA*
Greatheed, Samuel *Alli, BiDLA, BiDLA Sup*
Greatly, Spencer *Alli Sup*
Greatorex, Edward *Alli Sup*
Greatorex, Elizabeth Richmond *ConP 1970*
Greatorex, Henry Wellington 1816-1858
  DcNAA
Greatorex, Thomas 1758-1831 *Alli*
Greatorex, Wilfred 1921- *Au&Wr, ConDr*
Greatrakes, Valentine 1628- *Alli*
Greatrex, Charles Butler *Alli Sup, ChPo,*
  ChPo S1, ChPo S2
Greaves, Charles Augustus *Alli Sup*
Greaves, Charles Sprengel 1802-1881 *Alli Sup*
Greaves, Donald 1943- *BlkAW*
Greaves, Sir Edward d1680 *Alli*
Greaves, G H *Alli Sup*
Greaves, George *Alli Sup*
Greaves, Griselda *ChPo S2*
Greaves, H B *MnBBF*
Greaves, H R G 1907- *ConAu 5R*
Greaves, John *Alli, Alli Sup*
Greaves, John 1602-1652 *Alli*
Greaves, Jonathan *Alli*
Greaves, Margaret 1914- *Au&Wr, ConAu 25,*
  SmATA 7, WrD 1976
Greaves, Michael Roger 1941- *Au&Wr*
Greaves, Norman *MnBBF*
Greaves, Percy L, Jr. 1906- *ConAu 49*
Greaves, Ralph C J 1889- *Br&AmS*
Greaves, Richard *AmA&B*
Greaves, Richard L 1938- *ConAu 33*
Greaves, Thomas *Alli*
Greaves, Thomas d1676 *Alli*
Greaves, Thomas Berkeley *Alli, BiDLA*
Greaves, William *Alli, BiDLA Sup*
Greban, Arnoul 1420-1471? *CasWL, EvEuW,*
  OxFr, Pen Eur
Greban, Simon d1473 *CasWL, OxFr,*
  Pen Eur
Grebanier, Bernard 1903- *AmA&B, ConAu 23*
Grebe, Maria Ester 1928- *ConAu 25*
Grebenc, Lucile 1893- *WhWNAA*
Grebenik, Eugene 1919- *Au&Wr*
Grebenshchikov, Grigory Dmitrievich 1882-
  CasWL
Grebner, Ezekiel *Alli*
Grebstein, Lawrence C 1937- *ConAu 29*
Grebstein, Sheldon Norman 1928- *ConAu 1R,*
  WrD 1976
Grece, Charles Frederick 1771?-1844 *Alli,*
  BbtC, DcNAA
Grece, Clair James *Alli Sup*
Grech, Nikolay Ivanovich 1787-1867 *CasWL,*
  DcRusL
Greco, El 1541?-1614 *AtlBL, NewC, REn*
Greco, Armando 1926- *AmSCAP 66*
Greco, Margaret *ConAu XR*

Greditzer, Harry G 1889- *WhWNAA*
Gredy, Jean-Pierre 1920- *McGWD*
Greeley, Adolphus Washington 1844- *AmLY,*
  DcAmA, WhWNAA
Greeley, Andrew M 1928- *ConAu 5R*
Greeley, Emily Elmore 1886- *WhWNAA*
Greeley, Horace 1811-1872 *Alli, Alli Sup,*
  AmA, AmA&B, BbD, BiD&SB, CasWL,
  ChPo, Chmbr 3, CnDAL, CyAL 2,
  DcAmA, DcEnL, DcNAA, EvLB, OxAm,
  REn, REnAL
Greeley, Robert F *Alli Sup*
Greeley, Samuel Arnold 1882- *WhWNAA*
Greely, Adolphus Washington 1844-1935
  Alli Sup, AmA&B, BiD&SB, DcNAA,
  OxCan, REnAL
Greely, Rose Isobel *ChPo*
Green SEE ALSO Greene
Green *Alli, BiDLA*
Green, Miss *PoIre*
Green, A *DcRusL*
Green, A G *ChPo S1*
Green, A S 1880-1932 *TwCW*
Green, A Wingfall 1900-1971? *ConAu P-1*
Green, Abel 1900-1973 *AmSCAP 66,*
  ConAu 41
Green, Adam *ConAu XR, REnAL,*
  SmATA 2
Green, Adolph 1915- *AmA&B, AmSCAP 66,*
  ConDr
Green, Alan 1906-1975 *ConAu 53, ConAu 57*
Green, Alexander Henry *Alli Sup*
Green, Alexander Little Page 1806-1874 *BiDSA,*
  DcAmA, DcNAA
Green, Alice Stopford *Alli Sup, Chmbr 3*
Green, Alix *ChPo S1*
Green, Allen Ayrault 1878- *AmA&B*
Green, Andrew *Alli, BiDLA*
Green, Andrew 1865-1950 *CatA 1952*
Green, Anna Katharine 1846-1935 *Alli Sup,*
  AmA&B, BbD, BiD&SB, DcAmA,
  DcBiA, DcNAA, EncM&D, LongC,
  OxAm, REn, REnAL, TwCA,
  WhWNAA
Green, Anne 1891- *AmNov*
Green, Anne 1899- *AmA&B, CatA 1952,*
  ConAmA, DcLEnL, LongC, OxAm, REn,
  REnAL, TwCA, TwCA Sup
Green, Anne M 1922- *ConAu 1R*
Green, Anson 1801-1879 *BbtC, DcNAA*
Green, Arnold *Alli Sup*
Green, Arnold W 1914- *ConAu 5R*
Green, Arthur *ChPo, ChPo S1*
Green, Arthur George 1864- *WhLA*
Green, Arthur Octavius *Alli Sup*
Green, Arthur S 1927- *ConAu 5R*
Green, Asa 1789-1837? *AmA, CnDAL,*
  DcLEnL, DcNAA, REnAL
Green, Asa T 1846-1917 *Alli Sup, OhA&B*
Green, Ashbel 1762-1848 *Alli, CyAL 1,*
  DcAmA, DcNAA
Green, B *Alli, Alli Sup, BiDLA*
Green, Mrs. B R *Alli Sup*
Green, Bartholomew *OxAm*
Green, Bassett *ChPo S2*
Green, Ben K 1911-1974 *AuNews 1*
Green, Benjamin Edwards 1822-1907 *Alli Sup,*
  DcNAA
Green, Benny 1927- *ConAu XR, WrD 1976*
Green, Beriah 1795-1874 *DcAmA, DcNAA,*
  OhA&B
Green, Bernard 1908- *AmSCAP 66*
Green, Bernard 1927- *ConAu 25*
Green, Bertha E 1889- *WhWNAA*
Green, Bryan Stuart Westmacott 1901- *Au&Wr,*
  ConAu P-1
Green, Bud 1897- *AmSCAP 66*
Green, Burton *Alli Sup*
Green, Calvin E *AmSCAP 66*
Green, Celia Elizabeth 1935- *Au&Wr, BiDPar,*
  WrD 1976
Green, Chaile *MnBBF*
Green, Charles *Alli*
Green, Charles 1840-1898 *ChPo*
Green, Charles 1901- *Au&Wr*
Green, Charles Alfred Howell 1864- *WhLA*
Green, Charles Ewing *Alli Sup*
Green, Charles Frederick *Alli Sup*

Green, Charles M *Alli Sup, EncM&D*
Green, Charles Montraville 1850-1928 *DcNAA*
Green, Charles Ransley 1845-1915 *DcNAA,*
  OhA&B
Green, Claude B *ChPo S2*
Green, Constance McLaughlin 1897-1975
  AmA&B, ConAu 9R, ConAu 61, OxAm,
  WrD 1976
Green, D *ConAu XR, SmATA 4*
Green, David Bronte 1910- *Au&Wr,*
  ConAu 13R, WrD 1976
Green, David E 1942- *ConAu 33, WrD 1976*
Green, David M 1932- *ConAu 41*
Green, Donald *BlkAW*
Green, Donald E 1936- *ConAu 45*
Green, Donald Ross 1924- *ConAu 37,*
  WrD 1976
Green, Dorothy 1915- *Au&Wr, ConP 1970*
Green, Duff 1791?-1875 *Alli Sup, AmA&B,*
  BiDSA, DcAmA, DcNAA
Green, Edward *Alli, BiDLA*
Green, Edward 1920- *ConAu 13R*
Green, Edward Barnaby d1788 *Alli*
Green, Edward J 1924- *IndAu 1917*
Green, Edward Rodney Richey 1920-
  WrD 1976
Green, Edwin Luther 1870-1948 *AmA&B,*
  BiDSA
Green, Eleanor 1911- *AmA&B, AmNov*
Green, Elisabeth Sara 1940- *WrD 1976*
Green, Eliza Graves *ChPo S2*
Green, Elizabeth A H 1906- *ConAu 23,*
  WrD 1976
Green, Elizabeth H *Alli Sup*
Green, Elizabeth Shippen *ChPo, ConICB*
Green, Elmer S 1886-1947 *DcNAA*
Green, Emanuel *Alli Sup*
Green, Emma 1875- *AnMV 1926*
Green, Ernest 1885- *Au&Wr*
Green, Ernestene L 1939- *ConAu 57*
Green, Evelyn Everett *Alli Sup*
Green, Everard *Alli Sup*
Green, F C 1891-1964 *WorAu*
Green, F M *Alli Sup*
Green, F W Edridge- *Alli Sup*
Green, Fitzhugh 1888-1947 *AmA&B, CarSB,*
  DcNAA, WhWNAA
Green, Fletcher Melvin 1895- *Au&Wr,*
  ConAu 1R
Green, Frances Harriet 1805-1878 *Alli, AmA,*
  ChPo, ChPo S2, DcNAA
Green, Francis d1809 *Alli, BiDLA*
Green, Francis 1842-1909 *DcNAA*
Green, Francis Harvey 1861-1958 *AmA&B*
Green, Francis Marion 1836-1911 *OhA&B*
Green, Francis Matthews 1835-1902 *Alli Sup,*
  DcAmA, DcNAA
Green, Frank Russell *ChPo*
Green, Frank W 1842?-1884 *ChPo*
Green, Frederick 1868- *WhWNAA*
Green, Frederick Lawrence 1902-1953 *LongC,*
  REn, TwCA Sup
Green, Frederick Pratt 1903- *ConP 1970,*
  WrD 1976
Green, G *Alli*
Green, Gabriel Marcus 1891-1919 *DcNAA*
Green, Galen 1949- *ConAu 57, DrAF 1976,*
  DrAP 1975
Green, George *Alli Sup*
Green, George 1793-1841 *BrAu 19*
Green, George Clark *Alli Sup*
Green, George Rex 1884- *WhWNAA*
Green, George Walton 1854-1903 *Alli Sup,*
  DcAmA, DcNAA
Green, Gerald 1922- *AmA&B, ConAu 13R,*
  WorAu
Green, Gerald B *MnBBF*
Green, Gertrude Everett *ChPo S1*
Green, Gladys 1894- *WhWNAA*
Green, H *Alli Sup*
Green, H Gordon *OxCan, OxCan Sup*
Green, H Leland 1907- *AmSCAP 66*
Green, H W *Alli Sup*
Green, Hannah *ConAu 49, ConLC 3,*
  DrAF 1976
Green, Harold 1912- *AmSCAP 66*
Green, Harold P 1922- *ConAu 13R*
Green, Sir Henry *Alli Sup*

Green, Henry 1801-1873 *Alli Sup, ChPo S2*
Green, Henry 1905-1974 *CasWL, CnMWL, ConAu 49, ConLC 2, ConNov 1972, ConNov 1976, CyWA, DcLEnL, EncWL, EvLB, LongC, ModBL, ModBL Sup, NewC, OxEng, Pen Eng, RAdv 1, REn, TwCA Sup, TwCW, WebEAL, WhTwL*
Green, Henry And Wigram, Robert *Alli Sup*
Green, Henry Mackenzie 1881- *DcLEnL*
Green, Henry Martin *Alli Sup*
Green, Henry W *Alli*
Green, Horace 1802-1866 *Alli, Alli Sup, DcAmA, DcNAA*
Green, Horace 1885-1943 *AmA&B, DcNAA*
Green, Howard P, Sr. 1892- *AmSCAP 66*
Green, Invisible *OhA&B*
Green, Irene Smith *ChPo*
Green, J *Alli*
Green, J C R 1949- *WrD 1976*
Green, J F *Alli Sup, ChPo S1*
Green, J H *Alli, Alli Sup*
Green, J William *ChPo S1*
Green, Jacob 1722-1790 *DcNAA*
Green, Jacob 1790-1841 *DcAmA, DcNAA*
Green, James *Alli, Alli Sup, BiDLA*
Green, James d1757? *BkIE*
Green, James 1771-1834 *ChPo S1*
Green, James Albert 1862-1955 *OhA&B*
Green, James Frederick 1910- *AmA&B*
Green, James L 1919- *ConAu 17R, WrD 1976*
Green, James S *Alli*
Green, Jane 1937- *ConAu 61, SmATA 9*
Green, Jane Nugent 1918- *ConAu 61*
Green, John *Alli, Alli Sup*
Green, John 1706-1779 *Alli*
Green, John 1908- *AmSCAP 66*
Green, John Alden 1925- *ConAu 5R*
Green, John Calvin, Jr. 1894- *WhWNAA*
Green, John Henneberry 1822- *PoIre*
Green, John Henry *ChPo, ChPo S1*
Green, John L, Jr. 1929- *ConAu 45*
Green, John Orne *Alli Sup*
Green, John Richard 1837-1883 *Alli Sup, BbD, BiD&SB, BrAu 19, CasWL, DcEnA, DcEnA Ap, DcEnL, DcEnL, DcEuL, EvLB, NewC, OxEng, Pen Eng*
Green, John Richards 1758-1818 *Alli, DcEnL*
Green, Johnny L *BlkAW*
Green, Jonathan 1939- *ConAu 61*
Green, Jonathan Harrington 1812?- *IndAu 1816, OhA&B*
Green, Joseph *Alli Sup*
Green, Joseph 1706-1780 *Alli, AmA, AmA&B, BiD&SB, CyAL 1, DcAmA, DcNAA, REnAL*
Green, Joseph 1931- *ConAu 29*
Green, Joseph F, Jr. 1924- *ConAu 13R*
Green, Joseph Frederick 1855- *WhLA*
Green, Joseph Henry 1791-1863 *Alli Sup*
Green, Julia 1861- *ChPo, ChPo S1, DcAmA, WhWNAA*
Green, Julian 1900- *AmA&B, Au&Wr, CatA 1952, CyWA, DcLEnL, EvLB, LongC, ModRL, ModWD, OxAm, REn, REnAL, TwCA, TwCA Sup*
Green, Julien 1900- *CasWL, ClDMEuL, CnMWL, CnMD, ConAu 21, ConLC 3, EncWL, EvEuW, McGWD, OxFr, Pen Eur, REn, REnWD, TwCW, WhTwL*
Green, L Dunton 1872- *WhLA*
Green, Landis K 1940- *ConAu 57*
Green, Lawrence George 1900- *Au&Wr*
Green, Leon 1888- *Au&Wr*
Green, Leslie Claude 1920- *Au&Wr, ConAu 13R*
Green, Levi Worthington 1858-1932 *DcNAA*
Green, Lewis 1806-1863 *BiDSA*
Green, Lewis G 1909- *AmSCAP 66*
Green, Louis 1929- *ConAu 45*
Green, M *Alli Sup*
Green, M C *ChPo S1*
Green, Margaret Murphy 1926- *AuBYP, ConAu 1R*
Green, Marian *ChPo*
Green, Mark J 1945- *ConAu 41*
Green, Martin Burgess 1927- *ConAu 17R, WrD 1976*

Green, Martyn 1899-1975 *ConAu 57*
Green, Mary A *ChPo*
Green, Mary Anne Everett 1818-1895 *Alli, Alli Sup, BrAu 19, Chmbr 3, DcEnL, DcLEnL, OxEng*
Green, Mary McBurney 1896- *AuBYP, ConAu 29*
Green, Mary Moore 1906- *ConAu P-1*
Green, Mason Arnold 1850-1926 *Alli Sup, DcNAA*
Green, Matthew 1696-1737 *Alli, BiD&SB, BrAu, CasWL, ChPo S1, Chmbr 2, DcEnL, DcLEnL, EvLB, NewC, OxEng, Pen Eng, WebEAL*
Green, Maurice R 1922- *ConAu 13R*
Green, Maury 1916- *ConAu 29*
Green, Maxwell Revenell 1929- *Au&Wr*
Green, Michael Frederick 1927- *Au&Wr, WrD 1976*
Green, Milton D 1903- *ConAu 41*
Green, Morton 1937- *ConAu 57, SmATA 8*
Green, Murray J 1919- *AmSCAP 66*
Green, N E *Alli Sup*
Green, Nathan 1827-1919 *Alli Sup, BiDSA, DcAmA, DcNAA*
Green, Nelson Winch *Alli Sup*
Green, Nicholas St. John 1830-1876 *Alli Sup, DcNAA*
Green, Norma B 1925- *ConAu 41*
Green, O O *ConAu XR*
Green, Olive *DcNAA*
Green, Oliver *MnBBF*
Green, Otis Howard 1898- *ConAu 9R, DcSpL*
Green, Paul Eliot 1894- *AmA&B, AmSCAP 66, Au&Wr, AuNews 1, CnDAL, CnMD, CnThe, ConAmA, ConAmL, ConAu 5R, ConDr, DcLEnL, EncWL, LongC, McGWD, ModAL, ModWD, OxAm, Pen Am, REn, REnAL, REnWD, TwCA, TwCA Sup, WebEAL, WhWNAA, WrD 1976*
Green, Percy B *ChPo, ChPo S1*
Green, Peter *WhLA*
Green, Peter Morris 1924- *Au&Wr, ChPo, ConAu 5R, ConNov 1972, ConNov 1976, WrD 1976*
Green, Phyllis 1932- *ConAu 45*
Green, Ralph *Alli*
Green, Ray 1909- *AmSCAP 66*
Green, Reginald Herbold 1935- *ConAu 25*
Green, Richard *Alli, Alli Sup, AuNews 1*
Green, Richard W *Alli*
Green, Robert *Alli*
Green, Robert L 1933- *LivBA*
Green, Roger C 1932- *ConAu 45*
Green, Roger Lancelyn 1918- *Au&Wr, AuBYP, ChPo, ChPo S1, ChPo S2, ConAu 1R, SmATA 2, ThBJA, WhCL*
Green, Ron *DrAP 1975*
Green, Rosalie B 1917- *ConAu 1R*
Green, Rose Basile 1914- *ConAu 41*
Green, Rufus Smith 1848-1925 *Alli Sup, DcAmA, DcNAA*
Green, Rupert *Alli*
Green, S *Alli*
Green, Mrs. S *BiDLA*
Green, S W *Alli Sup*
Green, Samuel *Alli*
Green, Samuel 1615-1702 *REnAL*
Green, Samuel Abbott 1830-1918 *Alli Sup, DcAmA, DcNAA*
Green, Samuel Bowdlear 1859-1910 *DcNAA*
Green, Samuel Gosnell 1822- *Alli Sup*
Green, Samuel Swett 1837-1918 *Alli Sup, AmA&B, DcNAA*
Green, Sanford 1914- *AmSCAP 66*
Green, Sanford Moon 1807-1901 *Alli Sup, DcNAA*
Green, Septimus G *ChPo S1*
Green, Seth 1817-1888 *Alli Sup, DcAmA, DcNAA*
Green, Sharpless Dobson 1885- *WhWNAA*
Green, Sheila Ellen 1934- *ConAu 1R, SmATA 8*
Green, Stanley 1923- *ConAu 1R*
Green, T *BiDLA*
Green, T A *Alli Sup*
Green, T J *ChPo*

Green, Thomas *Alli, Alli Sup*
Green, Thomas 1658-1738 *Alli, DcEnL*
Green, Thomas 1769-1825 *Alli*
Green, Thomas, Jr. *Alli, BiDLA*
Green, Thomas Bowden *Alli Sup*
Green, Thomas Edward 1857-1940 *Alli Sup, AmA&B, DcNAA, WhWNAA*
Green, Thomas F 1927- *ConAu 57*
Green, Thomas Henry *Alli Sup*
Green, Thomas Hill 1836-1882 *Alli Sup, BbD, BiD&SB, BrAu 19, CasWL, Chmbr 3, DcEnA, DcEuL, EvLB, OxEng, Pen Eng, REn*
Green, Thomas Jefferson 1801-1863 *BiDSA, DcNAA*
Green, Thomas Louis 1799-1883 *Alli Sup*
Green, Thomas Marshall 1836-1904 *BiDSA, DcNAA*
Green, Thomas Michael Ramsay *Au&Wr*
Green, Thomas Sheldon *Alli Sup*
Green, Timothy 1936- *Au&Wr, ConAu 49, WrD 1976*
Green, Towneley *ChPo, ChPo S1*
Green, Ulysses *BlkAW*
Green, Upfield *Alli Sup*
Green, Urban Clifford 1926- *AmSCAP 66*
Green, Valentine *Alli*
Green, Victor 1905- *IndAu 1917*
Green, Vivian Hubert Howard 1915- *Au&Wr, ConAu 9R, WrD 1976*
Green, W *Alli, Alli Sup*
Green, W, And Penn, John *Alli*
Green, W C *ChPo S2*
Green, W H *Alli Sup*
Green, Walton 1881- *WhWNAA*
Green, William *Alli, BbtC, BiDLA, BiDSA, BkIE*
Green, William d1794 *Alli*
Green, William 1870-1952 *OhA&B*
Green, William 1913- *AmSCAP 66*
Green, William 1926- *ConAu 53*
Green, William 1927- *Au&Wr*
Green, William Charles *Alli Sup*
Green, William Henry 1825-1900 *Alli Sup, AmA, DcAmA, DcNAA*
Green, William Lowthian *Alli Sup*
Green, William Mark 1929- *ConAu 45*
Green, William Martin *BiDSA*
Green, William Mercer 1798-1887 *Alli Sup, BiDSA, DcAmA, DcNAA*
Green, William Pringle *BbtC*
Green, William Raymond 1856-1947 *DcNAA*
Green, William Spotswood *Alli Sup, OxCan*
Green, Winifred *ChPo S2*
Green-Price, Sir Richard Dansey 1872-1909 *Br&AmS*
Green-Wanstall, Kenneth 1915- *Au&Wr*
Green-Wanstall, Kenneth 1918- *ConAu 13R*
Greenacre, Phyllis 1894- *ConAu 5R*
Greenan, John T 1890- *WhWNAA*
Greenawalt, R Kent 1936- *ConAu 33*
Greenaway, Frank 1917- *Au&Wr*
Greenaway, Gladys 1901- *Au&Wr*
Greenaway, John *ChPo*
Greenaway, Kate 1846-1901 *AnCL, AuBYP, CarSB, ChPo, ChPo S1, ChPo S2, FamAI, JBA 1934, JBA 1951, NewC, OxEng, WhCL*
Greenaway, Stephen 1713-1795 *Alli*
Greenaway, Thomas 1819- *Alli Sup*
Greenbank, Anthony Hunt 1933- *ConAu 49*
Greenbank, Percy *ChPo, ChPo S1*
Greenbank, Richard Kelly 1924- *BiDPar*
Greenbaum, Fred 1930- *ConAu 37*
Greenbaum, Leonard 1930- *ConAu 21*
Greenbaum, Sidney 1929- *ConAu 33, WrD 1976*
Greenberg, Abner 1889-1959 *AmSCAP 66*
Greenberg, Alvin 1932- *ConAu 33, DrAF 1976, DrAP 1975, WrD 1976*
Greenberg, Barbara L 1932- *ConAu 53, DrAP 1975*
Greenberg, Bernard L 1917- *ConAu 41*
Greenberg, Clement 1909- *AmA&B, ConAu 1R, TwCA Sup, WrD 1976*
Greenberg, Daniel A 1934- *ConAu 5R*
Greenberg, Daniel S 1931- *ConAu 29*
Greenberg, Edward 1942- *ConAu 53*

Greenberg, Eliezer 1896- *CasWL*
Greenberg, Florence 1882- *Au&Wr*
Greenberg, Harvey R 1935- *ConAu 33,*
SmATA 5
Greenberg, Henry F 1912- *AmSCAP 66*
Greenberg, Herbert 1935- *ConAu 25,*
WrD 1976
Greenberg, Ira A 1924- *ConAu 49*
Greenberg, Jack *ChPo S2*
Greenberg, Joanne 1932- *AmA&B, ConAu 5R,*
DrAF 1976
Greenberg, Judith Anne *DrAP 1975*
Greenberg, Kenneth R 1930- *ConAu 57*
Greenberg, Martin Harry 1941- *ConAu 49*
Greenberg, Milton 1927- *ConAu 25*
Greenberg, Morrie *ConAu XR*
Greenberg, Morris S 1924- *ConAu 33*
Greenberg, Moshe 1928- *ConAu 13R*
Greenberg, Robert Arthur 1930- *ConAu 1R*
Greenberg, Samuel 1893-1917 *AmA&B, OxAm,*
Pen Am, REn, REnAL
Greenberg, Selig 1904- *ConAu 49*
Greenberg, Selma 1930- *ConAu 29*
Greenberg, Sidney 1917- *ConAu 9R*
Greenberg, Stanley Bernard 1945- *ConAu 53*
Greenberg, Uri Zevi 1891- *Pen Cl, Pen Eur*
Greenberg, Uri Zvi 1895- *CasWL*
Greenberger, Allen J 1937- *ConAu 41*
Greenberger, Howard 1924- *ConAu 45*
Greenberger, Martin 1931- *ConAu 61*
Greenbie, Marjorie Latta Barstow 1891-1976
AmA&B, AnMV 1926, ConAu 61,
WhWNAA
Greenbie, Sydney 1889-1960 *AmA&B,*
WhWNAA
Greenblatt, Augusta 1912- *ConAu 57*
Greenblatt, Edwin 1920- *ConAu 49*
Greenblatt, M H 1922- *ConAu 17*
Greenblatt, Robert Benjamin 1906- *ConAu P-1*
Greenblatt, Stephen J 1943- *ConAu 49*
Greenblum, Joseph 1925- *ConAu 23*
Greenburg, Dan 1936- *AmA&B, ConAu 13R*
Greenbury, Thomas *Alli Sup*
Greene SEE ALSO Green
Greene, Mrs. *CarSB*
Greene, A C 1923- *ConAu 37, WrD 1976*
Greene, Adam *ConAu XR*
Greene, Aella 1838-1903 *Alli Sup, BiD&SB,*
ChPo, ChPo S1, ChPo S2, DcAmA,
DcNAA
Greene, Albert C *DcEnL*
Greene, Albert Gorton 1802-1868 *Alli, AmA,*
AmA&B, BiD&SB, ChPo, CyAL 2,
DcAmA, DcNAA, EvLB, REnAL
Greene, Alexander *Alli*
Greene, Alma *OxCan Sup*
Greene, Anne Bosworth 1878-1961 *AmA&B,*
TwCA
Greene, Arthur Maurice, Jr. 1872- *WhWNAA*
Greene, Asa 1789?-1837 *Alli, BbD, BiD&SB,*
CyAL 2, DcAmA, DcNAA, OxAm,
REnAL
Greene, Bartholomew *Alli*
Greene, Batchelder *Alli Sup*
Greene, Belle C *DcAmA, DcNAA*
Greene, Bert 1923- *ConAu 57*
Greene, Bette 1934- *ChLR 2, ConAu 53,*
SmATA 8, WrD 1976
Greene, Carl H 1945- *BlkAW*
Greene, Carla 1916- *AuBYP, ConAu 1R,*
SmATA 1, WrD 1976
Greene, Charles *Alli Sup*
Greene, Charles Ezra 1842-1903 *Alli Sup,*
DcAmA, DcNAA
Greene, Charles Harwood *Alli Sup*
Greene, Charles Lyman 1862-1929 *DcNAA*
Greene, Charles Samuel 1856-1930 *ChPo,*
ChPo S1, DcNAA, WhWNAA
Greene, Charles Warren 1840-1920 *Alli Sup,*
AmA&B, DcAmA, DcNAA
Greene, Charles Wilson 1866- *IndAu 1917,*
WhWNAA
Greene, Clay Meredith 1850-1933 *AmA&B,*
DcNAA
Greene, Constance C 1924- *ConAu 61*
Greene, Daniel Howland 1807-1886 *DcNAA*
Greene, Dascom 1825-1900 *DcNAA*
Greene, David Herbert 1913- *Au&Wr,*

ConAu 23
Greene, David Maxson 1832-1905 *DcNAA*
Greene, Dominick Sarsfield *Alli Sup*
Greene, Donald J 1916- *ConAu 1R*
Greene, Duane Merritt *Alli Sup*
Greene, Edward Lee 1843-1915 *AmA, DcAmA,*
DcNAA
Greene, Emily Jane *BlkAW*
Greene, Evarts Boutell 1870-1947 *AmA&B,*
DcAmA, DcNAA, WhWNAA
Greene, Felix 1909- *Au&Wr, ConAu 1R*
Greene, Frances Harriet *DcAmA*
Greene, Frances Nimmo *AmA&B, BiDSA,*
CarSB
Greene, Francis Vinton 1850-1921 *Alli Sup,*
AmA, BiD&SB, DcAmA, DcNAA
Greene, Frederick Stuart 1870- *WhWNAA*
Greene, Gael *ConAu 13R*
Greene, George *Alli, BiDLA*
Greene, George Arthur 1853- *PoIre*
Greene, George E 1861-1917 *IndAu 1816*
Greene, George Francis 1858-1926 *DcNAA*
Greene, George Washington 1811-1883 *Alli,*
Alli Sup, AmA, AmA&B, BiD&SB,
CyAL 2, DcAmA, DcEnL, DcNAA
Greene, Georgia Hanley 1882- *WhWNAA*
Greene, Graham 1904- *Au&Wr, AuNews 2,*
CasWL, CatA 1947, ChPo S2, CnMD,
CnMWL, CnThe, ConAu 13R, ConDr,
ConLC 1, ConLC 3, ConLC 6,
ConNov 1972, ConNov 1976, CrCD,
CyWA, EncM&D, EncWL, LongC,
McGWD, ModBL, ModBL Sup, ModWD,
NewC, OxEng, Pen Eng, RAdv 1, REn,
TwCA, TwCA Sup, TwCW, WebEAL,
WhCL, WhTwL, WrD 1976
Greene, Harris 1921- *Au&Wr, ConAu 13R*
Greene, Harris Ray 1829-1892 *Alli Sup,*
DcNAA
Greene, Harry 1928- *AmSCAP 66*
Greene, Harry A 1889- *ConAu 17*
Greene, Harry J 1906- *ConAu 57*
Greene, Harry Plunket 1865- *WhLA*
Greene, Henry *Alli Sup*
Greene, Henry Copley 1871-1951 *AmA&B,*
DcAmA, WhWNAA
Greene, Henry Graham 1904- *DcLEnL, EvLB*
Greene, Herbert 1898- *Au&Wr, ChPo,*
ChPo S1, ChPo S2, ConAu P-1
Greene, Herbert Eveleth 1858-1942 *AmA&B*
Greene, Herbert Wilber 1851-1924 *DcNAA*
Greene, Homer 1853-1940 *Alli Sup, AmA&B,*
BiD&SB, ChPo, ChPo S1, DcAmA,
DcNAA
Greene, Howard R 1937- *ConAu 61*
Greene, Isabella Catherine 1842?- *Alli Sup,*
DcAmA, DcNAA
Greene, Jack Phillip 1931- *ConAu 9R,*
IndAu 1917
Greene, Jacob Wesley 1839-1916 *IndAu 1917*
Greene, James H 1915- *ConAu 17R,*
WrD 1976
Greene, James Hervey 1834-1890 *OhA&B*
Greene, Janet 1917- *ConAu 5R*
Greene, Jay E 1914- *ConAu 5R*
Greene, Jerome G J *Alli Sup*
Greene, Joe *BlkAW*
Greene, Joe 1915- *AmSCAP 66*
Greene, John *Alli*
Greene, John Baker Stafford *Alli Sup*
Greene, John Colton 1917- *IndAu 1917*
Greene, John L 1912- *AmSCAP 66*
Greene, John M *Alli Sup*
Greene, John Priest 1849-1933 *DcNAA,*
WhWNAA
Greene, John W 1836-1908 *OhA&B*
Greene, Jonathan Edward 1943- *ConAu 33,*
ConP 1970, ConP 1975, DrAP 1975,
WrD 1976
Greene, Joseph *Alli Sup*
Greene, Joseph Nelson 1868- *IndAu 1816*
Greene, Joseph Reay *Alli Sup*
Greene, Joshua *Alli*
Greene, Josiah E 1911- *AmA&B, AmNov*
Greene, Judith 1936- *WrD 1976*
Greene, Kathleen Conyngham *ChPo, ChPo S1,*
ChPo S2, PoIre
Greene, L Patrick *MnBBF*

Greene, Lee S 1905- *ConAu 13R*
Greene, Lorenzo J 1899- *LivBA*
Greene, Louisa Lelias 1833- *Alli Sup, BiD&SB*
Greene, Marian Eleanor Postlethwaite 1879-
ChPo
Greene, Mark R 1923- *ConAu 1R*
Greene, Mary *BiDSA*
Greene, Mary Frances *IndAu 1917*
Greene, Maurice d1755 *Alli*
Greene, Max *Alli*
Greene, Maxine 1917- *ConAu 23*
Greene, Millen Sanford 1825- *ChPo S1*
Greene, Milton L *AmSCAP 66*
Greene, Mort 1912- *AmSCAP 66*
Greene, Naomi 1942- *ConAu 45*
Greene, Nathanael 1935- *ConAu 25,*
WrD 1976
Greene, Nathaniel 1797-1877 *Alli, CyAL 2,*
DcAmA, DcNAA
Greene, Norman 1930- *AmSCAP 66*
Greene, Otis *BlkAW*
Greene, Parnell *Alli Sup*
Greene, Patricia L *DrAP 1975*
Greene, Mrs. Philipps *Alli Sup*
Greene, R A And Lumpkin, J W *Alli*
Greene, R H *Alli Sup*
Greene, R W *Alli*
Greene, Reuben *Alli Sup*
Greene, Reynolds W, Jr. 1924- *ConAu 5R*
Greene, Richard *Alli*
Greene, Richard Gleason 1829-1914 *Alli Sup,*
DcNAA
Greene, Richard Henry 1839-1926 *DcNAA*
Greene, Richard L 1904- *ConAu 5R*
Greene, Robert *Alli, Alli Sup*
Greene, Robert 1560?-1592 *Alli, AtlBL, BbD,*
BiD&SB, BrAu, CasWL, ChPo,
ChPo S1, Chmbr 1, CnE&AP, CnThe,
CrE&SL, CriT 1, CyWA, DcEnA,
DcEnL, DcEuL, DcLEnL, EvLB,
McGWD, MouLC 1, NewC, OxEng,
Pen Eng, REn, REnWD, WebEAL
Greene, Robert 1922- *ConAu XR*
Greene, Robert Berkeley *Alli*
Greene, Roy Farrell 1873- *ChPo, DcAmA*
Greene, Samuel D *Alli Sup*
Greene, Samuel Stillman 1810-1883 *Alli,*
CyAL 1, DcAmA, DcNAA
Greene, Sarah Pratt 1856?-1935 *Alli Sup,*
AmA&B, BiD&SB, DcAmA, DcBiA,
DcNAA, OxAm
Greene, Schuyler 1880-1927 *AmSCAP 66*
Greene, Shirley E 1911- *ConAu 1R*
Greene, Sigrid 1921- *WrD 1976*
Greene, Stephanie 1953- *ConAu 61*
Greene, Theodore Meyer 1897-1969 *AmA&B*
Greene, Thomas *Alli, Alli Sup*
Greene, Thomas d1901 *PoIre*
Greene, Thomas Huntley *Alli Sup*
Greene, Thomas Lyman 1851-1904 *DcNAA*
Greene, Thomas M 1926- *ConAu 9R*
Greene, Thomas Whitcombe 1842- *Alli Sup*
Greene, Victor R 1933- *ConAu 25, WrD 1976*
Greene, Vivian *AuNews 2*
Greene, W *Alli Sup*
Greene, W A *Alli Sup*
Greene, W T *MnBBF*
Greene, Walter E 1929- *ConAu 25*
Greene, Ward 1892-1956 *AmA&B, AmNov,*
REnAL, TwCA, TwCA Sup, WhWNAA
Greene, Wesley 1849-1935 *DcNAA*
Greene, Wilda 1911- *ConAu 23, WrD 1976*
Greene, William *Alli, Alli Sup, BiDLA*
Greene, William Batchelder 1819-1878 *Alli,*
Alli Sup, DcAmA, DcNAA
Greene, William Batchelder 1851- *AmA&B,*
DcNAA
Greene, William C 1933- *ConAu 13R*
Greene, William Chase 1890- *AmA&B,*
WhWNAA
Greene, William H *Alli Sup*
Greene, William Houston 1854-1918 *Alli Sup,*
DcAmA, DcNAA
Greene, William Howe *OxCan*
Greene, William Thomas *Alli Sup*
Greene, Zorika *ChPo S2*
Greener, Amy *ChPo S2*
Greener, Leslie 1900- *ConAu 21, WrD 1976*

Greener, Michael John 1931- *ConAu 25,*
WrD 1976
Greener, William Wellington *Alli Sup*
Greenewalt, Crawford Hallock 1902- *ConAu 1R*
Greenfield, Abraham Lincoln 1898-1941
DcNAA
Greenfield, Benjamin Wyatt *Alli Sup*
Greenfield, Eloise 1929- *BlkAW, ConAu 49,*
LivBAA, WrD 1976
Greenfield, Eric Viele 1881- *WhWNAA*
Greenfield, Irving A 1928- *ConAu 33*
Greenfield, Jeff 1943- *ConAu 37*
Greenfield, Jerome 1923- *ConAu 5R,*
WrD 1976
Greenfield, Jerry *ConAu XR*
Greenfield, M Rose *Alli Sup*
Greenfield, Marjorie M *ChPo*
Greenfield, Nathaniel *Alli*
Greenfield, Norman S 1923- *ConAu 41*
Greenfield, Patricia Marks 1940- *ConAu 21*
Greenfield, Sidney M 1932- *ConAu 21*
Greenfield, Stanley B 1922- *ConAu 9R*
Greenfield, Thelma N 1922- *ConAu 25*
Greenfield, Thomas *Alli, Alli Sup*
Greenfield, William *Alli*
Greenfield, William Smith *Alli Sup*
Greenhalgh, Joseph Dodson *Alli Sup*
Greenhalgh, P A L 1945- *ConAu 49*
Greenhalgh, Thomas *Alli Sup*
Greenham, Richard 1531-1591 *Alli*
Greenhaw, H Wayne 1940- *ConAu 23*
Greenhill, Alfred George *Alli Sup*
Greenhill, Basil Jack 1920- *Au&Wr,*
ConAu 5R, OxCan Sup
Greenhill, J, Harrison, W & Furnivall, F
Alli Sup
Greenhill, J P 1895- *Au&Wr*
Greenhill, Joseph *Alli*
Greenhill, Marion *Alli Sup*
Greenhill, Mitch 1944- *AmSCAP 66*
Greenhill, Ralph *OxCan Sup*
Greenhill, Thomas *Alli*
Greenhill, William d1677? *Alli*
Greenholz, Martin 1904- *AmSCAP 66*
Greenhood, David 1895- *ConAu 1R*
Greenhood, Elisha *Alli Sup*
Greenhorn *AmA&B*
Greenhow, Edward *Alli Sup*
Greenhow, Edward Headlam 1814-1888
Alli Sup
Greenhow, M H *Alli Sup*
Greenhow, Robert 1800-1854 *Alli, AmA,*
BiDSA, CyAL 2, DcAmA, DcNAA
Greenhow, Rose *Alli Sup*
Greenhow, T M *Alli Sup*
Greenhow, William Thomas 1831- *Alli Sup*
Greenhut, Melvin L 1921- *ConAu 13R*
Greenidge, Charles Wilton Wood 1889- *Au&Wr*
Greenidge, Edwin 1929- *LivBA*
Greening, Edward Owen *Alli Sup*
Greening, Hamilton *MnBBF*
Greening, Henry *Alli*
Greening, W H *Alli Sup*
Greenish, Henry G *Alli Sup*
Greenland, George *ChPo*
Greenland, Herbert G *ChPo*
Greenlaw, A *Alli*
Greenlaw, Alexander John *Alli Sup*
Greenlaw, Edwin Almiron 1874-1931 *DcNAA*
Greenlaw, John *MnBBF*
Greenlaw, Paul S 1930- *ConAu 1R*
Greenlaw, Walter 1900- *AmSCAP 66*
Greenleaf, A B *Alli Sup*
Greenleaf, Barbara Kaye 1942- *ConAu 29,*
SmATA 6
Greenleaf, Benjamin 1786-1864 *Alli, DcAmA,*
DcNAA
Greenleaf, Charles Ravenscroft 1838-1911
Alli Sup, DcNAA
Greenleaf, Elisabeth Bristol *ChPo S1*
Greenleaf, Elizabeth Bristol *OxCan*
Greenleaf, F *Alli*
Greenleaf, Mrs. Georgie H 1842-1913 *DcNAA*
Greenleaf, H M *ChPo*
Greenleaf, Mrs. J T *ChPo, ChPo S1*
Greenleaf, Jonathan 1785-1865 *Alli, DcAmA,*
DcNAA
Greenleaf, Lawrence N *Alli Sup*

Greenleaf, Lawrence Nichols 1838- *DcNAA*
Greenleaf, Moses 1777-1834 *Alli, AmA,*
DcAmA, DcNAA, REnAL
Greenleaf, Richard Edward 1930- *ConAu 25*
Greenleaf, Robert And Family *ChPo*
Greenleaf, Simon 1783-1853 *Alli, CyAL 1,*
DcAmA, DcNAA
Greenleaf, Thomas *Alli*
Greenleaf, Thomas 1755-1798 *AmA&B*
Greenleaf, William 1917- *ConAu 9R,*
WrD 1976
Greenlee, Douglas 1935- *ConAu 45*
Greenlee, J Harold 1918- *ConAu 17R,*
WrD 1976
Greenlee, Sam 1930- *BlkAW, LivBA*
Greenlees, Ian Gordon 1913- *WrD 1976*
Greenlick, Merwyn R 1935- *ConAu 41*
Greenlund, Alys 1902- *AmSCAP 66*
Greenly, A H *ChPo*
Greenly, Lady Coffin *Alli*
Greenough, Charles P *Alli Sup*
Greenough, Chester Noyes 1874-1938 *AmA&B,*
DcNAA
Greenough, David Stoddard 1752-1826 *EarAB*
Greenough, David Stoddard 1787-1830 *EarAB*
Greenough, Frances *Alli Sup*
Greenough, G B *Alli*
Greenough, Henry 1807-1883 *Alli Sup,*
AmA&B, DcAmA, DcNAA
Greenough, Horatio 1805-1852 *Alli, AmA,*
AmA&B, CyAL 2, DcNAA, OxAm,
REnAL
Greenough, James Bradstreet 1833-1901
Alli Sup, AmA&B, DcAmA, DcNAA,
REnAL
Greenough, James Carruthers 1829-1924
DcNAA
Greenough, Mrs. Richard *DcAmA*
Greenough, Richard S *ChPo*
Greenough, Sarah Dana 1827-1885 *Alli Sup,*
BiD&SB, DcAmA, DcNAA
Greenough, Walter Sidney 1887-1967
IndAu 1917
Greenough, William Croan 1914- *ConAu 13R,*
IndAu 1917
Greenough, William Parker *OxCan*
Greenshields, John Blackwood *Alli Sup*
Greensides, Henry *Alli Sup*
Greenslade, Stanley Lawrence 1905- *Au&Wr*
Greenslet, Ferris 1875-1959 *AmA&B, ChPo,*
ChPo S1, DcAmA, REnAL
Greenspan, Charlotte L 1921- *ConAu 33*
Greenspun, Hank *ConAu XR*
Greenspun, Herman M 1909- *AuNews 2,*
ConAu 21
Greensted, Frances *BiDLA*
Greensted, Francis *Alli*
Greenstein, Fred I 1930- *ConAu 49*
Greenstock, David Lionel 1912- *Au&Wr,*
ConAu 9R
Greenstone, J David 1937- *ConAu 25*
Greenstone, Julius H 1873- *WhWNAA*
Greenstreet, James *Alli Sup*
Greenstreet, William Lees *Alli Sup*
Greenup, Albert William 1866- *WhLA*
Greenup, J *Alli*
Greenup, Mrs. W T *Alli Sup*
Greenville, Denis d1703 *Alli*
Greenville, George *Alli*
Greenwald, Emanuel 1811-1885 *Alli Sup,*
BiDSA, DcAmA, DcNAA, OhA&B
Greenwald, Harold 1910- *AmA&B, Au&Wr,*
ConAu 1R, WrD 1976
Greenwald, Jerry 1923- *ConAu 57*
Greenwald, Joel 1938- *AmSCAP 66*
Greenwald, Leopold 1889-1955 *OhA&B*
Greenwald, Sheila 1934- *ChPo, ConAu XR,*
IlBYP, IlCB 1966, SmATA 8
Greenwalt, Mary Hallock 1872- *WhWNAA*
Greenwalt, Tibor J 1914- *WrD 1976*
Greenway, Grandfather 1800-1860 *AmA*
Greenway, J R *BiDSA*
Greenway, James *Alli*
Greenway, John 1919- *ChPo S1, ConAu 9R*
Greenway, Roger S 1934- *ConAu 53*
Greenway, Thomas 1838-1908 *OxCan*
Greenway, Walter Burton 1876-1940 *DcNAA*
Greenwell, Dora 1821-1882 *Alli Sup, ChPo,*

ChPo S1, DcEnL, NewC
Greenwell, George C *Alli Sup*
Greenwell, Nicholas *Alli Sup*
Greenwell, William *Alli Sup*
Greenwood *Alli*
Greenwood, Abraham *Alli, BiDLA*
Greenwood, Alice Davis Odekirk 1850-1936
IndAu 1816
Greenwood, Allen 1866-1942 *DcNAA*
Greenwood, Charles 1821- *Alli*
Greenwood, Daniel *Alli*
Greenwood, David Charles 1927- *ConAu 61*
Greenwood, Duncan 1919- *Au&Wr, ConAu 21*
WrD 1976
Greenwood, Edward Alister 1930- *ConAu 29*
Greenwood, Elisha 1863- *DcAmA*
Greenwood, Francis William Pitt 1797-1843 *Alli,*
CyAL 2, DcAmA, DcNAA
Greenwood, Frank *BlkAW*
Greenwood, Frank 1924- *ConAu 25*
Greenwood, Frederick 1830-1909 *Alli Sup,*
ChPo, DcEnL, NewC
Greenwood, George *Alli, Alli Sup*
Greenwood, Sir George 1850- *WhLA*
Greenwood, George Wright *Alli Sup*
Greenwood, Gertrude Shisler 1899- *OhA&B*
Greenwood, Gordon 1913- *ConAu 21*
Greenwood, Gordon E 1935- *ConAu 37*
Greenwood, Grace 1823-1904 *Alli, Alli Sup,*
AmA, AmA&B, BbD, BiD&SB, ChPo,
ChPo S2, DcAmA, DcEnL, DcNAA,
OxAm
Greenwood, Sir Granville George 1850-1928
ChPo S1
Greenwood, Guy *HsB&A*
Greenwood, Harry 1848- *Alli Sup*
Greenwood, Henry *Alli*
Greenwood, Henry Charles 1827- *Alli Sup*
Greenwood, Isaac 1702-1745 *Alli, DcNAA*
Greenwood, Isaac John 1833-1911 *Alli Sup,*
DcNAA
Greenwood, J B *Alli*
Greenwood, J M *Alli Sup*
Greenwood, Jabez *Alli Sup*
Greenwood, James *Alli, Alli Sup, DcEnL,*
MnBBF
Greenwood, James 1855- *Alli Sup*
Greenwood, James Mickleborough 1836-1914
Alli Sup, DcAmA, DcNAA
Greenwood, Jean Maury 1912- *TexWr*
Greenwood, Jessy E *Alli Sup*
Greenwood, John *Alli*
Greenwood, John Beswicke *Alli Sup*
Greenwood, John Ormerod 1907- *Au&Wr*
Greenwood, Joseph Albert 1906- *BiDPar*
Greenwood, Joseph Gouge 1821- *Alli Sup*
Greenwood, Julia Eileen Courtney 1910-
ConAu P-1, WrD 1976
Greenwood, Laura *Alli Sup, ChPo S1*
Greenwood, Major *Alli Sup*
Greenwood, Major 1880- *WhLA*
Greenwood, Marianne 1926- *ConAu 9R*
Greenwood, Nic *Alli*
Greenwood, Norman Neill 1925- *WrD 1976*
Greenwood, Robert 1897- *Au&Wr*
Greenwood, Robin *MnBBF*
Greenwood, Ted *ConAu XR*
Greenwood, Theresa 1936- *BlkAW, ConAu 29,*
WrD 1976
Greenwood, Thomas *Alli, Alli Sup, ChPo S1*
Greenwood, Walter 1903-1974 *Au&Wr,*
ConAu 53, ConDr, DcLEnL, EvLB,
LongC, NewC, Pen Eng, TwCA,
TwCA Sup, TwCW
Greenwood, Will *Alli*
Greenwood, William *Alli*
Greenwood, William 1845-1931 *DcNAA*
Greenwood, William Henry *Alli Sup*
Greep, Walter 1897- *TexWr*
Greepe, Thomas *Alli*
Greer, Ann Lennarson 1944- *ConAu 53*
Greer, Blanche 1884- *ChPo*
Greer, C Lee 1874- *TexWr, WhWNAA*
Greer, Carl Richard 1876-1946 *OhA&B*
Greer, Carlotta C 1879-1965 *ConAu P-1*
Greer, David Hummell 1844-1919 *ChPo,*
DcAmA, DcNAA
Greer, Edward *Alli Sup*

Greer, F H *Alli Sup*
Greer, Georgeanna H 1922- *ConAu 57*
Greer, Germaine 1939- *AuNews 1, WrD 1976*
Greer, Henry *Alli Sup*
Greer, Herb 1929- *Au&Wr, ConAu 5R*
Greer, Hilton Ross 1879-1949 *AmA&B, BiDSA, ChPo S1, DcNAA, TexWr, WhWNAA*
Greer, Mrs. J R *Alli*
Greer, James *Alli Sup*
Greer, James Kimmins 1896- *TexWr*
Greer, Jesse 1896- *AmSCAP 66*
Greer, John *PoIre*
Greer, John 1851-1895? *PoIre*
Greer, Louise 1899- *ConAu P-1*
Greer, Maria *Alli Sup*
Greer, Maria J *Alli Sup*
Greer, Sarah D *Alli Sup, PoIre*
Greer, Scott A 1922- *AmA&B, ConAu 45*
Greer, Thomas H 1914- *ConAu 23*
Greer, Tom *Alli Sup*
Greer-Petrie, Cordia *AmA&B, WhWNAA*
Greet, Ben 1857-1936 *LongC*
Greet, John *Alli Sup*
Greet, Kenneth Gerald 1918- *Au&Wr, ConAu 5R, WrD 1976*
Greet, T Y 1923- *ConAu 13R*
Greet, William Cabell 1901-1972 *AmA&B, ConAu 37*
Greever, Garland 1883- *WhWNAA*
Greever, William St. Clair 1916- *ConAu 5R, WhPNW*
Greeves, Edith *Alli Sup*
Greeves, Frederic 1903- *Au&Wr, WrD 1976*
Greey, Edward 1835-1888 *Alli Sup, BbD, BiD&SB, CarSB, DcAmA, DcNAA*
Greff, Joachim 1500?- *OxGer*
Grefflinger, Georg 1620?-1677? *CasWL*
Greffyn, W *Alli*
Greflinger, Georg 1620?-1677? *OxGer*
Greg, John *Alli*
Greg, John Anthony *Alli*
Greg, Percy 1836-1899 *Alli Sup, Chmbr 3*
Greg, Robert Philips And Lettsom, W G *Alli Sup*
Greg, Samuel 1804-1876 *Alli Sup, ChPo S1*
Greg, Thomas *Alli*
Greg, Sir Walter Wilson 1875-1959 *DcLEnL, OxEng, Pen Eng, REn*
Greg, William *Alli*
Greg, William Rathbone 1809-1881 *Alli, Alli Sup, BiD&SB, BrAu 19, Chmbr 3, DcEnL, DcLEnL, EvLB, NewC*
Gregan, Paul *ChPo S1, PoIre*
Gregg, Abraham *Alli Sup*
Gregg, Alexander 1819-1893 *Alli Sup, BiDSA, DcAmA, DcNAA*
Gregg, Andrew K 1929- *ConAu 29*
Gregg, David 1846-1919 *BiD&SB, DcAmA, DcNAA*
Gregg, David McMurtrie 1833-1916 *DcNAA*
Gregg, David Weinert 1918- *ConAu 17R, WrD 1976*
Gregg, Ernest *BlkAW*
Gregg, F *Alli*
Gregg, Florence *Alli Sup*
Gregg, Frank Moody 1864-1937 *OhA&B*
Gregg, Fred Marion 1867- *WhWNAA*
Gregg, Frederick J *PoIre*
Gregg, Hubert *WrD 1976*
Gregg, J Chandler *Alli Sup*
Gregg, J E *TexWr*
Gregg, James E 1927- *ConAu 23*
Gregg, James Edgar 1875-1946 *DcNAA*
Gregg, James R 1914- *ConAu 23*
Gregg, Jarvis 1808-1836 *DcNAA*
Gregg, Jess 1926- *ConAu 61*
Gregg, John *BiDLA*
Gregg, John 1798-1878 *Alli Sup*
Gregg, John Allen Fitzgerald 1873- *WhLA*
Gregg, John Anthony *Alli, BiDLA*
Gregg, John E 1925- *ConAu 45*
Gregg, John Robert 1867-1948 *AmA&B, AmLY, DcNAA, WhWNAA*
Gregg, Josiah 1806-1850 *Alli, AmA, AmA&B, DcLEnL, DcNAA, OxAm, REnAL*
Gregg, Lucinda J *ChPo*
Gregg, Lucy Brown 1833- *IndAu 1917*

Gregg, Martin *ConAu XR*
Gregg, Mary Kirby 1817-1893 *CarSB*
Gregg, Mary Louise 1921- *AmSCAP 66*
Gregg, Norma *ChPo S1*
Gregg, Pauline *Au&Wr, ConAu 5R, WrD 1976*
Gregg, Richard Alexander 1927- *ConAu 13R, WrD 1976*
Gregg, Robert Samuel 1834- *Alli Sup*
Gregg, Rollin Robinson 1828-1886 *Alli Sup, DcNAA*
Gregg, Samuel *Alli Sup*
Gregg, Sidney John 1902- *Au&Wr, WrD 1976*
Gregg, St. George d1840 *PoIre*
Gregg, T D d1881 *Alli*
Gregg, Thomas *BiDLA*
Gregg, Thomas 1808-1892 *Alli Sup, OhA&B*
Gregg, Tresham Dames d1881 *Alli Sup, PoIre*
Gregg, W T *Alli Sup*
Gregg, William 1817-1909 *Alli Sup, DcNAA*
Gregg, William Henry *Alli Sup*
Gregg, William Stephenson *Alli Sup*
Gregg, Willis Ray 1880-1938 *DcNAA, WhWNAA*
Gregg, Wilson d1899 *DcNAA*
Greggs, Herbert D 1931- *BlkAW*
Gregh, Fernand 1873-1960 *OxFr*
Grego, Joseph *Alli Sup*
Gregoire De Tours 538?-594 *OxFr*
Gregoire, Agnes *ChPo*
Gregoire, Georges Stanislas 1845-1928 *DcNAA*
Gregoire, Gilles *OxCan Sup*
Gregor, A James 1929- *ConAu 57*
Gregor, Arthur 1923- *ConAu 25, ConP 1970, ConP 1975, DrAP 1975, WrD 1976*
Gregor, Elmer Russell 1878-1954 *AmA&B, MnBBF, WhWNAA*
Gregor, Emmy S 1892- *OhA&B*
Gregor, Francis 1760-1815 *Alli, BiDLA, BiDLA Sup*
Gregor, Howard F 1920- *ConAu 5R*
Gregor, Ian 1926- *Au&Wr*
Gregor, Rex H 1922- *ConAu 13R*
Gregor, Walter *Alli Sup*
Gregor, William *Alli, BiDLA*
Gregor-Dellin, Martin 1926- *Au&Wr*
Gregor-Tajovsky, Jozef 1874-1940 *CasWL*
Gregoras, Nicephorus 1295?-1360 *CasWL, EuA, Pen Cl*
Gregorcic, Simon 1844-1906 *CasWL*
Gregorian, Vartan 1935- *ConAu 29*
Gregorovich, Andrew *OxCan Sup*
Gregorovius, Ferdinand Adolf 1821-1891 *BbD, BiD&SB, CasWL, EuA, OxGer*
Gregory Acindynus *CasWL*
Gregory Of Cyprus 1241?-1289? *Pen Cl*
Gregory Of Narek 950?-1010 *CasWL*
Gregory Of Nazianzus 329?-390? *CasWL, Pen Cl*
Gregory Of Nyssa 335?-394? *CasWL, Pen Cl*
Gregory Of Tours, Georgius Florentius 538?-594 *CasWL, Pen Eur*
Gregory Of Tours, Saint 538?-594 *NewC*
Gregory Palamas *CasWL, Pen Cl*
Gregory I, Saint 540?-604 *NewC, OxEng, PoCh, REn*
Gregory VII, Saint 1020?-1085 *NewC, REn*
Gregory The Great, Saint 540?-604 *CasWL, Pen Eur*
Gregory, Doctor *ChPo*
Gregory, Lady 1852-1932 *Chmbr 3, LongC, ModBL, ModBL Sup, ModWD*
Gregory, Lady ALSO Gregory, Augusta
Gregory, Lady ALSO Gregory, Isabella
Gregory, A E *Alli Sup*
Gregory, Alexander *Alli Sup*
Gregory, Alfred *Alli Sup*
Gregory, Alyse 1884- *ChPo S1, WhLA*
Gregory, Arthur *Alli*
Gregory, Lady Augusta 1852-1932 *CasWL, CnThe, CyWA, McGWD, NewC, OxEng, WhLA*
Gregory, Lady A ALSO Gregory, Lady
Gregory, Lady A ALSO Gregory, Isabella
Gregory, Augustus Charles And Francis T *Alli Sup*
Gregory, Benjamin *Alli Sup*
Gregory, Bobby 1900- *AmSCAP 66*

Gregory, Carole *BlkAW*
Gregory, Caspar Rene 1846-1917 *DcNAA*
Gregory, Cedric E 1908- *WrD 1976*
Gregory, Charles Noble 1851-1932 *DcNAA, WhWNAA*
Gregory, Charles William *Alli Sup*
Gregory, Chester Arthur 1880-1956 *IndAu 1917, OhA&B*
Gregory, Christine *ChPo S2*
Gregory, Claudius Jabez 1879?-1944 *DcNAA, OxCan*
Gregory, Daniel Seelye 1832-1915 *Alli Sup, AmA&B, DcAmA, DcNAA, OhA&B*
Gregory, Dave *MnBBF*
Gregory, David 1661-1708 *Alli*
Gregory, David 1932- *AmA&B, ConAu 45, LivBAA, WrD 1976*
Gregory, Dick 1932- *AmA&B, ConAu 45, LivBAA, WrD 1976*
Gregory, Duncan *MnBBF*
Gregory, Duncan Farquharson d1844 *Alli*
Gregory, Edmond *Alli*
Gregory, Edmund d1650 *DcEnL*
Gregory, Edmund Ironside *Alli Sup*
Gregory, Edward S 1843-1884 *BiDSA, DcNAA*
Gregory, Eliot 1854?-1915 *AmA&B, DcAmA, DcNAA*
Gregory, Elizabeth *ConAu XR*
Gregory, F *Alli*
Gregory, Francis *Alli*
Gregory, Frank M *ChPo S2*
Gregory, George *Alli*
Gregory, George d1853 *Alli*
Gregory, George 1754-1808 *Alli, PoIre*
Gregory, Georgiana *Alli Sup*
Gregory, Harry *ConAu XR, MnBBF*
Gregory, Herbert E 1869- *WhWNAA*
Gregory, Horace 1898- *AmA&B, ChPo, ChPo S1, ChPo S2, CnDAL, ConAmA, ConAu 5R, ConP 1970, ConP 1975, DcLEnL, DrAP 1975, ModAL, OxAm, Pen Am, RAdv 1, REn, REnAL, SixAP, TwCA, TwCA Sup, WrD 1976*
Gregory, Hylton *MnBBF*
Gregory, Isaac *Alli Sup*
Gregory, Lady Isabella Augusta 1852-1932 *AtlBL, ChPo, ChPo S2, DcLEnL, EvLB, Pen Eng, REn, REnWD, TwCA, TwCA Sup, TwCW, WebEAL, WhLA*
Gregory, I A ALSO Gregory, Lady
Gregory, I A ALSO Gregory, Augusta
Gregory, Jack Norman 1920- *WrD 1976*
Gregory, Jackson 1882-1943 *AmA&B, AmLY, DcNAA, REnAL, TwCA, TwCA Sup, WhWNAA*
Gregory, James 1639-1675 *Alli*
Gregory, James 1753-1821 *Alli, BiDLA*
Gregory, James Stothert 1912- *Au&Wr, WrD 1976*
Gregory, John *Alli, Alli Sup*
Gregory, John 1607-1646 *Alli*
Gregory, John 1724-1773 *Alli, DcEnL*
Gregory, John 1810-1881 *DcNAA*
Gregory, John George *Alli Sup*
Gregory, John Goadby 1856-1947 *AmA&B, DcAmA, DcNAA*
Gregory, John Herbert 1874- *WhWNAA*
Gregory, John Mark *Alli*
Gregory, John Milton 1822-1898 *Alli Sup, DcAmA, DcNAA*
Gregory, John Robinson *Alli Sup*
Gregory, John Uriah 1830-1913 *DcNAA*
Gregory, Joseph *Alli, BiDLA*
Gregory, Josiah *Alli Sup*
Gregory, Malcolm Spencer 1931- *WrD 1976*
Gregory, Maze William *Alli Sup*
Gregory, Octavia *ChPo S2*
Gregory, Olinthus Gilbert 1774-1841 *Alli, BiDLA*
Gregory, Oliver Fuller 1844- *AmLY*
Gregory, Padraic 1886- *CatA 1947, ChPo, ChPo S1, WhLA*
Gregory, Paul Roderick 1941- *ConAu 53*
Gregory, Peter 1924- *ConAu 41*
Gregory, Philip E 1886- *ChPo*
Gregory, R R C *ChPo S2*
Gregory, Richard Langton 1923- *ConAu 17R, ConAu 57, WrD 1976*
Gregory, Robert *Alli Sup*
Gregory, Robert 1819- *BiD&SB*

Grey, J R *ChPo*
Grey, Jane *DcNAA*
Grey, Lady Jane 1537-1554 *Alli, REn*
Grey, Jane Willis *ChPo S1*
Grey, Jeannie H *Alli Sup*
Grey, Jerry 1926- *ConAu 53*
Grey, John *Alli, BiDLA, MnBBF*
Grey, John 1812- *Alli Sup*
Grey, John Edward *Alli Sup*
Grey, John W *EncM&D*
Grey, Joseph W 1879-1956 *AmSCAP 66*
Grey, Katharine *DcNAA*
Grey, Lanny 1909- *AmSCAP 66*
Grey, Louis *EncM&D*
Grey, Margaret *Alli Sup*
Grey, Maria G, And Emily Shirreff *Alli*
Grey, Maria Georgina 1816- *Alli Sup*
Grey, Nicholas 1590-1660 *Alli*
Grey, Oliver *Alli Sup*
Grey, Pamela Genevieve Adelaid Tennant
    1871-1928 *ChPo, ChPo S1*
Grey, Richard 1694-1771 *Alli, DcEnL*
Grey, Robert Hyde *Alli*
Grey, Robert Waters 1943- *ConAu 49,
    DrAP 1975*
Grey, Rosamond S *Alli Sup*
Grey, Rowland 1863- *Alli Sup, WhLA*
Grey, Sidney *Alli Sup*
Grey, Simeon *Alli Sup*
Grey, Standish *Alli Sup*
Grey, Sydney *ChPo, ChPo S1, ChPo S2*
Grey, T Willis *ChPo S2*
Grey, Theresa *Alli Sup*
Grey, Thomas *Alli, NewC*
Grey, Thomas De *Alli*
Grey, Vere *Alli Sup*
Grey, Vivian *ConAu 17R*
Grey, William *Alli, Alli Sup, DcNAA*
Grey, Mrs. William *Alli Sup*
Grey, Sir William De *Alli*
Grey, Zachary 1687-1766 *Alli, DcEnL*
Grey, Zane 1875?-1939 *AmA&B, ArizL,
    DcLEnL, DcNAA, EvLB, LongC,
    MnBBF, OhA&B, OxAm, Pen Am, REn,
    REnAL, TwCA, TwCA Sup, TwCW,
    WebEAL, WhWNAA*
Grey Hawk *OxCan*
Grey Of Fallodon, Edward Grey, Viscount
    1862-1933 *DcLEnL, EvLB, LongC, OxEng,
    TwCA, TwCA Sup, WhLA*
Grey Owl 1888-1938 *CanWr, DcLEnL,
    DcNAA, OxCan, WhCL*
Greylock, Godfrey *DcAmA, DcNAA*
Greyser, Stephen A 1935- *ConAu 33*
Greysmith, David 1942- *WrD 1976*
Greyson, Emile 1823- *BbD, BiD&SB*
Greyson, M *Alli Sup*
Greyson, T *Alli, BiDLA*
Gribachev, Nikolai Matveyevich 1910- *CasWL*
Gribbel, John 1858-1936 *ChPo S1*
Gribbin, Henry *PoIre*
Gribbin, Lenore S 1922- *ConAu 33*
Gribbin, William James 1943- *ConAu 45*
Gribble, Charles E 1936- *ConAu 41*
Gribble, Francis Henry 1862- *ChPo S1*
Gribble, Francis Woodward *ChPo S2*
Gribble, James 1938- *ConAu 29*
Gribble, James Dunning Baker *Alli Sup*
Gribble, Joseph Besly *Alli Sup*
Gribble, Leonard Reginald 1908- *Au&Wr,
    ConAu 9R, EncM&D, LongC, MnBBF*
Gribble, Robert *Alli Sup*
Gribble, Thomas *Alli Sup*
Gribbons, Warren D 1921- *ConAu 29*
Gribelin, Simon 1661-1733 *BkIE*
Griboyedov, Aleksander Sergeyevich 1793-1829
    *BbD, BiD&SB, CasWL, CnThe, DcEuL,
    DcRusL, EuA, EvEuW, McGWD,
    Pen Eur, REn, REnWD*
Grice, Charles Valentine Le *Alli*
Grice, Frederick 1910- *Au&Wr, ConAu 9R,
    SmATA 6, WrD 1976*
Grice, Mary *ChPo S2*
Grice, Thomas *Alli*
Grider, Dorothy *ChPo, IlCB 1956*
Gridley, Albert Leverett 1839-1927 *DcNAA*
Gridley, Amos Delos 1819-1876 *DcNAA*
Gridley, Henry Amelius Adams *Alli Sup*

Gridley, Jeremiah d1767 *Alli*
Gridley, Marion E 1906- *ConAu 45*
Gridley, Selah 1767-1826? *DcNAA*
Grieb, Herbert C 1898- *AmSCAP 66*
Grieb, Kenneth J 1939- *ConAu 29, WrD 1976*
Grieb, Lyndal 1940- *ConAu 61*
Grieben, Hermann 1822-1890 *BiD&SB*
Griechen-Muller *OxGer*
Grieck, Claude De 1625-1670? *CasWL*
Grieder, Josephine 1939- *ConAu 53*
Grieder, Mrs. Paul A *AmNov XR*
Grieder, Theodore 1926- *ConAu 45*
Grieder, Walter 1924- *ConAu 41, SmATA 9*
Grieg, David Lundie *ChPo*
Grieg, Edvard Hagerup 1843-1907 *AtlBL, REn*
Grieg, Johan Nordahl Brun 1902-1943
    ClDMEuL, EvEuW
Grieg, Michael 1922- *ConAu 17R*
Grieg, Nordahl Brun 1902-1943 *CasWL, ChPo,
    ChPo S1, CnMD, CnThe, EncWL,
    McGWD, ModWD, Pen Eur, REn,
    REnWD, TwCW, WhTwL*
Griepenkerl, Robert 1810-1868 *OxGer*
Griepenkerl, Wolfgang Robert 1810-1868
    BiD&SB
Grier, B R 1913- *ConAu 25*
Grier, Eldon 1917- *CanWr, ConP 1970,
    OxCan, OxCan Sup*
Grier, J B *Alli Sup*
Grier, James Alexander 1846-1918 *DcAmA,
    DcNAA*
Grier, James W 1902-1959 *AmSCAP 66*
Grier, John William *Alli Sup*
Grier, Norman MacDowell 1890- *WhWNAA*
Grier, Richard *Alli, BiDLA*
Grier, Richard Macgregor *Alli Sup*
Grier, W W *Alli Sup*
Grier, William *Alli*
Grier, William H *LivBA*
Grierson, Constantia 1706-1733 *Alli, PoIre*
Grierson, Edward 1914- *Au&Wr, ConAu 1R,
    WrD 1976*
Grierson, Elizabeth Wilson *ChPo S2,
    JBA 1934, JBA 1951*
Grierson, Francis 1848-1927 *AmA&B, Au&Wr,
    DcNAA, OxAm, REn, TwCA,
    TwCA Sup*
Grierson, Francis ALSO Shepard, B
Grierson, Francis Durham *MnBBF*
Grierson, George Abraham *Alli Sup*
Grierson, Sir Herbert John Clifford 1866-1960
    *CasWL, ChPo, ChPo S2, Chmbr 3,
    DcLEnL, EvLB, LongC, ModBL, NewC,
    Pen Eng, REn, TwCA, TwCA Sup*
Grierson, James *Alli, Alli Sup, BiDLA*
Grierson, James Moncrieff *Alli Sup*
Grierson, John 1909- *ConAu 19, WrD 1976*
Grierson, Linden 1914- *Au&Wr, ConAu P-1*
Grierson, Thomas *Alli Sup*
Grierson, Thomas B *Alli Sup*
Gries, Johann Diederich 1775-1842 *OxGer*
Griesbach, William Antrobus 1878-1945
    DcNAA
Griesbaum, Leonard 1932- *AmSCAP 66*
Griese, Arnold A 1921- *ConAu 49, SmATA 9*
Griese, Friedrich 1890-1975 *ClDMEuL, CnMD,
    ModWD, OxGer*
Griesinger, Karl Theodor 1809-1884 *BbD,
    BiD&SB*
Grieson, Ronald Edward 1943- *ConAu 49*
Griessman, Benjamin Eugene 1934- *ConAu 41*
Griest, William A 1846-1926 *IndAu 1917*
Grieve, Alan Thomas 1928- *Au&Wr*
Grieve, Alison *MnBBF*
Grieve, Andrew W 1925- *ConAu 9R*
Grieve, Christopher Murray 1892- *Au&Wr,
    CasWL, ChPo, Chmbr 3, ConAu 5R,
    ConP 1970, ConP 1975, DcLEnL, EvLB,
    LongC, NewC, OxEng, Pen Eng, REn,
    TwCA, TwCA Sup, WebEAL, WhLA,
    WrD 1976*
Grieve, James *Alli*
Grieve, John *Alli, Alli Sup*
Grieve, Lucia Catherine Graeme 1862-1946
    DcNAA
Grieve, Peter *Alli Sup*
Grieve, R *Alli Sup*
Grieve, Robert 1855-1924 *DcNAA*

Grieve, Symington *Alli Sup*
Grieve, William *Alli*
Grieves, Forest L 1938- *ConAu 53*
Griew, Edward James 1930- *Au&Wr*
Grifalconi, Ann 1929- *BkP, ChPo S1,
    ConAu 5R, IlBYP, IlCB 1966,
    SmATA 2, ThBJA*
Griff *ConAu XR*
Griff, Alan *LongC*
Griffen, Annie M *Alli Sup*
Griffen, Jeff 1923- *ConAu 13R*
Griffes, Charles Tomlinson 1884-1920
    AmSCAP 66, OxAm
Griffies, Thomas *Alli, BiDLA*
Griffin, Mr. *Alli*
Griffin, A H 1911- *ConAu 21*
Griffin, A P C *BiDSA*
Griffin, Al 1919- *ConAu 33*
Griffin, Alice McClure *LivFWS*
Griffin, Amos *BlkAW*
Griffin, Annelle 1911- *TexWr*
Griffin, Anthony *Alli*
Griffin, Appleton Prentiss Clark 1852-1926
    Alli Sup, AmA&B, DcNAA
Griffin, Arthur J 1921- *ConAu 49*
Griffin, B *Chmbr 1*
Griffin, Barbara C 1945- *ConAu 53*
Griffin, Barrholomew d1602 *Alli*
Griffin, Bartholomew d1602 *BrAu, DcEnL,
    EvLB*
Griffin, Bryant Wade 1885- *WhWNAA*
Griffin, C F *ConAu XR*
Griffin, C W 1925- *ConAu 53*
Griffin, Charles Henry 1922- *ConAu 17R*
Griffin, Clare Elmer 1892- *AmA&B,
    WhWNAA*
Griffin, David *WrD 1976*
Griffin, Donald R 1915- *ConAu 37,
    WrD 1976*
Griffin, Edmund Dorr 1770-1837 *DcNAA*
Griffin, Edmund Dorr 1804-1830 *Alli, CyAL 2,
    DcNAA*
Griffin, Edward *Alli Sup*
Griffin, Edward Dorr 1770-1837 *Alli, CyAL 1,
    DcAmA*
Griffin, Edward Loggin *Alli*
Griffin, Edwin Ellis *Alli Sup*
Griffin, Elizabeth *Alli, BiDLA*
Griffin, Ella *AuBYP*
Griffin, Ernest G 1916- *ConAu 25*
Griffin, Ernest Harrison 1877- *WhLA*
Griffin, Eugene 1855-1907 *Alli Sup, DcNAA*
Griffin, Frank 1911- *Au&Wr*
Griffin, Frank Loxley 1881- *WhWNAA*
Griffin, Frederick *Alli, Alli Sup, BbtC*
Griffin, Frederick 1798-1879 *DcNAA*
Griffin, Frederick 1889-1946 *DcNAA*
Griffin, George *MnBBF, OxCan*
Griffin, George 1778-1860 *Alli, DcAmA,
    DcNAA*
Griffin, George Hermon 1839-1894 *DcNAA*
Griffin, Gerald *Chmbr 3, PoIre*
Griffin, Gerald 1803-1840 *Alli, BbD, BiD&SB,
    BrAu 19, CasWL, ChPo S1, CyWA,
    DcBiA, DcEnA, DcEnL, DcLEnL, EvLB,
    HsB&A, NewC, OxEng, PoIre*
Griffin, Gerald 1891-1962 *AmSCAP 66*
Griffin, Gerald G 1933- *ConAu 57*
Griffin, Gilderoy Wells 1840-1891 *Alli Sup,
    BiD&SB, BiDSA, DcAmA, DcNAA*
Griffin, Gillett Good 1928- *AuBYP, ChPo,
    IlCB 1956*
Griffin, Glen C 1934- *ConAu 29*
Griffin, Gregory *Alli, DcEnL*
Griffin, Gwyn 1922?-1967 *RAdv 1, WorAu*
Griffin, Harry 1911- *WrD 1976*
Griffin, J A *OxCan Sup*
Griffin, Jacqueline P 1927- *ConAu 33*
Griffin, James *Alli Sup*
Griffin, James A 1934- *ConAu 29*
Griffin, John 1769-1834 *Alli, BiDLA*
Griffin, John Howard 1902- *Pen Am, WhTwL*
Griffin, John Howard 1920- *AmA&B, Au&Wr,
    AuNews 1, ConAu 1R, WorAu,
    WrD 1976*
Griffin, John Joseph *Alli, Alli Sup*
Griffin, John Nash *Alli Sup*
Griffin, John Quincy Adams *Alli Sup*

DcAmA, DcNAA, OhA&B
Gross, Samuel Eberly 1843-1913 *DcNAA*
Gross, Samuel Weissell 1837-1889 *Alli Sup,*
DcAmA, DcNAA
Gross, Sarah Chokla 1906- *ConAu 61,*
SmATA 9
Gross, Seymour L 1926- *ConAu 1R*
Gross, Shelley 1938- *ConAu 21*
Gross, Stuart D 1914- *ConAu 57*
Gross, Suzanne 1933- *ConAu 17R*
Gross, Theodore L 1930- *ConAu 41*
Gross, Walter 1909- *AmSCAP 66*
Gross, Walter 1923- *ConAu 21*
Gross, Werter L *BlkAW*
Gross, William Joseph 1894- *ConAu P-1*
Grossack, Martin Myer 1928- *ConAu 9R*
Grossbach, Robert 1941- *ConAu 33*
Grosscup, Peter Strenger 1852-1921 *OhA&B*
Grosse, Alexander d1654 *Alli*
Grosse, Charles *MnBBF*
Grosse, Julius Waldemar 1828-1902 *BiD&SB,*
OxGer
Grosse, Robert *Alli*
Grosse, Robert Le *Alli*
Grosse, William *Alli*
Grosser, Alfred 1925- *ConAu 45*
Grosseteste, Robert 1175?-1253 *Alli, CasWL,*
Chmbr 1, DcSpL, EvLB, NewC, OxEng,
Pen Eng, REn
Grosshans, Henry 1921- *ConAu 29*
Grossholtz, Jean 1929- *ConAu 1R*
Grossi, Tommaso 1791?-1853 *BbD, BiD&SB,*
CasWL, DcBiA, DcEuL, Pen Eur, REn
Grossinger, Tania 1937- *ConAu 53,*
WrD 1976
Grosskopf, Charlotte D *IndAu 1917*
Grosskopf, Johannes Friedrich Wilhelm
1885-1948 *CasWL*
Grosskurth, Phyllis 1924- *ConAu 13R,*
OxCan Sup
Grossman, Alfred 1927- *Au&Wr, ConAu 5R,*
ConNov 1972, ConNov 1976, Pen Am,
WrD 1976
Grossman, Allen R 1932- *AmA&B,*
ConAu 1R
Grossman, Bernard 1885-1951 *AmSCAP 66*
Grossman, Edith Searle 1863-1931 *TwCW*
Grossman, Edward 1891- *AmSCAP 66*
Grossman, Frances Kaplan 1939- *ConAu 57*
Grossman, Herbert 1934- *ConAu 17R,*
WrD 1976
Grossman, Jean Schick 1894-1972 *ConAu 37*
Grossman, Julian 1931- *ConAu 53*
Grossman, Kurt R 1897-1972 *ConAu 33*
Grossman, Leonid Petrovich 1888-1966 *CasWL,*
EvEuW
Grossman, Morton Charles 1919- *ConAu 1R*
Grossman, Nancy S 1940- *IlBYP, IlCB 1966*
Grossman, Reinhardt 1931- *WrD 1976*
Grossman, Ronald P 1934- *ConAu 21*
Grossman, Samuel 1897- *ConAu 53*
Grossman, Sebastian P 1934- *ConAu 23,*
WrD 1976
Grossman, Shelly 1928?-1975 *ConAu 57*
Grossman, Vasili Semyonovich 1905-1964
CasWL, DcRusL, EvEuW
Grossman, William L 1906- *ConAu 23*
Grossmann, Edith Howitt 1865-1931 *DcLEnL*
Grossmann, Georg Martin 1823-1897 *DcNAA*
Grossmann, Gustav Friedrich Wilhelm 1746-1796
OxGer
Grossmann, Louis 1863-1926 *Alli Sup,*
DcNAA, OhA&B
Grossmann, Reinhardt S 1931- *ConAu 33*
Grossmith, George 1847-1912 *Alli Sup,*
CasWL, DcLEnL, EvLB, Pen Eng
Grossmith, George, Jr. *ChPo*
Grossmith, John *Alli Sup*
Grossmith, Walter Weedon 1854-1919 *DcLEnL*
Grossmith, Weedon 1854-1919 *Pen Eng*
Grossmith, William Robert *Alli Sup*
Grossteste, Robert 1175?-1253 *DcEuL*
Grossu, Sergiu 1920- *ConAu 57*
Grossvogel, David I 1925- *ConAu 1R*
Grosswirth, Marvin 1931- *ConAu 33*
Grostete, Robert 1175?-1253 *Alli*
Grosthead, Robert 1175?-1253 *Alli*
Grosvenor, Lord *Alli*

Grosvenor, Mrs. *Alli Sup*
Grosvenor, Abbie Johnston 1865- *AmA&B,*
IndAu 1816, WhWNAA
Grosvenor, Benjamin 1675-1758 *Alli*
Grosvenor, C P *Alli Sup*
Grosvenor, Charles Henry 1833-1917 *DcNAA,*
OhA&B
Grosvenor, Edwin Augustus 1845-1936 *AmLY,*
DcAmA, DcNAA, WhWNAA
Grosvenor, Elizabeth Mary 1797- *Alli Sup*
Grosvenor, Gilbert Hovey 1875-1966 *AmA&B,*
REnAL, WhWNAA
Grosvenor, Countess H *Alli*
Grosvenor, Mrs. H S *Alli Sup*
Grosvenor, Mrs. Ian *MnBBF*
Grosvenor, J DuV *Alli Sup*
Grosvenor, Kali *BlkAW, LivBA*
Grosvenor, Melville Bell 1901- *AmA&B*
Grosvenor, Ralph L 1893- *AmSCAP 66*
Grosvenor, Lady Theodora *Alli Sup*
Grosvenor, Verta Mae 1938- *BlkAW,*
DrAF 1976, DrAP 1975, LivBA
Grosvenor, William Mason 1835-1900 *Alli Sup,*
DcNAA
Grosz, Ferdinand 1849- *BiD&SB*
Grosz, George Ehrenfried 1893-1959 *AmA&B,*
AtlBL, OxGer, REn, WhGrA
Groszmann, Gustav Friedrich Wilhelm 1746-1796
BiD&SB
Groszmann, Maximilian Paul Eugen 1855-1922
AmLY, DcNAA
Grote, Augustus Radcliffe 1841-1903 *Alli Sup,*
DcAmA, DcNAA
Grote, George 1794-1871 *Alli, Alli Sup, BbD,*
BiD&SB, BrAu 19, Chmbr 3, DcEnA,
DcEnL, DcEuL, DcLEnL, EvLB, NewC,
OxEng, Pen Eng, REn
Grote, Harriet 1792-1878 *Alli Sup, NewC*
Grote, John 1813-1886? *Alli Sup, BrAu 19*
Grote, Mrs. S M *Alli Sup*
Groth, Alexander J 1932- *ConAu 41*
Groth, Klaus Johann 1819-1899 *CasWL, EuA,*
OxGer
Grotius *DcNAA*
Grotius, Hugo 1583-1645 *BbD, BiD&SB,*
CasWL, DcEuL, EuA, EvEuW, NewC,
OxEng, REn
Grotjahn, Martin 1904- *ConAu 41*
Groto, Luigi 1541-1585 *BbD, BiD&SB,*
McGWD, REn
Groton, William Mansfield 1850-1915 *DcNAA*
Grouard, Emile Jean Baptiste 1840-1931
DcNAA, OxCan
Groulx, Lionel-Adolphe 1878-1967 *CanWr,*
CasWL, OxCan, OxCan Sup
Groulx, Louis Thomas 1819- *BbtC*
Ground, William David *Alli Sup*
Grounds, Roger *WrD 1976*
Groupe, Darryl R *ConAu XR*
Groussac, Paul 1848-1929 *CasWL, Pen Am*
Groussard, Serge 1920- *REn*
Grousset, Paschal 1844-1909 *CarSB*
Grout, Henry *Alli Sup*
Grout, Josiah 1841-1925 *DcNAA*
Grout, Lewis 1815-1905 *Alli Sup, DcNAA*
Grout, Ruth E 1901- *ConAu 17*
Grouya, Theodor J 1910- *AmSCAP 66*
Grove, Miss *BbtC*
Grove, Alfred Thomas 1924- *Au&Wr*
Grove, Mrs. C *Alli*
Grove, Edward *Alli*
Grove, Eleanor *Alli Sup*
Grove, Eliza *Alli Sup, ChPo, ChPo S1*
Grove, Florence Craufurd *Alli Sup*
Grove, Fred 1913- *ConAu 1R*
Grove, Frederick Philip 1871?-1948 *CanNov,*
CanWr, CasWL, DcLEnL, LongC,
OxCan, OxCan Sup, Pen Eng, REnAL,
TwCW, WebEAL, WhWNAA
Grove, Sir George 1820-1900 *Alli Sup,*
BiD&SB, Chmbr 3, DcEnL, NewC,
OxEng, REn
Grove, Harriet Pyne 1866-1939 *OhA&B*
Grove, Helen Harriet 1917- *IndAu 1917*
Grove, Henry 1683-1738 *Alli*
Grove, Jack William 1920- *Au&Wr,*
ConAu 5R
Grove, John *Alli Sup*

Grove, Joseph *Alli*
Grove, Matthew *Alli*
Grove, Richard D 1927- *AmSCAP 66*
Grove, Robert d1696 *Alli*
Grove, W *Alli Sup*
Grove, W R *Alli*
Grove, Will O *ConAu XR*
Grove, William *ChPo*
Grove, William Bywater *Alli Sup*
Grove, Sir William Robert 1811?- *DcEnL*
Grovenor, Benjamin *Alli*
Grover, Albert *Alli Sup*
Grover, Arthur 1918- *AmSCAP 66*
Grover, Burton Baker 1858- *WhWNAA*
Grover, David H 1925- *ConAu 13R*
Grover, Delo Corydon 1869-1955 *OhA&B*
Grover, Edwin Osgood 1870- *AmA&B,*
AnMV 1926, ChPo, ChPo S1, ChPo S2,
WhWNAA
Grover, Eulalie Osgood 1873-1958 *AmA&B,*
AuBYP, ChPo, ChPo S1, OhA&B,
WhWNAA
Grover, Frederick Warren 1876- *WhWNAA*
Grover, Henry Montague 1791-1866 *Alli,*
Alli Sup, BrAu 19
Grover, John William *Alli Sup*
Grover, Linda 1934- *ConAu 29, WrD 1976*
Grover, Philip 1929- *WrD 1976*
Grover, W H *ChPo S2*
Groves, Charles Edward *Alli Sup*
Groves, Charles Pelham 1887- *Au&Wr*
Groves, Colin Peter 1942- *ConAu 61*
Groves, Edith Lelean 1870-1931 *ChPo,*
ChPo S1, DcNAA
Groves, Edward *PoIre*
Groves, Ernest Rutherford 1877-1946 *AmA&B,*
DcNAA, WhWNAA
Groves, Francis Richard 1889- *ConAu P-1*
Groves, Georgina *WrD 1976*
Groves, Gerald Vann 1927- *Au&Wr*
Groves, Gladys 1894- *AmA&B*
Groves, H E 1921- *ConAu 5R*
Groves, Harold M 1897- *ConAu 5R*
Groves, Harriet *Alli Sup*
Groves, Henry *Alli Sup*
Groves, Henry Charles *Alli Sup*
Groves, Mrs. James A *OhA&B*
Groves, John *Alli*
Groves, John Percy *Alli Sup*
Groves, Louis 1867- *ChPo S1*
Groves, Paul 1930- *Au&Wr*
Groves, Reginald 1908- *Au&Wr, ConAu 13R*
Groves, Ruth Clouse 1902- *ConAu 17*
Groves, Ryland *ChPo*
Groves, Sylvia Mary 1904- *Au&Wr,*
WrD 1976
Groves, W *Alli*
Groves, Webber 1697-1793 *Alli*
Groves, William E *MnBBF*
Groves, William John *Alli Sup*
Groves, William Kynaston *Alli Sup*
Groves-Raines, Antony 1913- *IlCB 1966*
Groves-Raines, Ralph Gore Antony 1913-
AuBYP
Grow, Lottie Lyons 1884- *IndAu 1917*
Growoll, Adolf 1850-1909 *AmA&B, DcNAA*
Growse, Frederic Salmon *Alli Sup*
Grozier, Edwin Atkins 1859-1924 *DcNAA*
Gruau, Rene 1910- *WhGrA*
Grub, George 1812-1893 *Alli Sup, EvLB*
Grub, Phillip D 1932- *ConAu 25*
Grubar, Francis S 1924- *ConAu 33*
Grubb, Davis Alexander 1919- *AmA&B,*
Au&Wr, ConAu 1R
Grubb, Dorothea *PoIre*
Grubb, Edward *Alli Sup*
Grubb, Edward 1854- *WhLA*
Grubb, Edward Burd 1841- *DcAmA*
Grubb, Eugene Housel 1850- *WhWNAA*
Grubb, Frederick 1930- *ChPo S2, ConP 1970,*
ConP 1975, WrD 1976
Grubb, Frederick 1932- *Au&Wr*
Grubb, Kenneth George 1900- *ConAu P-1,*
WrD 1976
Grubb, Mary B *IndAu 1917*
Grubb, Norman Percy 1895- *ConAu P-1,*
WrD 1976
Grubb, T H *Alli Sup*

Grubbs, Frank Leslie, Jr. 1931- *ConAu 29*
Grubbs, Robert L 1919- *ConAu 1R*
Grubbs, W H *TexWr*
Grube, Bernhard Adam 1715-1808 *DcAmA*
Grube, Georges M A 1899- *ConAu P-1*
Grube, John Deen 1930- *ConP 1970*
Grubel, Herbert G 1934- *ConAu 9R*
Grubel, Johann Konrad 1736-1809 *OxGer*
Grubel, Konrad 1736-1809 *BiD&SB*
Gruber, Frank 1904-1969 *AmA&B*, *ConAu 25*,
  ConAu P-1, *EncM&D*
Gruber, Frederick C 1903- *ConAu 49*
Gruber, Gary R 1940- *ConAu 53*
Gruber, Jacob W 1921- *ConAu 1R*
Gruber, Joseph John 1930- *ConAu 5R*,
  IndAu 1917
Gruber, Levi Franklin 1871-1941 *AmA&B*,
  DcNAA, *WhWNAA*
Gruber, Ludwig *McGWD*
Gruber, Martin Jay 1937- *ConAu 53*
Gruber, Ruth *ConAu 25*
Gruberg, Martin 1935- *ConAu 33*, *WrD 1976*
Grubinski, Waclaw 1883- *CasWL*, *ClDMEuL*
Grucci, Joseph Leonard *ChPo S1*
Gruchy, Martin *Alli*
Grudin, Louis 1898- *ConAu 1R*
Grueber, C S *Alli*
Grueber, Charles Stephen *Alli Sup*
Grueber, Erwin *Alli Sup*
Grueber, Herbert Appold *Alli Sup*
Gruelle, John Barton 1880?-1938 *ChPo S1*,
  ChPo S2, *DcNAA*, *IndAu 1816*, *OhA&B*
Gruelle, Johnny 1880?-1938 *AmA&B*,
  AmSCAP 66, *ChPo*, *REnAL*
Gruelle, Justin *ChPo S2*
Gruelle, Richard Buckner 1851-1914
  IndAu 1816
Gruelle, Worth *AuNews 2*
Gruen, John 1926- *ConAu 17R*
Gruen, Victor David 1903- *ConAu 13R*,
  WrD 1976
Gruenbaum, Adolf 1923- *ConAu 9R*
Gruenbaum, Ludwig *ConAu 49*
Gruenberg, Benjamin Charles 1875-1965
  ConAu P-1, *WhWNAA*
Gruenberg, Louis 1884?-1964 *AmSCAP 66*,
  OxAm
Gruenberg, Sidonie Matsner 1881-1974 *AmA&B*,
  AuBYP, *ChPo*, *ConAu 49*, *ConAu P-1*,
  SmATA 2, *WhWNAA*
Gruener, Hippolyte 1869- *WhWNAA*
Gruenhagen, Robert W 1932- *ConAu 29*
Gruening, Ernest Henry 1887-1974 *AmA&B*,
  ConAu 49, *TwCA*, *TwCA Sup*
Gruenwald, Alfred 1886-1951 *AmSCAP 66*
Gruffydd Ab Yr Ynad Coch *DcEnL*
Gruffydd, Owain Ab *NewC*
Gruffydd, Peter 1935- *ConP 1970*, *ConP 1975*,
  WrD 1976
Gruffydd, W J 1916- *Au&Wr*
Gruffydd, William John 1881-1954 *CasWL*,
  Pen Eng
Grugeon, Alfred *Alli Sup*
Gruger, Frederick Roderigo 1871- *ChPo*
Gruggen, F J *Alli*
Gruhn, Carrie Myers 1907- *ConAu P-1*
Grulee, Clifford Grosselle 1880- *WhWNAA*
Gruliow, Leo 1913- *ConAu 5R*
Grumbach, Doris 1918- *ConAu 5R*
Grumbine, E Evalyn 1900- *AuBYP*
Grumbine, Ezra Light 1845-1923 *DcNAA*
Grumbine, Harvey Carson 1869-1941 *AmA&B*,
  OhA&B, *WhWNAA*
Grumbine, J C F *Alli Sup*
Grumbkow, Friedrich Wilhelm Von 1678-1739
  OxGer
Grumbler, Anthony *DcNAA*
Grumelli, Antoino 1928- *ConAu 37*
Grumley, Michael 1941- *ConAu 29*,
  WrD 1976
Grummann, Paul Henry 1872- *IndAu 1816*,
  WhWNAA
Grumme, Marguerite *ConAu 5R*
Grun, Anastasius 1806-1876 *BbD*, *BiD&SB*,
  CasWL, *EvEuW*, *OxGer*, *Pen Eur*
Grun, Bernard 1901-1972 *Au&Wr*, *ConAu 37*
Grun, Max VonDer *OxGer*
Grunbaum, Adolf 1923- *WrD 1976*

Grunberg, Jacques *AmSCAP 66*
Grunberg, Karl 1891- *CnMD*
Grund, Francis Joseph 1805?-1863 *Alli*,
  Alli Sup, *DcAmA*, *DcNAA*, *OxAm*,
  REnAL
Grundgens, Gustaf 1899-1963 *CrCD*
Grundgens, Gustav 1899-1963 *OxGer*
Grundman, Clare Ewing 1913- *AmSCAP 66*
Grundstein, Nathan David 1913- *ConAu 37*,
  WrD 1976
Grundt, Leonard 1936- *ConAu 57*
Grundtvig, Nicolai Frederik Severin 1783-1872
  BbD, *BiD&SB*, *CasWL*, *DcEuL*, *EuA*,
  EvEuW, *Pen Eur*, *REn*
Grundtvig, Sven Hersleb 1824-1883 *CasWL*,
  DcEuL
Grundy, Charles Henry *Alli Sup*
Grundy, Cuthbert C *Alli Sup*
Grundy, Sir Cuthbert Cartwright *ChPo*
Grundy, Felix 1777-1840 *BiDSA*
Grundy, Francis H *Alli Sup*
Grundy, Fred 1905- *Au&Wr*
Grundy, George Beardoe 1861- *WhLA*
Grundy, John *Alli*, *BiDLA*
Grundy, John Brownsdon Clowes 1902- *Au&Wr*
Grundy, Rupert Francis Brooks 1903- *Au&Wr*,
  WrD 1976
Grundy, Sydney *ChPo*
Grundy, Sydney 1848-1914 *Alli Sup*, *BrAu 19*,
  Chmbr 3, *McGWD*, *NewC*
Grundy, Wilfred Walker 1884- *WhLA*
Gruneberg, Hans 1907- *Au&Wr*, *WrD 1976*
Gruneisen, Charles Lewis 1806-1879 *Alli Sup*,
  DcEnL
Gruner, Louis *Alli*
Grunewald, Matthias 1470?-1528 *AtlBL*,
  OxGer, *REn*
Grunfeld, Frederic V 1929- *WrD 1976*
Grunn, Homer 1880-1944 *AmSCAP 66*
Grunsky, Carl Ewald 1855-1934 *DcNAA*,
  WhWNAA
Grunwald, Henry Anatole 1922- *AmA&B*
Grunwald, Stefan 1933- *ConAu 29*
Grupp, Stanley E 1927- *ConAu 53*
Gruppe, Otto Friedrich 1804-1876 *BiD&SB*
Grusd, Edward Elihu 1904- *ConAu 19*
Gruskin, Alan D 1904-1970 *ConAu 29*,
  ConAu P-1
Gruson, Edward S 1929- *ConAu 45*
Gruss, Edmond C 1933- *ConAu 53*
Gruter, Janus 1560-1627 *DcEuL*
Grutzmacher, Harold M, Jr. 1930- *ConAu 29*
Gruver, William R, II 1929- *ConAu 45*
Gry, Leon P F 1879- *WhLA*
Grylls, Mary 1836-1863 *Alli Sup*
Grymeston, Elizabeth *Alli*
Grynaeus, Simon 1725-1799 *OxGer*
Grynberg, Henryk 1936- *ConAu 29*
Gryndall, Will *Alli*
Gryphius, Andreas 1616-1664 *BbD*, *BiD&SB*,
  CasWL, *CnThe*, *DcEuL*, *EuA*, *EvEuW*,
  McGWD, *OxGer*, *Pen Eur*, *REnWD*
Gryphius, Christian 1649-1706 *OxGer*
Gryst, Edward 1911- *ConAu 1R*
Grzanna, Donald E 1931- *AmSCAP 66*
Guadagnoli, Antonio 1798-1858 *BiD&SB*
Guadagnolo, Joseph F 1912- *ConAu 5R*
Guadaloupe, Brother Jose De 1896-1974
  ConAu XR
Guaiferius Of Salerno *CasWL*
Gualandi *BiD&SB*
Gualo 1150?- *BiB N*
Gualtieri, Luigi 1826-1901 *BiD&SB*
Guamani *PueRA*
Guandolo, John 1919- *ConAu 21*, *WrD 1976*
Guarcello, Giovanni *ChPo*
Guard, J *Alli Sup*
Guard, Theodore DeLa 1578?-1652 *AmA*,
  NewC
Guard, Thomas *Alli Sup*
Guardati, Tommaso *CasWL*
Guardi, Francesco 1712-1793 *AtlBL*, *REn*
Guardini, Romano 1885- *CatA 1947*
Guare, John 1938- *ConDr*, *WrD 1976*
Guareschi, Giovanni 1908-1968 *CatA 1952*,
  ConAu 25, *EncWL*, *ModRL*, *TwCA Sup*,
  TwCW
Guarini, Battista 1538-1612 *CasWL*, *EvEuW*

Guarini, Giambattista 1538-1612 *Pen Eur*,
  REn
Guarini, Gian Battista 1538-1612 *McGWD*
Guarini, Giovanni Battista 1538?-1612 *BbD*,
  BiD&SB, *CrE&SL*, *EuA*, *NewC*, *OxEng*,
  REnWD
Guarini, Guarino 1374-1460 *CasWL*
Guarino Da Verona 1374-1460 *DcEuL*
Guarino Of Verona 1374-1460 *REn*
Guarino, Battista 1434-1503 *CasWL*
Guarino, M Vincent 1939- *ConAu 41*
Guarinoni, Hippolyt 1571-1654 *OxGer*
Guarnieri, John Albert 1917- *AmSCAP 66*
Guatama, Prince Of India *ChPo*
Guay, Charles 1845-1922 *DcNAA*
Guazzo, Stefano 1530-1593 *DcEuL*, *REn*
Guback, Thomas H 1937- *ConAu 25*
Gubb, Alfred Samuel *Alli Sup*
Gubbins, Charlotte *PoIre*
Gubbins, Ellen *Alli Sup*
Gubbins, Florence Irene *ChPo S2*
Gubbins, John Harington *Alli Sup*
Gubbins, Martin R *Alli*
Guberlet, Muriel Lewin 1889- *WhPNW*
Gubern, Santiago 1933- *ConAu 45*
Gubernatis, Angelo De 1840- *Alli Sup*,
  BiD&SB
Gubrium, Jaber F 1943- *ConAu 53*
Gubser, Nicholas J 1938- *ConAu 17R*
Guccione, Robert, Jr. *AuNews 2*
Guck, Dorothy 1913- *ConAu 49*
Gudde, Erwin Gustav 1889- *AmA&B*,
  ConAu 5R
Gude, R *Alli*
Gudea 2144?BC-2124BC *DcOrL 3*
Gudeman, Alfred 1862- *WhWNAA*
Gudenian, Haig 1918- *Au&Wr*
Guder, Eileen 1919- *ConAu 17R*
Gudgeon, T W *Alli Sup*
Gudger, Eugene Willis 1866- *WhWNAA*
Gudmundson, Shirley M *AuBYP*
Gudmundsson, Kristmann Borgfjord 1902?-
  CasWL, *EncWL*
Gudmundsson, Tomas 1901- *CasWL*
Gudschinsky, Sarah Caroline 1919- *ConAu 33*,
  WrD 1976
Gudzenko, Semen Petrovich 1922-1953 *CasWL*
Gudzy, Nikolai Kalinnikovich 1887- *CasWL*
Gue, Belle Willey 1860- *AnMV 1926*,
  WhWNAA
Gue, Benjamin F 1828-1904 *AmA&B*, *DcNAA*
Guedalla, Philip 1889-1944 *ChPo*, *DcLEnL*,
  EvLB, *LongC*, *ModBL*, *NewC*, *OxEng*,
  REn, *TwCA*, *TwCA Sup*, *TwCW*,
  WhWNAA
Guede, Norina Lami 1913- *ConAu 9R*
Guedel, Arthur Ernest 1883-1956 *IndAu 1917*
Guehenno, Jean 1890- *EncWL*
Guehenno, Marcel 1890- *CasWL*
Guelfo Of Denmark *REn*
Guelich, Robert A 1939- *ConAu 45*
Guell Y Rente, Jose 1818-1884 *BbD*, *BiD&SB*
Guell Y Rente, Juan 1815-1875 *BbD*, *BiD&SB*
Guemple, Lee 1930- *ConAu 41*
Guenee, Antoine 1717-1803 *OxFr*
Guenette, Robert 1935- *ConAu 25*
Guenin, Emile *OxCan*
Guenther, Charles 1920- *ConAu 29*,
  DrAP 1975, *WrD 1976*
Guenther, Johannes Von 1866- *McGWD*
Guenther, John *ConAu 5R*
Gueorguievna, Marie, Grand Duchess *ChPo*
Guerard, Albert Joseph 1914- *AmA&B*,
  AmNov, *ConAu 1R*, *ConNov 1972*,
  ConNov 1976, *DrAF 1976*, *OxAm*,
  TwCA Sup, *WrD 1976*
Guerard, Albert Leon 1880-1959 *AmA&B*,
  REnAL, *TwCA*, *TwCA Sup*, *WhWNAA*
Guerau DeLiost 1877-1933 *CasWL*
Guerber, Helene Adeline 1859-1929 *AmLY*,
  BiD&SB, *DcAmA*, *DcNAA*, *WhWNAA*
Guercheville, A DePons, Marquise De 1570-1632
  OxCan
Guercino 1591-1666 *AtlBL*
Guercio, Claudia *ChPo*
Guerin, Charles 1873-1907 *CasWL*, *EuA*,
  EvEuW, *OxFr*
Guerin, Eugenie De 1805-1848 *BbD*, *BiD&SB*,

Guilloux, Louis 1899- CasWL, ClDMEuL, EncWL, EvEuW, TwCA, TwCA Sup
Guilmartin, John Francis, Jr. 1940- ConAu 53
Guilmette, Charles Alexander Alli Sup
Guilpin, Everard CasWL
Guimaraes, Afonso Henriquez DaCosta 1870-1921 Pen Am
Guimaraes, Bernardo 1825-1884 Pen Am
Guimaraes Rosa, Joao 1908-1967 CasWL, Pen Am, WhTwL, WorAu
Guimera, Angel 1847-1924 CasWL, ClDMEuL, McGWD, Pen Eur
Guimond, James 1936- ConAu 25
Guinagh, Kevin 1897- ConAu 17R
Guinee, W B Alli Sup
Guinee, William B d1901 PoIre
Guiness, Maurice AmA&B
Guiney, Louise Imogen 1861-1920 Alli Sup, AmA&B, BbD, BiD&SB, ChPo, ChPo S1, ChPo S2, DcAmA, DcLEnL, DcNAA, EvLB, LongC, OxAm, PoIre, PoIre, TwCA, TwCA Sup
Guiney, Mortimer 1930- ConAu 53
Guinicelli, Guido 1240?-1276? BiD&SB, DcEuL, REn
Guinizelli, Guido 1240?-1276? CasWL, EuA, Pen Eur, REn
Guinn, Paul 1928- ConAu 13R
Guinness, Sir Alec 1914- NewC, REn
Guinness, Bryan Walter 1905- Au&Wr, WrD 1976
Guinness, Claude Hugh Campbell Alli Sup
Guinness, Fanny E 1831- Alli Sup, BbD, BiD&SB
Guinness, Henry Grattan 1835-1910 Alli Sup, BbD, BiD&SB, PoIre
Guinness, Mrs. J G PoIre
Guinness, Jane Lucretia PoIre
Guinness, Maurice 1897- Au&Wr
Guinness, Richard PoIre
Guinon, Albert 1863-1923 OxFr
Guins, George Constantine 1887- Au&Wr
Guinzburg, Harold K 1899-1961 AmA&B
Guio, Carrie Abbot d1967 IndAu 1917
Guion, David 1895- OxAm
Guion, David W 1892- AmSCAP 66
Guion, Robert Morgan 1924- ConAu 17R, IndAu 1917
Guiot De Dijon CasWL
Guiot De Provins CasWL, OxFr
Guipon, Leon 1872-1910 ChPo
Guiraldes, Ricardo 1886-1927 CasWL, CnMWL, CyWA, DcSpL, EncWL, Pen Am, REn Am, TwCW, WorAu
Guirao, Ramon Pen Am
Guiraud, Baron Alexandre 1788-1847 BiD&SB, OxFr
Guiraut De Borneil 1165?-1220 CasWL
Guiraut De Bornelh 1165?-1220 CasWL, Pen Eur
Guiraut Riquier 1254?-1292 CasWL, Pen Eur
Guirdham, Arthur 1905- Au&Wr, WrD 1976
Guirey, George Alli Sup
Guiry, Michael Grace Alli Sup
Guiscard De Beaulieu Alli, BiB N
Guise, Cedric Hay 1890- OhA&B, WhWNAA
Guise, F Alli Sup
Guise, Mrs. Francis Alli Sup
Guise, Samuel Alli, BiDLA
Guise, William 1653-1684 Alli
Guisy, J Alli
Guiteau, Charles J Alli Sup
Guiterman, Arthur 1871-1943 AmA&B, AmLY, ChPo, ChPo S1, ChPo S2, CnDAL, DcNAA, EvLB, OxAm, REn, REnAL, St&VC, TwCA, TwCA Sup, WhWNAA
Guither, Harold D 1927- ConAu 29
Guiton, Jeremy David LeHardy 1933- WrD 1976
Guitry, Lucien 1860-1925 OxFr
Guitry, Sacha 1885-1957 CasWL, ClDMEuL, CnMD, EvEuW, McGWD, ModWD, OxFr, Pen Eur, REn, TwCA, TwCA Sup
Guitteau, William Backus 1877- OhA&B
Guittone D'Arezzo 1230?-1294? BiD&SB, CasWL, EuA, Pen Eur
Guittone Of Arezzo 1230-1294 DcEuL

Guizot, Madam 1773-1827 CarSB
Guizot, Francois Pierre Guillaume 1787-1874 BbD, DcEuL, EvEuW, NewC, OxEng, OxFr, REn
Gulbransen, Marie Helen 1897- WhWNAA
Gulbranssen, Trygve 1894- TwCA, TwCA Sup
Guldberg, Frederick Hoegh BiD&SB
Gulesian, Grace Warner AmSCAP 66
Gulia, Drmit 1874-1960 DcOrL 3
Gulick, Bill ConAu XR
Gulick, Charles Adams, Jr. 1896- WhWNAA
Gulick, Charles Burton 1868- DcAmA
Gulick, Edward Leeds 1862-1931 DcNAA
Gulick, Grover C 1916- ConAu 33, WhPNW
Gulick, John Thomas 1832-1923 BiD&SB, DcAmA, DcNAA
Gulick, Luther Halsey 1828-1891 Alli Sup, DcNAA
Gulick, Luther Halsey 1865-1918 AmA&B, DcNAA
Gulick, Luther Halsey 1892- WhWNAA
Gulick, Peggy 1918- AuBYP
Gulick, Sidney Lewis 1860-1945 AmA&B, AmLY, DcNAA, WhWNAA
Gulick, Sidney Lewis, Jr. 1902- WhWNAA
Gulielmus Peregrinus 1197?- DcEnL
Gulik, Robert H Van ConAu XR
Gull, Cyril Ranger 1875- MnBBF
Gull, G Eckford Alli Sup
Gull, William, And Baly, William Alli
Gullahorn, Genevieve AuBYP
Gulland, Charles Alli Sup
Gullans, Charles 1929- ConAu 1R, ConP 1970, ConP 1975, DrAP 1975, WrD 1976
Gullard, Charles 1840- ChPo
Gullason, Thomas A 1924- ConAu 23
Gullberg, Hjalmar Robert 1898-1961 CasWL, ClDMEuL, EncWL, Pen Eur
Gullet, Chris Alli
Gullett, D W OxCan Sup
Gulley, F A Alli Sup
Gulley, Halbert E 1919- ConAu 5R
Gulley, Norman 1920- ConAu 33
Gullick, Charles Francis William Rowley 1907- Au&Wr, ConAu 5R
Gullick, John Michael 1916- Au&Wr, ConAu 13R
Gullick, Thomas John Alli Sup
Gullifer, Helena Alli Sup
Gullifer, Joseph William Alli, BiDLA
Gulliford, Ronald 1920- ConAu 13R, WrD 1976
Gullins, D Edna BlkAW
Gulliver, Lemuel Alli
Gulliver, Lemuel 1909- ConAu XR, WrD 1976
Gulliver, Lemuel, Jr. Alli
Gulliver, Lucile 1882-1964 AmA&B, AmLY
Gullott, J L Alli Sup
Gully, James Manby 1808-1883 Alli, Alli Sup
Gully, Robert, And Capt Denham Alli
Gulson, Theodore Alli
Gulston, A J Alli Sup
Gulston, A S Alli Sup
Gulston, Ant Alli
Gulston, Charles 1913- Au&Wr
Gulston, Edward Alli
Gulube, D N AfA 1
Gulubov, Konstantin 1892- CasWL
Guma, Enoch Stephen 1901?-1918 AfA 1
Guma, Samson Mbizo 1923?- AfA 1
Gumble, Albert 1883-1946 AmSCAP 66
Gumble, Thomas Alli
Gumbleden, John Alli
Gumede BlkAW
Gumersall, L ChPo
Gumilyov, Nikolai Stepanovich 1886-1921 CasWL, ChPo, ClDMEuL, DcRusL, EncWL, EuA, EvEuW, ModSL 1, Pen Eur, REn, TwCW, WhTwL
Gumley, F W MnBBF
Gumley, J Alli
Gumley, Robert Alli Sup
Gummere, Amelia Mott 1859-1937 AmA&B, AmLY, DcNAA, WhWNAA
Gummere, Francis Barton 1855-1919 Alli Sup, AmA&B, BiD&SB, DcAmA, DcNAA, OxAm, REnAL, TwCA, TwCA Sup

Gummere, John 1784-1845 Alli, DcAmA, DcNAA
Gummere, Richard M, Jr. 1912- ConAu 45
Gummere, Richard Mott 1883- WhWNAA
Gummere, Samuel Rene 1789-1866 Alli, DcAmA, DcNAA
Gump, Richard 1906- AmSCAP 66, ConAu P-1
Gumpert, Thekla Von 1810-1897 BbD, BiD&SB
Gumpert, Traugott Ernest 1904- Au&Wr
Gumppenberg, Hanns, Freiherr Von 1866-1928 OxGer
Gumuchian, K A ChPo
Gunadhya DcOrL 2
Gunby, Andrew Augustus 1849- BiDSA
Gunckel, John Elstner 1846-1915 DcNAA, OhA&B
Gundacker Von Judenburg OxGer
Gundelfinger, Matthias OxGer
Gunder, Claude A 1873- IndAu 1917
Gunderode, Karoline Von 1780-1806 BiD&SB, OxGer
Gunders, Henry 1924- ConAu 29
Gundersheimer, Werner L 1937- ConAu 53
Gunderson, Doris V ConAu 29
Gunderson, Harvey L MnnWr
Gunderson, Keith 1935- ConAu 33, DrAP 1975
Gunderson, Robert Gray 1915- ConAu 1R
Gundling, Jakob Paul 1673-1731 OxGer
Gundolf, Friedrich 1880-1931 OxGer, REn
Gundrey, Elizabeth 1924- ConAu 13R
Gundry, Arthur W 1857- Alli Sup
Gundry, Dudley William 1916- Au&Wr, WrD 1976
Gundry, Frances Ruth Gilchrist 1875-1933 OhA&B
Gundry, Hamilton D Alli Sup
Gundry, Robert H 1932- ConAu 29
Gundulf d1108 BiB N
Gundulic, Franje Pen Eur
Gundulic, Ivan 1588-1638 BbD, BiD&SB, CasWL
Gundy, H Pearson 1905- ConAu 45p, OxCan Sup
Gunhill, D D Alli
Gunji, Masakatsu 1913- ConAu 29
Gunn, Sister Agnes Marie 1928- ConAu 17R
Gunn, Alexander d1829 Alli
Gunn, Alexander 1837-1901 OhA&B
Gunn, Mrs. Aneas 1870-1961 TwCW
Gunn, Anne Alli, BiDLA
Gunn, Barbara Alli Sup
Gunn, Bill 1934- AmA&B, AuNews 1, BlkAW, ConLC 5
Gunn, Charles Hains Alli Sup
Gunn, Donald 1797-1878 BbtC, DcNAA
Gunn, Douglas Alli Sup
Gunn, Drewey Wayne 1939- ConAu 57
Gunn, Geoffrey MnBBF
Gunn, Gilbert LongC
Gunn, Giles B 1938- ConAu 57
Gunn, Glenn Dillard 1874- WhWNAA
Gunn, J A W 1937- ConAu 25
Gunn, J C Alli
Gunn, James Edwin 1923- ConAu 9R, DrAF 1976, WrD 1976
Gunn, John Alli, BiDLA, BiDLA Sup, PoIre
Gunn, John 1925- Au&Wr
Gunn, John 1937- ConAu 49
Gunn, John C Alli Sup
Gunn, John William Cormack 1889- WhLA
Gunn, Neil Miller 1891-1973 Au&Wr, CasWL, ChPo, ConAu 37, ConNov 1972, DcLEnL, EvLB, LongC, NewC, Pen Eng, TwCA, TwCA Sup
Gunn, Otis Berthoude 1828-1901 DcNAA
Gunn, Peter 1914- ConAu 25
Gunn, Robert Alexander 1844- Alli Sup, DcNAA
Gunn, S Alli Sup
Gunn, Sidney Allan 1876- WhWNAA
Gunn, Thom 1924- CnE&AP, NewC
Gunn, Thom 1929- AmA&B, Au&Wr, CasWL, ChPo, ChPo S1, ChPo S2, ConAu 17R, ConLC 3, ConLC 6, ConP 1970, ConP 1975, DrAP 1975,

LongC, ModBL, ModBL Sup, Pen Eng, RAdv 1, REn, TwCW, WebEAL, WhTwL, WorAu, WrD 1976

Gunn, Thomas Butler *Alli Sup, ChPo, EarAB, EarAB Sup*

Gunn, Victor *MnBBF*

Gunn, W M *Alli*

Gunn, William *Alli*

Gunn, William A *Alli*

Gunn, William Harrison 1934- *AuNews 1, ConAu 13R*

Gunnarsson, Gunnar 1889-1975 *CasWL, ClDMEuL, ConAu 61, CyWA, EncWL, EvEuW, REn, TwCA, TwCA Sup, TwCW*

Gunnell, Bryn 1933- *WrD 1976*

Gunnell, John C 1933- *ConAu 25*

Gunneman, Louis Herman 1910- *IndAu 1917*

Gunning, Miss *Alli, BiDLA*

Gunning, Mrs. *Alli*

Gunning, Elizabeth 1734-1790 *NewC*

Gunning, Fred *Alli*

Gunning, H *Alli*

Gunning, Hugh 1902- *Au&Wr*

Gunning, Maria 1733-1760 *NewC*

Gunning, Peter 1613-1684 *Alli, DcEnL*

Gunning, Richard *Alli, BiDLA*

Gunning, Robert 1908- *ConAu 25*

Gunning, Susannah 1740?-1800 *BrAu, DcLEnL, NewC, OxEng*

Gunning, William D 1830-1888 *Alli Sup, DcNAA, OhA&B*

Gunnison, Almon 1844-1917 *Alli Sup, DcAmA, DcNAA*

Gunnison, Elisha Norman 1837-1880 *Alli Sup, ChPo, ChPo S1, DcAmA, DcNAA*

Gunnison, Herbert Foster 1858-1932 *DcNAA*

Gunnison, John Williams 1812-1853 *Alli, DcAmA, DcNAA*

Gunnison, Lynn *DcNAA*

Gunsaulus, Frank Wakeley 1856-1921 *Alli Sup, AmA&B, BiD&SB, ChPo, ChPo S2, DcAmA, DcNAA, OhA&B*

Gunsky, Maurice J 1888-1945 *AmSCAP 66*

Gunson, Georgianna Gordon *ChPo*

Gunston, Bill 1927- *Au&Wr, ConAu 49, SmATA XR, WrD 1976*

Gunston, David *Au&Wr*

Gunston, William Tudor 1927- *ConAu 49, SmATA 9, WrD 1976*

Gunstone, Frank Denby 1923- *Au&Wr, WrD 1976*

Guntekin, Resat Nuri 1892?-1956 *DcOrL 3, REnWD*

Guntekin, Reshad Nuri 1892?-1956 *Pen Cl*

Gunter, Archibald Clavering 1847-1907 *Alli Sup, AmA, AmA&B, BbD, BiD&SB, DcAmA, DcNAA, OxAm, REnAL*

Gunter, Bessie E *BiDSA*

Gunter, Bradley 1940- *ConAu 29*

Gunter, Edmund 1581-1626 *Alli*

Gunter, Edward C 1917- *AmSCAP 66*

Gunter, Pete Addison Yancey 1936- *ConAu 33, WrD 1976*

Gunter, Peter *Alli*

Gunther *CasWL*

Gunther Von Dem Forste *OxGer*

Gunther, Agnes 1863-1911 *ClDMEuL, OxGer*

Gunther, Albert Everard 1903- *Au&Wr, ConAu 29, WrD 1976*

Gunther, Albert Karl Ludwig Gotthelf 1830- *BiD&SB*

Gunther, Albrecht Carl Ludwig 1830- *Alli Sup*

Gunther, Bernard 1929- *Au&Wr, ConAu 45*

Gunther, Charles Godfrey 1880-1929 *DcNAA*

Gunther, Erna 1896- *OxCan Sup, WhPNW*

Gunther, Gerald 1927- *ConAu 33*

Gunther, Johann Christian 1695-1723 *BiD&SB, CasWL, DcEuL, EuA, EvEuW, OxGer, Pen Eur, REn*

Gunther, John 1901-1970 *AmA&B, AmNov, AuBYP, ConAu 9R, ConAu 25, EvLB, LongC, OxAm, Pen Am, REn, REnAL, SmATA 2, TwCA, TwCA Sup*

Gunther, Mavis 1903- *Au&Wr*

Gunther, Max 1927- *ConAu 13R*

Gunther, Peter F 1920- *ConAu 9R*

Gunther, Robert Theodore 1869- *WhLA*

Gunther, William 1924- *AmSCAP 66*

Gunthorpe, Louisa M *Alli Sup*

Gunton, David *Alli Sup*

Gunton, George 1845-1919 *Alli Sup, DcAmA, DcNAA*

Gunton, Symon *Alli*

Guntrip, Henry James Samuel 1901- *Au&Wr, ConAu 5R, WrD 1976*

Gunzburg, Isidore 1875- *WhLA*

Guomundsson, Kristmann Borgfjoro 1902- *ClDMEuL, EvEuW*

Guotaere, Der *OxGer*

Guppy, Mrs. *Alli, BiDLA*

Guppy, Henry 1861- *WhLA*

Guppy, Henry Brougham *Alli Sup*

Guppy, Nicholas 1925- *ConAu 5R*

Guppy, R *Alli*

Gupta, Bhairavprasad *DcOrL 2*

Gupta, Brijen Kishore 1929- *ConAu 45*

Gupta, Maithilisaran 1886-1964 *DcOrL 2*

Gupta, Marie 1946- *ConAu 57*

Gupta, Nagendranath 1862-1940 *DcLEnL*

Gupta, Ram Chandra 1927- *ConAu 23*

Gupta, S 1927- *ConAu 57*

Gupta, Shiv K 1930- *ConAu 57*

Gupta, Sulekh Chandra 1928- *ConAu 13R*

Guptill, Arthur L *WhWNAA*

Guptill, Nathanael M 1917- *ConAu 45*

Guramishvili, Davit 1705-1792 *DcOrL 3*

Gurd, C *OxCan Sup*

Gurd, Fraser Baillie 1883-1948 *DcNAA*

Gurd, Norman St. Clair 1870-1943 *DcNAA*

Gurdas Bhalla, Bhai d1637 *DcOrL 2*

Gurdjieff, George Ivanovitch 1868-1949 *LongC*

Gurdon, Brampton *Alli*

Gurdon, John *ChPo S1*

Gurdon, John Everard 1898- *MnBBF*

Gurdon, Philip *Alli*

Gurdon, Thornhagh *Alli*

Gurdon, W *Alli*

Gureh, Ali Abdullah *AfA 1*

Guri, Chaim 1923- *CasWL*

Gurian, Waldemar 1902- *BkC 3, CatA 1947*

Gurik, Robert 1932- *OxCan Sup*

Gurk, Paul 1880-1953 *OxGer*

Gurko, Leo 1914- *ConAu 5R, SmATA 9, ThBJA*

Gurko, Miriam *SmATA 9, ThBJA, WrD 1976*

Gurler, Henry Benjamin 1840-1928 *DcNAA*

Gurley, Mrs. E S *Alli Sup*

Gurley, Leonard B 1804-1880 *OhA&B*

Gurley, Ralph Randolph 1797-1872 *DcNAA*

Gurman, Alan S 1945- *ConAu 53*

Gurnall, William 1617-1679 *Alli, DcEnL*

Gurnay, Edmund *Alli*

Gurnell, Robert Molesworth *Alli Sup*

Gurnet *ChPo*

Gurnett, George 1791?- *BbtC*

Gurney, Alfred *Alli Sup, ChPo, ChPo S1*

Gurney, Antoinette *AmA&B, WhWNAA*

Gurney, Archer Thompson 1820-1887 *Alli, Alli Sup, ChPo, ChPo S1, PoCh*

Gurney, Arthur *Alli*

Gurney, Auber *Alli*

Gurney, Augustus *Alli Sup*

Gurney, Daniel *Alli*

Gurney, Diana *ChPo S2*

Gurney, Dorothy Frances *ChPo, ChPo S2*

Gurney, Edmund 1847-1888 *Alli, Alli Sup, BiDPar, BrAu 19*

Gurney, Elise Eleanor *ChPo S2*

Gurney, Eliza P *Alli Sup*

Gurney, Eric *ChPo S2*

Gurney, Gene 1924- *ConAu 5R*

Gurney, Henry Palin *Alli Sup*

Gurney, Hudson 1774?-1864 *Alli, BiDLA, DcEnL*

Gurney, Ivor 1890-1937 *ChPo S2*

Gurney, J Eric 1910- *AuBYP, ConAu 1R*

Gurney, J H, Jr., Russell, C & Coues, E *Alli Sup*

Gurney, James Hampden 1802-1862 *ChPo*

Gurney, John Hampden 1802-1862 *Alli, Alli Sup, ChPo S1, PoCh*

Gurney, John Henry *Alli Sup*

Gurney, Joseph *BiDLA*

Gurney, Joseph, & Gurney, William Brodie *Alli*

Gurney, Joseph John 1788-1847 *Alli, ChPo S1*

Gurney, Nancy Jack 1915?-1973 *AuBYP, ConAu 45*

Gurney, Priscilla *ChPo S1*

Gurney, Richard, Jr. *Alli, BiDLA*

Gurney, Somerville A *Alli Sup*

Gurney, Thomas 1705-1770 *Alli, BrAu, DcEnL, OxEng*

Gurney, W *ChPo S2*

Gurney, W B *Alli*

Gurney, William *Alli, Alli Sup, BiDLA*

Gurney-Salter, Emma 1875- *WhLA*

Gurnhill, James *Alli Sup*

Guro, Elena 1877-1913 *CasWL*

Gurowski, Count Adam 1805-1866 *Alli Sup, AmA&B, BiD&SB, DcAmA, DcNAA, REnAL*

Gurpinar, Huseyin Rahmi 1864-1944 *DcOrL 3*

Gurr, Andrew 1936- *ConAu 33*

Gurr, Edward 1905- *Au&Wr, WrD 1976*

Gurr, Harry *Alli Sup*

Gurr, Marjorie Ruth 1917- *Au&Wr*

Gurr, Ted Robert 1936- *ConAu 41*

Gurr, Thomas Stuart *MnBBF*

Gurteen, Stephen Humphreys V 1840-1898? *DcAmA, DcNAA*

Gurtler, Frederick H 1884- *WhWNAA*

Gurulugomi 1200?- *DcOrL 2*

Guruprasad *DcOrL 2*

Gurwitsch, Aron 1901-1973 *ConAu 41, ConAu P-1*

Gurwood, John d1845 *Alli*

Gusai *DcOrL 1*

Guseck, Bernd Von 1803-1871 *BiD&SB*

Gusev, Sergey Ivanovich 1867-1963 *DcRusL, TwCA, TwCA Sup*

Gusev-Orenburgski 1867-1963 *DcRusL*

Gusev-Orenburgsky, Sergey Ivanovich 1867-1963 *CasWL, EvEuW*

Gusfield, Joseph R 1923- *ConAu 53*

Gushington, Angelina *Alli Sup*

Gushington, Impulsia *NewC*

Gusikoff, Michel 1895- *AmSCAP 66*

Gusling, Kalfus Kurtz *WhWNAA*

Gusman, Alzira Jean *TexWr*

Gusman, Meyer 1894-1960 *AmSCAP 66*

Guss, Carolyn 1910- *IndAu 1917*

Guss, Donald L 1929- *ConAu 17R*

Guss, Leonard M 1926- *ConAu 21*

Gussin, David 1899- *AmSCAP 66*

Gussman, Boris 1914- *ConAu 5R*

Gussow, Joan Dye 1928- *ConAu 29*

Gustaf Adolf II 1594-1632 *NewC*

Gustaf VI, Adolf, King Of Sweden 1882-1973 *ConAu 45*

Gustaf-Janson, Gosta 1902- *CasWL, EvEuW*

Gustafson, Alrik 1903-1970 *AmA&B, ConAu 1R*

Gustafson, Axel 1849?- *Alli Sup, DcAmA*

Gustafson, Axel Ferdinand 1880- *WhWNAA*

Gustafson, Donald F 1934- *ConAu 9R*

Gustafson, Elton T *AuBYP*

Gustafson, James M 1925- *ConAu 25*

Gustafson, Ralph 1909- *CanWr, CasWL, ChPo S1, ConAu 23, ConP 1970, ConP 1975, DcLEnL, OxCan, OxCan Sup, TwCA Sup, WrD 1976*

Gustafson, Richard F 1934- *ConAu 17R*

Gustafson, Sarah R *SmATA 1*

Gustafson, Vera 1918- *AmSCAP 66*

Gustafson, W Eric 1933- *ConAu 57*

Gustafson, Zadel B 1841?-1917 *Alli Sup, BiD&SB, ChPo, ChPo S1, DcAmA, DcNAA*

Gustaitis, Rasa 1934- *ConAu 25*

Gustav III 1746-1792 *CasWL*

Gustav Vom See 1803-1875 *BiD&SB*

Gustavo *PueRA*

Gustavo Montiel *PueRA*

Gustavson, Carl G 1915- *ConAu 17R*

Gustavus I 1496-1560 *NewC*

Gustavus II 1594-1935 *REn*

Gustavus III 1746-1792 *DcEuL*

Gustavus Adolphus II 1594-1632 *NewC, OxGer*

Gustavus Adolphus, Lion Of The North 1594-1632 *NewC*

Gustavus Adolphus, The Snow King 1594-1632 *NewC*

Gustavus Ericksson 1496-1560 *NewC*

Gustavus Vasa 1496-1560 *NewC*
Gustin, Lawrence Robert 1937- *ConAu 57*
Gustkey, Earl 1940- *ConAu 57*
Gutch, J W G *Alli*
Gutch, John d1831 *Alli, BiDLA*
Gutch, John Mathew d1858 *Alli*
Gutch, Robert *Alli, BiDLA*
Gutcheon, Beth R 1945- *ConAu 49*
Gutenberg, Arthur W 1920- *ConAu 37*
Gutenberg, Johannes 1400?-1468? *NewC,*
    OxGer, REn
Guterman, Simeon L 1907- *ConAu 41*
Guterman, Stanley S 1934- *ConAu 29*
Gutermann, Sophie Von *OxGer*
Gutermuth, Clinton Raymond 1900- *AmA&B*
Gutersloh, Albert Paris 1887-1973 *CasWL,*
    EncWL, ModGL, OxGer
Guth, Oscar Alphons 1918- *Au&Wr*
Guth, William Westley 1871-1929 *DcNAA*
Guthe, Karl Eugen 1866-1915 *DcNAA*
Gutheim, Frederick 1908- *AmA&B, ConAu 23*
Gutheim, James Koppel 1817-1886 *Alli Sup,*
    BiDSA, DcAmA, DcNAA
Gutherie, Thomas Anstey 1856- *MnBBF*
Guthke, Karl S 1933- *ConAu 41*
Guthman, Edwin 1919- *ConAu 33*
Guthman, William H 1924- *ConAu 57*
Guthmann, Harry George 1896- *ConAu 1R,*
    WhWNAA
Guthrie, Alfred Bertram, Jr. 1901- *AmA&B,*
    AmNov, CnDAL, ConAu 57,
    ConNov 1972, ConNov 1976, CyWA,
    DrAF 1976, DcLEnL, IndAu 1917,
    ModAL, OxAm, REnAL, TwCA Sup,
    WhPNW, WrD 1976
Guthrie, Anna Lorraine d1936 *DcNAA*
Guthrie, Anne 1890- *AuBYP, ConAu 5R*
Guthrie, Archibald *MnBBF*
Guthrie, Arlo 1947- *AmA&B*
Guthrie, Arthur *Alli Sup, ChPo*
Guthrie, Charles Claude 1880- *WhWNAA*
Guthrie, Charles John 1849-1920 *ChPo S2*
Guthrie, Donald 1916- *ConAu 13R*
Guthrie, Douglas James 1885- *Au&Wr*
Guthrie, Ellen Emma *Alli Sup*
Guthrie, Ellen Jane *Alli Sup*
Guthrie, Francis *Alli Sup*
Guthrie, Frederick 1833-1886 *Alli Sup*
Guthrie, G J *Alli, BiDLA Sup*
Guthrie, George *Alli Sup*
Guthrie, Grace *TexWr*
Guthrie, Harvey Henry, Jr. 1924- *ConAu 13R*
Guthrie, Henry d1676? *Alli*
Guthrie, Hugh *ConAu XR*
Guthrie, Hunter 1901-1974 *ConAu 53*
Guthrie, James *Alli, Alli Sup*
Guthrie, James Cargill 1814?- *Alli Sup, BbD,*
    BiD&SB, ChPo
Guthrie, James Joshua 1874-1952 *ChPo,*
    ChPo S1
Guthrie, James Shields 1931- *ConAu 33*
Guthrie, James W 1936- *ConAu 41*
Guthrie, John *Alli, Alli Sup*
Guthrie, John 1908- *Au&Wr, WrD 1976*
Guthrie, John A 1907- *ConAu 1R*
Guthrie, Joseph Edward 1871-1935 *DcNAA,*
    WhWNAA
Guthrie, Judith Bretherton 1905-1972 *ConAu 37*
Guthrie, Katharine Blanche *Alli Sup*
Guthrie, Kathleen *Au&Wr*
Guthrie, Kenneth Sylvan 1871-1940 *AmLY,*
    AnMV 1926, DcNAA, WhWNAA
Guthrie, Lewis VanGilder 1868- *WhWNAA*
Guthrie, Malcolm *Alli Sup*
Guthrie, Maria *Alli*
Guthrie, Mary Jane 1895- *WhWNAA*
Guthrie, Mary Louise d1970 *IndAu 1917*
Guthrie, Matthew d1807 *Alli*
Guthrie, Max *ChPo*
Guthrie, Norman Gregor 1877-1929 *DcNAA,*
    OxCan
Guthrie, Ramon 1896-1973 *AmA&B, Au&Wr,*
    ConAu 5R, ConAu 45, ConP 1970,
    ConP 1975
Guthrie, Ramsay *WhLA*
Guthrie, Robert V 1930- *ConAu 53*
Guthrie, Samuel 1782-1848 *DcNAA*
Guthrie, Thomas *Chmbr 3*

Guthrie, Thomas 1803-1873 *Alli, Alli Sup,*
    BrAu 19, ChPo S1, DcEnL, EvLB
Guthrie, Thomas Anstey 1856-1934 *Alli Sup,*
    BiD&SB, ChPo, ChPo S1, ChPo S2,
    Chmbr 3, DcEnA Ap, DcLEnL, EvLB,
    LongC, NewC, OxEng, TwCA,
    TwCA Sup, WhCL
Guthrie, Sir Tyrone 1900-1971 *ConAu 29,*
    NewC
Guthrie, Vee *ChPo, ChPo S2*
Guthrie, W E *Alli Sup*
Guthrie, William *Alli, Chmbr 2*
Guthrie, William 1620-1665 *Alli*
Guthrie, William 1708-1770 *Alli, DcEnL*
Guthrie, William 1835- *Alli Sup*
Guthrie, William Buck 1869-1940 *DcNAA*
Guthrie, William Dameron 1859-1935 *DcAmA,*
    DcNAA
Guthrie, William Keith Chambers 1906-
    Au&Wr, WrD 1976
Guthrie, William Norman 1868-1944 *AmA&B,*
    BiD&SB, DcAmA, OhA&B
Guthrie, Woody 1912-1967 *AmA&B*
Guthrie-Smith, William Herbert 1861-1940
    CasWL, DcLEnL, TwCW
Guthry, Henry *Alli*
Gutierrez, Antonio Garcia 1812?-1884 *BiD&SB,*
    DcEuL
Gutierrez, Eduardo *REn*
Gutierrez, Juan Maria 1809-1878 *CasWL,*
    Pen Am
Gutierrez, Juan Rufo *DcEuL*
Gutierrez, Miguel 1940- *DcCLA*
Gutierrez DelArroyo, Isabel 1907- *PueRA*
Gutierrez Gonzalez, Gregorio 1826-1872 *CasWL,*
    Pen Am
Gutierrez Najera, Manuel 1859-1895 *CasWL,*
    DcSpL, Pen Am, REn
Gutierrez-Vega, Zenaida 1930- *ConAu 41*
Gutkelch, Walter 1901- *CnMD*
Gutkind, Erwin A 1901- *ConAu 5R*
Gutkind, Lee 1943- *ConAu 53*
Gutman, I 1907- *Au&Wr*
Gutman, Judith Mara 1928- *ConAu 21,*
    WrD 1976
Gutman, Robert 1926- *ConAu 45*
Gutman, Robert W 1925- *ConAu 25,*
    WrD 1976
Gutmann, Edward *Alli Sup*
Gutmann, James 1897- *ConAu 21*
Gutmann, Joseph 1923- *ConAu 49*
Gutnik, Martin J 1942- *ConAu 49*
Guto'r Glyn *CasWL*
Gutsche, Thelma 1915- *Au&Wr, ConAu 23*
Gutten, George Barton 1874- *WhWNAA*
Guttenbrunner, Michael 1919- *OxGer*
Guttentag, Marcia 1932- *ConAu 57*
Gutteridge, Bernard 1916- *ConP 1970*
Gutteridge, Donald George 1937- *ConP 1975,*
    OxCan Sup, WrD 1976
Gutteridge, John Rowton *Alli Sup*
Gutteridge, Joseph *Alli Sup*
Gutteridge, Lindsay 1923- *ConAu 49*
Gutteridge, M *Alli Sup*
Gutteridge, William Frank 1919- *ConAu 13R,*
    WrD 1976
Gutterson, Herbert 1915- *Au&Wr, ConAu 9R*
Guttinguer, Ulric 1785-1866 *BbD, BiD&SB,*
    OxFr
Guttmacher, Alan F 1898-1974 *ConAu 1R,*
    ConAu 49
Guttmacher, Manfred S 1898-1966 *ConAu 13,*
    ConAu P-1
Guttmann, Alexander *ConAu 29*
Guttmann, Allen 1932- *ConAu 1R, WrD 1976*
Guttsman, Wilhelm Leo 1920- *ConAu 9R*
Guttuso, Renato 1912- *WhGrA*
Gutwillig, Robert Alan 1931- *AmA&B,*
    Au&Wr
Gutzke, Manford G 1896- *ConAu 17R*
Gutzkow, Karl Ferdinand 1811-1878 *BbD,*
    BiD&SB, CasWL, DcEuL, EuA, EvEuW,
    McGWD, OxGer, Pen Eur, REn
Gutzlaff, Charles 1803-1851 *Alli*
Guy, Bishop Of Amiens d1076? *BiB N*
Guy De Bazoches 1146?-1203 *CasWL*
Guy Of Bazoches 1146?-1203 *Pen Eur*
Guy, Anne W *ConAu 5R*

Guy, Douglas Sherwood 1855- *WhLA*
Guy, Harold A 1904- *ConAu 17R*
Guy, J *Alli, BiDLA*
Guy, John d1628? *OxCan*
Guy, Joseph *Alli, BiDLA*
Guy, Joseph, Jr. *Alli, BiDLA*
Guy, Melmoth *Alli*
Guy, Richard *Alli*
Guy, Rosa 1925- *BlkAW*
Guy, Rosa 1928- *ConAu 17R*
Guy, Samuel *Alli Sup*
Guy, Seymour J 1824-1910 *EarAB*
Guy, Thomas 1645?-1724 *Alli, Alli Sup,*
    NewC
Guy, Violet M *ChPo*
Guy, William *Alli, Alli Sup*
Guy, William Augustus 1810-1885 *Alli,*
    Alli Sup
Guyal, Louise H *ChPo S2*
Guyau, Jean-Marie 1854-1898 *OxFr*
Guybon, Francis *Alli*
Guyer, William Harris 1870- *WhWNAA*
Guynes, Charlsa Anne 1933- *AmSCAP 66*
Guyon, Madame 1648-1717 *OxFr*
Guyon, Jeanne Marie Bouvier DeLaMotte
    1648-1717 *ChPo, DcEuL, PoCh*
Guyonvarch, Irene Cecilia 1915- *Au&Wr*
Guyot *DcEuL*
Guyot, Arnold Henry 1807-1884 *Alli Sup, BbD,*
    BiD&SB, CyAL 1, DcAmA, DcNAA
Guyot, James F 1932- *ConAu 53*
Guys, Constantin 1805-1892 *AtlBL, OxFr*
Guyse, John 1680-1761 *Alli*
Guyton, Arthur C 1919- *ConAu 17R*
Guyton, Emma Jane 1825-1887 *Alli Sup*
Guzie, Tad W 1934- *ConAu 13R*
Guzman, Augusto 1903- *DcCLA*
Guzman, Fernan Perez De 1376?-1460? *DcEuL*
Guzman, Martin Luis 1887- *CasWL, DcSpL,*
    Pen Am, REn
Guzzwell, John 1930- *ConAu 13R*
Gvadanyi, Count Jozsef 1725-1801 *CasWL*
Gwaitney, John Langston 1928- *LivBA*
Gwalachmai *DcEnL*
Gwalia, Alfred *WhLA*
Gwaltney, Francis Irby 1921- *ConAu 1R*
Gwaltney, John Langston 1928- *ConAu 33,*
    WrD 1976
Gwaltney, Leslie Lee 1876- *WhWNAA*
Gwathmey, Edward Moseley 1891-1956
    AmA&B
Gwathmey, James Tayloe 1865-1944 *DcNAA*
Gwathmey, John H 1886- *AmA&B*
Gwatkin, Richard *Alli Sup*
Gwent, Sarah *Alli Sup*
Gwilliam, Sir Henry *Alli*
Gwilliam, John *Alli, BiDLA*
Gwilliam, Kenneth M 1937- *ConAu 17R*
Gwillim, Sir Henry *BiDLA*
Gwillim, John *Alli*
Gwillum, Dafydd Ap *NewC*
Gwilt, Joseph *Alli, BiDLA*
Gwilym, Dafydd Ap 1340-1400 *NewC*
Gwilym, David Ap 1340-1400 *Alli*
Gwilym, Davydd Ab 1340-1400 *DcEnL*
Gwin, William McKendree 1805-1885 *BiDSA*
Gwinett, Ambrose *Alli*
Gwinn, Christine Margaret 1900- *WrD 1976*
Gwinn, Ralph Waldo 1884-1962 *IndAu 1917*
Gwinne, Matthew d1627 *Alli*
Gwinneth, John *Alli*
Gwirtz, Irvin R 1903-1957 *AmSCAP 66*
Gwirtzman, Milton S 1933- *ConAu 29*
Gwyer, Joseph *Alli Sup*
Gwylt, Hannah Jackson *Alli Sup*
Gwyn, David *Alli*
Gwyn, Eleanor 1650-1687 *REn*
Gwyn, H B 1873- *WhWNAA*
Gwyn, Julian 1937- *ConAu 57*
Gwyn, Laura 1833- *BiDSA, DcNAA,*
    LivFWS
Gwyn, Nell 1650-1687 *NewC*
Gwyn, Richard 1934- *ConAu 25, OxCan Sup,*
    WrD 1976
Gwyn, William Brent 1927- *ConAu 13R,*
    WrD 1976
Gwyne, Lawrence *Alli*
Gwyne, Reginald *MnBBF*

Gwyne, William *Alli*
Gwynn, Audrey Jean *Au&Wr*
Gwynn, Denis Rolleston 1893- *Au&Wr,*
 CatA 1947, ConAu P-1
Gwynn, Edward John 1868- *WhLA*
Gwynn, Heather *ChPo S2*
Gwynn, John *Alli*
Gwynn, Joseph 1835- *ChPo S1*
Gwynn, Stephen Lucius 1864-1950 *ChPo S1,*
 Chmbr 3, EvLB, LongC, ModBL, NewC,
 PoIre, TwCA, TwCA Sup, WhLA
Gwynne, Arthur *MnBBF*
Gwynne, Eleanor 1650-1687 *REn*
Gwynne, Enid *Au&Wr*
Gwynne, Erskine 1898?-1948 *DcNAA, WhLA*
Gwynne, Fanny Price *Alli Sup*
Gwynne, Fred *IlBYP*
Gwynne, George John *Alli Sup*
Gwynne, John *Alli*
Gwynne, John Harold 1899- *AuBYP*
Gwynne, Lawrence *BiDLA*
Gwynne, Matthew *Alli*
Gwynne, Nadolig Ximenes *Alli Sup*
Gwynne, Parry *Alli Sup*
Gwynne, Pryce *Alli Sup*
Gwynne, T *Alli*
Gwynne, Walker 1845-1931 *AmLY, DcNAA,*
 WhWNAA
Gwynne-Vaughan, Helen Charlotte Isabella 1879-
 WhLA
Gwynneth, John *Alli*
Gyanagyaw Ma Ma Lei *DcOrL 2*
Gyarfas, Miklos 1915- *CrCD*
Gybson *Alli*
Gybson, Thomas *Alli*
Gye, Hal *ChPo, ChPo S1*
Gyer, Nicholas *Alli*
Gyffard, George *Alli*
Gyfford, E *Alli, BiDLA*
Gyfford, R *Alli*
Gyges *NewC*
Gylby, Anthony *Alli*
Gylby, Goddred *Alli*
Gyldenvand, Lily M 1917- *ConAu 13R,*
 WrD 1976
Gylebie, Anthony *Alli*
Gyles, J F *Alli, BiDLA*
Gyles, John *OxCan*
Gyles, John 1678?-1755 *DcNAA*
Gyles, William *Alli*
Gyll, Gordon Willoughby James 1818-1878
 Alli Sup
Gyllembourg-Ehrensvard, Thomasine C
 1773-1856 *BiD&SB*
Gyllembourg-Ehrensvard, Countess T C
 1773-1856 *CasWL*
Gyllenborg, Count Carl 1679-1746 *CasWL*
Gyllenborg, Count Gustaf Fredrik 1731-1808
 CasWL, DcEuL
Gyllenborg, Thomasine Christine 1773-1856
 DcEuL
Gyllensten, Lars Johan Wictor 1921- *CasWL,*
 Pen Eur
Gyongyosi, Istvan 1629?-1704 *CasWL*
Gyp 1850-1932 *BiD&SB, EvEuW, OxFr*
Gysbers, Norman C 1932- *ConAu 61*
Gyulai, Pal 1826-1909 *BiD&SB, CasWL,*
 ClDMEuL, EuA

H

ModWD, OxAm, REnAL
Hackett, Buddy 1924- *AmSCAP 66*
Hackett, Byrne 1879-1953 *AmA&B*
Hackett, Cecil Arthur 1908- *Au&Wr,
ConAu 13R, WrD 1976*
Hackett, Charles Wilson 1888- *TexWr*
Hackett, Donald F 1918- *ConAu 29*
Hackett, Frances *AuBYP*
Hackett, Francis 1883-1962 *AmA&B, LongC,
OxAm, REnAL, TwCA, TwCA Sup*
Hackett, Frank Warren 1841-1926 *Alli Sup,
DcAmA, DcNAA*
Hackett, Herbert L 1917-1964 *ConAu 1R*
Hackett, Horatio Balch 1808-1875 *Alli,
Alli Sup, BiD&SB, DcAmA, DcNAA*
Hackett, James *Alli*
Hackett, James Dominick 1877-1936 *DcNAA*
Hackett, James Henry 1800-1871 *Alli Sup,
AmA&B, BiD&SB, DcAmA, DcNAA,
REnAL*
Hackett, James Thomas 1805- *Alli*
Hackett, James Thompson 1858- *ChPo S2*
Hackett, John *Alli*
Hackett, John W 1924- *ConAu 17R*
Hackett, Karleton Spalding 1867- *WhWNAA*
Hackett, Laura Lyman 1916- *ConAu 17R*
Hackett, M *Alli Sup*
Hackett, Marie G 1923- *ConAu 37*
Hackett, P *Pen Eng*
Hackett, Paul 1920- *ConAu 29*
Hackett, Richard R *Alli Sup*
Hackett, Roger *Alli*
Hackett, Thomas *Alli*
Hackett, Walter 1876-1944 *DcNAA*
Hackett, William *Alli, BiDLA*
Hackewill, William *Alli*
Hackforth-Jones, Gilbert 1900- *Au&Wr,
ConAu 13R*
Hackforth-Jones, Margaret S *WrD 1976*
Hackh, Ingo Waldemar Dagobert 1890-1938
DcNAA
Hackhouse, Alfred *Alli Sup*
Hackitt, Thomas *Alli*
Hacklander, Friedrich Wilhelm Von 1816-1877
BbD, BiD&SB, DcBiA, EvEuW, OxGer
Hackle, Palmer *Alli*
Hackleman, Wauneta 1915- *WrD 1976*
Hackleton, Mrs. M W *Alli Sup*
Hackleton, W M *ChPo S2*
Hackley, Charles Elihu 1836- *Alli Sup*
Hackley, Charles William 1808-1861 *Alli,
DcAmA, DcNAA*
Hackluyt, Richard *Alli*
Hackman, Alfred 1811-1874 *Alli Sup*
Hackman, J Richard 1940- *ConAu 49*
Hackman, James *Alli*
Hackman, Martha L 1912- *ConAu 29*
Hackman, Neil *DrAP 1975*
Hackmann, Heinrich Friedrich 1864- *WhLA*
Hackner, Willibald *Alli Sup*
Hackney, Alan Charles Langley 1924- *Au&Wr,
ConAu 5R*
Hackney, Louise Wallace d1945 *DcNAA*
Hackney, Sheldon 1933- *ConAu 41*
Hackney, Vivian 1914- *ConAu 23*
Hacks, Peter 1928- *CasWL, CnMD, CrCD,
EncWL Sup, McGWD, ModGL, ModWD,
OxGer, Pen Eur*
Hackwood, Frederick William *Alli Sup*
Hacohen, Shalom 1772-1845 *Pen Eur*
Hacon 1217-1263 *DcEuL*
Hadamar Von Laber 1300?-1360? *CasWL,
OxGer*
Hadank, O H W 1889- *WhGrA*
Hadas, Moses 1900-1966 *AmA&B, ConAu 1R,
ConAu 25, Pen Am, REnAL, WorAu*
Hadath, Gunby 1880?-1954 *ChPo, WhCL,
WhLA*
Hadath, John Edward Gunby *MnBBF*
Hadaway, W S *ChPo S2*
Hadawi, Sami 1904- *ConAu 23*
Haddad, George M 1910- *ConAu 17R*
Haddad, Malek 1927- *DcOrL 3*
Haddan, Arthur West 1816-1873 *Alli Sup*
Haddan, Eugene E 1918- *IndAu 1917*
Haddan, J L *Alli Sup*
Haddan, Thomas Henry 1814-1873 *Alli Sup*
Hadden, Anne *ChPo*

Hadden, Briton 1898-1929 *REnAL*
Hadden, Frances Roots 1910- *AmSCAP 66*
Hadden, J Cuthbert *Alli Sup, ChPo S2*
Hadden, James 1845-1923 *DcNAA*
Hadden, Maude Emma Miner 1880- *ChPo,
ConAu 17*
Hadden, Richard M 1910- *AmSCAP 66*
Hadden, Robert Henry *Alli Sup*
Hadden, William Baugh *Alli Sup*
Haddington, Thomas Hamilton d1637 *Alli*
Haddington, Thomas Hamilton d1785 *Alli*
Haddo, James *Alli*
Haddo, Oliver *ConAu XR*
Haddock, Albert *NewC*
Haddock, Charles Brickett 1796-1861 *Alli,
CyAL 1, DcAmA, DcNAA*
Haddock, Frank C *Alli Sup*
Haddock, Frank Channing 1853-1915 *DcNAA*
Haddock, Joseph W *Alli Sup*
Haddock, John A 1823- *DcNAA*
Haddon, Alfred Cort *Alli Sup*
Haddon, Archibald 1871- *WhLA*
Haddon, Caroline *Alli Sup*
Haddon, Christopher *LongC, TwCA,
TwCA Sup*
Haddon, John *Alli Sup*
Haddon, Walter 1516-1572 *Alli, DcEnL*
Haddox, John H 1929- *ConAu 45*
Haden, Charles Thomas *Alli*
Haden, Francis Seymour 1818- *Alli Sup*
Haden, Russell Landram 1888- *WhWNAA*
Haden, Thomas *Alli*
Hader, Berta *AmA&B, AuBYP, AuICB,
ConICB, IICB 1945, IICB 1956,
IICB 1966, JBA 1951, St&VC*
Hader, Berta And Elmer *BkP, Cald 1938,
IIBYP, JBA 1934*
Hader, Elmer Stanley 1889- *AmA&B, AuBYP,
AuICB, ConICB, IIBYP, IICB 1945,
IICB 1956, IICB 1966, JBA 1951,
St&VC*
Hadermann, Jeannette Ritchie *Alli Sup,
DcNAA, LivFWS*
Hadewijch *CasWL, EuA, Pen Eur*
Hadewijch *CasWL, EuA, Pen Eur*
Hadfield, Alan 1904- *Au&Wr*
Hadfield, Alice Mary 1908- *Au&Wr*
Hadfield, Mrs. E *Alli Sup*
Hadfield, E C R *ConAu XR*
Hadfield, Elizabeth *ChPo*
Hadfield, Ellis Charles Raymond 1909- *Au&Wr,
ConAu 13R*
Hadfield, H H *Alli Sup*
Hadfield, James *Alli*
Hadfield, John Charles Heywood 1907- *Au&Wr*
Hadfield, Joseph *OxCan*
Hadfield, Miles Heywood 1903- *Au&Wr,
ConAu P-1*
Hadfield, Robert L *MnBBF*
Hadfield, Stephen John 1908- *Au&Wr*
Hadfield, Thomas *Alli*
Hadfield, William 1800-1887 *Alli Sup*
Hadik, Laszlo 1932?-1973 *ConAu 45*
Hadingham, Evan 1951- *WrD 1976*
Hadlaub SEE ALSO Hadloub
Hadlaub, Johann *BbD, BiD&SB*
Hadlaub, Johannes *CasWL*
Hadlaub, Johans *OxGer*
Hadleigh, Alan *ChPo*
Hadley, Alden H 1877?-1951 *IndAu 1917*
Hadley, Almira Jane Harvey 1847-1923
IndAu 1917
Hadley, Amos *Alli Sup*
Hadley, Arthur Twining 1856-1930 *Alli Sup,
AmA&B, AmLY, BbD, BiD&SB,
DcAmA, DcNAA, REnAL*
Hadley, Caroline *Alli Sup*
Hadley, Chalmers 1872-1958 *IndAu 1816,
OhA&B*
Hadley, Drummond *DrAP 1975*
Hadley, Eleanor M 1916- *ConAu 29*
Hadley, Florence Jones *ChPo S2*
Hadley, Franklin *ConAu XR, SmATA XR*
Hadley, George *Alli*
Hadley, Grace Talbot *IndAu 1917*
Hadley, Hamilton 1896- *ConAu P-1*
Hadley, Henry 1871-1937 *AmSCAP 66*
Hadley, Herbert Spencer 1872-1927 *DcNAA*
Hadley, Hiram 1833-1922 *DcNAA*

Hadley, James 1821-1872 *Alli Sup, CyAL 1,
DcAmA, DcNAA*
Hadley, John *Alli*
Hadley, John d1744 *Alli*
Hadley, John Bell *Alli Sup*
Hadley, John Vestal 1842-1915 *DcNAA,
IndAu 1816*
Hadley, Leila 1926- *Au&Wr, ConAu 41*
Hadley, Leila E B 1929- *WrD 1976*
Hadley, Lizzie M *ChPo*
Hadley, Milton Herschel 1898- *IndAu 1917*
Hadley, Samuel Hopkins 1842-1906 *DcNAA*
Hadley Chase, James 1906- *WrD 1976*
Hadloub SEE ALSO Hadlaub
Hadloub, Johannes *DcEuL, Pen Eur*
Hadloub, Johans *OxGer*
Hadlow, Leonard Harold 1908- *Au&Wr,
ConAu P-1, WrD 1976*
Hadow, James *Alli*
Hadow, Maria Stephania Anna *Au&Wr*
Hadow, William Henry 1859- *WhLA*
Hadra, Berthold Ernest 1842-1903 *DcNAA*
Hadrian 076-138 *CasWL, NewC, Pen Cl,
REn*
Hadsell, O D *Alli Sup*
Hadwen, J Lovel *Alli Sup*
Hadwiger, Don F 1930- *ConAu 21*
Hadwiger, Viktor 1878-1911 *OxGer*
Hadzsits, George Depue 1875-1954 *AmA&B,
WhWNAA*
Haeberle, Erwin J 1936- *ConAu 29*
Haeberle, William L 1922- *IndAu 1917*
Haebich, Kathryn A 1899- *ConAu 5R*
Haecht, Willem Van 1530?-1585? *CasWL*
Haeckel, Ernst 1834-1919 *BbD, BiD&SB,
OxGer, REn*
Haecker, Hans Joachim 1910- *CnMD*
Haecker, Theodor 1879-1945 *CatA 1952*
Haeddi d705 *BiB S*
Haefele, John W 1913- *ConAu 1R*
Haegglund, Bengt 1920- *ConAu 25*
Haenicke, Diether H 1935- *ConAu 33*
Haenigsen, Harry William 1900- *AmA&B*
Haenschen, Gustave *AmSCAP 66*
Haentzschel, Adolph T 1881- *ConAu 1R*
Haering, Bernard 1912- *ConAu 5R*
Haering, Theodor L 1884- *WhLA*
Haeseler, Charles H *Alli Sup*
Haeussler, Paul 1895- *AmSCAP 66*
Hafen, LeRoy R 1893- *AmA&B, Au&Wr,
WhWNAA*
Hafenrichter, A L 1897- *WhWNAA*
Haferkorn, Henry Ernest 1859-1933 *DcNAA*
Hafez, Mohammad Shamsoddin 1320?-1389?
DcOrL 3
Haff, Carl 1879- *WhLA*
Haffenden, Philip Spencer 1926- *ConAu 61*
Haffert, John Mathias 1915- *BkC 4*
Haffkine, Waldemar Mordecai Wolff 1860-
WhLA
Haffner, James Wilson 1929- *IndAu 1917*
Haffner, Karl 1804-1876 *BiD&SB*
Haffner, Katherine Neuhaus 1909- *IndAu 1917*
Hafford, Ferris S 1857-1916 *OhA&B*
Hafiz 1320?-1389? *ChPo S1, ChPo S2,
CyWA, DcOrL 3, NewC, REn*
Hafiz, Khwaja Shams-Ad-Din Muhammad
1320?-1389? *BbD*
Hafiz, Khwaja Shams-Ad-Din Muhammad
1300?-1389? *BiD&SB*
Hafiz, Shams-Al-Din Muhammad 1320?-1389?
CasWL, Pen Cl
Hafiz, Shams-Ed-Din Muhammad 1320?-1389?
OxEng
Hafiz, Shams-Ud-Din Muhammad 1320?-1389?
RCom
Hafiz Ibrahim, Muhammad 1871?-1932 *CasWL*
Hafley, James 1928- *ConAu 17R, WrD 1976*
Hafner, Lawrence E 1924- *ConAu 25*
Hafner, Marilyn 1925- *IIBYP*
Hafner, Marylin 1925- *ChPo S1, SmATA 7*
Hafner, Philipp 1735?-1764 *CasWL, OxGer*
Hafstein, Hannes 1861-1922 *CasWL*
Hafter, Ernst 1876- *WhLA*
Haga, Enoch John 1931- *ConAu 25,
WrD 1976*
Hagalin, Gudmundur Gislason 1898- *CasWL,
ClDMEuL, EncWL*

Hailmann, William Nicholas 1836-1920
AmA&B, DcAmA, DcNAA, OhA&B
Hailperin, Herman 1899- *AmA&B, Au&Wr,*
ConAu 5R
Hails, W H *Alli, BiDLA*
Hails, William Anthony *Alli, BiDLA*
Hailsham Of Saint@ Marylebone, Lord 1907-
Au&Wr
Hailstone, Edward 1818-1890 *Alli Sup*
Hailstone, Herbert *Alli Sup*
Hailstone, John *Alli, BiDLA*
Hailstone, Thomas *Alli Sup*
Hailstones, Thomas J 1919- *ConAu 41*
Haiman, Franklyn S 1929- *ConAu 37*
Haiman, Miecislaus 1888- *BkC 2, CatA 1947*
Haimann, Theo 1911- *ConAu 5R*
Haime, Agnes Irvine Constance 1884- *Au&Wr,*
ChPo S2, ConAu P-1
Haimes, Norma *ConAu 53*
Haimon *NewC*
Haimowitz, Morris L 1918- *ConAu 37*
Haimowitz, Natalie Reader 1923- *ConAu 53*
Hainam, Richard *Alli*
Haindl, Marieluise 1901-1974 *ConAu 49*
Hainer, Bayard Taylor 1860- *DcAmA,*
WhWNAA
Haines, Alanson Austin 1830-1891 *Alli Sup,*
DcNAA
Haines, Alice Calhoun *ChPo, WhWNAA*
Haines, Aubrey Leon 1914- *WhPNW*
Haines, Benjamin H *Alli Sup*
Haines, C Grove 1906- *AmA&B*
Haines, C R *Alli Sup*
Haines, Charles 1928- *ConAu 41*
Haines, Charles Glidden 1792-1825 *Alli,*
DcNAA
Haines, Charles Grove 1879-1948 *DcNAA,*
WhWNAA
Haines, Donal Hamilton 1886- *WhWNAA*
Haines, E *MnBBF*
Haines, E Irvine 1877- *WhWNAA*
Haines, E J *ChPo S2*
Haines, Edmund 1914- *AmSCAP 66*
Haines, Elijah Middlebrook 1822-1889 *Alli Sup,*
DcNAA
Haines, Elwood Lindsay 1893-1949 *ChPo S1,*
DcNAA, OhA&B
Haines, Eva May *ChPo, ChPo S1, ChPo S2*
Haines, F E H *Alli Sup*
Haines, Francis 1899- *ConAu 5R*
Haines, Francis D, Jr. 1923- *ConAu 53,*
WhPNW
Haines, Gail Kay 1943- *ConAu 37, WrD 1976*
Haines, Geoffrey Colton 1899- *Au&Wr*
Haines, George H, Jr. 1937- *ConAu 33*
Haines, Helen Elizabeth 1872- *ChPo, REnAL*
Haines, Henry Stevens 1836-1923 *DcNAA*
Haines, Herbert 1826-1872 *Alli Sup*
Haines, Hiram *BiDSA*
Haines, James A 1925- *AmSCAP 66*
Haines, John 1924- *AmA&B, ConAu 17R,*
ConP 1970, ConP 1975, DrAP 1975,
WrD 1976
Haines, Lynn 1876-1929 *DcNAA*
Haines, Mabel Rainsford *AnMV 1926*
Haines, Pamela Mary 1929- *WrD 1976*
Haines, Perry Franklin 1889- *ConAu 5R*
Haines, Peter C 1840- *Alli Sup*
Haines, Philip Frost John Bird *Alli Sup*
Haines, R H *Alli Sup*
Haines, Richard *Alli*
Haines, Samuel Charles *Alli Sup*
Haines, Thomas Harvey 1871- *WhWNAA*
Haines, V G 1934- *Au&Wr*
Haines, Walter Stanley 1850-1923 *DcNAA*
Haines, Walter Wells 1918- *ConAu 1R,*
WrD 1976
Haines, William G *ChPo S1*
Haines, William T And Young, W V K *Alli Sup*
Haines, William Wister 1908- *AmA&B,*
Au&Wr, ConAu P-1, ModWD, REnAL,
TwCA Sup
Haines, Zenas T *Alli Sup*
Haining, John Allison 1885- *WhWNAA*
Haining, Peter Alexander 1940- *ConAu 45,*
WrD 1976
Hainisch, Michael 1858- *WhLA*
Hains, Thornton Jenkins 1866- *AmA&B,*

BiDSA, DcAmA, DcNAA
Hainsworth, Marguerite Dorothy *Au&Wr,*
WrD 1976
Hair, Adelbert 1871-1932 *OhA&B*
Hair, James *Alli Sup*
Hair, James T *Alli Sup*
Hair, P E H 1926- *ConAu 25*
Hair, William Ivy 1930- *ConAu 29*
Haire, Frances H 1894- *WhWNAA*
Haire, Wilson John 1932- *WrD 1976*
Hairston, Jester 1901- *AmSCAP 66*
Hairston, Loyle 1926- *BlkAW, LivBA*
Hairston, William *AmA&B, BlkAW*
Haisley, Lyra 1905- *TexWr*
Haislip, Harvey 1889- *ConAu 1R, WrD 1976*
Haislip, John 1925- *ConAu 33, DrAP 1975*
Haite, George Charles 1855- *ChPo S1*
Haithcox, John Patrick 1933- *ConAu 29*
Haiward, John *Alli*
Haj, Fareed 1935- *ConAu 29*
Hajek Z Libocan, Vaclav 1553- *CasWL*
Haji, Al-Ghassaniy *AfA 1*
Haji Khalfa 1609-1657 *CasWL*
Haji Khalfa 1609-1657 *CasWL*
Hajji Khalfah 1609-1657 *DcOrL 3, Pen Cl,*
REn
Hajos, Karl 1889-1950 *AmSCAP 66*
Hake, Alfred Egmont *Alli Sup*
Hake, Edward *Alli, CrE&SL*
Hake, Edward 1554?-1579 *DcEnL*
Hake, Thomas Gordon 1809-1895 *Alli Sup,*
BiD&SB, BrAu 19, ChPo, Chmbr 3,
DcEnA Ap, EvLB
Hake, Thomas St. Edmund *Alli Sup*
Hakem 985-1021? *NewC*
Hakes, Joseph Edward 1916- *ConAu 9R*
Hakewill, Arthur William 1808-1856 *Alli Sup*
Hakewill, Edward Charles 1812-1872 *Alli Sup*
Hakewill, George 1579-1649 *Alli, DcEnL*
Hakewill, James *Alli, BiDLA*
Hakewill, James Ridgway *Alli Sup*
Hakewill, William *Alli*
Hakim 985-1021? *NewC*
Hakim, Taufiq Al- 1902- *CasWL*
Hakim, Tawfiq Al- 1898?- *DcOrL 3*
Hakki, Yehia *CasWL*
Hakluyt, Richard 1552?-1616 *Alli, AnCL,*
AtlBL, BiD&SB, BiDSA, BrAu, CasWL,
Chmbr 1, CrE&SL, CyWA, DcEnA,
DcEnL, DcEuL, DcLEnL, EvLB, NewC,
OxAm, OxCan, OxEng, Pen Eng, REn,
REnAL, WebEAL
Hakobian, Hakob 1866-1937 *DcOrL 3*
Hakucho *DcOrL 1*
Hakushu *DcOrL 1*
Hala *DcOrL 2*
Halacy, Daniel Stephen 1919- *AuBYP,*
ConAu 5R
Halas, Frantisek 1901-1949 *CasWL, EncWL,*
EvEuW, ModSL 2, Pen Eur
Halas, John 1912- *WhGrA*
Halasz, Nicholas 1895- *ConAu 17R,*
WrD 1976
Halbe, Max 1865-1944 *ClDMEuL, CnMD,*
EncWL, McGWD, ModWD, OxGer,
Pen Eur, REn
Halberg, Catherine S *ChPo*
Halberstadt, John 1941- *ConAu 49*
Halberstadt, William Harold 1930- *ConAu 1R*
Halberstam, Alfred Peter 1926- *Au&Wr*
Halberstam, David 1934- *AmA&B, WrD 1976*
Halbert, Henry Sale 1837-1916 *BiDSA,*
DcNAA
Halbert, Homer Valmore 1858-1927 *DcNAA*
Halbert, William Morton *Alli Sup*
Halbertsma, Eeltsje 1797-1858 *CasWL*
Halbertsma, Joast 1789-1869 *CasWL*
Halbertsma, Tsjalling 1792-1852 *CasWL*
Halbrook, Brewster *WhWNAA*
Halbrooke, W *Alli*
Halck, Jorgen *Au&Wr*
Halcomb, J *Alli*
Halcombe, John, Jr. *Alli*
Halcombe, John Joseph *Alli Sup*
Halcrow, Harold Graham 1911- *ConAu 17R*
Haldane, Alexander *Alli*
Haldane, Charlotte *NewC*
Haldane, Henry *Alli, BiDLA*

Haldane, J W C *Alli Sup*
Haldane, James Alexander 1768-1851 *Alli,*
BiDLA, DcEnL
Haldane, James Robert Alexander Chinnery
Alli Sup
Haldane, John Burdon Sanderson 1892-1964
DcLEnL, EvLB, LongC, NewC, OxEng,
TwCA, TwCA Sup
Haldane, John Scott 1860- *WhLA*
Haldane, R C *Alli Sup*
Haldane, Richard Burdon, Viscount 1856-1928
Alli Sup, NewC, OxEng
Haldane, Robert *BiDLA, BiDLA Sup*
Haldane, Robert 1764-1842 *Alli, DcEnL*
Haldane, Sean *ChPo S1*
Haldane, Vere *Alli Sup*
Haldane-Duncan, Alison *ChPo S2*
Haldane-Stevenson, James Patrick 1910-
ConAu 45, WrD 1976
Haldeman, Charles 1931- *ConAu 5R*
Haldeman, Isaac Massey 1845-1933 *AmLY,*
DcNAA
Haldeman, Joe 1943- *ConAu 53*
Haldeman, Oakley 1909- *AmSCAP 66*
Haldeman, Samuel Stehman 1812-1880 *Alli,*
Alli Sup, AmA&B, DcAmA, DcNAA
Haldeman-Julius, E 1889-1951 *AmA&B,*
REnAL, WhWNAA
Halden, Charles Ab Der *OxCan*
Halderman, Samuel Stehman 1812-1880
BiD&SB
Haldimand, Sir Frederick 1718-1791 *OxCan*
Hale *Alli, MnBBF*
Hale, Judge *ChPo S2*
Hale, Mrs. *Alli, BiDLA*
Hale, A M *Alli Sup*
Hale, Albert Barlow 1860-1929 *DcNAA*
Hale, Allean Lemmon 1914- *ConAu 33,*
WrD 1976
Hale, Anne Gardner 1823-1914 *Alli Sup,*
ChPo S1, DcAmA, DcNAA
Hale, Annie Riley 1859-1944 *DcNAA*
Hale, Arlene 1924- *AuBYP, ConAu 1R*
Hale, Arthur *ChPo S2*
Hale, Beatrice Forbes-Robertson 1883-
WhWNAA
Hale, Benjamin 1797-1863 *Alli, DcAmA,*
DcNAA
Hale, C H *Alli Sup*
Hale, Charles 1831-1882 *Alli, DcNAA*
Hale, Charles A 1930- *ConAu 25*
Hale, Charles Leslie 1902- *Au&Wr*
Hale, Charles Reuben 1837-1900 *Alli Sup,*
DcAmA, DcNAA
Hale, Clement *MnBBF*
Hale, David 1791-1849 *Alli*
Hale, David G 1938- *ConAu 45*
Hale, Dennis 1944- *ConAu 25*
Hale, Edward *Alli Sup*
Hale, Edward 1858-1918 *DcNAA*
Hale, Edward Everett 1822-1909 *Alli, Alli Sup,*
AmA, AmA&B, BbD, BiD&SB, CarSB,
ChPo, ChPo S1, ChPo S2, Chmbr 3,
CnDAL, CyAL 2, CyWA, DcAmA,
DcEnL, DcLEnL, DcNAA, EvLB,
JBA 1934, OxAm, Pen Am, REn,
REnAL
Hale, Edward Everett, Jr. 1863-1932 *Alli Sup,*
AmA&B, AmLY, DcNAA, REnAL
Hale, Edwin Moses 1829-1899 *Alli Sup,*
DcAmA, DcNAA
Hale, Ellen D *ChPo*
Hale, Emma Tharp *ChPo*
Hale, Enoch 1790-1848 *Alli, DcAmA,*
DcNAA
Hale, Francis Joseph 1922- *ConAu 53*
Hale, Frank W, Jr. 1927- *LivBA*
Hale, Franklin Darius 1854-1940 *DcNAA*
Hale, Garth 1888-1962 *AmA&B, AmNov,*
OhA&B
Hale, Geoffrey *MnBBF*
Hale, George Ellery 1868-1938 *DcNAA,*
WhWNAA
Hale, George Silsbee 1825-1877 *Alli Sup,*
DcAmA
Hale, Gertrude Elizabeth *Alli Sup*
Hale, H *OxCan*
Hale, Harris Grafton 1865-1945 *DcNAA*

Hall, Amanda H *Alli Sup*
Hall, Andrew 1935- *ConAu 21*
Hall, Angus 1932- *Au&Wr, ConAu 21, WrD 1976*
Hall, Mrs. Angus W *Alli Sup*
Hall, Ann 1929- *ConAu XR*
Hall, Anna Camden *ChPo S1*
Hall, Anna Gertrude 1882-1967 *ConAu P-1, SmATA 8*
Hall, Anna Maria 1800-1881 *Alli, Alli Sup, BbD, BiD&SB, CarSB, DcEnL, DcLEnL, EvLB, NewC, PoIre*
Hall, Annie E *ChPo, ChPo S1*
Hall, Ansel Franklin 1894-1962 *AmA&B*
Hall, Anson *MnBBF*
Hall, Anthony 1679-1723 *Alli, DcEnL*
Hall, Anthony Stewart 1945- *WrD 1976*
Hall, Archibald *Alli*
Hall, Archibald 1812- *BbtC*
Hall, Arethusa 1802-1891 *Alli Sup, AmA&B, DcAmA, DcNAA*
Hall, Arlene Stevens 1923- *ConAu 17R*
Hall, Arnold Bennett 1881-1936 *DcNAA, IndAu 1816, WhWNAA*
Hall, Arthur *Alli, DcEnL*
Hall, Arthur Cleveland 1865-1910 *DcAmA Sup, DcNAA*
Hall, Arthur Crawshaw Alliston 1847-1910 *Alli Sup, DcAmA*
Hall, Arthur D *Alli Sup*
Hall, Arthur Dudley 1852-1912 *DcNAA*
Hall, Arthur Graham 1865-1925 *DcNAA*
Hall, Arthur Henry 1876- *WhLA*
Hall, Arthur Jackson 1874- *TexWr*
Hall, Arthur Vine 1862- *ChPo, ChPo S1, ChPo S2*
Hall, Asa Zadel 1875- *ConAu 1R*
Hall, Asaph 1829-1907 *DcNAA*
Hall, Lady Augusta *Alli Sup*
Hall, B Clarence, Jr. 1936- *ConAu 57, WrD 1976*
Hall, B M *Alli Sup*
Hall, Basil 1788-1844 *Alli, BbtC, BiD&SB, BrAu 19, Chmbr 3, DcEnL, EvLB, OxAm, OxCan*
Hall, Baynard Rush 1798-1863 *Alli, AmA&B, CyAL 2, DcAmA, DcLEnL, DcNAA*
Hall, Benjamin *Alli*
Hall, Benjamin Franklin 1814-1891 *Alli Sup, DcAmA, DcNAA*
Hall, Benjamin Homer 1830-1891? *Alli Sup, ChPo, DcAmA, DcNAA*
Hall, Bennie Caroline *ConAu 1R*
Hall, Bert *DcNAA*
Hall, Bolton 1854-1938 *AmLY, DcAmA, DcNAA, WhWNAA*
Hall, Brian P 1935- *ConAu 61*
Hall, C E *Alli Sup*
Hall, Calvin Springer, Jr. 1909- *AmA&B, ConAu 13R*
Hall, Cameron P 1898- *ConAu 49*
Hall, Cara D *EarAB*
Hall, Carlyle B *BlkAW*
Hall, Carolyn *ChPo*
Hall, Carolyn Vosburg 1927- *ConAu 61*
Hall, Mrs. Cecil A *OxCan*
Hall, Challis A, Jr. 1917- *ConAu 1R*
Hall, Charles *Alli, Alli Sup, BiDLA*
Hall, Mrs. Charles *Alli Sup*
Hall, Charles Albert 1872- *WhLA*
Hall, Charles Cuthbert 1852-1908 *Alli Sup, DcAmA, DcNAA*
Hall, Charles D *ChPo*
Hall, Charles E *Alli Sup*
Hall, Charles Francis 1821-1871 *Alli Sup, AmA&B, DcAmA, DcNAA, OhA&B, OxCan*
Hall, Charles Gilbert 1866-1947 *DcNAA, OhA&B*
Hall, Charles Henry *Alli, BiDLA*
Hall, Charles Henry 1820-1895 *Alli Sup, BiDSA, DcAmA, DcNAA*
Hall, Charles Mercer 1864-1929 *DcNAA, WhWNAA*
Hall, Charles Radclyffe *Alli Sup*
Hall, Charles Roswell 1853-1931 *DcNAA*
Hall, Charles Samuel 1827-1910 *DcNAA*
Hall, Charles Winslow 1843-1916 *Alli Sup,*

BbtC, BiD&SB, DcAmA, DcNAA
Hall, Charlotte *Alli Sup*
Hall, Christopher Newman 1816-1902 *Alli Sup, BiD&SB, ChPo, ChPo S1, PoCh*
Hall, Mrs. Christopher Newman *Alli Sup*
Hall, Christopher Webber 1845-1911 *DcAmA, DcNAA*
Hall, Clara *ChPo, ChPo S1*
Hall, Clara Oakey *Alli Sup*
Hall, Clarence W 1902- *AmA&B*
Hall, Claudia *ConAu XR, WrD 1976*
Hall, Clayton Colman 1847-1916 *DcNAA*
Hall, Clement d1759 *CnDAL*
Hall, Clifton L 1898- *ConAu P-1*
Hall, Clifton Rumery 1884-1945 *DcNAA*
Hall, Colby Dixon 1875- *AmA&B*
Hall, D *Alli Sup*
Hall, D J 1903- *ConAu 13R*
Hall, Daniel George Edward 1891- *Au&Wr, WhLA, WrD 1976*
Hall, David Oswald William *Au&Wr*
Hall, DeLou Perrin 1897- *IndAu 1917*
Hall, Dick Wick 1877-1926 *ArizL*
Hall, Donald Andrew 1928- *AmA&B, AuBYP, ChPo, ChPo S1, CnE&AP, ConAu 5R, ConLC 1, DcEnL, DrAF 1976, DrAP 1975, OxAm, Pen Am, RAdv 1, REn, REnAL, WorAu, WrD 1976*
Hall, Donald John 1903- *Au&Wr, ChPo S2, NewC, WrD 1976*
Hall, Donald Ray 1933- *ConAu 33*
Hall, Douglas *BlkAW*
Hall, Douglas 1931- *IICB 1966*
Hall, Douglas Kent 1938- *ConAu 33*
Hall, E *Alli Sup, ChPo S1*
Hall, E C S *Alli Sup*
Hall, E Garnett *Alli Sup*
Hall, E H *Alli*
Hall, Miss E M *Alli*
Hall, Edith Arlene Stevens 1923- *IndAu 1917*
Hall, Edith King *ChPo S2*
Hall, Edmond 1901- *AmSCAP 66*
Hall, Edmund *Alli*
Hall, Edward *Alli*
Hall, Edward 1498?-1547 *Alli, BrAu, CasWL, Chmbr 1, DcEnL, EvLB, NewC, OxEng, Pen Eng, WebEAL*
Hall, Edward Brooks 1800-1866 *Alli, Alli Sup, DcNAA*
Hall, Edward Hagaman 1858-1936 *DcNAA*
Hall, Edward Henry 1831-1912 *Alli Sup, DcAmA, DcNAA, OhA&B*
Hall, Edward Hepple *Alli Sup*
Hall, Edward Potter *Alli Sup*
Hall, Edward S 1840?- *EarAB*
Hall, Edward Twitchell 1914- *AmA&B*
Hall, Edward Vine *Alli Sup*
Hall, Edward Winslow 1840-1910 *DcNAA*
Hall, Edwin 1802-1877 *Alli, DcAmA, DcNAA*
Hall, Edwin Herbert 1855-1938 *DcNAA*
Hall, Eleanor F *ChPo*
Hall, Elfin *Alli Sup*
Hall, Elisa 1892- *DcCLA*
Hall, Eliza Calvert 1856- *BiDSA, ChPo, DcNAA*
Hall, Elizabeth Cornelia 1898- *ConAu 37*
Hall, Elizabeth Wason 1912- *ConAu 1R, IndAu 1917*
Hall, Ellyn *ChPo*
Hall, Elvajean 1910- *AuBYP, ConAu 13R, SmATA 6*
Hall, Emily *ChPo*
Hall, Esther Greenacre *AuBYP*
Hall, Eugene J 1845- *Alli Sup, ChPo, ChPo S2, DcNAA*
Hall, Evan *ConAu XR*
Hall, Everard *Alli*
Hall, Everett Wesley 1901-1960 *AmA&B*
Hall, Ezra Calvert *DcNAA*
Hall, Fannie M *ChPo S2*
Hall, Fanny W 1796?- *DcNAA*
Hall, Fernau *WrD 1976*
Hall, Fitzedward 1825-1901 *Alli Sup, AmA, AmA&B, BiD&SB, DcAmA, DcNAA*
Hall, Florence Marion Howe 1845-1922 *Alli Sup, AmA&B, AmLY, ChPo S1, ChPo S2, DcAmA, DcNAA, REnAL*

Hall, Francis *Alli, BbtC*
Hall, Francis Joseph 1857-1932 *AmLY, DcAmA, DcNAA, OhA&B, WhWNAA*
Hall, Francis Russell *Alli*
Hall, Frank 1836-1918 *DcNAA*
Hall, Frank Oliver 1860-1941 *DcNAA, WhWNAA*
Hall, Frank Richards 1900- *IndAu 1917*
Hall, Fred 1898-1964 *AmSCAP 66*
Hall, Frederic *Alli Sup*
Hall, Frederic 1825-1898 *DcNAA*
Hall, Frederic Aldin 1854-1925 *DcNAA*
Hall, Frederic T *Alli Sup*
Hall, Frederick *Alli Sup, ChPo, ChPo S1*
Hall, Frederick 1780-1843 *DcAmA, DcNAA*
Hall, Frederick Arthur Patrick 1932- *Au&Wr*
Hall, Mrs. Frederick J *Alli Sup*
Hall, Frederick James And Twells, Philip *Alli Sup*
Hall, G C *Alli Sup*
Hall, G K *OxCan Sup*
Hall, Gayl 1910- *TexWr*
Hall, Geoffrey 1901- *Au&Wr*
Hall, Geoffrey Fowler 1888-1970 *ConAu P-1*
Hall, George *Alli Sup*
Hall, George 1612-1668 *Alli, DcEnL*
Hall, George Barnes *Alli Sup*
Hall, George Berringer *Alli Sup*
Hall, George F 1908- *ConAu 45*
Hall, George Henry 1825-1913 *EarAB*
Hall, George James *Alli Sup*
Hall, Georgette Brockman 1915- *ConAu 57*
Hall, Geraldine M 1935- *ConAu 33*
Hall, Gertrude 1863- *AmA&B, BiD&SB, ChPo, DcAmA*
Hall, Gertrude 1912- *AmSCAP 66*
Hall, Gimone 1940- *ConAu 29, WrD 1976*
Hall, Goldan Orlando 1897- *WhWNAA*
Hall, Gordon d1826 *Alli*
Hall, Gordon Langley 1929- *Au&Wr, AuBYP, ConAu 1R*
Hall, Granville Stanley 1844?-1924 *Alli Sup, BiD&SB, DcAmA, DcNAA, OhA&B, OxAm, REnAL, TwCA, TwCA Sup*
Hall, Grover C 1888- *WhWNAA*
Hall, Guillermo Franklin 1866-1940 *DcNAA*
Hall, Gwendolyn Midlo 1929- *ConAu 41*
Hall, H Duncan 1891- *Au&Wr, ConAu 29, WrD 1976*
Hall, H Oliver *ChPo S1*
Hall, H T *Alli Sup*
Hall, Halbert Weldon 1941- *ConAu 53*
Hall, Harlan Page 1838-1907 *DcNAA, OhA&B*
Hall, Harold Fielding- *TwCA Sup*
Hall, Harrison 1785-1866 *Alli, BiDSA, DcAmA, DcNAA*
Hall, Harvey Monroe 1874-1932 *DcNAA*
Hall, Hattie Vose *ChPo*
Hall, Hazel 1886-1924 *AnMV 1926, ChPo, ChPo S1, ChPo S2, DcNAA*
Hall, Helen *AmSCAP 66*
Hall, Helen Jameson 1902- *ChPo S1*
Hall, Henry *Alli, Alli Sup*
Hall, Henry 1814-1889 *DcNAA*
Hall, Henry 1845-1920 *AmLY, DcNAA*
Hall, Henry Armstrong *Alli Sup*
Hall, Henry Clay *ChPo S2*
Hall, Henry F *OxCan Sup*
Hall, Henry Marion 1877- *ConAu 5R, WhWNAA*
Hall, Herbert Byng *Alli Sup*
Hall, Herbert James 1870-1923 *DcNAA*
Hall, Herman *MnBBF*
Hall, Herschel Salmon 1874-1921 *OhA&B*
Hall, Hiland 1795-1885 *Alli, Alli Sup, DcAmA, DcNAA*
Hall, Hilkiah Bedford *Alli Sup*
Hall, Holworthy *AmA&B, AmLY XR, DcNAA, TwCA, TwCA Sup, WhWNAA*
Hall, Howard d1921 *DcNAA*
Hall, Howard Judson 1869-1942 *AmA&B, WhWNAA*
Hall, Hubert 1857- *Alli Sup*
Hall, Irene *Au&Wr*
Hall, Isaac *Alli*
Hall, Isaac Freeman 1847-1928 *DcNAA*
Hall, Isaac Hollister 1837-1896 *Alli Sup,*

DcAmA, DcNAA
Hall, J *Alli Sup*
Hall, J A *Alli Sup*
Hall, J C *ChPo*
Hall, J Curtis 1926- *ConAu 53*
Hall, J DeP *ConAu XR*
Hall, J G *Alli Sup*
Hall, J Tillman 1916- *ConAu 1R*
Hall, J V *Alli*
Hall, James *Alli, Alli Sup, BiDLA*
Hall, James 1744-1826 *BiDSA, DcAmA,
 DcNAA*
Hall, Sir James 1761-1832 *Alli, BiDLA,
 DcEnL*
Hall, James 1793-1868 *Alli, AmA, AmA&B,
 CyAL 1, DcAmA, DcLEnL, DcNAA,
 OhA&B, OxAm, Pen Am, REnAL*
Hall, James 1811-1898 *Alli, DcAmA, DcNAA*
Hall, James 1869-1917 *DcNAA*
Hall, James 1918- *WrD 1976*
Hall, James 1933- *ConAu 53*
Hall, James A 1934- *BiDPar*
Hall, James B 1918- *ConAu 1R,
 ConNov 1972, ConNov 1976, DrAF 1976,
 DrAP 1975, WrD 1976*
Hall, James C, Jr. 1932- *LivBA*
Hall, James Norman 1887-1951 *AmA&B,
 AmNov, AuBYP, CyWA, DcLEnL,
 JBA 1934, MnBBF, OxAm, Pen Am,
 REn, REnAL, TwCA, TwCA Sup,
 WhWNAA*
Hall, James Parker 1871-1928 *DcNAA*
Hall, James W 1937- *ConAu 45*
Hall, Jarvis *AmA&B, WhWNAA*
Hall, Jay C *ConAu 57*
Hall, Jeannie Pendleton *ChPo, TexWr*
Hall, Jenni 1939- *WrD 1976*
Hall, Jennie 1875-1921 *AmLY, DcNAA*
Hall, Jerome 1901- *AmA&B, ConAu P-1,
 WrD 1976*
Hall, Jesse *ConAu XR*
Hall, John *Alli, Alli Sup, BrAu, ChPo S1,
 ChPo S2, DcEnL*
Hall, John 1627-1656 *Alli, CasWL*
Hall, John 1783-1847 *DcNAA*
Hall, John 1806-1894 *DcAmA, DcNAA*
Hall, John 1829-1898 *Alli Sup, BbD,
 BiD&SB, DcAmA, DcNAA*
Hall, John 1943- *BlkAW*
Hall, John Andrew 1852-1925 *OhA&B*
Hall, John B *ChPo S1*
Hall, John C 1915- *ConAu 57*
Hall, John Carey *Alli Sup*
Hall, John Charles *Alli Sup*
Hall, John Clive 1920- *ChPo S2, ConP 1970,
 ConP 1975, WrD 1976*
Hall, John E *BlkAW*
Hall, John Edward 1837- *Alli Sup*
Hall, John Elihu 1783-1829 *Alli, AmA&B,
 CyAL 1, DcAmA, DcNAA*
Hall, John F 1919- *ConAu 1R*
Hall, John H 1825?- *EarAB, EarAB Sup*
Hall, John K *Alli Sup*
Hall, John Leslie 1856-1928 *BiDSA, DcNAA*
Hall, John O P 1911- *ConAu 9R*
Hall, John Paxton *Alli Sup*
Hall, John Randolph 1892- *WhWNAA*
Hall, John Vine 1774-1860 *Alli Sup, NewC*
Hall, John Whitney 1916- *ConAu 25*
Hall, John William *Alli Sup, WhWNAA*
Hall, Jonathan Prescott *Alli*
Hall, Josef Washington 1894-1960 *AmA&B,
 AnMV 1926, EvLB, TwCA, TwCA Sup,
 WhWNAA*
Hall, Joseph *Alli, Alli Sup, Chmbr 1*
Hall, Joseph 1574-1656 *Alli, BrAu, CasWL,
 ChPo, CrE&SL, DcEnL, DcEuL,
 DcLEnL, EvLB, MouLC 1, NewC,
 OxEng, Pen Eng, REn, WebEAL*
Hall, Joseph 1906- *ConAu 41*
Hall, Joseph Sparkes *Alli Sup*
Hall, Josiah Newhall 1859-1939 *DcNAA,
 WhWNAA*
Hall, Julia G *Alli Sup*
Hall, Sir Julian Henry 1907- *Au&Wr*
Hall, Julius *Alli Sup*
Hall, Katharine Mason *ChPo S2*
Hall, Kathleen Mary 1924- *ConAu 5R,*

WrD 1976
Hall, Kenneth Franklin 1926- *ConAu 17R,
 IndAu 1917*
Hall, Kirkwood M 1944- *BlkAW*
Hall, L A *Alli Sup*
Hall, Lawrence Sargent 1915- *ConAu 1R,
 DrAF 1976*
Hall, Leland 1883-1957 *AmA&B, TwCA,
 TwCA Sup*
Hall, Lewis A *Alli Sup*
Hall, Lindsay Bernard 1859- *ChPo*
Hall, Livingston 1903- *ConAu 21*
Hall, Louis *ChPo*
Hall, Louisa Jane 1802-1892 *Alli, CyAL 2,
 DcAmA, DcNAA, FemPA*
Hall, Louise Gardiner *Alli Sup*
Hall, Luella J 1890- *ConAu 45*
Hall, Lydia H *ChPo S2*
Hall, Lyman 1859-1905 *BiDSA, DcNAA*
Hall, Lyman W *Alli Sup*
Hall, Lynn 1937- *ConAu 23, SmATA 2*
Hall, M *Alli Sup*
Hall, M D *Alli Sup*
Hall, Mrs. M G C *Alli Sup*
Hall, Madeline *ChPo*
Hall, Malcolm 1945- *ConAu 49, SmATA 7*
Hall, Manly Palmer 1901- *Au&Wr,
 WhWNAA, WrD 1976*
Hall, Lady Margaret *ChPo S2*
Hall, Margaret Scott 1864- *BiDSA*
Hall, Margaret Seymour *ChPo*
Hall, Marguerite Radclyffe 1888?-1943
 DcLEnL, EvLB
Hall, Maria *Alli Sup*
Hall, Marie *Alli Sup*
Hall, Marie Boas 1919- *Au&Wr, ConAu 1R,
 ConAu 9R, WrD 1976*
Hall, Marjory 1908- *AuBYP, ConAu XR,
 WrD 1976*
Hall, Mark W 1943- *ConAu 33*
Hall, Marshall d1857 *Alli*
Hall, Marshall Renwood 1889-1947 *OhA&B,
 WhWNAA*
Hall, Martin Hardwick 1925- *ConAu 33*
Hall, Mary Anne 1934- *ConAu 29*
Hall, Mary L *Alli Sup*
Hall, Mary Stuart *Alli Sup*
Hall, Mrs. Matthew *Alli, Alli Sup*
Hall, Maurice Crowther 1881-1938 *DcNAA*
Hall, Maurits Cornelis Van 1768-1858 *CasWL*
Hall, May F *ChPo S2*
Hall, Melville *MnBBF*
Hall, Michael Garibaldi 1926- *ConAu 13R*
Hall, Miranda *Alli Sup*
Hall, N John 1933- *ConAu 61*
Hall, Nancy Lee 1923- *ConAu 57*
Hall, Natalie Watson 1923- *ConAu 5R,
 IlCB 1966*
Hall, Nathaniel B 1916- *LivBA, WrD 1976*
Hall, Newman 1816-1902 *Alli, BbD, ChPo,
 ChPo S1, DcEnL*
Hall, Newton Marshall 1865-1926 *DcNAA*
Hall, O M *ConAu XR*
Hall, Oakley 1920- *ConAu 9R*
Hall, P W *Alli, BiDLA*
Hall, Patrick 1932- *ConAu 21*
Hall, Penelope C 1933- *ConAu 17R*
Hall, Percy *MnBBF*
Hall, Peter 1803-1849 *Alli*
Hall, Peter 1930- *CrCD*
Hall, Peter Geoffrey 1932- *Au&Wr,
 ConAu 17R, WrD 1976*
Hall, Prescott Farnsworth 1868-1921 *AmLY,
 BiDPar, DcAmA, DcNAA*
Hall, R *Alli Sup*
Hall, R A *Alli Sup*
Hall, R Cargill 1937- *ConAu 49*
Hall, R G *Alli*
Hall, Radclyffe 1886?-1943 *LongC, ModBL,
 NewC, REn, TwCA, TwCA Sup, TwCW,
 WhLA*
Hall, Randall Cooke 1842-1921 *DcNAA*
Hall, Raymond E 1903- *TexWr*
Hall, Richard *Alli, BiDLA, MnBBF*
Hall, Richard d1604 *Alli*
Hall, Richard 1925- *Au&Wr, ConAu 17R,
 WrD 1976*
Hall, Robert *Alli, Alli Sup, BiDLA,*

Chmbr 2
Hall, Robert d1791 *Alli*
Hall, Robert 1763-1824 *Alli*
Hall, Robert 1764-1831 *Alli, BrAu 19,
 DcEnL, EvLB*
Hall, Robert Anderson, Jr. 1911- *AmA&B,
 ConAu 13R*
Hall, Robert Benjamin 1918- *ConAu 57*
Hall, Robert E 1924- *ConAu 17R*
Hall, Robert King 1912- *AmA&B, WrD 1976*
Hall, Robert Pleasants 1825-1854 *BiDSA,
 DcNAA*
Hall, Robert W *Alli Sup*
Hall, Rodney 1935- *ConP 1970, ConP 1975,
 WrD 1976*
Hall, Roger Wolcott 1919- *Au&Wr,
 ConAu 29*
Hall, Rosalys Haskell 1914- *AuBYP,
 ConAu 9R, MorJA, SmATA 7*
Hall, Ross H 1926- *ConAu 61*
Hall, Rowland *DcEnL*
Hall, Rubylea 1910- *ConAu 17*
Hall, Rupert *MnBBF*
Hall, Ruth *ChPo*
Hall, Ruth 1858-1934 *AmA&B, BiD&SB,
 CarSB, ChPo S1, DcAmA, DcNAA,
 WhWNAA*
Hall, S *ChPo*
Hall, S J *Alli Sup*
Hall, S R *Alli, Alli Sup*
Hall, S S *Alli*
Hall, S W *Alli Sup*
Hall, Salem *Alli Sup*
Hall, Sam S 1838-1886 *HsB&A, REnAL*
Hall, Samuel *Alli Sup*
Hall, Samuel 1740-1809 *AmA&B, REnAL*
Hall, Samuel Carter 1800-1889 *Alli, Alli Sup,
 BbD, BiD&SB, ChPo, ChPo S1,
 ChPo S2, Chmbr 3, DcEnL, NewC,
 PoIre*
Hall, Mrs. Samuel Carter 1800-1881 *Alli,
 BrAu 19, CarSB, ChPo, ChPo S1,
 ChPo S2, Chmbr 3*
Hall, Samuel Read 1795-1877 *DcAmA,
 DcNAA*
Hall, Samuel Romilly d1876 *Alli Sup*
Hall, Samuel S *AmA&B*
Hall, Sarah Ewing 1761-1830 *Alli, AmA,
 AmA&B, CyAL 1, DcAmA, DcNAA,
 FemPA*
Hall, Sarah J *Alli Sup*
Hall, Sarah Sewell *TexWr*
Hall, Saville *MnBBF*
Hall, Sharlot Mabridth 1870- *AmLY, ArizL,
 ChPo S2*
Hall, Sidney *Alli*
Hall, Spencer 1806-1875 *Alli Sup, PoIre*
Hall, Spencer Timothy 1812-1885 *Alli Sup*
Hall, Susan 1940- *ConAu 57*
Hall, Sydney Prior *Alli Sup*
Hall, T *Alli Sup*
Hall, T Dwight *Alli Sup*
Hall, Ted Byron 1902- *ConAu 33*
Hall, Theodore Dana *DrAP 1975*
Hall, Theodore Hall 1854- *Alli Sup*
Hall, Theodore Parsons 1835-1909 *DcNAA*
Hall, Theophilus Parsons *Alli Sup*
Hall, Theresa Oakey *Alli Sup*
Hall, Thomas *Alli, BiDLA*
Hall, Thomas 1610-1665 *Alli*
Hall, Thomas Bartlett 1824-1903 *Alli Sup,
 DcAmA, DcNAA*
Hall, Thomas Cuming 1858-1936 *AmLY,
 DcAmA, DcNAA, WhWNAA*
Hall, Thomas Mifflin 1798-1828 *Alli, CyAL 1,
 DcAmA*
Hall, Thomas Mifflin 1806- *Alli Sup*
Hall, Thomas Proctor 1858-1931 *DcAmA,
 DcNAA*
Hall, Thomas Winthrop 1862-1900 *BiD&SB,
 DcAmA, DcNAA*
Hall, Thomas Wright *Alli Sup*
Hall, Thor 1927- *ConAu 37, WrD 1976*
Hall, Timothy d1690 *Alli*
Hall, Tom *ChPo, ChPo S2, DcAmA*
Hall, Tord 1910- *ConAu 29*
Hall, Townshend M *Alli Sup*
Hall, Trevor Henry 1910- *Au&Wr, BiDPar,*

ConAu 29
Hall, Valentine G *Alli Sup*
Hall, Van Beck 1934- *ConAu 45*
Hall, Vernon, Jr. 1913- *AmA&B, ConAu 5R*
Hall, Violette *DcAmA, WhWNAA*
Hall, W *Alli, EarAB Sup*
Hall, W C *PoIre*
Hall, W E *Alli Sup*
Hall, W J *Alli*
Hall, W Robert *ChPo S2*
Hall, Wade H 1934- *ConAu 5R, DrAP 1975*
Hall, Walter *DrAP 1975*
Hall, Walter 1940- *ConAu 21*
Hall, Walter G *Alli Sup*
Hall, Mrs. Walter G *Alli Sup*
Hall, Walter Henry 1862-1935 *DcNAA*
Hall, Walter Phelps 1884- *AmA&B*
Hall, Wendell Woods 1896- *AmSCAP 66*
Hall, Wendy *Au&Wr*
Hall, Weston B 1886-1948 *DcNAA*
Hall, Whitmore *Alli Sup*
Hall, Wilhelmina L *Alli Sup*
Hall, Willard *Alli*
Hall, William *Alli, Alli Sup*
Hall, William Champaign *Alli Sup*
Hall, William Charles 1870-1936 *ChPo S1, ChPo S2*
Hall, William David 1908- *TexWr*
Hall, William Douglas 1926- *Au&Wr*
Hall, William Edward 1836- *Alli Sup*
Hall, William H *Alli Sup*
Hall, William H, And W D Bernard *Alli*
Hall, William Henry d1807 *Alli*
Hall, William Henry Bullock 1837- *Alli Sup*
Hall, Sir William Hutcheon 1797?-1878
 Alli Sup
Hall, William Jared *HsB&A*
Hall, William John *Alli Sup*
Hall, William Norman 1915-1974 *AuBYP, ConAu 53*
Hall, William Shafer 1861-1948 *DcNAA, WhWNAA*
Hall, William Whitty 1810-1876 *Alli, Alli Sup, BiDSA, DcAmA, DcNAA*
Hall, William Winslow *ChPo S2*
Hall, Willis 1929- *CnMD, CnThe, ConDr, CrCD, LongC, ModWD, Pen Eng, WrD 1976*
Hall, Winfield Scott 1861-1942 *ChPo, DcAmA, DcNAA, WhWNAA*
Hall, Wraxall *Alli Sup*
Hall And Sellers *Alli*
Hall-Jones, Frederick George 1891- *WrD 1976*
Hall-Noonan, Laura Rita 1888- *WhWNAA*
Hall-Quest, Alfred Lawrence *AmA&B*
Hall-Quest, Edna Olga 1899- *AuBYP*
Hall-Quest, Olga Wilbourne 1899- *Au&Wr, ConAu 5R*
Hall-Stevenson, John *BrAu, NewC*
Hallack, Cecily 1898-1938 *CatA 1947*
Hallack, Rosemary Cecily 1798-1838 *ChPo*
Hallagan, Robert H 1926- *AmSCAP 66*
Hallaj, Husain Ibn Mansur 858?-922 *CasWL*
Hallam *WrD 1976*
Hallam, Arthur Henry 1811-1833 *Alli, BrAu 19, ChPo, Chmbr 3, DcEnA, DcEnL, DcLEnL, NewC, OxEng, REn*
Hallam, Atlantis 1915- *ConAu 5R*
Hallam, Douglas d1948 *DcNAA*
Hallam, Ebenezer Charles Bethlehem *Alli Sup*
Hallam, F H *Alli Sup*
Hallam, H E 1923- *ConAu 23*
Hallam, Henry 1777-1859 *Alli, BbD, BiD&SB, BrAu 19, CasWL, Chmbr 3, DcEnA, DcEnL, DcEuL, DcLEnL, EvLB, NewC, OxEng, Pen Eng*
Hallam, John Harvey 1917- *Au&Wr, ConAu 13R*
Hallam, Julia Kirkland Clark 1860-1927 *AmLY, DcAmA, DcNAA, WhWNAA*
Hallam, Robert Alexander 1807-1877 *Alli, Alli Sup, DcAmA*
Hallam, Robert Kay 1921- *ChPo S2*
Hallam, Thomas *Alli Sup*
Hallaran, William Saunders *Alli, BiDLA*
Hallard, Frederick *Alli Sup*
Hallard, James Henry 1861- *ChPo*
Hallard, Peter *SmATA 3*

Hallard, Peter J *MnBBF*
Hallas, Charles E *Alli Sup*
Hallatt, George Wilson Tuxford *Alli Sup*
Hallaway, John *Alli*
Hallberg, Charles William 1899- *ConAu P-1*
Hallberg, Peter 1916- *ConAu 53*
Halle, Edward *EvLB*
Halle, H Fraser *Alli*
Halle, Hughes R P Fraser *Alli Sup*
Halle, Katherine Murphy *ConAu 41*
Halle, Kay *ConAu XR*
Halle, Louis J 1901- *REnAL*
Halle, Louis Joseph, Jr. 1910- *AmA&B, ConAu 1R*
Halle, Mary *Alli Sup*
Halle, Rita Sulzbacher 1887- *OhA&B, WhWNAA*
Halle, Ruth 1918- *Au&Wr*
Halleck, Fitz-Greene 1790-1867 *Alli, Alli Sup, AmA, AmA&B, AtlBL, BbD, BiD&SB, CasWL, ChPo, ChPo S1, ChPo S2, Chmbr 3, CnDAL, CyAL 1, DcAmA, DcEnL, DcLEnL, DcNAA, EvLB, OxAm, Pen Am, REn, REnAL*
Halleck, Henry Wager 1815?-1872 *Alli, Alli Sup, DcAmA, DcNAA*
Halleck, Reuben Post 1859-1936 *AmA&B, AmLY, BiDSA, ChPo, DcAmA, DcNAA, WhWNAA*
Halleck, Seymour L 1929- *ConAu 21*
Hallen, Arthur Washington Cornelius *Alli Sup*
Hallen, Erik Gustaf *Au&Wr*
Hallenberg, Jonas 1748-1834 *DcEuL*
Haller, Adolf 1897- *AuBYP*
Haller, Albert Henry 1866-1906 *DcNAA*
Haller, Albrecht Von 1708-1777 *BiD&SB, CasWL, DcEuL, EuA, EvEuW, OxGer, Pen Eur*
Haller, Archibald O, Jr. 1926- *ConAu 45*
Haller, John S, Jr. 1940- *ConAu 61*
Haller, Joseph 1800-1843 *DcEnL*
Haller, Mark H 1928- *ConAu 9R*
Haller, P *Pen Eur*
Haller, Robert S 1933- *ConAu 1R*
Haller, William 1885-1974 *Au&Wr, ConAu 49*
Halleran, Eugene E 1905- *ConAu 1R*
Hallet, Doctor *Alli*
Hallet, Caroline *ChPo*
Hallet, Jean-Pierre 1927- *ConAu 17R*
Hallet, Joseph, Jr. 1692-1744 *Alli, DcEnL*
Hallet, Richard Matthews 1887-1967 *AmA&B*
Hallett, Benjamin Franklin 1797-1862 *DcNAA*
Hallett, Caroline M *Alli Sup*
Hallett, Miss E V *Alli Sup*
Hallett, Ellen Kathleen 1899- *ConAu P-1*
Hallett, George Hervey, Jr. 1895- *AmA&B*
Hallett, Gerard Ludlow *Alli Sup*
Hallett, Graham 1929- *ConAu 25, WrD 1976*
Hallett, John C *AmSCAP 66*
Hallett, Kathryn J 1937- *ConAu 57*
Hallett, Moses *Alli Sup*
Hallett, Paul Haberer 1911- *BkC 6*
Hallett, Richard Matthews 1887- *WhWNAA*
Hallett, Robert *Alli*
Hallett, Robin 1926- *Au&Wr, WrD 1976*
Hallett, Thomas George Palmer *Alli Sup*
Hallevi, Jehudah 1080?-1150? *BiD&SB*
Halley, Edmund 1656-1742 *Alli, DcEnL, NewC, REn*
Halley, Frances Nell 1914- *TexWr*
Halley, George *Alli*
Halley, Mabel Christie *TexWr*
Halley, Robert 1796-1876 *Alli, Alli Sup*
Halley, Robert, Jr. *Alli Sup*
Halley, William *BbtC*
Halley Mora, Mario 1924- *DcCLA*
Hallgarten, George W F 1901-1975 *ConAu 57*
Hallgarten, Siegfried Fritz 1902- *Au&Wr, ConAu 5R, WrD 1976*
Hallgren, Mauritz Alfred 1899-1956 *AmA&B, TwCA, TwCA Sup*
Hallgrim Pjetersson 1614?-1674 *DcEuL*
Hallgrimsson, Jonas 1807-1845 *CasWL, DcEuL, EuA, Pen Eur*
Hallgrimur Petursson 1614?-1674 *Pen Eur*
Halliburton, Sir Brenton 1775-1860 *Alli Sup, BbtC, DcNAA, OxCan*

Halliburton, Richard 1900-1939 *AmA&B, CnDAL, DcNAA, EvLB, OxAm, REnAL, TwCA, TwCA Sup, WhWNAA*
Halliburton, Warren J 1924- *ConAu 33, LivBAA*
Halliday, Alexander *Alli Sup, BiDLA, BiDLA Sup*
Halliday, Sir Andrew d1840 *Alli*
Halliday, Andrew *Alli Sup*
Halliday, Andrew 1830-1877 *DcEnL*
Halliday, Ben D *HsB&A*
Halliday, Brett 1904- *AmA&B, EncM&D, WorAu*
Halliday, Dorothy *WrD 1976*
Halliday, E M 1913- *ConAu 1R*
Halliday, Frank Ernest 1903- *Au&Wr, ConAu 1R*
Halliday, Fred 1937- *ConAu 53*
Halliday, G *Alli Sup*
Halliday, Gertrude *ChPo*
Halliday, Hugh *OxCan*
Halliday, James *ConAu XR*
Halliday, John *Alli, ChPo S1*
Halliday, John Gustavus *Alli Sup*
Halliday, Maria *Alli Sup*
Halliday, Michael *ConAu XR, EncM&D, LongC*
Halliday, Richard 1905-1973 *ConAu 41*
Halliday, Robert J *Alli Sup*
Halliday, Samuel Byram 1812-1897 *Alli Sup, BiD&SB, DcAmA, DcNAA*
Halliday, W M *OxCan*
Halliday, William Ross 1926- *ConAu 49, WhPNW*
Halliday, Winifred *ChPo*
Hallie, Philip P 1922- *ConAu 13R*
Hallifax *Alli*
Hallifax, Doctor *Alli*
Hallifax, Charles *Alli*
Hallifax, James *Alli*
Hallifax, Samuel 1733-1790 *Alli, DcEnL*
Hallifax, William *Alli*
Halligan, Nicholas 1917- *ConAu 13R*
Hallilay, Richard *Alli Sup*
Hallimond, John Greener 1852-1924 *DcNAA*
Hallin, Emily Watson 1919- *ConAu 25, SmATA 6, WrD 1976*
Hallinan, Nancy 1921- *Au&Wr, ConAu 9R, DrAF 1976*
Hallinan, Vincent 1896- *ConAu 1R*
Hallion, John *PoIre*
Hallion, Richard P 1948- *ConAu 41*
Halliwell, David 1936- *Au&Wr, ConDr, WrD 1976*
Halliwell, David 1937- *CrCD*
Halliwell, James Orchard 1820-1889 *Alli, CarSB, DcEnA, OxEng, St&VC*
Halliwell, Leslie 1929- *ConAu 49, WrD 1976*
Halliwell, T *Alli Sup*
Halliwell, William *Alli Sup*
Halliwell-Phillipps, James Orchard 1820-1889 *Alli Sup, BbD, BiD&SB, ChPo, ChPo S1, ChPo S2, DcEnA, DcEnL, DcLEnL, EvLB, NewC, OxEng*
Hallman, Adolf 1893- *WhGrA*
Hallman, Ralph J 1911- *ConAu 13R*
Hallmann, Johann Christian 1640?-1704? *OxGer*
Hallner, Andrew 1846-1930 *DcNAA*
Hallo, William W 1928- *ConAu 37, WrD 1976*
Hallock, Charles 1834-1917 *Alli Sup, AmA, AmA&B, BiD&SB, DcAmA, DcNAA*
Hallock, Ella 1861-1934 *DcNAA*
Hallock, Gerard Benjamin Fleet 1856- *AmLY, DcAmA, WhWNAA*
Hallock, Joseph Newton 1832?-1913 *DcAmA, DcNAA*
Hallock, Julia Isabel 1846- *DcAmA*
Hallock, Leavitt Homan 1842-1921 *DcNAA*
Hallock, Mary *ChPo*
Hallock, Mary Angeline 1810- *Alli Sup, DcAmA, DcNAA*
Hallock, R T *Alli Sup*
Hallock, Robert Crawford 1857-1932 *DcNAA*
Hallock, Ruth Mary 1876- *ChPo, ChPo S2*
Hallock, S W *ChPo*
Hallock, William 1857-1913 *DcNAA*
Hallock, William Allen 1794-1880 *Alli,*

Alli Sup, BiD&SB, DcAmA, DcNAA
Hallock, William H Alli Sup
Halloran, Alfred Laurence Alli Sup
Halloran, Edward G 1909- AmSCAP 66
Halloran, Henry 1811-1893 Alli Sup, ChPo, DcLEnL, PoIre
Halloran, Laurence Hynes 1766-1831 PoIre
Halloran, Lawrence Hynes 1766-1831 BiDLA
Halloran, Richard 1930- ConAu 29
Hallorom, L H DcEnL
Halloway, Benjamin Alli
Halloway, Vance 1916- ConAu 53
Hallowell, A Irving 1892-1974 ConAu 5R, ConAu 53, OxCan
Hallowell, Alice BiDSA
Hallowell, Anna Coffin Davis 1838- Alli Sup, DcAmA, DcNAA
Hallowell, Benjamin Alli Sup
Hallowell, Benjamin 1799-1877 DcNAA
Hallowell, Mrs. J L Alli Sup
Hallowell, J S Alli Sup, BbtC
Hallowell, John H 1913- ConAu 13R
Hallowell, John K Alli Sup
Hallowell, Richard Price 1835-1905 Alli Sup, BiD&SB, DcAmA, DcNAA
Hallowell, Mrs. Robert AmA&B
Hallowell, Russell F 1897-1965 AmSCAP 66
Hallowell, Sarah Catherine 1833- Alli Sup, DcAmA, DcNAA
Hallowes, John Francis Tooke Alli Sup
Hallpike, C R 1938- ConAu 41
Halls, John J ChPo S1
Halls, John James Alli Sup
Halls, Robert Alli, ChPo
Halls, Wilfred Douglas 1918- ConAu 1R, WrD 1976
Hallstead, William F, III 1924- ConAu 5R
Hallstrom, Per August Leonard 1866-1960 CasWL, ClDMEuL, EncWL, EvEuW, ModWD
Hallsworth, Thomas E ChPo S1
Hallum, John 1833- BiDSA, DcNAA
Hallum, Mattie A 1872- BiDSA
Hallward, F M ChPo
Hallward, John Alli
Hallward, Michael 1889- ConAu 49
Hallward, Rex ChPo S1
Hallworth, Joseph Bryant 1872- DcAmA
Hally, S Alli Sup
Hallywell, Henry Alli
Halm, Friedrich 1806-1871 BiD&SB, CasWL, EuA, EvEuW, OxGer
Halm, George N 1901- ConAu 23
Halm, George Robert 1850-1899 ChPo, ChPo S1
Halmael, Hendrik Van 1654-1718 CasWL
Halman, Talat Sait 1931- ConAu 53
Halmos, Paul 1911- Au&Wr, ConAu 17R, WrD 1976
Halmyr, H ChPo S1
Halpe, Ashley 1933- ConP 1970
Halper, Albert 1904- AmA&B, AmNov, Au&Wr, CnDAL, ConAmA, ConAu 5R, DcLEnL, OxAm, REn, REnAL, TwCA, TwCA Sup, WhWNAA
Halper, Thomas 1942- ConAu 41
Halperin, Don A 1925- ConAu 57
Halperin, Irving 1922- ConAu 29
Halperin, John 1941- ConAu 53
Halperin, Morton H 1938- ConAu 9R
Halperin, Samuel 1930- ConAu 1R
Halpern, A M 1914- ConAu 17R
Halpern, Daniel 1945- ConAu 33, DrAP 1975
Halpern, Joel M 1929- ConAu 5R
Halpern, Leivick McGWD, REnWD
Halpern, Leon 1908- AmSCAP 66
Halpern, Manfred 1924- ConAu 9R
Halpern, Martin 1929- AmA&B, ConAu 5R
Halpern, Moishe Leib 1886-1932 CasWL
Halpern, Paul G 1937- ConAu 45
Halpern, Paul J 1942- ConAu 57
Halpern, Stephen Mark 1940- ConAu 57
Halpert, Herbert OxCan, OxCan Sup
Halpert, Inge D 1926- ConAu 23
Halpert, Stephen 1941- ConAu 37
Halphen, Louis 1880-1950 OxFr
Halpin, Andrew Williams 1911- ConAu 17R, WrD 1976

Halpin, J EarAB, EarAB Sup
Halpin, John Nicholas 1790-1851 Alli
Halpin, Nicholas John 1790-1850 BiDLA, PoIre
Halpin, Patrick Albert 1847-1920 DcNAA
Halpin, William 1825-1892 PoIre
Halpin, William Henry PoIre
Halpine, Charles Graham 1829-1868 Alli Sup, AmA, AmA&B, BiD&SB, ChPo, CyAL 2, DcAmA, DcEnL, DcLEnL, DcNAA, OxAm, PoIre, REnAL
Halpine, Mary Grace d1892? HsB&A, HsB&A Sup
Halpine, Mary J Alli Sup
Halprin, Ann ConDr
Halprin, Lawrence 1916- ConAu 41
Hals, Frans 1580?-1666 AtlBL, REn
Hals, Ronald M 1926- ConAu 33
Halsall, Elizabeth 1916- ConAu 33, WrD 1976
Halsall, Eric 1920- Au&Wr, WrD 1976
Halsband, Robert 1914- ConAu 17R
Halse, Edward Alli Sup
Halse, George Alli Sup
Halse, Mrs. George Alli Sup
Halse, Harold MnBBF
Halsell, Grace 1923- AuBYP, AuNews 1, ConAu 23
Halsey, A H 1923- ConAu 17R, WrD 1976
Halsey, Calista Alli Sup
Halsey, Charles Storrs 1834-1933 Alli Sup, DcNAA
Halsey, Edmund Drake 1840-1896 DcNAA
Halsey, Elizabeth 1890- ConAu 17
Halsey, Forrest 1878- AmA&B
Halsey, Francis Whiting 1851-1919 AmA&B, ChPo S1, DcAmA, DcNAA
Halsey, Frank Davis 1890?-1941 AmA&B, DcNAA
Halsey, Frederick Arthur 1856-1935 AmLY, DcAmA, DcNAA
Halsey, Frederick Robert Alli Sup
Halsey, George Dawson 1889- ConAu 1R
Halsey, Harlan Page 1837-1898 DcAmA, EncM&D, DcNAA
Halsey, Joseph Alli Sup
Halsey, L Alli Sup
Halsey, Leroy Jones 1812-1896 Alli Sup, BiDSA, DcAmA, DcNAA
Halsey, Lewis 1843-1914 DcNAA, OhA&B
Halsey, Margaret 1910- AmA&B, REnAL
Halsey, Martha T 1932- ConAu 37
Halsey, Rena Isabelle 1860-1932 DcNAA, WhWNAA
Halsey, Richard Townley Haines 1865-1942 DcNAA
Halsey, Rosalie Vrylina ChPo, ChPo S1
Halsey, William BlkAW
Halsey, William Donaldson 1860-1939 DcNAA
Halsman, Philippe 1906- AmA&B, Au&Wr, AuBYP, ConAu 23
Halstead, Ada L DcNAA
Halstead, Byron David 1852- DcAmA
Halstead, David 1861- WhLA
Halstead, E Sinclair MnBBF
Halstead, George Bruce 1853- BiDSA
Halstead, Leonora B Alli Sup
Halstead, Murat 1829-1908 AmA, AmA&B, BbD, BiD&SB, DcAmA, DcNAA, OhA&B
Halstead, Oliver Spencer 1792-1877 DcNAA
Halstead, Robert Alli
Halstead, S B MnBBF
Halstead, William Perdue 1906- IndAu 1917
Halstead, William Riley 1848-1931 Alli Sup, AmLY, DcNAA, IndAu 1816, WhWNAA
Halsted, Anna Roosevelt 1906-1975 ConAu 61
Halsted, Byron David 1852-1919 Alli Sup, DcNAA
Halsted, Caroline Amelia d1851 Alli
Halsted, Edward Pellew Alli Sup
Halsted, George B Alli Sup
Halsted, George Bruce 1853-1922 Alli Sup, DcAmA, DcNAA
Halsted, H Alli Sup
Halsted, O Alli Sup
Halsted, Oliver Spencer 1792-1877 Alli Sup,

DcAmA
Halsted, Peter Alli
Halsted, Thomas Daniell Alli Sup
Halsted, William Alli
Halsted, William H Alli Sup
Halsted, William Stewart 1852-1922 DcNAA
Halswelle, Keeley 1832-1891 ChPo, ChPo S2
Halsy, James Alli
Halter, Carl 1915- ConAu 17R
Halter, Jon C 1941- ConAu 61
Halton, Richard Joseph Alli Sup
Haltrecht, Montague 1932- ConAu 29, WrD 1976
Halverson, Alton C O 1922- ConAu 61
Halverson, Richard C 1916- ConAu 1R
Halverson, William H 1930- ConAu 37
Halvey, Margaret 1859- PoIre
Halvorson, Arndt L 1915- ConAu 5R
Halward, John Alli
Halward, Leslie George 1905- Au&Wr
Haly, Aylmer Alli, BiDLA
Haly, Mrs. George Alli Sup
Haly, George Thomas Alli Sup
Haly, William W Alli
Halyard, Harry AmA&B
Halyburton, Thomas 1674-1712 Alli, DcEnL
Halyburton, William Alli
Halys, Nevin ChPo
Ham, Charles 1880- WhWNAA
Ham, Charles Henry 1831-1902 Alli Sup, DcAmA, DcNAA
Ham, George D Alli Sup
Ham, George Henry 1847-1926 DcNAA
Ham, James Panton Alli Sup
Ham, John Alli Sup
Ham, Marion Franklin 1867-1956 BiDSA, DcAmA, OhA&B, WhWNAA
Ham, Olive Mary 1918- Au&Wr, WrD 1976
Ham, Robert Alli
Ham, Wayne Albert 1938- ConAu 21, WrD 1976
Hamachek, Don E 1933- ConAu 17R
Hamada, Hirosuke 1893- ConAu 45
Hamadhani, Al- 969?-1007 CasWL, DcOrL 3
Hamadhani, Ahmad Ibn Al-Husain Al-969?-1007 Pen Cl
Hamady, Walter AuNews 1
Hamaker, Adda May 1885- WhWNAA
Hamaker, John Irvin 1869- WhWNAA
Hamalian, Leo 1920- ConAu 5R
Haman, Samuel Alli Sup
Hamann, Johann Georg 1697-1733 OxGer
Hamann, Johann Georg 1730-1788 CasWL, DcEuL, EuA, EvEuW, OxGer, Pen Eur, REn
Hamartolus CasWL
Hamawi Hames, Jack 1920- Au&Wr
Hamberg, Daniel 1924- ConAu 1R
Hamberg, John Alli Sup
Hamberg, Theodore Alli Sup
Hamberger, John F 1934- IlBYP, IlCB 1966
Hamberlin, LaFayette Rupert 1861-1902 AmA&B, BiDSA
Hambidge, Gove 1890- AmA&B
Hambidge, Jay 1867-1924 DcNAA
Hambidge, Ruth ChPo S2
Hamblen, Bernard 1877-1962 AmSCAP 66
Hamblen, Edwin Crowell 1900-1963 AmA&B
Hamblen, Emily S 1864- WhWNAA
Hamblen, Herbert Elliott 1849- AmA&B, BiD&SB, DcAmA, DcNAA
Hamblen, John Wesley 1924- IndAu 1917
Hamblen, Suzy AmSCAP 66
Hambleton, Godfrey William Alli Sup
Hambleton, Jack AuBYP
Hambleton, James P BiDSA
Hambleton, James Pinkney Alli Sup
Hambleton, John Alli, Alli Sup
Hambleton, Joseph Alli Sup
Hambleton, Ronald 1917- CanWr, ConP 1970, OxCan
Hambletonian WhLA, WhWNAA
Hamblett, Charles Au&Wr
Hamblin, C L 1922- ConAu 25
Hamblin, Dora Jane 1920- AuBYP, ConAu 37
Hamblin, Hazel TexWr
Hamblin, Ola 1903- TexWr
Hamblin, W K 1928- ConAu 53

Hambourg, Mark 1879- *WhLA*
Hambrecht, George P 1871- *WhWNAA*
Hambridge, J *ChPo*
Hamburg, Carl H 1915- *ConAu 37,*
WrD 1976
Hamburger, Anne Ellen *ConP 1970*
Hamburger, Kaete 1896- *ConAu 29*
Hamburger, Max 1897- *ConAu 17*
Hamburger, Michael J 1938- *ConAu 45*
Hamburger, Michael Peter Leopold 1924-
Au&Wr, ConAu 5R, ConLC 5,
ConP 1970, ConP 1975, WorAu,
WrD 1976
Hamburger, Philip 1914- *AmA&B, Au&Wr,*
ConAu 5R, WrD 1976
Hamburger, Robert 1943- *ConAu 61*
Hamburgh, Max 1922- *ConAu 61*
Hamby, Alonzo Lee 1940- *ConAu 37,*
WrD 1976
Hamby, Wallace Bernard 1903- *WrD 1976*
Hamby, William Henry 1875-1928 *DcNAA*
Hamdallah-I Mustaufi 1281?-1350 *CasWL*
Hamdi, Mehmed Hamdullah 1449?-1503
DcOrL 3
Hamdullah Mustawfi 1281?-1350 *Pen Cl*
Hameiri, Avigdor 1887?-1970 *CasWL, Pen Cl*
Hamel, Andre R *BbtC*
Hamel, Charles Dennis 1881- *WhWNAA*
Hamel, F L *BiDLA*
Hamel, Felix Hargrave De 1838- *Alli Sup*
Hamel, Felix John *Alli, Alli Sup*
Hamel, Frank *ChPo S2*
Hamel, Leopold *Alli Sup*
Hamel, N *BiDLA*
Hamel, Thomas Etienne 1830-1913 *DcNAA*
Hamele, Ottamar 1878-1964 *AmA&B*
Hamelin, Jean *OxCan, OxCan Sup*
Hamelin, Marcel *OxCan Sup*
Hamelin, Octave 1856-1907 *OxFr*
Hamelink, Jacques Marinus 1939- *CasWL*
Hamelinus Of Verulam *BiB N*
Hamell, Patrick Joseph 1910- *Au&Wr,*
ConAu P-1, WrD 1976
Hamelman, Paul W 1930- *ConAu 41*
Hamer, Charles John 1856- *WhLA*
Hamer, David Allan 1938- *ConAu 45*
Hamer, Edward And Lloyd, H W *Alli Sup*
Hamer, Enid *ChPo S2*
Hamer, John *Alli Sup*
Hamer, Martin J 1931- *BlkAW, LivBA*
Hamer, Philip May 1891- *AmA&B*
Hamer, Richard Frederick Sanger 1935-
Au&Wr
Hamer, Sam Hield 1869- *ChPo, ChPo S2,*
MnBBF
Hamer, Sarah Selina *Alli Sup*
Hamerling, Robert 1830-1889 *BiD&SB,*
EvEuW, OxGer
Hamermesh, Morton 1915- *ConAu 5R*
Hamerow, Theodore S 1920- *ConAu 49*
Hamersley, James Hooker 1844-1901 *ChPo,*
DcAmA, DcNAA
Hamersley, John William 1808-1889 *Alli Sup,*
DcAmA
Hamersley, Lewis Randolph 1847-1910 *DcAmA,*
DcNAA
Hamersley, Richard *Alli*
Hamersley, William 1835-1920 *DcNAA*
Hamersley, William James *ChPo S1*
Hamersly, Lewis Randolph *Alli Sup*
Hamersly, Thomas Holdup Stevens *Alli Sup*
Hamerton *PoIre*
Hamerton, Eugenie *Alli Sup*
Hamerton, Nora *ChPo S2*
Hamerton, Philip Gilbert 1834-1894 *Alli Sup,*
BbD, BiD&SB, BrAu 19, CarSB, ChPo,
ChPo S1, Chmbr 3, DcBiA, DcEnL,
EvLB, NewC
Hames, Inez 1892- *ConAu 29*
Hamey, Baldwin *Alli*
Hamid Kashmiri d1844 *DcOrL 3*
Hamidi, Mihdi 1914- *CasWL*
Hamieri, Avigdor 1886-1970 *Pen Eur*
Hamil, Fred C *OxCan*
Hamil, Thomas Arthur 1928- *AuBYP*
Hamilcar Barca 270?BC-228BC *REn*
Hamill, Ernest A *ChPo S1*
Hamill, Ethel *ConAu XR, WrD 1976*

Hamill, Howard M 1847- *BiDSA*
Hamill, Howard Melanchthon 1849-1915
DcNAA
Hamill, Katharine Forrest *ChPo S1*
Hamill, Pete 1935- *ConAu 25*
Hamill, Robert Hoffman 1912- *ConAu 33,*
IndAu 1917, WrD 1976
Hamill, S S *Alli Sup*
Hamilton, Duchess Of *NewC*
Hamilton, Lady *Alli*
Hamilton, Marquis Of *Alli*
Hamilton, Mrs. *Alli*
Hamilton, A *Alli*
Hamilton, Miss A *Alli, BiDLA*
Hamilton, A Charles *ChPo*
Hamilton, A E *ChPo S1*
Hamilton, A G *Alli, Alli Sup*
Hamilton, A W *ChPo S2*
Hamilton, Adelbert *Alli Sup*
Hamilton, Alex *Au&Wr*
Hamilton, Alexander *Alli, BiDLA, Chmbr 3*
Hamilton, Alexander 1712-1756 *AmA, DcNAA,*
OxAm, REnAL
Hamilton, Alexander 1757-1804 *Alli, AmA,*
AmA&B, BbD, BiD&SB, CyAL 1,
CyWA, DcAmA, DcEnL, DcLEnL,
DcNAA, EvLB, OxAm, REn, REnAL
Hamilton, Alexander 1809- *ChPo S1*
Hamilton, Alexander 1815-1907 *DcNAA*
Hamilton, Alexander Henry Abercromby 1829-
Alli Sup
Hamilton, Alexander V *Alli Sup*
Hamilton, Alfred Starr 1914- *ConAu 53,*
ConP 1970, DrAP 1975
Hamilton, Alice *ConAu XR*
Hamilton, Alice 1869- *WhWNAA*
Hamilton, Alice King *Alli Sup, DcAmA,*
DcNAA
Hamilton, Allan McLane 1848-1919 *Alli Sup,*
DcNAA
Hamilton, Allen McLane 1848-1919 *DcAmA*
Hamilton, Andrew *Alli, Alli Sup*
Hamilton, Andrew 1855- *ChPo S1*
Hamilton, Ann *ChPo S1, PoIre*
Hamilton, Anna *ChPo*
Hamilton, Anna Elizabeth *PoIre*
Hamilton, Anna Elizabeth 1843-1875 *PoIre*
Hamilton, Anne *WhWNAA*
Hamilton, Anthony *Alli*
Hamilton, Count Anthony 1646?-1720 *Alli,*
BbD, BiD&SB, BrAu, CasWL, DcEnL,
DcEuL, NewC, OxEng, OxFr, PoIre,
REn
Hamilton, Archibald *Alli*
Hamilton, Lord Archibald 1769- *Alli, BiDLA*
Hamilton, Arthur *Alli Sup, AmSCAP 66*
Hamilton, Arthur Douglas Bruce 1900- *Au&Wr*
Hamilton, Arthur Hayne *Alli Sup*
Hamilton, B L St. John 1914- *ConAu 13R*
Hamilton, Betsy *AmA&B, BiDSA, DcNAA*
Hamilton, Bob 1899- *AmSCAP 66*
Hamilton, Bobb 1928- *BlkAW*
Hamilton, Bruce 1900- *EncM&D*
Hamilton, Buzz *ConAu XR*
Hamilton, C G *Alli Sup*
Hamilton, Mrs. C G *Alli Sup*
Hamilton, C H H *Alli Sup*
Hamilton, C J *Alli Sup*
Hamilton, C T *Alli Sup*
Hamilton, Carl 1914- *ConAu 53*
Hamilton, Cecily 1872- *MnBBF*
Hamilton, Celia V *Alli Sup*
Hamilton, Charles *Alli, Alli Sup, ChPo S2,*
LongC
Hamilton, Sir Charles *BbtC*
Hamilton, Charles 1753-1792 *Alli, PoIre*
Hamilton, Charles 1875-1961 *OxEng*
Hamilton, Charles ALSO Richards, F
Hamilton, Charles 1913- *ConAu 5R*
Hamilton, Charles Claude *PoIre*
Hamilton, Charles Frederick 1869-1933 *DcNAA*
Hamilton, Charles G *Alli Sup*
Hamilton, Charles Granville 1905- *ConAu 41*
Hamilton, Charles Harold St. John 1876-1961
MnBBF, WhCL
Hamilton, Charles James *Alli Sup*
Hamilton, Mrs. Charles James *Alli Sup*
Hamilton, Charles Vernon 1929- *AmA&B,*

LivBAA
Hamilton, Charles W 1890- *ConAu 5R*
Hamilton, Christine H *ChPo*
Hamilton, Cicely 1872-1952 *LongC*
Hamilton, Clare *ConAu XR*
Hamilton, Clarence Grant 1865-1935 *DcNAA,*
WhWNAA
Hamilton, Clayton 1881-1946 *AmA&B, AmLY,*
DcNAA, REnAL, TwCA, TwCA Sup,
WhWNAA
Hamilton, Clive *EvLB, LongC, NewC,*
TwCA Sup
Hamilton, Cosmo 1872?-1942 *LongC, NewC,*
REn, TwCA, TwCA Sup
Hamilton, D Howland *Alli Sup*
Hamilton, David *Alli*
Hamilton, Sir David *Alli*
Hamilton, David 1916- *AmA&B*
Hamilton, David 1918- *ConAu 29, WrD 1976*
Hamilton, David Henry 1813-1879 *DcNAA*
Hamilton, David James *Alli Sup*
Hamilton, Donald 1916- *ConAu 1R,*
EncM&D
Hamilton, Dorothy 1906- *ConAu 33*
Hamilton, Douglas *Alli Sup*
Hamilton, E J *Alli Sup*
Hamilton, E P *Alli Sup*
Hamilton, Earl J 1899- *Au&Wr, ConAu P-1*
Hamilton, Edward G 1897- *ConAu P-1*
Hamilton, Edward John 1834-1918 *Alli Sup,*
AmA, AmLY, DcAmA, DcNAA,
OhA&B
Hamilton, Edward P *OxCan*
Hamilton, Edwin 1849-1919 *Alli Sup, ChPo,*
PoIre
Hamilton, Edwin Timothy 1898- *WhWNAA,*
OhA&B
Hamilton, Eleanor Poorman 1909- *ConAu 1R*
Hamilton, Eliza 1758-1816 *BiDLA*
Hamilton, Eliza Mary *Alli*
Hamilton, Elizabeth *Chmbr 2*
Hamilton, Elizabeth d1882 *Alli Sup*
Hamilton, Elizabeth 1758-1816 *Alli, BbD,*
BiD&SB, BrAu 19, ChPo, ChPo S2,
DcEnL, EvLB, NewC, PoIre
Hamilton, Elizabeth 1906- *Au&Wr,*
ConAu P-1, WrD 1976
Hamilton, Lady Elizabeth Emma 1821-
Alli Sup
Hamilton, Elizabeth Mary 1807-1851 *PoIre*
Hamilton, Emma *Alli, BiDLA*
Hamilton, Lady Emma 1761?-1815 *NewC,*
REn
Hamilton, Ernest *ConAu XR, MnBBF*
Hamilton, Eugene James Lee 1845- *Alli Sup*
Hamilton, Eugene Lee *DcEnA Ap*
Hamilton, F E *ChPo*
Hamilton, F H *Alli Sup*
Hamilton, F W *ChPo S1*
Hamilton, Flora Deshler Brent 1872-1933
DcNAA, OhA&B
Hamilton, Foreststorn 1921- *AmSCAP 66*
Hamilton, Franc *Alli*
Hamilton, Francis *Alli*
Hamilton, Francis Frazee 1891-1960
IndAu 1917
Hamilton, Frank 1883-1952 *IndAu 1917*
Hamilton, Frank Hastings 1813-1886 *Alli Sup,*
DcAmA, DcNAA
Hamilton, Franklin Elmer Ellsworth 1866-1918
DcNAA, OhA&B
Hamilton, Franklin Willard 1923- *ConAu 33,*
WrD 1976
Hamilton, Frederick J 1895- *AmSCAP 66*
Hamilton, Sir Frederick William 1815- *Alli Sup*
Hamilton, Frederick William 1860-1940
DcNAA
Hamilton, G *Alli Sup*
Hamilton, G Baldwin *Alli Sup*
Hamilton, Gail 1833-1896 *Alli Sup, AmA,*
AmA&B, BiD&SB, ChPo, DcAmA,
DcEnL, DcNAA, OxAm

Hamilton, Gavin *Alli Sup*
Hamilton, Gavin d1797 *Alli*
Hamilton, George *Alli, Alli Sup, BiDLA,*
MnBBF
Hamilton, George 1901-1957 *AmSCAP 66*
Hamilton, George A *ChPo S1*
Hamilton, George Burton *Alli Sup*
Hamilton, George Hall 1884- *WhLA,*
WhWNAA
Hamilton, George Livingstone 1874-1940
DcNAA
Hamilton, Sir George Rostrevor 1888-1967 *ChPo,*
ChPo S1, ChPo S2, CnE&AP, LongC,
ModBL, NewC
Hamilton, Gilbert VanTassel 1877-1943 *OhA&B*
Hamilton, Gladys I *ChPo*
Hamilton, Grace *Alli Sup*
Hamilton, H B *Alli Sup*
Hamilton, H L *Alli Sup*
Hamilton, Hans *Alli*
Hamilton, Hans Claude *Alli Sup*
Hamilton, Harriet *Alli Sup*
Hamilton, Harry *ChPo*
Hamilton, Helen *ChPo S1*
Hamilton, Henry *Alli Sup, DcNAA, PoIre*
Hamilton, Henry 1840-1916 *ChPo S2*
Hamilton, Henry R *Alli Sup*
Hamilton, Henry Raymond 1861-1940 *DcNAA*
Hamilton, Henry W 1898- *ConAu 33*
Hamilton, Holman 1910- *ConAu 13R,*
IndAu 1917
Hamilton, Horace Ernst 1911- *ChPo S2,*
ConAu 21, IndAu 1917
Hamilton, Howard Devon 1920- *ConAu 13R,*
IndAu 1917
Hamilton, Hugh 1729-1805 *Alli, DcEnL*
Hamilton, Iain Bertram 1920- *Au&Wr*
Hamilton, Ian 1938- *Au&Wr, ConP 1970,*
ConP 1975, WrD 1976
Hamilton, Ian Standish Monteith 1853-
Alli Sup, ChPo, ChPo S1
Hamilton, Islay *Alli Sup*
Hamilton, J A *Alli, Alli Sup*
Hamilton, J Benson *Alli Sup*
Hamilton, J P 1781?- *Alli*
Hamilton, J Wallace 1900-1968 *ConAu P-1*
Hamilton, Jack *ConAu XR, WrD 1976*
Hamilton, James *Alli, Alli Sup, BiDLA*
Hamilton, James 1793-1873 *Alli Sup*
Hamilton, James 1814-1867 *Alli, Alli Sup,*
DcEnL
Hamilton, James 1819-1878 *EarAB,*
EarAB Sup
Hamilton, James, Duke Of 1606-1649 *Alli*
Hamilton, James, Jr. *Alli*
Hamilton, James Alexander 1788-1878 *Alli Sup,*
AmA&B, DcAmA, DcNAA
Hamilton, James Archibald *Alli*
Hamilton, James Cleland 1836-1907 *DcNAA,*
OxCan
Hamilton, James Edward *Alli, BbtC, BiDLA*
Hamilton, James Henry 1861- *IndAu 1816*
Hamilton, James Robertson 1921- *WrD 1976*
Hamilton, Janet Thompson 1795-1873 *Alli Sup,*
ChPo, ChPo S1, ChPo S2
Hamilton, Jay Benson 1847-1920 *OhA&B*
Hamilton, Jean Tyree 1909- *ConAu 33*
Hamilton, Jessie *Alli Sup*
Hamilton, John *Alli, Alli Sup, ChPo*
Hamilton, John d1570 *Alli*
Hamilton, John 1761-1814 *NewC*
Hamilton, John 1800-1884 *PoIre*
Hamilton, John Brown 1847-1898 *DcNAA*
Hamilton, John Church 1792-1882 *Alli,*
Alli Sup, AmA&B, BiD&SB, DcAmA,
DcNAA
Hamilton, John James 1917- *Au&Wr*
Hamilton, John Judson 1854- *WhWNAA*
Hamilton, John McLure 1853-1936 *DcNAA,*
WhWNAA
Hamilton, John Potter 1781?- *Alli Sup,*
Br&AmS
Hamilton, John Sherman 1870- *IndAu 1816*
Hamilton, John Taylor 1859- *AmA&B,*
DcAmA
Hamilton, John William 1845-1934 *Alli Sup,*
BiDSA, DcAmA, DcNAA, WhWNAA
Hamilton, Joseph *Alli, Alli Sup*

Hamilton, Joseph Gregoire DeRoulhac 1878-
AmA&B, AmLY, BiDSA, WhWNAA
Hamilton, Julia *ConAu XR, WrD 1976*
Hamilton, K *Alli Sup*
Hamilton, Kate Livingston *Alli Sup*
Hamilton, Kate Waterman 1841-1934 *Alli Sup,*
AmA&B, ChPo, ChPo S2, DcAmA,
DcNAA
Hamilton, Katharine Olds *ChPo, ChPo S1*
Hamilton, Kay *AuBYP, ConAu XR, OhA&B*
Hamilton, Kenneth 1917- *ConAu 17R,*
WrD 1976
Hamilton, Ker Baillie 1804- *Alli Sup*
Hamilton, Kiilu Anthony *BlkAW*
Hamilton, L *Alli Sup*
Hamilton, L Hill 1917- *AmSCAP 66*
Hamilton, Laurentine 1826-1882 *DcNAA*
Hamilton, Leonidas LeCenci *Alli Sup*
Hamilton, Leveson Russell 1823-1869 *Alli Sup*
Hamilton, Lillias 1893-1894 *BbD*
Hamilton, Miss M *Alli*
Hamilton, Mrs. M J R *BiDSA*
Hamilton, Margaret *ChPo*
Hamilton, Marion Ethel 1881- *AnMV 1926,*
ChPo, WhWNAA
Hamilton, Marshall Lee 1937- *ConAu 37*
Hamilton, Mary *Alli Sup*
Hamilton, Mary Agnes 1884-1966 *EvLB,*
LongC, TwCA, TwCA Sup
Hamilton, Max 1912- *Au&Wr, MnBBF,*
WrD 1976
Hamilton, May Charlotte *PoIre*
Hamilton, Michael *ConAu XR*
Hamilton, Michael 1927- *ConAu 29*
Hamilton, Milton W 1901- *ConAu P-1*
Hamilton, Murray *MnBBF*
Hamilton, N Raphael *OxCan Sup*
Hamilton, Nancy 1908- *AmSCAP 66*
Hamilton, Neill Q 1925- *ConAu 61*
Hamilton, Newburgh *Alli*
Hamilton, Nicholas E Stephen Armytage
Alli Sup
Hamilton, P S *Alli Sup*
Hamilton, Patrick *Alli Sup*
Hamilton, Patrick 1503-1527 *Alli*
Hamilton, Patrick 1889- *WhWNAA*
Hamilton, Patrick 1904-1962 *CnMD, DcLEnL,*
EncM&D, LongC, ModWD, REn,
TwCA Sup, TwCW, WhTwL
Hamilton, Paul *ConAu 57, WrD 1976*
Hamilton, Peter 1817-1888 *BiDSA*
Hamilton, Peter 1947- *WrD 1976*
Hamilton, Peter Joseph 1859-1927 *BiDSA,*
DcAmA, DcNAA
Hamilton, Pierce Stevens 1826-1893 *BbtC,*
DcNAA, OxCan
Hamilton, R *Alli Sup*
Hamilton, Raphael N 1892- *ConAu 29*
Hamilton, Richard *Alli Sup*
Hamilton, Richard T 1869- *BlkAW*
Hamilton, Richard Winter 1794-1848 *Alli,*
DcEnL
Hamilton, Robert *Alli, Alli Sup*
Hamilton, Robert 1721-1793 *Alli*
Hamilton, Robert 1743?-1829 *Alli, BiDLA,*
DcEnL
Hamilton, Robert 1908- *CatA 1952*
Hamilton, Robert 1928- *LivBA*
Hamilton, Robert Douglas 1783-1857 *BbtC*
Hamilton, Robert S *Alli Sup, DcAmA*
Hamilton, Robert Scott *PoIre*
Hamilton, Robert W *ConAu XR*
Hamilton, Roland T *BlkAW*
Hamilton, Ronald 1909- *Au&Wr, ConAu 13R,*
WrD 1976
Hamilton, Rose L 1873- *WhWNAA*
Hamilton, Ross 1920- *ChPo S2*
Hamilton, Rowland *Alli Sup*
Hamilton, Rufus *AmA&B, DcNAA*
Hamilton, Russel *AuBYP*
Hamilton, Russell G 1934- *ConAu 61*
Hamilton, Samuel King 1837-1922 *DcNAA*
Hamilton, Sarah B Edmonds *BlkAW*
Hamilton, Schuyler 1822-1903 *Alli, DcAmA,*
DcNAA
Hamilton, Seena M 1926- *ConAu 17R*
Hamilton, Shearer *ChPo S2*
Hamilton, Sinclair *ChPo, ChPo S1*

Hamilton, Smith *Alli, BiDLA*
Hamilton, Stanislaus Murray 1855-1909
DcNAA
Hamilton, T *Alli Sup*
Hamilton, T C *Alli Sup*
Hamilton, T H *Alli Sup*
Hamilton, Terrick *Alli*
Hamilton, Thomas *Alli, Alli Sup, Chmbr 3,*
PoIre
Hamilton, Thomas 1789-1842 *Alli, BiD&SB,*
BrAu 19, DcEnL, EvLB, NewC
Hamilton, Thomas Hale 1914- *IndAu 1917*
Hamilton, Thomas Jefferson 1885- *WhWNAA*
Hamilton, Vereker M *PoIre*
Hamilton, Vereker M And Fasson, Stewart
Alli Sup
Hamilton, Virginia 1936- *AuBYP, AuICB,*
AuNews 1, BlkAW, ChLR 1, ChPo S2,
ConAu 25, MorBMP, NewbC 1966,
SmATA 4
Hamilton, W *PoIre*
Hamilton, W C *PoIre*
Hamilton, W D *OxCan Sup*
Hamilton, W G *Alli Sup*
Hamilton, W H *ChPo S2, PoIre*
Hamilton, W J *Alli*
Hamilton, W R *Alli Sup, BbtC*
Hamilton, W T *Alli*
Hamilton, Wade *ConAu XR, WrD 1976*
Hamilton, Walter *Alli, Alli Sup*
Hamilton, Walter 1844-1899 *ChPo, ChPo S1*
Hamilton, Walter Kerr 1808-1869 *Alli Sup*
Hamilton, Walter R *OxCan*
Hamilton, Walton Hale 1881- *WhWNAA*
Hamilton, William *Alli, Alli Sup, BiDLA,*
WrD 1976
Hamilton, Sir William *Chmbr 3*
Hamilton, William d1797 *Alli*
Hamilton, William d1808 *Alli*
Hamilton, Sir William 1730-1803 *Alli*
Hamilton, William 1751-1801 *BkIE*
Hamilton, Sir William 1788-1856 *Alli,*
BiD&SB, BrAu 19, CasWL, DcEnL,
EvLB, NewC, OxEng
Hamilton, William, Jr. 1924- *ConAu 53*
Hamilton, William, Of Bangour 1704-1754 *Alli,*
BbD, BiD&SB, BrAu, CasWL, ChPo,
ChPo S1, Chmbr 2, DcEnL, EvLB,
NewC, OxEng, Pen Eng
Hamilton, William, Of Gilbertfield 1665?-1751
BrAu, CasWL, Chmbr 2, EvLB, Pen Eng
Hamilton, William Alexander Baillie 1844-
Alli Sup
Hamilton, William B 1908-1972 *ConAu 37,*
ConAu P-1
Hamilton, William Douglas *Alli Sup*
Hamilton, William Douglas 1832-1916 *OhA&B*
Hamilton, William Gerard 1729-1796 *Alli,*
NewC
Hamilton, William Hamilton 1886- *ChPo,*
ChPo S1, WhLA
Hamilton, William J *HsB&A*
Hamilton, William James 1903- *Au&Wr*
Hamilton, William John, Jr. 1902- *AmA&B*
Hamilton, William Peter 1867-1929 *DcNAA*
Hamilton, William Reeve 1855-1914 *DcNAA*
Hamilton, Sir William Rowan 1805-1865 *Alli,*
NewC, OxEng, PoIre
Hamilton, William T *Alli Sup*
Hamilton, William T 1796-1884 *BiDSA*
Hamilton, William Thomas 1822-1908 *DcNAA*
Hamilton, William Tighe *Alli Sup*
Hamilton, William Wistar 1868-1960 *AmA&B*
Hamilton-Edwards, Gerald Kenneth Savery 1906-
Au&Wr, ConAu 21, WrD 1976
Hamilton-Gordon *Alli Sup*
Hamilton Hill, Margot 1921- *Au&Wr*
Hamilton-King, Harriet Eleanor *ChPo S2*
Hamilton-Wilkes, Edwin Montague 1914-
Au&Wr
Hamit, Abdulhak Tarhan 1852-1937 *DcOrL 3*
Hamlet, Ham *WhWNAA*
Hamlet, L Alton 1903- *WhWNAA*
Hamlett, Ermine Marie 1903- *TexWr*
Hamlett, Lizzie *BiDSA*
Hamley, Charles *Alli Sup*
Hamley, Dennis 1935- *ConAu 57*
Hamley, Edward *Alli, BiDLA*

Hamley, Sir Edward Bruce 1824-1893 *Alli,*
Alli Sup, BiD&SB, Chmbr 3
Hamley, William George *Alli Sup*
Hamlin, Alfred Dwight Foster 1855-1926
AmA&B, AmLY, DcAmA, DcNAA
Hamlin, Augustus Choate 1829-1905 *Alli Sup,*
DcAmA, DcNAA, EarAB Sup
Hamlin, Bruce Gordon 1929- *Au&Wr*
Hamlin, Charles 1837-1911 *Alli Sup, DcAmA,*
DcNAA
Hamlin, Charles Eugene 1861-1921 *DcNAA*
Hamlin, Cyrus 1811-1900 *Alli Sup, DcAmA,*
DcNAA
Hamlin, Fannie E *Alli Sup*
Hamlin, Gladys E *ConAu 37*
Hamlin, Griffith Askew 1919- *ConAu 37*
Hamlin, Howard Elroy 1888- *OhA&B*
Hamlin, John H 1880-1951 *AmA&B,*
WhWNAA
Hamlin, Kate L *ChPo*
Hamlin, Marie Caroline Watson *Alli Sup*
Hamlin, Mary T *ChPo*
Hamlin, Myra Louise 1856-1927 *DcNAA*
Hamlin, Myra Sawyer *Alli Sup*
Hamlin, Scoville 1889- *WhWNAA*
Hamlin, Talbot Faulkner 1889-1956 *AmA&B,*
OxAm
Hamlin, Teunis Slingerland 1847-1907 *DcAmA,*
DcNAA
Hamline, Leonidas Lent 1797?-1865 *Alli Sup,*
DcAmA, DcNAA, OhA&B
Hamlisch, Marvin 1944- *AmSCAP 66*
Hamlyn, George *Alli Sup*
Hamlyn, Harvey *ChPo S1, ChPo S2*
Hamm, Glenn B 1936- *ConAu 53*
Hamm, Jack 1916- *ConAu 5R*
Hamm, Margherita Arlina 1871-1907 *AmA&B,*
DcNAA
Hamm, Russell Leroy 1926- *ConAu 5R,*
IndAu 1917
Hammack, Bobby 1922- *AmSCAP 66*
Hammack, E B *Alli Sup*
Hamman, Louis 1877- *WhWNAA*
Hammarskjold, Dag 1905-1961 *REn*
Hammarskold, Lars 1785-1827 *CasWL*
Hammel, Claus 1932- *CrCD*
Hammel, Faye 1929- *ConAu 1R*
Hammel, Mamie L 1867-1943 *OhA&B*
Hammell, Agnes *WhWNAA*
Hammen, Carl Schlee 1923- *ConAu 53*
Hammen, Oscar J 1907- *ConAu 25*
Hammenhog, Waldemar 1902- *CasWL*
Hammer, Bonaventure 1842-1917 *DcNAA*
Hammer, Carl, Jr. 1910- *ConAu 53*
Hammer, Emanuel F 1926- *ConAu 29,*
WrD 1976
Hammer, Jeanne-Ruth 1912- *ConAu 9R*
Hammer, Jefferson J 1933- *ConAu 41*
Hammer, Joseph *Alli, BiDLA*
Hammer, Julius 1810-1862 *BiD&SB*
Hammer, Louis *DrAP 1975*
Hammer, Richard 1928- *ConAu 25,*
SmATA 6
Hammer, Robert 1930- *AmSCAP 66*
Hammer, Victor *ChPo S1*
Hammer, William Joseph 1858-1934 *DcNAA,*
WhWNAA
Hammer-Purgstall, Joseph, Freiherr Von
1774-1856 *OxGer*
Hammerich, Peter Frederik Adolf 1809-1877
BiD&SB
Hammerli-Marti, S *Pen Eur*
Hammerling, Robert 1830-1889 *BbD*
Hammerman, Donald R 1925- *ConAu 13R*
Hammerman, Gay M 1926- *ConAu 33,*
SmATA 9
Hammerman, Herman 1912- *AmSCAP 66*
Hammershaimb, Erling 1904- *Au&Wr*
Hammerskold, Lorenzo 1785-1827 *DcEuL*
Hammerstein, Alice 1921- *AmSCAP 66*
Hammerstein, Oscar 1847-1919 *OxAm*
Hammerstein, Oscar, II 1895-1960 *AmA&B,*
AmSCAP 66, ChPo S1, CnDAL,
McGWD, ModWD, OxAm, REn,
REnAL
Hammerstein-Equord, Hans August Von
1881-1947 *OxGer*
Hammerstein-Illing, Caecilie 1868- *WhWNAA*

Hammerton, Grenville *MnBBF*
Hammerton, Sir John Alexander 1871-1949
ChPo S1, ChPo S2, EvLB, WhLA
Hammes, John A 1924- *ConAu 13R,*
WrD 1976
Hammett, Charles Edward, Jr. *Alli Sup*
Hammett, Dashiell 1894-1961 *AuNews 1,*
CasWL, CnDAL, CnMWL, ConLC 3,
ConLC 5, CyWA, EncM&D, LongC,
ModAL, ModAL Sup, OxAm, OxEng,
Pen Am, REn, REnAL, TwCA,
TwCA Sup, TwCW, WebEAL, WhTwL
Hammett, Louis Plack 1894- *Au&Wr*
Hammett, Samuel Adams 1816-1865 *Alli, AmA,*
AmA&B, CnDAL, CyAL 2, DcAmA,
DcNAA, OxAm, REnAL
Hammett, Samuel Dashiell 1894-1961 *AmA&B,*
AuNews 1, DcLEnL, EvLB, MnBBF
Hammick, Horacio H *Alli Sup*
Hammick, James Thomas 1819- *Alli Sup*
Hammill, C H *ChPo S2*
Hamming, Richard W 1915- *ConAu 57*
Hammitt, Orlin 1916- *AmSCAP 66*
Hammon, Briton *BlkAW*
Hammon, George *Alli*
Hammon, John *Alli*
Hammon, Jupiter 1720?-1800? *AmA, AmA&B,*
BlkAW, DcNAA, OxAm, REnAL
Hammon, William *Alli*
Hammond, Adam *Alli Sup*
Hammond, Albert L 1892- *ConAu 1R*
Hammond, Anthony *Alli, DcAmA*
Hammond, Anthony 1668-1738 *Alli, DcEnL*
Hammond, Arthur 1882- *WhWNAA*
Hammond, Barbara 1873-1961 *LongC*
Hammond, Basil Calvin *BlkAW*
Hammond, Bray 1886-1968 *AmA&B, OxAm*
Hammond, C *ChPo S1*
Hammond, Caleb, Jr. 1915- *AmA&B*
Hammond, Carlos Conrad 1898- *IndAu 1917*
Hammond, Charles *Alli, Alli Sup*
Hammond, Charles 1779-1840 *BiDSA,*
OhA&B
Hammond, Charles 1813-1878 *DcNAA*
Hammond, Charles D 1818- *Alli, Alli Sup*
Hammond, Charles Edward *Alli Sup*
Hammond, Christopher *McGWD*
Hammond, Cleon E 1908- *AmSCAP 66*
Hammond, Cyril Oswald 1903- *Au&Wr*
Hammond, Dick E 1928- *IndAu 1917*
Hammond, Mrs. E H *Alli*
Hammond, Earl R 1886- *AmSCAP 66*
Hammond, Edward Payson 1831-1910 *Alli Sup,*
DcAmA, DcNAA
Hammond, Edwin Hughes 1919- *ConAu 13R*
Hammond, Egerton Douglas *Alli Sup*
Hammond, Elanor Prescott 1866-1934 *ChPo,*
ChPo S2, DcNAA, WhWNAA
Hammond, Elisha *Alli*
Hammond, George *Alli*
Hammond, George Peter 1896- *AmA&B*
Hammond, Gertrude Demain *ChPo S1*
Hammond, Guyton B 1930- *ConAu 17R*
Hammond, Hala Jean *WhWNAA*
Hammond, Harold 1874- *ChPo*
Hammond, Harriet *ChPo*
Hammond, Harriot Milton 1838-1903 *DcNAA*
Hammond, Helen Buis 1901- *IndAu 1917*
Hammond, Henrietta Hardy 1854-1883
AmA&B, BiD&SB, BiDSA, DcAmA,
DcNAA
Hammond, Henry *Alli Sup*
Hammond, Henry 1605-1660 *Alli, BrAu,*
DcEnL
Hammond, Henry L *Alli Sup*
Hammond, Herbert *ChPo S1*
Hammond, Hope 1877- *WhWNAA*
Hammond, Humphrey *Alli*
Hammond, J *Alli*
Hammond, J D 1933- *ConAu 45*
Hammond, J L 1872-1949 *LongC*
Hammond, Mrs. J W *BlkAW*
Hammond, Jabez Delano 1778-1855 *Alli, AmA,*
DcAmA, DcNAA
Hammond, James *Alli Sup, Chmbr 2*
Hammond, James 1710-1742 *Alli, ChPo,*
DcEnL
Hammond, James Henry 1807-1864 *Alli,*

Alli Sup, BiDSA, CyAL 2, DcAmA,
DcNAA
Hammond, Jane *WrD 1976*
Hammond, John *Alli, HsB&A, OxAm,*
REnAL
Hammond, John 1635-1712 *BiDSA*
Hammond, John Hays 1855-1936 *DcNAA*
Hammond, John Henry 1871-1949 *DcNAA*
Hammond, John Winthrop 1887-1934 *DcNAA*
Hammond, Jonathan Pinkney *Alli Sup*
Hammond, Joseph *Alli Sup*
Hammond, Mrs. L H *ChPo*
Hammond, Lawrence Victor Francis 1925-
Au&Wr
Hammond, Lily Hardy 1859-1925 *AmLY,*
DcNAA
Hammond, M E *Alli Sup*
Hammond, Mac 1926- *ConAu 17R,*
ConP 1970, DrAP 1975, WrD 1976
Hammond, Marcus Claudius Marcellus
1814-1876 *Alli, BiDSA, CyAL 2, DcAmA*
Hammond, Maria Johns 1862- *ChPo, ChPo S1*
Hammond, Martha Louise *ChPo*
Hammond, Matthew Brown 1868-1933 *DcNAA,*
IndAu 1816, WhWNAA
Hammond, Melvin Ormond 1876-1934 *DcNAA,*
OxCan
Hammond, Natalie d1931 *DcNAA*
Hammond, Natalie Hays 1904- *Au&Wr*
Hammond, Nathaniel Job 1833-1899 *DcNAA*
Hammond, Nicholas Geoffrey Lempriere 1907-
Au&Wr, ConAu 13R, WrD 1976
Hammond, Norman 1944- *ConAu 49*
Hammond, Otis Grant 1867-1944 *DcNAA,*
WhWNAA
Hammond, Paul 1947- *ConAu 57*
Hammond, Paul Y 1929- *ConAu 1R*
Hammond, Percival Hudson 1924- *Au&Wr*
Hammond, Percy Hunter 1873-1936 *DcNAA,*
OhA&B, REnAL, TwCA, TwCA Sup
Hammond, Peter 1921- *Au&Wr*
Hammond, Philip C 1924- *ConAu 5R*
Hammond, Phillip E 1931- *ConAu 17R*
Hammond, Ralph *AuBYP, ConAu XR,*
MnBBF, WrD 1976
Hammond, Richard J 1911- *ConAu 61*
Hammond, Robert *Alli, Alli Sup*
Hammond, Ross W 1918- *ConAu 33*
Hammond, Samuel *Alli*
Hammond, Samuel H 1809-1878 *Alli, Alli Sup,*
DcNAA, HsB&A
Hammond, Stephen Tillinghast 1831- *DcNAA*
Hammond, Thomas *Alli*
Hammond, Thomas T 1920- *ConAu 9R*
Hammond, W A *Alli Sup*
Hammond, W Rogers 1920- *ConAu 45*
Hammond, Wally *MnBBF*
Hammond, Walter *MnBBF*
Hammond, William *Alli, ChPo*
Hammond, William d1783 *PoCh*
Hammond, William Alexander 1828-1900
Alli Sup, AmA&B, BiD&SB, BiDSA,
DcAmA, DcNAA
Hammond, William Alexander 1861-1938
DcNAA
Hammond, William Andrew *Alli*
Hammond, William G 1874-1945 *AmSCAP 66*
Hammond, William Gardiner 1829-1894
DcNAA
Hammond, Winifred Graham 1899-
IndAu 1917
Hammond Innes, Ralph 1913- *Au&Wr,*
AuBYP, ConAu 5R, LongC, WrD 1976
Hammonde, Daphne *ChPo, ChPo S2*
Hammonds, Carsie 1894- *AmA&B*
Hammonds, Michael 1942- *ConAu 45*
Hammontree, Marie Gertrude 1913- *ConAu 5R,*
IndAu 1917, WrD 1976
Hammurabi, King Of Babylon 2067BC-2025BC
REn
Hamner, Earl, Jr. *AuNews 2*
Hamner, Laura V *TexWr*
Hamnett, Keith 1940- *Au&Wr*
Hamod, Sam 1936- *ConAu 45, DrAP 1975*
Hamon, Edouard 1841-1904 *DcNAA*
Hamon, Henry *Alli Sup*
Hamon, Jean 1618-1687 *OxFr*
Hamon, Peter Gustavus *Alli Sup*

Hamond, George *Alli*
Hamond, Thomas *Alli*
Hamond, Walter *Alli*
Hamor, Ralphe *Alli*
Hamor, William Allen 1887- *WhWNAA*
Hamori, Laszlo Dezso 1911- *ConAu 9R*
Hamp, Eric P 1920- *ConAu 17R*
Hamp, Pierre 1876-1962 *CasWL, ClDMEuL,*
 EvEuW, OxCan, OxFr
Hamp, Sidford Frederick 1855-1919 *AmA&B,*
 DcAmA, DcNAA
Hampden, The Spirit Of 1770-1847 *DcEnL*
Hampden, Allen *Alli Sup*
Hampden, Augustus Charles Hobart 1822-1886
 Alli Sup
Hampden, Baroness Catherine A Hobart-
 Alli Sup
Hampden, Henrietta *Alli Sup*
Hampden, John *Alli Sup*
Hampden, John 1594-1643 *Alli, NewC, REn*
Hampden, John 1898- *Au&Wr*
Hampden, Lucy Pauline Hobart- 1793-1868
 Alli Sup
Hampden, Renn Dickson 1793-1868 *Alli,*
 Alli Sup, DcEnL
Hampden, Rob *Alli*
Hampden, Sydney *Alli Sup*
Hampden, Baron Vere Henry Hobart- 1818-1875
 Alli Sup
Hampden, Walter 1879-1955 *REn, REnAL*
Hampden-Jones *Alli Sup*
Hampden-Turner, Charles M 1934- *ConAu 33*
Hampe, John Henry *Alli*
Hamper, William 1776-1831 *Alli*
Hample, Stoo 1926- *ChPo*
Hample, Stuart 1926- *AmSCAP 66*
Hampole, The Hermit Of *DcEnL*
Hampole, Richard *Alli*
Hampole, Richard Rolle Of *Chmbr 1*
Hampoole, Richard *Alli*
Hampsch, George Harold 1927- *ConAu 13R,*
 WrD 1976
Hampshire, A Cecil *Au&Wr*
Hampshire, Michael Allen *IlBYP*
Hampshire, Stuart 1914- *WorAu*
Hampson, Alfred Leete *ChPo*
Hampson, Sir G F *Alli*
Hampson, Sir George Francis 1860- *WhLA*
Hampson, John *Alli, BiDLA*
Hampson, Norman 1922- *ConAu 25,*
 WrD 1976
Hampson, P *Alli Sup*
Hampson, R T *Alli*
Hampson, Thomas *Alli Sup*
Hampson, Walter 1864-1932 *ChPo S1*
Hampson, William *Alli, BiDLA*
Hampstead, J *Alli*
Hampton *Alli*
Hampton, Benjamin Bowles 1875-1932 *DcNAA*
Hampton, Benjamin Bowles 1875- *WhWNAA*
Hampton, Christopher James 1946- *Au&Wr,*
 CnThe, ConAu 25, ConDr, ConLC 4
Hampton, Christopher James 1948- *CrCD*
Hampton, Christopher Martin 1929-
 Au&Wr   ConAu 53,
 ConP 1975, WrD 1976
Hampton, George *Alli*
Hampton, H Duane 1932- *ConAu 33*
Hampton, Isabel Adams *DcNAA*
Hampton, Jack Fitz-Gerald 1909- *Au&Wr,*
 WrD 1976
Hampton, James d1778 *Alli*
Hampton, James N *Alli*
Hampton, Kate Phelan *BiDSA*
Hampton, Kathleen 1923- *ConAu 1R*
Hampton, Lady Laura Elizabeth 1845- *Alli Sup*
Hampton, Mark *ConAu XR, WrD 1976*
Hampton, Richard *Alli Sup*
Hampton, Robert E 1924- *ConAu 33*
Hampton, Trevor Arthur 1912- *Au&Wr,*
 WrD 1976
Hampton, Valvera Moore *TexWr*
Hampton, Wade *BiDSA*
Hampton, William *Alli*
Hampton, William Albert 1929- *ConAu 33,*
 WrD 1976
Hampull, Richard *Alli*
Hamre, Leif 1914- *Au&Wr, ConAu 5R,*

SmATA 5, WrD 1976
Hamsby, Florence *ChPo*
Hamsher, J Herbert 1938- *ConAu 57*
Hamshere, Cyril 1912- *ConAu 41*
Hamst, Olphar *Alli Sup, DcEnL*
Hamstead, J *Alli, BiDLA*
Hamsun, Knut Pederson 1859-1952 *AtlBL,*
 CasWL, ClDMEuL, CnMD, CyWA,
 DcBiA, EncWL, EvEuW, LongC,
 Pen Eur, REn, REnWD, TwCA,
 TwCA Sup, TwCW, WhLA, WhTwL
Hamzah Fansuri *Pen Cl*
Hamzatov, Rasul 1923- *DcOrL 3*
Han, Fei-Tzu d233BC *CasWL, DcOrL 1*
Han, Seung Soo 1936- *ConAu 45*
Han, Shan *CasWL*
Han, Sor-Ya 1900- *DcOrL 1*
Han, Sungjoo 1940- *ConAu 53*
Han, Suyin 1917- *Au&Wr, ConAu 17R,*
 TwCW, WorAu, WrD 1976
Han, T'ai-Fu *DcOrL 1*
Han, Yon-Gun 1879-1944 *CasWL, DcOrL 1*
Han, Yu 768-824 *CasWL, DcOrL 1, Pen Cl*
Han-Mac-Tu 1912-1940 *DcOrL 2*
Han-Shan *DcOrL 1*
Hanaford, Mrs. J R *ChPo*
Hanaford, Jennie Estelle d1924 *DcNAA*
Hanaford, Phebe Ann 1829-1921 *Alli Sup,*
 AmA&B, BbD, BiD&SB, CarSB,
 DcAmA
Hanaford, Phoebe Ann 1829-1921 *ChPo S1,*
 DcNAA
Hanaghan, Jonathan 1887- *Au&Wr, ChPo S2*
Hanam, Richard *Alli*
Hanauer, Walter W 1915- *AmSCAP 66*
Hanburg, N *Alli*
Hanbury, Barnard, And George Waddington
 Alli
Hanbury, Benjamin 1778-1864 *Alli, Alli Sup*
Hanbury, Cornelius *Alli Sup*
Hanbury, Daniel 1825-1875 *Alli Sup*
Hanbury, David T *OxCan*
Hanbury, Harold Greville 1898- *Au&Wr,*
 WrD 1976
Hanbury, Lionel *Alli Sup*
Hanbury, William d1718 *Alli*
Hanbury, Baron William Bateman- 1826-
 Alli Sup
Hanbury-Tenison, Airling Robin 1936-
 ConAu 57, WrD 1976
Hanbury-Tenison, Marika 1938- *WrD 1976*
Hanby, Benjamin Russel 1833-1867 *AmA&B,*
 ChPo S1
Hanby, Harriet S *ChPo S1*
Hance, Alicia Mary *Alli Sup*
Hance, E H *Alli Sup*
Hance, Edward M And Morton, T N *Alli Sup*
Hance, William A 1916- *ConAu 9R,*
 WrD 1976
Hanchant, Wilfred Lewis *ChPo*
Hanchard, J *Alli Sup*
Hanchett, Francis Gilbert 1856- *ChPo S1*
Hanchett, Henry Granger 1853-1918 *Alli Sup,*
 DcAmA, DcNAA
Hanchett, William 1922- *ConAu 33*
Hanchev, Vesselin 1919-1966 *CasWL*
Hancock, Albert Elmer 1870-1915 *DcNAA*
Hancock, Alice Van Fossen 1890- *ConAu 1R*
Hancock, Almira Russell *Alli Sup*
Hancock, Anne *Alli Sup*
Hancock, Anson Uriel *DcAmA*
Hancock, Augusta *ChPo S1, ChPo S2*
Hancock, B J *ChPo S1*
Hancock, Blith *Alli*
Hancock, Charles *Alli Sup*
Hancock, Charles 1819-1868 *ChPo*
Hancock, Dorothy *BlkAW*
Hancock, E *Alli Sup*
Hancock, E Campbell *Alli Sup*
Hancock, Edward L 1930- *ConAu 45*
Hancock, Edward Lee 1873-1911 *DcNAA*
Hancock, Elizabeth Hazlewood 1871-1915
 BiDSA, DcNAA
Hancock, Frances *WhWNAA*
Hancock, H J B *Alli Sup*
Hancock, Harold B 1913- *ConAu 53*
Hancock, Harrie Irving 1868-1922 *DcNAA*
Hancock, Harris 1867-1944 *DcNAA*

Hancock, Henry d1880 *Alli Sup*
Hancock, Sir Henry James Burford- 1839-
 Alli Sup
Hancock, J Webster *BbtC*
Hancock, John *Alli, BiDLA*
Hancock, John d1744 *Alli*
Hancock, John 1670-1752 *Alli*
Hancock, John 1737-1793 *Alli, REn, REnAL*
Hancock, John 1825-1891 *OhA&B*
Hancock, John Coulter 1929- *IndAu 1917*
Hancock, John Webster *Alli Sup*
Hancock, Joseph Lane 1864-1922 *DcNAA*
Hancock, K 1935- *Au&Wr*
Hancock, Keith *ConAu XR*
Hancock, Mrs. LaTouche *Alli Sup*
Hancock, Leslie 1941- *ConAu 23*
Hancock, M Donald 1939- *ConAu 33*
Hancock, Malcolm 1936- *ConAu 25*
Hancock, Mary A 1923- *ConAu 37*
Hancock, Maxine 1942- *ConAu 61*
Hancock, Natalie Morris *ChPo S1*
Hancock, Norman 1894- *Au&Wr*
Hancock, Ralph Lowell 1903- *AmA&B,*
 Au&Wr, ConAu P-1, IndAu 1917
Hancock, Robert *Alli*
Hancock, S J *Alli Sup, BiDSA*
Hancock, Sallie J *Alli Sup*
Hancock, Samuel Farwell 1836-1905 *DcNAA*
Hancock, Selina *Alli Sup*
Hancock, Sheila 1942- *ConAu 49*
Hancock, Sibyl 1940- *ConAu 49, SmATA 9*
Hancock, Thomas *Alli, Alli Sup*
Hancock, Thomas 1783-1849 *PoIre*
Hancock, Thomas 1786-1865 *Alli Sup*
Hancock, Vesta Wills 1898- *WhWNAA*
Hancock, W K 1898- *ConAu 5R*
Hancock, William *Alli, Alli Sup*
Hancock, William Neilson *Alli Sup*
Hand, Geoffrey Joseph Philip 1931- *ConAu 25,*
 WrD 1976
Hand, George H *Alli Sup*
Hand, Harold Curtis 1901- *AmA&B*
Hand, Jackson 1913- *ConAu 61*
Hand, Joan Carole 1943- *ConAu 57,*
 DrAF 1976, DrAP 1975
Hand, John 1845-1903 *PoIre*
Hand, John Raymond 1886-1967 *IndAu 1917*
Hand, Learned 1872-1961 *AmA&B*
Hand, Marie Cutshall 1902- *IndAu 1917*
Hand, Q R, Jr. 1937- *BlkAW*
Hand, Samuel *Alli Sup*
Hand, Thomas A 1915- *ConAu 13R*
Hand, Thomas J *Alli Sup*
Hand, Wayland D 1907- *ConAu 41*
Handasyd, Talbot Blayney *Alli*
Handcock, William *Alli Sup*
Handcock, William 1761-1839 *PoIre*
Handcock, William Day 1899- *Au&Wr*
Handcock, William Domville *Alli Sup*
Handcock, William J *Alli Sup*
Handel, George Frederic 1685-1759 *AtlBL,*
 NewC, REn
Handel, Gerald 1924- *ConAu 23*
Handel, Samuel 1913- *Au&Wr*
Handel-Mazzetti, Enrica Von 1871-1955
 CatA 1947, ClDMEuL, EncWL, ModGL,
 OxGer
Handelman, Howard 1943- *ConAu 57*
Handelsman, Judith Florence 1948- *ConAu 61*
Handerson, Henry Ebenezer 1837-1918 *DcNAA,*
 OhA&B
Handford, Michael Anthony 1944- *WrD 1976*
Handford, Thomas *ChPo S2*
Handford, Thomas W d1904 *Alli Sup,*
 DcNAA
Handforth, Thomas S 1897-1948 *AmA&B,*
 AuBYP, Cald 1938, IlBYP, IlCB 1945,
 IlCB 1956, JBA 1951
Handke, Peter 1942- *CasWL, ConLC 5,*
 CrCD, DrAF 1976, EncWL Sup,
 McGWD, ModGL, OxGer
Handl, Irene 1912- *WrD 1976*
Handl, Jakob 1550-1591 *OxGer*
Handler, Jerome S 1933- *ConAu 53*
Handler, Julian Harris 1922- *ConAu 21*
Handler, Milton 1903- *ConAu 61*
Handler, Philip 1917- *ConAu 33*
Handley, Eric Walter 1926- *WrD 1976*

Handley, Graham Roderick 1926- *Au&Wr,*
WrD 1976
Handley, J E *Alli Sup*
Handley, James *Alli*
Handley-Taylor, Geoffrey 1920- *Au&Wr,*
ChPo S1, ConAu 5R, WrD 1976
Handlin, Mary 1913- *ConAu 33*
Handlin, Oscar 1915- *AmA&B, Au&Wr,*
ConAu 1R, OxAm, REnAL, TwCA Sup,
WrD 1976
Handlin, William Wallace 1830- *Alli Sup,*
BiDSA, DcNAA
Handman, Lou 1894-1956 *AmSCAP 66*
Handover, P M 1923-1974 *ConAu 9R,*
ConAu 53
Hands, Arthur *Alli Sup*
Hands, Elizabeth *Alli, BiDLA*
Hands, Joseph *Alli Sup*
Hands, Lydia *Alli Sup*
Hands, Thomas *Alli Sup*
Hands, William *Alli, BiDLA*
Hands, William John 1825-1913 *ChPo S1*
Handschin, Charles Hart 1873- *AmLY*
Handscombe, Richard 1935- *ConAu 37*
Handy, A H *ChPo S2*
Handy, Alexander Hamilton 1809-1883 *BiDSA*
Handy, Isaac William Kerr 1815-1878 *Alli Sup,*
DcNAA
Handy, J H *Alli Sup*
Handy, R D *Alli Sup*
Handy, Robert T 1918- *ConAu 5R*
Handy, Rollo 1927- *ConAu 9R, WrD 1976*
Handy, Washington R 1812- *Alli*
Handy, William Christopher 1873-1958
AmA&B, AmSCAP 66, OxAm, REnAL
Handy, William Henry 1843-1929 *OhA&B*
Handy, William J 1918- *ConAu 45*
Handyside, F D *Alli Sup*
Handyside, Henry *Alli Sup*
Handyside, Mrs. L *Alli Sup*
Haner, F T 1929- *ConAu 53*
Hanerfield, Thomas *Alli*
Hanes, Edward L 1871-1941 *DcNAA*
Hanes, Elizabeth Sill *ConAu 1R*
Hanes, Frank Borden 1920- *AmA&B,*
ConAu 1R, WrD 1976
Hanes, John L *Alli Sup*
Hanes, Leigh Buckner 1893- *AmA&B,*
AnMV 1926
Hanes, Leigh Buckner 1894- *ChPo, ChPo S1*
Haney, David 1938- *ConAu 57*
Haney, James Parton 1869-1923 *DcNAA*
Haney, John B 1931- *ConAu 29*
Haney, John Louis 1877- *WhWNAA*
Haney, Lewis Henry 1882- *WhWNAA*
Haney, Lynn 1941- *ConAu 49*
Haney, Ray 1921- *AmSCAP 66*
Haney, Thomas K 1936- *ConAu 13R*
Haney, Thomas R *ConAu 45*
Haney, William Valentine Patrick 1925-
ConAu 17R, WrD 1976
Hanff, Helene *ConAu 5R*
Hanford, Ben 1861-1910 *OhA&B*
Hanford, C J *Alli*
Hanford, Charles J *ChPo S1*
Hanford, Cornelius Holgate 1849-1926 *DcNAA*
Hanford, Helen Margaret Ellwanger 1882-1944
DcNAA, OhA&B, WhWNAA
Hanford, James Holly 1882-1969 *AmA&B,*
OhA&B, REnAL
Hanford, Lloyd D 1901- *ConAu 13R*
Hangen, Putnam Welles 1930- *AmA&B*
Hangen, Welles 1930- *ConAu 9R*
Hanger, Charles Henry *Alli Sup*
Hanger, George *Alli, BiDLA, BiDLA Sup*
Hanger, John Howard 1907-1965 *IndAu 1917*
Hanger, John Warren 1877-1973 *IndAu 1917*
Hanger, Philip *Alli*
Hangford, George Washington *ChPo*
Hanh, Nhat *ConP 1970*
Hanham, Frederick *Alli Sup*
Hanhart, M And N *Alli*
Hanhart, Nicholas *Alli Sup*
Hanifan, Lyda Judson 1879-1932 *DcNAA,*
WhWNAA
Hanifi, M Jamil 1935- *ConAu 61*
Hanighen, Bernard D *AmSCAP 66*
Haning, Bob *ConAu XR*

Haning, James R 1928- *ConAu 45*
Hanitsch, Karl Richard 1860- *WhLA*
Hanka, Vaclav 1791-1861 *CasWL, Pen Eur*
Hanke, Howard August 1911- *ConAu 1R*
Hanke, Lewis Ulysses 1905- *AmA&B*
Hanken, Edward *BiDLA Sup*
Hankey, Miss *Alli Sup*
Hankey, Arabella Katherine 1834-1911 *ChPo*
Hankey, Cyril Patrick 1886- *ConAu 1R*
Hankey, Donald 1884-1916 *LongC*
Hankey, Muriel W Arnold 1895- *BiDPar*
Hankey, Rosalie A *ConAu XR*
Hankey, Thomson *Alli Sup*
Hankey, William Lee 1869- *ChPo S2,*
IICB 1945
Hankin, Christiana C *Alli*
Hankin, E Hanbury 1865- *WhLA*
Hankin, Edward *Alli, BiDLA*
Hankin, St. John Emile Clavering 1869-1909
ChPo S1, CnMD, CnThe, McGWD,
ModWD, NewC, REnWD
Hankins, Arthur Preston 1880-1932 *DcNAA,*
WhWNAA
Hankins, Clabe *ConAu XR*
Hankins, Frank Hamilton 1877- *OhA&B,*
WhWNAA
Hankins, John Erskine 1905- *AmA&B,*
ConAu 49
Hankins, Marie Louise *EarAB Sup*
Hankins, Maude McGehee *ChPo*
Hankins, Norman E 1935- *ConAu 61*
Hankins, Paula *BlkAW*
Hankinson, Charles James 1866- *MnBBF,*
WhLA
Hankinson, Cyril Francis James 1895- *Au&Wr,*
ConAu P-1
Hankinson, Thomas Edwards *Alli, ChPo*
Hanks, Charles Stedman 1856-1908 *DcNAA*
Hanks, Henry *Alli Sup*
Hanks, Jervis F 1799- *EarAB*
Hanks, Lucien M 1910- *ConAu 37*
Hanks, Stedman W *Alli Sup*
Hanle, Dorothea Zack 1917- *ConAu 13R*
Hanley, Boniface Francis 1924- *ConAu 9R*
Hanley, Clifford 1922- *Au&Wr, ConAu 9R,*
ConNov 1972, ConNov 1976, WrD 1976
Hanley, Evelyn A *ConAu 41*
Hanley, Georgia Eldredge 1882- *WhWNAA*
Hanley, Gerald Anthony 1916- *Au&Wr,*
ConAu 1R, ConNov 1972, ConNov 1976,
LongC, TwCA Sup, TwCW
Hanley, Hope Anthony 1926- *ConAu 9R*
Hanley, Hugh 1902- *OhA&B, WhWNAA*
Hanley, Isabella *Alli Sup*
Hanley, James 1901- *Au&Wr, CnMD Sup,*
ConDr, ConLC 3, ConLC 5,
ConNov 1972, ConNov 1976, DcLEnL,
EvLB, LongC, ModBL, ModBL Sup,
NewC, Pen Eng, REn, TwCA,
TwCA Sup, TwCW, WhTwL, WrD 1976
Hanley, James Frederick 1892-1942
AmSCAP 66
Hanley, Katharine Rose 1932- *ConAu 37*
Hanley, Mary K *ChPo*
Hanley, P *Alli*
Hanley, Peter *Alli Sup*
Hanley, Sylvanus *Alli, Alli Sup*
Hanley, Theodore Dean 1915- *ConAu 5R*
Hanley, Thomas O'Brien 1918- *ConAu 1R*
Hanley, William 1931- *CnMD Sup,*
ConAu 41, ConDr, CrCD, DrAF 1976,
ModWD, WrD 1976
Hanlo, Jan Bernardus Maria Rafael 1912-1969
CasWL
Hanlon, Bert *AmSCAP 66*
Hanlon, John *Alli Sup*
Hanlon, John 1897- *WhWNAA*
Hanlon, John J 1912- *ConAu 57*
Hanly, James F 1863-1920 *DcNAA,*
IndAu 1816
Hanman, Bernard Leslie George 1913- *Au&Wr*
Hanmer, Anthony John *Alli Sup*
Hanmer, J W *Alli*
Hanmer, Sir John *Alli*
Hanmer, Jonathan d1687 *Alli*
Hanmer, Meredith 1543-1604 *Alli, DcEnL*
Hanmer, Sir Thomas 1676?-1746 *Alli*
Hann, James 1799-1856 *Alli Sup*

Hann, William *Alli Sup*
Hanna, Alfred Jackson 1893- *ConAu 45*
Hanna, Charles Augustus 1863-1950 *AmLY,*
OhA&B
Hanna, David 1917- *ConAu 57*
Hanna, David Blythe 1858-1938 *DcNAA*
Hanna, Edward Judson *ChPo*
Hanna, Elizabeth H *BiDSA*
Hanna, Geneva R *AuBYP*
Hanna, Guy Carleton 1879- *IndAu 1816*
Hanna, J Marshall *Alli Sup*
Hanna, J Marshall 1907- *ConAu 1R*
Hanna, John Paul 1932- *ConAu 45*
Hanna, Lavone Agnes 1896- *ConAu 13R,*
WrD 1976
Hanna, Marcus Alonzo 1837-1904 *OhA&B,*
OxAm
Hanna, Mark 1837-1904 *REnAL*
Hanna, Mary Carr 1905- *ConAu 45*
Hanna, Matthew Elting 1873-1936 *DcNAA*
Hanna, Paul R 1902- *ConAu 45, SmATA 9*
Hanna, Phil Townsend 1896- *WhWNAA*
Hanna, R Philip 1910-1957 *AmSCAP 66*
Hanna, Robert Edward 1887- *WhWNAA*
Hanna, Sarah R *Alli Sup*
Hanna, Thomas 1928- *ConAu 1R*
Hanna, Tom *DrAP 1975*
Hanna, W H *ChPo S1*
Hanna, Willard A 1911- *OhA&B*
Hanna, William 1808-1882 *Alli, Alli Sup,*
DcEnL, EvLB
Hanna, William John 1931- *ConAu 61*
Hannaford, Ebenezer 1840-1905 *Alli Sup,*
OhA&B
Hannaford, John 1918- *ConAu 45*
Hannaford, Samuel *Alli Sup*
Hannah, Annie L *ChPo, ChPo S1*
Hannah, Barry *DrAF 1976*
Hannah, Harvey L 1913- *IndAu 1917*
Hannah, Ian Campbell 1874-1944 *OhA&B,*
WhWNAA
Hannah, John *Alli Sup*
Hannah, John 1792-1867 *Alli Sup*
Hannah, John 1818-1888 *Alli Sup, DcEnL*
Hannah, Mary *Alli Sup*
Hannak, Johann Jacques 1892- *ConAu P-1*
Hannam, Charles Lewis 1925- *ConAu 61,*
WrD 1976
Hannam, Hattie Lloyd *ChPo*
Hannam, John *Alli*
Hannam, Richard *Alli*
Hannam, Thomas *Alli, BiDLA*
Hannan, Charles *Alli Sup*
Hannan, Edward James 1921- *WrD 1976*
Hannan, Frederick Watson 1866-1929 *DcNAA*
Hannan, Joseph F 1923- *ConAu 9R*
Hannan, Josephine *Alli Sup*
Hannau, Hans W 1904- *ConAu 23*
Hannaway, Patricia H 1929- *ConAu 61*
Hannaway, Patti 1929- *ConAu XR*
Hannay, Alexander *Alli Sup*
Hannay, Charles James Jenkins 1835- *Alli Sup*
Hannay, David *Alli, Alli Sup*
Hannay, George K *Alli*
Hannay, James *Chmbr 3*
Hannay, James 1827-1873 *Alli, Alli Sup,*
BiD&SB, BrAu 19, CasWL, DcEnL,
DcLEnL, EvLB, NewC
Hannay, James Henry 1842-1910 *Alli Sup,*
DcLEnL, DcNAA, OxCan
Hannay, James Owen 1865-1950 *DcRusL,*
EvLB, LongC, NewC, TwCA,
TwCA Sup, WhLA
Hannay, Patrick d1629? *Alli, BrAu, CasWL,*
DcLEnL
Hannay, Peter *Alli Sup*
Hannay, R *Alli*
Hannay, Robert *Alli*
Hannay, Robert d1894 *PoIre*
Hannay, Robert Cutlar Fergusson *Alli Sup*
Hanneman, Audre 1926- *ConAu 23*
Hannes, Edward *Alli*
Hannes, William *Alli*
Hannett, Edward *Alli*
Hanney, Peter 1930- *WrD 1976*
Hannibal, 247BC-183BC *REn*
Hannibal, Edward L 1936- *ConAu 29,*
DrAF 1976, WrD 1976

Harben, William Nathaniel 1858-1919 *AmA&B, AmLY, BiD&SB, BiDSA, DcAmA, DcBiA, DcNAA, OxAm, REnAL*

Harberger, Arnold C 1924- *ConAu 13R, WrD 1976*

Harbert, Earl N 1934- *ConAu 33*

Harbert, Elizabeth Morrisson Boynton 1845-1925 *DcNAA, IndAu 1816*

Harbert, James K 1930- *AmSCAP 66*

Harbert, Lizzie B *Alli Sup*

Harbert, Mary Ann 1945- *ConAu 61*

Harbert, Sir William *Alli*

Harberton, Viscount 1867- *WhLA*

Harbeson, Gladys Evans 1899- *ConAu 21, WrD 1976*

Harbeson, John Frederick 1888- *WhWNAA*

Harbeson, John Willis 1938- *ConAu 57*

Harbin, Calvin E 1916- *ConAu 23*

Harbin, George *Alli*

Harbin, Robert 1909- *Au&Wr*

Harbin, Thomas *Alli*

Harbinson, A Marshall 1896- *WhWNAA*

Harbinson, Robert *ConAu XR, WrD 1976*

Harbinson, W A 1941- *ConAu 61*

Harbison, E Harris 1907-1964 *AmA&B*

Harbison, J S *Alli Sup*

Harbison, Winfred Audif 1904- *IndAu 1917*

Harbord, James Guthrie 1866-1947 *DcNAA*

Harbord, John Bradley *Alli Sup*

Harbottle, Michael Neale 1917- *ConAu 29, WrD 1976*

Harbour, Jefferson Lee 1857-1931 *AmA&B, DcNAA*

Harbron, John Davison 1924- *Au&Wr, ConAu 9R, OxCan Sup*

Harburg, E Y 1898- *AmSCAP 66, ConDr*

Harbury, Colin Desmond 1922- *WrD 1976*

Harby, Isaac 1788-1828 *Alli, AmA&B, BiD&SB, BiDSA, CyAL 1, DcAmA, DcNAA*

Harby, Mrs. Lee 1859- *DcAmA*

Harby, Lee Cohen 1849- *BiDSA*

Harby, Thomas *Alli*

Harcave, Sidney S 1916- *ConAu 17R*

Harchar, Harry A 1912- *AmA&B*

Harcleroad, Fred F 1918- *ConAu 17R*

Harcourt, Alfred 1881-1954 *AmA&B*

Harcourt, Alfred Frederick Pollock *Alli Sup*

Harcourt, Augustus George Vernon 1834- *Alli Sup*

Harcourt, Bateman *Alli Sup*

Harcourt, C G Vernon *Alli Sup*

Harcourt, Edward Vernon *Alli Sup*

Harcourt, Edward William 1825- *Alli Sup*

Harcourt, Frederick C V *PoIre*

Harcourt, Geoffrey Colin 1931- *ConAu 25, WrD 1976*

Harcourt, George *MnBBF*

Harcourt, Helen *Alli Sup, DcNAA*

Harcourt, Henry 1873- *WhLA*

Harcourt, Mrs. J *Alli Sup*

Harcourt, James *Alli*

Harcourt, Leveson Francis Vernon- *Alli Sup*

Harcourt, Leveson Vernon 1788-1860 *Alli, Alli Sup*

Harcourt, Melville 1909- *ConAu 5R*

Harcourt, Palma *WrD 1976*

Harcourt, R *Alli Sup*

Harcourt, Richard 1840-1911 *DcNAA*

Harcourt, Robert *Alli*

Harcourt, Sir William George Granville 1827- *Alli Sup*

Harcourt, William Vernon- 1789-1871 *Alli Sup*

Harcourt-Reilly, Sir Henry *REn*

Harcus, William *Alli Sup*

Hard, Frederick 1897- *ConAu 25*

Hard, Margaret 1888?-1974 *ConAu 49*

Hard, Walter Rice 1882-1966 *AmA&B, ChPo S1, REnAL, WhWNAA*

Hard, William 1878- *AmLY*

Hard Pan *DcNAA*

Hardacre, Benjamin *Alli Sup, ChPo S2*

Hardaker, Joseph *ChPo S1*

Hardallo 1860?-1919 *AfA 1*

Hardaway, William Augustus 1850-1923 *Alli Sup, DcNAA*

Hardayal, Lala 1884-1939 *DcLEnL*

Hardcastle, Charlotte *Alli Sup*

Hardcastle, David, Jr. *Alli*

Hardcastle, George *Alli Sup*

Hardcastle, Henry 1841- *Alli Sup*

Hardcastle, Mark *Alli Sup*

Hardcastle, Michael 1933- *ConAu 25, WrD 1976*

Hardcastle, Thomas *Alli*

Hardcastle, William *Alli*

Hardeby, Geoffrey d1360 *Alli*

Hardecanute 1019?-1042 *NewC*

Hardee, William Joseph 1815-1873 *Alli Sup, BiDSA, DcAmA, DcNAA*

Hardekopf, Ferdinand 1876-1954 *OxGer*

Hardeman, Beaureguard, Jr. 1944- *BlkAW*

Hardeman, J J *Alli Sup*

Harden, Donald B 1901- *ConAu 5R, WrD 1976*

Harden, Edward Jenkins 1813-1873 *BiDSA, DcNAA*

Harden, John William *Alli Sup*

Harden, Maximilian 1861-1927 *OxGer*

Harden, Oleta Elizabeth 1935- *ConAu 37, WrD 1976*

Harden, Ralph William *Alli Sup*

Harden, Samuel 1831- *IndAu 1816*

Harden, William 1844-1936 *AmA&B, BiDSA, DcNAA*

Harden, William Dearing 1837- *BiDSA*

Hardenberg, Baron Friedrich Leopold Von 1772-1801 *BiD&SB, DcEuL, EuA, EvEuW, OxEng, OxGer, REn*

Hardenberg, Karl August, Furst Von 1750-1822 *OxGer*

Hardenbergh, Jacobus R d1792 *CyAL 1*

Hardenbrook, Ellie Lee *LivFWS*

Hardendorff, Jeanne B *ChPo S2*

Hardenstein, Ernest *Alli Sup*

Harder, Eleanor 1925- *ConAu 37*

Harder, Geraldine Gross 1926- *ConAu 53*

Harder, Oscar Edward 1883- *WhWNAA*

Hardess, George M *Alli Sup*

Hardesty, Irving 1866- *WhWNAA*

Hardesty, Nancy A 1941- *ConAu 57*

Hardgrave, Robert L, Jr. 1939- *ConAu 25*

Hardicanute 1019?-1042 *NewC*

Hardie, Alexander 1841-1936 *BbtC, DcNAA*

Hardie, Charles Dunn 1911- *Au&Wr, WrD 1976*

Hardie, David *Alli, BiDLA*

Hardie, Frank 1911- *Au&Wr, ConAu 33, WrD 1976*

Hardie, James *Alli Sup*

Hardie, James 1750?-1832 *DcAmA, DcNAA*

Hardie, Martin *ChPo S2*

Hardie, Norman David 1924- *WrD 1976*

Hardie, Thomas *Alli*

Hardie, W Auchterlonie 1897- *MnBBF*

Hardiman, J *Alli*

Hardiman, James W 1919- *ConAu 33*

Hardin, Charles M 1908- *ConAu 49*

Hardin, Charlotte Prentiss 1882- *BiDSA*

Hardin, Clement *AmA&B, ConAu XR*

Hardin, Clifford Morris 1915- *IndAu 1917, WrD 1976*

Hardin, Garrett James 1915- *ConAu 17R*

Hardin, George Anson 1832-1900 *DcNAA*

Hardin, Herschel *OxCan Sup*

Hardin, Martin D 1780-1823 *Alli, BiDSA*

Hardin, Mitch *ConAu XR*

Hardin, Paul, III 1931- *ConAu 25*

Hardin, Peter *ConAu XR*

Hardin, Richard F 1937- *ConAu 45*

Hardin, Tom *ConAu XR*

Hardin, Wes *ConAu XR*

Hardin, Willett Lepley 1868- *OhA&B, WhWNAA*

Harding *Alli*

Harding, A *Alli*

Harding, A E *ChPo S1*

Harding, Alfred 1892- *AmA&B*

Harding, Alice d1938 *DcNAA*

Harding, Arthur McCracken 1884-1947 *DcNAA, WhWNAA*

Harding, Arthur Robert 1871-1930 *OhA&B*

Harding, Austin *WhLA*

Harding, Barbara 1926- *ConAu 41*

Harding, Benjamin Fosdick 1857-1923 *DcNAA*

Harding, Bertita 1902- *ConAu 5R*

Harding, Bertita 1907- *AmA&B, TwCA, TwCA Sup*

Harding, C T *ChPo, ChPo S1*

Harding, Carl B *ConAu XR*

Harding, Caroline Hirst Brown *IndAu 1816*

Harding, Charles *Alli Sup*

Harding, Charlotte 1873- *IlCB 1945*

Harding, Chester 1792-1866 *Alli Sup, OxAm*

Harding, Chester 1843- *DcAmA*

Harding, Claud *Alli Sup*

Harding, D W 1906- *ConAu P-1*

Harding, D W 1940- *ConAu 41*

Harding, Donald Edward 1916- *ConAu 53*

Harding, E Hurren *Alli Sup*

Harding, Edward 1849- *PoIre*

Harding, Mrs. Edward *DcNAA*

Harding, Edward John 1851- *Alli Sup*

Harding, Edwin B 1887- *WhWNAA*

Harding, Emily Grace *Alli Sup*

Harding, Emily J *ChPo, ChPo S1, ChPo S2*

Harding, Esther A *ChPo*

Harding, F E *Alli Sup*

Harding, Florence *Alli Sup*

Harding, Gardner Ludwig 1887-1940 *DcNAA*

Harding, George *WrD 1976*

Harding, George Canady 1829-1881 *IndAu 1816*

Harding, George L *ChPo S2*

Harding, George Laban 1893- *IndAu 1917*

Harding, George Rogers 1840- *Alli Sup*

Harding, H A 1871- *WhWNAA*

Harding, H Rowland *Alli Sup*

Harding, Harold F 1903- *ConAu 37*

Harding, Helen J *ChPo S2*

Harding, J D 1797- *Alli, Alli Sup*

Harding, J W *Alli, BiDLA, BkIE*

Harding, Jack 1914- *ConAu 29, IndAu 1917*

Harding, James 1929- *Au&Wr, ConAu 33, WrD 1976*

Harding, Jesper 1799-1865 *AmA&B*

Harding, John *Alli, Alli Sup*

Harding, John 1378-1465 *Alli, DcEnL*

Harding, John 1805-1874 *Alli Sup*

Harding, John Duffield 1798-1863 *ChPo*

Harding, John George *Alli Sup*

Harding, John Milburn 1873-1934 *OhA&B*

Harding, John William 1864- *AmA&B, AmLY, WhWNAA*

Harding, Joseph Anthony 1924- *Au&Wr*

Harding, Katharine Washburn *WhWNAA*

Harding, Lewis Albert 1880-1944 *IndAu 1816*

Harding, Margaret Snodgrass 1885- *WhWNAA*

Harding, Matthew Whiteman *WrD 1976*

Harding, Nathaniel *Alli*

Harding, R Winbolt *ChPo S2*

Harding, Richard William 1939- *Au&Wr*

Harding, Robert *ChPo S1*

Harding, Ruth Guthrie 1882- *AnMV 1926, ChPo, ChPo S1*

Harding, S And E *Alli*

Harding, S Graham *MnBBF*

Harding, Samuel *Alli*

Harding, Samuel Bannister 1866-1927 *DcNAA, IndAu 1816*

Harding, Stanley *Alli Sup*

Harding, Sylvester 1745-1809 *BkIE*

Harding, Thomas *Alli, Alli Sup*

Harding, Thomas 1512-1572 *Alli, DcEnL*

Harding, Thomas G 1937- *ConAu 21*

Harding, Vincent 1931- *BlkAW, LivBA*

Harding, Virginia Hamlet 1909- *ConAu 45*

Harding, W M *Alli Sup*

Harding, Wallace J *Alli Sup*

Harding, Walter Roy 1917- *ChPo S1, ConAu 1R, WrD 1976*

Harding, Warren Gamaliel 1865-1923 *AmA&B, DcNAA, OhA&B, OxAm, REn, REnAL*

Harding, Warren Gamaliel, II 1905- *OhA&B*

Harding, William 1792-1886 *Alli Sup*

Harding, William E *Alli Sup*

Harding, William Procter Gould 1864-1930 *DcNAA, WhWNAA*

Hardinge, B *Alli Sup*

Hardinge, Belle Boyd *Alli Sup, BiD&SB, BiDSA*

Hardinge, C S *Alli*

Hardinge, E M *DcAmA, DcNAA*

Hardinge, Emma *Alli Sup*
Hardinge, George *BiDLA, BiDLA Sup, LongC*
Hardinge, George 1744-1816 *Alli, DcEnL*
Hardinge, H *Alli Sup*
Hardinge, Helen 1901- *ConAu 29, WrD 1976*
Hardinge, Nicholas 1700-1758 *Alli, DcEnL*
Hardinge, Rex 1904- *MnBBF*
Hardinge, W M *ChPo*
Hardinge, William Henry *Alli Sup*
Hardinge, William Money *Alli Sup*
Hardingham, George Gatton Melhuish *Alli Sup*
Hardingham, John Frederick Watson 1916- *Au&Wr, ConAu P-1, WrD 1976*
Hardison, Osborne B 1928- *ConAu 5R, WrD 1976*
Hardisway, Peter *Alli*
Hardman, David Rennie *WrD 1976*
Hardman, Ed *Alli*
Hardman, F *Alli*
Hardman, Frederick 1793-1864 *DcNAA*
Hardman, Frederick 1814-1874 *Alli Sup*
Hardman, John 1944- *ConAu 45*
Hardman, Joseph William *Alli Sup*
Hardman, Richards Lynden 1924- *ConAu 13R*
Hardman, William *Alli Sup*
Hardnett, Linda G *BlkAW*
Hardon, John Anthony 1914- *ConAu 1R, WrD 1976*
Hardouin, Jean 1646-1729 *DcEuL, REn*
Hardoy, Jorge Enrique 1926- *ConAu 33*
Hardress, Sir Thomas *Alli*
Hardt, Ernst 1876-1947 *ClDMEuL, McGWD, ModWD, OxGer*
Hardt, J Pearce 1922- *ConAu 5R*
Harduyn, Justus De 1582-1636 *CasWL*
Hardwich, Sara M *Alli Sup*
Hardwich, Thomas Frederick *Alli Sup*
Hardwick, Adam *ConAu XR*
Hardwick, Archer 1918- *AmSCAP 66*
Hardwick, Benjamin *Alli Sup*
Hardwick, Charles 1817-1889 *Alli Sup*
Hardwick, Charles 1821-1859 *Alli, Alli Sup*
Hardwick, Clyde T 1915- *ConAu 5R*
Hardwick, Elizabeth 1916- *AmA&B, ConAu 5R, WorAu, WrD 1976*
Hardwick, Homer *ConAu 41*
Hardwick, Humphrey *Alli*
Hardwick, Mary Elizabeth 1925- *Au&Wr*
Hardwick, Michael 1924- *Au&Wr, ConAu 49, WrD 1976*
Hardwick, Mollie *Au&Wr, ConAu 49, WrD 1976*
Hardwick, Richard Holmes, Jr. 1923- *ConAu 5R, WrD 1976*
Hardwick, Sylvia *ConAu XR*
Hardwick, William *Alli*
Hardwicke, Earls Of *Alli*
Hardwicke, Major-General, And Mr. Gray *Alli*
Hardwicke, Sir Cedric 1893-1964 *LongC, NewC*
Hardwicke, Henry 1861-1909 *DcNAA*
Hardwicke, Herbert Junius *Alli Sup*
Hardwicke, Josephine 1888- *WhWNAA*
Hardwicke, Philip Yorke, Earl Of 1720-1790 *DcEnL, NewC*
Hardwicke, Rita *TexWr*
Hardwicke, William *Alli Sup*
Hardy *Alli*
Hardy, Lieutenant *Alli*
Hardy, Miss *Alli*
Hardy, Mrs. *Alli Sup*
Hardy, A S *MnBBF*
Hardy, Adam *WrD 1976*
Hardy, Albert H *ChPo S1, ChPo S2*
Hardy, Alexander G 1920-1973 *ConAu 45*
Hardy, Alexandre 1570?-1632 *BiD&SB, CasWL, DcEuL, EuA, McGWD, OxFr, Pen Eur, REn*
Hardy, Alice Dale *ConAu 19, SmATA 1*
Hardy, Sir Alister Clavering 1896- *BiDPar*
Hardy, Arthur L *BiDSA*
Hardy, Arthur Sherburne 1847-1930 *Alli Sup, AmA&B, BbD, BiD&SB, DcAmA, DcBiA, DcLEnL, DcNAA, EncM&D, OxAm, REnAL, TwCA, WhWNAA*
Hardy, Arthur Steffens *MnBBF*
Hardy, Bobbie *WrD 1976*

Hardy, C Colburn 1910- *ConAu 53*
Hardy, Campbell C 1831-1919 *Alli Sup, BbtC, OxCan*
Hardy, Charles F *ChPo, ChPo S1*
Hardy, Charles Oscar 1884-1940 *DcNAA*
Hardy, Chester Ernest 1882- *WhWNAA*
Hardy, D, Jr. *ChPo S1*
Hardy, David 1829-1857 *BiDSA*
Hardy, David A 1936- *ConAu 61, SmATA 9*
Hardy, Douglas *ConAu XR*
Hardy, Dudley 1867-1922 *ChPo*
Hardy, E A *OxCan*
Hardy, E H *ChPo S1*
Hardy, E S *MnBBF*
Hardy, E Stuart *ChPo S1*
Hardy, Edmund Armitage *Alli Sup*
Hardy, Edward John *Alli Sup*
Hardy, Edward R 1908- *ConAu P-1*
Hardy, Edwin Noah 1861- *WhWNAA*
Hardy, Elizabeth 1794-1854 *Alli Sup*
Hardy, Emma 1840-1912 *ChPo S2*
Hardy, Eric *ConAu 61*
Hardy, Ernest George And Mann, J S *Alli Sup*
Hardy, Evan A 1890- *WhWNAA*
Hardy, Evelyn 1902- *Au&Wr, ConAu 23*
Hardy, Francis *Alli*
Hardy, Frank 1917- *TwCW, WebEAL*
Hardy, Frederic *Alli Sup*
Hardy, George 1904- *TexWr*
Hardy, H H *Alli*
Hardy, Henry *Alli, BiDLA*
Hardy, Henry Harrison 1882- *WhLA*
Hardy, Henry Reginald 1903- *WhWNAA*
Hardy, Horatio Charles *Alli, BiDLA*
Hardy, Horatio Nelson *Alli Sup*
Hardy, Iza Duffus *Alli Sup, BiD&SB*
Hardy, J *Alli*
Hardy, J P 1933- *ConAu 25*
Hardy, Jack 1909- *Au&Wr*
Hardy, James *Alli*
Hardy, Janet *Alli Sup*
Hardy, John *Alli, BiDSA*
Hardy, John Edward 1922- *AmA&B, ConAu 13R*
Hardy, John Philips 1933- *WrD 1976*
Hardy, John Stockdale *Alli*
Hardy, Joseph *Alli*
Hardy, Julia Dyer *ChPo S2*
Hardy, L R *ChPo*
Hardy, Leroy C 1927- *ConAu 29*
Hardy, Marjorie 1888-1948 *DcNAA*
Hardy, Marjorie Enid 1913- *Au&Wr, WrD 1976*
Hardy, Lady Mary *Alli Sup*
Hardy, Mary Earle 1846-1928 *AmLY, ChPo, DcNAA, WhWNAA*
Hardy, Michael 1933- *ConAu 25*
Hardy, Nathaniel 1618-1670 *Alli*
Hardy, Paul *ChPo, ChPo S1, ChPo S2*
Hardy, Philip *MnBBF*
Hardy, Philip Dixon 1794?-1875 *Alli, Alli Sup, BiDLA Sup, PoIre*
Hardy, Rene 1911- *REn*
Hardy, Richard Earl 1938- *ConAu 37, WrD 1976*
Hardy, Robert *Alli*
Hardy, Robert 1917- *WrD 1976*
Hardy, Robert Spence 1803-1868 *Alli, Alli Sup*
Hardy, Robert William Hale *Alli, Alli Sup*
Hardy, Robina F *Alli Sup, ChPo*
Hardy, Ronald Harold 1919- *Au&Wr, ConAu 5R*
Hardy, Samuel 1720-1793 *Alli*
Hardy, Mrs. Samuel *Alli Sup*
Hardy, Stuart 1901- *ConAu XR*
Hardy, Thomas *Alli*
Hardy, Thomas 1840-1928 *Alli Sup, AnCL, AtlBL, BbD, BiD&SB, BrAu 19, CasWL, ChPo, ChPo S1, ChPo S2, Chmbr 3, CnE&AP, CnMWL, CriT 3, CyWA, DcBiA, DcEnA, DcEnA Ap, DcEnL, DcEuL, DcLEnL, EncWL, EvLB, LongC, ModBL, ModBL Sup, ModWD, NewC, OxEng, Pen Eng, RAdv 1, RCom, REn, TwCW, WebEAL, WhCL, WhLA, WhTwL*
Hardy, Sir Thomas Duffus 1804-1878 *Alli, Alli Sup, DcEnL*

Hardy, W Auchterlonie *Alli Sup*
Hardy, William *Alli, Alli Sup*
Hardy, Sir William 1807-1887 *Alli Sup*
Hardy, William D 1913- *AmSCAP 66*
Hardy, William George 1895- *Au&Wr, ConAu 5R, WrD 1976*
Hardy, William George 1896- *CanNov, CanWr, DcLEnL, OxCan, WhWNAA*
Hardy, William Marion 1922- *ConAu 1R*
Hardyck, Curtis D 1929- *ConAu 29*
Hardyng, John 1378-1465? *Alli, CasWL*
Hare, Mrs. *Alli*
Hare, A Paul 1923- *ConAu 1R*
Hare, Amory 1885- *AmA&B, AnMV 1926, ChPo, ChPo S1*
Hare, Arley 1871- *WhWNAA*
Hare, Augustus And Julius *Chmbr 3*
Hare, Augustus John Cuthbert 1834-1903 *Alli, Alli Sup, BiD&SB, BrAu, CasWL, ChPo, DcEnA, DcEnA Ap, DcLEnL, EvLB, NewC*
Hare, Augustus William 1792-1834 *Alli, BiD&SB, DcEnA, DcEnL, DcEuL, EvLB*
Hare, C E 1893- *Br&AmS*
Hare, Cyril 1900-1958 *EncM&D, LongC*
Hare, David 1947- *CnThe, ConDr, WrD 1976*
Hare, Douglas Robert Adams 1929- *ConAu 45*
Hare, Edward Wesley *Alli*
Hare, Emily *Alli Sup, DcNAA*
Hare, Eric B 1894- *ConAu P-1*
Hare, F A C *Alli Sup*
Hare, F Kenneth 1919- *ConAu 37*
Hare, Francis 1688-1740 *Alli, DcEnL*
Hare, George Emlen 1808-1892 *DcAmA, DcNAA*
Hare, Henry *Alli*
Hare, Henry 1693-1749 *Alli*
Hare, Hobart Amory 1862-1931 *Alli Sup, DcAmA, DcNAA, WhWNAA*
Hare, Hugh *Alli*
Hare, Humphrey John 1909- *Au&Wr*
Hare, J I Clark And Wallace, Horace B *Alli*
Hare, James d1808 *Alli*
Hare, John *Alli*
Hare, John 1935- *ConAu 21, OxCan Sup, WrD 1976*
Hare, John Innes Clark 1816-1905 *DcAmA, DcNAA*
Hare, John Middleton *Alli Sup*
Hare, Julius Charles 1795-1855 *Alli, BiD&SB, BrAu 19, DcEnA, DcEnL, DcEuL, EvLB, NewC, OxEng*
Hare, Kenneth 1888- *ChPo S2, WhLA*
Hare, Maria d1870 *Alli Sup*
Hare, Martin *NewC*
Hare, Maud 1874-1936 *DcNAA*
Hare, Nathan 1934- *BlkAW, ConAu 41, LivBAA*
Hare, Peter H 1935- *ConAu 33*
Hare, Richard 1907-1966 *ConAu P-1*
Hare, Richard Mervyn 1919- *Au&Wr, ConAu 5R, WrD 1976*
Hare, Robert 1781-1858 *Alli, AmA&B, DcAmA, DcNAA, OxAm, REnAL*
Hare, Samuel *Alli*
Hare, T Truxton 1878-1956 *CarSB*
Hare, Thomas *Alli*
Hare, Thomas 1806- *Alli Sup*
Hare, Van Court, Jr. 1929- *ConAu 25*
Hare, W R *Alli Sup*
Hare, Walter Ben 1870-1950 *REnAL*
Hare, William Aldworth Home *Alli Sup*
Hare, William Hobart 1838-1909 *DcNAA*
Hare And Skinner *Alli*
Haren, Jonkheer Onno Zwier Van 1713-1779 *CasWL*
Haren, Jonkheer Willem Van 1710-1768 *CasWL*
Haren, Onno Zwier Van 1713-1779 *BiD&SB, DcEuL, EvEuW*
Haren, Willem Van 1710-1768 *BiD&SB, DcEuL*
Haresnape, Geoffrey Laurence 1939- *ConP 1970*
Hareven, Tamara K 1937- *ConAu 25*
Harewood, Earl Of 1923- *Au&Wr*
Harewood, Harry *Alli*
Harfield, Edmund *MnBBF*

Harflete, Henry *Alli*
Harford, Charles Joseph *Alli*
Harford, David K 1947- *ConAu 49*
Harford, Frederick Kill *Alli Sup*
Harford, John Battersby 1857- *WhLA*
Harford, John Scandrett 1785-1866 *Alli, Alli Sup*
Harford, Raph *Alli*
Hargadon, Michael 1888- *WhWNAA*
Hargens, Charles, Jr. *ConICB*
Harger, C M 1863- *HsB&A*
Harger, Lois *ChPo*
Harger, Oscar 1843-1887 *DcNAA*
Harger, Rolla Neil 1890- *IndAu 1917*
Harger, William Henderson 1936- *ConAu 57*
Hargis, Ed *ChPo*
Hargis, John Edwin 1914- *IlCB 1945*
Hargis, Robert Bell Smith 1818-1893 *Alli Sup, DcNAA*
Hargitt, Charles Wesley 1852-1927 *DcNAA, WhWNAA*
Hargrave, A *Alli*
Hargrave, Catherine Perry 1884-1953 *OhA&B*
Hargrave, Ely 1741- *Alli, BiDLA*
Hargrave, Francis 1741-1821 *Alli, BiDLA*
Hargrave, Frank Flavius 1878-1962 *IndAu 1917*
Hargrave, Hugh Dunbar 1854-1883 *ChPo S1*
Hargrave, J F *Alli*
Hargrave, James 1798-1865 *OxCan*
Hargrave, John 1894- *ChPo*
Hargrave, Joseph James 1841-1894 *DcNAA, OxCan*
Hargrave, Letitia 1813-1854 *OxCan*
Hargrave, O T 1936- *ConAu 33*
Hargrave, Richard 1803-1879 *IndAu 1917*
Hargrave, Rowena Hullett 1906- *ConAu 33, IndAu 1917*
Hargrave, Sidney *MnBBF*
Hargraves, Edmund Hammond *Alli*
Hargraves, James *Alli*
Hargray, Lorrence *BlkAW*
Hargreave, Charles James 1820-1866 *Alli Sup*
Hargreaves, Charles *Alli Sup*
Hargreaves, Elisabeth *Au&Wr*
Hargreaves, H *Alli Sup*
Hargreaves, Harry 1922- *ConAu 5R*
Hargreaves, James *Alli, BiDLA*
Hargreaves, John D 1924- *ConAu 9R*
Hargreaves, John George *Alli Sup*
Hargreaves, Mark Kippax *Alli Sup*
Hargreaves, Mary W M 1914- *ConAu 37*
Hargreaves, Peter Hickman 1927- *Au&Wr*
Hargreaves, Reginald Charles 1888- *Au&Wr, ConAu P-1*
Hargreaves, Robert *Alli*
Hargreaves, Robert Martin 1933- *Au&Wr*
Hargreaves, Thomas *Alli, Alli Sup*
Hargreaves, William *Alli Sup*
Hargreaves-Mawdsley, W Norman 1921- *ConAu 9R*
Hargrove, Barbara Watts 1924- *ConAu 33, WrD 1976*
Hargrove, Charles *Alli Sup*
Hargrove, Ely *Alli*
Hargrove, Erwin C 1930- *WrD 1976*
Hargrove, George *Alli, BiDLA*
Hargrove, Katharine T *ConAu 33*
Hargrove, Marion 1919- *AmA&B, REnAL, TwCA Sup*
Hargrove, Merwin Matthew 1910- *ConAu 9R, WrD 1976*
Hargrove, Robert Kenyon 1829- *DcAmA*
Hargrove, S H 1903- *AnMV 1926*
Hargrove, Tazewell L *Alli Sup*
Hargrove, W *Alli*
Hariaudh 1865-1941 *DcOrL 2*
Haribhadra *DcOrL 2*
Harik, Iliya F 1934- *ConAu 25*
Haring, Bernard 1912- *ConAu XR, WrD 1976*
Haring, Clarence Henry 1885-1960 *AmA&B, WhWNAA*
Haring, Douglas Gilbert 1894- *AmA&B*
Haring, Firth 1937- *ConAu 25*
Haring, Georg Wilhelm Heinrich 1797-1871 *DcEuL, EvEuW*
Haring, Joseph E 1931- *ConAu 33, WrD 1976*
Haring, Norris G 1923- *ConAu 1R*

Haring, Philip S 1915- *ConAu 37, WrD 1976*
Haring, Robert 1896- *AmSCAP 66*
Haring, Wilhelm *EuA*
Haringer, Jakob 1898-1948 *OxGer*
Harington SEE ALSO Harrington
Harington, Charles Sumner *Alli Sup*
Harington, Donald 1935- *ConAu 13R*
Harington, E C *Alli*
Harington, Henry 1727-1816 *Alli, BiDLA*
Harington, James 1611-1677 *BrAu, EvLB, NewC, OxEng*
Harington, John *Chmbr 1*
Harington, Sir John 1561-1612 *BiD&SB, BrAu, CasWL, Chmbr 1, CrE&SL, DcLEnL, EvLB, NewC, OxEng, Pen Eng, REn*
Harington, John ALSO Haryngton, John
Harington, John Herbert *Alli, BiDLA*
Harington, John R S *Alli Sup*
Harington, Joy Nora Pepys 1914- *Au&Wr, WrD 1976*
Harington, Sir Richard 1835- *Alli Sup*
Harington Zielinska, Brenda Stanley Ivy 1924- *Au&Wr*
Hariot, Thomas 1560-1621 *Alli, CnDAL, OxAm, REnAL*
Hariri, Al- 1054-1122 *CasWL*
Hariri, Abu Muhammad Al-Q B 'Ali Al- 1054-1122 *DcOrL 3*
Hariri, Abu Muhammad Al-Qasim Al- 1054-1122 *Pen Cl*
Hariscandra, 'Bhartendu' 1850-1885 *DcOrL 2*
Harison, Francis *Alli Sup*
Harizi, Judah Ben Solomon Al- 1165?-1235? *CasWL*
Harjo, Joy *DrAP 1975*
Harjo, Patty Leah *DrAP 1975*
Hark, Joseph Maximilian 1849-1930 *Alli Sup, DcAmA, DcNAA, WhWNAA*
Hark, Mildred *ConAu XR*
Harkavy, Alexander 1863-1939 *DcNAA*
Harkaway, Hal *ConAu XR*
Harker, Bailey J *Alli Sup*
Harker, David *ChPo S2*
Harker, George A *ChPo*
Harker, Herbert *OxCan Sup*
Harker, John *MnBBF*
Harker, Kenneth 1927- *Au&Wr*
Harker, Lizzie Allen 1863-1933 *EvLB, TwCA, WhLA*
Harker, Oliver Albert 1844?-1936 *DcNAA, IndAu 1917*
Harker, Ray Clarkson 1866- *AmLY, WhWNAA*
Harker, Samuel *DcNAA*
Harker, W *Alli Sup*
Harker, William *Alli Sup*
Harkey, Ira Brown, Jr. 1918- *ConAu 57, WrD 1976*
Harkey, Sidney Levi 1827- *DcAmA*
Harkey, Simeon Walcher 1811-1889 *Alli, Alli Sup, BiDSA, DcNAA*
Harkey, Simon Walcher 1811-1889 *DcAmA*
Harkey, William G 1914- *ConAu 25*
Harkin, Alexander 1818-1895? *Alli Sup, PoIre*
Harkin, Hugh 1791-1854 *PoIre*
Harkin, Thomas *OxCan Sup*
Harkins, Philip 1912- *AuBYP, ConAu 29, MorJA, SmATA 6*
Harkins, William E 1921- *ConAu 33*
Harkkon, Omar *BlkAW*
Harkness, Albert 1822-1907 *Alli, Alli Sup, CyAL 1, DcAmA, DcNAA*
Harkness, Bruce 1923- *ConAu 13R*
Harkness, David J 1913- *ConAu 9R*
Harkness, David W 1937- *ConAu 29, WrD 1976*
Harkness, Donna J *OhA&B*
Harkness, Georgia Elma 1891-1974 *AmA&B, Au&Wr, ConAu 1R, ConAu 53, WhWNAA*
Harkness, Gladys Estelle Suiter 1908?-1973 *ConAu 41*
Harkness, Henry Law *Alli Sup*
Harkness, James 1803-1878 *Alli, DcAmA, DcNAA*
Harkness, Margaret Elise *Alli Sup*
Harkness, Marjory Gane 1880- *ConAu 23*
Harkness, Rebekah 1915- *AmSCAP 66*

Harkness, Ruth 1901-1947 *DcNAA*
Harkness, Thomas And Nicholson, Henry A *Alli Sup*
Harkness, William 1837- *Alli Sup, DcAmA*
Harknett, Terry 1936- *ConAu 57*
Harlakenden, Roger *CyAL 1*
Harlan *ConAu XR*
Harlan, Caleb 1814-1902 *Alli Sup, AmA&B, DcNAA*
Harlan, Edgar Rubey 1869-1941 *DcNAA, IndAu 1917*
Harlan, George Cuvier 1835-1909 *Alli Sup, DcAmA, DcNAA*
Harlan, Glen *ConAu XR, SmATA XR, WrD 1976*
Harlan, J *Alli*
Harlan, Jacob Wright 1828- *IndAu 1816*
Harlan, John Marshall 1833-1911 *BiDSA, DcNAA*
Harlan, John Marshall 1899-1971 *ConAu 33*
Harlan, John Maynard 1864-1934 *DcNAA*
Harlan, Josiah 1799-1871 *DcNAA*
Harlan, Louis R 1922- *ConAu 23*
Harlan, Mary B *Alli Sup*
Harlan, Richard 1796-1843 *Alli, DcAmA, DcNAA*
Harlan, Rolvix 1876- *WhWNAA*
Harlan, William K 1938- *ConAu 45*
Harland, E *ChPo*
Harland, Henry 1861-1905 *Alli Sup, AmA, AmA&B, BbD, BiD&SB, CarSB, Chmbr 3, DcAmA, DcBiA, DcEnA Ap, DcNAA, EvLB, LongC, OxAm, OxEng, Pen Am, REnAL*
Harland, James Penrose 1891- *AmA&B*
Harland, John 1806-1868 *Alli Sup, ChPo S1*
Harland, Marion 1830-1922 *Alli, Alli Sup, AmA, AmA&B, BiD&SB, BiDSA, ChPo, DcAmA, DcBiA, DcNAA, OxAm, REnAL*
Harland, Sydney Cross 1891- *Au&Wr*
Harland, Walter Brian 1917- *Au&Wr*
Harle, Elizabeth *ConAu XR, WrD 1976*
Harle, Jonathan *Alli*
Harle, William Lockey *Alli Sup*
Harlequin *ConAu XR*
Harleston, Edward Nathaniel *BlkAW*
Harley *Alli*
Harley, A B *ChPo S1*
Harley, A J *Alli Sup*
Harley, Anne 1906- *WhWNAA*
Harley, Catherine Winifred 1895- *WhLA*
Harley, Edward *Alli*
Harley, Sir Edward *Alli*
Harley, Esther 1935- *Au&Wr*
Harley, George *Alli*
Harley, George 1829- *Alli Sup*
Harley, George Davies *Alli*
Harley, James Kimball 1828-1889 *EarAB Sup*
Harley, John *Alli Sup, ConAu XR, WrD 1976*
Harley, John Eugene 1892- *AmA&B*
Harley, John Hunter 1866- *WhLA*
Harley, John J *ChPo*
Harley, John Laker 1911- *Au&Wr*
Harley, Lewis Reifsnyder 1866- *DcAmA*
Harley, Robert, Earl Of Oxford 1661-1724 *Alli, NewC, REn*
Harley, Timothy *Alli Sup*
Harley, Walter S 1867- *WhWNAA*
Harley, William d1830 *Alli*
Harline, Leigh 1907- *AmSCAP 66*
Harling, W Franke 1887-1958 *AmSCAP 66*
Harling-Comyns, Francis Michel 1907- *Au&Wr*
Harlow, Alvin Fay 1875-1963 *AmA&B, AuBYP, WhWNAA*
Harlow, B F *Alli Sup*
Harlow, Francis H 1928- *ConAu 57*
Harlow, Henry Addison 1830-1913 *DcNAA*
Harlow, Mrs. Leo *CatA 1947*
Harlow, Lewis A 1901- *ConAu P-1*
Harlow, Lizzie K *Alli Sup*
Harlow, Louis Kinney 1850-1913 *ChPo S1*
Harlow, Neal Rotan 1908- *IndAu 1917*
Harlow, Ralph Volney 1884-1956 *AmA&B*
Harlow, Rex Frances 1892- *AmA&B, WhWNAA*
Harlow, Robert *OxCan, OxCan Sup*

Harlow, Samuel Ralph 1885-1972 *ChPo S2,*
ConAu 1R, ConAu 37
Harlow, Victor Emmanuel 1876-1958 *AmA&B,*
WhWNAA
Harlow, W M 1900- *ConAu 13R*
Harlow, William Burt 1856-1928 *DcAmA,*
DcNAA
Harlowe, George Henry 1787-1819 *ChPo S1*
Harlowe, Pedaell *Alli*
Harlwick, William *Alli*
Harm, J *Alli*
Harm, Marjorie Lea *ChPo S1*
Harman, Alec *ConAu XR*
Harman, Ephraim *Alli*
Harman, F E *Alli Sup*
Harman, Henry Elliott 1866-1927 *AmLY,*
BiDSA, DcNAA, WhWNAA
Harman, Henry Martyn 1822-1897 *Alli Sup,*
DcAmA, DcNAA
Harman, Ian Denis Anthony 1911- *Au&Wr*
Harman, Isaac *Alli*
Harman, Jane *ConAu 57*
Harman, John *Alli*
Harman, M F *ChPo*
Harman, Matthew 1822- *ChPo S1*
Harman, Paul *Alli*
Harman, Richard Alexander 1917- *ConAu 9R*
Harman, Thomas *Alli, CasWL, DcLEnL*
Harman, Thomas T *Alli Sup*
Harman, Willis W 1918- *ConAu 5R*
Harmand, T *Alli*
Harmar, John d1613 *Alli*
Harmar, John 1594?-1670 *Alli*
Harmati, Sandor 1892-1936 *AmSCAP 66*
Harmelink, Barbara *ConAu 61, SmATA 9*
Harmer, Anthony *Alli*
Harmer, Bertha d1934 *DcNAA*
Harmer, Jack P 1884-1962 *AmSCAP 66*
Harmer, James *Alli, BiDLA*
Harmer, Mabel 1894- *ConAu 9R*
Harmer, Ruth Mulvey 1919- *ConAu 9R*
Harmer, Sir S F 1862- *WhLA*
Harmer, Samuel Young 1809- *PoCh*
Harmer, T *Alli*
Harmer, Thomas 1715-1788 *Alli, DcEnL*
Harmodius d514BC *NewC*
Harmon, A J 1926- *ConAu 21*
Harmon, Daniel Williams 1778-1845? *Alli,*
AmA&B, BbtC, DcNAA, OxCan
Harmon, Gary L 1935- *ConAu 37*
Harmon, George Dewey 1896- *AmA&B*
Harmon, Glynn 1933- *ConAu 45*
Harmon, Henry C *Alli Sup*
Harmon, James Judson 1933- *ConAu 23*
Harmon, Jim *ConAu XR*
Harmon, Lyn S 1930- *ConAu 21*
Harmon, Marion Hicks *ChPo*
Harmon, Maurice 1930- *ConAu 23*
Harmon, Nolan Bailey 1892- *AmA&B*
Harmon, R Bartlett 1932- *ConAu 17R*
Harmon, Susanna M 1940- *ConAu 57*
Harmon, Thomas Dudley 1919- *IndAu 1917*
Harmon, William 1938- *ConAu 33,*
DrAP 1975
Harms, Ernest 1895-1974 *ConAu 49,*
ConAu P-1
Harms, John 1900- *ConAu 17R*
Harms, Leroy Stanley 1928- *ConAu 53*
Harms, Robert T 1932- *ConAu 37*
Harms, Valerie 1940- *ConAu 49*
Harmsworth, Alfred Charles William 1865-1922
LongC, MnBBF, NewC
Harmsworth, Cecil Bisshopp 1869-1948 *NewC*
Harmsworth, Harold Sidney 1868-1940 *LongC,*
NewC
Harmsworth, Sir Hildebrand Aubrey 1872-1929
NewC
Harmsworth, Sir Robert Leicester 1870-1937
NewC
Harnack, Curtis 1927- *AmA&B, ConAu 1R,*
DrAF 1976, WrD 1976
Harnack, R Victor 1927- *ConAu 13R*
Harnan, Terry 1920- *ConAu 45*
Harnden, Henry 1823-1900 *DcNAA*
Harnden, Ruth *ChPo S2*
Harned, William E 1883- *WhWNAA*
Harnell, Joseph 1924- *AmSCAP 66*
Harner, Herman Edwin 1898- *WhWNAA*

Harness, Alden 1874- *WhWNAA*
Harness, Alice Conner 1902- *ChPo S1*
Harness, John *Alli*
Harness, William *Alli*
Harnett, Cynthia Mary 1893- *Au&Wr,*
AuBYP, ConAu P-1, IlCB 1956,
SmATA 5, ThBJA, WhCL, WrD 1976
Harnett, Penelope Mary *PoIre*
Harnetty, Peter 1927- *ConAu 37*
Harney, George Edward 1840-1924 *Alli Sup,*
DcNAA
Harney, George Julian *Alli Sup*
Harney, George S 1866?- *IndAu 1917*
Harney, Gilbert L *Alli Sup*
Harney, John Hopkins 1806-1867 *BiDSA*
Harney, John Milton 1789?-1825? *Alli,*
AmA&B, BiDSA, DcAmA, DcNAA
Harney, Richard J *Alli Sup*
Harney, William Wallace *BiDSA*
Harney, William Wallace 1831-1912 *BiDSA,*
ChPo, ChPo S2, DcAmA, DcNAA,
IndAu 1816
Harnsberger, Caroline Thomas 1902- *ConAu 61*
Haro, Luis De d1532 *DcEuL*
Haro, Robert P 1936- *ConAu 33*
Harold I d1040 *NewC*
Harold II 1022?-1066 *NewC*
Harold Harefoot *NewC*
Harold, Childe *DcNAA*
Harold, John *Alli Sup*
Haroun-Al-Raschid *NewC, REn*
Haroutunian, Joseph 1904- *AmA&B*
Harpagus *REn*
Harpel, Oscar Henry *Alli Sup*
Harper Of Lincoln's Inn *Alli*
Harper, Alice 1883- *WhWNAA*
Harper, Andrew *Alli, BiDLA*
Harper, Carol Ely *ConAu 61*
Harper, Carrie Anna d1918 *AmLY, DcNAA*
Harper, Charles George 1863- *ChPo*
Harper, Clio 1872- *WhWNAA*
Harper, Daniel *ConAu XR, WrD 1976*
Harper, Edward *Alli Sup*
Harper, Edward d1902 *PoIre*
Harper, Eliza Elliott *LivFWS*
Harper, Fletcher 1806-1877 *AmA&B*
Harper, Floyd Arthur 1905- *AmA&B*
Harper, Fowler Vincent 1897- *OhA&B*
Harper, Frances Ellen Watkins 1825-1911
Alli Sup, BlkAW, ChPo S1, DcNAA
Harper, Francis B *Alli Sup*
Harper, Francis Whaley *Alli Sup*
Harper, Frederick *Alli Sup*
Harper, George Andrew 1879-1939 *DcNAA,*
WhWNAA
Harper, George McLean 1863-1947 *AmA&B,*
AmLY, DcAmA, DcNAA, REnAL,
TwCA, TwCA Sup, WhWNAA
Harper, Gillis *MnBBF*
Harper, Harry *Alli Sup, MnBBF*
Harper, Henry A *Alli Sup*
Harper, Henry Howard 1871- *AmA&B, ChPo,*
ChPo S1
Harper, Howard 1904- *ConAu 17R*
Harper, Howard M, Jr. 1930- *ConAu 21*
Harper, Ida Husted 1851-1931 *AmA&B,*
AmLY, DcNAA, IndAu 1816,
WhWNAA
Harper, Isabel Westcott *ChPo S2*
Harper, Jacob Chandler 1858-1939 *Alli Sup,*
DcNAA
Harper, James 1795-1869 *AmA&B*
Harper, James E 1927- *ConAu 41*
Harper, James P *Alli Sup*
Harper, John *Alli, Alli Sup*
Harper, John Charles 1917- *Au&Wr*
Harper, John Lyell 1873-1924 *DcNAA*
Harper, John Murdoch 1845-1919 *ChPo,*
DcNAA
Harper, John Russell 1914- *ConAu 33,*
OxCan Sup, WrD 1976
Harper, John Warren *ChPo S1*
Harper, Joseph Henry 1850-1938 *DcNAA*
Harper, L *Alli Sup*
Harper, Mrs. Lathrop Colgate *OhA&B,*
WhWNAA
Harper, Lawrence A 1901- *AmA&B*

Harper, Lizzie 1837-1916? *DcNAA*
Harper, Mabel Herbert *AmLY*
Harper, Malcolm McLachlan *Alli Sup, ChPo,*
ChPo S1
Harper, Marjorie *AmSCAP 66*
Harper, Marvin Henry 1901- *ConAu 49*
Harper, Merritt Wesley 1877-1938 *AmLY,*
DcNAA, WhWNAA
Harper, Michael Claude 1931- *Au&Wr*
Harper, Michael S 1938- *BlkAW, ConAu 33,*
ConP 1975, DrAP 1975, LivBA,
WrD 1976
Harper, Olive *Alli Sup, DcNAA*
Harper, Paul Tompkins 1881-1931 *DcNAA*
Harper, R D *Alli Sup*
Harper, Redd 1903- *AmSCAP 66*
Harper, Robert A 1924- *ConAu 17R*
Harper, Robert Francis 1864-1914 *DcNAA*
Harper, Robert Goodloe 1765-1825 *Alli,*
BiDSA, CyAL 1, DcAmA, DcNAA
Harper, Robert J C 1927- *ConAu 13R*
Harper, Robert Story 1899-1962 *AmA&B,*
Au&Wr, OhA&B
Harper, Roland M 1878- *WhWNAA*
Harper, Ruth *ChPo*
Harper, S *Alli*
Harper, Samuel Alain 1875- *IndAu 1917*
Harper, Samuel Brown *Alli Sup*
Harper, Samuel Northrup 1882-1943 *DcNAA*
Harper, T *Alli, BiDLA*
Harper, Theodore Acland 1871-1942 *AmA&B,*
DcNAA, WhWNAA
Harper, Thomas *Alli*
Harper, Thomas Norton 1821- *Alli Sup*
Harper, Walter *Alli, BiDLA*
Harper, Wilhelmina 1884-1973 *AmA&B,*
AuBYP, ConAu P-1, SmATA 4,
WhWNAA
Harper, William 1790-1847 *BiDSA, DcNAA*
Harper, William Allen 1880-1942 *AmA&B,*
AmLY, DcNAA, WhWNAA
Harper, William Hudson 1857-1946 *DcNAA*
Harper, William McL *ChPo*
Harper, William Rainey 1856-1906 *AmA&B,*
DcAmA, DcNAA, OhA&B, REnAL
Harper, William St. John 1851-1910 *ChPo,*
ChPo S1
Harpestraeng, Henrik d1244 *CasWL*
Harpignies, Henri 1819-1916 *OxFr*
Harpley, T *Alli, BiDLA*
Harpocration, Valerius *NewC*
Harpole, Patricia Chayne 1933- *ConAu 37*
Harpsfield, John d1578 *Alli*
Harpsfield, Nicholas d1583 *Alli*
Harpsfield, Nicholas 1519-1575 *CasWL*
Harpster, Hilda Thankful 1905- *OhA&B*
Harpur, Alexander *Alli Sup*
Harpur, Charles 1813?-1868 *Alli Sup, CasWL,*
ChPo, Chmbr 3, DcLEnL, OxEng,
WebEAL
Harpur, George *Alli Sup*
Harpur, Joseph *Alli, BiDLA*
Harr, Barbara *DrAP 1975*
Harr, Richard *Alli*
Harr, Wilber C 1908- *ConAu 1R*
Harraden, Beatrice 1864-1936 *BbD, BiD&SB,*
Chmbr 3, EvLB, LongC, NewC, REn,
TwCA, TwCA Sup, TwCW, WhLA
Harraden, Gertrude *Alli Sup, ChPo S1,*
ChPo S2
Harraden, R B *Alli*
Harradine, A C *ChPo S1*
Harrah, David 1926- *ConAu 5R, WrD 1976*
Harral, Alfred *Alli Sup*
Harral, Stewart 1906-1964 *ConAu 5R*
Harral, Thomas *Alli, BiDLA*
Harrar, E S 1905- *ConAu P-1*
Harrar, Thomas *Alli*
Harre, John 1931- *ConAu 23*
Harre, Rom 1927- *ConAu 5R, WrD 1976*
Harre, T Everett 1884- *AmA&B, AmLY*
Harreld, Claudia White *BlkAW*
Harrell, Allen W 1922- *ConAu 29*
Harrell, Costen J 1885- *ConAu 5R*
Harrell, David Edwin, Jr. 1930- *ConAu 37,*
WrD 1976
Harrell, Dennis 1949- *BlkAW*
Harrell, Irene Burk 1927- *ConAu 23,*

WrD 1976
Harrell, John G 1922- *ConAu 9R*
Harrell, John M *BiDSA*
Harrell, John Mortimer *DcNAA*
Harrell, Neva Yarbo *TexWr*
Harrell, Thomas Willard 1911- *ConAu 1R*
Harrelson, Walter Joseph 1919- *ConAu 9R,*
WrD 1976
Harrer, Charles *Alli Sup*
Harrer, Gustave Adolphus 1886-1943 *AmA&B,*
DcNAA, WhWNAA
Harrer, Heinrich 1912- *Au&Wr, ConAu 17R*
Harrey, Cyril *ChPo S1*
Harries, Arthur John *Alli Sup*
Harries, John *Alli Sup*
Harries, Karsten 1937- *ConAu 25*
Harries, Owen *Alli Sup*
Harriford, Daphne *WrD 1976*
Harrigan, Anthony 1925- *ConAu 21*
Harrigan, Edward 1845-1911 *AmA, AmA&B,*
BiD&SB, ChPo S2, CnThe, DcAmA,
DcNAA, McGWD, ModWD, OxAm,
PoIre, REnAL, REnWD
Harrigan, Ned 1845-1911 *AmA*
Harriman, Alice 1861-1925 *DcNAA*
Harriman, Blanche Avicestill *WhWNAA*
Harriman, Mrs. Borden *ChPo*
Harriman, Edward Avery 1869- *WhWNAA*
Harriman, Edward H 1848-1909 *REnAL*
Harriman, Eliza A *ChPo*
Harriman, Florence Jaffray 1870- *WhWNAA*
Harriman, Frances *ChPo*
Harriman, John 1904-1960 *AmA&B, AmNov,*
TwCA, TwCA Sup
Harriman, Karl Edwin 1875-1935 *AmA&B,*
DcAmA, DcNAA
Harriman, Margaret 1928- *ConAu 21*
Harriman, Margaret Case d1966 *AmA&B*
Harriman, Richard L 1944- *ConAu 33*
Harriman, Sarah 1942- *ConAu 57*
Harriman, Walter 1817-1884 *Alli Sup,*
DcAmA, DcNAA
Harring, Harro 1798-1870 *OxGer*
Harrington SEE ALSO Harington
Harrington, Countess Of *Alli Sup*
Harrington, Doctor *DcEnL*
Harrington, A W *ChPo*
Harrington, Adelaide L *Alli Sup*
Harrington, Alan 1919- *AmA&B, DrAF 1976,*
Pen Am
Harrington, Alan Stewart 1918- *Au&Wr*
Harrington, Alice H *ChPo*
Harrington, Anne Elizabeth *ChPo*
Harrington, Bernard James 1848-1907 *Alli Sup,*
DcNAA
Harrington, Mrs. C O *ChPo S2*
Harrington, Charles *Alli Sup*
Harrington, Charles 1856-1908 *DcNAA*
Harrington, Charles F *Alli Sup*
Harrington, Charles Kendall 1858-1920 *DcNAA*
Harrington, Charles Loammi 1847-1927
DcNAA
Harrington, Donald Szantho 1914- *ConAu 21*
Harrington, E B *Alli*
Harrington, Mrs. E D *Alli*
Harrington, Edith *ChPo S2*
Harrington, Sir Edward d1807 *Alli*
Harrington, Elbert Wellington 1901- *ConAu 37,*
IndAu 1917, WrD 1976
Harrington, Elizabeth D *ChPo*
Harrington, Florence *Alli Sup*
Harrington, Fred Harvey 1912- *AmA&B*
Harrington, George F 1825-1883 *Alli Sup,*
AmA, AmA&B, DcLEnL, DcNAA
Harrington, George Fellows *Alli Sup*
Harrington, George W *AnMV 1926*
Harrington, Geri *ConAu 57*
Harrington, Harold David 1903- *ConAu 25,*
IndAu 1917
Harrington, Harry Franklin 1882-1935 *ChPo S1,*
DcNAA, WhWNAA
Harrington, Henry *Alli*
Harrington, Henry 1729-1816 *Alli*
Harrington, Jack 1918- *ConAu 57*
Harrington, Sir James *Alli*
Harrington, James d1693 *Alli*
Harrington, James 1611-1677 *Alli, BrAu,*
CasWL, Chmbr 1, CrE&SL, DcEnA,

DcEnL, EvLB, NewC, Pen Eng, REn
Harrington, Jeremiah C 1882-1926 *DcNAA*
Harrington, Jeremy 1932- *ConAu 41*
Harrington, John 1534-1582 *Alli, Alli Sup,*
DcEnL
Harrington, Sir John 1561-1612 *Alli, Chmbr 1,*
NewC
Harrington, John ALSO Haryngton, John
Harrington, John A *Alli Sup*
Harrington, John Herbert *Alli*
Harrington, Joseph *Alli*
Harrington, Joseph 1903- *EncM&D*
Harrington, K *ConAu XR*
Harrington, Karl Pomeroy 1861-1953 *AmA&B,*
WhWNAA
Harrington, Kate *Alli Sup, ChPo*
Harrington, Lyn Davis 1911- *AuBYP,*
ConAu 5R, OxCan, OxCan Sup,
SmATA 5
Harrington, Mark Raymond 1882- *ConAu 17*
Harrington, Mark Walrod 1848-1926 *Alli Sup,*
DcAmA, DcNAA
Harrington, Mary Burton *ChPo*
Harrington, Michael *OxCan*
Harrington, Michael 1928- *AmA&B,*
ConAu 17R
Harrington, Mildred Priscilla 1886- *ChPo*
Harrington, Milton Alexander 1884-1942
DcNAA
Harrington, Ralph *Alli Sup*
Harrington, Robert *Alli, BiDLA*
Harrington, S M *Alli*
Harrington, Sarah Jane S *ChPo, ChPo S1*
Harrington, Thomas *Alli*
Harrington, Thomas Francis 1866-1919 *DcNAA*
Harrington, Victor B 1915- *AmSCAP 66*
Harrington, W Clark 1905- *AmSCAP 66*
Harrington, William *Alli, ChPo S1*
Harrington, William 1931- *AmA&B,*
ConAu 9R
Harrington, William O 1918- *AmSCAP 66*
Harriot *OxAm*
Harriot, John-Staples *Alli*
Harriot, Thomas *Alli Sup*
Harriot, Thomas 1560-1621 *Alli, CyAL 1,*
REnAL
Harriott, Clara Morris *AmA&B, DcNAA*
Harriott, John *Alli, BiDLA*
Harriott, Thomas 1560-1621 *Alli, DcEnL*
Harris, Miss *Alli*
Harris, A C *Alli Sup*
Harris, Ada Leonora *ChPo, ChPo S1,*
ChPo S2
Harris, Adah May Glasener 1881- *OhA&B*
Harris, Addison Clay 1840-1916 *IndAu 1917*
Harris, Agnes C *ChPo S2*
Harris, Agnes Olivia *ChPo S2*
Harris, Alan 1928- *ConAu 5R*
Harris, Albert J 1908- *ConAu 1R, WrD 1976*
Harris, Albert Mason 1868-1945 *DcNAA*
Harris, Alexander *Alli, Alli Sup*
Harris, Alexander 1805-1874 *WebEAL*
Harris, Alexander 1827- *DcNAA*
Harris, Alf 1928- *ConAu 53*
Harris, Alice Kessler 1941- *ConAu 37*
Harris, Amanda Bartlett 1824-1917 *Alli Sup,*
AmA&B, BiD&SB, DcAmA, DcNAA
Harris, Andrew *ConAu XR*
Harris, Annie Elizabeth 1877- *WhWNAA*
Harris, Sir Augustus Henry Glossop 1852-1896
BiD&SB
Harris, Barbara S 1927- *ConAu 49*
Harris, Barth *Alli*
Harris, Belle 1926- *AmSCAP 66*
Harris, Ben Charles 1907- *ConAu 57*
Harris, Ben M 1923- *ConAu 5R*
Harris, Benjamin d1716? *AmA, AmA&B,*
NewC, OxAm, REnAL
Harris, Bernice Kelly 1894?-1973 *AmA&B,*
AmNov, ConAu 5R, ConAu 45
Harris, Bertha 1937- *ConAu 29*
Harris, Bess *OxCan Sup*
Harris, Bill *BlkAW*
Harris, Branson L 1817-1901 *IndAu 1816*
Harris, Brice *ChPo S1*
Harris, Bruce Fairgray 1921- *WrD 1976*
Harris, Caleb Fiske 1818-1881 *ChPo, ChPo S1,*
REnAL

Harris, Carlton Danner 1864-1928 *DcNAA,*
WhWNAA
Harris, Caroline H *ChPo*
Harris, Catherine *Alli, BiDLA*
Harris, Chapin Aaron 1806-1866? *Alli,*
DcAmA, DcNAA
Harris, Charles 1859-1943 *DcNAA*
Harris, Sir Charles Alexander 1855- *WhLA*
Harris, Charles B 1940- *ConAu 53*
Harris, Charles H, III 1937- *ConAu 13R*
Harris, Charles Kassell 1865-1930 *AmA&B,*
AmLY, AmSCAP 66, DcNAA, OxAm,
REnAL
Harris, Chauncy D 1914- *ConAu 29,*
WrD 1976
Harris, Chester W 1910- *ConAu P-1*
Harris, Christie Irwin 1907- *ConAu 5R,*
OxCan Sup, SmATA 6
Harris, Christopher *LongC, WrD 1976*
Harris, Cicero Willis *BiDSA*
Harris, Clement Antrobus 1862- *ChPo*
Harris, Clyde E, Jr. *ConAu 23*
Harris, Colver *ConAu XR, OhA&B,*
SmATA 7
Harris, Cora May 1869-1935 *DcNAA*
Harris, Corinne Meredith 1888- *TexWr*
Harris, Corra 1869-1935 *AmA&B, BiDSA,*
WhWNAA
Harris, Credo Fitch d1956 *AmA&B*
Harris, Croasdaile Edward *Alli Sup*
Harris, Curtis C, Jr. 1930- *ConAu 53*
Harris, Cyril 1891- *AmA&B, ConAu P-1,*
OxCan
Harris, Dale Benner 1914- *ConAu 13R,*
IndAu 1917
Harris, Daniel *Alli*
Harris, Dave 1889- *AmSCAP 66*
Harris, David *Alli Sup*
Harris, David George *Alli Sup*
Harris, Delmer 1937- *ConAu 61*
Harris, Dorothy Joan 1931- *ConAu 45*
Harris, Douglas H 1930- *ConAu 25*
Harris, Dudley Arthur 1925- *WrD 1976*
Harris, E B *Alli Sup*
Harris, Edith *ChPo S2*
Harris, Edmund *Alli*
Harris, Edward C 1899- *AmSCAP 66*
Harris, Edward D *Alli Sup*
Harris, Edward William 1832-1925 *DcNAA*
Harris, Elijah Paddock 1832-1920 *DcNAA*
Harris, Elisha 1824-1884 *Alli Sup*
Harris, Ella Isabel 1859-1923 *DcNAA*
Harris, Elliot 1932- *ConAu 25*
Harris, Emerson Pitt 1853-1937 *DcNAA,*
WhWNAA
Harris, Emilia Marion *Alli Sup*
Harris, Emily Marion *ChPo, ChPo S1*
Harris, Emily T *Alli Sup*
Harris, Eric *OxCan*
Harris, Ernest E 1914- *ConAu 33, WrD 1976*
Harris, Ernest S *MnBBF*
Harris, Errol E 1908- *ConAu 49*
Harris, Ethel Grace *ChPo S2*
Harris, Ethel Ramos *AmSCAP 66*
Harris, Evelyn Marjorie 1919- *Au&Wr*
Harris, Everett Earl 1887- *WhWNAA*
Harris, F *Alli Sup*
Harris, F Brayton 1932- *ConAu 21*
Harris, Mrs. F McCready *Alli Sup*
Harris, Fay 1902- *WhWNAA*
Harris, Frances Allen *BiDSA*
Harris, Frank 1856-1931 *CnDAL, CnMD,*
ConAmL, EvLB, LongC, ModBL, NewC,
OxAm, OxEng, Pen Eng, RAdv 1,
TwCA, TwCA Sup, TwCW, WhTwL
Harris, Frank Burlingame *DcAmA*
Harris, Frank George 1899- *Au&Wr*
Harris, Frederic Robert 1875- *WhWNAA*
Harris, Frederick John 1943- *ConAu 57*
Harris, Mrs. G *Alli Sup*
Harris, G P *Alli*
Harris, G W *MnBBF*
Harris, Garrard 1875-1927 *DcNAA,*
WhWNAA
Harris, Gene Gray 1929- *ConAu 17R*
Harris, George d1796 *Alli*
Harris, George 1809-1890 *Alli, Alli Sup*
Harris, George 1844-1922 *DcAmA, DcNAA*

Harris, George, Tucker, W J & Glezen, E
Alli Sup
Harris, George Collyer 1834-1874 *Alli Sup*
Harris, George E *Alli Sup*
Harris, George F *Alli Sup*
Harris, George Frederick *Alli Sup*
Harris, George S *ChPo*
Harris, George W *Alli*
Harris, George Washington 1814-1869 *Alli Sup,*
AmA, AmA&B, BiD&SB, BiDSA,
CnDAL, DcAmA, DcLEnL, DcNAA,
OxAm, Pen Am, REnAL, WebEAL
Harris, Gertrude 1916- *ConAu 57*
Harris, Gilbert D *BiDSA*
Harris, Grace Mowry 1874- *WhWNAA*
Harris, H A *ChPo S1*
Harris, H A 1902- *ConAu 49*
Harris, Harold M 1915- *Au&Wr*
Harris, Harry 1901- *AmSCAP 66*
Harris, Hazel Harper 1906- *TexWr,*
WhWNAA
Harris, Helen 1927- *Au&Wr, ConAu 61,*
WrD 1976
Harris, Helen C *BlkAW*
Harris, Henrietta *Alli, BiDLA*
Harris, Henry *Alli, Alli Sup*
Harris, Henry Wilson 1883- *WhLA*
Harris, Herbert 1911- *Au&Wr, EncM&D,*
WrD 1976
Harris, Herbert 1914?-1974 *ConAu 49*
Harris, Herman K, II 1940- *BlkAW,*
DrAP 1975
Harris, Hope V *ChPo S1*
Harris, Hugh 1897- *Au&Wr*
Harris, Hunter Lee 1866-1893 *BiDSA, DcNAA*
Harris, Irving David 1914- *ConAu 13R*
Harris, Isaac *Au&Wr*
Harris, Isham Green 1818-1899 *BiDSA*
Harris, J *Alli, BiDLA*
Harris, J L *Alli Sup*
Harris, J W *Alli Sup*
Harris, James *Alli, Alli Sup, Chmbr 2*
Harris, James 1709-1780 *Alli, DcEnL, EvLB*
Harris, James 1746-1820 *Alli*
Harris, James Arthur 1880-1930 *DcNAA*
Harris, James Blair *TexWr*
Harris, James Coffee 1858- *WhWNAA*
Harris, James Howard, Earl Of Malmesbury
1807-1889 *Alli Sup*
Harris, James Leon 1934- *BlkAW*
Harris, James Rendel *Alli Sup*
Harris, James Thomas 1856-1931 *DcLEnL*
Harris, Jane Allen 1918- *ConAu 1R*
Harris, Janet 1932- *ConAu 33, SmATA 4*
Harris, Janette Hoston 1939- *LivBA*
Harris, Jay Morton *AmSCAP 66*
Harris, Jennie *ChPo S1*
Harris, Jerry Weseley 1933- *AmSCAP 66*
Harris, Jessica L 1939- *ConAu 33*
Harris, Joel Chandler 1848-1908 *Alli Sup,*
AmA, AmA&B, AnCL, AtlBL, AuBYP,
BbD, BiD&SB, BiDSA, CarSB, CasWL,
ChPo, ChPo S1, ChPo S2, Chmbr 3,
CnDAL, CyWA, DcAmA, DcBiA,
DcEnA Ap, DcLEnL, DcNAA, EvLB,
FamAYP, JBA 1934, OxAm, OxEng,
Pen Am, RAdv 1, REn, REnAL,
St&VC, WebEAL, WhCL, YABC 1
Harris, John *Alli, Alli Sup, Au&Wr,*
ChPo S1, ChPo S2
Harris, John 1667-1719 *Alli, DcEnL, NewC*
Harris, John 1766-1846 *ChPo*
Harris, John 1802?-1856 *Alli, DcEnL*
Harris, John 1820-1884 *Alli Sup*
Harris, John 1915- *ConAu 5R*
Harris, John 1916- *WrD 1976*
Harris, John 1931- *Au&Wr*
Harris, John Andrews 1834-1922 *Alli Sup,*
DcNAA
Harris, John B *MnBBF*
Harris, John B 1903-1922 *LongC, REn*
Harris, John H 1874- *WhLA*
Harris, John Howard *Alli Sup*
Harris, John Howard 1847-1925 *DcNAA*
Harris, John M *Alli Sup*
Harris, John Oberlin *Alli Sup*
Harris, John S 1917- *ConAu 29, WrD 1976*
Harris, John Tindall *Alli Sup*

Harris, John Wyndham Parkes Lucas Beynon
WorAu
Harris, Joseph *Alli*
Harris, Joseph d1764 *Alli*
Harris, Joseph 1758-1789 *Alli*
Harris, Joseph 1828-1892 *Alli Sup, DcNAA*
Harris, Joseph Hemington *Alli Sup*
Harris, Joseph Pratt 1896- *ConAu 1R*
Harris, Josiah 1821- *Alli Sup*
Harris, Julia Collier 1875- *AmA&B*
Harris, Julia M 1891- *WhWNAA*
Harris, Julia Mildred *ChPo S1*
Harris, Julian *BiDSA*
Harris, Julian 1896- *ConAu 1R*
Harris, Kathleen *ConAu XR*
Harris, L M, Mrs. *ChPo*
Harris, L P Mohun *Alli Sup*
Harris, Larry M *ConAu XR*
Harris, Laura B 1894- *AmA&B, IndAu 1917,*
OhA&B
Harris, Lee O 1839-1909 *Alli Sup, DcAmA,*
DcNAA, IndAu 1816
Harris, Leon A, Jr. 1926- *AmSCAP 66,*
AuBYP, ConAu 9R, SmATA 4
Harris, Leon R 1886?-1960 *BlkAW, OhA&B*
Harris, Leroy *BlkAW*
Harris, Lillie *Alli Sup*
Harris, Lily C *Alli Sup*
Harris, Lloyd J 1947- *ConAu 61*
Harris, Lorens Aikman 1903-1966 *IndAu 1917*
Harris, Louis 1921- *ConAu 13R*
Harris, Louisa *BiDSA*
Harris, Louise 1903- *ConAu 17R, WrD 1976*
Harris, Lundy H, Mrs. *BiDSA*
Harris, Luther Metcalf *Alli Sup*
Harris, Lynn H 1885- *WhWNAA*
Harris, M Anstice 1858- *AmLY*
Harris, MacDonald *ConAu XR*
Harris, Marguerite 1899- *ConP 1970,*
DrAP 1975
Harris, Marie *DrAP 1975*
Harris, Marie Calcote 1874- *TexWr*
Harris, Marilyn *ConAu XR*
Harris, Marion Rose 1925- *Au&Wr,*
ConAu P-1, WrD 1976
Harris, Marjorie 1919- *WrD 1976*
Harris, Marjorie Silliman 1890- *ConAu P-1*
Harris, Mark 1907- *WhWNAA*
Harris, Mark 1922- *AmA&B, Au&Wr,*
ConAu 5R, ConNov 1972, ConNov 1976,
DrAF 1976, OxAm, RAdv 1, WrD 1976
Harris, Marshall D 1903- *ConAu 1R*
Harris, Martin Douglas *OxCan*
Harris, Marvin 1927- *AmA&B*
Harris, Mary 1905- *CatA 1952*
Harris, Mary B 1943- *ConAu 53*
Harris, Mary Imogene *ConAu 49, WrD 1976*
Harris, Mary K 1905-1966 *ConAu P-1*
Harris, Mattie Anstice 1858- *WhWNAA*
Harris, Mattie Virginia *AmA&B*
Harris, Maurice Henry 1859-1930 *AmLY,*
DcNAA, WhWNAA
Harris, Max 1921- *ConP 1970, TwCW*
Harris, Merriman Colbert 1846-1921 *DcNAA,*
OhA&B
Harris, Merton L *TexWr*
Harris, Michael H 1941- *ConAu 57*
Harris, Michael R 1936- *ConAu 29,*
WrD 1976
Harris, Middleton 1908- *LivBA*
Harris, Mildred *ChPo S1*
Harris, Miles F 1913- *ConAu 5R*
Harris, Miriam Coles 1834-1925 *Alli Sup,*
AmA, AmA&B, AmLY, BiD&SB,
DcAmA, DcNAA
Harris, Moses *Alli*
Harris, Myron 1922- *AmSCAP 66*
Harris, Nathaniel Edwin 1846-1929 *Alli Sup,*
DcNAA
Harris, Ned Brunson *WhWNAA*
Harris, Neil 1936- *BlkAW*
Harris, Norman Alec 1918- *Au&Wr*
Harris, Norman Dwight 1870-1958 *OhA&B,*
WhWNAA
Harris, Patricia *ConAu 57*
Harris, Paula Josephine 1929- *Au&Wr*
Harris, Penelope *TexWr*
Harris, Peter 1923- *WrD 1976*

Harris, Peter Bernard 1929- *WrD 1976*
Harris, Philip Robert 1926- *ConAu 17R,*
WrD 1976
Harris, R *BiDLA*
Harris, R Laird 1911- *ConAu 1R*
Harris, Raymond *Alli*
Harris, Reginald Duckett 1920- *Au&Wr*
Harris, Reginald V *OxCan*
Harris, Remus Anthony 1916- *AmSCAP 66*
Harris, Rex 1904- *Au&Wr*
Harris, Richard *Alli, BbtC*
Harris, Richard 1833- *Alli Sup*
Harris, Richard Donald *Alli Sup*
Harris, Richard Julian *Alli Sup*
Harris, Robert *Alli Sup*
Harris, Robert 1578-1658 *Alli*
Harris, Robert 1907- *ConAu 5R*
Harris, Robert T 1912- *ConAu 5R*
Harris, Robin S 1919- *ConAu 21, OxCan Sup*
Harris, Roger *ConAu XR*
Harris, Roland *ChPo S2*
Harris, Rollin Arthur 1863-1918 *DcNAA*
Harris, Ronald Walter 1916- *ConAu 5R,*
WrD 1976
Harris, Rosemary Jeanne *Au&Wr, ConAu 33,*
SmATA 4, WrD 1976
Harris, Roy 1898- *OxAm, REn, REnAL*
Harris, S *Alli*
Harris, Samuel 1814-1899 *Alli Sup, DcAmA,*
DcNAA
Harris, Samuel Bache *Alli Sup*
Harris, Samuel Smith 1841-1888 *Alli Sup,*
BiDSA, DcAmA, DcNAA
Harris, Seale 1870- *WhWNAA*
Harris, Seymour Edwin 1897-1974 *AmA&B,*
ConAu 53, TwCA Sup
Harris, Seymour Frederick 1851- *Alli Sup*
Harris, Sheldon H 1928- *ConAu 37,*
WrD 1976
Harris, Stanley *Alli Sup*
Harris, Stephen L 1937- *ConAu 29*
Harris, Sydney Justin 1917- *ConAu 61*
Harris, Sydney Justin 1914- *AmA&B*
Harris, Sylvanus *Alli Sup*
Harris, T *Alli, ChPo S2*
Harris, Thaddeus *BiDSA*
Harris, Thaddeus Mason 1768-1842 *Alli,*
AmA&B, ChPo, CyAL 1, DcAmA,
DcNAA
Harris, Thaddeus William 1795-1856 *Alli,*
DcAmA, DcNAA
Harris, Theodore 1912- *AmSCAP 66*
Harris, Theodore Findley 1931- *AuNews 1*
Harris, Theodore Wilson 1921- *CasWL*
Harris, Thistle Y 1902- *WrD 1976*
Harris, Thom *Alli*
Harris, Thomas *Alli, Alli Sup*
Harris, Thomas 1784-1861 *DcNAA*
Harris, Thomas 1810-1877 *PoIre*
Harris, Thomas Frederick *Alli Sup*
Harris, Thomas Green 1854- *WhWNAA*
Harris, Thomas Lake 1823-1906 *Alli, Alli Sup,*
AmA, AmA&B, BiD&SB, ChPo,
ChPo S1, ChPo S2, DcAmA, DcNAA,
OxAm, REnAL
Harris, Thomas LeGrand 1863-1941 *DcAmA,*
DcNAA, IndAu 1816
Harris, Thomas Leonard *DcEnL*
Harris, Tom *BlkAW, OxCan Sup*
Harris, Tucker 1747-1821 *Alli*
Harris, Victor 1869-1943 *AmSCAP 66*
Harris, Vincent Dormer *Alli Sup*
Harris, W *Alli, Alli Sup*
Harris, W A *Alli Sup*
Harris, W S, Sir *Alli*
Harris, W S *Alli Sup*
Harris, W T *Alli Sup*
Harris, Walt *ChPo*
Harris, Walter *Alli*
Harris, Walter 1647?-1726? *Alli, DcEnL*
Harris, Walter A 1929- *ConAu 29, WrD 1976*
Harris, Walter Eric *OxCan Sup, WhWNAA*
Harris, Wendell W *BlkAW*
Harris, Will J 1900- *AmSCAP 66*
Harris, William *Alli, Alli Sup, BiDLA*
Harris, William 1675?-1740 *Alli, DcEnL*
Harris, William 1720-1770 *Alli, DcEnL*
Harris, William 1816- *BbtC*

Harris, William A *Alli*
Harris, William C 1933- *ConAu 23*
Harris, William Charles 1830-1905 *Alli Sup,
DcAmA, DcNAA*
Harris, Sir William Cornwallis *Alli*
Harris, William Harry *Alli Sup*
Harris, William Hetherington *Alli Sup*
Harris, William J 1942- *BlkAW, ConAu 53,
DrAP 1975*
Harris, William Logan 1817-1887 *Alli Sup,
DcAmA, DcNAA, OhA&B*
Harris, William M And Clarkson, Thomas
Alli Sup
Harris, William Mercer 1858- *BiDSA*
Harris, William Peter 1923- *Au&Wr*
Harris, William Richard 1847-1923 *DcNAA*
Harris, Sir William Snow 1792-1867 *Alli,
Alli Sup*
Harris, William Torrey 1835-1909 *Alli Sup,
AmA, AmA&B, BiD&SB, ChPo S1,
DcAmA, DcNAA, OxAm, REnAL*
Harris, William W *Alli Sup*
Harris, William Welton 1866- *WhWNAA*
Harris, Wilson 1883-1955 *LongC*
Harris, Wilson 1921- *Au&Wr, ConNov 1972,
ConNov 1976, ConP 1970, ConP 1975,
LongC, WebEAL, WhTwL, WrD 1976*
Harris, Woody 1911- *AmSCAP 66*
Harris, Worsley Poulett *Alli Sup*
Harris, Zellig S 1909- *AmA&B*
Harrison *BbtC*
Harrison, Doctor *Alli*
Harrison, A Stewart *Alli Sup*
Harrison, Agnes *Alli Sup*
Harrison, Albert Edward *Alli Sup*
Harrison, Alfred H *OxCan*
Harrison, Alice Morgan *ChPo*
Harrison, Allan E 1925- *ConAu 57*
Harrison, Amelia 1852-1903 *DcNAA*
Harrison, Amos *Alli*
Harrison, Anthony *Alli, BiDLA*
Harrison, Arthur 1902- *AmSCAP 66*
Harrison, Barbara 1941- *ConAu 29*
Harrison, Belle Richardson *BiDSA*
Harrison, Benjamin *Alli*
Harrison, Benjamin 1740?-1791 *BiDSA*
Harrison, Benjamin 1833-1901 *Alli Sup,
AmA&B, BiD&SB, DcAmA, DcNAA,
IndAu 1816, OhA&B, OxAm, REnAL*
Harrison, Bennett 1942- *ConAu 53*
Harrison, Bernard 1933- *WrD 1976*
Harrison, Bill *ConAu XR*
Harrison, Birge *DcNAA*
Harrison, Bob 1915- *AmSCAP 66*
Harrison, Brian 1909- *ConAu 13*
Harrison, Brian Fraser 1918- *Au&Wr,
WrD 1976*
Harrison, Mrs. Burton 1843?-1920 *AmA&B,
BbD, BiD&SB, DcAmA, DcNAA*
Harrison, C *Alli Sup*
Harrison, C William 1913- *AuBYP,
IndAu 1917*
Harrison, Carey 1944- *ConAu 61*
Harrison, Carter Henry 1825-1895 *ChPo,
DcNAA*
Harrison, Mrs. Carter Henry *ChPo*
Harrison, Cass 1922- *AmSCAP 66*
Harrison, Charles *Alli Sup, ChPo, OxCan*
Harrison, Charles F 1883-1955 *AmSCAP 66*
Harrison, Charles James 1828-1915 *OhA&B*
Harrison, Charles Yale 1898-1954 *AmA&B,
AmNov, REnAL, WhWNAA*
Harrison, Chip 1952- *ConAu 29*
Harrison, Clifford *Alli Sup, ChPo, ChPo S1*
Harrison, Constance Cary 1843?-1920 *Alli Sup,
AmA, AmA&B, BiDSA, Chmbr 3,
CnDAL, DcAmA, DcBiA, DcNAA,
LivFWS, OxAm, REnAL*
Harrison, Cynthia Ellen 1946- *ConAu 57*
Harrison, D Dex 1909- *Au&Wr*
Harrison, D J *Alli*
Harrison, David *Alli, Alli Sup*
Harrison, David Lakin 1926- *Au&Wr,
WrD 1976*
Harrison, DeLeon 1941- *BlkAW*
Harrison, Deloris 1938- *ConAu 61, SmATA 9*
Harrison, Earl Stanley 1871- *WhWNAA*
Harrison, Edith Ogden d1955 *AmA&B,*

BiDSA, WhWNAA
Harrison, Edward *Alli, BiDLA*
Harrison, Sir Edward Richard 1872- *WhLA*
Harrison, Edwin *MnBBF*
Harrison, Elizabeth 1849-1927 *AmA&B,
DcNAA*
Harrison, Elizabeth Cavanna 1909- *WrD 1976*
Harrison, Elizabeth Fancourt 1921- *Au&Wr*
Harrison, Ellenetta *BiDSA*
Harrison, Eunice B *BlkAW*
Harrison, Everett F 1902- *ConAu P-1,
WrD 1976*
Harrison, F Bayford *Alli Sup, MnBBF*
Harrison, Fairfax 1869-1938 *DcNAA*
Harrison, Fanny *Alli Sup*
Harrison, Faye M *ChPo S2*
Harrison, Florence 1884- *ChPo, ChPo S1,
ChPo S2*
Harrison, Francis *Alli Sup*
Harrison, Francis Burton 1873- *CatA 1952*
Harrison, Francis Llewellyn 1905- *Au&Wr*
Harrison, Frank R, III 1935- *ConAu 53*
Harrison, Fred 1917- *ConAu 29*
Harrison, Frederic 1831-1923 *Alli Sup,
BiD&SB, BrAu 19, ChPo S1, Chmbr 3,
DcEnA, DcEnA Ap, DcEnL, DcEuL,
DcLEnL, EvLB, LongC, NewC, OxEng*
Harrison, G H *ChPo*
Harrison, Gabriel 1818?-1902 *Alli Sup,
AmA&B, DcAmA, DcNAA*
Harrison, George *Alli, Alli Sup, BiDLA,
ChPo S2*
Harrison, Sir George *Alli*
Harrison, George Bagshawe 1894- *AmA&B,
CatA 1952, ConAu 1R, LongC,
TwCA Sup*
Harrison, George H DeStrabolgie N P *Alli Sup*
Harrison, George Harrison Rogers *Alli Sup*
Harrison, George Leib 1811-1885 *Alli Sup,
DcAmA, DcNAA*
Harrison, George Robert 1874- *WhWNAA*
Harrison, George Russell 1898- *ConAu 19*
Harrison, Gertrude F *ChPo*
Harrison, Gessner 1807-1862 *Alli, AmA,
BiDSA, DcAmA, DcNAA*
Harrison, Gilbert A 1915- *AmA&B*
Harrison, Gustavus *Alli*
Harrison, H *Alli Sup, MnBBF*
Harrison, Hall 1837-1900 *Alli Sup, BiDSA,
DcAmA, DcNAA*
Harrison, Hank 1940- *ConAu 41*
Harrison, Harry *Alli Sup*
Harrison, Harry 1925- *ConAu 1R, SmATA 4,
WrD 1976*
Harrison, Helga Susan Barbara 1924- *Au&Wr,
WrD 1976*
Harrison, Henry 1903- *AnMV 1926, ChPo S1,
WhWNAA*
Harrison, Henry Sydnor 1880-1930 *AmA&B,
DcNAA, LongC, OxAm, REnAL, TwCA*
Harrison, Henry William *Alli Sup*
Harrison, Herbert Eric 1899- *WhLA*
Harrison, Howard 1930- *ConAu 5R,
WrD 1976*
Harrison, I Henry *Alli Sup*
Harrison, Ida Withers 1851-1927 *DcNAA,
WhWNAA*
Harrison, J *Alli, Alli Sup*
Harrison, J B *Alli*
Harrison, J Bayford *Alli Sup*
Harrison, J J *Alli Sup*
Harrison, J P *MnBBF*
Harrison, Jack Lamar 1927- *IndAu 1917*
Harrison, Jake R *ChPo S2*
Harrison, James *Alli, Alli Sup, BiDLA Sup*
Harrison, James 1937- *ConAu 13R*
Harrison, James Albert 1848-1911 *Alli Sup,
AmA, AmA&B, BiD&SB, BiDSA,
ChPo S1, CnDAL, DcAmA, DcNAA*
Harrison, James Bower *Alli Sup*
Harrison, James Carter *Alli Sup*
Harrison, James Ernest *ChPo S2*
Harrison, James Hargrave *Alli Sup*
Harrison, James Maurice 1892- *Au&Wr*
Harrison, James Minnis 1873- *BlkAW*
Harrison, James Thomas *WrD 1976*
Harrison, Jane *ChPo, ChPo S1*
Harrison, Jane Ellen 1850-1928 *Alli Sup,*

BiD&SB, EvLB, NewC
Harrison, Jay S 1927-1974 *ConAu 53*
Harrison, Jeffery Graham 1922- *Au&Wr*
Harrison, Jennie 1841-1912 *Alli Sup, ChPo,
DcNAA*
Harrison, Jim 1937- *AmA&B, ConAu XR,
ConLC 6, ConP 1970, ConP 1975,
DrAF 1976, DrAP 1975, RAdv 1,
WrD 1976*
Harrison, Joanna *Alli Sup*
Harrison, John *Alli, Alli Sup, BiDLA, ChPo,
ConDr*
Harrison, John 1693-1776 *Alli*
Harrison, John Baughman 1907- *ConAu 1R*
Harrison, John Denby *Alli Sup*
Harrison, John Fletcher Clews 1921- *ConAu 25,
WrD 1976*
Harrison, John Hoffman 1808-1849 *BiDSA,
DcNAA*
Harrison, John M 1914- *ConAu 25*
Harrison, John Pollard 1796-1849 *DcNAA,
OhA&B*
Harrison, John Raymond *AuNews 2*
Harrison, John Smith 1877- *IndAu 1816,
OhA&B, WhWNAA*
Harrison, Jonathan Baxter 1835-1907 *Alli Sup,
DcAmA, DcNAA, OhA&B*
Harrison, Joseph *Alli*
Harrison, Joseph 1810-1874 *Alli Sup, DcAmA,
DcNAA*
Harrison, Joseph Graham 1912- *Au&Wr*
Harrison, Joseph LeRoy 1862-1950 *AmA&B,
AmLY, ChPo, ChPo S1, WhWNAA*
Harrison, Joseph T 1853-1940 *OhA&B*
Harrison, Joshua Clarkson *Alli Sup*
Harrison, Josiah *Alli*
Harrison, Keith Edward 1932- *ChPo S1,
ConP 1970, ConP 1975, WrD 1976*
Harrison, Kenneth Cecil 1915- *Au&Wr,
ConAu 9R, WrD 1976*
Harrison, Lawrence John *Alli Sup*
Harrison, Lawrence Whitaker 1876- *WhLA*
Harrison, Leon 1866-1928 *DcNAA*
Harrison, Louise C 1908- *ConAu P-1*
Harrison, Lovell Birge 1854-1929 *DcNAA*
Harrison, Lowell H 1922- *ConAu 37,
WrD 1976*
Harrison, Lucy 1844-1915 *ChPo S2*
Harrison, Luther 1877- *WhWNAA*
Harrison, Mrs. M B *Alli Sup*
Harrison, M John 1945- *ConAu 53*
Harrison, Marguerite E *AmA&B*
Harrison, Martin 1930- *ConAu 49*
Harrison, Mary *Alli Sup*
Harrison, Mary Bennett 1877- *WhWNAA*
Harrison, Mary St. Leger 1852-1931 *CatA 1947,
Chmbr 3, DcEnA Ap, LongC, TwCA,
TwCA Sup, WhLA*
Harrison, Matthew *Alli*
Harrison, Michael *Alli*
Harrison, Michael 1907- *Au&Wr, EncM&D*
Harrison, Molly 1909- *Au&Wr*
Harrison, Muriel Stevens 1906- *TexWr*
Harrison, Nan Hillary *TexWr*
Harrison, Nellie Fortescue *Alli Sup*
Harrison, Nicholas Bacon *Alli*
Harrison, Norman Kingsley 1891- *Au&Wr*
Harrison, Octavian Baxter Cameron 1819-
Alli Sup
Harrison, Oscar *Alli Sup*
Harrison, Paul Carter 1936- *BlkAW*
Harrison, Paul M 1923- *ConAu 53*
Harrison, R *Alli*
Harrison, R E *Alli Sup*
Harrison, R Tarrant *Alli*
Harrison, Ralph *Alli*
Harrison, Raymond H 1911- *ConAu 17R*
Harrison, Reginald *Alli Sup*
Harrison, Rex 1908- *NewC*
Harrison, Richard *Alli, Alli Sup*
Harrison, Richard G *EarAB Sup*
Harrison, Richard John 1920- *WrD 1976*
Harrison, Robert *Alli, Alli Sup*
Harrison, Robert 1932- *ConAu 25*
Harrison, Robert Alexander 1833-1878 *Alli Sup,
BbtC, DcNAA*
Harrison, Roland Kenneth 1920- *Au&Wr,
ConAu 49*

Hart, Johnny *AuNews 1, ConAu 49*
Hart, Joseph 1712-1768 *Alli, ChPo, ChPo S1,*
PoCh
Hart, Joseph C 1798-1855 *AmA&B, DcNAA,*
OxAm, REnAL
Hart, Joseph J *Alli Sup*
Hart, Joseph Kinmont 1876-1949 *AmA&B,*
DcNAA, IndAu 1816, WhWNAA
Hart, Judith 1924- *WrD 1976*
Hart, Julia Catherine 1796-1867 *AmA&B,*
DcLEnL, DcNAA, OxCan
Hart, Julia Duggan 1873- *TexWr*
Hart, Julius 1859-1930 *BiD&SB, ClDMEuL,*
OxGer
Hart, Katharine *ChPo*
Hart, Ken 1917- *AmSCAP 66*
Hart, Kenneth Richard Amiel 1900- *Au&Wr*
Hart, L W *Alli*
Hart, Larry 1920- *ConAu 33*
Hart, Leonard *MnBBF*
Hart, Levi d1808 *Alli*
Hart, Levi, And V R Osborn *Alli*
Hart, Liddell *Au&Wr, EvLB, TwCA,*
TwCA Sup
Hart, Lorenz 1895-1943 *AmSCAP 66,*
McGWD, REnAL
Hart, Louise 1911- *ChPo S2*
Hart, Ludovico Woolfgang *Alli Sup*
Hart, Luther 1783-1834 *DcNAA*
Hart, M O *BbtC*
Hart, Marie 1932- *ConAu 41*
Hart, Marilyn M 1926- *ConAu 45*
Hart, Mary H *Alli Sup*
Hart, Maurice 1909- *AmSCAP 66*
Hart, Moss 1904-1961 *AmA&B, CasWL,*
CnDAL, CnMD, CnThe, LongC,
McGWD, ModWD, OxAm, Pen Am,
REn, REnAL, REnWD, TwCA,
TwCA Sup, WebEAL
Hart, Oliver 1723-1795 *Alli*
Hart, Patrick 1925- *ConAu 53*
Hart, Ray L 1929- *ConAu 29*
Hart, Sir Reginald Clare 1848- *WhLA*
Hart, Richard *Alli Sup*
Hart, Richard 1908- *ConAu P-1*
Hart, Robert Allan 1929- *IndAu 1917*
Hart, S *ChPo*
Hart, Sackville *MnBBF*
Hart, Samuel 1845-1917 *Alli Sup, DcAmA,*
DcNAA
Hart, Sophie Chantal 1869- *WhWNAA*
Hart, Stephen 1782-1857 *DcNAA*
Hart, Tony *REnAL*
Hart, V Donn 1918- *ConAu 13R*
Hart, Virgil Chittenden 1840-1904 *Alli Sup,*
DcNAA
Hart, Walter 1906?-1973 *ConAu 45*
Hart, Walter Morris 1872- *AmA&B, ChPo S2,*
REnAL
Hart, William *Alli, BiDLA*
Hart, Sir William *Alli*
Hart, William Henry d1888 *Alli Sup*
Hart, William M 1823-1894 *EarAB,*
EarAB Sup
Hart, William Neville *Alli, BiDLA*
Hart, William Octave 1857-1929 *DcNAA*
Hart, William R *Alli Sup*
Hart, William S 1872-1946 *AmA&B, MnBBF*
Hart-Davis, Duff 1936- *ConAu 29, WrD 1976*
Hart-Davis, Sir Rupert 1907- *ChPo S1,*
WorAu
Hart-Smith, William 1911- *ConAu 23,*
ConP 1970, ConP 1975, WrD 1976
Hartcliffe, John *Alli*
Hartcup, Adeline 1918- *Au&Wr, WrD 1976*
Hartcup, Guy 1919- *ConAu 29, WrD 1976*
Hartcup, John 1915- *Au&Wr, WrD 1976*
Harte, Bret 1836?-1902 *AmA, AmA&B,*
AtlBL, AuBYP, BiD&SB, CasWL,
CnDAL, CriT 3, CyWA, DcAmA,
DcNAA, OxAm, Pen Am, RAdv 1, REn,
REnAL, WebEAL
Harte, Francis Bret 1836?-1902 *Alli Sup,*
AmA, BbD, ChPo, ChPo S1, ChPo S2,
Chmbr 3, CyAL 2, DcBiA, DcEnA,
DcEnA Ap, DcEnL, DcLEnL, EvLB,
MouLC 4, OxEng
Harte, George *Alli*

Harte, George C *Alli Sup*
Harte, J *ChPo*
Harte, Laurence 1863- *PoIre*
Harte, Lucy Cecil *DcAmA*
Harte, Marjorie *ConAu XR, WrD 1976*
Harte, Oliver *MnBBF*
Harte, Richard Hickman 1855-1925 *DcNAA*
Harte, Thomas Joseph 1914-1974 *ConAu 53*
Harte, Walter 1700?-1774 *DcEnL*
Harte, Walter Blackburn 1867?-1898 *ChPo S2,*
DcAmA, DcNAA
Harte, William *Alli Sup*
Harte, William Marshall *Alli*
Hartendorp, A V H 1893- *ConAu P-1,*
WrD 1976
Hartendorp, A V H 1903- *WhWNAA*
Harter, Helen 1905- *ConAu 5R*
Harter, Joseph 1837-1913 *OhA&B*
Harter, Lafayette George, Jr. 1918- *ConAu 9R*
Hartert, Ernst J O 1859- *WhLA*
Hartford, Claire 1913- *ConAu 29*
Hartford, Ellis F 1905- *ConAu P-1*
Hartford, Frances, Countess Of *Alli*
Hartford, Huntington, II 1911- *AmA&B,*
ConAu 17R
Hartford, Margaret E 1917- *ConAu 41*
Hartford, Nora B *ChPo S2*
Hartford, Via *ConAu XR*
Hartgill, George *Alli*
Hartgyll, George *Alli*
Harth, Robert 1940- *ConAu 33*
Harthill, Susanna *Alli Sup*
Harthoorn, Antonie Marinus 1923- *Au&Wr,*
ConAu 53, WrD 1976
Harthoorn, Susanne 1927- *Au&Wr*
Hartich, Alice 1888- *ConAu 17*
Hartig, Henry Edward 1892- *WhWNAA*
Hartig, Herbert 1930- *AmSCAP 66*
Hartigan, Patrick Joseph 1879- *ChPo,*
ChPo S1
Harting, James Edmund 1841- *Alli Sup,*
BiD&SB
Hartington, Marquis Of *Alli Sup*
Hartje, Robert G 1922- *ConAu 25*
Hartke, Vance 1919- *ConAu 25, IndAu 1917*
Hartland *Alli*
Hartland, Edwin 1848-1927 *CarSB*
Hartlaub, Felix 1913-1945 *EncWL, OxGer*
Hartlaub, Geno 1915- *Pen Eur*
Hartlaub, Gustav Friedrich 1884-1963 *BiDPar*
Hartleben, Otto Erich 1864-1905 *CasWL,*
ClDMEuL, EvEuW, ModWD, OxGer
Hartley, Mrs. *Alli Sup*
Hartley, Arthur Bamford 1909- *Au&Wr*
Hartley, Benjamin *Alli Sup*
Hartley, C P *Au&Wr*
Hartley, Cecil B *Alli Sup, BiD&SB, DcAmA,*
DcNAA
Hartley, Charles *Alli Sup*
Hartley, David *Chmbr 2*
Hartley, David d1813 *Alli*
Hartley, David 1705-1757 *Alli, BrAu, CasWL,*
DcEnA, DcEnL, EvLB, OxEng, Pen Eng,
REn, WebEAL
Hartley, Ellen R 1915- *ConAu 5R, WrD 1976*
Hartley, Emily *Alli Sup*
Hartley, F W *Alli Sup*
Hartley, Fountain J *Alli Sup*
Hartley, George Inness 1887-1949 *AmA&B,*
DcNAA
Hartley, Harald *ChPo S2*
Hartley, Sir Harold Brewer 1878- *Au&Wr,*
ChPo
Hartley, Helene Willey *AmA&B*
Hartley, Isaac Smithson 1830-1899 *Alli Sup,*
DcAmA, DcNAA
Hartley, J *Alli*
Hartley, James *Alli*
Hartley, John *Alli, Alli Sup*
Hartley, John 1839-1915 *Alli Sup, ChPo,*
ChPo S1, ChPo S2
Hartley, John I 1921- *ConAu 5R*
Hartley, Jonathan Scott 1845-1912 *DcNAA*
Hartley, Joseph Robert 1931- *IndAu 1917*
Hartley, L *Alli Sup*
Hartley, Leslie Poles 1895-1972 *Au&Wr,*
CasWL, ConAu 37, ConAu 45, ConLC 2,

ConNov 1972, ConNov 1976, DcLEnL,
EncWL, EvLB, LongC, ModBL,
ModBL Sup, NewC, Pen Eng, RAdv 1,
REn, TwCA Sup, TwCW, WebEAL,
WhTwL
Hartley, Livingston 1900- *ConAu 61*
Hartley, Lodwick 1906- *ConAu 1R,*
WrD 1976
Hartley, Marie 1905- *Au&Wr, ConAu 9R,*
WrD 1976
Hartley, Marsden 1877-1943 *AtlBL, OxAm,*
REnAL
Hartley, May *Alli Sup*
Hartley, Oliver Cromwell 1823-1850 *Alli Sup,*
DcNAA
Hartley, R K *Alli Sup*
Hartley, Rachel M 1895- *ConAu 5R*
Hartley, Ralph *Alli, BiDLA*
Hartley, Raymond Oswald 1929- *AmSCAP 66*
Hartley, Robert Milham 1796-1881 *Alli Sup,*
DcAmA, DcNAA
Hartley, Susan *ChPo, ChPo S1*
Hartley, Thomas 1707-1784 *Alli, BiDLA,*
BiDLA Sup
Hartley, W *Alli Sup*
Hartley, W G *Alli Sup*
Hartley, Walter Noel *Alli Sup*
Hartley, Walter S 1927- *AmSCAP 66*
Hartley, William B 1913- *ConAu 5R*
Hartley, William Douglas 1921- *IndAu 1917*
Hartley, Winchcombe Saville *Alli Sup*
Hartlib, Samuel 1596?-1662? *Alli, CasWL,*
CrE&SL
Hartlieb, Johann *OxGer*
Hartlieb, Johannes *CasWL*
Hartling, Peter 1933- *CasWL, ModGL,*
OxGer
Hartman, Blanche 1863-1946 *DcNAA*
Hartman, Carl G 1879- *WhWNAA*
Hartman, Chester W 1936- *ConAu 57*
Hartman, David N 1921- *ConAu 13R*
Hartman, Don 1900-1958 *AmSCAP 66*
Hartman, Frank 1881-1945 *OhA&B*
Hartman, G A *Alli Sup*
Hartman, George *Alli*
Hartman, George E 1926- *ConAu 41*
Hartman, Gertrude 1876-1955 *AmA&B,*
JBA 1951
Hartman, Henry G 1877-1952 *OhA&B*
Hartman, Herbert Weidler 1901-1945 *DcNAA*
Hartman, Howard Levi 1924- *IndAu 1917*
Hartman, John Clark 1861-1941 *DcNAA*
Hartman, John J 1942- *ConAu 49*
Hartman, Lee Foster 1879-1941 *AmA&B,*
DcNAA, IndAu 1917
Hartman, Leon Wilson 1876-1943 *DcNAA*
Hartman, Levi Balmer 1838-1907 *DcNAA*
Hartman, Lewis Oliver 1876-1955 *IndAu 1917*
Hartman, Louis F 1901- *ConAu 23*
Hartman, Nancy Carol 1942- *ConAu 53*
Hartman, Olov 1906- *ConAu 29*
Hartman, Patience *ConAu XR*
Hartman, Rachel 1920-1972 *ConAu 5R,*
ConAu 33
Hartman, Rhondda Evans 1934- *ConAu 61*
Hartman, Robert James 1906- *IndAu 1917*
Hartman, Robert K 1940- *ConAu 41*
Hartman, Robert S 1910-1973 *Au&Wr,*
ConAu 17, ConAu 45
Hartman, Roger *ConAu XR*
Hartman, Shirley 1929- *ConAu 57*
Hartman, Sylvester J 1877-1953 *IndAu 1917*
Hartman, Violet Thomas *ChPo*
Hartman, William D And Mechener, Ezra
Alli Sup
Hartman, William Dell 1817-1899 *DcNAA*
Hartmann, Der Arme *OxGer*
Hartmann Von Aue 1170?-1215? *BiD&SB,*
CasWL, CyWA, DcEuL, EuA, EvEuW,
OxGer, Pen Eur, REn
Hartmann Von Ouwe 1170?-1215? *OxGer*
Hartmann, Alfred 1814-1897 *BiD&SB*
Hartmann, Andreas *OxGer*
Hartmann, Arthur Martinus 1881-1956
AmSCAP 66
Hartmann, Carl Robert Eduard Von 1842-1906
EvEuW
Hartmann, Eduard Von 1842-1906 *BbD,*

BiD&SB, OxGer
Hartmann, Edward George 1912- *ConAu 41*
Hartmann, Ernest L 1934- *ConAu 21,*
WrD 1976
Hartmann, Francis M 1870-1932 *DcNAA*
Hartmann, Franz *Alli Sup*
Hartmann, Frederick Howard 1922- *ConAu 1R*
Hartmann, George 1852- *ArizL*
Hartmann, Helmut Henry 1931- *WrD 1976*
Hartmann, Jacob Wittmer 1881- *WhWNAA*
Hartmann, John William Christian 1905-
Au&Wr
Hartmann, Klaus 1925- *ConAu 21*
Hartmann, Moritz 1821-1872 *BiD&SB,*
CasWL, DcEuL, EvEuW, OxGer
Hartmann, Raye 1876- *OhA&B*
Hartmann, Sadakichi 1867?-1944 *AmA&B,*
DcNAA, DcAmA, OxAm, REnAL
Hartmann, Susan M 1940- *ConAu 41*
Hartmann, T *Alli Sup*
Hartmanni, Varuna *TexWr*
Hartnack, Justus 1912- *ConAu 41*
Hartnell, H C *Alli Sup*
Hartner, Eva 1850- *DcBiA*
Hartness, James 1861-1934 *DcNAA, OhA&B*
Hartnett, Laurence John 1898- *WrD 1976*
Hartnett, Michael 1941- *Au&Wr, ConP 1970,*
ConP 1975, WrD 1976
Hartnoll, Phyllis *ChPo*
Hartny, Tsishka 1887- *DcRusL*
Hartocollis, Peter 1922- *ConAu 45*
Hartog, Jan De 1914- *CasWL, EncWL,*
TwCA Sup
Hartog, Marcus Manuel *Alli Sup*
Hartog, Sir Philip Joseph 1864-1937 *ChPo S2*
Harton, Sibyl 1898- *Au&Wr*
Hartop, Martin *Alli*
Hartough, Mrs. S M *Alli Sup*
Hartranft, Rufus C *Alli Sup*
Hartridge, Clifford Wayne 1866-1937 *DcNAA*
Hartridge, Gustavus *Alli Sup*
Hartridge, Hamilton 1886- *Au&Wr*
Hartshorn, C W *Alli*
Hartshorn, Charles Warren 1814-1893 *DcNAA*
Hartshorn, Edwin Alonzo *DcNAA*
Hartshorn, John *Alli*
Hartshorn, Thomas C *Alli*
Hartshorn, William Newton 1843-1920 *DcNAA*
Hartshorne, B F *Alli Sup*
Hartshorne, Caroline Ellen *Alli*
Hartshorne, Charles 1897- *AmA&B, Au&Wr,*
ConAu 9R
Hartshorne, Charles Henry 1802-1865 *Alli,*
Alli Sup, ChPo, ChPo S1
Hartshorne, Charles Hopkins 1851-1918
DcNAA
Hartshorne, Edward 1818-1885 *Alli, DcAmA*
Hartshorne, Emily Sophia *Alli Sup*
Hartshorne, Esther Kimball *ChPo*
Hartshorne, Grace *ChPo*
Hartshorne, Henry 1823-1897 *Alli, Alli Sup,*
AmA&B, BiD&SB
Hartshorne, Henry 1823-1884 *ChPo*
Hartshorne, Henry 1823-1897 *DcAmA,*
DcNAA
Hartshorne, Hugh 1885-1967 *AmA&B,*
WhWNAA
Hartshorne, Joseph 1779-1850 *Alli, BiDSA*
Hartshorne, Oliver *Alli Sup*
Hartshorne, Richard 1899- *Au&Wr,*
ConAu 5R, WrD 1976
Hartshorne, Thomas L 1935- *ConAu 37,*
WrD 1976
Hartsock, Ernest Abner 1903-1930 *AmA&B,*
AnMV 1926, DcNAA, WhWNAA
Hartson, Hall 1739?-1773 *DcEnL, PoIre*
Hartson, William Roland 1947- *WrD 1976*
Hartsough, L *ChPo*
Hartston, Hall *Alli*
Hartston, William R 1947- *Au&Wr*
Hartstonge, Matthew Weld *Alli, BiDLA,*
PoIre
Hartsuch, Paul Jackson 1902- *ConAu 57,*
IndAu 1917
Hartswick, Jennie Betts *ChPo*
Hartt, Charles Frederick 1840-1878 *Alli Sup,*
DcAmA, DcNAA
Hartt, George Montgomery 1877- *WhWNAA*

Hartt, Irene Widdemar LeB *Alli Sup*
Hartt, Mabel F *Alli Sup*
Hartt, Rollin Lynde 1869-1946 *AmA&B,*
DcNAA
Hartung, Ernst Johannes 1893- *WrD 1976*
Hartup, Willard W 1927- *ConAu 25*
Hartweg, Raoul *OxCan Sup*
Hartwell, Abraham *Alli*
Hartwell, Alice Booth *WhWNAA*
Hartwell, Alonzo 1805-1873 *EarAB,*
EarAB Sup
Hartwell, Charles Stearns 1855-1931 *DcNAA*
Hartwell, Dickson Jay 1906- *ConAu P-1*
Hartwell, Mrs. Dickson Jay *OhA&B*
Hartwell, Edward Mussey 1850-1922 *DcNAA*
Hartwell, Herbert 1894- *Au&Wr, WrD 1976*
Hartwell, J M *MnBBF*
Hartwell, Jesse 1772-1860 *OhA&B*
Hartwell, Mary *Alli Sup, ChPo, DcNAA*
Hartwell, Nancy *AuBYP, ConAu XR*
Hartwell, Ronald Max 1921- *ConAu 25*
Hartwell, Samuel Willard 1882- *WhWNAA*
Hartwick, Harry *AmA&B*
Hartwig Von Raute *OxGer*
Hartwig Von Rute *OxGer*
Hartwig, George *Alli*
Hartwig, Gustave *ChPo S1*
Hartwig, Marie Dorothy 1906- *ConAu 1R*
Harty, William *Alli, BiDLA*
Hartz, Jim *AuNews 2*
Hartz, Mina Frasa 1903- *IndAu 1917*
Hartzel, J C *Alli Sup*
Hartzel, Jonas *Alli Sup*
Hartzell, Jonas Hazard 1830-1890 *Alli Sup,*
DcAmA, DcNAA
Hartzell, Josiah 1833-1914 *DcNAA, OhA&B*
Hartzenbusch, Juan Eugenio 1806-1880
BiD&SB, CasWL, DcEuL, DcSpL, EuA,
EvEuW, Pen Eur, REn
Hartzenbusch Y Martinez, Juan Eugenio
1806-1880 *McGWD*
Hartzler, Daniel David 1941- *ConAu 61*
Hartzler, Henry Burns 1840-1920 *DcNAA*
Hartzler, John Ellsworth 1879- *IndAu 1816,*
OhA&B, WhWNAA
Hartzler, Jonas Smucker 1857- *IndAu 1816*
Hartzog, William Benjamin 1863-1945 *OhA&B*
Harun Al-Rashid 763?-809 *NewC*
Harun Ar-Rashid 763?-809 *NewC*
Harvard, Charles *ConAu XR*
Harvard, John 1607-1638 *CyAL 1, REn*
Harvard, Senior *DcNAA*
Harvard, Stephen 1948- *ConAu 57*
Harvard, Stephen P *Alli Sup*
Harvard, W M *BbtC*
Harvard, William Martin 1790-1857 *DcNAA*
Harvest, George d1776 *Alli*
Harvest, William *Alli*
Harvester, Simon *Au&Wr, ConAu XR*
Harvey, Abraham *Alli Sup*
Harvey, Alexander *Alli Sup*
Harvey, Alexander 1868-1949 *AmA&B,*
AmLY, DcNAA, WhWNAA
Harvey, Alice G 1893- *WhWNAA*
Harvey, Alick *MnBBF*
Harvey, Annie Jane *Alli Sup*
Harvey, Arthur 1834- *BbtC*
Harvey, Bennett *Alli Sup*
Harvey, C H Fox *MnBBF*
Harvey, Charles John Derrick 1922- *ConAu 9R,*
ConP 1970
Harvey, Charles M 1848- *BiDSA*
Harvey, Charles Nigel 1916- *Au&Wr*
Harvey, Christopher 1597?-1663 *CasWL, ChPo,*
DcEnL
Harvey, D P *ChPo S2*
Harvey, D W *Alli*
Harvey, Daniel Cobb 1886- *OxCan*
Harvey, Donald J 1922- *ConAu 41*
Harvey, E Newton 1887- *WhWNAA*
Harvey, Edmund George 1828-1884 *Alli Sup*
Harvey, Edward Burns 1939- *ConAu 41*
Harvey, Ellen Louisa *Alli Sup*
Harvey, Everett Burton 1892- *WhWNAA*
Harvey, Fitzwilliam *Alli Sup*
Harvey, Francis *Alli Sup*
Harvey, Frank 1912- *Au&Wr, ConAu 5R*
Harvey, Frederick Burn *Alli Sup*

Harvey, Frederick William 1888- *CatA 1947,*
ChPo, ChPo S1, NewC
Harvey, G Bianca *Alli Sup*
Harvey, G H *ChPo, ChPo S1*
Harvey, Gabriel 1545?-1630? *Alli, BrAu,*
CasWL, Chmbr 1, CrE&SL, DcEnL,
DcEuL, DcLEnL, EvLB, NewC, OxEng,
Pen Eng, REn
Harvey, George *Alli, BiDLA Sup*
Harvey, Sir George 1805-1876 *Alli Sup*
Harvey, George Brinton McClellan 1864-1928
AmA&B, DcNAA
Harvey, George Cockburn 1858-1935 *AmA&B,*
DcNAA
Harvey, Gideon d1700 *Alli*
Harvey, Gina P 1922- *ConAu 45*
Harvey, H *MnBBF*
Harvey, H 1821- *Alli*
Harvey, Henry B *Alli Sup*
Harvey, Herbert J *ChPo S2*
Harvey, Hezekiah 1821-1893 *DcNAA*
Harvey, Hope 1877- *WhWNAA*
Harvey, Ian Douglas 1914- *Au&Wr,*
ConAu P-1
Harvey, Jack *MnBBF*
Harvey, Jack 1917- *Au&Wr*
Harvey, James *Alli, Alli Sup*
Harvey, James C 1925- *ConAu 45*
Harvey, James Clarence 1859-1917 *ChPo,*
ChPo S2, DcNAA
Harvey, James O 1926- *ConAu 17R*
Harvey, Jane *Alli, BiDLA*
Harvey, Jean-Charles 1891-1967 *CanWr,*
CasWL, OxCan
Harvey, John *Alli, Alli Sup*
Harvey, John 1680-1738? *ChPo, ChPo S1*
Harvey, Sir John 1778-1852 *OxCan*
Harvey, John Bawtree *ChPo S2*
Harvey, John F 1921- *ConAu 13R*
Harvey, John Henry 1891- *Au&Wr*
Harvey, John Hooper 1911- *Au&Wr,*
ConAu 5R, WrD 1976
Harvey, John LeGrand 1857- *DcAmA*
Harvey, John Robert 1942- *Au&Wr*
Harvey, Jonathan 1939- *ConAu 61*
Harvey, Lashley Grey 1900- *ConAu 37*
Harvey, Laurence 1928- *NewC*
Harvey, Lorenzo Dow 1848-1922 *DcNAA*
Harvey, Margaret Boyle d1912 *ChPo, DcNAA*
Harvey, Maria Luisa Alvarez 1938- *ConAu 53*
Harvey, Marion 1900- *OhA&B*
Harvey, Minnie L *Alli Sup*
Harvey, Moses 1820-1901 *Alli Sup, BbtC,*
DcNAA, OxCan
Harvey, Nigel 1916- *WrD 1976*
Harvey, Norman B 1931- *Au&Wr*
Harvey, O J 1927- *ConAu 37*
Harvey, Orlando Emery 1887-1952 *OhA&B*
Harvey, Oscar Jewell 1851-1922 *DcNAA*
Harvey, Paul *AmA&B*
Harvey, Peggy 1884- *WhWNAA*
Harvey, Peter 1810-1877 *Alli Sup, DcNAA*
Harvey, Peter Noel 1916- *Au&Wr*
Harvey, Philip *Alli Sup*
Harvey, Rachel *ConAu XR, WrD 1976*
Harvey, Richard *Alli*
Harvey, Richard B 1930- *ConAu 49*
Harvey, Robert *Alli Sup*
Harvey, Robert 1884- *ConAu 5R*
Harvey, Robert Cadzow *ChPo S2*
Harvey, Robert Otto 1923- *IndAu 1917*
Harvey, Rodney Beecher 1890-1945 *IndAu 1917*
Harvey, Ross *MnBBF*
Harvey, Rowland Hill 1889-1943 *DcNAA*
Harvey, Ruth C 1918- *ConAu 1R*
Harvey, T *Alli*
Harvey, Thomas *Alli, Alli Sup*
Harvey, Thomas 1812-1884 *Alli Sup*
Harvey, Thomas Chapman *Alli Sup*
Harvey, Thomas Edmund 1875- *WhLA*
Harvey, Thomas Hingston 1831-1872 *Alli Sup*
Harvey, Thomas Wadleigh 1821-1892 *DcNAA,*
OhA&B
Harvey, Van A 1926- *ConAu 33*
Harvey, Virginia I 1917- *ConAu 57*
Harvey, W *Alli Sup, BbtC*
Harvey, W C *Alli*
Harvey, W J *Alli Sup*

Harvey, Walter *Alli Sup*
Harvey, William *Alli, Alli Sup, BiDLA*
Harvey, William 1578-1657 *Alli, BrAu, DcEnL, NewC, OxEng, REn*
Harvey, William 1796-1866 *ChPo, ChPo S2*
Harvey, William 1874- *ChPo S2*
Harvey, William Burnett 1922- *ConAu 41*
Harvey, William Frederick 1853- *Alli Sup*
Harvey, William Henry 1811-1866 *Alli, Alli Sup*
Harvey, William Hope 1851-1936 *BiDSA, DcAmA, DcNAA, OhA&B, OxAm, REnAL, WhWNAA*
Harvey, William Marsh *Alli Sup*
Harvey, William Penn 1828-1917 *OhA&B*
Harvey, William Wigan 1810-1883 *Alli Sup*
Harvey-Gibson, Robert John 1860- *WhLA*
Harvie, John *Alli*
Harvie-Brown *Alli Sup*
Harvison, C W *OxCan Sup*
Harward, Simon *Alli*
Harward, Timothy Blake 1932- *ConAu 25*
Harwell, Ann J 1936- *ConAu 57*
Harwell, Richard Barksdale 1915- *AmA&B, ConAu 1R*
Harwin, Brian *AuBYP, ConAu XR, SmATA XR*
Harwood *Alli*
Harwood, Alice 1909- *Au&Wr, ConAu 5R, WrD 1976*
Harwood, Andrew Allen 1802-1884 *Alli Sup, DcAmA, DcNAA*
Harwood, Annie *Alli Sup*
Harwood, Anthony *ChPo S2*
Harwood, Sir Busick d1814 *Alli, BiDLA, BiDLA Sup*
Harwood, Caroline *Alli, BiDLA*
Harwood, Charlotte *Alli, BiDLA*
Harwood, David 1938- *Au&Wr, WrD 1976*
Harwood, Edward *Alli*
Harwood, Edward 1729-1794? *Alli, DcEnL*
Harwood, Edwin 1939- *ConAu 29*
Harwood, Edwin And Wildes, George D *Alli Sup*
Harwood, Elizabeth *OxCan Sup*
Harwood, F J *ChPo*
Harwood, Frederick *ChPo S1*
Harwood, G H *Alli*
Harwood, Gabriel H *Alli Sup*
Harwood, George 1845- *Alli Sup*
Harwood, Gina *ChPo S2, ConAu XR*
Harwood, Gwen 1920- *ConP 1970, ConP 1975, WhTwL, WrD 1976*
Harwood, Harold Marsh 1874-1959 *DcLEnL, NewC*
Harwood, Isabella 1840?-1888 *Alli Sup, BrAu 19*
Harwood, J A *Alli Sup*
Harwood, James *Alli*
Harwood, John *Alli, BiDLA*
Harwood, John Berwick *Alli Sup*
Harwood, John Edmund 1771-1809 *Alli, CyAL 1, DcAmA, DcNAA*
Harwood, Lee 1939- *ConAu 21, ConP 1970, ConP 1975*
Harwood, Pearl Augusta 1903- *ConAu 13R, SmATA 9*
Harwood, Richard *Alli*
Harwood, Ronald 1934- *Au&Wr, ConAu 1R, WrD 1976*
Harwood, Thomas *Alli, BiDLA*
Harwood, Uriel *Alli, BiDLA*
Harwood, William *Alli*
Harwood, William Sumner 1857-1908 *DcNAA*
Haryngton, Sir John 1561-1612 *DcEnL*
Haryngton ALSO Harington; Harrington
Has, Kunz *OxGer*
Hasam Sah 1735-1843 *DcOrL 2*
Hasan, Mahammed Abdille *AfA 1*
Hasan, S Z 1885- *WhLA*
Hasan Dihlavi 1253-1328 *DcOrL 2*
Hasan Khan, Shabir *DcOrL 2*
Hasbrouck, D C *ChPo*
Hasbrouck, J *Alli Sup*
Hasbrouck, Joseph *ChPo S2*
Hasbrouck, Joseph 1840- *DcNAA*
Hasbrouck, Kenneth E 1916- *ConAu 49*
Hasbrouck, Louise Seymour 1883- *AmA&B,*

ChPo, ChPo S2, WhWNAA
Hascall, Daniel 1782-1852 *DcAmA, DcNAA*
Hascard, Gregory d1708 *Alli*
Haschka, Laurenz L 1749-1827 *BiD&SB, ChPo*
Haschka, Lorenz Leopold 1749-1827 *OxGer*
Hasdeu, Bogdan Petriceicu 1838-1907 *CasWL*
Hasebroek, Johannes Petrus 1812-1896 *BiD&SB, CasWL*
Hasek, Jaroslav 1883-1923 *CasWL, ClDMEuL, EncWL, EvEuW, LongC, ModSL 2, Pen Eur, REn, TwCA, TwCA Sup, TwCW, WhTwL*
Hasel, Gerhard F 1935- *ConAu 41*
Haselden, Adolphus Frederick *Alli Sup*
Haselden, Kyle 1913-1968 *ConAu 5R*
Haselden, Percy *ChPo*
Haselden, Thomas *Alli*
Haseldine, G A *Alli Sup*
Haseldon, W S *Alli*
Haseler, Digby Bertram *ChPo S1*
Haselfoot, Frederick Kneller Haselfoot 1828- *Alli Sup*
Hasell, Elizabeth Julia 1830-1887 *Alli Sup*
Haseloff, Charles *DrAP 1975*
Haseltine, Blanche Sage 1889- *WhWNAA*
Haselwood, Cecil *Alli Sup*
Haselwood, Constance *ChPo*
Haseman, Leonard 1884- *IndAu 1917, WhWNAA*
Hasen, Syed J *Alli Sup*
Hasenclever, Walter 1890-1940 *CasWL, ClDMEuL, CnMD, EncWL, McGWD, ModGL, ModWD, OxGer, Pen Eur*
Haserick, E C *Alli Sup*
Hasham Shah 1735-1843 *CasWL*
Hashim, Makhdum Mahammad 1692-1761 *DcOrL 2*
Hashimi, Zahur Muhammad Shah Sa'id 1926- *DcOrL 2*
Hashr, Agha *REnWD*
Hasim, Ahmet 1885-1933 *DcOrL 3*
Haskel, Daniel 1784-1848 *AmA&B, DcNAA*
Haskel, Daniel ALSO Haskell, Daniel
Haskel, R M *Alli*
Haskell, Arnold Lionel 1903- *Au&Wr, ConAu 5R, SmATA 6*
Haskell, B D *Alli Sup*
Haskell, Charles Cheves 1880- *WhWNAA*
Haskell, Daniel 1784-1848 *CyAL 1, DcAmA, REnAL*
Haskell, Daniel ALSO Haskel, Daniel
Haskell, Daniel C 1883- *AmA&B*
Haskell, Mrs. E F *Alli Sup*
Haskell, Francis James Herbert 1928- *Au&Wr, ConAu 9R, WrD 1976*
Haskell, Helen Eggleston 1871- *AmA&B, JBA 1934, JBA 1951*
Haskell, Henry Joseph 1874-1952 *OhA&B*
Haskell, Lottie *ChPo S1, ChPo S2*
Haskell, Lucy *ChPo S1, ChPo S2*
Haskell, Martin R 1912- *ConAu 41*
Haskell, Peter Thomas 1923- *Au&Wr*
Haskell, Thomas Hawes 1842-1900 *Alli Sup, DcNAA*
Haskell, Thomas Nelson 1826-1906 *DcNAA*
Haskell, W G *ChPo S1*
Haskell, William B *OxCan*
Haskett, Edythe Rance 1915- *BlkAW, ConAu 23, LivBA*
Haskey, Henricus *Alli*
Haskin, Dorothy C 1905- *ConAu 5R, WrD 1976*
Haskin, Frederic Jennings 1872- *AmLY, DcNAA, WhWNAA*
Haskin, William Lawrence 1841-1931 *DcNAA*
Haskins, Alma Eunice 1875- *WhWNAA*
Haskins, C H *Alli Sup*
Haskins, Caryl Davis 1867-1911 *DcAmA, DcNAA*
Haskins, Charles Homer 1870-1937 *AmA&B, DcNAA, WhWNAA*
Haskins, Charles Nelson 1874-1942 *DcNAA*
Haskins, Charles Waldo 1852-1903 *DcNAA*
Haskins, David Greene 1818-1896 *Alli Sup, DcAmA, DcNAA*
Haskins, Edmund Henry *Alli Sup*
Haskins, Elizabeth *Alli*

Haskins, George Foxcroft 1806-1872 *Alli Sup, DcNAA*
Haskins, George Lee 1915- *ConAu 1R, WrD 1976*
Haskins, Howard Davis 1871-1933 *DcNAA*
Haskins, Ilma 1919- *ConAu 45*
Haskins, James 1805-1845 *BbtC, ChPo S2, PoIre*
Haskins, James 1941- *ConAu 33, SmATA 9*
Haskins, Jim 1941- *ConAu XR, LivBA, SmATA XR, WrD 1976*
Haskins, John *Alli, PoIre*
Haskins, Minnie Louise 1875-1957 *ChPo S1, EvLB*
Haskins, Robert Willson 1796-1870 *DcNAA*
Haskoll, W Davis *Alli Sup*
Haslam, Gerald William 1937- *ConAu 29, WrD 1976*
Haslam, Herbert 1928- *AmSCAP 66*
Haslam, John *Alli, Alli Sup, BiDLA*
Haslam, R T 1888- *WhWNAA*
Haslam, Samuel Holker & Edwards, Joseph *Alli Sup*
Haslam, Mrs. T J *Alli Sup*
Haslam, William *Alli, Alli Sup*
Haslam, William Saunders *BiDLA*
Haslar, John *MnBBF*
Haslehurst, George *Alli*
Haslehurst, W W *ChPo S2*
Haslem, John 1808-1884 *Alli Sup*
Haslem, William Saunders *Alli*
Hasler, Joan 1931- *ConAu 29*
Haslerigg, Sir Arthur *Alli*
Haslerud, George M 1906- *ConAu 45*
Hasleton, Richard *Alli*
Haslett, Charles *Alli Sup*
Haslett, Elmer 1894- *WhWNAA*
Haslewood, Frances C *Alli Sup*
Haslewood, Francis *Alli, Alli Sup*
Haslewood, John *Alli*
Haslewood, Joseph 1769-1833 *Alli, BiDLA, DcEnL*
Haslewood, William *Alli*
Hasley, Louis 1906- *ConAu 37*
Hasley, Lucile 1909- *BkC 5, CatA 1952, ConAu P-1, IndAu 1917*
Hasling, John 1928- *ConAu 33*
Hasloch, John *Alli*
Haslop, Alice *Alli Sup*
Haslope, L L *Alli Sup*
Hasluck, Alice *ChPo S1*
Hasluck, Paul N *Alli Sup*
Hasluck, Samuel L *Alli Sup*
Hasolle, James *Alli, DcEnL*
Hasrat Mohani, Sayyid Fazlu'l-Hasan 1850-1951 *DcOrL 2*
Hass, C Glen 1915- *ConAu 17R*
Hass, Hans 1919- *Au&Wr*
Hass, Robert *DrAP 1975*
Hassall, Arthur *Alli Sup*
Hassall, Arthur Hill *Alli, Alli Sup*
Hassall, Charles *Alli*
Hassall, Christopher Vernon 1912-1963 *ChPo, ChPo S1, ChPo S2, DcLEnL, LongC, ModBL, NewC, TwCW, WorAu*
Hassall, Ian *ChPo*
Hassall, Joan 1906- *ChPo, ChPo S1, ChPo S2, IlCB 1956, WhGrA*
Hassall, John 1868-1948 *ChPo, ChPo S1, LongC*
Hassall, Richard *Alli Sup*
Hassall, W J *Alli Sup*
Hassall, William Owen 1912- *Au&Wr, ConAu 13R, WrD 1976*
Hassam, A *Alli Sup*
Hassam, Childe 1859-1935 *OxAm*
Hassam, F Childe 1859-1935 *ChPo, ChPo S1*
Hassam, John Tyler 1841-1903 *DcNAA*
Hassan, A B *Alli Sup*
Hassan, Ihab Habib 1925- *ConAu 1R, ConAu 5R*
Hassan, William Ephraim, Jr. 1923- *ConAu 33*
Hassan B Thabit *DcOrL 3*
Hassan Ibn Thabit *CasWL*
Hassard, Albert Richard 1873-1940 *DcNAA*
Hassard, Annie *Alli Sup*
Hassard, Francis Charles *Alli Sup, PoIre*
Hassard, John Rose Greene 1836-1888 *Alli Sup,*

AmA&B, BiD&SB, DcAmA, DcNAA
Hassard, Richard Samuel *Alli Sup*
Hassaurek, Friedrich 1832-1885 *Alli Sup,*
BiD&SB, DcAmA, DcNAA, OhA&B
Hasse, Adelaide R *AmLY, WhWNAA*
Hassel, Richard *Alli*
Hasselgrew, Nicholas *Alli*
Hassell, Cushing Biggs 1808-1880 *BiDSA,*
DcNAA
Hassell, J *Alli, BiDLA*
Hassell, Joseph *Alli Sup*
Hassell, Kate Mary *TexWr*
Hasselriis, Else *ConICB, IlCB 1945*
Hasselt, Andre Henri Constant Van 1806-1874
BiD&SB, EuA, EvEuW
Hassenger, Robert 1937- *ConAu 21*
Hassenpflug, Hans Daniel 1794-1862 *OxGer*
Hasset-Blener, Thomas *Alli*
Hassing, Per 1916- *ConAu 37*
Hasskarl, Gottlieb Christopher Henry 1855-1929
DcNAA
Hassler, Charles William d1888 *DcNAA*
Hassler, Donald M 1937- *ConAu 41,*
DrAP 1975
Hassler, Edgar Wakefield 1859-1905 *DcNAA*
Hassler, Ferdinand Rudolph 1770-1843 *DcAmA,*
DcNAA
Hassler, Hans Leo 1564-1612 *AtlBL, CasWL*
Hassler, Russell Herman 1906- *IndAu 1917*
Hassler, Warren W, Jr. 1926- *ConAu 9R*
Hasson, James 1892- *Au&Wr*
Hassrick, Peter H 1941- *ConAu 49*
Hastain, Eugene *ChPo, ChPo S2*
Haste, Gwendolen 1889- *AnMV 1926, ChPo,*
WhWNAA
Hasted, Edward 1732-1812 *Alli*
Hasted, Henry *Alli Sup*
Hastie, W *Alli Sup*
Hastings, Adrian 1929- *ConAu 17R*
Hastings, Alan *ConAu XR*
Hastings, Anna *Alli Sup*
Hastings, Arthur Claude 1935- *BiDPar,*
ConAu 37
Hastings, Baird 1919- *Au&Wr*
Hastings, Cecily Mary Eleanor 1924- *Au&Wr,*
ConAu 5R
Hastings, Charles Sheldon 1848-1932 *DcAmA,*
DcNAA
Hastings, David R *Alli Sup*
Hastings, Elizabeth 1864-1955 *AmA&B,*
DcAmA
Hastings, Elizabeth 1913- *WhWNAA*
Hastings, Ernest Clement 1887?-1942 *DcNAA*
Hastings, Fanny DeGroot *ChPo, ChPo S1,*
ChPo S2
Hastings, Lady Flora Elizabeth Rawdon
1806-1839 *Alli, ChPo, ChPo S1, PoIre*
Hastings, Francis *Alli*
Hastings, Sir Francis *Alli*
Hastings, Francis Rawdon *Alli*
Hastings, Frank Warren 1856-1925 *DcNAA,*
WhWNAA
Hastings, Frederick *Alli Sup*
Hastings, George Everett *WhWNAA*
Hastings, George Woodyatt 1825- *Alli Sup*
Hastings, Graham *EncM&D*
Hastings, H L *ChPo S1*
Hastings, Harold 1916- *AmSCAP 66*
Hastings, Harrington *ConAu XR*
Hastings, Henry James *Alli*
Hastings, Horace Lorenzo 1831-1899 *Alli Sup,*
DcAmA, DcNAA
Hastings, Hudson Bridge 1885- *WhWNAA*
Hastings, Hugh *Alli Sup*
Hastings, Ian 1912- *ConAu 45*
Hastings, James *Alli Sup*
Hastings, James Syme 1870-1921 *OhA&B*
Hastings, John *Alli, Alli Sup*
Hastings, John K *Alli Sup*
Hastings, Lansford Warren 1818?-1870 *DcNAA,*
OhA&B
Hastings, Lewis M *Alli Sup*
Hastings, Lillian McKenney 1897- *WhWNAA*
Hastings, M Louise C *ChPo S2*
Hastings, Macdonald 1909- *Au&Wr,*
ConAu 53, EncM&D, WrD 1976
Hastings, Margaret 1910- *ConAu 41*

Hastings, Michael *MnBBF*
Hastings, Michael 1938- *Au&Wr, ConDr,*
WrD 1976
Hastings, Sir Patrick 1880-1952 *NewC*
Hastings, Paul Guiler 1914- *ConAu 1R,*
IndAu 1917
Hastings, Phyllis Dora Hodge 1904- *Au&Wr,*
ConAu 9R, WrD 1976
Hastings, Robert Paul 1933- *Au&Wr,*
WrD 1976
Hastings, Rosetta Butler 1844-1934 *ChPo,*
OhA&B
Hastings, Ross 1915- *AmSCAP 66*
Hastings, Sarah 1773-1812 *DcNAA*
Hastings, Sybil *Alli Sup*
Hastings, Sydney 1841- *Alli Sup*
Hastings, T *Alli, BiDLA*
Hastings, Thomas *PoIre*
Hastings, Thomas 1784-1872 *Alli, AmA&B,*
ChPo, DcNAA, OxAm, PoCh, REnAL
Hastings, Thomas S *Alli Sup*
Hastings, Thomas Samuel 1827-1911 *DcNAA*
Hastings, Truman *Alli Sup*
Hastings, Warren 1732?-1818 *Alli, BiDLA,*
NewC, REn
Hastings, Wells *ChPo*
Hastings, Wells Southworth 1878-1923 *DcNAA*
Hastings, William T 1881- *ConAu 5R*
Haston, Dougal 1940- *WrD 1976*
Hasty, John Eugene 1897- *IndAu 1917*
Hasty, Ronald W 1941- *ConAu 53*
Hasund, S 1868- *WhLA*
Haswell, Alanson Mason 1847- *AmA&B,*
DcNAA, WhWNAA
Haswell, Anthony 1756-1816 *AmA&B,*
DcNAA
Haswell, Charles Haynes 1809-1907 *Alli,*
DcAmA, DcNAA
Haswell, Chetwynd John Drake 1919-
ConAu 41, WrD 1976
Haswell, George C *Alli Sup*
Haswell, Harold Alanson, Jr. 1912- *ConAu 45*
Haswell, J B *Alli Sup*
Haswell, James M *Alli Sup*
Haswell, James M 1810-1876 *Alli Sup*
Haswell, Jock 1919- *Au&Wr, ConAu XR,*
WrD 1976
Haswell, John *ChPo, ChPo S2*
Haswell, Keeley *ChPo S1*
Haswell, Susannah *Alli*
Haswell, Thomas *Alli Sup*
Haswell, William A *Alli Sup*
Hasworth, H H *Alli, BiDLA*
Haszard, H *Alli Sup*
Hatar, Gyozo Victor John 1914- *Au&Wr*
Hatch, Alden 1898-1975 *AmA&B, Au&Wr,*
AuBYP, ConAu 57
Hatch, Beatrice *ChPo S1*
Hatch, Benjamin F *Alli Sup*
Hatch, David Patterson 1846-1912 *DcNAA*
Hatch, Denison 1935- *ConAu 33, WrD 1976*
Hatch, Edwin 1835-1889 *Alli Sup, ChPo S1,*
NewC
Hatch, Elvin 1937- *ConAu 45*
Hatch, Eric Stow 1901-1973 *AmA&B, AmNov,*
ConAu 41, TwCA, TwCA Sup
Hatch, Henry John *Alli Sup*
Hatch, James V 1928- *ConAu 41*
Hatch, John *Alli*
Hatch, John Charles 1917- *Au&Wr,*
ConAu 9R, WrD 1976
Hatch, K L 1871- *WhWNAA*
Hatch, Leonard 1882- *ChPo S1*
Hatch, Louis Clinton 1872-1931 *AmA&B,*
DcNAA
Hatch, Marion F *ChPo S1*
Hatch, Mary Cottam 1912- *AnCL, St&VC*
Hatch, Mary R Platt 1848-1935 *AmA&B,*
DcNAA, WhWNAA
Hatch, Preble D K 1898- *ConAu 23*
Hatch, Raymond N 1911- *ConAu 21*
Hatch, Reuben *Alli Sup*
Hatch, Richard A 1940- *ConAu 21*
Hatch, Richard Warren 1898- *AmA&B,*
WhCL, WhWNAA
Hatch, Susan L *Alli Sup*
Hatch, Vernie L Bosler 1888- *IndAu 1917*
Hatch, W *Alli Sup*

Hatch, Walter Mooney 1843-1879 *Alli Sup*
Hatch, William E *Alli Sup*
Hatch, William Henry Paine 1875-1972
AmA&B, ConAu 37, WhWNAA
Hatch, William Stanley 1789-1872 *Alli Sup,*
OhA&B
Hatchard, Fanny Vincent Steele d1880 *Alli Sup*
Hatchard, Louisa *Alli Sup*
Hatchard, Thomas Goodwin *Alli, Alli Sup*
Hatchell, John *Alli, BiDLA*
Hatchell, John P *Alli*
Hatcher, Eldridge Burwell 1865-1943 *BiDSA,*
DcNAA
Hatcher, Harlan Henthorne 1898- *AmA&B,*
Au&Wr, ConAu 19, OhA&B, REnAL,
TwCA, TwCA Sup
Hatcher, John 1942- *ConAu 33, WrD 1976*
Hatcher, John Bell 1861-1904 *DcNAA*
Hatcher, John E *BiDSA*
Hatcher, Mattie Austin *TexWr*
Hatcher, Nat B 1897- *ConAu 1R*
Hatcher, Orie Latham d1946 *DcNAA,*
WhWNAA
Hatcher, Sadie Bacon 1895?- *IndAu 1917*
Hatcher, Thomas *Alli*
Hatcher, William Bass 1888-1947 *DcNAA*
Hatcher, William Eldridge 1835-1912 *Alli Sup,*
BiDSA, DcNAA
Hatchet, Hiram *ChPo*
Hatchett, Charles *Alli*
Hatchett, Hiram *ChPo S1*
Hate, Gossinath Sadashivji *Alli Sup*
Hatefi, 'Abdollah 1440?-1521 *DcOrL 3*
Hately, T L *ChPo S2*
Hatfield, Miss *Alli, BiDLA*
Hatfield, C W 1877- *ChPo S1, WhLA*
Hatfield, Clarence E *AmA&B*
Hatfield, Dorothy B 1921- *ConAu 53*
Hatfield, Edwin Francis 1807-1883 *Alli Sup,*
AmA&B, ChPo, DcAmA, DcNAA
Hatfield, Henry Caraway 1912- *AmA&B*
Hatfield, Henry Rand 1866- *WhWNAA*
Hatfield, J F *Alli, BiDLA*
Hatfield, James Taft 1862-1945 *AmA&B,*
AmLY, DcNAA, WhWNAA
Hatfield, John 1933- *Au&Wr*
Hatfield, John Thomas 1851- *IndAu 1816*
Hatfield, Joseph Henry 1863-1928 *ChPo*
Hatfield, Julia *Alli Sup*
Hatfield, Malcolm Keith 1900-1962 *IndAu 1917*
Hatfield, Marcus Patten 1849-1909 *Alli Sup,*
DcNAA
Hatfield, Richard *AmLY XR*
Hatfield, Robert Griffith 1815-1879 *DcNAA*
Hatfield, Miss S E *ChPo S2*
Hatfield, Victor Murray 1859- *IndAu 1917*
Hatfield, W Wilbur 1882- *WhWNAA*
Hathaway, Anne 1556?-1623 *NewC, REn*
Hathaway, Arthur Stafford 1855-1934 *DcNAA,*
WhWNAA
Hathaway, B A *Alli Sup*
Hathaway, Baxter L 1909- *AmA&B,*
ConAu 1R
Hathaway, Benjamin 1822- *Alli Sup, AmA&B,*
BiD&SB, ChPo, ChPo S2, DcAmA,
DcNAA
Hathaway, Charles 1904-1966 *AmSCAP 66*
Hathaway, Dale E 1925- *ConAu 9R*
Hathaway, Ernest Jackson 1871-1930 *DcNAA,*
OxCan
Hathaway, Harle Wallace 1866- *WhWNAA*
Hathaway, Jan *ConAu XR*
Hathaway, Lulu 1903- *ConAu 13R*
Hathaway, M E N *ChPo*
Hathaway, Maurine *OhA&B*
Hathaway, Richard *DcEnL*
Hathaway, Rufus Hawten 1869- *ChPo*
Hathaway, Sibyl Collings 1884- *ConAu 1R*
Hathaway, Starke R 1903- *ConAu 5R*
Hathaway, Timothy *Alli Sup*
Hathaway, W J *Alli Sup*
Hathaway, W S *Alli, BiDLA*
Hathaway, Warren 1828-1909 *DcAmA,*
DcNAA
Hathaway, William *DrAP 1975*
Hathaway, William E 1844- *OhA&B*
Hathcock, Louise *ConAu 1R*
Hatherell, J W *Alli*

Hatherley, Captain *MnBBF*
Hatherway, Cyril *MnBBF*
Hatheway, Calvin 1796-1866 *BbtC, DcNAA, OxCan*
Hatheway, Joel 1878- *WhWNAA*
Hatheway, Mary E N *Alli Sup, ChPo S1, ChPo S2*
Hatheway, Warren Franklin 1850-1923 *AmLY, DcNAA*
Hathorn, F G *Alli Sup*
Hathorn, Richmond 1917- *ConAu 1R*
Hathornethwaite, Thomas *PoIre*
Hathornthwaite, Thomas *Alli Sup*
Hatif Of Isfahan, Sayid Ahmad d1784 *CasWL*
Hatifi, Maulana Abdallah d1520? *BiD&SB*
Hatim Al-Ta'i *CasWL*
Hatley, Griffith *Alli*
Hatley, T Marvin 1905- *AmSCAP 66*
Hatrak, Edward D 1920- *AmSCAP 66*
Hatsell, John 1742-1820 *Alli, BiDLA*
Hatt, Andrew *Alli*
Hatt, George *Alli Sup*
Hatt, Harold Ernest 1932- *ConAu 21, WrD 1976*
Hatt, Richard 1785- *Alli, BiDLA, BiDLA Sup*
Hatt, Robert Torrens 1902- *IndAu 1917*
Hatt, William Kendrick 1868- *WhWNAA*
Hattan, Anne Phillips *ChPo S2*
Hattecliffe, Vinc *Alli*
Hatten, William *PoIre*
Hatteras, Owen *ConAmA*
Hattersley, John *ChPo S2*
Hattersley, Mary Emma *Alli Sup*
Hattery, Lowell H 1916- *ConAu 17R*
Hatto I 871?-913 *NewC*
Hatto II 969?- *NewC*
Hatton, A L *Alli Sup*
Hatton, Alma W 1917- *AmSCAP 66*
Hatton, Charles *Au&Wr*
Hatton, Sir Christopher *Alli*
Hatton, Sir Christopher 1540-1591 *Alli, NewC, OxEng*
Hatton, E Finch- *Alli Sup*
Hatton, Edward *Alli*
Hatton, Fanny 1870?-1939 *AmA&B*
Hatton, Frank 1861-1883 *Alli Sup*
Hatton, Frederic 1879-1946 *AmA&B, DcNAA*
Hatton, G Noel *Alli Sup, NewC*
Hatton, George J F, Earl Of Winchilsea d1887 *Alli Sup*
Hatton, Harold Heneage Finch- 1856- *Alli Sup*
Hatton, John W *BiDSA*
Hatton, Joseph 1841?-1907? *Alli Sup, BbD, BiD&SB, BrAu 19, DcEnL, NewC, OxCan*
Hatton, Mark *Alli Sup*
Hatton, Murray E G F, Earl Of Winchilsea 1851- *Alli Sup*
Hatton, Ragnhild Marie 1913- *Au&Wr, ConAu 25, WrD 1976*
Hatton, Robert Wayland 1934- *ConAu 37*
Hatton, Thomas *Alli, Alli Sup*
Hatton, W H And Fox, Walter Edward *Alli Sup*
Hatvary, George Egon *ConAu 53*
Hatzfeld, Adolf Von 1892-1957 *OxGer*
Hatzfeld, Adolphe *OxFr*
Hatzfeld, Helmut A 1892- *DcSpL*
Hatzidakis, Nicholas 1872- *WhLA*
Hatzlerin, Clara *CasWL, OxGer*
Haub, Hattie D F *WhWNAA*
Hauberg, Clifford A 1906- *ConAu 37*
Haubiel, Charles 1892- *AmSCAP 66*
Haubold, Herman Arthur 1867-1931 *DcNAA*
Hauch Von Koln *OxGer*
Hauch, Carsten 1790-1872 *Pen Eur*
Hauch, Johannes Carsten 1790-1872 *BiD&SB, CasWL, DcEuL, EuA, EvEuW*
Hauck, Allan 1925- *ConAu 1R*
Hauck, Louise Platt 1883-1943 *AmA&B, DcNAA, WhWNAA*
Hauck, Paul A 1924- *ConAu 41*
Hauck, Richard Boyd 1936- *ConAu 53*
Hauenschild, Richard Georg Spiller Von *BiD&SB*
Hauerwas, Stanley Martin 1940- *ConAu 57*
Hauff, Wilhelm 1802-1827 *AuBYP, BiD&SB, CasWL, DcBiA, EuA, EvEuW, OxGer,*

Pen Eur, REn, WhCL
Hauffman *Alli*
Haug, Balthasar 1731-1792 *OxGer*
Haug, Friedrich 1761-1829 *OxGer*
Haug, Johann Cristoph Friedrich 1761-1829 *BiD&SB*
Haug, Martin 1827-1876 *Alli Sup*
Haugaard, Erik Christian 1923- *AuBYP, ConAu 5R, SmATA 4, ThBJA, WrD 1976*
Haugaard, William Paul 1929- *ConAu 25, WrD 1976*
Haugan, Randolph Edgar 1902- *ChPo*
Hauge, Eiliv Odde 1913- *Au&Wr*
Haugen, Edmund Bennett 1913- *ConAu 17R*
Haugen, Einar 1906- *ConAu 21, WrD 1976*
Haugen, Nils Pederson 1849-1931 *DcNAA*
Hauger, George 1921- *Au&Wr*
Haugh, Irene 1906- *CatA 1952*
Haugh, Richard 1942- *ConAu 57*
Haugh, Robert F 1910- *ConAu 61*
Haughton, Mrs. *Alli Sup*
Haughton, Edward *Alli, Alli Sup*
Haughton, G W *Alli Sup*
Haughton, George Dunbar *Alli Sup*
Haughton, Sir Graves Champney d1849 *Alli*
Haughton, John *Alli Sup*
Haughton, John Alan 1880-1951 *AmSCAP 66*
Haughton, John Colpoys 1817-1887 *Alli Sup*
Haughton, Julia *ChPo*
Haughton, Mary Arnold *Alli*
Haughton, Percy Duncan 1876-1924 *DcNAA*
Haughton, Ptolemy *Alli Sup*
Haughton, R B *BiDSA*
Haughton, Rosemary 1927- *Au&Wr, ConAu 5R, WrD 1976*
Haughton, S M *Alli Sup*
Haughton, Samuel *Alli, Alli Sup*
Haughton, Thomas *Alli Sup*
Haughton, William *Alli, BbtC, BrAu, DcEnL, NewC*
Haughton, William 1575?-1605 *CasWL*
Haughton, William 1811-1883 *Alli Sup*
Haugsted, Ejler 1875- *WhLA*
Haugwitz, August Adolf Von 1654-1706 *OxGer*
Haugwitz, Christian August, Graf Von 1752-1831 *OxGer*
Hauk, James G 1924- *IndAu 1917*
Hauk, Maung *ConAu XR*
Haukin, William *Alli*
Hauksbee, Francis *Alli*
Haulleville, Eric De 1900-1941 *ClDMEuL*
Haultain, Sir Frederick William Gordon 1857-1942 *OxCan*
Haultain, Theodore Arnold 1857-1941 *DcNAA, OxCan*
Hauman, Doris 1897- *IlCB 1956*
Hauman, George 1890- *IlCB 1956*
Haun, Paul 1906- *ConAu 17*
Haupt, Alexander James Derbyshire 1859-1934 *DcNAA*
Haupt, Charles Elvin 1852-1920 *DcAmA, DcNAA*
Haupt, Herman 1817-1905 *Alli, Alli Sup, DcAmA, DcNAA*
Haupt, Herman, Jr. *Alli Sup*
Haupt, Lewis Muhlenberg 1844-1937 *Alli Sup, DcAmA, DcNAA*
Haupt, Moritz 1808-1874 *OxGer*
Haupt, Paul 1858- *DcAmA*
Haupt, William Ayers 1846-1896 *AmA&B, BiD&SB*
Haupt, Zygmunt 1907?-1975 *ConAu 61*
Hauptman, Gerhart Johann Robert 1862-1946 *ChPo S2*
Hauptmann, Carl 1858-1921 *CasWL, ClDMEuL, CnMD, EncWL, EvEuW, McGWD, ModGL, ModWD, OxGer*
Hauptmann, Gerhart 1862-1946 *AtlBL, BiD&SB, CasWL, ClDMEuL, CnMD, CnThe, CyWA, EncWL, EvEuW, LongC, McGWD, ModGL, ModWD, NewC, OxEng, OxGer, Pen Eur, RCom, REn, REnWD, TwCA, TwCA Sup, TwCW, WhTwL*
Hausdorff, Don 1927- *ConAu 45*
Hausenstein, Wilhelm 1882-1957 *OxGer*
Hauser, Arnold 1892- *TwCA Sup*

Hauser, Conrad Augustine 1872-1943 *DcNAA*
Hauser, Harald 1912- *CnMD, CrCD*
Hauser, Heinrich 1901- *TwCA, TwCA Sup*
Hauser, Mrs. I L *Alli Sup*
Hauser, Jacob 1909- *WrD 1976*
Hauser, James Joseph 1854- *DcNAA*
Hauser, Kaspar 1812?-1833 *REn*
Hauser, Margaret L 1909- *ConAu P-1, SmATA 10*
Hauser, Marianne 1910- *ConAu P-1, WrD 1976*
Hauser, Phillip M 1909- *ConAu 17R*
Hauser, Richard *Au&Wr*
Hauser, W A *Alli Sup*
Hausgen, Mattie Lee *ChPo*
Haushofer, Albrecht 1903-1945 *ModGL, OxGer, Pen Eur*
Haushofer, Karl 1869-1946 *REn*
Hausknecht, Murray 1925- *ConAu 37*
Hausman, Gerald 1945- *ConAu 45, DrAP 1975*
Hausman, Warren H 1939- *ConAu 17R*
Hausmann, Bernard A 1899- *ConAu 23*
Hausmann, Manfred 1898- *CnMD, ModGL, OxGer*
Hausrath, Adolf 1837-1909 *OxGer*
Hausrath, Alfred Hartmann 1901- *ConAu 41*
Hausser, Freidrich 1875- *WhLA*
Haussig, Hans Wilhelm 1916- *ConAu 29*
Haussmann, Baron Eugene-Georges 1809-1891 *OxFr*
Haussonville, Gabriel P O D, Comte D' 1843-1924 *BiD&SB, OxFr*
Haussonville, J O B DeCleron, Comte D' 1809-1884 *BiD&SB*
Haussonville, Louise D' 1818-1882 *BiD&SB*
Hausted, Peter *Alli*
Hautenville, H B *Alli*
Hauteroche, Noel LeBreton, Sieur De 1617-1707 *OxFr*
Hauteville, Mary De *Alli Sup*
Hautleigh, John *Alli Sup*
Hautlein, Marquis De *NewC*
Hautpoul, Anne-M DeM DeC, Comtesse D' 1760-1837 *OxFr*
Hautzig, Esther Rudomin 1930- *AuBYP, ConAu 1R, MorBMP, SmATA 4, ThBJA, WrD 1976*
Havant, H *MnBBF*
Havard, John David Jayne 1924- *Au&Wr*
Havard, Neast *Alli*
Havard, Valery 1846-1927 *DcNAA*
Havard, William 1710?-1778 *Alli, PoIre*
Havard, William C, Jr. 1923- *ConAu 1R*
Havel, J E 1928- *ConAu 41*
Havel, Vaclav 1936- *Au&Wr, CasWL, CnThe, CrCD, EncWL Sup, ModSL 2, ModWD, REnWD*
Havell, Ernest B 1861- *WhLA*
Haveloch, Henry *Alli*
Havelock, Eric Alfred 1903- *AmA&B, Au&Wr, ConAu P-1*
Havelock-Allen *Alli Sup*
Haveman, Robert Henry 1936- *ConAu 17R, WrD 1976*
Havemann, Ernest 1912- *ConAu 1R*
Havemann, William G 1923- *AmSCAP 66*
Havemeyer, John Craig 1833-1922 *DcNAA*
Havemeyer, Loomis 1886-1971 *ConAu 33*
Haven, Alice Bradley Neal 1828-1863 *Alli, Alli Sup, AmA, AmA&B, CyAL 2, DcAmA, DcNAA*
Haven, Charles Chauncy d1874 *DcNAA*
Haven, Claris *Alli Sup*
Haven, Curtis *Alli Sup*
Haven, Emily Neal 1827-1863 *AmA, DcNAA*
Haven, Erastus Otis 1820-1881 *Alli, Alli Sup, CyAL 2, DcAmA, DcNAA*
Haven, Gilbert 1821-1880 *Alli Sup, BiD&SB, DcAmA, DcNAA*
Haven, Jason 1733-1803 *Alli*
Haven, Joseph 1816-1874 *Alli, Alli Sup, DcAmA, DcNAA*
Haven, Nathan Appleton 1790-1826 *Alli*
Haven, Nathaniel Appleton 1790-1826 *CyAL 1*
Haven, Richard 1924- *ConAu 25*
Haven, Samuel 1727-1806 *Alli*
Haven, Samuel Foster 1806-1881 *Alli Sup,*

DcAmA, DcNAA
Haven, Samuel Foster 1831-1862 DcNAA
Havenhand, John ConAu XR, SmATA XR
Havens, Alice ChPo S1
Havens, Catherine Elizabeth 1839-1939 DcNAA
Havens, George Remington 1890- AmA&B,
  ConAu 5R
Havens, Kate E ChPo S1
Havens, Munson Aldrich 1873-1942 OhA&B
Havens, Murray Clark 1932- ConAu 41
Havens, Raymond Dexter 1880-1958 AmA&B,
  ChPo, WhWNAA
Havens, Thomas R H 1939- ConAu 41
Haver-Schmidt, Francois 1835-1894 BiD&SB
Haverfield, Elna W Alli Sup
Haverfield, Thomas Tunstall 1798-1866 Alli,
  Alli Sup, BiDLA
Havergal, Cecilia Alli Sup, ChPo S1
Havergal, Frances Ridley 1836-1879 Alli Sup,
  BbD, BiD&SB, BrAu 19, ChPo,
  ChPo S1, ChPo S2
Havergal, Francis Tebbs 1829-1890 Alli Sup
Havergal, Maria Vernon Graham d1887
  Alli Sup
Havergal, William Henry 1793-1870 Alli Sup,
  ChPo, PoCh
Haverkamp-Begemann, Egbert 1923-
  ConAu 17R
Haverly, Charles OxCan
Haverly, Christopher 1837-1901 AmA&B,
  DcNAA
Havers, Alice Alli Sup, ChPo, ChPo S2
Havers, Clopton Alli
Havers, Dora Alli Sup
Havers, George Alli
Haverschmidt, Francois 1835-1894 CasWL,
  EvEuW
Haversham, Lord M Thomson Alli
Haverstick, John 1919- ConAu 25
Haverstock, Nathan Alfred 1931- ConAu 53
Haverty, Martin 1809-1887 Alli
Havez, Jean 1874-1925 AmSCAP 66
Havighurst, Alfred F 1904- ConAu 33,
  WrD 1976
Havighurst, Marion Boyd d1974 AuBYP,
  ConAu 49, ConAu P-1, MorJA, OhA&B
Havighurst, Robert James 1900- Au&Wr,
  ConAu 23
Havighurst, Mrs. Walter WhWNAA
Havighurst, Walter Edwin 1901- AmA&B,
  AmNov, Au&Wr, AuBYP, CnDAL,
  ConAu 1R, MorJA, OhA&B, OxAm,
  REnAL, SmATA 1, TwCA Sup,
  WrD 1976
Havil, Anthony WrD 1976
Haviland, Alfred Alli Sup
Haviland, C Augustus 1832-1918 DcNAA
Haviland, Clarence Floyd 1875-1930 DcNAA
Haviland, D Alli
Haviland, E W Alli Sup
Haviland, Fergus MnBBF
Haviland, J Alli
Haviland, John 1792-1852 Alli, DcNAA
Haviland, Laura S 1808-1898 Alli Sup,
  DcNAA
Haviland, Thomas Heath OxCan
Haviland, Virginia 1911- ChPo S1, ChPo S2,
  ConAu 17R, SmATA 6
Haviland-Taylor, Katharine AmA&B,
  WhWNAA
Havill, Edward 1907- AmA&B, AmNov
Havilton, Jeffrey MnBBF
Havinden, Ashley Eldrid 1903- WhGrA
Havins, Thomas Robert 1890- TexWr
Havlice, Patricia Pate 1943- ConAu 29
Havlicek, Karel 1821-1856 BiD&SB, EuA
Havlicek Borovsky, Karel 1821-1856 CasWL,
  Pen Eur
Havliczek, Karel 1821-1856 DcEuL
Havlik, John F 1917- ConAu 45
Havran, Martin Joseph 1929- ConAu 1R,
  WrD 1976
Havrilesky, Thomas M 1939- ConAu 53
Haw, Miss M J BiDSA, LivFWS
Haw, Reginald 1915- Au&Wr
Haw, Richard Claude 1913- Au&Wr,
  ConAu P-1
Haw, William Alli Sup, BbtC

Haw Haw, Lord LongC
Hawaja Musa CasWL
Haward, John Warrington Alli Sup
Haward, Lawrence 1878- WhLA
Haward, Lazarus Alli
Haward, Nicholas Alli
Hawarden, Doctor Alli
Hawarth, Ellen C Alli Sup
Hawe, Joseph Alli Sup, PoIre
Haweis, Hugh Reginald 1838-1901 Alli Sup,
  BbD, BiD&SB, ChPo, NewC
Haweis, Mrs. Hugh Reginald 1852-1898 ChPo
Haweis, John O W Alli
Haweis, Mary Eliza Alli Sup
Haweis, Thomas 1734-1820 Alli, BiDLA,
  PoCh
Hawes, Alfred T 1874- WhWNAA
Hawes, Angelica H Alli Sup
Hawes, Annie M L ChPo
Hawes, Arthur Briscoe Alli Sup
Hawes, Barbara Alli
Hawes, Benjamin, Jr. Alli
Hawes, Charles Boardman 1889-1923 AmA&B,
  AuBYP, DcNAA, JBA 1934, Newb 1922,
  REnAL, TwCA
Hawes, Charles Henry 1867-1943 AmA&B,
  DcNAA, WhWNAA
Hawes, Edward Alli
Hawes, Evelyn AuNews 1, ConAu 13R
Hawes, Frances Cooper 1897- Au&Wr,
  ConAu P-1
Hawes, Gene R 1922- ConAu 5R
Hawes, George Edward 1864-1937 OhA&B,
  WhWNAA
Hawes, Granville P Alli Sup
Hawes, Harriet Boyd 1871- AmLY
Hawes, Harry Bartow 1869-1947 DcNAA
Hawes, Herbert Bouldin 1872- WhWNAA
Hawes, Herbert H Alli Sup
Hawes, Horace Alli Sup
Hawes, J H Alli Sup
Hawes, James Anderson 1873-1936 DcNAA
Hawes, James William 1844-1918 DcNAA
Hawes, Jesse Alli Sup
Hawes, Joel 1789-1867 Alli, Alli Sup,
  BiD&SB, DcAmA, DcNAA
Hawes, John Bromham, II 1877-1938 DcNAA,
  WhWNAA
Hawes, Joseph M 1938- ConAu 53
Hawes, Judy 1913- ConAu 33, SmATA 4,
  WrD 1976
Hawes, M W ChPo
Hawes, Mary Virginia Alli
Hawes, Robert, And Robert Loder Alli
Hawes, Samuel Alli, BiDLA
Hawes, Stephen Alli, Alli Sup, ChPo,
  Chmbr 1
Hawes, Stephen 1475?-1523? BrAu, CasWL,
  DcEnA, DcEnL, DcEuL, DcLEnL, EvLB,
  NewC, OxEng, Pen Eng, REn, WebEAL
Hawes, William Alli Sup
Hawes, William 1736-1808 Alli
Hawes, William Post 1803-1842 Alli, AmA&B,
  CyAL 2, DcAmA, DcNAA
Hawgood, John Arkas 1905- Au&Wr
Hawi, Khalil 1925- DcOrL 3
Hawk, Affable LongC
Hawk, Alex WrD 1976
Hawk, Arsina And Grace Allen ChPo S2
Hawk, May ChPo
Hawk, Sir Mulberry REn
Hawk, Philip Bovier 1874- WhWNAA
Hawk, Sparrow MnBBF
Hawk, Virginia Driving SmATA 8
Hawke, Annabella Eliza Cassandra 1787- Alli,
  BiDLA
Hawke, Arabella Eliza Cassandra 1787- PoIre
Hawke, Captain Robert MnBBF
Hawke, David Martin 1917- Au&Wr
Hawke, G MnBBF
Hawke, Gary Richard 1942- Au&Wr,
  WrD 1976
Hawke, John 1846- WhLA
Hawke, Martin B 1777- Alli, BiDLA
Hawke, Michael Alli
Hawke, William H Alli Sup
Hawken, Joan Pamela Au&Wr
Hawken, William R 1917- ConAu 9R

Hawker, Captain BiDLA
Hawker, Beatrice 1910- Au&Wr
Hawker, Charles Alli Sup
Hawker, Edward Alli Sup
Hawker, Essex Alli
Hawker, John Alli Sup
Hawker, Mary Elizabeth 1848-1908 BrAu 19,
  NewC
Hawker, Morwenna Pauline 1865- BiD&SB
Hawker, P Alli
Hawker, R A Alli
Hawker, Robert 1753-1827 Alli, BiDLA
Hawker, Robert Stephen 1803-1875 Alli Sup,
  BrAu 19, CasWL, ChPo, ChPo S1,
  ChPo S2, Chmbr 3, CnE&AP, DcLEnL,
  EvLB, NewC, OxEng, WebEAL
Hawkeridge, William OxCan
Hawkes, Arthur 1871-1933 DcNAA
Hawkes, Catharine Moira 1917- Au&Wr
Hawkes, Clarence 1869-1954 AmA&B, AmLY,
  ChPo, ChPo S1, DcAmA, WhWNAA
Hawkes, Ernest William 1881- AmA&B,
  OxCan
Hawkes, George Alli Sup
Hawkes, Glenn R 1919- ConAu 17R
Hawkes, Henry Alli Sup
Hawkes, Herbert Edwin 1872-1943 DcNAA,
  WhWNAA
Hawkes, Hester 1900- AuBYP
Hawkes, Jacquetta 1910- Au&Wr, LongC,
  REn, TwCA Sup, WrD 1976
Hawkes, John Alli Sup, OxCan
Hawkes, John 1790?- Br&AmS
Hawkes, John 1925- AmA&B, CasWL,
  ConAu 1R, ConDr, ConLC 1, ConLC 2,
  ConLC 3, ConLC 4, ConNov 1972,
  ConNov 1976, CrCD, DrAF 1976,
  EncWL, ModAL, ModAL Sup, OxAm,
  Pen Am, RAdv 1, WebEAL, WhTwL,
  WorAu, WrD 1976
Hawkes, John Ryder 1910- Au&Wr
Hawkes, Mervyn L Alli Sup
Hawkes, Nathan Mortimer 1843-1919 DcNAA
Hawkes, Terence 1932- ConAu 17R
Hawkes, W J ChPo, ChPo S1
Hawkes, W R Alli
Hawkes, William Alli, PoIre
Hawkesbury, Lord Alli
Hawkesworth, Miss Alli, BiDLA
Hawkesworth, Mrs. ChPo S1
Hawkesworth, Alan Spencer 1867- WhWNAA
Hawkesworth, Eric William 1921- ConAu 29,
  WrD 1976
Hawkesworth, John Chmbr 2, PoIre
Hawkesworth, John 1715?-1773 Alli, BiD&SB,
  BrAu, CasWL, ChPo S1, DcEnL,
  DcLEnL, NewC
Hawkesworth, John 1920- Au&Wr
Hawkesworth, Richard Alli
Hawkey, C Alli Sup
Hawking, James Alli Sup
Hawkins, A Alli, ChPo S2
Hawkins, A E Alli Sup
Hawkins, Alfred 1802?-1854 BbtC, DcNAA
Hawkins, Sir Anthony Hope 1863-1933 BbD,
  BiD&SB, Chmbr 3, DcEnA Ap, DcLEnL,
  EvLB, LongC, NewC, OxEng, REn,
  TwCA, TwCA Sup, WhCL
Hawkins, Arthur 1903- ConAu 21, IlBYP
Hawkins, Benjamin 1754-1816 BiDSA,
  DcNAA
Hawkins, Benjamin Waterhouse 1807-1889
  Alli Sup, DcAmA
Hawkins, Bessie ChPo S2
Hawkins, Brett W 1937- ConAu 21
Hawkins, Caesar Alli
Hawkins, Caesar Henry 1798-1884 Alli Sup
Hawkins, Charles Halford Alli Sup
Hawkins, Charlotte AmSCAP 66
Hawkins, Chauncey Jeddie 1876-1930 DcNAA
Hawkins, Sir Christopher Alli, BiDLA
Hawkins, Daisy Waterhouss Alli Sup
Hawkins, Darnell 1946- BlkAW
Hawkins, Denis J B 1906- CatA 1952
Hawkins, Dexter Arnold 1825-1886 Alli Sup,
  DcAmA
Hawkins, Edward Alli Sup
Hawkins, Edward 1780-1867 Alli, Alli Sup

Hawkins, Edward 1789-1882 *Alli, Alli Sup*
Hawkins, Edwards Comerford *Alli Sup*
Hawkins, Ernest 1802-1868 *Alli, Alli Sup, BbtC*
Hawkins, Erskine 1914- *AmSCAP 66*
Hawkins, Floyd W 1904- *AmSCAP 66*
Hawkins, Francis *Alli*
Hawkins, Francis Vaughan 1833- *Alli Sup*
Hawkins, Frederick W 1849- *Alli Sup, BiD&SB*
Hawkins, G *ChPo S1*
Hawkins, Gaynelle *TexWr*
Hawkins, George *Alli*
Hawkins, Gerald Stanley 1928- *ConAu 17R, WrD 1976*
Hawkins, Gordon 1919- *ConAu 41*
Hawkins, Griffith *Alli, BiDLA*
Hawkins, H *Alli, BiDLA*
Hawkins, H P *ChPo*
Hawkins, Henry *Alli, Alli Sup, BiDLA Sup*
Hawkins, Henry 1572?-1646 *CasWL*
Hawkins, Hubert Howard 1916- *IndAu 1917*
Hawkins, Hugh 1929- *ConAu 1R*
Hawkins, I *Alli Sup*
Hawkins, Irene Beatrice 1906- *IlCB 1956*
Hawkins, Isaac *Alli*
Hawkins, J *Alli Sup*
Hawkins, James *Alli Sup*
Hawkins, James E *Alli Sup*
Hawkins, James Harold 1889- *WhWNAA*
Hawkins, Janet 1911- *TexWr*
Hawkins, Jeffery *BlkAW*
Hawkins, John *Alli, BiDLA Sup, MnBBF, OxCan Sup*
Hawkins, Sir John 1532-1595 *Alli, NewC, OxEng, REn*
Hawkins, Sir John 1719-1789 *Alli, ChPo S2, DcEnA, DcEnL, NewC, OxEng*
Hawkins, John Andrew 1855- *IndAu 1816*
Hawkins, John Noel 1944- *ConAu 61*
Hawkins, John Parker 1830-1914 *DcNAA, IndAu 1917*
Hawkins, John Sidney d1842 *Alli, BiDLA*
Hawkins, K J *MnBBF*
Hawkins, Kennith 1890- *WhWNAA*
Hawkins, Laetitia Matilda *Alli, BiDLA*
Hawkins, Micah 1777-1825 *AmA&B*
Hawkins, Michael *MnBBF*
Hawkins, Nehemiah 1833-1928 *DcNAA*
Hawkins, Odie 1937- *BlkAW, ConAu 57, LivBAA*
Hawkins, Quail 1905- *AuBYP, ConAu 17R, SmATA 6*
Hawkins, Sir Richard d1622 *Alli*
Hawkins, Robert *Alli*
Hawkins, Robert 1923- *ConAu 21*
Hawkins, Rush Christopher 1831-1920 *Alli Sup, AmA&B, DcAmA, DcNAA*
Hawkins, S W *ChPo S1*
Hawkins, Sheila 1905- *IlCB 1945*
Hawkins, Thomas *Alli*
Hawkins, Sir Thomas *Alli*
Hawkins, Thomas 1810-1889 *Alli Sup*
Hawkins, Thomas L 1783-1862 *OhA&B*
Hawkins, W *Alli*
Hawkins, W B *Alli*
Hawkins, W M *Alli Sup*
Hawkins, Walter Everette 1886- *BlkAW*
Hawkins, Walter T *ChPo*
Hawkins, Willard E 1887- *WhWNAA*
Hawkins, William *Alli, BiDLA, OxCan Sup*
Hawkins, William d1801 *Alli*
Hawkins, William 1912- *ConAu 1R*
Hawkins, William Bentinck Lethem *Alli Sup*
Hawkins, William Francis 1916- *Au&Wr*
Hawkins, William George 1823-1909 *Alli Sup, BiDSA, DcAmA, DcNAA*
Hawkins, Willis B *ChPo*
Hawkinson, John Samuel 1912- *AuBYP, ConAu 5R, ConAu 23, SmATA 4*
Hawkinson, Lucy 1924- *AuBYP*
Hawkridge, Emma *DcNAA*
Hawkridge, John *Alli*
Hawks, Miss *Alli*
Hawks, Cicero Stephens 1812-1868 *BiDSA*
Hawks, E R *Alli Sup*
Hawks, Edward 1878- *BkC 2, CatA 1947*
Hawks, Ellison 1889- *Au&Wr*

Hawks, Francis Lister 1798-1866 *Alli, Alli Sup, AmA, AmA&B, BiD&SB, BiDSA, CarSB, ChPo, ChPo S1, ChPo S2, CyAL 2, DcAmA, DcNAA*
Hawks, Isaac *HsB&A*
Hawks, Wells 1870-1941 *DcNAA*
Hawksford, C M *Alli Sup*
Hawkshaw, Ann *Alli Sup, ChPo, ChPo S1*
Hawkshaw, Benjamin 1670?-1724 *PoIre*
Hawkshaw, John *Alli*
Hawkshead, James *Alli*
Hawksley, Cordelia J *Alli Sup*
Hawksley, John *Alli, BiDLA*
Hawksley, Thomas *Alli Sup*
Hawksmoor, Nicholas 1666?-1736 *Alli, AtlBL*
Hawksworth, Hallam *DcNAA*
Hawksworth, John *Alli Sup*
Hawkwood, Allan *AmLY XR*
Hawkwood, Sir John De 1320-1394 *NewC, REn*
Hawkyns, George *Alli*
Hawkyns, Sir John 1532-1595 *NewC*
Hawles, John 1645-1716 *Alli*
Hawley, Amos H 1910- *ConAu 37*
Hawley, Antoinette A *ChPo*
Hawley, Blair 1924- *WrD 1976*
Hawley, Bostwick 1814-1910 *Alli Sup, DcAmA, DcNAA*
Hawley, C *Alli Sup*
Hawley, Cameron 1905-1969 *AmA&B, ConAu 1R, ConAu 25*
Hawley, Charles 1819-1885 *Alli Sup, DcAmA, DcNAA*
Hawley, Charles Beach 1858-1915 *AmSCAP 66*
Hawley, Ellis W 1929- *ConAu 17R*
Hawley, Florence M *ConAu XR*
Hawley, Frederick *Alli Sup*
Hawley, Frederick Barnard 1843-1929 *Alli Sup, DcNAA*
Hawley, George *MnBBF*
Hawley, Gideon d1807 *Alli*
Hawley, Gideon 1785-1870 *DcAmA, DcNAA*
Hawley, Giles P *Alli Sup*
Hawley, Graham Jenkins 1885- *WhWNAA*
Hawley, Hattie Louise 1890-1934 *DcNAA*
Hawley, Helen L *ChPo S1*
Hawley, Henrietta Ripperger 1890?-1974 *ConAu 49*
Hawley, Herbert *MnBBF*
Hawley, Hudson *ChPo S1*
Hawley, Isabel Lockwood 1935- *ConAu 57*
Hawley, James H 1847-1929 *DcNAA*
Hawley, Jane Stouder 1936- *ConAu 23*
Hawley, John Gardner 1845-1900 *Alli Sup, DcNAA*
Hawley, John Hugh *Alli Sup*
Hawley, L H *ChPo*
Hawley, Mabel C *ConAu 19, SmATA 1*
Hawley, Ralph Chipman 1880- *WhWNAA*
Hawley, Richard *Alli Sup*
Hawley, Robert Coit 1933- *ConAu 57*
Hawley, Thomas P *Alli Sup*
Hawley, Walter Augustus 1863-1920 *DcNAA*
Hawley, William Fitz 1804-1855 *BbtC, DcNAA, OxCan*
Hawley, William George 1903- *Au&Wr*
Hawley, Zerah 1781-1856 *DcNAA*
Hawley, Zerah Kent 1806-1869 *DcNAA*
Hawn, Henry Gaines 1864- *DcNAA*
Haworth, Adrian Hardy *Alli, BiDLA*
Haworth, Clarence Everett 1860- *BiDSA*
Haworth, Clarence V 1875- *IndAu 1917*
Haworth, Don *ConDr*
Haworth, Edith Stow *TexWr, WhWNAA*
Haworth, Euphrasia Fanny *Alli Sup*
Haworth, Frieda Mary 1898- *Au&Wr, WrD 1976*
Haworth, Lawrence 1926- *ConAu 5R*
Haworth, Martin E *Alli Sup*
Haworth, Paul Leland 1876-1938 *AmA&B, AmLY, DcNAA, IndAu 1816, OxCan*
Haworth, Samuel *Alli*
Haworth, William *Alli*
Haworth-Booth, Michael 1896- *Au&Wr, ConAu 5R*
Haworth-Booth, Michael 1906- *WrD 1976*
Hawrylo, Frank 1936- *AmSCAP 66*
Hawtayne, G H *Alli Sup*
Hawtayne, William *Alli, BiDLA*

Hawthorn, Audrey *OxCan Sup*
Hawthorn, Geoffrey 1941- *Au&Wr*
Hawthorn, Harry Bertram *OxCan Sup*
Hawthorn, Herbert J *ChPo, ChPo S1*
Hawthorn, J R H *Alli Sup*
Hawthorn, John *Alli*
Hawthorn, John Raymond 1911- *WrD 1976*
Hawthorn, Joseph *ChPo S1*
Hawthornden, Earl Of *CnE&AP*
Hawthorne, Alice *Alli Sup*
Hawthorne, Captain R M *HsB&A, YABC 1*
Hawthorne, Emily 1845- *Alli Sup, ChPo, DcNAA*
Hawthorne, Fred Lee 1880- *WhWNAA*
Hawthorne, George Stuart *Alli Sup*
Hawthorne, H B *OxCan*
Hawthorne, Hildegarde 1871-1952 *AmA&B, AuBYP, ChPo, DcAmA, JBA 1934, JBA 1951, REnAL, WhWNAA*
Hawthorne, James Boardman 1837-1910 *BiDSA*
Hawthorne, Jennie Crawley 1916- *ConAu P-1, WrD 1976*
Hawthorne, Julian 1846-1934 *Alli Sup, AmA&B, BbD, BiD&SB, CarSB, ChPo, ChPo S2, Chmbr 3, DcAmA, DcBiA, DcEnA, DcEnA Ap, DcEnL, DcNAA, EncM&D, OxAm, REnAL, TwCA, WhWNAA*
Hawthorne, L E Jennie 1916- *Au&Wr*
Hawthorne, Manning *ChPo*
Hawthorne, Nathaniel 1804-1864 *Alli, Alli Sup, AmA, AmA&B, AmWr, AtlBL, BbD, BiD&SB, CarSB, CasWL, ChPo S1, ChPo S2, Chmbr 3, CnDAL, CriT 3, CyAL 2, CyWA, DcAmA, DcBiA, DcEnA, DcEnA Ap, DcEnL, DcLEnL, DcNAA, EvLB, FamAYP, MouLC 3, OxAm, OxEng, Pen Am, RAdv 1, RCom, REn, REnAL, St&VC, WebEAL, WhCL*
Hawthorne, Rainey *Alli Sup*
Hawthorne, Robert *Alli Sup*
Hawthorne, Rose *AmA&B*
Hawthorne, Sophia 1810-1871 *Alli Sup, DcAmA*
Hawton, Hector 1901- *Au&Wr, ConAu 13R, MnBBF, WrD 1976*
Hawtrey, Mrs. *Alli Sup, ChPo*
Hawtrey, Charles *Alli*
Hawtrey, Charles S *Alli*
Hawtrey, Charles Sleech *BiDLA*
Hawtrey, Edith *Alli Sup*
Hawtrey, Edward M *Alli Sup*
Hawtrey, Louisa *Alli Sup*
Hawtrey, Montagu John Gregg *Alli, Alli Sup*
Hawtrey, Stephen Thomas *Alli Sup*
Hawys, John *Alli*
Haxby, John *Alli*
Hay, A Hamilton *ChPo S1*
Hay, Alexander *Alli*
Hay, Sir Alexander *Alli Sup*
Hay, Arthur 1824-1878 *Alli Sup*
Hay, C A And Jacobs, H E *Alli Sup*
Hay, Charles *Alli*
Hay, Charles Augustus 1821-1893 *DcNAA*
Hay, Charles Colcock *BiDSA*
Hay, Clarence Leonard *ChPo S2*
Hay, David *Alli Sup*
Hay, David M 1935- *ConAu 53*
Hay, David Ramsay 1798- *Alli*
Hay, Denys 1915- *Au&Wr, ConAu 13R, WrD 1976*
Hay, Ebenezer Story *Alli Sup*
Hay, Edward *Alli, BiDLA*
Hay, Elijah *ChPo*
Hay, Eloise K 1926- *ConAu 9R*
Hay, Elzey *Alli Sup, AmA&B, DcNAA*
Hay, George *Alli, Alli Sup, PoIre*
Hay, George 1765-1830 *Alli, BiDSA, DcNAA*
Hay, George 1831-1912 *ChPo*
Hay, George Campbell 1915- *CasWL, ChPo, ChPo S1, ChPo S2, ConP 1970, Pen Eng*
Hay, Gustavus 1866-1901 *DcAmA, DcNAA*
Hay, Gyula 1900- *CrCD, ModWD, Pen Eur*
Hay, Mrs. H H *Alli*
Hay, Helen *ChPo, DcAmA*
Hay, Helen Selina, Countess Of Gifford 1807-1867 *Alli Sup*

Hay, Henry Hanby *ChPo, ChPo S1*
Hay, Ian 1876-1952 *Chmbr 3, DcLEnL,*
 EvLB, LongC, NewC, REn, TwCA,
 TwCA Sup, TwCW
Hay, J B *Alli*
Hay, J Marley *Alli Sup*
Hay, Jacob 1920- *ConAu 25*
Hay, James *Alli Sup*
Hay, James, Jr. 1881-1936 *AmA&B, DcNAA,*
 WhWNAA
Hay, James G 1936- *ConAu 53*
Hay, James William *Alli Sup*
Hay, Jane Eleanor *Alli Sup*
Hay, Janet *ChPo*
Hay, John *Alli, Alli Sup, Chmbr 3*
Hay, John 1915- *AmA&B*
Hay, Sir John Charles Dalrymple 1821-
 Alli Sup, BiD&SB
Hay, John H Drummond *Alli*
Hay, John Milton 1838-1905 *Alli Sup, AmA,*
 AmA&B, BbD, BiD&SB, CasWL, ChPo,
 ChPo S1, ChPo S2, DcAmA, DcBiA,
 DcNAA, EvLB, IndAu 1816, OhA&B,
 OxAm, Pen Am, REn, REnAL
Hay, Julius 1900- *CnMD*
Hay, Sir Leith *Alli*
Hay, Leon Edwards *ConAu 25*
Hay, Mrs. M B *LivFWS*
Hay, Mrs. M H *BiDLA*
Hay, Malcolm *ChPo S2*
Hay, Margaret Hilda *WhWNAA*
Hay, Margaret W *WhWNAA*
Hay, Martyn *Alli Sup*
Hay, Mary Cecil 1840?-1886 *Alli Sup,*
 BiD&SB, DcBiA
Hay, Matthew *Alli Sup*
Hay, Montague *MnBBF*
Hay, Oliver Perry 1846-1930 *DcNAA,*
 IndAu 1917, WhWNAA
Hay, Peter *Alli*
Hay, Peter 1935- *ConAu 21*
Hay, Richard *Alli*
Hay, Richard Augustin *Alli*
Hay, Richard Carman 1893-1930 *DcNAA*
Hay, Richard LeRoy 1926- *IndAu 1917*
Hay, Robert *Alli Sup*
Hay, Robert Dean 1921- *ConAu 61,*
 IndAu 1917
Hay, Robert Edwin 1910- *Au&Wr*
Hay, Romanus *Alli*
Hay, Sara Henderson 1906- *AmA&B,*
 AmSCAP 66, ChPo, ChPo S1, ChPo S2
Hay, Sarah Henderson 1906- *ConAu P-1*
Hay, Stephen N 1925- *ConAu 5R, WrD 1976*
Hay, Stuart *ChPo S1*
Hay, Thomas *Alli, Alli Sup, ChPo*
Hay, Thomas Robson 1888-1974 *AmA&B,*
 ConAu 49, WhWNAA
Hay, Timothy *DcNAA*
Hay, W S *ChPo S2*
Hay, William *Alli Sup*
Hay, William 1700?-1755 *Alli*
Hay, William Delisle *Alli Sup*
Hay, William Gosse 1875-1945 *CasWL,*
 DcLEnL
Haya DeLaTorre, Victor Raul *DcSpL*
Hayakawa, Samuel Ichiye 1906- *AmA&B,*
 ConAu 13R, REn, REnAL, TwCA Sup,
 WrD 1976
Hayakawa, Yoshio 1917- *WhGrA*
Hayashi, Fumiko 1904-1951 *CasWL,*
 EncWL Sup, Pen Cl
Hayashi, Shuseki *ConAu XR*
Hayashi, Tadasu, Viscount 1850-1913 *DcLEnL*
Hayashi, Tetsumaro 1929- *ConAu 37,*
 WrD 1976
Hayata, Bunzo 1874- *WhLA*
Haycock, Ronald G *OxCan Sup*
Haycock, William d1872? *Alli Sup*
Haycox, Ernest 1899-1950 *AmA&B, MnBBF,*
 REnAL, TwCA Sup, WhWNAA
Haycraft, Howard 1905- *AmA&B, AuBYP,*
 ConAu 23, EncM&D, REnAL,
 SmATA 6
Haycraft, Margaret Scott *Alli Sup, ChPo S1,*
 ChPo S2
Haycraft, Molly Costain 1911- *ConAu 13R,*
 SmATA 6

Haycroft, Nathaniel *Alli Sup*
Haycroft, Pendleton *WhWNAA*
Hayden, Albert A 1923- *ConAu 33,*
 WrD 1976
Hayden, Amos Sutton 1813-1880 *OhA&B*
Hayden, Andrew *OxCan*
Hayden, Arthur G 1874- *WhWNAA*
Hayden, Mrs. C A *Alli*
Hayden, C Gervin *ConAu XR*
Hayden, Carl T 1877-1972 *ConAu 33*
Hayden, Donald E 1915- *ConAu 25,*
 WrD 1976
Hayden, Edward Everett 1858-1932 *DcNAA*
Hayden, Edward Parker d1922 *ChPo*
Hayden, Eric William 1919- *ConAu 5R,*
 WrD 1976
Hayden, Ferdinand V 1827-1888 *Alli Sup,*
 DcAmA, DcNAA
Hayden, H Henry *Alli Sup*
Hayden, Harold Arthur 1898- *Au&Wr*
Hayden, Henry *BbtC*
Hayden, Henry C *ChPo S1, ChPo S2*
Hayden, Horace Edwin 1837-1917 *AmA&B,*
 BiDSA, DcNAA
Hayden, Horace H 1769-1844 *Alli, BiDSA,*
 DcAmA, DcNAA
Hayden, Howard K 1930- *ConAu 17R*
Hayden, Jabez Haskell 1811-1902 *Alli Sup,*
 DcNAA
Hayden, Jay *ConAu XR*
Hayden, Jay G 1884- *WhWNAA*
Hayden, John *Alli, Alli Sup*
Hayden, John J 1859- *Alli Sup, PoIre*
Hayden, John O 1932- *ConAu 25*
Hayden, Julie *DrAF 1976*
Hayden, Katharine Shepard *ChPo*
Hayden, Marie L *Alli Sup*
Hayden, Morgan Parritt 1845-1928 *OhA&B*
Hayden, Robert C 1937- *WrD 1976*
Hayden, Robert Earl 1913- *AmA&B, BlkAW,*
 ChPo S1, ChPo S2, ConLC 5,
 ConP 1970, ConP 1975, CrCAP,
 DrAP 1975, LivBA, WrD 1976
Hayden, Sarah Marshall *IndAu 1816*
Hayden, Sidney *Alli Sup*
Hayden, Mrs. Sumner *Alli Sup*
Hayden, Thomas *Alli Sup*
Hayden, Thomas Emmett 1940?- *AmA&B*
Hayden, Warren Luce 1835-1918 *OhA&B*
Hayden, William *Alli Sup*
Hayden, William Benjamin 1816-1893 *Alli Sup,*
 DcAmA, DcNAA
Haydn, Franz Joseph 1732-1809 *AtlBL, REn*
Haydn, Hiram Collins 1831-1913 *Alli Sup,*
 AmA&B, DcAmA, DcNAA, OhA&B
Haydn, Hiram Collins 1907-1973 *AmA&B,*
 AmNov, Au&Wr, CnDAL, ConAu 45,
 ConAu P-1, ConNov 1972, OhA&B,
 OxAm, REnAL, TwCA Sup
Haydn, Joseph d1856 *Alli*
Haydn, Joseph 1732-1809 *NewC, OxGer*
Haydocke, Richard *Alli*
Haydon, A Eustace 1880-1975 *ConAu 61*
Haydon, Andrew 1867-1932 *DcNAA*
Haydon, Arthur Lincoln 1872- *ChPo, ChPo S1,*
 ChPo S2, MnBBF, OxCan, WhLA
Haydon, Benjamin Robert 1786-1846 *Alli,*
 BrAu 19, CasWL, ChPo, ChPo S1,
 DcLEnL, NewC, OxEng, REn
Haydon, Frank Scott 1822-1887 *Alli Sup*
Haydon, Frederick Wordsworth 1827-1886
 Alli Sup
Haydon, G H 1827-1886 *Alli Sup*
Haydon, Glen 1896-1966 *Au&Wr, ConAu P-1*
Haydon, John *Alli*
Haydon, N G *MnBBF*
Haydon, Percy Montague 1895- *MnBBF*
Haydon, Rex *MnBBF*
Haye, Anthony Oneal *Alli Sup*
Haye, Drummond George *Alli*
Haye, T D *Alli Sup*
Hayek, Friedrich August Von 1899- *LongC,*
 TwCA Sup, WrD 1976
Hayens, Herbert 1861- *MnBBF*
Hayes *Alli*
Hayes, Miss *Alli Sup*
Hayes, A A *BbtC*
Hayes, Abner Pierce 1876-1929 *DcNAA*

Hayes, Alden C 1916- *ConAu 57*
Hayes, Alfred *ChPo S1*
Hayes, Alfred 1857-1936 *Alli Sup, ChPo,*
 ChPo S1, WhLA
Hayes, Alfred 1911- *AmA&B, AmNov,*
 ModAL, OxAm, REn, REnAL,
 TwCA Sup
Hayes, Ann L 1924- *ConAu 25, DrAP 1975*
Hayes, Anna Hansen 1886- *ChPo, ConAu 1R,*
 WhPNW
Hayes, Augustus Allen 1837-1892 *Alli Sup,*
 AmA&B, BiD&SB, DcAmA, DcNAA
Hayes, Bartlett H 1904- *Au&Wr*
Hayes, Billy *AmSCAP 66*
Hayes, Carlton Joseph Huntley 1882-1964
 AmA&B, AmLY, CatA 1947, ConAu 1R,
 LongC, REnAL, TwCA Sup, WhWNAA
Hayes, Charles 1678-1760 *Alli*
Hayes, Charles Harris 1868-1910 *DcNAA*
Hayes, Charles R 1914- *AmSCAP 66*
Hayes, Charles Wells 1828-1908 *Alli Sup,*
 DcNAA
Hayes, Charles Willard 1859-1916 *DcNAA*
Hayes, Clair W *CarSB*
Hayes, Con F *Alli Sup*
Hayes, Cora Walker *ChPo*
Hayes, D *Alli*
Hayes, Daniel 1733?-1767 *PoIre*
Hayes, Donald Jeffrey 1904- *BlkAW*
Hayes, Doremus Almy 1863-1936 *AmLY,*
 DcNAA, OhA&B, WhWNAA
Hayes, Dorsha *AmA&B, AmNov*
Hayes, Douglas *Au&Wr*
Hayes, Douglas A 1918- *ConAu 1R*
Hayes, E *Alli, ChPo*
Hayes, E Nelson 1920- *ConAu 29*
Hayes, Edgar Junius 1905- *AmSCAP 66*
Hayes, Edward *OxCan, PoIre*
Hayes, Edward C 1937- *ConAu 45*
Hayes, Edward Cary 1868-1928 *AmLY,*
 DcNAA, WhWNAA
Hayes, Edward L 1931- *ConAu 29*
Hayes, Ellen 1851-1930 *DcNAA, OhA&B,*
 WhWNAA
Hayes, Evelyn *DcLEnL*
Hayes, Everis Anson *WhWNAA*
Hayes, F *PoIre*
Hayes, Fenno *ChPo*
Hayes, Florence 1895- *AuBYP*
Hayes, Francis Clement 1904- *ConAu 21*
Hayes, Grace Person 1919- *ConAu 33*
Hayes, H K 1884- *WhWNAA*
Hayes, Harry Gordon 1883- *OhA&B,*
 WhWNAA
Hayes, Helen 1900- *OxAm, REn*
Hayes, Henry *Alli Sup*
Hayes, Henry 1824-1904 *AmA, BiD&SB,*
 DcAmA, DcNAA
Hayes, Isaac Israel 1832-1881 *Alli Sup,*
 AmA&B, BbD, BiD&SB, DcAmA,
 DcNAA, OxCan, REnAL
Hayes, Ivor *MnBBF*
Hayes, J Milton *ChPo S1*
Hayes, J R *Alli Sup*
Hayes, J W *Alli Sup*
Hayes, James M *BkC 2*
Hayes, James T 1923- *ConAu 29*
Hayes, Jeff W 1858-1917 *DcNAA, OhA&B*
Hayes, John *Alli, BiDLA, OxCan Sup*
Hayes, John d1815 *AmA&B, DcNAA*
Hayes, John Alexander 1898- *IndAu 1917*
Hayes, John Clifford 1920- *IndAu 1917*
Hayes, John F 1904- *ConAu P-1*
Hayes, John Lord 1812-1887 *Alli Sup,*
 DcNAA
Hayes, John Russell 1866-1945 *AmA&B,*
 AmLY, ChPo, ChPo S1, DcAmA,
 DcNAA, WhWNAA
Hayes, John Trevor 1929- *Au&Wr*
Hayes, Joseph Arnold 1918-1968 *AmA&B,*
 ConAu 17R, ConNov 1972, ConNov 1976,
 IndAu 1917, REnAL, WrD 1976
Hayes, Juanita 1904- *Au&Wr*
Hayes, Justin *Alli Sup*
Hayes, Kate E 1856- *PoIre*
Hayes, Larry Ray 1940- *AmSCAP 66*
Hayes, Louis D 1940- *ConAu 29, WrD 1976*
Hayes, Lyman Simpson 1850-1935 *DcNAA*

Hayes, M Horace *Alli Sup, Br&AmS*
Hayes, Mabel *ChPo S2*
Hayes, Margaret 1925- *Au&Wr, ConAu 21*
Hayes, Margaret E *Alli Sup*
Hayes, Marjorie *AmA&B*
Hayes, Marrijane Johnston 1920- *IndAu 1917*
Hayes, Mrs. Meredith *OhA&B*
Hayes, Nancy M *ChPo, ChPo S1, ChPo S2*
Hayes, Nelson Taylor 1903-1971 *Au&Wr, ConAu 1R, ConAu 33*
Hayes, Paul J 1922- *ConAu 57*
Hayes, Paul Martin 1942- *WrD 1976*
Hayes, Peter Lind 1915- *AmA&B, AmSCAP 66*
Hayes, Philip Cornelius 1833-1916 *Alli Sup, DcNAA, OhA&B*
Hayes, Ralph Eugene 1927- *ConAu 21, IndAu 1917*
Hayes, Rea *AmSCAP 66*
Hayes, Richard *Alli*
Hayes, Richard 1930- *AmSCAP 66*
Hayes, Robert M 1926- *ConAu 9R*
Hayes, Rutherford Birchard 1822-1893 *AmA&B, OhA&B, OxAm, REnAL*
Hayes, S *PoIre*
Hayes, Samuel *Alli, BiDLA, PoIre*
Hayes, Samuel d1795? *PoIre*
Hayes, Samuel P 1910- *ConAu 5R*
Hayes, Stephen Quentin 1873-1936 *DcNAA*
Hayes, Thomas *Alli*
Hayes, W M 1857- *WhWNAA*
Hayes, Wayland Jackson 1893-1972 *Au&Wr, ConAu P-1*
Hayes, Will *ConAu 5R, SmATA 7*
Hayes, Will 1890- *WhLA*
Hayes, William 1708-1777 *Alli*
Hayes, William Allen 1843-1924 *DcNAA*
Hayes, William Dimitt 1913- *AuBYP, ConAu 5R, SmATA 8*
Hayes, William Edward 1897- *AmA&B, IndAu 1917*
Hayes, William Patrick 1887- *WhWNAA*
Hayford, Fred Kwesi 1937- *ConAu 45*
Hayford, Gladys May Casely 1904- *AfA 1, ChPo S1*
Hayford, J E *AfA 1*
Hayford, John Fillmore 1868-1925 *DcNAA*
Haygarth, Henry William *Alli*
Haygarth, John d1813 *Alli, BiDLA*
Haygarth, William *Alli, BiDLA Sup*
Haygood, Atticus Green 1839-1896 *Alli Sup, AmA&B, BiD&SB, BiDSA, DcAmA, DcNAA*
Hayhurst, John 1907- *Au&Wr*
Haykal, Muhammad Husayn 1888-1956 *DcOrL 3*
Hayler, Florena A 1875- *WhWNAA*
Hayler, Guy 1850- *WhLA*
Hayley, Herman Wadsworth 1867-1899 *DcNAA*
Hayley, John William 1834-1927 *DcNAA*
Hayley, R M *Alli Sup*
Hayley, Thomas *Alli*
Hayley, Vivian 1915- *TexWr*
Hayley, William *Alli, Chmbr 2*
Hayley, William 1745-1820 *Alli, BiD&SB, BiDLA, BrAu 19, CasWL, ChPo, ChPo S1, DcEnL, EvLB, NewC, OxEng, WebEAL*
Hayley Bell, Mary *ConAu 25*
Hayllar, Florence H *Alli Sup*
Haym, Rudolf 1821-1901 *OxGer*
Hayman *ConAu XR*
Hayman, Carol Bessent 1927- *ConAu 53, WrD 1976*
Hayman, David 1927- *ConAu 17R, WrD 1976*
Hayman, Francis 1708?-1776 *BkIE*
Hayman, Henry 1823- *Alli Sup*
Hayman, John L, Jr. 1929- *ConAu 25*
Hayman, Lee Richard 1922- *IndAu 1917, OhA&B*
Hayman, Mary *Alli Sup*
Hayman, Max 1908- *ConAu 17R*
Hayman, Richard 1920- *AmSCAP 66*
Hayman, Robert *ChPo*
Hayman, Robert d1631? *Alli, OxCan*
Hayman, Ronald 1932- *Au&Wr, ConAu 25, WrD 1976*

Hayman, Samuel *Alli Sup*
Hayman, Samuel 1818-1886 *Alli Sup, PoIre*
Hayman, Walter Kurt 1926- *Au&Wr, WrD 1976*
Haymes, Robert C 1931- *ConAu 33*
Haymo *BiB S*
Haymo Of Canterbury d1054 *BiB S*
Haymon *NewC*
Haymond, C And Burch, J C *Alli Sup*
Hayn, Annette *DrAP 1975*
Haynam *Alli*
Hayne, Coe 1875- *WhWNAA*
Hayne, David *OxCan Sup*
Hayne, Joseph E 1849-1911 *DcNAA*
Hayne, M H E *OxCan*
Hayne, Paul Hamilton 1830-1886 *Alli, Alli Sup, AmA, AmA&B, BbD, BiD&SB, BiDSA, CasWL, ChPo, ChPo S1, ChPo S2, Chmbr 3, CnDAL, CyAL 2, DcAmA, DcLEnL, DcNAA, EvLB, OxAm, Pen Am, REn, REnAL*
Hayne, Robert Y 1791-1839 *Alli, CyAL 1*
Hayne, Robert Young 1853-1903 *Alli Sup, BiDSA, DcNAA*
Hayne, Samuel *Alli*
Hayne, Thomas 1581-1645 *Alli*
Hayne, William Hamilton 1856-1929 *BiDSA, ChPo, ChPo S1, DcAmA, DcNAA*
Hayneccius, Martin 1544-1611 *OxGer*
Hayner, Rutherford 1877-1939 *DcNAA*
Haynes, Albert *BlkAW*
Haynes, Alfred H 1910- *ConAu 5R*
Haynes, Anna *ConAu XR*
Haynes, Anna Lee *ChPo*
Haynes, Betsy 1937- *ConAu 57*
Haynes, Miss C D *Alli*
Haynes, C M *Alli Sup*
Haynes, Carlyle Boynton 1882-1958 *AmA&B*
Haynes, Carol *ChPo*
Haynes, Christopher *Alli*
Haynes, D F *Alli, BiDLA*
Haynes, D H *Alli Sup*
Haynes, David C *Alli Sup*
Haynes, Dorothy K 1918- *Au&Wr, WrD 1976*
Haynes, Dudley Cammet 1809-1888 *DcNAA*
Haynes, E M *Alli Sup*
Haynes, Edward George Ambrose 1906- *Au&Wr*
Haynes, Edwin Mortimer 1836-1910 *DcNAA*
Haynes, Elizabeth Ross *WhWNAA*
Haynes, Emory J 1847?-1914 *Alli Sup, BiD&SB, DcAmA, DcNAA*
Haynes, F M F *ChPo S1*
Haynes, Freeman Oliver *Alli Sup*
Haynes, George Edmund 1880-1960 *AmA&B, WhWNAA*
Haynes, George Henry 1855-1912 *DcNAA*
Haynes, George Henry 1866- *WhWNAA*
Haynes, Gideon *Alli Sup*
Haynes, Hopton 1672-1749 *Alli*
Haynes, Irving Samuel 1851-1946 *DcNAA*
Haynes, J *Alli*
Haynes, James 1788-1851 *Alli, PoIre*
Haynes, John *Alli*
Haynes, John Bishop *Alli Sup*
Haynes, John Edward *Alli Sup*
Haynes, John Frederick *Alli Sup*
Haynes, Joseph *Alli*
Haynes, Landon Carter 1816-1875 *BiDSA*
Haynes, Laura Nixon 1876- *WhWNAA*
Haynes, Lemuel 1753-1834 *DcNAA*
Haynes, Linda *ConAu XR*
Haynes, Louise Marshall *AnMV 1926, ChPo, ChPo S2*
Haynes, M S *Alli Sup*
Haynes, Mae Elizabeth *ChPo*
Haynes, Maria S 1912- *ConAu 25*
Haynes, Mary F *ChPo*
Haynes, Mifflin A *Alli*
Haynes, Nancy M *MnBBF*
Haynes, Nathaniel Smith 1844-1925 *DcNAA*
Haynes, Pat *ConAu XR, MnBBF*
Haynes, Renee Oriana 1906- *ConAu 49, WrD 1976*
Haynes, Richard *Alli*
Haynes, Richard F 1935- *ConAu 49*
Haynes, Robert *IlBYP, MnBBF*
Haynes, Robert Talmadge, Jr. 1926- *ConAu 1R*

Haynes, Robert Vaughn 1929- *ConAu 41*
Haynes, Roy Asa 1881-1940 *DcNAA, OhA&B, WhWNAA*
Haynes, S R *Alli Sup*
Haynes, Samuel d1752 *Alli*
Haynes, Shirley *ChPo*
Haynes, Stanley *Alli Sup*
Haynes, Sybille Edith 1926- *ConAu 57, WrD 1976*
Haynes, Thomas *Alli, BiDLA*
Haynes, V A *MnBBF*
Haynes, William *Alli Sup*
Haynes, William Barber 1881- *OhA&B, WhWNAA*
Haynes, William Warren 1921- *ConAu 5R*
Haynes, Williams 1886- *AmA&B, WhWNAA*
Haynie, James Henry 1841-1912 *AmA&B, DcNAA*
Haynie, William S 1918- *AmSCAP 66*
Hays *Alli*
Hays, Agee 1900- *WhWNAA*
Hays, Arthur Garfield 1881-1954 *AmA&B, WhWNAA*
Hays, Arthur Homer 1881- *IndAu 1917, WhWNAA*
Hays, Billy Silas 1898- *AmSCAP 66*
Hays, Brooks 1898- *ConAu P-1, WrD 1976*
Hays, Calvin Cornwell 1861-1935 *DcNAA*
Hays, David G 1928- *ConAu 21*
Hays, Ebenezer Zane 1837-1909 *OhA&B*
Hays, Edward *Alli*
Hays, Elinor Rice *AmA&B, ConAu 1R*
Hays, Frances *Alli Sup*
Hays, Frank Alfred 1888- *WhWNAA*
Hays, George Peirce 1838-1897 *Alli Sup, DcAmA, DcNAA*
Hays, Gertrude *ChPo*
Hays, Harold Melvin 1880-1940 *DcNAA*
Hays, Helen *Alli Sup*
Hays, Helen Ireland 1903- *ChPo S2, ConAu 61*
Hays, Hobe *AuBYP*
Hays, Hoffman Reynolds 1904- *AmA&B, ConP 1970, ConP 1975, DrAP 1975, TwCA Sup, WrD 1976*
Hays, Isaac 1796-1879 *Alli, DcNAA*
Hays, Isaac Minis 1847-1925 *AmLY, DcNAA*
Hays, Janice Nicholson 1929- *WrD 1976*
Hays, Margaret G *ChPo*
Hays, Margaret Parker 1874-1925 *DcNAA*
Hays, Mary *Alli, BiDLA*
Hays, Matilda M *Alli Sup*
Hays, Paul R 1903- *ConAu 19*
Hays, Peter L 1938- *ConAu 33, WrD 1976*
Hays, Richard D 1942- *ConAu 37*
Hays, Robert Glenn 1935- *ConAu 53*
Hays, Samuel Pfrimmer 1921- *IndAu 1917*
Hays, Mrs. W J *Alli Sup*
Hays, Will H 1879-1954 *IndAu 1917*
Hays, Willet Martin 1859-1928 *DcNAA*
Hays, William Harrison 1915- *IndAu 1917*
Hays, William Shakespeare 1837-1907 *AmA, AmA&B, BiD&SB, BiDSA, ChPo, DcAmA, DcNAA*
Hays, Wilma Pitchford 1909- *AuBYP, ConAu 1R, SmATA 1, ThBJA, WrD 1976*
Haystead, Ladd 1900- *WhWNAA*
Haystead, Wesley 1942- *ConAu 57*
Hayter *Alli*
Hayter, Adrian *Au&Wr*
Hayter, Alethea 1911- *Au&Wr, ConAu 29, WrD 1976*
Hayter, Sir Arthur Divett 1835- *Alli Sup*
Hayter, Cecil Goodenough 1871-1922 *MnBBF*
Hayter, Earl W 1901- *ConAu 41*
Hayter, Flora *Alli Sup*
Hayter, Henry Heylyn 1821-1895 *Alli Sup, BiD&SB*
Hayter, John *Alli*
Hayter, John 1756-1818 *Alli, BiDLA, ChPo*
Hayter, Richard *Alli*
Hayter, Teresa *WrD 1976*
Hayter, Thomas d1762 *Alli*
Hayter, Thomas d1799 *Alli*
Hayter, Sir William Goodenough 1906- *Au&Wr, ConAu 21, WrD 1976*
Haythorne, George Vickers 1909- *WrD 1976*

Haythornthwaite, Philip John 1951- *WrD 1976*
Hayton, Leonard George 1908- *AmSCAP 66*
Hayton, Richard Neil 1916- *ConAu 57*
Haytov, Nikolay 1929- *CasWL*
Hayus, John *Alli*
Hayward, Abraham 1801-1884 *Alli, Alli Sup, BiD&SB, BrAu 19, Chmbr 3, DcEnL, DcLEnL, EvLB, NewC, OxEng*
Hayward, Adele M *ChPo*
Hayward, Almira L *Alli Sup*
Hayward, Arthur Lawrence 1885- *MnBBF, WhLA*
Hayward, Ben *Alli Sup*
Hayward, C *Alli*
Hayward, Caroline *Alli Sup*
Hayward, Catherine *BbtC*
Hayward, Charles, Jr. *Alli*
Hayward, Charles Harold 1898- *Au&Wr, ConAu 9R*
Hayward, Christopher R 1925- *AmSCAP 66*
Hayward, Dagney *MnBBF*
Hayward, Mrs. E *ChPo*
Hayward, Edward *Alli*
Hayward, Edward Dykes *Alli Sup*
Hayward, Edward Farwell 1851-1923 *Alli Sup, DcAmA, DcNAA*
Hayward, Elwes R C *Alli Sup*
Hayward, Emeroy *ChPo*
Hayward, Enid 1907- *WhWNAA*
Hayward, Enos F *ChPo, ChPo S1*
Hayward, George 1781-1862 *DcAmA*
Hayward, George 1791-1863 *Alli, DcAmA, DcNAA*
Hayward, H F *ChPo*
Hayward, H Richard *ChPo S1*
Hayward, Harrison Washburn 1873-1932 *DcNAA*
Hayward, Henry Howard *Alli Sup*
Hayward, J Henry *Alli Sup*
Hayward, Jack 1931- *ConAu 57*
Hayward, Jack W *ChPo S1*
Hayward, James 1786-1866 *DcNAA*
Hayward, John *Alli*
Hayward, Sir John 1564?-1627 *Alli, BrAu, Chmbr 1, DcEnL, DcLEnL, EvLB, NewC, OxEng*
Hayward, John 1781-1862 *DcNAA*
Hayward, John 1905-1965 *ChPo S1, ChPo S2, DcLEnL, LongC*
Hayward, John F 1918- *ConAu 5R*
Hayward, John Forrest 1916- *ConAu 9R, WrD 1976*
Hayward, John Williams 1828- *Alli Sup*
Hayward, Joseph *Alli*
Hayward, Maria L *Alli Sup*
Hayward, Marvin Leslie 1877- *WhWNAA*
Hayward, Max *ChPo S2*
Hayward, Percival *WhWNAA*
Hayward, Percy Roy 1884- *WhWNAA*
Hayward, Richard *ConAu XR*
Hayward, Richard 1818-1869 *AmA*
Hayward, Richard 1893- *ConAu P-1*
Hayward, Roger *Alli*
Hayward, Samuel *Alli*
Hayward, Silvanus 1828-1908 *DcNAA*
Hayward, Thomas *Alli*
Hayward, Victoria 1876- *WhWNAA*
Hayward, W *Alli Sup*
Hayward, W I *Alli Sup*
Hayward, W R *Alli Sup*
Hayward, Walter Brownell 1877- *AmA&B*
Hayward, William 1870-1945 *CatA 1952*
Hayward, William C 1847-1917 *DcNAA*
Hayward, William H 1813-1876 *Alli Sup, DcNAA*
Hayward, William Richart *WhWNAA*
Hayward, William Stephens *Alli Sup, MnBBF*
Haywarde, Sir John *Alli*
Haywarde, Richard *Alli, ChPo, DcNAA*
Haywarde, William *Alli*
Haywell, F *ChPo, ChPo S1*
Haywood *Alli*
Haywood, A G *Alli Sup*
Haywood, Carolyn 1898- *AmA&B, AuBYP, AuICB, ChPo, ConAu 5R, JBA 1951, MorBMP, SmATA 1*
Haywood, Charles 1904- *ConAu 1R, OxCan, WrD 1976*

Haywood, Eliza Fowler 1693?-1756 *Alli, BrAu, CasWL, DcEnA, DcEnL, DcLEnL, EvLB, NewC, OxEng, Pen Eng*
Haywood, F *Alli, Alli Sup*
Haywood, H Carl 1931- *ConAu 49*
Haywood, Harry LeRoy 1886-1955 *OhA&B, WhWNAA*
Haywood, Helen Riviere 1907- *Au&Wr*
Haywood, Henry d1755 *Alli*
Haywood, James *Alli*
Haywood, John *Alli Sup*
Haywood, John 1762?-1826 *Alli, BiDSA, DcAmA, DcNAA*
Haywood, John Alfred 1913- *ConAu 17R*
Haywood, John Campbell *ChPo S2*
Haywood, Marshall DeLancey 1871-1933 *AmLY, ChPo, DcNAA*
Haywood, P D *Alli Sup*
Haywood, Richard Mansfield 1905- *ConAu 33*
Haywood, Richard Mowbray 1933- *ConAu 25, WrD 1976*
Haywood, Thomas *Alli*
Haywood, William *Alli, ChPo S1*
Haywood, William Dudley 1869-1928 *DcNAA*
Haywood, William G *Alli Sup*
Haywood, X *Alli Sup*
Hayworth, Donald 1898- *WhWNAA*
Hazard, Ann *Alli*
Hazard, Buck *MnBBF*
Hazard, Caroline 1856-1945 *Alli Sup, AmA&B, AnMV 1926, BiD&SB, ChPo S1, DcAmA, DcNAA*
Hazard, Cora Lapham *ChPo, ChPo S1*
Hazard, Daniel Lyman 1865- *WhWNAA*
Hazard, Ebenezer 1744-1817 *Alli, DcAmA, DcNAA, OxAm, REnAL*
Hazard, Elizabeth 1799-1882 *Alli Sup, DcNAA*
Hazard, Harry *HsB&A*
Hazard, Jack *ConAu XR*
Hazard, John Newbold 1909- *ConAu 1R, WrD 1976*
Hazard, Joseph *Alli, BbtC*
Hazard, Joseph 1757-1817 *ChPo, DcNAA*
Hazard, Laurence *ConAu XR*
Hazard, Leland 1893- *ConAu 17R*
Hazard, Lucy Lockwood 1890- *AmA&B*
Hazard, Marshall Custiss 1839-1929 *DcAmA, DcNAA*
Hazard, Patrick D 1927- *ConAu 13R*
Hazard, Paul 1878-1944 *ChPo, ClDMEuL, OxFr, WhLA*
Hazard, Rowland Gibson 1801-1888 *Alli, Alli Sup, DcAmA, DcNAA*
Hazard, Samuel 1784-1870 *Alli, AmA&B, DcAmA, DcNAA*
Hazard, Samuel 1834-1876 *Alli Sup, BiD&SB, DcAmA, DcNAA*
Hazard, Shepherd Tom 1797-1886 *REnAL*
Hazard, Thomas Robinson 1784-1876 *Alli, Alli Sup, DcAmA*
Hazard, Thomas Robinson 1797-1886 *AmA&B, DcNAA, OxAm*
Hazard, Willis Pope 1825-1913 *Alli Sup, DcAmA, DcNAA*
Hazaz, Chaim 1898- *CasWL*
Hazel, Harry *Alli Sup, AmA&B, MnBBF*
Hazel, Joseph Clinton *AnMV 1926*
Hazel, Robert *DrAP 1975*
Hazel, Robert 1921- *AmA&B, IndAu 1917*
Hazeland, Mrs. E A *Alli Sup*
Hazeland, William *Alli*
Hazeldean, J O *Alli Sup*
Hazelius, Ernest Lewis 1777-1853 *Alli, DcAmA, DcNAA*
Hazelius, Ernest Williams *BiDSA*
Hazell, W Howard 1869- *WhLA*
Hazell, Walter And Hogkin, Howard *Alli Sup*
Hazelrigg, Meredith K 1942- *ConAu 33*
Hazeltine, Alice Isabel 1878- *AuBYP, ChPo*
Hazeltine, Horace *AmLY XR, DcNAA, WhWNAA*
Hazeltine, Lieutenant-Colonel *HsB&A*
Hazeltine, Mary Emogene 1868-1949 *AmA&B, DcNAA*
Hazeltine, Mayo Williamson 1841-1909 *Alli Sup, AmA&B, BbD, BiD&SB, ChPo S2, DcAmA, DcNAA, REnAL*

Hazeltine, Miron James 1824-1907 *Alli Sup, DcNAA, HsB&A*
Hazelton, Alexander *ConAu XR*
Hazelton, George Cochrane 1868-1921 *AmA&B, BiD&SB, DcNAA*
Hazelton, Harry *HsB&A*
Hazelton, John Hampden *AmLY, WhWNAA*
Hazelton, John Morton 1867-1940 *DcNAA*
Hazelton, Roger 1909- *AmA&B, ConAu 1R*
Hazelwood, Carey *Alli Sup*
Hazelwood, Rex *MnBBF*
Hazen, Allen 1869-1930 *DcNAA*
Hazen, Allen Tracy 1904- *Au&Wr, ConAu P-1*
Hazen, Charles Downer 1868-1941 *AmA&B, DcAmA, DcNAA*
Hazen, E *Alli*
Hazen, H A *Alli Sup*
Hazen, Henry Allen 1832-1900 *DcNAA*
Hazen, Henry Allen 1849-1900 *DcNAA*
Hazen, Henry Honeyman 1879- *WhWNAA*
Hazen, Jasper 1790?-1882 *DcNAA*
Hazen, John Munger 1838- *DcNAA*
Hazen, Marshman Williams 1845-1911 *DcAmA, DcNAA*
Hazen, Mary P *Alli Sup*
Hazen, W R *Alli Sup*
Hazen, William Babcock 1830-1887 *Alli Sup, DcAmA, DcNAA, OhA&B*
Hazhar 1920- *DcOrL 3*
Hazlehurst, Cameron 1941- *WrD 1976*
Hazlehurst, George S *Alli Sup*
Hazlerigg, Grey *Alli Sup*
Hazlett, Edward Everett 1892- *AuBYP*
Hazlett, Helen *Alli Sup*
Hazlewood, David *Alli Sup*
Hazlewood, Jeffrey Maison 1925- *Au&Wr*
Hazlewood, Lee 1929- *AmSCAP 66*
Hazlewood, Michael Edward 1944- *Au&Wr*
Hazlewood, Walter Gordon *WrD 1976*
Hazlitt, Henry 1894- *AmA&B, Au&Wr, ConAu 5R, REnAL, WhWNAA, WrD 1976*
Hazlitt, W I *Alli Sup*
Hazlitt, William 1778-1830 *Alli, AtlBL, BiD&SB, BiDLA, BrAu 19, CasWL, Chmbr 3, CriT 2, CyWA, DcEnA, DcEnA Ap, DcEnL, DcEuL, DcLEnL, EvLB, MouLC 3, NewC, OxEng, Pen Eng, RAdv 1, RCom, REn, WebEAL*
Hazlitt, William, Jr. 1811-1893 *Alli, NewC*
Hazlitt, William Carew 1834-1913 *Alli, Alli Sup, BbD, BbtC, BiD&SB, ChPo, ChPo S1, DcEnL, DcLEnL, NewC, OxCan, OxEng*
Hazo, Robert G 1931- *ConAu 23*
Hazo, Samuel John 1928- *ConAu 5R, ConP 1970, ConP 1975, DrAP 1975*
Hazoume, Paul 1890- *AfA 1*
Hazzard, Charles 1871-1938 *DcNAA*
Hazzard, George E 1845-1926 *IndAu 1816*
Hazzard, Jesse Charles 1871- *WhWNAA*
Hazzard, John Edward 1881-1935 *AmSCAP 66, ChPo, DcNAA*
Hazzard, Shirley 1931- *AmA&B, Au&Wr, ConAu 9R, ConNov 1972, ConNov 1976, DrAF 1976, WrD 1976*
Heacox, Arthur Edward *WhWNAA*
Head, Alice Maud *Au&Wr*
Head, Ann *ConAu XR*
Head, Barclay Vincent 1844- *Alli Sup, BiD&SB*
Head, Bessie 1937- *AfA 1, ConAu 29, ConNov 1972, ConNov 1976, WrD 1976*
Head, Charles *BbtC*
Head, Mrs. Cloyd *AmA&B, WhWNAA*
Head, Constance 1939- *ConAu 37, WrD 1976*
Head, David Henry George 1922- *Au&Wr*
Head, Sir Edmund Walker 1805-1868 *Alli, Alli Sup, BrAu 19, DcEnL, OxCan, REnAL*
Head, Edward Francis *Alli Sup*
Head, Erasmus *Alli*
Head, Eunice Tietjens *WhWNAA*
Head, Mrs. F E *Alli Sup*
Head, Sir Francis Bond 1793-1875 *Alli, Alli Sup, BbtC, BrAu 19, Chmbr 3,*

DcEnL, DcLEnL, EvLB, OxCan

Head, Franklin Harvey 1835-1914 *Alli Sup, DcAmA, DcNAA*

Head, Frederick William 1854- *Alli Sup*

Head, Gay *ConAu XR, SmATA XR*

Head, Sir George 1782-1855 *Alli, BbtC, Chmbr 3, DcEnL, OxCan*

Head, George E *Alli Sup*

Head, Sir Henry 1861-1940 *ChPo S1*

Head, J H *Alli Sup*

Head, James H *ChPo S1*

Head, James Roper *Alli, BiDLA*

Head, John *Alli Sup*

Head, Sir John *Alli, BiDLA*

Head, John W *Alli Sup*

Head, John Waldegrave 1912- *Au&Wr*

Head, June *ChPo*

Head, Matthew 1907- *AmA&B, ConAu XR, EncM&D, WorAu*

Head, Michael *Alli, BiDLA Sup*

Head, Nelson *Alli Sup*

Head, Percy Rendell *Alli Sup*

Head, Richard 1637?-1687? *Alli, CasWL, DcEnL, DcLEnL, NewC, PoIre*

Head, Richard G 1938- *ConAu 53*

Head, Robert *Alli Sup*

Head, Robert 1942- *AmA&B*

Head, Robert V 1929- *ConAu 41*

Head, Roy Burke 1886- *TexWr*

Head, Sylvia *ChPo S1*

Head, Mrs. Thomasen *Alli*

Head, Timothy E 1934- *ConAu 13R*

Headden, William Parker 1850- *WhWNAA*

Headen, John *WhWNAA*

Heading, Roger 1930- *WrD 1976*

Headingley, Adolphe S *Alli Sup*

Headings, Mildred J 1908- *ConAu 37*

Headington, Christopher John Magenis 1930- *WrD 1976*

Headington, J A And Franklin, Joseph *Alli Sup*

Headlam, Beatrice R *Alli Sup*

Headlam, Cecil 1872- *WhLA*

Headlam, John *Alli, BiDLA*

Headlam, Stewart Duckworth *Alli Sup*

Headlam, Thomas E *Alli*

Headlam, Walter George 1866-1908 *EvLB, TwCA*

Headland, Edward *Alli Sup*

Headland, Frederick William *Alli, Alli Sup*

Headland, Isaac Taylor 1859-1942 *AmA&B, AmLY, ChPo, ChPo S2, DcNAA, OhA&B, WhWNAA*

Headlee, Thomas J 1877-1946 *IndAu 1917*

Headley, Elizabeth 1909- *AuBYP, ConAu XR, MorJA, SmATA 1*

Headley, Henry 1766-1788 *Alli, ChPo S1, ChPo S2, DcEnL*

Headley, Joel Tyler 1813?-1897 *Alli, Alli Sup, AmA, AmA&B, BbtC, BiD&SB, ChPo S1, CyAL 2, DcAmA, DcNAA*

Headley, John W *BiDSA*

Headley, Leal A 1884- *WhWNAA*

Headley, Phineas Camp 1819-1903 *Alli, Alli Sup, AmA, AmA&B, BiD&SB, CyAL 2, DcAmA, DcNAA*

Headley, Tanfield George *Alli Sup*

Headley, Walter Balls *Alli Sup*

Headrick, James *Alli, BiDLA*

Headrick, John *Alli*

Headstrom, Birger Richard 1902- *AuBYP, WrD 1976*

Headstrom, Richard 1902- *ConAu 1R, SmATA 8*

Heady, Earl O 1916- *ConAu 17R*

Heady, Eleanor Butler 1917- *ConAu 41, SmATA 7, SmATA 8, WrD 1976*

Heady, Harold Franklin 1916- *ConAu 53, WrD 1976*

Heady, Morrison 1829-1915 *Alli Sup, BiDSA, DcNAA*

Heafford, Michael R 1938- *WrD 1976*

Heafford, Philip Ernest 1906- *Au&Wr*

Heaford, A S *Alli Sup*

Heagerty, John Joseph 1879-1946 *DcNAA*

Heagle, David 1836-1922 *DcNAA*

Heagney, Anne 1901- *BkC 6, ConAu 5R*

Heagney, Harold Jerome 1890- *BkC 1, CatA 1947*

Heagney, William H 1882-1955 *AmSCAP 66*

Heal, Edith 1903- *ConAu 1R, SmATA 7*

Heal, Gilbert B 1887- *WhWNAA*

Heal, Jeanne 1917- *Au&Wr, ConAu P-1, WrD 1976*

Heald, Charles Brehmer 1882-1974 *ConAu 49*

Heald, Edmund *Alli Sup*

Heald, Edward Thornton 1885- *ConAu 17R, OhA&B*

Heald, Frederick DeForest 1872- *WhWNAA*

Heald, Henry 1779- *AmA, REnAL*

Heald, Timothy 1944- *ConAu 49*

Heald, W M *Alli, BiDLA*

Healde, Thomas *Alli*

Heale, James Newton *Alli Sup*

Heale, William *Alli, DcEnL*

Heales, Alfred *Alli Sup*

Healey, Charles Heley Chadwyck 1845- *Alli Sup*

Healey, Denis Winston 1917- *Au&Wr*

Healey, F G 1903- *ConAu 21*

Healey, Francis *Alli Sup*

Healey, James 1936- *ConAu 53*

Healey, James Stewart 1931- *ConAu 57*

Healey, John *Alli, CasWL*

Healey, Robert 1921- *ConAu 61*

Health Doctor, The *WhWNAA*

Healy, Arthur K D *ChPo*

Healy, Cahir 1877- *Au&Wr, PoIre, WhLA*

Healy, David Frank 1926- *ConAu 17R, WrD 1976*

Healy, Fleming 1911- *ConAu 5R*

Healy, George Peter Alexander 1813-1894 *DcNAA*

Healy, George Robert 1923- *ConAu 17R*

Healy, John 1850- *WhLA*

Healy, John Francis 1926- *Au&Wr*

Healy, Sister Kathleen *ConAu 61*

Healy, Mary *Alli Sup*

Healy, Maurice *ChPo S2*

Healy, Maurice *PoIre*

Healy, Monica d1876 *PoIre*

Healy, Patrick Joseph 1871-1937 *DcNAA*

Healy, Paul Francis 1915- *AmA&B, ConAu 17R*

Healy, Richard J 1916- *ConAu 25, WrD 1976*

Healy, Sean D 1927- *ConAu 25*

Healy, Tim 1893-1947 *DcNAA*

Healy, Timothy Michael 1855- *Alli Sup*

Healy, Timothy S 1923- *ConAu 41*

Healy, W J *OxCan*

Healy, William 1869- *WhWNAA*

Heaney, J M P *Alli Sup*

Heaney, John J 1925- *ConAu 9R*

Heaney, Seamus 1939- *ChPo S2, ConLC 5, ConP 1970, ConP 1975, ModBL Sup, WrD 1976*

Heanley, K M *Alli Sup*

Heanley, Robert Marshall *Alli Sup*

Heap, David Porter 1843-1910 *Alli Sup, DcAmA, DcNAA*

Heap, Sir Desmond 1907- *Au&Wr, ConAu P-1, WrD 1976*

Heap, Gwynn Harris 1817-1887 *Alli Sup, DcAmA, DcNAA*

Heap, Harry Rupert 1917- *Au&Wr*

Heap, Henry *Alli*

Heap, Jean Walmsley 1920- *Au&Wr*

Heaphy, Musgrave *Alli Sup*

Heaphy, Thomas 1813-1873 *Alli Sup*

Heaps, Chris *ChPo S2*

Heaps, Leo *OxCan Sup*

Heaps, Willard Allison 1909- *AuBYP*

Heaps, William James 1868- *WhWNAA*

Heard, Albert F *Alli Sup*

Heard, Alexander 1917- *ConAu 17R*

Heard, Franklin Fiske 1825-1889 *Alli, Alli Sup, AmA&B, DcAmA, DcNAA*

Heard, G F 1889-1971 *LongC*

Heard, Gerald 1889-1971 *AmA&B, Au&Wr, ConAu 21, ConAu 29, EncM&D, LongC, NewC, REn, TwCA, TwCA Sup*

Heard, Henry FitzGerald 1889-1971 *BiDPar, ConAu XR, EncM&D, TwCA, TwCA Sup*

Heard, Isaac V D 1834-1913 *Alli Sup, DcNAA*

Heard, J Norman 1922- *ConAu 9R*

Heard, James Arthur *Alli Sup*

Heard, John, Jr. *ChPo S2*

Heard, John Bickford *Alli Sup*

Heard, Josephine Henderson 1861- *BlkAW*

Heard, Nathan Cliff 1936- *AmA&B, BlkAW, ConAu 53, LivBA*

Heard, Paul Leonard *TexWr*

Heard, Richard 1936- *AmSCAP 66*

Heard, Thomas Jefferson 1814- *BiDSA*

Heard, William *Alli*

Heard, William H 1850-1937 *DcNAA*

Hearder, Harry 1924- *ConAu 5R*

Hearn, Edward *Alli*

Hearn, Faith *ChPo*

Hearn, Ila *ChPo*

Hearn, John 1804?-1847 *PoIre*

Hearn, Lafcadio 1850-1904 *Alli Sup, AmA, AmA&B, AnCL, AtlBL, BbD, BiD&SB, BiDSA, CasWL, ChPo, Chmbr 3, CnDAL, CriT 3, CyWA, DcAmA, DcBiA, DcEuL, DcLEnL, DcNAA, EvLB, ModAL, NewC, OhA&B, OxAm, OxEng, Pen Am, Pen Eng, PoIre, RAdv 1, REn, REnAL*

Hearn, Michael Patrick *ChPo S2*

Hearn, Stanley *MnBBF*

Hearn, Thomas *Alli, BiDLA*

Hearn, William Edward 1826-1888 *Alli Sup*

Hearnden, Isaac *Alli Sup*

Hearne, Edwin *Alli Sup*

Hearne, Erasmus *Alli*

Hearne, George Richard Mant *MnBBF*

Hearne, Jack W *MnBBF*

Hearne, John 1926- *Au&Wr, CasWL, ConNov 1972, ConNov 1976, LongC, Pen Eng, WebEAL, WorAu, WrD 1976*

Hearne, Mary Anne *Alli Sup*

Hearne, Reginald 1919- *Au&Wr, WrD 1976*

Hearne, Samuel *Alli*

Hearne, Samuel 1745-1792 *Alli, BbtC, DcLEnL, OxCan*

Hearne, Thomas 1678-1735 *Alli, BrAu, CasWL, Chmbr 2, DcEnL, DcLEnL, EvLB, NewC, OxEng, Pen Eng*

Hearne, Urban *Alli*

Hearne, William T *BiDSA*

Hearnshaw, Fossey John Cobb 1869- *WhLA*

Hearon, Shelby 1931- *AuNews 2, ConAu 25*

Hearsey, John Edward Nicholl 1928- *Au&Wr, ConAu 5R, WrD 1976*

Hearst, James *DrAP 1975*

Hearst, James S *ChPo*

Hearst, William Randolph 1863-1951 *AmA&B, LongC, OxAm, REn, REnAL*

Hearst, William Randolph, Jr. 1908- *AmA&B*

Heart, Jonathan *Alli*

Hearten, Laura W *ChPo*

Heartfield, John 1891- *WhGrA*

Heartley, Charles Tebbott *Alli Sup*

Heartman, Charles F *ChPo*

Heartman, Harold *ConAu XR*

Heartwell, Henry *Alli, BiDLA*

Heasel, Anthony *Alli*

Heasell, Anne *Alli Sup*

Heasman, Alfred, Cane, E And Coote, G *Alli Sup*

Heasman, Kathleen Joan 1913- *Au&Wr, ConAu P-1, WrD 1976*

Heater, Derek Benjamin 1931- *ConAu 57, WrD 1976*

Heath, A S *Alli Sup*

Heath, Alfred *ChPo*

Heath, Arnold *Alli Sup*

Heath, Benjamin d1766 *Alli*

Heath, Bernard *MnBBF*

Heath, Blanche T *ChPo, ChPo S2*

Heath, Bobby 1889-1952 *AmSCAP 66*

Heath, Catherine 1924- *WrD 1976*

Heath, Charles *Alli, BiDLA*

Heath, Charles d1848 *Alli*

Heath, Christopher 1835- *Alli Sup*

Heath, Clara B 1837- *ChPo, ChPo S1*

Heath, D J *Alli*

Heath, Douglas Denon 1811- *Alli Sup*

Heath, Douglas H 1925- *ConAu 17R*

Heath, Douglass D *Alli*

Heath, Dunbar Isidore 1816-1888 *Alli Sup*

Heath, Dwight B 1930- *ConAu 17R, WrD 1976*

Heckman, Hazel Melissa 1904- *ConAu 21*,
WhPNW
Heckman, William O 1921- *ConAu 21*
Hecko, Frantisek 1905-1960 *CasWL*,
ModSL 2, *Pen Eur*
Heckscher, August 1913- *AmA&B*, *Au&Wr*,
ConAu 1R
Heckscher, Robert Valantine 1883- *AmA&B*
Heckstall-Smith, Hugh 1896- *Au&Wr*
Heckwelder, John 1743-1810 *Alli*
Heclawa *AmLY XR*
Hector, Annie 1825-1902 *Alli Sup*, *BiD&SB*,
NewC
Hector, James *BbtC*
Hector, John *Alli Sup*
Hector, William *Alli Sup*
Hedayat, Sadeq 1903-1951 *DcOrL 3*
Hedberg, Carl Olof 1899- *EncWL*, *EvEuW*
Hedberg, Frans Theodor 1828-1908 *BiD&SB*,
CasWL
Hedberg, Olle 1899- *CasWL*, *Pen Eur*
Hedberg, Tor Harald 1862-1931 *CasWL*,
ClDMEuL, *CnMD*, *MnBBF*
Hedborn, Samuel 1783-1849 *CasWL*
Hedbrook, Arthur *OhA&B*
Hedbrooke, Andrew 1841-1887 *AmA*
Hedda d705 *BiB S*
Hedde, Wilhelmina Genevava 1895- *ConAu 5R*,
IndAu 1917
Hedden, William D *Alli Sup*
Hedden, Worth Tuttle 1896- *AmA&B*, *AmNov*,
ConAu 21
Hedderwick, James 1814-1897 *Alli Sup*, *ChPo*,
ChPo S1, *DcEnL*
Hedderwick, T C H *Alli Sup*
Hedelin, Francois *BiD&SB*
Hedenstierna, Karl Joseph Alfred 1852-
BiD&SB
Hedenvind-Eriksson, Gustav 1880-1967 *CasWL*,
Pen Eur
Hedgcock, Frank Arthur 1875- *ChPo S1*
Hedgcock, George G 1863- *WhWNAA*
Hedge, Frederic Henry 1805-1890 *Alli*,
Alli Sup, *AmA*, *AmA&B*, *BbD*,
BiD&SB, *ChPo*, *ChPo S1*, *CyAL 2*,
DcAmA, *DcNAA*, *EarAB*, *OxAm*,
REnAL
Hedge, Leslie 1922- *ConAu 9R*
Hedge, Levi 1766?-1844? *Alli*, *AmA*, *DcAmA*,
DcNAA
Hedgecock, Thomas *Alli*, *BiDLA Sup*
Hedgeland, Isabella *Alli*, *BiDLA*
Hedgeman, Anna Arnold 1899- *ConAu P-1*
Hedges, Ada Hastings *WhWNAA*
Hedges, Bob A 1919- *ConAu 45*
Hedges, Sir Charles d1714 *Alli*
Hedges, David 1930- *ConAu 45*
Hedges, Elaine R 1927- *ConAu 57*
Hedges, Frank Hinckley 1895- *WhWNAA*
Hedges, Geoffrey C 1926- *Au&Wr*
Hedges, Gilbert Lawrence 1874-1929 *DcNAA*
Hedges, Henry Parsons 1817-1911 *DcNAA*
Hedges, Isaac A *Alli Sup*
Hedges, Job Elmer 1862-1925 *DcNAA*
Hedges, John *Alli*, *ChPo*
Hedges, John Kirby 1811- *Alli Sup*
Hedges, Joseph *ConAu 57*
Hedges, Killingworth 1852- *Alli Sup*, *WhLA*
Hedges, Marion Hawthorne 1888-1959
IndAu 1917
Hedges, Mary J *Alli Sup*
Hedges, Phineas *Alli*
Hedges, S P *Alli Sup*
Hedges, Samuel 1854-1916 *DcNAA*
Hedges, Sidney George 1897- *Au&Wr*, *ChPo*,
ChPo S1, *ConAu 9R*, *MnBBF*
Hedges, Trimble R 1906- *ConAu 21*
Hedges, Ursula M 1940- *ConAu 29*
Hedges, William L 1923- *ConAu 37*
Hedges, William S 1895- *WhWNAA*
Hedin, Sven Anders Von 1865-1952 *REn*,
TwCA, *TwCA Sup*, *WhLA*
Hedlamb, J *Alli*
Hedley, Alfred E *Alli Sup*
Hedley, Evalena Fryer *WhWNAA*
Hedley, George 1899- *ConAu 19*
Hedley, George Roberts *Alli Sup*
Hedley, James Alexander 1844-1916 *DcNAA*

Hedley, John *Alli Sup*
Hedley, John Cuthbert 1837- *Alli Sup*
Hedley, Olwen 1912- *ConAu 61*, *WrD 1976*
Hedley, Oswald Dodd *Alli Sup*
Hedley, Thomas Frederick *Alli Sup*
Hedley, William *Alli*, *BiDLA*
Hedlund, Ronald D 1941- *ConAu 33*
Hedly, Thomas *Alli*
Hedrich, Arthur William 1888- *WhWNAA*
Hedrich, Franz 1823?-1895 *OxGer*
Hedrick, Addie M 1903- *ConAu 25*,
WrD 1976
Hedrick, Basil C 1932- *ConAu 33*
Hedrick, Earle Raymond 1876-1943 *DcNAA*
Hedrick, Floyd Dudley 1927- *ConAu 33*,
WrD 1976
Hedrick, Mary A *Alli Sup*
Hedrick, Ulysses Prentiss 1870- *WhWNAA*
Hedwig, Heilige 1174-1243 *OxGer*
Hedwig, Herzogin Von Schwaben d994 *OxGer*
Heebner, Charles F *Alli Sup*
Heelu, Jan Van *CasWL*
Heely, Joseph *Alli*, *BiDLA*
Heemskerk, Johann Van 1597-1656 *BiD&SB*,
CasWL, *DcEuL*
Heenan, John Carmel 1905- *CatA 1952*
Heeney, Arnold *OxCan Sup*
Heeney, Bertal *OxCan*
Heeney, Brian *OxCan Sup*
Heer, David MacAlpine 1930- *ConAu 13R*,
WrD 1976
Heer, Friedrich 1916- *OxGer*
Heer, Jakob Christoph 1859-1925 *OxGer*
Heer, Nancy Whittier *ConAu 33*
Heere, Lucas De 1534-1584 *CasWL*
Heere, Lucas Van 1534-1584 *DcEuL*
Heeren, Arnold Hermann Ludwig 1760-1842
BiD&SB
Heeresma, Heere 1932- *CasWL*, *ConAu 25*
Heermance, Edgar Laing *WhWNAA*
Heermance, J Noel 1939- *ConAu 25*
Heermann, Johannes 1585-1647 *BbD*, *OxGer*
Heermans, Forbes 1856-1928 *AmA&B*,
DcAmA, *DcNAA*
Heermans, J *Alli Sup*
Heerwagen, Paul K 1895- *ConAu 29*,
WrD 1976
Heerwart, Eleanor Luden 1835- *ChPo S1*
Heever, C M VanDen 1902- *NewC*
Heezen, Bruce C 1924- *ConAu 49*
Hefelbower, Samuel Gring 1871- *WhWNAA*
Heffern, Richard 1950- *ConAu 61*
Heffernan, D Edward *Alli Sup*
Heffernan, James A W 1939- *ConAu 25*
Heffernan, Michael *DrAP 1975*
Heffernan, Michael J d1885 *PoIre*
Heffernan, Thomas *DrAP 1975*
Heffernan, William A 1937- *ConAu 25*
Heffley, Wayne 1927- *ConAu 9R*
Heffron, Dorris 1944- *ConAu 49*
Heflebower, Clara Keck 1871-1937 *OhA&B*
Hefley, James C 1930- *ConAu 13R*
Hefner, Hugh 1926- *AuNews 1*
Hefner, Keith 1929- *AmSCAP 66*
Hefner-Alteneck, Jacob Heinrich Von 1811-1903
BiD&SB
Hefti, Neal 1922- *AmSCAP 66*
Hegan, Alice Caldwell 1870-1942 *DcAmA*,
OxAm
Hegarty, Edward J 1891- *ConAu 1R*,
IndAu 1917
Hegarty, Sister M Loyola 1918- *ConAu 37*
Hegarty, Reginald Beaton 1906-1973 *AuBYP*,
ConAu 41, *ConAu P-1*, *SmATA 10*
Hegel, Georg Wilhelm Friedrich 1770-1831 *BbD*,
BiD&SB, *CasWL*, *DcEuL*, *EuA*, *EvEuW*,
NewC, *OxEng*, *OxGer*, *Pen Eur*, *REn*
Hegel, Richard 1927- *ConAu 57*
Hegeler, Sten 1923- *Au&Wr*, *WrD 1976*
Hegeman, Elizabeth Blair 1942- *ConAu 61*
Hegeman, Mary Theodore 1907- *WrD 1976*
Hegemon Of Thasos *CasWL*
Hegenbarth, Josef 1884- *WhGrA*
Heger, Theodore Ernest 1907- *ConAu 33*
Hegesias *Pen Cl*
Hegesippus *CasWL*, *ConAu XR*, *WrD 1976*
Hegge, Robert 1599-1629 *Alli*
Heggen, Thomas O 1919-1949 *AmA&B*,

CyWA, *DcNAA*, *McGWD*, *OxAm*,
Pen Am, *REn*, *REnAL*, *TwCA Sup*
Heggie, John 1859- *ChPo S1*
Heggoy, Alf Andrew 1938- *ConAu 37*
Hegias *Pen Cl*
Heginbothom, Ottiwell 1744-1768 *PoCh*
Hegius, Alexander 1433?-1498 *CasWL*, *DcEuL*
Hegland, Martin 1880- *WhWNAA*
Heglar, Mary Schnall 1934- *ConAu 49*
Hegner, Johann Ulrich 1759-1840 *OxGer*
Hegner, Robert 1880- *WhWNAA*
Hegner, Ulrich 1759-1840 *BiD&SB*
Hegstad, Roland R 1926- *ConAu 57*
Heiber, Helmut 1924- *ConAu 49*
Heiberg, Gunnar Edvard Rode 1857-1929
CasWL, *ClDMEuL*, *CnMD*, *CnThe*,
EncWL, *McGWD*, *ModWD*, *Pen Eur*,
REn, *REnWD*, *WorAu*
Heiberg, Hermann 1840-1910 *BiD&SB*, *OxGer*
Heiberg, Johan Ludvig 1791-1860 *BbD*,
BiD&SB, *CasWL*, *DcEuL*, *EuA*, *EvEuW*,
McGWD, *Pen Eur*, *REnWD*
Heiberg, Johanne Luise 1812-1890 *CasWL*
Heiberg, Peter Andreas 1758-1841 *BiD&SB*,
CasWL, *DcEuL*, *EuA*, *Pen Eur*
Heiby, Walter A 1918- *ConAu 21*
Heichberger, Robert Lee 1930- *ConAu 53*
Heicher, Merlo K W 1882-1967 *ConAu P-1*
Heidbreder, Margaret Ann 1933- *ConAu 37*
Heide, Florence Parry *ChPo S1*, *ChPo S2*
Heidegger, Gotthard 1666-1711 *OxGer*
Heidegger, Martin 1889- *CasWL*, *LongC*,
OxGer, *REn*, *TwCA Sup*, *TwCW*
Heidel, William Arthur 1868-1941 *AmA&B*,
DcNAA, *WhWNAA*
Heidelberg, Daniel W *Alli Sup*
Heiden, Carol A 1939- *ConAu 57*
Heidenberg, Johannes Von *OxGer*
Heidenreich, Charles A 1917- *ConAu 25*
Heidenstam, Carl Gustaf Verner Von 1859-1940
EvEuW
Heidenstam, Verner Von 1859-1940 *BiD&SB*,
CasWL, *ClDMEuL*, *CyWA*, *EncWL*,
Pen Eur, *REn*, *TwCA*, *TwCA Sup*
Heiderstadt, Dorothy 1907- *AuBYP*,
ConAu 1R, *SmATA 6*
Heidingsfield, Myron S 1914- *ConAu 1R*
Heiferman, Ronald Ian 1941- *ConAu 61*
Heifetz, Hank *DrAF 1976*
Heifetz, Harold 1919- *ConAu 25*, *WrD 1976*
Heifetz, Jascha 1901- *AmSCAP 66*, *REn*
Heifetz, Milton D 1921- *ConAu 57*
Heifetz, Vladimir 1893- *AmSCAP 66*
Heigel, Karl Von 1835- *BiD&SB*
Heiges, P Myers 1887-1968 *ConAu P-1*
Heighway, Osborn W Trenery *Alli*, *Alli Sup*
Heighway, William *Alli Sup*
Heije, Jan Pieter 1809-1876 *BiD&SB*
Heijermans, Herman 1864-1924 *CasWL*,
ClDMEuL, *CnMD*, *CnThe*, *EncWL*,
EuA, *McGWD*, *ModWD*, *Pen Eur*,
REnWD
Heijermans, Louis *WhLA*
Heijke, John 1927- *ConAu 21*
Heiland, Louis *ChPo S2*
Heiland, Samuel *Alli*
Heilbron, Bertha L *MnnWr*
Heilbron, J L 1934- *ConAu 53*
Heilbroner, Joan Knapp 1922- *ConAu 1R*
Heilbroner, Robert Louis 1919- *AmA&B*,
ConAu 1R
Heilbronner, Walter L 1924- *ConAu 25*
Heilbrun, Carolyn G 1926- *ConAu 45*
Heilbrunn, Otto 1906-1969 *ConAu P-1*
Heilig, Matthias R 1881- *ConAu 23*
Heiliger, Edward Martin 1909- *ConAu 13R*
Heilman, Arthur 1914- *ConAu 5R*
Heilman, Grant 1919- *ConAu 53*
Heilman, Joan Rattner *ConAu 57*
Heilman, Robert Bechtold 1906- *AmA&B*,
ConAu 13R, *WhPNW*, *WrD 1976*
Heilner, Van Campen 1899-1970 *ConAu 29*
Heilprin, Angelo 1853-1907 *Alli Sup*, *AmA*,
AmA&B, *DcAmA*, *DcNAA*, *REnAL*
Heilprin, Louis 1851-1914 *Alli Sup*, *DcAmA*,
DcNAA
Heilprin, Michael 1823-1888 *Alli Sup*,
AmA&B, *DcAmA*, *DcNAA*

Heim, Alice Winifred 1913- *ConAu 33,*
WrD 1976
Heim, Emery 1906-1946 *AmSCAP 66*
Heim, Ralph Daniel 1895- *ConAu 21,*
WrD 1976
Heim, Roger 1900- *BiDPar*
Heiman, Ernest J 1930- *ConAu 53, WrD 1976*
Heiman, Grover G 1920- *ConAu 5R*
Heiman, Judith 1935- *ConAu 1R*
Heimann, Ernest Max 1901- *Au&Wr*
Heimann, Susan 1940- *ConAu 33*
Heimarck, Theodore 1906- *ConAu 5R*
Heimbeck, Raeburne S 1930- *ConAu 29*
Heimburg, Wilhelmine 1850-1912 *BiD&SB,*
OxGer
Heimer, Melvin Lytton 1915-1971 *ConAu 1R,*
ConAu 29
Heimert, Alan 1928- *ConAu 5R*
Heimler, Eugene 1922- *Au&Wr, ConAu 13R*
Heimsath, Charles H 1928- *ConAu 17R*
Hein, Beverly J 1920- *AmSCAP 66*
Hein, Eleanor C 1933- *ConAu 61*
Hein, John 1921- *ConAu 45*
Hein, Leonard William 1916- *ConAu 53*
Hein, Lucille Eleanor 1915- *ConAu 5R,*
WrD 1976
Hein, Norvin 1914- *ConAu 61*
Hein, Otto Louis 1847- *WhWNAA*
Hein, Piet 1905- *CasWL, ConAu 49,*
Pen Eur
Hein, Silvio 1879-1928 *AmSCAP 66*
Heinberg, Paul 1924- *ConAu 45*
Heindel, Augusta Foss 1865-1949 *OhA&B,*
WhWNAA
Heindel, Margaret Foss *WhWNAA*
Heindel, Max 1865-1919 *DcNAA*
Heindorf, Ray John 1908- *AmSCAP 66*
Heine, A G E *Alli Sup*
Heine, Carl 1936- *ConAu 57*
Heine, Heinrich 1797-1856 *AtlBL, BbD,*
BiD&SB, CasWL, ChPo, ChPo S1,
ChPo S2, CyWA, DcEuL, EuA, EvEuW,
NewC, OxFr, OxGer, Pen Eur,
RCom, REn
Heine, Ralph W 1914- *ConAu 41*
Heine, William *Alli*
Heineman, John Louis 1865-1947 *IndAu 1917*
Heinemann, Margot Claire 1913- *Au&Wr*
Heinemann, William 1863-1920 *BiD&SB,*
LongC, NewC
Heinen, Hubert 1937- *ConAu 41*
Heiner, Jessie Margarethe 1874-1960 *OhA&B*
Heiner, Marie Hays 1907- *OhA&B*
Heinesen, Andreas William 1900- *CasWL*
Heinesen, Jens Pauli 1932- *CasWL*
Heinesen, William 1900- *Pen Eur*
Heiney, Donald 1921- *ConAu 1R*
Heiney, Enos Boyd 1868- *IndAu 1816*
Heinisch, Paul 1878- *CatA 1952*
Heinke, Clarence H 1912- *ConAu 53*
Heinl, Robert Debs, Jr. 1916- *ConAu 5R*
Heinlein, Robert A 1907- *AmA&B, Au&Wr,*
AuBYP, ConAu 1R, ConLC 1, ConLC 3,
ConNov 1972, ConNov 1976, DrAF 1976,
MorJA, Pen Am, REnAL, SmATA 9,
TwCA Sup, TwCW, WebEAL,
WrD 1976
Heinly, John *IlBYP*
Heinrich 1211-1242 *OxGer*
Heinrich VII 1275?-1313 *OxGer*
Heinrich Clusener *OxGer*
Heinrich Der Glichezaere *CasWL, OxGer*
Heinrich II, Der Heilige 973-1024 *OxGer*
Heinrich Der Lowe 1129-1195 *OxGer*
Heinrich Der Stolze d1139 *OxGer*
Heinrich Der Teichner d1377? *OxGer*
Heinrich Der Vogler *OxGer*
Heinrich I, Der Vogler, Deutscher Konig 876-936
OxGer
Heinrich Frauenlob, Meister d1318 *OxGer*
Heinrich Hetzbold Von Weissensee *OxGer*
Heinrich Julius, Duke Of Brunswick 1564-1613
BiD&SB, CasWL
Heinrich Julius, Herzog Von Braunschweig
1564-1613 *OxGer*
Heinrich III, Kaiser 1017-1056 *OxGer*
Heinrich IV, Kaiser 1050-1106 *OxGer*
Heinrich V, Kaiser 1081-1125 *OxGer*

Heinrich VI, Kaiser 1165-1197 *OxGer*
Heinrich, Prinz Von Preussen 1726-1802 *OxGer*
Heinrich Raspe d1247 *OxGer*
Heinrich Von Bergen *OxGer*
Heinrich Von Beringen *CasWL, OxGer*
Heinrich Von Breslau, Herzog *OxGer*
Heinrich Von Burgus, Bruder *OxGer*
Heinrich Von Dem Turlin *CasWL, OxGer*
Heinrich Von Der Muore *OxGer*
Heinrich Von Der Mure *OxGer*
Heinrich Von Freiberg *CasWL, OxGer,*
Pen Eur
Heinrich Von Hesler *OxGer*
Heinrich Von Krolewiz *OxGer*
Heinrich Von Laufenberg 1390?-1460 *OxGer*
Heinrich Von Meissen 1250?-1318 *CasWL,*
DcEuL, Pen Eur
Heinrich Von Meissen, Markgraf 1218-1288
OxGer
Heinrich Von Melk *CasWL, EvEuW, OxGer,*
Pen Eur
Heinrich Von Morungen d1222 *CasWL, EuA,*
OxGer, Pen Eur
Heinrich Von Mugeln 1320?-1372 *CasWL,*
OxGer
Heinrich Von Neustadt *CasWL, OxGer,*
Pen Eur
Heinrich Von Nordlingen *CasWL, OxGer*
Heinrich Von Ofterdingen *OxGer*
Heinrich Von Plauen 1370?-1429 *OxGer*
Heinrich Von Rugge d1191? *OxGer*
Heinrich Von Sax *OxGer*
Heinrich Von Stretelingen *OxGer*
Heinrich Von Veldecke *BiD&SB*
Heinrich Von Veldeke *CasWL, EuA, OxGer*
Heinrich Von Wittenweiler *Pen Eur*
Heinrich, Julius *Alli Sup*
Heinrich, Julius, Duke Of Brunswick 1564-1613
BbD, DcEuL
Heinrich, Max 1853-1916 *DcNAA*
Heinrich, Willi 1920- *Au&Wr, WorAu*
Heinrick, Hugh 1831-1877 *PoIre*
Heins, A James 1931- *ConAu 5R*
Heins, Ethel *ChPo S2*
Heinse, Johann Jakob Wilhelm 1749?-1803
CasWL, DcEuL, EvEuW, OxGer,
Pen Eur, REn
Heinse, Wilhelm 1749?-1803 *BiD&SB*
Heinsius, Daniel 1580-1655 *CasWL, DcEuL,*
EuA, OxEng, Pen Eur
Heinsius, Nicolaas, I 1620-1681 *DcEuL*
Heinsius, Nicolaas, II 1656- *DcEuL*
Heinsius, Nicolaes, Jr. 1656-1718 *CasWL*
Heinsohn, A G, Jr. 1896- *ConAu P-1*
Heinsohn, George Edwin 1933- *WrD 1976*
Heintz, Ann Christine 1930- *ConAu 61*
Heintz, John 1936- *ConAu 45*
Heintze, Carl 1922- *ConAu 57*
Heinz, G *ConAu XR*
Heinz, John F 1926- *AmSCAP 66*
Heinz, W C 1915- *ConAu 5R, WrD 1976*
Heinz, William Frederick 1899- *ConAu 61*
Heinzelin Von Konstanz *OxGer*
Heinzen, Karl 1809-1880 *CasWL*
Heinzman, George Melville 1916- *ConAu 1R,*
IndAu 1917
Heiremans, Luis Alberto 1928-1964 *CrCD*
Heirich, Max 1931- *ConAu 29*
Heironimus, Dorothy Helen 1899- *IndAu 1917*
Heironimus, Norval Chase 1864-1937
IndAu 1917
Heisch, C E *Alli Sup*
Heisch, Charles *Alli Sup*
Heise, Edward Tyler 1912- *ConAu 1R*
Heise, Kenan 1933- *ConAu 57*
Heise, Margaret Armstrong *ChPo*
Heiseler, Bernt Von 1907- *CnMD, ModWD,*
OxGer
Heiseler, Henry Von 1875-1928 *ClDMEuL,*
ModWD
Heiser, Alta Harvey 1877- *OhA&B*
Heiser, Charles B, Jr. 1920- *ConAu 45*
Heiser, Karl William 1878-1939 *OhA&B*
Heiser, Ruth Bishop 1909- *IndAu 1917*
Heiser, Victor George 1873-1972 *AmA&B,*
ConAu 33, WhWNAA
Heiserman, Arthur Ray 1929- *ConAu 1R,*
IndAu 1917, WrD 1976

Heiserman, David L 1940- *ConAu 61*
Heisey, Alan Milliken 1928- *ConAu 57*
Heiskell, Andrew 1915- *AmA&B*
Heiskell, Joseph B *Alli Sup*
Heiskell, Samuel Gordon 1858-1923 *DcNAA*
Heisler, Charles Washington 1857- *DcNAA*
Heisler, Daniel Yost 1820-1888 *DcNAA*
Heisler, John Clement 1862- *WhWNAA*
Heisler, Martin O 1938- *ConAu 45*
Heiss, Michael 1818-1890 *Alli Sup, DcNAA*
Heiss, Willard C 1921- *IndAu 1917*
Heissenbuttel, Helmut 1921- *CasWL, ModGL,*
OxGer, Pen Eur
Heistand, Henry Olcott Sheldon 1856-1924
AmA, DcNAA, OhA&B
Heiter, Guillermo 1915- *WhGrA*
Heitler, Walter 1904- *ConAu 13R, WrD 1976*
Heitman, Francis Bernard 1838-1926 *DcNAA*
Heitman, Sidney 1924- *ConAu 9R*
Heitmann, Hans 1904-1970 *CasWL*
Heitner, Robert R 1920- *ConAu 5R,*
WrD 1976
Heiton, John *Alli Sup*
Heitzman, Charles 1836-1896 *Alli Sup,*
DcAmA, DcNAA
Heizer, Robert F *OxCan Sup*
Hejazi, Mohammad 1900- *DcOrL 3*
Hejinian, John Paull 1941- *WrD 1976*
Hektor, Enno 1820-1874 *CasWL*
Hektorovic, Petar 1487-1572 *CasWL, Pen Eur*
Helali, Badroddin 1470?-1529 *DcOrL 3*
Helbemae, Gert 1913- *Au&Wr*
Helbig, Otto H 1914- *AmSCAP 66*
Helbling, Robert E 1923- *ConAu 49*
Helburn, Theresa 1887?-1959 *AmA&B, ChPo,*
REnAL
Helck, C Peter 1893- *ConAu 1R*
Held, Isidore William 1876-1947 *DcNAA*
Held, Jack Preston 1926- *ConAu 33*
Held, John, Jr. 1889-1958 *AmA&B, ChPo S1,*
OxAm, REnAL
Held, Joseph 1930- *ConAu 45*
Held, Omar Conrad 1896-1966 *IndAu 1917*
Held, R Burnell 1921- *ConAu 33*
Held, Ray E 1918- *ConAu 45*
Held, Richard 1922- *ConAu 41*
Held, Virginia P 1929- *ConAu 1R, WrD 1976*
Helder, Dom *ConAu XR*
Helder, Knute *ChPo*
Helderman, Leonard Clinton 1895-1943
IndAu 1917
Heldmann, Bernard *Alli Sup*
Hele, Arthur d1778 *Alli*
Hele, Nicholas Fenwick *Alli Sup*
Hele, Richard *Alli*
Hele, Thomas 1740-1780? *Alli*
Helena *NewC*
Helena, Saint 250?-330? *NewC*
Heley, A A *Alli Sup*
Helfen, Mathias 1889- *BkC 2*
Helfen, Matthias 1889- *WhWNAA*
Helfenstein, Ernest *AmA&B*
Helfenstein, Jacob *Alli Sup*
Helfer, Walter 1896-1959 *AmSCAP 66*
Helfert, Erich A 1931- *ConAu 9R*
Helfman, Elizabeth S 1911- *AuBYP,*
ConAu 5R, SmATA 3, WrD 1976
Helfman, Harry Carmozin 1910- *AuBYP,*
ConAu 25, SmATA 3, WrD 1976
Helfman, Max 1901-1963 *AmSCAP 66*
Helfritz, Hans 1902- *ConAu 41*
Helgason, Jon 1899- *CasWL*
Helgesen, Paul 1485?-1535? *CasWL, DcEuL*
Heliade-Radulescu, Ion 1802-1872 *CasWL*
Heliczer, Piero 1937- *Pen Am*
Helie, Paulus *CasWL*
Helinand De Froidmont 1160?-1229? *Pen Eur*
Heliodorus *BbD, BiD&SB, CasWL, DcSpL,*
NewC, OxEng, Pen Cl
Heliogabalus 204-222 *NewC, REn*
Helitzer, Florence 1928- *ConAu 17R*
Hell, Theodor 1775-1856 *OxGer*
Hellaakoski, Aaro Antti 1893-1952 *CasWL,*
EncWL, Pen Eur
Hellanicus 480?BC-405?BC *CasWL, Pen Cl*
Hellberg, Karl 1875- *WhWNAA*
Hellberg, Rolf 1908- *Au&Wr*
Helleberg, Carl Gustaf *Alli Sup*

Hellen, J A 1935- *ConAu 61*
Hellens, Franz 1881-1972 *CasWL, ClDMEuL*
Hellenthal, John Albertus 1874-1945 *AmA&B*
Heller *ConAu 49*
Heller, Abraham M 1898-1975 *ConAu 57*
Heller, Celia S *ConAu 37*
Heller, David 1922-1968 *ConAu P-1*
Heller, Deane 1924- *ConAu 9R*
Heller, Edmund 1875-1939 *AmA&B, DcNAA*
Heller, Erich 1911- *AmA&B, Au&Wr, ConAu 13R, WrD 1976*
Heller, Francis H 1917- *ConAu 1R*
Heller, Herbert Lynn 1908- *ConAu 21, IndAu 1917*
Heller, Isaac 1809-1836 *IndAu 1816*
Heller, John 1928- *AmSCAP 66*
Heller, Joseph 1923- *AmA&B, AuNews 1, CasWL, ConAu 5R, ConDr, ConLC 1, ConLC 3, ConLC 5, ConNov 1972, ConNov 1976, DrAF 1976, ModAL, ModAL Sup, OxAm, Pen Am, RAdv 1, TwCW, WebEAL, WhTwL, WorAu, WrD 1976*
Heller, Louise R 1870- *BiD&SB*
Heller, Mark 1914- *ConAu 61*
Heller, Maximilian 1860-1929 *DcNAA*
Heller, Michael 1937- *ConAu 45, DrAP 1975*
Heller, Otto 1863-1941 *AmLY, DcNAA, WhWNAA*
Heller, Peter 1920- *ConAu 41*
Heller, Richard H 1924- *AmA&B*
Heller, Robert 1812-1871 *BiD&SB*
Heller, Robert 1899?-1973 *ConAu 41*
Heller, Robert W 1933- *ConAu 25*
Heller, Samuel *AnMV 1926*
Heller, Thomas Edmund *Alli Sup*
Heller, Walter W 1915- *ConAu 21, WrD 1976*
Heller, William Jacob 1857-1920 *DcNAA*
Heller, Yomtob Lipmann 1579-1654 *CasWL*
Hellerman, Fred 1927- *AmSCAP 66*
Hellerman, Herbert 1927- *ConAu 53*
Hellerstein, Jerome R 1907- *ConAu P-1*
Helliar, A *Alli Sup*
Hellie, Richard 1937- *ConAu 33, WrD 1976*
Hellier, A M *Alli Sup*
Hellier, Benjamin *Alli Sup*
Hellier, Henry *Alli*
Hellinger, Mark 1903-1947 *AmA&B, DcNAA, REnAL*
Hellins, John *Alli, BiDLA*
Hellis, Nellie *Alli Sup*
Hellison, Donald R 1938- *ConAu 53*
Hellman, C Doris 1910-1973 *ConAu 41*
Hellman, Ellen 1908- *WrD 1976*
Hellman, Geoffrey T 1907- *AmA&B, REnAL*
Hellman, George Sidney 1878-1958 *AmA&B, ChPo, REnAL, WhWNAA*
Hellman, Hal 1927- *ConAu XR, SmATA 4, WrD 1976*
Hellman, Harold 1927- *ConAu 25, SmATA 4*
Hellman, Hugo E 1908- *ConAu 19*
Hellman, Lillian 1905- *AmA&B, AuNews 1, AuNews 2, CasWL, CnDAL, CnMD, CnThe, ConLC 2, ConLC 4, CrCD, CyWA, McGWD, ModAL, ModAL Sup, ModWD, OxAm, Pen Am, REn, REnAL, REnAL Sup, TwCA, TwCA Sup, WebEAL, WhTwL*
Hellman, Lillian 1906- *Au&Wr, ConAu 13R, EncWL Sup*
Hellman, Lillian 1907- *ConDr, LongC, WrD 1976*
Hellman, Robert 1919- *ConAu 17R*
Hellman, Sam 1885- *AmA&B*
Hellmann, Anna 1902?-1972 *ConAu 33*
Hellmann, Donald C 1933- *ConAu 45*
Hellmann, Ellen 1908- *Au&Wr*
Hellmuth, Isaac 1819- *Alli Sup, BbtC*
Hellmuth, Jerome 1911- *ConAu 13R*
Hellmuth, William Frederick, Jr. 1920- *ConAu 1R*
Hello, Ernest 1828-1885 *OxFr*
Hellon, Henry George *Alli Sup*
Hellowes, Edward *Alli, DcEuL*
Hellows, Edward *Alli*
Hellriegel, Martin B 1890- *CatA 1952*
Hellstrom, Eva Backstrom 1898- *BiDPar*

Hellstrom, Gustaf 1882-1953 *CasWL, ClDMEuL, Pen Eur, REn*
Hellstrom, Ward 1930- *ConAu 33, WrD 1976*
Hellwig, Monika Konrad 1929- *ConAu 37*
Hellyer, Arthur George Lee 1902- *Au&Wr, ConAu 9R, WrD 1976*
Hellyer, David Tirrell 1913- *ConAu 17R*
Hellyer, Jill 1925- *Au&Wr, WrD 1976*
Hellyer, Paul T 1923- *OxCan Sup, WrD 1976*
Hellyer, S Stevens *Alli Sup*
Helm, A Truman *ArizL*
Helm, Alfred *Alli Sup*
Helm, Bertrand P 1929- *ConAu 37*
Helm, E Eugene 1928- *ConAu 1R*
Helm, Everett 1913- *ConAu 49*
Helm, George Frederick *Alli Sup*
Helm, H J *Alli Sup*
Helm, James I *Alli Sup*
Helm, Mary 1845-1913 *DcNAA*
Helm, Peter James 1916- *Au&Wr, ConAu 9R*
Helm, Robert Meredith 1917- *ConAu 17R*
Helm, Thomas 1919- *ConAu 5R*
Helm, Thomas B 1822-1889 *Alli Sup, IndAu 1816*
Helm, William P 1883- *WhWNAA*
Helman, Albert 1903- *CasWL*
Helman, Edith F 1905- *DcSpL*
Helmbold, Ludwig 1532-1598 *BiD&SB, OxGer*
Helme, Elizabeth *Alli*
Helme, J *Alli*
Helme, William *Alli, BiDLA*
Helmer, Jean Cassels *IlBYP*
Helmer, John 1946- *ConAu 41*
Helmer, N *Alli Sup*
Helmer, William F 1926- *ConAu 33*
Helmericks, Bud *ConAu XR*
Helmericks, Constance Chittenden 1918- *AmA&B, ConAu 9R*
Helmericks, Harmon Robert 1917- *Au&Wr, ConAu 29*
Helmericks, Harmon Robert 1918- *AmA&B*
Helmers, Dow 1906- *ConAu 61*
Helmers, Jan Frederik 1767-1813 *BiD&SB, CasWL*
Helmholtz, Hermann Ludwig Ferdinand Von 1821-1894 *BbD, REn*
Helmholz, Henry F 1882- *WhWNAA*
Helmholz, R H 1940- *ConAu 61*
Helmi, Jack *ConAu XR*
Helmick, Eli Alva 1863-1945 *IndAu 1917*
Helming, Ann *ConAu 1R*
Helmker, Judith Anne 1940- *ConAu 33, WrD 1976*
Helmore, Frederick *Alli Sup*
Helmore, Geoffrey Anthony 1922- *ConAu 29, WrD 1976*
Helmore, Margaret C *Alli Sup*
Helmore, Thomas 1811-1890 *Alli, Alli Sup*
Helmreich, Ernst Christian 1902- *ConAu 1R, WrD 1976*
Helmreich, Paul C 1933- *ConAu 53*
Helms, Elmer Ellsworth 1863-1955 *OhA&B*
Helms, Lloyd Alvin 1902- *IndAu 1917*
Helms, Ludwig Verner *Alli Sup*
Helms, Randel 1942- *ConAu 49, WrD 1976*
Helms, W T *BiDSA*
Helms, William Thomas d1900 *DcNAA*
Helmstadter, Gerald C 1925- *ConAu 13R*
Helmsworth, Richard *Alli*
Helmuth, Justus Christian Henry 1745-1825 *Alli, DcAmA*
Helmuth, William Tod 1833-1902 *Alli, Alli Sup, AmA&B, DcAmA, DcNAA*
Heloise *ConAu XR*
Heloise 1101-1164 *OxFr, REn*
Helper, Hinton Rowan 1829-1909 *Alli, Alli Sup, AmA, AmA&B, BiD&SB, BiDSA, CnDAL, DcAmA, DcNAA, OxAm, REn, REnAL*
Helper, Maria Louisa *Alli Sup*
Helps, Sir Arthur 1813?-1875 *Alli, Alli Sup, BbD, BiD&SB, BrAu 19, Chmbr 3, DcEnA, DcEnL, DcEuL, DcLEnL, EvLB, NewC, OxEng*
Helps, Edmund Arthur *Alli Sup*
Helps, Racey 1913-1971 *ConAu 23, ConAu 29, SmATA 2*
Helser, Albert David 1897- *AmA&B, OhA&B*

Helsham, Henry *Alli*
Helsham, Richard d1738 *Alli*
Helson, Harry 1898- *ConAu P-1*
Helston, John 1877- *ChPo S2*
Heltai, Jeno 1871-1957 *CasWL, Pen Eur*
Helton, David 1940- *ConAu 25*
Helton, Roy Addison 1886- *AmA&B, AnMV 1926, ChPo, REnAL, WhWNAA*
Helton, Tinsley 1915- *ConAu 1R*
Helvetius, Claude Adrien 1715-1771 *BiD&SB, CasWL, DcEuL, EuA, EvEuW, NewC, OxEng, OxFr, Pen Eur, REn*
Helvick, James *WorAu*
Helweg, Hans H 1917- *IlCB 1956*
Helwig *OxGer*
Helwig, David 1938- *Au&Wr, ConAu 33, ConP 1970, ConP 1975, OxCan Sup, WrD 1976*
Helwig, Johann 1609-1674 *OxGer*
Helwig, John B 1833-1904 *OhA&B*
Helwys, Thomas *Alli*
Hely, James *Alli, BiDLA*
Helys Of Winchester *BiB N*
Hemacandra 1088?-1172 *CasWL, DcOrL 2*
Hemachandra *CasWL*
Hemans, Mrs. 1793-1835 *Chmbr 3, Pen Eng*
Hemans, Charles Isidore 1817-1876 *Alli Sup*
Hemans, Dorothea Browne 1793-1835 *ChPo, ChPo S1*
Hemans, Felicia Dorothea Browne 1793-1835 *Alli, BbD, BiD&SB, BrAu 19, CarSB, CasWL, ChPo S2, DcEnA, DcEnL, DcEuL, DcLEnL, EvLB, NewC, OxEng, PoCh, REn, WebEAL*
Hemans, George Willoughby And Hassard, R *Alli Sup*
Hemans, Lawton Thomas 1864-1916 *DcNAA*
Hemans, Willis J *ChPo*
Hembdt, Phil Harold 1875-1927 *DcNAA*
Hembel, William 1764-1851 *CyAL 2*
Hembling, Nina 1875- *WhWNAA*
Hembree, Charles R 1938- *ConAu 33*
Hembroff-Schleicher, Edythe *OxCan Sup*
Hemcandra Gosvami *DcOrL 2*
Hemdahl, Reuel Gustaf 1903- *ConAu 37*
Hemenway, Abby Maria 1828-1890 *Alli Sup, ChPo, DcAmA, DcNAA*
Hemenway, Asa 1810-1892 *Alli Sup, DcNAA*
Hemenway, C F *ChPo*
Hemenway, Henry Bixby 1856-1931 *DcNAA, WhWNAA*
Hemenway, Herbert Daniel 1873- *AmLY, WhWNAA*
Hemenway, Robert 1921- *Au&Wr, ConAu 33*
Hemery, Francis H *Alli Sup*
Hemery And Dumaresq *Alli*
Hemesath, Caroline 1899- *ConAu 61*
Hemet, John *BiDLA*
Heming *Alli*
Heming, Arthur 1870-1940 *CanNov, CanWr, DcNAA, OxCan*
Heming, Edward *Alli*
Heming, Jack Chetwynd Western 1899- *Au&Wr*
Heming, Jack Rupert Dempster 1925- *Au&Wr*
Heming, John 1556?-1630 *NewC*
Heming, S *Alli*
Heming, T *BiDLA*
Heming, Thomas *Alli*
Heming, William 1602-1651? *CasWL, DcLEnL*
Heminger, Isaac Newton 1868-1941 *OhA&B, WhWNAA*
Hemingford, Walter De d1347 *DcEnL*
Hemings, William *Alli*
Hemingus, Monachus Wigorniensis *Alli*
Hemingway, Ernest 1899?-1961 *AmA&B, AmNov, AmWr, ArizL, AuNews 2, CasWL, ChPo S1, ChPo S2, Chmbr 3, CnDAL, CnMD, CnMWL, ConAmA, ConAmL, ConLC 1, ConLC 3, ConLC 6, CyWA, DcLEnL, EncWL, EvLB, LongC, ModAL, ModAL Sup, ModWD, OxAm, OxEng, Pen Am, RAdv 1, RCom, REn, REnAL, TwCA, TwCA Sup, TwCW, WebEAL, WhTwL*
Hemingway, J B H *Alli Sup*
Hemingway, Taylor *ConAu XR*

Hemingway, Thomas Keith 1931- *Au&Wr*
Heminway, John Hylan, Jr. 1944- *ConAu 25,*
WrD 1976
Hemiup, Maria Remington *Alli Sup*
Hemleben, Sylvester John 1902- *ConAu 25*
Hemler, Opal Tafe 1890- *OhA&B*
Hemley, Cecil Herbert 1914-1966 *AmA&B,*
ConAu 1R, ConAu 25
Hemley, Elaine Gottlieb *ConAu XR*
Hemlow, Joyce 1906- *Au&Wr, ConAu 5R,*
WrD 1976
Hemment, Marguerite E 1908- *AmSCAP 66*
Hemmenway, Moses 1735-1811 *Alli, DcNAA*
Hemmeon, Morley DeWolfe 1868-1919 *DcNAA*
Hemmer, Eugene 1929- *AmSCAP 66*
Hemmer, Jarl Robert 1893-1944 *CasWL,*
ClDMEuL
Hemmerde, Edward George 1871- *WhLA*
Hemmeter, John C 1863?-1931 *DcAmA,*
DcNAA, WhWNAA
Hemming Of Worcester *BiB N*
Hemming, E J *BbtC*
Hemming, George Wirgman 1821- *Alli Sup*
Hemming, James 1909- *Au&Wr*
Hemming, John *Alli*
Hemming, John Henry 1935- *Au&Wr,*
ConAu 29, WrD 1976
Hemming, Roy 1928- *ConAu 61*
Hemming, S *Alli*
Hemming, William Douglas *Alli Sup*
Hemminge, John 1556?-1630 *NewC*
Hemminge, William 1602-1651 *DcLEnL*
Hemmingford, Walter De *Alli*
Hemmingsen, Niels 1513-1600 *CasWL, DcEuL*
Hemon, Louis 1880-1913 *CasWL, ClDMEuL,*
CyWA, LongC, OxAm, OxCan, OxFr,
Pen Eur, REn, REnAL, TwCA,
TwCA Sup
Hemon, Roparz *Pen Eur*
Hempel, Charles Julius 1811-1879 *Alli,*
Alli Sup, DcAmA
Hemphill, Barbara d1858 *Alli Sup*
Hemphill, Charles Robert 1852- *BiDSA*
Hemphill, George 1922- *ConAu 13R,*
WrD 1976
Hemphill, James Calvin 1850-1927 *BiDSA,*
DcNAA
Hemphill, John 1803-1862 *BiDSA*
Hemphill, John K 1919- *ConAu 53*
Hemphill, Martha Locke 1904- *ConAu 37*
Hemphill, Mary Louise 1877- *AnMV 1926*
Hemphill, Paul James 1936?- *AuNews 2,*
ConAu 49
Hemphill, Paul James 1938- *WrD 1976*
Hemphill, Richard *Alli Sup, PoIre*
Hemphill, Rosemary 1922- *Au&Wr*
Hemphill, Samuel *Alli Sup*
Hemphill, Vivia 1889-1934 *DcNAA*
Hemphill, W Edwin 1912- *ConAu 21*
Hemphill, William Despard *Alli Sup*
Hemphrey, Malcolm *ChPo S1*
Hempl, George 1859-1921 *DcNAA*
Hemple, Emma *ChPo S1*
Hempseed, Isabell *ChPo*
Hempstead, Edward *BiDSA*
Hempstead, Fay 1847-1934 *Alli Sup, AmA&B,*
BiDSA, DcNAA
Hempstead, Giles Samuel Booth 1794-1883
OhA&B
Hempstead, Junius Lackland 1842- *DcNAA*
Hempstead, Junius B *BiDSA*
Hempstead, Samuel H *Alli*
Hempstead, T *Alli Sup*
Hempstead, Thomas 1822-1886 *ChPo S1,*
DcNAA
Hempstone, Smith 1929- *ConAu 1R*
Hempton, John *Alli Sup*
Hemschemeyer, Judith 1935- *ConAu 49,*
DrAP 1975
Hemsley, Almon *ChPo*
Hemsley, J B *ChPo*
Hemsley, William *ChPo S2*
Hemsley, William Botting *Alli Sup*
Hemsterhuis, Francois 1721-1790 *CasWL,*
EvEuW
Hemstreet, Charles 1866- *AmA&B, ChPo S2,*
DcAmA, DcNAA
Hemstreet, William *Alli Sup*

Hemsworth, Richard *Alli*
Hemyng, Bracebridge 1841-1901 *EncM&D,*
HsB&A, MnBBF, WhCL
Hemyng, Philip B *MnBBF*
Hemyng, Philip H *Alli Sup*
Hemyng, Samuel Bracebridge 1841-1901
Alli Sup
Henault, Charles-Jean-Francois 1685-1770 *OxFr*
Henault, Gilles 1920- *CanWr, OxCan,*
OxCan Sup
Henault, Guy *OxCan*
Henault, Marie 1921- *ConAu 33, WrD 1976*
Henchard, Michael *REn*
Henchie, E J *Alli Sup*
Henchman, Humphrey *Alli*
Henchman, Richard *Alli*
Henck, John Benjamin 1815?-1903 *Alli,*
DcNAA, DcNAA
Henckell, Karl Friedrich 1864-1929 *OxGer*
Henday, Anthony *OxCan*
Hendel, Charles William 1890- *ConAu P-1*
Hendel, Samuel 1909- *ConAu 1R*
Henderick, George *Alli, BiDLA*
Henderley, Brooks *ConAu 19, SmATA 1*
Henderlite, Rachel 1905- *ConAu 1R*
Hendershot, Carl H *WrD 1976*
Henderson, Captain *Alli, BiDLA*
Henderson, Mrs. *Alli, Alli Sup*
Henderson, A G *Alli Sup*
Henderson, Alexander *Alli, BbtC, BiDLA,*
ChPo S2
Henderson, Alexander 1583-1646 *Alli*
Henderson, Alexander 1910- *ConAu P-1*
Henderson, Alexander Edward *Alli Sup*
Henderson, Alexander Ernest 1916- *WrD 1976*
Henderson, Alfred *Alli Sup, WhWNAA*
Henderson, Algo Donmyer 1897- *ConAu 1R,*
OhA&B
Henderson, Alice Corbin 1881-1949 *AmA&B,*
ChPo, CnDAL, ConAmL, DcNAA,
OxAm, REn, REnAL
Henderson, Andrew *Alli, Alli Sup*
Henderson, Andrew 1783-1835 *ChPo S2*
Henderson, Anna R *BiDSA, ChPo*
Henderson, Archibald *Alli Sup*
Henderson, Archibald 1877-1963 *AmA&B,*
AmLY, BiDSA, LongC, REnAL, TwCA,
TwCA Sup
Henderson, Archibald 1916- *ConAu 53*
Henderson, Arthur *ChPo*
Henderson, Arthur 1893- *WhLA*
Henderson, Bancroft Clinton 1924- *IndAu 1917*
Henderson, Bernard William 1871- *MnBBF*
Henderson, Bert C 1904- *ConAu P-1*
Henderson, Bill 1941- *ConAu 33*
Henderson, Charles, Jr. 1923- *ConAu 45*
Henderson, Charles E 1907- *AmSCAP 66*
Henderson, Charles Hanford 1861-1941
AmA&B, DcAmA, DcNAA
Henderson, Charles Richmond 1848-1915
AmA&B, DcAmA, DcNAA, IndAu 1816
Henderson, D M *Alli Sup*
Henderson, Dan Fenno 1921- *ConAu 17R,*
WrD 1976
Henderson, Daniel *Alli Sup*
Henderson, Daniel MacIntyre 1851-1906 *AmA,*
AmA&B, ChPo, ChPo S1, DcNAA,
REnAL
Henderson, Daniel MacIntyre 1880-1955
AmA&B, AnMV 1926, ChPo, ChPo S1,
ChPo S2, REnAL, WhWNAA
Henderson, David 1942- *BlkAW, ConAu 25,*
ConP 1970, DrAP 1975
Henderson, Dion 1921- *ConAu 9R*
Henderson, Dorothy *ChPo, OxCan*
Henderson, Dwight F 1937- *ConAu 41*
Henderson, E H *ChPo*
Henderson, Ebenezer *Alli, BiDLA*
Henderson, Ebenezer 1809-1879 *Alli Sup*
Henderson, Edwin 1844-1926 *OhA&B*
Henderson, Elliott Blaine 1877-1944 *OhA&B*
Henderson, Elsie M *ChPo S1*
Henderson, Emily *Alli Sup, ChPo, ChPo S2*
Henderson, Ernest Flagg 1861-1928 *DcAmA,*
DcNAA
Henderson, Ernest McKay 1879- *WhWNAA*
Henderson, Ernest Norton 1869-1938 *DcNAA*
Henderson, F L *ChPo S1*

Henderson, Fletcher 1897-1952 *AmSCAP 66*
Henderson, Florence Leslie 1859- *Alli Sup*
Henderson, Frances C *Alli Sup*
Henderson, Francis M 1921- *WrD 1976*
Henderson, Frank *Alli Sup*
Henderson, G F R *BiDSA*
Henderson, G P 1920- *ConAu 37*
Henderson, G R *Alli Sup*
Henderson, George *Alli, BiDLA, ChPo,*
ChPo S1
Henderson, George 1931- *ConAu 25*
Henderson, George And Hume, Allan O
Alli Sup
Henderson, George C 1891- *IndAu 1917*
Henderson, George Cockburn 1870- *WhLA*
Henderson, George J *Alli Sup*
Henderson, George Patrick 1915- *ConAu 29,*
WrD 1976
Henderson, George Wylie 1904- *AmA&B,*
BlkAW
Henderson, Gerard Carl 1891-1927 *DcNAA*
Henderson, Gilbert Stuart *Alli Sup*
Henderson, Gwen 1908- *AmSCAP 66*
Henderson, H O 1889- *WhWNAA*
Henderson, Hamish 1919- *ConP 1970,*
ConP 1975, WrD 1976
Henderson, Harold Gould 1889-1974 *ChPo,*
ChPo S1, ConAu 53
Henderson, Hattie Olds *ChPo S2*
Henderson, Helen *ChPo*
Henderson, Helen Weston 1874- *AmA&B,*
AmLY, WhWNAA
Henderson, Howard *Alli Sup*
Henderson, Howard Andrew Millet 1836-1912
DcNAA, OhA&B
Henderson, Hume *ChPo S2*
Henderson, Ian 1910- *ConAu 17*
Henderson, Ian Thomson 1908- *WrD 1976*
Henderson, Irving *MnBBF*
Henderson, Isaac 1850-1909 *Alli Sup,*
AmA&B, BiD&SB, DcAmA, DcNAA
Henderson, Isabel 1933- *ConAu 25*
Henderson, J *BiDLA*
Henderson, J E *ChPo, ChPo S1*
Henderson, J K *PoIre*
Henderson, J L H *OxCan Sup*
Henderson, Miss J P *BiDSA*
Henderson, J Raymond 1929- *AmSCAP 66*
Henderson, J Stanley *HsB&A*
Henderson, J T *Alli Sup*
Henderson, James *Alli Sup, MnBBF, PoIre*
Henderson, James 1783?-1848 *NewC*
Henderson, James 1824- *ChPo S1*
Henderson, James 1850- *PoIre*
Henderson, James 1934- *ConAu 33,*
WrD 1976
Henderson, James C 1858-1881 *ChPo,*
ChPo S1
Henderson, James L 1910- *Au&Wr*
Henderson, James Samuel *PoIre*
Henderson, John *Alli, Alli Sup, BiDLA*
Henderson, John 1747-1785 *Alli, ChPo S1,*
PoIre
Henderson, John 1757-1788 *Alli, DcEnL,*
PoIre
Henderson, John 1795- *BiDSA*
Henderson, John 1915- *ConAu 5R*
Henderson, John Brooks, Jr. 1870-1923 *BiDSA,*
DcAmA, DcNAA
Henderson, John Brooks, Sr. 1826- *BiDSA*
Henderson, John C, Jr. *Alli Sup*
Henderson, John Macdonald *Alli Sup*
Henderson, John S 1919- *ConAu 5R*
Henderson, John W 1910- *ConAu 25*
Henderson, Joseph Franklin 1852-1916 *HsB&A,*
OhA&B
Henderson, Joseph Lindsey 1869- *TexWr,*
WhWNAA
Henderson, Joseph W *Alli Sup*
Henderson, Julia Putnam *Alli Sup*
Henderson, Junius 1865-1937 *DcNAA*
Henderson, Katherine *Alli Sup*
Henderson, Keith 1883- *IICB 1945*
Henderson, Keith M 1934- *ConAu 23*
Henderson, Kenneth David Druitt 1903-
Au&Wr, ConAu P-1, WrD 1976
Henderson, Laurence 1928- *Au&Wr,*
ConAu 53, WrD 1976

DcNAA
Hennequin, Emile *Pen Eur*
Hennesey, James J 1926- *ConAu 33*
Hennessey, Caroline 1931- *ConAu XR*
Hennessey, Eileen *WhWNAA*
Hennessey, Henry *Alli Sup*
Hennessey, R A S 1937- *ConAu 29*
Hennessey, William John 1839-1917 *ChPo*
Hennessy, Bernard C 1924- *ConAu 13R*
Hennessy, Sir John Pope 1834- *Alli Sup*
Hennessy, Jossleyn 1903- *Au&Wr, ConAu 9R,*
WrD 1976
Hennessy, Mary L 1927- *ConAu 23*
Hennessy, Roland Burke 1870-1939 *AmA&B,*
DcNAA
Hennessy, William B d1921 *DcNAA*
Hennessy, William Charles 1860?-1898 *PoIre*
Hennessy, William John 1839-1917 *EarAB,*
EarAB Sup
Hennessy, William Maunsell 1828-1889
Alli Sup
Hennesy, James Albert 1863- *WhWNAA*
Henney, Nella 1894- *AmA&B*
Henney, William Franklin 1852-1928 *DcNAA,*
WhWNAA
Henni, John Martin 1805-1881 *OhA&B*
Henniker, Lord 1752- *BiDLA*
Henniker, Sir Frederick *Alli*
Henniker, Lord John *Alli*
Henniker, Sir Mark Chandos Auberon 1906-
Au&Wr
Henniker, Robert d1880 *Alli Sup*
Henning, Charles N 1915- *ConAu 1R*
Henning, Daniel H 1931- *ConAu 45*
Henning, E F *ChPo*
Henning, Edward B 1922- *ConAu 17R*
Henning, George *Alli*
Henning, Julia R *BiDSA*
Henning, Thomas *BbtC*
Henninger, George R 1895-1953 *AmSCAP 66*
Henninger, Joseph Burns 1847-1943 *IndAu 1816*
Hennings, Dorothy Grant 1935- *ConAu 53*
Henningsen, Agnes Kathinka Malling 1868-1962
CasWL, Pen Eur
Henningsen, Charles Frederick 1815-1877
Alli Sup, AmA, AmA&B, BbD, BiD&SB,
DcAmA, REnAL
Henningsen, Poul 1894-1967 *CasWL*
Hennique, Leon 1851-1935 *OxFr*
Hennissart, Martha *EncM&D*
Hennrich, Kilian Joseph 1880-1946 *BkC 2,*
DcNAA
Henrey, Madeleine 1906- *ConAu 13R,*
WrD 1976
Henrey, Mrs. Robert *ConAu XR*
Henri I 1005-1060 *OxFr*
Henri II 1519-1559 *OxFr*
Henri III 1551-1589 *OxFr*
Henri IV 1553-1610 *OxFr*
Henri V *OxFr*
Henri, Comte De Paris *OxFr*
Henri D'Andeli *OxFr*
Henri D'Andely *CasWL*
Henri De Mondeville *CasWL*
Henri De Valenciennes *OxFr*
Henri, Adrian 1932- *ConAu 25, ConP 1970,*
ConP 1975, WrD 1976
Henri, Florette *AmA&B*
Henri, G *ConAu XR*
Henri, Robert 1865-1929 *AtlBL, DcNAA,*
OhA&B, OxAm, REnAL, WhWNAA
Henric, James *Alli*
Henrich, Edith *ChPo*
Henrich, H R *MnBBF*
Henrici, Arthur Trautwein 1889- *WhWNAA*
Henrici, Christian Friedrich 1700-1764 *OxGer*
Henrici, Max 1884- *WhWNAA*
Henrici, Olaus *Alli Sup*
Henricks, Namee 1890- *AmA&B*
Henricus *PoIre*
Henricus, Huntindiensis *Alli*
Henries, A Doris Banks 1930?- *AfA 1*
Henrietta *PoIre*
Henrietta Maria 1609-1669 *REn*
Henriette D'Angleterre 1644-1670 *OxFr*
Henriksen, Agner Damgaard 1896- *Au&Wr*
Henriod, Lorraine 1925- *ConAu 45*
Henrion, F H K 1914- *WhGrA*

Henriot, Emile 1889-1961 *EvEuW*
Henrique, Louise *ChPo*
Henriques, Alfred Gutteres *Alli Sup*
Henriques, Robert David Quixano 1905-1967
LongC, NewC, REn, TwCA Sup
Henriques, Veronica 1931- *Au&Wr,*
WrD 1976
Henriquez Urena, Pedro 1884-1946 *DcSpL,*
Pen Am
Henrotin, Ellen M 1847-1922 *DcNAA*
Henry I 1068-1135? *BiB N, NewC*
Henry II 1133-1189 *NewC*
Henry III 1207-1272 *NewC*
Henry IV 1050-1106 *REn*
Henry IV 1367?-1413 *NewC, REn*
Henry IV 1553-1610 *NewC, REn*
Henry V 1387-1422 *NewC, REn*
Henry VI 1421-1471 *NewC*
Henry VII 1457-1509 *NewC, REn*
Henry, Archdeacon Of Huntington 1084?-1155
Alli
Henry Beauclerc 1068-1135 *NewC*
Henry Curtmantle 1133-1189 *NewC*
Henry Howard, Earl Of Surrey 1517?-1547
Henry IV, King Of England 1367?-1413 *Alli*
Henry VIII, King Of England 1491-1547 *Alli,*
CasWL, Chmbr 1, EvLB, NewC, REn
Henry, Marquis And Earl Of Worcester *Alli*
Henry Of Anjoy 1133-1189 *NewC*
Henry Of Avranches d1262? *CasWL*
Henry Of Bolingbroke 1367-1413 *NewC*
Henry Of Huntingdon 1084?-1155 *BiB N,*
BrAu, CasWL, Chmbr 1, DcEnL, EvLB,
NewC, OxEng
Henry Of Lancaster 1367-1413 *NewC*
Henry Of Navarre 1553-1610 *NewC*
Henry Of Saltrey *BiB N*
Henry Of Settimello *CasWL*
Henry Plantagenet 1133-1189 *NewC*
Henry The Great 1553-1610 *NewC*
Henry The Minstrel 1450?-1492? *Alli, BrAu,*
ChPo S1, DcEnL, EvLB, NewC, OxEng,
Pen Eng, REn
Henry The Navigator 1394-1460 *REn*
Henry Tudor 1457-1509 *NewC*
Henry, A L *MnBBF*
Henry, Alexander *Alli Sup*
Henry, Alexander 1739-1824 *Alli, BbtC,*
DcAmA, DcLEnL, DcNAA, OxCan
Henry, Alexander 1783-1882 *PoIre*
Henry, Alexander, The Younger d1814 *OxCan*
Henry, Alfred H 1865- *WhWNAA*
Henry, Alfred Judson 1858-1931 *DcNAA*
Henry, Ann *OxCan Sup*
Henry, Arthur 1867-1934 *AmA&B, DcAmA,*
DcNAA
Henry, Augustin 1857- *WhLA*
Henry, B C *Alli Sup*
Henry, Bernard 1902- *Au&Wr*
Henry, Bessie Walker 1921- *ConAu 9R*
Henry, Buck *ConDr*
Henry, Caleb Sprague 1804-1884 *Alli, Alli Sup,*
AmA&B, BiD&SB, CyAL 2, DcAmA,
DcNAA, REnAL
Henry, Carl F H 1913- *ConAu 13R*
Henry, Carol 1928- *BlkAW, DrAP 1975*
Henry, Charles *Alli Sup*
Henry, Claud 1914- *ConAu 45*
Henry, D S *Alli Sup*
Henry, Daniel *ConAu XR*
Henry, Daniel, Jr. 1851-1908 *Alli Sup, AmA,*
OhA&B, PoIre
Henry, David *Alli Sup*
Henry, David 1710-1792 *Alli*
Henry, David W 1852- *IndAu 1816*
Henry, DeWitt *DrAF 1976*
Henry, Mrs. E *Alli Sup*
Henry, Edgar *Alli Sup*
Henry, Edna G 1874- *IndAu 1917*
Henry, Baron Edouard *PoIre*
Henry, Francis 1905-1953 *AmSCAP 66*
Henry, Frederick August 1867-1948 *OhA&B*
Henry, Frederick P *Alli Sup*
Henry, George *BbtC*
Henry, Mrs. George *Alli Sup*
Henry, George William 1889-1964 *AmA&B*
Henry, Gerritt *DrAP 1975*
Henry, Grace Gilbert 1885- *WhWNAA*

Henry, Guy Vernor 1839-1899 *Alli Sup,*
DcAmA
Henry, H A *Alli Sup*
Henry, H L *Alli Sup*
Henry, Harold Wilkinson 1926- *ConAu 37*
Henry, Harriet *ConAu 49*
Henry, Howell Meadors 1879- *WhWNAA*
Henry, Hugh Thomas 1862-1946 *CatA 1947,*
ChPo S1, DcNAA
Henry, I M Porter *LivFWS*
Henry, Ina M *BiDSA*
Henry, J *Alli, PoIre*
Henry, J R *Alli*
Henry, J T *Alli Sup*
Henry, James 1798-1876 *Alli Sup, PoIre*
Henry, James 1809-1895 *Alli Sup, DcAmA,*
DcNAA
Henry, James Buchanan *Alli Sup*
Henry, James S 1950- *ConAu 49*
Henry, Jardine *Alli Sup*
Henry, Joanne Landers 1927- *ConAu 17R,*
IndAu 1917, SmATA 6
Henry, John *Alli, Alli Sup, BiDLA,*
EarAB Sup
Henry, John Flournoy 1793-1873 *BiDSA,*
DcAmA, DcNAA, OhA&B
Henry, John Joseph 1758-1810? *Alli, BbtC,*
DcAmA, DcNAA
Henry, John Robertson 1868- *WhWNAA*
Henry, Joseph 1797?-1878? *Alli, Alli Sup,*
DcAmA, DcNAA, OxAm, REnAL
Henry, Joseph B 1901- *ConAu 17, WrD 1976*
Henry, Kenneth 1920- *ConAu 57*
Henry, Laurin L 1921- *ConAu 1R*
Henry, Lucian Edward *Alli Sup*
Henry, Lucien *Alli Sup*
Henry, M H *Alli Sup*
Henry, Marguerite 1902- *AmA&B, Au&Wr,*
AuBYP, AuICB, BkCL, ConAu 17R,
JBA 1951, Newb 1922, WrD 1976
Henry, Martin Malousha 1867-1943
IndAu 1917, OhA&B
Henry, Mary H *Alli Sup, DcNAA*
Henry, Matthew 1662-1714 *Alli, CasWL,*
Chmbr 2, DcEnL, EvLB
Henry, Matthew Schropp 1790-1862 *DcNAA*
Henry, Mellinger Edward 1873-1946 *DcNAA*
Henry, O 1862-1910 *AmA&B, AtlBL, BiDSA,*
CasWL, ChPo, Chmbr 3, CnDAL,
CyWA, DcLEnL, DcNAA, EncM&D,
EncWL, EvLB, LongC, ModAL, OxAm,
OxEng, Pen Am, RAdv 1, REn, REnAL,
TwCA, TwCA Sup, TwCW, WebEAL,
WhTwL
Henry, O ALSO Porter, William Sydney
Henry, Patrick 1736-1799 *Alli, AmA,*
AmA&B, BbD, BiD&SB, BiDSA,
DcAmA, OxAm, REn, REnAL
Henry, Philip 1631-1696 *Alli*
Henry, Phineas *Alli Sup*
Henry, R *Alli Sup*
Henry, Ralph Chester 1912- *WhPNW*
Henry, Ralph L 1895- *WhWNAA*
Henry, Raymond Varo *PoIre*
Henry, Rene 1871- *ChPo S1*
Henry, Robert *Chmbr 2*
Henry, Robert 1718-1790 *Alli, DcEnL, EvLB*
Henry, Robert 1792-1856 *Alli, BiDSA,*
CyAL 2
Henry, Robert Llewellyn, Jr. 1882- *WhWNAA*
Henry, Robert Selph 1889- *ConAu 1R,*
WhWNAA
Henry, S E *ChPo*
Henry, Samuel J 1879- *Br&AmS*
Henry, Sarepta Myrenda Irish 1839-1900
Alli Sup, AmA&B, DcAmA, DcNAA
Henry, Shirley 1925?-1972 *ConAu 33*
Henry, Stuart Oliver 1860-1953 *AmA&B,*
AmLY, DcAmA, WhWNAA
Henry, T S *MnBBF*
Henry, Thomas *Alli, BiDLA, PoIre*
Henry, Thomas 1879-1962 *WhCL*
Henry, Thomas C 1790-1827 *Alli, DcAmA,*
DcNAA
Henry, Thomas Edward 1910- *Au&Wr*
Henry, Vera *ConAu 21, WrD 1976*
Henry, W M *PoIre*
Henry, W P 1929- *ConAu 17R*

Henry, W S *Alli*
Henry, Waights Gibbs 1879- *WhWNAA*
Henry, Walter 1791-1860 *Alli, BbtC, DcNAA*
Henry, Will *AmA&B*
Henry, William *Alli*
Henry, William 1775-1836 *Alli, BiDLA*
Henry, William A *OxCan*
Henry, William Arnon 1850-1932 *DcAmA, DcNAA, OhA&B*
Henry, William Elmer 1857-1936 *DcNAA, IndAu 1816*
Henry, William John Charles *Alli Sup*
Henry, William S *BlkAW*
Henry, William Seaton 1816-1851 *DcAmA, DcNAA*
Henry, William Wirt 1831-1900 *AmA, AmA&B, BiDSA, DcAmA, DcNAA*
Henry-Ruffin, M E *ChPo S1, DcNAA*
Henryson, Edward *Alli*
Henryson, Robert 1430?-1506? *Alli, AtlBL, BrAu, CasWL, Chmbr 1, CnE&AP, CriT 1, DcEuL, DcLEnL, EvLB, MouLC 1, NewC, OxEng, Pen Eng, REn, WebEAL*
Henrysoun, Robert 1430?-1506? *DcEnL*
Henschel, Elizabeth Georgie *Au&Wr, WrD 1976*
Henschke, Alfred *EvEuW, REn*
Hensel, George W, Jr. 1866- *WhWNAA*
Hensel, Luise 1798-1876 *BiD&SB, OxGer, PoCh*
Hensel, Octavia *Alli Sup, DcNAA*
Hensel, William Uhler 1836-1915 *DcNAA*
Hensel, William Uhler 1851- *Alli Sup, DcAmA*
Hensen, Herwig 1917- *CnMD, ModWD*
Hensey, Andrew Fitch 1880-1951 *OhA&B*
Henshall, Audrey Shore 1927- *ConAu 9R, WrD 1976*
Henshall, James Alexander 1836-1925 *Alli Sup, DcAmA, DcNAA, OhA&B*
Henshall. Samuel d1807 *Alli*
Henshaw, Annie B *Alli Sup*
Henshaw, David 1791-1852 *Alli, DcAmA, DcNAA*
Henshaw, Helen Manville 1876-1908 *DcNAA*
Henshaw, Henry Wetherbee 1850-1930 *DcNAA*
Henshaw, J Sidney 1814- *Alli*
Henshaw, James *REnWD*
Henshaw, James Ene 1924- *AfA 1, ConDr, TwCW, WrD 1976*
Henshaw, John Prentiss Kewley 1792-1852 *Alli, DcAmA, DcNAA*
Henshaw, Joseph d1678 *Alli*
Henshaw, Joshua Sidney 1811-1859 *DcAmA, DcNAA*
Henshaw, Julia Willmothe 1869-1937 *DcNAA, OxCan, WhWNAA*
Henshaw, Mrs. M E *ChPo*
Henshaw, Marshall 1820-1900 *DcNAA*
Henshaw, Nathaniel *Alli*
Henshaw, Nevil Gratiot 1880-1938 *BiDSA, DcNAA, WhWNAA*
Henshaw, Samuel *Alli Sup*
Henshaw, Sarah Edwards 1822- *Alli Sup, ChPo, ChPo S1*
Henshaw, T 1889- *Au&Wr*
Henshaw, Thomas *Alli*
Henshel, Richard L 1939- *ConAu 57*
Henshew, T W *Alli Sup*
Henshon, Gravenor *Alli*
Henslee, Mrs. J F *TexWr*
Hensler, Karl Friedrich 1759?-1825 *BiD&SB, OxGer*
Hensley, Charles S 1919- *ConAu 41*
Hensley, E G *ChPo*
Hensley, Jeannine *ChPo S2*
Hensley, Joe L 1926- *ConAu 33, DrAF 1976, IndAu 1917*
Hensley, Lewis *Alli Sup*
Hensley, Sophie M 1866- *DcAmA*
Henslin, James Marvin 1937- *ConAu 41*
Henslow, A F *Alli Sup*
Henslow, George *Alli Sup*
Henslow, John Stevens 1796-1861 *Alli, Alli Sup*
Henslowe, J R *Alli Sup*
Henslowe, Leonard *WhLA*

Henslowe, Philip d1616 *CrE&SL, NewC, Pen Eng, WebEAL*
Henslowe, William Henry *Alli*
Hensman, Alfred Peach *Alli Sup*
Hensman, Arthur *Alli Sup*
Hensman, C R 1923- *Au&Wr*
Hensman, Howard *Alli Sup*
Hensman, John *Alli Sup*
Henson, Clyde E 1914- *ConAu 5R*
Henson, Herbert Hensley 1863-1947 *CnMWL, LongC, WhLA, WorAu*
Henson, Josiah 1789-1883 *AmA, AmA&B, DcNAA, OxAm, OxCan, REnAL*
Henson, Lance *DrAP 1975*
Henson, Norris Christy 1918- *AmSCAP 66*
Henson, Philip Truman 1898-1968 *IndAu 1917*
Henson, Poindexter Smith 1831-1914 *DcNAA*
Henson, Robert 1934- *AmSCAP 66*
Henson, William *Alli Sup*
Henston, Mrs. *ChPo*
Henstra, Friso 1928- *IlBYP, SmATA 8*
Hent, R W *Alli Sup*
Henthorn, William E 1928- *ConAu 41*
Hentoff, Nat 1925- *AuBYP, ChLR 1, ChPo S2, ConAu 1R, REnAL, ThBJA, WrD 1976*
Hentoff, Nathan Irving 1925- *AmA&B*
Henton, Collett *MnBBF*
Henty, George Alfred 1832-1902 *Alli Sup, BbD, BiD&SB, BrAu 19, CarSB, CasWL, Chmbr 3, DcLEnL, EvLB, JBA 1934, LongC, MnBBF, NewC, OxEng, Pen Eng, WhCL*
Henty, Richmond *Alli Sup*
Hentz, Caroline Lee 1800-1856 *Alli, AmA, AmA&B, BiD&SB, BiDSA, CyAL 2, DcAmA, DcNAA, OhA&B, REnAL*
Hentz, Caroline Therese *Alli*
Hentz, John P 1832-1915 *OhA&B*
Hentz, Julia L 1829-1879 *BiDSA*
Hentz, Nicholas Marcellus 1797-1856 *Alli Sup, BiDSA, DcAmA, DcNAA, OhA&B, OxAm*
Henville, Philip *Alli*
Henwood, James N J 1932- *ConAu 29*
Henz, Rudolf 1897- *OxGer*
Henze, Donald F 1928- *ConAu 23*
Henze, Hans Werner 1926- *OxGer*
Henzen, Karl Georg Wilhelm 1850- *BiD&SB*
Henzi, Samuel 1701-1749 *OxGer*
Hepburn, A D *Alli Sup*
Hepburn, Alice *Alli Sup*
Hepburn, Alonzo Barton 1846-1922 *DcNAA*
Hepburn, Andrew Dousa 1830-1921 *DcNAA*
Hepburn, Andrew H 1899?-1975 *ConAu 57*
Hepburn, Charles McGuffey 1859-1929 *IndAu 1816*
Hepburn, David 1857- *PoIre*
Hepburn, Duncan D *Alli Sup*
Hepburn, Elizabeth Newport *AmA&B*
Hepburn, George *Alli*
Hepburn, George Buchan *Alli*
Hepburn, H P *Alli Sup*
Hepburn, James d1578 *NewC*
Hepburn, James Bonaventura 1573-1620? *Alli*
Hepburn, James Curtis 1815-1911 *Alli Sup, DcAmA, DcNAA*
Hepburn, John *Alli*
Hepburn, Mary Fishburn 1888- *ChPo*
Hepburn, Mitchell *OxCan*
Hepburn, Robert 1690- *Alli*
Hepburn, Ronald William 1927- *Au&Wr, ConAu 13R, WrD 1976*
Hepburn, Thomas Nicholl 1861- *ChPo, ChPo S1*
Hepburn, William Murray 1874-1963 *IndAu 1917, WhWNAA*
Hephaestus *CasWL*
Hepner, Harry W 1893- *ConAu 29*
Hepner, James O 1933- *ConAu 57*
Heppelwhite, George d1786 *NewC*
Heppenstall, Margit Strom 1913- *ConAu 23*
Heppenstall, Rayner 1911- *Au&Wr, ConAu 1R, ConNov 1972, ConNov 1976, ConP 1970, ConP 1975, DcLEnL, LongC, ModBL, ModBL Sup, Pen Eng, WorAu, WrD 1976*
Hepple, Bob Alexander 1934- *Au&Wr,*

ConAu 29
Hepple, Norman *ChPo S2*
Hepplestone, Jane *Alli Sup*
Heppner, Sam 1913- *Au&Wr, ConAu 25, WrD 1976*
Heptenstall, E *Alli Sup*
Hepwith, John *Alli*
Hepworth, Miss *ChPo S1*
Hepworth, Carrington *MnBBF*
Hepworth, E N Molesworth *Alli Sup*
Hepworth, George Hughes 1833-1902 *Alli Sup, AmA&B, BbD, BiD&SB, CyAL 2, DcAmA, DcNAA*
Hepworth, Mrs. George Hughes *Alli Sup*
Hepworth, James B 1910- *ConAu 1R*
Hepworth, Philip 1912- *ConAu 17R*
Hepworth, T C *Alli Sup*
Hequembourg, C L *Alli Sup*
Her, Erich *WhLA*
Heracleides Ponticus 390?BC-310?BC *Pen Cl*
Heraclides Ponticus 390?BC-310?BC *CasWL*
Heraclito 1864-1927 *PueRA*
Heraclitus *BbD, BiD&SB, CasWL, NewC, OxEng, Pen Cl, REn*
Heraclius, Emperor *CasWL*
Herald, Kathleen *ThBJA*
Herapath, Edwin John Moore 1822- *Alli*
Herapath, John 1793- *Alli*
Herapath, Thornton John 1830- *Alli*
Herapath, William 1796- *Alli*
Herapath, William Bird *Alli*
Herard, Moses *Alli*
Heraud, Edith *Alli Sup*
Heraud, J A *Alli, BiDLA*
Heraud, John Abraham 1799-1887 *Alli, Alli Sup, BiD&SB, BrAu 19, CasWL, Chmbr 3, DcEnL, EvLB*
Heraus, Karl Gustav 1671-1725? *OxGer*
Heraut Berry, Le *CasWL*
Heravi, Mehdi 1940- *ConAu 29*
Herbart, Johann Friedrich 1776-1841 *DcEuL*
Herbelot, Barthelemy *OxFr*
Herben, Beatrice Slayton *CarSB*
Herben, Jan 1857-1936 *CasWL*
Herben, Stephen Joseph 1861- *WhWNAA*
Herber, Bernard P 1929- *ConAu 21*
Herber, Lewis 1921- *ConAu 1R*
Herber, William Edward 1920- *IndAu 1917*
Herberay DesEssarts, Nicolas d1552? *DcEuL, OxFr*
Herberg, Will 1908- *AmA&B*
Herberger, Charles F 1920- *ConAu 41*
Herberger, Valerius 1562-1627 *OxGer*
Herbermann, Charles George 1840-1916 *Alli Sup, AmA&B, DcAmA, DcNAA*
Herbers, John N 1923- *ConAu 33*
Herbert, Mister *Alli, BiDLA*
Herbert Le Duc De Dammartin *CasWL*
Herbert, Agnes *WhLA*
Herbert, Sir Alan Patrick 1890-1971 *Au&Wr, ChPo, ChPo S1, ChPo S2, ConAu 33, ConNov 1972, DcLEnL, EvLB, LongC, ModBL, NewC, Pen Eng, REn, TwCA, TwCA Sup, TwCW*
Herbert, Alfred Francis Xavier 1901- *DcLEnL*
Herbert, Algernon 1792-1855 *Alli*
Herbert, Alice *ChPo, ChPo S1*
Herbert, Arthur *Alli, ConAu XR*
Herbert, Auberon Edward William Molyneux 1838- *Alli Sup*
Herbert, Caroline *Alli*
Herbert, Cecil *MnBBF*
Herbert, Cecil L 1926- *ConP 1970*
Herbert, Charles *Alli, MnBBF*
Herbert, Darkin Williams 1882- *WhLA*
Herbert, David *Alli Sup*
Herbert, David Thomas 1935- *ConAu 49*
Herbert, Don 1917- *AuBYP, ConAu 29, SmATA 8*
Herbert, Donald Jeffry 1917- *AmA&B*
Herbert, E *ChPo*
Herbert, Edward, Baron H Of Cherbury 1583?-1648 *Alli, BiD&SB, BrAu, CasWL, CnE&AP, CrE&SL, DcEnA, DcEnL, DcEuL, DcLEnL, NewC, OxEng, REn*
Herbert, Sir Edward *Alli*
Herbert, Evan *Alli*

Herbert, Evelyn *Au&Wr*
Herbert, Fanny 1871- *ChPo S1*
Herbert, Frances Georgiana *Alli Sup*
Herbert, Frank *MnBBF*
Herbert, Frank Patrick 1920- *AmA&B,
   ConAu 53, SmATA 9, WrD 1976*
Herbert, Frederick Hugh 1897-1958 *AmA&B,
   McGWD, TwCA Sup*
Herbert, George *Alli Sup, Chmbr 1*
Herbert, George 1593-1633? *Alli, AtlBL, BbD,
   BiD&SB, BrAu, CasWL, ChPo,
   ChPo S1, ChPo S2, CnE&AP, CrE&SL,
   CriT 1, CyWA, DcEnA, DcEnL, DcEuL,
   DcLEnL, EvLB, MouLC 1, NewC,
   OxEng, Pen Eng, RAdv 1, REn,
   WebEAL*
Herbert, George R C, Earl Of Pembroke
   1850-1895 *Alli Sup, NewC*
Herbert, Glen *ChPo S1*
Herbert, H S *Alli Sup*
Herbert, Henry *Alli*
Herbert, Henry H M, Earl Of Carnarvon
   1831-1890 *Alli Sup*
Herbert, Henry John George d1849 *Alli*
Herbert, Henry K *ChPo S2*
Herbert, Henry William 1807-1858 *Alli,
   Alli Sup, AmA, AmA&B, BbD, BbtC,
   BiD&SB, Br&AmS, ChPo, ChPo S1,
   CyAL 2, DcAmA, DcEnL, DcLEnL,
   DcNAA, EarAB, EarAB Sup, HsB&A,
   NewC, OxAm, REnAL*
Herbert, Herbert 1865- *WhLA*
Herbert, Hilary Abner 1834-1919 *BiDSA,
   DcAmA, DcNAA*
Herbert, Ivor 1925- *Au&Wr, ConAu 53,
   WrD 1976*
Herbert, James D d1837 *PoIre*
Herbert, Jane Emily d1886? *Alli Sup, PoIre*
Herbert, Jean 1905- *AmSCAP 66*
Herbert, Jean Daniel Fernand 1897- *Au&Wr,
   ConAu 17R*
Herbert, John *MnBBF*
Herbert, John 1924- *ConAu 23, WrD 1976*
Herbert, John 1926- *ConDr, OxCan Sup,
   WrD 1976*
Herbert, John Alexander 1862- *WhLA*
Herbert, John Beresford *Alli Sup*
Herbert, John Rogers 1810-1890 *ChPo*
Herbert, Kevin 1921- *ConAu 17R*
Herbert, Leila 1868-1897 *BiDSA, DcNAA*
Herbert, Lizzie Boynton *ChPo*
Herbert, M N *Alli Sup*
Herbert, Maria *Alli Sup*
Herbert, Martin 1933- *Au&Wr*
Herbert, Mary, Countess Of Pembroke
   1561-1621 *Alli, CasWL, DcEnL, EvLB,
   NewC*
Herbert, Lady Mary 1835- *Alli Sup*
Herbert, Mary Charlotte 1839- *Alli Sup*
Herbert, Mary E *BbtC, DcNAA, OxCan,
   PoIre*
Herbert, Lady Mary Elizabeth 1822- *Alli Sup*
Herbert, May *Alli Sup*
Herbert, Nellie Candee 1856- *ChPo*
Herbert, Nicholas *Alli Sup*
Herbert, Sir Percy *Alli*
Herbert, Philip 1584-1650 *Alli, NewC*
Herbert, Reginald 1841- *Br&AmS*
Herbert, Robert L 1929- *ConAu 9R*
Herbert, Samuel *Alli, BiDLA*
Herbert, Sarah 1824-1844 *BbtC, ChPo,
   DcNAA, OxCan, PoIre*
Herbert, Sarah A F *Alli Sup*
Herbert, Sarah And Mary E *Alli Sup*
Herbert, Solomon 1874- *WhLA*
Herbert, Stanley *Alli*
Herbert, Thomas *Alli, Alli Sup*
Herbert, Thomas 1597-1642? *NewC*
Herbert, Sir Thomas 1606?-1682? *Alli,
   Chmbr 1, DcEnL, EvLB, NewC*
Herbert, Thomas Martin *Alli Sup*
Herbert, Victor 1859-1924 *AmSCAP 66,
   McGWD, OxAm, REn, REnAL*
Herbert, W *Alli, Alli Sup*
Herbert, Wallace *Alli Sup*
Herbert, William *Alli, BiDLA, BiDLA Sup,
   Chmbr 2*
Herbert, William 1580-1630 *Alli, DcEnL,*

NewC
Herbert, William 1718-1795 *Alli, DcEnL*
Herbert, William 1778-1847 *BiDLA, ChPo S1*
Herbert, William 1869-1930 *DcNAA*
Herbert, Xavier 1901- *CasWL, ConNov 1972,
   ConNov 1976, WebEAL, WrD 1976*
Herbert, Xavier 1911- *TwCW*
Herbert, Zbigniew 1924- *CasWL, EncWL Sup,
   ModSL 2, ModWD, Pen Eur, WhTwL,
   WorAu*
Herbert Of Cherbury, Baron Edward 1583-1648
   *CasWL, Chmbr 1, DcLEnL, EvLB,
   Pen Eng, WebEAL*
Herbertson, Agnes Crozier 1800-1881 *ChPo,
   ChPo S2*
Herbertson, Gary J 1938- *ConAu 25*
Herbin, John Frederic 1860-1923 *DcLEnL,
   DcNAA*
Herbison, David 1800-1880 *ChPo S2, PoIre*
Herbort Von Fritzlar *CasWL, OxGer*
Herbrand, Jan 1931- *ConAu 49*
Herbruck, Edward 1849-1934 *OhA&B*
Herbruck, Emil Peter 1856-1940 *OhA&B*
Herbst, J *Alli*
Herbst, Josephine 1897-1969 *AmA&B, AmNov,
   ConAmA, ConAu 5R, ConAu 25, OxAm,
   REn, REnAL, TwCA, TwCA Sup,
   WebEAL, WhWNAA*
Herbst, Jurgen 1928- *ConAu 37, WrD 1976*
Herbst, Robert L 1935- *ConAu 61*
Herbst, Winfrid 1891- *BkC 1, CatA 1947*
Herchmer, W M *BbtC*
Herckeman, Elias *Alli*
Herculano, Alexandre 1810-1866 *Pen Eur*
Herculano DeCarvalho E Araujo, A 1810-1877
   BbD, BiD&SB, CasWL, EvEuW
Hercules, Frank 1917- *BlkAW, ConAu 1R,
   LivBAA*
Herczeg, Ferenc 1863-1954 *CasWL,
   ClDMEuL, Pen Eur*
Herd, Dale 1940- *ConAu 61*
Herd, David 1732-1810 *Alli, ChPo S2,
   Chmbr 2, DcEnL, EvLB, Pen Eng*
Herd, Harold 1893- *Au&Wr*
Herdal, Harald 1900- *CasWL, EncWL,
   Pen Eur*
Herdan, Gustav 1897- *ConAu 1R*
Herde, Rossiter *MnBBF*
Herdeck, Donald E 1924- *ConAu 53*
Herder, Johann Gottfried Von 1744-1803 *AtlBL,
   BbD, BiD&SB, CasWL, ChPo S1,
   DcEuL, EuA, EvEuW, NewC, OxEng,
   OxGer, Pen Eur, RCom, REn*
Herdman, John *Alli, BiDLA*
Herdman, M S S *Alli Sup*
Herdman, W A *Alli Sup*
Herdman, William *Alli*
Herdman, William Gawin 1805-1882 *Alli Sup*
Herdson, Hen *Alli*
Herdt, Sheryll Patterson 1941- *ConAu 57*
Herebert, Bishop Of Norwich d1119 *BiB N*
Herebert Of Bosham *BiB N*
Heredia, Jose Maria De 1803-1839 *BbD,
   CasWL, DcSpL, Pen Am, REn*
Heredia, Jose Maria De 1842-1905 *AtlBL, BbD,
   BiD&SB, CasWL, ClDMEuL, DcEuL,
   EuA, EvEuW, OxFr, Pen Eur, REn*
Hereford, Bishop *Alli*
Hereford, Bishop Of *ChPo*
Hereford, Charles *Alli, BiDLA*
Hereford, Elizabeth J *Alli Sup, BiDSA, ChPo*
Hereford, John *ConAu XR*
Hereford, Nicholas *Chmbr 1*
Hereford, Robert A 1902- *AuBYP*
Hereford, William R *BiDSA*
Hereford, William Richard 1871-1928 *DcNAA*
Hereford-Lambert, Johnny *AmSCAP 66*
Hereman d1077 *BiB S*
Heren, Louis 1919- *ConAu 25*
Herendeen, Frederick 1893-1962 *AmSCAP 66*
Hereward *NewC*
Herfindahl, Orris C 1918-1972 *ConAu 37,
   ConAu 41*
Herford, Brooke *Alli Sup*
Herford, Brooke 1830-1903 *ChPo S1*
Herford, Charles Harold 1853-1931 *Alli Sup,
   ChPo S2, Chmbr 3, TwCA, TwCA Sup,
   WhLA*

Herford, Ivan S Andrew *Alli Sup*
Herford, Oliver 1863-1935 *AmA&B, BiD&SB,
   CarSB, ChPo, ChPo S1, ChPo S2,
   DcAmA, DcNAA, EvLB, LongC, NewC,
   OxAm, REnAL, TwCA, TwCA Sup*
Herger *CasWL, OxGer*
Hergesheimer, Joseph 1880-1954 *AmA&B,
   CasWL, Chmbr 3, CnDAL, ConAmA,
   ConAmL, CyWA, DcBiA, DcLEnL,
   EvLB, LongC, OxAm, OxEng, Pen Am,
   REn, REnAL, TwCA, TwCA Sup,
   TwCW, WhWNAA*
Herget, William *Alli*
Herget, John Francis 1873-1960 *OhA&B*
Herian, V *ConAu XR*
Heriat, Philippe 1898-1971 *CasWL,
   ConAu XR, EvEuW*
Heribert Von Salurn 1637-1700 *OxGer*
Herick, Samuel Edward 1841-1904 *DcNAA*
Herillus *Pen Cl*
Hering, Agnes Brown 1883- *WhWNAA*
Hering, Carl 1860-1926 *Alli Sup, DcNAA*
Hering, Constantine 1800-1880 *Alli, DcAmA,
   DcNAA*
Hering, Daniel Webster 1850-1938 *DcNAA*
Hering, Francis *Alli*
Hering, Jeanie *Alli Sup*
Hering, Oswald Constantin 1874-1941 *DcNAA*
Hering, Rudolph 1847-1923 *DcAmA, DcNAA*
Herington, Cecil John 1924- *Au&Wr,
   ConAu 29*
Heriot, Angus 1927- *ConAu 5R*
Heriot, Cuthbert *Alli Sup*
Heriot, George 1759- *Alli, BbtC, BiDLA,
   OxCan*
Heriot, John 1760-1833 *Alli, BiDLA*
Herissant, Doctor *Alli*
Heritage, John *MnBBF*
Heritage, Martin *EncM&D*
Heriteau, Jacqueline 1925- *ConAu 45*
Herity, Michael 1929- *ConAu 49*
Herjolfsson, Bjarni *OxCan*
Herkless, W R *Alli Sup*
Herklots, Geoffrey Alton Craig 1902- *Au&Wr*
Herklots, Hugh Gerard Gibson 1903- *Au&Wr,
   OxCan*
Herle, Charles 1598-1659 *Alli*
Herlihy, David J 1930- *ConAu 41*
Herlihy, Francis 1912- *CatA 1952*
Herlihy, James Leo 1927- *AmA&B, Au&Wr,
   ConAu 1R, ConDr, ConLC 6,
   ConNov 1972, ConNov 1976, DrAF 1976,
   WorAu, WrD 1976*
Herlossohn, Karl 1804-1849 *OxGer*
Herloszsohn, Karl 1804-1849 *BiD&SB*
Herman *Alli, BiB N*
Herman De Valenciennes *OxFr*
Herman, Alan *OxCan*
Herman, Charlotte 1937- *ConAu 41*
Herman, Donald L 1928- *ConAu 53*
Herman, George Richard 1925- *ConAu 5R,
   WrD 1976*
Herman, Gordon Lee 1931- *Au&Wr,
   WrD 1976*
Herman, Henry 1832?-1894 *BbD, BiD&SB,
   EncM&D*
Herman, Henry M *Alli Sup*
Herman, J B *Alli Sup*
Herman, Jan 1942- *ConAu 45, DrAF 1976*
Herman, Jerry *AmSCAP 66*
Herman, Judith 1943- *ConAu 49*
Herman, Julius 1894-1955 *MnBBF*
Herman, Leonora *ChPo S1*
Herman, Louis Jay 1925- *ConAu 53*
Herman, Marguerite Shalett 1914- *ConAu 41*
Herman, Nikolaus 1480?-1561 *OxGer*
Herman, Pinky 1905- *AmSCAP 66*
Herman, Reinhold Ludwig 1849- *ChPo S1*
Herman, Samuel 1891- *AmSCAP 66*
Herman, Simon N 1912- *ConAu 29*
Herman, Sondra R 1932- *ConAu 25*
Herman, Stanley M 1928- *ConAu 25*
Herman, Thomas *Alli, BiDLA*
Herman, William *Alli Sup*
Herman, William 1915- *OhA&B*
Herman, Woodrow Wilson 1913- *AmSCAP 66*
Herman, Woody 1913- *AmSCAP 66*
Herman, Yuri Pavlovich 1910- *CasWL,*

DcRusL
Hermance, William Ellsworth 1862-1927 *DcNAA*
Hermand, Jost 1930- *ConAu 41*
Hermann *REn*
Hermann Der Cherusker *OxGer*
Hermann Der Damen *OxGer*
Hermann, Landgraf Von Thuringen d1217 *OxGer*
Hermann The German *DcEuL*
Hermann Von Fritzlar *OxGer*
Hermann Von Sachsenheim 1363?-1458 *OxGer*
Hermann Von Salzburg *OxGer*
Hermann, Donald H J 1943- *ConAu 45*
Hermann, Edward J 1919- *ConAu 17R*
Hermann, Georg 1871-1943 *OxGer*
Hermann, George R 1894- *TexWr*
Hermann, John 1917- *ConAu 49*
Hermann, Nikolaus 1480?-1561 *BiD&SB, OxGer*
Hermann, Ralph 1914- *AmSCAP 66*
Hermann, Theodore Placid 1909- *ConAu P-1, IndAu 1917*
Hermann-Neisse, Max 1886-1941 *ClDMEuL*
Hermanns, Peter *ConAu XR, WrD 1976*
Hermanns, William 1895- *ConAu 37, WrD 1976*
Hermannsson, Haldor 1878-1958 *REnAL*
Hermannsson, Halldor 1878-1958 *AmA&B*
Hermanovsky-Orlando, Fritz Von 1877-1954 *OxGer*
Hermans, Petrus Hendrik 1898- *Au&Wr*
Hermans, Willem Frederik 1921- *CasWL, ConAu P-1, Pen Eur*
Hermansen, John 1918- *ConAu 45*
Hermanson, Dennis 1947- *SmATA 10*
Hermant, Abel 1862-1950 *ClDMEuL, EvEuW, OxFr*
Hermens, Ferdinand Aloysius 1906- *AmA&B, CatA 1952*
Hermes *WrD 1976*
Hermes Trismegitus *CasWL*
Hermes, Johann Timotheus 1738-1821 *CasWL, DcEuL, EvEuW, OxGer*
Hermine 1835-1923 *AmA*
Hermlin, Stephan 1915- *CasWL, EncWL Sup, ModGL, OxGer, Pen Eur*
Hermon, Harry *Alli Sup*
Hermonyme, Georges *OxFr*
Hermonymus, Georgius *DcEuL*
Hermosilla, Jose Gomez 1771-1837 *DcEuL*
Herms, William Brodbeck 1876-1949 *OhA&B, WhWNAA*
Hern, Anthony 1916- *Au&Wr, ConAu 23*
Hernadi, Paul 1936- *ConAu 41*
Hernaman, Claudia Frances *Alli Sup, ChPo*
Hernandez, Al 1909- *ConAu 21, WrD 1976*
Hernandez, Alejandro Rene 1916- *AmSCAP 66*
Hernandez, Amado V 1903-1970 *DcOrL 2*
Hernandez, Barbara *DrAP 1975*
Hernandez, Frances 1926- *ConAu 37*
Hernandez, Jose 1834-1886 *CasWL, CyWA, DcSpL, Pen Am, REn*
Hernandez, Jose P H 1892-1922 *PueRA*
Hernandez, Juana Amelia *ConAu 45*
Hernandez, Luis F 1923- *ConAu 61*
Hernandez, Luisa Josefina 1928- *DcCLA*
Hernandez, Miguel 1910-1942 *CasWL, EncWL, EvEuW, Pen Eur, TwCW, WorAu*
Hernandez, Pedro F 1925- *ConAu 45*
Hernandez Aquino, Luis 1907- *PueRA*
Hernandez Cata, Alfonso 1885-1940 *CasWL, Pen Am*
Hernandez-Cruz, Victor *DrAP 1975*
Hernandez DeAraujo, Carmen 1832-1877 *PueRA*
Hernandez DeOviedo Y Valdes, Gonzalo *PueRA*
Hernandez Montis, Vicente 1925- *BiDPar*
Hernandez Vargas, Francisco 1914- *PueRA*
Herndl, George C 1927- *ConAu 33*
Herndon, Booton 1915- *ConAu 9R*
Herndon, John Goodwin 1856- *ChPo*
Herndon, Mary Eliza 1820- *Alli, BiDSA, DcAmA, DcNAA*
Herndon, William Henry 1818-1891 *AmA&B, BbD, BiD&SB, DcAmA, DcNAA, OxAm, REn, REnAL*
Herndon, William Lewis 1813-1857 *Alli,*

BiDSA, DcAmA, DcNAA
Herne, James A 1839-1901 *AmA, AmA&B, BiD&SB, CasWL, Chmbr 3, CnDAL, CnThe, DcAmA, DcLEnL, McGWD, ModWD, OxAm, REn, REnAL, REnWD*
Herne, John *Alli*
Herne, Niall *Alli Sup*
Herne, Samuel *Alli*
Herne, Thomas d1722 *Alli*
Herner, Charles H 1930- *ConAu 29*
Hernon, G D *Alli*
Hernon, John *Alli Sup*
Hernon, Peter 1944- *ConAu 61*
Hernton, Calvin C 1932- *AmA&B, BlkAW, ConAu 9R, ConP 1975, DrAF 1976, DrAP 1975, LivBA, WrD 1976*
Hero *CasWL*
Hero, Alfred O, Jr. 1924- *ConAu 21*
Herod I 073?BC-004BC *NewC*
Herod Agrippa I 011?BC-044AD *NewC*
Herod Antipas 004BC-039AD *REn*
Herod The Great 073?BC-004BC *NewC, REn*
Herodas *CasWL, NewC, OxEng, Pen Cl*
Herodes Atticus 101?-177 *Pen Cl*
Herodian *CasWL*
Herodian 180?-260? *CasWL, Pen Cl*
Herodianus *BbD, BiD&SB*
Herodias *NewC*
Herodotus 484?BC-425?BC *AtlBL, BbD, BiD&SB, CasWL, CyWA, DcEnL, DcEuL, NewC, OxEng, Pen Cl, RCom, REn*
Heroet, Antoine 1492?-1568 *DcEuL, EuA, OxFr*
Herold, Andre Ferdinand 1865- *ClDMEuL*
Herold, Brenda 1948- *ConAu 33, DrAP 1975*
Herold, Charles E 1862-1931 *IndAu 1917*
Herold, Don 1889-1966 *AmA&B, IndAu 1917, REnAL*
Herold, Jacob Brooks 1888- *WhWNAA*
Herold, Jean Christopher 1919-1964 *AmA&B, ConAu P-1*
Herold, Justin 1861-1942 *DcNAA*
Heron, Anne J *OhA&B*
Heron, Denis Caulfield *Alli Sup*
Heron, Emily Australie *Alli Sup*
Heron, Henrietta 1874?-1944 *OhA&B*
Heron, Herbert *ChPo*
Heron, Mrs. Hubert *PoIre*
Heron, James *Alli Sup*
Heron, James Henry 1877- *WhWNAA*
Heron, John *Alli*
Heron, John M *Alli Sup*
Heron, Laurence Tunstall 1902- *ConAu 49*
Heron, M Newcastle *Alli, BiDLA*
Heron, Sir Richard *Alli*
Heron, Robert 1758-1826 *Alli, DcEnL*
Heron, Robert 1764-1807 *Alli, DcEnL*
Heron, Robert M 1823- *Alli Sup, PoIre*
Heron, William *PoIre*
Heron-Allen, Edward 1861- *ChPo S1, ChPo S2*
Herondas *OxEng, Pen Cl*
Herostratus *NewC*
Heroux, Denis *OxCan Sup*
Herp, Henricus d1477 *CasWL*
Herpel, George L 1921- *ConAu 41*
Herpin, Luce *BiD&SB*
Herport, Brian *Alli*
Herr, Dan 1917- *ConAu 1R*
Herr, Edwin L 1933- *ConAu 37*
Herr, Isaac *ChPo*
Herr, J G *Alli Sup*
Herr, John 1781-1850 *DcNAA*
Herr, John 1872-1943 *IndAu 1917*
Herr, Laetitia Neff 1881- *ChPo*
Herr, Lucien 1864-1926 *OxFr*
Herr, Richard 1922- *ConAu 1R*
Herrad Von Landsberg d1195 *OxGer*
Herrad Von Landsperg d1195 *Pen Eur*
Herrand Von Wildonie *OxGer*
Herreid, Charles N 1857- *WhWNAA*
Herreken, N T *Alli*
Herrera, Alfonso L 1868- *WhWNAA*
Herrera, Antonio De 1559-1625 *DcEuL*
Herrera, Ernesto 1886-1917 *ModWD*
Herrera, Fernando De 1534-1597 *BbD, BiD&SB, CasWL, DcEuL, DcSpL, EuA,*

EvEuW, Pen Eur, REn
Herrera, Gabriel Alonso De 1470?-1539? *CasWL*
Herrera, Humberto 1900- *AmSCAP 66*
Herrera, Velino 1902- *IICB 1945*
Herrera Y Reissig, Julio 1875-1910 *CasWL, DcSpL, EncWL, Pen Am, REn*
Herrera Y Tordesillas, Antonio De 1559?-1625 *CasWL, OxAm*
Herrero, Abelardo 1936- *WhGrA*
Herreros *DcSpL*
Herreshoff, David 1921- *ConAu 21*
Herreshoff, Lewis Francis 1890-1972 *ConAu 37, ConAu P-1*
Herrey, Robert F *Alli*
Herrick, Bruce Hale 1936- *ConAu 17R*
Herrick, Charles Judson 1868- *OhA&B, WhWNAA*
Herrick, Cheesman Abiah 1866-1956 *AmA&B*
Herrick, Christine Terhune 1859-1944 *Alli Sup, AmLY, BiD&SB, DcAmA, DcNAA*
Herrick, Clarence Luther 1858-1904 *Alli Sup, DcAmA, DcNAA*
Herrick, Clay 1867-1935 *OhA&B*
Herrick, Clay, Jr. 1911- *OhA&B*
Herrick, Edward C d1862 *CyAL 1*
Herrick, Francis Hobart 1858-1940 *AmA&B, DcAmA, DcNAA, OhA&B*
Herrick, George Frederick 1834-1926 *DcNAA*
Herrick, Glenn Washington 1870- *WhWNAA*
Herrick, Henry Martyn 1861-1945 *DcNAA*
Herrick, Henry Walker 1824-1906 *DcNAA, EarAB, EarAB Sup*
Herrick, Huldah *DcNAA*
Herrick, Jean Mellin *ConAu 49*
Herrick, John Russell 1822-1912 *Alli Sup, DcAmA, DcNAA*
Herrick, Joseph *Alli*
Herrick, Lucius Carroll 1840-1903 *Alli Sup, DcNAA*
Herrick, M W And Doxsee, J W *Alli Sup*
Herrick, Marvin Theodore 1899-1966 *ConAu 1R*
Herrick, Myron Timothy 1854-1929 *DcNAA, OhA&B*
Herrick, Neal Q 1927- *ConAu 49*
Herrick, Paul Young 1910-1958 *AmSCAP 66*
Herrick, Robert 1591-1674 *Alli, AnCL, AtlBL, BbD, BiD&SB, BrAu, CasWL, ChPo, ChPo S1, ChPo S2, Chmbr 1, CnE&AP, CrE&SL, CriT 1, CyWA, DcEnA, DcEnL, DcEuL, DcLEnL, EvLB, LongC, MouLC 1, NewC, OxEng, Pen Eng, RAdv 1, REn, WebEAL*
Herrick, Robert 1868-1938 *AmA&B, AmLY, BbD, BiD&SB, CasWL, CnDAL, ConAmA, ConAmL, DcAmA, DcLEnL, DcNAA, EncWL Sup, EvLB, LongC, OxAm, OxEng, Pen Am, REn, REnAL, TwCA, TwCA Sup, TwCW, WebEAL, WhWNAA*
Herrick, Robert L 1930- *ConAu 61*
Herrick, Samuel 1880- *WhWNAA*
Herrick, Samuel Edward 1841-1904 *Alli Sup, DcAmA*
Herrick, Sophia McIlvaine Bledsoe 1837-1919 *Alli Sup, AmA&B, BiD&SB, BiDSA, DcAmA, DcNAA, OhA&B*
Herrick, Walter R, Jr. 1918- *ConAu 23*
Herrick, William 1915- *ConAu 23, WrD 1976*
Herrick, William Augustus 1831-1885 *Alli Sup, DcNAA*
Herrick, William Dodge 1831-1903 *DcNAA*
Herrick, William F *EarAB Sup*
Herrick, William Hale 1860-1887 *Alli Sup*
Herridge, William Thomas 1857-1929 *DcNAA*
Herries, Edward 1855- *Alli Sup*
Herries, J Forbes *ChPo S2*
Herries, John *Alli*
Herries, John Charles *Alli, BiDLA*
Herries, Maitland Stewart *ChPo*
Herrig, Hans 1845-1892 *BbD, BiD&SB*
Herrigan, Jackie *AuNews 1*
Herrigan, Jeff *AuNews 1*
Herriman, Abbie Frances Sampson 1854- *OhA&B*
Herriman, Dorothy Choate 1901- *ChPo*
Herriman, George 1880-1944 *ChPo, REnAL*

Herring, Armine Styleman *Alli Sup*
Herring, Francis *Alli*
Herring, George C, Jr. 1936- *ConAu 41*
Herring, Harriet Laura 1892- *WhWNAA*
Herring, Hubert 1889- *REnAL*
Herring, John *AmSCAP 66*
Herring, Mel *BlkAW*
Herring, Needham Bryan 1839-1923 *DcNAA*
Herring, Paul *MnBBF*
Herring, Pendleton 1903- *Au&Wr*
Herring, Ralph A 1901- *ConAu 21*
Herring, Reuben 1922- *ConAu 17R*
Herring, Richard *Alli, Alli Sup*
Herring, Richard Francis *Alli Sup*
Herring, Robert *ChPo*
Herring, Thomas *Alli*
Herring, Thomas 1691-1757 *Alli*
Herringham, W *Alli*
Herringshaw, Thomas William 1858- *DcAmA*
Herrington, Richard *BlkAW*
Herrington, Walter Stevens 1860-1947 *DcNAA*
Herriot, Edouard 1872-1957 *REn*
Herriot, James *WrD 1976*
Herriot, Peter 1939- *ConAu 29*
Herriott, George *Alli*
Herriott, M E 1897- *WhWNAA*
Herriott, Robert E 1929- *ConAu 17R*
Herrman, Daniel 1910- *AmSCAP 66*
Herrman, Josephine Herbst *WhWNAA*
Herrman, T C *Alli*
Herrmann, Alexander 1844-1896 *DcNAA*
Herrmann, Frank 1927- *ConAu 21*
Herrmann, George Rudolph 1894- *IndAu 1917, WhWNAA*
Herrmann, Ignat 1854-1935 *CasWL*
Herrmann, Mrs. John *AmNov XR*
Herrmann, Klaus 1903- *CnMD*
Herrmann, Klaus J 1929- *ConAu 37*
Herrmann, Lazar 1896-1961 *AmA&B*
Herrmann, Louis George 1900-1965 *IndAu 1917*
Herrmann, Luke John 1932- *Au&Wr, WrD 1976*
Herrmann, Robert O 1932- *ConAu 41*
Herrmann-Neisse, Max 1886-1941 *EncWL, OxGer, Pen Eur*
Herrmanns, Ralph 1933- *ConAu 9R, WrD 1976*
Herrnstadt, Richard L 1926- *ConAu 33*
Herrnstein, Barbara *ConAu XR, WrD 1976*
Herrod, Walter *MnBBF*
Herron, Edna *AnMV 1926*
Herron, Edward A 1912- *ConAu 5R, SmATA 4*
Herron, Fanny E *BiDSA, LivFWS*
Herron, George Davis 1862-1925 *BiD&SB, DcAmA, DcNAA, IndAu 1816*
Herron, Ima Honaker 1899- *ConAu 25*
Herron, Joel 1916- *AmSCAP 66*
Herron, Lowell William 1916- *ConAu 1R*
Herron, Orley Rufus, Jr. 1933- *ConAu 25, WrD 1976*
Herron, S P *Alli Sup*
Herron, Shaun 1912- *ConAu 29, WrD 1976*
Herron, W W *Alli Sup*
Herron, William George 1933- *ConAu 37, WrD 1976*
Herrtage, Sidney John Hervon *Alli Sup*
Hersam, Ernest Albion 1868- *WhWNAA*
Hersch, Virginia 1896- *AmA&B, AmNov, WhWNAA*
Herschberger, Ruth Margaret 1917- *AmA&B, ConAu 33, ConP 1970, DrAP 1975, REnAL, TwCA Sup*
Herschel, Caroline Lucretia 1750-1848 *Alli, DcEnL*
Herschel, Clemens 1842-1930 *DcAmA, DcNAA*
Herschel, Clement *Alli Sup*
Herschel, Frederick William 1738-1822 *BbD*
Herschel, Sir John Frederick William 1792-1871 *Alli, Alli Sup, BiD&SB, BrAu 19, Chmbr 3, DcEnL, EvLB, NewC*
Herschel, Mary Cornwallis *Alli Sup*
Herschel, Sir William 1738-1822 *Alli, NewC, REn*
Herschell, Philip *Alli*
Herschell, Ridley Haim 1807-1864 *Alli, Alli Sup*

Herschell, William 1738-1822 *BiDLA*
Herschell, William 1873-1939 *ChPo, ChPo S1, DcNAA, IndAu 1816*
Herscher, Louis 1894- *AmSCAP 66*
Hersee, S And E *ChPo S1*
Hersee, William *BiDLA*
Herser, T *Alli*
Hersey, Charles *Alli Sup*
Hersey, Frances Lester Warner 1888- *WhWNAA*
Hersey, George Dallas 1847- *DcAmA*
Hersey, George Leonard 1927- *ConAu 41*
Hersey, Geraldine 1931- *WrD 1976*
Hersey, Harold Brainerd 1893-1956 *AmA&B, AnMV 1926, REnAL, WhWNAA*
Hersey, Heloise Edwina 1855-1933 *DcAmA, DcNAA*
Hersey, Jean 1902- *ConAu 9R*
Hersey, John 1914- *AmA&B, AmNov, CasWL, CnDAL, ConAu 17R, ConLC 1, ConLC 2, ConNov 1972, ConNov 1976, CyWA, DrAF 1976, LongC, ModAL, OxAm, Pen Am, RAdv 1, REn, REnAL, TwCA Sup, WrD 1976*
Hersey, Marie Louise *ChPo S2*
Hersey, William Dearborn 1910- *ConAu P-1*
Hersh, Arthur B 1900- *AmSCAP 66*
Hersh, Evelyn S 1911- *AmSCAP 66*
Hersh, Seymour M 1936- *AmA&B, AuNews 1*
Hershan, Stella K 1915- *ConAu 33*
Hershaw, Fay McKeene *BlkAW*
Hershberg, David 1935- *ConAu 45*
Hershberger, Guy Franklin 1896- *IndAu 1917*
Hershberger, Hazel Kuhns *ConAu 5R*
Hershbergery Leander Leonard 1890-1950 *IndAu 1917*
Hershe, Harriet *ChPo*
Hershenson, David Bert 1933- *ConAu 41*
Hershenson, Maurice 1933- *ConAu 41*
Hersher, Leonard 1925- *ConAu 41*
Hershey, Amos Shartle 1867-1933 *DcNAA, IndAu 1816, WhWNAA*
Hershey, Burnet 1896-1971 *AmA&B, ConAu 25, ConAu 33*
Hershey, Gerald L 1931- *ConAu 53*
Hershey, Scott Funk 1852-1931 *DcNAA, IndAu 1917, OhA&B*
Hershfield, Harry 1885-1974 *ConAu 53*
Hershfield, Leo *ChPo, ChPo S1*
Hershkowitz, Joseph 1919- *WhWNAA*
Hershkowitz, Leo 1924- *ConAu 25*
Hershman, Morris 1920- *ConAu 53*
Hersholt, Jean 1886-1956 *ChPo*
Hershon, Paul Isaac 1817-1888 *Alli Sup*
Hershon, Robert 1936- *ConAu 33, DrAP 1975*
Herskovits, Frances Shapiro 1897-1972 *ConAu 33*
Herskovits, Melville Jean 1895-1963 *AmA&B, OhA&B, REnAL, TwCA Sup*
Herskowitz, Herbert Bennett 1925- *ConAu 17R*
Hersom, Frank E 1894-1941 *AmSCAP 66*
Herst, Herman, Jr. 1909- *ConAu 1R*
Herst, Jerry 1909- *AmSCAP 66*
Hertel, Francois 1905- *CanWr, CasWL, OxCan, OxCan Sup*
Hertell, Thomas *Alli*
Herter, Christian Archibald 1865-1910 *DcNAA*
Hertford, Marquis Of 1748- *Alli, BiDLA*
Hertford, A C *Alli Sup*
Hertford, Joseph *Alli Sup*
Hertfordshire Incumbent, A *DcEnL*
Hertling, G H 1930- *ConAu 41*
Hertog, Ary Den 1889-1958 *CnMD*
Hertor, Christian Archibald 1865- *DcAmA*
Herts, Benjamin Russell 1888-1954 *AmA&B, AmLY*
Hertsens, Marcel 1918- *ConAu 9R*
Hertslet, Charles John Belcher *Alli Sup*
Hertslet, Sir Edward 1824- *Alli Sup*
Hertslet, Laura *Alli Sup*
Hertslet, Lewis *Alli*
Hertslet, Reginald H *Alli Sup*
Herty, Charles Holmes 1867-1938 *DcNAA*
Herty, Thomas *Alli*
Hertz, Emanuel 1870-1940 *AmA&B, DcNAA, REnAL*
Hertz, Fred 1933- *AmSCAP 66*

Hertz, Heinrich Rudolf 1857-1894 *REn*
Hertz, Helen A *Alli Sup*
Hertz, Henrik 1798-1870 *BbD, BiD&SB, CasWL, DcEuL, EuA, EvEuW, McGWD, Pen Eur*
Hertz, K V 1945- *ConP 1970*
Hertz, Peter Donald 1933- *ConAu 37*
Hertz, Richard C 1916- *ConAu 21*
Hertz, Solange 1920- *ConAu 5R*
Hertz, Wilhelm 1835-1902 *BiD&SB, OxGer*
Hertzberg, Arthur 1921- *ConAu 17R*
Hertzberg, Hans Rudolph Reinhard 1871-1920 *BiDSA, ChPo S2, DcNAA*
Hertzberg, Nancy *ConP 1970*
Hertzberg, Nancy Florence 1923- *Au&Wr*
Hertzen, Aleksandr Ivanovich 1812-1870 *REn*
Hertzler, Arthur Emanuel 1870-1946 *AmA&B, DcNAA, REnAL, WhWNAA*
Hertzler, Edith DeVilliers 1878- *WhWNAA*
Hertzler, Joyce O 1895- *ConAu 1R*
Hertzler, Lois Shank 1927- *ConAu 57*
Hertzman, Lewis 1927- *ConAu 9R, OxCan Sup, WrD 1976*
Herum, John 1931- *ConAu 61*
Heruy, Sirek Walda Sellase 1878-1938 *AfA 1*
Hervas Y Cobo DeLaTorre, Jose De d1742 *CasWL, DcEuL*
Hervas Y Panduro, Lorenzo 1735-1809 *CasWL, DcEuL*
Herve, Jean-Luc *ConAu 49*
Herve, Julia Wright *BlkAW*
Herve, Peter *Alli*
Herve-Bazin, Jean-Pierre Marie *CasWL, WorAu*
Hervey, Lord *Chmbr 2*
Hervey, Mrs. *Alli, BiDLA*
Hervey, Albert *Alli Sup*
Hervey, Alpheus Baker 1839-1931 *Alli Sup, DcNAA*
Hervey, Lord Arthur *Alli*
Hervey, Charles *ChPo*
Hervey, Christopher *Alli*
Hervey, Eleanora Louisa 1811- *Alli, Alli Sup, ChPo, ChPo S1*
Hervey, Frederic *Alli*
Hervey, George Winfred *Alli, Alli Sup*
Hervey, H *ChPo*
Hervey, H M *Alli Sup*
Hervey, Harry Clay 1900-1951 *AmA&B, AmNov, REnAL, TexWr*
Hervey, Hedley *MnBBF*
Hervey, Henry Martyn 1838-1875 *OhA&B*
Hervey, J *Alli*
Hervey, J E *Alli Sup*
Hervey, James 1714-1758 *Alli, BbD, BrAu, CasWL, Chmbr 2, DcEnL, DcEuL, DcLEnL, EvLB, NewC, OxEng, PoCh*
Hervey, James Walter 1819-1905 *IndAu 1816*
Hervey, Jane *ConAu XR*
Hervey, John, Lord Hervey Of Ickworth 1696-1743 *Alli, BrAu, CasWL, DcEnL, DcLEnL, EvLB, NewC, OxEng, Pen Eng, REn*
Hervey, John Lewis 1870-1947 *DcNAA*
Hervey, John Russell *ChPo S1*
Hervey, M F S *Alli Sup*
Hervey, M H *MnBBF*
Hervey, Lady Mary *Alli*
Hervey, Mrs. Mayo D *AmA&B*
Hervey, Michael 1914- *Au&Wr*
Hervey, Michael 1920- *ConAu 9R*
Hervey, Rosamond *Alli Sup*
Hervey, Thomas *Alli, Alli Sup, BiDLA*
Hervey, Thomas Kibble 1799?-1859 *Alli, ChPo, ChPo S1, DcEnL, NewC*
Hervey, Mrs. Thomas Kibble 1811- *Alli, ChPo S1*
Hervieu, Paul Ernest 1857-1915 *ClDMEuL, EuA, EvEuW, McGWD, ModWD, OxFr*
Hervieux, J A *BbtC*
Hervilly, Ernest D' 1839- *BiD&SB*
Herwegen, Ildefons 1874-1946 *CatA 1947*
Herwegh, Georg 1817-1875 *BbD, BiD&SB, CasWL, DcEuL, EvEuW, OxGer, Pen Eur, REn*
Herwig, Holger H 1941- *ConAu 61*
Herwig, Rob 1935- *WrD 1976*
Herwig, Mrs. Robert J 1919- *AmNov XR*

Hewgill, Edwin *Alli*
Hewins, Caroline Maria 1846-1926 *Alli Sup,*
  ChPo, ChPo S2, DcAmA, DcNAA
Hewins, Elsie Vera *Au&Wr*
Hewins, Geoffrey Shaw 1889- *Au&Wr,*
  ConAu P-1
Hewins, Ralph Anthony 1909- *Au&Wr,*
  ConAu P-1
Hewison, F *ChPo S2*
Hewit, Alexander *Alli*
Hewit, Augustine Francis 1820-1897 *DcNAA*
Hewit, Augustus Francis 1820-1897 *BiD&SB*
Hewit, Nathaniel Augustus 1820-1897 *Alli Sup,*
  DcAmA, DcNAA
Hewit, S A *Alli*
Hewitson, Anthony *Alli Sup*
Hewitson, John Nelson 1917- *ConAu 29*
Hewitson, William Chapman 1806-1878 *Alli,*
  Alli Sup
Hewitson, William Hepburn *Alli Sup*
Hewitt, Alison Hope 1915- *WrD 1976*
Hewitt, Andrew *ChPo*
Hewitt, Arthur Wentworth 1883- *AmA&B*
Hewitt, Barnard 1906- *ConAu 13R*
Hewitt, C Rawleston *MnBBF*
Hewitt, Cecil Rolph 1901- *Au&Wr*
Hewitt, Charles David 1938- *Au&Wr*
Hewitt, Charles Gordon 1885-1920 *DcNAA*
Hewitt, D C *Alli Sup*
Hewitt, Edgar *Alli Sup*
Hewitt, Edward Crawford 1828- *Alli Sup*
Hewitt, Edward W And Coleman, W E *Alli Sup*
Hewitt, Emily Clark 1944- *ConAu 45*
Hewitt, Emma Churchman 1850- *BiDSA,*
  ChPo, DcAmA
Hewitt, G M A *ChPo S1*
Hewitt, Geof 1943- *ConAu 33, ConP 1970,*
  ConP 1975, DrAP 1975, WrD 1976
Hewitt, Graily *Alli Sup*
Hewitt, Henry Marmaduke *Alli Sup, PoIre*
Hewitt, Herbert James 1890- *Au&Wr,*
  ConAu 13R, WrD 1976
Hewitt, J *Alli*
Hewitt, J, Jr. *ChPo*
Hewitt, J A *Alli Sup*
Hewitt, J O M *Alli Sup*
Hewitt, James *Alli Sup*
Hewitt, James 1770-1827 *OxAm, REnAL*
Hewitt, James 1928- *Au&Wr, ConAu 57*
Hewitt, James Alexander *Alli Sup*
Hewitt, Jean 1929- *Au&Wr*
Hewitt, Joan Evelyne 1912- *Au&Wr*
Hewitt, John *Alli, Alli Sup, ChPo S1*
Hewitt, John 1907- *CasWL, ConP 1970,*
  ConP 1975, WrD 1976
Hewitt, John Haskell 1835-1920 *DcNAA*
Hewitt, John Henry 1801-1890 *BiDSA*
Hewitt, John Hill 1801-1890 *AmA, AmA&B,*
  BiD&SB, ChPo, DcAmA, DcNAA,
  REnAL
Hewitt, John P 1941- *ConAu 53*
Hewitt, Joseph F 1886-1957 *AmSCAP 66*
Hewitt, L E *ChPo S1*
Hewitt, Luisa *ChPo, ChPo S1*
Hewitt, Margaret *ChPo S1*
Hewitt, Mary Elizabeth 1818- *Alli, AmA&B,*
  BiD&SB, ChPo, ChPo S1, CyAL 2,
  DcAmA, DcNAA, FemPA
Hewitt, Oscar *Alli Sup*
Hewitt, R C *MnBBF*
Hewitt, Walter Charles 1859-1940 *DcNAA*
Hewitt, William *Alli*
Hewitt, William Henry 1936- *ConAu 17R*
Hewlett, Albion Walter 1874-1925 *DcNAA*
Hewlett, Alfred d1885 *Alli Sup*
Hewlett, Ebenezer *Alli, Alli Sup*
Hewlett, Edgar *Alli Sup*
Hewlett, Esther *Alli*
Hewlett, Henry Gay *Alli Sup*
Hewlett, J G *Alli*
Hewlett, James P *Alli*
Hewlett, John *Alli, BiDLA, BiDLA Sup*
Hewlett, John 1905- *AmA&B, AmNov*
Hewlett, John Grigg *Alli Sup*
Hewlett, Maurice Henry 1861-1923 *BbD,*
  BiD&SB, ChPo, ChPo S1, ChPo S2,
  Chmbr 3, DcBiA, DcEnA Ap, DcEuL,
  DcLEnL, EvLB, LongC, ModBL, NewC,

OxEng, Pen Eng, REn, TwCA,
  TwCA Sup, TwCW
Hewlett, Richard Greening 1923- *ConAu 9R*
Hewlett, Richard Whitfield *Alli Sup*
Hewlett, Miss S S *Alli Sup*
Hewlett, William Oxenham *Alli Sup*
Hewlings, A *Alli, BiDLA*
Hewnden, Anthony *Alli*
Hews, Mary Catherine *ChPo*
Hewson *Alli*
Hewson, Addinell 1828-1889 *Alli, Alli Sup,*
  DcNAA
Hewson, Sir Bushby 1902- *Au&Wr*
Hewson, John 1930- *ConAu 37, WrD 1976*
Hewson, Lionel Lloyd 1874- *WhLA*
Hewson, Thomas T 1773-1848 *Alli*
Hewson, William *Alli Sup*
Hewson, William 1739-1774 *Alli*
Hewson, William 1806-1870 *Alli Sup*
Hewytt, John *Alli*
Hexamer, Charles John 1862-1921 *DcNAA*
Hexham, Henry *Alli*
Hexham, Lionel J F *Alli Sup*
Hexner, Ervin Paul 1893- *ConAu 5R*
Hext, Harrington *EncM&D, LongC, NewC,*
  TwCA, TwCA Sup
Hextall, David *ConAu XR*
Hexter, J H 1910- *ConAu 13R*
Hexter, Maurice Beck 1891- *OhA&B*
Hey, J V D *Alli*
Hey, John *Alli, BiDLA*
Hey, John 1734-1815 *Alli, BiDLA Sup*
Hey, Nigel S 1936- *ConAu 33, WrD 1976*
Hey, Phillip H *DrAP 1975*
Hey, Rebecca *Alli Sup*
Hey, Richard *Alli, BiDLA, BiDLA Sup*
Hey, Richard 1926- *CnMD, CrCD*
Hey, Baron Victor Alexander Sereld K 1876-1928
  CnMWL
Hey, W *Alli, BiDLA*
Hey, Wilhelm 1789-1854 *BiD&SB, ChPo,*
  OxGer
Hey, William d1797 *BbtC*
Hey, William 1736-1819 *Alli, BiDLA*
Hey, Mrs. William *Alli*
Hey, William, Jr. *Alli*
Heycock, Edwin *Alli Sup*
Heydecker, Edward LeMoyne 1863- *DcAmA*
Heydecker, J J *Au&Wr*
Heyden, C, Jr. *Alli*
Heyden, Sir Christopher *Alli*
Heyden, Friedrich August Von 1789-1851
  BiD&SB, OxGer
Heyden, John *Alli*
Heyden, Thomas *Alli Sup*
Heydon, John *Alli*
Heydon, Joseph Kentigern 1884- *BkC 4*
Heydon, Sir Peter Richard 1913-1971 *Au&Wr,*
  ConAu P-1
Heydt, Herman August 1868-1941 *ChPo S2,*
  DcNAA
Heyduck-Huth, Hilde 1929- *ConAu 57,*
  SmATA 8
Heyduk, Adolf 1835-1923 *BiD&SB, CasWL*
Heye, Jan Pieter 1809-1876 *CasWL*
Heyel, Carl 1908- *ConAu 17R*
Heyen, William 1940- *ConAu 33, DrAP 1975*
Heyer, Georgette 1902-1974 *Au&Wr,*
  ConAu 49, DcLEnL, EncM&D, LongC,
  NewC, REn, TwCA, TwCA Sup, TwCW
Heyer, Herman *ChPo*
Heyer, Jane *ChPo*
Heyerdahl, Thor 1914- *Au&Wr, ConAu 5R,*
  LongC, SmATA 2, TwCA Sup, TwCW,
  WrD 1976
Heyerdahl, Vivian Hipple 1902- *IndAu 1917*
Heyermans, Herman 1864-1924 *CasWL, EuA,*
  EvEuW
Heygate, Sir John 1903- *Au&Wr*
Heygate, William Edward *Alli Sup*
Heyking, Elisabeth Von 1861-1925 *OxGer*
Heyl, Lewis *Alli Sup*
Heyl, Paul Renno 1872- *ChPo*
Heylen, Louis *Alli Sup*
Heyliger, William 1884-1955 *AmA&B,*
  AuBYP, CatA 1947, JBA 1934,
  JBA 1951, REnAL, YABC 1
Heylin, John d1760? *Alli*

Heylin, Peter 1600-1662 *Alli, DcEnL, EvLB,*
  NewC
Heylyn, John d1760? *Alli*
Heylyn, Peter 1600-1662 *Alli, BrAu, CasWL,*
  Chmbr 1, DcLEnL, NewC, OxEng
Heym, Georg 1887-1912 *CasWL, ClDMEuL,*
  EncWL, ModGL, OxGer, Pen Eur, REn,
  WhTwL
Heym, Stefan 1913- *AmA&B, AmNov,*
  Au&Wr, ConAu 9R, ModGL, OxGer,
  Pen Eur, REnAL, TwCA Sup
Heyman, Abigail 1942- *ConAu 57, WrD 1976*
Heyman, Edward 1907- *AmSCAP 66*
Heyman, Henrik *McGWD*
Heymann, Hans 1885-1949 *DcNAA*
Heymann, Lucie 1900- *Au&Wr*
Heymel, Alfred Walter Von 1878-1914 *OxGer*
Heyn, F A 1910- *BiDPar*
Heyne, Benjamin *Alli, BiDLA Sup*
Heyne, Christian Gottlob 1729-1812 *DcEuL*
Heyne, Christian Leberecht 1751-1821 *OxGer*
Heyneccius, Martin *OxGer*
Heyneman, Anne 1909- *ChPo, IlCB 1956*
Heyneman, Anne 1910- *IlCB 1945*
Heynes, Amy Elizabeth 1860- *WhLA*
Heynes, John *Alli*
Heynes, Matthew *Alli*
Heynes, Samuel *Alli*
Heynicke, Kurt 1891- *ModWD, OxGer*
Heynlin, J *CasWL*
Heyns, Maria 1621- *CasWL*
Heyns, Zacharias 1566-1638? *CasWL*
Heyrick, John, Jr. d1797 *Alli, BiDLA*
Heyrick, Samuel *Alli, BiDLA*
Heyrick, Thomas 1650?-1694 *Alli, CasWL*
Heyricke, Richard *Alli*
Heyricke, Thomas *Alli*
Heyse, Johann Ludwig Paul 1830-1914 *BbD,*
  BiD&SB, DcBiA
Heyse, Paul Johann Ludwig Von 1830-1914
  CasWL, ClDMEuL, EuA, EvEuW, OxGer,
  Pen Eur, REn
Heyser, K E *Alli Sup*
Heysham, John *Alli, BiDLA*
Heysham, Theodore 1864-1935 *DcNAA*
Heysham, W Nunez 1825?-1905 *Br&AmS*
Heysinger, Isaac Winter 1842-1917 *DcNAA*
Heyst, Axel *ConAu XR*
Heythuren, J Van *Alli*
Heyward *Alli*
Heyward, Dorothy Kuhns 1890-1961 *AmA&B,*
  ModWD, OhA&B, REnAL
Heyward, DuBose 1885-1940 *AmA&B,*
  AmSCAP 66, ChPo, CnDAL, CnMD,
  ConAmA, ConAmL, CyWA, DcLEnL,
  DcNAA, EvLB, LongC, McGWD,
  ModAL, ModWD, OxAm, Pen Am, REn,
  REnAL, TwCA, TwCA Sup, TwCW
Heyward, Janie Screven 1865-1939 *BiDSA,*
  ChPo, DcNAA
Heyward, Samuel Edwin, Jr. 1904-
  AmSCAP 66
Heywood, A Amy *ChPo S2*
Heywood, Benjamin Arthur *Alli Sup*
Heywood, Bernard Oliver Francis 1871- *WhLA*
Heywood, Christopher 1928- *ConAu 41*
Heywood, Donald *AmSCAP 66*
Heywood, Edmund *Alli Sup*
Heywood, Eliza 1693-1756 *Alli, DcEnL*
Heywood, Ellis d1572? *Alli*
Heywood, F M *ChPo S2*
Heywood, Florence *AmLY*
Heywood, George Washington *Alli Sup*
Heywood, Henry T *Alli Sup*
Heywood, Herbert *ChPo*
Heywood, J C *Alli Sup*
Heywood, James *Alli*
Heywood, James 1810- *Alli Sup*
Heywood, Jasper 1535?-1598 *Alli, CasWL,*
  DcEnL
Heywood, John *Alli Sup*
Heywood, John 1497?-1580? *Alli, BiD&SB,*
  BrAu, CasWL, ChPo, Chmbr 1, CnThe,
  CrE&SL, DcEnA, DcEnL, DcLEnL,
  EvLB, McGWD, NewC, OxEng,
  Pen Eng, REn, REnWD, WebEAL
Heywood, John Healy 1818-1880 *DcNAA*
Heywood, Joseph Converse d1900 *DcNAA*

Hiebert, Clarence 1927- *ConAu 61*
Hiebert, D Edmond 1910- *ConAu 17R,*
WrD 1976
Hiebert, Paul Gerhardt 1892- *CanWr,*
ConAu 23, OxCan, OxCan Sup, TwCW
Hiebert, Ray Eldon 1932- *AmA&B,*
ConAu 17R
Hiel, Emmanuel 1834-1899 *BiD&SB*
Hield, Mary *Alli Sup*
Hiemer, Franz Carl *ChPo*
Hiemstra, Mary *OxCan*
Hiener, Wilhelm 1926- *Au&Wr*
Hieng, Andrej 1925- *ModSL 2*
Hieover, Harry *Alli*
Hiernaux, Jean 1921- *ConAu 57*
Hierocles *OxEng*
Hieron, Samuel 1572-1617 *Alli*
Hieronymus *Pen Cl*
Hieronymus, Saint 348?-420 *CasWL, Pen Cl*
Hierro, Jose 1922- *CasWL, Pen Eur*
Hiers, Richard H 1932- *ConAu 53*
Hierta, Lars Johan 1801-1872 *CasWL*
Hiesberger, Jean Marie 1941- *ConAu 41*
Hiestand, Dale L 1925- *ConAu 41*
Hiffernan, John Michael *Alli Sup*
Hiffernan, Paul 1719-1777 *Alli, DcEnL, PoIre*
Hifler, Joyce 1925- *ConAu 21*
Hifni Nasif, Malak 1886-1918 *CasWL*
Higbee, Alma Robison *ChPo, ChPo S1*
Higbee, Dollie *BiDSA*
Higbee, Edward 1910- *ConAu 13R*
Higby, Chester Penn 1885-1966 *AmA&B*
Higby, Mary Jane *ConAu 25*
Higden, Henry *Alli*
Higden, Ralph 1299-1364? *Alli, DcEnL, EvLB*
Higden, Ranulf 1299?-1364? *Alli, BrAu,*
CasWL, EvLB, NewC, OxEng, Pen Eng,
REn
Higden, William *Alli*
Higdon, Hal 1931- *ConAu 9R, SmATA 4,*
WrD 1976
Higdon, Ranulf 1299?-1363? *NewC*
Higenbottam, Frank 1910- *ConAu 25*
Higford, William 1580-1657 *Alli*
Higgens, Charles *Alli Sup*
Higges, Joseph *Alli*
Higgeson *Alli*
Higgie, Lincoln William 1938- *ConAu 5R*
Higgin, George *Alli Sup*
Higgin, L *Alli Sup*
Higginbotham, C H *OxCan Sup*
Higginbotham, Irene 1918- *AmSCAP 66*
Higginbotham, J J *Alli Sup*
Higginbotham, John David 1864- *ChPo*
Higginbotham, John E 1933- *ConAu 29*
Higginbotham, R Don 1931- *ConAu 17R*
Higginbotham, Theophilus *ChPo*
Higginbottom, Frederick James 1859- *WhLA*
Higgins, A C 1930- *ConAu 37*
Higgins, Aidan 1927- *Au&Wr, CasWL,*
ConAu 9R, ConNov 1972, ConNov 1976,
ModBL Sup
Higgins, Aiden 1927- *WrD 1976*
Higgins, Aileen Cleveland 1882- *AmA&B*
Higgins, Alexander G McLellan Pearce
ChPo S2
Higgins, Alexander Pearce 1865- *WhLA*
Higgins, Alice *ChPo*
Higgins, Alice 1924?-1974 *ConAu 53*
Higgins, Alvin McCaslin 1866-1938 *DcNAA*
Higgins, Alvin S *Alli Sup*
Higgins, Angus John Brockhurst 1911- *Au&Wr,*
ConAu 13R, WrD 1976
Higgins, Bryan *Alli*
Higgins, Charles *Alli Sup*
Higgins, Charlotte M *Alli Sup, CarSB*
Higgins, Chester *LivBA*
Higgins, Clement 1844- *Alli Sup*
Higgins, Colin 1941- *ConAu 33, WrD 1976*
Higgins, D S 1938- *Au&Wr*
Higgins, David *Alli Sup*
Higgins, David William 1834-1917 *DcNAA*
Higgins, Dick 1938- *ConAu XR, ConDr,*
DrAF 1976, DrAP 1975, WrD 1976
Higgins, Don 1928- *ConAu 25*
Higgins, Edward *Alli Sup*
Higgins, Emily *Alli Sup*
Higgins, Eugene 1860?- *PoIre*

Higgins, Francis *Alli*
Higgins, Frederick Robert 1896-1941 *CasWL,*
ChPo, ChPo S1, ChPo S2, DcLEnL,
NewC, REn
Higgins, George V 1939- *ConLC 4,*
ConNov 1976, DrAF 1976, WrD 1976
Higgins, Godfrey *BiDLA Sup*
Higgins, Godfrey 1771-1833 *Alli*
Higgins, Helen Boyd 1892-1971 *IndAu 1917*
Higgins, Henry Hugh *Alli Sup*
Higgins, J A *Alli Sup*
Higgins, J C *ChPo S2*
Higgins, J Frederick *Alli Sup*
Higgins, Jack *WrD 1976*
Higgins, James Hart 1911- *MnBBF*
Higgins, Janet Gertrude *DcLEnL*
Higgins, Jean C 1932- *ConAu 29, WrD 1976*
Higgins, Jesse *Alli*
Higgins, John 1544-1605 *Alli, DcEnL*
Higgins, John 1934- *WrD 1976*
Higgins, John J 1935- *ConAu 45*
Higgins, John Lee *AnMV 1926*
Higgins, Katharine Elizabeth 1847-1925
DcNAA
Higgins, Lewis R d1916 *MnBBF*
Higgins, Lucy Porter *ChPo*
Higgins, Marguerite 1920-1966 *AmA&B,*
ConAu 5R, ConAu 25
Higgins, Matthew James 1810-1868 *Alli Sup,*
DcEnL, DcLEnL, OxEng
Higgins, Patrick J *PoIre*
Higgins, Patrick Philip 1829- *PoIre*
Higgins, Paul Lambourne 1916- *ConAu 1R*
Higgins, Raymond Aurelius 1916- *Au&Wr*
Higgins, Reynold Alleyne 1916- *ConAu 25,*
WrD 1976
Higgins, Richard C 1938- *AmA&B,*
ConAu 13R
Higgins, Richard Thomas *Alli Sup*
Higgins, Rosalyn 1937- *ConAu 9R,*
WrD 1976
Higgins, S And Brisbane, W H *Alli Sup*
Higgins, Sophia Elizabeth *Alli Sup*
Higgins, Thomas 1797-1879 *Alli Sup*
Higgins, Thomas Alfred 1823-1905 *DcNAA*
Higgins, Thomas Joseph 1899- *ConAu 1R,*
WrD 1976
Higgins, Tobias *Alli*
Higgins, Trumbull 1919- *ConAu 17R*
Higgins, W H *Alli Sup, OxCan*
Higgins, W Mullinger *Alli*
Higgins, W Robert 1938- *ConAu 37,*
WrD 1976
Higgins, Walter *MnBBF*
Higgins, William *Alli, BiDLA, PoIre*
Higgins, William Edward 1865-1920
IndAu 1917
Higgins, William Henry 1830- *BbtC, PoIre*
Higgins, William Mullinger *Alli Sup*
Higgins, William R 1838-1895 *IndAu 1816*
Higginson, Alexander Henry 1876- *Br&AmS*
Higginson, Charles F *Alli Sup*
Higginson, E C *Alli Sup*
Higginson, Edward 1807-1880 *Alli Sup*
Higginson, Ella 1862-1940 *AmA&B, AmLY,*
ChPo, ChPo S2, DcAmA, DcNAA
Higginson, Ellen *Alli Sup*
Higginson, Francis *Alli Sup*
Higginson, Francis d1670? *Alli*
Higginson, Francis 1586?-1630 *Alli, AmA&B,*
CyAL 2, DcAmA, OxAm, REnAL
Higginson, Francis John 1806-1872 *DcNAA*
Higginson, Fred H 1921- *Au&Wr, ConAu 1R*
Higginson, Henry Lee 1834-1919 *DcNAA*
Higginson, John 1616-1708 *Alli, AmA,*
CyAL 1, CyAL 2, DcAmA
Higginson, John A *MnBBF*
Higginson, Joseph Vincent 1896- *AmSCAP 66*
Higginson, Mary Potter Thacher 1844-1941
Alli Sup, AmA&B, BiD&SB, ChPo,
ChPo S1, DcAmA, DcNAA
Higginson, Mrs. S J 1840-1916 *Alli Sup*
Higginson, Sarah Jane 1840-1916 *BiD&SB,*
DcAmA, DcNAA
Higginson, Stephen 1743-1828 *CyAL 2,*
DcAmA, DcNAA
Higginson, Thomas Wentworth 1823-1911
Alli Sup, AmA, AmA&B, BbD, BiD&SB,

CasWL, ChPo, ChPo S1, ChPo S2,
Chmbr 3, CnDAL, CyAL 2, DcAmA,
DcLEnL, DcNAA, OxAm, REn, REnAL
Higginson, W G *Alli Sup*
Higgons, Bevil 1670-1735 *Alli*
Higgons, Theophilus d1659 *Alli*
Higgons, Sir Thomas 1624-1691 *Alli, DcEnL*
Higgs, Arthur Hibble *Alli Sup*
Higgs, David 1939- *ConAu 61*
Higgs, Eric Sidney 1908- *ConAu 9R,*
WrD 1976
Higgs, Gertrude M *ChPo S1, ChPo S2*
Higgs, Griffin 1589-1659 *Alli*
Higgs, Griffith 1589-1659 *Alli*
Higgs, J F *Alli Sup*
Higgs, James *Alli Sup*
Higgs, Joseph *Alli*
Higgs, Oliver *BlkAW*
Higgs, Paget *Alli Sup*
Higgs, W P *Alli Sup*
Higgs, William *Alli Sup*
Higgs-Walker, James Arthur 1892- *Au&Wr*
High, Dallas M 1931- *ConAu 21*
High, Edwin W 1841-1907 *IndAu 1917*
High, Freeman 1897- *AmSCAP 66*
High, James Lambert 1844-1898 *Alli Sup,*
DcNAA
High, Philip E 1914- *Au&Wr*
High, Stanley 1895-1961 *AmA&B*
Higham, Charles 1931- *Au&Wr, ConAu 33,*
ConP 1970, ConP 1975, WrD 1976
Higham, David 1895- *Au&Wr, ConAu 1R*
Higham, Florence May Greir 1896- *Au&Wr,*
WrD 1976
Higham, John *Alli*
Higham, John 1920- *ConAu 1R*
Higham, Mary R *Alli Sup*
Higham, Robert R A 1935- *Au&Wr,*
WrD 1976
Higham, Robin 1925- *ConAu 1R, WrD 1976*
Higham, Roger Stephen 1935- *Au&Wr,*
ConAu 33, WrD 1976
Higham, T F *ChPo*
Higham, Thomas *Alli Sup*
Higham, Thomas Farrant 1890- *Au&Wr,*
WrD 1976
Highet, Gilbert Arthur 1906- *AmA&B,*
Au&Wr, ChPo S2, ConAu 1R, LongC,
NewC, RAdv 1, REnAL, TwCA Sup,
WrD 1976
Highet, John 1918- *Au&Wr, WrD 1976*
Highland, Dora *WrD 1976*
Highley, Miss *Alli, BiDLA*
Highley, Samuel *Alli Sup*
Highmore, Anthony *Alli, BiDLA*
Highmore, Joseph 1692-1780 *Alli, BkIE*
Highmore, Nathaniel *Alli, BiDLA,*
BiDLA Sup
Highmore, Nathaniel 1613-1684? *Alli, DcEnL*
Highmore, Nathaniel Joseph 1844- *Alli Sup*
Highsmith, Patricia 1921- *Au&Wr,*
ConAu 1R, ConLC 2, ConLC 4,
ConNov 1972, ConNov 1976, EncM&D,
WhTwL, WorAu, WrD 1976
Highsmith, Richard Morgan, Jr. 1920-
ConAu 37, WhPNW
Hight, B W *Alli Sup*
Hight, James 1872-1958 *DcLEnL*
Hight, John J 1834-1886 *IndAu 1816, OhA&B*
Highton, E Gilbert *Alli Sup*
Highton, Edward *Alli Sup*
Highton, Henry *ChPo*
Highton, Henry 1816-1873 *Alli Sup*
Hightower, Charles *BlkAW*
Hightower, Florence Cole 1916- *Au&Wr,*
AuBYP, ConAu 1R, SmATA 4, ThBJA
Higinbotham, George *Alli Sup*
Higinbotham, Harlow Niles 1838-1919 *DcNAA*
Higinbotham, John D *OxCan*
Higinbotham, John U 1867- *AmA&B*
Higinbotham, Josephine M *Alli Sup*
Higins, John *Alli*
Higley, Charles 1866-1943 *DcNAA, OhA&B*
Higley, Louis Allen 1871-1955 *OhA&B*
Higman, Francis M 1935- *ConAu 25*
Hignett, George Edward *Alli Sup*
Hignett, Sean 1934- *Au&Wr, ConAu 49,*
WrD 1976

DcAmA, DcNAA
Hill, G D *Alli*
Hill, G F *ChPo*
Hill, G H *Alli Sup*
Hill, Geoffrey 1932- *CnE&AP, ConLC 5, ConP 1970, ConP 1975, ModBL Sup, WrD 1976*
Hill, George *Alli Sup*
Hill, George 1750-1819 *Alli, BiDLA, DcEnL*
Hill, George 1796-1871 *Alli, AmA&B, BiD&SB, ChPo, ChPo S1, ChPo S2, CyAL 2, DcAmA, DcNAA*
Hill, George 1810-1901 *PoIre*
Hill, George Anthony 1842-1916 *DcNAA*
Hill, George Birbeck Norman 1835-1903 *Alli Sup, BrAu 19, ChPo S1, Chmbr 3, DcLEnL, NewC, OxEng*
Hill, George Canning 1825-1898 *Alli, Alli Sup, BiD&SB*
Hill, George Canning 1825-1893 *CarSB*
Hill, George Canning 1825-1898 *DcAmA, DcNAA, HsB&A*
Hill, George Delgarno *Alli Sup*
Hill, George E 1907- *ConAu P-1*
Hill, George Francis 1867- *WhLA*
Hill, George Handel 1809-1849 *OxAm*
Hill, George Handel 1809-1848 *REnAL*
Hill, George James *Alli Sup*
Hill, George Nesse *Alli, BiDLA Sup*
Hill, George Rowley 1864- *ChPo*
Hill, George William 1823-1884 *Alli Sup, OhA&B*
Hill, George William 1824-1906 *Alli Sup, BbtC, DcNAA, OxCan*
Hill, George William 1838-1914 *DcNAA*
Hill, Georgiana *Alli Sup*
Hill, Gladwin 1914- *ConAu 25*
Hill, Grace Brooks *ConAu 19, SmATA 1*
Hill, Grace Livingston 1865-1947 *AmA&B, ChPo, DcAmA, DcNAA, REnAL, TwCA, TwCA Sup, WhWNAA*
Hill, Graham *ChPo*
Hill, H *Alli Sup*
Hill, H D N *ConAu XR*
Hill, H E *Alli Sup*
Hill, H Gregory *MnBBF*
Hill, Hamilton Andrews 1827-1895 *Alli Sup, DcAmA, DcNAA*
Hill, Hamlin 1931- *ConAu 9R*
Hill, Harriet S *Alli Sup*
Hill, Harry Egbert *MnBBF*
Hill, Harry Granison 1874-1951 *IndAu 1917, OhA&B*
Hill, Harry Gregory *MnBBF*
Hill, Hay *Alli Sup*
Hill, Headon 1857-1924 *EncM&D, MnBBF*
Hill, Helen *ConAu XR*
Hill, Helen d1942 *DcNAA*
Hill, Helen M 1915- *ConAu 57*
Hill, Henry *Alli*
Hill, Henry 1795-1889? *Alli Sup, DcAmA*
Hill, Henry 1895- *DcNAA*
Hill, Henry Barker 1849-1903 *Alli Sup, DcAmA, DcNAA*
Hill, Henry Bertram 1907- *ConAu 1R*
Hill, Henry David *Alli*
Hill, Henry F *Alli Sup*
Hill, Henry Thomas *Alli Sup*
Hill, Henry Wayland 1853-1929 *DcNAA*
Hill, Henry Wood *Alli Sup*
Hill, Herbert *Alli Sup*
Hill, Herbert Wynford 1875-1943 *AmA&B, WhWNAA*
Hill, Hinda Teague *WhWNAA*
Hill, Howard Copeland 1878-1940 *AmA&B, DcNAA, WhWNAA*
Hill, Hyacinthe *ConAu XR, WrD 1976*
Hill, Ira 1783-1838 *Alli, DcNAA*
Hill, Isabel 1800-1842 *ChPo, ChPo S2*
Hill, J Arthur 1872-1951 *BiDPar*
Hill, J B *Alli Sup*
Hill, Mrs. J B *Alli Sup*
Hill, J G *Alli Sup*
Hill, J H *Alli Sup*
Hill, James *Alli, ChPo S1, WrD 1976*
Hill, James Jerome 1838-1916 *BbtC, DcNAA*
Hill, James Langdon 1848-1931 *AmLY, DcNAA, WhWNAA*

Hill, James N 1934- *ConAu 33*
Hill, James Reginald 1906- *Au&Wr*
Hill, Sir James William Francis 1899- *Au&Wr*
Hill, James Woodward *Alli Sup*
Hill, Janet McKenzie 1852-1933 *AmLY, DcNAA*
Hill, Jeff *ChPo S2*
Hill, Jim *ChPo*
Hill, Jim Dan 1897- *AmA&B, ConAu P-1*
Hill, John *Alli, Alli Sup, BiDLA, BiDLA Sup*
Hill, Lady John *Alli*
Hill, John d1807 *Alli*
Hill, John d1904? *PoIre*
Hill, John 1711-1746 *Alli*
Hill, Sir John 1716-1775 *Alli, DcEnL*
Hill, John 1871- *ChPo S2*
Hill, John Alexander 1858-1916 *DcNAA, REnAL*
Hill, John Boynton 1796-1886 *DcNAA*
Hill, John C *Alli Sup*
Hill, John Calhoun *BlkAW*
Hill, John Campbell 1888- *ConAu 37, WrD 1976*
Hill, John Clarence 1876- *WhWNAA*
Hill, John Daniel *Alli Sup*
Hill, John Edward 1864-1934 *DcNAA*
Hill, John Edward Christopher 1912- *Au&Wr*
Hill, John Ethan 1865- *DcAmA*
Hill, John George Henry *Alli Sup*
Hill, John Godfrey 1870- *WhWNAA*
Hill, John Harwood 1809-1886 *Alli Sup*
Hill, John Henry 1839-1922 *EarAB, EarAB Sup*
Hill, John Hugh 1905- *ConAu 1R*
Hill, John M 1887- *WhWNAA*
Hill, John P 1936- *ConAu 29*
Hill, John S 1929- *ConAu 37*
Hill, John Spencer *Alli Sup*
Hill, John W *Alli Sup, MnBBF*
Hill, John Wesley 1831-1913 *OhA&B*
Hill, John Wesley 1863-1936 *DcNAA, OhA&B*
Hill, John Wiley 1890- *IndAu 1917*
Hill, John Woodroffe *Alli Sup*
Hill, Joseph 1625-1707 *Alli*
Hill, Joseph Abner 1877- *TexWr, WhWNAA*
Hill, Joseph Adna 1860- *DcAmA*
Hill, Julious C *BlkAW*
Hill, K F *HsB&A, HsB&A Sup*
Hill, Kate Neely *Alli Sup, DcNAA*
Hill, Kathleen Louise 1917- *ConAu 9R, SmATA 4*
Hill, Kay *ConAu XR, OxCan Sup, SmATA 4*
Hill, Kenneth 1937- *Au&Wr*
Hill, King *ConAu XR*
Hill, Knox C 1910- *ConAu P-1*
Hill, L C *Alli Sup*
Hill, L Draper 1935- *ConAu 17R, WrD 1976*
Hill, L J *Alli Sup*
Hill, L L *Alli Sup*
Hill, Laindon *Alli Sup*
Hill, Laurance Landreth 1887-1932 *DcNAA*
Hill, Lawrence Francis 1890- *OhA&B*
Hill, Lee H 1899- *ConAu 37*
Hill, Lee H 1899-1974 *ConAu 45*
Hill, Sir Leonard Erskine 1866- *WhLA*
Hill, Leslie Alexander 1918- *Au&Wr, ConAu 23, WrD 1976*
Hill, Leslie Pinckney 1880-1960 *BlkAW, ChPo, ChPo S2*
Hill, Leubrie 1873-1916 *BlkAW*
Hill, Lorna 1902- *Au&Wr, AuBYP, ConAu P-1, WrD 1976*
Hill, Lucie Haskell *TexWr*
Hill, Lucy *Alli Sup*
Hill, Lucy A *Alli Sup*
Hill, Lysander 1834-1914 *DcNAA*
Hill, Mabel 1864- *WhWNAA*
Hill, Mabel Betsey 1877- *ChPo*
Hill, Margaret 1915- *AuBYP, ConAu 1R*
Hill, Marion 1870-1918 *DcNAA*
Hill, Mars 1927- *BlkAW*
Hill, Martha S *ChPo S1*
Hill, Marvin Luter 1888- *TexWr*
Hill, Marvin S 1928- *ConAu 61*
Hill, Mary *ChPo S1*
Hill, Mary Anderson *ArizL*

Hill, Mary Carter d1890 *BiDSA*
Hill, Mary Raymond 1923- *ConAu 57*
Hill, Matthew Berkeley *Alli Sup*
Hill, Matthew Davenport 1792-1872 *Alli Sup, DcEnL*
Hill, May 1888- *AmSCAP 66*
Hill, Micaiah *Alli Sup*
Hill, Michael 1943- *WrD 1976*
Hill, Mildred 1859-1916 *AmSCAP 66, ChPo*
Hill, Mildred Martin *BlkAW, ChPo*
Hill, Monica *ConAu XR, SmATA 3*
Hill, N *Alli*
Hill, N N *Alli Sup*
Hill, Nathaniel *Alli*
Hill, Nathaniel Peter 1832-1900 *DcNAA*
Hill, Nicholas *Alli*
Hill, Nicholas, Jr. *Alli*
Hill, Noah 1739-1815 *Alli*
Hill, Norman Llewellyn 1895- *Au&Wr, ConAu 5R, WrD 1976*
Hill, Octavia 1838?- *Alli Sup*
Hill, O'Dell Travers *Alli Sup*
Hill, Oliver *Alli, ChPo, ChPo S1*
Hill, Pamela 1920- *ConAu 49, WrD 1976*
Hill, Pascoe Grenfell 1804-1882 *Alli, Alli Sup*
Hill, Patty Smith 1868-1946 *ChPo, ChPo S1, DcNAA*
Hill, Peter Proal 1926- *ConAu 33*
Hill, Philip Carteret *BbtC*
Hill, Philip G 1934- *ConAu 33*
Hill, Pierre Bernard 1877-1958 *ChPo S2*
Hill, Polly 1914- *ConAu XR*
Hill, Polly Knipp 1900- *ChPo, ChPo S1*
Hill, Quentin 1950- *BlkAW*
Hill, R *Alli*
Hill, R B *OxCan*
Hill, Ralph Nading 1917- *AuBYP, ConAu 1R*
Hill, Randolph *Alli Sup*
Hill, Reginald Charles 1936- *WrD 1976*
Hill, Richard *Alli, Alli Sup*
Hill, Sir Richard 1733-1808 *Alli, ChPo, DcEnL*
Hill, Richard 1901- *ConAu 1R*
Hill, Richard 1941- *ConAu 33, WrD 1976*
Hill, Richard Desmond 1920- *Au&Wr*
Hill, Richard E 1920- *ConAu 33*
Hill, Richard Johnson 1925- *ConAu 9R*
Hill, Robert *Alli*
Hill, Robert 1699-1777 *Alli*
Hill, Mrs. Robert *PoIre*
Hill, Robert Gardiner 1811-1878 *Alli Sup*
Hill, Robert Henry 1910- *Au&Wr*
Hill, Robert Thomas 1858- *Alli Sup, DcAmA, TexWr*
Hill, Robert W *DrAP 1975*
Hill, Robert W 1919- *AuBYP, ConAu 9R*
Hill, Roberta J *DrAP 1975*
Hill, Roland *ChPo S1*
Hill, Rosalind Mary Theodosia 1908- *ConAu P-1, WrD 1976*
Hill, Rosamond Davenport *Alli Sup*
Hill, Roscoe E 1936- *ConAu 37*
Hill, Roscoe R 1880-1960 *AmA&B*
Hill, Rowland *Alli*
Hill, Rowland 1744-1833? *Alli, BiDLA, BiDLA Sup, ChPo, DcEnL, PoCh*
Hill, Sir Rowland 1795-1879 *NewC, OxEng*
Hill, Rowley 1836-1887 *Alli Sup*
Hill, Roy L 1925- *BlkAW*
Hill, Ruth A *ConAu XR, SmATA 6*
Hill, Ruth Livingston *ConAu XR*
Hill, S S *Alli, Alli Sup, BbtC, OxCan*
Hill, Samuel *Alli, BiDLA, EarAB Sup*
Hill, Samuel E 1913- *ConAu 17R*
Hill, Samuel S, Jr. 1927- *ConAu 9R*
Hill, Stewart 1901- *Au&Wr*
Hill, Susan Elizabeth 1942- *ConAu 33, ConDr, ConNov 1976, ConLC 4, WrD 1976*
Hill, Sylvia 1908- *WhWNAA*
Hill, Theodore *Alli*
Hill, Theophilus Hunter 1836-1901 *Alli Sup, AmA&B, BiD&SB, BiDSA, DcAmA, DcNAA*
Hill, Thomas *Alli, Alli Sup*
Hill, Thomas d1860 *DcNAA*
Hill, Thomas 1818-1891 *Alli, AmA&B, BiD&SB, ChPo S1, CyAL 1, DcAmA, DcEnL, DcNAA, OhA&B*

Hino, Chikatsune *DcOrL 1*
Hinojosa, Rolando *DrAF 1976*
Hinostroza, Rodolfo 1941- *DcCLA*
Hinrichs, August 1879-1956 *CasWL, WhLA*
Hinrichs, Carl Detlef 1836- *DcAmA*
Hinrichs, Gustavus Detlef 1836-1923 *Alli Sup, DcNAA*
Hinrichsen, Ludwig 1872-1957 *CasWL*
Hinrichsen, Max 1901-1965 *ConAu P-1*
Hinscliff, M W *ChPo S2*
Hinsdale, Burke Aaron 1837-1900 *Alli Sup, AmA&B, DcAmA, DcNAA, OhA&B*
Hinsdale, Grace Webster 1832- *Alli Sup, DcAmA, PoCh*
Hinsdale, Guy 1858- *WhWNAA*
Hinsdale, Laura F *BiDSA, ChPo, ChPo S1*
Hinsdale, Richard L 1826-1856 *EarAB, EarAB Sup*
Hinsdale, Wilbert B 1854?-1944 *DcNAA, OhA&B*
Hinshaw, Cecil E 1911- *ConAu 13R*
Hinshaw, John E 1862- *WhWNAA*
Hinshaw, Randall 1915- *ConAu 41*
Hinshaw, Robert E 1933- *ConAu 57*
Hinsley, F H 1918- *ConAu 17R*
Hinson, E Glenn 1931- *ConAu 21, WrD 1976*
Hinson, Maurice 1930- *ConAu 45*
Hinson, Walter Benwell 1862-1926 *DcNAA*
Hint, Aadu 1910- *CasWL*
Hinterhoff, Eugene 1895- *ConAu P-1*
Hintikka, Kaarlo Jaakko Juhani 1929- *ConAu 1R, WrD 1976*
Hinton, A W *Alli Sup*
Hinton, Benjamin *Alli*
Hinton, Bernard L 1937- *ConAu 33*
Hinton, Charles Howard *Alli Sup*
Hinton, Charles Louis 1869- *ChPo, ChPo S2, IlCB 1945*
Hinton, Edward Wilcox 1868-1936 *DcNAA, WhWNAA*
Hinton, Harold C 1924- *Au&Wr, ConAu 17R*
Hinton, Henry *BlkAW*
Hinton, Henry L *Alli Sup*
Hinton, Herbert Allan 1888-1945 *MnBBF*
Hinton, Howard 1834-1920 *DcNAA*
Hinton, Isaac Taylor 1799-1847 *Alli, BiDSA, DcAmA, DcNAA*
Hinton, James *Alli, Alli Sup, BiDLA, Chmbr 3*
Hinton, James 1822-1875 *Alli Sup, BiD&SB, BrAu 19, EvLB*
Hinton, John *Alli*
Hinton, Sir John *Alli*
Hinton, John 1926- *ConAu 49*
Hinton, John Howard 1791-1873 *Alli, Alli Sup, ChPo S1*
Hinton, John William *Alli Sup*
Hinton, Phyllis *Au&Wr*
Hinton, Richard Josiah 1830-1901 *Alli Sup, BiD&SB, ChPo, DcAmA, DcNAA*
Hinton, Richard W *ConAu XR*
Hinton, Walter 1889- *OhA&B*
Hinton, William *Alli*
Hinton, William H 1919- *ConAu 25*
Hinton, Zebulon Wright *Alli Sup*
Hintz, Howard William 1903-1964 *AmA&B, REnAL*
Hintz, Loren E *WhWNAA*
Hintz, Orton Sutherland 1907- *WrD 1976*
Hintze, Guenther 1906- *ConAu 21*
Hintze, Naomi A 1909- *ConAu 45, WrD 1976*
Hinxman, Emmeline *Alli Sup*
Hinz, Francis Joseph 1923- *Au&Wr*
Hinz, Stella M *ChPo S1*
Hioan, G R *Alli, BiDLA*
Hiorns, Arthur H *Alli Sup*
Hipkins, Alfred James *Alli Sup*
Hipp, George *ConAu XR*
Hipparchus Of Nicaea *CasWL, Pen Cl*
Hippeau, Celestin 1803-1883 *BiD&SB*
Hippel, Theodor Gottlieb Von 1741-1796 *BiD&SB, CasWL, DcEuL, EvEuW, OxGer*
Hippel, Ursula Von *AuBYP*
Hippenstiel, Harold Franklin 1892- *WhWNAA*
Hipperson, Alfred John 1919- *Au&Wr*
Hippesley, George *Alli*
Hippesley, J H *Alli*

Hippias Of Elis *CasWL*
Hippisley *Alli*
Hippisley, George *AmA&B*
Hippisley, Sir John Coxe 1765-1825 *Alli, BiDLA*
Hippius, Zinaida Nikolayevna 1867?-1945 *CasWL, ClDMEuL, DcRusL, EncWL Sup, REn*
Hipple, Walter J, Jr. 1921- *ConAu 41*
Hippler, Arthur E 1935- *ConAu 57*
Hippocrates 460?BC-377?BC *CasWL, NewC, OxEng, Pen Cl, REn*
Hippolyta *REn*
Hipponax *CasWL, Pen Cl*
Hippopotamus, Eugene H *AuBYP, ThBJA*
Hipsher, Edward Ellsworth 1871?-1948 *DcNAA, OhA&B*
Hipshman, May 1919- *AuBYP*
Hipskind, Mildred 1903- *IndAu 1917*
Hipskind, Verne K 1925- *ConAu 21*
Hipsley, William *Alli Sup*
Hiquaeus, Antonius *Alli*
Hiraethoc, Gruffyd *Alli*
Hiraga, Gennai *DcOrL 1*
Hiraoka, Kimitake *WorAu*
Hirata, Atsutane *DcOrL 1*
Hirawa, Yasuko *ChPo S1*
Hirche, Peter 1923- *CnMD, CrCD*
Hird, James *Alli Sup*
Hird, W G *Alli Sup*
Hird, William *Alli*
Hire, Frank *ChPo S2*
Hires, Harrison 1887- *ChPo*
Hirn, Yrjo 1870-1952 *CasWL*
Hiro, Dilip *WrD 1976*
Hirohito 1901- *REn*
Hiroi, Isami *Alli Sup*
Hirons, Montague John David 1916- *Au&Wr, WrD 1976*
Hirsch, Abby 1946- *ConAu 45*
Hirsch, Alcan 1885-1938 *DcNAA*
Hirsch, Arthur Henry 1878- *OhA&B, WhWNAA*
Hirsch, E Donald, Jr. 1928- *ConAu 25*
Hirsch, Emil Gustav 1852-1923 *DcNAA*
Hirsch, Ernest A 1924- *ConAu 25, WrD 1976*
Hirsch, Foster 1943- *ConAu 45*
Hirsch, Fred 1931- *Au&Wr, ConAu 25*
Hirsch, Herbert 1941- *ConAu 41*
Hirsch, Joseph 1910- *ChPo S1*
Hirsch, Lester M 1925- *ConAu 17R*
Hirsch, Louis Achille 1887-1924 *AmSCAP 66*
Hirsch, Marilyn *ChPo S1*
Hirsch, Monroe J 1917- *ConAu 41*
Hirsch, Morris Isaac 1915- *WrD 1976*
Hirsch, S Carl 1913- *AnCL, ConAu 5R, SmATA 2, ThBJA, WrD 1976*
Hirsch, Seev 1931- *ConAu 33, WrD 1976*
Hirsch, Thomas L 1931- *ConAu 49*
Hirsch, Walter 1891- *AmSCAP 66*
Hirsch, Walter 1919- *ConAu 13R*
Hirsch, Werner Z 1920- *ConAu 17R, WrD 1976*
Hirsch, William Randolph *ConAu XR*
Hirschbein, Peretz 1880-1948 *CasWL, EncWL, McGWD*
Hirschberg, Alice Kerr-Helson 1852- *ChPo*
Hirschberg, Cornelius 1901- *ConAu 17*
Hirschel, Solomon 1762- *BiDLA*
Hirschensohn, Chajim 1856- *WhWNAA*
Hirschfeld, Albert 1903- *AmA&B, ConAu 1R*
Hirschfeld, Georg 1873-1942 *McGWD, ModWD, OxGer, REn*
Hirschfeld, Herman 1905- *ConAu P-1*
Hirschfelder, Jacob Maier 1819-1902 *BbtC, DcNAA*
Hirschfield *ChPo*
Hirschfield, Robert S 1928- *ConAu 45*
Hirschhorn, Clive 1940- *ConAu 57, WrD 1976*
Hirschl, Andrew Jackson 1852-1908 *Alli Sup, DcNAA*
Hirschman, Albert O 1915- *ConAu 1R*
Hirschman, Jack 1933- *ConP 1970, ConP 1975, DrAP 1975, WrD 1976*
Hirschmeier, Johannes 1921- *ConAu 13R, WrD 1976*
Hirsh, Alice *ChPo S2*

Hirsh, Marilyn 1944- *ConAu 49, SmATA 7*
Hirshbein, Peretz 1880-1948 *CnThe, ModWD, REnWD*
Hirshberg, Albert S 1909-1973 *AuBYP, ConAu 1R, ConAu 41*
Hirshberg, Leonard Keene 1877- *AmLY*
Hirshberg, Leonard Keene 1877- *WhWNAA*
Hirshfeld, Clarence Floyd 1881- *WhWNAA*
Hirshfield, Daniel S 1942- *ConAu 29*
Hirshhorn, Naomi Caryl *AmSCAP 66*
Hirshson, Stanley Philip 1928- *ConAu 1R*
Hirst, Alice Elizabeth 1898- *Au&Wr*
Hirst, Augusta Ann *Alli, BiDLA*
Hirst, Barton Cooke 1861-1935 *DcNAA*
Hirst, David W 1920- *ConAu 37*
Hirst, Francis W 1873-1953 *NewC, WhLA*
Hirst, Gillian Jose Charlotte 1938- *Au&Wr*
Hirst, Henry Beck 1813?-1874 *Alli, AmA, AmA&B, BiD&SB, ChPo S1, CnDAL, DcAmA, CyAL 2, DcNAA, OxAm, REnAL*
Hirst, J Crowther *Alli Sup*
Hirst, John *Alli Sup*
Hirst, Rodney Julian 1920- *Au&Wr, ConAu 9R, WrD 1976*
Hirst, Samuel *Alli Sup*
Hirst, Stephen M 1939- *ConAu 53*
Hirst, Thomas *Alli Sup*
Hirst, William *Alli*
Hirst, Wilma E 1914- *ConAu 13R*
Hirst-Smith, Ann 1945- *WrD 1976*
Hirt, Michael L 1934- *ConAu 9R*
Hirth, Friedrich 1845- *AmLY, DcAmA*
Hirtius, Aulus d043BC *CasWL, Pen Cl*
Hirzelin 1270?- *OxGer*
Hiscock, Eric C 1908- *WrD 1976*
Hiscocks, Charles Richard 1907- *ConAu 53, WrD 1976*
Hiscox, Edward Thurston 1814-1901 *Alli Sup, DcNAA*
Hiscox, Gardner Dexter 1822-1908 *DcNAA*
Hiser, Iona Seibert 1901- *ConAu 1R, SmATA 4*
Hisinger *Alli*
Hiskett, Mervyn 1920- *ConAu 61*
Hislop, Alexander *Alli Sup*
Hislop, Andrew *BrAu 19*
Hislop, Codman 1906- *ConAu 33*
Hislop, Dora *WhWNAA*
Hislop, J P *Alli Sup*
Hislop, James 1798-1827 *DcEnL*
Hislop, Stephen 1817-1863 *Alli Sup*
Hiss, Alger 1904- *Au&Wr, ConAu 33*
Hissey, James John *Alli Sup*
Historian *WhWNAA*
Historicus *DcNAA*
Historicus 1827- *DcEnL*
Hita, Archpriest Of *DcEuL, EvEuW*
Hita, Gines Perez De 1545?-1610? *BiD&SB, DcEuL*
Hitchcock, Albert Spear 1865-1935 *DcNAA*
Hitchcock, Albert Wellman 1861-1907 *DcNAA*
Hitchcock, Alfred 1813-1874 *Alli Sup, DcAmA, DcNAA*
Hitchcock, Alfred 1899- *Au&Wr, EncM&D, NewC, REnAL*
Hitchcock, Alfred Marshall 1868-1941 *AmA&B, AmLY, DcNAA, WhWNAA*
Hitchcock, Belle A *ChPo*
Hitchcock, Benjamin W *Alli Sup*
Hitchcock, Caroline Hanks 1863- *DcAmA*
Hitchcock, Charles Henry 1836-1919 , *DcAmA, DcNAA*
Hitchcock, Curtice 1892-1946 *AmA&B*
Hitchcock, David 1773- *Alli, CyAL 1, DcNAA*
Hitchcock, DeWitt C *EarAB, EarAB Sup*
Hitchcock, Edward 1793-1864 *Alli, Alli Sup, BbD, BiD&SB, CyAL 1, DcAmA, DcEnL, DcNAA, REnAL*
Hitchcock, Edward 1828-1911 *DcAmA, DcNAA*
Hitchcock, Edward 1854-1925 *DcNAA*
Hitchcock, Embury Asbury 1866-1948 *OhA&B*
Hitchcock, Enos 1744-1803 *Alli, AmA&B, DcAmA, DcNAA, OxAm, REnAL*
Hitchcock, Ethan Allen 1798-1870 *Alli, Alli Sup, AmA, AmA&B, BiD&SB,*

Hobbs, Jack *MnBBF*
Hobbs, James *Alli Sup*
Hobbs, John Leslie 1916-1964 *ConAu 5R*
Hobbs, John Sanders 1913- *Au&Wr*
Hobbs, Perry *ConAu XR*
Hobbs, Peter V 1936- *ConAu 53*
Hobbs, Roe Raymond 1871-1933 *BiDSA,
    DcNAA*
Hobbs, Samuel *Alli Sup*
Hobbs, Samuel W *Alli Sup*
Hobbs, Stephen *Alli, Alli Sup*
Hobbs, Thomas Francis *Alli Sup*
Hobbs, Valentine *ChPo*
Hobbs, W Fisher *Alli Sup*
Hobbs, William 1939- *ConAu 21*
Hobbs, William Herbert 1864-1953 *AmA&B,
    WhWNAA*
Hobby, A M *ChPo S1*
Hobby, Alfred M *BiDSA*
Hobby, Bertram Maurice 1905- *Au&Wr*
Hobby, Edwin *Alli Sup*
Hobby, Laura Aline *TexWr*
Hobby, Oveta Culp *TexWr*
Hobby, William 1707-1765 *Alli, DcAmA*
Hobday, Edward *Alli Sup*
Hobday, Frederick *WhLA*
Hobden, H F *ChPo, ChPo S2*
Hobden, Roger *MnBBF*
Hoben, Allan 1874-1935 *DcNAA*
Hoben, John B 1908- *ConAu 37*
Hoberecht, Earnest 1918- *AmA&B, ConAu 23*
Hoberman, Mary Ann 1930- *BkCL, ChPo S1,
    ChPo S2, ConAu 41, SmATA 5*
Hobhouse, Sir Arthur, Baron Hobhouse 1819-
    Alli Sup
Hobhouse, Sir Benjamin 1757-1831 *Alli,
    BiDLA*
Hobhouse, Christina 1941- *Au&Wr,
    ConAu 25, WrD 1976*
Hobhouse, Edmund *Alli Sup*
Hobhouse, Henry 1854- *Alli Sup*
Hobhouse, Hermione 1934- *ConAu 41*
Hobhouse, Janet 1948- *ConAu 57*
Hobhouse, Baron John Cam 1786-1869 *Alli,
    BbD, BiD&SB, BiDLA, CasWL, DcEnL,
    DcLEnL, EvLB, NewC, OxEng, Pen Eng*
Hobhouse, Leonard Trelawny 1864- *WhLA*
Hobhouse, Thomas *Alli, BiDLA*
Hobhouse, Walter *Alli Sup*
Hobkirk, Charles P *Alli Sup*
Hobkirk, William *Alli Sup*
Hobler, F *Alli*
Hobler, F, Jr. *Alli*
Hobler, Francis *Alli Sup*
Hobley, Henry *Alli Sup*
Hobley, Leonard Frank 1903- *Au&Wr,
    ConAu 13R, WrD 1976*
Hoblyn, Anna Margaret *Alli Sup*
Hoblyn, Maria Theresa *Alli Sup*
Hoblyn, Richard D *Alli*
Hobman, Daisy Lucie 1891- *WhLA*
Hobman, Joseph Burton 1872- *WhLA*
Hobsbaum, Philip 1932- *Au&Wr, ChPo S1,
    ConAu 9R, ConP 1970, ConP 1975,
    WrD 1976*
Hobsbawm, Eric John Ernest 1917- *Au&Wr,
    ConAu 5R, WrD 1976*
Hobson, Captain *Alli*
Hobson, Anne *BiDSA*
Hobson, Anthony Robert Alwyne 1921-
    ConAu 33, WrD 1976
Hobson, Archibald *ChPo*
Hobson, Arthur H B *Alli Sup*
Hobson, Benjamin *Alli Sup*
Hobson, Burton 1933- *ConAu 5R*
Hobson, Mrs. Carey *MnBBF*
Hobson, E S C 1850?- *Br&AmS*
Hobson, Edmund 1931- *ConAu 45*
Hobson, Edwin *Alli Sup*
Hobson, Francis Thayer 1897-1967 *AmA&B*
Hobson, Fred Colby, Jr. 1943- *ConAu 53,
    WrD 1976*
Hobson, George Carey 1890-1945 *CasWL*
Hobson, Hank *ConAu XR*
Hobson, Harold 1904- *CrCD, LongC*
Hobson, Harriet Malone *AmA&B*
Hobson, Harry 1907- *Au&Wr*
Hobson, Harry 1908- *ConAu P-1*

Hobson, J A *OxCan*
Hobson, John *Alli, Alli Sup, BiDLA*
Hobson, John Atkinson 1858-1940 *NewC*
Hobson, John P *ChPo*
Hobson, John Peyton 1850-1934 *DcNAA,
    WhWNAA*
Hobson, John Philip *Alli Sup*
Hobson, Jonathan Todd 1850-1923 *IndAu 1917*
Hobson, Joseph *Alli*
Hobson, Julius *LivBA*
Hobson, L J *Alli*
Hobson, Laura Keane Z 1900- *AmA&B,
    AmNov, Au&Wr, ConAu 17R,
    ConNov 1972, ConNov 1976, REn,
    REnAL, TwCA Sup, WrD 1976*
Hobson, Mrs. M A Carey *Alli Sup*
Hobson, M B *ChPo S2*
Hobson, Paul *Alli*
Hobson, Polly 1913- *AuBYP, ConAu XR,
    WrD 1976*
Hobson, Richard *Alli Sup*
Hobson, Richmond P, Jr. *OxCan*
Hobson, Richmond Pearson 1870-1937 *AmA&B,
    BiDSA, DcAmA, DcNAA*
Hobson, Samuel *Alli*
Hobson, Samuel Bonnin 1888-1967 *CasWL*
Hobson, Stanley *MnBBF*
Hobson, Thomas *Alli*
Hobson, Thomas 1544?-1630 *NewC*
Hobson, W R *OxCan*
Hobson, Wilder 1906-1964 *AmA&B*
Hobson, William 1911- *WrD 1976*
Hoby, Sir Edward *Alli*
Hoby, Sir Thomas 1530-1566 *Alli, BrAu,
    CasWL, Chmbr 1, CrE&SL, DcEuL,
    DcLEnL, EvLB, OxEng, REn*
Hocatius Jr. *WhWNAA*
Hoccham, William Of *Alli*
Hoccleve, John 1370?-1450? *Pen Eng*
Hoccleve, Thomas 1370?-1450? *Alli, BrAu,
    CasWL, Chmbr 1, CriT 1, DcEnL,
    DcLEnL, EvLB, MouLC 1, NewC,
    OxEng, REn*
Hoch, August 1868-1919 *DcNAA*
Hoch, Edward D 1930- *ConAu 29, EncM&D,
    WrD 1976*
Hochaday, John A *Alli Sup*
Hochdoerfer, K F Richard 1854- *AmLY*
Hoche, Louis-Lazare 1768-1797 *OxFr*
Hochfield, George 1926- *ConAu 1R*
Hochheimer, Louis *Alli Sup*
Hochhuth, Rolf 1931- *CasWL, CnMD,
    CnThe, ConAu 5R, ConLC 4, CrCD,
    EncWL Sup, McGWD, ModGL, ModWD,
    OxGer, Pen Eur, REnWD, TwCW,
    WorAu*
Hochin, John Pearce *Alli*
Hochman, Sandra 1936- *AmA&B, ConAu 5R,
    ConLC 3, ConP 1970, ConP 1975,
    DrAF 1976, DrAP 1975, WrD 1976*
Hochman, Shirley D 1917- *ConAu 61*
Hochschild, Arlie Russell 1940- *ConAu 57*
Hochstein, Rolaine *ConAu 45*
Hochsteller, C *Alli*
Hochstrasser, Henry De *Alli Sup*
Hochwaelder, Fritz 1911- *ConAu 29*
Hochwald, Werner 1910- *ConAu 17R*
Hochwalder, Fritz 1911- *CasWL, CnMD,
    CnThe, ConAu XR, CrCD, EncWL,
    McGWD, ModGL, ModWD, OxGer,
    Pen Eur, REnWD, TwCW, WorAu*
Hochwalt, Albert Frederick 1869-1938 *AmA&B,
    DcNAA, OhA&B, WhWNAA*
Hochwalt, Albert G 1893-1920 *DcNAA*
Hock, Theobald 1573-1618? *OxGer*
Hockaby, Stephen *ConAu XR, EncM&D,
    LongC*
Hockema, Frank C 1892-1956 *IndAu 1917*
Hocker, Karla *ConAu 49*
Hocket, Charles F 1916- *WrD 1976*
Hockett, Charles F 1916- *ConAu 17R*
Hockett, Homer Carey 1875- *AmA&B,
    WhWNAA*
Hockin, Frederick *Alli Sup*
Hockin, J P *BiDLA*
Hockin, John Brent *Alli Sup*
Hockin, Thomas A *OxCan Sup*
Hocking, Anthony 1938- *Au&Wr, WrD 1976*

Hocking, Brian 1914- *ConAu 17*
Hocking, Joseph 1860-1937 *Alli Sup, BbD,
    Chmbr 3, EvLB, LongC, NewC, TwCA,
    TwCA Sup*
Hocking, Mary 1921- *Au&Wr, WrD 1976*
Hocking, Salome *Alli Sup*
Hocking, Silas Kitto 1850-1935 *Alli Sup,
    Chmbr 3, EvLB, LongC, NewC*
Hocking, William Ernest 1873-1966 *AmA&B,
    ConAu P-1, OhA&B, OxAm, REnAL,
    TwCA Sup, WhWNAA*
Hockley, G C 1931- *ConAu 29*
Hockley, James Anthony 1913- *Au&Wr*
Hockley, Lewis *MnBBF*
Hockley, William Browne 1792-1860 *Alli Sup,
    DcLEnL, OxEng*
Hockliffe, Frederick 1833-1914 *ChPo S1*
Hockridge, Gertrude *ChPo S1*
Hodas, Dorothy Gertrude 1912- *AmSCAP 66*
Hodasevich, R *Alli Sup*
Hodden, Richard *Alli*
Hodder, Alfred 1866-1907 *DcAmA, DcNAA,
    OhA&B*
Hodder, Edward Mulberry 1810-1878 *BbtC,
    DcNAA*
Hodder, Edwin 1837?-1904 *Alli Sup, CarSB,
    ChPo S1, DcEnL*
Hodder, Frank Heywood 1860-1935 *DcNAA*
Hodder, George *Alli Sup*
Hodder, Grant *Alli Sup*
Hodder, James *Alli*
Hodder-Williams, Christopher 1927- *ConAu 1R*
Hoddesdon, Henry *Alli*
Hoddesdon, John *Alli*
Hoddis, Jakob Van 1887-1942 *OxGer, Pen Eur,
    WhTwL*
Hoddy, Robert *Alli Sup*
Hodell, Charles Wesley 1872- *IndAu 1816*
Hodell, Frans Oscar Leonard 1840-1890
    BiD&SB
Hodes, Arthur W 1904- *AmSCAP 66*
Hodes, Aubrey 1927- *ConAu 33*
Hodes, Scott 1937- *ConAu 49*
Hodgart, Matthew John Caldwell 1916-
    Au&Wr, ConAu 5R, WrD 1976
Hodgdon, N C *Alli Sup*
Hodge *Alli*
Hodge, A *Alli, BiDLA*
Hodge, Alan 1915- *Au&Wr*
Hodge, Archibald Alexander 1823-1886
    *Alli Sup, AmA&B, DcAmA, DcEnL,
    DcNAA*
Hodge, Caspar Wistar 1870- *WhWNAA*
Hodge, Charles 1797-1878 *Alli, Alli Sup,
    AmA, AmA&B, BbD, CyAL 2, DcAmA,
    DcEnL, DcNAA, REnAL*
Hodge, D M *Alli Sup*
Hodge, David *Alli Sup*
Hodge, David W 1935- *ConAu 61*
Hodge, E Chatterton *ConAu XR*
Hodge, F O *ChPo S1*
Hodge, Francis 1915- *ConAu 33, WrD 1976*
Hodge, Frederick Webb 1864-1956 *AmA&B,
    AmLY, DcAmA, OxAm, OxCan,
    REnAL*
Hodge, Gene 1898- *ConAu 45*
Hodge, Hiram C *Alli Sup*
Hodge, Horace Emerton 1904-1958 *DcLEnL*
Hodge, Hugh Lenox 1796-1873 *Alli Sup,
    DcAmA, DcNAA*
Hodge, James Hozier 1906- *Au&Wr*
Hodge, James L 1935- *ConAu 41*
Hodge, Jane Aiken 1917- *Au&Wr, AuBYP,
    ConAu 5R, WrD 1976*
Hodge, John *Alli, Alli Sup, ChPo*
Hodge, John Aspinwall 1831-1901 *Alli Sup,
    DcAmA, DcNAA*
Hodge, Katherine *Alli Sup*
Hodge, Marshall Bryant 1925- *ConAu 23*
Hodge, Merton *DcLEnL*
Hodge, Orlando J 1828-1912 *OhA&B*
Hodge, Paul R *Alli*
Hodge, Paul William 1934- *ConAu 33,
    WrD 1976*
Hodge, Richard Morse 1864- *WhWNAA*
Hodge, Samuel 1829- *Alli Sup, BiDSA*
Hodge, T Shirby *OhA&B*
Hodge, T Shirley *AmLY XR*

Hodge, Thomas *Alli Sup*
Hodge, Thomas Hounsell *BbtC*
Hodge, Tobe *Alli Sup*
Hodge, W *Alli Sup*
Hodge, Walter Roberts 1884- *WhWNAA*
Hodgen, Joseph Dupuy 1865- *WhWNAA*
Hodges, A D *Alli*
Hodges, Arthur 1868-1949 *DcNAA, WhWNAA*
Hodges, Barbara K 1893-1949 *LongC, TwCA, TwCA Sup*
Hodges, C B *Alli Sup*
Hodges, Carl G 1902-1964 *AuBYP, ConAu 5R, SmATA 10*
Hodges, Charles *Alli*
Hodges, Claire McClure *TexWr*
Hodges, Cyril 1915- *ConP 1970*
Hodges, Cyril Walter 1909- *AnCL, Au&Wr, AuBYP, ChPo S2, ConAu 13R, IlCB 1945, IlCB 1956, IlCB 1966, SmATA 2, ThBJA, WhCL*
Hodges, D F *ChPo*
Hodges, David *IlBYP*
Hodges, Donald Clark 1923- *ConAu 53, WrD 1976*
Hodges, Doris Marjorie 1915- *Au&Wr, ConAu 25, WrD 1976*
Hodges, Elizabeth Jamison *AuBYP, ConAu 9R, SmATA 1*
Hodges, Ellen G *Alli Sup*
Hodges, Fletcher 1906- *IndAu 1917*
Hodges, Fletcher, Jr. *ChPo S2*
Hodges, Fred Jenner 1895- *IndAu 1917*
Hodges, Frenchy Jolene 1940- *BlkAW*
Hodges, George 1856-1919 *AmA&B, AmLY, BiD&SB, DcAmA, DcNAA*
Hodges, George Samuel *Alli Sup*
Hodges, George Washington *BlkAW*
Hodges, Graham R 1915- *ConAu 5R*
Hodges, H A 1905- *Au&Wr*
Hodges, Harold Mellor 1922- *ConAu 17R*
Hodges, Henry 1920- *Au&Wr, ConAu 37*
Hodges, Henry G 1888- *ConAu 5R*
Hodges, James *Alli, Alli Sup, BbtC*
Hodges, James S 1885- *AmSCAP 66*
Hodges, John C 1892- *ConAu 5R*
Hodges, Mrs. John F *PoIre*
Hodges, John Frederick 1815-1899 *Alli Sup, PoIre*
Hodges, Johnny 1907- *AmSCAP 66*
Hodges, Laura Fletcher 1857-1923 *IndAu 1917*
Hodges, Leigh Mitchell 1876-1954 *AmA&B, ChPo*
Hodges, Louise T *BiDSA*
Hodges, Luther 1898-1974 *ConAu 53*
Hodges, Margaret Moore 1911- *ConAu 1R, IndAu 1917, SmATA 1, WrD 1976*
Hodges, Nathaniel 1630-1684 *DcEnL*
Hodges, Nicholas William *Alli, Alli Sup*
Hodges, Norman Edward 1939- *LivBA*
Hodges, Paul Chesley 1893- *IndAu 1917*
Hodges, Phineas *Alli, BiDLA*
Hodges, Richard *Alli, Alli Sup*
Hodges, Richard E 1928- *ConAu 41*
Hodges, Richard Manning 1827-1896 *Alli Sup, DcNAA*
Hodges, Sydney 1829-1900 *Alli Sup, ChPo S2*
Hodges, Thomas *Alli*
Hodges, Thomas Law *Alli*
Hodges, Turner *ConAu XR*
Hodges, W *Alli, BiDLA*
Hodges, Walter *Alli*
Hodges, Wickens *Alli*
Hodges, William *Alli, Alli Sup*
Hodges, Zane Clark 1932- *ConAu 41*
Hodgetts, E A Brayley *Alli Sup*
Hodgetts, J E 1917- *ConAu 13R, OxCan, OxCan Sup*
Hodgetts, James Frederick *Alli Sup, MnBBF*
Hodgetts, Richard M 1942- *ConAu 57*
Hodgin, Charles Elkanah 1858- *IndAu 1917*
Hodgin, Cyrus Wilburn 1842-1908 *DcAmA, DcNAA, IndAu 1816*
Hodgins, Bruce W 1931- *ConAu 37, OxCan Sup*
Hodgins, Eric 1899-1971 *AmA&B, ConAu 29, REnAL, WhWNAA, WorAu*

Hodgins, Frank E 1854- *WhWNAA*
Hodgins, Frederick B *ChPo*
Hodgins, John George 1821-1912 *Alli Sup, BbtC, DcNAA, OxCan*
Hodgins, Norris 1895- *WhWNAA*
Hodgins, Thomas 1828?-1910 *Alli Sup, BbtC, DcNAA*
Hodgkin, Henry Theodore 1877-1933 *DcNAA, WhWNAA*
Hodgkin, Howard 1857- *Alli Sup*
Hodgkin, John *Alli, BiDLA*
Hodgkin, John Eliot *Alli Sup*
Hodgkin, Louise Manning 1846- *DcAmA*
Hodgkin, Robert Allason 1916- *Au&Wr*
Hodgkin, Robin A 1916- *WrD 1976*
Hodgkin, Thomas *Alli, Alli Sup, BiDLA, Chmbr 3*
Hodgkin, Thomas 1831-1913 *Alli Sup, BrAu 19*
Hodgkins, E *Alli, BiDLA*
Hodgkins, George *Alli*
Hodgkins, Louise Manning 1846-1935 *AmA&B, ChPo, DcNAA*
Hodgkinson, Florence *Alli Sup*
Hodgkinson, John 1766-1805 *DcNAA*
Hodgkinson, W R *Alli Sup*
Hodgkiss, Alan Geoffrey 1921- *Au&Wr, WrD 1976*
Hodgman, Edwin Ruthven 1819-1900 *DcNAA*
Hodgman, Stephen A *Alli Sup*
Hodgskin, Thomas *Alli*
Hodgson *Alli*
Hodgson, Adam *Alli, BbtC*
Hodgson, Bernard *Alli*
Hodgson, Brian Houghton *Alli Sup*
Hodgson, Mrs. C Hunter *Alli Sup*
Hodgson, Charles *Alli Sup*
Hodgson, Christopher *Alli, BiDLA*
Hodgson, Christopher Pemberton *Alli Sup*
Hodgson, D H 1939- *ConAu 25*
Hodgson, D S *Alli Sup*
Hodgson, Decimus *Alli Sup*
Hodgson, E *Alli*
Hodgson, Elizabeth *Alli Sup*
Hodgson, Ellen *Alli Sup*
Hodgson, Frances Eliza *Chmbr 3*
Hodgson, Francis 1780-1852 *Alli, BiDLA, DcEnL*
Hodgson, Francis 1805-1877 *Alli, DcAmA, DcNAA*
Hodgson, Francis Cotterell *Alli Sup*
Hodgson, Frederick T *Alli Sup*
Hodgson, Frederick Thomas 1836- *DcNAA*
Hodgson, George *Alli*
Hodgson, Geraldine Emma 1865- *WhLA*
Hodgson, Godfrey 1934- *ConAu 25*
Hodgson, H J *Alli*
Hodgson, Henry 1753- *Alli, BiDLA*
Hodgson, Henry John *Alli Sup*
Hodgson, Isaac *Alli*
Hodgson, J *BiDLA*
Hodgson, J F *BbtC*
Hodgson, J G *ChPo*
Hodgson, James *Alli*
Hodgson, James Goodwin 1892- *WhWNAA*
Hodgson, James M *Alli Sup*
Hodgson, James Thomas 1846-1880 *Alli Sup*
Hodgson, Jane Ann *Alli Sup*
Hodgson, John *Alli, Alli Sup, BiDLA, BiDLA Sup*
Hodgson, John 1779-1845 *DcEnL*
Hodgson, John C L *OxCan*
Hodgson, John Evans *Alli Sup*
Hodgson, John Reed 1927- *Au&Wr*
Hodgson, John Studholme *Alli Sup*
Hodgson, John Syner 1917- *WrD 1976*
Hodgson, Joseph *Alli, BiDLA Sup*
Hodgson, Joseph 1838-1913 *Alli Sup, BiDSA, DcNAA*
Hodgson, Laurence Curran 1874-1937 *DcNAA*
Hodgson, Leonard 1889-1969 *ConAu P-1, WhLA*
Hodgson, Lucas *Alli*
Hodgson, Margaret *ConAu XR*
Hodgson, Marshall G S 1922- *ConAu 21, IndAu 1917*
Hodgson, Martha 1906- *ConAu 57*
Hodgson, May *Alli Sup*

Hodgson, Norma *ConAu XR*
Hodgson, Pat 1928- *ConAu 57*
Hodgson, Peter Crafts 1934- *ConAu 29, WrD 1976*
Hodgson, Peter Edward 1928- *ConAu 9R, WrD 1976*
Hodgson, Phyllis 1909- *ConAu P-1*
Hodgson, R R *Alli Sup*
Hodgson, Ralph 1871-1962 *AnCL, AtlBL, ChPo, ChPo S1, ChPo S2, Chmbr 3, CnE&AP, DcLEnL, EvLB, LongC, ModBL, NewC, OhA&B, OxEng, Pen Eng, REn, TwCA, TwCA Sup, WhTwL*
Hodgson, Read *Alli*
Hodgson, Richard 1855-1905 *BiDPar*
Hodgson, Richard Sargeant 1924- *ConAu 13R*
Hodgson, Robert d1844 *Alli, BiDLA, DcEnL*
Hodgson, Robert D 1923- *ConAu 5R*
Hodgson, Robert Willard 1893- *WhWNAA*
Hodgson, Shadworth Hollway 1832-1912 *Alli Sup, BrAu 19, NewC, OxEng*
Hodgson, Solomon *ChPo S1*
Hodgson, Studhome *Alli*
Hodgson, Thomas *Alli, BiDLA*
Hodgson, W E *MnBBF*
Hodgson, W J *ChPo*
Hodgson, William *Alli, Alli Sup, BiDLA*
Hodgson, William, Jr. *Alli*
Hodgson, William Archer 1887- *WhLA*
Hodgson, William Ballantyne 1815-1880 *Alli Sup, DcEnL*
Hodgson, William Brown 1801-1871 *DcNAA*
Hodgson, William Earl *Alli*
Hodgson, William Hope 1875-1918 *EncM&D*
Hodgson, William Noel 1893-1916 *ChPo, ChPo S2*
Hodgson, Mrs. Willoughby *WhLA*
Hodin, Joseph Paul 1905- *Au&Wr, ConAu 41*
Hodnett, Edward 1901- *AmA&B, ConAu 13R*
Hodows, Lewis 1872- *WhWNAA*
Hodowud, Edward Fred 1924- *AmSCAP 66*
Hodsdon, Nicholas E 1941- *ConAu 49*
Hodsdon, Nick *ConAu 49*
Hodskinson, Joseph *Alli, BiDLA*
Hodson, Mrs. *ChPo*
Hodson, Arnold Wienholt *WhLA*
Hodson, Frodsham *Alli, BiDLA*
Hodson, G *BiDLA*
Hodson, George *Alli*
Hodson, George Hewitt *Alli Sup*
Hodson, Henry Vincent 1906- *Au&Wr, ConAu 5R, WrD 1976*
Hodson, James *Alli, BiDLA*
Hodson, James Shirley *Alli Sup*
Hodson, John *Alli, PoIre*
Hodson, Joseph 1822-1912 *OhA&B*
Hodson, Margaret *Alli*
Hodson, Moses Mitchell 1855-1941 *IndAu 1917*
Hodson, Phineas *Alli*
Hodson, Richard Edmond *Alli Sup*
Hodson, Richard G *Alli Sup*
Hodson, Septimus *Alli, BiDLA*
Hodson, Thomas *Alli, Alli Sup, BiDLA*
Hodson, W *Alli, BiDLA*
Hodson, William *Alli, PoIre*
Hody, Edward *Alli*
Hody, Humphrey 1659-1706 *Alli, DcEnL*
Hodza, Michal Miloslav 1811-1870 *CasWL*
Hoe, J L *ChPo S1*
Hoe, Richard March 1812-1886 *OxAm*
Hoe, Robert 1784-1833 *REnAL*
Hoe, Robert 1839-1909 *Alli Sup, AmA&B, DcNAA, REnAL*
Hoe, William *Alli Sup*
Hoebel, Edward Adamson 1906- *ConAu 1R*
Hoeber, Arthur 1854-1915 *ChPo, DcNAA*
Hoeber, E W *Alli Sup*
Hoeck, Louis George 1863-1952 *OhA&B*
Hoeck, Theobald 1573-1618? *CasWL*
Hoecker, Karla 1901- *ConAu 49*
Hoefer, Edmund 1819-1882 *BiD&SB*
Hoeffer, Blanche Cummins 1881?-1938 *IndAu 1917*
Hoefkens, Laurence John 1907- *Au&Wr*
Hoegh-Guldberg, Frederick 1771-1852 *BiD&SB*
Hoehler, Fred Kenneth 1893- *OhA&B*
Hoehling, A A 1915- *ConAu 1R*

Hoehling, Mary 1914- *AuBYP*
Hoehn, Matthew 1883-1959 *REnAL*
Hoehner, Harold W 1935- *ConAu 37,
WrD 1976*
Hoekema, Anthony Andrew 1913- *Au&Wr,
ConAu 9R, WrD 1976*
Hoel, Adolf 1879- *WhLA*
Hoel, Isgurd 1890-1960 *Pen Eur*
Hoel, Robert F 1942- *ConAu 53*
Hoel, Sigurd 1890-1960 *CasWL, ClDMEuL,
EncWL, EvEuW*
Hoelzel, Alfred 1934- *ConAu 41*
Hoen, Pieter 't 1744?-1818 *CasWL*
Hoenig, J 1916- *ConAu 29, WrD 1976*
Hoenig, Sidney B 1907- *ConAu 45*
Hoeniger, F David 1921- *ConAu 41*
Hoenigswald, Henry M 1915- *ConAu 13R,
WrD 1976*
Hoerle, Helen 1895- *WhWNAA*
Hoernle, Augustus Frederick Rudolf *Alli Sup*
Hoernle, John Frederick David *Alli Sup*
Hoerschelmann, Fred Von 1910- *ModGL*
Hoetink, H 1931- *ConAu 23*
Hoexter, Corinne K 1927- *ConAu 49,
SmATA 6*
Hoey, A E B *Alli Sup*
Hoey, Christopher Clinton 1831?-1885 *PoIre*
Hoey, Frances Sarah 1830- *Alli Sup, BbD,
BiD&SB*
Hoey, John Cashel 1828-1892 *PoIre*
Hoey, John O'Reilly , *PoIre*
Hoey, William *Alli Sup*
Hofdijk, Willem Jakobszoon 1816-1888 *CasWL*
Hofdorp, Pim 1912- *Au&Wr*
Hofdyk, Willem Jakobsz 1816-1888 *BiD&SB*
Hofer, Andreas 1767-1810 *NewC, OxGer*
Hofer, Peter *WrD 1976*
Hofer, Philip 1898- *AmA&B, ChPo,
ChPo S1*
Hoff, Carol 1900- *ConAu 21*
Hoff, Ebbe Curtis 1906- *ConAu 57*
Hoff, Emanuel Buechley 1860-1928 *DcNAA,
OhA&B*
Hoff, Gertrud *CasWL*
Hoff, Harry Summerfield 1910- *ConAu 1R,
LongC, Pen Eng, WorAu*
Hoff, Hubert 1870- *WhLA*
Hoff, Marilyn 1942- *ConAu 17R*
Hoff, Mary Summerfield *NewC*
Hoff, Max 1905- *WhGrA*
Hoff, Rhoda *ChPo S1*
Hoff, Syd 1912- *AmA&B, Au&Wr, ChPo S1,
ConAu 5R, IlCB 1966, SmATA 9,
ThBJA*
Hoff, Sydney 1912- *AuBYP*
Hoff, Ursula 1909- *Au&Wr*
Hoff, Vivian Beaumont 1911- *AmSCAP 66*
Hoff, William Bainbridge 1846-1903 *Alli Sup,
DcAmA, DcNAA*
Hoffding, Harold 1843- *WhLA*
Hoffe, Monckton 1881?-1951 *DcLEnL, LongC*
Hoffecker, Savin 1908- *ConAu 5R*
Hoffeld, Donald R 1933- *ConAu 29*
Hoffenstein, Samuel 1890-1947 *AmA&B,
ChPo, DcNAA, REnAL, TwCA,
TwCA Sup*
Hoffer, Abram 1917- *BiDPar*
Hoffer, Charles R 1929- *ConAu 13R*
Hoffer, Charles Russell 1892- *IndAu 1917*
Hoffer, Clara *OxCan*
Hoffer, Eric 1902- *ConAu 13R, RAdv 1,
WorAu, WrD 1976*
Hofferbert, Richard I 1937- *ConAu 29*
Hoffert, H *Alli Sup*
Hoffham, Otto Christiaan Frederik 1744-1799
CasWL
Hoffine, Lyla *ConAu 1R*
Hoffman SEE ALSO Hoffmann, Hofman
Hoffman, Aaron 1880-1924 *DcNAA*
Hoffman, Abbie 1936- *AmA&B, ConAu 21*
Hoffman, Abram J *EarAB Sup*
Hoffman, Adeline M 1908- *ConAu 29*
Hoffman, Al 1902-1960 *AmSCAP 66*
Hoffman, Albert Frank 1867-1950 *OhA&B*
Hoffman, Alice Crowell *ChPo*
Hoffman, Alice Spencer *ChPo S1*
Hoffman, Annie E *Alli Sup*
Hoffman, Arthur A *Alli Sup*

Hoffman, Arthur Henry 1873- *WhWNAA*
Hoffman, Arthur S 1926- *ConAu 25*
Hoffman, Arthur Sullivant 1876- *AmA&B,
REnAL, WhWNAA*
Hoffman, Arthur W 1921- *ConAu 5R,
WrD 1976*
Hoffman, August Heinrich 1798-1874 *BbD,
DcEuL*
Hoffman, Bernard G 1925- *ConAu 41*
Hoffman, Betty Hannah 1918- *ConAu 9R*
Hoffman, Carl T *ChPo*
Hoffman, Charles Fenno 1806-1884 *Alli, AmA,
AmA&B, BiD&SB, CasWL, ChPo,
CnDAL, CyAL 2, DcAmA, DcBiA,
DcEnL, DcLEnL, DcNAA, EvLB, OxAm,
Pen Am, REnAL*
Hoffman, Charles Frederick 1830-1897 *Alli Sup,
DcAmA*
Hoffman, Charles Frederick 1843-1897 *DcNAA*
Hoffman, Charles W 1870- *OhA&B*
Hoffman, D T *ConAu XR*
Hoffman, Daniel 1923- *AmA&B, ConAu 1R,
ConLC 6, ConP 1970, ConP 1975,
DrAP 1975, WorAu, WrD 1976*
Hoffman, Dave A 1890-1958 *AmSCAP 66*
Hoffman, David *ChPo S2*
Hoffman, David 1784-1854 *Alli, AmA&B,
BiD&SB, BiDSA, CyAL 1, DcAmA,
DcNAA*
Hoffman, David Bancroft 1827- *Alli Sup,
DcAmA*
Hoffman, David Murray 1791-1878 *DcAmA,
DcNAA*
Hoffman, Donald 1933- *WrD 1976*
Hoffman, Donald S 1936- *ConAu 57*
Hoffman, Ernst Theodor Wilhelm 1776-1822
CasWL, DcEuL
Hoffman, Eugene Augustus 1829-1902 *Alli Sup,
ChPo, DcAmA, DcNAA*
Hoffman, Felix 1911- *IlCB 1956*
Hoffman, Frank Sargent 1852-1928 *AmLY,
DcAmA, DcNAA*
Hoffman, Franz 1814-1882 *CarSB*
Hoffman, Frederick J 1909-1967 *AmA&B,
ConAu 1R, WorAu*
Hoffman, Frederick Ludwig 1865-1946 *DcNAA*
Hoffman, Gail 1896- *ConAu 5R*
Hoffman, George W 1914- *ConAu 13R*
Hoffman, Gloria *AuBYP*
Hoffman, Heinrich 1809-1874 *DcEuL, OxEng*
Hoffman, H ALSO Hoffman-Donner, H
Hoffman, Helmut 1912- *ConAu 1R*
Hoffman, Hester Rosalyn 1895- *ConAu P-1,
IndAu 1917*
Hoffman, J Milton 1846-1928 *HsB&A*
Hoffman, Jack 1917- *AmSCAP 66*
Hoffman, James David 1868-1938 *IndAu 1917*
Hoffman, Jill *DrAP 1975*
Hoffman, John N 1804-1857 *Alli, DcAmA,
DcNAA*
Hoffman, John Thompson 1828- *Alli Sup*
Hoffman, Joseph G 1909-1974 *ConAu 53*
Hoffman, Kai 1874-1949 *Pen Eur*
Hoffman, L Richard 1930- *ConAu 13R*
Hoffman, Lee 1932- *ConAu 25*
Hoffman, Lisa 1919- *ConAu 29*
Hoffman, Lois Wladis 1929- *ConAu 13R*
Hoffman, Malvina 1887-1966 *AmA&B,
REnAL*
Hoffman, Mary Jane *Alli Sup*
Hoffman, Michael J 1939- *ConAu 29,
WrD 1976*
Hoffman, Murray 1791-1878 *Alli, Alli Sup,
DcNAA*
Hoffman, Olivia Watson *AmSCAP 66*
Hoffman, Paul 1934- *ConAu 45*
Hoffman, Phyllis M 1944- *ConAu 29,
SmATA 4*
Hoffman, Professor *MnBBF*
Hoffman, Richard *DrAP 1975*
Hoffman, Richard 1831-1909 *DcNAA*
Hoffman, Richard L 1937- *ConAu 29,
WrD 1976*
Hoffman, Robert Louis 1937- *ConAu 37,
WrD 1976*
Hoffman, Ross John Swartz 1902- *AmA&B,
BkC 3, CatA 1947*
Hoffman, Stanley 1928- *AmA&B*

Hoffman, Stanley 1944- *ConLC 5,
DrAF 1976*
Hoffman, Stanley D 1926- *AmSCAP 66*
Hoffman, Viktor Viktorovich 1884-1911 *DcRusL*
Hoffman, Wickham 1821-1900 *Alli Sup,
BiD&SB, DcAmA, DcNAA*
Hoffman, Willa M 1914- *ConAu 61*
Hoffman, William *MnnWr*
Hoffman, William 1925- *AmA&B, ConAu 21*
Hoffman, William Dawson 1884-1952 *AmA&B*
Hoffman, William M 1939- *ConAu 57, ConDr,
DrAP 1975, WrD 1976*
Hoffman-Donner, Heinrich 1809-1894 *ChPo*
Hoffman-Donner, H ALSO Hoffman, H
Hoffmann SEE ALSO Hoffman, Hofman
Hoffmann, Adolf G 1890- *AmSCAP 66*
Hoffmann, Alexius 1863-1940 *DcNAA*
Hoffmann, Ann Marie 1930- *ConAu 37,
WrD 1976*
Hoffmann, August Heinrich 1798-1874 *BiD&SB,
EvEuW, REn*
Hoffmann, A H ALSO Hoffmann VonF, A
Hoffmann, Banesh 1906- *ConAu 5R,
WrD 1976*
Hoffmann, Charles G 1921- *ConAu 13R*
Hoffmann, Christine *IlBYP*
Hoffmann, Donald 1933- *ConAu 25*
Hoffmann, Eleanor 1895- *ConAu P-1*
Hoffmann, Erik P 1939- *ConAu 33*
Hoffmann, Ernest Theodor Amadeus 1776-1822
*BiD&SB, CyWA, EuA, NewC, OxEng,
OxFr, OxGer, RCom, REn, WhCL*
Hoffmann, Ernst Theodor Wilhelm 1776-1822
BbD, EvEuW, Pen Eur
Hoffmann, Felix 1911-1975 *ChPo S1,
ConAu 29, ConAu 57, ConAu 61, IlBYP,
IlCB 1966, SmATA 9, ThBJA*
Hoffmann, Francois-Benoit 1760-1828 *OxFr*
Hoffmann, Franz 1814-1882 *BiD&SB*
Hoffmann, Frederick 1832-1904 *Alli Sup,
DcNAA*
Hoffmann, Frederick August *Alli Sup*
Hoffmann, Hans 1848-1909 *BiD&SB, OxGer*
Hoffmann, Heinrich 1809-1894 *BiD&SB,
EvEuW, WhCL*
Hoffmann, H ALSO Hoffmann-Donner, H
Hoffmann, Hilde 1927- *ConAu 25, IlBYP*
Hoffmann, Kai Anton Carl Nyholm 1874-1949
CasWL
Hoffmann, Leon-Francois 1932- *ConAu 49*
Hoffmann, Malcolm Arthur 1912- *WrD 1976*
Hoffmann, Margaret Jones 1910- *AuBYP,
ConAu 5R*
Hoffmann, Max 1873-1963 *AmSCAP 66*
Hoffmann, Peggy 1910- *AuBYP, ConAu XR,
WrD 1976*
Hoffmann, Phil 1868- *WhWNAA*
Hoffmann, Professor *Alli Sup*
Hoffmann, Ralph 1870-1932 *DcAmA, DcNAA*
Hoffmann, Stanley 1928- *ConAu 13R*
Hoffmann, U J *Alli Sup*
Hoffmann, William *Alli Sup*
Hoffmann-Donner, Heinrich 1809-1894 *CarSB,
ChPo S1*
Hoffmann-Donner, H ALSO Hoffmann, H
Hoffmann VonFallersleben, August H 1798-1874
CasWL, EuA, OxGer, Pen Eur
Hoffmann, VonF, A ALSO Hoffmann, Aug
Hoffmann VonHofmannswaldau, Christian
1617-1679 *BiD&SB*
Hoffmannswaldau, Christian Hoffmann Von
1617-1679 *DcEuL, EvEuW, OxGer*
Hoffmanowa, Klementyna 1798-1845 *CasWL*
Hoffmeister, Adolf 1902-1973 *ConAu 41,
Pen Eur, WhGrA*
Hoffmeister, Donald Frederick 1916- *ConAu 53,
WrD 1976*
Hoffner, Pelagie Doane *AuBYP*
Hoffnung, Gerard 1925-1959 *ChPo S1,
WhGrA*
Hofinger, Johannes 1905- *ConAu P-1*
Hofland, Mrs. B 1770-1844 *BiDLA*
Hofland, Barbara Hoole 1770-1844 *Alli,
BrAu 19, ChPo, ChPo S2, DcEnL*
Hofland, M A *ChPo, ChPo S1, ChPo S2*
Hofland, Thomas Christopher 1777-1843 *Alli,
ChPo*

Hofland, Mrs. Thomas Christopher 1770-1844 *Alli*

Hofland, Mrs. W H 1770-1844 *CarSB*

Hofling, Charles K 1920- *ConAu 41*

Hofman, Anton *ConAu XR*

Hofman, Caroline *ChPo, ChPo S1*

Hofman, David 1908- *Au&Wr*

Hofman, Heinrich Oscar 1852-1924 *DcAmA, DcNAA*

Hofman, Julius 1865- *AmLY*

Hofmann, Armin 1920- *WhGrA*

Hofmann, August Wilhelm 1818- *Alli, Alli Sup*

Hofmann, Friedrich 1813-1888 *BiD&SB*

Hofmann, Hans 1880- *REn*

Hofmann, Hans 1923- *ConAu 1R, WrD 1976*

Hofmann, Julius K 1865-1928 *DcNAA, WhWNAA*

Hofmann, Melita C *ConAu 5R*

Hofmann, Tabea *ChPo S1*

Hofmann VonHofmannswaldau, Christian 1617-1679 *CasWL, EuA, OxGer, Pen Eur, REn*

Hofmannsthal, Hugo Hofmann Von 1874-1929 *AtlBL, CasWL, ClDMEuL, CnMWL, CnThe, EncWL, EvEuW, McGWD, ModGL, ModWD, NewC, OxEng, OxGer, Pen Eur, REn, REnWD, TwCA, TwCA Sup, TwCW*

Hofprediger, Johannes Martin Vogel *WhLA*

Hofshteyn, David 1889-1952 *CasWL*

Hofsinde, Robert 1902-1973 *AuBYP, ConAu 45, IlCB 1956, ThBJA*

Hofstadter, Albert 1910- *ConAu 33*

Hofstadter, Richard 1916-1970 *AmA&B, ConAu 1R, ConAu 29, OxAm, Pen Am, REn, REnAL, WorAu*

Hofstead, John Andrew 1885- *ChPo S1*

Hofstede, Geert H 1928- *ConAu 41*

Hofstetter, Henry W 1914- *WrD 1976*

Hog, James *Alli*

Hog, Sir Roger *Alli*

Hogaeus, Gulielmus *Alli*

Hogan *Alli*

Hogan, Arthur Riky *Alli Sup*

Hogan, Bernice Harris 1929- *ChPo, ConAu 13R*

Hogan, E *Alli*

Hogan, Edmund *Alli Sup*

Hogan, Francis T 1916- *AmSCAP 66*

Hogan, George *MnBBF*

Hogan, Inez 1895- *AuBYP, ConAu 1R, MorJA, SmATA 2*

Hogan, Inez 1900- *IlCB 1945*

Hogan, James 1898- *CatA 1952*

Hogan, James Francis 1855- *Alli Sup, BbD, BiD&SB, Chmbr 3, PoIre*

Hogan, John *PoIre*

Hogan, John 1805-1892 *Alli Sup, AmA, BiDSA, DcAmA, DcNAA*

Hogan, John A *BiDSA*

Hogan, John Baptist 1829?-1901 *DcAmA, DcNAA*

Hogan, John Charles 1919- *ConAu 17R, WrD 1976*

Hogan, John D 1927- *ConAu 45*

Hogan, John Joseph 1829-1913 *DcNAA*

Hogan, John Sheridan 1815?-1859 *Alli, BbtC, DcNAA, PoIre*

Hogan, John V L 1890- *WhWNAA*

Hogan, Katherine E *Alli Sup*

Hogan, Louise E 1855-1929 *DcAmA, DcNAA*

Hogan, Michael 1832-1899 *Alli Sup, PoIre*

Hogan, Paul 1927- *ConAu 61*

Hogan, Ray 1908- *ConAu 9R*

Hogan, Ray 1918- *Au&Wr*

Hogan, Robert F 1927- *ConAu 41*

Hogan, Robert Goode 1930- *Au&Wr, ConAu 1R, WrD 1976*

Hogan, Robert J 1897- *WhWNAA*

Hogan, Thomas *EarAB, EarAB Sup*

Hogan, Ursula 1899- *ConAu 5R*

Hogan, W *Alli*

Hogan, Walter d1921 *DcNAA*

Hogan, Willard N 1909- *ConAu 21*

Hogan, William d1848 *Alli, DcNAA*

Hogan, William Francis 1930- *ConAu 25*

Hogan, William Ranson *TexWr*

Hogarth, Jr. *ConAu XR, SmATA 6*

Hogarth, Alfred Moore 1876- *WhLA*

Hogarth, David George 1862-1927 *DcLEnL, OxEng*

Hogarth, Douglas *ConAu XR*

Hogarth, George 1777-1870 *Alli, Alli Sup, DcEnL*

Hogarth, Grace Weston 1905- *Au&Wr*

Hogarth, Paul 1917- *Au&Wr, ConAu 49, WhGrA*

Hogarth, Richard *Alli*

Hogarth, William 1697-1764 *Alli, AtlBL, BkIE, ChPo, NewC, REn*

Hogarth, William, Jr. 1882- *ConAmA*

Hogas, Calistrat 1847-1917 *CasWL*

Hogben, James *Alli*

Hogben, John *ChPo*

Hogben, Lancelot Thomas 1895-1975 *Chmbr 3, ConAu 61, EvLB, LongC, NewC, TwCA, TwCA Sup*

Hogberg, Olof 1855-1932 *ClDMEuL, EncWL*

Hogbin, Alfred C *Alli Sup*

Hogbin, Herbert Ian Priestley 1904- *Au&Wr, ConAu 9R, WrD 1976*

Hoge, Mrs. A H *Alli Sup*

Hoge, Dean Richard 1937- *ConAu 53*

Hoge, Ellice *ChPo*

Hoge, James 1752-1820 *BiDSA*

Hoge, Moses 1752-1820 *Alli, DcAmA*

Hoge, Moses Drury *BiDSA*

Hoge, Peyton Harrison 1858-1940 *AmA&B, AmLY, BiDSA, DcNAA, WhWNAA*

Hoge, William James 1821-1864 *Alli Sup, BiDSA, DcAmA, DcNAA, OhA&B*

Hogeboom, Amy 1891- *AuBYP*

Hogendorn, Jan Stafford 1937- *ConAu 37, WrD 1976*

Hogg, Beth 1917- *AuBYP, ConAu 5R*

Hogg, Charles Edgar 1852-1935 *DcNAA*

Hogg, David *Alli Sup*

Hogg, Edward *Alli*

Hogg, Francis Roberts *Alli Sup*

Hogg, Garry Lester 1902- *Au&Wr, ConAu 23, SmATA 2, WhCL, WrD 1976*

Hogg, George Crawford *Alli Sup*

Hogg, Henry *Alli Sup*

Hogg, Ian V 1926- *ConAu 29*

Hogg, J J *Alli*

Hogg, Jabez *Alli, Alli Sup*

Hogg, James *Chmbr 3*

Hogg, James 1770-1835 *Alli, AtlBL, BbD, BiD&SB, BiDLA, BiDLA Sup, BrAu 19, CasWL, ChPo, ChPo S1, ChPo S2, DcEnA, DcEnL, DcEuL, DcLEnL, EvLB, MouLC 3, NewC, OxEng, Pen Eng, REn, WebEAL*

Hogg, James 1800-1866 *Alli Sup, BbtC, DcNAA, PoIre*

Hogg, John *Alli, Alli Sup, BbtC*

Hogg, John 1803-1880 *Alli Sup*

Hogg, John 1839- *ChPo S1*

Hogg, John Thomas 1907- *Au&Wr*

Hogg, John W *Alli Sup*

Hogg, Lewis Maydwell *Alli Sup*

Hogg, M G *Alli Sup*

Hogg, O F G *WrD 1976*

Hogg, Oliver Frederick Gillian 1887- *Au&Wr, WrD 1976*

Hogg, Quintin McGarel 1907- *ConAu P-1*

Hogg, Robert *Alli*

Hogg, Robert 1864- *ChPo, ChPo S1*

Hogg, Robert Lawrence 1942- *ConAu 53, ConP 1970, OxCan*

Hogg, Thomas *Alli, BiDLA*

Hogg, Thomas E *BiDSA*

Hogg, Thomas Jefferson 1792-1862 *CasWL, EvLB, NewC, OxEng, Pen Eng, REn*

Hogg, W Richey 1921- *ConAu 1R*

Hogg, W T M 1842- *ChPo*

Hogg, Walter *ChPo S1*

Hogg, Wilson Thomas 1852- *DcAmA*

Hogg, Wilson T ALSO Hogue, Wilson T

Hoggan, Frances Elizabeth 1843- *Alli Sup*

Hoggan, William Brooke *Alli Sup*

Hoggard, James 1941- *WrD 1976*

Hoggard, Miles *Alli*

Hoggart, Richard 1918- *Au&Wr, ConAu 9R, LongC, WorAu, WrD 1976*

Hogge, George *Alli Sup*

Hoghendorp, Gijsbrecht Van 1589-1639 *CasWL*

Hogins, James Burl 1936- *ConAu 53*

Hogner, Dorothy Childs *AmA&B, AuBYP, ConAu 33, JBA 1951, OxCan, SmATA 4, WhWNAA, WrD 1976*

Hogner, Nils 1893-1970 *AuBYP, IlCB 1945, IlCB 1956, IlCB 1966, JBA 1951*

Hogrefe, Pearl *ConAu P-1*

Hogrogian, Nancy *ChPo S1*

Hogrogian, Nonny 1932- *AuBYP, BkP, ChLR 2, ChPo S2, ConAu 45, IlBYP, IlCB 1966, NewbC 1966, SmATA 7, ThBJA*

Hogue, Arthur R 1906- *ConAu 37, WrD 1976*

Hogue, Richard 1946- *ConAu 49*

Hogue, Wilson Thomas 1852-1920 *DcNAA*

Hogue, Wilson T ALSO Hogg, Wilson T

Hogwood, Mackenzie *MnBBF*

Hohberg, Wolfgang Helmhard, Freiherr Von 1612-1688 *CasWL, OxGer*

Hohenberg, John 1906- *AmA&B, ConAu 13R, WrD 1976*

Hohenberg, Paul M 1933- *ConAu 25*

Hohenburg, Markgraf Von *OxGer*

Hohendahl, Peter Uwe 1936- *ConAu 45*

Hohengarten, Carl 1902- *AmSCAP 66*

Hohenhausen, Baroness Elizabeth P A 1789-1857 *BiD&SB*

Hohenheim, Franziska, Reichsgrafin Von 1748-1811 *OxGer*

Hohenlohe-Schillingsfurst, Chlodwig Zu 1819-1901 *OxGer*

Hohenstein, Henry John 1931- *ConAu 53, WrD 1976*

Hohenwarter, Peter 1894- *BiDPar*

Hohfeld, Wesley Newcomb 1879-1918 *DcNAA*

Hohimer, Frank 1928- *ConAu 57*

Hohlbaum, Robert 1886-1955 *OxGer*

Hohlfeld, Alexander Rudolf 1865- *WhWNAA*

Hohlfelder, Robert Lane 1938- *ConAu 45*

Hohman, Arthur Joseph 1886-1943 *DcNAA*

Hohn, Hazel *ConAu 5R, WrD 1976*

Hohnen, David 1925- *Au&Wr, ConAu 21, WrD 1976*

Hohoff, Tay *ConAu XR*

Hoiby, Lee 1926- *AmSCAP 66*

Hoig, Stan 1924- *ConAu 1R*

Hoijer, Benjamin 1767-1812 *CasWL*

Hoijer, Bjorn-Erik 1907- *CnMD*

Hoisington, Harland 1896?-1973 *ConAu 45*

Hoisington, Henry Richard 1801-1858 *DcNAA*

Hoisington, May Folwell 1874- *ChPo, WhWNAA*

Hojeda, Diego De 1571?-1615 *CasWL, DcEuL, DcSpL, EvEuW, Pen Am, Pen Eur*

Hokanson, Margrethe 1893- *AmSCAP 66*

Hoke, Helen L 1903- *AuBYP*

Hoke, Jacob 1825-1893 *Alli Sup, DcAmA, DcNAA*

Hoke, John Lindsay 1925- *ConAu 41, SmATA 7*

Hoke, Kremer Jacob 1878- *WhWNAA*

Hoke, Russell Allen 1896- *AmA&B, WhWNAA*

Hoke, Travis Henderson 1892-1947 *AmA&B*

Hoker, John *Alli*

Hokusai *REn*

Holabird, Samuel B 1824- *Alli Sup*

Holaday, Allan Gibson 1916- *ConAu 37*

Holahan, Martha Eileen 1863- *PoIre*

Holan, Vladimir 1905- *CasWL, ModSL 2, WhTwL, WorAu*

Holand, Hjalmar Rued 1872-1963 *AmA&B, WhWNAA*

Holbach, Baron Paul Heinrich Dietrich D' 1723-1789 *BiD&SB, CasWL, DcEuL, EvEuW, Pen Eur*

Holbach, Baron Paul Henri Thiry D' 1723-1789 *EuA, NewC, OxEng, OxFr*

Holbeach, Henry *Alli Sup, DcEnL, NewC*

Holbeche, Philippa Jack 1919- *Au&Wr, ConAu P-1*

Holbein, Hans 1497?-1543 *AtlBL, NewC, OxGer, REn*

Holberg, Ludvig, Baron Holberg 1684-1754 *BiD&SB, CasWL, CnThe, DcEuL, EuA, EvEuW, McGWD, Pen Eur, REnWD*

Holberg, Richard A 1889-1942 *AuBYP*,
JBA 1951
Holberg, Ruth Langland 1889- *ConAu 5R*,
JBA 1951, *SmATA 1*, *WrD 1976*
Holberry, Mark *Alli*
Holberton, Wakeman *Alli Sup*
Holbik, Karel 1920- *ConAu 37*, *WrD 1976*
Holbo, Paul Sothe 1929- *ConAu 25*,
WrD 1976
Holborn, Hajo 1902-1969 *ConAu 25*
Holborn, Ian Bernard Stoughton 1872-1925
ChPo, *ChPo S1*
Holborn, Louise W 1898- *ConAu 25*
Holborne, Anthony *Alli*
Holbourne, Sir Robert d1647 *Alli*
Holbrey, Joseph *Alli Sup*
Holbrook, Alfred 1816-1909 *Alli Sup*, *DcAmA*,
DcNAA, *OhA&B*
Holbrook, Anthony *Alli*
Holbrook, Bill 1921- *ConAu 61*
Holbrook, Brewster *WhWNAA*
Holbrook, Carey 1885- *ChPo*
Holbrook, David Kenneth 1923- *Au&Wr*,
ChPo, *ChPo S1*, *ConAu 5R*,
ConNov 1972, *ConP 1970*, *ConP 1975*,
NewC, *WorAu*, *WrD 1976*
Holbrook, Edmund S 1816-1897 *ChPo S1*
Holbrook, Edwin A *Alli Sup*
Holbrook, Evans 1875-1932 *DcNAA*,
WhWNAA
Holbrook, Florence 1860?-1932 *AmLY*,
DcAmA, *DcNAA*
Holbrook, J *Alli*
Holbrook, J P *Alli Sup*
Holbrook, James H 1812-1864 *Alli Sup*,
DcAmA, *DcNAA*
Holbrook, Jennifer Kearns 1931- *WrD 1976*
Holbrook, John *DrAP 1975*
Holbrook, John C *Alli Sup*, *DcNAA*
Holbrook, John Edwards 1794?-1871 *Alli*,
BiDSA, *CyAL 1*, *DcAmA*, *DcNAA*
Holbrook, Josiah 1788-1854 *AmA*, *ChPo S2*,
DcNAA, *OhA&B*, *OxAm*, *REnAL*
Holbrook, Kennedy *Alli Sup*
Holbrook, Martin Luther 1831-1902 *Alli Sup*,
DcAmA, *DcNAA*, *OhA&B*
Holbrook, Peter *ConAu XR*
Holbrook, Reginald Heber 1845-1910 *Alli Sup*,
OhA&B
Holbrook, Richard Thayer 1870-1934 *AmA&B*,
DcNAA
Holbrook, Richard Thayer 1870- *WhWNAA*
Holbrook, Ruth *ChPo*
Holbrook, Sabra *ConAu XR*
Holbrook, Silas Pinckney 1796-1835 *AmA&B*,
BiDSA, *CyAL 1*, *DcAmA*, *DcNAA*
Holbrook, Stewart Hall 1893-1964 *AmA&B*,
AuBYP, *ConAu P-1*, *OxAm*, *REnAL*,
SmATA 2, *ThBJA*, *TwCA Sup*,
WhPNW, *WhWNAA*
Holbrook, Zephaniah Swift 1847-1901 *DcNAA*
Holbrooke, W *Alli*
Holburn, James 1900- *Au&Wr*
Holby, John *MnBBF*
Holck, Manfred, Jr. 1930- *ConAu 17R*,
WrD 1976
Holcomb, Carlysle Henry 1888- *OhA&B*
Holcomb, George L 1911- *ConAu 45*
Holcomb, Helen H *Alli Sup*
Holcomb, Jerry 1927- *ConAu 25*
Holcomb, Thomas A E *Alli Sup*
Holcomb, Walter 1853-1938 *DcNAA*
Holcombe, Arthur Norman 1884- *AmA&B*,
ConAu 29, *WhWNAA*
Holcombe, Burton 1911- *WhWNAA*
Holcombe, Chester 1844-1912 *BiD&SB*,
DcAmA, *DcNAA*
Holcombe, Henry 1762-1826 *BiDSA*, *DcAmA*,
DcNAA
Holcombe, Hosea 1780-1841 *BiDSA*, *DcAmA*,
DcNAA
Holcombe, James Philemon 1820-1873 *Alli*,
Alli Sup, *BbtC*, *BiDSA*, *DcAmA*,
DcNAA
Holcombe, John Walker 1853-1940 *IndAu 1816*
Holcombe, Return Ira 1845-1916 *DcNAA*,
OhA&B
Holcombe, William *Alli*

Holcombe, William Frederick 1827-1904
Alli Sup, *DcAmA*, *DcNAA*
Holcombe, William Henry 1825-1893 *Alli*,
Alli Sup, *AmA&B*, *BiDSA*, *DcAmA*,
DcNAA, *OhA&B*
Holcot, Robert d1349 *Alli*, *DcEnL*
Holcroft, Fanny *Alli*, *BiDLA*
Holcroft, Montague Harry 1902- *DcLEnL*,
LongC
Holcroft, Montague Henry 1902- *TwCW*
Holcroft, Thomas 1745-1809 *Alli*, *BiD&SB*,
BrAu, *CasWL*, *ChPo S1*, *Chmbr 2*,
DcEnL, *DcEuL*, *DcLEnL*, *EvLB*, *NewC*,
OxEng, *REn*, *WebEAL*
Hold, Mrs. Roland *AmA&B*
Holden, Albert P *ChPo*
Holden, Anne Stratton 1887- *AmSCAP 66*
Holden, Arthur Cort 1890- *ChPo*, *ChPo S1*
Holden, Austin Wells *Alli Sup*
Holden, Beatrice 1873?- *Br&AmS*
Holden, C F *Alli Sup*
Holden, C W *PoIre*
Holden, David 1924- *Au&Wr*, *ConAu 41*
Holden, Donald 1931- *ConAu 45*
Holden, E M *ChPo S1*
Holden, Edgar 1838-1909 *DcNAA*
Holden, Edward Goodman 1839-1927 *DcNAA*
Holden, Edward Singleton 1846-1914 *Alli Sup*,
BiD&SB, *BiDSA*, *DcAmA*, *DcNAA*
Holden, Frances Viola *ChPo S1*
Holden, G d1793 *Alli*
Holden, George *Alli*, *Alli Sup*
Holden, George Henry 1848-1914 *Alli Sup*,
DcAmA, *DcNAA*
Holden, George Parker 1869-1935 *DcNAA*,
WhWNAA
Holden, Harrington William *Alli Sup*
Holden, Henry 1596-1662 *Alli*, *DcEnL*
Holden, Horace *Alli*
Holden, Hubert Ashton *Alli*
Holden, Inez 1906-1974 *ConAu 53*
Holden, J *Alli*, *BiDLA*
Holden, J W *Alli Sup*
Holden, James *Alli Sup*
Holden, James D 1846-1925 *DcNAA*
Holden, James Milnes 1918- *Au&Wr*,
WrD 1976
Holden, John *Alli*, *Alli Sup*
Holden, John A 1855-1941 *DcNAA*
Holden, John Jarvis *ChPo S1*
Holden, Jonathan 1941- *ConAu 45*,
DrAP 1975
Holden, Laurence 1710- *Alli*
Holden, Libby 1923- *AmSCAP 66*
Holden, Luther *Alli*, *Alli Sup*
Holden, Luther Loud *Alli Sup*, *DcAmA*
Holden, Martha Everts 1844-1896 *AmA&B*,
DcNAA
Holden, Matthew, Jr. 1931- *ConAu 57*,
LivBAA, *WrD 1976*
Holden, Molly 1927- *ConAu 25*, *ConP 1970*,
ConP 1975, *WrD 1976*
Holden, Oliver 1765-1844 *AmA&B*
Holden, Patrick F 1872- *PoIre*
Holden, R *Alli*, *Alli Sup*
Holden, R J *ChPo*
Holden, Raymond Peckham 1894-1972 *AmA&B*,
AuBYP, *ConAu 5R*, *ConAu 37*, *REnAL*,
TwCA, *TwCA Sup*
Holden, S *Alli Sup*
Holden, Samuel *Alli*
Holden, Sidney 1900-1947 *AmSCAP 66*
Holden, Thomas *Alli*
Holden, Vincent F 1911-1972 *ConAu 37*
Holden, W Sprague 1909-1973 *ChPo S1*,
ConAu 1R, *ConAu 45*
Holden, Ward Andrews 1886- *WhWNAA*
Holden, Warren *Alli Sup*
Holden, Warren 1817-1903 *DcNAA*
Holden, William Clifford *Alli*, *Alli Sup*
Holden, William Curry 1896- *AmA&B*,
Au&Wr
Holden, William Curry 1898- *TexWr*,
WhWNAA
Holder, Reverend *BiDLA*
Holder, Arthur Ernest 1860- *WhWNAA*
Holder, C S *ChPo*, *ChPo S1*
Holder, Charles Frederick 1851-1915 *Alli Sup*,

AmA&B, *BiD&SB*, *DcAmA*, *DcNAA*
Holder, Francis Jerome 1876- *WhWNAA*
Holder, Geoffrey Lamont 1931- *BlkAW*
Holder, Glenn 1906- *ConAu 41*
Holder, Henry Evans *Alli*
Holder, J N *BlkAW*
Holder, James Elliott *BlkAW*
Holder, Joseph Bassett 1824-1888 *Alli Sup*,
DcAmA, *DcNAA*
Holder, Lawrence *BlkAW*
Holder, Owen 1921- *Au&Wr*
Holder, P *OxCan Sup*
Holder, William d1697 *Alli*
Holder, William G 1937- *ConAu 25*
Holderlin, Friedrich 1770-1843 *AtlBL*,
BiD&SB, *DcEuL*, *EuA*, *McGWD*,
OxGer, *Pen Eur*, *RCom*, *REn*
Holderlin, Johann Christian Friedrich 1770-1843
CasWL, *EvEuW*
Holderness, Mary *Alli*
Holdgate, Martin Wyatt 1931- *Au&Wr*,
WrD 1976
Holdheim, William Wolfgang 1926- *ConAu 1R*,
WrD 1976
Holdich, Catherine *Alli Sup*
Holdich, Charles Walter *Alli Sup*
Holdich, Joseph 1804-1893 *Alli*, *DcAmA*,
DcNAA
Holding, Carlisle B 1849-1929 *Alli Sup*, *CarSB*,
OhA&B
Holding, Charles H 1897- *ConAu P-1*
Holding, Elisabeth Sanxay 1889-1955 *AmA&B*,
EncM&D, *WhWNAA*
Holding, Elizabeth E *BiDSA*
Holding, Ephraim *DcEnL*
Holding, James 1907- *AuBYP*, *ConAu 25*,
SmATA 3
Holding, John *Alli Sup*
Holding, Thomas Hiram *Alli Sup*
Holding, Val *MnBBF*
Holditch, Benjamin *Alli*
Holditch, Benjamin 1770-1824 *Alli*
Holditch, Rob *Alli*
Holdren, Bob Ray 1922- *ConAu 37*,
IndAu 1917
Holdren, John P 1944- *ConAu 33*
Holdreth, Lionel H *Alli*, *Alli Sup*
Holdsworth, Annie E *BbD*
Holdsworth, Edmund W H *Alli Sup*
Holdsworth, Edward 1688-1747 *Alli*, *DcEnL*
Holdsworth, Gladys Bronwyn *WhLA*
Holdsworth, Irene *Au&Wr*, *ConAu P-1*
Holdsworth, Joseph *Alli Sup*
Holdsworth, Mary 1908- *ConAu P-1*
Holdsworth, Philip J *Alli Sup*
Holdsworth, Richard 1590-1649 *Alli*, *DcEnL*
Holdsworth, W *Alli*
Holdsworth, William Andrews *Alli Sup*
Holdsworth, William Curtis *IlBYP*
Holdsworth, Richard 1590-1649 *Alli*, *DcEnL*
Holdsworth, Sir William Searle 1871- *WhLA*
Holdsworth, Winch *Alli*
Hole, Charles *Alli Sup*
Hole, Christina 1896- *Au&Wr*
Hole, E S *ChPo S2*
Hole, Hugh Marshall 1805- *WhLA*
Hole, James *Alli Sup*
Hole, John *Alli*, *BiDLA*
Hole, Matthew d1730? *Alli*
Hole, Richard 1750-1803 *Alli*, *DcEnL*
Hole, Robert *Alli*
Hole, Samuel Reynolds 1819-1904 *Alli Sup*,
BiD&SB, *DcLEnL*, *OxEng*
Hole, W G *Alli Sup*
Hole, William *Alli*, *Alli Sup*, *ChPo S2*
Holecek, Josef 1853-1929 *CasWL*, *ClDMEuL*,
EncWL
Holeman, F R *Alli Sup*
Holeman, Francis Rader d1913 *DcNAA*
Holford, Lord 1907- *Au&Wr*
Holford, Miss *BiDLA*
Holford, George *Alli*, *BiDLA*, *BiDLA Sup*
Holford, Ingrid 1920- *Au&Wr*, *WrD 1976*
Holford, John Henry 1830-1870 *Alli Sup*
Holford, Mrs. M *Alli*, *BiDLA*
Holford, Margaret 1778-1852 *Alli*, *ChPo*
Holgate, C W *Alli Sup*
Holgate, Jerome Bonaparte *Alli*, *Alli Sup*,
DcNAA

Holgate, Thomas Franklin 1859-1945 *DcNAA, WhWNAA*
Holger Danske *NewC, OxFr*
Holiband, Claudius *Alli*
Holiday, Barten *Alli*
Holiday, F W 1921- *ConAu 25*
Holiday, Henry 1839-1927 *ChPo, ChPo S2*
Holifield, Harold *BlkAW*
Holiner, Mann 1897-1958 *AmSCAP 66*
Holinshead, Raphael 1520?-1580? *Alli*
Holinshed, Raphael 1520?-1580? *Alli, AtlBL, BbD, BiD&SB, BrAu, CasWL, Chmbr 1, CrE&SL, DcEnA, DcEnL, DcLEnL, EvLB, NewC, OxEng, Pen Eng, REn, WebEAL*
Holisher, Desider 1901-1972 *ConAu 19, ConAu 37, SmATA 6*
Holiwell, Mrs. M J H *BbtC*
Holkot, Robert *Alli*
Holl, Adelaide Hinkle 1910- *AmA&B, ConAu 1R, SmATA 8*
Holl, Henry *Alli Sup*
Holl, Jack M 1937- *ConAu 57*
Holladay, Mrs. Lewis L *OhA&B*
Holladay, Sylvia A 1936- *ConAu 57*
Holladay, William L 1926- *ConAu 53*
Hollaender, Felix 1867-1931 *OxGer*
Holland *DcEnL*
Holland, Captain *Alli*
Holland, Lady *Alli*
Holland, Miss *Alli*
Holland, Mrs. *BiDPar*
Holland, Abraham *Alli*
Holland, Alma Boice *ConAu 29*
Holland, Barbara A 1925- *ConAu 57, DrAP 1975*
Holland, Bernard Henry 1856-1926 *ChPo*
Holland, C *Alli Sup*
Holland, Cecelia Anastasia 1943- *ConAu 17R, DrAF 1976, WrD 1976*
Holland, Charles *Alli Sup*
Holland, Claudia 1903- *AmA&B, AmNov*
Holland, Clive 1866- *Alli Sup, BiD&SB, MnBBF, WhLA*
Holland, Deborah Katherine 1947- *ConAu 57*
Holland, Denis 1826?-1872 *Alli Sup, PoIre*
Holland, DeWitte T 1923- *ConAu 45*
Holland, Edward *Alli Sup, ChPo, PoIre*
Holland, Edward Clifford 1794-1824 *BiDSA, DcAmA*
Holland, Edwin Clifford 1794-1824 *Alli, AmA, AmA&B, CnDAL, CyAL 1, DcNAA, OxAm, REnAL*
Holland, Elihu Goodwin 1817-1878 *Alli, CyAL 2, DcNAA*
Holland, Elizabeth Anne 1928- *Au&Wr, WrD 1976*
Holland, Ernest Otto 1874- *IndAu 1816, WhWNAA*
Holland, Francis *Alli*
Holland, Francis Ross, Jr. 1927- *ConAu 33, WrD 1976*
Holland, Frederick May 1836-1908 *Alli Sup, BiD&SB, DcAmA, DcNAA*
Holland, Frederick West 1811-1895 *Alli Sup, CyAL 2, DcAmA, DcNAA*
Holland, G *Alli*
Holland, G A *TexWr*
Holland, G Calvert *Alli, Alli Sup*
Holland, Glen A 1920- *ConAu 37*
Holland, H W *Alli Sup*
Holland, Henry *Alli, BbtC, BiDLA*
Holland, Sir Henry 1788-1873 *Alli, Alli Sup, BiDLA Sup, DcEnL*
Holland, Lord Henry Edward Fox 1802- *Alli*
Holland, Lord Henry Fox 1705-1774 *Alli*
Holland, Henry Rich, Earl Of d1648? *Alli*
Holland, Lord Henry Richard Vassal Fox 1773-1840 *Alli, BiDLA, BrAu 19, DcEnL*
Holland, Henry Scott 1847- *Alli Sup, BiD&SB*
Holland, Henry Ware 1844- *DcAmA*
Holland, Hezekiah *Alli*
Holland, Hilda 1901?-1975 *ConAu 57*
Holland, Hugh 1563?-1633 *Alli, ChPo*
Holland, Isabelle 1920- *ConAu 21, SmATA 8*
Holland, J Simon *Alli Sup*
Holland, James Gordon 1927- *ConAu 1R*
Holland, James R 1944- *ConAu 37,*

Holland, James William 1849-1922 *Alli Sup, DcNAA*
Holland, Janice 1913-1962 *IlBYP, IlCB 1956, IlCB 1966*
Holland, John *Alli, BiDLA, MnBBF, PoIre*
Holland, John 1794-1872 *Alli Sup, ChPo S1, ChPo S2*
Holland, John Douglas 1917-1936 *ChPo*
Holland, John L 1919- *ConAu 25*
Holland, Joseph *Alli*
Holland, Josiah Gilbert 1819-1881 *Alli, Alli Sup, AmA, AmA&B, BbD, BiD&SB, ChPo, ChPo S1, ChPo S2, Chmbr 3, CnDAL, CyAL 2, DcAmA, DcBiA, DcEnL, DcLEnL, DcNAA, EvLB, OxAm, REn, REnAL*
Holland, Joyce 1921- *ConAu 5R*
Holland, Katrin *AmA&B, ConAu XR, TwCA Sup*
Holland, Kel *ConAu XR*
Holland, Kenneth J 1918- *ConAu 33*
Holland, Kevin Crossley *ChPo S1*
Holland, Laurence Bedwell 1920- *ConAu 17R, WrD 1976*
Holland, Leslie Arthur 1921- *Au&Wr, WrD 1976*
Holland, Lynwood M 1905- *ConAu 41*
Holland, Marion 1908- *AuBYP, ConAu 61, SmATA 6*
Holland, Mary *Alli*
Holland, Mignon *BlkAW*
Holland, Muriel *Au&Wr*
Holland, Norah Mary d1925 *ChPo, ChPo S2, DcNAA*
Holland, Norman 1910- *Au&Wr*
Holland, Norman N 1927- *ConAu 17R, WrD 1976*
Holland, Penelope *Alli Sup*
Holland, Philemon 1552-1637 *Alli, BrAu, CasWL, Chmbr 1, DcEnL, EvLB, NewC, OxEng*
Holland, Philip *Alli*
Holland, R A *Alli Sup*
Holland, Ray P 1884- *AmA&B, WhWNAA*
Holland, Richard *Alli*
Holland, Sir Richard *Alli, BrAu, CasWL, EvLB*
Holland, Richard George d1871? *PoIre*
Holland, Robert *Alli, Alli Sup*
Holland, Robert 1940- *ConAu 33*
Holland, Robert Afton 1844-1909 *BiDSA, DcAmA, DcNAA*
Holland, Robert Emmet 1892-1946 *BkC 3, CatA 1947, DcNAA*
Holland, Rodney *MnBBF*
Holland, Rupert Sargent 1878-1952 *AmLY, ChPo, JBA 1934, JBA 1951, REnAL, WhWNAA*
Holland, Samuel *Alli, BiDLA Sup*
Holland, Samuel Jan 1728?-1801 *BbtC, OxCan*
Holland, Spencer Langton 1856- *Alli Sup*
Holland, Stephen Bainsbridge *MnBBF*
Holland, Susan *OxCan Sup*
Holland, Thomas *Alli*
Holland, Thomas 1908- *Au&Wr, WrD 1976*
Holland, Thomas Agar 1803-1888 *ChPo S2*
Holland, Thomas E 1934- *ConAu 53*
Holland, Thomas Erskine 1835- *Alli Sup, BiD&SB*
Holland, Tim 1931- *ConAu 57*
Holland, Trevenen J *Alli Sup*
Holland, Vyvyan 1886-1967 *ConAu 25, LongC*
Holland, W Bob 1868- *WhWNAA*
Holland, William Edward Sladen 1873- *WhLA*
Holland, William Jacob 1848-1932 *AmA&B, AmLY, DcAmA, DcNAA*
Hollander, A Nicolaas Jan Den 1906- *ConAu 29*
Hollander, Bernard 1864- *WhLA*
Hollander, Gwenda 1907- *Au&Wr*
Hollander, Hans 1899- *Au&Wr*
Hollander, Jacob Harry 1871-1940 *DcAmA, DcNAA*
Hollander, John 1929- *AmA&B, AuBYP, ChPo, ChPo S1, ConAu 1R, ConLC 2, ConLC 5, ConP 1970, ConP 1975, DrAP 1975, OxAm, Pen Am, REnAL,*

WhTwL, WorAu, WrD 1976
Hollander, Lee M 1880- *ConAu 1R, TexWr, WhWNAA*
Hollander, Paul *AuBYP*
Hollander, Paul 1932- *ConAu 37*
Hollander, Ralph 1916- *AmSCAP 66*
Hollander, Robert 1933- *ConAu 13R*
Hollander, Sophie Smith 1911- *ConAu 13R*
Hollander, Stanley C 1919- *ConAu 37, WrD 1976*
Hollands, Edmund H 1879- *WhWNAA*
Hollands, Hulda Theodate 1837-1910 *DcNAA*
Hollenweger, Walter J 1927- *ConAu 53*
Holler, John 1904- *AmSCAP 66*
Holler, Ronald F 1938- *ConAu 53*
Holleran, Eugene M 1922- *BiDPar*
Hollerer, Walter 1922- *OxGer, Pen Eur*
Holles, Lord Denzil 1597-1680 *Alli*
Holles, Robert Owen 1926- *ConAu 5R, ConDr, WrD 1976*
Holles, Thomas *Alli*
Holley, Alexander Lyman 1832-1882 *Alli Sup, DcAmA, DcNAA*
Holley, Bobbie Lee 1927- *ConAu 33*
Holley, Edward Gailon 1927- *ConAu 5R, WrD 1976*
Holley, George Washington 1810-1897 *Alli Sup, ChPo, DcAmA, DcNAA*
Holley, Henry Whitcomb 1828-1897 *DcNAA*
Holley, Horace 1781-1827 *Alli, CyAL 2*
Holley, Horace Hotchkiss 1887-1960 *AmA&B, ChPo S1*
Holley, Irving Brinton, Jr. 1919- *ConAu 37, WrD 1976*
Holley, Marietta 1836-1926 *Alli Sup, AmA, AmA&B, AmLY, BbD, BiD&SB, DcAmA, DcNAA, OxAm, REn, REnAL*
Holley, Mary Austin 1784-1846 *Alli, AmA, BiDSA, DcAmA, DcNAA, REnAL*
Holley, Mary T *ChPo S1*
Holley, Orville Luther 1791-1861 *Alli, DcAmA, DcNAA*
Holli, Melvin George 1933- *ConAu 25, WrD 1976*
Hollick, Ann L 1941- *ConAu 57*
Hollick, Arthur 1857- *WhWNAA*
Holliday, Carl 1879-1936 *AmA&B, AmLY, BiDSA, DcNAA, OhA&B, REnAL, WhWNAA*
Holliday, Ferdinand C 1814- *Alli Sup, IndAu 1816*
Holliday, Francis *Alli*
Holliday, George H 1847-1919 *OhA&B*
Holliday, H L *ChPo S2*
Holliday, James *ConAu XR*
Holliday, Joe 1910- *Au&Wr, ConAu XR*
Holliday, John *Alli, BiDLA*
Holliday, John d1801 *Alli*
Holliday, John Hampden 1846-1921 *IndAu 1816*
Holliday, Joseph 1910- *ConAu 29*
Holliday, Murray Lucas 1908- *IndAu 1917*
Holliday, Robert Cortes 1880-1946 *AmA&B, ChPo, ChPo S2, DcNAA, IndAu 1917, REnAL, TwCA, TwCA Sup, WhWNAA*
Holliday, Robert Reade 1908- *Au&Wr*
Hollier, Robert *OxCan Sup*
Hollindale, Peter 1936- *WrD 1976*
Holling, Clancy *IlBYP*
Holling, Holling Clancy 1900- *AmA&B, AuBYP, AuICB, IlCB 1956, IlCB 1966, JBA 1951, St&VC*
Holling, Lucille Webster 1900- *IlBYP, IlCB 1956, IlCB 1966, JBA 1951*
Hollingbery, R H *Alli Sup*
Hollingdale, Reginald John 1930- *Au&Wr, WrD 1976*
Hollingdale, Stuart Havelock 1910- *Au&Wr*
Hollings, Doctor *Alli*
Hollings, Mrs. *Alli Sup*
Hollings, F S *CarSB, ChPo S2*
Hollings, George Seymour *Alli Sup*
Hollings, James Francis 1806-1862 *ChPo, ChPo S1*
Hollingshead, August DeBelmont 1907- *ConAu 13R, WrD 1976*
Hollingshead, John 1827- *Alli Sup, BbD, BiD&SB, DcEnL*

Hollingshead, Kyle 1941- *ConAu 23,*
WrD 1976
Hollingshead, Raphael d1580? *CasWL, EvLB,*
NewC, REn
Hollingshead, William *Alli*
Hollingsworth, Alvin *IlBYP*
Hollingsworth, Harold M 1932- *ConAu 53*
Hollingsworth, J Rogers 1932- *ConAu 13R*
Hollingsworth, James Gentry *ChPo S2*
Hollingsworth, Lyman B 1919- *ConAu 45*
Hollingsworth, Nathaniel *Alli, BiDLA*
Hollingsworth, Paul M 1932- *ConAu 29,*
WrD 1976
Hollingsworth, S *Alli, BiDLA, OxCan*
Hollingsworth, Thelka *AmSCAP 66*
Hollington, Richard Deming 1870-1944 *OhA&B*
Hollingworth, Harry Levi 1880-1956 *AmA&B,*
AmLY, WhWNAA
Hollingworth, Henry *Alli Sup*
Hollingworth, J B *Alli, BiDLA*
Hollingworth, Leta 1886-1939 *DcNAA*
Hollingworth, Richard *Alli*
Hollingworth, Rudolph *Alli*
Hollingworth, S *BbtC*
Hollins, James *Alli Sup*
Hollis, Barbara Coonley 1922- *WrD 1976*
Hollis, Christopher 1902- *CatA 1947,*
WrD 1976
Hollis, Daniel W 1922- *ConAu 5R*
Hollis, Dorothea *ChPo S1*
Hollis, E B *Alli Sup*
Hollis, Gerald 1919- *Au&Wr*
Hollis, Harry Newcombe, Jr. 1938- *ConAu 57*
Hollis, Helen Rice 1908- *ConAu 61,*
WrD 1976
Hollis, Henry French 1869- *WhWNAA*
Hollis, Ira Nelson 1856-1930 *DcNAA,*
IndAu 1816
Hollis, James R 1940- *ConAu 41*
Hollis, Jim *ConAu XR, WrD 1976*
Hollis, John *Alli, BiDLA*
Hollis, Joseph W 1922- *ConAu 25*
Hollis, Lucile Ussery 1921- *ConAu 25,*
WrD 1976
Hollis, Maurice Christopher 1902- *Au&Wr,*
DcLEnL, EvLB
Hollis, Susan Barrett *ChPo*
Hollis, Thomas 1659-1731 *CyAL 1*
Hollis, Thomas 1720-1774 *Alli*
Hollis, William *Alli Sup*
Hollister, Bernard C 1938- *ConAu 49*
Hollister, C Warren 1930- *ConAu 1R*
Hollister, Charles A 1918- *ConAu 17R*
Hollister, Edward Payson 1839-1877 *HsB&A*
Hollister, George E 1905- *ConAu 17*
Hollister, Gideon Hiram 1817-1881 *Alli,*
Alli Sup, AmA, AmA&B, BiD&SB,
DcAmA, DcNAA, OxAm, REnAL
Hollister, Horace 1822-1893 *DcAmA, DcNAA*
Hollister, Horace Adelbert 1857-1931 *DcNAA*
Hollister, John Fletcher 1811-1882 *DcNAA*
Hollister, Leo E 1920- *ConAu 23*
Hollister, Mary Brewster 1891- *AmA&B,*
OhA&B, WhWNAA
Hollister, Ned 1876-1924 *DcNAA*
Hollister, O J *Alli Sup*
Hollister, Ovando James 1834-1892 *DcNAA*
Hollister, Richard Dennis Teall 1878-
WhWNAA
Hollister, W R *BiDSA*
Hollmann, Clide John 1896-1966 *ConAu 5R*
Hollo, Anselm 1934- *ConAu 21, ConP 1970,*
ConP 1975, DrAP 1975, WrD 1976
Hollom, Philip Arthur Dominic 1912- *Au&Wr,*
ConAu 13R
Hollon, William Eugene 1913- *AmA&B,*
AuNews 1, ConAu 1R
Hollond, E *Alli Sup*
Hollonius, Ludwig *CasWL, OxGer*
Hollopeter, William Clarence 1858-1927
DcNAA
Holloran, L *Alli*
Holloway, A H *Alli Sup*
Holloway, Anna *Alli Sup*
Holloway, B *Alli*
Holloway, Benjamin *Alli*
Holloway, Brenda Wilmar 1908- *Au&Wr,*
ConAu P-1

Holloway, Charlotte Molyneux *CarSB*
Holloway, David Richard 1924- *Au&Wr*
Holloway, E W *ChPo*
Holloway, Edward Stratton 1859-1939 *DcNAA,*
WhWNAA
Holloway, Elizabeth *BiDSA*
Holloway, Emory 1885- *AmA&B, ConAu 49,*
OxAm, REnAL, TwCA, TwCA Sup,
WhWNAA
Holloway, Ephraim S 1833-1895 *OhA&B*
Holloway, Francis A 1872- *ChPo S2*
Holloway, Geoffrey 1918- *ConAu 49*
Holloway, George *Alli Sup*
Holloway, George 1921- *ConAu 25*
Holloway, H *Alli Sup*
Holloway, H R *Alli*
Holloway, Harry 1925- *ConAu 9R,*
WrD 1976
Holloway, Henry H *Alli Sup*
Holloway, J *Alli Sup*
Holloway, James *Alli*
Holloway, James Thomas *Alli*
Holloway, James Y 1927- *ConAu 53*
Holloway, John *Alli, BiDLA, MnBBF*
Holloway, John 1920- *Au&Wr, ChPo S2,*
ConAu 5R, ConP 1970, ConP 1975,
ModBL, NewC, WorAu, WrD 1976
Holloway, John George *Alli*
Holloway, John Nelson 1839-1887 *IndAu 1816*
Holloway, John Wesley 1865- *BlkAW*
Holloway, Julia Herman *ChPo*
Holloway, Laura Carter 1848- *Alli Sup, BbD,*
BiD&SB, BiDSA, DcAmA
Holloway, Lucy Ariel Williams 1905- *BlkAW*
Holloway, Mark 1917- *Au&Wr, ConAu 21,*
WrD 1976
Holloway, Maurice 1920- *ConAu 9R*
Holloway, Maxine *TexWr*
Holloway, Pearl 1888- *WhWNAA*
Holloway, Robert *Alli, BiDLA*
Holloway, Robert J 1921- *ConAu 13R*
Holloway, Stanley 1890- *NewC*
Holloway, Teresa 1906- *ConAu 17R*
Holloway, Thomas *Alli Sup*
Holloway, Trevor *MnBBF*
Holloway, W V 1903- *ConAu 1R*
Holloway, William *Alli, Alli Sup, BiDLA,*
ChPo, ChPo S1
Holloway, William Robeson 1836-1911
IndAu 1816
Hollowell, J H *Alli Sup*
Hollowell, Lillian *ChPo*
Hollowood, Albert Bernard 1910- *Au&Wr,*
ConAu 9R
Hollowood, Jane Marian *Au&Wr*
Holls, Frederick William *Alli Sup*
Holls, George Frederick William 1857-1903
DcAmA, DcNAA
Hollway-Calthrop *Alli Sup*
Holly, H W *Alli Sup*
Holly, Henry Hudson 1834-1892 *Alli Sup,*
DcAmA, DcNAA
Holly, J Fred 1915- *ConAu 5R*
Holly, J Hunter *ConAu XR*
Holly, Jan 1785-1849 *CasWL*
Holly, Joan C 1932- *ConAu 1R*
Hollyband, Claudius *Alli*
Hollybushe, John *Alli*
Hollyday, Frederic B M 1928- *ConAu 45*
Hollyday, Mrs. R C *Alli Sup*
Hollyday, Robert H 1815-1905 *OhA&B*
Hollyngus, Edmond *Alli*
Holm, Anne 1922- *AnCL, ConAu 17R,*
SmATA 1
Holm, Don 1918- *ConAu 33*
Holm, Gert 1882- *WhWNAA*
Holm, H J Frits Vilhelm 1881- *WhLA*
Holm, Hannebo *AuBYP*
Holm, J *Alli Sup*
Holm, John Cecil 1904- *ModWD, REnAL*
Holm, John Cecil 1906- *CnMD*
Holm, Marilyn D 1944- *ConAu 17R*
Holm, Oscar William *WhPNW*
Holm, Saxe 1830?-1885 *Alli Sup, AmA,*
AmA&B, ChPo, ChPo S1, DcAmA,
DcNAA, OxAm
Holm, Sven Aage 1902- *Au&Wr, ConAu P-1*

Holm, Torfhildur Thorsteinsdottir 1845-1918
EuA
Holman, C Hugh 1914- *ConAu 5R*
Holman, Carrie Ellen *ChPo*
Holman, D A *Alli Sup*
Holman, Dennis 1915- *Au&Wr, ConAu 9R*
Holman, E S *MnBBF*
Holman, Edna Bourne *ChPo*
Holman, Edward Lee 1894- *WrD 1976*
Holman, Emile 1890- *WhWNAA*
Holman, Felice 1919- *AuBYP, ChPo S2,*
ConAu 5R, SmATA 7, WrD 1976
Holman, Frederick VanVoorhies 1852-1927
AmLY, DcNAA, WhWNAA
Holman, Harriet R 1912- *ChPo S1, ConAu 37*
Holman, Hugh 1914- *AmA&B*
Holman, J Alan 1931- *IndAu 1917*
Holman, J G 1764- *BiDLA*
Holman, James 1787-1857 *Alli, DcEnL*
Holman, Jesse Lynch 1784-1842 *IndAu 1816*
Holman, Joseph George 1764-1817 *Alli, DcEnL*
Holman, L Bruce 1939- *ConAu 61*
Holman, Louis A 1866-1939 *AmA&B, AmLY,*
DcNAA
Holman, M Carl 1919- *BlkAW*
Holman, Mary Velora 1901- *OhA&B*
Holman, Richard Morris 1886-1935 *DcNAA,*
WhWNAA
Holman, Silas Whitcomb 1856-1900 *DcNAA*
Holman, William R 1926- *ConAu 49*
Holmans, Alan Edward 1934- *ConAu 1R*
Holmberg, Gustaf Frederik 1872-1936 *DcNAA,*
WhWNAA
Holmden, Annie *Alli Sup*
Holme, Bryan 1913- *AuBYP*
Holme, C Geoffrey 1887- *ChPo, ChPo S1*
Holme, Cecil Frederick *Alli Sup*
Holme, Christopher *Alli Sup*
Holme, Constance 1881?-1955 *DcLEnL, EvLB,*
LongC, OxEng, TwCA, TwCA Sup
Holme, Daryl *Alli Sup*
Holme, Gordon *MnBBF*
Holme, J Stanford *Alli Sup*
Holme, Jamie Sexton 1893- *AnMV 1926*
Holme, John *Alli*
Holme, John Gunnlaugur 1878-1922 *DcNAA*
Holme, K E *ConAu XR, WrD 1976*
Holme, Randle *Alli*
Holme, T *Alli Sup*
Holme, Thea 1903- *ConAu 41*
Holme, Mrs. Torre *ChPo S1*
Holme, W *Alli Sup*
Holme, Wilfred *Alli*
Holmelund, Paul 1890- *ConAu 5R*
Holmer, Paul L 1916- *ConAu 37, WrD 1976*
Holmes, Major *Alli*
Holmes, A Bromley *Alli Sup*
Holmes, Abiel 1763-1837 *Alli, AmA,*
AmA&B, BiD&SB, BiDLA, CyAL 1,
DcAmA, DcNAA, OxAm, REnAL
Holmes, Abraham S *OxCan*
Holmes, Alan A 1821- *ChPo S1*
Holmes, Alice A 1821- *Alli Sup, DcNAA*
Holmes, Andrew *MnBBF*
Holmes, Andrew Fernando 1797-1860 *BbtC*
Holmes, Angus *MnBBF*
Holmes, Arthur *ChPo S1*
Holmes, Arthur 1872-1965 *AmA&B, AmLY,*
OhA&B, WhWNAA
Holmes, Arthur Frank 1924- *ConAu 33,*
WrD 1976
Holmes, Augustus *ChPo*
Holmes, Baptist James *Alli Sup*
Holmes, Bayard Taylor 1852-1924 *DcNAA*
Holmes, Burton 1870- *WhWNAA*
Holmes, C *Alli Sup*
Holmes, C Raymond 1929- *ConAu 57*
Holmes, Calvin Pratt 1839-1902 *DcNAA*
Holmes, Captain Howard *HsB&A*
Holmes, Charles John 1868-1936 *ChPo S1*
Holmes, Charles M 1923- *ConAu 29*
Holmes, Charles S 1916-1976 *ConAu 41,*
ConAu 61, WrD 1976
Holmes, Clarence 1879-1938 *DcNAA*
Holmes, Clellon 1926- *REnAL*
Holmes, Colin 1938- *ConAu 25*
Holmes, Con *MnBBF*

Holt, Gavin *ConAu XR*
Holt, Geoffrey B A *MnBBF*
Holt, Geoffrey Ogden 1910- *Au&Wr*
Holt, George Chandler 1843-1931 *DcNAA*
Holt, George Edmund 1881- *WhWNAA*
Holt, Guy 1892-1934 *AmA&B, DcNAA*
Holt, Hamilton 1872-1951 *AmA&B, AmLY, WhWNAA*
Holt, Hans 1909- *CnMD*
Holt, Harry Quentin 1896- *IndAu 1917*
Holt, Helen *ConAu XR*
Holt, Henry *Alli Sup, MnBBF*
Holt, Henry 1840-1926 *AmA&B, BiDPar, DcAmA, DcNAA*
Holt, Isabella 1892-1962 *AmA&B*
Holt, Jack *MnBBF*
Holt, James 1939- *ConAu 25*
Holt, John *Alli, AmA&B*
Holt, Sir John 1642-1710 *Alli*
Holt, John 1721-1784 *AmA&B*
Holt, John 1742-1801 *Alli, BiDLA*
Holt, John 1926- *ConAu 25*
Holt, John Agee 1920- *ConAu 1R*
Holt, John Saunders 1826-1886 *BiD&SB, BiDSA, DcAmA, DcNAA*
Holt, Joseph *Alli*
Holt, Kare 1917- *CasWL*
Holt, Lee E 1912- *ConAu 13R*
Holt, Len *LivBA*
Holt, Lucius Hudson 1881-1935 *AmA&B, WhWNAA*
Holt, Ludlow *Alli*
Holt, Luther Emmett 1855-1924 *DcNAA*
Holt, Luther Emmett, Jr. 1895-1974 *AmA&B, ConAu 53*
Holt, Mrs. M A *Alli Sup*
Holt, Margaret 1937- *AuBYP, ConAu 17R, SmATA 4*
Holt, Martin *DcNAA*
Holt, Marvell *WhLA*
Holt, Mary Helen *Alli Sup*
Holt, Michael Paul 1929- *Au&Wr, ConAu 53, WrD 1976*
Holt, R D 1897- *TexWr*
Holt, Richard *Alli, MnBBF*
Holt, Robert *Alli Sup*
Holt, Robert A *ChPo S1*
Holt, Robert B *Alli Sup*
Holt, Robert Edward Hallett 1853- *Alli Sup*
Holt, Robert Rutherford 1917- *Au&Wr, ConAu 41*
Holt, Robert T 1928- *ConAu 37*
Holt, Rochelle L 1946- *ConAu 57*
Holt, Roland 1867-1931 *DcNAA*
Holt, Sestertius *Alli Sup*
Holt, Simma *OxCan*
Holt, Stephen *AuBYP, ConAu XR, SmATA XR*
Holt, Tex *ConAu XR*
Holt, Thelma Jewett 1913- *ConAu 29*
Holt, Thomas *Alli*
Holt, Victoria 1906- *AmA&B, Au&Wr, ConAu XR, EncM&D, SmATA 2, WorAu, WrD 1976*
Holt, Vincent M *Alli Sup*
Holt, W *Alli Sup*
Holt, Walter J *MnBBF*
Holt, Will 1929- *AmSCAP 66*
Holt, William 1897- *Au&Wr, ConAu P-1, WrD 1976*
Holt, Winifred d1945 *AmA&B*
Holtan, Orley I 1933- *ConAu 33*
Holtby, Robert Tinsley 1921- *WrD 1976*
Holtby, Winifred 1898-1935 *ChPo S1, Chmbr 3, DcLEnL, EvLB, LongC, ModBL, NewC, REn, TwCA, TwCA Sup, TwCW*
Holte, F *Alli Sup*
Holte, John 1570?- *Alli, DcEnL*
Holtei, Karl Von 1798-1880 *BbD, BiD&SB, EvEuW, OxGer*
Holter, Don W 1905- *ConAu 37*
Holtham, E G *Alli Sup*
Holthausen, F *Alli Sup*
Holthouse, Carsten *Alli, Alli Sup*
Holthouse, Henry James *Alli*
Holthusen, Hans Egon 1913- *Au&Wr, ConAu 45, EvEuW, ModGL, OxGer,*

Pen Eur, TwCW, WorAu
Holtje, Herbert F 1931- *ConAu 61*
Holton, David Parsons 1812-1883 *DcNAA*
Holton, Edwin Lee 1876-1950 *IndAu 1917*
Holton, Gerald 1922- *ConAu 13R*
Holton, Henry *EarAB Sup*
Holton, Isaac Farwell 1812-1874 *Alli Sup, DcNAA*
Holton, Leonard 1915- *AuBYP, ConAu XR, EncM&D, SmATA 2, WorAu*
Holton, Martha Adelaide 1865- *WhWNAA*
Holton, Milne 1931- *ConAu 41*
Holton, Robert W 1922- *AmSCAP 66*
Holton, Walter H *MnBBF*
Holtrop, William Frans 1908- *ConAu 57*
Holttum, Richard Eric 1895- *Au&Wr, WrD 1976*
Holty, Hermann 1828-1887 *BiD&SB*
Holty, Ludwig Christoph Heinrich 1748-1776 *OxGer, Pen Eur*
Holty, Ludwig Heinrich Christoph 1748-1776 *BiD&SB, CasWL, ChPo S1, ChPo S2, DcEuL, EuA, EvEuW, REn*
Holtz, Avraham 1934- *ConAu 29*
Holtzclaw, Henry Fuller 1893- *WhWNAA*
Holtzman, Abraham 1921- *ConAu 1R, WrD 1976*
Holtzman, Jerome 1926- *ConAu 53*
Holtzman, Paul D 1918- *ConAu 33*
Holtzman, Wayne Harold 1923- *ConAu 37, WrD 1976*
Holub, Miroslav 1923- *CasWL, ConAu 21, ConLC 4, ModSL 2, WhTwL, WorAu*
Holway, Edward W D *OxCan*
Holway, Hope 1886- *WhWNAA*
Holway, John 1929- *ConAu 57*
Holway, Mary Gordon d1922 *DcNAA*
Holway, Ruth 1884- *WhWNAA*
Holwell, John d1685? *Alli*
Holwell, John Zephaniah 1711-1798 *Alli*
Holwell, Thomas *Alli*
Holwell, William d1798 *Alli*
Holworthy, Mercedes Claire 1890- *BkC 5*
Holworthy, S M *Alli Sup*
Holybush, John *Alli*
Holyday, Barten 1593-1661 *Alli, CasWL, DcEnL*
Holyer, Erna Maria 1925- *ConAu 29, WrD 1976*
Holyer, Ernie *ConAu XR, WrD 1976*
Holyfield, Rose *ChPo S2*
Holyoake, Austin And Watts, Charles *Alli Sup*
Holyoake, Francis 1567?-1653 *Alli*
Holyoake, George Jacob 1817-1906 *Alli Sup, BiD&SB, BrAu 19, Chmbr 3, DcEnL, NewC*
Holyoake, Manfred *Alli Sup*
Holyoake, Thomas 1616-1675 *Alli*
Holyoke, Edward 1689-1769 *Alli, DcAmA*
Holyoke, Edward Augustus 1728-1829 *Alli, CyAL 1, DcNAA*
Holyoke, Hetty *DcNAA*
Holyoke, Maria Ballard *Alli Sup*
Holyoke, Samuel Adams 1762-1820 *Alli, AmA&B, DcNAA*
Holywood, John d1235 *Alli, DcEnL*
Holz, Arno 1863-1929 *CasWL, ClDMEuL, CnMD, EncWL, EvEuW, ModGL, ModWD, OxGer, Pen Eur, REn*
Holz, Nicolaus 1868- *WhLA*
Holz, Robert K 1930- *ConAu 53*
Holzapfel, Rudi 1938- *ConP 1970*
Holzapfel, Rudolf Patrick 1938- *ConAu P-1*
Holzberger, William George 1932- *ConAu 53*
Holzer, Hans 1920- *AmSCAP 66, BiDPar, ConAu 13R*
Holzer, Lou 1913- *AmSCAP 66*
Holzinger, Karl John 1892- *WhWNAA*
Holzman, Franklyn Dunn 1918- *ConAu 61*
Holzman, Philip Seidman 1922- *ConAu 37*
Holzman, Robert Stuart 1907- *AmA&B, ConAu 1R*
Holzmann, Abraham 1874-1939 *AmSCAP 66*
Holzner, Joseph 1875-1947 *CatA 1952*
Holzworth, John Michael 1888- *OhA&B*
Homan, Helen Walker 1893- *AmA&B, CatA 1947*
Homan, Robert Anthony 1929- *ConAu 5R,*

WrD 1976
Homans, Benjamin *Alli*
Homans, Isaac Smith 1807-1879 *DcNAA*
Homans, Isaac Smith, Jr. *Alli Sup*
Homans, J S *Alli Sup*
Homans, J Smith *Alli*
Homans, J Smith, Jr. *Alli*
Homans, Peter 1930- *ConAu 23, WrD 1976*
Homar, Lorenzo 1913- *WhGrA*
Homberg, Hans 1903- *CnMD*
Homberg, Otto 1857- *WhLA*
Homberger, Conrad P 1900- *ConAu 13R*
Homburg, Ernst Christoph 1605-1681 *OxGer*
Homburger, Erik *ConAu XR*
Home *Alli*
Home, Alexander *Alli, EvLB, Pen Eng*
Home, Andrew 1864- *MnBBF*
Home, Athol *MnBBF*
Home, Cecil *Alli Sup, EvLB*
Home, Charles *Alli, BiDLA*
Home, Daniel Dunglas 1833-1886 *Alli Sup, BiDPar, NewC, OxEng, REn*
Home, Mrs. Daniel Dunglas *Alli Sup*
Home, David *Alli*
Home, David Milne *Alli Sup*
Home, Edwin *MnBBF*
Home, Ernest H A *ChPo S1*
Home, Sir Everard 1756-1832 *Alli, BiDLA*
Home, F Wyville *Alli Sup, ChPo S2*
Home, Francis *Alli*
Home, G Milne *Alli Sup*
Home, Henry, Lord Kames 1696-1782 *Alli, BiDLA, BrAu, Chmbr 2, DcEnL, EvLB, NewC, OxEng, Pen Eng*
Home, J *Alli Sup*
Home, James *Alli*
Home, John *Alli, Chmbr 2*
Home, John 1722-1808 *Alli, BiD&SB, BrAu, CasWL, DcEnA, DcEnL, DcEuL, DcLEnL, EvLB, NewC, OxEng, Pen Eng, REn*
Home, K *Alli Sup*
Home, R d1879 *Alli Sup*
Home, Robert *Alli*
Home, T *MnBBF*
Home, William Douglas 1912- *Au&Wr, CnMD, CnThe, ConDr, CrCD, ModWD, WrD 1976*
Home-Gall, Edward Reginald 1899- *MnBBF*
Home-Gall, Reginald *MnBBF*
Home-Gall, William Benjamin 1861-1936 *MnBBF*
Home-Gall, William Bolinbroke 1894- *MnBBF*
Home Goal *MnBBF*
Homeford, Caleb *Alli Sup*
Homei *DcOrL 1*
Homer *AtlBL, BbD, BiD&SB, CasWL, ChPo, CyWA, DcBiA, DcEnL, DcEuL, NewC, OxEng, Pen Cl, RCom*
Homer, A N *Alli Sup*
Homer, Benjamin 1917- *AmSCAP 66*
Homer, Henry 1752-1791 *Alli*
Homer, John *BbtC*
Homer, Joy 1915-1946 *DcNAA*
Homer, Louise, Jr. *ChPo*
Homer, Philip Brucebriges *Alli*
Homer, Sidney 1864-1953 *AmSCAP 66, OxAm, REnAL*
Homer, William *Alli*
Homer, William Innes 1929- *ConAu 13R, WrD 1976*
Homer, Winslow 1836-1910 *AtlBL, ChPo, ChPo S1, ChPo S2, EarAB, EarAB Sup, OxAm, REn, REnAL*
Homersham, E Margery *Alli Sup*
Homersham, Matilda *Alli Sup*
Homes, Geoffrey 1901- *EncM&D*
Homes, Henry Augustus 1812-1888? *Alli Sup, DcAmA*
Homes, Mary Sophie 1830?- *Alli Sup, AmA&B, BiD&SB, BiDSA, DcAmA, DcNAA, LivFWS*
Homes, Nathaniel d1679 *Alli*
Homes, William 1663-1746 *Alli, DcNAA*
Homewood, A S *ChPo S2*
Hommius, Festus 1567-1642 *CasWL*
Homoras *ConAu XR*
Hompson, Davi Det *DrAP 1975*

Hope, Keith 1936- *Au&Wr*
Hope, L *Alli*
Hope, Laura Lee *ConAu 17R, REnAL, SmATA 1, WhCL*
Hope, Laurence 1865-1904 *ChPo S1, ChPo S2, EvLB, LongC, TwCA, TwCA Sup*
Hope, Louisa Octavia *Alli Sup*
Hope, Lydia *Alli Sup*
Hope, M J *Alli Sup*
Hope, Marion Dominica *WrD 1976*
Hope, Marjorie 1923- *ConAu 29, WrD 1976*
Hope, Mark *Alli Sup*
Hope, Matthew Boyd 1812-1859 *DcAmA*
Hope, Quentin M 1923- *ConAu 13R*
Hope, Robert Charles *Alli Sup*
Hope, Ronald Sydney 1921- *Au&Wr, ConAu 9R, WrD 1976*
Hope, Stanley *Alli Sup*
Hope, T Radford *Alli Sup*
Hope, Thomas *Alli, Chmbr 2*
Hope, Sir Thomas d1646 *Alli, DcEnL*
Hope, Thomas 1770?-1831 *Alli, BbD, BiD&SB, BiDLA, BrAu 19, DcEnL, DcLEnL, EvLB, NewC, OxEng*
Hope, Thomas Charles *Alli*
Hope, Thomas Edward 1923- *Au&Wr*
Hope, Walter *MnBBF*
Hope, Welborn 1903- *ConAu 29*
Hope, Will *MnBBF*
Hope, William *Alli*
Hope, Sir William *Alli*
Hope, William Edward Stanton 1889-1961 *MnBBF*
Hope-Edwardes *Alli Sup*
Hope-Mason, Gordon Nisbett 1913- *Au&Wr*
Hope-Simpson, Jacynth Ann 1930- *Au&Wr, ConAu 13R, WrD 1976*
Hopewell, Anne Madge *ChPo S2*
Hopewell, Menra d1870? *HsB&A*
Hopewell, S 1924- *ConAu 25*
Hopf, Alice L 1904- *ConAu 17R, SmATA 5*
Hopf, Ludwig 1884- *WhLA*
Hopfen, Hans Von 1835-1904 *BiD&SB, OxGer*
Hopfinger, Kurt Bernard 1921- *Au&Wr*
Hopgood, James *Alli Sup*
Hopgood, Thomas Frederick *Alli Sup*
Hopke, William E 1918- *ConAu 21*
Hopken, Johan Von 1712-1789 *DcEuL*
Hopkins *Alli*
Hopkins, A *ChPo*
Hopkins, A T *AuBYP, ConAu XR*
Hopkins, Abel Grosvenor 1844-1899 *DcAmA*
Hopkins, Albert Allis 1869-1939 *DcNAA*
Hopkins, Alfred 1870-1941 *DcNAA*
Hopkins, Alonzo *Alli Sup*
Hopkins, Alphonso Alvah 1843-1918 *Alli Sup, AmA&B, BiD&SB, ChPo, DcAmA, DcNAA*
Hopkins, Andrew Winkle 1880- *WhWNAA*
Hopkins, Antony 1921- *Au&Wr, WrD 1976*
Hopkins, Archibald 1842-1926 *DcNAA, WhWNAA*
Hopkins, Arthur John *DcNAA*
Hopkins, Arthur Melancthon 1878-1950 *AmA&B, OhA&B, REn, REnAL*
Hopkins, B *MnBBF*
Hopkins, B Smith 1873- *WhWNAA*
Hopkins, Benjamin *Alli*
Hopkins, Bill 1928- *ConAu 9R*
Hopkins, Caspar Thomas 1826-1893 *Alli Sup, DcAmA, DcNAA*
Hopkins, Charles 1664-1699 *Alli, DcEnL, DcLEnL*
Hopkins, Charles Edwin 1886-1946 *OhA&B*
Hopkins, Charles Wyman 1839-1910 *DcNAA*
Hopkins, Clark 1895- *AuBYP*
Hopkins, Claude D 1906- *AmSCAP 66*
Hopkins, Cyril George 1866-1919 *AmLY, DcNAA*
Hopkins, D C *Alli Sup*
Hopkins, David d1814 *Alli, BiDLA, BiDLA Sup*
Hopkins, E Russell *OxCan Sup*
Hopkins, Edward John *Alli Sup*
Hopkins, Edward Washburn 1857-1932 *BiD&SB, DcAmA, DcNAA*
Hopkins, Erastus 1810-1872 *Alli, DcAmA, DcNAA*

Hopkins, Evan *Alli Sup*
Hopkins, Evan Henry *Alli Sup*
Hopkins, Ezekiel 1633-1690 *Alli*
Hopkins, Florence B 1887- *OhA&B*
Hopkins, Francis R C *ChPo*
Hopkins, Frank Lawrence *Alli Sup*
Hopkins, Frederick W *Alli Sup*
Hopkins, George *Alli Sup*
Hopkins, George Emil 1937- *ConAu 33, WrD 1976*
Hopkins, George Milton 1842-1902 *DcNAA*
Hopkins, Gerard Manley 1844-1889 *AnCL, AtlBL, BrAu 19, CasWL, ChPo, ChPo S1, ChPo S2, Chmbr 3, CnE&AP, CnMWL, CriT 3, CyWA, DcLEnL, EvLB, LongC, ModBL, ModBL Sup, NewC, OxEng, Pen Eng, RAdv 1, RCom, REn, WebEAL, WhTwL*
Hopkins, H W *Alli*
Hopkins, Hannah H *Alli Sup*
Hopkins, Harry 1913- *Au&Wr, ConAu 29, WrD 1976*
Hopkins, Harvey L *Alli Sup*
Hopkins, Helen *ChPo*
Hopkins, Henry *Alli Sup*
Hopkins, Herbert Muller 1870-1910 *ChPo, DcAmA, DcNAA*
Hopkins, Isaac Stiles 1841- *BiDSA*
Hopkins, Isabel Thompson *Alli Sup, DcNAA*
Hopkins, Jack W 1930- *ConAu 25*
Hopkins, James Franklin 1909- *ConAu 1R*
Hopkins, James Frederick 1868-1931 *DcNAA*
Hopkins, James Herron 1832-1904 *DcNAA*
Hopkins, James Love 1868-1931 *DcNAA*
Hopkins, Jane Ellice *Alli Sup*
Hopkins, Jasper Stephens, Jr. 1936- *ConAu 37, WrD 1976*
Hopkins, Jeremiah 1797-1837 *AmA*
Hopkins, Jerry 1935- *ConAu 25*
Hopkins, John *Chmbr 1*
Hopkins, John d1570 *Alli, CasWL, ChPo S1, DcEnL, DcEuL, EvLB*
Hopkins, John 1675-1701? *Alli, DcEnL, PoIre*
Hopkins, John 1931- *ConDr, ConLC 4, WrD 1976*
Hopkins, John Baker *Alli Sup*
Hopkins, John Castell 1864-1923 *AmLY, DcNAA, OxCan*
Hopkins, John Henry 1792-1868 *Alli, Alli Sup, AmA, AmA&B, BbD, BiD&SB, CyAL 2, DcAmA, DcNAA, PoIre*
Hopkins, John Henry 1820-1891 *Alli Sup, BiD&SB, ChPo, DcAmA, DcNAA, PoIre*
Hopkins, John Livingston 1828- *Alli Sup, BiDSA*
Hopkins, John Walter *Alli Sup*
Hopkins, Joseph *Alli, BiDLA*
Hopkins, Joseph G E 1909- *ConAu 1R*
Hopkins, Joseph Martin 1919- *ConAu 49*
Hopkins, Josiah 1786-1862 *DcNAA, PoCh*
Hopkins, Kenneth 1914- *Au&Wr, ChPo S1, ConAu 1R*
Hopkins, L *ChPo*
Hopkins, L Thomas 1889- *WhWNAA*
Hopkins, Lee 1934- *ConAu 57*
Hopkins, Lee Bennett 1938- *ChPo S1, ChPo S2, ConAu 25, SmATA 3, WrD 1976*
Hopkins, Lemuel 1750-1801 *Alli, AmA, AmA&B, CnDAL, CyAL 1, DcAmA, DcLEnL, DcNAA, OxAm, Pen Am, REn, REnAL*
Hopkins, Linton Cooke 1872-1943 *BiDSA, DcNAA*
Hopkins, Livingston 1846-1927 *Alli Sup, DcNAA, OhA&B*
Hopkins, Louisa Parsons 1834-1895 *Alli Sup, BiD&SB, DcAmA, DcNAA*
Hopkins, Louisa Payson 1812-1862 *Alli, DcAmA, DcNAA*
Hopkins, Louise Virginia Martin 1861- *AmA&B*
Hopkins, Lyman *AuBYP, ConAu XR, SmATA 5, WrD 1976*
Hopkins, Manley *Alli Sup*
Hopkins, Margaret Sutton Briscoe 1864- *AmA&B, BiD&SB, DcAmA, WhWNAA*
Hopkins, Marjorie 1911- *ConAu 21,*

SmATA 9
Hopkins, Mark 1802-1887 *Alli, Alli Sup, AmA, AmA&B, BbD, BiD&SB, CyAL 1, DcAmA, DcNAA, OxAm, REnAL*
Hopkins, Mark 1851-1935 *Alli Sup, BiD&SB, DcAmA, DcNAA*
Hopkins, Mark W 1931- *ConAu 29*
Hopkins, Marmaduke *Alli*
Hopkins, Mary Alden 1876-1960 *AmA&B, ChPo S1*
Hopkins, Matthew d1647 *Alli, BrAu, DcLEnL, OxEng*
Hopkins, Nevil Monroe 1873-1945 *DcNAA*
Hopkins, Pauline 1859-1930 *BlkAW*
Hopkins, Pauline Bradford Mackie 1874-1956 *AmA&B, DcAmA, OhA&B, WhWNAA*
Hopkins, Prynce C 1885- *ConAu 21*
Hopkins, Pryns *ConAu XR*
Hopkins, Puffer *AmA&B*
Hopkins, Raymond F 1939- *ConAu 49*
Hopkins, Richard *Alli*
Hopkins, Robert Thurston 1883- *MnBBF*
Hopkins, Rufus Clement 1816- *DcNAA*
Hopkins, Samuel 1693-1755 *Alli, DcNAA*
Hopkins, Samuel 1721-1803 *Alli, AmA, AmA&B, BiD&SB, CyAL 1, DcAmA, DcNAA, DcEnL, DcNAA, OxAm, REnAL*
Hopkins, Samuel 1807-1887 *Alli, Alli Sup, AmA&B, DcAmA, DcNAA*
Hopkins, Samuel Augustus 1858-1921 *DcNAA*
Hopkins, Samuel Miles 1772-1837 *Alli, DcAmA, DcNAA*
Hopkins, Samuel Miles 1813-1901 *Alli Sup, DcAmA*
Hopkins, Samuel Miles 1814-1901 *DcNAA*
Hopkins, Sarah W *Alli Sup*
Hopkins, Selden R *Alli Sup*
Hopkins, Stephen 1707-1785 *Alli, DcAmA, DcNAA, OxAm, REnAL*
Hopkins, Terence K 1928- *ConAu 9R*
Hopkins, Thomas d1864? *Alli, Alli Sup, BiDLA*
Hopkins, Thomas Cramer 1861-1935 *DcAmA, DcNAA, WhWNAA*
Hopkins, Thomas J 1930- *ConAu 37, WrD 1976*
Hopkins, Thomas M *IndAu 1816*
Hopkins, Thomas Marsland *Alli Sup*
Hopkins, Tighe *Alli Sup*
Hopkins, Vivian C 1909- *ConAu 33, WrD 1976*
Hopkins, William *Alli*
Hopkins, William 1647-1700 *Alli, DcEnL*
Hopkins, William 1706-1786 *Alli, BiDLA, DcEnL*
Hopkins, William Barton 1853-1904 *Alli Sup, DcNAA*
Hopkins, William Bonner *Alli Sup*
Hopkins, William John 1863-1926 *AmA&B, DcNAA*
Hopkins, William Rowland 1869- *OhA&B*
Hopkinson, Miss A M *Alli Sup*
Hopkinson, Sir Alfred *ChPo S2*
Hopkinson, Alfred 1851- *Alli Sup*
Hopkinson, Alfred Stephan 1908- *Au&Wr*
Hopkinson, Mrs. C A *Alli Sup*
Hopkinson, Cecil 1898- *Au&Wr*
Hopkinson, Clement Allan Slade 1934- *ConP 1970*
Hopkinson, Diana Mary 1912- *ConAu 29, WrD 1976*
Hopkinson, Francis 1737-1791 *Alli, AmA, AmA&B, BbD, BiD&SB, CasWL, ChPo, ChPo S1, CnDAL, CyAL 1, DcAmA, DcLEnL, DcNAA, EvLB, OxAm, Pen Am, REn, REnAL*
Hopkinson, H G M 1921- *Au&Wr*
Hopkinson, Henry *Alli Sup*
Hopkinson, Henry Thomas 1905- *ConAu 17R, WrD 1976*
Hopkinson, John *Alli*
Hopkinson, Joseph *Alli Sup*
Hopkinson, Joseph 1770-1842 *Alli, AmA&B, BiD&SB, ChPo, CyAL 1, DcAmA, DcEnL, EvLB, OxAm, OxEng, REnAL*
Hopkinson, Leslie W 1866- *WhWNAA*
Hopkinson, Samuel *Alli, BiDLA*
Hopkinson, Tom 1905- *ConNov 1972,*

ConNov 1976, WrD 1976
Hopkinson, William Alli
Hopkirk, Mary 1902- Au&Wr
Hopkirk, Thomas Alli, BiDLA
Hopley, Catherine Cooper Alli Sup
Hopley, Edward Alli Sup
Hopley, Esther Alli Sup
Hopley, George ConAu XR, EncM&D,
TwCA Sup
Hopley, Howard Alli Sup
Hopley, John Edward 1850-1927 DcNAA,
OhA&B
Hopley, Thomas Alli Sup
Hopley-Woolrich, Cornell George 1903-1968
ConAu P-1
Hopp, Signe Marie 1905- Au&Wr
Hoppe, Arthur Watterson 1925- AmA&B,
ConAu 5R, WrD 1976
Hoppe, Emil O 1878- Au&Wr, ConAu 9R
Hoppe, Ronald A 1931- ConAu 45
Hoppener, J Alli
Hoppenstedt, Elbert M 1917- ConAu 1R
Hopper, Anna Logan 1875- WhWNAA
Hopper, Clarence Alli Sup
Hopper, Columbus B 1931- ConAu 33
Hopper, David H 1927- ConAu 23
Hopper, DeWolf 1858-1935 DcNAA
Hopper, Edmund Charles Alli Sup
Hopper, Edward 1816-1888 Alli Sup, ChPo,
ChPo S1, DcAmA, DcNAA
Hopper, Edward 1882-1967 AtlBL, REn
Hopper, Eleanor Tileston ChPo
Hopper, Florence ChPo S1
Hopper, Franklin Ferguson 1878- WhWNAA
Hopper, Harold S 1912- AmSCAP 66
Hopper, Hedda 1890-1966 AmA&B
Hopper, James Marie 1876-1956 AmA&B
Hopper, Jane d1922 DcNAA
Hopper, John 1934- ConAu 17R
Hopper, M Alli Sup
Hopper, Margaretta Alli Sup
Hopper, Nora 1871-1906 ChPo, DcEnA Ap,
PoIre
Hopper, Stanley Romaine 1907- AmA&B
Hopper, Vincent Foster 1906-1976 ConAu 1R,
ConAu 61
Hopper, William DeWolf 1858-1935 AmA&B,
DcNAA
Hoppin, Augustus 1828-1896 Alli Sup,
AmA&B, BiD&SB, ChPo, DcAmA,
DcNAA, EarAB, EarAB Sup
Hoppin, Benjamin Alli Sup
Hoppin, Benjamin 1851-1923 DcNAA
Hoppin, Courtland EarAB, EarAB Sup
Hoppin, Frederick Street 1876-1946 DcNAA
Hoppin, James Mason 1820-1906 Alli Sup,
AmA&B, BiD&SB, DcAmA, DcNAA
Hoppin, Joseph Clark 1870-1925 AmLY,
DcNAA
Hoppin, Richard H 1913- ConAu 41
Hoppin, William J ChPo S2
Hoppner, John 1758-1810 AtlBL
Hoppner, Richard Belgrave Alli, BiDLA
Hoppock, Robert 1901- ConAu 1R,
WrD 1976
Hopps, John Page 1834-1911 Alli Sup,
BiD&SB, ChPo
Hoppus, John Alli
Hoppus, John Devenish Alli Sup
Hoppus, Mary A M Alli Sup, ChPo
Hopson, Charles R Alli
Hopson, Dan, Jr. 1930- ConAu 23
Hopson, Edmund BiDLA
Hopson, Edward Alli
Hopson, Ella Lord Alli Sup
Hopson, George Bailey 1838-1916 DcNAA
Hopson, Peregrine Thomas d1759 OxCan
Hopton, Arthur 1588-1614 Alli
Hopton, Richard Alli
Hopton, Susannah 1627-1709 Alli, DcEnL
Hopton, William 1823- Alli Sup
Hopwood, Avery 1882-1928 AmA&B, CnDAL,
DcNAA, EncM&D, McGWD, ModWD,
OhA&B, OxAm, REnAL
Hopwood, Charles Henry 1829- Alli Sup
Hopwood, Henry Alli
Hopwood, James 1752-1819 BkIE
Hopwood, John Alli

Hopwood, Josephus 1843-1935 DcNAA
Hopwood, Robert R 1910- ConAu P-1
Hopwood, Ronald Arthur 1868- ChPo S1,
ChPo S2, NewC
Hopwood, Victor G OxCan Sup
Hora, Josef 1891-1945 CasWL, CIDMEuL,
EncWL, EvEuW, ModSL 2, Pen Eur,
WhTwL
Horace 065BC-008BC AtlBL, BbD, BiD&SB,
CasWL, ChPo, CyWA, DcEnL, DcEuL,
NewC, OxEng, Pen Cl, RCom, REn
Horace, Young DcEnL
Horack, Frank Edward 1873- WhWNAA
Horack, H Claude 1877- WhWNAA
Horadam, Alwyn Francis 1923- WrD 1976
Horak, M Stephan 1920- ConAu 9R
Horan, James David 1914- AmA&B,
ConAu 13R
Horan, Kenneth 1890- AmA&B, AmNov
Horan, William D 1933- ConAu 25
Horatio PoIre
Horatio, Jane ConAu XR
Horatio-Jones, Edward Babatunde Bankole 1930-
AfA 1
Horbach, Michael 1924- ConAu 29
Horbery, Matthew 1707-1773 Alli, DcEnL
Horchler, Richard 1925- ConAu 5R
Horchow, Reuben 1895-1958 OhA&B
Hord, Parker 1883- AmA&B
Horde, Thomas Alli, BiDLA
Horden, John Alli, ChPo S2
Horder, John 1936- ConP 1970
Horder, Margaret L'Anson 1911- IlCB 1956
Horder, Mervyn 1910- Au&Wr, WrD 1976
Horder, W Garrett Alli Sup, ChPo S2
Hordern, Joseph Alli
Hordern, Joseph Calveley Alli Sup
Hordern, William 1920- ConAu 13R
Hordon, Harris E 1942- ConAu 53
Hore, Alexander Hugh Alli Sup
Hore, Annie Boyle Alli Sup
Hore, Charles Alli, BiDLA
Hore, Henry Francis Alli Sup
Hore, J P Alli Sup, Br&AmS
Hore, John Patrick 1840-1864 PoIre
Hore, Marcus PoIre
Hore, Philip H Alli Sup
Hore-Ruthven, Patrick ChPo S1
Horecky, Paul Louis 1913- ConAu 5R,
WrD 1976
Horelick, Arnold L 1928- ConAu 17R
Horetzky, Charles Alli Sup, OxCan
Horgan, John 1940- Au&Wr
Horgan, John J 1910- ConAu 61
Horgan, John Joseph 1881- CatA 1947,
WhLA
Horgan, Matthew d1849 PoIre
Horgan, Michael P 1846- PoIre
Horgan, Paul 1903- AmA&B, AmNov,
Au&Wr, AuBYP, CatA 1947, ChPo,
CnDAL, ConAu 13R, ConNov 1972,
ConNov 1976, DcLEnL, DrAF 1976,
IlCB 1945, OxAm, REnAL, TwCA Sup,
TwCA Sup, WhWNAA, WrD 1976
Horgan, Stephen Henry 1854-1941 DcNAA
Hori, Ichiro 1910- ConAu 25
Hori, Tsuneo 1896- WhLA
Horia, Vintila 1910?- TwCW
Horia, Vintila 1915- WorAu
Horie, Shigeo 1903- ConAu P-1
Horine, John 1869- WhWNAA
Horka-Follick, Lorayne Ann 1940- ConAu 29
Horkheimer, Max 1895-1973 ConAu 41
Horlacher, James Levi 1870-1942 IndAu 1917
Horlacher, Levi Jackson 1896- IndAu 1917,
WhWNAA
Horlacher, Walter Rawlins 1897- IndAu 1917
Horler, Sydney 1888-1954 EncM&D, EvLB,
LongC, MnBBF
Horlet, Joseph Alli
Horley, Cyril ChPo S1
Horley, Georgina Ursula Au&Wr
Horlock, John Harold 1928- WrD 1976
Horlock, K W 1800?- Alli Sup, Br&AmS
Horman, Richard E 1945- ConAu 29
Horman, William 1450?-1535 Alli, BrAu,
CasWL, OxEng
Hormanden, Daniel 1694-1778 DcNAA

Hormann, Ludwig Von 1837- BiD&SB
Hormayr, Joseph, Freiherr Von 1782-1848
OxGer
Hormell, Orren Chalmer 1879- IndAu 1917
Horn Alli
Horn, Alfred Aloysius 1861?-1931 CasWL,
LongC, TwCA, TwCA Sup
Horn, Charles Edward 1786-1849? Alli, NewC
Horn, D B 1901- ConAu 1R
Horn, Daniel 1934- ConAu 21
Horn, Edward Traill 1850-1915 Alli Sup,
DcAmA, DcNAA
Horn, Ernest 1882- WhWNAA
Horn, Francis H 1908- ConAu 53
Horn, Franz Christoph 1781-1837 BiD&SB,
OxGer
Horn, George Alli
Horn, George F 1917- ConAu 5R
Horn, George Thomas Alli Sup
Horn, Heinrich Moritz 1814-1874 OxGer
Horn, Henry BiDLA
Horn, Henry, And Edwin T Hurlstone Alli
Horn, Henry A Alli Sup
Horn, Henry Eyster 1913- ConAu 23
Horn, Jeanne P 1925- ConAu 5R
Horn, John Alli
Horn, John L 1928- ConAu 37
Horn, John Louis 1883- WhWNAA
Horn, Louise McCloy ChPo
Horn, Michiel OxCan Sup
Horn, Paul 1930- AmSCAP 66
Horn, Paul Whitfield 1870-1932 DcNAA,
WhWNAA
Horn, Peter 1934- WrD 1976
Horn, Robert Alli
Horn, Robert M 1933- ConAu 29
Horn, Mrs. S G Alli Sup
Horn, Siegfried Herbert 1908- ConAu 37,
WrD 1976
Horn, Stanley Fitzgerald 1889- AmA&B
Horn, Stefan F 1900- ConAu P-1
Horn, Stephen 1931- ConAu 13R, ConAu 45,
WrD 1976
Horn, Thomas Alli
Horn, Thomas D 1918- ConAu 13R
Horn, Trader TwCA, TwCA Sup
Horn, Ulric ChPo
Horn, Walter 1908- ConAu 23
Horn, William 1839-1917 OhA&B
Horn, William F REnAL
Hornaday, Mary 1906- WhWNAA
Hornaday, William Temple 1854-1937 Alli Sup,
AmA&B, AmLY, BiD&SB, ChPo,
DcAmA, DcNAA, IndAu 1816,
JBA 1934, OxCan, REnAL, TwCA,
TwCA Sup, WhWNAA
Hornadge, William 1918- Au&Wr
Hornback, Bert G 1935- ConAu 29
Hornback, Florence Mary 1892- OhA&B
Hornbeck, Cecil Alli Sup
Hornbeck, Stanley K 1883- WhWNAA
Hornbein, Thomas Frederic 1930- ConAu 53,
WhWNAA
Hornberger, Theodore 1906- ConAu 5R
Hornblow, Arthur 1865-1941? Alli Sup,
AmA&B, DcNAA
Hornblow, Leonora 1920- Au&Wr, AuBYP
Hornblower, Francis ChPo
Hornblower, J C Alli
Hornbook, Adam 1759-1839 AmA
Hornbook, Adam 1805- DcEnL
Hornburg VonRotenburg, Lupold OxGer
Hornby, Charles Alli
Hornby, Mrs. Edmund Alli
Hornby, Geoffrey Alli
Hornby, Geoffry BiDLA
Hornby, George S Alli Sup
Hornby, John 1880-1927 OxCan
Hornby, John 1913- Au&Wr, ConAu 9R
Hornby, Robert 1919- Au&Wr
Hornby, Thomas Alli, BiDLA
Hornby, William Alli
Horncastle, George MnBBF
Horne, Bishop ChPo
Horne, A H Alli Sup
Horne, Abraham Reeser 1834-1902 DcNAA
Horne, Alistair Allan 1925- Au&Wr,
ConAu 5R, OxCan, WrD 1976

Horne, Andrew *Alli, BiDLA*
Horne, Charles *Alli Sup*
Horne, Charles Francis 1870-1942 *AmA&B, AmLY, DcNAA, WhWNAA*
Horne, Cynthia Miriam 1939- *ConAu 5R*
Horne, Cyril Morton 1886-1916 *ChPo, ChPo S1*
Horne, David *ChPo, ChPo S1*
Horne, David Mark Kentigern 1923-1940 *ChPo S2*
Horne, Diantha W *ChPo*
Horne, Donald Richmond 1921- *Au&Wr, WrD 1976*
Horne, Fallon & Thornthwaite, William H *Alli Sup*
Horne, Frank S 1899-1974 *AnMV 1926, BlkAW, ChPo S1, ConAu 53*
Horne, Geoffrey 1916- *Au&Wr, ConAu 9R*
Horne, George *Alli Sup*
Horne, George 1730-1792 *Alli, DcEnL*
Horne, H P *Alli*
Horne, Henry *Alli*
Horne, Herbert Percy 1865-1916 *ChPo*
Horne, Herman Harrell 1874-1946 *AmLY, DcNAA, WhWNAA*
Horne, Howard *AmA&B, ConAu XR*
Horne, Hubert T M *Alli Sup*
Horne, Hugh Robert 1915- *ConAu 5R*
Horne, Ida Harrell *BiDSA*
Horne, J G *ChPo, ChPo S2*
Horne, J H *Alli Sup*
Horne, James *Alli Sup*
Horne, John *Alli, Alli Sup, BiDLA, NewC, OxEng*
Horne, John d1676 *Alli*
Horne, John d1934 *ChPo S1*
Horne, Mary Tracy Earle 1864- *AmA&B*
Horne, Massingberd *Alli Sup*
Horne, Melvil *BiDLA*
Horne, Melville *Alli*
Horne, Richard Hengist 1803-1884 *BbD, CasWL, ChPo, ChPo S2, DcEnL, DcLEnL, EvLB, OxEng*
Horne, Richard Henry 1803-1884 *Alli, Alli Sup, BiD&SB, BrAu 19, CarSB, CasWL, Chmbr 3, DcEnA, DcEuL, DcLEnL, EvLB, JBA 1934, NewC, OxEng*
Horne, Robert *Alli*
Horne, Robert d1580 *Alli*
Horne, Shirley 1919- *ConAu 49*
Horne, Thomas *Alli, BiDLA*
Horne, Thomas Hartwell 1780-1862 *Alli, BiDLA, Chmbr 2, DcEnL, EvLB*
Horne, W W *Alli, BiDLA*
Horne, William *Alli, Alli Sup*
Horne, William Titus 1876- *WhWNAA*
Horne Tooke, John *CasWL*
Horneck, Anthony 1641-1696 *Alli*
Horneck, William *Alli*
Hornem, Horace 1788-1824 *DcEnL*
Horner, Dave 1934- *ConAu 17R*
Horner, David *Au&Wr*
Horner, Francis *Alli Sup*
Horner, Francis 1778-1817 *Alli, DcEnL*
Horner, Francis Asbury 1849-1920 *IndAu 1816*
Horner, Francis D'Altry And Kidson, G *Alli Sup*
Horner, G R B *Alli*
Horner, George F 1899- *ConAu 33*
Horner, Hattie *Alli Sup*
Horner, John B 1856-1933 *Alli, DcNAA, WhWNAA*
Horner, John Curwen 1922- *Au&Wr, WrD 1976*
Horner, John Truman 1888- *WhWNAA*
Horner, Jonah *Alli, Alli Sup*
Horner, Joseph *Alli Sup*
Horner, Joseph Andrew *Alli Sup*
Horner, L David, III 1934- *WrD 1976*
Horner, Leonard *Alli*
Horner, S S *Alli Sup*
Horner, Susan *Alli Sup*
Horner, T *Alli, BiDLA*
Horner, Thomas Marland 1927- *ConAu 37*
Horner, W G *Alli*

Horner, William Edmunds 1793-1853 *Alli, DcAmA, DcNAA*
Horney, Karen 1885-1952 *AmA&B, TwCA Sup*
Horngren, Charles T 1926- *ConAu 57*
Hornibroke, J L *MnBBF*
Hornibrook, Emma E *Alli Sup*
Hornibrook, Isabel *Alli Sup, AmLY*
Hornibrook, J Laurence *Alli Sup*
Hornibrooke, Isabel *AmA&B*
Hornik, Edith Lynn 1930- *ConAu 61*
Horniman, Annie Elizabeth Fredericka 1860-1937 *LongC, NewC*
Horniman, Roy 1872-1907 *CnMWL*
Hornman, Henry *Alli*
Hornor, S Stockton *Alli, Alli Sup*
Hornos, Axel 1907- *ConAu 29*
Hornsbrugh, Wilma *ChPo S1*
Hornsby, Alton, Jr. 1940- *ConAu 37, LivBA, WrD 1976*
Hornsby, H W *ChPo S2*
Hornsby, John Allan 1859-1939 *DcNAA*
Hornsby, Robert Allen 1926- *WrD 1976*
Hornsby, Roger A 1926- *ConAu 21*
Hornsby, Samuel J *Alli Sup*
Hornsby, T N *Alli Sup*
Hornsby, Thomas *Alli*
Hornsey, John *Alli, BiDLA*
Hornsey, Richard *OxCan Sup*
Hornstein, Harvey A 1938- *ConAu 53*
Hornstein, Lillian Herlands 1909- *ConAu 45*
Hornung, Clarence Pearson 1899- *ConAu 17R*
Hornung, Ernest William 1866-1921 *BbD, BiD&SB, Chmbr 3, DcLEnL, EncM&D, EvLB, LongC, MnBBF, NewC, REn, TwCA, TwCA Sup, TwCW*
Hornyansky, Michael *OxCan*
Horovitz, Frances Margaret 1938- *ConP 1970*
Horovitz, Israel 1939- *ConAu 33, ConDr, CrCD, DrAF 1976, DrAP 1975, ModAL Sup, WrD 1976*
Horovitz, Michael 1935- *ConP 1970, ConP 1975, WrD 1976*
Horovitz, Yaakov 1901- *CasWL*
Horowitz, Al *ConAu XR*
Horowitz, David 1939- *Au&Wr, ConAu 13R*
Horowitz, Edward 1904- *ConAu 1R*
Horowitz, Esther 1920- *ConAu 49*
Horowitz, Gad *OxCan Sup*
Horowitz, I A 1907-1973 *ConAu 41*
Horowitz, Ira 1934- *ConAu 41*
Horowitz, Irving Louis 1929- *ConAu 41*
Horowitz, Leonard M 1937- *ConAu 37*
Horowitz, Mardi J 1934- *ConAu 33*
Horowitz, Michael M 1933- *ConAu 41*
Horowitz, Robert S 1924- *ConAu 9R*
Horozco, Sebastian De 1510?-1580? *CasWL, DcSpL*
Horr, Alfred Reuel 1875-1958 *OhA&B*
Horr, George Edwin 1856-1927 *DcNAA*
Horr, Grace H *ChPo*
Horr, Norton T And Bemis, Alton A *Alli Sup*
Horrabin, James Francis 1884-1962 *NewC, WhCL*
Horrall, Onis Harrison 1888- *IndAu 1917*
Horrall, Spillard F 1829-1911 *IndAu 1917*
Horrell, C William 1918- *ConAu 61*
Horrigan, L B And Thompson, Seymour *Alli Sup*
Horrock, Nicholas 1936- *ConAu 49*
Horrocks, Brian Gwynne 1895- *WrD 1976*
Horrocks, Charles *Alli Sup*
Horrocks, Edna M 1908- *ConAu 17*
Horrocks, James *CyAL 1*
Horrocks, James D *Alli Sup*
Horrocks, John E 1913- *ConAu 5R*
Horrocks, Joseph *Alli Sup*
Horrocks, William Heaton 1859- *WhLA*
Horrox, Jeremiah 1619-1641 *Alli*
Horrwitz, Ernest Philip 1866- *AmA&B*
Horry, Peter *BiDSA*
Horry, S C *Alli*
Horry, Sidney Calder *Alli Sup*
Horsborough, Wendy *ChPo S2*
Horsbrugh, Wilma *ChPo*
Horsburgh, Andrew *Alli Sup*
Horsburgh, Andrew 1827- *ChPo S1*
Horsburgh, H J N 1918- *ConAu 25*

Horsburgh, James *Alli, Alli Sup, BiDLA*
Horsburgh, John 1791-1869 *Alli Sup*
Horsburgh, Matilda *Alli Sup*
Horsburgh, William *Alli*
Horsefall, James *Alli*
Horsefield, Ethelyn *ChPo S1*
Horsefield, Frederic John 1859- *WhLA*
Horsefield, J W *Alli*
Horsefield, John Keith 1901- *ConAu 5R, WrD 1976*
Horsell, William *Alli Sup*
Horsely, David *ConAu XR*
Horsely, Ramsbottom *ConAu XR*
Horseman, Elaine Hall 1925- *ConAu 13R*
Horseman, John 1775-1844 *ChPo*
Horseman, Nicholas *Alli*
Horsey, George 1819- *Alli Sup*
Horsey, John *Alli*
Horsfall, Jack Campbell 1912- *Au&Wr*
Horsfall, John *Alli*
Horsfall, Magdalene 1884-1936 *CarSB*
Horsfall, Richard *Alli Sup*
Horsfall, Robert Bruce 1869- *ChPo, ChPo S1, IlCB 1945, WhWNAA*
Horsfall, T C *Alli Sup*
Horsfield, Louisa A *Alli Sup*
Horsfield, Thomas 1773-1859 *Alli, DcAmA*
Horsfield, Thomas Walker 1837- *DcEnL*
Horsford, Cornelia 1861- *DcAmA*
Horsford, Eben Norton 1818-1893 *Alli Sup, DcAmA, DcNAA*
Horsford, J *Alli*
Horsford, John *Alli Sup*
Horsford, Mrs. M G *ChPo S2*
Horsford, Mary L'Hommedieu Gardiner 1824-1855 *Alli, DcAmA, DcNAA*
Horsley, Charles Edward *Alli Sup*
Horsley, Heneage *BiDLA*
Horsley, Henry Sharpe *ChPo S1*
Horsley, James 1938- *ConAu 45*
Horsley, John *Alli, Alli Sup*
Horsley, John 1685-1731 *Alli, DcEnL*
Horsley, John Callcott 1817-1903 *ChPo, ChPo S1*
Horsley, John Shelton 1870- *WhWNAA*
Horsley, John William *Alli Sup*
Horsley, Phyllis Margaret 1903- *Au&Wr*
Horsley, Reginald Ernest 1863- *ChPo, MnBBF*
Horsley, Samuel 1733-1806 *Alli, Chmbr 2, DcEnL*
Horsley, Victor Alexander Haden *Alli Sup*
Horsley, William *Alli*
Horsman, Gallan *BlkAW*
Horsman, Gilbert *Alli*
Horsman, Reginald 1931- *Au&Wr, ConAu 1R, WrD 1976*
Horsmanden, Daniel 1691-1778 *Alli, DcAmA*
Horsnell, John *Alli*
Horsnell, William *Alli Sup, BbtC*
Horspool, A *ChPo, ChPo S1*
Horspool, Maurice Arthur Rupert 1905- *Au&Wr*
Horst, Ben *Alli Sup*
Horst, Irvin B 1915- *ConAu 41*
Horst, Rudolf H 1878- *WhWNAA*
Horst, Samuel 1919- *ConAu 21*
Horstmann, Carl *Alli Sup*
Horstmann, G Henry *Alli Sup*
Horstmann, Ignatius Frederick 1840-1908 *DcNAA, OhA&B*
Hort, Lieutenant Colonel *Alli*
Hort, Mrs. Alfred *Alli Sup*
Hort, Fenton John Anthony 1828-1892 *Alli Sup, BrAu 19, OxEng*
Hort, Josiah d1751 *Alli*
Hort, Richard *PoIre*
Hort, Robert *Alli*
Hort, William Jillard *Alli, BiDLA*
Horta, Maria Teresa *AuNews 1*
Hortatzis, Georgios *Pen Eur*
Horte, Josiah d1751 *Alli*
Horten, Hans Ernest 1914- *Au&Wr*
Hortensius 114BC-050BC *CasWL, Pen Cl*
Hortentius *Alli*
Horthouse, J Henry *ChPo S1*
Horton, Alice *ChPo*
Horton, Caroline W *Alli Sup*
Horton, Charles Marcus 1879- *WhWNAA*

Horton, Corinne Stocker *BiDSA*
Horton, Douglas 1891- *AmA&B*
Horton, Mrs. E N *Alli Sup*
Horton, Edward *Alli Sup*
Horton, Edward Augustus 1843-1931 *AmLY, BiD&SB, DcAmA, DcNAA*
Horton, Elizabeth 1902- *AmSCAP 66*
Horton, Ellis 1842-1900 *IndAu 1917*
Horton, F *MnBBF*
Horton, Feliz Lee *WrD 1976*
Horton, Francis Allen *Alli Sup*
Horton, Frank E 1939- *ConAu 29, WrD 1976*
Horton, George 1859-1942 *AmA&B, BiD&SB, ChPo, ChPo S1, DcAmA, DcNAA*
Horton, George Firman 1806-1886 *Alli Sup, DcAmA, DcNAA*
Horton, George Moses 1797?-1883? *BlkAW, ChPo S1, CnDAL*
Horton, James Africanus Beale 1832-1883 *AfA 1, Alli Sup*
Horton, John 1905- *ConAu 9R*
Horton, John S *EarAB Sup*
Horton, Joshua H 1835?-1907 *OhA&B*
Horton, Lance *MnBBF*
Horton, Lewis Henry 1898- *AmSCAP 66*
Horton, Louise 1916- *ConAu 49*
Horton, Lowell 1936- *ConAu 53*
Horton, Mrs. M B *Alli Sup*
Horton, Marcus 1879- *AmLY*
Horton, Marion *WhWNAA*
Horton, Mary-Louise *BlkAW*
Horton, Nancy Phyllis *ChPo S1*
Horton, Paul Burleigh 1916- *ConAu 1R, WrD 1976*
Horton, Philip 1912- *AmSCAP 66*
Horton, Sir R Wilmot *BbtC*
Horton, Richard *Alli Sup*
Horton, Robert Elmer 1875-1945 *DcNAA, WhWNAA*
Horton, Robert Forman 1855- *Alli Sup, WhLA*
Horton, Rod W 1910- *ConAu 49*
Horton, Rushmore G 1826- *Alli, DcNAA*
Horton, Samuel Dana 1844-1895 *Alli Sup, DcAmA, DcNAA, OhA&B*
Horton, Stanley M 1916- *ConAu 57*
Horton, Thomas d1673 *Alli*
Horton, Thomas Corwin 1848-1932 *DcNAA, OhA&B, WhWNAA*
Horton, Thomas Galland *Alli Sup*
Horton, Tudor *EarAB, EarAB Sup*
Horton, Vaughn 1911- *AmSCAP 66*
Horton, W Gray 1897- *Au&Wr*
Horton, Walter Marshall 1895-1966 *AmA&B, OhA&B, WhWNAA*
Horton-Smith, Lionel Graham Horton 1871- *WhLA*
Hortop, Job *Alli, DcEnL*
Horvat, Branko 1928- *ConAu 53*
Horvath, Andreas 1778-1839 *BiD&SB*
Horvath, Betty 1927- *ConAu 17R, SmATA 4, WrD 1976*
Horvath, Ferdinand Huszti 1891- *ConICB, IlCB 1945*
Horvath, Janos 1921- *ConAu 41*
Horvath, Odon Von 1901-1938 *CasWL, CnMD, CnThe, EncWL, McGWD, ModGL, ModWD, OxGer, REnWD, TwCA*
Horvath, Violet Mary 1924- *ConAu 29, WrD 1976*
Horwell, H W *Alli Sup*
Horwich, Frances R 1908- *AmA&B, ConAu P-1*
Horwitt, Arnold B 1918- *AmSCAP 66*
Horwitz, B *Alli Sup*
Horwitz, Carrie Norris *CarSB*
Horwitz, Julius 1920- *AmA&B, ConAu 9R, WrD 1976*
Horwitz, Orville *Alli Sup*
Horwitz, Sylvia L 1911- *ConAu 61*
Horwood, Alfred John *Alli Sup*
Horwood, Caroline *Alli, BiDLA, ChPo*
Horwood, Harold 1923- *ConAu 21, OxCan Sup*
Horwood, Murray Philip 1892- *WhWNAA*
Hosack, David 1769-1835 *Alli, CyAL 1, DcAmA, DcNAA*
Hosack, John d1887 *Alli, Alli Sup*

Hosack, William *Alli Sup*
Hoschna, Karl 1877-1911 *AmSCAP 66*
Hose, G *BbtC*
Hose, H J *Alli*
Hosea *DcOrL 3*
Hosea, Lucy Klinck Rice 1852-1921 *OhA&B*
Hosea, Robert 1811-1906 *OhA&B*
Hoseason, John Cochrane *Alli Sup*
Hoseido, Kisanji *DcOrL 1*
Hoselitz, Bert F 1913- *ConAu 1R*
Hoseman, Thomas *ChPo*
Hosemann, Theodor 1807-1875 *ChPo*
Hosey, Athena 1929- *AmSCAP 66*
Hoseyn Va'eze Kashefi d1505 *DcOrL 3*
Hosford, Benjamin Franklin 1817-1864 *DcNAA*
Hosford, Dorothy 1900-1952 *AnCL, BkCL, MorJA, St&VC*
Hosford, Frances Juliette 1853-1937 *DcNAA, OhA&B*
Hosford, Jessie 1892- *ConAu 41, SmATA 5*
Hosford, Oramel 1820-1893 *DcNAA*
Hosford, Philip L 1926- *ConAu 57*
Hoshaw, Robert William 1921- *IndAu 1917*
Hoshour, Samuel Klinefelter 1803-1883 *Alli Sup, AmA&B, DcNAA, IndAu 1816*
Hosic, James Fleming 1870-1959 *AmA&B, WhWNAA*
Hosie, Stanley W 1922- *ConAu 25*
Hosier, Helen Kooiman 1928- *ConAu 61*
Hosier, John *Alli*
Hosken, Alice Cecil Seymour *WhLA*
Hosken, Clifford *MnBBF*
Hosken, Clifford 1882- *WhLA*
Hosken, Ernest Charles Heath 1875- *MnBBF, WhLA*
Hosken, Fran P 1919- *ConAu 57*
Hosken, James Dryden *ChPo S2*
Hoskiaer, Otto Valdemar Von *Alli Sup*
Hoskin, A A *ChPo*
Hoskin, Arthur Joseph 1869- *WhWNAA*
Hosking, Arthur N *ChPo S2*
Hosking, Gordon Albert 1907- *Au&Wr*
Hosking, William *Alli, Alli Sup*
Hoskins, Mrs. A L *AmA&B*
Hoskins, Bradford S *BbtC*
Hoskins, C *ChPo S2*
Hoskins, Chapin 1891- *WhWNAA*
Hoskins, Franklin Evans 1858-1920 *DcNAA*
Hoskins, G A *Alli, Alli Sup*
Hoskins, George Gordon *Alli Sup*
Hoskins, H H *Alli*
Hoskins, Halford Lancaster 1891-1967 *AmA&B, IndAu 1917*
Hoskins, James Dickason 1870- *WhWNAA*
Hoskins, John *Alli Sup, ChPo*
Hoskins, John 1566-1638 *Alli, CasWL, DcEnL*
Hoskins, John 1827- *ChPo S2*
Hoskins, John, Jr. d1631 *Alli*
Hoskins, John Preston 1867- *WhWNAA*
Hoskins, Joseph 1745-1788 *Alli, PoCh*
Hoskins, Josephine R *BiDSA, LivFWS*
Hoskins, Katherine DeMontalant 1909- *AmA&B, Au&Wr, ConAu 25, ConP 1970, ConP 1975, WrD 1976*
Hoskins, Leander Miller 1860-1937 *DcNAA*
Hoskins, Mary Inge 1858- *WhWNAA*
Hoskins, Nathan 1795-1869 *DcAmA, DcNAA*
Hoskins, Robert 1933- *ConAu 29*
Hoskins, Samuel Elliot *Alli Sup*
Hoskins, Thomas H *Alli Sup*
Hoskins, William George 1908- *Au&Wr, ConAu 13R*
Hoskins, William Walton *BiDSA*
Hoskinson, W S *Alli Sup*
Hoskold, H D *Alli Sup*
Hoskyns, Chandos Wren *Alli, Alli Sup*
Hoskyns, John *Alli Sup*
Hoskyns, John, Jr. d1631 *Alli*
Hoskyns, John, Sr. d1638 *Alli*
Hoskyns-Abrahall *Alli Sup*
Hoskyns-Abrahall, Clare *Au&Wr, ConAu 29*
Hosley, Richard 1921- *ConAu 5R*
Hosman, Everett Mills 1888- *WhWNAA*
Hosmat, Hyton *DcNAA*
Hosmer, Arthur Henry *Alli Sup*
Hosmer, Burr Griswold *Alli Sup*
Hosmer, Charles B, Jr. 1932- *ConAu 13R*

Hosmer, Frederick Lucian 1840-1929 *Alli Sup, AmA&B, ChPo, ChPo S1, DcAmA, DcNAA, OhA&B, WebEAL, WhWNAA*
Hosmer, G H *Alli Sup*
Hosmer, George Leonard 1874-1935 *DcNAA, WhWNAA*
Hosmer, George Washington 1830?-1914 *Alli Sup, AmA&B, BiD&SB, DcAmA, DcNAA*
Hosmer, Hezekiah Lord 1814-1893 *Alli Sup, AmA, AmA&B, DcNAA, OhA&B*
Hosmer, James Kendall 1834-1927 *Alli Sup, AmA, AmA&B, BiD&SB, BiDSA, DcAmA, DcNAA, OhA&B, REnAL, WhWNAA*
Hosmer, John Allen 1850-1907 *AmA&B, DcNAA, OhA&B*
Hosmer, Lucius 1870-1935 *AmSCAP 66*
Hosmer, Margaret Kerr 1830-1889 *Alli Sup, AmA&B, BiD&SB, DcAmA, DcNAA*
Hosmer, Ralph Sheldon 1874- *WhWNAA*
Hosmer, Titus d1780 *CyAL 1*
Hosmer, William *Alli, DcNAA*
Hosmer, William H C 1814-1877 *Alli, AmA, AmA&B, BiD&SB, CyAL 2, DcAmA, DcLEnL, DcNAA, OxAm, REnAL*
Hosmon, Robert Stahr 1943- *ConAu 45*
Hosokawa, Bill *ConAu XR*
Hosokawa, William K 1915- *ConAu 29*
Hospers, John 1918- *AmA&B, ConAu 1R*
Hoss, Elijah Embree 1849-1919 *BiDSA, DcNAA*
Hoss, George Washington 1824-1906 *DcNAA*
Hoss, Margaret McBride *ChPo*
Hoss, Marvin Allen 1929- *ConAu 29*
Hossack, Annie Dennison *ChPo S1*
Hossack, Colin *Alli*
Hossent, Harry 1916- *Au&Wr, ConAu P-1, WrD 1976*
Hossfeld, C *Alli Sup*
Hoster, Constance 1864- *WhLA*
Hosterman, Arthur David 1860-1939 *OhA&B*
Hostetter, B Charles 1916- *ConAu 1R*
Hostler, Charles W 1919- *ConAu 23*
Hostos, Bonilla Eugenio Maria De 1839-1903 *Pen Am*
Hostos, Eugenio Maria De 1839-1903 *CasWL, DcSpL, PueRA, REn*
Hostovsky, Egon 1908-1973 *Au&Wr, CasWL, EncWL, EvEuW, ModSL 2, Pen Eur, TwCW, WorAu*
Hostrop, Richard Winfred 1925- *ConAu 25, WrD 1976*
Hostrup, Jens Christian 1818-1892 *BiD&SB, CasWL, DcEuL*
Hotchkin, B B *Alli Sup*
Hotchkin, James Harvey 1781-1851 *DcNAA*
Hotchkin, Samuel Fitch 1833-1912 *Alli Sup, DcAmA, DcNAA*
Hotchkin, Thomas *Alli*
Hotchkiss, Chauncey Crafts 1852-1920 *AmA&B, AmLY, DcAmA, DcNAA*
Hotchkiss, Christine Alexandra 1921- *Au&Wr*
Hotchkiss, Clarence Roland 1880- *WhWNAA*
Hotchkiss, George Woodward 1831-1926 *DcNAA*
Hotchkiss, James Harvey 1781-1851 *DcAmA, DcNAA*
Hotchkiss, Jeanette 1901- *ConAu 23*
Hotchkiss, Jedediah 1827-1899 *Alli Sup, BiDSA, DcNAA*
Hotchkiss, Philo Pratt *Alli Sup*
Hotchkiss, Ralf D 1947- *ConAu 33*
Hotchkiss, Willard E 1874- *WhWNAA*
Hotchkiss, William Otis 1878- *WhWNAA*
Hotchkiss, Willis Ray 1873-1948 *OhA&B*
Hotchner, Aaron Edward 1919- *AmA&B*
Hotckkin, James H d1851 *Alli*
Hotham, Charles *Alli*
Hotham, Durand *Alli*
Hotham, Sir John *Alli*
Hotham, Sir Richard *Alli*
Hothom, Walter *DcEnL*
Hotman, Francois 1524-1590 *DcEuL, OxFr*
Hotos, Adolfo De 1887- *PueRA*
Hotson, John Hargrove 1930- *ConAu 25, WrD 1976*
Hotson, John Leslie 1897- *TwCA Sup*

Hotson, Leslie 1897- *AmA&B*, *LongC*, *REn*
Hotspur *WrD 1976*
Hotspur, Paul *MnBBF*
Hott, James William 1844-1902 *DcAmA*,
 DcNAA, *OhA&B*
Hottel, Hoyt Clarke 1903- *IndAu 1917*
Hotten, John Camden 1832-1873 *Alli Sup*
Hou, Chi-Ming 1924- *ConAu 23*
Houblon, A G *MnBBF*
Houbraken, Arnold 1660-1719 *CasWL*
Houck, Frederick Alfons 1866-1954 *OhA&B*
Houck, George Francis 1847-1916 *OhA&B*
Houck, John W 1931- *ConAu 29*
Houck, Louis *Alli Sup*
Houck, Louis 1840-1925 *DcNAA*
Houdar DeLaMotte, Antoine 1672-1731 *CasWL*,
 OxFr, *Pen Eur*
Houdemius, Joh *Alli*
Houdetot, Elisabeth-Sophie, Comtesse D'
 1730-1813 *OxFr*
Houdini, Harry 1874-1926 *DcNAA*
Houdon, Jean Antoine 1741-1828 *AtlBL*, *OxFr*,
 REn
Houedard, Pierre-Sylvester 1924- *ConP 1970*,
 ConP 1975, *WrD 1976*
Houf, Horace Thomas 1889-1959 *OhA&B*
Hough, Alfred J 1848-1922 *ChPo*, *ChPo S1*,
 DcNAA
Hough, Charles *Alli Sup*
Hough, Charlotte 1924- *ChPo S2*, *ConAu 9R*,
 IlCB 1956, *SmATA 9*, *WrD 1976*
Hough, Clara Sharpe 1893- *AmA&B*
Hough, Clarence Augustus 1867?-1935
 IndAu 1917
Hough, Donald 1895-1965 *AmA&B*, *REnAL*
Hough, Edwin Leadman 1852- *BbD*
Hough, Emerson 1857-1923 *AmA&B*, *AmLY*,
 BiD&SB, *DcAmA*, *DcLEnL*, *DcNAA*,
 OxAm, *REn*, *REnAL*, *TwCA*,
 TwCA Sup
Hough, Florenz H *BlkAW*
Hough, Franklin Benjamin 1820?-1885 *Alli*,
 Alli Sup, *BbtC*, *CyAL 2*, *DcAmA*,
 DcNAA, *OhA&B*
Hough, George A 1868- *WhWNAA*
Hough, George Tanner *Alli Sup*
Hough, George Washington 1836-1909 *Alli Sup*,
 DcAmA, *DcNAA*
Hough, Graham Goulder 1908- *Au&Wr*,
 ConP 1970, *WorAu*
Hough, Helen Charlotte 1924- *Au&Wr*
Hough, Henry Beetle 1896- *AmA&B*, *AmNov*,
 ConAu 1R, *REnAL*, *TwCA Sup*
Hough, Henry W 1906- *ConAu 25*
Hough, James *Alli*
Hough, John 1651-1743 *Alli*
Hough, John T, Jr. 1946- *ConAu 33*
Hough, Joseph C, Jr. 1933- *ConAu 23*
Hough, Lewis *Alli Sup*, *MnBBF*
Hough, Lewis Sylvester 1819-1903 *DcNAA*
Hough, Lindy Downer 1944- *ConAu 61*
Hough, Louis 1914- *ConAu 37*, *IndAu 1917*
Hough, Lynn Harold 1877-1971 *AmA&B*,
 OhA&B, *WhWNAA*
Hough, Mary Paul 1858-1941 *DcNAA*
Hough, Nathaniel *Alli*
Hough, Richard Alexander 1922- *Au&Wr*,
 AuBYP, *ConAu 5R*
Hough, Romeyn Beck 1857-1924 *AmLY*,
 DcNAA
Hough, Stanley Bennett 1917- *Au&Wr*,
 ConAu 5R, *WrD 1976*
Hough, Theodore 1865-1924 *DcNAA*
Hough, W S *Alli Sup*
Hough, Walter 1859-1935 *DcNAA*
Hough, Will 1882-1962 *AmSCAP 66*
Hough, William *Alli*
Hough, William Samuel 1860-1912 *DcNAA*
Hougham, Arthur 1889- *WhLA*
Houghteling, James L, Jr. 1920- *ConAu 5R*
Houghton, Lord 1809-1885 *Alli Sup*, *BrAu 19*,
 ChPo, *ChPo S1*, *Chmbr 3*, *DcEnL*,
 DcLEnL, *NewC*, *OxEng*, *Pen Eng*
Houghton, Alfred Thomas 1896- *Au&Wr*,
 WrD 1976
Houghton, Arthur Amory *ChPo S1*
Houghton, Arthur Boyd 1836-1875 *ChPo*
Houghton, Aylmar *Alli*

Houghton, Carolyn Wells *WhWNAA*
Houghton, Charles Adams *Alli Sup*
Houghton, Charles Norris 1909- *Au&Wr*,
 IndAu 1917
Houghton, Claude 1889-1961 *ChPo S1*,
 ChPo S2, *LongC*, *TwCA*, *TwCA Sup*,
 WhLA
Houghton, Donald Herbert 1930- *Au&Wr*
Houghton, Douglass 1809-1845 *Alli*
Houghton, E H *Alli Sup*
Houghton, Edward L *Alli Sup*
Houghton, Edward P *Alli Sup*
Houghton, Edward Rittenhouse 1871-1955
 AmA&B
Houghton, Elizabeth *ConAu XR*
Houghton, Ellen *CarSB*
Houghton, Ellen E *Alli Sup*, *CarSB*, *ChPo*
Houghton, Eric 1930- *Au&Wr*, *AuBYP*,
 ConAu 1R, *SmATA 7*, *WrD 1976*
Houghton, Frederick Lowell 1859-1927 *DcNAA*
Houghton, George Washington Wright
 1850-1891 *Alli Sup*, *AmA&B*, *BiD&SB*,
 ChPo, *DcAmA*, *DcNAA*
Houghton, George William 1905- *Au&Wr*,
 ConAu 13R
Houghton, Georgiana *Alli Sup*
Houghton, H H *Alli Sup*
Houghton, Mrs. Hedwin *REnAL*
Houghton, Henry Clark 1837-1901 *Alli Sup*,
 DcAmA, *DcNAA*
Houghton, Henry Oscar 1823-1895 *AmA&B*
Houghton, J *Alli*, *BiDLA*
Houghton, John *Alli*
Houghton, Louise Seymour 1838-1920 *Alli Sup*,
 AmLY SR, *DcAmA*, *DcNAA*
Houghton, Mary *Alli*, *BiDLA*
Houghton, Neal D 1895- *ConAu 25*,
 WrD 1976
Houghton, Norris 1909- *AmA&B*, *ConAu 23*
Houghton, Pendlebury *Alli*, *BiDLA*
Houghton, Ptolemy *Alli Sup*
Houghton, Reginald Leighton 1910- *Au&Wr*
Houghton, Baron Richard Monckton Milnes
 1809-1885 *BiD&SB*, *CasWL*, *DcEnA*,
 EvLB
Houghton, R M ALSO Milnes, Richard M
Houghton, Robert Offley Ashburton Milnes
 1858-1945 *ChPo*, *ChPo S1*, *ChPo S2*
Houghton, Ross C *Alli Sup*
Houghton, S M *Alli Sup*
Houghton, Stanley 1881-1913 *Chmbr 3*,
 CnMD, *LongC*, *McGWD*, *ModWD*,
 NewC
Houghton, Thomas *Alli*
Houghton, Walter *Alli Sup*
Houghton, Walter E, Jr. 1904- *AmA&B*,
 ChPo S1
Houghton, Walter Edwards 1904- *ConAu P-1*
Houghton, Walter Raleigh *DcNAA*
Houghton, Walter Raleigh 1845-1929
 IndAu 1816
Houghton, William *Alli*, *Alli Sup*, *BiDLA*
Houghton, William 1812-1870 *Alli Sup*
Houghton, William Addison 1852-1917 *DcNAA*
Houghton, William Stanley 1881-1913 *DcLEnL*,
 EvLB, *OxEng*, *REn*, *TwCA*, *TwCW*
Hougron, Jean 1923- *REn*
Houk, Eliza Phillips Thruston 1833-1914
 DcNAA, *OhA&B*
Houk, Howard Jacob 1912- *IndAu 1917*
Houlbrook, William *Alli*
Houlbrooke, Theophilus *Alli*
Houlder, Charles Spencer *Alli Sup*
Houlder, J A *Alli Sup*
Houlder, Robert *Alli*
Houldey, William Ephraim *Alli Sup*
Houldin, Joseph Eric 1916- *Au&Wr*,
 WrD 1976
Houlding, Henry *Alli Sup*
Houlding, John Richard *Alli Sup*
Houle, Cyril O 1913- *ConAu 5R*, *WrD 1976*
Houle, Leopold *OxCan*
Houlehen, Robert J 1918- *ConAu 49*
Houlgate, Deke 1930- *ConAu 61*
Houlston, Thomas *Alli*
Houlston, William *Alli*, *Alli Sup*, *BiDLA*
Hoult, Norah 1898- *LongC*, *TwCA*,
 TwCA Sup, *WhTwL*

Houlton, Elisabeth 1919- *Au&Wr*
Houlton, Ella Catharine *Alli Sup*
Houlton, Robert *Alli*, *BiDLA*, *PoIre*
Houn, Franklin W 1920- *ConAu 23*,
 WrD 1976
Hounsom, Eric W *OxCan Sup*
Hourani, George F 1913- *ConAu 45*
Hourd, Marjorie Lovegrove 1903- *Au&Wr*
Hourihane, Ursula Mary 1902- *Au&Wr*
Hours, Madeleine 1915- *ConAu 49*
Hours-Miedan, Madeleine *ConAu 49*
Hours-Miedan, Magdeleine *ConAu 49*
Hourwich, Isaac Aaronovich 1860-1924 *AmLY*,
 DcNAA
Houschone, William *Alli*
House, Abigail 1790-1861 *OhA&B*
House, Anne W *ConAu XR*
House, Benjamin Davenport 1844-1887
 IndAu 1816
House, Boyce 1896-1961 *AmA&B*
House, Charles 1916- *ConAu 25*
House, Edward Howard 1836-1901 *Alli Sup*,
 AmA, *AmA&B*, *BiD&SB*, *DcAmA*,
 DcNAA
House, Edward Mandell 1858-1938 *AmA&B*,
 DcNAA, *OxAm*, *TexWr*
House, Elwin Lincoln 1861-1932 *DcNAA*,
 WhWNAA
House, Ernest R 1937- *ConAu 45*
House, Erwin 1824-1875 *Alli Sup*, *OhA&B*
House, Homer Clyde 1871-1939 *AmA&B*,
 ChPo S2, *DcNAA*, *WhWNAA*
House, Humphry 1908-1955 *WorAu*
House, Jay Elmer 1872-1936 *AmA&B*,
 DcNAA, *TwCA*
House, John William 1919- *WrD 1976*
House, Julius Temple *WhWNAA*
House, Ralph Emerson 1873-1940 *DcNAA*
House, Robert Burton 1892- *ConAu P-1*
House, Robert W 1920- *ConAu 53*
House, Roy Temple 1878-1963 *AmA&B*,
 ChPo S1, *WhWNAA*
House, Timothy d1865? *EarAB*
Household, Geoffrey 1900- *Au&Wr*,
 ConNov 1972, *ConNov 1976*, *EncM&D*,
 LongC, *NewC*, *TwCA*, *TwCA Sup*,
 WhCL, *WrD 1976*
Household, Henry Leonard Moore 1914-
 Au&Wr
Household, Humphrey George West 1906-
 Au&Wr, *WrD 1976*
Houselander, Caryll *CatA 1947*
Houseman, Barton L 1933- *ConAu 61*
Houseman, C *Alli*
Houseman, Clemence Annie 1863?- *ChPo*
Houseman, John *Alli*
Houseman, Laurence 1865-1959 *CnThe*
Houseman, L ALSO Housman, Laurence
Houseman, Lorna 1924- *Au&Wr*, *WrD 1976*
Housepian, Marjorie 1923- *ConAu 33*
Houser, Allan C 1914- *IlBYP*, *IlCB 1945*,
 IlCB 1956, *IlCB 1966*
Houser, James Alfred 1847-1916 *IndAu 1917*
Houser, John David 1888-1938 *DcNAA*
Houseworth, Henry *IndAu 1917*
Housh, Snow Longley *ChPo S2*
Houslop, Norman Louis 1906- *Au&Wr*
Housman, A E 1859-1936 *AnCL*, *AtlBL*,
 CnE&AP, *CnMWL*, *CyWA*, *EncWL*,
 LongC, *ModBL*, *ModBL Sup*, *Pen Eng*,
 RAdv 1, *REn*, *RCom*, *St&VC*, *TwCW*,
 WebEAL, *WhTwL*
Housman, Alfred Edward 1859-1936 *CasWL*,
 ChPo, *ChPo S1*, *ChPo S2*, *Chmbr 3*,
 DcLEnL, *EvLB*, *NewC*, *OxEng*, *TwCA*,
 TwCA Sup, *WhLA*
Housman, Francis *Alli Sup*
Housman, Henry *Alli Sup*
Housman, John *BiDLA*
Housman, Laurence 1865-1959 *ChPo*, *ChPo S1*,
 ChPo S2, *Chmbr 3*, *CnMD*, *DcEnA Ap*,
 DcLEnL, *EvLB*, *IlCB 1945*, *JBA 1934*,
 LongC, *McGWD*, *ModBL*, *ModWD*,
 NewC, *OxEng*, *Pen Eng*, *REn*, *TwCA*,
 TwCA Sup, *WhLA*
Housman, L ALSO Houseman, Laurence
Housman, R *BiDLA*
Housman, R T *ChPo S1*

Howard, Frederick *Alli, BrAu, DcEnL*
Howard, G Alvan *ChPo S1*
Howard, Geoffrey *ChPo, ChPo S1*
Howard, George *Alli*
Howard, George Arthur 1918- *WrD 1976*
Howard, George Broadley *Alli Sup*
Howard, George Edmund 1725-1786 *DcEnL*
Howard, George Elliott 1849-1928? *AmA&B, DcAmA, DcNAA*
Howard, George Fitzalan Bronson 1884-1922 *AmA&B, DcNAA, EncM&D, REnAL*
Howard, George Henry 1843-1917 *DcNAA*
Howard, George Henry 1844-1925 *DcNAA*
Howard, George Sallade 1903- *AmSCAP 66*
Howard, George W F, Earl Of Carlisle 1802-1864 *Alli, Alli Sup*
Howard, George Washington *Alli Sup*
Howard, Gilbert 1934- *ConAu 49*
Howard, Gorges Edmund 1715-1786 *Alli, PoIre*
Howard, H *BiDLA*
Howard, H L *NewC*
Howard, H R *AmA&B, BiDSA*
Howard, Harold P 1905- *ConAu 33*
Howard, Harry Clay 1866-1930 *DcNAA*
Howard, Harry Nicholas 1902- *AmA&B, ConAu 49, WhWNAA, WrD 1976*
Howard, Hartley *ConAu XR, WrD 1976*
Howard, Harvey J 1880- *WhWNAA*
Howard, Helen Addison 1904- *ConAu 5R, WhPNW, WrD 1976*
Howard, Helen Manley *ChPo S1*
Howard, Henry *Alli*
Howard, Henry 1539?-1614 *Alli, DcEnL*
Howard, Henry 1757-1842 *Alli*
Howard, Henry 1769-1847 *ChPo, ChPo S1p*
Howard, Henry 1815- *Alli Sup, BbtC*
Howard, Henry 1859-1933 *DcNAA, WhWNAA*
Howard, Henry, Earl Of Surrey 1517?-1547 *Alli, AtlBL, BrAu, CasWL, ChPo, CnE&AP, CrE&SL, CriT 1, DcEnL, DcLEnL, EvLB, NewC, Pen Eng*
Howard, Henry Charles, Earl Of Suffolk 1833- *Alli Sup*
Howard, Henry Edward John 1795-1868 *Alli, Alli Sup*
Howard, Henry Newman 1861- *ChPo S2*
Howard, Henry St. John *Alli Sup*
Howard, Herbert *ChPo, MnBBF*
Howard, Hilda *OxCan*
Howard, Horton *Alli Sup*
Howard, Hugh *ChPo*
Howard, Hugh 1675-1737 *BkIE*
Howard, Ian P 1927- *ConAu 23*
Howard, Irene *OxCan Sup*
Howard, J B *Alli, BiDLA*
Howard, J E *Alli Sup*
Howard, J H *Alli, BbtC*
Howard, J P *Alli Sup*
Howard, J R *ChPo*
Howard, J Woodford, Jr. 1931- *ConAu 33, WrD 1976*
Howard, Jacob M *Alli*
Howard, James *Alli, Alli Sup*
Howard, James A 1922- *ConAu 13R*
Howard, James H 1925- *ConAu 41*
Howard, James H W *BlkAW*
Howard, James Quay 1836-1912 *Alli Sup, AmA&B, DcNAA, OhA&B*
Howard, Jane Temple 1935- *ConAu 29, WrD 1976*
Howard, Jarrard John *BiDLA*
Howard, John *Alli, Alli Sup, BiDLA, NewC*
Howard, John 1726-1790 *Alli*
Howard, John 1838-1904 *DcNAA*
Howard, John 1916- *ConAu 41*
Howard, John Eldred 1913- *Au&Wr*
Howard, John Eliot *Alli Sup*
Howard, John Galen 1864-1931 *DcNAA*
Howard, John Gordon 1899- *AmA&B, OhA&B*
Howard, John H *Alli Sup*
Howard, John Harris 1861-1950 *OhA&B*
Howard, John Jarrard *Alli*
Howard, John M *MnBBF*
Howard, John Owens *Alli, PoIre*
Howard, John R 1933- *ConAu 53*
Howard, John Raymond 1837-1926 *AmA&B, DcNAA*

Howard, John Tasker 1890-1964 *AmA&B, AmSCAP 66, REnAL, TwCA Sup*
Howard, John Walter *Alli, BiDLA*
Howard, Joseph *Alli Sup*
Howard, Joseph, Jr. 1833-1908 *Alli Sup, DcAmA, DcNAA*
Howard, Joseph A 1928- *AmSCAP 66*
Howard, Joseph Edgar 1878-1961 *AmSCAP 66*
Howard, Joseph Jackson 1827- *Alli Sup*
Howard, Joseph Kinsey 1906-1951 *AmA&B, TwCA Sup*
Howard, Joseph Leon 1917- *ConAu 1R*
Howard, Joyce 1922- *ConAu 5R*
Howard, Justin H *ChPo, EarAB, EarAB Sup*
Howard, Katharine 1850- *ChPo S1*
Howard, Katherine Lane 1858-1929 *OhA&B*
Howard, Kathleen *WhWNAA*
Howard, Keble *MnBBF*
Howard, Kenneth Samuel 1882- *ConAu 9R*
Howard, Langley *MnBBF*
Howard, Leland Ossian 1857- *AmLY, DcAmA, WhWNAA*
Howard, Leon 1903- *AmA&B*
Howard, Leonard d1767 *Alli*
Howard, Leslie 1893-1943 *REn*
Howard, Louis G Redmond *MnBBF*
Howard, Louis Orrin 1884- *WhWNAA*
Howard, Lowell Bennett 1925- *ConAu 13R, WrD 1976*
Howard, Luke *Alli, BiDLA*
Howard, Mabel *ChPo*
Howard, Marion *Alli Sup*
Howard, Martin d1781 *OxAm, REnAL*
Howard, Mary 1907- *ConAu XR*
Howard, Mary Matilda *Alli Sup*
Howard, Matthew V *MnnWr*
Howard, Maureen 1930- *ConAu 53, ConLC 5*
Howard, Mel 1912- *AmSCAP 66*
Howard, Michael Eliot 1922- *Au&Wr, ConAu 1R*
Howard, Michael S 1922-1974 *ConAu 53*
Howard, Middleton *BbtC*
Howard, Milford W 1862- *BiDSA*
Howard, Munroe 1913- *ConAu 23*
Howard, Nathan, Jr. 1808- *Alli, Alli Sup*
Howard, Nathaniel *Alli, BiDLA*
Howard, Oliver *ChPo*
Howard, Oliver Otis 1830-1909 *Alli Sup, AmA&B, BiD&SB, DcAmA, DcNAA*
Howard, Patricia 1937- *ConAu 17R, WrD 1976*
Howard, Paul *WhWNAA*
Howard, Paul Mason 1909- *AmSCAP 66*
Howard, Pauline Stoddard *ChPo S2*
Howard, Pendleton 1894- *TexWr*
Howard, Percy *Alli Sup*
Howard, Peter D 1908-1965 *ConAu P-1*
Howard, Philip d1810 *Alli, BiDLA*
Howard, Philip Eugene 1870-1946 *AmA&B, DcNAA*
Howard, Philip Nicholas Charles 1933- *WrD 1976*
Howard, Police Captain *AmA&B*
Howard, Prosper *MnBBF*
Howard, R T *ChPo S2*
Howard, Richard 1929- *AmSCAP 66*
Howard, Richard 1929- *AmA&B, AuNews 1, ConAu 53, ConP 1970, ConP 1975, CrCAP, DrAP 1975, ModAL Sup, RAdv 1, WorAu, WrD 1976*
Howard, Rob *IlBYP*
Howard, Robert *Alli, Alli Sup*
Howard, Robert d1740? *Alli*
Howard, Sir Robert 1626-1698 *Alli, BrAu, CasWL, Chmbr 1, DcEnL, EvLB*
Howard, Robert 1926- *ConAu 41*
Howard, Robert Ervin 1906-1936 *ChPo, WhWNAA*
Howard, Robert West 1908- *AmA&B, Au&Wr, ConAu 1R, SmATA 5*
Howard, Roger 1938- *ConDr, WrD 1976*
Howard, Roland *MnBBF*
Howard, Ronnalie Roper 1936- *ConAu 41*
Howard, Rowland *MnBBF*
Howard, Roy Wilson 1883-1964 *AmA&B, WhWNAA*
Howard, Sallie *BlkAW*

Howard, Samuel d1783? *Alli*
Howard, Sarah *Alli*
Howard, Sarah Elizabeth *ChPo*
Howard, Sidney Coe 1891-1939 *AmA&B, CasWL, CnDAL, CnMD, CnThe, ConAmA, ConAmL, DcLEnL, DcNAA, LongC, McGWD, ModAL, ModWD, OxAm, Pen Am, REn, REnAL, REnWD, TwCA, TwCA Sup, WebEAL*
Howard, Simeon 1733-1804 *Alli*
Howard, Sylvanus *Alli*
Howard, Thomas *Alli, Alli Sup, NewC*
Howard, Thomas 1930- *ConAu 37*
Howard, Timothy Edward 1837-1916 *DcNAA, IndAu 1816*
Howard, Troy *ConAu XR*
Howard, V E *Alli*
Howard, Vanessa 1955- *BlkAW*
Howard, Vechel *ConAu XR*
Howard, Vernon Linwood 1918- *AuBYP*
Howard, W W *Alli*
Howard, Walter d1902 *BiDSA*
Howard, Warren *AmA&B*
Howard, Warren Starkie 1930- *ConAu 5R*
Howard, Wilbert Francis 1880- *WhLA*
Howard, Wilbert R *BlkAW*
Howard, William *Alli*
Howard, William E 1877- *TexWr*
Howard, William Lee 1860?-1918 *DcAmA, DcNAA*
Howard, William Marshall 1880-1889 *ChPo, ChPo S1*
Howard, Winifred Mary DeLisle d1909 *ChPo*
Howard-Gibbon, Amelia Frances 1826-1874 *ChPo S1*
Howard-Williams, Jeremy 1922- *WrD 1976*
Howarde, Will *Alli Sup*
Howarth, David 1912- *ConAu 13R, SmATA 6, WrD 1976*
Howarth, Donald 1931- *Au&Wr, ConAu 25, ConDr, WrD 1976*
Howarth, Ellen Clementine 1827-1899 *Alli Sup, BiD&SB, ChPo, DcAmA, DcNAA, PoIre*
Howarth, Henry *Alli*
Howarth, James 1866- *MnBBF*
Howarth, John *ConAu XR*
Howarth, Osbert John Radclyffe 1877- *WhLA*
Howarth, Patrick John Fielding 1916- *Au&Wr, WrD 1976*
Howarth, Thomas Edward Brodie 1914- *Au&Wr*
Howarth, W D 1922- *ConAu 45*
Howarth, William *Alli Sup*
Howarth, William Louis 1940- *ConAu 37, WrD 1976*
Howat, George Rutland *Alli Sup*
Howat, Gerald Malcolm David 1928- *Au&Wr, WrD 1976*
Howat, Hugh Taylor *Alli Sup*
Howat, John K 1937- *ConAu 49*
Howatch, Susan 1940- *AuNews 1, ConAu 45, WrD 1976*
Howatson, Bella 1863- *ChPo S1*
Howatt, J Reid *Alli Sup*
Howay, Frederick William 1867-1943 *DcNAA, OxCan, WhWNAA*
Howbert, Abraham R 1825-1895 *OhA&B*
Howbert, Irving 1846-1934 *IndAu 1816*
Howden, John Of d1275 *CasWL*
Howden, Molly *ChPo*
Howden, Peter *Alli Sup*
Howden, Roger Of d1201? *CasWL, NewC*
Howden, Walter Cranston 1851- *ChPo, ChPo S1*
Howe, Alexander Hamilton *Alli Sup*
Howe, Andrew Jackson 1825-1892 *Alli Sup, DcAmA, DcNAA, OhA&B*
Howe, Carl Ellis 1898- *WhWNAA*
Howe, Caroline Dana 1830?-1907 *DcAmA, DcNAA*
Howe, Carrol Bruce 1910- *WhPNW*
Howe, Charles *Alli Sup*
Howe, Charles 1661-1745 *Alli, DcEnL*
Howe, Charles B 1870- *WhWNAA*
Howe, Charles Horace 1912- *ConAu 53, WrD 1976*
Howe, Charles L 1932- *ConAu 17R*
Howe, Cupples *Alli Sup*

Howe, D P *Alli Sup*
Howe, Daniel Wait 1839-1921 *Alli Sup, AmLY, DcAmA, DcNAA, IndAu 1816*
Howe, Daniel Walker 1937- *ConAu 29*
Howe, Delia Akeley 1875- *AmA&B*
Howe, Doris Kathleen *ConAu 49, WrD 1976*
Howe, Eber D 1798- *OhA&B*
Howe, Edgar Watson 1853-1937 *Alli Sup, AmA&B, BiD&SB, CasWL, CnDAL, CyWA, DcAmA, DcNAA, IndAu 1816, OxAm, REn, REnAL, TwCA, TwCA Sup, WebEAL*
Howe, Edward *Alli Sup*
Howe, Edward Everett 1862-1913 *DcNAA*
Howe, Elias, Jr. *Alli*
Howe, Elisha P *Alli Sup*
Howe, Ellic Paul 1910- *Au&Wr, ConAu 25*
Howe, Fanny *DrAP 1975*
Howe, Fisher 1798-1871 *Alli, Alli Sup, DcAmA, DcNAA*
Howe, Frances R *Alli Sup*
Howe, Frances Rose 1851-1916 *IndAu 1917*
Howe, Frank *MnBBF*
Howe, Frank William 1865- *WhWNAA*
Howe, Frederic Clemson 1867-1940 *DcAmA, DcNAA, OhA&B, WhWNAA*
Howe, Frederick *ChPo, ChPo S1*
Howe, Gene Alexander 1886-1952 *REnAL, TexWr*
Howe, Geoffrey Leslie 1924- *Au&Wr*
Howe, George 1802-1883 *Alli Sup, BiDSA, DcAmA, DcNAA*
Howe, George 1876-1936 *DcNAA, WhWNAA*
Howe, George 1881- *AmA&B*
Howe, George 1898- *AmA&B, AmNov*
Howe, George Frederick 1901- *OhA&B*
Howe, George Warren 1909- *AmSCAP 66*
Howe, George William Osborn 1875- *WhLA*
Howe, Gertrude Herrick 1902- *IlCB 1956*
Howe, H *Alli*
Howe, Harriet D'Oyley *Alli, Alli Sup*
Howe, Harrison Estell 1881-1942 *DcNAA*
Howe, Harrison Estell 1881- *WhWNAA*
Howe, Helen Huntington 1905-1975 *AmA&B, Au&Wr, ConAu 23, ConAu 57, REnAL, TwCA Sup*
Howe, Henry 1816-1893 *Alli, Alli Sup, AmA, AmA&B, BiD&SB, DcAmA, DcNAA, EarAB, EarAB Sup, OhA&B*
Howe, Henry Marion 1848-1922 *DcAmA, DcNAA, WhWNAA*
Howe, Herbert Alonzo 1858-1926 *DcAmA, DcNAA, OhA&B*
Howe, Hubert S, Jr. 1942- *ConAu 57*
Howe, Irving 1920- *AmA&B, ConAu 9R, ModAL, RAdv 1, REnAL, TwCA Sup*
Howe, J Olin 1875- *WhWNAA*
Howe, James *Alli*
Howe, James Lewis 1859- *WhWNAA*
Howe, Jane Moore 1914- *IndAu 1917*
Howe, John *Chmbr 1, OxCan*
Howe, John d1721 *Alli*
Howe, John 1630-1705 *Alli, DcEnL, EvLB, NewC*
Howe, John Badlam 1813-1882 *Alli Sup, DcAmA, DcNAA, IndAu 1816*
Howe, John Benedict 1859-1943 *DcNAA*
Howe, Jonathan Trumbull 1935- *ConAu 29*
Howe, Joseph 1804-1873 *Alli, BbtC, BrAu 19, CanWr, Chmbr 3, DcLEnL, OxCan, REnAL*
Howe, Joseph William 1846-1890 *Alli Sup, DcNAA*
Howe, Josiah d1701 *Alli, DcEnL*
Howe, Julia Romana 1844-1886 *DcNAA*
Howe, Julia Ward 1819-1910 *Alli, Alli Sup, AmA, AmA&B, BbD, BiD&SB, ChPo, ChPo S1, ChPo S2, Chmbr 3, CnDAL, CyAL 2, DcAmA, DcEnL, DcLEnL, DcNAA, EvLB, FemPA, OxAm, OxEng, Pen Am, REn, REnAL, WebEAL*
Howe, Lina *Alli Sup*
Howe, Louis McHenry *ChPo*
Howe, Lucien 1848-1928 *DcNAA*
Howe, Malverd Abijah 1863- *Alli Sup, DcAmA, WhWNAA*
Howe, Marie d1934 *DcNAA*
Howe, Marie Jenney 1870- *WhWNAA*

Howe, Mark Anthony DeWolfe 1809-1895 *Alli Sup, DcAmA, DcNAA*
Howe, Mark Antony DeWolfe 1864-1960 *AmA&B, AmLY, ChPo, DcAmA, OxAm, REn, REnAL, TwCA, TwCA Sup, WhWNAA*
Howe, Mark DeWolfe 1906-1967 *AmA&B*
Howe, Marshall Avery 1867-1936 *DcNAA, WhWNAA*
Howe, Martha C *ChPo*
Howe, Mary 1882-1964 *AmSCAP 66*
Howe, Mary A *Alli Sup*
Howe, Maud *Alli Sup, DcAmA, WhWNAA*
Howe, Maude Johnson 1887- *AmSCAP 66*
Howe, Muriel *Au&Wr, WrD 1976*
Howe, Nathaniel 1764-1837 *Alli, CyAL 1*
Howe, Nelson S 1935- *ConAu 33, WrD 1976*
Howe, Obadiah d1682 *Alli*
Howe, Quincy 1900- *AmA&B, ConAu 49, REnAL*
Howe, R H *Alli Sup*
Howe, Reginald Heber 1846- *DcAmA*
Howe, Reginald Heber, Jr. 1875-1932 *AmLY, DcAmA, DcNAA, WhWNAA*
Howe, Reuel L 1905- *ConAu 1R, ConAu 23*
Howe, Richard, Viscount 1725-1799 *Alli*
Howe, Robert 1732-1785 *Alli*
Howe, Robin 1908- *Au&Wr, WrD 1976*
Howe, Russell Warren 1925- *Au&Wr, ConAu 49*
Howe, Samuel *Alli*
Howe, Samuel Burnett 1879-1941 *DcNAA, WhWNAA*
Howe, Samuel Gridley 1801-1876 *Alli, AmA, AmA&B, DcAmA, DcNAA, OxAm, REn, REnAL*
Howe, T H *Alli*
Howe, Thomas *Alli, BiDLA*
Howe, Thomas Carr 1904- *IndAu 1917*
Howe, W Asquith 1910- *ConAu 29*
Howe, Walter 1849-1890 *DcNAA*
Howe, Will David 1873-1946 *AmA&B, ChPo, DcNAA, IndAu 1917, REnAL*
Howe, William 1619-1656 *Alli*
Howe, Sir William 1729-1814 *Alli, OxAm, REnAL*
Howe, William F 1828-1902 *DcNAA*
Howe, William F And Hummel, A H *Alli Sup*
Howe, William Henry 1848- *ChPo S1*
Howe, William Stuart 1890- *WhWNAA*
Howe, William Thomas Hildrup 1874-1939 *AmA&B*
Howe, William Wirt 1833-1909 *Alli Sup, AmA&B, BiDSA, DcAmA, DcNAA*
Howe, Zadoc *EarAB*
Howel Ab Owain *DcEnL*
Howel The Good *Alli*
Howel, Laurence d1720 *Alli*
Howel, Thomas *Alli*
Howell, Mrs. *Alli, BiDLA*
Howell, A *Alli Sup*
Howell, Agnes Rous *Alli Sup, ChPo S2*
Howell, Alfred 1836-1911 *Alli Sup, DcNAA*
Howell, Alfred Brazier 1886- *WhWNAA*
Howell, Almonte Charles 1895- *WhWNAA*
Howell, Andrew Jackson, Jr. *BiDSA*
Howell, Annie *ChPo S1*
Howell, Anthony 1945- *ConP 1970, ConP 1975, WrD 1976*
Howell, Arthur Holmes 1872- *WhWNAA*
Howell, Arthur P *Alli Sup*
Howell, Barbara 1937- *ConAu 49*
Howell, C R *Alli Sup*
Howell, Caroline A *Alli*
Howell, Catharine Augusta *Alli Sup*
Howell, Charles *Alli Sup*
Howell, Charles Boynton 1840-1888 *Alli Sup, DcNAA*
Howell, Charles Fish 1868-1943 *DcNAA*
Howell, Clark 1863-1936 *BiDSA, DcNAA*
Howell, Clinton T 1913- *ConAu 29*
Howell, Constance *Alli Sup*
Howell, E J *Alli Sup*
Howell, Edward Alexander 1912- *Au&Wr*
Howell, Elizabeth Lloyd 1828- *Alli, BbD*
Howell, Eva *ChPo S1*
Howell, Fleming 1849-1941 *DcNAA*
Howell, George *Alli, Alli Sup*

Howell, George Rogers 1833-1899 *Alli Sup, DcAmA, DcNAA*
Howell, Helen 1934- *ConAu 57*
Howell, Henry Spencer 1857-1912 *DcNAA*
Howell, Inez Baker 1887- *TexWr*
Howell, J B *EarAB*
Howell, James *Alli, Alli Sup, Chmbr 1*
Howell, James 1594?-1666 *Alli, BiD&SB, BrAu, CrE&SL, DcEnA, DcEnL, EvLB, NewC, OxEng, REn*
Howell, James Edwin 1928- *ConAu 1R*
Howell, Jane L *Alli Sup*
Howell, John *Alli, Alli Sup*
Howell, John Adams 1840- *DcAmA*
Howell, John Christian 1924- *ConAu 21, WrD 1976*
Howell, John Edward *Alli Sup*
Howell, John M 1933- *ConAu 33*
Howell, Joseph B *EarAB Sup*
Howell, Joseph Morton 1863-1937 *OhA&B*
Howell, Joseph T 1942- *ConAu 45*
Howell, Laurence *Alli*
Howell, Leon 1936- *ConAu 25*
Howell, Mark Ian 1935- *Au&Wr*
Howell, Mary Hubbard *Alli Sup*
Howell, Maxwell *OxCan Sup*
Howell, Mortimer Sloper 1841- *Alli Sup*
Howell, Nancy *OxCan Sup*
Howell, Rednap *BiDSA*
Howell, Richard W 1926- *ConAu 57*
Howell, Robert B 1944- *AmSCAP 66*
Howell, Robert Boyte Crawford 1801-1868 *Alli Sup, BiDSA, DcAmA, DcNAA*
Howell, Robert Lee 1928- *ConAu 25*
Howell, Roger 1936- *ConAu 21, WrD 1976*
Howell, S *ConAu XR, SmATA XR*
Howell, Thomas *Alli, Alli Sup, BiDLA, CasWL, DcEnL*
Howell, Thomas B *Alli, BiDLA*
Howell, Thomas B 1921- *AmSCAP 66*
Howell, Thomas Jefferson 1842-1912 *DcNAA*
Howell, Thomas Jones *Alli*
Howell, Virginia Tier *ConAu XR, SmATA 4, WrD 1976*
Howell, Mrs. W May *Alli Sup*
Howell, Wilbur Samuel 1904- *AmA&B, ConAu 33*
Howell, William *Alli, Alli Sup*
Howell, William 1630-1683 *Alli, DcEnL*
Howell, William Henry 1860-1945 *Alli Sup, DcNAA, WhWNAA*
Howells, Annie T *Alli Sup*
Howells, John Gwilym 1918- *ConAu 23, WrD 1976*
Howells, Mary *ChPo S1*
Howells, Mildred 1872- *ChPo, WhWNAA*
Howells, William Cooper 1807-1894 *DcAmA, DcNAA, OhA&B*
Howells, William Dean 1837-1920 *Alli Sup, AmA, AmA&B, AmWr, AtlBL, BbD, BiD&SB, CarSB, CasWL, ChPo, ChPo S1, ChPo S2, Chmbr 3, CnDAL, CriT 3, CyAL 2, CyWA, DcAmA, DcBiA, DcEnA, DcEnA Ap, DcEnL, DcLEnL, DcNAA, EncWL Sup, EvLB, McGWD, ModAL, ModAL Sup, ModWD, OhA&B, OxAm, OxEng, Pen Am, RAdv 1, RCom, REn, REnAL, WebEAL*
Howells, William Hooper *ChPo S1*
Howells, William White 1908- *AmA&B, Au&Wr, ConAu 1R, WrD 1976*
Howells, Winifred 1863-1889 *ChPo*
Howels, William *Alli*
Howenstein, Emily Guillon Fuller *OhA&B*
Howenstine, E Jay, Jr. 1914- *OhA&B*
Hower, Frank Leslie 1903- *OhA&B*
Hower, Ralph M 1903-1973 *ConAu 1R, ConAu 45*
Hower, Ross L 1904- *WhWNAA*
Howerth, Ira Woods 1860-1938 *DcNAA, IndAu 1816, WhWNAA*
Howerton, James Robert 1861-1924 *DcNAA*
Howes, Barbara 1914- *AmA&B, ChPo, ConAu 9R, ConP 1970, ConP 1975, DrAP 1975, Pen Am, REnAL, SmATA 5, WorAu, WrD 1976*
Howes, Barnabas *Alli Sup*

Howes, Cecil 1880- *WhWNAA*
Howes, Clarence 1899- *Au&Wr, WrD 1976*
Howes, Edith *ChPo S2*
Howes, Edmund *Alli*
Howes, Ethel Puffer 1872- *WhWNAA*
Howes, Francis *Alli, BiDLA*
Howes, Frank 1891- *Au&Wr*
Howes, Frederick William *Alli Sup*
Howes, George Bond *Alli Sup*
Howes, George Edwin 1865- *WhWNAA*
Howes, Grace Clementine *ChPo*
Howes, Hannah Cushman 1896- *WhWNAA*
Howes, John *Alli*
Howes, Michael 1904- *ConAu 61*
Howes, Paul Griswold 1892- *ConAu 29*
Howes, Raymond Floyd 1903- *ConAu P-1, WrD 1976*
Howes, Robert *Alli*
Howes, Robert Gerard 1919- *ConAu 1R*
Howes, Royce B 1901-1973 *AmA&B, ConAu 19, ConAu 41*
Howes, T *Alli*
Howes, Thomas *Alli*
Howett, Samuel *Alli*
Howgate, H W *Alli Sup, OxCan*
Howgill, Francis *Alli*
Howgrave, Francis *Alli*
Howick, Viscount *Alli*
Howick, Daniel *Alli Sup*
Howick, David *Alli Sup*
Howick, William *PoIre*
Howick, William Henry 1924- *ConAu 33*
Howie, Carl G 1920- *ConAu 13R*
Howie, James *Alli Sup*
Howie, James Muir *Alli Sup*
Howie, John 1735-1791 *Alli, Chmbr 2, DcEnL, EvLB*
Howison, George Holmes 1834-1916 *AmA&B, DcAmA, DcNAA, OhA&B*
Howison, James *Alli, BiDLA*
Howison, John *Alli, BbtC, OxCan*
Howison, Robert Reid 1820-1906 *Alli, Alli Sup, BiD&SB, BiDSA, DcAmA, DcNAA*
Howison, William *Alli, BiDLA*
Howiston, Mary *ChPo*
Howith, Harry 1934- *ConAu 25, ConP 1970, ConP 1975, OxCan Sup, WrD 1976*
Howitt, Anna Mary *Alli*
Howitt, Ema *Alli*
Howitt, F H *Alli Sup*
Howitt, Margaret *Alli Sup*
Howitt, Mary 1799-1888 *Alli, Alli Sup, BbD, BiD&SB, BrAu 19, CarSB, CasWL, ChPo, ChPo S1, ChPo S2, DcEnA, DcEnL, DcEuL, EvLB, HsB&A, NewC*
Howitt, Richard 1792-1879 *Alli, Alli Sup, ChPo, ChPo S1, ChPo S2, DcLEnL*
Howitt, Samuel 1750-1823 *Alli, Br&AmS, ChPo*
Howitt, William 1792-1879 *Alli, Alli Sup, BbD, BiD&SB, BrAu 19, CarSB, CasWL, ChPo, ChPo S1, ChPo S2, DcEnA, DcEnL, DcEuL, EvLB, NewC*
Howitt, William And Mary *Chmbr 3*
Howitzer, Bronson *ConAu XR*
Howland, Alfred Cornelius 1838-1909 *EarAB*
Howland, Arthur Charles 1869-1952 *AmA&B*
Howland, Charles Roscoe 1871-1946 *OhA&B*
Howland, E T *ChPo*
Howland, Edward *Alli Sup*
Howland, Edward 1832-1890 *DcNAA*
Howland, Frances Louise Morse 1855-1944 *AmA&B, AmLY, DcNAA, WhWNAA*
Howland, Franklyn 1843-1907 *DcAmA, DcNAA*
Howland, George 1824-1892 *Alli Sup, ChPo, DcAmA, DcNAA*
Howland, Harold 1877-1966 *AmA&B*
Howland, Henry *ChPo, ChPo S1*
Howland, Henry Raymond 1844-1930 *DcNAA*
Howland, Hewitt Hanson 1863-1944 *AmA&B, ChPo, DcNAA, IndAu 1917*
Howland, Louis 1857-1934 *AmA&B, DcNAA, IndAu 1816*
Howland, Marie *Alli Sup*
Howland, Oliver Aiken 1847-1905 *DcNAA*
Howland, Mrs. R S *ChPo*
Howland, Robert S *Alli Sup*

Howland, William H 1831-1869 *HsB&A*
Howland, William P *OxCan*
Howland, Zoeth *ChPo*
Howldy, Thomas *Alli*
Howlett, Bart *Alli*
Howlett, Duncan 1906- *AmA&B, Au&Wr, WrD 1976*
Howlett, John *Alli*
Howlett, John d1804 *Alli*
Howlett, John Henry *Alli*
Howlett, John Reginald 1940- *Au&Wr*
Howlett, Martin 1863- *WhLA*
Howlett, Richard 1841- *Alli Sup*
Howlett, Robert *Alli Sup*
Howlett, Thomas Rosling 1827-1898 *DcAmA, DcNAA*
Howley, Edward *Alli Sup*
Howley, Frank Leo 1903- *AmA&B*
Howley, James Patrick *OxCan*
Howley, Michael Francis 1843-1914 *Alli Sup, DcNAA, OxCan*
Howley, William 1765-1848 *Alli, BiDLA*
Howman, Roger *Alli*
Howorth, Mrs. *Alli, BiDLA*
Howorth, George *Alli Sup*
Howorth, Sir Henry Hoyle 1842- *Alli Sup, BiD&SB*
Howorth, Muriel K *Au&Wr, ConAu XR, ConAu P-1*
Howorth, William *Alli*
Hows, John Augustus 1832-1874 *ChPo, ChPo S2, EarAB, EarAB Sup*
Hows, John William Stanhope 1797-1871 *Alli, Alli Sup, DcAmA, DcNAA*
Hows, R S *Alli Sup*
Howse, Ernest Marshall 1902- *ConAu 49, WrD 1976*
Howse, Isaac *Alli*
Howse, Joseph 1773-1852 *OxCan*
Howse, Philip Edwin 1937- *Au&Wr*
Howse, Richard And Kirby, J W *Alli Sup*
Howship, John *Alli*
Howson, Charles *Alli Sup*
Howson, Edmund Whytehead *ChPo S1*
Howson, Henry *Alli Sup*
Howson, John 1556-1631 *Alli*
Howson, John Saul 1816-1885 *Alli, Alli Sup, DcEnL*
Howson, Robert *Alli*
Howson, Walter *Alli Sup*
Howson, William *Alli*
Howth, Margaret *OxAm*
Howton, F William 1925- *ConAu 29*
Hoxie, George Luke 1872- *WhWNAA*
Hoxie, Robert Franklin 1868-1916 *DcNAA*
Hoxton, Walter *Alli*
Hoy, Albert Harris 1840?- *DcAmA*
Hoy, Cyrus H 1926- *ConAu 21*
Hoy, David 1930- *ConAu 17R, IndAu 1917*
Hoy, Ella Compton 1888- *WhWNAA*
Hoy, Mrs. Frank *BiDSA*
Hoy, James *Alli*
Hoy, James F 1939- *ConAu 57*
Hoy, John C 1933- *ConAu 21*
Hoy, Thomas *Alli*
Hoye, Anna Scott 1915- *ConAu 13R*
Hoyem, Andrew 1935- *Au&Wr, ConAu 9R, ConP 1970, ConP 1975, DrAP 1975, WrD 1976*
Hoyer, George W 1919- *ConAu 1R*
Hoyer, H Conrad 1907- *ConAu 33*
Hoyer, M A *Alli Sup*
Hoyer, Mildred N *ConAu 57, WrD 1976*
Hoyers, Anna Owena 1584-1655 *OxGer*
Hoyland, Mr. *Alli*
Hoyland, John *Alli*
Hoyland, John S *ChPo S2*
Hoyland, Michael David 1925- *ConAu 23, WrD 1976*
Hoyland, Rosemary Jean 1929- *IlCB 1956*
Hoyle, Charles *Alli, BiDLA, PoIre*
Hoyle, Edmond 1672-1769 *Alli, BiD&SB, BrAu, NewC, OxEng*
Hoyle, Edward *Alli Sup*
Hoyle, Fred 1915- *Au&Wr, ConAu 5R, ConNov 1972, TwCW, WorAu, WrD 1976*
Hoyle, Geoffrey 1942- *Au&Wr, ConAu 53,*

WrD 1976
Hoyle, John *Alli*
Hoyle, Martha Byrd 1930- *ConAu 29*
Hoyle, Raphael 1804-1838 *EarAB Sup*
Hoyle, Thomas, Jr. *Alli*
Hoyle, William 1831- *Alli Sup*
Hoyle, William Evans *Alli Sup*
Hoyles, J Arthur 1908- *ConAu 5R, WrD 1976*
Hoylus, Bill O'Th' *ChPo S2*
Hoyos, Juan Lopez De *DcEuL*
Hoyrup, Paul 1909- *WhGrA*
Hoys, Dudley *MnBBF*
Hoys, Frank Dudley 1897- *Au&Wr*
Hoyt, Arthur Stephen 1851-1924 *DcNAA*
Hoyt, Charles Alva 1931- *ConAu 33*
Hoyt, Charles Hale 1860-1900 *AmA, AmA&B, BiD&SB, CnThe, DcAmA, DcNAA, ModWD, OxAm, REnAL, REnWD*
Hoyt, Charles Oliver 1856-1927 *DcNAA*
Hoyt, Charles Wilson 1872-1928 *DcNAA*
Hoyt, David Webster 1833-1921 *DcNAA*
Hoyt, Deristhe L 1844?- *DcAmA, DcNAA*
Hoyt, Edwin Palmer 1923- *AuBYP, ConAu 1R*
Hoyt, Elizabeth Ellis 1893- *ConAu 37, WrD 1976*
Hoyt, Elizabeth Orpha 1834- *OhA&B*
Hoyt, Epaphras 1765-1850 *Alli, DcAmA, DcNAA*
Hoyt, Florence H *ChPo*
Hoyt, Francis Deming 1843-1922 *DcNAA*
Hoyt, Franklin Chase 1876-1937 *DcNAA, WhWNAA*
Hoyt, Franklin Sherman 1873- *WhWNAA*
Hoyt, Mrs. G S *Alli Sup*
Hoyt, Helen 1887- *ChPo, ChPo S2, WhWNAA*
Hoyt, Henry Franklin 1854-1930 *DcNAA*
Hoyt, Henry Martyn 1830-1892 *Alli Sup, DcAmA, DcNAA*
Hoyt, Henry Martyn 1887-1920 *DcNAA*
Hoyt, Herman Arthur 1909- *ConAu 29, IndAu 1917*
Hoyt, Homer 1896- *ConAu 1R*
Hoyt, J *Alli Sup*
Hoyt, J B *Alli*
Hoyt, J K And Ward, Anna L *Alli Sup*
Hoyt, Mrs. J W *ChPo*
Hoyt, James Humphrey 1852-1917 *OhA&B*
Hoyt, James Madison 1815-1895 *OhA&B*
Hoyt, James Philip 1844-1925 *DcNAA*
Hoyt, James S *Alli Sup*
Hoyt, Jehiel Keeler 1820-1895 *DcNAA*
Hoyt, Jo Wasson 1927- *ConAu 21, IndAu 1917*
Hoyt, John Clayton 1874- *WhWNAA*
Hoyt, John Wesley 1831-1912 *DcAmA, DcNAA, OhA&B*
Hoyt, John William 1903-1937 *DcNAA*
Hoyt, Joseph B 1913- *ConAu 5R, WrD 1976*
Hoyt, Joseph Gibson 1815-1862 *Alli Sup, DcNAA*
Hoyt, Juliet 1887-1947 *DcNAA*
Hoyt, K C *Alli Sup*
Hoyt, Kenneth B 1924- *ConAu 45*
Hoyt, Martin W 1850- *Alli Sup*
Hoyt, Mary Finch *AuBYP*
Hoyt, Murray 1904- *ConAu 9R*
Hoyt, Nancy 1902- *AmA&B*
Hoyt, Olga 1922- *ConAu 25*
Hoyt, Ralph 1806-1878 *Alli, AmA&B, ChPo, ChPo S1, ChPo S2, CyAL 2, DcAmA, DcNAA*
Hoyt, Rosamund 1868-1925 *ChPo*
Hoyt, Samuel *ChPo*
Hoyt, T C 1874- *ArizL*
Hoyt, Vance Joseph 1889- *AmA&B, WhWNAA*
Hoyt, Wayland 1838-1910 *Alli Sup, DcAmA, DcNAA, OhA&B*
Hoyt, Wilbur Franklin 1864-1930 *DcNAA, OhA&B, WhWNAA*
Hoyte, Henry *Alli, BiDLA*
Hoz Y Mota, Juan Claudio DeLa 1622-1714 *CasWL, DcEuL, McGWD*
Hozeny, Tony 1946- *ConAu 61*
Hozier, Henry Montague 1832- *Alli Sup*
Hozier, Pierre DeLaGarde D' 1592-1660 *OxFr*

Hozier, William W *Alli Sup*
Hozjusz *ConAu XR*
Hrabal, Bohumil 1914- *CasWL, ModSL 2, Pen Eur, WhTwL*
Hraban *CasWL*
Hrabanus Maurus 776?-856 *OxGer, Pen Eur*
Hrastnik, Franz 1904- *CnMD*
Hrbek, Jeffrey Dolezal 1882-1907 *DcNAA*
Hrdlicka, Ales 1869-1943 *AmA&B, AmLY, DcNAA, REnAL, WhWNAA*
Hristic, Jovan 1933- *CasWL*
Hristov, Kiril 1875-1944 *Pen Eur*
Hromadka, Josef L 1889-1971 *ConAu P-1*
Hronsky, Jozef Ciger 1896-1961 *CasWL*
Hrosvitha *REn, REnWD*
Hrothgar *REn*
Hrotsvith *OxGer, Pen Eur*
Hrotsvitha 935?-1001? *CasWL, CnThe, REn, REnWD*
Hrubin, Frantisek 1910-1971 *CasWL, ModSL 2*
Hrushevs'ky, Mykhaylo 1866-1934 *CasWL*
Hruska-Cortes, Elias 1943- *ConAu 45, DrAP 1975*
Hruza, Zdenek 1926- *ConAu 61*
Hsaung, U *DcOrL 2*
Hsi, Jung *DcOrL 1*
Hsi, K'ang 223-262? *CasWL, DcOrL 1, Pen Cl*
Hsia, C-T 1921- *ConAu 1R*
Hsia, David Yi-Yung 1925-1972 *ConAu 33*
Hsia, Hsiao *ConAu XR*
Hsia, Tseng-Yu *DcOrL 1*
Hsia, Tsi-An 1916-1965 *ConAu 25*
Hsia, Yen 1900- *CasWL, DcOrL 1*
Hsiang-Shan Chu-Shih *DcOrL 1*
Hsiao, Ch'ien 1911- *CasWL*
Hsiao, Chun 1908- *CasWL, DcOrL 1*
Hsiao, Hsia *WrD 1976*
Hsiao, Kung-Chuan 1897- *ConAu 1R, WrD 1976*
Hsiao, Tso-Liang 1910- *ConAu 1R*
Hsiao, T'ung 501-531 *CasWL, DcOrL 1*
Hsiao-Hsiao Sheng *DcOrL 1*
Hsiao-Hsueh *DcOrL 1*
Hsieh, Hun *DcOrL 1*
Hsieh, Lin-Ch'uan *DcOrL 1*
Hsieh, Ling-Yun 385-433 *CasWL, DcOrL 1*
Hsieh, Ping-Ying 1908- *CasWL*
Hsieh, Tiao *DcOrL 1*
Hsieh, T'iao *DcOrL 1*
Hsieh, T'iao 464-499 *CasWL*
Hsieh, Wan-Ying *DcOrL 1*
Hsin, Ch'i-Chi 1140-1207 *CasWL, DcOrL 1*
Hsin-Hai, Chang 1898?-1972 *ConAu 37*
Hsiung, Fu-Hsi 1900-1965 *CasWL*
Hsiung, James Chieh 1935- *ConAu 37*
Hsiung, Lung-Feng *DcOrL 1*
Hsu, Chih-Mo 1896?-1931 *CasWL, DcOrL 1, EncWL Sup, Pen Cl*
Hsu, Cho-Yun 1930- *ConAu 17R*
Hsu, Francis Lang Kwang 1909- *AmA&B, ConAu 1R*
Hsu, Hsia-K'o 1586-1641 *CasWL*
Hsu, Immanuel C Y 1923- *ConAu 1R*
Hsu, Kai-Yu 1922- *ConAu 21, WrD 1976*
Hsu, Kuang-Ch'i 1562-1633 *CasWL*
Hsu, Ling 507-581 *CasWL, DcOrL 1*
Hsu, Shen *CasWL, DcOrL 1*
Hsu, Ti-Shan 1893-1941 *CasWL, DcOrL 1*
Hsu, Yin-Fu *DcOrL 1*
Hsu, Yu-Sen *DcOrL 1*
Hsuan-Tsang 600-664 *DcOrL 1*
Hsueh, Ch'in *Pen Cl*
Hsueh, Chun-Tu 1922- *ConAu 41*
Hsueh, Fu-Ch'eng 1838-1894 *CasWL*
Hsun-Tzu 298BC-238BC *CasWL, DcOrL 1*
Htei Myain, U *DcOrL 2*
Htin, Maun 1909- *DcOrL 2*
Htin Aung, U *ConAu XR*
Hu, Feng 1903- *CasWL, DcOrL 1*
Hu, Hsien-Su *DcOrL 1*
Hu, Shih 1891-1962 *CasWL, DcOrL 1, REn*
Hu, Sze-Tsen 1914- *ConAu 41*
Hu, Yeh-P'in *DcOrL 1*
Hu-Shang Li-Weng *DcOrL 1*
Huaco, George A 1927- *ConAu 17R*
Huang, David S 1930- *ConAu 9R*

Huang, Kung-Tu *DcOrL 1*
Huang, Parker 1914- *ConAu 45*
Huang, Po-Fei *ConAu XR*
Huang, Ray 1918- *ConAu 61*
Huang, Ti *REn*
Huang, T'ing-Chien 1045-1105 *CasWL, DcOrL 1*
Huang, Tsun-Hsien 1848-1905 *CasWL, DcOrL 1*
Huang, Tsung-Hsi 1610-1695 *CasWL*
Huang-Fu, Mei *DcOrL 1*
Huard, L *ChPo S1, ChPo S2*
Huard, Victor Alphonse 1853-1929 *DcNAA, OxCan, WhWNAA*
Huarte DeSan Juan 1530?-1591? *CasWL, DcEuL*
Hubach, Robert R 1916- *ConAu 1R*
Hubalek, Claus 1926- *CnMD, ModWD*
Hubartt, Paul Leroy 1919- *ConAu 5R, IndAu 1917*
Hubback, Mrs. *Alli*
Hubback, Catherine Anne *Alli Sup*
Hubback, John *Alli*
Hubbard, Father *Alli*
Hubbard, Alice 1861-1915 *DcNAA*
Hubbard, Alice L *ChPo*
Hubbard, Arthur John 1856- *WhLA*
Hubbard, Bela 1814-1896 *Alli Sup, DcAmA, DcNAA*
Hubbard, Benjamin *Alli*
Hubbard, Bernard Rosecrans 1888-1962 *AmA&B, CatA 1947*
Hubbard, Charles Eustis *Alli Sup*
Hubbard, Clara E *ChPo S2*
Hubbard, D L 1929- *ConAu 21*
Hubbard, David Allan 1928- *ConAu 33*
Hubbard, David G 1920- *ConAu 33*
Hubbard, Elbert 1856-1915 *AmA&B, BbD, BiD&SB, ChPo S2, CnDAL, DcAmA, DcLEnL, DcNAA, EvLB, OxAm, REn, REnAL, TwCA, TwCA Sup*
Hubbard, Fordyce Mitchell 1809-1888 *Alli, BiDSA*
Hubbard, Frances Virginia B *WhWNAA*
Hubbard, Frank McKinney 1868-1930 *DcNAA, IndAu 1816, OhA&B, OxAm, TwCA, TwCA Sup, WhWNAA*
Hubbard, Frederick Heman *Alli Sup*
Hubbard, Freeman 1894- *ConAu 5R, WrD 1976*
Hubbard, Gardiner Greene *Alli Sup*
Hubbard, Gardiner Greene 1822-1897 *DcNAA*
Hubbard, George *Alli, BiDLA*
Hubbard, George 1859- *WhLA*
Hubbard, George 1871- *WhWNAA*
Hubbard, George David 1871- *WhWNAA*
Hubbard, George Henry 1857- *AmLY*
Hubbard, H *Alli*
Hubbard, Harvey d1862 *DcNAA*
Hubbard, Havrah William Lines 1867- *WhWNAA*
Hubbard, Henry *Alli*
Hubbard, Henry Vincent 1875-1947 *DcNAA, WhWNAA*
Hubbard, Hesketh 1892- *WhLA*
Hubbard, J G *Alli*
Hubbard, J P *Alli*
Hubbard, James Mascarene 1836- *Alli Sup*
Hubbard, Jeremiah 1837-1915 *IndAu 1917*
Hubbard, John *Alli*
Hubbard, John 1859-1910 *DcNAA*
Hubbard, John C d1805 *Alli*
Hubbard, John Niles 1815-1897 *DcNAA*
Hubbard, Joseph S 1823- *Alli*
Hubbard, Kin 1868-1930 *AmA&B, DcNAA, REnAL*
Hubbard, Lafayette Ronald 1911- *Au&Wr, WrD 1976*
Hubbard, Leonidas, Jr. *OxCan*
Hubbard, Leverett *Alli*
Hubbard, Louis Herman 1882- *TexWr*
Hubbard, Lucien 1889?-1971 *ConAu 33*
Hubbard, Lucius Lee 1849-1933 *Alli Sup, DcAmA, DcNAA, OhA&B, WhWNAA*
Hubbard, Luther Prescott *Alli Sup*
Hubbard, Margaret Ann 1909- *BkC 4, CatA 1947, ConAu XR, MnnWr*
Hubbard, Mina *OxCan*
Hubbard, Myla *ChPo S1*

Hubbard, Oliver Payson 1809-1900 *DcNAA*
Hubbard, Philip Maitland 1910- *Au&Wr*
Hubbard, Preston John 1918- *ConAu 5R*
Hubbard, Prevost 1881- *WhWNAA*
Hubbard, Richard Bennett 1835?-1901 *BiDSA, DcAmA, DcNAA*
Hubbard, Robert Hamilton 1916- *ConAu 1R, OxCan Sup, WrD 1976*
Hubbard, Rose *Alli Sup*
Hubbard, Sara Anderson 1832-1918 *DcNAA*
Hubbard, Stephen Grosvenor 1816-1905 *DcNAA*
Hubbard, Theodora 1887-1935 *DcNAA*
Hubbard, Thomas Leslie Wallan 1905- *ConAu P-1, WrD 1976*
Hubbard, Wales *Alli Sup*
Hubbard, William *Alli*
Hubbard, William 1621-1704 *Alli, AmA, AmA&B, BiD&SB, CyAL 1, DcAmA, DcNAA, OxAm, REnAL*
Hubbard, Wynant Davis 1900-1961 *AmA&B*
Hubbard-Kernan, Will 1845-1905 *DcNAA, OhA&B*
Hubbart, Henry Clyde 1882- *OhA&B*
Hubbell, Alvin Allace 1846-1911 *DcNAA*
Hubbell, Frank Allen 1907- *AmSCAP 66*
Hubbell, George Allen 1862-1943 *AmLY, BiDSA, OhA&B*
Hubbell, Harriet Weed 1909- *AuBYP, ConAu 5R*
Hubbell, Harry M 1881-1971 *ConAu 29*
Hubbell, J H *ChPo*
Hubbell, Jay Broadus 1885- *AmA&B, ChPo, ConAu 1R, WhWNAA*
Hubbell, Lindley Williams 1901- *AmA&B, ConAu P-1*
Hubbell, Martha Stone 1814-1856 *Alli, Alli Sup, AmA&B, BiD&SB, DcAmA, DcNAA*
Hubbell, Mary E *ChPo*
Hubbell, Mary Elizabeth 1833-1854 *AmA&B*
Hubbell, Patricia 1928- *BkCL, ChPo S1, ChPo S2, ConAu 17R, SmATA 8*
Hubbell, Raymond 1879-1954 *AmSCAP 66*
Hubbell, Richard Whittaker 1914- *Au&Wr, ConAu 13R, WrD 1976*
Hubbell, Rose Strong *ChPo, ChPo S2*
Hubbell, Walter 1851- *Alli Sup, DcAmA, DcNAA*
Hubbert, Marion King 1903- *WrD 1976*
Hubbert, Thomas *Alli*
Hubberthorne, Richard *Alli*
Hubble, Edwin Powell 1889-1953 *REnAL*
Hubble, Martie 1922- *AmSCAP 66*
Hubbocke, William *Alli*
Hubel, Eduard *WhLA*
Hubenka, Lloyd J 1931- *ConAu 49*
Huber, Charlotte *St&VC*
Huber, Florence M *WhWNAA*
Huber, Jack T 1918- *ConAu 23, WrD 1976*
Huber, John Bessner 1864-1924 *DcNAA*
Huber, K *EarAB*
Huber, Kurt 1893-1943 *OxGer*
Huber, Leonard Victor 1903- *ConAu 57*
Huber, Ludwig Ferdinand 1764-1804 *DcEuL, OxGer*
Huber, Mary Florence *WhWNAA*
Huber, Max 1919- *WhGrA*
Huber, Miriam Blanton *AmA&B*
Huber, Morton Wesley 1923- *ConAu 17R*
Huber, Richard Miller 1922- *ConAu 33, WrD 1976*
Huber, Therese 1764-1829 *OxGer*
Huber, Thomas 1937- *ConAu 29*
Huberich, Charles Henry 1877-1945 *DcNAA, OhA&B*
Huberman, Edward 1910- *ConAu 13R*
Huberman, Elizabeth Duncan Lyle 1915- *ConAu 13R*
Huberman, Leo 1903- *ConAu 1R*
Hubert, Saint 656?-727 *NewC, OxFr*
Hubert, Antonis De 1583-1636 *CasWL*
Hubert, Sir Francis 1568?-1629 *Alli, CasWL*
Hubert, Frank *MnBBF*
Hubert, Henry Samuel Musgrave *Alli Sup*
Hubert, J *Alli*
Hubert, L M *ChPo*
Hubert, Petrus 1810-1882 *DcNAA*
Hubert, Philip Gengembre 1852-1925 *DcNAA,*

OhA&B
Hubert, Renee Riese 1916- *ConAu 61*
Hubert, Robert *Alli*
Huberts, A *Alli*
Hubin, Allen J 1936- *ConAu 33, EncM&D*
Hubka, Betty 1924- *ConAu 13R*
Hublay, Miklos 1918- *CrCD*
Hubler, Edward L 1902-1965 *ConAu P-1*
Hubler, Richard Gibson 1912- *AmA&B, AmNov, ConAu 1R, WrD 1976*
Hubly, Barnard *Alli*
Hubner, Charles William 1835-1929 *Alli Sup, AmA, AmA&B, AmLY, BiD&SB, BiDSA, ChPo, DcAmA, DcNAA, WhWNAA*
Hubner, Tobias 1577-1636 *OxGer*
Huby, Pamela Margaret Clark 1922- *BiDPar, ConAu 21, WrD 1976*
Huc, Evariste Regis 1813-1860 *BbD, BiD&SB, CasWL*
Huc, Philippe *OxFr*
Hucarius *BiB S*
Hucbald Of St. Amand 840?-930 *Pen Eur*
Huch, Friedrich 1873-1913 *ClDMEuL, EncWL, EvEuW, OxGer*
Huch, Ricarda Octavia 1864-1947 *CasWL, ClDMEuL, EncWL, EvEuW, ModGL, OxGer, Pen Eur, REn, TwCA, TwCA Sup, WhLA*
Huch, Richard d1785 *Alli*
Huchel, Peter 1903- *CasWL, CnMD, EncWL, ModGL, OxGer, Pen Eur*
Hucheon *EvLB*
Huchoun *BrAu, EvLB, NewC, OxEng*
Huchown *CasWL, Chmbr 1, EvLB*
Huck, Arthur 1926- *WrD 1976*
Huck, Charlotte S *ChPo S1*
Huckaby, Gerald 1933- *ConAu 33*
Huckel, Oliver 1864-1940 *AmA&B, ChPo, DcNAA, WhWNAA*
Huckell, John *Alli, BiDLA*
Huckins, Wesley C 1918- *ConAu 23*
Huckleberry, Alan Wright 1912- *IndAu 1917*
Huckleberry, E R 1894- *ConAu 61*
Hucks, A Anthony *ChPo*
Hucks, J *Alli, BiDLA*
Hudak, Andrew, Jr. 1918- *AmSCAP 66*
Huddart, Joseph 1741-1816 *Alli, BiDLA*
Huddesford, G *Alli*
Huddesford, George 1749-1809 *Alli, ChPo, ChPo S1, CyAL 1, DcEnL*
Huddesford, William d1772 *Alli*
Huddilston, John Homer 1869-1956 *DcAmA, OhA&B*
Huddle, David 1942- *ConAu 57, DrAF 1976, DrAP 1975*
Huddle, Frank, Jr. 1943- *ConAu 37*
Huddleston, Miss *Alli Sup*
Huddleston, David R *MnBBF*
Huddleston, Floyd Houston 1919- *AmSCAP 66*
Huddleston, Mrs. G C *Alli Sup*
Huddleston, Hubbard *Alli Sup*
Huddleston, John *Alli*
Huddleston, John Homer 1869- *AmA&B*
Huddleston, Lawrence *Alli*
Huddleston, Lee Eldridge 1935- *ConAu 21*
Huddleston, Mabel P *AnMV 1926*
Huddleston, Robert *PoIre*
Huddleston, Robert 1776-1827 *Alli*
Huddleston, Rodney D 1937- *ConAu 33*
Huddleston, Samuel Brown 1843-1917 *IndAu 1917*
Huddleston, Sisley 1883-1952 *NewC, WhLA*
Huddleston, Trevor 1913- *WrD 1976*
Huddleston, William *Alli*
Huddy, Delia 1934- *ConAu 25*
Huddy, Xenophon Pearce 1878-1943 *DcNAA*
Hudelson, Earl 1888- *IndAu 1917, WhWNAA*
Hudemann, Ludwig Friedrich 1703-1770 *OxGer*
Hudgins, H C, Jr. 1932- *ConAu 33*
Hudig, Ferrand Whaley 1883- *WhLA*
Hudig-Frey, Margareta 1894- *WhLA*
Hudis, Norman Israel 1922- *Au&Wr*
Hudleston, John *BiDLA, MnBBF*
Hudleston, Richard *Alli*
Hudleston, Robert *MnBBF*
Hudley, George *Alli*
Hudnall, Richard Henry 1870- *BiDSA*

Hudnut, Robert K 1934- *ConAu 25, WrD 1976*
Hudon, Edward Gerard 1915- *ConAu 5R*
Hudon, Maxime 1841-1914 *DcNAA*
Hudson, Captain *Alli Sup*
Hudson, Mrs. *Alli*
Hudson, Alec *ConAu XR*
Hudson, Alfred *Alli Sup*
Hudson, Alfred Sereno 1839-1907 *DcNAA*
Hudson, Annie Cropsey *ChPo*
Hudson, Arthur Palmer 1892- *AmA&B*
Hudson, Charles 1795-1881 *Alli Sup, AmA, AmA&B, CyAL 2, DcAmA, DcNAA*
Hudson, Charles & Edward Shirley Kennedy *Alli*
Hudson, Charles F *Alli Sup*
Hudson, Charles M 1932- *ConAu 33, WrD 1976*
Hudson, Charles Thomas And Gosse, P H *Alli Sup*
Hudson, Corrie *Alli Sup*
Hudson, Darril 1931- *ConAu 45*
Hudson, David D *ChPo, ChPo S1*
Hudson, Derek 1911- *Au&Wr, ChPo, ChPo S2, ConAu 9R, WrD 1976*
Hudson, Edmund *Alli Sup*
Hudson, Edward 1743-1821 *PoIre*
Hudson, Elizabeth Harriot *Alli Sup*
Hudson, Erasmus Darwin 1805-1880 *DcAmA, DcNAA*
Hudson, Erasmus Darwin 1843-1887 *Alli Sup, DcAmA, DcNAA*
Hudson, Estelle *TexWr*
Hudson, F *Alli, Alli Sup*
Hudson, Fearnside *Alli Sup*
Hudson, Francis S Brereton *PoIre*
Hudson, Frank *Alli Sup, ChPo*
Hudson, Frank C *WhWNAA*
Hudson, Frederick 1819-1875 *Alli Sup, BiD&SB, CyAL 2, DcAmA, DcNAA*
Hudson, G M *ChPo S2*
Hudson, Geoffrey Francis 1903-1974 *ConAu 49*
Hudson, Gladys W 1926- *ConAu 33, WrD 1976*
Hudson, Hanna Reba *Alli Sup, ChPo*
Hudson, Helen *AmA&B*
Hudson, Henry *Alli*
Hudson, Henry d1611 *OxCan, REn, REnAL*
Hudson, Henry Norman 1814-1886 *Alli, Alli Sup, AmA, AmA&B, BbD, BiD&SB, Chmbr 3, CyAL 2, DcAmA, DcNAA, REnAL*
Hudson, Horace Bushnell 1861-1920 *DcNAA*
Hudson, Hosea *LivBA*
Hudson, Hoyt Hopewell 1893-1944 *ChPo S2, DcNAA*
Hudson, J *MnBBF*
Hudson, J C *Alli*
Hudson, J R *ChPo*
Hudson, J W *Alli*
Hudson, James A 1924- *ConAu 33, WrD 1976*
Hudson, James Fairchild 1846-1915 *Alli Sup, DcAmA, DcNAA, OhA&B*
Hudson, James Jackson 1919- *ConAu 25, WrD 1976*
Hudson, Jay William 1874-1958 *AmA&B, OhA&B, TwCA, TwCA Sup*
Hudson, Jeffery *ConAu XR, SmATA XR, WrD 1976*
Hudson, Sir Jeffrey 1619-1682 *NewC, REn*
Hudson, John *ChPo, ChPo S1*
Hudson, John 1662-1719 *Alli, DcEnL*
Hudson, John A 1927- *ConAu 25*
Hudson, John Christopher 1900- *Au&Wr*
Hudson, John Pilkington 1910- *Au&Wr*
Hudson, Joseph *Alli*
Hudson, Joseph Kennedy 1840-1907 *DcNAA*
Hudson, Joseph Magloire 1821- *BbtC*
Hudson, Joshua Hilary 1832-1909 *BiDSA*
Hudson, Kate *ChPo*
Hudson, Kenneth 1916- *Au&Wr*
Hudson, L *ChPo*
Hudson, Liam 1933- *ConAu 29, WrD 1976*
Hudson, Lois Phillips 1927- *ConAu 1R*
Hudson, Margaret 1906- *TexWr*
Hudson, Mary *PoIre*
Hudson, Mary Ann *Alli Sup*

Hudson, Mary Clemmer Ames 1839-1884 *Alli Sup, AmA&B, BiD&SB, DcAmA, DcNAA*
Hudson, Mary E *Alli Sup*
Hudson, Mary W *Alli Sup*
Hudson, Mary Worrall 1840- *ChPo S1*
Hudson, Michael *Alli*
Hudson, Michael C 1938- *ConAu 37*
Hudson, Michael Huckleberry 1939- *ConAu 33*
Hudson, Palmer 1892- *ConAu 19*
Hudson, Peggy 1936- *ConAu 37*
Hudson, R Lofton 1910- *ConAu 13R*
Hudson, Ralph Gorton 1885- *WhWNAA*
Hudson, Randolph H 1927- *ConAu 17R*
Hudson, Richard *Alli, BiDLA*
Hudson, Robert *ConAu XR*
Hudson, Robert Francis 1922- *Au&Wr*
Hudson, Robert Paine *ChPo, DcNAA*
Hudson, Robert Payne *BiDSA*
Hudson, Samuel *Alli*
Hudson, Sanford A *Alli Sup*
Hudson, Stephen 1869?-1944 *DcLEnL, LongC, ModBL, NewC, REn, TwCA, TwCA Sup, WhLA*
Hudson, T S *Alli Sup*
Hudson, Theodore R *ConAu 45*
Hudson, Thomas *Alli, Alli Sup, BrAu, DcEnL*
Hudson, Thomson Jay 1834-1903 *AmA, DcAmA, DcNAA, OhA&B*
Hudson, Tom *ChPo*
Hudson, W E d1853 *Alli*
Hudson, W J 1934- *Au&Wr*
Hudson, Washington *Alli Sup*
Hudson, Will 1908- *AmSCAP 66*
Hudson, William *Alli Sup*
Hudson, William 1730?-1793 *Alli*
Hudson, William Cadwalader 1843-1915 *AmA&B, DcNAA*
Hudson, William H *Alli Sup*
Hudson, William Henry *Chmbr 3*
Hudson, William Henry 1841-1922 *Alli Sup, AnCL, AtlBL, CarSB, CasWL, ChPo S1, ChPo S2, Chmbr 3, CyWA, DcBiA, DcEuL, DcLEnL, EvLB, LongC, ModBL, NewC, OxEng, Pen Eng, RAdv 1, REn, TwCA, TwCA Sup, TwCW, WebEAL*
Hudson, William Henry 1862-1918 *DcAmA, LongC, NewC, TwCA*
Hudson, William Sloane 1822-1861 *DcNAA*
Hudson, William Sloane 1850-1929 *DcNAA*
Hudson, William Smith 1810-1881 *DcNAA*
Hudson, Wilma Jones 1916- *ConAu 33, WrD 1976*
Hudson, Winthrop Still 1911- *AmA&B, ConAu 1R, WrD 1976*
Hudson-Williams, Thomas 1873- *WhLA*
Hue De Rotelande *CasWL*
Hue, Francis *BiDLA*
Huebner, Anna 1877?-1974 *ConAu 53*
Huebner, Francis Christian 1869-1954 *OhA&B*
Huebner, Ilse 1898- *AmSCAP 66*
Huebner, Russell Henry 1941- *IndAu 1917*
Huebner, Solomon Stephen 1882- *WhWNAA*
Huebsch, Samuel *Alli Sup*
Hueck, Catherine De 1900- *CatA 1952*
Hueffer, 1873-1939 *TwCA Sup*
Hueffer, Ford Madox 1873-1939 *CasWL, ChPo, Chmbr 3, EvLB, LongC, REn*
Hueffer, Franz 1845-1889 *Alli Sup*
Hueffer, Hermann *CasWL*
Huegli, A G 1913- *ConAu 13R*
Huelin, Gordon 1919- *Au&Wr*
Huelsenbeck, Richard 1892-1974 *EncWL, OxGer*
Huemann, G *Alli Sup*
Huerta, Vicente Garcia DeLa 1734-1787 *BiD&SB, DcEuL, DcSpL, REn*
Huerter, Charles 1885- *AmSCAP 66*
Hues, Robert *Alli*
Huessy, Hans R 1921- *ConAu 21*
Huestis *BbtC*
Huestis, Alexander Comstock 1819-1895 *DcAmA*
Huestis, Anne Campbell 1876- *ChPo*
Hueston, Billy 1896-1957 *AmSCAP 66*
Hueston, Ethel 1887- *AmA&B, AmNov, CarSB, REnAL*

Huet, Conrad Busken 1826-1886 *BiD&SB, CasWL, EuA, EvEuW, Pen Eur*
Huet, Pierre-Daniel 1630-1721 *DcEuL, OxFr*
Huether, Anne Frances *ConAu XR*
Huey, Edmund Burke 1870-1913 *DcNAA*
Huey, Maud Morrison *ChPo S2*
Huey, Pennock *Alli Sup*
Hufana, Alejandrino G 1926- *ConP 1970, ConP 1975, WrD 1976*
Hufbauer, G C 1939- *Au&Wr*
Hufeland, Christoph Wilhelm Friedrich 1762-1836 *OxGer*
Hufeland, Otto 1855-1940 *DcNAA*
Huff, Barbara A *ChPo, ChPo S1*
Huff, Bessie M 1892- *WhWNAA*
Huff, Betty Tracy *ConAu 25, WrD 1976*
Huff, Clay G 1900- *IndAu 1917*
Huff, Darrell 1913- *ConAu 1R*
Huff, Jacob K 1851-1910 *DcNAA*
Huff, Robert 1924- *ConAu 13R, ConP 1970, ConP 1975, DrAP 1975, WrD 1976*
Huff, Tom *AuNews 2*
Huff, Vaughn E 1935- *ConAu 29*
Huff, William Harper *ChPo, ChPo S1*
Huff, William Henry *BlkAW*
Huffaker, Carl L 1886- *WhWNAA*
Huffaker, Sandy 1943- *SmATA 10*
Huffard, Grace Thompson 1892- *ChPo, ConAu P-1*
Huffard, Grace Thompson 1894- *IndAu 1917*
Huffcut, Ernest Wilson 1860-1907 *DcAmA, DcNAA*
Huffert, Anton M 1912- *ConAu 13R*
Huffington, Agnes Maria 1859-1935 *IndAu 1816*
Huffman, Franklin E 1934- *ConAu 29*
Huffman, Jasper Abraham 1880- *IndAu 1816, OhA&B, WhWNAA*
Huffman, Laurie 1916- *ConAu 45*
Hufford, Lois Grosvenor 1845-1937 *IndAu 1816*
Hufford, Susan 1940- *ConAu 57*
Huford, Oliver *ChPo*
Hufschmidt, Maynard Michael 1912- *ConAu 41*
Hufton, Olwen H 1938- *ConAu 21*
Hug Von Werbenwag *OxGer*
Hug, Armand 1910- *AmSCAP 66*
Hug, Bernal D 1896- *ConAu 57*
Hugel, Friedrich, Freiherr Von 1852-1926 *OxGer*
Hugell, Mrs. *BiDLA*
Hugenberg, Alfred 1864-1951 *OxGer*
Hugentabler, Robert Campbell 1862-1936 *OhA&B*
Hugessen, Edward Hugessen Knatchbull- 1829- *Alli Sup*
Huggan, A *Alli*
Huggard, Eric Richard 1919- *Au&Wr*
Huggard, J J *Alli Sup*
Huggard, Miles *Alli*
Huggard, Samuel J *PoIre*
Huggenberger, Alfred 1867-1960 *OxGer*
Huggenvik, Theodore 1889- *AmA&B*
Hugget, Anthony *Alli*
Huggett, Frank Edward 1924- *Au&Wr, ConAu 9R, WrD 1976*
Huggett, Richard 1929- *Au&Wr, ConAu 53, WrD 1976*
Huggett, William Turner *ConAu 53*
Huggins, Alice Margaret 1891-1971 *ConAu P-1*
Huggins, Barber *CyAL 1*
Huggins, Eli Lundy 1842-1929 *DcNAA*
Huggins, Hastings Charles *Alli Sup*
Huggins, John Richard Desborus *REnAL*
Huggins, M B *ChPo*
Huggins, Nathan Irvin 1927- *ConAu 29, LivBAA*
Huggins, Samuel *Alli Sup*
Huggins, Sir William *Chmbr 3*
Huggins, William d1761 *Alli*
Huggins, William 1824- *Alli Sup*
Huggins, William Lloyd 1865-1941 *OhA&B*
Hugh, Abbot Of Reading d1164 *Alli, BiB N*
Hugh De Hoveden *BiB N*
Hugh De Nonant d1199 *BiB N*
Hugh De Rutland *Alli, BiB N*
Hugh Of Avalon, Saint 1135?-1200 *NewC*
Hugh Of Lincoln, Saint 1135?-1200 *NewC*
Hugh Of Lincoln, Saint 1246?-1255 *NewC, REn*

Hugh Of Rutland *DcEnL*
Hugh Of Saint Victor 1096-1141 *CasWL*
Hugh Primas *CasWL, Pen Eur*
Hugh, Philip *ChPo S1*
Hugh-Jones, Siriol 1924-1964 *LongC*
Hughan, Jessie Wallace 1875- *WhWNAA*
Hughan, Samuel *Alli Sup*
Hughan, William James 1841- *Alli Sup*
Hughe, William d1549 *Alli*
Hughes *Alli*
Hughes, Mrs. *Alli, BiDLA*
Hughes, A *Alli Sup*
Hughes, A McC *Alli Sup*
Hughes, A W *Alli Sup*
Hughes, Adelaide Manola 1884-1923 *DcNAA*
Hughes, Adella Prentiss 1869-1950 *OhA&B*
Hughes, Agnes Lockhart *AmA&B*
Hughes, Alfred *Alli*
Hughes, Allison *Alli Sup, ChPo S1*
Hughes, Andrew 1937- *ConAu 61*
Hughes, Anselm 1889- *Au&Wr*
Hughes, Anthony John 1933- *ConAu 9R*
Hughes, Arthur 1832-1915 *ChPo, ChPo S1, WhCL*
Hughes, Arthur Joseph 1928- *ConAu 17R*
Hughes, Arthur Montague D'Urban 1873-1974 *ConAu 49*
Hughes, B P 1903- *ConAu 61*
Hughes, Barbara *DrAP 1975*
Hughes, Basil *WhLA*
Hughes, Benjamin *Alli*
Hughes, Brenda *WrD 1976*
Hughes, C J 1918- *ConAu 17R*
Hughes, C J Pennethorne *ConAu XR*
Hughes, Catharine R 1935- *ConAu 41*
Hughes, Charles *Alli*
Hughes, Charles C 1929- *ConAu 41*
Hughes, Charles Evans 1862-1948 *AmA&B, DcNAA, REn, REnAL*
Hughes, Charles H 1877- *WhWNAA*
Hughes, Charles L 1933- *ConAu 17R*
Hughes, Christopher *Alli Sup*
Hughes, Cledwyn 1920- *Au&Wr, ConAu 13R, WrD 1976*
Hughes, Colin Anfield 1930- *ConAu 23, WrD 1976*
Hughes, Cornelius Jabez *Alli Sup*
Hughes, D *Alli*
Hughes, D L *Alli Sup*
Hughes, Daniel 1929- *ConAu 33, DrAP 1975*
Hughes, Daniel E 1851-1892 *Alli Sup, DcNAA*
Hughes, David 1930- *Au&Wr*
Hughes, David John 1820-1915 *DcNAA*
Hughes, Donald *ChPo S2*
Hughes, Dorothy Belle 1904- *AmA&B, EncM&D, REnAL, TwCA Sup*
Hughes, Dorothy Berry 1910- *ConAu 33, WrD 1976*
Hughes, Douglas A 1938- *ConAu 29*
Hughes, E *Alli Sup*
Hughes, E F *ChPo S1*
Hughes, E J *Alli Sup*
Hughes, Edward *Alli, ChPo*
Hughes, Edward Francis *Alli Sup*
Hughes, Edward Robert 1851-1914 *ChPo S1*
Hughes, Edward Stuart Reginald 1919- *WrD 1976*
Hughes, Edwin Holt 1866-1950 *AmA&B, WhWNAA*
Hughes, Elinor L 1906- *AmA&B*
Hughes, Emmet John 1920- *AmA&B*
Hughes, Ernest 1915- *AmSCAP 66*
Hughes, Everett C *OxCan*
Hughes, Miss F *Alli Sup*
Hughes, Felicity 1938- *ConAu 33*
Hughes, Fiona 1954- *Au&Wr*
Hughes, Francis *Alli Sup*
Hughes, Franklin *ChPo*
Hughes, G Bernard *Au&Wr*
Hughes, G E 1918- *ConAu 23*
Hughes, George *Alli Sup*
Hughes, George 1603-1667 *Alli*
Hughes, George 1828-1904 *DcNAA*
Hughes, George Charles *Alli Sup*
Hughes, George Shelley *WhWNAA*
Hughes, Gervase 1905- *Au&Wr, ConAu 9R, WrD 1976*
Hughes, Glenn Arthur 1894-1964 *AmA&B,*

REnAL, WhPNW
Hughes, Glyn 1935- *Au&Wr, ConAu 33, ConP 1975, WrD 1976*
Hughes, Graham 1928- *ConAu 57*
Hughes, Griffith *Alli*
Hughes, H *Alli, BiDLA*
Hughes, H G *Alli*
Hughes, H H *Alli*
Hughes, H M *Alli, Alli Sup*
Hughes, H N *ChPo S2*
Hughes, H Stuart 1916- *Au&Wr, ConAu 1R, WrD 1976*
Hughes, Harold K 1911- *ConAu 9R*
Hughes, Harry *MnBBF*
Hughes, Hatcher 1881?-1945 *AmA&B, CnDAL, CnMD, DcLEnL, DcNAA, ModWD, OxAm, REn, REnAL, TwCA, TwCA Sup*
Hughes, Hector James 1871- *WhWNAA*
Hughes, Helen 1928- *ConAu 13R*
Hughes, Henry *Alli, Alli Sup*
Hughes, Henry 1826?-1862 *DcNAA*
Hughes, Henry Maldwyn 1875- *WhLA*
Hughes, Henry Stuart 1916- *AmA&B*
Hughes, Herbert Delauney 1914- *Au&Wr*
Hughes, Hugh *Alli, Alli Sup*
Hughes, Isabel *OxCan*
Hughes, J G *Alli*
Hughes, J T *Alli, BiDLA*
Hughes, Jabez 1685-1731 *Alli*
Hughes, James *Alli*
Hughes, James d1870 *Alli Sup*
Hughes, James D *ChPo S2*
Hughes, James Langston 1902-1967 *CasWL, ChPo, ChPo S1, ChPo S2, DcLEnL*
Hughes, James L SEE Hughes, Langston
Hughes, James Laughlin 1846-1935 *AmLY, ChPo, DcNAA, WhWNAA*
Hughes, James Monroe 1890- *ConAu 1R, IndAu 1917*
Hughes, James Pennethorne *ConAu XR*
Hughes, James Quentin 1920- *Au&Wr, ConAu 13R, WrD 1976*
Hughes, James Stannus *Alli Sup*
Hughes, James Vaughan *Alli Sup*
Hughes, Jasper Seaton 1843-1926 *OhA&B*
Hughes, John *Alli, Alli Sup, BiDLA, Chmbr 2, DcEnL, OxCan*
Hughes, John 1677-1720 *Alli, CasWL, ChPo, ChPo S1, DcEnL, EvLB, NewC*
Hughes, John 1682-1710 *Alli*
Hughes, John 1776-1843 *DcEnL*
Hughes, John 1790-1858 *Alli Sup*
Hughes, John 1797-1864 *Alli, Alli Sup, AmA&B, BiD&SB, CyAL 2, DcAmA, PoIre*
Hughes, John 1832-1887 *Pen Eng*
Hughes, John 1930- *ConAu 1R*
Hughes, John A 1941- *ConAu 41*
Hughes, John Arthur *Alli Sup*
Hughes, John Ceiriog 1832-1887 *ChPo, NewC*
Hughes, John Jay 1928- *ConAu 57*
Hughes, John Joseph 1797-1864 *DcNAA*
Hughes, John Paul 1920-1974 *ConAu 1R, ConAu 53*
Hughes, John Scott 1893- *Au&Wr*
Hughes, John Stoddard 1894- *WhWNAA*
Hughes, John T *BiDSA*
Hughes, John William 1797-1850 *Alli Sup*
Hughes, Joseph *Alli, Alli Sup, BiDLA*
Hughes, Judith M 1941- *ConAu 33, WrD 1976*
Hughes, Julius Henry *Alli Sup*
Hughes, Katherine d1925 *DcNAA*
Hughes, Ken 1922- *Au&Wr, ConAu 5R, WrD 1976*
Hughes, Langston 1902-1967 *AmA&B, AmSCAP 66, AnCL, AuBYP, BkCL, BlkAW, ChPo, CnDAL, CnMD, ConAmA, ConAu 1R, ConAu 25, ConLC 1, ConLC 5, ConP 1975, CrCD, EncWL, LongC, McGWD, ModAL, ModAL Sup, ModWD, OxAm, Pen Am, RAdv 1, REn, REnAL, SixAP, SmATA 4, St&VC, TwCA, TwCA Sup, WebEAL, WhTwL*
Hughes, Langston SEE Hughes, James L
Hughes, LaVaughn Rachel 1919- *AmSCAP 66*

Hughes, Leo 1908- *ConAu 41*
Hughes, Lewis *Alli, Alli Sup, BiDLA*
Hughes, Mary *CarSB, ChPo*
Hughes, Mary Gray 1930- *ConAu 61*
Hughes, Mary Louise 1910- *ConAu 29*
Hughes, Matilda *ConAu XR*
Hughes, Matthew F 1834-1895 *PoIre*
Hughes, Matthew Simpson 1863-1920 *DcNAA*
Hughes, Merrit Y 1893-1970 *ConAu P-1*
Hughes, Michael *Alli*
Hughes, N C *Alli Sup*
Hughes, Nathaniel Cheairs, Jr. 1930-
  ConAu 17R
Hughes, Nicholas Collin 1822-1893 *DcAmA,
  DcNAA*
Hughes, Obadiah 1695-1744 *Alli*
Hughes, Owain 1943- *Au&Wr, ConAu 21*
Hughes, Patrick 1939- *ConAu 61*
Hughes, Paul L 1915- *ConAu 9R*
Hughes, Pennethorne 1907-1967 *ConAu 21*
Hughes, Percy 1872- *WhWNAA*
Hughes, Philip 1895- *CatA 1947, ConAu 17*
Hughes, Philip Edgcumbe 1915- *Au&Wr,
  ConAu 9R, WrD 1976*
Hughes, Phillip William 1926- *WrD 1976*
Hughes, Quentin 1920- *ConAu 29*
Hughes, R E *Alli*
Hughes, R E 1927- *ConAu 5R*
Hughes, R John 1930- *WrD 1976*
Hughes, R M *Alli*
Hughes, R S *ChPo S2*
Hughes, Rhoda *Alli Sup*
Hughes, Rice *Alli, BiDLA*
Hughes, Richard *Alli, Alli Sup*
Hughes, Richard Arthur Warren 1900- *Au&Wr,
  CasWL, ChPo, ChPo S2, ConAu 5R,
  ConLC 1, ConNov 1972, ConNov 1976,
  CyWA, DcLEnL, EncWL, EvLB, LongC,
  ModBL, ModBL Sup, NewC, OxEng,
  Pen Eng, RAdv 1, REn, SmATA 8,
  TwCA, TwCA Sup, TwCW, WhCL,
  WhLA, WhTwL, WrD 1976*
Hughes, Riley 1914- *BkC 5*
Hughes, Robert 1929?-1972 *ConAu 37*
Hughes, Robert J 1859- *PoIre*
Hughes, Robert J 1916- *AmSCAP 66*
Hughes, Robert Morton 1855-1940 *BiDSA,
  DcNAA, WhWNAA*
Hughes, Robert William 1821-1901 *Alli Sup,
  AmA, BiDSA, DcAmA, DcNAA*
Hughes, Rosalind *ChPo S1*
Hughes, Rupert 1872-1956 *AmA&B,
  AmSCAP 66, AnMV 1926, ChPo,
  ChPo S1, ChPo S2, ConAmL, DcAmA,
  OhA&B, OxAm, REnAL, TwCA,
  TwCA Sup, WhWNAA*
Hughes, Russell Meriwether 1900- *TexWr,
  WhWNAA*
Hughes, Mrs. S 1748- *Alli, BiDLA*
Hughes, Samuel *Alli, Alli Sup*
Hughes, Shirley 1929- *IlCB 1966, WrD 1976*
Hughes, Spike 1908- *Au&Wr, WrD 1976*
Hughes, Stephen Ormsby 1924- *ConAu 61*
Hughes, T *Alli*
Hughes, T B *Alli, BiDLA*
Hughes, T J *Alli Sup*
Hughes, T M *Alli*
Hughes, Ted 1930- *CasWL, ChPo, ChPo S1,
  ChPo S2, CnE&AP, ConAu 1R,
  ConLC 2, ConLC 4, ConP 1970,
  ConP 1975, EncWL Sup, LongC, ModBL,
  ModBL Sup, NewC, Pen Eng, RAdv 1,
  TwCW, WebEAL, WhTwL, WorAu,
  WrD 1976*
Hughes, Terence *Alli Sup*
Hughes, Terence McMahon 1812-1849 *PoIre*
Hughes, Thomas *Alli, Alli Sup, CasWL,
  Chmbr 1, Chmbr 3, DcEnL, REnWD*
Hughes, Thomas 1821- *Alli Sup*
Hughes, Thomas 1822-1896 *Alli Sup, BbD,
  BiD&SB, BrAu 19, CarSB, CasWL,
  CyWA, DcBiA, DcEnA, DcEnL, DcEuL,
  DcLEnL, EvLB, JBA 1934, MnBBF,
  MouLC 4, NewC, OxEng, Pen Eng,
  REn, WhCL*
Hughes, Thomas 1854-1934 *DcNAA*
Hughes, Thomas Aloysius 1849-1929 *AmA&B,
  DcAmA, DcNAA*

Hughes, Mrs. Thomas Francis *Alli Sup*
Hughes, Thomas Houghton 1884-1944 *DcNAA*
Hughes, Thomas J 1865-1934 *OhA&B*
Hughes, Thomas Lloyd 1806-1896 *OhA&B*
Hughes, Thomas P *Alli Sup*
Hughes, Thomas Parke 1923- *ConAu 29*
Hughes, Thomas Patrick 1838-1911 *Alli Sup,
  DcAmA, DcNAA*
Hughes, Thomas Rowland 1903-1949 *CasWL*
Hughes, Thomas Smart *Alli*
Hughes, Thomas Welburn 1853- *WhWNAA*
Hughes, Virginia *ConAu XR*
Hughes, W *Alli, BiDLA*
Hughes, W Hastings *Alli Sup*
Hughes, Walter *ChPo S1*
Hughes, Walter Dudley 1918- *Au&Wr*
Hughes, Walter Llewellyn 1910- *Au&Wr,
  ConAu 1R*
Hughes, Walter Oldham Hughes- *Alli Sup*
Hughes, William *Alli, Alli Sup, BiDLA*
Hughes, William 1803-1861 *Alli Sup*
Hughes, William Carter *Alli Sup*
Hughes, William Franklin 1913- *IndAu 1917*
Hughes, William J, Jr. 1897?-1974 *ConAu 45*
Hughes, William Jesse 1912- *Au&Wr,
  WrD 1976*
Hughes, William Joseph 1863-1939 *DcNAA*
Hughes, William R *Alli Sup, ChPo*
Hughes, William Taylor 1850-1925 *DcNAA*
Hughes, Zach *WrD 1976*
Hughes-Stanton, Blair Rowlands 1902- *ChPo*
Hughey, G W *Alli Sup, BiDSA*
Hughey, Ruth Willard 1899- *ConAu 1R*
Hughlings, J P *Alli Sup*
Hughlings-Jackson *Alli Sup*
Hughly, Young *BlkAW*
Hughs, Mary *Alli, ChPo, DcNAA*
Hughson, D *Alli*
Hughson, Shirley Carter 1867-1949 *BiDSA,
  DcNAA*
Hugill, R *MnBBF*
Hugill, Robert *Au&Wr, WrD 1976*
Hugill, Stan James 1906- *ConAu 23,
  WrD 1976*
Hugman, William Curtis *Alli Sup*
Hugo Candidus d1155? *Alli, BiB N*
Hugo, Count Of Montfort 1357-1423 *CasWL*
Hugo Of Lincoln *Alli*
Hugo Sotaevagina *BiB N*
Hugo Von Langenstein *OxGer*
Hugo Von Montfort 1357-1423 *DcEuL, OxGer,
  Pen Eur*
Hugo Von Trimberg 1230?-1313? *CasWL,
  DcEuL, OxGer, Pen Eur*
Hugo, Abel 1798-1855 *OxFr*
Hugo, Charles-Victor 1826-1871 *OxFr*
Hugo, Eugene 1800-1837 *OxFr*
Hugo, Grant 1920- *Au&Wr, WrD 1976*
Hugo, Mrs. Ian *AmNov XR*
Hugo, Jean 1894- *WhGrA*
Hugo, Jean-Francois-Victor 1828-1873 *OxFr*
Hugo, Minor *Alli*
Hugo, Richard Franklin 1923- *ConAu 49,
  ConLC 6, ConP 1970, ConP 1975,
  DrAP 1975, WhPNW, WrD 1976*
Hugo, T *Alli*
Hugo, Thomas 1820-1876 *Alli Sup, ChPo S1*
Hugo, Victor Marie 1802-1885 *AtlBL, BbD,
  BiD&SB, CasWL, ChPo, ChPo S1,
  ChPo S2, CnThe, CyWA, DcBiA,
  DcEnL, DcEuL, EncM&D, EuA, EvEuW,
  HsB&A, McGWD, MnBBF, NewC,
  OxEng, OxFr, Pen Eur, RCom, REn,
  REnWD*
Hugolin, Pere *DcNAA*
Hugot, Paul Charles Emile 1904- *Au&Wr*
Hugues Capet 938?-996 *OxFr*
Hugues De Berze 1150?-1219 *CasWL*
Hugues D'Oisy 1150?-1190? *CasWL*
Huguet-Latour, Louis A 1824?-1824 *DcNAA*
Huhn, Bruno 1871-1950 *AmSCAP 66*
Huhner, Leon 1871- *WhWNAA*
Huhner, Max 1873-1947 *DcNAA, WhWNAA*
Huhta, James K 1937- *ConAu 37*
Hui-Chiao 497-554 *DcOrL 1*
Hui-Yuan *DcOrL 1*
Huicke, William *Alli*
Huidekoper, Frederic 1817-1892 *Alli, Alli Sup,*

DcAmA, DcNAA
Huidekoper, Frederic Louis 1874-1940 *DcNAA,
  WhWNAA*
Huidekoper, Henry Shippen 1839-1918 *Alli Sup,
  DcAmA, DcNAA*
Huidekoper, Rush Shippen 1854-1901 *DcAmA,
  DcNAA*
Huidobro, Vicente 1893-1948 *CasWL, DcSpL,
  EncWL, Pen Am, TwCA, TwCA Sup,
  TwCW, WhTwL*
Huie, James *Alli*
Huie, James A *Alli, Alli Sup*
Huie, John 1887- *ChPo, ChPo S1, ChPo S2*
Huie, Richard *ChPo S1*
Huie, William Bradford 1910- *AmA&B,
  Au&Wr, AuNews 1, ConAu 9R,
  ConNov 1972, ConNov 1976, REnAL,
  TwCA Sup, WrD 1976*
Huie, William O 1911- *ConAu 23*
Huiginn, Eugene Joseph Vincent 1860-1927
  DcNAA
Huise, John *Alli*
Huish, Alexander *Alli*
Huish, Francis *Alli*
Huish, Marcus Bourne *Alli Sup*
Huish, Robert 1777-1850 *Alli, BiDLA,
  HsB&A*
Huit, Ephraim d1644 *Alli*
Huit, John *Alli*
Huitfeldt, Arild 1546-1609 *CasWL*
Huizinga, Arnold VanC P 1876-1953 *AmA&B*
Huizinga, Henry 1873-1945 *AmA&B, DcNAA,
  WhWNAA*
Huizinga, J H 1908- *Au&Wr*
Huizinga, Johan 1872-1945 *CasWL,
  TwCA Sup*
Hula, Harold L 1930- *ConAu 25*
Hulbert, Archer Butler 1873-1933 *AmA&B,
  DcAmA, DcNAA, OhA&B, WhWNAA*
Hulbert, Charles 1778-1857 *Alli, Alli Sup*
Hulbert, Charles Augustus *Alli Sup*
Hulbert, Daniel P M *Alli*
Hulbert, Edwin James 1829-1910 *DcNAA*
Hulbert, Henry Woodward 1858-1937 *DcNAA*
Hulbert, Homer Bezaleel 1863-1949 *DcNAA*
Hulbert, James A 1906- *LivBA*
Hulbert, Joan Margery 1911- *Au&Wr*
Hulbert, Lloyd *MnBBF*
Hulbert, Mary 1863-1939 *DcNAA*
Hulbert, William Davenport 1868-1913 *DcNAA*
Hulburt, Emma Kidd 1886- *WhWNAA*
Hulet, Claude Lyle 1920- *ConAu 53*
Hulet, James d1771 *BkIE*
Hulett, James d1771 *BkIE*
Hulfish, David Stephen 1873- *IndAu 1917*
Hulfish, Edwin E, Jr. 1842- *ChPo*
Hulfish, James D 1843- *ChPo*
Hulick, Elizabeth *ChPo S1*
Hulicka, Irene M 1927- *ConAu 37*
Hulicka, Karel 1913- *ConAu 41*
Huling, Alice B *ChPo*
Huling, Caroline Alden 1857-1941 *DcNAA,
  WhWNAA*
Hulit, Leonard 1856-1924 *DcNAA*
Hulke, John Whittaker *Alli Sup*
Hulke, Malcolm 1924- *Au&Wr, WrD 1976*
Hull, A Warner *Alli Sup*
Hull, Albert W 1880- *WhWNAA*
Hull, Alexander 1887-1953 *OhA&B,
  WhWNAA*
Hull, Amelia Matilda *Alli Sup*
Hull, Amos Girard 1815-1898 *Alli, DcNAA*
Hull, Asa *ChPo S1*
Hull, Augustus Longstreet 1847-1909 *BiDSA,
  DcNAA*
Hull, C *Alli Sup*
Hull, C F W *Alli Sup*
Hull, Charles Henry 1864-1936 *DcNAA*
Hull, D W *Alli Sup*
Hull, David Stewart 1938- *ConAu 25,
  WrD 1976*
Hull, Denison Bingham 1897- *ConAu 37*
Hull, E L *Alli Sup*
Hull, Edith Maude *DcLEnL, EvLB, LongC,
  NewC, REn, TwCA*
Hull, Edmund C P *Alli Sup*
Hull, Edna Mayne *AmA&B*
Hull, Edward 1829- *Alli Sup, BbD, BiD&SB*

Humphrey, Francis *Alli Sup*
Humphrey, Francis A *ChPo*
Humphrey, G H *Alli Sup*
Humphrey, George *Alli*
Humphrey, Grace 1882- *AmA&B, WhWNAA*
Humphrey, Heman 1779-1861 *Alli, CyAL 1, DcAmA, DcNAA*
Humphrey, James *ChPo*
Humphrey, James 1939- *ConAu 45, DrAP 1975, WrD 1976*
Humphrey, James H 1911- *ConAu 61*
Humphrey, Jennett *ChPo S1*
Humphrey, John *Alli*
Humphrey, Laurence 1527?-1590 *Alli*
Humphrey, Leonard J 1897- *WhWNAA*
Humphrey, Lillie Muse *BlkAW*
Humphrey, Lizbeth B *ChPo, ChPo S1, ChPo S2*
Humphrey, Lizzie B 1850- *EarAB, EarAB Sup*
Humphrey, Lucy H *DcNAA*
Humphrey, M *Alli Sup*
Humphrey, Malcolm *ChPo*
Humphrey, Marie E Ives *AmLY*
Humphrey, Mary A *Alli Sup*
Humphrey, Mary A P *ChPo*
Humphrey, Maud 1868- *ChPo*
Humphrey, Michael 1926- *ConAu 29*
Humphrey, Myrtle 'Moss' 1934- *BlkAW*
Humphrey, Old d1854 *Alli, ChPo S1, DcEnL*
Humphrey, Mrs. Robert *Alli Sup*
Humphrey, Robert L 1923- *ConAu 57*
Humphrey, Seth King 1864-1932 *DcNAA*
Humphrey, W C *Alli*
Humphrey, W D *ChPo S1*
Humphrey, W Desterling *Alli Sup*
Humphrey, W H *BbtC*
Humphrey, William 1839- *Alli Sup*
Humphrey, William 1924- *AmA&B, ConNov 1972, ConNov 1976, DrAF 1976, Pen Am, REnAL, WorAu, WrD 1976*
Humphrey, William Brewster 1867- *AmLY*
Humphrey, William Depue 1900- *OhA&B*
Humphrey, Willis C 1839-1888 *DcNAA*
Humphrey, Zephaniah Moore 1824-1881 *DcNAA*
Humphrey, Zephine 1874- *AmA&B, DcAmA*
Humphreys, Doctor *Alli Sup*
Humphreys, Alexander Crombie 1851-1927 *DcNAA*
Humphreys, Alexander J 1913- *ConAu 33, WrD 1976*
Humphreys, Alice Lee 1893- *ConAu 5R*
Humphreys, Andrew Atkinson 1810-1883 *Alli Sup, DcAmA, DcNAA*
Humphreys, Asher *Alli*
Humphreys, Betty Vance 1927- *Au&Wr, WrD 1976*
Humphreys, Cecil Frances *ChPo*
Humphreys, Charles John *Alli Sup*
Humphreys, Christmas 1901- *Au&Wr, ChPo S1, ChPo S2*
Humphreys, David *Alli, BiDSA*
Humphreys, David 1752-1818 *Alli, AmA, AmA&B, ChPo, CnDAL, CyAL 1, DcAmA, DcEnL, DcLEnL, DcNAA, OxAm, Pen Am, REnAL*
Humphreys, Mrs. Desmond *Chmbr 3*
Humphreys, Edward Rupert 1820-1893 *Alli, Alli Sup, CyAL 2, DcAmA, DcNAA*
Humphreys, Eliza *Alli Sup*
Humphreys, Eliza d1938 *EvLB, WhLA*
Humphreys, Emyr Owen 1919- *Au&Wr, ConAu 5R, ConNov 1972, ConNov 1976, WorAu, WrD 1976*
Humphreys, Evan Williams 1816-1884 *OhA&B*
Humphreys, Francis *Alli*
Humphreys, Francis Landon 1858-1937 *DcNAA*
Humphreys, Frank Landon 1858-1937 *DcAmA*
Humphreys, Frederick 1816-1900 *DcNAA*
Humphreys, George H & Hackley, Charles E *Alli Sup*
Humphreys, George W 1875-1949 *DcNAA*
Humphreys, Gordon *MnBBF*
Humphreys, Hector d1857 *CyAL 1*
Humphreys, Henry *Alli Sup*
Humphreys, Henry Noel 1810-1879 *Alli, Alli Sup*
Humphreys, Henry R Morin *Alli Sup*

Humphreys, Humphrey d1712 *Alli*
Humphreys, Ida Frances 1852- *DcNAA*
Humphreys, J R Adams 1918- *ConAu 1R*
Humphreys, James 1748-1810 *AmA&B*
Humphreys, James 1768-1830 *Alli, DcEnL*
Humphreys, Jennett *Alli Sup, ChPo S1*
Humphreys, John *Alli, BiDLA*
Humphreys, John Doddridge, Jr. *Alli, BiDLA*
Humphreys, John O 1927-1970 *IndAu 1917*
Humphreys, Joseph *PoIre*
Humphreys, Joseph 1720- *PoCh*
Humphreys, Laud 1930- *ConAu 29, WrD 1976*
Humphreys, Laura B *Alli Sup*
Humphreys, Mary Eglantyne Hill 1914- *ConAu 5R*
Humphreys, Mary Gay d1915 *DcNAA, OhA&B*
Humphreys, Milton Wylie 1844- *DcAmA*
Humphreys, Noel *ChPo S2*
Humphreys, Phebe Westcott 1868-1939 *DcNAA*
Humphreys, R *PoIre*
Humphreys, Rose *Alli Sup*
Humphreys, Ruth *TexWr*
Humphreys, Sam *Alli*
Humphreys, T *Alli*
Humphreys, Thomas *BiDLA*
Humphreys, Thomas Darwin *Alli Sup*
Humphreys, West Hughes 1806-1883 *Alli, BiDSA, DcNAA*
Humphreys, Willard Cunningham 1867-1902 *DcNAA*
Humphreys, Wilton Wylie 1844- *BiDSA*
Humphreyville, Theresa R 1918- *ConAu 13R*
Humphrie, Thomas *Alli*
Humphries, Adelaide Morris 1898- *ConAu P-1*
Humphries, Adelaide Morris 1899- *OhA&B*
Humphries, David *REn*
Humphries, Elsie Mary 1905- *Au&Wr, WrD 1976*
Humphries, George Rolfe 1894-1969 *ChPo S1*
Humphries, Helen Speirs Dickie 1915- *Au&Wr, ConAu P-1*
Humphries, Jack 1817-1855 *AmA, OhA&B*
Humphries, John 1922- *Au&Wr*
Humphries, John Thomas Conolly d1896 *PoIre*
Humphries, Mary 1905- *ConAu 53*
Humphries, Rolfe 1894-1969 *AmA&B, CnDAL, ConAu 5R, ConAu 25, OxAm, RAdv 1, REnAL, TwCA, TwCA Sup*
Humphries, Sydney Vernon 1907- *Au&Wr, WrD 1976*
Humphris, Francis Howard 1866- *WhLA*
Humphry, Alfred Paget *Alli Sup*
Humphry, Derek 1930- *ConAu 41*
Humphry, Sir George Murray 1820-1896 *Alli Sup, BiD&SB*
Humphry, Hugh McNab 1855- *Alli Sup*
Humphry, James, III *ChPo*
Humphry, Joseph Thomas 1816- *Alli Sup*
Humphry, W W *Alli*
Humphry, William Gilson 1815-1888 *Alli, Alli Sup*
Humphrys, Geoffrey *WrD 1976*
Humphrys, Leslie George 1921- *Au&Wr, WrD 1976*
Humphrys, Thomas *Alli*
Humpidge, Thomas Samuel d1887 *Alli Sup*
Humpstone, Charles Cheney 1931- *ConAu 49*
Humston, Robert *Alli*
Hun, Henry 1854-1924 *Alli Sup, DcNAA*
Hun, John Gale 1877-1945 *DcNAA*
Hun, M T *Alli Sup*
Hundley, Daniel Robinson 1832-1899 *Alli Sup, BiDSA, DcNAA*
Hundley, Joan Martin 1921- *ConAu 45*
Hundley, Norris C, Jr. 1935- *ConAu 17R, WrD 1976*
Hundley, P *ChPo*
Hundley, Richard 1931- *AmSCAP 66*
Hundley, Will M 1860?- *OhA&B*
Huneker, James Gibbons 1860?-1921 *AmA&B, CnDAL, ConAmL, DcAmA, DcLEnL, DcNAA, LongC, OxAm, Pen Am, RAdv 1, REn, REnAL, TwCA, TwCA Sup*
Huneryager, S G 1933- *ConAu 1R*
Hung, Mai *DcOrL 1*

Hung, P'ien *DcOrL 1*
Hung, Shen 1893-1955 *CasWL, DcOrL 1, REnWD*
Hung, Sheng 1645?-1704 *CasWL, DcOrL 1, Pen Cl*
Hungerford, Sir Anthony *Alli*
Hungerford, Edward 1875-1948 *AmA&B, AmLY, DcNAA*
Hungerford, Edward Buell 1900- *AuBYP, ConAu 37*
Hungerford, Harold R 1928- *ConAu 33*
Hungerford, Herbert Barker 1885- *WhWNAA*
Hungerford, James Edward 1814-1883 *Alli Sup, BiDSA, HsB&A*
Hungerford, M C *ChPo*
Hungerford, Margaret Wolfe 1855?-1897 *Alli Sup, BbD, BiD&SB, BrAu 19, Chmbr 3, NewC*
Hungerford, Mary 1832-1901 *DcNAA*
Hungerford, Pixie *ConAu XR*
Hungerford, T A G 1915- *Au&Wr*
Hunker, Henry L 1924- *ConAu 13R, WrD 1976*
Hunkin, Harry *OxCan Sup*
Hunkin, Tim Mark Trelawney 1950- *WrD 1976*
Hunkins, Eusebia Simpson 1902- *AmSCAP 66*
Hunkins, Francis P 1938- *ConAu 57*
Hunkins, Leecynth 1930- *BlkAW*
Hunn, Katharine *ChPo S2*
Hunnewell, James Frothingham 1832-1910 *Alli Sup, BiD&SB, DcAmA, DcNAA*
Hunnex, Milton D 1917- *ConAu 29*
Hunnicut, Clyde J 1889- *TexWr*
Hunnicutt, James W 1814- *Alli Sup, DcAmA, DcNAA*
Hunnicutt, William Littleton Clark 1834-1910 *DcNAA*
Hunningher, Benjamin 1903- *AmA&B*
Hunnings, Neville March 1929- *ConAu 25*
Hunnings, Thomas Neville March 1929- *Au&Wr, WrD 1976*
Hunnis, William d1597? *Alli, CasWL, Chmbr 1, DcEnL, EvLB*
Hunnius, Agidius 1555-1603 *OxGer*
Hunold, Christian Friedrich 1680-1721 *OxGer*
Hunsaker, David M 1944- *ConAu 33*
Hunsberger, Warren S 1911- *ConAu 41*
Hunscher, Helen Alvina 1904- *Au&Wr*
Hunsinger, Clarence S 1892- *OhA&B*
Hunsinger, Paul 1919- *ConAu 33*
Hunt *Alli*
Hunt, Sir A *ChPo*
Hunt, A B *Alli Sup*
Hunt, A Leigh *Alli Sup*
Hunt, Arthur Joseph 1835- *Alli Sup*
Hunt, Arthur Prince 1874-1925 *DcNAA*
Hunt, Arthur Surridge 1871- *WhLA*
Hunt, Sir Aubrey DeVere *Alli*
Hunt, Barbara 1907- *ConAu 5R*
Hunt, Ben *TexWr*
Hunt, Bernice Kohn *WrD 1976*
Hunt, Bristow *Alli Sup*
Hunt, Mrs. C W *ChPo S1*
Hunt, Carleton *BiDSA*
Hunt, Caroline Louisa 1865-1927 *DcNAA*
Hunt, Charles H *BiDSA*
Hunt, Charles Havens *Alli Sup*
Hunt, Charles Henry *Alli, BiDLA*
Hunt, Charles Warren 1858-1932 *DcNAA*
Hunt, Charlotte *ConAu XR, WrD 1976*
Hunt, Charlotte Matilda *Alli*
Hunt, Chester L 1912- *ConAu 13R*
Hunt, Chillingham *Alli Sup*
Hunt, Clara Whitehill 1871-1958 *AmA&B, JBA 1934, JBA 1951*
Hunt, Cornelius E *Alli Sup*
Hunt, Dave *ConAu 57*
Hunt, David *Alli Sup*
Hunt, David 1942- *ConAu 33*
Hunt, David C 1926- *ConAu 57*
Hunt, DeForest *Alli Sup*
Hunt, DeWitt Talmadge 1889- *WhWNAA*
Hunt, Donnell R 1926- *IndAu 1917*
Hunt, Dorothy Alice 1896- *Au&Wr*
Hunt, Douglas 1918- *ConAu 13R*
Hunt, E *Alli Sup*
Hunt, E Howard, Jr. 1918- *AmA&B, AmNov, AuNews 1, ConAu 45, ConLC 3,*

EncM&D

Hunt, Edgar Hubert 1909- *ConAu P-1, WrD 1976*

Hunt, Edward *Alli*

Hunt, Edward Bissell 1822-1863 *Alli Sup, DcAmA*

Hunt, Edward Thomas Eyre 1885-1953 *OhA&B, WhWNAA*

Hunt, Elgin Fraser 1895- *ConAu 1R, WrD 1976*

Hunt, Eliza Meadows Shepherd 1845- *Alli Sup*

Hunt, Ellen St. John *Alli Sup*

Hunt, Elwin 1888- *WhWNAA*

Hunt, Emily Honoria Leigh *Alli Sup*

Hunt, Erling Messer 1901- *AmA&B*

Hunt, Evelyn Tooley *BlkAW*

Hunt, Everette Howard, Jr. 1918- *AmA&B*

Hunt, Ezra Mundy 1830-1894 *Alli Sup, DcAmA, DcNAA*

Hunt, F W *Alli*

Hunt, Florine E 1928- *ConAu 13R*

Hunt, Francis *ConAu 19*

Hunt, Frazier 1885-1967 *AmA&B*

Hunt, Frederick Knight 1814-1855? *Alli, DcEnL*

Hunt, Freeman 1804-1858 *Alli, AmA&B, BiD&SB, DcAmA, DcNAA*

Hunt, G H *Alli Sup*

Hunt, G T *OxCan*

Hunt, Gaillard 1862-1924 *AmA&B, AmLY, BiDSA, DcAmA, DcNAA*

Hunt, George *Alli, OxCan*

Hunt, George Dillwyn 1819-1908 *Alli Sup, OhA&B*

Hunt, George Laird 1918- *ConAu 49*

Hunt, George Madden 1843-1919 *OhA&B*

Hunt, George Pinney 1918- *AuBYP*

Hunt, Gilbert J *Alli, BbtC*

Hunt, Gladys M 1926- *ConAu 29, WrD 1976*

Hunt, Gordon 1906-1970 *ConAu 29*

Hunt, Graham *MnBBF*

Hunt, H Draper 1935- *ConAu 37*

Hunt, H Lyons 1882- *WhWNAA*

Hunt, H M *ChPo*

Hunt, Harriot Kezia 1805-1875 *Alli, DcAmA, DcNAA*

Hunt, Harrison *ConAu XR, OhA&B, WrD 1976*

Hunt, Harrison Randall 1889- *OhA&B, WhWNAA*

Hunt, Helen Maria Fiske 1830-1885 *Alli Sup, AmA, CyAL 2, DcAmA, DcNAA, OxAm, REnAL*

Hunt, Henry *Alli, Alli Sup*

Hunt, Henry 1773-1835 *REn*

Hunt, Henry George Bonavia 1847- *Alli Sup, MnBBF*

Hunt, Henry Jackson 1819-1889 *DcAmA, DcNAA*

Hunt, Herbert James *Au&Wr*

Hunt, Holman 1827-1910 *AtlBL, REn*

Hunt, Howard 1918- *AmNov*

Hunt, Hugh 1911- *ConAu 5R*

Hunt, Ignatius 1920- *ConAu 17R*

Hunt, Inez Whitaker 1899- *ConAu P-1*

Hunt, Irene 1907- *AuBYP, ChLR 1, ConAu 17R, MorBMP, NewbC 1966, SmATA 2, ThBJA*

Hunt, Isaac 1742?-1809 *Alli, AmA, AmA&B, BiDLA, CnDAL, DcNAA, OxAm, REnAL*

Hunt, Isobel Violet *ChPo S1*

Hunt, J D S *MnBBF*

Hunt, J H *Alli*

Hunt, J McVicker 1906- *ConAu 37, WrD 1976*

Hunt, J P *Alli, BiDLA*

Hunt, J William, Jr. 1930- *ConAu 53*

Hunt, James *Alli, Alli Sup*

Hunt, James G 1870- *WhWNAA*

Hunt, James H *BiDSA*

Hunt, James Henry Leigh 1784-1859 *Alli, BbD, BiDLA, CasWL, ChPo, ChPo S1, ChPo S2, Chmbr 3, DcEnL, EvLB, MouLC 3, OxEng*

Hunt, Jedediah 1815-1860 *DcAmA, OhA&B, OxCan*

Hunt, Jeremiah 1678-1744 *Alli, DcEnL*

Hunt, John *Alli, BiDLA, ConAu XR*

Hunt, John 1827- *Alli Sup*

Hunt, John J 1929- *ConAu 33*

Hunt, John P 1915- *ConAu 33*

Hunt, John W 1927- *ConAu 21*

Hunt, John Warren *Alli Sup*

Hunt, Josie *ChPo S2*

Hunt, Kari 1920- *AuBYP, ConAu 41*

Hunt, Kellogg W 1912- *ConAu 5R*

Hunt, Kyle *ConAu XR, EncM&D, LongC*

Hunt, Lawrence J 1920- *ConAu 5R*

Hunt, Leigh 1784-1859 *Alli, AtlBL, BiD&SB, BrAu 19, CnE&AP, CriT 2, DcEuL, NewC, Pen Eng, RAdv 1, REn, WebEAL*

Hunt, Leigh H *Alli Sup*

Hunt, LeMesurier *Alli Sup*

Hunt, Louise Livingston *Alli Sup, BiDSA*

Hunt, Lucy B *Alli Sup*

Hunt, Mabel Leigh 1892-1971 *AmA&B, AuBYP, ConAu P-1, IndAu 1917, JBA 1951, SmATA 1*

Hunt, Madeline Bonavia *Alli Sup*

Hunt, Margaret 1831- *Alli Sup*

Hunt, Marigold 1905- *CatA 1952*

Hunt, Mary Alice 1928- *ChPo S2*

Hunt, Mary Hannah 1830-1906 *DcNAA*

Hunt, Maurice *MnBBF*

Hunt, Maurice Osborn 1912- *IndAu 1917*

Hunt, Maurice P 1915- *ConAu 25*

Hunt, Morton M 1920- *Au&Wr, ConAu 5R*

Hunt, Noreen 1931- *Au&Wr*

Hunt, Patricia Joan 1921- *Au&Wr, WrD 1976*

Hunt, Pauline Grace 1879- *WhWNAA*

Hunt, Penelope *ConAu XR*

Hunt, Peter 1922- *ConAu 5R*

Hunt, Philip *Alli*

Hunt, R *Alli, Alli Sup*

Hunt, R S And Randel, J F *Alli*

Hunt, R T *Alli Sup*

Hunt, Randall 1807-1892 *BiDSA*

Hunt, Raymond G 1928- *ConAu 9R*

Hunt, Richard *Alli*

Hunt, Richard Morris 1828-1895 *Alli Sup, OxAm*

Hunt, Richard N 1931- *ConAu 9R*

Hunt, Robert *Alli, Alli Sup*

Hunt, Robert 1807-1887 *Alli, Alli Sup, DcEnL*

Hunt, Robert 1907- *ChPo*

Hunt, Robert C 1934- *ConAu 21*

Hunt, Robert Shapland *Alli Sup*

Hunt, Robert William Gainer 1923- *Au&Wr, WrD 1976*

Hunt, Rockwell Dennis 1868- *WhWNAA*

Hunt, Rowland *Alli*

Hunt, Sam 1946- *ConP 1975, WrD 1976*

Hunt, Samuel 1810-1878 *DcAmA*

Hunt, Samuel Furman 1844-1907 *OhA&B*

Hunt, Sandford 1825-1896 *Alli Sup, DcAmA, DcNAA*

Hunt, Sanford Bebee 1825-1884 *DcAmA*

Hunt, Sara Keables *Alli Sup, ChPo*

Hunt, Shelley Leigh *Alli Sup*

Hunt, Suzanne 1942- *Au&Wr*

Hunt, T B *ChPo*

Hunt, T F *Alli*

Hunt, Ted *BlkAW*

Hunt, Theodore Whitefield 1844-1930 *Alli Sup, AmA&B, DcAmA, DcNAA, WhWNAA*

Hunt, Thomas *Alli*

Hunt, Thomas 1696-1774 *Alli, DcEnL*

Hunt, Thomas 1855-1933 *DcNAA*

Hunt, Thomas Forsyth 1862-1927 *DcNAA*

Hunt, Thomas Poage 1794-1876 *Alli, BiDSA, DcAmA, DcNAA*

Hunt, Thomas Sterry 1826-1892 *Alli, Alli Sup, DcAmA, DcNAA*

Hunt, Thornton Leigh 1810-1873 *Alli, Alli Sup*

Hunt, Timothy Dwight 1821-1895 *DcNAA*

Hunt, Todd T 1938- *ConAu 13R*

Hunt, Vere Dawson DeVere 1825?- *Alli Sup, Br&AmS*

Hunt, Violet 1866-1942 *EvLB, LongC, NewC, Pen Eng, REn, TwCA, TwCA Sup, TwCW*

Hunt, Virginia Lloyd 1888- *OhA&B*

Hunt, Walter F 1882- *WhWNAA*

Hunt, William *Alli, Alli Sup, BiDLA*

Hunt, William 1934- *ConAu 49, DrAP 1975*

Hunt, William Dudley, Jr. 1922- *ConAu 33, WrD 1976*

Hunt, William Ellis 1833-1919 *OhA&B*

Hunt, William F 1875-1963 *IndAu 1917*

Hunt, William Gibbes 1791-1833 *OxAm, REnAL*

Hunt, William Henry 1824-1884 *BiDSA*

Hunt, Mrs. William Holman *Alli Sup*

Hunt, William Morris 1824-1879 *DcNAA, OxAm*

Hunt, William Southworth 1879-1940 *AmA&B, DcNAA*

Hunt-Bode, Gisele *Au&Wr*

Huntar, Alex *Alli*

Hunter *Alli*

Hunter, Colonel d1734 *CyAL 1*

Hunter, Mrs. *BiDLA, Chmbr 2*

Hunter, A *Alli Sup*

Hunter, A C *MnBBF*

Hunter, Miss A S *Alli, BiDLA, ChPo*

Hunter, Adam *Alli Sup*

Hunter, Alan James Herbert 1922- *Au&Wr, ConAu 9R, EncM&D, WrD 1976*

Hunter, Alberta 1897- *AmSCAP 66*

Hunter, Alexander *Alli, BiDSA*

Hunter, Alexander 1729-1809 *Alli*

Hunter, Alexander 1843- *DcNAA*

Hunter, Alexander Stuart 1857-1926 *DcNAA, WhWNAA*

Hunter, Alfred John 1891-1961 *MnBBF*

Hunter, Allan Armstrong 1893- *ConAu 5R, WrD 1976*

Hunter, Andrew *ChPo*

Hunter, Andrew Frederick 1863-1940 *DcNAA*

Hunter, Anne 1742-1821 *Alli, ChPo S1, DcEnL*

Hunter, Anson *ConAu XR*

Hunter, Archibald MacBride 1906- *ConAu 9R, WrD 1976*

Hunter, Beatrice Trum 1918- *ConAu 17R*

Hunter, Benjamin *Alli Sup*

Hunter, Bettie Keyes *LivFWS*

Hunter, C Bruce 1917- *ConAu 61*

Hunter, C G *Alli*

Hunter, Cecilia Bull *ChPo*

Hunter, Charles *Alli Sup*

Hunter, Charles Fergus 1846- *ChPo S1*

Hunter, Christine 1910- *ConAu XR, WrD 1976*

Hunter, Christopher *Alli*

Hunter, Christopher 1675-1757 *Alli*

Hunter, Clingham *AmA&B, DcNAA*

Hunter, Cora Work 1880-1951 *OhA&B*

Hunter, Daniel J *Alli Sup*

Hunter, Dard 1883-1966 *AmA&B, ConAu 25, ConAu P-1, OhA&B, OxAm, REnAL, WhWNAA*

Hunter, David *Alli, Alli Sup*

Hunter, Donald 1898- *Au&Wr*

Hunter, Doris A Leenhouts 1929- *ConAu 37, WrD 1976*

Hunter, Eddie *BlkAW*

Hunter, Edward 1902- *AmA&B, Au&Wr, ConAu 5R, WrD 1976*

Hunter, Edward Thomas Gurney 1880- *WhLA*

Hunter, Eileen Helen 1905- *Au&Wr*

Hunter, Eleanor *BlkAW*

Hunter, Eleanor Augusta 1855- *ChPo, ChPo S1*

Hunter, Eliza B *Alli Sup*

Hunter, Ella *Alli Sup*

Hunter, Evan 1926- *AmA&B, AmSCAP 66, Au&Wr, AuBYP, ConAu 5R, ConNov 1972, ConNov 1976, DrAF 1976, EncM&D, Pen Am, REn, REnAL, WhTwL, WorAu, WrD 1976*

Hunter, Fred *AmA&B*

Hunter, Frederick J 1916- *ConAu 33*

Hunter, Frederick Mercer *Alli Sup*

Hunter, G M *Alli, BiDLA*

Hunter, Geoffrey Basil Bailey 1925- *Au&Wr, ConAu 33, WrD 1976*

Hunter, George 1835- *OhA&B*

Hunter, George Leland 1867-1927 *DcNAA, WhWNAA*

Hunter, George Washington *Alli Sup*
Hunter, George William 1873-1948 *DcNAA, WhWNAA*
Hunter, George Yeates *Alli Sup*
Hunter, Graham *AmA&B*
Hunter, H *MnBBF*
Hunter, H St. John *Alli Sup*
Hunter, Hall *ConAu XR*
Hunter, Harriett Eliza *Alli Sup, ChPo S1*
Hunter, Hay And White, Walter *Alli Sup*
Hunter, Henry 1741-1802 *Alli, DcEnL*
Hunter, Henry E *Alli Sup*
Hunter, Hilda 1921- *Au&Wr, ConAu 49, SmATA 7*
Hunter, Hiram A 1800-1883 *IndAu 1816*
Hunter, Howard Eugene 1929- *ConAu 41*
Hunter, J A H 1902- *ConAu P-1*
Hunter, J A W *Alli Sup*
Hunter, J F M 1924- *ConAu 37*
Hunter, J Marvin 1880- *TexWr*
Hunter, J Paul 1934- *ConAu 21, WrD 1976*
Hunter, J Walker *TexWr*
Hunter, Jac *Alli*
Hunter, Jack D 1921- *ConAu 5R*
Hunter, James *Alli, Alli Sup, BiDLA*
Hunter, James 1830- *ChPo*
Hunter, James J *Alli Sup*
Hunter, Jane Edna 1882- *OhA&B*
Hunter, Jim 1939- *Au&Wr, ConAu 9R, ConNov 1972, ConNov 1976, WrD 1976*
Hunter, Joel 1870- *WhWNAA*
Hunter, John *Alli, Alli Sup, BbtC, BiDLA, ConAu XR, MnBBF, WrD 1976*
Hunter, John 1728-1793 *Alli, NewC, OxEng*
Hunter, John 1747-1837 *Alli, DcEnL*
Hunter, Mrs. John *Alli, ChPo S1*
Hunter, John Dunn 1798-1827 *Alli, AmA&B, BiDSA, DcAmA, DcNAA*
Hunter, John Howard 1839-1911 *DcNAA*
Hunter, John Kelso 1802-1873 *Alli Sup*
Hunter, John M 1921- *ConAu 13R*
Hunter, Joseph *Alli, BiDLA*
Hunter, Joseph 1783-1861 *DcEnL*
Hunter, Kathleen *Au&Wr*
Hunter, Kermit 1910- *CnDAL, ModWD*
Hunter, Kim 1922- *ConAu 61*
Hunter, Kristin 1931- *AuBYP, AuICB, AuNews 1, BlkAW, ConAu 13R, ConNov 1972, ConNov 1976, DrAF 1976, LivBAA, WrD 1976*
Hunter, Leslie Stannard 1890- *Au&Wr, ConAu P-1, WhLA*
Hunter, Louise H *ConAu 41*
Hunter, Louise Olivia *ChPo, ChPo S2*
Hunter, Lydia 1827-1903 *ChPo*
Hunter, Maggie *ChPo S1*
Hunter, Maria *Alli, BiDLA*
Hunter, Martha Lavinia 1870- *TexWr, WhWNAA*
Hunter, Martha T *BiDSA*
Hunter, Martin *OxCan Sup*
Hunter, Mary Kate *TexWr*
Hunter, Maud Lily 1910- *Au&Wr, ConAu 9R*
Hunter, Merlin Harold 1887-1948 *DcNAA, WhWNAA*
Hunter, Minerva *ChPo S2*
Hunter, Mollie 1922- *AuBYP, ConAu XR, SmATA 2, ThBJA, WrD 1976*
Hunter, Ned *HsB&A*
Hunter, Norman Charles 1908-1971 *Au&Wr, CnMD, ConAu 29, CrCD*
Hunter, Norman George Lorimer 1899- *Au&Wr, ChPo S2, WhCL, WrD 1976*
Hunter, P H *Alli Sup*
Hunter, Paul *ConAu XR, DrAP 1975*
Hunter, Peter 1746-1805 *OxCan*
Hunter, R F *Alli Sup*
Hunter, R T *Alli Sup*
Hunter, Rachael d1813 *Alli, BiDLA Sup*
Hunter, Robbins 1880-1954 *OhA&B*
Hunter, Robert *Alli, Alli Sup, BbtC, OxCan Sup*
Hunter, Robert d1734 *Alli, DcEnL*
Hunter, Robert 1874-1942 *DcNAA, WhWNAA*
Hunter, Robert 1940- *Au&Wr*
Hunter, Robert, Jr. *OxCan*
Hunter, Robert Condie 1861- *ChPo*

Hunter, Robert E *Alli Sup*
Hunter, Robert E 1940- *ConAu 41*
Hunter, Robert Mercer Taliaferro 1809-1887 *BiDSA*
Hunter, Rowland *MnBBF*
Hunter, Sam 1923- *ConAu 13R*
Hunter, Samuel *Alli Sup*
Hunter, Samuel J *Alli Sup*
Hunter, Samuel John 1866-1946 *DcNAA, WhWNAA*
Hunter, Stephen Alexander 1851-1925 *DcNAA*
Hunter, Sylvester Joseph 1829- *Alli Sup*
Hunter, Theodore And Patten, Jarvis *Alli Sup*
Hunter, Theresa M 1877- *TexWr*
Hunter, Thomas *Alli Sup*
Hunter, Thomas d1777 *Alli*
Hunter, Thomas 1831-1915 *DcNAA*
Hunter, Thomas Lomax *AmA&B, ChPo*
Hunter, Vickie *ConAu XR*
Hunter, Victoria Alberta 1929- *ConAu 5R*
Hunter, W *ChPo S1*
Hunter, W P *Alli*
Hunter, W R G *ChPo S1*
Hunter, Walter King 1867- *WhLA*
Hunter, Walter Samuel 1889-1954 *AmA&B, WhWNAA*
Hunter, Wiles Robert 1874- *DcNAA, IndAu 1816*
Hunter, William *Alli, Alli Sup, BiDLA*
Hunter, William d1815 *Alli*
Hunter, William 1718-1783 *Alli, DcEnL, NewC*
Hunter, William 1811-1877 *PoIre*
Hunter, William A 1908- *ConAu 13R*
Hunter, William Alexander 1844- *Alli Sup*
Hunter, William Armstrong 1855-1920 *DcNAA*
Hunter, William B, Jr. *ChPo*
Hunter, William C 1812-1891 *Alli Sup, AmA, AmA&B, DcNAA*
Hunter, William F 1901- *WhWNAA*
Hunter, William Henry 1852-1906 *OhA&B*
Hunter, William King *Alli Sup*
Hunter, William Randolph 1843-1886 *DcAmA*
Hunter, William S *BbtC*
Hunter, Sir William Wilson 1840-1900 *Alli Sup, BbD, BiD&SB, BrAu 19, DcLEnL, NewC, OxEng*
Hunter Blair, Sir David Oswald 1853-1939 *CatA 1947*
Hunter-Blair, Norma 1932- *Au&Wr*
Hunter Blair, Pauline 1921- *ConAu 29, SmATA 3*
Hunter Blair, Peter 1912- *Au&Wr*
Hunter-Duvar, John 1830-1899 *BiD&SB, DcNAA, OxCan*
Hunter-Hodgson *Alli Sup*
Hunting, Constance 1925- *ConAu 45*
Hunting, Gardner 1872-1958 *AmA&B, WhWNAA*
Hunting, George Field 1836-1901 *ChPo*
Hunting, Mary Gardner *ChPo*
Huntingdon, A *MnBBF*
Huntingdon, Augusta *Alli Sup*
Huntingdon, D *ChPo*
Huntingdon, G *Alli Sup*
Huntingdon, Harry *MnBBF*
Huntingdon, Henry Of *Alli, DcEnL*
Huntingford, Edward *Alli Sup*
Huntingford, George Isaac 1748-1832 *Alli, BiDLA*
Huntingford, Henry *Alli*
Huntingford, John *Alli*
Huntingford, Thomas *Alli*
Huntington, Anna Hyatt 1876-1973 *ConAu 45*
Huntington, Annie *ChPo*
Huntington, Annie Oakes *DcAmA*
Huntington, Archer Milton 1870-1955 *AmA&B, DcAmA, DcSpL, REnAL*
Huntington, Arria Sargent 1848- *AmA&B, DcNAA*
Huntington, Charles Andrew 1822-1904 *DcNAA*
Huntington, Charles Clifford *WhWNAA*
Huntington, Dan 1774-1864 *DcNAA*
Huntington, Daniel 1788-1858 *DcNAA*
Huntington, Daniel 1816-1906 *EarAB*
Huntington, David Lynde 1870-1929 *DcNAA*
Huntington, DeWitt Clinton 1830-1912 *DcAmA, DcNAA*

Huntington, Dwight Williams 1851-1939 *DcNAA*
Huntington, E A *Alli*
Huntington, Ebenezer *Alli*
Huntington, Elijah Baldwin 1816-1877 *Alli Sup, DcNAA*
Huntington, Ellsworth 1876-1947 *AmA&B, AmLY, DcNAA, REnAL, WhWNAA*
Huntington, Emily 1841-1909 *Alli Sup, ChPo, DcNAA*
Huntington, Faye *Alli Sup, AmA&B, DcAmA, DcNAA*
Huntington, Frances Carpenter *AmA&B*
Huntington, Frances Irwin *BiDSA*
Huntington, Frank 1848- *WhWNAA*
Huntington, Bishop Frederic Dan 1819-1904 *Alli, Alli Sup, AmA&B, BiD&SB, ChPo S1, CyAL 2, DcAmA, DcEnL, DcNAA*
Huntington, Gale 1902- *ConAu 9R*
Huntington, George *ChPo*
Huntington, George 1824- *Alli Sup*
Huntington, George 1835-1916 *DcNAA*
Huntington, Gurdon 1818-1875 *DcNAA*
Huntington, H M *ChPo*
Huntington, H S *AmLY XR, DcNAA*
Huntington, Harriet Elizabeth 1909- *AmA&B, AuBYP, ConAu 5R, MorJA, SmATA 1, WrD 1976*
Huntington, Harwood 1861-1923 *DcNAA*
Huntington, Helen d1950 *AmA&B*
Huntington, Henry E 1850-1927 *REnAL*
Huntington, Henry Greenough *Alli Sup*
Huntington, Henry Strong 1836-1920 *DcNAA*
Huntington, J F *Alli*
Huntington, James Otis Sargent 1854-1938 *DcNAA*
Huntington, Jedediah Vincent 1815-1862 *Alli, Alli Sup, AmA, AmA&B, BbD, BiD&SB, CyAL 2, DcAmA, DcNAA*
Huntington, Joseph 1735-1794 *Alli, DcNAA*
Huntington, Joshua *Alli Sup*
Huntington, Joshua 1786-1819 *Alli, DcNAA*
Huntington, Lucius Seth 1827-1886 *Alli Sup, DcNAA, OxCan*
Huntington, Mary Clark *ChPo*
Huntington, Maud *ChPo*
Huntington, Mildred *ChPo*
Huntington, Robert 1636-1701 *Alli, DcEnL*
Huntington, Samuel Phillips 1927- *AmA&B, ConAu 1R*
Huntington, Susan 1791-1823 *Alli*
Huntington, Thomas Waterman 1893-1973 *ConAu 45, WhWNAA*
Huntington, Tuley Francis 1870-1938 *AmA&B, DcNAA*
Huntington, Virginia 1889- *ConAu 21*
Huntington, Webster Perit 1865-1946 *OhA&B*
Huntington, Whitney Clark 1887- *WhWNAA*
Huntington, Willard Vincent 1856-1915 *DcNAA*
Huntington, William 1744-1813 *Alli, DcEnL*
Huntington, William Clarence 1876- *WhPNW*
Huntington, William Reed 1838-1909 *Alli Sup, AmA&B, ChPo, ChPo S1, DcAmA, DcNAA*
Huntington-Wilson, Francis Mairs *DcNAA*
Huntley, Anna M *ChPo, ChPo S1*
Huntley, Chester Robert 1911-1974 *AuNews 1, ConAu 49*
Huntley, Chet *AuNews 1, ConAu 49*
Huntley, Elizabeth Maddox *BlkAW*
Huntley, Florence Chance 1860-1912 *DcNAA, OhA&B*
Huntley, Frank Livingstone 1902- *ConAu 33*
Huntley, George Ezra 1870- *WhWNAA*
Huntley, Henry *Alli*
Huntley, Sir Henry V *Alli*
Huntley, Herbert Edwin 1892- *Au&Wr, ConAu P-1*
Huntley, James Robert 1923- *ConAu 29, WrD 1976*
Huntley, Jobe 1918- *AmSCAP 66*
Huntley, Louis Grow 1885- *WhWNAA*
Huntley, Lydia Howard 1791-1865 *Alli, AmA, DcNAA, OxAm*
Huntley, Richard Webster 1793-1857 *Alli Sup*
Huntley, Rowland Webster 1793-1857 *ChPo*
Huntley, Stanley d1885 *Alli Sup, DcNAA*
Huntley, William *Alli*

Husk, William Henry *Alli Sup*
Huskell, John *Alli*
Huskinson, Eliza *Alli*
Huskisson, William 1770-1830 *Alli, BiDLA*
Husmann, George 1827-1902 *Alli Sup, DcNAA*
Huson, Paul 1942- *ConAu 29, WrD 1976*
Huss SEE ALSO Hus
Huss, Johannes 1369?-1415 *OxGer*
Huss, John 1369?-1415 *CasWL, NewC, REn*
Huss, Roy 1927- *ConAu 25*
Hussein, Nadir 1939- *ConP 1970*
Hussein, Taha 1889-1973 *ConAu 45*
Husserl, Edmund 1859-1938 *REn, WorAu*
Hussey, A *Alli*
Hussey, Christopher *Alli*
Hussey, David Edward 1934- *ConAu 57*
Hussey, Dynely 1893- *ChPo*
Hussey, E G *Alli Sup*
Hussey, Edward Law *Alli Sup*
Hussey, G *Alli*
Hussey, Garret *Alli, BiDLA*
Hussey, J R *Alli Sup*
Hussey, James McConnel *Alli Sup*
Hussey, Jennie Evelyn 1874- *WhWNAA*
Hussey, John A 1913- *ConAu 61*
Hussey, Joseph *Alli*
Hussey, Maurice Percival 1925- *Au&Wr, ConAu 9R*
Hussey, Norah E *ChPo*
Hussey, Robert 1801-1856 *Alli*
Hussey, Ruth Anne *ChPo*
Hussey, T J *Alli*
Hussey, Mrs. T J *Alli*
Hussey, Tacitus 1833- *DcNAA, IndAu 1917*
Hussey, Thomas *Alli*
Hussey, Walter *PoIre*
Hussey, William *Alli, BiDLA*
Hussey, William Joseph 1862-1926 *DcAmA, DcNAA*
Husslein, Joseph 1873-1952 *AmA&B, BkC 1, CatA 1947, WhWNAA*
Husson, Albert 1912- *McGWD*
Husson, Jules *OxFr*
Hussovius, Mikolaj 1475?-1533? *CasWL*
Hussowski, Mikolaj 1475?-1533? *CasWL*
Huste, Annemarie 1943- *ConAu 57*
Husted, Harry H 1886?-1972 *IndAu 1917*
Husted, Helen McLanahan *ChPo*
Husted, Mary Irving *WhWNAA*
Hustington, Harry *MnBBF*
Huston, C *Alli*
Huston, Charles d1849 *DcNAA*
Huston, Claudius Hart 1876-1952 *IndAu 1917*
Huston, Ethelyn Leslie 1869- *WhWNAA*
Huston, Fran *ConAu XR*
Huston, Frank C 1871-1959 *AmSCAP 66*
Huston, Henry Augustus 1858- *WhWNAA*
Huston, James 1820-1854 *BbtC, DcNAA, OxCan*
Huston, James Alvin 1918- *ConAu 41, IndAu 1917*
Huston, John 1906- *ConDr, REnAL*
Huston, Luther A 1888- *ConAu 21*
Huston, M M *TexWr*
Huston, Mary E *Alli Sup*
Huston, McCready 1891- *AmA&B, WhWNAA*
Huston, Mervyn James 1912- *ConAu 61, WrD 1976*
Huston, Paul Griswold 1873-1960 *OhA&B*
Huston, R G *Alli Sup*
Huston, Robert *Alli Sup*
Huston, William Dale 1918- *AmSCAP 66*
Hustvedt, Lloyd 1922- *ConAu 21*
Huszar, George B De 1919- *ConAu 19*
Hutch, William *Alli Sup*
Hutchens, Eleanor Newman 1919- *ConAu 13R*
Hutchens, John Kennedy 1905- *AmA&B, WhPNW*
Hutchens, Maurice 1893- *TexWr*
Hutchens, Paul 1902- *ConAu 61*
Hutcheon, Mrs. *Alli Sup*
Hutcheon, Rebecca 1851?- *ChPo S1*
Hutcheson, Archibald d1740 *Alli*
Hutcheson, C *Alli*
Hutcheson, Francis 1694-1746? *Alli, BiD&SB, BrAu, CasWL, Chmbr 2, DcEnA,*

DcEnL, DcEuL, NewC, OxEng, Pen Eng
Hutcheson, George *Alli*
Hutcheson, Gilbert *Alli, BiDLA*
Hutcheson, Helen Thayer 1860-1886 *ChPo*
Hutcheson, John Conroy *Alli Sup*
Hutcheson, Robert 1906- *Au&Wr*
Hutcheson, Robert Kyrle *Alli, BiDLA*
Hutcheson, T S *Alli Sup*
Hutcheson, Tom *ChPo*
Hutcheson, William *Alli Sup, ChPo S1*
Hutcheson, William J F *ChPo*
Hutchieson, J C *Alli Sup, ChPo, ChPo S1, ChPo S2*
Hutchin, Edward *Alli*
Hutchin, Kenneth Charles 1908- *Au&Wr, WrD 1976*
Hutchings, Mrs. *ChPo S2*
Hutchings, Alan Eric 1910- *Au&Wr, ConAu 1R*
Hutchings, Arthur James Bramwell 1906- *Au&Wr, ConAu 5R, WrD 1976*
Hutchings, Chesley Martin 1890- *OhA&B*
Hutchings, Donald William 1923- *Au&Wr*
Hutchings, Edward *Alli*
Hutchings, Ernest A D 1917- *Au&Wr*
Hutchings, Henry *Alli Sup*
Hutchings, James Mason 1820-1902 *Alli Sup, DcNAA*
Hutchings, Margaret 1918- *ConAu 9R*
Hutchings, Monica Mary 1917- *Au&Wr, ConAu 9R*
Hutchings, Patrick A 1929- *ConAu 53*
Hutchings, Raymond 1924- *ConAu 33*
Hutchings, Reginald Salis 1915- *Au&Wr*
Hutchings, Richard John 1922- *Au&Wr*
Hutchings, Sabra Palmer *OhA&B*
Hutchings, Samuel *Alli Sup*
Hutchings, Thomas *Alli*
Hutchings, William Henry *Alli Sup*
Hutchins, Carleen Maley 1911- *ConAu 17R, SmATA 9*
Hutchins, Charles Bowman *ChPo S1*
Hutchins, Daryl 1920- *AmSCAP 66*
Hutchins, Edward *Alli*
Hutchins, Francis Gilman 1939- *ConAu 21, WrD 1976*
Hutchins, Frank Wade 1858-1951 *OhA&B*
Hutchins, Harry Burns 1847-1930 *DcNAA*
Hutchins, James B *Alli Sup*
Hutchins, James H *BiDSA*
Hutchins, John 1698-1773 *Alli, DcEnL*
Hutchins, Louise Cortelle Jones *OhA&B*
Hutchins, M Patricia R 1911- *Au&Wr*
Hutchins, Maude 1889?- *AmA&B, ConAu 61, ConNov 1972, ConNov 1976, DrAF 1976, WorAu, WrD 1976*
Hutchins, Pat 1942- *IlBYP, WrD 1976*
Hutchins, Richard d1781 *Alli*
Hutchins, Robert Maynard 1899- *AmA&B, OxAm, REnAL, WhWNAA*
Hutchins, Ross Elliott 1906- *AuBYP, ConAu 9R, SmATA 4, ThBJA*
Hutchins, Stilson 1838-1912 *DcNAA*
Hutchins, Thomas *BbtC, BiDSA*
Hutchins, Thomas 1730?-1789 *Alli, DcAmA, DcNAA*
Hutchins, William *EvLB*
Hutchins, William James 1871-1958 *AmA&B, OhA&B, WhWNAA*
Hutchinson *Alli*
Hutchinson, Mrs. *Alli, Alli Sup*
Hutchinson, A *Alli*
Hutchinson, Miss A A *BiDLA*
Hutchinson, A H *ChPo S1*
Hutchinson, Aaron 1722-1800 *DcAmA*
Hutchinson, Alexander Copeland *Alli, BiDLA*
Hutchinson, Alexander Hadden *Alli Sup*
Hutchinson, Alfred 1924-1972 *AfA 1, RGAfl, TwCW*
Hutchinson, Anne 1591-1643 *OxAm, REn, REnAL*
Hutchinson, Arthur Blockley *Alli Sup*
Hutchinson, Arthur Stuart Menteth 1879-1971 *Au&Wr, Chmbr 3, ConAu 29, CyWA, DcBiA, DcLEnL, EvLB, LongC, REn, TwCA, TwCA Sup, TwCW*
Hutchinson, B *Alli*

Hutchinson, Benjamin *Alli, BiDLA*
Hutchinson, C Alan 1914- *ConAu 29*
Hutchinson, C C *Alli Sup*
Hutchinson, C F *Alli Sup*
Hutchinson, Cyril *Alli*
Hutchinson, Daniel Faloon *BbtC, PoIre*
Hutchinson, Mrs. E G *Alli Sup*
Hutchinson, Edward *Alli Sup*
Hutchinson, Edward Prince 1906- *AmA&B*
Hutchinson, Eliot Dole 1900- *ConAu 61*
Hutchinson, Eliza *Alli Sup*
Hutchinson, Ellen Mackay 1851- *Alli Sup, BbD, BiD&SB, DcAmA, DcNAA*
Hutchinson, Emilie Josephine 1877-1938 *DcNAA*
Hutchinson, Enoch *Alli, Alli Sup, ChPo S1*
Hutchinson, Frances E 1871- *WhLA*
Hutchinson, Frances Kinsley 1857- *AmA&B, DcNAA*
Hutchinson, Francis *Alli Sup*
Hutchinson, Francis d1739? *Alli*
Hutchinson, Frank Hubbard 1894-1934 *OhA&B*
Hutchinson, G Evelyn 1903- *AmA&B, ConAu P-1*
Hutchinson, G T 1880- *Br&AmS*
Hutchinson, G Thompson *Alli Sup*
Hutchinson, George *Alli Sup*
Hutchinson, George Andrew d1913 *MnBBF*
Hutchinson, H *Alli Sup*
Hutchinson, H Lester 1904- *ConAu 17R*
Hutchinson, Henry *Alli*
Hutchinson, Henry Doveton *Alli Sup*
Hutchinson, Henry Neville 1856- *WhLA*
Hutchinson, Hilda *ChPo S2*
Hutchinson, Horace G *Alli Sup*
Hutchinson, I R *BiDSA*
Hutchinson, J *BiDLA, ChPo S1*
Hutchinson, J H *Alli Sup*
Hutchinson, J P *Alli Sup*
Hutchinson, J R *MnBBF*
Hutchinson, J Robert *Alli Sup*
Hutchinson, Mrs. James Pemberton *AmA&B*
Hutchinson, Jesse, Jr. *ChPo S1*
Hutchinson, John *Alli, Alli Sup*
Hutchinson, John 1615-1664 *NewC, REn*
Hutchinson, John 1674-1737 *Alli, DcEnL*
Hutchinson, John 1884- *Au&Wr, WhLA*
Hutchinson, John 1921- *ConAu 45*
Hutchinson, John A *Alli Sup*
Hutchinson, John Alexander 1840-1896 *DcNAA*
Hutchinson, John Hely 1724-1794 *PoIre*
Hutchinson, John Irwin 1867- *WhWNAA*
Hutchinson, John Russell 1807-1878 *DcAmA, DcNAA*
Hutchinson, John Wallace 1821-1908 *DcAmA, DcNAA*
Hutchinson, Jonathan *Alli Sup*
Hutchinson, Joshua *Alli Sup*
Hutchinson, Julius *Alli, BiDLA*
Hutchinson, Lucy *Alli*
Hutchinson, Lucy 1620-1676? *Alli, BrAu, CasWL, Chmbr 1, DcEnL, DcEuL, DcLEnL, EvLB, OxEng, REn*
Hutchinson, Margaret Massey 1904- *Au&Wr, ChPo, ConAu P-1*
Hutchinson, Margarite *Alli Sup*
Hutchinson, Mary F K *ChPo*
Hutchinson, Michael *Alli*
Hutchinson, Michael E 1925- *ConAu 17R*
Hutchinson, Norman *ChPo S2*
Hutchinson, Paul 1890-1956 *AmA&B, WhWNAA*
Hutchinson, Pearse 1927- *ConP 1970, ConP 1975, WrD 1976*
Hutchinson, Peter 1943- *ConAu 61*
Hutchinson, Peter Orlando *Alli Sup*
Hutchinson, R *MnBBF*
Hutchinson, R J *ChPo*
Hutchinson, Ray Coryton 1907-1975 *Au&Wr, ConAu 1R, ConAu 61, ConNov 1972, ConNov 1976, LongC, ModBL, NewC, REn, TwCA, TwCA Sup, TwCW*
Hutchinson, Richard Hely *Alli*
Hutchinson, Richard Wyatt 1894- *ConAu 5R*
Hutchinson, Robert *Alli Sup*
Hutchinson, Robert 1924- *ConAu 13R, DrAF 1976, DrAP 1975, WrD 1976*
Hutchinson, Robert Fame *Alli Sup*

Hutchinson, Roger d1555 *Alli*
Hutchinson, Samuel d1780 *Alli*
Hutchinson, Sylvster *BlkAW*
Hutchinson, T J *Alli*
Hutchinson, Thomas *Alli, Alli Sup, ChPo, ChPo S2*
Hutchinson, Thomas 1711-1780 *Alli, AmA, AmA&B, CyAL 1, DcAmA, DcNAA, OxAm, Pen Am, REnAL*
Hutchinson, Thomas Joseph 1820- *Alli Sup*
Hutchinson, Vernal 1922- *ConAu 49*
Hutchinson, Veronica S 1895-1961 *ChPo S2, OhA&B*
Hutchinson, W M L *AnCL*
Hutchinson, W N *Alli*
Hutchinson, William *Alli, Alli Sup, BiDLA*
Hutchinson, William M 1916- *IlBYP, IlCB 1966*
Hutchinson, William Nelson *Alli Sup*
Hutchinson, Woods 1862-1930 *DcNAA*
Hutchison, Aeneas Barkly *Alli Sup*
Hutchison, Bruce 1901- *CanWr, CasWL, LongC, OxCan, OxCan Sup*
Hutchison, Chester Smith 1902- *ConAu 17*
Hutchison, Christine 1901- *TexWr*
Hutchison, Dwight 1890?-1975 *ConAu 57*
Hutchison, E R 1926- *ConAu 25*
Hutchison, Frederick J & Macgregor, H G *Alli Sup*
Hutchison, George *Alli Sup*
Hutchison, George Andrew 1842-1912 *Alli Sup, ChPo, ChPo S2*
Hutchison, Harold Frederick 1900- *Au&Wr, ConAu 1R, WrD 1976*
Hutchison, Harry *ChPo S1*
Hutchison, Hazel Collister *AnMV 1926, OhA&B*
Hutchison, Henry 1923- *WrD 1976*
Hutchison, Isobel Wylie 1889- *Au&Wr, ChPo, ChPo S2, OxCan*
Hutchison, Jane Campbell 1932- *ConAu 37*
Hutchison, John *Alli, Alli Sup*
Hutchison, John 1851- *ChPo S1*
Hutchison, John Alexander 1912- *AmA&B*
Hutchison, John Russell 1807-1878 *Alli Sup*
Hutchison, Joseph Chrisman 1822-1887 *Alli Sup, DcAmA, DcNAA*
Hutchison, Margaret *OxCan*
Hutchison, Paula 1905- *ChPo, IlBYP, IlCB 1956*
Hutchison, Robert *Alli*
Hutchison, Robert 1871- *WhLA*
Hutchison, Robert Allen 1862-1937 *DcNAA, WhWNAA*
Hutchison, Robert Pender *Alli Sup*
Hutchison, Sidney Charles 1912- *Au&Wr, ConAu 25, WrD 1976*
Hutchison, William *Alli Sup*
Hutchison, William Bruce 1901- *CanNov*
Hutchison, William M *ChPo, ChPo S1, ChPo S2*
Hutchison, William Robert 1930- *ConAu 21*
Hutchisson, W H Florio *Alli Sup*
Huth, Alfred Henry 1850- *Alli Sup*
Huth, Frederick Henry 1844- *Alli Sup*
Huth, Henry 1815-1878 *Alli Sup, OxEng*
Huthersall, John *Alli*
Huthmacher, J Joseph 1929- *ConAu 21, SmATA 5, WrD 1976*
Hutin, Serge Roger Jean 1929- *BiDPar*
Hutman, Norma Louise 1935- *ConAu 25*
Hutson, Anthony Brian Austen 1934- *WrD 1976*
Hutson, Charles Woodward 1840-1936 *Alli Sup, AmA&B, AmLY, BiDSA, DcAmA, DcNAA, WhWNAA*
Hutson, Harold Horton 1914- *AmA&B*
Hutt, Frank Walcott 1869- *ChPo, ChPo S1, ChPo S2*
Hutt, Hector *MnBBF*
Hutt, Maurice George 1928- *ConAu 13R*
Hutt, Max L 1908- *ConAu 57*
Hutt, W H 1899- *ConAu 57*
Hutt, William *Alli*
Hutten, Baroness Elizabeth Von *DcAmA*
Hutten, Henry *Alli*
Hutten, Leon *Alli*
Hutten, Robert *Alli*

Hutten, Ulrich Von 1488-1523 *BbD, BiD&SB, CasWL, DcEuL, DcNAA, EuA, EvEuW, NewC, OxEng, OxGer, Pen Eur, REn*
Huttenback, Robert A 1928- *ConAu 25*
Hutter, E W *Alli*
Huttig, Jack W 1919- *ConAu 53*
Huttman, William *Alli*
Hutto, John R 1879- *TexWr*
Hutto, Nelson 1904- *ConAu P-1*
Hutton *Alli*
Hutton, Albinia Catherine *ChPo S1*
Hutton, Alfred *Alli Sup*
Hutton, Arthur Wollaston *Alli Sup*
Hutton, Barbara *Alli Sup*
Hutton, Catherine 1756-1846 *Alli, BiDLA, BrAu 19*
Hutton, Charles *Alli*
Hutton, Charles 1737-1823 *Alli, BiDLA*
Hutton, Clarke 1898- *IlCB 1945, IlCB 1956, IlCB 1966*
Hutton, David Graham 1904- *ChPo S2*
Hutton, Edward 1875-1969 *CatA 1947, LongC, WhLA*
Hutton, Enoch *Alli Sup*
Hutton, F H *Alli*
Hutton, Frederick Remsen 1853-1918 *DcAmA, DcNAA*
Hutton, Geoffrey 1928- *ConAu 41*
Hutton, George *Alli, BiDLA*
Hutton, George Clark *Alli Sup*
Hutton, Henry *Alli, DcEnL*
Hutton, Henry 1815-1863 *Alli Sup*
Hutton, Henry Dix *Alli Sup*
Hutton, Hugh 1795-1871 *PoIre*
Hutton, J Bernard 1911- *ConAu 21, WrD 1976*
Hutton, James *Alli Sup*
Hutton, James 1726-1797 *Alli, BiDLA, BiDLA Sup, DcEnL*
Hutton, James Harriman *Alli, BiDLA*
Hutton, Joan *ChPo S2*
Hutton, John *ChPo S1*
Hutton, John Henry 1885-1968 *ConAu P-1, WhLA*
Hutton, Joseph 1787-1828 *Alli, AmA&B, DcNAA, REnAL*
Hutton, Joseph, Jr. *Alli*
Hutton, Joseph Henry *Alli Sup*
Hutton, Laurence 1843-1904 *Alli Sup, AmA, AmA&B, BbD, BiD&SB, DcAmA, DcNAA, OxAm, REnAL*
Hutton, Luke *Alli*
Hutton, Mark *Alli Sup*
Hutton, Mary A *PoIre*
Hutton, Matthew d1758 *Alli*
Hutton, Matthew 1546-1605 *Alli*
Hutton, Maurice 1856-1940 *CanWr, DcNAA, OxCan, WhWNAA*
Hutton, R N *Alli*
Hutton, Richard *Alli*
Hutton, Sir Richard d1639 *Alli*
Hutton, Richard Holt 1826-1897 *Alli Sup, BiD&SB, BrAu 19, CasWL, Chmbr 3, DcEnL, DcLEnL, EvLB, NewC, OxEng*
Hutton, Mrs. Richard Holt *Alli Sup*
Hutton, Robert *Alli*
Hutton, Robert Shaw *Alli Sup*
Hutton, S K *Alli Sup*
Hutton, Samuel King 1877- *OxCan*
Hutton, Thomas *Alli, Alli Sup*
Hutton, Vernon Wollaston *Alli Sup*
Hutton, W *Alli*
Hutton, Walter S *Alli Sup*
Hutton, Warwick 1939- *ConAu 61*
Hutton, William *Alli*
Hutton, William d1861 *Alli Sup, BbtC, DcNAA*
Hutton, William 1723?-1815 *Alli, BiDLA, BiDLA Sup, DcEnL*
Hutton, William Holden 1860- *Alli Sup, WhLA*
Hutton, William Pepperal *PoIre*
Hutton, William Rich 1826-1901 *DcNAA*
Hutton, Wyndham Madden 1831?-1882 *Alli Sup, PoIre*
Hutulia, R *ChPo*
Huus, Helen 1913- *ConAu 1R*
Huvos, Kornel 1913- *ConAu 49*

Huws, Daniel 1932- *ConP 1975, WrD 1976*
Hux, John Rodwell *Alli Sup*
Huxford, Alfred Lear And Way, J Albert *Alli Sup*
Huxham, John *Alli Sup*
Huxham, John 1694-1768 *Alli*
Huxhold, Harry N 1922- *ConAu 61*
Huxley, Aldous 1894-1963 *AmA&B, AtlBL, BiDPar, CasWL, ChPo, ChPo S1, ChPo S2, Chmbr 3, CnMD, CnMWL, ConLC 1, ConLC 3, ConLC 4, ConLC 5, CyWA, DcLEnL, EncWL, EvLB, LongC, ModBL, ModBL Sup, ModWD, NewC, OxEng, Pen Eng, RAdv 1, REn, TwCA, TwCA Sup, TwCW, WebEAL, WhTwL*
Huxley, Anthony Julian 1920- *Au&Wr, ConAu 9R, WrD 1976*
Huxley, Elspeth 1907- *Au&Wr, DcLEnL, EncM&D, LongC, TwCW, WorAu, WrD 1976*
Huxley, George *Alli*
Huxley, George Leonard 1932- *Au&Wr, ConAu 23, WrD 1976*
Huxley, Gervas 1894- *Au&Wr*
Huxley, Henrietta *ChPo S2*
Huxley, Herbert Henry 1916- *Au&Wr, ConAu 5R*
Huxley, Sir Julian Sorrell 1887-1975 *Au&Wr, Chmbr 3, ConAu 9R, ConAu 57, DcLEnL, EvLB, LongC, NewC, OxEng, Pen Eng, REn, TwCA, TwCA Sup, TwCW, WhLA*
Huxley, Laura Archera *AmA&B, ConAu 13R*
Huxley, Leonard 1860-1933 *ChPo S2, NewC*
Huxley, Marjorie *ChPo S2*
Huxley, Mildred *ChPo S2*
Huxley, Thomas Henry 1825-1895 *AHi, Alli Sup, AtlBL, BbD, BiD&SB, BrAu 19, CasWL, ChPo S2, Chmbr 3, CriT 3, CyWA, DcEnA, DcEnA Ap, DcEnL, DcEuL, DcLEnL, EvLB, MouLC 4, NewC, OxEng, Pen Eng, REn, WebEAL*
Huxley-Blythe, Peter J 1925- *ConAu 17R*
Huxtable, A *Alli*
Huxtable, Edgar *Alli, Alli Sup*
Huxtable, Marjorie *LongC*
Huxtable, William John Fairchild 1912- *Au&Wr, ConAu 13R, WrD 1976*
Huy-Can *DcOrL 2*
Huyck, Margaret Hellie 1939- *ConAu 49*
Huydecoper, Balthazar 1695-1778 *CasWL*
Huygens, Christian 1629-1693 *DcEuL*
Huygens, Constantijn 1596-1687 *BbD, BiD&SB, CasWL, DcEuL, EuA, Pen Eur*
Huyghue, Douglas S *BbtC*
Huyghue, S Douglas S *Alli Sup*
Huyke, Juan B 1880-1961 *PueRA*
Huyshe, Francis *Alli*
Huyshe, George Lightfoot *Alli Sup, OxCan*
Huyshe, J M *Alli*
Huyshe, John *Alli*
Huysman, Roelof *CasWL, EuA, OxGer*
Huysmann, Rudolf *DcEuL*
Huysmans, Charles Marie Georges 1848-1907 *EuA*
Huysmans, Georges Charles 1848-1907 *Pen Eur*
Huysmans, Joris Karl 1848-1907 *AtlBL, BbD, BiD&SB, CasWL, ClDMEuL, CyWA, EncWL, EvEuW, ModRL, OxFr, REn, WhTwL*
Hviezdoslav 1849-1921 *CasWL, ClDMEuL, DcEuL, EncWL, EuA, Pen Eur*
Hwang, Chin-I 1516- *DcOrL 1*
Hwetbert d732? *BiB S*
Hyacinth, The *ChPo*
Hyacinthe, Pere 1827- *BbD, BiD&SB*
Hyams, Barry 1911- *ConAu 13R*
Hyams, Edward 1910-1975 *Au&Wr, ConAu 5R, ConAu 61, LongC, TwCW, WorAu, WrD 1976*
Hyams, Joe 1923- *AmA&B, WrD 1976*
Hyams, Joseph 1923- *ConAu 17R*
Hyamson, Albert Montefiore 1875- *WhLA*
Hyamson, Moses 1862-1949 *DcNAA, WhWNAA*
Hyatt, Alpheus 1838-1902 *Alli Sup, BiD&SB,*

I

I, S *ConAmA*
I Chia *DcOrL 1*
I-Ching 635-713 *CasWL, DcOrL 1*
I H G 1860?- *Br&AmS*
I R V *WhWNAA*
I S *TwCA, TwCA Sup*
I-Tsing *DcOrL 1, DcOrL 2*
Iacopone Da Todi *McGWD*
Iager, G F *Alli*
Iamblichus 250?-330? *BbD, BiD&SB, CasWL, NewC, Pen Cl*
Iambulus *Pen Cl*
Iams, F M *Alli Sup*
Iams, Jack 1910- *AmA&B, AmNov, EncM&D*
Iams, Thomas M, Jr. 1928- *ConAu 9R*
Ian, Janis *ChPo S2*
Iannelli, Theresa Rose 1936- *AmSCAP 66*
Ianni, Francis A J 1926- *ConAu 45*
Ianniello, Lynne Young 1925- *ConAu 17R*
Iannone, Jeanne Koppel *SmATA 7*
Iannone, Ron 1940- *ConAu 53*
Ianora, Claudio *OxCan Sup*
Ianthe *DcEnL*
Iashvili, Paolo 1894-1937 *DcOrL 3*
Iasilli, Gerardo 1880- *AmSCAP 66*
Iatrides, John O 1932- *ConAu 25*
Ib *WhWNAA*
Ibanez, Vicente Blasco 1867-1928 *LongC, ModRL, OxEng, TwCA, TwCA Sup*
Ibara, Saikaku 1642-1693 *CasWL, CyWA*
Ibarbourou, Juana De 1895- *CasWL, DcSpL, EncWL, Pen Am, REn*
Ibberson, George *Alli Sup*
Ibbertson, Julius *BiDLA*
Ibbetson, Agnes 1757-1823 *Alli*
Ibbetson, James 1717-1781 *Alli*
Ibbetson, James 1755-1790 *Alli*
Ibbetson, Julius C d1817 *Alli*
Ibbetson, Laporte And J Hassell *Alli*
Ibbetson, Richard *Alli*
Ibbetson, William John *Alli Sup*
Ibbot, Benjamin 1680-1725 *Alli, DcEnL*
Ibbotson, H Walter *Alli Sup*
Ibbotson, Henry J *BbtC*
Ibbotson, Joseph Darling 1869- *WhWNAA*
Ibbotson, M C 1930- *ConAu 25, SmATA 5*
Iberville, Pierre LeMoyne, Sieur D' 1661-1706 *BiDSA, OxCan, REn, REnAL*
Ibid *WhWNAA*
Iblseng, Magnus Colbjorn 1852-1930 *DcNAA*
Ibn 'Abd Rabbihi, Ahmad B Muhammad 860-940 *CasWL, DcOrL 3*
Ibn 'Abdun d1134 *CasWL*
Ibn Al-'Arabi, Muhammad Ibn 'Ali 1165-1240 *Pen Cl*
Ibn Al-'Arabi, Muhyi-Al-Din 1165-1240 *CasWL*
Ibn Al-Athir, 'Izz Al-Din Abu Al-Husan 1160-1233 *CasWL*
Ibn Al-Farid, 'Umar 1181-1235 *CasWL*

Ibn Al-Farid Sharaf Ad-Din 'Umar 1181-1235 *DcOrL 3*
Ibn Al-Muqaffa' *CasWL*
Ibn Al-Mu'tazz 861-908 *CasWL*
Ibn Al-Nadim, Abu Al-Faraj Muhammad d995? *CasWL*
Ibn Al-Rumi 836-890? *CasWL*
Ibn Bajja, Abu Bakr Muhammad B Y B As-S d1138 *DcOrL 3*
Ibn Battuta, Muhammad Ibn 'Abdullah 1304-1377? *CasWL, DcOrL 3, Pen Cl*
Ibn Batuta 1304?-1377? *BiD&SB, NewC*
Ibn Danyal *DcOrL 3*
Ibn Da'ud, Abraham 1110-1180? *CasWL*
Ibn Doreid, Abubekr Mohammed 838-933 *BiD&SB*
Ibn Esra 1092-1167 *BiD&SB*
Ibn Ezra, Abraham Ben Me'ir 1092-1167 *CasWL, EuA, EvEuW, Pen Cl, Pen Eur*
Ibn Ezra, Moses Ben Jacob 1060-1139 *CasWL, EuA, EvEuW, Pen Eur*
Ibn Falaquera *CasWL*
Ibn Faris, Abu'l-Husayn d1004? *DcOrL 3*
Ibn Gabirol, Solomon Ben Judah 1021?-1058? *CasWL, EuA*
Ibn Gayyat *CasWL*
Ibn Hasdai, Abraham d1240 *Pen Eur*
Ibn Hazm, 'Ali Ibn Ahmad 994-1064 *CasWL, DcOrL 3, Pen Cl*
Ibn Hisham *DcOrL 3*
Ibn-I Yamin, Amir Mahmud 1367?- *CasWL*
Ibn Jubair, Abu Al-Hasan Ibn Ahmad Al-K 1145-1217 *CasWL*
Ibn Khaldun, 'Abd-Al-Rahman 1332-1406 *CasWL, Pen Cl*
Ibn Khaldun, Abderrahman 1332-1406 *BbD, BiD&SB*
Ibn Khaldun, Abu Zayd 'Abdarrahman B M 1332-1406 *DcOrL 3*
Ibn Khallikan, Ahmad Ibn Muhammad 1211-1282 *BiD&SB, DcOrL 3, Pen Cl*
Ibn Koteiba, Abdallah Ibn Muslim 828-890 *BiD&SB*
Ibn Muqaffa 720-757 *DcOrL 3*
Ibn Mu'tazz, Abu'l-'Abbas 'Abdallah 861-908 *DcOrL 3*
Ibn Pakuda, Bachya *CasWL*
Ibn Qutaibah, Abu Muhammad 'Abdullah 828-889? *CasWL*
Ibn Qutayba 828-889? *DcOrL 3*
Ibn Quzman d1160 *CasWL*
Ibn-Rushd, Abu'l-Walid M B A B Muhammad 1126-1198 *CasWL, DcOrL 3, EuA*
Ibn Sina, Abu 'Ali 980?-1037 *BiD&SB, CasWL, DcOrL 3, Pen Cl*
Ibn Taymiyya, Taqi Ad-Din Ahmad 1263-1328 *DcOrL 3*
Ibn Tofail, Abu B Muhammad B 'Abd Al-M 1105?-1185 *BbD, BiD&SB, CasWL, DcOrL 3*
Ibn Yamin *DcOrL 3*

Ibn Zaidun 394-463 *CasWL*
Ibrahim Of Aleppo 1490?-1549 *BiD&SB*
Ibrahim, Hafiz 1870-1932 *DcOrL 3*
Ibrahim, Ibrahim Abdelkader 1923- *ConAu 13R*
Ibrahim, Jussuf 1877- *WhLA*
Ibrahim Hilmy, Prince *Alli Sup*
Ibrahimi, Bashir Al- 1889-1965 *DcOrL 3*
Ibrahimov, Mirza 1911- *DcOrL 3*
Ibraileanu, Garabet 1871-1936 *CasWL*
Ibsen, Henrik 1828-1906 *AtlBL, BbD, BiD&SB, CasWL, ClDMEuL, CnMD, CnThe, CyWA, DcEuL, EncWL, EuA, EvEuW, LongC, McGWD, ModWD, NewC, OxEng, OxGer, Pen Eur, RCom, REn, REnWD*
Ibukun, Olu 1945?- *AfA 1*
Ibuse, Masuji 1898- *CasWL, DcOrL 1, EncWL Sup, Pen Cl, WhTwL*
Ibycus 560?BC-525? *BC BbD, BiD&SB, CasWL, Pen Cl, REn*
Icaza, Francisco A De 1863-1925 *CasWL, EncWL*
Icaza, Jorge 1906- *CasWL, CyWA, DcCLA, DcSpL, EncWL, Pen Am*
Ice, Jackson Lee 1925- *ConAu 25, WrD 1976*
Iceberg Slim *BlkAW*
Icenhower, Joseph Bryan 1913- *AuBYP, ConAu 5R*
Ichenhaeuser, Eliza 1869- *WhLA*
Ichijo, Kanera *DcOrL 1*
Ichikawa, Danjuro *DcOrL 1*
Ichikawa, Sanki 1886- *WhLA*
Ichiyo *CasWL, DcOrL 1*
Ickelsamer, Valentin *OxGer*
Ickes, Harold L 1874-1952 *AmA&B, REnAL*
Icks, Robert J 1900- *ConAu 41*
Icolari, Daniel Leonardo 1942- *ConAu 17R*
Iconoclast *TwCA, TwCA Sup*
'Id, Muhammad 'Ali Khalifa Al- 1904- *DcOrL 3*
Idamore *DcNAA*
Idank, Joseph Anthony 1904- *WhWNAA*
Iddesleigh, Earl Of *Alli Sup*
Iddings, Joseph Paxson 1857-1920 *DcNAA*
Ide, Esther Cary *WhWNAA*
Ide, Frances Otis Ogden 1853-1927 *AmA&B, BiD&SB, DcAmA, DcNAA*
Ide, George Barton 1804-1872 *Alli Sup, BiD&SB, DcAmA, DcNAA*
Ide, George Edward 1860-1919 *DcNAA*
Ide, Harold 1917- *AmSCAP 66*
Ide, Simeon 1794-1889 *Alli Sup, REnAL*
Ideen, Marie A *Alli Sup*
Idell, Albert Edward 1901-1958 *AmA&B, AmNov, REnAL, TwCA Sup*
Idelsohn, Abraham Zebi 1882-1938 *OhA&B*
Iden, Henry *Alli*
Iden, William *ConAu XR*
Idle, Christopher *Alli*
Idleman, Finis Schuyler 1875-1941 *DcNAA*

Inchaustegui Cabral, Hector 1912- *DcCLA*
Inchbald, Elizabeth Simpson 1753-1821 *Alli,*
BbD, BiD&SB, BiDLA, BrAu, CasWL,
Chmbr 2, DcEnA, DcEnL, DcLEnL,
EvLB, NewC, OxEng, Pen Eng
Inchbald, John *Alli Sup*
Inchbald, P *Alli, BiDLA*
Inchbold, John William 1830-1888 *Alli Sup*
Inchcliffe, Richard *ChPo S1*
Inchequin, Lord *Alli*
Inches, James *OxCan*
Inchfawn, Fay 1881- *ChPo, ChPo S1,*
ChPo S2, LongC
Inciardi, James A 1939- *ConAu 61*
Inclan, Ramon DelValle- 1866-1936 *ModRL,*
TwCA, TwCA Sup
Incledon, Benjamin *Alli*
Incledon, Philip *WrD 1976*
Incogniteau, Jean-Louis *ConAu XR*
Incognitus *PueRA*
Inconnue, L' 1825-1881 *AmA, AmA&B*
Ind, Allison 1903-1974 *ConAu P-1*
Indelli, William 1924- *AmSCAP 66*
Inderlied, Mary Elizabeth 1945- *ConAu 49*
Indermaur, John *Alli Sup*
Inderwick, Frederick Andrew 1836- *Alli Sup*
Indik, Bernard P 1932- *ConAu 33*
Indy, Paul-Marie-Theodore-Vincent D'
1851-1931 *OxFr*
Indy, Vincent D' 1851-1931 *AtlBL*
Ineichen, J *Pen Eur*
Ineson, George Hudswell 1914- *Au&Wr*
Inett, John *Alli*
Inez, Colette 1931- *ConAu 37, DrAP 1975,*
WrD 1976
Infans, Roger *BiB N*
Infant Garcia, Romanz Del *CasWL*
Infeld, Leopold 1898-1968 *AmA&B*
Infield, Georgina 1932- *Au&Wr*
Infield, Glenn B 1920- *ConAu 5R, WrD 1976*
Ing, Harry Raymond 1899- *Au&Wr*
Ingalesa, Isabella 1855- *DcNAA*
Ingalesa, Richard 1863- *DcNAA*
Ingalese, Isabella 1855- *WhWNAA*
Ingalese, Richard 1863- *WhWNAA*
Ingall *BbtC*
Ingall, Oswald Drew 1884-1938 *DcNAA*
Ingalls, Claude Eugene 1877- *WhWNAA*
Ingalls, Daniel H H 1916- *ConAu 17R*
Ingalls, Edith *ChPo*
Ingalls, Fay 1882- *OhA&B*
Ingalls, James Monroe 1837-1927 *DcNAA*
Ingalls, Jeremiah 1764-1838 *DcNAA*
Ingalls, Jeremy 1911- *ConAu 1R, DrAP 1975,*
REnAL, WrD 1976
Ingalls, John James 1833-1900 *AmA&B, ChPo,*
DcNAA
Ingalls, Joshua King 1816- *Alli Sup, BiD&SB,*
DcAmA, DcNAA
Ingalls, Leonard *AuBYP*
Ingalls, Lorna *ChPo*
Ingalls, Walter Renton 1886- *WhWNAA*
Ingalls, William 1769-1851 *DcAmA, DcNAA*
Ingals, Ephraim Fletcher 1848-1918 *Alli Sup,*
DcNAA
Ingamells, Rex 1913-1955 *TwCW*
Ingard, K Uno 1921- *ConAu 33*
Ingate, Mary 1912- *WrD 1976*
Ingate, Sophia *Alli Sup*
Ingbar, Mary Lee 1926- *ConAu 41*
Inge, Clinton Owen 1909- *AmSCAP 66*
Inge, M Thomas 1936- *ConAu 17R*
Inge, William 1913-1973 *AmA&B, CnMD,*
CnThe, ConAu 9R, ConDr, ConLC 1,
CrCD, McGWD, ModAL, ModWD,
OxAm, Pen Am, REn, REnAL, REnWD,
TwCA Sup, TwCW, WebEAL
Inge, William Ralph 1860-1954 *Alli Sup,*
Chmbr 3, DcLEnL, EvLB, LongC,
NewC, OxEng, TwCA, TwCA Sup,
WhLA
Ingeland, Thomas *Alli*
Ingelden *Alli*
Ingelend, Thomas *ChPo S1, DcEnL, DcLEnL*
Ingelgren, Georg 1782?-1813 *CasWL*
Ingelo, Nathaniel d1683 *Alli, DcEnL*
Ingelow, Jean 1820-1897 *Alli Sup, BbD,*
BiD&SB, BrAu 19, CarSB, CasWL,

ChPo, ChPo S1, ChPo S2, Chmbr 3,
DcBiA, DcEnA, DcEnL, DcEuL,
DcLEnL, EvLB, JBA 1934, NewC,
OxEng, Pen Eng, WhCL
Ingemann, Bernhard Severin 1789-1862 *BbD,*
BiD&SB, CasWL, ChPo, DcEuL, EuA,
EvEuW, Pen Eur, REn
Ingerman, Stryker *ChPo*
Ingersol, Jared *ConAu XR*
Ingersoll, A J *Alli Sup*
Ingersoll, Adele R *ChPo*
Ingersoll, C M *Alli*
Ingersoll, Charles Jared 1782-1862 *Alli,*
Alli Sup, AmA, AmA&B, BiD&SB,
CyAL 1, DcAmA, DcNAA, OxAm,
REnAL
Ingersoll, Charles Jared 1805-1882 *Alli Sup,*
BbtC, DcNAA
Ingersoll, David E 1939- *ConAu 41*
Ingersoll, Drake *WhWNAA*
Ingersoll, Edward *Alli*
Ingersoll, Edward 1782-1862 *CyAL 1*
Ingersoll, Edward 1790-1841 *DcNAA*
Ingersoll, Edward 1817-1893 *DcAmA, DcNAA*
Ingersoll, Elihu Parsons 1804-1887 *DcNAA*
Ingersoll, Ernest 1852-1946 *Alli Sup, AmA&B,*
AmLY, BbD, BiD&SB, CarSB, ChPo S1,
DcAmA, DcNAA, REnAL, WhWNAA
Ingersoll, Frances Evans *ChPo*
Ingersoll, Henry Hulbert 1844-1915 *BiDSA,*
DcNAA
Ingersoll, J M 1869- *WhWNAA*
Ingersoll, Jared *CyAL 1*
Ingersoll, Jared 1722-1781 *Alli*
Ingersoll, Joseph Reed 1786-1868 *Alli, CyAL 1,*
DcAmA, DcNAA
Ingersoll, Julia Harriet 1820?-1898 *DcAmA*
Ingersoll, L Dunham *Alli Sup, DcNAA,*
BiD&SB, DcAmA
Ingersoll, Marian C *ChPo*
Ingersoll, Ralph McAllister 1900- *Au&Wr,*
ChPo, ConAu P-1, REnAL, TwCA Sup,
WhWNAA
Ingersoll, Robert Green 1833-1899 *Alli Sup,*
AmA, AmA&B, BbD, BiD&SB, DcAmA,
DcNAA, OxAm, REn, REnAL
Ingersoll, Royal Rodney 1847-1931 *DcNAA*
Ingersoll, Will E *CanNov*
Ingham, Alfred *Alli Sup*
Ingham, Annie *ChPo S1*
Ingham, Daniel *WrD 1976*
Ingham, Edward And Davies, R *Alli Sup*
Ingham, Ellery Percy 1856-1926 *DcAmA,*
DcNAA
Ingham, Frederic *DcNAA*
Ingham, Harvey A *Alli Sup*
Ingham, Hastings *Alli Sup*
Ingham, Jane Sarson Cooper *Alli Sup*
Ingham, John *Alli Sup*
Ingham, John Hall 1860- *ChPo, ChPo S1*
Ingham, Kenneth 1921- *Au&Wr, WrD 1976*
Ingham, Mary Bigelow 1832-1924 *OhA&B*
Ingham, Nelson 1893- *AmSCAP 66*
Ingham, Richard *Alli Sup*
Ingham, Richard Arnison 1935- *WrD 1976*
Ingham, Samuel *Alli*
Ingham, Sarson C J *Alli Sup, ChPo, ChPo S1*
Ingham, William *Alli Sup*
Ingilby, Joan Alicia 1911- *Au&Wr, ConAu 9R,*
WrD 1976
Ingle, Clifford 1915- *ConAu 29*
Ingle, Dwight Joyce 1907- *ConAu P-1*
Ingle, Edward 1861-1924 *Alli Sup, BiDSA,*
DcAmA, DcNAA
Ingleby, Clement Mansfield 1823-1886 *Alli,*
Alli Sup, BbD, BiD&SB, DcEnL
Ingleby, Holcombe *Alli Sup*
Ingleby, John *Alli*
Ingledew, C J Davison *Alli Sup*
Inglefield, Captain *Alli*
Inglefield, Ann *Alli*
Inglefield, Sir Edward Augustus 1820-1894 *Alli,*
Alli Sup, OxCan
Inglehart, Fanny C G *BiDSA*
Inglehart, Frances 1851- *DcAmA*
Ingles, G Lloyd 1901- *ConAu P-1*
Ingles DeSousa, Herculano Marcos 1853-1918
Pen Am

Inglesant, John *MnBBF*
Inglesant, Paul *MnBBF*
Inglin, Meinrad 1893-1971 *CasWL, EncWL*
Inglis, A Percy *Alli Sup*
Inglis, Alex I *OxCan Sup*
Inglis, Alexander James 1879-1924 *AmA&B,*
DcNAA
Inglis, Andrew *Alli Sup*
Inglis, B D 1930- *Au&Wr*
Inglis, Brian St. John 1916- *Au&Wr,*
ConAu 17R, WrD 1976
Inglis, Catherine H 1815- *PoIre*
Inglis, Catherine Hart *Alli Sup*
Inglis, Charles *Alli Sup*
Inglis, Charles 1734-1816 *Alli, BbtC, BiDLA,*
DcAmA, DcNAA
Inglis, David *BbtC*
Inglis, David 1825-1877 *DcAmA*
Inglis, David Rittenhouse 1905- *ConAu 5R*
Inglis, Henry *Alli Sup*
Inglis, Henry David *Alli, BiDLA*
Inglis, Henry David 1795-1835 *Alli, BbD,*
BiD&SB, DcEnL
Inglis, James *Alli Sup*
Inglis, Sir James d1554 *Alli, DcEnL*
Inglis, James d1820 *Alli*
Inglis, James 1845- *ChPo*
Inglis, James 1927- *ConAu 21*
Inglis, James McDonald *Alli Sup*
Inglis, John *Alli Sup*
Inglis, John d1850 *BbtC*
Inglis, John 1763-1834 *Alli, DcEnL*
Inglis, John 1813- *ChPo S1*
Inglis, Mary *ChPo*
Inglis, Ralston *Alli Sup*
Inglis, Mrs. Richmond *Alli*
Inglis, Robert *ChPo S2*
Inglis, Sir Robert Harry 1786-1855 *Alli*
Inglis, Robert Morton Gall 1910- *Au&Wr,*
ConAu 13R
Inglis, Robert Stirling 1835-1886 *Alli Sup,*
ChPo S2
Inglis, Ross *MnBBF*
Inglis, Ruth Langdon 1927- *ConAu 49*
Inglis, Stuart J 1923- *ConAu 41*
Inglis, William 1872-1949 *DcNAA*
Inglis-Jones, Elisabeth 1900- *Au&Wr,*
WrD 1976
Inglisham, John *ChPo S1, ChPo S2*
Ingmethorpe, Thomas *Alli*
Ingmire, Katherine *Alli Sup*
Ingold, Meister *OxGer*
Ingold, Ernest 1885- *AmA&B*
Ingold, Klara 1913- *ConAu 61*
Ingoldsby *DcEnA*
Ingoldsby, Dalton *Alli Sup*
Ingoldsby, J *Alli Sup*
Ingoldsby, Thomas 1788-1845 *Alli, CasWL,*
ChPo, DcEnL, NewC
Ingpen, Abel *Alli*
Ingpen, Roger 1868-1936 *ChPo*
Ingpen, William *Alli*
Ingraham, Abijah *Alli Sup*
Ingraham, Charles Anson 1852-1935 *DcNAA*
Ingraham, Charles Anson 1852- *WhWNAA*
Ingraham, Edward D 1793-1854 *Alli, DcAmA,*
DcNAA
Ingraham, Ellen M 1832-1919 *Alli Sup,*
IndAu 1816
Ingraham, Herbert 1883-1910 *AmSCAP 66*
Ingraham, J H *Alli*
Ingraham, John Phillips Thurston 1817-1906
Alli Sup, DcAmA, DcNAA
Ingraham, Joseph Holt 1809-1860 *AmA,*
AmA&B, BbD, BiD&SB, BiDSA,
CnDAL, DcAmA, DcLEnL, DcNAA,
HsB&A, OxAm, REnAL
Ingraham, Leonard W 1913- *ConAu 25,*
SmATA 4
Ingraham, Mark H 1896- *ConAu 61*
Ingraham, Mary Kinley 1874- *WhWNAA*
Ingraham, Prentiss 1843-1904 *AmA&B,*
BiDSA, CarSB, DcAmA, DcNAA,
HsB&A, MnBBF, OxAm, REnAL
Ingraham, Roy 1895- *AmSCAP 66*
Ingraham, Ruth *ChPo*
Ingraham, Vernon L 1924- *ConAu 33*
Ingram, Alexander *Alli, BiDLA*

Ingram, Arthur Foley Winnington 1858-1946 NewC, WhLA
Ingram, Arthur Henry Winnington *Alli Sup*
Ingram, Bowen *ConAu 37*
Ingram, Sir Bruce 1877-1963 *LongC*
Ingram, Collingwood 1880- *ConAu 61*
Ingram, Cordie Webb 1880- *TexWr*
Ingram, Dale d1793 *Alli*
Ingram, Derek Thynne 1925- *Au&Wr, ConAu 9R, WrD 1976*
Ingram, Edward James *Alli, BiDLA*
Ingram, Edward Lovering 1862-1938 *DcNAA, WhWNAA*
Ingram, Eleanor Marie 1886-1921 *DcNAA*
Ingram, Forrest L 1938- *ConAu 53*
Ingram, George *ChPo*
Ingram, George 1892- *Au&Wr*
Ingram, George S *Alli Sup*
Ingram, Henry *Alli, BiDLA Sup*
Ingram, Henry Atlee 1858-1927 *Alli Sup, DcNAA*
Ingram, J K *Chmbr 3*
Ingram, J S *Alli Sup*
Ingram, James 1774-1850 *Alli, BiDLA, DcEnL*
Ingram, James C 1922- *ConAu 5R*
Ingram, John G *ChPo S1*
Ingram, John H 1849- *Alli Sup*
Ingram, John Kells 1823-1907 *Alli Sup, BrAu 19, ChPo S2, DcLEnL, NewC, PoIre*
Ingram, Joseph Forsyth *PoIre*
Ingram, Kenneth 1882-1965 *ConAu P-1*
Ingram, Madeline Dean 1901- *IndAu 1917*
Ingram, Maria *DrAP 1975*
Ingram, Marvin 1938- *AmSCAP 66*
Ingram, Percival H *MnBBF*
Ingram, Robert 1727-1804 *Alli, DcEnL*
Ingram, Robert Acklom d1809 *Alli*
Ingram, Rowland *Alli, BiDLA*
Ingram, Thomas Dunbar 1827- *Alli Sup*
Ingram, Thomas Henry 1924- *ConAu 49*
Ingram, Tom 1924- *ChPo, ConAu 49*
Ingram, Vernon Martin 1924- *WrD 1976*
Ingram, W J Evelyn *Alli Sup*
Ingram, William *Alli, BiDLA, ChPo S1*
Ingram, William 1930- *ConAu 41*
Ingram, Willis J *ConAu XR*
Ingram-Brown, Robert 1911- *Au&Wr*
Ingrams, Doreen Constance 1906- *Au&Wr, ConAu 33, WrD 1976*
Ingrams, Richard *WrD 1976*
Ingrams, William Harold 1897- *Au&Wr*
Ingres, Jean Auguste Dominique 1780-1867 *AtlBL, NewC, OxFr, REn*
Ingrey, Derek 1929- *Au&Wr*
Ings, E *Alli*
Ingstad, Helge Marcus *OxCan*
Ingulf 1030?-1109 *BiB N*
Ingulphus 1030?-1109 *Alli, DcEnL*
Injanashi 1837-1892 *DcOrL 1*
Ink, Evangeline 1883-1923 *OhA&B*
Ink Dabbler, The *WhWNAA*
Inkeles, Alex 1920- *ConAu 1R*
Inkersley, Thomas *Alli*
Inkster, John Gibson 1867-1946 *DcNAA*
Inlow, Gail M 1910- *ConAu 5R*
Inman *HsB&A Sup*
Inman, Arthur Crew 1895- *AmA&B, ChPo S1, WhWNAA*
Inman, Billie Andrew 1929- *ConAu 29*
Inman, Escott *MnBBF*
Inman, G E *ChPo*
Inman, Henry *ChPo*
Inman, Henry 1837-1899 *AmA, AmA&B, CnDAL, DcAmA, DcNAA, OxAm, REnAL*
Inman, Herbert Escott *MnBBF*
Inman, Isaac M *Alli Sup*
Inman, Jack 1919- *ConAu 25*
Inman, James *Alli, BiDLA*
Inman, James William *Alli Sup*
Inman, John 1805-1850 *CyAL 2*
Inman, Mary *Alli Sup*
Inman, Robert 1931- *ConAu 17R, WrD 1976*
Inman, Robert Randolph *HsB&A*
Inman, Samuel Guy 1877-1965 *AmA&B, REnAL, WhWNAA*

Inman, Thomas *Alli Sup*
Inman, Thomas 1830-1876 *Alli Sup*
Inman, Will *ConAu XR*
Innes, Alexander *Alli, Alli Sup*
Innes, Alexander Taylor *Alli Sup*
Innes, Arthur Charles 1834- *Alli Sup*
Innes, Brian 1928- *Au&Wr, ConAu 23*
Innes, C L *Alli Sup*
Innes, Catherine *ChPo S1*
Innes, Cosmo 1798-1874 *Alli Sup, BrAu 19, CasWL, Chmbr 3, EvLB*
Innes, Emily *Alli Sup*
Innes, F *MnBBF*
Innes, Frank C 1934- *ConAu 45*
Innes, George *Alli*
Innes, George Rose- *Alli Sup*
Innes, Hammond 1913- *AmA&B, ConAu XR, ConNov 1972, ConNov 1976, LongC, REn, TwCW, WorAu, WrD 1976*
Innes, Hugh *Alli*
Innes, Isabella *Alli Sup*
Innes, J C *Alli Sup*
Innes, J T *ChPo S2*
Innes, James *Alli*
Innes, James D *Alli*
Innes, James John McLeod *Alli Sup*
Innes, Jean *WrD 1976*
Innes, John *Alli*
Innes, John d1776 *Alli*
Innes, John Brodie *Alli Sup*
Innes, Lewis Charles *Alli Sup*
Innes, Louis 1650?- *Alli*
Innes, Mary *TexWr*
Innes, Michael 1906- *ConNov 1972, ConNov 1976, DcLEnL, EncM&D, EvLB, LongC, NewC, Pen Eng, REn, TwCA, TwCA Sup, TwCW, WrD 1976*
Innes, Peter R *Alli Sup*
Innes, Robert 1810- *ChPo S1*
Innes, Robert T A 1861- *WhLA*
Innes, Rosemary E *ConAu 25*
Innes, Thomas 1662-1744 *Alli, CasWL, Chmbr 2, DcEnL, EvLB*
Innes, William *Alli, BiDLA*
Innes Of Learney, Sir Thomas 1893- *Au&Wr*
Innes-Smith, Robert Stuart 1928- *Au&Wr*
Inness, George 1825-1894 *AtlBL, OxAm, REn*
Inness, George, Jr. 1854-1926 *DcNAA, WhWNAA*
Innis, Donald Quayle 1924- *ConAu 41*
Innis, Harold Adams 1894-1952 *CanWr, DcLEnL, OxCan*
Innis, Mary Quayle 1899- *CanNov, OxCan*
Innis, Pauline B 1918- *ConAu 1R*
Innsley, Owen *BiD&SB, DcAmA, DcNAA*
Innsly, Owen *Alli Sup*
Inoue, Yukitoshi 1945- *ConAu 25*
Inouye, Daniel K 1924- *ConAu 25*
Insall, Donald W 1926- *ConAu 61*
Insetta, Paul Peter 1915- *AmSCAP 66*
Insh, G P *OxCan*
Insha, Sayyid Insha'llah Khan 1757-1817 *DcOrL 2*
Insight, James *ConAu XR*
Inskeep, Annie Dolman *WhWNAA*
Inskip, Betty 1905- *WhLA*
Inskip, James Theodore 1868- *WhLA*
Inskip, John Swanel 1816-1884 *Alli, DcAmA, DcNAA, OhA&B*
Inskip, Robert Mills *Alli Sup*
Inskipp, James 1790-1868 *ChPo*
Inslow, Hope *Alli Sup*
Instone, Gordon 1916- *Au&Wr*
Intelligence Officer, The *WhLA*
Intert, G D *MnBBF*
Intra, Giambattista 1832- *BiD&SB*
Intriligator, Michael D 1938- *ConAu 53*
Invalid, An 1802-1876 *DcEnL*
Inverarity, Robert Bruce 1909- *AmA&B, WrD 1976*
Invincible Doctor, The 1270-1347 *DcEnL*
Inwards, Jabez *Alli Sup*
Inwards, James *Alli Sup*
Inwards, R *Alli Sup*
Inwood, Henry William *Alli*
Inwood, William *Alli, BiDLA*
Inyart, Gene 1927- *ConAu XR, SmATA 6*

Ioane-Zosime d978? *DcOrL 3*
Iolo Morganwg 1747-1826 *CasWL*
Ion Of Chios 484?BC-422?BC *BbD, BiD&SB, CasWL*
Iona, Andy 1902- *AmSCAP 66*
Ionesco, Eugene 1912- *CasWL, CnMD, CnMWL, CnThe, ConAu 9R, ConLC 1, ConLC 4, ConLC 6, CrCD, EncWL, EvEuW, LongC, McGWD, ModRL, ModWD, Pen Eur, RCom, REn, REnWD, SmATA 7, TwCW, WhTwL, WorAu*
Ionescu, Ghita J 1913- *Au&Wr, WrD 1976*
Ioor, William 1780?-1830 *AmA, AmA&B, DcNAA, OxAm, REnAL*
Iorga, Nicolae 1871-1940 *CasWL, ClDMEuL, CnMD, EncWL, Pen Eur*
Iorio, Adrian J *ChPo*
Iorio, James 1921- *ConAu 61*
Iorio, John 1925- *ConAu 49*
Iosif, Stefan Octavian 1875-1913 *CasWL, EvEuW*
Iota *Chmbr 3*
Ipcar, Dahlov 1917- *AuBYP, BkP, ChPo S1, ChPo S2, ConAu 17R, IlCB 1956, IlCB 1966, SmATA 1, ThBJA*
Ipsen, D C 1921- *ConAu 33, WrD 1976*
Ipsen, L S *ChPo*
Ipuwer *DcOrL 3*
Iqbal, Afzal 1919- *ConAu 61*
Iqbal, Sir Muhammad 1873-1938 *CasWL, DcLEnL, DcOrL 2, EncWL, Pen Cl*
Iqua *ConAu XR*
Iraiyanar *DcOrL 2*
Iraj, Jalal Al-Mamalik, Mirza 1874-1925? *CasWL*
Iraj Mirza 1874-1925? *DcOrL 3*
Iramalinka Pillai, Svami 1823-1874 *DcOrL 2*
Iranek-Osmecki, Kazimierz 1897- *ConAu 49*
'Iraqi, Ibrahim, Fakhr-Al-Din d1289 *CasWL*
Irbe, Andrejs *Pen Eur*
Irby, Augustus Henry *Alli Sup*
Irby, Charles Leonard And James Mangles *Alli*
Irby, F W *Alli Sup*
Irby, Kenneth 1936- *ConP 1970, ConP 1975, DrAP 1975, WrD 1976*
Irby, Leonard Howard L *Alli Sup*
Irby, Richard 1825-1902 *Alli Sup, BiDSA, DcAmA, DcNAA*
Iredell, James 1750-1799 *BiDSA*
Iredell, James 1788-1853 *Alli, BiDSA, DcAmA*
Irelan, Mrs. C E *ChPo S1*
Irelan, John Robert *Alli Sup*
Ireland *Alli*
Ireland, Baron *ChPo*
Ireland, Alan Stuart 1940- *ConP 1970*
Ireland, Alexander *Alli Sup*
Ireland, Alleyne 1871- *AmLY, BiD&SB, DcAmA*
Ireland, Arthur Joseph 1874- *MnBBF, WhLA*
Ireland, David 1927- *ConAu 25, ConNov 1976, WrD 1976*
Ireland, Doreen *ChPo S1, WrD 1976*
Ireland, Earl 1928- *ConAu 5R*
Ireland, F G *Alli Sup*
Ireland, George William *Au&Wr*
Ireland, J P *Alli*
Ireland, James *Alli Sup*
Ireland, John d1808 *Alli, NewC*
Ireland, John 1761-1842 *Alli, BiDLA, DcEnL*
Ireland, John 1828-1918 *DcNAA*
Ireland, John 1838- *BiD&SB, DcAmA*
Ireland, John And Nichols, John *Alli Sup*
Ireland, John B *Alli Sup*
Ireland, John Of 1435?-1496 *CasWL*
Ireland, Joseph Norton 1817-1898 *Alli Sup, AmA, AmA&B, DcAmA, DcNAA, REnAL*
Ireland, Kevin Mark 1933- *ConP 1970, ConP 1975, WrD 1976*
Ireland, Mary B 1834- *BiD&SB*
Ireland, Mary Eliza 1834- *Alli Sup, DcAmA, DcNAA*
Ireland, Michael *NewC*
Ireland, Norma Olin 1907- *ConAu 9R*
Ireland, Robert H *Alli Sup*
Ireland, Robert M 1937- *ConAu 45*

Ireland, Samuel 1750-1800 *Alli, BkIE, DcEnL*
Ireland, Sidney *Alli Sup*
Ireland, Thomas *Alli*
Ireland, Thomas Saxton 1895- *AmA&B, OhA&B*
Ireland, William Henry 1777-1835 *Alli, BiDLA, CasWL, ChPo, Chmbr 2, DcEnL, DcLEnL, EvLB, NewC, REn*
Ireland, William Wotherspoon *Alli Sup*
Iremonger, F A 1878- *WhLA*
Iremonger, Frederic *Alli, BiDLA*
Iremonger, Lucille *Au&Wr, BiDPar, ConAu 9R*
Iremonger, Thomas Lascelles *Au&Wr*
Iremonger, Valentin 1918- *ConP 1970, ConP 1975, WrD 1976*
Irenaeus 135?-202? *BbD, CasWL, Pen Cl*
Ireson, Anthony 1913- *Au&Wr*
Ireson, Barbara 1927- *Au&Wr, ChPo, ChPo S1, ConAu 5R*
Ireton, Henry *MnBBF*
Ireton, Henry 1611-1651 *REn*
Ireton, John *Alli*
Irgint, Wallace Admah 1875-1959 *ChPo*
Iriarte, Juan De *DcSpL*
Iriarte, Tomas De 1750-1791 *CasWL, DcEuL, DcSpL, EvEuW, Pen Eur, REn*
Iriarte Y Oropesa, Tomas De 1750-1791 *ChPo S1, EuA*
Irion, Alfred Briggs *BiDSA*
Irion, Mary Jean 1922- *ConAu 23, WrD 1976*
Irion, Paul E 1922- *ConAu 23*
Iris, Frederico Scharmel 1889- *ChPo, ChPo S1*
Irish, A B *Alli Sup*
Irish, David *Alli*
Irish, Donald P 1919- *ConAu 49*
Irish, Frank V 1848- *WhWNAA*
Irish, Marian D 1909- *ConAu 9R*
Irish, William *AmA&B, ConAu XR, EncM&D, TwCA Sup*
Irish, William N *Alli Sup*
Irishman, An *PoIre*
Iriye, Akira 1934- *ConAu 25*
Irland, David *ConAu XR*
Iroaganachi, J O 1940?- *AfA 1*
Iron, John *WhLA, WhWNAA*
Iron, Nathaniel Colchester *HsB&A*
Iron, Ralph *Alli Sup, BiD&SB, EvLB, LongC, NewC, OxEng, REn*
Iron Chancellor, The *NewC*
Iron Duke, The *NewC*
Iron Hand *OxCan*
Ironmaster, Maximus *ConAu XR*
Ironquill 1841-1911 *AmA, AmA&B, ChPo, ChPo S1, DcAmA*
Irons, Archie C *HsB&A, HsB&A Sup*
Irons, Earl D 1891- *AmSCAP 66*
Irons, James *BbtC*
Irons, Joseph *Alli*
Irons, L C *Alli Sup*
Irons, Lettie Artley *HsB&A*
Irons, W *Alli Sup*
Irons, William J 1812-1883 *Alli, Alli Sup*
Ironside, Lieutenant Colonel *Alli*
Ironside, Edward d1803 *Alli, BiDLA*
Ironside, F Gilbert *Alli*
Ironside, Henry Allan 1876- *WhWNAA*
Ironside, Margaret *Au&Wr*
Ironside, Matthew *MnBBF*
Ironside, Nestor *DcEnL, NewC*
Irrefragable Doctor, The *DcEnL*
Irregang, Meister *OxGer*
Irvin, Benjamin *Alli Sup*
Irvin, D, Lester, G N And Hill, W B *Alli Sup*
Irvin, Eric 1908- *ConP 1970*
Irvin, Margaret Elizabeth 1916- *ConP 1970*
Irvin, Mildred Leisure 1912- *IndAu 1917*
Irvin, Rea *ChPo S1*
Irvin, T C *Alli Sup*
Irvin, Will *ChPo S1*
Irvine, Alexander *Alli, Alli Sup, BiDLA*
Irvine, Alexander Fitzgerald 1863-1941 *ChPo, DcNAA*
Irvine, Alexander Forbes *Alli*
Irvine, Andrew *Alli*
Irvine, Andrew Leicester 1881- *ChPo*
Irvine, Benjamin Franklin *WhWNAA*
Irvine, C E *Alli Sup*

Irvine, Christopher *Alli*
Irvine, Demar 1908- *ConAu 33*
Irvine, Edward James 1896- *WhWNAA*
Irvine, Freda *Alli Sup*
Irvine, Gerard A D'Arcy *PoIre*
Irvine, Helen Douglas *CatA 1947, ChPo*
Irvine, James Pearson *Alli Sup*
Irvine, Keith 1924- *ConAu 29, WrD 1976*
Irvine, Mabel V *ChPo, ChPo S1*
Irvine, Mary Catharine *Alli Sup*
Irvine, Patrick *Alli*
Irvine, Paul 1891- *WhWNAA*
Irvine, Ralph *Alli*
Irvine, Sadie A E *ChPo*
Irvine, T A *OxCan*
Irvine, William *Alli, BiDLA*
Irvine, William 1882?- *OxCan*
Irvine, William 1906-1964 *AmA&B, REnAL, TwCA Sup*
Irvine-Pollock, Lillian 1856- *ChPo S2*
Irving, A *Alli*
Irving, Aemilius *BbtC*
Irving, Alexander *Alli Sup*
Irving, Benjamin Atkinson *Alli, Alli Sup*
Irving, Brian William 1932- *ConAu 53*
Irving, C *Alli*
Irving, Christopher *WhLA, WhWNAA*
Irving, Clifford Michael 1930- *Au&Wr, AuNews 1, ConAu 1R, WrD 1976*
Irving, Constance *ChPo*
Irving, David 1778-1860 *Alli, Alli Sup, BiDLA*
Irving, David John Cawdell 1938- *Au&Wr, ConAu 13R*
Irving, Eames *Alli Sup*
Irving, Ebenezer 1776-1868 *CyAL 1*
Irving, Edward 1792-1834 *Alli, BbD, BrAu 19, Chmbr 3, DcEnL, EvLB, NewC*
Irving, Elizabeth Jane *Alli Sup, ChPo*
Irving, Ethel *Alli Sup*
Irving, Fannie Belle *Alli Sup*
Irving, George Clerk d1866 *BbtC*
Irving, George Vere *Alli, Alli Sup*
Irving, Gordon 1918- *Au&Wr, ConAu 25*
Irving, Harold Rupert 1899- *WrD 1976*
Irving, Harriet *HsB&A*
Irving, Harry James 1908- *AmSCAP 66*
Irving, Helen *FemPA*
Irving, Helen W *Alli*
Irving, Sir Henry 1838-1905 *NewC, REn*
Irving, Horace *MnBBF*
Irving, John *DrAF 1976*
Irving, John 1942- *ConAu 25*
Irving, John A *OxCan*
Irving, John Beaufain 1800-1881 *DcNAA*
Irving, John Beaufain 1825-1877 *BiDSA, DcNAA*
Irving, John Henry Brodribb 1838- *Alli Sup*
Irving, John Treat 1778-1838 *Alli, CyAL 1*
Irving, John Treat, Jr. 1812-1906 *Alli, Alli Sup, AmA, AmA&B, BiD&SB, CyAL 1, DcAmA, DcNAA, OxAm, REnAL*
Irving, Joseph *Alli Sup*
Irving, Kate *Alli Sup*
Irving, L H *Alli*
Irving, Lukin Homfray 1855-1942 *DcNAA*
Irving, Maude A *ChPo S2*
Irving, Maxwell John *Alli*
Irving, Miles *WhWNAA*
Irving, Minna *AmA&B, DcNAA*
Irving, Nancy *AuBYP, ConAu XR*
Irving, Peter 1771-1838 *Alli, AmA, AmA&B, CyAL 1, DcAmA, DcNAA, OxAm, REnAL*
Irving, Peter Henry Howy 1914- *Au&Wr, WrD 1976*
Irving, Pierre Munroe 1803-1876 *Alli Sup, BiD&SB, CyAL 1, DcAmA, DcNAA, REnAL, OxAm*
Irving, R E *Alli Sup*
Irving, R L Graham 1877-1969 *ConAu P-1*
Irving, Ralph *Alli, BiDLA*
Irving, Reginald *WhLA, WhWNAA*
Irving, Robert 1913- *AmA&B, ConAu XR, ThBJA*
Irving, Roland Duer 1847-1888 *Alli Sup, DcAmA, DcNAA*
Irving, T B 1914- *ConAu 37*

Irving, Theodore 1809-1880 *Alli, Alli Sup, BiDSA, CyAL 1, DcAmA, DcEnL, DcNAA*
Irving, Thomas *Alli*
Irving, Thomas J *Alli Sup*
Irving, W Noel *ChPo*
Irving, Walter *Alli Sup*
Irving, Washington 1783-1859 *Alli, AmA, AmA&B, AmWr, AtlBL, BbD, BiD&SB, CarSB, CasWL, ChPo, ChPo S2, Chmbr 3, CnDAL, CriT 3, CyAL 1, CyWA, DcAmA, DcBiA, DcEnA, DcEnL, DcLEnL, DcNAA, DcSpL, EvLB, FamAYP, MouLC 3, OxAm, OxCan, OxEng, Pen Am, RAdv 1, REn, REnAL, WebEAL, WhCL, WiscW*
Irving, William *AuBYP, ConAu XR*
Irving, William 1766-1821 *Alli, AmA, BiD&SB, CyAL 1, DcAmA, OxAm, REnAL*
Irwin, Viscountess *Alli*
Irwin, Anne *Alli Sup, ChPo S1*
Irwin, Constance Frick 1913- *ConAu 1R, IndAu 1917, SmATA 6, WrD 1976*
Irwin, David *OxCan*
Irwin, David George 1933- *Au&Wr, ConAu 53, WrD 1976*
Irwin, Demaris 1851-1933 *OhA&B*
Irwin, Edward *Alli Sup, PoIre*
Irwin, Elisabeth Antoinette d1942 *DcNAA*
Irwin, Eyles 1748?-1817 *Alli, BiDLA, PoIre*
Irwin, F C *Alli*
Irwin, Florence 1869- *AmA&B, WhWNAA*
Irwin, Frederick Charles 1870- *WhWNAA*
Irwin, G *Alli*
Irwin, Gene 1916- *AmSCAP 66*
Irwin, George 1910-1971 *ConAu 41*
Irwin, Godfrey 1895- *WhWNAA*
Irwin, Grace Lilian 1907- *Au&Wr, AuBYP, ConAu 17R, OxCan, WrD 1976*
Irwin, H C *PoIre*
Irwin, Henry Crossley *Alli Sup*
Irwin, Inez Haynes 1873- *AmA&B, CarSB, REnAL, TwCA, TwCA Sup, WhWNAA*
Irwin, Isabel C *ChPo S1, PoIre*
Irwin, John 1817- *BbtC*
Irwin, John Arthur 1853-1912 *DcAmA, DcNAA*
Irwin, John Conran 1917- *Au&Wr, WrD 1976*
Irwin, John T 1940- *ConAu 53*
Irwin, John V 1917- *ConAu 45*
Irwin, Keith Gordon 1885-1964 *ConAu 5R*
Irwin, Lois 1926- *AmSCAP 66*
Irwin, M *ChPo S2*
Irwin, M E *Alli Sup*
Irwin, Margaret 1889-1967 *DcLEnL, LongC, TwCA Sup, TwCW, WhLA*
Irwin, Patricia Kathleen 1916- *ConAu XR, ConP 1970*
Irwin, Peter George 1925- *WrD 1976*
Irwin, Ray Watkins 1896- *WhWNAA*
Irwin, Raymond 1902- *Au&Wr, ConAu P-1*
Irwin, Rea *ChPo S2*
Irwin, Russell *ChPo, ChPo S1*
Irwin, Ruth Beckey 1906- *ConAu 29*
Irwin, Theodore 1907- *AmA&B*
Irwin, Thomas Caulfield 1823-1892 *Alli, Alli Sup, ChPo S1, PoIre*
Irwin, Vera Rushforth 1913- *ConAu 33*
Irwin, Violet 1881- *AmA&B, REnAL, WhWNAA*
Irwin, Mrs. Wallace *AmA&B*
Irwin, Wallace Admah 1875-1959 *AmA&B, ChPo S1, ChPo S2, CnDAL, ConAmL, DcAmA, OxAm, REn, REnAL, St&VC, TwCA, TwCA Sup*
Irwin, Will 1873-1948 *AmA&B, ChPo S1, EncM&D, OxAm, REnAL, WhWNAA*
Irwin, William 1923- *AmSCAP 66*
Irwin, Mrs. William Arthur 1916- *WrD 1976*
Irwin, William C K 1907- *AmSCAP 66*
Irwin, William H H 1841-1879 *OhA&B*
Irwin, William Henry 1873-1948 *DcNAA, TwCA, TwCA Sup*
Irwin-Williams, Cynthia 1936- *ConAu 45*
Iryon 1206-1289 *DcOrL 1*
Irzykowski, Karol 1873-1944 *CasWL, ModSL 2, Pen Eur*

DcAmA, DcNAA
Ives, Cornelius *Alli*
Ives, E *Alli*
Ives, Edward *Alli*
Ives, Edward D 1925- *ConAu 25, OxCan, OxCan Sup*
Ives, Edward Otto *Alli, BiDLA*
Ives, Eli 1779-1861 *CyAL 1*
Ives, Ella Gilbert 1847-1913 *ChPo, DcNAA*
Ives, Frederic Eugene 1856-1937 *DcNAA*
Ives, George Burnham 1856-1930 *DcNAA*
Ives, George Cecil 1867- *WhLA*
Ives, Howard Chapin 1878-1944 *DcNAA, WhWNAA*
Ives, Howard Colby *ChPo*
Ives, J *Alli Sup*
Ives, J M *Alli*
Ives, James Edmund 1865- *WhWNAA*
Ives, James Merritt 1824-1895 *AmA&B, REn, REnAL*
Ives, Jeremy *Alli*
Ives, John 1751-1776 *Alli*
Ives, Joseph Christmas 1828-1868 *Alli Sup, DcNAA*
Ives, Joseph Moss 1876-1939 *DcNAA*
Ives, Lawrence *ConAu XR*
Ives, Levi 1750-1826 *Alli*
Ives, Levi Silliman 1797-1867 *Alli, DcAmA, DcNAA*
Ives, Mabel Lorenz *AnMV 1926*
Ives, Paul Pomeroy 1877- *WhWNAA*
Ives, R A *Alli Sup*
Ives, Ruth *ChPo S2*
Ives, Sandy *ConAu XR*
Ives, Sarah Noble 1864- *AmA&B, ChPo, WhWNAA*
Ives, Sumner 1911- *ConAu 9R*
Ivey, Allen E 1933- *ConAu 49*
Ivey, Burnett Steele *ChPo, ChPo S2, TexWr*
Ivey, George James *Alli Sup*
Ivey, Thomas Neal 1860-1923 *DcNAA*
Ivie, Robert M 1930- *ConAu 9R*
Ivimey, Joseph *Alli, BiDLA*
Ivins, Anthony Woodward 1852-1934 *DcNAA*
Ivins, Florence Wyman *ChPo*
Ivins, Lester Sylvan 1878- *WhWNAA*
Ivins, William Mills 1851-1915 *Alli Sup, DcNAA*
Ivison, Elizabeth 1931- *Au&Wr*
Ivison, Ursula *Alli, BiDLA*
Ivnev, Ryurik 1893- *CasWL*
Ivnyov, Ryurik 1893- *DcRusL*
Ivo, Ledo 1924- *TwCW*
Ivor, Roderick *MnBBF*
Ivory, Bertha May *BiDSA, DcNAA*
Ivory, James 1765-1842 *Alli*
Ivoryy *Alli*
Ivry, Alfred Lyon 1935- *ConAu 45*
Ivs, Elam, Jr. *ChPo*
Iwamatsu, Jun 1908- *AuBYP*
Iwano, Homei 1873-1920 *DcOrL 1*
Iwaszkiewicz, Jaroslaw 1894- *CasWL, ClDMEuL, CnMD, EncWL, ModSL 2, ModWD, Pen Eur*
Iwata, Masakazu 1917- *ConAu 17R, WrD 1976*
Ixford, Noah *Alli*
Iyangar, Venkatesa 1891- *REn*
Iyengar, K R Srinivasa 1908- *ConAu 5R, DcLEnL, REn*
Iyengar, S Kesava 1894- *ConAu 17R*
Iyengar, V V Srinivasa 1871-1954 *DcLEnL*
Iyer, Baghavan Narashimhan 1930- *ConAu 57*
Izacke, Richard 1624-1700 *Alli*
Izant, Grace Goulder 1893- *ConAu P-1*
Izard, Barbara 1926- *ConAu 29*
Izard, Carroll E 1923- *ConAu 49*
Izard, George 1776-1828 *BbtC, DcNAA*
Izard, Ralph 1742-1804 *Alli, BiDSA*
Izax, Ikabod *ChPo S1, DcNAA*
Izban, Samuel 1905- *ConAu 49*
Izmailov, Alexander Yefimovich 1779-1831 *CasWL*
Izmaylov, Alexander Yefimovich 1779-1831 *DcRusL*
Izumi, Kyoka 1873-1939 *CasWL, DcOrL 1*
Izumi, Shikibu 974?-1030? *CasWL, DcOrL 1*
Izumo, Takeda 1691-1756 *CnThe, REnWD*

Izzard, Ralph William Burdick 1910- *Au&Wr*
Izzet Molla Kececizade 1785-1829 *DcOrL 3*
Izzo, Herbert J 1928- *ConAu 41*

J

Jackson, Dennis Barry 1929- *Au&Wr*
Jackson, Dennis Emerson 1878- *IndAu 1917,*
WhWNAA
Jackson, Don D 1920-1968 *ConAu P-1*
Jackson, Donald 1919- *ConAu 17R*
Jackson, Donald Dale 1935- *ConAu 49*
Jackson, Dorothy Virginia Steinhauer 1924-
Au&Wr, ConAu 13R
Jackson, Douglas N 1929- *ConAu 37*
Jackson, Dugald Caleb 1865- *DcAmA,*
WhWNAA
Jackson, Dugald Caleb, Jr. 1895- *WhWNAA*
Jackson, Dunham 1888-1946 *DcNAA*
Jackson, E A *Alli Sup*
Jackson, Edgar Stanaway *Alli Sup*
Jackson, Edward 1856-1942 *DcNAA*
Jackson, Edward Dudley 1808-1879 *Alli,*
Alli Sup, ChPo
Jackson, Edward Payson 1840-1905 *Alli Sup,*
BiD&SB, ChPo, DcAmA, DcNAA
Jackson, Edward Steane *Alli Sup*
Jackson, Elaine *BlkAW*
Jackson, Elmer Martin, Jr. 1906- *WhWNAA*
Jackson, Emma Lou *BlkAW*
Jackson, Eric *MnBBF*
Jackson, Erna *ChPo S1*
Jackson, Esther Merle 1922- *ConAu 13R*
Jackson, Ethel A *ChPo*
Jackson, Eugenia Lutcher *BlkAW*
Jackson, Eva E 1858-1956 *OhA&B*
Jackson, F S *ChPo S1*
Jackson, Francis 1789-1861 *Alli Sup, DcAmA,*
DcNAA
Jackson, Frank G *Alli Sup*
Jackson, Franklin *BlkAW*
Jackson, Franz 1912- *AmSCAP 66*
Jackson, Fred A *ChPo, ChPo S1*
Jackson, Fred Kinney 1874- *WhWNAA*
Jackson, Frederica *ChPo*
Jackson, Frederick *Alli, AmA&B*
Jackson, Frederick 1886-1953 *AmA&B*
Jackson, Frederick Ellsworth 1879-1963
IndAu 1917
Jackson, Frederick George 1860-1938 *NewC,*
WhLA
Jackson, Frederick J *Alli Sup*
Jackson, Frederick John Foakes 1855-1941
AmA&B, WhWNAA
Jackson, G Hunt *Alli Sup*
Jackson, Gabriel 1921- *ConAu 21*
Jackson, Gabriele Bernhard 1934- *ConAu 29*
Jackson, Gabrielle Emilie 1861- *AmA&B,*
DcAmA
Jackson, Gainor W 1926- *WrD 1976*
Jackson, Genevieve Vaughan *IlCB 1956*
Jackson, Geoffrey 1915- *ConAu 61,*
WrD 1976
Jackson, George *Alli, BbtC, BiDLA,*
ChPo S2
Jackson, George 1864- *WhLA*
Jackson, George Anson 1846-1907 *Alli Sup,*
DcAmA, DcNAA
Jackson, George Frederick 1836-1869 *Alli Sup*
Jackson, George Frederick 1906- *IndAu 1917*
Jackson, George Leroy 1875- *WhWNAA*
Jackson, George Pullen 1874-1953 *AmA&B,*
REnAL, WhWNAA
Jackson, George Russell *Alli Sup*
Jackson, George S 1906-1976 *ConAu 61,*
ConAu P-1
Jackson, George Thomas 1852-1916 *Alli Sup,*
DcAmA, DcNAA
Jackson, Georgina F *Alli Sup*
Jackson, Gordon Noel 1913- *WrD 1976*
Jackson, Greig Stewart 1918- *AmSCAP 66*
Jackson, H M *OxCan*
Jackson, Hall d1797 *Alli*
Jackson, Harold Thomas 1897- *Au&Wr,*
WrD 1976
Jackson, Harry *MnBBF*
Jackson, Harvey *MnBBF*
Jackson, Helen *ChPo S1*
Jackson, Helen Hunt 1831-1885 *Alli Sup,*
AmA, AmA&B, BbD, BiD&SB, CarSB,
CasWL, ChPo, ChPo S1, ChPo S2,
CnDAL, DcAmA, DcBiA, DcLEnL,
DcNAA, EvLB, JBA 1934, MouLC 4,
OxAm, REn, REnAL, St&VC

Jackson, Henry *Alli, Alli Sup*
Jackson, Henry 1798-1863 *Alli, DcNAA*
Jackson, Henry 1831-1879 *Alli Sup, BiD&SB*
Jackson, Henry Ezekiel 1869-1939 *DcNAA*
Jackson, Henry Martin 1912- *WhPNW*
Jackson, Henry Rootes 1820-1898 *Alli, AmA,*
AmA&B, BiDSA, ChPo, ChPo S1,
CyAL 2, DcAmA, DcNAA
Jackson, Herbert C 1917- *ConAu 9R,*
WrD 1976
Jackson, Herbert G, Jr. 1928- *ConAu 37,*
WrD 1976
Jackson, Holbrook 1874-1948 *ChPo, ChPo S2,*
DcLEnL, EvLB, LongC, NewC, REn,
TwCA, TwCA Sup
Jackson, Holmes Condict 1875-1927 *DcNAA*
Jackson, Howard *MnBBF*
Jackson, Howard Manucy 1900- *AmSCAP 66*
Jackson, Humphrey *Alli*
Jackson, I *ChPo S1*
Jackson, Isaac Rand d1845 *DcNAA*
Jackson, Isaac Wilber 1805?-1877 *Alli,*
CyAL 1, DcAmA, DcNAA
Jackson, J Denis *BlkAW*
Jackson, J F *Alli, BiDLA*
Jackson, J L *Alli*
Jackson, J M *Alli Sup*
Jackson, J R *Alli*
Jackson, Jacob Hugh 1891- *WhWNAA*
Jackson, Jacqueline 1928- *ConAu 45*
Jackson, Jacquelyne Johnson 1932- *ConAu 37*
Jackson, James *Alli, OxCan*
Jackson, James 1757-1806 *BiDSA*
Jackson, James 1777-1867 *DcAmA, DcNAA*
Jackson, James 1810-1834 *DcNAA*
Jackson, James 1819-1887 *BiDSA*
Jackson, James A *OxCan Sup*
Jackson, James Caleb 1811-1895 *Alli Sup,*
DcAmA, DcNAA
Jackson, James Charles 1936- *WrD 1976*
Jackson, James Grey *Alli, BiDLA*
Jackson, James Sutton *PoIre*
Jackson, James Thomas *BlkAW*
Jackson, Janet *ChPo S2*
Jackson, Jay *WhWNAA*
Jackson, Jeremiah *Alli, BiDLA*
Jackson, Jesse 1908- *AuBYP, BlkAW,*
ConAu 25, LivBA, OhA&B, SmATA 2
Jackson, Jill 1913- *AmSCAP 66*
Jackson, Jo *BlkAW*
Jackson, John *Alli, Alli Sup, BiDLA*
Jackson, John d1807 *Alli*
Jackson, John d1857 *PoIre*
Jackson, John 1686-1763 *Alli, DcEnL*
Jackson, John 1811-1885 *Alli Sup*
Jackson, John, Jr. *Alli, BiDLA*
Jackson, John Archer 1929- *ConAu 13R*
Jackson, John D 1834-1875 *Alli Sup, DcNAA*
Jackson, John Edward *Alli Sup, ChPo*
Jackson, John Glover 1907- *LivBA*
Jackson, John Howard 1932- *ConAu 41*
Jackson, John Hughlings *Alli Sup*
Jackson, John Mills *Alli, BbtC, BiDLA,*
OxCan
Jackson, John N 1925- *ConAu 37, WrD 1976*
Jackson, John Oswald *Alli Sup*
Jackson, John P *Alli Sup*
Jackson, John Price *WhWNAA*
Jackson, John Robert *BlkAW*
Jackson, John William *Alli, Alli Sup, PoIre*
Jackson, Jonathan 1743-1810 *DcAmA,*
DcNAA
Jackson, Joseph *Alli, BiDLA*
Jackson, Joseph 1847-1924 *DcNAA*
Jackson, Joseph 1867-1946 *AmA&B, DcNAA,*
WhWNAA
Jackson, Joseph 1924- *Au&Wr, ConAu P-1*
Jackson, Joseph Cooke 1835-1913 *DcNAA*
Jackson, Joseph Edward *Alli Sup*
Jackson, Joseph Henry 1894-1955 *AmA&B,*
REnAL, TwCA, TwCA Sup, WhWNAA
Jackson, Josephine *Alli Sup*
Jackson, Joy J 1928- *ConAu 29*
Jackson, Julian *MnBBF*
Jackson, Sir K A *Alli*
Jackson, Katherine Gauss 1904-1975 *ConAu 57*
Jackson, Kathryn 1907- *ChPo, ChPo S1*
Jackson, Keith 1928- *ConAu 61*

Jackson, Kenneth Terry 1939- *ConAu 21,*
WrD 1976
Jackson, Miss L E H *Alli Sup*
Jackson, Laura F *AmA&B*
Jackson, Laura Riding 1901- *AmA&B,*
ConP 1970, ConP 1975, TwCA Sup,
WrD 1976
Jackson, Laurence *Alli*
Jackson, Leguin Henry *BiDLA*
Jackson, LeRoy Freeman 1881- *ChPo*
Jackson, Lewis *MnBBF*
Jackson, Lewis Evans 1822- *DcAmA*
Jackson, Lewis D'Augilar *Alli Sup*
Jackson, Lucille *ConAu XR*
Jackson, Mae 1946- *BlkAW, ChPo S2,*
DrAP 1975
Jackson, Mahalia 1901-1972 *ConAu 33*
Jackson, Margaret Doyle 1868- *AmA&B,*
DcAmA
Jackson, Margaret Hastings 1861-1939 *DcNAA*
Jackson, Margaret Weymouth 1895- *AmA&B,*
AuNews 1, IndAu 1917
Jackson, Marian 1922- *Au&Wr*
Jackson, Mary 1924- *ConAu 61*
Jackson, Mary Anna d1915 *BiDSA, DcNAA*
Jackson, Mary Catherine *Alli Sup*
Jackson, Mary Coleman *AuBYP*
Jackson, Mason *Alli Sup*
Jackson, Matthew *Alli*
Jackson, Mike 1888-1945 *AmSCAP 66*
Jackson, Miles *Alli*
Jackson, Miles Merrill, Jr. 1929- *ConAu 41,*
LivBAA
Jackson, Moses *Alli Sup*
Jackson, Nell C 1929- *LivBA*
Jackson, Neville 1923- *ConAu XR,*
WrD 1976
Jackson, Nora 1915- *Au&Wr, ConAu XR,*
WrD 1976
Jackson, Norman 1932- *ConAu 25,*
ConP 1970
Jackson, Mrs. Nugent *ChPo S1*
Jackson, O B *AuBYP, SmATA 6*
Jackson, Orpha *AuBYP*
Jackson, Paul R 1905- *ConAu P-1*
Jackson, Percival Ephrates 1891- *ConAu 1R*
Jackson, Peter *Alli*
Jackson, Peter 1928- *ConP 1970*
Jackson, Peter William Russell 1926-
WrD 1976
Jackson, Philander *MnBBF*
Jackson, Philip W 1928- *ConAu 23*
Jackson, Phyllis *ChPo*
Jackson, Phyllis Wynn 1898-1959 *AmA&B,*
IndAu 1917
Jackson, Potter *BiDLA*
Jackson, R E *ConAu XR*
Jackson, R Orlando *BlkAW*
Jackson, R W *ChPo*
Jackson, Randle *Alli, BiDLA*
Jackson, Richard *Alli, BlkAW*
Jackson, Richard A *ChPo S2*
Jackson, Richard Charles *Alli Sup*
Jackson, Richard Meredith 1903- *Au&Wr*
Jackson, Robert 1751-1827 *Alli, BiDLA*
Jackson, Robert 1911- *Au&Wr, ConAu 9R*
Jackson, Robert Blake 1926- *AuBYP,*
ConAu 5R, SmATA 8
Jackson, Robert Edmund Scoresby- *Alli Sup*
Jackson, Robert J *Alli Sup*
Jackson, Robert J 1936- *ConAu 25,*
WrD 1976
Jackson, Robert Montgomery Smith 1815-1865
Alli Sup, DcNAA
Jackson, Robert S 1926- *ConAu 29*
Jackson, Robert Tracy 1861-1948 *DcNAA,*
WhWNAA
Jackson, Robert Wyse 1908- *Au&Wr*
Jackson, Rosemary Elizabeth 1917- *WrD 1976*
Jackson, Rowland *Alli, Alli Sup*
Jackson, Roy William 1907- *AmSCAP 66*
Jackson, Ruth A *ConAu 45*
Jackson, S Wesley 1936- *ConAu 33*
Jackson, Sally *ConAu XR, SmATA XR*
Jackson, Sam *ConAu XR*
Jackson, Samuel *Alli*
Jackson, Samuel 1787-1872 *DcAmA, DcNAA*
Jackson, Samuel Macauley 1851-1912 *AmA&B,*

DcAmA, DcNAA
Jackson, Samuel Trevena 1869- *ChPo*
Jackson, Sara *ChPo S1*
Jackson, Sarah *Alli*
Jackson, Seguin Henry *Alli*
Jackson, Sheldon 1834-1909 *Alli Sup,
BiD&SB, DcAmA, DcNAA*
Jackson, Shirley 1919-1965 *AmA&B, AmNov,
ConAu 1R, ConAu 25, ConNov 1976,
LongC, ModAL, OxAm, Pen Am,
RAdv 1, REn, REnAL, SmATA 2,
TwCA Sup*
Jackson, Spencer *Alli Sup, BlkAW*
Jackson, T *Alli, ChPo*
Jackson, Tatlow *Alli Sup, DcNAA*
Jackson, Theodore *Alli*
Jackson, Thomas *Alli*
Jackson, Thomas d1646 *Alli*
Jackson, Thomas 1579-1640 *Alli, DcEnL*
Jackson, Thomas 1773-1837 *DcEnL*
Jackson, Thomas 1783-1873 *Alli Sup*
Jackson, Thomas 1812-1886 *Alli Sup*
Jackson, Thomas Graham 1835- *Alli Sup*
Jackson, Thomas Jonathan 1824-1863 *REn,
REnAL*
Jackson, Thomas William 1867-1934 *DcNAA*
Jackson, Thomas Wright 1869-1925 *DcNAA,
OhA&B*
Jackson, Timothy *Alli*
Jackson, W *Alli*
Jackson, W A *Alli*
Jackson, W A Douglas 1923- *ConAu 45*
Jackson, W G F 1917- *ConAu 25*
Jackson, W R Hall *ChPo S2*
Jackson, W T *Alli Sup*
Jackson, W T H 1915- *ConAu 1R*
Jackson, W Turrentine 1915- *ConAu 13R*
Jackson, W Warner *BlkAW*
Jackson, Walter H *Alli Sup*
Jackson, Wes 1936- *ConAu 49*
Jackson, Wilfrid *ChPo S2*
Jackson, Will *BlkAW*
Jackson, William *Alli, Alli Sup, BbtC,
BiDLA*
Jackson, William d1795 *Alli*
Jackson, William 1730-1803 *Alli*
Jackson, William 1750-1815 *Alli, DcEnL*
Jackson, William C *ChPo*
Jackson, William Henry 1843-1942 *AmA&B,
DcNAA*
Jackson, William Keith 1928- *WrD 1976*
Jackson, William Peter Uprichard 1918-
WrD 1976
Jackson, William Robert *Alli Sup*
Jackson, William V *ChPo S1*
Jackson, William Vernon 1926- *ConAu 23*
Jackson, William Walrond *Alli Sup*
Jackson, Winifred Virginia *AnMV 1926,
ChPo S1*
Jackson, Z *Alli*
Jacno, Marcel 1904- *WhGrA*
Jaco, E Gartly 1923- *ConAu 1R, WrD 1976*
Jacob *Alli*
Jacob Ben Asher 1269?-1343 *CasWL*
Jacob Frances *CasWL*
Jacob Le Bibliophile *OxFr*
Jacob Of Serug *CasWL*
Jacob, Alaric 1909- *Au&Wr, ConAu 5R*
Jacob, Alexander *Alli*
Jacob, Archibald Hamilton *Alli Sup*
Jacob, Arthur *Alli, Alli Sup*
Jacob, Bruno 1881- *WhLA*
Jacob, Cary Franklin 1885- *AnMV 1926*
Jacob, Charles E 1931- *ConAu 13R*
Jacob, Edith S *Alli Sup*
Jacob, Edward d1788 *Alli*
Jacob, Edward d1841 *Alli*
Jacob, Edward Frederick Fulford 1882-1928
DcNAA
Jacob, Edwin Frederick Fulford 1882-1928
CanNov
Jacob, Ephraim A *Alli Sup*
Jacob, Ernest Fraser 1894- *ConAu 1R*
Jacob, Eustace Wilberforce *Alli Sup*
Jacob, Fred 1882-1926 *OxCan*
Jacob, G A *Alli*
Jacob, George Adolphus *Alli Sup*
Jacob, George Andrew *Alli Sup*

Jacob, Sir George LeGrand *Alli Sup*
Jacob, Gertrude L *Alli Sup*
Jacob, Giles 1686-1744 *Alli, DcEnL*
Jacob, Hans 1896- *WhLA*
Jacob, Henry *Alli*
Jacob, Henry 1563-1624 *Alli, BiDLA, DcEnL*
Jacob, Henry 1606?-1652 *Alli*
Jacob, Hildebrand *Alli*
Jacob, Isaac 1908- *Au&Wr*
Jacob, John *Alli*
Jacob, John 1812-1858 *Alli Sup*
Jacob, John Alexander *Alli Sup*
Jacob, John G *DcNAA*
Jacob, Joseph *Alli*
Jacob, M *Alli*
Jacob, Max 1876-1944 *CasWL, ClDMEuL,
CnMWL, EncWL, EvEuW, ModRL,
OxFr, Pen Eur, REn, WhTwL, WorAu*
Jacob, Michelle *OxCan Sup*
Jacob, Nancy L 1943- *ConAu 29*
Jacob, Naomi Ellington 1889?-1964 *CatA 1947,
DcLEnL, EvLB, LongC, NewC, Pen Eng,
TwCA, TwCA Sup, TwCW, WhWNAA*
Jacob, Paul 1940- *ConP 1970, ConP 1975,
WrD 1976*
Jacob, Philip E 1914- *ConAu 53*
Jacob, Philip Whittington d1890 *Alli Sup*
Jacob, Piers Anthony Dillingham 1934-
ConAu 23, WrD 1976
Jacob, T Evan *Alli Sup*
Jacob, Violet 1863-1946 *CasWL, ChPo, EvLB,
NewC, Pen Eng*
Jacob, W J *Alli Sup*
Jacob, W S *Alli*
Jacob, William d1851 *Alli, BiDLA,
BiDLA Sup*
Jacobi, Abraham 1830-1919 *Alli Sup, DcAmA,
DcNAA*
Jacobi, Carl 1908- *ConAu P-1*
Jacobi, Charles Thomas *Alli Sup*
Jacobi, Franz Ernst 1864- *WhLA*
Jacobi, Frederick 1891-1952 *AmSCAP 66*
Jacobi, Friedrich Heinrich 1743-1819 *BbD,
BiD&SB, CasWL, EvEuW, OxGer, REn*
Jacobi, Hermann Georg *Alli Sup*
Jacobi, Johann Carl 1807- *WhLA*
Jacobi, Johann Georg 1740-1814 *BiD&SB,
CasWL, OxGer, Pen Eur*
Jacobi, John Christian *ChPo S1*
Jacobi, Jolande Szekacs 1890- *Au&Wr,
BiDPar, ConAu 9R*
Jacobi, Mary 1842-1906 *Alli Sup, BiD&SB,
DcAmA, DcNAA*
Jacobs, A Gertrude *ChPo*
Jacobs, Al 1903- *AmSCAP 66*
Jacobs, Albert Poole 1853-1909 *Alli Sup,
DcNAA*
Jacobs, Allen S *WhWNAA*
Jacobs, Alma Sylvia *WhWNAA*
Jacobs, Anne Marguerite 1889- *OhA&B*
Jacobs, Arthur David 1922- *ConAu 5R,
WrD 1976*
Jacobs, Beth *AuBYP*
Jacobs, Caroline Elliott 1835-1916 *DcNAA*
Jacobs, Caroline Emilia 1872-1909 *DcNAA*
Jacobs, Charles Michael 1875-1938 *AmA&B,
DcNAA*
Jacobs, Clyde E 1925- *ConAu 37*
Jacobs, Dan N 1925- *ConAu 5R, WrD 1976*
Jacobs, David Michael 1942- *ConAu 57*
Jacobs, Dick 1918- *AmSCAP 66*
Jacobs, Edwin Elmore 1877- *WhWNAA*
Jacobs, Flora Gill 1918- *AuBYP, ConAu 1R,
SmATA 2*
Jacobs, Francine 1935- *ConAu 49*
Jacobs, Frank 1929- *AuBYP, ConAu 13R,
WrD 1976*
Jacobs, Frederic *Alli*
Jacobs, Frederick B 1880-1942 *OhA&B,
WhWNAA*
Jacobs, G Walker 1948- *ConAu 49*
Jacobs, Gabrielle M *ChPo S2*
Jacobs, Glenn 1940- *ConAu 29*
Jacobs, Harold 1941- *ConAu 45*
Jacobs, Harvey 1915- *ConAu 21, IndAu 1917*
Jacobs, Harvey 1929- *ConAu 29*
Jacobs, Hayes B 1919- *ConAu 9R*
Jacobs, Helen *ChPo S1*

Jacobs, Helen Hull 1908- *AmA&B, Au&Wr,
AuBYP, ConAu 9R, WrD 1976*
Jacobs, Henry Barton 1858- *WhWNAA*
Jacobs, Henry Eyster 1844-1932 *Alli Sup,
DcAmA, DcNAA*
Jacobs, Herbert A 1903- *ConAu 13R*
Jacobs, J C H *WrD 1976*
Jacobs, J H *Alli Sup*
Jacobs, Jane 1916- *AmA&B, ConAu 21*
Jacobs, Jerry 1932- *ConAu 29*
Jacobs, John 1918- *ConAu 23*
Jacobs, John Adamson 1806-1869 *DcAmA,
DcNAA*
Jacobs, Joseph 1854-1916 *Alli Sup, AmA&B,
AnCL, BiD&SB, BrAu 19, CarSB,
Chmbr 3, DcAmA, DcNAA, JBA 1934,
REnAL, St&VC, WhCL*
Jacobs, Leah *ConAu XR*
Jacobs, Leland B *AuBYP, ChPo, ChPo S1,
ChPo S2*
Jacobs, Leo 1879- *WhWNAA*
Jacobs, Leslie *ChPo*
Jacobs, Lou, Jr. 1921- *ConAu 23, SmATA 2*
Jacobs, Louis 1920- *ConAu 1R, WrD 1976*
Jacobs, Melville 1902- *AmA&B, ConAu 1R*
Jacobs, Melvin Clay 1885- *WhWNAA*
Jacobs, Michael 1808-1871 *Alli Sup, DcAmA*
Jacobs, Michael William 1850- *Alli Sup,
DcAmA*
Jacobs, Michel 1877- *WhWNAA*
Jacobs, Milton 1920- *ConAu 37*
Jacobs, Monty 1875- *WhLA*
Jacobs, Morton P 1917- *AmSCAP 66*
Jacobs, Orange 1827-1914 *DcNAA*
Jacobs, Paul 1918- *AmA&B, ConAu 13R*
Jacobs, Pepita Jimenez 1932- *ConAu 17R*
Jacobs, Peter *BbtC*
Jacobs, Philip Peter 1879-1940 *DcNAA*
Jacobs, Robert D 1918- *ConAu 41*
Jacobs, Robert L 1904- *Au&Wr*
Jacobs, Roderick A 1934- *ConAu 23*
Jacobs, Samuel 1821-1891 *IndAu 1816*
Jacobs, Samuel William 1871-1938 *DcNAA*
Jacobs, Sarah Sprague 1813- *Alli, Alli Sup,
CyAL 2, DcAmA, DcNAA*
Jacobs, T C *Au&Wr*
Jacobs, T C H *ConAu XR, MnBBF*
Jacobs, T G *Alli*
Jacobs, Thornwell 1877-1956 *AmA&B, BiDSA,
ChPo, ChPo S1, WhWNAA*
Jacobs, Walter Darnell 1922- *ConAu 17R,
WrD 1976*
Jacobs, Wilbur Ripley 1918- *AmA&B,
ConAu 13R, WrD 1976*
Jacobs, William *Alli*
Jacobs, William Jay 1933- *ConAu 57*
Jacobs, William Leroy 1869-1917 *ChPo*
Jacobs, William Wymark 1863-1943 *BbD,
BiD&SB, CasWL, Chmbr 3, DcBiA,
DcEnA Ap, DcLEnL, EncM&D, EvLB,
LongC, MnBBF, ModBL, NewC, OxEng,
Pen Eng, REn, TwCA, TwCA Sup,
TwCW, WhLA*
Jacobs-Bond, Carrie *AmA&B*
Jacobsen, Gertrude Ann 1895-1942 *DcNAA*
Jacobsen, Hermann Johannes Heinrich 1898-
Au&Wr
Jacobsen, Janet *ChPo S1*
Jacobsen, Jens Peter 1847-1885 *BiD&SB,
CasWL, ClDMEuL, CyWA, DcEuL,
EuA, EvEuW, Pen Eur, REn*
Jacobsen, Jerome Vincent 1894- *Au&Wr*
Jacobsen, Jorgen-Frantz 1900-1938 *CasWL,
EvEuW, Pen Eur*
Jacobsen, Josephine 1908- *ConAu 33,
ConP 1975, DrAF 1976, DrAP 1975,
WrD 1976*
Jacobsen, Julius *Alli Sup*
Jacobsen, Lyle E 1929- *ConAu 13R*
Jacobsen, Marion Leach 1908- *ConAu 61*
Jacobsen, O Irving 1896- *ConAu 25*
Jacobsen, Peder Wilhelm 1799-1848 *DcEuL*
Jacobsen, Rolf 1907- *CasWL*
Jacobsohn, Paul 1868- *WhLA*
Jacobson, Augustus *Alli Sup*
Jacobson, C A 1876- *WhWNAA*
Jacobson, Dan 1929- *Au&Wr, CasWL,
ConAu 1R, ConLC 4, ConNov 1972,*

James, Mrs. A G F Eliot *Alli Sup*
James, Alan 1943- *Au&Wr, WrD 1976*
James, Alexander *Alli Sup, BbtC*
James, Alice Archer Sewall 1870-1955 *AmA&B, DcAmA, OhA&B*
James, Allen *ConAu XR*
James, Andrew *ConAu XR*
James, Anne *Alli Sup*
James, Arabella M *Alli Sup*
James, Arthur C *ChPo S1*
James, Arthur Walter 1912- *Au&Wr*
James, B *Alli Sup*
James, Barbara Ethel *Au&Wr*
James, Bartlett B *WhWNAA*
James, Beauregard *BlkAW*
James, Benjamin 1768-1825 *BiDSA, DcNAA*
James, Bernard R *MnBBF*
James, Bertha TenEyck *ChPo S1*
James, Bessie Rowland 1895- *AmA&B, WhWNAA*
James, Billy 1895-1965 *AmSCAP 66*
James, Brian *ConAu XR*
James, Bruce *MnBBF*
James, Bruno S 1906- *ConAu 5R*
James, Burnett 1919- *ConAu 5R*
James, Bushrod Washington 1836-1903 *DcAmA, DcNAA*
James, C B *ConAu 57*
James, C E *ChPo S2*
James, C T C *Alli Sup*
James, Cary A 1935- *ConAu 29*
James, Charles *Alli, Alli Sup, BiDLA*
James, Charles Canniff 1863-1916 *DcNAA*
James, Charles Fenton 1844-1902 *DcAmA, DcNAA*
James, Charles J 1944- *ConAu 53*
James, Charles Lyman 1934- *ConAu 29, LivBAA, WrD 1976*
James, Charles Pinckney 1818-1899 *DcNAA*
James, Croake *Alli Sup*
James, Cyril L R 1901- *CasWL, ConNov 1972, ConNov 1976, DcLEnL, WebEAL, WrD 1976*
James, D Bloomfield *Alli Sup*
James, D Clayton 1931- *ConAu 29*
James, D G 1905- *ConAu 1R*
James, David *Alli, BiDLA, MnBBF*
James, David Burnett Stephen 1919- *Au&Wr*
James, David Edward 1937- *Au&Wr, WrD 1976*
James, David Geraint 1922- *Au&Wr, WrD 1976*
James, David Henry 1881- *Au&Wr*
James, David Pelham 1919- *Au&Wr*
James, Denise *ConAu 29*
James, Don 1905- *ConAu 1R*
James, Dynely *ConAu XR, SmATA 6, ThBJA, WrD 1976*
James, Edgar C 1933- *ConAu 13R*
James, Edmund Janes 1855- *Alli Sup, DcAmA*
James, Edmund Janes 1855-1925 *DcNAA*
James, Edward *Alli, Alli Sup*
James, Edward 1885- *Au&Wr*
James, Edward T 1917- *ConAu 33*
James, Edwin *ConAu XR*
James, Edwin 1797-1861 *Alli, AmA&B, DcAmA, DcNAA, REnAL*
James, Edwin 1812?-1882 *Alli, Alli Sup*
James, Mrs. Edwin *Alli Sup*
James, Edwin Oliver 1888-1972 *Au&Wr, ChPo, ConAu P-1*
James, Eleanor 1912- *ConAu 41*
James, Elizabeth Mary *Alli, BiDLA*
James, Ella *Alli Sup*
James, Eric Arthur 1925- *Au&Wr, ConAu P-1*
James, Ernest *MnBBF*
James, Estelle 1935- *ConAu 37*
James, F M *ChPo*
James, Fleming 1874?-1959 *AmA&B, OhA&B*
James, Fleming, Jr. 1904- *ConAu P-1*
James, Florence *DcEnA Ap*
James, Florence Alice *Alli Sup*
James, Francis *Alli*
James, Francis Bacon 1864-1924 *OhA&B*
James, Frank Linsly *Alli Sup*
James, Franklin *OhA&B*

James, Freeman Kelly, Jr. 1927- *AmSCAP 66*
James, G *ChPo S1*
James, George Francis 1867-1932 *DcAmA, DcNAA*
James, George Oscar 1873-1931 *DcNAA*
James, George Payne Rainsford 1799?-1860 *Alli, BbD, BiD&SB, BrAu 19, CasWL, ChPo S1, Chmbr 3, DcBiA, DcEnA, DcEnL, DcEuL, DcLEnL, EvLB, HsB&A, MnBBF, NewC, OxEng, WebEAL*
James, George Wharton 1858-1923 *AmA&B, AmLY, DcAmA, DcNAA*
James, Gilbert *ChPo, IlCB 1945*
James, H F *Alli Sup*
James, H Thomas 1915- *ConAu 25*
James, Harold *IlBYP*
James, Harry 1916- *AmSCAP 66*
James, Harry Clebourne 1896- *ConAu 5R*
James, Hartwell *DcAmA*
James, Heather 1914- *ConAu 45, WrD 1976*
James, Helen *OxCan*
James, Henry *Alli, Chmbr 3*
James, Sir Henry 1803-1877 *Alli Sup*
James, Henry 1811-1882 *Alli Sup, AmA, AmA&B, BbD, BiD&SB, CyAL 2, DcAmA, DcNAA, OxAm, Pen Am, REnAL*
James, Henry 1843-1916 *Alli Sup, AmA, AmA&B, AmWr, AtlBL, BbD, BiD&SB, CasWL, CnDAL, CnMD, CnMWL, CnThe, CriT 3, CyWA, DcAmA, DcBiA, DcEnA, DcEnA Ap, DcEnL, DcEuL, DcLEnL, DcNAA, EncWL, EvLB, LongC, McGWD, ModAL, ModAL Sup, ModBL, ModBL Sup, ModWD, NewC, OxAm, OxEng, Pen Am, Pen Eng, RAdv 1, RCom, REn, REnAL, REnWD, TwCW, WebEAL, WhTwL*
James, Henry 1879-1947 *AmA&B, DcNAA, TwCA, TwCA Sup, WhWNAA*
James, Henry Alfred *Alli Sup*
James, Henry Ammon 1854-1929 *Alli Sup, BiDSA, DcAmA, DcNAA*
James, Henry Evan Murchison *Alli Sup*
James, Herbert Armitage 1844- *Alli Sup*
James, Herbert Wentworth *MnBBF*
James, Herman Gerlach 1887- *AmLY, OhA&B, WhWNAA*
James, Horatio *Alli Sup*
James, Hugo *Alli Sup*
James, Inez Eleanor 1919- *AmSCAP 66*
James, Isaac *Alli, BiDLA*
James, J *Alli Sup*
James, J H *Alli*
James, J H, Jr. *Alli Sup*
James, James *DcLEnL*
James, James Alton 1864-1962 *AmA&B, AmLY, DcAmA, WhWNAA*
James, James Henry *Alli Sup*
James, Jean Eileen 1934- *AmSCAP 66*
James, Jesse 1847-1882 *OxAm, REn, REnAL*
James, John *Alli, Alli Sup, Au&Wr, BiDLA, ChPo, ChPo S1, ConAu 45*
James, John Angell 1785-1859 *Alli, DcEnL*
James, John Haddy 1789-1869 *Alli Sup*
James, John Hough 1800-1881 *OhA&B*
James, John Ivor Pulsford 1913- *WrD 1976*
James, Sir John Kingston 1816-1893 *Alli Sup, PoIre*
James, John Thomas 1786-1829? *Alli, DcEnL*
James, Josef C 1916?-1973 *ConAu 45*
James, Joseph B 1912- *ConAu 17R*
James, Joseph Brindley *Alli Sup*
James, Josephine *ConAu XR, SmATA 6*
James, Judith *ConAu XR*
James, L *Alli*
James, L W *OxCan Sup*
James, Leonard F 1904- *ConAu 49*
James, Leslie 1915- *Au&Wr*
James, Lionel 1868- *WhLA*
James, Lionel 1871- *ChPo S1, WhLA*
James, Lizzie *Alli Sup*
James, Louis 1933- *ChPo S1, ConAu 13R, WrD 1976*
James, M E *Alli Sup*
James, M R 1940- *ConAu 57*
James, Maria 1793-1868 *Alli, ChPo, DcNAA*

James, Marian *Alli, Alli Sup*
James, Marion 1913- *AmSCAP 66*
James, Marlise Ann 1945- *ConAu 57*
James, Marmaduke *Alli*
James, Marquis 1891-1955 *AmA&B, OxAm, REnAL, TwCA Sup, WhWNAA*
James, Martha *AmA&B*
James, Mary Dagworthy 1810-1883 *Alli Sup, DcNAA*
James, Matthew *ConAu XR, WrD 1976*
James, Maurice Theodore 1905- *IndAu 1917*
James, Michael 1932- *Au&Wr*
James, Montague Rhodes 1862-1936 *DcLEnL, EvLB, LongC, NewC, OxEng, Pen Eng, TwCA, TwCA Sup, TwCW, WhLA*
James, Moses Prosser *Alli Sup*
James, Neill 1902- *AmA&B*
James, Noel David Glaves 1911- *Au&Wr, WrD 1976*
James, Norah Cordner 1900- *Au&Wr, ConAu 29, LongC, TwCA, TwCA Sup*
James, Norma Wood *AuBYP*
James, Mrs. Orrin *Alli Sup, HsB&A, HsB&A Sup*
James, P D 1920- *ConAu 21, EncM&D*
James, Paul *Alli Sup, AmA&B, ConAu XR*
James, Peter N 1940- *ConAu 57*
James, Philip *Alli Sup*
James, Philip 1890- *AmSCAP 66*
James, Philip Brutton 1901- *ChPo, ChPo S1, ChPo S2*
James, Philip Seaforth 1914- *Au&Wr, ConAu P-1, WrD 1976*
James, Police Captain *DcNAA*
James, Preston E 1899- *Au&Wr, ConAu 45*
James, Richard 1592-1638 *Alli*
James, Richard Moore *Alli Sup*
James, Richard Sexton 1824- *DcAmA*
James, Robert 1703-1776 *Alli*
James, Robert C 1918- *ConAu 5R*
James, Robert Leigh 1918- *Au&Wr*
James, Robert Rhodes 1933- *Au&Wr, ConAu 17R*
James, Ronald *ConAu XR*
James, Roy *ChPo S2*
James, S *Alli*
James, S T *MnBBF*
James, Samuel *Alli, BiDLA*
James, Samuel Benjamin *Alli Sup*
James, Samuel Humphreys 1857- *AmA&B, BiDSA, DcAmA, DcNAA*
James, Silas *Alli*
James, Simon *ConAu XR*
James, Sophie A M *PoIre*
James, Stanley Bloomfield 1869- *CatA 1947*
James, Sydney V 1929- *ConAu 1R, WrD 1976*
James, T F *ConAu XR, SmATA 8*
James, T Horton *Alli*
James, T S *Alli Sup*
James, T W *Alli Sup*
James, Thelma Gray 1899- *ConAu 5R*
James, Theodore, Jr. 1934- *ConAu 33, WrD 1976*
James, Theodore E 1913- *ConAu 57*
James, Thomas *Alli, ChPo S1*
James, Thomas d1804 *Alli*
James, Thomas 1571-1629 *Alli, DcEnL*
James, Thomas 1593?-1635? *BbD, OxCan*
James, Thomas 1782-1847 *DcNAA, OxAm*
James, Thomas 1809-1863 *Alli Sup*
James, Thomas Chalkley 1766-1835 *Alli, DcAmA*
James, Thomas D *Alli Sup*
James, Thomas Henry *Alli Sup*
James, Thomas N *ConAu 57*
James, Thomas Potts 1803?-1882 *DcAmA, DcNAA*
James, U P And Joseph F *Alli Sup*
James, Vernon *MnBBF*
James, W *Alli Sup*
James, W, And Grassi, G *Alli*
James, W And Mole, A *Alli*
James, W F *Alli Sup*
James, Walter 1905- *Au&Wr*
James, Walter 1912- *Au&Wr, ConAu 5R*
James, Walter Herman 1873- *WhWNAA*
James, Warren E 1922- *ConAu 45*

James, Weldon 1912- *ConAu 1R*
James, Will 1892-1942 *AuBYP, DcNAA, JBA 1934, JBA 1951, Newb 1922, OxAm, REnAL, TwCA, TwCA Sup, WhWNAA*
James, Will 1896- *AmSCAP 66*
James, William *Alli, Alli Sup, BiDLA, Chmbr 3*
James, William d1827 *Alli, BbtC, DcEnL*
James, William 1787-1861 *Alli Sup*
James, William 1818-1864 *ChPo*
James, William 1842-1910 *AmA, AmA&B, AmWr, AtlBL, BiD&SB, BiDPar, CasWL, CyWA, DcAmA, DcEuL, DcLEnL, DcNAA, EvLB, LongC, ModAL, ModAL Sup, NewC, OxAm, OxEng, Pen Am, RCom, REn, REnAL, WebEAL, WhTwL*
James, William Bosville *Alli*
James, William M *ConAu 57*
James, Sir William Milbourne 1807-1881 *Alli Sup*
James, William Milbourne 1881- *ConAu P-1*
James, William Powell 1837-1885 *Alli Sup*
James, William Roderick 1892-1942 *AmA&B, DcNAA*
James Of Rusholme, Lord 1909- *Au&Wr*
Jameson *Alli*
Jameson, Mrs. 1797-1860 *DcEnL*
Jameson, Anna Brownell Murphy 1794-1860 *Alli, BbtC, BrAu 19, BiD&SB, CanWr, ChPo S1, Chmbr 3, DcEnA, EvLB, NewC, OxCan, OxEng*
Jameson, Annie Edith *WhLA*
Jameson, Ephraim Orcutt 1832?-1902 *DcAmA, DcNAA*
Jameson, Eric *ConAu XR, WrD 1976*
Jameson, Francis James *Alli Sup*
Jameson, Helen D *ChPo*
Jameson, Henry W *Alli Sup*
Jameson, Horatio Gates 1778-1855 *Alli Sup, DcNAA*
Jameson, James *Alli Sup*
Jameson, John Alexander 1824-1890 *Alli Sup, DcAmA, DcNAA*
Jameson, John Franklin 1859-1937 *Alli Sup, AmA&B, DcAmA, DcNAA, OxAm, REnAL*
Jameson, Sir Leander Starr 1853-1917 *NewC*
Jameson, Malcolm 1891-1945 *AuBYP*
Jameson, Margaret *Alli Sup*
Jameson, Margaret Storm 1897- *DcLEnL, EvLB*
Jameson, Marg Storm SEE Jameson, Storm
Jameson, Mary Booth Tarkington 1881-1937 *IndAu 1917*
Jameson, Newton Booth Tarkington 1908-1956 *IndAu 1917*
Jameson, R *Alli*
Jameson, R G *Alli*
Jameson, R S *Alli*
Jameson, Raymond Deloy 1896- *WhWNAA*
Jameson, Robert *Alli Sup, MnBBF*
Jameson, Robert 1773-1854 *Alli, BiDLA*
Jameson, Robert F *Alli*
Jameson, Robert William 1805-1856 *Alli*
Jameson, Robert William 1805-1868 *BiD&SB*
Jameson, Samuel H 1896- *ConAu 45*
Jameson, Storm 1897- *Au&Wr, ConNov 1972, ConNov 1976, LongC, ModBL, NewC, Pen Eng, REn, TwCA, TwCA Sup, TwCW, WrD 1976*
Jameson, Storm ALSO Jameson, M Storm
Jameson, Thomas *Alli, BiDLA*
Jameson, Vic 1924- *ConAu 17R*
Jameson, William *Alli*
Jamet, Albert 1883-1948 *DcNAA*
Jami, $'abd-Urrahman 1414-1492 *BbD, BiD&SB*
Jami, Moulana 'Abdorrahman 1414-1492 *DcOrL 3*
Jami, Nur-Al-Din 'Abd-Al-Rahman 1414-1492 *CasWL, Pen Cl*
Jamiaque, Yves 1922- *CnMD*
Jamie, William 1818-1864 *ChPo S1*
Jamieson, Mrs. *Alli*
Jamieson, Alexander *Alli, BiDLA Sup*
Jamieson, Andrew *Alli Sup*

Jamieson, David T *ChPo*
Jamieson, Eleanore *ChPo S2*
Jamieson, Frances *Alli Sup*
Jamieson, George *Alli Sup*
Jamieson, George Auldjo *Alli Sup*
Jamieson, James· *Alli*
Jamieson, Jane H *Alli Sup*
Jamieson, John *Alli Sup*
Jamieson, John 1759-1838 *Alli, BiDLA, DcEnL, EvLB, NewC, OxEng*
Jamieson, Leland Shattuck 1904-1941 *DcNAA, WhWNAA*
Jamieson, Michael 1938- *Au&Wr*
Jamieson, Nina Moore 1885-1932 *CanNov, DcNAA, OxCan, WhWNAA*
Jamieson, Paul F 1903- *ConAu P-1*
Jamieson, Peter *ConP 1970*
Jamieson, Robert *Alli, Alli Sup, BiDLA, ChPo S2, DcEnL*
Jamieson, Robert 1780?-1844 *ChPo*
Jamieson, Robert 1803-1880 *Alli Sup*
Jamieson, Robert Dickson 1834- *ChPo S1*
Jamieson, Stuart *OxCan Sup*
Jamieson, T F *Alli Sup*
Jamieson, Thomas *Alli Sup*
Jamieson, W F *Alli Sup*
Jamieson, William C E *Alli Sup*
Jamineau, I *Alli*
Jamison, Alcinous Berton 1851-1938 *OhA&B*
Jamison, Andrew 1948- *ConAu 29*
Jamison, Cecilia Viets 1837?-1909 *Alli Sup, AmA, AmA&B, BiD&SB, BiDSA, DcAmA, DcNAA*
Jamison, David d1909 *PoIre*
Jamison, David Flavel 1810-1864 *Alli Sup, AmA, BiDSA, DcNAA*
Jamison, F B *Alli Sup*
Jamison, Henrietta L *ChPo*
Jamison, Jane *WhWNAA*
Jamison, John Cary *ChPo*
Jamison, Minnie Lou 1866- *WhWNAA*
Jamison, Roscoe Conkling 1888-1918 *BlkAW*
Jamme, Albert 1916- *ConAu 5R, WrD 1976*
Jammes, Francis 1868-1938 *CasWL, CatA 1947, ChPo, ClDMEuL, EncWL, EvEuW, ModRL, NewC, OxEng, OxFr, Pen Eur, REn, TwCA, TwCA Sup, WhTwL*
Jammes, Jean Raymond Jules 1926- *Au&Wr*
Jamyn, Amadis 1538?-1585 *BiD&SB, DcEuL, OxFr*
Jan *ConAu XR*
Jan I 1252-1594 *DcEuL*
Jan De Rijmer *BiD&SB*
Jan Van Ruusbroec *EuA*
Jan, Arthur J *OxCan*
Jan, George P 1925- *ConAu 21*
Janakiraman, Ti 1921- *DcOrL 2*
Janayev, I V *DcOrL 3*
Janda, Bohumil 1831-1875 *BiD&SB*
Janda, Kenneth 1935- *ConAu 13R*
Janda, Victoria *ChPo S2*
Jandel, Ragnar 1895-1939 *ClDMEuL*
Jandl, Ernst 1925- *CasWL, OxGer*
Jandt, Fred E 1944- *ConAu 53*
Jane Seymour 1509?-1537 *REn*
Jane Shore *REn*
Jane, Joseph *Alli*
Jane, Mary Childs 1909- *AuBYP, ConAu 1R, SmATA 6*
Jane, V *Alli Sup*
Jane, William *Alli*
Janecek, Ota 1919- *WhGrA*
Janecke, Ernst Gustav Georg 1875- *WhLA*
Janelle, Pierre 1891- *CatA 1952*
Janes, E *Alli Sup*
Janes, Edward C 1908- *AuBYP*
Janes, Edwin Lines 1807-1875 *Alli Sup, DcAmA, DcNAA*
Janes, Frederic 1808- *ChPo S1*
Janes, Frederick *Alli Sup*
Janes, George Milton 1869-1936 *OhA&B*
Janes, Harold Davidson 1923- *IndAu 1917*
Janes, John *OxCan*
Janes, Lewis George 1844-1901 *AmA, DcAmA, DcNAA*
Janes, Margaret P *Alli Sup*
Janes, Robert *Alli*

Janes, Thomas *Alli, ChPo S1*
Janet, Lillian *WrD 1976*
Janet, Paul 1823-1899 *BiD&SB, OxFr*
Janevski, Slavko 1920- *ModSL 2*
Janeway, Eliot 1913- *AmA&B, WrD 1976*
Janeway, Elizabeth 1913- *AmA&B, AmNov, Au&Wr, AuBYP, AuNews 1, ChPo, ConAu 45, DrAF 1976, REnAL, TwCA Sup*
Janeway, Jacob Jones 1774-1858 *Alli, DcAmA*
Janeway, James 1636-1674 *Alli*
Janeway, Theodore Caldwell 1872-1917 *DcNAA*
Janeway, Thomas Leiper 1805-1895 *DcNAA*
Janey, Margaret *BlkAW*
Janger, Allen R 1932- *ConAu 29, WrD 1976*
Janice *AuBYP, ConAu XR*
Janicius, Klemens 1516-1543 *CasWL, EvEuW*
Janicki, Klemens 1516-1543 *CasWL*
Janifer, Laurence M 1933- *ConAu 9R*
Janik, Allan 1941- *ConAu 53*
Janin, Jules Gabriel 1804-1874 *BiD&SB, EvEuW, OxFr*
Janis, Elsie 1889-1956 *AmSCAP 66, OhA&B*
Janis, Irving L 1918- *ConAu 17R*
Janis, J Harold 1910- *ConAu 13R*
Janis, Joan Gardner 1926- *AmSCAP 66*
Janis, Sidney 1896- *AmA&B, Au&Wr*
Janis, Stephen 1907- *AmSCAP 66*
Janisch, Hudson Ralph *Alli Sup*
Janiver, Thomas A 1849-1913 *CarSB*
Jankowsky, Kurt Robert 1928- *ConAu 37*
Jannequin, Clement *OxFr*
Janner, Greville Ewan 1928- *Au&Wr, ConAu 13R*
Janney, Lucy N *Alli Sup*
Janney, Oliver Edward 1856-1930 *DcNAA*
Janney, Russell Dixon 1883?-1963 *AmA&B, AmNov, OhA&B, REnAL*
Janney, Samuel L *Alli*
Janney, Samuel Macpherson 1801-1880 *Alli, Alli Sup, AmA, AmA&B, BiDSA, ChPo S1, DcAmA, DcNAA*
Jannings, Emil 1887-1950 *REn*
Janoff, Ron *DrAP 1975*
Janosch 1931- *ChPo S1, ConAu XR, IlBYP, SmATA 8*
Janossy, Lajos 1912- *Au&Wr*
Janowitz, Maurice 1919- *AmA&B*
Janowitz, Morris 1919- *ConAu 13R*
Janowitz, Phyllis *DrAP 1975*
Janowski, Tadeus Marian 1923- *ConAu 53*
Janowski, Thaddeus-Marian 1923- *WrD 1976*
Janowsky, Oscar Isaiah 1900- *Au&Wr, ConAu 1R, ConAu 5R, WrD 1976*
Jans, Emerson *ConAu XR*
Jans, Zephyr *ConAu XR*
Jansen Enikel *OxGer*
Jansen, Bernhard 1877- *WhLA*
Jansen, Clifford J 1935- *ConAu 33*
Jansen, Cornelius 1585-1638 *DcEuL, OxFr, Pen Eur, REn*
Jansen, Jared *ConAu XR, SmATA XR, WrD 1976*
Jansen, John Frederick 1918- *ConAu 23, WrD 1976*
Jansen, Mogens B 1930- *Au&Wr*
Jansen, Reiner d1706 *AmA&B*
Jansenius 1585-1638 *OxFr*
Jansevskis, Jekabs 1865-1931 *CasWL*
Janson, Baldwin *Alli, BiDLA*
Janson, Charles William *Alli, BiDLA*
Janson, Donald 1921- *ConAu 5R*
Janson, Dora Jane *AuBYP*
Janson, Ellen *ChPo S2*
Janson, Hank *ConAu XR, WrD 1976*
Janson, Horst Woldemar 1913- *AuBYP, ConAu 1R, SmATA 9, WrD 1976*
Janson, Kristofer Nagel 1841-1917 *BiD&SB, ClDMEuL, EvEuW*
Janssen, Albrecht 1886- *WhLA*
Janssen, Frederick William *Alli Sup*
Janssen, Johann Theodor 1853- *WhLA*
Janssen, Johannes 1829-1891 *BiD&SB*
Janssen, Lawrence H 1921- *ConAu 13R*
Janssen, Milton W *BlkAW*
Janssen, Sir Stephen Theodore *Alli*
Janssen, Werner 1900- *AmSCAP 66*
Janssens, Paul Mary *ConAu 53*

Jefferys, C ChPo
Jefferys, Elizabeth Miller ChPo
Jefferys, John BiDLA
Jefferys, Nathaniel Alli, BiDLA
Jefferys, Thomas Alli
Jefferys, William Hamilton 1871-1945 AmA&B, AmLY, WhWNAA
Jeffray, James Alli, BiDLA
Jeffree, H W Alli Sup
Jeffrey, Adi-Kent Thomas 1916- ConAu 37, WrD 1976
Jeffrey, Agnes ChPo S1
Jeffrey, Alexander Alli
Jeffrey, David Lyle 1941- ConAu 57
Jeffrey, Edward Charles 1866- WhWNAA
Jeffrey, Ellen WhWNAA
Jeffrey, Lord Francis 1773-1850 Alli, BbD, BiD&SB, BrAu 19, CasWL, Chmbr 3, CriT 2, DcEnA, DcEnL, DcEuL, DcLEnL, EvLB, MouLC 3, NewC, OxEng, Pen Eng, WebEAL
Jeffrey, George Alli Sup
Jeffrey, Janet ChPo
Jeffrey, Lloyd Nicholas 1918- ConAu 37, WrD 1976
Jeffrey, Mildred ConAu 5R
Jeffrey, P Shaw ChPo
Jeffrey, Robert T Alli Sup
Jeffrey, Rosa Vertner 1828-1894 Alli Sup, AmA, AmA&B, BiD&SB, BiDSA, ChPo, DcAmA, DcNAA, LivFWS
Jeffrey, Russell Alli Sup
Jeffrey, Ruth ConAu XR
Jeffrey, William 1896-1946 ChPo, EvLB, Pen Eng
Jeffrey-Smith, May Thornton 1882- Au&Wr
Jeffreys, Lord d1703 Alli
Jeffreys, Mrs. Arnold Alli Sup
Jeffreys, C ChPo
Jeffreys, George 1678-1775 Alli, DcEnL
Jeffreys, Baron George Of Wem 1648-1689 REn
Jeffreys, H Alli
Jeffreys, Harold 1891- WhLA
Jeffreys, Henry Anthony Alli Sup
Jeffreys, John Gwyn 1809-1885 Alli Sup
Jeffreys, Julius Alli
Jeffreys, M E Alli Sup
Jeffreys, Montagu Vaughan Castelman 1900- Au&Wr, ConAu 5R, WrD 1976
Jeffreys, Raymond John 1896- OhA&B
Jeffreys, U M Grant 1864-1956 OhA&B
Jeffries, Benjamin Joy 1833-1915 Alli Sup, DcAmA, DcNAA
Jeffries, C IndAu 1816
Jeffries, Sir Charles Joseph 1896- Au&Wr, ConAu 5R
Jeffries, Charlie TexWr
Jeffries, Daniel Alli
Jeffries, Derwin J 1915- ConAu 57
Jeffries, Fayette BiDSA
Jeffries, George Fish Alli Sup
Jeffries, Graeme Montagu 1900- MnBBF
Jeffries, Graham Montague 1900- EncM&D
Jeffries, Guillane Lois 1933- Au&Wr
Jeffries, Herb AmSCAP 66
Jeffries, James Graydon 1901-1936 DcNAA, IndAu 1816, OhA&B
Jeffries, John 1744-1819 Alli
Jeffries, John Parsons 1815-1888 Alli Sup, OhA&B
Jeffries, Millard Dudley BiDSA
Jeffries, Ona 1893?-1973 ConAu 41
Jeffries, Richard 1848-1887 DcEuL, REn, WhCL
Jeffries, Roderic 1926- Au&Wr, AuBYP, ConAu 17R, EncM&D, SmATA 4
Jeffries, Virginia M 1911- ConAu 5R
Jeffries, Zay 1888- WhWNAA
Jeffs, Julian 1931- ConAu 37, WrD 1976
Jeffs, Rae 1921- ConAu 25, WrD 1976
Jefkins, Frank William 1920- Au&Wr, ConAu 13R, WrD 1976
Jege CasWL
Jegon, William Alli
Jehangir NewC
Jehudah Halevi 1086-1142? DcEuL
Jeitteles, Alois 1794-1858 OxGer
Jekyd, Nat Alli

Jekyl, Sir Joseph d1738 Alli
Jekyl, Thomas Alli
Jekyll, Gertrude 1843-1932 LongC, WhLA
Jekyll, Joseph Alli, BiDLA
Jekyll, Walter Alli Sup
Jelakomitch, Ivan EuA
Jelavich, Barbara 1923- ConAu 53
Jelesnik, Eugene 1914- AmSCAP 66
Jelf, Ernest Arthur 1868- WhLA
Jelf, George Edward Alli Sup
Jelf, Richard William 1798-1871 Alli, Alli Sup
Jelf, Wilfrid d1935 Br&AmS
Jelf, William Edward 1811-1875 Alli, Alli Sup
Jelf-Sharp, C ChPo
Jelinek, Ivan Maria Joseph 1909- Au&Wr
Jelinger, Christopher Alli
Jelks, John L 1870- WhWNAA
Jellacic, Josef 1801-1859 OxGer
Jellema, Roderick 1927- ConAu 41, DrAP 1975
Jellett, Henry Alli Sup
Jellett, Henry 1872- WhLA
Jellett, Hewitt Poole Alli Sup
Jellett, John Hewitt 1817-1888 Alli Sup
Jelley, Symmes M IndAu 1816
Jellicoe, A C M ChPo S1
Jellicoe, Ann 1927- CnThe, ConDr, CrCD, McGWD, ModWD, ModWD, NewC, REnWD, TwCW, WorAu, WrD 1976
Jellicoe, Geoffrey Alan 1900- Au&Wr, ConAu 13R
Jellicoe, John ChPo
Jellicoe, Sir John Rushworth 1859- WhLA
Jellicoe, S Charles d1902? PoIre
Jellicoe, Sidney 1906- ConAu 33
Jellicoe, Susan 1907- Au&Wr
Jellie, William Harvey Alli Sup
Jelliffe, Smith Ely 1866-1945 DcNAA, WhWNAA
Jellinek, Paul 1897- Au&Wr, ConAu 13R
Jellison, Charles Albert, Jr. 1924- ConAu 1R
Jelly, George Oliver 1909- WrD 1976
Jelly, Harry Alli
Jelly, Oliver 1909- Au&Wr
Jemison, Louisa BiDSA
Jemison, Mary 1743-1833 OxAm, REnAL
Jemmat, Mrs. Alli
Jemmat, William Alli
Jemmett, Charles Edward Alli Sup
Jemmett, William T Alli
Jemmott, Claudia E 1949- BlkAW
Jemne, Elsa Laubach 1888- IlCB 1945
Jenatsch, Georg 1596-1639 OxGer
Jencken, Ferdinand Edward d1881 Alli Sup
Jencken, Henry D Alli Sup
Jencks, Charles 1939- ConAu 49
Jencks, Chauncey C ChPo
Jencks, Christopher 1936- ConAu 49
Jenghiz Khan NewC
Jenings, Abraham Alli
Jenings, Edward Alli
Jenings, Elizabeth Janet Alli Sup
Jenings, John Alli
Jenison, Don P 1897- ConAu 17R
Jenison, Madge 1874-1960 AmA&B
Jenison, Robert Alli
Jenkin, Henrietta C 1807?-1885 Alli Sup, BiD&SB
Jenkin, Henry Charles Fleeming 1833-1885 Alli Sup
Jenkin, Robert 1656-1727 Alli
Jenkin, Thomas Alli
Jenkin, William Alli
Jenkins, A M Alli Sup
Jenkins, Alan 1914- Au&Wr, ConAu 57, WrD 1976
Jenkins, Alan C MnBBF
Jenkins, Alan Charles 1914- Au&Wr
Jenkins, Alexander Alli, BiDLA
Jenkins, Alexander Howell Alli Sup
Jenkins, Anne Alli Sup
Jenkins, Arthur Hugh 1880- WhWNAA
Jenkins, Brian OxCan Sup
Jenkins, Burris Atkins 1869-1945 AmA&B, BiDSA, DcNAA, WhWNAA
Jenkins, C Alli
Jenkins, C L 1940- Au&Wr
Jenkins, Charles 1786-1831 Alli

Jenkins, Charles Christopher 1882-1943 CanNov, DcNAA
Jenkins, Charles Francis 1865-1951 AmA&B, WhWNAA
Jenkins, Charles Francis 1867-1934 DcNAA, IndAu 1816, OhA&B
Jenkins, Clarke 1917- LivBA
Jenkins, Clive 1926- Au&Wr, ConAu 13R
Jenkins, D R Alli Sup
Jenkins, David 1586?-1667 Alli
Jenkins, Deaderick Franklin 1910- AmA&B, BlkAW
Jenkins, Dorothy Helen 1907-1972 ConAu 37
Jenkins, E J ChPo
Jenkins, Ebenezer Evans Alli Sup
Jenkins, Edward 1838- BbD, BiD&SB, DcEnL
Jenkins, Edward L 1866-1908 OhA&B
Jenkins, Eleanor B S ChPo S1
Jenkins, Eliza ChPo S1
Jenkins, Elizabeth ChPo S2
Jenkins, Elizabeth 1907- DcLEnL, WorAu
Jenkins, Ella 1924- AmSCAP 66
Jenkins, Ernest MnBBF
Jenkins, Ferrell 1936- ConAu 57
Jenkins, Frances 1872-1942 DcNAA, WhWNAA
Jenkins, Frances Briggs 1905- ConAu 25
Jenkins, Frank E 1854- WhWNAA
Jenkins, Geoffrey 1920- Au&Wr
Jenkins, George Alli Sup
Jenkins, Gladys Gardner 1901- ConAu 1R
Jenkins, Goeffrey 1920- ConAu 5R
Jenkins, Gordon 1910- AmSCAP 66
Jenkins, Gwyn 1919- ConAu 1R
Jenkins, H Campbell ChPo S2
Jenkins, Mrs. H E ChPo S2
Jenkins, Harold 1909- Au&Wr, ConAu 9R, WrD 1976
Jenkins, Henry Alli Sup
Jenkins, Herbert 1876-1923 NewC
Jenkins, Hermon Dutilh 1842-1918 OhA&B
Jenkins, Hester Donaldson 1869-1941 DcNAA
Jenkins, Holt M 1920- ConAu 17R
Jenkins, Howard Malcolm 1842-1902 Alli Sup, AmA&B, DcAmA, DcNAA
Jenkins, Iredell 1909- WrD 1976
Jenkins, Ivor 1913- Au&Wr
Jenkins, Jabez Alli Sup
Jenkins, James Archibald 1919- Au&Wr
Jenkins, James J 1923- ConAu 13R
Jenkins, Jennie ChPo
Jenkins, Jeremiah Alli
Jenkins, Jerry B 1949- ConAu 49
Jenkins, John Alli Sup, BbtC
Jenkins, John d1823 Alli
Jenkins, John 1813-1898 DcNAA
Jenkins, John 1928- ConAu 45
Jenkins, John David 1828-1876 Alli Sup
Jenkins, John Edward 1838- Alli Sup
Jenkins, John Geraint 1929- Au&Wr, ConAu 21, WrD 1976
Jenkins, John H ChPo S1
Jenkins, John Robin 1912- Au&Wr, ConAu 1R, WorAu
Jenkins, John Stilwell 1818-1852 Alli, AmA, AmA&B, BiD&SB, DcAmA, DcNAA
Jenkins, Joseph Alli, BiDLA
Jenkins, Joseph Willcox 1928- AmSCAP 66
Jenkins, Kenneth V 1930- ConAu 53
Jenkins, Sir Leoline 1623-1685 Alli
Jenkins, Louis 1942- ConAu 53, DrAP 1975
Jenkins, MacGregor 1869-1940 AmA&B, DcNAA, WhWNAA
Jenkins, Margaret Ezizabeth 1905- WorAu
Jenkins, Marie Magdalen 1909- ConAu 41, SmATA 7
Jenkins, Martin David 1904- IndAu 1917
Jenkins, Mary Alli Sup
Jenkins, May Carolyn Au&Wr
Jenkins, Michael 1936- ConAu 25, WrD 1976
Jenkins, Olaf Pitt 1889- IndAu 1917
Jenkins, Oliver ChPo
Jenkins, Oliver 1901- AnMV 1926
Jenkins, Oliver Louis d1869 Alli Sup, DcNAA
Jenkins, Oliver Peebles 1850-1935 DcNAA, OhA&B
Jenkins, Paul Burrill 1872-1936 AmLY,

DcNAA, WhWNAA
Jenkins, Ralph Carlton 1891-1946 *DcNAA*
Jenkins, Raymond Leonard 1935- *Au&Wr,*
WrD 1976
Jenkins, Robert C *Alli*
Jenkins, Robert Charles *Alli Sup*
Jenkins, Robert Smith 1870-1931 *DcNAA*
Jenkins, Robert Thomas 1881-1969 *CasWL*
Jenkins, Robin 1912- *CasWL, ConNov 1972,*
ConNov 1976, WorAu, WrD 1976
Jenkins, Romilly James Heald 1907- *ConAu 5R*
Jenkins, Roy Harris 1920- *Au&Wr,*
ConAu 9R, WorAu, WrD 1976
Jenkins, Samuel *Alli, Alli Sup*
Jenkins, Stephen 1857-1913 *DcNAA*
Jenkins, T *Alli*
Jenkins, T A *Alli*
Jenkins, Thomas *Alli, BiDLA*
Jenkins, Thomas Atkinson 1868-1935 *DcNAA*
Jenkins, Timothy *OhA&B*
Jenkins, Tudor Morgan 1894- *Au&Wr*
Jenkins, Vivian Gordon James 1911- *Au&Wr*
Jenkins, Warren *Alli*
Jenkins, Welborn Victor 1879- *BlkAW*
Jenkins, Will *ChPo*
Jenkins, Will F 1896-1975 *AmA&B,*
ConAu 9R, ConAu 57, WhWNAA
Jenkins, William *Alli*
Jenkins, William A 1922- *ConAu 61,*
SmATA 9
Jenkins, William H *BlkAW*
Jenkins, William Lemuel *Alli Sup*
Jenkins, William Still *Alli Sup*
Jenkinson, Anthony *Alli*
Jenkinson, Charles, Earl Of Liverpool 1727-1808
Alli
Jenkinson, Daniel *Alli*
Jenkinson, Edward B 1930- *ConAu 23*
Jenkinson, Henry Irwin *Alli Sup*
Jenkinson, Isaac 1825-1911 *IndAu 1816,*
OhA&B
Jenkinson, J *ChPo*
Jenkinson, J S *Alli*
Jenkinson, James *Alli*
Jenkinson, John Banks 1781-1840 *Alli*
Jenkinson, Michael 1938- *ConAu 25*
Jenkinson, Richard *Alli*
Jenkinson, Thomas Barge *Alli Sup*
Jenko, Simon 1835-1869 *CasWL*
Jenks, Albert Ernest 1869-1953 *AmA&B*
Jenks, Almet 1892-1966 *ConAu P-1,*
WhWNAA
Jenks, Arthur Whipple 1863-1923 *DcNAA*
Jenks, Benjamin 1646-1724 *Alli, DcEnL*
Jenks, Clarence Wilfred 1909- *Au&Wr,*
ConAu 9R
Jenks, Cornelia H *Alli Sup*
Jenks, Edward *Alli Sup*
Jenks, Edward A *Alli Sup*
Jenks, Edward Augustus 1830-1908 *ChPo S2,*
DcNAA
Jenks, Edward Watrous 1833-1903 *DcNAA*
Jenks, George Charles 1850-1929 *AmA&B,*
DcNAA, HsB&A, REnAL
Jenks, H N *ChPo S2*
Jenks, Henry Fitch 1842-1920 *DcNAA*
Jenks, Jacquetta Agneta Mariana *Alli, BiDLA*
Jenks, James *Alli*
Jenks, Jeremiah Whipple 1856- *DcAmA*
Jenks, Jeremiah Whipple 1856-1929 *DcNAA*
Jenks, John Edward 1866- *WhWNAA*
Jenks, John Whipple Porter 1819-1894 *DcAmA,*
DcNAA
Jenks, Jorian Edward Forwood *ChPo S2*
Jenks, Joseph William 1808-1884 *Alli, DcNAA*
Jenks, Louis G 1875- *WhWNAA*
Jenks, R W *Alli*
Jenks, Randolph 1912- *ConAu 9R*
Jenks, Richard *Alli*
Jenks, S *Alli*
Jenks, Tudor 1857-1922 *AmA&B, AmLY,*
BiD&SB, CarSB, ChPo, DcAmA,
DcNAA, REnAL
Jenks, William 1778-1866 *Alli, DcAmA,*
DcNAA
Jenks, William Lee 1856-1936 *DcNAA*
Jenkyn, Thomas W *Alli*
Jenkyn, William 1612-1662 *Alli*

Jenkyns, Chris 1924- *IlBYP, IlCB 1956*
Jennens, Charles d1773 *Alli, DcEnL*
Jenner, Charles *Alli*
Jenner, Charles 1737-1774 *Alli*
Jenner, David *Alli*
Jenner, Delia 1944- *ConAu 23*
Jenner, Edward 1749-1823 *Alli, BiDLA,*
NewC, REn
Jenner, Edward 1803-1872 *ChPo*
Jenner, G *Alli Sup*
Jenner, G C *Alli*
Jenner, H Penfold *ChPo*
Jenner, Heather *ConAu XR, WrD 1976*
Jenner, Henry *Alli, BiDLA, Pen Eng*
Jenner, Katharine Amabel *Alli Sup*
Jenner, Katharine Lee 1853- *Alli Sup, WhLA*
Jenner, R *Alli Sup*
Jenner, S *Alli*
Jenner, Stephen d1880 *Alli Sup, ChPo,*
ChPo S1
Jenner, Thomas *Alli, Alli Sup, NewC*
Jenner, W *Alli*
Jenner, W J F 1940- *ConAu 29*
Jenner, Sir William 1815- *Alli Sup*
Jenner, William A 1868- *WhWNAA*
Jenness, A *Alli Sup*
Jenness, Aylette 1934- *ConAu 25*
Jenness, Burt Franklin 1876- *TexWr*
Jenness, Diamond 1886- *OxCan*
Jenness, John Scribner 1827-1879 *Alli Sup,*
DcAmA, DcNAA
Jenness, Mary d1947 *DcNAA*
Jenness, Theodora R 1847- *Alli Sup, DcNAA*
Jennett, Sean 1912- *ConP 1970*
Jenneval 1808-1830 *BiD&SB*
Jenney, Charles Elmer 1872-1919 *ChPo S2,*
DcNAA
Jenney, George *Alli*
Jenney, Mary Perry 1845-1928 *OhA&B*
Jenney, S M *Alli Sup*
Jenney, W P *Alli Sup*
Jenney, William LeBaron 1832-1907 *DcNAA*
Jennings, Anne *ChPo S2*
Jennings, Arthur Charles *Alli Sup*
Jennings, C *Alli Sup*
Jennings, Charles Egerton *Alli Sup*
Jennings, Charles Godwin *Alli Sup*
Jennings, Clotilda d1895 *Alli Sup, BbtC,*
DcNAA, OxCan
Jennings, Dana Close 1923- *ConAu 53*
Jennings, David 1691-1762 *Alli, DcEnL*
Jennings, Dean Southern 1905- *AmA&B*
Jennings, Edward M 1936- *ConAu 29*
Jennings, Elizabeth 1926- *Au&Wr, ChPo,*
ChPo S1, ChPo S2, ConAu 61, ConLC 5,
ConP 1970, ConP 1975, LongC, ModBL,
ModBL Sup, NewC, Pen Eng, RAdv 1,
TwCW, WebEAL, WhTwL, WorAu,
WrD 1976
Jennings, Fabian *OxCan Sup*
Jennings, Francis 1808-1891 *DcNAA*
Jennings, Francis M *Alli Sup*
Jennings, Frank 1890- *WrD 1976*
Jennings, Gary 1928- *AuBYP, ConAu 5R,*
SmATA 9
Jennings, George *PoIre*
Jennings, George Henry *Alli Sup*
Jennings, Gertrude *DcLEnL*
Jennings, H A *BlkAW*
Jennings, Hargrave d1890 *Alli Sup*
Jennings, Henry *Alli Sup, ChPo*
Jennings, Henry C 1850-1927 *DcNAA*
Jennings, Henry Constantine 1731-1819 *Alli,*
DcEnL
Jennings, Henry James *Alli Sup*
Jennings, Herbert Spencer 1868-1947 *AmA&B,*
DcNAA, WhWNAA
Jennings, I H *Alli Sup*
Jennings, Isaac 1789-1874 *Alli Sup, DcNAA,*
OhA&B
Jennings, Isaac 1816-1887 *DcNAA*
Jennings, Ivor 1903-1965 *ConAu 5R*
Jennings, J *Alli*
Jennings, J A *ChPo*
Jennings, James *Alli*
Jennings, James 1772- *BiDLA, ChPo*
Jennings, James Hennen 1854-1920 *DcNAA*
Jennings, James M 1924- *ConAu 37*

Jennings, Jerry 1935- *ConAu 53*
Jennings, Jesse David 1909- *ConAu 33*
Jennings, John *Alli*
Jennings, John 1814- *BbtC*
Jennings, John 1933- *AmSCAP 66*
Jennings, John Andrew 1855- *Alli Sup, PoIre*
Jennings, John Edward, Jr. 1906-1973 *AmA&B,*
AmNov, AuBYP, ConAu 45, ConAu P-1,
REnAL, TwCA Sup
Jennings, John Joseph 1853-1909 *BiDSA,*
DcNAA
Jennings, Jonathan 1784-1834 *IndAu 1917*
Jennings, Kate Vaughan *Alli Sup*
Jennings, Leslie Nelson 1890-1972 *ConAu P-1*
Jennings, Louis John 1837- *Alli Sup*
Jennings, Napoleon Augustus 1856-1918 *BiDSA,*
DcAmA, DcNAA
Jennings, Nathaniel *Alli*
Jennings, Otto Emery 1877- *OhA&B,*
WhWNAA
Jennings, Paul *Alli Sup*
Jennings, Paul Francis 1918- *Au&Wr,*
ConAu 9R, NewC
Jennings, Richard *Alli, Alli Sup*
Jennings, Richard 1907- *ConAu 17R*
Jennings, Robert *Alli Sup, MnBBF*
Jennings, Robert E 1931- *ConAu 61*
Jennings, S M *ConAu 57, SmATA 3*
Jennings, Samuel *Alli Sup*
Jennings, Samuel Kennedy 1771-1854 *DcNAA*
Jennings, Sarah, Duchess Of Marlborough *Alli*
Jennings, Vivien *ConAu 61*
Jennings, Walter Wilson 1887- *WhWNAA*
Jennings, William *Alli, BiDLA*
Jennings, William Dale 1917- *ConAu 25*
Jennings, William S 1942- *AmSCAP 66*
Jennings, Winifred *Alli Sup*
Jennings And Heckford *Alli*
Jennison, C S *AuBYP, ConAu XR,*
SmATA 6
Jennison, Christopher 1938- *ConAu 53*
Jennison, Keith Warren 1911- *AmA&B,*
AuBYP
Jennison, Lucy White 1850- *Alli Sup,*
BiD&SB, DcAmA, DcNAA
Jennison, Peter S 1922- *ConAu 9R*
Jennison, William *Alli Sup*
Jenny, Charles Francis 1860-1923 *DcNAA*
Jennyngs, Radulphus *Alli*
Jennyns, Joseph Clayton *Alli, BiDLA*
Jenour, Alfred *Alli*
Jenour, Matthew *Alli, BiDLA*
Jenrette, Corinne McLemore 1903- *BlkAW*
Jens, Walter 1923- *EncWL, ModGL, OxGer,*
Pen Eur
Jense, William 1870- *WhLA*
Jensen, Ad E 1899- *ConAu 19*
Jensen, Alan F 1938- *ConAu 53*
Jensen, Andrew F, Jr. 1929- *ConAu 57*
Jensen, Ann 1902- *ConAu 23, TexWr*
Jensen, Arthur Robert 1923- *ConAu 1R,*
WrD 1976
Jensen, Axel 1932- *CasWL*
Jensen, Clayne R 1930- *ConAu 17R,*
WrD 1976
Jensen, David E *AuBYP*
Jensen, DeLamar 1925- *ConAu 9R,*
WrD 1976
Jensen, Erik Aalbaek 1923- *CasWL*
Jensen, Frede 1926- *ConAu 57*
Jensen, Gwendolyn Evans 1936- *ConAu 57*
Jensen, H James 1933- *ConAu 25*
Jensen, Irving L 1920- *ConAu 17R*
Jensen, J Vernon 1922- *ConAu 49*
Jensen, Jens Peter 1883- *WhWNAA*
Jensen, Jo *ConAu 49*
Jensen, Johannes Vilhelm 1873-1950 *CasWL,*
ClDMEuL, CyWA, EncWL, EvEuW,
Pen Eur, REn, TwCA, TwCA Sup,
TwCW
Jensen, John H 1929- *ConAu 23*
Jensen, John Martin 1893- *ConAu P-1*
Jensen, Julie *ConAu XR*
Jensen, Lawrence N 1924- *ConAu 17R*
Jensen, Lloyd 1936- *ConAu 61*
Jensen, Mary Fassett 1919- *Au&Wr*
Jensen, Mary Ten Eyck Bard 1904-1970
ConAu 5R, ConAu 29

Jensen, Merrill 1905- *AmA&B*
Jensen, Michael C 1939- *ConAu 49*
Jensen, Niels 1927- *ConAu 49*
Jensen, Oliver 1914- *ConAu 25*
Jensen, Paul K 1916- *ConAu 17R*
Jensen, Paul M 1944- *ConAu 53*
Jensen, Pauline Marie 1900- *ConAu 17*
Jensen, Richard C 1936- *ConAu 49*
Jensen, Richard J 1941- *ConAu 33, WrD 1976*
Jensen, Rolf 1912- *ConAu 21*
Jensen, Rosalie 1938- *ConAu 57*
Jensen, Thit Maria Kirstine Dorothea 1876-1957 *CasWL, REn*
Jensen, Virginia Allen 1927- *ConAu 45, SmATA 8*
Jensen, Wiers 1866-1925 *BiDPar*
Jensen, Wilhelm 1837-1911 *BiD&SB, CasWL, EvEuW, OxGer*
Jenson, Robert W 1930- *ConAu 5R*
Jent, John William 1877- *WhWNAA*
Jentes, Harry 1897-1958 *AmSCAP 66*
Jenty, Charles N *Alli*
Jentz, Gaylord A 1931- *ConAu 25*
Jenynges, Edward *Alli*
Jenyns, F G *Alli Sup*
Jenyns, Leonard *Alli, Alli Sup*
Jenyns, Roger *Alli Sup*
Jenyns, Soame 1704-1787 *Alli, BrAu, ChPo S1, DcEnL, DcLEnL, NewC, OxEng, Pen Eng*
Jephcock, E Woodward *ChPo*
Jephcott, Agnes Pearl 1900- *Au&Wr*
Jephcott, Sydney Wheeler 1860-1951 *DcLEnL*
Jephson, Alexander *Alli*
Jephson, Sir Charles Denham Norreys 1799-1888 *PoIre*
Jephson, D L A *ChPo*
Jephson, Henry L *Alli Sup*
Jephson, Ina *BiDPar*
Jephson, John *Alli*
Jephson, John Mounteney 1819-1865 *Alli Sup, PoIre*
Jephson, Lina *ChPo*
Jephson, Philippa Prittie *Alli Sup*
Jephson, Richard Mounteney 1842- *Alli Sup*
Jephson, Robert 1736-1803 *Alli, DcEnL, PoIre*
Jeppson, Janet O 1926- *ConAu 49, WrD 1976*
Jeppson, Lee Ralph 1910- *Au&Wr*
Jepsen, Hans Lyngby 1920- *CasWL*
Jepson, Arthur 1854- *Alli Sup*
Jepson, Edgar Alfred 1863-1938 *EvLB, NewC, WhLA*
Jepson, Selwyn 1899- *Au&Wr, EncM&D*
Jepson, Willis Linn 1867- *AmLY, WhWNAA*
Jerabek, Frantisek 1836-1893 *BiD&SB*
Jerauld, Charlotte Ann Fille-Brown 1820-1845 *Alli Sup, AmA&B, DcNAA*
Jerdan, Maxwell *Alli Sup*
Jerdan, William 1782-1869 *Alli, Alli Sup, BiDLA Sup, ChPo, ChPo S1, ChPo S2, DcEnL*
Jerdein, Arthur *Alli Sup*
Jerdon, Gertrude *Alli Sup*
Jerdon, Thomas Caverhill *Alli Sup*
Jeremiah *DcOrL 3, NewC*
Jeremiah, John *Alli Sup*
Jeremias, Joachim 1900- *ConAu 5R*
Jeremie, James Ameriaux *Alli*
Jeremie, Nicolas 1669-1732 *OxCan*
Jeremie, Peter *Alli Sup*
Jeremy, George *Alli*
Jeremy, Henry *Alli, BiDLA*
Jeremy, Sister Mary *CatA 1952, ConAu 5R*
Jeremy, Walter D *Alli Sup*
Jermain, Frances Delavan Page 1829-1905 *OhA&B*
Jerman, Sylvia Paul *ConAu XR*
Jermann, Edward *Alli Sup*
Jerment, George *Alli, BiDLA*
Jermin, Michael d1659 *Alli*
Jermon, J Wagner *Alli Sup*
Jermyn, L E *Alli Sup*
Jermyn, R Gordon *MnBBF*
Jernegan, Charles *Alli*
Jernegan, Marcus Wilson 1872-1949 *AmA&B, DcNAA*
Jernegan, Prescott F 1866- *WhWNAA*

Jerningham, Edward 1727-1812 *Alli, ChPo S1, DcEnL*
Jerningham, Hubert Edward Henry 1842- *Alli Sup*
Jerningham, John *ChPo S2*
Jerome, Father 1885- *AnMV 1926, ChPo*
Jerome, Saint 342?-420 *CasWL, NewC, OxEng, Pen Cl, RCom, REn*
Jerome, Annie E *ChPo S2*
Jerome, Chauncey 1793-1868 *DcNAA*
Jerome, Duncan I *Alli Sup*
Jerome, Ferris *Alli Sup*
Jerome, Henry 1917- *AmSCAP 66*
Jerome, Irene Elizabeth 1858- *Alli Sup, CarSB, ChPo*
Jerome, Jerome 1906-1964 *AmSCAP 66*
Jerome, Jerome Klapka 1859-1927 *Alli Sup, BbD, BiD&SB, CasWL, Chmbr 3, CyWA, DcBiA, DcEnA Ap, DcLEnL, EvLB, LongC, McGWD, MnBBF, ModBL, ModWD, NewC, OxEng, Pen Eng, REn, TwCA, TwCW*
Jerome, John 1932- *ConAu 45*
Jerome, Judson Blair 1927- *ConAu 9R, ConP 1970, ConP 1975, DrAF 1976, DrAP 1975, WrD 1976*
Jerome, M K 1893- *AmSCAP 66*
Jerome, Mark *ConAu XR*
Jerome, Maude Nugent 1877-1958 *AmSCAP 66*
Jerome, Owen Fox *AmA&B*
Jerome, Pierre *OxCan*
Jerome, Stephen *Alli, BrAu*
Jerome, Thomas Spencer 1864-1914 *DcNAA*
Jerome, William 1865-1932 *AmSCAP 66*
Jerome, William Travers 1850-1934 *DcNAA*
Jerr, William A *AuBYP*
Jerram, Charles 1770-1853 *Alli, BiDLA, DcEnL*
Jerram, Jane Elizabeth *ChPo S1*
Jerram, Samuel John *Alli Sup*
Jerrard, George B *Alli Sup*
Jerrard, Harold George 1921- *Au&Wr*
Jerrard, Paul *Alli Sup*
Jerrell, Annie R *Alli Sup*
Jerrett, Jean 1924- *AmSCAP 66*
Jerringham, Sir William *Alli*
Jerrod *BlkAW*
Jerrold, A *Alli Sup*
Jerrold, Blanchard 1826-1884 *ChPo, ChPo S1*
Jerrold, Daphne *ChPo, ChPo S2*
Jerrold, Douglas *Chmbr 3*
Jerrold, Douglas 1893-1964 *CatA 1947, EvLB, LongC*
Jerrold, Douglas E *BbtC*
Jerrold, Douglas William 1803-1857 *Alli, BbD, BiD&SB, BrAu 19, DcEnA, DcEnL, DcEuL, DcLEnL, EvLB, McGWD, NewC, OxEng, Pen Eng*
Jerrold, Evelyn Douglas *Alli Sup*
Jerrold, Fanny *Alli Sup*
Jerrold, Ianthe 1897- *Au&Wr, ChPo, ChPo S1, ChPo S2, WrD 1976*
Jerrold, Louise *WhWNAA*
Jerrold, Sidney 1857- *Alli Sup*
Jerrold, Mrs. T S *ChPo S1*
Jerrold, Tom *Alli Sup*
Jerrold, Walter Copeland 1865-1929 *ChPo, ChPo S1, ChPo S2*
Jerrold, William Blanchard 1826-1884 *Alli, Alli Sup, BbD, BiD&SB, BrAu 19, Chmbr 3, DcEnA, DcEnL, NewC*
Jerschke, Oskar 1861-1928 *OxGer*
Jersey, Countess Of 1849- *CarSB*
Jersey Lily, The *NewC*
Jersild, Arthur T 1902- *ConAu 1R*
Jersild, Paul T 1931- *ConAu 37*
Jerusalem, Karl Wilhelm 1747-1772 *OxGer*
Jervais, T *Alli*
Jervas, Charles *Alli*
Jervell, Jacob 1925- *ConAu 61*
Jervey, Caroline Howard Gilman 1823-1877 *AmA&B, BiD&SB, BiDSA, ChPo, DcAmA, DcNAA, LivFWS*
Jervey, Henry 1866-1942 *DcNAA*
Jervey, Theodore Dehon 1859- *BiDSA*
Jervis, William *Alli*
Jervis, David *Alli Sup*
Jervis, Frank Robert Joseph 1906- *WrD 1976*

Jervis, Henry Jervis White d1881 *Alli, Alli Sup*
Jervis, Sir J *Alli*
Jervis, J W *Alli*
Jervis, John Bloomfield 1795-1885 *Alli Sup, DcAmA, DcNAA*
Jervis, Sir John White *Alli, BiDLA*
Jervis, M L *ChPo S1*
Jervis, Lady Marian *Alli Sup*
Jervis, Swynfen *Alli, Alli Sup*
Jervis, Thomas 1748-1833 *Alli, BiDLA, PoCh*
Jervis, William George *Alli Sup*
Jervis, William Henley 1813-1883 *Alli Sup*
Jervis, William Paget *Alli Sup*
Jervis, William Percival 1850-1925 *DcNAA*
Jervise, Andrew 1820-1878 *Alli Sup*
Jervoise, Mrs. Arthur Tristram *Alli Sup*
Jerwood, James *Alli*
Jeschke, H Jewett 1873- *WhWNAA*
Jeschke, Marlin 1929- *ConAu 45*
Jesensky, Janko 1874-1945 *CasWL, EncWL, ModSL 2, Pen Eur, TwCW*
Jesmanyjasita *DcOrL 2*
Jesmer, Elaine 1939- *AuNews 1, ConAu 49, WrD 1976*
Jesness, Oscar Bernard 1889- *WhWNAA*
Jespersen, Jens Otto Harry 1860-1943 *OxEng, WhLA*
Jesse *Alli*
Jesse, Edward 1780-1868 *Alli, Alli Sup, EvLB*
Jesse, Friniwyd Tennyson 1895?-1958 *ChPo, ChPo S1, EncM&D, EvLB, LongC, NewC, REn, TwCA, TwCA Sup*
Jesse, George Richard 1820- *Alli Sup*
Jesse, J *Alli*
Jesse, John Heneage 1815-1874 *Alli, Alli Sup, BiD&SB, DcEnL, EvLB*
Jesse, Michael *ConAu XR*
Jesse, Richard Henry 1853- *BiDSA*
Jesse, William *Alli*
Jesse, William d1814 *Alli, BiDLA, BiDLA Sup*
Jessel, George 1898- *AmSCAP 66*
Jessel, John *WorAu*
Jessett, Frederick Bowreman *Alli Sup*
Jessey, Cornelia 1910- *AmA&B, AmA&B, AmNov*
Jessey, Henry 1601-1663 *Alli*
Jessop, Charles Moore *Alli Sup*
Jessop, Constantius *Alli*
Jessop, Ernest H *ChPo*
Jessop, Francis *Alli*
Jessop, Francis H *Alli Sup*
Jessop, George H *PoIre*
Jessop, Gilbert L *MnBBF*
Jessop, Joseph Chasser 1892- *Au&Wr*
Jessop, M K *Alli Sup, ChPo, PoIre*
Jessop, Thomas Edmund 1896- *Au&Wr, ConAu 9R, WrD 1976*
Jessop, William *Alli Sup*
Jessop, William Henry Bowlestone *Alli Sup*
Jessopp, Augustus 1824-1914 *Alli Sup, BrAu 19, Chmbr 3, DcEnA Ap*
Jessopp, C S *Alli Sup*
Jessopp, John *Alli Sup*
Jessor, Richard 1924- *ConAu 41*
Jessup, Alfred Claude 1891-1953 *ChPo*
Jessup, Charles Lee 1865-1938 *IndAu 1917*
Jessup, Ernest Maurice *ChPo S2*
Jessup, Frances *ConAu XR*
Jessup, Frank W 1909- *Au&Wr, WrD 1976*
Jessup, Henry Harris 1832-1910 *Alli Sup, BbD, BiD&SB, DcAmA, DcNAA*
Jessup, Henry Wynans 1864-1934 *AmLY, DcNAA, WhWNAA*
Jessup, Philip C 1897- *AmA&B, REnAL*
Jessup, Richard 1925- *AmA&B*
Jessup, Walter A 1877-1944 *AmLY, DcNAA, IndAu 1917*
Jessye, Eva Alberta 1895- *AmSCAP 66*
Jessye, Eva Alberta 1897- *BlkAW*
Jesten, H *Alli*
Jester, Eleanore Livingston 1914- *IndAu 1917*
Jester, George *ChPo S1*
Jester, Lewis T 1893- *WhWNAA*
Jesup, Edward *Alli*
Jesup, Henry Griswold 1826-1903 *Alli Sup, DcNAA*
Jesus 004?BC-028?AD *REn*

Johann Von Soest 1448-1506 *OxGer*
Johann Von Tepl 1350?-1415? *CasWL, EuA, EvEuW*
Johann Von Wurzburg *CasWL, OxGer*
Johann, Fischer 1881- *WhLA*
Johannes *WhWNAA*
Johannes A Lapide 1430?-1496 *CasWL*
Johannes De Alta Silva *CasWL, Pen Eur*
Johannes Grammaticus *BiB N*
Johannes Magnus 1488-1544 *CasWL*
Johannes Scotus Erigena 810?-860? *BiB S, CasWL*
Johannes Scotus ALSO John Scotus
Johannes Secundus 1511-1536 *Pen Eur*
Johannes Ur Kotlum *CasWL*
Johannes Von Der Ostsee *OxGer*
Johannes Von Frankenstein *OxGer*
Johannes Von Freiberg *OxGer*
Johannes Von Indersdorf *OxGer*
Johannes Von Posilge 1340?-1405 *OxGer*
Johannes Von Ringgenberg *OxGer*
Johannes Von Tepl 1360?-1414? *OxGer, Pen Eur*
Johannes Von Winterthur 1300?-1348? *OxGer*
Johannes, R *ConAu 49*
Johannesen, Richard L 1937- *ConAu 17R*
Johannesson, Olof *ConAu XR*
Johannis, Theodore B, Jr. 1914- *ConAu 33*
Johannot, Alfred 1800-1837 *OxFr*
Johannot, Tony 1803-1852 *ChPo S1, OxFr*
Johannsen, Albert 1871- *WhWNAA*
Johannsen, Hano D 1933- *ConAu 29*
Johannsen, Michael 1615-1679 *OxGer*
Johannsen, Oskar Augustus 1870- *WhWNAA*
Johannsen, Robert Walter 1925- *ConAu 1R*
Johannsen Wagner, Else 1894- *Au&Wr*
Johannssen, Michael 1615-1679 *OxGer*
Johansen, Andrew *Alli, BiDLA*
Johansen, Dorothy O 1904- *ConAu P-1, WhPNW*
Johansen, Margaret Alison 1896- *AuBYP, TexWr*
Johanson, Klara 1875-1948 *CasWL*
Johanson, Stanley Morris 1933- *ConAu 45*
Johansson, Lars 1638?-1674 *CasWL, EvEuW*
John 1167-1216 *NewC*
John II 1404-1454 *DcEuL*
John, Abbot Of Forde *BiB N*
John Argyropulos d1487 *Pen Cl*
John Beccus d1293 *CasWL*
John Cameniates *Pen Cl*
John VI Cantacuzenus 1292?-1383? *CasWL, EuA, Pen Cl*
John Chrysostom 344?-407 *CasWL*
John Cinnamus 1143?-1195? *CasWL, Pen Cl*
John Climacus *CasWL*
John Climax d670? *Pen Cl*
John Cumyn *BiB N*
John Cyparissiotes *CasWL*
John De Hauteville *Alli, BiB N*
John De Saint Omer *BiB N*
John Doxopatres, The Sicilian *CasWL*
John Geometres *CasWL*
John Hancock *REn*
John Italus *CasWL, Pen Cl*
John, King Of England 1167-1216 *REn*
John Kyriotes Geometres *CasWL, Pen Cl*
John Lackland *NewC*
John Malalas 491?-578? *CasWL, Pen Cl*
John Mauropous, Of Euchaita *CasWL*
John Mauropus *Pen Cl*
John Moschus d619? *CasWL, Pen Cl*
John Of Arderne 1307-1380? *CasWL*
John Of Beverley *Alli*
John Of Beverley d721 *Alli, BiB S*
John Of Brompton *Alli, BiB N*
John Of Bromyard *DcEnL*
John Of Capua *CasWL*
John Of Cornwall *Alli, BiB N*
John Of Corvei *BiB S*
John Of Damascus 675?-749? *CasWL, Pen Cl*
John Of Euchaita *CasWL*
John Of Fordun *CasWL, DcEnL*
John Of Gaddesden *Alli, DcEnL*
John Of Gaunt 1340-1399 *NewC, REn*
John Of Hanville *Pen Eur*
John Of Hauteville *Pen Eur*
John Of Hexham *BiB N, DcEnL*

John Of Hoveden d1275 *Pen Eng*
John Of Howden d1275 *Pen Eng*
John Of Ireland *CasWL*
John Of Oxnead *DcEnL*
John Of Saint Omer *DcEnL*
John Of Salisbury 1120?-1180 *Alli, BiB N, BrAu, CasWL, DcEnL, DcEuL, EvLB, NewC, OxEng, Pen Eng*
John Of The Cross, Saint 1542-1591 *AtlBL, CasWL, EvEuW, NewC, Pen Eur, RCom, REn*
John Of Tilbury *BiB N*
John Of Trevisa 1326-1402 *EvLB, Pen Eng*
John Of Trokelowe *DcEnL*
John Of Wallingford *BiB N*
John Pecham d1292 *CasWL*
John Philoponus *CasWL, Pen Cl*
John, Saint *REn*
John Scotus Erigena 810?-877? *Pen Eur*
John Scylitzes *CasWL, Pen Cl*
John Stobaeus *CasWL*
John The Baptist, Saint *REn*
John The Exarch *Pen Eur*
John The Lydian 490?- *CasWL*
John Tzetzes 1110?-1180? *CasWL, Pen Cl*
John Xiphilinus 1010?-1075 *CasWL*
John Zonaras *CasWL, Pen Cl*
John, Alix *OxCan*
John, Augustus Edwin 1878-1961? *AtlBL, ChPo, OxEng*
John, B *ConAu XR*
John, Betty 1907- *ConAu XR, WrD 1976*
John, Chris Sam. *Alli, BiDLA*
John, Dane *ConAu 57*
John, Edmund *ChPo S1*
John, Elizabeth Beaman 1907- *ConAu 5R*
John, Errol 1925?- *CnMD, ConDr, ModWD, WrD 1976*
John, Eugenie *BiD&SB*
John, Evan *NewC*
John, Gabriel *Alli*
John, Gwendolyn Mary d1934 *ChPo*
John, Hedley *BlkAW*
John, Helen James 1930- *ConAu 61*
John, I G *BiDSA*
John, John Price Durbin 1843-1916 *DcNAA, IndAu 1816*
John, June 1925- *WrD 1976*
John, Owen 1918- *Au&Wr*
John, Robert *ConAu 29, WrD 1976*
John, T B *Alli*
John, William Mestrezat 1888-1962 *AmA&B, WhWNAA*
Johnes, Arthur James *Alli*
Johnes, Edward Rodolph 1852-1903 *Alli Sup, DcAmA, DcNAA*
Johnes, Meredith *Alli Sup*
Johnes, Thomas *Alli*
Johnes, Thomas 1748?-1816 *Alli, BiDLA, DcEnL*
Johnie Armstrong *NewC*
Johnn, David *ConAu 57*
Johnpoll, Bernard K 1926- *ConAu 21*
Johns, Al 1878-1928 *AmSCAP 66*
Johns, Albert Cameron 1914- *ConAu 49*
Johns, Annie *BiDSA*
Johns, Avery 1905- *ConAu XR, SmATA 2, WrD 1976*
Johns, Bennett George 1820-1891 *Alli, Alli Sup*
Johns, Bernard George 1820-1891 *ChPo S2*
Johns, Charles Alexander 1811-1874 *Alli, Alli Sup, ChPo, ChPo S1, ChPo S2, PoIre*
Johns, Charles Rowland 1882- *WhLA*
Johns, Clayton 1857-1932 *DcNAA*
Johns, Edna *WhWNAA*
Johns, Edward Alistair 1936- *ConAu 45, WrD 1976*
Johns, Foster *ConAu XR*
Johns, Francis A *ChPo S1*
Johns, Frederic 1868- *WhLA*
Johns, Geoffrey *ConAu XR, WrD 1976*
Johns, George S *Alli Sup*
Johns, Gilbert *MnBBF*
Johns, Henry D *Alli*
Johns, Henry T *Alli Sup*
Johns, John *ChPo S2*

Johns, John 1796-1876 *Alli Sup, BiDSA, DcNAA*
Johns, John E 1921- *ConAu 9R*
Johns, June 1925- *ConAu 57*
Johns, Kenneth *ConAu XR*
Johns, Montgomery *Alli*
Johns, Orrick 1887-1946 *AmA&B, ChPo, ChPo S1, ConAmL, REn, REnAL, TwCA, TwCA Sup*
Johns, Ray E 1900- *ConAu 41*
Johns, Richard A 1929- *ConAu 17R, WrD 1976*
Johns, Richard And Nicolas, P H *Alli Sup*
Johns, Robert Magrath *Alli Sup*
Johns, Thompson *WhWNAA*
Johns, Veronica Parker 1907- *EncM&D*
Johns, W E 1893-1968 *LongC*
Johns, Warren L 1929- *ConAu 23*
Johns, Whitey *ConAu 57*
Johns, William *Alli, BiDLA, BiDLA Sup*
Johns, William Earl 1893-1968 *MnBBF, WhCL*
Johns Smith, June 1925- *Au&Wr*
Johnsen, Erik Kristian 1863-1923 *DcNAA*
Johnsen, H *Alli*
Johnsgard, Paul A 1931- *ConAu 49, WrD 1976*
Johnson *Alli*
Johnson, Major *Alli, BiDLA*
Johnson, Mrs. *Alli Sup*
Johnson, A *ConAu XR*
Johnson, A E *ConAu XR, SmATA 2*
Johnson, Mrs. A M *Alli, BiDLA*
Johnson, Abraham *Alli*
Johnson, Adolphus *BlkAW*
Johnson, Alan P 1929- *ConAu 17R*
Johnson, Albert 1904- *ConAu 9R*
Johnson, Albinus Alonzo 1852- *IndAu 1917*
Johnson, Alec Albert 1897- *Au&Wr*
Johnson, Alexander 1847-1941 *DcNAA, IndAu 1816*
Johnson, Alexander Bryan 1786-1867 *Alli, AmA&B, DcAmA, DcNAA*
Johnson, Alexander Bryan 1860-1917 *DcNAA*
Johnson, Alfred Challice *Alli Sup*
Johnson, Alfred E *Alli Sup*
Johnson, Alice *OxCan Sup*
Johnson, Alice 186-?-1940 *BiDPar*
Johnson, Alicia L 1944- *BlkAW, LivBA*
Johnson, Allen 1870-1931 *AmA&B, AmLY, DcNAA, OxAm, REnAL*
Johnson, Allison H 1910- *ConAu 41*
Johnson, Alvin Saunders 1874-1971 *AmA&B, ConAu 29, REnAL, TwCA Sup*
Johnson, Amanda *WhWNAA*
Johnson, Amandus 1877-1974 *AmA&B, ConAu 49, WhWNAA*
Johnson, Amelia E 1859- *BlkAW*
Johnson, Andrew *Alli Sup, BiDSA*
Johnson, Andrew 1808-1870 *AmA&B*
Johnson, Andrew 1808-1875 *DcNAA, OxAm, REn, REnAL*
Johnson, Andrew 1875- *WhWNAA*
Johnson, Andrew N 1887- *ConAu 61*
Johnson, Anna *Alli Sup*
Johnson, Anna C *Alli, Alli Sup, DcEnL, DcNAA*
Johnson, Anna J *Alli Sup*
Johnson, Anna M 1860- *AmA&B, AmLY*
Johnson, Annabel Jones 1921- *AmA&B, AuBYP, ConAu 9R, SmATA 2, ThBJA*
Johnson, Anne Porter *ChPo, ChPo S2*
Johnson, Annie June *ChPo S1*
Johnson, Anthony *Alli*
Johnson, Arnold 1893- *AmSCAP 66*
Johnson, Arnold W 1900- *ConAu P-1*
Johnson, Artemas Nixon 1817- *Alli, DcNAA*
Johnson, Arthur *Alli*
Johnson, Arthur Henry *Alli Sup*
Johnson, Arthur Menzies 1921- *ConAu 21*
Johnson, Aubrey Rodway 1901- *Au&Wr, WrD 1976*
Johnson, Avery F 1906- *IlCB 1945, IlCB 1956*
Johnson, B Pauline 1905- *WhPNW*
Johnson, Barry L 1934- *ConAu 33*
Johnson, Barry L 1943- *ConAu 61*
Johnson, Barton W 1833-1894 *DcAmA, DcNAA*

Johnson, Ben *Alli*
Johnson, Ben, Jr. *Alli*
Johnson, Ben E 1940- *ConAu 61*
Johnson, Benjamin *Alli, BiDLA*
Johnson, Benjamin A 1937- *ConAu 23*
Johnson, Benjamin F 1849-1916 *Alli Sup, AmA, DcAmA, DcNAA*
Johnson, Benjamin Franklin 1856-1921 *DcNAA*
Johnson, Benjamin Pierce 1793-1869 *Alli, DcAmA, DcNAA*
Johnson, Bernard 1933- *ConAu 33*
Johnson, Bernard H, Jr. 1920- *LivBA*
Johnson, Bertha French 1906- *ConAu 41*
Johnson, Bradford 1937- *ConAu 57*
Johnson, Bradley T *Alli Sup*
Johnson, Bradley Tyler 1829-1903 *BiDSA, DcAmA, DcNAA*
Johnson, Bryan Stanley 1933-1973 *Au&Wr, ConAu 9R, ConAu 49, ConAu 53, ConLC 6, ConNov 1972, ConP 1970, ConP 1975, ModBL Sup*
Johnson, Brian Stanley 1933-1974 *NewC, TwCW*
Johnson, Bruce 1933- *ConAu 33*
Johnson, Buddy 1915- *AmSCAP 66*
Johnson, Buford Jeanette 1880- *WhWNAA*
Johnson, Burges 1877-1963 *AmA&B, AmLY, ChPo, ChPo S1, ChPo S2, REnAL, WhWNAA*
Johnson, Burt Parker 1905- *IndAu 1917*
Johnson, Byron Lindberg 1917- *ConAu 21*
Johnson, Mrs. C *Alli Sup*
Johnson, C Edward *ConAu XR*
Johnson, C F *ConAu 57*
Johnson, C F T *Alli*
Johnson, C H *Alli, BiDLA*
Johnson, Caleb *WhWNAA*
Johnson, Captain Charles *Alli, NewC*
Johnson, Carl E 1937- *ConAu 25*
Johnson, Carol Virginia 1928- *ConAu 9R*
Johnson, Cecil *ChPo S1*
Johnson, Cecil Edward 1927- *ConAu 33*
Johnson, Chalmers A 1931- *ConAu 5R*
Johnson, Charlene *ConAu 57*
Johnson, Charles *Alli Sup, DrAF 1976*
Johnson, Charles 1679-1748 *Alli, DcEnL, NewC*
Johnson, Charles 1928- *AmSCAP 66*
Johnson, Charles 1949- *BlkAW*
Johnson, Charles Beneulyn 1843-1928 *DcNAA*
Johnson, Charles Benjamin 1928- *ConAu 5R*
Johnson, Charles Bertram 1880- *BlkAW*
Johnson, Charles Earl 1812-1876 *DcNAA*
Johnson, Charles Ellicott 1920- *ConAu 1R*
Johnson, Charles Frederick *AuBYP*
Johnson, Charles Frederick 1836-1931 *Alli Sup, AmA&B, BbD, BiD&SB, ChPo, DcAmA, DcNAA*
Johnson, Charles Henry 1870-1948 *DcNAA*
Johnson, Charles Howard *ChPo*
Johnson, Charles L 1876-1950 *AmSCAP 66*
Johnson, Charles Morris 1869- *WhWNAA*
Johnson, Charles Nelson 1860- *AmLY, DcAmA, WhWNAA*
Johnson, Charles Plumptre 1853- *Alli Sup, ChPo, WhLA*
Johnson, Charles S *ConAu XR*
Johnson, Charles Spurgeon 1893-1956 *AmA&B, REnAL*
Johnson, Charles W 1843-1905 *DcNAA*
Johnson, Christine C *BlkAW*
Johnson, Christopher *Alli, BiDLA*
Johnson, Christopher G A Y Johnson 1903- *Au&Wr*
Johnson, Christopher Louis McIntosh 1931- *Au&Wr, ConAu 13R*
Johnson, Clarence C 1882-1953 *IndAu 1917*
Johnson, Claude Ellsworth 1867-1943 *DcNAA*
Johnson, Claudius Osborne 1894- *WhPNW*
Johnson, Clifford Vincent 1936- *BlkAW*
Johnson, Clifton 1865-1940 *AmA&B, BiD&SB, ChPo S1, DcAmA, DcNAA, REnAL, WhWNAA*
Johnson, Clive 1930- *ConAu 29*
Johnson, Constance Fuller Wheeler 1879- *AmA&B, AmLY, ChPo, WhWNAA*
Johnson, Crisfield *Alli Sup*
Johnson, Crockett 1906-1975 *Au&Wr, AuBYP,*

BkP, ConAu 57, IlCB 1956, IlCB 1966, SmATA 1, ThBJA
Johnson, Curt 1928- *ConAu 33*
Johnson, Curtiss Sherman 1899- *ConAu 45*
Johnson, Cuthbert *Alli*
Johnson, Cuthbert W *Alli*
Johnson, Cyril LaFawn 1907- *IndAu 1917*
Johnson, Cyrus Caswell 1886- *WhWNAA*
Johnson, D *Alli*
Johnson, Mrs. D *Alli, BiDLA*
Johnson, D Barton 1933- *ConAu 33*
Johnson, D Bruce 1942- *ConAu 61*
Johnson, D Gale 1916- *ConAu 17R*
Johnson, Dale A 1936- *ConAu 37*
Johnson, Daniel *Alli Sup*
Johnson, David 1927- *Au&Wr, ConAu 13R*
Johnson, David George 1906- *Au&Wr, ConAu 9R*
Johnson, David Newhall 1824-1906 *DcNAA*
Johnson, Davis Ben 1880-1952 *OhA&B*
Johnson, Denis *DrAP 1975*
Johnson, Diane 1934- *Au&Wr, ConAu 41, ConLC 5, DrAF 1976, WrD 1976*
Johnson, Don Allen 1942- *BlkAW*
Johnson, Donald Bruce 1921- *ConAu 1R, WrD 1976*
Johnson, Donald Edwin 1920- *Au&Wr*
Johnson, Donald M 1909- *ConAu 1R*
Johnson, Donald McIntosh 1903- *Au&Wr, ConAu 5R, WrD 1976*
Johnson, Donovan A 1910- *ConAu 1R, ConAu 5R*
Johnson, Doris J *BlkAW*
Johnson, Dorothy *NewC*
Johnson, Dorothy Biddle 1887?-1974 *ConAu 53*
Johnson, Dorothy Cooper 1890- *TexWr*
Johnson, Dorothy E 1920- *ConAu 53*
Johnson, Dorothy Marie 1905- *Au&Wr, ConAu 5R, SmATA 6, WhPNW*
Johnson, Dorothy Vena d1970 *BlkAW*
Johnson, Douglas 1925- *Au&Wr*
Johnson, Douglas W 1934- *ConAu 57*
Johnson, Douglas Wilson 1878-1944 *DcNAA, WhWNAA*
Johnson, Dudley Vaughan *MnBBF*
Johnson, Duncan Starr 1867-1937 *DcNAA*
Johnson, E *Alli Sup, ChPo S1*
Johnson, E A *Alli*
Johnson, E A J 1900-1972 *ConAu 37, ConAu P-1*
Johnson, E Ashby 1917- *ConAu 33*
Johnson, E C *Alli Sup*
Johnson, E K *ChPo*
Johnson, E W 1941- *ConAu 29*
Johnson, Earl, Jr. 1933- *ConAu 61*
Johnson, Eastman 1824-1906 *OxAm*
Johnson, Edd *BlkAW*
Johnson, Edgar 1901- *AmA&B, AuBYP, ConAu 9R, REnAL, TwCA Sup*
Johnson, Edgar Raymond 1912- *ConAu 9R, SmATA 2, ThBJA*
Johnson, Edith Cherry 1879- *OhA&B, WhWNAA*
Johnson, Edmund Charles *Alli Sup*
Johnson, Edna *ChPo, ChPo S2*
Johnson, Edward *Alli*
Johnson, Edward 1598-1672 *AmA, AmA&B, CnDAL, CyAL 1, OxAm, Pen Am, REnAL*
Johnson, Edward 1600-1682 *DcAmA*
Johnson, Edward 1910-1961 *AmSCAP 66*
Johnson, Edward A *Alli Sup*
Johnson, Edward A 1915- *ConAu 37*
Johnson, Edward Augustus 1860-1944 *DcNAA*
Johnson, Edward Carl 1880- *WhWNAA*
Johnson, Edward Lewis *Alli Sup*
Johnson, Edward Woodward 1876-1954 *OhA&B*
Johnson, Edwin *Alli Sup*
Johnson, Edwin A 1829- *Alli Sup, DcAmA, DcNAA*
Johnson, Edwin Ferry 1803-1872 *DcNAA*
Johnson, Edwin Rossiter 1840- *Alli Sup*
Johnson, Effie *DcNAA*
Johnson, Elden *OxCan Sup*
Johnson, Eldon Lee 1908- *IndAu 1917*
Johnson, Eleanor Shipp *WhWNAA*
Johnson, Electa Search 1909- *ConAu 1R*
Johnson, Elias Finley 1861-1933 *AmLY,*

DcNAA
Johnson, Elias H 1841-1906 *DcAmA, DcNAA*
Johnson, Elizabeth 1911- *ConAu 1R, SmATA 7*
Johnson, Elizabeth Winthrop 1850- *Alli Sup, AmA&B, DcNAA*
Johnson, Ellen d1873 *Alli Sup*
Johnson, Ellen H 1910- *ConAu 37*
Johnson, Elmer Douglas 1915- *ConAu 9R*
Johnson, Elmer Hubert 1917- *ConAu 13R, WrD 1976*
Johnson, Elwin Bird 1865-1928 *DcNAA*
Johnson, Emily Pauline 1862-1913 *BbD, BiD&SB, BrAu 19, ChPo, ChPo S1, Chmbr 3, DcLEnL, DcNAA*
Johnson, Emily S *ChPo S1*
Johnson, Emma B *Alli Sup*
Johnson, Emory Richard 1864- *DcAmA*
Johnson, Enid 1892- *AuBYP, JBA 1934*
Johnson, Eola 1909- *ConAu 49*
Johnson, Eric W 1918- *ConAu 5R, SmATA 8, WrD 1976*
Johnson, Ernest Clifton 1851-1933 *DcNAA*
Johnson, Ernle Sacheverell Wilberforce *Alli Sup*
Johnson, Esther 1681-1728 *DcEnL, NewC, REn*
Johnson, Eugene *BlkAW*
Johnson, Eugene Harper *IlBYP, IlCB 1956, IlCB 1966*
Johnson, Evangeline Maria *Alli Sup*
Johnson, Evans *Alli Sup*
Johnson, Evelyn Allen *BlkAW*
Johnson, Everett Herschel 1903- *IndAu 1917*
Johnson, Eyvind 1900- *CasWL, EncWL, EvEuW, Pen Eur*
Johnson, F Henry *OxCan Sup*
Johnson, Fabian *Alli*
Johnson, Falk S 1903- *WrD 1976*
Johnson, Falk S 1913- *ConAu 17R*
Johnson, Fenton 1888-1958 *BlkAW, ChPo*
Johnson, Finley *ChPo*
Johnson, Florence Miriam *WhWNAA*
Johnson, Francis *Alli, Alli Sup*
Johnson, Francis 1837-1908 *HsB&A, HsB&A Sup, IndAu 1816*
Johnson, Francis Howe 1835-1920 *DcAmA, DcNAA*
Johnson, Frank *Alli Sup, BbtC*
Johnson, Frank Arthur *BlkAW*
Johnson, Frank Grant 1825- *Alli, DcNAA*
Johnson, Frank Grant 1835- *Alli Sup, DcAmA*
Johnson, Franklin 1836-1916 *Alli Sup, DcAmA, DcNAA, OhA&B*
Johnson, Franklin Winslow 1870- *AmLY, WhWNAA*
Johnson, Franklyn A 1921- *ConAu 1R*
Johnson, Fred 1940- *BlkAW*
Johnson, Frederick Charles 1853-1913 *DcNAA*
Johnson, Frederick E *Alli Sup*
Johnson, Frederick Green 1890- *WhWNAA*
Johnson, Frederick H *Alli Sup*
Johnson, G Orville 1915- *ConAu 1R*
Johnson, G T *ChPo S1*
Johnson, G W *Alli*
Johnson, Gaylord 1884- *ConAu P-1, SmATA 7*
Johnson, Geoffrey 1893-1966 *Au&Wr, ChPo, ChPo S1, ChPo S2, ConAu P-1*
Johnson, George *Alli Sup*
Johnson, George 1818- *Alli Sup*
Johnson, George 1837-1911 *DcNAA*
Johnson, George 1889-1944 *DcNAA*
Johnson, George 1917- *ConAu 5R, IndAu 1917*
Johnson, George B *Alli Sup*
Johnson, George Ellsworth 1862-1931 *DcNAA*
Johnson, George Henry 1850- *WhWNAA*
Johnson, George Henry Sacheverell 1808-1881 *Alli Sup*
Johnson, George J *Alli Sup*
Johnson, George Lindsay *Alli Sup*
Johnson, George M *MnBBF*
Johnson, George Metcalf 1885- *AmA&B, WhWNAA*
Johnson, George Washington 1839-1917 *BbtC, DcNAA*
Johnson, George William *Alli*

Johnson, Georgia Douglas 1886-1966
*AnMV 1926, BlkAW, ChPo S1,
WhWNAA*
Johnson, Georgiana *Alli Sup*
Johnson, Gerald White 1890- *AmA&B, AnCL,
AuBYP, CnDAL, OxAm, REnAL,
ThBJA, TwCA Sup, WhWNAA*
Johnson, Gertrude F 1929- *ConAu 57*
Johnson, Grace Fitch 1871-1952 *IndAu 1917*
Johnson, Greer 1920?-1974 *ConAu 53*
Johnson, Guion Griffis 1900- *TexWr,
WhWNAA*
Johnson, Guy Benton 1901- *TexWr,
WhWNAA*
Johnson, H A *Alli Sup*
Johnson, H B *WhWNAA*
Johnson, H B, Jr. 1931- *ConAu 29*
Johnson, H C Ross *Alli Sup*
Johnson, H T *Alli Sup*
Johnson, Hall 1888-1970 *AmSCAP 66,
BlkAW*
Johnson, Halvard 1936- *ConAu 33,
DrAP 1975, WrD 1976*
Johnson, Hammel *OhA&B*
Johnson, Hannah More *Alli Sup, ChPo*
Johnson, Harold L 1924- *ConAu 13R*
Johnson, Harold Scholl 1929- *ConAu 37,
WrD 1976*
Johnson, Harold V 1897- *ConAu 1R*
Johnson, Harold Victor 1918- *AmSCAP 66*
Johnson, Harriet Merrill 1867-1934 *DcNAA*
Johnson, Harrison *Alli Sup*
Johnson, Harry Alleyn 1920- *LivBA*
Johnson, Harry Alleyn 1921- *ConAu 45*
Johnson, Harry G 1923- *ConAu 5R, OxCan,
WrD 1976*
Johnson, Harry L 1929- *ConAu 29*
Johnson, Harry Morton 1917- *ConAu 9R*
Johnson, Harvey L 1904- *ConAu 37*
Johnson, Haymond Nathaniel *MnnWr*
Johnson, Haynes Bonner 1931- *AmA&B,
ConAu 5R*
Johnson, Helen 1835-1863 *BbtC*
Johnson, Helen Aurelia *BlkAW*
Johnson, Helen Louise Kendrick 1843-1917
*Alli Sup, AmA, AmA&B, BiD&SB,
CarSB, ChPo S1, DcAmA, DcNAA*
Johnson, Helen Lessing 1865-1934 *ChPo S1*
Johnson, Helen Lossing 1865-1946 *DcNAA*
Johnson, Helen Mar 1835-1863 *DcNAA,
OxCan*
Johnson, Helene V 1907- *AnMV 1926,
BlkAW*
Johnson, Henry *Alli, Alli Sup*
Johnson, Henry 1855-1918 *AmA&B, AmLY,
DcNAA*
Johnson, Henry Luttman *Alli Sup*
Johnson, Henry Robert Vaughan 1820- *Alli Sup*
Johnson, Henry T 1858-1930 *MnBBF*
Johnson, Henry Theodore 1857-1910 *BlkAW*
Johnson, Herbert 1878-1946 *AmA&B*
Johnson, Herbert A 1934- *ConAu 5R*
Johnson, Herbert Clark 1911- *BlkAW*
Johnson, Herbert J 1933- *ConAu 29*
Johnson, Herbert Webster 1906- *ConAu 5R,
WrD 1976*
Johnson, Herman M 1815- *Alli*
Johnson, Herrick 1832-1913 *Alli Sup, DcAmA,
DcNAA*
Johnson, Mrs. Herrick *ChPo*
Johnson, Herschel Vespasian 1812-1880 *BiDSA*
Johnson, Herschell 1948- *BlkAW*
Johnson, Hewlett 1874-1966 *LongC*
Johnson, Hilda *ChPo*
Johnson, Hildegard Binder 1908- *ConAu 9R*
Johnson, Homer Preston *BlkAW*
Johnson, Homer Uri 1830-1901 *DcNAA,
OhA&B*
Johnson, Horace 1893-1964 *AmSCAP 66*
Johnson, Howard 1873- *IndAu 1917*
Johnson, Howard 1888-1941 *AmA&B*
Johnson, Howard Albert 1915-1974 *ConAu 1R,
ConAu 49*
Johnson, Howard E 1887-1941 *AmSCAP 66*
Johnson, Hugh G *BlkAW*
Johnson, Hugh Samuel 1882-1942 *AmA&B,
DcNAA*
Johnson, Humphrey *Alli*

Johnson, Humphrey Wynne 1925-1976
ConAu 61
Johnson, Hunter 1906- *AmSCAP 66*
Johnson, I D *Alli Sup*
Johnson, Irma Bolan 1903- *ConAu 1R*
Johnson, Irving McClure 1905- *Au&Wr,
ConAu 1R*
Johnson, Irving Peake 1866- *WhWNAA*
Johnson, Isaac *Alli*
Johnson, J *Alli, BiDLA*
Johnson, J C 1896- *AmSCAP 66*
Johnson, J E *Alli, Alli Sup*
Johnson, J E 1916- *Au&Wr*
Johnson, J George 1913- *AmSCAP 66*
Johnson, J K *OxCan Sup*
Johnson, J M *Alli Sup*
Johnson, J Rosamond 1873-1954 *AmSCAP 66*
Johnson, Jalmar Edwin 1905- *ConAu 5R*
Johnson, James *Alli, Alli Sup, BiDLA,
ChPo, DcEnL*
Johnson, James d1774 *Alli*
Johnson, James d1811 *BrAu 19*
Johnson, James And John Henry *Alli Sup*
Johnson, James A 1917- *AmSCAP 66*
Johnson, James Bowen 1830-1899 *DcNAA*
Johnson, James C *ChPo, ChPo S1*
Johnson, James Craig 1944- *ConAu 53*
Johnson, James Henry 1930- *ConAu 25,
WrD 1976*
Johnson, James J 1939- *ConAu 33*
Johnson, James L 1927- *ConAu 21*
Johnson, James P 1891-1955 *AmSCAP 66*
Johnson, James R *Alli*
Johnson, James Ralph 1922- *AuBYP,
ConAu 1R, SmATA 1, WrD 1976*
Johnson, James Rosser 1916- *ConAu 9R*
Johnson, James Turner 1938- *ConAu 61*
Johnson, James Weldon 1871-1938 *AmA&B,
AmSCAP 66, AnCL, AnMV 1926,
BlkAW, CasWL, ChPo, ChPo S1,
ChPo S2, ConAmA, ConAmL, DcLEnL,
DcNAA, ModAL Sup, OxAm, Pen Am,
RAdv 1, REn, REnAL, SixAP, TwCA,
TwCA Sup, WebEAL, WhWNAA*
Johnson, James William 1927- *ConAu 53*
Johnson, Jane M 1914- *ConAu 49*
Johnson, Jasper W *Alli Sup*
Johnson, Jay W 1903- *AmSCAP 66*
Johnson, Jean Dye 1920- *ConAu 23*
Johnson, Jennie LaRue *ChPo*
Johnson, Jerry Mack 1927- *ConAu 53*
Johnson, Jesse 1842-1918 *DcNAA*
Johnson, Jesse J 1914- *BlkAW, LivBA,
WrD 1976*
Johnson, Jessie Davis *BlkAW*
Johnson, Jinna *ConAu XR*
Johnson, Joan Helen 1931- *ConAu 61*
Johnson, Joe 1940- *BlkAW, DrAF 1976,
DrAP 1975, LivBA*
Johnson, Joe Donald 1943- *ConAu 57*
Johnson, John *Alli, BiDLA*
Johnson, John 1662-1725 *Alli, DcEnL*
Johnson, Sir John 1742-1830 *OxCan*
Johnson, John 1829-1907 *BiDSA, DcAmA,
DcNAA*
Johnson, John 1861- *Alli Sup*
Johnson, John Alexander 1849-1929 *OhA&B*
Johnson, John B *Alli, Alli Sup*
Johnson, John Butler 1850-1902 *Alli Sup,
DcAmA, DcNAA*
Johnson, John E 1929- *ChPo S1, IlBYP,
IICB 1966*
Johnson, John Edgar *Alli Sup*
Johnson, John G *Alli Sup*
Johnson, John H 1826- *BbtC*
Johnson, John J 1912- *ConAu 9R*
Johnson, John Lipscomb *Alli Sup*
Johnson, John M *OxCan*
Johnson, Johnni 1922- *ConAu 13R*
Johnson, Jonathan 1874- *WhWNAA*
Johnson, Jonathan Eastman 1824-1906 *EarAB*
Johnson, Joseph *Alli Sup, ChPo S1*
Johnson, Joseph 1776-1862 *BiDSA, DcAmA,
DcNAA*
Johnson, Joseph 1822- *Alli Sup*
Johnson, Joseph E 1946- *ConAu 37,
WrD 1976*
Johnson, Joseph Forsyth *Alli Sup*

Johnson, Joseph French 1853-1925 *AmA&B,
AmLY, DcAmA, DcNAA*
Johnson, Joseph M 1883?-1973 *ConAu 45*
Johnson, Josephine Winslow 1910- *AmA&B,
AmNov, AnMV 1926, ChPo, CnDAL,
ConAmA, ConAu 25, ConNov 1972,
ConNov 1976, DcLEnL, DrAF 1976,
OxAm, REnAL, TwCA, TwCA Sup,
WhWNAA, WrD 1976*
Johnson, Kathryn 1929- *ConAu 33*
Johnson, Keith B 1933- *ConAu 29*
Johnson, Kenneth G 1922- *ConAu 41*
Johnson, Kenneth M 1903- *ConAu 5R*
Johnson, Kristi Planck 1944- *ConAu 57*
Johnson, L D *Alli*
Johnson, L D 1916- *ConAu 33*
Johnson, Laura 1825-1889 *Alli, Alli Sup,
DcAmA, DcNAA*
Johnson, Laurence 1845-1893 *Alli Sup,
DcNAA*
Johnson, Leanna F *BlkAW*
Johnson, Lemuel A 1941- *AfA 1, ConAu 53*
Johnson, Lena Agnes 1911- *TexWr*
Johnson, Lena Williams 1884- *TexWr*
Johnson, Lewis Franklin 1859-1931 *DcNAA*
Johnson, Lewis Jerome 1867- *DcAmA*
Johnson, Lewis Kerr 1904- *ConAu 1R*
Johnson, Lionel Pigot 1867-1902 *AtlBL,
BrAu 19, CasWL, ChPo, ChPo S2,
Chmbr 3, CnE&AP, DcEnA Ap, DcEuL,
DcLEnL, EvLB, LongC, NewC, OxEng,
Pen Eng, PoIre, REn, WebEAL*
Johnson, Lois Smith 1894- *ConAu P-1,
SmATA 6*
Johnson, Lois Walfrid 1936- *ConAu 57*
Johnson, Lorenzo Dow 1805-1867 *DcNAA*
Johnson, Louis 1924- *ChPo S1, ConP 1970,
ConP 1975, LongC, TwCW, WrD 1976*
Johnson, Louisa *Alli*
Johnson, Lucile 1907- *AmSCAP 66*
Johnson, Lucius Henry 1863- *WhWNAA*
Johnson, Lute H *WhWNAA*
Johnson, Luther Appeles 1858-1900 *BiDSA,
DcNAA*
Johnson, Luther R *ChPo S1*
Johnson, Lyndon Baines 1908-1973 *AmA&B,
ConAu 41, ConAu 53, OxAm, REn*
Johnson, Mrs. M A *ChPo S1*
Johnson, Mrs. M B *ChPo S1*
Johnson, M Glen 1936- *ConAu 41*
Johnson, M J *Alli*
Johnson, Mrs. M O *Alli Sup, ChPo*
Johnson, Mabel Hubbard *ChPo*
Johnson, Mae Smith 1890- *BlkAW*
Johnson, Maggie Pogue *BlkAW*
Johnson, Margaret 1860- *Alli Sup, AmA&B,
ChPo, ChPo S1, ChPo S2, DcAmA,
WhWNAA*
Johnson, Margaret 1926- *ConAu 37*
Johnson, Margaret Sweet 1893- *AuBYP,
JBA 1951*
Johnson, Maria L *Alli Sup*
Johnson, Marilue Carolyn 1931- *ConAu 45*
Johnson, Marion Georgina Wikeley 1912-
Au&Wr, ConAu 9R
Johnson, Marjorie Cecil 1904- *DcSpL*
Johnson, Marmaduke d1674 *AmA&B*
Johnson, Marshall *ChPo S1*
Johnson, Marshall D 1935- *ConAu 33*
Johnson, Martin Elmer 1884-1937 *AmA&B,
DcNAA, REnAL*
Johnson, Mary *ChPo S1*
Johnson, Mary A *Alli Sup*
Johnson, Mary Anne 1943- *ConAu 53*
Johnson, Mary Eugenia *Alli Sup*
Johnson, Mary F *Alli, BiDLA*
Johnson, Mary Louise *ConAu XR*
Johnson, Mary Kitz 1904- *ConAu P-1*
Johnson, Mary Walley *TexWr*
Johnson, Maryanna 1925- *ConAu 33*
Johnson, Matthew *Alli, BlkAW*
Johnson, Matthias *OxGer*
Johnson, Maud Marian *ChPo S1, ChPo S2*
Johnson, Maurice d1755 *Alli*
Johnson, Maurice 1913- *ConAu 1R*
Johnson, Mauritz 1922- *ConAu 41*
Johnson, Merle Allison 1934- *ConAu 37*
Johnson, Merle DeVore 1874-1935 *AmA&B,*

AmLY, ChPo, ChPo S1, DcNAA,
OxAm
Johnson, Michael Henderson Flowers 1928-
WrD 1976
Johnson, Michael L 1943- ConAu 53
Johnson, Milton 1932- IlCB 1966
Johnson, Myron ChPo
Johnson, Miss N C ChPo
Johnson, Nathaniel Emmons d1847 DcNAA
Johnson, Nicholas 1934- AmA&B, ConAu 29,
WrD 1976
Johnson, Niel M 1931- ConAu 41
Johnson, Nora 1933- Au&Wr
Johnson, Norman M ChPo
Johnson, Nunnally 1897- AmA&B, ChPo,
REnAL
Johnson, O W And W Winfield Alli
Johnson, Olga Weydemeyer 1901- ConAu 29,
OxCan Sup
Johnson, Olive McClintic TexWr
Johnson, Oliver 1809-1889 Alli Sup, AmA&B,
BiD&SB, ChPo, DcAmA, DcNAA,
OxAm
Johnson, Oliver A 1923- ConAu 29
Johnson, Osa Helen 1894-1953 AmA&B,
AuBYP, REnAL
Johnson, Otis Coe 1839-1912 DcNAA
Johnson, Overton d1849 IndAu 1816
Johnson, Owen McMahon 1878-1952 AmA&B,
ConAmL, DcAmA, EncM&D, OxAm,
REnAL, TwCA, TwCA Sup
Johnson, Pamela Hansford 1912- Au&Wr,
ConAu 1R, ConLC 1, ConNov 1972,
ConNov 1976, DcLEnL, EncWL Sup,
EvLB, LongC, ModBL, ModBL Sup,
NewC, REn, TwCA Sup, TwCW,
WebEAL, WrD 1976
Johnson, Patrick Spencer 1938- ConAu 9R
Johnson, Paul Alli Sup
Johnson, Paul Bede 1928- Au&Wr,
ConAu 17R, WrD 1976
Johnson, Paul Emanuel 1898- Au&Wr,
ConAu 13R
Johnson, Paul Victor 1920- ConAu 1R,
IndAu 1917, WrD 1976
Johnson, Pauline 1862?-1913 CanWr, OxCan
Johnson, Pauline B ConAu 1R
Johnson, Percy John William 1895- Au&Wr
Johnson, Pete K H 1904- AmSCAP 66
Johnson, Peter Jeffrey 1946- Au&Wr,
WrD 1976
Johnson, Peter Leo 1888- BkC 6
Johnson, Philander Chase 1866-1939 AmA&B,
ChPo, DcAmA, DcNAA, REnAL
Johnson, Philip A 1915- ConAu 13R
Johnson, Pierce 1921- ConAu 41
Johnson, Quentin G 1930- ConAu 9R
Johnson, R Alli, Alli Sup
Johnson, R S 1946- ConAu 29
Johnson, Ralph Alli
Johnson, Randall BlkAW
Johnson, Ray BlkAW
Johnson, Ray 1927- AmA&B, ConAu 17R
Johnson, Raynor Carey 1901- Au&Wr, BiDPar
Johnson, Reginald Brimley 1867-1932 ChPo
Johnson, Reverdy 1796-1876 BiDSA
Johnson, Richard Alli Sup, ChPo, OxCan
Johnson, Richard d1720 Alli
Johnson, Richard 1573-1659? Alli, BrAu,
CasWL, DcEnA, DcEnL, EvLB, NewC,
OxEng
Johnson, Richard 1734-1793 CarSB
Johnson, Richard 1939- ConAu 57
Johnson, Richard A 1937- ConAu 37,
WrD 1976
Johnson, Richard B 1914- ConAu 41
Johnson, Richard Byron Alli Sup, OxCan
Johnson, Richard C 1919- ConAu 33
Johnson, Richard Francis Alli Sup
Johnson, Richard Locke Alli Sup
Johnson, Richard M 1934- ConAu 23
Johnson, Richard Mentor 1781-1850 BiDSA
Johnson, Richard Otto 1859-1928 IndAu 1816
Johnson, Richard T 1938- ConAu 53,
WrD 1976
Johnson, Richard W 1827-1897 Alli Sup,
BiDSA, DcAmA, DcNAA
Johnson, Robert Alli, BiDLA

Johnson, Robert A 1921- ConAu 61
Johnson, Robert Clyde 1919- ConAu 5R,
WrD 1976
Johnson, Robert E AuBYP
Johnson, Robert Erwin 1923- ConAu 37,
WrD 1976
Johnson, Robert Gibbon d1850 Alli, DcNAA
Johnson, Robert Ivar 1933- AmA&B,
ConAu 53
Johnson, Robert J 1933- ConAu 23
Johnson, Robert L 1919- ConAu 33
Johnson, Robert Leon 1930- ConAu 33,
WrD 1976
Johnson, Robert Owen 1926- ConAu 33
Johnson, Robert Sherlaw 1932- ConAu 61,
WrD 1976
Johnson, Robert U And Buel, Clarence C
Alli Sup
Johnson, Robert Underwood 1853-1937
AmA&B, AmLY, BbD, BiD&SB, ChPo,
ChPo S1, ChPo S2, DcAmA, DcNAA,
IndAu 1816, OxAm, REn, REnAL,
TwCA, TwCA Sup, WhWNAA
Johnson, Robert Vincent 1927- WrD 1976
Johnson, Robert Wallace Alli, BiDLA
Johnson, Robert Willard 1921- ConAu 17R,
WrD 1976
Johnson, Robert William Alli Sup
Johnson, Roger N 1939- ConAu 53
Johnson, Ronald 1935- ConAu 9R,
ConP 1970, ConP 1975, DrAP 1975,
WrD 1976
Johnson, Rosa Vertner Alli Sup, AmA&B,
DcAmA
Johnson, Rose DcNAA
Johnson, Rossall J 1917- ConAu 21
Johnson, Rossiter 1840-1931 AmA&B, BbD,
BiD&SB, CarSB, ChPo, ChPo S1,
DcAmA, DcNAA, OxCan, REnAL,
WhWNAA
Johnson, Mrs. Rossiter AmA&B
Johnson, Roswell Hill 1877- WhWNAA
Johnson, Ruby Kelley 1928- ConAu 33
Johnson, Ruie WhWNAA
Johnson, Ruth Brownlee BlkAW
Johnson, Ryerson 1901- ConAu 5R,
SmATA 10
Johnson, S Alli
Johnson, S Lawrence 1909- ConAu 29,
WrD 1976
Johnson, Mrs. S O Alli Sup
Johnson, Samuel Alli, Chmbr 2
Johnson, Samuel 1649-1703 Alli, EvLB,
NewC
Johnson, Samuel 1696-1772 Alli, AmA,
AmA&B, CnDAL, CyAL 1, DcAmA,
DcLEnL, DcNAA, OxAm, REn, REnAL
Johnson, Samuel 1705-1773 Alli, DcEnL
Johnson, Samuel 1709-1784 Alli, AtlBL, BbD,
BiD&SB, BrAu, CasWL, ChPo,
ChPo S1, ChPo S2, CnE&AP, CriT 2,
CyWA, DcBiA, DcEnA, DcEnA Ap,
DcEnL, DcEuL, DcLEnL, EvLB,
MouLC 2, NewC, OxAm, OxEng,
Pen Eng, RCom, REn, WebEAL
Johnson, Samuel 1757-1836 DcNAA
Johnson, Samuel 1763-1843 DcNAA
Johnson, Samuel 1822-1882 Alli Sup, AmA,
DcAmA, DcNAA, PoCh, WebEAL
Johnson, Samuel A 1895- ConAu 17R
Johnson, Samuel B d1820 Alli
Johnson, Samuel Jenkins Alli Sup
Johnson, Samuel Lewis ChPo, ChPo S1
Johnson, Samuel M 1899- BlkAW
Johnson, Samuel William 1830-1909 Alli Sup,
DcAmA, DcNAA
Johnson, Sarah Barclay 1837-1885 Alli,
DcAmA, DcNAA
Johnson, Searcy Lee 1908- AmSCAP 66
Johnson, Sherman E 1908- Au&Wr,
ConAu 53
Johnson, Shirley King 1927- ConAu 9R,
SmATA 10, WrD 1976
Johnson, Siddie Joe 1905- AuBYP, ChPo S1,
JBA 1951, TexWr
Johnson, Sol C 1868- WhWNAA
Johnson, Solomon 1850-1918 OhA&B
Johnson, Stanley L 1920- ConAu 17R

Johnson, Stanley Patrick 1940- ConAu 23
Johnson, Stephen Philip Lowthian 1912-
Au&Wr
Johnson, Stowers Au&Wr, ConAu 5R,
WrD 1976
Johnson, Susannah Alli Sup
Johnson, T Alli
Johnson, T B BiDLA
Johnson, Theodore Alli Sup
Johnson, Theodore Taylor 1818- Alli, DcNAA
Johnson, Thomas Alli, DrAP 1975
Johnson, Thomas d1644 Alli
Johnson, Thomas 1675-1750 DcEnL
Johnson, Thomas 1732-1819 BiDSA
Johnson, Thomas 1760?-1825? BiDSA,
DcNAA
Johnson, Thomas Burgland d1840 Alli,
Br&AmS
Johnson, Thomas Cary 1859-1936 AmLY,
BiDSA, DcAmA, DcNAA, WhWNAA
Johnson, Thomas Frank 1920- ConAu 9R
Johnson, Thomas Herbert ChPo, ChPo S1
Johnson, Thomas M Alli Sup
Johnson, Thomas Marvin 1889- AmA&B
Johnson, Thomas R BbtC
Johnson, Tom Loftin 1854-1911 OhA&B
Johnson, Uwe 1934- Au&Wr, CasWL,
ConAu 1R, ConLC 5, EncWL, ModGL,
OxGer, Pen Eur, TwCW, WorAu
Johnson, Van L 1908- ConAu 37
Johnson, Vernon Cecil 1886- CatA 1947
Johnson, Victor Hugo 1912- Au&Wr
Johnson, Virginia 1914- ConAu 33
Johnson, Virginia Eshelman 1925- AmA&B,
AuNews 1, ConAu 21
Johnson, Virginia Wales 1849-1916 Alli Sup,
AmA, AmA&B, BiD&SB, DcAmA,
DcNAA
Johnson, Virginia Weisel 1910- ConAu 17R,
WhPNW
Johnson, Vlyn ChPo S2
Johnson, W B Alli, Alli Sup, BiDLA
Johnson, W Bolingbroke ConAu XR
Johnson, W G Alli
Johnson, W R Alli, BbtC, BiDLA, ChPo S2
Johnson, Walter Alli Sup
Johnson, Walter Frank, Jr. 1914- ConAu 5R
Johnson, Walter Rogers 1794-1852 Alli,
DcAmA, DcNAA
Johnson, Warren Arthur 1937- ConAu 33,
WrD 1976
Johnson, Wendell A L 1906-1965 AmA&B,
ConAu 1R
Johnson, Wendell F 1893- OhA&B
Johnson, Wendell Stacy 1927- ConAu 1R,
WrD 1976
Johnson, William Alli, Alli Sup, BiDLA,
BrAu 19, CasWL
Johnson, William d1666 Alli
Johnson, William d1848 Alli
Johnson, Sir William 1715-1774 Alli, OxAm,
OxCan, REnAL
Johnson, William 1771-1834 BiDSA, DcNAA
Johnson, William 1811- Alli
Johnson, William 1912-1960 AmSCAP 66
Johnson, William, And Nicholson, Peter Alli
Johnson, William Alexander 1931?-
AmSCAP 66, ConAu 5R
Johnson, William Alfred Alli Sup
Johnson, William Branch 1893- Au&Wr,
ConAu 5R
Johnson, William Bullien 1782-1862 BiDSA
Johnson, William C 1945- ConAu 61
Johnson, William Eugene 1862-1945 AmLY,
OhA&B, WhWNAA
Johnson, William Forbes Alli Sup
Johnson, William Hallock 1865- AmLY,
WhWNAA
Johnson, William Hannibal 1860-1934 OhA&B
Johnson, William Henry 1833-1901 DcNAA
Johnson, William Henry 1845-1907 BiDSA,
DcAmA, DcNAA
Johnson, William Hilton 1935- IndAu 1917
Johnson, William Knox 1868-1906 PoIre
Johnson, William Martin d1796 Alli, CyAL 1
Johnson, William Matthews 1905- BlkAW,
LivBAA, WrD 1976
Johnson, William Moore, & Exley, Thomas Alli,

BiDLA
Johnson, William R *ConAu 17R*
Johnson, William Samuel *ChPo S2*
Johnson, William Samuel 1727-1819 *AmA&B,*
CyAL 1
Johnson, William Samuel 1859-1937 *AmA&B,*
AmLY, DcNAA
Johnson, William Savage 1877-1942 *DcNAA,*
OhA&B, WhWNAA
Johnson, William Weber 1909- *AmA&B,*
AuBYP, ConAu 17R, SmATA 7,
WrD 1976
Johnson, William Woolsey 1841-1927 *Alli Sup,*
AmLY, CyAL 1, DcAmA, DcNAA
Johnson, Willis Ernest 1869- *WhWNAA*
Johnson, Willis Fletcher 1857-1931 *AmA&B,*
DcNAA
Johnson, Willis Grant 1866-1908 *DcNAA*
Johnson, Willis Hugh 1902- *IndAu 1917*
Johnson, Winifred 1905- *ConAu 5R*
Johnson, Wolcott *WhWNAA*
Johnson, Yvette *BlkAW*
Johnson, Zachariah d1892 *Polre*
Johnson-Marshall, Percy E A 1915- *ConAu 23*
Johnson Of Boone, Benjamin *AmA&B*
Johnsoe, Fowler De *Alli*
Johnston, A J *Alli*
Johnston, A Montgomery 1915- *ConAu 29*
Johnston, A R Campbell 1812-1888 *Alli Sup*
Johnston, Agnes Christine *ConAu XR,*
SmATA 2
Johnston, Albert C, Jr. 1925- *AmSCAP 66*
Johnston, Alexander *Alli*
Johnston, Alexander d1799 *Alli*
Johnston, Alexander 1849-1889 *Alli Sup, AmA,*
AmA&B, DcAmA, DcNAA, REnAL
Johnston, Alexander Keith 1804-1871 *Alli,*
Alli Sup
Johnston, Alexander Keith 1846-1879 *Alli Sup*
Johnston, Alfred Wintle 1859- *WhLA*
Johnston, Alma Calder *Alli Sup*
Johnston, Alva 1888-1950 *REnAL*
Johnston, Andrew *Alli*
Johnston, Angus James, II 1916- *ConAu 9R*
Johnston, Anna Isabel *Polre*
Johnston, Annie Fellows 1863-1931 *AmA&B,*
ArizL, BiDSA, CarSB, ChPo, DcAmA,
DcNAA, IndAu 1816, JBA 1934, OxAm,
REnAL, TwCA, TwCA Sup
Johnston, Arthur 1587-1641 *Alli, CasWL,*
Chmbr 1, DcEnL, EvLB
Johnston, Arthur 1841-1919 *DcNAA*
Johnston, Arthur 1924- *ConAu 23*
Johnston, Arthur E 1895- *OhA&B*
Johnston, Arthur James 1898-1954
AmSCAP 66
Johnston, Avin Harry 1906- *ConAu 1R*
Johnston, Bernard 1934- *ConAu 17R*
Johnston, Bernice Houle 1914- *ConAu 33*
Johnston, Bert 1898-1952 *OhA&B*
Johnston, Bill 1782-1870 *OxCan*
Johnston, Brenda A 1944- *ConAu 57*
Johnston, Bruce F 1919- *ConAu 41*
Johnston, Bryce 1747-1805 *Alli*
Johnston, C F T *Alli*
Johnston, Charles *Alli, Alli Sup*
Johnston, Charles d1800 *DcEnL*
Johnston, Charles 1867-1931 *DcAmA, DcNAA,*
WhWNAA
Johnston, Charles Haven Ladd 1877-1943
AmA&B, AmLY, WhWNAA
Johnston, Charles Hepburn 1912- *ConAu 13R,*
WrD 1976
Johnston, Charles Hughes 1877-1917 *DcNAA*
Johnston, Christopher 1856-1914 *DcNAA*
Johnston, Christopher N *Alli Sup*
Johnston, David *Alli*
Johnston, David 1802-1879 *Alli Sup*
Johnston, David Claypoole 1799-1865 *AmA&B,*
EarAB, EarAB Sup
Johnston, David Emmons 1845-1917 *DcNAA*
Johnston, Denis 1901- *Au&Wr, CasWL,*
CnMD, CnThe, ConAu 21, ConDr,
LongC, McGWD, ModBL, ModBL Sup,
ModWD, NewC, REnWD, TwCA Sup,
WrD 1976
Johnston, Donald Kent 1881-1944 *DcNAA*
Johnston, Dorothy Grunbock 1915- *ConAu 5R*

Johnston, Edith Constance Farrington 1890-
IlCB 1945, IlCB 1956
Johnston, Edward William *BiDSA*
Johnston, Elias *Alli, BiDLA Sup*
Johnston, Elizabeth Bryant 1833-1907 *Alli Sup,*
BiDSA, DcNAA
Johnston, Ella Bond 1860- *IndAu 1917*
Johnston, Ellen *Alli Sup*
Johnston, Eugene T *Alli Sup, Polre*
Johnston, Fran 1925- *ConAu 13R*
Johnston, Francis E 1931- *ConAu 53*
Johnston, Frederick *ChPo S2*
Johnston, Frederick 1811-1894 *BiDSA,*
DcNAA
Johnston, Gary *BlkAW*
Johnston, Gene 1908- *AmSCAP 66*
Johnston, George *Alli, Alli Sup, BiDSA*
Johnston, George d1855 *Alli*
Johnston, George 1829-1891 *DcNAA*
Johnston, George 1913- *CanWr, ConAu 1R,*
ConP 1975, OxCan, OxCan Sup,
WrD 1976
Johnston, George Alexander 1888- *WhLA*
Johnston, George Benson 1913- *ConP 1970*
Johnston, George Burke 1907- *ConAu P-1*
Johnston, George Doherty 1832- *BiDSA*
Johnston, Grace Keith *Alli Sup*
Johnston, H A S 1913-1967 *ConAu 21*
Johnston, H J M 1939- *ConAu 41,*
OxCan Sup
Johnston, Haidee *Polre*
Johnston, Hamilton Charles Phillott 1915-
Au&Wr
Johnston, Hank *ConAu XR*
Johnston, Harold Whetstone 1859-1912 *DcAmA,*
DcNAA
Johnston, Harriet *Polre*
Johnston, Sir Harry Hamilton 1858-1927
Chmbr 3, EvLB, LongC, NewC, TwCA
Johnston, Henry *Alli, Alli Sup, BiDLA,*
ChPo S1, ChPo S2
Johnston, Henry 1922- *ConAu 25*
Johnston, Henry Halcro 1856- *WhLA*
Johnston, Henry Hamilton *Alli Sup*
Johnston, Henry Phelps 1842-1923 *Alli Sup,*
AmA&B, DcAmA, DcNAA
Johnston, Henry William *Alli Sup*
Johnston, Herbert 1912- *ConAu 5R*
Johnston, Howard A 1860-1936 *DcNAA,*
OhA&B
Johnston, Hugh 1840-1922 *Alli Sup, DcAmA,*
DcNAA
Johnston, J Field *Alli Sup*
Johnston, J P *Alli Sup*
Johnston, J W *ChPo S1*
Johnston, James *Alli, Alli Sup, OxCan Sup,*
Polre
Johnston, James Brown 1862- *WhLA*
Johnston, James D *Alli Sup*
Johnston, James Finlay Weir 1796-1855 *Alli,*
BbtC, OxCan
Johnston, James John 1862- *ChPo S1*
Johnston, James M *Polre*
Johnston, James Nicholl *Polre*
Johnston, James Nicoll 1831-1918 *ChPo S1*
Johnston, James Weir 1796-1853 *DcEnL*
Johnston, James Wesley 1847?-1936 *AmA&B,*
DcNAA
Johnston, James William 1792-1873 *OxCan*
Johnston, Jill 1929- *ConAu 53, WrD 1976*
Johnston, Jocelyn 1855- *Polre*
Johnston, Johanna *AuBYP, ConAu 57*
Johnston, John *Alli, Alli Sup*
Johnston, John d1612 *Alli, DcEnL*
Johnston, John 1603-1675 *Alli*
Johnston, John 1748-1827 *Polre*
Johnston, John 1757-1820 *Alli*
Johnston, John 1775-1861 *BiDLA, OhA&B*
Johnston, John 1806-1879 *Alli, Alli Sup,*
DcAmA, DcNAA
Johnston, John A *Polre*
Johnston, John Black 1802-1882 *OhA&B*
Johnston, John Black 1868-1939 *DcNAA,*
OhA&B
Johnston, John Brown *Alli Sup*
Johnston, John H 1921- *ConAu 9R*
Johnston, John Moore 1747- *Polre*

Johnston, John Thomas Morris 1856-1930
DcNAA
Johnston, John Wilson *Alli Sup*
Johnston, Joseph *Alli, Alli Sup*
Johnston, Joseph Eggleston 1807-1891 *Alli Sup,*
BiDSA, DcAmA, DcNAA
Johnston, Josiah Stoddard *BiDSA*
Johnston, Josiah Stoddard 1784-1833 *DcNAA*
Johnston, Josiah Stoddard 1833-1913 *DcAmA,*
DcNAA
Johnston, Julia Harriette 1849-1919 *Alli Sup,*
AmLY, ChPo S1, DcNAA, OhA&B
Johnston, L C *Polre*
Johnston, L F C *Alli*
Johnston, Laurie *AuBYP*
Johnston, Leonard 1920- *ConAu 13R*
Johnston, Louisa Mae *AuBYP*
Johnston, Lukin *OxCan*
Johnston, Mother M Francis 1900- *CatA 1947*
Johnston, Mrs. M L *Alli Sup*
Johnston, Mabel A d1945 *DcNAA*
Johnston, Mabel Lauer 1886- *WhWNAA*
Johnston, Margaret A *BiDSA*
Johnston, Maria Isabella 1835- *DcNAA*
Johnston, Marianne C *Alli Sup*
Johnston, Mary 1870-1936 *AmA&B, BbD,*
BiD&SB, BiDSA, ChPo, Chmbr 3,
CnDAL, ConAmL, CyWA, DcAmA,
DcBiA, DcEnA Ap, DcNAA, LongC,
OxAm, REn, REnAL, TwCA
Johnston, Mary 1925- *AmSCAP 66*
Johnston, Minton C 1900- *ConAu 5R*
Johnston, Mireille 1940- *ConAu 49*
Johnston, Myrtle 1909- *TwCA, TwCA Sup*
Johnston, Nathan Robinson 1820-1904 *DcAmA,*
OhA&B
Johnston, Nathaniel *Alli*
Johnston, Patricia 1922-1953 *AmSCAP 66*
Johnston, Patrick *DcEnL*
Johnston, Percy 1930- *BlkAW*
Johnston, Priscilla 1910- *Au&Wr*
Johnston, R *Alli Sup*
Johnston, Ralph E 1902- *AuBYP*
Johnston, Sir Reginald Fleming 1874- *WhLA*
Johnston, Remington Allen 1875-1946
IndAu 1816
Johnston, Richard H 1868- *WhWNAA*
Johnston, Richard James Humphreys 1910-
AmA&B
Johnston, Richard Malcolm 1822-1898 *Alli Sup,*
AmA, AmA&B, BiD&SB, BiDSA,
DcAmA, DcBiA, DcLEnL, DcNAA,
OxAm, REnAL
Johnston, Robert *Alli, Alli Sup*
Johnston, Robert d1639? *Alli, DcEnL*
Johnston, Robert Matteson 1867-1920 *AmA&B,*
AmLY, DcNAA
Johnston, Robert W *Alli Sup*
Johnston, Ronald 1926- *Au&Wr, ConAu 13R,*
WrD 1976
Johnston, Ruth *ChPo S1*
Johnston, Samuel F 1830-1861 *BbtC*
Johnston, Sue Mildred Lee 1896- *WhWNAA*
Johnston, T *Alli Sup*
Johnston, T B And Robertson, James A *Alli Sup*
Johnston, T P *Alli Sup, ChPo S1*
Johnston, T R 1893- *WhWNAA*
Johnston, Thomas *Alli, BbtC*
Johnston, Thomas E 1931- *ConAu 13R*
Johnston, Thomas T *AnMV 1926*
Johnston, Thomas Todd *WhWNAA*
Johnston, Tony 1942- *ConAu 41, SmATA 8*
Johnston, W And A K *Alli*
Johnston, W Corrie *Alli Sup*
Johnston, W V *OxCan Sup*
Johnston, Wijnant 1890- *IndAu 1917*
Johnston, William *Alli, Alli Sup, ChPo S2,*
Polre
Johnston, William 1804-1892? *DcNAA,*
OhA&B
Johnston, William 1829-1902 *Alli Sup, Polre*
Johnston, William 1840-1917 *DcNAA*
Johnston, William 1871- *MnBBF*
Johnston, William 1871-1929 *AmA&B, AmLY*
Johnston, William 1901- *WrD 1976*
Johnston, William 1925- *ConAu 33,*
WrD 1976

Johnston, William Alexander 1864-1946 *OhA&B*

Johnston, William Allen 1876- *AmLY*

Johnston, William Andrew 1871-1929 *DcNAA*

Johnston, William Atkinson 1868-1937 *DcNAA*

Johnston, William Dawson 1871-1928 *AmLY, DcNAA*

Johnston, William Denis 1901- *DcLEnL*

Johnston, William Drumm 1899-1972 *IndAu 1917*

Johnston, William Harris *Alli Sup*

Johnston, William Murray 1936- *ConAu 37, WrD 1976*

Johnston, William Preston 1831-1899 *Alli Sup, AmA, BiD&SB, BiDSA, ChPo S2, DcAmA, DcNAA*

Johnston-Saint, Peter 1889-1974 *Au&Wr, ConAu 53*

Johnstone, Mrs. *Alli*

Johnstone, Alexander *ChPo*

Johnstone, Alfred S *ChPo S1*

Johnstone, Andrew Cochrane *Alli, BiDLA*

Johnstone, Anne *IlBYP*

Johnstone, Arthur Edward 1860-1944 *DcNAA*

Johnstone, Athol A *Alli Sup*

Johnstone, Augusta *Alli Sup*

Johnstone, C E *ChPo*

Johnstone, C F *Alli Sup*

Johnstone, C L *Alli Sup*

Johnstone, C Laura *Alli Sup*

Johnstone, Charles 1719?-1800? *Alli, BbD, BiD&SB, CasWL, Chmbr 2, DcEuL, DcLEnL, EvLB, NewC, OxEng*

Johnstone, Charlotte Stuart *Alli Sup*

Johnstone, Chevalier De *Alli*

Johnstone, Christian Isobel 1781-1857 *BiD&SB, Chmbr 2, NewC*

Johnstone, D Lawson *Alli Sup*

Johnstone, David *ChPo*

Johnstone, Edward *Alli*

Johnstone, George *Alli*

Johnstone, George d1787 *Alli*

Johnstone, Gordon 1876-1926 *AmSCAP 66*

Johnstone, Henry *ChPo, ChPo S2*

Johnstone, Henry 1844- *ChPo*

Johnstone, Henry Alexander Munro Butler- 1837- *Alli Sup*

Johnstone, Henry W, Jr. 1920- *ConAu 1R*

Johnstone, Herrick *HsB&A*

Johnstone, Hilda 1882- *WhLA*

Johnstone, Ian Anthony 1935- *WrD 1976*

Johnstone, J *ChPo*

Johnstone, J Alfred 1861- *WhLA*

Johnstone, J C *Alli Sup*

Johnstone, James *Alli, Alli Sup*

Johnstone, James 1730-1802 *Alli*

Johnstone, James, Chevalier De 1719-1800? *OxCan*

Johnstone, James Barbour *Alli Sup*

Johnstone, Janet *IlBYP*

Johnstone, Job 1793-1862 *BiDSA*

Johnstone, John *Alli, BiDLA, OxCan Sup*

Johnstone, John d1836 *Alli*

Johnstone, Kathleen Yerger 1906- *ConAu 9R*

Johnstone, Keith *ConDr, WrD 1976*

Johnstone, Laurence *Alli Sup*

Johnstone, Mary Pauline 1919- *Au&Wr*

Johnstone, Richard *Alli Sup*

Johnstone, Robert *Alli Sup*

Johnstone, T Boston *Alli Sup*

Johnstone, Ted *ConAu XR*

Johnstone, Thomas 1812-1870 *ChPo*

Johnstone, Thomas A 1888- *AmSCAP 66*

Johnstone, Viola Mary 1915- *Au&Wr*

Johnstone, W D *Alli*

Johnstone, Walter *BbtC, OxCan*

Johnstone, William *Alli, BiDLA*

Johnstone, William Borthwick 1813-1868 *Alli Sup*

Johnstone, William G & Croall, Alexander *Alli Sup*

Johnstone, William Henry *Alli, Alli Sup*

Johnstone, William Jackson 1867-1939? *DcNAA, IndAu 1816, WhWNAA*

Johnstoun, James *Alli*

Johonnot, James 1823-1888 *Alli, Alli Sup, DcAmA, DcNAA*

Johst, Hanns 1890- *ClDMEuL, CnMD,*

ModWD, OxGer

Join-Lambert, Michel 1919- *Au&Wr*

Joiner, C L 1923- *Au&Wr*

Joiner, Charles W 1916- *ConAu 1R*

Joiner, Edward Earl 1924- *ConAu 49*

Joiner, Verna J 1896- *ConAu 1R*

Joinville, Jean, Sire De 1224?-1317 *AtlBL, BbD, BiD&SB, CasWL, DcEuL, EuA, EvEuW, NewC, OxEng, OxFr, Pen Eur, REn*

Jokai, Maurice 1825-1904 *BiD&SB*

Jokai, Maurus 1825-1904 *BbD, CyWA, DcEuL, EvEuW*

Jokai, Mor 1825-1904 *CasWL, DcBiA, EuA, Pen Eur*

Jokai, Moricz 1825-1904 *ClDMEuL*

Jokostra, Peter 1912- *OxGer*

Jolande Von Vianden, Grafin 1230?-1283 *OxGer*

Jolas, Eugene 1894-1952 *OxAm, REn, REnAL*

Jole, William *Alli*

Jolgar Cacho, Manuel 1898- *PueRA*

Joliat, Eugene 1910- *ConAu 49*

Jolicoeur, Catherine *OxCan Sup*

Joliet, Charles 1832- *BiD&SB*

Joliet, Louis 1645-1700 *REn*

Joliffe, Henry *Alli*

Jolin, Johan Kristofer 1818-1884 *BiD&SB*

Jolin, Stephen Towne 1941- *ConAu 45*

Joline, Adrian Hoffman 1850-1912 *AmA&B, ChPo, ChPo S1, DcNAA*

Joliph, William *Alli*

Jolivet, Alfred 1885- *WhLA*

Jolivet, R 1891-1966 *ConAu P-1*

Joll, Boyd Burnett *Alli Sup*

Joll, Edna Casler d1963 *WhPNW*

Joll, James Bysse 1918- *Au&Wr, ConAu 5R*

Jolles, Benjamin Abraham 1906- *Au&Wr, WrD 1976*

Jolley, Derrick Alan 1928- *Au&Wr*

Jolley, Florence W 1917- *AmSCAP 66*

Jollie, F *Alli, BiDLA*

Jollie, T *Alli*

Jolliet, Adrien *OxCan*

Jolliet, Louis 1645-1700 *OxCan, REn*

Jollife, T R *Alli*

Jolliffe, Edward B *OxCan Sup*

Jolliffe, H R 1904- *ConAu 1R*

Jolliffe, John 1804-1868 *DcNAA*

Jolliffe, John E A 1891-1964 *ConAu 5R*

Jolling, Jack *MnBBF*

Jolly, Alexander 1756-1838 *Alli*

Jolly, Alison 1937- *ConAu 41*

Jolly, Cyril Arthur 1910- *Au&Wr, ConAu P-1, WrD 1976*

Jolly, Emily *Alli Sup, HsB&A*

Jolly, Hugh Reginald 1918- *WrD 1976*

Jolly, J B F *Alli*

Jolly, Julius *Alli Sup*

Jolly, Pete 1932- *AmSCAP 66*

Jolly, Sarah *Alli Sup*

Jolly, William *Alli Sup*

Jolly, William Percy 1922- *Au&Wr, ConAu 53, WrD 1976*

Jolobe, James Ranisi 1902- *AfA 1, Pen Cl*

Jolson, Al 1886-1950 *AmSCAP 66*

Jolson, Marvin A 1922- *ConAu 49*

Joly, Cyril Bencraft 1918- *ConAu P-1*

Joly, Eugene 1901- *Au&Wr*

Joly, Guy *BiD&SB, OxFr*

Joly, John Swift 1818-1887 *PoIre*

Joly DeLotbiniere, Sir Henri-Gustave 1829-1908 *OxCan*

Jolys, Jean Marie Arthur d1926 *DcNAA*

Jon Eiriksson 1727-1787 *DcEuL*

Jon Thorlaksson 1744-1819 *DcEuL*

Jonas *DcEnL*

Jonas Hallgrimsson 1807-1845 *Pen Eur*

Jonas, A *Alli*

Jonas, Alberto 1868-1943 *DcNAA*

Jonas, Arthur 1930- *ConAu 13R*

Jonas, Carl 1913- *AmA&B, ConAu 9R, REnAL, TwCA Sup*

Jonas, Doris F 1916- *ConAu 61*

Jonas, Edward James *Alli Sup*

Jonas, George 1935- *ConAu 29, ConP 1970, ConP 1975, DrAP 1975, OxCan Sup, WrD 1976*

Jonas, Gerald *DrAP 1975*

Jonas, Hans 1903- *ConAu 61*

Jonas, Ilsedore B *ConAu 33*

Jonas, Justus 1493-1555 *OxGer*

Jonas, Klaus W 1920- *Au&Wr, ConAu 1R*

Jonas, Manfred 1927- *ConAu 21, WrD 1976*

Jonas, Nita *AmSCAP 66, ChPo*

Jonas, Peter *Alli, BiDLA*

Jonas, Rosalie M *ChPo, ChPo S1*

Jonas, Ruth *ChPo*

Jonas, S A *BiDSA*

Jonas, Sylvia Lucile Reiss 1895- *IndAu 1917*

Jonassen, Christen T 1912- *ConAu 41*

Jonasson, Johannes, Ur Kotlum 1899- *CasWL*

Jonathan *CasWL*

Joncaire, Louis Thomas De 1670-1739 *OxCan*

Joncas, Louis Zephirin 1846-1903 *DcNAA*

Joncich, Geraldine 1931- *ConAu 25*

Jonckbloet, Willem Jozef A 1817-1885 *BbD, BiD&SB, CasWL*

Jonckheere, Karel 1906- *CasWL*

Jonctijs, Daniel Ewoutsz 1611-1654 *CasWL*

Jones *Alli*

Jones, Captain *Alli*

Jones, Mrs. *Alli*

Jones, Mrs. A *ChPo S1*

Jones, A B *Alli Sup*

Jones, A C H *Alli Sup*

Jones, A E *Alli Sup, OxCan*

Jones, A Kate *ChPo*

Jones, A Morris 1899- *ConAu P-1*

Jones, Abner 1772-1841 *DcNAA*

Jones, Abner Dumont 1807-1872 *Alli, DcNAA*

Jones, Abraham *Alli, BiDLA*

Jones, Adam Leroy 1873-1934 *AmA&B, DcNAA*

Jones, Adolphus Eberhardt 1819-1889 *OhA&B*

Jones, Adrienne 1915- *ConAu 33, SmATA 7, WrD 1976*

Jones, Agnes Elizabeth *Alli Sup*

Jones, Alan Griffith 1943- *Au&Wr, WrD 1976*

Jones, Alan Moore, Jr. 1942- *ConAu 53*

Jones, Alexander 1802?-1863? *Alli, BiDSA, DcAmA, DcNAA*

Jones, Alexander 1906- *ConAu 1R*

Jones, Alfred *Alli, Alli Sup*

Jones, Alfred B *Alli*

Jones, Alfred Ernest 1879-1958 *WorAu*

Jones, Alfred Orlando *Alli Sup*

Jones, Alice 1853?-1933 *DcNAA, OxCan*

Jones, Alice Danner 1854-1926 *ChPo S2, OhA&B*

Jones, Alice H *BlkAW*

Jones, Alice Ilgenfritz d1906 *BiDSA, DcNAA*

Jones, Alonzo T *Alli Sup*

Jones, Alun Richard 1929- *Au&Wr*

Jones, Amanda Theodosia 1835-1914 *Alli Sup, AmA, AmA&B, BiD&SB, ChPo, ChPo S1, DcAmA, DcNAA*

Jones, Amos 1821-1903 *IndAu 1816*

Jones, Annie B *ChPo*

Jones, Anson 1798-1858 *BiDSA, DcNAA*

Jones, Archer 1926- *ConAu 1R*

Jones, Archibald Bence- 1857- *Alli Sup*

Jones, Archie N 1900- *ConAu P-1*

Jones, Arnold Hugh Martin 1904- *Au&Wr*

Jones, Arthur 1909- *AmSCAP 66*

Jones, Arthur Edward 1838-1918 *DcNAA*

Jones, Arthur Julius 1871- *WhWNAA*

Jones, Arthur Llwellyn *DcLEnL*

Jones, Augustine 1835-1925 *AmLY, DcAmA, DcNAA*

Jones, Barbara A *ChPo*

Jones, Barbara Ann 1948- *AmSCAP 66*

Jones, Barbara Mildred 1917- *Au&Wr, ConAu 1R, WrD 1976*

Jones, Barry *MnBBF*

Jones, Barry Owen 1932- *Au&Wr*

Jones, Basset *Alli*

Jones, Bayard Hale 1887-1957 *AmA&B*

Jones, Benjamin Charles *Alli Sup*

Jones, Bennett Melvill 1887- *WhLA*

Jones, Bernard *Au&Wr*

Jones, Berta B And Blakeley, Harriette *Alli Sup*

Jones, Beryl Bailey- *IlCB 1956*

Jones, Biff 1930- *AmSCAP 66*

Jones, Billy M 1925- *ConAu 21*

Jones, Bob 1911- *ConAu 25, WrD 1976*

Jones, Brian 1938- *Au&Wr, ChPo S1, ConP 1970, ConP 1975, WrD 1976*
Jones, Buehring H 1823- *BiDSA*
Jones, Burr W 1846-1935 *AmLY, DcNAA*
Jones, Byron Del Norte 1866- *IndAu 1917*
Jones, C *Alli Sup*
Jones, C d1792 *Alli*
Jones, C A *CarSB*
Jones, C C *Alli*
Jones, C Davenport *Alli Sup*
Jones, C David A 1921- *WrD 1976*
Jones, C Handfield, And E H Sieveking *Alli*
Jones, C J *Alli*
Jones, C Rachel *Alli Sup*
Jones, Cadwallader *BiDSA*
Jones, Carol Ann 1942- *IlCB 1966*
Jones, Carolyn 1932- *ConAu 29*
Jones, Carter Helm 1861-1946 *DcNAA*
Jones, Cave 1869-1929 *DcNAA*
Jones, Cecilia Anne *Alli Sup*
Jones, Charles *Alli*
Jones, Charles 1906- *WrD 1976*
Jones, Charles 1910- *AmSCAP 66, Au&Wr, ConAu P-1*
Jones, Charles A *TexWr*
Jones, Charles A 1815?-1851 *Alli, DcNAA, OhA&B*
Jones, Charles Alfred *Alli Sup*
Jones, Charles Colcock 1804-1863 *Alli, Alli Sup, BiDSA, DcAmA, DcNAA*
Jones, Charles Colcock, Jr. 1831-1893 *Alli Sup, AmA, AmA&B, BiD&SB, BiDSA, DcAmA, DcNAA*
Jones, Charles Edgeworth 1867- *BiDSA*
Jones, Charles Edward 1867-1941 *DcNAA*
Jones, Charles Edwin 1932- *ConAu 49*
Jones, Charles H *ChPo S2*
Jones, Charles Handfield *Alli Sup*
Jones, Charles Henry 1837-1911 *Alli Sup, DcAmA, DcNAA*
Jones, Charles J *Alli Sup*
Jones, Charles O 1931- *ConAu 17R*
Jones, Charles W 1905- *ConAu 13R, WrD 1976*
Jones, Charles William *Alli Sup*
Jones, Chaucer *Alli Sup*
Jones, Chester Lloyd 1881-1941 *AmLY, DcNAA*
Jones, Christine 1937- *ConAu 61*
Jones, Christopher William 1937- *ConAu 23, WrD 1976*
Jones, Clara Augusta *ChPo, DcNAA, HsB&A*
Jones, Clarence M 1889-1949 *AmSCAP 66*
Jones, Clifford M 1902- *ConAu 17R, WrD 1976*
Jones, Colin Seymour 1938- *Au&Wr*
Jones, Cornelia *Alli Sup, BlkAW*
Jones, Cranston E 1918- *ConAu 1R*
Jones, Cyril Meredith 1904- *ConAu 23, WrD 1976*
Jones, D *Alli, BiDLA*
Jones, D E *Alli Sup*
Jones, D L 1925- *ConAu 25*
Jones, D M *PoIre*
Jones, D Mervyn 1922- *ConAu 21*
Jones, Daisy Marvel 1906- *ConAu 17R, IndAu 1917*
Jones, Daniel 1881-1967 *ConAu 5R*
Jones, David *Alli, Alli Sup*
Jones, David d1780? *Alli*
Jones, David 1736-1820 *DcNAA*
Jones, David 1815-1896 *OhA&B*
Jones, David 1895-1974 *CasWL, CnE&AP, CnMWL, ConAu 9R, ConAu 53, ConLC 2, ConLC 4, ConP 1970, ConP 1975, LongC, ModBL, ModBL Sup, NewC, OxEng, Pen Eng, RAdv 1, REn, TwCW, WhTwL, WorAu*
Jones, David F *Alli*
Jones, David Griffiths *Alli Sup*
Jones, David Gwenallt 1899-1968 *CasWL*
Jones, David Hugh 1900- *AmSCAP 66*
Jones, David Michael 1895-1974 *ChPo, ChPo S2*
Jones, David Morgan 1843-1915 *Alli Sup, DcNAA*
Jones, David Rice- *Alli Sup*

Jones, David Russell *Alli Sup*
Jones, DeLancey Floyd- *Alli Sup*
Jones, Diana Wynne 1934- *Au&Wr, ConAu 49, SmATA 9, WrD 1976*
Jones, Donald 1938- *ChPo S1, ConAu 17R, DrAP 1975, WrD 1976*
Jones, Donald Forsha 1890- *WhWNAA*
Jones, Dorothy Holder *ConAu 9R*
Jones, Douglas C 1924- *ConAu 21*
Jones, Douglas F *Alli Sup*
Jones, Douglas Gordon 1929- *CanWr, CasWL, ConAu 29, ConP 1970, ConP 1975, OxCan, OxCan Sup, WrD 1976*
Jones, Duane *ConAu XR*
Jones, DuPre Anderson 1937- *ConAu 21*
Jones, Dwight Arven 1854-1913 *Alli Sup, DcNAA*
Jones, E Alfred 1872- *WhLA*
Jones, E B B H *AfA 1*
Jones, E B C d1966 *LongC*
Jones, E Brandram *Alli Sup*
Jones, E D *Alli Sup*
Jones, E H 1925- *BlkAW, LongC*
Jones, E J *Alli Sup*
Jones, E K *Alli Sup*
Jones, E Lloyd *Alli Sup*
Jones, E Neville *ChPo*
Jones, E O *Alli*
Jones, E T *Alli*
Jones, E Terrence 1941- *ConAu 33, WrD 1976*
Jones, E W *Alli Sup*
Jones, E Winston 1911- *ConAu 13R*
Jones, Easley Stephen 1884-1947 *DcNAA*
Jones, Ebenezer 1820-1860 *Alli, BbD, BiD&SB, BrAu 19, CasWL, ChPo, ChPo S1, Chmbr 3, DcLEnL, EvLB, NewC, WebEAL*
Jones, Edgar DeWitt 1876-1956 *AmA&B*
Jones, Sir Edgar Rees 1878- *WhLA*
Jones, Edmund *Alli*
Jones, Edmund 1722-1765 *PoCh*
Jones, Edmund Adams 1842- *AmLY*
Jones, Edward *Alli, BiDLA*
Jones, Edward A 1903- *ConAu 25*
Jones, Edward C *BbtC*
Jones, Edward Conway 1820-1865 *ChPo, DcNAA, PoIre*
Jones, Edward David 1870- *AmLY, WhWNAA*
Jones, Edward E 1926- *ConAu 17R*
Jones, Edward Godden *Alli, BiDLA Sup*
Jones, Edward G ALSO Jones, Edwin G
Jones, Edward Groves 1874-1921 *DcNAA*
Jones, Edward H, Jr. 1922- *ConAu 13R*
Jones, Edward James *Alli Sup*
Jones, Edward Monckton *Alli Sup*
Jones, Edward Smyth 1881- *BlkAW, ChPo S1*
Jones, Edwin Godden *BiDLA*
Jones, Edwin G ALSO Jones Edward G
Jones, Edwin Owen *Alli Sup*
Jones, Edwyn *Alli Sup*
Jones, Eldred D 1925- *ConAu 45*
Jones, Eli Stanley 1884- *AmA&B, ConAu 41, TwCA Sup, WhWNAA*
Jones, Elijah *ChPo S2*
Jones, Eliot 1887- *WhWNAA*
Jones, Elisha 1832-1888 *DcNAA*
Jones, Elizabeth B 1907- *ConAu 61*
Jones, Elizabeth C *ChPo S1*
Jones, Elizabeth Ivins *ChPo S1*
Jones, Elizabeth Mohr 1927- *IndAu 1917*
Jones, Elizabeth Orton 1910- *AuBYP, Cald 1938, ChPo, ChPo S1, IlBYP, IlCB 1945, IlCB 1956, JBA 1951, St&VC*
Jones, Elizabeth Warren *ChPo S1*
Jones, Ellis O *ChPo*
Jones, Elmer Ellsworth 1876?- *IndAu 1917, WhWNAA*
Jones, Elwyn 1923- *Au&Wr, WrD 1976*
Jones, Emlyn 1912- *ConAu 23*
Jones, Emma Garrison 1833-1898 *HsB&A*
Jones, Emrys 1920- *Au&Wr, ConAu 17R, WrD 1976*
Jones, Lady Enid 1889- *Au&Wr*
Jones, Enid Huws 1911- *ConAu 49*
Jones, Epaphras *IndAu 1816*

Jones, Erasmus W 1817- *DcNAA*
Jones, Eric Lionel 1936- *Au&Wr, WrD 1976*
Jones, Ernest *Chmbr 3*
Jones, Ernest 1879-1958 *WhLA, WorAu*
Jones, Ernest Charles 1819-1868? *Alli, Alli Sup, BiD&SB, BrAu 19, CasWL, EvLB, NewC*
Jones, Evan 1820-1852 *BbD, BiD&SB*
Jones, Evan 1915- *AmA&B, Au&Wr, ConAu 9R, SmATA 3*
Jones, Evan 1927- *AmA&B, ConP 1970*
Jones, Evan Gordon 1927- *Au&Wr*
Jones, Evan Lloyd 1931- *ConP 1970, ConP 1975, WrD 1976*
Jones, Evan Rowland *Alli Sup*
Jones, Eve 1924- *ConAu 1R*
Jones, Everett L 1915- *ConAu 13R*
Jones, Everett LeRoi 1934- *AmA&B, WorAu*
Jones, E LeRoi ALSO Jones, LeRoi
Jones, Ezra Earl 1939- *ConAu 57*
Jones, F A *Alli Sup*
Jones, F Bolton *ChPo*
Jones, F O *Alli Sup*
Jones, F W *Alli Sup*
Jones, Felix Edward Aylmer 1889- *ConAu P-1*
Jones, Florence A *ChPo*
Jones, Frances P 1890- *ConAu 9R*
Jones, Francis Arthur *ChPo S1, ChPo S2*
Jones, Francis Avery 1910- *Au&Wr*
Jones, Francis Henry *Alli Sup*
Jones, Frank *Alli Sup*
Jones, Frank 1873- *WhLA*
Jones, Frank E 1917- *ConAu 13R*
Jones, Frank H 1899- *Au&Wr, WrD 1976*
Jones, Frank Lancaster 1937- *ConAu 29, WrD 1976*
Jones, Frank Leonard 1872-1953 *IndAu 1917*
Jones, Frank Llewellyn 1907- *WrD 1976*
Jones, Franklin 1939- *WrD 1976*
Jones, Franklin Daniel 1887-1929 *DcNAA*
Jones, Franklin Ross 1921- *ConAu 53*
Jones, Fred Rufus 1893- *WhWNAA*
Jones, Frederic *BiDLA*
Jones, Frederic Coningesby *BiDLA*
Jones, Frederick *Alli*
Jones, Frederick Coningesby *Alli*
Jones, Frederick E 1759?-1834 *PoIre*
Jones, Frederick Lafayette 1901- *AmA&B, Au&Wr*
Jones, Frederick Robertson 1872-1941 *AmLY, DcNAA*
Jones, Frederick Warner *Alli Sup*
Jones, G *Alli*
Jones, G Curtis 1911- *ConAu 5R*
Jones, G F *Alli*
Jones, G William 1931- *ConAu 21*
Jones, Gary M 1925- *ConAu 17R*
Jones, Gayl 1949- *BlkAW, ConLC 6, DrAF 1976*
Jones, Gene 1928- *ConAu 21*
Jones, Gene-Olivar *BlkAW*
Jones, Genevieve Estelle *OhA&B*
Jones, George *Alli, Alli Sup*
Jones, George 1786-1869 *ChPo, ChPo S1*
Jones, George 1800-1870 *Alli, Alli Sup, AmA&B, DcAmA, DcNAA*
Jones, George 1810-1879 *DcAmA*
Jones, George Fenwick 1916- *ConAu 13R*
Jones, George Heber 1867-1919 *AmLY, DcNAA*
Jones, George Hilton 1924- *ConAu 33, WrD 1976*
Jones, George James 1856- *DcAmA*
Jones, George Mallory 1873-1940 *DcNAA, OxCan, WhWNAA*
Jones, George Matthew d1831 *Alli*
Jones, George Morgan Edwardes 1858- *Alli Sup*
Jones, George Thaddeus 1917- *AmSCAP 66, ConAu 53*
Jones, George William *Alli Sup*
Jones, George William 1837-1911 *DcNAA*
Jones, Georgia Holloway *BlkAW*
Jones, Gerald Norman *MnBBF*
Jones, Gibbon *Alli*
Jones, Giles *Alli*
Jones, Gillingham *MnBBF*
Jones, Glyn 1905- *Au&Wr, CnMWL, ConAu 9R, ConNov 1972, ConNov 1976,*

Jones, Lloyd S 1931- *ConAu 1R*
Jones, Louis C 1908- *ConAu 5R*
Jones, Lucy *Alli Sup*
Jones, Lyndon Hamer 1927- *Au&Wr,*
 WrD 1976
Jones, Lynds 1865- *AmLY, WhWNAA*
Jones, Lynds E *Alli Sup*
Jones, Mabel Cronise 1860-1920 *AmLY,*
 DcNAA, OhA&B
Jones, Madeline Adams 1913- *ConAu 23*
Jones, Madison Percy 1925- *Au&Wr,*
 ConAu 13R, ConLC 4, ConNov 1972,
 ConNov 1976, WrD 1976
Jones, Major 1812-1882 *AmA, OxAm*
Jones, Major J *ConAu 33, LivBA*
Jones, Maldwyn Allen 1922- *ConAu 1R*
Jones, Marc Edmund 1888- *ConAu 33,*
 WrD 1976
Jones, Marcus Eugene 1852-1934 *DcAmA,*
 DcNAA, WhWNAA
Jones, Margaret Boone 1924- *ConAu 25*
Jones, Margaret Charlotte *Alli Sup*
Jones, Margaret E W 1938- *ConAu 37,*
 WrD 1976
Jones, Margaret Lawrence *Alli Sup*
Jones, Margaret Wynne *ChPo*
Jones, Maria W *ChPo*
Jones, Mary *Alli, Alli Sup, BiDSA*
Jones, Mary Alice 1898- *AuBYP, ChPo S2,*
 ConAu 17R, MorJA, SmATA 6
Jones, Mary Brush 1925- *ConAu 25*
Jones, Mary Cadwalader 1850-1935 *DcNAA*
Jones, Mary Chandler 1871- *ChPo S1*
Jones, Mary S W *ChPo*
Jones, Mary Voell 1933- *ConAu 21,*
 WrD 1976
Jones, Maryer *BlkAW*
Jones, Matt Bushnell 1871-1940 *DcNAA*
Jones, Matthew Henry *Alli Sup*
Jones, Mattie M *Alli Sup*
Jones, Maurice 1863- *WhLA*
Jones, Maurice Bethell *ChPo S2*
Jones, Maxwell 1907- *ConAu 25*
Jones, Melville *WrD 1976*
Jones, Meredith *Alli Sup*
Jones, Mervyn 1922- *Au&Wr, ConAu 45,*
 ConNov 1972, ConNov 1976, WrD 1976
Jones, Morris Charles 1819- *Alli Sup*
Jones, Morris Val 1914- *ConAu 5R*
Jones, Nard 1904- *AmA&B, AmNov,*
 REnAL, WhPNW, WhWNAA
Jones, Nelson Edwards 1821-1901 *DcAmA,*
 DcNAA, OhA&B
Jones, O *Alli, DcEnL*
Jones, Oakah L, Jr. 1930- *ConAu 17R*
Jones, Oliver J *Alli*
Jones, Orlando *ConAu XR*
Jones, Oswald *BlkAW*
Jones, Owen *Alli Sup*
Jones, Owen 1740-1814 *Alli*
Jones, Owen 1809?-1874 *Alli, ChPo*
Jones, Owen Rogers 1922- *ConAu 1R,*
 WrD 1976
Jones, Pamelia Pearl 1877- *WhWNAA*
Jones, Pascal *Alli*
Jones, Pat *ConAu XR*
Jones, Paul 1897- *ChPo S2, WhWNAA*
Jones, Paul Barrington *Alli Sup*
Jones, Paul Davis 1940- *ConAu 49*
Jones, Paul J 1897?-1974 *ConAu 53*
Jones, Paul VanBrunt 1882- *WhWNAA*
Jones, Paulette *BlkAW*
Jones, Peter 1802-1856 *Alli Sup, BbtC,*
 DcNAA
Jones, Peter 1920- *Au&Wr*
Jones, Peter 1921- *Au&Wr, ConAu 5R*
Jones, Peter 1929- *ConAu 53, WrD 1976*
Jones, Peter D'Alroy 1931- *ConAu 5R*
Jones, Philip *Alli*
Jones, Philip Lovering 1838-1913 *DcNAA*
Jones, Pirkle 1914- *ConAu 29*
Jones, Pleasant *Alli Sup, DcNAA*
Jones, Plummer F 1875- *BiDSA*
Jones, Putnam Fennell 1902- *Au&Wr*
Jones, Quincy 1933- *AmSCAP 66*
Jones, R *Alli, ChPo*
Jones, R Harries *Alli Sup*

Jones, R J Cornewall *Alli Sup*
Jones, R J Hampden- *Alli Sup*
Jones, R M Hugh *Alli Sup*
Jones, R P 1933- *Au&Wr*
Jones, R W *Alli Sup*
Jones, Ralph H 1906- *BlkAW*
Jones, Ralph M *ChPo S1, ChPo S2*
Jones, Randolph *Alli Sup*
Jones, Reginald L 1931- *ConAu 45, LivBA*
Jones, Rice 1715-1801 *Alli*
Jones, Rice 1716-1801 *DcEnL*
Jones, Richard *Alli, BiDLA*
Jones, Richard d1652 *DcEnL*
Jones, Richard 1779-1851 *NewC*
Jones, Richard 1790-1855 *BrAu 19*
Jones, Richard 1855-1923 *BiDSA, DcAmA,*
 DcNAA
Jones, Richard 1926- *Au&Wr, ConAu 49,*
 WrD 1976
Jones, Mrs. Richard *OhA&B*
Jones, Richard Allan 1943- *OxCan Sup,*
 WrD 1976
Jones, Richard Benjamin 1933- *Au&Wr,*
 ConAu 25, WrD 1976
Jones, Richard C 1906- *AmSCAP 66*
Jones, Richard C 1910- *IlCB 1945, IlCB 1956*
Jones, Richard Foster 1886- *AmA&B*
Jones, Richard Granville 1926- *WrD 1976*
Jones, Richard H 1914- *ConAu 49*
Jones, Richard Lloyd 1873- *WhWNAA*
Jones, Richard M 1892-1945 *AmSCAP 66*
Jones, Richard Uriah 1877-1941 *DcNAA*
Jones, Richard Watson 1837- *BiDSA*
Jones, Robert *Alli, Alli Sup, BlkAW*
Jones, Robert 1809-1879 *Alli Sup*
Jones, Robert 1875?-1917? *ChPo*
Jones, Robert A *ChPo*
Jones, Robert Baker *Alli Sup*
Jones, Robert Crompton *Alli Sup, ChPo S2*
Jones, Robert Edmond 1887-1954 *OxAm, REn,*
 REnAL
Jones, Robert Emmet 1928- *ConAu 1R*
Jones, Robert Epes 1908- *ConAu P-1*
Jones, Robert F 1934- *ConAu 49*
Jones, Robert H *Alli Sup*
Jones, Robert H 1927- *ConAu 5R*
Jones, Robert L *DrAP 1975*
Jones, Robert Leslie *OxCan*
Jones, Robert O 1928- *ConAu 29*
Jones, Robert Ralston 1850-1930 *OhA&B*
Jones, Robert Saint Clair *Alli Sup*
Jones, Robert William 1884- *WhWNAA*
Jones, Lady Roderick *REn*
Jones, Roger *BlkAW*
Jones, Rosaline E *ChPo S1*
Jones, Rosie Lee Logan 1924- *BlkAW,*
 LivBAA
Jones, Rowland *Alli*
Jones, Ruby Aileen Hiday 1908- *ConAu P-1,*
 IndAu 1917
Jones, Rufus Matthew 1863-1948 *AmA&B,*
 AmLY, DcNAA, LongC, REnAL,
 TwCA Sup, WhWNAA
Jones, Russell Bradley 1894- *ConAu 1R*
Jones, Ruth Lambert 1896- *WhWNAA*
Jones, S A *Alli Sup*
Jones, S Jennie *ChPo S1*
Jones, Sally *WrD 1976*
Jones, Samuel *Alli, BiDLA*
Jones, Samuel 1735-1814 *DcNAA*
Jones, Samuel 1778-1862 *DcNAA*
Jones, Samuel, And Varick, R *Alli*
Jones, Samuel And Spencer, J C *Alli Sup*
Jones, Samuel Arthur 1834-1912 *DcNAA*
Jones, Samuel Flood *Alli Sup*
Jones, Samuel Milton 1846-1904 *DcNAA,*
 OhA&B
Jones, Samuel Porter 1847-1906 *Alli Sup,*
 BiDSA, DcAmA, DcNAA
Jones, Sarah J *Alli Sup*
Jones, Sarah L *Alli Sup*
Jones, Sarah Smith *Alli Sup*
Jones, Scott N 1929- *ConAu 29*
Jones, Sheridan *LongC*
Jones, Sibella *Alli Sup*
Jones, Sidney 1869-1946 *NewC*
Jones, Silas *Alli*
Jones, Silas 1942- *BlkAW*

Jones, Spencer 1857- *WhLA*
Jones, Spike 1911-1964 *AmSCAP 66*
Jones, Stacy V 1894- *ConAu 1R*
Jones, Stan 1914-1963 *AmSCAP 66*
Jones, Stanley Bruce 1927- *WrD 1976*
Jones, Stanley L 1918- *ConAu 9R*
Jones, Stead 1922- *Au&Wr*
Jones, Stephen 1763-1827 *Alli, BiDLA,*
 DcEnL
Jones, Stephen 1935- *ConAu 49*
Jones, Stephen Oscar 1880- *AmSCAP 66*
Jones, Mrs. Sutton 1927- *AmSCAP 66*
Jones, T *Alli, BiDLA*
Jones, T H *ChPo S1*
Jones, T Mason *Alli Sup*
Jones, T Percy *Alli, ChPo, DcEnL*
Jones, T Rupert *Alli*
Jones, Thelma Foght *MnnWr*
Jones, Thelma Hamilton *ChPo S2*
Jones, Theodore *Alli Sup*
Jones, Theophilus *Alli, BiDLA*
Jones, Thomas *Alli, Alli Sup, BiDLA*
Jones, Sir Thomas *Alli*
Jones, Thomas d1882 *ChPo*
Jones, Thomas 1731-1792 *DcAmA*
Jones, Thomas 1750?- *Br&AmS*
Jones, Thomas 1756-1807 *Alli*
Jones, Thomas 1777- *BiDLA Sup*
Jones, Thomas 1810-1875 *Alli Sup*
Jones, Thomas B 1929- *ConAu 25*
Jones, Thomas David 1811-1881 *OhA&B*
Jones, Thomas Elsa 1888-1973 *IndAu 1917*
Jones, Thomas Goode 1844- *Alli Sup, BiDSA*
Jones, Thomas Gwynn 1871-1949 *CasWL,*
 ChPo S2, WebEAL Eng, WhLA
Jones, Thomas M 1916- *ConAu 29*
Jones, Thomas Rupert *Alli Sup*
Jones, Thomas Rymer d1880 *Alli, Alli Sup*
Jones, Thomas Samuel, Jr. 1882-1932
 AnMV 1926, AmA&B, ChPo, ChPo S2,
 DcNAA, REnAL, WhWNAA
Jones, Thomas Snell *Alli*
Jones, Thomas W 1947- *ConAu 53*
Jones, Thomas Wharton 1808- *Alli, Alli Sup*
Jones, Tilford *BlkAW*
Jones, Tom *MnBBF*
Jones, Tom 1928- *AmA&B, AmSCAP 66,*
 ConAu 53, ConDr
Jones, Uriah James 1818-1864 *DcNAA*
Jones, Vane A 1917- *ConAu 21*
Jones, Vernon 1897- *ConAu 53, WrD 1976*
Jones, Victor 1919- *Au&Wr, ConAu 5R*
Jones, Vincent 1872- *WhWNAA*
Jones, Virgil Carrington 1906- *AmA&B,*
 ConAu 1R
Jones, Virginia Smith 1827- *DcAmA, OhA&B*
Jones, W *Alli*
Jones, W C *Alli*
Jones, W Glyn 1928- *ConAu 49*
Jones, W L *ChPo, ChPo S1*
Jones, W M *ChPo, ChPo S1*
Jones, W R D 1924- *Au&Wr*
Jones, W T 1910- *ConAu 37, WrD 1976*
Jones, Walter *Alli, BlkAW*
Jones, Walter 1693?-1756 *PoIre*
Jones, Walter 1865-1935 *DcNAA*
Jones, Walter Benton 1893- *ConAu 1R*
Jones, Walter Clyde 1870-1928 *DcNAA*
Jones, Walter Paul 1891- *ConAu P-1,*
 IndAu 1917
Jones, Walter Whitmore *Alli Sup*
Jones, Webb *ConAu XR*
Jones, Wellington D 1886- *WhWNAA*
Jones, Weyman 1928- *AuBYP, ConAu 17R,*
 SmATA 4
Jones, Wharton Stewart 1849-1936 *DcNAA*
Jones, Miss Whitmore *Alli Sup*
Jones, Wilbur *ConAu XR*
Jones, Wilbur Devereux 1916- *ConAu 1R,*
 WrD 1976
Jones, Wiley *Alli Sup, BiDSA*
Jones, Wilfred *ConICB*
Jones, Wilfred J 1888- *IlCB 1945*
Jones, Willa Saunders 1904- *BlkAW*
Jones, William *Alli, Alli Sup, BiDLA,*
 OxCan
Jones, Sir William *Chmbr 2*
Jones, Sir William 1566-1640 *Alli*

Jones, William 1680-1749 *Alli*
Jones, William 1726-1800 *Alli, ChPo S1, ChPo S2, NewC*
Jones, Sir William 1746-1794 *Alli, BrAu, CasWL, ChPo, ChPo S1, ChPo S2, DcEnA, DcEnL, DcEuL, EvLB, NewC, OxEng*
Jones, William 1760-1831 *DcNAA*
Jones, William 1762-1846 *Alli*
Jones, William 1871-1909 *AmA&B*
Jones, William Alfred 1817-1900 *Alli, AmA, AmA&B, CyAL 2, DcAmA, DcNAA*
Jones, William Arthur *Alli Sup*
Jones, William Basil Tickell 1822- *Alli, Alli Sup*
Jones, William Bence- d1882 *Alli Sup*
Jones, William C & Cunningham, Joseph O *Alli Sup*
Jones, William Carey 1814-1867 *OhA&B*
Jones, William Cary 1854-1923 *DcNAA*
Jones, William Caswell 1848-1915 *DcNAA*
Jones, William D *Alli Sup*
Jones, William Daniel *Alli Sup*
Jones, William Garmon 1884- *WhLA*
Jones, William Glynne *ConAu XR*
Jones, William H *Alli Sup, BlkAW*
Jones, William Hanbury *Alli Sup*
Jones, William Henry Rich- 1817-1885 *Alli Sup*
Jones, William Hite *BiDSA*
Jones, William James *Alli Sup*
Jones, William Louis 1827- *BiDSA*
Jones, William M 1927- *ConAu 33, ConAu 61*
Jones, William Palmer *Alli Sup*
Jones, William Patterson 1831-1886 *DcNAA*
Jones, William Powell 1901- *ConAu 1R, OhA&B*
Jones, William Prime *Alli Sup*
Jones, William R 1889- *WhWNAA*
Jones, William Russell 1870- *WhWNAA*
Jones, William Todd 1759?-1818 *Alli, BiDLA, PoIre*
Jones, Willis Knapp 1895- *AmA&B, ConAu 13R, DcSpL, OhA&B, WhWNAA*
Jones, Yorke 1860- *BlkAW*
Jones-Evans, Eric 1898- *Au&Wr, ConAu 21, WrD 1976*
Jones-Foster, Ardennes *ChPo S2*
Jones Minor Of St. Agnes School *MnBBF*
Jones-Parry *Alli Sup*
Jong *TwCA, TwCA Sup*
Jong, Adrianus Michael De 1888-1943 *CasWL*
Jong, Erica 1942- *AuNews 1, ConAu 6, ConP 1975, CrCAP, DrAF 1976, DrAP 1975, RAdv 1, WrD 1976*
Jong, Erica 1943?- *ConLC 4*
Jonge, Johan Karel Jacob De 1827-1880 *BiD&SB*
Jonge, Johannes Cornelis De 1793-1853 *BiD&SB*
Jongeward, Dorothy 1925- *ConAu 49*
Jongh Osborne, Lilly De 1882- *DcCLA*
Jongkind, Johan Barthold 1819-1891 *AtlBL*
Jongleur *ChPo S1*
Jonk, Clarence 1906- *ConAu 5R, SmATA 10*
Jonker, Ingrid 1933-1965 *WhTwL*
Jonklaas, David 1932- *ConP 1970*
Jonsen, Albert R 1931- *ConAu 25*
Jonson, Ben 1572?-1637 *Alli, AtlBL, BbD, BiD&SB, BrAu, CasWL, ChPo, Chmbr 1, CnE&AP, CnThe, CrE&SL, CriT 1, CyWA, DcEnA, DcEnL, DcEuL, DcLEnL, EvLB, McGWD, MouLC 1, NewC, OxEng, Pen Eng, PoLE, RAdv 1, RCom, REn, REnWD, WebEAL*
Jonson, Robert *OxAm*
Jonsson, Bolu Hjalmar *CasWL*
Jonsson, Karl d1212? *CasWL*
Jonston, John *Alli*
Joos, Martin 1907- *ConAu P-1*
Joost, Nicholas Teynac 1916- *AmA&B, ConAu 13R*
Joplin, Scott 1868-1919? *AmSCAP 66*
Joplin, Scott 1868-1917 *BlkAW*
Joplin, Thomas *Alli*
Jopling, Joseph *Alli*
Jopling, Louise 1843- *WhLA*
Joporkoff, Theodor 1887- *WhLA*

Jopp, Hal *ConAu 57*
Jopp, Harold Dowling, Jr. 1946- *ConAu 57*
Jopp, James *BiDLA*
Jopp, Thomas *Alli*
Joralemon, Ira B 1884-1975 *ConAu 61*
Joravsky, David 1925- *ConAu 1R*
Jordaens, Jacob 1593-1678 *AtlBL*
Jordan Fantosme *BiB N*
Jordan, A *Alli Sup*
Jordan, Agnes C *Alli Sup*
Jordan, Albert Tate *TexWr*
Jordan, Alice Mabel *ChPo*
Jordan, Alma Theodora 1929- *ConAu 33, WrD 1976*
Jordan, Amos A 1922- *ConAu 33*
Jordan, Archibald Campbell 1906-1968 *AfA 1, Pen Cl*
Jordan, Arthur Melville 1888- *WhWNAA*
Jordan, Barbara Leslie 1915- *WrD 1976*
Jordan, Bessie Q *ChPo S1*
Jordan, Charles Bernard 1878-1941 *DcNAA*
Jordan, Charles H *Alli Sup*
Jordan, Charlotte Brewster *ChPo, ChPo S1, ChPo S2*
Jordan, Clarence L 1912- *ConAu 23*
Jordan, Cordelia Jane 1830-1898 *DcNAA*
Jordan, Cornelia Jane Matthews 1830-1898 *Alli Sup, AmA&B, BiD&SB, BiDSA, ChPo, DcAmA, LivFWS*
Jordan, Dale R 1931- *ConAu 45*
Jordan, David Francis 1890-1942 *DcNAA*
Jordan, David K 1942- *ConAu 61*
Jordan, David M 1935- *ConAu 33*
Jordan, David P 1939- *ConAu 57*
Jordan, David Starr 1851-1931 *Alli Sup, AmA&B, AmLY, BbD, BiD&SB, ChPo, ChPo S1, ChPo S2, DcAmA, DcNAA, OxAm, REnAL*
Jordan, Dorothea 1762?-1816 *NewC*
Jordan, Dorothy 1762?-1816 *NewC*
Jordan, Dulcie 1835-1895 *DcAmA*
Jordan, Dulcina Mason 1833-1895 *Alli Sup, DcNAA, IndAu 1816, OhA&B*
Jordan, Edwin Oakes 1866-1936 *AmLY, DcNAA, WhWNAA*
Jordan, Elijah 1875-1953 *IndAu 1917*
Jordan, Elizabeth Garver 1867-1947 *AmA&B, BkC 2, CarSB, CatA 1947, DcAmA, DcNAA, REnAL, WhWNAA, WiscW*
Jordan, Elsie *BlkAW*
Jordan, F *Alli Sup*
Jordan, Floyd 1900-1959 *IndAu 1917*
Jordan, Francis 1843-1911 *DcNAA*
Jordan, Frank *Alli Sup*
Jordan, Frank Marion *BiDSA*
Jordan, Frederick Samuel James 1908- *Au&Wr*
Jordan, Furneaux *Alli Sup*
Jordan, G W *Alli, BiDLA*
Jordan, Gail *ConAu XR*
Jordan, Gerald Ray 1896-1964 *Au&Wr, ConAu 5R, ConAu P-1*
Jordan, Gilbert John 1902- *ConAu 49*
Jordan, Grace Edgington *ConAu 1R, WhPNW*
Jordan, H B *Alli Sup*
Jordan, Harvey Ernest 1878- *WhWNAA*
Jordan, Helen Rosaline *TwCA, TwCA Sup*
Jordan, Henry *Alli, Alli Sup*
Jordan, Israel *ChPo*
Jordan, J A *MnBBF*
Jordan, James B *Alli Sup*
Jordan, James C *Alli Sup*
Jordan, James R *Alli Sup*
Jordan, Joe 1882- *AmSCAP 66*
Jordan, Joel *ChPo S1*
Jordan, John *Alli, Alli Sup*
Jordan, John 1805- *PoIre*
Jordan, John, Jr. *Alli*
Jordan, John A 1843-1917 *DcNAA*
Jordan, John Clark 1883- *WhWNAA*
Jordan, John E 1919- *ConAu 1R, WrD 1976*
Jordan, John Packard 1877-1932 *DcNAA*
Jordan, John Woolf 1840-1921 *Alli Sup, AmA&B, AmLY, DcAmA, DcNAA*
Jordan, Jules 1850-1927 *DcNAA*
Jordan, Juletta A 1855- *ArizL*
Jordan, June Meyer 1936- *BlkAW, ChPo S1, ChPo S2, ConAu 33, ConLC 5,*

DrAF 1976, DrAP 1975, LivBA, SmATA 4, WrD 1976
Jordan, Kate 1862-1926 *AmA&B, AmLY XR, DcNAA*
Jordan, Lois B 1912- *ConAu 57*
Jordan, Louis Henry 1855-1923 *DcNAA*
Jordan, Marcia 1855- *ChPo*
Jordan, Margaret E *PoIre*
Jordan, Mary Augusta 1855-1941 *AmA&B, DcNAA*
Jordan, Max 1895- *CatA 1947*
Jordan, Mildred A 1901- *AmA&B, AmNov, ConAu 25, SmATA 5, TwCA Sup*
Jordan, Nell *WrD 1976*
Jordan, Norman 1938- *BlkAW, ConAu 33, DrAP 1975, LivBA*
Jordan, Orvis Fairlee 1877- *WhWNAA*
Jordan, Pascual 1902- *BiDPar*
Jordan, Pat 1941- *ConAu 33*
Jordan, Philip 1902- *WhLA*
Jordan, Philip Dillon 1903- *AuBYP, ConAu 9R, MnnWr, OhA&B*
Jordan, Phyllis P *AfA 1*
Jordan, Ralph W 1891- *WhWNAA*
Jordan, Richard 1756-1826 *Alli Sup, BiDSA, DcNAA*
Jordan, Riverda Harding 1873- *WhWNAA*
Jordan, Robert Jacob *Alli Sup*
Jordan, Robert Paul 1921- *ConAu 29*
Jordan, Robert Smith 1929- *ConAu 45, WrD 1976*
Jordan, Roy 1916- *AmSCAP 66*
Jordan, Ruth 1926- *ConAu 57, WrD 1976*
Jordan, Stello 1914- *ConAu 29*
Jordan, Terry G 1938- *ConAu 21*
Jordan, Thomas *Alli Sup*
Jordan, Thomas 1612?-1685? *Alli, ChPo, DcEnL, DcLEnL, NewC*
Jordan, Thomas 1819-1895 *Alli Sup, BiDSA, DcAmA*
Jordan, Thomas 1832-1895 *DcNAA*
Jordan, Thurston C, Jr. 1940- *ConAu 25*
Jordan, W Clarence *BlkAW*
Jordan, Weymouth T 1912- *ConAu 17*
Jordan, Whitman Howard 1851-1931 *AmLY, DcNAA*
Jordan, Wilbur Kitchener 1902- *Au&Wr, ConAu 5R, IndAu 1917*
Jordan, Wilhelm 1819-1904 *BbD, BiD&SB, EvEuW, OxGer*
Jordan, William *BiDLA*
Jordan, William A 1928- *ConAu 33*
Jordan, William Frederick 1867-1926 *DcNAA*
Jordan, William George 1852-1939 *DcNAA*
Jordan, William George 1864-1928 *AmA&B, DcAmA, DcNAA*
Jordan, William Leighton *Alli Sup*
Jordan, William Mark 1909- *Au&Wr*
Jordan, William S, Jr. 1917- *ConAu 13R*
Jordan, Winifred Virginia *BlkAW*
Jordan, Winthrop D 1931- *ConAu 25*
Jordan, Zbigniew Antoni 1911- *Au&Wr, ConAu 25, WrD 1976*
Jordan-Smith, Paul 1885- *ChPo S2, WhWNAA*
Jordanes *CasWL, Pen Eur*
Jorden, Edward 1569-1632 *Alli*
Jorden, Eleanor Harz *ConAu 5R*
Jordy, William H 1917- *ConAu 1R*
Jorge Pill *PueRA*
Jorge-Cardoso, Onelio 1914- *DcCLA*
Jorgensen, A *BbtC*
Jorgensen, James D 1932- *ConAu 41*
Jorgensen, Jens Johannes 1866-1956 *CasWL, ClDMEuL*
Jorgensen, Johannes 1866-1956 *CatA 1947, EncWL, Pen Eur*
Jorgensen, Joseph G 1934- *ConAu 61*
Jorgensen, M *BiDLA*
Jorgensen, Mary Venn *AuBYP, ConAu 1R*
Jorgensen, Neil 1934- *ConAu 53*
Jorgensen, Paul A 1916- *WrD 1976*
Jorgensen, Richard E *DrAP 1975*
Jorgenson, Ivar *AuBYP, ConAu XR, ThBJA*
Jorgenson, Theodore 1894- *AmA&B, WhWNAA*
Joris, Francoise Mallet- *ModRL*
Jorisz, David 1501-1556 *CasWL*

Jorn, Asger 1914-1973 *ConAu 41*
Jorstad, Erling 1930- *ConAu 29*
Jortin, John 1698-1770 *Alli, Chmbr 2, DcEnL, EvLB*
Josa, Fortunato Pietro Luigi *Alli Sup*
Josaphare, Lionel 1876- *AmA&B*
Joscelin De Brakelonde *Alli, BiB N*
Joscelin ALSO Jocelin De Brakelonde
Joscelyn, Archie Lynn 1899- *Au&Wr, ConAu 1R, WhPNW*
Joscelyn, Jep *BiDSA*
Joscelyn, John 1529-1603 *NewC*
Joscelyne, Ida *Alli Sup*
Jose Balsamo *PueRA*
Jose Ben Jose *CasWL*
Jose, Arthur Wilberforce 1863-1934 *DcLEnL*
Jose, James R 1939- *ConAu 29*
Josefovits, Teri 1909-1958 *AmSCAP 66*
Joseloff, Stanley 1907- *AmSCAP 66*
Joseph, Chief 1840?-1904 *REnAL*
Joseph Genesius *CasWL, Pen Cl*
Joseph I, Kaiser 1678-1711 *OxGer*
Joseph II, Kaiser 1741-1790 *OxGer, REn*
Joseph Of Arimathea *REn*
Joseph Of Exeter 1180?-1210? *Alli, BiB N, CasWL, DcEnL, DcEuL, NewC*
Joseph Of Oxford *Alli*
Joseph Of Sicily *CasWL*
Joseph Of Volokolamsk 1440?-1515 *Pen Eur*
Joseph, Saint *REn*
Joseph Volotsky *CasWL*
Joseph, Alexander 1907- *AuBYP, ConAu 13R*
Joseph, Arthur *BlkAW*
Joseph, Bertram Leon 1915- *Au&Wr, ConAu 5R*
Joseph, David I 1941- *ConAu 9R*
Joseph, Donald 1898- *AmA&B, AmNov, TexWr*
Joseph, Fitzroy G *BlkAW*
Joseph, George *Alli Sup*
Joseph, Helen Haimon 1888- *OhA&B*
Joseph, Henry Samuel *Alli Sup*
Joseph, James Herz 1924- *ConAu 1R, IndAu 1917*
Joseph, Jesse Montefiore 1884- *OhA&B*
Joseph, Joan 1939- *ConAu 25*
Joseph, John 1923- *ConAu 1R*
Joseph, Jonathan *ConAu XR*
Joseph, Joseph M 1903- *ConAu 5R*
Joseph, Michael Kennedy 1914- *Au&Wr, ChPo S2, ConAu 9R, ConNov 1972, ConNov 1976, ConP 1970, ConP 1975, LongC, TwCW, WrD 1976*
Joseph, Morris 1848- *WhLA*
Joseph, N S *Alli Sup*
Joseph, Nahum *Alli, BiDLA*
Joseph, Raymond A *BlkAW*
Joseph, Richard 1910- *AmA&B, ConAu 1R*
Joseph, Stephen 1921- *ConAu 9R*
Joseph, Stephen M 1938- *ConAu 25, DrAF 1976, WrD 1976*
Joseph, W F G *ChPo*
Josephare, Lionel 1876- *DcAmA*
Josephine *ChPo S2*
Josephs, Laurence *DrAP 1975*
Josephs, Matthew *Alli Sup*
Josephs, Ray 1912- *ConAu 9R, WrD 1976*
Josephs, Stephen *ConAu XR*
Josephson, Aksel Gustav Salomon 1860-1944 *AmLY, DcNAA, WhWNAA*
Josephson, Clifford A 1922- *ConAu 17R*
Josephson, Emanuel M 1895- *WhWNAA*
Josephson, Hannah 1900- *ConAu 29*
Josephson, Harold 1942- *ConAu 61*
Josephson, Matthew 1899- *AmA&B, ConAmA, OxAm, Pen Am, REn, REnAL, TwCA, TwCA Sup*
Josephson, Ragnar 1891-1966 *CasWL, CnMD, ModWD*
Josephus Iscanus *Alli*
Josephus, Flavius 037?-095 *AtlBL, BbD, BiD&SB, CasWL, NewC, OxEng, Pen Cl, RCom, REn*
Josephy, Alvin M, Jr. 1915- *ConAu 17R, OxCan Sup, WrD 1976*
Josey, Alex 1910- *Au&Wr*
Josey, Charles Conant 1893- *WhWNAA*
Josey, E J 1924- *ConAu 29, LivBA*

Josh Billings *DcEnL, OxEng*
Josh Malihabadi 1894- *DcOrL 2*
Joshi, Gaurishankar Govardhandas 1892- *REn*
Joshua, Wynfred 1930- *ConAu 29*
Josi, Ilacandra 1902- *DcOrL 2*
Josi, Sures *DcOrL 2*
Josi, Umasankar 1911- *DcOrL 2*
Josiah Allen's Wife 1836-1926 *AmA, REn*
Josika, Baron Miklos 1794-1865 *CasWL, EvEuW, Pen Eur*
Josika, Baron Nikolas 1794-1865 *BbD, BiD&SB*
Josipovici, Gabriel David 1940- *ConAu 37, ConLC 6, WrD 1976*
Joslin, Mrs. B F *Alli*
Joslin, Benjamin Franklin 1796-1861 *Alli, CyAL 2, DcNAA*
Joslin, Sesyle 1929- *Au&Wr, AuBYP, ConAu XR, SmATA 2, ThBJA*
Joslin, Theodore Goldsmith 1890-1944 *DcNAA*
Josling, Harold *MnBBF*
Josquin Des Pres 1445?-1521 *AtlBL, REn*
Joss, Catherine 1818-1907 *OhA&B*
Josse, Monsieur *OxFr*
Josse, Augustin E *Alli*
Josse, Augustine Louis *BiDLA*
Josseline, John *Alli*
Josselyn, Mrs. C R *Alli Sup*
Josselyn, Charles 1847-1925 *DcAmA, DcNAA*
Josselyn, Freeman Marshall 1866-1916 *DcNAA*
Josselyn, John *Alli, AmA&B, CyAL 1, OxAm, Pen Am*
Josselyn, Robert 1810-1884 *Alli, BiDSA, ChPo, ChPo S1, DcNAA*
Josset, Christopher 1906- *Au&Wr*
Jossy *Alli*
Jost, Arthur C 1874- *WhWNAA*
Josten, Werner 1885-1963 *AmSCAP 66*
Jot, Joe, Jr. *HsB&A*
Jotuni, Maria 1880-1943 *CasWL, CrCD, Pen Eur, REn*
Jouard, Paul E 1928- *AmSCAP 66*
Joubert, Andre J 1924- *ConAu 49*
Joubert, Joseph 1754-1824 *BbD, BiD&SB, DcEuL, OxFr*
Joubert, Leo 1826- *BiD&SB*
Joudry, Patricia *OxCan*
Jouffroy, Simon-Theodore 1796-1843? *OxFr*
Jouffroy, Theodore Simon 1796-1843? *DcEuL*
Joughlin, Clueas *MnBBF*
Jouhandeau, Marcel Henri 1888- *Au&Wr, CasWL, ClDMEuL, EncWL, EvEuW, OxFr, Pen Eur, REn, WhTwL, WorAu*
Jouin, Louis 1818-1899 *Alli Sup, DcAmA, DcNAA*
Joule, Benjamin Saint John Baptist *Alli Sup*
Joule, Francis *Alli Sup*
Joule, James Prescott 1817-1889 *Alli Sup*
Jourard, Sidney M 1926-1974 *ConAu 5R, ConAu 53*
Jourdain, Monsieur *OxFr*
Jourdain, Alice M 1923- *ConAu 53*
Jourdain, Beatrice Alsager *Alli Sup*
Jourdain, Eleanor *LongC*
Jourdain, Francis Charles Robert 1865- *WhLA*
Jourdain, Henry Francis Newdigate 1872- *WhLA*
Jourdan, Jean-Baptiste *OxFr*
Jourdan, Mary Jane d1865 *Alli Sup*
Jourdan, Sil *Alli*
Journet, Cardinal Charles 1891?-1975 *ConAu 57*
Journeyman *AmA&B*
Joutel, Henri *OxCan*
Jouve, Odoric-Martin *OxCan*
Jouve, Pierre Jean 1887- *Au&Wr, CasWL, ClDMEuL, CnMWL, EncWL, EvEuW, OxFr, Pen Eur, REn, WhTwL, WorAu*
Jouvenat, Mrs. M M *BiDSA*
Jouvenel DesUrsins, Jean 1388-1473 *CasWL*
Jouvet, Louis 1885?-1951 *ClDMEuL, EncWL, OxFr, REn*
Jouy, Joseph-Etienne 1764-1846 *OxFr*
Jouy, Victor Joseph Etienne 1764-1846 *BbD, BiD&SB*
Jovanovic, Jovan 1833-1904 *BbD, BiD&SB*
Jovanovic, Zmaj Jovan 1833-1904 *CasWL*

Jovellanos, Gaspar Melchor De 1744-1811 *BbD, BiD&SB, CasWL, DcEuL, DcSpL, EuA, EvEuW, Pen Eur, REn*
Jovine, Francesco 1902-1950 *CasWL, EncWL, EvEuW, Pen Eur*
Jovino *DcSpL*
Jovius, Paulus *CasWL*
Jowett, Benjamin 1817-1893 *Alli, Alli Sup, BiD&SB, BrAu 19, CasWL, Chmbr 3, DcEnA, DcEnA Ap, DcEuL*
Jowett, Benjamin 1817-1929 *DcLEnL*
Jowett, Benjamin 1817-1893 *EvLB, MouLC 4, NewC, OxEng*
Jowett, Joseph *Alli*
Jowett, William *Alli, Alli Sup*
Joy, Lord *Alli*
Joy, Barbara Ellen 1898- *ConAu 5R*
Joy, Bernard 1911- *Au&Wr*
Joy, Charles Rhind 1885- *AuBYP*
Joy, David Anthony Welton 1942- *WrD 1976*
Joy, Dickson *MnBBF*
Joy, Donald Marvin 1928- *ConAu 13R, WrD 1976*
Joy, Edward Thomas 1909- *Au&Wr, ConAu 9R, WrD 1976*
Joy, Elisabeth 1886- *WhWNAA*
Joy, G F *ChPo S1*
Joy, George d1550 *Alli*
Joy, Sir George Andrew 1896- *BiDPar*
Joy, H H *Alli*
Joy, J M *Alli Sup, PoIre*
Joy, James Richard 1863-1957 *AmA&B, DcAmA, WhWNAA*
Joy, Jane Ellis *ChPo, ChPo S1*
Joy, Jennie *ChPo*
Joy, Kenneth Ernest 1908- *ConAu 23*
Joy, Leonard W 1894-1961 *AmSCAP 66*
Joy, Sarah L *ChPo*
Joy, Thomas Alfred 1904- *WrD 1976*
Joy, Thomas Musgrave 1882-1941 *ChPo*
Joyce, Arthur J *Alli Sup*
Joyce, Beatrice 1900- *AmSCAP 66*
Joyce, Cara *ChPo S2*
Joyce, Ernest *MnBBF*
Joyce, Ernest 1899- *ConAu 33*
Joyce, George Hayward 1864-1943 *CatA 1947*
Joyce, James *Alli, PoIre*
Joyce, James 1882-1941 *AtlBL, CasWL, ChPo, ChPo S1, Chmbr 3, CnMD, CnMWL, CyWA, DcLEnL, EncWL, EvLB, LongC, McGWD, ModBL, ModBL Sup, ModWD, NewC, OxEng, Pen Eng, PoIre, RAdv 1, RCom, REn, TwCA, TwCA Sup, TwCW, WebEAL, WhTwL*
Joyce, James Avery *Au&Wr*
Joyce, James Daniel 1921- *ConAu 9R*
Joyce, James Wayland 1812-1887 *Alli Sup*
Joyce, Jeremiah 1764-1816 *Alli, BiDLA, DcEnL*
Joyce, John Alexander 1842-1915 *Alli Sup, AmA, AmA&B, ChPo, ChPo S1, ChPo S2, DcNAA, PoIre*
Joyce, Lillian Elwyn Elliott *AmA&B*
Joyce, Mary Rosera 1930- *ConAu 29, WrD 1976*
Joyce, Mathias 1754-1814 *PoIre*
Joyce, Michael 1903- *Au&Wr, WrD 1976*
Joyce, Patrick Weston 1827-1914 *Alli Sup, BrAu 19, NewC, OxEng, PoIre*
Joyce, R B 1924- *ConAu 45*
Joyce, Robert Dwyer 1836-1883 *Alli Sup, AmA&B, BbD, BiD&SB, ChPo, ChPo S1, DcAmA, DcLEnL, DcNAA, PoIre*
Joyce, Robert E 1934- *ConAu 29, WrD 1976*
Joyce, T H *Alli Sup*
Joyce, Thomas *PoIre*
Joyce, Trevor 1947- *ConP 1970*
Joyce, W H H *BiDSA*
Joyce, William *Alli Sup, LongC*
Joyce-Prendergast, Kathleen M *CatA 1952*
Joye, George d1550 *Alli*
Joyner, Charles W 1935- *ConAu 37*
Joyner, Fred Bunyan 1895- *OhA&B*
Joyner, James Yadkin 1862- *BiDSA*
Joyner, Jerry *IlBYP*
Joyner, Mary Anne *Alli Sup*

Jungle Doctor *ConAu XR*
Jungmann, Josef Jakub 1773-1847 *CasWL,*
  DcEuL, EuA, Pen Eur
Jungmann, Joseph A 1889-1975 *Au&Wr,*
  CatA 1952, OxGer
Junian, T *Alli Sup*
Junior, Thomas C *Alli Sup*
Juniper, William *Alli*
Junius *Alli, AmA&B, BiD&SB, BrAu,*
  CasWL, Chmbr 2, DcEnL, DcEuL,
  DcLEnL, DcNAA, EvLB, NewC, OxEng,
  Pen Eng, WhWNAA
Junius Anonymous *DcEnL*
Junius, Francis 1589-1677 *BrAu, OxEng*
Junius, Franciscus 1589-1677 *BrAu, CasWL*
Junius, Franz 1589-1677 *BrAu*
Junius, Franziskus 1589-1677 *NewC*
Junius, Hadrianus 1511-1575 *CasWL*
Junius, Patrick *Alli*
Junius, R *Alli*
Junius Americanus *AmA&B*
Junker, Karin Stensland 1916- *ConAu 9R*
Junkin, Charles Irwin *ChPo, ChPo S2*
Junkin, David Xavier 1808-1880 *Alli, Alli Sup,*
  DcAmA, DcNAA
Junkin, George 1790-1868 *Alli, Alli Sup,*
  DcAmA, DcNAA, OhA&B
Junkin, Harry W *EncM&D*
Junkin, Margaret *Alli, DcAmA, FemPA*
Junkins, Donald 1931- *AmA&B, ConAu 33,*
  DrAP 1975, WrD 1976
Junner, Gordon Mackenzie *Au&Wr*
Junner, Robert Gordon *Alli Sup*
Junor, John 1919- *Au&Wr*
Junot, Madame 1784-1838 *BiD&SB*
Junqueira Freire, Luis Jose 1832-1855 *Pen Am*
Junqueira Freire, Luiz Jose 1832-1855 *BbD,*
  BiD&SB
Junqueiro, Abilio Manuel Guerra 1850-1923
  ClDMEuL, EvEuW, Pen Eur
Jupo, Frank J 1904- *AuBYP, ConAu 5R,*
  IlCB 1956, SmATA 7, WrD 1976
Jupp, Edward Basil d1877 *Alli Sup*
Jupp, Edward Kaye *Alli Sup*
Jupp, James 1932- *ConAu 23*
Juptner, Joseph Paul 1913- *ConAu 5R*
Jur'at, Shaikh Qalandar Bakhsh d1810
  DcOrL 2
Jurcic, Josip 1844-1881 *CasWL*
Jurgens, Dick 1911- *AmSCAP 66*
Jurgens, W A 1928- *ConAu 41*
Jurgensen, Barbara 1928- *ConAu 17R,*
  WrD 1976
Jurieu, Pierre 1637-1713 *OxFr*
Jurin, James 1684-1750 *Alli*
Juris, Hervey A 1938- *ConAu 53*
Juriscola *DcNAA*
Jurjevich, Ratibor-Ray M 1915- *ConAu 37,*
  WrD 1976
Jurji, Edward J 1907- *ConAu 13R*
Jurkowski, John *DrAF 1976*
Jurmann, Walter 1903- *AmSCAP 66*
Jury, Elsie McLeod *OxCan*
Jury, Wilfrid *OxCan*
Jussawalla, Adil Jehangir 1940- *ConP 1970*
Jusserand, Jean Adrien Antoine Jules 1855-1932
  BbD, BiD&SB, DcAmA, DcLEnL, LongC,
  OxAm, REn, REnAL, TwCA
Jussieu, Antoine De 1686-1758 *OxFr*
Jussieu, Bernard De 1699-1777 *OxFr*
Jussieu, Joseph De 1704-1779 *OxFr*
Just, Bela 1906-1954 *EncWL*
Just, Ernest Everett 1883-1941 *DcNAA*
Just, Ward 1935- *ConAu 25, ConLC 4,*
  DrAF 1976
Justamond, John O d1786 *Alli*
Juste, Michael *ChPo S2*
Justel *Alli*
Justen, Joseph *Alli Sup*
Juster, F Thomas 1926- *ConAu 45*
Juster, Norton 1929- *Au&Wr, AuBYP,*
  ConAu 13R, SmATA 3, WhCL
Justice, Alexander *Alli*
Justice, Blair 1927- *ConAu 45*
Justice, Donald 1925- *AmA&B, ConAu 5R,*
  ConLC 6, ConP 1970, ConP 1975,
  DrAP 1975, Pen Am, WorAu, WrD 1976
Justice, Elizabeth *Alli*

Justice, James *Alli*
Justice, Maibelle Heicks Monroe 1871-
  IndAu 1816
Justice, Marion T *ChPo*
Justice, William G, Jr. 1930- *ConAu 53*
Justiciar *ConAu XR*
Justificus *WrD 1976*
Justified Sinner, A *DcEnL*
Justin *CasWL*
Justin Martyr 100?-162? *BbD, CasWL*
Justin, Mother Marie St. *CatA 1952*
Justinger, Konrad d1425? *OxGer*
Justinian I 483-565 *NewC, REn*
Justinian The Great 483-565 *NewC*
Justo Derecho *PueRA*
Justus, May 1898- *AmA&B, AuBYP, ChPo,*
  ChPo S1, ChPo S2, ConAu 9R,
  JBA 1951, SmATA 1
Justyne, William *ChPo S1*
Juta, Jan 1895- *ConAu 49*
Juta, Rene *ConAu 49*
Jutikkala, Eino Kaarlo Ilmari 1907- *ConAu P-1*
Juvaini *CasWL*
Juvenal *DcEnL*
Juvenal 060?-140? *AtlBL, BbD, BiD&SB,*
  CasWL, CyWA, NewC, Pen Cl, RCom,
  REn
Juvenal DesUrsins, Jean 1388-1473 *BiD&SB,*
  OxFr
Juvencus, Gaius Vettius Aquilinus *CasWL*
Juvenio *WhLA*
Juvonen, Helvi 1919-1959 *Pen Eur*
Juwayni 1226-1283 *Pen Cl*
Juxon, William 1582-1663 *Alli*
Jyl Of Breyntford *Alli*

K

K, C H *PoIre*
K, H *PoIre*
K, R *ConAmA*
K, Sharon *ChPo*
K O S 1881- *ConICB*
K R *CasWL, DcRusL*
Ka, Abdou Anta *AfA 1*
Ka-Tzetnik 135633 *ConAu 29*
Kaalund, Hans Vilhelm 1818-1885 *BbD, BiD&SB, CasWL*
Kaapuni, Sam 1915- *AmSCAP 66*
Ka'b Ibn Zahir *BiD&SB*
Ka'b Ibn Zuhair *CasWL*
Kaba, Lansine 1941- *ConAu 61*
Kabak, Abraham Aba 1881?-1944 *CasWL, Pen Eur*
Kabak, Milton 1926- *AmSCAP 66*
Kabaphes, Konstantinos Petrou *AtlBL*
Kabat, Elvin Abraham 1914- *WrD 1976*
Kabbada, Mika'el 1915- *AfA 1*
Kabdebo, Tamas 1934- *ConAu XR, SmATA XR*
Kabdebo, Thomas George 1934- *ConAu 53, SmATA 10, WrD 1976*
Kabir 1440-1518 *CasWL, DcOrL 2, NewC, Pen Ind*
Kabir, Humayan 1906- *REn*
Kabraji, Fredoon 1897- *Au&Wr, ConAu P-1*
Kacew, Romain *WorAu*
Kachingwe, Aubrey 1926- *AfA 1*
Kachmar, Jessie *DrAP 1975*
Kachru, Braj Behari 1932- *ConAu 61*
Kacic-Miosic, Andrija 1690?-1760 *BbD, BiD&SB, CasWL, Pen Eur*
Kaciyappa Civaccariyar *DcOrL 2*
Kacyzne, Alter 1885-1941 *CasWL*
Kaczer, Illes 1887- *Au&Wr, ConAu P-1*
Kadai, Heino Olavi 1931- *ConAu 21*
Kadar Yar 1802-1850? *DcOrL 2*
Kaden, Juljusz *ClDMEuL*
Kaden, Woldemar 1838- *BiD&SB*
Kaden-Bandrowski, Juliusz 1885-1944 *CasWL, EncWL, EvEuW, ModSL 2, Pen Eur*
Kadesch, Robert R 1922- *ConAu 57*
Kadiri, Abdullo *DcOrL 3*
Kadish, Ferne 1940- *ConAu 61*
Kadish, I *WhWNAA*
Kadison, Philip 1919- *AmSCAP 66*
Kadler, H Eric 1922- *ConAu 29*
Kadlubek, Wincenty 1150?-1223 *CasWL*
Kadmus, G *DcNAA*
Kadushin, Alfred 1916- *ConAu 25, WrD 1976*
Kadushin, Charles 1932- *ConAu 25*
Kaeck, Alexander Paki 1926- *AmSCAP 66*
Kaegi, Walter Emil, Jr. 1937- *ConAu 25*
Kael, Pauline 1919- *AmA&B, Au&Wr, ConAu 45, WrD 1976*
Kaelbling, Rudolf 1928- *ConAu 17R*
Kaelin, Eugene F 1926- *ConAu 45*
Kaemer, Francis *Alli*
Kaemmerer, Ludwig 1862- *WhLA*

Kaempfen, Albert 1826- *BiD&SB*
Kaempfer, Engelbert 1651-1716 *BbD, BiD&SB*
Kaempffert, Waldemar B 1877-1956 *BiDPar*
Kaese, Harold 1909?-1975 *ConAu 57*
Kaestner, Abraham Gotthelf 1717-1800 *DcEuL*
Kaestner, Dorothy 1920- *ConAu 61, WrD 1976*
Kaestner, Erich 1899-1974 *ConAu 49*
Kafe, Joseph Kofi Thompson 1933- *ConAu 49*
Kaffka, Margit 1880-1918 *CasWL, ClDMEuL, Pen Eur*
Kafka, Franz 1883-1924 *AtlBL, CasWL, ClDMEuL, CnMD, CnMWL, CyWA, EncWL, EvEuW, LongC, ModGL, OxEng, OxGer, Pen Eur, RCom, REn, TwCA, TwCA Sup, TwCW, WhTwL*
Kafka, Gustav 1883- *WhLA*
Kafka, John 1905- *AmA&B, AmNov*
Kafka, Sherry 1937- *ConAu 21*
Kafka, Vincent W 1924- *ConAu 61*
Kafker, Frank A 1931- *ConAu 37*
Kafu *CasWL, DcOrL 1*
Kaga, Chiyo *DcOrL 1*
Kaga No Chiyo 1703-1775 *CasWL*
Kagame, Alegisi 1912- *Pen Cl*
Kagame, Alexis 1912- *AfA 1, Pen Cl*
Kagami, Shiko *DcOrL 1*
Kagan, Benjamin 1914- *ConAu 21*
Kagan, Donald 1932- *ConAu 23*
Kagan, Jerome 1929- *ConAu 5R*
Kagan, Richard 1943- *ConAu 57*
Kagan, Richard C 1938- *ConAu 53*
Kagan-Kans, Eva 1928- *ConAu 49*
Kagara, Malam Abubakar Imam 1910?- *AfA 1*
Kagara, Malam Muhammadu Bello 1905?- *AfA 1*
Kagawa, Toyohiko 1888-1960 *ChPo, TwCA, TwCA Sup*
Kagey, Rudolf 1904-1946 *AmA&B, DcNAA*
Kagin, Edwin *MnnWr*
Kagy, Frederick D 1917- *ConAu 13R*
Kah-Ge-Ga-Gah-Bowh, Chief 1818-1863 *REnAL*
Kahal, Irving 1903-1942 *AmSCAP 66*
Kahan, Gerald 1923- *ConAu 33, WrD 1976*
Kahan, John Hans 1903- *Au&Wr*
Kahan, Stanley 1931- *ConAu 5R*
Kahana-Karmon, Amaliah 1920?- *CasWL*
Kahane, Howard 1928- *ConAu 49*
Kahiga, Samuel 1940?- *AfA 1*
Kahiramdas *CasWL*
Kahl, Ann Hammel 1929- *ConAu 17R*
Kahl, Virginia 1919- *AuBYP, BkP, ChPo, ChPo S1, ConAu 49, IlCB 1956, IlCB 1966, MorJA*
Kahle, Clara M *ChPo*
Kahle, Paul E 1875- *WhLA*
Kahle, Roger 1943- *ConAu 33*
Kahlenberg, Louis Albert 1870-1941 *AmLY, DcNAA, WhWNAA*
Kahlenberg, Mary Hunt 1940- *ConAu 45*
Kahler, Erich Gabriel 1885-1970 *ConAu 5R,*

ConAu 29
Kahler, Hugh MacNair 1883- *AmA&B, MnBBF, REnAL, WhWNAA*
Kahler, Woodland 1895- *ConAu 1R, WrD 1976*
Kahm, Harold S *MnBBF*
Kahn, Alfred E 1917- *ConAu 41*
Kahn, Alfred J 1919- *ConAu 5R*
Kahn, Balthazar 1944- *ConAu XR*
Kahn, Bernard M 1930- *AmSCAP 66*
Kahn, Dave 1910- *AmSCAP 66*
Kahn, David 1930- *ConAu 25, WrD 1976*
Kahn, Donald 1918- *AmSCAP 66*
Kahn, Ely Jacques 1884-1972 *ConAu 37*
Kahn, Ely Jacques, Jr. 1916- *AmA&B, Au&Wr, TwCA Sup*
Kahn, Frank J 1938- *ConAu 33*
Kahn, Gilbert 1912- *ConAu 1R*
Kahn, Grace LeBoy 1891- *AmSCAP 66*
Kahn, Gus 1886-1941 *AmSCAP 66*
Kahn, Gustave 1859-1936 *CasWL, ClDMEuL, EvEuW, OxFr, Pen Eur, REn*
Kahn, Hannah Abrahams 1911- *AuNews 2, WrD 1976*
Kahn, Herman 1922- *AmA&B*
Kahn, Isador William 1890- *WhWNAA*
Kahn, Itzhak 1908- *Au&Wr*
Kahn, Jack Harold 1904- *Au&Wr*
Kahn, Joseph d1940 *DcNAA*
Kahn, Kathy 1945- *ConAu 41*
Kahn, Lothar 1922- *ConAu 25*
Kahn, Louis I 1901-1974 *ConAu 49*
Kahn, Ludwig W 1910- *ConAu 41*
Kahn, Marvin Irving 1915- *AmSCAP 66*
Kahn, Max 1887-1926 *DcNAA*
Kahn, Otto Hermann 1867-1934 *AmLY, DcNAA, REnAL*
Kahn, Robert I 1910- *ConAu 5R*
Kahn, Robert L 1918- *ConAu 17R*
Kahn, Roger 1927- *AuBYP, ConAu 25*
Kahn, Roger Wolfe 1907-1962 *AmSCAP 66*
Kahn, Ruth 1872- *DcAmA*
Kahn, S David 1929- *BiDPar*
Kahn, Sherman 1934- *AmSCAP 66*
Kahn, Si 1944- *ConAu 33*
Kahn, Stephen 1940- *ConAu 5R*
Kahn, Steve *ConAu XR*
Kahn, Sy M 1924- *ChPo S1, ConAu 25, WrD 1976*
Kahn, Theodore C 1912- *ConAu 33*
Kahn-Freund, Otto 1900- *WrD 1976*
Kahnweiler, Daniel-Henry 1884- *ConAu 29*
Kahrl, Stanley J 1931- *ConAu 9R*
Kahrstedt, Ulrich 1888- *WhLA*
Kaikavus Ibn Iskandar, 'Unsur Al-Ma'ali *CasWL*
Kaikini, P R 1912- *ConAu 61*
Kail, Mary E 1827-1890 *OhA&B*
Kailas, Uuno 1901-1933 *Pen Eur*
Kailasam *DcOrL 2*
Kaim-Caudle, Peter Robert 1916- *ConAu 23,*

Pen Cl
Kampelman, Max M 1920- *ConAu 41*
Kampen, Irene Trepel 1922- *ConAu 1R*
Kampen, Nikolaas Godfried Van 1776-1839 *BbD, BiD&SB*
Kampen, Owen *IlBYP*
Kampf, Abraham 1920- *ConAu 23*
Kampf, Avram *ConAu XR*
Kampf, Louis 1929- *ConAu 33, WrD 1976*
Kamphausen, Hugo 1863- *WhWNAA*
Kampmeier, August 1856- *WhWNAA*
Kampmeier, Otto Frederic 1888- *WhWNAA*
Kampov, Boris Nikolayevich 1908- *DcRusL*
Kamrany, Nake M 1934- *ConAu 37*
Kan, Pao *CasWL, DcOrL 1*
Kanagaki, Robun 1829-1894 *DcOrL 1*
Kanakadasa *DcOrL 2*
Kan'ami, Kiyotsugu 1333-1384 *CasWL, DcOrL 1*
Kanavel, Allen Buckner 1874-1938 *AmLY, DcNAA, WhWNAA*
Kanazawa, Masakata 1934- *ConAu 25*
Kanazawa, Roger *ConAu XR*
Kandaouroff, Berice 1912- *ConAu 33*
Kandel, Denise Bystryn 1933- *ConAu 13R*
Kandel, I L 1881- *ConAu 1R*
Kandel, Lenore *ConP 1970, ConP 1975, WrD 1976*
Kandell, Alice S 1938- *ConAu 33, WrD 1976*
Kander, Lizzie Black 1858-1940 *DcNAA, WhWNAA*
Kander, Mrs. Simon *DcNAA*
Kandinsky, Wassily 1866-1944 *AtlBL, REn*
Kando, Thomas M 1941- *ConAu 49*
Kane, Al Philip *ChPo S1*
Kane, Annie 1839- *ChPo S2*
Kane, Bernie 1906- *AmSCAP 66*
Kane, Bob *EncM&D*
Kane, Dennis Cornelius 1918- *ConAu 41*
Kane, E B 1944- *ConAu 57*
Kane, Edward *Alli Sup, PoIre*
Kane, Edward C *PoIre*
Kane, Edward J 1935- *ConAu 41*
Kane, Elisha Kent 1820-1857 *Alli, AmA, BbD, BiD&SB, CyAL 2, DcAmA, DcNAA, EarAB Sup, OxAm, OxCan, REnAL*
Kane, Frank 1912-1968 *AmA&B, ConAu 5R, ConAu 25*
Kane, H H *Alli Sup*
Kane, H Victor 1906- *ConAu 29*
Kane, Harnett Thomas 1910- *AmA&B, AmNov, CatA 1952, REn, REnAL, TwCA Sup*
Kane, Henry 1918- *AmA&B, EncM&D*
Kane, Henry Bugbee 1902- *AuBYP, ChPo, ChPo S1, ChPo S2, IlCB 1945, IlCB 1956, IlCB 1966*
Kane, Henry Hubbell 1854- *DcNAA*
Kane, J Blackburne *Alli Sup*
Kane, James J *Alli Sup*
Kane, James Johnson 1837-1921 *DcNAA*
Kane, John Joseph 1909- *ConAu 13*
Kane, John Kintzing 1795-1858 *DcNAA*
Kane, John P 1860- *PoIre*
Kane, Julia *WrD 1976*
Kane, Margaret 1836- *Alli Sup*
Kane, Patrick *ChPo S1*
Kane, Paul 1810-1871 *Alli, BbtC, DcNAA, OxCan*
Kane, Philip *WhWNAA*
Kane, Sir Robert John 1810- *Alli*
Kane, Robert S 1925- *ConAu 9R*
Kane, Robert William 1910- *IlCB 1956*
Kane, Sheikh Hamidou 1928- *AfA 1, Pen Cl*
Kane, Thomas Leiper 1822-1883 *Alli Sup, DcAmA, DcNAA*
Kane, Thomas P 1848-1923 *DcNAA*
Kane, W F DeVismes *Alli Sup*
Kane, William Everett 1943- *ConAu 49*
Kanet, Roger E 1936- *ConAu 33*
Kanfer, Frederick H 1925- *ConAu 41*
K'ang, Chin-Chih *REnWD*
Kang, Shin T 1935- *ConAu 33*
Kang, Younghill 1903-1972 *AmA&B, ConAu 37, REnAL, TwCA, TwCA Sup*
K'ang, Yu-Wei 1858-1927 *CasWL, DcOrL 1*
Kangro, Bernard 1910- *CasWL*
Kani, Abu Bekir 1712-1792 *DcOrL 3*

Kanik, Orhan Veli 1914-1950 *DcOrL 3*
Kanin, Garson 1912- *AmA&B, AmSCAP 66, AuNews 1, CnMD, ConAu 5R, ConDr, ModWD, OxAm, Pen Am, REnAL, WorAu, WrD 1976*
Kanin, Michael 1910- *ConAu 61*
Kanitz, Ernest 1894- *AmSCAP 66*
Kanitz, Philipp Felix 1829-1904 *BbD, BiD&SB*
Kanmacher, Frederick *BiDLA*
Kannegiesser, Karl Ludwig 1781-1861 *BiD&SB*
Kanner, Heinrich 1864- *WhLA*
Kanner, Jerome H 1903- *AmSCAP 66*
Kanner, Leo 1894- *ConAu 17R*
Kanof, Abram 1903- *ConAu 29*
Kanovsky, Eliyahu 1922- *ConAu 33*
Kant, Hermann 1926- *CasWL*
Kant, Immanuel 1724-1804 *BbD, BiD&SB, CasWL, CyWA, DcEuL, EvEuW, NewC, OxEng, OxGer, Pen Eur, REn*
Kantar, Edwin B 1932- *ConAu 41*
Kantemir, Prince Antiochus Dmitrievich 1709?-1744 *BbD, BiD&SB, CasWL, DcEuL, DcRusL, EuA, REn*
Kantemir, Dimitrie, Hospodar Of Moldavia 1673-1723 *EuA*
Kanto, Peter 1932- *ConAu 23, WrD 1976*
Kantonen, Taito Almar 1900- *ConAu 33, OhA&B, WrD 1976*
Kantor, Harry 1911- *ConAu 1R, WrD 1976*
Kantor, Herman I 1909- *ConAu 57*
Kantor, Jacob Robert 1888- *IndAu 1917, WhWNAA*
Kantor, James 1927- *ConAu 21*
Kantor, John Leonard 1890- *WhWNAA*
Kantor, MacKinlay 1904- *AmA&B, AmNov, AuBYP, ChPo S1, CnDAL, ConAmA, ConAu 61, ConNov 1972, ConNov 1976, DcLEnL, EncM&D, ModAL, OxAm, Pen Am, REn, REnAL, TwCA, TwCA Sup, TwCW, WrD 1976*
Kantor, Marvin 1934- *ConAu 49*
Kantorowicz, Hermann 1877- *WhLA*
Kantzow, Thomas 1505?-1542 *OxGer*
Kanwa *DcOrL 2*
Kanwar, Mahfooz A 1939- *ConAu 37*
Kany, Charles Emil 1895- *ConAu 1R, DcSpL*
Kanya-Forstner, A S 1940- *ConAu 25*
Kanza, Thomas R 1933- *ConAu 53*
Kanzawa, Toshiko *ConAu XR*
Kanze, Motokiyo *CasWL*
Kanzer, Mark 1908- *ConAu 37*
Kanzler, Der *OxGer*
Kao, Ch'i 1336-1374 *CasWL*
Kao, Ming *CasWL, DcOrL 1*
Kao, Ngo *DcOrL 1*
Kao, Shih 707?-765 *CasWL*
Kao, Tse-Ch'eng *CyWA, DcOrL 1, REnWD*
Kao, Yu *DcOrL 1*
Kapek, Karel *LongC, TwCA, TwCA Sup*
Kapelner, Alan *AmA&B, ConAu 5R*
Kapelrud, Arvid Schou 1912- *Au&Wr, WrD 1976*
Kaper, Bronislaw 1902- *AmSCAP 66*
Kapfer, Miriam B 1935- *ConAu 33*
Kapfer, Philip G 1936- *ConAu 33*
Kapilar *DcOrL 2*
Kaplan, Abraham 1918- *AmA&B, ConAu 13R*
Kaplan, Albert A *AuBYP*
Kaplan, Allan 1932- *ConAu 33, DrAP 1975*
Kaplan, Anne Bernays 1930- *ConAu 1R*
Kaplan, Arthur 1925- *ConAu 5R*
Kaplan, Benjamin 1911- *ConAu 1R*
Kaplan, Bernard 1944- *ConAu 49, DrAF 1976*
Kaplan, Berton H 1930- *ConAu 61*
Kaplan, Boche 1926- *ConAu 23, IlBYP*
Kaplan, Charles 1919- *ConAu 9R*
Kaplan, David Gordon 1908- *ConAu 61*
Kaplan, Fred 1937- *ConAu 41*
Kaplan, Frederick I 1920- *ConAu 23*
Kaplan, Harold 1916- *ConAu 17R*
Kaplan, Harold J 1918- *AmA&B, TwCA Sup*
Kaplan, Helen Singer 1929- *AuNews 1*
Kaplan, Howard N 1932- *ConAu 61*
Kaplan, Irma 1900- *ConAu 29, SmATA 10*
Kaplan, Jack A 1947- *ConAu 57*
Kaplan, Jacob J 1920- *ConAu 23*
Kaplan, Jean Caryl Korn 1926- *ConAu 5R,*

SmATA 10
Kaplan, Johanna *DrAF 1976*
Kaplan, Justin 1925- *AmA&B, Au&Wr, AuNews 1, ConAu 17R, WrD 1976*
Kaplan, Lawrence Jay 1915- *ConAu 21*
Kaplan, Lawrence S 1924- *ConAu 33*
Kaplan, Margaret *AuBYP*
Kaplan, Max 1911- *ConAu 1R*
Kaplan, Milton *DrAP 1975*
Kaplan, Moise N 1893- *WhWNAA*
Kaplan, Mordecai 1881- *AmA&B*
Kaplan, Morton A 1921- *ConAu 5R, WrD 1976*
Kaplan, Philip 1916- *ConAu 13R*
Kaplan, Robert B 1928- *ConAu 13R, WrD 1976*
Kaplan, Roche *ChPo S1*
Kaplan, S Howard 1938- *ConAu 25*
Kaplan, Samuel 1935- *ConAu 21*
Kaplan, Sheldon Z 1911- *AmSCAP 66*
Kaplan, Sidney *ChPo*
Kaplan, Stuart R 1932- *ConAu 49*
Kaplan, Ysabel DeWitt 1877- *ChPo*
Kaplansky, Irving 1917- *WrD 1976*
Kaplon, Morton F 1921- *ConAu 23*
Kaplow, Jeffry 1937- *ConAu 17R*
Kapnist, Basil 1756-1823 *DcEuL*
Kapnist, Vasili Vasilievich 1757-1824? *BbD, BiD&SB, CasWL, DcRusL*
Kapp, David 1904- *AmSCAP 66*
Kapp, Frederick *Alli*
Kapp, Friedrich 1824-1884 *Alli Sup, BiD&SB*
Kapp, Gisbert *Alli Sup*
Kapp, K William 1910- *ConAu 5R, WrD 1976*
Kapp, Paul 1907- *AmSCAP 66, AuBYP, ChPo, ChPo S1, ChPo S2*
Kapp, Reginald Otto 1885-1966 *ConAu 5R*
Kapp, Wolfgang 1858-1922 *OxGer*
Kapp, Yvonne 1903- *Au&Wr*
Kappel, Philip 1901- *ConAu P-1*
Kappen, Charles Vaughan 1910- *ConAu 9R*
Kappers, Jan 1914- *BiDPar*
Kappes, Alfred 1850-1894 *ChPo*
Kappis, Max 1881- *WhLA*
Kapr, Albert 1918- *WhGrA*
Kaprow, Allan 1927- *AmA&B, ConDr*
Kapsas, Vincas *CasWL*
Kapusta, Paul *ConAu XR*
Kaputikian, Silva 1919- *DcOrL 3*
Kara Giorg 1826-1903 *CasWL, OhA&B*
Karacaoglan *CasWL, DcOrL 3*
Karadzic, Vuk Stefanovic 1787-1864 *BbD, BiD&SB, CasWL, EuA, Pen Eur*
Karagatses, M 1908-1960 *EncWL Sup*
Karai, Senryu 1718-1790 *CasWL, DcOrL 1*
Karaka, D Framji *Alli Sup*
Karaka, Dosabhai Framji 1911- *DcLEnL*
Karaliychev, Angel 1902- *CasWL*
Karamisin *ChPo*
Karamzin, Nikolay Mikhaylovich 1765?-1826 *BbD, BiD&SB, CasWL, DcEuL, DcRusL, EuA, EvEuW, Pen Eur, REn*
Karanikas, Alexander 1916- *ConAu 33, WrD 1976*
Karanta, Kota Sivarama 1902- *DcOrL 2*
Karaosmanoglu, Yakub Kadri 1888?-1974 *Pen Cl*
Karaosmanoglu, Yakup Kadri 1888?-1974 *DcOrL 3, EncWL Sup*
Karapetoff, Vladimir 1876- *AmLY, WhWNAA*
Karasek Ze Lvovic, Jiri 1871-1951 *CasWL*
Karaslavov, Georgi 1904- *CasWL*
Karasoutzas, John 1824-1873 *BiD&SB*
Karasz, Ilonka 1896- *ChPo, IlBYP, IlCB 1956*
Karavayeva, Anna 1893- *CasWL*
Karavelov, Lyuben 1835?-1879 *BiD&SB, CasWL, Pen Eur*
Kardatzke, Carl Henry 1904-1959 *IndAu 1917*
Kardiner, Abram 1891- *AmA&B*
Kardish, Laurence 1945- *ConAu 49*
Kardouche, G Khalil 1935- *ConAu 17R*
Karel Havlicek *EuA*
Karel, Leonard 1912- *ConAu 49*
Karelitz, George Boris 1895-1943 *DcNAA*
Karelitz, Samuel 1900- *Au&Wr*

Karen, Ruth 1922- *AuBYP*, *ConAu 17R*,
  SmATA 9, *WrD 1976*
Kareyev, Nikolay Ivanovich 1850-1931 *DcRusL*
Karg, Elissa Jane 1951- *ConAu 23*
Karger, Alfred Gus 1901- *OhA&B*
Karger, Delmar William 1913- *ConAu 17R*,
  WrD 1976
Kargon, Robert Hugh 1938- *ConAu 45*
Kariel, Henry S 1924- *AmA&B*, *ConAu 13R*
Karig, Walter 1898-1956 *AmA&B*, *AmNov*,
  ChPo, *REnAL*, *TwCA Sup*
Karim, Ahmed Awad 1890?- *AfA 1*
Karim, Walidin 1951- *BlkAW*
Karina *ConAu XR*
Karinthy, Ferenc 1921- *CrCD*
Karinthy, Frigyes 1887-1938 *CasWL*, *EncWL*,
  EvEuW, *Pen Eur*
Karishka, Paul *DcNAA*
Kariuki, Joseph E 1931- *AfA 1*, *BlkAW*
Kariuki, Josiah Mwangi 1931- *ConP 1970*
Kariv, Abraham 1900- *CasWL*
Kark, Leslie 1910- *Au&Wr*
Kark, Nina Mary 1925- *ConAu 17R*,
  SmATA 4
Kark, Norman 1898- *Au&Wr*
Karklins, Valdemars *Pen Eur*
Karkoschka, Erhard 1923- *ConAu 45*
Karl SEE ALSO Charles
Karl August, Herzog Von Sachsen-Weimar
  1757-1828 *OxGer*
Karl III, Der Dicke 839-888 *OxGer*
Karl I, Der Grosse 742-814 *OxGer*
Karl II, Der Kahle 823-877 *OxGer*
Karl, Erzherzog 1771-1847 *OxGer*
Karl Eugen, Herzog Von Wurttemberg 1728-1794
  OxGer
Karl Friedrich, Markgraf Von Baden 1728-1811
  OxGer
Karl I, Herzog Von Braunschweig 1713-1780
  OxGer
Karl IV, Kaiser 1316-1378 *OxGer*
Karl V, Kaiser 1500-1558 *OxGer*
Karl VII, Kaiser 1697-1745 *OxGer*
Karl VI, Kaiser Und Konig Karl III 1685-1740
  OxGer
Karl Theodor, Kurfurst Von Pfalz-Bayern
  1724-1799 *OxGer*
Karl, Frederick Robert 1927- *Au&Wr*,
  ConAu 5R
Karl, Jean E 1927- *ChPo S1*, *ConAu 29*
Karlan, Richard 1919- *ConAu 17R*
Karlee, Varfelli 1900?- *AfA 1*
Karlen, Arno M 1937- *ConAu 1R*, *DrAF 1976*,
  DrAP 1975
Karlen, Delmar 1912- *ConAu 5R*, *WrD 1976*
Karlfeldt, Erik Axel 1864-1931 *CasWL*,
  ClDMEuL, *EncWL*, *EvEuW*, *Pen Eur*,
  REn, *TwCA Sup*, *TwCW*
Karlgren, Bernhard 1889- *ConAu P-1*
Karlin, Eugene 1918- *IlBYP*, *IlCB 1966*,
  SmATA 10
Karlin, Frederick James 1936- *AmSCAP 66*
Karlin, Jules 1899- *ConAu 25*
Karlin, Robert 1918- *ConAu 9R*
Karling, Eva Hill LeSeuer *TexWr*
Karling, John Sidney 1899- *Au&Wr*
Karlins, Marvin 1941- *ConAu 25*
Karlmann 829?-880 *OxGer*
Karlsson, Elis 1905- *ConAu P-1*
Karlstadt 1480?-1541 *OxGer*
Karlweis, C 1850-1901 *OxGer*
Karmel, Alex 1931- *ConAu 23*, *DrAF 1976*
Karmel, Peter Henry 1922- *WrD 1976*
Karmel-Wolfe, Henia 1923- *ConAu 49*
Karmi, Hasan Said 1908- *ConAu 45*
Karn, Esther Nelson 1880-1935? *IndAu 1816*,
  OhA&B, *WhWNAA*
Karnad, Giris 1937- *DcOrL 2*
Karnes, Thomas L 1914- *ConAu 23*
Karney, Beulah Mullen *ConAu 13R*
Karniewski, Janusz *ConAu XR*, *WrD 1976*
Karnovitch, Evgenij Petrovitch 1823- *BbD*,
  BiD&SB
Karnow, Stanley 1925- *ConAu 57*
Karns, Thomas C *BiDSA*
Karo, Henry Arnold 1903- *Au&Wr*
Karo, Joseph 1488-1575 *CasWL*, *EuA*
Karol, Alexander *WrD 1976*

Karol, K S *ConAu XR*
Karolevitz, Bob *ConAu XR*
Karolevitz, Robert F 1922- *ConAu 17R*
Karolides, Nicholas J 1928- *ConAu 21*
Karolides, Paul *WhLA*
Karoly, Akin *Alli Sup*
Karolyi, Erna M *ChPo S2*
Karon, Bertram Paul 1930- *ConAu 61*
Karoniaktatie *DrAP 1975*
Karonin 1857-1892 *CasWL*
Karp, Abraham J 1921- *ConAu 5R*,
  WrD 1976
Karp, David 1922- *AmA&B*, *Au&Wr*,
  ConAu 1R, *ConNov 1972*, *ConNov 1976*,
  WrD 1976
Karp, Ivan C 1926- *ConAu 17R*
Karp, Lila 1933- *ConAu 25*, *DrAF 1976*
Karp, Mark 1922- *ConAu 1R*
Karp, Stephen A 1928- *ConAu 1R*
Karpat, Kemal H 1925- *ConAu 23*, *WrD 1976*
Karpatkin, Marvin M 1926-1975 *ConAu 53*
Karpeles, Maud 1885- *Au&Wr*, *ConAu 25*,
  OxCan, *OxCan Sup*, *WrD 1976*
Karpenko-Karyy, I 1845-1907 *ModSL 2*
Karpf, Holly W 1946- *ConAu 37*
Karpin, Fred L 1913- *ConAu 13R*
Karpinski, Franciszek 1741-1825 *BiD&SB*,
  CasWL, *Pen Eur*
Karpinski, Louis Charles 1878- *AmLY*,
  WhWNAA
Karplus, Walter J 1927- *ConAu 21*,
  WrD 1976
Karpowicz, Tymoteusz 1921- *CasWL*
Karr, Alphonse 1808-1890 *BbD*, *BiD&SB*,
  OxFr
Karr, E R 1918- *ConAu 1R*
Karr, Elizabeth *Alli Sup*
Karr, Elizabeth Platt *OhA&B*
Karr, Elizabeth R 1925- *AmSCAP 66*
Karr, Ethel *Alli Sup*
Karr, H W Seton- *Alli Sup*
Karr, Harold 1921- *AmSCAP 66*
Karr, Jean-Baptiste Alphonse 1808-1890 *CasWL*,
  EvEuW
Karr, Walter Scott Seton- 1822- *Alli Sup*
Karrer, Otto 1888- *CatA 1952*
Karris, Robert J 1938- *ConAu 53*
Karsavin, Lev Platonovich 1882- *CasWL*
Karsch, Anna Luisa 1722-1791 *DcEuL*
Karsch, Anne Luise 1722-1791 *CasWL*
Karschin, Anna Luise 1722-1791 *OxGer*
Karsen, Sonja 1919- *ConAu 41*
Karsh, Anna Luise 1722-1791 *BiD&SB*
Karsh, Yousuf 1908- *ConAu 33*
Karshin, Anna Luise 1722-1791 *BiD&SB*
Karshner, Roger 1928- *ConAu 33*
Karslake, William Henry *Alli Sup*
Karsner, David 1889-1941 *AmA&B*, *DcNAA*
Karsner, Howard T 1879- *WhWNAA*
Karsten, Karl G 1891-1968 *IndAu 1917*,
  WhWNAA
Karsten, Peter 1938- *ConAu 37*
Karta, Nat *ConAu XR*, *WrD 1976*
Kartack, Elsie *ChPo*
Karvas, Peter 1920- *CnThe*, *CrCD*, *ModSL 2*,
  REnWD
Karve, Dinakar Dhondo 1899- *ConAu 5R*
Karve, Irawati 1905-1970 *ConAu P-1*
Karyotakis, Costas 1896-1928 *Pen Eur*
Kasack, Hermann 1896-1966 *CasWL*, *EncWL*,
  ModGL, *OxGer*, *Pen Eur*
Kasai, Zenzo 1887-1928 *DcOrL 1*
Kaschnitz, Marie Luise 1901-1974 *CasWL*,
  EncWL, *ModGL*, *OxGer*, *Pen Eur*
Kasdan, Sara 1911- *ConAu 1R*
Kase, Francis J 1910- *ConAu 23*
Kasenkina, Oksana Stepanovna 1896-
  CatA 1952
Kaser, David 1924- *ConAu 17R*, *IndAu 1917*
Kaser, Margaret Katharine 1895- *OhA&B*
Kaser, Michael Charles 1926- *Au&Wr*,
  ConAu 17R, *WrD 1976*
Kasey, J W *Alli Sup*
Kash, Don E 1934- *ConAu 23*, *WrD 1976*
Kashefi, Hoseyn Va'ez *DcOrL 3*
Kashevaroff, Andrew P 1863- *WhWNAA*
Kashiwagi, Hiroshi *DrAF 1976*
Kashiwagi, Isami 1925- *IlBYP*, *IlCB 1956*,

  SmATA 10
Kashiwagi, Kiroshi *DrAP 1975*
Kasic, Bartulo *Pen Eur*
Kasimi *DcOrL 2*
Kaslow, Florence Whiteman 1930- *ConAu 45*
Kasner, Edward 1878- *WhWNAA*
Kasper, Sydney H 1911- *ConAu 1R*
Kasperson, Roger E 1938- *ConAu 29*,
  WrD 1976
Kasprowicz, Jan 1860-1926 *CasWL*, *ClDMEuL*,
  EncWL, *EvEuW*, *ModSL 2*, *ModWD*,
  Pen Eur, *TwCW*
Kasra'i, Siyavush 1925- *CasWL*
Kasrils, Ronald 1938- *ConAu 29*
Kass, Janos 1927- *WhGrA*
Kass, Jerome 1937- *ConAu 57*
Kass, Norman 1934- *ConAu 29*
Kassak, Lajos 1887-1967 *CasWL*, *EncWL*,
  Pen Eur, *WhTwL*
Kassalow, Everett M 1918- *ConAu 45*
Kassam, Yusuf O 1943- *ConP 1970*
Kassebaum, Gene G 1929- *ConAu 17R*
Kassel, Art 1896-1965 *AmSCAP 66*
Kassel, Charles 1877- *TexWr*, *WhWNAA*
Kassil, Lev 1905- *TwCW*
Kassin, Arthur Robert 1917- *AmSCAP 66*
Kassirer, Norma *AuBYP*
Kassner, Rudolf 1873-1959 *CasWL*, *EncWL*,
  ModGL, *OxGer*, *Pen Eur*
Kassof, Allen 1930- *ConAu 23*
Kasson, John Adam 1822-1910 *DcAmA*,
  DcNAA
Kast, Fremont E 1926- *ConAu 23*
Kastelan, Jure 1919- *CasWL*, *ModSL 2*,
  Pen Eur
Kastelle, Pieter Leonard VanDe 1748-1810
  CasWL
Kastenbaum, Robert 1932- *ConAu 13R*
Kaster, Joseph 1912- *ConAu P-1*
Kastl, Albert J 1939- *ConAu 57*
Kastl, Lena 1942- *ConAu 61*
Kastle, Herbert D 1924- *ConAu 1R*
Kastle, Joseph Hoeing 1864-1916 *DcNAA*
Kastle, Leonard 1929- *AmSCAP 66*
Kastner, Abraham Gotthelf 1719-1800 *BbD*,
  BiD&SB
Kastner, Erhart 1904- *EncWL*, *OxGer*
Kastner, Erich 1899-1974 *AuBYP*, *CasWL*,
  ClDMEuL, *CnMD*, *EncWL*, *EvEuW*,
  ModGL, *ModWD*, *OxGer*, *Pen Eur*,
  ThBJA, *WhCL*, *WorAu*
Kastner, Jonathan 1937- *ConAu 25*
Kastner, Marianna 1940- *ConAu 25*
Kat, Willem 1902- *BiDPar*
Kataev, Valentin Petrovich 1897- *CnMD*,
  ModWD, *TwCA*, *TwCA Sup*
Katai *DcOrL 1*
Katayama, Toshihiro 1928- *WhGrA*
Katayev, Evgeny *CasWL*
Katayev, Valentin Petrovich 1897- *CasWL*,
  ClDMEuL, *DcRusL*, *EncWL*, *EvEuW*,
  McGWD, *ModSL 1*, *Pen Eur*, *REn*,
  TwCW
Katayev, Yevgeni Petrovich 1903-1942
  ClDMEuL, *DcRusL*
Katcha, Vahe 1928- *ConAu XR*
Katchadourian, Vahe 1928- *ConAu 29*
Katchamakoff, Atanas 1898- *IlCB 1945*
Katchen, Carole 1944- *ConAu 61*, *SmATA 9*
Katchmer, George Andrew 1916- *ConAu 1R*,
  WrD 1976
Kate, Cousin *DcEnL*
Kate, Jan Jakob Lodewijk Ten 1819-1889 *BbD*,
  BiD&SB, *CasWL*
Kateb, Yacine 1929- *DcOrL 3*, *EncWL Sup*,
  REnWD
Katebi Torshizi d1434 *DcOrL 3*
Katen, Thomas Ellis 1931- *ConAu 53*
Katenin, Pavel Alexandrovich 1792-1853 *CasWL*,
  DcRusL, *EuA*
Kater, Henry 1777-1835 *Alli*
Katerla, Jozef *CasWL*, *EvEuW*
Kates, George Whitfield *ChPo*
Kates, Philip 1883-1935 *OhA&B*
Kates, Robert W 1929- *ConAu 17R*
Katharine *DcNAA*
Katherine, Queen Of England *Alli*
Kathman, J C *Alli Sup*

Kathrens, Richard Donland 1866- *AmLY*
Kathryn *ConAu XR, SmATA XR*
Kati, Mahmud 1468?-1570? *AfA 1*
Katia Baden *WhWNAA*
Katib Celebi, Mustafa 1608-1657 *CasWL, DcOrL 3*
Katib Chelebi *Pen Cl*
Katibu, Cheo *BlkAW*
Katibu, Mwanifunzi *BlkAW*
Katibu, Sultani 1949- *BlkAW*
Katicic, Radoslav 1930- *ConAu 37*
Katkov, Mikhail Nikiforovich 1818-1887 *CasWL, DcEuL, DcRusL, EvEuW*
Katkov, Norman 1918- *AmA&B, AmNov, ConAu 13R*
Kato, Genchi 1873- *WhLA*
Kato, Gyotai *DcOrL 1*
Kato, Shuichi 1919- *ConAu 37, WrD 1976*
Kato, Shuson *DcOrL 1*
Katona, Joseph 1791?-1830 *BbD, BiD&SB*
Katona, Jozsef 1791?-1830 *CasWL, EvEuW, McGWD, Pen Eur*
Katope, Christopher G 1918- *ConAu 21*
Katrak, Kersy Dady 1936- *ConP 1970*
Katsaros, Thomas 1926- *ConAu 57*
Katscher, Robert 1894-1942 *AmSCAP 66*
Katsh, Abraham Isaac 1908- *ConAu 5R*
Katsumoto, Masakira 1895- *WhLA*
Katsushika, Hokusai 1760-1849 *REn*
Kattan, Naim *OxCan Sup*
Katte, Hans Hermann Von 1704-1730 *OxGer*
Katterhenry, Edwin A 1900- *OhA&B*
Katterhenry, Rose Carolyn Byers 1878- *IndAu 1917*
Katterjohn, Monte Melchior 1891- *IndAu 1816*
Katterns, Daniel *Alli*
Katydid *AmLY XR, WhWNAA*
Katyrev-Rostovsky, Prince Ivan M d1640 *CasWL, DcRusL, Pen Eur*
Katz, Abraham 1926- *ConAu 49*
Katz, Alfred *ConAu XR*
Katz, Sir Bernard 1911- *Au&Wr*
Katz, Bobbi 1933- *ChPo S2, ConAu 37, WrD 1976*
Katz, Daniel 1903- *ConAu 41*
Katz, Elia *DrAF 1976*
Katz, Elias 1912- *ConAu 29*
Katz, Ellis 1938- *ConAu 29*
Katz, Eve 1938- *ConAu 45*
Katz, Fred 1919- *AmSCAP 66*
Katz, Fred 1938- *ConAu 49, SmATA 6*
Katz, H W 1906- *TwCA*
Katz, Irving I 1907- *ConAu 1R*
Katz, Jacob 1904- *ConAu 1R*
Katz, John Stuart 1938- *ConAu 37*
Katz, Josef 1918- *ConAu 53*
Katz, Joseph *ChPo S1*
Katz, Joseph 1910- *ConAu 1R*
Katz, Leandro *DrAP 1975*
Katz, Leon 1919- *ConAu 49*
Katz, Leonard 1926- *ConAu 21*
Katz, Martin 1929- *ConAu 23, WrD 1976*
Katz, Marvin C 1930- *ConAu 25*
Katz, Menke 1906- *ConAu 13R, DrAP 1975, WrD 1976*
Katz, Michael B 1939- *ConAu 33*
Katz, Milton 1907- *Au&Wr, ConAu P-1*
Katz, Mort 1925- *ConAu 61*
Katz, Naomi Corrine *TexWr*
Katz, Robert 1933- *ConAu 25*
Katz, Robert L 1917- *ConAu 9R*
Katz, Ronald Stanley 1945- *Au&Wr*
Katz, Samuel 1914- *ConAu 25*
Katz, Sanford N 1933- *ConAu 33, WrD 1976*
Katz, Stanley Nider 1934- *ConAu 9R*
Katz, Steve *DrAF 1976, DrAP 1975*
Katz, Steven 1935- *ConAu 25*
Katz, William 1922- *AmSCAP 66*
Katz, William A 1924- *ConAu 25*
Katz, William Loren 1927- *ConAu 21*
Katzenbach, William E 1904-1975 *ConAu 61*
Katzenberger, Frances Isabelle 1861-1938 *OhA&B*
Katzin, Olga *LongC*
Katzman, Allen 1937- *ConAu 29, DrAP 1975, WrD 1976*
Katzman, Anita 1920- *ConAu 57*

Katzman, David Manners 1941- *ConAu 53*
Katzmann, Mary J *BbtC*
Katznelson, Jehuda Loeb 1847-1917 *Pen Eur*
Katznelson-Shazar, Rachel 1888-1975 *ConAu 61*
Katzner, Kenneth 1930- *ConAu 5R*
Kaucher, Harriet *ChPo*
Kauder, Emil 1901- *ConAu 17R*
Kaudzite, Matiss 1848-1926 *CasWL*
Kaudzite, Reinis 1839-1920 *CasWL*
Kaufelt, David Allan 1939- *ConAu 45, WrD 1976*
Kauffeld, Carl F 1911-1974 *ConAu 49*
Kauffer, Edward McKnight 1891- *IlCB 1945*
Kauffman SEE ALSO Kaufman
Kauffman, Angelica 1740-1807 *BkIE*
Kauffman, C H *BiDLA*
Kauffman, Calvin Henry 1869-1931 *DcNAA, WhWNAA*
Kauffman, Catherine 1859-1948 *OhA&B*
Kauffman, Christmas Carol Miller 1902- *ConAu 1R, IndAu 1917*
Kauffman, Donald T 1920- *ChPo S2, ConAu 25*
Kauffman, Dorotha S 1925- *ConAu 17R*
Kauffman, George B 1930- *ConAu 17R*
Kauffman, Helen Reed *AmSCAP 66*
Kauffman, Henry J 1908- *ConAu 13R*
Kauffman, James M 1940- *ConAu 57*
Kauffman, Joseph F 1921- *ConAu 45*
Kauffman, Luther S *Alli Sup*
Kauffman, Reginald Wright 1877-1959 *AmA&B, ChPo, ChPo S1, ChPo S2, REnAL, WhWNAA*
Kauffman, Ruth d1952 *AmA&B*
Kauffman, Stanley 1916- *AmA&B, AmNov*
Kauffmann, Georg 1925- *ConAu 49*
Kauffmann, Lane 1921- *Au&Wr, ConAu 17R*
Kauffmann, Stanley 1916- *Au&Wr, ConAu 5R, LongC, Pen Am, WorAu, WrD 1976*
Kaufman SEE ALSO Kauffman
Kaufman, Alfred 1878- *WhWNAA*
Kaufman, Alvin S *AmSCAP 66*
Kaufman, Anton 1882- *WhWNAA*
Kaufman, Arnold S 1927- *ConAu 25*
Kaufman, Bel *AmA&B, ConAu 13R, DrAF 1976, WrD 1976*
Kaufman, Bill M 1930- *AmSCAP 66*
Kaufman, Bob 1925- *BlkAW, ConAu 41, ConP 1970, DrAP 1975, LivBA, Pen Am, RAdv 1*
Kaufman, Burton I 1940- *ConAu 33*
Kaufman, Donald D 1933- *ConAu 29*
Kaufman, Edmund George 1891- *ConAu 21*
Kaufman, George Simon 1889-1961 *AmA&B, CasWL, CnDAL, CnMD, CnThe, ConAmA, ConAmL, DcLEnL, EvLB, LongC, McGWD, ModWD, OxAm, Pen Am, REn, REnAL, REnWD, TwCA, TwCA Sup, TwCW, WebEAL*
Kaufman, Gerald Bernard 1930- *ConAu 23, WrD 1976*
Kaufman, Gerald Lynton 1893- *ChPo*
Kaufman, Gordon Dester 1925- *ConAu 13R*
Kaufman, Helen Andrews 1889- *IndAu 1917*
Kaufman, Herbert 1878-1947 *AmA&B, AmLY, ChPo, ChPo S2, DcNAA*
Kaufman, Irving 1920- *ConAu 21*
Kaufman, Jacob J 1914- *ConAu 41*
Kaufman, Kenneth *ChPo*
Kaufman, Kenneth Carlyle 1887-1945 *AmA&B*
Kaufman, Lenard 1913- *AmA&B, AmNov, TwCA Sup*
Kaufman, Martin Ellis 1899- *AmSCAP 66*
Kaufman, Mel B 1879-1932 *AmSCAP 66*
Kaufman, Mervyn D 1932- *ConAu 5R, SmATA 4*
Kaufman, Morris 1919- *Au&Wr, WrD 1976*
Kaufman, Paul 1886- *AmA&B, WhWNAA*
Kaufman, Reginald Wright 1877-1959 *DcAmA*
Kaufman, Robert 1931- *ConAu 17R*
Kaufman, Roger 1932- *ConAu 53*
Kaufman, Rosalie *Alli Sup*
Kaufman, Rosamond V P 1923- *ConAu 9R*
Kaufman, Sherwin A 1920- *ConAu 25*
Kaufman, Shirley 1923- *ConAu 49, DrAP 1975*

Kaufman, Sue 1926- *ConAu XR, ConLC 3, DrAF 1976, WrD 1976*
Kaufman, Wallace 1939- *ConAu 25*
Kaufman, William I 1922- *ConAu 13R*
Kaufman, Wolfe 1905?-1970 *ConAu 29*
Kaufmann, Alexander 1817-1893 *BbD, BiD&SB*
Kaufmann, Christoph 1753-1795 *OxGer*
Kaufmann, Harry 1927- *ConAu 45*
Kaufmann, Helen L 1887- *ConAu 5R*
Kaufmann, Henry William 1913- *ConAu 41*
Kaufmann, John 1931- *IlBYP, IlCB 1966*
Kaufmann, Mathilde *BiD&SB*
Kaufmann, Moritz *Alli Sup*
Kaufmann, Myron S 1921- *ConAu 25*
Kaufmann, Peter 1800-1869? *OhA&B*
Kaufmann, R James 1924- *ConAu 13R*
Kaufmann, R T *Alli Sup*
Kaufmann, U Milo 1934- *ConAu 41*
Kaufmann, Ulrich George 1920- *ConAu 23*
Kaufmann, Walter 1921- *AmA&B, ConAu 1R, WrD 1976*
Kaufmann, Walter 1933- *ConAu 61*
Kaufmann, William W 1918- *ConAu 13R*
Kaufringer, Heinrich *OxGer*
Kaula, Edna Mason 1906- *AuBYP, ConAu 5R*
Kaulitz-Niedeck, R 1881- *WhLA*
Kaun, Alexander Samuel 1889-1944 *AnMV 1926, DcNAA*
Kaunitz, Wenzel Anton, Graf Von 1711-1794 *OxGer*
Kaup, Elizabeth Bartol Dewing 1885- *AmA&B, AmNov*
Kauper, Paul Gerhardt 1907-1974 *ConAu 1R, ConAu 49, IndAu 1917*
Kausler, Donald H 1927- *ConAu 17R*
Kauth, Benjamin 1914- *Au&Wr, ConAu 5R, WrD 1976*
Kautilya *DcOrL 2, Pen Cl*
Kautsky, Karl 1854-1938 *REn, WhLA*
Kautz, August Valentine 1828-1895 *Alli Sup, DcAmA, DcNAA*
Kautz, John Iden 1896- *IndAu 1917*
Kauvar, Gerald B 1938- *ConAu 45*
Kavafis SEE ALSO Cavafy; Kavaphes
Kavafis, Konstantinos 1863-1933 *CasWL, TwCA Sup, WhTwL*
Kavaler, Lucy 1930- *AuBYP, ConAu 57*
Kavan, Anna 1904-1968 *ConAu XR, ConLC 5, ConNov 1976*
Kavanagh, Arthur *Alli, Alli Sup*
Kavanagh, Bridget *Alli Sup*
Kavanagh, Henry 1823- *PoIre*
Kavanagh, James W *Alli*
Kavanagh, Mrs. James W *Alli Sup*
Kavanagh, Julia 1824-1877 *Alli, Alli Sup, BbD, BiD&SB, BrAu 19, Chmbr 3, DcEnA, DcEnL, DcLEnL, EvLB, NewC, OxEng*
Kavanagh, M D *Alli*
Kavanagh, Marcus A 1859-1937 *DcNAA*
Kavanagh, Matthew *Alli*
Kavanagh, Maurice Dennis *Alli Sup*
Kavanagh, Morgan Peter d1874 *Alli, Alli Sup, PoIre*
Kavanagh, Patrick 1905?-1967 *CasWL, ChPo, ConAu 25, ConP 1970, LongC, ModBL Sup, Pen Eng, REn, TwCW, WhTwL, WorAu*
Kavanagh, Patrick Fidelis *PoIre*
Kavanagh, Patrick Joseph 1931- *Au&Wr, ConP 1970, ConP 1975, WrD 1976*
Kavanagh, Rose 1859-1891 *PoIre*
Kavanagh, T Henry *Alli*
Kavanaugh, Benjamin Taylor 1805-1888 *Alli Sup, BiDSA, DcNAA*
Kavanaugh, James J 1929- *ConAu 13R*
Kavanaugh, Kieran 1928- *ConAu 25*
Kavanaugh, Robert E 1926- *ConAu 29*
Kavanaugh, Mrs. Russell *Alli Sup*
Kavaphes SEE ALSO Cavafy; Kavafis
Kavaphes, Konstantinos 1863-1933 *EvEuW, LongC*
Kavaugh, Thomas Henry *Alli Sup*
Kavelin, Konstantin Dmitrievich 1818-1885 *CasWL, DcRusL*
Kavenagh, W Keith 1926- *ConAu 37, WrD 1976*

Kaverin, Veniamin 1902- *DcRusL, EncWL, Pen Eur*
Kaverin, Venyamin 1902- *CasWL, ClDMEuL, EvEuW, ModSL 1, REn, TwCW*
Kavesh, Robert A 1927- *ConAu 17R*
Kavet, Robert 1924- *ConAu 37*
Kavi, Nanalal *DcOrL 2*
Kavic, Lorne John 1936- *WrD 1976*
Kavli, Guthorm 1917- *Au&Wr, ConAu P-1*
Kavolis, Vytautas 1930- *ConAu 25*
Kawabata, Yasunari 1899-1972 *CasWL, CnMWL, ConAu 33, ConLC 2, ConLC 5, DcOrL 1, EncWL, Pen Cl, RCom, REn, WhTwL, WorAu*
Kawahigashi, Hekigodo *DcOrL 1*
Kawahito, Kiyoshi 1939- *ConAu 37*
Kawai, Kazuo 1904-1963 *ConAu 1R*
Kawajima, Onitsura 1661-1738 *CasWL*
Kawakami, K K 1874- *AmLY*
Kawakami, Toyo S 1916- *ConAu 33*
Kawakibi, 'Abd Ar-Rahman Al- 1849-1902? *DcOrL 3*
Kawatake, Mokuami *CasWL, DcOrL 1*
Kawin, Bruce F 1945- *ConAu 37, WrD 1976*
Kawin, Ethel d1969 *ConAu P-1*
Kay Clement *WhWNAA*
Kay, A K Clark *MnBBF*
Kay, Albert William 1931- *Au&Wr*
Kay, Alexander *Alli Sup*
Kay, Alexander J *Alli Sup*
Kay, Barbara Ann 1929- *ConAu 13R, WhWNAA*
Kay, Bernard *MnBBF*
Kay, Brian Ross 1924- *ConAu 1R*
Kay, David *Alli Sup*
Kay, Donald 1939- *ConAu 57*
Kay, E H D And Simonet, Emma *Alli Sup*
Kay, Sir Edward Ebenezer 1822- *Alli Sup*
Kay, Edward J 1898- *AmSCAP 66*
Kay, Ernest 1915- *Au&Wr, ConAu 13R, WrD 1976*
Kay, Fred Hall *WhWNAA*
Kay, George *Alli, ConAu XR*
Kay, George 1924- *ConP 1970*
Kay, George 1936- *ConAu 21, WrD 1976*
Kay, Gertrude Alice 1884-1939 *AmA&B, ChPo, ConICB, DcNAA, OhA&B, WhWNAA*
Kay, Harry 1919- *ConAu 25*
Kay, Helen *AuBYP, ConAu XR, SmATA 6*
Kay, Hershy 1919- *AmSCAP 66*
Kay, James *Alli*
Kay, John *Alli, DcEnL, PoLE*
Kay, Jonathan *Alli*
Kay, Joseph 1821-1878 *Alli, Alli Sup*
Kay, Julian 1910- *AmSCAP 66*
Kay, Kenneth 1915- *ConAu 9R*
Kay, Kwesi 1940?- *AfA 1*
Kay, Lester Williams 1921- *WrD 1976*
Kay, Mack H 1917- *AmSCAP 66*
Kay, Mara *ConAu 5R, WrD 1976*
Kay, Matthew *Alli*
Kay, Norman 1929- *ConAu 45*
Kay, Paul 1934- *ConAu 41*
Kay, Ray *MnBBF*
Kay, Robin Langford 1919- *WrD 1976*
Kay, Stephen *Alli*
Kay, Terence 1918- *ConAu 17R*
Kay, Terry *ConAu XR*
Kay, Thomas *Alli*
Kay, Thomas d1572 *DcEnL*
Kay, Thomas 1841-1914 *ChPo S2*
Kay, Thomas O 1932- *ConAu 1R*
Kay, W *Alli*
Kay, Wallace *MnBBF*
Kay, Wilbur W *ChPo S1*
Kay, William *ChPo S1*
Kay, William 1820-1886 *Alli Sup*
Kay, William 1930- *ConAu 29*
Kay, William E *Alli Sup*
Kay, William Henry *Alli Sup*
Kay, Zell *ConAu XR*
Kay-Shuttleworth *Alli Sup*
Kayal, Joseph M 1942- *ConAu 57*
Kayal, Philip M 1943- *ConAu 57*
Kayat, Asaad Yacoob *Alli Sup*
Kayden, Eugene Mark 1886- *WhWNAA*
Kayden, Mildred *AmSCAP 66*
Kaye, Aaron M *ChPo*

Kaye, Anstey *MnBBF*
Kaye, Barbara 1908- *ConAu XR, WrD 1976*
Kaye, Barrington 1924- *Au&Wr, WrD 1976*
Kaye, Benjamin M 1883- *AmSCAP 66*
Kaye, Benny 1915- *AmSCAP 66*
Kaye, Buddy 1918- *AmSCAP 66*
Kaye, Crawford *MnBBF*
Kaye, Evelyn 1937- *ConAu 57*
Kaye, Frederick Benjamin 1892-1930 *AmA&B, DcNAA*
Kaye, Geraldine Hughesdon 1925- *Au&Wr, ConAu 13R, SmATA 10, WrD 1976*
Kaye, James R 1929- *AmSCAP 66*
Kaye, John 1784-1853 *Alli*
Kaye, John Brayshaw *Alli Sup*
Kaye, Sir John William 1814-1876 *Alli, Alli Sup, BiD&SB, BrAu 19, ChPo, ChPo S1, Chmbr 3, DcEnA, DcEnL, EvLB, NewC*
Kaye, John William 1840-1895 *PoIre*
Kaye, John William 1846- *DcAmA*
Kaye, Julian Bertram 1925- *ConAu 1R, WrD 1976*
Kaye, Lady Lister *Alli*
Kaye, Marvin 1938- *ConAu 53, WrD 1976*
Kaye, Mary Margaret 1909- *Au&Wr*
Kaye, Myrna 1957- *ConAu 57*
Kaye, Norman 1922- *AmSCAP 66*
Kaye, Peter 1918- *AmSCAP 66*
Kaye, Philip A 1920- *ConAu 37*
Kaye, Philip B *AmA&B, BlkAW*
Kaye, Richard *Alli*
Kaye, Sammy 1910- *AmSCAP 66*
Kaye, Tom *WrD 1976*
Kaye, Walter Jenkinson *ChPo S1, ChPo S2*
Kaye, William 1917- *AmSCAP 66*
Kaye-Cook, L *MnBBF*
Kaye-Kysilevs'kyj, V J *OxCan*
Kaye-Smith, Sheila 1887?-1956 *BkC 4, CatA 1947, ChPo S1, CyWA, DcLEnL, EvLB, LongC, ModBL, NewC, Pen Eng, REn, TwCA, TwCA Sup, TwCW*
Kayes, Cornelius 1810-1868 *PoIre*
Kayira, Legson Didimu 1940?- *AfA 1, ConAu 17R, RGAfl*
Kayira, Legson Didimu 1942- *Au&Wr*
Kayo, Patrice 1940?- *AfA 1*
Kayper-Mensah, Albert William 1923- *AfA 1*
Kays, William *Alli*
Kaysen, Carl 1920- *ConAu 17R*
Kayser, Edna James *ChPo S1*
Kayser, Elmer Louis 1896- *ConAu 37*
Kayser, J *Alli*
Kaysing, Bill 1922- *ConAu 33*
Kazakevich, Emmanuil Jenrikhovich 1913-1949 *CasWL*
Kazakov, Yuri Pavlovich 1927- *ConAu 5R, ModSL 1, Pen Eur, TwCW, WorAu*
Kazamias, Andreas M 1927- *ConAu 17R*
Kazan, Elia 1909- *ConAu 21, ConLC 6, OxAm, REnAL, WrD 1976*
Kazantzakis, Nikos 1883?-1957 *AtlBL, CasWL, CnMD, EncWL, OxEng, Pen Eur, REn, TwCA Sup, TwCW, WhTwL*
Kazarian, Edward A 1931- *ConAu 53*
Kazemzadeh, Firuz 1924- *ConAu 23, WrD 1976*
Kazim Khan Khatak, Shayda 1725?-1780? *DcOrL 3*
Kazin, Alfred 1915- *AmA&B, Au&Wr, CasWL, ConAu 1R, OxAm, Pen Am, RAdv 1, REn, REnAL, TwCA Sup*
Kazin, Vasili Vasilievich 1898- *CasWL, ClDMEuL, DcRusL*
Kazinczy, Ferenc 1759-1831 *CasWL, Pen Eur*
Keable, John Edward 1903- *Au&Wr*
Keable, Robert 1887-1927 *EvLB, LongC, NewC, REn, TwCA*
Keach, Benjamin 1640-1704 *Alli, ChPo, DcEnL*
Keach, Elias *Alli*
Keagy, John Milton 1795-1837 *DcNAA*
Kealey, Edward J 1936- *WrD 1976*
Kealing, Ethel Black *IndAu 1917*
Kealy, Edward Herbert 1873- *WhLA*
Kealy, Edward J 1936- *ConAu 37*
Kealy, J D F *OxCan Sup*
Kean, Abram *OxCan*

Kean, Arthur *Alli Sup*
Kean, Charles Duell 1910-1963 *AmA&B, ConAu 5R*
Kean, Charles John 1811-1868 *NewC*
Kean, Edmund 1787-1833 *NewC, REn*
Kean, Edward George 1924- *AmSCAP 66*
Kean, H A *ChPo*
Kean, James *Alli Sup*
Kean, Martha *OhA&B*
Kean, T *Alli*
Keane, Augustus Henry 1835- *Alli Sup*
Keane, Bil 1922- *ConAu 33, SmATA 4*
Keane, David Deady *Alli, Alli Sup*
Keane, Ellsworth McGranahan 1927- *ConP 1970*
Keane, John B 1928- *ConAu 29*
Keane, John Friar Thomas 1854- *Alli Sup*
Keane, Sir John Henry 1816-1881 *Alli Sup, PoIre*
Keane, John Joseph 1839-1918 *DcNAA*
Keane, M J *PoIre*
Keane, Marcus *Alli Sup*
Keane, Moira *Au&Wr*
Keane, Patrick J 1939- *ConAu 45*
Keane, William *Alli Sup*
Kearey, Charles 1916- *ConAu 45*
Kearley, F Furman 1932- *ConAu 57*
Kearley, George *Alli Sup*
Kearney, Belle *BiDSA*
Kearney, George Fairchild 1895- *WhWNAA*
Kearney, Hugh Francis 1924- *Au&Wr, ConAu 5R*
Kearney, James d1876? *PoIre*
Kearney, James R 1929- *ConAu 25*
Kearney, John *PoIre*
Kearney, John 1865-1941 *CatA 1947*
Kearney, John Watts *Alli Sup*
Kearney, Michael *Alli, PoIre*
Kearney, Patrick 1848-1900? *PoIre*
Kearney, Ruth Elizabeth *ConAu XR*
Kearney, Stephen Watts 1794-1848 *DcAmA*
Kearney, W J d1852? *PoIre*
Kearns, Francis E 1931- *ConAu 29*
Kearns, J F *Alli Sup*
Kearns, James A, III 1949- *ConAu 29*
Kearns, Lionel John 1937- *ConAu 17R, ConP 1970, ConP 1975, OxCan Sup, WrD 1976*
Kearns, Martha 1945- *ConAu 57*
Kearny, Edward 1936- *WrD 1976*
Kearny, John *Alli*
Kearny, Thomas 1878-1942 *DcNAA*
Kearsley, C And G *Alli*
Kearsley, George *Alli, ChPo*
Kearsley, Harriet *Alli Sup*
Keary, Anna Maria 1825-1879 *Alli Sup*
Keary, Annie 1825-1879 *BbD, BiD&SB, BrAu 19, CasWL, ChPo, ChPo S1, EvLB, St&VC*
Keary, Charles Francis *Alli Sup, BbD*
Keary, E M *ChPo S1*
Keary, Eliza *Alli Sup*
Keary, Elizabeth *PoIre*
Keary, Mary *Alli Sup*
Keary, Maud *ChPo*
Keary, Peter 1865-1915 *MnBBF*
Keary, William *Alli*
Keasberry, Benjamin Peach *Alli Sup*
Keasbey, Edward Quinton 1849-1925 *AmLY, DcNAA*
Keasbey, Lindley Miller 1867- *DcAmA*
Keasby, Anthony Q *Alli Sup*
Keast, James D 1930- *ConAu 25*
Keast, William R 1914- *ConAu 13R, Pen Am*
Keate, George 1729-1797 *Alli, DcEnL*
Keate, T W *Alli Sup*
Keate, Thomas d1821 *Alli, BiDLA*
Keate, William *Alli*
Keating, Bern 1915- *ConAu XR, SmATA XR, WrD 1976*
Keating, Charlotte M 1927- *ConAu 33, WrD 1976*
Keating, Edward M 1925- *ConAu 13R*
Keating, Eliza H *Alli, Alli Sup, ChPo, ChPo S2*
Keating, Geoffry 1570-1625? *Alli, Pen Eng*
Keating, George *Alli Sup*
Keating, H S And J S Willis *Alli*

Keating, Henry Reymond Fitzwalter 1926-
Au&Wr, ConAu 33, EncM&D, WrD 1976
Keating, John Henry 1870-1963 AmSCAP 66
Keating, John J 1918?-1975 ConAu 61
Keating, John Marie 1852-1893 Alli Sup,
DcAmA, DcNAA
Keating, John McLeod 1830-1906 AmA,
AmA&B, DcNAA
Keating, Joseph 1871- WhLA
Keating, Joseph Ignatius Patrick 1865-1939
CatA 1947, WhLA
Keating, L Clark 1907- ConAu 21, WrD 1976
Keating, Lawrence Alfred 1903-1966 AuBYP,
ConAu 5R
Keating, Leo Bernard 1915- ConAu 29,
SmATA 10
Keating, Michael 1932- ConAu 49
Keating, Norma AuBYP
Keating, Reginald James Thomas 1910-
Au&Wr
Keating, Sally Sayward DcNAA
Keating, William Alli
Keating, William Hypolitus 1799-1840 Alli,
BbtC, DcNAA
Keating, William V Alli
Keatinge, J J Alli
Keatinge, Maurice Alli, BiDLA
Keatinge, Mrs. Richard Harte Alli Sup
Keatinge, Thomas Alli, BiDLA
Keatley, Sheila Marjorie 1912- Au&Wr
Keator, Alfred Decker 1886- WhWNAA
Keats, Charles B 1905- ConAu P-1
Keats, Donald 1929- AmSCAP 66
Keats, Eleanor B DrAP 1975
Keats, Ezra Jack 1916- AuBYP, AuICB,
AuNews 1, BkP, ChLR 1, ChPo S1,
ChPo S2, IlBYP, IlCB 1956, IlCB 1966,
MorJA, NewbC 1956, WrD 1976
Keats, Gwendoline BbD, BiD&SB
Keats, John 1795-1821 Alli, AnCL, AtlBL,
BiD&SB, BrAu 19, CasWL, ChPo,
ChPo S1, ChPo S2, Chmbr 3, CnE&AP,
CriT 2, CyWA, DcEnA, DcEnL,
DcLEnL, EvLB, MouLC 2, NewC,
OxEng, Pen Eng, RAdv 1, RCom, REn,
St&VC, WebEAL
Keats, John C 1920- AmA&B, REnAL
Keats, Myron AmA&B, WhWNAA
Keaveney, Sydney Starr 1939- ConAu 53
Keay Alli
Keay, Andrew Alli Sup
Keay, Frederick 1915- ConAu 33
Keay, J Seymour Alli Sup
Keay, John 1941- WrD 1976
Keays, Hersilia A Mitchell 1861-1910 DcNAA
Kebbel, Carston Dirs Alli Sup
Kebbel, Thomas Edward 1828- Alli Sup,
BiD&SB
Kebbell, William Alli Sup
Kebede, Mikael AfA 1
Keble, J A ChPo S2
Keble, John 1792-1866 Alli, Alli Sup, BbD,
BiD&SB, BrAu 19, CasWL, ChPo,
ChPo S1, ChPo S2, Chmbr 3, DcEnA,
DcEnL, DcEuL, DcLEnL, EvLB, NewC,
OxEng, Pen Eng, PoCh, REn, WebEAL
Keble, Joseph 1632-1710 Alli
Keble, Thomas 1793-1875 BrAu 19
Kebschull, Harvey G 1932- ConAu 41
Kechley, Gerald 1919- AmSCAP 66
Keckeler, Mrs. T H Alli Sup
Keckley, Elizabeth 1825?-1907? Alli Sup,
BlkAW, DcNAA
Kedar, Obed OhA&B
Keddell, Georgina 1913- ConAu 25
Keddie, Henrietta 1827-1914 Alli Sup,
BiD&SB, ChPo
Keddie, James 1883-1942 DcNAA
Keddie, James Alfred Grant 1900- Au&Wr,
WrD 1976
Keddie, Nikki R 1930- ConAu 25
Keddie, William d1877 Alli, Alli Sup
Keddington, R d1760 Alli
Keddle, Charlotte E Alli Sup
Keden, Joe 1898- AmSCAP 66
Kedgley, Susan 1948- ConAu 61
Kedington, R d1760 Alli
Kedney, John Steinfort 1819-1911 Alli Sup,

ChPo, DcAmA, DcNAA
Kedourie, Elie 1926- Au&Wr, ConAu 21
Kedrin, Dmitry 1907-1945 Pen Eur
Kedward, H R 1937- Au&Wr
Kedzie, Daniel Peter 1930- ConAu 17R,
WrD 1976
Kedzie, J H Alli Sup
Kedzie, John Hume 1815-1903 DcNAA
Kedzie, William K Alli Sup
Kee, Howard Clark 1920- ConAu 23
Kee, John 1842?- PoIre
Kee, Robert 1919- Au&Wr, WrD 1976
Keeble, Sir Frederick William 1870- WhLA
Keeble, Henry Alli Sup
Keeble, John Alli
Keeble, John 1944- ConAu 29
Keeble, Leslie Arthur James 1904- Au&Wr
Keech, B B ChPo
Keech, Lilian Sue WhWNAA
Keech, R B ChPo
Keech, Roy Adelbert WhWNAA
Keech, William J 1904- ConAu P-1
Keech, William R 1939- ConAu 25
Keedy, Charles Cochran 1891-1934 DcNAA
Keedy, Edward Everett 1869-1931 DcNAA
Keedy, Mervin L 1920- ConAu 53
Keefe, Carolyn 1928- ConAu 57
Keefe, Donald Joseph 1924- ConAu 37
Keefe, Jack REnAL
Keefe, Mildred Jones 1896- WrD 1976
Keefer, T C OxCan Sup
Keefer, T Frederick 1930- ConAu 23
Keefer, Thomas Coltrin 1821-1915 Alli Sup,
BbtC, DcNAA
Keegan, Arthur J 1895- AmSCAP 66
Keegan, D F Alli Sup
Keegan, Frank L 1925- ConAu 45
Keegan, James 1860-1894 PoIre
Keegan, John 1809-1849 ChPo S1, PoIre
Keegan, John Curran 1854- PoIre
Keegan, Marcia 1943- ConAu 49, SmATA 9
Keegan, Martha ChPo
Keegan, Mary Heathcott 1914- ConAu 5R
Keegan, Warren J 1936- ConAu 57
Keegan, William Alli, BiDLA
Keel, Laura ConAu XR
Keelan PoIre
Keelan, Grace 1893- TexWr
Keele, Kenneth David 1909- Au&Wr,
ConAu 5R, WrD 1976
Keele, W C BbtC
Keele, William Conway 1798-1872 DcNAA
Keeler, Andrew S Alli Sup
Keeler, Bronson C d1909 Alli Sup, DcNAA
Keeler, Charles Augustus 1871-1937 AmA&B,
ChPo, ChPo S2, DcAmA, DcNAA,
WhWNAA
Keeler, Clyde Edgar 1900- OhA&B
Keeler, Harriet Louise 1846-1921 DcNAA,
OhA&B
Keeler, Harry Stephen 1894?-1967 AmA&B,
EncM&D, WhWNAA
Keeler, Sister Jerome 1895- CatA 1947
Keeler, Katherine 1887- AuBYP
Keeler, Lucy Elliott 1864-1930 OhA&B
Keeler, Miriam Brown TexWr
Keeler, O B 1882- WhWNAA
Keeler, Ralph Olmstead 1840-1873 Alli Sup,
AmA&B, DcAmA, DcNAA, OhA&B,
OxAm
Keeley, Edmund Leroy 1928- AmA&B,
ConAu 1R, DrAF 1976, DrAP 1975,
WorAu, WrD 1976
Keeley, James 1867-1934 AmA&B
Keeley, Joseph Charles 1907- AmA&B,
ConAu 25
Keeley, Leslie E 1832-1900 DcNAA
Keeling, Annie E Alli Sup
Keeling, Bartholomew Alli
Keeling, Cecil Frank 1912- WhGrA
Keeling, Clinton Harry 1932- Au&Wr,
ConAu 9R
Keeling, E B ConAu XR
Keeling, Elsa D'Esterre 1860?- Alli Sup, PoIre
Keeling, Jill Annette 1923- Au&Wr,
ConAu P-1, WrD 1976
Keeling, William Alli
Keely, Robert Neff 1860- DcAmA

Keen, Benjamin Alli
Keen, Ernest 1937- ConAu 33, WrD 1976
Keen, J Osborne Alli Sup
Keen, Martin Leon 1913- ConAu 33,
SmATA 4, WrD 1976
Keen, Samuel Ashton 1842-1895? DcNAA,
OhA&B
Keen, William Williams 1837-1932 Alli Sup,
AmLY, DcAmA, DcNAA
Keenan, Alan 1920- CatA 1952
Keenan, Angela Elizabeth 1890- ConAu 61
Keenan, Boyd R 1928- ConAu 17R
Keenan, Henry Francis 1850?-1928 Alli Sup,
AmA&B, AmLY, BiD&SB, DcAmA,
DcBiA, DcNAA, OxAm, REnAL
Keenan, Sir Patrick Joseph 1826- Alli Sup
Keene, Burt ConAu XR
Keene, Carolina E Alli
Keene, Caroline AmNov XR
Keene, Carolyn AmA&B, ConAu 17,
EncM&D, SmATA 1
Keene, Charles Samuel 1823-1891 ChPo
Keene, Donald 1922- AmA&B, ConAu 1R
Keene, Edmund 1713-1781 Alli
Keene, Edward Spencer 1864-1928 AmLY,
DcNAA
Keene, Edwin 1826-1857 Alli Sup
Keene, Faraday EncM&D, TwCA,
TwCA Sup
Keene, Florence Rosina WhWNAA
Keene, Foxhall Parker 1867-1941 Br&AmS,
DcNAA
Keene, G Alli
Keene, Henry George 1825- Alli Sup
Keene, J Calvin 1908- ConAu P-1
Keene, James Alli Sup
Keene, James Boddely Alli Sup
Keene, John Baptist Alli Sup
Keene, John Harrington Alli Sup
Keene, Kahn 1909- AmSCAP 66
Keene, Katherine Alli Sup
Keene, King HsB&A
Keene, Luther Alli Sup
Keene, Mrs. Luther ChPo
Keene, Martin A Alli Sup
Keene, Nancy Beatrice 1923- Au&Wr,
WrD 1976
Keene, Ralph ChPo
Keene, Roy MnBBF
Keene, Mrs. S F Alli Sup
Keene, William Alli Sup
Keener, Frederick M 1937- ConAu 53
Keener, John Christian 1819-1906 BiDSA,
DcAmA, DcNAA
Keener, William Albert 1856-1913 Alli Sup,
DcAmA, DcNAA
Keeney, Charles James 1912- ConAu 5R
Keeney, Chuck ConAu XR
Keeney, Eldora Nelson 1878- IndAu 1917
Keeney, Ella B And Noble, Annette L Alli Sup
Keeney, Louella ChPo S2
Keeney, William 1922- ConAu 41
Keenleyside, Hugh Llewellyn 1898- ConAu P-1,
OxCan, WrD 1976
Keens, Michael Alli
Keep, Austin Baxter 1875-1932 DcNAA
Keep, David 1936- ConAu 61
Keep, John 1781-1870 Alli Sup, OhA&B
Keep, John 1926- ConAu 9R
Keep, Josiah 1849-1911 Alli Sup, DcAmA,
DcNAA
Keep, Robert Porter 1844-1904 Alli Sup,
DcAmA, DcNAA
Keep, Virginia ChPo
Keepe, Henry Alli
Keepe, W A Alli
Keeper, John Alli
Keepers, W Floyd 1896- WhWNAA
Keeping, Charles William James 1924- Au&Wr,
ConAu 21, IlBYP, IlCB 1966, PiP,
SmATA 9, ThBJA
Keeping, Walker Alli Sup
Keer, William Brown Alli Sup
Kees, Weldon 1914-1955? CrCAP, Pen Am,
WorAu
Keese, Harvey AmLY XR
Keese, John 1805-1856 Alli Sup, AmA&B,
ChPo, ChPo S1, DcNAA

Keese, Oline *Alli Sup*
Keese, William Linn 1835-1904 *Alli Sup,*
  DcAmA, DcNAA
Keesecker, William Francis 1918- *ConAu 33,*
  WrD 1976
Keeshan, Robert J 1927- *ConAu 5R*
Keesing, Felix Maxwell 1902-1961 *AmA&B*
Keesing, Nancy 1923- *ConAu 9R, ConP 1970,*
  TwCW
Keeslar, Oreon 1907- *ConAu P-1*
Keeson, Alfred *Alli Sup*
Keesy, William Allen 1843?-1910 *OhA&B*
Keetley, Charles Robert Bell *Alli Sup*
Keeton, Elizabeth B 1919- *ConAu 29*
Keeton, George Williams 1902- *Au&Wr,*
  ConAu 13R, WrD 1976
Keeton, Kathy *AuNews 2*
Keeton, Morris Teuton 1917- *ConAu 1R,*
  WrD 1976
Keeton, Robert E 1919- *ConAu 5R*
Keever, Edward W 1889- *OhA&B*
Keever, Jack 1938- *ConAu 53*
Keevill, Henry J 1914- *ConAu P-1*
Keezer, Dexter Merriam 1865- *ConAu 1R*
Keezer, Dexter Merriam 1896- *AmA&B,*
  Au&Wr
Kefauver, Estes 1903-1963 *AmA&B*
Keffer, Charles Albert 1861-1935 *DcNAA*
Kefferstan, Jean *ConAu 57*
Kegan, Adrienne Koch 1912-1971 *ConAu 33*
Kegel, Charles H 1924- *ConAu 1R*
Kegley, Charles William 1912- *AmA&B,*
  ConAu 5R
Kegley, Howard C *ChPo*
Kehl, D G 1936- *ConAu 33*
Kehm, Freda S *ConAu 29*
Kehner, Clarence Way 1926- *AmSCAP 66*
Kehoe, Alice B *OxCan Sup*
Kehoe, Constance 1933- *ConAu 13R*
Kehoe, James *Alli Sup*
Kehoe, Monika 1909- *ConAu 21*
Kehoe, Patrick E 1941- *ConAu 57*
Kehoe, Simon D *Alli Sup*
Kehoe, William F 1933- *ConAu 13R*
Kehr, Cyrus 1856-1941 *IndAu 1917*
Keich, Gideon 1923- *WhGrA*
Keichu, *DcOrL 1*
Keidel, George Charles 1868- *AmLY*
Keif, Aubrey *WhWNAA*
Keifer, Joseph Warren 1836-1932 *AmLY,*
  DcAmA, DcNAA, OhA&B
Keiffer, Aldine S *BiDSA*
Keighly, Henry Peach *Alli Sup*
Keighly, Walker *Alli, BiDLA*
Keightley, Rideal Eric 1890- *WhLA*
Keightley, Sir Samuel Robert 1859- *PoIre,*
  WhLA
Keightley, Thomas 1789-1872 *Alli, BiD&SB,*
  BrAu 19, Chmbr 3, DcEnA, DcEnL,
  EvLB, NewC
Keigwin, Albert Edwin 1861?-1937 *AmLY,*
  DcNAA
Keigwin, Richard Prescott 1883- *ChPo*
Keil, Frederick William 1830-1909 *OhA&B*
Keil, H H J 1930- *BiDPar*
Keiler, Ralph *MnBBF*
Keiley, A M *Alli Sup*
Keiley, Anthony M *BiDSA*
Keiley, Jarvis *ChPo*
Keiley, William S *Alli Sup*
Keilholz, Frederick Johnson 1898- *WhWNAA*
Keill, James 1673-1719 *Alli*
Keill, John 1671-1721 *Alli*
Keiller, William 1861-1931 *DcNAA*
Keillor, Garrison *DrAP 1975*
Keilly, Anne 1850?- *PoIre*
Keilwey, Robert *Alli*
Keily, John *Alli Sup*
Keim, Charles J 1922- *ConAu 33*
Keim, DeBenneville Randolph 1841-1914
  Alli Sup, DcNAA
Keim, Karl Theodor 1825-1878 *BiD&SB*
Keimberg, Allyn *ConAu XR*
Keimer, Samuel 1688-1739 *Alli, AmA,*
  AmA&B, CyAL 1, DcAmA, EarAB,
  OxAm, REnAL
Keimes, Lawrence *Alli*
Keir, Archibald *Alli, BiDLA*

Keir, Christine *ConAu XR, SmATA 3*
Keir, David E 1906-1969 *ChPo S2, ConAu P-1,*
  OxCan, WhLA
Keir, David Lindsay 1895- *ConAu 21*
Keir, Ennis *Alli Sup*
Keir, James *Alli, BiDLA*
Keir, Malcolm 1887- *WhWNAA*
Keir, P *Alli*
Keir, Peter *Alli*
Keirstead, Burton Seely 1907- *Au&Wr,*
  ConAu 5R
Keiser, Albert 1887-1959 *AmA&B, REnAL*
Keiser, Edna Louise Frankman 1894-
  IndAu 1917
Keiser, Norman F 1930- *ConAu 13R*
Keislar, Evan R 1913- *ConAu 23*
Keisman, Michael E 1932- *ConAu 25*
Keita, Fodeba 1921- *AfA 1*
Keith X *ConAu XR*
Keith, Adolphus 1939- *BlkAW*
Keith, Agnes Newton 1901- *AmA&B, Au&Wr,*
  ConAu 17R, REnAL, TwCA Sup,
  WrD 1976
Keith, Alexander *Alli*
Keith, Alexander 1799-1880 *Alli Sup*
Keith, Alexander 1811- *ChPo S1*
Keith, Alexander 1895- *WhLA*
Keith, Alexander, Jr. *Alli*
Keith, Alyn Yates *DcAmA, DcNAA*
Keith, Sir Arthur 1866-1955 *DcLEnL,*
  TwCA Sup, WhLA
Keith, Arthur Berriedale 1879-1944 *NewC,*
  WhLA
Keith, Arthur Leslie 1874-1942 *IndAu 1816,*
  WhWNAA
Keith, Benjamin F 1825- *IndAu 1816*
Keith, Carlton *AuBYP, ConAu XR,*
  SmATA 1
Keith, Charles *Alli Sup*
Keith, Charles 1749- *ChPo*
Keith, Charles Penrose 1854-1939 *Alli Sup,*
  AmLY, DcAmA, DcNAA, WhWNAA
Keith, Conway *Alli Sup*
Keith, David *AmA&B, ConAu 49,*
  WrD 1976
Keith, Donald *ConAu XR*
Keith, Duncan *Alli Sup*
Keith, Edson 1863-1939 *DcNAA*
Keith, Eros *ChPo S2, IlBYP*
Keith, Florence Frances *ChPo*
Keith, Frances Guignard Gibbes *WhWNAA*
Keith, George *PoCh*
Keith, George 1638?-1716 *Alli, DcEnL,*
  OxAm, REnAL
Keith, Sir George Mouat *Alli*
Keith, George S *Alli, BiDLA*
Keith, Harold Verne 1903- *AmA&B, AuBYP,*
  ConAu 5R, MorBMP, MorJA,
  NewbC 1956, SmATA 2, WhWNAA
Keith, Herbert F 1895- *ConAu 37*
Keith, Ian L 1911- *AmSCAP 66*
Keith, Isaac Stockton 1755-1813 *Alli, BiDSA*
Keith, James *Alli, Alli Sup, BiDLA*
Keith, James d1719 *Alli*
Keith, John Alexander Hull 1869-1931 *DcNAA*
Keith, Joseph Joel *ChPo S2*
Keith, Judith 1923- *ConAu 49*
Keith, K Wymand 1924- *ConAu 33*
Keith, Lee *ConAu XR*
Keith, Leslie *Alli Sup, BbD*
Keith, Louis *MnBBF*
Keith, Marian *OxCan*
Keith, Marion 1876- *CanNov*
Keith, Maurice *Alli Sup*
Keith, Melville Cox 1835-1903 *DcNAA*
Keith, Merton Spencer 1851-1920 *DcNAA*
Keith, Nathaniel S And Neymann, Percy
  Alli Sup
Keith, Noel L 1903- *ConAu 57*
Keith, Mrs. Oscar L *AmA&B*
Keith, Patrick *Alli*
Keith, Reuel d1842 *Alli*
Keith, Robert 1681-1757 *Alli, Chmbr 2,*
  DcEnL, EvLB
Keith, Sir Robert Murray *Alli*
Keith, Ronald *OxCan Sup*
Keith, T J *Alli Sup*
Keith, Thomas *Alli, Alli Sup*

Keith, Thomas 1759-1824 *Alli, BiDLA*
Keith, W J 1934- *ConAu 17R, OxCan Sup*
Keith, William *Alli*
Keith, Sir William 1680-1749 *Alli, DcAmA*
Keith, William 1839-1911 *ChPo, EarAB,*
  EarAB Sup
Keith-Falconer *Alli Sup*
Keith-Lucas, Alan 1910- *ConAu 5R*
Keith-Lucas, Bryan 1912- *Au&Wr, WrD 1976*
Keith-Spiegel, Patricia 1939- *ConAu 41*
Keithley, E Clinton 1880-1955 *AmSCAP 66*
Keithley, Erwin M 1905- *ConAu 23*
Keithley, George 1935- *ConAu 37,*
  DrAF 1976, DrAP 1975
Kekewich, George *Alli, BiDLA*
Kekkonen, Sylvi 1900?-1974 *ConAu 53*
Kelaart, Edward Frederick *Alli Sup*
Kelber, Magda 1908- *Au&Wr, ConAu 5R*
Kelder, Diane 1934- *ConAu 25*
Keleher, Will 1886-1972 *ConAu 37*
Kelen, Emery 1896- *ConAu 9R, IlCB 1945*
Kelen, Stephen 1902- *WrD 1976*
Kelen, Stephen 1912- *Au&Wr*
Kelf-Cohen, Reuben 1895- *Au&Wr,*
  ConAu 49, WrD 1976
Kelham, Robert *Alli*
Kelk, T *Alli, BiDLA*
Kelke, William Hastings *Alli Sup*
Kell, James H 1930- *IndAu 1917*
Kell, John *Alli, BiDLA*
Kell, John McIntosh 1823-1900 *BiDSA,*
  DcNAA
Kell, Joseph *AuNews 1, ConAu XR, LongC,*
  WorAu, WrD 1976
Kell, Richard Alexander 1927- *ConAu 5R,*
  ConP 1970, ConP 1975, WrD 1976
Kelland, Clarence Budington 1881-1964
  AmA&B, AmNov, OxAm, REn, REnAL,
  TwCA, TwCA Sup, WhWNAA
Kelland, Philip 1808-1879 *Alli, Alli Sup*
Kellar, Harry 1849-1922 *DcNAA, OhA&B*
Kellar, James Harley 1922- *IndAu 1917*
Kellar, Kenneth C 1906- *ConAu 45*
Kellaway, Frank Gerald 1922- *Au&Wr,*
  ConAu 9R
Kellaway, George Percival 1909- *ConAu 23,*
  WrD 1976
Kellaway, William 1926- *Au&Wr*
Kelle, John *Alli*
Kelleher, Daniel Lawrence 1883- *CatA 1952,*
  ChPo, ChPo S1, PoIre
Kellem, Craig C 1943- *AmSCAP 66*
Kellem, Milton 1911- *AmSCAP 66*
Kellen, William V *Alli Sup*
Keller, Albert Galloway 1874-1956 *AmA&B,*
  DcAmA, OhA&B, TwCA, TwCA Sup,
  WhWNAA
Keller, Allan 1904- *ConAu 29*
Keller, Allen 1925- *AmSCAP 66*
Keller, Arthur Ignatius 1867-1924 *AmA&B*
Keller, B L *ConAu 49*
Keller, Charles 1942- *ConAu 49, SmATA 8*
Keller, Charles Walter, Jr. 1898- *WhWNAA*
Keller, Clair W 1932- *ConAu 53*
Keller, David H 1880- *REnAL*
Keller, Dean H 1933- *ConAu 53*
Keller, Ernst 1891- *WhGrA*
Keller, Ethel May 1878- *AmA&B*
Keller, Eva M *ChPo*
Keller, Ezra 1812-1848 *Alli*
Keller, Frances Ruth 1911- *AuBYP*
Keller, Gail Faithfull *ConAu 57, SmATA 8*
Keller, Gerard 1829-1899 *BiD&SB, CasWL*
Keller, Gottfried 1819-1890 *BbD, BiD&SB,*
  CasWL, ChPo S2, ClDMEuL, CyWA,
  DcEuL, EuA, EvEuW, OxGer, Pen Eur,
  REn
Keller, H A 1894- *WhWNAA*
Keller, H S *ChPo*
Keller, Harry Bert 1924- *IndAu 1917*
Keller, Helen Adams 1880-1968 *AmA&B,*
  BiDSA, ChPo S1, DcLEnL, LongC,
  OxAm, REn, REnAL, WhWNAA
Keller, Howard H 1941- *ConAu 45*
Keller, James Gregory 1900- *AmA&B,*
  CatA 1952
Keller, Jerry 1937- *AmSCAP 66*
Keller, John E 1917- *ConAu 45*

Keller, John W *Alli Sup*
Keller, Joseph Edward 1827-1886 *Alli Sup,
DcAmA*
Keller, Karl 1933- *ConAu 57*
Keller, M C *Alli Sup*
Keller, M J *Alli Sup*
Keller, Matthias 1813-1875 *DcNAA*
Keller, Morton 1929- *ConAu 5R*
Keller, Paul 1873-1932 *OxGer*
Keller, Philip W *OxCan*
Keller, Sheldon B 1923- *AmSCAP 66*
Keller, Thomas F 1931- *ConAu 9R*
Keller, W D 1900- *ConAu 41*
Keller, Werner Rudolf 1909- *Au&Wr,
ConAu 23*
Kellerman, Ivy 1877- *ChPo*
Kellerman, William Ashbrook 1850-1908
DcAmA, DcNAA, OhA&B
Kellermann, Bernhard 1879-1951 *OxGer*
Kellermann, Francois-Christophe *OxFr*
Kellet, Alexander *Alli*
Kellet, Edward *Alli*
Kellett, Arnold 1926- *WrD 1976*
Kellett, Ernest Edward 1864-1950 *EvLB*
Kellett, Sir Henry 1806?-1875 *Alli Sup, OxCan*
Kelley *Au&Wr*
Kelley, Adelaide 1852-1928 *DcNAA*
Kelley, Alden D 1903- *ConAu 1R*
Kelley, Ben 1936- *ConAu 45*
Kelley, Caroline E *Alli Sup*
Kelley, Datus *Alli Sup*
Kelley, David Campbell 1833-1909 *BiDSA,
DcAmA*
Kelley, Donald R 1931- *ConAu 29*
Kelley, E G *Alli Sup*
Kelley, Earl Clarence 1895- *ConAu 5R*
Kelley, Edgar Stillman 1857-1944 *AmLY,
AmSCAP 66, DcNAA, OhA&B, REnAL*
Kelley, Edward 1555-1595 *Alli*
Kelley, Emma Dunham *BlkAW*
Kelley, Ethel May 1878- *AmLY, ChPo,
ChPo S2, WhWNAA*
Kelley, Eugene J 1922- *ConAu 13R*
Kelley, Florence 1859-1932 *DcNAA*
Kelley, Francis Beverly 1905- *OhA&B*
Kelley, Francis Clement 1870-1948 *AmA&B,
AmLY, BkC 2, CatA 1947, WhWNAA*
Kelley, George W 1879- *WhWNAA*
Kelley, Grace G *ChPo*
Kelley, H N 1911- *ConAu 45*
Kelley, Hall Jackson 1790-1874 *Alli Sup,
DcAmA, DcNAA*
Kelley, Henry Smith 1832-1911 *Alli Sup,
DcNAA*
Kelley, Hubert, Jr. 1926- *ConAu 5R*
Kelley, Irad 1791-1875 *OhA&B*
Kelley, James Douglas Jerrold 1847-1922
*Alli Sup, AmA, AmA&B, BiD&SB,
DcAmA, DcNAA*
Kelley, Jane Holden 1928- *ConAu 45*
Kelley, Jay George 1838-1899 *DcAmA,
DcNAA*
Kelley, Jesse Fillmore And Mackie, Adam
Alli Sup
Kelley, Joanna 1910- *ConAu 23*
Kelley, Jonathan F 1817-1855 *OhA&B*
Kelley, Joseph J, Jr. 1914- *ConAu 61*
Kelley, Leon 1895- *WhWNAA*
Kelley, Lilla Elizabeth 1872- *AmLY,
WhWNAA*
Kelley, Martha Mott *EncM&D*
Kelley, Oliver Hudson 1826-1913 *Alli Sup,
DcNAA*
Kelley, Page H 1924- *ConAu 25*
Kelley, Reeve Spencer 1912- *AnCL*
Kelley, Robert 1925- *ConAu 25, WrD 1976*
Kelley, Robert E 1938- *ConAu 53*
Kelley, Ruth Edna 1893- *WhWNAA*
Kelley, Samuel Walter 1855-1929 *DcNAA,
OhA&B*
Kelley, Stanley, Jr. 1926- *ConAu 13R*
Kelley, W P 1878- *WhWNAA*
Kelley, William 1929- *ConAu 5R*
Kelley, William Darrah 1814-1890 *Alli Sup,
BiD&SB, DcAmA, DcNAA*
Kelley, William Melvin 1937- *AmA&B,
BlkAW, ConNov 1972, ConNov 1976,
DrAF 1976, LivBA, Pen Am, WorAu,*

WrD 1976
Kelley, William T 1917- *ConAu 37*
Kelley, William Valentine 1843-1927 *DcNAA*
Kellgren, Johan Henrik 1751-1795 *BbD,
BiD&SB, CasWL, DcEuL, EuA, EvEuW*
Kellicott, William Erskine 1878-1919 *DcNAA*
Kellie, Alexander *Alli, BiDLA*
Kellie, George *Alli*
Kellie, Sir Thomas *Alli*
Kellin, Sally Moffet 1932- *ConAu 61,
SmATA 9*
Kelling, Furn L 1914- *ConAu 17R*
Kelling, George W 1944- *ConAu 57*
Kelling, Hans-Wilhelm 1932- *ConAu 37,
WrD 1976*
Kelling, Simon *Alli*
Kellison, Matthew 1560-1641 *Alli, DcEnL*
Kellison, Stephen G 1942- *ConAu 53*
Kellner, Bruce 1930- *ConAu 29*
Kellner, Elisabeth Willard d1916 *DcNAA*
Kellner, Esther Armacost 1909- *ConAu 13R,
IndAu 1917*
Kellner, L 1904- *ConAu 5R*
Kellner, Max 1861-1935 *DcNAA*
Kello, John *Alli*
Kellock, H A *ChPo*
Kellogg, Abner Otis 1818-1888 *Alli Sup,
DcNAA*
Kellogg, Albert 1813-1887 *DcNAA*
Kellogg, Alfred Hosea 1837-1906 *Alli Sup,
DcAmA, DcNAA*
Kellogg, Alfred Latimer 1915- *ConAu 41*
Kellogg, Alice Maud 1862-1911 *DcNAA*
Kellogg, Allyn S *Alli Sup*
Kellogg, Amos Markham 1832-1914 *Alli Sup,
ChPo, DcAmA, DcNAA*
Kellogg, Brainerd d1930 *DcNAA*
Kellogg, Celia *DcNAA*
Kellogg, Charles Flint 1909- *ConAu 23*
Kellogg, Charlotte Hoffman 1864-1946 *AmA&B,
ChPo S1, OhA&B, WhWNAA*
Kellogg, Clara Louise 1842-1916 *DcNAA*
Kellogg, Mrs. E S *ChPo*
Kellogg, Edward 1790-1858 *AmA, AmA&B,
DcNAA*
Kellogg, Elijah 1813-1901 *Alli Sup, AmA,
AmA&B, BiD&SB, CarSB, DcAmA,
DcNAA, OxAm, REnAL*
Kellogg, Elizabeth Rockey 1870- *OhA&B*
Kellogg, Ensign Hosmer 1812-1882 *Alli Sup*
Kellogg, Eva D *ChPo S2*
Kellogg, Eva Mary 1860- *DcAmA*
Kellogg, Frank Eugene 1854- *DcNAA*
Kellogg, Gene 1916- *SmATA XR, ConAu 9R*
Kellogg, Grace *WhWNAA*
Kellogg, James Lawrence 1866-1938 *DcNAA*
Kellogg, Jean 1916- *AuBYP, ConAu XR,
SmATA 10*
Kellogg, John Harvey 1852-1904? *Alli Sup,
DcAmA*
Kellogg, John Harvey 1852-1943 *DcNAA*
Kellogg, Kate *ChPo, ChPo S1*
Kellogg, Kay 1901- *AmSCAP 66*
Kellogg, Laura Cornelius 1881- *WhWNAA*
Kellogg, Lavinia Steele *Alli Sup*
Kellogg, Lester Stanley 1903- *Au&Wr*
Kellogg, Louise Phelps 1872?-1942 *AmA&B,
DcNAA, OxCan, WhWNAA, WiscW*
Kellogg, Marjorie 1922- *AmA&B, ConLC 2*
Kellogg, Miner Kilbourne 1814-1889 *Alli Sup,
OhA&B*
Kellogg, Olin Clay 1870- *DcAmA*
Kellogg, Paul Underwood 1879-1958 *AmA&B,
WhWNAA*
Kellogg, Robert H *Alli Sup*
Kellogg, Samuel Henry 1839-1899 *Alli Sup,
DcAmA, DcNAA*
Kellogg, Sanford Cobb 1842- *BiDSA, DcNAA*
Kellogg, Sarah Prescott 1829-1895 *ChPo,
ChPo S1, DcNAA*
Kellogg, Sarah Winter *Alli Sup*
Kellogg, Steven 1941- *ConAu 49, IlBYP,
SmATA 8, WrD 1976*
Kellogg, Theodore H *DcNAA*
Kellogg, Vernon Lyman 1867-1937 *AmA&B,
AmLY, CarSB, DcAmA, DcNAA,
WhWNAA*
Kellogg, Warren Franklin 1860- *Alli Sup,*

DcAmA
Kellogg, Winthrop Niles 1898- *ConAu 1R,
WhWNAA*
Kellor, Frances Alice 1873-1952 *OhA&B,
WhWNAA*
Kellough, Richard Dean 1935- *ConAu 53*
Kellow, Henry Arthur *ChPo*
Kellow, Kathleen *ConAu XR, EncM&D,
SmATA 2, WorAu, WrD 1976*
Kellow, Norman B 1914- *ConAu 21*
Kellum, D F 1936- *ConAu 61*
Kellum-Rose, Matthew *BlkAW*
Kellus, Samuel *Alli*
Kellwaye, Simon *Alli*
Kelly *Alli*
Kelly, Lady *Au&Wr*
Kelly, A C *Alli Sup*
Kelly, Alfred H 1907- *ConAu 5R*
Kelly, Alison 1913- *WrD 1976*
Kelly, Allen 1852-1916 *DcNAA*
Kelly, Aloysius Oliver Joseph 1870-1911
DcNAA
Kelly, Amy 1877- *OhA&B*
Kelly, Averill Alison 1913- *Au&Wr,
ConAu 13R*
Kelly, Balmer H 1914- *ConAu 17R*
Kelly, Bernard Joseph 1910- *BkC 6,
CatA 1952*
Kelly, Bernard W 1872- *CatA 1947*
Kelly, Blanche Mary 1881- *BkC 4, CatA 1947,
ChPo*
Kelly, Charles *Alli, Alli Sup*
Kelly, Charles 1889- *WhWNAA*
Kelly, Charles Arthur d1907 *Alli Sup,
ChPo S2, PoIre*
Kelly, Charles Patrick Bernard 1891?-1971
ConAu 29
Kelly, Charlotte M *BkC 5*
Kelly, Christopher *Alli*
Kelly, Clarence 1941- *ConAu 61*
Kelly, Clyde 1883-1935 *DcNAA, WhWNAA*
Kelly, D *Alli*
Kelly, Dave *DrAP 1975*
Kelly, David M 1938- *ConAu 29*
Kelly, Denis *Alli*
Kelly, Denis 1841-1870? *PoIre*
Kelly, Denis Henry 1797?-1877 *PoIre*
Kelly, Dennis *Alli Sup*
Kelly, Dominick d1806? *PoIre*
Kelly, Mrs. E C d1840? *PoIre*
Kelly, Edmond 1851-1909 *DcAmA, DcNAA*
Kelly, Edmund *Alli Sup*
Kelly, Edward H 1930- *ConAu 37*
Kelly, Edward M *Alli*
Kelly, Eleanor F *PoIre*
Kelly, Eleanor Mercein 1880- *AmA&B, TwCA,
TwCA Sup, WhWNAA*
Kelly, Ellinor J *Alli Sup, PoIre*
Kelly, Eric Philbrook 1884-1960 *AmA&B,
AnCL, AuBYP, JBA 1934, JBA 1951,
Newb 1922, REnAL, WhWNAA,
YABC 1*
Kelly, Ernece Beverly *LivBA*
Kelly, Ernest 1883- *WhWNAA*
Kelly, Evander Francis 1879- *WhWNAA*
Kelly, Fanny *Alli Sup*
Kelly, Faye L 1914- *ConAu 23*
Kelly, Florence Finch 1858-1939 *AmA&B,
DcAmA, DcNAA, WhWNAA*
Kelly, Frances Maria 1790-1882 *PoIre*
Kelly, Francis Clement *ChPo*
Kelly, Frank A 1879- *ChPo S1*
Kelly, Frank K 1914- *ConAu 1R*
Kelly, Fred Charters 1882-1959 *AmA&B,
OhA&B, WhWNAA*
Kelly, Frederic Festus *Alli Sup*
Kelly, Frederic Joseph 1922- *ConAu 53*
Kelly, Frederick James 1880- *WhWNAA*
Kelly, George A 1916- *ConAu 17R*
Kelly, George C 1849?-1895 *DcNAA, HsB&A*
Kelly, George Edward 1887-1974? *AmA&B,
AuNews 1, CnDAL, CnMD, ConAmA,
ConAmL, ConAu 49, ConDr, DcLEnL,
LongC, McGWD, ModAL, ModWD,
OxAm, REn, REnAL, TwCA,
TwCA Sup*
Kelly, George Fox *Alli Sup*
Kelly, Gerald R 1930- *ConAu 29*

Kelly, Glenn *AmA&B, AmNov XR*
Kelly, Gul *Alli*
Kelly, Gwen Nita 1922- *Au&Wr*
Kelly, Harold Edward 1864- *AmA&B*
Kelly, Harry Eugene 1870-1936 *DcNAA*
Kelly, Henry Ansgar 1934- *ConAu 25*
Kelly, Herbert Hamilton 1860- *WhLA*
Kelly, Howard Atwood 1858-1943 *DcNAA,
   WhWNAA*
Kelly, Hugh 1739-1777 *Alli, BrAu, Chmbr 2,
   DcEnL, DcLEnL, EvLB, NewC, OxEng,
   PoIre*
Kelly, Isabella *Alli, BiDLA, PoIre*
Kelly, J *Alli Sup, PoIre*
Kelly, J J *Alli Sup*
Kelly, James *Alli, Alli Sup, WhWNAA*
Kelly, James d1881 *PoIre*
Kelly, James 1829-1907 *DcNAA*
Kelly, James 1855- *ChPo*
Kelly, James 1912- *AmA&B*
Kelly, James A 1891- *AmSCAP 66*
Kelly, James B 1905- *ConAu 49*
Kelly, James Edward 1855-1933 *ChPo S1*
Kelly, James Fitzmaurice- *TwCA, TwCA Sup*
Kelly, James Henry *Alli Sup*
Kelly, James J 1845?- *PoIre*
Kelly, James Madison 1795-1849 *BiDSA*
Kelly, James Plunkett 1920- *ConAu 53*
Kelly, Jennie J *ChPo S1*
Kelly, Jo-Ann 1949- *BlkAW*
Kelly, John *Alli, Alli Sup, ChPo, ChPo S1,
   ChPo S2, PoIre*
Kelly, John d1751 *PoIre*
Kelly, John 1750-1809 *Alli*
Kelly, John 1801-1876 *Alli Sup*
Kelly, John 1809-1875 *PoIre*
Kelly, John 1857- *ChPo S1*
Kelly, John 1913-1966 *AmA&B, AmNov*
Kelly, Father John Bernard 1888-1957 *AmA&B,
   CatA 1947, ChPo S1*
Kelly, John Francis *Alli Sup*
Kelly, John Frederick 1888-1947 *DcNAA*
Kelly, John Liddell 1850- *Alli Sup*
Kelly, John M, Jr. 1919- *ChPo S1,
   ConAu 13R*
Kelly, John N D 1909- *ConAu 5R*
Kelly, John Tarpey 1864-1899 *PoIre*
Kelly, Jonathan Falconbridge 1817-1855 *Alli,
   AmA, AmA&B, BiD&SB, DcNAA,
   OxAm, REnAL*
Kelly, Judith 1908- *AmNov*
Kelly, Kathleen Sheridan White 1945-
   ConAu 49
Kelly, L V *OxCan*
Kelly, Lawrence C 1932- *ConAu 23*
Kelly, Leo J 1925- *ConAu 41*
Kelly, Louis Gerard 1935- *WrD 1976*
Kelly, Lucile Rood *WhWNAA*
Kelly, Luther Sage 1849-1928 *AmA&B,
   DcNAA*
Kelly, Mahlon 1939- *ConAu 53*
Kelly, Margaret Ricaud 1910- *WrD 1976*
Kelly, Marie-Noele 1907- *WrD 1976*
Kelly, Mary *Alli Sup*
Kelly, Mary Anne 1825?-1910 *PoIre*
Kelly, Mary E *Alli Sup*
Kelly, Mary I 1856-1884 *PoIre*
Kelly, Mary Theresa Coolican 1927- *Au&Wr,
   ConAu 1R*
Kelly, Matthew *Alli Sup*
Kelly, Maurice Anthony 1931- *ConAu 53*
Kelly, Maurice Nugent 1919- *Au&Wr,
   ConAu 23, WrD 1976*
Kelly, Melville Clyde 1883-1935 *DcNAA,
   OhA&B*
Kelly, Meriba Ada B *ChPo, ChPo S1*
Kelly, Michael 1762-1826 *Alli*
Kelly, Michael 1937- *Au&Wr*
Kelly, Michael J 1857-1894 *DcNAA*
Kelly, Myra 1875-1910 *AmA&B, CarSB,
   DcAmA, DcNAA*
Kelly, Nora Hickson 1910- *OxCan, WrD 1976*
Kelly, Patrick *Alli, BiDLA*
Kelly, Pauline Agnes 1936- *ConAu 45*
Kelly, Peter Burrowes 1811-1883 *PoIre*
Kelly, Philip John 1896-1972 *ConAu 5R,
   ConAu 37*
Kelly, Ralph *ConAu XR, SmATA 7*

Kelly, Ray *ConAu XR*
Kelly, Regina Z *ConAu 1R, SmATA 5*
Kelly, Richard *DrAP 1975*
Kelly, Richard J *WhLA*
Kelly, Richard J 1938- *ConAu 41*
Kelly, Robert 1935- *Au&Wr, ConAu 17R,
   ConP 1970, ConP 1975, CrCAP,
   DrAF 1976, DrAP 1975, Pen Am,
   WrD 1976*
Kelly, Robert Glynn 1920- *ConAu 1R*
Kelly, Robert James 1877- *WhWNAA*
Kelly, Robert Lincoln 1865- *WhWNAA*
Kelly, Rosalie *ConAu 61*
Kelly, Roy Willmarth 1888- *WhWNAA*
Kelly, Samuel Jewett 1866-1948 *OhA&B*
Kelly, Sophia *Alli, Alli Sup*
Kelly, T *Alli Sup*
Kelly, T W *ChPo S1*
Kelly, Terence 1920- *Au&Wr*
Kelly, Thomas *Alli, Alli Sup, BiDLA*
Kelly, Thomas 1769-1855 *ChPo, PoCh, PoIre*
Kelly, Thomas 1863- *AmA&B*
Kelly, Thomas 1909- *Au&Wr, ConAu P-1*
Kelly, Thomas 1919- *WrD 1976*
Kelly, Thomas Howard 1895- *AmA&B,
   Au&Wr*
Kelly, Thomas Raymond 1893-1941 *OhA&B*
Kelly, Thomas W *PoIre*
Kelly, Thomas W 1800?- *Alli Sup, PoIre*
Kelly, Tim 1935- *ConAu 13R*
Kelly, Tim 1937- *WrD 1976*
Kelly, Tom *ChPo S1*
Kelly, W *Alli*
Kelly, Walt 1913-1973 *AmA&B, AmSCAP 66,
   ConAu 45, IlBYP, REnAL*
Kelly, Walter Crawford, Jr. 1913-1973 *ChPo S1*
Kelly, Walter Keating *Alli, Alli Sup, PoIre*
Kelly, William *Alli Sup, BbtC, ChPo S2*
Kelly, William d1909 *PoIre*
Kelly, William D d1900 *PoIre*
Kelly, William J 1862- *PoIre*
Kelly, William Leo 1924- *ConAu 13R*
Kelly, William Louis 1837- *PoIre*
Kelly, William W 1928- *ConAu 9R*
Kelly-Gadol, Joan 1928- *ConAu 61*
Kelly, James B *Alli*
Kelman, Herbert Chanoch 1927- *ConAu 13R,
   WrD 1976*
Kelman, John *Alli Sup*
Kelman, John 1864-1929 *DcNAA, WhLA*
Kelman, Steven 1948- *ConAu 29*
Kelpius, Johann 1673-1708 *CasWL*
Kelsal, Edward *Alli*
Kelsall, Charles *Alli, BiDLA*
Kelsall, Henry *Alli Sup*
Kelsey, Alice Geer 1896- *AnCL, Au&Wr,
   AuBYP, ConAu 5R, MorJA, SmATA 1,
   WrD 1976*
Kelsey, Andrea J *DrAP 1975*
Kelsey, Carl 1870- *AmLY, WhWNAA*
Kelsey, Charles Boyd 1850-1917 *Alli Sup,
   DcAmA, DcNAA*
Kelsey, Mrs. Charles E *Alli Sup*
Kelsey, Francis Willey 1858-1927 *AmA&B,
   DcNAA*
Kelsey, Frederick Wallace 1850-1935 *DcNAA*
Kelsey, Henry 1670?-1724? *OxCan*
Kelsey, Jeannette Garr 1850- *DcNAA*
Kelsey, Joan Marshall 1907- *ConAu 5R*
Kelsey, Joseph *Alli*
Kelsey, Kate *ChPo S1*
Kelsey, Leroy Huron *ChPo, ChPo S1*
Kelsey, Morton T 1917- *ConAu 23,
   WrD 1976*
Kelsey, Rayner Wickersham 1879-1934 *DcNAA*
Kelsey, Richard *Alli Sup*
Kelsey, Vera *OxCan*
Kelshall, T M *ChPo S1*
Kelso, Charles D 1928- *IndAu 1917*
Kelso, Hamilton *Alli*
Kelso, Isaac *Alli Sup, IndAu 1816, OhA&B*
Kelso, James Anderson 1873- *AmLY*
Kelso, John Johnston *Alli Sup*
Kelso, John Russell 1831-1891 *Alli Sup,
   DcNAA*
Kelso, Louis O 1913- *ConAu 25*
Kelso, Reuben Edgar 1871-1956 *IndAu 1917*

Kelso, Robert Wilson 1880- *WhWNAA*
Kelso, Ruth 1885- *WhWNAA*
Kelson, T M *Alli, BiDLA*
Kelt, Thomas *Alli*
Keltie, John Scott *Alli Sup*
Keltner, John W 1918- *ConAu 29*
Kelton, Arthur *Alli, DcEnL*
Kelton, Charlotte 1899- *TexWr*
Kelton, Dwight H 1843-1906 *Alli Sup, DcNAA*
Kelton, Elmer 1926- *AuNews 1, ConAu 21,
   WrD 1976*
Kelton, John Cunningham 1828-1893 *Alli Sup,
   DcAmA, DcNAA*
Keltridge, John *Alli*
Kelty, Mary Anne *Alli, Alli Sup*
Kelvin, Baron 1824-1907 *BbD, BiD&SB,
   BrAu 19, Chmbr 3, NewC, OxEng*
Kelway, Christine 1900- *Au&Wr, WrD 1976*
Kelway, Thomas *Alli*
Kelynack, Theo N 1866- *WhLA*
Kelyng, Sir John *Alli*
Kelynge, William *Alli*
Kem, Samuel *Alli*
Kemal, Namik 1840-1888 *CasWL*
Kemal, Orhan 1914-1970 *DcOrL 3*
Kemal, Yasar 1922- *DcOrL 3, WhTwL*
Kemal, Yashar 1922- *TwCW, WorAu*
Kemal Tahir 1910- *CasWL*
Kemble, Adelaide d1879 *DcEuL*
Kemble, C *Alli*
Kemble, Charles 1775-1854 *Alli, Alli Sup,
   BiDLA, DcEuL, NewC, REn*
Kemble, Edward Cleveland 1827-1886 *DcNAA*
Kemble, Edward Windsor 1861-1933 *ChPo,
   DcNAA, OxAm, REnAL*
Kemble, Fanny 1809-1893 *AmA, REnAL*
Kemble, Frances *Alli Sup*
Kemble, Frances Anne 1809-1893 *Alli, Alli Sup,
   AmA, AmA&B, BiD&SB, BiDSA,
   BrAu 19, ChPo, ChPo S2, DcEnA,
   DcEnL, DcEuL, DcLEnL, NewC, OxAm,
   OxEng*
Kemble, George Stephen 1758-1822 *Alli,
   DcEuL*
Kemble, James *Au&Wr, ConAu 29,
   WrD 1976*
Kemble, John Mitchell 1807-1857 *Alli,
   BrAu 19, DcEnL, DcEuL, NewC, OxEng*
Kemble, John Philip 1757-1823 *Alli, BiDLA,
   DcEuL, NewC*
Kemble, Marie-Therese 1774-1838 *Alli, BiDLA*
Kemble, Marion *Alli Sup*
Kemble, Roger 1721-1802 *DcEuL*
Kemble, Sarah 1755-1831 *DcEuL*
Kemelman, Harry 1908- *AmA&B, AuNews 1,
   ConAu 9R, ConLC 2, EncM&D,
   WrD 1976*
Kemeny, John George 1926- *Au&Wr,
   ConAu 33, WrD 1976*
Kemeny, Peter 1938- *ConAu 53*
Kemeny, Baron Zsigmond 1814-1875 *BiD&SB,
   CasWL, Pen Eur*
Kemeys, John G *Alli*
Kemisch, S B *Alli Sup*
Kemler, Edgar J 1906-1960 *AmA&B*
Kemlo, F *Alli Sup*
Kemm, Robert F *ChPo S1*
Kemmer, George W 1890- *AmSCAP 66*
Kemmerer, Donald Lorenzo 1905- *Au&Wr,
   ConAu 1R*
Kemmerer, Edwin Walter 1875-1945 *AmLY,
   DcNAA, WhWNAA*
Kemmis, William *Alli Sup*
Kemnitius, Mart *Alli*
Kemp, Mrs. *Alli Sup*
Kemp, Abraham *CasWL*
Kemp, Alec M *MnBBF*
Kemp, Alexander Ferrie 1822-1884 *BbtC,
   DcNAA*
Kemp, Alvin F 1876- *WhWNAA*
Kemp, Arnold *BlkAW, LivBA*
Kemp, Betty 1916- *Au&Wr, ConAu 9R,
   WrD 1976*
Kemp, Charles F 1912- *ConAu 9R, WrD 1976*
Kemp, David Ashton McIntyre 1921- *Au&Wr*
Kemp, Diana Moyle 1919- *ConAu P-1*
Kemp, Dixon *Alli Sup*
Kemp, E B L *ChPo*

Kemp, E C *Alli*
Kemp, Edward *Alli*
Kemp, Edward Curtis *Alli Sup*
Kemp, Eric Waldram 1915- *Au&Wr*
Kemp, Gene 1926- *WrD 1976*
Kemp, George *Alli Sup*
Kemp, George Baring *Alli*
Kemp, H S M *OxCan*
Kemp, Harold 1896- *Au&Wr*
Kemp, Harry Hibbard 1883-1960 *AmA&B,
   ChPo, ChPo S2, ConAmL, OhA&B,
   OxAm, REn, REnAL*
Kemp, Henry L *Alli Sup*
Kemp, Henry William *Alli Sup*
Kemp, James *Alli, BiDLA*
Kemp, James Furman 1859-1926 *DcAmA,
   DcNAA*
Kemp, John *Alli, Alli Sup*
Kemp, John d1717 *Alli*
Kemp, John d1812 *CyAL 1*
Kemp, Joseph 1778-1824 *Alli, BiDLA*
Kemp, Joyce Lindley 1926- *Au&Wr*
Kemp, Louis Wiltz *TexWr*
Kemp, Lysander 1920- *AmA&B, ConAu 45*
Kemp, Margaret Sylvia 1923- *Au&Wr*
Kemp, Norman Frederick 1925- *Au&Wr*
Kemp, Patrick S 1932- *ConAu 53*
Kemp, Peter Mant Macintyre 1915- *Au&Wr,
   ConAu 25*
Kemp, Philip 1887- *Au&Wr, WrD 1976*
Kemp, Robert 1856-1915 *ChPo S1*
Kemp, Robert 1908-1967 *ConAu P-1*
Kemp, Robert H 1820-1897 *DcNAA*
Kemp, Roy Z 1910- *ConAu 9R*
Kemp, T Lindley *Alli*
Kemp, Thomas Richardson *Alli Sup*
Kemp, Tom 1921- *Au&Wr, ConAu 25*
Kemp, Vernon *OxCan*
Kemp, W *Alli*
Kemp, Walter *Alli Sup*
Kemp, William *Alli, CasWL, ChPo S2, REn*
Kemp, William Webb 1873-1946 *DcNAA,
   WhWNAA*
Kempe, A J *Alli*
Kempe, Alfred Bray 1849- *Alli Sup*
Kempe, Anna Eliza *NewC*
Kempe, Harry Robert *Alli Sup*
Kempe, John Edward 1810- *Alli Sup*
Kempe, John William *Alli Sup*
Kempe, Margery 1373?-1440? *Alli, CasWL,
   NewC, OxEng, Pen Eng*
Kempenfelt, Richard 1718-1782 *NewC, PoCh*
Kemper, Andrew Carr 1832-1905 *OhA&B*
Kemper, Charles Pendleton *BiDSA*
Kemper, Donald J 1929- *ConAu 21,
   WrD 1976*
Kemper, Frederick Augustus 1799-1851 *OhA&B*
Kemper, Inez 1906- *ConAu P-1*
Kemper, James Lawson 1823- *BiDSA*
Kemper, Ronnie 1912- *AmSCAP 66*
Kemper, William Harrison 1839-1927 *AmLY,
   DcNAA, IndAu 1816*
Kempers, Mart 1924- *WhGrA*
Kempf, Edward John 1885- *IndAu 1917,
   WhWNAA*
Kempf, Joseph George 1893- *CatA 1947,
   IndAu 1917*
Kempf, Paul 1883- *WhWNAA*
Kempfer, Lester Leroy 1932- *ConAu 49*
Kempferhausen *DcEnL*
Kempher, Ruth Moon 1934- *ConAu 25*
Kempinski, Leo A 1891-1958 *AmSCAP 66*
Kempis, Thomas A' 1380-1471 *AtlBL, BbD,
   BiD&SB, ChPo, DcEnL, DcSpL, EuA,
   EvEuW, NewC, OxEng, REn*
Kemplay, Christopher *Alli Sup*
Kempling, William Bailey 1869- *WhLA*
Kempner, Alfred *REn*
Kempner, Lydia Rabinowitsch 1871- *WhLA*
Kempner, Mary Jean 1913-1969 *ConAu 29,
   SmATA 10*
Kempner, N *Alli Sup*
Kempson, F Claude 1860?- *Br&AmS*
Kempson, M *Alli Sup*
Kempster, Bartholomew *Alli*
Kempster, Bert *MnBBF*
Kempster, Jim *MnBBF*
Kempster, Mary Yates 1911- *Au&Wr,*

ConAu P-1
Kempt, Sir James 1764-1854 *OxCan*
Kempt, Robert *Alli Sup*
Kempthorne, John *Alli Sup*
Kempthorne, John 1775-1838 *Alli, BiDLA,
   PoCh*
Kempthorne, John Augustine 1864- *WhLA*
Kempton, Mrs. C B *ChPo*
Kempton, Henry Tattershall Knowles *Alli Sup*
Kempton, J H 1891- *WhWNAA*
Kempton, James Murray, Jr. 1945?-1971
   ConAu 33
Kempton, Jean Goldschmidt 1946?-1971
   ConAu 33
Kempton, Jean Welch 1914- *ConAu 49,
   SmATA 10*
Kempton, Kenneth Payson 1891- *WhWNAA*
Kempton, Murray 1918- *AmA&B, WorAu*
Kemshead, W B *Alli Sup*
Ken, Thomas 1637-1711 *Alli, BbD, BrAu,
   CasWL, ChPo, ChPo S1, Chmbr 2,
   DcEnA, DcEnL, DcLEnL, EvLB, NewC,
   OxEng, PoCh*
Kenan, Amos 1927- *CnMD Sup*
Kenan, Kate Clifford *LivFWS*
Kenan, Thomas S *Alli Sup*
Kenawell, William Wooding 1920- *BiDPar*
Kenchio, Suyematz *Alli Sup*
Kendal, Mrs. *Alli, BiDLA*
Kendal, Mrs. 1849-1935 *ChPo S1*
Kendal, John *Alli*
Kendal, Samuel 1753-1815 *Alli*
Kendale *DcEnL*
Kendall, A *Alli, BiDLA*
Kendall, A F *Alli*
Kendall, Amos 1789-1869 *Alli, Alli Sup,
   AmA&B, BiD&SB, BiDSA, DcAmA,
   DcNAA*
Kendall, Arthur Isaac 1877- *WhWNAA*
Kendall, B J *Alli Sup*
Kendall, Calvin Noyes 1858-1921 *DcNAA*
Kendall, Carlton 1895- *WhWNAA*
Kendall, Carol Seeger 1917- *AuBYP,
   ConAu 5R, OhA&B, ThBJA*
Kendall, Charles *Alli Sup*
Kendall, David *ChPo S2*
Kendall, David Evan 1944- *ConAu 29*
Kendall, Dorothy Steinbomer 1912- *ConAu 57*
Kendall, Mrs. E D *Alli Sup*
Kendall, E K *BbtC*
Kendall, E Lorna 1921- *ConAu 5R*
Kendall, E Otis *Alli*
Kendall, Edmund Hale *Alli Sup*
Kendall, Edward Augustus 1776?-1842 *Alli,
   BiDLA, CarSB*
Kendall, Elaine 1929- *ConAu 17R*
Kendall, Elizabeth Kimball 1855- *DcNAA,
   WhWNAA*
Kendall, Elsie D *ChPo, ChPo S1*
Kendall, Enion d1856 *IndAu 1816*
Kendall, Ezra Fremont 1861-1910 *DcNAA,
   OhA&B*
Kendall, Ezra Otis 1818-1899 *DcNAA*
Kendall, G E *ChPo*
Kendall, George d1663 *Alli*
Kendall, George Wilkins 1809-1867 *Alli, AmA,
   AmA&B, BiD&SB, BiDSA, DcAmA,
   DcNAA, OxAm, REnAL*
Kendall, Guy 1906- *ChPo S2*
Kendall, Harriet *Alli Sup, ChPo S2*
Kendall, Henry *Alli Sup*
Kendall, Henry Clarence 1841?-1882 *Alli Sup,
   BbD, BiD&SB, BrAu 19, ChPo S1,
   Chmbr 3, DcLEnL, EvLB, NewC,
   OxEng, WebEAL*
Kendall, Henry Madison 1901-1966 *ConAu 5R*
Kendall, Isoline Rodd 1873- *BiDSA*
Kendall, J *Alli*
Kendall, James *Alli Sup*
Kendall, John *Alli*
Kendall, John d1814 *Alli, BiDLA,
   BiDLA Sup*
Kendall, John Jennings *Alli Sup*
Kendall, John Kaye *ChPo, ChPo S1,
   ChPo S2, WhLA*
Kendall, John Smith 1874- *AmA&B, AmLY,
   BiDSA, WhWNAA*
Kendall, Josepha *ChPo S1*

Kendall, Kenneth E 1913- *ConAu 45*
Kendall, Lace *AmA&B, ConAu XR,
   SmATA 3, ThBJA*
Kendall, Laura E *Alli Sup*
Kendall, Lyle H, Jr. 1919- *ConAu 17R*
Kendall, Margaret M *ChPo*
Kendall, Maurice George 1907- *Au&Wr*
Kendall, May 1861-1943 *Alli Sup, ChPo S1*
Kendall, Oswald *MnBBF, WhLA*
Kendall, Paul Murray 1911-1973 *ConAu P-1*
Kendall, Robert 1934- *ConAu 13R*
Kendall, Ross C 1886- *AmSCAP 66*
Kendall, Thomas Henry 1839-1882 *CasWL*
Kendall, Timothy *Alli*
Kendall, W S d1876 *AmA&B*
Kendall, William *Alli, BiDLA*
Kendall, Willmoore 1909- *ConAu 5R*
Kenderdine, Thaddeus S 1836-1922 *DcNAA*
Kendig, A B *Alli Sup*
Kendirck, Asahel C 1809- *Alli*
Kendis, James 1883-1946 *AmSCAP 66*
Kendle, John Edward 1937- *ConAu 61*
Kendler, Howard H 1919- *ConAu 17R*
Kendo, T A *Alli Sup*
Kendon, Frank 1893-1959 *ChPo, ChPo S1,
   ChPo S2, NewC*
Kendrake, Carleton *ConAu XR, EncM&D*
Kendrew, Mary E *ChPo S1, ChPo S2*
Kendrick *BiDLA*
Kendrick, Asahel Clark 1809-1895 *Alli Sup,
   AmA&B, ChPo S1, DcAmA, DcNAA*
Kendrick, Ashael Clark 1809-1895 *BiD&SB*
Kendrick, Baynard Hardwick 1894- *AmA&B,
   AmNov, Au&Wr, ConAu 1R, EncM&D,
   REnAL, WorAu*
Kendrick, Benjamin Burks 1884-1946 *DcNAA*
Kendrick, Charles d1914 *ChPo*
Kendrick, Clark 1775-1824 *DcAmA*
Kendrick, David Andrew 1937- *ConAu 23*
Kendrick, Delores *BlkAW*
Kendrick, Mrs. E C *ChPo*
Kendrick, Eliza Hall 1863-1940 *DcNAA*
Kendrick, Florence H *ChPo S1*
Kendrick, Frank J 1928- *ConAu 41*
Kendrick, James d1882 *Alli Sup*
Kendrick, James And Robert M Morris *Alli*
Kendrick, John B 1851-1931 *DcNAA*
Kendrick, John William 1853-1924 *DcNAA*
Kendrick, Michael *MnBBF*
Kendrick, William K F *OxCan*
Kendricke, John *Alli*
Kendricks, James *ConAu XR*
Kendris, Christopher 1923- *ConAu 5R*
Keneally, Thomas 1935- *CasWL, ConLC 5,
   ConNov 1972, ConNov 1976, WrD 1976*
Kenealy, Ahmed John 1854- *DcAmA*
Kenealy, Arabella *BbD*
Kenealy, Edward Vaughan Hyde 1819-1880 *Alli,
   Alli Sup, PoIre*
Kenealy, William 1828-1876 *PoIre*
Kenelly, John W 1935- *ConAu 25*
Kenelm, Saint *REn*
Kenelski, Maurice *IlBYP*
Kenen, Peter B 1932- *ConAu 5R*
Kenez, Peter 1937- *ConAu 29*
Keng, Chi-Chih *DcOrL 1*
Kenian, Paul Roger *ConAu XR*
Kenin, Richard M 1947- *WrD 1976*
Kenington, T, Lockyer, J F & Leach, C W
   Alli Sup
Kenison, Ervin M 1869-1942 *DcNAA*
Kenison, Gloria *DrAP 1975*
Keniston, James Mortimer 1848-1927 *DcNAA*
Keniston, Kenneth 1930- *AmA&B, ConAu 25*
Kenkel, Joseph Bernard 1894- *IndAu 1917*
Kenkel, William F 1925- *ConAu 61*
Kenko *CasWL, DcOrL 1*
Kenko-Hoshi *Pen Cl*
Kenlon, John 1859-1940 *AmLY, DcNAA*
Kenly, John Reese 1822-1891 *Alli Sup, BiDSA,
   DcAmA, DcNAA*
Kenly, Julie Woodbridge Terry Closson
   1869-1943 *AmA&B, OhA&B*
Kenman, George 1845- *AmLY*
Kenmare, Dallas *ChPo S2*
Kenn, Clevedone *ChPo*
Kenn, Thomas 1637-1711? *BrAu, CasWL,
   EvLB*

Kenna, Ella *Alli Sup*
Kenna, Peter 1930- *ConAu 61*
Kennamer, Lorrin, Jr. 1924- *ConAu 5R*
Kennan, George 1845-1924 *Alli Sup, AmA&B, BbD, BiD&SB, DcAmA, DcNAA, OhA&B, OxAm, REn, REnAL*
Kennan, George Frost 1904- *AmA&B, Au&Wr, ConAu 1R, OxAm, REnAL, WorAu*
Kennan, Kent Wheeler 1913- *AmSCAP 66, ConAu 1R, WrD 1976*
Kennard, Adam Steinmetz *Alli*
Kennard, Agnes *Alli Sup*
Kennard, Edward 1842- *Alli Sup*
Kennard, Mrs. Edward 1850?-1914? *Br&AmS*
Kennard, George *Alli*
Kennard, Joseph Spencer 1859-1944 *Alli Sup, AmA&B, DcAmA, DcNAA, WhWNAA*
Kennard, Mary E *Alli Sup, BbD*
Kennard, Nina H *Alli Sup*
Kennard, Robert Bruce *Alli Sup*
Kennard-Davis, Arthur 1910- *ConAu P-1*
Kennaway, Charles Edward *Alli, Alli Sup*
Kennaway, James 1928-1968 *AmA&B, WorAu*
Kennaway, Sir John Henry 1837- *Alli Sup*
Kennaway, Laurence J *Alli Sup*
Kennebeck, Edwin 1924- *ConAu 41*
Kennebeck, Paul 1943- *ConAu 53*
Kennedy, Captain *Alli*
Kennedy, A *Alli*
Kennedy, A E *ChPo S2*
Kennedy, A J *Alli Sup*
Kennedy, A S *Alli Sup*
Kennedy, Adam *AuNews 1*
Kennedy, Adrienne 1931- *BlkAW, ConDr, CrCD, LivBA, WrD 1976*
Kennedy, Albert Joseph 1879- *WhWNAA*
Kennedy, Alexander *Alli Sup*
Kennedy, Alexander B W *Alli Sup*
Kennedy, Alexander Ralph *ChPo*
Kennedy, Alexander William Maxwell Clark 1851- *Alli Sup*
Kennedy, Alfred James 1921- *Au&Wr*
Kennedy, Andrew *Alli*
Kennedy, Andrew 1931- *ConAu 61*
Kennedy, Annie Richardson 1868- *WhWNAA*
Kennedy, Archibald 1685-1763 *Alli, DcNAA*
Kennedy, Arnold *Alli Sup*
Kennedy, Arthur Garfield 1880-1954 *AmA&B*
Kennedy, Benjamin E *Alli Sup*
Kennedy, Benjamin F 1832-1916 *IndAu 1917*
Kennedy, Benjamin Hall 1804-1889 *Alli, Alli Sup*
Kennedy, Bruce M 1929- *ConAu 57*
Kennedy, C M *Alli*
Kennedy, Charles *PoIre*
Kennedy, Charles E 1856-1929 *OhA&B, WhWNAA*
Kennedy, Charles Egbert *Alli Sup*
Kennedy, Charles Rann 1808-1867 *Alli, Alli Sup, BrAu 19, ChPo, ChPo S1*
Kennedy, Charles Rann 1871-1950 *AmA&B, AmLY, ConAmL, LongC, OxAm, REnAL, TwCA, TwCA Sup, WhWNAA*
Kennedy, Charles William 1882-1969 *AmA&B, ChPo, ChPo S1*
Kennedy, Clarence Hamilton 1879- *IndAu 1917*
Kennedy, Crammond 1842-1918? *Alli Sup, AmA&B, BiD&SB, ChPo, ChPo S1, DcAmA, DcNAA*
Kennedy, D James 1930- *ConAu 61*
Kennedy, D S 1856- *WhWNAA*
Kennedy, Daniel Joseph 1862-1930 *DcNAA, WhWNAA*
Kennedy, David d1886 *Alli Sup*
Kennedy, David 1849-1885 *ChPo S1*
Kennedy, David Brian 1937- *Au&Wr*
Kennedy, David Michael 1941- *ConAu 29, WrD 1976*
Kennedy, Don H 1911- *ConAu 61*
Kennedy, E B *Alli Sup*
Kennedy, E C *Alli Sup*
Kennedy, E E *Alli Sup*
Kennedy, Edward Shirley *Alli Sup*
Kennedy, Elijah Robinson 1846?-1926 *AmLY, DcNAA*
Kennedy, Emily *TexWr*
Kennedy, Eugene C 1928- *ConAu 25*

Kennedy, Evory d1887 *Alli Sup*
Kennedy, Florynce R 1916- *LivBA*
Kennedy, Foster 1884- *WhWNAA*
Kennedy, Gail 1900-1972 *ConAu 33*
Kennedy, Gavin 1940- *ConAu 61, WrD 1976*
Kennedy, Geoffrey Anketell Studdert *ChPo S1, ChPo S2*
Kennedy, George 1928- *ConAu 5R*
Kennedy, Gerald 1907- *ConAu 5R, WrD 1976*
Kennedy, Gerta *ChPo S1*
Kennedy, Gilbert George 1844- *Alli Sup*
Kennedy, Grace 1782-1825 *Alli, BiD&SB, DcEnL*
Kennedy, H *Alli Sup*
Kennedy, H E *ChPo S1*
Kennedy, Harry *ChPo*
Kennedy, Henry Dawson 1869-1925 *DcNAA*
Kennedy, Herbert Lennard Goodrich 1892-1910 *ChPo*
Kennedy, Horace Milton 1852- *Alli Sup*
Kennedy, Howard *AmA&B*
Kennedy, Howard Angus 1861-1938 *CanNov, DcNAA, OxCan, WhWNAA*
Kennedy, Hugh *Alli*
Kennedy, Hugh A *Alli Sup*
Kennedy, Mrs. Hugh A *Alli Sup*
Kennedy, J *Alli, Alli Sup, BiDLA*
Kennedy, J Hardee 1915- *ConAu 13R*
Kennedy, J R *Alli Sup*
Kennedy, James *Alli, Alli Sup, PoIre*
Kennedy, James d1827 *Alli*
Kennedy, James d1859 *PoIre*
Kennedy, James 1405?-1466 *Alli*
Kennedy, James 1798-1868 *PoIre*
Kennedy, James 1850-1922 *AmLY, DcNAA*
Kennedy, James Christopher 1844- *ChPo S1*
Kennedy, James Frederick Shaw *Alli Sup*
Kennedy, James Harrison *Alli Sup*
Kennedy, James Henry 1849-1934 *DcNAA, OhA&B*
Kennedy, James Houghton *Alli Sup*
Kennedy, James Macintosh 1848-1922 *ChPo*
Kennedy, Sir James Shaw 1788-1865 *Alli Sup*
Kennedy, James William 1905- *Au&Wr, ConAu 1R*
Kennedy, Jane *Alli, Alli Sup*
Kennedy, Jay Byron 1931- *IndAu 1917*
Kennedy, Jay Richard 1904- *AmSCAP 66*
Kennedy, John *Alli, Alli Sup, DcLEnL*
Kennedy, John d1760 *Alli*
Kennedy, John 1700-1770 *Alli, DcEnL*
Kennedy, John 1789- *ChPo*
Kennedy, John 1819-1884 *Alli Sup*
Kennedy, John Fitzgerald 1917-1963 *AmA&B, AnCL, ChPo, ConAu 1R, OxAm, REn, REnAL*
Kennedy, John H *OxCan*
Kennedy, John J 1914- *ConAu 57*
Kennedy, Sir John Noble 1893- *Au&Wr*
Kennedy, John Pendleton 1795-1870 *Alli, Alli Sup, AmA, AmA&B, BbD, BiD&SB, BiDSA, CasWL, Chmbr 3, CnDAL, CyAL 1, CyWA, DcAmA, DcBiA, DcLEnL, DcNAA, EvLB, OxAm, OxEng, Pen Am, REnAL, WebEAL*
Kennedy, Joseph 1858-1937 *AmLY, DcNAA, WhWNAA*
Kennedy, Joseph 1923- *Au&Wr, WrD 1976*
Kennedy, Joseph 1929- *ConAu 1R*
Kennedy, Joseph Camp Griffith 1813-1887 *Alli Sup, DcNAA*
Kennedy, Judith M 1935- *ConAu 41*
Kennedy, Kathleen 1947?-1975 *ConAu 57*
Kennedy, Kenneth A R 1930- *ConAu 45*
Kennedy, Kieran A 1935- *ConAu 37*
Kennedy, L D 1924- *ConAu 45*
Kennedy, Leo 1907- *CanWr, DcLEnL, OxCan, WebEAL*
Kennedy, Leonard Anthony 1922- *ConAu 37*
Kennedy, Leslie *ChPo S2*
Kennedy, Lewis And T B Grainger *Alli*
Kennedy, Ludovic Henry Coverley 1919- *Au&Wr, WrD 1976*
Kennedy, M G *Alli Sup, PoIre*
Kennedy, Mrs. M G *ChPo*
Kennedy, M V *Alli*
Kennedy, Malcolm Duncan 1895- *ConAu 9R, WrD 1976*

Kennedy, Margaret 1896-1967 *ChPo S2, Chmbr 3, ConAu 25, DcLEnL, EvLB, LongC, McGWD, ModBL, ModWD, NewC, OxEng, Pen Eng, REn, TwCA, TwCA Sup, TwCW*
Kennedy, Marjory *Alli Sup*
Kennedy, Mark *BlkAW*
Kennedy, Mary *DrAP 1975*
Kennedy, Mary J *Alli Sup*
Kennedy, Matthew *Alli*
Kennedy, Mervyn LeBan 1858?-1907 *PoIre*
Kennedy, Michael 1926- *ConAu 13R, WrD 1976*
Kennedy, Millard Fillmore 1863- *IndAu 1917*
Kennedy, Milward 1894-1968 *EncM&D*
Kennedy, Mollie *ChPo*
Kennedy, Patrick 1801-1873 *Alli Sup, BiD&SB, BrAu 19, PoIre*
Kennedy, Paul *ChPo S1*
Kennedy, Paul Edward 1929- *IlCB 1966*
Kennedy, Pendleton *Alli*
Kennedy, Peter *Alli*
Kennedy, Philip Pendleton 1808?-1864 *DcNAA*
Kennedy, Quintin *Chmbr 1*
Kennedy, Quintine *Alli*
Kennedy, R *Alli*
Kennedy, Ralph Dale 1897-1965 *ConAu 1R*
Kennedy, Rann 1772-1851 *Alli, ChPo S1, NewC*
Kennedy, Raymond A 1934- *ConAu 5R*
Kennedy, Reginald Frank 1897- *Au&Wr*
Kennedy, Richard 1910- *IlBYP, IlCB 1956, IlCB 1966*
Kennedy, Richard 1932- *ConAu 57*
Kennedy, Richard Hartley d1865 *Alli, PoIre*
Kennedy, Richard S 1920- *ConAu 5R*
Kennedy, Robert *Alli*
Kennedy, Robert E, Jr. 1937- *ConAu 37*
Kennedy, Robert Emmet 1877-1941 *AmA&B, DcNAA*
Kennedy, Robert Francis 1925-1968 *AmA&B, ConAu 1R*
Kennedy, Robert L 1930- *ConAu 57*
Kennedy, Robert Patterson 1840-1918 *DcNAA*
Kennedy, Robert Woods 1911- *ConAu 49*
Kennedy, Roderick Stuart 1889- *WhWNAA*
Kennedy, Rose 1890- *ConAu 53, HsB&A, OhA&B*
Kennedy, Ruth Lee 1895- *DcSpL*
Kennedy, S M *Alli Sup*
Kennedy, Saidee E *ChPo*
Kennedy, Sara Beaumont d1921 *AmA&B, AmLY, BiDSA, DcAmA, DcNAA*
Kennedy, Sarah Lehr 1874- *OhA&B*
Kennedy, Sidney Robinson 1875- *AmLY*
Kennedy, Sighle Aileen 1919- *ConAu 53*
Kennedy, Sinclair 1875-1947 *DcNAA*
Kennedy, Stetson 1916- *ConAu 5R*
Kennedy, Susan Estabrook 1942- *ConAu 45*
Kennedy, T *ChPo, ChPo S2*
Kennedy, T F 1921- *ConAu 53*
Kennedy, Theodora *Alli Sup*
Kennedy, Thomas *Alli*
Kennedy, Thomas d1842 *PoIre*
Kennedy, Thomas 1776-1832 *ChPo, DcNAA*
Kennedy, Vallejo Ryan *BlkAW*
Kennedy, Vans *Alli*
Kennedy, W G *PoIre*
Kennedy, W P M 1881-1963 *OxCan*
Kennedy, W R *OxCan*
Kennedy, W W *MnBBF*
Kennedy, Walker 1857-1909 *BiDSA, DcAmA, DcNAA*
Kennedy, Walter 1460?-1508? *Alli, BrAu, Chmbr 1, DcEnL, EvLB, NewC, OxEng*
Kennedy, Walter Wallace 1898- *Au&Wr*
Kennedy, William *Alli, Alli Sup*
Kennedy, William 1799-1871 *BiD&SB, BiDSA, ChPo, ChPo S1, ChPo S2, PoIre*
Kennedy, William 1814-1890 *OxCan*
Kennedy, William 1928- *ConLC 6*
Kennedy, William G 1829-1893 *DcNAA*
Kennedy, William Henry John 1888-1948 *DcNAA*
Kennedy, William Of Whistle Binkie *ChPo*
Kennedy, William Paul McClure 1881- *WhWNAA*
Kennedy, William Rann 1846- *Alli Sup*

Kennedy, William Robert *Alli Sup*
Kennedy, William Sloane 1822-1861 *DcAmA, OhA&B*
Kennedy, William Sloane 1850-1929 *Alli Sup, AmA&B, BbD, BiD&SB, ChPo S1, DcAmA, DcNAA, OhA&B*
Kennedy, X J 1929- *AmA&B, ChPo, ChPo S2, ConAu XR, ConP 1970, ConP 1975, DrAP 1975, Pen Am, WorAu, WrD 1976*
Kennedy-Bell, Douglas *MnBBF*
Kennedy-Fraser, Marjory 1857- *ChPo*
Kenneggy, Richard *ConAu XR, WrD 1976*
Kennell, Ruth Epperson 1893- *ConAu 29, SmATA 6*
Kennelly, Ardyth Matilda 1912- *AmA&B, Au&Wr*
Kennelly, Arthur Edwin 1861-1939 *DcNAA, WhWNAA*
Kennelly, Brendan 1936- *ConAu 9R, ConP 1970, ConP 1975, WrD 1976*
Kenner, Charles Leroy 1933- *ConAu 25*
Kenner, Hugh 1923- *ConAu 23, WorAu*
Kenner, Peggy 1937- *BlkAW*
Kennerley, Mitchell 1878- *AmA&B*
Kennerly, David *AuNews 2*
Kennerly, Karen 1940- *ConAu 33*
Kennet, Basil 1674-1714 *DcEnL*
Kennet, Charles Egbert *Alli Sup*
Kennet, White 1660-1728 *DcEnL*
Kenneth, Mister *ConAu XR*
Kennett, Basil 1674-1714? *Alli*
Kennett, John Edward 1920- *Au&Wr*
Kennett, Lee 1931- *ConAu 23*
Kennett, Robert Hatch 1864- *WhLA*
Kennett, White 1660-1728 *Alli, BiD&SB, NewC*
Kenneway, E *Alli Sup*
Kenney, Alice P 1937- *ConAu 25, WrD 1976*
Kenney, Antony Reginald 1931- *Au&Wr*
Kenney, Arthur H *Alli*
Kenney, Charles Lamb 1823-1881 *Alli Sup, BiD&SB, PoIre*
Kenney, Edward *Alli*
Kenney, Edwin James, Jr. 1942- *ConAu 53*
Kenney, George Churchill 1889- *ConAu P-1*
Kenney, James 1780-1849 *Alli, BbD, BiD&SB, BiDLA, BiDLA Sup, ChPo, DcEnL, PoIre*
Kenney, James Francis 1884-1946 *CatA 1947, DcNAA, WhWNAA*
Kenney, John Henry *Alli, BiDLA, PoIre*
Kenney, John Paul 1920- *ConAu 17R*
Kenney, M M *BiDSA*
Kenney, Minnie E *Alli Sup, ChPo*
Kenney, Sylvia W 1922- *ConAu P-1*
Kenney, William Francis 1865- *AmLY*
Kenngott, George Frederick *WhWNAA*
Kennick, Thomas *Alli Sup*
Kennick, W E 1923- *ConAu 13R*
Kennicott, B *Alli*
Kennicott, Benjamin 1718-1783 *Alli, DcEnL*
Kennicott, Donald 1881-1965 *AmA&B*
Kennion, Alfred *Alli Sup*
Kennion, Edward *Alli*
Kennion, George *Alli Sup*
Kennion, Mary *Alli Sup*
Kennion, Robert Winter *Alli Sup*
Kennion, Roger Lloyd 1866- *WhLA*
Kenniston, Ida *ChPo*
Kenny, Alexander S *Alli Sup*
Kenny, Annie M *PoIre*
Kenny, Anthony John Patrick 1931- *WrD 1976*
Kenny, Charles *Alli, Alli Sup*
Kenny, Charles F 1898- *AmSCAP 66*
Kenny, Charles J *ConAu XR, EncM&D, LongC*
Kenny, Courtney Stanhope 1847- *Alli Sup*
Kenny, Daniel J *Alli Sup*
Kenny, E E C *Alli*
Kenny, Ellsworth Newcomb 1909- *AuBYP, ConAu 5R*
Kenny, Herbert Andrew 1912- *ConAu 41*
Kenny, Hugh *AuBYP*
Kenny, John P 1909- *ConAu 17R*
Kenny, John Peter 1916- *ConAu 45*
Kenny, Kathryn *ConAu XR*
Kenny, M L *Alli Sup*

Kenny, Maurice *DrAP 1975*
Kenny, Michael 1863-1946 *BkC 2, CatA 1947, DcNAA*
Kenny, Michael 1923- *ConAu 1R*
Kenny, Nicholas Napoleon 1895- *AmA&B*
Kenny, Nick A 1895- *AmSCAP 66, ChPo, ChPo S1*
Kenny, Robert *Alli, BiDLA, BiDLA Sup*
Kenny, Shirley Strum 1934- *ConAu 45*
Kenny, Stan *MnBBF*
Kenny, Thomas *Alli Sup*
Kenny, Vincent 1919- *ConAu 45*
Kenny, W Henry 1918- *ConAu 37*
Kenny, W S *Alli*
Kenoyer, Natlee Peoples 1907- *ConAu 5R*
Kenrick, Charles William Herbert *Alli Sup*
Kenrick, Francis Patrick 1797-1863 *Alli, AmA&B, BiD&SB, BiDSA, CyAL 2, DcAmA, DcNAA*
Kenrick, John *Alli*
Kenrick, John d1877 *Alli Sup*
Kenrick, Peter Richard 1806-1896 *Alli Sup, BiD&SB, BiDSA, DcAmA*
Kenrick, Timothy 1759-1804 *Alli*
Kenrick, Tony 1935- *Au&Wr*
Kenrick, William *Alli Sup*
Kenrick, William 1720-1779 *Alli, DcEnL*
Kenrick, William 1789-1872 *DcNAA*
Kenroy, Henry *Alli*
Kensai *DcOrL 1*
Kensett, John Frederick 1816-1872 *EarAB*
Kenshalo, Daniel R 1922- *ConAu 41*
Kensington, E T *Alli Sup*
Kent, Abraham *Alli*
Kent, Adolphus *Alli*
Kent, Alexander 1924- *Au&Wr, ConAu XR, WrD 1976*
Kent, Allen 1921- *ConAu 9R*
Kent, Arden *ConAu XR*
Kent, Arthur 1920- *AmSCAP 66*
Kent, Arthur William Charles 1925- *Au&Wr, MnBBF, WrD 1976*
Kent, Benjamin *Alli Sup*
Kent, Beverley *MnBBF*
Kent, C H *Alli Sup*
Kent, Charles 1823-1902 *ChPo, ChPo S1*
Kent, Charles Foster 1867-1925 *AmA&B, AmLY, DcAmA, DcNAA, REnAL*
Kent, Charles William 1860-1917 *AmA&B, BiDSA, ChPo, ChPo S1, DcNAA*
Kent, Charlotte 1907- *AmSCAP 66*
Kent, Corita 1918- *AmA&B*
Kent, Cromwell *OxCan Sup*
Kent, Donald P 1916- *ConAu 17R*
Kent, Dorothy S *Alli Sup*
Kent, Edward Allen 1933- *ConAu 45*
Kent, Edward George *Alli Sup*
Kent, Edwin Newell 1875-1947 *DcNAA*
Kent, Elizabeth Talbot d1651 *Alli*
Kent, Frank Richardson 1877-1958 *AmA&B, REnAL, WhWNAA*
Kent, George *Alli*
Kent, George 1796-1884 *ChPo*
Kent, George Edward 1920- *BlkAW, LivBA*
Kent, George O 1919- *ConAu 37*
Kent, George W 1928- *ConAu 25*
Kent, Gertrude Hall 1874-1956 *ChPo S2*
Kent, Graeme 1933- *Au&Wr*
Kent, Helen Elise *ChPo S1*
Kent, Henry S *ChPo S2*
Kent, Herbert Vaughan 1863- *WhLA*
Kent, Homer Austin, Jr. 1926- *ConAu 9R, WrD 1976*
Kent, Ira Rich 1876-1945 *AmA&B, ChPo*
Kent, J T *Alli Sup*
Kent, Jack 1920- *AmA&B*
Kent, James *Alli Sup, DcNAA*
Kent, James 1700-1776 *Alli*
Kent, James 1763-1847 *Alli, AmA, AmA&B, BbD, BiD&SB, CyAL 1, DcAmA, DcEnL, DcNAA, OxAm, REnAL*
Kent, James Tyler 1849-1916 *DcNAA*
Kent, John 1820?- *Br&AmS*
Kent, John 1860- *ChPo*
Kent, Mrs. John *Alli Sup*
Kent, John Henry Somerset 1923- *Au&Wr, ConAu 9R*
Kent, Karlene *DcNAA*

Kent, Lewis Edward 1906- *Au&Wr*
Kent, Louis *ChPo*
Kent, Louise Andrews 1886-1969 *AmA&B, AmNov, AuBYP, ConAu 1R, ConAu 25, JBA 1951, REnAL, TwCA Sup*
Kent, Lucien Hervey 1816-1900 *DcNAA*
Kent, Malcolm 1932- *ConAu 45*
Kent, Margaret 1894- *Au&Wr, ConAu 25, SmATA 2*
Kent, Marianne *Alli Sup*
Kent, Marvin 1816-1908 *OhA&B*
Kent, Michael *CatA 1952*
Kent, Nathaniel *Alli*
Kent, Nora 1899- *Au&Wr, ConAu P-1, WrD 1976*
Kent, Norton A 1873- *WhWNAA*
Kent, Paul *ChPo*
Kent, Philip *Alli Sup, ChPo, ConAu XR*
Kent, Phillip *MnBBF*
Kent, Raymond Asa 1883-1943 *DcNAA, WhWNAA*
Kent, Robert *Alli Sup*
Kent, Robert Thurston 1860-1947 *DcNAA*
Kent, Rockwell 1882-1971 *AmA&B, ChPo, ConAmA, ConAu 5R, ConAu 29, IlBYP, IlCB 1945, OxAm, REnAL, SmATA 6, TwCA, TwCA Sup*
Kent, Roland Grubb 1877- *WhWNAA*
Kent, S H *Alli Sup*
Kent, Sadie Trezevant *WhWNAA*
Kent, Samuel *Alli*
Kent, Sandra 1927- *AmSCAP 66*
Kent, Sherman 1903- *ConAu 53*
Kent, Tony *ConAu XR*
Kent, Walter 1911- *AmSCAP 66*
Kent, William *Alli, Alli Sup*
Kent, William 1685-1748 *Alli, AtlBL, BkIE, ChPo*
Kent, William 1851-1918 *DcAmA, DcNAA*
Kent, William 1864-1928 *DcNAA*
Kent, William Charles Mark 1823-1902 *Alli Sup, BbD, BiD&SB, ChPo, DcEnL*
Kent, William H B 1878-1947 *DcNAA*
Kent, William Henry *Alli Sup*
Kent, William Saville *Alli Sup*
Kent, Willis *DcNAA, OhA&B*
Kent, Wyndham *Alli Sup*
Kent & Strathern, Edward A, Duke Of 1767-1820 *OxCan*
Kentfield, Calvin Brice 1924- *Au&Wr, ConAu 5R, DrAF 1976*
Kentigern, Saint 510?-601? *NewC, REn*
Kentish, Edward *Alli, BiDLA, BiDLA Sup*
Kentish, John *Alli, BiDLA*
Kentish, Richard *Alli, BiDLA*
Kentish, Thomas *Alli, Alli Sup*
Kenton, James *Alli*
Kenton, Maxwell *ConAu XR, WrD 1976*
Kenton, Simon 1755-1836 *AmA&B, OxAm, REn, REnAL*
Kenton, Stanley Newcomb 1912- *AmSCAP 66*
Kenton, Warren 1933- *ConAu 29, WrD 1976*
Kenulf *BiB S*
Kenward, James *Alli Sup*
Kenward, James Macara 1908- *Au&Wr, ConAu 5R, WrD 1976*
Kenward, Jean *ChPo S1, WrD 1976*
Kenwood, Henry Richard 1862- *WhLA*
Kenwood, J *Alli Sup*
Kenworth, Brian J 1920- *WrD 1976*
Kenworthy, Brian John 1920- *Au&Wr*
Kenworthy, Leonard Stout 1912- *ConAu 1R, IndAu 1917, SmATA 6*
Kenwrick, George *Alli*
Kenyatta, Damon *BlkAW*
Kenyatta, Jomo 1893?- *AfA 1, Au&Wr*
Kenyon *AmLY XR*
Kenyon, Alfred Monroe 1869-1921 *DcNAA*
Kenyon, Arthur *Alli*
Kenyon, Bernice Lesbia 1897- *AmA&B, ChPo, ChPo S2, WhWNAA*
Kenyon, Charles 1880- *AmA&B, AmLY*
Kenyon, Doris *ChPo*
Kenyon, Edith C *Alli Sup*
Kenyon, Frank Wilson 1912- *Au&Wr, ConAu 1R*
Kenyon, Sir Frederic George 1863-1952 *ChPo, ChPo S1, ChPo S2, NewC, WhLA*

Kenyon, Lord George 1776- *Alli, BiDLA*
Kenyon, George Thomas 1840- *Alli Sup*
Kenyon, Ira A 1884- *WiscW*
Kenyon, James Benjamin 1858-1924 *Alli Sup, AmA&B, AmLY, BbD, BiD&SB, ChPo, ChPo S1, ChPo S2, DcAmA, DcNAA*
Kenyon, James William 1910- *Au&Wr, ConAu P-1*
Kenyon, John 1783?-1856 *Alli, DcEnL, NewC*
Kenyon, John 1812-1869 *PoIre*
Kenyon, John Philipps 1927- *Au&Wr, ConAu 9R*
Kenyon, John Samuel 1874- *WhWNAA*
Kenyon, Kathleen Mary 1906- *Au&Wr, ConAu 21, WrD 1976*
Kenyon, Ley 1913- *Au&Wr, ConAu 13R, SmATA 6*
Kenyon, Lord Lloyd 1733-1802 *Alli*
Kenyon, Michael 1931- *ConAu 13R, WrD 1976*
Kenyon, Nellis Douglas *WhWNAA*
Kenyon, Oliver C *Alli Sup*
Kenyon, Orr *DcNAA*
Kenyon, Raymond G 1922- *AuBYP*
Kenyon, Robert Lloyd 1848- *Alli Sup, WhLA*
Kenyon, S C *ChPo S1*
Kenyon, Theda *AmA&B, AmNov, WhWNAA*
Kenyon, W A *OxCan Sup*
Kenyon, William Asbury 1817-1862 *DcNAA*
Kenyon, William Trevor 1847- *Alli Sup*
Kenzel, Francis LaFayette 1863-1943 *DcNAA*
Keogh *Alli*
Keogh, Andrew 1869-1953 *AmA&B*
Keogh, Cornelius *Alli, BiDLA*
Keogh, James 1916- *ConAu 45*
Keogh, John *Alli, BiDLA*
Keogh, John 1650?-1725 *PoIre*
Keogh, Lilian Gilmore 1927- *ConAu 9R*
Keohane, Robert O 1941- *ConAu 45*
Keohler, Thomas G *PoIre*
Keon, Miles Gerald 1821-1875 *Alli, Alli Sup, PoIre*
Keough *PoIre*
Keough, Hugh Edmond *ChPo S1*
Keown, Anna Gordon 1897-1957 *NewC*
Keown, Eric 1904-1963 *LongC*
Kepes, Gyorgy 1906- *AmA&B, Au&Wr*
Kepes, Juliet 1919- *AuBYP, ChPo, IlCB 1956, IlCB 1966, ThBJA*
Kephale, Richard *Alli*
Kephart, Cyrus Jeffries 1852-1932 *AmLY, DcAmA, DcNAA, OhA&B, WhWNAA*
Kephart, Ezekiel Boring 1834-1906 *DcAmA, DcNAA*
Kephart, Horace 1862-1931 *AmA&B, CnDAL, DcNAA*
Kephart, Isaiah Lafayette 1832-1908 *DcNAA, OhA&B*
Kephart, Newell C 1911- *ConAu 17*
Kephart, William M 1921- *ConAu 41*
Kepler, Alexander *Alli Sup*
Kepler, Johannes 1571-1630 *BbD, BiD&SB, NewC, REn*
Kepler, Thomas Samuel 1897-1963 *AmA&B, ConAu 1R*
Kepler, William M 1841-1909 *OhA&B*
Keplinger, Mrs. E M *BiDSA, LivFWS*
Kepner, Fred 1921- *AmSCAP 66*
Keppel, F H *Alli Sup*
Keppel, Frederick d1777 *Alli*
Keppel, Frederick 1845-1912 *AmA&B, ChPo, DcNAA, PoIre*
Keppel, Frederick Paul 1875-1943 *AmA&B, DcNAA*
Keppel, George Thomas, Earl Of Albemarle 1799-1891 *Alli, Alli Sup, BrAu 19*
Keppel, Henry *Alli*
Keppel, Joseph *Alli*
Keppel, Sarah *ChPo S1*
Keppel, Sonia 1900- *WrD 1976*
Keppel, Thomas *Alli*
Keppel, William Coutts 1832- *Alli Sup*
Keppel-Jones, Arthur Mervyn 1909- *Au&Wr*
Keppell, Charlotte *WrD 1976*
Kepple, Ella Huff 1902- *ConAu 17*
Keppler, C F 1909- *ConAu 17R*
Keppler, Joseph 1838-1894 *AmA&B, REnAL*

Ker, Alan *ChPo*
Ker, Alice Jane Shannan *Alli Sup*
Ker, Anne *Alli, BiDLA*
Ker, Bruce Stanley 1925- *Au&Wr*
Ker, David 1842-1914 *Alli Sup, BbD, BiD&SB, ChPo, DcAmA, DcNAA, MnBBF*
Ker, George *Alli*
Ker, H Bellenden *Alli*
Ker, Henry 1785?- *DcNAA*
Ker, John d1741 *Alli*
Ker, John d1886 *Alli Sup*
Ker, John Bellenden 1765-1842 *Alli, ChPo*
Ker, John Of Kersland *Alli*
Ker, M E S *ChPo*
Ker, Mary Sigsbee *ChPo*
Ker, Robert *Alli*
Ker, Robert 1578-1654 *ChPo*
Ker, Thomas Forster 1830- *Alli Sup*
Ker, William *Alli, Alli Sup*
Ker, William Paton 1855-1923 *Chmbr 3, DcEuL, DcLEnL, EvLB, LongC, ModBL, OxEng, Pen Eng, TwCA, TwCA Sup*
Ker, William T *Alli Sup*
Ker Wilson, Barbara 1929- *Au&Wr, ConAu 5R*
Kerallain, Rene De *OxCan*
Keramopullos, Antonios D 1870- *WhLA*
Keratry, Auguste Hilarion De 1769-1859 *BiD&SB*
Kerba, Buck *WhWNAA*
Kerbabayev, Berdi 1894- *DcOrL 3*
Kerber, August Frank 1917- *ConAu 23*
Kerbey, Joseph Orton d1913 *DcNAA*
Kerby, George William 1860-1944 *DcNAA, WhWNAA*
Kerby, Jeremiah *Alli, BiDLA*
Kerby, Joe Kent 1933- *ConAu 53*
Kerby, Paul 1903- *AmSCAP 66*
Kerby, Robert L 1934- *ConAu 41*
Kerby, William Joseph 1870-1936 *CatA 1947, DcNAA*
Kercheval, Albert F 1829-1893 *DcNAA, OhA&B*
Kercheval, George Truman *Alli Sup*
Kercheval, Samuel 1786-1845? *BiDSA, DcNAA*
Kercheville, F M 1901- *TexWr*
Kerekes, Frank 1896- *WhWNAA*
Kerekes, Tibor 1893- *ConAu 17*
Kerem, A *DcOrL 3*
Kerenski, Aleksandr Feodorovich 1881-1970 *REn*
Kerensky, Oleg 1930- *ConAu 29, WrD 1976*
Kerensky, V M 1930- *ConAu 53*
Keres, Paul 1916-1975 *ConAu 57*
Kereszty, Roch A 1933- *ConAu 29, WrD 1976*
Kerfoot, John Barrett 1865-1927 *DcNAA*
Kerger, Ann 1894- *AmSCAP 66*
Kerhuel, John *Alli*
Kerigan, Florence 1896- *ChPo, ConAu 29, WhWNAA, WrD 1976*
Kerker, Ann Elizabeth 1912- *IndAu 1917*
Kerker, Gustave A 1857-1923 *AmSCAP 66*
Kerkhoven, Petrus Frans Van 1818-1857 *BiD&SB*
Kerl, Simon *DcNAA*
Kerlan, Irvin 1912-1963 *ChPo, ConAu 5R*
Kerlan, Milton 1901- *WhWNAA*
Kerley, Charles Gilmore 1863-1945 *DcNAA, WhWNAA*
Kerlin, Isaac Newton 1834-1893 *DcNAA*
Kerlin, Robert Thomas 1866-1950 *AmA&B, BiDSA*
Kerlinger, Fred N 1910- *ConAu 49*
Kermack, Stuart Grace 1888- *Au&Wr*
Kermack, William Ogilvy 1898- *Au&Wr*
Kerman, Cynthia Earl 1923- *ConAu 57*
Kerman, Gertrude Lerner 1909- *ConAu 5R*
Kerman, Joseph Wilfred 1924- *AmA&B, WrD 1976*
Kermani, Taghi Thomas 1929- *ConAu 25*
Kermode, Frank 1919- *ConAu 1R, NewC, WorAu, WrD 1976*
Kermode, John Frank 1919- *Au&Wr*
Kermode, M E *Alli Sup*
Kermode, Tamar A *LivFWS*

Kermode, William *Alli Sup*
Kermond, Evelyn Carolyn Conway 1927- *Au&Wr, WrD 1976*
Kern, Alfred 1924- *ConAu 33*
Kern, Alfred Allan 1879- *BiDSA, WhWNAA*
Kern, E R *ConAu XR*
Kern, G M *Alli*
Kern, Horatio G d1889 *Alli Sup*
Kern, James V 1909- *AmSCAP 66*
Kern, Janet 1924- *ConAu 5R*
Kern, Jerome David 1885-1945 *AmSCAP 66, McGWD, OxAm, REn, REnAL*
Kern, Johan Hendrick Caspar *Alli Sup*
Kern, John Adam 1846-1926 *AmLY, BiDSA, DcAmA, DcNAA*
Kern, John Dwight 1900-1948 *DcNAA*
Kern, John W *Alli Sup*
Kern, Maximilian 1890- *WhWNAA*
Kern, Maximilian G *Alli Sup*
Kern, Olly J 1861- *AmLY*
Kern, Robert W 1934- *ConAu 61*
Kern, Sergius *Alli Sup*
Kern, W Bliem *DrAP 1975*
Kernahan, Arthur Earl 1888-1944 *OhA&B*
Kernahan, Coulson 1856-1943 *BbD, BiD&SB, ChPo, ChPo S1, ChPo S2, NewC, PoIre, WhLA*
Kernahan, Mrs. Coulson 1856- *WhLA*
Kernahan, Mary Jean Hickling Bettany 1857-1941 *ChPo, NewC*
Kernan, Alvin B 1923- *ConAu 49*
Kernan, Francis *Alli*
Kernan, J Frank *Alli Sup*
Kernan, Jerome B 1932- *ConAu 25*
Kernan, Julie K *Au&Wr, BkC 2*
Kernan, Plowden *ChPo*
Kernan, Thomas Dickenson 1903- *CatA 1947*
Kernan, Will Hubbard 1845-1905 *BiDSA, DcAmA, DcNAA, OhA&B*
Kernan, William Fergus 1892- *CatA 1947*
Kerndl, Rainer 1928- *CrCD*
Kernell, William B 1891-1963 *AmSCAP 66*
Kerner, Andreas Justinus 1786-1862 *DcEuL*
Kerner, Ben *AuBYP*
Kerner, Fred 1921- *AmA&B, ConAu 9R, WrD 1976*
Kerner, Justinus Andreas Christian 1786-1862 *BbD, BiD&SB, CasWL, EuA, EvEuW, OxGer, REn*
Kerner, Robert Joseph 1887-1956 *AmA&B, WhWNAA*
Kerner, Theobald 1817- *BiD&SB*
Kerney, James 1873-1934 *DcNAA*
Kerney, John *Alli*
Kerney, Martin Joseph 1819-1861 *BiDSA, DcNAA*
Kernighan, Robert Kirkland 1857-1926 *ChPo, ChPo S1, DcNAA, PoIre*
Kernochan, Marshall 1880-1955 *AmSCAP 66*
Kernot, Henry 1806-1874 *DcNAA*
Kerns, Gerald H *ChPo S1*
Kerns, Thomas *Alli*
Kerouac, Jack 1922-1969 *AmA&B, AuNews 1, CasWL, CnMWL, ConAu XR, ConLC 1, ConLC 2, ConLC 3, ConLC 5, ConNov 1976, ConP 1970, EncWL, LongC, ModAL, ModAL Sup, OxAm, Pen Am, RAdv 1, REn, REnAL, TwCW, WebEAL, WhTwL, WorAu*
Kerouac, Jean-Louis Lebrid De 1922-1969 *AuNews 1, ConAu 5R, ConAu 25*
Kerouac, John *ConAu XR*
Kerpelman, Larry C 1939- *ConAu 37, WrD 1976*
Kerr *DcNAA*
Kerr, Albert Boardman 1875-1945 *DcNAA*
Kerr, Mrs. Alexander *Alli*
Kerr, Alexander McBride 1921- *Au&Wr, ConAu 61, WrD 1976*
Kerr, Alexander Walter 1920- *Au&Wr*
Kerr, Alfred 1867?-1948 *EncWL, OxGer, Pen Eur, REn*
Kerr, Alva Martin 1875-1928 *DcNAA, OhA&B*
Kerr, Alvah Milton 1858-1924 *AmA&B, OhA&B*
Kerr, Lady Amabell *Alli Sup*
Kerr, Andrew William *Alli Sup*

Kerr, Lady Anne 1883-1941 *CatA 1947*

Kerr, Ben *ConAu XR*

Kerr, Charles 1863- *WhWNAA*

Kerr, Clark 1911- *AmA&B, ConAu 45*

Kerr, D G G 1913- *ConAu 1R, OxCan*

Kerr, David *CyAL 1*

Kerr, David S *Alli*

Kerr, E W 1874- *WhWNAA*

Kerr, Eliza *Alli Sup*

Kerr, Elizabeth Margaret 1905- *ConAu 37, WrD 1976*

Kerr, Ella Johnson *ChPo*

Kerr, Frank Robison 1889- *Au&Wr, WrD 1976*

Kerr, Frederick *ConAu XR, WrD 1976*

Kerr, Geoffrey 1895- *Au&Wr*

Kerr, George *Alli*

Kerr, H B *Alli Sup*

Kerr, Harry D 1880-1957 *AmSCAP 66*

Kerr, Harry P 1928- *ConAu 5R*

Kerr, Hugh d1843 *BiDSA, DcNAA*

Kerr, Hugh Thomson 1871- *ChPo S1, WhWNAA*

Kerr, J *Alli*

Kerr, J George *ChPo, ChPo S1*

Kerr, James *Alli, Alli Sup, BiDLA*

Kerr, James 1805-1855 *OhA&B*

Kerr, James 1918- *Au&Wr*

Kerr, James Edwin *BiDSA*

Kerr, James Edwin 1867- *ChPo S1*

Kerr, James Manford 1851-1929 *DcNAA*

Kerr, James Stolee 1928- *ConAu 17R*

Kerr, Jean 1923- *AmA&B, AmSCAP 66, ConAu 5R, OxAm, WorAu, WrD 1976*

Kerr, Jessica 1901- *ConAu 29*

Kerr, John *Alli Sup, PoIre*

Kerr, John 1859- *ChPo*

Kerr, John Glasgow 1824-1901 *OhA&B*

Kerr, John Graham 1869- *WhLA*

Kerr, John Henry 1858-1936 *DcNAA*

Kerr, John Leeds 1780-1844 *BiDSA*

Kerr, K Austin 1938- *ConAu 25, WrD 1976*

Kerr, L *Alli*

Kerr, Laura 1904- *AuBYP*

Kerr, Lois *ConAu XR*

Kerr, Louisa Hay *Alli Sup*

Kerr, Mabel E *ChPo S2*

Kerr, Michael Crawford 1827-1876 *Alli Sup*

Kerr, Mina 1878- *AmLY*

Kerr, Minnie Markham 1879-1951 *OhA&B*

Kerr, Myra Wehrly 1885- *OhA&B*

Kerr, Norman D *ConAu XR*

Kerr, Norman Shanks *Alli Sup*

Kerr, Orpheus C 1836-1901 *Alli Sup, AmA, AmA&B, BbD, BiD&SB, ChPo, ChPo S1, CnDAL, DcAmA, DcEnL, DcLEnL, DcNAA, OxAm, REn*

Kerr, Phil 1906-1960 *AmSCAP 66*

Kerr, R H *Alli, BiDLA*

Kerr, R W *Alli Sup*

Kerr, R Watson 1895- *WhLA*

Kerr, Ralph *ChPo*

Kerr, Robert *Alli, Alli Sup*

Kerr, Robert 1755-1814? *Alli, BiDLA, BiDLA Sup, DcEnL, NewC*

Kerr, Robert 1811-1848 *ChPo S1*

Kerr, Robert 1823- *Alli Sup*

Kerr, Robert 1899- *WrD 1976*

Kerr, Robert J *PoIre*

Kerr, Robert Malcolm *Alli*

Kerr, Robert Pollok 1850-1923 *Alli Sup, BiDSA, DcAmA, DcNAA*

Kerr, Rose Netzorg 1892- *ChPo S2, ConAu 23*

Kerr, Samuel C *Alli Sup*

Kerr, Simon *Alli, BiDLA*

Kerr, Sophie 1880-1965 *AmA&B, AmNov, TwCA, TwCA Sup, WhWNAA*

Kerr, Thomas *Alli Sup*

Kerr, Walter Francis 1913- *AmA&B, AmSCAP 66, Au&Wr, ConAu 5R, OxAm, REnAL, WorAu, WrD 1976*

Kerr, Walter Montagu d1888 *Alli Sup*

Kerr, Washington Caruthers 1827-1885 *Alli Sup, BiDSA*

Kerr, William *Alli, BbtC, ChPo*

Kerr, William C *Alli Sup*

Kerr, William H C *BbtC*

Kerr, William Hastings *Alli Sup*

Kerr, William Henry 1852-1932 *IndAu 1917*

Kerr, William J 1890- *AmSCAP 66*

Kerr, William Of Glasgow *ChPo*

Kerr, William Schomberg Robert 1832-1870 *Alli Sup*

Kerr, William Williamson 1820- *Alli Sup*

Kerr, Winfield Scott 1852-1917 *OhA&B*

Kerr-Smith *Alli Sup*

Kerrich, Thomas d1828 *Alli*

Kerrick, Harrison Summers 1873-1939 *DcNAA*

Kerrick, Samuel *Alli*

Kerrick, Walter d1803 *Alli*

Kerridge, W T *MnBBF*

Kerrigan, Anthony 1918- *Au&Wr, ConAu 49, ConLC 4, ConLC 6, WrD 1976*

Kerrigan, William J *ConAu 49*

Kerrison, Lady Caroline M *Alli Sup*

Kerrison, Robert *Alli, BiDLA*

Kerry, Charles *Alli Sup*

Kerry, Frances *ConAu XR*

Kerry, Lois *SmATA 1*

Kerry-Nichols *Alli Sup*

Kersell, John E 1930- *ConAu 45*

Kersey, Jesse *Alli, BiDLA Sup*

Kersey, John *Alli*

Kersh, Cyril 1925- *Au&Wr, WrD 1976*

Kersh, Gerald 1911?-1968 *ConAu 25, EncM&D, LongC, TwCA Sup*

Kershaw, Mrs. *BbtC*

Kershaw, Alister 1921- *Au&Wr, ConAu 5R*

Kershaw, Arthur *Alli, BiDLA*

Kershaw, Frances I M *Alli Sup*

Kershaw, J Martine *Alli Sup*

Kershaw, James *Alli*

Kershaw, John Hugh D'Allenger 1931- *Au&Wr*

Kershaw, Mark *Alli Sup*

Kershaw, Peter *WrD 1976*

Kershaw, Philip G *BbtC*

Kershaw, S Wayland *Alli Sup*

Kershaw, Tom *Alli Sup*

Kershner, Frederick Doyle 1875- *AmLY, WhWNAA*

Kershner, Glenn Robert 1884- *OhA&B*

Kershner, Howard Eldred 1891- *AmA&B, ConAu 23*

Kerslake, Rosina *Alli Sup*

Kerslake, Thomas 1813-1891 *Alli Sup*

Kersley, George Herbert *Alli Sup*

Kersnik, Janko 1852-1897 *CasWL*

Kersnowski, Frank L 1934- *ConAu 41*

Kersting, Anthony Frank 1916- *Au&Wr*

Kersting, Friedrich Georg 1785-1847 *OxGer*

Kertesz, Stephen D 1904- *ConAu 21*

Kertland, William *PoIre*

Kerton, Henry *Alli*

Kertoon, J W *Alli Sup*

Kertz, J P *Alli*

Kertzer, Morris Norman 1910- *ConAu 1R*

Kervan, Alte Stillwell *ChPo*

Kervyn DeLettenhove, Josef Marie B K 1817-1891 *BiD&SB*

Kerwood, John R 1942- *ConAu 53*

Kesa'i, Abu 'l-Hasan 953-1002? *DcOrL 3*

Kesava Dev, P 1905- *DcOrL 2*

Kesavsut 1866-1905 *DcOrL 2*

Kesey, Ken 1935- *AmA&B, CasWL, ConAu 1R, ConLC 1, ConLC 3, ConLC 6, ConNov 1972, ConNov 1976, DrAF 1976, EncWL Sup, ModAL Sup, Pen Am, RAdv 1, WebEAL, WhTwL, WrD 1976*

Kesham, D *Alli*

Keshav Das 1555-1617 *CasWL*

Keshishian, John M 1923- *ConAu 25*

Kesler, Jay 1935- *ConAu 61*

Kesler, Lew 1915- *AmSCAP 66*

Kesling, Robert Vernon 1917- *IndAu 1917*

Kesnar, Maurits 1900-1957 *AmSCAP 66*

Kessel, Barney 1923- *AmSCAP 66*

Kessel, John Howard 1928- *ConAu 23, WrD 1976*

Kessel, Joseph 1898- *CasWL, ClDMEuL, EncWL, REn, WorAu*

Kessel, Lipmann 1914- *Au&Wr, ConAu 13R*

Kessel, Marcel 1899- *ChPo*

Kessel, Martin 1901- *TwCW*

Kessel, Maurice *REn*

Kessell, Mary M *ChPo S1*

Kesselman, Judi R 1934- *ConAu 61*

Kesselman, Mark J *ConAu 37*

Kesselring, Joseph O 1902-1967 *AmA&B, LongC, McGWD, ModWD*

Kessen, William 1925- *ConAu 1R, WrD 1976*

Kessing, C R *ChPo S2*

Kessler, Clara Louise *ChPo*

Kessler, Diane Cooksey 1947- *ConAu 57*

Kessler, Edward 1927- *ConAu 61*

Kessler, Jascha Frederick 1929- *AmSCAP 66, ConAu 17R, ConLC 4, ConP 1970, DrAF 1976, DrAP 1975, WrD 1976*

Kessler, Julius *Alli Sup*

Kessler, Leonard P 1921- *AuBYP, ChPo, IlCB 1956, IlCB 1966*

Kessler, Mary 1916- *TexWr*

Kessler, Milton 1930- *ConAu 1R, ConP 1970, ConP 1975, DrAP 1975, WrD 1976*

Kessler, Ralph 1919- *AmSCAP 66*

Kessler, Raymond Wilke 1905- *IndAu 1917*

Kessler, Sheila *ConAu 57*

Kesson, John *Alli Sup*

Kesten, Hermann 1900- *ClDMEuL, ModGL, ModWD, OxGer, Pen Eur, REn, TwCA, TwCA Sup, WhTwL, WrD 1976*

Kester, Paul 1870-1933 *AmA&B, DcNAA, OhA&B, REnAL*

Kester, Vaughan 1869-1911 *AmA&B, BiDSA, DcAmA, DcNAA, OhA&B, TwCA*

Kesterson, David B 1938- *ConAu 41*

Kesterton, Wilfred Harold 1914- *ConAu 41, OxCan Sup, WrD 1976*

Kesteven, Raymond 1922- *Au&Wr*

Kesteven, W B *Alli*

Kestner, Johann Georg Christian 1741-1800 *OxGer*

Ketch, John d1686 *NewC, REn*

Ketcham, Bryan Ellsworth 1898- *OhA&B*

Ketcham, Carl H 1923- *ConAu 29*

Ketcham, Charles B 1926- *ConAu 29*

Ketcham, Henry King 1920- *AmA&B*

Ketcham, John 1782-1865 *IndAu 1816*

Ketcham, Orman W 1918- *ConAu 23*

Ketcham, Ralph Louis 1927- *ConAu 9R, WrD 1976*

Ketcham, Rodney K 1909- *ConAu 1R*

Ketcham, Victor Alvin 1883-1947 *DcNAA*

Ketcham, William Ezra 1837-1903 *DcNAA*

Ketcham, Wilmot A 1860-1928 *OhA&B*

Ketchum, Alton Harrington 1904- *OhA&B*

Ketchum, Annie Chambers 1824-1904 *Alli Sup, AmA&B, BiD&SB, BiDSA, ChPo, ChPo S1, DcAmA, DcNAA, LivFWS*

Ketchum, Arthur 1878- *ChPo*

Ketchum, Carleton J 1897- *WhWNAA*

Ketchum, Creston Donald 1922- *ConAu 9R*

Ketchum, Jack *ConAu XR*

Ketchum, Jesse *OxCan*

Ketchum, John Buckhout 1837-1914 *ChPo, DcAmA, DcNAA*

Ketchum, Marshall D 1905- *ConAu P-1*

Ketchum, Milo Smith 1872-1934 *DcNAA, WhWNAA*

Ketchum, Richard M 1922- *ConAu 25, WrD 1976*

Ketchum, Silas 1835-1880 *DcNAA*

Ketchum, Thomas Carleton Lee 1862?-1927 *DcNAA*

Ketchum, William 1798-1876 *Alli Sup, DcNAA*

Ketchum, William C 1931- *ConAu 33, WrD 1976*

Ketchum, William Quintard 1818-1901 *DcNAA*

Ketchum, William Quintard 1898- *WhWNAA*

Ketel, Cornelis 1548-1616 *CasWL*

Ketelaar, Jan Arnold Albert 1908- *Au&Wr*

Ketelbey, Caroline 1896- *Au&Wr*

Ketelbey, D M 1896- *WhLA*

Keteltas, Abraham d1798 *Alli*

Kethe, William *Alli, ChPo, PoCh*

Ketler, Isaac Conrad 1853-1913 *DcNAA*

Ketley, Joseph *Alli*

Ketrick, Michael J 1857- *PoIre*

Kett, Charles W *Alli Sup*

Kett, Franc *Alli*

Kett, Henry 1761-1825 *Alli, BiDLA, ChPo S2, DcEnL*

Kett, Joseph F 1938- *ConAu 25*
Kette, Dragotin 1876-1899 *CasWL*
Kettel, Samuel 1800-1855 *ChPo, ChPo S1*
Ketteler, Wilhelm Emanuel Von 1811-1877 *BbD, BiD&SB*
Kettelkamp, Larry Dale 1933- *AuBYP, ConAu 29, IlCB 1966, SmATA 2, ThBJA, WrD 1976*
Kettell, Samuel 1800-1855 *Alli, AmA&B, BiD&SB, CyAL 2, DcAmA, DcNAA, OxAm, REnAL*
Kettell, Thomas Prentice *Alli Sup*
Kettenfeier, Petri *EvEuW*
Ketterer, David 1942- *ConAu 53*
Kettle, Arnold Charles 1916- *ConAu 9R, WrD 1976*
Kettle, Jocelyn Pamela 1934- *ConAu 25*
Kettle, Mary Rosa Stuart d1895 *Alli Sup, BiD&SB*
Kettle, Pamela *ConAu XR*
Kettle, Robert *Alli*
Kettle, Rosa Mackenzie d1895 *BbD*
Kettle, Thomas Michael 1880-1916 *ChPo, NewC*
Kettleborough, Charles 1878-1938 *IndAu 1816*
Kettlewell, Gover *ChPo*
Kettlewell, John 1653-1695 *Alli, DcEnL*
Kettlewell, Samuel *Alli Sup*
Kettlewell, W W *Alli Sup*
Kettner, Elmer Arthur 1906-1964 *ConAu 1R*
Keucher, William F 1918- *ConAu 49*
Keve, Paul W 1913- *ConAu 9R, WrD 1976*
Keveren, A G *MnBBF*
Kevern, Barbara *ConAu XR*
Keveson, Peter 1919- *AmSCAP 66*
Kevess, Arthur S 1916- *AmSCAP 66*
Kevin, Saint *REn*
Kevin, Neil 1903- *CatA 1952*
Kewen, Edward John Cage 1825-1879 *DcNAA*
Kewes, Karol 1924- *ConAu 9R*
Kewley, Thomas Henry 1911- *Au&Wr*
Kexel, Olof 1748-1796 *BiD&SB, CasWL*
Key, Alexander Hill 1904- *AuBYP, ConAu 5R, SmATA 8, WrD 1976*
Key, Amy *Alli Sup*
Key, Benjamin H *Alli Sup*
Key, Ellen 1849-1926 *CasWL, ClDMEuL, REn*
Key, Francis Scott 1779?-1843 *Alli, AmA, AmA&B, BbD, BiD&SB, BiDSA, ChPo, ChPo S2, CnDAL, CyAL 1, DcAmA, DcLEnL, DcNAA, EvLB, OxAm, OxEng, PoCh, REn, REnAL*
Key, George *Alli*
Key, Julian *WhGrA*
Key, Mary Ritchie 1924- *ConAu 45*
Key, Naiad Cresap *TexWr*
Key, Pierre VanRensselaer 1872-1945 *AmA&B, DcNAA, WhWNAA*
Key, Robert E *ChPo, ChPo S2*
Key, Mrs. Scott *TexWr*
Key, Ted 1912- *AmA&B, ConAu XR*
Key, Theodore 1912- *ConAu 13R*
Key, Thomas 1833- *Alli Sup*
Key, Thomas Hewitt 1799-1875 *Alli, Alli Sup*
Key, V O, Jr. 1908-1963 *Au&Wr, ConAu 1R*
Key, William H 1919- *ConAu 45*
Key, William S *Alli Sup*
Key, Wilson Bryan 1925- *ConAu 49*
Keyawa, Stanley J 1920- *AmSCAP 66*
Keyes, Asa 1787-1880 *DcNAA*
Keyes, Baron 1898- *AmSCAP 66*
Keyes, Benjamin F *Alli Sup*
Keyes, Charles Henry 1858-1925 *DcNAA*
Keyes, Charles M 1840-1902 *OhA&B*
Keyes, Charles Reuben 1871- *WhWNAA*
Keyes, Charles Rollin 1864- *AmLY*
Keyes, Clinton Walker 1888-1943 *DcNAA*
Keyes, Daniel 1927- *ConAu 17R, WrD 1976*
Keyes, Donald C *AmSCAP 66*
Keyes, E R *Alli Sup*
Keyes, Edward L *ChPo*
Keyes, Edward Lawrence 1843-1924 *Alli Sup, BiDSA, DcAmA, DcNAA*
Keyes, Edward Loughborough 1874?-1949 *DcNAA, WhWNAA*
Keyes, Emerson Willard 1828-1897 *Alli Sup, DcAmA, DcNAA*

Keyes, Erasmus Darwin 1810-1895 *Alli Sup, BiD&SB, DcAmA, DcNAA*
Keyes, F J *Alli Sup*
Keyes, Frances Parkinson 1885-1970 *AmA&B, AmNov, BkC 5, CatA 1947, ConAu 5R, ConAu 25, EvLB, LongC, Pen Am, REn, TwCA, TwCA Sup, TwCW, WhWNAA*
Keyes, Frederick George 1885- *Au&Wr*
Keyes, Frederick J *ChPo S2*
Keyes, Homer Eaton 1875- *WhWNAA*
Keyes, Isaiah Waterloo Nicholson 1818- *Alli Sup*
Keyes, James 1801-1883 *OhA&B*
Keyes, John *Alli*
Keyes, Julia L *LivFWS*
Keyes, Kenneth S, Jr. 1921- *ConAu 17R*
Keyes, Langley Carleton, Jr. 1938- *ConAu 25*
Keyes, Laurence 1914- *AmSCAP 66*
Keyes, Margaret Frings 1929- *ConAu 57, WrD 1976*
Keyes, Nelson Beecher 1894- *AuBYP*
Keyes, Ralph 1945- *ConAu 49*
Keyes, Rowena Keith 1880-1948 *DcNAA, WhWNAA*
Keyes, Sidney Arthur Kilworth 1922-1943 *CasWL, DcLEnL, EvLB, LongC, OxEng, Pen Eng, REn, TwCW, WebEAL, WhTwL, WorAu*
Keyes, Thomas Bassett 1874-1938 *DcNAA*
Keyes, Wade 1821-1879 *Alli Sup, BiDSA, DcNAA*
Keyes, Winfield Scott 1834- *DcAmA*
Keyfitz, Nathan 1913- *ConAu 25, WrD 1976*
Keyhoe, Donald Edward 1897- *AmA&B*
Keyishian, Harry 1932- *ConAu 61*
Keyl, E G W *Alli*
Keyl, F W *ChPo*
Keylinge, Sir John *Alli*
Keymer, Nathaniel *Alli Sup*
Keymis, Lawrence *Alli*
Keymolen, Julien 1930- *WhGrA*
Keymor, John *Alli*
Keyne, Saint *REn*
Keyne, Ada *Alli Sup*
Keynes, Sir Geoffrey Langdon 1887- *Au&Wr, ChPo, ChPo S1, ChPo S2*
Keynes, Baron John Maynard 1883-1946 *DcLEnL, EvLB, LongC, NewC, OxEng, REn, TwCA, TwCA Sup, WebEAL*
Keynes, John Neville *Alli Sup*
Keynes, R *Alli*
Keys, Ancel 1904- *ConAu 61*
Keys, J K *Alli Sup*
Keys, John *Alli*
Keys, John D 1938- *ConAu 9R*
Keys, Thomas Edward 1908- *ConAu P-1, WrD 1976*
Keys, William W *Alli Sup*
Keysall, John *Alli, BiDLA*
Keyser, Arthur *Alli Sup*
Keyser, Cassius Jackson 1862-1947 *DcNAA, OhA&B, WhWNAA*
Keyser, Charles Edward *Alli Sup*
Keyser, Charles Shearer 1825-1904 *Alli Sup, DcNAA*
Keyser, Harriete A *Alli Sup*
Keyser, Henry *Alli*
Keyser, Jakob Rudolph 1803-1864 *BiD&SB*
Keyser, James William 1917- *Au&Wr*
Keyser, Leander Sylvester 1856-1937 *AmLY, DcAmA, DcNAA, OhA&B, WhWNAA*
Keyser, Minna *ChPo S1*
Keyser, Peter Dirck 1835-1897 *Alli Sup, DcAmA, DcNAA*
Keyserling, Eduard, Graf Von 1855-1918 *ClDMEuL, EncWL, OxGer*
Keyserling, Hermann Alexander Von 1880-1946 *EvEuW, LongC, OxGer, Pen Eur, REn, TwCA, TwCA Sup*
Keyserling, Leon H 1908- *ConAu 61, WrD 1976*
Keyserlingk, Robert Wendelin 1905- *CatA 1952*
Keysner, Blanche Whiting *ChPo S1*
Keyt, Alonzo Thrasher 1827-1885 *Alli Sup, DcNAA, OhA&B*
Keyt, David 1930- *ConAu 1R*
Keyt, George 1901- *ConP 1970*
Keyt, William Edward *Alli, BiDLA*

Keyts *Alli*
Keyworth, J W *Alli Sup*
Keyworth, Maurice Reed 1884-1935 *DcNAA*
Keyworth, Thomas *Alli, Alli Sup*
Kgositsile, Keorapetse William 1938- *BlkAW, ConP 1975, DrAP 1975, WrD 1976*
Kgositsile, Melba *BlkAW*
Kgositsile, William Keorapetse 1938- *AfA 1*
Khadduri, Majid 1909- *ConAu 1R, WrD 1976*
Khadilkar, Krsnaji Prabhakar 1872-1948 *DcOrL 2*
Khadim, Qiyamuddin 1912- *DcOrL 3*
Khai-Hung 1896-1947 *DcOrL 2*
Khaketla, Bennett Makalo 1913- *AfA 1*
Khaketla, Caroline N 'm Ramolahloane 1918?- *AfA 1*
Khalid, Khalid Muhammad 1920- *CasWL*
Khalili, Khalilullah 1907- *DcOrL 3*
Khamisi, 'Abdarrahman Al- 1920- *DcOrL 3*
Khan, Zillur Rahman 1938- *ConAu 41*
Khandekar, Visnu Sakharam 1898- *DcOrL 2*
Khani, Ahmade 1650-1707 *DcOrL 3*
Khanlari, Parviz Natel 1914- *CasWL*
Khanna, J L 1925- *ConAu 23*
Khanshendel, Chiron 1948- *ConAu XR*
Khaqani, Afzal-Al-Din Ibrahim 1126-1198 *CasWL*
Khaqani, Afzaloddin Badil B 'Ali 1121?-1199 *DcOrL 3*
Khare, Narayan Bhaskar 1882- *ConAu P-1*
Khatchadourian, Haig 1925- *ConAu 53*
Khayyam, Omar 1050?-1125? *BbD, BiD&SB, ChPo S1, ChPo S2, DcOrL 3, NewC*
Khayyam, Omar SEE ALSO Omar Khayyam
Khazzoom, J Daniel 1932- *ConAu 17R*
Khemnitser, Ivan Ivanovich 1745-1784 *CasWL, DcRusL*
Khera, S S 1903- *ConAu 13R*
Kheraskov, Mikhail Matveyevich 1733-1807 *BiD&SB, CasWL, DcRusL*
Kherdian, David 1931- *ConAu 21, ConLC 6, DrAP 1975, WrD 1976*
Khersakov, Michael 1733-1807 *DcEuL*
Kherumian, Raphael 1903- *BiDPar*
Khetaegkaty, Kosta 1859-1906 *DcOrL 3*
Khetagurov, Kosta *CasWL*
Khety *DcOrL 3*
Khiengsiri, Kanha *DcOrL 2*
Khin Hnin Ju 1925- *DcOrL 2*
Khizhinsky, Leonid Semyonovich 1896- *WhGrA*
Khlebnikov, Velemir Vladimirovich 1885-1922 *CasWL, ClDMEuL, EncWL, ModSL 1, REn, WhTwL, WorAu*
Khlebnikov, Viktor Vladimirovich 1885-1922 *DcRusL, Pen Eur*
Khlesl, Melchior 1553-1630 *OxGer*
Khmelnitski, Nikolay Ivanovich 1789-1846 *DcRusL*
Khodasevich, Vladislav Felitsianovich 1886-1939 *CasWL, ClDMEuL, DcRusL, EncWL, REn, WorAu*
Khomyakov, Aleksey Stepanovich 1804-1860 *CasWL, DcEuL, DcRusL, EuA, EvEuW, Pen Eur*
Khosla, Gopal Das 1901- *Au&Wr, WrD 1976*
Khosrow, Khusraw *DcOrL 3*
Khouri, Fred John 1916- *ConAu 25, WrD 1976*
Khoury, Edward A 1916- *AmSCAP 66*
Khrabr The Monk *Pen Eur*
Khraief, Al-Bashir 1917- *DcOrL 3*
Khrakhuni, Zareh 1926- *DcOrL 3*
Khrushchev, Nikita Sergeyevich 1884-1971 *ConAu 29, REn*
Khuen, Johann 1606-1675 *OxGer*
Khu'krit Pramoj, Mom Ratchawong 1912- *Pen Cl*
Khumalo, J M *AfA 1*
Khushhal Khan K 1613-1689 *CasWL, DcOrL 3*
Khusrau Dihlavi, Abu'l-Hasan, Amir 1253-1325 *CasWL*
Khuulich Sandag *DcOrL 1*
Khvajuye Kermani, Kamaloddin Abo'l-'Ata 1281-1352 *DcOrL 3*
Khvorostinin, Prince Ivan Andreyevich d1625 *DcRusL*

DcEnL, EvLB, NewC, OxEng, REn, REnWD
Killigrew, Thomas 1657-1719 *Alli, BrAu, NewC, OxEng*
Killigrew, William *Alli*
Killigrew, Sir William 1606?-1695 *Alli*
Killigrew, Sir William 1606?-1695? *BiD&SB, BrAu, CasWL, Chmbr 1, DcEnL, DcLEnL, NewC, OxEng*
Killikelly, Sarah Hutchins 1840-1912 *AmA&B, DcNAA, IndAu 1816*
Killilea, Marie 1913- *ConAu 5R, SmATA 2*
Killinbeck, John *Alli*
Killingsworth, W *MnBBF*
Killingworth, Grantham *Alli*
Killion, Carl Everest 1899- *IndAu 1917*
Killion, Katheryn L 1936- *ConAu 17R*
Killion, Ronald G 1931- *ConAu 61*
Killits, John Milton 1858-1938 *OhA&B*
Kilmartin, Edward J 1923- *ConAu 17R*
Kilmer, Alfred Joyce 1886-1918 *ChPo S1, DcNAA, EvLB*
Kilmer, Aline 1888-1941 *AmA&B, CatA 1947, ChPo, ChPo S1, ChPo S2, DcNAA, REnAL, WhWNAA*
Kilmer, Annie Kilburn d1932 *AmA&B, ChPo, ChPo S1, ChPo S2, DcNAA*
Kilmer, Joyce 1886-1918 *AmA&B, AmLY, AmSCAP 66, ChPo, ChPo S2, CnDAL, ConAmL, DcLEnL, DcNAA, LongC, OxAm, REn, REnAL, St&VC, TwCA*
Kilmer, Kenton *ChPo*
Kilmer, Kenton 1909- *ConAu 1R*
Kilmer, Theron Wendell 1872-1946 *AmLY, DcNAA, WhWNAA*
Kilmister, Clive William 1924- *Au&Wr, WrD 1976*
Kilner, Colleen Browne *ChPo*
Kilner, Dorothy 1755-1836 *CarSB, ChPo*
Kilner, James *Alli*
Kilner, Joseph *Alli*
Kilner, W B *Alli Sup*
Kiloh, M A *Alli*
Kilonfe, Oba 1940- *BlkAW*
Kilpatrick, F P 1920- *ConAu 21*
Kilpatrick, George A 1941- *BlkAW*
Kilpatrick, James *Alli*
Kilpatrick, James Jackson 1920- *AmA&B, AuNews 1, AuNews 2, ConAu 1R*
Kilpatrick, Lincoln *BlkAW*
Kilpatrick, Sir T *Alli*
Kilpatrick, Thomas Buchanan 1857-1930 *DcNAA*
Kilpatrick, Una Pierce *TexWr*
Kilpatrick, William Heard 1871-1965 *AmA&B, REnAL, WhWNAA*
Kilpi, Volter Adalbert 1874-1939 *EncWL, Pen Eur*
Kilpin, Lisa *Alli Sup*
Kilpin, Samuel *Alli*
Kilreon, Beth *ConAu XR, SmATA 4*
Kilroy, Thomas 1934- *ConAu 53*
Kilson, Marion 1936- *ConAu 37, WrD 1976*
Kilson, Martin L 1931- *LivBA*
Kilson, Roger *Alli*
Kilty, John *Alli*
Kilty, W, T Harris, And J N Watkins *Alli*
Kilty, William 1757-1821 *Alli, AmA, DcNAA*
Kiltz, Rita 1895- *AmSCAP 66*
Kilvert, B Cory, Jr. 1930- *ConAu 45, WrD 1976*
Kilvert, Francis 1793-1863 *Alli Sup*
Kilvert, Mrs. M A *DcNAA*
Kilvert, Margaret Cameron 1867- *AmA&B, WhWNAA*
Kilvert, Robert Francis 1840-1879 *OxEng*
Kim, C I Eugene 1930- *ConAu 37*
Kim, Chin W 1936- *ConAu 37*
Kim, Ch'on-T'aek *DcOrL 1*
Kim, Chong-Sik *DcOrL 1*
Kim, Hae-Gyong *DcOrL 1*
Kim, Helen 1899-1970 *ConAu P-1*
Kim, Hyung-Chan 1938- *ConAu 57*
Kim, Ilpyong J 1931- *ConAu 53*
Kim, Jung-Gun 1933- *ConAu 53*
Kim, K H 1936- *ConAu 29*
Kim, Kwan-Bong 1936- *ConAu 37*
Kim, Kyon-Myong *DcOrL 1*

Kim, Kyung-Won 1936- *ConAu 29*
Kim, Man-Jung 1637-1692 *DcOrL 1*
Kim, Pu-Sik 1075-1151 *DcOrL 1*
Kim, Richard C C 1923- *ConAu 29*
Kim, Richard E 1932- *ConAu 5R, ConNov 1972, ConNov 1976, DrAF 1976, WrD 1976*
Kim, Se-Jin 1933- *ConAu 53*
Kim, Seung Hee 1936- *ConAu 29*
Kim, Si-Sup 1435-1493 *DcOrL 1*
Kim, Sowol 1903-1934 *DcOrL 1*
Kim, Su-Jang *DcOrL 1*
Kim, Tong-In 1900-1951 *DcOrL 1*
Kim, Yong Choon 1935- *ConAu 57*
Kim, Yong-Ik 1920- *ConAu 17R*
Kim, Yoon Hough 1934- *ConAu 33*
Kim, Young Hum 1920- *ConAu 23, WrD 1976*
Kim Set *DcOrL 2*
Kimball, Alice W *ChPo*
Kimball, Arthur G 1927- *ConAu 41*
Kimball, Arthur Lalanne 1856-1922 *AmLY, DcAmA, DcNAA*
Kimball, Arthur Livingstone 1886-1943 *DcNAA*
Kimball, Arthur Reed 1855-1933 *DcNAA*
Kimball, C *Alli*
Kimball, Dexter Simpson 1865- *AmLY*
Kimball, Edwin Coolidge *Alli Sup*
Kimball, Elijah H *Alli Sup*
Kimball, Emma Adeline 1847- *ChPo S1, DcAmA*
Kimball, Everett 1873- *WhWNAA*
Kimball, Fiske 1888-1955 *AmA&B*
Kimball, George 1943- *ConAu 53*
Kimball, George Selwyn 1846-1909 *DcNAA*
Kimball, Gertrude Selwyn 1863-1910 *DcNAA*
Kimball, Gustavus Sylvester 1860-1937 *DcNAA, WhWNAA*
Kimball, H E *ChPo S1*
Kimball, H I *Alli Sup*
Kimball, Hannah Parker 1861- *BiD&SB, ChPo S1, DcAmA*
Kimball, Harriet McEwen 1834-1917 *Alli Sup, AmA&B, BiD&SB, ChPo, ChPo S1, DcAmA, DcNAA*
Kimball, Heber Chase 1801-1868 *OhA&B*
Kimball, Henry Dox 1841-1915 *DcNAA*
Kimball, Herbert Harvey 1862- *WhWNAA*
Kimball, James William 1812-1885 *Alli, Alli Sup, DcAmA, DcNAA*
Kimball, John Calvin 1832-1910 *DcAmA, DcNAA*
Kimball, John P 1941- *ConAu 45*
Kimball, Kate Fisher 1860-1917 *DcNAA*
Kimball, Lucia E F *Alli Sup*
Kimball, Maria Porter 1852-1933 *DcNAA*
Kimball, Miriam Irene *ChPo*
Kimball, Nancy *ConAu XR*
Kimball, Richard Burleigh 1816-1892 *Alli, Alli Sup, AmA, BbD, BiD&SB, BiDSA, CyAL 2, DcAmA, DcBiA, DcNAA, OxAm*
Kimball, Richard Laurance 1939- *ConAu 53*
Kimball, Solon T 1909- *ConAu 21*
Kimball, Spencer L 1918- *ConAu 1R*
Kimball, Spencer W 1895- *ConAu 45*
Kimball, Stanley B 1926- *ConAu 17R*
Kimball, Sumner Increase 1834-1923 *DcAmA, DcNAA*
Kimball, T J *Alli*
Kimball, Warren F 1935- *ConAu 25*
Kimball, William Wirt 1848-1930 *DcNAA*
Kimball, Yeffe 1914- *IlCB 1966*
Kimbel, Harry Milton 1877-1956 *OhA&B*
Kimber, Edward d1769 *Alli*
Kimber, Harry Hubert 1903- *IndAu 1917*
Kimber, Isaac 1692-1758 *Alli, DcEnL*
Kimber, Thomas *Alli*
Kimberley, Jonathan *Alli*
Kimberling, Hadley Siegel 1862-1920 *IndAu 1816*
Kimberly, Robert L 1836-1913 *OhA&B*
Kimble, Daniel Porter 1934- *ConAu 41*
Kimble, David 1921- *ConAu 13R*
Kimble, George Herbert Tinley 1908- *AmA&B, Au&Wr*
Kimble, Gregory A 1917- *ConAu 21*
Kimble, Vesta Baker 1900- *WrD 1976*

Kimbrell, Grady 1933- *ConAu 33*
Kimbro, John M 1929- *ConAu 45*
Kimbrough, Edward 1918- *AmA&B, AmNov*
Kimbrough, Emily 1899- *AmA&B, Au&Wr, ConAu 17R, IndAu 1917, OxAm, REnAL, SmATA 2, WorAu, WrD 1976*
Kimbrough, Jess *BlkAW*
Kimbrough, Katheryn *ConAu XR*
Kimbrough, Richard B 1931- *ConAu 41*
Kimbrough, Robert Alexander, III 1929- *ConAu 9R, WrD 1976*
Kimbugwe, Henry S *AfA 1*
Kimche, David *Au&Wr*
Kime, W T *Alli*
Kimenye, Barbara 1940?- *AfA 1*
Kimes, Kenneth F 1920- *AmSCAP 66*
Kimhi, David 1160?-1235 *CasWL*
Kimmel, Arthur S 1930- *ConAu 41*
Kimmel, Douglas C 1943- *ConAu 53*
Kimmel, Edwin H 1926- *AmSCAP 66*
Kimmel, Eric A 1946- *ConAu 49, WrD 1976*
Kimmel, Jo 1931- *ConAu 53*
Kimmel, Melvin 1930- *ConAu 25*
Kimmell, Susan C 1894- *BiDPar*
Kimmelman, Burt *DrAP 1975*
Kimmins, Anthony 1901-1964 *LongC*
Kimmins, Charles William 1856- *ChPo S1*
Kimpel, Ben D 1915- *ConAu 57*
Kimpel, Ben F 1905- *ConAu 1R*
Kimpel, Benjamin Franklin 1909- *WrD 1976*
Kimpton, *Alli*
Kimrey, Grace Saunders 1910- *ConAu 45*
Kimsey, Mrs. Homer Lee *OhA&B*
Kimura, Keichi *ChPo S1*
Kimura, Tsunehisa 1928- *WhGrA*
Kimzey, Ardis *DrAP 1975*
Kin-Wun Min-Gyi U Kaung 1821-1908 *Pen Cl*
Kinahan, A M R *Alli Sup, PoIre*
Kinahan, D *Alli*
Kinahan, Gerard Henry d1886 *Alli Sup*
Kinamo, Hodari *BlkAW*
Kinane, C H *Alli Sup*
Kinane, James d1868 *PoIre*
Kinard, Epsie *TexWr*
Kinard, James Pinckney 1864-1951 *AmA&B*
Kinaston, Sir Francis *BrAu*
Kinau, Hans *OxGer*
Kinau, Rudolf 1887- *CasWL, OxGer*
Kincadius, Thomas *Alli*
Kincaid, Alan *ConAu XR*
Kincaid, Alexander *Alli*
Kincaid, Alice *ChPo*
Kincaid, Charles Augustus 1870- *WhLA*
Kincaid, Edgar B *TexWr*
Kincaid, Sir John *Chmbr 3*
Kincaid, Michael *DrAP 1975*
Kincaid, Sidney Bolton *Alli Sup*
Kincaid, Suzanne 1936- *ConAu 9R*
Kinch, Sam E, Jr. 1940- *ConAu 45*
Kincheloe, Raymond McFarland 1909- *ConAu 61*
Kincheloe, Samuel Clarence 1890- *OhA&B*
Kinchen, Oscar A *OxCan*
Kinck, Hans Ernst 1865-1926 *CasWL, ClDMEuL, Pen Eur*
Kinck, Peter *Alli*
Kind, Edmund J 1914- *ConAu 5R*
Kind, Friedrich 1768-1843 *OxGer*
Kind, Johann Friedrich 1768-1843 *BiD&SB*
Kind, M *Alli*
Kindall, Alva Frederick 1906- *ConAu 1R*
Kinder, *Alli*
Kinder, Faye 1902- *ConAu 5R*
Kinder, Francis S *ChPo S2*
Kinder, Henry *Alli*
Kinder, James S 1895- *ConAu 13R*
Kinder, Marsha 1940- *ConAu 41*
Kinder, Martin *ChPo S1, ChPo S2*
Kindermann, Balthasar 1629-1706 *OxGer*
Kindersley, Mrs. *BiDLA*
Kindersley, Edward C *Alli*
Kindersley, N E *Alli, BiDLA*
Kindersley, Mrs. N E *Alli*
Kindi, Al- d870? *CasWL*
Kindi, Abu Yusuf Ya'qub B Ishaq Al- d870? *DcOrL 3*
Kindle, Edward Martin 1869-1940 *IndAu 1917*
Kindleberger, Charles P, II 1910- *AmA&B*

King, John Henry 1843- *DcNAA*
King, John L 1917- *ConAu 41*
King, John Lyle 1823-1892 *Alli Sup, IndAu 1917*
King, John Mark 1829-1899 *DcNAA*
King, John Myers *Alli Sup*
King, John Q Taylor 1921- *ConAu 25*
King, John Reginald 1934- *Au&Wr*
King, John Richard *Alli Sup*
King, John William *Alli Sup*
King, Jonas 1792-1869 *DcAmA*
King, Joseph *Alli, BiDLA*
King, Joseph E *ChPo*
King, Josiah *Alli*
King, Julia Anne d1919 *DcNAA*
King, K DeWayne 1925- *ConAu 13R*
King, Katherine 1850- *Alli Sup, HsB&A, HsB&A Sup*
King, Katherine Douglas *DcNAA*
King, Kennedy *EvLB, MnBBF*
King, Kenneth Moffat 1906- *Au&Wr*
King, Larry L 1929- *ConAu 13R*
King, Lawrence J 1915- *IndAu 1917*
King, Lester S 1908- *ConAu 33*
King, Leyland *BlkAW*
King, Louis Joseph *Alli Sup*
King, Louisa Yeomans 1863-1948 *AmLY, DcNAA*
King, Louise W *ConAu 13R*
King, Lucille Mabel *ChPo*
King, Mrs. M *Alli Sup*
King, M P *Alli, BiDLA*
King, M R *Alli Sup*
King, Marcet 1922- *ConAu 25*
King, Margaret Rives 1819-1898 *OhA&B*
King, Maria M *Alli Sup*
King, Marian *AmA&B, Au&Wr, ConAu 5R, WrD 1976*
King, Marie Burnadette *ChPo*
King, Marjorie Cameron 1909- *ConAu 33*
King, Mark 1945- *ConAu 61*
King, Marquis Fayette 1835-1904 *DcNAA*
King, Martha Bennett *AuBYP*
King, Martin *ConAu XR*
King, Martin Luther, Jr. 1929-1968 *AmA&B, BlkAW, ConAu 25, OxAm, REnAL*
King, Mary 1865- *DcAmA*
King, Mary Ada *Alli Sup*
King, Mary B *Alli Sup*
King, Mary Louise 1911- *ConAu 23*
King, Mildred *AmSCAP 66*
King, Moses 1853-1909 *Alli Sup, DcNAA*
King, Myron *ChPo*
King, N Q 1922- *ConAu 1R*
King, Netti *ChPo S1*
King, Nicholas *Alli*
King, Norman A *ConAu XR, WrD 1976*
King, O H P 1902- *ConAu 1R*
King, Oscar Benjamin 1889- *WhWNAA*
King, Oswin Kerryn 1889- *WhWNAA*
King, Patricia 1930- *ConAu 5R*
King, Patrick Martin *PoIre*
King, Paul *ConAu XR, OxCan, WrD 1976*
King, Pauline *ChPo*
King, Peggy Cameron *ConAu XR*
King, Pendleton *Alli Sup*
King, Pete 1914- *AmSCAP 66*
King, Peter 1669-1733? *Alli, DcEnL*
King, Lord Peter 1775-1833 *Alli, BiDLA*
King, Peter John Locke 1811-1885 *Alli Sup*
King, Peter Kenneth 1922- *Au&Wr*
King, Philip 1904- *Au&Wr, CnThe, WrD 1976*
King, Philip Burke 1903- *IndAu 1917*
King, Philip Parker *Alli*
King, Preston 1936- *ConAu 23*
King, Ralph 1928- *Au&Wr*
King, Ray A 1933- *ConAu 21*
King, Reefe *SmATA 8*
King, Reginald *MnBBF*
King, Richard *Alli, Alli Sup*
King, Richard 1749-1810 *Alli, BiDLA, DcEnL*
King, Richard 1811?-1876 *OxCan*
King, Richard A 1929- *ConAu 23*
King, Richard Ashe 1839- *Alli Sup*
King, Richard G 1922- *ConAu 37*
King, Richard John 1811?-1879 *Alli, Alli Sup, DcEnL*

King, Richard L 1937- *ConAu 45*
King, Robert *Alli, Alli Sup, DrAP 1975, MnBBF*
King, Sir Robert *Alli*
King, Robert 1862-1932 *AmSCAP 66*
King, Robert Charles 1928- *ConAu 17R, WrD 1976*
King, Robert G 1929- *ConAu 23*
King, Robert H 1935- *ConAu 45*
King, Mrs. Robert Moss *Alli Sup*
King, Robert R 1942- *ConAu 61*
King, Roberta Walton *TexWr*
King, Robin 1919- *ConAu 5R, IlCB 1956*
King, Roma Alvah, Jr. 1914- *ConAu 1R*
King, Rufus 1755-1827 *AmA&B*
King, Rufus 1817-1891 *Alli Sup, DcNAA, OhA&B*
King, Rufus 1893-1966 *AmA&B, EncM&D*
King, Rufus 1917- *ConAu 25*
King, Rupert Wearing 1911- *Au&Wr*
King, Ruth *ConICB*
King, Ruth Rodney *ConAu XR*
King, Samuel *Alli, Alli Sup, BiDLA*
King, Samuel C *Alli*
King, Samuel William *Alli Sup*
King, Seth S *AuBYP*
King, Sophia *Alli, BiDLA*
King, Spencer Bidwell, Jr. 1904- *ConAu P-1, WrD 1976*
King, Stanton Henry 1868- *DcAmA*
King, Stella *Au&Wr*
King, Stephen 1947- *ConAu 61, SmATA 9*
King, Stephen W 1947- *ConAu 61*
King, Stoddard 1889-1933 *AmA&B, AmSCAP 66, ChPo, DcNAA, REnAL*
King, Susan Petigru 1826-1875 *Alli Sup, BiDSA, DcAmA, DcNAA, LivFWS*
King, T S *Alli*
King, T Staneyan *MnBBF*
King, Talbert *MnBBF*
King, Teri 1940- *WrD 1976*
King, Terry Johnson 1929- *ConAu 17R*
King, Thomas *Alli, Alli Sup*
King, Thomas 1781-1805 *Alli*
King, Thomas Davies 1819-1884 *DcNAA*
King, Thomas H *Alli Sup*
King, Thomas J 1925- *ConAu 37, WrD 1976*
King, Thomas M 1929- *ConAu 57*
King, Thomas Starr 1824-1864? *Alli Sup, AmA&B, BbD, BiD&SB, ChPo S1, CyAL 2, DcAmA, DcNAA, OxAm, REnAL*
King, Thorold *Alli Sup, DcNAA, OhA&B*
King, Toler *Alli Sup, DcNAA*
King, Tom *MnBBF*
King, Tom W *HsB&A*
King, Veronica *AuNews 1*
King, Violet *CanNov*
King, Violet M *ChPo S2*
King, W *Alli, BiDLA*
King, W J *Alli Sup*
King, Walker d1827 *Alli, BiDLA*
King, Wayne 1901- *AmSCAP 66*
King, Wilburn Hill 1839- *BiDSA*
King, Willard L 1893- *ConAu 1R, WrD 1976*
King, Willard Vinton 1868- *WhWNAA*
King, Willford Isbell 1880- *WhWNAA*
King, William *Alli, BiDSA, Chmbr 2*
King, William 1650-1729 *Alli, BrAu, DcEnL, OxEng*
King, William 1663-1712 *Alli, BrAu, CasWL, ChPo S2, DcEnL, DcLEnL, OxEng*
King, William 1685-1763 *Alli, DcEnL, NewC*
King, William 1830-1917 *DcNAA*
King, William And Rowney, Thomas H *Alli Sup*
King, William Benjamin Basil 1859-1928 *BiD&SB, CanNov, DcAmA, DcNAA, OxCan*
King, William Croker *Alli Sup*
King, William Donald Aelian *ConAu 57*
King, William Fletcher 1830-1921 *DcNAA, OhA&B*
King, William Francis Henry *Alli Sup*
King, William H d1883 *Alli Sup*
King, William Joseph Harding 1869- *WhLA*
King, William L *Alli Sup*

King, William Lyon Mackenzie 1874-1950 *OxCan, WhWNAA*
King, William Peter 1871- *WhWNAA*
King, William Richard 1938- *ConAu 23, WrD 1976*
King, William Ross 1822- *Alli Sup, BbtC*
King, William Rufus 1786-1853 *BiDSA*
King, William Rufus 1839-1898 *Alli Sup, DcAmA, DcNAA*
King, Willis Percival 1839-1909 *BiDSA, DcNAA*
King, Winston Lee 1907- *ConAu 41, IndAu 1917*
King, Woodie, Jr. 1937- *BlkAW, LivBA*
King, Mrs. Wyncie *AmA&B*
King-Hall, Magdalen 1904-1971 *Au&Wr, ConAu 29, ConAu P-1*
King-Hall, Sir Stephen 1893-1966 *ChPo S2, ConAu 5R, LongC, WhLA*
King-Hele, Desmond George 1927- *Au&Wr, ConAu 1R, ConAu 29, WrD 1976*
King Of Bath *NewC*
King Philip d1676 *OxAm, REn*
Kingdom, William, Jr. *Alli, BbtC*
Kingdon, Abraham *Alli Sup*
Kingdon, Broughton *Alli*
Kingdon, Frank 1894-1972 *ConAu 33, REnAL*
Kingdon, H D *Alli Sup*
Kingdon, Hollingworth Tully *Alli Sup*
Kingdon, John Abernethy *Alli Sup*
Kingdon, John W 1940- *ConAu 25, WrD 1976*
Kingdon, Robert McCune 1927- *ConAu 21, WrD 1976*
Kingdon, Roger *Alli, BiDLA*
Kingdon, Samuel Nicholson 1805-1872 *Alli Sup*
Kingdon-Ward, Jean 1921- *Au&Wr, WrD 1976*
Kingdon-Ward, Winifred Mary 1884- *Au&Wr*
Kingery, Robert E 1913- *ConAu 9R*
Kingesmil, Andrew *Alli*
Kingham, Richard *Alli Sup*
Kinghorn, Joseph *Alli, BiDLA*
Kinghorn, Kenneth Cain 1930- *ConAu 41*
Kinghorne, Joseph William 1890- *WhWNAA*
Kinglake, Alexander William 1809-1891 *Alli Sup, BiD&SB, BrAu 19, CasWL, Chmbr 3, DcEnA, DcEnL, DcLEnL, EvLB, NewC, OxEng, Pen Eng, REn, WebEAL*
Kinglake, Arthur *Alli Sup*
Kinglake, John Alexander 1802- *Alli*
Kinglake, Robert *Alli, BiDLA*
Kingmaker 1420-1471 *REn*
Kingman, Bradford 1831-1903 *Alli Sup, DcNAA*
Kingman, Dong 1911- *IlCB 1956*
Kingman, Frances *Alli Sup*
Kingman, Henry 1863-1921 *DcNAA*
Kingman, Lee 1919- *AuBYP, ChPo, ChPo S1, ConAu 5R, MorJA, SmATA 1, WrD 1976*
Kingo, Thomas Hansen 1634-1703 *BbD, BiD&SB, CasWL, DcEuL, EvEuW, Pen Eur*
Kingry, Philip L 1942- *ConAu 53*
Kings, Leslie *MnBBF*
King's Norton, Lord 1902- *Au&Wr*
Kingsborough, Edward King, Viscount 1795-1837 *Alli*
Kingsbury, Alice *Alli Sup*
Kingsbury, Alison Mason 1898- *ChPo, ChPo S1*
Kingsbury, Arthur 1939- *ConAu 29*
Kingsbury, B *Alli Sup*
Kingsbury, Benjamin *Alli, BiDLA*
Kingsbury, Benjamin 1813-1886 *DcNAA*
Kingsbury, Benjamin Freeman 1872-1946 *DcNAA*
Kingsbury, Charles People 1818-1879 *Alli, DcAmA, DcNAA*
Kingsbury, Elizabeth 1865-1922 *Alli Sup, OhA&B*
Kingsbury, Frederick *Alli Sup*
Kingsbury, Harmon d1868 *Alli, Alli Sup, DcNAA*
Kingsbury, Mrs. Howard *ChPo*
Kingsbury, Mrs. J D *Alli Sup*
Kingsbury, Jack Dean 1934- *ConAu 37*

Kinsey-Jones, Brian *ConAu XR*
Kinsley, Albert Thomas 1877- *AmLY,*
  WhWNAA
Kinsley, D A 1939- *ConAu 45*
Kinsley, James 1922- *ConAu 1R*
Kinsley, William Wirt 1837-1923 *Alli Sup,*
  AmLY, DcNAA
Kinsman, Ed *Alli*
Kinsman, Frederick Joseph 1868-1944 *AmLY,*
  CatA 1947, OhA&B, WhWNAA
Kinsman, J B *Alli Sup*
Kinsman, John *Alli Sup*
Kinsman, Josiah Burnham d1912 *DcNAA*
Kinsolving, Anne 1906- *WhWNAA*
Kinsolving, George Herbert 1849- *DcAmA*
Kinsolving, Sally Bruce 1876-1962 *AmA&B,*
  AnMV 1926, CatA 1947, WhWNAA
Kinstler, Everett Raymond 1926- *ConAu 33*
Kintner, Earl Wilson 1912- *ConAu 45,*
  IndAu 1917
Kintner, William R 1915- *ConAu 5R*
Kinto *CasWL*
Kinton, Jack F 1939- *ConAu 57*
Kintsch, Walter 1932- *ConAu 29*
Kintzing, Pearce 1861-1917 *DcNAA*
Kinver, Richard *WhLA*
Kinwelmarsh, Francis 1546?-1580 *CrE&SL*
Kinwelmersh, Francis 1546?-1580 *DcEnL*
Kinyanjui, Peter 1940?- *AfA 1*
Kinyon, John 1918- *AmSCAP 66*
Kinzer, Betty 1922- *ConAu 21*
Kinzer, Donald Louis 1914- *ConAu 53*
Kinzer, H M 1923?-1975 *ConAu 57*
Kinzie, Mrs. John H *Alli*
Kinzie, Juliette Augusta 1806-1870 *Alli Sup,*
  DcAmA, DcNAA
Kip, F M *Alli*
Kip, J *Alli*
Kip, Lawrence *Alli Sup*
Kip, Leonard 1826-1906? *Alli Sup, AmA&B,*
  BiD&SB, DcAmA, DcNAA
Kip, William Ingraham 1811-1893 *Alli,*
  Alli Sup, AmA&B, BiD&SB, CyAL 2,
  DcAmA, DcNAA
Kip, William T *Alli Sup*
Kiparsky, Valentin Julius Alexander 1904-
  Au&Wr, ConAu 17R
Kipling, John Lockwood 1837-1911 *ChPo,*
  NewC
Kipling, Mrs. John Lockwood *ChPo, ChPo S2*
Kipling, Rudyard 1865-1936 *Alli Sup, AnCL,*
  AtlBL, AuBYP, BbD, BiD&SB, CarSB,
  CasWL, ChPo, ChPo S1, ChPo S2,
  Chmbr 3, CnE&AP, CnMWL, CriT 3,
  CyWA, DcAmA, DcBiA, DcEnA,
  DcEnA Ap, DcEuL, DcLEnL, EncWL,
  EvLB, FamAYP, FamSYP, JBA 1934,
  LongC, MnBBF, ModBL, ModBL Sup,
  NewC, OxAm, OxCan, OxEng, Pen Eng,
  RAdv 1, RCom, REn, St&VC, TwCA,
  TwCA Sup, TwCW, WebEAL, WhCL,
  WhLA, WhTwL
Kipling, Thomas d1822 *Alli, BiDLA*
Kiplinger, Austin Huntington 1918- *AmA&B,*
  ConAu 57
Kiplinger, Willard Monroe 1891-1967 *AmA&B,*
  OhA&B
Kipniss, Robert *IlBYP*
Kippax, John *Alli*
Kippax, John Robert 1849-1922 *Alli Sup,*
  DcNAA
Kippen, Jane M *Alli Sup*
Kipphardt, Heinar 1922- *CasWL, CnMD,*
  CnThe, CrCD, McGWD, ModWD,
  OxGer, REnWD
Kipping, Robert *Alli Sup*
Kippis, Andrew 1725-1795 *Alli, DcEnL, PoCh*
Kippley, John F 1930- *ConAu 29*
Kippley, Sheila K 1939- *ConAu 61*
Kips, Joseph *Alli Sup*
Kirack, Alex *DrAF 1976, DrAP 1975*
Kiraly, Bela 1912- *ConAu 61*
Kirby, Alfred F P *Alli Sup*
Kirby, Amos 1889- *WhWNAA*
Kirby, Arthur *MnBBF*
Kirby, Bernard C 1907- *BiDPar*
Kirby, C F *Alli Sup*
Kirby, Charles *Alli Sup*

Kirby, Clarence Valentine 1875-1947 *DcNAA*
Kirby, David K 1944- *ConAu 53*
Kirby, David Peter 1936- *Au&Wr, ConAu 25,*
  WrD 1976
Kirby, Douglas James 1929- *Au&Wr,*
  ChPo S1, ConAu 25
Kirby, E Stuart 1909- *ConAu 13R*
Kirby, Edmund Adolphus *Alli Sup*
Kirby, Elizabeth 1823-1873 *CarSB*
Kirby, Ephraim d1804 *Alli*
Kirby, George *Alli*
Kirby, Georgiana 1818- *Alli Sup, DcAmA,*
  DcNAA
Kirby, Gilbert Walter 1914- *Au&Wr,*
  WrD 1976
Kirby, Jack Temple 1938- *ConAu 25*
Kirby, James *BbtC*
Kirby, Jean *ConAu XR*
Kirby, Jeannie *ChPo*
Kirby, Jeremiah *Alli*
Kirby, John *Alli, PoIre*
Kirby, John 1690- *Alli*
Kirby, John Joshua 1716-1774 *Alli*
Kirby, Joshua *Alli*
Kirby, Joshua 1716-1774 *BkIE*
Kirby, K O *Alli Sup*
Kirby, M Sheelah Flanagan 1916- *ConAu 5R*
Kirby, Margaret *ChPo S1*
Kirby, Margaret Butler 1913- *Au&Wr*
Kirby, Mary *Alli Sup*
Kirby, Maurice B *ChPo S1*
Kirby, R S *Alli*
Kirby, Richard *Alli*
Kirby, Richard Shelton 1874- *WhWNAA*
Kirby, Robert *TexWr*
Kirby, Rollin 1875-1952 *AmA&B*
Kirby, Rosalba B *ChPo*
Kirby, Sheelah 1916- *Au&Wr, WrD 1976*
Kirby, Thomas *Alli, BiDLA*
Kirby, Thomas Austin 1904- *Au&Wr,*
  ConAu 5R
Kirby, Thomas Frederick *Alli Sup*
Kirby, William *Alli, BiDLA, BiDLA Sup,*
  Chmbr 3
Kirby, William 1759-1850 *Alli*
Kirby, William 1817-1906 *Alli Sup, BbtC,*
  BiD&SB, CanWr, CasWL, DcLEnL,
  DcNAA, OxAm, OxCan, OxCan Sup,
  REn, REnAL
Kirby, William Forsell *Alli Sup*
Kirbye, George *Alli*
Kirbye, J Edward 1873- *AmLY, WhWNAA*
Kirch, Patti 1942-1963 *ChPo S1*
Kirchbach, Wolfgang 1857- *BiD&SB*
Kirchberg, Conrad V *ChPo*
Kircher, Ralf Charles 1907- *OhA&B*
Kirchhof, Hans Wilhelm 1525?-1603? *OxGer*
Kirchhoff, Charles William Henry 1853-1916
  DcNAA
Kirchhoff, Gustav Robert 1824-1887 *REn*
Kirchhoff, Hans Wilhelm 1525?-1603? *OxGer*
Kirchhoff, Theodor 1828-1899 *BiD&SB,*
  CasWL
Kirchhoffer, Henry *PoIre*
Kirchhoffer, Julia Georgiana Mary 1855-1878
  Alli Sup, PoIre
Kirchmayer, Thomas 1511-1563 *DcEuL*
Kirchner, Ernst Ludwig 1880-1938 *AtlBL,*
  OxGer
Kirchner, Glenn 1930- *ConAu 29*
Kirchner, Theodore *ChPo S1*
Kirchner, Walther 1905- *ConAu 1R*
Kirchwey, Freda 1893-1976 *AmA&B,*
  ConAu 61
Kirchwey, George Washington 1855-1942
  DcNAA
Kirdar, Uner 1933- *ConAu 23*
Kireevsky, Ivan Vasilyevich 1806-1856 *CasWL*
Kireyevski, Ivan Vasilyevich 1806-1856 *DcRusL*
Kireyevsky, Ivan Vasilyevich 1806-1856 *CasWL*
Kireyevsky, Pyotr Vasilyevich 1808-1856 *CasWL*
Kirill Of Turov *Pen Eur*
Kirill Turovski *DcRusL*
Kirillov, Vladimir Timofeyevich 1889- *DcRusL*
Kirk *Alli*
Kirk, Abdier *BbtC*
Kirk, Alexander Carnegie *Alli Sup*
Kirk, Andrew D 1898- *AmSCAP 66*

Kirk, B Reid *Alli Sup*
Kirk, Charles D *Alli Sup*
Kirk, Clara M 1898- *ConAu P-1*
Kirk, David 1935- *ConAu 29*
Kirk, Donald 1938- *ConAu 37, WrD 1976*
Kirk, Donald R 1935- *ConAu 57*
Kirk, Edward *Alli Sup*
Kirk, Edward 1846- *DcNAA*
Kirk, Edward Cameron 1856- *WhWNAA*
Kirk, Edward Norris 1802-1874 *Alli, Alli Sup,*
  DcAmA, DcNAA
Kirk, Eleanor 1831- *Alli Sup, AmA&B,*
  ChPo, DcAmA, DcNAA
Kirk, Elizabeth D 1937- *ConAu 53*
Kirk, Ellen Warner Olney 1842-1928 *Alli Sup,*
  AmA&B, BbD, BiD&SB, CarSB,
  DcAmA, DcBiA, DcNAA
Kirk, Florence *ChPo S1*
Kirk, Geoffrey Stephen 1921- *ConAu 5R,*
  WrD 1976
Kirk, George Eden 1911- *Au&Wr, ConAu 1R*
Kirk, George Harley 1831- *Alli Sup, PoIre*
Kirk, Grayson Louis 1903- *AmA&B, OhA&B*
Kirk, H David 1918- *ConAu 17R*
Kirk, Hans Rudolf 1898-1962 *CasWL,*
  ClDMEuL, EncWL, Pen Eur
Kirk, Harris Elliott 1872-1953 *AmA&B,*
  WhWNAA
Kirk, Helen *Alli Sup*
Kirk, Henry *ChPo S2*
Kirk, Hyland Clare 1846-1917 *Alli Sup,*
  DcNAA
Kirk, Irene 1926- *ConAu 5R*
Kirk, Irina *ConAu XR*
Kirk, J S *Alli Sup*
Kirk, James A 1929- *ConAu 37*
Kirk, James Hobert 1923- *IndAu 1917*
Kirk, Jerome 1937- *ConAu 49*
Kirk, John 1813-1886 *Alli Sup*
Kirk, Sir John 1832-1922 *NewC*
Kirk, John Esben 1905-1975 *ConAu 57,*
  WrD 1976
Kirk, John Foster 1824-1904 *Alli Sup, AmA,*
  AmA&B, BbtC, BiD&SB, CyAL 2,
  DcAmA, DcNAA
Kirk, John T 1933- *ConAu 49*
Kirk, Margaret Locke 1896- *TexWr*
Kirk, Maria Louise 1860?- *ChPo S1, ConICB*
Kirk, Mary Wallace 1889- *ConAu 57*
Kirk, Paul *BlkAW*
Kirk, R G 1881- *WhWNAA*
Kirk, Rey John *Alli*
Kirk, Richard 1931- *ConAu 13R*
Kirk, Richard Ray 1877- *ChPo S1, ChPo S2,*
  WhWNAA
Kirk, Robert *OxCan*
Kirk, Robert Warner *ConAu 9R*
Kirk, Roger E 1930- *ConAu 41*
Kirk, Russell Amos 1918- *AmA&B, Au&Wr,*
  AuNews 1, ChPo S2, ConAu 1R, WorAu,
  WrD 1976
Kirk, Ruth Eleanor 1925- *AuBYP,*
  ConAu 13R, SmATA 5, WhPNW
Kirk, Samuel A 1904- *ConAu 45*
Kirk, Ted *ConAu XR*
Kirk, Theron 1919- *AmSCAP 66*
Kirk, Thomas 1765-1797 *BkIE*
Kirk, Thomas Hobson 1899- *Au&Wr,*
  ConAu 23, WrD 1976
Kirk, William 1880- *AmLY, WhWNAA*
Kirk, William Boyton *Alli Sup*
Kirk, William Frederick 1877-1927 *ChPo,*
  ChPo S1, DcNAA, WiscW
Kirk-Greene, Anthony Hamilton Millard 1925-
  Au&Wr, ConAu 61, WrD 1976
Kirk-Greene, Christopher Walter Edward 1926-
  Au&Wr, ConAu 13R, WrD 1976
Kirkaldy, Adam Willis 1867- *WhLA*
Kirkaldy, David *Alli Sup*
Kirkaldy, John Francis 1908- *Au&Wr,*
  WrD 1976
Kirkall, Viscount *Alli Sup*
Kirkall, Elisha 1685-1742 *BkIE*
Kirkbride, Sir Alec Seath 1897- *Au&Wr,*
  WrD 1976
Kirkbride, Franklin Butler 1867- *WhWNAA*
Kirkbride, John *Alli*
Kirkbride, Ronald 1912- *AmA&B, AmNov,*

Au&Wr, ConAu 1R, WhWNAA
Kirkbride, Thomas Story 1809-1883 *Alli, DcAmA, DcNAA*
Kirkby, Christopher *Alli*
Kirkby, John *Alli, DcEnL*
Kirkcaldy, Agnes *Alli Sup*
Kirkconnell, Watson 1895- *Au&Wr, CanWr, CasWL, ChPo, ConP 1970, DcLEnL, OxCan, OxCan Sup, WhWNAA*
Kirke, Sir David 1597?-1654 *OxCan*
Kirke, Edmund *Alli Sup, AmA&B, DcAmA, DcEnL, DcNAA*
Kirke, Edward 1553-1613 *BrAu, NewC, OxEng*
Kirke, Henry 1842- *Alli Sup, OxCan*
Kirke, John *Alli, BiDLA*
Kirke, Percy 1646?-1691 *NewC*
Kirke, Robert *Alli*
Kirke, T *Alli*
Kirke, Thomas *Alli*
Kirke White, Henry *DcEnL*
Kirkeby, Wallace T 1891- *AmSCAP 66*
Kirkendall, Don 1923- *ConAu 49*
Kirkendall, Lester A 1903- *ConAu 1R, WrD 1976*
Kirkes, William Senhouse And James Paget *Alli*
Kirkham, Charles J *Alli Sup*
Kirkham, E Bruce 1938- *ConAu 37, WrD 1976*
Kirkham, Michael Campbell 1934- *Au&Wr, ConAu 25, WrD 1976*
Kirkham, Nellie *Au&Wr, WrD 1976*
Kirkham, Reginald S *MnBBF*
Kirkham, Samuel *Alli, DcNAA*
Kirkham, Stanton Davis 1868-1944 *AmA&B, DcNAA, WhWNAA*
Kirkhoffer, Clara *ChPo*
Kirkland, Bryant M 1914- *ConAu 21*
Kirkland, Captain *MnBBF*
Kirkland, Caroline Matilda Stansbury 1801-1864 *Alli, Alli Sup, AmA, AmA&B, BbD, BiD&SB, ChPo, CyAL 2, DcAmA, DcNAA, OxAm, REn, REnAL*
Kirkland, Charles P *Alli Sup*
Kirkland, Daniel 1833- *ChPo*
Kirkland, Edward Chase 1894- *Au&Wr, ConAu 1R, WhWNAA, WrD 1976*
Kirkland, Edwin C *ChPo S1*
Kirkland, Elizabeth Stansbury 1828-1896 *Alli Sup, DcAmA, DcNAA*
Kirkland, Frances *ChPo*
Kirkland, Frazar *Alli Sup*
Kirkland, Jack 1901?-1969 *CnMD, McGWD, ModWD*
Kirkland, James *Alli, BiDLA*
Kirkland, James 1721-1798 *Alli*
Kirkland, James Hampton 1859-1939 *AmA&B, BiDSA*
Kirkland, John Thornton 1770-1840 *AmA&B, BiD&SB, DcAmA*
Kirkland, Joseph 1830-1894 *Alli Sup, AmA, AmA&B, BbD, BiD&SB, CasWL, DcAmA, DcLEnL, DcNAA, EvLB, OxAm, REn, REnAL*
Kirkland, Samuel 1744-1808 *CyAL 2*
Kirkland, T H *BiDSA*
Kirkland, Thomas 1835-1898 *DcNAA*
Kirkland, William 1800-1846 *Alli, CyAL 2*
Kirkland, Winifred Margaretta 1872-1943 *AmA&B, AmLY, DcNAA, WhWNAA*
Kirkman, Francis *Alli, DcEnL*
Kirkman, Francis 1632?- *CasWL*
Kirkman, Frederick Bernulf Beever 1869- *WhLA*
Kirkman, James Thomas *Alli, BiDLA*
Kirkman, Marshall Monroe 1842-1921 *Alli Sup, AmA&B, DcAmA, DcNAA*
Kirkman, Thomas Penyngton *Alli Sup*
Kirkman, William *Alli Sup*
Kirkman, William Patrick 1932- *Au&Wr, WrD 1976*
Kirkpatrick, Alexander T *Alli Sup*
Kirkpatrick, Blaine Evron 1887-1959 *IndAu 1917*
Kirkpatrick, Charles Milton 1915- *IndAu 1917*
Kirkpatrick, Clifford 1898- *WhWNAA*
Kirkpatrick, Cynthia Cole 1811-1888 *OhA&B*
Kirkpatrick, Diane 1933- *ConAu 53*

Kirkpatrick, Donald A 1928- *AmSCAP 66*
Kirkpatrick, Donald L 1924- *ConAu 41*
Kirkpatrick, Dow 1917- *ConAu 23*
Kirkpatrick, E A *Alli Sup*
Kirkpatrick, Edward *Alli Sup*
Kirkpatrick, Edwin Asbury 1862-1937 *AmLY, DcNAA, WhWNAA*
Kirkpatrick, Elenita T *TexWr*
Kirkpatrick, Evron M 1911- *ConAu 57*
Kirkpatrick, Francis *PoIre*
Kirkpatrick, Frank Home 1874-1940 *DcNAA*
Kirkpatrick, Frederick Alexander 1861-1953 *NewC*
Kirkpatrick, George Ross 1867-1937 *OhA&B*
Kirkpatrick, H *Alli, BiDLA*
Kirkpatrick, Ivone Augustine 1897-1964 *ConAu P-1*
Kirkpatrick, J *Alli*
Kirkpatrick, James *Alli, PoIre*
Kirkpatrick, Jane 1772-1850 *DcNAA*
Kirkpatrick, Jeane D J 1926- *ConAu 53*
Kirkpatrick, John *Alli, Alli Sup, BiDLA, PoIre*
Kirkpatrick, John 1905- *ConAu 45*
Kirkpatrick, John Ervin 1869-1931 *DcNAA*
Kirkpatrick, L *Alli Sup*
Kirkpatrick, Lyman B, Jr. 1916- *ConAu 33*
Kirkpatrick, M Glen 1889- *WhWNAA*
Kirkpatrick, Oliver Austin 1911- *ConAu 49, LivBAA*
Kirkpatrick, Ralph 1911- *ConAu 49*
Kirkpatrick, Samuel A, III 1943- *ConAu 41*
Kirkpatrick, Smith 1922- *ConAu 49, DrAF 1976*
Kirkpatrick, Thomas Percy Claude 1869- *WhLA*
Kirkpatrick, Thomas Winfrid 1896- *Au&Wr*
Kirkpatrick, William *Alli, BiDLA*
Kirkpatrick, William Arber Brown 1880- *ChPo S1*
Kirkpatrick, William B *Alli Sup*
Kirksey, Van *BlkAW*
Kirkton, James d1699 *Alli, DcEnL*
Kirkup, James Falconer 1918- *ChPo, ChPo S2, WorAu*
Kirkup, James Falconer 1923- *ConP 1970, ConP 1975, LongC, Pen Eng, REn, WrD 1976*
Kirkup, James Falconer 1924- *Au&Wr, NewC*
Kirkup, James Falconer 1927- *ConAu 1R, ConLC 1*
Kirkup, Thomas *Alli Sup*
Kirkus, Virginia 1893- *AmA&B, ConAu XR*
Kirkus, William 1830- *Alli, Alli Sup, DcAmA*
Kirkwall, Victor *Alli Sup*
Kirkwood, Alexander *BbtC*
Kirkwood, Arthur *Alli Sup*
Kirkwood, Daniel 1814-1895 *Alli Sup, BiDSA, DcAmA, DcNAA, IndAu 1816*
Kirkwood, Ellen Swan 1904- *ConAu 25*
Kirkwood, James *Alli*
Kirkwood, James 1930- *Au&Wr, AuNews 2, ConAu 1R*
Kirkwood, Jim *ConAu XR*
Kirkwood, John *Alli Sup*
Kirkwood, Joseph Edward 1872-1928 *DcNAA*
Kirkwood, Joyce Irving 1912- *Au&Wr*
Kirkwood, Kenneth P 1899-1968 *ConAu 37*
Kirkwood, Marie *WhWNAA*
Kirkwood, R *Alli, BiDLA*
Kirkwood, Robert 1793-1866 *Alli Sup, DcAmA*
Kirkwood, William Paul 1867- *WhWNAA*
Kirle, R *Alli*
Kirliak, Illia *OxCan*
Kirlin, Joseph Louis Jerome 1868-1926 *DcNAA*
Kirmse, Marguerite 1885-1954 *ConICB, IlBYP, IlCB 1945, IlCB 1956*
Kirn, Ann Minette 1910- *AuBYP, ChPo S1, IlCB 1966*
Kirn, George John 1863- *WhWNAA*
Kironde, Erisa 1940?- *AfA 1*
Kirouac, Conrad *OxCan*
Kirov, Sergei Mironovich 1886-1934 *REn*
Kirsanov, Semen Isaakovich 1906- *CasWL*
Kirsanov, Semyon 1906- *Pen Eur*
Kirsap, Joseph *Alli Sup*

Kirsch, Arthur C 1932- *ConAu 13R*
Kirsch, Felix Marie 1884-1945 *CatA 1947, DcNAA*
Kirsch, Leonard Joel 1934- *ConAu 37*
Kirsch, Robert 1922- *AmA&B, ConAu 33*
Kirschbaum, Joseph M *OxCan Sup*
Kirschbaum, Richard Warren 1894-1948 *DcNAA*
Kirschenbaum, Aaron 1926- *ConAu 33*
Kirschner, Allen 1930- *ConAu 29*
Kirschner, Aloysia *OxGer*
Kirschner, Fritz *ConAu XR*
Kirschner, Linda Rae 1939- *ConAu 33*
Kirschten, Ernest 1902-1974 *ConAu 49, ConAu P-1*
Kirshaw, S D *Alli*
Kirshner, Gloria Ifland *ConAu 41*
Kirshon, Vladimir Mikhaylovich 1902-1938? *CasWL, ClDMEuL, CnMD, DcRusL, EvEuW, ModWD, Pen Eur, REn*
Kirsner, Robert 1921- *ConAu 23*
Kirson, Alice Atkinson 1868- *AmLY*
Kirst, Hans Hellmut 1914- *CasWL, ModGL, TwCW, WorAu*
Kirst, Michael W 1939- *ConAu 45*
Kirstein, George Garland 1909- *AmA&B*
Kirstein, Lincoln 1907- *AmA&B*
Kirtland, Dorrance *Alli*
Kirtland, Ethel Schwartz 1881-1963 *IndAu 1917*
Kirtland, G B *ConAu XR, SmATA 2, ThBJA*
Kirtland, John Copeland 1870- *WhWNAA*
Kirtland, Lucian Swift 1881-1965 *AmA&B, OhA&B, WhWNAA*
Kirtley, James Addison 1822- *BiDSA*
Kirtley, James Samuel *WhWNAA*
Kirton, Henry *Alli*
Kirton, John Williams 1831-1892 *Alli Sup, ChPo S1*
Kirton, St. Clair *BlkAW*
Kirttivasa 1385- *CasWL*
Kirusna Pillai, Henry Alfred 1827-1900 *DcOrL 2*
Kirusnamurtti, R 1899-1954 *DcOrL 2*
Kirvan, John J 1932- *ConAu 23*
Kirwan *Alli, BiD&SB, DcAmA, DcEnL, DcNAA*
Kirwan, Achille *PoIre*
Kirwan, Albert Dennis 1904- *ConAu 1R*
Kirwan, Andrew Valentine *Alli Sup*
Kirwan, Archibald William L Patrick 1907- *Au&Wr*
Kirwan, Edward Dominic Geoffry Martin *Alli Sup*
Kirwan, F D *Alli, BiDLA*
Kirwan, Sir John Waters 1869- *WhLA*
Kirwan, Laurence Patrick 1907- *ConAu 1R*
Kirwan, M W *Alli Sup*
Kirwan, Molly 1906- *Au&Wr, ConAu P-1*
Kirwan, Richard d1812 *Alli*
Kirwan, Rose *PoIre*
Kirwan, Thomas 1829-1911 *Alli Sup, DcNAA*
Kirwan, Walter Blake 1754-1805 *Alli*
Kirwan-Ward, Bernard Edward 1909- *Au&Wr*
Kirwin, Harry Wynne 1911-1963 *ConAu 1R*
Kirzner, Israel M 1930- *ConAu 1R*
Kis, Danilo 1935- *CasWL*
Kisamore, Norman D 1928- *ConAu 5R*
Kisbey, W H *Alli Sup*
Kisbey, William 1828-1910 *PoIre*
Kisch, Egon Erwin 1885-1948 *Pen Eur*
Kisco, Charles W 1896- *AmSCAP 66*
Kiseki *CasWL*
Kiser, Clyde V 1904- *ConAu 25*
Kiser, Irene Denman 1884- *TexWr*
Kiser, Martha Gwinn *AuBYP*
Kiser, Samuel Ellsworth 1862-1942 *AmA&B, ChPo, ChPo S1, ChPo S2, DcAmA, DcNAA, OhA&B, WhWNAA*
Kisfaludy, Karoly 1788-1830 *BbD, BiD&SB, CasWL, EuA, McGWD, Pen Eur*
Kisfaludy, Sandor 1772-1844 *BbD, BiD&SB, CasWL, EuA, Pen Eur*
Kish, G Hobab *ConAu XR*
Kish, George 1914- *ConAu 1R*
Kish, Leslie 1910- *ConAu P-1, WrD 1976*
Kishida, Eriko 1929- *ConAu 53*
Kishon, Ephraim 1924- *Au&Wr, ConAu 49,*

REnWD
Kisich, Mrs. Oliver Michael *AmNov XR*
Kisielewski, Jan August 1876-1918 *CasWL*
Kisinger, Grace Gelvin 1913-1960? *AuBYP,*
 ConAu P-1, SmATA 10
Kisker, George W 1912- *ConAu 21*
Kismaric, Carole 1942- *ConAu 33*
Kiss, Josef 1843-1921 *BbD, BiD&SB*
Kiss, Jozsef 1843-1921 *ClDMEuL, Pen Eur*
Kissam, Edward 1943- *ConAu 61, DrAP 1975*
Kissam, Philip 1896- *Au&Wr, WrD 1976*
Kissam, Richard Sharpe 1806-1861 *DcNAA*
Kissam, Samuel 1796-1868 *DcNAA*
Kissane, John M 1928- *ConAu 53*
Kissane, Leedice McAnelly 1905- *ConAu 25*
Kissen, David Morris 1916- *Au&Wr*
Kissen, Fan 1904- *ConAu P-1*
Kissin, Eva H 1923- *ConAu 29, SmATA 10*
Kissinger, Henry Alfred 1923- *AmA&B,*
 ConAu 1R, WrD 1976
Kissling, Fred R, Jr. 1930- *ConAu 23,*
 WrD 1976
Kissling, Henry Robert 1904- *IndAu 1917*
Kissling, Mrs. Robert C *AmNov XR*
Kist, Willem 1758-1841 *CasWL*
Kiste, Robert Carl 1936- *ConAu 61*
Kistemaeckers, Henry 1872- *ClDMEuL*
Kister, Kenneth F 1935- *ConAu 25*
Kistner, Robert William 1917- *Au&Wr,*
 ConAu 61, WrD 1976
Kita, Morio 1927- *DcOrL 1*
Kitagawa, Daisuke 1910- *ConAu 17*
Kitagawa, Fuyuhiko 1900- *DcOrL 1*
Kitagawa, Joseph M 1915- *ConAu 1R*
Kitahara, Hakushu 1885-1942 *DcOrL 1*
Kitano, Harry H L 1926- *ConAu 29,*
 WrD 1976
Kitch, John Walter 1866-1946 *IndAu 1816*
Kitchel, Courtney Smith 1843-1931 *DcNAA*
Kitchell, Joseph Gray 1862-1947 *OhA&B*
Kitchen, Fred *ChPo S2*
Kitchen, Helen 1920- *ConAu 9R*
Kitchen, Herminie B 1901-1973 *Au&Wr,*
 ConAu P-1
Kitchen, J M W *Alli Sup*
Kitchen, James Howard 1902- *Au&Wr,*
 WrD 1976
Kitchen, Joseph Moses Ward 1846-1931 *DcNAA*
Kitchen, Karl Kingsley 1885-1935 *AmA&B,*
 DcNAA, OhA&B
Kitchen, Martin 1936- *ConAu 61, WrD 1976*
Kitchen, Paddy 1934- *ConAu 25, WrD 1976*
Kitchen, Thomas *Alli*
Kitchener, Henry Thomas *Alli, BiDLA*
Kitchener, William 1775-1827 *Alli, DcEnL*
Kitchin, C H B 1895-1967 *EncM&D, LongC*
Kitchin, Darcy Butterworth *Alli Sup*
Kitchin, George William 1827- *Alli Sup*
Kitchin, John *Alli*
Kitchin, Shepherd Braithwaite *WhLA*
Kitchin, William Copeman 1855-1920 *DcNAA*
Kitching, George *Alli Sup*
Kitching, Wilfred 1893- *WrD 1976*
Kite, Charles d1811 *Alli, BiDLA,*
 BiDLA Sup
Kite, Edward *Alli Sup*
Kite, Elizabeth 1864- *CatA 1947*
Kite, Frederick Robert *Alli Sup*
Kite, Larry *ConAu XR*
Kite, Shirley *ChPo*
Kite, William 1810- *Alli Sup*
Kitereza, Aniceti 1900?- *AfA 1*
Kith, William *Alli*
Kitman, Marvin 1929- *AmA&B*
Kitowicz, Jedrzej 1728-1804 *CasWL*
Kitselman, Leslie Curtis 1892- *IndAu 1816*
Kitson, Charles Herbert 1874- *WhLA*
Kitson, Harry Dexter 1886- *IndAu 1816,*
 WhWNAA
Kitson, Jack William 1940- *ConAu 25*
Kitson, Roger *Alli, BiDLA*
Kitson Clark, George Sydney Roberts 1900-
 Au&Wr, ConAu 23
Kitt, Eartha Mae 1928- *LivBA*
Kitt, Jessie Weber *AnMV 1926*
Kittermaster, Arthur Michael 1918- *Au&Wr*
Kittermaster, Frederick Wilson *Alli Sup*
Kittle, Samuel *Alli*

Kitto, H D F 1897- *ConAu P-1, WrD 1976*
Kitto, John 1804-1854 *Alli, BiD&SB,*
 Chmbr 3, DcEnL, EvLB, NewC
Kitto, R L M *Alli Sup*
Kittoe, Captain *Alli*
Kittoe, W H *Alli*
Kitton, Frederick *Alli Sup*
Kitton, Frederick G *Alli Sup*
Kitton, Frederick George 1856-1904 *ChPo*
Kittowe, Robert *Alli*
Kittredge, A O *Alli Sup*
Kittredge, Daniel Wright 1879-1958 *OhA&B*
Kittredge, Elizabeth *OhA&B*
Kittredge, George F *Alli Sup*
Kittredge, George Lyman 1860-1941 *AmA&B,*
 ChPo, CnDAL, DcLEnL, DcNAA,
 LongC, NewC, OxAm, REn, REnAL,
 TwCA, TwCA Sup
Kittredge, Henry Crocker 1890- *ChPo*
Kittredge, Henry Grattan 1845-1909 *DcNAA*
Kittredge, Walter 1834-1905 *ChPo, DcAmA,*
 DcNAA, OxAm
Kittredge, William *DrAF 1976*
Kittrell, Norman Goree 1849-1927 *BiDSA,*
 DcNAA
Kittridge, Walter 1832-1905 *ChPo S2*
Kitts, Eustace J *Alli Sup*
Kitzberg, August 1855-1927 *CasWL*
Kitzinger, Sheila 1929- *ConAu 37, WrD 1976*
Kitzinger, Uwe W 1928- *ConAu 1R,*
 WrD 1976
Kivi, Aleksis 1834-1872 *CasWL, EuA, REn,*
 REnWD
Kivi, Alexis 1834-1872 *Pen Eur*
Kivimaa, Kaarlo Arvi 1904- *Pen Eur*
KixMiller, William 1885-1945 *DcNAA,*
 IndAu 1917
Kiyokawa, Shoichi *DrAP 1975*
Kiyooka, Roy *OxCan Sup*
Kiyotsuga, Kwanami *REnWD*
Kizer, Carolyn 1925- *ConP 1970, ConP 1975,*
 CrCAP, DrAP 1975, Pen Am, WorAu
Kizer, Carolyn 1926- *WrD 1976*
Kjaer, Nils 1870-1924 *CasWL*
Kjelgaard, James Arthur 1910-1959 *AuBYP*
Kjelgaard, Jim 1910-1959 *JBA 1951, St&VC*
Kjelland, Alexander Lange 1849-1906 *BbD,*
 DcBiA
Kjellgren, Josef 1907-1948 *CasWL*
Kjellin, John J 1904- *AmSCAP 66*
Kjerkegaard, Soren Aabye 1813-1855 *BiD&SB*
Kjerkegaard SEE ALSO Kierkegaard
Kjome, June C 1920- *ConAu 5R*
Klaas, Joe 1920- *ConAu 29, WrD 1976*
Klaasse, Piet *ChPo S1*
Klaassen, Leo H 1920- *ConAu 23*
Klabund 1890-1928 *ClDMEuL, CnMD,*
 EncWL, EvEuW, ModGL, ModWD,
 OxGer, Pen Eur, REn
Klaczko, Julian 1828- *BiD&SB*
Klaeber, Frederick 1863- *WhWNAA*
Klaeber, Friederich 1863- *AmA&B*
Klaer, Fred Harlen 1878-1915 *DcNAA*
Klafs, Carl E 1911- *ConAu 13R*
Klages, Raymond W 1888-1947 *AmSCAP 66*
Klages, Theodore 1911- *AmSCAP 66*
Klagsbrun, Francine *ConAu 21*
Klahr, Myra *DrAP 1975*
Klaich, Dolores 1936- *ConAu 49*
Klainikite, Anne *ConAu XR*
Klaj, Johann 1616-1656 *CasWL, DcEuL,*
 OxGer, Pen Eur
Klamkin, Charles 1923- *ConAu 61*
Klamkin, Lynn 1950- *ConAu 45*
Klamkin, Marian 1926- *ConAu 49, WrD 1976*
Klapatch, Ahdell LaVaque 1916- *ChPo*
Klaperman, Gilbert 1921- *ConAu 49*
Klaperman, Libby Mindlin 1921- *ConAu 9R*
Klapp, H Milnor 1810?-1872 *Alli Sup, HsB&A,*
 HsB&A Sup
Klapp, Michael 1834-1888 *BiD&SB*
Klapp, Orrin E 1915- *ConAu 9R*
Klapper, Charles Frederick 1905- *Au&Wr,*
 ConAu P-1, WrD 1976
Klapper, M Roxana 1937- *ConAu 53*
Klapper, Marvin 1922- *ConAu 17R*
Klapper, Paul 1885- *AmLY, WhWNAA*
Klappert, Peter 1942- *ConAu 33, DrAP 1975,*

WrD 1976
Klappholz, Kurt 1913-1975 *ConAu 61*
Klaproth, Heinrich Julius Von 1783-1835 *BbD,*
 BiD&SB
Klare, George Roger 1922- *ConAu 5R,*
 WrD 1976
Klare, Hugh J 1916- *WrD 1976*
Klaren, Peter F 1938- *ConAu 57*
Klarmann, Andrew Francis 1866-1931
 CatA 1947, ChPo S2, DcNAA
Klass, Morton 1927- *ConAu 1R*
Klass, Philip J 1919- *ConAu 25*
Klass, Sheila Solomon 1927- *ConAu 37,*
 WrD 1976
Klass, Sholom 1916- *ConAu 23*
Klassen, Peter J 1930- *ConAu 45*
Klassen, Randolph Jacob 1933- *ConAu 61*
Klassen, William 1930- *ConAu 25*
Klatzkin, Leon 1914- *AmSCAP 66*
Klauber, Marcy 1896-1960 *AmSCAP 66*
Klauder, Francis John 1918- *ConAu 53*
Klaue, Lola Shelton 1903- *ConAu 5R*
Klauke, *BbtC*
Klauprecht, Emil 1815-1896 *OhA&B*
Klaus, Bruder *OxGer*
Klaus, Eugenia *Alli Sup*
Klauser, Julius 1854-1907 *DcNAA*
Klausler, Alfred P 1910- *ConAu 23*
Klausmeier, Herbert John 1915- *ConAu 1R,*
 IndAu 1917
Klausner, Joseph 1874-1958 *CasWL*
Klausner, Margot 1905-1976? *ConAu 61*
Klausner, Samuel Z 1923- *ConAu 17R*
Klauss, Noah 1901- *AmSCAP 66*
Klaver, Martin Arnold 1900- *AmA&B*
Klaw, Spencer 1920- *ConAu 25*
Klayman, Maxwell Irving 1917- *ConAu 29,*
 WrD 1976
Kldiashvili, Sergo 1893- *DcOrL 3*
Klebe, Charles Eugene 1907- *ConAu 23*
Klebe, Gene *ConAu XR*
Kleber, Albert 1881-1958 *IndAu 1917*
Kleber, Jean-Baptiste 1753-1800 *OxFr*
Kleberger, Ilse 1921- *ConAu 41, SmATA 5*
Klee, Paul 1879-1940 *AtlBL, OxGer, REn*
Klee, W G *Alli Sup*
Kleeberg, Irene Cumming 1932- *ConAu 61*
Kleeberg, Minna 1841-1878 *DcNAA*
Kleeberger, Jessie G 1893- *WhWNAA*
Kleehoven, Hans Ankwicz 1883- *WhLA*
Kleeman, Rita Sulzbacher Halle 1887-1971
 AmA&B, Au&Wr, OhA&B, WhWNAA
Kleene, Stephen Cole 1909- *ConAu 41,*
 WrD 1976
Klees, Fredric 1901- *ConAu 19*
Kleiman, Robert 1918- *ConAu 13R*
Klein, Aaron E 1930- *ConAu 25*
Klein, Abraham Moses 1909-1972 *CanWr,*
 CasWL, ConAu 37, ConP 1970, DcLEnL,
 EncWL Sup, LongC, OxCan, OxCan Sup,
 Pen Eng, REnAL, TwCA Sup, WebEAL
Klein, Alan F 1911- *ConAu 57*
Klein, Alexander 1918- *AmA&B, ConAu 5R*
Klein, Alexander 1923- *WrD 1976*
Klein, Arnold William 1945- *ConAu 37*
Klein, Arthur Jay 1884- *WhWNAA*
Klein, Bernard 1921- *ConAu 17R*
Klein, Bert Howard *ChPo, ChPo S1*
Klein, Charles 1867-1915 *AmA&B, Chmbr 3,*
 DcNAA, OxAm, REnAL
Klein, Daniel Martin 1939- *ConAu 61*
Klein, David 1919- *AuBYP, ConAu 1R*
Klein, David Ballin 1897- *ConAu 41*
Klein, Deanne Arkus 1934- *AmSCAP 66*
Klein, Donald C 1923- *ConAu 25*
Klein, Doris F *ConAu XR*
Klein, Edward Emanuel *Alli Sup*
Klein, Ernest 1899- *ConAu 21*
Klein, Felix 1862- *CatA 1947, WhLA*
Klein, Frederic Shriver 1904- *ConAu 13R,*
 WrD 1976
Klein, Gerard 1937- *ConAu 49*
Klein, H Arthur *AuBYP, ConAu 13R,*
 SmATA 8
Klein, Harry 1912- *Au&Wr*
Klein, Harry Martin John 1873- *WhWNAA*
Klein, Herman 1856- *WhLA*

Klein, Isaac 1905- *ConAu 57*
Klein, J *Alli Sup*
Klein, J F *Alli Sup*
Klein, Johann August 1778-1831 *OxGer*
Klein, John 1915- *AmSCAP 66*
Klein, John J 1929- *ConAu 17R*
Klein, Joseph Frederic 1849-1918 *DcNAA*
Klein, Joseph Jerome 1885- *AmLY*
Klein, Josephine 1926- *ConAu 1R*, *WrD 1976*
Klein, Julius *WhWNAA*
Klein, Julius Leopold 1810-1876 *BiD&SB*,
  OxGer
Klein, K K *ConAu XR*
Klein, Leonore 1916- *AuBYP*, *ConAu 1R*,
  SmATA 6
Klein, Lothar 1932- *AmSCAP 66*
Klein, Lou 1888-1945 *AmSCAP 66*
Klein, Manuel 1876-1919 *AmSCAP 66*
Klein, Marcus 1928- *ConAu 9R*, *WrD 1976*
Klein, Martin A 1934- *ConAu 23*
Klein, Maury 1939- *ConAu 33*
Klein, Maxine 1934- *ConAu 61*
Klein, Mina C *ConAu 37*, *SmATA 8*
Klein, Muriel Walzer 1920- *ConAu 29*
Klein, Norma 1938- *ChLR 2*, *ConAu 41*,
  DrAF 1976, *SmATA 7*
Klein, Norman 1897-1948 *DcNAA*,
  WhWNAA
Klein, Philip Alexander 1927- *ConAu 17R*,
  WrD 1976
Klein, Philip Shriver 1909- *ConAu 1R*
Klein, Rose 1918- *ConAu 21*
Klein, Stanley 1930- *ConAu 57*
Klein, Suzanne Marie 1940- *ConAu 57*
Klein, Ted U 1926- *ConAu 25*
Klein, Thomas D 1941- *ConAu 61*
Klein, William Livingston 1851-1931 *DcNAA*
Klein, Woody 1929- *ConAu 13R*
Kleinbauer, W Eugene 1937- *ConAu 37*
Kleine-Ahlbrandt, William Laird 1932-
  ConAu 29, *WrD 1976*
Kleinecke, August 1881-1944 *AmSCAP 66*
Kleineidam, Horst 1932- *CrCD*
Kleiner, Richard 1921- *AmSCAP 66*
Kleinfeld, Vincent A 1907- *ConAu 17R*
Kleinhans, Theodore John 1924- *Au&Wr*,
  ConAu 5R, *WrD 1976*
Kleinman, Bertha A 1877- *ArizL*
Kleinman, Isador I 1913- *AmSCAP 66*
Kleinmann, Jack H 1932- *ConAu 21*
Kleinmuntz, Benjamin 1930- *ConAu 33*
Kleinpaul, Rudolph 1845- *BiD&SB*
Kleinschmidt, Rudolph August 1878-
  WhWNAA
Kleinsinger, George 1914- *AmSCAP 66*
Kleinsmid, Rufus Bernhard Von 1875-
  WhWNAA
Kleiser, Grenville 1868-1953 *AmA&B*, *AmLY*,
  ChPo S1
Kleist, Ewald Christian Von 1715-1759 *BiD&SB*,
  CasWL, *DcEuL*, *EvEuW*, *OxGer*,
  Pen Eur, *REn*
Kleist, Heinrich Von 1777-1811 *AtlBL*,
  BiD&SB, *CasWL*, *CnThe*, *CyWA*,
  DcEuL, *EuA*, *EvEuW*, *McGWD*, *OxGer*,
  Pen Eur, *RCom*, *REn*, *REnWD*
Kleist, James Aloysius 1873- *WhWNAA*
Klement, Frank L 1908- *ConAu 9R*,
  WrD 1976
Klemer, Richard Hudson 1918-1972 *Au&Wr*,
  ConAu 5R, *ConAu 37*
Klemin, Diana *ChPo S2*, *ConAu 49*
Klemke, E D 1926- *ConAu 25*
Klemke, Werner 1917- *WhGrA*
Klemm, C *Alli Sup*
Klemm, Edward G, Jr. 1910- *ConAu 57*
Klemm, Friedrich Gustav 1802-1867 *BiD&SB*
Klemm, Gustav 1897-1947 *AmSCAP 66*
Klemm, Louis Richard 1845-1916 *Alli Sup*,
  DcAmA, *DcNAA*, *OhA&B*
Klemm, Roberta K 1884- *ConAu 61*
Klemm, William Robert 1934- *IndAu 1917*
Klempner, Irving M 1924- *ConAu 53*
Klempner, John 1898-1972 *AmA&B*, *AmNov*,
  ConAu 37
Klen, Yuriy 1891-1947 *ModSL 2*
Klenk, Robert W 1934- *ConAu 29*
Klenner, John 1899-1955 *AmSCAP 66*

Klenz, William 1915- *ConAu 5R*
Klepper, Jochen 1903-1942 *EncWL*, *OxGer*
Klepper, Michael M 1934- *AmSCAP 66*
Klerer, Melvin 1926- *ConAu 21*
Klesel, Melchior *OxGer*
Klestadt, Albert 1913- *Au&Wr*
Klett, Guy S 1897- *ConAu P-1*
Klettenberg, Susanna Katharina Von 1723-1774
  OxGer
Klewin, W Thomas 1921- *ConAu 29*
Kleyman, Paul 1945- *ConAu 57*
Kleyn, Johannes Petrus 1760-1805 *CasWL*
Klibansky, Raymond *Au&Wr*
Klickmann, F Henri 1885- *AmSCAP 66*
Klickmann, Flora *ChPo*, *ChPo S1*
Klicpera, Vaclav Kliment 1792-1859 *BiD&SB*,
  CasWL, *CnThe*, *REnWD*
Klier, Heinrich 1926- *Au&Wr*
Kliever, Lonnie D 1931- *ConAu 29*
Kliewer, Warren 1931- *ConAu 45*, *DrAP 1975*
Klijn, Hendrik Harmsen 1773-1856 *CasWL*
Klikspaan *CasWL*, *EuA*, *EvEuW*
Klima, Ivan 1931- *ConAu 25*, *ModSL 2*
Klimas, Antanas 1924- *ConAu 41*
Kliment, Metropolitan Of Turnovo *CasWL*
Kliment Of Ohrid 840?-916 *CasWL*
Kliment Smolyatich *DcRusL*
Klimes, Robert 1926- *AmSCAP 66*
Klimisch, Sister Mary Jane 1920- *ConAu 17R*
Klimo, Jon *DrAP 1975*
Klimowicz, Barbara 1927- *ConAu 21*,
  SmATA 10
Klimt, Gustav 1862-1918 *AtlBL*, *OxGer*
Klin, George 1931- *ConAu 53*
Klinck, Carl Frederick 1908- *CanWr*, *CasWL*,
  ConAu 17R, *OxCan*, *OxCan Sup*,
  REnAL
Klinck, George Alfred 1903- *Au&Wr*,
  ConAu 9R
Klinckowstroem, Carl Graf Von 1884- *BiDPar*
Klindt-Jensen, Ole 1918- *Au&Wr*, *ConAu 21*
Kline, A C *Alli Sup*
Kline, Burton 1877- *AmA&B*, *AmLY*,
  WhWNAA
Kline, Franz 1910-1962 *REn*
Kline, George 1757?-1820 *AmA&B*
Kline, George L 1921- *AuNews 1*,
  ConAu 17R
Kline, Lloyd W 1931- *ConAu 33*, *WrD 1976*
Kline, Magdalena 1838-1921 *OhA&B*
Kline, Marion Justus 1871-1934 *DcNAA*
Kline, Morris 1908- *ConAu 5R*, *WrD 1976*
Kline, Nancy Meadors 1946- *ConAu 57*
Kline, Norman 1935- *ConAu 25*
Kline, Otis Adelbert 1891-1946 *DcNAA*
Kline, Peter 1936- *ConAu 25*, *WrD 1976*
Kline, William Jay 1848- *WhWNAA*
Klineberg, Otto 1899- *AmA&B*
Klinefelter, Lee M 1892- *WhWNAA*
Klinefelter, Walter 1899- *ConAu 9R*
Kling, Robert E, Jr. 1920- *ConAu 29*
Kling, Simcha 1922- *ConAu 13R*
Klingaman, Orie Erb 1874-1941 *IndAu 1917*
Klingberg, Frank Joseph 1883- *WhWNAA*
Klingemann, Carl *Alli Sup*
Klingemann, Ernst August Friedrich 1777-1831
  BbD, *BiD&SB*, *OxGer*
Klingensmith, Don Joseph 1901- *WrD 1976*
Klinger, Eric 1933- *ConAu 33*, *WrD 1976*
Klinger, Friedrich Maximilian Von 1752-1831
  BbD, *BiD&SB*, *CasWL*, *DcEuL*, *EuA*,
  EvEuW, *McGWD*, *OxGer*, *Pen Eur*,
  REn
Klinger, Kurt 1914- *ConAu 17R*
Klinger, Kurt 1928- *CnMD*, *CrCD*
Klingle, George *Alli Sup*, *ChPo*, *ChPo S1*,
  DcAmA
Klingsor, Tristan 1874- *OxFr*, *Pen Eur*
Klingstedt, Joe Lars 1938- *ConAu 53*
Klink, Johanna L 1918- *ChPo S1*, *ConAu 61*
Klinkner, Anthony Ferdinand 1880- *CatA 1947*,
  WhWNAA
Klinkowitz, Jerome 1943- *ConAu 45*
Klippart, John Hancock 1823-1878 *Alli Sup*,
  DcNAA, *OhA&B*
Klipstein, Louis Frederick 1813-1878 *AmA*,
  DcNAA, *REnAL*
Klise, Eugene Storm 1908- *ConAu 5R*

Klise, Thomas S 1928- *ConAu 57*
Klitgaard, Mogens 1906-1945 *CasWL*, *EncWL*,
  Pen Eur
Klock, G C *ChPo*
Kloefkorn, William *DrAP 1975*
Kloetzli, Walter 1921- *ConAu 1R*
Klohr, John N 1869-1956 *AmSCAP 66*
Kloman, William C And Miles, T F *Alli Sup*
Klonglan, Gerald E 1936- *ConAu 41*
Klonowic, Sebastian Fabian 1545?-1602 *CasWL*,
  Pen Eur
Klonowicz, Sebastian Fabian 1545?-1602 *BbD*,
  BiD&SB
Kloos, Willem Johannes Theodorus 1859-1938
  CasWL, *ClDMEuL*, *Pen Eur*
Klooster, Fred H 1922- *ConAu 1R*,
  IndAu 1917
Klopp, Onno 1822-1903 *BiD&SB*
Kloppenburg, Boaventura 1919- *BiDPar*
Klopper, Harry 1920- *Au&Wr*
Klopstock, Friedrich Gottlieb 1724-1803 *BbD*,
  BiD&SB, *CasWL*, *ChPo*, *DcEuL*, *EuA*,
  EvEuW, *McGWD*, *NewC*, *OxEng*,
  OxGer, *Pen Eur*, *RCom*, *REn*
Klopstock, Meta 1728-1758 *OxGer*
Klos, Frank W, Jr. 1924- *ConAu 13R*
Klose, C L *Alli*
Klose, F G d1830 *Alli*
Klose, Kevin 1940- *ConAu 53*
Klose, Norma Cline 1936- *ConAu 17R*
Kloss, Charles Luther 1862-1931 *DcNAA*
Kloss, Phillips Wray 1902-1933 *ConAu P-1*,
  DcNAA
Kloss, Robert J 1935- *ConAu 45*
Klotman, Robert Howard 1918- *AmSCAP 66*,
  ConAu 53
Klotsche, Ernest Heinrich 1875- *WhWNAA*
Klotz, Christian Adolf 1738-1771 *OxGer*
Klotz, Leora 1928- *AmSCAP 66*
Klotz, Oscar 1878-1936 *DcNAA*
Klotz, Oskar 1878-1936 *AmLY*
Klubertanz, George Peter 1912- *AmA&B*,
  ConAu 5R
Kluckhohn, Clyde Kay Maben 1905-1960
  AmA&B, *REnAL*, *TwCA Sup*
Kluckhohn, Frank L 1907-1970 *ConAu 5R*,
  ConAu 29
Klug, Eugene F 1917- *ConAu 45*
Kluge, Alexander 1932- *AmA&B*, *ModGL*
Kluge, Eike-Henner W 1942- *ConAu 61*
Kluge, Kurt 1886-1940 *EvEuW*, *OxGer*
Kluger, James R 1939- *ConAu 29*
Kluger, Richard 1934- *ConAu 9R*
Klugh, Henry E 1927- *ConAu 53*
Kluibenschadel, Tuifelermaler Kassian *OxGer*
Kluwe, Mary Jean 1905- *ConAu 23*
Klyce, Scudder 1897-1933 *DcNAA*
Klychkov, Sergei Antonovich 1889- *EncWL*
Klychkov, Sergey 1889- *CasWL*, *DcRusL*
Klymasz, Robert B *OxCan Sup*
Klyuchevsky, Vasily Osipovich 1842-1911
  CasWL
Klyushnikov, Ivan Pavlovich 1811-1895 *CasWL*
Klyushnikov, Victor Petrovich 1841-1892 *CasWL*
Klyuyev, Nikolay Alexeyevich 1887-1937
  CasWL, *DcRusL*, *EncWL*, *EvEuW*,
  Pen Eur, *TwCW*
Kmoch, George *OxCan*
Kmoch, Hans 1897?-1973 *ConAu 41*
Knab, Frederick 1865-1918 *DcNAA*
Knachel, Philip A 1926- *ConAu 23*
Knaggs, Henry Guard *Alli Sup*
Knaggs, Nelson S 1907- *OhA&B*
Knaggs, Samuel *Alli*
Knaggs, Thomas *Alli*
Knapen, D M *Alli*
Knaplund, Paul Alexander 1885-1964 *AmA&B*,
  ConAu P-1
Knapp, Adeline 1860-1909 *ChPo*, *DcAmA*,
  DcNAA
Knapp, Albert 1798-1864 *BiD&SB*, *DcEuL*
Knapp, Arthur John *Alli Sup*
Knapp, Arthur May 1841-1921 *BiD&SB*,
  DcAmA, *DcNAA*
Knapp, Bettina *ConAu 13R*
Knapp, Bradford 1870- *TexWr*
Knapp, Charles 1868-1936 *DcNAA*
Knapp, Clarence Hollister *ChPo*, *ChPo S1*

Knapp, Clark D *Alli Sup*
Knapp, David A 1938- *ConAu 41*
Knapp, Ethel Marjorie *ChPo*
Knapp, F H *Alli*
Knapp, Francis 1672- *CyAL 1*
Knapp, Frederick H *Alli Sup*
Knapp, George Leonard 1872- *AmA&B*
Knapp, Grace Higley 1870- *WhWNAA*
Knapp, H J *Alli, BiDLA*
Knapp, H S *Alli Sup*
Knapp, Halsey B 1888- *WhWNAA*
Knapp, Horace S *DcNAA*
Knapp, J A *ChPo*
Knapp, J L *Alli, BiDLA*
Knapp, J Merrill 1914- *ConAu 53*
Knapp, J W *Alli*
Knapp, Jacob 1799-1874 *Alli Sup, DcNAA*
Knapp, Jacob Hermann 1832- *Alli Sup*
Knapp, John George Francis Henry *Alli Sup*
Knapp, John Leonard 1767-1845 *ChPo*
Knapp, Joseph G 1900- *ConAu 37*
Knapp, Joseph G 1924- *ConAu 41*
Knapp, Lewis M 1894- *ConAu 23*
Knapp, M L *Alli Sup*
Knapp, Martin Wells 1853-1901 *Alli Sup, DcNAA*
Knapp, Moses L 1799-1879 *DcNAA*
Knapp, N P *Alli Sup*
Knapp, Philip Coombs 1858- *AmLY*
Knapp, Robert Hampden 1915-1974 *ConAu 15, ConAu 53*
Knapp, Samuel Lorenzo 1783?-1838 *Alli, AmA, AmA&B, BiD&SB, CyAL 1, DcAmA, DcNAA, OxAm, REnAL*
Knapp, Samuel Lorenzo 1821-1888 *BbD*
Knapp, Shepherd 1873-1946 *DcNAA*
Knapp, Thad Johnson 1876-1933 *DcNAA*
Knapp, William Henry *Alli Sup*
Knapp, William Ireland 1835-1908 *Alli Sup, AmA&B, DcNAA*
Knapp-Fisher, Edward George 1915- *WrD 1976*
Knappen, Theodore M 1871- *WhWNAA*
Knapper, Christopher 1940- *ConAu 29*
Knapton, Ernest John 1902- *ConAu 1R, WrD 1976*
Knatchbull, Sir Edward *Alli*
Knatchbull, Sir Norton d1684 *Alli*
Knatchbull-Hugessen, Edward Hugessen 1829-1893 *Alli Sup, ChPo, ChPo S1, DcEnL, NewC, WhCL*
Knaub, Richard K 1928- *ConAu 41*
Knauff, Ellen Raphael *WrD 1976*
Knauss, William H 1839-1917 *OhA&B*
Knaust, Heinrich 1522?-1577 *OxGer*
Knauth, Joachim 1931- *CnMD*
Knauth, Percy 1914- *ConAu 57*
Knayston, Joannes *Alli*
Kneale, Martha Hurst 1909- *BiDPar*
Kneale, Nigel *ConDr*
Kneale, Thomas Nigel 1922- *Au&Wr*
Kneass, Strickland Landis 1861-1928 *DcNAA*
Kneass, William 1780-1840 *REnAL*
Knebel, Aaron G 1874-1938 *OhA&B*
Knebel, Fletcher 1911- *AmA&B, Au&Wr, AuNews 1, ConAu 1R, ConNov 1972, ConNov 1976, WrD 1976*
Knebel, Karl Ludwig Von 1744-1834 *OxGer*
Knecht, Edmund *Alli Sup*
Knecht, Karl Kae 1883- *WhWNAA*
Knecht, Robert Jean 1926- *ConAu 33, WrD 1976*
Kneebone, Geoffrey Thomas 1918- *ConAu 5R*
Kneebone, Peter *ChPo S1*
Kneeland, Abner 1774-1844 *Alli, DcAmA, DcNAA, OxAm*
Kneeland, Clarissa A 1873- *WhWNAA*
Kneeland, Samuel 1697-1769 *AmA&B*
Kneeland, Samuel 1821-1888 *Alli, Alli Sup, AmA&B, BiD&SB, DcAmA, DcNAA*
Kneeland, Samuel F *Alli Sup*
Kneeland, Stillman Foster 1845-1926 *AmA&B, DcNAA*
Kneer, Leo B *ChPo S1*
Kneese, Allen V 1930- *ConAu 13R*
Knef, Hildegard 1925- *ConAu 45*
Kneip, Jakob 1881-1958 *OxGer*
Kneipple, Edith Elizabeth 1902- *AmA&B*
Knell, Henry *Alli Sup*

Knell, John George *Alli Sup*
Knell, Paul *Alli*
Knell, Thomas *Alli*
Kneller, Sir Godfrey 1649?-1723 *AtlBL, REn*
Kneller, John W 1916- *ConAu 17R*
Knepler, Henry 1922- *ConAu 23*
Kneppelhout, Johannes 1814-1885 *CasWL, EuA, EvEuW*
Knepper, Mamie C 1884- *OhA&B*
Knevels, Mrs. D C *Alli Sup*
Knevels, Gertrude 1881-1962 *AmA&B, REnAL, WhWNAA*
Knevet, Ralph -1671? *Alli, CasWL, ChPo*
Knew, George *MnBBF*
Knewstub, John *Alli*
Knezevich, Stephen J 1920- *ConAu 5R*
Kniashnin, Jakov Borissovitch 1742-1791 *BbD, BiD&SB*
Kniaznin, Franciszek Dionizy 1750-1807 *BiD&SB, CasWL, EvEuW, Pen Eur*
Knibbs, Harry Herbert 1874-1945 *AmA&B, NewC, TwCA, TwCA Sup*
Knibbs, Henry Herbert 1874-1945 *ChPo, ChPo S1, ChPo S2, DcNAA, WhWNAA*
Knickerbacker, Joseph Foster 1824-1882 *DcNAA*
Knickerbocker, Charles Herrick 1922- *AmA&B, Au&Wr, ConAu 13R*
Knickerbocker, Cholly *AmA&B*
Knickerbocker, Diedrich 1783-1859 *AmA&B, DcEnL, DcNAA, EvLB, OxAm, OxEng*
Knickerbocker, Hubert Renfro 1898-1949 *AmA&B, DcNAA, REnAL*
Knickerbocker, Joseph Foster *Alli Sup*
Knickerbocker, Junior *DcNAA*
Knickerbocker, Kenneth L 1905- *ConAu 5R*
Knickerbocker, William Skinkle 1892- *AmA&B, WhWNAA*
Kniel, S M *ChPo*
Knieste, Adam 1917- *AmSCAP 66*
Knifesmith *ConAu XR*
Kniffen, Fred B 1900- *ConAu 1R*
Kniffin, William Henry 1874- *WhWNAA*
Knigge, Baron Adolf Franz Heinrich Von 1752-1796 *BiD&SB, CasWL, DcEuL, EvEuW, OxGer*
Knight *Alli*
Knight, Madam *Alli*
Knight, A G *ChPo S1*
Knight, Adam *AmA&B, ConAu XR*
Knight, Adele Ferguson 1867- *AmLY, WhWNAA*
Knight, Alfred E *Alli Sup*
Knight, Ann C *Alli, OxCan*
Knight, Anne Katherine 1933- *WrD 1976*
Knight, Annette F C *Alli Sup*
Knight, Archibald Patterson 1849-1935 *DcNAA*
Knight, Arthur 1916- *ConAu 41*
Knight, Arthur George *Alli Sup*
Knight, Arthur Lee *Alli Sup, MnBBF*
Knight, Arthur Winfield 1937- *ConAu 53, DrAF 1976, DrAP 1975*
Knight, Austin Melvin 1854-1927 *DcNAA*
Knight, Barbara Jean *BlkAW*
Knight, Beatrice 1925- *AmSCAP 66*
Knight, Bernard 1931- *Au&Wr, ConAu 49, WrD 1976*
Knight, Bertram 1904- *Au&Wr, WrD 1976*
Knight, Brook J *Alli Sup*
Knight, C *Alli, Alli Sup, BiDLA*
Knight, Cameron *Alli Sup*
Knight, Camilla J *ChPo*
Knight, Charles *Alli Sup*
Knight, Charles 1791-1873 *Alli, Alli Sup, BbD, BiD&SB, BrAu 19, CasWL, ChPo, Chmbr 3, DcEnA, DcEnL, DcLEnL, EvLB, NewC, OxEng*
Knight, Charles D *Alli Sup*
Knight, Charles Henry *Alli*
Knight, Charles Landon 1867-1933 *AuNews 2, OhA&B*
Knight, Charles Robert 1874-1953 *IlCB 1956*
Knight, Charles W 1891- *ConAu P-1*
Knight, Clayton 1891-1969 *AuBYP, ConAu P-1*
Knight, Clifford 1886- *AmA&B, WhWNAA*
Knight, Cornelia 1757-1837 *DcEnL*
Knight, Cuthbert *Alli*

Knight, D *Alli Sup*
Knight, D M *Alli*
Knight, Damon 1922- *ConAu 49, SmATA 9, WorAu, WrD 1976*
Knight, David *ConAu XR*
Knight, David C *AuBYP*
Knight, David Marcus 1936- *ConAu 57*
Knight, Derek *MnBBF*
Knight, Douglas M 1921- *ConAu 49*
Knight, E A Lampriere *ChPo S1*
Knight, E Cornelia *Alli, BiDLA*
Knight, E P H *Alli*
Knight, Edgar Wallace 1886-1953 *AmA&B*
Knight, Edward *Alli, ChPo*
Knight, Edward Frederick 1853- *Alli Sup*
Knight, Edward Henry 1824-1883 *Alli Sup, DcAmA, DcNAA*
Knight, Enoch *Alli Sup*
Knight, Eric Mowbray 1897-1943 *AuBYP, CnDAL, CyWA, REn, REnAL, TwCA, TwCA Sup, WhCL*
Knight, Etheridge 1931- *BlkAW, ConAu 23, ConP 1975, DrAP 1975, LivBA, WrD 1976*
Knight, Etheridge 1933- *ConP 1970*
Knight, Everett Warren 1919- *Au&Wr, ConAu 33*
Knight, Francis *Alli*
Knight, Francis Arnold 1852- *BiD&SB*
Knight, Francis Edgar 1905- *Au&Wr*
Knight, Frank 1905- *WhCL*
Knight, Frank H 1885-1972 *ConAu 33*
Knight, Frederick 1791-1849 *CyAL 1, DcAmA, DcNAA*
Knight, Frederick Butterfield 1891-1948 *DcNAA, WhWNAA*
Knight, Frederick Winn *Alli Sup*
Knight, Frida 1910- *ConAu 49*
Knight, Frideswide Frances Emma 1910- *Au&Wr*
Knight, G B *Alli*
Knight, G Norman 1891- *ConAu 25*
Knight, Gareth *WrD 1976*
Knight, George Angus Fulton 1909- *ConAu 1R, WrD 1976*
Knight, George Thomson 1850-1911 *DcNAA*
Knight, George Wells 1858-1932 *Alli Sup, DcAmA, DcNAA, OhA&B*
Knight, George Wilson 1897- *Au&Wr, ChPo S1, ConAu 13R, DcLEnL, NewC, Pen Eng, REn, REnAL, TwCA, TwCA Sup, WrD 1976*
Knight, Glee 1947- *ConAu 57, DrAP 1975*
Knight, Gowen *Alli*
Knight, Grant Cochran 1893-1956 *AmA&B*
Knight, Mrs. H C *Alli*
Knight, H H *Alli Sup*
Knight, H Lady Luxborough *Alli*
Knight, H Ralph 1895- *ConAu 25*
Knight, Harold V 1907- *ConAu 23*
Knight, Hattie M 1908- *ConAu 29*
Knight, Helen Cross *Alli Sup, AmA&B, ChPo S2, DcNAA*
Knight, Henry *Alli, Alli Sup*
Knight, Henry Cogswell 1788?-1835 *Alli, AmA, AmA&B, ChPo, CyAL 1, DcAmA, DcNAA, REnAL*
Knight, Henry DeBoyne 1898- *Au&Wr*
Knight, Henry Gally 1786-1846 *Alli, ChPo, Chmbr 2, EvLB*
Knight, Henry H *Alli Sup*
Knight, Hester 1920- *Au&Wr*
Knight, Hilary 1926- *AuBYP, ChPo, ChPo S1, ChPo S2, IlCB 1966*
Knight, Holford 1877- *WhLA*
Knight, Hugh McCown 1905- *ConAu 5R*
Knight, Ione Kemp 1922- *ConAu 37*
Knight, Isabel F 1930- *ConAu 25*
Knight, J A *Alli*
Knight, James *Alli, BiDLA, ConAu XR*
Knight, James 1650?-1720 *OxCan*
Knight, James 1793-1863 *Alli Sup*
Knight, James 1810-1887 *Alli Sup, BiDSA, DcAmA, DcNAA*
Knight, James Allen 1918- *ConAu 13R, WrD 1976*
Knight, James B 1929- *AmSCAP 66*
Knight, John *Alli, BiDLA*

Knight, John 1852- *ChPo S1*
Knight, John 1906- *Au&Wr, WrD 1976*
Knight, John Collyer *Alli, Alli Sup*
Knight, John S, III *AuNews 2*
Knight, John Shively *AuNews 2*
Knight, Jonathan 1789- *CyAL 1*
Knight, Joseph *Alli, BiDLA*
Knight, Joseph 1829-1907 *Alli Sup, BrAu 19, DcEnA Ap, NewC*
Knight, Joseph Philip 1812-1887 *NewC*
Knight, Julia *ChPo*
Knight, K G 1921- *ConAu 25*
Knight, Karl Frederick 1930- *ConAu 17R, WrD 1976*
Knight, Katharine *ChPo*
Knight, Laura 1877- *ChPo*
Knight, Legh *Alli Sup*
Knight, Lewis Washington 1816-1904 *DcNAA*
Knight, Lucian Lamar 1868-1933 *AmA&B, BiDSA, ChPo, DcNAA, WhWNAA*
Knight, Mallory T *ConAu XR*
Knight, Marcia *ChPo S1*
Knight, Marcus 1903- *Au&Wr*
Knight, Margaret Kennedy Horsey 1903- *Au&Wr, ConAu P-1, WrD 1976*
Knight, Matthew Richey *Alli Sup*
Knight, Maude *ChPo S2*
Knight, Maxwell 1900- *ConAu P-1*
Knight, Miriam S *Alli Sup*
Knight, Nicholas 1861- *WhWNAA*
Knight, Norman 1891- *WrD 1976*
Knight, Norman L 1895- *ConAu 23*
Knight, Oliver 1919- *ConAu 21*
Knight, Olivia 1830?- *PoIre*
Knight, Ora Willis 1874-1913 *DcNAA*
Knight, Paul Emerson 1925- *ConAu 13R*
Knight, Peter *AuBYP*
Knight, R *BbtC*
Knight, Richard Donald 1913- *Au&Wr*
Knight, Richard Payne 1750-1824 *Alli, BiDLA, Chmbr 2, DcEnL*
Knight, Robert *Alli, Alli Sup, BiDLA*
Knight, Robert S *Alli Sup*
Knight, Roderic C 1942- *ConAu 61*
Knight, Roger *Alli*
Knight, Roy Clement 1907- *Au&Wr, ConAu 13R*
Knight, Roy Gaveston *ChPo S2*
Knight, Ruth Adams 1898-1974 *AuBYP, ConAu 5R, ConAu 49, MorJA, OhA&B*
Knight, Mrs. S G *Alli Sup*
Knight, Samuel 1674-1746 *Alli, BiDLA, DcEnL*
Knight, Sarah Kemble 1666-1727 *AmA, AmA&B, CnDAL, DcAmA, EvLB, OxAm, Pen Am, REn, REnAL*
Knight, Thomas *Alli, BiDLA*
Knight, Thomas d1820 *Alli*
Knight, Thomas Andrew 1758-1838 *Alli, BiDLA*
Knight, Thomas Arthur 1876-1946 *OhA&B*
Knight, Thomas Frederick *BbtC*
Knight, Thomas S 1921- *ConAu 17R*
Knight, Titus *Alli*
Knight, Valentine Catherwood *Alli Sup*
Knight, Vick 1908- *AmSCAP 66*
Knight, Vick R, Jr. 1928- *ConAu 45*
Knight, Virginia *OxCan*
Knight, W H *Alli Sup*
Knight, Walker L 1924- *ConAu 37*
Knight, Wallace E *DrRAF 1976*
Knight, William *Alli, Alli Sup, ChPo S1*
Knight, William 1790-1878 *Alli Sup*
Knight, William Allen 1863-1957 *AmA&B*
Knight, William Allen 1869- *ChPo S1*
Knight, William Angus 1836-1916 *Alli Sup, BiD&SB, ChPo, DcEuL, NewC*
Knight, William Henry *Alli Sup, ChPo S2*
Knight, William Nicholas 1939- *ConAu 37, WrD 1976*
Knight, William P *Alli*
Knight, William Stanley Macbean 1869- *WhLA*
Knight, William Thomas *Alli Sup*
Knight, Wilson 1897- *LongC*
Knight, Wynter Frore *Alli Sup*
Knight-Adkin, James Harry 1879- *WhLA*
Knight-Patterson, W M *ConAu XR, WrD 1976*

Knightley, Miss D G *MnBBF*
Knightley, Phillip 1929- *ConAu 25*
Knightley, Thomas Edward *Alli Sup*
Knighton, F *Alli*
Knighton, Henry *Alli, DcEnL*
Knighton, Sir William d1836 *Alli*
Knighton, William 1834- *Alli, Alli Sup*
Knights, Helen C *Alli*
Knights, Leslie Douglas 1914- *Au&Wr*
Knights, Lionel Charles 1906- *Au&Wr, ConAu 5R, DcLEnL, Pen Eng, TwCA Sup, WrD 1976*
Knights, Peter R 1938- *ConAu 37*
Knipe, Alden Arthur 1870-1950 *AmA&B, AmLY, JBA 1934, JBA 1951, WhWNAA*
Knipe, Arthur Alden 1870-1950 *ChPo, ChPo S1*
Knipe, Eliza *Alli, BiDLA*
Knipe, Emilie Benson 1870-1958 *AmA&B, AmLY, ChPo, JBA 1934, JBA 1951, WhWNAA*
Knipe, Humphry 1941- *ConAu 37*
Knipe, Rest *Alli*
Knipe, Wayne Bishop, III 1946- *ConAu 53*
Knipp, Charles T 1869- *WhWNAA*
Knipperdollink, Bernhard d1536 *OxGer*
Knipschield, Don 1940- *ConAu 5R*
Knish, Ann *AmA&B, ChPo, WhWNAA*
Knist, F Emma 1948- *ConAu 53*
Knister, Raymond 1900-1932 *CanNov, CanWr, ChPo, DcLEnL, DcNAA, OxCan*
Knittel, John 1891- *Au&Wr, TwCA, TwCA Sup*
Knittermeyer, Hinrich Johann 1891- *WhLA*
Knittle, Rhea Mansfield 1883-1955 *OhA&B*
Knivelton, Sayntlowe *Alli*
Knobel, Elizabeth *WhWNAA*
Knobelsdorff, Georg Wenzeslaus Von 1699-1753 *OxGer*
Knoblaugh, Edward G *ChPo S1*
Knoblaugh, H Edward 1904- *CatA 1947*
Knoble, Cliff 1892- *OhA&B, WhWNAA*
Knobler, Nathan 1926- *ConAu 33*
Knobloch, Arthur Frederick *Alli Sup*
Knobloch, Edgar *Au&Wr*
Knoblock, Edward 1874-1945 *AmA&B, EvLB, ModWD, NewC, REn, REnAL*
Knocker, Edward *Alli Sup*
Knodt, William Charles 1936- *BiDPar*
Knoebl, Kuno 1936- *ConAu 25*
Knoefel, Peter Klerner 1906- *IndAu 1917*
Knoepfle, John 1923- *ConAu 13R, ConP 1970, ConP 1975, DrAP 1975, WrD 1976*
Knoepflmacher, U C 1931- *ConAu 13R*
Knoeppel, Charles Edward 1881-1936 *DcNAA*
Knoerle, Jeanne 1928- *ConAu 45*
Knokes, John *Alli*
Knoles, George Harmon 1907- *AmA&B, ConAu 5R*
Knoll, Gerald M 1942- *ConAu 29*
Knoll, Horton Budd 1906- *IndAu 1917*
Knoll, Robert Edwin 1922- *ConAu 1R*
Knollenberg, Bernhard 1892-1973 *AmA&B, ConAu 21, ConAu 41, IndAu 1917*
Knolles, Richard 1525?-1610 *Alli, BrAu, CasWL, Chmbr 1, DcEnA, DcEnL, DcEuL, EvLB, NewC, OxEng*
Knollis, Francis d1596 *Alli*
Knollis, Francis M *Alli*
Knollys, Bodley *MnBBF*
Knollys, Hanserd *Alli*
Knollys, Henry *Alli Sup*
Knollys, Wilfred E *ChPo*
Knollys, William Wallingford *Alli Sup*
Knoop, Wera Ouckama 1902-1921 *OxGer*
Knop, Werner 1912?-1970 *ConAu 29*
Knopf, Alfred A 1892- *AmA&B, REnAL*
Knopf, Blanche d1966 *AmA&B*
Knopf, Carl Sumner 1889-1942 *DcNAA, OhA&B, WhWNAA*
Knopf, Edwin H 1899- *AmSCAP 66*
Knopf, Sigard Adolphus 1857-1940 *AmLY, DcNAA*
Knopf, Terry Ann 1940- *ConAu 25, WrD 1976*
Knorr, Albert Scofield 1929- *ConAu 25*

Knorr VonRosenroth, Christian 1636-1689 *OxGer*
Knorring, Baroness Sofia Margareta Von 1797-1848 *BbD, BiD&SB, CasWL, EuA, EvEuW*
Knortz, Karl 1841-1918 *Alli Sup, AmLY, BiD&SB, CasWL, DcAmA, OhA&B*
Knot, G C P *Alli, BiDLA*
Knott, Alfred *Alli Sup, ChPo*
Knott, Bill 1927- *ConAu XR, SmATA 3, WrD 1976*
Knott, Bill 1940- *AmA&B, ConP 1975, RAdv 1, WrD 1976*
Knott, Edward 1580-1656? *Alli, DcEnL*
Knott, Frederick M P 1918- *EncM&D*
Knott, Henry *Alli Sup*
Knott, Herman *NewC*
Knott, Jean 1883- *WhWNAA*
Knott, John *Alli*
Knott, John F *Alli Sup*
Knott, John R, Jr. 1937- *ConAu 57*
Knott, John William 1822-1870 *Alli Sup*
Knott, Laura A *WhWNAA*
Knott, Luella *ChPo S1*
Knott, M O'Malley 1876?- *Br&AmS*
Knott, Peter N *PoIre*
Knott, Suie E S *ChPo S2*
Knott, Thomas Albert 1880-1945 *AmA&B, REnAL, WhWNAA*
Knott, William Cecil, Jr. 1927- *AmA&B, ConAu 5R, SmATA 3, WrD 1976*
Knott, William Kilborn 1940- *ConP 1970, CrCAP, WrD 1976*
Knowler, William d1767 *Alli*
Knowler, William d1773 *Alli*
Knowles, Alison 1933- *ConAu 17R*
Knowles, Ansel Merton 1874-1956 *IndAu 1917*
Knowles, Asa S 1909- *ConAu 29*
Knowles, Cecilia 1899- *Au&Wr*
Knowles, Charles *Alli*
Knowles, Daniel Clark 1836-1913 *DcNAA*
Knowles, Daniel Clarke *Alli Sup*
Knowles, David 1896-1974 *Au&Wr, ConAu 5R, ConAu 53, WorAu*
Knowles, Davidson *ChPo, ChPo S1*
Knowles, Dorothy 1906- *ConAu 25, WrD 1976*
Knowles, Edward Hadarezer *Alli Sup*
Knowles, Ellin J 1835?-1929 *AmLY, DcNAA*
Knowles, Elsie A G 1908- *BiDPar*
Knowles, Frederick Lawrence 1869-1905 *ChPo, ChPo S1, ChPo S2, DcAmA, DcNAA*
Knowles, Frederick W 1911- *BiDPar*
Knowles, G H *MnBBF*
Knowles, Gaye 1905- *Au&Wr*
Knowles, George *Alli*
Knowles, George Parker 1797- *Alli*
Knowles, Henry *Alli Sup*
Knowles, Henry P 1912- *ConAu 61*
Knowles, Herbert 1798-1817 *Alli, BbD, BiD&SB, ChPo S1, Chmbr 2, DcEnL, EvLB*
Knowles, Horace J *ChPo*
Knowles, J C *Alli*
Knowles, James *Alli*
Knowles, James Davis 1798-1838 *Alli, DcAmA, DcNAA*
Knowles, James Hinton *Alli Sup*
Knowles, James Sheridan 1784-1862 *Alli, BbD, BiD&SB, BrAu 19, CasWL, ChPo, Chmbr 2, DcEnA, DcEnL, DcLEnL, EvLB, McGWD, MouLC 3, NewC, OxEng, PoIre, REn*
Knowles, Sir James Thomas 1831-1908 *DcEuL, NewC*
Knowles, John *Alli*
Knowles, John 1926- *AmA&B, Au&Wr, CasWL, ConAu 17R, ConLC 1, ConLC 4, ConNov 1972, ConNov 1976, DrAF 1976, RAdv 1, SmATA 8, WorAu, WrD 1976*
Knowles, John Dickinson *Alli Sup*
Knowles, John Harris 1832-1908 *DcNAA*
Knowles, Joseph W 1922- *ConAu 23*
Knowles, Louis L 1947- *ConAu 29*
Knowles, Mabel Winifred 1875- *MnBBF, WhLA*
Knowles, Malcolm Shepherd 1913- *ConAu 5R*

Knowles, Michael Clive David 1906- *WrD 1976*
Knowles, Morris 1869- *WhWNAA*
Knowles, N K *Alli Sup*
Knowles, Redvers Victor 1900- *Au&Wr*
Knowles, Richard *Alli, BiDLA*
Knowles, Richard Brinsley 1820-1882 *Alli, Alli Sup, PoIre*
Knowles, Robert Edward 1868-1946 *DcNAA, OxCan, WhWNAA*
Knowles, Sarah E *Alli Sup*
Knowles, Susanne 1911- *Au&Wr, ChPo S2, WrD 1976*
Knowles, Sylvia H *ChPo*
Knowles, Thomas *Alli, BiDLA*
Knowles, Thomas 1723?-1802 *Alli, DcEnL*
Knowles, Thomas E *MnBBF*
Knowles, Vernon 1890- *ChPo S2*
Knowles, W E *ChPo S1*
Knowles, William 1806-1889 *OhA&B*
Knowlles, Richard *Alli*
Knowls, Thomas *Alli*
Knowlton, Charles 1800-1850 *DcNAA*
Knowlton, Daniel Chauncey 1876- *WhWNAA*
Knowlton, Derrick 1921- *ConAu 57, WrD 1976*
Knowlton, Donald Snow 1892- *ChPo, OhA&B, WhWNAA*
Knowlton, Edgar C, Jr. 1921- *ConAu 41*
Knowlton, Frank Hall 1860-1926 *AmLY, DcAmA, DcNAA*
Knowlton, Miss H O *ChPo*
Knowlton, Helen Mary 1832-1918 *Alli Sup, DcAmA, DcNAA*
Knowlton, I C *Alli Sup*
Knowlton, Isaac Case 1820-1894 *DcNAA*
Knowlton, J B *ChPo*
Knowlton, J Burnett *ChPo S2*
Knowlton, J M *Alli Sup*
Knowlton, James Albert 1855?-1937 *IndAu 1917*
Knowlton, Miles Justin 1825-1874 *Alli Sup, DcAmA, DcNAA*
Knowlton, Robert A 1914- *ConAu 1R*
Knowlton, Thomas d1782 *Alli*
Knowlton, William Augustus 1838-1933 *OhA&B*
Knowlton, William H 1927- *ConAu 17R, WrD 1976*
Knowlton, William Smith *ChPo, ChPo S1*
Knox, Doctor *Alli*
Knox, A A *Alli*
Knox, A E *Alli*
Knox, Adeline 1845- *BiD&SB, DcAmA, DcNAA*
Knox, Alexander *Alli Sup*
Knox, Alexander 1757-1831 *Alli, BiDLA, BrAu 19*
Knox, Alexander 1907- *CanNov*
Knox, Alexander A *Alli Sup*
Knox, Alexander Andrew 1818-1891 *PoIre*
Knox, Ann *ChPo S1*
Knox, Arthur Edward 1809?- *Alli Sup*
Knox, Bill 1928- *Au&Wr, ConAu XR, WrD 1976*
Knox, Calvin M *AuBYP, ConAu XR, ThBJA*
Knox, Charles *Alli*
Knox, Charles Eugene 1833-1900 *Alli Sup, DcAmA, DcNAA*
Knox, Cleone *ConAu XR*
Knox, Collie 1897- *Au&Wr, WrD 1976*
Knox, Mrs. Craig *DcEnL*
Knox, David B *PoIre*
Knox, David Broughton 1916- *Au&Wr, WrD 1976*
Knox, David H, Jr. 1943- *ConAu 41*
Knox, Donald E 1936- *ConAu 45*
Knox, Edmund Arbuthnott 1847- *WhLA*
Knox, Edmund George Valpy 1881- *Au&Wr, ChPo, ChPo S1, ChPo S2, ConAu 29, DcLEnL, EvLB, LongC, NewC, TwCA, TwCA Sup*
Knox, Etta Duncan 1892- *TexWr*
Knox, Franklin 1874-1944 *AmA&B*
Knox, George *Alli, BiDLA*
Knox, George Alexander 1919- *WrD 1976*
Knox, George Edward *Alli Sup*
Knox, George William 1853-1912 *DcAmA, DcNAA*
Knox, Gilbert *OxCan*

Knox, Helen Ada *ChPo S2*
Knox, Helen Boardman 1870-1947 *AmSCAP 66*
Knox, Henry Macdonald 1916- *Au&Wr, ConAu 13R, WrD 1976*
Knox, Hugh *Alli*
Knox, Isa Craig 1831-1903 *Alli Sup, BrAu 19, ChPo, ChPo S1, ChPo S2, HsB&A*
Knox, J H *Alli Sup, PoIre*
Knox, J H Mason 1872- *WhWNAA*
Knox, J Mason *ChPo S2*
Knox, Jackson *HsB&A*
Knox, Jacqueline Lloyd *BlkAW*
Knox, James *ChPo, ChPo S1*
Knox, James Samuel 1872- *WhWNAA*
Knox, Jean Lindsay *BlkAW*
Knox, Jessie Juliet *AmLY*
Knox, John *Alli, BbtC, Chmbr 1, OxCan*
Knox, John d1790 *Alli*
Knox, John 1505?-1572 *Alli, BbD, BiD&SB, BrAu, CasWL, DcEnA, DcEnL, EvLB, NewC, OxEng, Pen Eng, RCom, REn*
Knox, John 1900- *AmA&B, Au&Wr, ConAu 13R, WrD 1976*
Knox, John 1905- *TexWr*
Knox, John Armoy 1850-1906 *Alli Sup, DcNAA*
Knox, John Ballenger 1909- *ConAu P-1*
Knox, John Clark 1881-1966 *AmA&B*
Knox, John D *Alli Sup*
Knox, John H *Alli Sup*
Knox, John Jay 1828-1892 *Alli Sup, DcAmA, DcNAA*
Knox, John P *Alli*
Knox, Julie LeClerc *IndAu 1917*
Knox, Kathleen *Alli Sup, ChPo S2, PoIre*
Knox, Loren L *Alli Sup*
Knox, Lucy 1845-1884 *Alli Sup, PoIre*
Knox, Martin VanBuren 1841- *DcAmA, DcNAA*
Knox, Mertice M C Buck 1870- *WhWNAA*
Knox, Minnie Faegre *WhWNAA*
Knox, Ned *ChPo*
Knox, Robert *Alli*
Knox, Robert 1641?-1720 *Alli, DcLEnL*
Knox, Robert 1791-1862 *Alli Sup*
Knox, Robert Buick 1918- *ConAu 25, WrD 1976*
Knox, Ronald Arbuthnott 1888-1957 *BkC 6, CatA 1947, ChPo S2, DcLEnL, EncM&D, EvLB, LongC, NewC, OxEng, TwCA, TwCA Sup, TwCW*
Knox, Rose Bell 1879- *AmA&B, JBA 1934, JBA 1951, WhWNAA*
Knox, Samuel 1756-1832 *DcNAA*
Knox, Samuel James 1918- *Au&Wr, WrD 1976*
Knox, T *Alli, BiDLA*
Knox, T W *BiDSA*
Knox, Thomas *Alli, Alli Sup, BiDLA*
Knox, Thomas 1818-1879 *ChPo S1*
Knox, Thomas Francis 1822-1882 *Alli Sup*
Knox, Thomas Wallace 1835-1896 *Alli Sup, AmA, AmA&B, BbD, BiD&SB, CarSB, DcAmA, DcNAA, MnBBF, REnAL*
Knox, Vera Huntingdon *ConAu 9R*
Knox, Vicesimus 1752-1821 *Alli, BiDLA, CasWL, ChPo, Chmbr 2, DcEnL, EvLB, OxEng*
Knox, W J *BbtC*
Knox, W Mayne *PoIre*
Knox, Walter 1863-1892 *IndAu 1816*
Knox, Warren Barr 1925- *ConAu 49*
Knox, William *Alli, BiDLA, BiDLA Sup, Chmbr 2*
Knox, William 1789-1825 *Alli, BiD&SB, ChPo, ChPo S2, DcEnL, EvLB*
Knox, William 1928- *ConAu 1R, WrD 1976*
Knox, William, Bishop Of Derry *BiDLA*
Knox-Johnston, Robin 1939- *Au&Wr, ConAu 29, WrD 1976*
Knox-Johnston, William Robert Patrick 1939- *WrD 1976*
Knox-Little *Alli Sup*
Knubel, Frederick Hermann 1870-1945 *DcNAA*
Knudsen, Carl Wilhelm 1818-1896 *DcNAA*
Knudsen, Erik 1922- *CasWL, Pen Eur*
Knudsen, Hans August Heinrich 1886-1971 *ConAu 29*

Knudsen, Jakob Christian Lindberg 1858-1917 *CasWL, ClDMEuL, EncWL, EuA, Pen Eur*
Knudsen, K *BlkAW*
Knudsen, Margrethe June 1934- *WrD 1976*
Knudsen, Peter Axel 1934- *WrD 1976*
Knudsen, R R *ConAu XR*
Knudson, Albert Cornelius 1873- *AmLY, WhWNAA*
Knudson, Danny Alan 1940- *ConAu 61, WrD 1976*
Knudson, Harris R, Jr. *WhPNW*
Knudson, R R *SmATA 7*
Knudson, Rozanne R 1932- *ConAu 33, SmATA 7, WrD 1976*
Knusel, Jack Leonard 1923- *ConAu 25, WrD 1976*
Knut *NewC*
Knuth, Helen 1912- *ConAu 53*
Knutson, Jeanne N 1934- *ConAu 41*
Knutson, Kent S 1924-1973 *ConAu 33, ConAu 41*
Knutt, Mrs. *Alli Sup*
Knyazhnin, Yakov Borisovich 1742-1791 *CasWL, DcRusL*
Knyvett, Sir Henry d1598 *OxEng*
Ko, Hung 253?-333? *CasWL*
K'o, Ling *DcOrL 1*
Ko, Won 1925- *ConAu 61, DrAP 1975*
Kobal, John 1943- *ConAu 61*
Kobayashi, Issa 1763-1828 *CasWL, DcOrL 1, REn*
Kobayashi, Masako Matsuno 1935- *AuBYP, ConAu 5R*
Kobayashi, Noritake 1932- *ConAu 53*
Kobayashi, Takiji 1903-1933 *CasWL, DcOrL 1, EncWL Sup, Pen Cl*
Kobbe, Gustav 1857-1918 *Alli Sup, AmA&B, AmLY, BiD&SB, ChPo, DcAmA, DcNAA*
Kobbe, M O *ChPo*
Kobbe, Theodor Christoph August Von 1798-1845 *BiD&SB*
Kobell, Franz Von 1803-1882 *BbD, BiD&SB, OxGer*
Kober, Arthur 1900-1975 *AmA&B, Au&Wr, ConAu 57, ConAu P-1, ModWD, OxAm, REn, REnAL, TwCA, TwCA Sup*
Kober, George Martin 1850-1931 *DcNAA*
Kober, Tobias *OxGer*
Kobler, Arthur Leon 1920- *ConAu 13R, WhPNW*
Kobler, Turner S 1930- *ConAu 37*
Kobrick, Leonard 1912- *AmSCAP 66*
Kobrin, David 1941- *ConAu 41*
Kobrin, Janet 1942- *ConAu 57*
Kobrin, Leon 1873-1946 *AmA&B, WhWNAA*
Kobylyans'ka, Ol'ha 1863?-1942 *ModSL 2, Pen Eur*
Kocbek, Edvard 1904- *CasWL*
Koch, Adrienne 1912- *AmA&B*
Koch, Christine 1869-1951 *CasWL*
Koch, Claude Francis 1918- *CatA 1952, ConAu 9R, WrD 1976*
Koch, Dorothy Clarke 1924- *AuBYP, ConAu 5R, SmATA 6*
Koch, Eric *OxCan, OxCan Sup*
Koch, Felix John 1882-1933 *DcNAA, OhA&B*
Koch, Frederick 1923- *AmSCAP 66*
Koch, Frederick Conrad 1876-1948 *DcNAA, WhWNAA*
Koch, Frederick Henry 1877-1944 *AmA&B, CnDAL, DcNAA, OxAm, WhWNAA*
Koch, Hans-Gerhard 1913- *ConAu 17R*
Koch, Helen L 1895- *ConAu 21*
Koch, Herbie 1903- *AmSCAP 66*
Koch, Howard *AmA&B, ConDr*
Koch, John James, Jr. 1920- *AmSCAP 66*
Koch, Julius Arnold 1864- *AmLY, WhWNAA*
Koch, Katharine Isabel 1898- *OhA&B*
Koch, Kenneth 1925- *AmA&B, ChPo S1, ChPo S2, ConAu 1R, ConDr, ConLC 5, ConP 1970, ConP 1975, CrCAP, DrAF 1976, DrAP 1975, Pen Am, RAdv 1, WebEAL, WorAu, WrD 1976*
Koch, Ludwig 1881- *Au&Wr*
Koch, Marie 1912- *AmSCAP 66*
Koch, Martin 1882-1940 *CasWL, ClDMEuL,*

Pen Eur, REn
Koch, Richard 1921- *ConAu 29*
Koch, Robert 1843-1910 *REn*
Koch, Robert 1918- *ConAu 9R*
Koch, Theodore Wesley 1871-1941 *AmA&B, AmLY, DcNAA*
Koch, Thilo 1920- *ConAu 25*
Koch, Thomas J 1947- *ConAu 61*
Koch, Thomas Walter 1933- *ConAu 17R*
Koch, Tom *IndAu 1917*
Koch, Vivienne 1914-1961 *AmA&B, TwCA Sup*
Koch, Walter A 1895- *BiDPar*
Koch, William H, Jr. 1923- *ConAu 17R*
Kochan, Lionel Edmund 1922- *Au&Wr*
Kochan, Paul C 1906- *ConAu 45*
Kochanovski, Jan 1530-1584 *BbD, BiD&SB*
Kochanowski, Jan 1530-1584 *CasWL, EuA, EvEuW, Pen Eur*
Kochanowski, Piotr 1566-1620 *CasWL*
Kochen, Manfred 1928- *ConAu 21*
Kochenburger, Ralph J 1919- *ConAu 53*
Kocher, Eric 1912- *ConAu 57*
Kochetov, Vsevolod A 1912-1973 *ConAu 45*
Kochkurov, Nikolay Ivanovich 1899- *CasWL, DcRusL*
Kochman, Thomas 1936- *ConAu 37*
Kochovski, Hieronymus Vespasian 1633-1699 *BbD, BiD&SB*
Kochowski, Wespazjan 1633-1700 *CasWL, Pen Eur*
Kocic, Petar 1877-1916 *CasWL, Pen Eur*
Kock, Charles Paul De 1794?-1871 *BbD, BiD&SB, CasWL, EuA, EvEuW, OxFr, Pen Eur*
Kock, Paul De 1794-1871 *DcEuL*
Kock, Paul Henri De 1819-1892 *BbD, BiD&SB*
Kocsis, James C 1936- *IlBYP, IlCB 1966*
Koda, Rohan 1867-1947 *CasWL, DcOrL 1*
Kodanda Rao, Pandurangi 1889- *ConAu 13R*
Koebner, Richard 1910- *AmSCAP 66*
Koecker, Leonard 1785-1850 *Alli*
Koefoed, Hans Anton 1922- *Au&Wr*
Koegel, Otto Erwin 1891- *IndAu 1917*
Koehler, Alan 1928- *ConAu 13R*
Koehler, Arthur 1885- *WhWNAA*
Koehler, Augustus *Alli Sup*
Koehler, Benjamin 1890- *WhWNAA*
Koehler, Emily W *ChPo*
Koehler, G Stanley 1915- *ConAu 37, WrD 1976*
Koehler, George *Alli Sup*
Koehler, George E 1930- *ConAu 25*
Koehler, Ludmila 1917- *ConAu 53*
Koehler, Nikki 1951- *ConAu 25*
Koehler, Stanley *DrAP 1975*
Koehler, Sylvester Rosa 1837-1900 *Alli Sup, AmA&B, BiD&SB, DcAmA, DcNAA*
Koehler, Ted 1894- *AmSCAP 66*
Koehler, W R 1914- *ConAu 9R*
Koelbing, Eugen *Alli Sup*
Koelle, L L Carmela *Alli Sup*
Koelle, Sigismund Wilhelm *Alli Sup*
Koeman, Jacob *CasWL*
Koen, Ross Y 1918- *ConAu 1R*
Koenen, Hendrik Jacob 1809-1874 *CasWL*
Koenerdingh, Jan 1632-1705 *CasWL*
Koenig, Allen Edward 1939- *ConAu 23*
Koenig, C Eldo 1919- *ConAu 21*
Koenig, Duane 1918- *ConAu 37*
Koenig, Fritz H 1940- *ConAu 53*
Koenig, George Augustus 1844-1913 *DcNAA*
Koenig, Laird *BlkAW, ConAu 29*
Koenig, Leo 1889-1970 *CasWL*
Koenig, Louis William 1916- *ConAu 1R*
Koenig, Samuel 1899-1972 *ConAu 17, ConAu 37*
Koenigsberg, Moses 1878-1945 *AmA&B, BiDSA, DcNAA, REnAL, WhWNAA*
Koenigsberger, Helmut Georg 1918- *ConAu 33, WrD 1976*
Koepke, Charles Augustus 1893-1966 *IndAu 1917*
Koeppel, Gary 1938- *ConAu 49*
Koeppen, Adolphus Louis 1804-1873 *Alli, DcNAA*
Koeppen, Wolfgang 1906- *CasWL, EncWL, ModGL, OxGer*

Koering, Ursula 1921- *IlBYP, IlCB 1956, MorJA*
Koerner, Gustav Philipp 1809-1896 *DcAmA, DcNAA*
Koerner, James D 1923- *ConAu 9R, WrD 1976*
Koerner, Stephan 1913- *ConAu 1R*
Koertge, Ronald *DrAP 1975*
Koesis, Robert 1935- *ConAu 29*
Koestenbaum, Peter *ConAu 29*
Koester, Frank 1876-1927 *DcNAA*
Koestler, Arthur 1905- *Au&Wr, CasWL, CnMWL, ConAu 1R, ConLC 1, ConLC 3, ConLC 6, ConNov 1972, ConNov 1976, CyWA, EncWL, LongC, ModBL, NewC, OxEng, Pen Eng, REn, TwCA Sup, TwCW, WebEAL, WhTwL, WrD 1976*
Koethe, John 1945- *ConAu 49, DrAP 1975*
Koetsveld, Cornelis Eliza Van 1807-1893 *CasWL*
Koff, Charles 1909- *AmSCAP 66*
Koffi, Raphael Atta 1935?- *AfA 1*
Koffka, Kurt 1886-1941 *DcNAA*
Koffler, Camilla d1955 *AuBYP*
Koffolt, Joseph Howard 1902- *WhWNAA*
Kofler, Leo *Alli Sup*
Kofoed, Jack *ConAu XR*
Kofoed, John C 1894- *ConAu 5R*
Kofron, Frank *ChPo*
Kofsky, Frank 1935- *ConAu 57*
Kogalniceanu, Mihail 1817-1891 *CasWL*
Kogan, Bernard Robert 1920- *ConAu 9R*
Kogan, Herman 1914- *ConAu 9R*
Kogan, Norman 1919- *ConAu 1R, WrD 1976*
Kogawa, Joy Nozomi 1935- *ConP 1970, WrD 1976*
Kogen, Harry 1895- *AmSCAP 66*
Koger, Earl, Sr. *BlkAW*
Kogiku, Kiichiro Chris 1927- *ConAu 33, WrD 1976*
Koginos, Manny T 1933- *ConAu 21*
Koglin, Anna Emilie 1891- *WhWNAA*
Kogos, Frederick 1907-1974 *ConAu 29, ConAu 53*
Koh, Byung Chul 1936- *ConAu 17R*
Koh, Sung Jae 1917- *ConAu 17R*
Kohak, Erazim V 1933- *ConAu 37*
Kohan, Charles Mendel 1884- *Au&Wr*
Kohavi, Y *ConAu XR*
Kohen-Raz, Reuven 1921- *ConAu 37*
Kohl, Herbert R *AmA&B*
Kohl, James 1942- *ConAu 57*
Kohl, Johann Georg 1808-1878 *AmA&B, BbD, BbtC, BiD&SB*
Kohl, Marguerite *AuBYP*
Kohler, D *Alli*
Kohler, Donna Jeane 1937- *AmSCAP 66*
Kohler, Foy David 1908- *ConAu 29, WrD 1976*
Kohler, Heinz 1934- *ConAu 23*
Kohler, Julilly House 1908- *AmA&B, OhA&B*
Kohler, Kaufmann 1843-1926 *AmA&B, DcNAA, OhA&B*
Kohler, Sister Mary Hortense 1892- *ConAu 5R, WrD 1976*
Kohler, Max James 1871-1934 *AmLY, DcNAA, WhWNAA*
Kohler, Wolfgang 1887-1967 *AmA&B, TwCA Sup*
Kohlhaas, Michael *REn*
Kohlman, Charles *Alli Sup*
Kohlman, Churchill 1906- *AmSCAP 66*
Kohlmann, Anthony 1771-1838 *DcAmA, DcNAA*
Kohlmann, Clarence 1891-1944 *AmSCAP 66*
Kohlmeier, Albert Ludwig 1883-1964 *IndAu 1917*
Kohlmeier, Louis M, Jr. 1926- *ConAu 49*
Kohlmeister, Benjamin *BbtC, OxCan*
Kohls, Richard Louis 1921- *IndAu 1917*
Kohlsaat, Herman Henry 1853-1924 *AmA&B, DcNAA*
Kohn, August 1868-1930 *AmLY, DcNAA, WhWNAA*
Kohn, Bernice Herstein 1920- *AuBYP, ConAu 9R, SmATA 4, WrD 1976*
Kohn, Ferdinand *Alli Sup*
Kohn, Hans 1891-1971 *AmA&B, ConAu 1R,*

ConAu 29, REnAL, TwCA Sup
Kohn, Jacob 1881- *ConAu 5R*
Kohn, Melvin L 1928- *ConAu 41*
Kohn, Salomon 1825- *BiD&SB*
Kohner, Frederick 1905- *AmA&B, Au&Wr, ConAu 1R, SmATA 10, TwCW*
Kohnstamm, Philipp Abraham 1875- *WhLA*
Kohon, Ethel 1890-1946 *DcNAA*
Kohout, Pavel 1928- *ConAu 45*
Kohr *Alli*
Kohr, Herbert O 1875- *OhA&B*
Kohr, Louise Hannah 1903- *ConAu 41*
Kohut, Alexander 1842-1894 *AmA&B, BbD, BiD&SB*
Kohut, George Alexander 1874-1933 *DcNAA*
Kohut, Heinz 1913- *ConAu 45*
Kohut, Les *ConAu XR*
Kohut, Nester C 1925- *ConAu 45*
Koi Hai *ConAu XR*
Koidula 1843-1886 *CasWL*
Koikawa, Harumachi *DcOrL 1*
Koilpillai, Charles *ConAu 41*
Koilpillai, Das *ConAu XR*
Koiner, Richard B 1929- *ConAu 17R*
Koizumi, Yakumo *DcLEnL*
Kojima, Takashi 1902- *ConAu P-1*
Kojiro, Nobumitsu *DcOrL 1*
Kokhanovskaya 1825?-1884 *CasWL, DcRusL*
Kokko, Yrjo Olavi 1903- *Au&Wr*
Kokkonen, Lauri 1918- *CrCD*
Kokkoris, Lycurgus 1877- *WhLA*
Kokoschka, Oskar 1886- *CnMD, EncWL, EvEuW, McGWD, ModGL, ModWD, OxGer, REn, REnWD, WhGrA*
Kolachine, Duke Of *WhLA*
Kolaja, Jiri Thomas 1919- *ConAu 9R, WrD 1976*
Kolakowski, Leszek 1927- *ConAu 49*
Kolar, Josef Jiri 1812- *BiD&SB*
Kolar, Slavko 1891-1963 *CasWL, CnMD, Pen Eur*
Kolars, Frank 1899-1972 *ConAu 5R, ConAu 37*
Kolarz, Walter d1962 *AmA&B*
Kolas, Jakub 1882-1956 *CasWL*
Kolas, Yakub 1882-1956 *DcRusL*
Kolasky, John 1915- *ConAu 25*
Kolatch, Jonathan 1943- *ConAu 41*
Kolb, Annette 1875-1967 *EncWL, EvEuW, ModGL, OxGer*
Kolb, Erwin J 1924- *ConAu 37*
Kolb, Gwin Jackson 1919- *ConAu 1R*
Kolb, Harold H, Jr. 1933- *ConAu 29*
Kolb, John F 1916?-1974 *ConAu 53*
Kolb, Ken 1926- *ConAu 21*
Kolb, Lawrence 1911-1972 *ConAu 37*
Kolb, Philip 1907- *ConAu 53*
Kolbe, F C *Alli Sup*
Kolbe, F W *Alli Sup*
Kolbe, Henry E 1907- *ConAu 5R*
Kolbe, J S *Alli Sup*
Kolbe, Parke Rexford 1881-1942 *OhA&B*
Kolbenheyer, Erwin Guido 1878-1962 *ClDMEuL, EncWL, EvEuW, ModWD, OxGer*
Kolbenhoff, Walter 1908- *OxGer*
Kolbrek, Loyal 1914- *ConAu 29*
Kolchak, Aleksandr Vasilyevich 1874-1920 *REn*
Kolchin, Peter 1943- *ConAu 41*
Kolcsey, Ferenc 1790-1838 *CasWL, Pen Eur*
Kolcsey, Ferencz 1790-1838 *BbD, BiD&SB*
Kolde, Endel Jakob 1917- *ConAu 45*
Kolenda, Konstantin 1923- *ConAu 13R*
Kolesnik, Walter B 1923- *ConAu 5R*
Kolhatkar, Sripad Krsna 1871-1934 *DcOrL 2*
Kolinski, Charles J 1916- *ConAu 17R*
Kolinsky, Martin 1936- *ConAu 61*
Koliqi, E *Pen Eur*
Koljevic, Svetozar 1930- *ConAu 17R*
Kolko, Gabriel 1932- *ConAu 5R*
Koll, Kilian *OxGer*
Kollar, Jan 1793-1852 *BiD&SB, CasWL, DcEuL, EuA, Pen Eur*
Kollat, David T 1938- *ConAu 41*
Kollataj, Hugo 1750-1812 *CasWL*
Kollbrunner, Oskar 1895-1932 *CasWL*
Kolle, Frederick Strange 1872?-1929 *DcAmA, DcNAA*
Kollek, Teddy *ConAu XR*

Kollek, Theodore 1911- *ConAu 29*
Koller, Armin Hajman 1878- *WhWNAA*
Koller, Charles W *ConAu 61*
Koller, James 1936- *ConAu 49, ConP 1970, ConP 1975, DrAP 1975, WrD 1976*
Koller, John M 1938- *ConAu 33*
Koller, Lawrence Robert 1912- *ConAu 1R*
Koller, Marvin Robert 1919- *ConAu 13R, WrD 1976*
Kollmyer, A H *Alli Sup*
Kollock, Henry *Alli Sup*
Kollock, Henry 1778-1819 *Alli, BiDSA, DcAmA*
Kollock, Shepard 1750-1839 *AmA&B*
Kollock, Sheppard Kosciuszko 1795-1865 *Alli, DcAmA, DcNAA*
Kollock, William 1940- *ConAu 33, WrD 1976*
Kollontay, Alexandra *WhLA*
Kollwitz, Kathe 1867-1945 *AtlBL, OxGer*
Kolman-Cassius, Jaroslav 1883-1951 *CasWL*
Kolmar, Gertrud 1894-1943 *EncWL, ModGL, OxGer, Pen Eur*
Kolmer, John Albert 1886- *WhWNAA*
Kolmodin, Olof 1690-1753 *CasWL*
Kolodin, Irving 1908- *AmA&B, REnAL*
Kolodin, Robert 1932- *AmSCAP 66*
Kolodny, Annette 1941- *ConAu 61*
Kolosimo, Peter 1922- *ConAu 53*
Kolross, Johannes 1500?-1558 *OxGer*
Kolsen, Helmut Max 1926- *WrD 1976*
Kolson, Clifford J 1920- *ConAu 9R*
Kolstoe, Oliver Paul 1920- *ConAu 17R, WrD 1976*
Kolthoff, Isaac Maurits 1894- *WhWNAA*
Koltsov, Alexey Vasilyevich 1809-1842 *BbD, BiD&SB, CasWL, DcEuL, DcRusL, EuA*
Koltun, Frances *ConAu 23*
Kolumbo, Kristofer *WhWNAA*
Kolup, Tile *OxGer*
Kolzov, Aleksei Vasilievitch 1809-1842 *BiD&SB*
Komachi *CasWL*
Komachiya, Sozo 1893- *WhLA*
Komai, Gonnosuke *DcLEnL*
Komarnicki, Titus 1896- *Au&Wr*
Komarnicki, Tytus 1896- *ConAu P-1*
Komarov, Matvey *CasWL*
Komarovsky, Mirra 1906- *AmA&B, ConAu P-1*
Komed *WhLA*
Komensky, Jan Amos 1592-1670 *CasWL, DcEuL, EuA, EvEuW*
Komey, Ellis Ayetey 1927-1972 *AfA 1, ConP 1970*
Komis, Alexander 1903- *Au&Wr*
Komisar, Lucy 1942- *ConAu 33, SmATA 9, WrD 1976*
Kommerell, Max 1902-1944 *CnMD, EncWL, ModGL*
Komoda, Kiyo 1937- *IlCB 1966, SmATA 9*
Kompert, Leopold 1822-1886 *OxGer*
Komroff, Manuel 1890-1974 *AmA&B, AmNov, AuBYP, CnDAL, ConAu 1R, ConAu 53, OxAm, REnAL, SmATA 2, TwCA, TwCA Sup, WrD 1976*
Konadu, Asare 1932- *ConAu XR, RGAfl*
Konadu, Samuel Asare 1932- *AfA 1, ConAu 23*
Konarski, Hieronim Stanislaw 1700-1773 *CasWL*
Konczacki, Zbigniew Andrzej 1917- *ConAu 21*
Kondratowicz, Vladislav 1823-1862 *BbD, BiD&SB*
Kone, Maurice 1932- *AfA 1*
Konecky, Eugene 1898- *WhWNAA*
Konecsni, Gyorgy 1908- *WhGrA*
Konefsky, Samuel J 1915-1970 *ConAu 29*
Konemann Von Jerxheim d1316 *CasWL*
Konemann, Pfaffe *OxGer*
Koner, Richard B 1929- *LivBA*
Koneski, Blaze 1921- *CasWL, ModSL 2*
Konevskoy, Ivan Ivanovich 1877-1901 *CasWL, DcRusL, EvEuW*
Konevsky, Ivan Ivanovich 1877-1901 *CasWL*
Koni, Anatoly Fedorovich 1844-1927 *CasWL*
Konick, Marcus 1914- *ConAu 37*
Konig, Charles 1774-1851 *Alli, BiDLA*
Konig, Ewald August 1833-1888 *BiD&SB*
Konig, Heinrich Joseph 1790-1869 *BiD&SB*

Konig, Johann Ulrich 1688-1744 *CasWL, OxGer*
Konig, Sigismund *Alli*
Konig, Ulrich Von 1688-1744 *DcEuL*
Konig Rother *CasWL*
Konig Vom Odenwald, Der *OxGer*
Konigsberg, Conrad Isidore 1916- *ConAu 23*
Konigsberg, Isidore 1916- *Au&Wr*
Konigsberger, Hans 1912- *WrD 1976*
Konigsburg, Elaine L 1930- *AnCL, AuBYP, AuICB, ChLR 1, ConAu 21, MorBMP, NewbC 1966, SmATA 4, ThBJA, WrD 1976*
Konigsmarck, Maria Aurora, Grafin Von 1662-1728 *OxGer*
Koning, Hans 1921- *DrAF 1976, SmATA 5, WorAu, WrD 1976*
Koningh, Abraham De 1587-1619 *CasWL*
Koningsberger, Hans 1921- *AmA&B, Au&Wr, ConAu 1R, SmATA 5, WorAu*
Konishi, Shigenao 1873- *WhLA*
Konkle, Burton Alva 1861-1944 *AmA&B, DcNAA, IndAu 1816*
Konkle, Janet Everest 1917- *ConAu 1R, WrD 1976*
Konley, Jeannette Vaughn *IndAu 1917*
Konnyu, Leslie 1914- *ConAu 13R*
Kono, Takashi 1906- *WhGrA*
Konody, Paul George 1872- *WhLA*
Konopak, Farona 1895- *OhA&B*
Konopinski, Emil Jan 1911- *IndAu 1917*
Konopka, Gisela 1910- *ConAu 9R*
Konopnicka, Maria 1842-1910 *CasWL, ClDMEuL, EuA, Pen Eur*
Konovalov, Serge 1899- *Au&Wr*
Konrad *Pen Eur*
Konrad IV 1228-1254 *OxGer*
Konrad, Der Junge, Konig *OxGer*
Konrad II, Kaiser 990?-1039 *OxGer*
Konrad I, Konig d918 *OxGer*
Konrad III, Konig 1093?-1152 *OxGer*
Konrad Von Ammenhusen *CasWL, OxGer*
Konrad Von Fussesbrunnen *CasWL, OxGer*
Konrad Von Haslau *OxGer*
Konrad Von Heimesfurt *CasWL, OxGer*
Konrad Von Helmsdorf *OxGer*
Konrad Von Kilchberg *OxGer*
Konrad Von Landeck *OxGer*
Konrad Von Marburg 1180?-1233 *OxGer*
Konrad Von Megenberg 1309?-1374 *CasWL, OxGer*
Konrad Von Stoffeln *OxGer*
Konrad Von Wurzburg 1220?-1287 *BiD&SB, CasWL, EvEuW, Pen Eur, OxGer*
Konrad, Evelyn 1930- *ConAu 33*
Konrad, Gyorgy 1933- *ConLC 4*
Konrad, Pfaffe *CasWL, OxGer*
Konrad, Wurzburg Von d1827 *DcEuL*
Konradin 1252-1268 *OxGer*
Konstam, Edwin Max 1870- *WhLA*
Konstam, Gertrude A *ChPo S1*
Konstantin Filozof *CasWL, Pen Eur*
Konstantinov, Aleko 1863-1897 *CasWL, Pen Eur*
Konstantinov, Fyodor Denisovich 1910- *WhGrA*
Konstantinov, Georgi 1902-1970 *CasWL*
Konstantinov, Konstantin 1890-1970 *CasWL*
Konstantinovic, Radomir 1928- *CasWL, Pen Eur*
Kontos, Peter G 1935- *ConAu 25*
Konviser, Maurice 1902- *Au&Wr*
Konvitz, Jeffrey 1944- *ConAu 53*
Konvitz, Milton Ridvas 1908- *AmA&B, ConAu 1R, WrD 1976*
Koo, Anthony Y C 1918- *ConAu 57*
Koo, Vi Kyuin Wellington 1887- *REn*
Koo, Vi Kyuin Wellington 1888- *WhLA*
Koob, C Albert 1920- *ConAu 41*
Koob, Derry D 1933- *ConAu 37*
Koob, Theodora 1918- *AuBYP, ConAu 5R*
Kooiman, Helen W *ConAu XR*
Kook, Elset *ChPo S1*
Kookogey, William P *Alli Sup*
Koolish, Lynda *DrAP 1975*
Koonce, Charles *TexWr*
Koonce, Ray F 1913- *ConAu 9R*
Koonts, Jones Calvin 1924- *ConAu 49, DrAP 1975*

Koontz, Harold 1908- *ConAu 41*
Koontz, Mary E *Alli Sup*
Koop, Katherine C 1923- *ConAu 17R*
Koopman, Harry Lyman 1860-1937? *Alli Sup, AmA&B, BiD&SB, ChPo, ChPo S1, DcAmA, DcNAA*
Koops, Mathias *Alli, BiDLA*
Koos, Leonard Vincent 1881- *WhWNAA*
Kooser, Ted 1939- *ConAu XR, DrAP 1975, WrD 1976*
Kooser, Theodore 1939- *ConAu 33*
Kooy, J M J 1902- *BiDPar*
Kopas, Cliff *OxCan Sup*
Kopecky, Oldrich 1923- *WhGrA*
Kopelke, Johannes 1854- *IndAu 1816*
Kopisch, August 1799-1853 *BiD&SB, OxGer*
Kopit, Arthur L 1937- *AmA&B, AuNews 1, CasWL, ConDr, ConLC 1, CrCD, McGWD, OxAm, Pen Am, REn, WebEAL, WorAu, WrD 1976*
Kopit, Arthur L 1938- *CnMD, ModWD*
Kopita, Murray 1903- *AmSCAP 66*
Kopkind, Andrew David 1935- *AmA&B, ConAu 29, WrD 1976*
Koplin, H T 1923- *ConAu 33, WrD 1976*
Koplitz, Eugene D 1928- *ConAu 37*
Koplow, Donald H 1935- *AmSCAP 66*
Kopp, Anatole 1915- *ConAu 29*
Kopp, Frederick 1914- *AmSCAP 66*
Kopp, Harriet Green *ConAu 41*
Kopp, Josef Eutychius 1793-1866 *BiD&SB*
Kopp, O W 1918- *ConAu 33*
Kopp, Richard L 1934- *ConAu 33, WrD 1976*
Kopp, Sheldon B 1929- *ConAu 37*
Koppanyi, Theodore 1901- *Au&Wr*
Koppel, Franz 1840- *BiD&SB*
Koppell, Alfred Baldwin 1898-1963 *AmSCAP 66*
Koppett, Leonard 1923- *ConAu 25*
Koppitz, Elizabeth M 1919- *ConAu 13R, WrD 1976*
Koppman, Lionel 1920- *ConAu 9R*
Koprowski, Kenneth *DrAP 1975*
Koprulu, Mehmed Fuad 1890-1966 *CasWL*
Kops, Bernard 1926- *ChPo, CnMD, ConAu 5R, ConDr, ConLC 4, ConNov 1972, ConNov 1976, ConP 1970, ConP 1975, ModWD, NewC, RAdv 1, TwCW, WorAu, WrD 1976*
Kops, Bernard 1928- *CrCD, ModBL Sup*
Kopsen, Dorothy Blaxland *Au&Wr*
Kopta, Josef 1894-1962 *CasWL*
Kopulos, Stella 1906- *ConAu 49*
Kopycinski, Joseph V 1923- *ConAu 33*
Korach, Mimi 1922- *SmATA 9*
Koraes, Adamantios 1748-1833 *EuA*
Korais, Adamantios 1748-1833 *CasWL, Pen Eur*
Korb, Arthur 1909- *AmSCAP 66*
Korbel, John 1918- *ConAu 9R*
Korbel, Josef 1909- *ConAu 37*
Korber, Friedrich 1887- *WhLA*
Korbonski, Andrzej 1927- *ConAu 9R*
Korbonski, Stefan 1903- *ConAu 5R*
Koreff, David Ferdinand 1783-1851 *OxGer*
Koren, Edward 1935- *ConAu 25, SmATA 5*
Koren, Henry Joseph 1912- *ConAu 9R, WrD 1976*
Koren, John 1861-1923 *DcAmA, DcNAA*
Korenbaum, Myrtle 1915- *ConAu 57*
Koresh *DcNAA*
Korff, Hermann August 1882- *WhLA*
Korff, Sergius Alexander 1876-1924 *DcNAA*
Korfker, Dena 1908- *ConAu 1R, WrD 1976*
Korg, Jacob 1922- *ConAu 5R, WrD 1976*
Korges, James 1930- *ConAu 25*
Korinetz, Yuri 1923- *ConAu 61, SmATA 9*
Korinfsky, Apollon Apollonovich 1868-1937 *CasWL*
Koriun *DcOrL 3*
Koriyama, Naoshi 1926- *ConP 1970*
Korman, A Gerd 1928- *ConAu 53*
Korman, Gerald 1936- *AmSCAP 66*
Kormendi, Ferenc 1900-1972 *AmA&B, AmNov, ConAu 37, WorAu*
Kormondy, Edward John 1926- *ConAu 33, WrD 1976*
Korn, Bertram Wallace 1918- *AmA&B,*

ConAu 1R

Korn, Peggy *ConAu XR*

Korn, Peter Jona 1922- *AmSCAP 66*

Kornacki, Jerzy *CasWL*

Kornaros, Vincenzo *REnWD*

Kornaros, Vitzentzos *CasWL*

Kornblum, Isidore Benjamin 1895- *AmSCAP 66*

Kornblum, Sylvan 1927- *ConAu 41*

Kornbluth, Cyril M 1922?-1958 *WorAu*

Kornbluth, Jesse 1946- *ConAu 25*

Korneichuk SEE ALSO Korniychuk

Korneichuk, Aleksandr Yevdokimovich 1905-1972 *ClDMEuL, CnMD, ConAu 33, CrCD, ModWD, REn*

Korneichuk, Nikolai Ivanovich *WorAu*

Korner, Christian Gottfried 1756-1831 *DcEuL, OxGer*

Korner, Emil 1884- *Au&Wr*

Korner, Karl Theodor 1791-1813 *BbD, BiD&SB, DcEuL, EvEuW*

Korner, Stephan 1913- *Au&Wr, ConAu XR, WrD 1976*

Korner, Theodor 1791-1813 *CasWL, ChPo, ChPo S2, EuA, OxGer, REn*

Kornfeld, Joseph Saul 1876-1943 *OhA&B*

Kornfeld, Paul 1889-1942 *CnMD, EncWL, McGWD, ModWD, OxGer*

Korngold, Erich Wolfgang 1897-1957 *AmSCAP 66*

Kornhauser, Arthur W 1896- *WhWNAA*

Kornhauser, David H 1918- *ConAu 41*

Kornhauser, William 1925- *ConAu 1R, WrD 1976*

Kornilov, Boris 1907-1939 *Pen Eur*

Kornilov, Lavr Georgyevich 1870-1918 *REn*

Kornitzer, Margaret Hester *Au&Wr*

Korniychuk SEE ALSO Korneichuk

Korniychuk, Alexander Evdokimovich 1905-1972 *DcRusL, EvEuW*

Korniychuk, Olexander 1905-1972 *CasWL, Pen Eur*

Kornrich, Milton 1933- *ConAu 17R*

Korol, Alexander G 1900- *ConAu 5R*

Korolenko, Vladimir Galaktionovich 1853-1921 *BiD&SB, CasWL, ClDMEuL, DcRusL, EncWL, EuA, EvEuW, ModSL 1, Pen Eur, REn*

Koroleva, Natalena 1888-1966 *ModSL 2*

Koromilas, Demetrios *REnWD*

Korotkin, Judith 1931- *ConAu 53*

Korsmo, Emil 1863- *WhLA*

Korson, George Gershon 1899- *ChPo S1, ChPo S2*

Kort, Wesley A 1935- *ConAu 37, WrD 1976*

Korte, Karl 1928- *AmSCAP 66*

Korte, Mary Norbert *ConP 1975, DrAP 1975, WrD 1976*

Korten, David C 1937- *ConAu 41*

Kortepeter, Max 1928- *ConAu 41*

Korth, Francis N 1912- *ConAu 25*

Korth, Leslie Oswald 1887- *Au&Wr, WrD 1976*

Korting, Gustav 1845- *BiD&SB*

Kortlander, Max 1890-1961 *AmSCAP 66*

Kortner, Fritz 1892-1970 *CrCD*

Kortner, Peter 1924- *ConAu 33, WrD 1976*

Kortner, Peter 1926- *Au&Wr*

Kortrecht, Augusta *ChPo*

Kortuem, Gustav Ferdinard Albert 1904- *Au&Wr*

Kortum, Karl Arnold 1745-1824 *BbD, BiD&SB, CasWL, DcEuL, OxGer*

Kortwright, Fanny Aikin 1821- *Alli Sup*

Korzeniowski, Jozef 1797-1863 *CasWL*

Korzeniowski, Jozef Teodor Konrad *EncM&D, LongC*

Korzybski, Alfred 1879-1950 *AmA&B, REn, REnAL, TwCA Sup*

Kos, Erih 1913- *CasWL, ModSL 2*

Kos-Rabcewicz-Zubowski, Ludwik *OxCan Sup*

Kosa, John 1914- *ConAu 5R, OxCan*

Kosak, Grega 1932- *WhGrA*

Kosakoff, Reuven 1898- *AmSCAP 66*

Kosan *DcOrL 1*

Koschade, Alfred 1928- *ConAu 21, WrD 1976*

Kosegarten, Ludwig Theobul 1758-1818 *BiD&SB, DcEuL, OxGer*

Kosel, Hermann 1896- *WhGrA*

Koser, Stewart Arment 1894- *WhWNAA*

Koshi, George M 1911- *ConAu 29*

Koshland, Ellen 1947- *ConAu 33*

Kosinski, Jerzy 1933- *AmA&B, ConAu 17R, ConLC 1, ConLC 2, ConLC 3, ConLC 6, ConNov 1972, ConNov 1976, DrAF 1976, EncWL Sup, ModAL Sup, RAdv 1, WorAu, WrD 1976*

Kosinski, Leonard V 1923- *ConAu 25*

Koskenniemi, Veikko Antero 1885-1962 *CasWL, Pen Eur, REn*

Koskoff, David E 1939- *ConAu 49, WrD 1976*

Kosloff, Lou 1904- *AmSCAP 66*

Koslow, Jules 1916- *ConAu 1R*

Kosmac, Ciril 1910- *Au&Wr, ModSL 2*

Kosor, Josip 1879-1961 *CasWL, CnMD, EvEuW, Pen Eur, WhLA*

Kosovel, Srecko 1904-1926 *CasWL*

Koss, Stephen Edward 1940- *ConAu 25, WrD 1976*

Kossack, Karl Ludwig Ernst 1814-1880 *BiD&SB*

Kossak, Zofia 1890-1968 *CatA 1952, ClDMEuL*

Kossak-Szczucka, Zofia 1890-1968 *CasWL, EvEuW, TwCA Sup*

Kossin, Sandy 1926- *SmATA 10*

Kossmann, Rudolf Richard 1934- *ConAu 37, WrD 1976*

Kossoff, David 1919- *ConAu 61, WrD 1976*

Kossuth, Lajos 1802-1894 *OxGer, Pen Eur*

Kost, John 1819-1904 *Alli Sup, DcAmA, DcNAA*

Kost, Mary Lu 1924- *ConAu 45*

Kost, Robert John 1913- *ConAu 1R, IndAu 1917*

Kostandin Yerznkatsi 1250?-1336? *DcOrL 3*

Kostelanetz, Richard C 1940- *AmA&B, ConAu 13R, ConP 1975, DrAF 1976, DrAP 1975, WrD 1976*

Kosten, Andrew 1921- *ConAu 1R*

Kostenko, Lina 1930- *ModSL 2*

Koster, Donald Nelson 1910- *ConAu 53, WrD 1976*

Koster, Hans 1818- *BbD, BiD&SB*

Koster, Henry *Alli*

Koster, John 1945- *ConAu 53*

Koster, John Theodore *Alli, BiDLA*

Koster, R M 1934- *ConAu 37*

Koster, Samuel *BiD&SB*

Kostic, Laza 1841-1910 *CasWL, Pen Eur*

Kostich, Dragos D 1921- *AuBYP, ConAu 5R*

Kostka, Edmund Karl 1915- *ConAu 17R*

Kostlin, Christian Reinhold 1813-1856 *BiD&SB*

Kostomarov, Nikolai Ivanovich 1817-1885 *BbD, BiD&SB, CasWL*

Kostov, Stefan 1879-1939 *CasWL*

Kostra, Jan 1910- *CasWL, ModSL 2*

Kostrov, Efim Ivanovich 1752-1796 *CasWL*

Kostrowitzky, Wilhelm Apollinaris *OxFr*

Kostylev, Valentin Ivanovich 1888-1950 *CasWL*

Kostylyev, Valentin Ivanovich 1888-1950 *EvEuW*

Kostylyov, Valentin Ivanovich 1888-1950 *DcRusL*

Kostyu, Frank A 1919- *ConAu 49*

Kosztolanyi, Dezso 1885-1936 *CasWL, ClDMEuL, EncWL, Pen Eur*

Kot-Murlyka *DcRusL*

Kothari, Hemraj 1933- *Au&Wr*

Kothari, Rajni 1928- *ConAu 33*

Kothen, Robert 1900- *CatA 1952*

Kotker, Norman R 1931- *ConAu 25, DrAF 1976, WrD 1976*

Kotker, Zane 1934- *ConAu 49, DrAF 1976*

Kotler, Milton 1935- *ConAu 29, WrD 1976*

Kotler, Philip 1931- *ConAu 33, WrD 1976*

Kotliarevsky, Ivan Petrovitch 1769-1838 *BiD&SB*

Kotlowitz, Robert 1924- *ConAu 33, ConLC 4, DrAF 1976*

Kotlyarevsky, Ivan 1769-1838 *CasWL, DcRusL, Pen Eur*

Kotlyarevsky, Nestor Alexandrovich 1863-1925 *CasWL*

Kotoshikhin, Grigory Karpovich 1630-1667 *CasWL*

Kotowicz, Caroline S 1918- *WrD 1976*

Kotowski, Joanne 1930- *ConAu 57*

Kotschevar, Lendal H 1908- *ConAu 17R*

Kotsuji, Abraham S 1899-1973 *ConAu 45, ConAu P-1*

Kotsyubinsky, Mykhaylo 1864-1913 *CasWL, DcRusL, ModSL 2, Pen Eur*

Kott, Jan 1914- *ConAu 13R, WorAu*

Kottlowski, Frank Edward 1921- *IndAu 1917*

Kottman, Richard N 1932- *ConAu 25, OxCan Sup*

Kotz, Nick 1932- *ConAu 29*

Kotz, Samuel 1930- *ConAu 13R*

Kotze, John Gilbert 1850- *Alli Sup*

Kotzebue, August Friedrich Ferdinand Von 1761-1819 *AtlBL, BbD, BiD&SB, CasWL, CnThe, DcEuL, EuA, EvEuW, McGWD, NewC, OxEng, OxFr, OxGer, Pen Eur, REn, REnWD*

Kotzebue, Otto Von 1787-1846 *OxGer*

Kotzebue, Wilhelm Von 1813-1887 *BiD&SB*

Kotzin, Michael C 1941- *ConAu 37, WrD 1976*

Kotzwinkle, William 1938- *ConAu 45, ConLC 5*

Kouadio-Tiacoh, Gabriel 1920?- *AfA 1*

Koubourlis, Demetrius J 1938- *ConAu 57*

Koudelka, Joseph Maria 1852- *AmLY*

Koues, Helen *WhWNAA*

Kouguell, Arkadie 1897- *AmSCAP 66*

Koujto Hmain *DcOrL 2*

Koumaris, John 1879- *WhLA*

Koumjian, Vaughn *DrAF 1976*

Koumoulides, John 1938- *ConAu 41*

Koun *DcOrL 1*

Kouns, Nathan Chapman 1833-1890 *Alli Sup, BiD&SB, BiDSA, DcAmA, DcNAA*

Kountz, Richard 1896-1950 *AmSCAP 66*

Koupernik, Cyrille 1917- *ConAu 57*

Kousoulas, D George 1923- *ConAu 17R*

Kousser, J Morgan 1943- *ConAu 57*

Koussevitzky, Sergey Alexandrovitch 1874-1951 *REn*

Koutoukas, H M *ConDr, SmATA XR, WrD 1976*

Kouts, Anne 1945- *ConAu 29, SmATA 8*

Kouts, Hertha Pretorius 1922- *ConAu 1R*

Koutzen, Boris 1901- *AmSCAP 66*

Kouwenaar, Gerrit 1923- *CasWL*

Kouwenhoven, John Atlee 1909- *AmA&B, ConAu 1R, WrD 1976*

Kouwenhoven, William Bennett 1886- *WhWNAA*

Kouyate, Seydou *AfA 1*

Kouyoumdjian, Dikran *LongC*

Kovac, Mirko 1938- *CasWL*

Kovacevic, Zivojin 1928- *WhGrA*

Kovach, Francis J 1918- *ConAu 61*

Kovacic, Ante 1854?-1889 *CasWL, Pen Eur*

Kovacic, Goran Ivan 1913-1943 *Pen Eur*

Kovacic, Ivan Goran 1913-1943 *CasWL*

Kovacs, Ernie 1919-1962 *AmA&B, AmSCAP 66*

Kovacs, Imre 1913- *ConAu 23*

Kovacs, Joseph 1912- *AmSCAP 66*

Kovak, Teri *DrAF 1976*

Kovalevskaya, Sofya Vasilyevna 1850-1891 *CasWL*

Kovalevsky, Sonya 1850-1891 *BiD&SB*

Kovalik, Nada 1926- *AuBYP, ConAu 25*

Kovalik, Vladimir 1928- *ConAu 25*

Kovarsky, Irving 1918- *ConAu 29*

Kovel, Joel S 1936- *Au&Wr, ConAu 29, WrD 1976*

Kovel, Ralph Mallory 1920- *ConAu 17R, WrD 1976*

Kovel, Terry Horvitz 1928- *ConAu 17R, WrD 1976*

Koven, Anna Farwell *WhWNAA*

Kovner, B 1874?-1974 *ConAu XR, WhWNAA*

Kovrig, Bennett 1940- *ConAu 29*

Kowalski, Frank 1907- *ConAu 37*

Kowet, Don 1937- *ConAu 57*

Kowitz, Gerald T 1928- *ConAu 33*

Kownslar, Allan O 1935- *ConAu 61*

Koyama, Kosuke 1929- *ConAu 57*

Koyi, Haji Kadyr 1817-1897 *DcOrL 3*

Koyo *DcOrL 1*

Kozak, Jan B 1889?-1974 *ConAu 45*

Kozak, Jus 1892-1964 *CasWL*

Kravchinsky, Sergey Mikhaylovich 1851-1895 *CasWL, DcRusL, EvEuW*
Kravetz, Nathan 1921- *AmA&B, ConAu 9R*
Kravis, Irving B 1916- *ConAu 17R*
Kravitz, Nathan *ConAu 49*
Kravitz, Nathaniel 1905- *ConAu 49*
Krawiec, T S 1913- *ConAu 25*
Krawitz, Henry 1947- *ConAu 45*
Krawitz, Herman E 1925- *ConAu 61*
Krawitz, Ruth 1929- *ConAu 9R*
Krayni, Anton *DcRusL*
Krcmery, Stefan 1892-1955 *CasWL*
Krebs, Alfred H 1920- *ConAu 23*
Krebs, Elvira 1869- *WhLA*
Krebs, John Michael 1804-1867 *Alli, BiDSA, DcAmA, DcNAA*
Krebs, Richard Julius Herman *TwCA Sup*
Krebs, Stanley LeFevre 1864-1935 *DcNAA*
Krebs, Theodore Luther 1860- *WhWNAA*
Krech, Mrs. George W *TexWr*
Krechmer, William 1909- *AmSCAP 66*
Kredel, Fritz 1900-1973 *ChPo, ConAu 41, IIBYP, IICB 1945, IICB 1956, IICB 1966, MorJA*
Kredenser, Gail 1936- *ConAu 21*
Kreeger, Irving Seymour 1924- *Au&Wr*
Krefetz, Gerald Saul 1932- *ConAu 33, WrD 1976*
Krefetz, Ruth Marossi 1923?-1972 *ConAu 37*
Krefft, Johann Ludwig Gerhard 1830- *Alli Sup*
Kregel, J A 1944- *ConAu 41, WrD 1976*
Kreh, Bernard 1925- *ConAu 57*
Krehbiel, Henry Edward 1854-1923 *AmA&B, BiD&SB, DcAmA, OhA&B*
Kreider, Barbara 1942- *ConAu 41*
Kreider, Carl Jonas 1914- *ConAu 37, IndAu 1917*
Kreig, Margaret B 1922- *ConAu 13R*
Kreindler, Lee S 1924- *ConAu 17R, WrD 1976*
Kreingold, Shana 1889?-1972 *ConAu 37*
Kreinin, Mordechai 1930- *ConAu 9R, WrD 1976*
Kreis, Dorothea Beeby 1900- *WhWNAA*
Kreis, Hans *ChPo*
Kreisel, Henry 1922- *CanWr, ConAu 61, OxCan, WrD 1976*
Kreisler, Fritz 1875-1962 *AmSCAP 66, REn*
Kreisman, Leonard T 1925- *ConAu 13R*
Kreitler, Hans 1916- *ConAu 45*
Kreitler, Shulamith 1938- *ConAu 45*
Krejci, Jaroslav 1916- *ConAu 41*
Kremen, Bennett 1936- *ConAu 57*
Kremenliev, Boris A 1911- *ConAu 45*
Krementz, Jill 1940- *AuNews 1, AuNews 2, ConAu 49*
Kremer, Alfred Von 1828-1889 *BiD&SB*
Kremer, R E *Alli Sup*
Kremers, Edward 1865- *WhWNAA*
Kremers, Harry C 1889- *WhWNAA*
Kreml, Anne Lee 1930- *ConAu 21*
Kremnitz, Mite 1852- *BiD&SB*
Krempel, Daniel S 1926- *ConAu 33*
Krenek, Ernst 1900- *ConAu 57*
Krengel, Joseph 1915- *AmSCAP 66*
Krenkel, John H 1906- *ConAu 33, WrD 1976*
Krentel, Mildred White 1921- *ConAu 5R*
Krents, Harold Eliot 1943- *ConAu 37*
Krentz, Edgar Martin 1928- *ConAu 23, WrD 1976*
Krenz, William F 1899- *AmSCAP 66*
Krepp, Frederick Charles *Alli Sup*
Krepps, Patrice *ChPo S2*
Krepps, Robert Wilson 1919- *Au&Wr, ConAu 1R*
Kresa, Helmy 1904- *AmSCAP 66*
Kresensky, Raymond 1897- *AnMV 1926, WhWNAA*
Kresge, Elijah Everitt 1875- *WhWNAA*
Kresh, Paul 1919- *ConAu 13R, WrD 1976*
Kresken, H Acosta *Alli Sup*
Kress, George Henry 1874- *AmLY, WhWNAA*
Kress, Paul F 1935- *ConAu 29*
Kress, Robert 1932- *ConAu 61*
Kressy, Michael 1936- *ConAu 61*
Krestovsky, V *BiD&SB*

Krestovsky, Vsevolod Vladmirovich 1840-1895 *BiD&SB, CasWL, DcRusL, EvEuW*
Kretschmann, Karl Friedrich 1738-1809 *DcEuL, OxGer*
Kretzer, Max 1854-1941 *BiD&SB, ClDMEuL, EvEuW, OxGer, REn*
Kretzmann, Adalbert Raphael Alexander 1903- *Au&Wr, ConAu P-1*
Kretzmann, Karl 1877-1949 *IndAu 1917*
Kretzmann, Norman 1928- *ConAu 49*
Kretzmann, Paul Edward 1883- *AmA&B, IndAu 1816, WhWNAA*
Kretzschmar, Karl 1877- *WhWNAA*
Kreuder, Ernst 1903-1972 *ModGL, OxGer*
Kreuter, Kent 1932- *ConAu 29*
Kreuttner, Mrs. C D McAllister *WhWNAA*
Kreutz, Arthur 1906- *AmSCAP 66*
Kreutzer, William *Alli Sup*
Kreutzwald, Friedrich Reinhold 1803-1882 *CasWL*
Kreuzer, James R 1913-1971 *ConAu P-1*
Kreve-Mickievicius, Vincas 1882-1954 *CasWL*
Krevitsky, Nathan I 1914- *ConAu 9R*
Krevitsky, Nik *ConAu XR*
Krevolin, Nathan 1927- *ConAu 41*
Krey, August Charles 1887-1961 *AmA&B*
Krey, Laura Lettie 1890- *AmA&B, REnAL, TwCA, TwCA Sup*
Kreyche, Gerald F 1927- *ConAu 37*
Kreyche, Robert J 1920- *ConAu 13R*
Kreymborg, Alfred 1883-1966 *AmA&B, AmSCAP 66, ChPo, ChPo S2, CnDAL, ConAmA, ConAmL, ConAu 25, LongC, ModAL, OxAm, REnAL, SixAP, TwCA, TwCA Sup*
Krez, Konrad 1828-1897 *CasWL*
Krickberg, Walter *OxCan Sup*
Kriebel, Oscar Schultz 1863-1932 *DcNAA*
Krieg, David *Alli*
Kriegbaum, Hillier 1902- *WrD 1976*
Kriege, Matilda H *ChPo*
Kriegel, Leonard 1933- *ConAu 33, WrD 1976*
Krieger, Leonard 1918- *AmA&B, ConAu 17R, WrD 1976*
Krieger, Murray 1923- *AmA&B, ConAu 1R, WrD 1976*
Krieghbaum, Hillier Hiram 1902- *ConAu 5R, IndAu 1917*
Kriegman, Oscar M 1930- *ConAu 9R*
Kriehn, George 1868- *DcAmA*
Kriensky, Morris 1917- *ConAu 57*
Kriesberg, Louis 1926- *ConAu 29, WrD 1976*
Krieze, Mrs. M *Alli Sup*
Krige, Uys 1910- *CasWL, ConNov 1972, ConNov 1976, Pen Cl, Pen Eng, TwCW, WrD 1976*
Krikorian, Jessie *Alli Sup*
Krikorian, Yervant H 1892- *ConAu 45*
Krilof, Ivan Andreevitch 1769-1844 *ChPo S2*
Krim, Seymour M 1922- *ConAu 5R, WrD 1976*
Krimerman, Leonard Isaiah 1934- *ConAu 17R*
Krimm, Hans 1875- *WhLA*
Kringle, Karan *OhA&B*
Kringsteiner, Joseph Ferdinand 1775-1810 *OxGer*
Krinitz, Elise *OxGer*
Krinsky, Carol Herselle 1937- *ConAu 37*
Kripke, Dorothy Karp *ConAu 17R*
Krippner, Stanley Curtis 1932- *BiDPar*
Krishnamurti, G *ChPo S1*
Krishnamurti, Jiddu 1891- *DcLEnL*
Krishnamurti, Jiddu 1895- *ConAu 61*
Krishnamurti, R 1899-1954 *CasWL*
Krislov, Joseph 1927- *ConAu 41*
Krislov, Samuel 1929- *ConAu 9R, WrD 1976*
Krispyn, Egbert 1930- *ConAu 13R*
Kristan Von Hamle *OxGer*
Kristan Von Luppin *OxGer*
Kristein, Marvin M 1926- *ConAu 29, WrD 1976*
Kristeller, Paul Oskar 1905- *AmA&B, ConAu 9R*
Kristensen, Aage Tom 1893- *CasWL*
Kristensen, H Kromann 1903- *BiDPar*
Kristensen, Tom 1893- *EncWL, Pen Eur, WhTwL*
Kristian Pagan *WhLA*

Kristof, Jane 1932- *ConAu 29, SmATA 8*
Kristof, Ladis K D 1918- *ConAu 61*
Kristoffersen, Eva M 1901- *AuBYP*
Kristoforidhi, K *Pen Eur*
Kristol, Irving 1920- *ConAu 25*
Kriton, Kate *ChPo*
Kritzeck, James 1930- *ConAu 5R*
Krizay, John 1926- *ConAu 61*
Krklec, Gustav 1899- *CasWL, Pen Eur*
Krleza, Miroslav 1893- *CasWL, ClDMEuL, CnMD, EncWL, ModSL 2, ModWD, Pen Eur, TwCW, WorAu*
Krochmal, Connie 1949- *ConAu 41*
Krochmal, Nachman 1785-1840 *CasWL*
Krock, Arthur 1887?-1974 *AmA&B, AuNews 1, ConAu 33, ConAu 49, WhWNAA*
Krock, George L 1908-1955 *OhA&B*
Krodel, Gerhard 1926- *ConAu 61*
Kroeber, Alfred L 1876-1960 *AmA&B*
Kroeber, Karl 1926- *ConAu 57*
Kroeber, Theodora Kracaw 1897- *AmA&B, ConAu 5R, SmATA 1, WrD 1976*
Kroeger, Adolph Ernst 1837-1882 *Alli Sup, BiD&SB, BiDSA, DcAmA, DcNAA*
Kroeger, Alice Bertha d1909 *DcNAA*
Kroeger, Arthur 1908- *ConAu 13R*
Kroeger, Frederick P 1921- *ConAu 33*
Kroeh, Charles Frederick 1846- *AmLY, DcAmA*
Kroeker, Kathe Freiligrath- *Alli Sup*
Kroetsch, Robert Paul 1927- *Au&Wr, ConAu 17R, ConLC 5, ConNov 1976, OxCan Sup, WrD 1976*
Krog, Helge 1889-1962 *CasWL, CnMD, EvEuW, McGWD, ModWD, Pen Eur, REnWD, TwCW*
Kroger, William S 1906- *ConAu P-1*
Krohn, Ernst C 1888- *AuNews 1, ConAu 37, WrD 1976*
Krohn, Henry *Alli*
Krohn, Herbert *DrAP 1975*
Krohn, Robert 1937- *ConAu 45*
Krohn, Sven I 1903- *BiDPar*
Krohn, William Otterbein 1868-1927 *DcNAA, OhA&B*
Kroll, Adam *Alli*
Kroll, Burt *ConAu XR*
Kroll, Francis Lynde 1904-1973 *ConAu P-1, SmATA 10*
Kroll, Harry Harrison 1888- *AmA&B, AmNov, IndAu 1917, REnAL, TwCA Sup*
Kroll, Judith *DrAP 1975*
Kroll, Morton 1923- *ConAu 49*
Kroll, William 1901- *AmSCAP 66*
Krollmann, Gustav W *ChPo*
Krolow, Karl 1915- *CasWL, EncWL, EvEuW, ModGL, OxGer, Pen Eur*
Kromer, Marcin 1512-1589 *CasWL*
Kron, Karl *Alli Sup, DcAmA, DcNAA*
Kronchmal, Nachman 1785-1840 *Pen Eur*
Krondes, Jimmy 1925- *AmSCAP 66*
Kronegger, Maria Elisabeth 1932- *ConAu 25, WrD 1976*
Kronenberg, Henry Harold 1902- *ConAu 1R*
Kronenberger, Louis 1904- *AmA&B, Au&Wr, ChPo, ConAu 1R, OhA&B, OxAm, REnAL, TwCA Sup, WrD 1976*
Kroner, Richard 1884- *ConAu 9R*
Kronhausen, Eberhard W 1915- *ConAu 9R*
Kronhausen, Phyllis C 1929- *ConAu 9R*
Kronick, David A 1917- *ConAu 9R*
Kroninger, Robert H 1923- *ConAu 13R*
Krook, Dorothea 1920- *Au&Wr*
Krooss, Herman E 1912-1975 *ConAu 17, ConAu 57*
Kropf, Linda S 1947- *ConAu 49*
Kropinski, Ludwik 1767-1844 *EvEuW*
Kropotkin, Prince Peter Alekseyevich 1842-1921 *BiD&SB, CasWL, ClDMEuL, EuA*
Kropotkin, Prince Pyotr Alekseyevich 1842-1921 *DcRusL, REn*
Kropp, Lloyd 1931- *ConAu 25, WrD 1976*
Krosby, H Peter *OxCan Sup*
Krosney, Mary Stewart 1939- *ConAu 17R*
Krotel, Gottlob Frederick 1826- *Alli, DcAmA*
Krotki, Karol J 1922- *ConAu 41*
Krouse, H Sylvester 1853-1940 *AmSCAP 66*

KEY TO TITLE CODES FOR USE IN LOCATING SOURCES

Detailed bibliographical information about the sources
listed below appears in the front of each volume.

AfA	African Authors	*CatA*	Catholic Authors
Alli	Allibone, S. Austin: A Critical Dictionary of English Literature and British and American Authors	*ChLR*	Children's Literature Review
		ChPo	Childhood in Poetry
Alli Sup	A Supplement to Allibone's Critical Dictionary of English Literature and British and American Authors	*Chmbr*	Chambers's Cyclopaedia of English Literature
		ClDMEuL	Columbia Dictionary of Modern European Literature
AmA	American Authors	*CnDAL*	Concise Dictionary of American Literature
AmA&B	American Authors and Books	*CnE&AP*	The Concise Encyclopedia of English and American Poets and Poetry
AmLY	The American Literary Yearbook		
AmNov	American Novelists of Today	*CnMD*	The Concise Encyclopedia of Modern Drama
AmSCAP 66	The ASCAP Biographical Dictionary of Composers, Authors and Publishers	*CnMWL*	The Concise Encyclopedia of Modern World Literature
AmWr	American Writers	*CnThe*	A Concise Encyclopedia of the Theatre
AnCL	Anthology of Children's Literature	*ConAmA*	Contemporary American Authors
AnMV 1926	Anthology of Magazine Verse for 1926 and Yearbook of American Poetry	*ConAmL*	Contemporary American Literature
		ConAu	Contemporary Authors
ArizL	Arizona in Literature	*ConDr*	Contemporary Dramatists
AtlBL	Atlantic Brief Lives	*ConICB*	Contemporary Illustrators of Children's Books
Au&Wr	The Author's and Writer's Who's Who (Sixth edition)	*ConLC*	Contemporary Literary Criticism
AuBYP	Authors of Books for Young People	*ConNOV*	Contemporary Novelists
AuICB	Authors and Illustrators of Children's Books	*ConP*	Contemporary Poets
AuNews	Authors in the News	*CrCAP*	Crowell's Handbook of Contemporary American Poetry
BbD	The Bibliophile Dictionary		
BbtC	Bibliotheca Canadensis	*CrCD*	Crowell's Handbook of Contemporary Drama
BiB	Biographia Britannica Literaria	*CrE&SL*	Crowell's Handbook of Elizabethan and Stuart Literature
BiD&SB	Biographical Dictionary and Synopsis of Books		
BiDLA	A Biographical Dictionary of the Living Authors of Great Britain and Ireland	*CriT*	The Critical Temper
		CyAL	Cyclopaedia of American Literature
BiDPar	Biographical Dictionary of Parapsychology	*CyWA*	Cyclopedia of World Authors
BiDSA	Biographical Dictionary of Southern Authors	*DcAmA*	A Dictionary of American Authors
BkC	The Book of Catholic Authors	*DcBiA*	A Dictionary of Biographies of Authors Represented in the Authors Digest Series
BkCL	A Book of Children's Literature		
BkIE	Book Illustrators in Eighteenth-Century England	*DcCLA*	A Dictionary of Contemporary Latin American Authors
BkP	Books are by People		
BlkAW	Black American Writers	*DcEnA*	A Dictionary of English Authors
Br&AmS	British and American Sporting Authors	*DcEnL*	Dictionary of English Literature
BrAu	British Authors Before 1800	*DcEuL*	A Dictionary of European Literature
BrAu 19	British Authors of the Nineteenth Century	*DcLEnL*	A Dictionary of Literature in the English Language
Cald 1938	Caldecott Medal Books, 1938-1957	*DcNAA*	A Dictionary of North American Authors Deceased Before 1950
CanNov	Canadian Novelists, 1920-1945		
CanWr	Canadian Writers	*DcOrL*	Dictionary of Oriental Literatures
CarSB	The Carolyn Sherwin Bailey Historical Collection of Children's Books	*DcRusL*	Dictionary of Russian Literature
		DcSpL	Dictionary of Spanish Literature
CasWL	Cassell's Encyclopaedia of World Literature	*DrAF 1976*	A Directory of American Fiction Writers (1976 edition)